includes the resources most appropriate for each type of paper. [watermark obscures] ...nce in
Chapter 53, Reading and Writing, on choosing a topic, developing a thesis, arguing about literature,
organizing a paper, writing a draft, revising and editing, and formatting a manuscript.

CASE STUDIES IN READING AND WRITING	COMPANION WEB SITE RESOURCES	SAMPLE PAPERS
Ch. 14, A Critical Case Study: William Faulkner's "Barn Burning," 492 Ch. 34, A Critical Case Study: T. S. Eliot's "The Love Song of J. Alfred Prufrock," 1067 Ch. 46, A Critical Case Study: Henrik Ibsen's *A Doll House*, 1626	VirtuaLit Interactive Poetry Tutorial	*The A & P as a State of Mind*, 2155 *Tossing Metaphors Together in "Catch,"* 678 *Memory in Elizabeth Bishop's "Manners,"* 712
A Poet's Explication: "A Personal Analysis of 'J. Alfred Prufrock'" with questions, 1079	VirtuaLit Interactive Poetry Tutorial	*A Reading of Dickinson's "There's a certain Slant of light,"* 2150 *The Use of Conventional Metaphors for Death in John Donne's "Death Be Not Proud,"* 943
Ch. 16, A Thematic Case Study: The Nature of Storytelling, 536 Ch. 36, Two Thematic Case Studies: The Love Poem and Teaching and Learning, 1098	VirtuaLit Interactive Poetry Tutorial	*Differences in Responses to Kate Chopin's "The Story of an Hour,"* 16 *Fulfillment or Failure? Marriage in* A Secret Sorrow *and "A Sorrowful Woman,"* 59 *The Struggle for Women's Self-Definition in* A Doll House *and* M. Butterfly, 2160
Ch. 14, A Critical Case Study: William Faulkner's "Barn Burning," 492 Ch. 34, A Critical Case Study: T. S. Eliot's "The Love Song of J. Alfred Prufrock," 1067 Ch. 46, A Critical Case Study: Henrik Ibsen's *A Doll House*, 1626	VirtuaLit Interactive Poetry Tutorial Multimedia Project Guides Online	*The Fires of Class Conflict in "Barn Burning,"* 516 *The Feminist Evidence in* Trifles, 1278 *On the Other Side of the Slammed Door in* A Doll House, 1638
Ch. 11, A Study of Nathaniel Hawthorne, 327 Ch. 12, A Study of Flannery O'Connor, 380 Ch. 13, A Study of Alice Munro, 447 Ch. 31, A Study of Emily Dickinson, 949 Ch. 32, A Study of Robert Frost, 995 Ch. 33, A Study of Langston Hughes, 1032 Ch. 43, A Study of Sophocles, 1282 Ch. 44, A Study of William Shakespeare, 1383	LitLinks VirtuaLit Interactive Poetry Tutorial	*Religious Faith in Four Poems by Emily Dickinson*, 991
Ch. 37, Brief Biographies of Selected Poets, 1116	LitLinks Multimedia Project Guides Online	*How the Narrator Cultivates a Rose for Emily*, 2180

THE BEDFORD
INTRODUCTION TO
LITERATURE

Reading · Thinking · Writing

SIXTH EDITION

THE BEDFORD INTRODUCTION TO LITERATURE

Reading · Thinking · Writing

Michael Meyer
University of Connecticut

BEDFORD/ST. MARTIN'S   Boston ◆ New York

For Bedford/St. Martin's

Developmental Editor: Aron Keesbury
Production Editor: Stasia Zomkowski
Senior Production Supervisor: Dennis Conroy
Marketing Manager: Richard Cadman
Editorial Assistant: Joshua Levy
Production Assistant: Kerri Cardone
Copyeditor: Jane Zanichkowsky
Text Design: Claire Seng-Niemoeller
Cover Design: Donna Lee Dennison
Cover Art: Pablo Picasso. *Girl Reading at a Table.* The Metropolitan Museum of Art, Bequest of
Florene M. Schoenborn, in honor of William S. Lieberman, 1995. (1996. 403.1) Photograph ©
1996 The Metropolitan Museum of Art.
Composition: Stratford Publishing Services, Inc.
Printing and Binding: Quebecor World/Hawkins

President: Charles H. Christensen
Editorial Director: Joan E. Feinberg
Editor in Chief: Karen S. Henry
Director of Marketing: Karen Melton
Director of Editing, Design, and Production: Marcia Cohen
Managing Editor: Elizabeth M. Schaaf

Library of Congress Control Number: 2001087441

Manufactured in the United States of America.

6 5 4 3 2 1

f e d c b a

For information, write: Bedford/St. Martin's, 75 Arlington Street, Boston, MA 02116
(617-399-4000)

ISBN: 0-312-25918-2

Acknowledgments

FICTION

Sherman Alexie. "Class" from *The Toughest Indian in the World* by Sherman Alexie. Copyright © 2000 by Sherman Alexie. Used by permission of Grove/Atlantic, Inc.
Isabel Allende. "The Judge's Wife" from *The Stories of Eva Luna* by Isabel Allende, translated from the Spanish
by Margaret Sayers Peden. Copyright © 1989 by Isabel Allende. English translation copyright © 1991 by Macmillan Publishing Company. Reprinted with permission of Scribner, A Division of Simon & Schuster.

*Acknowledgments and copyrights are continued at the back of the book on pages 2215–2228, which constitute an extension of
the copyright page. It is a violation of the law to reproduce these selections by any means whatsoever without the written
permission of the copyright holder.*

For My Wife
Regina Barreca

About Michael Meyer

Michael Meyer has taught introductory writing and literature courses for more than thirty years — since 1981 at the University of Connecticut and before that at the University of North Carolina at Charlotte and the College of William and Mary.

In addition to being an experienced teacher, Meyer is a highly regarded literary scholar. His scholarly articles have appeared in distinguished journals such as *American Literature, Studies in the American Renaissance,* and *Virginia Quarterly Review.* An internationally recognized authority on Henry David Thoreau, Meyer is a former president of the Thoreau Society and coauthor (with Walter Harding) of *The New Thoreau Handbook,* a standard reference source. His first book, *Several More Lives to Live: Thoreau's Political Reputation in America,* was awarded the Ralph Henry Gabriel Prize by the American Studies Association. He is also the editor of *Frederick Douglass: The Narrative and Selected Writings* and the author of *The Little, Brown Guide to Writing Research Papers,* Third Edition. His other books for Bedford / St. Martin's include *The Compact Bedford Introduction to Literature,* Fifth Edition; *Poetry: An Introduction,* Third Edition; and *Thinking and Writing about Literature,* Second Edition.

Preface for Instructors

The sixth edition of *The Bedford Introduction to Literature* incorporates a wide range of distinctive features that have been class-tested in thousands of literature courses and carefully revised over six editions. With its balance of classic and contemporary, traditional, and multicultural works, along with its in-depth treatment of selected writers, provocative secondary materials, and pervasive concern with critical reading, thinking, and writing, this text-anthology addresses all the requirements of the contemporary introductory literature course.

Like its predecessors, the sixth edition of *The Bedford Introduction to Literature* reflects the assumptions that understanding enhances the enjoyment of literature and that reading literature offers a valuable and unique means of apprehending life in its richness and diversity. The book also reflects the hope that the selections included will encourage students to become lifelong readers of imaginative literature. Designed to accommodate a variety of teaching styles, this rich collection of 65 stories (21 of them new to the sixth edition), 422 poems (101 of them new), and 24 plays (5 of them new) represents a wide range of periods, nationalities, and voices. Each selection has been carefully chosen for its appeal to students today and for its usefulness in demonstrating the effects, significance, and pleasures of literature. To enhance these selections, this edition includes many images and photographs of selected authors, a portfolio of photographs of plays in performance, and, new to this edition, a separate chapter consisting of concise biographies of selected poets that provide valuable background information.

Again, like its predecessors, the sixth edition of *The Bedford Introduction to Literature* is designed for the introductory course as it is taught today, which varies — from school to school and from instructor to instructor — more than ever before. Even the traditional course emphasizing the elements of literature and a broad range of works from the Western canon is changing in response to important developments in literary studies and, more generally, in higher education and in American society. The course is now viewed by many teachers as a rich opportunity to supplement classics of Western literature with the work of writers previously excluded from the traditional canon. Increasingly, it now also serves as an introduction to the discipline of literary study, a challenging development that brings to the undergraduate classroom important trends in literary theory and provocative new readings of both familiar and unfamiliar texts. Finally, and perhaps most often, the introduction to literature course is now also taught as a second course in composition in which the critical thinking and writing that students do are as important as the reading that they do. The sixth edition of *The Bedford Introduction to Literature* responds to these developments and the increase in the use of technology in teaching literature with distinctive features that address the needs of instructors who teach a traditional course but who are also concerned about canonical issues, literary theory, and writing about literature.

New to the Sixth Edition

In addition to the 21 new stories, 101 new poems, and 5 new plays, this edition offers strengthened coverage of the elements of literature as well as deeper coverage of the critical approaches taught in today's courses:

- **New chapters, Combining the Elements,** in both Fiction and Poetry, guide students through the essential process of understanding—and writing about—how the elements of literature combine to create an experience of literary meanings and effects.
- **Two new sample papers-in-process** model the stages of developing a thesis and writing an explication.
- **New Thematic Case Studies** in Fiction and Poetry build on the success of the Authors in Depth and on the Critical and Cultural Case Studies to focus students' attention on important and engaging themes that encourage them to draw on their own experience.
- **New "Suggested Topics for Longer Papers"** following every casebook chapter help students use the Authors in Depth, the Critical and Cultural Case Studies, and the Thematic Case Studies as sources for longer papers.
- **New biographical notes** for more than 80 of the most frequently assigned poets provide background information, including provocative comments on poetry by many of the poets.

In addition to the new features in the book, this edition keeps up with a changing student body and with new modes of teaching literature by integrating a new Web site with the book, using a variety of new media to expand the world of literature for students. Links throughout the book lead to relevant, informative, and stimulating resources available on the Web.

- **The new VirtuaLit Interactive Poetry Tutorial** guides students through a series of interactive exercises that get them to actively engage in the close reading of a poem's elements and a study of its cultural and critical texts.
- **New LitQuiz online quizzes** for every story, every play, and every element of poetry can be used either by students for self-study with im-

mediate feedback or by instructors for assessment, with results collated automatically and available online.

- **LitLinks** supplement the book's biographical and contextual coverage and provide annotated links to carefully chosen Web sites, including biographical, critical, and cultural information for every fiction writer, every playwright, and many of the book's celebrated poets.
- **Interactive Multimedia Project Guides** help students with the book's new multimedia project assignments by taking them step by step through the process of finding, evaluating, and incorporating Web resources into their projects.

A Flexible and Teachable Organization

To be flexible enough to support a wide range of teaching styles while simultaneously providing a solid framework for understanding and enjoying literature, the sixth edition of *The Bedford Introduction to Literature* is organized into four principal parts: Fiction, Poetry, Drama, and Critical Thinking and Writing. The four parts are designed to be taught either in order or separately. Each genre section begins with discussions of literary elements and then moves to a variety of critical approaches, concluding with an extensive collection of literary works. The fourth part provides four detailed chapters on critical thinking, reading, and writing that can be assigned at any point during the course.

Writing about Literature

The book's concern with helping students write about literature is pervasive. The sixth edition of *The Bedford Introduction to Literature* is especially suited for courses in which writing in response to literature is a central component. Seven chapters cover every step of the writing process — from generating topics to documenting sources — and offer advice on different kinds of writing assignments. Two extensive chapters — "Reading and Writing" and "The Literary Research Paper" — discuss and illustrate the writing process while offering models of the different types of papers usually assigned in an introductory course, including explication, analysis, and comparison-contrast. A detailed chapter on the literary research paper, including a student model (with discussion of using and documenting online sources in the most recent MLA style), provides the necessary information for finding, evaluating, and documenting sources.

In addition, three chapters — "Writing about Fiction," "Writing about Poetry," and "Writing about Drama" — focus on genre-specific writing assignments, each with Questions for Responsive reading and Writing along with sample student papers. The first of these chapters, "Writing about Fiction," includes a model of every stage of a student's paper in progress, leading from a reader's initial responses to the final draft. New to this edition are two chapters (10 and 30) combining the elements of literature for fiction and poetry that guide students through the complex process of synthesizing their understanding of how literary elements contribute to the effects and meanings of a work. For fiction the emphasis is on how to develop a thesis for a paper, and for poetry the focus is on writing an explication of a poem.

Also integrated throughout the book are seven "Questions for Writing" units, one on response reading and writing for each genre, one on incorporating outside sources, one on writing about an author covered in depth, one on developing a topic into a revised thesis, and one on applying a critical strategy to a work. Many of these units are illustrated by a sample paper. The book includes a total of fourteen sample papers that provide concrete, accessible models for a wide range of assignments. Students will also find useful a chapter on developing strategies for taking essay examinations assigned in literature courses.

Finally, a new and useful reference chart of all the writing-about-literature features is provided on the front endpapers of the book to help students (and instructors) find the writing advice they need. In sum, this expanded coverage offers a comprehensive overview of writing about literature.

Focus on Critical Reading and Thinking

To encourage the critical reading and thinking that are an integral part of the writing process, advice on how to read imaginative literature appears at the beginning of each genre section. It offers practical advice about the kinds of questions active readers ask themselves as they read. To provoke students' interest, sharpen their thinking, and help them improve their discussion and writing skills, the number and variety of questions related to the readings have been increased in the sixth edition. "First Response" questions can be used as in-class or at-home writing prompts as well as provocative means of generating the kind of critical thinking that promotes class discussion. New to this edition are "Critical Strategies" questions following many of the selections; these questions suggest avenues of critical inquiry for discussion and writing. In addition to the more than two thousand questions that comprise the "Considerations for Critical Thinking and Writing" and "Connections to Other Selections" (questions and suggestions useful for class discussion or writing assignments), the chapter titled "Reading and Writing" describes how to read a work closely, annotate a text, take notes, keep a reading journal, and develop a topic into a thesis. This chapter also includes a section on arguing about literature that discusses how to generate arguments on literary topics and make those arguments persuasive. A list of questions based on the critical approaches covered in the chapter "Critical Strategies for Reading" helps students to discover the significant issues regarding a short story, poem, or play that may be arguable. In addition, an annotated list of important reference sources for literary research is provided.

Selected Major Authors Treated in Depth

For each genre, the book includes chapters focusing on two or more major figures. There are four stories each by Nathaniel Hawthorne, Flannery O'Connor, and Alice Munro; an extensive selection of poems by Emily Dickinson, Robert Frost, and Langston Hughes; and two plays by Sophocles and two by Shakespeare. Substantial introductions provide useful biographical and critical information about each of these important writers, and photographs of the writers help to engage students more fully with the writers' works. A selection of "Perspectives" — excerpts from letters, journals, and critical commentaries — follows each writer's works to provide a context for discussion and writing. In addition, "Considerations for Critical Thinking and Writing" follow both selections and "Perspectives"; these questions for discussion or writing encourage critical thinking and provide stimulating opportunities for student essays.

Also included are chronologies summarizing important dates for the eight major writers featured and complementary critical readings on a particular work by each of the eight authors. These critical readings offer students examples of the variety of approaches they can take in reading and writing about literature. The two readings on Hawthorne, for instance, focus on feminist and psychological approaches to "The Birthmark." By reading commentaries by two critics who argue competing ideas about one text or who illuminate different aspects of that text, students can see immediately that there is no single way to read a work of literature, an important and necessary step for learning how to formulate their own critical approaches in their essays.

Critical, Cultural, and Thematic Case Studies

A "Critical Case Study" chapter in each genre section gathers four or more critical analyses of a single work — such as T. S. Eliot's "The Love Song of J. Alfred Prufrock" — to illustrate the variety of approaches covered in Chapter 52. The questions following these readings encourage students to analyze a particular critical strategy. Included in the critical case study on Ibsen's *A Doll House* is a "Questions for Writing" unit that shows students how to draw on critical approaches in their own writing and features a sample paper.

A "Cultural Case Study" for each genre invites students to practice cultural criticism by using cultural and historical documents to ask new questions of a text. For fiction, the focus is on James Joyce's "Eveline"; for poetry, Julia Alvarez's "Queens, 1963"; and for drama, David Henry Hwang's *M. Butterfly*. The accompanying documents range from photographs and advertisements to interviews, letters, popular arts, and newspaper stories, all followed by questions designed to shed light on the literary work under consideration.

New to this edition is a "Thematic Case Study" for fiction and poetry. In fiction, four stories exploring the nature of storytelling are grouped together to produce important and fascinating insights into fiction. In poetry, poems are clustered around two different themes: poems about love and poems about teaching and learning. These student-friendly chapters invite readers to consider significant themes that cut across literary tradition, culture, and history. At the end of each of the case study chapters (including the authors treated in depth) are new suggested topics for longer papers and research projects that include online documents as well as multimedia sources.

Albums of Contemporary and World Literature

For each genre an album of contemporary selections offers some of the most interesting and lively stories, poems, and plays published in the recent past, including works by E. Annie Proulx, Amy Bloom, Sherman Alexie, Martín Espada, Donald Hall, Billy Collins, Mary Oliver, Wendy Wasserstein, and August Wilson. Biographical information about the album authors is included in the text to introduce instructors and students to these important but, perhaps, unfamiliar writers.

In addition, albums of world literature in each genre section offer students a sampling of stories, poems, and plays from other cultures, including the work of Isabel Allende (Chile), Tadeusz Borowski (Poland), Naguib Mahfouz (Egypt), Claribel Alegría (El Salvador), Octavio Paz (Mexico), Yehuda Amichai (Israel), Tomas Transtromer (Sweden), Vaclav Havel (Czech Republic), and Wole Soyinka (Nigeria), among many others. Half the stories and a third of the poems and plays in this edition are by women and minority writers and writers from other cultures. Related to this multicultural emphasis is a section on poetry in translation in Chapter 22, "Word Choice, Word Order, and Tone." This section presents different versions of poems that help students understand the significance of a translator's choices concerning diction and tone. The translated poems encourage students to explore the nuances of poetic language as well as larger issues related to translation. This is complemented in the fiction section by two translations of a portion of a Chekhov story, and in the drama section by a translation of a scene from *Oedipus the King*.

"Connections to Other Selections" consist of questions that link the selections in the albums of contemporary and world literature to more traditional selections in the text. For example, August Wilson's *The Piano Lesson* is linked with Arthur Miller's *Death of a Salesman* and Ralph Ellison's "Battle Royal," while Wole Soyinka's play *The Strong Breed* is connected to Sophocles' *Oedipus the King*. These questions provide engaging writing opportunities and provocative topics for class discussion. "Connections to Other Selections" questions also appear after most of the works in the chapters on the elements of fiction, poetry, and drama.

Sensible and Useful Coverage of Literary Theory

Chapter 52, "Critical Strategies for Reading," deepens the introductory discussions of active reading by focusing on the different reading strategies employed by contemporary literary theorists. This chapter, which can be assigned at any point in the course, introduces students to a wide variety of major contemporary theoretical approaches — formalist, biographical, psychological, historical (including literary history criticism, Marxist criticism, new historicist criticism, and cultural criticism), gender strategies (including feminist criticism and gay and lesbian criticism), mythological, reader-response, and deconstructionist. In brief examples the approaches are applied in analyzing Kate Chopin's "The Story of an Hour," as well as other works, so that students will have a sense of how to use these strategies in their own reading and writing. A selected bibliography for the approaches and a set of "Perspectives" by contemporary literary critics conclude this important chapter.

Although the emphasis in this text is on critical reading and understanding rather than on critical terminology, terms such as *symbol, irony,* and *metaphor* are defined and illustrated to equip students with a basic working vocabulary for discussing and writing about literature. When first defined in the text, these terms appear in boldface italic type. An "Index of Terms" appears inside the back cover of the book for easy reference, and a "Glossary of Literary Terms" provides thorough explanations of more than two hundred terms central to the study of literature.

Perspectives on Literature

This popular feature consists of 134 "Perspectives" — journal notes, letters, classic and contemporary theoretical essays, interviews, and student responses — useful for class discussion and student writing. "Perspectives" are included in five different places in the text: in the chapters treating major authors in depth; in the three "Critical Case Study" chapters focusing on a particular work in each genre; in the "Cultural Case Study" chapters in each genre; at the end of Chapter 52, on literary theory; and, finally, throughout the text's discussion chapters. Individual "Perspectives" in these chapters follow the works to which they refer and, in many cases, discuss a literary work in terms of the elements of literature for which they serve as illustrations. A variety of "Perspectives" are integrated throughout the book to teach students how to think critically and write effectively about literature.

Connections between "Popular" and "Literary" Culture

As in previous editions, *The Bedford Introduction to Literature,* Sixth Edition, features introductions to each genre section that draw on carefully chosen examples from popular culture to explain the elements of the genre, inviting students to make connections between what they already know and what they will encounter in subsequent selections. Comparisons between popular culture and more canonical literary selections offer excellent writing opportunities, and suggestions are provided after each popular culture example. The examples include excerpts from a romance novel and from *Tarzan of the*

Apes, greeting-card verse, and, new to this edition, Saundra Sharp's rap poem "It's the Law," as well as scenes from a television script for *Seinfeld.*

Resources for Teaching THE BEDFORD INTRODUCTION TO LITERATURE, *Sixth Edition*

This thorough and practical instructor's manual — more than 500 pages long and spiral bound — discusses every selection, suggests responses to many of the questions posed in the text, and provides teaching tips from instructors who have taught from previous editions. The manual also offers questions and writing assignments for the selections in the collection chapter at the end of each genre section. It includes biographical information for authors whose backgrounds are not discussed in the text and offers selected bibliographies for authors treated in depth, as well as a bibliography of articles on teaching literature. The manual also gives several suggestions for teaching thematic units, a list of selections linked by "Connections" questions, and an annotated list of videos, films, and recordings related to the works of literature in the text.

Moreover, additional works of literature from any of Bedford/St. Martin's literary reprint series are available at a special price with *The Bedford Introduction to Literature.* Titles from the highly praised Case Studies in Contemporary Criticism include *The Awakening, The Dead, Death in Venice, Emma, Frankenstein, Great Expectations, Gulliver's Travels, Hamlet, Heart of Darkness, The House of Mirth, Howards End, Jane Eyre, A Portrait of the Artist as a Young Man, The Scarlet Letter, The Secret Sharer, Tess of the D'Urbervilles, The Turn of the Screw, The Wife of Bath,* and *Wuthering Heights.* Volumes from the Bedford Cultural Editions, the Bedford Shakespeare Series, and Case Studies in Critical Controversy include *Adventures of Huckleberry Finn, Benito Cereno, The Blithedale Romance, Clotel, The Commerce of Everyday Life: Selections from THE SPECTATOR and THE TATLER, Death in Venice, Evelina, The First Part of King Henry the Fourth, Life in the Iron-Mills, Oroonoko, The Rape of the Lock, Reading the West: An Anthology of Dime Westerns, The Rime of the Ancient Mariner, The Taming of the Shrew, The Tempest, Three Lives, Twelfth Night,* and *The Yellow Wallpaper.*

Literature Aloud and Videotapes

A CD of selected poems, stories, and scenes is available to instructors who adopt *The Bedford Introduction to Literature,* Sixth Edition. This rich resource for instructors and students offers the voice of literature as read by celebrated writers and actors. A selection of videotapes of plays and short stories are also available to qualified adopters.

Robert Frost: Poems, Life, Legacy

This comprehensive CD-ROM on the life and works of Robert Frost includes searchable text of his poetry, audio performances of Frost reading sixty-nine of his finest poems, over 1,500 pages of biography and literary criticism, and a new documentary film narrated by Richard Wilbur. It is available to qualified adopters of *The Bedford Introduction to Literature.*

Acknowledgments

This book has benefited from the ideas, suggestions, and corrections of scores of careful readers who helped transform various stages of an evolving manuscript into a finished book and into subsequent editions. I remain grateful to those I have thanked in previous prefaces, particularly the late Robert Wallace of Case Western Reserve University. In addition, many instructors who used the fifth edition of *The Bedford Introduction to Literature* responded to a questionnaire on the book. For their valuable comments and advice I am grateful to Alan K. Bickford, Macon State College; Betsy A. Bowen, Fairfield University; Elizabeth Breen, Pierce College; Stephen C. Brennan, Louisiana State University; Jon W. Brooks, Okaloosa-Walton Community College; Robin Calitri, Merced College; Cynthia Cox, Belmont University; Charles Fisher, Aims Community College; Claire Kamasaki, Middlesex Community College; David McDowell, Anne Arundel Community College; Jim Read, Allan Hancock College; David A. Salomon, Black Hills State University; Pam Sutton, Union University; Jack E. Trotter, Trident Technical College; Kellie Wells, Georgia College and State University; and Arthur G. Wemple, Bloomsburg University.

I would also like to give special thanks to the following instructors who have contributed teaching tips to *Resources for Teaching THE BEDFORD INTRODUCTION TO LITERATURE:* Sandra Adickes, Winona State University; Helen J. Aling, Northwestern College; Sr. Anne Denise Brennan, College of Mt. St. Vincent; Robin Calitri, Merced College; James H. Clemmer, Austin Peay State University; Robert Croft, Gainesville College; Thomas Edwards, Westbrook College; Elizabeth Kleinfeld, Red Rocks Community College; Olga Lyles, University of Nevada; Timothy Peters, Boston University; Catherine Rusco, Muskegon Community College; Robert M. St. John, De Paul University; Richard Stoner, Broome Community College; Nancy Veiga, Modesto Junior College; Karla Walters, University of New Mexico; and Joseph Zeppetello, Ulster Community College.

I am also indebted to those who cheerfully answered questions and generously provided miscellaneous bits of information. What might have seemed to them like inconsequential conversations turned out to be important leads. Among these friends and colleagues are Raymond Anselment, Ann Charters, Karen Chow, John Christie, Eleni Coundouriotis, Irving Cummings, William Curtin, Patrick Hogan, Lee Jacobus, Thomas Jambeck, Bonnie Januszewski-Ytuarte, Greta Little, George Monteiro, Brenda Murphy, Joel Myerson, Thomas Recchio, William Sheidley, Stephanie Smith, Milton Stern, Kenneth Wilson, and the dedicated reference librarians at the Homer Babbidge Library, University of Connecticut.

I continue to be grateful for what I have learned from teaching my students and for the many student papers I have received over the years that I have used in various forms to serve as good and accessible models of student writing. I am also indebted to Julie Nash and Jill McDonough for their extensive work on the sixth edition of *Resources for Teaching THE BEDFORD INTRODUCTION TO LITERATURE*.

At Bedford/St. Martin's, my debts once again require more time to acknowledge than the deadline allows. Charles H. Christensen and Joan E. Feinberg initiated this project and launched it with their intelligence, energy, and sound advice. Karen Henry, Kathy Retan, and Alanya Harter tirelessly steered earlier editions through rough as well as becalmed moments; their work was as first-rate as it was essential. Aron Keesbury splendidly carried on that tradition as developmental editor for this edition; his solid contributions and poetic sensibilities made this project both a success and a pleasure. Editorial assistant Josh Levy, with the help of Donna Ashley, oversaw *Resources for Teaching THE BEDFORD INTRODUCTION TO LITERATURE* with clearheaded intelligence, meticulous attention, and welcome enthusiasm. He also handily juggled a variety of other tasks, including reviewing, researching, preparing the indexes, and developing the audio CD that accompanies the text, *Lit. Aloud*. Amy Thomas shared the Herculean labor of clearing permissions with the unflappable Arthur Johnson. The difficult tasks of production were skillfully managed by Stasia Zomkowski, whose attention to details and deadlines was essential to the completion of this project. She was ably assisted by Kerri Cardone. Jane Zanichkowsky provided careful copyediting, and Janet Cocker and Mary Lou Wilshaw-Watts proofread. Numerous other people at Bedford Books — including Amanda Bristow and Donna Lee Dennison — helped to make this enormous project a manageable one.

Finally, I am grateful to my sons Timothy and Matthew for all kinds of help, but mostly I'm just grateful they're my sons. And always for making all the difference, I dedicate this book to my wife, Regina Barreca.

Brief Contents

Contents

POETRY   667

The Elements of Poetry   669

24. Figures of Speech   777

25. Symbol, Allegory, and Irony 801

Symbol 801

Allegory 803

Irony 806

Poems for Further Study 810

26. Sounds 832

Listening to Poetry 832

ANONYMOUS, *Scarborough Fair* 833
JOHN UPDIKE, *Player Piano* 834
MAY SWENSON, *A Nosty Fright* 835
EMILY DICKINSON, *A Bird came down the Walk—* 836
GALWAY KINNELL, *Blackberry Eating* 838

Rhyme 839

RICHARD ARMOUR, *Going to Extremes* 839
ROBERT SOUTHEY, *From "The Cataract of Lodore"* 839
PERSPECTIVE: DAVID LENSON, *On the Contemporary Use of Rhyme* 842

Sound and Meaning 843

GERARD MANLEY HOPKINS, *God's Grandeur* 843

Poems for Further Study 845

EDGAR ALLAN POE, *The Bells* 845
PAULA GUNN ALLEN, *Hoop Dancer* 847
LEWIS CARROLL [Charles Lutwidge Dodgson], *Jabberwocky* 848
SYLVIA PLATH, *Mushrooms* 849
WILLIAM HEYEN, *The Trains* 850
VIRGINIA HAMILTON ADAIR, *Dirty Old Man* 851
JOHN DONNE, *Song* 851
MONA VAN DUYN, *What the Motorcycle Said* 852
ALEXANDER POPE, *From An Essay on Criticism* 853
GWENDOLYN BROOKS, *Sadie and Maud* 855
MAXINE HONG KINGSTON, *Restaurant* 855
PAUL HUMPHREY, *Blow* 856
ROBERT FRANCIS, *The Pitcher* 857
HELEN CHASIN, *The Word* Plum 857
JOHN KEATS, *Ode to a Nightingale* 858
PERSPECTIVE: DYLAN THOMAS, *On the Words in Poetry* 861

27. Patterns of Rhythm 863

Some Principles of Meter 863

WALT WHITMAN, *From "Song of the Open Road"* 864
WILLIAM WORDSWORTH, *My Heart Leaps Up* 867

Suggestions for Scanning a Poem 868

TIMOTHY STEELE, *Waiting for the Storm* 868
WILLIAM BUTLER YEATS, *That the Night Come* 869

Poems for Further Study 870

ALICE JONES, *The Foot* 870
A. E. HOUSMAN, *When I was one-and-twenty* 871
NIKKI GIOVANNI, *Clouds* 872

28. Poetic Forms 885

Some Common Poetic Forms 885

Sonnet 888

Villanelle 894

Sestina 896

Epigram 899

Limerick 900

Haiku 902

33. A Study of Langston Hughes 1032

34. A Critical Case Study: T. S. Eliot's "The Love Song of J. Alfred Prufrock" 1067

35. A Cultural Case Study: Julia Alvarez's "Queens, 1963" 1084

39. An Album of World Literature 1198

40. An Album of Contemporary Poems 1211

DRAMA 1231
The Study of Drama 1233

41. Reading Drama 1235

Reading Drama Responsively 1235

Elements of Drama 1250

Drama in Popular Forms 1261

42. Writing about Drama 1275

From Reading to Writing 1275
Questions for Responsive Reading and Writing 1276

43. A Study of Sophocles 1282

Chronology 1283

Theatrical Conventions of Greek Drama 1283

A Collection of Plays   1727

INTRODUCTION
Reading
Imaginative Literature

THE NATURE OF LITERATURE

Literature does not lend itself to a single tidy definition because the making of it over the centuries has been as complex, unwieldy, and natural as life itself. Is literature everything that has been written, from ancient prayers to graffiti? Does it include songs and stories that were not written down until many years after they were recited? Does literature include the television scripts from *Seinfeld* as well as Shakespeare's *King Lear*? Is literature only writing that has permanent value and continues to move people? Must literature be true or beautiful or moral? Should it be socially useful?

Although these kinds of questions are not conclusively answered in this book, they are implicitly raised by the stories, poems, and plays included here. No definition of literature, particularly a brief one, is likely to satisfy everyone because definitions tend to weaken and require qualification when confronted by the uniqueness of individual works. In this context it is worth recalling Herman Melville's humorous use of a definition of a whale in *Moby-Dick* (1851). In the course of the novel Melville presents his imaginative and symbolic whale as inscrutable, but he begins with a quotation from Georges Cuvier, a French naturalist who defines a whale in his nineteenth-century study *The Animal Kingdom* this way: "The whale is a mammiferous animal without hind feet." Cuvier's description is technically correct, of course, but there is little wisdom in it. Melville understood that the reality of the whale (which he describes as the "ungraspable phantom of life") cannot be caught by isolated facts. If the full meaning of the whale is to be understood, it must be sought on the open sea of experience, where the whale itself is, rather than in exclusionary definitions. Facts and definitions are helpful; however, they do not always reveal the whole truth.

Despite Melville's reminder that a definition can be too limiting and even comical, it is useful for our purposes to describe literature as a fiction consisting of carefully arranged words designed to stir the imagination. Stories, poems, and plays are fictional. They are made up — imagined — even when based on actual historic events. Such imaginative writing differs from other kinds of writing because its purpose is not primarily to transmit facts or ideas. Imaginative literature is a source more of pleasure than of information, and we read it for basically the same reasons we listen to music or view a dance: enjoyment, delight, and satisfaction. Like other art forms, imaginative literature offers pleasure and usually attempts to convey a perspective, mood, feeling, or experience. Writers transform the facts the world provides — people, places, and objects — into experiences that suggest meanings.

Consider, for example, the difference between the following factual description of a snake and a poem on the same subject. Here is *Webster's Tenth New Collegiate Dictionary* definition:

> any of numerous limbless scaled reptiles (suborder Serpentes syn. Ophidia) with a long tapering body and with salivary glands often modified to produce venom which is injected through grooved or tubular fangs.

Contrast this matter-of-fact definition with Emily Dickinson's poetic evocation of a snake in "A narrow Fellow in the Grass":

> A narrow Fellow in the Grass
> Occasionally rides —
> You may have met Him — did you not
> His notice sudden is —
>
> The Grass divides as with a Comb —   5
> A spotted shaft is seen —
> And then it closes at your feet
> And opens further on —
>
> He likes a Boggy Acre
> A floor too cool for Corn —   10
> Yet when a Boy, and Barefoot —
> I more than once at Noon
> Have passed, I thought, a Whip lash
> Unbraiding in the Sun
> When stooping to secure it   15
> It wrinkled, and was gone —
>
> Several of Nature's People
> I know, and they know me —
> I feel for them a transport
> Of cordiality —   20
>
> But never met this Fellow
> Attended, or alone
> Without a tighter breathing
> And Zero at the Bone —

The dictionary provides a succinct, anatomical description of what a snake is, while Dickinson's poem suggests what a snake can mean. The definition offers facts; the poem offers an experience. The dictionary would probably allow someone who had never seen a snake to sketch one with reasonable accuracy. The poem also provides some vivid subjective descriptions — for example, the snake dividing the grass "as with a Comb" — yet it offers more than a picture of serpentine movements. The poem conveys the ambivalence many people have about snakes — the kind of feeling, for example, so evident on the faces of visitors viewing the snakes at a zoo. In the poem there is both a fascination with and a horror of what might be called snakehood; this combination of feelings has been coiled in most of us since Adam and Eve.

That "narrow Fellow" so cordially introduced by way of a riddle (the word *snake* is never used in the poem) is, by the final stanza, revealed as a snake in the grass. In between, Dickinson uses language expressively to convey her meaning. For instance, in the line "His notice sudden is," listen to the *s* sound in each word and note how the verb *is* unexpectedly appears at the end, making the snake's hissing presence all the more "sudden." And anyone who has ever been surprised by a snake knows the "tighter breathing / And Zero at the Bone" that Dickinson evokes so successfully by the rhythm of her word choices and line breaks. Perhaps even more significant, Dickinson's poem allows those who have never encountered a snake to imagine such an experience.

A good deal more could be said about the numbing fear that undercuts the affection for nature at the beginning of this poem, but the point here is that imaginative literature gives us not so much the full, factual proportions of the world as some of its experiences and meanings. Instead of defining the world, literature encourages us to try it out in our imaginations.

THE VALUE OF LITERATURE

Mark Twain once shrewdly observed that a person who chooses not to read has no advantage over a person who is unable to read. In industrialized societies today, however, the question is not who reads, because nearly everyone can and does, but what is read. Why should anyone spend precious time with literature when there is so much reading material available that provides useful information about everything from the daily news to personal computers? Why should a literary artist's imagination compete for attention that could be spent on the firm realities that constitute everyday life? In fact, national best-seller lists much less often include collections of stories, poems, or plays than they do cookbooks and, not surprisingly, diet books. Although such fare may be filling, it doesn't stay with you. Most people have other appetites too.

Certainly one of the most important values of literature is that it nourishes our emotional lives. An effective literary work may seem to speak directly to us, especially if we are ripe for it. The inner life that good writers reveal in their characters often gives us glimpses of some portion of ourselves. We can be moved to laugh, cry, tremble, dream, ponder, shriek, or rage with a character by simply turning a page instead of turning our lives upside down. Although the experience itself is imagined, the emotion is real. That's why the final chapters of a good adventure novel can make a reader's heart race as much as a 100-yard dash or why the repressed love of Hester Prynne in *The Scarlet Letter* by Nathaniel Hawthorne is painful to a sympathetic reader. Human emotions speak a universal language regardless of when or where a work was written.

In addition to appealing to our emotions, literature broadens our perspectives on the world. Most of the people we meet are pretty much like ourselves, and what we can see of the world even in a lifetime is astonishingly limited. Literature allows us to move beyond the inevitable boundaries of our own lives and culture because it introduces us to people different from ourselves, places remote from our neighborhoods, and times other than our own. Reading makes us more aware of life's possibilities as well as its subtleties and ambiguities. Put simply, people who read literature experience more life and have a keener sense of a common human identity than those who do not. It is true, of course, that many people go through life without reading imaginative literature, but that is a loss rather than a gain. They may find themselves troubled by the same kinds of questions that reveal Daisy Buchanan's restless, vague discontentment in F. Scott Fitzgerald's *The Great Gatsby:* "What'll we do with ourselves this afternoon?" cried Daisy, "and the day after that, and the next thirty years?"

Sometimes students mistakenly associate literature more with school than with life. Accustomed to reading it in order to write a paper or pass an examination, students may perceive such reading as a chore instead of a pleasurable opportunity, something considerably less important than studying for the "practical" courses that prepare them for a career. The study of literature, however, is also practical because it engages you in the kinds of problem solving important in a variety of fields, from philosophy to science and technology. The interpretation of literary texts requires you to deal with uncertainties, value judgments, and emotions; these are unavoidable aspects of life.

People who make the most significant contributions to their professions — whether in business, engineering, teaching, or some other area — tend to be challenged rather than threatened by multiple possibilities. Instead of retreating to the way things have always been done, they bring freshness and creativity to their work. F. Scott Fitzgerald once astutely described the "test of a first-rate intelligence" as "the ability to hold two opposed ideas in the mind at the same time, and still retain the ability to function." People with such intelligence know how to read situations, shape questions, interpret details, and evaluate competing points of view.

Equipped with a healthy respect for facts, they also understand the value of pursuing hunches and exercising their imaginations. Reading literature encourages a suppleness of mind that is helpful in any discipline or work.

Once the requirements for your degree are completed, what ultimately matters are not the courses listed on your transcript but the sensibilities and habits of mind that you bring to your work, friends, family, and, indeed, the rest of your life. A healthy economy changes and grows with the times; people do too if they are prepared for more than simply filling a job description. The range and variety of life that literature affords can help you to interpret your own experiences and the world in which you live.

To discover the insights that literature reveals requires careful reading and sensitivity. One of the purposes of a college introduction to literature class is to cultivate the analytic skills necessary for reading well. Class discussions often help establish a dialogue with a work that perhaps otherwise would not speak to you. Analytic skills can also be developed by writing about what you read. Writing is an effective means of clarifying your responses and ideas because it requires you to account for the author's use of language as well as your own. This book is based on two premises: that reading literature is pleasurable and that reading and understanding a work sensitively by thinking, talking, or writing about it increase the pleasure of the experience of it.

Understanding its basic elements — such as point of view, symbol, theme, tone, irony, and so on — is a prerequisite to an informed appreciation of literature. This kind of understanding allows you to perceive more in a literary work in much the same way that a spectator at a tennis match sees more if he or she understands the rules and conventions of the game. But literature is not simply a spectator sport. The analytic skills that open up literature also have their uses when you watch a television program or film and, more important, when you attempt to sort out the significance of the people, places, and events that constitute your own life. Literature enhances and sharpens your perceptions. What could be more lastingly practical as well as satisfying?

THE CHANGING LITERARY CANON

Perhaps the best reading creates some kind of change in us: we see more clearly; we're alert to nuances; we ask questions that previously didn't occur to us. Henry David Thoreau had that sort of reading in mind when he remarked in *Walden* that the books he valued most were those that caused him to date "a new era in his life from the reading." Readers are sometimes changed by literature, but it is also worth noting that the life of a literary work can also be affected by its readers. Melville's *Moby-Dick,* for example, was not valued as a classic until the 1920s, when critics rescued the novel from the obscurity of being cataloged in many libraries (including Yale's) not under fiction but under cetology, the study of whales. Indeed, many writers contemporary to Melville who were important and popular in the nineteenth century — William Cullen Bryant, Henry Wadsworth Longfellow, and James Russell Lowell, to name a few — are now mostly unread; their names appear more often on elementary schools built early in this century than in anthologies. Clearly, literary reputations and what is valued as great literature change over time and in the eyes of readers.

Such changes have accelerated during the past thirty years as the literary *canon* — those works considered by scholars, critics, and teachers to be the most important to read and study — has undergone a significant series of shifts. Writers who previously were overlooked, undervalued, neglected, or studiously ignored have been brought into focus in an effort to create a more diverse literary canon, one that recognizes the contributions of the many cultures that make up American society. Since the 1960s, for example, some critics have reassessed writings by women who had been left out of the standard literary traditions dominated by male writers. Many more female writers are now read alongside the male writers who traditionally populated literary history. Hence, a reader of Mark Twain and Stephen Crane is now just as likely to encounter Kate Chopin in a literary anthology. Until fairly recently Chopin was mostly regarded as a minor local colorist of Louisiana life. In the 1960s, however, the feminist movement helped to establish her present reputation as a significant voice in American literature owing to the feminist concerns so compellingly articulated by her female characters. This kind of enlargement of the canon also resulted from another reform movement of the 1960s. The civil rights movement sensitized literary critics to the political, moral, and aesthetic necessity of rediscovering African American literature, and more recently Asian and Hispanic writers have been making their way into the canon. Moreover, on a broader scale the canon is being revised and enlarged to include the works of writers from parts of the world other than the West, a development that reflects the changing values, concerns, and complexities of the past several years, when literary landscapes have shifted as dramatically as the political boundaries of Eastern Europe and the former Soviet Union.

No semester's reading list — or anthology — can adequately or accurately echo all the new voices competing to be heard as part of the mainstream literary canon, but recent efforts to open up the canon attempt to sensitize readers to the voices of women, minorities, and writers from all over the world. This development has not occurred without its urgent advocates or passionate dissenters. It's no surprise that issues about race, gender, and class often get people off the fence and on their feet (these controversies are discussed further in Chapter 52, "Critical Strategies for Reading"). Although what we regard as literature — whether it's called great, classic, or canonical — continues to generate debate, there is no question that such controversy will continue to reflect readers' values as well as the writers they admire.

FICTION

FICTION

The Elements
of Fiction

1

Reading Fiction

READING FICTION RESPONSIVELY

Reading a literary work responsively can be an intensely demanding activity. Henry David Thoreau — about as intense and demanding a reader and writer as they come — insists that "books must be read as deliberately and reservedly as they were written." Thoreau is right about the necessity for a conscious, sustained involvement with a literary work. Imaginative literature does demand more from us than, say, browsing through *People* magazine in a dentist's waiting room, but Thoreau makes the process sound a little more daunting than it really is. For when we respond to the demands of responsive reading, our efforts are usually rewarded with pleasure as well as understanding. Careful, deliberate reading — the kind that engages a reader's imagination as it calls forth the writer's — is a means of exploration that can take a reader outside whatever circumstance or experience previously defined his or her world. Just as we respond moment by moment to people and situations in our lives, we also respond to literary works as we read them, though we may not be fully aware of how we are affected at each point along the way. The more conscious we are of how and why we respond to works in particular ways, the more likely we are to be imaginatively engaged in our reading.

In a very real sense both the reader and the author create the literary work. How a reader responds to a story, poem, or play will help to determine its meaning. The author arranges the various elements that constitute his or her craft — elements such as plot, character, setting, point of view, symbolism, theme, and style, which you will be examining in subsequent chapters and which are defined in the Glossary of Literary Terms (p. 2190) — but the author cannot completely control the reader's response any more than a person can absolutely predict how a remark or action will be received by a stranger, a friend, or even a family member. Few authors *tell* readers how to respond. Our sympathy, anger, confusion, laughter, sadness, or whatever the feeling might be is left up to us to experience. Writers may have the talent to evoke such feelings, but they don't have the power and authority to enforce them. Because of the range of possible responses produced by imaginative literature, there is no single, correct, definitive response or interpretation. There can be readings that are wrongheaded or foolish, and some readings are better than others — that is, more responsive to a work's details and more persuasive — but that doesn't mean there is only one possible reading of a work (see Chapter 2, "Writing about Fiction").

Experience tells us that different people respond differently to the same work. Consider, for example, how often you've heard Melville's *Moby-Dick* described as one of the greatest American novels. This, however, is how a reviewer in *New Monthly Magazine* described the book when it was published in 1851: it is "a huge dose of hyperbolical slang, maudlin sentimentalism and tragic-comic bubble and squeak." Melville surely did not intend or desire this response; but there it is, and it was not a singular, isolated reaction. This reading — like any reading — was influenced by the values, assumptions, and expectations that the readers brought to the novel from both previous readings and life experiences. The reviewer's refusal to take the book seriously may have caused him to miss the boat from the perspective of many other readers of *Moby-Dick,* but it indicates that even "classics" (perhaps especially those kinds of works) can generate disparate readings.

Consider the following brief story by Kate Chopin, a writer whose fiction (like Melville's) sometimes met with indifference or hostility in her own time. As you read, keep track of your responses to the central character, Mrs. Mallard. Write down your feelings about her in a substantial paragraph when you finish the story. Think, for example, about how you respond to the emotions she expresses concerning news of her husband's death. What do you think of her feelings about marriage? Do you think you would react the way she does under similar circumstances?

KATE CHOPIN (1851–1904)

Web *Research Kate Chopin with LitLinks at*
http://www.bedfordstmartins.com/meyer/bedintrolit

The Story of an Hour   1894

Knowing that Mrs. Mallard was afflicted with a heart trouble, great care was taken to break to her as gently as possible the news of her husband's death.

It was her sister Josephine who told her, in broken sentences; veiled hints that revealed in half concealing. Her husband's friend Richards was there, too, near her. It was he who had been in the newspaper office when intelligence of the railroad disaster was received, with Brently Mallard's name leading the list of "killed." He had only taken the time to assure himself of its truth by a second telegram, and had hastened to forestall any less careful, less tender friend in bearing the sad message.

She did not hear the story as many women have heard the same, with a paralyzed inability to accept its significance. She wept at once, with sudden, wild abandonment, in her sister's arms. When the storm of grief had spent itself she went away to her room alone. She would have no one follow her.

There stood, facing the open window, a comfortable, roomy armchair. Into this she sank, pressed down by a physical exhaustion that haunted her body and seemed to reach into her soul.

She could see in the open square before her house the tops of trees that were all aquiver with the new spring life. The delicious breath of rain was in the air. In the street below a peddler was crying his wares. The notes of a distant song which some one was singing reached her faintly, and countless sparrows were twittering in the eaves.

There were patches of blue sky showing here and there through the clouds that had met and piled one above the other in the west facing her window.

She sat with her head thrown back upon the cushion of the chair, quite motionless, except when a sob came up into her throat and shook her, as a child who has cried itself to sleep continues to sob in its dreams.

She was young, with a fair, calm face, whose lines bespoke repression and even a certain strength. But now there was a dull stare in her eyes, whose gaze was fixed away off yonder on one of those patches of blue sky. It was not a glance of reflection, but rather indicated a suspension of intelligent thought.

There was something coming to her and she was waiting for it, fearfully. What was it? She did not know; it was too subtle and elusive to name. But she felt it, creeping out of the sky, reaching toward her through the sounds, the scents, the color that filled the air.

Now her bosom rose and fell tumultuously. She was beginning to recognize this thing that was approaching to possess her, and she was striving to beat it back with her will—as powerless as her two white slender hands would have been.

When she abandoned herself a little whispered word escaped her slightly parted lips. She said it over and over under her breath: "free, free, free!" The vacant stare and the look of terror that had followed it went from her eyes. They stayed keen and bright. Her pulses beat fast, and the coursing blood warmed and relaxed every inch of her body.

She did not stop to ask if it were or were not a monstrous joy that held her. A clear and exalted perception enabled her to dismiss the suggestion as trivial.

She knew that she would weep again when she saw the kind, tender hands folded in death; the face that had never looked save with love upon her, fixed and gray and dead. But she saw beyond that bitter moment a long procession of years to come that would belong to her absolutely. And she opened and spread her arms out to them in welcome.

There would be no one to live for her during those coming years; she would live for herself. There would be no powerful will bending hers in that blind persistence with which men and women believe they have a right to impose a private will upon a fellow-creature. A kind intention or a cruel intention made the act seem no less a crime as she looked upon it in that brief moment of illumination.

And yet she had loved him — sometimes. Often she had not. What did it 15
matter! What could love, the unsolved mystery, count for in face of this possession of self-assertion which she suddenly recognized as the strongest impulse of her being!

"Free! Body and soul free!" she kept whispering.

Josephine was kneeling before the closed door with her lips to the keyhole,
imploring for admission. "Louise, open the door! I beg; open the door — you
will make yourself ill. What are you doing, Louise? For heaven's sake open the
door."

"Go away. I am not making myself ill." No; she was drinking in a very elixir
of life through that open window.

Her fancy was running riot along those days ahead of her. Spring days,
and summer days, and all sorts of days that would be her own. She breathed a
quick prayer that life might be long. It was only yesterday she had thought
with a shudder that life might be long.

She arose at length and opened the door to her sister's importunities. 20
There was a feverish triumph in her eyes, and she carried herself unwittingly
like a goddess of Victory. She clasped her sister's waist, and together they descended the stairs. Richards stood waiting for them at the bottom.

Some one was opening the front door with a latchkey. It was Brently Mallard who entered, a little travel-stained, composedly carrying his gripsack and
umbrella. He had been far from the scene of accident, and did not even know
there had been one. He stood amazed at Josephine's piercing cry; at Richards'
quick motion to screen him from the view of his wife.

But Richards was too late.

When the doctors came they said she had died of heart disease — of joy
that kills.

Did you find Mrs. Mallard a sympathetic character? Some readers think
that she is callous, selfish, and unnatural — even monstrous — because she
ecstatically revels in her newly discovered sense of freedom so soon after
learning of her husband's presumed death. Others read her as a victim of
her inability to control her own life in a repressive, male-dominated society.
Is it possible to hold both views simultaneously, or are they mutually exclusive? Are your views in any way influenced by your being male or female?
Does your age affect your perception? What about your social and economic background? Does your nationality, race, or religion in any way
shape your attitudes? Do you have particular views about the institution of
marriage that inform your assessment of Mrs. Mallard's character? Have
other reading experiences — perhaps a familiarity with some of Chopin's
other stories — predisposed you one way or another to Mrs. Mallard?

Understanding potential influences might be useful in determining
whether a particular response to Mrs. Mallard is based primarily on the
story's details and their arrangement or on an overt or subtle bias that
is brought to the story. If you unconsciously project your beliefs and
assumptions onto a literary work, you run the risk of distorting it to
accommodate your prejudice. Your feelings can be a reliable guide to interpretation, but you should be aware of what those feelings are based on.

Often specific questions about literary works cannot be answered definitively. For example, Chopin does not explain why Mrs. Mallard suffers a heart attack at the end of this story. Is the shock of seeing her "dead" husband simply too much for this woman "afflicted with a heart trouble"? Does she die of what the doctors call a "joy that kills" because she is so glad to see her husband? Is she so profoundly guilty about feeling "free" at her husband's expense that she has a heart attack? Is her death a kind of willed suicide in reaction to her loss of freedom? Your answers to these questions will depend on which details you emphasize in your interpretation of the story and the kinds of perspectives and values you bring to it. If, for example, you read the story from a feminist perspective, you would be likely to pay close attention to Chopin's comments about marriage in paragraph 14. Or if you read the story as an oblique attack on the insensitivity of physicians of the period, you might want to find out whether Chopin wrote elsewhere about doctors (she did) and compare her comments with historic sources. (A number of "Critical Strategies for Reading," including feminist and historical approaches, appear in Chapter 52.)

Reading responsively makes you an active participant in the process of creating meaning in a literary work. The experience that you and the author create will most likely not be identical to another reader's encounter with the same work, but then that's true of nearly any experience you'll have, and it is part of the pleasure of reading. Indeed, talking and writing about literature is a way of sharing responses so that they can be enriched and deepened.

A SAMPLE PAPER

Differences in Responses to Kate Chopin's "The Story of an Hour"

The following paper was written in response to an assignment that called for a three- to four-page discussion of how different readers might interpret Mrs. Mallard's character. The paper is based on the story as well as on the discussion of reader-response criticism (pp. 2109–11) in Chapter 52, "Critical Strategies for Reading." As that discussion indicates, reader-response criticism is a critical approach that focuses on the reader rather than on the work itself in order to describe how the reader creates meaning from the text.

Wally Villa
Professor Brian
English 210
March 12, 20--

Differences in Responses to
Kate Chopin's "The Story of an Hour"

Kate Chopin's "The Story of an Hour" appears merely
to explore a woman's unpredictable reaction to her husband's assumed death and reappearance, but actually Chopin
offers Mrs. Mallard's bizarre story to reveal problems
that are inherent in the institution of marriage. By offering this depiction of a marriage that stifles the woman
to the point that she celebrates the death of her kind and
loving husband, Chopin challenges her readers to examine
their own views of marriage and relationships between men
and women. Each reader's judgment of Mrs. Mallard and her
behavior inevitably stems from his or her own personal
feelings about marriage and the influences of societal
expectations. Readers of differing genders, ages, and
marital experiences are, therefore, likely to react differently to Chopin's startling portrayal of the Mallards'
marriage, and that certainly is true of my response to
the story compared to my father's and grandmother's
responses.

 Marriage often establishes boundaries between people
that make them unable to communicate with each other. The
Mallards' marriage was evidently crippled by both their
inability to talk to one another and Mrs. Mallard's conviction that her marriage was defined by a "powerful will
bending hers in that blind persistence with which men and
women believe they have a right to impose a private will
upon a fellow-creature." Yet she does not recognize that
it is not just men who impose their will upon women and

that the problems inherent in marriage affect men and women
equally. To me, Mrs. Mallard is a somewhat sympathetic
character, and I appreciate her longing to live out the
"years to come that would belong to her absolutely." However, I also believe that she could have tried to improve
her own situation somehow, either by reaching out to her
husband or by abandoning the marriage altogether. Chopin
uses Mrs. Mallard's tragedy to illuminate aspects of marriage that are harmful and, in this case, even deadly.
Perhaps the Mallards' relationship should be taken as a
warning to others: sacrificing one's own happiness in order
to satisfy societal expectations can poison one's life and
even destroy entire families.

  When my father read "The Story of an Hour," his reaction to Mrs. Mallard was more antagonistic than my own. He
sees Chopin's story as a timeless "battle of the sexes,"
serving as further proof that men will never really be able
to understand what it is that women want. Mrs. Mallard
endures an obviously unsatisfying marriage without ever
explaining to her husband that she feels trapped and unfulfilled. Mrs. Mallard dismisses the question of whether or
not she is experiencing a "monstrous joy" as trivial, but
my father does not think that this is a trivial question.
He believes Mrs. Mallard is guilty of a monstrous joy because she selfishly celebrates the death of her husband
without ever allowing him the opportunity to understand her
feelings. He believes that, above all, Brently Mallard
should be seen as the most victimized character in the
story. Mr. Mallard is a good, kind man, with friends who
care about him and a marriage that he thinks he can depend
on. He "never looked save with love" upon his wife, his
only "crime" was coming home from work one day, and yet he
is the one who is bereaved at the end of the story, for

reasons he will never understand. Mrs. Mallard's passion
for her newly discovered freedom is perhaps understandable, but according to my father, Mr. Mallard is the character most deserving of sympathy.

Maybe not surprisingly, my grandmother's interpretation of "The Story of an Hour" was radically different
from both mine and my father's. My grandmother was married
in 1936 and widowed in 1959 and therefore can identify
with Chopin's characters, who live at the turn of the century. Her first reaction, aside from her unwavering support for Mrs. Mallard and her predicament, was that this
story demonstrates the differences between the ways men
and women related to each other a century ago and the way
they relate today. Unlike my father, who thinks Mrs. Mallard is too passive, my grandmother believes that Mrs.
Mallard doesn't even know that she is feeling repressed
until after she is told that Brently is dead. In 1894,
divorce was so scandalous and stigmatized that it simply
wouldn't have been an option for Mrs. Mallard, and so her
only way "out" of the marriage would have been one of
their deaths. Being relatively young, Mrs. Mallard probably considered herself doomed to a long life in an unhappy
marriage. My grandmother also feels that, in spite of all
we know of Mrs. Mallard's feelings about her husband and
her marriage, she still manages to live up to everyone's
expectations of her as a woman both in life and in death.
She is a dutiful wife to Brently, as she is expected to
be, she weeps "with sudden, wild abandonment" when she
hears the news of his death, she locks herself in her room
to cope with her new situation, and she has a fatal heart
attack upon seeing her husband arrive home. Naturally the
male doctors would think that she died of the "joy that
kills"; nobody could have guessed that she was unhappy

Villa 4

with her life, and she would never have wanted them to
know.

    Interpretations of "The Story of an Hour" seem to
vary according to the gender, age, and experience of the
reader. While both male and female readers can certainly
sympathize with Mrs. Mallard's plight, female readers--as
was evident in our class discussions--seem to relate more
easily to her predicament and are quicker to exonerate her
of any responsibility for her unhappy situation. Conversely, male readers are more likely to feel compassion
for Mr. Mallard, who loses his wife for reasons that will
always remain entirely unknown to him. Older readers probably understand more readily the strength of social forces
and the difficulty of trying to deny societal expectations
concerning gender roles in general and marriage in particular. Younger readers seem to feel that Mrs. Mallard is too
passive and that she could have improved her domestic life
immeasurably if she had taken the initiative to either improve or end her relationship with her husband. Ultimately,
how each individual reader responds to Mrs. Mallard's story
reveals his or her own ideas about marriage, society, and
how men and women communicate with each other.

    Before beginning your own writing assignment on fiction, you should review Chapter 2, "Writing about Fiction," as well as Chapter 53, "Reading and Writing," which provides a step-by-step explanation of how to choose a topic, develop a thesis, and organize various types of writing assignments. If you use outside sources, you should also be familiar with the conventional documentation procedures described in Chapter 54, "The Literary Research Paper."

EXPLORATIONS AND FORMULAS

Each time we pick up a work of fiction, go to the theater, or turn on the television, we have a trace of the same magical expectation that can be heard in the voice of a child who begs, "Tell me a story." Human beings have enjoyed stories ever since they learned to speak. Whatever the motive for creating stories — even if simply to delight or instruct — the basic human impulse to tell and hear stories existed long before the development of written language. Myths about the origins of the world and legends about the heroic exploits of demigods were among the earliest forms of storytelling to develop into oral traditions, which were eventually written down. These narratives are the ancestors of the stories we read on the printed page today. Unlike the early listeners to ancient myths and legends, we read our stories silently, but the pleasure derived from the mysterious power of someone else's artfully arranged words remains largely the same. Every one of us likes a good story.

The stories that appear in anthologies for college students are generally chosen for their high literary quality. Such stories can affect us at the deepest emotional level, reveal new insights into ourselves or the world, and stretch us by exercising our imaginations. They warrant careful reading and close study to appreciate the art that has gone into creating them. The following chapters on plot, character, setting, and the other elements of literature are designed to provide the terms and concepts that can help you understand how a work of fiction achieves its effects and meanings. It is worth acknowledging, however, that many people buy and read fiction that is quite different from the stories usually anthologized in college texts. What about all those paperbacks with exciting, colorful covers near the cash registers in shopping malls and corner drugstores?

These books, known as *formula fiction,* are the adventure, western, detective, science fiction, and romance novels that entertain millions of readers annually. What makes them so popular? What do their characters, plots, and themes offer readers that accounts for the tremendous sales of stories with titles like *Caves of Doom, Silent Scream, Colt .45,* and *Forbidden Ecstasy?* Many of the writers included in this book have enjoyed wide popularity and written best-sellers, but there are more readers of formula fiction than there are readers of Hemingway, Faulkner, or Oates, to name only a few. Formula novels do, of course, provide entertainment, but that makes them no different from serious stories, if entertainment means pleasure. Any of the stories in this or any other anthology can be read for pleasure.

Formula fiction, though, is usually characterized as escape literature. There are sensible reasons for this description. Adventure stories about soldiers of fortune are eagerly read by men who live pretty average lives doing ordinary jobs. Romance novels about attractive young women falling in love with tall, dark, handsome men are read mostly by women who dream themselves out of their familiar existences. The excitement, violence, and passion that such stories provide are a kind of reprieve from everyday experience.

And yet readers of serious fiction may also use it as a refuge, a liberation from monotony and boredom. Mark Twain's humorous stories have, for example, given countless hours of pleasurable relief to readers who would rather spend time in Twain's light and funny world than in their own. Others might prefer the terror of Edgar Allan Poe's fiction or the painful predicament of two lovers in a Joyce Carol Oates story.

Thus, to get at some of the differences between formula fiction and serious literature, it is necessary to go beyond the motives of the reader to the motives of the writer and the qualities of the work itself.

Unlike serious fiction, the books displayed next to the cash registers (and their short story equivalents on the magazine racks) are written with only one object: to be sold. They are aimed at specific consumer markets that can be counted on to buy them. This does not mean that all serious writers must live in cold garrets writing for audiences who have not yet discovered their work. No one writes to make a career of poverty. It does mean, however, that if a writer's primary purpose is to anticipate readers' generic expectations about when the next torrid love scene, bloody gunfight, or thrilling chase is due, there is little room to be original or to have something significant to say. There is little if any chance to explore seriously a character, idea, or incident if the major focus is not on the integrity of the work itself.

Although the specific elements of formula fiction differ depending on the type of story, some basic ingredients go into all westerns, mysteries, adventures, science fiction, and romances. From the very start, a reader can anticipate a happy ending for the central character, with whom he or she will identify. There may be suspense, but no matter what or how many the obstacles, complications, or near defeats, the hero or heroine succeeds and reaffirms the values and attitudes the reader brings to the story. Virtue triumphs, love conquers all, honesty is the best policy, and hard work guarantees success. Hence, the villains are corralled, the wedding vows are exchanged, the butler confesses, and gold is discovered at the last moment. The visual equivalents of such formula stories are readily available at movie theaters and in television series. Some are better than others, but all are relatively limited by the writer's goal of giving an audience what will sell.

Although formula fiction may not offer many surprises, it provides pleasure to a wide variety of readers. College professors, for example, are just as likely to be charmed by formula stories as anyone else. Readers of serious fiction who revel in exploring more challenging imaginative worlds can also enjoy formulaic stories, which offer little more than an image of the world as a simple place in which our assumptions and desires are confirmed. The familiarity of a given formula is emotionally satisfying because we are secure in our expectations of it. We know at the start of a Sherlock Holmes story that the mystery will be solved by that famous detective's relentless scientific analysis of the clues, but we take pleasure in seeing how Holmes unravels the mystery before us. Similarly, we know that James Bond's wit, grace, charm, courage, and skill will ultimately prevail over the diabolic schemes of eccentric villains, but we volunteer for the mission anyway.

Perhaps that happens for the same reason that we climb aboard a roller coaster: no matter how steep and sharp the curves, we stay on a track that is both exciting and safe. Although excitement, adventure, mystery, and romance are major routes to escape in formula fiction, most of us make that trip only temporarily, for a little relaxation and fun. Momentary relief from our everyday concerns is as healthy and desirable as an occasional daydream or fantasy. Such reading is a form of play because we — like spectators of or participants in a game — experience a formula of excitement, tension, and then release that can fascinate us regardless of how many times the game is played.

Many publishers of formula fiction — such as romance, adventure, or detective stories — issue a set number of new novels each month. Readers can buy them in stores or subscribe to them through the mail. These same publishers send "tip sheets" on request to authors who want to write for a particular series. The details of the formula differ from one series to another, but each tip sheet covers the basic elements that go into a story.

There are many kinds of formulaic romance novels; some include psychological terrors, some use historical settings, and some even incorporate time travel so that the hero or heroine can travel back in time and fall in love, and still others create mystery and suspense. Several publishers have recently released romances that reflect contemporary social concerns and issues; multicultural couples and gay and lesbian relationships as well as more explicit descriptions of sexual activities are now sometimes featured in these books. In general, however, the majority of romance novels are written to appeal to a readership that embraces more traditional societal expectations and values.

The following composite tip sheet summarizes the typical advice offered by publishers of romance novels. These are among the most popular titles published in the United States; it has been estimated that four out of every ten paperbacks sold are romance novels. The categories and the tone of the language in this composite tip sheet are derived from a number of publishers and provide a glimpse of how formula fiction is written and what the readers of romance novels are looking for in their escape literature.

A Composite of a Romance Tip Sheet

Plot

The story focuses on the growing relationship between the heroine and hero. After a number of complications, they discover lasting love and make a permanent commitment to each other in marriage. The plot should move quickly. Background information about the heroine should be kept to a minimum. The hero should appear as early as possible (preferably in the first chapter and no later than the second), so that the hero's and heroine's feelings about each other are in the foreground as they cope with misperceptions that keep them apart until the final pages of the story. The more tension created by their uncertainty about each other's love, the greater the excitement and anticipation for the reader.

Love is the major interest. Do not inject murder, extortion, international intrigue, hijacking, horror, or supernatural elements into the plot. Controversial social issues and politics, if mentioned at all, should never be allowed a significant role. Once the heroine and hero meet, they should clearly be interested in each other, but that interest should be complicated by some kind of misunderstanding. He, for example, might find her too ambitious, an opportunist, cold, or flirtatious; or he might assume that she is attached to someone else. She might think he is haughty, snobbish, power hungry, indifferent, or contemptuous of her. The reader knows what they do not: that eventually these obstacles will be overcome. Interest is sustained by keeping the lovers apart until very near the end so that the reader will stay with the plot to see how they get together.

Heroine

The heroine is a modern American woman between the ages of nineteen and twenty-eight who reflects today's concerns. The story is told in the third person from her point of view. She is attractive and nicely dressed but not glamorous; glitter and sophistication should be reserved for the other woman (the heroine's rival for the hero), whose flashiness will compare unfavorably with the heroine's modesty. When the heroine does dress up, however, her beauty should be stunningly apparent. Her trim figure is appealing but not abundant; a petite healthy appearance is desirable. Both her looks and her clothes should be generously detailed.

Her personality is spirited and independent without being pushy or stubborn because she knows when to give in. Although sensitive, she doesn't cry every time she is confronted with a problem (though she might cry in private moments). A sense of humor is helpful. Because she is on her own, away from parents (usually deceased) or other protective relationships, she is self-reliant as well as vulnerable. The story may begin with her on the verge of an important decision about her life. She is clearly competent but not entirely certain of her own qualities. She does not take her attractiveness for granted or realize how much the hero is drawn to her.

Common careers for the heroine include executive secretary, nurse, 5 teacher, interior designer, assistant manager, department store buyer, travel agent, or struggling photographer (no menial work). She can also be a doctor, lawyer, or other professional. Her job can be described in some detail and made exciting, but it must not dominate her life. Although she is smart, she is not extremely intellectual or defined by her work. Often she meets the hero through work, but her major concerns center on love, marriage, home, and family. White wine is okay, but she never drinks alone — or uses drugs. She may be troubled, frustrated, threatened, and momentarily thwarted in the course of the story, but she never totally gives in to despair or desperation. She has strengths that the hero recognizes and admires.

Hero

The hero should be about ten years older than the heroine and can be foreign or American. He needn't be handsome in a traditional sense, but he must be strongly masculine. Always tall and well built (not brawny or thick) and usually dark, he looks as terrific in a three-piece suit as he does in sports clothes. His clothes reflect good taste and an affluent life-style. Very successful professionally and financially, he is a man in charge of whatever work he's engaged in (financier, doctor, publisher, architect, business executive, airline pilot, artist, etc.). His wealth is manifested in his sophistication and experience.

His past may be slightly mysterious or shrouded by some painful moment (perhaps with a woman) that he doesn't want to discuss. Whatever the circumstance—his wife's death or divorce are common—it was not his fault. Avoid chronic problems such as alcoholism, drug addiction, or sexual dysfunctions. To others he may appear moody, angry, unpredictable, and explosively passionate, but the heroine eventually comes to realize his warm, tender side. He should be attractive not only as a lover but also as a potential husband and father.

Secondary Characters

Because the major interest is in how the heroine will eventually get together with the hero, the other characters are used to advance the action. There are three major types:

(1) *The Other Woman:* Her vices serve to accent the virtues of the heroine; immediately beneath her glamorous sophistication is a deceptive, selfish, mean-spirited, rapacious predator. She may seem to have the hero in her clutches, but she never wins him in the end.

(2) *The Other Man:* He usually falls into two types: (a) the decent sort who is [10] there when the hero isn't around and (b) the selfish sort who schemes rather than loves. Neither is a match for the hero.

(3) *Other Characters:* Like furniture, they fill in the background and are useful for positioning the hero and heroine. These characters are familiar types such as the hero's snobbish aunt, the heroine's troubled younger siblings, the loyal friend, or the office gossip. They should be realistic, but they must not be allowed to obscure the emphasis on the lovers. The hero may have children from a previous marriage, but they should rarely be seen or heard. It's usually simpler and better not to include them.

Setting

The setting is usually contemporary. Romantic, exciting places are best: New York City, London, Paris, Rio, the mountains, the ocean—wherever it is exotic and love's possibilities are the greatest. Marriage may take the heroine and hero to a pretty suburb or small town.

Love Scenes

The hero and heroine may make love before marriage. The choice will depend largely on the heroine's sensibilities and circumstances. She should reflect modern attitudes. If the lovers do engage in premarital sex, it should be made clear that neither is promiscuous, especially the heroine. Even if their relationship is consummated before marriage, their lovemaking should not occur until late in the story. There should be at least several passionate scenes, but complications, misunderstandings, and interruptions should keep the couple from actually making love until they have made a firm commitment to each other. Descriptions should appeal to the senses; however, detailed, graphic close-ups are unacceptable. Passion can be presented sensually but not clinically; the lovemaking should be seen through a soft romantic lens.

Violence and any out-of-the-way sexual acts should not even be hinted at. No coarse language.

Writing

Avoid extremely complex sentences, very long paragraphs, and lengthy descriptions. Use concise, vivid details to create the heroine's world. Be sure to include full descriptions of the hero's and heroine's physical features and clothes. Allow the reader to experience the romantic mood surrounding the lovers. Show how the heroine feels; do not simply report her feelings. Dialogue should sound like ordinary conversation, and the overall writing should be contemporary English without slang, difficult foreign expressions, strange dialects, racial epithets, or obscenities (*hell, damn,* and a few other mild swears are all right).

Length

55,000 to 65,000 words in ten to twelve chapters.

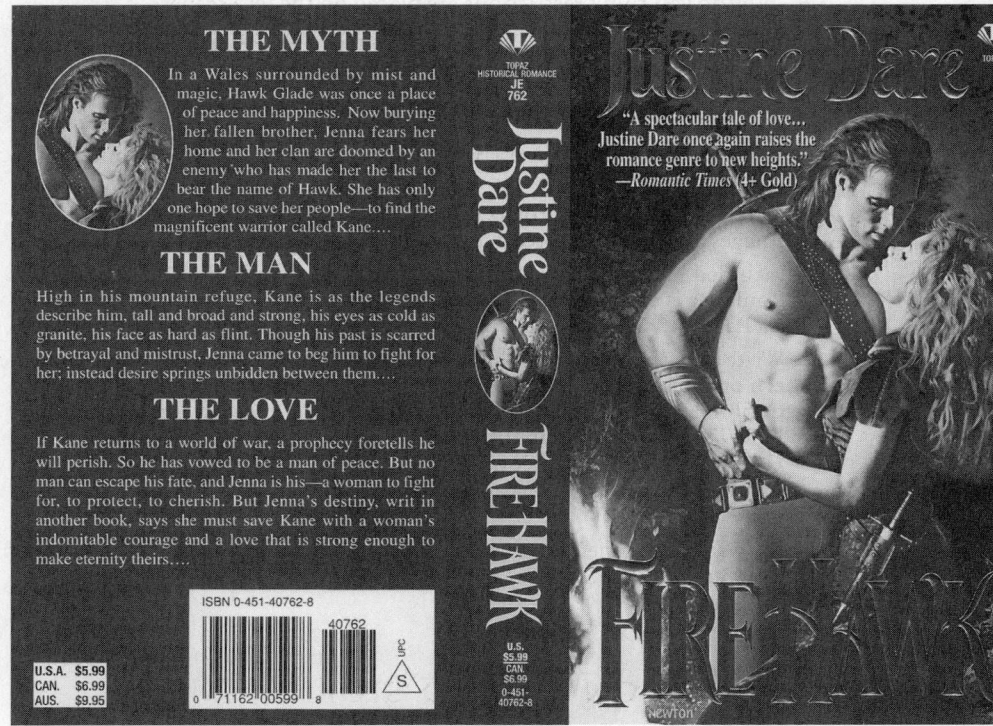

The cover for FireHawk (Penguin, 1997) illustrates another convention of romance formula fiction: its packaging demands an image of a man clasping a passionate beauty to his manly chest. As the back-cover copy suggests, this Topaz novel is a historical romance — a subcategory of the romance formula — and so a few of the guidelines on the tip sheet are modified (the setting is medieval Wales rather than contemporary America, for example). But most of the guidelines apply: Kane is strong and so is Jenna's powerful love.

CONSIDERATIONS FOR CRITICAL THINKING AND WRITING

1. FIRST RESPONSE. Given the expectations implied by the tip sheet, what generalizations can you make about those likely to write formula fiction? Does the tip sheet change the way you think about romantic fiction or other kinds of formula fiction?

2. Who is the intended audience for this type of romance? Try to describe the audience in detail: How does a romance novel provide escape for these readers?

3. Why is it best that the heroine be "attractive and nicely dressed but not glamorous"? Why do you think publishers advise writers to include detailed descriptions of her clothes? Do you find the heroine appealing? Why or why not?

4. Why should the hero be "about ten years older than the heroine"? If he is divorced, why is it significant that "it was not his fault"?

5. Why do you think the hero and heroine are kept apart by complications until the end of the story? Does the outline of the plot sound familiar to you or remind you of any other stories?

6. Why do you think restrictions are placed on the love scenes?

7. Why are "extremely complex sentences, very long paragraphs, and lengthy descriptions" discouraged?

8. To what extent does the tip sheet describe the strategies used in popular television soap operas? How do you account for the appeal of these shows?

9. Explain how the tip sheet confirms traditional views of male and female roles in society. Does it accommodate any broken traditions?

10. Carefully examine the Topaz Historical Romance cover. How do the cover's images and copy reinforce what readers can expect from a romance novel?

11. Included in the marketing material that accompanies the Topaz Historical Romance is this notation: "Topaz is an Official Sponsor of the Mrs. America Pageant." Why do you suppose the publishers support this contest?

12. Write a tip sheet for another kind of popular formula story, such as a western or a detective story, that you have observed in a novel, television show, or film. How is the plot patterned? How are the characters made familiar? How is the setting related to the story? What are the obligatory scenes? How is the overall style consistent? To get started, you might consider an Agatha Christie novel, an episode from a police series on television, or a James Bond film.

13. Try writing a scene for a formula romance, or read the excerpt from Edgar Rice Burroughs's *Tarzan of the Apes* (p. 66) and try an adventure scene.

A COMPARISON OF TWO STORIES

Each of the following contemporary pieces of fiction is about a woman who experiences deep sorrow. The first, from *A Secret Sorrow* by Karen van der Zee, is an excerpt from a romance by Harlequin Books, a major publisher of formula fiction that has sold well over a billion copies of its romance titles — enough for about 20 percent of the world's population. The second piece, Gail Godwin's "A Sorrowful Woman," is a complete short story that originally appeared in *Esquire;* it is not a formula story. Unlike *A Secret Sorrow,* Godwin's story does not have a standard plot pattern employing familiar character types that appear in a series of separate but similar works.

Read each selection carefully and look for evidence of formulaic writing in the chapters from *A Secret Sorrow.* Pay particular attention to the advice on plotting and characterization offered in the composite tip sheet. As you read Godwin's short story, think about how it is different from van der Zee's excerpt; note also any similarities. The questions that follow the stories should help you consider how the experiences of reading the two are different.

KAREN VAN DER ZEE (B. 1947)

Born and raised in Holland, Karen van der Zee lives in the United States, where she has become a successful romance writer, contributing more than fifteen novels to the popular Harlequin series. This excerpt consists of the final two chapters of *A Secret Sorrow.* This is what has happened so far: the central character, Faye, is recuperating from the psychological effects of a serious car accident in which she received a permanent internal injury. After the accident, she quits her job and breaks her engagement to Greg. She moves into her brother Chuck's house and falls in love with Kai, a visiting Texan and good friend of her brother. At the end of Chapter 10, Kai insists on knowing why she will not marry him and asks, "Who is Doctor Jaworski?"

Neb *Research Karen van der Zee with LitLinks at*
http://www.bedfordstmartins.com/meyer/bedintrolit

From A Secret Sorrow   *1981*

Chapter Eleven

Faye could feel the blood drain from her face and for one horrifying moment she thought she was going to faint right in Kai's arms. The room tilted and everything swirled around in a wild madman's dance. She clutched at him for support, fighting for control, trying to focus at some point beyond his shoulder. Slowly, everything steadied.

"I . . . I don't know him," she murmured at last. "I. . . ."

He reached in the breast pocket of his shirt, took out a slip of paper, and held it out for her to see. One glance and Faye recognized it as the note from Doctor Martin with Doctor Jaworski's name scrawled on it, thickly underlined.

"How did you get that?" Her voice was a terrified whisper. She was still holding on, afraid she would fall if she let go.

"I found it on the floor in my bedroom. It must have fallen out of your 5 wallet along with everything else on Saturday morning."

Yes — oh God! Her legs were shaking so badly, she knew it was only his arms that kept her from falling.

"Who is Doctor Jaworski, Faye?" His voice was patiently persistent.

"I . . . he. . . ." Her voice broke. "Let me go, please let me go." She felt as if she were suffocating in his embrace and she struggled against him, feebly, but it was no use.

"He's a psychiatrist, isn't he?" His voice was gentle, very gentle, and she looked up at him in stunned surprise.

He knew, oh God, he knew. She closed her eyes, a helpless sense of in- 10
evitability engulfing her.

"You know," she whispered. "How do you know?"

"Simple. Two minutes on the phone to Chicago." He paused. "Doctor Martin — was he one of the doctors who treated you at the hospital?"

"Yes."

"Why did he give you Doctor Jaworski's name? Did he want you to make an appointment with him?"

"Yes." Despondency overtook her. There was no going back now. No es- 15
cape from the truth. No escape from his arms. Resistance faded and she felt numbed and lifeless. It didn't matter any more. Nothing mattered.

"Did you?" Kai repeated.

"Did I what?"

"See him — Doctor Jaworski."

"No."

"Why did Doctor Martin want you to see a psychiatrist?" 20

"I. . . ." Faye swallowed miserably. "It's . . . it's therapy for grieving . . . mourning." She made a helpless gesture with her hand. "When people lose a . . . a wife, or husband for instance, they go through a more or less pre-dictable pattern of emotions. . . ." She gave him a quick glance, then looked away. "Like denial, anger. . . ."

". . . depression, mourning, acceptance," Kai finished for her, and she looked back at him in surprise.

"Yes."

His mouth twisted in a little smile. "I'm not totally ignorant about sub-jects other than agronomy." There was a momentary pause as he scrutinized her face. "Why did you need that kind of therapy, Faye?"

And then it was back again, the resistance, the revolt against his probing 25
questions. She stiffened in defense — her whole body growing rigid with in-stinctive rebellion.

"It's none of your business!"

"Oh, yes, it is. We're talking about our life together. Your life and mine."

She strained against him, hands pushing against his chest. "Let me go! Please let me go!" Panic changed into tears. She couldn't take his nearness any more, the feel of his hard body touching hers, the strength of him.

"No, Faye, no. You're going to tell me. Now. I'm not letting you go until you've told me everything. Everything, you hear?"

"I can't!" she sobbed. "I can't!" 30

"Faye," he said slowly, "you'll *have* to. You told me you love me, but you don't want to marry me. You have given me no satisfactory reasons, and I'll be damned if I'm going to accept your lack of explanations."

"You have no right to demand an explanation!"

"Oh, yes, I have. You're part of me, Faye. Part of my life."

"You talk as if you own me!" She was trembling, struggling to get away from him. She couldn't stand there, so close to him with all the pent-up despair inside her, the anger, the fear of what she knew not how to tell him.

His hands were warm and strong on her back, holding her steady. Then, with one hand, he tilted back her head and made her look at him. "You gave me your love—I own that," he said softly. "True loving involves commitment, vulnerability, trust. Don't you trust me, Faye?"

New tears ran silently down her cheeks. "If I told you," she blurted out, "you wouldn't . . . you wouldn't. . . ."

"I wouldn't *what?*"

"You wouldn't want me any more!" The words were wrenched from her in blind, agonizing grief. "You wouldn't *want* me any more!"

He shook his head incredulously. "What makes you think you can make that decision for me? Do you have so little trust in my love for you?"

Faye didn't answer, couldn't answer. Through a mist of tears he was nothing but a blur in front of her eyes.

"What is so terrible that you can't tell me?"

She shrank inwardly, as if shriveling away in pain. "Let me go," she whispered. "Please let me go and I'll tell you."

After a moment's hesitation Kai released her. Faye backed away from him, feeling like a terrified animal. She stood with her back against the wall, glad for the support, her whole body shaking. She took a deep breath and wiped her face dry with her hand.

"I'm afraid . . . afraid to marry you."

"Afraid?" He looked perplexed. "Afraid of what? Of me? Of marriage?"

Faye closed her eyes, taking another deep breath. "I can't be what you want me to be. We can't have the kind of life you want." She looked at him, standing only a few feet away, anguish tearing through her. "I'm so afraid . . . you'll be disappointed," she whispered.

"Oh God, Faye," he groaned, "I love you." He came toward her and panic surged through her as he held her against the wall, his hands reaching up to catch her face between them.

"Don't," she whispered. "Please, don't touch me." But it was no use. His mouth came down on hers and he kissed her with a hard, desperate passion.

"I love you," he said huskily. "I love you."

Faye wrenched her face free from his hands. "Don't touch me! Please don't touch me!" She was sobbing now, her words barely audible. Her knees gave way and her back slid down along the wall until she crumpled on to the floor, face in her hands.

Kai took a step backward and pulled her up. "Stand up, Faye. For God's sake stand up!" He held her against the wall and she looked at him, seeing every line in his dark face, the intense blue of his eyes, and knew that this was the moment, that there was no more waiting.

And Kai knew it too. His eyes held hers locked in unrelenting demand. "Why should I be disappointed, Faye? *Why?*"

Her heart was thundering in her ears and it seemed as if she couldn't breathe, as if she were going to drown.

"Because . . . because I can't give you children! Because I can't get pregnant! I can't have babies! That's why!" Her voice was an agonized cry, torn from the depths of her misery. She yanked down his arms that held her locked against the wall and moved away from him. And then she saw his face.

It was ashen, gray under his tan. He stared at her as if he had never seen 55 her before.

"Oh my God, Faye. . . ." His voice was low and hoarse. "Why didn't you tell me, why. . . ."

Faye heard no more. She ran out the door, snatching her bag off the chair as she went by. The only thought in her mind was to get away — away from Kai and what was in his eyes.

She reached for Kai's spare set of car keys in her bag, doing it instinctively, knowing she couldn't walk home alone in the dark. How she managed to get the keys in the door lock and in the ignition she never knew. Somehow, she made it home.

The phone rang as Faye opened the front door and she heard Chuck answer it in the kitchen.

"She's just got in," he said into the mouthpiece, smiling at Faye as she 60 came into view. He listened for a moment, nodded. "Okay, fine with me."

Faye turned and walked up the stairs, taking deep breaths to calm her shattered nerves. Kai hadn't wasted any time checking up on her. She didn't care what he was telling Chuck, but she wasn't going to stand there listening to a one-sided conversation. But only a second later Chuck was behind her on the stairs.

"Kai wanted to know whether you'd arrived safely."

"I did, thank you," she said levelly, her voice surprisingly steady.

"I take it you ran out and took off with his car?"

"Did he say that?" 65

"No. He was *worried* about you. He wanted to make sure you went home." He sounded impatient, and she couldn't blame him. She was making life unbearable for everyone around her. Everybody worried about her. Everybody loved her. Everything should be right. Only it wasn't.

"Well, I'm home now, and I'm going to bed. Good night."

"Good night, Faye."

Faye lay in bed without any hope of sleep. Mechanically she started to sort through her thoughts and emotions, preparing mentally for the next confrontation. There would be one, she didn't doubt it for a moment. But she needed time — time to clear her head, time to look at everything in a reasonable, unemotional way.

It was a temptation to run — get in the car and keep driving, but it would 70 be a stupid thing to do. There was no place for her to go, and Kai would find her, no matter what. If there was one thing she knew about Kai it was his stubbornness and his persistence. She had to stick it out, right here, get it over with, deal with it. Only she didn't know how.

She lay listening to the stillness, just a few sounds here and there — the house creaking, a car somewhere in the distance, a dog barking. She had to think, but her mind refused to cooperate. She *had* to think, decide what to say to Kai the next time she saw him, but she couldn't think, she *couldn't think*.

And then, as she heard the door open in the silence, the quiet footsteps coming up the stairs, she knew it was too late, that time had run out.

Without even knocking he came into her room and walked over to the bed. She could feel the mattress sag as his weight came down on it. Her heart was pounding like a sledgehammer, and then his arms came around her and he drew her against him.

"Faye," he said quietly, "please marry me."

"No," she said thickly. "No." She could feel him stiffen against her and she   75
released herself from his arms and slid off the bed. She switched on the light and stood near the window, far from the bed, far from Kai. "I don't expect you to play the gentleman, I don't expect you to throw out a life of dreams just for the sake of chivalry. You don't have to marry me, Kai." She barely recognized her own voice. It was like the cool calm sound of a stranger, unemotional, cold. "You don't have to marry me," she repeated levelly, giving him a steady look.

Her words were underlined by the silence that followed, a silence loaded with a strange, vibrating energy, a force in itself, filling the room.

Kai rose to his feet, slowly, and the face that looked at her was like that of a stranger, a dangerous, angry stranger. Never before had she seen him so angry, so full of hot, fuming fury.

"Shut up," he said in a low, tight voice. "Shut up and stop playing the martyr!"

The sound of his voice and the words he said shocked Faye into silence. She stared at him open-mouthed, and then a slow, burning anger arose inside her.

"How dare you! How. . . ."   80

He strode toward her and took her upper arms and shook her. "Shut up and listen to me! What the hell are you thinking? What the hell did you expect me to do when you told me? You throw me a bomb and then walk out on me! What did you expect my reaction to be? Was I supposed to stay cool and calm and tell you it didn't matter? Would you have married me then? Well, let me tell you something! It matters! It matters to me! I am not apologizing for my reaction!" He paused, breathing hard. "You know I always wanted children, but what in God's name makes you think you're the only one who has the right to feel bad about it? I have that right too, you hear! I love you, dammit, and I want to marry you, and if we can't have children I have all the right in the world to feel bad about it!"

He stopped talking. He was still breathing hard and he looked at her with stormy blue eyes. Faye felt paralyzed by his tirade and she stared at him, incapable of speech. She couldn't move, she couldn't think.

"Why do you think I want you for my wife?" he continued on a calmer note. "Because you're some kind of baby factory? What kind of man do you think I am? I love *you*, not your procreating ability. So we have a problem. Well, we'll learn to deal with it, one way or another."

There was another silence, and still Faye didn't speak, and she realized she was crying, soundlessly, tears slowly dripping down her cheeks. She was staring at his chest, blindly, not knowing what to think, not thinking at all.

He lifted her chin, gently. "Look at me, Faye."   85

She did, but his face was only a blur.

"Faye, we're in this together—you and I. Don't you see that? It's not just *your* problem, it's *ours*."

"No," she whispered. "No!" She shook her head wildly. "You have a choice, don't you see that? You don't have to marry me. You could marry someone else and have children of your own."

"Oh, God, Faye," he groaned, "you're wrong. Don't you know? Don't you see? I *don't* have a choice. I never did have a choice, or a chance. Not since I met you and fell in love with you. I don't *want* anybody else, don't you understand that? I want you, only you."

She wanted to believe it, give in to him. Never before had she wanted any- 90 thing more desperately than she wanted to give in to him now. But she couldn't, she couldn't. . . . She closed her eyes, briefly, fighting for reason, common sense.

"Kai, I . . . I can't live all my life with your regret and your disappointment. Every time we see some pregnant woman, every time we're with somebody else's children I'll feel I've failed you! I. . . ." Her voice broke and new sobs came unchecked.

He held her very tightly until she calmed down and then he put her from him a little and gave her a dark, compelling look.

"It's not *my* regret, or *my* disappointment," he said with quiet emphasis. "It's *ours*. We're not talking about *you* or *me*. We're talking about *us*. I love you, and you love me, and that's the starting point, that comes first. From then on we're in it together."

Faye moved out of his arms, away from him, but her legs wouldn't carry her and she sank into a chair. She covered her face with her hands and tried desperately to stop the crying, to stop the tears from coming and coming as if they would never end.

"How . . . how can I ever believe it?"   95

"Because I'm asking you to," he said quietly. He knelt in front of her, took her hands away from her wet face. "Look at me, Faye. No other woman can give me what you can — yourself, your love, your warmth, your sense of humor. All the facets of your personality that make up the final you. I've known other women, Faye, but none of them have ever stirred in me any feelings that come close to what I feel for you. You're an original, remember? There's no replacement for an original. There are only copies, and I don't want a copy. To me you're special, and you'll have to believe it, take it on faith. That's what love is all about."

He was holding her hands in his, strong brown hands, and she was look- ing down on them, fighting with herself, fighting with everything inside her to believe what he was saying, to accept it, to give in to it.

Leaning forward, Kai kissed her gently on the mouth and smiled. "It's all been too much too soon for you, hasn't it? You never really got a chance to get over the shock, and when I fell in love with you it only made things worse." He smiled ruefully and Faye was surprised at his insight.

"Yes," she said. "It all happened too fast."

"Bad timing. If only we could have met later, after you'd sorted it all out in 100 your mind, then it would never have been such a crisis."

She looked at him doubtfully. "It wouldn't have changed the facts."

"No, but it might have changed your perspective."

Would it have? she wondered. Could she ever feel confident and secure in her worth as a woman? Or was she at this moment too emotionally bruised to accept that possibility?

"I don't understand," he said, "why I never guessed what was wrong. Now that I know, it all seems so obvious." He looked at her thoughtfully. "Faye," he said gently, "I want you to tell me exactly what happened to you, what Doctor Martin told you."

She stared at him, surprised a little. A thought stirred in the back of her 105 mind. Greg. He had never even asked. The why and the what had not interested

him. But Kai, he wanted to know. She swallowed nervously and began the
story, slowly, word for word, everything Doctor Martin had said. And he listened, quietly, not interrupting. "So you see," she said at last, "we don't have to
hope for any miracles either."

"We'll make our own miracles," he said, and smiled. "Come here," he said
then, "kiss me."

She did, shyly almost, until he took over and lifted her up and carried her
to the bed. He looked down on her, eyes thoughtful. "I won't pretend I understand your feelings about this, the feelings you have about yourself as a
woman, but I'll try." He paused for a moment. "Faye," he said then, speaking
with slow emphasis, "don't *ever,* not for a single moment, think that you're not
good enough for me. You're the best there is, Faye, the very best."

His mouth sought hers and he kissed her with gentle reassurance at first,
then with rising ardor. His hands moved over her body, touching her with sensual, intimate caresses.

"You're my woman, Faye, you're mine. . . ."

Her senses reeled. She could never love anyone like she loved him. No one   110
had ever evoked in her this depth of emotion. This was real, this was forever.
Kai wanted her as much as ever. No chivalry, this, no game of pretense, she was
very sure of that. And when he lifted his face and looked at her, it was all there
in his eyes and the wonder of it filled her with joy.

"Do you believe me now?" he whispered huskily. "Do you believe I love you
and want you and need you?"

She nodded wordlessly, incapable of uttering a sound.

"And do you love me?"

Again she nodded, her eyes in his.

"Okay, then." In one smooth flowing movement he got to his feet. He   115
crossed to the closet, opened it, and took out her suitcases. He put one on the
end of the bed and began to pile her clothes in it, taking armfuls out of the
closet.

Faye watched incredulously. "What are you doing?" she managed at last.

Kai kept on moving around, opening drawers, taking out her things, filling the suitcase until it could hold no more. "Get dressed. We're going home."

"Home . . . ?"

For a moment he stopped and he looked at her with a deep blue glitter in
his eyes. "Yes, *home*—where you belong. With me, in my house, in my bed, in
my arms."

"Oh, Kai," she said tremulously, smiling suddenly. "It's midnight!"   120

His eyes were very dark. "I've waited long enough, I'm not waiting any
more. You're coming with me, now. And I'm not letting you out of my sight
until we're safely married. I don't want you getting any crazy ideas about running off to save me from myself, or some such notion."

Her throat was dry. "Please, let's not rush into it! Let's think about it
first!"

Calmly he zipped up the full suitcase, swung it off the bed, and put it near
the door. "I'm not rushing into anything," he said levelly. "I've wanted to
marry you for quite a while, remember?"

He crossed to the bed, sat down next to her, and put his arm around her.
"Faye, I wish you wouldn't worry so. I'm not going to change my mind. And I
haven't shelved my hopes for a family, either." There was a brief silence. "When

we're ready to have kids, we'll have them. We'll adopt them. There are orphanages the world over, full of children in need of love and care. We'll do whatever it takes. We'll get them, one way or another."

Faye searched his face, faint hope flickering deep inside her. 125

"Would you want that?"

"Why not?"

"I don't know, really. I thought you . . . it isn't the same."

"No," he said levelly, "it isn't. Adoption is a different process from pregnancy and birth, but the kids will be ours just the same and we'll love them no less."

"Yes," she said, "yes." And suddenly it seemed as if a light had been turned 130 on inside her, as if suddenly she could see again, a future with Kai, a future with children.

A bronzed hand lifted her face. "Look, Faye, I'll always be sorry. I'll always be sorry not to see you pregnant, not to see you with a big stomach knowing you're carrying my child, but I'll live."

Faye lowered her eyes and tears threatened again. With both his hands he cupped her face.

"Look at me, Faye. I want you to stop thinking of yourself as a machine with a defect. You're not a damaged piece of merchandise, you hear? You're a living, breathing human being, a warm-blooded female, and I love you."

Through a haze of tears she looked at him, giving a weak smile. "I love you too." She put her arms around him and he heaved an unsteady breath.

"Faye," he said huskily, "you're my first and only choice." 135

Chapter Twelve

Kai and Faye had their family, two girls and a boy. They came to them one at a time, from faraway places, with small faces and large dark eyes full of fear. In their faces Faye could read the tragedies of war and death and poverty. They were hungry for love, hungry for nourishment and care. At night they woke in terror, screaming, their memories alive in sleep.

Time passed, and in the low white ranch house under the blue skies of Texas they flourished like the crops in the fields. They grew tall and straight and healthy and the fear in the dark eyes faded. Like their father they wore jeans and boots and large-brimmed hats, and they rode horses and played the guitar. They learned to speak English with a Southern twang.

One day Kai and Faye watched them as they played in the garden, and joy and gratitude overflowed in Faye's heart. Life was good and filled with love.

"They're all ours," she said. Even now after all these years she sometimes still couldn't believe it was really so.

Kai smiled at her. His eyes, still very blue, crinkled at the corners. "Yes, and 140 you're all mine."

"They don't even look like us," she said. "Not even a tiny little bit." No blondes, no redheads.

Taking her in his arms, Kai kissed her. "They're true originals, like their mother. I wouldn't want it any other way."

There was love in his embrace and love in his words and in her heart there was no room now for doubt, no room for sorrow.

Sometimes in the night he would reach for her and she would wake to his touch, his hands on her breast, her stomach, searching. In the warm darkness of their bed she would come to him and they would hold each other close and she knew he had been dreaming.

She knew the dream. She was walking away from him, calling out that she couldn't marry him, the words echoing all around. *"I can't marry you! I can't marry you!"* And Kai was standing there watching her go, terrified, unable to move, his legs frozen to the ground. He wanted to follow her, keep her from leaving, but his legs wouldn't move. 145

Kai had told her of the dream, of the panic that clutched at him as he watched her walk out of his life. And always he would wake and search for her in the big bed, and she knew of only one way to reassure him. And in the warm afterglow of lovemaking, their bodies close together, she knew that to him she was everything, to him she was the only woman, beautiful, complete, whole.

GAIL GODWIN (B. 1937)

Born in Birmingham, Alabama, Gail Godwin was educated at the University of North Carolina and the University of Iowa, where she earned a Ph.D. in English in 1971. She is a full-time writer who has won grants from the National Endowment for the Arts, the Guggenheim Foundation, and the American Institute for the Arts and Letters. Among her novels are *Glass People* (1971), *A Mother and Two Daughters* (1981), *The Finishing School* (1985), and *Evensong* (1999). Her short stories have been collected in several volumes including *Dream Children* (1976) and *Mr. Bedford and the Muses* (1983).

Web   *Research Gail Godwin with LitLinks at*
http://www.bedfordstmartins.com/meyer/bedintrolit

A Sorrowful Woman   *1971*

Once upon a time there was a wife and mother one too many times

One winter evening she looked at them: the husband durable, receptive, gentle; the child a tender golden three. The sight of them made her so sad and sick she did not want to see them ever again.

She told the husband these thoughts. He was attuned to her; he understood such things. He said he understood. What would she like him to do? "If you could put the boy to bed and read him the story about the monkey who ate too many bananas, I would be grateful." "Of course," he said. "Why, that's a pleasure." And he sent her off to bed.

The next night it happened again. Putting the warm dishes away in the cupboard, she turned and saw the child's gray eyes approving her movements. In the next room was the man, his chin sunk in the open collar of his favorite wool shirt. He was dozing after her good supper. The shirt was the gray of the child's trusting gaze. She began yelping without tears, retching in between. The man woke in alarm and carried her in his arms to bed. The boy followed them up the stairs, saying, "It's all right, Mommy," but this made her scream. "Mommy is sick," the father said, "go wait for me in your room."

The husband undressed her, abandoning her only long enough to root beneath the eiderdown for her flannel gown. She stood naked except for her bra, which hung by one strap down the side of her body; she had not the impetus to shrug it off. She looked down at the right nipple, shriveled with chill, and thought, How absurd, a vertical bra. "If only there were instant sleep," she said, hiccuping, and the husband bundled her into the gown and went out and came back with a sleeping draught guaranteed swift. She was to drink a little glass of cognac followed by a big glass of dark liquid and afterwards there was just time to say Thank you and could you get him a clean pair of pajamas out of the laundry, it came back today.

The next day was Sunday and the husband brought her breakfast in bed 5 and let her sleep until it grew dark again. He took the child for a walk, and when they returned, red-cheeked and boisterous, the father made supper. She heard them laughing in the kitchen. He brought her up a tray of buttered toast, celery sticks, and black bean soup. "I am the luckiest woman," she said, crying real tears. "Nonsense," he said. "You need a rest from us," and went to prepare the sleeping draught, find the child's pajamas, select the story for the night.

She got up on Monday and moved about the house till noon. The boy, delighted to have her back, pretended he was a vicious tiger and followed her from room to room, growling and scratching. Whenever she came close, he would growl and scratch at her. One of his sharp little claws ripped her flesh, just above the wrist, and together they paused to watch a thin red line materialize on the inside of her pale arm and spill over in little beads. "Go away," she said. She got herself upstairs and locked the door. She called the husband's office and said, "I've locked myself away from him. I'm afraid." The husband told her in his richest voice to lie down, take it easy, and he was already on the phone to call one of the baby-sitters they often employed. Shortly after, she heard the girl let herself in, heard the girl coaxing the frightened child to come and play.

After supper several nights later, she hit the child. She had known she was going to do it when the father would see. "I'm sorry," she said, collapsing on the floor. The weeping child had run to hide. "What has happened to me, I'm not myself anymore." The man picked her tenderly from the floor and looked at her with much concern. "Would it help if we got, you know, a girl in? We could fix the room downstairs. I want you to feel freer," he said, understanding these things. "We have the money for a girl. I want you to think about it."

And now the sleeping draught was a nightly thing, she did not have to ask. He went down to the kitchen to mix it, he set it nightly beside her bed. The little glass and the big one, amber and deep rich brown, the flannel gown and the eiderdown.

The man put out the word and found the perfect girl. She was young, dynamic, and not pretty. "Don't bother with the room, I'll fix it up myself." Laughing, she employed her thousand energies. She painted the room white, fed the child lunch, read edifying books, raced the boy to the mailbox, hung her own watercolors on the fresh-painted walls, made spinach soufflé, cleaned a spot from the mother's coat, made them all laugh, danced in stocking feet to music in the white room after reading the child to sleep. She knitted dresses for herself and played chess with the husband. She washed and set the mother's soft ash-blonde hair and gave her neck rubs, offered to.

The woman now spent her winter afternoons in the big bedroom. She 10 made a fire in the hearth and put on slacks and an old sweater she had loved at school, and sat in the big chair and stared out the window at snow-ridden branches, or went away into long novels about other people moving through other winters.

The girl brought the child in twice a day, once in the later afternoon when he would tell of his day, all of it tumbling out quickly because there was not much time, and before he went to bed. Often now, the man took his wife to dinner. He made a courtship ceremony of it, inviting her beforehand so she could get used to the idea. They dressed and were beautiful together again and went out into the frosty night. Over candlelight he would say, "I think you are better, you know." "Perhaps I am," she would murmur. "You look . . . like a cloistered queen," he said once, his voice breaking curiously.

One afternoon the girl brought the child into the bedroom. "We've been out playing in the park. He found something he wants to give you, a surprise." The little boy approached her, smiling mysteriously. He placed his cupped hands in hers and left a live dry thing that spat brown juice in her palm and leapt away. She screamed and wrung her hands to be rid of the brown juice. "Oh, it was only a grasshopper," said the girl. Nimbly she crept to the edge of the curtain, did a quick knee bend, and reclaimed the creature, led the boy competently from the room.

"The girl upsets me," said the woman to her husband. He sat frowning on the side of the bed he had not entered for so long. "I'm sorry, but there it is." The husband stroked his creased brow and said he was sorry too. He really did not know what they would do without that treasure of a girl. "Why don't you stay here with me in bed," the woman said.

Next morning she fired the girl who cried and said, "I loved the little boy, what will become of him now?" But the mother turned away her face and the girl took down the watercolors from the walls, sheathed the records she had danced to, and went away.

"I don't know what we'll do. It's all my fault, I know. I'm such a burden, I 15 know that."

"Let me think. I'll think of something." (Still understanding these things.)

"I know you will. You always do," she said.

With great care he rearranged his life. He got up hours early, did the shopping, cooked the breakfast, took the boy to nursery school. "We will manage," he said, "until you're better, however long that is." He did his work, collected the boy from the school, came home and made the supper, washed the dishes, got the child to bed. He managed everything. One evening, just as she was on the verge of swallowing her draught, there was a timid knock on her door. The little boy came in wearing his pajamas. "Daddy has fallen asleep on my bed and I can't get in. There's not room."

Very sedately she left her bed and went to the child's room. Things were much changed. Books were rearranged, toys. He'd done some new drawings. She came as a visitor to her son's room, wakened the father and helped him to bed. "Ah, he shouldn't have bothered you," said the man, leaning on his wife. "I've told him not to." He dropped into his own bed and fell asleep with a moan. Meticulously she undressed him. She folded and hung his clothes. She covered his body with the bedclothes. She flicked off the light that shone in his face.

The next day she moved her things into the girl's white room. She put her   20 hairbrush on the dresser; she put a note pad and pen beside the bed. She stocked the little room with cigarettes, books, bread, and cheese. She didn't need much.

At first the husband was dismayed. But he was receptive to her needs. He understood these things. "Perhaps the best thing is for you to follow it through," he said. "I want to be big enough to contain whatever you must do."

All day long she stayed in the white room. She was a young queen, a virgin in a tower; she was the previous inhabitant, the girl with all the energies. She tried these personalities on like costumes, then discarded them. The room had a new view of streets she'd never seen that way before. The sun hit the room in late afternoon and she took to brushing her hair in the sun. One day she decided to write a poem. "Perhaps a sonnet." She took up her pen and pad and began working from words that had lately lain in her mind. She had choices for the sonnet, ABAB or ABBA for a start. She pondered these possibilities until she tottered into a larger choice: she did not have to write a sonnet. Her poem could be six, eight, ten, thirteen lines, it could be any number of lines, and it did not even have to rhyme.

She put down the pen on top of the pad.

In the evenings, very briefly, she saw the two of them. They knocked on her door, a big knock and a little, and she would call Come in, and the husband would smile though he looked a bit tired, yet somehow this tiredness suited him. He would put her sleeping draught on the bedside table and say, "The boy and I have done all right today," and the child would kiss her. One night she tasted for the first time the power of his baby spit.

"I don't think I can see him anymore," she whispered sadly to the man. And   25 the husband turned away, but recovered admirably and said, "Of course, I see."

So the husband came alone. "I have explained to the boy," he said. "And we are doing fine. We are managing." He squeezed his wife's pale arm and put the two glasses on her table. After he had gone, she sat looking at the arm.

"I'm afraid it's come to that," she said. "Just push the notes under the door; I'll read them. And don't forget to leave the draught outside."

The man sat for a long time with his head in his hands. Then he rose and went away from her. She heard him in the kitchen where he mixed the draught in batches now to last a week at a time, storing it in a corner of the cupboard. She heard him come back, leave the big glass and the little one outside on the floor.

Outside her window the snow was melting from the branches, there were more people on the streets. She brushed her hair a lot and seldom read anymore. She sat in her window and brushed her hair for hours, and saw a boy fall off his new bicycle again and again, a dog chasing a squirrel, an old woman peek slyly over her shoulder and then extract a parcel from a garbage can.

In the evening she read the notes they slipped under her door. The child   30 could not write, so he drew and sometimes painted his. The notes were painstaking at first; the man and boy offering the final strength of their day to her. But sometimes, when they seemed to have had a bad day, there were only hurried scrawls.

One night, when the husband's note had been extremely short, loving but short, and there had been nothing from the boy, she stole out of her room as she often did to get more supplies, but crept upstairs instead and stood outside their doors, listening to the regular breathing of the man and boy asleep. She hurried back to her room and drank the draught.

She woke earlier now. It was spring, there were birds. She listened for sounds of the man and the boy eating breakfast; she listened for the roar of the motor when they drove away. One beautiful noon, she went out to look at her kitchen in the daylight. Things were changed. He had bought some new dish towels. Had the old ones worn out? The canisters seemed closer to the sink. She got out flour, baking powder, salt, milk (he bought a different brand of butter), and baked a loaf of bread and left it cooling on the table.

The force of the two joyful notes slipped under her door that evening pressed her into the corner of the little room; she had hardly space to breathe. As soon as possible, she drank the draught.

Now the days were too short. She was always busy. She woke with the first bird. Worked till the sun set. No time for hair brushing. Her fingers raced the hours.

Finally, in the nick of time, it was finished one late afternoon. Her veins 35 pumped and her forehead sparkled. She went to the cupboard, took what was hers, closed herself into the little white room and brushed her hair for a while.

The man and boy came home and found: five loaves of warm bread, a roast stuffed turkey, a glazed ham, three pies of different fillings, eight molds of the boy's favorite custard, two weeks' supply of fresh-laundered sheets and shirts and towels, two hand-knitted sweaters (both of the same gray color), a sheath of marvelous watercolor beasts accompanied by mad and fanciful stories nobody could ever make up again, and a tablet full of love sonnets addressed to the man. The house smelled redolently of renewal and spring. The man ran to the little room, could not contain himself to knock, flung back the door.

"Look, Mommy is sleeping," said the boy. "She's tired from doing all our things again." He dawdled in a stream of the last sun for that day and watched his father roll tenderly back her eyelids, lay his ear softly to her breast, test the delicate bones of her wrist. The father put down his face into her fresh-washed hair.

"Can we eat the turkey for supper?" the boy asked.

CONSIDERATIONS FOR CRITICAL THINKING AND WRITING

1. FIRST RESPONSE. How did you respond to the excerpt from *A Secret Sorrow* and to "A Sorrowful Woman"? Do you like one more than the other? Is one of the women — Faye or Godwin's unnamed wife — more likable than the other? Why do you think you respond the way you do to the characters and the stories — is your response intellectual, emotional, a result of authorial intent, a mix of these, or something else entirely?

2. Describe what you found appealing in each story. Can you point to passages in both that strike you as especially well written or interesting? Was there anything in either story that did not appeal to you? Why?

3. How do the two women's attitudes toward family life differ? How does that difference constitute the problem in each story?

4. How is the woman's problem in "A Sorrowful Woman" made more complex than Faye's in *A Secret Sorrow*? What is the purpose of the husband and child in Godwin's story?

5. How would you describe the theme — the central point and meaning — in each story?

6. To what extent might "A Sorrowful Woman" be regarded as an unromantic sequel to *A Secret Sorrow*?

7. Can both stories be read a second or third time and still be interesting? Why or why not?

8. Explain how you think a romance formula writer would end "A Sorrowful Woman," or write the ending yourself.

9. Contrast what marriage means in the two stories.

10. Discuss your feelings about the woman in "A Sorrowful Woman." How does she remain a sympathetic character in spite of her refusal to be a traditional wife and mother? (It may take more than one reading of the story to see that Godwin does sympathize with her.)

11. The happy ending of *A Secret Sorrow* may seem like that of a fairy tale, but it is realistically presented because there is nothing strange, mysterious, or fabulous that strains our ability to believe it could happen. In contrast, "A Sorrowful Woman" begins with an epigraph (*"Once upon a time . . ."*) that causes us to expect a fairy-tale ending, but that story is clearly a fairy tale gone wrong. Consider the two stories as fairy tales. How might "A Sorrowful Woman" be read as a dark version of "Sleeping Beauty"?

12. CRITICAL STRATEGIES. Read the section on feminist criticism in Chapter 52, "Critical Strategies for Reading." Based on that discussion, what do you think a feminist critic might have to say about these two stories?

PERSPECTIVES

KAY MUSSELL (B. 1943)

Are Feminism and Romance Novels Mutually Exclusive?   1997

If feminism and romance are mutually exclusive, a lot of romance writers and readers haven't heard the news yet. In my experience, the only people who think they are mutually exclusive are people who don't know much about romances — or about women, or dare I add about feminism? That last point may be provocative and subject to real debate.

Twenty years ago, when romance novels were getting a lot of attention in the media, I thought that their increased popularity and changing content had something to do with the challenge mounted by feminism to more traditional women. I saw romances back then as a kind of backlash against the more aggressive and controversial aspects of feminism — something that reaffirmed traditional values and made women who hadn't bought into the feminist critique feel validated about their own choices. I also expected romances to fade away as more and more women entered the labor force and became practical feminists if not theoretical or political feminists.

Was I ever wrong! Instead of quietly going the way of the Western (which is much less popular now than it was a few decades ago), romances have become one of the hottest areas of publishing. One reason, of course, is that romances have changed with the times. The newer romances incorporate feminist themes while still reaffirming more traditional notions about love and family. Moreover, many romance writers have openly claimed feminist values and, in the process, rejected easy stereotypes about themselves and their work. For example, see the essays by romance writers collected in Jayne Ann Krentz's *Dangerous Men & Adventurous Women.*

More difficult to illustrate, but I think equally important, is change in feminist thinking itself. Twenty or so years ago, when academic feminists first became interested in the romance genre, there was wider agreement among feminists themselves on what the feminist agenda should be — and conventional romantic relationships, widely assumed to be discriminatory toward women, were not part of it. Thus romances were seen as threatening to female autonomy. But as feminism has matured — and as feminist scholars have come to recognize a broader range of female experience — some scholars have challenged those earlier notions in productive ways.

I don't know how you can read many romances today as anything but feminist. To take just one issue: Heroes and heroines meet each other on a much more equal playing field. Heroes don't always dominate and heroines are frequently right. Heroines have expertise and aren't afraid to show it. Heroes aren't the fount of all wisdom and they actually have things to learn from heroines. This is true of both contemporary and historical romances. I'm not trying to argue that all romances before the 1990s featured unequal relationships or that all romances today are based on equality. That's clearly not the case. But in general heroines today have a lot more independence and authority than their counterparts did in earlier romances. I think that's clear evidence of the influence of feminism on romances and of the ability of romance novels to address contemporary concerns that women share.

From "All About Romance: The Back-Fence for Lovers of Romance Novels" accessed at **<http://www.likesbooks.com/mussell.html>.**

CONSIDERATIONS FOR CRITICAL THINKING AND WRITING

1. How might the excerpt from *A Secret Sorrow* be read "as a kind of backlash against the more aggressive and controversial aspects of feminism"?
2. Examine some recent romance novel covers and back-cover copy in a bookstore. What evidence is there to support or refute Mussell's claim that "newer romances incorporate feminist themes while still reaffirming more traditional notions about love and family"?
3. Write an essay in which you consider a book, film, or television program that seems to appeal to male fantasies, and explore some of the similarities and differences between male and female tastes in popular fiction.

THOMAS JEFFERSON (1743–1826)

On the Dangers of Reading Fiction   *1818*

A great obstacle to good education is the inordinate passion prevalent for novels, and the time lost in that reading which should be instructively employed. When this poison infects the mind, it destroys its tone and revolts it against wholesome reading. Reason and fact, plain and unadorned, are rejected. Nothing can engage attention unless dressed in all the figments of fancy, and nothing so bedecked comes amiss. The result is a bloated imagination, sickly judgment, and disgust towards all the real businesses of life. This mass of trash, however, is not without some distinction; some few modeling their narratives, although fictitious, on the incidents of real life, have been able to make them interesting and useful vehicles of a sound morality. . . . For a like reason, too, much poetry should not be indulged. Some is useful for forming style and taste. Pope, Dryden, Thompson, Shakespeare, and of the French, Molière, Racine, the Corneilles, may be read with pleasure and improvement.

Letter to Nathaniel Burwell, March 14, 1818,
in The Writings of Thomas Jefferson

CONSIDERATIONS FOR CRITICAL THINKING AND WRITING

1. Jefferson voices several common objections to fiction. What, according to him, are the changes associated with reading fiction? Are these concerns still expressed today? Why or why not? To what extent are Jefferson's arguments similar to twentieth-century objections to watching television?

2. Explain why you agree or disagree that works of fiction should serve as "useful vehicles of a sound morality."

3. How do you think Jefferson would regard Harlequin romances?

2

Writing about
Fiction

FROM READING TO WRITING

There's no question about it: writing about fiction is a different experience
than reading it. The novelist William Styron amply concedes that writing
to him is not so much about pleasure as it is about work: "Let's face it, writing is hell." Although Styron's lament concerns his own feelings about
writing prose fiction, he no doubt speaks for many other writers, including
essayists. Writing is, of course, work, but it is also a pleasure when it goes
well — when ideas feel solid and the writing is fluid. You can experience
that pleasure as well, if you approach writing as an intellectual and emotional opportunity rather than merely a sentence.

Just as reading fiction requires an imaginative, conscious response, so
does writing about fiction. Composing an essay is not just recording your
interpretive response to a work because the act of writing can change your
response as you explore, clarify, and discover relationships you hadn't
previously considered or recognized. Most writers discover new ideas and
connections as they move through the process of rereading and annotating the text, taking notes, generating ideas, developing a thesis, and organizing an argumentative essay (these matters are detailed in Chapter 53,
"Reading and Writing"). To become more conscious of the writing process,
first study the following questions specifically aimed at sharpening your
response to reading and writing about fiction. Then examine the case
study of a student's paper in progress that takes you through writing a
first response to reading, brainstorming for a paper topic, writing a first
draft, revising, and writing the final paper.

QUESTIONS FOR RESPONSIVE READING AND WRITING

The following questions can help you consider important elements of fiction that reveal your responses to a story's effects and meanings. The questions are general, so they will not always be relevant to a particular story. Many of them, however, should prove useful for thinking, talking, and writing about a work of fiction. If you are uncertain about the meaning of a term used in a question, consult the Glossary of Literary Terms beginning on page 2190 of this book. You should also find useful the discussion of various critical approaches to literature in Chapter 52, "Critical Strategies for Reading."

Plot

1. Does the plot conform to a formula? Is it like those of any other stories you have read? Did you find it predictable?
2. What is the source and nature of the conflict for the protagonist? Was your major interest in the story based on what happens next or on some other concern? What does the title reveal now that you've finished the story?
3. Is the story told chronologically? If not, in what order are its events told, and what is the effect of that order on your response to the action?
4. What does the exposition reveal? Are flashbacks used? Did you see any foreshadowings? Where is the climax?
5. Is the conflict resolved at the end? Would you characterize the ending as happy, unhappy, or somewhere in between?
6. Is the plot unified? Is each incident somehow related to some other element in the story?

Character

7. Do you identify with the protagonist? Who (or what) is the antagonist?
8. Did your response to any characters change as you read? What do you think caused the change? Do any characters change and develop in the course of the story? How?
9. Are round, flat, or stock characters used? Is their behavior motivated and plausible?
10. How does the author reveal characters? Are they directly described or indirectly presented? Are the characters' names used to convey something about them?
11. What is the purpose of the minor characters? Are they individualized, or do they primarily represent ideas or attitudes?

Setting

12. Is the setting important in shaping your response? If it were changed, would your response to the story's action and meaning be significantly different?
13. Is the setting used symbolically? Are the time, place, and atmosphere related to the theme?
14. Is the setting used as an antagonist?

Point of View

15. Who tells the story? Is it a first-person or third-person narrator? Is it a major or minor character or one who does not participate in the action at all? How much does the narrator know? Does the point of view change at all in the course of the story?
16. Is the narrator reliable and objective? Does the narrator appear too innocent, emotional, or self-deluded to be trusted?
17. Does the author directly comment on the action?
18. If told from a different point of view, how would your response to the story change? Would anything be lost?

Symbolism

19. Did you notice any symbols in the story? Are they actions, characters, settings, objects, or words?
20. How do the symbols contribute to your understanding of the story?

Theme

21. Did you find a theme? If so, what is it?
22. Is the theme stated directly, or is it developed implicitly through the plot, characters, or some other element?
23. Is the theme a confirmation of your values, or does it challenge them?

Style, Tone, and Irony

24. Do you think the style is consistent and appropriate throughout the story? Do all the characters use the same kind of language, or did you hear different voices?
25. Would you describe the level of diction as formal or informal? Are the sentences short and simple, long and complex, or some combination?
26. How does the author's use of language contribute to the tone of the story? Did it seem, for example, intense, relaxed, sentimental, nostalgic, humorous, angry, sad, or remote?
27. Do you think the story is worth reading more than once? Does the author's use of language bear close scrutiny so that you feel and experience more with each reading?

Critical Strategies

28. Is there a particular critical approach that seems especially appropriate for this story? (See the discussion of "Critical Strategies for Reading" beginning on p. 2091.)
29. How might biographical information about the author help you to determine the central concerns of the story?
30. How might historical information about the story provide a useful context for interpretation?
31. What kinds of evidence from the story are you focusing on to support your interpretation? Does your interpretation leave out any important elements that might undercut or qualify your interpretation?
32. To what extent do your own experiences, values, beliefs, and assumptions inform your interpretation?
33. Given that there are a variety of ways to interpret the story, which one seems the most useful to you?

A SAMPLE PAPER IN PROGRESS

The following student paper was written in response to an assignment that asked for a comparison and contrast of the treatment of marriage in the excerpt from Karen van der Zee's novel *A Secret Sorrow* (p. 27) and in Gail Godwin's short story "A Sorrowful Woman" (p. 35). The final draft of the paper is preceded by four distinct phases of composition: (1) an initial response, (2) a brainstorming exercise, (3) a preliminary draft of the paper, and (4) an annotated version of the preliminary draft that shows how the student thought about revising the paper. Maya Leigh's First Response is an informal paper based on questions supplied by the instructor: "How did you respond to each story? Do you like one more than the other? Is one of the women more likable than the other? Why do you think you respond the way you do? Is your response to the characters and the stories primarily intellectual, emotional, a result of authorial intention, a mix of these, or something else entirely?" (Spelling and grammatical errors in Maya's preliminary drafts have been silently corrected so as not to distract from her developing argument.)

First Response:

```
Reading the excerpt from the Harlequin I was irritated by
the seeming helplessness of Faye; in the first chapter she
is constantly on the edge of hysteria and can hardly stand
up. I could do without all of the fainting, gasping, and
```

general theatrics. I've read Harlequins before, and I
usually skim through that stuff to get to the good romantic
parts and the happy ending. What I like about these kinds of
romance novels is the happy ending. Even though the ending
is kind of clichéd with the white fence and blue skies,
there is still something satisfying about having everything
work out okay.

The Godwin story, of course, does not have a happy
ending. It is a much more powerful story, and it is one
that I could read several times, unlike the Harlequin. The
Godwin woman bothers me too, because I can't really see
what she has to complain about. Her husband is perfectly
accommodating and understanding. It seems that if she were
unhappy with her life as a wife and mother and wanted to
work or do something else, he wouldn't have a problem with
it. She seems to throw away her life and hurt her family
for nothing.

I enjoyed reading the Godwin story more just because it
is well written and more complex, but I liked the ending of
the Harlequin more. I think on an emotional level I liked
the Harlequin better, and on an intellectual level I liked
the Godwin story more. It is more satisfying emotionally to
see a romance develop and end happily than it is to see the
deterioration of a marriage and the suicide of a depressed
woman. I don't really find either character particularly
likable; toward the end when the Godwin woman comes out
of her room and starts doing things again I begin to feel
sympathy for her--I can understand her having a period of
depression, but I want her to pull herself out of it, and
when she doesn't, I am disappointed. Even though Faye is
annoying in the beginning, because everything ends happily
I am almost willing to forgive and forget my previous annoyance with her. If the Godwin woman hadn't killed herself
and had returned to her family life, I would have liked her
better, but because she doesn't I leave the story feeling
discouraged.

Brainstorming

By listing these parallel but alternate treatments of marriage in each story, Maya begins to assemble an inventory of relevant topics related to the assignment. What becomes clear to her is that her approach will emphasize the differences in each story's portrayal of marriage.

Marriage

Godwin	Harlequin
marriage as *end* of life — confining, weighty	marriage as end, goal — dreamlike, idyllic
husband — durable, receptive, understanding	husband — understanding, manly
p. 35 sight of family makes her sad and sick	p. 34 watching kids she feels that life is good + filled with love
house in winter — girl paints room white	white house in Texas under blue skies
the power of his baby spit and looking at arm p. 38	in husband's embrace no room for doubt or sorrow p. 34
family makes her sad	family makes her happy
weight pressing on her	weight lifted off her
impersonal — the husband, the child emphasis on roles	Kai, Faye, our children
dead in the end	beautiful, whole, complete in the end
crisis due to fear of always having husband and kid	crisis due to fear of never having husband and kids
feels incomplete and depressed as only wife and mother	feels incomplete and depressed not being wife and mother

Revising: First and Second Drafts

Maya's first draft of the paper pursues and develops many of the topics she noted while brainstorming. She explores the differences between each story's treatment of marriage in detail by examining each protagonist's role as wife and mother, her husband's response, the role played by her children, and the ending of each story. The second draft's annotations indicate that Maya has been able to distance herself enough from her first draft to critique its weak moments. In the annotations she recognizes, for example, that she needs a clearer thesis, some stronger transitions between paragraphs, some crisper and more detailed sentences to clarify points, and a more convincing conclusion as well as a more pointed title.

Separate Sorrows

In both the excerpt from A Secret Sorrow and "A Sorrowful Woman," by Gail Godwin, the story is centered
around ideas of marriage and family. However, marriage and
family are presented in very different lights in the two
stories. Karen van der Zee presents marriage with children
as perfect and somewhat dream-like; it is what Faye, the
heroine of A Secret Sorrow, wants, and what is necessary
for her happiness. For Godwin's heroine, marriage and family are almost the antithesis of happiness; her home life
seems to suffocate her and eventually leads her to commit
suicide.

Both of the female protagonists in the two stories
experience a crisis of sorts. In A Secret Sorrow Faye's
crisis comes before marriage. She is distraught and upset
because she cannot have children and fears that this will
prevent her from marrying the man she loves. Both she
and her beloved, Kai, have always wanted a marriage with
children, and it is assumed that only under these circumstances will they truly be happy. Faye feels that her inability to have children is a fatal flaw. "Every time we
see some pregnant woman, every time we're with somebody
else's children I'll feel I've failed you!" (32). In "A
Sorrowful Woman," however, the crisis comes after the
marriage, when the woman has already procured her husband
and child. Faye would be ecstatic in this woman's situation. The protagonist of the Godwin story, however, is
not. Her husband and son bring her such sorrow that eventually she is unable to see them at all, and communicates
only through notes stuck under her bedroom door. Faye's
anxiety and fear is based on the thought of losing her man
and never having children. In contrast, Godwin's character
has a loving husband and child and is still filled with
grief. In a Harlequin such as A Secret Sorrow, this is

unimaginable; it goes against every formula of romance
writing, where books always end with a wedding, and happiness after that is just assumed.

In A Secret Sorrow, marriage is portrayed as the end,
as in the goal. It is what the heroine wants. The author
works to let the reader know that only in this way will
Faye be fulfilled and happy; it is what the entire story,
with all the plot twists and romantic interludes, has been
working toward. In "A Sorrowful Woman," marriage is the
end, but not as in the goal--it is quite literally the end
of the woman's life. Though we don't see what her life was
like before her emotional crisis, there are hints of it.
When she moves into the new room she mentions seeing the
streets from a whole new perspective, suggesting the previous monotony of her daily life. In addition, in the
final paragraphs of the story when the character bakes
pies and bread and washes and folds the laundry, her son
says, "she's tired from doing all our things again," (39)
giving us an idea of what "our things" were, and what the
woman did with her time before becoming ill.

In A Secret Sorrow Faye's inability to have children does not end Kai's love for her, and the two go on
to get married and adopt children. Faye's married life
is described in a very idyllic way--she raises her son and
two daughters in a "white ranch house under the blue skies
of Texas" (34). In other words, once she is married and
has children there is no more anxiety, nothing more to
fear. The author leads us to the conclusion that marriage
solves all problems and is a source of unending happiness
for all. This is a great difference from the Godwin tale,
which takes place in the winter and maintains a sense of
cold throughout the whole thing. Whenever Godwin describes
the family it is not in the light, glowing terms of van der
Zee, but always with a sense of weight or guilt or failure

about it. The child's trusting gaze makes the protagonist begin "yelping without tears" (35). Any sign of life or love increases her sorrow and makes her want to be rid of it. For example, when the hired girl brings her son to visit her with a grasshopper he's found--something both alive and from the outside world--she gets very upset and forces her husband to fire her. The girl is too much of an infringement on her space, and too much of a reminder of what she can no longer be.

Never is the difference between the two authors' portrayals of marriage more apparent than when both the women are viewing their families. Faye, sitting with her husband and watching her children play, felt that "life was good and filled with love" (34). Godwin's protagonist, on the other hand, says, "The sight of them made her so sad and sick she did not want to see them ever again" (35). When Kai, now her husband, embraces Faye, she feels that, "There was love in his embrace and love in his words and in her heart there was no room now for doubt, no room for sorrow" (34). When Godwin's heroine feels the loving touch of her husband's arm and the kiss of her child she cannot bear it and cuts off all direct contact with them. The situation of her marriage pushes her into a self-imposed imprisonment and lethargy. She feels unbearably sad because she can no longer be who they want and need her to be. She avoids them not because she does not love them, but rather because she loves them so much that it is too painful to see them and feel her failure.

When Faye's fears of losing Kai are assuaged, and she is happily married, it is as though a great weight has been lifted off of her. Godwin's character, on the other hand, feels her marriage as a great weight pressing in on her. The love of her husband and child weighs on her and immobilizes her. When she leaves her room for a day and leaves out freshly baked bread for her husband and son, they express their happiness in the notes they write to her that night, and "the force of the two joyful notes . . . pressed her into the corner of the little room; she hardly had space to breathe" (39). Faye can be a traditional wife and mother, so her family is a source of joy. Godwin's character can no longer do this, and so her family is a representation of her failure, and the guilt presses her further and further into herself, until she can retreat no further and ends her life.

The endings of the two stories are powerful illustrations of the differences between them. In the end of A Secret Sorrow the author shows us Faye feeling "beautiful, complete, whole" (35) in her role as wife and mother. Godwin, on the other hand, shows us her heroine dead on her bed. Godwin first gives the reader hope, by showing all that the woman has done, and saying that "the house smelled redolently of renewal and spring" (39). This makes the blow even harder when we then discover, along with the husband and child, the woman's suicide.

Karen van der Zee creates a story full of emotional highs and lows, but one that leads up to--and ends with-- marriage. After the marriage all plot twists and traumas come to a halt. Faye is brought to new life by her marriage and children; in it she finds completion of herself and total happiness. Godwin's tale, on the other hand, is full of anguish and emotion, but it all takes place after the marriage. The character she creates is stifled and killed by her marriage. There is no portrayal of unending happiness in her tale, but rather unending woe.

Maya Leigh
Professor Herlin
English 104
October 10, 20--

title works for Godwin—but does it for van der Zee?

Separate Sorrows)→

Karen van der Zee's novel   *Gail Godwin's short story*

In both the excerpt from A Secret Sorrow and "A Sor-

plot   *s*

rowful Woman," ~~by Gail Godwin,~~ the ~~story is~~ centered

around ideas of marriage and family. However, marriage and

family are presented in very different lights in the two

stories. Karen van der Zee presents marriage with children

totally fulfilling

as perfect and ~~somewhat dream-like~~; it is what Faye, the

protagonist

~~heroine~~ of A Secret Sorrow, wants / and what is necessary

unnamed protagonist

for her happiness. For Godwin's ~~heroine~~, marriage and

family are almost the antithesis of happiness; her

home life seems to suffocate her and eventually leads

her to commit suicide.

need a clear thesis here—is it that SS endorses marriage while SW problematizes it?

Both of the female protagonists in the two stories

experience a crisis ~~of sorts~~. In A Secret Sorrow Faye's

crisis comes before marriage. She is distraught and upset

because she cannot have children and fears that this will

prevent her from marrying the man she loves. Both she and

her beloved, Kai, have always wanted a marriage with

unclear referent

children, and ⓘ(it) is assumed that only under these circum-

stances will they truly be happy. Faye feels that her

that cuts her off from Kai's love

inability to have children is a fatal flaw. "Every time

we see some pregnant woman, every time we're with some-

body else's children I'll feel I've failed you!" (32).

from page

In "A Sorrowful Woman," however, the crisis comes after

secured

the marriage, when the woman has already ~~procured~~ her

Unlike   *who*

husband and child. Faye would be ecstatic in this woman's

Leigh 2

situation. ~~T~~he protagonist of ~~the~~ Godwin's story~~,~~ ~~however,~~
Inexplicably,
is not. ~~H~~er husband and son bring her such sorrow that

eventually she is unable to see them at all, ~~and~~ communi-
~~c~~ing
cates only through notes stuck under her bedroom door.

Faye's anxiety and fear is based on the thought of losing
her man and never having children. ~~In contrast,~~ Godwin's
yet she
character has a loving husband and child ~~and~~ is still

filled with grief. ~~In a Harlequin such as A Secret Sorrow,~~
sense of defeat would be *in a Harlequin romance because* *one of the most popular*
this ~~is~~ unimaginable it goes against ~~every~~ formulas~~of~~
the plot
romance writing~~;~~ ~~where books~~ always end's with a wedding,
with the assumption that the rest is happily ever after.
~~and happiness after that is just assumed.~~

In A Secret Sorrow, marriage is portrayed as ~~the end,~~
Van der Zee
~~as in~~ the goal. ~~It is what the heroine wants.~~ ~~The author~~
works to let the reader know that only in this way will
Faye be fulfilled and happy; it is what the entire story,
with all the plot twists and romantic interludes, ~~has been~~
working toward. ~~I~~n "A Sorrowful Woman," marriage is the end,
also
but not as in the goal: it is quite literally the end of
the woman's life. Though we don't see what her life was
like before her emotional crisis, there are hints of it.
When she moves into the new room, she mentions seeing the
need p. ref
streets from a whole new perspective, suggesting the previous monotony of her daily life. In addition, in the
final paragraphs of the story--when the character bakes
pies and bread and washes and folds the laundry--her son
says, "She's tired from doing all our things again," (39)
giving us an idea of what "our things" were and what the
woman did with her time before becoming ill.

insert on new page

I like this!

is she really ill? or just withdrawing from her life?

*need
transition* | In <u>A Secret Sorrow</u> Faye's inability to have children

does not end Kai's love for her, and the two go on to get

married and adopt children. Faye's married life is

described in a very idyllic way--she raises her son and two

daughters in a "white ranch house under the blue skies of

Texas" (34). ~~In other words,~~ <u>o</u>nce she is married and has

because the plot
children there is no more anxiety, ~~nothing more to fear.~~

~~The author~~ leads us to the conclusion that marriage solves

all problems and is a source of unending happiness₍₎ ~~for~~

ly *rs*
~~all.~~ This ~~is a~~ great_^ differ_^ence from ~~the~~ Godwin_^'s tale,

which takes place in the winter and maintains a sense of

cold₍₎ ~~throughout the whole thing.~~ Whenever Godwin

describes the family it is ~~not~~ in ~~the light, glowing~~ terms
that suggest
~~of van der Zee, but always with a sense of~~ weight_, ~~or~~

guilt_, or failure₍₎ ~~about it.~~ The child's trusting gaze

makes the protagonist begin "yelping without tears" (35)_,
while
_^ ~~A~~ny sign of life or love increases her sorrow and makes
unclear referent
her want to be rid of (it). For example, when the hired

girl brings her son to visit her with a grasshopper he's
--
found _^something both alive and from the outside world _^
--
the girl.
she gets very upset and forces her husband to fire ~~her.~~
Apparently,
~~T~~he girl is too much of an infringement on her space, ~~and~~

too much of a reminder of what she can no longer be.

Never is the difference between the two authors' por-

trayals of marriage more apparent than when both the women

are viewing their families. Faye, sitting with her husband

and watching her children play, felt that "life was good

and filled with love" (34). Godwin's protagonist, on the

other hand, says, "The sight of them made her so sad and sick she did not want to see them ever again" (35). When Kai, now her husband, embraces Faye, she feels, "There was love in his embrace and love in his words and in her heart there was no room now for doubt, no room for sorrow" (34). When Godwin's heroine feels the loving touch of her husband's arm and the kiss of her child, she cannot bear it and cuts off all direct contact with them. The situation of her marriage pushes her into a self-imposed imprisonment and lethargy. She feels unbearably sad because she can no longer be who they want and need her to be. She avoids them not because she does not love them but rather because she loves them so much that it is too painful to see them and feel her failure.

should I use epigram here? or work into the thesis?

need →
transition   When Faye's fears of losing Kai are assuaged, and she is happily married, it is as though a great weight has been lifted off her. Godwin's character, on the other hand, feels her marriage as a great weight pressing in on her~~.~~ *and* ~~The love of her husband and child weighs on her and~~ immobiliz~~es~~ *cing* her. When she leaves her room for a day and *puts* ~~leaves~~ out freshly baked bread for her husband and son, they express their happiness in the notes they write to her that night, and "the force of the two joyful notes . . . pressed her into the corner of the little room; she had hardly space to breathe" (39). Faye can be ~~a~~ *the* traditional wife and mother, so her family is a source of joy. Godwin's character can no longer do this, and so her family ~~is a~~ representation*s* ~~of~~ her *own* failure, and the guilt

Leigh 5

presses her further and further into herself/ until she

can retreat no further and ends her life.

The endings of the two stories are powerful illus-

trations of the differences between them. In the end of

A Secret Sorrow the author shows us Faye feeling "beauti-

ful, complete, whole" (35) in her role as wife and mother.

protagonist

Godwin, on the other hand, shows us her ~~heroine~~ dead on

seems to

her bed. Godwin ~~first~~ give/ the reader hope/ by showing

all that the woman has done/ and saying that "the house

smelled redolently of renewal and spring" (39). This makes

the blow even harder when we then discover, along with the

death

husband and child, the woman's ~~suicide~~.

same idyllic surroundings as VDZ's blue skies?

Karen van der Zee creates a story full of emotional

highs and lows/ but one that leads up to--and ends with--

marriage. After the marriage all plot twists and traumas

come to a halt. Faye is brought to new life by her mar-

fulfillment

riage and children; ~~in it~~ she finds ~~completion of herself~~

story, however,

and total happiness. Godwin's ~~tale, on the other hand,~~ is

confusion (?) that

full of anguish and ~~emotion, but it~~ all takes/ place after

the marriage. The character she creates is stifled and

killed by her marriage. There is no portrayal of unending

happiness in her tale, but rather unending ⟨woe.⟩ *is this the right word, since she dies?*

Final Draft

The changes noted in Maya's annotations on her second draft are put to good use in the following final draft. By not insisting that Godwin's protagonist actually commits suicide, Maya shifts her attention away from this indeterminable death to the causes and effects of it. This shift leads her to a stronger thesis—that Godwin raises questions about the efficacy of marriage rather than endorsing it as a certain recipe for happiness the way van der Zee does. Maya also incorporates additional revisions, such as transitions (see, for example, the revision between paragraphs 3 and 4), sentence clarity, and a fuller and more persuasive concluding paragraph.

Maya Leigh
Professor Herlin
English 104
October 10, 20--

Fulfillment or Failure?
Marriage in A Secret Sorrow and "A Sorrowful Woman"

In both the excerpt from Karen van der Zee's novel
A Secret Sorrow and in Gail Godwin's short story "A Sorrowful Woman," the plots center around ideas of marriage
and family. However, marriage and family are presented
in very different lights in the two stories. Karen van
der Zee presents marriage with children as perfect and
totally fulfilling; it is what Faye, the protagonist of
A Secret Sorrow, wants and what is necessary for her happiness. For Godwin's unnamed protagonist marriage and family are almost the antithesis of happiness; her home life
seems to suffocate her and eventually leads to her death.
A Secret Sorrow directly endorses and encourages marriage,
whereas "A Sorrowful Woman" indirectly questions and dis-
courages it.

Both of the female protagonists in the two stories
experience a crisis. In A Secret Sorrow Faye's crisis
comes before the marriage. She is distraught and upset
because she cannot have children and fears that this will
prevent her from marrying the man she loves. Both she and
her beloved, Kai, desire marriage with children, and van
der Zee suggests that only with these things will they
truly be happy. Faye feels that her inability to have
children is a fatal flaw that cuts her off from Kai's love.
"Every time we see some pregnant woman, every time we're
with somebody else's children I'll feel I've failed
you!" (32). Faye's anxiety and fear are based on the

thought of losing her man and never having children. In "A
Sorrowful Woman," however, the crisis comes after the marriage, when the woman has already secured her husband and
child. Unlike Faye, who would be ecstatic in this woman's
situation, the protagonist of Godwin's story is not. Inexplicably, her husband and son bring her such sorrow that
eventually she is unable to see them at all, communicating
only through notes stuck under her bedroom door. Godwin's
character has a loving husband and child, yet she is still
filled with grief. This sense of defeat would be unimaginable in a Harlequin romance because it goes against one of
the most popular formulas of romance writing: the plot
always ends with a wedding, with the assumption that the
rest is happily ever after.

In A Secret Sorrow, marriage is portrayed as the
goal. Van der Zee works to let the reader know that only
in this way will Faye be fulfilled and happy; it is what
the entire story, with all the plot twists and romantic
interludes, works toward. Marriage is also the end in "A
Sorrowful Woman" but not as in the goal: it is quite literally the end of the woman's life. Though we don't see
what her life was like before her emotional crisis, there
are hints of it. When she moves into a new bedroom--away
from her husband--she mentions seeing the streets from a
whole new perspective (38), suggesting the previous monotony of her daily life. In addition, in the final paragraphs
of the story--when the character bakes pies and bread and
washes and folds the laundry--her son says, "She's tired
from doing all our things again," (39) giving us an idea
of what "our things" were and what the woman did with her
time before her crisis.

This monotony of marriage is absent in A Secret Sorrow. Faye's inability to have children does not end Kai's

love for her, and the two go on to marry and adopt children. Faye's married life is described in a very idyllic
way: she raises her son and two daughters in a "white
ranch house under the blue skies of Texas" (34). Once she
is married and has children, there is no more anxiety because the plot leads us to the conclusion that marriage
solves all problems and is a source of unending happiness.
This greatly differs from Godwin's tale, which takes place
in winter and maintains a sense of cold. Whenever Godwin
describes the family, it is in terms that suggest weight,
guilt, or failure. The child's trusting gaze makes the
protagonist begin "yelping without tears" (35), and any
sign of life or love increases her sorrow and makes her
want to be alone. For example, when the hired girl brings
her son to visit her with a grasshopper he's found (37)--
something both alive and from the outside world--she gets
very upset and forces her husband to fire the girl. Apparently, the girl is too much of an infringement on
her space, too much of a reminder of what she can no
longer be.

Never is the difference between the two authors' portrayals of marriage more apparent than when both women are
viewing their families. Faye, sitting with her husband and
watching her children play, feels that "life was good and
filled with love" (34). Godwin's protagonist, on the other
hand, says, "The sight of them made her so sad and sick
she did not want to see them ever again" (35). When Kai,
now her husband, embraces Faye, she feels, "There was love
in his embrace and love in his words and in her heart
there was no room now for doubt, no room for sorrow" (34).
When Godwin's heroine feels the loving touch of her husband's arm and the kiss of her child, she cannot bear it
and cuts off all direct contact with them. The situation

of her marriage pushes her into a self-imposed imprisonment and lethargy. She feels unbearably sad because she can
no longer be who they want and need her to be. She avoids
them not because she does not love them but rather because
she loves them so much that it is too painful to see them
and feel her failure. The epigram to Godwin's story tells
us that "Once upon a time there was a wife and a mother
one too many times" (35). The addition of "one too many
times" to this traditional story opening forces the idea
of repetition and monotony: it suggests that it is not
that state of being a wife and mother that is inherently
bad but rather the fact that that is all Godwin's character is. Day in and day out, too many times over, the woman
is just a wife and a mother, and it isn't enough for her.

In van der Zee's story there could be no such thing
as too much motherhood or too much of being a wife. When
Faye's fears of losing Kai are assuaged, and she is happily married, it is as though a great weight has been
lifted off her. Godwin's character, on the other hand,
feels her marriage as a great weight pressing on her and
immobilizing her. When she leaves her room for a day and
puts out freshly baked bread for her husband and son, they
express their happiness in the notes they write to her
that night, and "the force of the two joyful notes . . .
pressed her into the corner of the little room; she hardly
had space to breathe" (39). Faye can be a traditional wife
and mother, so her family is a source of joy. Godwin's
character can no longer be the traditional wife and
mother, and so her family represents her own failure, and
the guilt presses her further and further into herself
until she can retreat no further and ends her life.

The endings of the two stories are powerful illustrations of the differences between them. In the end of

A Secret Sorrow the author shows us Faye feeling "beautiful, complete, whole" (35) in her role as wife and mother.
Godwin, on the other hand, shows us her protagonist dead
on her bed. Godwin seems to give the reader hope by showing all that the woman has done and saying that "the house
smelled redolently of renewal and spring" (39). This makes
the blow even harder when we then discover, along with the
husband and child, the woman's death. The ambiguous way
the death of Godwin's unnamed protagonist is dealt with
reinforces the author's negative portrayal of marriage. It
isn't explicitly written as a suicide, and Godwin seems to
encourage her readers to see it as the inevitable consequence of her marriage.

Van der Zee creates a story full of emotional highs
and lows, but one that leads up to and ends with marriage.
After the marriage all of the plot twists and traumas
come to a halt, replaced with peace and happiness. Faye
is brought to new life by her marriage and children; she
finds fulfillment of all of her desires in them. Godwin's
story, however, is full of postmarital anguish and confusion. The character she creates is stifled and most definitely unfulfilled by her marriage. A burst of creative
energy right before her death produces, among other
things, "a sheath of marvelous watercolor beasts accompanied by mad and fanciful stories nobody could ever
make up again, and a tablet full of love sonnets addressed to the man" (39). It is clear that the woman had
talents and desires not met by the routine duties of her
marital life. For Faye, the protagonist of A Secret
Sorrow, marriage is the happily-ever-after ending she has
wanted all of her life; for Godwin's protagonist, on the
other hand, marriage is just a monotonous and interminable
ever after.

3

Plot

Created by a writer's imagination, a work of fiction need not be factual or historically accurate. Although actual people, places, and events may be included in fiction, facts are not as important as is the writer's use of them. We can learn much about Russian life in the early part of the nineteenth century from Leo Tolstoy's *War and Peace,* but that historical information is incidental to Tolstoy's exploration of human nature. Tolstoy, like most successful writers, makes us accept as real the world in his novel no matter how foreign it may be to our own reality. One of the ways a writer achieves this acceptance and engagement — and one of a writer's few obligations — is to interest us in what is happening in the story. We are carried into the writer's fictional world by the plot.

Plot is the author's arrangement of incidents in a story. It is the organizing principle that controls the order of events. This structure is, in a sense, what remains after a writer edits out what is irrelevant to the story being told. We don't need to know, for example, what happens to Rip Van Winkle's faithful dog, Wolf, during his amiable master's twenty-year nap in the Catskill Mountains in order to be enchanted by Washington Irving's story of a henpecked husband. Instead, what is told takes on meaning as it is brought into focus by a skillful writer who selects and orders the events that constitute the story's plot.

Events can be presented in a variety of orders. A chronological arrangement begins with what happens first, then second, and so on, until the last incident is related. That is how "Rip Van Winkle" is told. The events in William Faulkner's "A Rose for Emily," however, are not arranged in chronological order because that would give away the story's surprise ending; instead, Faulkner moves back and forth between the past and present to provide information that leads up to the final startling moment (which won't be given away here either; the story begins on p. 75).

Some stories begin at the end and then lead up to why or how events worked out as they did. If you read the first paragraph of Ralph Ellison's "Battle Royal" (p. 231), you'll find an example of this arrangement that will make it difficult for you to stop reading. Stories can also begin in the middle of things (the Latin term for this common plot strategy is *in medias res*). In this kind of plot we enter the story on the verge of some important moment. John Updike's "A & P" (p. 606) begins with the narrator, a teenager working at a checkout counter in a supermarket, telling us: "In walks these three girls in nothing but bathing suits." Right away we are brought into the middle of a situation that will ultimately create the conflict in the story.

Another common strategy is the *flashback,* a device that informs us about events that happened before the opening scene of a work. Nearly all of Ellison's "Battle Royal" takes the form of a flashback as the narrator recounts how his identity as a black man was shaped by the circumstances that attended a high-school graduation speech he delivered twenty years earlier in a hotel ballroom before a gathering of the town's leading white citizens, most of whom were "quite tipsy." Whatever the plot arrangement, you should be aware of how the writer's conscious ordering of events affects your responses to the action.

EDGAR RICE BURROUGHS (1875–1950)

A great many stories share a standard plot pattern. The following excerpt from Edgar Rice Burroughs's novel *Tarzan of the Apes* provides a conventional plot pattern in which the *character,* an imagined person in the story, is confronted with a problem leading to a climactic struggle that is followed by a resolution of the problem. The elements of a conventional plot are easily recognizable to readers familiar with fast-paced, action-packed mysteries, spy thrillers, westerns, or adventure stories. These page-turners are carefully plotted so that the reader is swept up by the action. More serious writers sometimes use similar strategies, but they do so with greater subtlety and for some purpose that goes beyond providing a thrill a minute. The writer of serious fiction is usually less concerned with what happens next to the central character than with why it happens. In Burroughs's adventure story, however, the emphasis is clearly on action. *Tarzan of the Apes* may add little or nothing to our understanding of life, but it is useful for delineating some important elements of plot. Moreover, it is great fun.

Burroughs's novel, published in 1914 and the first of a series of enormously popular Tarzan books and films, charts the growth to manhood of a child raised in the African jungle by great apes. Tarzan struggles to survive his primitive beginnings and to reconcile what he has learned in the jungle with his equally powerful instincts to be a civilized human being. One of the more exciting moments in Tarzan's development is his final confrontation with his old enemy, Terkoz, a huge tyrannical ape that has kidnapped Jane, a pretty nineteen-year-old from Baltimore, Maryland, who has accompanied her father on an expedition to the jungle.

In the chapter preceding this excerpt, Tarzan falls in love with Jane and writes this pointed, if not eloquent, note to her: "I am Tarzan of the Apes. I want you. I am yours. You are mine." Just as he finishes the note, he hears "the agonized screams of a woman" and rushes to their source to find Esmeralda, Jane's maid, hysterical with fear and grief. She reports that Jane, the fair and gentle embodiment of civilization in the story, has been carried off by a gorilla. Here is the first half of the next chapter, which illustrates how Burroughs plots the sequence of events so that the emphasis is on physical action.

Web   *Research Edgar Rice Burroughs with LitLinks at*
http://www.bedfordstmartins.com/meyer/bedintrolit

From Tarzan of the Apes   *1914*

From the time Tarzan left the tribe of great anthropoids in which he had been raised, it was torn by continual strife and discord. Terkoz proved a cruel and capricious king, so that, one by one, many of the older and weaker apes, upon whom he was particularly prone to vent his brutish nature, took their families and sought the quiet and safety of the far interior.

But at last those who remained were driven to desperation by the continued truculence of Terkoz, and it so happened that one of them recalled the parting admonition of Tarzan:

"If you have a chief who is cruel, do not do as the other apes do, and attempt, any one of you, to pit yourself against him alone. But, instead, let two or three or four of you attack him together. Then, if you will do this, no chief will dare to be other than he should be, for four of you can kill any chief who may ever be over you."

And the ape who recalled this wise counsel repeated it to several of his fellows, so that when Terkoz returned to the tribe that day he found a warm reception awaiting him.

There were no formalities. As Terkoz reached the group, five huge, hairy   5
beasts sprang upon him.

At heart he was an arrant coward, which is the way with bullies among apes as well as among men; so he did not remain to fight and die, but tore himself away from them as quickly as he could and fled into the sheltering boughs of the forest.

Two more attempts he made to rejoin the tribe, but on each occasion he was set upon and driven away. At last he gave it up, and turned, foaming with rage and hatred, into the jungle.

For several days he wandered aimlessly, nursing his spite and looking for some weak thing on which to vent his pent anger.

It was in this state of mind that the horrible, manlike beast, swinging from tree to tree, came suddenly upon two women in the jungle.

He was right above them when he discovered them. The first intimation   10
Jane Porter had of his presence was when the great hairy body dropped to the
earth beside her, and she saw the awful face and the snarling, hideous mouth
thrust within a foot of her.

One piercing scream escaped her lips as the brute hand clutched her arm.
Then she was dragged toward those awful fangs which yawned at her throat.
But ere they touched that fair skin another mood claimed the anthropoid.

The tribe had kept his women. He must find others to replace them. This
hairless white ape would be the first of his new household, and so he threw her
roughly across his broad, hairy shoulders and leaped back into the trees, bearing Jane away.

Esmeralda's scream of terror had mingled once with that of Jane, and
then, as was Esmeralda's manner under stress of emergency which required
presence of mind, she swooned.

But Jane did not once lose consciousness. It is true that that awful face,
pressing close to hers, and the stench of the foul breath beating upon her nostrils, paralyzed her with terror; but her brain was clear, and she comprehended
all that transpired.

With what seemed to her marvelous rapidity the brute bore her through   15
the forest, but still she did not cry out or struggle. The sudden advent of the
ape had confused her to such an extent that she thought now that he was bearing her toward the beach.

For this reason she conserved her energies and her voice until she could
see that they had approached near enough to the camp to attract the succor
she craved.

She could not have known it, but she was being borne farther and farther
into the impenetrable jungle.

The scream that had brought Clayton and the two older men stumbling
through the undergrowth had led Tarzan of the Apes straight to where Esmeralda lay, but it was not Esmeralda in whom his interest centered, though pausing over her he saw that she was unhurt.

For a moment he scrutinized the ground below and the trees above, until
the ape that was in him by virtue of training and environment, combined with
the intelligence that was his by right of birth, told his wondrous woodcraft the
whole story as plainly as though he had seen the thing happen with his own
eyes.

And then he was gone again into the swaying trees, following the high-flung   20
spoor which no other human eye could have detected, much less translated.

At boughs' ends, where the anthropoid swings from one tree to another,
there is most to mark the trail, but least to point the direction of the quarry;
for there the pressure is downward always, toward the small end of the branch,
whether the ape be leaving or entering a tree. Nearer the center of the tree,
where the signs of passage are fainter, the direction is plainly marked.

Here, on this branch, a caterpillar has been crushed by the fugitive's great
foot, and Tarzan knows instinctively where that same foot would touch in the
next stride. Here he looks to find a tiny particle of the demolished larva, oft-
times not more than a speck of moisture.

Again, a minute bit of bark has been upturned by the scraping hand, and
the direction of the break indicates the direction of the passage. Or some great
limb, or the stem of the tree itself has been brushed by the hairy body, and a

tiny shred of hair tells him by the direction from which it is wedged beneath the bark that he is on the right trail.

Nor does he need to check his speed to catch these seemingly faint records of the fleeing beast.

To Tarzan they stand out boldly against all the myriad other scars and 25 bruises and signs upon the leafy way. But strongest of all is the scent, for Tarzan is pursuing up the wind, and his trained nostrils are as sensitive as a hound's.

There are those who believe that the lower orders are specially endowed by nature with better olfactory nerves than man, but it is merely a matter of development.

Man's survival does not hinge so greatly upon the perfection of his senses. His power to reason has relieved them of many of their duties, and so they have, to some extent, atrophied, as have the muscles which move the ears and scalp, merely from disuse.

The muscles are there, about the ears and beneath the scalp, and so are the nerves which transmit sensations to the brain, but they are underdeveloped because they are not needed.

Not so with Tarzan of the Apes. From early infancy his survival had depended upon acuteness of eyesight, hearing, smell, touch, and taste far more than upon the more slowly developed organ of reason.

The least developed of all in Tarzan was the sense of taste, for he could eat 30 luscious fruits, or raw flesh, long buried, with almost equal appreciation; but in that he differed but slightly from more civilized epicures.

Almost silently the ape-man sped on in the track of Terkoz and his prey, but the sound of his approach reached the ears of the fleeing beast and spurred it on to greater speed.

Three miles were covered before Tarzan overtook them, and then Terkoz, seeing that further flight was futile, dropped to the ground in a small open glade, that he might turn and fight for his prize or be free to escape unhampered if he saw that the pursuer was more than a match for him.

He still grasped Jane in one great arm as Tarzan bounded like a leopard into the arena which nature had provided for this primeval-like battle.

When Terkoz saw that it was Tarzan who pursued him, he jumped to the conclusion that this was Tarzan's woman, since they were of the same kind — white and hairless — and so he rejoiced at this opportunity for double revenge upon his hated enemy.

To Jane the strange apparition of this godlike man was as wine to sick 35 nerves.

From the description which Clayton and her father and Mr. Philander had given her, she knew that it must be the same wonderful creature who had saved them, and she saw in him only a protector and a friend.

But as Terkoz pushed her roughly aside to meet Tarzan's charge, and she saw the great proportions of the ape and the mighty muscles and the fierce fangs, her heart quailed. How could any vanquish such a mighty antagonist?

Like two charging bulls they came together, and like two wolves sought each other's throat. Against the long canines of the ape was pitted the thin blade of the man's knife.

Jane — her lithe, young form flattened against the trunk of a great tree, her hands tight pressed against her rising and falling bosom, and her eyes wide

with mingled horror, fascination, fear, and admiration—watched the primor-
dial ape battle with the primeval man for possession of a woman—for her.

As the great muscles of the man's back and shoulders knotted beneath   40
the tension of his efforts, and the huge biceps and forearm held at bay those
mighty tusks, the veil of centuries of civilization and culture were swept from
the blurred vision of the Baltimore girl.

When the long knife drank deep a dozen times of Terkoz's heart's blood,
and the great carcass rolled lifeless upon the ground, it was a primeval woman
who sprang forward with outstretched arms toward the primeval man who
had fought for her and won.

And Tarzan?

He did what no red-blooded man needs lessons in doing. He took his
woman in his arms and smothered her upturned, panting lips with kisses.

For a moment Jane lay there with half-closed eyes. For a moment—the
first in her young life—she knew the meaning of love.

But as suddenly as the veil had been withdrawn it dropped again, and an   45
outraged conscience suffused her face with its scarlet mantle, and a mortified
woman thrust Tarzan of the Apes from her and buried her face in her hands.

Tarzan had been surprised when he had found the girl he had learned to
love after a vague and abstract manner a willing prisoner in his arms. Now he
was surprised that she repulsed him.

He came close to her once more and took hold of her arm. She turned
upon him like a tigress, striking his great breast with her tiny hands.

Tarzan could not understand it.

A moment ago, and it had been his intention to hasten Jane back to her
people, but that little moment was lost now in the dim and distant past of
things which were but can never be again, and with it the good intention had
gone to join the impossible.

Since then Tarzan of the Apes had felt a warm, lithe form close pressed to   50
his. Hot, sweet breath against his cheek and mouth had fanned a new flame to
life within his breast, and perfect lips had clung to his in burning kisses that
had seared a deep brand into his soul—a brand which marked a new Tarzan.

Again he laid his hand upon her arm. Again she repulsed him. And then
Tarzan of the Apes did just what his first ancestor would have done.

He took his woman in his arms and carried her into the jungle.

This episode begins with **exposition,** the background information the
reader needs to make sense of the situation in which the characters are
placed. The first eight paragraphs let us know that Terkoz has been overthrown as leader of the ape tribe and that he is roaming the jungle "looking for some weak thing on which to vent his pent anger." This exposition
is in the form of a flashback. (Recall that the previous chapter ended with
Esmeralda's report of the kidnapping; now we will see what happened.)

Once this information supplies a context for the characters, the plot
gains momentum with the **rising action,** a complication that intensifies the
situation: Terkoz, looking for a victim, discovers the vulnerable Esmeralda
and Jane. His first impulse is to kill Jane, but his "mood" changes when he
remembers that he has no woman of his own after having been forced to
leave the tribe (more exposition). Hence, there is a further complication in

the rising action when he decides to carry her off. Just when it seems that the situation could not get any worse, it does. The reader is invited to shudder even more than if Terkoz had made a meal of Jane because she may have to endure the "awful face," "foul breath," and lust of this beast.

At this point we are brought up to the action that ended the preceding chapter. Tarzan races to the rescue by unerringly following the trail from the place where Jane was kidnapped. He relentlessly tracks Terkoz. Unfortunately, Burroughs slows down the pursuit here by including several paragraphs that abstractly consider the evolutionary development of human reliance on reason more than on their senses for survival. This discussion offers a rationale for Tarzan's remarkable ability to track Jane, but it is an interruption in the chase.

When Tarzan finally catches up to Terkoz, the **conflict** of this episode fully emerges. Tarzan must save the woman he loves by defeating his long-standing enemy. For Terkoz seeks to achieve a "double revenge" by killing Tarzan and taking his woman. Terkoz's assumption that Jane is Tarzan's woman is a **foreshadowing,** a suggestion of what is yet to come. In this conflict Tarzan is the **protagonist** or **hero,** the central character who engages our interest and empathy. *Protagonist* is often a more useful term than hero or **heroine,** however, because the central character of a story can be despicable as well as heroic. In Edgar Allan Poe's "The Tell-Tale Heart," for example, the central character is a madman and murderer. Terkoz is the **antagonist,** the force that opposes the protagonist.

The battle between Tarzan and Terkoz creates **suspense** because the reader is made anxious about what is going to happen. Burroughs makes certain that the reader will worry about the outcome by having Jane wonder, "How could any vanquish such a mighty antagonist?" If we are caught up in the moment, we watch the battle, as Jane does, with "mingled horror, fascination, fear, and admiration" to see what will happen next. The moment of greatest emotional tension, the **climax,** occurs when Tarzan kills Terkoz. Tarzan's victory is the **resolution** of the conflict, also known as the **dénouement** (a French word meaning the "untying of the knot"). This could have been the conclusion to the episode except that Jane and Tarzan simultaneously discover their "primeval" selves sexually drawn to each other. Burroughs resolves one conflict — the battle with Terkoz — but then immediately creates another — by raising the question of what a respectable professor's daughter from Baltimore is doing in the sweaty arms of a panting, half-naked man.

For a brief moment the cycle of conflict, suspense, and resolution begins again as Jane passionately kisses Tarzan; then her "outraged conscience" causes her to regain her sense of propriety and she pushes him away. Although Tarzan succeeds in the encounter with Terkoz, he is not successful with Jane. However, Burroughs creates suspense for a third time at the very end of the episode, when the "new Tarzan," having been transformed by this sexual awakening, "took his woman in his arms and carried her into the jungle." What will he do next? Despite the novel's implausibility (beginning with the premise that apes could raise a human child) and its heavy use of coincidences (not the least of which is Tarzan's donning a loincloth for the first time only four pages before he meets Jane), the story is difficult to put down. The plot swings us swiftly and smoothly from incident to incident, even if there is an occasional interruption, such as Burroughs's discussion of evolution, in the flow of the action.

Although this pattern of exposition, rising action, conflict, suspense, climax, and resolution provides a useful outline of many plots that emphasize physical action, a greater value of this pattern is that it helps us to see how innovative artists move beyond formula fiction by manipulating and changing the pattern for their own purposes. At the furthest extreme are those modern storytellers who reject traditional plotting techniques in favor of experimental approaches. Instead of including characters who wrestle with conflicts, experimental fiction frequently may concern the writer's own efforts to create a story. Rather than ordering experience, such writers disrupt it by insisting that meanings in fiction are as elusive — or nonexistent — as meanings in life; they are likely to reject both traditional values and traditional forms of writing. Most writers, however, use conflicts in their plots to reveal characters and convey meanings. The nature of those conflicts can help determine how important physical action is to the plot.

The primary conflict that Tarzan experiences in his battle with Terkoz is external. External conflict is popular in adventure stories because the protagonist's physical struggles with a formidable foe or the ever-present dangers of a dense jungle echoing wild screams provide plenty of excitement. External conflicts may place the protagonist in opposition to another individual, nature, or society. Tarzan's battle with societal values begins the moment he instinctively takes Jane in his arms to carry her off into the jungle. He will learn that an individual's conflict with society can be as frustrating as it is complex, which is why so many plots in serious fiction focus on this conflict. It can be seen, to cite only two examples, in a mysterious stranger's alienation from a materialistic culture in Herman Melville's "Bartleby, the Scrivener" (p. 116) and in a young black man's struggle with racism in Ellison's "Battle Royal" (p. 231).

Conflict may also be internal; in such a case some moral or psychological issue must be resolved within the protagonist. Inner conflicts frequently accompany external ones, as in Godwin's "A Sorrowful Woman" (p. 35). Godwin's story is quiet and almost uneventful compared with *Tarzan of the Apes.* The conflict, though puzzling, is more significant in "A Sorrowful Woman" because that story subtly explores some troubling issues that cannot be resolved simply by "huge biceps" or a "lithe, young form." The protagonist struggles with both internal and external forces. We are not told why she withdraws from her considerate husband and beautiful son. There is no exposition to explain why she is hopelessly "sad and sick" of them. There is no readily identifiable antagonist in her way, but there are several possibilities. Her antagonist is some part of herself that cannot find satisfaction in playing the roles of wife and mother, yet her husband and child also seem to bear some of the responsibility, as does the domestic environment that defines her.

Godwin creates questions for the reader rather than suspense. We are compelled to keep asking why the protagonist in her story is so unhappy instead of what is going to happen next. The story ends with her flurry of domestic activity and her death, but we do not feel as if we have come to a resolution. "A Sorrowful Woman" will not let us go because we keep coming back to what causes the protagonist's rejection of her role. Has she gone mad? Are the husband and child not what they seem to be? Is her domestic life stifling rather than nourishing? Does her family destroy rather than support her? Who or what is to blame? No one is able to rescue the sorrowful woman from her conflict, nor does the design of Godwin's plot relieve the reader of the questions the story raises. The meaning of the action is not self-evident as it is in *Tarzan of the Apes*. It must be drawn from a careful reading of the interrelated details and dialogues that constitute this story's action.

Although Burroughs makes enormous demands on Tarzan to survive the perils of the jungle, the author makes few demands on the reader. In part, that's why *Tarzan of the Apes* is so much fun: we sit back while Tarzan does all the work, struggling heroically through all the conflicts Burroughs has planted along his jungle paths. Godwin's story, in contrast, illustrates that there are other kinds of plots, less dependent on action but equally full of conflict. This kind of reading is more demanding, but ultimately more satisfying, because as we confront conflicts in serious fiction we read not only absorbing stories but also ourselves. We are invited not to escape life but to look long and hard at it. Although serious fiction can be as diverting and pleasurable as most standard action-packed plots, serious fiction offers an additional important element: a perspective on experience that reflects rather than deflects life.

The following three stories—Alice Walker's "The Flowers," William Faulkner's "A Rose for Emily," and Andre Dubus's "Killings"—are remarkable for the different kinds of tension produced in each by a subtle use of plot.

ALICE WALKER (B. 1944)

Novelist, poet, and political activist, Alice Walker was born in 1944 to Minnie Tallulah Grant Walker and Willie Lee Walker, sharecroppers in Eatonton, Georgia. A promising student from the beginning, Walker started her collegiate career at Spelman College in Atlanta, but graduated from Sarah Lawrence College in New York in 1965. After teaching history in Mississippi, she won a fellowship from the Radcliffe Institute and went on to teach at Wellesley College, where she pioneered one of the first women's studies courses in the country. Walker has published three volumes of poetry, *Once* (1968), *Revolutionary Petunias and Other Poems* (1973), and *Horses*

Make a Landscape Look More Beautiful (1984), and a book of essays, *Living by the Word* (1988). Her numerous works of fiction include *In Love and Trouble: Stories of Black Women* (1973), *The Temple of My Familiar* (1989), *By the Light of My Father's Smile* (1998), *Possessing the Secret of Joy* (1998), and *The Color Purple* (1982), which was made into a major motion picture. The acclaim for her novel *Meridian* (1982) won her a Guggenheim Fellowship and led her to San Francisco, where she still lives. Walker's writing career has been defined largely by political interests that have not waned since the sixties, and she has contributed substantially to the antinuclear and environmental movements, women's rights, and the movement for the protection of indigenous peoples.

Web *Research Alice Walker with LitLinks at*
http://www.bedfordstmartins.com/meyer/bedintrolit

The Flowers   1973

It seemed to Myop as she skipped lightly from hen house to pigpen to smokehouse that the days had never been as beautiful as these. The air held a keenness that made her nose twitch. The harvesting of the corn and cotton, peanuts and squash, made each day a golden surprise that caused excited little tremors to run up her jaws.

Myop carried a short, knobby stick. She struck out at random at chickens she liked, and worked out the beat of a song on the fence around the pigpen. She felt light and good in the warm sun. She was ten, and nothing existed for her but her song, the stick clutched in her dark brown hand, and the tat-de-ta-ta-ta of accompaniment.

Turning her back on the rusty boards of her family's sharecropper cabin, Myop walked along the fence till it ran into the stream made by the spring. Around the spring, where the family got drinking water, silver ferns and wildflowers grew. Along the shallow banks pigs rooted. Myop watched the tiny white bubbles disrupt the thin black scale of soil and the water that silently rose and slid away down the stream.

She had explored the woods behind the house many times. Often, in late autumn, her mother took her to gather nuts among the fallen leaves. Today she made her own path, bouncing this way and that way, vaguely keeping an eye out for snakes. She found, in addition to various common but pretty ferns and leaves, an armful of strange blue flowers with velvety ridges and a sweet-suds bush full of the brown, fragrant buds.

By twelve o'clock, her arms laden with sprigs of her findings, she was a 5 mile or more from home. She had often been as far before, but the strangeness of the land made it not as pleasant as her usual haunts. It seemed gloomy in the little cove in which she found herself. The air was damp, the silence close and deep.

Myop began to circle back to the house, back to the peacefulness of the morning. It was then she stepped smack into his eyes. Her heel became lodged in the broken ridge between brow and nose, and she reached down quickly, unafraid, to free herself. It was only when she saw his naked grin that she gave a little yelp of surprise.

He had been a tall man. From feet to neck covered a long space. His head lay beside him. When she pushed back the leaves and layers of earth and debris Myop saw that he'd had large white teeth, all of them cracked or broken, long fingers, and very big bones. All his clothes had rotted away except some threads of blue denim from his overalls. The buckles of the overalls had turned green.

Myop gazed around the spot with interest. Very near where she'd stepped into the head was a wild pink rose. As she picked it to add to her bundle she noticed a raised mound, a ring, around the rose's root. It was the rotted remains of a noose, a bit of shredding plowline, now blending benignly into the soil. Around an overhanging limb of a great spreading oak clung another piece. Frayed, rotted, bleached, and frazzled—barely there—but spinning restlessly in the breeze. Myop laid down her flowers.

And the summer was over.

CONSIDERATIONS FOR CRITICAL THINKING AND WRITING

1. FIRST RESPONSE. How do you interpret the final line of the story? What is the effect of the brevity of that sentence?
2. Describe the atmosphere and tone of the first three paragraphs. What emotions do they produce concerning Myop's childhood?
3. How might paragraph 5 be described as an example of foreshadowing?
4. What is the conflict in the story? What is its climax? Is there a resolution to the conflict? Explain.
5. What do you think is the central point of this story?

CONNECTIONS TO OTHER SELECTIONS

1. Discuss the significance of Myop's experience and that of the narrator in Ralph Ellison's "Battle Royal" (p. 231).
2. Write an essay comparing the ending of Walker's story with that of Raymond Carver's "Popular Mechanics" (p. 286). What is the effect of the ending on your reading of each story?

WILLIAM FAULKNER (1897–1962)

Born into an old Mississippi family that had lost its influence and wealth during the Civil War, William Faulkner lived nearly all his life in the South writing about Yoknapatawpha County, an imagined Mississippi county similar to his home in Oxford. Among his novels based on this fictional location are *The Sound and the Fury* (1929), *As I Lay Dying* (1930), *Light in August* (1932), and *Absalom, Absalom!* (1936). Although his writings are regional in their emphasis on local social history, his concerns are broader. In his 1950 acceptance speech for the Nobel Prize for literature, he insisted that the "problems of the human heart in conflict with itself . . . alone can make good writing because only that is worth writing about, worth the agony and the sweat." This commitment is evident in his novels and in *The Collected Stories of William Faulkner* (1950). "A

Rose for Emily," about the mysterious life of Emily Grierson, presents a personal conflict rooted in her southern identity. It also contains a grim surprise.

Web   *Research William Faulkner with LitLinks at*
http://www.bedfordstmartins.com/meyer/bedintrolit

A Rose for Emily   *1931*

I

When Miss Emily Grierson died, our whole town went to her funeral: the men through a sort of respectful affection for a fallen monument, the women mostly out of curiosity to see the inside of her house, which no one save an old manservant — a combined gardener and cook — had seen in at least ten years.

It was a big, squarish frame house that had once been white, decorated with cupolas and spires and scrolled balconies in the heavily lightsome style of the seventies, set on what had once been our most select street. But garages and cotton gins had encroached and obliterated even the august names of that neighborhood; only Miss Emily's house was left, lifting its stubborn and coquettish decay above the cotton wagons and the gasoline pumps — an eyesore among eyesores. And now Miss Emily had gone to join the representatives of those august names where they lay in the cedar-bemused cemetery among the ranked and anonymous graves of Union and Confederate soldiers who fell at the battle of Jefferson.

Alive, Miss Emily had been a tradition, a duty, and a care; a sort of hereditary obligation upon the town, dating from that day in 1894 when Colonel Sartoris, the mayor — he who fathered the edict that no Negro woman should appear on the streets without an apron — remitted her taxes, the dispensation dating from the death of her father on into perpetuity. Not that Miss Emily would have accepted charity. Colonel Sartoris invented an involved tale to the effect that Miss Emily's father had loaned money to the town, which the town, as a matter of business, preferred this way of repaying. Only a man of Colonel Sartoris' generation and thought could have invented it, and only a woman could have believed it.

When the next generation, with its more modern ideas, became mayors and aldermen, this arrangement created some little dissatisfaction. On the first of the year they mailed her a tax notice. February came, and there was no reply. They wrote her a formal letter, asking her to call at the sheriff's office at her convenience. A week later the mayor wrote her himself, offering to call or to send his car for her, and received in reply a note on paper of an archaic shape, in a thin, flowing calligraphy in faded ink, to the effect that she no longer went out at all. The tax notice was also enclosed, without comment.

They called a special meeting of the Board of Aldermen. A deputation 5 waited upon her, knocked at the door through which no visitor had passed since she ceased giving china-painting lessons eight or ten years earlier. They were admitted by the old Negro into a dim hall from which a stairway mounted into still more shadow. It smelled of dust and disuse — a close, dank smell. The Negro led them into the parlor. It was furnished in heavy, leather-covered furniture. When the Negro opened the blinds of one window, they could see that the leather was cracked; and when they sat down, a faint dust rose sluggishly about their thighs, spinning with slow motes in the single sun-ray. On a tarnished gilt easel before the fireplace stood a crayon portrait of Miss Emily's father.

They rose when she entered—a small, fat woman in black, with a thin gold chain descending to her waist and vanishing into her belt, leaning on an ebony cane with a tarnished gold head. Her skeleton was small and spare; perhaps that was why what would have been merely plumpness in another was obesity in her. She looked bloated, like a body long submerged in motionless water, and of that pallid hue. Her eyes, lost in the fatty ridges of her face, looked like two small pieces of coal pressed into a lump of dough as they moved from one face to another while the visitors stated their errand.

She did not ask them to sit. She just stood in the door and listened quietly until the spokesman came to a stumbling halt. Then they could hear the invisible watch ticking at the end of the gold chain.

Her voice was dry and cold. "I have no taxes in Jefferson. Colonel Sartoris explained it to me. Perhaps one of you can gain access to the city records and satisfy yourselves."

"But we have. We are the city authorities, Miss Emily. Didn't you get a notice from the sheriff, signed by him?"

"I received a paper, yes," Miss Emily said. "Perhaps he considers himself 10
the sheriff . . . I have no taxes in Jefferson."

"But there is nothing on the books to show that, you see. We must go by the—"

"See Colonel Sartoris. I have no taxes in Jefferson."

"But, Miss Emily—"

"See Colonel Sartoris." (Colonel Sartoris had been dead almost ten years.) "I have no taxes in Jefferson. Tobe!" The Negro appeared. "Show these gentlemen out."

II

So she vanquished them, horse and foot, just as she had vanquished their 15
fathers thirty years before about the smell. That was two years after her father's death and a short time after her sweetheart—the one we believed would marry her—had deserted her. After her father's death she went out very little; after her sweetheart went away, people hardly saw her at all. A few of the ladies had the temerity to call, but were not received, and the only sign of life about the place was the Negro man—a young man then—going in and out with a market basket.

"Just as if a man—any man—could keep a kitchen properly," the ladies said; so they were not surprised when the smell developed. It was another link between the gross, teeming world and the high and mighty Griersons.

A neighbor, a woman, complained to the mayor, Judge Stevens, eighty years old.

"But what will you have me do about it, madam?" he said.

"Why, send her word to stop it," the woman said. "Isn't there a law?"

"I'm sure that won't be necessary," Judge Stevens said. "It's probably just a 20
snake or a rat that nigger of hers killed in the yard. I'll speak to him about it."

The next day he received two more complaints, one from a man who came in diffident deprecation. "We really must do something about it, Judge. I'd be the last one in the world to bother Miss Emily, but we've got to do something." That night the Board of Aldermen met — three graybeards and one younger man, a member of the rising generation.

"It's simple enough," he said. "Send her word to have her place cleaned up. Give her a certain time to do it in, and if she don't . . ."

"Dammit, sir," Judge Stevens said, "will you accuse a lady to her face of smelling bad?"

So the next night, after midnight, four men crossed Miss Emily's lawn and slunk about the house like burglars, sniffing along the base of the brickwork and at the cellar openings while one of them performed a regular sowing motion with his hand out of a sack slung from his shoulder. They broke open the cellar door and sprinkled lime there, and in all the outbuildings. As they recrossed the lawn, a window that had been dark was lighted and Miss Emily sat in it, the light behind her, and her upright torso motionless as that of an idol. They crept quietly across the lawn and into the shadow of the locusts that lined the street. After a week or two the smell went away.

That was when people had begun to feel really sorry for her. People in our town, remembering how old lady Wyatt, her great-aunt, had gone completely crazy at last, believed that the Griersons held themselves a little too high for what they really were. None of the young men were quite good enough for Miss Emily and such. We had long thought of them as a tableau, Miss Emily a slender figure in white in the background, her father a spraddled silhouette in the foreground, his back to her and clutching a horsewhip, the two of them framed by the back-flung front door. So when she got to be thirty and was still single, we were not pleased exactly, but vindicated; even with insanity in the family she wouldn't have turned down all of her chances if they had really materialized.

When her father died, it got about that the house was all that was left to her; and in a way, people were glad. At last they could pity Miss Emily. Being left alone, and a pauper, she had become humanized. Now she too would know the old thrill and the old despair of a penny more or less.

The day after his death all the ladies prepared to call at the house and offer condolence and aid, as is our custom. Miss Emily met them at the door, dressed as usual and with no trace of grief on her face. She told them that her father was not dead. She did that for three days, with the ministers calling on her, and the doctors, trying to persuade her to let them dispose of the body. Just as they were about to resort to law and force, she broke down, and they buried her father quickly.

We did not say she was crazy then. We believed she had to do that. We remembered all the young men her father had driven away, and we knew that with nothing left, she would have to cling to that which had robbed her, as people will.

III

She was sick for a long time. When we saw her again, her hair was cut short, making her look like a girl, with a vague resemblance to those angels in colored church windows — sort of tragic and serene.

The town had just let the contracts for paving the sidewalks, and in the 30
summer after her father's death they began the work. The construction company came with niggers and mules and machinery, and a foreman named
Homer Barron, a Yankee — a big, dark, ready man, with a big voice and eyes
lighter than his face. The little boys would follow in groups to hear him cuss
the niggers, and the niggers singing in time to the rise and fall of picks. Pretty
soon he knew everybody in town. Whenever you heard a lot of laughing anywhere about the square, Homer Barron would be in the center of the group.
Presently we began to see him and Miss Emily on Sunday afternoons driving in
the yellow-wheeled buggy and the matched team of bays from the livery stable.

At first we were glad that Miss Emily would have an interest, because the
ladies all said, "Of course a Grierson would not think seriously of a Northerner, a day laborer." But there were still others, older people, who said that
even grief could not cause a real lady to forget *noblesse oblige*° — without calling
it *noblesse oblige*. They just said, "Poor Emily. Her kinsfolk should come to her."
She had some kin in Alabama; but years ago her father had fallen out with
them over the estate of old lady Wyatt, the crazy woman, and there was no
communication between the two families. They had not even been represented
at the funeral.

And as soon as the old people said, "Poor Emily," the whispering began.
"Do you suppose it's really so?" they said to one another. "Of course it is. What
else could . . ." This behind their hands; rustling of craned silk and satin behind jalousies closed upon the sun of Sunday afternoon as the thin, swift
clop-clop-clop of the matched team passed: "Poor Emily."

She carried her head high enough — even when we believed that she was
fallen. It was as if she demanded more than ever the recognition of her dignity
as the last Grierson; as if it had wanted that touch of earthiness to reaffirm her
imperviousness. Like when she bought the rat poison, the arsenic. That was
over a year after they had begun to say "Poor Emily," and while the two female
cousins were visiting her.

"I want some poison," she said to the druggist. She was over thirty then,
still a slight woman, though thinner than usual, with cold, haughty black eyes
in a face the flesh of which was strained across the temples and about the eye-
sockets as you imagine a lighthouse-keeper's face ought to look. "I want some
poison," she said.

"Yes, Miss Emily. What kind? For rats and such? I'd recom —"   35
"I want the best you have. I don't care what kind."
The druggist named several. "They'll kill anything up to an elephant. But
what you want is —"
"Arsenic," Miss Emily said. "Is that a good one?"
"Is . . . arsenic? Yes, ma'am. But what you want —"
"I want arsenic."   40
The druggist looked down at her. She looked back at him, erect, her face
like a strained flag. "Why, of course," the druggist said. "If that's what you
want. But the law requires you to tell what you are going to use it for."
Miss Emily just stared at him, her head tilted back in order to look him eye
for eye, until he looked away and went and got the arsenic and wrapped it up.
The Negro delivery boy brought her the package; the druggist didn't come

noblesse oblige: The obligation of people of high social position.

back. When she opened the package at home there was written on the box, under the skull and bones: "For rats."

IV

So the next day we all said, "She will kill herself"; and we said it would be the best thing. When she had first begun to be seen with Homer Barron, we had said, "She will marry him." Then we said, "She will persuade him yet," because Homer himself had remarked—he liked men, and it was known that he drank with the younger men in the Elks' Club—that he was not a marrying man. Later we said, "Poor Emily" behind the jalousies as they passed on Sunday afternoon in the glittering buggy, Miss Emily with her head high and Homer Barron with his hat cocked and a cigar in his teeth, reins and whip in a yellow glove.

Then some of the ladies began to say that it was a disgrace to the town and a bad example to the young people. The men did not want to interfere, but at last the ladies forced the Baptist minister—Miss Emily's people were Episcopal—to call upon her. He would never divulge what happened during that interview, but he refused to go back again. The next Sunday they again drove about the streets, and the following day the minister's wife wrote to Miss Emily's relations in Alabama.

So she had blood-kin under her roof again and we sat back to watch developments. At first nothing happened. Then we were sure that they were to be married. We learned that Miss Emily had been to the jeweler's and ordered a man's toilet set in silver, with the letters H. B. on each piece. Two days later we learned that she had bought a complete outfit of men's clothing, including a nightshirt, and we said, "They are married." We were really glad. We were glad because the two female cousins were even more Grierson than Miss Emily had ever been. 45

So we were not surprised when Homer Barron—the streets had been finished some time since—was gone. We were a little disappointed that there was not a public blowing-off, but we believed that he had gone on to prepare for Miss Emily's coming, or to give her a chance to get rid of the cousins. (By that time it was a cabal, and we were all Miss Emily's allies to help circumvent the cousins.) Sure enough, after another week they departed. And, as we had expected all along, within three days Homer Barron was back in town. A neighbor saw the Negro man admit him at the kitchen door at dusk one evening.

And that was the last we saw of Homer Barron. And of Miss Emily for some time. The Negro man went in and out with the market basket, but the front door remained closed. Now and then we would see her at a window for a moment, as the men did that night when they sprinkled the lime, but for almost six months she did not appear on the streets. Then we knew that this was to be expected too; as if that quality of her father which had thwarted her woman's life so many times had been too virulent and too furious to die.

When we next saw Miss Emily, she had grown fat and her hair was turning gray. During the next few years it grew grayer and grayer until it attained an even pepper-and-salt iron-gray, when it ceased turning. Up to the day of her death at seventy-four it was still that vigorous iron-gray, like the hair of an active man.

From that time on her front door remained closed, save for a period of six or seven years, when she was about forty, during which she gave lessons in china-painting. She fitted up a studio in one of the downstairs rooms, where the daughters and granddaughters of Colonel Sartoris' contemporaries were sent to her with the same regularity and in the same spirit that they were sent to church on Sundays with a twenty-five-cent piece for the collection plate. Meanwhile her taxes had been remitted.

Then the newer generation became the backbone and the spirit of the 50 town, and the painting pupils grew up and fell away and did not send their children to her with boxes of color and tedious brushes and pictures cut from the ladies' magazines. The front door closed upon the last one and remained closed for good. When the town got free postal delivery, Miss Emily alone refused to let them fasten the metal numbers above her door and attach a mailbox to it. She would not listen to them.

Daily, monthly, yearly we watched the Negro grow grayer and more stooped, going in and out with the market basket. Each December we sent her a tax notice, which would be returned by the post office a week later, unclaimed. Now and then we would see her in one of the downstairs windows — she had evidently shut up the top floor of the house — like the carven torso of an idol in a niche, looking or not looking at us, we could never tell which. Thus she passed from generation to generation — dear, inescapable, impervious, tranquil, and perverse.

And so she died. Fell ill in the house filled with dust and shadows, with only a doddering Negro man to wait on her. We did not even know she was sick; we had long since given up trying to get information from the Negro. He talked to no one, probably not even to her, for his voice had grown harsh and rusty, as if from disuse.

She died in one of the downstairs rooms, in a heavy walnut bed with a curtain, her gray head propped on a pillow yellow and moldy with age and lack of sunlight.

V

The Negro met the first of the ladies at the front door and let them in, with their hushed, sibilant voices and their quick, curious glances, and then he disappeared. He walked right through the house and out the back and was not seen again.

The two female cousins came at once. They held the funeral on the second 55 day, with the town coming to look at Miss Emily beneath a mass of bought flowers, with the crayon face of her father musing profoundly above the bier and the ladies sibilant and macabre; and the very old men — some in their brushed Confederate uniforms — on the porch and the lawn, talking of Miss Emily as if she had been a contemporary of theirs, believing that they had danced with her and courted her perhaps, confusing time with its mathematical progression, as the old do, to whom all the past is not a diminishing road but, instead, a huge meadow which no winter ever quite touches, divided from them now by the narrow bottle-neck of the most recent decade of years.

Already we knew that there was one room in that region above stairs which no one had seen in forty years, and which would have to be forced. They waited until Miss Emily was decently in the ground before they opened it.

The violence of breaking down the door seemed to fill this room with pervading dust. A thin, acrid pall as of the tomb seemed to lie everywhere upon this room decked and furnished as for a bridal: upon the valance curtains of faded rose color, upon the rose-shaded lights, upon the dressing table, upon the delicate array of crystal and the man's toilet things backed with tarnished silver, silver so tarnished that the monogram was obscured. Among them lay a collar and tie, as if they had just been removed, which, lifted, left upon the surface a pale crescent in the dust. Upon a chair hung the suit, carefully folded; beneath it the two mute shoes and the discarded socks.

The man himself lay in the bed.

For a long while we just stood there, looking down at the profound and fleshless grin. The body had apparently once lain in the attitude of an embrace, but now the long sleep that outlasts love, that conquers even the grimace of love, had cuckolded him. What was left of him, rotted beneath what was left of the nightshirt, had become inextricable from the bed in which he lay; and upon him and upon the pillow beside him lay that even coating of the patient and biding dust.

Then we noticed that in the second pillow was the indentation of a 60 head. One of us lifted something from it, and leaning forward, that faint and invisible dust dry and acrid in the nostrils, we saw a long strand of iron-gray hair.

CONSIDERATIONS FOR CRITICAL THINKING AND WRITING

1. FIRST RESPONSE. How might this story be rewritten as a piece of formula fiction? You could write it as a romance, detective, or horror story — whatever strikes your fancy. Does Faulkner's version have elements of formulaic fiction?

2. What is the effect of the final paragraph of the story? How does it contribute to your understanding of Emily? Why is it important that we get this information last rather than at the beginning of the story?

3. What details foreshadow the conclusion of the story? Did you anticipate the ending?

4. Contrast the order of events as they happen in the story with the order in which they are told. How does this plotting create interest and suspense?

5. Faulkner uses a number of gothic elements in this plot: the imposing decrepit house, the decayed corpse, and the mysterious secret horrors connected with Emily's life. How do these elements forward the plot and establish the atmosphere?

6. How does the information provided by the exposition indicate the nature of the conflict in the story? What does Emily's southern heritage contribute to the story?

7. Who or what is the antagonist of the story? Why is it significant that Homer Barron is a construction foreman and a northerner?

8. In what sense does the narrator's telling of the story serve as "A Rose for Emily"? Why do you think the narrator uses *we* rather than *I*?

9. Explain how Emily's reasons for murdering Homer are related to her personal history and to the ways she handled previous conflicts.

10. Discuss how Faulkner's treatment of the North and South contributes to the meaning of the story.

11. Provide an alternative title and explain how the emphasis in your title is reflected in the story.

1. Contrast Faulkner's ordering of events with Tim O'Brien's "How to Tell a True War Story" (p. 548). How does each author's arrangement of incidents create different effects on the reader?

2. To what extent do concepts of honor and tradition influence the action in "A Rose for Emily" and "How to Tell a True War Story"?

PERSPECTIVE

WILLIAM FAULKNER (1897–1962)

On "A Rose for Emily"   1959

Q. What is the meaning of the title "A Rose for Emily"?

A. Oh, it's simply the poor woman had had no life at all. Her father had kept her more or less locked up and then she had a lover who was about to quit her, she had to murder him. It was just "A Rose for Emily" — that's all.

Q. . . . What ever inspired you to write this story?

A. That to me was another sad and tragic manifestation of man's condition in which he dreams and hopes, in which he is in conflict with himself or with his environment or with others. In this case there was the young girl with a young girl's normal aspirations to find love and then a husband and a family, who was brow-beaten and kept down by her father, a selfish man who didn't want her to leave home because he wanted a housekeeper, and it was a natural instinct of — repressed which — you can't repress it — you can mash it down but it comes up somewhere else and very likely in a tragic form, and that was simply another manifestation of man's injustice to man, of the poor tragic human being struggling with its own heart, with others, with its environment, for the simple things which all human beings want. In that case it was a young girl that just wanted to be loved and to love and to have a husband and a family.

Q. And that purely came from your imagination?

A. Well, the story did but the condition is there. It exists. I didn't invent that condition, I didn't invent the fact that young girls dream of someone to love and children and a home, but the story of what her own particular tragedy was was invented, yes. . . .

Q. Sir, it has been argued that "A Rose for Emily" is a criticism of the North, and others have argued saying that it is a criticism of the South. Now, could this story, shall we say, be more properly classified as a criticism of the times?

A. Now that I don't know, because I was simply trying to write about people. The writer uses environment — what he knows — and if there's a symbolism in which the lover represented the North and the woman who murdered him represents the South, I don't say that's not valid and not there, but it was no intention of the writer to say, Now let's see, I'm going to write a piece in which I will use a symbolism for the North and another symbol for the South, that he was simply writing about people, a story which he thought was tragic and true, because it came out of the human heart, the human aspiration, the human — the conflict of conscience with glands, with the Old Adam. It was a conflict not between North and the South so much as between, well you might say, God and Satan.

Q. Sir, just a little more on that thing. You say it's a conflict between God and Satan. Well, I don't quite understand what you mean. Who is — did one represent the —

A. The conflict was in Miss Emily, that she knew that you do not murder people. She had been trained that you do not take a lover. You marry, you don't take a lover. She had broken all the laws of her tradition, her background, and she had finally broken the law of God too, which says you do not take human life. And she knew she was doing wrong, and that's why her own life was wrecked. Instead of murdering one lover, and then to go and take another and when she used him up to murder him, she was expiating her crime.

Q. Was the "Rose for Emily" an idea or a character? Just how did you go about it?

A. That came from a picture of the strand of hair on the pillow. It was a ghost story. Simply a picture of a strand of hair on the pillow in the abandoned house.

From *Faulkner in the University*, edited by
Frederick Gwynn and Joseph Blotner

CONSIDERATIONS FOR CRITICAL THINKING AND WRITING

1. Discuss whether you think Faulkner's explanation of the conflict between "God and Satan" limits or expands the meaning of the story for you.

2. In what sense is "A Rose for Emily" a ghost story?

3. Compare Faulkner's account of how he conceived "A Rose for Emily" with Flannery O'Connor's description of "Good Country People" in the Perspective on page 438. To what extent are their attitudes about symbolism similar?

ANDRE DUBUS (1936–1999)

Though a native of Louisiana, where he attended the Christian Brothers School and McNeese State College, Andre Dubus lived much of his life in Massachusetts; many of his stories are set in the Merrimack Valley north of Boston. After college Dubus served as an officer for five years in the Marine Corps. He then took an M.F.A. at the University of Iowa in 1966 and began teaching at Bradford College in Massachusetts. His fiction earned him numerous awards, and he was both a Guggenheim and a MacArthur Fellow. Among his collections of fiction are *Separate Flights* (1975); *Adultery and Other Choices* (1977); *Finding a Girl in America* (1980), from which "Killings" is taken; *The Last Worthless Evening* (1986); *Collected Stories* (1988); and *Dancing after Hours* (1996). In 1991 he published *Broken Vessels,* a collection of autobiographical essays. His stories are often tense with violence, anger, tenderness, and guilt; they are populated by characters who struggle to understand and survive their experiences, painful with failure and the weight of imperfect relationships. In "Killings" Dubus offers a powerful blend of intimate domestic life and shocking violence.

Web   *Research Andre Dubus with LitLinks at*
http://www.bedfordstmartins.com/meyer/bedintrolit

Killings   1979

On the August morning when Matt Fowler buried his youngest son, Frank, who had lived for twenty-one years, eight months, and four days, Matt's older son, Steve, turned to him as the family left the grave and walked between their friends, and said: "I should kill him." He was twenty-eight, his brown hair starting to thin in front where he used to have a cowlick. He bit his lower lip, wiped his eyes, then said it again. Ruth's arm, linked with Matt's, tightened; he looked at her. Beneath her eyes there was swelling from the three days she had suffered. At the limousine Matt stopped and looked back at the grave, the casket, and the Congregationalist minister who he thought had probably had a difficult job with the eulogy though he hadn't seemed to, and the old funeral director who was saying something to the six young pallbearers. The grave was on a hill and overlooked the Merrimack, which he could not see from where he stood; he looked at the opposite bank, at the apple orchard with its symmetrically planted trees going up a hill.

Next day Steve drove with his wife back to Baltimore where he managed the branch office of a bank, and Cathleen, the middle child, drove with her husband back to Syracuse. They had left the grandchildren with friends. A month after the funeral Matt played poker at Willis Trottier's because Ruth, who knew this was the second time he had been invited, told him to go, he couldn't sit home with her for the rest of her life, she was all right. After the game Willis went outside to tell everyone good night and, when the others had driven away, he walked with Matt to his car. Willis was a short, silver-haired man who had opened a diner after World War II, his trade then mostly very early breakfast, which he cooked, and then lunch for the men who worked at the leather and shoe factories. He now owned a large restaurant.

"He walks the Goddamn streets," Matt said.

"I know. He was in my place last night, at the bar. With a girl."

"I don't see him. I'm in the store all the time. Ruth sees him. She sees him   5 too much. She was at Sunnyhurst today getting cigarettes and aspirin, and there he was. She can't even go out for cigarettes and aspirin. It's killing her."

"Come back in for a drink."

Matt looked at his watch. Ruth would be asleep. He walked with Willis back into the house, pausing at the steps to look at the starlit sky. It was a cool summer night; he thought vaguely of the Red Sox, did not even know if they were at home tonight; since it happened he had not been able to think about any of the small pleasures he believed he had earned, as he had earned also what was shattered now forever: the quietly harried and quietly pleasurable days of fatherhood. They went inside. Willis's wife, Martha, had gone to bed hours ago, in the rear of the large house which was rigged with burglar and fire alarms. They went downstairs to the game room: the television set suspended from the ceiling, the pool table, the poker table with beer cans, cards, chips, filled ashtrays, and the six chairs where Matt and his friends had sat, the friends picking up the old banter as though he had only been away on vacation; but he could see the affection and courtesy in their eyes. Willis went behind the bar and mixed them each a Scotch and soda; he stayed behind the bar and looked at Matt sitting on the stool.

"How often have you thought about it?" Willis said.

"Every day since he got out. I didn't think about bail. I thought I wouldn't have to worry about him for years. She sees him all the time. It makes her cry."

"He was in my place a long time last night. He'll be back." 10

"Maybe he won't."

"The band. He likes the band."

"What's he doing now?"

"He's tending bar up to Hampton Beach. For a friend. Ever notice even the worst bastard always has friends? He couldn't get work in town. It's just tourists and kids up to Hampton. Nobody knows him. If they do, they don't care. They drink what he mixes."

"Nobody tells me about him." 15

"I hate him, Matt. My boys went to school with him. He was the same then. Know what he'll do? Five at the most. Remember that woman about seven years ago? Shot her husband and dropped him off the bridge in the Merrimack with a hundred-pound sack of cement and said all the way through it that nobody helped her. Know where she is now? She's in Lawrence now, a secretary. And whoever helped her, where the hell is he?"

"I've got a .38 I've had for years, I take it to the store now. I tell Ruth it's for the night deposits. I tell her things have changed: we got junkies here now too. Lots of people without jobs. She knows though."

"What does she know?"

"She knows I started carrying it after the first time she saw him in town. She knows it's in case I see him, and there's some kind of a situation—"

He stopped, looked at Willis, and finished his drink. Willis mixed him another. 20

"What kind of situation?"

"Where he did something to me. Where I could get away with it."

"How does Ruth feel about that?"

"She doesn't know."

"You said she does, she's got it figured out." 25

He thought of her that afternoon: when she went into Sunnyhurst, Strout was waiting at the counter while the clerk bagged the things he had bought; she turned down an aisle and looked at soup cans until he left.

"Ruth would shoot him herself, if she thought she could hit him."

"You got a permit?"

"No."

"I do. You could get a year for that." 30

"Maybe I'll get one. Or maybe I won't. Maybe I'll just stop bringing it to the store."

Richard Strout was twenty-six years old, a high school athlete, football scholarship to the University of Massachusetts where he lasted for almost two semesters before quitting in advance of the final grades that would have forced him not to return. People then said: Dickie can do the work; he just doesn't want to. He came home and did construction work for his father but refused his father's offer to learn the business; his two older brothers had learned it, so that Strout and Sons trucks going about town, and signs on construction sites, now slashed wounds into Matt Fowler's life. Then Richard married a young girl and became a bartender, his salary and tips augmented and perhaps sometimes matched by his father, who also posted his bond. So his friends, his enemies (he had those: fist fights or, more often, boys and then young men who had not fought him when they thought they should have), and those who simply knew him by face and name, had a series of images of him which they recalled when they heard of the killing: the high school running back, the young drunk in bars, the oblivious hard-hatted young man eating lunch at a counter, the bartender who could perhaps be called courteous but not more than that: as he tended bar, his dark eyes and dark, wide-jawed face appeared less sullen, near blank.

One night he beat Frank. Frank was living at home and waiting for September, for graduate school in economics, and working as a lifeguard at Salisbury Beach, where he met Mary Ann Strout, in her first month of separation. She spent most days at the beach with her two sons. Before ten o'clock one night Frank came home; he had driven to the hospital first, and he walked into the living room with stitches over his right eye and both lips bright and swollen.

"I'm all right," he said, when Matt and Ruth stood up, and Matt turned off the television, letting Ruth get to him first: the tall, muscled but slender suntanned boy. Frank tried to smile at them but couldn't because of his lips.

"It was her husband, wasn't it?" Ruth said. 35

"Ex," Frank said. "He dropped in."

Matt gently held Frank's jaw and turned his face to the light, looked at the stitches, the blood under the white of the eye, the bruised flesh.

"Press charges," Matt said.

"No."

"What's to stop him from doing it again? Did you hit him at all? Enough 40 so he won't want to next time?"

"I don't think I touched him."

"So what are you going to do?"

"Take karate," Frank said, and tried again to smile.

"That's not the problem," Ruth said.

"You know you like her," Frank said. 45

"I like a lot of people. What about the boys? Did they see it?"

"They were asleep."

"Did you leave her alone with him?"

"He left first. She was yelling at him. I believe she had a skillet in her hand."

"Oh for God's sake," Ruth said. 50

Matt had been dealing with that too: at the dinner table on evenings when Frank wasn't home, was eating with Mary Ann; or, on the other nights—and Frank was with her every night—he talked with Ruth while they watched television, or lay in bed with the windows open and he smelled the night air and imagined, with both pride and muted sorrow, Frank in Mary Ann's arms. Ruth didn't like it because Mary Ann was in the process of divorce, because she had two children, because she was four years older than Frank, and finally—she told this in bed, where she had during all of their marriage told him of her deepest feelings: of love, of passion, of fears about one of the children, of pain Matt had caused her or she had caused him—she was against it because of what she had heard: that the marriage had gone bad early, and for most of it Richard and Mary Ann had both played around.

"That can't be true," Matt said. "Strout wouldn't have stood for it."

"Maybe he loves her."

"He's too hot-tempered. He couldn't have taken that."

But Matt knew Strout had taken it, for he had heard the stories too. He wondered who had told them to Ruth; and he felt vaguely annoyed and iso-lated: living with her for thirty-one years and still not knowing what she talked about with her friends. On these summer nights he did not so much argue with her as try to comfort her, but finally there was no difference between the two: she had concrete objections, which he tried to overcome. And in his at-tempt to do this, he neglected his own objections, which were the same as hers, so that as he spoke to her he felt as disembodied as he sometimes did in the store when he helped a man choose a blouse or dress or piece of costume jew-elry for his wife.

"The divorce doesn't mean anything," he said. "She was young and maybe she liked his looks and then after a while she realized she was living with a bas-tard. I see it as a positive thing."

"She's not divorced yet."

"It's the same thing. Massachusetts has crazy laws, that's all. Her age is no problem. What's it matter when she was born? And that other business: even if it's true, which it probably isn't, it's got nothing to do with Frank, and it's in the past. And the kids are no problem. She's been married six years; she ought to have kids. Frank likes them. He plays with them. And he's not going to marry her anyway, so it's not a problem of money."

"Then what's he doing with her?"

"She probably loves him, Ruth. Girls always have. Why can't we just leave it at that?"

"He got home at six o'clock Tuesday morning."

"I didn't know you knew. I've already talked to him about it."

Which he had: since he believed almost nothing he told Ruth, he went to Frank with what he believed. The night before, he had followed Frank to the car after dinner.

"You wouldn't make much of a burglar," he said.

"How's that?"

Matt was looking up at him; Frank was six feet tall, an inch and a half taller than Matt, who had been proud when Frank at seventeen outgrew him; he had only felt uncomfortable when he had to reprimand or caution him. He touched Frank's bicep, thought of the young taut passionate body, believed he could sense the desire, and again he felt the pride and sorrow and envy too, not knowing whether he was envious of Frank or Mary Ann.

"When you came in yesterday morning, I woke up. One of these mornings your mother will. And I'm the one who'll have to talk to her. She won't inter-fere with you. Okay? I know it means—" But he stopped, thinking: I know it means getting up and leaving that suntanned girl and going sleepy to the car, I know—

"Okay," Frank said, and touched Matt's shoulder and got into the car.

There had been other talks, but the only long one was their first one: a night driving to Fenway Park, Matt having ordered the tickets so they could talk, and knowing when Frank said yes, he would go, that he knew the talk was coming too. It took them forty minutes to get to Boston, and they talked about Mary Ann until they joined the city traffic along the Charles River, blue in the late sun. Frank told him all the things that Matt would later pretend to believe when he told them to Ruth.

"It seems like a lot for a young guy to take on," Matt finally said. 70

"Sometimes it is. But she's worth it."

"Are you thinking about getting married?"

"We haven't talked about it. She can't for over a year. I've got school."

"I *do* like her," Matt said.

He did. Some evenings, when the long summer sun was still low in the sky, 75 Frank brought her home; they came into the house smelling of suntan lotion and the sea, and Matt gave them gin and tonics and started the charcoal in the backyard, and looked at Mary Ann in the lawn chair: long and very light brown hair (Matt thinking that twenty years ago she would have dyed it blonde), and the long brown legs he loved to look at; her face was pretty; she had probably never in her adult life gone unnoticed into a public place. It was in her wide brown eyes that she looked older than Frank; after a few drinks Matt thought what he saw in her eyes was something erotic, testament to the rumors about her; but he knew it wasn't that, or all that: she had, very young, been through a sort of pain that his children, and he and Ruth, had been spared. In the moments of his recognizing that pain, he wanted to tenderly touch her hair, wanted with some gesture to give her solace and hope. And he would glance at Frank, and hope they would love each other, hope Frank would soothe that pain in her heart, take it from her eyes; and her divorce, her age, and her children did not matter at all. On the first two evenings she did not bring her boys, and then Ruth asked her to bring them the next time. In bed that night Ruth said, "She hasn't brought them because she's embarrassed. She shouldn't feel embarrassed."

Richard Strout shot Frank in front of the boys. They were sitting on the living room floor watching television, Frank sitting on the couch, and Mary Ann just returning from the kitchen with a tray of sandwiches. Strout came in the front door and shot Frank twice in the chest and once in the face with a 9 mm automatic. Then he looked at the boys and Mary Ann, and went home to wait for the police.

It seemed to Matt that from the time Mary Ann called weeping to tell him until now, a Saturday night in September, sitting in the car with Willis, parked beside Strout's car, waiting for the bar to close, that he had not so much moved through his life as wandered through it, his spirits like a dazed body bumping into furniture and corners. He had always been a fearful father: when his children were young, at the start of each summer he thought of them drowning in a pond or the sea, and he was relieved when he came home in the evenings and they were there; usually that relief was his only acknowledgment of his fear, which he never spoke of, and which he controlled within his heart. As he had when they were very young and all of them in turn, Cathleen too, were drawn to the high oak in the backyard, and had to climb it. Smiling, he

watched them, imagining the fall: and he was poised to catch the small body
before it hit the earth. Or his legs were poised; his hands were in his pockets or
his arms were folded and, for the child looking down, he appeared relaxed and
confident while his heart beat with the two words he wanted to call out but did
not: *Don't fall.* In winter he was less afraid: he made sure the ice would hold him
before they skated, and he brought or sent them to places where they could
sled without ending in the street. So he and his children had survived their
childhood, and he only worried about them when he knew they were driving a
long distance, and then he lost Frank in a way no father expected to lose his
son, and he felt that all the fears he had borne while they were growing up, and
all the grief he had been afraid of, had backed up like a huge wave and struck
him on the beach and swept him out to sea. Each day he felt the same and
when he was able to forget how he felt, when he was able to force himself not
to feel that way, the eyes of his clerks and customers defeated him. He wished
those eyes were oblivious, even cold; he felt he was withering in their tenderness. And beneath his listless wandering, every day in his soul he shot Richard
Strout in the face; while Ruth, going about town on errands, kept seeing him.
And at nights in bed she would hold Matt and cry, or sometimes she was silent
and Matt would touch her tightening arm, her clenched fist.

As his own right fist was now, squeezing the butt of the revolver, the last of
the drinkers having left the bar, talking to each other, going to their separate
cars which were in the lot in front of the bar, out of Matt's vision. He heard
their voices, their cars, and then the ocean again, across the street. The tide was
in and sometimes it smacked the sea wall. Through the windshield he looked
at the dark red side wall of the bar, and then to his left, past Willis, at Strout's
car, and through its windows he could see the now-emptied parking lot, the
road, the sea wall. He could smell the sea.

The front door of the bar opened and closed again and Willis looked at
Matt then at the corner of the building; when Strout came around it alone
Matt got out of the car, giving up the hope he had kept all night (and for the
past week) that Strout would come out with friends, and Willis would simply
drive away; thinking: *All right then. All right;* and he went around the front of
Willis's car, and at Strout's he stopped and aimed over the hood at Strout's
blue shirt ten feet away. Willis was aiming too, crouched on Matt's left, his
elbow resting on the hood.

"Mr. Fowler," Strout said. He looked at each of them, and at the guns. 80
"Mr. Trottier."

Then Matt, watching the parking lot and the road, walked quickly between the car and the building and stood behind Strout. He took one leather
glove from his pocket and put it on his left hand.

"Don't talk. Unlock the front and back and get in."

Strout unlocked the front door, reached in and unlocked the back, then
got in, and Matt slid into the back seat, closed the door with his gloved hand,
and touched Strout's head once with the muzzle.

"It's cocked. Drive to your house."

When Strout looked over his shoulder to back the car, Matt aimed at his 85
temple and did not look at his eyes.

"Drive slowly," he said. "Don't try to get stopped."

They drove across the empty front lot and onto the road, Willis's headlights shining into the car; then back through town, the sea wall on the left

hiding the beach, though far out Matt could see the ocean; he uncocked the re-volver; on the right were the places, most with their neon signs off, that did so much business in summer: the lounges and cafés and pizza houses, the street itself empty of traffic, the way he and Willis had known it would be when they decided to take Strout at the bar rather than knock on his door at two o'clock one morning and risk that one insomniac neighbor. Matt had not told Willis he was afraid he could not be alone with Strout for very long, smell his smells, feel the presence of his flesh, hear his voice, and then shoot him. They left the beach town and then were on the high bridge over the channel: to the left the smacking curling white at the breakwater and beyond that the dark sea and the full moon, and down to his right the small fishing boats bobbing at anchor in the cove. When they left the bridge, the sea was blocked by abandoned beach cottages, and Matt's left hand was sweating in the glove. Out here in the dark in the car he believed Ruth knew. Willis had come to his house at eleven and asked if he wanted a nightcap; Matt went to the bedroom for his wallet, put the gloves in one trouser pocket and the .38 in the other and went back to the living room, his hand in his pocket covering the bulge of the cool cylinder pressed against his fingers, the butt against his palm. When Ruth said good night she looked at his face, and he felt she could see in his eyes the gun, and the night he was going to. But he knew he couldn't trust what he saw. Willis's wife had taken her sleeping pill, which gave her eight hours — the reason, Willis had told Matt, he had the alarms installed, for nights when he was late at the restaurant — and when it was all done and Willis got home he would leave ice and a trace of Scotch and soda in two glasses in the game room and tell Martha in the morning that he had left the restaurant early and brought Matt home for a drink.

"He was making it with my wife." Strout's voice was careful, not pleading.

Matt pressed the muzzle against Strout's head, pressed it harder than he wanted to, feeling through the gun Strout's head flinching and moving forward; then he lowered the gun to his lap.

"Don't talk," he said.

Strout did not speak again. They turned west, drove past the Dairy Queen closed until spring, and the two lobster restaurants that faced each other and were crowded all summer and were now also closed, onto the short bridge crossing the tidal stream, and over the engine Matt could hear through his open window the water rushing inland under the bridge; looking to his left he saw its swift moonlit current going back into the marsh which, leaving the bridge, they entered: the salt marsh stretching out on both sides, the grass tall in patches but mostly low and leaning earthward as though windblown, a large dark rock sitting as though it rested on nothing but itself, and shallow pools reflecting the bright moon.

Beyond the marsh they drove through woods, Matt thinking now of the hole he and Willis had dug last Sunday afternoon after telling their wives they were going to Fenway Park. They listened to the game on a transistor radio, but heard none of it as they dug into the soft earth on the knoll they had chosen because elms and maples sheltered it. Already some leaves had fallen. When the hole was deep enough they covered it and the piled earth with dead branches, then cleaned their shoes and pants and went to a restaurant farther up in New Hampshire where they ate sandwiches and drank beer and watched the rest of the game on television. Looking at the back of Strout's head he thought of Frank's grave; he had not been back to it; but he would go before winter, and its second burial of snow.

He thought of Frank sitting on the couch and perhaps talking to the children as they watched television, imagined him feeling young and strong, still warmed from the sun at the beach, and feeling loved, hearing Mary Ann moving about in the kitchen, hearing her walking into the living room; maybe he looked up at her and maybe she said something, looking at him over the tray of sandwiches, smiling at him, saying something the way women do when they offer food as a gift, then the front door opening and this son of a bitch coming in and Frank seeing that he meant the gun in his hand, this son of a bitch and his gun the last person and thing Frank saw on earth.

When they drove into town the streets were nearly empty: a few slow cars, a policeman walking his beat past the darkened fronts of stores. Strout and Matt both glanced at him as they drove by. They were on the main street, and all the stoplights were blinking yellow. Willis and Matt had talked about that too: the lights changed at midnight, so there would be no place Strout had to stop and where he might try to run. Strout turned down the block where he lived and Willis's headlights were no longer with Matt in the back seat. They had planned that too, had decided it was best for just the one car to go to the house, and again Matt had said nothing about his fear of being alone with Strout, especially in his house: a duplex, dark as all the houses on the street were, the street itself lit at the corner of each block. As Strout turned into the driveway Matt thought of the one insomniac neighbor, thought of some man or woman sitting alone in the dark living room, watching the all-night channel from Boston. When Strout stopped the car near the front of the house, Matt said: "Drive it to the back."

He touched Strout's head with the muzzle. 95

"You wouldn't have it cocked, would you? For when I put on the brakes."

Matt cocked it, and said: "It is now."

Strout waited a moment; then he eased the car forward, the engine doing little more than idling, and as they approached the garage he gently braked. Matt opened the door, then took off the glove and put it in his pocket. He stepped out and shut the door with his hip and said: "All right."

Strout looked at the gun, then got out, and Matt followed him across the grass, and as Strout unlocked the door Matt looked quickly at the row of small backyards on either side, and scattered tall trees, some evergreens, others not, and he thought of the red and yellow leaves on the trees over the hole, saw them falling soon, probably in two weeks, dropping slowly, covering. Strout stepped into the kitchen.

"Turn on the light." 100

Strout reached to the wall switch, and in the light Matt looked at his wide back, the dark blue shirt, the white belt, the red plaid pants.

"Where's your suitcase?"

"My suitcase?"

"Where is it?"

"In the bedroom closet." 105

"That's where we're going then. When we get to a door you stop and turn on the light."

They crossed the kitchen, Matt glancing at the sink and stove and refrigerator: no dishes in the sink or even the dish rack beside it, no grease splashings on the stove, the refrigerator door clean and white. He did not want to look at any more but he looked quickly at all he could see: in the living room magazines and newspapers in a wicker basket, clean ashtrays, a record player, the records shelved next to it, then down the hall where, near the bedroom door, hung a color photograph of Mary Ann and the two boys sitting on a lawn — there was no house in the picture — Mary Ann smiling at the camera or Strout or whoever held the camera, smiling as she had on Matt's lawn this summer while he waited for the charcoal and they all talked and he looked at her brown legs and at Frank touching her arm, her shoulder, her hair; he moved down the hall with her smile in his mind, wondering: was that when they were both playing around and she was smiling like that at him and they were happy, even sometimes, making it worth it? He recalled her eyes, the pain in them, and he was conscious of the circles of love he was touching with the hand that held the revolver so tightly now as Strout stopped at the door at the end of the hall.

"There's no wall switch."

"Where's the light?"

"By the bed." 110

"Let's go."

Matt stayed a pace behind, then Strout leaned over and the room was lighted: the bed, a double one, was neatly made; the ashtray on the bedside table clean, the bureau top dustless, and no photographs; probably so the girl — who *was* she? — would not have to see Mary Ann in the bedroom she believed was theirs. But because Matt was a father and a husband, though never an ex-husband, he knew (and did not want to know) that this bedroom had never been theirs alone. Strout turned around; Matt looked at his lips, his wide jaw, and thought of Frank's doomed and fearful eyes looking up from the couch.

"Where's Mr. Trottier?"

"He's waiting. Pack clothes for warm weather."

"What's going on?" 115

"You're jumping bail."

"Mr. Fowler —"

He pointed the cocked revolver at Strout's face. The barrel trembled but not much, not as much as he had expected. Strout went to the closet and got the suitcase from the floor and opened it on the bed. As he went to the bureau, he said: "He was making it with my wife. I'd go pick up my kids and he'd be there. Sometimes he spent the night. My boys told me."

He did not look at Matt as he spoke. He opened the top drawer and Matt stepped closer so he could see Strout's hands: underwear and socks, the socks rolled, the underwear folded and stacked. He took them back to the bed, arranged them neatly in the suitcase, then from the closet he was taking shirts and trousers and a jacket; he laid them on the bed and Matt followed him to the bathroom and watched from the door while he packed those things a person accumulated and that became part of him so that at times in the store Matt felt he was selling more than clothes.

"I wanted to try to get together with her again." He was bent over the suit- 120 case. "I couldn't even talk to her. He was always with her. I'm going to jail for it; if I ever get out I'll be an old man. Isn't that enough?"

"You're not going to jail."

Strout closed the suitcase and faced Matt, looking at the gun. Matt went to his rear, so Strout was between him and the lighted hall; then using his handkerchief he turned off the lamp and said: "Let's go."

They went down the hall, Matt looking again at the photograph, and through the living room and kitchen, Matt turning off the lights and talking, frightened that he was talking, that he was telling this lie he had not planned: "It's the trial. We can't go through that, my wife and me. So you're leaving. We've got you a ticket, and a job. A friend of Mr. Trottier's. Out west. My wife keeps seeing you. We can't have that anymore."

Matt turned out the kitchen light and put the handkerchief in his pocket, and they went down the two brick steps and across the lawn. Strout put the suitcase on the floor of the back seat, then got into the front seat and Matt got in the back and put on his glove and shut the door.

"They'll catch me. They'll check passenger lists."   125

"We didn't use your name."

"They'll figure that out too. You think I wouldn't have done it myself if it was that easy?"

He backed into the street, Matt looking down the gun barrel but not at the profiled face beyond it.

"You were alone," Matt said. "We've got it worked out."

"There's no planes this time of night, Mr. Fowler."   130

"Go back through town. Then north on 125."

They came to the corner and turned, and now Willis's headlights were in the car with Matt.

"Why north, Mr. Fowler?"

"Somebody's going to keep you for a while. They'll take you to the airport." He uncocked the hammer and lowered the revolver to his lap and said wearily: "No more talking."

As they drove back through town, Matt's body sagged, going limp with his   135
spirit and its new and false bond with Strout, the hope his lie had given Strout. He had grown up in this town whose streets had become places of apprehension and pain for Ruth as she drove and walked, doing what she had to do; and for him too, if only in his mind as he worked and chatted six days a week in his store; he wondered now if his lie would have worked, if sending Strout away would have been enough; but then he knew that just thinking of Strout in Montana or whatever place lay at the end of the lie he had told, thinking of him walking the streets there, loving a girl there (who *was* she?) would be enough to slowly rot the rest of his days. And Ruth's. Again he was certain that she knew, that she was waiting for him.

They were in New Hampshire now, on the narrow highway, passing the shopping center at the state line, and then houses and small stores and sandwich shops. There were few cars on the road. After ten minutes he raised his trembling hand, touched Strout's neck with the gun, and said: "Turn in up here. At the dirt road."

Strout flicked on the indicator and slowed.

"Mr. Fowler?"

"They're waiting here."

Strout turned very slowly, easing his neck away from the gun. In the moon-   140
light the road was light brown, lighter and yellowed where the headlights shone; weeds and a few trees grew on either side of it, and ahead of them were the woods.

"There's nothing back here, Mr. Fowler."

"It's for your car. You don't think we'd leave it at the airport, do you?"

He watched Strout's large, big-knuckled hands tighten on the wheel, saw Frank's face that night: not the stitches and bruised eye and swollen lips, but his own hand gently touching Frank's jaw, turning his wounds to the light. They rounded a bend in the road and were out of sight of the highway: tall trees all around them now, hiding the moon. When they reached the abandoned gravel pit on the left, the bare flat earth and steep pale embankment behind it, and the black crowns of trees at its top, Matt said: "Stop here."

Strout stopped but did not turn off the engine. Matt pressed the gun hard against his neck, and he straightened in the seat and looked in the rearview mirror, Matt's eyes meeting his in the glass for an instant before looking at the hair at the end of the gun barrel.

"Turn it off."   145

Strout did, then held the wheel with two hands, and looked in the mirror.

"I'll do twenty years, Mr. Fowler; at least. I'll be forty-six years old."

"That's nine years younger than I am," Matt said, and got out and took off the glove and kicked the door shut. He aimed at Strout's ear and pulled back the hammer. Willis's headlights were off and Matt heard him walking on the soft thin layer of dust, the hard earth beneath it. Strout opened the door, sat for a moment in the interior light, then stepped out onto the road. Now his face was pleading. Matt did not look at his eyes, but he could see it in the lips.

"Just get the suitcase. They're right up the road."

Willis was beside him now, to his left. Strout looked at both guns. Then he   150
opened the back door, leaned in, and with a jerk brought the suitcase out. He was turning to face them when Matt said: "Just walk up the road. Just ahead."

Strout turned to walk, the suitcase in his right hand, and Matt and Willis followed; as Strout cleared the front of his car he dropped the suitcase and, ducking, took one step that was the beginning of a sprint to his right. The gun kicked in Matt's hand, and the explosion of the shot surrounded him, isolated him in a nimbus of sound that cut him off from all his time, all his history, isolated him standing absolutely still on the dirt road with the gun in his hand, looking down at Richard Strout squirming on his belly, kicking one leg behind him, pushing himself forward, toward the woods. Then Matt went to him and shot him once in the back of the head.

Driving south to Boston, wearing both gloves now, staying in the middle lane and looking often in the rearview mirror at Willis's headlights, he relived the suitcase dropping, the quick dip and turn of Strout's back, and the kick of the gun, the sound of the shot. When he walked to Strout, he still existed within the first shot, still trembled and breathed with it. The second shot and the burial seemed to be happening to someone else, someone he was watching. He and Willis each held an arm and pulled Strout face-down off the road and into the woods, his bouncing sliding belt white under the trees where it was so dark that when they stopped at the top of the knoll, panting and sweating, Matt could not see where Strout's blue shirt ended and the earth began. They pulled off the branches then dragged Strout to the edge of the hole and went behind him and lifted his legs and pushed him in. They stood still for a moment. The woods were quiet save for their breathing, and Matt remembered hearing the movements of birds and small animals after the first shot. Or maybe he had not heard them. Willis went down to the road. Matt could see him clearly out on the tan dirt, could see the glint of Strout's car and, beyond the road, the gravel pit. Willis came back up the knoll with the suitcase. He dropped it in the hole and took off his gloves and they went down to his car for the spades. They worked quietly. Sometimes they paused to listen to the woods. When they were finished Willis turned on his flashlight and they covered the earth with leaves and branches and then went down to the spot in front of the car, and while Matt held the light Willis crouched and sprinkled dust on the blood, backing up till he reached the grass and leaves, then he used leaves until they had worked up to the grave again. They did not stop. They walked around the grave and through the woods, using the light on the ground, looking up through the trees to where they ended at the lake. Neither of them spoke above the sounds of their heavy and clumsy strides through low brush and over fallen branches. Then they reached it: wide and dark, lapping softly at the bank, pine needles smooth under Matt's feet, moonlight on the lake, a small island near its middle, with black, tall evergreens. He took out the gun and threw for the island: taking two steps back on the pine needles, striding with the throw and going to one knee as he followed through, looking up to see the dark shapeless object arcing downward, splashing.

They left Strout's car in Boston, in front of an apartment building on Commonwealth Avenue. When they got back to town Willis drove slowly over the bridge and Matt threw the keys into the Merrimack. The sky was turning light. Willis let him out a block from his house, and walking home he listened for sounds from the houses he passed. They were quiet. A light was on in his living room. He turned it off and undressed in there, and went softly toward the bedroom; in the hall he smelled the smoke, and he stood in the bedroom doorway and looked at the orange of her cigarette in the dark. The curtains were closed. He went to the closet and put his shoes on the floor and felt for a hanger.

"Did you do it?" she said.

He went down the hall to the bathroom and in the dark he washed his 155 hands and face. Then he went to her, lay on his back, and pulled the sheet up to his throat.

"Are you all right?" she said.

"I think so."

Now she touched him, lying on her side, her hand on his belly, his thigh.

"Tell me," she said.

He started from the beginning, in the parking lot at the bar; but soon with 160 his eyes closed and Ruth petting him, he spoke of Strout's house: the order, the woman presence, the picture on the wall.

"The way she was smiling," he said.

"What about it?"

"I don't know. Did you ever see Strout's girl? When you saw him in town?"

"No."

"I wonder who she was." 165

Then he thought: *not was: is. Sleeping now she is his girl.* He opened his eyes, then closed them again. There was more light beyond the curtains. With Ruth now he left Strout's house and told again his lie to Strout, gave him again that hope that Strout must have for a while believed, else he would have to believe only the gun pointed at him for the last two hours of his life. And with Ruth he saw again the dropping suitcase, the darting move to the right: and he told of the first shot, feeling her hand on him but his heart isolated still, beating on the road still in that explosion like thunder. He told her the rest, but the words had no images for him, he did not see himself doing what the words said he had done; he only saw himself on that road.

"We can't tell the other kids," she said. "It'll hurt them, thinking he got away. But we mustn't."

"No."

She was holding him, wanting him, and he wished he could make love with her but he could not. He saw Frank and Mary Ann making love in her bed, their eyes closed, their bodies brown and smelling of the sea; the other girl was faceless, bodiless, but he felt her sleeping now; and he saw Frank and Strout, their faces alive; he saw red and yellow leaves falling on the earth, then snow: falling and freezing and falling; and holding Ruth, his cheek touching her breast, he shuddered with a sob that he kept silent in his heart.

CONSIDERATIONS FOR CRITICAL THINKING AND WRITING

1. FIRST RESPONSE. How do you feel about Matt's act of revenge? Trace the emotions his character produces in you as the plot unfolds.

2. Discuss the significance of the title. Why is "Killings" a more appropriate title than "Killers"?

3. What are the effects of Dubus's ordering of events in the story? How would the effects be different if the story were told in a chronological order?

4. Describe the Fowler family before Frank's murder. How does the murder affect Matt?

5. What is learned about Richard from the flashback in paragraphs 32 through 75? How does this information affect your attitude toward him?

6. What is the effect of the description of Richard shooting Frank in paragraph 76?

7. How well planned is Matt's revenge? Why does he lie to Richard about sending him out west?

8. Describe Matt at the end of the story when he tells his wife about the killing. How do you think this revenge killing will affect the Fowler family?

9. How might "Killings" be considered a love story as well as a murder story?

10. CRITICAL STRATEGIES. Read the section on psychological criticism (pp. 2099–101) in Chapter 52, "Critical Strategies for Reading." How do the details of the killing and the disposal of Richard's body reveal Matt's emotions? What is he thinking and feeling as he performs these actions? How did you feel as you read about them?

CONNECTIONS TO OTHER SELECTIONS

1. Compare and contrast Matt's motivation for murder with Emily's in "A Rose for Emily." Which character made you feel more empathy and sympathy for his or her actions? Why?

2. Explore the father-son relationships in "Killings" and William Faulkner's "Barn Burning" (p. 493). Read the section on psychological criticism in Chapter 52, "Critical Strategies for Reading." How do you think a psychological critic would interpret these relationships in each story?

3. In an essay discuss the respective treatments of family life in "Killings" and Gish Jen's "Who's Irish?" (p. 178). Do these very different stories have anything in common?

PERSPECTIVES

THOMAS E. KENNEDY (B. 1944)

On Morality and Revenge in "Killings"   1988

When Fowler fires at the younger man, "the explosion of the shot surrounded him, isolated him in a nimbus of sound that cut him off from all his time, all his history, isolated him standing absolutely still on the dirt road. . . . The second shot . . . seemed to be happening to someone else, someone he was watching." When Fowler returns home after he and his friend have buried Strout's body, his wife is waiting for him in the dark bedroom. She knows, without having been told, what he has done, and she tries to make love to him while he relates the details, but he cannot make love, for he has isolated himself by his act. The final irony occurs when they realize they will be unable to tell their other children about it, that the children will believe their brother's murderer has escaped trial and punishment and has run off. Thus, we see the first consequence of Fowler's unnatural act, the profound isolation he must suffer for it. Even his sob at the close of the story is one of isolation, "silent in his heart."

The story's point is clear: the blade of murder cuts both ways. Victim and killer are united and isolated, one in death, the other in the ultimate breach of respect for human life. Like Cain, the killer has distinguished himself from humankind and presumably must suffer that distinction for the rest of his days. An intriguing question that follows from the story is whether the act of murder affects all men equally. Will a person of inferior morality suffer equally with a person of more sensitive humanity like Matt Fowler? Throughout Fowler's abduction of Strout, he must fight to prevent himself from witnessing Strout's humanity, must forbid him from speaking lest he become too close to the sound of his voice, must prevent himself from smelling the man's smells. When, finally, he must lie to Strout to accomplish the abduction, giving the younger man hope that he is not to be killed, Fowler suffers for his cruelty. Thus, there is not even a moment's satisfaction of vengeance for Fowler; his is a rational act, an extermination to eliminate Strout from their world and end Ruth's pain. Strout, presumably, killed Fowler's son in passion. It is interesting to compare the two acts and to compare the fate of suffering attached to each.

A profound lifelong isolation awaits Fowler as a result of his act of premeditated murder. It is intriguing to consider what Strout's fate might have been had he stood trial and gone to prison for his act. The suggestion is that Strout was a man of inferior morality, the son of an affluent family who pampered him, a violent husband. Might the culmination of his weakness in murder and the suffering imposed on him for it, the experience of finally having to account for his actions, have resulted in his moral development and growth?

What then, finally, is the meaning for human society of Fowler's homicidal revenge? We understand Fowler. We follow him through his deed not without the desire for him to complete it, to succeed, to rid the world of this killer. We note his reluctance, his moral hesitation, the morality he must overcome, and we urge him, on some level, to overcome it. Once he has begun the action, abducted Strout, we know he *must* complete it, even if we share his mixed feelings about the choice he has made. Yet what is the final result for the world?

Strout is eliminated, but Fowler is left morally wounded to walk the earth, and his suffering will spread, has already begun to spread to his children.

From *Andre Dubus: A Study of the Short Fiction*

CONSIDERATIONS FOR CRITICAL THINKING AND WRITING

1. Explain how you would answer the following question raised by Kennedy: "Will a person of inferior morality suffer equally with a person of more sensitive humanity like Matt Fowler?"

2. Discuss why and how profound isolation affects nearly all the characters in this story.

A. L. BADER (B. 1902)
Nothing Happens in Modern Short Stories   1945

Any teacher who has ever confronted a class with representative modern short stories will remember the disappointment, the puzzled "so-what" attitude, of certain members of the group. "Nothing happens in some of these stories," "They just end," or "They're not real stories" are frequent criticisms. . . . Sometimes the phrase "Nothing happens" seems to mean that nothing significant happens, but in a great many cases it means that the modern short story is charged with a lack of narrative structure. Readers and critics accustomed to an older type of story are baffled by a newer type. They sense the underlying and unifying design of the one, but they find nothing equivalent to it in the other. Hence they maintain that the modern short story is plotless, static, fragmentary, amorphous — frequently a mere character sketch or vignette, or a mere reporting of a transient moment, or the capturing of a mood or nuance — everything, in fact, except a story.

From "The Structure of the Modern Story" in *College English*

CONSIDERATIONS FOR CRITICAL THINKING AND WRITING

1. What is the basic objection to the "newer type" of short story? How does it differ from the "older type"?

2. Consider any one of the stories from the Album of Contemporary Stories (pp. 637–66) as an example of the newer type. Does anything "happen" in the story? How does it differ from the excerpt from Edgar Rice Burroughs's *Tarzan of the Apes* (p. 66)?

3. Read a recent story published in *The New Yorker* or the *Atlantic Monthly* and compare its narrative structure with that of Faulkner's "A Rose for Emily" (p. 75).

4

Character

Character is essential to plot. Without characters Burroughs's *Tarzan of the Apes* would be a travelogue through the jungle and Faulkner's "A Rose for Emily" little more than a faded history of a sleepy town in the South. If stories were depopulated, the plots would disappear because characters and plots are interrelated. A dangerous jungle is important only because we care what effect it has on a character. Characters are influenced by events just as events are shaped by characters. Tarzan's physical strength is the result of his growing up in the jungle, and his strength, along with his inherited intelligence, allows him to be master there.

The methods by which a writer creates people in a story so that they seem actually to exist are called **characterization.** Huck Finn never lived, yet those who have read Mark Twain's novel about his adventures along the Mississippi River feel as if they know him. A good writer gives us the illusion that a character is real, but we should also remember that a character is not an actual person but instead has been created by the author. Though we might walk out of a room in which Huck Finn's Pap talks racist nonsense, we would not throw away the book in a similar fit of anger. This illusion of reality is the magic that allows us to move beyond the circumstances of our own lives into a writer's fictional world, where we can encounter everyone from royalty to paupers, murderers, lovers, cheaters, martyrs, artists, destroyers, and, nearly always, some part of ourselves. The life that a writer breathes into a character adds to our own experiences and enlarges our view of the world.

A character is usually but not always a person. In Jack London's *Call of the Wild*, the protagonist is a devoted sled dog; in Herman Melville's *Moby-Dick*, the antagonist is an unfathomable whale. Perhaps the only possible qualification to be placed on character is that whatever it is — whether an animal or even an inanimate object, such as a robot — it must have some recognizable human qualities. The action of the plot interests us primarily because we care about what happens to people and what they do. We may identify with a character's desires and aspirations, or we may be disgusted by his or her viciousness and selfishness. To understand our response to a story, we should be able to recognize the methods of characterization the author uses.

CHARLES DICKENS (1812–1870)

Charles Dickens is well known for creating characters who have stepped off the pages of his fictions into the imaginations and memories of his readers. His characters are successful not because readers might have encountered such people in their own lives, but because his characterizations are vivid and convincing. He manages to make strange and eccentric people appear familiar. The following excerpt from *Hard Times* is the novel's entire first chapter. In it Dickens introduces and characterizes a school principal addressing a classroom full of children.

Web   *Research Charles Dickens with LitLinks at*
       http://www.bedfordstmartins.com/meyer/bedintrolit

From Hard Times   *1854*

"Now, what I want is, Facts. Teach these boys and girls nothing but Facts. Facts alone are wanted in life. Plant nothing else, and root out everything else. You can only form the minds of reasoning animals upon Facts: nothing else will ever be of any service to them. This is the principle on which I bring up my own children, and this is the principle on which I bring up these children. Stick to Facts, sir!"

The scene was a plain, bare, monotonous vault of a schoolroom, and the speaker's square forefinger emphasized his observations by underscoring every sentence with a line on the schoolmaster's sleeve. The emphasis was helped by the speaker's square wall of a forehead, which had his eyebrows for its base, while his eyes found commodious cellarage in two dark caves, overshadowed by the wall. The emphasis was helped by the speaker's mouth, which was wide, thin, and hard set. The emphasis was helped by the speaker's voice, which was inflexible, dry, and dictatorial. The emphasis was helped by the speaker's hair, which bristled on the skirts of his bald head, a plantation of firs to keep the wind from its shining surface, all covered with knobs, like the crust of a plum pie, as if the head had scarcely warehouse-room for the hard facts stored inside. The speaker's obstinate carriage, square coat, square legs, square shoulders — nay, his very neckcloth, trained to take him by the throat with an unaccommodating grasp, like a stubborn fact, as it was — all helped the emphasis.

"In this life, we want nothing but Facts, sir; nothing but Facts!"

The speaker, and the schoolmaster, and the third grown person present, all backed a little, and swept with their eyes the inclined plane of little vessels then and there arranged in order, ready to have imperial gallons of facts poured into them until they were full to the brim.

Dickens withholds his character's name until the beginning of the second chapter; he calls this fact-bound educator Mr. Gradgrind. Authors sometimes put as much time and effort into naming their characters as parents invest in naming their children. Names can be used to indicate qualities that the writer associates with the characters. Mr. Gradgrind is precisely what his name suggests. The "schoolmaster" employed by Gradgrind is Mr. M'Choakumchild. Pronounce this name aloud and you have the essence of this teacher's educational philosophy. In Nathaniel Hawthorne's *The Scarlet Letter*, Chillingworth is cold and relentless in his single-minded quest for revenge. The innocent and youthful protagonist in Herman Melville's *Billy Budd* is nipped in the bud by the evil Claggart, whose name simply sounds unpleasant.

Names are also used in films to suggest a character's nature. One example that is destined to be a classic is the infamous villain Darth Vader, whose name identifies his role as an invader allied with the dark and death. On the heroic side, it makes sense that Marion Morrison decided to change his box-office name to John Wayne in order to play tough, masculine roles because both the first and last of his chosen names are unambiguously male and to the point, while his given name is androgynous. There may also be some significance to the lack of a specific identity. In Godwin's "A Sorrowful Woman" (p. 35) the woman, man, boy, and girl are reduced to a set of domestic functions, and their not being named emphasizes their roles as opposed to their individual identities. Of course, not every name is suggestive of the qualities a character may embody, but it is frequently worth determining what is in a name.

The only way to tell whether a name reveals character is to look at the other information the author supplies about the character. We evaluate fictional characters in much the same way we understand people in our own lives. By piecing together bits of information, we create a context that allows us to interpret their behavior. We can predict, for instance, that an acquaintance who is a chronic complainer is not likely to have anything good to say about a roommate. We interpret words and actions in the light of what we already know about someone, and that is why keeping track of what characters say (and how they say it) along with what they do (and don't do) is important.

Authors reveal characters by other means too. Physical descriptions can indicate important inner qualities; disheveled clothing, a crafty smile, or a blush might communicate as much as or more than what a character says. Characters can also be revealed by the words and actions of others who respond to them. In literature, moreover, we have one great advantage that life cannot offer; a work of fiction can give us access to a person's thoughts. Although in Herman Melville's "Bartleby, the Scrivener" (p. 116) we learn about Bartleby primarily through descriptive details, words, actions, and his relationships with the other characters, Melville allows us to enter the lawyer's consciousness.

Authors have two major methods of presenting characters: ***showing*** and ***telling.*** Characters shown in dramatic situations reveal themselves indirectly by what they say and do. In the first paragraph of the excerpt from *Hard Times*, Dickens shows us some of Gradgrind's utilitarian educational principles by having him speak. We can infer the kind of person he is from his reference to boys and girls as "reasoning animals," but we are not told what to think of him until the second paragraph. It would be impossible to admire Gradgrind after reading the physical description of him and the school that he oversees. The adjectives in the second paragraph make the author's evaluation of Gradgrind's values and personality clear: everything about him is rigidly "square"; his mouth is "thin, and hard set"; his voice is "inflexible, dry, and dictatorial"; and he presides over a "plain, bare, monotonous vault of a schoolroom." Dickens directly lets us know how to feel about Gradgrind, but he does so artistically. Instead of simply being presented with a statement that Gradgrind is destructively practical, we get a detailed and amusing description.

We can contrast Dickens's direct presentation in this paragraph with the indirect showing that Gail Godwin uses in "A Sorrowful Woman." Godwin avoids telling us how we should think about the characters. Their story includes little description and no evaluations or interpretations by the author. To determine the significance of the events, the reader must pay close attention to what the characters say and do. Like Godwin, many twentieth-century authors favor showing over telling because showing allows readers to discover the meanings, which modern authors are often reluctant to impose on an audience for whom fixed meanings and values are not as strong as they once were. However, most writers continue to reveal characters by telling as well as showing when the technique suits their purposes — when, for example, a minor character must be sketched economically or when a long time has elapsed, causing changes in a major character. Telling and showing complement each other.

Characters can be convincing whether they are presented by telling or showing, provided their actions are ***motivated.*** There must be reasons for how they behave and what they say. If adequate motivation is offered, we can understand and find ***plausible*** their actions no matter how bizarre. In "A Rose for Emily" (p. 75), Faulkner makes Emily Grierson's intimacy with a corpse credible by preparing us with information about her father's death along with her inability to leave the past and live in the present. Emily turns out to be ***consistent.*** Although we are surprised by the ending of the story, the behavior it reveals is compatible with her temperament.

Some kinds of fiction consciously break away from our expectations of traditional realistic stories. Consistency, plausibility, and motivation are not very useful concepts for understanding and evaluating characterizations in modern ***absurdist literature,*** for instance, in which characters are often alienated from themselves and their environment in an irrational world. In this world there is no possibility for traditional heroic action; instead we find an *antihero* who has little control over events. Yossarian from Joseph Heller's *Catch-22* is an example of a protagonist who is thwarted by the absurd terms on which life offers itself to many twentieth-century characters.

In most stories we expect characters to act plausibly and in ways consistent with their personalities, but that does not mean that characters cannot develop and change. A *dynamic* character undergoes some kind of change because of the action of the plot. Huck Finn's view of Jim, the runaway slave in Mark Twain's novel, develops during their experiences on the raft. Huck discovers Jim's humanity and, therefore, cannot betray him because Huck no longer sees his companion as merely the property of a white owner. On the other hand, Huck's friend, Tom Sawyer, is a *static* character because he does not change. He remains interested only in high adventure, even at the risk of Jim's life. As static characters often do, Tom serves as a foil to Huck; his frivolous concerns are contrasted with Huck's serious development. A *foil* helps to reveal by contrast the distinctive qualities of another character.

The protagonist in a story is usually a dynamic character who experiences some conflict that makes an impact on his or her life. Less commonly, static characters can also be protagonists. Rip Van Winkle wakes up from his twenty-year sleep in Washington Irving's story to discover his family dramatically changed and his country no longer a British colony, but none of these important events has an impact on his character; he continues to be the same shiftless and idle man that he was before he fell asleep. The protagonist in Faulkner's "A Rose for Emily" is also a static character; indeed, she rejects all change. Our understanding of her changes, but she does not. Ordinarily, however, a plot contains one or two dynamic characters with any number of static characters in supporting roles. This is especially true of short stories, in which brevity limits the possibilities of character development.

The extent to which a character is developed is another means by which character can be analyzed. The novelist E. M. Forster coined the terms *flat* and *round* to distinguish degrees of character development. A *flat character* embodies one or two qualities, ideas, or traits that can be readily described in a brief summary. For instance, Mr. M'Choakumchild in Dickens's *Hard Times* stifles students instead of encouraging them to grow. Flat characters tend to be one-dimensional. They are readily accessible because their characteristics are few and simple; they are not created to be psychologically complex.

Some flat characters are immediately recognizable as *stock characters.* These stereotypes are particularly popular in formula fiction, television programs, and action movies. Stock characters are types rather than individuals. The poor but dedicated writer falls in love with a hard-working understudy, who gets nowhere because the corrupt producer favors his boozy, pampered mistress for the leading role. Characters such as these — the loyal servant, the mean stepfather, the henpecked husband, the dumb blonde, the sadistic army officer, the dotty grandmother — are prepackaged; they lack individuality because their authors have, in a sense, not imaginatively created them but simply summoned them from a warehouse of clichés and social prejudices. Stock characters can become fresh if a good writer makes them vivid, interesting, or memorable, but too often a writer's use of these stereotypes is simply weak characterization.

Round characters are more complex than flat or stock characters. Round characters have more depth and require more attention. They may surprise us or puzzle us. Although they are more fully developed, round characters are also more difficult to summarize because we are aware of competing ideas, values, and possibilities in their lives. As a flat character, Huck Finn's alcoholic, bigoted father is clear to us; we know that Pap is the embodiment of racism and irrationality. But Huck is considerably less predictable because he struggles with what Twain calls a "sound heart and a deformed conscience."

In making distinctions between flat and round characters, you must understand that an author's use of a flat character — even as a protagonist — does not necessarily represent an artistic flaw. Moreover, both flat and round characters can be either dynamic or static. Each plot can be made most effective by its own special kind of characterization. Terms such as *round* and *flat* are helpful tools to use to determine what we know about a character, but they are not an infallible measurement of the quality of a story.

The next three stories — Jhumpa Lahiri's "When Mr. Pirzada Came to Dine," Herman Melville's "Bartleby, the Scrivener," and Alice McDermott's "Enough" — offer character studies worthy of close analysis. As you read them, notice the methods of characterization used to bring each to life.

JHUMPA LAHIRI (B. 1967)

Born in London and raised in Rhode Island, Jhumpa Lahiri is the daughter of Bengali parents. She graduated from Barnard College with a B.A. in English and went on to earn four degrees from Boston University — master's degrees in English, creative writing, and comparative studies in literature and the arts, and a Ph.D. in Renaissance studies. In 1998 Lahiri published three stories in *The New Yorker*, and the following year published her first book, the short story collection *The Interpreter of Maladies* (1999), which won her the 2000 Pulitzer Prize for fiction. She currently resides in New York City. Lahiri locates her stories between the cultures of the United States and India, using lavish description of setting and the elaboration of cultural traditions to illuminate her characters' inner worlds.

Web *Research Jhumpa Lahiri with LitLinks at*
http://www.bedfordstmartins.com/meyer/bedintrolit

When Mr. Pirzada Came to Dine　　　　　　　*1999*

In the autumn of 1971 a man used to come to our house, bearing confections in his pocket and hopes of ascertaining the life or death of his family. His name was Mr. Pirzada, and he came from Dacca, now the capital of Bangladesh, but then a part of Pakistan. That year Pakistan was engaged in civil war. The eastern frontier, where Dacca was located, was fighting for autonomy from the ruling regime in the west. In March, Dacca had been invaded, torched, and shelled by the Pakistani army. Teachers were dragged onto streets and shot, women dragged into barracks and raped. By the end of the summer, three hundred thousand people were said to have died. In Dacca Mr. Pirzada had a three-story home, a lectureship in botany at the university, a wife of twenty years, and seven daughters between the ages of six and sixteen whose names all began with the letter A. "Their mother's idea," he explained one day, producing from his wallet a black-and-white picture of seven girls at a picnic, their braids tied with ribbons, sitting cross-legged in a row, eating chicken curry off of banana leaves. "How am I to distinguish? Ayesha, Amira, Amina, Aziza, you see the difficulty."

Each week Mr. Pirzada wrote letters to his wife, and sent comic books to each of his seven daughters, but the postal system, along with most everything else in Dacca, had collapsed, and he had not heard word of them in over six months. Mr. Pirzada, meanwhile, was in America for the year, for he had been awarded a grant from the government of Pakistan to study the foliage of New England. In spring and summer he had gathered data in Vermont and Maine, and in autumn he moved to a university north of Boston, where we lived, to write a short book about his discoveries. The grant was a great honor, but when converted into dollars it was not generous. As a result, Mr. Pirzada lived in a room in a graduate dormitory, and did not own a proper stove or a television set. And so he came to our house to eat dinner and watch the evening news.

At first I knew nothing of the reason for his visits. I was ten years old, and was not surprised that my parents, who were from India, and had a number of Indian acquaintances at the university, should ask Mr. Pirzada to share our meals. It was a small campus, with narrow brick walkways and white pillared buildings, located on the fringes of what seemed to be an even smaller town. The supermarket did not carry mustard oil, doctors did not make house calls, neighbors never dropped by without an invitation, and of these things, every so often, my parents complained. In search of compatriots, they used to trail their fingers, at the start of each new semester, through the columns of the university directory, circling surnames familiar to their part of the world. It was in this manner that they discovered Mr. Pirzada, and phoned him, and invited him to our home.

I have no memory of his first visit, or of his second or his third, but by the end of September I had grown so accustomed to Mr. Pirzada's presence in our living room that one evening, as I was dropping ice cubes into the water pitcher, I asked my mother to hand me a fourth glass from a cupboard still out of my reach. She was busy at the stove, presiding over a skillet of fried spinach with radishes, and could not hear me because of the drone of the exhaust fan and the fierce scrapes of her spatula. I turned to my father, who was leaning against the refrigerator, eating spiced cashews from a cupped fist.

"What is it, Lilia?"　　　　　　　　　　　　　　　　　　　　　　　　　5

"A glass for the Indian man."

"Mr. Pirzada won't be coming today. More importantly, Mr. Pirzada is no longer considered Indian," my father announced, brushing salt from the cashews out of his trim black beard. "Not since Partition. Our country was divided. 1947."

When I said I thought that was the date of India's independence from Britain, my father said, "That too. One moment we were free and then we were sliced up," he explained, drawing an X with his finger on the countertop, "like a pie. Hindus here, Muslims there. Dacca no longer belongs to us." He told me that during Partition Hindus and Muslims had set fire to each other's homes. For many, the idea of eating in the other's company was still unthinkable.

It made no sense to me. Mr. Pirzada and my parents spoke the same language, laughed at the same jokes, looked more or less the same. They ate pickled mangoes with their meals, ate rice every night for supper with their hands. Like my parents, Mr. Pirzada took off his shoes before entering a room, chewed fennel seeds after meals as a digestive, drank no alcohol, for dessert dipped austere biscuits into successive cups of tea. Nevertheless my father insisted that I understand the difference, and he led me to a map of the world taped to the wall over his desk. He seemed concerned that Mr. Pirzada might take offense if I accidentally referred to him as an Indian, though I could not really imagine Mr. Pirzada being offended by much of anything. "Mr. Pirzada is Bengali, but he is a Muslim," my father informed me. "Therefore he lives in East Pakistan, not India." His finger trailed across the Atlantic, through Europe, the Mediterranean, the Middle East, and finally to the sprawling orange diamond that my mother once told me resembled a woman wearing a sari with her left arm extended. Various cities had been circled with lines drawn between them to indicate my parents' travels, and the place of their birth, Calcutta, was signified by a small silver star. I had been there only once and had no memory of the trip. "As you see, Lilia, it is a different country, a different color," my father said. Pakistan was yellow, not orange. I noticed that there were two distinct parts to it, one much larger than the other, separated by an expanse of Indian territory; it was as if California and Connecticut constituted a nation apart from the U.S.

My father rapped his knuckles on top of my head. "You are, of course, 10 aware of the current situation? Aware of East Pakistan's fight for sovereignty?"

I nodded, unaware of the situation.

We returned to the kitchen, where my mother was draining a pot of boiled rice into a colander. My father opened up the can on the counter and eyed me sharply over the frames of his glasses as he ate some more cashews. "What exactly do they teach you at school? Do you study history? Geography?"

"Lilia has plenty to learn at school," my mother said. "We live here now, she was born here." She seemed genuinely proud of the fact, as if it were a reflection of my character. In her estimation, I knew, I was assured a safe life, an easy life, a fine education, every opportunity. I would never have to eat rationed food, or obey curfews, or watch riots from my rooftop, or hide neighbors in water tanks to prevent them from being shot, as she and my father had. "Imagine having to place her in a decent school. Imagine her having to read during power failures, by the light of kerosene lamps. Imagine the pressures, the tutors, the constant exams." She ran a hand through her hair, bobbed to a suitable length for her part-time job as a bank teller. "How can you possibly expect her to know about Partition? Put those nuts away."

"But what does she learn about the world?" My father rattled the cashew can in his hand. "What is she learning?"

We learned American history, of course, and American geography. That year, and every year, it seemed, we began by studying the Revolutionary War. We were taken in school buses on field trips to visit Plymouth Rock, and to walk the Freedom Trail, and to climb to the top of the Bunker Hill Monument. We made dioramas out of colored construction paper depicting George Washington crossing the choppy waters of the Delaware River, and we made puppets of King George wearing white tights and a black bow in his hair. During tests we were given blank maps of the thirteen colonies, and asked to fill in names, dates, capitals. I could do it with my eyes closed.

The next evening Mr. Pirzada arrived, as usual, at six o'clock. Though they were no longer strangers, upon first greeting each other, he and my father maintained the habit of shaking hands.

"Come in, sir. Lilia, Mr. Pirzada's coat, please."

He stepped into the foyer, impeccably suited and scarved, with a silk tie knotted at his collar. Each evening he appeared in ensembles of plums, olives, and chocolate browns. He was a compact man, and though his feet were perpetually splayed, and his belly slightly wide, he nevertheless maintained an efficient posture, as if balancing in either hand two suitcases of equal weight. His ears were insulated by tufts of graying hair that seemed to block out the unpleasant traffic of life. He had thickly lashed eyes shaded with a trace of camphor, a generous mustache that turned up playfully at the ends, and a mole shaped like a flattened raisin in the very center of his left cheek. On his head he wore a black fez made from the wool of Persian lambs, secured by bobby pins, without which I was never to see him. Though my father always offered to fetch him in our car, Mr. Pirzada preferred to walk from his dormitory to our neighborhood, a distance of about twenty minutes on foot, studying trees and shrubs on his way, and when he entered our house his knuckles were pink with the effects of crisp autumn air.

"Another refugee, I am afraid, on Indian territory."

"They are estimating nine million at the last count," my father said.

Mr. Pirzada handed me his coat, for it was my job to hang it on the rack at the bottom of the stairs. It was made of finely checkered gray-and-blue wool, with a striped lining and horn buttons, and carried in its weave the faint smell of limes. There were no recognizable tags inside, only a hand-stitched label with the phrase "Z. Sayeed, Suitors" embroidered on it in cursive with glossy black thread. On certain days a birch or maple leaf was tucked into a pocket. He unlaced his shoes and lined them against the baseboard; a golden paste clung to the toes and heels, the result of walking through our damp, unraked lawn. Relieved of his trappings, he grazed my throat with his short, restless fingers, the way a person feels for solidity behind a wall before driving in a nail. Then he followed my father to the living room, where the television was tuned to the local news. As soon as they were seated my mother appeared from the kitchen with a plate of mincemeat kebabs with coriander chutney. Mr. Pirzada popped one into his mouth.

"One can only hope," he said, reaching for another, "that Dacca's refugees are as heartily fed. Which reminds me." He reached into his suit pocket and gave me a small plastic egg filled with cinnamon hearts. "For the lady of the house," he said with an almost imperceptible splay-footed bow.

"Really, Mr. Pirzada," my mother protested. "Night after night. You spoil her."

"I only spoil children who are incapable of spoiling."

It was an awkward moment for me, one which I awaited in part with 25 dread, in part with delight. I was charmed by the presence of Mr. Pirzada's rotund elegance, and flattered by the faint theatricality of his attentions, yet unsettled by the superb ease of his gestures, which made me feel, for an instant, like a stranger in my own home. It had become our ritual, and for several weeks, before we grew more comfortable with one another, it was the only time he spoke to me directly. I had no response, offered no comment, betrayed no visible reaction to the steady stream of honey-filled lozenges, the raspberry truffles, the slender rolls of sour pastilles. I could not even thank him, for once, when I did, for an especially spectacular peppermint lollipop wrapped in a spray of purple cellophane, he had demanded, "What is this thank-you? The lady at the bank thanks me, the cashier at the shop thanks me, the librarian thanks me when I return an overdue book, the overseas operator thanks me as she tries to connect me to Dacca and fails. If I am buried in this country I will be thanked, no doubt, at my funeral."

It was inappropriate, in my opinion, to consume the candy Mr. Pirzada gave me in a casual manner. I coveted each evening's treasure as I would a jewel, or a coin from a buried kingdom, and I would place it in a small keepsake box made of carved sandalwood beside my bed, in which, long ago in India, my father's mother used to store the ground areca nuts she ate after her morning bath. It was my only memento of a grandmother I had never known, and until Mr. Pirzada came to our lives I could find nothing to put inside it. Every so often before brushing my teeth and laying out my clothes for school the next day, I opened the lid of the box and ate one of his treats.

That night, like every night, we did not eat at the dining table, because it did not provide an unobstructed view of the television set. Instead we huddled around the coffee table, without conversing, our plates perched on the edges of our knees. From the kitchen my mother brought forth the succession of dishes: lentils with fried onions, green beans with coconut, fish cooked with raisins in a yogurt sauce. I followed with the water glasses, and the plate of lemon wedges, and the chili peppers, purchased on monthly trips to Chinatown and stored by the pound in the freezer, which they liked to snap open and crush into their food.

Before eating Mr. Pirzada always did a curious thing. He took out a plain silver watch without a band, which he kept in his breast pocket, held it briefly to one of his tufted ears, and wound it with three swift flicks of his thumb and forefinger. Unlike the watch on his wrist, the pocket watch, he had explained to me, was set to the local time in Dacca, eleven hours ahead. For the duration of the meal the watch rested on his folded paper napkin on the coffee table. He never seemed to consult it.

Now that I had learned Mr. Pirzada was not an Indian, I began to study him with extra care, to try to figure out what made him different. I decided that the pocket watch was one of those things. When I saw it that night, as he wound it and arranged it on the coffee table, an uneasiness possessed me; life, I realized, was being lived in Dacca first. I imagined Mr. Pirzada's daughters rising from sleep, tying ribbons in their hair, anticipating breakfast, preparing for school. Our meals, our actions, were only a shadow of what had already happened there, a lagging ghost of where Mr. Pirzada really belonged.

At six-thirty, which was when the national news began, my father raised 30 the volume and adjusted the antennas. Usually I occupied myself with a book, but that night my father insisted that I pay attention. On the screen I saw tanks rolling through dusty streets, and fallen buildings, and forests of unfamiliar trees into which East Pakistani refugees had fled, seeking safety over the Indian border. I saw boats with fan-shaped sails floating on wide coffee-colored rivers, a barricaded university, newspaper offices burnt to the ground. I turned to look at Mr. Pirzada; the images flashed in miniature across his eyes. As he watched he had an immovable expression on his face, composed but alert, as if someone were giving him directions to an unknown destination.

During the commercial my mother went to the kitchen to get more rice, and my father and Mr. Pirzada deplored the policies of a general named Yahyah Khan. They discussed intrigues I did not know, a catastrophe I could not comprehend. "See, children your age, what they do to survive," my father said as he served me another piece of fish. But I could no longer eat. I could only steal glances at Mr. Pirzada, sitting beside me in his olive green jacket, calmly creating a well in his rice to make room for a second helping of lentils. He was not my notion of a man burdened by such grave concerns. I wondered if the reason he was always so smartly dressed was in preparation to endure with dignity whatever news assailed him, perhaps even to attend a funeral at a moment's notice. I wondered, too, what would happen if suddenly his seven daughters were to appear on television, smiling and waving and blowing kisses to Mr. Pirzada from a balcony. I imagined how relieved he would be. But this never happened.

That night when I placed the plastic egg filled with cinnamon hearts in the box beside my bed, I did not feel the ceremonious satisfaction I normally did. I tried not to think about Mr. Pirzada, in his lime-scented overcoat, connected to the unruly, sweltering world we had viewed a few hours ago in our bright, carpeted living room. And yet for several moments that was all I could think about. My stomach tightened as I worried whether his wife and seven daughters were now members of the drifting, clamoring crowd that had flashed at intervals on the screen. In an effort to banish the image I looked around my room, at the yellow canopied bed with matching flounced curtains, at framed class pictures mounted on white and violet papered walls, at the penciled inscriptions by the closet door where my father recorded my height on each of my birthdays. But the more I tried to distract myself, the more I began to convince myself that Mr. Pirzada's family was in all likelihood dead. Eventually I took a square of white chocolate out of the box, and unwrapped it, and then I did something I had never done before. I put the chocolate in my mouth, letting it soften until the last possible moment, and then as I chewed it slowly, I prayed that Mr. Pirzada's family was safe and sound. I had never prayed for anything before, had never been taught or told to, but I decided, given the circumstances, that it was something I should do. That night when I went to the bathroom I only pretended to brush my teeth, for I feared that I would somehow rinse the prayer out as well. I wet the brush and rearranged the tube of paste to prevent my parents from asking any questions, and fell asleep with sugar on my tongue.

* * *

No one at school talked about the war followed so faithfully in my living room. We continued to study the American Revolution, and learned about the injustices of taxation without representation, and memorized passages from the Declaration of Independence. During recess the boys would divide in two groups, chasing each other wildly around the swings and seesaws, Redcoats against the colonies. In the classroom our teacher, Mrs. Kenyon, pointed frequently to a map that emerged like a movie screen from the top of the chalkboard, charting the route of the *Mayflower,* or showing us the location of the Liberty Bell. Each week two members of the class gave a report on a particular aspect of the Revolution, and so one day I was sent to the school library with my friend Dora to learn about the surrender at Yorktown. Mrs. Kenyon handed us a slip of paper with the names of three books to look up in the card catalogue. We found them right away, and sat down at a low round table to read and take notes. But I could not concentrate. I returned to the blond-wood shelves, to a section I had noticed labeled "Asia." I saw books about China, India, Indonesia, Korea. Eventually I found a book titled *Pakistan: A Land and Its People.* I sat on a footstool and opened the book. The laminated jacket crackled in my grip. I began turning the pages, filled with photos of rivers and rice fields and men in military uniforms. There was a chapter about Dacca, and I began to read about its rainfall, and its jute production. I was studying a population chart when Dora appeared in the aisle.

"What are you doing back here? Mrs. Kenyon's in the library. She came to check up on us."

I slammed the book shut, too loudly. Mrs. Kenyon emerged, the aroma of her perfume filling up the tiny aisle, and lifted the book by the tip of its spine as if it were a hair clinging to my sweater. She glanced at the cover, then at me.

"Is this book a part of your report, Lilia?"

"No, Mrs. Kenyon."

"Then I see no reason to consult it," she said, replacing it in the slim gap on the shelf. "Do you?"

As weeks passed it grew more and more rare to see any footage from Dacca on the news. The report came after the first set of commercials, sometimes the second. The press had been censored, removed, restricted, rerouted. Some days, many days, only a death toll was announced, prefaced by a reiteration of the general situation. More poets were executed, more villages set ablaze. In spite of it all, night after night, my parents and Mr. Pirzada enjoyed long, leisurely meals. After the television was shut off, and the dishes washed and dried, they joked, and told stories, and dipped biscuits in their tea. When they tired of discussing political matters they discussed, instead, the progress of Mr. Pirzada's book about the deciduous trees of New England, and my father's nomination for tenure, and the peculiar eating habits of my mother's American coworkers at the bank. Eventually I was sent upstairs to do my homework, but through the carpet I heard them as they drank more tea, and listened to cassettes of Kishore Kumar, and played Scrabble on the coffee table, laughing and arguing long into the night about the spellings of English words. I wanted to join them, wanted, above all, to console Mr. Pirzada somehow. But apart from eating a piece of candy for the sake of his family and praying for their safety, there was nothing I could do. They played Scrabble until the eleven o'clock news, and then, sometime around midnight, Mr. Pirzada walked back to his dormitory. For this reason I never saw him leave, but each night as I drifted off to sleep I would hear them, anticipating the birth of a nation on the other side of the world.

One day in October Mr. Pirzada asked upon arrival, "What are these large orange vegetables on people's doorsteps? A type of squash?" 40

"Pumpkins," my mother replied. "Lilia, remind me to pick one up at the supermarket."

"And the purpose? It indicates what?"

"You make a jack-o'-lantern," I said, grinning ferociously. "Like this. To scare people away."

"I see," Mr. Pirzada said, grinning back. "Very useful."

The next day my mother bought a ten-pound pumpkin, fat and round, and placed it on the dining table. Before supper, while my father and Mr. Pirzada were watching the local news, she told me to decorate it with markers, but I wanted to carve it properly like others I had noticed in the neighborhood. 45

"Yes, let's carve it," Mr. Pirzada agreed, and rose from the sofa. "Hang the news tonight." Asking no questions, he walked into the kitchen, opened a drawer, and returned, bearing a long serrated knife. He glanced at me for approval. "Shall I?"

I nodded. For the first time we all gathered around the dining table, my mother, my father, Mr. Pirzada, and I. While the television aired unattended we covered the tabletop with newspapers. Mr. Pirzada draped his jacket over the chair behind him, removed a pair of opal cuff links, and rolled up the starched sleeves of his shirt.

"First go around the top, like this," I instructed, demonstrating with my index finger.

He made an initial incision and drew the knife around. When he had come full circle he lifted the cap by the stem; it loosened effortlessly, and Mr. Pirzada leaned over the pumpkin for a moment to inspect and inhale its contents. My mother gave him a long metal spoon with which he gutted the interior until the last bits of string and seeds were gone. My father, meanwhile, separated the seeds from the pulp and set them out to dry on a cookie sheet, so that we could roast them later on. I drew two triangles against the ridged surface for the eyes, which Mr. Pirzada dutifully carved, and crescents for eyebrows, and another triangle for the nose. The mouth was all that remained, and the teeth posed a challenge. I hesitated.

"Smile or frown?" I asked. 50

"You choose," Mr. Pirzada said.

As a compromise I drew a kind of grimace, straight across, neither mournful nor friendly. Mr. Pirzada began carving, without the least bit of intimidation, as if he had been carving jack-o'-lanterns his whole life. He had nearly finished when the national news began. The reporter mentioned Dacca, and we all turned to listen: An Indian official announced that unless the world helped to relieve the burden of East Pakistani refugees, India would have to go to war against Pakistan. The reporter's face dripped with sweat as he relayed the information. He did not wear a tie or a jacket, dressed instead as if he himself were about to take part in the battle. He shielded his scorched face as he hollered things to the cameraman. The knife slipped from Mr. Pirzada's hand and made a gash dipping toward the base of the pumpkin.

"Please forgive me." He raised a hand to one side of his face, as if someone had slapped him there. "I am — it is terrible. I will buy another. We will try again."

"Not at all, not at all," my father said. He took the knife from Mr. Pirzada, and carved around the gash, evening it out, dispensing altogether with the teeth I had drawn. What resulted was a disproportionately large hole the size of a lemon, so that our jack-o'-lantern wore an expression of placid astonishment, the eyebrows no longer fierce, floating in frozen surprise above a vacant, geometric gaze.

For Halloween I was a witch. Dora, my trick-or-treating partner, was a witch 55 too. We wore black capes fashioned from dyed pillowcases and conical hats with wide cardboard brims. We shaded our faces green with a broken eye shadow that belonged to Dora's mother, and my mother gave us two burlap sacks that had once contained basmati rice, for collecting candy. That year our parents decided that we were old enough to roam the neighborhood unattended. Our plan was to walk from my house to Dora's, from where I was to call to say I had arrived safely, and then Dora's mother would drive me home. My father equipped us with flashlights, and I had to wear my watch and synchronize it with his. We were to return no later than nine o'clock.

When Mr. Pirzada arrived that evening he presented me with a box of chocolate-covered mints.

"In here," I told him, and opened up the burlap sack. "Trick or treat!"

"I understand that you don't really need my contribution this evening," he said, depositing the box. He gazed at my green face, and the hat secured by a string under my chin. Gingerly he lifted the hem of the cape, under which I was wearing a sweater and a zipped fleece jacket. "Will you be warm enough?"

I nodded, causing the hat to tip to one side.

He set it right. "Perhaps it is best to stand still." 60

The bottom of our staircase was lined with baskets of miniature candy, and when Mr. Pirzada removed his shoes he did not place them there as he normally did, but inside the closet instead. He began to unbutton his coat, and I waited to take it from him, but Dora called me from the bathroom to say that she needed my help drawing a mole on her chin. When we were finally ready my mother took a picture of us in front of the fireplace, and then I opened the front door to leave. Mr. Pirzada and my father, who had not gone into the living room yet, hovered in the foyer. Outside it was already dark. The air smelled of wet leaves, and our carved jack-o'-lantern flickered impressively against the shrubbery by the door. In the distance came the sounds of scampering feet, and the howls of the older boys who wore no costume at all other than a rubber mask, and the rustling apparel of the youngest children, some so young that they were carried from door to door in the arms of their parents.

"Don't go into any of the houses you don't know," my father warned.

Mr. Pirzada knit his brows together. "Is there any danger?"

"No, no," my mother assured him. "All the children will be out. It's a tradition."

"Perhaps I should accompany them?" Mr. Pirzada suggested. He looked 65 suddenly tired and small, standing there in his splayed, stockinged feet, and his eyes contained a panic I had never seen before. In spite of the cold I began to sweat inside my pillowcase.

"Really, Mr. Pirzada," my mother said, "Lilia will be perfectly safe with her friend."

"But if it rains? If they lose their way?"

"Don't worry," I said. It was the first time I had uttered those words to Mr. Pirzada, two simple words I had tried but failed to tell him for weeks, had said only in my prayers. It shamed me now that I had said them for my own sake.

He placed one of his stocky fingers on my cheek, then pressed it to the back of his own hand, leaving a faint green smear. "If the lady insists," he conceded, and offered a small bow.

We left, stumbling slightly in our black pointy thrift-store shoes, and when we turned at the end of the driveway to wave good-bye, Mr. Pirzada was standing in the frame of the doorway, a short figure between my parents, waving back. 70

"Why did that man want to come with us?" Dora asked.

"His daughters are missing." As soon as I said it, I wished I had not. I felt that my saying it made it true, that Mr. Pirzada's daughters really were missing, and that he would never see them again.

"You mean they were kidnapped?" Dora continued. "From a park or something?"

"I didn't mean they were missing. I meant, he misses them. They live in a different country, and he hasn't seen them in a while, that's all."

We went from house to house, walking along pathways and pressing door- 75 bells. Some people had switched off all their lights for effect, or strung rubber bats in their windows. At the McIntyres' a coffin was placed in front of the door, and Mr. McIntyre rose from it in silence, his face covered with chalk, and deposited a fistful of candy corns into our sacks. Several people told me that they had never seen an Indian witch before. Others performed the transaction without comment. As we paved our way with the parallel beams of our flashlights we saw eggs cracked in the middle of the road, and cars covered with shaving cream, and toilet paper garlanding the branches of trees. By the time we reached Dora's house our hands were chapped from carrying our bulging burlap bags, and our feet were sore and swollen. Her mother gave us bandages for our blisters and served us warm cider and caramel popcorn. She reminded me to call my parents to tell them I had arrived safely, and when I did I could hear the television in the background. My mother did not seem particularly relieved to hear from me. When I replaced the phone on the receiver it occurred to me that the television wasn't on at Dora's house at all. Her father was lying on the couch, reading a magazine, with a glass of wine on the coffee table, and there was saxophone music playing on the stereo.

After Dora and I had sorted through our plunder, and counted and sampled and traded until we were satisfied, her mother drove me back to my house. I thanked her for the ride, and she waited in the driveway until I made it to the door. In the glare of her headlights I saw that our pumpkin had been shattered, its thick shell strewn in chunks across the grass. I felt the sting of tears in my eyes, and a sudden pain in my throat, as if it had been stuffed with the sharp tiny pebbles that crunched with each step under my aching feet. I opened the door, expecting the three of them to be standing in the foyer, waiting to receive me, and to grieve for our ruined pumpkin, but there was no one. In the living room Mr. Pirzada, my father, and mother were sitting side by side on the sofa. The television was turned off, and Mr. Pirzada had his head in his hands.

What they heard that evening, and for many evenings after that, was that India and Pakistan were drawing closer and closer to war. Troops from both sides lined the border, and Dacca was insisting on nothing short of independence. The war was to be waged on East Pakistani soil. The United States was siding with West Pakistan, the Soviet Union with India and what was soon to be Bangladesh. War was declared officially on December 4, and twelve days later, the Pakistani army, weakened by having to fight three thousand miles from their source of supplies, surrendered in Dacca. All of these facts I know only now, for they are available to me in any history book, in any library. But then it remained, for the most part, a remote mystery with haphazard clues. What I remember during those twelve days of the war was that my father no longer asked me to watch the news with them, and that Mr. Pirzada stopped bringing me candy, and that my mother refused to serve anything other than boiled eggs with rice for dinner. I remember some nights helping my mother spread a sheet and blankets on the couch so that Mr. Pirzada could sleep there, and high-pitched voices hollering in the middle of the night when my parents called our relatives in Calcutta to learn more details about the situation. Most of all I remember the three of them operating during that time as if they were a single person, sharing a single meal, a single body, a single silence, and a single fear.

In January, Mr. Pirzada flew back to his three-story home in Dacca, to discover what was left of it. We did not see much of him in those final weeks of the year; he was busy finishing his manuscript, and we went to Philadelphia to spend Christmas with friends of my parents. Just as I have no memory of his first visit, I have no memory of his last. My father drove him to the airport one afternoon while I was at school. For a long time we did not hear from him. Our evenings went on as usual, with dinners in front of the news. The only difference was that Mr. Pirzada and his extra watch were not there to accompany us. According to reports Dacca was repairing itself slowly, with a newly formed parliamentary government. The new leader, Sheikh Mujib Rahman, recently released from prison, asked countries for building materials to replace more than one million houses that had been destroyed in the war. Countless refugees returned from India, greeted, we learned, by unemployment and the threat of famine. Every now and then I studied the map above my father's desk and pictured Mr. Pirzada on that small patch of yellow, perspiring heavily, I imagined, in one of his suits, searching for his family. Of course, the map was outdated by then.

Finally, several months later, we received a card from Mr. Pirzada commemorating the Muslim New Year, along with a short letter. He was reunited, he wrote, with his wife and children. All were well, having survived the events of the past year at an estate belonging to his wife's grandparents in the mountains of Shillong. His seven daughters were a bit taller, he wrote, but otherwise they were the same, and he still could not keep their names in order. At the end of the letter he thanked us for our hospitality, adding that although he now understood the meaning of the words "thank you" they still were not adequate to express his gratitude. To celebrate the good news my mother prepared a special dinner that evening, and when we sat down to eat at the coffee table we toasted our water glasses, but I did not feel like celebrating. Though I had not seen him for months, it was only then that I felt Mr. Pirzada's absence. It was only then, raising my water glass in his name, that I knew what it meant to miss someone who was so many miles and hours away, just as he had missed his wife and daughters for so many months. He had no reason to return to us, and my parents predicted, correctly, that we would never see him again. Since January, each night before bed, I had continued to eat, for the sake of Mr. Pirzada's family, a piece of candy I had saved from Halloween. That night there was no need to. Eventually, I threw them away.

CONSIDERATIONS FOR CRITICAL THINKING AND WRITING

1. FIRST RESPONSE. How does Lahiri contrast life in East Pakistan with life in America?

2. How does Lahiri provide background exposition about the civil war in Pakistan? What comments in the story about the teaching of history in American schools suggest that such exposition is necessary?

3. To what extent is the behavior of the adults and of Lilia determined by their cultural backgrounds? What evidence in the story supports this?

4. Characterize Mr. Pirzada. Why do you think he keeps his watch set to the local time in Dacca?

5. What do you think is the story's major conflict? Who or what is the antagonist? Explain.

6. What is the effect of the story being told from the perspective of a ten-year-old Indian girl born in the United States?

7. How is Lilia affected by Mr. Pirzada's visits to her house?

8. Explain why you think Lilia or Mr. Pirzada is the central character in the story.

9. CRITICAL STRATEGIES. Read the section on Marxist criticism (p. 2103) in Chapter 52, "Critical Strategies for Reading," and read some background information on the Pakistan war of 1971. How do you think a Marxist critic might approach this story?

CONNECTIONS TO OTHER SELECTIONS

1. Compare the use of exposition to reveal character in this story and in Raymond Carver's "Popular Mechanics" (p. 286). How does exposition or its relative absence affect your understanding of and response to the characters in each story?

2. Write an essay comparing the characters' efforts to be American in Lahiri's story and in Gish Jen's "Who's Irish?" (p. 178).

HERMAN MELVILLE (1819–1891)

Hoping to improve his distressed financial situation, Herman Melville left New York and went to sea as a young common sailor. He returned to become an uncommon writer. His experiences at sea became the basis for his early novels: *Typee* (1846), *Omoo* (1847), *Mardi* (1849), *Redburn* (1849), and

White-Jacket (1850). Ironically, with the publication of his masterpiece, *Moby-Dick* (1851), Melville lost the popular success he had enjoyed with his earlier books because his readers were not ready for its philosophical complexity. Although he wrote more, Melville's works were read less and slipped into obscurity. His final short novel, *Billy Budd,* was not published until the 1920s, when critics rediscovered him. In "Bartleby, the Scrivener," Melville presents a quiet clerk in a law office whose baffling "passive resistance" disrupts the life of his employer, a man who attempts to make sense of Bartleby's refusal to behave reasonably.

Web   *Research Herman Melville with LitLinks at*
http://www.bedfordstmartins.com/meyer/bedintrolit

Bartleby, the Scrivener   *1853*
A Story of Wall Street

I am a rather elderly man. The nature of my avocations, for the last thirty years, has brought me into more than ordinary contact with what would seem an interesting and somewhat singular set of men, of whom, as yet, nothing, that I know of, has ever been written — I mean, the law-copyists, or scriveners. I have known very many of them, professionally and privately, and, if I pleased, could relate divers histories, at which good-natured gentlemen might smile, and sentimental souls might weep. But I waive the biographies of all other scriveners, for a few passages in the life of Bartleby, who was a scrivener, the strangest I ever saw, or heard of. While, of other law-copyists, I might write the complete life, of Bartleby nothing of that sort can be done. I believe that no materials exist, for a full and satisfactory biography of this man. It is an irreparable loss to literature. Bartleby was one of those beings of whom nothing is ascertainable, except from the original sources, and, in his case, those are very small. What my own astonished eyes saw of Bartleby, *that* is all I know of him, except, indeed, one vague report, which will appear in the sequel.

Ere introducing the scrivener, as he first appeared to me, it is fit I make some mention of myself, my *employés,* my business, my chambers, and general surroundings, because some such description is indispensable to an adequate understanding of the chief character about to be presented. Imprimis:° I am a man who, from his youth upwards, has been filled with a profound conviction that the easiest way of life is the best. Hence, though I belong to a profession proverbially energetic and nervous, even to turbulence, at times, yet nothing of that sort have I ever suffered to invade my peace. I am one of those unambitious lawyers who never address a jury, or in any way draw down public applause; but, in the cool tranquillity of a snug retreat, do a snug business among rich men's bonds, and mortgages, and title-deeds. All who know me, consider me an eminently *safe* man. The late John Jacob Astor,° a personage little given to poetic enthusiasm, had no hesitation in pronouncing my first

---

Imprimis: In the first place.
John Jacob Astor (1763–1848): An enormously wealthy American capitalist.

grand point to be prudence; my next, method. I do not speak it in vanity, but simply record the fact, that I was not unemployed in my profession by the late John Jacob Astor; a name which, I admit, I love to repeat; for it hath a rounded and orbicular sound to it, and rings like unto bullion. I will freely add, that I was not insensible to the late John Jacob Astor's good opinion.

Some time prior to the period at which this little history begins, my avocations had been largely increased. The good old office, now extinct in the State of New York, of a Master in Chancery, had been conferred upon me. It was not a very arduous office, but very pleasantly remunerative. I seldom lose my temper; much more seldom indulge in dangerous indignation at wrongs and outrages; but I must be permitted to be rash here and declare, that I consider the sudden and violent abrogation of the office of Master in Chancery, by the new Constitution, as a —— premature act; inasmuch as I had counted upon a lifelease of the profits, whereas I only received those of a few short years. But this is by the way.

My chambers were up stairs, at No. — Wall Street. At one end, they looked upon the white wall of the interior of a spacious skylight shaft, penetrating the building from top to bottom.

This view might have been considered rather tame than otherwise, deficient in what landscape painters call "life." But, if so, the view from the other end of my chambers offered, at least, a contrast, if nothing more. In that direction, my windows commanded an unobstructed view of a lofty brick wall, black by age and everlasting shade; which wall required no spyglass to bring out its lurking beauties, but, for the benefit of all near-sighted spectators, was pushed up to within ten feet of my window-panes. Owing to the great height of the surrounding buildings, and my chambers being on the second floor, the interval between this wall and mine not a little resembled a huge square cistern. 5

At the period just preceding the advent of Bartleby, I had two persons as copyists in my employment, and a promising lad as an office-boy. First, Turkey; second, Nippers; third, Ginger Nut. These may seem names, the like of which are not usually found in the Directory. In truth, they were nicknames, mutually conferred upon each other by my three clerks, and were deemed expressive of their respective persons or characters. Turkey was a short, pursy Englishman, of about my own age — that is, somewhere not far from sixty. In the morning, one might say, his face was of a fine florid hue, but after twelve o'clock, meridian — his dinner hour — it blazed like a grate full of Christmas coals; and continued blazing — but, as it were, with a gradual wane — till six o'clock, P.M., or thereabouts; after which, I saw no more of the proprietor of the face, which, gaining its meridian with the sun, seemed to set with it, to rise, culminate, and decline the following day, with the like regularity and undiminished glory. There are many singular coincidences I have known in the course of my life, not the least among which was the fact, that, exactly when Turkey displayed his fullest beams from his red and radiant countenance, just then, too, at that critical moment, began the daily period when I considered his business capacities as seriously disturbed for the remainder of the twenty-four hours. Not that he was absolutely idle, or averse to business then; far from it. The difficulty was, he was apt to be altogether too energetic. There was a strange, inflamed, flurried, flighty recklessness of activity about him. He would be incautious in dipping his pen into his inkstand. All his blots upon my documents were dropped there after twelve o'clock, meridian. Indeed, not only would he be reckless, and sadly given to making blots in the afternoon, but, some days, he went further, and was rather noisy. At such times, too, his face flamed with augmented blazonry, as if cannel coal had been heaped on anthracite. He made an unpleasant racket with his chair; spilled his sand-box; in mending his pens, impatiently split them all to pieces, and threw them on the floor in a sudden passion; stood up, and leaned over his table, boxing his papers about in a most indecorous manner, very sad to behold in an elderly man like him. Nevertheless, as he was in many ways a most valuable person to me, and all the time before twelve o'clock, meridian, was the quickest, steadiest creature, too, accomplishing a great deal of work in a style not easily to be matched — for these reasons, I was willing to overlook his eccentricities, though, indeed, occasionally, I remonstrated with him. I did this very gently, however, because, though the civilest, nay, the blandest and most reverential of men in the morning, yet, in the afternoon, he was disposed, upon provocation, to be slightly rash with his tongue — in fact, insolent. Now, valuing his morning services as I did, and resolved not to lose them — yet, at the same time, made uncomfortable by his inflamed ways after twelve o'clock — and being a man of peace, unwilling by my admonitions to call forth unseemly retorts from him, I took upon me, one Saturday noon (he was always worse on Saturdays) to hint to him, very kindly, that, perhaps, now that he was growing old, it might be well to abridge his labors; in short, he need not come to my chambers after twelve o'clock, but, dinner over, had best go home to his lodgings, and rest himself till tea-time. But no; he insisted upon his afternoon devotions. His countenance became intolerably fervid, as he oratorically assured me — gesticulating with a long ruler at the other end of the room — that if his services in the morning were useful, how indispensable, then, in the afternoon?

"With submission, sir," said Turkey, on this occasion, "I consider myself your right-hand man. In the morning I but marshal and deploy my columns; but in the afternoon I put myself at their head, and gallantly charge the foe, thus" — and he made a violent thrust with the ruler.

"But the blots, Turkey," intimated I.

"True; but, with submission, sir, behold these hairs! I am getting old. Surely, sir, a blot or two of a warm afternoon is not to be severely urged against gray hairs. Old age — even if it blot the page — is honorable. With submission, sir, we *both* are getting old."

This appeal to my fellow-feeling was hardly to be resisted. At all events, I 10 saw that go he would not. So, I made up my mind to let him stay, resolving, nevertheless, to see to it that, during the afternoon, he had to do with my less important papers.

Nippers, the second on my list, was a whiskered, sallow, and, upon the whole, rather piratical-looking young man, of about five-and-twenty. I always deemed him the victim of two evil powers — ambition and indigestion. The ambition was evinced by a certain impatience of the duties of a mere copyist, an unwarrantable usurpation of strictly professional affairs such as the original drawing up of legal documents. The indigestion seemed betokened in an occasional nervous testiness and grinning irritability, causing the teeth to audibly grind together over mistakes committed in copying; unnecessary maledictions, hissed, rather than spoken, in the heat of business; and especially by a continual discontent with the height of the table where he worked. Though of a very ingenious mechanical turn, Nippers could never get this table to suit him. He put chips under it, blocks of various sorts, bits of pasteboard, and at last went so far as to attempt an exquisite adjustment, by final pieces of folded blotting-paper. But no invention would answer. If, for the sake of easing his back, he brought the table-lid at a sharp angle well up towards his chin, and wrote there like a man using the steep roof of a Dutch house for his desk, then he declared that it stopped the circulation in his arms. If now he lowered the table to his waistbands, and stooped over it in writing, then there was a sore aching in his back. In short, the truth of the matter was, Nippers knew not what he wanted. Or, if he wanted anything, it was to be rid of a scrivener's table altogether. Among the manifestations of his diseased ambition was a fondness he had for receiving visits from certain ambiguous-looking fellows in seedy coats, whom he called his clients. Indeed, I was aware that not only was he, at times, considerable of a ward-politician, but he occasionally did a little business at the justices' courts, and was not unknown on the steps of the Tombs.° I have good reason to believe, however, that one individual who called upon him at my chambers, and who, with a grand air, he insisted was his client, was no other than a dun, and the alleged title-deed, a bill. But, with all his failings, and the annoyances he caused me, Nippers, like his compatriot Turkey, was a very useful man to me; wrote a neat, swift hand; and, when he chose, was not deficient in a gentlemanly sort of deportment. Added to this, he always dressed in a gentlemanly sort of way; and so, incidentally, reflected credit upon my chambers. Whereas, with respect to Turkey, I had much ado to keep him from being a reproach to me. His clothes were apt to look oily, a smell of eating-houses. He wore his pantaloons very loose and baggy in summer. His coats were execrable, his hat not to be handled. But while the hat was a thing of indifference to me, inasmuch as his natural civility and deference, as a dependent Englishman, always led him to doff it the moment he entered the room, yet his coat was another matter. Concerning his coats, I reasoned with him; but with no effect. The truth was, I suppose, that a man with so small an income could not afford to sport such a lustrous face and a lustrous coat at one and the same time. As Nippers once observed, Turkey's money went chiefly for red ink. One winter day, I presented Turkey with a highly respectable-looking coat of my own — a padded gray coat, of a most comfortable warmth, and which buttoned straight up from the knee to the neck. I thought Turkey would appreciate the favor, and abate his rashness and obstreperousness of afternoons. But no; I verily believe that buttoning himself up in so downy and blanket-like a coat had a pernicious effect upon him — upon the same principle that too much oats are bad for horses. In fact, precisely as a rash, restive horse is said to feel his oats, so Turkey felt his coat. It made him insolent. He was a man whom prosperity harmed.

Though, concerning the self-indulgent habits of Turkey, I had my own private surmises, yet, touching Nippers, I was well persuaded that, whatever might be his faults in other respects, he was, at least, a temperate young man. But indeed, nature herself seemed to have been his vintner, and, at his birth, charged him so thoroughly with an irritable, brandy-like disposition, that all subsequent potations were needless. When I consider how, amid the stillness of my chambers, Nippers would sometimes impatiently rise from his seat, and

the Tombs: A jail in New York City.

stooping over his table, spread his arms wide apart, seize the whole desk, and move it, and jerk it, with a grim, grinding motion on the floor, as if the table were a perverse voluntary agent, intent on thwarting and vexing him, I plainly perceive that, for Nippers, brandy-and-water were altogether superfluous.

It was fortunate for me that, owing to its peculiar cause—indigestion— the irritability and consequent nervousness of Nippers were mainly observable in the morning, while in the afternoon he was comparatively mild. So that, Turkey's paroxysms only coming on about twelve o'clock, I never had to do with their eccentricities at one time. Their fits relieved each other, like guards. When Nippers' was on, Turkey's was off; and *vice versa*. This was a good natural arrangement, under the circumstances.

Ginger Nut, the third on my list, was a lad, some twelve years old. His fa- ther was a carman, ambitious of seeing his son on the bench instead of a cart, before he died. So he sent him to my office, as student at law, errand-boy, cleaner, and sweeper, at the rate of one dollar a week. He had a little desk to himself, but he did not use it much. Upon inspection, the drawer exhibited a great array of the shells of various sorts of nuts. Indeed, to this quick-witted youth, the whole noble science of the law was contained in a nutshell. Not the least among the employments of Ginger Nut, as well as one which he dis- charged with the most alacrity, was his duty as cake and apple purveyor for Turkey and Nippers. Copying lawpapers being proverbially a dry, husky sort of business, my two scriveners were fain to moisten their mouths very often with Spitzenbergs, to be had at the numerous stalls nigh the Custom House and Post Office. Also, they sent Ginger Nut very frequently for that peculiar cake— small, flat, round, and very spicy—after which he had been named by them. Of a cold morning, when business was but dull, Turkey would gobble up scores of these cakes, as if they were mere wafers—indeed, they sell them at the rate of six or eight for a penny—the scrape of his pen blending with the crunching of the crisp particles in his mouth. Of all the fiery afternoon blunders and flurried rashness of Turkey, was his once moistening a ginger-cake between his lips, and clapping it on to a mortgage, for a seal. I came within an ace of dis- missing him then. But he mollified me by making an oriental bow, and saying—

"With submission, sir, it was generous of me to find you in stationery on my own account." 15

Now my original business—that of a conveyancer and title hunter, and drawer-up of recondite documents of all sorts—was considerably increased by receiving the Master's office. There was now great work for scriveners. Not only must I push the clerks already with me, but I must have additional help.

In answer to my advertisement, a motionless young man one morning stood upon my office threshold, the door being open, for it was summer. I can see that figure now—pallidly neat, pitiably respectable, incurably forlorn! It was Bartleby.

After a few words touching his qualifications, I engaged him, glad to have among my corps of copyists a man of so singularly sedate an aspect, which I thought might operate beneficially upon the flighty temper of Turkey, and the fiery one of Nippers.

I should have stated before that ground-glass folding-doors divided my premises into two parts, one of which was occupied by my scriveners, the other by myself. According to my humor, I threw open these doors, or closed them. I resolved to assign Bartleby a corner by the folding-doors, but on my side of them, so as to have this quiet man within easy call, in case any trifling thing was to be done. I placed his desk close up to a small side-window in that part of the room, a window which originally had afforded a lateral view of certain grimy brickyards and bricks, but which, owing to subsequent erections, commanded at present no view at all, though it gave some light. Within three feet of the panes was a wall, and the light came down from far above, between two lofty buildings, as from a very small opening in a dome. Still further to a satisfactory arrangement, I procured a high green folding screen, which might entirely isolate Bartleby from my sight, though not remove him from my voice. And thus, in a manner, privacy and society were conjoined.

At first, Bartleby did an extraordinary quantity of writing. As if long famishing for something to copy, he seemed to gorge himself on my documents. There was no pause for digestion. He ran a day and night line, copying by sunlight and by candle-light. I should have been quite delighted with his application, had he been cheerfully industrious. But he wrote on silently, palely, mechanically. 20

It is, of course, an indispensable part of a scrivener's business to verify the accuracy of his copy, word by word. Where there are two or more scriveners in an office, they assist each other in this examination, one reading from the copy, the other holding the original. It is a very dull, wearisome, and lethargic affair. I can readily imagine that, to some sanguine temperaments, it would be altogether intolerable. For example, I cannot credit that the mettlesome poet, Byron, would have contentedly sat down with Bartleby to examine a law document of, say five hundred pages, closely written in a crimpy hand.

Now and then, in the haste of business, it had been my habit to assist in comparing some brief document myself, calling Turkey or Nippers for this purpose. One object I had, in placing Bartleby so handy to me behind the screen, was, to avail myself of his services on such trivial occasions. It was on the third day, I think, of his being with me, and before any necessity had arisen for having his own writing examined, that, being much hurried to complete a small affair I had in hand, I abruptly called to Bartleby. In my haste and natural expectancy of instant compliance, I sat with my head bent over the original on my desk, and my right hand sideways, and somewhat nervously extended with the copy, so that, immediately upon emerging from his retreat, Bartleby might snatch it and proceed to business without the least delay.

In this very attitude did I sit when I called to him, rapidly stating what it was I wanted him to do — namely, to examine a small paper with me. Imagine my surprise, nay, my consternation, when, without moving from his privacy, Bartleby, in a singularly mild, firm voice, replied, "I would prefer not to."

I sat awhile in perfect silence, rallying my stunned faculties. Immediately it occurred to me that my ears had deceived me, or Bartleby had entirely misunderstood my meaning. I repeated my request in the clearest tone I could assume; but in quite as clear a one came the previous reply, "I would prefer not to."

"Prefer not to," echoed I, rising in high excitement, and crossing the room 25 with a stride. "What do you mean? Are you moonstruck? I want you to help me compare this sheet here — take it," and I thrust it towards him.

"I would prefer not to," said he.

I looked at him steadfastly. His face was leanly composed; his gray eye dimly calm. Not a wrinkle of agitation rippled him. Had there been the least uneasiness, anger, impatience, or impertinence in his manner; in other words, had there been anything ordinarily human about him, doubtless I should have violently dismissed him from the premises. But as it was, I should have as soon thought of turning my pale plaster-of-paris bust of Cicero out of doors. I stood gazing at him awhile, as he went on with his own writing, and then re-seated myself at my desk. This is very strange, thought I. What had one best do? But my business hurried me. I concluded to forget the matter for the present, reserving it for my future leisure. So, calling Nippers from the other room, the paper was speedily examined.

A few days after this, Bartleby concluded four lengthy documents, being quadruplicates of a week's testimony taken before me in my High Court of Chancery. It became necessary to examine them. It was an important suit, and great accuracy was imperative. Having all things arranged, I called Turkey, Nippers, and Ginger Nut, from the next room, meaning to place the four copies in the hands of my four clerks, while I should read from the original. Accordingly, Turkey, Nippers, and Ginger Nut had taken their seats in a row, each with his document in his hand, when I called to Bartleby to join this interesting group.

"Bartleby! quick, I am waiting."

I heard a slow scrape of his chair legs on the uncarpeted floor, and soon he 30
appeared standing at the entrance of his hermitage.

"What is wanted?" said he, mildly.

"The copies, the copies," said I, hurriedly. "We are going to examine them. There" — and I held towards him the fourth quadruplicate.

"I would prefer not to," he said, and gently disappeared behind the screen.

For a few moments I was turned into a pillar of salt, standing at the head of my seated column of clerks. Recovering myself, I advanced towards the screen, and demanded the reason for such extraordinary conduct.

"*Why* do you refuse?" 35

"I would prefer not to."

With any other man I should have flown outright into a dreadful passion, scorned all further words, and thrust him ignominiously from my presence. But there was something about Bartleby that not only strangely disarmed me, but, in a wonderful manner, touched and disconcerted me. I began to reason with him.

"These are your own copies we are about to examine. It is labor saving to you, because one examination will answer for your four papers. It is common usage. Every copyist is bound to help examine his copy. Is it not so? Will you not speak? Answer!"

"I prefer not to," he replied in a flute-like tone. It seemed to me that, while I had been addressing him, he carefully revolved every statement that I made; fully comprehended the meaning; could not gainsay the irresistible conclusion; but, at the same time, some paramount consideration prevailed with him to reply as he did.

"You are decided, then, not to comply with my request — a request made 40
according to common usage and common sense?"

He briefly gave me to understand, that on that point my judgment was sound. Yes: his decision was irreversible.

It is not seldom the case that, when a man is browbeaten in some unprecedented and violently unreasonable way, he begins to stagger in his own plainest faith. He begins, as it were, vaguely to surmise that, wonderful as it may be, all the justice and all the reason is on the other side. Accordingly, if any disinterested persons are present, he turns to them for some reinforcement for his own faltering mind.

"Turkey," said I, "what do you think of this? Am I not right?"

"With submission, sir," said Turkey, in his blandest tone, "I think that you are."

"Nippers," said I, "what do *you* think of it?" 45

"I think I should kick him out of the office."

(The reader of nice perceptions will have perceived that, it being morning, Turkey's answer is couched in polite and tranquil terms, but Nippers replies in ill-tempered ones. Or, to repeat a previous sentence, Nippers' ugly mood was on duty, and Turkey's off.)

"Ginger Nut," said I, willing to enlist the smallest suffrage in my behalf, "what do *you* think of it?"

"I think, sir, he's a little *luny*," replied Ginger Nut, with a grin.

"You hear what they say," said I, turning towards the screen, "come forth 50 and do your duty."

But he vouchsafed no reply. I pondered a moment in sore perplexity. But once more business hurried me. I determined again to postpone the consideration of this dilemma to my future leisure. With a little trouble we made out to examine the papers without Bartleby, though at every page or two Turkey deferentially dropped his opinion, that this proceeding was quite out of the common; while Nippers, twitching in his chair with a dyspeptic nervousness, ground out, between his set teeth, occasional hissing maledictions against the stubborn oaf behind the screen. And for his (Nippers') part, this was the first and the last time he would do another man's business without pay.

Meanwhile Bartleby sat in his hermitage, oblivious to everything but his own peculiar business there.

Some days passed, the scrivener being employed upon another lengthy work. His late remarkable conduct led me to regard his ways narrowly. I observed that he never went to dinner; indeed, that he never went anywhere. As yet I had never, of my personal knowledge, known him to be outside of my office. He was a perpetual sentry in the corner. At about eleven o'clock though, in the morning, I noticed that Ginger Nut would advance toward the opening in Bartleby's screen, as if silently beckoned thither by a gesture invisible to me where I sat. The boy would then leave the office, jingling a few pence, and reappear with a handful of ginger-nuts, which he delivered in the hermitage, receiving two of the cakes for his trouble.

He lives, then, on ginger-nuts, thought I; never eats a dinner, properly speaking; he must be a vegetarian, then, but no; he never eats even vegetables, he eats nothing but ginger-nuts. My mind then ran on in reveries concerning the probable effects upon the human constitution of living entirely on ginger-nuts. Ginger-nuts are so called, because they contain ginger as one of their peculiar constituents, and the final flavoring one. Now, what was ginger? A hot, spicy thing. Was Bartleby hot and spicy? Not at all. Ginger, then, had no effect upon Bartleby. Probably he preferred it should have none.

Nothing so aggravates an earnest person as a passive resistance. If the indi- 55 vidual so resisted be of a not inhumane temper, and the resisting one perfectly harmless in his passivity, then, in the better moods of the former, he will endeavor charitably to construe to his imagination what proves impossible to be solved by his judgment. Even so, for the most part, I regarded Bartleby and his ways. Poor fellow! thought I, he means no mischief; it is plain he intends no insolence; his aspect sufficiently evinces that his eccentricities are involuntary. He is useful to me. I can get along with him. If I turn him away, the chances are he will fall in with some less indulgent employer, and then he will be rudely treated, and perhaps driven forth miserably to starve. Yes. Here I can cheaply purchase a delicious self-approval. To befriend Bartleby; to humor him in his strange wilfulness, will cost me little or nothing, while I lay up in my soul what will eventually prove a sweet morsel for my conscience. But this mood was not invariable with me. The passiveness of Bartleby sometimes irritated me. I felt strangely goaded on to encounter him in new opposition — to elicit some angry spark from him answerable to my own. But, indeed, I might as well have essayed to strike fire with my knuckles against a bit of Windsor soap. But one afternoon the evil impulse in me mastered me, and the following little scene ensued:

"Bartleby," said I, "when those papers are all copied, I will compare them with you."

"I would prefer not to."

"How? Surely you do not mean to persist in that mulish vagary?"

No answer.

I threw open the folding-doors nearby, and turning upon Turkey and Nip- 60
pers, exclaimed:

"Bartleby a second time says, he won't examine his papers. What do you think of it, Turkey?"

It was afternoon, be it remembered. Turkey sat glowing like a brass boiler; his bald head steaming; his hands reeling among his blotted papers.

"Think of it?" roared Turkey. "I think I'll just step behind his screen, and black his eyes for him!"

So saying, Turkey rose to his feet and threw his arms into a pugilistic position. He was hurrying away to make good his promise, when I detained him, alarmed at the effect of incautiously rousing Turkey's combativeness after dinner.

"Sit down, Turkey," said I, "and hear what Nippers has to say. What do you 65
think of it, Nippers? Would I not be justified in immediately dismissing Bartleby?"

"Excuse me, that is for you to decide, sir. I think his conduct quite un-usual, and, indeed, unjust, as regards Turkey and myself. But it may only be a passing whim."

"Ah," exclaimed I, "you have strangely changed your mind, then — you speak very gently of him now."

"All beer," cried Turkey; "gentleness is effects of beer — Nippers and I dined together to-day. You see how gentle *I* am, sir. Shall I go and black his eyes?"

"You refer to Bartleby, I suppose. No, not to-day, Turkey," I replied; "pray, put up your fists."

I closed the doors, and again advanced towards Bartleby. I felt additional 70
incentives tempting me to my fate. I burned to be rebelled against again. I re-membered that Bartleby never left the office.

"Bartleby," said I, "Ginger Nut is away; just step around to the Post Office, won't you?" (it was but a three minutes' walk) "and see if there is anything for me."

"I would prefer not to."

"You *will* not?"

"I *prefer* not."

I staggered to my desk, and sat there in a deep study. My blind inveteracy 75
returned. Was there any other thing in which I could procure myself to be ignominiously repulsed by this lean, penniless wight? — my hired clerk? What
added thing is there, perfectly reasonable, that he will be sure to refuse to do?

"Bartleby!"

No answer.

"Bartleby," in a louder tone.

No answer.

"Bartleby," I roared. 80

Like a very ghost, agreeably to the laws of magical invocation, at the third
summons, he appeared at the entrance of his hermitage.

"Go to the next room, and tell Nippers to come to me."

"I prefer not to," he respectfully and slowly said, and mildly disappeared.

"Very good, Bartleby," said I, in a quiet sort of serenely-severe self-
possessed tone, intimating the unalterable purpose of some terrible retribution very close at hand. At the moment I half intended something of the kind.
But upon the whole, as it was drawing towards my dinner-hour, I thought it
best to put on my hat and walk home for the day, suffering much from perplexity and distress of mind.

Shall I acknowledge it? The conclusion of this whole business was, that it 85
soon became a fixed fact of my chambers, that a pale young scrivener, by the
name of Bartleby, had a desk there; that he copied for me at the usual rate of
four cents a folio (one hundred words); but he was permanently exempt from
examining the work done by him, that duty being transferred to Turkey and
Nippers, out of compliment, doubtless, to their superior acuteness; moreover,
said Bartleby was never, on any account, to be dispatched on the most trivial
errand of any sort; and that even if entreated to take upon him such a matter,
it was generally understood that he would "prefer not to" — in other words,
that he would refuse point-blank.

As days passed on, I became considerably reconciled to Bartleby. His
steadiness, his freedom from all dissipation, his incessant industry (except
when he chose to throw himself into a standing revery behind his screen), his
great stillness, his unalterableness of demeanor under all circumstances, made
him a valuable acquisition. One prime thing was this — *he was always there* —
first in the morning, continually through the day, and the last at night. I had a
singular confidence in his honesty. I felt my most precious papers perfectly safe
in his hands. Sometimes, to be sure, I could not, for the very soul of me, avoid
falling into sudden spasmodic passions with him. For it was exceeding difficult
to bear in mind all the time those strange peculiarities, privileges, and unheard-
of exemptions, forming the tacit stipulations on Bartleby's part under which
he remained in my office. Now and then, in the eagerness of dispatching pressing business, I would inadvertently summon Bartleby, in a short, rapid tone, to
put his finger, say, on the incipient tie of a bit of red tape with which I was
about compressing some papers. Of course, from behind the screen the usual
answer, "I prefer not to," was sure to come; and then, how could a human creature, with the common infirmities of our nature, refrain from bitterly exclaiming upon such perverseness — such unreasonableness? However, every added

repulse of this sort which I received only tended to lessen the probability of my repeating the inadvertence.

Here it must be said, that, according to the custom of most legal gentlemen occupying chambers in densely populated law buildings, there were several keys to my door. One was kept by a woman residing in the attic, which person weekly scrubbed and daily swept and dusted my apartments. Another was kept by Turkey for convenience sake. The third I sometimes carried in my own pocket. The fourth I knew not who had.

Now, one Sunday morning I happened to go to Trinity Church, to hear a celebrated preacher, and finding myself rather early on the ground I thought I would walk round to my chambers for a while. Luckily I had my key with me; but upon applying it to the lock, I found it resisted by something inserted from the inside. Quite surprised, I called out; when to my consternation a key was turned from within; and thrusting his lean visage at me, and holding the door ajar, the apparition of Bartleby appeared, in his shirt-sleeves, and otherwise in a strangely tattered *deshabille*, saying quietly that he was sorry, but he was deeply engaged just then, and — preferred not admitting me at present. In a brief word or two, he moreover added, that perhaps I had better walk round the block two or three times, and by that time he would probably have concluded his affairs.

Now, the utterly unsurmised appearance of Bartleby, tenanting my law-chambers of a Sunday morning, with his cadaverously gentlemanly *nonchalance*, yet withal firm and self-possessed, had such a strange effect upon me, that incontinently I slunk away from my own door, and did as desired. But not without sundry twinges of impotent rebellion against the mild effrontery of this unaccountable scrivener. Indeed, it was his wonderful mildness chiefly, which not only disarmed me, but unmanned me, as it were. For I consider that one, for the time, is sort of unmanned when he tranquilly permits his hired clerk to dictate to him, and order him away from his own premises. Furthermore, I was full of uneasiness as to what Bartleby could possibly be doing in my office in his shirt-sleeves, and in an otherwise dismantled condition of a Sunday morning. Was anything amiss going on? Nay, that was out of the question. It was not to be thought of for a moment that Bartleby was an immoral person. But what could he be doing there? — copying? Nay again, whatever might be his eccentricities, Bartleby was an eminently decorous person. He would be the last man to sit down to his desk in any state approaching to nudity. Besides, it was Sunday; and there was something about Bartleby that forbade the supposition that he would by any secular occupation violate the proprieties of the day.

Nevertheless, my mind was not pacified; and full of a restless curiosity, at last I returned to the door. Without hindrance I inserted my key, opened it, and entered. Bartleby was not to be seen. I looked round anxiously, peeped behind his screen; but it was very plain that he was gone. Upon more closely examining the place, I surmised that for an indefinite period Bartleby must have ate, dressed, and slept in my office, and that too without plate, mirror, or bed. The cushioned seat of a rickety old sofa in one corner bore the faint impress of a lean, reclining form. Rolled away under his desk, I found a blanket; under the empty grate, a blacking box and brush; on a chair, a tin basin, with soap and a ragged towel; in a newspaper a few crumbs of ginger-nuts and a morsel of cheese. Yes, thought I, it is evident enough that Bartleby has been making his home here, keeping bachelor's hall all by himself. Immediately then the thought came sweeping across me, what miserable friendlessness and loneliness are here revealed! His poverty is great; but his solitude, how horrible! Think of it. Of a Sunday, Wall Street is deserted as Petra;° and every night of every day it is an emptiness. This building, too, which of week-days hums with industry and life, at nightfall echoes with sheer vacancy, and all through Sunday is forlorn. And here Bartleby makes his home; sole spectator of a solitude which he has seen all populous—a sort of innocent and transformed Marius brooding among the ruins of Carthage?°

For the first time in my life a feeling of overpowering stinging melancholy seized me. Before, I had never experienced aught but a not unpleasing sadness. The bond of a common humanity now drew me irresistibly to gloom. A fraternal melancholy! For both I and Bartleby were sons of Adam. I remembered the bright silks and sparkling faces I had seen that day, in gala trim, swan-like sailing down the Mississippi of Broadway; and I contrasted them with the pallid copyist, and thought to myself, Ah, happiness courts the light, so we deem the world is gay; but misery hides aloof, so we deem that misery there is none. These sad fancyings—chimeras, doubtless, of a sick and silly brain—led on to other and more special thoughts, concerning the eccentricities of Bartleby. Presentiments of strange discoveries hovered round me. The scrivener's pale form appeared to me laid out, among uncaring strangers, in its shivering winding-sheet.

Suddenly I was attracted by Bartleby's closed desk, the key in open sight left in the lock.

I mean no mischief, seek the gratification of no heartless curiosity, thought I; besides, the desk is mine, and its contents, too, so I will make bold to look within. Everything was methodically arranged, the papers smoothly placed. The pigeon-holes were deep, and removing the files of documents, I groped into their recesses. Presently I felt something there, and dragged it out. It was an old bandanna handkerchief, heavy and knotted. I opened it, and saw it was a saving's bank.

I now recalled all the quiet mysteries which I had noted in the man. I remembered that he never spoke but to answer; that, though at intervals he had considerable time to himself, yet I had never seen him reading—no, not even a newspaper; that for long periods he would stand looking out, at his pale window behind the screen, upon the dead brick wall; I was quite sure he never visited any refectory or eating-house; while his pale face clearly indicated that he never drank beer like Turkey; or tea and coffee even, like other men; that he never went anywhere in particular that I could learn; never went out for a walk, unless, indeed, that was the case at present; that he had declined telling who he was, or whence he came, or whether he had any relatives in the world; that though so thin and pale, he never complained of ill-health. And more than all, I remembered a certain unconscious air of pallid—how shall I call it?—of pallid haughtiness, say, or rather an austere reserve about him, which had positively awed me into my tame compliance with his eccentricities, when I had feared to ask him to do the slightest incidental thing for me, even though

Petra: An ancient Arabian city whose ruins were discovered in 1812.
Marius . . . of Carthage: Gaius Marius (157–86 B.C.), an exiled Roman general, sought refuge in the African city-state of Carthage, which was destroyed by the Romans in the Third Punic War.

I might know, from his long-continued motionlessness, that behind his screen he must be standing in one of those dead-wall reveries of his.

Revolving all these things, and coupling them with the recently discovered 95 fact, that he made my office his constant abiding place and home, and not forgetful of his morbid moodiness; revolving all these things, a prudential feeling began to steal over me. My first emotions had been those of pure melancholy and sincerest pity; but just in proportion as the forlornness of Bartleby grew and grew to my imagination, did that same melancholy merge into fear, that pity into repulsion. So true it is, and so terrible, too, that up to a certain point the thought or sight of misery enlists our best affections; but, in certain special cases, beyond that point it does not. They err who would assert that invariably this is owing to the inherent selfishness of the human heart. It rather proceeds from a certain hopelessness of remedying excessive and organic ill. To a sensitive being, pity is not seldom pain. And when at last it is perceived that such pity cannot lead to effectual succor, common sense bids the soul be rid of it. What I saw that morning persuaded me that the scrivener was the victim of innate and incurable disorder. I might give alms to his body; but his body did not pain him; it was his soul that suffered, and his soul I could not reach.

I did not accomplish the purpose of going to Trinity Church that morning. Somehow, the things I had seen disqualified me for the time from churchgoing. I walked homeward, thinking what I would do with Bartleby. Finally, I resolved upon this — I would put certain calm questions to him the next morning, touching his history, etc., and if he declined to answer them openly and unreservedly (and I supposed he would prefer not), then to give him a twenty dollar bill over and above whatever I might owe him, and tell him his services were no longer required; but that if in any other way I could assist him, I would be happy to do so, especially if he desired to return to his native place, wherever that might be, I would willingly help to defray the expenses. Moreover, if, after reaching home, he found himself at any time in want of aid, a letter from him would be sure of a reply.

The next morning came.

"Bartleby," said I, gently calling to him behind his screen.

No reply.

"Bartleby," said I, in a still gentler tone, "come here; I am not going to ask 100 you to do anything you would prefer not to do — I simply wish to speak to you."

Upon this he noiselessly slid into view.

"Will you tell me, Bartleby, where you were born?"

"I would prefer not to."

"Will you tell me *anything* about yourself?"

"I would prefer not to." 105

"But what reasonable objection can you have to speak to me? I feel friendly towards you."

He did not look at me while I spoke, but kept his glance fixed upon my bust of Cicero, which, as I then sat, was directly behind me, some six inches above my head.

"What is your answer, Bartleby?" said I, after waiting a considerable time for a reply, during which his countenance remained immovable, only there was the faintest conceivable tremor of the white attenuated mouth.

"At present I prefer to give no answer," he said, and retired into his hermitage.

It was rather weak in me I confess, but his manner, on this occasion, nettled 110
me. Not only did there seem to lurk in it a certain calm disdain, but his perverseness seemed ungrateful, considering the undeniable good usage and indulgence
he had received from me.

Again I sat ruminating what I should do. Mortified as I was at his behavior,
and resolved as I had been to dismiss him when I entered my office, nevertheless
I strangely felt something superstitious knocking at my heart, and forbidding
me to carry out my purpose, and denouncing me for a villain if I dared to
breathe one bitter word against this forlornest of mankind. At last, familiarly
drawing my chair behind his screen, I sat down and said: "Bartleby, never
mind, then, about revealing your history; but let me entreat you, as a friend, to
comply as far as may be with the usages of this office. Say now, you will help to
examine papers tomorrow or next day: in short, say now, that in a day or two
you will begin to be a little reasonable: — say so, Bartleby."

"At present I would prefer not to be a little reasonable," was his mildly cadaverous reply.

Just then the folding-doors opened, and Nippers approached. He seemed
suffering from an unusually bad night's rest, induced by severer indigestion
than common. He overheard those final words of Bartleby.

"*Prefer not*, eh?" gritted Nippers — "I'd *prefer* him, if I were you, sir," addressing me — "I'd *prefer* him; I'd give him preferences, the stubborn mule!
What is it, sir, pray, that he *prefers* not to do now?"

Bartleby moved not a limb.   115

"Mr. Nippers," said I, "I'd prefer that you would withdraw for the present."

Somehow, of late, I had got into the way of involuntarily using this word
"prefer" upon all sorts of not exactly suitable occasions. And I trembled to
think that my contact with the scrivener had already and seriously affected me
in a mental way. And what further and deeper aberration might it not yet produce? This apprehension had not been without efficacy in determining me to
summary measures.

As Nippers, looking very sour and sulky, was departing, Turkey blandly
and deferentially approached.

"With submission, sir," said he, "yesterday I was thinking about Bartleby
here, and I think that if he would but prefer to take a quart of good ale every
day, it would do much towards mending him, and enabling him to assist in examining his papers."

"So you have got the word, too," said I, slightly excited.   120

"With submission, what word, sir?" asked Turkey, respectfully crowding
himself into the contracted space behind the screen, and by so doing, making
me jostle the scrivener. "What word, sir?"

"I would prefer to be left alone here," said Bartleby, as if offended at being
mobbed in his privacy.

"*That's* the word, Turkey," said I — "*that's* it."

"Oh, *prefer*? oh yes — queer word. I never use it myself. But, sir, as I was saying, if he would but prefer — "

"Turkey," interrupted I, "you will please withdraw."   125

"Oh certainly, sir, if you prefer that I should."

As he opened the folding-door to retire, Nippers at his desk caught a
glimpse of me, and asked whether I would prefer to have a certain paper
copied on blue paper or white. He did not in the least roguishly accent the

word "prefer." It was plain that it involuntarily rolled from his tongue. I thought to myself, surely I must get rid of a demented man, who already has in some degree turned the tongues, if not the heads of myself and clerks. But I thought it prudent not to break the dismission at once.

The next day I noticed that Bartleby did nothing but stand at his window in his dead-wall revery. Upon asking him why he did not write, he said that he had decided upon doing no more writing.

"Why, how now? what next?" exclaimed I, "do no more writing?"

"No more."

"And what is the reason?"

"Do you not see the reason for yourself?" he indifferently replied.

I looked steadfastly at him, and perceived that his eyes looked dull and glazed. Instantly it occurred to me, that his unexampled diligence in copying by his dim window for the first few weeks of his stay with me might have temporarily impaired his vision.

I was touched. I said something in condolence with him. I hinted that of course he did wisely in abstaining from writing for a while; and urged him to embrace that opportunity of taking wholesome exercise in the open air. This, however, he did not do. A few days after this, my other clerks being absent, and being in a great hurry to dispatch certain letters by the mail, I thought that, having nothing else earthly to do, Bartleby would surely be less inflexible than usual, and carry these letters to the Post Office. But he blankly declined. So, much to my inconvenience, I went myself.

Still added days went by. Whether Bartleby's eyes improved or not, I could not say. To all appearance, I thought they did. But when I asked him if they did, he vouchsafed no answer. At all events, he would do no copying. At last, in replying to my urgings, he informed me that he had permanently given up copying.

"What!" exclaimed I; "suppose your eyes should get entirely well—better than ever before—would you not copy then?"

"I have given up copying," he answered, and slid aside.

He remained as ever, a fixture in my chamber. Nay—if that were possible—he became still more of a fixture than before. What was to be done? He would do nothing in the office; why should he stay there? In plain fact, he had now become a millstone to me, not only useless as a necklace, but afflictive to bear. Yet I was sorry for him. I speak less than truth when I say that, on his own account, he occasioned me uneasiness. If he would but have named a single relative or friend, I would instantly have written, and urged their taking the poor fellow away to some convenient retreat. But he seemed alone, absolutely alone in the universe. A bit of wreck in the mid-Atlantic. At length, necessities connected with my business tyrannized over all other considerations. Decently as I could, I told Bartleby that in six days' time he must unconditionally leave the office. I warned him to take measures, in the interval, for procuring some other abode. I offered to assist him in this endeavor, if he himself would but take the first step towards a removal. "And when you finally quit me, Bartleby," added I, "I shall see that you go not away entirely unprovided. Six days from this hour, remember."

At the expiration of that period, I peeped behind the screen, and lo! Bartleby was there.

I buttoned up my coat, balanced myself; advanced slowly towards him, touched his shoulder, and said, "The time has come; you must quit this place; I am sorry for you; here is money; but you must go."

"I would prefer not," he replied, with his back still towards me.

"You *must.*"

He remained silent.

Now I had an unbounded confidence in this man's common honesty. He had frequently restored to me sixpences and shillings carelessly dropped upon the floor, for I am apt to be very reckless in such shirt-button affairs. The proceeding, then, which followed will not be deemed extraordinary.

"Bartleby," said I, "I owe you twelve dollars on account; here are thirty-two, the odd twenty are yours — Will you take it?" and I handed the bills towards him.   145

But he made no motion.

"I will leave them here, then," putting them under a weight on the table. Then taking my hat and cane and going to the door, I tranquilly turned and added — "After you have removed your things from these offices, Bartleby, you will of course lock the door — since every one is now gone for the day but you — and if you please, slip your key underneath the mat, so that I may have it in the morning. I shall not see you again; so good-bye to you. If, hereafter, in your new place of abode, I can be of any service to you, do not fail to advise me by letter. Good-bye, Bartleby, and fare you well."

But he answered not a word; like the last column of some ruined temple, he remained standing mute and solitary in the middle of the otherwise deserted room.

As I walked home in a pensive mood, my vanity got the better of my pity. I could not but highly plume myself on my masterly management in getting rid of Bartleby. Masterly I call it, and such it must appear to any dispassionate thinker. The beauty of my procedure seemed to consist in its perfect quietness. There was no vulgar bullying, no bravado of any sort, no choleric hectoring, and striding to and fro across the apartment, jerking out vehement commands for Bartleby to bundle himself off with his beggarly traps. Nothing of the kind. Without loudly bidding Bartleby depart — as an inferior genius might have done — I *assumed* the ground that depart he must; and upon that assumption built all I had to say. The more I thought over my procedure, the more I was charmed with it. Nevertheless, next morning, upon awakening, I had my doubts — I had somehow slept off the fumes of vanity. One of the coolest and wisest hours a man has, is just after he awakes in the morning. My procedure seemed as sagacious as ever — but only in theory. How it would prove in practice — there was the rub. It was truly a beautiful thought to have assumed Bartleby's departure; but, after all, that assumption was simply my own, and none of Bartleby's. The great point was, not whether I had assumed that he would quit me, but whether he would prefer to do so. He was more a man of preferences than assumptions.

After breakfast, I walked down town, arguing the probabilities *pro* and *con.*   150 One moment I thought it would prove a miserable failure, and Bartleby would be found all alive at my office as usual; the next moment it seemed certain that I should find his chair empty. And so I kept veering about. At the corner of Broadway and Canal Street, I saw quite an excited group of people standing in earnest conversation.

"I'll take odds he doesn't," said a voice as I passed.

"Doesn't go? — done!" said I, "put up your money."

I was instinctively putting my hand in my pocket to produce my own, when I remembered that this was an election day. The words I had overheard

bore no reference to Bartleby, but to the success or non-success of some candidate for the mayoralty. In my intent frame of mind, I had, as it were, imagined
that all Broadway shared in my excitement, and were debating the same question with me. I passed on, very thankful that the uproar of the street screened
my momentary absent-mindedness.

As I had intended, I was earlier than usual at my office door. I stood listening for a moment. All was still. He must be gone. I tried the knob. The door
was locked. Yes, my procedure had worked to a charm; he indeed must be vanished. Yet a certain melancholy mixed with this: I was almost sorry for my brilliant success. I was fumbling under the door mat for the key, which Bartleby
was to have left there for me, when accidentally my knee knocked against a
panel, producing a summoning sound, and in response a voice came to me
from within — "Not yet; I am occupied."

It was Bartleby.   155

I was thunderstruck. For an instant I stood like the man who, pipe in
mouth, was killed one cloudless afternoon long ago in Virginia, by summer
lightning; at his own warm open window he was killed, and remained leaning
out there upon the dreamy afternoon, till some one touched him, when he fell.

"Not gone!" I murmured at last. But again obeying that wondrous ascendancy which the inscrutable scrivener had over me, and from which ascendancy,
for all my chafing, I could not completely escape, I slowly went down stairs and
out into the street, and while walking round the block, considered what I should
next do in this unheard-of perplexity. Turn the man out by an actual thrusting I
could not; to drive him away by calling him hard names would not do; calling in
the police was an unpleasant idea; and yet, permit him to enjoy his cadaverous
triumph over me — this, too, I could not think of. What was to be done? or, if
nothing could be done, was there anything further that I could *assume* in the
matter? Yes, as before I had prospectively assumed that Bartleby would depart, so
now I might retrospectively assume that departed he was. In the legitimate carrying out of this assumption, I might enter my office in a great hurry, and pretending not to see Bartleby at all, walk straight against him as if he were air. Such a
proceeding would in a singular degree have the appearance of a home-thrust. It
was hardly possible that Bartleby could withstand such an application of the
doctrine of assumption. But upon second thoughts the success of the plan
seemed rather dubious. I resolved to argue the matter over with him again.

"Bartleby," said I, entering the office, with a quietly severe expression, "I
am seriously displeased. I am pained, Bartleby. I had thought better of you. I
had imagined you of such a gentlemanly organization, that in any delicate
dilemma a slight hint would suffice — in short, an assumption. But it appears I
am deceived. Why," I added, unaffectedly starting, "you have not even touched
that money yet," pointing to it, just where I had left it the evening previous.

He answered nothing.

"Will you, or will you not, quit me?" I now demanded in a sudden passion,   160
advancing close to him.

"I would prefer *not* to quit you," he replied, gently emphasizing the *not*.

"What earthly right have you to stay here? Do you pay any rent? Do you
pay my taxes? Or is this property yours?"

He answered nothing.

"Are you ready to go on and write now? Are your eyes recovered? Could
you copy a small paper for me this morning? or help examine a few lines? or

step round to the Post Office? In a word, will you do anything at all, to give a coloring to your refusal to depart the premises?"

He silently retired into his hermitage.   165

I was now in such a state of nervous resentment that I thought it but prudent to check myself at present from further demonstrations. Bartleby and I were alone. I remembered the tragedy of the unfortunate Adams and the still more unfortunate Colt° in the solitary office of the latter; and how poor Colt, being dreadfully incensed by Adams, and imprudently permitting himself to get wildly excited, was at unawares hurried into his fatal act—an act which certainly no man could possibly deplore more than the actor himself. Often it had occurred to me in my ponderings upon the subject that had that altercation taken place in the public street, or at a private residence, it would not have terminated as it did. It was the circumstance of being alone in a solitary office, up stairs, of a building entirely unhallowed by humanizing domestic associations—an uncarpeted office, doubtless, of a dusty, haggard sort of appearance—this it must have been, which greatly helped to enhance the irritable desperation of the hapless Colt.

But when this old Adam of resentment rose in me and tempted me concerning Bartleby, I grappled him and threw him. How? Why, simply by recalling the divine injunction: "A new commandment give I unto you, that ye love one another." Yes, this it was that saved me. Aside from higher considerations, charity often operates as a vastly wise and prudent principle—a great safeguard to its possessor. Men have committed murder for jealousy's sake, and anger's sake, and hatred's sake, and selfishness' sake, and spiritual pride's sake; but no man, that ever I heard of, ever committed a diabolical murder for sweet charity's sake. Mere self-interest, then, if no better motive can be enlisted, should, especially with high-tempered men, prompt all beings to charity and philanthropy. At any rate, upon the occasion in question, I strove to drown my exasperated feelings towards the scrivener by benevolently construing his conduct. Poor fellow, poor fellow! thought I, he don't mean anything; and besides, he has seen hard times, and ought to be indulged.

I endeavored, also, immediately to occupy myself, and at the same time to comfort my despondency. I tried to fancy, that in the course of the morning, at such time as might prove agreeable to him, Bartleby, of his own free accord, would emerge from his hermitage and take up some decided line of march in the direction of the door. But no. Half-past twelve o'clock came; Turkey began to glow in the face, overturn his inkstand, and become generally obstreperous; Nippers abated down into quietude and courtesy; Ginger Nut munched his noon apple; and Bartleby remained standing at his window in one of his profoundest dead-wall reveries. Will it be credited? Ought I to acknowledge it? That afternoon I left the office without saying one further word to him.

Some days now passed, during which, at leisure intervals I looked a little into "Edwards on the Will," and "Priestley on Necessity."° Under the circumstances, those books induced a salutary feeling. Gradually I slid into the persuasion that these troubles of mine, touching the scrivener, had been all predestined from

---

Adams . . . Colt: Samuel Adams was killed by John C. Colt, brother of the gun maker, during a quarrel in 1842. After a sensational court case, Colt committed suicide just before he was to be hanged.

"Edwards . . . Necessity": Jonathan Edwards, in *Freedom of the Will* (1754), and Joseph Priestley, in *Doctrine of Philosophical Necessity* (1777), both argued that human beings do not have free will.

eternity, and Bartleby was billeted upon me for some mysterious purpose of an all-wise Providence, which it was not for a mere mortal like me to fathom. Yes, Bartleby, stay there behind your screen, thought I; I shall persecute you no more; you are harmless and noiseless as any of these old chairs; in short, I never feel so private as when I know you are here. At last I see it, I feel it; I penetrate to the predestined purpose of my life. I am content. Others may have loftier parts to enact; but my mission in this world, Bartleby, is to furnish you with office-room for such period as you may see fit to remain.

I believe that this wise and blessed frame of mind would have continued 170 with me, had it not been for the unsolicited and uncharitable remarks obtruded upon me by my professional friends who visited the rooms. But thus it often is, that the constant friction of illiberal minds wears out at last the best resolves of the more generous. Though to be sure, when I reflected upon it, it was not strange that people entering my office should be struck by the peculiar aspect of the unaccountable Bartleby, and so be tempted to throw out some sinister observations concerning him. Sometimes an attorney, having business with me, and calling at my office, and finding no one but the scrivener there, would undertake to obtain some sort of precise information from him touching my whereabouts; but without heeding his idle talk, Bartleby would remain standing immovable in the middle of the room. So after contemplating him in that position for a time, the attorney would depart, no wiser than he came.

Also, when a reference was going on, and the room full of lawyers and witnesses, and business driving fast, some deeply-occupied legal gentleman present, seeing Bartleby wholly unemployed, would request him to run round to his (the legal gentleman's) office and fetch some papers for him. Thereupon, Bartleby would tranquilly decline, and yet remain idle as before. Then the lawyer would give a great stare, and turn to me. And what could I say? At last I was made aware that all through the circle of my professional acquaintance, a whisper of wonder was running round, having reference to the strange creature I kept at my office. This worried me very much. And as the idea came upon me of his possibly turning out a long-lived man, and keeping occupying my chambers, and denying my authority; and perplexing my visitors; and scandalizing my professional reputation; and casting a general gloom over the premises; keeping soul and body together to the last upon his savings (for doubtless he spent but half a dime a day), and in the end perhaps outlive me, and claim possession of my office by right of his perpetual occupancy: as all these dark anticipations crowded upon me more and more, and my friends continually intruded their relentless remarks upon the apparition in my room; a great change was wrought in me. I resolved to gather all my faculties together, and forever rid me of this intolerable incubus.

Ere revolving any complicated project, however, adapted to this end, I first simply suggested to Bartleby the propriety of his permanent departure. In a calm and serious tone, I commended the idea to his careful and mature consideration. But, having taken three days to meditate upon it, he apprised me, that his original determination remained the same; in short, that he still preferred to abide with me.

What shall I do? I now said to myself, buttoning up my coat to the last button. What shall I do? what ought I to do? what does conscience say I *should* do with this man, or, rather, ghost. Rid myself of him, I must; go, he shall. But how? You will not thrust him, the poor, pale, passive mortal—you will not thrust such a helpless creature out of your door? you will not dishonor yourself by such cruelty? No, I will not, I cannot do that. Rather would I let him live and die here, and then mason up his remains in the wall. What, then, will you do? For all your coaxing, he will not budge. Bribes he leaves under your own paperweight on your table; in short, it is quite plain that he prefers to cling to you.

Then something severe, something unusual must be done. What! surely you will not have him collared by a constable, and commit his innocent pallor to the common jail? And upon what ground could you procure such a thing to be done? — a vagrant, is he? What! he a vagrant, a wanderer, who refuses to budge? It is because he will *not* be a vagrant, then, that you seek to count him *as* a vagrant. That is too absurd. No visible means of support: there I have him. Wrong again: for indubitably he *does* support himself, and that is the only unanswerable proof that any man can show of his possessing the means so to do. No more, then. Since he will not quit me, I must quit him. I will change my offices; I will move elsewhere, and give him fair notice, that if I find him on my new premises I will then proceed against him as a common trespasser.

Acting accordingly, next day I thus addressed him: "I find these chambers 175 too far from the City Hall; the air is unwholesome. In a word, I propose to remove my offices next week, and shall no longer require your services. I tell you this now, in order that you may seek another place."

He made no reply, and nothing more was said.

On the appointed day I engaged carts and men, proceeded to my chambers, and having but little furniture, everything was removed in a few hours. Throughout, the scrivener remained standing behind the screen, which I directed to be removed the last thing. It was withdrawn; and, being folded up like a huge folio, left him the motionless occupant of a naked room. I stood in the entry watching him a moment, while something from within me upbraided me.

I re-entered, with my hand in my pocket — and — and my heart in my mouth.

"Good-bye, Bartleby; I am going — good-bye, and God some way bless you; and take that," slipping something in his hand. But it dropped upon the floor, and then — strange to say — I tore myself from him whom I had so longed to be rid of.

Established in my new quarters, for a day or two I kept the door locked, 180 and started at every footfall in the passages. When I returned to my rooms, after any little absence, I would pause at the threshold for an instant, and attentively listen, ere applying my key. But these fears were needless. Bartleby never came nigh me.

I thought all was going well, when a perturbed-looking stranger visited me, inquiring whether I was the person who had recently occupied rooms at No. — Wall Street.

Full of forebodings, I replied that I was.

"Then, sir," said the stranger, who proved a lawyer, "you are responsible for the man you left there. He refuses to do any copying; he refuses to do anything; he says he prefers not to; and he refuses to quit the premises."

"I am very sorry, sir," said I, with assumed tranquillity, but an inward tremor, "but, really, the man you allude to is nothing to me — he is no relation or apprentice of mine, that you should hold me responsible for him."

"In mercy's name, who is he?"   185

"I certainly cannot inform you. I know nothing about him. Formerly I employed him as a copyist; but he has done nothing for me now for some time past."

"I shall settle him, then — good morning, sir."

Several days passed, and I heard nothing more; and, though I often felt a charitable prompting to call at the place and see poor Bartleby, yet a certain squeamishness, of I know not what, withheld me.

All is over with him, by this time, thought I, at last, when, through another week, no further intelligence reached me. But, coming to my room the day after, I found several persons waiting at my door in a high state of nervous excitement.

"That's the man — here he comes," cried the foremost one, whom I recognized as the lawyer who had previously called upon me alone.   190

"You must take him away, sir, at once," cried a portly person among them, advancing upon me, and whom I knew to be the landlord of No. — Wall Street. "These gentlemen, my tenants, cannot stand it any longer; Mr. B——," pointing to the lawyer, "has turned him out of his room, and he now persists in haunting the building generally, sitting upon the banisters of the stairs by day, and sleeping in the entry by night. Everybody is concerned; clients are leaving the offices; some fears are entertained of a mob; something you must do, and that without delay."

Aghast at this torrent, I fell back before it, and would fain have locked myself in my new quarters. In vain I persisted that Bartleby was nothing to me — no more than to any one else. In vain — I was the last person known to have anything to do with him, and they held me to the terrible account. Fearful, then, of being exposed in the papers (as one person present obscurely threatened), I considered the matter, and, at length, said, that if the lawyer would give me a confidential interview with the scrivener, in his (the lawyer's) own room, I would, that afternoon, strive my best to rid them of the nuisance they complained of.

Going up stairs to my old haunt, there was Bartleby silently sitting upon the banister at the landing.

"What are you doing here, Bartleby?" said I.

"Sitting upon the banister," he mildly replied.   195

I motioned him into the lawyer's room, who then left us.

"Bartleby," said I, "are you aware that you are the cause of great tribulation to me, by persisting in occupying the entry after being dismissed from the office?"

No answer.

"Now one of two things must take place. Either you must do something, or something must be done to you. Now what sort of business would you like to engage in? Would you like to re-engage in copying for some one?"

"No; I would prefer not to make any change."   200

"Would you like a clerkship in a dry-goods store?"

"There is too much confinement about that. No, I would not like a clerkship; but I am not particular."

"Too much confinement," I cried, "why, you keep yourself confined all the time!"

"I would prefer not to take a clerkship," he rejoined, as if to settle that little item at once.

"How would a bar-tender's business suit you? There is no trying of the 205
eye-sight in that."

"I would not like it at all; though, as I said before, I am not particular."

His unwonted wordiness inspirited me. I returned to the charge.

"Well, then, would you like to travel through the country collecting bills
for the merchants? That would improve your health."

"No, I would prefer to be doing something else."

"How, then, would going as a companion to Europe, to entertain some 210
young gentleman with your conversation — how would that suit you?"

"Not at all. It does not strike me that there is anything definite about that.
I like to be stationary. But I am not particular."

"Stationary you shall be, then," I cried, now losing all patience, and, for
the first time in all my exasperating connection with him, fairly flying into a
passion. "If you do not go away from these premises before night, I shall feel
bound — indeed, I *am* bound — to — to quit the premises myself!" I rather absurdly concluded, knowing not with what possible threat to try to frighten his
immobility into compliance. Despairing of all further efforts, I was precipi-
tately leaving him, when a final thought occurred to me — one which had not
been wholly unindulged before.

"Bartleby," said I, in the kindest tone I could assume under such exciting
circumstances, "will you go home with me now — not to my office, but my
dwelling — and remain there till we can conclude upon some convenient
arrangement for you at our leisure? Come, let us start now, right away."

"No: at present I would prefer not to make any change at all."

I answered nothing; but, effectually dodging every one by the suddenness 215
and rapidity of my flight, rushed from the building, ran up Wall Street towards
Broadway, and, jumping into the first omnibus, was soon removed from pursuit.
As soon as tranquillity returned, I distinctly perceived that I had now done all
that I possibly could, both in respect to the demands of the landlord and his tenants, and with regard to my own desire and sense of duty, to benefit Bartleby, and
shield him from rude persecution. I now strove to be entirely care-free and quies-
cent; and my conscience justified me in the attempt; though, indeed, it was not
so successful as I could have wished. So fearful was I of being again hunted out
by the incensed landlord and his exasperated tenants, that, surrendering my
business to Nippers, for a few days, I drove about the upper part of the town and
through the suburbs, in my rockaway; crossed over to Jersey City and Hoboken,
and paid fugitive visits to Manhattanville and Astoria. In fact, I almost lived in
my rockaway for the time.

When again I entered my office, lo, a note from the landlord lay upon the
desk. I opened it with trembling hands. It informed me that the writer had sent
to the police, and had Bartleby removed to the Tombs as a vagrant. Moreover,
since I knew more about him than any one else, he wished me to appear at that
place, and make a suitable statement of the facts. These tidings had a conflicting
effect upon me. At first I was indignant; but, at last, almost approved. The landlord's energetic, summary disposition, had led him to adopt a procedure which I
do not think I would have decided upon myself; and yet, as a last resort, under
such peculiar circumstances, it seemed the only plan.

As I afterwards learned, the poor scrivener, when told that he must be conducted to the Tombs, offered not the slightest obstacle, but, in his pale, unmoving way, silently acquiesced.

Some of the compassionate and curious by-standers joined the party; and headed by one of the constables arm-in-arm with Bartleby, the silent procession filed its way through all the noise, and heat, and joy of the roaring thoroughfares at noon.

The same day I received the note, I went to the Tombs, or, to speak more properly, the Halls of Justice. Seeking the right officer, I stated the purpose of my call, and was informed that the individual I described was, indeed, within. I then assured the functionary that Bartleby was a perfectly honest man, and greatly to be compassionated, however unaccountably eccentric. I narrated all I knew, and closed by suggesting the idea of letting him remain in as indulgent confinement as possible, till something less harsh might be done — though, indeed, I hardly knew what. At all events, if nothing else could be decided upon, the almshouse must receive him. I then begged to have an interview.

Being under no disgraceful charge, and quite serene and harmless in all   220
his ways, they had permitted him freely to wander about the prison, and, especially, in the inclosed grass-platted yards thereof. And so I found him there, standing all alone in the quietest of the yards, his face towards a high wall, while all around, from the narrow slits of the jail windows, I thought I saw peering out upon him the eyes of murderers and thieves.

"Bartleby!"

"I know you," he said, without looking round — "and I want nothing to say to you."

"It was not I that brought you here, Bartleby," said I, keenly pained at his implied suspicion. "And to you, this should not be so vile a place. Nothing reproachful attaches to you by being here. And see, it is not so sad a place as one might think. Look, there is the sky, and here is the grass."

"I know where I am," he replied, but would say nothing more, and so I left him.

As I entered the corridor again, a broad meat-like man, in an apron, accosted   225
me, and, jerking his thumb over his shoulder, said — "Is that your friend?"

"Yes."

"Does he want to starve? If he does, let him live on the prison fare, that's all."

"Who are you?" asked I, not knowing what to make of such an unofficially speaking person in such a place.

"I am the grub-man. Such gentlemen as have friends here, hire me to provide them with something good to eat."

"Is this so?" said I, turning the turnkey.   230

He said it was.

"Well, then," said I, slipping some silver into the grub-man's hands (for so they called him), "I want you to give particular attention to my friend there; let him have the best dinner you can get. And you must be as polite to him as possible."

"Introduce me, will you?" said the grub-man, looking at me with an expression which seemed to say he was all impatience for an opportunity to give a specimen of his breeding.

Thinking it would prove of benefit to the scrivener, I acquiesced; and, asking the grub-man his name, went up with him to Bartleby.

"Bartleby, this is a friend; you will find him very useful to you."   235

"Your sarvant, sir, your sarvant," said the grub-man, making a low salutation behind his apron. "Hope you find it pleasant here, sir; nice grounds — cool apartments — hope you'll stay with us some time — try to make it agreeable. What will you have for dinner to-day?"

"I prefer not to dine to-day," said Bartleby, turning away. "It would disagree with me; I am unused to dinners." So saying, he slowly moved to the other side of the inclosure, and took up a position fronting the deadwall.

"How's this?" said the grub-man, addressing me with a stare of astonishment. "He's odd, ain't he?"

"I think he is a little deranged," said I, sadly.

"Deranged? deranged is it? Well, now, upon my word, I thought that friend of yourn was a gentleman forger; they are always pale and genteel-like, them forgers. I can't help pity 'em — can't help it, sir. Did you know Monroe Edwards?" he added, touchingly, and paused. Then, laying his hand piteously on my shoulder, sighed, "he died of consumption at Sing-Sing. So you weren't acquainted with Monroe?"

"No, I was never socially acquainted with any forgers. But I cannot stop longer. Look to my friend yonder. You will not lose by it. I will see you again."

Some few days after this, I again obtained admission to the Tombs, and went through the corridors in quest of Bartleby; but without finding him.

"I saw him coming from his cell not long ago," said a turnkey, "may be he's gone to loiter in the yards."

So I went in that direction.

"Are you looking for the silent man?" said another turnkey, passing me. "Yonder he lies — sleeping in the yard there. 'Tis not twenty minutes since I saw him lie down."

The yard was entirely quiet. It was not accessible to the common prisoners. The surrounding walls, of amazing thickness, kept off all sounds behind them. The Egyptian character of the masonry weighed upon me with its gloom. But a soft imprisoned turf grew under foot. The heart of the eternal pyramids, it seemed, wherein, by some strange magic, through the clefts, grass-seed, dropped by birds, had sprung.

Strangely huddled at the base of the wall, his knees drawn up, and lying on his side, his head touching the cold stones, I saw the wasted Bartleby. But nothing stirred. I paused; then went close up to him; stooped over, and saw that his dim eyes were open; otherwise he seemed profoundly sleeping. Something prompted me to touch him. I felt his hand, when a tingling shiver ran up my arm and down my spine to my feet.

The round face of the grub-man peered upon me now. "His dinner is ready. Won't he dine to-day, either? Or does he live without dining?"

"Lives without dining," said I, and closed the eyes.

"Eh! — He's asleep, ain't he?"

"With kings and counselors," ° murmured I.

There would seem little need for proceeding further in this history. Imagination will readily supply the meagre recital of poor Bartleby's interment. But, ere parting with the reader, let me say, that if this little narrative has sufficiently

240

245

250

°*"With kings and counselors"*: From Job 3:13–14: "then had I been at rest, / With kings and counselors of the earth, / which built desolate places for themselves."

interested him, to awaken curiosity as to who Bartleby was, and what manner of life he led prior to the present narrator's making his acquaintance, I can only reply, that in such curiosity I fully share, but am wholly unable to gratify it. Yet here I hardly know whether I should divulge one little item of rumor, which came to my ear a few months after the scrivener's decease. Upon what basis it rested, I could never ascertain; and hence, how true it is I cannot now tell. But, inasmuch as this vague report has not been without a certain suggestive interest to me, however sad, it may prove the same with some others; and so I will briefly mention it. The report was this: that Bartleby had been a subordinate clerk in the Dead Letter Office at Washington, from which he had been suddenly removed by a change in the administration. When I think over this rumor, hardly can I express the emotions which seize me. Dead letters! does it not sound like dead men? Conceive a man by nature and misfortune prone to a pallid hopelessness, can any business seem more fitted to heighten it than that of continually handling these dead letters, and assorting them for the flames? For by the cart-load they are annually burned. Sometimes from out the folded paper the pale clerk takes a ring — the finger it was meant for, perhaps, moulders in the grave; a bank-note sent in swiftest charity — he whom it would relieve, nor eats nor hungers any more; pardon for those who died despairing; hope for those who died unhoping; good tidings for those who died stifled by unrelieved calamities. On errands of life, these letters speed to death.

Ah, Bartleby! Ah, humanity!

CONSIDERATIONS FOR CRITICAL THINKING AND WRITING

1. FIRST RESPONSE. How does the lawyer's description of himself serve to characterize him? Why is it significant that he is a lawyer? Are his understandings and judgments about Bartleby and himself always sound?

2. Why do you think Turkey, Nippers, and Ginger Nut are introduced to the reader before Bartleby?

3. Describe Bartleby's physical characteristics. How is his physical description a foreshadowing of what happens to him?

4. How does Bartleby's "I would prefer not to" affect the routine of the lawyer and his employees?

5. What is the significance of the subtitle: "A Story of Wall Street"?

6. Who is the protagonist? Whose story is it?

7. Does the lawyer change during the story? Does Bartleby? Who is the antagonist?

8. What motivates Bartleby's behavior? Why do you think Melville withholds the information about the Dead Letter Office until the end of the story? Does this background adequately explain Bartleby?

9. Does Bartleby have any lasting impact on the lawyer?

10. Do you think Melville sympathizes more with Bartleby or with the lawyer?

11. Describe the lawyer's changing attitudes toward Bartleby.

12. Consider how this story could be regarded as a kind of protest with nonnegotiable demands.

13. Discuss the story's humor and how it affects your response to Bartleby.

14. Trace your emotional reaction to Bartleby as he is revealed in the story.

15. CRITICAL STRATEGIES. Read the section on biographical criticism (pp. 0000–00) in Chapter 52, "Critical Strategies for Reading," and use the library to learn about Melville's reputation as a writer at the time of his writing "Bartleby." How might this information produce a provocative biographical approach to the story?

CONNECTIONS TO OTHER SELECTIONS

1. Compare Bartleby's withdrawal from life with that of the protagonist in Gail Godwin's "A Sorrowful Woman" (p. 35). Why does each character choose death?

2. How is Melville's use of Bartleby's experience in the Dead Letter Office similar to Nathaniel Hawthorne's use of Brown's forest encounter with the devil in "Young Goodman Brown" (p. 331)? Why is each experience crucial to an understanding of what informs the behavior of these characters?

3. Discuss the significant parallels between "Bartleby, the Scrivener" and Franz Kafka's "A Hunger Artist" (p. 577), both stories about self-denial and isolation. Explain whether you think Bartleby's and the hunger artist's responses to their environments are similar or different.

PERSPECTIVES ON MELVILLE

NATHANIEL HAWTHORNE (1804–1864)

On Herman Melville's Philosophic Stance 1856

[Melville] stayed with us from Tuesday till Thursday; and, on the intervening day, we took a pretty long walk together, and sat down in a hollow among the sand hills (sheltering ourselves from the high, cool wind) and smoked a cigar. Melville, as he always does, began to reason of Providence and futurity, and of everything that lies beyond human ken, and informed me that he had "pretty much made up his mind to be annihilated"; but still he does not seem to rest in that anticipation; and, I think, will never rest until he gets hold of a definite belief. It is strange how he persists—and has persisted ever since I knew him, and probably long before—in wandering to-and-fro over these deserts, as dismal and monotonous as the sand hills amid which we were sitting. He can neither believe, nor be comfortable in his unbelief; and he is too honest and courageous not to try to do one or the other. If he were a religious man, he would be one of the most truly religious and reverential; he has a very high and noble nature, and better worth immortality than most of us.

From *The American Notebooks*

CONSIDERATIONS FOR CRITICAL THINKING AND WRITING

1. How does this description of Melville shed light on the central concerns of "Bartleby, the Scrivener"?

2. Which side does Hawthorne seem to be on — "belief" or "unbelief"? Why?

3. Compare Hawthorne's description with Melville's view of Hawthorne (p. 374). What attitudes about life do they share?

4. Write an essay about the issue of "belief" and "unbelief" in "Bartleby, the Scrivener" and Ernest Hemingway's "Soldier's Home" (p. 152).

DAN McCALL (b. 1940)

On the Lawyer's Character in "Bartleby, the Scrivener"   1989

The overwhelming majority of the Bartleby Industry reads the narrator of the story in a way that is not only different from mine but quite incompatible with mine. Every virtue I see in the man, they see as a vice; where I see his strength, they see his weakness; what I see as his genuine responsiveness, they see as his cold self-absorption. Some critics read the story as I do, but we are in a distinct minority. There are several reasons this should be so, and I think I understand at least some of them, but first I should like to present as fairly as I can the majority opinion.

Robert Weisbuch, who has said the Lawyer is Charles Dickens, refers to the Lawyer as "unnatural," "anti-natural," "lifeless," "self-satisfied," "pompous," and "rationalizing." The Lawyer "investigates Bartleby but refuses authentic emotional commitment in so doing," and "Bartleby rightly refuses to credit the Lawyer's false commitment." The Lawyer is guilty of "toadyism" and his final heartbroken outburst, "Ah, Bartleby! Ah, humanity!" is no more than "a someways hollow and unfeeling exclamation."[1] Another critic calls the Lawyer a "smug fool" who is "terribly unkind to a very sick man."[2] I had always thought of the Lawyer as a kind of stand-in for us, a figure we could identify with as we struggled to understand Bartleby. On the contrary, the narrator is "deficient in humanity and quite obtuse towards human beings." I must have had it backwards, for "surely this was Melville's intention: to have his reader *not* sympathize with the Lawyer, *not* to identify with him, *not* to put himself in the Lawyer's place" (*his* italics, not mine).[3] Another critic says, "The narrator attains new heights of vague sentimentality rather than a peak of awareness in his climactic and highly revealing sigh: 'Ah, Bartleby! Ah, humanity!'" This reader provides dismissive certainty in answering the question

> Who then is Melville's narrator? He is the sort of man one tends to find in high places: the snug man whose worldly success has convinced him that this is the "best of all possible worlds," and whose virtues cluster around a "prudential" concern for maintaining his own situation. The narrator can never fully understand or truly befriend Bartleby because the narrator is simply too complacent, both philosophically and morally, to sympathize with human dissatisfaction and despair.[4]

[1] Robert Weisbuch, "Melville's 'Bartleby' and the Dead Letter of Charles Dickens," *Atlantic Double-Cross: American Literature and British Influence in the Age of Emerson* (Chicago: University of Chicago Press, 1986), pp. 44, 45–47.
[2] David Shusterman, "The 'Reader Fallacy' and 'Bartleby, the Scrivener,'" *New England Quarterly*, 45 (March 1972), 118–24, pp. 122–23.
[3] Ibid., p. 121.
[4] Allan Emery, "The Alternatives of Melville's 'Bartleby,'" *Nineteenth-Century Fiction*, 31 (1976), 170–87, pp. 186–87.

Still another reader tells us the Lawyer's commentary "rings with blasphemy" and demonstrates "grotesque manifestations of diseased conscience."[5]

Authority is the enemy here. In the extended quotation just above it is taken for granted that the "sort of man one tends to find in high places" is superficial and selfish. Worldly success is bad for the character. The Lawyer has to be bad, or he wouldn't be in an office on Wall Street. Hershel Parker tells us that "our ultimate opinion" of the Lawyer "is not contempt so much as bleak astonishment at his secure blindness. With a bitterer irony than the narrator is capable of, we murmur something like 'Ah, narrator! Ah, humanity!' In his self-consciously eloquent sequel, after all, the lawyer has merely made his last cheap purchase of a 'delicious self-approval.'" Parker maintains that when "this easy-conscienced" man speaks of kings and counselors, "he is experiencing a comfortable, self-indulgent variety of melancholy"; when he quotes words from the Book of Job he does so "with prideful aptness," and "characteristically perverts them from profound lament to sonorous urbanity."[6]

This last feature of Parker's argument is interesting to me because it reminds me of the first time I read the story, at eighteen. I was overwhelmed by the discovery that Bartleby had died, and I didn't know that "With kings and counselors" was a quotation from the Book of Job. The phrase "With kings and counselors" seemed to me majestic and solemn and final. That "murmured I" put a deep hush around it. But it never occurred to me that the man who said those words was "easy-conscienced" or "self-indulgent" or the sort of man who "characteristically perverts" a "profound lament to sonorous urbanity." The figure of Bartleby seemed so weird and funny and painful, his death at once inevitable and shocking, that I did not see it as an occasion for the man who was telling me about it to make a "last cheap purchase" of "delicious self-approval." I trusted that Lawyer.

Thirty years later, I still do. He seems to me extremely intelligent, whimsical and ironic, generous, self-aware, passionate, and thoroughly competent.

From The Silence of Bartleby

[5] William Bysshe Stein, "Bartleby: The Christian Conscience," in *Melville Annual 1965, A Symposium: "Bartleby, the Scrivener,"* ed. Howard P. Vincent (Kent, Ohio: Kent State University Press, 1966), p. 107.
[6] Hershel Parker, "The Sequel in 'Bartleby,'" in *Bartleby the Inscrutable: A Collection of Commentary on Herman Melville's Tale "Bartleby, the Scrivener,"* ed. M. Thomas Inge (Hamden, Conn.: Archon Books, 1979), 159–65, pp. 163–64.

CONSIDERATIONS FOR CRITICAL THINKING AND WRITING

1. How does McCall characterize the "majority opinion" on the lawyer's character? What is his opinion of the lawyer?

2. How does McCall's opinion of the lawyer compare with Hawthorne's opinion of Herman Melville in the preceding Perspective?

3. Write an essay explaining whether you find the "majority opinion" or McCall's view of the lawyer more convincing.

ALICE McDERMOTT (B. 1953)

Alice McDermott was born in Brooklyn and raised on Long Island, New York, in a Catholic family of Irish origin. She received a B.A. from the State University of New York at Oswego in 1975 and an M.A. from the University of New Hampshire in 1978. McDermott published her first novel, *A Bigamist's Daughter,* in 1982, and has since completed three more, *That Night* (1987), *At Weddings and Wakes* (1992), and *Charming Billy* (1998), winner of the National Book Award. She has taught at the University of California at San Diego and at American University, lectured at the University of New Hampshire, and been writer-in-residence at Lynchburg and Hollins Colleges in Virginia. Currently, she is a writer-in-residence at Johns Hopkins University in Baltimore. McDermott's fiction frequently derives from her own experience, often focusing on Irish American characters, though she claims, "It's not so much what happens to us, it's what we say about it."

Web   *Research Alice McDermott with LitLinks at*
       http://www.bedfordstmartins.com/meyer/bedintrolit

Enough   *2000*

Begin, then, with the ice-cream dishes, carried from the dining room into the narrow kitchen on a Sunday night, the rest of the family still sitting contented around the lace-covered table, her father's cigarette smoke just beginning to drift into the air that was still rich from the smell of the roast, and the roasted potatoes, the turnips and carrots and green beans, the biscuits and the Sunday-only perfume of her mother and sisters. Carried just two dishes at a time because this was the good set, cabbage roses with gold trim. Two bowls at a time, silver spoons inside, carried carefully and carefully placed on the drainboard beside the soapy water where the dinner plates were already soaking, her mother being a great believer in soaking, whether children or dishes or clothes, or souls. Let it soak: the stained blouse, the bruised knee, the sin — sending them into their rooms with a whole rosary to pray, on their knees, and a full hour in which to do it.

   She was the youngest child, the third girl with three brothers, and since the boys were excused and the kitchen too small, their mother said, to hold a pair of sisters in it together, this final task, the clearing of the ice-cream dishes, was hers alone. Two at a time, she gathered the plates while the others sat, contented, limp, stupefied with food, while she herself felt her stomach straining against the now tight waist of her good dress, felt her legs grown heavy from all she had eaten. Sunday dinner was the only meal they had with their father, who worked two jobs to keep them all fed (that was the way it was put by mother and father both, without variance), and the bounty of the spread seemed to be their parents' defiant proof of the man's long week of labor. They always ate too much at Sunday dinner and they always had dessert. Pie on the first Sunday of the month, then cake, ice cream, stewed fruit — one Sunday after the other and always in that same rotation. Ice cream being the pinnacle for her, stewed fruit the depths from which she would have to rise, through pie (if mincemeat, hardly a step in the right direction, if blueberry, more encouraging), then cake — always yellow with eggs and dusted with powdered sugar — and then at last, again, ice cream, store-bought or homemade, it hardly made a difference to she who was told once a month that a lady takes a small spoonful, swallows it, and then takes another. She does *not* load the spoon up and then run the stuff in and out of her mouth, studying each time the shape her lips have made ("Look how cross-eyed she gets when she's gazing at it"). A lady doesn't want to show her tongue at the dinner table.

Carefully, she collected the bowls and carried them two by two into the narrow kitchen. She placed one on the drainboard and then lifted the spoon out of the other and, always, with a glance over her shoulder, licked the spoon, front and back, and then raised the delicate bowl to her chin and licked that, too, licked the cabbage roses and the pale spaces in between, long strokes of the tongue from gold-edged rim to gold-edged rim and then another tour around the middle. Place it down softly and pick up the next. The creamy dregs spotting her nose and her cheeks, vanilla or chocolate, peach or strawberry — strawberry the best because her brothers and a sister always left behind any big pieces of the fruit. Heel of her hand to the sticky tip of her nose (lick that, too) and then back into the dining room again for the next two bowls. Oh, it was good, as good as the whole heaping bowl that had been filled by her father at the head of the table, passed hand to hand by her sisters and brothers, and set before her.

Extrapolate, then, from the girlhood ritual (not to say, of course, that it ended with her girlhood) to what came to be known as her trouble with the couch. Trouble *on* the couch would have been more accurate, she understood later, when she had a sense of humor about these things that at the time had no humor in them at all. But such precision was the last thing her family would have sought, not in these matters. Her trouble with the couch, it was called. Mother walking into what should have been the empty apartment except that the boiler at the school had broken and the pastor had sent them all home and here she was with the boy from upstairs, side by side on the couch, her two cheeks flushed fever pink and her mouth a bleary, full-blown rose, and her mother would have her know (once the boy had slipped out the door) that she wasn't born yesterday and Glory Be to God fourteen years old was a fine age to be starting this nonsense and wasn't it a good thing that tomorrow was Saturday and the confessionals at church would be fully manned. She'd had a good soaking in recriminations all that evening and well into Saturday afternoon when she finished the rosary the priest himself had prescribed, the end coming only after she returned from the Communion rail on Sunday morning and her mother caught and held her eye. A stewed-fruit Sunday no doubt.

Her oldest sister found her next, on the couch with her high-school sweet- 5 heart, midafternoon once again — their mother, widowed now, off working in an office — and the first four buttons of her dress undone, the lace bodice of her pale-pink slip all exposed, And then not a month or two later that same sister found her there with another boy, his head in her lap and his hand brushing up and down from her ankle to her knees.

Then there was that Saturday night during the war when her oldest brother, too drunk to go home to his new wife on the next block, let himself in and found her stretched out on the couch in the embrace of some midshipman who, it was clear, despite their quick rearranging of clothes, had his fingers tangled up in her garter. There were buttons undone that time, too, and yet again when she was spied on by the second sister, who never did marry herself but who had an eyeful, let me tell you — a marine, this time, his mouth, to put it delicately, where her corsage should have been and her own hands twisted into his hair as if to hold him there — which led to such a harangue about her trouble with the couch that, finally, even her old mother was moved to say that there was a war on, after all.

Later, her best girlfriend joked that maybe she would want to bring that couch along with her on her wedding night. And joked again, nine months to the week later, when her first son was born, that she didn't seem to need that old couch after all.

There were seven children born altogether, the first followed and each of the others preceded by a miscarriage, so that there were thirteen pregnancies in all, every loss mourned so ferociously that both her husband and her mother advised, each time, not to try again, each birth celebrated with a christening party that packed the small house — made smaller by the oversized floral couch and high-backed chairs and elaborate lamps she had chosen — and spilled out into the narrow yard and breezeway, where there would be dancing, if the weather allowed. A phonograph placed behind the screen in the kitchen window and the records going all through the long afternoon, and on into the evening. You'd see her there after the last guest had gone, the baby on her shoulder and maybe another child on her hip, dancing to something slow and reluctant and melancholy ("One for my baby, and one more for the road"). Lipstick and face powder on the white christening gown that night, as well as the scent of the party itself, cigarette smoke and perfume and the cocktails on her breath.

She was a mother forever rubbing a licked finger to her children's cheeks, scrubbing at the pink traces of her own kisses, forever swelling up again with the next birth. Kids in her lap and her arms wrapped around them even after their limbs had grown longer than her own. The boys, before she knew it, lifting her off her feet when she took them in her arms.

She was forty-six when she gave birth to the last, and he was eighteen and on a   10 weekend home from college when he recognized, for the first time in his life, what the sighs and the stirrings coming from his parents' bedroom on that Saturday morning actually signified. (He did a quick calculation of their ages, just to be sure he had it right and then thought, Still?, amazed and a little daunted.) For the rest of the weekend, he imagined ways he might rib them about it, although he couldn't bring himself to come out with anything, knowing full well that even the most good-natured mention of what went on behind their bedroom door could get him the back of his father's hand — or, worse yet, cause a blush to rise from his own cheeks well before he'd managed to raise any kind of glow in theirs.

And there was the Christmas, some years later, when one of them had given their parents a nostalgic collection of forties music and, listening to Bing Crosby sing in his slow, sleepy way, "Kiss me once and kiss me twice (and kiss me once again)," hadn't their mother said, for all assembled to hear, "If you don't turn this off, I'm going to have to find a place to be alone with your father." And hadn't he and his siblings, every one of them well versed by then in matters of love and sex, sat dumbfounded, calculating, no doubt . . . seventy-one, seventy-two . . . still?

Shades of the trouble with the couch, she took her husband's hand in his last days and unbuttoned her blouse and didn't seem to care a bit who saw her, doctor or nurse, son or daughter or grandchild — or older sister who'd never married herself and couldn't help but say, out in the waiting room, "Now, really." She leaned forward, now and again, to whisper to him, even after he was well past hearing, her open lips brushing both the surgical tape that se- cured the respirator in his mouth and the stubbly gray beard of his cheek.

Growing plump in her widowhood, though she was the first to admit she'd never been what you would call thin, she travelled in busloads of retirees — mostly widows, although there was the occasional man or two — only missing a museum trip or a foliage tour or a luncheon (with a cocktail) at this or that historic site or country inn if a grandchild was in need of minding. What she could do best — her own daughters marvelled at it, who else would have the patience — was sit for hours and hours at a time with a colicky baby over her shoulder or a worn-out toddler on her knee and talk or sing. She told nonsense stories, more sound than substance, or sang every tune in her lifetime repertoire, from Beatles songs to ancient hymns, hypnotizing the children somehow (her sons and daughters were sure of it) into sleep, or sometimes just a dazed contentedness, tucked under her arm or under her chin, seconds, min- utes, then hours ticking by, the bars of summer or winter, late-afternoon or early-morning sunlight moving across them, across the length of a room, and neither of them, adult or child, seeming to mark the time gone by.

But take a look in your freezer after she's gone, the daughters reported to one another and to the better-liked sisters-in-law as well. Nearly a full gallon eaten — or all but a final spoonful so she didn't have to put the carton in the trash and give herself away. She's welcome to it, of course, but at her age it's a weight thing. She needs to watch her weight. It's the deceptiveness, too, don't you see. What does she eat when she's alone?

Alone, in an apartment now, ever since the night a stranger crept up the 15 breezeway, broke the kitchen window, and made off with her purse, the portable TV, and the boxed silver in the dining room which had been her mother's, she licked chocolate pudding from the back of a spoon, sherbet, gelato, sorbet, ice cream, of course. She scraped the sides of the carton, ran a finger around the rim.

On visits to her out-of-state children she'd get up in the night, stand by the light of the refrigerator, take a few tablespoons from the gallon, or a single ice-cream bar, but always end up going back for more. A daughter-in-law found her one morning, 2 A.M., with the last chocolate/vanilla ice-cream cup and a tiny wooden spoon — leftovers from the grandchild's birthday party she had made the trip specifically to attend — and gave her such a lecture, as she put it when she got home, that you'd think she'd been shooting heroin.

It was the weight that concerned them, said her children, conferring. They were afraid it was the weight that was keeping her these days from those senior trips she used to love, from the winter vacations in Florida she'd once looked forward to. Now that the grandchildren were grown out of the need for a sitter, she should be doing more of those things, not fewer. They solicited a talking-to for their mother from her doctor, who instead reminded them all that she was past eighty and healthy enough and free to do, or not do, what she liked.

They took to stopping by to see her, on lunch hours, or before going to the grocery store, keeping their car keys in their hands, and urging her to turn off the television, to plan something, to do something. Her grandchildren, driving cars now, asked her out to their kinds of places, treated her to frothy lattes topped with whipped cream that would repeat on her the rest of the afternoon and on into the evening, despite bicarbs and antacids, until she brought herself to tell them when they called, "Thank you, dear, but I'm quite content at home."

Peach, strawberry, and reliable vanilla. Rocky road and butter pecan and mint chocolate chip. Looking at ninety and still, still, the last thing she feels at the end of each day is that longing to wrap her legs around him, around someone. The pleasure of the taste, of loading up a spoon and finishing it bit by bit, and then taking another spoonful and another—one kind of pleasure, enhanced by stealth and guilt, when it is someone else's carton, someone else's home in the middle of the night, another kind when it's her own and she carries her bowl, in full light, to the couch before the television in the living room. Forbidden youthful passion and domestic married love, something like that, anyway, if you want to extrapolate. If you want to begin with the ice-cream dishes licked clean by a girl who is now the old woman past all usefulness, closing her eyes at the first taste. If you want to make a metaphor out of her lifelong cravings, something she is not inclined to do. Pleasure is pleasure. A remnant of strawberries, a young man's hands, a newborn in your arms, or your own child's changing face. Your lips to the familiar stubble of your husband's cheek. Your tongue to the last vein of fudge in the empty carton. Pleasure is pleasure. If you have an appetite for it, you'll find there's plenty. Plenty to satisfy you—lick the back of the spoon. Take another, and another. Plenty. Never enough.

CONSIDERATIONS FOR CRITICAL THINKING AND WRITING

1. FIRST RESPONSE. What do you think of the protagonist's appetite for pleasure? Explain why you find her character to be attractive or unattractive.
2. In what sense is there coherence and continuity in the protagonist's life?
3. What do you think is the narrator's attitude toward her? What specific passage or passages support your assessment?
4. How do you think this story might read differently if it were told by the protagonist rather than a third-person narrator (see the glossary for a definition of a third-person narrator)?
5. How would you characterize the narrator?
6. What do you take to be the story's conflict? Is there a resolution?
7. What do you think is the central point of the story? In what passage or passages does it seem most apparent to you?
8. Try writing a physical description of the protagonist (at any age) that you think reflects her sensibilities.

CONNECTIONS TO OTHER SELECTIONS

1. Read A. L. Bader's "Nothing Happens in Modern Short Stories" (p. 98). To what extent are Bader's comments relevant to "Enough"?

2. Discuss the treatment and significance of eating in "Enough" and in Lahiri's "When Mr. Pirzada Came to Dine" (p. 105) or Melville's "Bartleby, the Scrivener" (p. 116).

5

Setting

Setting is the context in which the action of a story occurs. The major elements of setting are time, place, and social environment that frame the characters. These elements establish the world in which the characters act. In most stories they also serve as more than backgrounds and furnishings. If we are sensitive to the contexts provided by setting, we are better able to understand the behavior of the characters and the significance of their actions. It may be tempting to read quickly through a writer's descriptions and ignore the details of the setting once a geographic location and a historic period are established. But if you read a story so impatiently, the significance of the setting may slip by you. That kind of reading is similar to traveling on interstate highways: a lot of ground gets covered, but very little is seen along the way.

Settings can be used to evoke a mood or atmosphere that will prepare the reader for what is to come. In "Young Goodman Brown" (p. 331), Nathaniel Hawthorne has his pious protagonist leave his wife and village one night to keep an appointment in a New England forest near the site of the seventeenth-century witch trials. This is Hawthorne's description of Brown entering the forest:

> He had taken a dreary road, darkened by all the gloomiest trees of the forest, which barely stood aside to let the narrow path creep through, and closed immediately behind. It was all as lonely as could be; and there is this peculiarity in such a solitude, that the traveler knows not who may be concealed by the innumerable trunks and the thick boughs overhead; so that with lonely footsteps he may yet be passing through an unseen multitude.

The atmosphere established in this descriptive setting is somber and threatening. Careful reading reveals that the forest is not simply the woods; it is a moral wilderness, where anything can happen.

If we ask why a writer chooses to include certain details in a work, then we are likely to make connections that relate the details to some larger purpose, such as the story's meaning. The final scene in Godwin's "A Sorrowful Woman" (p. 35) occurs in the spring, an ironic time for the action to be set because instead of rebirth for the protagonist there is only death. There is usually a reason for placing a story in a particular time or location. Katherine Mansfield has the protagonist in "Miss Brill" (p. 259) discover her loneliness and old age in a French vacation town, a lively atmosphere that serves as a cruel contrast to an elderly (and foreign) lady's painful realization.

Melville's "Bartleby, the Scrivener" (p. 116) takes on meaning as Bartleby's "dead-wall reveries" begin to reflect his shattered vision of life. He is surrounded by walls. A folding screen separates him from others in the office; he is isolated. The office window faces walls; there is no view to relieve the deadening work. Bartleby faces a wall at the prison where he dies; the final wall is death. As the subtitle indicates, this is "A Story of Wall Street." Unless the geographic location or the physical details of a story are used merely as necessary props, they frequently shed light on character and action. All offices have walls, but Melville transforms the walls into an antagonist that represents the limitations Bartleby sees and feels all around him but does not speak of.

Time, location, and the physical features of a setting can all be relevant to the overall purpose of a story. So too is the social environment in which the characters are developed. In Faulkner's "A Rose for Emily" (p. 75) the changes in her southern town serve as a foil for Emily's tenacious hold on a lost past. She is regarded as a "fallen monument," as old-fashioned and peculiar as the "stubborn and coquettish decay" of her house. Neither she nor her house fits into the modern changes that are paving and transforming the town. Without the social context, this story would be mostly an account of a bizarre murder rather than an exploration of the conflicts Faulkner associated with the changing South. Setting enlarges the meaning of Emily's actions.

Some settings have traditional associations that are closely related to the action of a story. Adventure and romance, for example, flourish in the fertile soil of most exotic settings: the film version of Isak Dinesen's novel *Out of Africa* is a lush visual demonstration of how setting can play a significant role in generating the audience's expectations of love and excitement.

Sometimes, writers reverse traditional expectations. When a tranquil garden is the scene for a horrendously bloody murder, we are as much taken by surprise as the victim is. In John Updike's "A & P" (p. 606) there seems to be little possibility for heroic action in so mundane a place as a supermarket, but the setting turns out to be appropriate for the important, unexpected decision the protagonist makes about life. Traditional associations are also disrupted in "A Sorrowful Woman," in which Godwin disassociates home from the safety, security, and comfort usually connected with it by presenting the protagonist's home as a deadly trap. By drawing on traditional associations, a writer can fulfill or disrupt a reader's expectations about a setting in order to complement the elements of the story.

Not every story uses setting as a means of revealing mood, idea, meaning, or characters' actions. Some stories have no particularly significant setting. It is entirely possible to envision a story in which two characters speak to each other about a conflict between them and little or no mention is made of the time or place they inhabit. If, however, a shift in setting would make a serious difference to our understanding of a story, then the setting is probably an important element in the work. Consider how different "Bartleby, the Scrivener" would be if it were set in a relaxed, pleasant, sunny town in the South rather than in the grinding, limiting materialism of Wall Street. Bartleby's withdrawal from life would be less comprehensible and meaningful in such a setting. The setting is integral to that story.

The following three stories — Ernest Hemingway's "Soldier's Home," Ron Hansen's "Nebraska," and Fay Weldon's "IND AFF, or Out of Love in Sarajevo" — include settings that serve to shape their meanings.

ERNEST HEMINGWAY (1899–1961)

In 1918, a year after graduating from high school in Oak Park, Illinois, Ernest Hemingway volunteered as an ambulance driver in World War I. At the Italian front, he was seriously wounded. This experience haunted him and many of the characters in his short stories and novels. *In Our Time* (1925) is a collection of short stories, including "Soldier's Home," that reflect some of Hemingway's own attempts to readjust to life back home after the war. *The Sun Also Rises* (1926), *A Farewell to Arms* (1929), and *For Whom the Bell Tolls* (1940) are also about war and its impact on people's lives. Hemingway courted violence all his life in war, the bullring, the boxing ring, and big game hunting. When he was sixty-two years old and terminally ill with cancer, he committed suicide by shooting himself with a shotgun. "Soldier's Home" takes place in a small town in Oklahoma; the war, however, is never distant from the protagonist's mind as he struggles to come home again.

Web *Research Ernest Hemingway with LitLinks at*
http://www.bedfordstmartins.com/meyer/bedintrolit

Soldier's Home   1925

Krebs went to the war from a Methodist college in Kansas. There is a picture which shows him among his fraternity brothers, all of them wearing exactly the same height and style collar. He enlisted in the Marines in 1917 and did not return to the United States until the second division returned from the Rhine in the summer of 1919.

There is a picture which shows him on the Rhine with two German girls and another corporal. Krebs and the corporal look too big for their uniforms. The German girls are not beautiful. The Rhine does not show in the picture.

By the time Krebs returned to his home town in Oklahoma the greeting of heroes was over. He came back much too late. The men from the town who had been drafted had all been welcomed elaborately on their return. There had been a great deal of hysteria. Now the reaction had set in. People seemed to think it was rather ridiculous for Krebs to be getting back so late, years after the war was over.

At first Krebs, who had been at Belleau Wood, Soissons, the Champagne, St. Mihiel, and in the Argonne° did not want to talk about the war at all. Later he felt the need to talk but no one wanted to hear about it. His town had heard too many atrocity stories to be thrilled by actualities. Krebs found that to be listened to at all he had to lie, and after he had done this twice he, too, had a re-action against the war and against talking about it. A distaste for everything that had happened to him in the war set in because of the lies he had told. All of the times that had been able to make him feel cool and clear inside himself when he thought of them; the times so long back when he had done the one thing, the only thing for a man to do, easily and naturally, when he might have done something else, now lost their cool, valuable quality and then were lost themselves.

His lies were quite unimportant lies and consisted in attributing to himself things other men had seen, done, or heard of, and stating as facts certain apoc-ryphal incidents familiar to all soldiers. Even his lies were not sensational at the pool room. His acquaintances, who had heard detailed accounts of German women found chained to machine guns in the Argonne forest and who could not comprehend, or were barred by their patriotism from interest in, any Ger-man machine gunners who were not chained, were not thrilled by his stories.

Krebs acquired the nausea in regard to experience that is the result of un-truth or exaggeration, and when he occasionally met another man who had really been a soldier and they talked a few minutes in the dressing room at a dance he fell into the easy pose of the old soldier among other soldiers: that he had been badly, sickeningly frightened all the time. In this way he lost everything.

During this time, it was late summer, he was sleeping late in bed, getting up to walk down town to the library to get a book, eating lunch at home, read-ing on the front porch until he became bored, and then walking down through the town to spend the hottest hours of the day in the cool dark of the pool room. He loved to play pool.

In the evening he practiced on his clarinet, strolled down town, read, and went to bed. He was still a hero to his two young sisters. His mother would have given him breakfast in bed if he had wanted it. She often came in when he was in bed and asked him to tell her about the war, but her attention always wandered. His father was noncommittal.

Before Krebs went away to the war he had never been allowed to drive the family motor car. His father was in the real estate business and always wanted the car to be at his command when he required it to take clients out into the

Belleau Wood . . . Argonne: Sites of battles in World War I in which American troops were in-strumental in pushing back the Germans.

country to show them a piece of farm property. The car always stood outside the First National Bank building where his father had an office on the second floor. Now, after the war, it was still the same car.

Nothing was changed in the town except that the young girls had grown 10 up. But they lived in such a complicated world of already defined alliances and shifting feuds that Krebs did not feel the energy or the courage to break into it. He liked to look at them, though. There were so many good-looking young girls. Most of them had their hair cut short. When he went away only little girls wore their hair like that or girls that were fast. They all wore sweaters and shirt waists with round Dutch collars. It was a pattern. He liked to look at them from the front porch as they walked on the other side of the street. He liked to watch them walking under the shade of the trees. He liked the round Dutch collars above their sweaters. He liked their silk stockings and flat shoes. He liked their bobbed hair and the way they walked.

When he was in town their appeal to him was not very strong. He did not like them when he saw them in the Greek's ice cream parlor. He did not want them themselves really. They were too complicated. There was something else. Vaguely he wanted a girl but he did not want to have to work to get her. He would have liked to have a girl but he did not want to have to spend a long time getting her. He did not want to get into the intrigue and the politics. He did not want to have to do any courting. He did not want to tell any more lies. It wasn't worth it.

He did not want any consequences. He did not want any consequences ever again. He wanted to live along without consequences. Besides he did not really need a girl. The army had taught him that. It was all right to pose as though you had to have a girl. Nearly everybody did that. But it wasn't true. You did not need a girl. That was the funny thing. First a fellow boasted how girls mean nothing to him, that he never thought of them, that they could not touch him. Then a fellow boasted that he could not get along without girls, that he had to have them all the time, that he could not go to sleep without them.

That was all a lie. It was all a lie both ways. You did not need a girl unless you thought about them. He learned that in the army. Then sooner or later you always got one. When you were really ripe for a girl you always got one. You did not have to think about it. Sooner or later it would come. He had learned that in the army.

Now he would have liked a girl if she had come to him and not wanted to talk. But here at home it was all too complicated. He knew he could never get through it all again. It was not worth the trouble. That was the thing about French girls and German girls. There was not all this talking. You couldn't talk much and you did not need to talk. It was simple and you were friends. He thought about France and then he began to think about Germany. On the whole he had liked Germany better. He did not want to leave Germany. He did not want to come home. Still, he had come home. He sat on the front porch.

He liked the girls that were walking along the other side of the street. He 15 liked the look of them much better than the French girls or the German girls. But the world they were in was not the world he was in. He would like to have one of them. But it was not worth it. They were such a nice pattern. He liked the pattern. It was exciting. But he would not go through all the talking. He did not want one badly enough. He liked to look at them all, though. It was not worth it. Not now when things were getting good again.

He sat there on the porch reading a book on the war. It was a history and he was reading about all the engagements he had been in. It was the most interesting reading he had ever done. He wished there were more maps. He looked forward with a good feeling to reading all the really good histories when they would come out with good detail maps. Now he was really learning about the war. He had been a good soldier. That made a difference.

One morning after he had been home about a month his mother came into his bedroom and sat on the bed. She smoothed her apron.

"I had a talk with your father last night, Harold," she said, "and he is willing for you to take the car out in the evenings."

"Yeah?" said Krebs, who was not fully awake. "Take the car out? Yeah?"

"Yes. Your father has felt for some time that you should be able to take the car out in the evenings whenever you wished but we only talked it over last night." 20

"I'll bet you made him," Krebs said.

"No. It was your father's suggestion that we talk the matter over."

"Yeah. I'll bet you made him," Krebs sat up in bed.

"Will you come down to breakfast, Harold?" his mother said.

"As soon as I get my clothes on," Krebs said. 25

His mother went out of the room and he could hear her frying something downstairs while he washed, shaved, and dressed to go down into the diningroom for breakfast. While he was eating breakfast his sister brought in the mail.

"Well, Hare," she said. "You old sleepyhead. What do you ever get up for?"

Krebs looked at her. He liked her. She was his best sister.

"Have you got the paper?" he asked.

She handed him the Kansas City *Star* and he shucked off its brown wrap- 30
per and opened it to the sporting page. He folded the *Star* open and propped it against the water pitcher with his cereal dish to steady it, so he could read while he ate.

"Harold," his mother stood in the kitchen doorway, "Harold, please don't muss up the paper. Your father can't read his *Star* if it's been mussed."

"I won't muss it," Krebs said.

His sister sat down at the table and watched him while he read.

"We're playing indoor over at school this afternoon," she said. "I'm going to pitch."

"Good," said Krebs. "How's the old wing?" 35

"I can pitch better than lots of the boys. I tell them all you taught me. The other girls aren't much good."

"Yeah?" said Krebs.

"I tell them all you're my beau. Aren't you my beau, Hare?"

"You bet."

"Couldn't your brother really be your beau just because he's your brother?" 40

"I don't know."

"Sure you know. Couldn't you be my beau, Hare, if I was old enough and if you wanted to?"

"Sure. You're my girl now."

"Am I really your girl?"

"Sure." 45

"Do you love me?"

"Uh, huh."

"Will you love me always?"

"Sure."

"Will you come over and watch me play indoor?" 50

"Maybe."

"Aw, Hare, you don't love me. If you loved me, you'd want to come over and watch me play indoor."

Krebs's mother came into the dining-room from the kitchen. She carried a plate with two fried eggs and some crisp bacon on it and a plate of buckwheat cakes.

"You run along, Helen," she said. "I want to talk to Harold."

She put the eggs and bacon down in front of him and brought in a jug of 55 maple syrup for the buckwheat cakes. Then she sat down across the table from Krebs.

"I wish you'd put down the paper a minute, Harold," she said.

Krebs took down the paper and folded it.

"Have you decided what you are going to do yet, Harold?" his mother said, taking off her glasses.

"No," said Krebs.

"Don't you think it's about time?" His mother did not say this in a mean 60 way. She seemed worried.

"I hadn't thought about it," Krebs said.

"God has some work for everyone to do," his mother said. "There can be no idle hands in His Kingdom."

"I'm not in His Kingdom," Krebs said.

"We are all of us in His Kingdom."

Krebs felt embarrassed and resentful as always. 65

"I've worried about you so much, Harold," his mother went on. "I know the temptations you must have been exposed to. I know how weak men are. I know what your own dear grandfather, my own father, told us about the Civil War and I have prayed for you. I pray for you all day long, Harold."

Krebs looked at the bacon fat hardening on his plate.

"Your father is worried, too," his mother went on. "He thinks you have lost your ambition, that you haven't got a definite aim in life. Charley Simmons, who is just your age, has a good job and is going to be married. The boys are all settling down; they're all determined to get somewhere; you can see that boys like Charley Simmons are on their way to being really a credit to the community."

Krebs said nothing.

"Don't look that way, Harold," his mother said. "You know we love you and 70 I want to tell you for your own good how matters stand. Your father does not want to hamper your freedom. He thinks you should be allowed to drive the car. If you want to take some of the nice girls out riding with you, we are only too pleased. We want you to enjoy yourself. But you are going to have to settle down to work, Harold. Your father doesn't care what you start in at. All work is honorable as he says. But you've got to make a start at something. He asked me to speak to you this morning and then you can stop in and see him at his office."

"Is that all?" Krebs said.

"Yes. Don't you love your mother, dear boy?"

"No," Krebs said.

His mother looked at him across the table. Her eyes were shiny. She started crying.

"I don't love anybody," Krebs said.   75

It wasn't any good. He couldn't tell her, he couldn't make her see it. It was silly to have said it. He had only hurt her. He went over and took hold of her arm. She was crying with her head in her hands.

"I didn't mean it," he said. "I was just angry at something. I didn't mean I didn't love you."

His mother went on crying. Krebs put his arm on her shoulder.

"Can't you believe me, mother?"

His mother shook her head.   80

"Please, please, mother. Please believe me."

"All right," his mother said chokily. She looked up at him. "I believe you, Harold."

Krebs kissed her hair. She put her face up to him.

"I'm your mother," she said. "I held you next to my heart when you were a tiny baby."

Krebs felt sick and vaguely nauseated.   85

"I know, Mummy," he said. "I'll try and be a good boy for you."

"Would you kneel and pray with me, Harold?" his mother asked.

They knelt down beside the dining-room table and Krebs's mother prayed.

"Now, you pray, Harold," she said.

"I can't," Krebs said.   90

"Try, Harold."

"I can't."

"Do you want me to pray for you?"

"Yes."

So his mother prayed for him and then they stood up and Krebs kissed his   95
mother and went out of the house. He had tried so to keep his life from being complicated. Still, none of it had touched him. He had felt sorry for his mother and she had made him lie. He would go to Kansas City and get a job and she would feel all right about it. There would be one more scene maybe before he got away. He would not go down to his father's office. He would miss that one. He wanted his life to go smoothly. It had just gotten going that way. Well, that was all over now, anyway. He would go over to the schoolyard and watch Helen play indoor baseball.

CONSIDERATIONS FOR CRITICAL THINKING AND WRITING

1. FIRST RESPONSE. The title, "Soldier's Home," focuses on the setting. Do you have a clear picture of Krebs's home? Describe it, filling in missing details from your associations of home, Krebs's routine, or anything else you can use.

2. What does the photograph of Krebs, the corporal, and the German girls reveal?

3. Belleau Wood, Soissons, the Champagne, St. Mihiel, and the Argonne were the sites of fierce and bloody fighting. What effect have these battles had on Krebs? Why do you think he won't talk about them to the people at home?

4. Why does Krebs avoid complications and consequences? How has the war changed his attitudes toward work and women? How is his hometown different from Germany and France? What is the conflict in the story?

5. Why do you think Hemingway refers to the protagonist as Krebs rather than Harold? What is the significance of his sister calling him "Hare"?

6. How does Krebs's mother embody the community's values? What does Krebs think of those values?

7. Why can't Krebs pray with his mother?

8. What is the resolution to Krebs's conflict?

9. Comment on the appropriateness of the story's title.

10. Explain how Krebs's war experiences are present throughout the story even though we get no details about them.

11. CRITICAL STRATEGIES. Read the section on reader-response criticism (pp. 2109–11) in Chapter 52, "Critical Strategies for Reading," and consider the following: Perhaps, after having been away from home for a time, you have returned to find yourself alienated from your family or friends. Describe your experience. What caused the change? How does this experience affect your understanding of Krebs? Alternately, if alienation hasn't been your experience, how does that difference affect your reading of Krebs?

CONNECTIONS TO OTHER SELECTIONS

1. Contrast the attitudes toward patriotism implicit in this story with those in Tim O'Brien's "How to Tell a True War Story" (p. 548). How do the stories' settings help to account for the differences between them?

2. How might Krebs's rejection of his community's values be related to Sammy's relationship to his supermarket job in John Updike's "A & P" (p. 606)? What details does Updike use to make the setting in "A & P" a comic, though nonetheless serious, version of Krebs's hometown?

3. Explain how the violent details that Tim O'Brien uses to establish the setting in "How to Tell a True War Story" (p. 548) can be considered representative of the kinds of horrors that haunt Krebs after he returns home.

PERSPECTIVES

E. E. CUMMINGS (1894–1962)

my sweet old etcetera   1926

my sweet old etcetera
aunt lucy during the recent

war could and what
is more did tell you just
what everybody was fighting   5

for,
my sister

isabel created hundreds
(and
hundreds) of socks not to   10

mention shirts fleaproof earwarmers

etcetera wristers etcetera, my

mother hoped that

i would die etcetera
bravely of course my father used   15
to become hoarse talking about how it was
a privilege and if only he
could meanwhile my

self etcetera lay quietly
in the deep mud et   20

cetera
(dreaming,
et
   cetera, of
Your smile   25
eyes knees and of your Etcetera)

CONSIDERATIONS FOR CRITICAL THINKING AND WRITING

1. Compare and contrast the narrator's view of the home front with
   Krebs's in "Soldier's Home." To what extent does he sound like Krebs?
   Are there any significant differences between the narrator's voice and
   Krebs's?

2. Write an essay on images of home in "my sweet old etcetera" and "Soldier's
   Home." Consider how the setting is used in each work to suggest the nature of the conflict.

ERNEST HEMINGWAY (1899–1961)
On What Every Writer Needs   *1954*

The most essential gift for a good writer is a built-in, shock-proof, shit detector. This is the writer's radar and all great writers have had it.

From *Writers at Work: The Paris Review Interviews* (Second Series)

CONSIDERATIONS FOR CRITICAL THINKING AND WRITING

1. Hemingway is typically forthright here, but it is tempting to dismiss his
   point as simply humorous. Take him seriously. What does he insist a good
   writer must be able to do?

2. How might Krebs in Hemingway's "Soldier's Home" (p. 152) be seen as having a similar kind of "shit detector" and "radar"?

3. Try writing a pithy, quotable statement that makes an observation about
   reading or writing.

Ron Hansen (b. 1947)

Born in Omaha, Nebraska, Ron Hansen holds a B.A. from Creighton University, an M.F.A. from the University of Iowa, and an M.A. in spirituality from Santa Clara University. He has received numerous fellowships and awards, including the Award in Literature from the American Academy and Institute of Arts and Letters. Hansen has taught writing and literature at Stanford, the University of Michigan, Cornell, and the University of Iowa, and is currently the Gerard Manley Hopkins, S.J., Professor in the Arts and Humanities at Santa Clara University. He is the author of five novels — *Desperadoes: A Novel* (1979), *Mariette in Ecstasy* (1992), *Atticus* (1996), *The Assassination of Jesse James by the Coward Robert Ford* (1997), and *Hitler's Niece* (1999) — a collection of short fiction, *Nebraska: Stories* (1989), and a children's book, *The Shadowmaker* (1989). Hansen's works tend to smudge generic lines, partaking freely of popular modes such as the murder mystery and the western, and to emphasize spiritual conflicts within his characters.

Web *Research Ron Hansen with LitLinks at*
http://www.bedfordstmartins.com/meyer/bedintrolit

Nebraska   *1989*

The town is Americus, Covenant, Denmark, Grange, Hooray, Jerusalem, Sweetwater — one of the lesser-known moons of the Platte, conceived in sickness and misery by European pioneers who took the path of least resistance and put down roots in an emptiness like the one they kept secret in their youth. In Swedish and Danish and German and Polish, in anxiety and fury and God's providence, they chopped at the Great Plains with spades, creating green sod houses that crumbled and collapsed in the rain and disappeared in the first persuasive snow and were so low the grown-ups stooped to go inside; and yet were places of ownership and a hard kind of happiness, the places their occupants gravely stood before on those plenary occasions when photographs were taken.

    And then the Union Pacific stopped by, just a camp of white campaign tents and a boy playing his Harpoon° at night, and then a supply store, a depot, a pine water tank, stockyards, and the mean prosperity of the twentieth century. The trains strolling into town to shed a boxcar in the depot sideyard, or crying past at sixty miles per hour, possibly interrupting a girl in her high-wire act, her arms looping up when she tips to one side, the railtop as slippery as a silver spoon. And then the yellow and red locomotive rises up from the heat shimmer over a mile away, the August noonday warping the sight of it, but cinders tapping away from the spikes and the iron rails already vibrating up inside the girl's shoes. She steps down to the roadbed and then into high weeds as the Union Pacific pulls Wyoming coal and Georgia-Pacific lumber and snowplow blades and aslant Japanese pickup trucks through the open

---

Harpoon: A brand-name harmonica.

countryside and on to Omaha. And when it passes by, a worker she knows is opposite her, like a pedestrian at a stoplight, the sun not letting up, the plainsong of grasshoppers going on and on between them until the worker says, "Hot."

Twice the Union Pacific tracks cross over the sidewinding Democrat, the water slow as an oxcart, green as silage, croplands to the east, yards and houses to the west, a green ceiling of leaves in some places, whirlpools showing up in it like spinning plates that lose speed and disappear. In winter and a week or more of just above zero, high-school couples walk the gray ice, kicking up snow as quiet words are passed between them, opinions are mildly compromised, sorrows are apportioned. And Emil Jedlicka unslings his blue-stocked .22 and slogs through high brown weeds and snow, hunting ring-necked pheasant, sidelong rabbits, and — always suddenly — quail, as his little brother Orin sprints across the Democrat in order to slide like an otter.

July in town is a gray highway and a Ford hay truck spraying by, the hay sailing like a yellow ribbon caught in the mouth of a prancing dog, and Billy Awalt up there on the camel's hump, eighteen years old and sweaty and dirty, peppered and dappled with hay dust, a lump of chew like an extra thumb under his lower lip, his blue eyes happening on a Dairy Queen and a pretty girl licking a pale trickle of ice cream from the cone. And Billy slaps his heart and cries, "Oh! I am pierced!"

And late October is orange on the ground and blue overhead and grain 5
silos stacked up like white poker chips, and a high silver water tower belittled one night by the sloppy tattoo of one year's class at George W. Norris High. And below the silos and water tower are stripped treetops, their gray limbs still lifted up in alleluia, their yellow leaves crowding along yard fences and sheeping along the sidewalks and alleys under the shepherding wind.

Or January and a heavy snow partitioning the landscape, whiting out the highways and woods and cattle lots until there are only open spaces and steamed-up windowpanes, and a Nordstrom boy limping pitifully in the hard plaster of his clothes, the snow as deep as his hips when the boy tips over and cannot get up until a little Schumacher girl sitting by the stoop window, a spoon in her mouth, a bowl of Cheerios in her lap, says in plain voice, "There's a boy," and her mother looks out to the sidewalk.

Houses are big and white and two stories high, each a cousin to the next, with pigeon roosts in the attic gables, green storm windows on the upper floor, and a green screened porch, some as pillowed and couched as parlors or made into sleeping rooms for the boy whose next step will be the Navy and days spent on a ship with his hometown's own population, on gray water that rises up and is allayed like a geography of cornfields, sugar beets, soybeans, wheat, that stays there and says, in its own way, "Stay." Houses are turned away from the land and toward whatever is not always, sitting across from each other like dressed-up children at a party in daylight, their parents looking on with hopes and fond expectations. Overgrown elm and sycamore trees poach the sunlight from the lawns and keep petticoats of snow around them into April. In the deep lots out back are wire clotheslines with flapping white sheets pinned to them, property lines are hedged with sour green and purple grapes, or with rabbit wire and gardens of peonies, roses, gladiola, irises, marigolds, pansies. Fruit trees are so closely planted that they cannot sway without knitting. The apples and cherries drop and sweetly decompose until they're only slight brown bumps in the yards, but the pears stay up in the wind, drooping under the pecks of birds, withering down like peppers until their sorrow is justly noticed and they one day disappear.

Aligned against an alley of blue shale rock is a garage whose doors slash weeds and scrape up pebbles as an old man pokily swings them open, teetering with his last weak push. And then Victor Johnson rummages inside, being cautious about his gray sweater and high-topped shoes, looking over paint cans, junked electric motors, grass rakes and garden rakes and a pitchfork and sickles, gray doors and ladders piled overhead in the rafters, and an old windup Victrola and heavy platter records from the twenties, on one of them a soprano singing "I'm a Lonesome Melody." Under a green tarpaulin is a wooden movie projector he painted silver and big cans of tan celluloid, much of it orange and green with age, but one strip of it preserved: of an Army pilot in jodhpurs hopping from one biplane onto another's upper wing. Country people who'd paid to see the movie had been spellbound by the slight dip of the wings at the pilot's jump, the slap of his leather jacket, and how his hair strayed wild and was promptly sleeked back by the wind. But looking at the strip now, pulling a ribbon of it up to a windowpane and letting it unspool to the ground, Victor can make out only twenty frames of the leap, and then snapshot after snapshot of an Army pilot clinging to the biplane's wing. And yet Victor stays with it, as though that scene of one man staying alive were what he'd paid his nickel for.

Main Street is just a block away. Pickup trucks stop in it so their drivers can angle out over their brown left arms and speak about crops or praise the weather or make up sentences whose only real point is their lack of complication. And then a cattle truck comes up and they mosey along with a touch of their cap bills or a slap of the door metal. High-school girls in skin-tight jeans stay in one place on weekends, and jacked-up cars cruise past, rowdy farmboys overlapping inside, pulling over now and then in order to give the girls cigarettes and sips of pop and grief about their lipstick. And when the cars peel out, the girls say how a particular boy measured up or they swap gossip about Donna Moriarity and the scope she permitted Randy when he came back from boot camp.

Everyone is famous in this town. And everyone is necessary. Townspeople   10 go to the Vaughn Grocery Store for the daily news, and to the Home Restaurant for history class, especially at evensong when the old people eat graveled pot roast and lemon meringue pie and calmly sip coffee from cups they tip to their mouths with both hands. The Kiwanis Club meets here on Tuesday nights, and hopes are made public, petty sins are tidily dispatched, the proceeds from the gumball machines are tallied up and poured into the upkeep of a playground. Yutesler's Hardware has picnic items and kitchen appliances in its one window, in the manner of those prosperous men who would prefer to be known for their hobbies. And there is one crisp, white, Protestant church with a steeple, of the sort pictured on calendars; and the Immaculate Conception Catholic Church, grayly holding the town at bay like a Gothic wolfhound. And there is an insurance agency, a county coroner and justice of the peace, a secondhand shop, a handsome chiropractor named Koch who coaches the Pony League baseball team, a post office approached on unpainted wood steps outside of a cheap mobile home, the Nighthawk tavern where there's Falstaff tap beer, a green pool table, a poster recording the Cornhuskers scores, a crazy man patiently tolerated, a gray-haired woman with an unmoored eye, a boy in spectacles thick as paperweights, a carpenter missing one index finger, a plump waitress whose day job is in a basement beauty shop, an old woman who creeps up to the side door at eight in order to purchase one shot glass of whiskey.

And yet passing by, and paying attention, an outsider is only aware of what isn't, that there's no bookshop, no picture show, no pharmacy or dry cleaners, no cocktail parties, extreme opinions, jewelry or piano stores, motels, hotels, hospital, political headquarters, philosophical theories about Being and the soul.

High importance is only attached to practicalities, and so there is the Batchelor Funeral Home, where a proud old gentleman is on display in a dark brown suit, his yellow fingernails finally clean, his smeared eyeglasses in his coat pocket, a grandchild on tiptoes by the casket, peering at the lips that will not move, the sparrow chest that will not rise. And there's Tommy Seymour's for Sinclair gasoline and mechanical repairs, a green balloon dinosaur bobbing from a string over the cash register, old tires piled beneath the cottonwood, For Sale in the sideyard a Case tractor, a John Deere reaper, a hay mower, a red manure spreader, and a rusty grain conveyor, green weeds overcoming them, standing up inside them, trying slyly and little by little to inherit machinery for the earth.

And beyond that are woods, a slope of pasture, six empty cattle pens, a driveway made of limestone pebbles, and the house where Alice Sorensen pages through a child's World Book Encyclopedia, stopping at the descriptions of California, Capetown, Ceylon, Colorado, Copenhagen, Corpus Christi, Costa Rica, Cyprus.

Widow Dworak has been watering the lawn in an open raincoat and apron, but at nine she walks the green hose around to the spigot and screws down the nozzle so that the spray is a misty crystal bowl softly baptizing the ivy. She says, "How about some camomile tea?" And she says, "Yum. Oh, boy. That hits the spot." And bends to shut the water off.

The Union Pacific night train rolls through town just after ten o'clock 15 when a sixty-year-old man named Adolf Schooley is a boy again in bed, and when the huge weight of forty or fifty cars jostles his upstairs room like a motor he'd put a quarter in. And over the sighing industry of the train, he can hear the train saying *Nebraska, Nebraska, Nebraska, Nebraska.* And he cannot sleep.

Mrs. Antoinette Heft is at the Home Restaurant, placing frozen meat patties on waxed paper, pausing at times to clamp her fingers under her arms and press the sting from them. She stops when the Union Pacific passes, then picks a cigarette out of a pack of Kools and smokes it on the back porch, smelling air as crisp as Oxydol, looking up at stars the Pawnee Indians looked at, hearing the low harmonica of big rigs on the highway, in the town she knows like the palm of her hand, in the country she knows by heart.

CONSIDERATIONS FOR CRITICAL THINKING AND WRITING

1. FIRST RESPONSE. How does the author's treatment of setting make you feel about the small Nebraska town described in the story?

2. In what sense is this piece of writing a *story*? Is there a conflict and a plot? Explain.

3. A number of people populate this story; describe the story's central character.

4. Comment on the author's use of detail to convey emotions and values. Use specific passages to illustrate your points.

5. How does the author organize his description of this Nebraska town?

6. Try writing a description of a place you know well that strongly conveys some kind of emotion or idea about it.

CONNECTIONS TO OTHER SELECTIONS

1. How is the meaning of "home" essential to the meanings of "Nebraska" and Hemingway's "Soldier's Home" (p. 152)?

2. Compare and contrast the tone of the setting in "Nebraska" with that of David Updike's in "Summer" (p. 316).

PERSPECTIVE

RON HANSEN (B. 1947)

On "Nebraska" as an Unconventional Short Story

An editor at *Prairie Schooner* asked if I'd written a short story with a Nebraska setting, for there was going to be a special anniversary issue of the literary quarterly celebrating its many years in the state. Although I'd grown up in Nebraska, I hadn't written any fiction specifically about it and decided it was high time I did. And so I began jotting down snapshot memories of things I'd seen, small towns I'd visited, and strangers with whom I'd had brief encounters as a child. The helter-skelter of memory meant there was no chronological sequence to the scenes and thus no plot except for the mystery of why one sudden glimpse or description seemed to invite and connect to another. I gradually began thinking of "Nebraska" as a hybrid of fiction and poetry and finally let it unfasten itself from the rules and limitations of the short story form.

From a correspondence to Michael Meyer,
December 19, 2000

CONSIDERATIONS FOR CRITICAL THINKING AND WRITING

1. In what sense can "Nebraska" be accurately described as a collection of "snapshot memories"? What makes it more than a series of photographs?

2. What, in your view, connects the various scenes presented in "Nebraska"? What do you think Hansen means by the phrase "helter-skelter of memory"?

3. How is "Nebraska" a "hybrid of fiction and poetry"? Choose a passage and explain why it seems especially poetic to you.

FAY WELDON (B. 1933)

Born in England and raised in New Zealand, Fay Weldon graduated from St. Andrew's University in Scotland. She wrote advertising copy for various companies and was a propaganda writer for the British Foreign Office before turning to fiction. She has written novels, short stories, plays, and radio scripts. In 1971 her script for an episode of "Upstairs, Downstairs" won an award from the Society of Film and Television Arts. She has written more than a score of novels, including *The Fat Woman's Joke* (1967), *Down Among the Women* (1971), *Praxis* (1978), *The Life and Loves of a She-Devil* (1983), and *Life Force* (1991), and an equal number of plays and scripts. Her collections of short stories include *Moon Over Minneapolis* (1992), *Wicked Women* (American edition, 1997), and *A Hard Time to Be a Father* (1998). Weldon often uses ironic humor to portray carefully drawn female characters coming to terms with the facts of their lives.

Web   *Research Fay Weldon with LitLinks at*
http://www.bedfordstmartins.com/meyer/bedintrolit

IND AFF   1988
or Out of Love in Sarajevo

This is a sad story. It has to be. It rained in Sarajevo, and we had expected fine weather.

The rain filled up Sarajevo's pride, two footprints set into a pavement which mark the spot where the young assassin Princip stood to shoot the Archduke Franz Ferdinand and his wife. (Don't forget his wife: everyone forgets his wife, the archduchess.) That was in the summer of 1914. Sarajevo is a pretty town, Balkan style, mountain-rimmed. A broad, swift, shallow river runs through its center, carrying the mountain snow away, arched by many bridges. The one nearest the two footprints has been named the Princip Bridge. The young man is a hero in these parts. Not only does he bring in the tourists — look, look, the spot, the very spot! — but by his action, as everyone knows, he lit a spark which fired the timber which caused World War I which crumbled the Austro-Hungarian Empire, the crumbling of which made modern Yugoslavia possible. Forty million dead (or was it thirty?) but who cares? So long as he loved his country.

The river, they say, can run so shallow in the summer it's known derisively as "the wet road." Today, from what I could see through the sheets of falling rain, it seemed full enough. Yugoslavian streets are always busy — no one stays home if they can help it (thus can an indecent shortage of housing space create a sociable nation) and it seemed as if by common consent a shield of bobbing umbrellas had been erected two meters high to keep the rain off the streets. It just hadn't worked around Princip's corner.

"Come all this way," said Peter, who was a professor of classical history, "and you can't even see the footprints properly, just two undistinguished puddles." Ah, but I loved him. I shivered for his disappointment. He was supervising my thesis on varying concepts of morality and duty in the early Greek States as evidenced in their poetry and drama. I was dependent upon him for my academic future. He said I had a good mind but not a first-class mind and somehow I didn't take it as an insult. I had a feeling first-class minds weren't all that good in bed.

Sarajevo is in Bosnia, in the center of Yugoslavia, that grouping of un- 5
likely states, that distillation of languages into the phonetic reasonableness of

Serbo-Croatian. We'd sheltered from the rain in an ancient mosque in Serbian Belgrade; done the same in a monastery in Croatia; now we spent a wet couple of days in Sarajevo beneath other people's umbrellas. We planned to go on to Montenegro, on the coast, where the fish and the artists come from, to swim and lie in the sun, and recover from the exhaustion caused by the sexual and moral torments of the last year. It couldn't possibly go on raining forever. Could it? Satellite pictures showed black clouds swishing gently all over Europe, over the Balkans, into Asia—practically all the way from Moscow to London, in fact. It wasn't that Peter and myself were being singled out. No. It was raining on his wife, too, back in Cambridge.

Peter was trying to decide, as he had been for the past year, between his wife and myself as his permanent life partner. To this end we had gone away, off the beaten track, for a holiday; if not with his wife's blessing, at least with her knowledge. Were we really, truly suited? We had to be sure, you see, that this was more than just any old professor-student romance; that it was the Real Thing, because the longer the indecision went on the longer Mrs. Piper would be left dangling in uncertainty and distress. They had been married for twenty-four years; they had stopped loving each other a long time ago, of course—but there would be a fearful personal and practical upheaval entailed if he decided to leave permanently and shack up, as he put it, with me. Which I certainly wanted him to do. I loved him. And so far I was winning hands down. It didn't seem much of a contest at all, in fact. I'd been cool and thin and informed on the seat next to him in a Zagreb theater (Mrs. Piper was sweaty and only liked telly); was now eager and anxious for social and political instruction in Sarajevo (Mrs. Piper spat in the face of knowledge, he'd once told me); and planned to be lissome (and I thought topless but I hadn't quite decided: this might be the area where the age difference showed) while I splashed and shrieked like a bathing belle in the shallows of the Montenegrin coast. (Mrs. Piper was a swimming coach: I imagined she smelt permanently of chlorine.)

In fact so far as I could see, it was no contest at all between his wife and myself. But Peter liked to luxuriate in guilt and indecision. And I loved him with an inordinate affection.

Princip's prints are a meter apart, placed as a modern cop on a training shoot-out would place his feet—the left in front at a slight outward angle, the right behind, facing forward. There seemed great energy focused here. Both hands on the gun, run, stop, plant the feet, aim, fire! I could see the footprints well enough, in spite of Peter's complaint. They were clear enough to me.

We went to a restaurant for lunch, since it was too wet to do what we loved to do: that is, buy bread, cheese, sausage, wine, and go off somewhere in our hired car, into the woods or the hills, and picnic and make love. It was a private restaurant—Yugoslavia went over to a mixed capitalist-communist economy years back, so you get either the best or worst of both systems, depending on your mood—that is to say, we knew we would pay more but be given a choice. We chose the wild boar.

"Probably ordinary pork soaked in red cabbage water to darken it," said   10 Peter. He was not in a good mood.

Cucumber salad was served first.

"Everything in this country comes with cucumber salad," complained Peter. I noticed I had become used to his complaining. I supposed that when you had been married a little you simply wouldn't hear it. He was forty-six and I was twenty-five.

"They grow a lot of cucumber," I said.

"If they can grow cucumbers," Peter then asked, "why can't they grow *mange-tout°?*" It seemed a why-can't-they-eat-cake sort of argument to me, but not knowing enough about horticulture not to be outflanked if I debated the point, I moved the subject on to safer ground.

"I suppose Princip's action couldn't really have started World War I," I re- 15 marked. "Otherwise, what a thing to have on your conscience! One little shot and the deaths of thirty million."

"Forty," he corrected me. Though how they reckon these things and get them right I can't imagine. "Of course he didn't start the war. That's just a simple tale to keep the children quiet. It takes more than an assassination to start a war. What happened was that the buildup of political and economic tensions in the Balkans was such that it had to find some release."

"So it was merely the shot that lit the spark that fired the timber that started the war, et cetera?"

"Quite," he said. "World War I would have had to have started sooner or later."

"A bit later or a bit sooner," I said, "might have made the difference of a million or so; if it was you on the battlefield in the mud and the rain you'd notice; exactly when they fired the starting-pistol; exactly when they blew the final whistle. Is that what they do when a war ends; blow a whistle? So that everyone just comes in from the trenches."

But he wasn't listening. He was parting the flesh of the soft collapsed 20 orangey-red pepper which sat in the middle of his cucumber salad; he was carefully extracting the pips. His nan had once told him they could never be digested, would stick inside and do terrible damage. I loved him for his dexterity and patience with his knife and fork. I'd finished my salad yonks ago, pips and all. I was hungry. I wanted my wild boar.

Peter might be forty-six, but he was six foot two and grizzled and muscled with it, in a dark-eyed, intelligent, broad-jawed kind of way. I adored him. I loved to be seen with him. "Muscular academic, not weedy academic" as my younger sister Clare once said. "Muscular academic is just a generally superior human being: everything works well from the brain to the toes. Weedy academic is when there isn't enough vital energy in the person, and the brain drains all the strength from the other parts." Well, Clare should know. Clare is only twenty-three, but of the superior human variety kind herself, vividly pretty, bright and competent — somewhere behind a heavy curtain of vibrant red hair, which she only parts for effect. She had her first degree at twenty. Now she's married to a Harvard professor of economics seconded to the United Nations. She can even cook. I gave up competing yonks ago. Though she too is capable of self-deception. I would say her husband was definitely of the weedy academic rather than the muscular academic type. And they have to live in Brussels.

mange-tout: A sugar pea or bean (French).

The archduke's chauffeur had lost his way, and was parked on the corner trying to recover his nerve when Princip came running out of a café, planted his feet, aimed, and fired. Princip was nineteen — too young to hang. But they sent him to prison for life and, since he had TB to begin with, he only lasted three years. He died in 1918, in an Austrian prison. Or perhaps it was more than TB: perhaps they gave him a hard time, not learning till later, when the Austro-Hungarian Empire collapsed, that he was a hero. Poor Princip, too young to die — like so many other millions. Dying for love of a country.

"I love you," I said to Peter, my living man, progenitor already of three children by his chlorinated, swimming-coach wife.

"How much do you love me?"

"Inordinately! I love you with inordinate affection." It was a joke between 25 us. Ind Aff!

"Inordinate affection is a sin," he'd told me. "According to the Wesleyans. John Wesley° himself worried about it to such a degree he ended up abbreviating it in his diaries, Ind Aff. He maintained that what he felt for young Sophy, the eighteen-year-old in his congregation, was not Ind Aff, which bears the spirit away from God towards the flesh: he insisted that what he felt was a pure and spiritual, if passionate, concern for her soul."

Peter said now, as we waited for our wild boar, and he picked over his pepper, "Your Ind Aff is my wife's sorrow, that's the trouble." He wanted, I knew, one of the long half-wrangles, half soul-sharings that we could keep going for hours, and led to piercing pains in the heart which could only be made better in bed. But our bedroom at the Hotel Europa was small and dark and looked out into the well of the building — a punishment room if ever there was one. (Reception staff did sometimes take against us.) When Peter had tried to change it in his quasi-Serbo-Croatian, they'd shrugged their Bosnian shoulders and pretended not to understand, so we'd decided to put up with it. I did not fancy pushing hard single beds together — it seemed easier not to have the pain in the heart in the first place. "Look," I said, "this holiday is supposed to be just the two of us, not Mrs. Piper as well. Shall we talk about something else?"

Do not think that the archduke's chauffeur was merely careless, an inefficient chauffeur, when he took the wrong turning. He was, I imagine, in a state of shock, fright, and confusion. There had been two previous attempts on the archduke's life since the cavalcade had entered town. The first was a bomb which got the car in front and killed its driver. The second was a shot fired by none other than young Princip, which had missed. Princip had vanished into the crowd and gone to sit down in a corner café and ordered coffee to calm his nerves. I expect his hand trembled at the best of times — he did have TB. (Not the best choice of assassin, but no doubt those who arrange these things have to make do with what they can get.) The archduke's chauffeur panicked, took the wrong road, realized what he'd done, and stopped to await rescue and instructions just outside the café where Princip sat drinking his coffee.

"What shall we talk about?" asked Peter, in even less of a good mood.

John Wesley (1703-1791): English religious leader and founder of Methodism.

"The collapse of the Austro-Hungarian Empire?" I suggested. "How does 30 an empire collapse? Is there no money to pay the military or the police, so everyone goes home? Or what?" He liked to be asked questions.

"The Hungro-Austrarian Empire," said Peter to me, "didn't so much collapse as fail to exist any more. War destroys social organizations. The same thing happened after World War II. There being no organized bodies left between Moscow and London—and for London read Washington, then as now—it was left to these two to put in their own puppet governments. Yalta, 1944. It's taken the best part of forty-five years for nations of West and East Europe to remember who they are."

"Austro-Hungarian," I said, "not Hungro-Austrarian."

"I didn't say Hungro-Austrarian," he said.

"You did," I said.

"Didn't," he said. "What the hell are they doing about our wild boar? Are 35 they out in the hills shooting it?"

My sister Clare had been surprisingly understanding about Peter. When I worried about him being older, she pooh-poohed it; when I worried about him being married, she said, "Just go for it, sister. If you can unhinge a marriage, it's ripe for unhinging, it would happen sooner or later, it might as well be you. See a catch, go ahead and catch! Go for it!"

Princip saw the archduke's car parked outside, and went for it. Second chances are rare in life: they must be responded to. Except perhaps his second chance was missing in the first place? Should he have taken his cue from fate, and just sat and finished his coffee, and gone home to his mother? But what's a man to do when he loves his country? Fate delivered the archduke into his hands: how could he resist it? A parked car, a uniformed and medaled chest, the persecutor of his country—how could Princip not, believing God to be on his side, but see this as His intervention, push his coffee aside and leap to his feet?

Two waiters stood idly by and watched us waiting for our wild boar. One was young and handsome in a mountainous Bosnian way—flashing eyes, hooked nose, luxuriant black hair, sensuous mouth. He was about my age. He smiled. His teeth were even and white. I smiled back, and instead of the pain in the heart I'd become accustomed to as an erotic sensation, now felt, quite violently, an associated yet different pang which got my lower stomach. The true, the real pain of Ind Aff!

"Fancy him?" asked Peter.

"No," I said. "I just thought if I smiled the wild boar might come quicker." 40

The other waiter was older and gentler: his eyes were soft and kind. I thought he looked at me reproachfully. I could see why. In a world which for once, after centuries of savagery, was finally full of young men, unslaughtered, what was I doing with this man with thinning hair?

"What are you thinking of?" Professor Piper asked me. He liked to be in my head.

"How much I love you," I said automatically, and was finally aware how much I lied. "And about the archduke's assassination," I went on, to cover the kind of tremble in my head as I came to my senses, "and let's not forget his wife, she died too—how can you say World War I would have happened anyway. If Princip hadn't shot the archduke, something else, some undisclosed, unsuspected variable, might have come along and defused the whole political/military situation, and neither World War I nor II ever happened. We'll just never know, will we?"

I had my passport and my travelers' checks with me. (Peter felt it was less confusing if we each paid our own way.) I stood up, and took my raincoat from the peg.

"Where are you going?" he asked, startled. 45

"Home," I said. I kissed the top of his head, where it was balding. It smelt gently of chlorine, which may have come from thinking about his wife so much, but might merely have been that he'd taken a shower that morning. ("The water all over Yugoslavia, though safe to drink, is unusually chlorinated": Guide Book.) As I left to catch a taxi to the airport the younger of the two waiters emerged from the kitchen with two piled plates of roasted wild boar, potatoes duchesse, and stewed peppers. ("Yugoslavian diet is unusually rich in proteins and fats": Guide Book.) I could tell from the glisten of oil that the food was no longer hot, and I was not tempted to stay, hungry though I was. Thus fate—or was it Bosnian willfulness?—confirmed the wisdom of my intent.

And that was how I fell out of love with my professor, in Sarajevo, a city to which I am grateful to this day, though I never got to see very much of it, because of the rain.

It was a silly sad thing to do, in the first place, to confuse mere passing academic ambition with love: to try and outdo my sister Clare. (Professor Piper was spiteful, as it happened, and did his best to have my thesis refused, but I went to appeal, which he never thought I'd dare, and won. I had a first-class mind after all.) A silly sad episode, which I regret. As silly and sad as Princip, poor young man, with his feverish mind, his bright tubercular cheeks, and his inordinate affection for his country, pushing aside his cup of coffee, leaping to his feet, taking his gun in both hands, planting his feet, aiming, and firing—one, two, three shots—and starting World War I. The first one missed, the second got the wife (never forget the wife), and the third got the archduke and a whole generation, and their children, and their children's children, and on and on forever. If he'd just hung on a bit, there in Sarajevo, that June day, he might have come to his senses. People do, sometimes quite quickly.

CONSIDERATIONS FOR CRITICAL THINKING AND WRITING

1. FIRST RESPONSE. Do you agree with Weldon's first line, "This is a sad story"? Explain why or why not.

2. How does the rain establish the mood for the story in the first five paragraphs?

3. Characterize Peter. What details concerning him reveal his personality?

4. Describe the narrator's relationship with Peter. How do you think he regards her? Why is she attracted to him?

5. Why is Sarajevo important for the story's setting? What is the effect of having the story of Princip's assassination of the Archduke Franz Ferdinand and his wife woven through the plot?

6. Describe Mrs. Piper. Though she doesn't appear in the story, she does have an important role. What do you think her role is?

7. What is "Ind Aff"? Why is it an important element of this story?

8. What is the significance of the two waiters (paras. 38–40)? How do they affect the narrator?

9. Why does the narrator decide to go home (para. 46)? Do you think she makes a reasoned or an impulsive decision? Explain why you think so.

10. Discuss the relationship between the personal history and the public history recounted in the story. How are the two interconnected? Explain whether you think it is necessary to be familiar with the assassinations in Sarajevo before reading the story.

11. CRITICAL STRATEGIES. Read the section on cultural criticism (pp. 2104–05) in Chapter 52, "Critical Strategies for Reading." How do you think a cultural critic might describe the nature of the narrator's relationship with her professor given the current attitudes on college campuses concerning teacher-student affairs?

CONNECTIONS TO OTHER SELECTIONS

1. Compare and contrast "IND AFF" and Joyce Carol Oates's "The Lady with the Pet Dog" (p. 201) as love stories. Do you think that the stories end happily, or the way you would want them to end? Are the endings problematic?

2. Explain how Weldon's concept of "Ind Aff" — "inordinate affection" — can be used to make sense of the relationship between Georgiana and Aylmer in Nathaniel Hawthorne's "The Birthmark" (p. 359).

3. How does passion figure in "IND AFF" and in D. H. Lawrence's "The Horse Dealer's Daughter" (p. 585)? Explain how Weldon's and Lawrence's perspectives on passion suggest differing views of love and human relationships.

PERSPECTIVE

FAY WELDON (B. 1933)

On the Importance of Place in "IND AFF"   *1997*

I'm the kind of writer who lives mostly in her head, looking inwards not outwards, more sensitive to people than places, unless the place turns out to be some useful metaphor. In Sarajevo, on a book tour, brooding about Ind. Aff., inordinate affection, these days more unkindly known as neurotic dependency, I was taken to see Princip's footsteps in the sidewalk. Fancy fell away. Here was the metaphor taken physical form — chance and death, so like chance and love. Then later we went up into the hills to eat wild boar and the intellectual Englishmen I was with seemed so pallid and absurd compared to the here-and-now mountain men: people came into perspective inside a landscape. I have a kind of rule of thumb: three preoccupations make a story. I interweaved them, delivered them into paper, and fell back into jet-lagged torpor.

From an interview with Michael Meyer, November 15, 1997

CONSIDERATIONS FOR CRITICAL THINKING AND WRITING

1. Weldon's description of how she began "IND AFF" draws on her personal experience in Sarajevo. How does that experience make its way into the story?

2. Consider Weldon's observation that "Here was the metaphor taken physical form — chance and death, so like chance and love." Do you think her observation works as a summary of the story?

3. Choose any other story in this anthology that can serve as an example of how "people come into perspective inside a landscape," and write an essay about it.

6

Point of View

Because one of the pleasures of reading fiction consists of seeing the world through someone else's eyes, it is easy to overlook the eyes that control our view of the plot, characters, and setting. *Point of view* refers to who tells us the story and how it is told. What we know and how we feel about the events in a story are shaped by the author's choice of a point of view. The teller of a story, the *narrator,* inevitably affects our understanding of the characters' actions by filtering what is told through his or her own perspective. The narrator should not be confused with the author who has created the narrative voice because the two are usually distinct (more on this point later).

If the narrative voice is changed, the story will change. Consider, for example, how different "Bartleby, the Scrivener" (p. 116) would be if Melville had chosen to tell the story from Bartleby's point of view instead of the lawyer's. With Bartleby as narrator, much of the mystery concerning his behavior would be lost. The peculiar force of his saying "I would prefer not to" would be lessened amid all the other things he would have to say as narrator. Moreover, the lawyer's reaction — puzzled, upset, outraged, and finally sympathetic to Bartleby — would be lost too. It would be entirely possible, of course, to write a story from Bartleby's point of view, but it would not be the story Melville wrote.

The possible ways of telling a story are many, and more than one point of view can be worked into a single story. However, the various points of view that storytellers draw on can be conveniently grouped into two broad categories: (1) the third-person narrator and (2) the first-person narrator. The third-person narrator uses *he, she,* or *they* to tell the story and does not participate in the action. The first-person narrator uses *I* and is a major or minor participant in the action. A second-person narrator, *you,* is possible but rarely used because of the awkwardness in thrusting the reader into the story, as in "You are minding your own business on a park bench when a drunk steps out of the bushes and demands your lunch bag."

Let's look now at the most important and most often used variations within first- and third-person narrations.

THIRD-PERSON NARRATOR (Nonparticipant)

1. Omniscient (the narrator takes us inside the character[s])
2. Limited omniscient (the narrator takes us inside one or two characters)
3. Objective (the narrator is outside the character[s])

No type of third-person narrator appears as a character in a story. The *omniscient narrator* is all-knowing. From this point of view, the narrator can move from place to place and pass back and forth through time, slipping into and out of characters as no human being possibly could in real life. This narrator can report the characters' thoughts and feelings as well as what they say and do. In the excerpt from *Tarzan of the Apes* (p. 66), Burroughs's narrator tells us about events concerning Terkoz in another part of the jungle that long preceded the battle between Terkoz and Tarzan. We also learn Tarzan's and Jane's inner thoughts and emotions during the episode. And Burroughs's narrator describes Terkoz as "an arrant coward" and a bully, thereby evaluating the character for the reader. This kind of intrusion is called *editorial omniscience.* In contrast, narration that allows characters' actions and thoughts to speak for themselves is known as *neutral omniscience.* Most modern writers use neutral omniscience so that readers can reach their own conclusions.

The *limited omniscient narrator* is much more confined than the omniscient narrator. With limited omniscience the author very often restricts the narrator to the single perspective of either a major or a minor character. Sometimes a narrator can see into more than one character, particularly in a longer work that focuses, for example, on two characters alternately from one chapter to the next. Short stories, however, frequently are restricted by length to a single character's point of view. The way people, places, and events appear to that character is the way they appear to the reader. The reader has access to the thoughts and feelings of the characters revealed by the narrator, but neither the reader nor the character has access to the inner lives of any of the other characters in the story. The events in Katherine Mansfield's "Miss Brill" (p. 259) are viewed entirely through the protagonist's eyes; we see a French vacation town as an elderly woman does. Miss Brill represents the central consciousness of the story. She unifies the story by being present through all the action. We are not told of anything that happens away from the character because the narration is based on her perception of things.

The most intense use of a central consciousness in narration can be seen in the *stream-of-consciousness technique* developed by modern writers such as James Joyce, Virginia Woolf, and William Faulkner. This technique takes a reader inside a character's mind to reveal perceptions, thoughts, and feelings on a conscious or unconscious level. A stream of consciousness suggests the flow of thought as well as its content; hence, complete sentences may give way to fragments as the character's mind makes rapid associations free of conventional logic or transitions.

The following passage is from Joyce's *Ulysses,* a novel famous for its extended use of this technique. In this paragraph Joyce takes us inside the mind of a character who is describing a funeral:

> Coffin now. Got here before us, dead as he is. Horse looking round at it with his plume skeowways [askew]. Dull eye: collar tight on his neck, pressing on a bloodvessel or something. Do they know what they cart out of here every day? Must be twenty or thirty funerals every day. Then Mount Jerome for the protestants. Funerals all over the world everywhere every minute. Shovelling them under by the cartload doublequick. Thousands every hour. Too many in the world.

The character's thoughts range from specific observations to speculations about death. Joyce creates the illusion that we are reading the character's thoughts as they occur. The stream-of-consciousness technique provides an intimate perspective on a character's thoughts.

In contrast, the ***objective point of view*** employs a narrator who does not see into the mind of any character. From this detached and impersonal perspective, the narrator reports action and dialogue without telling us directly what the character feels and thinks. We observe the characters in much the same way we would perceive events in a film or play: we supply the meanings; no analysis or interpretation is provided by the narrator. This point of view places a heavy premium on dialogue, actions, and details to reveal character.

In Hemingway's "Soldier's Home" (p. 152), a limited omniscient narration is the predominant point of view. Krebs's thoughts and reaction to being home from the war are made available to the reader by the narrator, who tells us that Krebs "felt embarrassed and resentful" or "sick and vaguely nauseated" by the small-town life he has reentered. Occasionally, however, Hemingway uses an objective point of view when he dramatizes particularly tense moments between Krebs and his mother. In the following excerpt, Hemingway's narrator shows us Krebs's feelings instead of telling us what they are. Krebs's response to his mother's concerns is presented without comment. The external details of the scene reveal his inner feelings.

> "I've worried about you so much, Harold," his mother went on. "I know the temptations you must have been exposed to. I know how weak men are. I know what your own dear grandfather, my own father, told us about the Civil War and I have prayed for you. I pray for you all day long, Harold."
> Krebs looked at the bacon fat hardening on his plate.
> "Your father is worried, too," his mother went on. "He thinks you have lost your ambition, that you haven't got a definite aim in life. Charley Simmons,

who is just your age, has a good job and is going to be married. The boys are all settling down; they're all determined to get somewhere; you can see that boys like Charley Simmons are on their way to being really a credit to the community."

Krebs said nothing.

"Don't look that way, Harold. . . ."

When Krebs looks at the bacon fat we can see him cooling and hardening too. Hemingway does not describe the expression on Krebs's face, yet we know it is a look that disturbs his mother as she goes on about what she thinks she knows. Krebs and his mother are clearly tense and upset; the details, action, and dialogue reveal that without the narrator telling the reader how each character feels.

FIRST-PERSON NARRATOR (Participant)

1. Major character
2. Minor character

With a *first-person narrator,* the *I* presents the point of view of only one character's consciousness. The reader is restricted to the perceptions, thoughts, and feelings of that single character. This is Melville's technique with the lawyer in "Bartleby, the Scrivener" (p. 116). Everything learned about the characters, action, and plot comes from the unnamed lawyer. Bartleby remains a mystery because we are limited to what the lawyer knows and reports. The lawyer cannot explain what Bartleby means because he does not entirely know himself. Melville's use of the first person encourages us to identify with the lawyer's confused reaction to Bartleby so that we pay attention not only to the scrivener but to the lawyer's response to him. We are as perplexed as the lawyer and share his effort to make sense of Bartleby.

The lawyer is a major character in Melville's story; indeed, many readers take him to be the protagonist. A first-person narrator can, however, also be a minor character (imagine how different the story would be if it were told by, say, Ginger Nut or by an observer who had little or nothing to do with the action). Faulkner uses an observer in "A Rose for Emily" (p. 75). His *we,* though plural and representative of the town's view of Emily, is nonetheless a first-person narrator.

One of the primary reasons for identifying the point of view in a story is to determine where the author stands in relation to the story. Behind the narrative voice of any story is the author, manipulating events and providing or withholding information. It is a mistake to assume that the narrative voice of a story is the author. The narrator, whether a first-person participant or a third-person nonparticipant, is a creation of the writer. A narrator's perceptions may be accepted, rejected, or modified by an author, depending on how the narrative voice is articulated.

Faulkner seems to have shared the fascination, sympathy, and horror of the narrator in "A Rose for Emily," but Melville must not be so readily identified with the lawyer in "Bartleby, the Scrivener." The lawyer's description of himself as "an eminently *safe* man," convinced "that the easiest way of life is the best," raises the question of how well equipped he is to fathom Bartleby's protest. To make sense of Bartleby, it is also necessary to understand the lawyer's point of view. Until the conclusion of the story, this "*safe* man" is too self-serving, defensive, and obtuse to comprehend the despair embodied in Bartleby and the deadening meaninglessness of Wall Street life.

The lawyer is an ***unreliable narrator,*** whose interpretation of events is different from the author's. We cannot entirely accept the lawyer's assessment of Bartleby because we see that the lawyer's perceptions are not totally to be trusted. Melville does not expect us, for example, to agree with the lawyer's suggestion that the solution to Bartleby's situation might be to "entertain some young gentleman with your conversation" on a trip to Europe. Given Bartleby's awful silences, this absurd suggestion reveals the lawyer's superficial understanding. The lawyer's perceptions frequently do not coincide with those Melville expects his readers to share. Hence, the lawyer's unreliability preserves Bartleby's mysterious nature while revealing the lawyer's sensibilities. The point of view is artistically appropriate for Melville's purposes because the eyes through which we perceive the plot, characters, and setting are also the subject of the story.

Narrators can be unreliable for a variety of reasons: they might lack self-knowledge, like Melville's lawyer, or they might be innocent and inexperienced, like Ralph Ellison's young narrator in "Battle Royal" (p. 231). Youthful innocence frequently characterizes a ***naive narrator*** such as Mark Twain's Huck Finn or Holden Caulfield, J. D. Salinger's twentieth-century version of Huck in *The Catcher in the Rye*. These narrators lack the sophistication to interpret accurately what they see; they are unreliable because the reader must go beyond their understanding of events to comprehend the situations described. Huck and Holden describe their respective social environments, but the reader, with more experience, supplies the critical perspective that each boy lacks. In "Battle Royal" that perspective is supplemented by Ellison's dividing the narration between the young man who experiences events and the mature man who reflects back on those events.

Few generalizations can be made about the advantages or disadvantages of using a specific point of view. What can be said with confidence, however, is that writers choose a point of view to achieve particular effects because point of view determines what we know about the characters and events in a story. We should, therefore, be aware of who is telling the story and whether the narrator sees things clearly and reliably.

The next three works warrant a careful examination of their points of view. In Gish Jen's "Who's Irish?," we hear the voice of a Chinese grandmother attempting to make sense of her daughter's family life. In Anton Chekhov's and Joyce Carol Oates's versions of "The Lady with the Pet Dog," we are presented with similar stories told from two different perspectives that make for intriguing comparisons and contrasts. And in Edwidge Danticat's

"New York Day Women," we are presented with competing points of view by a mother and daughter.

GISH JEN (B. 1956)

The daughter of Chinese immigrants, Gish Jen grew up in Yonkers and Scarsdale, New York, and was educated at Harvard, Stanford, and the Iowa Writers' Workshop. A fellowship at Radcliffe's Bunting Institute led to her first novel, *Typical American* (1991), which describes how Chinese immigrants in the United States are transformed by their efforts to pursue the American dream. Her second novel, *Mona in the Promised Land*, appeared in 1996. Of her own family's experience as immigrants she says, "My parents were born into a culture that puts society first," but "I was born into a culture that puts the individual first. This forced me to carve out a balance for myself." Jen's concern about her characters' identities is close to her own heart: her real name is Lillian but in high school she adopted Gish — after the actress Lillian Gish — because that "was part of becoming a writer" rather than "becoming the person I was supposed to be." Jen's fiction enlarges her readers' sense of what constitutes a "typical American." Her first collection of stories, *Imagining America: Stories from the Promised Land*, appeared in 1991. "Who's Irish?," which first appeared in *The New Yorker*, is collected in *Who's Irish? Stories* (1999); it explores both the difficulties and the humor associated with her characters' struggles with their identities.

Web   *Research Gish Jen with LitLinks at*
http://www.bedfordstmartins.com/meyer/bedintrolit

Who's Irish?   *1998*

In China, people say mixed children are supposed to be smart, and definitely my granddaughter Sophie is smart. But Sophie is wild, Sophie is not like my daughter Natalie, or like me. I am work hard my whole life, and fierce besides. My husband always used to say he is afraid of me, and in our restaurant, busboys and cooks all afraid of me too. Even the gang members come for protection money, they try to talk to my husband. When I am there, they stay away. If they come by mistake, they pretend they are come to eat. They hide behind the menu, they order a lot of food. They talk about their mothers. Oh, my mother have some arthritis, need to take herbal medicine, they say. Oh, my mother getting old, her hair all white now.

I say, Your mother's hair used to be white, but since she dye it, it become black again. Why don't you go home once in a while and take a look? I tell them, Confucius say a filial son knows what color his mother's hair is.

My daughter is fierce too, she is vice president in the bank now. Her new house is big enough for everybody to have their own room, including me. But

Sophie take after Natalie's husband's family, their name is Shea. Irish. I always thought Irish people are like Chinese people, work so hard on the railroad, but now I know why the Chinese beat the Irish. Of course, not all Irish are like the Shea family, of course not. My daughter tell me I should not say Irish this, Irish that.

How do you like it when people say the Chinese this, the Chinese that, she say.

You know, the British call the Irish heathen, just like they call the Chinese, 5 she say.

You think the Opium War was bad, how would you like to live right next door to the British, she say.

And that is that. My daughter have a funny habit when she win an argument, she take a sip of something and look away, so the other person is not embarrassed. So I am not embarrassed. I do not call anybody anything either. I just happen to mention about the Shea family, an interesting fact: four brothers in the family, and not one of them work. The mother, Bess, have a job before she got sick, she was executive secretary in a big company. She is handle everything for a big shot, you would be surprised how complicated her job is, not just type this, type that. Now she is a nice woman with a clean house. But her boys, every one of them is on welfare, or so-called severance pay, or so-called disability pay. Something. They say they cannot find work, this is not the economy of the fifties, but I say, Even the black people doing better these days, some of them live so fancy, you'd be surprised. Why the Shea family have so much trouble? They are white people, they speak English. When I come to this country, I have no money and do not speak English. But my husband and I own our restaurant before he die. Free and clear, no mortgage. Of course, I understand I am just lucky, come from a country where the food is popular all over the world. I understand it is not the Shea family's fault they come from a country where everything is boiled. Still, I say.

She's right, we should broaden our horizons, say one brother, Jim, at Thanksgiving. Forget about the car business. Think about egg rolls.

Pad thai, say another brother, Mike. I'm going to make my fortune in pad thai. It's going to be the new pizza.

I say, You people too picky about what you sell. Selling egg rolls not good 10 enough for you, but at least my husband and I can say, We made it. What can you say? Tell me. What can you say?

Everybody chew their tough turkey.

I especially cannot understand my daughter's husband John, who has no job but cannot take care of Sophie either. Because he is a man, he say, and that's the end of the sentence.

Plain boiled food, plain boiled thinking. Even his name is plain boiled: John. Maybe because I grew up with black bean sauce and hoisin sauce and garlic sauce, I always feel something is missing when my son-in-law talk.

But, okay: so my son-in-law can be man, I am baby-sitter. Six hours a day, same as the old sitter, crazy Amy, who quit. This is not so easy, now that I am sixty-eight, Chinese age almost seventy. Still, I try. In China, daughter take care of mother. Here it is the other way around. Mother help daughter, mother ask, Anything else I can do? Otherwise daughter complain mother is not supportive. I tell daughter, We do not have this word in Chinese, *supportive*. But my daughter too busy to listen, she has to go to meeting, she has to write memo while her husband go to the gym to be a man. My daughter say otherwise he will be depressed. Seems like all his life he has this trouble, depression.

No one wants to hire someone who is depressed, she say. It is important 15 for him to keep his spirits up.

Beautiful wife, beautiful daughter, beautiful house, oven can clean itself automatically. No money left over, because only one income, but lucky enough, got the baby-sitter for free. If John lived in China, he would be very happy. But he is not happy. Even at the gym things go wrong. One day, he pull a muscle. Another day, weight room too crowded. Always something.

Until finally, hooray, he has a job. Then he feel pressure.

I need to concentrate, he say. I need to focus.

He is going to work for insurance company. Salesman job. A paycheck, he say, and at least he will wear clothes instead of gym shorts. My daughter buy him some special candy bars from the health-food store. They say THINK! on them, and are supposed to help John think.

John is a good-looking boy, you have to say that, especially now that he 20 shave so you can see his face.

I am an old man in a young man's game, say John.

I will need a new suit, say John.

This time I am not going to shoot myself in the foot, say John.

Good, I say.

She means to be supportive, my daughter say. Don't start the send her 25 back to China thing, because we can't.

Sophie is three years old American age, but already I see her nice Chinese side swallowed up by her wild Shea side. She looks like mostly Chinese. Beautiful black hair, beautiful black eyes. Nose perfect size, not so flat looks like something fell down, not so large looks like some big deal got stuck in wrong face. Everything just right, only her skin is a brown surprise to John's family. So brown, they say. Even John say it. She never goes in the sun, still she is that color, he say. Brown. They say, Nothing the matter with brown. They are just surprised. So brown. Nattie is not that brown, they say. They say, It seems like Sophie should be a color in between Nattie and John. Seems funny, a girl named Sophie Shea be brown. But she is brown, maybe her name should be Sophie Brown. She never go in the sun, still she is that color, they say. Nothing the matter with brown. They are just surprised.

The Shea family talk is like this sometimes, going around and around like a Christmas-tree train.

Maybe John is not her father, I say one day, to stop the train. And sure enough, train wreck. None of the brothers ever say the word *brown* to me again.

Instead, John's mother, Bess, say, I hope you are not offended.

She say, I did my best on those boys. But raising four boys with no father is 30 no picnic.

You have a beautiful family, I say.

I'm getting old, she say.

You deserve a rest, I say. Too many boys make you old.

I never had a daughter, she say. You have a daughter.

I have a daughter, I say. Chinese people don't think a daughter is so great, 35 but you're right. I have a daughter.

I was never against the marriage, you know, she say. I never thought John was marrying down. I always thought Nattie was just as good as white.

I was never against the marriage either, I say. I just wonder if they look at the whole problem.

Of course you pointed out the problem, you are a mother, she say. And now we both have a granddaughter. A little brown granddaughter, she is so precious to me.

I laugh. A little brown granddaughter, I say. To tell you the truth, I don't know how she came out so brown.

We laugh some more. These days Bess need a walker to walk. She take so 40 many pills, she need two glasses of water to get them all down. Her favorite TV show is about bloopers, and she love her bird feeder. All day long, she can watch that bird feeder, like a cat.

I can't wait for her to grow up, Bess say. I could use some female company.

Too many boys, I say.

Boys are fine, she say. But they do surround you after a while.

You should take a break, come live with us, I say. Lots of girls at our house.

Be careful what you offer, say Bess with a wink. Where I come from, people 45 mean for you to move in when they say a thing like that.

Nothing the matter with Sophie's outside, that's the truth. It is inside that she is like not any Chinese girl I ever see. We go to the park, and this is what she does. She stand up in the stroller. She take off all her clothes and throw them in the fountain.

Sophie! I say. Stop!

But she just laugh like a crazy person. Before I take over as baby-sitter, Sophie has that crazy-person sitter, Amy the guitar player. My daughter thought this Amy very creative — another word we do not talk about in China. In China, we talk about whether we have difficulty or no difficulty. We talk about whether life is bitter or not bitter. In America, all day long, people talk about creative. Never mind that I cannot even look at this Amy, with her shirt so short that her belly button showing. This Amy think Sophie should love her body. So when Sophie take off her diaper, Amy laugh. When Sophie run around naked, Amy say she wouldn't want to wear a diaper either. When Sophie go *shu-shu*, in her lap, Amy laugh and say there are no germs in pee. When Sophie take off her shoes, Amy say bare feet is best, even the pediatrician say so. That is why Sophie now walk around with no shoes like a beggar child. Also why Sophie love to take off her clothes.

Turn around! say the boys in the park. Let's see that ass!

Of course, Sophie does not understand, Sophie clap her hands, I am the 50 only one to say, No! This is not a game.

It has nothing to do with John's family, my daughter say. Amy was too permissive, that's all.

But I think if Sophie was not wild inside, she would not take off her shoes and clothes to begin with.

You never take off your clothes when you were little, I say. All my Chinese friends had babies, I never saw one of them act wild like that.

Look, my daughter say. I have a big presentation tomorrow.

John and my daughter agree Sophie is a problem, but they don't know 55 what to do.

You spank her, she'll stop, I say another day.

But they say, Oh no.

In America, parents not supposed to spank the child.

It gives them low self-esteem, my daughter say. And that leads to problems later, as I happen to know.

My daughter never have big presentation the next day when the subject of spanking come up. 60

I don't want you to touch Sophie, she say. No spanking, period.

Don't tell me what to do, I say.

I'm not telling you what to do, say my daughter. I'm telling you how I feel.

I am not your servant, I say. Don't you dare talk to me like that.

My daughter have another funny habit when she lose an argument. She spread out all her fingers and look at them, as if she like to make sure they are still there. 65

My daughter is fierce like me, but she and John think it is better to explain to Sophie that clothes are a good idea. This is not so hard in the cold weather. In the warm weather, it is very hard.

Use your words, my daughter say. That's what we tell Sophie. How about if you set a good example.

As if good example mean anything to Sophie. I am so fierce, the gang members who used to come to the restaurant all afraid of me, but Sophie is not afraid.

I say, Sophie, if you take off your clothes, no snack.

I say, Sophie, if you take off your clothes, no lunch. 70

I say, Sophie, if you take off your clothes, no park.

Pretty soon we are stay home all day, and by the end of six hours she still did not have one thing to eat. You never saw a child stubborn like that.

I'm hungry! she cry when my daughter come home.

What's the matter, doesn't your grandmother feed you? My daughter laugh.

No! Sophie say. She doesn't feed me anything! 75

My daughter laugh again. Here you go, she say.

She say to John, Sophie must be growing.

Growing like a weed, I say.

Still Sophie take off her clothes, until one day I spank her. Not too hard, but she cry and cry, and when I tell her if she doesn't put her clothes back on I'll spank her again, she put her clothes back on. Then I tell her she is good girl, and give her some food to eat. The next day we go to the park and, like a nice Chinese girl, she does not take off her clothes.

She stop taking off her clothes, I report. Finally! 80

How did you do it? my daughter ask.

After twenty-eight years experience with you, I guess I learn something, I say.

It must have been a phase, John say, and his voice is suddenly like an expert.

His voice is like an expert about everything these days, now that he carry a leather briefcase, and wear shiny shoes, and can go shopping for a new car. On the company, he say. The company will pay for it, but he will be able to drive it whenever he want.

A free car, he say. How do you like that. 85

It's good to see you in the saddle again, my daughter say. Some of your family patterns are scary.

At least I don't drink, he say. He say, And I'm not the only one with scary family patterns.

That's for sure, say my daughter.

Everyone is happy. Even I am happy, because there is more trouble with Sophie, but now I think I can help her Chinese side fight against her wild side. I teach her to eat food with fork or spoon or chopsticks, she cannot just grab into the middle of a bowl of noodles. I teach her not to play with garbage cans. Sometimes I spank her, but not too often, and not too hard.

Still, there are problems. Sophie like to climb everything. If there is a railing, she is never next to it. Always she is on top of it. Also, Sophie like to hit the mommies of her friends. She learn this from her playground best friend, Sinbad, who is four. Sinbad wear army clothes every day and like to ambush his mommy. He is the one who dug a big hole under the play structure, a foxhole he call it, all by himself. Very hardworking. Now he wait in the foxhole with a shovel full of wet sand. When his mommy come, he throw it right at her.

Oh, it's all right, his mommy say. You can't get rid of war games, it's part of their imaginative play. All the boys go through it.

Also, he like to kick his mommy, and one day he tell Sophie to kick his mommy too.

I wish this story is not true.

Kick her, kick her! Sinbad say.

Sophie kick her. A little kick, as if she just so happened was swinging her little leg and didn't realize that big mommy leg was in the way. Still I spank Sophie and make Sophie say sorry, and what does the mommy say?

Really, it's all right, she say. It didn't hurt.

After that, Sophie learn she can attack mommies in the playground, and some will say, Stop, but others will say, Oh, she didn't mean it, especially if they realize Sophie will be punished.

This is how, one day, bigger trouble come. The bigger trouble start when Sophie hide in the foxhole with that shovel full of sand. She wait, and when I come look for her, she throw it at me. All over my nice clean clothes.

Did you ever see a Chinese girl act this way?

Sophie! I say. Come out of there, say you're sorry.

But she does not come out. Instead, she laugh. Naaah, naah-na, naaa-naaa, she say.

I am not exaggerate: millions of children in China, not one act like this.

Sophie! I say. Now! Come out now!

But she know she is in big trouble. She know if she come out, what will happen next. So she does not come out. I am sixty-eight, Chinese age almost seventy, how can I crawl under there to catch her? Impossible. So I yell, yell, yell, and what happen? Nothing. A Chinese mother would help, but American mothers, they look at you, they shake their head, they go home. And, of course, a Chinese child would give up, but not Sophie.

I hate you! she yell. I hate you, Meanie!

Meanie is my new name these days.

Long time this goes on, long long time. The foxhole is deep, you cannot see too much, you don't know where is the bottom. You cannot hear too much either. If she does not yell, you cannot even know she is still there or not. After a while, getting cold out, getting dark out. No one left in the playground, only us.

Sophie, I say. How did you become stubborn like this? I am go home without you now.

I try to use a stick, chase her out of there, and once or twice I hit her, but still she does not come out. So finally I leave. I go outside the gate.

Bye-bye! I say. I'm go home now. 110

But still she does not come out and does not come out. Now it is dinner-time, the sky is black. I think I should maybe go get help, but how can I leave a little girl by herself in the playground? A bad man could come. A rat could come. I go back in to see what is happen to Sophie. What if she have a shovel and is making a tunnel to escape?

Sophie! I say.

No answer.

Sophie!

I don't know if she is alive. I don't know if she is fall asleep down there. If 115 she is crying, I cannot hear her.

So I take the stick and poke.

Sophie! I say. I promise I no hit you. If you come out, I give you a lollipop.

No answer. By now I worried. What to do, what to do, what to do? I poke some more, even harder, so that I am poking and poking when my daughter and John suddenly appear.

What are you doing? What is going on? say my daughter.

Put down that stick! say my daughter. 120

You are crazy! say my daughter.

John wiggle under the structure, into the foxhole, to rescue Sophie.

She fell asleep, say John the expert. She's okay. That is one big hole.

Now Sophie is crying and crying.

Sophia, my daughter say, hugging her. Are you okay, peanut? Are you okay? 125

She's just scared, say John.

Are you okay? I say too. I don't know what happen, I say.

She's okay, say John. He is not like my daughter, full of questions. He is full of answers until we get home and can see by the lamplight.

Will you look at her? he yell then. What the hell happened?

Bruises all over her brown skin, and a swollen-up eye. 130

You are crazy! say my daughter. Look at what you did! You are crazy!

I try very hard, I say.

How could you use a stick? I told you to use your words!

She is hard to handle, I say.

She's three years old! You cannot use a stick! say my daughter. 135

She is not like any Chinese girl I ever saw, I say.

I brush some sand off my clothes. Sophie's clothes are dirty too, but at least she has her clothes on.

Has she done this before? ask my daughter. Has she hit you before?

She hits me all the time, Sophie say, eating ice cream.

Your family, say John. 140

Believe me, say my daughter.

A daughter I have, a beautiful daughter. I took care of her when she could not hold her head up. I took care of her before she could argue with me, when she was a little girl with two pigtails, one of them always crooked. I took care of her when we have to escape from China, I took care of her when suddenly we live in a country with cars everywhere, if you are not careful your little girl get run over. When my husband die, I promise him I will keep the family together, even though it was just two of us, hardly a family at all.

But now my daughter take me around to look at apartments. After all, I can cook, I can clean, there's no reason I cannot live by myself, all I need is a telephone. Of course, she is sorry. Sometimes she cry, I am the one to say everything will be okay. She say she have no choice, she doesn't want to end up divorced. I say divorce is terrible, I don't know who invented this terrible idea. Instead of live with a telephone, though, surprise, I come to live with Bess. Imagine that. Bess make an offer and, sure enough, where she come from, people mean for you to move in when they say things like that. A crazy idea, go to live with someone else's family, but she like to have some female company, not like my daughter, who does not believe in company. These days when my daughter visit, she does not bring Sophie. Bess say we should give Nattie time, we will see Sophie again soon. But seems like my daughter have more presentation than ever before, every time she come she have to leave.

I have a family to support, she say, and her voice is heavy, as if soaking wet. I have a young daughter and a depressed husband and no one to turn to.

When she say no one to turn to, she mean me.   145

These days my beautiful daughter is so tired she can just sit there in a chair and fall asleep. John lost his job again, already, but still they rather hire a baby-sitter than ask me to help, even they can't afford it. Of course, the new baby-sitter is much younger, can run around. I don't know if Sophie these days is wild or not wild. She call me Meanie, but she like to kiss me too, sometimes. I remember that every time I see a child on TV. Sophie like to grab my hair, a fistful in each hand, and then kiss me smack on the nose. I never see any other child kiss that way.

The satellite TV has so many channels, more channels than I can count, including a Chinese channel from the Mainland and a Chinese channel from Taiwan, but most of the time I watch bloopers with Bess. Also, I watch the bird feeder — so many, many kinds of birds come. The Shea sons hang around all the time, asking when will I go home, but Bess tell them, Get lost.

She's a permanent resident, say Bess. She isn't going anywhere.

Then she wink at me, and switch the channel with the remote control.

Of course, I shouldn't say Irish this, Irish that, especially now I am become   150
honorary Irish myself, according to Bess. Me! Who's Irish? I say, and she laugh. All the same, if I could mention one thing about some of the Irish, not all of them of course, I like to mention this: Their talk just stick. I don't know how Bess Shea learn to use her words, but sometimes I hear what she say a long time later. *Permanent resident. Not going anywhere.* Over and over I hear it, the voice of Bess.

CONSIDERATIONS FOR CRITICAL THINKING AND WRITING

   1. FIRST RESPONSE. How sympathetic are you to the grandmother? What did you find likeable about her? Was there anything about her that you didn't like?

2. Imagine this story with an editorial omniscient point of view. How would your response to the protagonist significantly change?

3. Characterize John and Natalie. Do they strike you as familiar types or do they seem as foreign to you as they do to the protagonist? Explain why or why not.

4. What is the conflict in the story? Is there more than one? How are these conflicts resolved?

5. How does the grandmother's use of language serve to characterize her?

6. How are racial stereotypes used in this story for the purposes of humor as well as for making serious points? What are those points?

7. Write a paragraph characterizing the grandmother's view of herself. Then write a descriptive paragraph about the grandmother from Natalie's point of view. Try to capture their voices in your descriptions.

8. Discuss Sinbad's function in the story.

9. How do you interpret the story's final paragraph? What sort of relationship does the grandmother have with Bess?

CONNECTIONS TO OTHER SELECTIONS

1. Compare and contrast the mother/daughter relationship in this story and in Edwidge Danticat's "New York Day Women" (p. 216).

2. Read Mark Twain's "The Story of the Good Little Boy" (p. 603). Based on your reading, what do you think Twain would have to say about Sophie in Jen's story?

ANTON CHEKHOV (1860–1904)

Born in a small town in Russia, Anton Chekhov gave up the career his medical degree prepared him for in order to devote himself to writing. His concentration on realistic detail in the hundreds of short stories he published has had an important influence on fiction writing. Modern drama has also been strengthened by his plays, among them these classics: *The Seagull* (1896), *Uncle Vanya* (1899), *The Three Sisters* (1901), and *The Cherry Orchard* (1904). Chekhov was a close observer of people in ordinary situations who struggle to live their lives as best they can. They are not very often completely successful. Chekhov's compassion, however, makes their failures less significant than their humanity. In "The Lady with the Pet Dog," love is at the heart of a struggle that begins in Yalta, a resort town on the Black Sea.

Web *Research Anton Chekhov with LitLinks at*
http://www.bedfordstmartins.com/meyer/bedintrolit

The Lady with the Pet Dog   *1899*

TRANSLATED BY AVRAHM YARMOLINSKY (1947)

I

A new person, it was said, had appeared on the esplanade: a lady with a pet dog. Dmitry Dmitrich Gurov, who had spent a fortnight at Yalta and had got used to the place, had also begun to take an interest in new arrivals. As he sat in Vernet's confectionery shop, he saw, walking on the esplanade, a fair-haired young woman of medium height, wearing a beret; a white Pomeranian was trotting behind her.

And afterwards he met her in the public garden and in the square several times a day. She walked alone, always wearing the same beret and always with the white dog; no one knew who she was and everyone called her simply "the lady with the pet dog."

"If she is here alone without husband or friends," Gurov reflected, "it wouldn't be a bad thing to make her acquaintance."

He was under forty, but he already had a daughter twelve years old, and two sons at school. They had found a wife for him when he was very young, a student in his second year, and by now she seemed half as old again as he. She was a tall, erect woman with dark eyebrows, stately and dignified and, as she said of herself, intellectual. She read a great deal, used simplified spelling in her letters, called her husband, not Dmitry, but Dimitry, while he privately considered her of limited intelligence, narrow-minded, dowdy, was afraid of her, and did not like to be at home. He had begun being unfaithful to her long ago—had been unfaithful to her often and, probably for that reason, almost always spoke ill of women, and when they were talked of in his presence used to call them "the inferior race."

It seemed to him that he had been sufficiently tutored by bitter experience to call them what he pleased, and yet he could not have lived without "the inferior race" for two days together. In the company of men he was bored and ill at ease, he was chilly and uncommunicative with them; but when he was among women he felt free, and knew what to speak to them about and how to comport himself; and even to be silent with them was no strain on him. In his appearance, in his character, in his whole makeup there was something attractive and elusive that disposed women in his favor and allured them. He knew that, and some force seemed to draw him to them, too.

Oft-repeated and really bitter experience had taught him long ago that with decent people—particularly Moscow people—who are irresolute and slow to move, every affair which at first seems a light and charming adventure inevitably grows into a whole problem of extreme complexity, and in the end a painful situation is created. But at every new meeting with an interesting woman this lesson of experience seemed to slip from his memory, and he was eager for life, and everything seemed so simple and diverting.

One evening while he was dining in the public garden the lady in the beret walked up without haste to take the next table. Her expression, her gait, her dress, and the way she did her hair told him that she belonged to the upper class, that she was married, that she was in Yalta for the first time and alone, and that she was bored there. The stories told of the immorality in Yalta are to a great extent untrue; he despised them, and knew that such stories were made up for the most part by persons who would have been glad to sin themselves if they had had the chance; but when the lady sat down at the next table three paces from him, he recalled these stories of easy conquests, of trips to the mountains, and the tempting thought of swift, fleeting liaison, a romance with an unknown woman of whose very name he was ignorant suddenly took hold of him.

He beckoned invitingly to the Pomeranian, and when the dog approached him, shook his finger at it. The Pomeranian growled; Gurov threatened it again.

The lady glanced at him and at once dropped her eyes.

"He doesn't bite," she said and blushed.   10

"May I give him a bone?" he asked; and when she nodded he inquired affably, "Have you been in Yalta long?"

"About five days."

"And I am dragging out the second week here."

There was a short silence.

"Time passes quickly, and yet it is so dull here!" she said, not looking at him. 15

"It's only the fashion to say it's dull here. A provincial will live in Belyov or Zhizdra and not be bored, but when he comes here it's 'Oh, the dullness! Oh, the dust!' One would think he came from Granada."

She laughed. Then both continued eating in silence, like strangers, but after dinner they walked together and there sprang up between them the light banter of people who are free and contented, to whom it does not matter where they go or what they talk about. They walked and talked of the strange light on the sea: the water was a soft, warm, lilac color, and there was a golden band of moonlight upon it. They talked of how sultry it was after a hot day. Gurov told her that he was a native of Moscow, that he had studied languages and literature at the university, but had a post in a bank; that at one time he had trained to become an opera singer but had given it up, that he owned two houses in Moscow. And he learned from her that she had grown up in Petersburg, but had lived in S—— since her marriage two years previously, that she was going to stay in Yalta for about another month, and that her husband, who needed a rest, too, might perhaps come to fetch her. She was not certain whether her husband was a member of a Government Board or served on a Zemstvo Council,° and this amused her. And Gurov learned too that her name was Anna Sergeyevna.

Afterwards in his room at the hotel he thought about her — and was certain that he would meet her the next day. It was bound to happen. Getting into bed he recalled that she had been a schoolgirl only recently, doing lessons like his own daughter; he thought how much timidity and angularity there was still in her laugh and her manner of talking with a stranger. It must have been the first time in her life that she was alone in a setting in which she was followed, looked at, and spoken to for one secret purpose alone, which she could hardly fail to guess. He thought of her slim, delicate throat, her lovely gray eyes.

"There's something pathetic about her, though," he thought, and dropped off.

Zemstvo Council: A district council.

II

A week had passed since they had struck up an acquaintance. It was a holiday. 20
It was close indoors, while in the street the wind whirled the dust about and
blew people's hats off. One was thirsty all day, and Gurov often went into the
restaurant and offered Anna Sergeyevna a soft drink or ice cream. One did not
know what to do with oneself.

In the evening when the wind had abated they went out on the pier to
watch the steamer come in. There were a great many people walking about the
dock; they had come to welcome someone and they were carrying bunches of
flowers. And two peculiarities of a festive Yalta crowd stood out: the elderly
ladies were dressed like young ones and there were many generals.

Owing to the choppy sea, the steamer arrived late, after sunset, and it was
a long time tacking about before it put in at the pier. Anna Sergeyevna peered
at the steamer and the passengers through her lorgnette as though looking for
acquaintances, and whenever she turned to Gurov her eyes were shining. She
talked a great deal and asked questions jerkily, forgetting the next moment
what she had asked; then she lost her lorgnette in the crush.

The festive crowd began to disperse; it was now too dark to see people's
faces; there was no wind any more, but Gurov and Anna Sergeyevna still stood
as though waiting to see someone else come off the steamer. Anna Sergeyevna
was silent now, and sniffed her flowers without looking at Gurov.

"The weather has improved this evening," he said. "Where shall we go
now? Shall we drive somewhere?"

She did not reply. 25

Then he looked at her intently, and suddenly embraced her and kissed her
on the lips, and the moist fragrance of her flowers enveloped him; and at once
he looked round him anxiously, wondering if anyone had seen them.

"Let us go to your place," he said softly. And they walked off together
rapidly.

The air in her room was close and there was the smell of the perfume she
had bought at the Japanese shop. Looking at her, Gurov thought: "What encounters life offers!" From the past he preserved the memory of carefree,
good-natured women whom love made gay and who were grateful to him for
the happiness he gave them, however brief it might be; and of women like his
wife who loved without sincerity, with too many words, affectedly, hysterically,
with an expression that it was not love or passion that engaged them but
something more significant; and of two or three others, very beautiful, frigid
women, across whose faces would suddenly flit a rapacious expression — an obstinate desire to take from life more than it could give, and these were women
no longer young, capricious, unreflecting, domineering, unintelligent, and
when Gurov grew cold to them their beauty aroused his hatred, and the lace
on their lingerie seemed to him to resemble scales.

But here there was the timidity, the angularity of inexperienced youth, a
feeling of awkwardness; and there was a sense of embarrassment, as though
someone had suddenly knocked at the door. Anna Sergeyevna, "the lady with
the pet dog," treated what had happened in a peculiar way, very seriously, as
though it were her fall — so it seemed, and this was odd and inappropriate. Her
features drooped and faded, and her long hair hung down sadly on either side

of her face; she grew pensive and her dejected pose was that of a Magdalene in a picture by an old master.

"It's not right," she said. "You don't respect me now, you first of all."   30

There was a watermelon on the table. Gurov cut himself a slice and began eating it without haste. They were silent for at least half an hour.

There was something touching about Anna Sergeyevna; she had the purity of a well-bred, naive woman who has seen little of life. The single candle burning on the table barely illumined her face, yet it was clear that she was unhappy.

"Why should I stop respecting you, darling?" asked Gurov. "You don't know what you're saying."

"God forgive me," she said, and her eyes filled with tears. "It's terrible."

"It's as though you were trying to exonerate yourself."   35

"How can I exonerate myself? No. I am a bad, low woman; I despise myself and I have no thought of exonerating myself. It's not my husband but myself I have deceived. And not only just now; I have been deceiving myself for a long time. My husband may be a good, honest man, but he is a flunkey! I don't know what he does, what his work is, but I know he is a flunkey! I was twenty when I married him. I was tormented by curiosity; I wanted something better. 'There must be a different sort of life,' I said to myself. I wanted to live! To live, to live! Curiosity kept eating at me — you don't understand it, but I swear to God I could no longer control myself; something was going on in me: I could not be held back. I told my husband I was ill, and came here. And here I have been walking about as though in a daze, as though I were mad; and now I have become a vulgar, vile woman whom anyone may despise."

Gurov was already bored with her; he was irritated by her naive tone, by her repentance, so unexpected and so out of place; but for the tears in her eyes he might have thought she was joking or play-acting.

"I don't understand, my dear," he said softly. "What do you want?"

She hid her face on his breast and pressed close to him.

"Believe me, believe me, I beg you," she said, "I love honesty and purity,   40
and sin is loathsome to me; I don't know what I'm doing. Simple people say, 'The Evil One has led me astray.' And I may say of myself now that the Evil One has led me astray."

"Quiet, quiet," he murmured.

He looked into her fixed, frightened eyes, kissed her, spoke to her softly and affectionately, and by degrees she calmed down, and her gaiety returned; both began laughing.

Afterwards when they went out there was not a soul on the esplanade. The town with its cypresses looked quite dead, but the sea was still sounding as it broke upon the beach; a single launch was rocking on the waves and on it a lantern was blinking sleepily.

They found a cab and drove to Oreanda.

"I found out your surname in the hall just now: it was written on the   45
board — von Dideritz," said Gurov. "Is your husband German?"

"No; I believe his grandfather was German, but he is Greek Orthodox himself."

At Oreanda they sat on a bench not far from the church, looked down at the sea, and were silent. Yalta was barely visible through the morning mist; white clouds rested motionlessly on the mountaintops. The leaves did not stir

on the trees, cicadas twanged, and the monotonous muffled sound of the sea
that rose from below spoke of the peace, the eternal sleep awaiting us. So it
rumbled below when there was no Yalta, no Oreanda here; so it rumbles now,
and it will rumble as indifferently and as hollowly when we are no more. And
in this constancy, in this complete indifference to the life and death of each of
us, there lies, perhaps, a pledge of our eternal salvation, of the unceasing advance of life upon earth, of unceasing movement towards perfection. Sitting
beside a young woman who in the dawn seemed so lovely, Gurov, soothed and
spellbound by these magical surroundings — the sea, the mountains, the
clouds, the wide sky — thought how everything is really beautiful in this world
when one reflects: everything except what we think or do ourselves when we
forget the higher aims of life and our own human dignity.

A man strolled up to them — probably a guard — looked at them and
walked away. And this detail, too, seemed so mysterious and beautiful. They saw
a steamer arrive from Feodosia, its lights extinguished in the glow of dawn.

"There is dew on the grass," said Anna Sergeyevna, after a silence.

"Yes, it's time to go home."   50

They returned to the city.

Then they met every day at twelve o'clock on the esplanade, lunched and
dined together, took walks, admired the sea. She complained that she slept
badly, that she had palpitations, asked the same questions, troubled now by
jealousy and now by the fear that he did not respect her sufficiently. And often
in the square or the public garden, when there was no one near them, he suddenly drew her to him and kissed her passionately. Complete idleness, these
kisses in broad daylight exchanged furtively in dread of someone's seeing
them, the heat, the smell of the sea, and the continual flitting before his eyes of
idle, well-dressed, well-fed people, worked a complete change in him; he kept
telling Anna Sergeyevna how beautiful she was, how seductive, was urgently
passionate; he would not move a step away from her, while she was often pensive and continually pressed him to confess that he did not respect her, did not
love her in the least, and saw in her nothing but a common woman. Almost
every evening rather late they drove somewhere out of town, to Oreanda or to
the waterfall; and the excursion was always a success, the scenery invariably
impressed them as beautiful and magnificent.

They were expecting her husband, but a letter came from him saying that
he had eye-trouble, and begging his wife to return home as soon as possible.
Anna Sergeyevna made haste to go.

"It's a good thing I am leaving," she said to Gurov. "It's the hand of Fate!"

She took a carriage to the railway station, and he went with her. They were   55
driving the whole day. When she had taken her place in the express, and when
the second bell had rung, she said, "Let me look at you once more — let me
look at you again. Like this."

She was not crying but was so sad that she seemed ill, and her face was
quivering.

"I shall be thinking of you — remembering you," she said. "God bless you;
be happy. Don't remember evil against me. We are parting forever — it has to
be, for we ought never to have met. Well, God bless you."

The train moved off rapidly, its lights soon vanished, and a minute later
there was no sound of it, as though everything had conspired to end as quickly
as possible that sweet trance, that madness. Left alone on the platform, and

gazing into the dark distance, Gurov listened to the twang of the grasshoppers and the hum of the telegraph wires, feeling as though he had just waked up. And he reflected, musing, that there had now been another episode or adventure in his life, and it, too, was at an end, and nothing was left of it but a memory. He was moved, sad, and slightly remorseful: this young woman whom he would never meet again had not been happy with him; he had been warm and affectionate with her, but yet in his manner, his tone, and his caresses there had been a shade of light irony, the slightly coarse arrogance of a happy male who was, besides, almost twice her age. She had constantly called him kind, exceptional, high-minded; obviously he had seemed to her different from what he really was, so he had involuntarily deceived her.

Here at the station there was already a scent of autumn in the air; it was a chilly evening.

"It is time for me to go north, too," thought Gurov as he left the platform. 60 "High time!"

III

At home in Moscow the winter routine was already established: the stoves were heated, and in the morning it was still dark when the children were having breakfast and getting ready for school, and the nurse would light the lamp for a short time. There were frosts already. When the first snow falls, on the first day the sleighs are out, it is pleasant to see the white earth, the white roofs; one draws easy, delicious breaths, and the season brings back the days of one's youth. The old limes and birches, white with hoar-frost, have a good-natured look; they are closer to one's heart than cypresses and palms, and near them one no longer wants to think of mountains and the sea.

Gurov, a native of Moscow, arrived there on a fine frosty day, and when he put on his fur coat and warm gloves and took a walk along Petrovka, and when on Saturday night he heard the bells ringing, his recent trip and the places he had visited lost all charm for him. Little by little he became immersed in Moscow life, greedily read three newspapers a day, and declared that he did not read the Moscow papers on principle. He already felt a longing for restaurants, clubs, formal dinners, anniversary celebrations, and it flattered him to entertain distinguished lawyers and actors, and to play cards with a professor at the physicians' club. He could eat a whole portion of meat stewed with pickled cabbage and served in a pan, Moscow style.

A month or so would pass and the image of Anna Sergeyevna, it seemed to him, would become misty in his memory, and only from time to time he would dream of her with her touching smile as he dreamed of others. But more than a month went by, winter came into its own, and everything was still clear in his memory as though he had parted from Anna Sergeyevna only yesterday. And his memories glowed more and more vividly. When in the evening stillness the voices of his children preparing their lessons reached his study, or when he listened to a song or to an organ playing in a restaurant, or when the storm howled in the chimney, suddenly everything would rise up in his memory: what had happened on the pier and the early morning with the mist on the mountains, and the steamer coming from Feodosia, and the kisses. He would pace about his room a long time, remembering and smiling; then his memories passed into reveries, and in his imagination the past would mingle with what was to come. He did not dream of Anna Sergeyevna, but she followed him about everywhere and watched him. When he shut his eyes he saw her before him as though she were there in the flesh; and she seemed to him lovelier, younger, tenderer than she had been, and he imagined himself a finer man than he had been in Yalta. Of evenings she peered out at him from the bookcase, from the fireplace, from the corner — he heard her breathing, the caressing rustle of her clothes. In the street he followed the women with his eyes, looking for someone who resembled her.

Already he was tormented by a strong desire to share his memories with someone. But in his home it was impossible to talk of his love, and he had no one to talk to outside; certainly he could not confide in his tenants or in anyone at the bank. And what was there to talk about? He hadn't loved her then, had he? Had there been anything beautiful, poetical, edifying, or simply interesting in his relations with Anna Sergeyevna? And he was forced to talk vaguely of love, of women, and no one guessed what he meant; only his wife would twitch her black eyebrows and say, "The part of a philanderer does not suit you at all, Dimitry."

One evening, coming out of the physicians' club with an official with 65
whom he had been playing cards, he could not resist saying:

"If you only knew what a fascinating woman I became acquainted with at Yalta!"

The official got into his sledge and was driving away, but turned suddenly and shouted: "Dmitry Dmitrich!"

"What is it?"

"You were right this evening: the sturgeon was a bit high."

These words, so commonplace, for some reason moved Gurov to indigna- 70
tion, and struck him as degrading and unclean. What savage manners, what mugs! What stupid nights, what dull, humdrum days! Frenzied gambling, gluttony, drunkenness, continual talk always about the same things! Futile pursuits and conversations always about the same topics take up the better part of one's time, the better part of one's strength, and in the end there is left a life clipped and wingless, an absurd mess, and there is no escaping or getting away from it — just as though one were in a madhouse or a prison.

Gurov, boiling with indignation, did not sleep all night. And he had a headache all the next day. And the following nights too he slept badly; he sat up in bed, thinking, or paced up and down his room. He was fed up with his children, fed up with the bank; he had no desire to go anywhere or to talk of anything.

In December during the holidays he prepared to take a trip and told his wife he was going to Petersburg to do what he could for a young friend — and he set off for S——. What for? He did not know, himself. He wanted to see Anna Sergeyevna and talk with her, to arrange a rendezvous if possible.

He arrived at S—— in the morning, and at the hotel took the best room, in which the floor was covered with gray army cloth, and on the table there was an inkstand, gray with dust and topped by a figure on horseback, its hat in its raised hand and its head broken off. The porter gave him the necessary information: von Dideritz lived in a house of his own on Staro-Goncharnaya Street, not far from the hotel: he was rich and lived well and kept his own horses; everyone in the town knew him. The porter pronounced the name: "Dridiritz."

Without haste Gurov made his way to Staro-Goncharnaya Street and found the house. Directly opposite the house stretched a long gray fence studded with nails.

"A fence like that would make one run away," thought Gurov, looking now 75 at the fence, now at the windows of the house.

He reflected: this was a holiday, and the husband was apt to be at home. And in any case, it would be tactless to go into the house and disturb her. If he were to send her a note, it might fall into her husband's hands, and that might spoil everything. The best thing was to rely on chance. And he kept walking up and down the street and along the fence, waiting for the chance. He saw a beggar go in at the gate and heard the dogs attack him; then an hour later he heard a piano, and the sound came to him faintly and indistinctly. Probably it was Anna Sergeyevna playing. The front door opened suddenly, and an old woman came out, followed by the familiar white Pomeranian. Gurov was on the point of calling to the dog, but his heart began beating violently, and in his excitement he could not remember the Pomeranian's name.

He kept walking up and down, and hated the gray fence more and more, and by now he thought irritably that Anna Sergeyevna had forgotten him, and was perhaps already diverting herself with another man, and that that was very natural in a young woman who from morning till night had to look at that damn fence. He went back to his hotel room and sat on the couch for a long while, not knowing what to do, then he had dinner and a long nap.

"How stupid and annoying all this is!" he thought when he woke and looked at the dark windows: it was already evening. "Here I've had a good sleep for some reason. What am I going to do at night?"

He sat on the bed, which was covered with a cheap gray blanket of the kind seen in hospitals, and he twitted himself in his vexation:

"So there's your lady with the pet dog. There's your adventure. A nice 80 place to cool your heels in."

That morning at the station a playbill in large letters had caught his eye. *The Geisha* was to be given for the first time. He thought of this and drove to the theater.

"It's quite possible that she goes to first nights," he thought.

The theater was full. As in all provincial theaters, there was a haze above the chandelier, the gallery was noisy and restless; in the front row, before the beginning of the performance the local dandies were standing with their hands clasped behind their backs; in the Governor's box the Governor's daughter, wearing a boa, occupied the front seat, while the Governor himself hid modestly behind the portiere and only his hands were visible; the curtain swayed; the orchestra was a long time tuning up. While the audience were coming in and taking their seats, Gurov scanned the faces eagerly.

Anna Sergeyevna, too, came in. She sat down in the third row, and when Gurov looked at her his heart contracted, and he understood clearly that in the whole world there was no human being so near, so precious, and so important to him; she, this little, undistinguished woman, lost in a provincial crowd, with a vulgar lorgnette in her hand, filled his whole life now, was his sorrow and his joy, the only happiness that he now desired for himself, and to the sounds of the bad orchestra, of the miserable local violins, he thought how lovely she was. He thought and dreamed.

A young man with small side-whiskers, very tall and stooped, came in with 85 Anna Sergeyevna and sat down beside her; he nodded his head at every step and seemed to be bowing continually. Probably this was the husband whom at Yalta, in an excess of bitter feeling, she had called a flunkey. And there really was in his lanky figure, his side-whiskers, his small bald patch, something of a flunkey's retiring manner; his smile was mawkish, and in his buttonhole there was an academic badge like a waiter's number.

During the first intermission the husband went out to have a smoke; she remained in her seat. Gurov, who was also sitting in the orchestra, went up to her and said in a shaky voice, with a forced smile:

"Good evening!"

She glanced at him and turned pale, then looked at him again in horror, unable to believe her eyes, and gripped the fan and the lorgnette tightly together in her hands, evidently trying to keep herself from fainting. Both were silent. She was sitting, he was standing, frightened by her distress and not daring to take a seat beside her. The violins and the flute that were being tuned up sang out. He suddenly felt frightened: it seemed as if all the people in the boxes were looking at them. She got up and went hurriedly to the exit; he followed her, and both of them walked blindly along the corridors and up and down stairs, and figures in the uniforms prescribed for magistrates, teachers, and officials of the Department of Crown Lands, all wearing badges, flitted before their eyes, as did also ladies, and fur coats on hangers; they were conscious of drafts and the smell of stale tobacco. And Gurov, whose heart was beating violently, thought:

"Oh, Lord! Why are these people here and this orchestra!"

And at that instant he suddenly recalled how when he had seen Anna 90 Sergeyevna off at the station he had said to himself that all was over between them and that they would never meet again. But how distant the end still was!

On the narrow, gloomy staircase over which it said "To the Amphitheatre," she stopped.

"How you frightened me!" she said, breathing hard, still pale and stunned. "Oh, how you frightened me! I am barely alive. Why did you come? Why?"

"But do understand, Anna, do understand —" he said hurriedly, under his breath. "I implore you, do understand —"

She looked at him with fear, with entreaty, with love; she looked at him intently, to keep his features more distinctly in her memory.

"I suffer so," she went on, not listening to him. "All this time I have been 95 thinking of nothing but you; I live only by the thought of you. And I wanted to forget, to forget; but why, oh, why have you come?"

On the landing above them two high school boys were looking down and smoking, but it was all the same to Gurov; he drew Anna Sergeyevna to him and began kissing her face and her hands.

"What are you doing, what are you doing!" she was saying in horror, pushing him away. "We have lost our senses. Go away today; go away at once — I conjure you by all that is sacred, I implore you — People are coming this way!"

Someone was walking up the stairs.

"You must leave," Anna Sergeyevna went on in a whisper. "Do you hear, Dmitry Dmitrich? I will come and see you in Moscow. I have never been happy; I am unhappy now, and I never, never shall be happy, never! So don't make me suffer still more! I swear I'll come to Moscow. But now let us part. My dear, good, precious one, let us part!"

She pressed his hand and walked rapidly downstairs, turning to look 100 round at him, and from her eyes he could see that she really was unhappy. Gurov stood for a while, listening, then when all grew quiet, he found his coat and left the theater.

IV

And Anna Sergeyevna began coming to see him in Moscow. Once every two or three months she left S——, telling her husband that she was going to consult a doctor about a woman's ailment from which she was suffering — and her husband did and did not believe her. When she arrived in Moscow she would stop at the Slavyansky Bazar Hotel, and at once send a man in a red cap to Gurov. Gurov came to see her, and no one in Moscow knew of it.

Once he was going to see her in this way on a winter morning (the messenger had come the evening before and not found him in). With him walked his daughter, whom he wanted to take to school: it was on the way. Snow was coming down in big wet flakes.

"It's three degrees above zero,° and yet it's snowing," Gurov was saying to his daughter. "But this temperature prevails only on the surface of the earth; in the upper layers of the atmosphere there is quite a different temperature."

"And why doesn't it thunder in winter, papa?"

He explained that, too. He talked, thinking all the while that he was on his   105
way to a rendezvous, and no living soul knew of it, and probably no one would ever know. He had two lives: an open one, seen and known by all who needed to know it, full of conventional truth and conventional falsehood, exactly like the lives of his friends and acquaintances; and another life that went on in secret. And through some strange, perhaps accidental, combination of circumstances, everything that was of interest and importance to him, everything that was essential to him, everything about which he felt sincerely and did not deceive himself, everything that constituted the core of his life, was going on concealed from others; while all that was false, the shell in which he hid to cover the truth — his work at the bank, for instance, his discussions at the club, his references to the "inferior race," his appearances at anniversary celebrations with his wife — all that went on in the open. Judging others by himself, he did not believe what he saw, and always fancied that every man led his real, most interesting life under cover of secrecy as under cover of night. The personal life of every individual is based on secrecy, and perhaps it is partly for that reason that civilized man is so nervously anxious that personal privacy should be respected.

Having taken his daughter to school, Gurov went on to the Slavyansky Bazar Hotel. He took off his fur coat in the lobby, went upstairs, and knocked gently at the door. Anna Sergeyevna, wearing his favorite gray dress, exhausted by the journey and by waiting, had been expecting him since the previous evening. She was pale, and looked at him without a smile, and he had hardly entered when she flung herself on his breast. Their kiss was a long, lingering one, as though they had not seen one another for two years.

"Well, darling, how are you getting on there?" he asked. "What news?"

"Wait; I'll tell you in a moment — I can't speak."

She could not speak; she was crying. She turned away from him, and pressed her handkerchief to her eyes.

"Let her have her cry; meanwhile I'll sit down," he thought, and he seated   110
himself in an armchair.

Then he rang and ordered tea, and while he was having his tea she remained standing at the window with her back to him. She was crying out of sheer agitation, in the sorrowful consciousness that their life was so sad; that

---

three degrees above zero: On the Celsius scale; about thirty-eight degrees Fahrenheit.

they could only see each other in secret and had to hide from people like thieves! Was it not a broken life?

"Come, stop now, dear!" he said.

It was plain to him that this love of theirs would not be over soon, that the end of it was not in sight. Anna Sergeyevna was growing more and more attached to him. She adored him, and it was unthinkable to tell her that their love was bound to come to an end some day; besides, she would not have believed it!

He went up to her and took her by the shoulders, to fondle her and say something diverting, and at that moment he caught sight of himself in the mirror.

His hair was already beginning to turn gray. And it seemed odd to him that he had grown so much older in the last few years, and lost his looks. The shoulders on which his hands rested were warm and heaving. He felt compassion for this life, still so warm and lovely, but probably already about to begin to fade and wither like his own. Why did she love him so much? He always seemed to women different from what he was, and they loved in him not himself, but the man whom their imagination created and whom they had been eagerly seeking all their lives; and afterwards, when they saw their mistake, they loved him nevertheless. And not one of them had been happy with him. In the past he had met women, come together with them, parted from them, but he had never once loved; it was anything you please, but not love. And only now when his head was gray he had fallen in love, really, truly—for the first time in his life.

Anna Sergeyevna and he loved each other as people do who are very close and intimate, like man and wife, like tender friends; it seemed to them that Fate itself had meant them for one another, and they could not understand why he had a wife and she a husband; and it was as though they were a pair of migratory birds, male and female, caught and forced to live in different cages. They forgave each other what they were ashamed of in their past, they forgave everything in the present, and felt that this love of theirs had altered them both.

Formerly in moments of sadness he had soothed himself with whatever logical arguments came into his head, but now he no longer cared for logic; he felt profound compassion, he wanted to be sincere and tender.

"Give it up now, my darling," he said. "You've had your cry; that's enough. Let us have a talk now, we'll think up something."

Then they spent a long time taking counsel together, they talked of how to avoid the necessity for secrecy, for deception, for living in different cities, and not seeing one another for long stretches of time. How could they free themselves from these intolerable fetters?

"How? How?" he asked, clutching his head. "How?"

And it seemed as though in a little while the solution would be found, and then a new and glorious life would begin; and it was clear to both of them that the end was still far off, and that what was to be most complicated and difficult for them was only just beginning.

CONSIDERATIONS FOR CRITICAL THINKING AND WRITING

1. FIRST RESPONSE. Consider the following assessment of the story: "No excuses can be made for the lovers' adulterous affair. They behave selfishly and irresponsibly. They are immoral—and so is the story." Explain what you think Chekhov's response to this view would be, given his treatment of the lovers. How does this compare with your own views?

2. Why is it significant that the setting of this story is a resort town? How does the vacation atmosphere affect the action?

3. What does Gurov's view of women reveal about him? Why does he regard them as an "inferior race"?

4. What do we learn about Gurov's wife and Anna's husband? Why do you think Chekhov includes this exposition? How does it affect our view of the lovers?

5. When and why do Gurov's feelings about Anna begin to change? Is he really in love with her?

6. Who or what is the antagonist in this story? What is the nature of the conflict?

7. What is the effect of having Gurov as the central consciousness? How would the story be different if it were told from Anna's perspective?

8. Why do you think Chekhov does not report what ultimately becomes of the lovers? Is there a resolution to the conflict? Is the ending of the story effective?

9. Discuss the validity of Gurov's belief that people lead their real lives in private rather than in public: "The personal life of every individual is based on secrecy, and perhaps it is partly for that reason that civilized man is so nervously anxious that personal privacy should be respected."

10. Describe your response to Gurov in Parts I and II, and discuss how your judgment of him changes in the last two parts of the story.

11. Based on your understanding of the characterizations of Gurov and Anna, consider the final paragraph of the story and summarize what you think will happen to them.

PERSPECTIVE
Two Additional Translations of the Final Paragraphs of Anton Chekhov's "The Lady with the Pet Dog"

"A Note on Reading Translations" appears on page 750. Because different translators of the same work make various choices in diction, phrasing, images, and tone as they interpret both the language and the work, they often produce subtly different translations. Compare the following two versions of the final six paragraphs of Chekhov's story with Avrahm Yarmolinsky's 1947 translation, reprinted in this anthology on pages 187–197.

ANTON CHEKHOV (1860–1904)
From "The Lady and the Dog"   *1899*
TRANSLATED BY CONSTANCE GARNETT (1963)

Anna Sergeyevna and he loved each other like people very close and akin, like husband and wife, like tender friends; it seemed to them that fate itself had meant them for one another, and they could not understand why he had a wife and she a husband; and it was as though they were a pair of birds of passage, caught and forced to live in different cages. They forgave each other for what they were ashamed of in their past, they forgave everything in the present, and felt that this love of theirs had changed them both.

In moments of depression in the past he had comforted himself with any arguments that came into his mind, but now he no longer cared for arguments; he felt profound compassion, he wanted to be sincere and tender. . . .

"Don't cry, my darling," he said. "You've had your cry; that's enough. . . . Let us talk now, let us think of some plan."

Then they spent a long while taking counsel together, talked of how to avoid the necessity for secrecy, for deception, for living in different towns and not seeing each other for long at a time. How could they be free from this intolerable bondage?

"How? How?" he asked, clutching his head. "How?"

And it seemed as though in a little while the solution would be found, and then a new and splendid life would begin; and it was clear to both of them that they had still a long, long way to go, and that the most complicated and difficult part of it was only just beginning.

From *My Life and Other Stories*

ANTON CHEKHOV (1860–1904)
From "A Lady with a Dog"   *1899*

TRANSLATED BY RONALD HINGLEY (1975)

Anne and he loved each other very, very dearly, like man and wife or bosom friends. They felt themselves predestined for each other. That he should have a wife, and she a husband . . . it seemed to make no sense. They were like two migratory birds, a male and a female, caught and put in separate cages. They had forgiven each other the shameful episodes of their past, they forgave each other for the present too, and they felt that their love had transformed them both.

Once, in moments of depression, he had tried to console himself with any argument which came into his head—but now he had no use for arguments. His deepest sympathies were stirred, he only wanted to be sincere and tender.

"Stop, darling," he said. "You've had your cry—that's enough. Now let's talk, let's think of something."

Then they consulted at length about avoiding the need for concealment and deception, for living in different towns, for meeting only at rare intervals. How could they break these intolerable bonds? How, how, how?

He clutched his head and asked the question again and again.

Soon, it seemed, the solution would be found and a wonderful new life would begin. But both could see that they still had a long, long way to travel— and that the most complicated and difficult part was only just beginning.

From *The Oxford Chekhov*, Vol. IX

PERSPECTIVE

ANTON CHEKHOV (1860–1904)

On Morality in Fiction 1890

You abuse me for objectivity, calling it indifference to good and evil, lack of ideals and ideas, and so on. You would have me, when I describe horse-thieves, say: "Stealing horses is an evil." But that has been known for ages without my saying so. Let the jury judge them; it's my job simply to show what sort of people they are. I write: You are dealing with horse-thieves, so let me tell you that they are not beggars but well-fed people, that they are people of a special cult, and that horse-stealing is not simply theft but a passion. Of course it would be pleasant to combine art with a sermon, but for me personally it is extremely difficult and almost impossible, owing to the conditions of technique. You see, to depict horse-thieves in seven hundred lines I must all the time speak and think in their tone and feel in their spirit, otherwise, if I introduce subjectivity, the image becomes blurred and the story will not be as compact as all short stories ought to be. When I write, I reckon entirely upon the reader to add for himself the subjective elements that are lacking in the story.

From a letter to Aleksey S. Suvorin in *Letters on the Short Story, the Drama, and Other Literary Topics* by Anton Chekhov

CONSIDERATIONS FOR CRITICAL THINKING AND WRITING

1. Why does Chekhov reject sermonizing in his fiction?
2. How does his "objectivity" affect your reading of "The Lady with the Pet Dog"?
3. Compare and contrast Chekhov's views with Thomas Jefferson's belief that fiction should offer "sound morality" (p. 42).

JOYCE CAROL OATES (B. 1938)

Raised in upstate New York, Joyce Carol Oates earned degrees at Syracuse University and the University of Wisconsin. Both the range and volume of her writing are extensive. A writer of novels, plays, short stories, poetry, and literary criticism, she has published some eighty books. Oates has described the subject matter of her fiction as "real people in a real society," but her method of expression ranges from the realistic to the experimental. Her novels include *them* (1969), *Do with Me What You Will* (1973), *Childwold* (1976), *Bellefleur* (1980), *A Bloodsmoor Romance* (1982), *Marya: A Life* (1986), *You Must Remember This* (1987), and *Black Water* (1992). Among her collections of short stories are *Marriages and Infidelities* (1972), which includes "The Lady with the Pet Dog," *Raven's Wing* (1986), *The Assignation* (1988), *Heat* (1991), *Haunted: Tales of the Grotesque* (1994), *Will You Always Love Me? and Other Stories* (1996), and *The Collector of Hearts* (1998). This story is

her modern version of the Chekhov story of the same title, this time told
from the woman's perspective.

Web *Research Joyce Carol Oates with LitLinks at*
http://www.bedfordstmartins.com/meyer/bedintrolit

The Lady with the Pet Dog   1972

I

Strangers parted as if to make way for him.

There he stood. He was there in the aisle, a few yards away, watching her.

She leaned forward at once in her seat, her hand jerked up to her face as if
to ward off a blow—but then the crowd in the aisle hid him, he was gone. She
pressed both hands against her cheeks. He was not here, she had imagined him.

"My God," she whispered.

She was alone. Her husband had gone out to the foyer to make a tele- 5
phone call; it was intermission at the concert, a Thursday evening.

Now she saw him again, clearly. He was standing there. He was staring at
her. Her blood rocked in her body, draining out of her head . . . she was going
to faint . . . They stared at each other. They gave no sign of recognition. Only
when he took a step forward did she shake her head *no—no—keep away*. It was
not possible.

When her husband returned, she was staring at the place in the aisle where
her lover had been standing. Her husband leaned forward to interrupt that
stare.

"What's wrong?" he said. "Are you sick?"

Panic rose in her in long shuddering waves. She tried to get to her feet,
panicked at the thought of fainting here, and her husband took hold of her.
She stood like an aged woman, clutching the seat before her.

At home he helped her up the stairs and she lay down. Her head was like a 10
large piece of crockery that had to be held still, it was so heavy. She was still
panicked. She felt it in the shallows of her face, behind her knees, in the pit of
her stomach. It sickened her, it made her think of mucus, of something thick
and gray congested inside her, stuck to her, that was herself and yet not herself—a poison.

She lay with her knees drawn up toward her chest, her eyes hotly open,
while her husband spoke to her. She imagined that other man saying, *Why did
you run away from me?* Her husband was saying other words. She tried to listen
to them. He was going to call the doctor, he said, and she tried to sit up. "No,
I'm all right now," she said quickly. The panic was like lead inside her, so
thickly congested. How slow love was to drain out of her, how fluid and sticky
it was inside her head!

Her husband believed her. No doctor. No threat. Grateful, she drew her
husband down to her. They embraced, not comfortably. For years now they
had not been comfortable together, in their intimacy and at a distance, and
now they struggled gently as if the paces of this dance were too rigorous for

them. It was something they might have known once, but had now outgrown. The panic in her thickened at this double betrayal: she drew her husband to her, she caressed him wildly, she shut her eyes to think about that other man.

A crowd of men and women parting, unexpectedly, and there he stood — there he stood — she kept seeing him, and yet her vision blotched at the memory. It had been finished between them, six months before, but he had come out here . . . and she had escaped him, now she was lying in her husband's arms, in his embrace, her face pressed against his. It was a kind of sleep, this love-making. She felt herself falling asleep, her body falling from her. Her eyes shut.

"I love you," her husband said fiercely, angrily.

She shut her eyes and thought of that other man, as if betraying him 15 would give her life a center.

"Did I hurt you? Are you — ?" Her husband whispered.

Always this hot flashing of shame between them, the shame of her husband's near failure, the clumsiness of his love —

"You didn't hurt me," she said.

II

They had said good-by six months before. He drove her from Nantucket, where they had met, to Albany, New York, where she visited her sister. The hours of intimacy in the car had sealed something between them, a vow of silence and impersonality: she recalled the movement of the highways, the passing of other cars, the natural rhythms of the day hypnotizing her toward sleep while he drove. She trusted him, she could sleep in his presence. Yet she could not really fall asleep in spite of her exhaustion, and she kept jerking awake, frightened, to discover that nothing had changed — still the stranger who was driving her to Albany, still the highway, the sky, the antiseptic odor of the rented car, the sense of a rhythm behind the rhythm of the air that might unleash itself at any second. Everywhere on this highway, at this moment, there were men and women driving together, bonded together — what did that mean, to be together? What did it mean to enter into a bond with another person?

No, she did not really trust him; she did not really trust men. He would 20 glance at her with his small cautious smile and she felt a declaration of shame between them.

Shame.

In her head she rehearsed conversations. She said bitterly, "You'll be relieved when we get to Albany. Relieved to get rid of me." They had spent so many days talking, confessing too much, driven to a pitch of childish excitement, laughing together on the beach, breaking into that pose of laughter that seems to eradicate the soul, so many days of this that the silence of the trip was like the silence of a hospital — all these surface noises, these rattles and hums, but an interior silence, a befuddlement. She said to him in her imagination, "One of us should die." Then she leaned over to touch him. She caressed the back of his neck. She said, aloud, "Would you like me to drive for a while?"

They stopped at a picnic area where other cars were stopped — couples, families — and walked together, smiling at their good luck. He put his arm around her shoulders and she sensed how they were in a posture together, a man and a woman forming a posture, a figure, that someone might sketch and show to them. She said slowly, "I don't want to go back. . . ."

Silence. She looked up at him. His face was heavy with her words, as if she had pulled at his skin with her fingers. Children ran nearby and distracted him—yes, he was a father too, his children ran like that, they tugged at his skin with their light, busy fingers.

"Are you so unhappy?" he said.   25

"I'm not unhappy, back there. I'm nothing. There's nothing to me," she said.

They stared at each other. The sensation between them was intense, exhausting. She thought that this man was her savior, that he had come to her at a time in her life when her life demanded completion, an end, a permanent fixing of all that was troubled and shifting and deadly. And yet it was absurd to think this. No person could save another. So she drew back from him and released him.

A few hours later they stopped at a gas station in a small city. She went to the women's rest room, having to ask the attendant for a key, and when she came back her eye jumped nervously onto the rented car—why? did she think he might have driven off without her?—onto the man, her friend, standing in conversation with the young attendant. Her friend was as old as her husband, over forty, with lanky, sloping shoulders, a full body, his hair thick, a dark, burnished brown, a festive color that made her eye twitch a little—and his hands were always moving, always those rapid conversational circles, going nowhere, gestures that were at once a little aggressive and apologetic.

She put her hand on his arm, a claim. He turned to her and smiled and she felt that she loved him, that everything in her life had forced her to this moment and that she had no choice about it.

They sat in the car for two hours, in Albany, in the parking lot of a Howard   30 Johnson's restaurant, talking, trying to figure out their past. There was no future. They concentrated on the past, the several days behind them, lit up with a hot, dazzling August sun, like explosions that already belonged to other people, to strangers. Her face was faintly reflected in the green-tinted curve of the windshield, but she could not have recognized that face. She began to cry; she told herself: *I am not here, this will pass, this is nothing.* Still, she could not stop crying. The muscles of her face were springy, like a child's, unpredictable muscles. He stroked her arms, her shoulders, trying to comfort her. "This is so hard . . . this is impossible . . ." he said. She felt panic for the world outside this car, all that was not herself and this man, and at the same time she understood that she was free of him, as people are free of other people, she would leave him soon, safely, and within a few days he would have fallen into the past, the impersonal past. . . .

"I'm so ashamed of myself!" she said finally.

She returned to her husband and saw that another woman, a shadow-woman, had taken her place—noiseless and convincing, like a dancer performing certain difficult steps. Her husband folded her in his arms and talked to her of his own loneliness, his worries about his business, his health, his mother, kept tranquilized and mute in a nursing home, and her spirit detached itself from her and drifted about the rooms of the large house she lived in with her husband, a shadow-woman delicate and imprecise. There was no boundary to her, no edge. Alone, she took hot baths and sat exhausted in the steaming water, wondering at her perpetual exhaustion. All that winter she noticed the limp, languid weight of her arms, her veins bulging slightly with the pressure of her extreme weariness. *This is fate,* she thought, to be here and not there, to be one person and not another, a certain man's wife and not the wife of another man. The long, slow pain of this certainty rose in her, but it never became clear, it was baffling and imprecise. She could not be serious about it; she kept congratulating herself on her own good luck, to have escaped so easily, to have freed herself. So much love had gone into the first several years of her marriage that there wasn't much left, now, for another man. . . . She was certain of that. But the bath water made her dizzy, all that perpetual heat, and one day in January she drew a razor blade lightly across the inside of her arm, near the elbow, to see what would happen.

Afterward she wrapped a small towel around it, to stop the bleeding. The towel soaked through. She wrapped a bath towel around that and walked through the empty rooms of her home, lightheaded, hardly aware of the stubborn seeping of blood. There was no boundary to her in this house, no precise limit. She could flow out like her own blood and come to no end.

She sat for a while on a blue love seat, her mind empty. Her husband telephoned her when he would be staying late at the plant. He talked to her always about his plans, his problems, his business friends, his future. It was obvious that he had a future. As he spoke she nodded to encourage him, and her heartbeat quickened with the memory of her own, personal shame, the shame of this man's particular, private wife. One evening at dinner he leaned forward and put his head in his arms and fell asleep, like a child. She sat at the table with him for a while, watching him. His hair had gone gray, almost white, at the temples — no one would guess that he was so quick, so careful a man, still fairly young about the eyes. She put her hand on his head, lightly, as if to prove to herself that he was real. He slept, exhausted.

One evening they went to a concert and she looked up to see her lover 35 there, in the crowded aisle, in this city, watching her. He was standing there, with his overcoat on, watching her. She went cold. That morning the telephone had rung while her husband was still home, and she had heard him answer it, heard him hang up — it must have been a wrong number — and when the telephone rang again, at 9:30, she had been afraid to answer it. She had left home to be out of the range of that ringing, but now, in this public place, in this busy auditorium, she found herself staring at that man, unable to make any sign to him, any gesture of recognition. . . .

He would have come to her but she shook her head. *No. Stay away.*

Her husband helped her out of the row of seats, saying, "Excuse us, please. Excuse us," so that strangers got to their feet, quickly, alarmed, to let them pass. Was that woman about to faint? What was wrong?

At home she felt the blood drain slowly back into her head. Her husband embraced her hips, pressing his face against her, in that silence that belonged to the earliest days of their marriage. She thought, *He will drive it out of me.* He made love to her and she was back in the auditorium again, sitting alone, now that the concert was over. The stage was empty; the heavy velvet curtains had not been drawn; the musicians' chairs were empty, everything was silent and expectant; in the aisle her lover stood and smiled at her — Her husband was impatient. He was apart from her, working on her, operating on her; and then, stricken, he whispered, "Did I hurt you?"

The telephone rang the next morning. Dully, sluggishly, she answered it. She recognized his voice at once — that "Anna?" with its lifting of the second syllable, questioning and apologetic and making its claim—"Yes, what do you want?" she said.

"Just to see you. Please—"   40

"I can't."

"Anna, I'm sorry, I didn't mean to upset you—"

"I can't see you."

"Just for a few minutes—I have to talk to you—"

"But why, why now? Why now?" she said.   45

She heard her voice rising, but she could not stop it. He began to talk again, drowning her out. She remembered his rapid conversation. She remembered his gestures, the witty energetic circling of his hands.

"Please don't hang up!" he cried.

"I can't—I don't want to go through it again—"

"I'm not going to hurt you. Just tell me how you are."

"Everything is the same."   50

"Everything is the same with me."

She looked up at the ceiling, shyly. "Your wife? Your children?"

"The same."

"Your son?"

"He's fine—"   55

"I'm so glad to hear that. I—"

"Is it still the same with you, your marriage? Tell me what you feel. What are you thinking?"

"I don't know. . . ."

She remembered his intense, eager words, the movement of his hands, that impatient precise fixing of the air by his hands, the jabbing of his fingers.

"Do you love me?" he said.   60

She could not answer.

"I'll come over to see you," he said.

"No," she said.

What will come next, what will happen?

Flesh hardening on his body, aging. Shrinking. He will grow old, but not   65
soft like her husband. They are two different types: he is nervous, lean, energetic, wise. She will grow thinner, as the tension radiates out from her backbone, wearing down her flesh. Her collarbones will jut out of her skin. Her husband, caressing her in their bed, will discover that she is another woman—she is not there with him—instead she is rising in an elevator in a downtown hotel, carrying a book as a prop, or walking quickly away from that hotel, her head bent and filled with secrets. Love, what to do with it? . . . Useless as moths' wings, as moths' fluttering. . . . She feels the flutterings of silky, crazy wings in her chest.

He flew out to visit her every several weeks, staying at a different hotel each time. He telephoned her, and she drove down to park in an underground garage at the very center of the city.

She lay in his arms while her husband talked to her, miles away, one body fading into another. He will grow old, his body will change, she thought, pressing her cheek against the back of one of these men. If it was her lover, they were in a hotel room: always the propped-up little booklet describing the hotel's many services, with color photographs of its cocktail lounge and dining room and coffee shop. Grow old, leave me, die, go back to your neurotic wife and your sad, ordinary children, she thought, but still her eyes closed gratefully against his skin and she felt how complete their silence was, how they had come to rest in each other.

"Tell me about your life here. The people who love you," he said, as he always did.

One afternoon they lay together for four hours. It was her birthday and she was intoxicated with her good fortune, this prize of the afternoon, this man in her arms! She was a little giddy, she talked too much. She told him about her parents, about her husband. . . . "They were all people I believed in, but it turned out wrong. Now, I believe in you. . . ." He laughed as if shocked by her words. She did not understand. Then she understood. "But I believe truly in you. I can't think of myself without you," she said. . . . He spoke of his wife, her ambitions, her intelligence, her use of the children against him, her use of his younger son's blindness, all of his words gentle and hypnotic and convincing in the late afternoon peace of this hotel room . . . and she felt the terror of laughter, threatening laughter. Their words, like their bodies, were aging.

She dressed quickly in the bathroom, drawing her long hair up around the   70 back of her head, fixing it as always, anxious that everything be the same. Her face was slightly raw, from his face. The rubbing of his skin. Her eyes were too bright, wearily bright. Her hair was blond but not so blond as it had been that summer in the white Nantucket air.

She ran water and splashed it on her face. She blinked at the water. Blind. Drowning. She thought with satisfaction that soon, soon, he would be back home, in that house on Long Island she had never seen, with that woman she had never seen, sitting on the edge of another bed, putting on his shoes. She wanted nothing except to be free of him. Why not be free? *Oh*, she thought suddenly, *I will follow you back and kill you. You and her and the little boy. What is there to stop me?*

She left him. Everyone on the street pitied her, that look of absolute zero.

III

A man and a child, approaching her. The sharp acrid smell of fish. The crashing of waves. Anna pretended not to notice the father with his son — there was something strange about them. That frank, silent intimacy, too gentle, the man's bare feet in the water and the boy a few feet away, leaning away from his father. He was about nine years old and still his father held his hand.

A small yipping dog, a golden dog, bounded near them.

Anna turned shyly back to her reading; she did not want to have to speak   75 to these neighbors. She saw the man's shadow falling over her legs, then over the pages of her book, and she had the idea that he wanted to see what she was reading. The dog nuzzled her; the man called him away.

She watched them walk down the beach. She was relieved that the man had not spoken to her.

She saw them in town later that day, the two of them brown-haired and patient, now wearing sandals, walking with that same look of care. The man's white shorts were soiled and a little baggy. His pullover shirt was a faded green. His face was broad, the cheekbones wide, spaced widely apart, the eyes stark in their sockets, as if they fastened onto objects for no reason, ponderous and edgy. The little boy's face was pale and sharp; his lips were perpetually parted.

Anna realized that the child was blind.

The next morning, early, she caught sight of them again. For some reason she went to the back door of her cottage. She faced the sea breeze eagerly. Her heart hammered. . . . She had been here, in her family's old house, for three days, alone, bitterly satisfied at being alone, and now it was a puzzle to her how her soul strained to fly outward, to meet with another person. She watched the man with his son, his cautious, rather stooped shoulders above the child's small shoulders.

The man was carrying something, it looked like a notebook. He sat on the 80 sand, not far from Anna's spot of the day before, and the dog rushed up to them. The child approached the edge of the ocean, timidly. He moved in short jerky steps, his legs stiff. The dog ran around him. Anna heard the child crying out a word that sounded like "Ty"—it must have been the dog's name—and then the man joined in, his voice heavy and firm.

"Ty—"

Anna tied her hair back with a yellow scarf and went down to the beach.

The man glanced around at her. He smiled. She stared past him at the waves. To talk to him or not to talk—she had the freedom of that choice. For a moment she felt that she had made a mistake, that the child and the dog would not protect her, that behind this man's ordinary, friendly face there was a certain arrogant maleness—then she relented, she smiled shyly.

"A nice house you've got there," the man said.

She nodded her thanks.   85

The man pushed his sunglasses up on his forehead. Yes, she recognized the eyes of the day before—intelligent and nervous, the sockets pale, untanned.

"Is that your telephone ringing?" he said.

She did not bother to listen. "It's a wrong number," she said.

Her husband calling: she had left home for a few days, to be alone.

But the man, settling himself on the sand, seemed to misinterpret this. He 90 smiled in surprise, one corner of his mouth higher than the other. He said nothing. Anna wondered: *What is he thinking?* The dog was leaping about her, panting against her legs, and she laughed in embarrassment. She bent to pet it, grateful for its busyness. "Don't let him jump up on you," the man said. "He's a nuisance."

The dog was a small golden retriever, a young dog. The blind child, standing now in the water, turned to call the dog to him. His voice was shrill and impatient.

"Our house is the third one down—the white one," the man said.

She turned, startled. "Oh, did you buy it from Dr. Patrick? Did he die?"

"Yes, finally. . . ."

Her eyes wandered nervously over the child and the dog. She felt the ner- 95 vous beat of her heart out to the very tips of her fingers, the fleshy tips of her fingers: little hearts were there, pulsing. *What is he thinking?* The man had opened his notebook. He had a piece of charcoal and he began to sketch something.

Anna looked down at him. She saw the top of his head, his thick brown hair, the freckles on his shoulders, the quick, deft movement of his hand. Upside down, Anna herself being drawn. She smiled in surprise.

"Let me draw you. Sit down," he said.

She knelt awkwardly a few yards away. He turned the page of the sketch pad. The dog ran to her and she sat, straightening out her skirt beneath her, flinching from the dog's tongue. "Ty!" cried the child. Anna sat, and slowly the pleasure of the moment began to glow in her; her skin flushed with gratitude.

She sat there for nearly an hour. The man did not talk much. Back and forth the dog bounded, shaking itself. The child came to sit near them, in silence. Anna felt that she was drifting into a kind of trance while the man sketched her, half a dozen rapid sketches, the surface of her face given up to him. "Where are you from?" the man asked.

"Ohio. My husband lives in Ohio."   100

She wore no wedding band.

"Your wife—" Anna began.

"Yes?"

"Is she here?"

"Not right now."   105

She was silent, ashamed. She had asked an improper question. But the man did not seem to notice. He continued drawing her, bent over the sketch pad. When Anna said she had to go, he showed her the drawings—one after another of her, Anna, recognizably Anna, a woman in her early thirties, her hair smooth and flat across the top of her head, tied behind by a scarf. "Take the one you like best," he said, and she picked one of her with the dog in her lap, sitting very straight, her brows and eyes clearly defined, her lips girlishly pursed, the dog and her dress suggested by a few quick irregular lines.

"Lady with pet dog," the man said.

She spent the rest of that day reading, nearer her cottage. It was not really a cottage—it was a two-story house, large and ungainly and weathered. It was mixed up in her mind with her family, her own childhood, and she glanced up from her book, perplexed, as if waiting for one of her parents or her sister to come up to her. Then she thought of that man, the man with the blind child, the man with the dog, and she could not concentrate on her reading. Someone—probably her father—had marked a passage that must be important, but she kept reading and rereading it: *We try to discover in things, endeared to us on that account, the spiritual glamour which we ourselves have cast upon them; we are disillusioned, and learn that they are in themselves barren and devoid of the charm that they owed, in our minds, to the association of certain ideas. . . .*

She thought again of the man on the beach. She lay the book aside and thought of him: his eyes, his aloneness, his drawings of her.

They began seeing each other after that. He came to her front door in the   110
evening, without the child; he drove her into town for dinner. She was shy and extremely pleased. The darkness of the expensive restaurant released her; she heard herself chatter; she leaned forward and seemed to be offering her face up to him, listening to him. He talked about his work on a Long Island newspaper and she seemed to be listening to him, as she stared at his face, arranging her own face into the expression she had seen in that charcoal drawing. Did he see her like that, then?—girlish and withdrawn and patrician? She felt the weight of his interest in her, a force that fell upon her like a blow. A repeated blow. Of course he was married, he had children—of course she was married, permanently married. This flight from her husband was not important. She had left him before, to be alone, it was not important. Everything in her was slender and delicate and not important.

They walked for hours after dinner, looking at the other strollers, the weekend visitors, the tourists, the couples like themselves. Surely they were mistaken for a couple, a married couple. *This is the hour in which everything is decided,* Anna thought. They had both had several drinks and they talked a great deal. Anna found herself saying too much, stopping and starting giddily. She put her hand to her forehead, feeling faint.

"It's from the sun—you've had too much sun—" he said.

At the door to her cottage, on the front porch, she heard herself asking him if he would like to come in. She allowed him to lead her inside, to close the door. *This is not important,* she thought clearly, *he doesn't mean it, he doesn't love me, nothing will come of it.* She was frightened, yet it seemed to her necessary to give in; she had to leave Nantucket with that act completed, an act of adultery, an accomplishment she would take back to Ohio and to her marriage.

Later, incredibly, she heard herself asking: "Do you . . . do you love me?"

"You're so beautiful!" he said, amazed.   115

She felt this beauty, shy and glowing and centered in her eyes. He stared at her. In this large, drafty house, alone together, they were like accomplices, conspirators. She could not think: how old was she? which year was this? They had done something unforgivable together, and the knowledge of it was tugging at their faces. A cloud seemed to pass over her. She felt herself smiling shrilly.

Afterward, a peculiar raspiness, a dryness of breath. He was silent. She felt a strange, idle fear, a sense of the danger outside this room and this old comfortable bed—a danger that would not recognize her as the lady in that drawing, the lady with the pet dog. There was nothing to say to this man, this stranger. She felt the beauty draining out of her face, her eyes fading.

"I've got to be alone," she told him.

He left, and she understood that she would not see him again. She stood by the window of the room, watching the ocean. A sense of shame overpowered her: it was smeared everywhere on her body, the smell of it, the richness of it. She tried to recall him, and his face was confused in her memory: she would have to shout to him across a jumbled space, she would have to wave her arms wildly. *You love me! You must love me!* But she knew he did not love her, and she did not love him; he was a man who drew everything up into himself, like all men, walking away, free to walk away, free to have his own thoughts, free to envision her body, all the secrets of her body. . . . And she lay down again in the bed, feeling how heavy this body had become, her insides heavy with shame, the very backs of her eyelids coated with shame.

"This is the end of one part of my life," she thought.   120

But in the morning the telephone rang. She answered it. It was her lover: they talked brightly and happily. She could hear the eagerness in his voice, the love in his voice, that same still, sad amazement—she understood how simple life was, there were no problems.

They spent most of their time on the beach, with the child and the dog. He joked and was serious at the same time. He said, once, "You have defined my soul for me," and she laughed to hide her alarm. In a few days it was time for her to leave. He got a sitter for the boy and took the ferry with her to the mainland, then rented a car to drive her up to Albany. She kept thinking: *Now something will happen. It will come to an end.* But most of the drive was silent and hypnotic. She wanted him to joke with her, to say again that she had defined his soul for him, but he drove fast, he was serious, she distrusted the hawkish look of his profile — she did not know him at all. At a gas station she splashed her face with cold water. Alone in the grubby little rest room, shaky and very much alone. In such places are women totally alone with their bodies. The body grows heavier, more evil, in such silence. . . . On the beach everything had been noisy with sunlight and gulls and waves; here, as if run to earth, everything was cramped and silent and dead.

She went outside, squinting. There he was, talking with the station attendant. She could not think as she returned to him whether she wanted to live or not.

She stayed in Albany for a few days, then flew home to her husband. He met her at the airport, near the luggage counter, where her three pieces of pale-brown luggage were brought to him on a conveyer belt, to be claimed by him. He kissed her on the cheek. They shook hands, a little embarrassed. She had come home again.

"How will I live out the rest of my life?" she wondered.   125

In January her lover spied on her: she glanced up and saw him, in a public place, in the DeRoy Symphony Hall. She was paralyzed with fear. She nearly fainted. In this faint she felt her husband's body, loving her, working its love upon her, and she shut her eyes harder to keep out the certainty of his love — sometimes he failed at loving her, sometimes he succeeded, it had nothing to do with her or her pity or her ten years of love for him, it had nothing to do with a woman at all. It was a private act accomplished by a man, a husband, or a lover, in communion with his own soul, his manhood.

Her husband was forty-two years old now, growing slowly into middle age, getting heavier, softer. Her lover was about the same age, narrower in the shoulders, with a full, solid chest, yet lean, nervous. She thought, in her paralysis, of men and how they love freely and eagerly so long as their bodies are capable of love, love for a woman; and then, as love fades in their bodies, it fades from their souls and they become immune and immortal and ready to die.

Her husband was a little rough with her, as if impatient with himself. "I love you," he said fiercely, angrily. And then, ashamed, he said, "Did I hurt you? . . ."

"You didn't hurt me," she said.

Her voice was too shrill for their embrace.   130

While he was in the bathroom she went to her closet and took out that drawing of the summer before. There she was, on the beach at Nantucket, a lady with a pet dog, her eyes large and defined, the dog in her lap hardly more than a few snarls, a few coarse soft lines of charcoal . . . her dress smeared, her arms oddly limp . . . her hands not well drawn at all. . . . She tried to think: did she love the man who had drawn this? did he love her? The fever in her husband's body had touched her and driven her temperature up, and now she stared at the drawing with a kind of lust, fearful of seeing an ugly soul in that woman's face, fearful of seeing the face suddenly through her lover's eyes. She breathed quickly and harshly, staring at the drawing.

And so, the next day, she went to him at his hotel. She wept, pressing against him, demanding of him, "What do you want? Why are you here? Why don't you let me alone?" He told her that he wanted nothing. He expected nothing. He would not cause trouble.

"I want to talk about last August," he said.

"Don't—" she said.

She was hypnotized by his gesturing hands, his nervousness, his obvious 135 agitation. He kept saying, "I understand. I'm making no claims upon you."

They became lovers again.

He called room service for something to drink and they sat side by side on his bed, looking through a copy of *The New Yorker,* laughing at the cartoons. It was so peaceful in this room, so complete. They were on a holiday. It was a secret holiday. Four-thirty in the afternoon, on a Friday, an ordinary Friday: a secret holiday.

"I won't bother you again," he said.

He flew back to see her again in March, and in late April. He telephoned her from his hotel—a different hotel each time—and she came down to him at once. She rose to him in various elevators, she knocked on the doors of various rooms, she stepped into his embrace, breathless and guilty and already angry with him, pleading with him. One morning in May, when he telephoned, she pressed her forehead against the doorframe and could not speak. He kept saying, "What's wrong? Can't you talk? Aren't you alone?" She felt that she was going insane. Her head would burst. Why, why did he love her, why did he pursue her? Why did he want her to die?

She went to him in the hotel room. A familiar room: had they been here 140 before? "Everything is repeating itself. Everything is stuck," she said. He framed her face in his hands and said that she looked thinner—was she sick?—what was wrong? She shook herself free. He, her lover, looked about the same. There was a small, angry pimple on his neck. He stared at her, eagerly and suspiciously. Did she bring bad news?

"So you love me? You love me?" she asked.

"Why are you so angry?"

"I want to be free of you. The two of us free of each other."

"That isn't true—you don't want that—"

He embraced her. She was wild with that old, familiar passion for him, her 145 body clinging to his, her arms not strong enough to hold him. Ah, what despair!—what bitter hatred she felt!—she needed this man for her salvation, he was all she had to live for, and yet she could not believe in him. He embraced her thighs, her hips, kissing her, pressing his warm face against her, and yet she could not believe in him, not really. She needed him in order to live, but he was not worth her love, he was not worth her dying. . . . She promised herself this: when she got back home, when she was alone, she would draw the razor more deeply across her arm.

The telephone rang and he answered it: a wrong number.

"Jesus," he said.

They lay together, still. She imagined their posture like this, the two of them one figure, one substance; and outside this room and this bed there was a universe of disjointed, separate things, blank things, that had nothing to do with them. She would not be Anna out there, the lady in the drawing. He would not be her lover.

"I love you so much . . ." she whispered.

"Please don't cry! We have only a few hours, please. . . ."   150

It was absurd, their clinging together like this. She saw them as a single figure in a drawing, their arms and legs entwined, their heads pressing mutely together. Helpless substance, so heavy and warm and doomed. It was absurd that any human being should be so important to another human being. She wanted to laugh: a laugh might free them both.

She could not laugh.

Sometime later he said, as if they had been arguing, "Look. It's you. You're the one who doesn't want to get married. You lie to me—"

"Lie to you?"

"You love me but you won't marry me, because you want something left 155 over—Something not finished—All your life you can attribute your misery to me, to our not being married—you are using me—"

"Stop it! You'll make me hate you!" she cried.

"You can say to yourself that you're miserable because of *me*. We will never be married, you will never be happy, neither one of us will ever be happy—"

"I don't want to hear this!" she said.

She pressed her hands flatly against her face.

She went to the bathroom to get dressed. She washed her face and part of 160 her body, quickly. The fever was in her, in the pit of her belly. She would rush home and strike a razor across the inside of her arm and free that pressure, that fever.

The impatient bulging of the veins: an ordeal over.

The demand of the telephone's ringing: that ordeal over.

The nuisance of getting the car and driving home in all that five o'clock traffic: an ordeal too much for a woman.

The movement of this stranger's body in hers: over, finished.

Now, dressed, a little calmer, they held hands and talked. They had to talk 165 swiftly, to get all their news in: he did not trust the people who worked for him, he had faith in no one, his wife had moved to a textbook publishing company and was doing well, she had inherited a Ben Shahn painting from her father and wanted to "touch it up a little"—she was crazy!—his blind son was at another school, doing fairly well, in fact his children were all doing fairly well in spite of the stupid mistake of their parents' marriage—and what about her? what about her life? She told him in a rush the one thing he wanted to hear: that she lived with her husband lovelessly, the two of them polite strangers, sharing a bed, lying side by side in the night in that bed, bodies out of which souls had fled. There was no longer even any shame between them.

"And what about me? Do you feel shame with me still?" he asked.

She did not answer. She moved away from him and prepared to leave.

Then, a minute later, she happened to catch sight of his reflection in the bureau mirror—he was glancing down at himself, checking himself mechanically, impersonally, preparing also to leave. He too would leave this room: he too was headed somewhere else.

She stared at him. It seemed to her that in this instant he was breaking from her, the image of her lover fell free of her, breaking from her . . . and she realized that he existed in a dimension quite apart from her, a mysterious being. And suddenly, joyfully, she felt a miraculous calm. This man was her husband, truly—they were truly married, here in this room—they had been married haphazardly and accidentally for a long time. In another part of the city she had another husband, a "husband," but she had not betrayed that man, not really. This man, whom she loved above any other person in the world, above even her own self-pitying sorrow and her own life, was her truest lover, her destiny. And she did not hate him, she did not hate herself any longer; she did not wish to die; she was flooded with a strange certainty, a sense of gratitude, of pure selfless energy. It was obvious to her that she had, all along, been behaving correctly; out of instinct.

What triumph, to love like this in any room, anywhere, risking even the 170 craziest of accidents!

"Why are you so happy? What's wrong?" he asked, startled. He stared at her. She felt the abrupt concentration in him, the focusing of his vision on her, almost a bitterness in his face, as if he feared her. What, was it beginning all over again? Their love beginning again, in spite of them? "How can you look so happy?" he asked. "We don't have any right to it. Is it because . . . ?"

"Yes," she said.

CONSIDERATIONS FOR CRITICAL THINKING AND WRITING

1. FIRST RESPONSE. Which version do you like better — Chekhov's story or Oates's? What's the point of retelling the story?

2. How would this story be different if it were told only in chronological order as it is in Part III? What do Parts I and II contribute to the details and information provided in Part III?

3. Why are Anna and her lover drawn to each other? What do we learn about their spouses that helps explain their attraction? Are there any other explanations?

4. Why is Anna so unhappy after the affair on Nantucket begins? Why does she think of suicide?

5. What is Anna's attitude toward men? Does it change during the story?

6. What details in the story make the narration particularly convincing from a woman's perspective? How might a man tell the story differently?

7. "What triumph, to love like this in any room, anywhere, risking even the craziest of accidents!" Explain this reflection of Anna's (para. 170) and relate it to her character.

8. How does Oates's arrangement of incidents validate Anna's feeling that "everything is repeating itself. Everything is stuck" (para. 140)?

9. Consider whether Anna reaches any kind of resolution to her problems by the end of the story. Is she merely "repeating" herself, or do you think she develops?

10. At the end of paragraph 19, Oates has Anna ask herself the question "What did it mean to enter into a bond with another person?" Write an essay explaining how the story answers that question.

11. CRITICAL STRATEGIES. Read the section on new historicist criticism (pp. 2103–04) in Chapter 52, "Critical Strategies for Reading," and consider how the institution of marriage was generally regarded when Chekhov and Oates wrote their respective stories. How do these two different perspectives on marriage compare with your own twenty-first-century point of view? How do you think a new historicist would weight the similarities and differences between these perspectives when comparing these two stories?

CONNECTION TO ANOTHER SELECTION

1. What similarities in setting, plot, and character are there between Oates's version and Chekhov's story? Are there any significant differences?

2. Describe how a familiarity with Chekhov's story affected your reading and expectations of Oates's version. Choose one version of the story and write an essay explaining why you prefer it over the other.

PERSPECTIVE

MATTHEW C. BRENNAN (B. 1955)

Point of View and Plotting in Chekhov's and Oates's "The Lady with the Pet Dog"   1985

Oates . . . retains Chekhov's third-person point of view. But unlike Chekhov, who focuses on the male lover, Gurov, Oates makes Anna S., the female lover, the center of consciousness. Because Chekhov privileges Gurov, he represents Anna's feelings only when she speaks to Gurov. In fact, when Anna S. expresses her shame to Gurov, Chekhov says, "The solitary candle on the table scarcely lit up her face"; and rather than reveal her inner thoughts he merely tells us, "it was obvious that her heart was heavy." So, by subordinating Anna S. to Gurov, Chekhov gives readers no way to understand the feminine side of a masculine story. In contrast, Oates presents what Chekhov leaves out — the female's experience — and so relegates the male lover (who in her version is nameless) to the limited status Chekhov relegates Anna S.: Oates privileges the point of view of Anna. Furthermore, because Anna S. says she feels "like a madwoman," Oates fragments Chekhov's traditionally chronological plot, which becomes a subtext against which Oates can foreground Anna's confusion, doubt, and struggle to find an identity. . . .

Chekhov develops a conventional, sequential plot. He spreads the five-step plot through the four formal divisions of his story. Part I consists of the exposition, during which Gurov and Anna S. meet at the resort, Yalta. Part II continues the exposition, as the characters become lovers, and it also introduces the rising action as they separate at the train station, Anna S. returning to her home in the town of S——, Gurov to his in Moscow. Then, in Part III, the action continues to rise as Gurov misses Anna and eventually goes to the town of S——. Here, at a concert, the two climactically meet again, and, as Part III ends, Anna S. agrees to come to Moscow. Finally, in Part IV, the action falls as Chekhov describes their affair and dramatizes it in a scene that forms the resolution, through which Gurov realizes, after looking in a mirror, that he is in love for the first time: he and Anna S. really are "as husband and wife" though separated by law.

Oates borrows all these events for her plot, but if Chekhov's is linear, hers is circular. Oates breaks her story into three parts. Part I depicts the climax, immediately giving her version the intensity that the high-strung center of consciousness, Anna, is experiencing. We are with her at the concert hall, where her lover appears and she faints, and then with her back home, where her husband clumsily makes love to her while she thinks of her lover. Part II opens with a flashback to the rising action — when the lover drives Anna to Albany where they separate, just as Chekhov's lovers separate at the train station; next, Part II both repeats the climax (at the concert and in the bedroom) and relates, for the first time, the falling action in which the lovers continue the affair. Part I, then, presents only the climax, and Part II widens the plot to record not just the center, the climax, but also the rising and falling actions that surround it. Part III, however, widens the circular plot still further. Expanding outward from the climactic center, first the plot regresses to embrace the exposition (in which the lovers meet and make love at the resort, in this version Nantucket); then it moves inward again, retracing chronologically the rising action, climax, and falling action; and finally, as Part III concludes, the plot introduces the resolution, rounding out its pattern.

Before the resolution, however, as we witness the falling action (the resumption of the affair) for the second time, Oates stresses the lack of development: Anna says, "'Everything is repeating itself. Everything is stuck.'" By having the plot repeat itself, and so fail to progress toward resolution, Oates conveys Anna's lack of identity: Anna is trapped between two relationships, two "husbands," and hence wavers throughout this version between feeling like "nothing" in her legal husband's house where "there was no boundary to her," "no precise limit," and feeling defined — as "recognizably Anna" — by her illicit lover, her true "husband," who has sketched her portrait, to which she continually refers as if grasping for a rope.

Here, then, with the climax repeated three times and the rising and falling actions twice, the plot finally progresses from this impasse to its resolution. And, appropriately, as the plot finally achieves its completion, so too does Anna, discovering as she symbolically looks into the mirror,

> this man was her husband, truly — they were truly married, here in this room — they had been married haphazardly and accidentally for a long time. In another part of the city she had another husband, a "husband," but she had not betrayed that man, not really. This man, whom she loved above any other person in the world . . . was her truest lover, her destiny.

Oates allows the plot to progress sequentially to the resolution — to integrity — only as Anna's consciousness discovers its true identity, its integration.

From Notes on Modern American Literature

CONSIDERATIONS FOR CRITICAL THINKING AND WRITING

1. What does Brennan mean by characterizing Chekhov's story as "masculine" and Oates's as "feminine"? How is each writer's use of point of view related to this question?

2. Brennan describes Chekhov's plot as "linear" and Oates's as "circular." How is this contrast influenced by the writer's use of point of view?

3. Brennan asserts that in Oates's story, "Anna's consciousness discovers its true identity, its integration." Write an essay explaining whether you agree or disagree with this assessment. In your response, consider how Oates's use of point of view affects your reading of Anna's character.

EDWIDGE DANTICAT (B. 1969)

Edwidge Danticat was raised by her uncle in her birthplace of Port-au-Prince, Haiti, until she joined her parents in Brooklyn at the age of twelve. Danticat showed promise as a writer in high school, and after taking a B.A. in French literature from Barnard College in 1990, she attended Brown

University's creative writing program, and published her first book, *Breath, Eyes, Memory*, in 1994. "New York Day Women" comes from the story collection *Krik? Krak!* (1995), a finalist for the National Book Award. The Haitian style of storytelling had a strong influence on Danticat; *Krik? Krak!* is named for a call-and-response practice that begins a story in the Haitian oral tradition. Danticat's latest publication, *The Farming of Bones* (1998), is a work of historical fiction set in her home country in 1937, a time of turmoil between Haiti and the Dominican Republic.

Web *Research Edwidge Danticat with LitLinks at*
http://www.bedfordstmartins.com/meyer/bedintrolit

New York Day Women   1995

Today, walking down the street, I see my mother. She is strolling with a happy gait, her body thrust toward the DON'T WALK sign and the yellow taxicabs that make forty-five-degree turns on the corner of Madison and Fifty-seventh Street.

I have never seen her in this kind of neighborhood, peering into Chanel and Tiffany's and gawking at the jewels glowing in the Bulgari windows. My mother never shops outside of Brooklyn. She has never seen the advertising office where I work. She is afraid to take the subway, where you may meet those young black militant street preachers who curse black women for straightening their hair.

Yet, here she is, my mother, who I left at home that morning in her bathrobe, with pieces of newspapers twisted like rollers in her hair. My mother, who accuses me of random offenses as I dash out of the house.

Would you get up and give an old lady like me your subway seat? In this state of mind, I bet you don't even give up your seat to a pregnant lady.

My mother, who is often right about that. Sometimes I get up and give my   5
seat. Other times, I don't. It all depends on how pregnant the woman is and whether or not she is with her boyfriend or husband and whether or not *he* is sitting down.

As my mother stands in front of Carnegie Hall, one taxi driver yells to another, "What do you think this is, a dance floor?"

My mother waits patiently for this dispute to be settled before crossing the street.

In Haiti when you get hit by a car, the owner of the car gets out and kicks you for getting blood on his bumper.

My mother who laughs when she says this and shows a large gap in her mouth where she lost three more molars to the dentist last week. My mother, who at fifty-nine, says dentures are okay.

You can take them out when they bother you. I'll like them. I'll like them fine.   10

Will it feel empty when Papa kisses you?

Oh no, he doesn't kiss me that way anymore.

My mother, who watches the lottery drawing every night on channel 11 without ever having played the numbers.

A third of that money is all I would need. We would pay the mortgage, and your father could stop driving that taxicab all over Brooklyn.

I follow my mother, mesmerized by the many possibilities of her journey. Even 15 in a flowered dress, she is lost in a sea of pinstripes and gray suits, high heels and elegant short skirts, Reebok sneakers, dashing from building to building.

My mother, who won't go out to dinner with anyone.

If they want to eat with me, let them come to my house, even if I boil water and give it to them.

My mother, who talks to herself when she peels the skin off poultry.

Fat, you know, and cholesterol. Fat and cholesterol killed your aunt Hermine.

My mother, who makes jam with dried grapefruit peel and then puts in cinna- 20 mon bark that I always think is cockroaches in the jam. My mother, whom I have always bought household appliances for, on her birthday. A nice rice cooker, a blender.

I trail the red orchids in her dress and the heavy faux leather bag on her shoulders. Realizing the ferocious pace of my pursuit, I stop against a wall to rest. My mother keeps on walking as though she owns the sidewalk under her feet.

As she heads toward the Plaza Hotel, a bicycle messenger swings so close to her that I want to dash forward and rescue her, but she stands dead in her tracks and lets him ride around her and then goes on.

My mother stops at a corner hot-dog stand and asks for something. The vendor hands her a can of soda that she slips into her bag. She stops by another vendor selling sundresses for seven dollars each. I can tell that she is looking at an African print dress, contemplating my size. I think to myself, Please Ma, don't buy it. It would be just another thing that I would bury in the garage or give to Goodwill.

Why should we give to Goodwill when there are so many people back home who need clothes? We save our clothes for the relatives in Haiti.

Twenty years we have been saving all kinds of things for the relatives in Haiti. I 25 need the place in the garage for an exercise bike.

You are pretty enough to be a stewardess. Only dogs like bones.

This mother of mine, she stops at another hot-dog vendor's and buys a frankfurter that she eats on the street. I never knew that she ate frankfurters. With her blood pressure, she shouldn't eat anything with sodium. She has to be careful with her heart, this day woman.

I cannot just swallow salt. Salt is heavier than a hundred bags of shame.

She is slowing her pace, and now I am too close. If she turns around, she might see me. I let her walk into the park before I start to follow again.

My mother walks toward the sandbox in the middle of the park. There a 30 woman is waiting with a child. The woman is wearing a leotard with biker's shorts and has small weights in her hands. The woman kisses the child good-bye and surrenders him to my mother; then she bolts off, running on the cemented stretches in the park.

The child given to my mother has frizzy blond hair. His hand slips into hers easily, like he's known her for a long time. When he raises his face to look at my mother, it is as though he is looking at the sky.

My mother gives this child the soda that she bought from the vendor on the street corner. The child's face lights up as she puts in a straw in the can for him. This seems to be a conspiracy just between the two of them.

My mother and the child sit and watch the other children play in the sandbox. The child pulls out a comic book from a knapsack with Big Bird on the back. My mother peers into his comic book. My mother, who taught herself to read as a little girl in Haiti from the books that her brothers brought home from school.

My mother, who has now lost six of her seven sisters in Ville Rose and has never had the strength to return for their funerals.

Many graves to kiss when I go back. Many graves to kiss. 35

She throws away the empty soda can when the child is done with it. I wait and watch from a corner until the woman in the leotard and biker's shorts returns, sweaty and breathless, an hour later. My mother gives the woman back her child and strolls farther into the park.

I turn around and start to walk out of the park before my mother can see me. My lunch hour is long since gone. I have to hurry back to work. I walk through a cluster of joggers, then race to a *Sweden Tours* bus. I stand behind the bus and take a peek at my mother in the park. She is standing in a circle, chatting with a group of women who are taking other people's children on an afternoon outing. They look like a Third World Parent-Teacher Association meeting.

I quickly jump into a cab heading back to the office. Would Ma have said hello had she been the one to see me first?

As the cab races away from the park, it occurs to me that perhaps one day I would chase an old woman down a street by mistake and that old woman would be somebody else's mother, who I would have mistaken for mine.

Day women come out when nobody expects them. 40

Tonight on the subway, I will get up and give my seat to a pregnant woman or a lady about Ma's age.

My mother, who stuffs thimbles in her mouth and then blows up her cheeks like Dizzy Gillespie while sewing yet another Raggedy Ann doll that she names Suzette after me.

I will have all these little Suzettes in case you never have any babies, which looks more and more like it is going to happen.

My mother who had me when she was thirty-three — *l'âge du Christ* — at the age that Christ died on the cross.

That's a blessing, believe you me, even if American doctors say by that time 45 you can make retarded babies.

My mother, who sews lace collars on my company softball T-shirts when she does my laundry.

Why, you can't you look like a lady playing softball?

My mother, who never went to any of my Parent-Teacher Association meetings when I was in school.

You're so good anyway. What are they going to tell me? I don't want to make you ashamed of this day woman. Shame is heavier than a hundred bags of salt.

CONSIDERATIONS FOR CRITICAL THINKING AND WRITING

1. FIRST RESPONSE. What is the effect of having two first-person points of view instead of having the story told exclusively from either the daughter's or mother's perspective?
2. The daughter frequently repeats the phrase "My mother." What does this suggest to you about the daughter's feelings for her mother?
3. Why does the daughter follow her mother? What does she learn about her?
4. How is the mother's world different from her daughter's?
5. How is the daughter's perspective on the mother different as a result of observing her on the street?
6. Although the story is set on New York City streets, Haiti is, in a sense, a part of the setting too. How is this effect achieved in the story?
7. What do you make of the mother's final words?
8. Describe what you think is the central point of the story.

CONNECTION TO ANOTHER SELECTION

1. Compare and contrast the mother's attitude toward Haiti with the grandmother's attitude toward China in Gish Jen's "Who's Irish?" (p. 178).

7

Symbolism

A *symbol* is a person, object, or event that suggests more than its literal meaning. This basic definition is simple enough, but the use of symbol in literature makes some students slightly nervous because they tend to regard it as a booby trap, a hidden device that can go off during a seemingly harmless class discussion. "I didn't see that when I was reading the story" is a frequently heard comment. This sort of surprise and recognition is both natural and common. Most readers go through a story for the first time getting their bearings, figuring out what is happening to whom and so on. Patterns and significant details often require a second or third reading before they become evident — before a symbol sheds light on a story. Then the details of a work may suddenly fit together, and its meaning may be reinforced, clarified, or enlarged by the symbol. Symbolic meanings are usually embedded in the texture of a story, but they are not "hidden"; instead, they are carefully placed. Reading between the lines (where there is only space) is unnecessary. What is needed is a careful consideration of the elements of the story, a sensitivity to its language, and some common sense.

Common sense is a good place to begin. Symbols appear all around us; anything can be given symbolic significance. Without symbols our lives would be stark and vacant. Awareness of a writer's use of symbols is not all that different from the kinds of perceptions and interpretations that allow us to make sense of our daily lives. We know, for example, that a ring used in a wedding is more than just a piece of jewelry because it suggests the unity and intimacy of a closed circle. The bride's gown may be white because we tend to associate innocence and purity with that color. Or consider the meaning of a small alligator sewn on a shirt or some other article of clothing. What started as a company trademark has gathered around it a range of meanings suggesting everything from quality and money to preppiness and silliness. The ring, the white gown, and the alligator trademark are symbolic because each has meanings that go beyond its specific qualities and functions.

Symbols such as these that are widely recognized by a society or culture are called *conventional symbols*. The Christian cross, the Star of David, a swastika, or a nation's flag all have meanings understood by large groups of people. Certain kinds of experiences also have traditional meanings in Western cultures. Winter, the setting sun, and the color black suggest death, while spring, the rising sun, and the color green evoke images of youth and new beginnings. (It is worth noting, however, that individual cultures sometimes have their own conventions; some Eastern cultures associate white rather than black with death and mourning. And obviously the polo player trademark would mean nothing to anyone totally unfamiliar with American culture.) These broadly shared symbolic meanings are second nature to us.

Writers use conventional symbols to reinforce meanings. Kate Chopin, for example, emphasizes the spring setting in "The Story of an Hour" (p. 12) as a way of suggesting the renewed sense of life that Mrs. Mallard feels when she thinks herself free from her husband.

A *literary symbol* can include traditional, conventional, or public meanings, but it may also be established internally by the total context of the work in which it appears. In "Soldier's Home" (p. 152), Hemingway does not use Krebs's family home as a conventional symbol of safety, comfort, and refuge from the war. Instead, Krebs's home becomes symbolic of provincial, erroneous presuppositions compounded by blind innocence, sentimentality, and smug middle-class respectability. The symbolic meaning of his home reveals that Krebs no longer shares his family's and town's view of the world. Their notions of love, the value of a respectable job, and a belief in God seem to him petty, complicated, and meaningless. The significance of Krebs's home is determined by the events within the story, which reverse and subvert the traditional associations readers might bring to it. Krebs's interactions with his family and the people in town reveal what home has come to mean to him.

A literary symbol can be a setting, character, action, object, name, or anything else in a work that maintains its literal significance while suggesting other meanings. Symbols cannot be restricted to a single meaning; they are suggestive rather than definitive. Their evocation of multiple meanings allows a writer to say more with less. Symbols are economical devices for evoking complex ideas without having to resort to painstaking explanations that would make a story more like an essay than an experience. The many walls in Melville's "Bartleby, the Scrivener" (p. 116) cannot be reduced to one idea. They have multiple meanings that unify the story. The walls are symbols of the deadening, dehumanizing, restrictive repetitiveness of the office routine, as well as of the confining, materialistic sensibilities of Wall Street. They suggest whatever limits and thwarts human aspirations, including death itself. We don't know precisely what shatters Bartleby's will to live, but the walls in the story, through their symbolic suggestiveness, indicate the nature of the limitations that cause the scrivener to slip into hopelessness and his "dead-wall reveries."

When a character, object, or incident indicates a single, fixed meaning, the writer is using *allegory* rather than symbol. Whereas symbols have literal functions as well as multiple meanings, the primary focus in allegory is on the abstract idea called forth by the concrete object. John Bunyan's *Pilgrim's Progress,* published during the seventeenth century, is a classic example of allegory because the characters, action, and setting have no existence beyond their abstract meanings. Bunyan's purpose is to teach his readers the exemplary way to salvation and heaven. The protagonist, named Christian, flees the City of Destruction in search of the Celestial City. Along the way he encounters characters who either help or hinder his spiritual journey. Among them are Mr. Worldly Wiseman, Faithful, Prudence, Piety, and a host of others named after the virtues or vices they display. These characters, places, and actions exist solely to illustrate religious doctrine. Allegory tends to be definitive rather than suggestive. It drives meaning into a corner and keeps it there. Most modern writers prefer the exploratory nature of symbol to the reductive nature of pure allegory.

Stories often include symbols that you may or may not perceive on a first reading. Their subtle use is a sign of a writer's skill in weaving symbols into the fabric of the characters' lives. Symbols may sometimes escape you, but that is probably better than finding symbols where only literal meanings are intended. Allow the text to help you determine whether a symbolic reading is appropriate. Once you are clear about what literally happens, read carefully and notice the placement of details that are emphasized. The pervasive references to time in Faulkner's "A Rose for Emily" (p. 75) and the many kinds of walls that appear throughout "Bartleby, the Scrivener" call attention to themselves and warrant symbolic readings. A symbol, however, need not be repeated to have an important purpose in a story. We don't learn until the very end of "Bartleby, the Scrivener" that Bartleby once worked as a clerk in the Dead Letter Office in Washington, D.C. This information is offered as merely an offhand rumor by the narrator, but its symbolic value is essential for understanding what motivates Bartleby's behavior. Indeed, Bartleby's experiences in the Dead Letter Office suggest enough about the nature of his thwarted hopes and desires to account for Bartleby's rejection of life.

By keeping track of the total context of the story, you should be able to decide whether your reading is reasonable and consistent with the other facts; plenty of lemons in literature yield no symbolic meaning even if they are squeezed. Be sensitive to the meanings that the author associates with people, places, objects, and actions. You may not associate home with provincial innocence as Hemingway does in "Soldier's Home," but a close reading of the story will permit you to see how and why he constructs that symbolic meaning. If you treat stories like people — with tact and care — they ordinarily are accessible and enjoyable.

The next four stories — Alberto Alvaro Ríos's "The Secret Lion," Colette's "The Hand," Ralph Ellison's "Battle Royal," and Gabriel García Márquez's "The Handsomest Drowned Man in the World" — rely on symbols to convey meanings that go far beyond the specific incidents described in their plots.

ALBERTO ALVARO RÍOS (B. 1952)

On the U.S. side of the border town of Nogales, Arizona, poet and fiction writer Alberto Alvaro Ríos was born to an English mother and a father from the Chiapas region of Mexico. As he grew up in Nogales, Ríos was discouraged from speaking Spanish in school and had to relearn the language in high school classes. Ríos took a B.A. from the University of Arizona in 1974, completed an M.F.A. there in 1979, and in 1982 published his first book, *Whispering to Fool the Wind: Poems,* which received the Walt Whitman Award from the Academy of American Poets. His other publications include *The Iguana Killer: Twelve Stories of the Heart* (1984), *Five Indiscretions: A Book of Poems* (1985), *The Lime Orchard Woman: Poems* (1988), *Teodora Luna's Two Kisses: Poems* (1990), and *Pig Cookies and Other Stories* (1995). A professor of English at Arizona State University, Ríos likes to write stories with inflections of Mexico, England, and the United States, claiming to use a personal "alphabet" consisting of cross-cultural words and images.

Web *Research Alberto Alvaro Ríos with LitLinks at*
http://www.bedfordstmartins.com/meyer/bedintrolit

The Secret Lion   1984

I was twelve and in junior high school and something happened that we didn't have a name for, but it was there nonetheless like a lion, and roaring, roaring that way the biggest things do. Everything changed. Just that. Like the rug, the one that gets pulled — or better, like the tablecloth those magicians pull where the stuff on the table stays the same but the gasp! from the audience makes the staying-the-same part not matter. Like that.

What happened was there were teachers now, not just one teacher, teacherz, and we felt personally abandoned somehow. When a person had all these teachers now, he didn't get taken care of the same way, even though six was more than one. Arithmetic went out the door when we walked in. And we saw girls now, but they weren't the same girls we used to know because we couldn't talk to them anymore, not the same way we used to, certainly not to Sandy, even though she was my neighbor, too. Not even to her. She just played the piano all the time. And there were words, oh there were words in junior high school, and we wanted to know what they were, and how a person did them — that's what school was supposed to be for. Only, in junior high school, school wasn't school, everything was backward-like. If you went up to a teacher and said the word to try and find out what it meant you got in trouble for saying it. So we didn't. And we figured it must have been that way about other stuff, too, so we never said anything about anything—we weren't stupid.

But my friend Sergio and I, we solved junior high school. We would come home from school on the bus, put our books away, change shoes, and go across the highway to the arroyo.° It was the one place we were not supposed to go. So we did. This was, after all, what junior high had at least shown us. It was our river, though, our personal Mississippi, our friend from long back, and it was full of stories and all the branch forts we had built in it when we were still the Vikings of America, with our own symbol, which we had carved everywhere, even in the sand, which let the water take it. That was good, we had decided; whoever was at the end of this river would know about us.

At the very very top of our growing lungs, what we would do down there was shout every dirty word we could think of, in every combination we could come up with, and we would yell about girls, and all the things we wanted to do with them, as loud as we could—we didn't know what we wanted to do with them, just things—and we would yell about teachers, and how we loved some of them, like Miss Crevelone, and how we wanted to dissect some of them, making signs of the cross, like priests, and we would yell this stuff over and over because it felt good, we couldn't explain why, it just felt good and for the first time in our lives there was nobody to tell us we couldn't. So we did.

One Thursday we were walking along shouting this way, and the railroad, the Southern Pacific, which ran above and along the far side of the arroyo, had dropped a grinding ball down there, which was, we found out later, a cannon-ball thing used in mining. A bunch of them were put in a big vat which turned around and crushed the ore. One had been dropped, or thrown—what do ca-boose men do when they get bored—but it got down there regardless and as we were walking along yelling about one girl or another, a particular Claudia, we found it, one of these things, looked at it, picked it up, and got very very excited, and held it and passed it back and forth, and we were saying "Guythisis, this is, geeGuythis . . .": we had this perception about nature then, that nature is imper-fect and that round things are perfect: we said "GuyGodthis is perfect, thisisthis is perfect, it's round, round and heavy, it'sit's the best thing we'veeverseen. Whatisit?" We didn't know. We just knew it was great. We just, whatever, we played with it, held it some more.

And then we had to decide what to do with it. We knew, because of a lot of things, that if we were going to take this and show it to anybody, this discovery, this best thing, was going to be taken away from us. That's the way it works with little kids, like all the polished quartz, the tons of it we had collected piece by piece over the years. Junior high kids too. If we took it home, my mother, we knew, was going to look at it and say "throw that dirty thing in the, get rid of it." Simple like, like that. "But ma it's the best thing I" "Getridofit." Simple.

So we didn't. Take it home. Instead, we came up with the answer. We dug a hole and buried it. And we marked it secretly. Lots of secret signs. And came back the next week to dig it up and, we didn't know, pass it around some more or something, but we didn't find it. We dug up that whole bank, and we never found it again. We tried.

arroyo: A small stream that rises and falls.

Sergio and I talked about that ball or whatever it was when we couldn't find it. All we used were small words, neat, good. Kid words. What we were really saying, but didn't know the words, was how much that ball was like that place, that whole arroyo: couldn't tell anybody about it, didn't understand what it was, didn't have a name for it. It just felt good. It was just perfect in the way it was that place, that whole going to that place, that whole junior high school lion. It was just iron-heavy, it had no name, it felt good or not, we couldn't take it home to show our mothers, and once we buried it, it was gone forever.

The ball was gone, like the first reasons we had come to that arroyo years earlier, like the first time we had seen the arroyo, it was gone like everything else that had been taken away. This was not our first lesson. We stopped going to the arroyo after not finding the thing, the same way we had stopped going there years earlier and headed for the mountains. Nature seemed to keep pushing us around one way or another, teaching us the same thing every place we ended up. Nature's gang was tough that way, teaching us stuff.

When we were young we moved away from town, me and my family. Ser- 10 gio's was already out there. Out in the wilds. Or at least the new place seemed like the wilds since everything looks bigger the smaller a man is. I was five, I guess, and we had moved three miles north of Nogales where we had lived, three miles north of the Mexican border. We looked across the highway in one direction and there was the arroyo; hills stood up in the other direction. Mountains, for a small man.

When the first summer came the very first place we went to was of course the one place we weren't supposed to go, the arroyo. We went down in there and found water running, summer rain water mostly, and we went swimming. But every third or fourth or fifth day, the sewage treatment plant that was, we found out, upstream, would release whatever it was that it released, and we would never know exactly what day that was, and a person really couldn't tell right off by looking at the water, not every time, not so a person could get out in time. So, we went swimming that summer and some days we had a lot of fun. Some days we didn't. We found a thousand ways to explain what happened on those other days, constructing elaborate stories about the neighborhood dogs, and hadn't she, my mother, miscalculated her step before, too? But she knew something was up because we'd come running into the house those days, wanting to take a shower, even — if this can be imagined — in the middle of the day.

That was the first time we stopped going to the arroyo. It taught us to look the other way. We decided, as the second side of summer came, we wanted to go into the mountains. They were still mountains then. We went running in one summer Thursday morning, my friend Sergio and I, into my mother's kitchen, and said, well, what'zin, what'zin those hills over there — we used her word so she'd understand us — and she said nothingdon'tworryaboutit. So we went out, and we weren't dumb, we thought with our eyes to each other, ohhoshe'stryingtokeepsomethingfromus. We knew adults.

We had read the books, after all; we knew about bridges and castles and wildtreacherousraging alligatormouth rivers. We wanted them. So we were going to go out and get them. We went back that morning into that kitchen and we said, "We're going out there, we're going into the hills, we're going away for three days, don't worry." She said, "All right."

"You know," I said to Sergio, "if we're going to go away for three days, well, we ought to at least pack a lunch."

But we were two young boys with no patience for what we thought at the time was mom-stuff: making sa-and-wiches. My mother didn't offer. So we got out little kid knapsacks that my mother had sewn for us, and into them we put the jar of mustard. A loaf of bread. Knivesforksplates, bottles of Coke, a can opener. This was lunch for the two of us. And we were weighed down, humped over to be strong enough to carry this stuff. But we started walking anyway, into the hills. We were going to eat berries and stuff otherwise. "Goodbye." My mom said that.

After the first hill we were dead. But we walked. My mother could still see us. And we kept walking. We walked until we got to where the sun is straight overhead, noon. That place. Where that is doesn't matter; it's time to eat. The truth is we weren't anywhere close to that place. We just agreed that the sun was overhead and that it was time to eat, and by tilting our heads a little we could make that the truth.

"We really ought to start looking for a place to eat."

"Yeah. Let's look for a good place to eat." We went back and forth saying that for fifteen minutes, making it lunchtime because that's what we always said back and forth before lunchtimes at home. "Yeah, I'm hungry all right." I nodded my head. "Yeah, I'm hungry all right too. I'm hungry." He nodded his head. I nodded my head back. After a good deal more nodding, we were ready, just as we came over a little hill. We hadn't found the mountains yet. This was a little hill.

And on the other side of this hill we found heaven.

It was just what we thought it would be.

Perfect. Heaven was green, like nothing else in Arizona. And it wasn't a cemetery or like that because we had seen cemeteries and they had gravestones and stuff and this didn't. This was perfect, had trees, lots of trees, had birds, like we had never seen before. It was like "The Wizard of Oz," like when they got to Oz and everything was so green, so emerald, they had to wear those glasses, and we ran just like them, laughing, laughing that way we did that moment, and we went running down to this clearing in it all, hitting each other that good way we did.

We got down there, we kept laughing, we kept hitting each other, we unpacked our stuff, and we started acting "rich." We knew all about how to do that, like blowing on our nails, then rubbing them on our chests for the shine. We made our sandwiches, opened our Cokes, got out the rest of the stuff, the salt and pepper shakers. I found this particular hole and I put my Coke right into it, a perfect fit, and I called it my Coke-holder. I got down next to it on my back, because everyone knows that rich people eat lying down, and I got my sandwich in one hand and put my other arm around the Coke in its holder. When I wanted a drink, I lifted my neck a little, put out my lips, and tipped my Coke a little with the crook of my elbow. Ah.

We were there, lying down, eating our sandwiches, laughing, throwing bread at each other and out for the birds. This was heaven. We were laughing and we couldn't believe it. My mother was keeping something from us, ah ha, but we had found her out. We even found water over at the side of the clearing to wash our plates with—we had brought plates. Sergio started washing his plates when he was done, and I was being rich with my Coke, and this day in summer was right.

When suddenly these two men came, from around a corner of trees and the tallest grass we had ever seen. They had bags on their backs, leather bags, bags and sticks.

We didn't know what clubs were, but I learned later, like I learned about 25 the grinding balls. The two men yelled at us. Most specifically, one wanted me to take my Coke out of my Coke-holder so he could sink his golf ball into it.

Something got taken away from us that moment. Heaven. We grew up a little bit, and couldn't go backward. We learned. No one had ever told us about golf. They had told us about heaven. And it went away. We got golf in exchange.

We went back to the arroyo for the rest of that summer, and tried to have fun the best we could. We learned to be ready for finding the grinding ball. We loved it, and when we buried it we knew what would happen. The truth is, we didn't look so hard for it. We were two boys and twelve summers then, and not stupid. Things get taken away.

We buried it because it was perfect. We didn't tell my mother, but together it was all we talked about, till we forgot. It was the lion.

Considerations for Critical Thinking and Writing

1. FIRST RESPONSE. How do the narrator's experiences in junior high school compare with your own? In what sense has "Everything changed"?

2. What is the effect of the narrator's running words and phrases together?

3. Describe the central conflict in the story. Who or what is the antagonist?

4. Discuss the symbolic significance(s) of the arroyo, the grinding ball, and the golf course. How are they related to one another, and how is meaning associated with each?

5. Discuss the significance of the title. In what sense can the secret lion be regarded as the central, controlling symbol?

6. What do you think is the major point of the story?

7. How do the boys' view of life develop and change over the course of the story?

Connections to Other Selections

1. How might "The Secret Lion" and Ralph Ellison's "Battle Royal" (p. 231) be compared and contrasted in terms of each narrator's sense that life doesn't always offer up what is expected of it?

2. Consider the ending of "The Secret Lion" and of Colette's "The Hand" (following). Is either conclusion a "happy ending"?

COLETTE (SIDONIE-GABRIELLE COLETTE / 1873–1954)

Born in Burgundy, France, Sidonie-Gabrielle Colette lived a long and remarkably diverse life. At various points during her career she supported herself as a novelist, music hall performer, and journalist. Her professional life and three marriages helped to shape her keen insights into modern love and women's lives. She is regarded as a significant feminist voice in the twentieth century, and her reputation is firmly fixed by her having been the first woman admitted to the Goncourt Academy and by the continued popularity of her work among readers internationally. Her best-known works include *Mitsou, or, How Girls Grow Wise* (1919), *Chéri* (1920), *Claudine's House* (1922), and *Gigi* (1944). "The Hand" signals a telling moment in the life of a young bride.

Web *Research Colette with LitLinks at*
http://www.bedfordstmartins.com/meyer/bedintrolit

The Hand   1924

He had fallen asleep on his young wife's shoulder, and she proudly bore the weight of the man's head, blond, ruddy-complexioned, eyes closed. He had slipped his big arm under the small of her slim, adolescent back, and his strong hand lay on the sheet next to the young woman's right elbow. She smiled to see the man's hand emerging there, all by itself and far away from its owner. Then she let her eyes wander over the half-lit room. A veiled conch shed a light across the bed the color of periwinkle.

"Too happy to sleep," she thought.

Too excited also, and often surprised by her new state. It had been only two weeks since she had begun to live the scandalous life of a newlywed who tastes the joys of living with someone unknown and with whom she is in love. To meet a handsome, blond young man, recently widowed, good at tennis and rowing, to marry him a month later: her conjugal adventure had been little more than a kidnapping. So that whenever she lay awake beside her husband, like tonight, she still kept her eyes closed for a long time, then opened them again in order to savor, with astonishment, the blue of the brand-new curtains, instead of the apricot-pink through which the first light of day filtered into the room where she had slept as a little girl.

A quiver ran through the sleeping body lying next to her, and she tightened her left arm around her husband's neck with the charming authority exercised by weak creatures. He did not wake up.

"His eyelashes are so long," she said to herself.   5

To herself she also praised his mouth, full and likable, his skin the color of pink brick, and even his forehead, neither noble nor broad, but still smooth and unwrinkled.

Her husband's right hand, lying beside her, quivered in turn, and beneath the curve of her back she felt the right arm, on which her whole weight was resting, come to life.

"I'm so heavy . . . I wish I could get up and turn the light off. But he's sleeping so well . . ."

The arm twisted again, feebly, and she arched her back to make herself lighter.

"It's as if I were lying on some animal," she thought.   10

She turned her head a little on the pillow and looked at the hand lying there next to her.

"It's so big! It really is bigger than my whole head."

The light, flowing out from under the edge of a parasol of bluish crystal, spilled up against the hand, and made every contour of the skin apparent, exaggerating the powerful knuckles and the veins engorged by the pressure on the arm. A few red hairs, at the base of the fingers, all curved in the same direction, like ears of wheat in the wind, and the flat nails, whose ridges the nail buffer had not smoothed out, gleamed, coated with pink varnish.

"I'll tell him not to varnish his nails," thought the young wife. "Varnish and pink polish don't go with a hand so . . . a hand that's so . . ."

An electric jolt ran through the hand and spared the young woman from having to find the right adjective. The thumb stiffened itself out, horribly long and spatulate, and pressed tightly against the index finger, so that the hand suddenly took on a vile, apelike appearance.

"Oh!" whispered the young woman, as though faced with something slightly indecent.

The sound of a passing car pierced the silence with a shrillness that seemed luminous. The sleeping man did not wake, but the hand, offended, reared back and tensed up in the shape of a crab and waited, ready for battle. The screeching sound died down and the hand, relaxing gradually, lowered its claws, and became a pliant beast, awkwardly bent, shaken by faint jerks which resembled some sort of agony. The flat, cruel nail of the overlong thumb glistened. A curve in the little finger, which the young woman had never noticed, appeared, and the wallowing hand revealed its fleshy palm like a red belly.

"And I've kissed that hand! . . . How horrible! Haven't I ever looked at it?"

The hand, disturbed by a bad dream, appeared to respond to this startling discovery, this disgust. It regrouped its forces, opened wide, and splayed its tendons, lumps, and red fur like battle dress, then slowly drawing itself in again, grabbed a fistful of the sheet, dug into it with its curved fingers, and squeezed, squeezed with the methodical pleasure of a strangler.

"Oh!" cried the young woman.

The hand disappeared and a moment later the big arm, relieved of its burden, became a protective belt, a warm bulwark against all the terrors of night. But the next morning, when it was time for breakfast in bed — hot chocolate and toast — she saw the hand again, with its red hair and red skin, and the ghastly thumb curving out over the handle of a knife.

"Do you want this slice, darling? I'll butter it for you."

She shuddered and felt her skin crawl on the back of her arms and down her back.

"Oh, no . . . no . . ."

Then she concealed her fear, bravely subdued herself, and, beginning her life of duplicity, of resignation, and of a lowly, delicate diplomacy, she leaned over and humbly kissed the monstrous hand.

CONSIDERATIONS FOR CRITICAL THINKING AND WRITING

1. FIRST RESPONSE. Where is "The Hand" set? How significant is the setting of the story?
2. How well did the young woman know her husband before she married him? What attracted her to him?
3. How does the wife regard the hand at the very beginning of the story? At what point does she begin to change her attitude?
4. Explain how the wife's description of the hand affects your own response to it. What prompts her "Oh!" in paragraphs 16 and 20? What do you suppose the wife is thinking at these moments?

5. What powerful feelings does the hand evoke in the wife? How do her descriptions of the hand suggest symbolic readings of it?

6. Describe the conflict in the story. Explain whether there is a resolution to this conflict.

7. Do you think the story is more about the husband or about the wife? Who is the central character? Explain your choice. Consider also whether the characters are static or dynamic.

8. Why do you think the narrator mentions that the husband was "recently widowed"?

9. Why do you think the wife kisses her husband's hand in the final paragraph? Write an essay explaining how the kiss symbolizes the nature of their relationship.

10. Describe the point of view in the story. Why do you suppose Colette doesn't use a first-person perspective that would reveal more intimately the wife's perceptions and concerns?

CONNECTIONS TO OTHER SELECTIONS

1. In "The Birthmark" (p. 359) Nathaniel Hawthorne also uses a hand for symbolic purposes. Compare the meanings he associates with the hand in his story with Colette's. How does each writer invest meanings in a central symbol? What are the significant similarities and differences in meanings? Write an essay explaining why you find one story more effective than the other.

2. Compare the use of settings in "The Hand" and in John Updike's "A & P" (p. 606). To what extent does each story attach meaning to its setting?

3. How might Gail Godwin's "A Sorrowful Woman" (p. 35) be read as a kind of sequel to "The Hand"?

RALPH ELLISON (1914–1994)

Born in Oklahoma and educated at the Tuskegee Institute in Alabama, where he studied music, Ralph Ellison gained his reputation as a writer on the strength of his only published novel, *Invisible Man* (1952). He also published some scattered short stories and two collections of essays, *Shadow and Act* (1964) and *Going to the Territory* (1986). Although his writing was not extensive, it is important because Ellison wrote about race relations in the context of universal human concerns. *Invisible Man* is the story of a young black man who moves from the South to the North and discovers what it means to be black in America. "Battle Royal," published in 1947 as a short story, became the first chapter of *Invisible Man*. It concerns the beginning of the protagonist's long struggle for an adult identity in a world made corrupt by racial prejudice.

Web *Research Ralph Ellison with LitLinks at*
http://www.bedfordstmartins.com/meyer/bedintrolit

Battle Royal   1947

It goes a long way back, some twenty years. All my life I had been looking for something, and everywhere I turned someone tried to tell me what it was. I accepted their answers too, though they were often in contradiction and even self-contradictory. I was naive. I was looking for myself and asking everyone except myself questions which I, and only I, could answer. It took me a long time and much painful boomeranging of my expectations to achieve a realization everyone else appears to have been born with: That I am nobody but myself. But first I had to discover that I am an invisible man!

And yet I am no freak of nature, nor of history. I was in the cards, other things having been equal (or unequal) eighty-five years ago. I am not ashamed of my grandparents for having been slaves. I am only ashamed of myself for having at one time been ashamed. About eighty-five years ago they were told that they were free, united with others of our country in everything pertaining to the common good, and, in everything social, separate like the fingers of the hand. And they believed it. They exulted in it. They stayed in their place, worked hard, and brought up my father to do the same. But my grandfather is the one. He was an odd old guy, my grandfather, and I am told I take after him. It was he who caused the trouble. On his deathbed he called my father to him and said, "Son, after I'm gone I want you to keep up the good fight. I never told you, but our life is a war and I have been a traitor all my born days, a spy in the enemy's country ever since I gave up my gun back in the Reconstruction. Live with your head in the lion's mouth. I want you to overcome 'em with yeses, undermine 'em with grins, agree 'em to death and destruction, let 'em swoller you till they vomit or bust wide open." They thought the old man had gone out of his mind. He had been the meekest of men. The younger children were rushed from the room, the shades drawn and the flame of the lamp turned so low that it sputtered on the wick like the old man's breathing. "Learn it to the young-uns," he whispered fiercely; then he died.

But my folks were more alarmed over his last words than over his dying. It was as though he had not died at all, his words caused so much anxiety. I was warned emphatically to forget what he had said and, indeed, this is the first time it has been mentioned outside the family circle. It had a tremendous effect upon me, however. I could never be sure of what he meant. Grandfather had been a quiet old man who never made any trouble, yet on his deathbed he had called himself a traitor and a spy, and he had spoken of his meekness as a dangerous activity. It became a constant puzzle which lay unanswered in the back of my mind. And whenever things went well for me I remembered my grandfather and felt guilty and uncomfortable. It was as though I was carrying out his advice in spite of myself. And to make it worse, everyone loved me for it. I was praised by the most lily-white men of the town. I was considered an example of desirable conduct—just as my grandfather had been. And what puzzled me was that the old man had defined it as *treachery*. When I was praised for my conduct I felt a guilt that in some way I was doing something that was really against the wishes of the white folks, that if they had understood they would have desired me to act just the opposite, that I should have been sulky and mean, and that that really would have been what they wanted, even though they were fooled and thought they wanted me to act as I did. It made me afraid that some day they would look upon me as a traitor and I would be lost. Still I was more afraid to act any other way because they didn't like that at all. The old man's words were like a curse. On my graduation day I delivered an oration in which I showed that humility was the secret, indeed, the very essence of progress. (Not that I believed this—how could I, remembering my grandfather?—I only believed that it worked.) It was a great success. Everyone praised me and I was invited to give the speech at a gathering of the town's leading white citizens. It was a triumph for our whole community.

It was in the main ballroom of the leading hotel. When I got there I discovered that it was on the occasion of a smoker, and I was told that since I was to be there anyway I might as well take part in the battle royal to be fought by some of my schoolmates as part of the entertainment. The battle royal came first.

All of the town's big shots were there in their tuxedoes, wolfing down the buffet foods, drinking beer and whiskey and smoking black cigars. It was a large room with a high ceiling. Chairs were arranged in neat rows around three sides of a portable boxing ring. The fourth side was clear, revealing a gleaming space of polished floor. I had some misgivings over the battle royal, by the way. Not from a distaste for fighting, but because I didn't care too much for the other fellows who were to take part. They were tough guys who seemed to have no grandfather's curse worrying their minds. No one could mistake their toughness. And besides, I suspected that fighting a battle royal might detract from the dignity of my speech. In those pre-invisible days I visualized myself as a potential Booker T. Washington. But the other fellows didn't care too much for me either, and there were nine of them. I felt superior to them in my way, and I didn't like the manner in which we were all crowded together into the servants' elevator. Nor did they like my being there. In fact, as the warmly lighted floors flashed past the elevator we had words over the fact that I, by taking part in the fight, had knocked one of their friends out of a night's work.

We were led out of the elevator through a rococo hall into an anteroom and told to get into our fighting togs. Each of us was issued a pair of boxing gloves and ushered out into the big mirrored hall, which we entered looking cautiously about us and whispering, lest we might accidentally be heard above the noise of the room. It was foggy with cigar smoke. And already the whiskey was taking effect. I was shocked to see some of the most important men of the town quite tipsy. They were all there—bankers, lawyers, judges, doctors, fire chiefs, teachers, merchants. Even one of the more fashionable pastors. Something we could not see was going on up front. A clarinet was vibrating sensuously and the men were standing up and moving eagerly forward. We were a small tight group, clustered together, our bare upper bodies touching and shining with anticipatory sweat; while up front the big shots were becoming increasingly excited over something we still could not see. Suddenly I heard the school superintendent, who had told me to come, yell, "Bring up the shines, gentlemen! Bring up the little shines!"

We were rushed up to the front of the ballroom, where it smelled even more strongly of tobacco and whiskey. Then we were pushed into place. I almost wet my pants. A sea of faces, some hostile, some amused, ringed around us, and in the center, facing us, stood a magnificent blonde—stark naked. There was dead silence. I felt a blast of cold air chill me. I tried to back away, but they were behind me and around me. Some of the boys stood with lowered heads, trembling. I felt a wave of irrational guilt and fear. My teeth chattered, my skin turned to goose flesh, my knees knocked. Yet I was strongly attracted

5

and looked in spite of myself. Had the price of looking been blindness, I would have looked. The hair was yellow like that of a circus kewpie doll, the face heavily powdered and rouged, as though to form an abstract mask, the eyes hollow and smeared a cool blue, the color of a baboon's butt. I felt a desire to spit upon her as my eyes brushed slowly over her body. Her breasts were firm and round as the domes of East Indian temples, and I stood so close as to see the fine skin texture and beads of pearly perspiration glistening like dew around the pink and erected buds of her nipples. I wanted at one and the same time to run from the room, to sink through the floor, or go to her and cover her from my eyes and the eyes of the others with my body; to feel the soft thighs, to caress her and destroy her, to love her and murder her, to hide from her, and yet to stroke where below the small American flag tattooed upon her belly her thighs formed a capital V. I had a notion that of all in the room she saw only me with her impersonal eyes.

And then she began to dance, a slow sensuous movement; the smoke of a hundred cigars clinging to her like the thinnest of veils. She seemed like a fair bird-girl girdled in veils calling to me from the angry surface of some gray and threatening sea. I was transported. Then I became aware of the clarinet playing and the big shots yelling at us. Some threatened us if we looked and others if we did not. On my right I saw one boy faint. And now a man grabbed a silver pitcher from a table and stepped close as he dashed ice water upon him and stood him up and forced two of us to support him as his head hung and moans issued from his thick bluish lips. Another boy began to plead to go home. He was the largest of the group, wearing dark red fighting trunks much too small to conceal the erection which projected from him as though in answer to the insinuating low-registered moaning of the clarinet. He tried to hide himself with his boxing gloves.

And all the while the blonde continued dancing, smiling faintly at the big shots who watched her with fascination, and faintly smiling at our fear. I noticed a certain merchant who followed her hungrily, his lips loose and drooling. He was a large man who wore diamond studs in a shirtfront which swelled with the ample paunch underneath, and each time the blonde swayed her undulating hips he ran his hand through the thin hair of his bald head and, with his arms upheld, his posture clumsy like that of an intoxicated panda, wound his belly in a slow and obscene grind. This creature was completely hypnotized. The music had quickened. As the dancer flung herself about with a detached expression on her face, the men began reaching out to touch her. I could see their beefy fingers sink into the soft flesh. Some of the others tried to stop them as she began to move around the floor in graceful circles, as they gave chase, slipping and sliding over the polished floor. It was mad. Chairs went crashing, drinks were spilt, as they ran laughing and howling after her. They caught her just as she reached a door, raised her from the floor, and tossed her as college boys are tossed at a hazing, and above her red, fixed-smiling lips I saw the terror and disgust in her eyes, almost like my own terror and that which I saw in some of the other boys. As I watched, they tossed her twice and her soft breasts seemed to flatten against the air and her legs flung wildly as she spun. Some of the more sober ones helped her to escape. And I started off the floor, heading for the anteroom with the rest of the boys.

Some were still crying in hysteria. But as we tried to leave we were stopped and ordered to get into the ring. There was nothing to do but what we were   10 told. All ten of us climbed under the ropes and allowed ourselves to be blind-folded with broad bands of white cloth. One of the men seemed to feel a bit sympathetic and tried to cheer us up as we stood with our backs against the ropes. Some of us tried to grin. "See that boy over there?" one of the men said. "I want you to run across at the bell and give it to him right in the belly. If you don't get him, I'm going to get you. I don't like his looks." Each of us was told the same. The blindfolds were put on. Yet even then I had been going over my speech. In my mind each word was as bright as flame. I felt the cloth pressed into place, and frowned so that it would be loosened when I relaxed.

But now I felt a sudden fit of blind terror. I was unused to darkness. It was as though I had suddenly found myself in a dark room filled with poisonous cottonmouths. I could hear the bleary voices yelling insistently for the battle royal to begin.

"Get going in there!"

"Let me at that big nigger!"

I strained to pick up the school superintendent's voice, as though to squeeze some security out of that slightly more familiar sound.

"Let me at those black sonsabitches!" someone yelled.   15

"No, Jackson, no!" another voice yelled. "Here, somebody, help me hold Jack."

"I want to get at that ginger-colored nigger. Tear him limb from limb," the first voice yelled.

I stood against the ropes trembling. For in those days I was what they called ginger-colored, and he sounded as though he might crunch me between his teeth like a crisp ginger cookie.

Quite a struggle was going on. Chairs were being kicked about and I could hear voices grunting as with a terrific effort. I wanted to see, to see more des-perately than ever before. But the blindfold was tight as a thick skin-puckering scab and when I raised my gloved hands to push the layers of white aside a voice yelled, "Oh, no you don't, black bastard! Leave that alone!"

"Ring the bell before Jackson kills him a coon!" someone boomed in the   20
sudden silence. And I heard the bell clang and the sound of the feet scuffling forward.

A glove smacked against my head. I pivoted, striking out stiffly as someone went past, and felt the jar ripple along the length of my arm to my shoulder. Then it seemed as though all nine of the boys had turned upon me at once. Blows pounded me from all sides while I struck out as best I could. So many blows landed upon me that I wondered if I were not the only blindfolded fighter in the ring, or if the man called Jackson hadn't succeeded in getting me after all.

Blindfolded, I could no longer control my motions. I had no dignity. I stumbled about like a baby or a drunken man. The smoke had become thicker and with each new blow it seemed to sear and further restrict my lungs. My saliva became like hot bitter glue. A glove connected with my head, filling my mouth with warm blood. It was everywhere. I could not tell if the moisture I felt upon my body was sweat or blood. A blow landed hard against the nape of my neck. I felt myself going over, my head hitting the floor. Streaks of blue light filled the black world behind the blindfold. I lay prone, pretending that I was knocked out, but felt myself seized by hands and yanked to my feet. "Get going, black boy! Mix it up!" My arms were like lead, my head smarting from blows. I managed to feel my way to the ropes and held on, trying to catch my breath. A glove landed in my mid-section and I went over again, feeling as though the smoke had become a knife jabbed into my guts. Pushed this way and that by the legs milling around me, I finally pulled erect and discovered that I could see the black, sweat-washed forms weaving in the smoky-blue atmosphere like drunken dancers weaving to the rapid drumlike thuds of blows.

Everyone fought hysterically. It was complete anarchy. Everybody fought everybody else. No group fought together for long. Two, three, four, fought one, then turned to fight each other, were themselves attacked. Blows landed below the belt and in the kidney, with the gloves open as well as closed, and with my eye partly opened now there was not so much terror. I moved carefully, avoiding blows, although not too many to attract attention, fighting from group to group. The boys groped about like blind, cautious crabs crouching to protect their mid-sections, their heads pulled in short against their shoulders, their arms stretched nervously before them, with their fists testing the smoke-filled air like the knobbed feelers of hypersensitive snails. In one corner I glimpsed a boy violently punching the air and heard him scream in pain as he smashed his hand against a ring post. For a second I saw him bent over holding his hand, then going down as a blow caught his unprotected head. I played one group against the other, slipping in and throwing a punch then stepping out of range while pushing the others into the melee to take the blows blindly aimed at me. The smoke was agonizing and there were no rounds, no bells at three minute intervals to relieve our exhaustion. The room spun round me, a swirl of lights, smoke, sweating bodies surrounded by tense white faces. I bled from both nose and mouth, the blood spattering upon my chest.

The men kept yelling, "Slug him, black boy! Knock his guts out!"

"Uppercut him! Kill him! Kill that big boy!"   25

Taking a fake fall, I saw a boy going down heavily beside me as though we were felled by a single blow, saw a sneaker-clad foot shoot into his groin as the two who had knocked him down stumbled upon him. I rolled out of range, feeling a twinge of nausea.

The harder we fought the more threatening the men became. And yet, I had begun to worry about my speech again. How would it go? Would they recognize my ability? What would they give me?

I was fighting automatically when suddenly I noticed that one after another of the boys was leaving the ring. I was surprised, filled with panic, as though I had been left alone with an unknown danger. Then I understood. The boys had arranged it among themselves. It was the custom for the two men left in the ring to slug it out for the winner's prize. I discovered this too late. When the bell sounded two men in tuxedoes leaped into the ring and removed the blindfold. I found myself facing Tatlock, the biggest of the gang. I felt sick at my stomach. Hardly had the bell stopped ringing in my ears than it clanged again and I saw him moving swiftly toward me. Thinking of nothing else to do I hit him smash on the nose. He kept coming, bringing the rank sharp violence of stale sweat. His face was a black blank of a face, only his eyes alive — with hate of me and aglow with a feverish terror from what had happened to us all. I became anxious. I wanted to deliver my speech and he came at me as though he meant to beat it out of me. I smashed him again and again, taking his blows as they came. Then on a sudden impulse I struck him lightly and as we clinched, I whispered, "Fake like I knocked you out, you can have the prize."

"I'll break your behind," he whispered hoarsely.

"For *them?*"

"For *me*, sonofabitch!"

They were yelling for us to break it up and Tatlock spun me half around with a blow, and as a joggled camera sweeps in a reeling scene, I saw the howling red faces crouching tense beneath the cloud of blue-gray smoke. For a moment the world wavered, unraveled, flowed, then my head cleared and Tatlock bounced before me. That fluttering shadow before my eyes was his jabbing left hand. Then falling forward, my head against his damp shoulder, I whispered,

"I'll make it five dollars more."

"Go to hell!"

But his muscles relaxed a trifle beneath my pressure and I breathed, "Seven?"

"Give it to your ma," he said, ripping me beneath the heart.

And while I still held him I butted him and moved away. I felt myself bombarded with punches. I fought back with hopeless desperation. I wanted to deliver my speech more than anything else in the world, because I felt that only these men could judge truly my ability, and now this stupid clown was ruining my chances. I began fighting carefully now, moving in to punch him and out again with my greater speed. A lucky blow to his chin and I had him going too — until I heard a loud voice yell, "I got my money on the big boy."

Hearing this, I almost dropped my guard. I was confused: Should I try to win against the voice out there? Would not this go against my speech, and was not this a moment for humility, for nonresistance? A blow to my head as I danced about sent my right eye popping like a jack-in-the-box and settled my dilemma. The room went red as I fell. It was a dream fall, my body languid and fastidious as to where to land, until the floor became impatient and smashed up to meet me. A moment later I came to. An hypnotic voice said FIVE emphatically. And I lay there, hazily watching a dark red spot of my own blood shaping itself into a butterfly, glistening and soaking into the soiled gray world of the canvas.

When the voice drawled TEN I was lifted up and dragged to a chair. I sat dazed. My eye pained and swelled with each throb of my pounding heart and I wondered if now I would be allowed to speak. I was wringing wet, my mouth still bleeding. We were grouped along the wall now. The other boys ignored me as they congratulated Tatlock and speculated as to how much they would be paid. One boy whimpered over his smashed hand. Looking up front, I saw attendants in white jackets rolling the portable ring away and placing a small square rug in the vacant space surrounded by chairs. Perhaps, I thought, I will stand on the rug to deliver my speech.

Then the M.C. called to us, "Come on up here boys and get your money." We ran forward to where the men laughed and talked in their chairs, waiting. Everyone seemed friendly now.

"There it is on the rug," the man said. I saw the rug covered with coins of all dimensions and a few crumpled bills. But what excited me, scattered here and there, were the gold pieces.

"Boys, it's all yours," the man said. "You get all you grab."

"That's right, Sambo," a blond man said, winking at me confidentially.

I trembled with excitement, forgetting my pain. I would get the gold and the bills, I thought. I would use both hands. I would throw my body against the boys nearest me to block them from the gold.

"Get down around the rug now," the man commanded, "and don't anyone 45
touch it until I give the signal."

"This ought to be good," I heard.

As told, we got around the square rug on our knees. Slowly the man raised
his freckled hand as we followed it upward with our eyes.

I heard, "These niggers look like they're about to pray!"

Then, "Ready," the man said. "Go!"

I lunged for a yellow coin lying on the blue design of the carpet, touching 50
it and sending a surprised shriek to join those rising around me. I tried frantically to remove my hand but could not let go. A hot, violent force tore through
my body, shaking me like a wet rat. The rug was electrified. The hair bristled up
on my head as I shook myself free. My muscles jumped, my nerves jangled,
writhed. But I saw that this was not stopping the other boys. Laughing in fear
and embarrassment, some were holding back and scooping up the coins
knocked off by the painful contortions of the others. The men roared above us
as we struggled.

"Pick it up, goddamnit, pick it up!" someone called like a bass-voiced par-
rot. "Go on, get it!"

I crawled rapidly around the floor, picking up the coins, trying to avoid
the coppers and to get greenbacks and the gold. Ignoring the shock by laughing, as I brushed the coins off quickly, I discovered that I could contain the
electricity—a contradiction, but it works. Then the men began to push us
onto the rug. Laughing embarrassedly, we struggled out of their hands and
kept after the coins. We were all wet and slippery and hard to hold. Suddenly I
saw a boy lifted into the air, glistening with sweat like a circus seal, and
dropped, his wet back landing flush upon the charged rug, heard him yell and
saw him literally dance upon his back, his elbows beating a frenzied tattoo
upon the floor, his muscles twitching like the flesh of a horse stung by many
flies. When he finally rolled off, his face was gray and no one stopped him
when he ran from the floor amid booming laughter.

"Get the money," the M.C. called. "That's good hard American cash!"

And we snatched and grabbed, snatched and grabbed. I was careful not to
come too close to the rug now, and when I felt the hot whiskey breath descend
upon me like a cloud of foul air I reached out and grabbed the leg of a chair. It
was occupied and I held on desperately.

"Leggo, nigger! Leggo!" 55

The huge face wavered down to mine as he tried to push me free. But my
body was slippery and he was too drunk. It was Mr. Colcord, who owned a
chain of movie houses and "entertainment palaces." Each time he grabbed me
I slipped out of his hands. It became a real struggle. I feared the rug more than
I did the drunk, so I held on, surprising myself for a moment by trying to top-
ple *him* upon the rug. It was such an enormous idea that I found myself actually carrying it out. I tried not to be obvious, yet when I grabbed his leg, trying
to tumble him out of the chair, he raised up roaring with laughter, and, looking at me with soberness dead in the eye, kicked me viciously in the chest. The
chair leg flew out of my hand and I felt myself going and rolled. It was as
though I had rolled through a bed of hot coals. It seemed a whole century
would pass before I would roll free, a century in which I was seared through
the deepest levels of my body to the fearful breath within me and the breath
seared and heated to the point of explosion. It'll all be over in a flash, I thought
as I rolled clear. It'll all be over in a flash.

But not yet, the men on the other side were waiting, red faces swollen as though from apoplexy as they bent forward in their chairs. Seeing their fingers coming toward me I rolled away as a fumbled football rolls off the receiver's fingertips, back into the coals. That time I luckily sent the rug sliding out of place and heard the coins ringing against the floor and the boys scuffling to pick them up and the M.C. calling, "All right, boys, that's all. Go get dressed and get your money."

I was limp as a dish rag. My back felt as though it had been beaten with wires.

When we had dressed the M.C. came in and gave us each five dollars, except Tatlock, who got ten for being last in the ring. Then he told us to leave. I was not to get a chance to deliver my speech, I thought. I was going out into the dim alley in despair when I was stopped and told to go back. I returned to the ballroom, where the men were pushing back their chairs and gathering in groups to talk.

The M.C. knocked on a table for quiet. "Gentlemen," he said, "we almost 60 forgot an important part of the program. A most serious part, gentlemen. This boy was brought here to deliver a speech which he made at his graduation yesterday . . ."

"Bravo!"

"I'm told that he is the smartest boy we've got out there in Greenwood. I'm told that he knows more big words than a pocket-sized dictionary."

Much applause and laughter.

"So now, gentlemen, I want you to give him your attention."

There was still laughter as I faced them, my mouth dry, my eye throbbing. 65 I began slowly, but evidently my throat was tense, because they began shouting, "Louder! Louder!"

"We of the younger generation extol the wisdom of that great leader and educator," I shouted, "who first spoke these flaming words of wisdom: 'A ship lost at sea for many days suddenly sighted a friendly vessel. From the mast of the unfortunate vessel was seen a signal: "Water, water; we die of thirst!" The answer from the friendly vessel came back: "Cast down your bucket where you are." The captain of the distressed vessel, at last heeding the injunction, cast down his bucket, and it came up full of fresh sparkling water from the mouth of the Amazon River.' And like him I say, and in his words, 'To those of my race who depend upon bettering their condition in a foreign land, or who underestimate the importance of cultivating friendly relations with the Southern white man, who is his next-door neighbor, I would say: "Cast down your bucket where you are" — cast it down in making friends in every manly way of the people of all races by whom we are surrounded . . .'"

I spoke automatically and with such fervor that I did not realize that the men were still talking and laughing until my dry mouth, filling up with blood from the cut, almost strangled me. I coughed, wanting to stop and go to one of the tall brass, sand-filled spittoons to relieve myself, but a few of the men, especially the superintendent, were listening and I was afraid. So I gulped it down, blood, saliva, and all, and continued. (What powers of endurance I had during those days! What enthusiasm! What a belief in the rightness of things!) I spoke even louder in spite of the pain. But still they talked and still they laughed, as though deaf with cotton in dirty ears. So I spoke with greater emotional emphasis. I closed my ears and swallowed blood until I was nauseated. The speech seemed a hundred times as long as before, but I could not leave out a single word. All had to be said, each memorized nuance considered, rendered. Nor was that all. Whenever I uttered a word of three or more syllables a group of voices would yell for me to repeat it. I used the phrase "social responsibility" and they yelled:

"What's that word you say, boy?"

"Social responsibility," I said.

"What?" 70

"Social . . ."

"Louder."

". . . responsibility."

"More!"

"Respon—" 75

"Repeat!"

"—sibility."

The room filled with the uproar of laughter until, no doubt, distracted by having to gulp down my blood, I made a mistake and yelled a phrase I had often seen denounced in newspaper editorials, heard debated in private.

"Social . . ."

"What?" they yelled. 80

". . . equality—"

The laughter hung smokelike in the sudden stillness. I opened my eyes, puzzled. Sounds of displeasure filled the room. The M.C. rushed forward. They shouted hostile phrases at me. But I did not understand.

A small dry mustached man in the front row blared out, "Say that slowly, son!"

"What, sir?"

"What you just said!" 85

"Social responsibility, sir," I said.

"You weren't being smart, were you, boy?" he said, not unkindly.

"No, sir!"

"You sure that about 'equality' was a mistake?"

"Oh, yes, sir," I said. "I was swallowing blood." 90

"Well, you had better speak more slowly so we can understand. We mean to do right by you, but you've got to know your place at all times. All right, now, go on with your speech."

I was afraid. I wanted to leave but I wanted also to speak and I was afraid they'd snatch me down.

"Thank you, sir," I said, beginning where I had left off, and having them ignore me as before.

Yet when I finished there was a thunderous applause. I was surprised to see the superintendent come forth with a package wrapped in white tissue paper, and, gesturing for quiet, address the men.

"Gentlemen, you see that I did not overpraise this boy. He makes a good 95 speech and some day he'll lead his people in the proper paths. And I don't have to tell you that that is important in these days and times. This is a good, smart boy, and so to encourage him in the right direction, in the name of the Board of Education I wish to present him a prize in the form of this . . ."

He paused, removing the tissue paper and revealing a gleaming calfskin brief case.

". . . in the form of this first-class article from Shad Whitmore's shop."

"Boy," he said, addressing me, "take this prize and keep it well. Consider it a badge of office. Prize it. Keep developing as you are and some day it will be filled with important papers that will help shape the destiny of your people."

I was so moved that I could hardly express my thanks. A rope of bloody saliva forming a shape like an undiscovered continent drooled upon the leather and I wiped it quickly away. I felt an importance that I had never dreamed.

"Open it and see what's inside," I was told.   100

My fingers a-tremble, I complied, smelling the fresh leather and finding an official-looking document inside. It was a scholarship to the state college for Negroes. My eyes filled with tears and I ran awkwardly off the floor.

I was overjoyed; I did not even mind when I discovered that the gold pieces I had scrambled for were brass pocket tokens advertising a certain make of automobile.

When I reached home everyone was excited. Next day the neighbors came to congratulate me. I even felt safe from grandfather, whose deathbed curse usually spoiled my triumphs. I stood beneath his photograph with my brief case in hand and smiled triumphantly into his stolid black peasant's face. It was a face that fascinated me. The eyes seemed to follow everywhere I went.

That night I dreamed I was at a circus with him and that he refused to laugh at the clowns no matter what they did. Then later he told me to open my brief case and read what was inside and I did, finding an official envelope stamped with the state seal; and inside the envelope I found another and another, endlessly, and I thought I would fall of weariness. "Them's years," he said. "Now open that one." And I did and in it I found an engraved document containing a short message in letters of gold. "Read it," my grandfather said. "Out loud!"

"To Whom It May Concern," I intoned. "Keep This Nigger-Boy Running."   105
I awoke with the old man's laughter ringing in my ears.

(It was a dream I was to remember and dream again for many years after. But at that time I had no insight into its meaning. First I had to attend college.)

CONSIDERATIONS FOR CRITICAL THINKING AND WRITING

1. FIRST RESPONSE. Discuss how the protagonist's expectations are similar to what has come to be known as the American dream — the assumption that ambition, hard work, perseverance, intelligence, and virtue always lead to success. Do you believe in the American dream?

2. How does the first paragraph of the story sum up the conflict that the narrator confronts? In what sense is he "invisible"?

3. Why do his grandfather's last words cause so much anxiety in the family? What does his grandfather mean when he says, "I want you to overcome 'em with yeses, undermine 'em with grins, agree 'em to death"?

4. What is the symbolic significance of the naked blonde? What details reveal that she represents more than a sexual tease in the story?

5. How does the battle in the boxing ring and the scramble for money afterward suggest the kind of control whites have over blacks in the story?

6. Why is it significant that the town is named Greenwood and that the brief-case award comes from Shad Whitmore's shop? Can you find any other details that serve to reinforce the meaning of the story?

7. What is the narrator's perspective as an educated adult telling the story, in contrast to his assumptions and beliefs as a recent high school graduate? How is this contrast especially evident in the speech before the "leading white citizens" of the town?

8. How can the dream at the end of the story be related to the major incidents that precede it?

9. Given the grandfather's advice, explain how "meekness" can be a "dangerous activity" and a weapon against oppression.

10. Imagine the story as told from a third-person point of view. How would this change the story? Do you think the story would be more or less effective told from a third-person point of view? Explain your answer.

11. CRITICAL STRATEGIES. Read the section on mythological criticism (pp. 2107–09) in Chapter 52, "Critical Strategies for Reading," and "What Is an Initiation Story?" by Mordecai Marcus (following). Discuss "Battle Royal" as an archetypal initiation story.

CONNECTIONS TO OTHER SELECTIONS

1. Compare and contrast Ellison's view of the South with William Faulkner's in "A Rose for Emily" (p. 75).

2. Compare and contrast this story with M. Carl Holman's poem "Mr. Z" (p. 1162).

PERSPECTIVE

MORDECAI MARCUS (B. 1925)

What Is an Initiation Story? 1960

An initiation story may be said to show its young protagonist experiencing a significant change of knowledge about the world or himself, or a change of character, or of both, and this change must point or lead him toward an adult world. It may or may not contain some form of ritual, but it should give some evidence that the change is at least likely to have permanent effects.

Initiation stories obviously center on a variety of experiences and the initiations vary in effect. It will be useful, therefore, to divide initiations into types according to their power and effect. First, some initiations lead only to the threshold of maturity and understanding but do not definitely cross it. Such stories emphasize the shocking effect of experience, and their protagonists tend to be distinctly young. Second, some initiations take their protagonists across a threshold of maturity and understanding but leave them enmeshed in a struggle for certainty. These initiations sometimes involve self-discovery. Third, the most decisive initiations carry their protagonists firmly into maturity and understanding, or at least show them decisively embarked toward maturity. These initiations usually center on self-discovery. For convenience, I will call these types tentative, uncompleted, and decisive initiations.

From "What Is an Initiation Story?" in *The Journal of Aesthetics and Art Criticism*

CONSIDERATIONS FOR CRITICAL THINKING AND WRITING

1. For a work to be classified as an initiation story, why should it "give some evidence that the change [in the protagonist] is at least likely to have permanent effects"?

2. Marcus divides initiations into three broad types: tentative, uncompleted, and decisive. Explain how you would categorize the initiation in Ellison's "Battle Royal."

GABRIEL GARCÍA MÁRQUEZ (B. 1927)

Fiction writer, essayist, journalist, and writer of scripts for screen and stage, Gabriel García Márquez is one of the most widely read and discussed authors in the history of Latin American literature. Born in Aracataca, Colombia, Márquez spent his first eight years listening to his grandmother weave matter-of-fact stories in which the living and the dead coexisted without distinction, a style that profoundly influenced the magic realism of his work years later. In 1936, Márquez moved to Sucre and lived with his parents for four years before going on to secondary school in Zipaquira, and then to study law at the Universidad Nacional in the capital city of Bogotá. The young Márquez's talents were recognized early. At the age of nineteen, he published his first story, "The Third Resignation," in the newspaper *El Espectador,* and it appeared with an introductory note hailing him as the "new genius of Colombian letters." This recognition allowed Márquez to abandon his university course and pursue a career in journalism that took him to Rome in 1954 as the European correspondent for *El Espectador.* The following year, he published a short story collection, *Leafstorm and Other Stories,* and later wrote the novel *In Evil Hour* (1962) while working for the Cuban news agency La Prensa in Colombia, Havana, and New York City. Later the author moved to Mexico City, where a gust of inspiration led him to risk financial ruin and write for a year in seclusion. The result was the 1967 publication of his masterpiece, *One Hundred Years of Solitude,* which brought him international fame and the ability to use his journalism in the service of left-wing causes worldwide. His other publications include *The Autumn of the Patriarch* (1975), *Chronicle of a Death Foretold* (1982), *Love in the Time of Cholera* (1985), *The General in His Labyrinth* (1990), and *Strange Pilgrims* (1993). Márquez was awarded the Nobel Prize for Literature in 1982.

Web   *Research Gabriel García Márquez with LitLinks at*
http://www.bedfordstmartins.com/meyer/bedintrolit

The Handsomest Drowned Man in the World   1968
A Tale for Children

TRANSLATED BY GREGORY RABASSA AND J. S. BERNSTEIN

The first children who saw the dark and slinky bulge approaching through the sea let themselves think it was an enemy ship. Then they saw it had no flags or masts and they thought it was a whale. But when it was washed up on the beach, they removed the clumps of seaweed, the jellyfish tentacles, and the remains of fish and flotsam, and only then did they see that it was a drowned man.

They had been playing with him all afternoon, burying him in the sand and digging him up again, when someone chanced to see them and spread the alarm in the village. The men who carried him to the nearest house noticed that he weighed more than any dead man they had ever known, almost as much as a horse, and they said to each other that maybe he'd been floating too long and the water had got into his bones. When they laid him on the floor they said he'd been taller than all other men because there was barely enough room for him in the house, but they thought that maybe the ability to keep on growing after death was part of the nature of certain drowned men. He had the smell of the sea about him and only his shape gave one to suppose that it was the corpse of a human being, because the skin was covered with a crust of mud and scales.

They did not even have to clean off his face to know that the dead man was a stranger. The village was made up of only twenty-odd wooden houses that had stone courtyards with no flowers and which were spread about on the end of a desertlike cape. There was so little land that mothers always went about with the fear that the wind would carry off their children and the few dead that the years had caused among them had to be thrown off the cliffs. But the sea was calm and bountiful and all the men fit into seven boats. So when they found the drowned man they simply had to look at one another to see that they were all there.

That night they did not go out to work at sea. While the men went to find out if anyone was missing in neighboring villages, the women stayed behind to care for the drowned man. They took the mud off with grass swabs, they removed the underwater stones entangled in his hair, and they scraped the crust off with tools used for scaling fish. As they were doing that they noticed that the vegetation on him came from faraway oceans and deep water and that his clothes were in tatters, as if he had sailed through labyrinths of coral. They noticed too that he bore his death with pride, for he did not have the lonely look of other drowned men who came out of the sea or that haggard, needy look of men who drowned in rivers. But only when they finished cleaning him off did they become aware of the kind of man he was and it left them breathless. Not only was he the tallest, strongest, most virile, and best built man they had ever seen, but even though they were looking at him there was no room for him in their imagination.

They could not find a bed in the village large enough to lay him on nor was   5 there a table solid enough to use for his wake. The tallest men's holiday pants would not fit him, nor the fattest ones' Sunday shirts, nor the shoes of the one with the biggest feet. Fascinated by his huge size and his beauty, the women then decided to make him some pants from a large piece of sail and a shirt from some bridal brabant linen so that he could continue through his death with dignity. As they sewed, sitting in a circle and gazing at the corpse between stitches, it seemed to them that the wind had never been so steady nor the sea so restless as on that night and they supposed that the change had something to do with the dead man. They thought that if that magnificent man had lived in the village, his house would have had the widest doors, the highest ceiling, and the strongest floor, his bedstead would have been made from a midship frame held together by iron bolts, and his wife would have been the happiest woman. They thought that he would have had so much authority that he could have drawn fish out of the sea simply by calling their names and that he would have put so much work into his land that spring would have burst forth from among the rocks so that he would have been able to plant flowers on the cliffs. They secretly compared him to their own men, thinking that for all their lives theirs were incapable of doing what he could do in one night, and they ended up dismissing them deep in their hearts as the weakest, meanest, and most useless creatures on earth. They were wandering through that maze of fantasy when the oldest woman, who as the oldest had looked upon the drowned man with more compassion than passion, sighed:

"He has the face of someone called Esteban."

It was true. Most of them had only to take another look at him to see that he could not have any other name. The more stubborn among them, who were the youngest, still lived for a few hours with the illusion that when they put his clothes on and he lay among the flowers in patent leather shoes his name might be Lautaro. But it was a vain illusion. There had not been enough canvas, the poorly cut and worse sewn pants were too tight, and the hidden strength of his heart popped the buttons on his shirt. After midnight the whistling of the wind died down and the sea fell into its Wednesday drowsiness. The silence put an end to any last doubts: he was Esteban. The women who had dressed him, who had combed his hair, had cut his nails and shaved him were unable to hold back a shudder of pity when they had to resign themselves to his being dragged along the ground. It was then that they understood how unhappy he must have been with that huge body since it bothered him even after death. They could see him in life, condemned to going through doors sideways, cracking his head on crossbeams, remaining on his feet during visits, not knowing what to do with his soft, pink, sea lion hands while the lady of the house looked for her most resistant chair and begged him, frightened to death, sit here, Esteban, please, and he, leaning against the wall, smiling, don't bother, ma'am, I'm fine where I am, his heels raw and his back roasted from having done the same thing so many times whenever he paid a visit, don't bother, ma'am, I'm fine where I am, just to avoid the embarrassment of breaking up the chair, and never knowing perhaps the ones who said don't go, Esteban, at least wait till the coffee's ready, were the ones who later on would whisper the big boob finally left, how nice, the handsome fool has gone. That was what the women were thinking beside the body a little before dawn. Later, when they covered his face with a handkerchief so that the light would not bother him, he looked so forever dead, so defenseless, so much like their men that the first furrows of tears opened in their hearts. It was one of the younger ones who began the weeping. The others, coming to, went from sighs to wails, and the more they sobbed the more they felt like weeping, because the drowned man was becoming all the more Esteban for them, and so they wept so much, for he was the most destitute, most peaceful, and most obliging man on earth, poor Esteban. So when the men returned with the news that the drowned man was not from the neighboring villages either, the women felt an opening of jubilation in the midst of their tears.

"Praise the Lord," they sighed, "he's ours!"

The men thought the fuss was only womanish frivolity. Fatigued because of the difficult nighttime inquiries, all they wanted was to get rid of the bother of the newcomer once and for all before the sun grew strong on that arid, windless day. They improvised a litter with the remains of foremasts and gaffs, tying it together with rigging so that it would bear the weight of the body until they reached the cliffs. They wanted to tie the anchor from a cargo ship to him so that he would sink easily into the deepest waves, where fish are blind and divers die of nostalgia, and bad currents would not bring him back to shore, as had happened with other bodies. But the more they hurried, the more the women thought of ways to waste time. They walked about like startled hens, pecking with the sea charms on their breasts, some interfering on one side to put a scapular of the good wind on the drowned man, some on the other side to put a wrist compass on him, and after a great deal of *get away from there, woman, stay out of the way, look, you almost made me fall on top of the dead man,* the men began to feel mistrust in their livers and started grumbling about why so many main-altar decorations for a stranger, because no matter how many nails and holy-water jars he had on him, the sharks would chew him all the same, but the women kept piling on their junk relics, running back and forth, stumbling, while they released in sighs what they did not in tears, so that the men finally exploded with *since when has there ever been such a fuss over a drifting corpse, a drowned nobody, a piece of cold Wednesday meat.* One of the women, mortified by so much lack of care, then removed the handkerchief from the dead man's face and the men were left breathless too.

He was Esteban. It was not necessary to repeat it for them to recognize him.   10 If they had been told Sir Walter Raleigh, even they might have been impressed with his gringo accent, the macaw on his shoulder, his cannibal-killing blunderbuss, but there could be only one Esteban in the world and there he was, stretched out like a sperm whale, shoeless, wearing the pants of an undersized child, and with those stony nails that had to be cut with a knife. They only had to take the handkerchief off his face to see that he was ashamed, that it was not his fault that he was so big or so heavy or so handsome, and if he had known that this was going to happen, he would have looked for a more discreet place to drown in, seriously, I even would have tied the anchor off a galleon around my neck and staggered off a cliff like someone who doesn't like things in order not to be upsetting people now with this Wednesday dead body, as you people say, in order not to be bothering anyone with this filthy piece of cold meat that doesn't have anything to do with me. There was so much truth in his manner that even the most mistrustful men, the ones who felt the bitterness of endless nights at sea fearing that their women would tire of dreaming about them and begin to dream of drowned men, even they and others who were harder still shuddered in the marrow of their bones at Esteban's sincerity.

That was how they came to hold the most splendid funeral they could conceive of for an abandoned drowned man. Some women who had gone to get flowers in the neighboring villages returned with other women who could not believe what they had been told, and those women went back for more flowers when they saw the dead man, and they brought more and more until there were so many flowers and so many people that it was hard to walk about. At the final moment it pained them to return him to the waters as an orphan and they chose a father and mother from among the best people, and aunts and uncles and cousins, so that through him all the inhabitants of the village became kinsmen. Some sailors who heard the weeping from a distance went off course and people heard of one who had himself tied to the mainmast, remembering ancient fables about sirens. While they fought for the privilege of carrying him on their shoulders along the steep escarpment by the cliffs, men and women became aware for the first time of the desolation of their streets, the dryness of their courtyards, the narrowness of their dreams as they faced the splendor and beauty of their drowned man. They let him go without an anchor so that he could come back if he wished and whenever he wished, and they all held their breath for the fraction of centuries the body took to fall into the abyss. They did not need to look at one another to realize that they were no longer all present, that they would never be. But they also knew that everything would be different from then on, that their houses would have wider doors, higher ceilings, and stronger floors so that Esteban's memory could go everywhere without bumping into beams and so that no one in the future would dare whisper the big boob finally died, too bad, the handsome fool has finally died, because they were going to paint their house fronts gay colors to make Esteban's memory eternal and they were going to break their backs digging for springs among the stones and planting flowers on the cliffs so that in future years at dawn the passengers on great liners would awaken, suffocated by the smell of gardens on the high seas, and the captain would have to come down from the bridge in his dress uniform, with his astrolabe, his pole star, and his row of war medals and, pointing to the promontory of roses on the horizon, he would say in fourteen languages, look there, where the wind is so peaceful now that it's gone to sleep beneath the beds, over there, where the sun's so bright that the sunflowers don't know which way to turn, yes, over there, that's Esteban's village.

CONSIDERATIONS FOR CRITICAL THINKING AND WRITING

1. FIRST RESPONSE. What did you make of this story on the first reading? What is it about the story that makes it difficult for a reader to have a firm sense of what is going on?

2. Why is it especially appropriate that it is the children who discover the drowned man? Consider also the story's subtitle.

3. Discuss the significance of how the village goes about naming Esteban.

4. How does Esteban's presence change relationships between men and women in the village? What determines their respective reactions to him?

5. What qualities of this story seem to invite a symbolic reading of Esteban? What kinds of meanings does the village associate with him? The outsiders? How does meaning evolve over the course of the story?

6. In what sense has the community become "Esteban's village"?

7. CRITICAL STRATEGIES. Read the section on mythological criticism (pp. 2107–09) in Chapter 52, "Critical Strategies for Reading," and discuss this story as a version of modern myth-making.

CONNECTION TO ANOTHER SELECTION

1. Discuss the symbolic nature of this story and Franz Kafka's "A Hunger Artist" (p. 577). What significant similarities and differences do you find?

8

Theme

Theme is the central idea or meaning of a story. It provides a unifying point around which the plot, characters, setting, point of view, symbols, and other elements of a story are organized. In some works the theme is explicitly stated. Nathaniel Hawthorne's "Wakefield," for example, begins with the author telling the reader that the point of his story is "done up neatly, and condensed into the final sentence." Most modern writers, however, present their themes implicitly (as Hawthorne does in the majority of his stories), so determining the underlying meaning of a work often requires more effort than it does from the reader of "Wakefield." One reason for the difficulty is that the theme is fused into the elements of the story, and these must be carefully examined in relation to one another as well as to the work as a whole. But then that's the value of determining the theme, for it requires a close analysis of all the elements of a work. Such a close reading often results in sharper insights into this overlooked character or that seemingly unrelated incident. Accounting for the details and seeing how they fit together result in greater understanding of the story. Such familiarity creates pleasure in much the same way that a musical piece heard more than once becomes a rich experience rather than simply a repetitive one.

Themes are not always easy to express, but some principles can aid you in articulating the central meaning of a work. First distinguish between the theme of a story and its subject. They are not equivalents. Many stories share identical subjects, such as fate, death, innocence, youth, loneliness, racial prejudice, and disillusionment. Yet each story usually makes its own statement about the subject and expresses some view of life. Hemingway's "Soldier's Home" (p. 152) and Faulkner's "Barn Burning" (p. 493) both describe young men who are unhappy at home and decide that they must leave, but the meaning of each story is quite different. A thematic generalization about "Soldier's Home" could be something like this: "The brutal experience of war can alienate a person from those — even family and friends — who are innocent of war's reality." The theme of Faulkner's story could be stated this way: "No matter how much one might love one's father, there comes a time when family loyalties must be left behind in order to be true to one's self."

These two statements of theme do not definitively sum up each story — there is no single, absolute way of expressing a work's theme — but they do describe a central idea in each. Furthermore, the emphasis in each of these themes could be modified or expanded because interpretations of interesting, complex works are always subject to revision. People have different responses to life, and so it is hardly surprising that responses to literature are not identical. When theme is considered, the possibilities for meaning are usually expanded and not reduced to categories such as "right" or "wrong."

Although readers may differ in their interpretations of a story, that does not mean that *any* interpretation is valid. If we were to assert that the soldier's dissatisfactions in Hemingway's story could be readily eliminated by his settling down to marriage and a decent job (his mother's solution), we would have missed Hemingway's purposes in writing the story; we would have failed to see how Krebs's war experiences have caused him to reexamine the assumptions and beliefs that previously nurtured him but now seem unreal to him. We would have to ignore much in the story in order to arrive at such a reading. To be valid, the statement of the theme should be responsive to the details of the story. It must be based on evidence within the story rather than solely on experiences, attitudes, or values the reader brings to the work — such as personally knowing a war veteran who successfully adjusted to civilian life after getting a good job and marrying. Familiarity with the subject matter of a story can certainly be an aid to interpretation, but it should not get in the way of seeing the author's perspective.

Sometimes readers too hastily conclude that a story's theme always consists of a moral, some kind of lesson that is dramatized by the various elements of the work. There are stories that do this — Hawthorne's "Wakefield," for example. Here are the final sentences in his story about a middle-aged man who drops out of life for twenty years:

> He has left us much food for thought, a portion of which shall lend its wisdom to a moral, and be shaped into a figure. Amid the seeming confusion of our mysterious world, individuals are so nicely adjusted to a system, and systems to one another and to a whole, that, by stepping aside for a moment, a man exposes himself to a fearful risk of losing his place forever. Like Wakefield, he may become, as it were, the Outcast of the Universe.

Most stories, however, do not include such direct caveats about the conduct of life. A tendency to look for a lesson in a story can produce a reductive and inaccurate formulation of its theme. Consider the damage done to Colette's "The Hand" (p. 228) if its theme is described as this:

"Adolescents are too young to cope with the responsibilities of marriage." Colette's focus in this story is on the young woman's response to her husband's powerful sexuality and dominance rather than on her inability to be a good wife.

In fact, a good many stories go beyond traditional moral values to explore human behavior instead of condemning or endorsing it. Chekhov's treatment of the adulterous affair between Gurov and Anna in "The Lady with the Pet Dog" (p. 187) portrays a love that is valuable and true despite the conventional moral codes it violates. That is not to say that the reader must agree with Chekhov's attitude that such love has a validity of its own. We are obligated to see that Chekhov is sympathetic to the lovers but not necessarily obligated to approve of their actions. All that is required is our willingness to explore with the author the issues set before us. The themes we encounter in literature may challenge as well as reassure us.

Determining the theme of a story can be a difficult task because all the story's elements may contribute to its central idea. Indeed, you may discover that finding the theme is more challenging than coming to grips with the author's values as they are revealed in the story. There is no precise formula that can take you to the center of a story's meaning and help you to articulate it. However, several strategies are practical and useful once you have read the story. Apply these pointers during a second or third reading:

1. Pay attention to the title of the story. It often provides a lead to a major symbol (Faulkner's "Barn Burning," p. 493) or to the subject around which the theme develops (Godwin's "A Sorrowful Woman," p. 35).
2. Look for details in the story that have potential for symbolic meanings. Careful consideration of names, places, objects, minor characters, and incidents can lead you to the central meaning — for example, think of the stripper in Ellison's "Battle Royal" (p. 231). Be especially attentive to elements you did not understand on the first reading.
3. Decide whether the protagonist changes or develops some important insight as a result of the action. Carefully examine any generalizations the protagonist or narrator makes about the events in the story.
4. When you formulate the theme of the story in your own words, write it down in one or two complete sentences that make some point about the subject matter. Revenge may be the subject of a story, but its theme should make a statement about revenge: "Instead of providing satisfaction, revenge defeats the best in one's self" is one possibility.
5. Be certain that your expression of the theme is a generalized statement rather than a specific description of particular people, places, and incidents in the story. Contrast the preceding statement of a theme on revenge with this too-specific one: "In Nathaniel Hawthorne's *The Scarlet Letter*, Roger Chillingworth loses his humanity owing to his single-minded attempts to punish Arthur Dimmesdale for fathering a child with Chillingworth's wife, Hester." Hawthorne's theme is not restricted to a single fictional character named Chillingworth but to anyone whose

life is ruined by revenge. Be certain that your statement of theme does not focus on only part of the story. The theme just cited for *The Scarlet Letter,* for example, relegates Hester to the status of a minor character. What it says about Chillingworth is true, but the statement is incomplete as a generalization about the novel.

6. Be wary of using clichés as a way of stating theme. They tend to short-circuit ideas instead of generating them. It may be tempting to resort to something like "Love conquers all" as a statement of the theme of Chekhov's "The Lady with the Pet Dog" (p. 187); however, even the slightest second thought reveals how much more ambiguous the ending of that story is.

7. Be aware that some stories emphasize theme less than others. Stories that have as their major purpose adventure, humor, mystery, or terror may have little or no theme. In Edgar Allan Poe's "The Pit and the Pendulum," for example, the protagonist is not used to condemn torture; instead, he becomes a sensitive gauge to measure the pain and horror he endures at the hands of his captors.

What is most valuable about articulating the theme of a work is the process by which the theme is determined. Ultimately, the theme is expressed by the story itself and is inseparable from the experience of reading the story. Tim O'Brien's explanation of "How to Tell a True War Story" (p. 548) is probably true of most kinds of stories: "In a true war story, if there's a moral [or theme] at all, it's like the thread that makes the cloth. You can't tease it out. You can't extract the meaning without unraveling the deeper meaning." Describing the theme should not be a way to consume a story, to be done with it. It is a means of clarifying our thinking about what we've read and probably felt intuitively.

Stephen Crane's "The Bride Comes to Yellow Sky," Katherine Mansfield's "Miss Brill," Dagoberto Gilb's "Love in L.A.," and Alison Baker's "Better Be Ready 'Bout Half Past Eight" are four stories whose respective themes emerge from the authors' skillful use of plot, character, setting, and symbol.

STEPHEN CRANE (1871–1900)

Born in Newark, New Jersey, Stephen Crane attended Lafayette College and Syracuse University and then worked as a free-lance journalist in New York City. He wrote newspaper pieces, short stories, poems, and novels for his entire, brief adult life. His first book, *Maggie: A Girl of the Streets* (1893), is a story about New York slum life and prostitution. His most famous novel, *The Red Badge of Courage* (1895), gives readers a vivid, convincing re-creation of Civil War battles, even though Crane had never been to war. However, Crane was personally familiar with the American West, where he traveled as a reporter. "The Bride Comes to Yellow Sky" includes some of the ingredients of a typical popular western—a confrontation between a marshal and a drunk who shoots up the town—but the story's theme is less predictable and more serious than the plot seems to suggest.

Web *Research Stephen Crane with LitLinks at*
http://www.bedfordstmartins.com/meyer/bedintrolit

The Bride Comes to Yellow Sky   *1898*

I

The great Pullman was whirling onward with such dignity of motion that a glance from the window seemed simply to prove that the plains of Texas were pouring eastward. Vast flats of green grass, dull-hued spaces of mesquit and cactus, little groups of frame houses, woods of light and tender trees, all were sweeping into the east, sweeping over the horizon, a precipice.

A newly married pair had boarded this coach at San Antonio. The man's face was reddened from many days in the wind and sun, and a direct result of his new black clothes was that his brick-colored hands were constantly performing in a most conscious fashion. From time to time he looked down respectfully at his attire. He sat with a hand on each knee, like a man waiting in a barber's shop. The glances he devoted to other passengers were furtive and shy.

The bride was not pretty, nor was she very young. She wore a dress of blue cashmere, with small reservations of velvet here and there, and with steel buttons abounding. She continually twisted her head to regard her puff sleeves, very stiff, straight, and high. They embarrassed her. It was quite apparent that she had cooked, and that she expected to cook, dutifully. The blushes caused by the careless scrutiny of some passengers as she had entered the car were strange to see upon this plain, under-class countenance, which was drawn in placid, almost emotionless lines.

They were evidently very happy. "Ever been in a parlor-car before?" he asked, smiling with delight.

"No," she answered; "I never was. It's fine, ain't it?"   5

"Great! And then after a while we'll go forward to the diner, and get a big lay-out. Finest meal in the world. Charge a dollar."

"Oh, do they?" cried the bride. "Charge a dollar? Why, that's too much—for us—ain't it, Jack?"

"Not this trip, anyhow," he answered bravely. "We're going to go the whole thing."

Later he explained to her about the trains. "You see, it's a thousand miles from one end of Texas to the other; and this train runs right across it, and never stops but four times." He had the pride of an owner. He pointed out to her the dazzling fittings of the coach; and in truth her eyes opened wider as she contemplated the sea-green figured velvet, the shining brass, silver, and glass, the wood that gleamed as darkly brilliant as the surface of a pool of oil. At one end a bronze figure sturdily held a support for a separated chamber, and at convenient places on the ceiling were frescoes in olive and silver.

To the minds of the pair, their surroundings reflected the glory of their 10
marriage that morning in San Antonio; this was the environment of their new
estate; and the man's face in particular beamed with an elation that made him
appear ridiculous to the negro porter. This individual at times surveyed them
from afar with an amused and superior grin. On other occasions he bullied
them with skill in ways that did not make it exactly plain to them that they
were being bullied. He subtly used all the manners of the most unconquerable
kind of snobbery. He oppressed them; but of this oppression they had small
knowledge, and they speedily forgot that infrequently a number of travelers
covered them with stares of derisive enjoyment. Historically there was supposed to be something infinitely humorous in their situation.

"We are due in Yellow Sky at 3:42," he said, looking tenderly into her eyes.

"Oh, are we?" she said, as if she had not been aware of it. To evince surprise at her husband's statement was part of her wifely amiability. She took
from a pocket a little silver watch; and as she held it before her, and stared at it
with a frown of attention, the new husband's face shone.

"I bought it in San Anton' from a friend of mine," he told her gleefully.

"It's seventeen minutes past twelve," she said, looking up at him with a
kind of shy and clumsy coquetry. A passenger, noting this play, grew excessively sardonic, and winked at himself in one of the numerous mirrors.

At last they went to the dining-car. Two rows of negro waiters, in glowing 15
white suits, surveyed their entrance with the interest, and also the equanimity,
of men who had been forewarned. The pair fell to the lot of a waiter who happened to feel pleasure in steering them through their meal. He viewed them
with the manner of a fatherly pilot, his countenance radiant with benevolence.
The patronage, entwined with the ordinary deference, was not plain to them.
And yet, as they returned to their coach, they showed in their faces a sense of
escape.

To the left, miles down a long purple slope, was a little ribbon of mist
where moved the keening Rio Grande. The train was approaching it at an
angle, and the apex was Yellow Sky. Presently it was apparent that, as the distance from Yellow Sky grew shorter, the husband became commensurately
restless. His brick-red hands were more insistent in their prominence. Occasionally he was even rather absent-minded and far-away when the bride leaned
forward and addressed him.

As a matter of truth, Jack Potter was beginning to find the shadow of a
deed weigh upon him like a leaden slab. He, the town marshal of Yellow Sky, a
man known, liked, and feared in his corner, a prominent person, had gone to
San Antonio to meet a girl he believed he loved, and there, after the usual
prayers, had actually induced her to marry him, without consulting Yellow Sky
for any part of the transaction. He was now bringing his bride before an innocent and unsuspecting community.

Of course people in Yellow Sky married as it pleased them in accordance
with a general custom; but such was Potter's thought of his duty to his
friends, or of their idea of his duty, or of an unspoken form which does not
control men in these matters, that he felt he was heinous. He had committed
an extraordinary crime. Face to face with this girl in San Antonio, and spurred
by his sharp impulse, he had gone headlong over all the social hedges. At San
Antonio he was like a man hidden in the dark. A knife to sever any friendly

duty, any form, was easy to his hand in that remote city. But the hour of Yellow Sky — the hour of daylight — was approaching.

He knew full well that his marriage was an important thing to his town. It could only be exceeded by the burning of the new hotel. His friends could not forgive him. Frequently he had reflected on the advisability of telling them by telegraph, but a new cowardice had been upon him. He feared to do it. And now the train was hurrying him toward a scene of amazement, glee, and reproach. He glanced out of the window at the line of haze swinging slowly in toward the train.

Yellow Sky had a kind of brass band, which played painfully, to the delight   20 of the populace. He laughed without heart as he thought of it. If the citizens could dream of his prospective arrival with his bride, they would parade the band at the station and escort them, amid cheers and laughing congratulations, to his adobe home.

He resolved that he would use all the devices of speed and plainscraft in making the journey from the station to his house. Once within that safe citadel, he could issue some sort of vocal bulletin, and then not go among the citizens until they had time to wear off a little of their enthusiasm.

The bride looked anxiously at him. "What's worrying you, Jack?"

He laughed again. "I'm not worrying, girl; I'm only thinking of Yellow Sky."

She flushed in comprehension.

A sense of mutual guilt invaded their minds and developed a finer tender-   25 ness. They looked at each other with eyes softly aglow. But Potter often laughed the same nervous laugh; the flush upon the bride's face seemed quite permanent. *JACK*

The traitor to the feelings of Yellow Sky narrowly watched the speeding landscape. "We're nearly there," he said.

Presently the porter came and announced the proximity of Potter's home. He held a brush in his hand, and, with all his airy superiority gone, he brushed Potter's new clothes as the latter slowly turned this way and that way. Potter fumbled out a coin and gave it to the porter, as he had seen others do. It was a heavy and muscle-bound business, as that of a man shoeing his first horse.

The porter took their bag, and as the train began to slow they moved forward to the hooded platform of the car. Presently the two engines and their long string of coaches rushed into the station of Yellow Sky.

"They have to take water here," said Potter, from a constricted throat and in mournful cadence, as one announcing death. Before the train stopped his eye had swept the length of the platform, and he was glad and astonished to see there was none upon it but the station-agent, who, with a slightly hurried and anxious air, was walking toward the water-tanks. When the train had halted, the porter alighted first, and placed in position a little temporary step.

"Come on, girl," said Potter, hoarsely. As he helped her down they each   30 laughed on a false note. He took the bag from the negro, and bade his wife cling to his arm. As they slunk rapidly away, his hang-dog glance perceived that they were unloading the two trunks, and also that the station-agent, far ahead near the baggage-car, had turned and was running toward him, making gestures. He laughed, and groaned as he laughed, when he noted the first effect of his marital bliss upon Yellow Sky. He gripped his wife's arm firmly to his side, and they fled. Behind them the porter stood, chuckling fatuously.

II

The California express on the Southern Railway was due at Yellow Sky in twenty-one minutes. There were six men at the bar of the Weary Gentleman saloon. One was a drummer° who talked a great deal and rapidly; three were Texans who did not care to talk at that time; and two were Mexican sheep-herders, who did not talk as a general practice in the Weary Gentleman saloon. The barkeeper's dog lay on the board walk that crossed in front of the door. His head was on his paws, and he glanced drowsily here and there with the constant vigilance of a dog that is kicked on occasion. Across the sandy street were some vivid green grass-plots, so wonderful in appearance, amid the sands that burned near them in a blazing sun, that they caused a doubt in the mind. They exactly resembled the grass mats used to represent lawns on the stage. At the cooler end of the railway station, a man without a coat sat in a tilted chair and smoked his pipe. The fresh-cut bank of the Rio Grande circled near the town, and there could be seen beyond it a great plum-colored plain of mesquit.

Save for the busy drummer and his companions in the saloon, Yellow Sky was dozing. The new-comer leaned gracefully upon the bar, and recited many tales with the confidence of a bard who has come upon a new field.

"— and at the moment that the old man fell downstairs with the bureau in his arms, the old woman was coming up with two scuttles of coal, and of course —"

The drummer's tale was interrupted by a young man who suddenly appeared in the open door. He cried: "Scratchy Wilson's drunk, and has turned loose with both hands." The two Mexicans at once set down their glasses and faded out of the rear entrance of the saloon.

The drummer, innocent and jocular, answered: "All right, old man. S'pose   35 he has? Come in and have a drink, anyhow."

But the information had made such an obvious cleft in every skull in the room that the drummer was obliged to see its importance. All had become instantly solemn. "Say," said he, mystified, "what is this?" His three companions made the introductory gesture of eloquent speech; but the young man at the door forestalled them.

"It means, my friend," he answered, as he came into the saloon, "that for the next two hours this town won't be a health resort."

The barkeeper went to the door, and locked and barred it; reaching out of the window, he pulled in heavy wooden shutters, and barred them. Immediately a solemn, chapel-like gloom was upon the place. The drummer was looking from one to another.

"But, say," he cried, "what is this, anyhow? You don't mean there is going to be a gun-fight?"

"Don't know whether there'll be a fight or not," answered one man,   40 grimly; "but there'll be some shootin' — some good shootin'."

The young man who had warned them waved his hand. "Oh, there'll be a fight fast enough, if any one wants it. Anybody can get a fight out there in the street. There's a fight just waiting."

The drummer seemed to be swayed between the interest of a foreigner and a perception of personal danger.

drummer: Traveling salesman.

"What did you say his name was?" he asked.

"Scratchy Wilson," they answered in chorus.

"And will he kill anybody? What are you going to do? Does this happen 45 often? Does he rampage around like this once a week or so? Can he break in that door?"

"No; he can't break down that door," replied the barkeeper. "He's tried it three times. But when he comes you'd better lay down on the floor, stranger. He's dead sure to shoot at it, and a bullet may come through."

Thereafter the drummer kept a strict eye upon the door. The time had not yet called for him to hug the floor, but, as a minor precaution, he sidled near the wall. "Will he kill anybody?" he said again.

The men laughed low and scornfully at the question.

"He's out to shoot, and he's out for trouble. Don't see any good in experimentin' with him."

"But what do you do in a case like this? What do you do?" 50

A man responded: "Why, he and Jack Potter — "

"But," in chorus the other men interrupted, "Jack Potter's in San Anton'."

"Well, who is he? What's he got to do with it?"

"Oh, he's the town marshal. He goes out and fights Scratchy when he gets on one of these tears."

"Wow!" said the drummer, mopping his brow. "Nice job he's got." 55

The voices had toned away to mere whisperings. The drummer wished to ask further questions, which were born of an increasing anxiety and bewilderment; but when he attempted them, the men merely looked at him in irritation and motioned him to remain silent. A tense waiting hush was upon them. In the deep shadows of the room their eyes shone as they listened for sounds from the street. One man made three gestures at the barkeeper; and the latter, moving like a ghost, handed him a glass and a bottle. The man poured a full glass of whisky, and set down the bottle noiselessly. He gulped the whisky in a swallow, and turned again toward the door in immovable silence. The drummer saw that the barkeeper, without a sound, had taken a Winchester from beneath the bar. Later he saw this individual beckoning to him, so he tiptoed across the room.

"You better come with me back of the bar."

"No thanks," said the drummer, perspiring; "I'd rather be where I can make a break for the back door."

Whereupon the man of bottles made a kindly but peremptory gesture. The drummer obeyed it, and, finding himself seated on a box with his head below the level of the bar, balm was laid upon his soul at sight of various zinc and copper fittings that bore a resemblance to armor-plate. The barkeeper took a seat comfortably upon an adjacent box.

"You see," he whispered, "this here Scratchy Wilson is a wonder with a 60 gun — a perfect wonder; and when he goes on the war-trail, we hunt our holes — naturally. He's about the last one of the old gang that used to hang out along the river here. He's a terror when he's drunk. When he's sober he's all right — kind of simple — wouldn't hurt a fly — nicest fellow in town. But when he's drunk — whoo!"

There were periods of stillness. "I wish Jack Potter was back from San Anton'," said the barkeeper. "He shot Wilson up once — in the leg — and he would sail in and pull out the kinks in this thing."

Presently they heard from a distance the sound of a shot, followed by three wild yowls. It instantly removed a bond from the men in the darkened saloon. There was a shuffling of feet. They looked at each other. "Here he comes," they said.

III

SCRATCHY

A man in a maroon-colored flannel shirt, which had been purchased for purposes of decoration, and made principally by some Jewish women on the East Side of New York, rounded a corner and walked into the middle of the main street of Yellow Sky. In either hand the man held a long, heavy, blue-black revolver. Often he yelled, and these cries rang through a semblance of a deserted village, shrilly flying over the roofs in a volume that seemed to have no relation to the ordinary vocal strength of a man. It was as if the surrounding stillness formed the arch of a tomb over him. These cries of ferocious challenge rang against walls of silence. And his boots had red tops with gilded imprints, of the kind beloved in winter by little sledding boys on the hillsides of New England.

The man's face flamed in a rage begot of whisky. His eyes, rolling, and yet keen for ambush, hunted the still doorways and windows. He walked with the creeping movement of the midnight cat. As it occurred to him, he roared menacing information. The long revolvers in his hands were as easy as straws; they were removed with an electric swiftness. The little fingers of each hand played sometimes in a musician's way. Plain from the low collar of the shirt, the cords of his neck straightened and sank, straightened and sank, as passion moved him. The only sounds were his terrible invitations. The calm adobes preserved their demeanor at the passing of this small thing in the middle of the street.

There was no offer of fight — no offer of fight. The man called to the sky. 65 There were no attractions. He bellowed and fumed and swayed his revolvers here and everywhere.

dog dance

The dog of the barkeeper of the Weary Gentleman saloon had not appreciated the advance of events. He yet lay dozing in front of his master's door. At sight of the dog, the man paused and raised his revolver humorously. At sight of the man, the dog sprang up and walked diagonally away, with a sullen head, and growling. The man yelled, and the dog broke into a gallop. As it was about to enter the alley, there was a loud noise, a whistling, and something spat the ground directly before it. The dog screamed, and, wheeling in terror, galloped headlong in a new direction. Again there was a noise, a whistling, and sand was kicked viciously before it. Fear-stricken, the dog turned and flurried like an animal in a pen. The man stood laughing, his weapons at his hips.

Ultimately the man was attracted by the closed door of the Weary Gentleman saloon. He went to it and, hammering with a revolver, demanded drink.

The door remaining imperturbable, he picked a bit of paper from the walk, and nailed it to the framework with a knife. He then turned his back contemptuously upon this popular resort and, walking to the opposite side of the street and spinning there on his heel quickly and lithely, fired at the bit of paper. He missed it by a half inch. He swore at himself, and went away. Later he comfortably fusilladed the windows of his most intimate friend. The man was playing with this town; it was a toy for him.

But still there was no offer of fight. The name of Jack Potter, his ancient antagonist, entered his mind, and he concluded that it would be a glad thing if he should go to Potter's house, and by bombardment induce him to come out and fight. He moved in the direction of his desire, chanting Apache scalp-music.

When he arrived at it, Potter's house presented the same still front as had ⁊₀ the other adobes. Taking up a strategic position, the man howled a challenge. But this house regarded him as might a great stone god. It gave no sign. After a decent wait, the man howled further challenges, mingling with them wonderful epithets.

Presently there came the spectacle of a man churning himself into deepest rage over the immobility of a house. He fumed at it as the winter wind attacks a prairie cabin in the North. To the distance there should have gone the sound of a tumult like the fighting of two hundred Mexicans. As necessity bade him, he paused for breath or to reload his revolvers.

IV

Potter and his bride walked sheepishly and with speed. Sometimes they laughed together shamefacedly and low.

"Next corner, dear," he said finally.

They put forth the efforts of a pair walking bowed against a strong wind. Potter was about to raise a finger to point the first appearance of the new home when, as they circled the corner, they came face to face with a man in a maroon-colored shirt, who was feverishly pushing cartridges into a large revolver. Upon the instant the man dropped his revolver to the ground and, like lightning, whipped another from its holster. The second weapon was aimed at the bridegroom's chest.

There was a silence. Potter's mouth seemed to be merely a grave for his ⁊₅ tongue. He exhibited an instinct to at once loosen his arm from the woman's grip, and he dropped the bag to the sand. As for the bride, her face had gone as yellow as old cloth. She was a slave to hideous rites, gazing at the apparitional snake.

The two men faced each other at a distance of three paces. He of the revolver smiled with a new and quiet ferocity.

"Tried to sneak up on me," he said. "Tried to sneak up on me!" His eyes grew more baleful. As Potter made a slight movement, the man thrust his revolver venomously forward. "No, don't you do it, Jack Potter. Don't you move a finger toward a gun just yet. Don't you move an eyelash. The time has come for me to settle with you and I'm goin' to do it my own way, and loaf along with no interferin'. So if you don't want a gun bent on you, just mind what I tell you."

Potter looked at his enemy. "I ain't got a gun on me, Scratchy," he said. "Honest, I ain't." He was stiffening and steadying, but yet somewhere at the back of his mind a vision of the Pullman floated: the sea-green figured velvet, the shining brass, silver, and glass, the wood that gleamed as darkly brilliant as the surface of a pool of oil—all the glory of marriage, the environment of the new estate. "You know I fight when it comes to fighting, Scratchy Wilson; but I ain't got a gun on me. You'll have to do all the shootin' yourself."

His enemy's face went livid. He stepped forward, and lashed his weapon to and fro before Potter's chest. "Don't you tell me you ain't got no gun on you, you whelp. Don't tell me no lie like that. There ain't a man in Texas ever seen you without no gun. Don't take me for no kid." His eyes blazed with light, and his throat worked like a pump.

"I ain't takin' you for no kid," answered Potter. His heels had not moved 80
an inch backward. "I'm takin' you for a damn fool. I tell you I ain't got a gun,
and I ain't. If you're goin' to shoot me up, you better begin now; you'll never
get a chance like this again."

So much enforced reasoning had told on Wilson's rage; he was calmer. "If
you ain't got a gun, why ain't you got a gun?" he sneered. "Been to Sunday-
school?"

"I ain't got a gun because I've just come from San Anton' with my wife. I'm
married," said Potter. "And if I'd thought there was going to be any galoots like
you prowling around when I brought my wife home, I'd had a gun, and don't
you forget it."

"Married!" said Scratchy, not at all comprehending.

"Yes, married. I'm married," said Potter, distinctly.

"Married?" said Scratchy. Seemingly for the first time, he saw the droop- 85
ing, drowning woman at the other man's side. "No!" he said. He was like a
creature allowed a glimpse of another world. He moved a pace backward, and
his arm, with the revolver, dropped to his side. "Is this the lady?" he asked.

"Yes; this is the lady," answered Potter.

There was another period of silence.

"Well," said Wilson at last, slowly, "I s'pose it's all off now."

"It's all off if you say so, Scratchy. You know I didn't make the trouble."
Potter lifted his valise.

"Well, I 'low it's off, Jack," said Wilson. He was looking at the ground. 90
"Married!" He was not a student of chivalry; it was merely that in the presence
of this foreign condition he was a simple child of the earlier plains. He picked
up his starboard revolver, and, placing both weapons in their holsters, he went
away. His feet made funnel-shaped tracks in the heavy sand.

Considerations for Critical Thinking and Writing

1. FIRST RESPONSE. Think of a western you've read or seen: any of Larry
   McMurtry's books would work, such as *Lonesome Dove* or *Evening Star.*
   Compare and contrast the setting, characters, action, and theme in Crane's
   story with your western.

2. What is the nature of the conflict Marshal Potter feels on the train in Part
   I? Why does he feel that he committed a "crime" in bringing home a bride
   to Yellow Sky?

3. What is the function of the "drummer," the traveling salesman, in Part II?

4. How do Mrs. Potter and Scratchy Wilson serve as foils for each other?
   What does each represent in the story?

5. What is the significance of the setting?

6. How does Crane create suspense about what will happen when Marshal
   Potter meets Scratchy Wilson? Is suspense the major point of the story?

7. Is Scratchy Wilson too drunk, comical, and ineffective to be a sympathetic
   character? What is the meaning of his conceding that "I s'pose it's all off
   now" at the end of Part IV? Is he a dynamic or a static character?

8. What details seem to support the story's theme? Consider, for example, the
   descriptions of the bride's clothes and Scratchy Wilson's shirt and boots.

9. Explain why the heroes in western stories are rarely married and why
   Crane's use of marriage is central to his theme.

10. CRITICAL STRATEGIES. Read the section on gender strategies (pp. 2105–06) in Chapter 52, "Critical Strategies for Reading." Explore the heterosexual and potentialy homosexual issues that a gender critic might discover in the story.

CONNECTIONS TO OTHER SELECTIONS

1. Although Scratchy Wilson and Katherine Mansfield's "Miss Brill" (p. 259) are radically different kinds of people, they share a painful recognition at the end of their stories. What does each of them learn? Discuss whether you think what each of them learns is of equal importance in changing his or her life.

2. Write an essay comparing Crane's use of suspense with William Faulkner's in "A Rose for Emily" (p. 75).

KATHERINE MANSFIELD (1888–1923)

Born in New Zealand, Katherine Mansfield moved to London when she was a young woman and began writing short stories. Her first collection, *In a German Pension,* appeared in 1911. Subsequent publications, which include *Bliss and Other Stories* (1920) and *The Garden Party* (1922), secured her reputation as an important writer. The full range of her short stories is available in *The Collected Short Stories of Katherine Mansfield* (1945). Mansfield tends to focus her stories on intelligent, sensitive protagonists who undergo subtle but important changes in their lives. In "Miss Brill," an aging Englishwoman spends the afternoon in a park located in an unnamed French vacation town watching the activities of the people around her. Through those observations, Mansfield characterizes Miss Brill and permits us to see her experience a moment that changes her view of the world as well as of herself.

Web *Research Katherine Mansfield with LitLinks at* http://www.bedfordstmartins.com/meyer/bedintrolit

Miss Brill   1922

Although it was so brilliantly fine — the blue sky powdered with gold and great spots of light like white wine splashed over the Jardins Publiques — Miss Brill was glad that she had decided on her fur. The air was motionless, but when you opened your mouth there was just a faint chill, like a chill from a glass of iced water before you sip, and now and again a leaf came drifting — from nowhere, from the sky. Miss Brill put up her hand and touched her fur. Dear little thing! It was nice to feel it again. She had taken it out of its box that afternoon, shaken out the moth-powder, given it a good brush, and rubbed the life back into the dim little eyes. "What has been happening to me?" said the sad little eyes. Oh, how sweet it was to see them snap at her again from the red eiderdown! . . . But the nose, which was of some black composition, wasn't at all firm. It must have had a knock, somehow. Never mind—a little dab of black sealing-wax when the time came—when it was absolutely necessary. . . . Little rogue! Yes, she really felt like that about it. Little rogue biting its tail just by her left ear. She could have taken it off and laid it on her lap and stroked it. She felt a tingling in her hands and arms, but that came from walking, she supposed. And when she breathed, something light and sad—no, not sad, exactly—something gentle seemed to move in her bosom.

There were a number of people out this afternoon, far more than last Sunday. And the band sounded louder and gayer. That was because the Season had begun. For although the band played all the year round on Sundays, out of season it was never the same. It was like someone playing with only the family to listen; it didn't care how it played if there weren't any strangers present. Wasn't the conductor wearing a new coat, too? She was sure it was new. He scraped with his foot and flapped his arms like a rooster about to crow, and the bandsmen sitting in the green rotunda blew out their cheeks and glared at the music. Now there came a little "flutey" bit—very pretty!—a little chain of bright drops. She was sure it would be repeated. It was; she lifted her head and smiled.

Only two people shared her "special" seat: a fine old man in a velvet coat, his hands clasped over a huge carved walking-stick, and a big old woman, sitting upright, with a roll of knitting on her embroidered apron. They did not speak. This was disappointing, for Miss Brill always looked forward to the conversation. She had become really quite expert, she thought, at listening as though she didn't listen, at sitting in other people's lives just for a minute while they talked around her.

She glanced, sideways, at the old couple. Perhaps they would go soon. Last Sunday, too, hadn't been as interesting as usual. An Englishman and his wife, he wearing a dreadful Panama hat and she button boots. And she'd gone on the whole time about how she ought to wear spectacles; she knew she needed them; but that it was no good getting any; they'd be sure to break and they'd never keep on. And he'd been so patient. He'd suggested everything—gold rims, the kind that curved round your ears, little pads inside the bridge. No, nothing would please her. "They'll always be sliding down my nose!" Miss Brill had wanted to shake her.

The old people sat on the bench, still as statues. Never mind, there was always the crowd to watch. To and fro, in front of the flower-beds and the band rotunda, the couples and groups paraded, stopped to talk, to greet, to buy a handful of flowers from the old beggar who had his tray fixed to the railings. Little children ran among them, swooping and laughing; little boys with big white silk bows under their chins, little girls, little French dolls, dressed up in velvet and lace. And sometimes a tiny staggerer came suddenly rocking into the open from under the trees, stopped, stared, as suddenly sat down "flop," until its small high-stepping mother, like a young hen, rushed scolding to its rescue. Other people sat on the benches and green chairs, but they were nearly always the same, Sunday after Sunday, and—Miss Brill had often noticed—there was something funny about nearly all of them. They were odd, silent, nearly all old, and from the way they stared they looked as though they'd just come from dark little rooms or even—even cupboards!

Behind the rotunda the slender trees with yellow leaves down drooping, and through them just a line of sea, and beyond the blue sky with gold-veined clouds.

Tum-tum-tum tiddle-um! tiddle-um! tum tiddley-um tum ta! blew the band.

Two young girls in red came by and two young soldiers in blue met them, and they laughed and paired and went off arm-in-arm. Two peasant women with funny straw hats passed, gravely, leading beautiful smoke-colored donkeys. A cold, pale nun hurried by. A beautiful woman came along and dropped her bunch of violets, and a little boy ran after to hand them to her, and she took them and threw them away as if they'd been poisoned. Dear me! Miss Brill didn't know whether to admire that or not! And now an ermine toque and a gentleman in grey met just in front of her. He was tall, stiff, dignified, and she was wearing the ermine toque she'd bought when her hair was yellow. Now everything, her hair, her face, even her eyes, was the same color as the shabby ermine, and her hand, in its cleaned glove, lifted to dab her lips, was a tiny yellowish paw. Oh, she was so pleased to see him — delighted! She rather thought they were going to meet that afternoon. She described where she'd been — everywhere, here, there, along by the sea. The day was so charming — didn't he agree? And wouldn't he, perhaps? . . . But he shook his head, lighted a cigarette, slowly breathed a great deep puff into her face, and, even while she was still talking and laughing, flicked the match away and walked on. The ermine toque was alone; she smiled more brightly than ever. But even the band seemed to know what she was feeling and played more softly, played tenderly, and the drum beat, "The Brute! The Brute!" over and over. What would she do? What was going to happen now? But as Miss Brill wondered, the ermine toque turned, raised her hand as though she'd seen some one else, much nicer, just over there, and pattered away. And the band changed again and played more quickly, more gaily than ever, and the old couple on Miss Brill's seat got up and marched away, and such a funny old man with long whiskers hobbled along in time to the music and was nearly knocked over by four girls walking abreast.

Oh, how fascinating it was! How she enjoyed it! How she loved sitting here, watching it all! It was like a play. It was exactly like a play. Who could believe the sky at the back wasn't painted? But it wasn't till a little brown dog trotted on solemn and then slowly trotted off, like a little "theatre" dog, a little dog that had been drugged, that Miss Brill discovered what it was that made it so exciting. They were all on the stage. They weren't only the audience, not only looking on; they were acting. Even she had a part and came every Sunday. No doubt somebody would have noticed if she hadn't been there; she was part of the performance after all. How strange she'd never thought of it like that before! And yet it explained why she made such a point of starting from home at just the same time each week — so as not to be late for the performance — and it also explained why she had quite a queer, shy feeling at telling her English pupils how she spent her Sunday afternoons. No wonder! Miss Brill nearly laughed out loud. She was on the stage. She thought of the old invalid gentleman to whom she read the newspaper four afternoons a week while he slept in the garden. She had got quite used to the frail head on the cotton pillow, the hollowed eyes, the open mouth, and the high pinched nose. If he'd been dead she mightn't have noticed for weeks; she wouldn't have minded. But suddenly he knew he was having the paper read to him by an actress! "An actress!" The old head lifted; two points of light quivered in the old eyes. "An actress — are ye?" And Miss Brill smoothed the newspaper as though it were the manuscript of her part and said gently: "Yes, I have been an actress for a long time."

The band had been having a rest. Now they started again. And what they 10
played was warm, sunny, yet there was just a faint chill—a something, what
was it?—not sadness—no, not sadness—a something that made you want to
sing. The tune lifted, lifted, the light shone; and it seemed to Miss Brill that in
another moment all of them, all the whole company, would begin singing. The
young ones, the laughing ones who were moving together, they would begin,
and the men's voices, very resolute and brave, would join them. And then she
too, she too, and the others on the benches—they would come in with a kind
of accompaniment—something low, that scarcely rose or fell, something so
beautiful—moving. . . . And Miss Brill's eyes filled with tears and she looked
smiling at all the other members of the company. Yes, we understand, we understand, she thought—though what they understood she didn't know.

Just at that moment a boy and a girl came and sat down where the old
couple had been. They were beautifully dressed; they were in love. The hero and
heroine, of course, just arrived from his father's yacht. And still soundlessly
singing, still with that trembling smile, Miss Brill prepared to listen.

"No, not now," said the girl. "Not here, I can't."

"But why? Because of that stupid old thing at the end there?" asked the
boy. "Why does she come here at all—who wants her? Why doesn't she keep
her silly old mug at home?"

"It's her fu-fur which is so funny," giggled the girl. "It's exactly like a fried
whiting."

"Ah, be off with you!" said the boy in an angry whisper. Then: "Tell me, ma 15
petite chère——"

"No, not here," said the girl. "Not *yet*."

On her way home she usually bought a slice of honey-cake at the baker's. It
was her Sunday treat. Sometimes there was an almond in her slice, sometimes
not. It made a great difference. If there was an almond it was like carrying
home a tiny present—a surprise—something that might very well not have
been there. She hurried on the almond Sundays and struck the match for the
kettle in quite a dashing way.

But today she passed the baker's by, climbed the stairs, went into the little
dark room—her room like a cupboard—and sat down on the red eiderdown.
She sat there for a long time. The box that the fur came out of was on the bed.
She unclasped the necklet quickly; quickly, without looking, laid it inside. But
when she put the lid on she thought she heard something crying.

CONSIDERATIONS FOR CRITICAL THINKING AND WRITING

1. FIRST RESPONSE. There is almost no physical description of Miss Brill in
   the story. What do you think she looks like? Develop a detailed description
   that would be consistent with her behavior.

2. How does the calculated omission of Miss Brill's first name contribute to
   her characterization?

3. What details make Miss Brill more than a stock characterization of a frail
   old lady?

4. What do Miss Brill's observations about the people she encounters reveal
   about her?

5. What is the conflict in the story? Who or what is the antagonist?

6. Locate the climax of the story. How is it resolved?

7. What is the purpose of the fur piece? What is the source of the crying in the final sentence of the story?

8. Is Miss Brill a static or a dynamic character?

9. Describe Miss Brill's sense of herself at the end of the story.

10. Discuss the function of the minor characters mentioned in the story. Analyze how Katherine Mansfield used them to reveal Miss Brill's character.

CONNECTIONS TO OTHER SELECTIONS

1. Compare Miss Brill's recognition with that of the narrator in Fay Weldon's "IND AFF, or Out of Love in Sarajevo" (p. 165).

2. Write an essay comparing the themes in "Miss Brill" and James Joyce's "Eveline" (p. 524).

DAGOBERTO GILB (B. 1950)

Born in Los Angeles, Dagoberto Gilb is a journeyman carpenter who considers both Los Angeles and El Paso to be home. He has been a visiting writer at the University of Texas and the University of Arizona. Among his literary prizes are the James D. Phelan Award in literature and the Whiting Award; he has also won a National Endowment for the Arts Creative Writing Fellowship. Gilb's fiction has been published in a variety of journals including the *Threepenny Review, ZYZZYVA,* and *American Short Fiction.* His stories, collected in *The Magic of Blood* (1993), from which "Love in L.A." is taken, often reflect his experiences as a worker moving between Los Angeles and El Paso. In 1994 he published his first novel, *The Last Known Residence of Mickey Acuña.*

Web   *Research Dagoberto Gilb with LitLinks at*
http://www.bedfordstmartins.com/meyer/bedintrolit

Love in L.A.   *1993*

Jake slouched in a clot of near motionless traffic, in the peculiar gray of concrete, smog, and early morning beneath the overpass of the Hollywood Freeway on Alvarado Street. He didn't really mind because he knew how much worse it could be trying to make a left onto the onramp. He certainly didn't do that every day of his life, and he'd assure anyone who'd ask that he never would either. A steady occupation had its advantages and he couldn't deny thinking about that too. He needed an FM radio in something better than this '58 Buick he drove. It would have crushed velvet interior with electric controls for the L.A. summer, a nice warm heater and defroster for the winter drives at the beach, a cruise control for those longer trips, mellow speakers front and rear of course, windows that hum closed, snuffing out that nasty exterior noise of freeways. The fact was that he'd probably have to change his whole style. Exotic colognes, plush, dark nightclubs, maitais and daiquiris, necklaced ladies in satin gowns, misty and sexy like in a tequila ad. Jake could imagine lots of possibilities when he let himself, but none that ended up with him pressed onto a stalled freeway.

Jake was thinking about this freedom of his so much that when he glimpsed its green light he just went ahead and stared bye bye to the steadily employed. When he turned his head the same direction his windshield faced, it was maybe one second too late. He pounced the brake pedal and steered the front wheels away from the tiny brakelights but the smack was unavoidable. Just one second sooner and it would only have been close. One second more and he'd be crawling up the Toyota's trunk. As it was, it seemed like only a harmless smack, much less solid than the one against his back bumper.

Jake considered driving past the Toyota but was afraid the traffic ahead would make it too difficult. As he pulled up against the curb a few carlengths ahead, it occurred to him that the traffic might have helped him get away too. He slammed the car door twice to make sure it was closed fully and to give himself another second more, then toured front and rear of his Buick for damage on or near the bumpers. Not an impressionable scratch even in the chrome. He perked up. Though the car's beauty was secondary to its ability to start and move, the body and paint were clean except for a few minor dings. This stood out as one of his few clearcut accomplishments over the years.

Before he spoke to the driver of the Toyota, whose looks he could see might present him with an added complication, he signaled to the driver of the car that hit him, still in his car and stopped behind the Toyota, and waved his hands and shook his head to let the man know there was no problem as far as he was concerned. The driver waved back and started his engine.

"It didn't even scratch my paint," Jake told her in that way of his. "So how   5 you doin? Any damage to the car? I'm kinda hoping so, just so it takes a little more time and we can talk some. Or else you can give me your phone number now and I won't have to lay my regular b.s. on you to get it later."

He took her smile as a good sign and relaxed. He inhaled her scent like it was clean air and straightened out his less than new but not unhip clothes.

"You've got Florida plates. You look like you must be Cuban."

"My parents are from Venezuela."

"My name's Jake." He held out his hand.

"Mariana."   10

They shook hands like she'd never done it before in her life.

"I really am sorry about hitting you like that." He sounded genuine. He fondled the wide dimple near the cracked taillight. "It's amazing how easy it is to put a dent in these new cars. They're so soft they might replace waterbeds soon." Jake was confused about how to proceed with this. So much seemed so unlikely, but there was always possibility. "So maybe we should go out to breakfast somewhere and talk it over."

"I don't eat breakfast."

"Some coffee then."

"Thanks, but I really can't."   15

"You're not married, are you? Not that that would matter that much to me. I'm an openminded kinda guy."

She was smiling. "I have to get to work."

"That sounds boring."

"I better get your driver's license," she said.

Jake nodded, disappointed. "One little problem," he said. "I didn't bring 20
it. I just forgot it this morning. I'm a musician," he exaggerated greatly, "and,
well, I dunno, I left my wallet in the pants I was wearing last night. If you have
some paper and a pen I'll give you my address and all that."

He followed her to the glove compartment side of her car.

"What if we don't report it to the insurance companies? I'll just get it fixed
for you."

"I don't think my dad would let me do that."

"Your dad? It's not your car?"

"He bought it for me. And I live at home."   25

"Right." She was slipping away from him. He went back around to the
back of her new Toyota and looked over the damage again. There was the
trunk lid, the bumper, a rear panel, a taillight.

"You do have insurance?" she asked, suspicious, as she came around the
back of the car.

"Oh yeah," he lied.

"I guess you better write the name of that down too."

He made up a last name and address and wrote down the name of an in- 30
surance company an old girlfriend once belonged to. He considered giving a
real phone number but went against that idea and made one up.

"I act too," he lied to enhance the effect more. "Been in a couple of
movies."

She smiled like a fan.

"So how about your phone number?" He was rebounding maturely.

She gave it to him.

"Mariana, you are beautiful," he said in his most sincere voice.   35

"Call me," she said timidly.

Jake beamed. "We'll see you, Mariana," he said holding out his hand. Her
hand felt so warm and soft he felt like he'd been kissed.

Back in his car he took a moment or two to feel both proud and sad about
his performance. Then he watched the rear view mirror as Mariana pulled up
behind him. She was writing down the license plate numbers on his Buick,
ones that he'd taken off a junk because the ones that belonged to his had ex-
pired so long ago. He turned the ignition key and revved the big engine and
clicked into drive. His sense of freedom swelled as he drove into the now moving street traffic, though he couldn't stop the thought about that FM stereo
radio and crushed velvet interior and the new car smell that would even make
it better.

CONSIDERATIONS FOR CRITICAL THINKING AND WRITING

1. FIRST RESPONSE. Is "Love in L.A." a love story? Try to argue that it is. (If the
   story ended with paragraph 37, how would your interpretation of the story
   be affected?)
2. What is the effect of setting the story's action in a Los Angeles traffic jam
   on the Hollywood Freeway?
3. Characterize Jake. What do his thoughts in the first two paragraphs reveal
   about him? About how old do you think he is?

4. There is little physical description of Jake in the story, but given what you learn about him, how would you describe his physical features and the way he dresses?

5. What causes Jake to smack into the back of Mariana's car? What is revealed about his character by the manner in which he has the accident?

6. Describe how Jake responds to Mariana when he introduces himself to her, especially in paragraph 12. What does his behavior reveal about his character?

7. How does Mariana respond to Jake? Explain whether you think she is a round or flat character.

8. Explain how their respective cars serve to characterize Jake and Mariana.

9. What does the final paragraph reveal about each character?

10. In a sentence or two write down what you think the story's theme is. How does the title contribute to that theme?

CONNECTIONS TO OTHER SELECTIONS

1. Compare and contrast the themes in "Love in L.A." and Fay Weldon's "IND AFF, or Out of Love in Sarajevo" (p. 165).

2. Consider Jake's relationship with his car and the narrator's relationship with his car in E. E. Cummings's poem "she being Brand" (p. 720). In an essay explore how the cars reveal each character's aspirations.

ALISON BAKER (B. 1953)

Born in Pennsylvania, Alison Baker was raised in Indiana and has subsequently lived in Chicago, Maine, and Utah. After graduating from Reed College, she worked in a hospital as a library assistant and earned a master's degree in library science. She now lives and writes in Oregon. Her stories are collected in *How I Came West and Why I Stayed* (1993) and in *Loving Wanda Beaver: Novella and Stories* (1995). "Better Be Ready 'Bout Half Past Eight" originally appeared in the *Atlantic Monthly* and was awarded first prize in the 1994 competition for the O. Henry Awards. Baker describes her fiction writing as "a comforting way of revising both my own past and the apparent present, as well as foretelling the unlikeliest of much-to-be-desired futures."

Web *Research Alison Baker with LitLinks at*
http://www.bedfordstmartins.com/meyer/bedintrolit

Better Be Ready 'Bout Half Past Eight   1993

"I'm changing sex," Zach said.

Byron looked up from his lab notebook. "For the better, I hope."

"This is something I've never discussed with you," Zach said, stepping back and leaning against the office door. "I need to. Do you want to get a beer or something?"

"I have to transcribe this data," Byron said. "What do you need to discuss?"
"My sexuality," Zach said. "The way I feel trapped in the wrong body." 5
"Well, I suppose you were right," Byron said.
"Right?" Zach said.
"Not to discuss it with me," Byron said. "It's none of my business, is it?"
"We've been friends a long time," Zach said.
"Have you always felt this way?" Byron said. 10
Zach nodded. "I didn't know it was this I was feeling," he said. "But I've been in therapy for over a year now, and I'm sure."
"You've been seeing Terry about *this?*"
Byron had given Zach the name of Terry Wu, whom he himself had once consulted professionally.
Zach nodded again.
"He's terrific. He knew the first time he met me what I was." 15
"What were you?" Byron said.
"A woman," Zach said.
Had he missed any signs? Byron sat frowning at the computer screen. Then he stood, shoved his hands into his pockets, and stared out the window. He could see the sky and the top of the snow-covered hills. On this floor all the windows started at chin level, so you couldn't see the parking lot or the ground outside; you could see only distances, clouds, and sections of sunrise.
He walked up and down the hall for a while. The surrounding labs buzzed with action, students leaning intently over whirring equipment, technicians laughing over coffee. Secretaries clopped through the hall and said, "Hi, Dr. Glass," when they passed him. He could ignore them, because he had a reputation for being absentminded; he was absorbed in his research, or perhaps in a new poem. He was well known, particularly in scientific circles, for his poetry. He edited the poetry column of a major scientific research journal. He judged many poetry-writing competitions, and he had edited anthologies.
What had he missed? 20
Worrying about it was useless. Zach's sexuality wasn't his concern. "Just as long as it doesn't interfere with work," he would say. "I can't have people's personal lives taking over the lab."
But in fact he didn't believe in the separation of work and home. "If your love life's screwed up, you're probably going to screw up the science," he'd said more than once when he sent a sobbing technician home, or gave a distraught graduate student the name of a counselor. As a result, his workers did sacrifice, to some extent, their personal lives; they came in on weekends or at night to see to an experiment. The dictum, even if artificial, seemed to work.
"Go on home," he imagined himself saying to Zach, patting him on the shoulder. "Come back when it's all over."
But that wouldn't work. For one thing, the fretting wouldn't end. For another thing, Zach wouldn't be Zach when he came back. He would be a woman Byron had never met.

"He's putting you on," Emily said. She was sitting at the table, ostensibly edit- 25 ing a paper on the synthesis of mRNA at the transcriptional level in the Drosophila Per protein, but whenever the spoon Byron held approached Toby's mouth, her own mouth opened in anticipation.
"Nope," Byron said, spooning more applesauce from the jar. "He wanted to tell me before he started wearing makeup."

"If Zach thinks that's the definition of women, he's headed for trouble," Emily said. "I suppose he's shaving his legs and getting silicone implants too."

"Not to mention waxing his bikini line," Byron said.

"Oh, God," Emily said, laughing. "I don't want to hear any more." She handed Byron a washcloth, and Byron carefully wiped applesauce off Toby's chin. "How would you know you were the wrong sex?"

"Women's intuition?" Byron said.   30

"Very attractive," he said the next morning, when Zach walked into the lab wearing eye shadow.

"Don't make fun of me, okay?" Zach said.

Byron felt embarrassed. "I didn't mean anything," he said. "I mean, it's subtle and everything."

Zach looked pleased. "I've been practicing," he said. "You know what? My younger brother wears more makeup than I do. Is this a crazy world or what?"

"Yeah," Byron said. He'd met Zach's brother, whose makeup was usually 35 black. "Are you doing this gradually? Or are you sort of going cold turkey? I mean, will you come in in nylons and spike heels some morning?"

"Babe," Zach said, "I've been getting hormones for six months. Don't you notice anything different?"

He put his hands on his hips and turned slowly around, and Byron saw discernible breasts pushing up the cloth of Zach's rugby shirt. Byron felt a little faint, but he managed to say, "You're wearing a bra."

Zach went over to look in the mirror behind the door. He stood on tiptoe, staring intently at his breasts for a moment, and then, as he took his lab coat off the hook, he said, "God, I'm starting to feel good."

"You are?" was all Byron could manage. He was wondering how to say, without hurting Zach's new feelings, Don't call me babe.

All day he tried not to look at Zach's breasts, but there they were, right in 40 front of him, as Zach bent over the bench, or peered into the microscope, or leaned back with his hands behind his neck, staring at the ceiling, thinking.

"I'm heading out," Byron said to Sarah in midafternoon.

"Are you okay?" she said, looking up from the bench. "You look a little peaked."

"I'm fine," Byron said. "I'll be back in the morning."

But once out in the parking lot, sitting in his car, he could think of no place he wanted to go. He hung on to the steering wheel and stared at the Mercedes in front of him, which had a Utah license plate that read IMAQT. A woman, of course.

Well, it's not *my* life, he thought. Nothing has changed for me.   45

"I haven't had this much trouble with breasts since I was sixteen," he said to Emily as they sat at the kitchen table watching the sunset.

"How big are they?" Emily said.

"Jesus, I don't know," Byron said.

"Bigger than mine?" she said.

Byron looked at Emily's breasts, which were bigger since she'd had Toby. 50 "No," he said. "But I think they've just started."

"You mean he'll keep taking hormones till they're the size he wants?" Emily said. "I should do that."

"You know," Byron said, "what I don't understand is why it bothers me so much. You'd think he's doing it to spite me."

"Going to meetings will be more expensive," she said.

"What do you mean?" Byron said.

"Honey," Emily said, "if Zach's a woman, you won't be sharing a room. 55 Will you?"

"Oh," Byron said. "Do you think it will make that much difference?"

"You're already obsessed with his breasts," Emily said. "Wait till he's fully equipped."

Byron leaned his head on his hand. He hadn't even *thought* about the surgical procedure.

"I think you're letting this come between us," Zach said the next day.

"What?" Byron said. 60

"We've been friends a long time. I don't want to lose that."

"Zach," Byron said, "I don't see how things can stay the same."

"But I'm still the same person," Zach said.

Byron was not at all sure of that. "Well, how's it going?" he finally said.

Zach seemed pleased to be asked. He sat down on the desk and folded his 65 arms. "Really well," he said. "The surgeon says the physiological changes are right on schedule. I'm scheduled for surgery starting next month."

"Starting?" Byron said.

"I'm going to have a series of operations," Zach said. "Over several months. Cosmetic surgery for the most part."

"Zach," Byron said, "maybe it's none of my business, but don't you feel —" He cast about for the right way to say it. "Won't the operations make you feel, uh, mutilated?"

Zach shook his head. "That's what it's all about," he said. "They won't. To tell you the truth, in the past year or two I've come to feel as if my penis is an alien growth on my body. It's my *enemy*, Byron. This surgery's going to liberate me."

Byron crossed his legs. "I don't think I can relate to that," he said. 70

"I know," Zach said. "My support group says nobody really understands."

"Your support group?" Byron said.

"Women who've had the operation," Zach said, "or are in the process. We meet every week."

"How many are there?"

"More than you'd think," Zach said. 75

"So," Byron said. "Are you — I mean, should I call you 'she' now?"

Zach grinned. "I've been calling myself 'she' for a while. But so far nobody outside my group has."

"Well," Byron said. He tried to look at Zach and smile, but he couldn't do both at once. He smiled first, and then looked. "I'll work on it," he said. "But it's not exactly easy for me either, you know."

"I know," Zach said. "I really appreciate your trying to understand." He stood up. "Back to work," he said. "Oh." He turned around with his hand on the doorknob. "I'm changing my name, too. As of next month I'll be Zoe."

"Zoe," Byron said. 80

"It means 'life,'" Zach said. "Mine is finally beginning."

"It means 'life,'" Byron said mincingly to Toby as he pulled the soggy diaper out from under him. "'Life,' for Christ's sake."

Toby smiled.

"What's he been for thirty-eight years—dead?" Byron said. He dried Toby and sprinkled him with powder, smoothing it into the soft creases. As he lifted Toby's feet to slide a clean diaper underneath him, a stream of pee arced gracefully into the air and hit Byron in the chest, leaving a trail of droplets across Toby's powdered thighs.

"Oh, geez," Byron said. "Couldn't you wait ten seconds?" He reached for   85
the washcloth and wiped the baby off. Then he wiggled the little penis between his thumb and forefinger. "You know what you are, don't you?" he said, leaning over and peering into Toby's face. "A little man. No question about that."

Toby laughed.

After he'd put Toby into the crib, Byron went into the bathroom, pulling his T-shirt off. He caught sight of himself in the mirror and stood still. With the neckband of the shirt stuck on his head, framing his face, the shirt hung from his head like a wig of green hair.

He took his glasses off to blur the details and moved close to the mirror, looking at the line of his jaw. Was his jaw strong? Some women who had what were called "strong features" were quite attractive. Byron's mother used to say that Emily was built like a football player, but Byron had always thought she was sexy.

He put his glasses on and stepped back, bending his knees so that only his shoulders showed in the glass. With long hair around his face, and a few hormones to change his shape a little, he'd make a terrific woman.

He opened the medicine cabinet and took out one of Emily's lipsticks. He   90
leaned forward and spread it on his mouth, and as he pressed his lips together, a woman's face materialized in the mirror. Byron's heart came to a standstill.

It was his mother.

"It was the weirdest thing," he said. "I never looked like her before. Never."

"You never cross-dressed before," Zach said, continuing to stare at the computer screen. "What's going on with this data?"

"Of course I never cross-dressed," Byron said. "I still don't cross-dress. I just happened to look in the mirror when my shirt was on my head."

Zach looked up at him and grinned. "And there she was," he said. "You   95
would be amazed what we find out about ourselves when we come to terms with our sexuality."

"Oh, for God's sake," Byron said. "I was taking my shirt off. I wasn't coming to terms with anything."

"That's fairly obvious," Zach said, tapping at the keyboard.

"Jesus!" Byron said. "Do those hormones come complete with bitchiness? Or is your period starting?"

Zach stared at him. "I can't believe you said that," he said.

Byron couldn't believe he'd said it either, but he went on. "Everything's   100
sexuality with you these days," he said crossly. "I'm trying to tell you about my mother and you tell me it's my goddamn sexuality."

Zach stood up and stepped away from the desk. "Look," he said, folding his arms, "it's called the Tiresias° syndrome. You're jealous because I understand both sexes. By cross-dressing—whether you go around in Emily's underwear or just pretend you've got a wig on—you're trying to identify with me."

For a long moment Byron was unable to move. "What?" he finally said.

Tiresias: A blind prophet from Greek legend.

"You can't handle talking about the things that really matter, can you?" Zach said. "As soon as we get close to personal feelings, you back off."

"Feelings," Byron said.

"You're a typical man when it comes to emotions," Zach said. 105

"And you're a typical woman," Byron said.

Zach shook his head. "You are in trouble, boy."

"*I'm* in trouble?" Byron said. "Looks to me like you're the one with the problem."

"That's the difference between us," Zach said. "I'm taking steps to correct my problem. You won't even admit yours."

"My problem is you," Byron said. "You are a fucking prick." 110

"Not for long," Zach said.

"Once a prick, always a prick," Byron shouted.

After Zach walked out the door, Byron sat down at his desk and stared at the data Zach had pulled up on the screen, but its sense eluded him. Finally he spun his chair around and put his feet up on the bookcase behind him, and reached for a legal pad.

He always wrote his poetry on long yellow legal pads. He had once tried to jot down some poetic thoughts on the computer, but they had slipped out of his poem and insinuated themselves into a new idea for a research project, which in fact developed into a grant proposal that was later funded. The experience had scared him.

He stared up at the slice of sky that was visible from where he sat, and held 115 the legal pad on his lap for more than an hour, during which time he wrote down thirteen words. When Sarah stuck her head into the office and said, "See you tomorrow," he put the pad down and left work for the day.

Driving home, he thought about his dead mother, Melba Glass. She had never liked Emily, but once Byron was married, his mother stopped saying snide things about her. She asked them instead. "Honey," she'd say, "isn't Emily a little *strident?*"

"What do you mean, 'strident'?" Byron would snarl, and she would say she'd meant nothing at all, really, young women were just *different* these days. Byron would narrow his eyes at her, but later, when he'd driven his mother to the train station and waved her off, the idea would come back to him. Emily *was* vociferous in her opinions. And not particularly tolerant of her mother-in-law's old-fashioned tendencies.

"Why doesn't your mother *drive?*" she'd say.

"Why should she?" he'd say. "She never needed to."

"She needs to now, doesn't she?" Emily would say. 120

"Why should she?" Byron would repeat, and for a couple of days he would react to everything Emily said as if she were being highly unreasonable, and *strident.*

What would Emily say if he told her that his dead mother had appeared to him? Worse, that he had appeared to himself as his dead mother?

Emily would lean over Toby's crib in the dark. "I'll be Don Ameche in a taxi, honey," she'd sing. "Better be ready 'bout half past eight."

"How are you? Three of you now. Ha!" Terry Wu said.

"Three of me?" Byron said. 125

"You have a little baby?" Terry said.

"Oh! Toby! Terrific! And Emily. I see. Sure, we're fine. Really. Everything's terrific."

A concerned look seized Terry Wu's face. "Do you protest too much?" he said, and he leaned forward, pressing his fingertips together.

"Protest?" Byron said. "That's not why I'm here."

"Maybe no, maybe yes," Terry said, but he leaned back again.   130

"No, it's my, uh, colleague. You know, Zach."

"Ah," Terry said.

"I seem obsessed," Byron said weakly.

"You are obsessed with your colleague?"

"With his sex," Byron said.   135

"*His* sex?" Terry said.

Byron felt himself blushing. "I can't get used to the idea that he's a woman."

Terry nodded again. "Each one is a mystery."

"No, it's just — why didn't I know?"

"Did you know your wife was pregnant when she conceived?"   140

"What does that have to do with it?" Byron said.

"Well," Terry said, "you were there when it happened, in fact you did the deed, and yet you didn't know about it."

"Terry, I think that's something else."

Terry shrugged. "Are you in love with your colleague?"

"Of course not." He was becoming angry. "What are you getting at?"   145

"I am trying to elicit a coherent statement from you," Terry said. "So far all you have managed to tell me is that you are obsessed with your colleague and are not in love with her. I am having trouble following your flight of ideas."

"Look." Byron stared down at his feet. "Someone whom I have known for more than twenty years has overnight turned into a woman. It's shaken my understanding of reality. I can no longer trust what I see before my eyes."

"Yet you call yourself a scientist," Terry said thoughtfully. "It is simply a matter of surgery and hormonal therapy, isn't it? Changing one form into another by a well-documented protocol?"

Byron stared at him. "That's not what I mean," he said.

Terry clasped his hands together happily. "Yet a magical process is in-   150
volved as well! An invisible and powerful force! Something that is beyond our understanding! But"—he put his hands on his desk and stared into Byron's eyes—"even your poetic license will not allow you to accept it?"

"My poetic license?" Byron said.

"Are man and woman so different, so unrelated, that no transformation is possible? It's this Western culture," Terry said in disgust. "In my country, people exchange sexes every day."

Byron wondered if he had understood Terry correctly.

"Suppose your little baby comes to you in twenty years and says, 'Daddy, I am now Chinese.' Will you disown the child, after twenty years of paternity? No! He will still be the son you love."

"Chinese?" Byron said.   155

"I fear our time is up," Terry said. He stood up and held his hand out. Byron stood too, and shook it. "Good to see you again. Would you like to resume these discussions on a regular basis? I can see you at this time every week."

"I don't think so," Byron said. "I just wanted this one consultation."

"Glad to be of service," Terry said. "No charge, no charge. Professional courtesy. Someday I may need an experiment!" He chuckled. "Or a poem."

"A shower?" Byron said.

"Isn't it a kick?" Emily said. "Gifts like garter belts and strawberry douches." 160

"That's sick," he said.

"Oh, come on, honey. His men friends are invited too." She put down the screwdriver she'd been using to put together Toby's Baby Bouncer and leaned over to kiss Byron's knee. "It'll be fun."

"Why don't we just play red rover?" Byron said. "All the girls can stand on one side and yell, 'Let Zach come on over.'"

"You act as if you've lost your best friend," Emily said.

"I *am* losing him. I've known him for twenty years and suddenly I find out 165 he's the opposite of what I thought he was."

"Ah," Emily said, and she sat back against the sofa. "Here we go. Men and women are the exact opposite."

"Don't you start," he said. "I don't need an attack on the home front."

"I'm supposed to comfort you, I suppose," Emily said. "Sympathize with you because your good buddy's going over to the enemy."

"Well?" Byron said. "Aren't you secretly glad? Having a celebration? Letting him in on all your girlish secrets?"

Emily shook her head. "We're talking about a human being who has suf- 170 fered for forty years, and you're jealous because we're giving him some lacy underpants? You're welcome to some of mine, if that's what you want." She smiled at him.

"Suffered?" Byron said. "The dire fate of living in a male body? A fate worse than death, clearly."

"Why are you attacking *me?*" Emily said.

"I'm not attacking you," he said. "I'm just upset." He scooted closer to her and put his arms around her, laying his head against her breasts. "What if I lost you, too?"

"Sweetheart," Emily said, "you're stuck with me for the duration."

"I hope so," Byron said. He turned his head and pressed his face against 175 her. "I certainly hope so." His voice, caught in her cleavage, sounded very far away.

"Nearly twenty years ago," Byron said softly, holding Toby in his arms as he rocked in the dark, "when Daddy and Uncle Zach were very young—"

Toby, who was gazing at his eyes as he spoke, flung out a fist.

"He was still Uncle Zach at the time," Byron said. He tucked the fist into his armpit. "Anyway, we used to ride out to the quarries outside Bloomington to go swimming. You've never been swimming, but it's a lot like bobbing around in Mummy's uterus."

Toby's eyes closed.

"We used to ride our bikes out there after we'd finished our lab work," 180 Byron said. "Riding a bike in the summertime in southern Indiana is a lot like swimming too. The air is so full of humidity you can hardly push the sweat out your pores.

"So we would ride out there in the late afternoon, and hide our bikes in the trees, and go out to our favorite jumping-off place," Byron said. "And

Daddy and Uncle Zach would take off all their clothes, and get a running start, and jump right off the edge of the cliff into space!"

Toby made a sound.

"Yes, the final frontier," Byron said. "And we would hit the water at the same instant, and sink nearly to the bottom of the bottomless pit, and bob up without any breath. It was so cold."

He frowned. What kind of story was this to tell his son? Toby was asleep now, but in a few years he'd complain. He'd want plot, and character development.

"That was poetry, son," Byron whispered. He stood up and laid the sleep- 185 ing baby on his stomach in the crib. Tomorrow morning Emily would put Toby in his new Baby Bouncer, and Toby Glass would begin to move through the world on his own.

"What are you giving her?" Sarah said.

"Who?" Byron said, looking up from his calculations.

"Zoe," Sarah said. "We're giving her silk underwear from Frederick's of Hollywood. Do you know her bra size?"

"Sarah," Byron said, pushing his chair back and crossing his arms, "why on earth would I know Zach's bra size?"

"Oooh," Sarah said. "Touchy, aren't we? You *are* friends." She stood there 190 watching him as if, Byron thought, she was daring him to deny it.

"There are some things you just don't discuss in the locker room," he said.

"Oh," Sarah said. "Well, what are you getting her?"

"I haven't thought about it," Byron said.

"Don't you think you *ought* to think about it?"

It was his mother's voice, and for a moment Byron thought his mother 195 had spoken, there in his office. It was just what she would have said. She would look at him over her glasses, a long, questioning look. "Why not something personal? Intimate? You two have known each other a long time."

"Mom, you don't get something intimate for another guy," he would say.

"Oh, Byron, Byron. You should be more flexible, dear. You sound like your father." Every time she had said it she meant it as a reproach, but Byron was always rather pleased.

He wished sadly that he *could* talk to his mother. She never even knew that he had a son of his own. He looked at the picture of Toby on the desk and thought, she would be disappointed to see how much he looks like Emily's father.

He pictured her sitting in the chair beside his desk, her legs crossed. She had had very nice legs. She always insisted on buying expensive stockings at Dellekamps'. "When I worked at Du Pont," she told him more than once, holding out her foot and gazing at her delicately pointed toes, "they gave us all the stockings we wanted, but they were nylon."

"Mom," Byron said aloud, "I don't want to give him anything." 200

And as if he had disappointed her again, he saw her sadly pick up her purse from the floor and stand up.

"Just let me tell you this, Byron," she said. "If you don't support Zoe at this time in her life, you'll regret it forever."

She stepped toward him, shaking her finger at him.

"Forever, Byron."

He sighed, and looked at the legal pad lying in wait on the desk. His mother   205
had once told him she used to write poetry, but he had never read any of it.

"I wonder what happened to all my mother's poems," Byron said.

Emily looked up from the paper she was reading and stared at him thoughtfully, chewing on the end of her red pencil. "It wasn't very *good* poetry," she said.

"How do you know?" he said.

She frowned. "Byron, sometimes I think you live in a cocoon."

"You read it?" Byron said in amazement.   210

"Sure," she said. "You know, little poems about love, flowers, the moon." She shook her head, looking at the paper in her lap. "This guy should try poetry," she said.

"Why didn't she let me read it?" Byron said. He glanced at the television screen, where a woman was talking about teenage reproductive strategies in abusive households. "Em. What happened to it?"

"She threw it away," Emily said. "She thought it was too embarrassing to keep."

"Why did she talk to *you* about it?" Byron said.

"We had to talk about something," Emily said.   215

"Maybe your mother is right," Byron said. "Maybe I have no idea what's going on in the world." He peered into the rearview mirror at Toby, who was snoring softly in his car seat and paying no attention.

Byron had thought in the beginning that being a scientist would increase his understanding of the world, and the world's understanding of itself. But instead, as his work grew more specialized over the years and his expertise became narrower, his brain seemed to be purging its data banks of extraneous information and shutting down, one after another, his receptors for external stimuli. He had been so caught up in chronicling the minuscule changes taking place in the gels and tubes of his laboratory that the universe had changed its very nature without his even noticing. The world had a new arrangement that everyone else seemed to understand very well; even his poetry had simply served to keep him self-absorbed, oblivious of what must be reality.

Actually, he rather liked the idea of living in a cocoon while the world became a wilder and more exotic place. Sirens wailed, cars throbbing with bass notes roared past him with mere children at the wheel, dead women appeared in mirrors, and men changed into women; but Byron and Toby Glass putted across town safe and snug inside a cocoon.

"What do *I* know?" Byron thought. "What *do* I know?"

"Can I help you?" said a heavily scented woman with beige hair. Her lips were a   220
carnivorous shade of red, and her eyelids were a remarkable magenta.

"I'm looking for a gift," Byron said.

"For Baby's mother?" the woman said.

"Who?" Byron said.

"Baby's mother," she said, and with a long scarlet fingernail she poked at the Snugli where Toby Glass was sleeping peacefully against Byron's stomach.

"Oh," Byron said. "No. This is for a shower." 225
"Oh, I love showers!" the woman said. "What kind?"
"Sort of a coming-out shower."
"We don't see many of those," she said. She turned to survey her wares. "Are you close to the young lady?"
"I used to be," Byron said. "But she's changed."
"*Plus ça change,*" the woman said. "Something to remember you by. Some- 230 thing in leather?"
"Well, I don't know," Byron said, nervously stroking the warm curve of Toby's back. "I thought maybe stockings?"
The woman frowned. "You mean like pantyhose?"
"I guess not," he said.
"I know." The woman tapped Byron's lower lip with the red fingernail. "Follow me." She led him to the back of the store and leaned down to pull open a drawer. "For our discerning customers. A Merry Widow." She held up a lacy black item covered with ribbons and zippers.
"Wow," Byron said. "I didn't know they still made those." 235
"They are *hot,*" the saleswoman said. She held it up against her body. "Imagine your friend in this!"
"I can't," Byron said.
"Do you know her bra size?" the woman asked.
"I'm not sure it's final yet," Byron said.
"Oh," the woman said. "Well. Maybe some perfume." Byron followed her 240 back to the front of the store, where she waved her hand grandly at a locked glass cabinet. "These are very fine perfumes, from the perfume capitals of the world. Paris, Hong Kong, Aspen. This one is very popular—La Différence."
"That's good," Byron said. "I'll take some of that."
"Oh, excellent choice!" The woman patted his cheek before she reached into her cleavage and drew out a golden key to unlock the perfume cabinet.
"While Ginny rings that up, would you like to try on some of our makeup?" said another salesperson.
"No, thanks," Byron said.
The woman pouted at him. "You *should,*" she said. "Lots of men wear it. 245 Girls go crazy for it." She patted a stool in front of the counter. "Sit down."
Byron sat, and she removed his glasses. "You'll look *terrific,*" she said. She leaned toward him, her lips parted, and gently massaged his eyelid with a colorful finger. "'Scuse me while I kiss the sky," she sang softly, stroking the other one. Then she drew on his eyelid with a long black instrument. "This is Creem-So-Soft," she told him. "It is *so* easy to put on." She drew it across the other eyelid, and finally she brushed his eyelashes with a little brush and stood back. "There," she said. "You are a *killer.*"
Toby began to gasp into Byron's shirt. The makeup woman swooped down. "Oooh," she said. "Little booper's making hungry noises." She lifted her eyes to Byron. "Bet I can stall him."
"You can?" Byron said.
"Babies *love* this," she said. She maneuvered Toby out of the Snugli and sat him down facing her on Byron's lap. She began to sketch on his face with the Creem-So-Soft while Toby stared silently at her nose. "There!" She picked Toby up and held him for Byron to examine.

Toby beamed and waved his limbs. He was adorned with a black mous- 250
tache and a pointy black goatee.

"Oh, how darling," Ginny said, coming back from the cash register. "Will
this be cash or charge?"

Byron looked at the bill she handed him. "Charge," he said. "I thought
this store went out of business a long time ago."

"Lots of people say that," Ginny said.

"What have you done to the baby?" Emily said when Byron walked in the door.

"Babies like this," Byron said. "It's a preview of what he'll look like in 255
twenty years."

"He's going to be a beatnik?" Emily said. She took Toby from Byron's
arms. "Don't you think you're rushing things a little?"

Byron sighed. "They grow up so fast," he said. He kissed the top of Toby's
head, and then kissed Emily. "How do you like the new me?"

Emily looked at him. "Did you get your hair cut?" she said.

"Em, I'm wearing makeup," Byron said.

"Oh," she said. "So you are." She held Toby up and sniffed at his bottom. 260
"Daddy didn't change your dipes," she said, and she carried him off to his
room.

Byron went into the bathroom to look at himself. His eyelids were a very
bright purple. He picked up Emily's Barn Red lipstick and carefully covered his
lips with it. Then he took off his glasses.

"You know who you look like?" Emily said, appearing beside him in the
mirror. "Your mother. Honest to God. If you had one of those curly little
perms, you could pass for your own mother." She peered into the mirror,
stretching her upper lip with her forefinger. "Do you think I should shave my
moustache?"

"No," Byron said. "It's sexy." He slid his hands under her arms and over
her breasts. "Let's go to bed."

"No, thanks," Emily said. She picked up her Creem-So-Soft and started to
outline her eyes. "I have no desire to sleep with your mother."

"You never did like my mother," Byron said. 265

"Not a lot," Emily said.

"I think I'll go over to the lab," Byron said. He kissed her cheek, leaving a
large red lip print.

"Hold still," Emily said. She wet a washcloth, and as she scrubbed his lips
he had a sudden vision of his mother scrubbing at grape juice the same way
thirty-five years ago. "There. Now you look like my husband again."

He looked in the mirror. His stinging lips were still pinker than normal.
"Is wearing makeup always so painful?"

"Always," she said. "We do it for love." 270

Byron liked weekends at the lab. He liked weekdays, too, when students and
technicians wandered in and out of one another's labs borrowing chemicals,
and all the world seemed engaged in analyzing the structures and chemical interactions of various tissues. But weekends, when the offices were empty and
the halls were quiet, and only the odd student padded back and forth from the
bathroom, had a cozy, private feeling. Byron could think better in the silence,

and he felt close to other scientists, who had given up time in the outside world to bend lovingly over their benches and peer into microscopes, hoping to add to the world's slim store of truth. Both the lab work he did and the poetry he wrote on weekends seemed to spring from a deeper level: a place of intuition and hope that was inaccessible when he was distracted by bustle. On weekends he caught glimpses of the world he hoped to find, where poetry and science were one, and could explain the meaning of life.

"The meaning of life," he said aloud, and wrote it down on his legal pad. Then he turned and typed it on the keyboard, and it appeared in amber letters on the screen in front of him. He smiled and pushed back in his chair, and put his feet on the desk. Poem or experiment? Either one!

He felt that he was on the threshold of an important discovery.

"Why are you doing this?"

Byron opened his eyes. It was Zoe, leaning against the doorjamb. It was 275 definitely and absolutely Zoe; she could no longer be mistaken for a man. He stared at her; what *was* it? The hair, the clothes, the jaw, the way the arms were folded: all were utterly familiar. What had happened?

"The makeup," Zoe said. She shook her head. "You're trying to be something you're not."

He had forgotten about the purple eye shadow and the mascara, but he said, "How do you know what I'm not?"

"It's just that you're so conservative," Zoe said.

"No," he said. "I'm really quite wild. I'm just handicapped by my many fears."

"You?" Zoe said. 280

He nodded. "But you're wild through and through."

Zoe shook her head. "I'm conservative at the core. That's always been my major problem." She gazed out the window at the white hills. "You know the only thing I regret? I'll never have any children now."

"You could adopt."

She shook her head. "They won't have my genes."

"You never really know your children anyway," Byron said. 285

Zoe sighed. "Tell me honestly. Did Emily teach you how to put that eyeliner on?"

Byron smiled. "No," he said. "In fact she learned from me."

Zoe narrowed her eyes and stared at him for a moment, and then sat down on a stool. "I'm thinking of going to law school."

"Are you serious?" he said. "You'd leave the lab?"

"Sure. Patents is the way to go." 290

"You'd leave me?"

Zoe reached over and seized the tablet. "Poetry, poetry, poetry," she said. "Always with you it's the poetry. Anyone would think you're too distracted to work."

"You think any of this is easy?" Byron said.

"None of it," she said, and they sat together for a while without talking. "Are you coming to my shower?"

"Aren't showers supposed to be a surprise?" Byron said. 295

Zoe shrugged. "I hate surprises. I told Sarah she could give me a shower only if she invited men, too."

"I got you a gift." Byron was surprised to feel suddenly shy. "But is there anything you'd really like?"

"Will you come see me in the hospital?"

Byron nodded.

Zoe smiled. "Actually, you look good in makeup," she said. "It redefines 300 your features. You look stronger."

"It's the same old me, though," Byron said. "I'm not any stronger than before."

"I really am thinking of law school," Zoe said. "I need to change my life."

"Changing your sex isn't enough?"

"No. That's who I've been all along."

"Oh," Byron said, and all at once he felt very sad, and exhausted. He put 305 his feet up on the desk, and they sat there in silence, gazing at the part of the world they could see through the window.

After a while he told Zoe about Toby's trip to Dellekamps'. "And then," he said, "I'm sitting on a bench in the mall giving him his bottle, and I look up and these two old ladies are staring at him. 'That is dis*gust*ing,' one of them says. And then the other one gasps and grabs her arm and points at me. And they both back away looking horrified."

Zoe began to laugh.

"And then a man and a little girl walk by, and the little girl says, 'Daddy, is that a homeless person?' And the father says, 'No, dear, that's a man with problems.'"

"Oh," Zoe gasped, holding her ribs.

Byron wiped the tears from his own cheeks, and when he looked at his 310 hand, he saw that it was smeared with mascara. "I had no idea," he said, "no idea why these people were saying these things. I'd forgotten about my makeup. And Toby just looked normal to me."

"Stop," Zoe said, bending over and clutching her stomach.

"And finally a man comes up to me with his hands on his hips and says, 'You ought to be ashamed.'"

"I'm dying," Zoe croaked. "I can't breathe. Oh." She jumped from the stool and ran through the door. "I have to pee."

"You," Byron called after her, "should be ashamed." He listened to the squeegeeing of her sneakers as she ran down the empty hall, and to the familiar creak of the hinges as she pushed open the door to the men's room.

"Glad you could make it, glad you could make it," Terry Wu said, shaking 315 Byron's hand vigorously.

"Did you doubt that I would?" Byron said.

"You're a busy man," Terry said. "So often the cells can't wait." He leaned forward and whispered, "I am giving her a vibrator." Aloud, he said, "The muscles of the calves ache when one first wears high heels."

"That is so true," Emily said. She smiled at Terry Wu and pulled Byron away. "That guy gives me the creeps," she said.

"Honey, you're being xenophobic," Byron said. "Things are different in his country."

They pushed their way through the crowd, Byron cupping one hand 320 protectively around Toby's head to keep him from being squashed in his Snugli.

"There you are!" Sarah appeared in front of them. "Isn't the turnout great?" She waved her arm at the crowd.

Emily hugged her. "Did you get it?" she said.

Sarah nodded. "I never spent that much on a bra in my life."

"How did you know what size to get?" Byron asked.

"I asked her," Sarah said. She led them over to where Zoe stood beside a gift-covered table. "Here are the Glasses!" 325

"I'm so glad you could come," Zoe said. She kissed Emily on the cheek and prodded Toby's bottom with a glistening red-tipped forefinger. "How's my little beatnik godbaby?"

"Zoe, you look gorgeous," Emily said. "Really. You look so — you."

"Next I'm going to have electrolysis on my facial hair," Zoe said.

"You look pretty good as you are," Byron said. He wondered when the time would come that Zoe would kiss *his* cheek. "I bought you some perfume, but I ended up giving it to Emily."

"Thank goodness," Zoe said. "I'm allergic to everything but La Différence, 330 anyway."

"One of these days," Byron said, "I'll write you a poem."

"He's never done that for me." Emily waved her hand at the table in front of them. "Look at all this loot."

They stared at the pile of presents. "I can't wait to open them," Zoe said. "I've always wanted a shower."

"Isn't it wonderful to get what you always wanted?" Byron put his arm through hers and squeezed it, and he could feel her breast against his triceps as she squeezed back, her muscles hardening briefly against his own.

He felt a rush of pleasure. On his left Emily reached for a bacon-wrapped 335 chicken liver; on his right his oldest friend in the world gently disengaged her arm from his to touch the hands of the dozens of people who had come to wish her well; and from his shoulders, like a newly discovered organ of delight, hung the little bag full of Toby Glass.

Toby Glass, who could grow up to be anything!

The musicians in the string quartet hired for the occasion began to tune their instruments, leaning toward each other, listening, nodding gravely. The cellist moved her stool a little closer to the violinist; the violinist held her instrument away from her neck as she shook back her long red hair, and then replaced it firmly under her chin. Suddenly, as if spontaneously, each player lifted her bow and held it poised in the air for a long moment, until at some prearranged and invisible signal they plunged their bows toward the strings of their various instruments and began to play.

CONSIDERATIONS FOR CRITICAL THINKING AND WRITING

1. FIRST RESPONSE. "You would be amazed what we find out about ourselves when we come to terms with our sexuality" (para. 95). Reflect on this observation made by Zach/Zoe and respond to it.

2. Describe Byron's assumptions about what constitutes femininity and masculinity.

3. How does Byron react to Zach's announcement about his sex change operation?

4. Trace Byron's gradual shift in attitude toward Zach/Zoe.

5. How does Baker challenge readers' assumptions about gender roles?
6. Byron struggles with his interests in science and poetry. How is this related to the story's central conflict?
7. What do you think is Emily's function in the story?
8. Analyze the significance of the final paragraph. Given that most of the story consists of dialogue, why do you suppose there is none in this paragraph?
9. Compare the opening line of this story with several others in this anthology, and discuss how their respective writers attempt to engage their readers' interest.
10. CRITICAL STRATEGIES. Read the discussion of gender criticism (pp. 2105–2107) in Chapter 52, "Critical Strategies for Reading," and describe how a gender critic might use this story to explore contemporary masculine and feminine behavior in the United States.

CONNECTIONS TO OTHER SELECTIONS

1. Compare the opening line of this story with several others in this anthology. Discuss how their respective writers immediately engage their readers' interest.
2. Discuss how the endings of Baker's story and Andre Dubus's "Killings" (p. 84) affect your understanding of and emotional response to the events in each story.

9

Style, Tone,
and Irony

STYLE

Style is a concept that everyone understands on some level because in its broadest sense it refers to the particular way in which anything is made or done. Style is everywhere around us. The world is saturated with styles in cars, clothing, buildings, teaching, dancing, music, politics — in anything that reflects a distinctive manner of expression or design. Consider, for example, how a tune sung by the Beatles differs from the same tune performed by a string orchestra. There's no mistaking the two styles.

Authors also have different characteristic styles. *Style* refers to the distinctive manner in which a writer arranges words to achieve particular effects. That arrangement includes individual word choices and matters such as the length of sentences, their structure and tone, and the use of irony.

Diction refers to a writer's choice of words. Because different words evoke different associations in a reader's mind, the writer's choice of words is crucial in controlling a reader's response. The diction must be appropriate for the characters and the situations in which the author places them. Consider how inappropriate it would have been if Melville had had Bartleby respond to the lawyer's requests with "Hell no!" instead of "I would prefer not to." The word *prefer* and the tentativeness of *would* help reinforce the scrivener's mildness, his dignity, and even his seeming reasonableness — all of which frustrate the lawyer's efforts to get rid of him. Bartleby, despite his passivity, seems to be in control of the situation. If he were to shout "Hell no!" he would appear angry, aggressive, desperate, and too informal, none of which would fit with his solemn, conscious decision to die. Melville makes the lawyer the desperate party by carefully choosing Bartleby's words.

Sentence structure is another element of a writer's style. Hemingway's terse, economical sentences are frequently noted and readily perceived. Here are the concluding sentences of Hemingway's "Soldier's Home" (p. 152), in which Krebs decides to leave home:

> He had tried so to keep his life from being complicated. Still, none of it had touched him. He had felt sorry for his mother and she had made him lie. He would go to Kansas City and get a job and she would feel all right about it. There would be one more scene maybe before he got away. He would not go down to his father's office. He would miss that one. He wanted his life to go smoothly. It had just gotten going that way. Well, that was all over now, anyway. He would go over to the schoolyard and watch Helen play indoor baseball.

Hemingway expresses Krebs's thought the way Krebs thinks. The style avoids any "complicated" sentence structures. Seven of the eleven sentences begin with the word *He.* There are no abstractions or qualifications. We feel as if we are listening not only to *what* Krebs thinks but to *how* he thinks. The style reflects his firm determination to make, one step at a time, a clean, unobstructed break from his family and the entangling complications they would impose on him.

Contrast this straightforward style with Vladimir Nabokov's description of a woman in his short story "The Vane Sisters." The sophisticated narrator teaches French literature at a women's college and is as observant as he is icily critical of the woman he describes in this passage:

> Her fingernails were gaudily painted, but badly bitten and not clean. Her lovers were a silent young photographer with a sudden laugh and two older men, brothers, who owned a small printing establishment across the street. I wondered at their tastes whenever I glimpsed, with a secret shudder, the higgledy-piggledy striation of black hairs that showed all along her pale shins through the nylon of her stockings with the scientific distinctness of a preparation flattened under glass; or when I felt, at her every movement, the dullish, stalish, not particularly conspicuous but all-pervading and depressing emanation that her seldom bathed flesh spread from under weary perfumes and creams.

This portrait—etched with a razor blade—is restrained but devastating. The woman's fingernails are "gaudily painted." She has no taste in men either. One of her lovers is "silent" except for a "sudden laugh," a telling detail that suggests a strikingly odd personality. Her other lovers, the two brothers (!), run a "small" business. We are invited to "shudder" along with the narrator as he vividly describes the "striation of black hairs" on her legs; we see the woman as if she were displayed under a microscope, an appropriate perspective given the narrator's close inspection. His scrutiny is relentless, and its object smells as awful as it looks (notice the difference in the language between this blunt description and the narrator's elegant distaste). He finds the woman "depressing" because the weight of her unpleasantness oppresses him.

The narrator reveals nearly as much about himself as about the woman, but Nabokov leaves the reader with the task of assessing the narrator's fastidious reactions. The formal style of this description is appropriately that of an educated, highly critical, close observer of life who knows how to convey the "dullish, stalish" essence of this woman. But, you might ask, what about the curious informality of "higgledy-piggledy"? Does that fit the formal professorial voice? Given Nabokov's well-known fascination with wit and, more important, the narrator's obvious relish for verbally slicing this woman into a slide specimen, the term is revealed as appropriately chosen once the reader sees the subtle, if brutal, pun on *piggledy*.

Hemingway's and Nabokov's uses of language are very different, yet each style successfully fuses what is said with how it is said. We could write summaries of both passages, but our summaries, owing to their styles, would not have the same effect as the originals. And that makes all the difference.

TONE

Style reveals ***tone,*** the author's implicit attitude toward the people, places, and events in a story. When we speak, tone is conveyed by our voice inflections, our wink of an eye, or some other gesture. A professor who says "You're going to fail the next exam" may be indicating concern, frustration, sympathy, alarm, humor, or indifference, depending on the tone of voice. In a literary work that spoken voice is unavailable; instead we must rely on the context in which a statement appears to interpret it correctly.

In Chopin's "The Story of an Hour" (p. 12), for example, we can determine that the author sympathizes with Mrs. Mallard despite the fact that her grief over her husband's assumed death is mixed with joy. Though Mrs. Mallard thinks she's lost her husband, she experiences relief because she feels liberated from an oppressive male-dominated life. That's why she collapses when she sees her husband alive at the end of the story. Chopin makes clear by the tone of the final line ("When the doctors came they said she had died of heart disease — of joy that kills") that the men misinterpret both her grief and joy, for in the larger context of Mrs. Mallard's emotions we see, unlike the doctors, that her death may well have been caused not by a shock of joy but by an overwhelming recognition of her lost freedom.

If we are sensitive to tone, we can get behind a character and see him or her from the author's perspective. In Melville's "Bartleby, the Scrivener" (p. 116) everything is told from the lawyer's point of view, but the tone of his remarks often separates him from the author's values and attitudes. When the lawyer characterizes himself at the beginning of the story, his use of language effectively allows us to see Melville disapproving of what the lawyer takes pride in:

> The late John Jacob Astor, a personage little given to poetic enthusiasm, had no hesitation in pronouncing my first grand point to be prudence; my next, method. I do not speak it in vanity.

But, of course, he is vain and a name-dropper as well. He likes the "rounded and orbicular sound" of Astor's name because it "rings like unto bullion." Tone, here, helps to characterize the lawyer. Melville doesn't tell us that the lawyer is status conscious and materialistic; instead, we discover that through the tone. This stylistic technique is frequently an important element for interpreting a story. An insensitivity to tone can lead a reader astray in determining the theme of a work. Regardless of who is speaking in a story, it is wise to listen for the author's voice too.

IRONY

One of the enduring themes in literature is that things are not always what they seem to be. What we see — or think we see — is not always what we get. The unexpected complexity that often surprises us in life — what Herman Melville in *Moby-Dick* called the "universal thump" — is fertile ground for writers of imaginative literature. They cultivate that ground through the use of *irony,* a device that reveals a reality different from what appears to be true.

Verbal irony consists of a person saying one thing but meaning the opposite. If a student driver smashes into a parked car and the angry instructor turns to say "You sure did well today," the statement is an example of verbal irony. What is meant is not what is said. Verbal irony that is calculated to hurt someone by false praise is commonly known as *sarcasm.* In literature, however, verbal irony is usually not openly aggressive; instead, it is more subtle and restrained though no less intense.

In Godwin's "A Sorrowful Woman" (p. 35), a woman retreats from her family because she cannot live in the traditional role that her husband and son expect of her. When the husband tries to be sympathetic about her withdrawal from family life, the narrator tells us three times that "he understood such things" and that in "understanding these things" he tried to be patient by "[s]till understanding these things." The narrator's repetition of these phrases constitutes verbal irony because they call attention to the fact that the husband doesn't understand his wife at all. His "understanding" is really only a form of condescension that represents part of her problem rather than a solution.

Situational irony exists when there is an incongruity between what is expected to happen and what actually happens. For instance, at the climactic showdown between Marshal Potter and Scratchy Wilson in Crane's "The Bride Comes to Yellow Sky" (p. 251), there are no gunshots, only talk — and what subdues Wilson is not Potter's strength and heroism but the fact that the marshal is now married. To take one more example, the protagonist in Godwin's "A Sorrowful Woman" seems, by traditional societal standards, to have all that a wife and mother could desire in a family, but, given her needs, that turns out not to be enough to sustain even her life, let alone her happiness. In each of these instances the ironic situation creates a distinction between appearances and realities and brings the reader closer to the central meaning of the story.

Another form of irony occurs when an author allows the reader to know more about a situation than a character knows. ***Dramatic irony*** creates a discrepancy between what a character believes or says and what the reader understands to be true. In Flannery O'Connor's "Revelation" (p. 410) the insecure Mrs. Turpin, as a member of "the home-and-land owner" class, believes herself to be superior to "niggers," "white-trash," and mere "home owners." She takes pride in her position in the community and in what she perceives to be her privileged position in relation to God. The reader, however, knows that her remarks underscore her failings rather than any superiority. Dramatic irony can be an effective way for an author to have a character unwittingly reveal himself or herself.

As you read Raymond Carver's "Popular Mechanics," T. Coraghessan Boyle's "Carnal Knowledge," Susan Minot's "Lust," and Punyakante Wijenaike's "Anoma," pay attention to the authors' artful use of style, tone, and irony to convey meanings.

RAYMOND CARVER (1938–1988)

Born in 1938 in Clatskanie, Oregon, to working-class parents, Carver grew up in Yakima, Washington, was educated at Humboldt State College in California, and did graduate work at the University of Iowa. He married at age nineteen and during his college years worked at a series of low-paying jobs to help support his family. These difficult years eventually ended in divorce. He taught at a number of universities, among them the University of California at Berkeley, the University of Iowa, the University of Texas at El Paso, and Syracuse University. Carver's collections of stories include *Will You Please Be Quiet, Please?* (1976), *What We Talk about When We Talk about Love* (1981), from which "Popular Mechanics" is taken, *Cathedral* (1984), and *Where I'm Calling From: New and Selected Stories* (1988). Though extremely brief, "Popular Mechanics" describes a stark domestic situation with a startling conclusion.

Web *Research Raymond Carver with LitLinks at*
http://www.bedfordstmartins.com/meyer/bedintrolit

Popular Mechanics   *1981*

Early that day the weather turned and the snow was melting into dirty water. Streaks of it ran down from the little shoulder-high window that faced the backyard. Cars slushed by on the street outside, where it was getting dark. But it was getting dark on the inside too.

He was in the bedroom pushing clothes into a suitcase when she came to the door.

I'm glad you're leaving! I'm glad you're leaving! she said. Do you hear?

He kept on putting his things into the suitcase.

Son of a bitch! I'm so glad you're leaving! She began to cry. You can't even   5
look me in the face, can you?

Then she noticed the baby's picture on the bed and picked it up.

He looked at her and she wiped her eyes and stared at him before turning
and going back to the living room.

Bring that back, he said.

Just get your things and get out, she said.

He did not answer. He fastened the suitcase, put on his coat, looked around   10
the bedroom before turning off the light. Then he went out to the living room.

She stood in the doorway of the little kitchen, holding the baby.

I want the baby, he said.

Are you crazy?

No, but I want the baby. I'll get someone to come by for his things.

You're not touching this baby, she said.   15

The baby had begun to cry and she uncovered the blanket from around his
head.

Oh, oh, she said, looking at the baby.

He moved toward her.

For God's sake! she said. She took a step back into the kitchen.

I want the baby.   20

Get out of here!

She turned and tried to hold the baby over in a corner behind the stove.

But he came up. He reached across the stove and tightened his hands on
the baby.

Let go of him, he said.

Get away, get away! she cried.   25

The baby was red-faced and screaming. In the scuffle they knocked down a
flowerpot that hung behind the stove.

He crowded her into the wall then, trying to break her grip. He held on to
the baby and pushed with all his weight.

Let go of him, he said.

Don't, she said. You're hurting the baby, she said.

I'm not hurting the baby, he said.   30

The kitchen window gave no light. In the near-dark he worked on her
fisted fingers with one hand and with the other hand he gripped the screaming
baby up under an arm near the shoulder.

She felt her fingers being forced open. She felt the baby going from her.

No! she screamed just as her hands came loose.

She would have it, this baby. She grabbed for the baby's other arm. She
caught the baby around the wrist and leaned back.

But he would not let go. He felt the baby slipping out of his hands and he   35
pulled back very hard.

In this manner, the issue was decided.

CONSIDERATIONS FOR CRITICAL THINKING AND WRITING

1. FIRST RESPONSE. Discuss the story's final lines. What is the "issue" that is
   "decided"?

2. Though there is little description of the setting in this story, how do the
   few details that are provided help to establish the tone?

3. How do small actions take on larger significance in the story? Consider the woman picking up the baby's picture and the knocked-down flowerpot.

4. Why is this couple splitting up? Do we know? Does it matter? Explain your response.

5. Discuss the title of the story. The original title was "Mine." Which do you think is more effective?

6. What is the conflict? How is it resolved?

7. Read I Kings 3 in the Bible for the story of Solomon. How might "Popular Mechanics" be read as a retelling of this story? What significant differences do you find in the endings of each?

8. Explain how Carver uses irony to convey theme.

Connections to Other Selections

1. Compare Carver's style with Ernest Hemingway's in "Soldier's Home" (p. 152).

2. How is the ending of "Popular Mechanics" similar to the ending of Nathaniel Hawthorne's "The Birthmark" (p. 359)?

PERSPECTIVE

John Barth (b. 1930)

On Minimalist Fiction 1987

Minimalism (of one sort or another) is the principle (one of the principles, anyhow) underlying (what I and many another interested observer consider to be perhaps) the most impressive phenomenon on the current (North American, especially the United States) literary scene (the gringo equivalent of *el boom* in the Latin American novel): I mean the new flowering of the (North) American short story (in particular the kind of terse, oblique, realistic or hyperrealistic, slightly plotted, extrospective, cool-surfaced fiction associated in the last five or ten years with such excellent writers as Frederick Barthelme, Ann Beattie, Raymond Carver, Bobbie Ann Mason, James Robison, Mary Robison, and Tobias Wolff, and both praised and damned under such labels as "K-Mart realism," "hick chic," "Diet-Pepsi minimalism" and "post-Vietnam, post-literary, postmodernist blue-collar neo-early-Hemingwayism"). . . .

The genre of the short story, as Poe distinguished it from the traditional tale in his 1842 review of Hawthorne's first collection of stories, is an early manifesto of modern narrative minimalism: "In the whole composition there should be no word written, of which the tendency . . . is not to the pre-established design. . . . Undue length is . . . to be avoided." Poe's codification informs such later nineteenth-century masters of terseness, selectivity, and implicitness (as opposed to leisurely once-upon-a-timelessness, luxuriant abundance, explicit and extended analysis) as Guy de Maupassant and Anton Chekhov. Show, don't tell, said Henry James in effect and at length in his prefaces to the 1908 New York edition of his novels. And don't tell a word more than you absolutely need to, added young Ernest Hemingway, who thus described his "new theory" in the early 1920's: "You could omit anything if you knew that you omitted, and the omitted part would strengthen the story and make people feel something more than they understood. . . ."

Old or new, fiction can be minimalist in any or all of several ways. There are minimalisms of unit, form, and scale: short words, short sentences and paragraphs, [and] super-short stories. . . . There are minimalisms of style: a stripped-down vocabulary; a stripped-down syntax that avoids periodic sentences, serial predications, and complex subordinating constructions; a stripped-down rhetoric that may eschew figurative language altogether; a stripped-down, non-emotive tone. And there are minimalisms of material: minimal characters, minimal exposition ("all that David Copperfield kind of crap," says J. D. Salinger's catcher in the rye), minimal *mises en scène,* minimal action, minimal plot.

From *Weber Studies*

CONSIDERATIONS FOR CRITICAL THINKING AND WRITING

1. To what extent do Ernest Hemingway's "Soldier's Home" (p. 152) and Raymond Carver's "Popular Mechanics" fulfill Barth's description of minimalist fiction? How does each story suggest that less is more?

2. Write an essay explaining why one of the short stories by Nathaniel Hawthorne, Flannery O'Connor, or Alice Munro in this anthology is not a minimalist story.

T. CORAGHESSAN BOYLE (B. 1948)

Born in Peekskill, New York, T. Coraghessan Boyle earned a doctorate at the University of Iowa and has taught at the University of Southern California. Among his literary awards is a National Endowment for the Arts Creative Writing Fellowship and the PEN/Faulkner Award for fiction. His fiction has appeared in a variety of periodicals including the *North American Review, The New Yorker, Harper's,* the *Atlantic Monthly,* and *Playboy.* His novels include *Water Music* (1981), *Budding Projects* (1984), *World's End* (1987), *East Is East* (1990), and *The Road to Wellville* (1993), recently made into a film. His short stories are collected in *Descent of Man* (1979), *Greasy Lake and Other Stories* (1985), *If the River Was Whiskey* (1989), and *Without a Hero and Other Stories* (1994), from which "Carnal Knowledge," a story characteristic of Boyle's ironic humor, is reprinted. His most recent collection is *T. C. Boyle Stories: The Collected Stories of T. Coraghessan Boyle* (1998).

Research T. Coraghessan Boyle with LitLinks at
http://www.bedfordstmartins.com/meyer/bedintrolit

Carnal Knowledge 1994

I'd never really thought much about meat. It was there in the supermarket in a plastic wrapper; it came between slices of bread with mayo and mustard and a dill pickle on the side; it sputtered and smoked on the grill till somebody flipped it over, and then it appeared on the plate, between the baked potato and the julienne carrots, neatly cross-hatched and floating in a puddle of red juice. Beef, mutton, pork, venison, dripping burgers, and greasy ribs — it was all the same to me, food, the body's fuel, something to savor a moment on the tongue before the digestive system went to work on it. Which is not to say I was totally unconscious of the deeper implications. Every once in a while I'd eat at home, a quartered chicken, a package of Shake 'n Bake, Stove Top stuffing, and frozen peas, and as I hacked away at the stippled yellow skin and pink flesh of the sanitized bird I'd wonder at the darkish bits of organ clinging to the ribs — what was that, liver? kidney? — but in the end it didn't make me any less fond of Kentucky Fried or Chicken McNuggets. I saw those ads in the magazines, too, the ones that showed the veal calves penned up in their own waste, their limbs atrophied and their veins so pumped full of antibiotics they couldn't control their bowels, but when I took a date to Anna Maria's, I could never resist the veal scallopini.

And then I met Alena Jorgensen.

It was a year ago, two weeks before Thanksgiving — I remember the date because it was my birthday, my thirtieth, and I'd called in sick and gone to the beach to warm my face, read a book, and feel a little sorry for myself. The Santa Anas were blowing and it was clear all the way to Catalina, but there was an edge to the air, a scent of winter hanging over Utah, and as far as I could see in either direction I had the beach pretty much to myself. I found a sheltered spot in a tumble of boulders, spread a blanket, and settled down to attack the pastrami on rye I'd brought along for nourishment. Then I turned to my book — a comfortingly apocalyptic tract about the demise of the planet — and let the sun warm me as I read about the denuding of the rain forest, the poisoning of the atmosphere, and the swift silent eradication of species. Gulls coasted by overhead. I saw the distant glint of jetliners.

I must have dozed, my head thrown back, the book spread open in my lap, because the next thing I remember, a strange dog was hovering over me and the sun had dipped behind the rocks. The dog was big, wild-haired, with one staring blue eye, and it just looked at me, ears slightly cocked, as if it expected a Milk-Bone or something. I was startled — not that I don't like dogs, but here was this woolly thing poking its snout in my face — and I guess that I must have made some sort of defensive gesture, because the dog staggered back a step and froze. Even in the confusion of the moment I could see that there was something wrong with this dog, an unsteadiness, a gimp, a wobble to its legs. I felt a mixture of pity and revulsion — had it been hit by a car, was that it? — when all at once I became aware of a wetness on the breast of my windbreaker, and an unmistakable odor rose to my nostrils: I'd been pissed on.

Pissed on. As I lay there unsuspecting, enjoying the sun, the beach, the solitude, this stupid beast had lifted its leg and used me as a pissoir — and now it was poised there on the edge of the blanket as if it expected a reward. A sudden rage seized me. I came up off the blanket with a curse, and it was only then that a dim apprehension seemed to seep into the dog's other eye, the brown one, and   5 it lurched back and fell on its face, just out of reach. And then it lurched and fell again, bobbing and weaving across the sand like a seal out of water. I was on my feet now, murderous, glad to see that the thing was hobbled — it would simplify the task of running it down and beating it to death.

"Alf!" a voice called, and as the dog floundered in the sand, I turned and saw Alena Jorgensen poised on the boulder behind me. I don't want to make too much of the moment, don't want to mythologize it or clutter the scene with allusions to Aphrodite rising from the waves or accepting the golden apple from Paris, but she was a pretty impressive sight. Bare-legged, fluid, as tall and uncompromising as her Nordic ancestors, and dressed in a Gore-Tex bikini and hooded sweatshirt unzipped to the waist, she blew me away, in any event. Piss-spattered and stupefied, I could only gape up at her.

"You bad boy," she said, scolding, "you get out of there." She glanced from the dog to me and back again. "Oh, you bad boy, what have you done?" she demanded, and I was ready to admit to anything, but it was the dog she was addressing, and the dog flopped over in the sand as if it had been shot. Alena skipped lightly down from the rock, and in the next moment, before I could protest, she was rubbing at the stain on my windbreaker with the wadded-up hem of her sweatshirt.

I tried to stop her — "It's all right," I said, "it's nothing," as if dogs routinely pissed on my wardrobe — but she wouldn't hear of it.

"No," she said, rubbing, her hair flying in my face, the naked skin of her thigh pressing unconsciously to my own, "no, this is terrible, I'm so embarrassed — Alf, you bad boy — I'll clean it for you, I will, it's the least — oh, look at that, it's stained right through to your T-shirt — "

I could smell her, the mousse she used in her hair, a lilac soap or perfume, 10 the salt-sweet odor of her sweat — she'd been jogging, that was it. I murmured something about taking it to the cleaner's myself.

She stopped rubbing and straightened up. She was my height, maybe even a fraction taller, and her eyes were ever so slightly mismatched, like the dog's: a deep earnest blue in the right iris, shading to sea-green and turquoise in the left. We were so close we might have been dancing. "Tell you what," she said, and her face lit with a smile, "since you're so nice about the whole thing, and most people wouldn't be, even if they knew what poor Alf has been through, why don't you let me wash it for you — and the T-shirt too?"

I was a little disconcerted at this point — I was the one who'd been pissed on, after all — but my anger was gone. I felt weightless, adrift, like a piece of fluff floating on the breeze. "Listen," I said, and for the moment I couldn't look her in the eye, "I don't want to put you to any trouble . . ."

"I'm ten minutes up the beach, and I've got a washer and dryer. Come on, it's no trouble at all. Or do you have plans? I mean, I could just pay for the cleaner's if you want . . ."

I was between relationships — the person I'd been seeing off and on for the past year wouldn't even return my calls — and my plans consisted of taking a solitary late-afternoon movie as a birthday treat, then heading over to my mother's for dinner and the cake with the candles. My Aunt Irene would be there, and so would my grandmother. They would exclaim over how big I was and how handsome and then they would begin to contrast my present self with my previous, more diminutive incarnations, and finally work themselves up to a spate of reminiscence that would continue unabated till my mother drove them home. And then, if I was lucky, I'd go out to a singles bar and make the acquaintance of a divorced computer programmer in her mid-thirties with three kids and bad breath.

I shrugged. "Plans? No, not really. I mean, nothing in particular." 15

Alena was housesitting a one-room bungalow that rose stumplike from the sand, no more than fifty feet from the tide line. There were trees in the yard behind it and the place was sandwiched between glass fortresses with crenellated decks, whipping flags, and great hulking concrete pylons. Sitting on the couch inside, you could feel the dull reverberation of each wave hitting the shore, a slow steady pulse that forever defined the place for me. Alena gave me a faded UC Davis sweatshirt that nearly fit, sprayed a stain remover on my T-shirt and windbreaker, and in a single fluid motion flipped down the lid of the washer and extracted two beers from the refrigerator beside it.

There was an awkward moment as she settled into the chair opposite me and we concentrated on our beers. I didn't know what to say. I was disoriented, giddy, still struggling to grasp what had happened. Fifteen minutes earlier I'd been dozing on the beach, alone on my birthday and feeling sorry for myself, and now I was ensconced in a cozy beach house, in the presence of Alena Jorgensen and her naked spill of leg, drinking a beer. "So what do you do?" she said, setting her beer down on the coffee table.

I was grateful for the question, too grateful maybe. I described to her at length how dull my job was, nearly ten years with the same agency, writing ad copy, my brain gone numb with disuse. I was somewhere in the middle of a blow-by-blow account of our current campaign for a Ghanian vodka distilled from calabash husks when she said, "I know what you mean," and told me she'd dropped out of veterinary school herself. "After I saw what they did to the animals. I mean, can you see neutering a dog just for our convenience, just because it's easier for us if they don't have a sex life?" Her voice grew hot. "It's the same old story, species fascism at its worst."

Alf was lying at my feet, grunting softly and looking up mournfully out of his staring blue eye, as blameless a creature as ever lived. I made a small noise of agreement and then focused on Alf. "And your dog," I said, "he's arthritic? Or is it hip dysplasia or what?" I was pleased with myself for the question — aside from "tapeworm," "hip dysplasia" was the only veterinary term I could dredge up from the memory bank, and I could see that Alf's problems ran deeper than worms.

Alena looked angry suddenly. "Don't I wish," she said. She paused to draw 20 a bitter breath. "There's nothing wrong with Alf that wasn't inflicted on him. They tortured him, maimed him, mutilated him."

"Tortured him?" I echoed, feeling the indignation rise in me — this beautiful girl, this innocent beast. "Who?"

Alena leaned forward and there was real hate in her eyes. She mentioned a prominent shoe company — spat out the name, actually. It was an ordinary name, a familiar one, and it hung in the air between us, suddenly sinister. Alf had been part of an experiment to market booties for dogs — suede, cordovan, patent leather, the works. The dogs were made to pace a treadmill in their booties, to assess wear; Alf was part of the control group.

"Control group?" I could feel the hackles rising on the back of my neck.

"They used eighty-grit sandpaper on the treads, to accelerate the process." Alena shot a glance out the window to where the surf pounded the shore; she bit her lip. "Alf was one of the dogs without booties."

I was stunned. I wanted to get up and comfort her, but I might as well have been grafted to the chair. "I don't believe it," I said. "How could anybody — " 25

"Believe it," she said. She studied me a moment, then set down her beer and crossed the room to dig through a cardboard box in the corner. If I was moved by the emotion she'd called up, I was moved even more by the sight of her bending over the box in her Gore-Tex bikini; I clung to the edge of the chair as if it were a plunging roller coaster. A moment later she dropped a dozen file folders in my lap. The uppermost bore the name of the shoe company, and it was crammed with news clippings, several pages of a diary relating to plant operations and workers' shifts at the Grand Rapids facility, and a floor plan of the laboratories. The folders beneath it were inscribed with the names of cosmetics firms, biomedical research centers, furriers, tanners, meatpackers. Alena perched on the edge of the coffee table and watched as I shuffled through them.

"You know the Draize test?"

I gave her a blank look.

"They inject chemicals into rabbits' eyes to see how much it'll take before they go blind. The rabbits are in cages, thousands of them, and they take a needle and jab it into their eyes — and you know why, you know in the name of what great humanitarian cause this is going on, even as we speak?"

I didn't know. The surf pounded at my feet. I glanced at Alf and then back 30 into her angry eyes.

"Mascara, that's what. Mascara. They torture countless thousands of rabbits so women can look like sluts."

I thought the characterization a bit harsh, but when I studied her pale lashes and tight lipstickless mouth, I saw that she meant it. At any rate, the notion set her off, and she launched into a two-hour lecture, gesturing with her flawless hands, quoting figures, digging through her files for the odd photo of legless mice or morphine-addicted gerbils. She told me how she'd rescued Alf herself, raiding the laboratory with six other members of the Animal Liberation Front, the militant group in honor of which Alf had been named. At first, she'd been content to write letters and carry placards, but now, with the lives of so many animals at stake, she'd turned to more direct action: harassment, vandalism, sabotage. She described how she'd spiked trees with Earth-First!ers in Oregon, cut miles of barbed-wire fence on cattle ranches in Nevada, destroyed records in biomedical research labs up and down the coast and insinuated herself between the hunters and the bighorn sheep in the mountains of Arizona. I could only nod and exclaim, smile ruefully and whistle in a low "holy cow!'" sort of way. Finally, she paused to level her unsettling eyes on me. "You know what Isaac Bashevis Singer said?"

We were on our third beer. The sun was gone. I didn't have a clue.

Alena leaned forward. "'Every day is Auschwitz for the animals.'"

I looked down into the amber aperture of my beer bottle and nodded my 35 head sadly. The dryer had stopped an hour and a half ago. I wondered if she'd go out to dinner with me, and what she could eat if she did. "Uh, I was wondering," I said, "if . . . if you might want to go out for something to eat — "

Alf chose that moment to heave himself up from the floor and urinate on the wall behind me. My dinner proposal hung in the balance as Alena shot up off the edge of the table to scold him and then gently usher him out the door. "Poor Alf," she sighed, turning back to me with a shrug. "But listen, I'm sorry if I talked your head off—I didn't mean to, but it's rare to find somebody on your own wavelength."

She smiled. *On your own wavelength:* the words illuminated me, excited me, sent up a tremor I could feel all the way down in the deepest nodes of my reproductive tract. "So how about dinner?" I persisted. Restaurants were running through my head—would it have to be veggie? Could there be even a whiff of grilled flesh on the air? Curdled goat's milk and tabbouleh, tofu, lentil soup, sprouts: *Every day is Auschwitz for the animals.* "No place with meat, of course."

She just looked at me.

"I mean, I don't eat meat myself," I lied, "or actually, not anymore"—since the pastrami sandwich, that is—"but I don't really know any place that . . ." I trailed off lamely.

"I'm a Vegan," she said.   40

After two hours of blind bunnies, butchered calves and mutilated pups, I couldn't resist the joke. "I'm from Venus myself."

She laughed, but I could see she didn't find it all that funny. Vegans didn't eat meat or fish, she explained, or milk or cheese or eggs, and they didn't wear wool or leather—or fur, of course.

"Of course," I said. We were both standing there, hovering over the coffee table. I was beginning to feel a little foolish.

"Why don't we just eat here," she said.

The deep throb of the ocean seemed to settle in my bones as we lay there in bed   45
that night, Alena and I, and I learned all about the fluency of her limbs and the sweetness of her vegetable tongue. Alf sprawled on the floor beneath us, wheezing and groaning in his sleep, and I blessed him for his incontinence and his doggy stupidity. Something was happening to me—I could feel it in the way the boards shifted under me, feel it with each beat of the surf—and I was ready to go along with it. In the morning, I called in sick again.

Alena was watching me from bed as I dialed the office and described how the flu had migrated from my head to my gut and beyond, and there was a look in her eye that told me I would spend the rest of the day right there beside her, peeling grapes and dropping them one by one between her parted and expectant lips. I was wrong. Half an hour later, after a breakfast of brewer's yeast and what appeared to be some sort of bark marinated in yogurt, I found myself marching up and down the sidewalk in front of a fur emporium in Beverly Hills, waving a placard that read HOW DOES IT FEEL TO WEAR A CORPSE? in letters that dripped like blood.

It was a shock. I'd seen protest marches on TV, antiwar rallies and civil rights demonstrations and all that, but I'd never warmed my heels on the pavement or chanted slogans or felt the naked stick in my hand. There were maybe forty of us in all, mostly women, and we waved our placards at passing cars and blocked traffic on the sidewalk. One woman had smeared her face and hands with cold cream steeped in red dye, and Alena had found a ratty mink stole somewhere—the kind that features whole animals sewed together, snout to tail, their miniature limbs dangling—and she'd taken a can of crimson spray paint to their muzzles so that they looked freshly killed. She brandished this grisly banner on a stick high above her head, whooping like a savage and chanting, "Fur is death, fur is death," over and over again till it became a mantra for the crowd. The day was unseasonably warm, the Jaguars glinted in the sun and the palms nodded in the breeze, and no one, but for a single tight-lipped salesman glowering from behind the store's immaculate windows, paid the slightest bit of attention to us.

I marched out there on the street, feeling exposed and conspicuous, but marching nonetheless—for Alena's sake and for the sake of the foxes and martens and all the rest, and for my own sake too: with each step I took I could feel my consciousness expanding like a balloon, the breath of saintliness seeping steadily into me. Up to this point I'd worn suede and leather like anybody else, ankle boots and Air Jordans, a bombardier jacket I'd had since high school. If I'd drawn the line with fur, it was only because I'd never had any use for it. If I lived in the Yukon—and sometimes, drowsing through a meeting at work, I found myself fantasizing about it—I would have worn fur, no compunction, no second thoughts.

But not anymore. Now I was the protestor, a placard waver, now I was fighting for the right of every last weasel and lynx to grow old and die gracefully, now I was Alena Jorgensen's lover and a force to be reckoned with. Of course, my feet hurt and I was running sweat and praying that no one from work would drive by and see me there on the sidewalk with my crazy cohorts and denunciatory sign.

We marched for hours, back and forth, till I thought we'd wear a groove in 50 the pavement. We chanted and jeered and nobody so much as looked at us twice. We could have been Hare Krishnas, bums, antiabortionists, or lepers, what did it matter? To the rest of the world, to the uninitiated masses to whose sorry number I'd belonged just twenty-four hours earlier, we were invisible. I was hungry, tired, discouraged. Alena was ignoring me. Even the woman in redface was slowing down, her chant a hoarse whisper that was sucked up and obliterated in the roar of traffic. And then, as the afternoon faded toward rush hour, a wizened silvery old woman who might have been an aging star or a star's mother or even the first dimly remembered wife of a studio exec got out of a long white car at the curb and strode fearlessly toward us. Despite the heat—it must have been eighty degrees at this point—she was wearing an ankle-length silver fox coat, a bristling shouldery wafting mass of peltry that must have decimated every burrow on the tundra. It was the moment we'd been waiting for.

A cry went up, shrill and ululating, and we converged on the lone old woman like a Cheyenne war party scouring the plains. The man beside me went down on all fours and howled like a dog. Alena slashed the air with her limp mink, and the blood sang in my ears. "Murderer!" I screamed, getting into it. "Torturer! Nazi!" The strings in my neck were tight. I didn't know what I was saying. The crowd gibbered. The placards danced. I was so close to the old woman I could smell her—her perfume, a whiff of mothballs from the coat—and it intoxicated me, maddened me, and I stepped in front of her to block her path with all the seething militant bulk of my one hundred eighty-five pounds of sinew and muscle.

I never saw the chauffeur. Alena told me afterward that he was a former kickboxing champion who'd been banned from the sport for excessive brutality.

The first blow seemed to drop down from above, a shell lobbed from deep within enemy territory; the others came at me like a windmill churning in a storm. Someone screamed. I remember focusing on the flawless rigid pleats of the chauffeur's trousers, and then things got a bit hazy.

I woke to the dull thump of the surf slamming at the shore and the touch of Alena's lips on my own. I felt as if I'd been broken on the wheel, dismantled, and put back together again. "Lie still," she said, and her tongue moved against my swollen cheek. Stricken, I could only drag my head across the pillow and gaze into the depths of her parti-colored eyes. "You're one of us now," she whispered.

Next morning I didn't even bother to call in sick.

By the end of the week I'd recovered enough to crave meat, for which I felt 55 deeply ashamed, and to wear out a pair of vinyl huaraches on the picket line. Together, and with various coalitions of antivivisectionists, militant Vegans, and cat lovers, Alena and I tramped a hundred miles of sidewalk, spray-painted inflammatory slogans across the windows of supermarkets and burger stands, denounced tanners, furriers, poulterers, and sausage makers, and somehow found time to break up a cockfight in Pacoima. It was exhilarating, heady, dangerous. If I'd been disconnected in the past, I was plugged in now. I felt righteous — for the first time in my life I had a cause — and I had Alena, Alena above all. She fascinated me, fixated me, made me feel like a tomcat leaping in and out of second-story windows, oblivious to the free-fall and the picket fence below. There was her beauty, of course, a triumph of evolution and the happy interchange of genes going all the way back to the cavemen, but it was more than that — it was her commitment to animals, to the righting of wrongs, to morality that made her irresistible. Was it love? The term is something I've always had difficulty with, but I suppose it was. Sure it was. Love, pure and simple. I had it, it had me.

"You know what?" Alena said one night as she stood over the miniature stove, searing tofu in oil and garlic. We'd spent the afternoon demonstrating out front of a tortilla factory that used rendered animal fat as a congealing agent, after which we'd been chased three blocks by an overweight assistant manager at Von's who objected to Alena's spray-painting MEAT IS DEATH over the specials in the front window. I was giddy with the adolescent joy of it. I sank into the couch with a beer and watched Alf limp across the floor to fling himself down and lick at a suspicious spot on the floor. The surf boomed like thunder.

"What?" I said.

"Thanksgiving's coming."

I let it ride a moment, wondering if I should invite Alena to my mother's for the big basted bird stuffed with canned oysters and buttered bread crumbs, and then realized it probably wouldn't be such a great idea. I said nothing.

She glanced over her shoulder. "The animals don't have a whole lot to be 60 thankful for, that's for sure. It's just an excuse for the meat industry to butcher a couple million turkeys, is all it is." She paused; hot safflower oil popped in the pan. "I think it's time for a little road trip," she said. "Can we take your car?"

"Sure, but where are we going?"

She gave me her Gioconda smile. "To liberate some turkeys."

* * *

In the morning I called my boss to tell him I had pancreatic cancer and wouldn't be in for a while, then we threw some things in the car, helped Alf scrabble into the back seat, and headed up Route 5 for the San Joaquin Valley. We drove for three hours through a fog so dense the windows might as well have been packed with cotton. Alena was secretive, but I could see she was excited. I knew only that we were on our way to rendezvous with a certain "Rolfe," a longtime friend of hers and a big name in the world of ecotage and animal rights, after which we would commit some desperate and illegal act, for which the turkeys would be eternally grateful.

There was a truck stalled in front of the sign for our exit at Calpurnia Springs, and I had to brake hard and jerk the wheel around twice to keep the tires on the pavement. Alena came up out of her seat and Alf slammed into the armrest like a sack of meal, but we made it. A few minutes later we were gliding through the ghostly vacancy of the town itself, lights drifting past in a nimbus of fog, glowing pink, yellow, and white, and then there was only the blacktop road and the pale void that engulfed it. We'd gone ten miles or so when Alena instructed me to slow down and began to study the right-hand shoulder with a keen, unwavering eye.

The earth breathed in and out. I squinted hard into the soft drifting glow   65
of the headlights. "There, there!" she cried and I swung the wheel to the right, and suddenly we were lurching along a pitted dirt road that rose up from the blacktop like a goat path worn into the side of a mountain. Five minutes later Alf sat up in the back seat and began to whine, and then a crude unpainted shack began to detach itself from the vagueness around us.

Rolfe met us on the porch. He was tall and leathery, in his fifties, I guessed, with a shock of hair and rutted features that brought Samuel Beckett to mind. He was wearing gumboots and jeans and a faded lumberjack shirt that looked as if it had been washed a hundred times. Alf took a quick pee against the side of the house, then fumbled up the steps to roll over and fawn at his feet.

"Rolfe!" Alena called, and there was too much animation in her voice, too much familiarity, for my taste. She took the steps in a bound and threw herself in his arms. I watched them kiss, and it wasn't a fatherly-daughterly sort of kiss, not at all. It was a kiss with some meaning behind it, and I didn't like it. Rolfe, I thought: What kind of name is that?

"Rolfe," Alena gasped, still a little breathless from bouncing up the steps like a cheerleader, "I'd like you to meet Jim."

That was my signal. I ascended the porch steps and held out my hand. Rolfe gave me a look out of the hooded depths of his eyes and then took my hand in a hard calloused grip, the grip of the wood splitter, the fence mender, the liberator of hothouse turkeys and laboratory mice. "A pleasure," he said, and his voice rasped like sandpaper.

There was a fire going inside, and Alena and I sat before it and warmed our   70
hands while Alf whined and sniffed and Rolfe served Red Zinger tea in Japanese cups the size of thimbles. Alena hadn't stopped chattering since we stepped through the door, and Rolfe came right back at her in his woodsy rasp, the two of them exchanging names and news and gossip as if they were talking in code. I studied the reproductions of teal and widgeon that hung from the peeling walls, noted the case of Heinz vegetarian beans in the corner and the half-gallon of Jack Daniel's on the mantel. Finally, after the third cup of tea,

Alena settled back in her chair—a huge old Salvation Army sort of thing with a soiled antimacassar—and said, "So what's the plan?"

Rolfe gave me another look, a quick predatory darting of the eyes, as if he weren't sure I could be trusted, and then turned back to Alena. "Hedda Gabler's Range-Fed Turkey Ranch," he said. "And no, I don't find the name cute, not at all." He looked at me now, a long steady assay. "They grind up the heads for cat food, and the neck, the organs, and the rest, that they wrap up in paper and stuff back in the body cavity like it was a war atrocity or something. Whatever did a turkey go and do to us to deserve a fate like that?"

The question was rhetorical, even if it seemed to have been aimed at me, and I made no response other than to compose my face in a look that wedded grief, outrage, and resolve. I was thinking of all the turkeys I'd sent to their doom, of the plucked wishbones, the pope's noses,° and the crisp browned skin I used to relish as a kid. It brought a lump to my throat, and something more: I realized I was hungry.

"Ben Franklin wanted to make them our national symbol," Alena chimed in, "did you know that? But the meat eaters won out."

"Fifty thousand birds," Rolfe said, glancing at Alena and bringing his incendiary gaze back to rest on me. "I have information they're going to start slaughtering them tomorrow, for the fresh-not-frozen market."

"Yuppie poultry," Alena's voice was drenched in disgust.   75

For a moment, no one spoke. I became aware of the crackling of the fire. The fog pressed at the windows. It was getting dark.

"You can see the place from the highway," Rolfe said finally, "but the only access is through Calpurnia Springs. It's about twenty miles—twenty-two point three, to be exact."

Alena's eyes were bright. She was gazing on Rolfe as if he'd just dropped down from heaven. I felt something heave in my stomach.

"We strike tonight."

Rolfe insisted that we take my car—"Everybody around here knows my   80
pickup, and I can't take any chances on a little operation like this"—but we did mask the plates, front and back, with an inch-thick smear of mud. We blackened our faces like commandos and collected our tools from the shed out back—tin snips, a crowbar, and two five-gallon cans of gasoline. "Gasoline?" I said, trying the heft of the can. Rolfe gave me a craggy look. "To create a diversion," he said. Alf, for obvious reasons, stayed behind in the shack.

If the fog had been thick in daylight, it was impenetrable now, the sky collapsed upon the earth. It took hold of the headlights and threw them back at me till my eyes began to water from the effort of keeping the car on the road. But for the ruts and bumps we might have been floating in space. Alena sat up front between Rolfe and me, curiously silent. Rolfe didn't have much to say either, save for the occasional grunted command: "Hang a right here"; "Hard left"; "Easy, easy." I thought about meat and jail and the heroic proportions to which I was about to swell in Alena's eyes and what I intended to do to her when we finally got to bed. It was 2:00 A.M. by the dashboard clock.

"Okay," Rolfe said, and his voice came at me so suddenly it startled me, "pull over here—and kill the lights."

pope's noses: Slang for the fleshy tail sections of turkeys and other poultry.

We stepped out into the hush of night and eased the doors shut behind us. I couldn't see a thing, but I could hear the not-so-distant hiss of traffic on the highway, and another sound, too, muffled and indistinct, the gentle unconscious suspiration of thousands upon thousands of my fellow creatures. And I could smell them, a seething rancid odor of feces and feathers and naked scaly feet that crawled down my throat and burned my nostrils. "Whew," I said in a whisper, "I can smell them."

Rolfe and Alena were vague presences at my side. Rolfe flipped open the trunk and in the next moment I felt the heft of a crowbar and a pair of tin snips in my hand. "Listen, you, Jim," Rolfe whispered, taking me by the wrist in his iron grip and leading me half-a-dozen steps forward. "Feel this?"

I felt a grid of wire, which he promptly cut: *snip, snip, snip.* 85

"This is their enclosure—they're out there in the day, scratching around in the dirt. You get lost, you follow this wire. Now, you're going to take a section out of this side, Alena's got the west side and I've got the south. Once that's done I signal with the flashlight and we bust open the doors to the turkey houses—they're these big low white buildings, you'll see them when you get close—and flush the birds out. Don't worry about me or Alena. Just worry about getting as many birds out as you can."

I was worried. Worried about everything, from some half-crazed farmer with a shotgun or AK-47 or whatever they carried these days, to losing Alena in the fog, to the turkeys themselves: How big were they? Were they violent? They had claws and beaks, didn't they? And how were they going to feel about me bursting into their bedroom in the middle of the night?

"And when the gas cans go up, you hightail it back to the car, got it?"

I could hear the turkeys tossing in their sleep. A truck shifted gears out on the highway. "I think so," I whispered.

"And one more thing—be sure to leave the keys in the ignition." 90

This gave me pause. "But—"

"The getaway." Alena was so close I could feel her breath on my ear. "I mean, we don't want to be fumbling around for the keys when all hell is breaking loose out there, do we?"

I eased open the door and reinserted the keys in the ignition, even though the automatic buzzer warned me against it. "Okay," I murmured, but they were already gone, soaked up in the shadows and the mist. At this point my heart was hammering so loudly I could barely hear the rustling of the turkeys—this is crazy, I told myself, it's hurtful and wrong, not to mention illegal. Spray-painting slogans was one thing, but this was something else altogether. I thought of the turkey farmer asleep in his bed, an entrepreneur working to make America strong, a man with a wife and kids and a mortgage . . . but then I thought of all those innocent turkeys consigned to death, and finally I thought of Alena, long-legged and loving, and the way she came to me out of the darkness of the bathroom and the boom of the surf. I took the tin snips to the wire.

I must have been at it half an hour, forty-five minutes, gradually working my way toward the big white sheds that had begun to emerge from the gloom up ahead, when I saw Rolfe's flashlight blinking off to my left. This was my signal to head to the nearest shed, snap off the padlock with my crowbar, fling open the doors, and herd a bunch of cranky suspicious gobblers out into the night. It was now or never. I looked twice round me and then broke for the near shed in an awkward crouching gait. The turkeys must have sensed that something was up — from behind the long white windowless wall there arose a watchful gabbling, a soughing of feathers that fanned up like a breeze in the treetops. *Hold on, you toms and hens,* I thought, *freedom is at hand.* A jerk of the wrist, and the padlock fell to the ground. Blood pounded in my ears, I took hold of the sliding door and jerked it open with a great dull booming reverberation — and suddenly, there they were, turkeys, thousands upon thousands of them, cloaked in white feathers under a string of dim yellow bulbs. The light glinted in their reptilian eyes. Somewhere a dog began to bark.

I steeled myself and sprang through the door with a shout, whirling the 95 crowbar over my head, "All right!" I boomed, and the echo gave it back to me a hundred times over, "this is it! Turkeys, on your feet!" Nothing. No response. But for the whisper of rustling feathers and the alertly cocked heads, they might have been sculptures, throw pillows, they might as well have been dead and butchered and served up with yams and onions and all the trimmings. The barking of the dog went up a notch. I thought I heard voices.

The turkeys crouched on the concrete floor, wave upon wave of them, stupid and immovable; they perched in the rafters, on shelves and platforms, huddled in wooden stalls. Desperate, I rushed into the front rank of them, swinging my crowbar, stamping my feet, and howling like the wishbone plucker I once was. That did it. There was a shriek from the nearest bird and the others took it up till an unholy racket filled the place, and now they were moving, tumbling down from their perches, flapping their wings in a storm of dried excrement and pecked-over grain, pouring across the concrete floor till it vanished beneath them. Encouraged, I screamed again — "Yeeee-ha-ha-ha-ha!" — and beat at the aluminum walls with the crowbar as the turkeys shot through the doorway and out into the night.

It was then that the black mouth of the doorway erupted with light and the *ka-boom!* of the gas cans sent a tremor through the earth. *Run!* a voice screamed in my head, and the adrenaline kicked in and all of a sudden I was scrambling for the door in a hurricane of turkeys. They were everywhere, flapping their wings, gobbling and screeching, loosing their bowels in panic. Something hit the back of my legs and all at once I was down amongst them, on the floor, in the dirt and feathers and wet turkey shit. I was a roadbed, a turkey expressway. Their claws dug at my back, my shoulders, the crown of my head. Panicked now, choking on feathers and dust and worse, I fought to my feet as the big screeching birds launched themselves round me, and staggered out into the barnyard. "There! Who's that there?" a voice roared, and I was off and running.

What can I say? I vaulted turkeys, kicked them aside like so many footballs, slashed and tore at them as they sailed through the air. I ran till my lungs felt as if they were burning right through my chest, disoriented, bewildered, terrified of the shotgun blast I was sure would cut me down at any moment. Behind me the fire raged and lit the fog till it glowed blood-red and hellish. But where was the fence? And where the car?

I got control of my feet then and stood stock-still in a flurry of turkeys, squinting into the wall of fog. Was that it? Was that the car over there? At that moment I heard an engine start up somewhere behind me — a familiar engine with a familiar coughing gurgle in the throat of the carburetor — and then the lights blinked on briefly three hundred yards away. I heard the engine race and listened, helpless, as the car roared off in the opposite direction. I stood there a moment longer, forlorn and forsaken, and then I ran blindly off into the night, putting the fire and the shouts and the barking and the incessant mindless squawking of the turkeys as far behind me as I could.

When dawn finally broke, it was only just perceptibly, so thick was the fog. I'd 100 made my way to a blacktop road — which road and where it led I didn't know — and sat crouched and shivering in a clump of weed just off the shoulder. Alena wouldn't desert me, I was sure of that — she loved me, as I loved her; needed me, as I needed her — and I was sure she'd be cruising along the back roads looking for me. My pride was wounded, of course, and if I never laid eyes on Rolfe again I felt I wouldn't be missing much, but at least I hadn't been drilled full of shot, savaged by farm dogs, or pecked to death by irate turkeys. I was sore all over, my shin throbbed where I'd slammed into something substantial while vaulting through the night, there were feathers in my hair, and my face and arms were a mosaic of cuts and scratches and long trailing fissures of dirt. I'd been sitting there for what seemed like hours, cursing Rolfe, developing suspicions about Alena and unflattering theories about environmentalists in general, when finally I heard the familiar slurp and roar of my Chevy Citation cutting through the mist ahead of me.

Rolfe was driving, his face impassive. I flung myself into the road like a tattered beggar, waving my arms over my head and giving vent to my joy, and he very nearly ran me down. Alena was out of the car before it stopped, wrapping me up in her arms, and then she was bundling me into the rear seat with Alf and we were on our way back to the hideaway. "What happened?" she cried, as if she couldn't have guessed. "Where were you? We waited as long as we could."

I was feeling sulky, betrayed, feeling as if I was owed a whole lot more than a perfunctory hug and a string of insipid questions. Still, as I told my tale I began to warm to it — they'd got away in the car with the heater going, and I'd stayed behind to fight the turkeys, the farmers, and the elements, too, and if that wasn't heroic, I'd like to know what was. I looked into Alena's admiring eyes and pictured Rolfe's shack, a nip or two from the bottle of Jack Daniel's, maybe a peanut-butter-and-tofu sandwich, and then the bed, with Alena in it. Rolfe said nothing.

Back at Rolfe's, I took a shower and scrubbed the turkey droppings from my pores, then helped myself to the bourbon. It was ten in the morning and the house was dark — if the world had ever been without fog, there was no sign of it here. When Rolfe stepped out on the porch to fetch an armload of firewood, I pulled Alena down into my lap. "Hey," she murmured, "I thought you were an invalid."

She was wearing a pair of too-tight jeans and an oversize sweater with nothing underneath it. I slipped my hand inside the sweater and found something to hold on to. "Invalid?" I said, nuzzling at her sleeve. "Hell, I'm a turkey liberator, an ecoguerrilla, a friend of the animals and the environment, too."

She laughed, but she pushed herself up and crossed the room to stare out 105 the occluded window. "Listen, Jim," she said, "what we did last night was great, really great, but it's just the beginning." Alf looked up at her expectantly. I heard Rolfe fumbling around on the porch, the thump of wood on wood. She turned around to face me now. "What I mean is, Rolfe wants me to go up to Wyoming for a little bit, just outside of Yellowstone — "

Me? Rolfe wants me? There was no invitation in that, no plurality, no ac-knowledgment of all we'd done and meant to each other. "For what?" I said. "What do you mean?"

"There's this grizzly — a pair of them, actually — and they've been raiding places outside the park. One of them made off with the mayor's Doberman the other night and the people are up in arms. We — I mean Rolfe and me and some other people from the old Bolt Weevils in Minnesota? — we're going to go up there and make sure the Park Service — or the local yahoos — don't elim-inate them. The bears, I mean."

My tone was corrosive. "You and Rolfe?"

"There's nothing between us, if that's what you're thinking. This has to do with animals, that's all."

"Like us?" 110

She shook her head slowly. "Not like us, no. We're the plague on this planet, don't you know that?"

Suddenly I was angry. Seething. Here I'd crouched in the bushes all night, covered in turkey crap, and now I was part of a plague. I was on my feet. "No, I don't know that."

She gave me a look that let me know it didn't matter, that she was already gone, that her agenda, at least for the moment, didn't include me and there was no use arguing about it. "Look," she said, her voice dropping as Rolfe slammed back through the door with a load of wood, "I'll see you in L.A. in a month or so, okay?" She gave me an apologetic smile. "Water the plants for me?"

An hour later I was on the road again. I'd helped Rolfe stack the wood beside the fireplace, allowed Alena to brush my lips with a good-bye kiss, and then stood there on the porch while Rolfe locked up, lifted Alf into the bed of his pickup, and rumbled down the rutted dirt road with Alena at his side. I watched till their brake lights dissolved in the drifting gray mist, then fired up the Citation and lurched down the road behind them. *A month or so:* I felt hol-low inside. I pictured her with Rolfe, eating yogurt and wheat germ, stopping at motels, wrestling grizzlies, and spiking trees. The hollowness opened up, cored me out till I felt as if I'd been plucked and gutted and served up on a platter myself.

I found my way back through Calpurnia Springs without incident — there 115 were no roadblocks, no flashing lights and grim-looking troopers searching trunks and back seats for a tallish thirty-year-old ecoterrorist with turkey tracks down his back — but after I turned onto the highway for Los Angeles, I had a shock. Ten miles up the road my nightmare materialized out of the gloom: red lights everywhere, signal flares and police cars lined up on the shoulder. I was on the very edge of panicking, a beat away from cutting across the median and giving them a run for it, when I saw the truck jackknifed up ahead. I slowed to forty, thirty, and then hit the brakes again. In a moment I was stalled in a line of cars and there was something all over the road, ghostly and white in the fog. At first I thought it must have been flung from the truck, rolls of toilet paper or crates of soap powder ruptured on the pavement. It was neither. As I inched closer, the tires creeping now, the pulse of the lights in my face, I saw that the road was coated in feathers, turkey feathers. A storm of them. A blizzard. And more: there was flesh there too, slick and greasy, a red pulp ground into the surface of the road, thrown up like slush from the tires of the car ahead of me, ground beneath the massive wheels of the truck. Turkeys. Turkeys everywhere.

The car crept forward. I flicked on the windshield wipers, hit the washer button, and for a moment a scrim of diluted blood obscured the windows and the hollowness opened up inside of me till I thought it would suck me inside out. Behind me, someone was leaning on his horn. A trooper loomed up out of the gloom, waving me on with the dead yellow eye of his flashlight. I thought of Alena and felt sick. All there was between us had come to this, expectations gone sour, a smear on the road. I wanted to get out and shoot myself, turn myself in, close my eyes, and wake up in jail, in a hair shirt, in a straitjacket, anything. It went on. Time passed. Nothing moved. And then, miraculously, a vision began to emerge from behind the smeared glass and the gray belly of the fog, lights glowing golden in the waste. I saw the sign, Gas/Food/Lodging, and my hand was on the blinker.

It took me a moment, picturing the place, the generic tile, the false cheer of the lights, the odor of charred flesh hanging heavy on the air, Big Mac, three-piece dark meat, carne asada, cheeseburger. The engine coughed. The lights glowed. I didn't think of Alena then, didn't think of Rolfe or grizzlies or the doomed bleating flocks and herds, or of the blind bunnies and cancerous mice—I thought only of the cavern opening inside me and how to fill it. "Meat," and I spoke the word aloud, talking to calm myself as if I'd awakened from a bad dream, "it's only meat."

CONSIDERATIONS FOR CRITICAL THINKING AND WRITING

1. FIRST RESPONSE. How do your own views of vegetarianism and animal rights' groups influence your response to this story?

2. Comment on how Boyle achieves humorous effects through his first-person narrator in the story's first paragraph.

3. Describe the tone of the first-person narrator. How does he regard the world — the people, situations, and events — he encounters? Why is it especially appropriate that he has a job writing copy for an advertising agency?

4. How does Boyle's style reveal the narrator's character? Select several paragraphs to illustrate your points.

5. How does the narrator use irony? Select three instances of his use of irony, and discuss their effects and what they reveal about him.

6. How does Boyle create a genuinely comic character with Alf? What is the narrator's relationship with Alf?

7. Characterize Alena. Why is the narrator both attracted to her and puzzled by her?

8. How do you think the story would differ if it were told from Alena's point of view?

9. What is your response to Alena's descriptions of commercial experiments on animals? How does the narrator respond to them?

10. What is the narrator's view of the protests he engages in with Alena? Discuss specific passages to support your answer.

11. How does paragraph 93 explain the narrator's willingness to go along with the raid on the turkey farm?

12. Describe the narrator's response to Rolfe. How does Boyle make Rolfe into a comic figure?

13. What is the major conflict in the story? How is it resolved in the story's final paragraphs?

14. How do the story's last words, "it's only meat," shed light on the significance of the title? What does a dictionary tell you about possible readings of the title?

15. CRITICAL STRATEGIES. Read the discussion on new historicist criticism (pp. 2103–04) in Chapter 52, "Critical Strategies for Reading," and describe how a new historicist might use "Carnal Knowledge" to describe aspects of American life in the early 1990s.

CONNECTIONS TO OTHER SELECTIONS

1. What do Alena and Nathaniel Hawthorne's Young Goodman Brown (p. 331) have in common as reformers? Are there also significant differences?

2. Write an essay comparing Boyle's humorous treatment of animal rights issues with Alison Baker's humorous approach to sex and gender issues in "Better Be Ready 'Bout Half Past Eight" (p. 266).

SUSAN MINOT (B. 1956)

Born and raised in Massachusetts, Susan Minot earned a B.A. at Brown University and an M.F.A. at Columbia University. Before devoting herself full-time to writing, Minot worked as an assistant editor at *Grand Street* magazine. Her stories have appeared in the *Atlantic Monthly, Harper's, The New Yorker, Mademoiselle,* and *Paris Review.* Her short stories have been collected in *Lust and Other Stories* (1989), and she has published three novels — *Monkeys* (1986), *Folly* (1992), and *Evening* (1998).

Web   *Research Susan Minot with LitLinks at*
http://www.bedfordstmartins.com/meyer/bedintrolit

Lust   *1984*

Leo was from a long time ago, the first one I ever saw nude. In the spring before the Hellmans filled their pool, we'd go down there in the deep end, with baby oil, and like that. I met him the first month away at boarding school. He had a halo from the campus light behind him. I flipped.

Roger was fast. In his illegal car, we drove to the reservoir, the radio blaring, talking fast, fast, fast. He was always going for my zipper. He got kicked out sophomore year.

By the time the band got around to playing "Wild Horses," I had tasted Bruce's tongue. We were clicking in the shadows on the other side of the amplifier, out of Mrs. Donovan's line of vision. It tasted like salt, with my neck bent back, because we had been dancing so hard before.

Tim's line: "I'd like to see you in a bathing suit." I knew it was his line when he said the exact same thing to Annie Hines.

You'd go on walks to get off campus. It was raining like hell, my sweater as 5 sopped as a wet sheep. Tim pinned me to a tree, the woods light brown and dark brown, a white house half hidden with the lights already on. The water was as loud as a crowd hissing. He made certain comments about my forehead, about my cheeks.

We started off sitting at one end of the couch and then our feet were squished against the armrest and then he went over to turn off the TV and came back after he had taken off his shirt and then we slid onto the floor and he got up again to close the door, then came back to me, a body waiting on the rug.

You'd try to wipe off the table or to do the dishes and Willie would untuck your shirt and get his hands up under in front, standing behind you, making puffy noises in your ear.

He likes it when I wash my hair. He covers his face with it and if I start to say something, he goes, "Shush."

For a long time, I had Philip on the brain. The less they noticed you, the more you got them on the brain.

My parents had no idea. Parents never really know what's going on, espe- 10 cially when you're away at school most of the time. If she met them, my mother might say, "Oliver seems nice" or "I like that one" without much of an opinion. If she didn't like them, "He's a funny fellow, isn't he?" or "Johnny's perfectly nice but a drink of water." My father was too shy to talk to them at all unless they played sports and he'd ask them about that.

The sand was almost cold underneath because the sun was long gone. Eben piled a mound over my feet, patting around my ankles, the ghostly surf rumbling behind him in the dark. He was the first person I ever knew who died, later that summer, in a car crash. I thought about it for a long time.

"Come here," he says on the porch.
I go over to the hammock and he takes my wrist with two fingers.
"What?"
He kisses my palm then directs my hand to his fly. 15

Songs went with whichever boy it was. "Sugar Magnolia" was Tim, with the line "Rolling in the rushes/down by the riverside." With "Darkness Darkness," I'd picture Philip with his long hair. Hearing "Under My Thumb" there'd be the smell of Jamie's suede jacket.

We hid in the listening rooms during study hall. With a record cover over the door's window, the teacher on duty couldn't look in. I came out flushed and heady and back at the dorm was surprised how red my lips were in the mirror.

One weekend at Simon's brother's, we stayed inside all day with the shades down, in bed, then went out to Store 24 to get some ice cream. He stood at the magazine rack and read through *MAD* while I got butterscotch sauce, craving something sweet.

I could do some things well. Some things I was good at, like math or painting or even sports, but the second a boy put his arm around me, I forgot about wanting to do anything else, which felt like a relief at first until it became like sinking into a muck.

It was different for a girl.   20

When we were little, the brothers next door tied up our ankles. They held the door of the goat house and wouldn't let us out till we showed them our underpants. Then they'd forget about being after us and when we played whiffle ball, I'd be just as good as they were.

Then it got to be different. Just because you have on a short skirt, they yell from the cars, slowing down for a while, and if you don't look, they screech off and call you a bitch.

"What's the matter with me?" they say, point-blank.

Or else, "Why won't you go out with me? I'm not asking you to get married," about to get mad.

Or it'd be, trying to be reasonable, in a regular voice, "Listen, I just want to   25 have a good time."

So I'd go because I couldn't think of something to say back that wouldn't be obvious, and if you go out with them, you sort of have to do something.

I sat between Mack and Eddie in the front seat of the pickup. They were having a fight about something. I've a feeling about me.

Certain nights you'd feel a certain surrender, maybe if you'd had wine. The surrender would be forgetting yourself and you'd put your nose to his neck and feel like a squirrel, safe, at rest, in a restful dream. But then you'd start to slip from that and the dark would come in and there'd be a cave. You make out the dim shape of the windows and feel yourself become a cave, filled absolutely with air, or with a sadness that wouldn't stop.

Teenage years. You know just what you're doing and don't see the things that start to get in the way.

Lots of boys, but never two at the same time. One was plenty to keep you   30 in a state. You'd start to see a boy and something would rush over you like a fast storm cloud and you couldn't possibly think of anyone else. Boys took it differently. Their eyes perked up at any little number that walked by. You'd act like you weren't noticing.

The joke was that the school doctor gave out the pill like aspirin. He didn't ask you anything. I was fifteen. We had a picture of him in assembly, holding up an IUD shaped like a T. Most girls were on the pill, if anything, because they couldn't handle a diaphragm. I kept the dial in my top drawer like my mother and thought of her each time I tipped out the yellow tablets in the morning before chapel.

If they were too shy, I'd be more so. Andrew was nervous. We stayed up with his family album, sharing a pack of Old Golds. Before it got light, we turned on the TV. A man was explaining how to plant seedlings. His mouth jerked to the side in a tic. Andrew thought it was a riot and kept imitating him. I laughed to be polite. When we finally dozed off, he dared to put his arm around me, but that was it.

You wait till they come to you. With half fright, half swagger, they stand one step down. They dare to touch the button on your coat then lose their nerve and quickly drop their hand so you—you'd do anything for them. You touch their cheek.

The girls sit around in the common room and talk about boys, smoking their heads off.

"What are you complaining about?" says Jill to me when we talk about 35 problems.

"Yeah," says Giddy. "You always have a boyfriend."

I look at them and think, As if.

I thought the worst thing anyone could call you was a cock-teaser. So, if you flirted, you had to be prepared to go through with it. Sleeping with someone was perfectly normal once you had done it. You didn't really worry about it. But there were other problems. The problems had to do with something else entirely.

Mack was during the hottest summer ever recorded. We were renting a house on an island with all sorts of other people. No one slept during the heat wave, walking around the house with nothing on which we were used to because of the nude beach. In the living room, Eddie lay on top of a coffee table to cool off. Mack and I, with the bedroom door open for air, sweated and sweated all night.

"I can't take this," he said at three A.M. "I'm going for a swim." He and 40 some guys down the hall went to the beach. The heat put me on edge. I sat on a cracked chest by the open window and smoked and smoked till I felt even worse, waiting for something—I guess for him to get back.

One was on a camping trip in Colorado. We zipped our sleeping bags together, the coyotes' hysterical chatter far away. Other couples murmured in other tents. Paul was up before sunrise, starting a fire for breakfast. He wasn't much of a talker in the daytime. At night, his hand leafed about in the hair at my neck.

There'd be times when you overdid it. You'd get carried away. All the next day, you'd be in a total fog, delirious, absent-minded, crossing the street and nearly getting run over.

The more girls a boy has, the better. He has a bright look, having reaped fruits, blooming. He stalks around, sure-shouldered, and you have the feeling he's got more in him, a fatter heart, more stories to tell. For a girl, with each boy it's as though a petal gets plucked each time.

Then you start to get tired. You begin to feel diluted, like watered-down stew.

Oliver came skiing with us. We lolled by the fire after everyone had gone to 45 bed. Each creak you'd think was someone coming downstairs. The silver loop bracelet he gave me had been a present from his girlfriend before.

On vacations, we went skiing, or you'd go south if someone invited you. Some people had apartments in New York that their families hardly ever used. Or summer houses, or older sisters. We always managed to find someplace to go.

We made the plan at coffee hour. Simon snuck out and met me at Main Gate after lights-out. We crept to the chapel and spent the night in the balcony. He tasted like onions from a submarine sandwich.

The boys are one of two ways: either they can't sit still or they don't move. In front of the TV, they won't budge. On weekends they play touch football while we sit on the sidelines, picking blades of grass to chew on, and watch. We're always watching them run around. We shiver in the stands, knocking our boots together to keep our toes warm, and they whizz across the ice, chopping their sticks around the puck. When they're in the rink, they refuse to look at you, only eyeing each other beneath low helmets. You cheer for them but they don't look up, even if it's a face-off when nothing's happening, even if they're doing drills before any game has started at all.

Dancing under the pink tent, he bent down and whispered in my ear. We slipped away to the lawn on the other side of the hedge. Much later, as he was leaving the buffet with two plates of eggs and sausage, I saw the grass stains on the knees of his white pants.

Tim's was shaped like a banana, with a graceful curve to it. They're all dif- 50 ferent. Willie's like a bunch of walnuts when nothing was happening, another's as thin as a thin hot dog. But it's like faces; you're never really surprised.

Still, you're not sure what to expect.

I look into his face and he looks back. I look into his eyes and they look back at mine. Then they look down at my mouth so I look at his mouth, then back to his eyes then, backing up, at his whole face. I think, Who? Who are you? His head tilts to one side.

I say, "Who are you?"

"What do you mean?"

"Nothing."   55

I look at his eyes again, deeper. Can't tell who he is, what he thinks.

"What?" he says. I look at his mouth.

"I'm just wondering," I say and go wandering across his face. Study the chin line. It's shaped like a persimmon.

"Who are you? What are you thinking?"

He says, "What the hell are you talking about?"   60

Then they get mad after, when you say enough is enough. After, when it's easier to explain that you don't want to. You wouldn't dream of saying that maybe you weren't really ready to in the first place.

Gentle Eddie. We waded into the sea, the waves round and plowing in, buffalo-headed, slapping our thighs. I put my arms around his freckled shoulders and he held me up, buoyed by the water, and rocked me like a sea shell.

I had no idea whose party it was, the apartment jam-packed, stepping over people in the hallway. The room with the music was practically empty, the bare floor, me in red shoes. This fellow slides onto one knee and takes me around the waist and we rock to jazzy tunes, with my toes pointing heavenward, and waltz and spin and dip to "Smoke Gets in Your Eyes" or "I'll Love You Just for Now." He puts his head to my chest, runs a sweeping hand down my inside thigh and we go loose-limbed and sultry and as smooth as silk and I stamp my red heels and he takes me into a swoon. I never saw him again after that but I thought, I could have loved that one.

You wonder how long you can keep it up. You begin to feel as if you're showing through, like a bathroom window that only lets in grey light, the kind you can't see out of.

They keep coming around. Johnny drives up at Easter vacation from Balti- 65
more and I let him in the kitchen with everyone sound asleep. He has friends waiting in the car.

"What are you, crazy? It's pouring out there," I say.

"It's okay," he says. "They understand."

So he gets some long kisses from me, against the refrigerator, before he goes because I hate those girls who push away a boy's face as if she were made out of Ivory soap, as if she's that much greater than he is.

The note on my cubby told me to see the headmaster. I had no idea for what. He had received complaints about my amorous displays on the town green. It was Willie that spring. The headmaster told me he didn't care what I did but that Casey Academy had a reputation to uphold in the town. He lowered his glasses on his nose. "We've got twenty acres of woods on this campus," he said. "If you want to smooch with your boyfriend, there are twenty acres for you to do it out of the public eye. You read me?"

Everybody'd get weekend permissions for different places, then we'd all go   70
to someone's house whose parents were away. Usually there'd be more boys than girls. We raided the liquor closet and smoked pot at the kitchen table and you'd never know who would end up where, or with whom. There were always disasters. Ceci got bombed and cracked her head open on the banister and needed stitches. Then there was the time Wendel Blair walked through the picture window at the Lowes' and got slashed to ribbons.

He scared me. In bed, I didn't dare look at him. I lay back with my eyes closed, luxuriating because he knew all sorts of expert angles, his hands never fumbling, going over my whole body, pressing the hair up and off the back of my head, giving an extra hip shove, as if to say *There*. I parted my eyes slightly, keeping the screen of my lashes low because it was too much to look at him, his mouth loose and pink and parted, his eyes looking through my forehead, or kneeling up, looking through my throat. I was ashamed but couldn't look him in the eye.

You wonder about things feeling a little off-kilter. You begin to feel like a piece of pounded veal.

At boarding school, everyone gets depressed. We go in and see the housemother, Mrs. Gunther. She got married when she was eighteen. Mr. Gunther was her high school sweetheart, the only boyfriend she ever had.
"And you knew you wanted to marry him right off?" we ask her.
She smiles and says, "Yes."   75
"They always want something from you," says Jill, complaining about her boyfriend.
"Yeah," says Giddy. "You always feel like you have to deliver something."
"You do," says Mrs. Gunther. "Babies."

After sex, you curl up like a shrimp, something deep inside you ruined, slammed in a place that sickens at slamming, and slowly you fill up with an overwhelming sadness, an elusive gaping worry. You don't try to explain it, filled with the knowledge that it's nothing after all, everything filling up finally and absolutely with death. After the briskness of loving, loving stops. And you roll over with death stretched out alongside you like a feather boa, or a snake, light as air, and you . . . you don't even ask for anything or try to say something to him because it's obviously your own damn fault. You haven't been able to — to what? To open your heart. You open your legs but can't, or don't dare anymore, to open your heart.

It starts this way: 80
You stare into their eyes. They flash like all the stars are out. They look at you seriously, their eyes at a low burn and their hands no matter what starting off shy and with such a gentle touch that the only thing you can do is take that tenderness and let yourself be swept away. When, with one attentive finger they tuck the hair behind your ear, you —

You do everything they want.

Then comes after. After when they don't look at you. They scratch their balls, stare at the ceiling. Or if they do turn, their gaze is altogether changed. They are surprised. They turn casually to look at you, distracted, and get a mild distracted surprise. You're gone. Their blank look tells you that the girl they were fucking is not there anymore. You seem to have disappeared.

CONSIDERATIONS FOR CRITICAL THINKING AND WRITING

1. FIRST RESPONSE. What do you think of the narrator? Why? Do you agree with the definition the story offers for *lust?*

2. Do you think that the narrator's depiction of male and female responses to sex are accurate? Explain why or why not.

3. How effective is the narrator's description of teenage sex? What do you think she means when she says "You know just what you're doing and don't see the things that start to get in the way" (para. 29)?

4. What is the story's conflict? Explain whether you think the conflict is resolved.

5. Discuss the story's tone. Is it what you expected from the title?

6. What do you think is the theme of "Lust"? Does its style carry its theme?

7. What is the primary setting for the story? What does it reveal about the nature of the narrator's economic and social class?

8. In a *Publisher's Weekly* interview (November 6, 1992), Minot observed, "There's more fictional material in unhappiness and disappointment and frustration than there is in happiness. Who was it said, 'Happiness is like a blank page'?" What do you think of this observation?

CONNECTIONS TO OTHER SELECTIONS

1. Compare the treatments of youthful sexuality in "Lust" and David Updike's "Summer" (p. 316). Do you prefer one story to the other? Why?

2. Compare the narrators of "Lust" and Alice Munro's "An Ounce of Cure" (p. 451). What significant similarities and differences do you see between the narrators?

3. Write an essay explaining the sort of advice the narrator of Fay Weldon's "IND AFF, or Out of Love in Sarajevo" (p. 165) might give to the narrator of "Lust." You might try writing this in the form of a letter.

PUNYAKANTE WIJENAIKE (B. 1933)

One of Sri Lanka's most accomplished novelists, Punyakante Wijenaike was born in 1933 in the city of Colombo, where she has lived most of her life and has published all of her works. When she was young, her grandmother scolded her for reading books, claiming it was not an activity for girls, but her mother encouraged her to read, and her lonely childhood led her to develop an active imagination. Her first book, the short story collection *The Third Woman,* appeared in 1963, and she now has twelve publications to her credit, including the novels *The Waiting Earth* (1966), *Giraya*

(1971), *The Betel Vine* (1972), *The Rebel* (1979), and *A Way of Life* (1987). Her latest novel, *Amulet* (1994), won a literary prize for the best Sri Lankan book in English. Wijenaike's work exhibits a robust social consciousness, often focusing on issues of minority oppression and ethnic tension in Colombo.

Web   *Research Punyakante Wijenaike with LitLinks at*
http://www.bedfordstmartins.com/meyer/bedintrolit

Anoma   1996

— I have got an idea.
— Why don't I call you Anoma?
— Then you are identified.
— Anoma — a girl, my friend and confidante.
— After all, we are both in this together, are we not?   5
— My grandmother keeps asking why I talk to myself.
— My grandmother, my archi-amma, does not know of your existence.
— I am talking to you because only you are in a position to understand what I am talking about. The Story behind your creation.
— You are still an embryo. Nature protects you from outside harm.
— When I talk you will listen but it will not disturb your sleep the way mine is   10
disturbed. You will not be disturbed by the nightmares I suffer.
— But can you feel me toss and turn in our bed at night?
— Unfortunately, I am neither child nor woman. If I were as small as you, still an embryo curled in my mother's womb, I would be yet untouched by anyone.
— I would have not the need to talk to anyone.
— I am fourteen years old and missing from my mother far away in the Middle East.
— Why did she have to go?   15
— She went to earn a pot of gold for us.
— Was money more important than being together?
— I remember mother before she went away. She used to comb my hair, wash my face clean, and starch my one and only white school uniform.
— Now I don't need the white uniform any more because I no longer go to school.
— My brother still goes to school.   20
— He is eleven years old but he does not miss mother the way I do because I wash his school clothes for him and cook his lunch. But he will not look me in the face nor talk to me.
— This hurts but I know why he avoids me. He thinks I have robbed mother of her place with father. He does not go anywhere near father at all.
— Archi-amma, my grandmother, cannot hear nor see very well. She never asks why I don't go to school any more. She is only glad I am at home to help her scrape a coconut or grind the chilly into a paste.
— You are the only one I can talk to, Anoma. I need to talk to someone.
— I am sick and afraid all the time.   25
— What will mother say, what will mother do when she finds out?

— I have to do something before she returns and finds out.
— During the day father neither looks at me nor comes near me.
— It is only at night, when he misses mother, that he calls for me.
— He does not think of my loneliness, only his.   30
— I can see brother does not sleep well at night either. Both of us wait night after night, dreading father's call. Often he smells of alcohol.
— Grandmother is too old to look after this household. Mother should have left someone younger in charge, like mother's sister, my Punchi-amma, my aunt. Someone who could cope with father's needs. Did she forget father's needs?
— I must warn you, Anoma, that it will not be by appointment that I disturb you when I need to communicate. It will be solely through my need to cry, to talk to someone when I cannot sleep at night. After all, it is not only father who needs comforting. His needs are physical. My need is to communicate.
— I am sure mother never wanted this to happen to me. She wanted me to remain chaste, a virgin until her return. When I attained age I remember her shielding me from the eyes of men. Even father and brother were not permitted near me until I ceased to menstruate and she had bathed me, pouring potful after potful of water over my head. She had gifted me with gold ear-studs and washed my soiled garment clean. That is why it is all so confusing. Why did she leave me unprotected after all that care?
— It is that pot of gold. It has ruined us.   35
— For evil crept into the house after she left. I cannot get rid of the smell of soiled garments in the night. Father's and mine.
— However much I bathe, pouring potful after potful of water over me, I cannot get rid of this dirty smell.
— Anoma, Anoma, where are you? Are you hiding from me? Of late it is as if you are not there, safe and warm, within me, consoling me. It seems the more I talk to you, the more you withdraw from me. Have I touched you, even in the womb? Is that why you lie so still and quiet, not moving any more, within me?
— Anoma, you are making me afraid. It is as if suddenly you have identified yourself and you have become suspicious of my talking to you.
— You are no longer an embryo, a silent, sympathetic listener. You are challeng-   40
ing me. You have escaped your protective shell.
— You are hurt and accusing me.
— You are asking, without being a silent listener, "Have I got a future? Will I be born or are you contemplating my destruction before birth?"
— Anoma, you are not giving me time to come to terms with the situation.
— By talking you have roused my conscience.
— This is terrible, I feel betrayed, destroyed. Why can't you remain a silent listener?   45
— Please understand I did not create you willingly.
— Father created you within me.
— You are his grandchild, not my child.
— I need to grow into full womanhood and carry my own child from a man who is not my father.
— There, I have hurt and confused you again.   50
— You can no longer remain silent within me now. You ask, "Will I be born?" How can I answer that, Anoma?
— It's your life against mine.
— If you are born I will die. In shame.

CONSIDERATIONS FOR CRITICAL THINKING AND WRITING

1. FIRST RESPONSE. What is the story behind the creation of Anoma? Why is she essential to the narrator and yet simultaneously unwanted?

2. Describe the effect of the fragmentary nature of this monologue. Explain why you think you know more or less about the narrator owning to this technique.

3. How do you feel about the girl's mother for leaving her unprotected? What complicates your attitudes toward the mother?

4. Discuss the younger brother's and the grandmother's response to the narrator's problem.

5. What do you think of the father? Is he in any way sympathetic? Explain why or why not.

6. How does the narrator's relationship with Anoma change over the course of the monologue?

7. Describe the dimensions of the narrator's dilemma in dealing with her family and with the prospect of giving birth to Anoma. What do you think she should do?

8. How do you respond to the subject matter of this story? What feelings does it evoke in you?

CONNECTION TO ANOTHER SELECTION

1. What thematic similarities do you find in this story and in Susan Minot's "Lust" (p. 304)? What, if anything, do the narrators have in common?

10

Combining the Elements of Fiction

THE ELEMENTS TOGETHER

The elements of fiction that you have examined in Chapters 1–9 provide terms and concepts that enable you to think, talk, and write about fiction in a variety of ways. As those chapters have indicated, there are many means available to you for determining a story's effects and meanings. By considering elements of fiction such as characterization, conflict, setting, point of view, symbolism, style, and theme, you can better articulate your understanding of a particular work. A careful reading of the work's elements allows you to see how the parts contribute to the whole.

The parts or elements of a story work together rather than in isolation to create a particular kind of experience, emotion, or insight for a reader. The symbolic significance of the free and easy Mississippi River setting of *The Adventures of Huckleberry Finn,* for example, cannot be excavated from Huck's first-person point of view. Nor can the "smothery" ways of the corrupt towns along the river be understood without the pious frauds, hypocrites, cowards, and other sordid characters that populate them. Add the plot that has Jim on the run from slavery and the unconscious ironic tone that Mark Twain invests in Huck — all constitute interrelated elements that add up to serious themes commenting on nineteenth-century society. Understanding the ways in which these elements work together produces a richer and more satisfying reading of a plot that might otherwise be read simply as a children's story.

MAPPING THE STORY

Writing about a story requires your creation of a clear path that a reader can take in order to follow your experience and understanding of the work. The path offers perspectives and directions that are informed by what caught your attention along the way. Your paper points out what you thought worth revisiting and taking the reader to see. Whatever the thesis of the paper, your role as a guide remains the same as you move from one element of the story to the next, offering an overall impression about the story. And as you already know, the best tours are always guided by informed and interesting voices.

This chapter presents an example of how one student, Janice Reardon, arrived at a thesis, combining her understanding of several elements of fiction for an assigned topic on David Updike's short story "Summer." After reviewing the elements of fiction covered in Chapters 1–9, Janice read the story several times, paying careful attention to plot, character, setting, point of view, symbolism, and so on. She then developed her ideas by brainstorming, drafting, and using the Questions for Writing (listed after the story) to develop her thesis into a statement that makes a definite claim about a specific idea and provides a clear sense of direction for the paper to come. As you read "Summer," think about what you might want to say about the relationship—or lack thereof—between Homer and Sandra. Pay attention to how the various elements of fiction work together to establish or reinforce that relationship.

DAVID UPDIKE (B. 1957)

Born in Ipswich, Massachusetts, David Updike is the son of John Updike. David received his B.A. in art history at Harvard and his M.A. from Teachers College, Columbia University. His acclaimed children's books include *An Autumn Tale* (1988), *A Spring Story* (1989), *Seven Times Eight* (1990), *The Sounds of Summer* (1993), and *A Helpful Alphabet of Friendly Objects* (1998), which he co-authored with his father. "Summer," a poignant tale for adults, is part of *Out on the Marsh: Stories* (1988), a collection of his short fiction; his short stories have also appeared in *The New Yorker.* Updike resides in Cambridge, Massachusetts.

Web Research David Updike with LitLinks at
http://www.bedfordstmartins.com/meyer/bedintrolit

Summer

1985

It was the first week in August, the time when summer briefly pauses, shifting between its beginning and its end: the light had not yet begun to change, the leaves were still full and green on the trees, the nights were still warm. From the woods and fields came the hiss of crickets; the line of distant mountains was still dulled by the edge of summer haze, the echo of fireworks was replaced by the rumble of thunder and the hollow premonition of school, too far off to imagine though dimly, dully felt. His senses were consumed by the joy of their own fulfillment: the satisfying swat of a tennis ball, the dappled damp and light of the dirt road after rain, the alternating sensations of sand, mossy stone, and pine needles under bare feet. His days were spent in the adolescent pursuit of childhood pleasures: tennis, a haphazard round of golf, a variant of baseball adapted to the local geography: two pine trees as foul poles, a broomstick as the bat, the apex of the small, secluded house the dividing line between home runs and outs. On rainy days they swatted bottle tops across the living room floor, and at night vented budding cerebral energy with games of chess thoughtfully played over glasses of iced tea. After dinner they would paddle the canoe to the middle of the lake, and drift beneath the vast, blue-black dome of sky, looking at the stars and speaking softly in tones which, with the waning summer, became increasingly philosophical: the sky's blue vastness, the distance and magnitude of stars, an endless succession of numbers, gave way to a rising sensation of infinity, eternity, an imagined universe with no bounds. But the sound of the paddle hitting against the side of the canoe, the faint shadow of surrounding mountains, the cry of a nocturnal bird brought them back to the happy, cloistered finity of their world, and they paddled slowly home and went to bed.

Homer woke to the slant and shadow of a summer morning, dressed in their shared cabin, and went into the house where Mrs. Thyme sat alone, looking out across the flat blue stillness of the lake. She poured him a cup of coffee and they quietly talked, and it was then that his happiness seemed most tangible. In this summer month with the Thymes, freed from the complications of his own family, he had released himself to them and, as interim member — friend, brother, surrogate son — he lived in a blessed realm between two worlds.

From the cool darkness of the porch, smelling faintly of moldy books and kerosene and the tobacco of burning pipes, he sat looking through the screen to the lake, shimmering beneath the heat of a summer afternoon: a dog lay sleeping in the sun, a bird hopped along a swaying branch, sunlight came in through the trees and collapsed on the sandy soil beside a patch of moss, or mimicked the shade and cadence of stones as they stepped to the edge of a lake where small waves lapped a damp rock and washed onto a sandy shore. An inverted boat lay decaying under a tree, a drooping American flag hung from its gnarled pole, a haphazard dock started out across the cove toward distant islands through which the white triangle of a sail silently moved.

The yellowed pages of the book from which he occasionally read swam before him: ". . . Holmes clapped the hat upon his head. It came right over the forehead and settled on the bridge of his nose. 'It is a question of cubic capacity' said he . . ." Homer looked up. The texture of the smooth, unbroken air was cleanly divided by the sound of a slamming door, echoing up into the woods around him. Through the screen he watched Fred's sister Sandra as she came ambling down the path, stepping lightly between the stones in her bare feet. She held a towel in one hand, a book in the other, and wore a pair of pale blue shorts — faded relics of another era. At the end of the dock she stopped, raised her hands above her head, stretching, and then sat down. She rolled over onto her stomach and, using the book as a pillow, fell asleep.

Homer was amused by the fact, that although she did this every day, she 5 didn't get any tanner. When she first came in her face was faintly flushed, and there was a pinkish line around the snowy band where her bathing suit strap had been, but the back of her legs remained an endearing, pale white, the color of eggshells, and her back acquired only the softest, brownish blur. Sometimes she kept her shoes on, other times a shirt, or sweater, or just collapsed onto the seat of the boat, her pale eyelids turned upward toward the pale sun; and as silently as she arrived, she would leave, walking back through the stones with the same, casual sway of indifference. He would watch her, hear the distant door slam, the shower running in the far corner of the house. Other times he would just look up and she would be gone.

On the tennis court she was strangely indifferent to his heroics. When the crucial moment arrived — Homer serving in the final game of the final set — the match would pause while she left, walking across the court, stopping to call the dog, swaying out through the gate. Homer watched her as she went down the path, and, impetus suddenly lost, he double faulted, stroked a routine backhand over the back fence, and the match was over.

When he arrived back at the house she asked him who won, but didn't seem to hear his answer. "I wish I could go sailing," she said, looking distractedly out over the lake.

At night, when he went out to the cottage where he and Fred slept, he could see her through the window as she lay on her bed, reading, her arm folded beneath her head like a leaf. Her nightgown, pulled and buttoned to her chin, pierced him with a regret that had no source or resolution, and its imagined texture floated in the air above him as he lay in bed at night, suspended in the surrounding darkness, the scent of pine, the hypnotic cadence of his best friend's breathing.

Was it that he had known her all his life, and as such had grown up in the shadow of her subtle beauty? Was it the condensed world of the lake, the silent reverence of surrounding woods, mountains, which heightened his sense of her and brought the warm glow of her presence into soft, amorous focus? She had the hair of a baby, the freckles of a child, and the sway of motherhood. Like his love, her beauty rose up in the world which spawned and nurtured it, and found in the family the medium in which it thrived, and in Homer distilled to a pure distant longing for something he had never had.

One day they climbed a mountain, and as the components of family and 10 friends strung out along the path on their laborious upward hike, he found himself tromping along through the woods with her with nobody else in sight. Now and then they would stop by a stream, or sit on a stump, or stone, and he would speak to her, and then they would set off again, he following her. But in the end this day exhausted him, following her pale legs and tripping sneakers over the ruts and stones and a thousand roots, all the while trying to suppress a wordless, inarticulate passion, and the last mile or so he left her, sprinting down the path in a reckless, solitary release, howling into the woods around him. He was lying on the grass, staring up into the patterns of drifting clouds when she came ambling down. "Wher'd you go? I thought I'd lost you," she said, and sat heavily down in the seat of the car. On the ride home, his elbow hopelessly held in the warm crook of her arm, he resolved to release his love, give it up, on the grounds that it was too disruptive to his otherwise placid life. But in the days to follow he discovered that his resolution had done little to change her, and her life went on its oblivious, happy course without him.

His friendship with Fred, meanwhile, continued on its course of athletic and boyhood fulfillment. Alcohol seeped into their diet, and an occasional cigarette, and at night they would drive into town, buy two enormous cans of Australian beer and sit at a small cove by the lake, talking. One night on the ride home Fred accelerated over a small bridge, and as the family station wagon left the ground their heads floated up to the ceiling, touched, and then came crashing down as the car landed and Fred wrestled the car back onto course. Other times they would take the motorboat out onto the lake and make sudden racing turns around buoys, sending a plume of water into the air and everything in the boat crashing to one side. But always with these adventures Homer felt a pang of absence, and was always relieved when they headed back toward the familiar cove, and home.

As August ran its merciless succession of beautiful days, Sandra drifted in and out of his presence in rising oscillations of sorrow and desire. She worked at a bowling alley on the other side of the lake, and in the evening Homer and Fred would drive the boat over, bowl a couple of strings, and wait for her to get off work. Homer sat at the counter and watched her serve up sloshing cups of coffee, secretly loathing the leering gazes of whiskered truck drivers, and loving her oblivious, vacant stare in answer, hip cocked, hand on counter, gazing up into the neon air above their heads. When she was finished, they would pile into the boat and skim through darkness the four or five miles home, and it was then, bundled beneath sweaters and blankets, the white hem of her waitressing dress showing through the darkness, their hair swept in the wind and their voices swallowed by the engine's slow, steady growl, that he felt most powerless to her attraction. As the boat rounded corners he would close his eyes and release himself to gravity, his body's warmth swaying into hers, guising his attraction in the thin veil of centrifugal force. Now and then he would lean into the floating strands of her hair and speak into her fragrance, watching her smile swell in the pale half-light of the moon, the umber glow of the boat's rear light, her laughter spilling backward over the swirling "V" of wake.

Into the humid days of August a sudden rain fell, leaving the sky a hard, unbroken blue and the nights clear and cool. In the morning when he woke, leaving Fred a heap of sighing covers in his bed, he stepped out into the first rays of sunlight that came through the branches of the trees and sensed, in the cool vapor that rose from damp pine needles, the piercing cry of a blue jay, that something had changed. That night as they ate dinner — hamburgers and squash and corn-on-the-cob — everyone wore sweaters, and as the sun set behind the undulating line of distant mountains — burnt, like a filament of summer into his blinking eyes — it was with an autumnal tint, a reddish glow. Several days later the tree at the end of the point bloomed with a sprig of russet leaves, one or two of which occasionally fell, and their lives became filled with an unspoken urgency. Life of summer went on in the silent knowledge that, with the slow, inexorable seepage of an hourglass, it was turning into fall. Another mountain was climbed, annual tennis matches were arranged and played. Homer and Fred became unofficial champions of the lake by trouncing the elder Dewitt boys, unbeaten in several years. "Youth, youth," glum Billy

Dewitt kept saying over iced tea afterward, in jest, though Homer could tell he was hiding some greater sense of loss.

And the moment, the conjunction of circumstance that, through the steady exertion of will, minor adjustments of time and place, he had often tried to induce, never happened. She received his veiled attentions with a kind of amused curiosity, as if smiling back on innocence. One night they had been the last ones up, and there was a fleeting, shuddering moment before he stepped through the woods to his cabin and she went to her bed that he recognized, in a distant sort of way, as the moment of truth. But to touch her, or kiss her, seemed suddenly incongruous, absurd, contrary to something he could not put his finger on. He looked down at the floor and softly said goodnight. The screen door shut quietly behind him and he went out into the darkness and made his way through the unseen sticks and stones, and it was only then, tripping drunkenly on a fallen branch, that he realized he had never been able to imagine the moment he distantly longed for.

The Preacher gave a familiar sermon about another summer having run   15 its course, the harvest of friendship reaped, and a concluding prayer that, "God willing, we will all meet again in June." That afternoon Homer and Fred went sailing, and as they swept past a neighboring cove Homer saw in its sullen shadows a girl sitting alone in a canoe, and in an eternal, melancholy signal of parting, she waved to them as they passed. And there was something in the way that she raised her arm which, when added to the distant impression of her fullness, beauty, youth, filled him with longing as their boat moved inexorably past, slapping the waves, and she disappeared behind a crop of trees.

The night before they were to leave they were all sitting in the living room after dinner — Mrs. Thyme sewing, Fred folded up with the morning paper, Homer reading on the other end of the couch where Sandra was lying — when the dog leapt up and things shifted in such a way that Sandra's bare foot was lightly touching Homer's back. Mrs. Thyme came over with a roll of newspaper, hit the dog on the head and he leapt off. But to Homer's surprise Sandra's foot remained, and he felt, in the faint sensation of exerted pressure, the passive emanation of its warmth, a distant signal of acquiescence. And as the family scene continued as before it was with the accompanying drama of Homer's hand, shielded from the family by a haphazard wall of pillows, migrating over the couch to where, in a moment of breathless abandon, settled softly on the cool hollow of her arch. She laughed at something her mother had said, her toe twitched, but her foot remained. It was only then, in the presence of the family, that he realized she was his accomplice, and that, though this was as far as it would ever go, his love had been returned.

CONSIDERATIONS FOR CRITICAL THINKING AND WRITING

1. FIRST RESPONSE. How do you respond to this love story? Would the story be more satisfying if Homer and Sandra openly acknowledged their feelings for each other and kissed at the end? Why or why not?

2. What details in the first paragraph evoke particular feelings about August? What sort of mood is created by these details?

3. How is Homer's attraction to Sandra made evident in paragraphs 5 through 9?

4. Why do you think August is described as a "merciless succession of beautiful days" (para. 12)?
5. Analyze the images in paragraph 13 that evoke the impending autumn. What does Billy Dewitt's lament about "youth, youth" add to this description?
6. Discuss the transition between paragraphs 14 and 15. How is the mood effectively changed between the night and the next day?
7. What effect does Homer's friendship with Fred and his relationship with the Thyme family have on your understanding of his reticent attraction to Sandra?
8. What, if any, significance can you attach to the names of Homer, Sandra, Thyme, and the Dewitt boys?
9. How successful do you think Updike is in evoking youthful feeling about summer in this story? Explain why you responded positively or negatively to this evocation of summer.

CONNECTIONS TO OTHER SELECTIONS

1. Compare David Updike's treatment of summer as the setting of his story with John Updike's use of summer as the setting in "A & P" (p. 606).
2. Discuss "Summer" and Dagoberto Gilb's "Love in L.A." (p. 263) as love stories. Explain why you might prefer one over the other.
3. Write an essay comparing how August is represented in "Summer" and in Sophie Cabot Black's poem "August" (p. 788).

As you read "Summer" what potential paper topics occurred to you? Annotating the text and brainstorming are both good ways to identify moments in a text that you will feel moved to write about if your instructor does not assign a paper topic to you. Even after you come up with a topic — say, the relationship between Homer and Sandra — you still need to turn it into a thesis. The following questions should prove useful in choosing a topic that you can develop into a thesis, the central idea of your paper. As you become increasingly engaged in your topic, you're likely to discover and perhaps change your ideas, so at the beginning stages it's best to regard your thesis as tentative. This will allow you to remain open to unexpected insights along the way.

QUESTIONS FOR WRITING
Developing a Topic into a Revised Thesis

1. If the topic is assigned, have you specifically addressed the prescribed subject matter?
2. If you choose your own topic, have you used your annotations, notes, and first response writing to help you find a suitable topic?
3. Is the topic too broad or too narrow? Is the topic focused enough to be feasible and manageable for the assigned length of the paper?

4. Is the topic too difficult or specialized for you to write about successfully? If you need information and expertise that goes well beyond the scope of the assignment, would it be better to choose another topic?
5. Is the topic too simple or obvious to allow you to develop a strong thesis?
6. Once you have focused your topic, what do you think you want to say about it? What is the central idea — the tentative thesis — of the paper?
7. Have you asked questions about the topic to help generate a thesis?
8. Have you tried brainstorming or freewriting as a means of producing ideas that would lead to a thesis?
9. Have you tried writing a rough outline or simply jotting down ideas to see if your tentative thesis can be supported or qualified and made firmer?
10. Is your thesis statement precise or vague? What is the central argument that your thesis makes?
11. Does the thesis help provide an organizing principle — a sense of direction — for the paper?
12. Does the thesis statement consist of one or more complete declarative sentences (not framed as a question) written in clear language that express a complete idea?
13. Is the thesis supported by specific references to the text you are discussing? Have you used brief quotations to illustrate important points and provide evidence for the argument?
14. Is everything included in the paper in some way related to the thesis? Should any sentences or paragraphs be deleted because they are irrelevant to the central point?
15. Does the thesis appear in the introductory paragraph? If not, is there a particular reason for including it later in the paper?
16. If during the course of writing the paper you shifted direction or change your mind about its central point, have you revised (or completely revamped) your thesis to reflect that change?
17. Have you developed a thesis that genuinely interests you? Are you interested enough in the thesis to write a paper that will also engage your reader?

A Sample of Brainstorming

After Janice has read the story twice carefully, she is ready to start working on turning the assigned topic into a defined thesis. Her instructor asked the class to answer the first question in the Considerations for Critical Thinking and Writing: *Would the story be more satisfying if Homer and Sandra openly acknowledged their feelings for each other and kissed at the end?* Janice uses the technique of brainstorming to come up with a more specific approach to the topic, thinking carefully about elements of the story like plot, setting, action, character, symbolism, tone, and theme.

— plot with subtle drama — why?

— "blessed realm between two worlds" — adolescence, the school years, real home-life (Homer with another family), state of desire before culmination

— *action*: regular, familiar, relatively uneventful, savoring state of vague desire

— *setting*: tranquil, idyllic, familiar, warm, unabrasive "happy, cloistered finity of their world" — unthreatening, known; things happen as they're expected to; navigable, happy, image of summer

— *character*: Homer is shy but sensitive; Sandra seems a little more in control; both are on the threshold of adulthood

— *symbolism*: "blessed realm between two worlds" — adolescent summer life on the lake vs. school and the adult world, summer month with Thymes vs. real home life

— *tone*: easy, light tone, vague but pleasant romantic longing

— *theme*: love acknowledged but kept as part of summer life

A Sample First Thesis

Reviewing her brainstorming list, Janice sees a connection between the plot and the setting that helps her to address the question and to draft a thesis.

David Updike's short story "Summer" is a love story with little drama or complication. This lack of action in the plot is mirrored by Updike's rendering of the setting and general atmosphere, which are evoked by the description of the picturesque cabin on a lake, the season of summer, and the symbolic "season" of adolescence. The fact that there is no great culmination to Homer's reticent attraction to Sandra is not a failure of the characters or of the fiction's drama. Instead, this nearly actionless plot captures and reflects the sense of adolescence and summer as a state of protected happiness.

A Sample Revised Thesis

After this initial attempt at a thesis, Janice asks herself several of the Questions for Writing on pages 321–22 and writes out her responses, realizing along the way how she needs to revise her thesis.

Is the topic (that the action reflects the setting to create a sense of "happy, cloistered finity") too simple? I could discuss whether the story succeeds in creating this sense. It does — through description of setting and of Homer's thoughts.

Is the thesis statement precise? Not quite; I think I need to say in the thesis what would be appealing about "between two worlds." Updike describes it in positive tones, but suggests with the word "cloistered" that there's

something they're closing themselves away from, implies there's a world outside. Why is the cloistered state happy and blessed? (I should also comment on the religious terminology, but maybe not in the thesis statement, since it's not the most important descriptive technique in the story.)

Does my thesis offer a direction for the paper, an organizing principle? I think that if I add onto the last sentence something about why the "realm between two worlds" is blessed, I'd be able to organize the paper as a discussion moving between action and setting to argue that the lack of action isn't a failure but a kind of fulfillment or contentment.

Is the thesis supported by specific references to the text you are discussing? Instead of saying "protected happiness" I should use one of the quotes I've been mentioning: "the happy, cloistered finity of their world" (para. 1) and "a blessed realm between two worlds" (para. 2).

David Updike's short story "Summer" involves little action or complication, but this lack of action in the plot is made meaningful by the rendering of the idyllic setting. Combined, these create a particular sense of summer, the symbolic "season" of adolescence, and of adolescent love. The fact that there is no great culmination to Homer's reticent attraction to Sandra is not a failure of the characters or of the plot. Instead, the light tone of this nearly actionless plot captures and reflects the theme—a sense of adolescence and summer as a "blessed realm between two worlds" (para. 2), in which the characters are relatively free of the constraints of more complex adult relationships but may enjoy something of adult consciousness of feeling.

Compare the two thesis statements. Does the revised version seem more effective to you? Why or why not? Can you think of ways of further improving the revised version? Do you think the thesis would be more effective if more or fewer elements were included in it?

Before you begin writing your own paper, review the Questions for Responsive Reading and Writing (pp. 44-45) in Chapter 2, "Writing about Fiction." These questions will help you to focus and sharpen your critical thinking and writing. You'll also find help in Chapter 53, "Reading and Writing," which offers a systematic overview of choosing a topic, developing a thesis, and organizing various types of assignments. If you use outside sources for the paper, be sure to acknowledge them adequately by using the conventional documentation procedures detailed in Chapter 54, "The Literary Research Paper."

Approaches
to Fiction

11

A Study of
Nathaniel Hawthorne

The four short stories by Nathaniel Hawthorne included in this chapter provide an opportunity to study a major fiction writer in depth. Getting to know an author's work is similar to developing a friendship with someone: the more encounters, the more intimate the relationship becomes. Familiarity with a writer's concerns and methods in one story can help to illuminate another story. As we become accustomed to someone's voice — a friend's or a writer's — we become attuned to nuances in tone and meaning. The nuances in Hawthorne's fiction warrant close analysis. Although the stories included are not wholly representative of his work, they suggest some of the techniques and concerns that characterize it. The four stories provide a useful context for reading individual stories. Moreover, the works invite comparisons and contrasts in their styles and themes. Following the four stories are some brief commentaries by and about Hawthorne that establish additional contexts for understanding his fiction.

A BRIEF BIOGRAPHY AND INTRODUCTION

Nathaniel Hawthorne (1804–1864) once described himself as "the obscurest man of letters in America." During the early years of his career, this self-assessment was mostly accurate, but the publication of *The Scarlet Letter* in 1850 marked the beginning of Hawthorne's reputation as a major American writer. His novels and short stories have entertained and challenged generations of readers; they have wide appeal because they can be read on many levels. Hawthorne skillfully creates an atmosphere of complexity and ambiguity that makes it difficult to reduce his stories to a simple view of life. The moral and psychological issues that he examines through the conflicts his characters experience are often intricate and mysterious. Readers are frequently made to feel that in exploring Hawthorne's characters they are also encountering some part of themselves.

Hawthorne achieved success as a writer only after a steady and intense struggle. His personal history was hardly conducive to producing a professional writer. Born in Salem, Massachusetts, Hawthorne came from a Puritan family of declining fortunes that prided itself on an energetic pursuit of practical matters such as law and commerce. He never knew his father, a sea captain who died in Dutch Guiana when Hawthorne was only four years old, but he did have a strong imaginative sense of an early ancestor, who as a Puritan judge persecuted Quakers, and of a later ancestor, who was a judge during the Salem witchcraft trials. His forebears seemed to haunt Hawthorne, so that in some ways he felt more involved in the past than in the present.

In "The Custom-House," the introduction to *The Scarlet Letter,* Hawthorne considers himself in relation to his severe Puritan ancestors:

> No aim, that I have ever cherished, would they recognize as laudable; no success of mine . . . would they deem otherwise than worthless, if not positively disgraceful. "What is he?" murmurs one gray shadow of my forefathers to the other. "A writer of story-books! What kind of a business in life, — what mode of glorifying God, or being serviceable to mankind in his day and generation, — may that be? Why, the degenerate fellow might as well have been a fiddler!" Such are the compliments bandied between my great-grandsires and myself, across the gulf of time! And yet, let them scorn me as they will, strong traits of their nature have intertwined with mine.

Hawthorne's sense of what his forebears might think of his work caused him to worry that the utilitarian world was more real and important than his imaginative creations. This issue became a recurring theme in his work.

Despite the Puritan strain in Hawthorne's sensibilities and his own deep suspicion that a literary vocation was not serious or productive work, Hawthorne was determined to become a writer. He found encouragement at Bowdoin College in Maine and graduated in 1825 with a class that included the poet Henry Wadsworth Longfellow and Franklin Pierce, who would be elected president of the United States in the early 1850s. After

PHOTO ABOVE: *Nathaniel Hawthorne in an undated photograph, probably taken — judging from his hollow cheeks and gray hair — near the end of his life. Reprinted by permission of Corbis-Bettmann.*

graduation Hawthorne returned to his mother's house in Salem, where for the next twelve years he read New England history as well as writers such as John Milton, William Shakespeare, and John Bunyan. During this time he lived a relatively withdrawn life devoted to developing his literary art. Hawthorne wrote and revised stories as he sought a style that would express his creative energies. Many of these early efforts were destroyed when they did not meet his high standards. His first novel, *Fanshawe*, was published anonymously in 1828; it concerns a solitary young man who fails to realize his potential and dies young. Hawthorne very nearly succeeded in reclaiming and destroying all the published copies of this work. It was not attributed to the author until after his death; not even his wife was aware that he had written it. The stories eventually published as *Twice-Told Tales* (1837) represent work that was carefully revised and survived Hawthorne's critical judgments.

Writing did not provide an adequate income, so like nearly all nineteenth-century American writers, Hawthorne had to take on other employment. He worked in the Boston Custom House from 1839 through 1840 to save money to marry Sophia Peabody, but he lost that politically appointed job when administrations changed. In 1841 he lived at Brook Farm, a utopian community founded by idealists who hoped to combine manual labor with art and philosophy. Finding that monotonous physical labor left little time for thinking and writing, Hawthorne departed after seven months. The experience failed to improve his financial situation, but it did eventually serve as the basis for a novel, *The Blithedale Romance* (1852).

Married in the summer of 1842, Hawthorne and his wife moved to the Old Manse in Concord, Massachusetts, where their neighbors included Ralph Waldo Emerson, Henry David Thoreau, Amos Bronson Alcott, and other writers and thinkers who contributed to the lively literary environment of that small town. Although Hawthorne was on friendly terms with these men, his skepticism concerning human nature prevented him from sharing either their optimism or their faith in radical reform of individuals or society. Hawthorne's view of life was chastened by a sense of what he called in "Wakefield" the "iron tissue of necessity." His sensibilities were more akin to Herman Melville's. When Melville and Hawthorne met while Hawthorne was living in the Berkshires of western Massachusetts, they responded to each other intensely. Melville admired the "power of blackness" he discovered in Hawthorne's writings and dedicated *Moby-Dick* to him.

During the several years he lived in the Old Manse, Hawthorne published a second collection of *Twice-Told Tales* (1842) and additional stories in *Mosses from an Old Manse* (1846). To keep afloat financially, he worked in the Salem Custom House from 1846 until 1849, when he again lost his job through a change in administrations. This time, however, he discovered that by leaving the oppressive materialism of the Custom House he found more energy to write: "So little adapted is the atmosphere of a Custom

House to the delicate harvest of fancy and sensibility, that, had I remained there through ten Presidencies yet to come, I doubt whether the tale of 'The Scarlet Letter' would ever have been brought before the public. My imagination was a tarnished mirror [there.]" Free of the Custom House, Hawthorne was at the height of his creativity and productivity during the early 1850s. In addition to *The Scarlet Letter* and *The Blithedale Romance*, he wrote *The House of the Seven Gables* (1851); *The Snow-Image, and Other Twice-Told Tales* (1852); a campaign biography of his Bowdoin classmate, *The Life of Franklin Pierce* (1852); and two collections of stories for children, *A Wonder Book* (1852) and *Tanglewood Tales* (1853).

Hawthorne's financial situation improved during the final decade of his life. In 1853 his friend President Pierce appointed him to the U.S. consulship in Liverpool, where he remained for the next four years. Following a tour of Europe from 1858 to 1860, Hawthorne and his family returned to Concord, and he published *The Marble Faun* (1860), his final completed work of fiction. He died while traveling through New Hampshire with former President Pierce.

Hawthorne's stories are much more complex than the melodramatic but usually optimistic fiction published in many magazines contemporary to him. Instead of cheerfully confirming public values and attitudes, his work tends to be dark and brooding. Modern readers remain responsive to Hawthorne's work — despite the fact that his nineteenth-century style takes some getting used to — because his psychological themes are as fascinating as they are disturbing. The range of his themes is not broad, but their treatment is remarkable for its insights.

Hawthorne wrote about individuals who suffer from inner conflicts caused by sin, pride, untested innocence, hidden guilt, perverse secrecy, cold intellectuality, and isolation. His characters are often consumed by their own passions, whether those passions are motivated by an obsession with goodness or evil. He looks inside his characters and reveals to us that portion of their hearts, minds, and souls that they keep from the world and even from themselves. This emphasis accounts for the private, interior, and sometimes gloomy atmosphere in Hawthorne's works. His stories rarely end on a happy note because the questions his characters raise are almost never completely answered. Rather than positing solutions to the problems and issues his characters encounter, Hawthorne leaves us with ambiguities suggesting that experience cannot always be fully understood and controlled. Beneath the surface appearances in his stories lurk ironies and shifting meanings that point to many complex truths instead of a single simple moral.

The following four Hawthorne stories provide an opportunity to study this writer in some depth. These stories are not intended to be entirely representative of the 120 or so that Hawthorne wrote, but they do offer some sense of the range of his techniques and themes. Hawthorne's fictional world of mysterious incidents and sometimes bizarre characters increases in meaning the more his stories are read in the context of one another.

CHRONOLOGY

1804	Born on July 4 in Salem, Massachusetts.
1808	Hawthorne's father, a sea captain, dies in Surinam, Dutch Guiana, leaving the family dependent on relatives.
1821–25	Attends Bowdoin College in Maine. Franklin Pierce (later to become president) and Henry Wadsworth Longfellow are classmates. Graduates eighteenth in a class of thirty-eight.
1828	Publishes *Fanshawe: A Tale* anonymously at his own expense.
1830–37	Publishes numerous stories in periodicals anonymously or pseudonymously, collected in *Twice-Told Tales.*
1838	Becomes engaged to Sophia Peabody.
1839–40	Works in Boston Custom House.
1841	From April to November, lives at the utopian Brook Farm Community.
1842–45	Marries (eventually has three children) and lives at the Old Manse in Concord, Massachusetts, where he meets Ralph Waldo Emerson and Henry David Thoreau.
1846	Publishes his second collection of stories, *Mosses from an Old Manse.*
1846–49	Works as a surveyor in the Salem Custom House.
1850	Publishes *The Scarlet Letter;* becomes a friend of Herman Melville.
1851	Publishes *The House of the Seven Gables; The Snow-Image, and Other Twice-Told Tales;* and *True Stories from History and Biography.*
1852	Publishes *The Blithedale Romance; A Wonder Book for Girls and Boys;* and *The Life of Franklin Pierce,* a campaign biography.
1853–57	Serves as United States Consul at Liverpool on appointment by President Pierce.
1857–59	Lives in Rome and Florence.
1860	Publishes *The Marble Faun;* returns to Concord.
1863	Publishes *Our Old Home: A Series of English Sketches.*
1864	Dies on May 19 at Plymouth, New Hampshire.

Research Nathaniel Hawthorne with LitLinks at
http://www.bedfordstmartins.com/meyer/bedintrolit

Young Goodman Brown   1835

Young Goodman Brown came forth at sunset into the street at Salem village; but put his head back, after crossing the threshold, to exchange a parting kiss with his young wife. And Faith, as the wife was aptly named, thrust her own pretty head into the street, letting the wind play with the pink ribbons of her cap while she called to Goodman Brown.

"Dearest heart," whispered she, softly and rather sadly, when her lips were close to his ear, "prithee put off your journey until sunrise and sleep in your own bed tonight. A lone woman is troubled with such dreams and such thoughts that she's afeared of herself sometimes. Pray tarry with me this night, dear husband, of all nights in the year."

"My love and my Faith," replied young Goodman Brown, "of all nights in the year, this one night must I tarry away from thee. My journey, as thou callest it, forth and back again, must needs be done 'twixt now and sunrise. What, my sweet, pretty wife, dost thou doubt me already, and we but three months married?"

"Then God bless you!" said Faith, with the pink ribbons; "and may you find all well when you come back."

"Amen!" cried Goodman Brown. "Say thy prayers, dear Faith, and go to 5
bed at dusk, and no harm will come to thee."

So they parted; and the young man pursued his way until, being about to turn the corner by the meeting-house, he looked back and saw the head of Faith still peeping after him with a melancholy air, in spite of her pink ribbons.

"Poor little Faith!" thought he, for his heart smote him. "What a wretch am I to leave her on such an errand! She talks of dreams, too. Methought as she spoke there was trouble in her face, as if a dream had warned her what work is to be done tonight. But no, no; 't would kill her to think it. Well, she's a blessed angel on earth; and after this one night I'll cling to her skirts and follow her to heaven."

With this excellent resolve for the future, Goodman Brown felt himself justified in making more haste on his present evil purpose. He had taken a dreary road, darkened by all the gloomiest trees of the forest, which barely stood aside to let the narrow path creep through, and closed immediately behind. It was all as lonely as could be; and there is this peculiarity in such a solitude, that the traveler knows not who may be concealed by the innumerable trunks and the thick boughs overhead; so that with lonely footsteps he may yet be passing through an unseen multitude.

"There may be a devilish Indian behind every tree," said Goodman Brown to himself; and he glanced fearfully behind him as he added, "What if the devil himself should be at my very elbow!"

His head being turned back, he passed a crook of the road, and, looking 10
forward again, beheld the figure of a man, in grave and decent attire, seated at the foot of an old tree. He arose at Goodman Brown's approach and walked onward side by side with him.

"You are late, Goodman Brown," said he. "The clock of the Old South was striking as I came through Boston, and that is full fifteen minutes agone."

"Faith kept me back a while," replied the young man, with a tremor in his voice, caused by the sudden appearance of his companion, though not wholly unexpected.

It was now deep dusk in the forest, and deepest in that part of it where these two were journeying. As nearly as could be discerned, the second traveler was about fifty years old, apparently in the same rank of life as Goodman Brown, and bearing a considerable resemblance to him, though perhaps more in expression than features. Still they might have been taken for father and son. And yet, though the elder person was as simply clad as the younger, and as simple in manner too, he had an indescribable air of one who knew the world, and who would not have felt abashed at the governor's dinner table or in King William's court, were it possible that his affairs should call him thither. But the only thing about him that could be fixed upon as remarkable was his staff, which bore the likeness of a great black snake, so curiously wrought that it might almost be seen to twist and wriggle itself like a living serpent. This, of course, must have been an ocular deception, assisted by the uncertain light.

"Come, Goodman Brown," cried his fellow-traveler, "this is a dull pace for the beginning of a journey. Take my staff, if you are so soon weary."

"Friend," said the other, exchanging his slow pace for a full stop, "having 15 kept covenant by meeting thee here, it is my purpose now to return whence I came. I have scruples touching the matter thou wot'st° of."

"Sayest thou so?" replied he of the serpent, smiling apart. "Let us walk on, nevertheless, reasoning as we go; and if I convince thee not thou shalt turn back. We are but a little way in the forest yet."

"Too far! too far!" exclaimed the goodman, unconsciously resuming his walk. "My father never went into the woods on such an errand, nor his father before him. We have been a race of honest men and good Christians since the days of the martyrs; and shall I be the first of the name of Brown that ever took this path and kept" —

"Such company, thou wouldst say," observed the elder person, interpreting his pause. "Well said, Goodman Brown! I have been as well acquainted with your family as with ever a one among the Puritans; and that's no trifle to say. I helped your grandfather, the constable, when he lashed the Quaker woman so smartly through the streets of Salem; and it was I that brought your father a pitch-pine knot, kindled at my own hearth, to set fire to an Indian village, in King Philip's war.° They were my good friends, both; and many a pleasant walk have we had along this path, and returned merrily after midnight. I would fain be friends with you for their sake."

"If it be as thou sayest," replied Goodman Brown, "I marvel they never spoke of these matters; or, verily, I marvel not, seeing that the least rumor of the sort would have driven them from New England. We are a people of prayer, and good works to boot, and abide no such wickedness."

"Wickedness or not," said the traveler with the twisted staff, "I have a very 20 general acquaintance here in New England. The deacons of many a church have drunk the communion wine with me; the selectmen of divers towns make me their chairman; and a majority of the Great and General Court are firm supporters of my interest. The governor and I, too — But these are state secrets."

"Can this be so?" cried Goodman Brown, with a stare of amazement at his undisturbed companion. "Howbeit, I have nothing to do with the governor and council; they have their own ways, and are no rule for a simple husbandman like me. But, were I to go on with thee, how should I meet the eye of that good old man, our minister, at Salem village? Oh, his voice would make me tremble both Sabbath day and lecture day."

wot'st: Know.
King Philip's war (1675–76): War between the colonists and an alliance of Indian tribes led by Metacan (also known as Metacomet), leader of the Wampanoags, who was called King Philip by the colonists.

Thus far the elder traveler had listened with due gravity; but now burst into a fit of irrepressible mirth, shaking himself so violently that his snakelike staff actually seemed to wriggle in sympathy.

"Ha! ha! ha!" shouted he again and again; then composing himself, "Well, go on, Goodman Brown, go on; but, prithee, don't kill me with laughing."

"Well, then, to end the matter at once," said Goodman Brown, considerably nettled, "there is my wife, Faith. It would break her dear little heart; and I'd rather break my own."

"Nay, if that be the case," answered the other, "e'en go thy ways, Goodman 25 Brown. I would not for twenty old women like the one hobbling before us that Faith should come to any harm."

As he spoke he pointed his staff at a female figure on the path, in whom Goodman Brown recognized a very pious and exemplary dame, who had taught him his catechism in youth, and was still his moral and spiritual adviser, jointly with the minister and Deacon Gookin.

"A marvel, truly that Goody Cloyse should be so far in the wilderness at nightfall," said he. "But with your leave, friend, I shall take a cut through the woods until we have left this Christian woman behind. Being a stranger to you, she might ask whom I was consorting with and whither I was going."

"Be it so," said his fellow-traveler. "Betake you to the woods, and let me keep the path."

Accordingly the young man turned aside, but took care to watch his companion, who advanced softly along the road until he had come within a staff's length of the old dame. She, meanwhile, was making the best of her way, with singular speed for so aged a woman, and mumbling some indistinct words — a prayer, doubtless — as she went. The traveler put forth his staff and touched her withered neck with what seemed the serpent's tail.

"The devil!" screamed the pious old lady. 30

"Then Goody Cloyse knows her old friend?" observed the traveler, confronting her and leaning on his writhing stick.

"Ah, forsooth, and is it your worship indeed?" cried the good dame. "Yea, truly is it, and in the very image of my old gossip, Goodman Brown, the grandfather of the silly fellow that now is. But — would your worship believe it? — my broomstick hath strangely disappeared, stolen, as I suspect, by that unhanged witch, Goody Cory, and that, too, when I was all anointed with the juice of smallage, and cinquefoil, and wolfsbane" —

"Mingled with fine wheat and the fat of a newborn babe," said the shape of old Goodman Brown.

"Ah, your worship knows the recipe," cried the old lady, cackling aloud. "So, as I was saying, being all ready for the meeting, and no horse to ride on, I made up my mind to foot it; for they tell me there is a nice young man to be taken into communion tonight. But now your good worship will lend me your arm, and we shall be there in a twinkling."

"That can hardly be," answered her friend. "I may not spare you my arm, 35 Goody Cloyse; but here is my staff, if you will."

So saying, he threw it down at her feet, where, perhaps, it assumed life, being one of the rods which its owner had formerly lent to the Egyptian magi. Of this fact, however, Goodman Brown could not take cognizance. He had cast up his eyes in astonishment, and, looking down again, beheld neither Goody

Cloyse nor the serpentine staff, but his fellow-traveler alone, who waited for him as calmly as if nothing had happened.

"That old woman taught me my catechism," said the young man; and there was a world of meaning in this simple comment. *multiple*

They continued to walk onward, while the elder traveler exhorted his companion to make good speed and persevere in the path, discoursing so aptly that his arguments seemed rather to spring up in the bosom of his auditor than to be suggested by himself. As they went, he plucked a branch of maple to serve for a walking stick, and began to strip it of the twigs and little boughs, which were wet with evening dew. The moment his fingers touched them they became strangely withered and dried up as with a week's sunshine. Thus the pair proceeded, at a good free pace, until suddenly, in a gloomy hollow of the road, Goodman Brown sat himself down on the stump of a tree and refused to go any farther.

"Friend," he said, stubbornly, "my mind is made up. Not another step will I budge on this errand. What if a wretched old woman do choose to go to the devil when I thought she was going to heaven: is that any reason why I should quit my dear Faith and go after her?"

"You will think better of this by and by," said his acquaintance, compos- 40
edly. "Sit here and rest yourself a while; and when you feel like moving again, there is my staff to help you along."

Without more words, he threw his companion the maple stick, and was as speedily out of sight as if he had vanished into the deepening gloom. The young man sat a few moments by the roadside, applauding himself greatly, and thinking with how clear a conscience he should meet the minister in his morning walk, nor shrink from the eye of good old Deacon Gookin. And what calm sleep would be his that very night, which was to have been spent so wickedly, but so purely and sweetly now, in the arms of Faith! Amidst these pleasant and praiseworthy meditations, Goodman Brown heard the tramp of horses along the road, and deemed it advisable to conceal himself within the verge of the forest, conscious of the guilty purpose that had brought him thither, though now so happily turned from it.

On came the hoof tramps and the voices of the riders, two grave old voices, conversing soberly as they drew near. These mingled sounds appeared to pass along the road, within a few yards of the young man's hiding-place; but, owing doubtless to the depth of the gloom at that particular spot, neither the travelers nor their steeds were visible. Though their figures brushed the small boughs by the wayside, it could not be seen that they intercepted, even for a moment, the faint gleam from the strip of bright sky athwart which they must have passed. Goodman Brown alternately crouched and stood on tiptoe, pulling aside the branches and thrusting forth his head as far as he durst without discerning so much as a shadow. It vexed him the more, because he could have sworn, were such a thing possible, that he recognized the voices of the minister and Deacon Gookin, jogging along quietly, as they were wont to do, when bound to some ordination or ecclesiastical council. While yet within hearing, one of the riders stopped to pluck a switch.

"Of the two, reverend sir," said the voice like the deacon's, "I had rather miss an ordination dinner than tonight's meeting. They tell me that some of our community are to be here from Falmouth and beyond, and others from Connecticut and Rhode Island, besides several of the Indian powwows, who, after their fashion, know almost as much deviltry as the best of us. Moreover, there is a goodly young woman to be taken into communion."

"Mighty well, Deacon Gookin!" replied the solemn old tones of the minister. "Spur up, or we shall be late. Nothing can be done, you know, until I get on the ground."

The hoofs clattered again; and the voices, talking so strangely in the empty air, passed on through the forest, where no church had ever been gathered or solitary Christian prayed. Whither, then, could these holy men be journeying so deep into the heathen wilderness? Young Goodman Brown caught hold of a tree for support, being ready to sink down on the ground, faint and overburdened with the heavy sickness of his heart. He looked up to the sky, doubting whether there really was a heaven above him. Yet there was the blue arch, and the stars brightening in it.

"With heaven above and Faith below, I will yet stand firm against the devil!" cried Goodman Brown.

While he still gazed upward into the deep arch of the firmament and had lifted his hands to pray, a cloud, though no wind was stirring, hurried across the zenith and hid the brightening stars. The blue sky was still visible, except directly overhead, where this black mass of cloud was sweeping swiftly northward. Aloft in the air, as if from the depths of the cloud, came a confused and doubtful sound of voices. Once the listener fancied that he could distinguish the accents of townspeople of his own, men and women, both pious and ungodly, many of whom he had met at the communion table, and had seen others rioting at the tavern. The next moment, so indistinct were the sounds, he doubted whether he had heard aught but the murmur of the old forest, whispering without a wind. Then came a stronger swell of those familiar tones, heard daily in the sunshine at Salem village, but never until now from a cloud of night. There was one voice, of a young woman, uttering lamentations, yet with an uncertain sorrow, and entreating for some favor, which, perhaps, it would grieve her to obtain; and all the unseen multitude, both saints and sinners, seemed to encourage her onward.

"Faith!" shouted Goodman Brown, in a voice of agony and desperation; and the echoes of the forest mocked him, crying, "Faith! Faith!" as if bewildered wretches were seeking her all through the wilderness.

The cry of grief, rage, and terror was yet piercing the night, when the unhappy husband held his breath for a response. There was a scream, drowned immediately in a louder murmur of voices, fading into far-off laughter, as the dark cloud swept away, leaving the clear and silent sky above Goodman Brown. But something fluttered lightly down through the air and caught on the branch of a tree. The young man seized it, and beheld a pink ribbon.

"My Faith is gone!" cried he after one stupefied moment. "There is no good on earth; and sin is but a name. Come, devil; for to thee is this world given."

And, maddened with despair, so that he laughed loud and long, did Goodman Brown grasp his staff and set forth again, at such a rate that he seemed to fly along the forest path rather than to walk or run. The road grew wilder and drearier and more faintly traced, and vanished at length, leaving him in the heart of the dark wilderness, still rushing onward with the instinct that guides mortal man to evil. The whole forest was peopled with frightful sounds—the creaking of the trees, the howling of wild beasts, and the yell of Indians; while sometimes the wind tolled like a distant church bell, and sometimes gave a broad roar around the traveler, as if all Nature were laughing him to scorn. But he was himself the chief horror of the scene, and shrank not from its other horrors. *↳ worse than all !*

"Ha! ha! ha!" roared Goodman Brown when the wind laughed at him. "Let us hear which will laugh loudest. Think not to frighten me with your deviltry. Come witch, come wizard, come Indian powwow, come devil himself, and here comes Goodman Brown. You may as well fear him as he fear you."

In truth, all through the haunted forest there could be nothing more frightful than the figure of Goodman Brown. On he flew among the black pines, brandishing his staff with frenzied gestures, now giving vent to an inspiration of horrid blasphemy, and now shouting forth such laughter as set all the echoes of the forest laughing like demons around him. The fiend in his own shape is less hideous than when he rages in the breast of man. Thus sped the demoniac on his course, until, quivering among the trees, he saw a red light before him, as when the felled trunks and branches of a clearing have been set on fire, and throw up their lurid blaze against the sky, at the hour of midnight. He paused, in a lull of the tempest that had driven him onward, and heard the swell of what seemed a hymn, rolling solemnly from a distance with the weight of many voices. He knew the tune; it was a familiar one in the choir of the village meeting-house. The verse died heavily away, and was lengthened by a chorus, not of human voices, but of all the sounds of the benighted wilderness pealing in awful harmony together. Goodman Brown cried out, and his cry was lost to his own ear by its unison with the cry of the desert.

In the interval of silence he stole forward until the light glared full upon his eyes. At one extremity of an open space, hemmed in by the dark wall of the forest, arose a rock, bearing some rude, natural resemblance either to an altar or a pulpit, and surrounded by four blazing pines, their tops aflame, their stems untouched, like candles at an evening meeting. The mass of foliage that had overgrown the summit of the rock was all on fire, blazing high into the night and fitfully illuminating the whole field. Each pendent twig and leafy festoon was in a blaze. As the red light arose and fell, a numerous congregation alternately shone forth, then disappeared in shadow, and again grew, as it were, out of the darkness, peopling the heart of the solitary woods at once.

"A grave and dark-clad company," quoth Goodman Brown.   55

In truth they were such. Among them, quivering to and fro between gloom and splendor, appeared faces that would be seen next day at the council board of the province, and others which, Sabbath after Sabbath, looked devoutly heavenward, and benignantly over the crowded pews, from the holiest pulpits in the land. Some affirm that the lady of the governor was there. At least there were high dames well known to her, and wives of honored husbands, and widows, a great multitude, and ancient maidens, all of excellent repute, and fair young girls, who trembled lest their mothers should espy them. Either the sudden gleams of light flashing over the obscure field bedazzled Goodman Brown, or he recognized a score of the church members of Salem village famous for their especial sanctity. Good old Deacon Gookin had arrived, and waited at the skirts of that venerable saint, his revered pastor. But, irreverently consorting with these grave, reputable, and pious people, these elders of the church, these chaste dames and dewy virgins, there were men of dissolute lives and women of spotted fame, wretches given over to all mean and filthy vice, and suspected even of horrid crimes. It was strange to see that the good shrank not from the wicked, nor were the sinners abashed by the saints. Scattered also among their pale-faced enemies were the Indian priests, or powwows, who had often scared their native forest with more hideous incantations than any known to English witchcraft.

"But where is Faith?" thought Goodman Brown; and, as hope came into his heart, he trembled.

Another verse of the hymn arose, a slow and mournful strain, such as the pious love, but joined to words which expressed all that our nature can conceive of sin, and darkly hinted at far more. Unfathomable to mere mortals is the lore of fiends. Verse after verse was sung; and still the chorus of the desert swelled between like the deepest tone of a mighty organ; and with the final peal of that dreadful anthem there came a sound, as if the roaring wind, the rushing streams, the howling beasts, and every other voice of the unconcerted wilderness were mingling and according with the voice of guilty man in homage to the prince of all. The four blazing pines threw up a loftier flame, and obscurely discovered shapes and visages of horror on the smoke wreaths above the impious assembly. At the same moment the fire on the rock shot redly forth and formed a glowing arch above its base, where now appeared a figure. With reverence be it spoken, the figure bore no slight similitude, both in garb and manner, to some grave divine of the New England churches.

"Bring forth the converts!" cried a voice that echoed through the field and rolled into the forest.

At the word, Goodman Brown stepped forth from the shadow of the trees 60 and approached the congregation, with whom he felt a loathful brotherhood by the sympathy of all that was wicked in his heart. He could have well-nigh sworn that the shape of his own dead father beckoned him to advance, looking downward from a smoke wreath, while a woman, with dim features of despair, threw out her hand to warn him back. Was it his mother? But he had no power to retreat one step, nor to resist, even in thought, when the minister and good old Deacon Gookin seized his arms and led him to the blazing rock. Thither came also the slender form of a veiled female, led between Goody Cloyse, that pious teacher of the catechism, and Martha Carrier, who had received the devil's promise to be queen of hell. A rampant hag was she. And there stood the proselytes beneath the canopy of fire.

"Welcome, my children," said the dark figure, "to the communion of your race. Ye have found thus young your nature and your destiny. My children, look behind you!"

They turned; and flashing forth, as it were, in a sheet of flame, the fiend worshipers were seen; the smile of welcome gleamed darkly on every visage.

"There," resumed the sable form, "are all whom ye have reverenced from youth. Ye deemed them holier than yourselves and shrank from your own sin, contrasting it with their lives of righteousness and prayerful aspirations heavenward. Yet here are they all in my worshiping assembly. This night it shall be granted you to know their secret deeds: how hoary-bearded elders of the church have whispered wanton words to the young maids of their households; how many a woman, eager for widows' weeds, has given her husband a drink at bedtime and let him sleep his last sleep in her bosom; how beardless youths have made haste to inherit their fathers' wealth; and how fair damsels — blush not, sweet ones — have dug little graves in the garden, and bidden me, the sole guest, to an infant's funeral. By the sympathy of your human hearts for sin ye shall scent out all the places — whether in church, bedchamber, street, field, or forest — where crime has been committed, and shall exult to behold the whole earth one stain of guilt, one mighty blood spot. Far more than this. It shall be yours to penetrate, in every bosom, the deep mystery of sin, the fountain of all wicked arts, and which inexhaustibly supplies more evil impulses than human power — than my power at its utmost — can make manifest in deeds. And now, my children, look upon each other."

They did so; and, by the blaze of the hell-kindled torches, the wretched man beheld his Faith, and the wife her husband, trembling before that unhallowed altar.

"Lo, there ye stand, my children," said the figure, in a deep and solemn 65 tone, almost sad with its despairing awfulness, as if his once angelic nature could yet mourn for our miserable race. "Depending upon one another's hearts, ye had still hoped that virtue were not all a dream. Now are ye undeceived. Evil is the nature of mankind. Evil must be your only happiness. Welcome again, my children, to the communion of your race."

"Welcome," repeated the fiend worshipers; in one cry of despair and triumph.

And there they stood, the only pair, as it seemed, who were yet hesitating on the verge of wickedness in this dark world. A basin was hollowed, naturally, in the rock. Did it contain water, reddened by the lurid light? or was it blood? or, perchance, a liquid flame? Herein did the shape of evil dip his hand and prepare to lay the mark of baptism upon their foreheads, that they might be partakers of the mystery of sin, more conscious of the secret guilt of others, both in deed and thought, than they could now be of their own. The husband cast one look at his pale wife, and Faith at him. What polluted wretches would the next glance show them to each other, shuddering alike at what they disclosed and what they saw!

"Faith! Faith!" cried the husband, "look up to heaven, and resist the wicked one."

Whether Faith obeyed he knew not. Hardly had he spoken when he found himself amid calm night and solitude, listening to a roar of the wind which died heavily away through the forest. He staggered against the rock, and felt it chill and damp; while a hanging twig, that had been all on fire, besprinkled his cheek with the coldest dew.

The next morning young Goodman Brown came slowly into the street of 70 Salem village, staring around him like a bewildered man. The good old minister was taking a walk along the graveyard to get an appetite for breakfast and meditate his sermon, and bestowed a blessing, as he passed, on Goodman Brown. He shrank from the venerable saint as if to avoid an anathema. Old Deacon Gookin was at domestic worship, and the holy words of his prayer were heard through the open window. "What God doth the wizard pray to?" quoth Goodman Brown. Goody Cloyse, that excellent old Christian, stood in the early sunshine at her own lattice, catechizing a little girl who had brought her a pint of morning's milk. Goodman Brown snatched away the child as from the grasp of the fiend himself. Turning the corner by the meeting-house, he spied the head of Faith, with the pink ribbons, gazing anxiously forth, and bursting into such joy at sight of him that she skipped along the street and almost kissed her husband before the whole village. But Goodman Brown looked sternly and sadly into her face, and passed on without a greeting.

Had Goodman Brown fallen asleep in the forest and only dreamed a wild dream of a witch-meeting?

Be it so if you will; but, alas! it was a dream of evil omen for young Goodman Brown. A stern, a sad, a darkly meditative, a distrustful, if not a desperate man did he become from the night of that fearful dream. On the Sabbath day, when the congregation were singing a holy psalm, he could not listen because an anthem of sin rushed loudly upon his ear and drowned all the blessed strain. When the minister spoke from the pulpit with power and fervid eloquence, and, with his hand on the open Bible, of the sacred truths of our religion, and of saintlike lives and triumphant deaths, and of future bliss or misery unutterable, then did Goodman Brown turn pale, dreading lest the roof should thunder down upon the gray blasphemer and his hearers. Often, awaking suddenly at midnight, he shrank from the bosom of Faith; and at morning or eventide, when the family knelt down at prayer, he scowled and muttered to himself, and gazed sternly at his wife, and turned away. And when he had lived long, and was borne to his grave a hoary corpse, followed by Faith, an aged woman, and children and grandchildren, a goodly procession, besides neighbors not a few, they carved no hopeful verse upon his tombstone, for his dying hour was gloom.

CONSIDERATIONS FOR CRITICAL THINKING AND WRITING

1. FIRST RESPONSE. Try to summarize "Young Goodman Brown" with a tidy moral. Is it possible? What makes this story complex?

2. What is the significance of Young Goodman Brown's name?

3. What is the symbolic value of the forest in this story? How are the descriptions of the forest contrasted with those of Salem village?

4. Characterize Young Goodman Brown at the beginning of the story. Why does he go into the forest? What does he mean when he says "Faith kept me back a while" (para. 12)?

5. What function do Faith's ribbons have in the story?

6. What foreshadows Young Goodman Brown's meeting with his "fellow-traveler" (para. 14)? Who is he? How do we know that Brown is keeping an appointment with a supernatural being?

7. The narrator describes the fellow-traveler's staff wriggling like a snake but then says, "This, of course, must have been an ocular deception, assisted by the uncertain light" (para. 13). What is the effect of this and other instances of ambiguity in the story?

8. What does Young Goodman Brown discover in the forest? What does he come to think of his ancestors, the church and state, Goody Cloyse, and even his wife?

9. Is Salem populated by hypocrites who cover hideous crimes with a veneer of piety and respectability? Do Faith and the other characters Brown sees when he returns from the forest appear corrupt to you?

10. Near the end of the story the narrator asks, "Had Goodman Brown fallen asleep in the forest and only dreamed a wild dream of a witch-meeting?" (para. 71). Was it a dream, or did the meeting actually happen? How does the answer to this question affect your reading of the story? Write an essay giving an answer to the narrator's question.

11. How is Young Goodman Brown changed by his experience in the forest? Does the narrator endorse Brown's unwillingness to trust anyone?

12. Consider the story as a criticism of the village's hypocrisy.

13. CRITICAL STRATEGIES. Read the section on psychological criticism (pp. 2099–101) in Chapter 52, "Critical Strategies for Reading," and discuss this story as an inward, psychological journey in which Young Goodman Brown discovers the power of blackness in himself but refuses to acknowledge that dimension of his personality.

CONNECTIONS TO OTHER SELECTIONS

1. Compare and contrast Young Goodman Brown's reasons for withdrawal with those of Melville's Bartleby, the Scrivener (p. 116). Do you find yourself more sympathetic with one character than the other? Explain.

2. To what extent is Hawthorne's use of dreams crucial in this story and in "The Birthmark" (p. 359)? Explain how Hawthorne uses dreams as a means to complicate our view of his characters.

3. What does Young Goodman Brown's pursuit of sin have in common with Aylmer's quest for perfection in "The Birthmark"? How do these pursuits reveal the characters' personalities and shed light on the theme of each story?

The Minister's Black Veil   *1836*
A Parable°

The sexton stood in the porch of Milford meeting-house, pulling lustily at the bell-rope. The old people of the village came stooping along the street. Children, with bright faces, tript merrily beside their parents, or mimicked a graver gait, in the conscious dignity of their Sunday clothes. Spruce bachelors looked sidelong at the pretty maidens, and fancied that the Sabbath sunshine made them prettier than on weekdays. When the throng had mostly streamed into the porch, the sexton began to toll the bell, keeping his eye on the Reverend Mr. Hooper's door. The first glimpse of the clergyman's figure was the signal for the bell to cease its summons.

"But what has good Parson Hooper got upon his face?" cried the sexton in astonishment.

All within hearing immediately turned about, and beheld the semblance of Mr. Hooper, pacing slowly his meditative way towards the meeting-house. With one accord they started, expressing more wonder than if some strange minister were coming to dust the cushions of Mr. Hooper's pulpit.

"Are you sure it is our parson?" inquired Goodman Gray of the sexton.

"Of a certainty it is good Mr. Hooper," replied the sexton. "He was to have   5 exchanged pulpits with Parson Shute of Westbury; but Parson Shute sent to excuse himself yesterday, being to preach a funeral sermon."

Another clergyman in New England, Mr. Joseph Moody, of York, Maine, who died about eighty years since, made himself remarkable by the same eccentricity that is here related of the Reverend Mr. Hooper. In his case, however, the symbol had a different import. In early life he had accidentally killed a beloved friend; and from that day till the hour of his own death, he hid his face from men. [Hawthorne's note.]

The cause of so much amazement may appear sufficiently slight. Mr. Hooper, a gentlemanly person of about thirty, though still a bachelor, was dressed with due clerical neatness, as if a careful wife had starched his band, and brushed the weekly dust from his Sunday's garb. There was but one thing remarkable in his appearance. Swathed about his forehead, and hanging down over his face, so low as to be shaken by his breath, Mr. Hooper had on a black veil. On a nearer view, it seemed to consist of two folds of crape, which entirely concealed his features, except the mouth and chin, but probably did not inter-cept his sight, farther than to give a darkened aspect to all living and inani-mate things. With this gloomy shade before him, good Mr. Hooper walked on-ward, at a slow and quiet pace, stooping somewhat and looking on the ground, as is customary with abstracted men, yet nodding kindly to those of his parishioners who still waited on the meeting-house steps. But so wonder-struck were they, that his greeting hardly met with a return.

"I can't really feel as if good Mr. Hooper's face was behind that piece of crape," said the sexton.

"I don't like it," muttered an old woman, as she hobbled into the meeting-house. "He has changed himself into something awful, only by hiding his face."

"Our parson has gone mad!" cried Goodman Gray, following him across the threshold.

A rumor of some unaccountable phenomenon had preceded Mr. Hooper 10 into the meeting-house, and set all the congregation astir. Few could refrain from twisting their heads towards the door; many stood upright, and turned directly about; while several little boys clambered upon the seats, and came down again with a terrible racket. There was a general bustle, a rustling of the women's gowns and shuffling of the men's feet, greatly at variance with that hushed repose which should attend the entrance of the minister. But Mr. Hooper appeared not to notice the perturbation of his people. He entered with an almost noiseless step, bent his head mildly to the pews on each side, and bowed as he passed his oldest parishioner, a white-haired great-grandsire, who occupied an arm-chair in the center of the aisle. It was strange to observe, how slowly this venerable man became conscious of something singular in the ap-pearance of his pastor. He seemed not fully to partake of the prevailing won-der, till Mr. Hooper had ascended the stairs, and showed himself in the pulpit, face to face with his congregation, except for the black veil. That mysterious emblem was never once withdrawn. It shook with his measured breath as he gave out the psalm; it threw its obscurity between him and the holy page, as he read the Scriptures; and while he prayed, the veil lay heavily on his uplifted countenance. Did he seek to hide it from the dread Being whom he was ad-dressing?

Such was the effect of this simple piece of crape, that more than one woman of delicate nerves was forced to leave the meeting-house. Yet perhaps the pale-faced congregation was almost as fearful a sight to the minister, as his black veil to them.

Mr. Hooper had the reputation of a good preacher, but not an energetic one: he strove to win his people heavenward, by mild persuasive influences, rather than to drive them thither, by the thunders of the Word. The sermon which he now delivered, was marked by the same characteristics of style and manner, as the general series of his pulpit oratory. But there was something, either in the sentiment of the discourse itself, or in the imagination of the auditors, which made it greatly the most powerful effort that they had ever heard from their pastor's lips. It was tinged, rather more darkly than usual, with the gentle gloom of Mr. Hooper's temperament. The subject had reference to secret sin, and those sad mysteries which we hide from our nearest and dearest, and would fain conceal from our own consciousness, even forgetting that the Omniscient can detect them. A subtle power was breathed into his words. Each member of the congregation, the most innocent girl, and the man of hardened breast, felt as if the preacher had crept upon them, behind his awful veil, and discovered their hoarded iniquity of deed or thought. Many spread their clasped hands on their bosoms. There was nothing terrible in what Mr. Hooper said; at least, no violence; and yet, with every tremor of his melancholy voice, the hearers quaked. An unsought pathos came hand in hand with awe. So sensible were the audience of some unwonted attribute in their minister, that they longed for a breath of wind to blow aside the veil, almost believing that a stranger's visage would be discovered, though the form, gesture, and voice were those of Mr. Hooper.

At the close of the services, the people hurried out with indecorous confusion, eager to communicate their pent-up amazement, and conscious of lighter spirits, the moment they lost sight of the black veil. Some gathered in little circles, huddled closely together, with their mouths all whispering in the center; some went homeward alone, wrapt in silent meditation; some talked loudly, and profaned the Sabbath-day with ostentatious laughter. A few shook their sagacious heads, intimating that they could penetrate the mystery; while one or two affirmed that there was no mystery at all, but only that Mr. Hooper's eyes were so weakened by the midnight lamp, as to require a shade. After a brief interval, forth came good Mr. Hooper also, in the rear of his flock. Turning his veiled face from one group to another, he paid due reverence to the hoary heads, saluted the middle-aged with kind dignity, as their friend and spiritual guide, greeted the young with mingled authority and love, and laid his hands on the little children's heads to bless them. Such was always his custom on the Sabbath-day. Strange and bewildered looks repaid him for his courtesy. None, as on former occasions, aspired to the honor of walking by their pastor's side. Old Squire Saunders, doubtless by an accidental lapse of memory, neglected to invite Mr. Hooper to his table, where the good clergyman had been wont to bless the food, almost every Sunday since his settlement. He returned, therefore, to the parsonage, and, at the moment of closing the door, was observed to look back upon the people, all of whom had their eyes fixed upon the minister. A sad smile gleamed faintly from beneath the black veil, and flickered about his mouth, glimmering as he disappeared.

"How strange," said a lady, "that a simple black veil, such as any woman might wear on her bonnet, should become such a terrible thing on Mr. Hooper's face!"

"Something must surely be amiss with Mr. Hooper's intellects," observed 15 her husband, the physician of the village. "But the strangest part of the affair is the effect of this vagary, even on a sober-minded man like myself. The black veil, though it covers only our pastor's face, throws its influence over his whole person, and makes him ghost-like from head to foot. Do you not feel it so?"

"Truly do I," replied the lady; "and I would not be alone with him for the world. I wonder he is not afraid to be alone with himself!"

"Men sometimes are so," said her husband.

That afternoon service was attended with similar circumstances. At its conclusion, the bell tolled for the funeral of a young lady. The relatives and friends were assembled in the house, and the more distant acquaintances stood about the door, speaking of the good qualities of the deceased, when their talk was interrupted by the appearance of Mr. Hooper, still covered with his black veil. It was now an appropriate emblem. The clergyman stepped into the room where the corpse was laid, and bent over the coffin, to take a last farewell of his deceased parishioner. As he stooped, the veil hung straight down from his forehead, so that, if her eye-lids had not been closed for ever, the dead maiden might have seen his face. Could Mr. Hooper be fearful of her glance, that he so hastily caught back the black veil? A person, who watched the interview between the dead and living, scrupled not to affirm, that, at the instant when the clergyman's features were disclosed, the corpse had slightly shuddered, rustling the shroud and muslin cap, though the countenance retained the composure of death. A superstitious old woman was the only witness of this prodigy. From the coffin, Mr. Hooper passed into the chamber of the mourners, and thence to the head of the staircase, to make the funeral prayer. It was a tender and heart-dissolving prayer, full of sorrow, yet so imbued with celestial hopes, that the music of a heavenly harp, swept by the fingers of the dead, seemed faintly to be heard among the saddest accents of the minister. The people trembled, though they but darkly understood him, when he prayed that they, and himself, and all of mortal race, might be ready, as he trusted this young maiden had been, for the dreadful hour that should snatch the veil from their faces. The bearers went heavily forth, and the mourners followed, saddening all the street, with the dead before them, and Mr. Hooper in his black veil behind.

"Why do you look back?" said one in the procession to his partner.

"I had a fancy," replied she, "that the minister and the maiden's spirit were walking hand in hand." 20

"And so had I, at the same moment," said the other.

That night, the handsomest couple in Milford village were to be joined in wedlock. Though reckoned a melancholy man, Mr. Hooper had a placid cheerfulness for such occasions, which often excited a sympathetic smile, where livelier merriment would have been thrown away. There was no quality of his disposition which made him more beloved than this. The company at the wedding awaited his arrival with impatience, trusting that the strange awe, which had gathered over him throughout the day, would now be dispelled. But such was not the result. When Mr. Hooper came, the first thing that their eyes rested on was the same horrible black veil, which had added deeper gloom to the funeral, and could portend nothing but evil to the wedding. Such was its immediate effect on the guests, that a cloud seemed to have rolled duskily from beneath the black crape, and dimmed the light of the candles. The bridal pair stood up before the minister. But the bride's cold fingers quivered in the tremulous hand of the bridegroom, and her death-like paleness caused a whisper, that the maiden who had been buried a few hours before, was come from her grave to be married. If ever another wedding were so dismal, it was that famous one, where they tolled the wedding-knell. After performing the ceremony, Mr. Hooper raised a glass of wine to his lips, wishing happiness to the new-married couple, in a strain of mild pleasantry that ought to have brightened the features of the guests, like a cheerful gleam from the hearth. At that instant, catching a glimpse of his figure in the looking-glass, the black veil involved his own spirit in the horror with which it overwhelmed all others. His frame shuddered—his lips grew white—he spilt the untasted wine upon the carpet—and rushed forth into the darkness. For the Earth, too, had on her Black Veil.

The next day, the whole village of Milford talked of little else than Parson Hooper's black veil. That, and the mystery concealed behind it, supplied a topic for discussion between acquaintances meeting in the street, and good women gossiping at their open windows. It was the first item of news that the tavernkeeper told to his guests. The children babbled of it on their way to school. One imitative little imp covered his face with an old black handkerchief, thereby so affrighting his playmates, that the panic seized himself, and he well nigh lost his wits by his own waggery.

It was remarkable, that, of all the busy-bodies and impertinent people in the parish, not one ventured to put the plain question to Mr. Hooper, wherefore he did this thing. Hitherto, whenever there appeared the slightest call for such interference, he had never lacked advisers, nor shown himself averse to be guided by their judgment. If he erred at all, it was by so painful a degree of self-distrust, that even the mildest censure would lead him to consider an indifferent action as a crime. Yet, though so well acquainted with this amiable weakness, no individual among his parishioners chose to make the black veil a subject of friendly remonstrance. There was a feeling of dread, neither plainly confessed nor carefully concealed, which caused each to shift the responsibility upon another, till at length it was found expedient to send a deputation of the church, in order to deal with Mr. Hooper about the mystery, before it should grow into a scandal. Never did an embassy so ill discharge its duties. The minister received them with friendly courtesy, but became silent, after they were seated, leaving to his visitors the whole burthen of introducing their important business. The topic, it might be supposed, was obvious enough. There was the black veil, swathed round Mr. Hooper's forehead, and concealing every feature above his placid mouth, on which, at times, they could perceive the glimmering of a melancholy smile. But that piece of crape, to their imagination, seemed to hang down before his heart, the symbol of a fearful secret between him and them. Were the veil but cast aside, they might speak freely of it, but not till then. Thus they sat a considerable time, speechless, confused, and shrinking uneasily from Mr. Hooper's eye, which they felt to be fixed upon them with an invisible glance. Finally, the deputies returned abashed to their constituents, pronouncing the matter too weighty to be handled, except by a council of the churches, if, indeed, it might not require a general synod.

But there was one person in the village, unappalled by the awe with which 25 the black veil had impressed all beside herself. When the deputies returned without an explanation, or even venturing to demand one, she, with the calm energy of her character, determined to chase away the strange cloud that appeared to be settling round Mr. Hooper, every moment more darkly than before. As his plighted wife, it should be her privilege to know what the black veil concealed. At the minister's first visit, therefore, she entered upon the subject, with a direct simplicity, which made the task easier both for him and her. After he had seated himself, she fixed her eyes steadfastly upon the veil, but could discern nothing of the dreadful gloom that had so overawed the multitude: it was but a double fold of crape, hanging down from his forehead to his mouth, and slightly stirring with his breath.

"No," said she aloud, and smiling, "there is nothing terrible in this piece of crape, except that it hides a face which I am always glad to look upon. Come, good sir, let the sun shine from behind the cloud. First lay aside your black veil: then tell me why you put it on."

Mr. Hooper's smile glimmered faintly.

"There is an hour to come," said he, "when all of us shall cast aside our veils. Take it not amiss, beloved friend, if I wear this piece of crape till then."

"Your words are a mystery too," returned the young lady. "Take away the veil for them, at least."

"Elizabeth, I will," said he, "so far as my vow may suffer me. Know, then, 30 this veil is a type and a symbol, and I am bound to wear it ever, both in light and darkness, in solitude and before the gaze of multitudes, and as with strangers, so with my familiar friends. No mortal eye will see it withdrawn. This dismal shade must separate me from the world: even you, Elizabeth, can never come behind it!"

"What grievous affliction hath befallen you," she earnestly inquired, "that you should thus darken your eyes for ever?"

"If it be a sign of mourning," replied Mr. Hooper, "I, perhaps, like most other mortals, have sorrows dark enough to be typified by a black veil."

"But what if the world will not believe that it is the type of an innocent sorrow?" urged Elizabeth. "Beloved and respected as you are, there may be whispers, that you hide your face under the consciousness of secret sin. For the sake of your holy office, do away this scandal!"

The color rose into her cheeks, as she intimated the nature of the rumors that were already abroad in the village. But Mr. Hooper's mildness did not forsake him. He even smiled again—that same sad smile, which always appeared like a faint glimmering of light, proceeding from the obscurity beneath the veil.

"If I hide my face for sorrow, there is cause enough," he merely replied; 35 "and if I cover it for secret sin, what mortal might not do the same?"

And with this gentle, but unconquerable obstinacy, did he resist all her entreaties. At length Elizabeth sat silent. For a few moments she appeared lost in thought, considering, probably, what new methods might be tried, to withdraw her lover from so dark a fantasy, which, if it had no other meaning, was perhaps a symptom of mental disease. Though of a firmer character than his own, the tears rolled down her cheeks. But, in an instant, as it were, a new feeling took the place of sorrow: her eyes were fixed insensibly on the black veil, when, like a sudden twilight in the air, its terrors fell around her. She arose, and stood trembling before him.

"And do you feel it then at last?" said he mournfully.

She made no reply, but covered her eyes with her hand, and turned to leave the room. He rushed forward and caught her arm.

"Have patience with me, Elizabeth!" cried he passionately. "Do not desert me, though this veil must be between us here on earth. Be mine, and hereafter there shall be no veil over my face, no darkness between our souls! It is but a mortal veil—it is not for eternity! Oh! you know not how lonely I am, and how frightened to be alone behind my black veil. Do not leave me in this miserable obscurity for ever!"

"Lift the veil but once, and look me in the face," said she.   40
"Never! It cannot be!" replied Mr. Hooper.
"Then, farewell!" said Elizabeth.

She withdrew her arm from his grasp, and slowly departed, pausing at the door, to give one long, shuddering gaze, that seemed almost to penetrate the mystery of the black veil. But, even amid his grief, Mr. Hooper smiled to think that only a material emblem had separated him from happiness, though the horrors which it shadowed forth, must be drawn darkly between the fondest of lovers.

From that time no attempts were made to remove Mr. Hooper's black veil, or, by a direct appeal, to discover the secret which it was supposed to hide. By persons who claimed a superiority to popular prejudice, it was reckoned merely an eccentric whim, such as often mingles with the sober actions of men otherwise rational, and tinges them all with its own semblance of insanity. But with the multitude, good Mr. Hooper was irreparably a bugbear. He could not walk the streets with any peace of mind, so conscious was he that the gentle and timid would turn aside to avoid him, and that others would make it a point of hardihood to throw themselves in his way. The impertinence of the latter class compelled him to give up his customary walk, at sunset, to the burial ground, for when he leaned pensively over the gate, there would always be faces behind the grave-stones, peeping at his black veil. A fable went the rounds that the stare of the dead people drove him thence. It grieved him, to the very depth of his kind heart, to observe how the children fled from his approach, breaking up their merriest sports, while his melancholy figure was yet afar off. Their instinctive dread caused him to feel, more strongly than aught else, that a preternatural horror was interwoven with the threads of the black crape. In truth, his own antipathy to the veil was known to be so great, that he never willingly passed before a mirror, nor stooped to drink at a still fountain, lest, in its peaceful bosom, he should be affrighted by himself. This was what gave plausibility to the whispers, that Mr. Hooper's conscience tortured him for some great crime, too horrible to be entirely concealed, or otherwise than so obscurely intimated. Thus, from beneath the black veil, there rolled a cloud into the sunshine, an ambiguity of sin or sorrow, which enveloped the poor minister, so that love or sympathy could never reach him. It was said, that ghost and fiend consorted with him there. With self-shudderings and outward terrors, he walked continually in its shadow, groping darkly within his own soul, or gazing through a medium that saddened the whole world. Even the lawless wind, it was believed, respected his dreadful secret, and never blew aside the veil. But still good Mr. Hooper sadly smiled, at the pale visages of the worldly throng as he passed by.

Among all its bad influences, the black veil had the one desirable effect, of   45
making its wearer a very efficient clergyman. By the aid of his mysterious emblem—for there was no other apparent cause—he became a man of awful power, over souls that were in agony for sin. His converts always regarded him with a dread peculiar to themselves, affirming, though but figuratively, that, before he brought them to celestial light, they had been with him behind the black veil. Its gloom, indeed, enabled him to sympathize with all dark affections. Dying sinners cried aloud for Mr. Hooper, and would not yield their breath till he appeared; though ever, as he stooped to whisper consolation, they shuddered at the veiled face so near their own. Such were the terrors of

the black veil, even when Death had bared his visage! Strangers came long distances to attend service at his church, with the mere idle purpose of gazing at his figure, because it was forbidden them to behold his face. But many were made to quake ere they departed! Once, during Governor Belcher's administration, Mr. Hooper was appointed to preach the election sermon. Covered with his black veil, he stood before the chief magistrate, the council, and the representatives, and wrought so deep an impression, that the legislative measures of that year were characterized by all the gloom and piety of our earliest ancestral sway.

In this manner Mr. Hooper spent a long life, irreproachable in outward act, yet shrouded in dismal suspicions; kind and loving, though unloved, and dimly feared; a man apart from men, shunned in their health and joy, but ever summoned to their aid in mortal anguish. As years wore on, shedding their snows above his sable veil, he acquired a name throughout the New-England churches, and they called him Father Hooper. Nearly all his parishioners, who were of mature age when he was settled, had been borne away by many a funeral: he had one congregation in the church, and a more crowded one in the churchyard; and having wrought so late into the evening, and done his work so well, it was now good Father Hooper's turn to rest.

Several persons were visible by the shaded candlelight, in the death-chamber of the old clergyman. Natural connections he had none. But there was the decorously grave, though unmoved physician, seeking only to mitigate the last pangs of the patient whom he could not save. There were the deacons, and other eminently pious members of his church. There, also, was the Reverend Mr. Clark, of Westbury, a young and zealous divine, who had ridden in haste to pray by the bedside of the expiring minister. There was the nurse, no hired handmaiden of death, but one whose calm affection had endured thus long, in secrecy, in solitude, amid the chill of age, and would not perish, even at the dying hour. Who, but Elizabeth! And there lay the hoary head of good Father Hooper upon the death-pillow, with the black veil still swathed about his brow and reaching down over his face, so that each more difficult gasp of his faint breath caused it to stir. All through life that piece of crape had hung between him and the world: it had separated him from cheerful brotherhood and woman's love, and kept him in that saddest of all prisons, his own heart; and still it lay upon his face, as if to deepen the gloom of his darksome chamber, and shade him from the sunshine of eternity.

For some time previous, his mind had been confused, wavering doubtfully between the past and the present, and hovering forward, as it were, at intervals, into the indistinctness of the world to come. There had been feverish turns, which tossed him from side to side, and wore away what little strength he had. But in his most convulsive struggles, and in the wildest vagaries of his intellect, when no other thought retained its sober influence, he still showed an awful solicitude lest the black veil should slip aside. Even if his bewildered soul could have forgotten, there was a faithful woman at his pillow, who, with averted eyes, would have covered that aged face, which she had last beheld in the comeliness of manhood. At length the death-stricken old man lay quietly in the torpor of mental and bodily exhaustion, with an imperceptible pulse, and breath that grew fainter and fainter, except when a long, deep, and irregular inspiration seemed to prelude the flight of his spirit.

The minister of Westbury approached the bedside.

"Venerable Father Hooper," said he, "the moment of your release is at 50 hand. Are you ready for the lifting of the veil, that shuts in time from eternity?"

Father Hooper at first replied merely by a feeble motion of his head; then, apprehensive, perhaps, that his meaning might be doubtful, he exerted himself to speak.

"Yea," said he, in faint accents, "my soul hath a patient weariness until that veil be lifted."

"And is it fitting," resumed the Reverend Mr. Clark, "that a man so given to prayer, of such a blameless example, holy in deed and thought, so far as mortal judgment may pronounce; is it fitting that a father in the church should leave a shadow on his memory, that may seem to blacken a life so pure? I pray you, my venerable brother, let not this thing be! Suffer us to be gladdened by your triumphant aspect, as you go to your reward. Before the veil of eternity be lifted, let me cast aside this black veil from your face!"

And thus speaking, the Reverend Mr. Clark bent forward to reveal the mystery of so many years. But, exerting a sudden energy, that made all the beholders stand aghast, Father Hooper snatched both his hands from beneath the bedclothes, and pressed them strongly on the black veil, resolute to struggle, if the minister of Westbury would contend with a dying man.

"Never!" cried the veiled clergyman. "On earth, never!"   55

"Dark old man!" exclaimed the affrighted minister, "with what horrible crime upon your soul are you now passing to the judgment?"

Father Hooper's breath heaved; it rattled in his throat; but, with a mighty effort, grasping forward with his hands, he caught hold of life, and held it back till he should speak. He even raised himself in bed; and there he sat, shivering with the arms of death around him, while the black veil hung down, awful, at that last moment, in the gathered terrors of a life-time. And yet the faint, sad smile, so often there, now seemed to glimmer from its obscurity, and linger on Father Hooper's lips.

"Why do you tremble at me alone?" cried he, turning his veiled face round the circle of pale spectators. "Tremble also at each other! Have men avoided me, and women shown no pity, and children screamed and fled, only for my black veil? What, but the mystery which it obscurely typifies, has made this piece of crape so awful? When the friend shows his inmost heart to his friend; the lover to his best-beloved; when man does not vainly shrink from the eye of his Creator, loathsomely treasuring up the secret of his sin; then deem me a monster, for the symbol beneath which I have lived, and die! I look around me, and, lo! on every visage a Black Veil!"

While his auditors shrank from one another, in mutual affright, Father Hooper fell back upon his pillow, a veiled corpse, with a faint smile lingering on the lips. Still veiled, they laid him in his coffin, and a veiled corpse they bore him to the grave. The grass of many years has sprung up and withered on that grave, the burial-stone is moss-grown, and good Mr. Hooper's face is dust; but awful is still the thought, that it moldered beneath the Black Veil!

CONSIDERATIONS FOR CRITICAL THINKING AND WRITING

1. FIRST RESPONSE. Why do you think Hooper wears the veil? Explain whether you think Hooper is right or wrong to wear it.

2. Describe the veil Hooper wears. How does it affect his vision?
3. Characterize the townspeople. How does the community react to the veil?
4. What is Hooper's explanation for why he wears the veil? Is he more or less effective as a minister because he wears it?
5. What is the one feature of Hooper's face that we see? What does that feature reveal about him?
6. Describe what happens at the funeral and wedding ceremonies at which Hooper officiates. How are the incidents at these events organized around the veil?
7. Why does Elizabeth think "it should be her privilege to know what the black veil concealed" (para. 25)? Why doesn't Hooper remove it at her request?
8. How does Elizabeth react to Hooper's refusal to take off the veil? Why is her response especially significant?
9. How do others in town explain why Hooper wears the veil? Do these explanations seem adequate to you? Why or why not?
10. Why is Hooper buried with the veil? Of what significance is it that grass "withered" on his grave (para. 59)?
11. Describe the story's point of view. How would a first-person narrative change the story dramatically?

CONNECTIONS TO OTHER SELECTIONS

1. How might this story be regarded as a sequel to "Young Goodman Brown"? How are the themes similar?
2. Explain how Faith in "Young Goodman Brown" (p. 331), Georgiana in "The Birthmark," and Elizabeth in "The Minister's Black Veil" are used to reveal the central male characters in each story. Describe the similarities that you see among these women characters.
3. Compare Hawthorne's use of symbol in "The Minister's Black Veil" and "The Birthmark." Write an essay explaining which symbol you think works more effectively to evoke the theme of its story.

Lady Eleanore's Mantle   1838

Not long after Colonel Shute had assumed the government of Massachusetts Bay, now nearly a hundred and twenty years ago, a young lady of rank and fortune arrived from England, to claim his protection as her guardian. He was her distant relative, but the nearest who had survived the gradual extinction of her family; so that no more eligible shelter could be found for the rich and highborn Lady Eleanore Rochcliffe than within the Province House of a transatlantic colony. The consort of Governor Shute, moreover, had been as a mother to her childhood, and was now anxious to receive her, in the hope that a beautiful young woman would be exposed to infinitely less peril from the primitive society of New England than amid the artifices and corruptions of a court. If either the Governor or his lady had especially consulted their own comfort, they would probably have sought to devolve the responsibility on other hands;

since, with some noble and splendid traits of character, Lady Eleanore was remarkable for a harsh, unyielding pride, a haughty consciousness of her hereditary and personal advantages, which made her almost incapable of control. Judging from many traditionary anecdotes, this peculiar temper was hardly less than a monomania; or, if the acts which it inspired were those of a sane person, it seemed due from Providence that pride so sinful should be followed by as severe a retribution. That tinge of the marvellous, which is thrown over so many of these half-forgotten legends, has probably imparted an additional wildness to the strange story of Lady Eleanore Rochcliffe.

The ship in which she came passenger had arrived at Newport, whence Lady Eleanore was conveyed to Boston in the Governor's coach, attended by a small escort of gentlemen on horseback. The ponderous equipage, with its four black horses, attracted much notice as it rumbled through Cornhill, surrounded by the prancing steeds of half a dozen cavaliers, with swords dangling to their stirrups and pistols at their holsters. Through the large glass windows of the coach, as it rolled along, the people could discern the figure of Lady Eleanore, strangely combining an almost queenly stateliness with the grace and beauty of a maiden in her teens. A singular tale had gone abroad among the ladies of the province, that their fair rival was indebted for much of the irresistible charm of her appearance to a certain article of dress—an embroidered mantle—which had been wrought by the most skilful artist in London, and possessed even magical properties of adornment. On the present occasion, however, she owed nothing to the witchery of dress, being clad in a riding habit of velvet, which would have appeared stiff and ungraceful on any other form.

The coachman reined in his four black steeds, and the whole cavalcade came to a pause in front of the contorted iron balustrade that fenced the Province House from the public street. It was an awkward coincidence that the bell of the Old South was just then tolling for a funeral; so that, instead of gladsome peal with which it was customary to announce the arrival of distinguished strangers, Lady Eleanore Rochcliffe was ushered by a doleful clang, as if calamity had come embodied in her beautiful person.

"A very great disrespect!" exclaimed Captain Langford, an English officer, who had recently brought dispatches to Governor Shute. "The funeral should have been deferred, lest Lady Eleanore's spirits be affected by such a dismal welcome."

"With your pardon, sir," replied Doctor Clarke, a physician, and a famous 5 champion of the popular party, "whatever the heralds may pretend, a dead beggar must have precedence of a living queen. King Death confers high privileges."

These remarks were interchanged while the speakers waited a passage through the crowd, which had gathered on each side of the gateway, leaving an open avenue to the portal of the Province House. A black slave in livery now leaped from behind the coach, and threw open the door; while at the same moment Governor Shute descended the flight of steps from his mansion, to assist Lady Eleanore in alighting. But the Governor's stately approach was anticipated in a manner that excited general astonishment. A pale young man, with his black hair all in disorder, rushed from the throng, and prostrated himself beside the coach, thus offering his person as a footstool for Lady Eleanore Rochcliffe to tread upon. She held back an instant, yet with an expression as if doubting whether the young man were worthy to bear the weight of her footstep, rather than dissatisfied to receive such awful reverence from a fellow-mortal.

"Up, sir," said the Governor, sternly, at the same time lifting his cane over the intruder. "What means the Bedlamite° by this freak?"

"Nay," answered Lady Eleanore playfully, but with more scorn than pity in her tone, "your Excellency shall not strike him. When men seek only to be trampled upon, it were a pity to deny them a favor so easily granted — and so well deserved!"

Then, though as lightly as a sunbeam on a cloud, she placed her foot upon the cowering form, and extended her hand to meet that of the Governor. There was a brief interval, during which Lady Eleanore retained this attitude; and never, surely, was there an apter emblem of aristocracy and hereditary pride trampling on human sympathies and the kindred of nature, than these two figures presented at that moment. Yet the spectators were so smitten with her beauty, and so essential did pride seem to the existence of such a creature, that they gave a simultaneous acclamation of applause.

"Who is this insolent young fellow?" inquired Captain Langford, who still 10 remained beside Doctor Clarke. "If he be in his senses, his impertinence demands the bastinado.° If mad, Lady Eleanore should be secured from further inconvenience, by his confinement."

"His name is Jervase Helwyse," answered the Doctor; "a youth of no birth or fortune, or other advantages, save the mind and soul that nature gave him; and being secretary to our colonial agent in London, it was his misfortune to meet this Lady Eleanore Rochcliffe. He loved her — and her scorn has driven him mad."

"He was mad so to aspire," observed the English officer.

"It may be so," said Doctor Clarke, frowning as he spoke. "But I tell you, sir, I could well-nigh doubt the justice of the Heaven above us if no signal humiliation overtake this lady, who now treads so haughtily into yonder mansion. She seeks to place herself above the sympathies of our common nature, which envelops all human souls. See, if that nature do not assert its claim over her in some mode that shall bring her level with the lowest!"

"Never!" cried Captain Langford indignantly — "neither in life, nor when they lay her with her ancestors."

Not many days afterwards the Governor gave a ball in honor of Lady 15 Eleanore Rochcliffe. The principal gentry of the colony received invitations, which were distributed to their residences, far and near, by messengers on horseback, bearing missives sealed with all the formality of official dispatches. In obedience to the summons, there was a general gathering of rank, wealth, and beauty; and the wide door of the Province House had seldom given admittance to more numerous and honorable guests than on the evening of Lady Eleanore's ball. Without much extravagance of eulogy, the spectacle might even be termed splendid; for, according to the fashion of the times, the ladies shone in rich silks and satins, outspread over wide-projecting hoops; and the gentlemen glittered in gold embroidery, laid unsparingly upon the purple, or scarlet, or sky-blue velvet, which was the material of their coats and waistcoats. The latter article of dress was of great importance, since it enveloped the wearer's body nearly to the knees, and was perhaps bedizened° with the amount

Bedlamite: Madman.
bastinado: A stick for beating.
bedizened: Tastelessly ornamented.

of his whole year's income, in golden flowers and foliage. The altered taste of the present day — a taste symbolic of a deep change in the whole system of society — would look upon almost any of those gorgeous figures as ridiculous; although that evening the guests sought their reflections in the pier-glasses, and rejoiced to catch their own glitter amid the glittering crowd. What a pity that one of the stately mirrors has not preserved a picture of the scene, which, by the very traits that were so transitory, might have taught us much that would be worth knowing and remembering!

Would, at least, that either painter or mirror could convey to us some faint idea of a garment, already noticed in this legend, — the Lady Eleanore's embroidered mantle, — which the gossips whispered was invested with magic properties, so as to lend a new and untried grace to her figure each time that she put it on! Idle fancy as it is, this mysterious mantle has thrown an awe around my image of her, partly from its fabled virtues, and partly because it was the handiwork of a dying woman, and, perchance, owed the fantastic grace of its conception to the delirium of approaching death.

After the ceremonial greetings had been paid, Lady Eleanore Rochcliffe stood apart from the mob of guests, insulating herself within a small and distinguished circle, to whom she accorded a more cordial favor than to the general throng. The waxen torches threw their radiance vividly over the scene, bringing out its brilliant points in strong relief; but she gazed carelessly, and with now and then an expression of weariness or scorn, tempered with such feminine grace that her auditors scarcely perceived the moral deformity of which it was the utterance. She beheld the spectacle not with vulgar ridicule, as disdaining to be pleased with the provincial mockery of a court festival, but with the deeper scorn of one whose spirit held itself too high to participate in the enjoyment of other human souls. Whether or no the recollections of those who saw her that evening were influenced by the strange events with which she was subsequently connected, so it was that her figure ever after recurred to them as marked by something wild and unnatural, — although, at the time, the general whisper was of her exceeding beauty, and of the indescribable charm which her mantle threw around her. Some close observers, indeed, detected a feverish flush and alternate paleness of countenance, with corresponding flow and revulsion of spirits, and once or twice a painful and helpless betrayal of lassitude, as if she were on the point of sinking to the ground. Then, with a nervous shudder, she seemed to arouse her energies and threw some bright and playful yet half-wicked sarcasm into the conversation. There was so strange a characteristic in her manners and sentiments that it astonished every right-minded listener; till looking in her face, a lurking and incomprehensible glance and smile perplexed them with doubts both as to her seriousness and sanity. Gradually, Lady Eleanore Rochcliffe's circle grew smaller, till only four gentlemen remained in it. These were Captain Langford, the English officer before mentioned; a Virginian planter, who had come to Massachusetts on some political errand; a young Episcopal clergyman, the grandson of a British earl; and, lastly, the private secretary of Governor Shute, whose obsequiousness had won a sort of tolerance from Lady Eleanore.

At different periods of the evening the liveried servants of the Province House passed among the guests, bearing huge trays of refreshments and French and Spanish wines. Lady Eleanore Rochcliffe, who refused to wet her beautiful lips even with a bubble of Champagne, had sunk back into a large damask chair, apparently overwearied either with the excitement of the scene or its tedium, and while, for an instant, she was unconscious of voices, laughter, and music, a young man stole forward, and knelt down at her feet. He bore a salver° in his hand, on which was a chased silver goblet, filled to the brim with wine, which he offered as reverentially as to a crowned queen, or rather with the awful devotion of a priest doing sacrifice to his idol. Conscious that some one touched her robe, Lady Eleanore started, and unclosed her eyes upon the pale, wild features and dishevelled hair of Jervase Helwyse.

"Why do you haunt me thus?" said she, in a languid tone, but with a kindlier feeling than she ordinarily permitted herself to express. "They tell me that I have done you harm."

"Heaven knows if that be so," replied the young man solemnly. "But, Lady   20
Eleanore, in requital of that harm, if such there be, and for your own earthly and heavenly welfare, I pray you to take one sip of this holy wine, and then to pass the goblet round among the guests. And this shall be a symbol that you have not sought to withdraw yourself from the chain of human sympathies — which whoso would shake off must keep company with fallen angels."

"Where has this mad fellow stolen that sacramental vessel?" exclaimed the Episcopal clergyman.

This question drew the notice of the guests to the silver cup, which was recognized as appertaining to the communion plate of the Old South Church; and, for aught that could be known, it was brimming over with the consecrated wine.

"Perhaps it is poisoned," half whispered the Governor's secretary.

"Pour it down the villain's throat!" cried the Virginian fiercely.

"Turn him out of the house!" cried Captain Langford, seizing Jervase Hel-   25
wyse so roughly by the shoulder that the sacramental cup was overturned, and its contents sprinkled upon Lady Eleanore's mantle. "Whether knave, fool, or Bedlamite, it is intolerable that the fellow should go at large."

"Pray, gentlemen, do my poor admirer no harm," said Lady Eleanore, with a faint and weary smile. "Take him out of my sight, if such be your pleasure; for I can find in my heart to do nothing but laugh at him; whereas, in all decency and conscience, it would become me to weep for the mischief I have wrought!"

But while the by-standers were attempting to lead away the unfortunate young man, he broke from them, and with a wild impassioned earnestness, offered a new and equally strange petition to Lady Eleanore. It was no other than that she should throw off the mantle, which, while he pressed the silver cup of wine upon her, she had drawn more closely around her form, so as almost to shroud herself within it.

"Cast it from you!" exclaimed Jervase Helwyse, clasping his hands in an agony of entreaty. "It may not yet be too late! Give the accursed garment to the flames!"

But Lady Eleanore, with a laugh of scorn, drew the rich folds of the embroidered mantle over her head, in such a fashion as to give a completely new aspect to her beautiful face, which — half hidden, half revealed — seemed to belong to some being of mysterious character and purposes.

"Farewell, Jervase Helwyse!" said she. "Keep my image in your remem-   30
brance, as you behold it now."

salver: A tray.

"Alas, lady!" he replied, in a tone no longer wild, but sad as a funeral bell. "We must meet shortly, when your face may wear another aspect—and that shall be the image that must abide within me."

He made no more resistance to the violent efforts of the gentlemen and servants, who almost dragged him out of the apartment, and dismissed him roughly from the iron gate of the Province House. Captain Langford, who had been very active in this affair, was returning to the presence of Lady Eleanore Rochcliffe, when he encountered the physician, Doctor Clarke, with whom he had held some casual talk on the day of her arrival. The Doctor stood apart, separated from Lady Eleanore by the width of the room, but eying her with such keen sagacity that Captain Langford involuntarily gave him credit for the discovery of some deep secret.

"You appear to be smitten, after all, with the charms of this queenly maiden," said he, hoping thus to draw forth the physician's hidden knowledge.

"God forbid!" answered Doctor Clarke, with a grave smile; "and if you be wise you will put up the same prayer for yourself. Woe to those who shall be smitten by this beautiful Lady Eleanore! But yonder stands the Governor—and I have a word or two for his private ear. Good night!"

He accordingly advanced to Governor Shute, and addressed him in so low 35 a tone that none of the by-standers could catch a word of what he said, although the sudden change of his Excellency's hitherto cheerful visage betokened that the communication could be of no agreeable import. A very few moments afterwards it was announced to the guests that an unforeseen circumstance rendered it necessary to put a premature close to the festival.

The ball at the Province House supplied a topic of conversation for the colonial metropolis for some days after its occurrence, and might still longer have been the general theme, only that a subject of all-engrossing interest thrust it, for a time, from the public recollection. This was the appearance of a dreadful epidemic, which, in that age and long before and afterwards, was wont to slay its hundreds and thousands on both sides of the Atlantic. On the occasion of which we speak, it was distinguished by a peculiar virulence, insomuch that it has left its traces—its pit-marks, to use an appropriate figure—on the history of the country, the affairs of which were thrown into confusion by its ravages. At first, unlike its ordinary course, the disease seemed to confine itself to the higher circles of society, selecting its victims from among the proud, the well-born, and the wealthy, entering unabashed into stately chambers, and lying down with the slumberers in silken beds. Some of the most distinguished guests of the Province House—even those whom the haughty Lady Eleanore Rochcliffe had deemed not unworthy of her favor—were stricken by this fatal scourge. It was noticed, with an ungenerous bitterness of feeling, that the four gentlemen—the Virginian, the British officer, the young clergyman, and the Governor's secretary—who had been her most devoted attendants on the evening of the ball, were the foremost on whom the plague stroke fell. But the disease, pursuing its onward progress, soon ceased to be exclusively a prerogative of aristocracy. Its red brand was no longer conferred like a noble's star, or an order of knighthood. It threaded its way through the narrow and crooked streets, and entered the low, mean, darksome dwellings, and laid its hand of death upon the artisans and laboring classes of the town. It compelled rich and poor to feel themselves brethren then; and stalking to and fro across the Three Hills, with a fierceness which made it almost a new pestilence, there was that mighty conqueror—that scourge and horror of our forefathers—the Small-Pox!

We cannot estimate the affright which this plague inspired of yore, by contemplating it as the fangless monster of the present day. We must remember, rather, with what awe we watched the gigantic footsteps of the Asiatic cholera, striding from shore to shore of the Atlantic, and marching like destiny upon cities far remote which flight had already half depopulated. There is no other fear so horrible and unhumanizing as that which makes man dread to breathe heaven's vital air lest it be poison, or to grasp the hand of a brother or friend lest the grip of the pestilence should clutch him. Such was the dismay that now followed in the track of the disease, or ran before it throughout the town. Graves were hastily dug, and the pestilential relics as hastily covered, because the dead were enemies of the living, and strove to draw them headlong, as it were, into their own dismal pit. The public councils were suspended, as if mortal wisdom might relinquish its devices, now that an unearthly usurper had found his way into the ruler's mansion. Had an enemy's fleet been hovering on the coast, or his armies trampling on our soil, the people would probably have committed their defence to that same direful conqueror who had wrought their own calamity, and would permit no interference with his sway. This conqueror had a symbol of his triumphs. It was a blood-red flag, that fluttered in the tainted air, over the door of every dwelling into which the Small-Pox had entered.

Such a banner was long since waving over the portal of the Province House; for thence, as was proved by tracking its footsteps back, had all this dreadful mischief issued. It had been traced back to a lady's luxurious chamber—to the proudest of the proud—to her that was so delicate, and hardly owned herself of earthly mould—to the haughty one, who took her stand above human sympathies—to Lady Eleanore! There remained no room for doubt that the contagion had lurked in that gorgeous mantle, which threw so strange a grace around her at the festival. Its fantastic splendor had been conceived in the delirious brain of a woman on her death-bed, and was the last toil of her stiffening fingers, which had interwoven fate and misery with its golden threads. This dark tale, whispered at first, was now bruited far and wide. The people raved against the Lady Eleanore, and cried out that her pride and scorn had evoked a fiend, and that, between them both, this monstrous evil had been born. At times, their rage and despair took the semblance of grinning mirth; and whenever the red flag of the pestilence was hoisted over another and yet another door, they clapped their hands and shouted through the streets, in bitter mockery: "Behold a new triumph for the Lady Eleanore!"

One day, in the midst of these dismal times, a wild figure approached the portal of the Province House, and folding his arms, stood contemplating the scarlet banner which a passing breeze shook fitfully, as if to fling abroad the contagion that it typified. At length, climbing one of the pillars by means of the iron balustrade, he took down the flag and entered the mansion, waving it above his head. At the foot of the staircase he met the Governor, booted and spurred, with his cloak drawn around him, evidently on the point of setting forth upon a journey.

"Wretched lunatic, what do you seek here?" exclaimed Shute, extending 40 his cane to guard himself from contact. "There is nothing here but Death. Back—or you will meet him!"

"Death will not touch me, the banner-bearer of the pestilence!" cried Jervase Helwyse, shaking the red flag aloft. "Death, and the Pestilence, who wears the aspect of the Lady Eleanore, will walk through the streets to-night, and I must march before them with this banner!"

"Why do I waste words on the fellow?" muttered the Governor, drawing his cloak across his mouth. "What matters his miserable life, when none of us are sure of twelve hours' breath? On, fool, to your own destruction!"

He made way for Jervase Helwyse, who immediately ascended the staircase, but, on the first landing place, was arrested by the firm grasp of a hand upon his shoulder. Looking fiercely up, with a madman's impulse to struggle with and rend asunder his opponent, he found himself powerless beneath a calm, stern eye, which possessed the mysterious property of quelling frenzy at its height. The person whom he had now encountered was the physician, Doctor Clarke, the duties of whose sad profession had led him to the Province House, where he was an infrequent guest in more prosperous times.

"Young man, what is your purpose?" demanded he.

"I seek the Lady Eleanore," answered Jervase Helwyse, submissively.   45

"All have fled from her," said the physician. "Why do you seek her now? I tell you, youth, her nurse fell death-stricken on the threshold of that fatal chamber. Know ye not, that never came such a curse to our shores as this lovely Lady Eleanore?—that her breath has filled the air with poison?—that she has shaken pestilence and death upon the land, from the folds of her accursed mantle?"

"Let me look upon her!" rejoined the mad youth, more wildly. "Let me behold her, in her awful beauty, clad in the regal garments of the pestilence! She and Death sit on a throne together. Let me kneel down before them!"

"Poor youth!" said Doctor Clarke; and, moved by a deep sense of human weakness, a smile of caustic humor curled his lip even then. "Wilt thou still worship the destroyer and surround her image with fantasies the more magnificent, the more evil she has wrought? Thus man doth ever to his tyrants. Approach, then! Madness, as I have noted, has that good efficacy, that it will guard you from contagion—and perchance its own cure may be found in yonder chamber."

Ascending another flight of stairs, he threw open a door and signed to Jervase Helwyse that he should enter. The poor lunatic, it seems probable, had cherished a delusion that his haughty mistress sat in state, unharmed herself by the pestilential influence, which, as by enchantment, she scattered round about her. He dreamed, no doubt, that her beauty was not dimmed, but brightened into superhuman splendor. With such anticipations, he stole reverentially to the door at which the physician stood, but paused upon the threshold, gazing fearfully into the gloom of the darkened chamber.

"Where is the Lady Eleanore?" whispered he.   50

"Call her," replied the physician.

"Lady Eleanore!—Princess!—Queen of Death!" cried Jervase Helwyse, advancing three steps into the chamber. "She is not here! There, on yonder table, I behold the sparkle of a diamond which once she wore upon her bosom. There"—and he shuddered—"there hangs her mantle, on which a dead woman embroidered a spell of dreadful potency. But where is the Lady Eleanore?"

Something stirred within the silken curtains of a canopied bed; and a low moan was uttered, which, listening intently, Jervase Helwyse began to distinguish as a woman's voice, complaining dolefully of thirst. He fancied, even, that he recognized its tones.

"My throat! — my throat is scorched," murmured the voice. "A drop of water!"

"What thing art thou?" said the brain-stricken youth, drawing near the 55 bed and tearing asunder its curtains. "Whose voice hast thou stolen for thy murmurs and miserable petitions, as if Lady Eleanore could be conscious of mortal infirmity? Fie! Heap of diseased mortality, why lurkest thou in my lady's chamber?"

"O Jervase Helwyse," said the voice — and as it spoke the figure contorted itself, struggling to hide its blasted face — "look not now on the woman you once loved! The curse of Heaven hath stricken me, because I would not call man my brother, nor woman sister. I wrapped myself in PRIDE as in a MANTLE, and scorned the sympathies of nature; and therefore has nature made this wretched body the medium of a dreadful sympathy. You are avenged — they are all avenged — Nature is avenged — for I am Eleanore Rochcliffe!"

The malice of his mental disease, the bitterness lurking at the bottom of his heart, mad as he was, for a blighted and ruined life, and love that had been paid with cruel scorn, awoke within the breast of Jervase Helwyse. He shook his finger at the wretched girl, and the chamber echoed, the curtains of the bed were shaken, with his outburst of insane merriment.

"Another triumph for the Lady Eleanore!" he cried. "All have been her victims! Who so worthy to be the final victim as herself?"

Impelled by some new fantasy of his crazed intellect, he snatched the fatal mantle and rushed from the chamber and the house. That night a procession passed, by torchlight, through the streets, bearing in the midst the figure of a woman, enveloped with a richly embroidered mantle; while in advance stalked Jervase Helwyse, waving the red flag of the pestilence. Arriving opposite the Province House, the mob burned the effigy, and a strong wind came and swept away the ashes. It was said that, from that very hour, the pestilence abated, as if its sway had some mysterious connection, from the first plague stroke to the last, with Lady Eleanore's Mantle. A remarkable uncertainty broods over that unhappy lady's fate. There is a belief, however, that in a certain chamber of this mansion a female form may sometimes be duskily discerned, shrinking into the darkest corner and muffling her face within an embroidered mantle. Supposing the legend true, can this be other than the once proud Lady Eleanore?

CONSIDERATIONS FOR CRITICAL THINKING AND WRITING

1. FIRST RESPONSE. In what sense does Hawthorne's first paragraph essentially reveal the plot of the story? Explain why this information enhances or diminishes your experience of reading the story.

2. Identify instances of foreshadowing throughout the story. Do the foreshadowings make the story more or less suspenseful for you?

3. What do you think is the theme? Point to paragraphs in the story that directly state the theme. Explain why you think this is or is not an effective strategy for conveying the story's theme.

4. What is a "monomania"? Which passages specifically indicate Lady Eleanore's "peculiar temper"?

5. What values are associated with England as opposed to the Massachusetts Bay Colony? How are these settings related to Lady Eleanore's character?

6. What kinds of "magic properties" does the mantle have?

7. Explain why you think the mantle is most accurately described as an allegory or symbol.

8. What does Jervase Helwyse reveal about Lady Eleanore's character?

9. What details associated with Dr. Clarke make him a particularly appropriate commentator on her behavior?

10. Comment on the appropriateness of Lady Eleanore's and Jervase's last names. How are they related to the theme?

11. CRITICAL STRATEGIES. Read the section on formalist criticism (pp. 2095–97) in Chapter 52, "Critical Strategies for Reading," and discuss Hawthorne's use of irony in this story.

CONNECTIONS TO OTHER SELECTIONS

1. Discuss the significance of Lady Eleanore's mantle and the veil in "The Minister's Black Veil" (p. 341). Which piece of cloth do you find more fascinating? Explain why.

2. Discuss the treatment of pride in "Lady Eleanore's Mantle" and in "The Birthmark" (below). Explain which protagonist seems more plausibly motivated to you.

3. In an essay explore the themes of isolation in this story and in one other Hawthorne story in this chapter.

The Birthmark   *1843*

In the latter part of the last century there lived a man of science, an eminent proficient in every branch of natural philosophy, who not long before our story opens had made experience of a spiritual affinity more attractive than any chemical one. He had left his laboratory to the care of an assistant, cleared his fine countenance from the furnace smoke, washed the stain of acids from his fingers, and persuaded a beautiful woman to become his wife. In those days when the comparatively recent discovery of electricity and other kindred mysteries of Nature seemed to open paths into the region of miracle, it was not unusual for the love of science to rival the love of woman in its depth and absorbing energy. The higher intellect, the imagination, the spirit, and even the heart might all find their congenial aliment in pursuits which, as some of their ardent votaries believed, would ascend from one step of powerful intelligence to another, until the philosopher should lay his hand on the secret of creative force and perhaps make new worlds for himself. We know not whether Aylmer possessed this degree of faith in man's ultimate control over Nature. He had devoted himself, however, too unreservedly to scientific studies ever to be weaned from them by any second passion. His love for his young wife might prove the stronger of the two; but it could only be by intertwining itself with his love of science, and uniting the strength of the latter to his own.

Such a union accordingly took place, and was attended with truly remarkable consequences and a deeply impressive moral. One day, very soon after their marriage, Aylmer sat gazing at his wife with a trouble in his countenance that grew stronger until he spoke.

"Georgiana," said he, "has it never occurred to you that the mark upon your cheek might be removed?"

"No, indeed," said she, smiling; but perceiving the seriousness of his manner, she blushed deeply. "To tell you the truth it has been so often called a charm that I was simple enough to imagine it might be so."

"Ah, upon another face perhaps it might," replied her husband; "but never on yours. No, dearest Georgiana, you came so nearly perfect from the hand of Nature that this slightest possible defect, which we hesitate whether to term a defect or a beauty, shocks me, as being the visible mark of earthly imperfection."

"Shocks you, my husband!" cried Georgiana, deeply hurt; at first reddening with momentary anger, but then bursting into tears. "Then why did you take me from my mother's side? You cannot love what shocks you!"

To explain this conversation it must be mentioned that in the center of Georgiana's left cheek there was a singular mark, deeply interwoven, as it were, with the texture and substance of her face. In the usual state of her complexion — a healthy though delicate bloom — the mark wore a tint of deeper crimson, which imperfectly defined its shape amid the surrounding rosiness. When she blushed it gradually became more indistinct, and finally vanished amid the triumphant rush of blood that bathed the whole cheek with its brilliant glow. But if any shifting motion caused her to turn pale, there was the mark again, a crimson stain upon the snow, in what Aylmer sometimes deemed an almost fearful distinctness. Its shape bore not a little similarity to the human hand, though of the smallest pygmy size. Georgiana's lovers were wont to say that some fairy at her birth hour had laid her tiny hand upon the infant's cheek, and left this impress there in token of the magic endowments that were to give her such sway over all hearts. Many a desperate swain would have risked life for the privilege of pressing his lips to the mysterious hand. It must not be concealed, however, that the impression wrought by this fairy sign manual varied exceedingly, according to the difference of temperament in the beholders. Some fastidious persons — but they were exclusively of her own sex — affirmed that the bloody hand, as they chose to call it, quite destroyed the effect of Georgiana's beauty, and rendered her countenance even hideous. But it would be as reasonable to say that one of those small blue stains which sometimes occur in the purest statuary marble would convert the Eve of Powers to a monster. Masculine observers, if the birthmark did not heighten their admiration, contented themselves with wishing it away, that the world might possess one living specimen of ideal loveliness without the semblance of a flaw. After his marriage, — for he thought little or nothing of the matter before, — Aylmer discovered that this was the case with himself.

Had she been less beautiful, — if Envy's self could have found aught else to sneer at, — he might have felt his affection heightened by the prettiness of this mimic hand, now vaguely portrayed, now lost, now stealing forth again and glimmering to and fro with every pulse of emotion that throbbed within her heart; but seeing her otherwise so perfect, he found this one defect grow more and more intolerable with every moment of their united lives. It was the fatal flaw of humanity which Nature, in one shape or another, stamps ineffaceably on all her productions, either to imply that they are temporary and finite, or that their perfection must be wrought by toil and pain. The crimson hand expressed the ineludible gripe° in which mortality clutches the highest and purest of earthly mold, degrading them into kindred with the lowest, and even with the very brutes, like whom their visible frames return to dust. In this manner, selecting it as the symbol of his wife's liability to sin, sorrow, decay, and death, Aylmer's somber imagination was not long in rendering the birthmark a frightful object, causing him more trouble and horror than ever Georgiana's beauty, whether of soul or sense, had given him delight.

At all the seasons which should have been their happiest, he invariably and without intending it, nay, in spite of a purpose to the contrary, reverted to this one disastrous topic. Trifling as it at first appeared, it so connected itself with innumerable trains of thought and modes of feeling that it became the central point of all. With the morning twilight Aylmer opened his eyes upon his wife's face and recognized the symbol of imperfection; and when they sat together at the evening hearth his eyes wandered stealthily to her cheek, and beheld, flickering with the blaze of the wood fire, the spectral hand that wrote mortality where he would fain have worshiped. Georgiana soon learned to shudder at his gaze. It needed but a glance with the peculiar expression that his face often wore to change the roses of her cheek into a deathlike paleness, amid which the crimson hand was brought strongly out, like a bas-relief of ruby on the whitest marble.

Late one night when the lights were growing dim, so as hardly to betray   10
the stain on the poor wife's cheek, she herself, for the first time, voluntarily took up the subject.

"Do you remember, my dear Aylmer," said she, with a feeble attempt at a smile, "have you any recollection of a dream last night about this odious hand?"

"None! none whatever!" replied Aylmer, starting; but then he added, in a dry, cold tone, affected for the sake of concealing the real depth of his emotion, "I might well dream of it; for before I fell asleep it had taken a pretty firm hold of my fancy."

"And you did dream of it?" continued Georgiana hastily, for she dreaded lest a gush of tears should interrupt what she had to say. "A terrible dream! I wonder that you can forget it. Is it possible to forget this one expression? — 'It is in her heart now; we must have it out!' Reflect, my husband; for by all means I would have you recall that dream."

The mind is in a sad state when Sleep, the all-involving, cannot confine her specters within the dim region of her sway, but suffers them to break forth, affrighting this actual life with secrets that perchance belong to a deeper one. Aylmer now remembered his dream. He had fancied himself with his servant Aminadab, attempting an operation for the removal of the birthmark; but the deeper went the knife, the deeper sank the hand, until at length its tiny grasp appeared to have caught hold of Georgiana's heart; whence, however, her husband was inexorably resolved to cut or wrench it away.

When the dream had shaped itself perfectly in his memory, Aylmer sat in   15
his wife's presence with a guilty feeling. Truth often finds its way to the mind close muffled in robes of sleep, and then speaks with uncompromising directness of matters in regard to which we practice an unconscious self-deception

---

gripe: Grip.

during our waking moments. Until now he had not been aware of the tyrannizing influence acquired by one idea over his mind, and of the lengths which he might find in his heart to go for the sake of giving himself peace.

"Aylmer," resumed Georgiana solemnly, "I know not what may be the cost to both of us to rid me of this fatal birthmark. Perhaps its removal may cause cureless deformity; or it may be the stain goes as deep as life itself. Again: do we know that there is a possibility, on any terms, of unclasping the firm grip of this little hand which was laid upon me before I came into the world?"

"Dearest Georgiana, I have spent much thought upon the subject," hastily interrupted Aylmer. "I am convinced of the perfect practicability of its removal."

"If there be the remotest possibility of it," continued Georgiana, "let the attempt be made at whatever risk. Danger is nothing to me; for life, while this hateful mark makes me the object of your horror and disgust, — life is a burden which I would fling down with joy. Either remove this dreadful hand, or take my wretched life! You have deep science. All the world bears witness of it. You have achieved great wonders. Cannot you remove this little, little mark, which I cover with the tips of two small fingers? Is this beyond your power, for the sake of your own peace, and to save your poor wife from madness?"

"Noblest, dearest, tenderest wife," cried Aylmer rapturously, "doubt not my power. I have already given this matter the deepest thought — thought which might almost have enlightened me to create a being less perfect than yourself. Georgiana, you have led me deeper than ever into the heart of science. I feel myself fully competent to render this dear cheek as faultless as its fellow; and then, most beloved, what will be my triumph when I shall have corrected what Nature left imperfect in her fairest work! Even Pygmalion, when his sculptured woman assumed life, felt not greater ecstasy than mine will be."

"It is resolved, then," said Georgiana, faintly smiling. "And, Aylmer, spare 20 me not, though you should find the birthmark take refuge in my heart at last."

Her husband tenderly kissed her cheek — her right cheek — not that which bore the impress of the crimson hand.

The next day Aylmer apprised his wife of a plan that he had formed whereby he might have opportunity for the intense thought and constant watchfulness which the proposed operation would require; while Georgiana, likewise, would enjoy the perfect repose essential to its success. They were to seclude themselves in the extensive apartments occupied by Aylmer as a laboratory, and where, during his toilsome youth, he had made discoveries in the elemental powers of Nature that had roused the admiration of all the learned societies in Europe. Seated calmly in this laboratory, the pale philosopher had investigated the secrets of the highest cloud region and of the profoundest mines; he had satisfied himself of the causes that kindled and kept alive the fires of the volcano; and had explained the mystery of fountains, and how it is that they gush forth, some so bright and pure, and others with such rich medicinal virtues, from the dark bosom of the earth. Here, too, at an earlier period, he had studied the wonders of the human frame, and attempted to fathom the very process by which Nature assimilates all her precious influences from earth and air, and from the spiritual world, to create and foster man, her masterpiece. The latter pursuit, however, Aylmer had long laid aside in unwilling recognition of the truth — against which all seekers sooner or later stumble — that our great creative Mother, while she amuses us with apparently working in the broadest sunshine, is yet severely careful to keep her own secrets, and, in spite of her pretended openness, shows us nothing but results. She permits us, indeed, to mar, but seldom to mend, and, like a jealous patentee, on no account to make. Now, however, Aylmer resumed these half-forgotten investigations, — not, of course, with such hopes or wishes as first suggested them, but because they involved much physiological truth and lay in the path of his proposed scheme for the treatment of Georgiana.

As he led her over the threshold of the laboratory, Georgiana was cold and tremulous. Aylmer looked cheerfully into her face, with intent to reassure her, but was so startled with the intense glow of the birthmark upon the whiteness of her cheek that he could not restrain a strong convulsive shudder. His wife fainted.

"Aminadab! Aminadab!" shouted Aylmer, stamping violently on the floor.

Forthwith there issued from an inner apartment a man of low stature, but 25 bulky frame, with shaggy hair hanging about his visage, which was grimed with the vapors of the furnace. This personage had been Aylmer's underworker during his whole scientific career, and was admirably fitted for that office by his great mechanical readiness, and the skill with which, while incapable of comprehending a single principle, he executed all the details of his master's experiments. With his vast strength, his shaggy hair, his smoky aspect, and the indescribable earthiness that encrusted him, he seemed to represent man's physical nature; while Aylmer's slender figure, and pale, intellectual face, were no less apt a type of the spiritual element.

"Throw open the door of the boudoir, Aminadab," said Aylmer, "and burn a pastille."

"Yes, master," answered Aminadab, looking intently at the lifeless form of Georgiana; and then he muttered to himself, "If she were my wife, I'd never part with that birthmark."

When Georgiana recovered consciousness she found herself breathing an atmosphere of penetrating fragrance, the gentle potency of which had recalled her from her deathlike faintness. The scene around her looked like enchantment. Aylmer had converted those smoky, dingy, somber rooms, where he had spent his brightest years in recondite pursuits, into a series of beautiful apartments not unfit to be the secluded abode of a lovely woman. The walls were hung with gorgeous curtains, which imparted the combination of grandeur and grace that no other species of adornment can achieve; and as they fell from the ceiling to the floor, their rich and ponderous folds, concealing all angles and straight lines, appeared to shut in the scene from infinite space. For aught Georgiana knew, it might be a pavilion among the clouds. And Aylmer, excluding the sunshine, which would have interfered with his chemical processes, had supplied its place with perfumed lamps, emitting flames of various hue, but all uniting in a soft, empurpled radiance. He now knelt by his wife's side, watching her earnestly, but without alarm; for he was confident in his science, and felt that he could draw a magic circle round her within which no evil might intrude.

"Where am I? Ah, I remember," said Georgiana faintly; and she placed her hand over her cheek to hide the terrible mark from her husband's eyes.

"Fear not, dearest!" exclaimed he. "Do not shrink from me! Believe me, 30 Georgiana, I even rejoice in this single imperfection, since it will be such a rapture to remove it."

"Oh, spare me!" sadly replied his wife. "Pray do not look at it again. I never can forget that convulsive shudder."

In order to soothe Georgiana, and, as it were, to release her mind from the burden of actual things, Aylmer now put in practice some of the light and playful secrets which science had taught him among its profounder lore. Airy figures, absolutely bodiless ideas, and forms of unsubstantial beauty came and danced before her, imprinting their momentary footsteps on beams of light. Though she had some indistinct idea of the method of these optical phenomena, still the illusion was almost perfect enough to warrant the belief that her husband possessed sway over the spiritual world. Then again, when she felt a wish to look forth from her seclusion, immediately, as if her thoughts were answered, the procession of external existence flitted across a screen. The scenery and the figures of actual life were perfectly represented, but with that bewitching, yet indescribable difference which always makes a picture, an image, or a shadow so much more attractive than the original. When wearied of this, Aylmer bade her cast her eyes upon a vessel containing a quantity of earth. She did so, with little interest at first; but was soon startled to perceive the germ of a plant shooting upward from the soil. Then came the slender stalk; the leaves gradually unfolded themselves; and amid them was a perfect and lovely flower.

"It is magical!" cried Georgiana. "I dare not touch it."

"Nay, pluck it," answered Aylmer: "pluck it, and inhale its brief perfume while you may. The flower will wither in a few moments and leave nothing save its brown seed vessels; but thence may be perpetuated a race as ephemeral as itself."

But Georgiana had no sooner touched the flower than the whole plant 35 suffered a blight, its leaves turning coal-black as if by the agency of fire.

"There was too powerful a stimulus," said Aylmer thoughtfully.

To make up for this abortive experiment, he proposed to take her portrait by a scientific process of his own invention. It was to be effected by rays of light striking upon a polished plate of metal. Georgiana assented; but, on looking at the result, was affrighted to find the features of the portrait blurred and indefinable; while the minute figure of a hand appeared where the cheek should have been. Aylmer snatched the metallic plate and threw it into a jar of corrosive acid.

Soon, however, he forgot these mortifying failures. In the intervals of study and chemical experiment he came to her flushed and exhausted, but seemed invigorated by her presence, and spoke in glowing language of the resources of his art. He gave a history of the long dynasty of the alchemists, who spent so many ages in quest of the universal solvent by which the golden principle might be elicited from all things vile and base. Aylmer appeared to believe that, by the plainest scientific logic, it was altogether within the limits of possibility to discover this long-sought medium; "but," he added, "a philosopher who should go deep enough to acquire the power would attain too lofty a wisdom to stoop to the exercise of it." Not less singular were his opinions in regard to the elixir vitae. He more than intimated that it was at his option to concoct a liquid that should prolong life for years, perhaps interminably; but that it would produce a discord in Nature which all the world, and chiefly the quaffer of the immortal nostrum, would find cause to curse.

"Aylmer, are you in earnest?" asked Georgiana, looking at him with amazement and fear. "It is terrible to possess such power, or even to dream of possessing it."

"Oh, do not tremble, my love," said her husband. "I would not wrong 40 either you or myself by working such inharmonious effects upon our lives; but

I would have you consider how trifling, in comparison, is the skill requisite to remove this little hand."

At the mention of the birthmark, Georgiana, as usual, shrank as if a red-hot iron had touched her cheek.

Again Aylmer applied himself to his labors. She could hear his voice in the distant furnace-room giving directions to Aminadab, whose harsh, uncouth, misshapen tones were audible in response, more like the grunt or growl of a brute than human speech. After hours of absence, Aylmer reappeared and proposed that she should now examine his cabinet of chemical products and natural treasures of the earth. Among the former he showed her a small vial, in which, he remarked, was contained a gentle yet most powerful fragrance, capable of impregnating all the breezes that blow across a kingdom. They were of inestimable value, the contents of that little vial; and, as he said so, he threw some of the perfume into the air and filled the room with piercing and invigorating delight.

"And what is this?" asked Georgiana, pointing to a small crystal globe containing a gold-colored liquid. "It is so beautiful to the eye that I could imagine it the elixir of life."

"In one sense it is," replied Aylmer; "or rather, the elixir of immortality. It is the most precious poison that ever was concocted in this world. By its aid I could apportion the lifetime of any mortal at whom you might point your finger. The strength of the dose would determine whether he were to linger out years, or drop dead in the midst of a breath. No king on his guarded throne could keep his life if I, in my private station, should deem that the welfare of millions justified me in depriving him of it."

"Why do you keep such a terrific drug?" inquired Georgiana in horror. 45

"Do not mistrust me, dearest," said her husband, smiling; "its virtuous potency is yet greater than its harmful one. But see! here is a powerful cosmetic. With a few drops of this in a vase of water, freckles may be washed away as easily as the hands are cleansed. A stronger infusion would take the blood out of the cheek, and leave the rosiest beauty a pale ghost."

"Is it with this lotion that you intend to bathe my cheek?" asked Georgiana, anxiously.

"Oh, no," hastily replied her husband; "this is merely superficial. Your case demands a remedy that shall go deeper."

In his interviews with Georgiana, Aylmer generally made minute inquiries as to her sensations and whether the confinement of the rooms and the temperature of the atmosphere agreed with her. These questions had such a particular drift that Georgiana began to conjecture that she was already subjected to certain physical influences, either breathed in with the fragrant air or taken with her food. She fancied likewise, but it might be altogether fancy, that there was a stirring up of her system — a strange, indefinite sensation creeping through her veins, and tingling, half painfully, half pleasurably, at her heart. Still, whenever she dared to look into the mirror, there she beheld herself pale as a white rose and with the crimson birthmark stamped upon her cheek. Not even Aylmer now hated it so much as she.

To dispel the tedium of the hours which her husband found it necessary 50 to devote to the processes of combination and analysis, Georgiana turned over the volumes of his scientific library. In many dark old tomes she met with chapters full of romance and poetry. They were the works of the philosophers of the middle ages, such as Albertus Magnus, Cornelius Agrippa, Paracelsus, and the famous friar who created the prophetic Brazen Head. All these antique naturalists stood in advance of their centuries, yet were imbued with some of their credulity, and therefore were believed, and perhaps imagined themselves to have acquired from the investigation of Nature a power above Nature, and from physics a sway over the spiritual world. Hardly less curious and imaginative were the early volumes of the Transactions of the Royal Society, in which the members, knowing little of the limits of natural possibility, were continually recording wonders or proposing methods whereby wonders might be wrought.

But to Georgiana the most engrossing volume was a large folio from her husband's own hand, in which he had recorded every experiment of his scientific career, its original aim, the methods adopted for its development, and its final success or failure, with the circumstances to which either event was attributable. The book, in truth, was both the history and emblem of his ardent, ambitious, imaginative, yet practical and laborious life. He handled physical details as if there were nothing beyond them; yet spiritualized them all, and redeemed himself from materialism by his strong and eager aspiration towards the infinite. In his grasp the veriest clod of earth assumed a soul. Georgiana, as she read, reverenced Aylmer and loved him more profoundly than ever, but with a less entire dependence on his judgment than heretofore. Much as he had accomplished, she could not but observe that his most splendid successes were almost invariably failures, if compared with the ideal at which he aimed. His brightest diamonds were the merest pebbles, and felt to be so by himself, in comparison with the inestimable gems which lay hidden beyond his reach. The volume, rich with achievements that had won renown for its author, was yet as melancholy a record as ever mortal hand had penned. It was the sad confession and continual exemplification of the shortcomings of the composite man, the spirit burdened with clay and working in matter, and of the despair that assails the higher nature at finding itself so miserably thwarted by the earthly part. Perhaps every man of genius in whatever sphere might recognize the image of his own experience in Aylmer's journal.

So deeply did these reflections affect Georgiana that she laid her face upon the open volume and burst into tears. In this situation she was found by her husband.

"It is dangerous to read in a sorcerer's books," said he with a smile, though his countenance was uneasy and displeased. "Georgiana, there are pages in that volume which I can scarcely glance over and keep my senses. Take heed lest it prove as detrimental to you."

"It has made me worship you more than ever," said she.

"Ah, wait for this one success," rejoined he, "then worship me if you will. I shall deem myself hardly unworthy of it. But come, I have sought you for the luxury of your voice. Sing to me, dearest." 55

So she poured out the liquid music of her voice to quench the thirst of his spirit. He then took his leave with a boyish exuberance of gaiety, assuring her that her seclusion would endure but a little longer, and that the result was already certain. Scarcely had he departed when Georgiana felt irresistibly impelled to follow him. She had forgotten to inform Aylmer of a symptom which for two or three hours past had begun to excite her attention. It was a sensation in the fatal birthmark, not painful, but which induced a restlessness throughout her system. Hastening after her husband, she intruded for the first time into the laboratory.

The first thing that struck her eye was the furnace, that hot and feverish worker, with the intense glow of its fire, which by the quantities of soot clustered above it seemed to have been burning for ages. There was a distilling apparatus in full operation. Around the room were retorts, tubes, cylinders, crucibles, and other apparatus of chemical research. An electrical machine stood ready for immediate use. The atmosphere felt oppressively close, and was tainted with gaseous odors which had been tormented forth by the processes of science. The severe and homely simplicity of the apartment, with its naked walls and brick pavement, looked strange, accustomed as Georgiana had become to the fantastic elegance of her boudoir. But what chiefly, indeed almost solely, drew her attention, was the aspect of Aylmer himself.

He was pale as death, anxious and absorbed, and hung over the furnace as if it depended upon his utmost watchfulness whether the liquid which it was distilling should be the draught of immortal happiness or misery. How different from the sanguine and joyous mien that he had assumed for Georgiana's encouragement!

"Carefully now, Aminadab; carefully, thou human machine; carefully, thou man of clay!" muttered Aylmer, more to himself than his assistant. "Now, if there be a thought too much or too little, it is all over."

"Ho! ho!" mumbled Aminadab. "Look, master! look!"   60

Aylmer raised his eyes hastily, and at first reddened, then grew paler than ever, on beholding Georgiana. He rushed towards her and seized her arm with a gripe that left the print of his fingers upon it.

"Why do you come hither? Have you no trust in your husband?" cried he impetuously. "Would you throw the blight of that fatal birthmark over my labors? It is not well done. Go, prying woman, go!"

"Nay, Aylmer," said Georgiana with the firmness of which she possessed no stinted endowment, "it is not you that have a right to complain. You mistrust your wife; you have concealed the anxiety with which you watch the development of this experiment. Think not so unworthily of me, my husband. Tell me all the risk we run, and fear not that I shall shrink; for my share in it is far less than your own."

"No, no, Georgiana!" said Aylmer impatiently; "it must not be."

"I submit," replied she calmly. "And, Aylmer, I shall quaff whatever   65
draught you bring me; but it will be on the same principle that would induce me to take a dose of poison if offered by your hand."

"My noble wife," said Aylmer, deeply moved, "I knew not the height and depth of your nature until now. Nothing shall be concealed. Know, then, that this crimson hand, superficial as it seems, has clutched its grasp into your being with a strength of which I had no previous conception. I have already administered agents powerful enough to do aught except to change your entire physical system. Only one thing remains to be tried. If that fails us we are ruined."

"Why did you hesitate to tell me this?" asked she.

"Because, Georgiana," said Aylmer in a low voice, "there is danger."

"Danger? There is but one danger — that this horrible stigma shall be left upon my cheek!" cried Georgiana. "Remove it, remove it, whatever be the cost, or we shall both go mad!"

"Heaven knows your words are too true," said Aylmer sadly. "And now, 70 dearest, return to your boudoir. In a little while all will be tested."

He conducted her back and took leave of her with a solemn tenderness which spoke far more than his words how much was now at stake. After his departure Georgiana became rapt in musings. She considered the character of Aylmer, and did it completer justice than at any previous moment. Her heart exulted, while it trembled, at his honorable love — so pure and lofty that it would accept nothing less than perfection nor miserably make itself contented with an earthlier nature than he had dreamed of. She felt how much more precious was such a sentiment than that meaner kind which would have borne with the imperfection for her sake, and have been guilty of treason to holy love by degrading its perfect idea to the level of the actual; and with her whole spirit she prayed that, for a single moment, she might satisfy his highest and deepest conception. Longer than one moment she well knew it could not be; for his spirit was ever on the march, ever ascending, and each instant required something that was beyond the scope of the instant before.

The sound of her husband's footsteps aroused her. He bore a crystal goblet containing a liquor colorless as water, but bright enough to be the draught of immortality. Aylmer was pale; but it seemed rather the consequence of a highly wrought state of mind and tension of spirit than of fear or doubt.

"The concoction of the draught has been perfect," said he, in answer to Georgiana's look. "Unless all my science have deceived me, it cannot fail."

"Save on your account, my dearest Aylmer," observed his wife, "I might wish to put off this birthmark of mortality by relinquishing mortality itself in preference to any other mode. Life is but a sad possession to those who have attained precisely the degree of moral advancement at which I stand. Were I weaker and blinder it might be happiness. Were I stronger, it might be endured hopefully. But, being what I find myself, methinks I am of all mortals the most fit to die."

"You are fit for heaven without tasting death!" replied her husband. "But 75 why do we speak of dying? The draught cannot fail. Behold its effect upon this plant."

On the window seat there stood a geranium diseased with yellow blotches, which had overspread all its leaves. Aylmer poured a small quantity of the liquid upon the soil in which it grew. In a little time, when the roots of the plant had taken up the moisture, the unsightly blotches began to be extinguished in a living verdure.

"There needed no proof," said Georgiana quietly. "Give me the goblet. I joyfully stake all upon your word."

"Drink, then, thou lofty creature!" exclaimed Aylmer, with fervid admiration. "There is no taint of imperfection on thy spirit. Thy sensible frame, too, shall soon be all perfect."

She quaffed the liquid and returned the goblet to his hand.

"It is grateful," said she, with a placid smile. "Methinks it is like water 80 from a heavenly fountain; for it contains I know not what of unobtrusive fragrance and deliciousness. It allays a feverish thirst that had parched me for many days. Now, dearest, let me sleep. My earthly senses are closing over my spirit like the leaves around the heart of a rose at sunset."

She spoke the last words with a gentle reluctance, as if it required almost more energy than she could command to pronounce the faint and lingering syllables. Scarcely had they loitered through her lips ere she was lost in slumber. Aylmer sat by her side, watching her aspect with the emotions proper to a man the whole value of whose existence was involved in the process now to be tested. Mingled with this mood, however, was the philosophic investigation characteristic of the man of science. Not the minutest symptom escaped him. A heightened flush of the cheek, a slight irregularity of breath, a quiver of the eyelid, a hardly perceptible tremor through the frame, — such were the details which, as the moments passed, he wrote down in his folio volume. Intense thought had set its stamp upon every previous page of that volume, but the thoughts of years were all concentrated upon the last.

While thus employed, he failed not to gaze often at the fatal hand, and not without a shudder. Yet once, by a strange and unaccountable impulse, he pressed it with his lips. His spirit recoiled, however, in the very act; and Georgiana, out of the midst of her deep sleep, moved uneasily and murmured as if in remonstrance. Again Aylmer resumed his watch. Nor was it without avail. The crimson hand, which at first had been strongly visible upon the marble paleness of Georgiana's cheek, now grew more faintly outlined. She remained not less pale than ever; but the birthmark, with every breath that came and went, lost somewhat of its former distinctness. Its presence had been awful; its departure was more awful still. Watch the stain of the rainbow fading out of the sky, and you will know how that mysterious symbol passed away.

"By Heaven! it is well-nigh gone!" said Aylmer to himself, in almost irrepressible ecstasy. "I can scarcely trace it now. Success! success! And now it is like the faintest rose color. The lightest flush of blood across her cheek would overcome it. But she is so pale!"

He drew aside the window curtain and suffered the light of natural day to fall into the room and rest upon her cheek. At the same time he heard a gross, hoarse chuckle, which he had long known as his servant Aminadab's expression of delight.

"Ah, clod! ah, earthly mass!" cried Aylmer, laughing in a sort of frenzy, 85 "you have served me well! Matter and spirit — earth and heaven — have both done their part in this! Laugh, thing of the senses! You have earned the right to laugh."

These exclamations broke Georgiana's sleep. She slowly unclosed her eyes and gazed into the mirror which her husband had arranged for that purpose. A faint smile flitted over her lips when she recognized how barely perceptible was now that crimson hand which had once blazed forth with such disastrous brilliancy as to scare away all their happiness. But then her eyes sought Aylmer's face with a trouble and anxiety that he could by no means account for.

"My poor Aylmer!" murmured she.

"Poor? Nay, richest, happiest, most favored!" exclaimed he. "My peerless bride, it is successful! You are perfect!"

"My poor Aylmer," she repeated, with a more than human tenderness, "you have aimed loftily; you have done nobly. Do not repent that with so high and pure a feeling, you have rejected the best the earth could offer. Aylmer, dearest Aylmer, I am dying!"

Alas! it was too true! The fatal hand had grappled with the mystery of life, 90 and was the bond by which an angelic spirit kept itself in union with a mortal frame. As the last crimson tint of the birthmark — that sole token of human imperfection — faded from her cheek, the parting breath of the now perfect woman passed into the atmosphere, and her soul, lingering a moment near her husband, took its heavenward flight. Then a hoarse, chuckling laugh was heard again! Thus ever does the gross fatality of earth exult in its invariable triumph over the immortal essence which, in this dim sphere of half development, demands the completeness of a higher state. Yet, had Aylmer reached a profounder wisdom, he need not thus have flung away the happiness which would have woven his mortal life of the selfsame texture with the celestial. The momentary circumstance was too strong for him; he failed to look beyond the shadowy scope of time, and, living once for all in eternity, to find the perfect future in the present.

CONSIDERATIONS FOR CRITICAL THINKING AND WRITING

1. FIRST RESPONSE. Consider this story as an early version of our contemporary obsession with physical perfection. What significant similarities — and differences — do you find?

2. Is Aylmer evil? Is he simply a stock version of a mad scientist? In what sense might he be regarded as an idealist?

3. What does the birthmark symbolize? How does Aylmer's view of it differ from the other perspectives provided in the story? What is the significance of its handlike shape?

4. Does Aylmer love Georgiana? Why does she allow him to risk her life to remove the birthmark?

5. In what sense can Aylmer be characterized as guilty of the sin of pride?

6. How is Aminadab a foil for Aylmer?

7. What is the significance of the descriptions of Aylmer's laboratory?

8. What do Aylmer's other experiments reveal about the nature of his work? How do they constitute foreshadowings of what will happen to Georgiana?

9. What is the theme of the story? What point is made about what it means to be a human being?

10. Despite the risks to Georgiana, Aylmer conducts his experiments in the hope and expectation of achieving a higher good. He devotes his life to science, and yet he is an egotist. Explain.

11. Discuss the extent to which Georgiana is responsible for her own death.

CONNECTIONS TO OTHER SELECTIONS

1. Compare Aylmer's unwillingness to accept things as they are with Young Goodman Brown's refusal to be a part of a community he regards as fallen.

2. What similarities do you see in Aylmer's growing feelings about the "crimson hand" on Georgiana's cheek and the young wife's feelings about her husband's hand in Colette's "The Hand" (p. 228)? How do Aylmer and the young wife cope with these feelings? How do you account for the differences between them?

PERSPECTIVES ON HAWTHORNE

Hawthorne on Solitude   *1837*

Dear Sir,

    Not to burthen you with my correspondence, I have delayed a rejoinder to your very kind and cordial letter, until now. It gratifies me to find that you have occasionally felt an interest in my situation. . . . You would have been nearer the truth if you had pictured me as dwelling in an owl's nest; for mine is about as dismal; and, like the owl I seldom venture abroad till after dark. By some witchcraft or other — for I really cannot assign any reasonable why and wherefore — I have been carried apart from the main current of life, and find it impossible to get back again. Since we last met . . . I have secluded myself from society; and yet I never meant any such thing, nor dreamed what sort of life I was going to lead. I have made a captive of myself and put me into a dungeon, and now I cannot find the key to let myself out — and if the door were open, I should be almost afraid to come out. You tell me that you have met with troubles and changes. I know not what they may have been; but I can assure you that trouble is the next best thing to enjoyment, and that there is no fate in this world so horrible as to have no share in either its joys or sorrows. For the last ten years, I have not lived, but only dreamed about living. It may be true that there have been some unsubstantial pleasures here in the shade, which I should have missed in the sunshine, but you cannot conceive how utterly devoid of satisfaction all my retrospects are. I have laid up no treasure of pleasant remembrances, against old age; but there is some comfort in thinking that my future years can hardly fail to be more varied, and therefore more tolerable, than the past.

    You give me more credit than I deserve, in supposing that I have led a studious life. I have, indeed, turned over a good many books, but in so desultory a way that it cannot be called study, nor has it left me the fruits of study. As to my literary efforts, I do not think much of them — neither is it worth while to be ashamed of them. They would have been better, I trust, if written under more favorable circumstances. I have had no external excitement — no consciousness that the public would like what I wrote, nor much hope nor a very passionate desire that they should do so. Nevertheless, having nothing else to be ambitious of, I have felt considerably interested in literature; and if my writings had made any decided impression, I should probably have been stimulated to greater exertions; but there has been no warmth of approbation, so that I have always written with benumbed fingers. I have another great difficulty, in the lack of materials; for I have seen so little of the world, that I have nothing but thin air to concoct my stories of, and it is not easy to give a lifelike semblance to such shadowy stuff. Sometimes, through a peep-hole, I have caught a glimpse of the real world; and the two or three articles, in which I have portrayed such glimpses, please me better than the others. I have now, or shall soon have, one sharp spur to exertion, which I lacked at an earlier period; for I see little prospect but that I must scribble for a living. But this troubles me much less than you would suppose. I can turn my pen to all sorts of drudgery, such as children's books, etc., and by and by, I shall get some editorship that will answer my purpose. Frank Pierce, who was with us at college, offered me his influence to obtain an office in the Exploring Expedition; but I believe that he was mistaken in supposing that a vacancy existed. If such a post were attainable, I should certainly accept it; for, though fixed so long to one spot, I have always had a desire to run around the world.

The copy of my Tales was sent to Mr. Owen's, the bookseller's in Cambridge. I am glad to find that you had read and liked some of the stories. To be sure, you could not well help flattering me a little; but I value your praise too highly not to have faith in its sincerity. When I last heard from the publisher — which was not very recently — the book was doing pretty well. Six or seven hundred copies had been sold. I suppose, however, these awful times have now stopped the sale.

I intend in a week or two to come out of my owl's nest, and not return to it till late in the summer — employing the interval in making a tour somewhere in New England. You, who have the dust of distant countries on your "sandal-shoon," cannot imagine how much enjoyment I shall have in this little excursion. Whenever I get abroad, I feel just as young as I did, ten years ago. What a letter I am inflicting on you! I trust you will answer it.

Yours sincerely,
Nath. Hawthorne.

From a letter to Henry Wadsworth Longfellow, June 4, 1837

CONSIDERATIONS FOR CRITICAL THINKING AND WRITING

1. How does Hawthorne regard his solitude? How does he feel it has affected his life and writing?

2. Hawthorne explains to Longfellow, one of his Bowdoin classmates, that "there is no fate in this world so horrible as to have no share in either its joys or sorrows" (para. 1). Explain how this idea is worked into "Young Goodman Brown" (p. 331).

3. Does Hawthorne indicate any positive results for having lived in his "owl's nest" (para. 1)? Consider how "The Minister's Black Veil" (p. 341) and this letter shed light on each other.

Hawthorne on the Power of the Writer's Imagination   *1850*

. . . Moonlight, in a familiar room, falling so white upon the carpet, and showing all its figures so distinctly — making every object so minutely visible, yet so unlike a morning or noontide visibility — is a medium the most suitable for a romance-writer° to get acquainted with his illusive guests. There is the little domestic scenery of the well-known apartment; the chairs, with each its separate

romance-writer: Hawthorne distinguished romance writing from novel writing. In the preface to *The House of the Seven Gables* he writes:

> The latter form of composition is presumed to aim at a very minute fidelity, not merely to the possible, but to the probable and ordinary course of man's experience. The former — while, as a work of art, it must rigidly subject itself to laws, and while it sins unpardonably so far as it may swerve aside from the truth of the human heart — has fairly a right to present that truth under circumstances, to a great extent, of the writer's own choosing or creation.

individuality; the center-table, sustaining a work-basket, a volume or two, and an extinguished lamp; the sofa; the book-case; the picture on the wall—all these details, so completely seen, are so spiritualized by the unusual light, that they seem to lose their actual substance, and become things of intellect. Nothing is too small or too trifling to undergo this change, and acquire dignity thereby. A child's shoe; the doll, seated in her little wicker carriage; the hobbyhorse— whatever, in a word, has been used or played with, during the day, is now invested with a quality of strangeness and remoteness, though still almost as vividly present as by daylight. Thus, therefore, the floor of our familiar room has become a neutral territory, somewhere between the real world and fairy-land, where the Actual and the Imaginary may meet, and each imbue itself with the nature of the other. Ghosts might enter here, without affrighting us. It would be too much in keeping with the scene to excite surprise, were we to look about us and discover a form, beloved, but gone hence, now sitting quietly in a streak of this magic moonshine, with an aspect that would make us doubt whether it had returned from afar, or had never once stirred from our fireside.

The somewhat dim coal-fire has an essential influence in producing the effect which I would describe. It throws its unobtrusive tinge throughout the room, with a faint ruddiness upon the walls and ceiling, and a reflected gleam from the polish of the furniture. This warmer light mingles itself with the cold spirituality of the moonbeams, and communicates, as it were, a heart and sensibilities of human tenderness to the forms which fancy summons up. It converts them from snow-images into men and women. Glancing at the looking-glass, we behold—deep within its haunted verge—the smouldering glow of the half-extinguished anthracite, the white moonbeams on the floor, and a repetition of all the gleam and shadow of the picture, with one remove farther from the actual, and nearer to the imaginative. Then, at such an hour, and with this scene before him, if a man, sitting all alone, cannot dream strange things, and make them look like truth, he need never try to write romances.

From *The Scarlet Letter*

CONSIDERATIONS FOR CRITICAL THINKING AND WRITING

1. Explain how Hawthorne uses light as a means of invoking the transforming powers of the imagination.

2. How do Hawthorne's stories fulfill his definition of romance writing? Why can't they be regarded as realistic?

3. Choose one story and discuss it as an attempt to evoke "the truth of the human heart."

Hawthorne on His Short Stories   *1851*

[These stories] have the pale tint of flowers that blossomed in too retired a shade—the coolness of a meditative habit, which diffuses itself through the feeling and observation of every sketch. Instead of passion there is sentiment; and, even in what purport to be pictures of actual life, we have allegory, not always warmly dressed in its habiliments of flesh and blood as to be taken into

the reader's mind without a shiver. Whether from lack of power, or an unconquerable reserve, the Author's touches have often an effect of tameness; the
merriest man can hardly contrive to laugh at his broadest humor; the tenderest woman, one would suppose, will hardly shed warm tears at his deepest
pathos. The book, if you would see anything in it, requires to be read in the
clear brown, twilight atmosphere in which it was written; if opened in the sunshine, it is apt to look exceedingly like a volume of blank pages.

From the preface to the 1851 edition of *Twice-Told Tales*

CONSIDERATIONS FOR CRITICAL THINKING AND WRITING

1. How does Hawthorne characterize his stories? Does his assessment accurately describe the stories you've read?

2. Why is a "twilight atmosphere" more conducive to an appreciation of
   Hawthorne's art than "sunshine"?

3. Write a one-page description of Hawthorne's stories in which you generalize about his characteristic approach to one of these elements: plot, character, setting, symbol, theme, tone.

HERMAN MELVILLE (1819–1891)
On Nathaniel Hawthorne's Tragic Vision   1851

There is a certain tragic phase of humanity which, in our opinion, was never
more powerfully embodied than by Hawthorne. We mean the tragicalness of
human thought in its own unbiased, native, and profounder workings. We
think that in no recorded mind has the intense feeling of the visable truth ever
entered more deeply than into this man's. By visable truth, we mean the apprehension of the absolute condition of present things as they strike the eye of the
man who fears them not, though they do their worst to him — the man who,
like Russia or the British Empire, declares himself a sovereign nature (in himself) amid the powers of heaven, hell, and earth. He may perish; but so long as
he exists he insists upon treating with all Powers upon an equal basis. If any of
those other Powers choose to withhold certain secrets, let them; that does not
impair my sovereignty in myself; that does not make me tributary. And perhaps,
after all, there is *no* secret. We incline to think that the Problem of the Universe
is like the Freemason's° mighty secret, so terrible to all children. It turns out, at
last, to consist in a triangle, a mallet, and an apron — nothing more! . . . There is
the grand truth about Nathaniel Hawthorne. He says NO! in thunder; but the
Devil himself cannot make him say *yes.* For all men who say *yes,* lie; and all men
who say *no* — why, they are in the happy condition of judicious, unincumbered
travelers in Europe; they cross the frontiers into Eternity with nothing but a
carpetbag — that is to say, the Ego. Whereas those *yes*-gentry, they travel with
heaps of baggage, and, damn them! they will never get through the Custom
House. What's the reason, Mr. Hawthorne, that in the last stages of meta-
physics a fellow always falls to *swearing* so? I could rip an hour.

From a letter to Hawthorne, April 16(?), 1851

Freemason: A member of the secret fraternity of Freemasonry.

CONSIDERATIONS FOR CRITICAL THINKING AND WRITING

1. What qualities in Hawthorne does Melville admire?
2. Explain how these qualities are embodied in one of the Hawthorne stories.
3. How might Melville's lawyer in "Bartleby, the Scrivener" (p. 116) be characterized as one of "those *yes*-gentry"?

TWO COMPLEMENTARY CRITICAL READINGS

JUDITH FETTERLEY (B. 1938)

A Feminist Reading of "The Birthmark"   *1978*

It is testimony at once to Hawthorne's ambivalence, his seeking to cover with one hand what he uncovers with the other; and to the pervasive sexism of our culture that most readers would describe "The Birthmark" as a story of failure rather than as the success story it really is — the demonstration of how to murder your wife and get away with it. It is, of course, possible to read "The Birthmark" as a story of misguided idealism, a tale of the unhappy consequences of man's nevertheless worthy passion for perfecting and transcending nature; and this is the reading usually given it. This reading, however, ignores the significance of the form idealism takes in the story. It is not irrelevant that "The Birthmark" is about a man's desire to perfect his wife, nor is it accidental that the consequence of this idealism is the wife's death. In fact, "The Birthmark" provides a brilliant analysis of the sexual politics of idealization and a brilliant exposure of the mechanisms whereby hatred can be disguised as love, neurosis can be disguised as science, murder can be disguised as idealization, and success can be disguised as failure. Thus, Hawthorne's insistence in his story on the metaphor of disguise serves as both warning and clue to a feminist reading. . . .

One cannot imagine this story in reverse — that is, a woman's discovering an obsessive need to perfect her husband and deciding to perform experiments on him — nor can one imagine the story being about a man's conceiving such an obsession for another man. It is woman, and specifically woman as wife, who elicits the obsession with imperfection and the compulsion to achieve perfection, just as it is man, and specifically man as husband, who is thus obsessed and compelled. In addition, it is clear from the summary that the imagined perfection is purely physical. Aylmer is not concerned with the quality of Georgiana's character or with the state of her soul, for he considers her "fit for heaven without tasting death." Rather, he is absorbed in her physical appearance, and perfection for him is equivalent to physical beauty. Georgiana is an exemplum of woman as beautiful object, reduced to and defined by her body. . . . "The Birthmark" demonstrates the fact that the idealization of women has its source in a profound hostility toward women and that it is at once a disguise for this hostility and the fullest expression of it. . . .

* * *

. . . Unable to accept himself for what he is, Aylmer constructs a mythology of science and adopts the character of a scientist to disguise his true nature and to hide his real motives, from himself as well as others. As a consequence, he acquires a way of acting out these motives without in fact having to be aware of them. One might describe "The Birthmark" as an exposé of science because it demonstrates the ease with which science can be invoked to conceal highly subjective motives. "The Birthmark" is an exposure of the realities that underlie the scientist's posture of objectivity and rationality and the claims of science to operate in an amoral and value-free world. Pale Aylmer, the intellectual scientist, is a mask for the brutish, earthy, soot-smeared Aminadab, just as the mythology of scientific research and objectivity finally masks murder, disguising Georgiana's death as just one more experiment that failed. . . .

The implicit feminism in "The Birthmark" is considerable. On one level the story is a study of sexual politics, of the powerlessness of women and of the psychology which results from that powerlessness. Hawthorne dramatizes the fact that woman's identity is a product of men's responses to her: "It must not be concealed, however, that the impression wrought by this fairy sign manual varied exceedingly, according to the difference of temperament in the beholders." To those who love Georgiana, her birthmark is evidence of her beauty; to those who envy or hate her, it is an object of disgust. It is Aylmer's repugnance for the birthmark that makes Georgiana blanch, thus causing the mark to emerge as a sharply defined blemish against the whiteness of her cheek. Clearly, the birthmark takes on its character from the eye of the beholder. And just as clearly Georgiana's attitude toward her birthmark varies in response to different observers and definers. Her self-image derives from internalizing the attitudes toward her of the man or men around her. Since what surrounds Georgiana is an obsessional attraction expressed as a total revulsion, the result is not surprising: continual self-consciousness that leads to a pervasive sense of shame and a self-hatred that terminates in an utter readiness to be killed. "The Birthmark" demonstrates the consequences to women of being trapped in the laboratory of man's mind, the object of unrelenting scrutiny, examination, and experimentation.

From *The Resisting Reader: A Feminist Approach to American Fiction*

CONSIDERATIONS FOR CRITICAL THINKING AND WRITING

1. In what sense does Fetterley regard "The Birthmark" as a "success story" (para. 1)? How does her feminist perspective inform this view?

2. Why do you think Fetterley argues that it is impossible to imagine reversing the male-female roles in this story?

3. How does Fetterley make a case for reading the story as an "exposé of science" (para. 3)? Explain why science is described as an essentially male activity.

4. Although Fetterley does not include "The Minister's Black Veil" (p. 341) in her discussion, might it not be argued that it too harbors an "implicit feminism" (para. 4)? Write an analysis of the Reverend Mr. Hooper from a feminist perspective.

JAMES QUINN (B. 1937) AND ROSS BALDESSARINI (B. 1937)

A Psychological Reading of "The Birthmark"   1981

Hawthorne's art in the creation of character in many ways anticipates modern psychoanalytic psychology. As a literary psychologist, he excels at revealing unconscious sources of obsessed behavior. In "The Birthmark," Aylmer, a scientist whose ambition may be to control nature, provides an exceptionally good example of an obsessive character. He is obsessed with imperfection in human nature and is unable to achieve a mature human relationship. . . .

. . . What has happened to make Aylmer feel this way? What indeed ails him? The question is a natural one, but useless. Hawthorne does not supply an answer and by this omission seems to suggest that insights into human behavior are likely to be subjective, imperfect, unsatisfying. What is important is not the cause of obsessive thought or compulsive behavior but the effects.

The dramatic situation here is that Aylmer, by marrying Georgiana, is forced to deal with a conflict between his earlier, somewhat distant view of her as an intellectualized feminine ideal and her present tangible reality. Clearly one meaning of the red hand is a mark of her accessibility to touch, that is, of her sexuality. It also includes conflict between personal idealization and reality — a classical and ubiquitous obsessional neurotic conflict. While Aylmer's struggle is virtually universal, his fixation on Georgiana's blemish approaches a symptom that is considered characteristic of obsessive-compulsive neurosis in modern-day psychopathological terms.[1] The function of such neurotic symptoms in the psychic economy is to inhibit intolerable anxiety by focusing on an isolated and somewhat concrete representation so as to avoid a larger emotional conflict.

The psychoanalytic theorist Fenichel has written, "Many compulsive neurotics have to worry very much about small and apparently insignificant things. In analysis, these small things turn out to be substitutes for important ones."[2] And further: "Compulsive neurotics try to use external objects for the solution or relief of their inner conflicts" (p. 293). As "the compulsive neurotic tends . . . to extend the range of his symptoms . . ." (p. 294), so Aylmer's reaction to the birthmark grew "more and more intolerable with every moment of their . . . lives," presumably as a result of Georgiana's unavoidable presence. What at first seemed a trifling matter "so connected itself with innumerable trains of thought and modes of feeling that it became the *central point of all*" [stress added]. Like Parson Hooper [in "The Minister's Black Veil"], Aylmer is

---

[1] Most of the characteristics of the illness can be found in the official definition of obsessive-compulsive disorder stated in the third edition of the American Psychiatric Association's (1980) *Diagnostic and Statistical Manual of Mental Disorders* (DSM-III):

> The essential features are recurrent obsessions and/or compulsions. Obsessions are defined as recurrent, persistent ideas, thoughts, images, or impulses which are ego-alien; that is, they are not experienced as voluntarily produced, but rather as ideas that invade the field of consciousness. Attempts are made to ignore or suppress them. Compulsions are behaviors which are not experienced as the outcome of the individual's own volition, but are accompanied by both a sense of subjective compulsion and a desire to resist (at least initially). (p. 234)

[2] Otto Fenichel, *The Psychoanalytic Theory of Neurosis* (New York, 1945), p. 290.

another Hawthornian victim of morbid forces, largely internal, beyond his control. Surely Aylmer's aversion owes its intensity and its obsessive character precisely to the fact that it is not accessible to conscious examination.[3] . . .

He draws distinct lines between good and bad as does . . . Young Goodman Brown, who must see Faith, indeed all women, as Madonna or whore and who therefore remains immature and uncommitted. Aylmer, too, is like an adolescent, unable to find a point of equilibrium between two poles of thought, not realizing that "to be is to be imperfect, that the price of human existence is imperfection."[4]

An ironic aspect of such obsessed and morbid behavior so often seen in Hawthorne's works is that the more one struggles to attain perfection or to retain an unreasonable fixed idea, the more one is caught up in dealing with its opposite — imperfection and destruction. . . .

Up to this point we have been concerned with Hawthorne's presentation of Aylmer as one more neurotic and troubled obsessional soul. More important, however, is Aylmer's dramatically exaggerated representation of a more general struggle to adjust the ideal and the real. Likewise the birthmark can be viewed on more than one level. It is a mark of Georgiana's accessibility to touch, of her sexuality. It is suggestive of the scarlet letter — another public sign of secret and lustful sin, of "putting hands upon" in a sexual sense, of being touched, tainted, having sexuality and womanly characteristics. And, within the Judeo-Christian tradition . . . it seems to Hawthorne to symbolize the fallen and sinful nature of man. In an even wider application, it symbolizes the mortality of all mankind.

We miss the point, however, if we connect the birthmark solely with neurotic conflicts of atypical individuals or even with the hold death has on everyone, for the mark is also connected with sexuality and new life, indeed with aspiration to beauty and achievement and with the joy and energy for living. The importance of Hawthorne's psychological symbol is not the susceptibility of man to sin and death, but the special manner in which the marked woman suffers her fate: it is Aylmer who kills her. When the inward life concentrates narcissistically on self, demonic violence flares up in the lust to control and possess another person. Yet the first to be destroyed is Aylmer himself, who steps out of the procession of life, suffering from an incapacity to accept and integrate human emotions.

From *University of Hartford Studies in Literature:*
A Journal of Interdisciplinary Criticism

[3] In Freudian theory, certain ideas heavily charged or invested with affect or emotion constantly press toward conscious recognition or awareness, and certain impulses toward overt satisfaction or fulfillment. What we note in this tale is something close to "isolation of affect" or suppression and limitation or restriction of a highly charged emotion. The feeling and its source seem to be a form of anxiety, fear of being harmed through intimacy — metaphorically a problem in the category of castration anxiety or fear of being found wanting (already castrated). The idea that the birthmark is a castration symbol has already been suggested by Simon Lesser, *Fiction and the Unconscious,* p. 88.

[4] Terence Martin, *Nathaniel Hawthorne* (New Haven, 1965), p. 70.

CONSIDERATIONS FOR CRITICAL THINKING AND WRITING

1. According to Quinn and Baldessarini, why isn't it fruitful to inquire into the causes of Aylmer's obsession? Explain why you agree or disagree with their assessment.

2. How might Aylmer, Parson Hooper, Lady Eleanore, and Young Goodman Brown all be regarded as exhibiting obsessive behavior?

3. Write an essay that discusses how and why this psychoanalytic reading leads to a focus on Aylmer while Judith Fetterley's feminist reading (p. 375) leads to an emphasis on Georgiana. For a discussion of psychological and feminist readings see Chapter 52, "Critical Strategies for Reading."

4. Explain what you think a psychological reading of Georgiana would make of her character.

SUGGESTED TOPICS FOR LONGER PAPERS
---

1. Consider the setting of each of the Hawthorne stories in this chapter. Why are they significant? How are they related to the stories' respective themes? In your essay, determine which story relies most heavily on setting to convey its meanings.

2. Read the perspective concerning Hawthorne and solitude (p. 371) and do some biographical research on Hawthorne's attitudes toward solitude and human isolation. How do details about his life shed light on the solitary or isolated characters in the four stories you have read in this chapter?

3. MULTIMEDIA PROJECT. How does Hawthorne's presentation of American Puritan culture in "Young Goodman Brown" compare with our contemporary perception of the Puritans? Using whatever media you prefer — books, articles, the Internet, television, films, music, etc. — gather images of Puritan culture to compare with Hawthorne's vision of the Puritans. Be sure to address how the nature of your sources — whether they are popular, scholarly, or artistic representations — affects the comparison.

Web   *For help with this project, use the Multimedia Project Guides Online at*
http://www.bedfordstmartins.com/meyer/bedintrolit

12

A Study of Flannery O'Connor

When Flannery O'Connor (1925–1964) died of lupus before her fortieth birthday, her work was cruelly cut short. Nevertheless, she had completed two novels, *Wise Blood* (1952) and *The Violent Bear It Away* (1960), as well as thirty-one short stories. Despite her brief life and relatively modest output,

Flannery O'Connor (undated photograph) in front of an accurate, if rather fierce self-portrait with one of her beloved peacocks. Reprinted by permission of Corbis-Bettmann.

her work is regarded as among the most distinguished American fiction of the mid-twentieth century. Her two collections of short stories, *A Good Man Is Hard to Find* (1955) and *Everything That Rises Must Converge* (1965), were included in *The Complete Stories of Flannery O'Connor* (1971), which won the National Book Award. The stories included in this chapter offer a glimpse into the work of this important twentieth-century writer.

A BRIEF BIOGRAPHY AND INTRODUCTION

O'Connor's fiction grapples with living a spiritual life in a secular world. Although this major concern is worked into each of her stories, she takes a broad approach to spiritual issues by providing moral, social, and psychological contexts that offer a wealth of insights and passion that her readers have found both startling and absorbing. Her stories are challenging because her characters, who initially seem radically different from people we know, turn out to be, by the end of each story, somehow familiar — somehow connected to us.

O'Connor inhabited simultaneously two radically different worlds. The world she created in her stories is populated with bratty children, malcontents, incompetents, pious frauds, bewildered intellectuals, deformed cynics, rednecks, hucksters, racists, perverts, and murderers who experience dramatically intense moments that surprise and shock readers. Her personal life, however, was largely uneventful. She humorously acknowledged its quiet nature in 1958 when she claimed that "there won't be any biographies of me because, for only one reason, lives spent between the house and the chicken yard do not make exciting copy."

A broad outline of O'Connor's life may not offer very much "exciting copy," but it does provide clues about why she wrote such powerful fiction. The only child of Catholic parents, O'Connor was born in Savannah, Georgia, where she attended a parochial grammar school and high school. When she was thirteen, her father became ill with disseminated lupus, a rare, incurable blood disease, and had to abandon his real-estate business. The family moved to Milledgeville in central Georgia, where her mother's family had lived for generations. Because there were no Catholic schools in Milledgeville, O'Connor attended a public high school. In 1942, the year after her father died of lupus, O'Connor graduated from high school and enrolled in Georgia State College for Women. There she wrote for the literary magazine until receiving her diploma in 1945. Her stories earned her a fellowship to the Writers' Workshop at the University of Iowa, and for two years she learned to write steadily and seriously. She sold her first story to *Accent* in 1946 and earned her master of fine arts degree in 1947. She wrote stories about life in the rural South, and this subject matter, along with her devout Catholic perspective, became central to her fiction.

With her formal education behind her, O'Connor was ready to begin her professional career at the age of twenty-two. Equipped with determination ("No one can convince me that I shouldn't rewrite as much as I do") and offered the opportunity to be around other practicing writers, she moved to New York, where she worked on her first novel, *Wise Blood*. In 1950, however, she was diagnosed as having lupus, and, returning to Georgia for treatment, she took up permanent residence on her mother's farm in Milledgeville. There she lived a severely restricted but productive life, writing stories and raising peacocks.

With the exception of O'Connor's early years in Iowa and New York and some short lecture trips to other states, she traveled little. Although she made a pilgrimage to Lourdes (apparently more for her mother's sake than for her own) and then to Rome for an audience with the pope, her life was centered in the South. Like those of William Faulkner and many other southern writers, O'Connor's stories evoke the rhythms of rural southern speech and manners in insulated settings where widely diverse characters mingle. Also like Faulkner, she created works whose meanings go beyond their settings. She did not want her fiction to be seen in the context of narrowly defined regionalism: she complained that "in almost every hamlet you'll find at least one old lady writing epics in Negro dialect and probably two or three old gentlemen who have impossible historical novels on the way." Refusing to be caricatured, she knew that "the woods are full of regional writers, and it is the great horror of every serious Southern writer that he will become one of them." O'Connor's stories are rooted in rural southern culture, but in a larger sense they are set within the psychological and spiritual landscapes of the human soul. This interior setting universalizes local materials in much the same way that Nathaniel Hawthorne's New England stories do. Indeed, O'Connor once described herself as "one of his descendants": "I feel more of a kinship with him than any other American."

O'Connor's deep spiritual convictions coincide with the traditional emphasis on religion in the South, where, she said, there is still the belief "that man has fallen and that he is only perfectible by God's grace, not by his own unaided efforts." Although O'Connor's Catholicism differs from the prevailing Protestant fundamentalism of the South, the religious ethos so pervasive even in rural southern areas provided fertile ground for the spiritual crises her characters experience. In a posthumous collection of her articles, essays, and reviews aptly titled *Mystery and Manners* (1969), she summarized her basic religious convictions:

> I am no disbeliever in spiritual purpose and no vague believer. I see from the standpoint of Christian orthodoxy. This means that for me the meaning of life is centered in our Redemption by Christ and what I see in the world I see in its relation to that. I don't think that this is a position that can be taken halfway or one that is particularly easy in these times to make transparent in fiction.

O'Connor realized that she was writing against the grain of the readers who discovered her stories in the *Partisan Review, Sewanee Review, Made-*

moiselle, or *Harper's Bazaar.* Many readers thought that Christian dogma would make her writing doctrinaire, but she insisted that the perspective of Christianity allowed her to interpret the details of life and guaranteed her "respect for [life's] mystery." O'Connor's stories contain no prepackaged prescriptions for living, no catechisms that lay out all the answers. Instead, her characters struggle with spiritual questions in bizarre, incongruous situations. Their lives are grotesque — even comic — precisely because they do not understand their own spiritual natures. Their actions are extreme and abnormal. O'Connor explains the reasons for this in *Mystery and Manners;* she says she sought to expose the "distortions" of "modern life" that appear "normal" to her audience. Hence, she used "violent means" to convey her vision to a "hostile audience." "When you can assume that your audience holds the same beliefs you do, you can relax a little and use more normal means of talking to it." But when the audience holds different values, "you have to make your vision apparent by shock — to the hard of hearing you shout, and for the almost-blind you draw large and startling figures." O'Connor's characters lose or find their soul-saving grace in painful, chaotic circumstances that bear little or no resemblance to the slow but sure progress to the Celestial City of repentant pilgrims in traditional religious stories.

Because her characters are powerful creations who live convincing, even if ugly, lives, O'Connor's religious beliefs never supersede her storytelling. One need not be either Christian or Catholic to appreciate her concerns about human failure and degradation and her artistic ability to render fictional lives that are alternately absurdly comic and tragic. The ironies that abound in her work leave plenty of room for readers of all persuasions. O'Connor's work is narrow in the sense that her concerns are emphatically spiritual, but her compassion and her belief in human possibilities — even among the most unlikely characters — afford her fictions a capacity for wonder that is exhilarating. Her precise, deft use of language always reveals more than it seems to tell.

Like Hawthorne's fiction, O'Connor's stories present complex experiences that cannot be tidily summarized; it takes the entire story to suggest the meanings. Read the following four stories for the pleasure of entering the remarkable world O'Connor creates. You're in for some surprises.

CHRONOLOGY

1925	Born on March 25 in Savannah, Georgia.
1938	Moves with family to Milledgeville, Georgia; enters the public Peabody High School.
1941	Father dies of lupus.

1942   Graduates from Peabody High School; enters Georgia State College for Women (now Georgia College and State University).

1943-45   Writes stories and poems for college literary magazine; graduates from Georgia State with an undergraduate degree in English.

1945-47   Enters writing program at the University of Iowa and earns a master of fine arts degree in creative writing.

1948-49   Attends Yaddo artists' colony near Saratoga Springs, New York, for several months; lives in New York and Connecticut.

1950   After an illness, returns to Milledgeville and is diagnosed as suffering from lupus, an incurable disease. Lives on her family's dairy farm the rest of her life.

1952   *Wise Blood* receives mixed reviews and upsets some Milledgeville residents.

1955   *A Good Man Is Hard to Find and Other Stories* receives critical praise; the Guggenheim foundation rejects her fellowship application for a second time.

1956   A degenerating hip forces her to use crutches; the first telephone is installed on the farm.

1957   Lectures at several universities; dislikes a television version of the short story "The Life You Save May Be Your Own"; receives a grant from the National Institute of Arts and Letters.

1958   Visits Lourdes and Rome.

1960   Publishes *The Violent Bear It Away*.

1962-63   Receives honorary doctorate from Saint Mary's women's college of the University of Notre Dame; speaks at a number of colleges in the South about her writing.

1964   Dies on August 3, 1964.

1965   *Everything That Rises Must Converge* published posthumously.

Web *Research Flannery O'Connor with LitLinks at*
http://www.bedfordstmartins.com/meyer/bedintrolit

A Good Man Is Hard to Find   1953

The grandmother didn't want to go to Florida. She wanted to visit some of her connections in east Tennessee and she was seizing at every chance to change Bailey's mind. Bailey was the son she lived with, her only boy. He was sitting on the edge of his chair at the table, bent over the orange sports section of the *Journal.* "Now look here, Bailey," she said, "see here, read this," and she stood with one hand on her thin hip and the other rattling the newspaper at his bald head. "Here this fellow that calls himself The Misfit is aloose from the Federal Pen and headed toward Florida and you read here what it says he did to these people. Just you read it. I wouldn't take my children in any direction with a criminal like that aloose in it. I couldn't answer to my conscience if I did."

Bailey didn't look up from his reading so she wheeled around then and faced the children's mother, a young woman in slacks, whose face was as broad and innocent as a cabbage and was tied around with a green headkerchief that had two points on the top like a rabbit's ears. She was sitting on the sofa, feeding the baby his apricots out of a jar. "The children have been to Florida before," the old lady said. "You all ought to take them somewhere else for a change so they would see different parts of the world and be broad. They never have been to east Tennessee."

The children's mother didn't seem to hear her but the eight-year-old boy, John Wesley, a stocky child with glasses, said, "If you don't want to go to Florida, why dontcha stay at home?" He and the little girl, June Star, were reading the funny papers on the floor.

"She wouldn't stay at home to be queen for a day," June Star said without raising her yellow head.

"Yes and what would you do if this fellow, The Misfit, caught you?" the grandmother asked. 5

"I'd smack his face," John Wesley said.

"She wouldn't stay at home for a million bucks," June Star said. "Afraid she'd miss something. She has to go everywhere we go."

"All right, Miss," the grandmother said. "Just remember that the next time you want me to curl your hair."

June Star said her hair was naturally curly.

The next morning the grandmother was the first one in the car, ready to go. 10 She had her big black valise that looked like the head of a hippopotamus in one corner, and underneath it she was hiding a basket with Pitty Sing, the cat, in it. She didn't intend for the cat to be left alone in the house for three days because he would miss her too much and she was afraid he might brush against one of the gas burners and accidentally asphyxiate himself. Her son, Bailey, didn't like to arrive at a motel with a cat.

She sat in the middle of the back seat with John Wesley and June Star on either side of her. Bailey and the children's mother and the baby sat in front and they left Atlanta at eight forty-five with the mileage on the car at 55890. The grandmother wrote this down because she thought it would be interesting to say how many miles they had been when they got back. It took them twenty minutes to reach the outskirts of the city.

The old lady settled herself comfortably, removing her white cotton gloves and putting them up with her purse on the shelf in front of the back window. The children's mother still had on slacks and still had her head tied up in a green kerchief, but the grandmother had on a navy blue straw sailor hat with a bunch of white violets on the brim and a navy blue dress with a small white dot in the print. Her collars and cuffs were white organdy trimmed with lace and at her neckline she had pinned a purple spray of cloth violets containing a sachet. In case of an accident, anyone seeing her dead on the highway would know at once that she was a lady.

She said she thought it was going to be a good day for driving, neither too hot nor too cold, and she cautioned Bailey that the speed limit was fifty-five miles an hour and that the patrolmen hid themselves behind billboards and small clumps of trees and sped out after you before you had a chance to slow down. She pointed out interesting details of the scenery: Stone Mountain; the blue granite that in some places came up to both sides of the highway; the brilliant red clay banks slightly streaked with purple; and the various crops that made rows of green lace-work on the ground. The trees were full of silver-white sunlight and the meanest of them sparkled. The children were reading comic magazines and their mother had gone back to sleep.

"Let's go through Georgia fast so we won't have to look at it much," John Wesley said.

"If I were a little boy," said the grandmother, "I wouldn't talk about my native state that way. Tennessee has the mountains and Georgia has the hills." 15

"Tennessee is just a hillbilly dumping ground," John Wesley said, "and Georgia is a lousy state too."

"You said it," June Star said.

"In my time," said the grandmother, folding her thin veined fingers, "children were more respectful of their native states and their parents and everything else. People did right then. Oh look at the cute little pickaninny!" she said and pointed to a Negro child standing in the door of a shack. "Wouldn't that make a picture, now?" she asked and they all turned and looked at the little Negro out of the back window. He waved.

"He didn't have any britches on," June Star said.

"He probably didn't have any," the grandmother explained. "Little niggers 20 in the country don't have things like we do. If I could paint, I'd paint that picture," she said.

The children exchanged comic books.

The grandmother offered to hold the baby and the children's mother passed him over the front seat to her. She set him on her knee and bounced him and told him about the things they were passing. She rolled her eyes and screwed up her mouth and stuck her leathery thin face into his smooth bland one. Occasionally he gave her a faraway smile. They passed a large cotton field with five or six graves fenced in the middle of it, like a small island. "Look at the graveyard!" the grandmother said, pointing it out. "That was the old family burying ground. That belonged to the plantation."

"Where's the plantation?" John Wesley asked.

"Gone With the Wind," said the grandmother. "Ha. Ha."

When the children finished all the comic books they had brought, they 25 opened the lunch and ate it. The grandmother ate a peanut butter sandwich and an olive and would not let the children throw the box and the paper napkins out the window. When there was nothing else to do they played a game by choosing a cloud and making the other two guess what shape it suggested. John Wesley took one the shape of a cow and June Star guessed a cow and John Wesley said, no, an automobile, and June Star said he didn't play fair, and they began to slap each other over the grandmother.

The grandmother said she would tell them a story if they would keep quiet. When she told a story, she rolled her eyes and waved her head and was very dramatic. She said once when she was a maiden lady she had been courted by a Mr. Edgar Atkins Teagarden from Jasper, Georgia. She said he was a very goodlooking man and a gentleman and that he brought her a watermelon every Saturday afternoon with his initials cut in it, E.A.T. Well, one Saturday, she said, Mr. Teagarden brought the watermelon and there was nobody at home and he left it on the front porch and returned in his buggy to Jasper, but she never got the watermelon, she said, because a nigger boy ate it when he saw the initials, E.A.T.! This story tickled John Wesley's funny bone and he giggled and giggled but June Star didn't think it was any good. She said she wouldn't marry a man that just brought her a watermelon on Saturday. The grandmother said she would have done well to marry Mr. Teagarden because he was a gentleman and had bought Coca-Cola stock when it first came out and that he had died only a few years ago, a very wealthy man.

They stopped at The Tower for barbecued sandwiches. The Tower was a part stucco and part wood filling station and dance hall set in a clearing outside of Timothy. A fat man named Red Sammy Butts ran it and there were signs stuck here and there on the building and for miles up and down the highway saying, TRY RED SAMMY'S FAMOUS BARBECUE. NONE LIKE FAMOUS RED SAMMY'S! RED SAM! THE FAT BOY WITH THE HAPPY LAUGH. A VETERAN! RED SAMMY'S YOUR MAN!

Red Sammy was lying on the bare ground outside The Tower with his head under a truck while a gray monkey about a foot high, chained to a small chinaberry tree, chattered nearby. The monkey sprang back into the tree and got on the highest limb as soon as he saw the children jump out of the car and run toward him.

Inside, The Tower was a long dark room with a counter at one end and tables at the other and dancing space in the middle. They all sat down at a board table next to the nickelodeon and Red Sam's wife, a tall burnt-brown woman with hair and eyes lighter than her skin, came and took their order. The children's mother put a dime in the machine and played "The Tennessee Waltz," and the grandmother said that tune always made her want to dance. She asked Bailey if he would like to dance but he only glared at her. He didn't have a naturally sunny disposition like she did and trips made him nervous. The grandmother's brown eyes were very bright. She swayed her head from side to side and pretended she was dancing in her chair. June Star said play something she could tap to so the children's mother put in another dime and played a fast number and June Star stepped out onto the dance floor and did her tap routine.

"Ain't she cute?" Red Sam's wife said, leaning over the counter. "Would you like to come be my little girl?"   30

"No I certainly wouldn't," June Star said. "I wouldn't live in a broken-down place like this for a million bucks!" and she ran back to the table.

"Ain't she cute?" the woman repeated, stretching her mouth politely.

"Aren't you ashamed?" hissed the grandmother.

Red Sam came in and told his wife to quit lounging on the counter and hurry up with these people's order. His khaki trousers reached just to his hip bones and his stomach hung over them like a sack of meal swaying under his shirt. He came over and sat down at a table nearby and let out a combination sigh and yodel. "You can't win," he said. "You can't win," and he wiped his sweating red face off with a gray handkerchief. "These days you don't know who to trust," he said. "Ain't that the truth?"

"People are certainly not nice like they used to be," said the grandmother.   35

"Two fellers come in here last week," Red Sammy said, "driving a Chrysler. It was a old beat-up car but it was a good one and these boys looked all right to me. Said they worked at the mill and you know I let them fellers charge the gas they bought? Now why did I do that?"

"Because you're a good man!" the grandmother said at once.

"Yes'm, I suppose so," Red Sam said as if he were struck with this answer.

His wife brought the orders, carrying the five plates all at once without a tray, two in each hand and one balanced on her arm. "It isn't a soul in this green world of God's that you can trust," she said. "And I don't count nobody out of that, not nobody," she repeated, looking at Red Sammy.

"Did you read about that criminal, The Misfit, that's escaped?" asked the 40
grandmother.

"I wouldn't be a bit surprised if he didn't attack this place right here," said the woman. "If he hears about it being here, I wouldn't be none surprised to see him. If he hears it's two cent in the cash register, I wouldn't be a tall surprised if he. . . ."

"That'll do," Red Sam said. "Go bring these people their Co'-Colas," and the woman went off to get the rest of the order.

"A good man is hard to find," Red Sammy said. "Everything is getting terrible. I remember the day you could go off and leave your screen door unlatched. Not no more."

He and the grandmother discussed better times. The old lady said that in her opinion Europe was entirely to blame for the way things were now. She said the way Europe acted you would think we were made of money and Red Sam said it was no use talking about it, she was exactly right. The children ran outside into the white sunlight and looked at the monkey in the lacy chinaberry tree. He was busy catching fleas on himself and biting each one carefully between his teeth as if it were a delicacy.

They drove off again into the hot afternoon. The grandmother took cat naps 45
and woke up every few minutes with her own snoring. Outside of Toombsboro she woke up and recalled an old plantation that she had visited in this neighborhood once when she was a young lady. She said the house had six white columns across the front and that there was an avenue of oaks leading up to it and two little wooden trellis arbors on either side in front where you sat down with your suitor after a stroll in the garden. She recalled exactly which road to turn off to get to it. She knew that Bailey would not be willing to lose any time looking at an old house, but the more she talked about it, the more she wanted to see it once again and find out if the little twin arbors were still standing. "There was a secret panel in this house," she said craftily, not telling the truth but wishing that she were, "and the story went that all the family silver was hidden in it when Sherman° came through but it was never found. . . ."

"Hey!" John Wesley said. "Let's go see it! We'll find it! We'll poke all the woodwork and find it! Who lives there? Where do you turn off at? Hey Pop, can't we turn off there?"

"We never have seen a house with a secret panel!" June Star shrieked. "Let's go to the house with the secret panel! Hey Pop, can't we go see the house with the secret panel!"

"It's not far from here, I know," the grandmother said. "It won't take over twenty minutes."

Sherman: William Tecumseh Sherman (1820–1891), Union Army commander who led infamous marches through the South during the Civil War.

Bailey was looking straight ahead. His jaw was as rigid as a horseshoe. "No," he said.

The children began to yell and scream that they wanted to see the house   50 with the secret panel. John Wesley kicked the back of the front seat and June Star hung over her mother's shoulder and whined desperately into her ear that they never had any fun even on their vacation, that they could never do what THEY wanted to do. The baby began to scream and John Wesley kicked the back of the seat so hard that his father could feel the blows in his kidney.

"All right!" he shouted and drew the car to a stop at the side of the road. "Will you all shut up? Will you all just shut up for one second? If you don't shut up, we won't go anywhere."

"It would be very educational for them," the grandmother murmured.

"All right," Bailey said, "but get this: this is the only time we're going to stop for anything like this. This is the one and only time."

"The dirt road that you have to turn down is about a mile back," the grandmother directed. "I marked it when we passed."

"A dirt road," Bailey groaned.   55

After they had turned around and were headed toward the dirt road, the grandmother recalled other points about the house, the beautiful glass over the front doorway and the candle-lamp in the hall. John Wesley said that the secret panel was probably in the fireplace.

"You can't go inside this house," Bailey said. "You don't know who lives there."

"While you all talk to the people in front, I'll run around behind and get in a window," John Wesley suggested.

"We'll all stay in the car," his mother said.

They turned onto the dirt road and the car raced roughly along in a swirl   60 of pink dust. The grandmother recalled the times when there were no paved roads and thirty miles was a day's journey. The dirt road was hilly and there were sudden washes in it and sharp curves on dangerous embankments. All at once they would be on a hill, looking down over the blue tops of trees for miles around, then the next minute, they would be in a red depression with the dust-coated trees looking down on them.

"This place had better turn up in a minute," Bailey said, "or I'm going to turn around."

The road looked as if no one had traveled on it for months.

"It's not much farther," the grandmother said and just as she said it, a horrible thought came to her. The thought was so embarrassing that she turned red in the face and her eyes dilated and her feet jumped up, upsetting her valise in the corner. The instant the valise moved, the newspaper top she had over the basket under it rose with a snarl and Pitty Sing, the cat, sprang onto Bailey's shoulder.

The children were thrown to the floor and their mother, clutching the baby, was thrown out the door onto the ground; the old lady was thrown into the front seat. The car turned over once and landed right-side-up in a gulch off the side of the road. Bailey remained in the driver's seat with the cat—gray-striped with a broad white face and an orange nose—clinging to his neck like a caterpillar.

As soon as the children saw they could move their arms and legs, they   65 scrambled out of the car, shouting, "We've had an ACCIDENT!" The grandmother was curled up under the dashboard, hoping she was injured so that

Bailey's wrath would not come down on her all at once. The horrible thought she had before the accident was that the house she had remembered so vividly was not in Georgia but in Tennessee.

Bailey removed the cat from his neck with both hands and flung it out the window against the side of a pine tree. Then he got out of the car and started looking for the children's mother. She was sitting against the side of the red gutted ditch, holding the screaming baby, but she only had a cut down her face and a broken shoulder. "We've had an ACCIDENT!" the children screamed in a frenzy of delight.

"But nobody's killed," June Star said with disappointment as the grandmother limped out of the car, her hat still pinned to her head but the broken front brim standing up at a jaunty angle and the violet spray hanging off the side. They all sat down in the ditch, except the children, to recover from the shock. They were all shaking.

"Maybe a car will come along," said the children's mother hoarsely.

"I believe I have injured an organ," said the grandmother, pressing her side, but no one answered her. Bailey's teeth were clattering. He had on a yellow sport shirt with bright blue parrots designed in it and his face was as yellow as the shirt. The grandmother decided that she would not mention that the house was in Tennessee.

The road was about ten feet above and they could see only the tops of the trees on the other side of it. Behind the ditch they were sitting in there were more woods, tall and dark and deep. In a few minutes they saw a car some distance away on top of a hill, coming slowly as if the occupants were watching them. The grandmother stood up and waved both arms dramatically to attract their attention. The car continued to come on slowly, disappeared around a bend and appeared again, moving even slower, on top of the hill they had gone over. It was a big black battered hearse-like automobile. There were three men in it.

It came to a stop just over them and for some minutes, the driver looked down with a steady expressionless gaze to where they were sitting, and didn't speak. Then he turned his head and muttered something to the other two and they got out. One was a fat boy in black trousers and a red sweat shirt with a silver stallion embossed on the front of it. He moved around on the right side of them and stood staring, his mouth partly open in a kind of loose grin. The other had on khaki pants and a blue striped coat and a gray hat pulled down very low, hiding most of his face. He came around slowly on the left side. Neither spoke.

The driver got out of the car and stood by the side of it, looking down at them. He was an older man than the other two. His hair was just beginning to gray and he wore silver-rimmed spectacles that gave him a scholarly look. He had a long creased face and didn't have on any shirt or undershirt. He had on blue jeans that were too tight for him and was holding a black hat and a gun. The two boys also had guns.

"We've had an ACCIDENT!" the children screamed.

The grandmother had the peculiar feeling that the bespectacled man was someone she knew. His face was as familiar to her as if she had known him all her life but she could not recall who he was. He moved away from the car and began to come down the embankment, placing his feet carefully so that he wouldn't slip. He had on tan and white shoes and no socks, and his ankles were red and thin. "Good afternoon," he said. "I see you all had you a little spill."

"We turned over twice!" said the grandmother.   75

"Oncet," he corrected. "We seen it happen. Try their car and see will it run, Hiram," he said quietly to the boy with the gray hat.

"What you got that gun for?" John Wesley asked. "Whatcha gonna do with that gun?"

"Lady," the man said to the children's mother, "would you mind calling them children to sit down by you? Children make me nervous. I want all you all to sit down right together there where you're at."

"What are you telling US what to do for?" June Star asked.

Behind them the line of woods gaped like a dark open mouth. "Come   80
here," said their mother.

"Look here now," Bailey said suddenly, "we're in a predicament! We're in. . . ."

The grandmother shrieked. She scrambled to her feet and stood staring. "You're The Misfit!" she said. "I recognized you at once!"

"Yes'm," the man said, smiling slightly as if he were pleased in spite of himself to be known, "but it would have been better for all of you, lady, if you hadn't of reckernized me."

Bailey turned his head sharply and said something to his mother that shocked even the children. The old lady began to cry and The Misfit reddened.

"Lady," he said, "don't you get upset. Sometimes a man says things he   85
don't mean. I don't reckon he meant to talk to you thataway."

"You wouldn't shoot a lady, would you?" the grandmother said and removed a clean handkerchief from her cuff and began to slap at her eyes with it.

The Misfit pointed the toe of his shoe into the ground and made a little hole and then covered it up again. "I would hate to have to," he said.

"Listen," the grandmother almost screamed, "I know you're a good man. You don't look a bit like you have common blood. I know you must come from nice people!"

"Yes mam," he said, "finest people in the world." When he smiled he showed a row of strong white teeth. "God never made a finer woman than my mother and my daddy's heart was pure gold," he said. The boy with the red sweat shirt had come around behind them and was standing with his gun at his hip. The Misfit squatted down on the ground. "Watch them children, Bobby Lee," he said. "You know they make me nervous." He looked at the six of them huddled together in front of him and he seemed to be embarrassed as if he couldn't think of anything to say. "Ain't a cloud in the sky," he remarked, looking up at it. "Don't see no sun but don't see no cloud neither."

"Yes, it's a beautiful day," said the grandmother. "Listen," she said, "you   90
shouldn't call yourself The Misfit because I know you're a good man at heart. I can just look at you and tell."

"Hush!" Bailey yelled. "Hush! Everybody shut up and let me handle this!" He was squatting in the position of a runner about to sprint forward but he didn't move.

"I pre-chate that, lady," The Misfit said and drew a little circle in the ground with the butt of his gun.

"It'll take a half a hour to fix this here car," Hiram called, looking over the raised hood of it.

"Well, first you and Bobby Lee get him and that little boy to step over yonder with you," The Misfit said, pointing to Bailey and John Wesley. "The boys want to ast you something," he said to Bailey. "Would you mind stepping back in them woods there with them?"

"Listen," Bailey began, "we're in a terrible predicament! Nobody realizes 95 what this is," and his voice cracked. His eyes were as blue and intense as the parrots in his shirt and he remained perfectly still.

The grandmother reached up to adjust her hat brim as if she were going to the woods with him but it came off in her hand. She stood staring at it and after a second she let it fall to the ground. Hiram pulled Bailey up by the arm as if he were assisting an old man. John Wesley caught hold of his father's hand and Bobby Lee followed. They went off toward the woods and just as they reached the dark edge, Bailey turned and supporting himself against a gray naked pine trunk, he shouted, "I'll be back in a minute, Mamma, wait on me!"

"Come back this instant!" his mother shrilled but they all disappeared into the woods.

"Bailey Boy!" the grandmother called in a tragic voice but she found she was looking at The Misfit squatting on the ground in front of her. "I just know you're a good man," she said desperately. "You're not a bit common!"

"Nome, I ain't a good man," The Misfit said after a second as if he had considered her statement carefully, "but I ain't the worst in the world neither. My daddy said I was a different breed of dog from my brothers and sisters. 'You know,' Daddy said, 'it's some that can live their whole life out without asking about it and it's others has to know why it is, and this boy is one of the latters. He's going to be into everything!'" He put on his black hat and looked up suddenly and then away deep into the woods as if he were embarrassed again. "I'm sorry I don't have on a shirt before you ladies," he said, hunching his shoulders slightly. "We buried our clothes that we had on when we escaped and we're just making do until we can get better. We borrowed these from some folks we met," he explained.

"That's perfectly all right," the grandmother said. "Maybe Bailey has an 100 extra shirt in his suitcase."

"I'll look and see terrectly," The Misfit said.

"Where are they taking him?" the children's mother screamed.

"Daddy was a card himself," The Misfit said. "You couldn't put anything over on him. He never got in trouble with the Authorities though. Just had the knack of handling them."

"You could be honest too if you'd only try," said the grandmother. "Think how wonderful it would be to settle down and live a comfortable life and not have to think about somebody chasing you all the time."

The Misfit kept scratching in the ground with the butt of his gun as if he 105 were thinking about it. "Yes'm, somebody is always after you," he murmured.

The grandmother noticed how thin his shoulder blades were just behind his hat because she was standing up looking down on him. "Do you ever pray?" she asked.

He shook his head. All she saw was the black hat wiggle between his shoulder blades. "Nome," he said.

There was a pistol shot from the woods, followed closely by another. Then silence. The old lady's head jerked around. She could hear the wind move through the tree tops like a long satisfied insuck of breath. "Bailey Boy!" she called.

"I was a gospel singer for a while," The Misfit said. "I been most everything. Been in the arm service, both land and sea, at home and abroad, been twict married, been an undertaker, been with the railroads, plowed Mother Earth, been in a tornado, seen a man burnt alive oncet," and he looked up at the children's mother and the little girl who were sitting close together, their faces white and their eyes glassy; "I even seen a woman flogged," he said.

"Pray, pray," the grandmother began, "pray, pray. . . ."   110

"I never was a bad boy that I remember of," The Misfit said in an almost dreamy voice, "but somewheres along the line I done something wrong and got sent to the penitentiary. I was buried alive," and he looked up and held her attention to him by a steady stare.

"That's when you should have started to pray," she said. "What did you do to get sent to the penitentiary that first time?"

"Turn to the right, it was a wall," The Misfit said, looking up again at the cloudless sky. "Turn to the left, it was a wall. Look up it was a ceiling, look down it was a floor. I forget what I done, lady. I set there and set there, trying to remember what it was I done and I ain't recalled it to this day. Oncet in a while, I would think it was coming to me, but it never come."

"Maybe they put you in by mistake," the old lady said vaguely.

"Nome," he said. "It wasn't no mistake. They had the papers on me."   115

"You must have stolen something," she said.

The Misfit sneered slightly. "Nobody had nothing I wanted," he said. "It was a head-doctor at the penitentiary said what I had done was kill my daddy but I known that for a lie. My daddy died in nineteen ought nineteen of the epidemic flu and I never had a thing to do with it. He was buried in the Mount Hopewell Baptist churchyard and you can see for yourself."

"If you would pray," the old lady said, "Jesus would help you."

"That's right," The Misfit said.

"Well then, why don't you pray?" she asked trembling with delight suddenly.   120

"I don't want no hep," he said. "I'm doing all right by myself."

Bobby Lee and Hiram came ambling back from the woods. Bobby Lee was dragging a yellow shirt with bright blue parrots in it.

"Throw me that shirt, Bobby Lee," The Misfit said. The shirt came flying at him and landed on his shoulder and he put it on. The grandmother couldn't name what the shirt reminded her of. "No, lady," The Misfit said while he was buttoning it up, "I found out the crime don't matter. You can do one thing or you can do another, kill a man or take a tire off his car, because sooner or later you're going to forget what it was you done and just be punished for it."

The children's mother had begun to make heaving noises as if she couldn't get her breath. "Lady," he asked, "would you and that little girl like to step off yonder with Bobby Lee and Hiram and join your husband?"

"Yes, thank you," the mother said faintly. Her left arm dangled helplessly   125 and she was holding the baby, who had gone to sleep, in the other. "Hep that lady up, Hiram," The Misfit said as she struggled to climb out of the ditch, "and Bobby Lee, you hold onto that little girl's hand."

"I don't want to hold hands with him," June Star said. "He reminds me of a pig."

The fat boy blushed and laughed and caught her by the arm and pulled her off into the woods after Hiram and her mother.

Alone with The Misfit, the grandmother found that she had lost her voice. There was not a cloud in the sky nor any sun. There was nothing around her but woods. She wanted to tell him that he must pray. She opened and closed her mouth several times before anything came out. Finally she found herself saying, "Jesus, Jesus," meaning Jesus will help you, but the way she was saying it, it sounded as if she might be cursing.

"Yes'm," The Misfit said as if he agreed. "Jesus thown everything off balance. It was the same case with Him as with me except He hadn't committed any crime and they could prove I had committed one because they had the papers on me. Of course," he said, "they never shown me my papers. That's why I sign myself now. I said long ago, you get your signature and sign everything you do and keep a copy of it. Then you'll know what you done and you can hold up the crime to the punishment and see do they match and in the end you'll have something to prove you ain't been treated right. I call myself The Misfit," he said, "because I can't make what all I done wrong fit what all I gone through in punishment."

There was a piercing scream from the woods, followed closely by a pistol   130
report. "Does it seem right to you, lady, that one is punished a heap and another ain't punished at all?"

"Jesus!" the old lady cried. "You've got good blood! I know you wouldn't shoot a lady! I know you come from nice people! Pray! Jesus, you ought not to shoot a lady. I'll give you all the money I've got!"

"Lady," The Misfit said, looking beyond her far into the woods, "there never was a body that give the undertaker a tip."

There were two more pistol reports and the grandmother raised her head like a parched old turkey hen crying for water and called, "Bailey Boy, Bailey Boy!" as if her heart would break.

"Jesus was the only One that ever raised the dead," The Misfit continued, "and He shouldn't have done it. He thown everything off balance. If He did what He said, then it's nothing for you to do but thow away everything and follow Him, and if He didn't, then it's nothing for you to do but enjoy the few minutes you got left the best way you can—by killing somebody or burning down his house or doing some other meanness to him. No pleasure but meanness," he said and his voice had become almost a snarl.

"Maybe He didn't raise the dead," the old lady mumbled, not knowing   135
what she was saying and feeling so dizzy that she sank down in the ditch with her legs twisted under her.

"I wasn't there so I can't say He didn't," The Misfit said. "I wisht I had of been there," he said, hitting the ground with his fist. "It ain't right I wasn't there because if I had of been there I would of known. Listen lady," he said in a high voice, "if I had of been there I would of known and I wouldn't be like I am now." His voice seemed about to crack and the grandmother's head cleared for an instant. She saw the man's face twisted close to her own as if he were going to cry and she murmured, "Why you're one of my babies. You're one of my own children!" She reached out and touched him on the shoulder. The Misfit sprang back as if a snake had bitten him and shot her three times through the chest. Then he put his gun down on the ground and took off his glasses and began to clean them.

Hiram and Bobby Lee returned from the woods and stood over the ditch, looking down at the grandmother who half sat and half lay in a puddle of blood with her legs crossed under her like a child's and her face smiling up at the cloudless sky.

Without his glasses, The Misfit's eyes were red-rimmed and pale and defenseless-looking. "Take her off and thow her where you thown the others," he said, picking up the cat that was rubbing itself against his leg.

"She was a talker, wasn't she?" Bobby Lee said, sliding down the ditch with a yodel.

"She would of been a good woman," The Misfit said, "if it had been some-   140
body there to shoot her every minute of her life."

"Some fun!" Bobby Lee said.

"Shut up, Bobby Lee," The Misfit said. "It's no real pleasure in life."

CONSIDERATIONS FOR CRITICAL THINKING AND WRITING

1. FIRST RESPONSE. How does O'Connor portray the family? What is comic about them? What qualities about them are we meant to take seriously? Are you shocked by what happens to them? Does your attitude toward them remain constant during the course of the story?

2. How do the grandmother's concerns about the trip to Florida foreshadow events in the story?

3. Describe the grandmother. How does O'Connor make her the central character?

4. What is Red Sammy's purpose in the story? Relate his view of life to the story's conflicts.

5. Characterize The Misfit. What makes him so? Can he be written off as simply insane? How does the grandmother respond to him?

6. Why does The Misfit say that "Jesus thown everything off balance" (para. 129)? What does religion have to do with the brutal action of this story?

7. What does The Misfit mean at the end when he says about the grandmother, "She would of been a good woman . . . if it had been somebody there to shoot her every minute of her life"?

8. Describe the story's tone. Is it consistent? What is the effect of O'Connor's use of tone?

9. How is coincidence used to advance the plot? How do coincidences lead to ironies in the story?

10. Explain how the title points to the story's theme.

CONNECTIONS TO OTHER SELECTIONS

1. What makes "A Good Man Is Hard to Find" so difficult to interpret in contrast, say, to reading Hawthorne's "The Birthmark" (p. 359)?

2. How does this family compare with the Snopeses in Faulkner's "Barn Burning" (p. 493)? Which family are you more sympathetic to?

3. Consider the criminal behavior of The Misfit and Abner Snopes. What motivates each character? Explain the significant similarities and differences between them.

Good Country People   1955

Besides the neutral expression that she wore when she was alone, Mrs. Freeman had two others, forward and reverse, that she used for all her human dealings. Her forward expression was steady and driving like the advance of a heavy truck. Her eyes never swerved to left or right but turned as the story turned as if they followed a yellow line down the center of it. She seldom used the other expression because it was not often necessary for her to retract a statement, but when she did, her face came to a complete stop, there was an almost imperceptible movement of her black eyes, during which they seemed to be receding, and then the observer would see that Mrs. Freeman, though she might stand there as real as several grain sacks thrown on top of each other, was no longer there in spirit. As for getting anything across to her when this was the case, Mrs. Hopewell had given it up. She might talk her head off. Mrs. Freeman could never be brought to admit herself wrong on any point. She would stand there and if she could be brought to say anything, it was something like, "Well, I wouldn't of said it was and I wouldn't of said it wasn't," or letting her gaze range over the top kitchen shelf where there was an assortment of dusty bottles, she might remark, "I see you ain't ate many of them figs you put up last summer."

They carried on their most important business in the kitchen at breakfast. Every morning Mrs. Hopewell got up at seven o'clock and lit her gas heater and Joy's. Joy was her daughter, a large blonde girl who had an artificial leg. Mrs. Hopewell thought of her as a child though she was thirty-two years old and highly educated. Joy would get up while her mother was eating and lumber into the bathroom and slam the door, and before long, Mrs. Freeman would arrive at the back door. Joy would hear her mother call, "Come on in," and then they would talk for a while in low voices that were indistinguishable in the bathroom. By the time Joy came in, they had usually finished the weather report and were on one or the other of Mrs. Freeman's daughters, Glynese or Carramae, Joy called them Glycerin and Caramel. Glynese, a redhead, was eighteen and had many admirers; Carramae, a blonde, was only fifteen but already married and pregnant. She could not keep anything in her stomach. Every morning Mrs. Freeman told Mrs. Hopewell how many times she had vomited since the last report.

Mrs. Hopewell liked to tell people that Glynese and Carramae were two of the finest girls she knew and that Mrs. Freeman was a *lady* and that she was never ashamed to take her anywhere or introduce her to anybody they might meet. Then she would tell how she had happened to hire the Freemans in the first place and how they were a godsend to her and how she had had them four years. The reason for her keeping them so long was that they were not trash. They were good country people. She had telephoned the man whose name they had given as a reference and he had told her that Mr. Freeman was a good farmer but that his wife was the nosiest woman ever to walk the earth. "She's got to be into everything," the man said. "If she don't get there before the dust settles, you can bet she's dead, that's all. She'll want to know all your business. I can stand him real good," he had said, "but me nor my wife neither could have stood that woman one more minute on this place." That had put Mrs. Hopewell off for a few days.

She had hired them in the end because there were no other applicants but she had made up her mind beforehand exactly how she would handle the woman. Since she was the type who had to be into everything, then, Mrs. Hopewell decided, she would not only let her be into everything, she would *see to it* that she was into everything—she would give her the responsibility of everything, she would put her in charge. Mrs. Hopewell had no bad qualities of her own but she was able to use other people's in such a constructive way that she never felt the lack. She had hired the Freemans and she had kept them four years.

Nothing is perfect. This was one of Mrs. Hopewell's favorite sayings. Another was: that is life! And still another, the most important, was: well, other people have their opinions too. She would make these statements, usually at the table, in a tone of gentle insistence as if no one held them but her, and the large hulking Joy, whose constant outrage had obliterated every expression from her face, would stare just a little to the side of her, her eyes icy blue, with the look of someone who has achieved blindness by an act of will and means to keep it.

When Mrs. Hopewell said to Mrs. Freeman that life was like that, Mrs. Freeman would say, "I always said so myself." Nothing had been arrived at by anyone that had not first been arrived at by her. She was quicker than Mr. Freeman. When Mrs. Hopewell said to her after they had been on the place a while, "You know, you're the wheel behind the wheel," and winked, Mrs. Freeman had said, "I know it. I've always been quick. It's some that are quicker than others."

"Everybody is different," Mrs. Hopewell said.

"Yes, most people is," Mrs. Freeman said.

"It takes all kinds to make the world."

"I always said it did myself."

The girl was used to this kind of dialogue for breakfast and more of it for dinner; sometimes they had it for supper too. When they had no guest they ate in the kitchen because that was easier. Mrs. Freeman always managed to arrive at some point during the meal and to watch them finish it. She would stand in the doorway if it were summer but in the winter she would stand with one elbow on top of the refrigerator and look down on them, or she would stand by the gas heater, lifting the back of her skirt slightly. Occasionally she would stand against the wall and roll her head from side to side. At no time was she in any hurry to leave. All this was very trying on Mrs. Hopewell but she was a woman of great patience. She realized that nothing is perfect and that in the Freemans she had good country people and that if, in this day and age, you get good country people, you had better hang onto them.

She had had plenty of experience with trash. Before the Freemans she had averaged one tenant family a year. The wives of these farmers were not the kind you would want to be around you for very long. Mrs. Hopewell, who had divorced her husband long ago, needed someone to walk over the fields with her; and when Joy had to be impressed for these services, her remarks were usually so ugly and her face so glum that Mrs. Hopewell would say, "If you can't come pleasantly, I don't want you at all," to which the girl, standing square and rigid-shouldered with her neck thrust slightly forward, would reply, "If you want me, here I am — LIKE I AM."

Mrs. Hopewell excused this attitude because of the leg (which had been shot off in a hunting accident when Joy was ten). It was hard for Mrs. Hopewell to realize that her child was thirty-two now and that for more than twenty years she had had only one leg. She thought of her still as a child because it tore her heart to think instead of the poor stout girl in her thirties who had never danced a step or had any *normal* good times. Her name was really Joy but as soon as she was twenty-one and away from home, she had had it legally changed. Mrs. Hopewell was certain that she had thought and thought until she had hit upon the ugliest name in any language. Then she had gone and had the beautiful name, Joy, changed without telling her mother until after she had done it. Her legal name was Hulga.

When Mrs. Hopewell thought the name, Hulga, she thought of the broad blank hull of a battleship. She would not use it. She continued to call her Joy to which the girl responded but in a purely mechanical way.

Hulga had learned to tolerate Mrs. Freeman who saved her from taking 15 walks with her mother. Even Glynese and Carramae were useful when they occupied attention that might otherwise have been directed at her. At first she had thought she could not stand Mrs. Freeman for she had found that it was not possible to be rude to her. Mrs. Freeman would take on strange resentments and for days together she would be sullen but the source of her displeasure was always obscure; a direct attack, a positive leer, blatant ugliness to her face — these never touched her. And without warning one day, she began calling her Hulga.

She did not call her that in front of Mrs. Hopewell who would have been incensed but when she and the girl happened to be out of the house together, she would say something and add the name Hulga to the end of it, and the big spectacled Joy-Hulga would scowl and redden as if her privacy had been intruded upon. She considered the name her personal affair. She had arrived at it first purely on the basis of its ugly sound and then the full genius of its fitness had struck her. She had a vision of the name working like the ugly sweating Vulcan° who stayed in the furnace and to whom, presumably, the goddess had to come when called. She saw it as the name of her highest creative act. One of her major triumphs was that her mother had not been able to turn her dust into Joy, but the greater one was that she had been able to turn it herself into Hulga. However, Mrs. Freeman's relish for using the name only irritated her. It was as if Mrs. Freeman's beady steel-pointed eyes had penetrated far enough behind her face to reach some secret fact. Something about her seemed to fascinate Mrs. Freeman and then one day Hulga realized that it was the artificial leg. Mrs. Freeman had a special fondness for the details of secret infections, hidden deformities, assaults upon children. Of diseases, she preferred the lingering or incurable. Hulga had heard Mrs. Hopewell give her the details of the hunting accident, how the leg had been literally blasted off, how she had never lost consciousness. Mrs. Freeman could listen to it any time as if it had happened an hour ago.

When Hulga stumped into the kitchen in the morning (she could walk without making the awful noise but she made it — Mrs. Hopewell was certain — because it was ugly-sounding), she glanced at them and did not speak. Mrs. Hopewell would be in her red kimono with her hair tied around her head in rags. She would be sitting at the table, finishing her breakfast and Mrs. Freeman would be hanging by her elbow outward from the refrigerator, looking down at the table. Hulga always put her eggs on the stove to boil and then stood over them with her arms folded, and Mrs. Hopewell would look at her — a kind of indirect gaze divided between her and Mrs. Freeman — and would think that if she would only keep herself up a little, she wouldn't be so bad looking. There was nothing wrong with her face that a pleasant expression wouldn't help. Mrs. Hopewell said that people who looked on the bright side of things would be beautiful even if they were not.

Vulcan: Roman god of fire.

Whenever she looked at Joy this way, she could not help but feel that it would have been better if the child had not taken the Ph.D. It had certainly not brought her out any and now that she had it, there was no more excuse for her to go to school again. Mrs. Hopewell thought it was nice for girls to go to school to have a good time but Joy had "gone through." Anyhow, she would not have been strong enough to go again. The doctors had told Mrs. Hopewell that with the best of care, Joy might see forty-five. She had a weak heart. Joy had made it plain that if it had not been for this condition, she would be far from these red hills and good country people. She would be in a university lecturing to people who knew what she was talking about. And Mrs. Hopewell could very well picture her there, looking like a scarecrow and lecturing to more of the same. Here she went about all day in a six-year-old skirt and a yellow sweat shirt with a faded cowboy on a horse embossed on it. She thought this was funny; Mrs. Hopewell thought it was idiotic and showed simply that she was still a child. She was brilliant but she didn't have a grain of sense. It seemed to Mrs. Hopewell that every year she grew less like other people and more like herself—bloated, rude, and squint-eyed. And she said such strange things! To her own mother she had said—without warning, without excuse, standing up in the middle of a meal with her face purple and her mouth half full—"Woman! do you ever look inside? Do you ever look inside and see what you are *not*? God!" she had cried sinking down again and staring at her plate, "Malebranche° was right: we are not our own light. We are not our own light!" Mrs. Hopewell had no idea to this day what brought that on. She had only made the remark, hoping Joy would take it in, that a smile never hurt anyone.

The girl had taken the Ph.D. in philosophy and this left Mrs. Hopewell at a complete loss. You could say, "My daughter is a nurse," or "My daughter is a schoolteacher," or even, "My daughter is a chemical engineer." You could not say, "My daughter is a philosopher." That was something that had ended with the Greeks and Romans. All day Joy sat on her neck in a deep chair, reading. Sometimes she went for walks but she didn't like dogs or cats or birds or flowers or nature or nice young men. She looked at nice young men as if she could smell their stupidity.

One day Mrs. Hopewell had picked up one of the books the girl had just 20 put down and opening it at random, she read, "Science, on the other hand, has to assert its soberness and seriousness afresh and declare that it is concerned solely with what-is. Nothing—how can it be for science anything but a horror and a phantasm? If science is right, then one thing stands firm: science wishes to know nothing of nothing. Such is after all the strictly scientific approach to Nothing. We know it by wishing to know nothing of Nothing." These words had been underlined with a blue pencil and they worked on Mrs. Hopewell like some evil incantation in gibberish. She shut the book quickly and went out of the room as if she were having a chill.

This morning when the girl came in, Mrs. Freeman was on Carramae. "She thrown up four times after supper," she said, "and was up twict in the night after three o'clock. Yesterday she didn't do nothing but ramble in the bureau drawer. All she did. Stand up there and see what she could run up on."

"She's got to eat," Mrs. Hopewell muttered, sipping her coffee, while she watched Joy's back at the stove. She was wondering what the child had said to

Malebranche: Nicolas Malebranche (1638–1715), a French philosopher.

the Bible salesman. She could not imagine what kind of a conversation she could possibly have had with him.

He was a tall gaunt hatless youth who had called yesterday to sell them a Bible. He had appeared at the door, carrying a large black suitcase that weighted him so heavily on one side that he had to brace himself against the door facing. He seemed on the point of collapse but he said in a cheerful voice, "Good morning, Mrs. Cedars!" and set the suitcase down on the mat. He was not a bad-looking young man though he had on a bright blue suit and yellow socks that were not pulled up far enough. He had prominent face bones and a streak of sticky-looking brown hair falling across his forehead.

"I'm Mrs. Hopewell," she said.

"Oh!" he said, pretending to look puzzled but with his eyes sparkling, "I saw it said 'The Cedars' on the mailbox so I thought you was Mrs. Cedars!" and he burst out in a pleasant laugh. He picked up the satchel and under cover of a pant, he fell forward into her hall. It was rather as if the suitcase had moved first, jerking him after it. "Mrs. Hopewell!" he said and grabbed her hand. "I hope you are well!" and he laughed again and then all at once his face sobered completely. He paused and gave her a straight earnest look and said, "Lady, I've come to speak of serious things." 25

"Well, come in," she muttered, none too pleased because her dinner was almost ready. He came into the parlor and sat down on the edge of a straight chair and put the suitcase between his feet and glanced around the room as if he were sizing her up by it. Her silver gleamed on the two sideboards; she decided he had never been in a room as elegant as this.

"Mrs. Hopewell," he began, using her name in a way that sounded almost intimate, "I know you believe in Chrustian service."

"Well yes," she murmured.

"I know," he said and paused, looking very wise with his head cocked on one side, "that you're a good woman. Friends have told me."

Mrs. Hopewell never liked to be taken for a fool. "What are you selling?" she asked. 30

"Bibles," the young man said and his eye raced around the room before he added, "I see you have no family Bible in your parlor, I see that is the one lack you got!"

Mrs. Hopewell could not say, "My daughter is an atheist and won't let me keep the Bible in the parlor." She said, stiffening slightly, "I keep my Bible by my bedside." This was not the truth. It was in the attic somewhere.

"Lady," he said, "the word of God ought to be in the parlor."

"Well, I think that's a matter of taste," she began. "I think . . ."

"Lady," he said, "for a Chrustian, the word of God ought to be in every room in the house besides in his heart. I know you're a Chrustian because I can see it in every line of your face." 35

She stood up and said, "Well, young man, I don't want to buy a Bible and I smell my dinner burning."

He didn't get up. He began to twist his hands and looking down at them, he said softly, "Well lady, I'll tell you the truth — not many people want to buy one nowadays and besides, I know I'm real simple. I don't know how to say a thing but to say it. I'm just a country boy." He glanced up into her unfriendly face. "People like you don't like to fool with country people like me!"

"Why!" she cried, "good country people are the salt of the earth! Besides, we all have different ways of doing, it takes all kinds to make the world go 'round. That's life!"

"You said a mouthful," he said.

"Why, I think there aren't enough good people in the world!" she said, 40 stirred. "I think that's what's wrong with it!"

His face had brightened. "I didn't introduce myself," he said. "I'm Manley Pointer from out in the country around Willohobie, not even from a place, just from near a place."

"You wait a minute," she said. "I have to see about my dinner." She went out to the kitchen and found Joy standing near the door where she had been listening.

"Get rid of the salt of the earth," she said, "and let's eat."

Mrs. Hopewell gave her a pained look and turned the heat down under the vegetables. "*I* can't be rude to anybody," she murmured and went back into the parlor.

He had opened the suitcase and was sitting with a Bible on each knee. 45

"You might as well put those up," she told him. "I don't want one."

"I appreciate your honesty," he said. "You don't see any more real honest people unless you go way out in the country."

"I know," she said, "real genuine folks!" Through the crack in the door she heard a groan.

"I guess a lot of boys come telling you they're working their way through college," he said, "but I'm not going to tell you that. Somehow," he said, "I don't want to go to college. I want to devote my life to Chrustian service. See," he said, lowering his voice, "I got this heart condition. I may not live long. When you know it's something wrong with you and you may not live long, well then, lady . . ." He paused, with his mouth open, and stared at her.

He and Joy had the same condition! She knew that her eyes were filling 50 with tears but she collected herself quickly and murmured, "Won't you stay for dinner? We'd love to have you!" and was sorry the instant she heard herself say it.

"Yes mam," he said in an abashed voice, "I would sher love to do that!"

Joy had given him one look on being introduced to him and then throughout the meal had not glanced at him again. He had addressed several remarks to her, which she had pretended not to hear. Mrs. Hopewell could not understand deliberate rudeness, although she lived with it, and she felt she had always to overflow with hospitality to make up for Joy's lack of courtesy. She urged him to talk about himself and he did. He said he was the seventh child of twelve and that his father had been crushed under a tree when he himself was eight years old. He had been crushed very badly, in fact, almost cut in two and was practically not recognizable. His mother had got along the best she could by hard working and she had always seen that her children went to Sunday School and that they read the Bible every evening. He was now nineteen years old and he had been selling Bibles for four months. In that time he had sold seventy-seven Bibles and had the promise of two more sales. He wanted to become a missionary because he thought that was the way you could do most for people. "He who losest his life shall find it," he said simply and he was so sincere, so genuine and earnest that Mrs. Hopewell would not for the world have smiled. He prevented his peas from sliding onto the table by blocking them with a piece of bread which he later cleaned his plate with. She could see Joy observing sidewise how he handled his knife and fork and she saw too that every few minutes, the boy would dart a keen appraising glance at the girl as if he were trying to attract her attention.

After dinner Joy cleared the dishes off the table and disappeared and Mrs. Hopewell was left to talk with him. He told her again about his childhood and his father's accident and about various things that had happened to him. Every five minutes or so she would stifle a yawn. He sat for two hours until finally she told him she must go because she had an appointment in town. He packed his Bibles and thanked her and prepared to leave, but in the doorway he stopped and wrung her hand and said that not on any of his trips had he met a lady as nice as her and he asked if he could come again. She had said she would always be happy to see him.

Joy had been standing in the road, apparently looking at something in the distance, when he came down the steps toward her, bent to the side with his heavy valise. He stopped where she was standing and confronted her directly. Mrs. Hopewell could not hear what he said but she trembled to think what Joy would say to him. She could see that after a minute Joy said something and that then the boy began to speak again, making an excited gesture with his free hand. After a minute Joy said something else at which the boy began to speak once more. Then to her amazement, Mrs. Hopewell saw the two of them walk off together, toward the gate. Joy had walked all the way to the gate with him and Mrs. Hopewell could not imagine what they had said to each other, and she had not yet dared to ask.

Mrs. Freeman was insisting upon her attention. She had moved from the 55 refrigerator to the heater so that Mrs. Hopewell had to turn and face her in order to seem to be listening. "Glynese gone out with Harvey Hill again last night," she said. "She had this sty."

"Hill," Mrs. Hopewell said absently, "is the one who works in the garage?"

"Nome, he's the one that goes to chiropracter school," Mrs. Freeman said. "She had this sty. Been had it two days. So she says when he brought her in the other night he says, 'Lemme get rid of that sty for you,' and she says, 'How?' and he says, 'You just lay yourself down acrost the seat of that car and I'll show you.' So she done it and he popped her neck. Kept on a-popping it several times until she made him quit. This morning," Mrs. Freeman said, "she ain't got no sty. She ain't got no traces of a sty."

"I never heard of that before," Mrs. Hopewell said.

"He ast her to marry him before the Ordinary,"° Mrs. Freeman went on, "and she told him she wasn't going to be married in no *office*."

"Well, Glynese is a fine girl," Mrs. Hopewell said. "Glynese and Carramae 60 are both fine girls."

"Carramae said when her and Lyman was married Lyman said it sure felt sacred to him. She said he said he wouldn't take five hundred dollars for being married by a preacher."

"How much would he take?" the girl asked from the stove.

"He said he wouldn't take five hundred dollars," Mrs. Freeman repeated.

"Well we all have work to do," Mrs. Hopewell said.

"Lyman said it just felt more sacred to him," Mrs. Freeman said. "The doc- 65 tor wants Carramae to eat prunes. Says instead of medicine. Says them cramps is coming from pressure. You know where I think it is?"

Ordinary: Justice of the peace.

"She'll be better in a few weeks," Mrs. Hopewell said.

"In the tube," Mrs. Freeman said. "Else she wouldn't be as sick as she is."

Hulga had cracked her two eggs into a saucer and was bringing them to the table along with a cup of coffee that she had filled too full. She sat down carefully and began to eat, meaning to keep Mrs. Freeman there by questions if for any reason she showed an inclination to leave. She could perceive her mother's eye on her. The first round-about question would be about the Bible salesman and she did not wish to bring it on. "How did he pop her neck?" she asked.

Mrs. Freeman went into a description of how he had popped her neck. She said he owned a '55 Mercury but that Glynese said she would rather marry a man with only a '36 Plymouth who would be married by a preacher. The girl asked what if he had a '32 Plymouth and Mrs. Freeman said what Glynese had said was a '36 Plymouth.

Mrs. Hopewell said there were not many girls with Glynese's common 70 sense. She said what she admired in those girls was their common sense. She said that reminded her that they had had a nice visitor yesterday, a young man selling Bibles. "Lord," she said, "he bored me to death but he was so sincere and genuine I couldn't be rude to him. He was just good country people, you know," she said, "—just the salt of the earth."

"I seen him walk up," Mrs. Freeman said, "and then later—I seen him walk off," and Hulga could feel the slight shift in her voice, the slight insinuation, that he had not walked off alone, had he? Her face remained expressionless but the color rose into her neck and she seemed to swallow it down with the next spoonful of egg. Mrs. Freeman was looking at her as if they had a secret together.

"Well, it takes all kinds of people to make the world go 'round," Mrs. Hopewell said. "It's very good we aren't all alike."

"Some people are more alike than others," Mrs. Freeman said.

Hulga got up and stumped, with about twice the noise that was necessary, into her room and locked the door. She was to meet the Bible salesman at ten o'clock at the gate. She had thought about it half the night. She had started thinking of it as a great joke and then she had begun to see profound implications in it. She had lain in bed imagining dialogues for them that were insane on the surface but that reached below to depths that no Bible salesman would be aware of. Their conversation yesterday had been of this kind.

He had stopped in front of her and had simply stood there. His face was 75 bony and sweaty and bright, with a little pointed nose in the center of it, and his look was different from what it had been at the dinner table. He was gazing at her with open curiosity, with fascination, like a child watching a new fantastic animal at the zoo, and he was breathing as if he had run a great distance to reach her. His gaze seemed somehow familiar but she could not think where she had been regarded with it before. For almost a minute he didn't say anything. Then on what seemed an insuck of breath, he whispered, "You ever ate a chicken that was two days old?"

The girl looked at him stonily. He might have just put this question up for consideration at the meeting of a philosophical association. "Yes," she presently replied as if she had considered it from all angles.

"It must have been mighty small!" he said triumphantly and shook all over with little nervous giggles, getting very red in the face, and subsiding finally into his gaze of complete admiration, while the girl's expression remained exactly the same.

"How old are you?" he asked softly.

She waited some time before she answered. Then in a flat voice she said, "Seventeen."

His smiles came in succession like waves breaking on the surface of a little 80 lake. "I see you got a wooden leg," he said. "I think you're brave. I think you're real sweet."

The girl stood blank and solid and silent.

"Walk to the gate with me," he said. "You're a brave sweet little thing and I liked you the minute I seen you walk in the door."

Hulga began to move forward.

"What's your name?" he asked, smiling down on the top of her head.

"Hulga," she said. 85

"Hulga," he murmured, "Hulga. Hulga. I never heard of anybody name Hulga before. You're shy, aren't you, Hulga?" he asked.

She nodded, watching his large red hand on the handle of the giant valise.

"I like girls that wear glasses," he said. "I think a lot. I'm not like these people that a serious thought don't ever enter their heads. It's because I may die."

"I may die too," she said suddenly and looked up at him. His eyes were very small and brown, glittering feverishly.

"Listen," he said, "don't you think some people was meant to meet on ac- 90 count of what all they got in common and all? Like they both think serious thoughts and all?" He shifted the valise to his other hand so that the hand nearest her was free. He caught hold of her elbow and shook it a little. "I don't work on Saturday," he said. "I like to walk in the woods and see what Mother Nature is wearing. O'er the hills and far away. Pic-nics and things. Couldn't we go on a pic-nic tomorrow? Say yes, Hulga," he said and gave her a dying look as if he felt his insides about to drop out of him. He had even seemed to sway slightly toward her.

During the night she had imagined that she seduced him. She imagined that the two of them walked on the place until they came to the storage barn beyond the two back fields and there, she imagined, that things came to such a pass that she very easily seduced him and that then, of course, she had to reckon with his remorse. True genius can get an idea across even to an inferior mind. She imagined that she took his remorse in hand and changed it into a deeper understanding of life. She took all his shame away and turned it into something useful.

She set off for the gate at exactly ten o'clock, escaping without drawing Mrs. Hopewell's attention. She didn't take anything to eat, forgetting that food is usually taken on a picnic. She wore a pair of slacks and a dirty white shirt, and as an afterthought, she had put some Vapex° on the collar of it since she did not own any perfume. When she reached the gate no one was there.

She looked up and down the empty highway and had the furious feeling that she had been tricked, that he had only meant to make her walk to the gate after the idea of him. Then suddenly he stood up, very tall, from behind a bush on the opposite embankment. Smiling, he lifted his hat which was new and wide-brimmed. He had not worn it yesterday and she wondered if he had bought it for the occasion. It was toast-colored with a red and white band around it and was slightly too large for him. He stepped from behind the bush

---

Vapex: Trade name for a nasal spray.

still carrying the black valise. He had on the same suit and the same yellow socks sucked down in his shoes from walking. He crossed the highway and said, "I knew you'd come!"

The girl wondered acidly how he had known this. She pointed to the valise and asked, "Why did you bring your Bibles?"

He took her elbow, smiling down on her as if he could not stop. "You can 95 never tell when you'll need the word of God, Hulga," he said. She had a moment in which she doubted that this was actually happening and then they began to climb the embankment. They went down into the pasture toward the woods. The boy walked lightly by her side, bouncing on his toes. The valise did not seem to be heavy today; he even swung it. They crossed half the pasture without saying anything and then, putting his hand easily on the small of her back, he asked softly, "Where does your wooden leg join on?"

She turned an ugly red and glared at him and for an instant the boy looked abashed. "I didn't mean you no harm," he said. "I only meant you're so brave and all. I guess God takes care of you."

"No," she said, looking forward and walking fast, "I don't even believe in God."

At this he stopped and whistled. "No!" he exclaimed as if he were too astonished to say anything else.

She walked on and in a second he was bouncing at her side, fanning with his hat. "That's very unusual for a girl," he remarked, watching her out of the corner of his eye. When they reached the edge of the wood, he put his hand on her back again and drew her against him without a word and kissed her heavily.

The kiss, which had more pressure than feeling behind it, produced that 100 extra surge of adrenaline in the girl that enables one to carry a packed trunk out of a burning house, but in her, the power went at once to the brain. Even before he released her, her mind, clear and detached and ironic anyway, was regarding him from a great distance, with amusement but with pity. She had never been kissed before and she was pleased to discover that it was an unexceptional experience and all a matter of the mind's control. Some people might enjoy drain water if they were told it was vodka. When the boy, looking expectant but uncertain, pushed her gently away, she turned and walked on, saying nothing as if such business, for her, were common enough.

He came along panting at her side, trying to help her when he saw a root that she might trip over. He caught and held back the long swaying blades of thorn vine until she had passed beyond them. She led the way and he came breathing heavily behind her. Then they came out on a sunlit hillside, sloping softly into another one a little smaller. Beyond, they could see the rusted top of the old barn where the extra hay was stored.

The hill was sprinkled with small pink weeds. "Then you ain't saved?" he asked suddenly, stopping.

The girl smiled. It was the first time she had smiled at him at all. "In my economy," she said, "I'm saved and you are damned but I told you I didn't believe in God."

Nothing seemed to destroy the boy's look of admiration. He gazed at her now as if the fantastic animal at the zoo had put its paw through the bars and given him a loving poke. She thought he looked as if he wanted to kiss her again and she walked on before he had the chance.

"Ain't there somewheres we can sit down sometime?" he murmured, his   105
voice softening toward the end of the sentence.

"In that barn," she said.

They made for it rapidly as if it might slide away like a train. It was a large
two-story barn, cool and dark inside. The boy pointed up the ladder that led
into the loft and said, "It's too bad we can't go up there."

"Why can't we?" she asked.

"Yer leg," he said reverently.

The girl gave him a contemptuous look and putting both hands on the   110
ladder, she climbed it while he stood below, apparently awestruck. She pulled
herself expertly through the opening and then looked down at him and said,
"Well, come on if you're coming," and he began to climb the ladder, awkwardly
bringing the suitcase with him.

"We won't need the Bible," she observed.

"You never can tell," he said, panting. After he had got into the loft, he was
a few seconds catching his breath. She had sat down in a pile of straw. A wide
sheath of sunlight, filled with dust particles, slanted over her. She lay back
against a bale, her face turned away, looking out the front opening of the barn
where hay was thrown from a wagon into the loft. The two pink-speckled hillsides lay back against a dark ridge of woods. The sky was cloudless and cold
blue. The boy dropped down by her side and put one arm under her and the
other over her and began methodically kissing her face, making little noises
like a fish. He did not remove his hat but it was pushed far enough back not to
interfere. When her glasses got in his way, he took them off of her and slipped
them into his pocket.

The girl at first did not return any of the kisses but presently she began to
and after she had put several on his cheek, she reached his lips and remained
there, kissing him again and again as if she were trying to draw all the breath
out of him. His breath was clear and sweet like a child's and the kisses were
sticky like a child's. He mumbled about loving her and about knowing when he
first seen her that he loved her, but the mumbling was like the sleepy fretting of
a child being put to sleep by his mother. Her mind, throughout this, never
stopped or lost itself for a second to her feelings. "You ain't said you loved me
none," he whispered finally, pulling back from her. "You got to say that."

She looked away from him off into the hollow sky and then down at a
black ridge and then down farther into what appeared to be two green swelling
lakes. She didn't realize he had taken her glasses but this landscape could not
seem exceptional to her for she seldom paid any close attention to her surroundings.

"You got to say it," he repeated. "You got to say you love me."   115

She was always careful how she committed herself. "In a sense," she began,
"if you use the word loosely, you might say that. But it's not a word I use. I
don't have illusions. I'm one of those people who see *through* to nothing."

The boy was frowning. "You got to say it. I said it and you got to say it," he
said.

The girl looked at him almost tenderly. "You poor baby," she murmured.
"It's just as well you don't understand," and she pulled him by the neck,
face-down, against her. "We are all damned," she said, "but some of us have
taken off our blindfolds and see that there's nothing to see. It's a kind of
salvation."

The boy's astonished eyes looked blankly through the ends of her hair. "Okay," he almost whined, "but do you love me or don'tcher?"

"Yes," she said and added, "in a sense. But I must tell you something. There mustn't be anything dishonest between us." She lifted his head and looked him in the eye. "I am thirty years old," she said. "I have a number of degrees."

The boy's look was irritated but dogged. "I don't care," he said. "I don't care a thing about what all you done. I just want to know if you love me or don'tcher?" and he caught her to him and wildly planted her face with kisses until she said, "Yes, yes."

"Okay then," he said, letting her go. "Prove it."

She smiled, looking dreamily out on the shifty landscape. She had seduced him without even making up her mind to try. "How?" she asked, feeling that he should be delayed a little.

He leaned over and put his lips to her ear. "Show me where your wooden leg joins on," he whispered.

The girl uttered a sharp little cry and her face instantly drained of color. The obscenity of the suggestion was not what shocked her. As a child she had sometimes been subject to feelings of shame but education had removed the last traces of that as a good surgeon scrapes for cancer; she would no more have felt it over what he was asking than she would have believed in his Bible. But she was as sensitive about the artificial leg as a peacock about his tail. No one ever touched it but her. She took care of it as someone else would his soul, in private and almost with her own eyes turned away. "No," she said.

"I known it," he muttered, sitting up. "You're just playing me for a sucker."

"Oh no no!" she cried. "It joins on at the knee. Only at the knee. Why do you want to see it?"

The boy gave her a long penetrating look. "Because," he said, "it's what makes you different. You ain't like anybody else."

She sat staring at him. There was nothing about her face or her round freezing-blue eyes to indicate that this had moved her; but she felt as if her heart had stopped and left her mind to pump her blood. She decided that for the first time in her life she was face to face with real innocence. This boy, with an instinct that came from beyond wisdom, had touched the truth about her. When after a minute, she said in a hoarse high voice, "All right," it was like surrendering to him completely. It was like losing her own life and finding it again, miraculously, in his.

Very gently he began to roll the slack leg up. The artificial limb, in a white sock and brown flat shoe, was bound in a heavy material like canvas and ended in an ugly jointure where it was attached to the stump. The boy's face and his voice were entirely reverent as he uncovered it and said, "Now show me how to take it off and on."

She took it off for him and put it back on again and then he took it off himself, handling it as tenderly as if it were a real one. "See!" he said with a delighted child's face. "Now I can do it myself!"

"Put it back on," she said. She was thinking that she would run away with him and that every night he would take the leg off and every morning put it back on again. "Put it back on," she said.

"Not yet," he murmured, setting it on its foot out of her reach. "Leave it off for a while. You got me instead."

She gave a little cry of alarm but he pushed her down and began to kiss her again. Without the leg she felt entirely dependent on him. Her brain seemed to have stopped thinking altogether and to be about some other function that it was not very good at. Different expressions raced back and forth over her face. Every now and then the boy, his eyes like two steel spikes, would glance behind him where the leg stood. Finally she pushed him off and said, "Put it back on me now."

"Wait," he said. He leaned the other way and pulled the valise toward him 135 and opened it. It had a pale blue spotted lining and there were only two Bibles in it. He took one of these out and opened the cover of it. It was hollow and contained a pocket flask of whiskey, a pack of cards, and a small blue box with printing on it. He laid these out in front of her one at a time in an evenly-spaced row, like one presenting offerings at the shrine of a goddess. He put the blue box in her hand. THIS PRODUCT TO BE USED ONLY FOR THE PRE-VENTION OF DISEASE, she read, and dropped it. The boy was unscrewing the top of the flask. He stopped and pointed, with a smile, to the deck of cards. It was not an ordinary deck but one with an obscene picture on the back of each card. "Take a swig," he said, offering her the bottle first. He held it in front of her, but like one mesmerized, she did not move.

Her voice when she spoke had an almost pleading sound. "Aren't you," she murmured, "aren't you just good country people?"

The boy cocked his head. He looked as if he were just beginning to understand that she might be trying to insult him. "Yeah," he said, curling his lip slightly, "but it ain't held me back none. I'm as good as you any day in the week."

"Give me my leg," she said.

He pushed it farther away with his foot. "Come on now, let's begin to have us a good time," he said coaxingly. "We ain't got to know one another good yet."

"Give me my leg!" she screamed and tried to lunge for it but he pushed her 140 down easily.

"What's the matter with you all of a sudden?" he asked, frowning as he screwed the top on the flask and put it quickly back inside the Bible. "You just a while ago said you didn't believe in nothing. I thought you was some girl!"

Her face was almost purple. "You're a Christian!" she hissed. "You're a fine Christian! You're just like them all—say one thing and do another. You're a perfect Christian, you're . . ."

The boy's mouth was set angrily. "I hope you don't think," he said in a lofty indignant tone, "that I believe in that crap! I may sell Bibles but I know which end is up and I wasn't born yesterday and I know where I'm going!"

"Give me my leg!" she screeched. He jumped up so quickly that she barely saw him sweep the cards and the blue box into the Bible and throw the Bible into his valise. She saw him grab the leg and then she saw it for an instant slanted forlornly across the inside of the suitcase with a Bible at either side of its opposite ends. He slammed the lid shut and snatched up the valise and swung it down the hole and then stepped through himself.

When all of him had passed but his head, he turned and regarded her with 145 a look that no longer had any admiration in it. "I've gotten a lot of interesting things," he said. "One time I got a woman's glass eye this way. And you needn't to think you'll catch me because Pointer ain't really my name. I use a different name at every house I call at and don't stay nowhere long. And I'll tell you another thing, Hulga," he said, using the name as if he didn't think much of it, "you ain't so smart. I been believing in nothing ever since I was born!" and then the toast-colored hat disappeared down the hole and the girl was left, sitting on the straw in the dusty sunlight. When she turned her churning face toward the opening, she saw his blue figure struggling successfully over the green speckled lake.

Mrs. Hopewell and Mrs. Freeman, who were in the back pasture, digging up onions, saw him emerge a little later from the woods and head across the meadow toward the highway. "Why, that looks like that nice dull young man that tried to sell me a Bible yesterday," Mrs. Hopewell said, squinting. "He must have been selling them to the Negroes back in there. He was so simple," she said, "but I guess the world would be better off if we were all that simple."

Mrs. Freeman's gaze drove forward and just touched him before he disappeared under the hill. Then she returned her attention to the evil-smelling onion shoot she was lifting from the ground. "Some can't be that simple," she said. "I know I never could."

CONSIDERATIONS FOR CRITICAL THINKING AND WRITING

1. FIRST RESPONSE. What do you think of Hulga's conviction that intelligence and education are incompatible with religious faith?

2. Why is it significant that Mrs. Hopewell's daughter has two names? How do the other characters' names serve to characterize them?

3. Why do you think Mrs. Freeman and Mrs. Hopewell are introduced before Hulga? What do they contribute to Hulga's story?

4. Identify the conflict in this story. How is it resolved?

5. Hulga and the Bible salesman play a series of jokes on each other. How are these deceptions related to the theme?

6. What is the effect of O'Connor's use of the phrase "good country people" throughout the story? Why is it an appropriate title?

7. The Bible salesman's final words to Hulga are "You ain't so smart. I been believing in nothing ever since I was born!" What religious values are expressed in the story?

8. After the Bible salesman leaves Hulga at the end of the story, O'Connor adds two more paragraphs concerning Mrs. Hopewell and Mrs. Freeman. What is the purpose of these final paragraphs?

9. Hulga's perspective on life is ironic, but she is also the subject of O'Connor's irony. Explain how O'Connor uses irony to reveal Hulga's character.

10. This story would be different if told from Hulga's point of view. Describe how the use of a limited omniscient narrator contributes to the story's effects.

CONNECTIONS TO OTHER SELECTIONS

1. How do Mrs. Hopewell's assumptions about life compare with those of Krebs's mother in Hemingway's "Soldier's Home" (p. 152)? Explain how the conflict in each story is related to what the mothers come to represent in the eyes of the central characters.

2. Discuss the treatment of faith in this story and in Hawthorne's "Young Goodman Brown" (p. 331).

Revelation   1964

The doctor's waiting room, which was very small, was almost full when the Turpins entered and Mrs. Turpin, who was very large, made it look even smaller by her presence. She stood looming at the head of the magazine table set in the center of it, a living demonstration that the room was inadequate and ridiculous. Her little bright black eyes took in all the patients as she sized up the seating situation. There was one vacant chair and a place on the sofa occupied by a blond child in a dirty blue romper who should have been told to move over and make room for the lady. He was five or six, but Mrs. Turpin saw at once that no one was going to tell him to move over. He was slumped down in the seat, his arms idle at his sides and his eyes idle in his head; his nose ran unchecked.

Mrs. Turpin put a firm hand on Claud's shoulder and said in a voice that included anyone who wanted to listen, "Claud, you sit in that chair there," and gave him a push down into the vacant one. Claud was florid and bald and sturdy, somewhat shorter than Mrs. Turpin, but he sat down as if he were accustomed to doing what she told him to.

Mrs. Turpin remained standing. The only man in the room besides Claud was a lean stringy old fellow with a rusty hand spread out on each knee, whose eyes were closed as if he were asleep or dead or pretending to be so as not to get up and offer her his seat. Her gaze settled agreeably on a well-dressed gray-haired lady whose eyes met hers and whose expression said: if that child belonged to me, he would have some manners and move over — there's plenty of room there for you and him too.

Claud looked up with a sigh and made as if to rise.

"Sit down," Mrs. Turpin said. "You know you're not supposed to stand on   5 that leg. He has an ulcer on his leg," she explained.

Claud lifted his foot onto the magazine table and rolled his trouser leg up to reveal a purple swelling on a plump marble-white calf.

"My!" the pleasant lady said. "How did you do that?"

"A cow kicked him," Mrs. Turpin said.

"Goodness!" said the lady.

Claud rolled his trouser leg down.   10

"Maybe the little boy would move over," the lady suggested, but the child did not stir.

"Somebody will be leaving in a minute," Mrs. Turpin said. She could not understand why a doctor — with as much money as they made charging five dollars a day to just stick their head in the hospital door and look at you — couldn't afford a decent-sized waiting room. This one was hardly bigger than a garage. The table was cluttered with limp-looking magazines and at one end of it there was a big green glass ash tray full of cigarette butts and cotton wads with little blood spots on them. If she had had anything to do with the running of the place, that would have been emptied every so often. There were no chairs against the wall at the head of the room. It had a rectangular-shaped panel in it that permitted a view of the office where the nurse came and went and the secretary listened to the radio. A plastic fern in a gold pot sat in the opening and trailed its fronds down almost to the floor. The radio was softly playing gospel music.

Just then the inner door opened and a nurse with the highest stack of yellow hair Mrs. Turpin had ever seen put her face in the crack and called for the next patient. The woman sitting beside Claud grasped the two arms of her chair and hoisted herself up; she pulled her dress free from her legs and lumbered through the door where the nurse had disappeared.

Mrs. Turpin eased into the vacant chair, which held her tight as a corset. "I wish I could reduce," she said, and rolled her eyes and gave a comic sigh.

"Oh, *you* aren't fat," the stylish lady said.   15

"Ooooo I am too," Mrs. Turpin said. "Claud he eats all he wants to and never weighs over one hundred and seventy-five pounds, but me I just look at something good to eat and I gain some weight," and her stomach and shoulders shook with laughter. "You can eat all you want to, can't you, Claud?" she asked, turning to him.

Claud only grinned.

"Well, as long as you have such a good disposition," the stylish lady said, "I don't think it makes a bit of difference what size you are. You just can't beat a good disposition."

Next to her was a fat girl of eighteen or nineteen, scowling into a thick blue book which Mrs. Turpin saw was entitled *Human Development.* The girl raised her head and directed her scowl at Mrs. Turpin as if she did not like her looks. She appeared annoyed that anyone should speak while she tried to read. The poor girl's face was blue with acne and Mrs. Turpin thought how pitiful it was to have a face like that at that age. She gave the girl a friendly smile but the girl only scowled the harder. Mrs. Turpin herself was fat but she had always had good skin, and though she was forty-seven years old, there was not a wrinkle in her face except around her eyes from laughing too much.

Next to the ugly girl was the child, still in exactly the same position, and 20 next to him was a thin leathery old woman in a cotton print dress. She and Claud had three sacks of chicken feed in their pump house that was in the same print. She had seen from the first that the child belonged with the old woman. She could tell by the way they sat—kind of vacant and white-trashy, as if they would sit there until Doomsday if nobody called and told them to get up. And at right angles but next to the well-dressed pleasant lady was a lank-faced woman who was certainly the child's mother. She had on a yellow sweat shirt and wine-colored slacks, both gritty-looking, and the rims of her lips were stained with snuff. Her dirty yellow hair was tied behind with a little piece of red paper ribbon. Worse than niggers any day, Mrs. Turpin thought.

The gospel hymn playing was, "When I looked up and He looked down," and Mrs. Turpin, who knew it, supplied the last line mentally, "And wona these days I know I'll we-eara crown."

Without appearing to, Mrs. Turpin always noticed people's feet. The well-dressed lady had on red and gray suede shoes to match her dress. Mrs. Turpin had on her good black patent leather pumps. The ugly girl had on Girl Scout shoes and heavy socks. The old woman had on tennis shoes and the white-trashy mother had on what appeared to be bedroom slippers, black straw with gold braid threaded through them—exactly what you would have expected her to have on.

Sometimes at night when she couldn't go to sleep, Mrs. Turpin would occupy herself with the question of who she would have chosen to be if she couldn't have been herself. If Jesus had said to her before he made her, "There's

only two places available for you. You can either be a nigger or white-trash,"
what would she have said? "Please, Jesus, please," she would have said, "just let
me wait until there's another place available," and he would have said, "No,
you have to go right now and I have only those two places so make up your
mind." She would have wiggled and squirmed and begged and pleaded but it
would have been no use and finally she would have said, "All right, make me a
nigger then—but that don't mean a trashy one." And he would have made her
a neat clean respectable Negro woman, herself but black.

Next to the child's mother was a red-headed youngish woman, reading
one of the magazines and working a piece of chewing gum, hell for leather, as
Claud would say. Mrs. Turpin could not see the woman's feet. She was not
white-trash, just common. Sometimes Mrs. Turpin occupied herself at night
naming the classes of people. On the bottom of the heap were most colored
people, not the kind she would have been if she had been one, but most of
them; then next to them—not above, just away from—were the white-trash;
then above them were the homeowners, and above them the home-and-land
owners, to which she and Claud belonged. Above she and Claud were people
with a lot of money and much bigger houses and much more land. But here
the complexity of it would begin to bear in on her, for some of the people with
a lot of money were common and ought to be below she and Claud and some
of the people who had good blood had lost their money and had to rent and
then there were colored people who owned their homes and land as well. There
was a colored dentist in town who had two red Lincolns and a swimming pool
and a farm with registered white-face cattle on it. Usually by the time she had
fallen asleep all the classes of people were moiling and roiling around in her
head, and she would dream they were all crammed in together in a box car,
being ridden off to be put in a gas oven.

"That's a beautiful clock," she said and nodded to her right. It was a big   25
wall clock, the face encased in a brass sunburst.

"Yes, it's very pretty," the stylish lady said agreeably. "And right on the dot
too," she added, glancing at her watch.

The ugly girl beside her cast an eye upward at the clock, smirked, then
looked directly at Mrs. Turpin and smirked again. Then she returned her eyes
to her book. She was obviously the lady's daughter because, although they
didn't look anything alike as to disposition, they both had the same shape of
face and the same blue eyes. On the lady they sparkled pleasantly but in the
girl's seared face they appeared alternately to smolder and to blaze.

What if Jesus had said, "All right, you can be white-trash or a nigger or
ugly"!

Mrs. Turpin felt an awful pity for the girl, though she thought it was one
thing to be ugly and another to act ugly.

The woman with the snuff-stained lips turned around in her chair and   30
looked up at the clock. Then she turned back and appeared to look a little to
the side of Mrs. Turpin. There was a cast in one of her eyes. "You want to know
wher you can get you one of themther clocks?" she asked in a loud voice.

"No, I already have a nice clock," Mrs. Turpin said. Once somebody like
her got a leg in the conversation, she would be all over it.

"You can get you one with green stamps," the woman said. "That's most
likely wher he got hisn. Save you up enough, you can get you most anythang. I
got me some joo'ry."

Ought to have got you a wash rag and some soap, Mrs. Turpin thought.

"I get contour sheets with mine," the pleasant lady said.

The daughter slammed her book shut. She looked straight in front of her, directly through Mrs. Turpin and on through the yellow curtain and the plate glass window which made the wall behind her. The girl's eyes seemed lit all of a sudden with a peculiar light, an unnatural light like night road signs give. Mrs. Turpin turned her head to see if there was anything going on outside that she should see, but she could not see anything. Figures passing cast only a pale shadow through the curtain. There was no reason the girl should single her out for her ugly looks.

"Miss Finley," the nurse said, cracking the door. The gum-chewing woman got up and passed in front of her and Claud and went into the office. She had on red high-heeled shoes.

Directly across the table, the ugly girl's eyes were fixed on Mrs. Turpin as if she had some very special reason for disliking her.

"This is wonderful weather, isn't it?" the girl's mother said.

"It's good weather for cotton if you can get the niggers to pick it," Mrs. Turpin said, "but niggers don't want to pick cotton any more. You can't get the white folks to pick it and now you can't get the niggers — because they got to be right up there with the white folks."

"They gonna *try* anyways," the white-trash woman said, leaning forward.

"Do you have one of the cotton-picking machines?" the pleasant lady asked.

"No," Mrs. Turpin said, "they leave half the cotton in the field. We don't have much cotton anyway. If you want to make it farming now, you have to have a little of everything. We got a couple of acres of cotton and a few hogs and chickens and just enough white-face that Claud can look after them himself."

"One thang I don't want," the white-trash woman said, wiping her mouth with the back of her hand. "Hogs. Nasty stinking things, a-gruntin and a-rootin all over the place."

Mrs. Turpin gave her the merest edge of her attention. "Our hogs are not dirty and they don't stink," she said. "They're cleaner than some children I've seen. Their feet never touch the ground. We have a pig parlor — that's where you raise them on concrete," she explained to the pleasant lady, "and Claud scoots them down with the hose every afternoon and washes off the floor." Cleaner by far than that child right there, she thought. Poor nasty little thing. He had not moved except to put the thumb of his dirty hand into his mouth.

The woman turned her face away from Mrs. Turpin. "I know I wouldn't scoot down no hog with no hose," she said to the wall.

You wouldn't have no hog to scoot down, Mrs. Turpin said to herself.

"A-gruntin and a-rootin and a-groanin," the woman muttered.

"We got a little of everything," Mrs. Turpin said to the pleasant lady. "It's no use in having more than you can handle yourself with help like it is. We found enough niggers to pick our cotton this year but Claud he has to go after them and take them home again in the evening. They can't walk that half a mile. No they can't. I tell you," she said and laughed merrily, "I sure am tired of buttering up niggers, but you got to love em if you want em to work for you. When they come in the morning, I run out and I say, 'Hi yawl this morning?' and when Claud drives them off to the field I just wave to beat the band and they just wave back." And she waved her hand rapidly to illustrate.

"Like you read out of the same book," the lady said, showing she understood perfectly.

"Child, yes," Mrs. Turpin said. "And when they come in from the field, 50 I run out with a bucket of icewater. That's the way it's going to be from now on," she said. "You may as well face it."

"One thang I know," the white-trash woman said. "Two thangs I ain't going to do: love no niggers or scoot down no hog with no hose." And she let out a bark of contempt.

The look that Mrs. Turpin and the pleasant lady exchanged indicated they both understood that you had to *have* certain things before you could *know* certain things. But every time Mrs. Turpin exchanged a look with the lady, she was aware that the ugly girl's peculiar eyes were still on her, and she had trouble bringing her attention back to the conversation.

"When you got something," she said, "you got to look after it." And when you ain't got a thing but breath and britches, she added to herself, you can afford to come to town every morning and just sit on the Court House coping and spit.

A grotesque revolving shadow passed across the curtain behind her and was thrown palely on the opposite wall. Then a bicycle clattered down against the outside of the building. The door opened and a colored boy glided in with a tray from the drugstore. It had two large red and white paper cups on it with tops on them. He was a tall, very black boy in discolored white pants and a green nylon shirt. He was chewing gum slowly, as if to music. He set the tray down in the office opening next to the fern and stuck his head through to look for the secretary. She was not in there. He rested his arms on the ledge and waited, his narrow bottom stuck out, swaying to the left and right. He raised a hand over his head and scratched the base of his skull.

"You see that button there, boy?" Mrs. Turpin said. "You can punch 55 that and she'll come. She's probably in the back somewhere."

"Is that right?" the boy said agreeably, as if he had never seen the button before. He leaned to the right and put his finger on it. "She sometime out," he said and twisted around to face his audience, his elbows behind him on the counter. The nurse appeared and he twisted back again. She handed him a dollar and he rooted in his pocket and made the change and counted it out to her. She gave him fifteen cents for a tip and he went out with the empty tray. The heavy door swung to slowly and closed at length with the sound of suction. For a moment no one spoke.

"They ought to send all them niggers back to Africa," the white-trash woman said. "That's wher they come from in the first place."

"Oh, I couldn't do without my good colored friends," the pleasant lady said.

"There's a heap of things worse than a nigger," Mrs. Turpin agreed. "It's all kinds of them just like it's all kinds of us."

"Yes, and it takes all kinds to make the world go round," the lady said 60 in her musical voice.

As she said it, the raw-complexioned girl snapped her teeth together. Her lower lip turned downwards and inside out, revealing the pale pink inside of her mouth. After a second it rolled back up. It was the ugliest face

Mrs. Turpin had ever seen anyone make and for a moment she was certain that the girl had made it at her. She was looking at her as if she had known and disliked her all her life — all of Mrs. Turpin's life, it seemed too, not just all the girl's life. Why, girl, I don't even know you, Mrs. Turpin said silently.

She forced her attention back to the discussion. "It wouldn't be practical to send them back to Africa," she said. "They wouldn't want to go. They got it too good here."

"Wouldn't be what they wanted — if I had anythang to do with it," the woman said.

"It wouldn't be a way in the world you could get all the niggers back over there," Mrs. Turpin said. "They'd be hiding out and lying down and turning sick on you and wailing and hollering and raring and pitching. It wouldn't be a way in the world to get them over there."

"They got over here," the trashy woman said. "Get back like they got 65
over."

"It wasn't so many of them then," Mrs. Turpin explained.

The woman looked at Mrs. Turpin as if here was an idiot indeed but Mrs. Turpin was not bothered by the look, considering where it came from.

"Nooo," she said, "they're going to stay here where they can go to New York and marry white folks and improve their color. That's what they all want to do, every one of them, improve their color."

"You know what comes of that, don't you?" Claud asked.

"No, Claud, what?" Mrs. Turpin said. 70

Claud's eyes twinkled. "White-faced niggers," he said with never a smile.

Everybody in the office laughed except the white-trash and the ugly girl. The girl gripped the book in her lap with white fingers. The trashy woman looked around her from face to face as if she thought they were all idiots. The old woman in the feed sack dress continued to gaze expressionless across the floor at the high-top shoes of the man opposite her, the one who had been pretending to be asleep when the Turpins came in. He was laughing heartily, his hands still spread out on his knees. The child had fallen to the side and was lying now almost face down in the old woman's lap.

While they recovered from their laughter, the nasal chorus on the radio kept the room from silence.

"You go to blank blank
And I'll go to mine
But we'll all blank along
To-geth-er,
And all along the blank
We'll hep each other out
Smile-ling in any kind of
Weath-ther!"

Mrs. Turpin didn't catch every word but she caught enough to agree with the spirit of the song and it turned her thoughts sober. To help anybody out that needed it was her philosophy of life. She never spared herself when she found somebody in need, whether they were white or black, trash or decent. And of all she had to be thankful for, she was most thankful that this was so. If Jesus had said, "You can be high society and have all the money you want and be thin and svelte-like, but you can't be a good woman with it," she would have had to say, "Well don't make me that then. Make me a good woman and it don't matter what else, how fat or how ugly or how poor!" Her heart rose. He had not made her a nigger or white-trash or ugly! He had made her herself and given her a little of everything. Jesus, thank you! she said. Thank you thank you thank you! Whenever she counted her blessings she felt as buoyant as if she weighed one hundred and twenty-five pounds instead of one hundred and eighty.

"What's wrong with your little boy?" the pleasant lady asked the white-trashy woman. 75

"He has a ulcer," the woman said proudly. "He ain't give me a minute's peace since he was born. Him and her are just alike," she said, nodding at the old woman, who was running her leathery fingers through the child's pale hair. "Look like I can't get nothing down them two but Co' Cola and candy."

That's all you try to get down em, Mrs. Turpin said to herself. Too lazy to light the fire. There was nothing you could tell her about people like them that she didn't know already. And it was not just that they didn't have anything. Because if you gave them everything, in two weeks it would all be broken or filthy or they would have chopped it up for lightwood. She knew all this from her own experience. Help them you must, but help them you couldn't.

All at once the ugly girl turned her lips inside out again. Her eyes fixed like two drills on Mrs. Turpin. This time there was no mistaking that there was something urgent behind them.

Girl, Mrs. Turpin exclaimed silently, I haven't done a thing to you! The girl might be confusing her with somebody else. There was no need to sit by and let herself be intimidated. "You must be in college," she said boldly, looking directly at the girl. "I see you reading a book there."

The girl continued to stare and pointedly did not answer. 80

Her mother blushed at this rudeness. "The lady asked you a question, Mary Grace," she said under her breath.

"I have ears," Mary Grace said.

The poor mother blushed again. "Mary Grace goes to Wellesley College," she explained. She twisted one of the buttons on her dress. "In Massachusetts," she added with a grimace. "And in the summer she just keeps right on studying. Just reads all the time, a real book worm. She's done real well at Wellesley; she's taking English and Math and History and Psychology and Social Studies," she rattled on, "and I think it's too much. I think she ought to get out and have fun."

The girl looked as if she would like to hurl them all through the plate glass window.

"Way up north," Mrs. Turpin murmured and thought, well, it hasn't done much for her manners. 85

"I'd almost rather to have him sick," the white-trash woman said, wrenching the attention back to herself. "He's so mean when he ain't. Look like some children just take natural to meanness. It's some gets bad when they get sick but he was the opposite. Took sick and turned good. He don't give me no trouble now. It's me waitin to see the doctor," she said.

If I was going to send anybody back to Africa, Mrs. Turpin thought, it would be your kind, woman. "Yes, indeed," she said aloud, but looking up at the ceiling, "it's a heap of things worse than a nigger." And dirtier than a hog, she added to herself.

"I think people with bad dispositions are more to be pitied than anyone on earth," the pleasant lady said in a voice that was decidedly thin.

"I thank the Lord he has blessed me with a good one," Mrs. Turpin said. "The day has never dawned that I couldn't find something to laugh at."

"Not since she married me anyways," Claud said with a comical straight   90
face.

Everybody laughed except the girl and the white-trash.

Mrs. Turpin's stomach shook. "He's such a caution," she said, "that I can't help but laugh at him."

The girl made a loud ugly noise through her teeth.

Her mother's mouth grew thin and tight. "I think the worst thing in the world," she said, "is an ungrateful person. To have everything and not appreciate it. I know a girl," she said, "who has parents who would give her anything, a little brother who loves her dearly, who is getting a good education, who wears the best clothes, but who can never say a kind word to anyone, who never smiles, who just criticizes and complains all day long."

"Is she too old to paddle?" Claud asked.   95

The girl's face was almost purple.

"Yes," the lady said, "I'm afraid there's nothing to do but leave her to her folly. Some day she'll wake up and it'll be too late."

"It never hurt anyone to smile," Mrs. Turpin said. "It just makes you feel better all over."

"Of course," the lady said sadly, "but there are just some people you can't tell anything to. They can't take criticism."

"If it's one thing I am," Mrs. Turpin said with feeling, "it's grateful. When   100
I think who all I could have been besides myself and what all I got, a little of everything, and a good disposition besides, I just feel like shouting, 'Thank you, Jesus, for making everything the way it is!' It could have been different!" For one thing, somebody else could have got Claud. At the thought of this, she was flooded with gratitude and a terrible pang of joy ran through her. "Oh thank you, Jesus, Jesus, thank you!" she cried aloud.

The book struck her directly over her left eye. It struck almost at the same instant that she realized the girl was about to hurl it. Before she could utter a sound, the raw face came crashing across the table toward her, howling. The girl's fingers sank like clamps into the soft flesh of her neck. She heard the mother cry out and Claud shout, "Whoa!" There was an instant when she was certain that she was about to be in an earthquake.

All at once her vision narrowed and she saw everything as if it were happening in a small room far away, or as if she were looking at it through the wrong end of a telescope. Claud's face crumpled and fell out of sight. The nurse ran in, then out, then in again. Then the gangling figure of the doctor rushed out of the inner door. Magazines flew this way and that as the table turned over. The girl fell with a thud and Mrs. Turpin's vision suddenly reversed itself and she saw everything large instead of small. The eyes of the white-trashy woman were staring hugely at the floor. There the girl, held down on one side by the nurse and on the other by her mother, was wrenching and turning in their grasp. The doctor was kneeling astride her, trying to hold her arm down. He managed after a second to sink a long needle into it.

Mrs. Turpin felt entirely hollow except for her heart which swung from side to side as if it were agitated in a great empty drum of flesh.

"Somebody that's not busy call for the ambulance," the doctor said in the off-hand voice young doctors adopt for terrible occasions.

Mrs. Turpin could not have moved a finger. The old man who had been 105 sitting next to her skipped nimbly into the office and made the call, for the secretary still seemed to be gone.

"Claud!" Mrs. Turpin called.

He was not in his chair. She knew she must jump up and find him but she felt like some one trying to catch a train in a dream, when everything moves in slow motion and the faster you try to run the slower you go.

"Here I am," a suffocated voice, very unlike Claud's, said.

He was doubled up in the corner on the floor, pale as paper, holding his leg. She wanted to get up and go to him but she could not move. Instead, her gaze was drawn slowly downward to the churning face on the floor, which she could see over the doctor's shoulder.

The girl's eyes stopped rolling and focused on her. They seemed a much 110 lighter blue than before, as if a door that had been tightly closed behind them was now open to admit light and air.

Mrs. Turpin's head cleared and her power of motion returned. She leaned forward until she was looking directly into the fierce brilliant eyes. There was no doubt in her mind that the girl did know her, knew her in some intense and personal way, beyond time and place and condition. "What you got to say to me?" she asked hoarsely and held her breath, waiting, as for a revelation.

The girl raised her head. Her gaze locked with Mrs. Turpin's. "Go back to hell where you came from, you old wart hog," she whispered. Her voice was low but clear. Her eyes burned for a moment as if she saw with pleasure that her message had struck its target.

Mrs. Turpin sank back in her chair.

After a moment the girl's eyes closed and she turned her head wearily to the side.

The doctor rose and handed the nurse the empty syringe. He leaned over 115 and put both hands for a moment on the mother's shoulders, which were shaking. She was sitting on the floor, her lips pressed together, holding Mary Grace's hand in her lap. The girl's fingers were gripped like a baby's around her thumb. "Go on to the hospital," he said. "I'll call and make the arrangements."

"Now let's see that neck," he said in a jovial voice to Mrs. Turpin. He began to inspect her neck with his first two fingers. Two little moon-shaped lines like pink fish bones were indented over her windpipe. There was the beginning of an angry red swelling above her eye. His fingers passed over this also.

"Lea' me be," she said thickly and shook him off. "See about Claud. She kicked him."

"I'll see about him in a minute," he said and felt her pulse. He was a thin gray-haired man, given to pleasantries. "Go home and have yourself a vacation the rest of the day," he said and patted her on the shoulder.

Quit your pattin me, Mrs. Turpin growled to herself.

"And put an ice pack over that eye," he said. Then he went and squatted 120 down beside Claud and looked at his leg. After a moment he pulled him up and Claud limped after him into the office.

Until the ambulance came, the only sounds in the room were the tremulous moans of the girl's mother, who continued to sit on the floor. The white-trash woman did not take her eyes off the girl. Mrs. Turpin looked straight ahead at nothing. Presently the ambulance drew up, a long dark shadow, behind the curtain. The attendants came in and set the stretcher down beside the girl and lifted her expertly onto it and carried her out. The nurse helped the mother gather up her things. The shadow of the ambulance moved silently away and the nurse came back in the office.

"That ther girl is going to be a lunatic, ain't she?" the white-trash woman asked the nurse, but the nurse kept on to the back and never answered her.

"Yes, she's going to be a lunatic," the white-trash woman said to the rest of them.

"Po' critter," the old woman murmured. The child's face was still in her lap. His eyes looked idly out over her knees. He had not moved during the disturbance except to draw one leg up under him.

"I thank Gawd," the white-trash woman said fervently, "I ain't a lunatic." 125

Claud came limping out and the Turpins went home.

As their pick-up truck turned into their own dirt road and made the crest of the hill, Mrs. Turpin gripped the window ledge and looked out suspiciously. The land sloped gracefully down through a field dotted with lavender weeds and at the start of the rise their small yellow frame house, with its little flower beds spread out around it like a fancy apron, sat primly in its accustomed place between two giant hickory trees. She would not have been startled to see a burnt wound between two blackened chimneys.

Neither of them felt like eating so they put on their house clothes and lowered the shade in the bedroom and lay down, Claud with his leg on a pillow and herself with a damp washcloth over her eye. The instant she was flat on her back, the image of a razor-backed hog with warts on its face and horns coming out behind its ears snorted into her head. She moaned, a low quiet moan.

"I am not," she said tearfully, "a wart hog. From hell." But the denial had no force. The girl's eyes and her words, even the tone of her voice, low but clear, directed only to her, brooked no repudiation. She had been singled out for the message, though there was trash in the room to whom it might justly have been applied. The full force of this fact struck her only now. There was a woman there who was neglecting her own child but she had been overlooked. The message had been given to Ruby Turpin, a respectable, hard-working, church-going woman. The tears dried. Her eyes began to burn instead with wrath.

She rose on her elbow and the washcloth fell into her hand. Claud was 130 lying on his back, snoring. She wanted to tell him what the girl had said. At the same time, she did not wish to put the image of herself as a wart hog from hell into his mind.

"Hey, Claud," she muttered and pushed his shoulder.

Claud opened one pale baby blue eye.

She looked into it warily. He did not think about anything. He just went his way.

"Wha, whasit?" he said and closed the eye again.

"Nothing," she said. "Does your leg pain you?" 135

"Hurts like hell," Claud said.

"It'll quit terreckly," she said and lay back down. In a moment Claud was snoring again. For the rest of the afternoon they lay there. Claud slept. She scowled at the ceiling. Occasionally she raised her fist and made a small stabbing motion over her chest as if she was defending her innocence to invisible guests who were like the comforters of Job, reasonable-seeming but wrong.

About five-thirty Claud stirred. "Got to go after those niggers," he sighed, not moving.

She was looking straight up as if there were unintelligible handwriting on the ceiling. The protuberance over her eye had turned a greenish-blue. "Listen here," she said.

"What?"   140

"Kiss me."

Claud leaned over and kissed her loudly on the mouth. He pinched her side and their hands interlocked. Her expression of ferocious concentration did not change. Claud got up, groaning and growling, and limped off. She continued to study the ceiling.

She did not get up until she heard the pick-up truck coming back with the Negroes. Then she rose and thrust her feet in her brown oxfords, which she did not bother to lace, and stumped out onto the back porch and got her red plastic bucket. She emptied a tray of ice cubes into it and filled it half full of water and went out into the back yard. Every afternoon after Claud brought the hands in, one of the boys helped him put out hay and the rest waited in the back of the truck until he was ready to take them home. The truck was parked in the shade under one of the hickory trees.

"Hi yawl this evening?" Mrs. Turpin asked grimly, appearing with the bucket and the dipper. There were three women and a boy in the truck.

"Us doin nicely," the oldest woman said. "Hi you doin?" and her gaze   145
struck immediately on the dark lump on Mrs. Turpin's forehead. "You done fell down, ain't you?" she asked in a solicitous voice. The old woman was dark and almost toothless. She had on an old felt hat of Claud's set back on her head. The other two women were younger and lighter and they both had new bright green sunhats. One of them had hers on her head; the other had taken hers off and the boy was grinning beneath it.

Mrs. Turpin set the bucket down on the floor of the truck. "Yawl hep yourselves," she said. She looked around to make sure Claud had gone. "No, I didn't fall down," she said, folding her arms. "It was something worse than that."

"Ain't nothing bad happen to you!" the old woman said. She said it as if they all knew that Mrs. Turpin was protected in some special way by Divine Providence. "You just had you a little fall."

"We were in town at the doctor's office for where the cow kicked Mr. Turpin," Mrs. Turpin said in a flat tone that indicated they could leave off their foolishness. "And there was this girl there. A big fat girl with her face all broke out. I could look at that girl and tell she was peculiar but I couldn't tell how. And me and her mama was just talking and going along and all of a sudden WHAM! She throws this big book she was reading at me and . . ."

"Naw!" the old woman cried out.

"And then she jumps over the table and commences to choke me."   150

"Naw!" they all exclaimed, "naw!"

"Hi come she do that?" the old woman asked. "What ail her?"

Mrs. Turpin only glared in front of her.

"Somethin ail her," the old woman said.

"They carried her off in an ambulance," Mrs. Turpin continued, "but be-   155
fore she went she was rolling on the floor and they were trying to hold her down to give her a shot and she said something to me." She paused. "You know what she said to me?"

"What she say?" they asked.

"She said," Mrs. Turpin began, and stopped, her face very dark and heavy. The sun was getting whiter and whiter, blanching the sky overhead so that the leaves of the hickory tree were black in the face of it. She could not bring forth the words. "Something real ugly," she muttered.

"She sho shouldn't said nothin ugly to you," the old woman said. "You so sweet. You the sweetest lady I know."

"She pretty too," the one with the hat on said.

"And stout," the other one said. "I never knowed no sweeter white lady."   160

"That's the truth befo' Jesus," the old woman said. "Amen! You des as sweet and pretty as you can be."

Mrs. Turpin knew exactly how much Negro flattery was worth and it added to her rage. "She said," she began again and finished this time with a fierce rush of breath, "that I was an old wart hog from hell."

There was an astounded silence.

"Where she at?" the youngest woman cried in a piercing voice.

"Lemme see her. I'll kill her!"   165

"I'll kill her with you!" the other one cried.

"She b'long in the sylum," the old woman said emphatically. "You the sweetest white lady I know."

"She pretty too," the other two said. "Stout as she can be and sweet. Jesus satisfied with her!"

"Deed he is," the woman declared.

Idiots! Mrs. Turpin growled to herself. You could never say anything intel-   170
ligent to a nigger. You could talk at them but not with them. "Yawl ain't drunk your water," she said shortly. "Leave the bucket in the truck when you're finished with it. I got more to do than just stand around and pass the time of day," and she moved off and into the house.

She stood for a moment in the middle of the kitchen. The dark protuber- ance over her eye looked like a miniature tornado cloud which might any moment sweep across the horizon of her brow. Her lower lip protruded dan- gerously. She squared her massive shoulders. Then she marched into the front of the house and out the side door and started down the road to the pig parlor. She had the look of a woman going single-handed, weaponless, into battle.

The sun was deep yellow now like a harvest moon and was riding westward very fast over the far tree line as if it meant to reach the hogs before she did. The road was rutted and she kicked several good-sized stones out of her path as she strode along. The pig parlor was on a little knoll at the end of a lane that ran off from the side of the barn. It was a square of concrete as large as a small room, with a board fence about four feet high around it. The concrete floor sloped slightly so that the hog wash could drain off into a trench where it was carried to the field for fertilizer. Claud was standing on the outside, on the edge of the concrete, hanging onto the top board, hosing down the floor in- side. The hose was connected to the faucet of a water trough nearby.

Mrs. Turpin climbed up beside him and glowered down at the hogs inside. There were seven long-snouted bristly shoats in it—tan with liver-colored spots—and an old sow a few weeks off from farrowing. She was lying on her side grunting. The shoats were running about shaking themselves like idiot children, their little slit pig eyes searching the floor for anything left. She had read that pigs were the most intelligent animal. She doubted it. They were supposed to be smarter than dogs. There had even been a pig astronaut. He had performed his assignment perfectly but died of a heart attack afterwards because they left him in his electric suit, sitting upright throughout his examination when naturally a hog should be on all fours.

A-gruntin and a-rootin and a-groanin.

"Gimme that hose," she said, yanking it away from Claud. "Go on and 175 carry them niggers home and then get off that leg."

"You look like you might have swallowed a mad dog," Claud observed, but he got down and limped off. He paid no attention to her humors.

Until he was out of earshot, Mrs. Turpin stood on the side of the pen, holding the hose and pointing the stream of water at the hind quarters of any shoat that looked as if it might try to lie down. When he had had time to get over the hill, she turned her head slightly and her wrathful eyes scanned the path. He was nowhere in sight. She turned back again and seemed to gather herself up. Her shoulders rose and she drew in her breath.

"What do you send me a message like that for?" she said in a low fierce voice, barely above a whisper but with the force of a shout in its concentrated fury. "How am I a hog and me both? How am I saved and from hell too?" Her free fist was knotted and with the other she gripped the hose, blindly pointing the stream of water in and out of the eye of the old sow whose outraged squeal she did not hear.

The pig parlor commanded a view of the back pasture where their twenty beef cows were gathered around the hay-bales Claud and the boy had put out. The freshly cut pasture sloped down to the highway. Across it was their cotton field and beyond that a dark green dusty wood which they owned as well. The sun was behind the wood, very red, looking over the paling of the trees like a farmer inspecting his own hogs.

"Why me?" she rumbled. "It's no trash around here, black or white, that I 180 haven't given to. And break my back to the bone every day working. And do for the church."

She appeared to be the right size woman to command the arena before her. "How am I a hog?" she demanded. "Exactly how am I like them?" and she jabbed the stream of water at the shoats. "There was plenty of trash there. It didn't have to be me.

"If you like trash better, go get yourself some trash then," she railed. "You could have made me trash. Or a nigger. If trash is what you wanted why didn't you make me trash?" She shook her fist with the hose in it and a watery snake appeared momentarily in the air. "I could quit working and take it easy and be filthy," she growled. "Lounge about the sidewalks all day drinking root beer. Dip snuff and spit in every puddle and have it all over my face. I could be nasty.

"Or you could have made me a nigger. It's too late for me to be a nigger," she said with deep sarcasm, "but I could act like one. Lay down in the middle of the road and stop traffic. Roll on the ground."

In the deepening light everything was taking on a mysterious hue. The pasture was growing a peculiar glassy green and the streak of highway had turned lavender. She braced herself for a final assault and this time her voice rolled out over the pasture. "Go on," she yelled, "call me a hog! Call me a hog again. From hell. Call me a wart hog from hell. Put that bottom rail on top. There'll still be a top and bottom!"

A garbled echo returned to her. 185

A final surge of fury shook her and she roared, "Who do you think you are?"

The color of everything, field and crimson sky, burned for a moment with a transparent intensity. The question carried over the pasture and across the highway and the cotton field and returned to her clearly like an answer from beyond the wood.

She opened her mouth but no sound came out of it.

A tiny truck, Claud's, appeared on the highway, heading rapidly out of sight. Its gears scraped thinly. It looked like a child's toy. At any moment a bigger truck might smash into it and scatter Claud's and the niggers' brains all over the road.

Mrs. Turpin stood there, her gaze fixed on the highway, all her muscles rigid, until in five or six minutes the truck reappeared, returning. She waited until it had had time to turn into their own road. Then like a monumental statue coming to life, she bent her head slowly and gazed, as if through the very heart of mystery, down into the pig parlor at the hogs. They had settled all in one corner around the old sow who was grunting softly. A red glow suffused them. They appeared to pant with a secret life.

Until the sun slipped finally behind the tree line, Mrs. Turpin remained there with her gaze bent to them as if she were absorbing some abysmal life-giving knowledge. At last she lifted her head. There was only a purple streak in the sky, cutting through a field of crimson and leading, like an extension of the highway, into the descending dusk. She raised her hands from the side of the pen in a gesture hieratic and profound. A visionary light settled in her eyes. She saw the streak as a vast swinging bridge extending upward from the earth through a field of living fire. Upon it a vast horde of souls were rumbling toward heaven. There were whole companies of white-trash, clean for the first time in their lives, and bands of black niggers in white robes, and battalions of freaks and lunatics shouting and clapping and leaping like frogs. And bringing up the end of the procession was a tribe of people whom she recognized at once as those who, like herself and Claud, had always had a little of everything and the God-given wit to use it right. She leaned forward to observe them closer. They were marching behind the others with great dignity, accountable as they had always been for good order and common sense and respectable behavior. They alone were on key. Yet she could see by their shocked and altered faces that even their virtues were being burned away. She lowered her hands and gripped the rail of the hog pen, her eyes small but fixed unblinkingly on what lay ahead. In a moment the vision faded but she remained where she was, immobile.

At length she got down and turned off the faucet and made her slow way on the darkening path to the house. In the woods around her the invisible cricket choruses had struck up, but what she heard were the voices of the souls climbing upward into the starry field and shouting hallelujah.

CONSIDERATIONS FOR CRITICAL THINKING AND WRITING

1. FIRST RESPONSE. Does your attitude toward Mrs. Turpin change or remain the same during the story? Do you *like* her more at some points than at others? Explain why.

2. Why is it appropriate that the two major settings for the action in this story are a doctor's waiting room and a "pig parlor"?

3. How does Mrs. Turpin's treatment of her husband help to characterize her?

4. Mrs. Turpin notices people's shoes. What does this and her thoughts about "classes of people" (para. 24) reveal about her? How does she see herself in relation to other people?

5. Why does Mary Grace attack Mrs. Turpin?

6. Why is it significant that the book Mary Grace reads is *Human Development*? What is the significance of her name?

7. What does the background music played on the radio contribute to the story?

8. To whom does Mrs. Turpin address this anguished question: "What do you send me a message [Mary Grace's whispered words telling her "Go back to hell where you came from, you old wart hog"] like that for?" (para. 178). Why is Mrs. Turpin so angry and bewildered?

9. What is the "abysmal life-giving knowledge" that Mrs. Turpin discovers in the next to the last paragraph? Why is it "abysmal"? How is it "life-giving"?

10. Given the serious theme, consider whether the story's humor is appropriate.

11. When Mrs. Turpin returns home bruised, a hired African American woman tells her that nothing really "bad" happened: "You just had you a little fall" (para. 147). Pay particular attention to the suggestive language of this sentence, and discuss its significance in relation to the rest of the story.

12. CRITICAL STRATEGIES. Choose a critical approach from Chapter 52, "Critical Strategies for Reading," that you think is particularly useful for explaining the themes of this story.

CONNECTIONS TO OTHER SELECTIONS

1. Compare and contrast Mary Grace with Hulga of "Good Country People" (p. 395).

2. Explain how "Revelation" could be used as a title for any of the O'Connor stories you have read.

3. Discuss Mrs. Turpin's prideful hypocrisy in connection with the racial attitudes expressed by the white men at the "smoker" in Ellison's "Battle Royal" (p. 231). How do pride and personal illusions inform these characters' racial attitudes?

4. Explore the nature of the "revelation" in O'Connor's story and in John Updike's "A & P" (p. 606).

Parker's Back   *1965*

Parker's wife was sitting on the front porch floor, snapping beans. Parker was sitting on the step, some distance away, watching her sullenly. She was plain, plain. The skin on her face was thin and drawn as tight as the skin on an onion and her eyes were gray and sharp like the points of two icepicks. Parker understood why he had married her — he couldn't have got her any other way — but he couldn't understand why he stayed with her now. She was pregnant and pregnant women were not his favorite kind. Nonetheless, he stayed as if she had him conjured. He was puzzled and ashamed of himself.

The house they rented sat alone save for a single tall pecan tree on a high embankment overlooking a highway. At intervals a car would shoot past below and his wife's eyes would swerve suspiciously after the sound of it and then come back to rest on the newspaper full of beans in her lap. One of the things she did not approve of was automobiles. In addition to her other bad qualities, she was forever sniffing up sin. She did not smoke or dip, drink whiskey, use bad language, or paint her face, and God knew some paint would have improved it, Parker thought. Her being against color, it was the more remarkable that she had married him. Sometimes he supposed that she had married him because she meant to save him. At other times he had a suspicion that she actually liked everything she said she didn't. He could account for her one way or another; it was himself he could not understand.

She turned her head in his direction and said, "It's no reason you can't work for a man. It don't have to be a woman."

"Aw shut your mouth for a change," Parker muttered.

If he had been certain she was jealous of the woman he worked for he would 5 have been pleased but more likely she was concerned with the sin that would result if he and the woman took a liking to each other. He had told her that the woman was a hefty young blonde; in fact she was nearly seventy years old and too dried up to have an interest in anything except getting as much work out of him as she could. Not that an old woman didn't sometimes get an interest in a young man, particularly if he was as attractive as Parker felt he was, but this old woman looked at him the same way she looked at her old tractor—as if she had to put up with it because it was all she had. The tractor had broken down the second day Parker was on it and she had set him at once to cutting bushes, saying out of the side of her mouth to the nigger, "Everything he touches, he breaks." She also asked him to wear his shirt when he worked; Parker had removed it even though the day was not sultry; he put it back on reluctantly.

This ugly woman Parker married was his first wife. He had had other women but he had planned never to get himself tied up legally. He had first seen her one morning when his truck broke down on the highway. He had managed to pull it off the road into a neatly swept yard on which sat a peeling two-room house. He got out and opened the hood of the truck and began to study the motor. Parker had an extra sense that told him when there was a woman nearby watching him. After he had leaned over the motor a few minutes, his neck began to prickle. He cast his eye over the empty yard and porch of the house. A woman he could not see was either nearby beyond a clump of honeysuckle or in the house, watching him out the window.

Suddenly Parker began to jump up and down and fling his hand about as if he had mashed it in the machinery. He doubled over and held his hand close to his chest. "God dammit!" he hollered, "Jesus Christ in hell! Jesus God Almighty damm! God dammit to hell!" he went on, flinging out the same few oaths over and over as loud as he could.

Without warning a terrible bristly claw slammed the side of his face and he fell backwards on the hood of the truck. "You don't talk no filth here!" a voice close to him shrilled.

Parker's vision was so blurred that for an instant he thought he had been attacked by some creature from above, a giant hawk-eyed angel wielding a hoary weapon. As his sight cleared, he saw before him a tall raw-boned girl with a broom,

"I hurt my hand," he said. "I HURT my hand." He was so incensed that he 10 forgot that he hadn't hurt his hand. "My hand may be broke," he growled although his voice was still unsteady.

"Lemme see it," the girl demanded.

Parker stuck out his hand and she came closer and looked at it. There was no mark on the palm and she took the hand and turned it over. Her own hand was dry and hot and rough and Parker felt himself jolted back to life by her touch. He looked more closely at her. I don't want nothing to do with this one, he thought.

The girl's sharp eyes peered at the back of the stubby reddish hand she held. There emblazoned in red and blue was a tattooed eagle perched on a cannon. Parker's sleeve was rolled to the elbow. Above the eagle a serpent was coiled about a shield and in the spaces between the eagle and the serpent there were hearts, some with arrows through them. Above the serpent there was a spread hand of cards. Every space on the skin of Parker's arm, from wrist to elbow, was covered in some loud design. The girl gazed at this with an almost stupefied smile of shock, as if she had accidentally grasped a poisonous snake; she dropped the hand.

"I got most of my other ones in foreign parts," Parker said. "These here I mostly got in the United States. I got my first one when I was only fifteen year old."

"Don't tell me," the girl said. "I don't like it. I ain't got any use for it." 15

"You ought to see to ones you can't see," Parker said and winked.

Two circles of red appeared like apples on the girl's cheeks and softened her appearance. Parker was intrigued. He did not for a minute think that she didn't like the tattoos. He had never yet met a woman who was not attracted to them.

Parker was fourteen when he saw a man in a fair, tattooed from head to foot. Except for his loins, which were girded with a panther hide, the man's skin was patterned in what seemed from Parker's distance—he was near the back of the tent, standing on a bench—a single intricate design of brilliant color. The man, who was small and sturdy, moved about on the platform, flexing his muscles so that the arabesque of men and beasts and flowers on his skin appeared to have a subtle motion of its own. Parker was filled with emotion, lifted up as some people are when the flag passes. He was a boy whose mouth habitually hung open. He was heavy and earnest, as ordinary as a loaf of bread. When the show was over, he had remained standing on the bench, staring where the tattooed man had been, until the tent was almost empty.

Parker had never before felt the least motion of wonder in himself. Until he saw the man at the fair, it did not enter his head that there was anything out of the ordinary about the fact that he existed. Even then it did not enter his head, but a peculiar unease settled in him. It was as if a blind boy had been turned so gently in a different direction that he did not know his destination had been changed.

He had his first tattoo some time after—the eagle perched on the cannon. 20 It was done by a local artist. It hurt very little, just enough to make it appear to Parker to be worth doing. This was peculiar too for before he had thought that only what did not hurt was worth doing. The next year he quit school because he was sixteen and could. He went to the trade school for a while, then he quit the trade school and worked for six months in a garage. The only reason he worked at all was to pay for more tattoos. His mother worked in a laundry and could support him, but she would not pay for any tattoo except her name on a heart, which he had put on, grumbling. However, her name was Betty Jean and nobody had to know it was his mother. He found out that the tattoos were attractive to the kind of girls he liked but who had never liked him before. He began to drink beer and get in fights. His mother wept over what was becoming of him. One night she dragged him off to a revival with her, not telling him where they were going. When he saw the big lighted church, he jerked out of her grasp and ran. The next day he lied about his age and joined the navy.

Parker was large for the tight sailor's pants but the silly white cap, sitting low on his forehead, made his face by contrast look thoughtful and almost intense. After a month or two in the navy, his mouth ceased to hang open. His features hardened into the features of a man. He stayed in the navy five years and seemed a natural part of the gray mechanical ship, except for his eyes, which were the same pale slate-color as the ocean and reflected the immense spaces around him as if they were a microcosm of the mysterious sea. In port Parker wandered about comparing the run-down places he was in to Birmingham, Alabama. Everywhere he went he picked up more tattoos.

He had stopped having lifeless ones like anchors and crossed rifles. He had a tiger and a panther on each shoulder, a cobra coiled about a torch on his chest, hawks on his thighs, Elizabeth II and Philip over where his stomach and liver were respectively. He did not care much what the subject was so long as it was colorful; on his abdomen he had a few obscenities but only because that seemed the proper place for them. Parker would be satisfied with each tattoo about a month, then something about it that had attracted him would wear off. Whenever a decent-sized mirror was available, he would get in front of it and study his overall look. The effect was not of one intricate arabesque of colors but of something haphazard and botched. A huge dissatisfaction would come over him and he would go off and find another tattooist and have another space filled up. The front of Parker was almost completely covered but there were no tattoos on his back. He had no desire for one anywhere he could not readily see it himself. As the space on the front of him for tattoos decreased, his dissatisfaction grew and became general.

After one of his furloughs, he didn't go back to the navy but remained away without official leave, drunk, in a rooming house in a city he did not know. His dissatisfaction, from being chronic and latent, had suddenly become acute and raged in him. It was as if the panther and the lion and the serpents and the eagles and the hawks had penetrated his skin and lived inside him in a raging warfare. The navy caught up with him, put him in the brig for nine months and then gave him a dishonorable discharge.

After that Parker decided that country air was the only kind fit to breathe. He rented the shack on the embankment and bought the old truck and took various jobs which he kept as long as it suited him. At the time he met his future wife, he was buying apples by the bushel and selling them for the same price by the pound to isolated homesteaders on back country roads.

"All that there," the woman said, pointing to his arm, "is no better than 25 what a fool Indian would do. It's a heap of vanity." She seemed to have found the word she wanted. "Vanity of vanities," she said.

Well what the hell do I care what she thinks of it? Parker asked himself, but he was plainly bewildered. "I reckon you like one of these better than another anyway," he said, dallying until he thought of something that would impress her. He thrust the arm back at her. "Which you like best?"

"None of them," she said, "but the chicken is not as bad as the rest."

"What chicken?" Parker almost yelled.

She pointed to the eagle.

"That's an eagle," Parker said. "What fool would waste their time having a 30 chicken put on themself?"

"What fool would have any of it?" the girl said and turned away. She went slowly back to the house and left him there to get going. Parker remained for almost five minutes, looking agape at the dark door she had entered.

The next day he returned with a bushel of apples. He was not one to be outdone by anything that looked like her. He liked women with meat on them, so you didn't feel their muscles, much less their bones. When he arrived, she was sitting on the top step and the yard was full of children, all as thin and poor as herself; Parker remembered it was Saturday. He hated to be making up to a woman when there were children around, but it was fortunate he had brought the bushel of apples off the truck. As the children approached him to see what he carried, he gave each child an apple and told it to get lost; in that way he cleared out the whole crowd.

The girl did nothing to acknowledge his presence. He might have been a stray pig or goat that had wandered into the yard and she too tired to take up the broom and send it off. He set the bushel of apples down next to her on the step. He sat down on a lower step.

"Hep yourself," he said, nodding at the basket; then he lapsed into silence.

She took an apple quickly as if the basket might disappear if she didn't 35 make haste. Hungry people made Parker nervous. He had always had plenty to eat himself. He grew very uncomfortable. He reasoned he had nothing to say so why should he say it? He could not think now why he had come or why he didn't go before he wasted another bushel of apples on the crowd of children. He supposed they were her brothers and sisters.

She chewed the apple slowly but with a kind of relish of concentration, bent slightly but looking out ahead. The view from the porch stretched off across a long incline studded with ironweed and across the highway to a vast vista of hills and one small mountain. Long views depressed Parker. You look out into space like that and you begin to feel as if someone were after you, the navy or the government or religion.

"Who them children belong to, you?" he said at length.

"I ain't married yet," she said. "They belong to momma." She said it as if it were only a matter of time before she would be married.

Who in God's name would marry her? Parker thought.

A large barefooted woman with a wide gap-toothed face appeared in the 40 door behind Parker. She had apparently been there for several minutes.

"Good evening," Parker said.

The woman crossed the porch and picked up what was left of the bushel of apples. "We thank you," she said and returned with it into the house.

"That your old woman?" Parker muttered.

The girl nodded. Parker knew a lot of sharp things he could have said like "You got my sympathy," but he was gloomily silent. He just sat there, looking at the view. He thought he must be coming down with something.

"If I pick up some peaches tomorrow I'll bring you some," he said.   45

"I'll be much obliged to you," the girl said.

Parker had no intention of taking any basket of peaches back there but the next day he found himself doing it. He and the girl had almost nothing to say to each other. One thing he did say was "I ain't got any tattoo on my back."

"What you got on it?" the girl said.

"My shirt," Parker said. "Haw."

"Haw, Haw," the girl said politely.   50

Parker thought he was losing his mind. He could not believe for a minute that he was attracted to a woman like this. She showed not the least interest in anything but what he brought until he appeared the third time with two cantaloups. "What's your name?" she asked.

"O. E. Parker," he said.

"What does the O. E. stand for?"

"You can just call me O. E.," Parker said. "Or Parker. Don't nobody call me by my name."

"What's it stand for?" she persisted.   55

"Never mind," Parker said. "What's yours?"

"I'll tell you when you tell me what them letters are the short of," she said. There was just a hint of flirtatiousness in her tone and it went rapidly to Parker's head. He had never revealed the name to any man or woman, only to the files of the navy and the government, and it was on his baptismal record, which he got at the age of a month; his mother was a Methodist. When the name leaked out of the navy files, Parker narrowly missed killing the man who used it.

"You'll go blab it around," he said.

"I'll swear I'll never tell nobody," she said. "On God's holy word I swear it."

Parker sat for a few minutes in silence. Then he reached for the girl's neck,   60 drew her ear close to his mouth and revealed the name in a low voice.

"Obadiah," she whispered. Her face slowly brightened as if the name came as a sign to her. "Obadiah," she said.

The name still stank in Parker's estimation.

"Obadiah Elihue," she said in a reverent voice.

"If you call me that aloud, I'll bust your head open," Parker said. "What's yours?"

"Sarah Ruth Cates," she said.   65

"Glad to meet you, Sarah Ruth," Parker said.

Sarah Ruth's father was a Straight Gospel preacher but he was away, spreading it in Florida. Her mother did not seem to mind his attention to the girl so long as he brought a basket of something with him when he came. As for Sarah Ruth herself, it was plain to Parker after he had visited three times that she was crazy about him. She liked him even though she insisted that pictures on the skin were vanity of vanities and even after hearing him curse, and even after she had asked him if he was saved and he had replied that he didn't see it was anything in particular to save him from. After that, inspired, Parker had said, "I'd be saved enough if you was to kiss me."

She scowled. "That ain't being saved," she said.

Not long after that she agreed to take a ride in his truck. Parker parked it on a deserted road and suggested to her that they lie down together in the back of it.

"Not until after we're married," she said—just like that.   70

"Oh, that ain't necessary," Parker said and as he reached for her, she thrust him away with such force that the door of the truck came off and he found himself flat on his back on the ground. He made up his mind then and there to have nothing further to do with her.

They were married in the County Ordinary's° office because Sarah Ruth thought churches were idolatrous. Parker had no opinion about that one way or the other. The Ordinary's office was lined with cardboard file boxes and record books with dusty yellow slips of paper hanging on out of them. The Ordinary was an old woman with red hair who had held office for forty years and looked as dusty as her books. She married them from behind the iron-grill of a standup desk and when she finished, she said with a flourish, "Three dollars and fifty cents and till death do you part!" and yanked some forms out of a machine.

Marriage did not change Sarah Ruth a jot and it made Parker gloomier than ever. Every morning he decided he had had enough and would not return that night; every night he returned. Whenever Parker couldn't stand the way he felt, he would have another tattoo, but the only surface left on him now was his back. To see a tattoo on his own back he would have to get two mirrors and stand between them in just the correct position and this seemed to Parker a good way to make an idiot of himself. Sarah Ruth who, if she had had better sense, could have enjoyed a tattoo on his back, would not even look at the ones he had elsewhere. When he attempted to point out especial details of them, she would shut her eyes tight and turn her back as well. Except in total darkness, she preferred Parker dressed and with his sleeves rolled down.

"At the judgment seat of God, Jesus is going to say to you, 'What you been doing all your life besides have pictures drawn all over you?'" she said.

"You don't fool me none," Parker said, "you're just afraid that hefty girl I   75
work for'll like me so much she'll say, 'Come on, Mr. Parker, let's you and me . . .'"

"You're tempting sin," she said, "and at the judgment seat of God you'll have to answer for that too. You ought to go back to selling the fruits of the earth."

Parker did nothing much when he was at home but listen to what the judgment seat of God would be like for him if he didn't change his ways. When he could, he broke in with tales of the hefty girl he worked for. "'Mr. Parker,'" he said she said, 'I hired you for your brains.'" (She had added, "So why don't you use them?")

"And you should have seen her face the first time she saw me without my shirt," he said. "'Mr. Parker,' she said, 'you're a walking panner-rammer!'" This had, in fact, been her remark but it had been delivered out of one side of her mouth.

Dissatisfaction began to grow so great in Parker that there was no containing it outside of a tattoo. It had to be his back. There was no help for it. A dim half-formed inspiration began to work in his mind. He visualized having a tattoo put there that Sarah Ruth would not be able to resist—a religious subject. He thought of an open book with HOLY BIBLE tattooed under it and an actual verse printed on the page. This seemed just the thing for a while; then he began to hear her say, "Ain't I already got a real Bible? What you think I want to read the same verse over and over for when I can read it all?" He needed something better even than the Bible! He thought about it so much that he began

---

Ordinary: Justice of the peace.

to lose sleep. He was already losing flesh—Sarah Ruth just threw food in the pot and let it boil. Not knowing for certain why he continued to stay with a woman who was both ugly and pregnant and no cook made him generally nervous and irritable, and he developed a little tic in the side of his face.

Once or twice he found himself turning around abruptly as if someone 80 were trailing him. He had had a granddaddy who had ended in the state mental hospital, although not until he was seventy-five, but as urgent as it might be for him to get a tattoo, it was just as urgent that he get exactly the right one to bring Sarah Ruth to heel. As he continued to worry over it, his eyes took on a hollow preoccupied expression. The old woman he worked for told him that if he couldn't keep his mind on what he was doing, she knew where she could find a fourteen-year-old colored boy who could. Parker was too preoccupied even to be offended. At any time previous, he would have left her then and there, saying drily, "Well, you go ahead on and get him then."

Two or three mornings later he was baling hay with the old woman's sorry baler and her broken-down tractor in a large field, cleared save for one enormous old tree standing in the middle of it. The old woman was the kind who would not cut down a large old tree because it was a large old tree. She had pointed it out to Parker as if he didn't have eyes and told him to be careful not to hit it as the machine picked up hay near it. Parker began at the outside of the field and made circles inward toward it. He had to get off the tractor every now and then and untangle the baling cord or kick a rock out of the way. The old woman had told him to carry the rocks to the edge of the field, which he did when she was there watching. When he thought he could make it, he ran over them. As he circled the field his mind was on a suitable design for his back. The sun, the size of a golf ball, began to switch regularly from in front to behind him, but he appeared to see it both places as if he had eyes in the back of his head. All at once he saw the tree reaching out to grasp him. A ferocious thud propelled him into the air, and he heard himself yelling in an unbelievably loud voice, "GOD ABOVE!"

He landed on his back while the tractor crashed upside-down into the tree and burst into flame. The first thing Parker saw were his shoes, quickly being eaten by the fire; one was caught under the tractor, the other was some distance away, burning by itself. He was not in them. He could feel the hot breath of the burning tree on his face. He scrambled backwards, still sitting, his eyes cavernous, and if he had known how to cross himself he would have done it.

His truck was on a dirt road at the edge of the field. He moved toward it, still sitting, still backwards, but faster and faster; halfway to it he got up and began a kind of forward-bent run from which he collapsed on his knees twice. His legs felt like two old rusted rain gutters. He reached the truck finally and took off in it, zigzagging up the road. He drove past his house on the embankment and straight for the city, fifty miles distant.

Parker did not allow himself to think on the way to the city. He only knew that there had been a great change in his life, a leap forward into a worse unknown, and that there was nothing he could do about it. It was for all intents accomplished.

The artist had two large cluttered rooms over a chiropodist's office on a 85 back street. Parker, still barefooted, burst silently in on him at a little after three in the afternoon. The artist, who was about Parker's own age—twenty-eight—but thin and bald, was behind a small drawing table, tracing a design in green ink. He looked up with an annoyed glance and did not seem to recognize Parker in the hollow-eyed creature before him.

"Let me see the book you got with all the pictures of God in it," Parker said breathlessly. "The religious one."

The artist continued to look at him with his intellectual, superior stare. "I don't put tattoos on drunks," he said.

"You know me!" Parker cried indignantly. "I'm O. E. Parker! You done work for me before and I always paid!"

The artist looked at him another moment as if he were not altogether sure. "You've fallen off some," he said. "You must have been in jail."

"Married," Parker said. 90

"Oh," said the artist. With the aid of mirrors the artist had tattooed on the top of his head a miniature owl, perfect in every detail. It was about the size of a half-dollar and served him as a show piece. There were cheaper artists in town but Parker had never wanted anything but the best. The artist went over to a cabinet at the back of the room and began to look over some art books. "Who are you interested in?" he said, "saints, angels, Christs or what?"

"God," Parker said.

"Father, Son, or Spirit?"

"Just God," Parker said impatiently. "Christ. I don't care. Just so it's God."

The artist returned with a book. He moved some papers off another table 95 and put the book down on it and told Parker to sit down and see what he liked. "The up-to-date ones are in the back," he said.

Parker sat down with the book and with his thumb. He began to go through it, beginning at the back where the up-to-date pictures were. Some of them he recognized — The Good Shepherd, Forbid Them Not, The Smiling Jesus, Jesus the Physician's Friend, but he kept turning rapidly backwards and the pictures became less and less reassuring. One showed a gaunt green dead face streaked with blood. One was yellow with sagging purple eyes. Parker's heart began to beat faster and faster until it appeared to be roaring inside him like a great generator. He flipped the pages quickly, feeling that when he reached the one ordained, a sign would come. He continued to flip through until he had almost reached the front of the book. On one of the pages a pair of eyes glanced at him swiftly. Parker sped on, then stopped. His heart too appeared to cut off; there was absolute silence. It said as plainly as if silence were a language itself, GO BACK.

Parker returned to the picture — the haloed head of a flat stern Byzantine Christ with all-demanding eyes. He sat there trembling; his heart began slowly to beat again as if it were being brought to life by a subtle power.

"You found what you want?" the artist asked.

Parker's throat was too dry to speak. He got up and thrust the book at the artist, opened at the picture.

"That'll cost you plenty," the artist said. "You don't want all those little 100 blocks though, just the outline and some better features."

"Just like it is," Parker said, "just like it is or nothing."

"It's your funeral," the artist said, "but I don't do that kind of work for nothing."

"How much?" Parker asked.

"It'll take maybe two days work."

"How much?" Parker said. 105

"On time or cash?" the artist asked. Parker's other jobs had been on time, but he had paid.

"Ten down and ten for every day it takes," the artist said.

Parker drew ten dollar bills out of his wallet; he had three left in.

"You come back in the morning," the artist said, putting the money in his own pocket. "First I'll have to trace that out of the book."

"No, no!" Parker said. "Trace it now or gimme my money back," and his 110 eyes blared as if he were ready for a fight.

The artist agreed. Anyone stupid enough to want a Christ on his back, he reasoned, would be just as likely as not to change his mind the next minute, but once the work was begun he could hardly do so.

While he worked on the tracing, he told Parker to go wash his back at the sink with the special soap he used there. Parker did it and returned to pace back and forth across the room, nervously flexing his shoulders. He wanted to go look at the picture again but at the same time he did not want to. The artist got up finally and had Parker lie down on the table. He swabbed his back with ethyl chloride and then began to outline the head on it with his iodine pencil. Another hour passed before he took up his electric instrument. Parker felt no particular pain. In Japan he had had a tattoo of the Buddha done on his upper arm with ivory needles; in Burma, a little brown root of a man had made a peacock on each of his knees using thin pointed sticks, two feet long; amateurs had worked on him with pins and soot. Parker was usually so relaxed and easy under the hand of the artist that he often went to sleep, but this time he remained awake, every muscle taut.

At midnight the artist said he was ready to quit. He propped one mirror, four feet square, on a table by the wall and took a smaller mirror off the lavatory wall and put it in Parker's hands. Parker stood with his back to the one on the table and moved the other until he saw a flashing burst of color reflected from his back. It was almost completely covered with little red and blue and ivory and saffron squares; from them he made out the lineaments of the face — a mouth, the beginning of heavy brows, a straight nose, but the face was empty; the eyes had not yet been put in. The impression for the moment was almost as if the artist had tricked him and done the Physician's Friend.

"It don't have eyes," Parker cried out.

"That'll come," the artist said, "in due time. We have another day to go on 115 it yet."

Parker spent the night on a cot at the Haven of Light Christian Mission. He found these the best places to stay in the city because they were free and included a meal of sorts. He got the last available cot and because he was still barefooted, he accepted a pair of second-hand shoes which, in his confusion, he put on to go to bed; he was still shocked from all that had happened to him. All night he lay awake in the long dormitory of cots with lumpy figures on them. The only light was from a phosphorescent cross glowing at the end of the room. The tree reached out to grasp him again, then burst into flame; the shoe burned quietly by itself; the eyes in the book said to him distinctly GO BACK and at the same time did not utter a sound. He wished that he were not in this city, not in this Haven of Light Mission, not in a bed by himself. He longed miserably for Sarah Ruth. Her sharp tongue and icepick eyes were the only comfort he could bring to mind. He decided he was losing it. Her eyes appeared soft and dilatory compared with the eyes in the book, for even though he could not summon up the exact look of those eyes, he could still feel their penetration. He felt as though, under their gaze, he was as transparent as the wing of a fly.

The tattooist had told him not to come until ten in the morning, but when he arrived at that hour, Parker was sitting in the dark hallway on the floor, waiting for him. He had decided upon getting up that, once the tattoo was on him, he would not look at it, that all his sensations of the day and night before were those of a crazy man and that he would return to doing things according to his own sound judgment.

The artist began where he left off. "One thing I want to know," he said presently as he worked over Parker's back, "why do you want this on you? Have you gone and got religion? Are you saved?" he asked in a mocking voice.

Parker's throat felt salty and dry. "Naw," he said, "I ain't got no use for none of that. A man can't save his self from whatever it is he don't deserve none of my sympathy." These words seemed to leave his mouth like wraiths and to evaporate at once as if he had never uttered them.

"Then why . . ."   120

"I married this woman that's saved," Parker said. "I never should have done it. I ought to leave her. She's done gone and got pregnant."

"That's too bad," the artist said. "Then it's her making you have this tattoo."

"Naw," Parker said, "she don't know nothing about it. It's a surprise for her."

"You think she'll like it and lay off you a while?"

"She can't help herself," Parker said. "She can't say she don't like the looks   125 of God." He decided he had told the artist enough of his business. Artists were all right in their place but he didn't like them poking their noses into the affairs of regular people. "I didn't get no sleep last night," he said. "I think I'll get some now."

That closed the mouth of the artist but it did not bring him any sleep. He lay there, imagining how Sarah Ruth would be struck speechless by the face on his back and every now and then this would be interrupted by a vision of the tree of fire and his empty shoe burning beneath it.

The artist worked steadily until nearly four o'clock, not stopping to have lunch, hardly pausing with the electric instrument except to wipe the dripping dye off Parker's back as he went along. Finally he finished. "You can get up and look at it now," he said.

Parker sat up but he remained on the edge of the table.

The artist was pleased with his work and wanted Parker to look at it at once. Instead Parker continued to sit on the edge of the table, bent forward slightly but with a vacant look. "What ails you?" the artist said. "Go look at it."

"Ain't nothing ail me," Parker said in a sudden belligerent voice. "That tat-   130 too ain't going nowhere. It'll be there when I get there." He reached for his shirt and began gingerly to put it on.

The artist took him roughly by the arm and propelled him between the two mirrors. "Now *look,*" he said, angry at having his work ignored.

Parker looked, turned white, and moved away. The eyes in the reflected face continued to look at him — still, straight, all-demanding, enclosed in silence.

"It was your idea, remember," the artist said. "I would have advised something else."

Parker said nothing. He put on his shirt and went out the door while the artist shouted, "I'll expect all of my money!"

Parker headed toward a package shop on the corner. He bought a pint of 135 whiskey and took it into a nearby alley and drank it all in five minutes. Then he moved on to a pool hall nearby which he frequented when he came to the city. It was a well-lighted barnlike place with a bar up one side and gambling machines on the other and pool tables in the back. As soon as Parker entered, a large man in a red and black checkered shirt hailed him by slapping him on the back and yelling, "Yeyyyyyy boy! O. E. Parker!"

Parker was not yet ready to be struck on the back. "Lay off," he said, "I got a fresh tattoo there."

"What you got this time?" the man asked and then yelled to a few at the machines. "O. E.'s got him another tattoo."

"Nothing special this time," Parker said and slunk over to a machine that was not being used.

"Come on," the big man said, "let's have a look at O. E.'s tattoo," and while Parker squirmed in their hands, they pulled up his shirt. Parker felt all the hands drop away instantly and his shirt fell again like a veil over the face. There was a silence in the pool room which seemed to Parker to grow from the circle around him until it extended to the foundations under the building and upward through the beams of the roof.

Finally some one said, "Christ!" Then they all broke into noise at once. 140 Parker turned around, an uncertain grin on his face.

"Leave it to O. E.!" the man in the checkered shirt said, "That boy's a real card!"

"Maybe he's gone and got religion," some one yelled.

"Not on your life," Parker said.

"O. E.'s got religion and is witnessing for Jesus, ain't you, O. E.?" a little man with a piece of cigar in his mouth said wryly. "An o-riginal way to do it if I ever saw one."

"Leave it to Parker to think of a new one!" the fat man said. 145

"Yyeeeeeeyyyyyyy boy!" someone yelled and they all began to whistle and curse in compliment until Parker said, "Aaa shut up."

"What'd you do it for?" somebody asked.

"For laughs," Parker said. "What's it to you?"

"Why ain't you laughing then?" somebody yelled. Parker lunged into the midst of them and like a whirlwind on a summer's day there began a fight that raged amid overturned tables and swinging fists until two of them grabbed him and ran to the door with him and threw him out. Then a calm descended on the pool hall as nerve shattering as if the long barnlike room were the ship from which Jonah had been cast into the sea.

Parker sat for a long time on the ground in the alley behind the pool hall, 150 examining his soul. He saw it as a spider web of facts and lies that was not at all important to him but which appeared to be necessary in spite of his opinion. The eyes that were now forever on his back were eyes to be obeyed. He was as certain of it as he had ever been of anything. Throughout his life, grumbling and sometimes cursing, often afraid, once in rapture, Parker had obeyed whatever instinct of this kind had come to him—in rapture when his spirit had lifted at the sight of the tattooed man at the fair, afraid when he had joined the navy, grumbling when he had married Sarah Ruth.

The thought of her brought him slowly to his feet. She would know what he had to do. She would clear up the rest of it, and she would at least be pleased. It seemed to him that, all along, that was what he wanted, to please her. His truck was still parked in front of the building where the artist had his place, but it was not far away. He got in it and drove out of the city and into the country night. His head was almost clear of liquor and he observed that his dissatisfaction was gone, but he felt not quite like himself. It was as if he were himself but a stranger to himself, driving into a new country though everything he saw was familiar to him, even at night.

He arrived finally at the house on the embankment, pulled the truck under the pecan tree, and got out. He made as much noise as possible to assert that he was still in charge here, that his leaving her for a night without word meant nothing except it was the way he did things. He slammed the car door, stamped up the two steps and across the porch and rattled the door knob. It did not respond to his touch. "Sarah Ruth!" he yelled, "let me in."

There was no lock on the door and she had evidently placed the back of a chair against the knob. He began to beat on the door and rattle the knob at the same time.

He heard the bed springs screak and bent down and put his head to the keyhole, but it was stopped up with paper. "Let me in!" he hollered, bamming on the door again. "What you got me locked out for?"

A sharp voice close to the door said, "Who's there?"   155

"Me," Parker said, "O. E."

He waited a moment.

"Me," he said impatiently, "O. E."

Still no sound from inside.

He tried once more. "O. E.," he said, bamming the door two or three more   160
times. "O. E. Parker. You know me."

There was a silence. Then the voice said slowly, "I don't know no O. E."

"Quit fooling," Parker pleaded. "You ain't got any business doing me this way. It's me, old O. E., I'm back. You ain't afraid of me."

"Who's there?" the same unfeeling voice said.

Parker turned his head as if he expected someone behind him to give him the answer. The sky had lightened slightly and there were two or three streaks of yellow floating above the horizon. Then as he stood there, a tree of light burst over the skyline.

Parker fell back against the door as if he had been pinned there by a lance.   165

"Who's there?" the voice from inside said and there was a quality about it now that seemed final. The knob rattled and the voice said peremptorily, "Who's there, I ast you?"

Parker bent down and put his mouth near the stuffed keyhole. "Obadiah," he whispered and all at once he felt the light pouring through him, turning his spider web soul into a perfect arabesque of colors, a garden of trees and birds and beasts.

"Obadiah Elihue!" he whispered.

The door opened and he stumbled in. Sarah Ruth loomed there, hands on her hips. She began at once, "That was no hefty blonde woman you was working for and you'll have to pay her every penny on her tractor you busted up. She don't keep insurance on it. She came here and her and me had us a long talk and I . . ."

Trembling, Parker set about lighting the kerosene lamp.   170

"What's the matter with you, wasting that keresene this near daylight?" she demanded. "I ain't got to look at you."

A yellow glow enveloped them. Parker put the match down and began to unbutton his shirt.

"And you ain't going to have none of me this near morning," she said.

"Shut your mouth," he said quietly. "Look at this and then I don't want to hear no more out of you." He removed the shirt and turned his back to her.

"Another picture," Sarah Ruth growled, "I might have known you was off after putting some more trash on yourself." 175

Parker's knees went hollow under him. He wheeled around and cried, "Look at it! Don't just say that! *Look* at it!"

"I done looked," she said.

"Don't you know who it is?" he cried in anguish.

"No, who is it?" Sarah Ruth said. "It ain't anybody I know."

"It's him," Parker said. 180

"Him who?"

"God!" Parker cried.

"God? God don't look like that!"

"What do you know how he looks?" Parker moaned. "You ain't seen him."

"He don't *look,*" Sarah Ruth said. "He's a spirit. No man shall see his face." 185

"Aw listen," Parker groaned, "this is just a picture of him."

"Idolatry!" Sarah Ruth screamed. "Idolatry! Enflaming yourself with idiots under every green tree! I can put up with lies and vanity but I don't want no idolator in this house!" and she grabbed up the broom and began to thrash him across the shoulders with it.

Parker was too stunned to resist. He sat there and let her beat him until she had nearly knocked him senseless and large welts had formed on the face of the tattooed Christ. Then he staggered up and made for the door.

She stamped the broom two or three times on the floor and went to the window and shook it out to get the taint of him off it. Still gripping it, she looked toward the pecan tree and her eyes hardened still more. There he was—who called himself Obadiah Elihue—leaning against the tree, crying like a baby.

Considerations for Critical Thinking and Writing

1. FIRST RESPONSE. Would you ever consider getting a tattoo for yourself? Why or why not?

2. How was Parker affected as a boy by seeing the tattooed man at the fair? Why does he continue to have himself tattooed?

3. How does Parker's wife regard his tattoos?

4. Why did Parker marry his wife? Why did she marry him? What keeps them together in the marriage? Which one of them seems more powerful in the relationship?

5. What is Parker's view of his wife's "forever sniffing up sin"?

6. What is Parker's attitude toward the navy, the government, and religion?

7. Why and how is Parker changed by crashing the tractor into the tree? Why does he subsequently decide to get a tattoo on his back?

8. How is Parker affected by the tattoo on his back? How does he think his wife will respond? How does she actually react to it?

9. What is the significance of Parker calling himself Obadiah Elihue when he returns home to his wife?

10. Why does Obadiah Elihue cry like a baby in the final scene?

11. Discuss the significance of the title.

12. How does humor contribute to the characterization of Parker? Do you think humor is appropriate for this story?

CONNECTIONS TO OTHER SELECTIONS

1. Compare the protagonists' attitudes toward religion in "Parker's Back" and Hawthorne's "Young Goodman Brown" (p. 331).

2. Compare the symbolic value of Parker's tattoo with the crimson hand in Hawthorne's "The Birthmark" (p. 359).

3. Write an essay that compares the themes of "Parker's Back" and "Revelation" (p. 410).

PERSPECTIVES ON O'CONNOR

O'Connor on Faith   *1955*

I write the way I do because (not though) I am a Catholic. This is a fact and nothing covers it like the bald statement. However, I am a Catholic peculiarly possessed of the modern consciousness, the thing Jung° describes as unhistorical, solitary, and guilty. To possess this within the Church is to bear a burden, the necessary burden for the conscious Catholic. It's to feel the contemporary situation at the ultimate level. I think that the Church is the only thing that is going to make the terrible world we are coming to endurable; the only thing that makes the Church endurable is that it is somehow the body of Christ and that on this we are fed. It seems to be a fact that you suffer as much from the Church as for it but if you believe in the divinity of Christ, you have to cherish the world at the same time that you struggle to endure it. This may explain the lack of bitterness in the stories.

From a letter to "A," July 20, 1955, in The Habit of Being

Jung: Carl Jung (1875–1961), a Swiss psychiatrist.

CONSIDERATIONS FOR CRITICAL THINKING AND WRITING

1. Consider how O'Connor's fiction expresses her belief that "you have to cherish the world at the same time that you struggle to endure it."

2. Do you agree that "bitterness" is absent from O'Connor's stories? Explain why or why not.

O'Connor on the Materials of Fiction   *1969*

The beginning of human knowledge is through the senses, and the fiction writer begins where human perception begins. He appeals through the senses, and you cannot appeal to the senses with abstractions. It is a good deal easier for most people to state an abstract idea than to describe and thus re-create some object that they actually see. But the world of the fiction writer is full of matter, and this is what the beginning fiction writers are very loath to create. They are concerned primarily with unfleshed ideas and emotions. They are apt to be reformers and to want to write because they are possessed not by a story but by the bare bones of some abstract notion. They are conscious of problems, not of people, of questions and issues, not of the texture of existence, of case histories and of everything that has a sociological smack, instead of with all those concrete details of life that make actual the mystery of our position on earth. . . .

One of the most common and saddest spectacles is that of a person of really fine sensibility and acute psychological perception trying to write fiction by using these [abstract] qualities alone. This type of writer will put down one intensely emotional or keenly perceptive sentence after the other, and the result will be complete dullness. The fact is that the materials of the fiction writer are the humblest. Fiction is about everything human and we are made out of dust, and if you scorn getting yourself dusty, then you shouldn't try to write fiction. It's not a grand enough job for you.

From "The Nature and Aim of Fiction" in *Mystery and Manners*

CONSIDERATIONS FOR CRITICAL THINKING AND WRITING

1. Explain O'Connor's idea that "the materials of the fiction writer are the humblest" (para. 2) by reference to the materials and details of her stories.

2. Choose a substantial paragraph from an O'Connor story and describe how it "appeals through the senses" (para. 1).

3. Write an essay in which you agree or disagree with the following statement: Hawthorne's fiction is a good example of the kinds of mistakes that O'Connor attributes to a beginning fiction writer.

O'Connor on the Use of Exaggeration and Distortion   1969

When I write a novel in which the central action is a baptism, I am very well aware that for a majority of my readers, baptism is a meaningless rite, and so in my novel I have to see that this baptism carries enough awe and mystery to jar the reader into some kind of emotional recognition of its significance. To this end I have to bend the whole novel — its language, its structure, its action. I have to make the reader feel, in his bones if nowhere else, that something is going on here that counts. Distortion in this case is an instrument; exaggeration has a purpose, and the whole structure of the story or novel has been made what it is because of belief. This is not the kind of distortion that destroys; it is the kind that reveals, or should reveal.

From "Novelist and Believer" in *Mystery and Manners*

CONSIDERATIONS FOR CRITICAL THINKING AND WRITING

1. It has been observed that in many of O'Connor's works the central action takes the form of some kind of "baptism" that initiates, tests, or purifies a character. Select a story that illustrates this generalization, and explain how the conflict results in a kind of baptism.

2. O'Connor says that exaggeration and distortion reveal something in her stories. What is the effect of such exaggeration and distortion? Typically, what is revealed by it? Focus your comments on a single story to illustrate your points.

3. Do you think that O'Connor's stories have anything to offer a reader who has no religious faith? Explain why or why not.

O'Connor on Theme and Symbol   *1969*

When you can state the theme of a story, when you can separate it from the story itself, then you can be sure the story is not a very good one. The meaning of a story has to be embodied in it, has to be made concrete in it. A story is a way to say something that can't be said any other way, and it takes every word in the story to say what the meaning is. You tell a story because a statement would be inadequate. When anybody asks what a story is about, the only proper thing is to tell him to read the story. The meaning of fiction is not abstract meaning but experienced meaning, and the purpose of making statements about the meaning of a story is only to help you to experience that meaning more fully.

The peculiar problem of the short-story writer is how to make the action he describes reveal as much of the mystery of existence as possible. He has only a short space to do it in and he can't do it by statement. He has to do it by showing, not by saying, and by showing the concrete—so that his problem is really how to make the concrete work double time for him.

In good fiction, certain of the details will tend to accumulate meaning from the action of the story itself, and when this happens they become symbolic in the way they work. I once wrote a story called "Good Country People," in which a lady Ph.D. has her wooden leg stolen by a Bible salesman whom she has tried to seduce. Now I'll admit that, paraphrased in this way, the situation is simply a low joke. The average reader is pleased to observe anybody's wooden leg being stolen. But without ceasing to appeal to him and without making any statements of high intention, this story does manage to operate at another level of experience, by letting the wooden leg accumulate meaning. Early in the story, we're presented with the fact that the Ph.D. is spiritually as well as physically crippled. She believes in nothing but her own belief in nothing, and we perceive that there is a wooden part of her soul that corresponds to her wooden leg. Now of course this is never stated. The fiction writer states as little as possible. The reader makes this connection from things he is shown. He may not even know that he makes the connection, but the connection is there nevertheless and it has its effect on him. As the story goes on, the wooden leg continues to accumulate meaning. The reader learns how the girl feels about her leg, how her mother feels about it, and how the country woman on the place feels about it; and finally, by the time the Bible salesman comes along, the leg has accumulated so much meaning that it is, as the saying goes, loaded. And when the Bible salesman steals it, the reader realizes that he has taken away part of the girl's personality and has revealed her deeper affliction to her for the first time.

If you want to say that the wooden leg is a symbol, you can say that. But it is a wooden leg first, and as a wooden leg it is absolutely necessary to the story. It has its place on the literal level of the story, but it operates in depth as well as on the surface. It increases the story in every direction, and this is essentially the way a story escapes being short.

Now a little might be said about the way in which this happens. I wouldn't want you to think that in that story I sat down and said, "I am now going to write a story about a Ph.D. with a wooden leg, using the wooden leg as a symbol for another kind of affliction." I doubt myself if many writers know what they are going to do when they start out. When I started writing that story, I didn't know there was going to be a Ph.D. with a wooden leg in it. I merely found myself one morning writing a description of two women that I knew something about, and before I realized it, I had equipped one of them with a daughter with a wooden leg. As the story progressed, I brought in the Bible salesman, but I had no idea what I was going to do with him. I didn't know he was going to steal that wooden leg until ten or twelve lines before he did it, but when I found out that this was what was going to happen, I realized that it was inevitable. This is a story that produces a shock for the reader, and I think one reason for this is that it produced a shock for the writer.

Now despite the fact that this story came about in this seemingly mindless fashion, it is a story that almost no rewriting was done on. It is a story that was under control throughout the writing of it, and it might be asked how this kind of control comes about, since it is not entirely conscious.

From "Writing Short Stories" in *Mystery and Manners*

CONSIDERATIONS FOR CRITICAL THINKING AND WRITING

1. Why is a "statement" (para. 1) inadequate to convey the meaning of a story?

2. O'Connor describes how the wooden leg "continues to accumulate meaning" (para. 3) in "Good Country People" (p. 395). Choose another story by O'Connor and explain how something specific and concrete is invested with symbolic meaning.

JOSEPHINE HENDIN (B. 1946)

On O'Connor's Refusal to "Do Pretty" 1970

There is, in the memory of one Milledgeville matron, the image of O'Connor at nineteen or twenty who, when invited to a wedding shower for an old family friend, remained standing, her back pressed against the wall, scowling at the group of women who had sat down to lunch. Neither the devil nor her mother could make her say yes to this fiercely gracious female society, but Flannery O'Connor could not say no even in a whisper. She could not refuse the invitation but she would not accept it either. She did not exactly "fuss" but neither did she "do pretty."

From *The World of Flannery O'Connor*

CONSIDERATIONS FOR CRITICAL THINKING AND WRITING

1. How is O'Connor's personality revealed in this anecdote about her ambivalent response to society? Allow the description to be suggestive for you, and flesh out a brief portrait of her.

2. Consider how this personality makes itself apparent in any one of O'Connor's stories you have read. How does the anecdote help to characterize the narrator's voice in the story?

3. To what extent do you think biographical details such as this — assuming the Milledgeville matron's memory to be accurate — can shed light on a writer's works?

CLAIRE KAHANE (B. 1935)

The Function of Violence in O'Connor's Fiction   1974

From the moment the reader enters O'Connor's backwoods, he is poised on the edge of a pervasive violence. Characters barely contain their rage; images reflect a hostile nature; and even the Christ to whom the characters are ultimately driven is a threatening figure . . . full of the apocalyptic wrath of the Old Testament.

O'Connor's conscious purpose is evident enough . . . : to reveal the need for grace in a world grotesque without a transcendent context. "I have found that my subject in fiction is the action of grace in territory largely held by the devil," she wrote [in *Mystery and Manners*], and she was not vague about what the devil is: "an evil intelligence determined on its own supremacy." It would seem that for O'Connor, given the fact of original Sin, any intelligence determined on its own supremacy was intrinsically evil. For in each work, it is the impulse toward secular autonomy, the smug confidence that human nature is perfectible by its own efforts, that she sets out to destroy, through an act of violence so intense that the character is rendered helpless, a passive victim of a superior power. Again and again she creates a fiction in which a character attempts to live autonomously, to define himself and his values, only to be jarred back to what she calls "reality" — the recognition of helplessness in the face of contingency, and the need for absolute submission to the power of Christ.

From "Flannery O'Connor's Rage of Vision" in *American Literature*

CONSIDERATIONS FOR CRITICAL THINKING AND WRITING

1. Choose an O'Connor story, and explain how grace — the divine influence from God that redeems a person — is used in it to transform a character.

2. Which O'Connor characters can be accurately described as having an "evil intelligence determined on its own supremacy" (para. 2)? Choose one character, and write an essay explaining how this description is central to the conflict of the story.

3. Compare an O'Connor story with one of Hawthorne's "in which a character attempts to live autonomously, to define himself and his values, only to be jarred back to . . . 'reality' — the recognition of helplessness in the face of contingency . . ." (para. 2).

EDWARD KESSLER (B. 1927)

On O'Connor's Use of History   1986

In company with other Southern writers . . . who aspire to embrace a lost tradition and look on history as a repository of value, Flannery O'Connor seems
a curious anomaly. She wrote of herself: "I am a Catholic peculiarly possessed
of the modern consciousness . . . unhistorical, solitary, and guilty." Likewise
her characters comprise a gallery of misfits isolated in a present and sentenced
to a lifetime of exile from the human community. In O'Connor's fiction, the
past neither justifies nor even explains what is happening. If she believed, for
example, in the importance of the past accident that maimed Joy in "Good
Country People," she could have demonstrated how the event predetermined
her present rejection of both human and external nature; but Joy's past is parenthetical: "Mrs. Hopewell excused this attitude because of the leg (which had
been shot off in a hunting accident when Joy was ten)." Believing that humankind is fundamentally flawed, O'Connor spends very little time constructing a past for her characters. The cure is neither behind us nor before us but
within us; therefore, the past — even historical time itself — supplies only a limited base for self-discovery.

From *Flannery O'Connor and the Language of Apocalypse*

CONSIDERATIONS FOR CRITICAL THINKING AND WRITING

1. Consider how O'Connor uses history in any one of her stories in this anthology and compare that "unhistorical" vision with Hawthorne's in
   "Young Goodman Brown" (p. 331) or "The Minister's Black Veil" (p. 341).

2. Write an essay in which you discuss Kessler's assertion that for O'Connor
   the "past is parenthetical," in contrast to most southern writers, who "embrace a lost tradition and look on history as a repository of value." For your
   point of comparison choose either William Faulkner's "A Rose for Emily"
   (p. 75) or "Barn Burning" (p. 493).

TWO COMPLEMENTARY
CRITICAL READINGS

A. R. COULTHARD (B. 1940)

On the Visionary Ending of "Revelation"   1983

The second part of the story does not keep pace with its rollicking opening,
but its psychological realism gives Mrs. Turpin's ultimate redemption a hard-
edged credibility. When the protagonist returns home, her first impulse is,
quite naturally, to resist the message of grace brought by the girl: " 'I am
not,' she said tearfully, 'a wart hog. From hell.' But the denial had no force."
Unable to reject the charge, Mrs. Turpin turns to resentment: "The message
had been given to Ruby Turpin, a respectable, hard-working, church-going
woman. The tears dried. Her eyes began to burn instead with wrath." Next

she attempts to exorcise the girl's demonic words by confessing them to her black fieldhands:

> "She said," she began again and finished this time with a fierce rush of breath, "that I was an old wart hog from hell."
>
> There was an astounded silence.
>
> "Where she at?" the youngest woman cried in a piercing voice.
>
> "Lemme see her. I'll kill her!"
>
> "I'll kill her with you!" the other one cried.
>
> "She b'long in the sylum," the old woman said emphatically. "You the sweetest white lady I know."
>
> "She pretty too," the other two said. "Stout as she can be and sweet. Jesus satisfied with her!"
>
> "Deed he is," the woman declared.
>
> Idiots! Mrs. Turpin growled to herself.

This little scene is both funny and thematically significant. Mrs. Turpin's refusal to accept the phony image of herself as a good woman offered by the blacks is a step toward facing the truth.

Mrs. Turpin's next step is literal. She climbs the hill to the hogpen, apparently considering it the appropriate place to reason out the meaning of being called a wart hog from hell. Once there, Ruby gets right down to business: "What do you send me a message like that for?" she demands. "How am I a hog and me both?" Then she yells, "Go on, call me a hog! Call me a hog again. From hell. Call me a wart hog from hell." She ends her harangue by hilariously roaring at God, "Who do you think you are?" In this scene, Ruby begins to grow into a sympathetic, even lovable, character. As O'Connor said, "You got to be a very big woman to shout at the Lord across a hogpen." You also got to believe.

God answers Mrs. Turpin by sending her an epiphany which is so unobtrusively presented that at first it seems to be only description: "A tiny truck, Claud's, appeared on the highway, heading rapidly out of sight. Its gears scraped thinly. It looked like a child's toy. At any moment a bigger truck might smash into it and scatter Claud's and the niggers' brains all over the road." The answer to Ruby's question is that God is omnipotent and that Ruby, like all mortals, is an insignificant, vulnerable creature whose life can end at any moment. Her response to this new knowledge is immediate: "Then like a monumental statue coming to life, she bent her head slowly and gazed, as if through the very heart of mystery, down into the pig parlor at the hogs."

The story originally ended at this point, but O'Connor decided that "something else was needed." Fortunately, what she added is not a concluding mini-sermon but a supernatural vision which is perfectly in keeping with the seriocomic tone of the story:

> A visionary light settled in her eyes . . . a vast horde of souls were rumbling toward heaven. There were whole companies of white-trash, clean for the first time in their lives, and bands of black niggers in white robes, and battalions of freaks and lunatics shouting and clapping and leaping like frogs. And bringing up the end of the procession was a tribe of people whom she recognized at once as those . . . like herself and Claud. . . . They were marching behind the others with great dignity. . . . They alone were on key. Yet she could see by their shocked and altered faces that even their virtues were being burned away.

This vision demolishes Ruby's earlier neat ranking of people, and its concluding sentence, which could have quotation marks around "virtues," completes her education by telling her that no one deserves grace and that we receive it only because of God's mysterious mercy. The epiphany takes, and the story ends with Ruby, "her eyes small but fixed unblinkingly on what lay ahead," prepared to face a humbler and more demanding life.

Though at least one reader whom O'Connor respected found "Revelation" pessimistic and considered the protagonist evil, O'Connor's main worry was that the story would "be taken to be one designed to make fun of Ruby," probably because her weaknesses are so vividly shown. But the great achievement of the protagonist's characterization is that Ruby Turpin retains her humanity to the end and does not, upon receiving grace, turn into an inspirational symbol. At the same time, O'Connor has made her conversion believable by dramatizing it in action and dialogue consistent with both Mrs. Turpin's humorous traits and her serious role in the story. "Revelation" is not only a delightful comedy but a profound dramatization of redemption as well.

From *American Literature*

CONSIDERATIONS FOR CRITICAL THINKING AND WRITING

1. According to Coulthard, how does O'Connor avoid turning the end of the story into a "mini-sermon" (para. 5)?

2. How would your response to the story be different if it ended as O'Connor first intended it to — without the concluding paragraph? How would you regard Mrs. Turpin if this paragraph did not appear in the story?

3. Write an essay in response to this judgment of "Revelation": "Religion and comedy don't mix; therefore, the comic tone of 'Revelation' is inappropriate to the concluding religious epiphany."

MARSHALL BRUCE GENTRY (B. 1953)
On the Revised Ending of "Revelation"   *1986*

The precise significance of Mrs. Turpin's vision of hordes on a fiery bridge is not altogether a matter of critical agreement. And O'Connor's letters show her to have been inconsistent in her opinion of "Revelation" while she was writing it. It was the ending of the story that most troubled her, and the sequence of versions shows O'Connor trying to make clear that Ruby is not entirely corrupt. In a letter dated 25 December 1963, O'Connor mentioned that a friend who had read a draft of "Revelation" had called Mrs. Turpin "evil" and had suggested that O'Connor omit the final vision, which the friend considered to be a confirmation of Mrs. Turpin's evilness. O'Connor's reaction was, "I am not going to leave it out. I am going to deepen it so that there'll be no mistaking Ruby is not just an evil Glad Annie." As she finished revising the story, O'Connor made the final vision less obviously of Mrs. Turpin's making. One late draft, for example, contains the statement that the Turpins, "marching behind the others" toward heaven "with great dignity," were "driving them, in fact, ahead of themselves, still responsible as they had always been for good order and common sense and respectable behavior." In the published text, the Turpins are still at the end of the procession, but there is no mention of them "driving" the others on, and they are "accountable" rather than "still responsible." Another significant difference between the draft and the published text is the addition in the final version of the fact that Mrs. Turpin sees that her "virtues" are "being burned away." In both these revisions there is less emphasis on Mrs. Turpin's smug perspective, more emphasis on what shocks her.

The final version makes the vision more clearly redemptive, and one apparent implication of the revisions is that Mrs. Turpin's revelation is supernatural in origin. This implication is misleading, however; there is still much in Mrs. Turpin's vision to suggest that she produces it, and the primary effect of O'Connor's revisions is to make Mrs. Turpin's unconscious more clearly responsible for her vision of entry into a heavenly community. This view may seem peculiar when one considers Mrs. Turpin's bigotry and banality, but one's impression of that bigotry and banality is the result of the narrator's emphasis in describing Mrs. Turpin. The narrator emphasizes the ridiculous aspects of Mrs. Turpin rather than making fully apparent the tracks she has laid to carry herself to the oven in which individuality is renounced and the ideal of heavenly community achieved.

From *Flannery O'Connor's Religion of the Grotesque*

CONSIDERATIONS FOR CRITICAL THINKING AND WRITING

1. What reservations, according to Gentry, did O'Connor have about the story's ending? For what purpose did O'Connor revise the manuscript?

2. How does Gentry's reading of the ending compare with Coulthard's? Which reading do you find closer to your own? Why?

3. Write an essay that considers Gentry's final charge that Mrs. Turpin appears "ridiculous" at the end of the story in contrast to Coulthard's assessment that she "retains her humanity."

--- SUGGESTED TOPICS FOR LONGER PAPERS ---

1. Discuss O'Connor's use of humor in the stories you've read in this chapter. As the basis of your discussion consider at least one humorous moment or scene in each story and characterize the tone of her humor. What generalizations can you make about the tone of the humor in her stories? How does O'Connor use humor to affect the reader's understanding of her themes?

2. O'Connor's fiction is often populated with peculiar characters who seem to demand psychological interpretation. O'Connor, however, made clear in a March 28, 1961, letter that "I am not interested in abnormal psychology." Research psychological readings of one of the stories in this chapter and argue for or against reading her characters from a psychological point of view. You may need to do your own psychological analysis of a character or two to argue for or against its relevance to the story.

3. MULTIMEDIA PROJECT. Quite a lot has been documented about tattoos in the recent past. Books, articles, and film documentaries have described the history and culture associated with tattoos. Explore some of this material in various media and write an essay that discusses why it is or isn't relevant to a reading of "Parker's Back."

Web   *For help with this project, use the Multimedia Project Guides Online at*
      http://www.bedfordstmartins.com/meyer/bedintrolit

13

A Study of Alice Monro

A BRIEF BIOGRAPHY AND INTRODUCTION

Nearly all of the fiction by Alice Munro (b. 1931) is set in southwestern Ontario, but her reputation as a brilliant short story writer goes far beyond the borders of her native Canada. Bharati Mukherjee, the novelist and short story writer, echoes many writers' opinions in noting that "Munro ranks among the finest short story writers in the English language." Her accessible and moving stories offer immediate pleasures while simultaneously exploring human complexities in what appear to be effortless anecdotal re-creations of everyday life. In one novel and seven collections of stories she has established herself as a major voice among fiction writers.

Munro began writing in her teens in the small rural town of Wingham, Ontario. She published her first story in 1950 while a student at Western Ontario University, but she left school to marry and moved to British Columbia, where she had three children and helped her husband establish a bookstore. This marriage broke up in 1972 when she returned to Ontario, and she remarried in 1976. Her first collection of stories, *Dance of the Happy Shades,* was not published until 1968, but it was highly acclaimed and won that year's Governor General's Award, Canada's highest literary prize. This success was followed by *Lives of Girls and Women* (1971), a collection of

PHOTO ABOVE: *Reprinted by permission of Canapress Photo Service.*

447

interlinked stories that was published as a novel and won the Canadian Booksellers Association International Book Year Award. This is the only novel Munro has published because she prefers the compression and brevity of short story writing. As she explains in a 1982 interview with Geoff Hancock for *Canadian Fiction Magazine,* she likes catching people in "snapshots": "I think this is why I'm not drawn to writing novels. Because I don't see that people develop and arrive somewhere. I just see people living in flashes." The form of the short story captures for Munro the fragmentary nature of her characters' experiences.

Her remaining six books are all short story collections, two of which also won the Governor General's Award in 1978 and 1986: *Something I've Been Meaning to Tell You* (1974); *Who Do You Think You Are?* (1978, titled *The Beggar Maid* in English and American editions); *The Moons of Jupiter* (1982); *The Progress of Love* (1986); *Friend of My Youth* (1990); and *Open Secrets* (1994). In addition, her stories are regularly printed in such publications as *The New Yorker,* the *Atlantic Monthly, Grand Street, Mademoiselle,* and *The Paris Review.*

The subject matter of Munro's stories has clearly developed from her own experience. She has explained in various interviews that her stories are not autobiographical, but she does claim an "emotional reality" for her characters that is drawn from her own life. Munro's experience of growing up in a relatively poor provincial southwestern Ontario town during the depression, negotiating the rebelliousness and idealism of adolescence, discovering sex, leaving home, testing herself at university, falling in love, getting married, having children, getting divorced, making a living, and getting along in a variety of complicated relationships all inform the fiction she creates.

Munro's fictional world ranges across the breadth of Canada from Ontario to British Columbia, but most readers agree that her Ontario stories, rooted as they are in her own formative past, represent more evocative settings experienced in childhood and recollected by a perceptive adult memory. Munro is repeatedly drawn back in her stories to rural Ontario despite the provincial and crabbed atmosphere of its small towns: "It's just that it's so basic like my own flesh or something that I can't be separated from." Many commentators compare Munro's interest in small-town settings to the use that American regional writers make of the rural South. Her admiration for American writers such as William Faulkner, Flannery O'Connor, Eudora Welty, and Carson McCullers has been frequently noted, and, as she has pointed out, "If I'm a regional writer, the region I'm writing about has many things in common with the American South." Munro's version of small-town Ontario, like O'Connor's version of the rural South, is one of a "closed rural society with a pretty homogeneous Scotch-Irish racial strain going slowly to decay."

Munro's characters, like Faulkner's or O'Connor's, often find themselves confronting entrenched customs and traditions, but their behavior is usually less overtly desperate and violently intense than that of their southern counterparts. To be sure there are drunks, suicides, molesters, lunatics, and bizarre eccentrics in Munro's stories, but Faulkner's Emily Grierson (p. 75) and Abner Snopes (p. 493) or O'Connor's Misfit (p. 384) represent more extreme character types than the more ordinary men and women who populate Munro's fictions. Perhaps Munro's description of the protagonist in "Prue" (p. 467) best describes her own strategies as a short story writer:

> She presents her life in anecdotes, and though it is the point of most of her anecdotes that hopes are dashed, dreams ridiculed, things never turn out as expected, everything is altered in a bizarre way and there is no explanation ever, people always feel cheered up after listening to her; they say of her that it is a relief to meet somebody who doesn't take herself too seriously, who is so unintense, and civilized, and never makes any real demands or complaints.

Given the intricacies and subtleties of Munro's stories, this description may seem overly simplistic, but it does suggest the modest and quiet wisdom to be found in her fiction. Good readers take Munro seriously.

Munro's realistic style is comfortably familiar. As she has noted, "I've never been an innovator or an experimental writer. I'm not very clever that way. I'm never ahead of what's being done at the time." Her prose is not informed by elaborate theoretical principles; instead she remembers and invents details that create a vivid character, moment, or setting that suggests larger meanings. Consider, for example the following passage from "How I Met My Husband," in which Munro's protagonist, a fifteen-year-old live-in cleaning girl, admires the bathroom in the house where she works:

> I had a bath in there once a week. They wouldn't have minded if I took one oftener, but to me it seemed like asking too much, or maybe risking making it less wonderful. The basin and the tub and the toilet were all pink, and there were glass doors with flamingos painted on them, to shut off the tub. The light had a rosy cast and the mat sank under your feet like snow, except that it was warm. The mirror was three-way. With the mirror all steamed up and the air like a perfume cloud, from things I was allowed to use, I stood up on the side of the tub and admired myself naked, from three directions. Sometimes I thought about the way we lived out at home and the way we lived here and how one way was so hard to imagine when you were living the other way. But I thought it was still a lot easier, living the way we lived at home, to picture something like this, the painted flamingos and the warmth and the soft mat, than it was anybody knowing only things like this to picture how it was the other way. And why was that?

Although Munro has described her own realistic sensibilities as being "very excited by what you might call the surface of life," in this passage she moves us beyond the pink surfaces of a bathroom toward an exploration of her protagonist's complex response to those surfaces. Her vivid description of the bathroom through her use of detail also works to reveal character.

In *Lives of Girls and Women* Munro has a character, Del Jordon, explain what she hopes to achieve in writing a work of fiction about small-town life in Ontario. Del works hard to portray not only what is actually "real" about the town, but what is meaningfully "true," and in order to do so she must capture the dull, ordinary simplicity of her neighbors' daily lives. Del's description of her efforts has often — and rightly — been used by critics to describe Munro's own intentions as a writer: "What I wanted was every last thing, every layer of speech and thought, stroke of light on bark or walls, every smell, pothole, pain, crack, delusion, held still and held together — radiant, everlasting." And that's really the point to be made about Munro's realistic technique: what is "everlasting," what is remembered and transformed into meaning, are details made "radiant," details that have been arranged and illuminated with meaning.

Like O'Connor's fiction, Munro's stories are filled with glimpses of what she describes in "An Ounce of Cure" (p. 451) as the "shameless, marvelous, shattering absurdity" of life. Although Munro's fictional world is easily distinguished from O'Connor's owing to its realistic texture and everyday qualities, hovering among the quotidian details of Munro's depiction of small-town life and commonplace relationships are explorations of uncertainties, illusions, and indeterminacies.

The following four stories are characteristic of much of Munro's fiction in their treatment of female characters who both long to be part of a relationship or community and need to stand on their own in order to discover what is truly valuable to them. While reading these stories, you may find yourself surprised and puzzled by the protagonist's experiences, and you may feel, like them, that you are on the threshold of making some discovery.

CHRONOLOGY

1931   Born on July 10 in Wingham, Ontario.

1949   Graduates from Wingham and District High School.

1949–51   Attends University of Western Ontario.

1950   Publishes her first short story, "The Dimensions of a Shadow."

1951   Marries James Munro and moves to Vancouver, British Columbia.

1953   Daughter Sheila born.

1957   Daughter Jenny born.

1963   Moves to Victoria and establishes Munro Books.

1966   Daughter Sarah born.

1968   Publishes first collection of stories, *Dance of the Happy Shades;* wins Governor General's Literary Award.

1971   *Lives of Girls and Women* is published.

1972   Divorces James Munro; writer-in-residence, University of Western Ontario.

1973   *Something I've Been Meaning to Tell You* is published.

1976   Marries Gerald Fremlin and moves to a farm outside Clinton, Ontario.

1978   *Who Do You Think You Are?* (titled *Beggar Maid* in American editions) is published; wins Governor General's Literary Award.

1979–82   Tours in Australia, China, and Scandinavia.

1980   Writer-in-residence at University of British Columbia and University of Queensland.

1982   *Moons of Jupiter* is published.

1986   *The Progress of Love* is published; wins Governor General's Literary Award and Marian Engel Prize.

1990   *Friend of My Youth* is published; wins Canada Council Molson Prize.

1994   *Open Secrets* is published.

1996   *Selected Stories* is published.

Web   *Research Alice Munro with LitLinks at*
http://www.bedfordstmartins.com/meyer/bedintrolit

An Ounce of Cure   *1968*

My parents didn't drink. They weren't rabid about it, and in fact I remember that when I signed the pledge in grade seven, with the rest of that superbly if impermanently indoctrinated class, my mother said, "It's just nonsense and fanaticism, children of that age." My father would drink a beer on a hot day, but my mother did not join him, and—whether accidentally or symbolically—this drink was always consumed *outside* the house. Most of the people we knew were the same way, in the small town where we lived. I ought not to say that it was this which got me into difficulties, because the difficulties I got into were a faithful expression of my own incommodious nature—the same nature that caused my mother to look at me, on any occasion which traditionally calls for feelings of pride and maternal accomplishment (my departure for my first formal dance, I mean, or my hellbent preparations for a descent on college) with an expression of brooding and fascinated despair, as if she could not possibly expect, did not ask, that it should go with me as it did with other girls; the dreamed-of spoils of daughters—orchids, nice boys, diamond rings—would be borne home in due course by the daughters of her friends, but not by me; all she could do was hope for a lesser rather than a greater disaster—an elopement, say, with a boy who could never earn his living, rather than an abduction into the White Slave trade.

But ignorance, my mother said, ignorance, or innocence if you like, is not always such a fine thing as people think and I am not sure it may not be dangerous for a girl like you; then she emphasized her point, as she had a habit of doing, with some quotation which had an innocent pomposity and odor of mothballs. I didn't even wince at it, knowing full well how it must have worked wonders with Mr. Berryman.

The evening I baby-sat for the Berrymans must have been in April. I had been in love all year, or at least since the first week in September, when a boy named Martin Collingwood had given me a surprised, appreciative, and rather ominously complacent smile in the school assembly. I never knew what surprised him; I was not looking like anybody but me; I had an old blouse on and my home-permanent had turned out badly. A few weeks after that he took me out for the first time, and kissed me on the dark side of the porch—also, I ought to say, on the mouth; I am sure it was the first time anybody had ever kissed me effectively, and I know that I did not wash my face that night or the next morning, in order to keep the imprint of those kisses intact. (I showed the most painful banality in the conduct of this whole affair, as you will see.) Two months, and a few amatory stages later, he dropped me. He had fallen for the girl who played opposite him in the Christmas production of *Pride and Prejudice.*

I said I was not going to have anything to do with that play, and I got another girl to work on Makeup in my place, but of course I went to it after all, and sat down in front with my girl friend Joyce, who pressed my hand when I was overcome with pain and delight at the sight of Mr. Darcy° in white breeches, silk waistcoat, and sideburns. It was surely seeing Martin as Darcy that did it for me; every girl is in love with Darcy anyway, and the part gave Martin an arrogance and male splendor in my eyes which made it impossible to remember that he was simply a high-school senior, passably good-looking and of medium intelligence (and with a reputation slightly tainted, at that, by such preferences as the Drama Club and the Cadet *Band*) who happened to be the first boy, the first really presentable boy, to take an interest in me. In the last act they gave him a chance to embrace Elizabeth (Mary Bishop, with a sallow complexion and no figure, but big vivacious eyes) and during this realistic encounter I dug my nails bitterly into Joyce's sympathetic palm.

That night was the beginning of months of real, if more or less self-   5
inflicted, misery for me. Why is it a temptation to refer to this sort of thing lightly, with irony, with amazement even, at finding oneself involved with such preposterous emotions in the unaccountable past? That is what we are apt to do, speaking of love; with adolescent love, of course, it's practically obligatory; you would think we sat around, dull afternoons, amusing ourselves with these tidbit recollections of pain. But it really doesn't make me feel very gay—worse still, it doesn't really surprise me—to remember all the stupid, sad, half-ashamed things I did, that people in love always do. I hung around the places where he might be seen, and then pretended not to see him; I made absurdly roundabout approaches, in conversation, to the bitter pleasure of casually mentioning his name. I daydreamed endlessly; in fact if you want to put it mathematically, I spent perhaps ten times as many hours thinking about Martin Collingwood—yes, pining and weeping for him—as I ever spent with him; the idea of him dominated my mind relentlessly and, after a while, against my will. For if at first I had dramatized my feelings, the time came when I would have been glad to escape them; my well-worn daydreams had become depressing and not even temporarily consoling. As I worked my math problems I would torture myself, quite mechanically and helplessly, with an exact recollection of Martin kissing my throat. I had an exact recollection of *everything*. One

---

Darcy: The hero of Jane Austen's (1775–1817) *Pride and Prejudice.*

night I had an impulse to swallow all the aspirins in the bathroom cabinet, but stopped after I had taken six.

My mother noticed that something was wrong and got me some iron pills. She said, "Are you sure everything is going all right at school?" *School!* When I told her that Martin and I had broken up all she said was, "Well so much the better for that. I never saw a boy so stuck on himself." "Martin has enough conceit to sink a battleship," I said morosely and went upstairs and cried.

The night I went to the Berrymans was a Saturday night. I baby-sat for them quite often on Saturday nights because they liked to drive over to Baileyville, a much bigger, livelier town about twenty miles away, and perhaps have supper and go to a show. They had been living in our town only two or three years — Mr. Berryman had been brought in as plant manager of the new doorfactory — and they remained, I suppose by choice, on the fringes of its society; most of their friends were youngish couples like themselves, born in other places, who lived in new ranch-style houses on a hill outside town where we used to go tobogganing. This Saturday night they had two other couples in for drinks before they all drove over to Baileyville for the opening of a new supperclub; they were all rather festive. I sat in the kitchen and pretended to do Latin. Last night had been the Spring Dance at the high school. I had not gone, since the only boy who had asked me was Millerd Crompton, who asked so many girls that he was suspected of working his way through the whole class alphabetically. But the dance was held in the Armories, which was only half a block away from our house; I had been able to see the boys in dark suits, the girls in long pale formals under their coats, passing gravely under the street-lights, stepping around the last patches of snow. I could even hear the music and I have not forgotten to this day that they played "Ballerina," and — oh, song of my aching heart — "Slow Boat to China." Joyce had phoned me up this morning and told me in her hushed way (we might have been discussing an incurable disease I had) that yes, M.C. *had* been there with M.B., and she had on a formal that must have been made out of somebody's old lace tablecloth, it just *hung*.

When the Berrymans and their friends had gone I went into the living room and read a magazine. I was mortally depressed. The big softly lit room, with its green and leaf-brown colors, made an uncluttered setting for the development of the emotions, such as you would get on a stage. At home the life of the emotions went on all right, but it always seemed to get buried under the piles of mending to be done, the ironing, the children's jigsaw puzzles and rock collections. It was the sort of house where people were always colliding with one another on the stairs and listening to hockey games and Superman on the radio.

I got up and found the Berrymans' "Danse Macabre" and put it on the record player and turned out the living-room lights. The curtains were only partly drawn. A street light shone obliquely on the windowpane, making a rectangle of thin dusty gold, in which the shadows of bare branches moved, caught in the huge sweet winds of spring. It was a mild black night when the last snow was melting. A year ago all this — the music, the wind and darkness, the shadows of the branches — would have given me tremendous happiness; when they did not do so now, but only called up tediously familiar, somehow humiliatingly personal thoughts, I gave up my soul for dead and walked into the kitchen and decided to get drunk.

No, it was not like that. I walked into the kitchen to look for a coke or 10
something in the refrigerator, and there on the front of the counter were three
tall beautiful bottles, all about half full of gold. But even after I had looked at
them and lifted them to feel their weight I had not decided to get drunk; I had
decided to have a drink.

Now here is where my ignorance, my disastrous innocence, comes in. It is
true that I had seen the Berrymans and their friends drinking their highballs
as casually as I would drink a coke, but I did not apply this attitude to myself.
No; I thought of hard liquor as something to be taken in extremities, and re-
lied upon for extravagant results, one way or another. My approach could not
have been less casual if I had been the Little Mermaid drinking the witch's
crystal potion. Gravely, with a glance at my set face in the black window above
the sink, I poured a little whisky from each of the bottles (I think now there
were two brands of rye and an expensive Scotch) until I had my glass full. For I
had never in my life seen anyone pour a drink and I had no idea that people
frequently diluted their liquor with water, soda, et cetera, and I had seen that
the glasses the Berrymans' guests were holding when I came through the living
room were nearly full.

I drank it off as quickly as possible. I set the glass down and stood looking
at my face in the window, half expecting to see it altered. My throat was burning, but I felt nothing else. It was very disappointing, when I had worked myself up to it. But I was not going to let it go at that. I poured another full glass,
then filled each of the bottles with water to approximately the level I had seen
when I came in. I drank the second glass only a little more slowly than the first.
I put the empty glass down on the counter with care, perhaps feeling in my
head a rustle of things to come, and went and sat down on a chair in the living
room. I reached up and turned on a floor lamp beside the chair, and the room
jumped on me.

When I say I was expecting extravagant results I do not mean that I was expecting this. I had thought of some sweeping emotional change, an upsurge of gaiety and irresponsibility, a feeling of lawlessness and escape, accompanied by a
little dizziness and perhaps a tendency to giggle out loud. I did not have in
mind the ceiling spinning like a great plate somebody had thrown at me, nor
the pale green blobs of the chairs swelling, converging, disintegrating, playing
with me a game full of enormous senseless inanimate malice. My head sank
back; I closed my eyes. And at once opened them, opened them wide, threw
myself out of the chair and down the hall and reached — thank God, thank
God! — the Berrymans' bathroom, where I was sick everywhere, everywhere,
and dropped like a stone.

From this point on I have no continuous picture of what happened; my
memories of the next hour or two are split into vivid and improbable segments, with nothing but murk and uncertainty between. I do remember lying
on the bathroom floor looking sideways at the little six-sided white tiles, which
lay together in such an admirable and logical pattern, seeing them with the
brief broken gratitude and sanity of one who has just been torn to pieces with
vomiting. Then I remember sitting on the stool in front of the hall phone, asking weakly for Joyce's number. Joyce was not home. I was told by her mother (a
rather rattlebrained woman, who didn't seem to notice a thing the matter —
for which I felt weakly, mechanically grateful) that she was at Kay Stringer's

house. I didn't know Kay's number so I just asked the operator; I felt I couldn't risk looking down at the telephone book.

Kay Stringer was not a friend of mine but a new friend of Joyce's. She had a vague reputation for wildness and a long switch of hair, very oddly, though naturally, colored — from soap-yellow to caramel-brown. She knew a lot of boys more exciting than Martin Collingwood, boys who had quit school or been imported into town to play on the hockey team. She and Joyce rode around in these boys' cars, and sometimes went with them — having lied of course to their mothers — to the Gay-la dance hall on the highway north of town.

I got Joyce on the phone. She was very keyed-up, as she always was with boys around, and she hardly seemed to hear what I was saying.

"Oh, I can't tonight," she said. "Some kids are here. We're going to play cards. You know Bill Kline? He's here. Ross Armour —"

"I'm *sick*," I said trying to speak distinctly; it came out an inhuman croak. "I'm *drunk* Joyce!" Then I fell off the stool and the receiver dropped out of my hand and banged for a while dismally against the wall.

I had not told Joyce where I was, so after thinking about it for a moment she phoned my mother, and using the elaborate and unnecessary subterfuge that young girls delight in, she found out. She and Kay and the boys — there were three of them — told some story about where they were going to Kay's mother, and got into the car and drove out. They found me still lying on the broadloom carpet in the hall; I had been sick again, and this time I had not made it to the bathroom.

It turned out that Kay Stringer, who arrived on this scene only by accident, was exactly the person I needed. She loved a crisis, particularly one like this, which had a shady and scandalous aspect and which must be kept secret from the adult world. She became excited, aggressive, efficient; that energy which was termed wildness was simply the overflow of a great female instinct to manage, comfort, and control. I could hear her voice coming at me from all directions, telling me not to worry, telling Joyce to find the biggest coffeepot they had and make it full of coffee (*strong* coffee, she said), telling the boys to pick me up and carry me to the sofa. Later, in the fog beyond my reach, she was calling for a scrub-brush.

Then I was lying on the sofa, covered with some kind of crocheted throw they had found in the bedroom. I didn't want to lift my head. The house was full of the smell of coffee. Joyce came in, looking very pale; she said that the Berryman kids had wakened up but she had given them a cookie and told them to go back to bed, it was all right; she hadn't let them out of their room and she didn't believe they'd remember. She said that she and Kay had cleaned up the bathroom and the hall though she was afraid there was still a spot on the rug. The coffee was ready. I didn't understand anything very well. The boys had turned on the radio and were going through the Berrymans' record collection; they had it out on the floor. I felt there was something odd about this but I could not think what it was.

Kay brought me a huge breakfast mug full of coffee.

"I don't know if I can," I said. "Thanks."

"Sit up," she said briskly, as if dealing with drunks was an everyday business for her, I had no need to feel myself important. (I met, and recognized, that tone of voice years later, in the maternity ward.) "Now drink," she said. I drank and at the same time realized that I was wearing only my slip. Joyce and Kay had taken off my blouse and skirt. They had brushed off the skirt and washed out the blouse, since it was nylon; it was hanging in the bathroom. I pulled the throw up under my arms and Kay laughed. She got everybody coffee. Joyce brought in the coffeepot and on Kay's instruction she kept filling my cup whenever I drank from it. Somebody said to me with interest, "You must have really wanted to tie one on."

"No," I said rather sulkily, obediently drinking my coffee. "I only had two   25 drinks."

Kay laughed, "Well it certainly gets to you, I'll say that. What time do you expect *they'll* be back?" she said.

"Late. After one I think."

"You should be all right by that time. Have some more coffee."

Kay and one of the boys began dancing to the radio. Kay danced very sexily, but her face had the gently superior and indulgent, rather cold look it had when she was lifting me up to drink the coffee. The boy was whispering to her and she was smiling, shaking her head. Joyce said she was hungry, and she went out to the kitchen to see what there was—potato chips or crackers, or something like that, that you could eat without making too noticeable a dint. Bill Kline came over and sat on the sofa beside me and patted my legs through the crocheted throw. He didn't say anything to me, just patted my legs and looked at me with what seemed to me a very stupid, half-sick, absurd, and alarming expression. I felt very uncomfortable; I wondered how it had ever got around that Bill Kline was so good looking, with an expression like that. I moved my legs nervously and he gave me a look of contempt, not ceasing to pat me. Then I scrambled off the sofa, pulling the throw around me, with the idea of going to the bathroom to see if my blouse was dry. I lurched a little when I started to walk, and for some reason—probably to show Bill Kline that he had not panicked me—I immediately exaggerated this, and calling out, "Watch me walk a straight line!" I lurched and stumbled, to the accompaniment of everyone's laughter, towards the hall. I was standing in the archway between the hall and the living room when the knob of the front door turned with a small matter-of-fact click and everything became silent behind me except the radio of course and the crocheted throw inspired by some delicate malice of its own slithered down around my feet and there—oh, delicious moment in a well-organized farce!—there stood the Berrymans, Mr. and Mrs., with expressions on their faces as appropriate to the occasion as any old-fashioned director of farces could wish. They must have been preparing those expressions, of course; they could not have produced them in the first moment of shock; with the noise we were making, they had no doubt heard us as soon as they got out of the car; for the same reason, we had not heard them. I don't think I ever knew what brought them home so early—a headache, an argument—and I was not really in a position to ask.

Mr. Berryman drove me home. I don't remember how I got into that car, or   30 how I found my clothes and put them on, or what kind of a good-night, if any, I said to Mrs. Berryman. I don't remember what happened to my friends, though I imagine they gathered up their coats and fled, covering up the ignominy of their departure with a mechanical roar of defiance. I remember

Joyce with a box of crackers in her hand, saying that I had become terribly sick from eating—I think she said *sauerkraut*—for supper, and that I had called them for help. (When I asked her later what they made of this she said, "It wasn't any use. You *reeked.*") I remember also her saying, "Oh, no, Mr. Berryman I beg of you, my mother is a terribly nervous person I don't know what the shock might do to her. I will go down on my knees to you if you like but *you must not phone my mother.*" I have no picture of her down on her knees—and she would have done it in a minute—so it seems this threat was not carried out.

Mr. Berryman said to me, "Well I guess you know your behavior tonight is a pretty serious thing." He made it sound as if I might be charged with criminal negligence or something worse. "It would be very wrong of me to overlook it," he said. I suppose that besides being angry and disgusted with *me,* he was worried about taking me home in this condition to my strait-laced parents, who could always say I got the liquor in his house. Plenty of Temperance people would think that enough to hold him responsible, and the town was full of Temperance people. Good relations with the town were very important to him from a business point of view.

"I have an idea it wasn't the first time," he said. "If it was the first time, would a girl be smart enough to fill three bottles up with water? No. Well in this case, she *was* smart enough, but not smart enough to know I could spot it. What do you say to that?" I opened my mouth to answer and although I was feeling quite sober the only sound that came out was a loud, desolate-sounding giggle. He stopped in front of our house. "Light's on," he said. "Now go in and tell your parents the straight truth. And if you don't, remember I will." He did not mention paying me for my baby-sitting services of the evening and the subject did not occur to me either.

I went into the house and tried to go straight upstairs but my mother called to me. She came into the front hall, where I had not turned on the light, and she must have smelled me at once for she ran forward with a cry of pure amazement, as if she had seen somebody falling, and caught me by the shoulders, as I did indeed fall down against the banister, overwhelmed by my fantastic lucklessness, and I told her everything from the start, not omitting even the name of Martin Collingwood and my flirtation with the aspirin bottle, which was a mistake.

On Monday morning my mother took the bus over to Baileyville and found the liquor store and bought a bottle of Scotch whisky. Then she had to wait for a bus back, and she met some people she knew and she was not quite able to hide the bottle in her bag; she was furious with herself for not bringing a proper shopping-bag. As soon as she got back she walked out to the Berrymans'; she had not even had lunch. Mr. Berryman had not gone back to the factory. My mother went in and had a talk with both of them and made an excellent impression and then Mr. Berryman drove her home. She talked to them in the forthright and unemotional way she had, which was always agreeably surprising to people prepared to deal with a mother, and she told them that although I seemed to do well enough at school I was extremely backward—or perhaps eccentric—in my emotional development. I imagine that this analysis of my behavior was especially effective with Mrs. Berryman, a great reader of Child Guidance books. Relations between them warmed to the point where my mother brought up a specific instance of my difficulties, and disarmingly related the whole story of Martin Collingwood.

Within a few days it was all over town and the school that I had tried to 35 commit suicide over Martin Collingwood. But it was already all over school and the town that the Berrymans had come home on Saturday night to find me drunk, staggering, wearing nothing but my slip, in a room with three boys, one of whom was Bill Kline. My mother had said that I was to pay for the bottle she had taken the Berrymans out of my baby-sitting earnings, but my clients melted away like the last April snow, and it would not be paid for yet if newcomers to town had not moved in across the street in July, and needed a baby sitter before they talked to any of their neighbors.

My mother also said that it had been a great mistake to let me go out with boys and that I would not be going out again until well after my sixteenth birthday, if then. This did not prove to be a concrete hardship at all, because it was at least that long before anybody asked me. If you think that news of the Berrymans' adventure would put me in demand for whatever gambols and orgies were going on in and around that town, you could not be more mistaken. The extraordinary publicity which attended my first debauch may have made me seem marked for a special kind of ill luck, like the girl whose illegitimate baby turns out to be triplets: nobody wants to have anything to do with her. At any rate I had at the same time one of the most silent telephones and positively the most sinful reputation in the whole high school. I had to put up with this until the next fall, when a fat blonde girl in grade ten ran away with a married man and was picked up two months later, living in sin — though not with the same man — in the city of Saulte Ste. Marie. Then everybody forgot about me.

But there was a positive, a splendidly unexpected, result of this affair: I got completely over Martin Collingwood. It was not only that he at once said, publicly, that he had always thought I was a nut; where he was concerned I had no pride, and my tender fancy could have found a way around that, a month, a week, before. What was it that brought me back into the world again? It was the terrible and fascinating reality of my disaster; it was *the way things happened*. Not that I enjoyed it; I was a self-conscious girl and I suffered a good deal from all this exposure. But the development of events on that Saturday night — that fascinated me; I felt that I had had a glimpse of the shameless, marvelous, shattering absurdity with which the plots of life, though not of fiction, are improvised. I could not take my eyes off it.

And of course Martin Collingwood wrote his Senior Matric that June, and went away to the city to take a course at a school for Morticians, as I think it is called, and when he came back he went into his uncle's undertaking business. We lived in the same town and we would hear most things that happened to each other but I do not think we met face to face or saw one another, except at a distance, for years. I went to a shower for the girl he married, but then everybody went to everybody else's showers. No, I do not think I really saw him again until I came home after I had been married several years, to attend a relative's funeral. Then I saw him; not quite Mr. Darcy but still very nice-looking in those black clothes. And I saw him looking over at me with an expression as close to a reminiscent smile as the occasion would permit, and I knew that he had been surprised by a memory either of my devotion or my little buried catastrophe. I gave him a gentle, uncomprehending look in return. I am a grown-up woman now; let him unbury his own catastrophes.

CONSIDERATIONS FOR CRITICAL THINKING AND WRITING

1. FIRST RESPONSE. Would you call the protagonist a typical teenager? What details make her unique?

2. How important is the setting for this story? Describe the values the narrator associates with "the small town where we lived" (para. 1).

3. Discuss the narrator's sense of humor. How does her humor affect your attitude toward her?

4. Describe the differences in perspective and sensibilities between the teenager who experiences the events in the story and the adult who recounts them.

5. How does the narrator's drunken baby-sitting episode affect her reputation? What does this reveal about her and the town?

6. Why is the narrator "fascinated" by the "events on that Saturday night" (para. 37)? Why is the episode she recounts important to her?

7. How convincing are the narrator's descriptions of the effects of alcohol on her? Cite specific passages to illustrate your points.

8. How would you describe the conflict in the story? How is it resolved?

9. How do you think this story would be different if the protagonist/narrator were male rather than female?

10. Discuss the significance of the title.

CONNECTIONS TO OTHER SELECTIONS

1. In an essay compare the use of point of view in "An Ounce of Cure" with Ralph Ellison's strategies in "Battle Royal" (p. 231). How is the point of view from which each story is told connected to the story's themes?

2. In an essay discuss the narrators' humor in "An Ounce of Cure" and John Updike's "A & P" (p. 606). How does the humor affect your response to each narrator?

Wild Swans   *1978*

Flo said to watch for White Slavers. She said this was how they operated: an old woman, a motherly or grandmotherly sort, made friends while riding beside you on a bus or train. She offered you candy, which was drugged. Pretty soon you began to droop and mumble, were in no condition to speak for yourself. Oh, help, the woman said, my daughter (granddaughter) is sick, please somebody help me get her off so that she can recover in the fresh air. Up stepped a polite gentleman, pretending to be a stranger, offering assistance. Together, at the next stop, they hustled you off the train or bus, and that was the last the ordinary world ever saw of you. They kept you a prisoner in the White Slave place (to which you had been transported drugged and bound so you wouldn't even know where you were), until such time as you were thoroughly degraded and in despair, your insides torn up by drunken men and invested with vile disease, your mind destroyed by drugs, your hair and teeth fallen out. It took about three years for you to get to this state. You wouldn't want to go home then; maybe couldn't remember home, or find your way if you did. So they let you out on the streets.

Flo took ten dollars and put it in a little cloth bag, which she sewed to the strap of Rose's slip. Another thing likely to happen was that Rose would get her purse stolen.

Watch out, Flo said as well, for people dressed up as ministers. They were the worst. That disguise was commonly adopted by White Slavers, as well as those after your money.

Rose said she didn't see how she could tell which ones were disguised.

Flo had worked in Toronto once. She had worked as a waitress in a coffee shop in Union Station. That was how she knew all she knew. She never saw sunlight, in those days, except on her days off. But she saw plenty else. She saw a man cut another man's stomach with a knife, just pull out his shirt and do a tidy cut, as if it was a watermelon not a stomach. The stomach's owner just sat looking down surprised, with no time to protest. Flo implied that that was nothing, in Toronto. She saw two bad women (that was what Flo called whores, running the two words together, like badminton) get into a fight, and a man laughed at them, other men stopped and laughed and egged them on, and they had their fists full of each other's hair. At last the police came and took them away, still howling and yelping.

She saw a child die of a fit too. Its face was black as ink.

"Well, I'm not scared," said Rose provokingly. "There's the police, anyway."

"Oh, them! They'd be the first ones to diddle you!"

She did not believe anything Flo said on the subject of sex. Consider the undertaker.

A little bald man, very neatly dressed, would come into the store sometimes and speak to Flo with a placating expression.

"I only wanted a bag of candy. And maybe a few packages of gum. And one or two chocolate bars. Could you go to the trouble of wrapping them?"

Flo in her mock-deferential tone would assure him that she could. She wrapped them in heavy-duty white paper, so they were something like presents. He took his time with the selection, humming and chatting, then dawdled for a while. He might ask how Flo was feeling. And how Rose was, if she was there.

"You look pale. Young girls need fresh air." To Flo he would say, "You work too hard. You've worked hard all your life."

"No rest for the wicked," Flo would say agreeably.

When he went out she hurried to the window. There it was — the old black hearse with its purple curtains.

"He'll be after them today!" Flo would say as the hearse rolled away at a gentle pace, almost a funeral pace. The little man had been an undertaker, but he was retired now. The hearse was retired too. His sons had taken over the undertaking and bought a new one. He drove the old hearse all over the country, looking for women. So Flo said. Rose could not believe it. Flo said he gave them the gum and the candy. Rose said he probably ate them himself. Flo said he had been seen, he had been heard. In mild weather he drove with the windows down, singing, to himself or to somebody out of sight in the back.

"Her brow is like the snowdrift
Her throat is like the swan . . ."

Flo imitated him singing. Gently overtaking some woman walking on a back road, or resting at a country crossroads. All compliments and courtesy and chocolate bars, offering a ride. Of course every woman who reported being asked said she had turned him down. He never pestered anybody, drove politely on. He called in at houses, and if the husband was home he seemed to like just as well as anything to sit and chat. Wives said that was all he ever did anyway but Flo did not believe it.

"Some women are taken in," she said. "A number." She liked to speculate on what the hearse was like inside. Plush. Plush on the walls and the roof and the floor. Soft purple, the color of the curtains, the color of dark lilacs.

All nonsense, Rose thought. Who could believe it, of a man that age?

Rose was going to Toronto on the train for the first time by herself. She had been once before, but that was with Flo, long before her father died. They took along their own sandwiches and bought milk from the vendor on the train. It was sour. Sour chocolate milk. Rose kept taking tiny sips, unwilling to admit that something so much desired could fail her. Flo sniffed it, then hunted up and down the train until she found the old man in his red jacket, with no teeth and the tray hanging around his neck. She invited him to sample the chocolate milk. She invited people nearby to smell it. He let her have some ginger ale for nothing. It was slightly warm.

"I let him know," Flo said, looking around after he had left. "You have to let them know." 20

A woman agreed with her but most people looked out the window. Rose drank the warm ginger ale. Either that, or the scene with the vendor, or the conversation Flo and the agreeing woman now got into about where they came from, why they were going to Toronto, and Rose's morning constipation which was why she was lacking color, or the small amount of chocolate milk she had got inside her, caused her to throw up in the train toilet. All day long she was afraid people in Toronto could smell vomit on her coat.

This time Flo started the trip off by saying, "Keep an eye on her, she's never been away from home before!" to the conductor, then looking around and laughing, to show that was jokingly meant. Then she had to get off. It seemed the conductor had no more need for jokes than Rose had, and no intention of keeping an eye on anybody. He never spoke to Rose except to ask for her ticket. She had a window seat, and was soon extraordinarily happy. She felt Flo receding, West Hanratty flying away from her, her own wearying self discarded as easily as everything else. She loved the towns less and less known. A woman was standing at her back door in her nightgown, not caring if everybody on the train saw her. They were travelling south, out of the snowbelt, into an earlier spring, a tenderer sort of landscape. People could grow peach trees in their back yards.

Rose collected in her mind the things she had to look for in Toronto. First, things for Flo. Special stockings for her varicose veins. A special kind of cement for sticking handles on pots. And a full set of dominoes.

For herself Rose wanted to buy hair-remover to put on her arms and legs, and if possible an arrangement of inflatable cushions, supposed to reduce your hips and thighs. She thought they probably had hair-remover in the drugstore in Hanratty, but the woman in there was a friend of Flo's and told everything. She told Flo who bought hair dye and slimming medicine and

French safes. As for the cushion business, you could send away for it but there was sure to be a comment at the Post Office, and Flo knew people there as well. She also planned to buy some bangles, and an angora sweater. She had great hopes of silver bangles and powder-blue angora. She thought they could transform her, make her calm and slender and take the frizz out of her hair, dry her underarms and turn her complexion to pearl.

The money for these things, as well as the money for the trip, came from a 25 prize Rose had won, for writing an essay called "Art and Science in the World of Tomorrow." To her surprise, Flo asked if she could read it, and while she was reading it, she remarked that they must have thought they had to give Rose the prize for swallowing the dictionary. Then she said shyly, "It's very interesting."

She would have to spend the night at Cela McKinney's. Cela McKinney was her father's cousin. She had married a hotel manager and thought she had gone up in the world. But the hotel manager came home one day and sat down on the dining-room floor between two chairs and said, "I am never going to leave this house again." Nothing unusual had happened, he had just decided not to go out of the house again, and he didn't, until he died. That had made Cela McKinney odd and nervous. She locked her doors at eight o'clock. She was also very stingy. Supper was usually oatmeal porridge, with raisins. Her house was dark and narrow and smelled like a bank.

The train was filling up. At Brantford a man asked if she would mind if he sat down beside her.

"It's cooler out than you'd think," he said. He offered her part of his newspaper. She said no thanks.

Then, lest he think her rude, she said it really was cooler. She went on looking out the window at the spring morning. There was no snow left, down here. The trees and bushes seemed to have a paler bark than they did at home. Even the sunlight looked different. It was as different from home, here, as the coast of the Mediterranean would be, or the valleys of California.

"Filthy windows, you'd think they'd take more care," the man said. "Do 30 you travel much by train?"

She said no.

Water was lying in the fields. He nodded at it and said there was a lot this year.

"Heavy snows."

She noticed his saying "snows," a poetic-sounding word. Anyone at home would have said "snow."

"I had an unusual experience the other day. I was driving out in the coun- 35 try. In fact, I was on my way to see one of my parishioners, a lady with a heart condition —"

She looked quickly at his collar. He was wearing an ordinary shirt and tie and a dark-blue suit.

"Oh, yes," he said. "I'm a United Church minister. But I don't always wear my uniform. I wear it for preaching in. I'm off duty today.

"Well, as I said, I was driving through the country and I saw some Canada geese down on a pond, and I took another look, and there were some swans down with them. A whole great flock of swans. What a lovely sight they were. They would be on their spring migration, I expect, heading up North. What a spectacle. I never saw anything like it."

Rose was unable to think appreciatively of the wild swans because she was afraid he was going to lead the conversation from them to Nature in general and then to God, the way a minister would feel obliged to do. But he did not, he stopped with the swans.

"A very fine sight. You would have enjoyed them."   40

He was between fifty and sixty years old, Rose thought. He was short, and energetic-looking, with a square ruddy face and bright waves of gray hair combed straight up from his forehead. When she realized he was not going to mention God she felt she ought to show her gratitude.

She said they must have been lovely.

"It wasn't even a regular pond, it was only some water lying in a field. It was just luck the water was lying there and they came down and I came driving by at the right time. Just luck. They come in at the east end of Lake Erie, I think. But I never was lucky enough to see them before."

She turned by degrees to the window, and he returned to his paper. She remained slightly smiling, so as not to seem rude, not to seem to be rejecting conversation altogether. The morning really was cool, and she had taken down her coat off the hook where she put it when she first got on the train; she had spread it over herself, like a lap robe. She had set her purse on the floor when the minister sat down, to give him room. He took the sections of the paper apart, shaking and rustling them in a leisurely, rather showy way. He seemed to her the sort of person who does everything in a showy way. A ministerial way. He brushed aside the sections he didn't want at the moment. A corner of newspaper touched her leg, just at the edge of her coat.

She thought for some time that it was the paper. Then she said to herself, 45 What if it is a hand? That was the kind of thing she could imagine. She would sometimes look at men's hands, at the fuzz on their forearms, their concentrating profiles. She would think about everything they could do. Even the stupid ones. For instance, the driver-salesman who brought the bread to Flo's store. The ripeness and confidence of manner, the settled mixture of ease and alertness with which he handled the bread truck. A fold of mature belly over the belt did not displease her. Another time she had her eye on the French teacher at school. Not a Frenchman at all, really, his name was McLaren, but Rose thought teaching French had rubbed off on him, made him look like one. Quick and sallow; sharp shoulders; hooked nose and sad eyes. She saw him lapping and coiling his way through slow pleasures, a perfect autocrat of indulgences. She had a considerable longing to be somebody's object. Pounded, pleasured, reduced, exhausted.

But what if it was a hand? What if it really was a hand? She shifted slightly, moved as much as she could toward the window. Her imagination seemed to have created this reality, a reality she was not prepared for at all. She found it alarming. She was concentrating on that leg, that bit of skin with the stocking over it. She could not bring herself to look. Was there a pressure, or was there not? She shifted again. Her legs had been, and remained, tightly closed. It was. It was a hand. It was a hand's pressure.

Please don't. That was what she tried to say. She shaped the words in her mind, tried them out, then couldn't get them past her lips. Why was that? The embarrassment, was it, the fear that people might hear? People were all around them, the seats were full.

It was not only that.

She did manage to look at him, not raising her head but turning it cautiously. He had tilted his seat back and closed his eyes. There was his dark-blue suit sleeve, disappearing under the newspaper. He had arranged the paper so that it overlapped Rose's coat. His hand was underneath, simply resting, as if flung out in sleep.

Now, Rose could have shifted the newspaper and removed her coat. If he 50 was not asleep, he would have been obliged to draw back his hand. If he was asleep, if he did not draw it back, she could have whispered *Excuse me* and set his hand firmly on his own knee. This solution, so obvious and foolproof, did not occur to her. And she would have to wonder, Why not? The minister's hand was not, or not yet, at all welcome to her. It made her feel uncomfortable, resentful, slightly disgusted, trapped, and wary. But she could not take charge of it, to reject it. She could not insist that it was there, when he seemed to be insisting that it was not. How could she declare him responsible, when he lay there so harmless and trusting, resting himself before his busy day, with such a pleased and healthy face? A man older than her father would be, if he were living, a man used to deference, an appreciator of Nature, delighter in wild swans. If she did say *Please don't* she was sure he would ignore her, as if overlooking some silliness or impoliteness on her part. She knew that as soon as she said it she would hope he had not heard.

But there was more to it than that. Curiosity. More constant, more imperious, than any lust. A lust in itself, that will make you draw back and wait, wait too long, risk almost anything, just to see what will happen. *To see what will happen.*

The hand began, over the next several miles, the most delicate, the most timid, pressures and investigations. Not asleep. Or if he was, his hand wasn't. She did feel disgust. She felt a faint, wandering nausea. She thought of flesh: lumps of flesh, pink snouts, fat tongues, blunt fingers, all on their way trotting and creeping and lolling and rubbing, looking for their comfort. She thought of cats in heat rubbing themselves along the top of board fences, yowling with their miserable complaint. It was pitiful, infantile, this itching and shoving and squeezing. Spongy tissues, inflamed membranes, tormented nerve-ends, shameful smells; humiliation.

All that was starting. His hand, that she wouldn't ever have wanted to hold, that she wouldn't have squeezed back, his stubborn patient hand was able, after all, to get the ferns to rustle and the streams to flow, to waken a sly luxuriance.

Nevertheless, she would rather not. She would still rather not. Please remove this, she said out the window. Stop it, please, she said to the stumps and barns. The hand moved up her leg past the top of her stocking to her bare skin, had moved higher, under her suspender, reached her underpants and the lower part of her belly. Her legs were still crossed, pinched together. While her legs stayed crossed she could lay claim to innocence, she had not admitted anything. She could still believe that she would stop this in a minute. Nothing was going to happen, nothing more. Her legs were never going to open.

But they were. They were. As the train crossed the Niagara Escarpment 55 above Dundas, as they looked down at the preglacial valley, the silver-wooded rubble of little hills, as they came sliding down to the shores of Lake Ontario, she would make this slow, and silent, and definite declaration, perhaps disappointing as much as satisfying the hand's owner. He would not lift his eyelids, his face would not alter, his fingers would not hesitate, but would go powerfully and discreetly to work. Invasion, and welcome, and sunlight flashing far and wide on the lake water; miles of bare orchards stirring round Burlington.

This was disgrace, this was beggary. But what harm in that, we say to ourselves at such moments, what harm in anything, the worse the better, as we ride the cold wave of greed, of greedy assent. A stranger's hand, or root vegetables or humble kitchen tools that people tell jokes about; the world is tumbling with innocent-seeming objects ready to declare themselves, slippery and obliging. She was careful of her breathing. She could not believe this. Victim and accomplice she was borne past Glassco's Jams and Marmalades, past the big pulsating pipes of oil refineries. They glided into suburbs where bedsheets, and towels used to wipe up intimate stains, flapped leeringly on the clotheslines, where even the children seemed to be frolicking lewdly in the schoolyards, and the very truck drivers stopped at the railway crossings must be thrusting their thumbs gleefully into curled hands. Such cunning antics now, such popular visions. The gates and towers of the Exhibition Grounds came into view, the painted domes and pillars floated marvellously against her eyelids' rosy sky. Then flew apart in celebration. You could have had such a flock of birds, wild swans, even, wakened under one big dome together, exploding from it, taking to the sky.

She bit the edge of her tongue. Very soon the conductor passed through the train, to stir the travellers, warn them back to life.

In the darkness under the station the United Church minister, refreshed, opened his eyes and got his paper folded together, then asked if she would like some help with her coat. His gallantry was self-satisfied, dismissive. No, said Rose, with a sore tongue. He hurried out of the train ahead of her. She did not see him in the station. She never saw him again in her life. But he remained on call, so to speak, for years and years, ready to slip into place at a critical moment, without even any regard, later on, for husband or lovers. What recommended him? She could never understand it. His simplicity, his arrogance, his perversely appealing lack of handsomeness, even of ordinary grown-up masculinity? When he stood up she saw that he was shorter even than she had thought, that his face was pink and shiny, that there was something crude and pushy and childish about him.

Was he a minister, really, or was that only what he said? Flo had mentioned people who were not ministers, dressed up as if they were. Not real ministers dressed as if they were not. Or, stranger still, men who were not real ministers pretending to be real but dressed as if they were not. But that she had come as close as she had, to what could happen, was an unwelcome thing. Rose walked through Union Station feeling the little bag with the ten dollars rubbing at her, knew she would feel it all day long, rubbing its reminder against her skin.

She couldn't stop getting Flo's messages, even with that. She remembered, 60 because she was in Union Station, that there was a girl named Mavis working here, in the gift shop, when Flo was working in the coffee shop. Mavis had warts on her eyelids that looked like they were going to turn into sties but they didn't, they went away. Maybe she had them removed, Flo didn't ask. She was very good-looking, without them. There was a movie star in those days she looked a lot like. The movie star's name was Frances Farmer.°

Frances Farmer (1904–1970): A Hollywood film star of the late 1930s and early 1940s.

Frances Farmer. Rose had never heard of her.

That was the name. And Mavis went and bought herself a big hat that dipped over one eye and a dress entirely made of lace. She went off for the weekend to Georgian Bay, to a resort up there. She booked herself in under the name of Florence Farmer. To give everybody the idea she was really the other one, Frances Farmer, but calling herself Florence because she was on holiday and didn't want to be recognized. She had a little cigarette holder that was black and mother-of-pearl. She could have been arrested, Flo said. For the *nerve*.

Rose almost went over to the gift shop to see if Mavis was still there and if she could recognize her, She thought it would be an especially fine thing to manage a transformation like that. To dare it; to get away with it, to enter on preposterous adventures in your own, but newly named, skin.

CONSIDERATIONS FOR CRITICAL THINKING AND WRITING

1. FIRST RESPONSE. Did you find Rose to be a sympathetic character? Were you surprised by her behavior? Was it credible? Explain why or why not.

2. Describe Flo's view of the world. How does Rose respond to her warnings about life?

3. How is Rose's experience on her trip to Toronto with Flo (paragraphs 19–22) relevant to her subsequent trip by herself?

4. How is West Hanratty implicitly contrasted with Toronto? What is the significance of these two settings?

5. Choose a passage that you think especially reveals Rose's character and explain what it indicates about her.

6. Why do you think Rose does not ask the minister to withdraw his hand? What explanation does the narrator offer?

7. The narrator describes Rose as both a "victim" and an "accomplice" (para. 56). Discuss this assessment and indicate whether you agree.

8. What do you think is the story's theme?

9. How is the story about Mavis related to Rose's story?

10. Comment on the story's title. Why do you suppose Munro chose "Wild Swans" rather than, say, "Victim and Accomplice"?

11. CRITICAL STRATEGIES. Read the section on psychological criticism (pp. 2099–102) in Chapter 52, "Critical Strategies for Reading." How would a psychological critic would discuss Rose's behavior.

CONNECTIONS TO OTHER SELECTIONS

1. Discuss the treatment of desire and passion in this story and in Susan Minot's "Lust" (p. 304). What important similarities and differences do you see?

2. Consider the endings of "Wild Swans" and Coltette's "The Hand" (p. 228), paying attention to the tone of each ending. In what ways do the endings resemble each other? How do they differ?

3. Discuss the characterization of men in "Wild Swans" and in one other Munro story chosen from this chapter. What, if any, generalizations can you make about Munro's treatment of men in the two stories?

Prue

Prue used to live with Gordon. This was after Gordon had left his wife and before he went back to her—a year and four months in all. Some time later, he and
his wife were divorced. After that came a period of indecision, of living together
off and on; then the wife went away to New Zealand, most likely for good.

Prue did not go back to Vancouver Island, where Gordon had met her
when she was working as a dining-room hostess in a resort hotel. She got a job
in Toronto, working in a plant shop. She had many friends in Toronto by that
time, most of them Gordon's friends and his wife's friends. They liked Prue
and were ready to feel sorry for her, but she laughed them out of it. She is very
likable. She has what eastern Canadians call an English accent, though she was
born in Canada—in Duncan, on Vancouver Island. This accent helps her to say
the most cynical things in a winning and lighthearted way. She presents her
life in anecdotes, and though it is the point of most of her anecdotes that
hopes are dashed, dreams ridiculed, things never turn out as expected, everything is altered in a bizarre way and there is no explanation ever, people always
feel cheered up after listening to her; they say of her that it is a relief to meet
somebody who doesn't take herself too seriously, who is so unintense, and civilized, and never makes any real demands or complaints.

The only thing she complains about readily is her name. Prue is a schoolgirl,
she says, and Prudence is an old virgin; the parents who gave her that name must
have been too shortsighted even to take account of puberty. What if she had
grown a great bosom, she says, or developed a sultry look? Or was the name itself
a guarantee that she wouldn't? In her late forties now, slight and fair, attending
to customers with a dutiful vivacity, giving pleasure to dinner guests, she might
not be far from what those parents had in mind: bright and thoughtful, a cheerful spectator. It is hard to grant her maturity, maternity, real troubles.

Her grownup children, the products of an early Vancouver Island marriage
she calls a cosmic disaster, come to see her, and instead of wanting money, like
other people's children, they bring presents, try to do her accounts, arrange to
have her house insulated. She is delighted with their presents, listens to their
advice, and, like a flighty daughter, neglects to answer their letters.

Her children hope she is not staying on in Toronto because of Gordon. ₅
Everybody hopes that. She would laugh at the idea. She gives parties and goes to
parties; she goes out sometimes with other men. Her attitude toward sex is very
comforting to those of her friends who get into terrible states of passion and
jealousy, and feel cut loose from their moorings. She seems to regard sex as a
wholesome, slightly silly indulgence, like dancing and nice dinners—something
that shouldn't interfere with people's being kind and cheerful to each other.

Now that his wife is gone for good, Gordon comes to see Prue occasionally, and sometimes asks her out for dinner. They may not go to a restaurant;
they may go to his house. Gordon is a good cook. When Prue or his wife lived
with him he couldn't cook at all, but as soon as he put his mind to it he became—he says truthfully—better than either of them.

Recently he and Prue were having dinner at his house. He had made
Chicken Kiev, and crème brûlée for dessert. Like most new, serious cooks, he
talked about food.

Gordon is rich, by Prue's — and most people's — standards. He is a neurologist. His house is new, built on a hillside north of the city, where there used to be picturesque, unprofitable farms. Now there are one-of-a-kind, architect-designed, very expensive houses on half-acre lots. Prue, describing Gordon's house, will say, "Do you know there are four bathrooms? So that if four people want to have baths at the same time there's no problem. It seems a bit much, but it's very nice, really, and you'd never have to go through the hall."

Gordon's house has a raised dining area — a sort of platform, surrounded by a conversation pit, a music pit, and a bank of heavy greenery under sloping glass. You can't see the entrance area from the dining area, but there are no intervening walls, so that from one area you can hear something of what is going on in the other.

During dinner the doorbell rang. Gordon excused himself and went down 10 the steps. Prue heard a female voice. The person it belonged to was still outside, so she could not hear the words. She heard Gordon's voice, pitched low, cautioning. The door didn't close — it seemed the person had not been invited in — but the voices went on, muted and angry. Suddenly there was a cry from Gordon, and he appeared halfway up the steps, waving his arms.

"The crème brûlée," he said. "Could you?" He ran back down as Prue got up and went into the kitchen to save the dessert. When she returned he was climbing the stairs more slowly, looking both agitated and tired.

"A friend," he said gloomily. "Was it all right?"

Prue realized he was speaking of the crème brûlée, and she said yes, it was perfect, she had got it just in time. He thanked her but did not cheer up. It seemed it was not the dessert he was troubled over but whatever had happened at the door. To take his mind off it, Prue started asking him professional questions about the plants.

"I don't know a thing about them," he said. "You know that."

"I thought you might have picked it up. Like the cooking." 15

"She takes care of them."

"Mrs. Carr?" said Prue, naming his housekeeper.

"Who did you think?"

Prue blushed. She hated to be thought suspicious.

"The problem is that I think I would like to marry you," said Gordon, with 20 no noticeable lightening of his spirits. Gordon is a large man, with heavy features. He likes to wear thick clothing, bulky sweaters. His blue eyes are often bloodshot, and their expression indicates that there is a helpless, baffled soul squirming around inside this doughty fortress.

"What a problem," said Prue lightly, though she knew Gordon well enough to know that it was.

The doorbell rang again, rang twice, three times, before Gordon could get to it. This time there was a crash, as of something flung and landing hard. The door slammed and Gordon was immediately back in view. He staggered on the steps and held his hand to his head, meanwhile making a gesture with the other hand to signify that nothing serious had happened, Prue was to sit down.

"Bloody overnight bag," he said. "She threw it at me."

"Did it hit you?"

"Glancing." 25

"It made a hard sound for an overnight bag. Were there rocks in it?"

"Probably cans. Her deodorant and so forth."
"Oh."
Prue watched him pour himself a drink. "I'd like some coffee, if I might,"
she said. She went to the kitchen to put the water on, and Gordon followed her.
"I think I'm in love with this person," he said.   30
"Who is she?"
"You don't know her. She's quite young."
"Oh."
"But I do think I want to marry you, in a few years' time."
"After you get over being in love?"   35
"Yes."
"Well. I guess nobody knows what can happen in a few years' time."

When Prue tells about this, she says, "I think he was afraid I was going to
laugh. He doesn't know why people laugh or throw their overnight bags at
him, but he's noticed they do. He's such a proper person, really. The lovely dinner. Then she comes and throws her overnight bag. And it's quite reasonable to
think of marrying me in a few years' time, when he gets over being in love. I
think he first thought of telling me to sort of put my mind at rest."

She doesn't mention that the next morning she picked up one of Gordon's cufflinks from his dresser. The cufflinks are made of amber and he
bought them in Russia, on the holiday he and wife took when they got back
together again. They look like squares of candy, golden, translucent, and this
one warms quickly in her hand. She drops it into the pocket of her jacket. Taking one is not a real theft. It could be a reminder, an intimate prank, a piece of
nonsense.

She is alone in Gordon's house; he has gone off early, as he always does. 40
The housekeeper does not come till nine. Prue doesn't have to be at the shop
until ten; she could make herself breakfast, stay and have coffee with the
housekeeper, who is her friend from olden times. But once she has the cufflink in her pocket she doesn't linger. The house seems too bleak a place to
spend an extra moment in. It was Prue, actually, who helped choose the building lot. But she's not responsible for approving the plans—the wife was back
by that time.

When she gets home she puts the cufflink in an old tobacco tin. The
children bought this tobacco tin in a junk shop years ago, and gave it to her for
a present. She used to smoke, in those days, and the children were worried
about her, so they gave her this tin full of toffees, jelly beans, and gumdrops,
with a note saying, "Please get fat instead." That was for her birthday. Now the
tin has in it several things besides the cufflink—all small things, not of
great value but not worthless, either. A little enameled dish, a sterling-
silver spoon for salt, a crystal fish. These are not sentimental keepsakes. She
never looks at them, and often forgets what she has there. They are not
booty, they don't have ritualistic significance. She does not take something
every time she goes to Gordon's house, or every time she stays over, or to mark
what she might call memorable visits. She doesn't do it in a daze and she
doesn't seem to be under a compulsion. She just takes something, every now
and then, and puts it away in the dark of the old tobacco tin, and more or less
forgets about it.

CONSIDERATIONS FOR CRITICAL THINKING AND WRITING

1. FIRST RESPONSE. Do you think Gordon and Prue will get married? Explain your answer.

2. Characterize Gordon. Why do you think Prue is attracted to him?

3. Do you think the description of Prue in the second paragraph adequately characterizes her? Explain why or why not.

4. What does Prue's response to Gordon's two encounters with the woman at the door reveal about Prue?

5. Reread paragraph 3 and discuss the appropriateness of Prue's name.

6. Discuss what you think is the conflict of this story. How do Gordon and Prue handle conflict?

7. Describe what you take to be the story's theme.

8. Why do you think Prue takes Gordon's cufflink? Why do you suppose she takes only one?

9. Consider the symbolic significance of the "old tobacco tin" by carefully analyzing the final paragraph of the story.

CONNECTIONS TO OTHER SELECTIONS

1. In an essay compare the themes of "Prue" and Katherine Mansfield's "Miss Brill" (p. 259).

2. Write an essay that compares the endings of "Prue" and Colette's "The Hand" (p. 228). What significant differences and similarities do you see between the central relationships portrayed in each story?

Miles City, Montana   *1985*

My father came across the field carrying the body of the boy who had been drowned. There were several men together, returning from the search, but he was the one carrying the body. The men were muddy and exhausted, and walked with their heads down, as if they were ashamed. Even the dogs were dispirited, dripping from the cold river. When they all set out, hours before, the dogs were nervy and yelping, the men tense and determined, and there was a constrained, unspeakable excitement about the whole scene. It was understood that they might find something horrible.

The boy's name was Steve Gauley. He was eight years old. His hair and clothes were mud-colored now and carried some bits of dead leaves, twigs, and grass. He was like a heap of refuse that had been left out all winter. His face was turned in to my father's chest, but I could see a nostril, an ear, plugged up with greenish mud.

I don't think so. I don't think I really saw all this. Perhaps I saw my father carrying him, and the other men following along, and the dogs, but I would not have been allowed to get close enough to see something like mud in his nostril. I must have heard someone talking about that and imagined that I saw it. I see his face unaltered except for the mud—Steve Gauley's familiar, sharp-honed, sneaky-looking face—and it wouldn't have been like that; it would have been bloated and changed and perhaps muddied all over after so many hours in the water.

To have to bring back such news, such evidence, to a waiting family, particularly a mother, would have made searchers move heavily, but what was happening here was worse. It seemed a worse shame (to hear people talk) that there was no mother, no woman at all — no grandmother or aunt, or even a sister — to receive Steve Gauley and give him his due of grief. His father was a hired man, a drinker but not a drunk, an erratic man without being entertaining, not friendly but not exactly a troublemaker. His fatherhood seemed accidental, and the fact that the child had been left with him when the mother went away, and that they continued living together, seemed accidental. They lived in a steep-roofed, gray-shingled hillbilly sort of house that was just a bit better than a shack — the father fixed the roof and put supports under the porch, just enough and just in time — and their life was held together in a similar manner; that is, just well enough to keep the Children's Aid at bay. They didn't eat meals together or cook for each other, but there was food. Sometimes the father would give Steve money to buy food at the store, and Steve was seen to buy quite sensible things, such as pancake mix and macaroni dinner.

I had known Steve Gauley fairly well. I had not liked him more often than I 5 had liked him. He was two years older than I was. He would hang around our place on Saturdays, scornful of whatever I was doing but unable to leave me alone. I couldn't be on the swing without him wanting to try it, and if I wouldn't give it up he came and pushed me so that I went crooked. He teased the dog. He got me into trouble — deliberately and maliciously, it seemed to me afterward — by daring me to do things I wouldn't have thought of on my own: digging up the potatoes to see how big they were when they were still only the size of marbles, and pushing over the stacked firewood to make a pile we could jump off. At school, we never spoke to each other. He was solitary, though not tormented. But on Saturday mornings, when I saw his thin, self-possessed figure sliding through the cedar hedge, I knew I was in for something and he would decide what. Sometimes it was all right. We pretended we were cowboys who had to tame wild horses. We played in the pasture by the river, not far from the place where Steve drowned. We were horses and riders both, screaming and neighing and bucking and waving whips of tree branches beside a little nameless river that flows into the Saugeen in southern Ontario.

The funeral was held in our house. There was not enough room at Steve's father's place for the large crowd that was expected because of the circumstances. I have a memory of the crowded room but no picture of Steve in his coffin, or of the minister, or of wreaths of flowers. I remember that I was holding one flower, a white narcissus, which must have come from a pot somebody forced indoors, because it was too early for even the forsythia bush or the trilliums and marsh marigolds in the woods. I stood in a row of children, each of us holding a narcissus. We sang a children's hymn, which somebody played on our piano: "When He Cometh, When He Cometh, to Make Up His Jewels." I was wearing white ribbed stockings, which were disgustingly itchy, and wrinkled at the knees and ankles. The feeling of these stockings on my legs is mixed up with another feeling in my memory. It is hard to describe. It had to do with my parents. Adults in general but my parents in particular. My father, who had carried Steve's body from the river, and my mother, who must have done most of the arranging of this funeral. My father in his dark-blue suit and my mother in her brown velvet dress with the creamy satin collar. They stood side by side opening and closing their mouths for the hymn, and I stood removed from them, in the row of children, watching. I felt a furious and sickening disgust. Children sometimes have an excess of disgust concerning adults. The size, the lumpy shapes, the bloated power. The breath, the coarseness, the hairiness, the horrid secretions. But this was more. And the accompanying anger had nothing sharp and self-respecting about it. There was no release, as when I would finally bend and pick up a stone and throw it at Steve Gauley. It could not be understood or expressed, though it died down after a while into a heaviness, then just a taste, an occasional taste — a thin, familiar misgiving.

Twenty years or so later, in 1961, my husband, Andrew, and I got a brand-new car, our first — that is, our first brand-new. It was a Morris Oxford, oyster-colored (the dealer had some fancier name for the color) — a big small car, with plenty of room for us and our two children. Cynthia was six and Meg three and a half.

Andrew took a picture of me standing beside the car. I was wearing white pants, a black turtleneck, and sunglasses. I lounged against the car door, canting my hips to make myself look slim.

"Wonderful," Andrew said. "Great. You look like Jackie Kennedy." All over this continent probably, dark-haired, reasonably slender young women were told, when they were stylishly dressed or getting their pictures taken, that they looked like Jackie Kennedy.

Andrew took a lot of pictures of me, and of the children, our house, our 10 garden, our excursions and possessions. He got copies made, labeled them carefully, and sent them back to his mother and his aunt and uncle in Ontario. He got copies for me to send to my father, who also lived in Ontario, and I did so, but less regularly than he sent his. When he saw pictures he thought I had already sent lying around the house, Andrew was perplexed and annoyed. He liked to have this record go forth.

That summer, we were presenting ourselves, not pictures. We were driving back from Vancouver, where we lived, to Ontario, which we still called "home," in our new car. Five days to get there, ten days there, five days back. For the first time, Andrew had three weeks' holiday. He worked in the legal department at B. C. Hydro.

On a Saturday morning, we loaded suitcases, two thermos bottles — one filled with coffee and one with lemonade — some fruit and sandwiches, picture books and coloring books, crayons, drawing pads, insect repellent, sweaters (in case it got cold in the mountains), and our two children into the car. Andrew locked the house, and Cynthia said ceremoniously, "Good-bye, house."

Meg said, "Goodbye, house." Then she said, "Where will we live now?"

"It's not goodbye forever," said Cynthia. "We're coming back. Mother! Meg thought we weren't ever coming back!"

"I did not," said Meg, kicking the back of my seat.   15

Andrew and I put on our sunglasses, and we drove away, over the Lions Gate Bridge and through the main part of Vancouver. We shed our house, the neighborhood, the city, and — at the crossing point between Washington and British Columbia — our country. We were driving east across the United States, taking the most northerly route, and would cross into Canada again at Sarnia, Ontario. I don't know if we chose this route because the Trans-Canada Highway was not completely finished at the time or if we just wanted the feeling of driving through a foreign, a very slightly foreign, country—that extra bit of interest and adventure.

We were both in high spirits. Andrew congratulated the car several times. He said he felt so much better driving it than our old car, a 1951 Austin that slowed down dismally on the hills and had a fussy-old-lady image. So Andrew said now.

"What kind of image does this one have?" said Cynthia. She listened to us carefully and liked to try out new words such as *image.* Usually she got them right.

"Lively," I said. "Slightly sporty. It's not show-off."

"It's sensible, but it has class," Andrew said. "Like my image."   20

Cynthia thought that over and said with a cautious pride, "That means like you think you want to be, Daddy?"

As for me, I was happy because of the shedding. I loved taking off. In my own house, I seemed to be often looking for a place to hide—sometimes from the children but more often from the jobs to be done and the phone ringing and the sociability of the neighborhood. I wanted to hide so that I could get busy at my real work, which was a sort of wooing of distant parts of myself. I lived in a state of siege, always losing just what I wanted to hold on to. But on trips there was no difficulty. I could be talking to Andrew, talking to the children and looking at whatever they wanted me to look at—a pig on a sign, a pony in a field, a Volkswagen on a revolving stand—and pouring lemonade into plastic cups, and all the time those bits and pieces would be flying together inside me. The essential composition would be achieved. This made me hopeful and lighthearted. It was being a watcher that did it. A watcher, not a keeper.

We turned east at Everett and climbed into the Cascades. I showed Cynthia our route on the map. First I showed her the map of the whole United States, which showed also the bottom part of Canada. Then I turned to the separate maps of each of the states we were going to pass through. Washington, Idaho, Montana, North Dakota, Minnesota, Wisconsin. I showed her the dotted line across Lake Michigan, which was the route of the ferry we would take. Then we would drive across Michigan to the bridge that linked the United States and Canada at Sarnia, Ontario. Home.

Meg wanted to see too.

"You won't understand," said Cynthia. But she took the road atlas into   25 the back seat.

"Sit back," she said to Meg. "Sit still. I'll show you."

I could hear her tracing the route for Meg, very accurately, just as I had done it for her. She looked up all the states' maps, knowing how to find them in alphabetical order.

"You know what that line is?" she said. "It's the road. That line is the road we're driving on. We're going right along this line."

Meg did not say anything.

"Mother, show me where we are right this minute," said Cynthia.   30

I took the atlas and pointed out the road through the mountains, and she took it back and showed it to Meg. "See where the road is all wiggly?" she said. "It's wiggly because there are so many turns in it. The wiggles are the turns." She flipped some pages and waited a moment. "Now," she said, "show me where we are." Then she called to me, "Mother, she understands! She pointed to it! Meg understands maps!"

It seems to me now that we invented characters for our children. We had them firmly set to play their parts. Cynthia was bright and diligent, sensitive, courteous, watchful. Sometimes we teased her for being too conscientious, too eager to be what we in fact depended on her to be. Any reproach or failure, any rebuff, went terribly deep with her. She was fair-haired, fair-skinned, easily showing the effects of the sun, raw winds, pride, or humiliation. Meg was more solidly built, more reticent—not rebellious but stubborn sometimes, mysterious. Her silences seemed to us to show her strength of character, and her negatives were taken as signs of an imperturbable independence. Her hair was brown, and we cut it in straight bangs. Her eyes were a light hazel, clear and dazzling.

We were entirely pleased with these characters, enjoying their contradictions as well as the confirmations of them. We disliked the heavy, the uninventive, approach to being parents. I had a dread of turning into a certain kind of mother—the kind whose body sagged, who moved in a woolly-smelling, milky-smelling fog, solemn with trivial burdens. I believed that all the attention these mothers paid, their need to be burdened, was the cause of colic, bed-wetting, asthma. I favored another approach—the mock desperation, the inflated irony of the professional mothers who wrote for magazines. In those magazine pieces, the children were splendidly self-willed, hard-edged, perverse, indomitable. So were the mothers, through their wit, indomitable. The real-life mothers I warmed to were the sort who would phone up and say, "Is my embryo Hitler by any chance over at your house?" They cackled clear above the milky fog.

We saw a dead deer strapped across the front of a pickup truck.

"Somebody shot it," Cynthia said. "Hunters shoot the deer." 35

"It's not hunting season yet," Andrew said. "They may have hit it on the road. See the sign for deer crossing?"

"I would cry if we hit one," Cynthia said sternly.

I had made peanut-butter-and-marmalade sandwiches for the children and salmon-and-mayonnaise for us. But I had not put any lettuce in, and Andrew was disappointed.

"I didn't have any," I said.

"Couldn't you have got some?" 40

"I'd have had to buy a whole head of lettuce just to get enough for sandwiches, and I decided it wasn't worth it."

This was a lie. I had forgotten.

"They're a lot better with lettuce."

"I didn't think it made that much difference." After a silence, I said, "Don't be mad."

"I'm not mad. I like lettuce on sandwiches." 45

"I just didn't think it mattered that much."

"How would it be if I didn't bother to fill up the gas tank?"

"That's not the same thing."

"Sing a song," said Cynthia. She started to sing:

"Five little ducks went out one day,
Over the hills and far away.
One little duck went
'Quack-quack-quack.'
Four little ducks came swimming back."

Andrew squeezed my hand and said, "Let's not fight."

"You're right. I should have got lettuce."   50
"It doesn't matter that much."

I wished that I could get my feelings about Andrew to come together into a serviceable and dependable feeling. I had even tried writing two lists, one of things I liked about him, one of things I disliked — in the cauldron of intimate life, things I loved and things I hated — as if I hoped by this to prove something, to come to a conclusion one way or the other. But I gave it up when I saw that all it proved was what I already knew — that I had violent contradictions. Sometimes the very sound of his footsteps seemed to me tyrannical, the set of his mouth smug and mean, his hard, straight body a barrier interposed — quite consciously, even dutifully, and with a nasty pleasure in its masculine authority — between me and whatever joy or lightness I could get in life. Then, with not much warning, he became my good friend and most essential companion. I felt the sweetness of his light bones and serious ideas, the vulnerability of his love, which I imagined to be much purer and more straightforward than my own. I could be greatly moved by an inflexibility, a harsh propriety, that at other times I scorned. I would think how humble he was, really, taking on such a ready-made role of husband, father, breadwinner, and how I myself in comparison was really a secret monster of egotism. Not so secret, either — not from him.

At the bottom of our fights, we served up what we thought were the ugliest truths. "I know there is something basically selfish and basically untrustworthy about you," Andrew once said. "I've always known it. I also know that that is why I fell in love with you."

"Yes," I said, feeling sorrowful but complacent.

"I know that I'd be better off without you."   55

"Yes. You would."

"You'd be happier without me."

"Yes."

And finally — finally — wracked and purged, we clasped hands and laughed, laughed at those two benighted people, ourselves. Their grudges, their grievances, their self-justification. We leapfrogged over them. We declared them liars. We would have wine with dinner, or decide to give a party.

I haven't seen Andrew for years, don't know if he is still thin, has gone completely gray, insists on lettuce, tells the truth, or is hearty and disappointed.   60

We stayed the night in Wenatchee, Washington, where it hadn't rained for weeks. We ate dinner in a restaurant built about a tree — not a sapling in a tub but a tall, sturdy cottonwood. In the early-morning light, we climbed out of the irrigated valley, up dry, rocky, very steep hillsides that would seem to lead to more hills, and there on the top was a wide plateau, cut by the great Spokane and Columbia rivers. Grainland and grassland, mile after mile. There were straight roads here, and little farming towns with grain elevators. In fact, there was a sign announcing that this county we were going through, Douglas County, had the second-highest wheat yield of any county in the United States. The towns had planted shade trees. At least, I thought they had been planted, because there were no such big trees in the countryside.

All this was marvelously welcome to me. "Why do I love it so much?" I said to Andrew. "Is it because it isn't scenery?"

"It reminds you of home," said Andrew. "A bout of severe nostalgia." But he said this kindly.

When we said "home" and meant Ontario, we had very different places in mind. My home was a turkey farm, where my father lived as a widower, and though it was the same house my mother had lived in, had papered, painted, cleaned, furnished, it showed the effects now of neglect and of some wild sociability. A life went on in it that my mother could not have predicted or condoned. There were parties for the turkey crew, the gutters and pluckers, and sometimes one or two of the young men would be living there temporarily, inviting their own friends and having their own impromptu parties. This life, I thought, was better for my father than being lonely, and I did not disapprove, had certainly no right to disapprove. Andrew did not like to go there, naturally enough, because he was not the sort who could sit around the kitchen table with the turkey crew, telling jokes. They were intimidated by him and contemptuous of him, and it seemed to me that my father, when they were around, had to be on their side. And it wasn't only Andrew who had trouble. I could manage those jokes, but it was an effort.

I wished for the days when I was little, before we had the turkeys. We had 65 cows, and sold the milk to the cheese factory. A turkey farm is nothing like as pretty as a dairy farm or a sheep farm. You can see that the turkeys are on a straight path to becoming frozen carcasses and table meat. They don't have the pretense of a life of their own, a browsing idyll, that cattle have, or pigs in the dappled orchard. Turkey barns are long, efficient buildings — tin sheds. No beams or hay or warm stables. Even the smell of guano seems thinner and more offensive than the usual smell of stable manure. No hints there of hay coils and rail fences and songbirds and the flowering hawthorn. The turkeys were all let out into one long field, which they picked clean. They didn't look like great birds there but like fluttering laundry.

Once, shortly after my mother died, and after I was married — in fact, I was packing to join Andrew in Vancouver — I was at home alone for a couple of days with my father. There was a freakishly heavy rain all night. In the early light, we saw that the turkey field was flooded. At least, the low-lying parts of it were flooded — it was like a lake with many islands. The turkeys were huddled on these islands. Turkeys are very stupid. (My father would say, "You know a chicken? You know how stupid a chicken is? Well, a chicken is an Einstein compared with a turkey.") But they had managed to crowd to higher ground and avoid drowning. Now they might push each other off, suffocate each other, get cold and die. We couldn't wait for the water to go down. We went out in an old rowboat we had. I rowed and my father pulled the heavy, wet turkeys into the boat and we took them to the barn. It was still raining a little. The job was difficult and absurd and very uncomfortable. We were laughing. I was happy to be working with my father. I felt close to all hard, repetitive, appalling work, in which the body is finally worn out, the mind sunk (though sometimes the spirit can stay marvelously light), and I was homesick in advance for this life and this place. I thought that if Andrew could see me there in the rain, redhanded, muddy, trying to hold on to turkey legs and row the boat at the same time, he would only want to get me out of there and make me forget about it. This raw life angered him. My attachment to it angered him. I thought that I shouldn't have married him. But who else? One of the turkey crew?

And I didn't want to stay there. I might feel bad about leaving, but I would feel worse if somebody made me stay.

Andrew's mother lived in Toronto, in an apartment building looking out on Muir Park. When Andrew and his sister were both at home, his mother slept in the living room. Her husband, a doctor, had died when the children were still too young to go to school. She took a secretarial course and sold her house at Depression prices, moved to this apartment, managed to raise her children, with some help from relatives—her sister Caroline, her brother-in-law Roger. Andrew and his sister went to private schools and to camp in the summer.

"I suppose that was courtesy of the Fresh Air Fund?" I said once, scornful of his claim that he had been poor. To my mind, Andrew's urban life had been sheltered and fussy. His mother came home with a headache from working all day in the noise, the harsh light of a department-store office, but it did not occur to me that hers was a hard or admirable life. I don't think she herself believed that she was admirable—only unlucky. She worried about her work in the office, her clothes, her cooking, her children. She worried most of all about what Roger and Caroline would think.

Caroline and Roger lived on the east side of the park, in a handsome stone 70 house. Roger was a tall man with a bald, freckled head, a fat, firm stomach. Some operation on his throat had deprived him of his voice—he spoke in a rough whisper. But everybody paid attention. At dinner once in the stone house—where all the dining-room furniture was enormous, darkly glowing, palatial—I asked him a question. I think it had to do with Whittaker Chambers, whose story was then appearing in the *Saturday Evening Post.* The question was mild in tone, but he guessed its subversive intent and took to calling me Mrs. Gromyko, referring to what he alleged to be my "sympathies." Perhaps he really craved an adversary, and could not find one. At that dinner, I saw Andrew's hand tremble as he lit his mother's cigarette. His Uncle Roger had paid for Andrew's education, and was on the board of directors of several companies.

"He is just an opinionated old man," Andrew said to me later. "What is the point of arguing with him?"

Before we left Vancouver, Andrew's mother had written, *Roger seems quite intrigued by the idea of your buying a small car!* Her exclamation mark showed apprehension. At that time, particularly in Ontario, the choice of a small European car over a large American car could be seen as some sort of declaration—a declaration of tendencies Roger had been sniffing after all along.

"It isn't that small a car," said Andrew huffily.

"That's not the point," I said. "The point is, it isn't any of his business!"

We spent the second night in Missoula. We had been told in Spokane, at a gas 75 station, that there was a lot of repair work going on along Highway 2, and that we were in for a very hot, dusty drive, with long waits, so we turned onto the interstate and drove through Coeur d'Alene and Kellogg into Montana. After Missoula, we turned south toward Butte, but detoured to see Helena, the state capital. In the car, we played Who Am I?

Cynthia was somebody dead, and an American, and a girl. Possibly a lady. She was not in a story. She had not been seen on television. Cynthia had not read about her in a book. She was not anybody who had come to the kindergarten, or a relative of any of Cynthia's friends.

"Is she human?" said Andrew, with a sudden shrewdness.

"No! That's what you forgot to ask!"

"An animal," I said reflectively.

"Is that a question? Sixteen questions!"   80

"No, it is not a question. I'm thinking. A dead animal."

"It's the deer," said Meg, who hadn't been playing.

"That's not fair!" said Cynthia. "She's not playing!"

"What deer?" said Andrew.

I said, "Yesterday."   85

"The day before," said Cynthia. "Meg wasn't playing. Nobody got it."

"The deer on the truck," said Andrew.

"It was a lady deer, because it didn't have antlers, and it was an American and it was dead," Cynthia said.

Andrew said, "I think it's kind of morbid, being a dead deer."

"I got it," said Meg.   90

Cynthia said, "I think I know what morbid is. It's depressing."

Helena, an old silver-mining town, looked forlorn to us even in the morning sunlight. Then Bozeman and Billings, not forlorn in the slightest — energetic, strung-out towns, with miles of blinding tinsel fluttering over used-car lots. We got too tired and hot even to play Who Am I? These busy, prosaic cities reminded me of similar places in Ontario, and I thought about what was really waiting there — the great tombstone furniture of Roger and Caroline's dining room, the dinners for which I must iron the children's dresses and warn them about forks, and then the other table a hundred miles away, the jokes of my father's crew. The pleasures I had been thinking of — looking at the countryside or drinking a Coke in an old-fashioned drugstore with fans and a high, pressed-tin ceiling — would have to be snatched in between.

"Meg's asleep," Cynthia said. "She's so hot. She makes me hot in the same seat with her."

"I hope she isn't feverish," I said, not turning around.

What are we doing this for, I thought, and the answer came — to show off.   95
To give Andrew's mother and my father the pleasure of seeing their grandchildren. That was our duty. But beyond that we wanted to show them something. What strenuous children we were, Andrew and I, what relentless seekers of approbation. It was as if at some point we had received an unforgettable, indigestible message — that we were far from satisfactory, and that the most commonplace success in life was probably beyond us. Roger dealt out such messages, of course — that was his style — but Andrew's mother, my own mother and father couldn't have meant to do so. All they meant to tell us was "Watch out. Get along." My father, when I was in high school, teased me that I was getting to think I was so smart I would never find a boyfriend. He would have forgotten that in a week. I never forgot it. Andrew and I didn't forget things. We took umbrage.

"I wish there was a beach," said Cynthia.

"There probably is one," Andrew said. "Right around the next curve."

"There isn't any curve," she said, sounding insulted.

"That's what I mean."

"I wish there was some more lemonade."   100

"I will just wave my magic wand and produce some," I said. "Okay, Cynthia? Would you rather have grape juice? Will I do a beach while I'm at it?"

She was silent, and soon I felt repentant. "Maybe in the next town there might be a pool," I said. I looked at the map. "In Miles City. Anyway, there'll be something cool to drink."

"How far is it?" Andrew said.

"Not so far," I said. "Thirty miles, about."

"In Miles City," said Cynthia, in the tones of an incantation, "there is a   105 beautiful blue swimming pool for children, and a park with lovely trees."

Andrew said to me, "You could have started something."

But there was a pool. There was a park too, though not quite the oasis of Cynthia's fantasy. Prairie trees with thin leaves — cottonwoods and poplars — worn grass, and a high wire fence around the pool. Within this fence, a wall, not yet completed, of cement blocks. There were no shouts or splashes; over the entrance I saw a sign that said the pool was closed every day from noon until two o'clock. It was then twenty-five after twelve.

Nevertheless I called out, "Is anybody there?" I thought somebody must be around, because there was a small truck parked near the entrance. On the side of the truck were these words: *We have Brains, to fix your Drains. (We have Roto-Rooter too.)*

A girl came out, wearing a red lifeguard's shirt over her bathing suit. "Sorry, we're closed."

"We were just driving through," I said.   110

"We close every day from twelve until two. It's on the sign." She was eating a sandwich.

"I saw the sign," I said. "But this is the first water we've seen for so long, and the children are awfully hot, and I wondered if they could just dip in and out — just five minutes. We'd watch them."

A boy came into sight behind her. He was wearing jeans and a T-shirt with the words *Roto-Rooter* on it.

I was going to say that we were driving from British Columbia to Ontario, but I remembered that Canadian place names usually meant nothing to Americans. "We're driving right across the country," I said. "We haven't time to wait for the pool to open. We were just hoping the children could get cooled off."

Cynthia came running up barefoot behind me. "Mother. Mother, where is   115 my bathing suit?" Then she stopped, sensing the serious adult negotiations. Meg was climbing out of the car — just wakened, with her top pulled up and her shorts pulled down, showing her pink stomach.

"Is it just those two?" the girl said.

"Just the two. We'll watch them."

"I can't let any adults in. If it's just the two, I guess I could watch them. I'm having my lunch." She said to Cynthia, "Do you want to come in the pool?"

"Yes, please," said Cynthia firmly.

Meg looked at the ground.   120

"Just a short time, because the pool is really closed," I said. "We appreciate this very much," I said to the girl.

"Well, I can eat my lunch out there, if it's just the two of them." She looked toward the car as if she thought I might try to spring some more children on her.

When I found Cynthia's bathing suit, she took it into the changing room. She would not permit anybody, even Meg, to see her naked. I changed Meg, who stood on the front seat of the car. She had a pink cotton bathing suit with straps that crossed and buttoned. There were ruffles across the bottom.

"She *is* hot," I said. "But I don't think she's feverish."

I loved helping Meg to dress or undress, because her body still had the 125 solid unself-consciousness, the sweet indifference, something of the milky smell, of a baby's body. Cynthia's body had long ago been pared down, shaped and altered, into Cynthia. We all liked to hug Meg, press and nuzzle her. Sometimes she would scowl and beat us off, and this forthright independence, this ferocious bashfulness, simply made her more appealing, more apt to be tormented and tickled in the way of family love.

Andrew and I sat in the car with the windows open. I could hear a radio playing, and thought it must belong to the girl or her boyfriend. I was thirsty, and got out of the car to look for a concession stand, or perhaps a soft-drink machine, somewhere in the park. I was wearing shorts, and the backs of my legs were slick with sweat. I saw a drinking fountain at the other side of the park and was walking toward it in a roundabout way, keeping to the shade of the trees. No place became real till you got out of the car. Dazed with the heat, with the sun on the blistered houses, the pavement, the burnt grass, I walked slowly. I paid attention to a squashed leaf, ground a Popsicle stick under the heel of my sandal, squinted at a trash can strapped to a tree. This is the way you look at the poorest details of the world resurfaced, after you've been driving for a long time — you feel their singleness and precise location and the forlorn coincidence of your being there to see them.

Where are the children?

I turned around and moved quickly, not quite running, to a part of the fence beyond which the cement wall was not completed. I could see some of the pool. I saw Cynthia, standing about waist-deep in the water, fluttering her hands on the surface and discreetly watching something at the end of the pool, which I could not see. I thought by her pose, her discretion, the look on her face, that she must be watching some byplay between the lifeguard and her boyfriend. I couldn't see Meg. But I thought she must be playing in the shallow water — both the shallow and deep ends of the pool were out of my sight.

"Cynthia!" I had to call twice before she knew where my voice was coming from. "Cynthia! Where's Meg?"

It always seems to me, when I recall this scene, that Cynthia turns very 130 gracefully toward me, then turns all around in the water — making me think of a ballerina on pointe — and spreads her arms in a gesture of the stage. "Dis-appeared!"

Cynthia was naturally graceful, and she did take dancing lessons, so these movements may have been as I have described. She did say "Disappeared" after looking all around the pool, but the strangely artificial style of speech and gesture, the lack of urgency, is more likely my invention. The fear I felt instantly when I couldn't see Meg — even while I was telling myself she must be in the shallower water — must have made Cynthia's movements seem unbearably slow and inappropriate to me, and the tone in which she could say "Disappeared" before the implications struck her (or was she covering, at once, some ever-ready guilt?) was heard by me as quite exquisitely, monstrously self-possessed.

I cried out for Andrew, and the lifeguard came into view. She was pointing toward the deep end of the pool, saying, "What's that?"

There, just within my view, a cluster of pink ruffles appeared, a bouquet, beneath the surface of the water. Why would a lifeguard stop and point, why would she ask what that was, why didn't she just dive into the water and swim to it? She didn't swim; she ran all the way around the edge of the pool. But by that time Andrew was over the fence. So many things seemed not quite plausible—Cynthia's behavior, then the lifeguard's—and now I had the impression that Andrew jumped with one bound over this fence, which seemed about seven feet high. He must have climbed it very quickly, getting a grip on the wire.

I could not jump or climb it, so I ran to the entrance, where there was a sort of lattice gate, locked. It was not very high, and I did pull myself over it. I ran through the cement corridors, through the disinfectant pool for your feet, and came out on the edge of the pool.

The drama was over.   135

Andrew had got to Meg first, and had pulled her out of the water. He just had to reach over and grab her, because she was swimming somehow, with her head underwater—she was moving toward the edge of the pool. He was carrying her now, and the lifeguard was trotting along behind. Cynthia had climbed out of the water and was running to meet them. The only person aloof from the situation was the boyfriend, who had stayed on the bench at the shallow end, drinking a milkshake. He smiled at me, and I thought that unfeeling of him, even though the danger was past. He may have meant it kindly. I noticed that he had not turned the radio off, just down.

Meg had not swallowed any water. She hadn't even scared herself. Her hair was plastered to her head and her eyes were wide open, golden with amazement. "I was getting the comb," she said. "I didn't know it was deep."

Andrew said, "She was swimming! She was swimming by herself. I saw her bathing suit in the water and then I saw her swimming."

"She nearly drowned," Cynthia said. "Didn't she? Meg nearly drowned."   140

"I don't know how it could have happened," said the lifeguard. "One moment she was there, and the next she wasn't."

What had happened was that Meg had climbed out of the water at the shallow end and run along the edge of the pool toward the deep end. She saw a comb that somebody had dropped lying on the bottom. She crouched down and reached in to pick it up, quite deceived about the depth of the water. She went over the edge and slipped into the pool, making such a light splash that nobody heard—not the lifeguard, who was kissing her boyfriend, or Cynthia, who was watching them. That must have been the moment under the trees when I thought, Where are the children? It must have been the same moment. At that moment, Meg was slipping, surprised, into the treacherously clear blue water.

"It's okay," I said to the lifeguard, who was nearly crying. "She can move pretty fast." (Though that wasn't what we usually said about Meg at all. We said she thought everything over and took her time.)

"You swam, Meg," said Cynthia, in a congratulatory way. (She told us about the kissing later.)

"I didn't know it was deep," Meg said. "I didn't drown."   145

We had lunch at a takeout place, eating hamburgers and fries at a picnic table not far from the highway. In my excitement, I forgot to get Meg a plain hamburger, and had to scrape off the relish and mustard with plastic spoons, then wipe the meat with a paper napkin, before she would eat it. I took advantage of the trash can there to clean out the car. Then we resumed driving east, with the car windows open in front. Cynthia and Meg fell asleep in the back seat.

Andrew and I talked quietly about what had happened. Suppose I hadn't had the impulse just at that moment to check on the children? Suppose we had gone uptown to get drinks, as we had thought of doing? How had Andrew got over the fence? Did he jump or climb? (He couldn't remember.) How had he reached Meg so quickly? And think of the lifeguard not watching. And Cynthia, taken up with the kissing. Not seeing anything else. Not seeing Meg drop over the edge.

Disappeared.

But she swam. She held her breath and came up swimming.

What a chain of lucky links.

150

That was all we spoke about — luck. But I was compelled to picture the opposite. At this moment, we could have been filling out forms. Meg removed from us, Meg's body being prepared for shipment. To Vancouver — where we had never noticed such a thing as a graveyard — or to Ontario? The scribbled drawings she had made this morning would still be in the back seat of the car. How could this be borne all at once, how did people bear it? The plump, sweet shoulders and hands and feet, the fine brown hair, the rather satisfied, secretive expression — all exactly the same as when she had been alive. The most ordinary tragedy. A child drowned in a swimming pool at noon on a sunny day. Things tidied up quickly. The pool opens as usual at two o'clock. The lifeguard is a bit shaken up and gets the afternoon off. She drives away with her boyfriend in the Roto-Rooter truck. The body sealed away in some kind of shipping coffin. Sedatives, phone calls, arrangements. Such a sudden vacancy, a blind sinking and shifting. Waking up groggy from the pills, thinking for a moment it wasn't true. Thinking if only we hadn't stopped, if only we hadn't taken this route, if only they hadn't let us use the pool. Probably no one would ever have known about the comb.

There's something trashy about this kind of imagining, isn't there? Something shameful. Laying your finger on the wire to get the safe shock, feeling a bit of what it's like, then pulling back. I believed that Andrew was more scrupulous than I about such things, and that at this moment he was really trying to think about something else.

When I stood apart from my parents at Steve Gauley's funeral and watched them, and had this new, unpleasant feeling about them, I thought that I was understanding something about them for the first time. It was a deadly serious thing. I was understanding that they were implicated. Their big, stiff, dressed-up bodies did not stand between me and sudden death, or any kind of death. They gave consent. So it seemed. They gave consent to the death of children and to my death not by anything they said or thought but by the very fact that they had made children — they had made me. They had made me, and for that reason my death — however grieved they were, however they carried on — would seem to them anything but impossible or unnatural. This was a fact, and even then I knew they were not to blame.

But I did blame them. I charged them with effrontery, hypocrisy. On Steve Gauley's behalf, and on behalf of all children, who knew that by rights they should have sprung up free, to live a new, superior kind of life, not to be caught in the snares of vanquished grownups, with their sex and funerals.

Steve Gauley drowned, people said, because he was next thing to an or-   155
phan and was let run free. If he had been warned enough and given chores to
do and kept in check, he wouldn't have fallen from an untrustworthy tree
branch into a spring pond, a full gravel pit near the river — he wouldn't have
drowned. He was neglected, he was free, so he drowned. And his father took it
as an accident, such as might happen to a dog. He didn't have a good suit for
the funeral, and he didn't bow his head for the prayers. But he was the only
grownup that I let off the hook. He was the only one I didn't see giving consent.
He couldn't prevent anything, but he wasn't implicated in anything, either —
not like the others, saying the Lord's Prayer in their unnaturally weighted
voices, oozing religion and dishonor.

At Glendive, not far from the North Dakota border, we had a choice — either to
continue on the interstate or head northeast, toward Williston, taking Route
16, then some secondary roads that would get us back to Highway 2.

We agreed that the interstate would be faster, and that it was important
for us not to spend too much time — that is, money — on the road. Nevertheless we decided to cut back to Highway 2.

"I just like the idea of it better," I said.

Andrew said, "That's because it's what we planned to do in the beginning."

"We missed seeing Kalispell and Havre. And Wolf Point. I like the name."   160

"We'll see them on the way back."

Andrew's saying "on the way back" was a surprising pleasure to me. Of
course, I had believed that we would be coming back, with our car and our lives
and our family intact, having covered all that distance, having dealt somehow
with those loyalties and problems, held ourselves up for inspection in such a
foolhardy way. But it was a relief to hear him say it.

"What I can't get over," said Andrew, "is how you got the signal. It's got to
be some kind of extra sense that mothers have."

Partly I wanted to believe that, to bask in my extra sense. Partly I wanted to
warn him — to warn everybody — never to count on it.

"What I can't understand," I said, "is how you got over the fence."   165

"Neither can I."

So we went on, with the two in the back seat trusting us, because of no
choice, and we ourselves trusting to be forgiven, in time, for everything that
had first to be seen and condemned by those children: whatever was flippant,
arbitrary, careless, callous — all our natural, and particular, mistakes.

CONSIDERATIONS FOR CRITICAL THINKING AND WRITING

1. FIRST RESPONSE. What's the tone of "Miles City, Montana"? Did you expect
the narrator to find Meg alive in the pool? How did you feel when you realized that Meg hadn't drowned?

2. How do the opening paragraphs describing Steve Gauley's death and funeral set the tone for the story? Which details of the description seem especially effective to you?

3. How does the funeral make the narrator feel? Why does she feel that way?

4. Describe the narrator's marriage to Andrew. How do they get along? How
do they regard each other? How do they handle their differences? Were you
surprised to learn that they no longer live together? Why or why not?

5. At one point in the story, the narrator describes herself as a "watcher, not a keeper" (para. 22). Is this an accurate self-assessment? What does this tell us about the narrator?

6. How does the car trip from Vancouver to Ontario serve as a structural device for the story?

7. What do you think is the central conflict in the story? Are additional related conflicts presented?

8. How is the theme of the story related to the narrator's response to Steve Gauley's drowning and Meg's near-drowning? What do you think is the theme?

9. Analyze the "Who Am I?" game played in the car (paras. 75–91). What purpose do you think this scene serves? How is it related to the story's theme?

10. Why does the narrator not blame Steve Gauley's father for Steve's drowning? Why does she instead blame her own parents?

11. How does knowing that the narrator no longer lives with her husband affect your reading of the story's final paragraphs (162–167)?

CONNECTIONS TO OTHER SELECTIONS

1. Compare the narrator in this story with the narrator in Munro's "An Ounce of Cure." Explain why you think their retrospective narrations are different from or similar to each other.

2. Write an essay that compares the fathers in this story with the father in Amy Bloom's "Hold Tight" (p. 650). What are some significant differences and similarities in the authors' respective treatments of fatherhood?

PERSPECTIVES ON MUNRO

GRAEME GIBSON (B. 1934)

An Interview with Munro on Writing   1973

Gibson: I'll begin with a general question: do you think writers know something special, in the way physicists or anthropologists do?

Munro: You mean probably that writers are . . . have just seen something special. I don't think they *know* something special. I do think that they, perhaps, just perhaps they see things differently. Well I know to me, just things in themselves are very important. I'm not a writer who is very concerned with ideas. I'm not an intellectual writer. I'm very, very excited by what you might call the surface of life, and it must be that this seems to me meaningful in a way I can't analyze or describe.

Gibson: Now when you say it's not that they know something special but, they see something special . . . what kinds of things?

Munro: Well for me it's just things about people, the way they look, the way they sound, the way things smell, the way everything is that you go through every day. It seems to me very important to do something with this.

Gibson: Yes. I mean, perhaps one of the most exciting things I found in reading your stuff was an incredible kind of recognition of how things are.

Munro: It seems to me very important to be able to get at the exact tone or texture of how things are. I can't really claim that it is linked to any kind of a religious feeling about the world, and yet that might come closest to describing it.

Gibson: A slightly different kind of question: In what way is writing important to you?

Munro: God . . . do you mean why do I do it? I don't know if I can get at that. I always have done it. It's . . . do you mean is it important as a kind of therapy? No, that's not it. I don't know why it's important. I don't understand this. I know that I'm never not writing, so that I'm not just sort of turning out one book and then taking a rest and then turning out another book. I'll never live long enough to deal with all the ideas that are—things that are working, because I write very slowly and things, with me, things sort of jell very slowly. But there are always things there that just—well I'm thinking of a thing I'm working on now which I haven't really begun to write much of at all, and it just, it exists and so I'm going to have to put it down or forget it. If I can.

Gibson: You say it exists. So then is your writing a response to something that is simply there?

Munro: Not there in the external world. It's there in my head, this story, if you want to call it that, the characters, the relationship, the lives of these people. I can now see it in my mind, not very well, rather dimly, and things will change as I work it out, but something is there that I'm probably going to have to deal with. Though other things are also there that I have failed to deal with. Often I fail to deal with things several times before I work them out successfully. But it's all there, and of course it comes from the external world. Where else would it come from? But I'm not the kind of writer that says: Now I've got to do something, I've got to write something about this existing problem or this relationship or this experience I've had. I don't work that directly.

Gibson: It's not problem solving then?

Munro: No. . . .

Gibson: You said you've always been writing. How really did you start writing?

Munro: I started writing things down when I was about fourteen or fifteen, and earlier than that I made up stories all the time. But I think they were the things that—I think many children do this, and I don't know, maybe loneliness in adolescence is one of the things that makes it persist.

Gibson: And insisting on your own view of the world too, I guess.

Munro: Yes, perhaps it helps to grow up feeling very alienated from the environment you happen to live in, which is another thing that happened to me.

Gibson: Where did the alienation come from?

Munro: Well I grew up in a rural community, a very traditional community. I almost always felt it. I find it still when I go back. The concern of everyone else I knew was dealing with life on a very practical level, and this is very understandable, because my family are farmers and they are two or three generations away from being pioneers. In order to survive it's necessary to be very good at making things with your hands, and always to think practically, and not to see more than is obviously there, not to see what we call beauty or—oh I'm not doing very well here, but I always realized that I had a different view of the world, and one that would bring me into great trouble and ridicule if it were exposed. I learned very early to disguise everything, and perhaps the escape into making stories was necessary.

Gibson: It's an extremely impractical kind of a thing to be doing.

Munro: To most of my relatives the work I do is still a very meaningless, useless type of work.

Gibson: A frill, if anything.

Munro: Not even a frill, almost a wrong thing to be doing, because it is so — if I were hooking rugs though, it would be all right, you see, because you put the rugs on the floor and people walk on them, but what do you do with books? In the community where I grew up, books were a time-waster and reading is a bad habit, and so if even reading is a bad habit, writing is an incomprehensible thing to do.

From *Eleven Canadian Novelists*

CONSIDERATIONS FOR CRITICAL THINKING AND WRITING

1. What do you think Munro means when she says "I'm not a writer who is very concerned with ideas" (para. 2)? Do you think this sensibility is made apparent in her fiction? Explain your response with reference to the four stories reprinted in this book.

2. What causes Munro to feel alienated from her environment? How do you think her sense of alienation is reflected in her writing?

3. Try conducting your own "interview" with Munro. Make up a few questions about some aspect of her work and attempt to write responses based on your reading of her stories.

BENJAMIN DeMOTT (B. 1924)

On Munro's Female Protagonists   1983

Shrewd, amused, self-aware, each of [Munro's] heroines is perfectly capable of recognizing and regretting a mistake or indiscretion. . . . But Mrs. Munro's women are also capable of relishing an indiscretion. They're risk takers at heart, plucky, independent, sexually vibrant. They're people one knows exist even though, for some reason, they fail to surface at parties, mixed doubles, carol sings, or during office hours. One knows they exist in number because one keeps seeing them clearly two rows ahead on airplanes, or way over in the back on the right, in somebody else's lecture room. Their intelligence beckons, not merely their recklessness; they're likable not alone for the dangers they have passed but for their alertness to the pleasures of the passage itself, both the before and after.

From *The New York Times Book Review*, March 20, 1983

CONSIDERATIONS FOR CRITICAL THINKING AND WRITING

1. How do the protagonists in "An Ounce of Cure" (p. 451), "Wild Swans" (p. 459), "Prue" (p. 467), and "Miles City, Montana" (p. 470) indicate that they know they have made a "mistake" or committed an "indiscretion"? Which protagonists, if any, seem to regret their experiences?

2. Explain how one of the four Munro stories illustrates DeMott's observation that Munro's women are capable of "relishing an indiscretion." Discuss why you agree or disagree that such relish is an appealing quality in a character.

3. In an essay discuss both the "intelligence" and the "recklessness" of the protagonist in "Prue." In your response, consider whether or not both terms apply equally to her character.

CATHERINE SHELDRICK ROSS

On the Reader's Experience in Reading Munro's Stories   1986

The reader's experience in reading Munro's stories is one of recognition. We say, yes, that is how life is; we recognize and acknowledge discoveries about our deepest selves. And this recognition is the purpose of the author's journeys into the past, undertaken with compassion and determination to "get it right," to get down the tones, textures, and appearances of things. Instead of plots, Munro's work offers arrangements of materials that shift our perceptions of ordinary events and make us see the ordinary in an extraordinary way. Her books are a demonstration of her sense that "at some level these things open; fragments, moments, suggestions, open full of power."

From "Alice Munro," in *Canadian Writers Since 1960,*
First Series, edited by W. H. New

CONSIDERATIONS FOR CRITICAL THINKING AND WRITING

1. Is your own experience in reading Munro's stories one of recognition? Explain why or why not. If not, what do you consider to be the primary experience of reading Munro's stories?

2. What does Munro's fiction offer instead of "plots," according to Ross? Choose a story and write an essay that either refutes or demonstrates Ross's perspective on Munro's fiction.

W. R. MARTIN (B. 1920)

On Prue's Suppressed Passions   1987

"Prue" is slight and cryptic. Alice Munro has described it as "a neater story than I usually write"; its neatness goes with the wry irony that informs it. Now the protagonist is well into middle-age — in her "late forties." For some years she has had a partly-on-but-mainly-off affair with Gordon, who is a shilly-shallier, a "helpless, baffled soul, squirming around inside his doughty fortress"; it is ironical that he is a "neurologist." He seems to have allowed his interest in food and comforts — his house has four bathrooms — to supplant his sex drive. A "quite young" and vigorous woman, whom Gordon thinks he loves, denied ingress to Gordon's house on a night when Prue is his guest to dinner, hurls her overnight bag at him, apparently out of frustration.

Gordon claims that he wants to marry Prue after he has got over "being in love" with the younger woman; perhaps he is attracted to Prue because she is habitually "cynical" and "lighthearted," "doesn't take herself too seriously," is "unintense, and civilized," "bright," and a "cheerful spectator" who can speak "lightly" of important matters; above all, "she seems to regard sex as a wholesome, slightly silly indulgence."

Throughout the story the short clipped sentences generate a dry ironic humor, and the joke is largely at the expense of Prue, who is more aptly named than she admits. When Gordon leaves her alone early in the morning, she picks up a single amber cufflink from his dresser and carries it off before the arrival of Gordon's housekeeper, her "friend from olden times." She possesses herself of the cufflink not for sentimental reasons, not as "booty," nor for its "ritualistic significance"; and she drops it into an old tobacco tin, where it joins several other ambiguous trophies, and "more or less forgets about it." She does not have the passion to throw an overnight bag at Gordon, so her response takes a devious form, apparently obscure even to herself because she shows no sign of recognising it for the revenge it is. She so slenderly knows herself that her attitudes, and even her "English accent," are artificially cultivated poses: she tells their friends that Gordon's attitude is "quite reasonable," but her suppressed passions tell a quite different story.

From *Alice Munro: Paradox and Parallel*

CONSIDERATIONS FOR CRITICAL THINKING AND WRITING

1. Explain why you agree or disagree with Martin's suggestion that "Prue" is a "slight and cryptic" story (para. 1).

2. Explain whether you agree with Martin that Prue's theft of the cufflink is a sign of "suppressed passions" (para. 3). Is there any other way to interpret her behavior?

3. Martin carefully works into his own writing brief quoted passages from "Prue" to make his points. Using Martin's paragraphs as a model, write a substantial one-paragraph analysis of Prue that describes something about her that you think is important for understanding her character.

GEORGE WOODCOCK (B. 1912)

On Symbolism in Munro's Fiction   1987

Alice Munro has always been rightly reluctant to offer theoretical explanations of her methods, for she is quite obviously an antidogmatic, the kind of writer who works with feeling ahead of theory. But even on the theoretical level she is shrewd in defining the perimeters of her approach, perhaps negatively rather than positively. She once, for example, in an essay written for John Metcalf's *The Narrative Voice* — entitled "The Colonel's Hash Resettled" — cautioned against attempts to read symbolism excessively into her stories. And she was right, for essentially her stories are what they say, offering their meaning with often stark directness and gaining their effect from their intense visuality, so that they are always vivid in the mind's eye, which is another way of saying that she has learnt the power of the image and how to turn it to the purposes of prose.

Her visuality is not merely a matter of rendering the surface, the realm of mere perception, for she has understood that one of the great advantages of any effective imagist technique is that the image not merely presents itself. It reverberates with the power of its associations, and even with the intensity of its own isolated and illuminated presence. Munro herself conveyed something of this when John Metcalf, remarking on the fact that she seemed to *"glory* in the surfaces and the textures," asked whether she did not in fact feel "'surfaces' not to be surfaces," and she answered that there was "a kind of magic . . . about everything . . . a feeling about the intensity of what is *there.*"

From *Northern Spring: The Flowering of Canadian Literature*

CONSIDERATIONS FOR CRITICAL THINKING AND WRITING

1. Woodcock cautions readers not to read excessive symbolism into Munro's stories, and yet he also argues that "her visuality is not merely a matter of rendering the surface" (para. 2). Can these two seemingly different perspectives be reconciled? Explain why or why not.

2. In an essay, discuss Munro's use of symbolism in "Prue" (p. 467) or "Miles City, Montana" (p. 470), and explain whether you feel it supports Woodcock's arguments in the above excerpt.

TWO COMPLEMENTARY CRITICAL READINGS

Munro on Narration in "An Ounce of Cure"   1970

One thing in ["An Ounce of Cure"] I think is interesting, now that I look back on it: when the girl's circumstances become hopelessly messy, when nothing is going to go right for her, she gets out of it by looking at the way things happen — by changing from a participant to an observer. This is what I used to do myself, it is what a writer does; I think it may be one of the things that make a writer in the first place. When I started to write the dreadful things I did write when I was about fifteen, I made the glorious leap from being a victim of my own ineptness and self-conscious miseries to being a godlike arranger of patterns and destinies, even if they were all in my head; I have never leapt back.

From "Author's Commentary" in *Sixteen by Twelve:*
Short Stories by Canadian Writers, edited by John Metcalf

CONSIDERATIONS FOR CRITICAL THINKING AND WRITING

1. Discuss the narrator's shift from participant to observer in "An Ounce of Cure" (p. 451).

2. Why do you think Munro describes her movement from participant to observer as a "glorious leap"?

3. Write an essay in which you consider an additional quality, attribute, strategy, or sensibility that you think is "one of the things that make a writer in the first place."

LORRAINE MCMULLEN (B. 1926)

On Munro's Ironic Humor
in "An Ounce of Cure"   1983

Munro is a satirist for whom disorder, chance happenings and meetings, and the bizarre characters who reveal us to ourselves are all parts of an absurd yet real world. Irony is at the core of Munro's view of humanity and events, a view she expresses with wit and humour, mixing paradoxes, startling comparisons, and unexpectedly incisive details with farcical scenes and eccentric or contradictory personalities. In her use of comic devices, Munro goes beyond the clever and the humorous. Her careful and accurate structuring of situations and juxtaposition of incidents reveal the coexistence of the bizarre with the ordinary, the genuine with the fraudulent, the immutable with the transient. Her ironically perceived characters, whether appearing to us as outlandish or ordinary, reveal to us our own contradictory impulses and ambivalent feelings, and through their weaknesses and vulnerability remind us of our own weaknesses, our own vulnerability. Challenging myths and sweeping away stereotypes, Munro induces us to recognize, with her, the "shameless, marvellous, shattering absurdity" around and within us.

From "'Shameless, Marvellous, Shattering Absurdity':
The Humour of Paradox in Alice Munro" in *Probable Fictions:
Alice Munro's Narrative Acts,* edited by Louis K. MacKendrick

CONSIDERATIONS FOR CRITICAL THINKING AND WRITING

1. Explain why you agree or disagree with McMullen's assertion that "irony is at the core of Munro's view of humanity and events."

2. Locate and describe the kinds of comic devices Munro uses in "An Ounce of Cure" (p. 451). What are the effects of those comic devices?

3. In an essay discuss how McMullen's claim that "An Ounce of Cure" "remind[s] us of our own weaknesses, our own vulnerability" can be reconciled with Munro's assertion that becoming an "observer" rather than a "participant" allowed her to feel like a "godlike arranger of patterns and destinies" instead of a victim. Explain why you think the narrator of "An Ounce of Cure" is a weak or a triumphant character.

SUGGESTED TOPICS FOR LONGER PAPERS

1. The endings of each of these four stories reveal something significant about their respective protagonists. Examine the endings closely and discuss whether or not the stories' conflicts are resolved. Would you characterize the endings as happy or unhappy?

2. How are men portrayed in Munro's stories? What purpose do they serve in the stories? What kinds of generalizations can you make about them? Write an essay that explores the thematic significance of the men in these stories.

(Text continues on page 491.)

3. **MULTIMEDIA PROJECT.** Research attitudes towards teen drinking in 1968, when "An Ounce of Cure" was published. Use any media ranging from magazine articles to health pamphlets or films for students as your sources of information. How do those attitudes compare with responses to teenage drinking today? Explain why you think Munro might or might not revise her treatment of drinking if she were writing the story now rather than in 1968.

Web   *For help with this project, use the Multimedia Project Guides Online at*
        http://www.bedfordstmartins.com/meyer/bedintrolit

14

A Critical Case Study:
William Faulkner's
"Barn Burning"

This chapter offers several critical approaches to a well-known short story by William Faulkner. Though there are many possible critical approaches to any given work (see Chapter 52, "Critical Strategies for Reading," for a discussion of a variety of methods), and there are numerous studies of Faulkner from formalist, biographical, historical, mythological, psychological, sociological, and other perspectives, it is worth noting that each reading of a work or writer is predicated on accepting certain assumptions about literature and life. Those assumptions or premises may be complementary or mutually exclusive, and they may appeal to you or appall you. What is interesting, however, is how various approaches reveal the text (as well as its readers and critics) by calling attention to certain elements or leaving others out. The following critical excerpts suggest only a portion of the range of possibilities, but even a small representation of approaches can help you to raise new questions, develop insights, recognize problems, and suggest additional ways of reading the text.

WILLIAM FAULKNER (1897–1962)

A biographical note for William Faulkner appears on page 74, before his story "A Rose for Emily." In "Barn Burning" Faulkner portrays a young boy's love and revulsion for his father, a frightening man who lives by a "ferocious conviction in the rightness of his own actions."

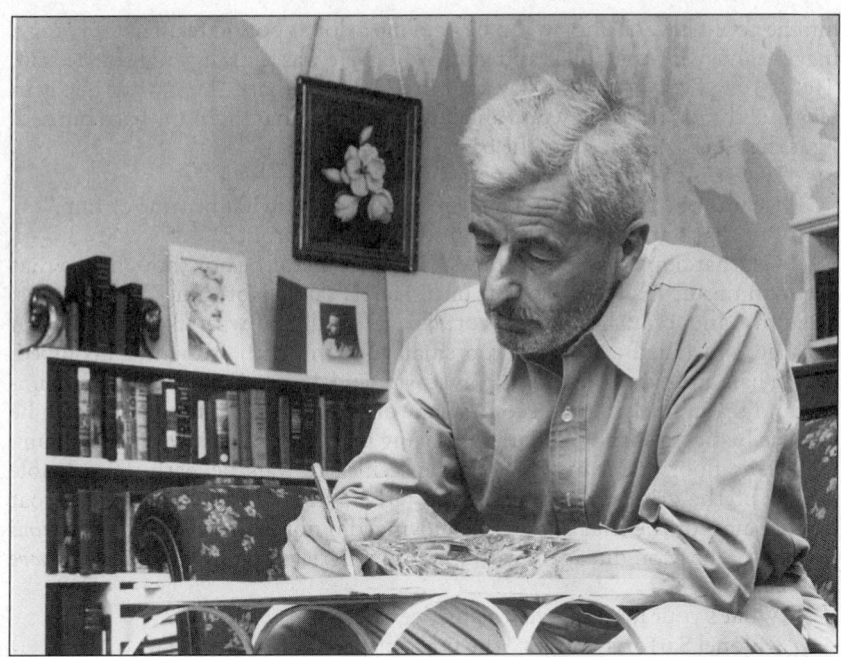

William Faulkner (May 6, 1955) in the spot where he did most of his writing—his living room—bent over a glass-topped table with a pen. Reprinted by permission of Corbis-Bettmann.

Barn Burning   *1939*

The store in which the Justice of the Peace's court was sitting smelled of cheese. The boy, crouched on his nail keg at the back of the crowded room, knew he smelled cheese, and more: from where he sat he could see the ranked shelves close-packed with the solid, squat, dynamic shapes of tin cans whose labels his stomach read, not from the lettering which meant nothing to his mind but from the scarlet devils and the silver curve of fish—this, the cheese which he knew he smelled and the hermetic meat which his intestines believed he smelled coming in intermittent gusts momentary and brief between the other constant one, the smell and sense just a little of fear because mostly of despair and grief, the old fierce pull of blood. He could not see the table where the Justice sat and before which his father and his father's enemy (*our enemy* he thought in that despair; *ourn! mine and hisn both! He's my father!*) stood, but he could hear them, the two of them that is, because his father had said no word yet:

"But what proof have you, Mr. Harris?"

"I told you. The hog got into my corn. I caught it up and sent it back to him. He had no fence that would hold it. I told him so, warned him. The next time I put the hog in my pen. When he came to get it I gave him enough wire to patch up his pen. The next time I put the hog up and kept it. I rode down to his house and saw the wire I gave him still rolled on to the spool in his yard. I told

him he could have the hog when he paid me a dollar pound fee. That evening a
nigger came with the dollar and got the hog. He was a strange nigger. He said,
'He say to tell you wood and hay kin burn.' I said, 'What?' 'That whut he say to
tell you,' the nigger said. 'Wood and hay kin burn.' That night my barn burned.
I got the stock out but I lost the barn."

"Where is the nigger? Have you got him?"

"He was a strange nigger, I tell you. I don't know what became of him."   5

"But that's not proof. Don't you see that's not proof?"

"Get that boy up here. He knows." For a moment the boy thought too that
the man meant his older brother until Harris said, "Not him. The little one.
The boy," and, crouching, small for his age, small and wiry like his father, in
patched and faded jeans even too small for him, with straight, uncombed,
brown hair and eyes gray and wild as storm scud, he saw the men between himself and the table part and become a lane of grim faces, at the end of which he
saw the Justice, a shabby, collarless, graying man in spectacles, beckoning him.
He felt no floor under his bare feet; he seemed to walk beneath the palpable
weight of the grim turning faces. His father, stiff in his black Sunday coat
donned not for the trial but for the moving, did not even look at him. *He aims
for me to lie*, he thought, again with that frantic grief and despair. *And I will have
to do hit.*

"What's your name, boy?" the Justice said.

"Colonel Sartoris Snopes," the boy whispered.

"Hey?" the Justice said. "Talk louder. Colonel Sartoris? I reckon anybody   10
named for Colonel Sartoris in this country can't help but tell the truth, can
they?" The boy said nothing. *Enemy! Enemy!* he thought; for a moment he
could not even see, could not see that the Justice's face was kindly nor discern
that his voice was troubled when he spoke to the man named Harris: "Do you
want me to question this boy?" But he could hear, and during those subsequent long seconds while there was absolutely no sound in the crowded little
room save that of quiet and intent breathing it was as if he had swung outward at the end of a grape vine, over a ravine, and at the top of the swing had
been caught in a prolonged instant of mesmerized gravity, weightless in time.

"No!" Harris said violently, explosively. "Damnation! Send him out of
here!" Now time, the fluid world, rushed beneath him again, the voices coming
to him again through the smell of cheese and sealed meat, the fear and despair
and the old grief of blood:

"This case is closed. I can't find against you, Snopes, but I can give you advice. Leave this country and don't come back to it."

His father spoke for the first time, his voice cold and harsh, level, without
emphasis: "I aim to. I don't figure to stay in a country among people who . . ."
he said something unprintable and vile, addressed to no one.

"That'll do," the Justice said. "Take your wagon and get out of this country before dark. Case dismissed."

His father turned, and he followed the stiff black coat, the wiry figure   15
walking a little stiffly from where a Confederate provost's man's musket ball
had taken him in the heel on a stolen horse thirty years ago, followed the two
backs now, since his older brother had appeared from somewhere in the crowd,
no taller than the father but thicker, chewing tobacco steadily, between the
two lines of grim-faced men and out of the store and across the worn gallery
and down the sagging steps and among the dogs and half-grown boys in the
mild May dust, where as he passed a voice hissed:

"Barn burner!"

Again he could not see, whirling; there was a face in a red haze, moonlike, bigger than the full moon, the owner of it half again his size, he leaping in the red haze toward the face, feeling no blow, feeling no shock when his head struck the earth, scrabbling up and leaping again, feeling no blow this time either and tasting no blood, scrabbling up to see the other boy in full flight and himself already leaping into pursuit as his father's hand jerked him back, the harsh, cold voice speaking above him: "Go get in the wagon."

It stood in a grove of locusts and mulberries across the road. His two hulking sisters in their Sunday dresses and his mother and her sister in calico and sunbonnets were already in it, sitting on or among the sorry residue of the dozen and more movings which even the boy could remember — the battered stove, the broken beds and chairs, the clock inlaid with mother-of-pearl, which would not run, stopped at some fourteen minutes past two o'clock of a dead and forgotten day and time, which had been his mother's dowry. She was crying, though when she saw him she drew her sleeve across her face and began to descend from the wagon. "Get back," the father said.

"He's hurt. I got to get some water and wash his . . ."

"Get back in the wagon," his father said. He got in too, over the tail-gate. 20 His father mounted to the seat where the older brother already sat and struck the gaunt mules two savage blows with the peeled willow, but without heat. It was not even sadistic; it was exactly that same quality which in later years would cause his descendants to over-run the engine before putting a motor car in motion, striking and reining back in the same movement. The wagon went on, the store with its quiet crowd of grimly watching men dropped behind; a curve in the road hid it. *Forever* he thought. *Maybe he's done satisfied now, now that he has . . .* stopping himself, not to say it aloud even to himself. His mother's hand touched his shoulder.

"Does hit hurt?" she said.

"Naw," he said. "Hit don't hurt. Lemme be."

"Can't you wipe some of the blood off before hit dries?"

"I'll wash to-night," he said. "Lemme be, I tell you."

The wagon went on. He did not know where they were going. None of 25 them ever did or ever asked, because it was always somewhere, always a house of sorts waiting for them a day or two days or even three days away. Likely his father had already arranged to make a crop on another farm before he . . . Again he had to stop himself. He (the father) always did. There was something about his wolflike independence and even courage when the advantage was at least neutral which impressed strangers, as if they got from his latent ravening ferocity not so much a sense of dependability as a feeling that his ferocious conviction in the rightness of his own actions would be of advantage to all whose interest lay with his.

That night they camped, in a grove of oaks and beeches where a spring ran. The nights were still cool and they had a fire against it, of a rail lifted from a nearby fence and cut into lengths — a small fire, neat, niggard almost, a shrewd fire; such fires were his father's habit and custom always, even in freezing weather. Older, the boy might have remarked this and wondered why not a big one; why should not a man who had not only seen the waste and extravagance of war, but who had in his blood an inherent voracious prodigality with material not his own, have burned everything in sight? Then he might have gone a step farther and thought that that was the reason: that niggard blaze was the living fruit of nights passed during those four years in the woods hiding from all men, blue or gray, with his strings of horses (captured horses, he called them). And older still, he might have divined the true reason: that the element of fire spoke to some deep mainspring of his father's being, as the element of steel or of powder spoke to other men, as the one weapon for the preservation of integrity, else breath were not worth the breathing, and hence to be regarded with respect and used with discretion.

But he did not think this now and he had seen those same niggard blazes all his life. He merely ate his supper beside it and was already half asleep over his iron plate when his father called him, and once more he followed the stiff back, the stiff and ruthless limp, up the slope and on to the starlit road where, turning, he could see his father against the stars but without face or depth—a shape black, flat, and bloodless as though cut from tin in the iron folds of the frockcoat which had not been made for him, the voice harsh like tin and without heat like tin:

"You were fixing to tell them. You would have told him."

He didn't answer. His father struck him with the flat of his hand on the side of the head, hard but without heat, exactly as he had struck the two mules at the store, exactly as he would strike either of them with any stick in order to kill a horse fly, his voice still without heat or anger. "You're getting to be a man. You got to learn. You got to learn to stick to your own blood or you ain't going to have any blood to stick to you. Do you think either of them, any man there this morning, would? Don't you know all they wanted was a chance to get at me because they knew I had them beat? Eh?" Later, twenty years later, he was to tell himself, "If I had said they wanted only truth, justice, he would have hit me again." But now he said nothing. He was not crying. He just stood there. "Answer me," his father said.

"Yes," he whispered. His father turned.   30

"Get on to bed. We'll be there tomorrow."

Tomorrow they were there. In the early afternoon the wagon stopped before a paintless two-room house identical almost with the dozen others it had stopped before even in the boy's ten years, and again, as on the other dozen occasions, his mother and aunt got down and began to unload the wagon, although his two sisters and his father and brother had not moved.

"Likely hit ain't fitten for hawgs," one of the sisters said.

"Nevertheless, fit it will and you'll hog it and like it," his father said. "Get out of them chairs and help your Ma unload."

The two sisters got down, big, bovine, in a flutter of cheap ribbons; one of   35
them drew from the jumbled wagon bed a battered lantern, the other a worn broom. His father handed the reins to the older son and began to climb stiffly over the wheel. "When they get unloaded, take the team to the barn and feed them." Then he said, and at first the boy thought he was still speaking to his brother: "Come with me."

"Me?" he said.

"Yes," his father said. "You."

"Abner," his mother said. His father paused and looked back—the harsh level stare beneath the shaggy, graying, irascible brows.

"I reckon I'll have a word with the man that aims to begin tomorrow owning me body and soul for the next eight months."

They went back up the road. A week ago—or before last night, that is—he   40
would have asked where they were going, but not now. His father had struck

him before last night but never before had he paused afterward to explain why; it was as if the blow and the following calm, outrageous voice still rang, repercussed, divulging nothing to him save the terrible handicap of being young, the light weight of his few years, just heavy enough to prevent his soaring free of the world as it seemed to be ordered but not heavy enough to keep him footed solid in it, to resist it and try to change the course of events.

Presently he could see the grove of oaks and cedars and the other flowering trees and shrubs where the house would be, though not the house yet. They walked beside a fence massed with honeysuckle and Cherokee roses and came to a gate swinging open between two brick pillars, and now, beyond a sweep of drive, he saw the house for the first time and at that instant he forgot his father and the terror and despair both, and even when he remembered his father again (who had not stopped) the terror and despair did not return. Because, for all the twelve movings, they had sojourned until now in a poor country, a land of small farms and fields and houses, and he had never seen a house like this before. *Hit's big as a courthouse* he thought quietly, with a surge of peace and joy whose reason he could not have thought into words, being too young for that: *They are safe from him. People whose lives are a part of this peace and dignity are beyond his touch, he no more to them than a buzzing wasp: capable of stinging for a little moment but that's all; the spell of this peace and dignity rendering even the barns and stable and cribs which belong to it impervious to the puny flames he might contrive* . . . this, the peace and joy, ebbing for an instant as he looked again at the stiff black back, the stiff and implacable limp of the figure which was not dwarfed by the house, for the reason that it had never looked big anywhere and which now, against the serene columned backdrop, had more than ever that impervious quality of something cut ruthlessly from tin, depthless, as though, sidewise to the sun, it would cast no shadow. Watching him, the boy remarked the absolutely undeviating course which his father held and saw the stiff foot come squarely down in a pile of fresh droppings where a horse had stood in the drive and which his father could have avoided by a simple change of stride. But it ebbed only for a moment, though he could not have thought this into words either, walking on in the spell of the house, which he could even want but without envy, without sorrow, certainly never with that ravening and jealous rage which unknown to him walked in the ironlike black coat before him: *Maybe he will feel it too. Maybe it will even change him now from what maybe he couldn't help but be.*

They crossed the portico. Now he could hear his father's stiff foot as it came down on the boards with clocklike finality, a sound out of all proportion to the displacement of the body it bore and which was not dwarfed either by the white door before it, as though it had attained to a sort of vicious and ravening minimum not to be dwarfed by anything—the flat, wide, black hat, the formal coat of broadcloth which had once been black but which had now that friction-glazed greenish cast of the bodies of old house flies, the lifted sleeve which was too large, the lifted hand like a curled claw. The door opened so promptly that the boy knew the Negro must have been watching them all the time, an old man with neat grizzled hair, in a linen jacket, who stood barring the door with his body, saying, "Wipe yo foots, white man, fo you come in here. Major ain't home nohow."

"Get out of my way, nigger," his father said, without heat too, flinging the door back and the Negro also and entering, his hat still on his head. And now the boy saw the prints of the stiff foot on the doorjamb and saw them appear on the pale rug behind the machinelike deliberation of the foot which seemed to bear (or transmit) twice the weight which the body compassed. The Negro was shouting "Miss Lula! Miss Lula!" somewhere behind them, then the boy, deluged as though by a warm wave by a suave turn of the carpeted stair and a pendant glitter of chandeliers and a mute gleam of gold frames, heard the swift feet and saw her too, a lady—perhaps he had never seen her like before either—in a gray, smooth gown with lace at the throat and an apron tied at the waist and the sleeves turned back, wiping cake or biscuit dough from her hands with a towel as she came up the hall, looking not at his father at all but at the tracks on the blond rug with an expression of incredulous amazement.

"I tried," the Negro cried. "I tole him to . . ."

"Will you please go away?" she said in a shaking voice. "Major de Spain is 45 not at home. Will you please go away?"

His father had not spoken again. He did not speak again. He did not even look at her. He just stood stiff in the center of the rug, in his hat, the shaggy iron-gray brows twitching slightly above the pebble-colored eyes as he appeared to examine the house with brief deliberation. Then with the same deliberation he turned; the boy watched him pivot on the good leg and saw the stiff foot drag round the arc of the turning, leaving a final long and fading smear. His father never looked at it, he never once looked down at the rug. The Negro held the door. It closed behind them, upon the hysteric and indistinguishable woman-wail. His father stopped at the top of the steps and scraped his boot clean on the edge of it. At the gate he stopped again. He stood for a moment, planted stiffly on the stiff foot, looking back at the house. "Pretty and white, ain't it?" he said. "That's sweat. Nigger sweat. Maybe it ain't white enough yet to suit him. Maybe he wants to mix some white sweat with it."

Two hours later the boy was chopping wood behind the house within which his mother and aunt and the two sisters (the mother and aunt, not the two girls, he knew that; even at this distance and muffled by walls the flat loud voices of the two girls emanated an incorrigible idle inertia) were setting up the stove to prepare a meal; when he heard the hooves and saw the linen-clad man on a fine sorrel mare, whom he recognized even before he saw the rolled rug in front of the Negro youth following on a fat bay carriage horse—a suffused, angry face vanishing, still at full gallop, beyond the corner of the house where his father and brother were sitting in the two tilted chairs; and a moment later, almost before he could have put the axe down, he heard the hooves again and watched the sorrel mare go back out of the yard, already galloping again. Then his father began to shout one of the sisters' names, who presently emerged backward from the kitchen door dragging the rolled rug along the ground by one end while the other sister walked behind it.

"If you ain't going to tote, go on and set up the wash pot," the first said.

"You, Sarty!" the second shouted. "Set up the wash pot!" His father appeared at the door, framed against that shabbiness, as he had been against that other bland perfection, impervious to either, the mother's anxious face at his shoulder.

"Go on," the father said. "Pick it up." The two sisters stopped, broad, 50 lethargic; stooping, they presented an incredible expanse of pale cloth and a flutter of tawdry ribbons.

"If I thought enough of a rug to have to git hit all the way from France I wouldn't keep hit where folks coming in would have to tromp on hit," the first said. They raised the rug.

"Abner," the mother said. "Let me do it."

"You go back and git dinner," his father said. "I'll tend to this."

From the woodpile through the rest of the afternoon the boy watched them, the rug spread flat in the dust beside the bubbling wash pot, the two sisters stooping over it with that profound and lethargic reluctance, while the father stood over them in turn, implacable and grim, driving them though never raising his voice again. He could smell the harsh homemade lye they were using; he saw his mother come to the door once and look toward them with an expression not anxious now but very like despair; he saw his father turn, and he fell to with the axe and saw from the corner of his eye his father raise from the ground a flattish fragment of field stone and examine it and return to the pot, and this time his mother actually spoke: "Abner. Abner. Please don't. Please, Abner."

Then he was done too. It was dusk; the whippoorwills had already begun. 55 He could smell coffee from the room where they would presently eat the cold food remaining from the midafternoon meal, though when he entered the house he realized they were having coffee again probably because there was a fire on the hearth, before which the rug now lay spread over the backs of the two chairs. The tracks of his father's foot were gone. Where they had been were now long, water-cloudy scoriations resembling the sporadic course of a lilliputian mowing machine.

It still hung there while they ate the cold food and then went to bed, scattered without order or claim up and down the two rooms, his mother in one bed, where his father would later lie, the older brother in the other, himself, the aunt, and the two sisters on pallets on the floor. But his father was not in bed yet. The last thing the boy remembered was the depthless, harsh silhouette of the hat and coat bending over the rug and it seemed to him that he had not even closed his eyes when the silhouette was standing over him, the fire almost dead behind it, the stiff foot prodding him awake. "Catch up the mule," his father said.

When he returned with the mule his father was standing in the black door, the rolled rug over his shoulder. "Ain't you going to ride?" he said.

"No. Give me your foot."

He bent his knee into his father's hand, the wiry, surprising power flowed smoothly, rising, he rising with it, on to the mule's bare back (they had owned a saddle once; the boy could remember it though not when or where) and with the same effortlessness his father swung the rug up in front of him. Now in the starlight they retraced the afternoon's path, up the dusty road rife with honeysuckle, through the gate and up the black tunnel of the drive to the lightless house, where he sat on the mule and felt the rough warp of the rug drag across his thighs and vanish.

"Don't you want me to help?" he whispered. His father did not answer and 60 now he heard again that stiff foot striking the hollow portico with that wooden and clocklike deliberation, that outrageous overstatement of the weight it carried. The rug, hunched, not flung (the boy could tell that even in the darkness) from his father's shoulder struck the angle of wall and floor with a sound unbelievably loud, thunderous, then the foot again, unhurried and enormous; a light came on in the house and the boy sat, tense, breathing steadily and quietly and just a little fast, though the foot itself did not increase its beat at all, descending the steps now; now the boy could see him.

"Don't you want to ride now?" he whispered. "We kin both ride now," the light within the house altering now, flaring up and sinking. *He's coming down the stairs now,* he thought. He had already ridden the mule up beside the horse block; presently his father was up behind him and he doubled the reins over and slashed the mule across the neck, but before the animal could begin to trot the hard, thin arm came around him, the hard, knotted hand jerking the mule back to a walk.

In the first red rays of the sun they were in the lot, putting plow gear on the mules. This time the sorrel mare was in the lot before he heard it at all, the rider collarless and even bareheaded, trembling, speaking in a shaking voice as the woman in the house had done, his father merely looking up once before stooping again to the hame he was buckling, so that the man on the mare spoke to his stooping back:

"You must realize you have ruined that rug. Wasn't there anybody here, any of your women . . ." he ceased, shaking, the boy watching him, the older brother leaning now in the stable door, chewing, blinking slowly and steadily at nothing apparently. "It cost a hundred dollars. But you never had a hundred dollars. You never will. So I'm going to charge you twenty bushels of corn against your crop. I'll add it in your contract and when you come to the commissary you can sign it. That won't keep Mrs. de Spain quiet but maybe it will teach you to wipe your feet before you enter her house again."

Then he was gone. The boy looked at his father, who still had not spoken or even looked up again, who was now adjusting the logger-head in the hame.

"Pap," he said. His father looked at him — the inscrutable face, the shaggy 65
brows beneath which the gray eyes glinted coldly. Suddenly the boy went toward him, fast, stopping as suddenly. "You done the best you could!" he cried. "If he wanted hit done different why didn't he wait and tell you how? He won't git no twenty bushels! He won't git none! We'll gether hit and hide hit! I kin watch . . ."

"Did you put the cutter back in that straight stock like I told you?"

"No, sir," he said.

"Then go do it."

That was Wednesday. During the rest of that week he worked steadily, at what was within his scope and some which was beyond it, with an industry that did not need to be driven nor even commanded twice; he had this from his mother, with the difference that some at least of what he did he liked to do, such as splitting wood with the half-size axe which his mother and aunt had earned, or saved money somehow, to present him with at Christmas. In company with the two older women (and on one afternoon, even one of the sisters), he built pens for the shoat and the cow which were part of his father's contract with the landlord, and one afternoon, his father being absent, gone somewhere on one of the mules, he went to the field.

They were running a middle buster now, his brother holding the plow 70
straight while he handled the reins, and walking beside the straining mule, the rich black soil shearing cool and damp against his bare ankles, he thought *Maybe this is the end of it. Maybe even that twenty bushels that seems hard to have to pay for just a rug will be a cheap price for him to stop forever and always from being what he*

used to be; thinking, dreaming now, so that his brother had to speak sharply to him to mind the mule: *Maybe he even won't collect the twenty bushels. Maybe it will all add up and balance and vanish—corn, rug, fire; the terror and grief, the being pulled two ways like between two teams of horses—gone,* done with for ever and ever.

Then it was Saturday; he looked up from beneath the mule he was harnessing and saw his father in the black coat and hat. "Not that," his father said. "The wagon gear." And then, two hours later, sitting in the wagon bed behind his father and brother on the seat, the wagon accomplished a final curve, and he saw the weathered paintless store with its tattered tobacco- and patent-medicine posters and the tethered wagons and saddle animals below the gallery. He mounted the gnawed steps behind his father and brother, and there again was the lane of quiet, watching faces for the three of them to walk through. He saw the man in spectacles sitting at the plank table and he did not need to be told this was a Justice of the Peace; he sent one glare of fierce, exultant, partisan defiance at the man in collar and cravat now, whom he had seen but twice before in his life, and that on a galloping horse, who now wore on his face an expression not of rage but of amazed unbelief which the boy could not have known was at the incredible circumstance of being sued by one of his own tenants, and came and stood against his father and cried at the Justice: "He ain't done it! He aint' burnt . . ."

"Go back to the wagon," his father said.

"Burnt?" the Justice said. "Do I understand this rug was burned too?"

"Does anybody here claim it was?" his father said. "Go back to the wagon." But he did not, he merely retreated to the rear of the room, crowded as that other had been, but not to sit down this time, instead, to stand pressing among the motionless bodies, listening to the voices:

"And you claim twenty bushels of corn is too high for the damage you did to the rug?" 75

"He brought the rug to me and said he wanted the tracks washed out of it. I washed the tracks out and took the rug back to him."

"But you didn't carry the rug back to him in the same condition it was in before you made the tracks on it."

His father did not answer, and now for perhaps half a minute there was no sound at all save that of breathing, the faint, steady suspiration of complete and intent listening.

"You decline to answer that, Mr. Snopes?" Again his father did not answer. "I'm going to find against you, Mr. Snopes. I'm going to find that you were responsible for the injury to Major de Spain's rug and hold you liable for it. But twenty bushels of corn seems a little high for a man in your circumstances to have to pay. Major de Spain claims it cost a hundred dollars. October corn will be worth about fifty cents. I figure that if Major de Spain can stand a ninety-five dollar loss on something he paid cash for, you can stand a five-dollar loss you haven't earned yet. I hold you in damages to Major de Spain to the amount of ten bushels of corn over and above your contract with him, to be paid to him out of your crop at gathering time. Court adjourned."

It had taken no time hardly, the morning was but half begun. He thought 80 they would return home and perhaps back to the field, since they were late, far behind all other farmers. But instead his father passed on behind the wagon, merely indicating with his hand for the older brother to follow with it, and crossed the road toward the blacksmith shop opposite, pressing on after his

father, overtaking him, speaking, whispering up at the harsh, calm face beneath the weathered hat: "He won't git no ten bushels neither. He won't git
one. We'll . . ." until his father glanced for an instant down at him, the face absolutely calm, the grizzled eyebrows tangled above the cold eyes, the voice almost pleasant, almost gentle:

"You think so? Well, we'll wait till October anyway."

The matter of the wagon—the setting of a spoke or two and the tightening of the tires—did not take long either, the business of the tires accomplished by driving the wagon into the spring branch behind the shop and letting it stand there, the mules nuzzling into the water from time to time, and
the boy on the seat with the idle reins, looking up the slope and through the
sooty tunnel of the shed where the slow hammer rang and where his father sat
on an upended cypress bolt, easily, either talking or listening, still sitting there
when the boy brought the dripping wagon up out of the branch and halted it
before the door.

"Take them on to the shade and hitch," his father said. He did so and returned. His father and the smith and a third man squatting on his heels inside
the door were talking, about crops and animals; the boy, squatting too in the
ammoniac dust and hoof-parings and scales of rust, heard his father tell a
long and unhurried story out of the time before the birth of the older brother
even when he had been a professional horsetrader. And then his father came
up beside him where he stood before a tattered last year's circus poster on the
other side of the store, gazing rapt and quiet at the scarlet horses, the incredible poisings and convolutions of tulle and tights and the painted leers of co-
medians, and said, "It's time to eat."

But not at home. Squatting beside his brother against the front wall, he
watched his father emerge from the store and produce from a paper sack a
segment of cheese and divide it carefully and deliberately into three with his
pocket knife and produce crackers from the same sack. They all three squatted
on the gallery and ate, slowly, without talking; then in the store again, they
drank from a tin dipper tepid water smelling of the cedar bucket and of
living beech trees. And still they did not go home. It was a horse lot this time, a
tall rail fence upon and along which men stood and sat and out of which one
by one horses were led, to be walked and trotted and then cantered back and
forth along the road while the slow swapping and buying went on and the
sun began to slant westward, they—the three of them—watching and listening, the older brother with his muddy eyes and his steady, inevitable tobacco,
the father commenting now and then on certain of the animals, to no one in
particular.

It was after sundown when they reached home. They ate supper by lamp- 85
light, then, sitting on the doorstep, the boy watched the night fully accomplish, listening to the whippoorwills and the frogs, when he heard his
mother's voice: "Abner! No! No! Oh, God. Oh, God. Abner!" and he rose,
whirled, and saw the altered light through the door where a candle stub now
burned in a bottle neck on the table and his father, still in the hat and coat, at
once formal and burlesque as though dressed carefully for some shabby and
ceremonial violence, emptying the reservoir of the lamp back into the five-
gallon kerosene can from which it had been filled, while the mother tugged at
his arm until he shifted the lamp to the other hand and flung her back, not
savagely or viciously, just hard, into the wall, her hands flung out against the

wall for balance, her mouth open and in her face the same quality of hopeless despair as had been in her voice. Then his father saw him standing in the door.

"Go to the barn and get that can of oil we were oiling the wagon with," he said. The boy did not move. Then he could speak.

"What . . ." he cried. "What are you . . ."

"Go get that oil," his father said. "Go."

Then he was moving, running, outside the house, toward the stable: this the old habit, the old blood which he had not been permitted to choose for himself, which had been bequeathed him willy nilly and which had run for so long (and who knew where, battening on what of outrage and savagery and lust) before it came to him. *I could keep on,* he thought. *I could run on and on and never look back, never need to see his face again. Only I can't. I can't,* the rusted can in his hand now, the liquid sploshing in it as he ran back to the house and into it, into the sound of his mother's weeping in the next room, and handed the can to his father.

"Ain't you going to even send a nigger?" he cried. "At least you sent a nig-   90 ger before!"

This time his father didn't strike him. The hand came even faster than the blow had, the same hand which had set the can on the table with almost excruciating care flashing from the can toward him too quick for him to follow it, gripping him by the back of his shirt and on to tiptoe before he had seen it quit the can, the face stooping at him in breathless and frozen ferocity, the cold, dead voice speaking over him to the older brother who leaned against the table, chewing with that steady, curious, sidewise motion of cows:

"Empty the can into the big one and go on. I'll catch up with you."

"Better tie him up to the bedpost," the brother said.

"Do like I told you," the father said. Then the boy was moving, his bunched shirt and the hard, bony hand between his shoulder-blades, his toes just touching the floor, across the room and into the other one, past the sisters sitting with spread heavy thighs in the two chairs over the cold hearth, and to where his mother and aunt sat side by side on the bed, the aunt's arms about his mother's shoulders.

"Hold him," the father said. The aunt made a startled movement. "Not   95 you," the father said. "Lennie. Take hold of him. I want to see you do it." His mother took him by the wrist. "You'll hold him better than that. If he gets loose don't you know what he is going to do? He will go up yonder." He jerked his head toward the road. "Maybe I'd better tie him."

"I'll hold him," his mother whispered.

"See you do then." Then his father was gone, the stiff foot heavy and measured upon the boards, ceasing at last.

Then he began to struggle. His mother caught him in both arms, he jerking and wrenching at them. He would be stronger in the end, he knew that. But he had no time to wait for it. "Lemme go!" he cried. "I don't want to have to hit you!"

"Let him go!" the aunt said. "If he don't go, before God, I am going up there myself!"

"Don't you see I can't?" his mother cried. "Sarty! Sarty! No! No! Help me,   100 Lizzie!"

Then he was free. His aunt grasped at him but it was too late. He whirled, running, his mother stumbled forward on to her knees behind him, crying to the nearer sister. "Catch him, Net! Catch him!" But that was too late too, the sister (the sisters were twins, born at the same time, yet either of them now gave the impression of being, encompassing as much living meat and volume and weight as any other two of the family) not yet having begun to rise from the chair, her head, face, alone merely turned, presenting to him in the flying instant an astonishing expanse of young female features untroubled by any surprise even, wearing only an expression of bovine interest. Then he was out of the room, out of the house, in the mild dust of the starlit road and the heavy rifeness of honeysuckle, the pale ribbon unspooling with terrific slowness under his running feet, reaching the gate at last and turning in, running, his heart and lungs drumming, on up the drive toward the lighted house, the lighted door. He did not knock, he burst in, sobbing for breath, incapable for the moment of speech; he saw the astonished face of the Negro in the linen jacket without knowing when the Negro had appeared.

"De Spain!" he cried, panted. "Where's . . ." then he saw the white man too emerging from a white door down the hall. "Barn!" he cried. "Barn!"

"What?" the white man said. "Barn?"

"Yes!" the boy cried. "Barn!"

"Catch him!" the white man shouted.   105

But it was too late this time too. The Negro grasped his shirt, but the entire sleeve, rotten with washing, carried away, and he was out that door too and in the drive again, and had actually never ceased to run even while he was screaming into the white man's face.

Behind him the white man was shouting, "My horse! Fetch my horse!" and he thought for an instant of cutting across the park and climbing the fence into the road, but he did not know the park nor how high the vine-massed fence might be and he dared not risk it. So he ran on down the drive, blood and breath roaring; presently he was in the road again though he could not see it. He could not hear either: the galloping mare was almost upon him before he heard her, and even then he held his course, as if the very urgency of his wild grief and need must in a moment more find him wings, waiting until the ultimate instant to hurl himself aside and into the weed-choked roadside ditch as the horse thundered past and on, for an instant in furious silhouette against the stars, the tranquil early summer night sky which, even before the shape of the horse and rider vanished, strained abruptly and violently upward: a long, swirling roar incredible and soundless, blotting the stars, and he springing up and into the road again, running again, knowing it was too late yet still running even after he heard the shot and, an instant later, two shots, pausing now without knowing he had ceased to run, crying "Pap! Pap!," running again before he knew he had begun to run, stumbling, tripping over something and scrabbling up again without ceasing to run, looking backward over his shoulder at the glare as he got up, running on among the invisible trees, panting, sobbing, "Father! Father!"

At midnight he was sitting on the crest of a hill. He did not know it was midnight and he did not know how far he had come. But there was no glare behind him now and he sat now, his back toward what he had called home for four days anyhow, his face toward the dark woods which he would enter when breath was strong again, small, shaking steadily in the chill darkness, hugging himself into the remainder of his thin, rotten shirt, the grief and despair now no longer terror and fear but just grief and despair. *Father. My father,* he thought. "He was brave!" he cried suddenly, aloud but not loud, no more than a whisper: "He was! He was in the war! He was in Colonel Sartoris' cav'ry!" not knowing that his father had gone to that war a private in the fine old European sense, wearing no uniform, admitting the authority of and giving fidelity to no man or army or flag, going to war as Malbrouck° himself did: for booty — it meant nothing and less than nothing to him if it were enemy booty or his own.

The slow constellations wheeled on. It would be dawn and then sun-up after a while and he would be hungry. But that would be tomorrow and now he was only cold, and walking would cure that. His breathing was easier now and he decided to get up and go on, and then he found that he had been asleep because he knew it was almost dawn, the night almost over. He could tell that from the whippoorwills. They were everywhere now among the dark trees below him, constant and inflectioned and ceaseless, so that, as the instant for giving over to the day birds drew nearer and nearer, there was no interval at all between them. He got up. He was a little stiff, but walking would cure that too as it would the cold, and soon there would be the sun. He went on down the hill, toward the dark woods within which the liquid silver voices of the birds called unceasing — the rapid and urgent beating of the urgent and quiring heart of the late spring night. He did not look back.

Malbrouck: John Churchill, duke of Marlborough (1650-1722), English military commander who led the armies of England and Holland in the War of Spanish Succession.

CONSIDERATIONS FOR CRITICAL THINKING AND WRITING

1. FIRST RESPONSE. Who is "Barn Burning" about? Explain your choice.

2. Explain why Sarty is a dynamic or a static character. Which term best describes his father? Why?

3. Who is the central character in this story? Explain your choice.

4. How are Sarty's emotions revealed in the story's opening paragraphs? What seems to be the function of the italicized passages there and elsewhere?

5. What do we learn from the story's exposition that helps us understand Abner's character? How does his behavior reveal his character? What do other people say about him?

6. How does Faulkner's physical description of Abner further our understanding of his personality?

7. Explain how the justice of the peace, Mr. Harris, and Major de Spain serve as foils to Abner. Discuss whether you think they are round or flat characters.

8. Who are the story's stock characters? What is their purpose?

9. Explain how the description of Major de Spain's house helps to frame the main conflicts that Sarty experiences in his efforts to remain loyal to his father.

10. Write an essay describing Sarty's attitudes toward his father as they develop and change throughout the story.

11. What do you think happens to Sarty's father and brother at the end of the story? How does your response to this question affect your reading of the last paragraph?

12. How does the language of the final paragraph suggest a kind of resolution to the conflicts Sarty has experienced?

CONNECTIONS TO OTHER SELECTIONS

1. Compare and contrast Faulkner's characterizations of Abner Snopes in this story and Miss Emily in "A Rose for Emily" (p. 75). How does the author generate sympathy for each character even though both are guilty of terrible crimes? Which character do you find more sympathetic? Explain why.

2. How does Abner Snopes's motivation for revenge compare with Matt Fowler's in Andre Dubus's "Killings" (p. 84)? How do the victims of each character's revenge differ and thereby help to shape the meanings of each story?

3. Read the section on mythological criticism in Chapter 52, "Critical Strategies for Reading." How do you think a mythological critic would make sense of Sarty Snopes and Matt Fowler?

PERSPECTIVES ON FAULKNER

JANE HILES (B. 1951)

Hiles uses a biographical approach (see pp. 2097–99 in Chapter 52, "Critical Strategies for Reading") to determine Faulkner's intentions in his characterization of how Sarty responds to the conflicts he feels about his father.

Blood Ties in "Barn Burning"   1985

" 'You're getting to be a man. . . . You got to learn to stick to your own blood or you ain't going to have any blood to stick to you' ": Abner Snopes's admonition to his son, Colonel Sartoris (or "Sarty"), introduces a central issue in Faulkner's "Barn Burning" — the kinship bond, which the story's narrator calls the "old fierce pull of blood." The interpretive crux of the work is a conflict between determinism, represented by the blood tie that binds Sarty to his clan, and free will, dramatized by the boy's ultimate repudiation of family ties and his decampment. Dissonances between the structure and the imagery of the work develop and amplify Sarty's conflict: viewed in the light of the narrator's deterministic assumptions, the story's denouement is a red herring which only appears to resolve the complexities created by evocative language. Sarty's seeming interruption of the antisocial pattern established by his father is actually a continuation of it, and the ostensible resolution of his moral dilemma actually no resolution at all. . . .

In an interview in Japan sixteen years after the publication of "Barn Burning," Faulkner delivered an appraisal of the phenomenon of clannishness that bears considerable relevance to Abner Snopes's defensive posture in "Barn Burning":

Yes, we are country people and we have never had too much in material possessions because 60 or 70 years ago we were invaded and we were conquered.

So we have been thrown back on our selves not only for entertainment but certain [sic] amount of defense. We have to be clannish just like the people in the Scottish highlands, each springing to defend his own blood whether it be right or wrong. Just a matter of custom and habit, we have to do it; interrelated that way, and usually there is hereditary head [sic] of the whole lot, as usually, the oldest son of the oldest son and each looked upon as chief of his own particular clan. That is the tone they live by. But I am sure it is because only a comparatively short time ago we were invaded by our own people — speaking in our own language which is always a pretty savage sort of warfare.

In Faulkner's estimation, the old pull of blood transcends considerations of caste, class, and occupation:

> . . . [I]t is regional. It is through what we call the "South." It doesn't matter what the people do. They can be land people, farmers, and industrialists, but there still exists the feeling of blood, of clan, blood for blood. It is pretty general through all the classes.[1]

Faulkner's explanation of the phenomenon of Southern clannishness touches upon a number of the issues that arise in "Barn Burning." In each case, alienation from the politically and economically dominant group leads to dependence upon an alternative source of security. Just as beleaguered Southerners, Faulkner suggests, have had to look to themselves for "defense" since the South was defeated, so Ab Snopes must turn to his kin for defense not only from Union troops but also from the landed Southern aristocrat who, in what Ab perceives as a failure of paternalism, "aims to begin . . . owning [him] body and soul." The clan's identifying characteristic, then, is its orientation to survival. Perhaps most interestingly, the comments made in the interview impinge upon the central issue of the morality of Sarty's choice. Faulkner's recognition here of a private code of honor suggests that Sarty's conduct is somewhat more questionable than is generally recognized, and his articulation in the interview of a necessity for clannishness suggests at least a modicum of sympathy for the "custom and habit" of "each springing to defend his own blood whether it be right or wrong."

From *Mississippi Quarterly: The Journal of Southern Culture*

[1]James B. Meriwether and Michael Millgate, eds., *Lion in the Garden* (New York: Random House, 1968), p. 191.

CONSIDERATIONS FOR CRITICAL THINKING AND WRITING

1. To what extent does Faulkner's description of clannishness in the South affect your understanding of whether Sarty resolves his dilemma at the end of the story?

2. Do you agree with Hiles that "Sarty's conduct is somewhat more questionable than is generally recognized" (para. 4)?

BENJAMIN DEMOTT (B. 1924)

DeMott pays close attention to matters of culture, race, class, and power that affect Abner Snopes, and from those perspectives Abner is seen as more than simply malevolent.

Abner Snopes as a Victim of Class   1988

We know that Ab Snopes is harsh to his wife, his sons, and his daughters, and that he is particularly cruel to his stock. We know that his hatred of the planters with whom he enters into sharecropping agreements repeatedly issues in acts of wanton destruction. We know that he's ridden with suspicion of his own closest kin, expecting them to betray him. And we know that — worse than any of this — he often behaves with fearful coldness to those who try desperately to communicate the loving respect they feel for him.

Given such a combination of racism, destructiveness, and blank insensitivity, it's tempting to imagine Ab as a figure in whom ignorance and brutality obliterate every sympathetic impulse, every normative response to peace, dignity, or beauty. Major de Spain seems to reach something close to that conclusion after the rug-laundering episode ("Wasn't there anybody here, any of your women . . ."). And although Ab's son is intensely loyal to his father and indignant at the injustice of the Major's twenty-bushel "charge" for the destruction of the rug, Sarty clearly has a conviction that "peace and dignity" are somehow *"beyond his [father's] touch, he no more to them than a buzzing wasp."* Is there anything to be made of Ab Snopes except a person whose raging malevolence has badly stunted if not crippled his humanity?

Denying the force of the malevolence is impossible — but tracing it solely to ignorance and insensitivity falsifies Ab's nature. Uneducated, probably illiterate, schooled in none of the revolutionary traditions which, in urban settings, were shaping popular protests against "economic injustice" when this story was written in the late 1930s, Ab nevertheless has managed, through the exercise of his own primitive intelligence, to make sense of his world, to arrive at a vision of the relations between labor, money, and the beautiful. It's a vision that's miles away from transforming itself into a broadly historical account of capital accumulation. Ab Snopes can't frame a theory to himself about, say, proletarian enslavement; he has no language in which to imagine a class solidarity leading to political action aimed at securing justice and truth. Indeed, he would explode at the notion that considerations of truth and justice have any pertinence either to the interests of the authorities opposing him or to his own interests in defying them. ("Later, twenty years later, [Sarty] was to tell himself, 'If I had said they wanted only truth, justice, he would have hit me again.'") For Ab Snopes the only principle lending significance to his war with the de Spains of this world is that of blood loyalty — determination to beat your personal enemy if you can and keep faith, at all costs, with your clan.

Yet despite all this, Ab does see that part of the power of the beautiful and the orderly to command our respect depends upon our refusal to remind ourselves that they have been brought into existence by other people's labor — by effort that often in history has been slave labor and has seldom been fairly recompensed. Sarty Snopes, grown up, presumably arrives finally at an understanding both that his father's situation was one of economic oppression and that the oppressors, when sitting in a court of law, are capable of attempting to reach beyond selfishness to a decent distribution of justice. But his father had, at the time, no grip on any of this.

Yet Ab is not a fool, and brutality and insensitivity are not the only features of character that we can make out in him. What we need also to summon is the terrible frustration of an undeveloped mind — aware of the weight of an immense unfairness, aware of the habit of the weak perpetually to behave as though the elegance, grace, beauty, and order found often in the neighborhoods of the rich somehow were traceable exclusively to the superior nature of the rich — and yet unable to move forward from either awareness to anything approaching rational protest. His rage cannot become a force leading toward any positive principle; it has no way to express itself except in viciousness to those closest at hand. It can't begin to make a serious bid for admiration, because whatever inclination we might have to admire it is instantly crossed by repugnance at the cruelty inherent in it.

But it remains true that, together with the ignorance and brutality in Ab Snopes, there is a ferocious, primitive undeceivedness in his reading of the terms of the relationship between rich and poor, lucky and unlucky, advantaged and disadvantaged. Ab Snopes has seen a portion of the truth of the world that many on his level, and most who are luckier, never see. We can damn him for allowing that truth to wreck his humanity, but when we fully bring him to life as a character, it's impossible not to include with our indictment a sense of pity.

From *Close Imagining: An Introduction to Literature*

CONSIDERATIONS FOR CRITICAL THINKING AND WRITING

1. DeMott acknowledges Abner's ignorance and brutality, but he also presents him as a man who suffers injustices. What are those injustices? Discuss whether you think they warrant a more balanced assessment of Abner's character.

2. Why doesn't Abner protest his "oppression" (para. 4)? Given DeMott's perspective on him, how might Abner — in another story — have been the hero rather than a terrible source of conflict?

3. To what extent can DeMott's approach to Abner's circumstances be described as a Marxist perspective? (For a discussion of Marxist criticism see p. 2103.)

GAYLE EDWARD WILSON (B. 1931)

The following analysis combines psychology and myth as a means of understanding the conflicts in "Barn Burning." The "Apollonian man" alluded to in the discussion (para. 1) refers to the myth of Apollo and implies a person who values order, community, balance, and self-knowledge to establish true relations between the individual and his world.

Conflict in "Barn Burning"   1990

Ruth Benedict's descriptions of two major patterns of culture provide an advantageous starting point for a discussion of the way in which Faulkner develops the content of "Barn Burning." The Paranoid way of life, she comments, has "no political organization. In a strict sense it has no legality."[1] As a consequence of the Paranoid man's adherence to this life-style, he is "lawless," and is feared as a warrior who will hesitate "at no treachery" (p. 121). In such a culture, "every man's

[1] *Patterns of Culture* (New York, 1959), p. 122.

hand is against every other man," and as a result each man relies upon blood ties to form social alliances and to sanction his actions (pp. 122–123). The Apollonian man, on the other hand, "keeps to the middle of the road, stays within the known map," and strives to fulfill his civic role in terms of the expectations of the community at large (p. 70). Men in such a society, although the blood tie is relatively important as a bond, turn to the community and its collected wisdom, as it is embodied in the law, for the approval of their actions and for their security. Thus the sanction for a man's "acts comes from the formal structure, not the individual" (p. 99) — from the community, not the blood kin. In "Barn Burning" Faulkner develops the ideas contained in these descriptions of dissimilar life-styles in a way which creates the central tension in the story and keeps it constantly before the reader. The reader is thus made aware of the pervasiveness of Sarty's *"terror and the grief, the being pulled two ways like between two teams of horses."*

The tension is made evident by the presence of effects which follow from actions taken in accord with the dominant characteristic of each life-style. Abner's "wolflike independence . . . his latent ravening ferocity . . . [and] conviction in the rightness of his own actions," which have frequently manifested themselves in acts of destruction against the property of an established community, clearly mark him as a follower of the Paranoid way. As such, his actions inevitably, and repeatedly, alienate him from each settled society into which he moves. His disregard for a "formal structure" of any kind is indicated by such a minor detail as that which occurs when Abner fuels his fire with "a rail lifted from a nearby fence and cut into lengths," an act which is symbolic of his rejection of any societally imposed limits. It is by burning barns, however, that Abner's Paranoid life-style and its consequences are most forcefully dramatized. At Abner's trial for barn burning, Sarty sees the men "between himself and the table part and become a lane of grim faces." Abner and Sarty then walk between the "two lines of grim-faced men" and they leave a "quiet crowd of grimly watching men." This separation of the Snopes family from the larger society as a consequence of acts motivated by Abner's "ravening ferocity" is underscored by the Justice's command to Abner: "Take your wagon and get out of this country before dark." The Snopes's wagon, containing "the sorry residue of the dozen and more movings," becomes, therefore, a symbol of the transient and nomadic way of life which the Snopes family is forced to adopt because of Abner's adherence to the Paranoid way. The de Spain tenant house and the manner in which the Snopes family lives in it are also effects of a life-style which is not concerned with permanence or order or boundaries or limits. The house is a "paintless two-room" structure "identical almost with the dozen others" in which the family has lived as a result of its nomadic existence, and the members of the family are found "scattered without order or claim up and down the two rooms."

On the other hand, the Harris and de Spain barns represent productivity and fertility, permanence and continuity, because they house the equipment, stock, and seed by which a society produces the goods to sustain and perpetuate itself. A barn and its contents are the effects of a society which is built upon the willingness of men to subordinate their unfettered desires to a communal consensus in order to develop a permanent community. The importance of a barn to the Apollonian way is illustrated by Sarty's thoughts when he sees the effect brought about by what a barn symbolizes. When he comes upon the de Spain house for the first time, he feels that *"the spell"* of *"peace and dignity"* cast by the magnificent house will render *"even the barns and stable and cribs which belong to it impervious to the puny flames he* [Abner] *might contrive.*" The sight of this apotheosis of the Apollonian way has a profound effect on Sarty: he "at that instant . . . forgot his father. . . ." It is most revealing that Sartoris should compare this house which symbolizes the *"peace and dignity"* of the Apollonian way with another kind of building which, because of what it represents, embodies the very essence of an ordered society: *"Hit's big as a courthouse* he thought quietly, with a surge of peace and joy."

Essentially, it is the concept of law, as symbolized by the de Spain house, that gives Sarty his sense of "peace and joy," for it is the law that provides man with the peace necessary to develop the "formal structure" of a communal, stable society. Without law, as Hobbes tells us, "there is no place for Industry; because the fruit thereof is uncertain: and consequently no Culture of the Earth; . . . no commodius Building; . . . no Society; and which is worst of all, continuall feare, and danger of violent death; And the life of man, solitary, poore, nasty, brutish, and short."[2] At its best, the law is moderate, even, and impartial. It protects as well as punishes; it is an elaborately worked out system designed to join men together in a common purpose, to insure the presumption of innocence until guilt is proved, and to make the punishment commensurate with the crime. In "Barn Burning" the primacy of the law in an Apollonian society is made quite evident. It is represented in a minor way by the contract in which Snopes engages with de Spain to work for eight months in return for a share of the crop. It is developed in a major way in the two trials which take place. In the first trial, the law protects Abner from unwarranted conclusions. Concerning the charge that Abner burned Harris's barn, the Justice asks Harris, "But what proof have you, Mr. Harris?" Harris tells of the Negro who appeared and gave him the cryptic message, "'wood and hay kin burn,'" to which the Justice replies, "But that's not proof. Don't you see that's not proof?" In the second trial, de Spain's unreasonable assessment of twenty bushels of corn in payment for the rug Abner ruined is not allowed. Abner is fined ten bushels, not twenty, as de Spain had wanted. For the men in "Barn Burning," . . . then, the law and its equitable application to all men is the *sine qua non* of the Apollonian way. . . . It is this belief in the law and its extensions of "justice" and "civilization" which guides and controls the behavior of the Apollonian man. This is the same realization that young Sarty is only able to articulate "twenty years" after Abner strikes him for not being willing to lie in his defense at the trial. " 'If I had said they only wanted truth, justice, he would have hit me again.' "

From *Mississippi Quarterly*

[2] Chapter XIII, "*Of the NATURAL CONDITION of Mankind, as concerning their Felicity, and Misery,*" *Leviathan* . . . (1651) in *Seventeenth-Century Verse and Prose,* ed. Helen White, Ruth Wallerstein, and Ricardo Quintana (New York, 1967), I, 223.

CONSIDERATIONS FOR CRITICAL THINKING AND WRITING

1. What distinctions are drawn between the "Paranoid man" and the "Apollonian man" (para. 1)? How do these two different types serve to frame the conflicts in "Barn Burning"?

2. How is Snopes's wagon an appropriate symbol of the "Paranoid way" (para. 1), and how are the Harris and de Spain barns fitting symbols of the "Apollonian way" (para. 3)?

3. In an essay explain why you think Sarty chooses one way of life over the other at the end of the story.

4. Compare Wilson's description of the story's conflicts with Hiles's and DeMott's.

JAMES FERGUSON (B. 1928)

Ferguson's formalist approach (see pp. 2095–97 in Chapter 52, "Critical Strategies for Reading") relates Faulkner's use of point of view to his thematic concerns in the story.

Narrative Strategy in "Barn Burning"   1991

The point of view is largely limited to the consciousness of Sarty Snopes, but in spite of his sensitivity and his intuitive sense of right and wrong, the little boy is far too young to understand his father and the complexities of the moral choice he must make. To enhance the pathos of his situation and the drama of Sarty's initiation into life, Faulkner felt the need for the occasional intrusion of an authorial voice giving the reader insights far beyond the capabilities of the youthful protagonist. A passage, for example, about the fires Abner Snopes builds affords us a sense of the rationale for the man's actions, of his strangely perverse integrity, which could not be supplied to us by the consciousness of his son:

> The nights were still cool and they had a fire against it, of a rail lifted from a nearby fence and cut into lengths — a small fire, neat, niggard almost, a shrewd fire; such fires were his father's habit and custom always, even in freezing weather. Older, the boy might have remarked this and wondered why not a big one; why should not a man who had not only seen the waste and extravagance of war, but who had in his blood an inherent voracious prodigality with material not his own, have burned everything in sight? Then he might have gone a step farther and thought that that was the reason: that niggard blaze was the living fruit of nights passed during those four years in the woods hiding from all men, blue or gray, with his strings of horses (captured horses, he called them). And older still, he might have divined the true reason: that the element of fire spoke to some deep mainspring of his father's being, as the element of steel or of powder spoke to other men, as the one weapon for the preservation of integrity, else breath were not worth the breathing, and hence to be regarded with respect and used with discretion.

Again, near the end of the story, after Sarty has betrayed his father, there is another brief shift away from the consciousness of the protagonist:

> "He was brave!" he cried suddenly, aloud but not loud, no more than a whisper: "He was! He was in the war! He was in Colonel Sartoris' cav'ry!" not knowing that his father had gone to that war a private in the fine old European sense, wearing no uniform, admitting the authority of and giving fidelity to no man or army or flag, going to war as Malbrouck himself did: for booty — it meant nothing and less than nothing to him if it were enemy booty or his own.

"Barn Burning" is incomparably richer than it would have been without such additions not only because they supply us with ironies otherwise unavailable to us but also because these manipulations of point of view dramatize *on the level of technique* the thematic matter of the story. The tensions between the awareness of the boy and the information supplied us by the authorial voice undergird and emphasize the conflicts between youth and age, innocence and sophistication, intuition and abstraction, decency and corruption, all of which lie at the core of the work.

From *Faulkner's Short Fiction*

CONSIDERATIONS FOR CRITICAL THINKING AND WRITING

1. In the first passage quoted by Ferguson how does the narrator's analysis of Abner Snopes become progressively sophisticated in explaining his reasons for building a small fire?

2. What other examples of shifts away from the consciousness of Sarty to a more informed point of view can you find in the story? Choose what you judge to be a significant example and write an essay about how Faulkner's use of point of view contributes to the story's themes.

QUESTIONS FOR WRITING
Incorporating the Critics

The following questions can help you to incorporate materials from critical essays into your own writing about a literary work. You may initially feel intimidated by the prospect of responding to the arguments of professional critics in your own paper. However, the process will not defeat you if you have clearly formulated your own response to the literary work and are able to distinguish it from the critics' perspectives. Reading the critics can help you to develop your own thesis — perhaps, to cite just two examples, by using them as supporting evidence or by arguing with them in order to clarify or qualify their points about the literary work. As you write and discover how to advance your thesis, you'll find yourself participating in a dialogue with the critics. This sort of conversation will help you to improve your thinking and hone your argument.

Keep in mind that the work of professional critics is a means of enriching your understanding of a literary work rather than a substitution for your own analysis and interpretation of that work. Quoting, paraphrasing, or summarizing a critic's perspective does not relieve you of the obligation of choosing a topic, organizing information, developing a thesis, and arguing your point of view by citing sufficient evidence from the text you are examining. These matters are discussed in further detail in Chapter 53, "Reading and Writing." You should also be familiar with the methods for documenting sources that are explained in Chapter 54, "The Literary Research Paper"; this chapter also contains important information about how to avoid plagiarism.

No doubt you won't find all literary criticism equally useful: some critics' arguments won't address your own areas of concern; some will be too difficult for you to get a handle on; and some will seem wrong-headed. However, much of the criticism you read will serve to make a literary work more accessible and interesting to you, and disagreeing with others' arguments will often help you to develop your own ideas about a work. When you use the work of critics in your own writing, you should consider the following questions. Responding to these questions will help you to ensure that you have a clear understanding of what a critic is arguing about a work, to what extent you agree with that argument, and how you plan to incorporate and respond to the critic's reading in your own paper. The more questions you can ask yourself in response to this list or as a result of your own reading, the more you'll be able to think critically about how you are approaching both the critics and the literary work under consideration.

1. Have you read the literary work carefully and taken notes of your own impressions before reading any critical perspectives so that your initial insights are not lost to the arguments made by the critics? Have you articulated your own responses to the work in a journal entry prior to reading the critics?

2. Are you sufficiently familiar with the literary work that you can determine the accuracy, fairness, and thoroughness of the critic's use of evidence from the work?

3. Have you read the critic's piece carefully? Try summarizing the critic's argument in a brief paragraph. Do you understand the nature and purpose of the critic's argument? Which passages are especially helpful to you? Which seem unclear? Why?

4. Is the critic's reading of the literary work similar to or different from your own reading? Why do you agree or disagree? What generational, historical, cultural, or biographical considerations might help to account for any differences between the critic's responses and your own?

5. How has your reading of the critic influenced your understanding of the literary work? Do issues that previously seemed unimportant now seem significant? What are these issues, and how does a consideration of them affect your reading of the work?

6. Are you too quickly revising or even discarding your own reading because the critic's perspective seems so polished and persuasive? Are you making use of your reading notes and the responses in your journal entries?

7. How would you classify the critic's approach? Through what kind of lens does the critic view the literary work? Is the critical approach formalist, biographical, psychological, sociological, mythological, reader-response, deconstructionist, or some combination of these or possibly other strategies? (For a discussion of these approaches, see Chapter 52, "Critical Strategies for Reading.")

8. What biases, if any, can you detect in the critic's approach? How might, for example, a southern critic's reading of "Barn Burning" differ from a northern critic's?

9. Can you determine how other critics have responded to the critic's work? Is the critic's work cited and taken seriously in other critics'

books and articles? Is the work dated by having been superseded by subsequent studies?

10. Are any passages or topics that you deem important left out by the critic? Do these omissions qualify or refute the critic's argument?

11. What judgments does the critic seem to make about the work? Is the work regarded, for example, as significant, unified, representative, trivial, inept, or irresponsible? Do you agree with these judgments? If not, can you develop and support a thesis about your difference of opinion?

12. What important disagreements do critics reveal in their approaches to the work? Do you find one perspective more convincing than another? Why? Is there a way of resolving their conflicting views that could serve as a thesis for your paper?

13. Can you extend or qualify the critic's argument to matters in the literary text that are not covered by the critic's perspective? Will this allow you to develop your own topic while acknowledging the critic's useful insights?

14. Have you quoted, paraphrased, or summarized the critic accurately and fairly? Have you avoided misrepresenting the critic's arguments in any way?

15. Are the critic's words, ideas, opinions, and insights adequately acknowledged and documented in the correct format? Do you understand the difference between common knowledge and plagiarism? Have you avoided quoting excessively? Are the quotations smoothly integrated into your own text?

16. Are you certain that your incorporation of the critic's work is for the purpose of developing your paper's thesis rather than for name-dropping or padding your paper? How can you explain to yourself why the critic's work is useful for your argument?

AN EXCERPT FROM A SAMPLE PAPER

The Fires of Class Conflict in "Barn Burning"

The following excerpt consists of the first few paragraphs of a sample student paper in which the student develops a thesis based on her reading of critical perspectives by Benjamin DeMott (p. 508) and Gayle Edward Wilson (p. 509). Sonia Metzger uses the two critics' different approaches to "Barn Burning" to develop a thesis that goes beyond either critic's perspective. The rest of her paper (not included) argues her thesis that a recognition of the class conflicts suppressed by Faulkner in the story makes Abner Snopes's violent response to the economic power inherent in Major de Spain's Apollonian values appear to be justifiable, rather than merely the desperate activity of a Paranoid man. Abner has good reason to fear Apollonian values because de Spain's world is carefully constructed to exclude him while simultaneously exploiting him.

Sonia Metzger
Professor Wolf
English 109
April 15, 20--

The Fires of Class Conflict in

"Barn Burning"

The central conflict in William Faulkner's "Barn Burning" concerns a young boy named Sarty Snopes who must
choose between loyalty to his father and his family and
loyalty to society and humanity. A first reading of the
story probably leaves most readers with the sense that the
boy must turn away from his father's vicious sensibilities
if he is to grow into a responsible adult. Sarty faces
tremendous pressure from his father to lie in court so
that his father will not be convicted of barn burning. He
knows his father wants him "to stick to your own blood or
you ain't going to have any blood to stick to you" (496;
all page references are to the class text, The Bedford
Introduction to Literature, 6th ed.).

Unlike the selfish, mean, vengeful father who despises
the wealth and gentility of the southern aristocracy and
is relentless in his contempt for the upper-class world of
Major de Spain, Sarty is a gentle, vulnerable character
who engages our sympathy. He is divided between wanting
his father's love and loving the "peace and dignity" (497)
that de Spain's house evokes within him. Gayle Edward Wilson, one of the critics I've read, mostly agrees with this
view of the story's conflict, but Benjamin DeMott goes beyond the focus on Sarty's conflicted conscience to examine
another, more subtle dimension of the story--the reasons
for Abner Snopes's ferocious rejection of the world he
wants to burn down.

Our understanding of Abner and his son is, according

to Wilson, deepened by employing two concepts from Ruth
Benedict's <u>Patterns of Culture</u> that she calls the "Paranoid man" and the "Apollonian man." Abner is a version of
the Paranoid man. His culture consists of a lawless, clannish, fierce world in which his nomadic, lonely existence
is characterized by violence, hatred, force, and destruction. Except for blood ties, he rejects forms of any kind:
the stability created by the Apollonian man (Major de
Spain) through law and order in a community is his enemy.
He will not be bound by any societal regulations; instead,
he destroys any sense of community through his barn burning and his erratic antisocial behavior. For Wilson, Sarty
must turn away from the Paranoid man to the Apollonian man
if he is to pledge his loyalty to justice and civilization
(511). This conflict is also recognized by Benjamin DeMott,
who acknowledges Abner's harshness, cruelty, destructiveness, paranoia, and coldness but who also raises an important question that shifts some of our focus from Sarty
onto Abner: "Is there anything to be made of Ab Snopes
except a person whose raging malevolence has badly stunted
if not crippled his humanity?" (508).

By considering when "Barn Burning" was written--
during the depression of the late 1930s--DeMott suggests a
kind of defense for understanding and even sympathizing
with Abner by pointing to issues of class and power embedded in the capitalistic culture and the nearly slave-labor
conditions endured by Abner. This version of Abner is not
merely brutish but also suffering from "the terrible frustration of an undeveloped mind--aware of the weight of an
immense unfairness . . . and yet unable to move forward . . .
to anything approaching rational protest" (508-09). DeMott
suggests that Abner warrants our pity rather than total
repudiation and that he, however imperfectly, does feel

(even if he doesn't comprehend) the pain produced by the miserable gap between the rich and the poor. With this gap in mind, I want to go further than DeMott goes and argue, using Wilson's categories, that Faulkner's portrayal of Apollonian values avoids confronting the economic oppression that Abner experiences but that neither he nor Sarty can articulate. Abner may fit much of the description associated with the Paranoid man, but there are important social reasons for his rightfully fearing the economic power of the Apollonian man.

SUGGESTED TOPICS FOR LONGER PAPERS

1. Write a character analysis of Abner Snopes. Does he change or develop through the course of the story? Do you identify with him in any way? Think about whether or not his behavior is criminal, insane, or heroic.

2. A great many articles and portions of books have been written about "Barn Burning." Scan these sources to get an overview of the kinds of critical approaches that have been applied to the story, and write a selective survey of how criticism about "Barn Burning" has evolved over the past three or four decades. Which approaches seem the most useful and revealing to you?

3. MULTIMEDIA PROJECT. Look for photographs, paintings, drawings, and written descriptions of the kind of grand late nineteenth-century house that Major de Spain lives in and compare those treatments with the thematic significance that Faulkner invests in the house in paragraph 41 of the story. To what extent does Faulkner reflect, idealize, or qualify the representations of such southern houses in his story?

Web *For help with this project, use the Multimedia Project Guides Online at* http://www.bedfordstmartins.com/meyer/bedintrolit

15

A Cultural Case Study: James Joyce's "Eveline"

Close reading is an essential and important means of appreciating the literary art of a text. This formalist approach to literature explores the subtle, complex relationships between how a work is constructed using elements such as plot, characterization, point of view, diction, metaphor, symbol, irony, and other literary techniques to create a coherent structure that contributes to a work's meaning. (For a more detailed discussion of formalistic approaches to literary works, see Chapter 52, "Critical Strategies for Reading.") The formalist focuses on the text itself rather than the historical, political, economic, and other contexts of a text. A formalist reading of *The Scarlet Letter*, for example, is more likely to examine how the book is structured around a series of scenes in which the main characters appear on or near the town scaffold than to analyze how the text portrays the social and religious values of Nathaniel Hawthorne or of seventeenth-century Puritan New Englanders. Although recent literary criticism has continued to demonstrate the importance of close readings to discover how a text creates its effects on a reader, scholars also have made a sustained effort to place literary texts in their historical and cultural contexts.

Cultural critics, like literary historians, place literary works in the contexts of their times, but they do not restrict themselves to major historical moments or figures. Instead of focusing on, perhaps, Hawthorne's friendship with Herman Melville, a cultural critic might examine the relationship between Hawthorne's writing and popular contemporary domestic novels that are now obscure. Cultural critics might even examine the Classic Comic book version of *The Scarlet Letter* or one of its many film versions to gain insight into how our culture has reinterpreted Hawthorne's writing. The materials used by cultural critics are taken from both "high culture" and popular culture. A cultural critic's approach to James Joyce's work might include discussions of Dublin's saloons, political pamphlets, and Catholic sexual mores as well as connections to Ezra Pound or T. S. Eliot.

The documents that follow Joyce's "Eveline" in this chapter offer a glimpse of how cultural criticism can be used to provide a rich and revealing historical context for a literary work. They include an early twentieth-century photograph of Dublin, a portion of a temperance tract, a letter from an Irish woman who emigrated to Australia, and a plot synopsis of the opera *The Bohemian Girl:* all these documents figure in one way or another in "Eveline." These documents are suggestive rather than exhaustive, but they do evoke some of the culture contemporary to Joyce that informs the world he creates in "Eveline" and thereby allow readers to gain a broader and deeper understanding of the story itself.

JAMES JOYCE (1882–1941)

James Joyce was born in Dublin, Ireland, during a time of political upheaval. The country had endured nearly a century of economic depression and terrible famine and continued to suffer under what many Irish regarded as British oppression. Irish nationalism and independence movements attempted to counter British economic exploitation and cultural arrogance. Joyce, influenced by a climate in which ecclesiastical privilege and governmental authority were at once powerful and suspect, believed the Irish were also unable to free themselves from the Catholic Church's compromises and their own political ineptitude. Change was in the air, but Ireland was slow to be moved by the reform currents already rippling through the Continent.

Modernism, as it was developing on the Continent, challenged traditional attitudes about God, humanity, and society. Scientific and industrial advances created not only material progress but also tremendous social upheaval, which sometimes produced a sense of discontinuity, fragmentation, alienation, and despair. Firm certainties gave way to anxious doubts, and the past was considered more as something to be overcome than as something to revere. Heroic action seemed remote and theatrical to a writer like Joyce, who rejected the use of remarkable historic events in his fiction and instead focused on the everyday lives of ordinary people trying to make sense of themselves.

Joyce himself came from a declining middle-class family of more than a dozen children, eventually reduced to poverty by his father's drinking. Nevertheless, Joyce received a fine classical education at Jesuit schools, including University College, Dublin. His strict early education was strongly traditional in its Catholicism, but when he entered University College, he rejected both his religion and his national heritage. By the time he took his undergraduate degree in 1902, he was more comfortable casting himself as an alienated writer than as a typical citizen of Dublin, who he thought

*James Joyce and Sylvia Beach, proprietor of the Parisian bookstore Shakespeare &
Company, together in Paris during the "roaring twenties." In 1920 James Joyce and his
family relocated to Paris, and in 1922 Beach published the first edition of* Ulysses.
Reprinted by permission of Corbis-Bettmann.

lived a life of mediocrity, sentimentality, and self-deception. While at college he studied modern languages and taught himself Norwegian so he
could read the plays of Henrik Ibsen in their original language (see p. 1568
for Ibsen's *A Doll House*). Joyce responded deeply to Ibsen's dramatizations
of troubled individuals who repudiate public morality and social values in

their efforts to create lives of integrity amid stifling families, institutions, and cultures.

After graduation Joyce left Dublin for Paris to study medicine, but that career soon ended when he dropped out of the single course for which he had registered. Instead, he wrote poetry, which was eventually published in 1907 as *Chamber Music*. In 1903 he returned to Dublin to be with his mother, then dying of cancer. The next summer he met Nora Barnacle, while she was working in a Dublin boardinghouse. After leaving Dublin with Nora in 1905 to return to the Continent, he visited his native city only a few times (the final visit was in 1912), and he lived the rest of his life in Europe. From 1920 until shortly before his death, Joyce settled in Paris, where he enjoyed the stimulation of living amid writers and artists. He lived with Nora his entire life, having two children and eventually marrying her in 1931.

Joyce earned a living by teaching at a Berlitz language school, tutoring, and working in a bank, but mostly he gathered impressions of the world around him — whether in Trieste, Zurich, Rome, or Paris — that he would incorporate into his literary work. His writings, however, were always about life in Ireland rather than the European cities in which he lived. Fortunately, Joyce's talents attracted several patrons who subsidized his income and helped him to publish.

Dubliners, Joyce's first major publication in fiction, was a collection of stories that he published in 1914 and that included "Eveline." Two years later Joyce published *A Portrait of the Artist as a Young Man,* a novel. Joyce strongly identified with the protagonist, who, like Joyce, rejected custom and tradition. If the price of independence from deadening sensibilities, crass materialism, and a circumscribed life was alienation, then so be it. Joyce believed that if the artist was to see clearly and report what he saw freshly, it was necessary to stand outside the commonplace responses to experience derived from family, church, or country. His next novel, *Ulysses* (1922), is regarded by many readers as Joyce's masterpiece. This remarkably innovative novel is an account of one day in the life of an Irish Jew named Leopold Bloom, who, despite his rather ordinary life in Dublin, represents a microcosm of all human experience. Joyce's stream-of-consciousness technique revealed the characters' thoughts as they experienced them (see pp. 174–75 for a discussion of this technique). These uninhibited thoughts were censored in the United States until 1933, when a judge ruled in a celebrated court case that the book was not obscene. Though *Ulysses* is Joyce's most famous book, *Finnegans Wake* (1939) is his most challenging. Even more unconventional and experimental than *Ulysses,* it endlessly plays with language within a fluid dream world in which the characters' experiences evolve into continuously expanding meanings produced through complex allusions and elaborate puns in multiple languages. The novel's plot defies summation, but its language warrants exploration, which is perhaps best begun by hearing a recording of Joyce reading aloud from the book. His stylistic innovations in *Ulysses* and *Finnegans Wake* had as great an influence on literature as the automobile and the radio did on people's daily lives, when people started covering more ground and hearing more voices than ever before.

Dubliners is Joyce's quarrel with his native city, and his homage to it. Written between 1904 and 1907, it is the most accessible of Joyce's works. It consists of a series of fifteen stories about characters who struggle with oppressive morality, plodding routines, somber shadows, self-conscious decency, restless desires, and frail gestures toward freedom. These stories contain no conventional high drama or action-filled episodes; instead, they are made up of small, quiet moments that turn out to be important in their characters' lives. Most of the characters are on the brink of discovering something, such as loss, shame, failure, or death. Typically, the protagonist suddenly experiences a deep realization about himself or herself, a truth that is grasped in an ordinary rather than melodramatic moment. Joyce called such a moment—when a character is overcome by a flash of recognition—an *epiphany* and defined it as "sudden spiritual manifestation, whether in the vulgarity of speech or gesture or in a memorable phase of the mind itself." Even the most commonplace experience might yield a spontaneous insight into the essential nature of a person or situation. Joyce's characters may live ordinary lives cluttered with mundane details, but their lives have significance. Indeed, they seem to stumble onto significance when they least expect it.

Joyce weaves his characters' dreams and longings into the texture of Dublin life, a social fabric that appears to limit his characters' options. He once explained to his publisher that his intention in *Dubliners* "was to write a chapter of the moral history of my country," and he focused on Dublin because that city seemed to him "the center of paralysis." The major causes of his characters' paralysis are transmitted by their family life, Catholicism, economic situations, and vulnerability to political forces. His characters have lives consisting largely of self-denial and drab duties, but they also have an irrepressible desire for something more—as in "Eveline," which focuses on a dutiful daughter's efforts to run away with her lover.

CHRONOLOGY

1882   Born on February 2 in Dublin, Ireland.

1888–98   Studies at Jesuit schools in preparation for university.

1898–1902   Attends University College, Dublin, another Jesuit school, and graduates with a degree in modern languages.

1902   Studies medicine in Paris but soon abandons it for writing.

1903   Returns to be at his mother's deathbed in Dublin.

1904   Meets Nora Barnacle, with whom he will have two children and live his entire life.

1905	Moves to the Continent to teach at the Berlitz school in Trieste and write.
1907	After working in a bank for a year in Rome, he returns to Trieste; publishes *Chamber Music*, a volume of poems.
1912	Makes his final visit to Ireland.
1914	Publishes *Dubliners* after eight years of censorship battles.
1916	Publishes *A Portrait of the Artist as a Young Man*.
1917	Has the first of a series of debilitating eye operations.
1918	Publishes *Exiles*, a play.
1920	Settles in Paris with his family.
1922	Publishes *Ulysses* amid controversy concerning its alleged obscenity.
1927	Publishes *Pomes Penyeach*.
1931	Marries Nora Barnacle.
1934	Publishes *Collected Poems*.
1939	Publishes *Finnegans Wake*.
1940	After the German occupation of Paris, the Joyces move to Zurich.
1941	Dies of a perforated ulcer on January 13 at Zurich.

Web *Research James Joyce with LitLinks at*
http://www.bedfordstmartins.com/meyer/bedintrolit

Eveline   1914

She sat at the window watching the evening invade the avenue. Her head was leaned against the window curtains and in her nostrils was the odor of dusty cretonne. She was tired.

Few people passed. The man out of the last house passed on his way home; she heard his footsteps clacking along the concrete pavement and afterwards crunching on the cinder path before the new red houses. One time there used to be a field there in which they used to play every evening with other people's children. Then a man from Belfast bought the field and built houses in it — not like their little brown houses but bright brick houses with shining roofs. The children of the avenue used to play together in that field — the Devines, the Waters, the Dunns, little Keogh the cripple, she and her brothers and sisters. Ernest, however, never played: he was too grown up. Her father used often to hunt them in out of the field with his blackthorn stick; but usually little Keogh used to keep *nix* and call out when he saw her father coming. Still they seemed to have been rather happy then. Her father was not so bad then; and besides, her mother was alive. That was a long time ago; she and her brothers and sisters were all grown up; her mother was dead. Tizzie Dunn was dead, too, and the Waters had gone back to England. Everything changes. Now she was going to go away like the others, to leave her home.

Home! She looked round the room, reviewing all its familiar objects which she had dusted once a week for so many years, wondering where on earth all the dust came from. Perhaps she would never see again those familiar objects from which she had never dreamed of being divided. And yet during all those years she had never found out the name of the priest whose yellowing photograph hung on the wall above the broken harmonium beside the colored print of the promises made to Blessed Margaret Mary Alacoque. He had been a school friend of her father. Whenever he showed the photograph to a visitor her father used to pass it with a casual word:

— He is in Melbourne now.

She had consented to go away, to leave her home. Was that wise? She tried 5 to weigh each side of the question. In her home anyway she had shelter and food; she had those whom she had known all her life about her. Of course she had to work hard both in the house and at business. What would they say of her in the Stores when they found out that she had run away with a fellow? Say she was a fool, perhaps; and her place would be filled up by advertisement. Miss Gavan would be glad. She had always had an edge on her, especially whenever there were people listening.

— Miss Hill, don't you see these ladies are waiting?

— Look lively, Miss Hill, please.

She would not cry many tears at leaving the Stores.

But in her new home, in a distant unknown country, it would not be like that. Then she would be married — she, Eveline. People would treat her with respect then. She would not be treated as her mother had been. Even now, though she was over nineteen, she sometimes felt herself in danger of her father's violence. She knew it was that that had given her the palpitations. When they were growing up he had never gone for her, like he used to go for Harry and Ernest, because she was a girl; but latterly he had begun to threaten her and say what he would do to her only for her dead mother's sake. And now she had nobody to protect her. Ernest was dead and Harry, who was in the church decorating business, was nearly always down somewhere in the country. Besides, the invariable squabble for money on Saturday nights had begun to weary her unspeakably. She always gave her entire wages — seven shillings — and Harry always sent up what he could but the trouble was to get any money from her father. He said she used to squander the money, that she had no head, that he wasn't going to give her his hard-earned money to throw about the streets, and much more, for he was usually fairly bad of a Saturday night. In the end he would give her the money and ask her had she any intention of buying Sunday's dinner. Then she had to rush out as quickly as she could and do her marketing, holding her black leather purse tightly in her hand as she elbowed her way through the crowds and returning home late under her load of provisions. She had hard work to keep the house together and to see that the two young children who had been left to her charge went to school regularly and got their meals regularly. It was hard work — a hard life — but now that she was about to leave it she did not find it a wholly undesirable life.

She was about to explore another life with Frank. Frank was very kind, 10 manly, open-hearted. She was to go away with him by the night-boat to be his wife and to live with him in Buenos Aires where he had a home waiting for her.

How well she remembered the first time she had seen him; he was lodging in a house on the main road where she used to visit. It seemed a few weeks ago. He was standing at the gate, his peaked cap pushed back on his head and his hair tumbled forward over a face of bronze. Then they had come to know each other. He used to meet her outside the Stores every evening and see her home. He took her to see *The Bohemian Girl* and she felt elated as she sat in an unaccustomed part of the theater with him. He was awfully fond of music and sang a little. People knew that they were courting and, when he sang about the lass that loves a sailor, she always felt pleasantly confused. He used to call her Poppens out of fun. First of all it had been an excitement for her to have a fellow and then she had begun to like him. He had tales of distant countries. He had started as a deck boy at a pound a month on a ship of the Allan Line going out to Canada. He told her the names of the ships he had been on and the names of the different services. He had sailed through the Straits of Magellan and he told her stories of the terrible Patagonians. He had fallen on his feet in Buenos Aires, he said, and had come over to the old country just for a holiday. Of course, her father had found out the affair and had forbidden her to have anything to say to him.

— I know these sailor chaps, he said.

One day he had quarreled with Frank and after that she had to meet her lover secretly.

The evening deepened in the avenue. The white of two letters in her lap grew indistinct. One was to Harry; the other was to her father. Ernest had been her favorite but she liked Harry too. Her father was becoming old lately, she noticed; he would miss her. Sometimes he could be very nice. Not long before, when she had been laid up for a day, he had read her out a ghost story and made toast for her at the fire. Another day, when their mother was alive, they had all gone for a picnic to the Hill of Howth. She remembered her father putting on her mother's bonnet to make the children laugh.

Her time was running out but she continued to sit by the window, leaning her head against the window curtain, inhaling the odor of dusty cretonne. Down far in the avenue she could hear a street organ playing. She knew the air. Strange that it should come that very night to remind her of the promise to her mother, her promise to keep the home together as long as she could. She remembered the last night of her mother's illness; she was again in the close dark room at the other side of the hall and outside she heard a melancholy air of Italy. The organ-player had been ordered to go away and given sixpence. She remembered her father strutting back into the sickroom saying:

— Damned Italians! coming over here! 15

As she mused the pitiful vision of her mother's life laid its spell on the very quick of her being — that life of commonplace sacrifices closing in final craziness. She trembled as she heard again her mother's voice saying constantly with foolish insistence:

— Derevaun Seraun! Derevaun Seraun!°

She stood up in a sudden impulse of terror. Escape! She must escape! Frank would save her. He would give her life, perhaps love, too. But she wanted to live. Why should she be unhappy? She had a right to happiness. Frank would take her in his arms, fold her in his arms. He would save her.

Derevaun Seraun!: "The end of pleasure is pain!" (Gaelic).

She stood among the swaying crowd in the station at the North Wall. He held her hand and she knew that he was speaking to her, saying something about the passage over and over again. The station was full of soldiers with brown baggages. Through the wide doors of the sheds she caught a glimpse of the black mass of the boat, lying in beside the quay wall, with illumined portholes. She answered nothing. She felt her cheek pale and cold and, out of a maze of distress, she prayed to God to direct her, to show her what was her duty. The boat blew a long mournful whistle into the mist. If she went, tomorrow she would be on the sea with Frank, steaming toward Buenos Aires. Their passage had been booked. Could she still draw back after all he had done for her? Her distress awoke a nausea in her body and she kept moving her lips in silent fervent prayer.

A bell clanged upon her heart. She felt him seize her hand: 20
—Come!

All the seas of the world tumbled about her heart. He was drawing her into them: he would drown her. She gripped with both hands at the iron railing.
—Come!

No! No! No! It was impossible. Her hands clutched the iron in frenzy. Amid the seas she sent a cry of anguish!
—Eveline! Evvy!   25

He rushed beyond the barrier and called to her to follow. He was shouted at to go on but he still called to her. She set her white face to him, passive, like a helpless animal. Her eyes gave him no sign of love or farewell or recognition.

CONSIDERATIONS FOR CRITICAL THINKING AND WRITING

1. FIRST RESPONSE. Explain why you agree or disagree with Eveline's decision.

2. Describe the character of Eveline. What do you think she looks like? Though there are no physical details about her in the story, write a one-page description of her as you think she would appear at the beginning of the story looking out the window.

3. Describe the physical setting of Eveline's home. How does she feel about living at home?

4. What sort of relationship does Eveline have with her father? Describe the range of her feelings toward him.

5. How is Frank characterized? Why does Eveline's father forbid them to see each other?

6. Why does thinking of her mother make Eveline want to "escape"?

7. Before she meets him at the dock, how does Eveline expect Frank to change her life?

8. Why doesn't she go with Frank to Buenos Aires?

9. What associations do you have about Buenos Aires? What symbolic value does this Argentine city have in the story?

10. Read carefully the water imagery in the final paragraphs of the story. How does this imagery help to suggest Eveline's reasons for not leaving with Frank?

11. Write a one-page physical description of Eveline as you think she would be thirty years after her decision to remain at home.

CONNECTIONS TO OTHER SELECTIONS

1. How does Eveline's response to her life at home compare with that of the narrator in Punyakante Wijenaike's "Anoma" (p. 312)? Write an essay that explores the similarities and differences in their efforts to escape to something better.

2. Write an essay about the meaning of "home" to the protagonists in "Eveline" and Ernest Hemingway's "Soldier's Home" (p. 152).

DOCUMENTS

CONSIDERATIONS FOR CRITICAL THINKING AND WRITING

1. Describe what this photograph tells you. What does it tell you about life in Dublin? Explain whether you think this photograph confirms or challenges the view of Dublin presented by Joyce in "Eveline."

2. Write an essay describing the mood evoked by this photograph, and compare it with the tone associated with urban life in "Eveline."

Photograph of Poole Street in Dublin, taken during the period 1880–1914. This street gives a sense of the "little brown house" that Eveline calls home. Reproduced by permission of The National Library of Ireland.

Resources of Ireland

The Alliance Temperance Almanack was published in London. The following excerpt describes the cost of Ireland's drinking habits in economic terms.

Much of the public attention is at this time drawn to the wants of the labour-ing poor of Ireland, and the great decay of her trade and manufactures. It may therefore be worth while to lay before our countrymen some calculations of the quantity of produce and employment which might arise from the whole population of that country agreeing to apply the vast sum, which, as stated below, is spent annually on whiskey in Ireland, to the encouragement of home manufactures, and the employment of the people. These advantages would follow in the most simple and natural course from the purchase of those articles of prime necessity, or of substantial comfort, the desire for which arises in the mind of every poor man whose habits do not lead him to prefer whiskey to domestic happiness. The Linen Manufacture, which *was* the staple trade of that island, the woollen trade, and the other more useful and indis-pensable occupations in a civilized community, are chiefly referred to; and the observer will be struck with the immense loss which that country sustains from the propensity to the use of Distilled Spirits.

"It appears from parliamentary returns, that the average quantity of Whiskey which paid excise duty in Ireland for each of the years 1826, 1827, 1828, and 1829, was Ten millions of Gallons. To this, if there be added one-sixth for reduction of strength by retailers, and also about Two Millions, Five Hundred Thousand Gallons made, but which did not pay duty, we shall have a total of upwards of *Fourteen Millions of Gallons, costing, at nine shillings per gallon, by retail, Six Millions Three Hundred Thousand Pounds sterling;* and being equal to a yearly consumption of more than Two Gallons for every man, woman, and child of our population."

*   *   *

The above remarks, though intended exclusively for Ireland, apply with great force to the United Kingdom generally. The ardent spirits, at full proof, on which duty was paid for home consumption in the year ending January 6, 1830, amounted to *twenty-seven millions five hundred and thirteen thousand two hundred and sixty gallons,* imperial measure. To this if we add, at a very low estimate as above, one-sixth, for the reduction of strength by retailers, without computing either the adulterations notoriously made, the spirits smuggled from the conti-nent, or the still greater quantity produced by illicit distillation in Scotland and Ireland, we find that we have expended in one year for ardent spirits, *eighteen millions nine hundred and eleven thousand six hundred and fifty-eight pounds, ten shillings.*

Table I. Shewing that the sum of Six Millions Three Hundred Thousand Pounds, which the People of Ireland pay annually for Whiskey, if expended as follows, would provide

1.	The population of Ireland, (computed at eight millions) with 2½ yards of linen each, amounting to 20,000,000 yards, at 1s. 3d. per yard	£1,250,000
2.	Ten thousand men in each county in Ireland with 3½ yards of Corduroy each, amounting to 1,120,000 yards, at 1s. per yard	56,000
3.	Four thousand men in each county with 3 yards of Kersey each, amounting to 384,000 yards, at 2s. 4d. per yard	44,800
4.	Ten thousand men in each county with 2½ yards of Broad Cloth, amounting to 720,000 yards, at 4s. per yard	144,000
5.	Four thousand men in each county with one hat each, amounting to 128,000 hats, at 5s. per hat	32,000
6.	Three millions of women and children with 1¼ yard of Check, amounting to 3,750,000 yards, at 10d. per yard.	156,250
7.	One million of women and children with 6 yards of stuff each, amounting to 6,000,000 yards, at 8d. per yard	200,000
8.	Three millions of women and children with 6 yards of printed calico, each, amounting to 18,000,000 yards, at 8d. per yard	600,000
9.	Three hundred and twenty thousand women with 2¼ yards of grey cloaking, amounting to 720,000 yards, at 2s. 8d. per yard	96,000
10.	Four millions of men, women, and children, with 2½ yards of Flannel each, amounting to 10,000,000 yards, at 1s. per yard	500,000
11.	Four millions of men, women, and children, with one pair of shoes each, at 5s. per pair	1,000,000
12.	Four millions of men, women and children, with one pair of stockings each, at 1s. 3d. per pair	250,000
13.	Ten thousand families in each county with one pair of blankets each, amounting to 320,000 pair, at 10s. per pair	160,000
14.	Four hundred tons of oatmeal for each county, amounting to 12,800 tons, at £15 per ton	192,000
15.	Three hundred tons of wheat meal for each county, amounting to 9,600 tons, at £18 per ton	172,800
16.	Two thousand pigs for each county, amounting to 64,000 pigs at £2 per pig	128,000
17.	Two thousand sheep for each county, amounting to 64,000 sheep, at £1 5s. per sheep	80,000
18.	Five hundred cows for each county, amounting to 16,000 cows, at £10 per cow	160,000
19.	And pay one thousand labourers in each county, (reclaiming land, &c.) amounting to 32,000 labourers, at 6s. per week each, or £15 12s. per year	499,200
20.	And support 1,000 aged and infirm in each county, amounting to 32,000 at 6d. per day, or £9 per year each	288,000
21.	And build fifty school-houses in each county, amounting to 1,600 at £100 each	160,000
22.	And pay fifty school-masters at £50, and fifty school-mistresses at £30 per year, in each county, amounting to 3,200 teachers, at an average salary of £40 each	128,000
23.	Leaving for other charitable purposes	2,950
	Total	£6,300,000

Let us now see what might be done by a proper application of the money, which the most moderate habitual tippler spends on whiskey in the course of a year.

One glass of whiskey per day, commonly called by drinking men *"their morning,"* costs (at three half-pence per glass) Two pounds Five Shillings and Seven-pence Half-penny, yearly! which sum, if laid by, would provide the following clothing, viz.:—

Three yards of Kersey for great coat, at 2s. 4d. per yard	£0	7	0
Two yards and a quarter of Broad Cloth for coat and waistcoat, at			
5s. 4d. per yard	0	12	0
Three yards and a half of Corduroy for Trowsers, at 1s. per yard	0	3	6
Two Neck Handkerchiefs	0	1	7½
One Hat	0	5	0
One Pair of Shoes	0	7	0
Two Pair of Stockings	0	8	0
Two Shirts	0	8	6
	£2	5	7½

Six million three hundred thousand sovereigns in gold would extend in a line from the town of Roscommon to the Circular Road of Dublin, being a distance of 66¼ Irish miles, or 85 English miles, and would require 49 horses and carts to draw them, at one ton weight each draft.

The same sum, if laid down in shillings, would extend in a line of 1442 Irish miles, or 1835 English miles, and would require 669 horses and carts to draw them, at one ton weight each draft.

The same sum, if laid down in penny pieces, would extend in a line of 25,000 miles, equal to the computed distance round the globe!

The three last year's expenditure on whiskey, say £18,900,000, would afford nine guineas for each family (four persons), in Ireland, allowing the population as already stated, at eight millions of souls!

Note.—The cost of ardent spirits in the United Kingdom which exceeds *eighteen millions nine hundred and eleven thousand pounds sterling, yearly,* would, on the calculations given, afford employment to *four hundred and twenty-eight thousand seven hundred and fifty men;* circulating among them nearly *six million pounds sterling* in wages only.

Our magistrates have already publicly declared that this enormous expenditure of £18,911,658 10s. is not to be regarded as merely useless, but horribly injurious; and their testimony is amply supported by the voice of *ninety five thousand offenders* committed within the past year to the prisons of England and Wales only. On high authority it is asserted that four-fifths of the crimes, three-fourths of the beggary, and one-half of all the madness of our countrymen arise from drinking. Have we nothing to learn from America, where, by the associated efforts of the sober and intelligent for the purpose of discouraging the use of ardent spirits, their consumption is already diminished one-third throughout the whole Union?

From *The Alliance Temperance Almanack* for 1910

Considerations for Critical Thinking and Writing

1. Describe the tone of this analysis of Ireland's consumption of alcohol. Why is it significant that this temperance publication originates from England?

2. What sort of economic argument is made here? Explain why you find it convincing or not.

3. How does this document speak to the conditions of Eveline Hill's life? Pay particular attention to paragraph 9 of the story.

A Letter Home from an Irish Emigrant in Australia   1882

The excerpt below comes from a letter written by Bridget Burke, who, at the age of twenty-one, emigrated from Galway, Ireland, to Brisbane, Australia. Though her spelling is rough, her affection for her brother John is clear.

Dear John

I am 40 Miles from My uncle. I feal Quare without a Home to goe to when on My sunday out. I often wish to Have you out Heare. I ame verry strange out Here. I cannot make free with any body. I often Have a Walk with Patt [her brother] & Has a long yarn of Home. He is verry Kind became a steady fellow since He Left Home & also I could not expect My father to be a bit better than My Uncle. His wife & children is all right it is a nice place to go but it is to [too] far away but My brother is near me & comes to see me 2 or 3 times a week. We often Have some fun talking of the Old times at Home.

Dear John you wanted to know How do I Like the Country or what sort of people are heare. John that Queston I cannot answer. There is all sortes black & white misted & married together & Living in pretty Cotages Just the same as the white people. Thire is English Irish French German Italian black Chineease and not forgetin the Juse [Jews]. There are verry rich fancy John white girls marrid to a black man & Irish girls to [too] & to Yellow Chinaman with their Hair platted down there[?] black back. Sow [so] you see that girls dont care what the do in this Country. The would do anny think [anything] before the worke & a great Lot of them does worse[?] than that same. & this is a fine Country for a Young person that can take care of himselfe.

Now John I must ask you for all my Aunts & Uncles Cousins friends & Neighbours sweet Harts & all also did Cannopy die yet. Now John I must Conclude Hoping that You will send me as Long a Letter as I have send you & Lett me know all about Home. Dirrect Your Letter as[?] Patt told you for me, I Have more[?] to say but remaning yours fond sister for ever

BDB

From David Fitzpatrick, *Oceans of Consolation: Personal Accounts of Irish Migration to Australia*, Cornell University Press (1994)

Considerations for Critical Thinking and Writing

1. How does Bridget feel about living in Australia? How does she feel about Ireland?

2. How is Australia's social structure different from Ireland's?

3. How does this letter help to fill in Eveline's feelings about leaving Ireland for Buenos Aires?

4. Research life in Buenos Aires during the first fifteen years of the twentieth century. What would it have been like to live there then? How would it be different from Ireland?

A Plot Synopsis of The Bohemian Girl
1843

The following synopsis recounts the story of The Bohemian Girl, *a well-loved opera by Michael William Balfe that played in the principal capitals of Europe, North America, and South America. It gives a sense of the romantic narrative Eveline and Frank would have seen at the opera.*

The action of this drama commences at the chateau of Count Arnheim, in Austria. The peasantry and retainers of the Count are making preparations for the chase, when Thaddeus, a Polish exile and fugitive from the Austrian troops, arrives in search of shelter and concealment. Here he encounters a band of Gipsies, headed by one Devilshoof, who, learning from Thaddeus that he is pursued by soldiers, gives him a disguise, conceals him, and puts the pursuing troops on the wrong track. Just at this time, shouts of distress are heard, and Florestein appears surrounded by huntsmen. The Count's child and her attendant have been attacked by an infuriated stag in the forest, and are probably destroyed. Hearing this, Thaddeus seizes a rifle, and hastens to their relief, and by a well-aimed shot kills the animal, and saves them from destruction. The Count now returns in time to hear of the peril of his darling child, and to see Thaddeus bearing her wounded form in his arms. Overjoyed to find her still alive, the Count overwhelms Thaddeus with grateful thanks, and invites him to join in the festivities about to take place. Thaddeus at first declines, but being warmly entreated to remain, at length consents to do so. They seat themselves at table, and the Count proposes as a toast, "Health and long life to the Emperor!" All except Thaddeus do honor to the toast, and his silence being observed, the Count challenges him to empty his goblet as the rest have done. Thaddeus, to the surprise of all, dashes the wine to the earth; this, of course, produces a burst of indignation. The assembled guests are infuriated by such an indignity to their monarch, and threaten the life of Thaddeus. At this moment Devilshoof returns, and at once takes sides with Thaddeus. The Count orders Devilshoof to be secured. The attendants seize and carry him into the castle. Thaddeus departs, and festivities are resumed. During the *fête*, Devilshoof escapes, taking with him the Count's infant daughter, Arline; and his flight being almost immediately discovered, the greatest excitement prevails. Peasants, huntsmen, and attendants hasten in search of the daring fugitive, and he is seen bearing the child across a dangerous precipice; he escapes, and the unhappy father sinks in despair as the First Act ends.

Twelve years are supposed to elapse, and we are transported to the city of Presburg, in the suburbs of which the Gipsies are encamped with the Queen of their tribe in whose tent dwells the Count's daughter, Arline, now a fine young woman. Florestein, a foppish *attaché* to the Court, is met by Devilshoof and his companions, who relieve him of his jewelry, among which is a medallion, which Devilshoof carries off. Thaddeus, who has joined the tribe, is now enamored of Arline, and he tells her that it was he who saved her life in infancy, but he still carefully conceals from her the secret of her birth. Arline confesses her love for Thaddeus, and they are betrothed according to the custom of the Gipsy tribe.

A grand fair is in progress in the plaza of the city, and hither, of course, come all the Gipsies, who add to the gayety and life of the scene by their peculiar dances, songs, etc. Florestein appears, and is quite fascinated by the beauty of Arline. While trying to engage her attention, he perceives his medallion hanging on her neck and claims it, charging her with having stolen it. This leads to great excitement: the guard is called, Arline is arrested, and the crowd dispersed by the soldiery. The supposed culprit is brought before Count Arnheim; Florestein presses the charge, and circumstances strengthen the appearance of guilt against Arline, when the Count perceives the mark left by the wound inflicted by the deer on Arline's arm. He asks its origin. She repeats the story as related to her by Thaddeus. The Count recognizes his long-lost child, and the Act ends with an effective *tableau*.

In the Third Act we find Arline restored to her rank and the home of her father; but the change in her prospects does not diminish her love for Thaddeus. He, daring all dangers for an interview, seeks and finds her here. He comes to bid her farewell, and prays that she will, even when surrounded by other admirers, give a thought to him who saved her life, and who loves her. She promises fidelity, and declares herself his and his only. Here we find that the Gipsy Queen, who also loves Thaddeus, has been plotting to take him from Arline. By her device the medallion was discovered in the possession of Arline. Even now she is conspiring to separate the lovers, but her plots fail. Thaddeus relates his history to Count Arnheim, who, in gratitude to the preserver of his child, bestows her upon him. Desire for vengeance now fills the heart of the Gipsy Queen; she induces one of her tribe to fire at Thaddeus as he is embracing Arline, but by a timely movement of Devilshoof the bullet reaches her own heart.

From *The Bohemian Girl*, edited by Richard Aldrich (1902)

CONSIDERATIONS FOR CRITICAL THINKING AND WRITING

1. Describe the action of this opera. How does its plot compare with Eveline's life?

2. Why do you suppose Joyce has Frank take Eveline to this particular opera?

3. One of the songs of *The Bohemian Girl* is titled "Tis Sad to Leave Our Fatherland" and contains these verses: "Without/friends, and without a home, my country too! yes, I'm exiled from thee; what/fate, what fate awaits me here, now! Pity, Heav'n! oh calm my despair!" How do these lines shed light on Eveline's situation?

SUGGESTED TOPICS FOR LONGER PAPERS

1. Write an essay that discusses the theme(s) of this story. Is the theme presented directly or is it offered implicitly through other elements of the story? Explain whether the theme reinforces your own values or challenges them.

2. Research biographical resources to describe in detail Joyce's attitudes toward Dublin, and explain how they are reflected in "Eveline."

3. **MULTIMEDIA PROJECT.** Review the cultural documents presented in this chapter and explain which one you find most revealing, and then use the library or the Internet to find an additional document that you think equally reveals the historical context for "Eveline."

Web *For help with this project, use the Multimedia Project Guides Online at* http://www.bedfordstmartins.com/meyer/bedintrolit

16

A Thematic Case Study:
The Nature of Storytelling

This chapter offers four stories that are thematically related. *Theme* is the central idea, the focal point of a story around which various elements such as plot, character, setting, and point of view revolve. Ultimately, what a text suggests about its main theme is what we respond to—or fail to respond to. Themes may be presented explicitly or implicitly. More often than not, you're likely to find yourself reading the elements of a given story very closely in order to determine the work's themes, because they are woven into the elements rather than embroidered by the author as a direct message in a concluding paragraph. Themes are most often found in the fabric of a story's elements, not in an attached label. For a detailed discussion of theme and some strategies for determining theme, see Chapter 8.

METAFICTION

The stories in this chapter by Margaret Atwood, George Bowering, Tim O'Brien, and Don DeLillo focus on the nature of storytelling. This single topic yields a wide range of fascinating, complex, and provocative themes owing to the unique perspective each story provides on the subject. These works are fictions about fiction. They self-consciously consider the nature of storytelling. The literary term used to describe a work that explores the nature, structure, logic, status, and function of storytelling is *metafiction*. The following metafictions raise significant questions and issues about how and why stories are told. In addition, these stories include other themes that reach beyond the immediate topic of storytelling to connect with other selections included in this anthology, so approach them as you would any story. Read carefully and deliberately to enhance your understanding and pleasure.

Margaret Atwood's "There Was Once" begins with the makings of a traditional kind of story—a fairy tale—but then quickly becomes fraught with issues of political correctness applied to storytelling. In the story, how does Atwood raise questions about the relationship between politics and fiction writing?

MARGARET ATWOOD (B. 1939)

Born in Ottawa, Ontario, Margaret Atwood was educated at the University of Toronto and Harvard University. She has been writing fiction and poetry since she was a child; along the way she has done odd jobs and been a screenwriter and a teacher. Among her collections of short stories are *Dancing Girls* (1977), *Bluebird's Egg* (1983), and *Wilderness Tips* (1991). Her highly successful novels include *Surfacing* (1972), *The Handmaid's Tale* (1986), *Cat's Eye* (1989), and *The Robber Bride* (1993), *Alias Grace* (1995), and *The Blind Assassin* (2000). She has also written twelve books of poetry. Atwood has enhanced the appreciation of Canadian literature through her editing of *The New Oxford Book of Canadian Verse in English* (1982) and *The Oxford Book of Canadian Short Stories in English* (1986). Her own work closely examines the weight of the complex human relationships that complicate her characters' lives. In "There Was Once," taken from her collection of short works, *Good Bones and Simple Murders* (1994), Atwood has fun with some of the demands placed on contemporary writers.

Web *Research Margaret Atwood with LitLinks at*
http://www.bedfordstmartins.com/meyer/bedintrolit

There Was Once   *1992*

—There was once a poor girl, as beautiful as she was good, who lived with her wicked stepmother in a house in the forest.

—Forest? *Forest* is passé, I mean, I've had it with all this wilderness stuff. It's not the right image of our society, today. Let's have some *urban* for a change.

—There was once a poor girl, as beautiful as she was good, who lived with her wicked stepmother in a house in the suburbs.

—That's better. But I have to seriously query this word *poor.*

—But she *was* poor!   5

—Poor is relative. She lived in a house, didn't she?

—Yes.

— Then socioeconomically speaking, she was not poor.

— But none of the money was *hers!* The whole point of the story is that the wicked stepmother makes her wear old clothes and sleep in the fireplace —

— Aha! They had a *fireplace!* With *poor,* let me tell you, there's no fireplace. 10 Come down to the park, come to the subway stations after dark, come down to where they sleep in cardboard boxes, and I'll show you *poor!*

— There was once a middle-class girl, as beautiful as she was good —

— Stop right there. I think we can cut the *beautiful,* don't you? Women these days have to deal with too many intimidating physical role models as it is, what with those bimbos in the ads. Can't you make her, well, more average?

— There was once a girl who was a little overweight and whose front teeth stuck out, who —

— I don't think it's nice to make fun of people's appearances. Plus, you're encouraging anorexia.

— I wasn't making fun! I was just describing —   15

— Skip the description. Description oppresses. But you can say what color she was.

— What color?

— You know. Black, white, red, brown, yellow. Those are the choices. And I'm telling you right now, I've had enough of white. Dominant culture this, dominant culture that —

— I don't know what color.

— Well, it would probably be *your* color, wouldn't it?   20

— But this isn't *about* me! It's about this girl —

— Everything is about you.

— Sounds to me like you don't want to hear this story at all.

— Oh well, go on. You could make her ethnic. That might help.

— There was once a girl of indeterminate descent, as average-looking as she 25 was good, who lived with her wicked —

— Another thing. *Good* and *wicked.* Don't you think you should transcend those puritanical judgmental moralistic epithets? I mean, so much of that is conditioning, isn't it?

—There was once a girl, as average-looking as she was well-adjusted, who lived with her stepmother, who was not a very open and loving person because she herself had been abused in childhood.

—Better. But I am so *tired* of negative female images! And stepmothers—they always get it in the neck! Change it to step*father*, why don't you? That would make more sense anyway, considering the bad behavior you're about to describe. And throw in some whips and chains. We all know what those twisted, repressed, middle-aged men are like—

—*Hey, just a minute!* I'm *a middle-aged*—

—Stuff it, Mister Nosy Parker. Nobody asked you to stick in your oar, or what-   30
ever you want to call that thing. This is between the two of us. Go on.

—There was once a girl—

—How old was she?

—I don't know. She was young.

—This ends with a marriage, right?

—Well, not to blow the plot, but—yes.   35

—Then you can scratch the condescending paternalistic terminology. It's *woman*, pal. *Woman.*

—There was once—

—What's this *was, once?* Enough of the dead past. Tell me about *now.*

—There—

—So?   40

—So, what?

—So, why not *here?*

Considerations for Critical Thinking and Writing

1. FIRST RESPONSE. Atwood plays with the conventions of the fairy tale in "There Was Once." Pick a familiar fairy tale and critique it as the second speaker might. Are such tales enjoyable, do you think? Or can they harm the children they're meant to entertain?

2. Describe the two speakers. How does Atwood individualize them even though she provides no physical descriptions of the two characters?

3. What does the second speaker object to in how the story writer tells the tale? Do you agree with any of the objections? Why or why not?

4. What does Atwood satirize in this story?

5. What is the theme of "There Was Once"? How does the title contribute to the theme?

6. Try writing a one-paragraph version of the story as you think the second speaker would want it to be.

CONNECTIONS TO OTHER SELECTIONS

1. Discuss the use of satire in "There Was Once" and in T. Coraghessan Boyle's "Carnal Knowledge" (p. 290). Though these are very different types of stories, how are the themes somewhat similar?

2. Write an essay that compares the treatment of fiction writing in "There Was Once" and in George Bowering's "A Short Story"(below).

If the problems confronted by Atwood's storyteller are external social and political issues, George Bowering's writer is a narrator with internal issues — an omniscient narrator "know-it-all" discovers that he experiences competing points of view within himself that cause him to warn the reader that he's not "God-like." Bowering clearly emphasizes the elements of fiction the way he organizes his story with headings and, for that matter, by providing the generic title "A Short Story." What's going on here?

GEORGE BOWERING (B. 1935)

Born in Penticon, British Columbia, George Bowering earned degrees at the University of British Columbia and has taught at Simon Fraser University. A poet, fiction writer, and literary critic, he is a two-time winner of the Governor General's Award — for poetry (1969) and fiction (1980). Among his collections of poems are *Touch: Selected Poems 1960–1970* (1971), *Particular Accidents: Selected Poems* (1980), and *West Window: Selected Poetry by George Bowering* (1982). His novels include *Burning Water* (1980), *Shoot!* (1984), and *Caprice* (1988). He has also published a collection of critical pieces, *The Mask in Place: Essays on Fiction in North America* (1983).

Web   *Research George Bowering with LitLinks at*
http://www.bedfordstmartins.com/meyer/bedintrolit

A Short Story   1983

Setting

It was that slightly disappointing moment in the year when the cherry blossoms have been blown off the trees, or shrunken to brown lace out of which little hard green pebbles are beginning to appear. The orchardists were running tractors between the rows of trees, disking the late spring weeds into the precious topsoil left there by the glacier that long ago receded from the desert valley.

Starlings were growing impatient with the season, tired of competing for scraps behind the Safeway store in town, eager for those high blue days when the cherries would be plump & pink, when they could laugh at the sunburnt men in high gum boots, who would again try to deceive them with fake cannons & old shirts stretcht between the branches.

High over Dog Lake a jet contrail was widening & drifting south. The orchards on the west bank were in shadow already, & sunlight sparkled off windows of the new housing development on the other shore. The lake was spotted with brown weeds dying underwater, where the newest poison had been dumpt by the government two weeks before.

Evening swallows were already dipping & soaring around the Jacobsen house, nabbing insects in their first minutes of activity after a warm day's sleep. The house was like many of the remodelled orchard homes in the southern part of the valley, its shiplap sides now covered with pastel aluminum, metallic screen doors here & there, a stone chimney marking the outside end of the living-room. Fifteen years ago the living-room had been used only when relatives from other valley towns came to visit. Now it was panelled with knotty cedar, animal heads looking across at one another from the walls, & the Jacobsens sat there after all the evening chores were done, watching Spokane television in color, and reading this week's paper, or perhaps having some toast & raspberry jam.

The rug was a pastel shade fairly close to that of the outside surface. The   5
Jacobsens lived with it, though neither of them particularly liked it. One of them had, once, when it was new; the other never thought of offering an opinion, or holding one.

Characters

The Jacobsens did not discuss things. They spoke short sentences to one another in the course of a card game, or while deciding which re-run was more worth watching on the mammoth television set parkt under a deer head on the west wall of the living-room.

"We haven't seen this Carol show, have we?" suggested Mrs Jacobsen. "I think it must have been on the night we played bridge with Stu & Ronnie."

"No, we saw it," said Mr Jacobsen from behind his sixteen-page newspaper. "This is the one where her & Harvey are on that jet plane that gets highjackt to South America."

"Sky-jackt."

"The same thing. But if you want to watch it again, go ahead."   10

"I cant remember a sky-jack one."

"Go ahead. I'll probably fall asleep in the middle, anyway," said Mr Jacobsen.

Art Jacobsen was tired every night. As soon as the after-supper card game was over, & his short legs were up on the aquamarine hassock, his eyes would begin to droop. He was 61 years old, & still working eleven hours a day in the orchard. Like most valley orchardists, he wore a shirt only during the early hours of the morning, when the dew was still on every leaf. His body was tanned & muscled, but it was getting more rectangular every year.

Audrey Jacobsen was ten years younger. She had only recently taken to coloring her hair, often a kind of brownish-red she mistakenly remembered from her youth. Her first husband used to tease her about having red hair, though it wasnt true. By the time that Ordie Michaels had died & Art Jacobsen had started courting her on rainy days, her hair was a good plain brown, usually under a kerchief.

She'd taken to wearing the kerchief, as all the women did, while sorting 15 fruit at the Coop packing-house. By the time Donna was five, Audrey had assumed the habit of wearing it all the time, except when she went for drives with Art Jacobsen.

They had been watching Carol on television for five years now, & she didn't know whether she liked the show.

It is not that I know all about the Jacobsens & Donna Michaels before I start telling you about them. I am what they call omniscient, all right, but there isnt any Jacobsen family until I commit them to this medium. I have some hazy ideas or images, rather, of their story, a sort of past & a present, I suppose, but really, for me the story is waiting somewhere in the future. Or I should say that I'm waiting for a time in the future when I will have the time to come to it, here. As a matter of fact, you dont have to, now, wait as long for it as I do.

So I am in the position ascribed to the narrator with the totally omniscient point of view. A know-it-all. Dont you believe it! "God-like." Dont you believe it!

For instance, I've been thinking about writing this story for two years. Just a month ago I began to imagine a woman visiting her mother & stepfather at their orchard home, & that common emotional violence later on. But I just got the names while I was writing the first parts of the story, & I didn't imagine the Jacobsen house near the lake — I thought it would be 40 kilometers farther south.

Do I have to mention that there is something difficult to explain about a 20 third-person omniscient narrative having all these "I's" in it? Point of view dictates distance. Well, I would like to keep you closer than your usual "god" will allow (except for people such as yourself, Leda) (no, that's not what I'm trying to do to you, reader: dont be so suspicious).

From up here I can see the Jacobsen house as a little square surrounded by trees that have nearly lost their blossoms & are just producing leaves. I have good eyes; I need them to see all that thru the drifting jet contrail.

By the way, have you noticed that when the narrator speaks in the first person, he makes you the second person? When he speaks of others in the third person, you are perhaps standing beside him, only the parallax preventing your seeing exactly what he is seeing. That makes for a greater distance produced by the first-person narrative. You must have noticed that.

Protagonist

Donna Michaels, an attractive honey-blonde in her early twenties, was about four kilometers from the Jacobsen house, driving along the lakeside road in her dented Morris Minor convertible. She had already gone thru her rite of passage between innocent childhood & knowledgeable maturity, involving strong Freudian implications. Now she was driving thru a warm valley evening, wishing that she had come a week ago, when the cherry blossoms were still at the beginning of their decline.

She had not been home during blossom time for seven years, & perhaps this more than anything else told her that she had really ceast to be a valley kid, that she was a Coast person. Looking to her right she could see, even in the shadows made by the hills over the water, splotches of brown weeds under the surface of the lake. A part of her that still wanted to be a valley person was hurt by that.

She thought about taking a Valium before she got there, only two kilome- 25 ters to go now. It was not really the time to appear. She should have arrived while Art was still out in the orchard, so she could have a calm talk with her mother. When Art was there, making his blustery remarks or criticisms about her language, her mother could be depended on to remain silent, just as she had always done during family hassles, just as she had done then.

"I love him, Donna. What am I supposed to do?" she had said.

"More than you love me?" That newcomer.

"I *chose* him."

That was the last time her mother had ever said anything so devastatingly open.

She got out of the car & took a Valium. One gets adept at swallowing 30 them without water. She was mildly surprised that she was walking slowly toward the single little ponderosa pine that used to be her going-to-be-alone place in the far corner of their orchard. It had perhaps grown four inches taller. Looking, farther up, she could see Star Bright. She made a trivial wish & walkt slowly back to the dusty car.

What a beautiful sight she was, with her long legs & summer dress, sunglasses percht on top of her short feathery blondish hair.

Symbolism

Donna got back into the dented Morris Minor, & before she let the clutch out, she unaccountably thought about the animal heads protruding from her stepfather's walls. The first time she had seen one, she had gone to the room next door, to see whether the elk's body stuck out from that side. What had ever been done with the bodies, she wondered now. Were they discarded, left on the forest floor for the delectation of ants? Did the family eat them? She couldn't remember eating mountain goat or moose, & she had been a picky eater as a child.

She decided that whatever had been done with the torso & legs, Art was only really interested in the trophy. He talkt about nature a lot, but he was quite comfortable under the stare of the big glass eyes.

Her dog Bridey passed away after a fit when she was twelve. Quickly, before he would have a chance to take her to the taxidermist, Donna put the heavy & limp body along with an adult's shovel into a wheelbarrow & pusht it for half an hour thru the crumbling earth, to the ponderosa. There she wasted no time looking at Bridey's fur & tight-closed eyes. She dug a deep hole & dropt her in & covered her up, without looking. She left no marker. She knew where Bridey was, & that was all that was necessary.

Now, she reflected, looking at the sagebrush growing around her tree, they 35 probably knew too, he probably saw the wheel tracks the next morning.

She let out the clutch & drove the last kilometer slowly, having pulled on the lights. Just in time, a mother quail & her five little ones raced in a line to the safety of the roadside weeds. She smiled as she imagined the mother there, counting them.

Then she was at the turn just before their driveway, where the truck & the new Toyota were parkt in a sharp vee. People here along Rawleigh Road never pulled their drapes. Thru the window she could see Mr & Mrs Jacobsen, an over-coloured Carol, & a deer she used to call Bambi, first childishly, then later to needle her stepfather.

Her car's wheels cruncht over the driveway. Before she got out she did up her two top buttons.

Conflict

Donna had driven 400 kilometers to be there, but she didn't want to go inside the house. Of course in a setting such as this, they would know that somebody had driven up the gravel driveway, & one of them, probably her mother, would be walking to the door at this moment.

Donna wanted to be with her mother, & especially because she never wrote 40 letters home. She did not even imagine writing "Mrs A. Jacobsen" on an envelope. She felt as if, yes, she still loved her mother, that strange older woman in polyester slacks, though they had not once spoken to each other on the telephone since Jacobsen had mounted her as his casual season's trophy. What ambiguity in the delivery of the thought. When it was accomplisht, & all three knew, what depressing decisions & solitudes.

Donna could not stay in that family where her first love, her first world face, lost all hope & fell in, decided to stay with the bringer of death. What polluted language in the formerly unchallenged eden. Why? How, rather.

"But I chose him. I made my choice."

"Do you love him? Can you?"

"I chose him."

She was not a woman then, but she was not a valley girl, either. She left 45 Dog Lake, she had to, & there was no question but the city on the coast, several ruinous jobs & some solitary education.

Now the door opened & it was Audrey who was illuminated by the porch light. Donna was momentarily ashamed with disappointment that her mother, Mrs Michaels, was not the picture of a defeated lustreless farm wife, the sensitive buffeted by life, such as one expected to find in the Canadian novels she had been reading.

"Donna! For the Lord's sake! Why didnt you tell us you were coming? Come in, you rascal," the woman said, her arms outstretcht as if offering the red knitting she had been doing while watching television.

Donna held her mother's elbows & kissed her nose as she felt the screen door bat against her rear. Her mother chattered with a little confusion as the pretty blonde deposited her purse & a book & something wrapt in party paper on the telephone table.

"Well, well," said Art Jacobsen, looking up from his paper, his feet still stretcht out on the hassock.

Dialogue

"I wish I'd gotten here while the blossoms were in full bloom," said Donna. It was 50 the perfect little bit of business to get thru the awkwardness of their surprise.

"Oh, we had a wonderful year for blossoms," said her mother. "When a breeze came up the whole valley smelled like a garden."

"It *is* a garden," said Donna, getting herself a cup of coffee from the pot on the stove. She came back thru the arch into the living-room, where her mother was still standing with the knitting in her hands. "At least that's how we Coast people think of it."

Art shook his paper to a new page.

"It's not the blossoms that count. It's the bees."

"The workers, you mean," said Donna, a little edge on her voice. She sat down with her coffee, not looking at him.

"Yeah, the queen sits at home, getting fatter & fatter, while the workers bring her the honey," said Art, his eyes looking at a news photo of the local skeet-shooting champs.

"Have you had any supper, dear?" Audrey piped in.

"Yes, I stopt at the Princeton bus station cafe, for old times sake," said Donna.

That was a nice shot. It was there that she had abandoned Art's truck that night, with the keys in the dash. She'd taken the bus to Vancouver with no baggage, not even clean underwear. Just two apples & her purse.

Art didn't say a word now.

"Well, well," said Audrey Jacobsen.

There was a silence. Even the knitting-needles crost & opened without a sound. It was pitch dark outside. A mirrored deer lookt in from between two young Lombardy poplars.

"How are all your aches & pains, Mom?" Donna askt at last, idly looking at snapshots from a glass bowl on the table beside her chair. Carol was over, & Art raised his remote control & shot the set off.

"Oh, the osteopath in Penticton said I did something to my lower spine when I was a girl, & I can never expect to be a hundred percent."

"Does that mean you're not all there?" askt Art.

Flashback

When he seemed absolutely ready to give it up, give up on it, to settle for some costly talk then, she offered him a cigarette, which he took politely, & lit one herself. It was the only sort of occasion upon which she smoked, anything. They were always grateful, the talkers, when she by her gestures allowed them a certain comfort, a freedom from embarrassment.

"Thank you," he said, & lay on his back beside her, carefully sharing the ashtray she kept on her belly.

"You needn't feel badly." Her voice was soft & sure, caring & casual, it seemed. "You might be surprised how often it happens. You had a lot to drink, I would imagine, it was only enough to make you think you wanted me. Happens quite a lot."

"No, that's not it. Well, it might be a little, but that's not really it. It's . . ."

She did not offer the interruption he was waiting for. She just smoked her cigarette. She butted it out in the ashtray, & handed the ashtray to him. So he had something to do with his free hand.

"It's just that you are about exactly the age of my daughter," he said.

"No kidding," she said, with a twiggy edge to her voice, & that was his first hint that it was time to go back to his hotel.

Foreshadowing

After he had left, she got the scissors & clipped her toenails. Having done five, she lay back & imagined the john walking back to his hotel. He did not seem like the taxi-taking kind.

She pictured him lying on her, brought by her to the margin of success. Then she yanked the scissors toward her, fetching a jolt as they sank into the flesh of his back. It was not an old movie on midnight television. The points of her scissors were just below the joining of her ribcage, forcing the skin a little.

I wonder whether I could just throw a few clothes into the car & drive to 75 Montreal, she thought.

Maybe you could work your way across the country, she replied.

She clipped five toenails again. They were the same ones.

Plot

The spare bedroom of the Jacobsen house was also a kind of store-room. It contained a gun-rack in which one could find a pump-action shotgun, a .22 caliber repeater rifle, an old .303 that once belonged to the Canadian Army, a .44 handgun in a tooled holster, a 30-30 with a scope sight, & a collector's .30 caliber machine-gun with a plugged barrel. This is where Donna was, taking off her light cardigan & shoes, finding the toothbrush & dental floss in the bottom of her big-city street bag, looking at herself, untanned, in the vanity mirror. A severed goat head lookt over her shoulder.

Thru two walls she could hear the Jacobsens disputing. Art's voice rose & rose, & at the end of a declarative sentence fragment it uttered the word "slut," followed by an exclamation point.

One would expect the ammunition to be lockt up, & it was, in a cabinet 80 with glass-panel doors. Donna shook the pillow out of one of the pillowcases, wrapt the pillowcase around her fist, & puncht one of the glass panels three times, each time with greater force.

The male voice rose to the word "hell!" & stopt. A door banged against a wall, & heavy footsteps approacht. Donna threw the pillowcase onto the bed beside her sweater. When Art propelled the bedroom door open, Donna was pointing a loaded shotgun at his head.

Art backt out of the bedroom & walkt backward all the way to the living-room. There he observed a slight movement of the dark holes he had wiped clean just the night before, & sat down in his favorite chair. He was on top of Audrey's knitting, but he felt convinced that he should not bring attention to such a minor problem.

Audrey Jacobsen, usually a chatterbox, found it hard to find the words she should say.

She said, "Donna . . ."

It was very frightening that Donna did not say a word. Art looked de- 85 pressed. He was a heavy man in his chair. Donna blew out her breath.

"For God's sake, girl, that's my husband!"

Donna did not breathe in.

"He's my husband, he's all I have!"

Donna turned a smooth quick arc, & shot her mother's face off.

Theme

Donna walkt from the house & into the orchard, the shotgun still dangling. 90
She had no shoes on. No-one followed her, & she did not look behind. She was
walking between two rows of cherry trees, so that when a quick hard breeze
came around a rock outface it blew a snow of exhausted blossoms over her
head.

Donna walkt down the slope, not flinching when a clacking sprinkler spun
slowly & soakt her dress from the waist down. It was really dark out now, & she
could see the lights of the retirement village on the far side of the lake.

The gun had made a dreadful noise. But now the night life was speaking
again, crickets nearby & frogs from down by the lake. They were calling each
other to come & do it.

Donna walkt till she came to the dirt road with the row of couchgrass
down the middle, & followed it till she arrived at her ponderosa. There she sat
down with her back to its narrow trunk, & dropt the shotgun to the dry
ground. The sky was filled with bright stars that seemed to have edges, & black
behind them. One never saw anything like that from the streets in Vancouver.
She thought of the universality speaking thru her condition.

Nearby, her dog lay curled, waiting for her to signal something to her. But
she ignored her, as she fought to remember what had happened in the last
hour, or was it some years? An airline jet with powerful landing lights appeared
from the other side of the hills & descended over the lake, heavily pulling back
on its fall toward the airstrip at the end.

Now that her eyes were adjusted to the late spring darkness of the valley, 95
she saw a bat flipping from direction to direction above her. She remembered
the fear that it might get caught in your hair. Bats dont get caught in your hair.

I'm not very old, Donna thought, I'm not very old & here I am already.
She pickt up the shotgun & fired the other barrel, & threw it over the side of
the hill.

Considerations for Critical Thinking and Writing

1. FIRST RESPONSE. Why do you suppose Bowering arranges the story in sections under headings such as Setting, Characters, Protagonist, and so on?
   What is the effect of this organizing principle on your reading?

2. If you were to go beyond the generic title of "A Short Story," what would
   you title it? Why?

3. What information do you get from the Setting section that is useful in understanding the story?

4. What do you make of the narrator's discussion of point of view in the
   Characters section? How does it affect your reading of the story?

5. Describe the Jacobsens' marriage. Do you think they are happy together?
   Explain your response.

6. Characterize Donna's past. What sort of life has she lived?

7. What is symbolic in the Symbolism section? Are there any other important
   symbols in the story?

8. What is the conflict in the Conflict section? Is it also the major conflict in
   the story?

9. What do the Flashback and Foreshadowing sections tell you about Donna?

10. Why does Donna shoot her mother? Explain why you think the shooting is ironic or not.

11. What do you think is the theme of the story? Can it be found tidily wrapped up in the Theme section?

CONNECTIONS TO OTHER SELECTIONS

1. Compare the motives for the killings in this story and in Andre Dubus's "Killings" (p. 84).

2. Write an essay on the narration of "A Short Story" and Tim O'Brien's "How to Tell a True War Story." In what sense is each story, in part, about telling stories?

Tim O'Brien's "How to Tell a True War Story" explores the tensions that exist between truth and fiction. Like Bowering's narration in "A Short Story," the narrator in O'Brien's story seems to be a work in progress, a work that perhaps can never be satisfactorily completed because the narrator cannot stop telling it. Moreover, like Bowering and Atwood, O'Brien seems keenly aware of his audience and includes his audience as one of his characters. As you read, try to determine what part you play in O'Brien's story.

TIM O'BRIEN (B. 1946)

Born in Austin, Minnesota, Tim O'Brien was educated at Macalester College and Harvard University. He was drafted to serve in the Vietnam War and received a Purple Heart. His work is heavily influenced by his service in the war. His first book, *If I Die in a Combat Zone, Box Me Up and Ship Me Home* (1973), is a blend of fiction and actual experiences during his tour of duty. *Going after Cacciato,* judged by many critics to be the best work of American fiction about the Vietnam War, won the National Book Award in 1978. He has also published four other novels, *Northern Lights* (1974), *The Nuclear Age* (1985), *In the Lake of the Woods* (1994), and *Tomcat in Love* (1998). "How to Tell a True War Story" is from a collection of interrelated stories titled *The Things They Carried* (1990). Originally published in *Esquire,* this story is at once grotesque and beautiful in its attempt to be true to experience.

Research Tim O'Brien with LitLinks at
http://www.bedfordstmartins.com/meyer/bedintrolit

How to Tell a True War Story   1987

This is true.

I had a buddy in Vietnam. His name was Bob Kiley, but everybody called him Rat.

A friend of his gets killed, so about a week later Rat sits down and writes a letter to the guy's sister. Rat tells her what a great brother she had, how strack° the guy was, a number one pal and comrade. A real soldier's soldier, Rat says. Then he tells a few stories to make the point, how her brother would always volunteer for stuff nobody else would volunteer for in a million years, dangerous stuff, like doing recon° or going out on these really badass night patrols. Stainless steel balls, Rat tells her. The guy was a little crazy, for sure, but crazy in a good way, a real daredevil, because he liked the challenge of it, he liked testing himself, just man against gook. A great, great guy, Rat says.

Anyway, it's a terrific letter, very personal and touching. Rat almost bawls writing it. He gets all teary telling about the good times they had together, how her brother made the war seem almost fun, always raising hell and lighting up villes° and bringing smoke to bear every which way. A great sense of humor, too. Like the time at this river when he went fishing with a whole damn crate of hand grenades. Probably the funniest thing in world history, Rat says, all that gore, about twenty zillion dead gook fish. Her brother, he had the right attitude. He knew how to have a good time. On Halloween, this real hot spooky night, the dude paints up his body all different colors and puts on this weird mask and goes out on ambush almost stark naked, just boots and balls and an M-16. A tremendous human being, Rat says. Pretty nutso sometimes, but you could trust him with your life.

And then the letter gets very sad and serious. Rat pours his heart out. He 5 says he loved the guy. He says the guy was his best friend in the world. They were like soul mates, he says, like twins or something, they had a whole lot in common. He tells the guy's sister he'll look her up when the war's over.

So what happens?

Rat mails the letter. He waits two months. The dumb cooze never writes back.

A true war story is never moral. It does not instruct, nor encourage virtue, nor suggest models of proper human behavior, nor restrain men from doing the things they have always done. If a story seems moral, do not believe it. If at the end of a war story you feel uplifted, or if you feel that some small bit of rectitude has been salvaged from the larger waste, then you have been made the victim of a very old and terrible lie. There is no rectitude whatsoever. There is no virtue. As a first rule of thumb, therefore, you can tell a true war story by its absolute and uncompromising allegiance to obscenity and evil. Listen to Rat Kiley. *Cooze*, he says. He does not say *bitch*. He certainly does not say *woman*, or *girl*. He says *cooze*. Then he spits and stares. He's nineteen years old — it's too much for him — so he looks at you with those big gentle killer eyes and says *cooze*, because his friend is dead, and because it's so incredibly sad and true: she never wrote back.

You can tell a true war story if it embarrasses you. If you don't care for obscenity, you don't care for the truth; if you don't care for the truth, watch how you vote. Send guys to war, they come home talking dirty.

Listen to Rat: "Jesus Christ, man, I write this beautiful fucking letter, I 10 slave over it, and what happens? The dumb cooze never writes back."

The dead guy's name was Curt Lemon. What happened was, we crossed a muddy river and marched west into the mountains, and on the third day we

strack: A strict military appearance.
doing recon: Reconnaissance, or exploratory survey of enemy territory.
villes: Villages.

took a break along a trail junction in deep jungle. Right away, Lemon and Rat Kiley started goofing off. They didn't understand about the spookiness. They were kids; they just didn't know. A nature hike, they thought, not even a war, so they went off into the shade of some giant trees—quadruple canopy, no sunlight at all—and they were giggling and calling each other motherfucker and playing a silly game they'd invented. The game involved smoke grenades, which were harmless unless you did stupid things, and what they did was pull out the pin and stand a few feet apart and play catch under the shade of those huge trees. Whoever chickened out was a motherfucker. And if nobody chickened out, the grenade would make a light popping sound and they'd be covered with smoke and they'd laugh and dance around and then do it again.

It's all exactly true.

It happened nearly twenty years ago, but I still remember that trail junction and the giant trees and a soft dripping sound somewhere beyond the trees. I remember the smell of moss. Up in the canopy there were tiny white blossoms, but no sunlight at all, and I remember the shadows spreading out under the trees where Lemon and Rat Kiley were playing catch with smoke grenades. Mitchell Sanders sat flipping his yo-yo. Norman Bowker and Kiowa and Dave Jensen were dozing, or half-dozing, and all around us were those ragged green mountains.

Except for the laughter things were quiet.

At one point, I remember, Mitchell Sanders turned and looked at me, not quite nodding, then after a while he rolled up his yo-yo and moved away.   15

It's hard to tell what happened next.

They were just goofing. There was a noise, I suppose, which must've been the detonator, so I glanced behind me and watched Lemon step from the shade into bright sunlight. His face was suddenly brown and shining. A handsome kid, really. Sharp gray eyes, lean and narrow-waisted, and when he died it was almost beautiful, the way the sunlight came around him and lifted him up and sucked him high into a tree full of moss and vines and white blossoms.

In any war story, but especially a true one, it's difficult to separate what happened from what seemed to happen. What seems to happen becomes its own happening and has to be told that way. The angles of vision are skewed. When a booby trap explodes, you close your eyes and duck and float outside yourself. When a guy dies, like Lemon, you look away and then look back for a moment and then look away again. The pictures get jumbled; you tend to miss a lot. And then afterward, when you go to tell about it, there is always that surreal seemingness, which makes the story seem untrue, but which in fact represents the hard and exact truth as it seemed.

In many cases a true war story cannot be believed. If you believe it, be skeptical. It's a question of credibility. Often the crazy stuff is true and the normal stuff isn't because the normal stuff is necessary to make you believe the truly incredible craziness.

In other cases you can't even tell a true war story. Sometimes it's just beyond telling.   20

I heard this one, for example, from Mitchell Sanders. It was near dusk and we were sitting at my foxhole along a wide, muddy river north of Quang Ngai. I remember how peaceful the twilight was. A deep pinkish red spilled out on the river, which moved without sound, and in the morning we would cross the river and march west into the mountains. The occasion was right for a good story.

"God's truth," Mitchell Sanders said. "A six-man patrol goes up into the mountains on a basic listening-post operation. The idea's to spend a week up there, just lie low and listen for enemy movement. They've got a radio along, so if they hear anything suspicious — anything — they're supposed to call in artillery or gunships, whatever it takes. Otherwise they keep strict field discipline. Absolute silence. They just listen."

He glanced at me to make sure I had the scenario. He was playing with his yo-yo, making it dance with short, tight little strokes of the wrist.

His face was blank in the dusk.

"We're talking hardass LP.° These six guys, they don't say boo for a solid week. They don't got tongues. *All* ears."

"Right," I said.

"Understand me?"

"Invisible."

Sanders nodded.

"Affirm," he said. "Invisible. So what happens is, these guys get themselves deep in the bush, all camouflaged up, and they lie down and wait and that's all they do, nothing else, they lie there for seven straight days and just listen. And man, I'll tell you — it's spooky. This is mountains. You don't *know* spooky till you been there. Jungle, sort of, except it's way up in the clouds and there's always this fog — like rain, except it's not raining — everything's all wet and swirly and tangled up and you can't see jack, you can't find your own pecker to piss with. Like you don't even have a body. Serious spooky. You just go with the vapors — the fog sort of takes you in. . . . And the sounds, man. The sounds carry forever. You hear shit nobody should *ever* hear."

Sanders was quiet for a second, just working the yo-yo, then he smiled at me. "So, after a couple days the guys start hearing this real soft, kind of wacked-out music. Weird echoes and stuff. Like a radio or something, but it's not a radio, it's this strange gook music that comes right out of the rocks. Faraway, sort of, but right up close, too. They try to ignore it. But it's a listening post, right? So they listen. And every night they keep hearing this crazyass gook concert. All kinds of chimes and xylophones. I mean, this is wilderness — no way, it can't be real — but there it *is,* like the mountains are tuned in to Radio Fucking Hanoi. Naturally they get nervous. One guy sticks Juicy Fruit in his ears. Another guy almost flips. Thing is, though, they can't report music. They can't get on the horn and call back to base and say, 'Hey, listen, we need some firepower, we got to blow away this weirdo gook rock band.' They can't do that. It wouldn't go down. So they lie there in the fog and keep their mouths shut. And what makes it extra bad, see, is the poor dudes can't horse around like normal. Can't joke it away. Can't even talk to each other except maybe in whispers, all hush-hush, and that just revs up the willies. All they do is listen."

Again there was some silence as Mitchell Sanders looked out on the river. The dark was coming on hard now, and off to the west I could see the mountains rising in silhouette, all the mysteries and unknowns.

LP: Listening post.

"This next part," Sanders said quietly, "you won't believe."

"Probably not," I said.

"You won't. And you know why?"

"Why?" 35

He gave me a tired smile. "Because it happened. Because every word is absolutely dead-on true."

Sanders made a little sound in his throat, like a sigh, as if to say he didn't care if I believed it or not. But he did care. He wanted me to believe, I could tell. He seemed sad, in a way.

"These six guys, they're pretty fried out by now, and one night they start hearing voices. Like at a cocktail party. That's what it sounds like, this big swank gook cocktail party somewhere out there in the fog. Music and chitchat and stuff. It's crazy, I know, but they hear the champagne corks. They hear the actual martini glasses. Real hoity-toity, all very civilized, except this isn't civilization. This is Nam.

"Anyway, the guys try to be cool. They just lie there and groove, but after a 40 while they start hearing—you won't believe this—they hear chamber music. They hear violins and shit. They hear this terrific mama-san soprano. Then after a while they hear gook opera and a glee club and the Haiphong Boys Choir and a barbershop quartet and all kinds of weird chanting and Buddha-Buddha stuff. The whole time, in the background, there's still that cocktail party going on. All these different voices. Not human voices, though. Because it's the mountains. Follow me? The rock—it's *talking*. And the fog, too, and the grass and the goddamn mongooses. Everything talks. The trees talk politics, the monkeys talk religion. The whole country. Vietnam, the place talks.

"The guys can't cope. They lose it. They get on the radio and report enemy movement—a whole army, they say—and they order up the firepower. They get arty° and gunships. They call in air strikes. And I'll tell you, they fuckin' crash that cocktail party. All night long, they just smoke those mountains. They make jungle juice. They blow away trees and glee clubs and whatever else there is to blow away. Scorch time. They walk napalm up and down the ridges. They bring in the Cobras and F-4s, they use Willie Peter and HE° and incendiaries. It's all fire. They make those mountains burn.

"Around dawn things finally get quiet. Like you never even *heard* quiet before. One of those real thick, real misty days—just clouds and fog, they're off in this special zone—and the mountains are absolutely dead-flat silent. Like Brigadoon°—pure vapor, you know? Everything's all sucked up inside the fog. Not a single sound, except they still *hear* it.

"So they pack up and start humping. They head down the mountain, back to base camp, and when they get there they don't say diddly. They don't talk. Not a word, like they're deaf and dumb. Later on this fat bird colonel comes up and asks what the hell happened out there. What'd they hear? Why all the ordnance? The man's ragged out, he gets down tight on their case. I mean, they spent six trillion dollars on firepower, and this fatass colonel wants answers, he wants to know what the fuckin' story is.

"But the guys don't say zip. They just look at him for a while, sort of funny-like, sort of amazed, and the whole war is right there in that stare. It

---

arty: Artillery.

Willie Peter and HE: White phosphorus, an incendiary substance, and high explosives.

Brigadoon: A fictional village in Scotland that only appears once every one hundred years; subject of a popular American musical (1947).

says everything you can't ever say. It says, man, you got *wax* in your ears. It says, poor bastard, you'll never know—wrong frequency—you don't *even* want to hear this. Then they salute the fucker and walk away, because certain stories you don't ever tell."

You can tell a true war story by the way it never seems to end. Not then, not 45 ever. Not when Mitchell Sanders stood up and moved off into the dark.

It all happened.

Even now I remember that yo-yo. In a way, I suppose, you had to be there, you had to hear it, but I could tell how desperately Sanders wanted me to believe him, his frustration at not quite getting the details right, not quite pinning down the final and definitive truth.

And I remember sitting at my foxhole that night, watching the shadows of Quang Ngai, thinking about the coming day and how we would cross the river and march west into the mountains, all the ways I might die, all the things I did not understand.

Late in the night Mitchell Sanders touched my shoulder.

"Just came to me," he whispered. "The moral, I mean. Nobody listens. No- 50 body hears nothing. Like that fatass colonel. The politicians, all the civilian types, what they need is to go out on LP. The vapors, man. Trees and rocks— you got to *listen* to your enemy."

And then again, in the morning, Sanders came up to me. The platoon was preparing to move out, checking weapons, going through all the little rituals that preceded a day's march. Already the lead squad had crossed the river and was filing off toward the west.

"I got a confession to make," Sanders said. "Last night, man, I had to make up a few things."

"I know that."

"The glee club. There wasn't any glee club."

"Right." 55

"No opera."

"Forget it, I understand."

"Yeah, but listen, it's still true. Those six guys, they heard wicked sound out there. They heard sound you just plain won't believe."

Sanders pulled on his rucksack, closed his eyes for a moment, then almost smiled at me.

I knew what was coming but I beat him to it. 60

"All right," I said, "what's the moral?"

"Forget it."

"No, go ahead."

For a long while he was quiet, looking away, and the silence kept stretching out until it was almost embarrassing. Then he shrugged and gave me a stare that lasted all day.

"Hear that quiet, man?" he said. "There's your moral." 65

In a true war story, if there's a moral at all, it's like the thread that makes the cloth. You can't tease it out. You can't extract the meaning without unraveling the deeper meaning. And in the end, really, there's nothing much to say about a true war story, except maybe "Oh."

True war stories do not generalize. They do not indulge in abstraction or analysis.

For example: War is hell. As a moral declaration the old truism seems perfectly true, and yet because it abstracts, because it generalizes, I can't believe it with my stomach. Nothing turns inside.

It comes down to gut instinct. A true war story, if truly told, makes the stomach believe.

This one does it for me. I've told it before — many times, many versions — but   70
here's what actually happened.

We crossed the river and marched west into the mountains. On the third day, Curt Lemon stepped on a booby-trapped 105 round. He was playing catch with Rat Kiley, laughing, and then he was dead. The trees were thick; it took nearly an hour to cut an LZ for the dustoff.°

Later, higher in the mountains, we came across a baby VC° water buffalo. What it was doing there I don't know — no farms or paddies — but we chased it down and got a rope around it and led it along to a deserted village where we set for the night. After supper Rat Kiley went over and stroked its nose.

He opened up a can of C rations, pork and beans, but the baby buffalo wasn't interested.

Rat shrugged.

He stepped back and shot it through the right front knee. The animal did   75
not make a sound. It went down hard, then got up again, and Rat took careful aim and shot off an ear. He shot it in the hindquarters and in the little hump at its back. He shot it twice in the flanks. It wasn't to kill; it was just to hurt. He put the rifle muzzle up against the mouth and shot the mouth away. Nobody said much. The whole platoon stood there watching, feeling all kinds of things, but there wasn't a great deal of pity for the baby water buffalo. Lemon was dead. Rat Kiley had lost his best friend in the world. Later in the week he would write a long personal letter to the guy's sister, who would not write back, but for now it was a question of pain. He shot off the tail. He shot away chunks of meat below the ribs. All around us there was the smell of smoke and filth, and deep greenery, and the evening was humid and very hot. Rat went to automatic. He shot randomly, almost casually, quick little spurts in the belly and butt. Then he reloaded, squatted down, and shot it in the left front knee. Again the animal fell hard and tried to get up, but this time it couldn't quite make it. It wobbled and went down sideways. Rat shot it in the nose. He bent forward and whispered something, as if talking to a pet, then he shot it in the throat. All the while the baby buffalo was silent, or almost silent, just a light bubbling sound where the nose had been. It lay very still. Nothing moved except the eyes, which were enormous, the pupils shiny black and dumb.

Rat Kiley was crying. He tried to say something, but then cradled his rifle and went off by himself.

The rest of us stood in a ragged circle around the baby buffalo. For a time no one spoke. We had witnessed something essential, something brand-new and profound, a piece of the world so startling there was not yet a name for it.

Somebody kicked the baby buffalo.

It was still alive, though just barely, just in the eyes.

"Amazing," Dave Jensen said. "My whole life, I never seen anything like it."   80

LZ for the dustoff: Landing zone for a helicopter evacuation of a casualty.
VC: Vietcong (North Vietnamese).

"Never?"

"Not hardly. Not once."

Kiowa and Mitchell Sanders picked up the baby buffalo. They hauled it across the open square, hoisted it up, and dumped it in the village well.

Afterward, we sat waiting for Rat to get himself together.

"Amazing," Dave Jensen kept saying.   85

"For sure."

"A new wrinkle. I never seen it before."

Mitchell Sanders took out his yo-yo.

"Well, that's Nam," he said. "Garden of Evil. Over here, man, every sin's real fresh and original."

How do you generalize?   90

War is hell, but that's not the half of it, because war is also mystery and terror and adventure and courage and discovery and holiness and pity and despair and longing and love. War is nasty; war is fun. War is thrilling; war is drudgery. War makes you a man; war makes you dead.

The truths are contradictory. It can be argued, for instance, that war is grotesque. But in truth war is also beauty. For all its horror, you can't help but gape at the awful majesty of combat. You stare out at tracer rounds unwinding through the dark like brilliant red ribbons. You crouch in ambush as a cool, impassive moon rises over the nighttime paddies. You admire the fluid symmetries of troops on the move, the harmonies of sound and shape and proportion, the great sheets of metal-fire streaming down from a gunship, the illumination rounds, the white phosphorous, the purply black glow of napalm, the rocket's red glare. It's not pretty, exactly. It's astonishing. It fills the eye. It commands you. You hate it, yes, but your eyes do not. Like a killer forest fire, like cancer under a microscope, any battle or bombing raid or artillery barrage has the aesthetic purity of absolute moral indifference — a powerful, implacable beauty — and a true war story will tell the truth about this, though the truth is ugly.

To generalize about war is like generalizing about peace. Almost everything is true. Almost nothing is true. At its core, perhaps, war is just another name for death, and yet any soldier will tell you, if he tells the truth, that proximity to death brings with it a corresponding proximity to life. After a fire fight, there is always the immense pleasure of aliveness. The trees are alive. The grass, the soil — everything. All around you things are purely living, and you among them, and the aliveness makes you tremble. You feel an intense, out-of-the-skin awareness of your living self — your truest self, the human being you want to be and then become by the force of wanting it. In the midst of evil you want to be a good man. You want decency. You want justice and courtesy and human concord, things you never knew you wanted. There is a kind of largeness to it; a kind of godliness. Though it's odd, you're never more alive than when you're almost dead. You recognize what's valuable. Freshly, as if for the first time, you love what's best in yourself and in the world, all that might be lost. At the hour of dusk you sit at your foxhole and look out on a wide river turning pinkish red, and at the mountains beyond, and although in the morning you must cross the river and go into the mountains and do terrible things and maybe die, even so, you find yourself studying the fine colors on the river, you feel wonder and awe at the setting of the sun, and you are filled with a hard, aching love for how the world could be and always should be, but now is not.

Mitchell Sanders was right. For the common soldier, at least, war has the feel — the spiritual texture — of a great ghostly fog, thick and permanent. There is no clarity. Everything swirls. The old rules are no longer binding, the old truths no longer true. Right spills over into wrong. Order blends into chaos, love into hate, ugliness into beauty, law into anarchy, civility into savagery. The vapors suck you in. You can't tell where you are, or why you're there, and the only certainty is absolute ambiguity.

In war you lose your sense of the definite, hence your sense of truth itself, and therefore it's safe to say that in a true war story nothing much is ever very true.   95

Often in a true war story there is not even a point, or else the point doesn't hit you until twenty years later, in your sleep, and you wake up and shake your wife and start telling the story to her, except when you get to the end you've forgotten the point again. And then for a long time you lie there watching the story happen in your head. You listen to your wife's breathing. The war's over. You close your eyes. You smile and think, Christ, what's the *point?*

This one wakes me up.

In the mountains that day, I watched Lemon turn sideways. He laughed and said something to Rat Kiley. Then he took a peculiar half step, moving from shade into bright sunlight, and the booby-trapped 105 round blew him into a tree. The parts were just hanging there, so Norman Bowker and I were ordered to shinny up and peel him off. I remember the white bone of an arm. I remember pieces of skin and something wet and yellow that must've been the intestines. The gore was horrible, and stays with me, but what wakes me up twenty years later is Norman Bowker singing "Lemon Tree" as we threw down the parts.

You can tell a true war story by the questions you ask. Somebody tells a story, let's say, and afterward you ask, "Is it true?" and if the answer matters, you've got your answer.

For example, we've all heard this one. Four guys go down a trail. A grenade   100 sails out. One guy jumps on it and takes the blast and saves his three buddies.

Is it true?

The answer matters.

You'd feel cheated if it never happened. Without the grounding reality, it's just a trite bit of puffery, pure Hollywood, untrue in the way all such stories are untrue. Yet even if it did happen — and maybe it did, anything's possible — even then you know it can't be true, because a true war story does not depend upon that kind of truth. Happeningness is irrelevant. A thing may happen and be a total lie; another thing may not happen and be truer than the truth. For example: four guys go down a trail. A grenade sails out. One guy jumps on it and takes the blast, but it's a killer grenade and everybody dies anyway. Before they die, though, one of the dead guys says, "The fuck you do *that* for?" and the jumper says, "Story of my life, man," and the other guy starts to smile but he's dead.

That's a true story that never happened.

Twenty years later, I can still see the sunlight on Lemon's face. I can see him   105 turning, looking back at Rat Kiley, then he laughed and took that curious half step from shade into sunlight, his face suddenly brown and shining, and when his foot touched down, in that instant, he must've thought it was the sunlight that was killing him. It was not the sunlight. It was a rigged 105 round. But if I could ever get the story right, how the sun seemed to gather around him and pick him up and lift him into a tree, if I could somehow recreate the fatal whiteness of that light, the quick glare, the obvious cause and effect, then you would believe the last thing Lemon believed, which for him must've been the final truth.

Now and then, when I tell this story, someone will come up to me afterward and say she liked it. It's always a woman. Usually it's an older woman of kindly temperament and humane politics. She'll explain that as a rule she hates war stories, she can't understand why people want to wallow in blood and gore. But this one she liked. Sometimes, even, there are little tears. What I should do, she'll say, is put it all behind me. Find new stories to tell.

I won't say it but I'll think it.

I'll picture Rat Kiley's face, his grief, and I'll think, *You dumb cooze.*

Because she wasn't listening.

It wasn't a war story. It was a love story. It was a ghost story.   110

But you can't say that. All you can do is tell it one more time, patiently, adding and subtracting, making up a few things to get at the real truth. No Mitchell Sanders, you tell her. No Lemon, no Rat Kiley. And it didn't happen in the mountains, it happened in this little village on the Batangan Peninsula, and it was raining like crazy, and one night a guy named Stink Harris woke up screaming with a leech on his tongue. You can tell a true war story if you just keep on telling it.

In the end, of course, a true war story is never about war. It's about the special way that dawn spreads out on a river when you know you must cross the river and march into the mountains and do things you are afraid to do. It's about love and memory. It's about sorrow. It's about sisters who never write back and people who never listen.

CONSIDERATIONS FOR CRITICAL THINKING AND WRITING

1. FIRST RESPONSE. What implicit problem is created about the story by its first line, "This is true"? How is the notion of "truth" problematized throughout the story?

2. Why is Rat Kiley so upset over Curt Lemon's sister not writing back?

3. How are you affected by the descriptions of Curt Lemon being blown up in paragraphs 17, 98, and 105?

4. Analyze the story told about the six-man patrol in paragraphs 19–65. How is this story relevant to the rest of the plot?

5. What emotions did you feel as you read about the shooting of the water buffalo? How does paragraph 75 achieve these effects?

6. Explain what you think O'Brien means when he writes "After a fire fight, there is always the immense pleasure of aliveness" (para. 93).

7. Trace the narrator's comments about what constitutes a true war story. What do you think these competing and contradictory ideas finally add up to?

8. Characterize the narrator. Why must he repeatedly "keep on telling" his war story?

9. Consider O'Brien's use of profanity and violence in this story. Do you think they are essential or merely sensational?

10. CRITICAL STRATEGIES. Read the discussion concerning historical criticism (pp. 2101–02) in Chapter 52, "Critical Strategies for Reading," and research American protests and reactions to the war in Vietnam. How are these responses relevant to O'Brien's story, particularly paragraphs 1–10 and 106–111?

CONNECTIONS TO OTHER SELECTIONS

1. Imagine Krebs from Ernest Hemingway's "Soldier's Home" (p. 152) writing a letter home recommending "How to Tell a True War Story" to his parents. Write that letter from Krebs's point of view.

2. How does the treatment of violence in O'Brien's story compare with that in Andre Dubus's "Killings" (p. 84)? Write an essay that points to specific descriptions and explains the fuction of the violence in each story.

Although Don DeLillo's "Videotape" is technically about television rather than writing, his story produces fundamental questions about what contemporary culture finds compelling and entertaining as well as how fiction can provide a commentary about that culture. In what sense can DeLillo's story serve as an enclosing summation of the many issues raised in the stories written by Atwood, Bowering, and O'Brien?

DON DELILLO (B. 1936)

Born in 1936, Don DeLillo grew up in an Italian American community in the Bronx, where he studied communication arts at Fordham College before beginning a short-lived career writing copy for an advertising agency. He published his first story in 1960, and four years later quit his job to devote himself fully to writing. His first novel, *Americana,* appeared in 1971, and he has since published eleven novels including *Libra* (1988), *Mao II* (1991), *Underworld* (1997), *The Body Artist* (2001), and *White Noise* (1985), which won the National Book Award. He is also the author of numerous essays, short stories, and plays, including *Valparaiso* (1999). DeLillo's work is defined by a sense of apocalyptic urgency, a postmodern preoccupation with spectacle and fragmentary perception, and an interest in mass media and the collective American experience.

Web   *Research Don DeLillo with LitLinks at*
http://www.bedfordstmartins.com/meyer/bedintrolit

Videotape   *1984*

It shows a man driving a car. It is the simplest sort of family video. You see a man at the wheel of a medium Dodge.

It is just a kid aiming her camera through the rear window of the family car at the windshield of the car behind her.

You know about families and their video cameras. You know how kids get involved, how the camera shows them that every subject is potentially charged, a million things they never see with the unaided eye. They investigate the meaning of inert objects and dumb pets and they poke at family privacy. They learn to see things twice.

It is the kid's own privacy that is being protected here. She is twelve years old and her name is being withheld even though she is neither the victim nor the perpetrator of the crime but only the means of recording it.

It shows a man in a sport shirt at the wheel of his car. There is nothing else 5 to see. The car approaches briefly, then falls back.

You know how children with cameras learn to work the exposed moments that define the family cluster. They break every trust, spy out the undefended space, catching Mom coming out of the bathroom in her cumbrous robe and turbaned towel, looking bloodless and plucked. It is not a joke. They will shoot you sitting on the pot if they can manage a suitable vantage.

The tape has the jostled sort of noneventness that marks the family product. Of course the man in this case is not a member of the family but a stranger in a car, a random figure, someone who has happened along in the slow lane.

It shows a man in his forties wearing a pale shirt open at the throat, the image washed by reflections and sunglint, with many jostled moments.

It is not just another video homicide. It is a homicide recorded by a child who thought she was doing something simple and maybe halfway clever, shooting some tape of a man in a car.

He sees the girl and waves briefly, wagging a hand without taking it off the 10 wheel—an underplayed reaction that makes you like him.

It is unrelenting footage that rolls on and on. It has an aimless determination, a persistence that lives outside the subject matter. You are looking into the mind of home video. It is innocent, it is aimless, it is determined, it is real.

He is bald up the middle of his head, a nice guy in his forties whose whole life seems open to the handheld camera.

But there is also an element of suspense. You keep on looking not because you know something is going to happen—of course you do know something is going to happen and you do look for that reason but you might also keep on looking if you came across this footage for the first time without knowing the outcome. There is a crude power operating here. You keep on looking because things combine to hold you fast—a sense of the random, the amateurish, the accidental, the impending. You don't think of the tape as boring or interesting. It is crude, it is blunt, it is relentless. It is the jostled part of your mind, the film that runs through your hotel brain under all the thoughts you know you're thinking.

The world is lurking in the camera, already framed, waiting for the boy or girl who will come along and take up the device, learn the instrument, shooting old Granddad at breakfast, all stroked out so his nostrils gape, the cereal spoon baby-gripped in his pale fist.

It shows a man alone in a medium Dodge. It seems to go on forever. 15

There's something about the nature of the tape, the grain of the image, the sputtering black-and-white tones, the starkness—you think this is more real, truer to life than anything around you. The things around you have a re-hearsed and layered and cosmetic look. The tape is superreal, or maybe under-real is the way you want to put it. It is what lies at the scraped bottom of all the layers you have added. And this is another reason why you keep on looking. The tape has a searing realness.

It shows him giving an abbreviated wave, stiff-palmed, like a signal flag at a siding.

You know how families make up games. This is just another game in which the child invents the rules as she goes along. She likes the idea of video-taping a man in his car. She has probably never done it before and she sees no reason to vary the format or terminate early or pan to another car. This is her game and she is learning it and playing it at the same time. She feels halfway clever and inventive and maybe slightly intrusive as well, a little bit of brazen-ness that spices any game.

And you keep on looking. You look because this is the nature of the footage, to make a channeled path through time, to give things a shape and a destiny.

Of course if she had panned to another car, the right car at the precise   20
time, she would have caught the gunman as he fired.

The chance quality of the encounter. The victim, the killer, and the child with a camera. Random energies that approach a common point. There's something here that speaks to you directly, saying terrible things about forces beyond your control, lines of intersection that cut through history and logic and every reasonable layer of human expectation.

She wandered into it. The girl got lost and wandered clear-eyed into hor-ror. This is a children's story about straying too far from home. But it isn't the family car that serves as the instrument of the child's curiosity, her inclination to explore. It is the camera that puts her in the tale.

You know about holidays and family celebrations and how somebody shows up with a camcorder and the relatives stand around and barely react be-cause they're numbingly accustomed to the process of being taped and decked and shown on the VCR with the coffee and cake.

He is hit soon after. If you've seen the tape many times you know from the handwave exactly when he will be hit. It is something, naturally, that you wait for. You say to your wife, if you're at home and she is there, Now here is where he gets it. You say, Janet, hurry up, this is where it happens.

Now here is where he gets it. You see him jolted, sort of wire shocked —   25
then he seizes up and falls toward the door or maybe leans or slides into the door is the proper way to put it. It is awful and unremarkable at the same time. The car stays in the slow lane. It approaches briefly, then falls back.

You don't usually call your wife over to the TV set. She has her programs, you have yours. But there's a certain urgency here. You want her to see how it looks. The tape has been running forever and now the thing is finally going to happen and you want her to be here when he's shot.

Here it comes, all right. He is shot, head-shot, and the camera reacts, the child reacts — there is a jolting movement but she keeps on taping, there is a sympathetic response, a nerve response, her heart is beating faster but she keeps the camera trained on the subject as he slides into the door and even as you see him die you're thinking of the girl. At some level the girl has to be pres-ent here, watching what you're watching, unprepared — the girl is seeing this cold and you have to marvel at the fact that she keeps the tape rolling.

It shows something awful and unaccompanied. You want your wife to see it because it is real this time, not fancy movie violence — the realness beneath the layers of cosmetic perception. Hurry up, Janet, here it comes. He dies so fast. There is no accompaniment of any kind. It is very stripped. You want to tell her it is realer than real but then she will ask what that means.

The way the camera reacts to the gunshot—a startle reaction that brings pity and terror into the frame, the girl's own shock, the girl's identification with the victim.

You don't see the blood, which is probably trickling behind his ear and down the back of his neck. The way his head is twisted away from the door, the twist of the head gives you only a partial profile and it's the wrong side, it's not the side where he was hit.

And maybe you're being a little aggressive here, practically forcing your wife to watch. Why? What are you telling her? Are you making a little statement? Like I'm going to ruin your day out of ordinary spite. Or a big statement? Like this is the risk of existing. Either way you're rubbing her face in this tape and you don't know why.

It shows the car drifting toward the guardrail and then there's a jostling sense of two other lanes and part of another car, a split-second blur, and the tape ends here, either because the girl stopped shooting or because some central authority, the police or the district attorney or the TV station, decided there was nothing else you had to see.

This is either the tenth or eleventh homicide committed by the Texas Highway Killer. The number is uncertain because the police believe that one of the shootings may have been a copycat crime.

And there is something about videotape, isn't there, and this particular kind of serial crime? This is a crime designed for random taping and immediate playing. You sit there and wonder if this kind of crime became more possible when the means of taping and playing an event—playing it immediately after the taping—became part of the culture. The principal doesn't necessarily commit the sequence of crimes in order to see them taped and played. He commits the crimes as if they were a form of taped-and-played event. The crimes are inseparable from the idea of taping and playing. You sit there thinking that this is a crime that has found its medium, or vice versa—cheap mass production, the sequence of repeated images and victims, stark and glary and more or less unremarkable.

It shows very little in the end. It is a famous murder because it is on tape and because the murderer has done it many times and because the crime was recorded by a child. So the child is involved, the Video Kid as she is sometimes called because they have to call her something. The tape is famous and so is she. She is famous in the modern manner of people whose names are strategically withheld. They are famous without names or faces, spirits living apart from their bodies, the victims and witnesses, the underage criminals, out there somewhere at the edges of perception.

Seeing someone at the moment he dies, dying unexpectedly. This is reason alone to stay fixed to the screen. It is instructional, watching a man shot dead as he drives along on a sunny day. It demonstrates an elemental truth, that every breath you take has two possible endings. And that's another thing. There's a joke locked away here, a note of cruel slapstick that you are completely willing to appreciate. Maybe the victim's a chump, a dope, classically unlucky. He had it coming, in a way, like an innocent fool in a silent movie.

You don't want Janet to give you any crap about it's on all the time, they show it a thousand times a day. They show it because it exists, because they have to show it, because this is why they're out there. The horror freezes your soul but this doesn't mean that you want them to stop.

CONSIDERATIONS FOR CRITICAL THINKING AND WRITING

1. FIRST RESPONSE. Probably just about everyone has had the experience of repeatedly watching "Real TV" videotapes of crimes, natural disasters, or terrible accidents. How does your experience compare with the narrator's? Did you find yourself identifying with him? Why or why not?

2. Who is the protagonist — the narrator or the girl? What do we learn about each of them?

3. What function do you think the wife, Janet, serves in the story?

4. What is the effect of the second-person narration? How do you think the story would be different if it were told from a first- or third-person point of view?

5. How does DeLillo create suspense in the story?

6. Notice how frequently the videotape is described by the phrase "It shows . . . ." How does this affect your response to the videotape?

7. What do you think the narrator means when he says that the "nature of the tape" seems "more real, truer to life than anything around you" (para. 16)? Consider other moments in the story when the "nature of the tape" is discussed as having a "searing realness," and explain why you agree or disagree.

8. The narrator claims that the video camera shows us "that every subject is potentially charged, a million things" never seen "with the unaided eye" (para. 3). Does that strike you as true? Do you think it is equally true of literature? Explain why or why not.

9. The narrator concludes with this assertion about videotapes: "The horror freezes your soul but this doesn't mean that you want them to stop." What do you think he means by this assessment? Explain why you agree or disagree.

CONNECTIONS TO OTHER SELECTIONS

1. How might "Videotape" and Margaret Atwood's "There Was Once" (p. 537) be regarded as critiques of contemporary culture? What do these works suggest to you about our expectations as readers and viewers of stories?

2. The narrator describes the videotape as a "sequence of repeated images and victims, stark and glary and more or less unremarkable" (para. 34). Explain why you think this description applies (or doesn't) to Tim O'Brien's "How to Tell a True War Story" (p. 548).

3. Comment on the thematic significance of violence in "Videotape" and in George Bowering's "A Short Story" (p. 540).

SUGGESTED TOPICS FOR LONGER PAPERS

1. Which of these four stories serves as the most interesting and provocative example of metafiction for you? What issues and themes about storytelling are raised by the story, and how do they affect your reading of fiction in general?

2. Choose any one of the stories and compare some element of it with Nathaniel Hawthorne's "Lady Eleanore's Mantle" (p. 350). How do the narrative techniques of the two stories differ, and what do they suggest about the nature of storytelling in our time and in Hawthorne's?

3. **MULTIMEDIA PROJECT.** Watch television news and look for a substantial story about crime, politics, disaster, or any topic that is presented with dramatic images. If possible, tape the segment and apply the "Questions for Responsive Reading and Writing" for fiction (p. 44) to the segment. Decide which questions are relevant and write an essay that considers how your examination of the segment's elements affects your response and your understanding of how the news story is told to you.

Web *For help with this project, use the Multimedia Project Guides Online at* http://www.bedfordstmartins.com/meyer/bedintrolit

A Collection
of Stories

17

Stories for Further Reading

The sixteen short stories in this collection represent a broad variety of styles and themes. They are written by men and women from a number of countries whose lives collectively span the nineteenth and twentieth centuries. The four stories in Chapter 18, "An Album of World Literature," by writers from Chile, Poland, Botswana, and Egypt, introduce themes and styles from traditions that might differ quite a bit from your own. The four stories in Chapter 19, "An Album of Contemporary Stories" — each written within the past ten years — offer a sustained opportunity to explore the fiction being produced today. Inevitably, you will find some of the following stories more appealing than others, but every one of them is worth a careful reading, the kind of reading rewarded by pleasure and understanding.

ANGELA CARTER (1940–1992)

Angela Carter was born Angela Olive Stalker in Eastbourne, England, and spent a "ludicrously overprotected" childhood in South London before marrying in 1960 and moving to Bristol. In 1965, she graduated from Bristol University with a degree in English, and in the following three years, published three novels, *Shadow Dance* (1966), *The Magic Toyshop* (1967), and *Several Perceptions* (1968), for which she received the Somerset Maugham Award. Carter used the prize money to travel to Japan, where, she once wrote, "I learned what it is to be a woman and became radicalized." Radical feminism and subversive humor are prime components of Carter's vivid style, which has been called gothic, antirealist, even magic realist because of the fantastic extremes of plot, setting, and character that appear in her novels and short fiction. Her other works include several short story collections, the novels *Love* (1971), *The Infernal Desire Machines of Doctor Hoffman*

(1972), *The Passion of New Eve* (1977), *Nights at the Circus* (1985), *Wise Children* (1991), and a controversial work of nonfiction, *The Sadeian Woman* (1979).

Web *Research Angela Carter with LitLinks at*
http://www.bedfordstmartins.com/meyer/bedintrolit

A Souvenir of Japan   1974

When I went outside to see if he was coming home, some children dressed ready for bed in cotton nightgowns were playing with sparklers in the vacant lot on the corner. When the sparks fell down in beards of stars, the smiling children cooed softly. Their pleasure was very pure because it was so restrained. An old woman said: "And so they pestered their father until he bought them fireworks." In this language, fireworks are called *hannabi*, which means "flower fire." All through summer, every evening, you can see all kinds of fireworks, from the humblest to the most elaborate, and once we rode the train out of Shinjuku for an hour to watch one of the public displays which are held over rivers so that the dark water multiplies the reflections.

By the time we arrived at our destination, night had already fallen. We were in the suburbs. Many families were on their way to enjoy the fireworks. Their mothers had scrubbed and dressed up the smallest children to celebrate the treat. The little girls were especially immaculate in pink and white cotton kimonos tied with fluffy sashes like swatches of candy floss. Their hair had been most beautifully brushed, arranged in sleek, twin bunches and decorated with twists of gold and silver thread. These children were all on their best behaviour because they were staying up late and held their parents' hands with a charming propriety. We followed the family parties until we came to some fields by the river and saw, high in the air, fireworks already opening out like variegated parasols. They were visible from far away and as we took the path that led through the fields towards their source they seemed to occupy more and more of the sky.

Along the path were stalls where shirtless cooks with sweatbands round their heads roasted corncobs and cuttlefish over charcoal. We bought cuttlefish on skewers and ate them as we walked along. They had been basted with soy sauce and were very good. There were also stalls selling goldfish in plastic bags and others for big balloons with rabbit ears. It was like a fairground — but such a well-ordered fair! Even the patrolling policemen carried coloured paper lanterns instead of torches. Everything was altogether quietly festive. Ice-cream sellers wandered among the crowd, ringing handbells. Their boxes of wares smoked with cold and they called out in plaintive voices, "Icy, icy, icy cream!" When young lovers dispersed discreetly down the tracks in the sedge, the shadowy, indefatigable salesmen pursued them with bells, lamps and mournful cries.

By now, a great many people were walking towards the fireworks but their steps fell so softly and they chatted in such gentle voices there was no more noise than a warm, continual, murmurous humming, the cosy sound of shared happiness, and the night filled with a muted, bourgeois yet authentic magic. Above our heads, the fireworks hung dissolving earrings on the night. Soon we lay down in a stubbled field to watch the fireworks. But, as I expected, he very quickly grew restive.

"Are you happy?" he asked. "Are you sure you're happy?" I was watching 5 the fireworks and did not reply at first although I knew how bored he was and, if he was himself enjoying anything, it was only the idea of my pleasure — or, rather, the idea that he enjoyed my pleasure, since this would be a proof of love. I became guilty and suggested we return to the heart of the city. We fought a silent battle of self-abnegation and I won it, for I had the stronger character. Yet the last thing in the world that I wanted was to leave the scintillating river and the gentle crowd. But I knew his real desire was to return and so return we did, although I do not know if it was worth my small victory of selflessness to bear his remorse at cutting short my pleasure, even if to engineer this remorse had, at some subterranean level, been the whole object of the outing.

Nevertheless, as the slow train nosed back into the thickets of neon, his natural liveliness returned. He could not lose his old habit of walking through the streets with a sense of expectation, as if a fateful encounter might be just around the corner, for, the longer one stayed out, the longer something remarkable might happen and, even if nothing ever did, the chance of it appeased the sweet ache of his boredom for a little while. Besides, his duty by me was done. He had taken me out for the evening and now he wanted to be rid of me. Or so I saw it. The word for wife, *okusan,* means the person who occupies the inner room and rarely, if ever, comes out of it. Since I often appeared to be his wife, I was frequently subjected to this treatment, though I fought against it bitterly.

But I usually found myself waiting for him to come home knowing, with a certain resentment, that he would not; and that he would not even telephone me to tell me he would be late, either, for he was far too guilty to do so. I had nothing better to do than to watch the neighbourhood children light their sparklers and giggle; the old woman stood beside me and I knew she disapproved of me. The entire street politely disapproved of me. Perhaps they thought I was contributing to the delinquency of a juvenile for he was obviously younger than I. The old woman's back was bowed almost to a circle from carrying, when he was a baby, the father who now supervised the domestic fireworks in his evening undress of loose, white drawers, naked to the waist. Her face had the seamed reserve of the old in this country. It was a neighbourhood poignantly rich in old ladies.

At the corner shop, they put an old lady outside on an upturned beer crate each morning, to air. I think she must have been the household grandmother. She was so old she had lapsed almost entirely into a somnolent plant life. She was of neither more nor less significance to herself or to the world than the pot of morning glories which blossomed beside her and perhaps she had less significance than the flowers, which would fade before lunch was ready. They kept her very clean. They covered her pale cotton kimono with a spotless pinafore trimmed with coarse lace and she never dirtied it because she did not move. Now and then, a child came out to comb her hair. Her consciousness was quite beclouded by time and, when I passed by, her rheumy eyes settled upon me always with the same, vague, disinterested wonder, like that of an Eskimo watching a train. When she whispered, *Irrasyaimase,* the shopkeeper's word of welcome, in the ghostliest of whispers, like the rustle of a paper bag, I saw her teeth were rimmed with gold.

The children lit sparklers under a mouse-coloured sky and, due to the pollution in the atmosphere, the moon was mauve. The cicadas throbbed and shrieked in the backyards. When I think of this city, I shall always remember the cicadas who whirr relentlessly all through the summer nights, rising to a piercing crescendo in the subfusc dawn. I have heard cicadas even in the busiest streets, though they thrive best in the back alleys, where they ceaselessly emit that scarcely tolerable susurration which is like a shrill intensification of extreme heat.

A year before, on such a throbbing, voluptuous, platitudinous, subtropical 10 night, we had been walking down one of these shady streets together, in and out of the shadows of the willow trees, looking for somewhere to make love. Morning glories climbed the lattices which screened the low, wooden houses, but the darkness hid the tender colours of these flowers, which the Japanese prize because they fade so quickly. He soon found a hotel, for the city is hospitable to lovers. We were shown into a room like a paper box. It contained nothing but a mattress spread on the floor. We lay down immediately and began to kiss one another. Then a maid soundlessly opened the sliding door and, stepping out of her slippers, crept in on stockinged feet, breathing apologies. She carried a tray which contained two cups of tea and a plate of candies. She put the tray down on the matted floor beside us and backed, bowing and apologizing, from the room whilst our uninterrupted kiss continued. He started to unfasten my shirt and then she came back again. This time, she carried an armful of towels. I was stripped stark naked when she returned for a third time to bring the receipt for his money. She was clearly a most respectable woman and, if she was embarrassed, she did not show it by a single word or gesture.

I learned his name was Taro. In a toy store, I saw one of those books for children with pictures which are cunningly made of paper cut-outs so that, when you turn the page, the picture springs up in the three stylised dimensions of a back-drop in Kabuki. It was the story of Momotaro, who was born from a peach. Before my eyes, the paper peach split open and there was the baby, where the stone should have been. He, too, had the inhuman sweetness of a child born from something other than a mother, a passive, cruel sweetness I did not immediately understand, for it was that of the repressed masochism which, in my country, is usually confined to women.

Sometimes he seemed to possess a curiously unearthly quality when he perched upon the mattress with his knees drawn up beneath his chin in the attitude of a pixy on a door-knocker. At these times, his face seemed somehow both too flat and too large for his elegant body which had such curious, androgynous grace with its svelte, elongated spine, wide shoulders and unusually well-developed pectorals, almost like the breasts of a girl approaching puberty. There was a subtle lack of alignment between face and body and he seemed almost goblin, as if he might have borrowed another person's head, as Japanese goblins do, in order to perform some devious trick. These impressions of a weird visitor were fleeting yet haunting. Sometimes, it was possible for me to believe he had practised an enchantment upon me, as foxes in this country may, for, here, a fox can masquerade as human and at the best of times the high cheekbones gave to his face the aspect of a mask.

His hair was so heavy his neck drooped under its weight and was of a black so deep it turned purple in sunlight. His mouth also was purplish and his blunt, bee-stung lips those of Gauguin's Tahitians. The touch of his skin was as smooth as water as it flows through the fingers. His eyelids were retractable, like those of a cat, and sometimes disappeared completely. I should have liked to have had him embalmed and been able to keep him beside me in a glass coffin, so that I could watch him all the time and he would not have been able to get away from me.

As they say, Japan is a man's country. When I first came to Tokyo, cloth carps fluttered from poles in the gardens of the families fortunate enough to have borne boy children, for it was the time of the annual festival, Boys' Day. At least they do not disguise the situation. At least one knows where one is. Our polarity was publicly acknowledged and socially sanctioned. As an example of the use of the word *dewa*, which occasionally means, as far as I can gather, "in", I found in a textbook a sentence which, when translated, read: "In a society where men dominate, they value women only as the object of men's passions." If the only conjunction possible to us was that of the death-defying double-somersault of love, it is, perhaps, a better thing to be valued only as an object of passion than never to be valued at all. I had never been so absolutely the mysterious other. I had become a kind of phoenix, a fabulous beast; I was an outlandish jewel. He found me, I think, inexpressibly exotic. But I often felt like a female impersonator.

In the department store there was a rack of dresses labelled: "For Young and Cute Girls Only". When I looked at them, I felt as gross as Glumdalclitch. I wore men's sandals because they were the only kind that fitted me and, even so, I had to take the largest size. My pink cheeks, blue eyes and blatant yellow hair made of me, in the visual orchestration of this city in which all heads were dark, eyes brown and skin monotone, an instrument which played upon an alien scale. In a sober harmony of subtle plucked instruments and wistful flutes, I blared. I proclaimed myself like a perpetual fanfare. He was so delicately put together that I thought his skeleton must have the airy elegance of a bird's and I was sometimes afraid that I might smash him. He told me that when he was in bed with me, he felt like a small boat upon a wide, stormy sea.

We pitched our tent in the most unlikely surroundings. We were living in a room furnished only by passion amongst homes of the most astounding respectability. The sounds around us were the swish of brooms upon *tatami* matting and the clatter of demotic Japanese. On all the windowledges, prim flowers bloomed in pots. Every morning, the washing came out on the balconies at seven. Early one morning, I saw a man washing the leaves of his tree. Quilts and mattresses went out to air at eight. The sunlight lay thick enough on these unpaved alleys to lay the dust and somebody always seemed to be practising Chopin in one or another of the flimsy houses, so lightly glued together from plywood it seemed they were sustained only by willpower. Once I was at home, however, it was as if I occupied the inner room and he did not expect me to go out of it, although it was I who paid the rent.

Yet, when he was away from me, he spent much of the time savouring the most annihilating remorse. But this remorse or regret was the stuff of life to him and out he would go again the next night, or, if I had been particularly angry, he would wait until the night after that. And, even if he fully intended to come back early and had promised me he would do so, circumstances always somehow denied him and once more he would contrive to miss the last train. He and his friends spent their nights in a desultory progression from coffee shop to bar to *pachinko*° parlour to coffee shop, again, with the radiant aimlessness of the pure existential hero. They were connoisseurs of boredom. They savoured the various bouquets of the subtly differentiated boredoms which rose from the long, wasted hours at the dead end of night. When it was time for the first train in the morning, he would go back to the mysteriously deserted, Piranesi perspectives of the station, discoloured by dawn, exquisitely tortured by the notion — which probably contained within it a damped-down spark of hope — that, this time, he might have done something irreparable.

I speak as if he had no secrets from me. Well, then, you must realise that I was suffering from love and I knew him as intimately as I knew my own image in a mirror. In other words, I knew him only in relation to myself. Yet, on those terms, I knew him perfectly. At times, I thought I was inventing him as I went along, however, so you will have to take my word for it that we existed. But I do not want to paint our circumstantial portraits so that we both emerge with enough well-rounded, spuriously detailed actuality that you are forced to believe in us. I do not want to practice such sleight of hand. You must be content only with glimpses of our outlines, as if you had caught sight of our reflections in the looking-glass of somebody else's house as you passed by the window. His name was not Taro. I only called him Taro so that I could use the conceit of the peach boy, because it seemed appropriate.

Speaking of mirrors, the Japanese have a great respect for them and, in old-fashioned inns, one often finds them hooded with fabric covers when not in use. He said: 'Mirrors make a room uncozy.' I am sure there is more to it than that although they love to be cozy. One must love coziness if one is to live so close together. But, as if in celebration of the thing they feared, they seemed to have made the entire city into a cold hall of mirrors which continually proliferated whole galleries of constantly changing appearances, all marvelous but none tangible. If they did not lock up the real looking-glasses, it would be hard to tell what was real and what was not. Even buildings one had taken for substantial had a trick of disappearance overnight. One morning, we woke to find the house next door reduced to nothing but a heap of sticks and a pile of newspaper neatly tied with string, left out for the garbage collector.

I would not say that he seemed to me to possess the same kind of insub- 20 stantiality although his departure usually seemed imminent, until I realised he was as erratic but as inevitable as the weather. If you plan to come and live in Japan, you must be sure you are stoical enough to endure the weather. No, it was not insubstantiality; it was a rhetoric valid only on its own terms. When I listened to his protestations, I was prepared to believe he believed in them, although I knew perfectly well they meant nothing. And that isn't fair. When he made them, he believed in them implicitly. Then, he was utterly consumed by conviction. But his dedication was primarily to the idea of himself in love. This idea seemed to him magnificent, even sublime. He was prepared to die for it, as one of Baudelaire's dandies might have been prepared to kill himself in order to preserve himself in the condition of a work of art, for he wanted to make this experience a masterpiece of experience which absolutely transcended the everyday. And this would annihilate the effects of the cruel drug, boredom, to which

pachinko: A Japanese game similar to pinball.

he was addicted although, perhaps, the element of boredom which is implicit in an affair so isolated from the real world was its principal appeal for him. But I had no means of knowing how far his conviction would take him. And I used to turn over in my mind from time to time the question: how far does a pretense of feeling, maintained with absolute conviction, become authentic?

This country has elevated hypocrisy to the level of the highest style. To look at a samurai, you would not know him for a murderer, or a geisha for a whore. The magnificence of such objects hardly pertains to the human. They live only in a world of icons and there they participate in rituals which transmute life itself to a series of grand gestures, as moving as they are absurd. It was as if they all thought, if we believe in something hard enough, it will come true and, lo and behold! they had done and it did. Our street was in essence a slum but, in appearance, it was a little enclave of harmonious quiet and, *mirabile dictu*, it was the appearance which was the reality, because they all behaved so well, kept everything so clean and lived with such rigorous civility. What terrible discipline it takes to live harmoniously. They had crushed all their vigor in order to live harmoniously and now they had the wistful beauty of flowers pressed dry in an enormous book.

But repression does not necessarily give birth only to severe beauties. In its programmed interstices, monstrous passions bloom. They torture trees to make them look more like the formal notion of a tree. They paint amazing pictures on their skins with awl and gouge, sponging away the blood as they go; a tatooed man is a walking masterpiece of remembered pain. They boast the most passionate puppets in the world who mimic love suicides in a stylized fashion, for here there is no such comfortable formula as 'happy ever after'. And, when I remembered the finale of the puppet tragedies, how the wooden lovers cut their throats together, I felt the beginnings of unease, as if the hieratic imagery of the country might overwhelm me, for his boredom had reached such a degree that he was insulated against everything except the irritation of anguish. If he valued me as an object of passion, he had reduced the word to its roots, which derives from the Latin, *patior*, I suffer. He valued me as an instrument which would cause him pain.

So we lived under a disorientated moon which was as angry a purple as if the sky had bruised its eye, and, if we made certain genuine intersections, these only took place in darkness. His contagious conviction that our love was unique and desperate infected me with an anxious sickness; soon we would learn to treat one another with the circumspect tenderness of comrades who are amputees, for we were surrounded by the most moving images of evanescence, fireworks, morning glories, the old, children. But the most moving of these images were the intangible reflections of ourselves we saw in one another's eyes, reflections of nothing but appearances, in a city dedicated to seeming, and, try as we might to possess the essence of each other's otherness, we would inevitably fail.

LANGSTON HUGHES (1902–1967)

A biographical overview of Langston Hughes begins on p. 1032 at the beginning of Chapter 33, "A Study of Langston Hughes."

On the Road

He was not interested in the snow. When he got off the freight, one early evening during the depression, Sargeant never even noticed the snow. But he must have felt it seeping down his neck, cold, wet, sopping in his shoes. But if you had asked him, he wouldn't have known it was snowing. Sargeant didn't see the snow, not even under the bright lights of the main street, falling white and flaky against the night. He was too hungry, too sleepy, too tired.

The Reverend Mr. Dorset, however, saw the snow when he switched on his porch light, opened the front door of his parsonage, and found standing there before him a big black man with snow on his face, a human piece of night with snow on his face — obviously unemployed.

Said the Reverend Mr. Dorset before Sargeant even realized he'd opened his mouth: "I'm sorry. No! Go right on down this street four blocks and turn to your left, walk up seven and you'll see the Relief Shelter. I'm sorry. No!" He shut the door.

Sargeant wanted to tell the holy man that he had already been to the Relief Shelter, been to hundreds of relief shelters during the depression years, the beds were always gone and supper was over, the place was full, and they drew the color line anyhow. But the minister said, "No," and shut the door. Evidently he didn't want to hear about it. And he *had* a door to shut.

The big black man turned away. And even yet he didn't see the snow, walking right into it. Maybe he sensed it, cold, wet, sticking to his jaws, wet on his black hands, sopping in his shoes. He stopped and stood on the sidewalk hunched over — hungry, sleepy, cold — looking up and down. Then he looked right where he was — in front of a church. Of course! A church! Sure, right next to a parsonage, certainly a church. 5

It had *two* doors.

Broad white steps in the night all snowy white. Two high arched doors with slender stone pillars on either side. And way up, a round lacy window with a stone crucifix in the middle and Christ on the crucifix in stone. All this was pale in the street lights, solid and stony pale in the snow.

Sargeant blinked. When he looked up, the snow fell into his eyes. For the first time that night he *saw* the snow. He shook his head. He shook the snow from his coat sleeves, felt hungry, felt lost, felt not lost, felt cold. He walked up the steps of the church. He knocked at the door. No answer. He tried the handle. Locked. He put his shoulder against the door and his long black body slanted like a ramrod. He pushed. With loud rhythmic grunts, like the grunts in a chain-gang song, he pushed against the door.

"I'm tired . . . Huh! . . . Hongry . . . Uh! . . . I'm sleepy . . . Huh! I'm cold . . . I got to sleep somewheres," Sargeant said. "This here is a church, ain't it? Well, uh!"

He pushed against the door. 10

Suddenly, with an undue cracking and screaking, the door began to give way to the tall black Negro who pushed ferociously against it.

By now two or three white people had stopped in the street, and Sargeant was vaguely aware of some of them yelling at him concerning the door. Three or four more came running, yelling at him.

"Hey!" they said. "Hey!"

"Uh-huh," answered the big tall Negro, "I know it's a white folks' church, but I got to sleep somewhere." He gave another lunge at the door. "Huh!"

And the door broke open.   15

But just when the door gave way, two white cops arrived in a car, ran up the steps with their clubs, and grabbed Sargeant. But Sargeant for once had no intention of being pulled or pushed away from the door.

Sargeant grabbed, but not for anything so weak as a broken door. He grabbed for one of the tall stone pillars beside the door, grabbed at it and caught it. And held it. The cops pulled and Sargeant pulled. Most of the people in the street got behind the cops and helped them pull.

"A big black unemployed Negro holding onto our church!" thought the people. "The idea!"

The cops began to beat Sargeant over the head, and nobody protested. But he held on.

And then the church fell down.   20

Gradually, the big stone front of the church fell down, the walls and the rafters, the crucifix and the Christ. Then the whole thing fell down, covering the cops and the people with bricks and stones and debris. The whole church fell down in the snow.

Sargeant got out from under the church and went walking on up the street with the stone pillar on his shoulder. He was under the impression that he had buried the parsonage and the Reverend Mr. Dorset who said, "No!" So he laughed, and threw the pillar six blocks up the street and went on.

Sargeant thought he was alone, but listening to the *crunch, crunch, crunch* on the snow of his own footsteps, he heard other footsteps, too, doubling his own. He looked around, and there was Christ walking along beside him, the same Christ that had been on the cross on the church—still stone with a rough stone surface, walking along beside him just like he was broken off the cross when the church fell down.

"Well, I'll be dogged," said Sargeant. "This here's the first time I ever seed you off the cross."

"Yes," said Christ, crunching his feet in the snow. "You had to pull the   25
church down to get me off the cross."

"You glad?" said Sargeant.

"I sure am," said Christ.

They both laughed.

"I'm a hell of a fellow, ain't I?" said Sargeant. "Done pulled the church down!"

"You did a good job," said Christ. "They have kept me nailed on a cross for 30
nearly two thousand years."

"Whee-ee-e!" said Sargeant. "I know you are glad to get off."

"I sure am," said Christ.

They walked on in the snow. Sargeant looked at the man of stone.

"And you have been up there two thousand years?"

"I sure have," said Christ.   35

"Well, if I had a little cash," said Sargeant, "I'd show you around a bit."

"I been around," said Christ.

"Yeah, but that was a long time ago."

"All the same," said Christ, "I've been around."

They walked on in the snow until they came to the railroad yards. 40
Sargeant was tired, sweating and tired.

"Where you goin'?" Sargeant said, stopping by the tracks. He looked at
Christ. Sargeant said, "I'm just a bum on the road. How about you? Where you
goin'?"

"God knows," Christ said, "but I'm leavin' here."

They saw the red and green lights of the railroad yard half veiled by the
snow that fell out of the night. Away down the track they saw a fire in a hobo
jungle.

"I can go there and sleep," Sargeant said.

"You can?" 45

"Sure," said Sargeant. "That place ain't got no doors."

Outside the town, along the tracks, there were barren trees and bushes
below the embankment, snow-gray in the dark. And down among the trees
and bushes there were makeshift houses made out of boxes and tin and old
pieces of wood and canvas. You couldn't see them in the dark, but you knew
they were there if you'd ever been on the road, if you had ever lived with the
homeless and hungry in a depression.

"I'm side-tracking," Sargeant said. "I'm tired."

"I'm gonna make it on to Kansas City," said Christ.

"O.K.," Sargeant said. "So long!" 50

He went down into the hobo jungle and found himself a place to sleep. He
never did see Christ no more. About 6:00 A.M. a freight came by. Sargeant
scrambled out of the jungle with a dozen or so more hobos and ran along the
track, grabbing at the freight. It was dawn, early dawn, cold and gray.

"Wonder where Christ is by now?" Sargeant thought. "He musta gone on
way on down the road. He didn't sleep in this jungle."

Sargeant grabbed the train and started to pull himself up into a moving
coal car, over the edge of a wheeling coal car. But strangely enough, the car was
full of cops. The nearest cop rapped Sargeant soundly across the knuckles
with his night stick. Wham! Rapped his big black hands for clinging to the top
of the car. Wham! But Sargeant did not turn loose. He clung on and tried to
pull himself into the car. He hollered at the top of his voice, "Damn it, lemme
in this car!"

"Shut up," barked the cop. "You crazy coon!" He rapped Sargeant across
the knuckles and punched him in the stomach. "You ain't out in no jungle
now. This ain't no train. You in jail."

Wham! across his bare black fingers clinging to the bars of his cell. 55
Wham! between the steel bars low down against his shins.

Suddenly Sargeant realized that he really was in jail. He wasn't on no train.
The blood of the night before had dried on his face, his head hurt terribly, and
a cop outside in the corridor was hitting him across the knuckles for holding
onto the door, yelling and shaking the cell door.

"They musta took me to jail for breaking down the door last night,"
Sargeant thought, "that church door."

Sargeant went over and sat on a wooden bench against the cold stone wall.
He was emptier than ever. His clothes were wet, clammy cold wet, and shoes

sloppy with snow water. It was just about dawn. There he was, locked up behind a cell door, nursing his bruised fingers.

The bruised fingers were his, but not the *door.*

Not the *club,* but the fingers.   60

"You wait," mumbled Sargeant, black against the jail wall. "I'm gonna
break down this door, too."

"Shut up — or I'll paste you one," said the cop.

"I'm gonna break down this door," yelled Sargeant as he stood up in his cell.

Then he must have been talking to himself because he said, "I wonder
where Christ's gone? I wonder if he's gone to Kansas City?"

FRANZ KAFKA (1883–1924)

German-language author Franz Kafka was born in 1883 to middle-class
Jewish parents in Prague, Czechoslovakia. He spoke Czech in his childhood, but later attended German schools and studied law in the German
half of Prague's Charles-Ferdinand University, finishing his doctorate in
1907. Kafka found work with the semigovernmental agency Worker's Accident Insurance Institute, a job that afforded him ample time to write, and
his first published prose appeared in 1908 under the title "Meditation."
Kafka went on to publish many novels and short stories, including
The Metamorphosis (1915), *The Judgment* (1916), and *In the Penal Colony* (1919).
He died of tuberculosis in 1924, and three posthumous publications immediately followed, *The Trial* (1925), *The Castle* (1926), and *America* (1927).
Kafka's stories and novels reveal deep anxieties about his own identity: psychological, rooted in the authoritarian dominance of his father, and social, prompted by his isolation from Prague's German population and his
lack of identification with his own Jewish background.

Web *Research Franz Kafka with LitLinks at*
http://www.bedfordstmartins.com/meyer/bedintrolit

A Hunger Artist   *1924*

TRANSLATED BY EDWIN AND WILLA MUIR

During these last decades the interest in professional fasting has markedly diminished. It used to pay very well to stage such great performances under
one's own management, but today that is quite impossible. We live in a different world now. At one time the whole town took a lively interest in the hunger
artist; from day to day of his fast the excitement mounted; everybody wanted
to see him at least once a day; there were people who bought season tickets for
the last few days and sat from morning till night in front of his small barred
cage; even in the nighttime there were visiting hours, when the whole effect

was heightened by torch flares; on fine days the cage was set out in the open air, and then it was the children's special treat to see the hunger artist; for their elders he was often just a joke that happened to be in fashion, but the children stood open-mouthed, holding each other's hands for greater security, marveling at him as he sat there pallid in black tights, with his ribs sticking out so prominently, not even on a seat but down among straw on the ground, sometimes giving a courteous nod, answering questions with a constrained smile, or perhaps stretching an arm through the bars so that one might feel how thin it was, and then again withdrawing deep into himself, paying no attention to anyone or anything, not even to the all-important striking of the clock that was the only piece of furniture in his cage, but merely staring into vacancy with half shut eyes, now and then taking a sip from a tiny glass of water to moisten his lips.

Besides casual onlookers there were also relays of permanent watchers selected by the public, usually butchers, strangely enough, and it was their task to watch the hunger artist day and night, three of them at a time, in case he should have some secret recourse to nourishment. This was nothing but a formality, instituted to reassure the masses, for the initiates knew well enough that during his fast the artist would never in any circumstances, not even under forcible compulsion, swallow the smallest morsel of food; the honor of his profession forbade it. Not every watcher, of course, was capable of understanding this; there were often groups of night watchers who were very lax in carrying out their duties and deliberately huddled together in a retired corner to play cards with great absorption, obviously intending to give the hunger artist the chance of a little refreshment, which they supposed he could draw from some private hoard. Nothing annoyed the artist more than such watchers; they made him miserable; they made his fast seem unendurable; sometimes he mastered his feebleness sufficiently to sing during their watch for as long as he could keep going, to show them how unjust their suspicions were. But that was of little use; they only wondered at his cleverness in being able to fill his mouth even while singing. Much more to his taste were the watchers who sat close up to the bars, who were not content with the dim night lighting of the hall but focused him in the full glare of the electric pocket torch given them by the impresario. The harsh light did not trouble him at all, in any case he could never sleep properly, and he could always drowse a little, whatever the light, at any hour, even when the hall was thronged with noisy onlookers. He was quite happy at the prospect of spending a sleepless night with such watchers; he was ready to exchange jokes with them, to tell them stories out of his nomadic life, anything at all to keep them awake and demonstrate to them again that he had no eatables in his cage and that he was fasting as not one of them could fast. But his happiest moment was when the morning came and an enormous breakfast was brought them, at his expense, on which they flung themselves with the keen appetite of healthy men after a weary night of wakefulness. Of course there were people who argued that this breakfast was an unfair attempt to bribe the watchers, but that was going rather too far, and when they were invited to take on a night's vigil without a breakfast, merely for the sake of the cause, they made themselves scarce, although they stuck stubbornly to their suspicions.

Such suspicions, anyhow, were a necessary accompaniment to the profession of fasting. No one could possibly watch the hunger artist continuously, day and night, and so no one could produce first-hand evidence that the fast had really been rigorous and continuous; only the artist himself could know that, he was therefore bound to be the sole completely satisfied spectator of his own fast. Yet for other reasons he was never satisfied; it was not perhaps mere fasting that had brought him to such skeleton thinness that many people had regretfully to keep away from his exhibitions, because the sight of him was too much for them, perhaps it was dissatisfaction with himself that had worn him down. For he alone knew, what no other initiate knew, how easy it was to fast. It was the easiest thing in the world. He made no secret of this, yet people did not believe him, at the best they set him down as modest; most of them, however, thought he was out for publicity or else was some kind of cheat who found it easy to fast because he had discovered a way of making it easy, and then had the impudence to admit the fact, more or less. He had to put up with all that, and in the course of time had got used to it, but his inner dissatisfaction always rankled, and never yet, after any term of fasting — this must be granted to his credit — had he left the cage of his own free will. The longest period of fasting was fixed by his impresario at forty days, beyond that term he was not allowed to go, not even in great cities, and there was good reason for it, too. Experience had proved that for about forty days the interest of the public could be stimulated by a steadily increasing pressure of advertisement, but after that the town began to lose interest, sympathetic support began notably to fall off; there were of course local variations as between one town and another or one country and another, but as a general rule forty days marked the limit. So on the fortieth day the flower bedecked cage was opened, enthusiastic spectators filled the hall, a military band played, two doctors entered the cage to measure the results of the fast, which were announced through a megaphone, and finally two young ladies appeared, blissful at having been selected for the honor, to help the hunger artist down the few steps leading to a small table on which was spread a carefully chosen invalid repast. And at this very moment the artist always turned stubborn. True, he would entrust his bony arms to the outstretched helping hands of the ladies bending over him, but stand up he would not. Why stop fasting at this particular moment, after forty days of it? He had held out for a long time, an illimitably long time; why stop now, when he was in his best fasting form, or rather, not yet quite in his best fasting form? Why should he be cheated of the fame he would get for fasting longer, for being not only the record hunger artist of all time, which presumably he was already, but for beating his own record by a performance beyond human imagination, since he felt that there were no limits to his capacity for fasting? His public pretended to admire him so much, why should it have so little patience with him; if he could endure fasting longer, why shouldn't the public endure it? Besides, he was tired, he was comfortable sitting in the straw, and now he was supposed to lift himself to his full height and go down to a meal the very thought of which gave him a nausea that only the presence of the ladies kept him from betraying, and even that with an effort. And he looked up into the eyes of the ladies who were apparently so friendly and in reality so cruel, and shook his head, which felt too heavy on its strengthless neck. But then there happened yet again what always happened. The impresario came forward, without a word — for the band made speech impossible — lifted his arms in the air above the artist, as if inviting Heaven to look down upon its creature here in the straw, this suffering martyr, which indeed he was, although in quite another sense; grasped him round the emaciated waist, with exaggerated caution, so that the frail condition he was in might be appreciated; and committed him to the care of the blenching ladies, not without secretly giving him a shaking so that his legs and body tottered and swayed. The artist now submitted completely; his head lolled on his breast as if it had landed there by chance; his body was hollowed out; his legs in a spasm of self-preservation clung close to each other at the knees, yet scraped on the ground as if it were not really solid ground, as if they were only trying to find solid ground; and the whole weight of his body, a feather-weight after all, relapsed onto one of the ladies, who, looking round for help and panting a little — this post of honor was not at all what she had expected it to be — first stretched her neck as far as she could to keep her face at least free from contact with the artist, when finding this impossible, and her more fortunate companion not coming to her aid but merely holding extended on her own trembling hand the little bunch of knucklebones that was the artist's, to the great delight of the spectators burst into tears and had to be replaced by an attendant who had long been stationed in readiness. Then came the food, a little of which the impresario managed to get between the artist's lips, while he sat in a kind of half-fainting trance, to the accompaniment of cheerful patter designed to distract the public's attention from the artist's condition; after that a toast was drunk to the public, supposedly prompted by a whisper from the artist in the impresario's ear; the band confirmed it with a mighty flourish, the spectators melted away, and no one had any cause to be dissatisfied with the proceedings, no one except the hunger artist himself, he only, as always.

So he lived for many years, with small regular intervals of recuperation, in visible glory, honored by the world, yet in spite of that troubled in spirit, and all the more troubled because no one would take his trouble seriously. What comfort could he possibly need? What more could he possibly wish for? And if some good-natured person, feeling sorry for him, tried to console him by pointing out that his melancholy was probably caused by fasting; it could happen, especially when he had been fasting for some time, that he reacted with an outburst of fury and to the general alarm began to shake the bars of his cage like a wild animal. Yet the impresario had a way of punishing these outbreaks which he rather enjoyed putting into operation. He would apologize publicly for the artist's behavior, which was only to be excused, he admitted, because of the irritability caused by fasting; a condition hardly to be understood by well-fed people; then by natural transition he went on to mention the artist's equally incomprehensible boast that he could fast for much longer than he was doing; he praised the high ambition, the good will, the great self-denial undoubtedly implicit in such a statement; and then quite simply countered it by bringing out photographs, which were also on sale to the public, showing the artist on the fortieth day of a fast lying in bed almost dead from exhaustion. This perversion of the truth, familiar to the artist though it was, always unnerved him afresh and proved too much for him. What was a consequence of the premature ending of his fast was here presented as the cause of it! To fight against this lack of understanding, against a whole world of nonunderstanding, was impossible. Time and again in good faith he stood by the bars listening to the impresario, but as soon as the photographs appeared he always let go and sank with a groan back on to his straw, and the reassured public could once more come close and gaze at him.

A few years later when the witnesses of such scenes called them to mind, 5 they often failed to understand themselves at all. For meanwhile the aforementioned change in public interest had set in; it seemed to happen almost overnight; there may have been profound causes for it, but who was going to bother about that; at any rate the pampered hunger artist suddenly found himself deserted one fine day by the amusement seekers, who were streaming past him to other more favored attractions. For the last time the impresario hurried him over half Europe to discover whether the old interest might still survive here and there; all in vain; everywhere, as if by secret agreement, a positive revulsion from professional fasting was in evidence. Of course it could not really have sprung up so suddenly as all that, and many premonitory symptoms which had not been sufficiently remarked or suppressed during the rush and glitter of success now came retrospectively to mind, but it was now too late to take any countermeasures. Fasting would surely come into fashion again at some future date, yet that was no comfort for those living in the present. What, then, was the hunger artist to do? He had been applauded by thousands in his time and could hardly come down to showing himself in a street booth at village fairs, and as for adopting another profession, he was not only too old for that but too frantically devoted to fasting. So he took leave of the impresario, his partner in an unparalleled career, and hired himself to a large circus; in order to spare his own feelings he avoided reading the conditions of his contract.

A large circus with its enormous traffic in replacing and recruiting men, animals, and apparatus can always find a use for people at any time, even for a hunger artist, provided of course that he does not ask too much, and in this particular case anyhow it was not only the artist who was taken on but his famous and long-known name as well, indeed considering the peculiar nature of his performance, which was not impaired by advancing age, it could not be objected that there was an artist past his prime, no longer at the height of his professional skill, seeking a refuge in some quiet corner of a circus; on the contrary, the hunger artist averred that he could fast as well as ever, which was entirely credible; he even alleged that if he were allowed to fast as he liked, and this was at once promised him without more ado, he could astound the world by establishing a record never yet achieved, a statement which certainly provoked a smile among the other professionals, since it left out of account the change in public opinion, which the hunger artist in his zeal conveniently forgot.

He had not, however, actually lost his sense of the real situation and took it as a matter of course that he and his cage should be stationed, not in the middle of the ring as a main attraction, but outside, near the animal cages, on a site that was after all easily accessible. Large and gaily painted placards made a frame for the cage and announced what was to be seen inside it. When the public came thronging out in the intervals to see the animals, they could hardly avoid passing the hunger artist's cage and stopping there for a moment; perhaps they might even have stayed longer had not those pressing behind them in the narrow gangway, who did not understand why they should be held up on their way toward the excitements of the menagerie, made it impossible for anyone to stand gazing quietly for any length of time. And that was the reason why the hunger artist, who had of course been looking forward to these visiting hours as the main achievement of his life, began instead to shrink from them. At first he could hardly wait for the intervals; it was exhilarating to watch the crowds come streaming his way, until only too soon—not even the most obstinate self-deception, clung to almost consciously, could hold out against the fact—the conviction was borne in upon him that these people, most of them, to judge from their actions, again and again, without exception, were all on their way to the menagerie. And the first sight of them from the distance remained the best. For when they reached his cage he was at once deafened by the storm of shouting and abuse that arose from the two contending factions, which renewed themselves continuously, of those who wanted to stop and stare at him—he soon began to dislike them more than the others—not out of real interest but only out of obstinate self-assertiveness, and those who wanted to go straight on to the animals. When the first great rush was past, the stragglers came along, and these, whom nothing could have prevented from stopping to look at him as long as they had breath, raced past with long strides, hardly even glancing at him, in their haste to get to the menagerie in time. And all too rarely did it happen that he had a stroke of luck, when some father of a family fetched up before him with his children, pointed a finger at the hunger artist, and explained at length what the phenomenon meant, telling stories of earlier years when he himself had watched similar but much more thrilling performances, and the children, still rather uncomprehending, since neither inside nor outside school had they been sufficiently prepared for this lesson—what did they care about fasting?—yet showed by the brightness of their intent eyes that new and better times might be coming. Perhaps, said the hunger artist to himself many a time, things would be a little better if his cage were set not quite so near the menagerie. That made it too easy for people to make their choice, to say nothing of what he suffered from the stench of the menagerie, the animals' restlessness by night, the carrying past of raw lumps of flesh for the beasts of prey, the roaring at feeding times, which depressed him continually. But he did not dare to lodge a complaint with the management; after all, he had the animals to thank for the troops of people who passed his cage, among whom there might always be one here and there to take an interest in him, and who could tell where they might seclude him if he called attention to his existence and thereby to the fact that, strictly speaking, he was only an impediment on the way to the menagerie.

A small impediment, to be sure, one that grew steadily less. People grew familiar with the strange idea that they could be expected, in times like these, to take an interest in a hunger artist, and with this familiarity the verdict went out against him. He might fast as much as he could, and he did so; but nothing could save him now, people passed him by. Just try to explain to anyone the art of fasting! Anyone who has no feeling for it cannot be made to understand it. The fine placards grew dirty and illegible, they were torn down; the little notice board telling the number of fast days achieved, which at first was changed carefully every day, had long stayed at the same figure, for after the first few weeks even this small task seemed pointless to the staff; and so the artist simply fasted on and on, as he had once dreamed of doing, and it was no trouble to him, just as he had always foretold, but no one counted the days, no one, not even the artist himself, knew what records he was already breaking, and his heart grew heavy. And when once in a time some leisurely passerby stopped, made merry over the old figure on the board, and spoke of swindling, that was in its way the stupidest lie ever invented by indifference and inborn malice, since it was not the hunger artist who was cheating; he was working honestly, but the world was cheating him of his reward.

Many more days went by, however, and that too came to an end. An overseer's eye fell on the cage one day and asked the attendants why this perfectly good cage should be left standing there unused with dirty straw inside it; nobody knew, until one man, helped out by the notice board, remembered about the hunger artist. They poked into the straw with sticks and found him in it. "Are you still fasting?" asked the overseer. "When on earth do you mean to stop?" "Forgive me, everybody," whispered the hunger artist; only the overseer, who had his ear to the bars, understood him. "Of course," said the overseer, and tapped his forehead with a finger to let the attendants know what state the man was in, "we forgive you." "I always wanted you to admire my fasting," said the hunger artist. "We do admire it," said the overseer, affably. "But you shouldn't admire it," said the hunger artist. "Well, then we don't admire it," said the overseer, "but why shouldn't we admire it?" "Because I have to fast, I can't help it," said the hunger artist. "What a fellow you are," said the overseer, "and why can't you help it?" "Because," said the hunger artist, lifting his head a little and speaking, with his lips pursed, as if for a kiss, right into the overseer's ear, so that no syllable might be lost, "because I couldn't find the food I liked. If I had found it, believe me, I should have made no fuss and stuffed myself like you or anyone else." These were his last words, but in his dimming eyes remained the firm though no longer proud persuasion that he was still continuing to fast.

"Well, clear this out now!" said the overseer, and they buried the hunger 10 artist, straw and all. Into the cage they put a young panther. Even the most insensitive felt it refreshing to see this wild creature leaping around the cage that had so long been dreary. The panther was all right. The food he liked was brought him without hesitation by the attendants; he seemed not even to miss his freedom; his noble body, furnished almost to the bursting point with all that it needed, seemed to carry freedom around with it too; somewhere in his jaws it seemed to lurk; and the joy of life streamed with such ardent passion from his throat that for the onlookers it was not easy to stand the shock of it. But they braced themselves, crowded round the cage, and did not want ever to move away.

JAMAICA KINCAID (B. 1949)

Jamaica Kincaid was born Elaine Potter Richardson on the Caribbean island of Antigua. She moved to New York in 1965 to work as an au pair, studied photography at both the New School for Social Research and Franconia College, and changed her name to Jamaica Kincaid in 1973 with her first publication, "When I Was 17," a series of interviews. Over the next few years, she wrote for *The New Yorker* magazine, first as a freelancer and then as a staff writer. In 1978, Kincaid wrote her first piece of fiction, "Girl," published in *The New Yorker* and included in her debut short story collection, *At the Bottom of the River* (1983), which won an award from the Academy and Institute of Arts and Letters and was nominated for the PEN/Faulkner Award. Her other work includes *Annie John* (1985),

Lucy (1990), *Autobiography of My Mother* (1994), and two nonfiction books, *A Small Place* (1988) and *My Brother* (1997). Whether autobiographical fiction or nonfiction, her work usually focuses on the perils of postcolonial society, paralleled by an examination of rifts in mother-daughter relationships.

Web *Research Jamaica Kincaid with LitLinks at*
http://www.bedfordstmartins.com/meyer/bedintrolit

Girl   *1978*

Wash the white clothes on Monday and put them on the stone heap; wash the color clothes on Tuesday and put them on the clothesline to dry; don't walk barehead in the hot sun; cook pumpkin fritters in very hot sweet oil; soak your little cloths right after you take them off; when buying cotton to make yourself a nice blouse, be sure that it doesn't have gum on it, because that way it won't hold up well after a wash; soak salt fish overnight before you cook it; is it true that you sing benna° in Sunday school?; always eat your food in such a way that it won't turn someone else's stomach; on Sundays try to walk like a lady and not like the slut you are so bent on becoming; don't sing benna in Sunday school; you mustn't speak to wharf-rat boys, not even to give directions; don't eat fruits on the street—flies will follow you; *but I don't sing benna on Sundays at all and never in Sunday school;* this is how to sew on a button; this is how to make a buttonhole for the button you have just sewed on; this is how to hem a dress when you see the hem coming down and so to prevent yourself from looking like the slut I know you are so bent on becoming; this is how you iron your father's khaki shirt so that it doesn't have a crease; this is how you iron your father's khaki pants so that they don't have a crease; this is how you grow okra—far from the house, because okra tree harbors red ants; when you are growing dasheen,° make sure it gets plenty of water or else it makes your throat itch when you are eating it; this is how you sweep a corner; this is how you sweep a whole house; this is how you sweep a yard; this is how you smile to someone you don't like too much; this is how you smile to someone you don't like at all; this is how you smile to someone you like completely; this is how you set a table for tea; this is how you set a table for dinner; this is how you set a table for dinner with an important guest; this is how you set a table for lunch; this is how you set a table for breakfast; this is how to behave in the presence of men who don't know you very well, and this way they won't recognize immediately the slut I have warned you against becoming; be sure to wash every day, even if it is with your own spit; don't squat down to play marbles—you are not a boy, you know; don't pick people's flowers—you might catch something; don't throw stones at blackbirds, because it might not be a blackbird at all; this is how to make a bread pudding; this is how to make

benna: Calypso music.
dasheen: The edible rootstock of taro, a tropical plant.

doukona;° this is how to make pepper pot;° this is how to make a good medicine for a cold; this is how to make a good medicine to throw away a child before it even becomes a child; this is how to catch a fish; this is how to throw back a fish you don't like, and that way something bad won't fall on you; this is how to bully a man; this is how a man bullies you; this is how to love a man, and if this doesn't work there are other ways, and if they don't work don't feel too bad about giving up; this is how to spit up in the air if you feel like it, and this is how to move quick so that it doesn't fall on you; this is how to make ends meet; always squeeze bread to make sure it's fresh; *but what if the baker won't let me feel the bread?*; you mean to say that after all you are really going to be the kind of woman who the baker won't let near the bread?

doukona: A spicy plantain pudding.
pepper pot: A stew.

D. H. LAWRENCE (1885–1930)

David Herbert Lawrence was born near Nottingham, England, in 1885. As a teenager, he worked as a factory clerk but became ill and, during his recuperation, became drawn to writing and teaching. He received a teaching certificate from University College, Nottingham, in 1908, having already published his first story. Lawrence achieved literary success early, publishing poems in the prestigious *English Review*, whose editor helped him to publish his first novel, *The White Peacock* (1911), which he followed with *The Trespasser* (1912) and *Sons and Lovers* (1913). In the meantime, he eloped with Freida Weekly, the German wife of a professor in Nottingham, and they were married in 1914. After World War I, Lawrence and his wife left England and never again resided there. The couple lived in Italy and traveled and lived in Ceylon, Australia, the United States, and Mexico. Lawrence published several novels and books of nonfiction along the way, including *The Rainbow* (1915), *Women in Love* (1920), *Lost Girl* (1920), *Aaron's Rod* (1922), *The Plumed Serpent* (1926), *Movements in European History* (1921), *Studies in Classic American Literature* (1923), and two books on psychoanalysis. Lawrence had already transgressed norms of decency with *The Rainbow*, considered obscene in England, and his next work, *Lady Chatterly's Lover*, was published privately in 1928 because of its explicit sexual descriptions. Also the author of plays, poems, and such famous short stories as "The Odour of Chrysanthemums" and "Daughters of the Vicar," Lawrence innovated in ways that go far beyond his challenge to standards of obscenity. His works characteristically probe the nature of unconscious experience and promote a new receptiveness to sexuality, intuition, and emotion. In 1930, Lawrence died of tuberculosis in the south of France.

Research D. H. Lawrence with LitLinks at
 http://www.bedfordstmartins.com/meyer/bedintrolit

The Horse Dealer's Daughter   1922

"Well, Mabel, and what are you going to do with yourself?" asked Joe, with foolish flippancy. He felt quite safe himself. Without listening for an answer, he turned aside, worked a grain of tobacco to the tip of his tongue, and spat it out. He did not care about anything, since he felt safe himself.

The three brothers and the sister sat round the desolate breakfast-table, attempting some sort of desultory consultation. The morning's post had given the final tap to the family fortunes, and all was over. The dreary dining-room itself, with its heavy mahogany furniture, looked as if it were waiting to be done away with.

But the consultation amounted to nothing. There was a strange air of in-effectuality about the three men, as they sprawled at table, smoking and re-flecting vaguely on their own condition. The girl was alone, a rather short, sullen-looking young woman of twenty-seven. She did not share the same life as her brothers. She would have been good-looking, save for the impressive fix-ity of her face, "bull-dog," as her brothers called it.

There was a confused tramping of horses' feet outside. The three men all sprawled round in their chairs to watch. Beyond the dark holly bushes that separated the strip of lawn from the high-road, they could see a cavalcade of shire horses swinging out of their own yard, being taken for exercise. This was the last time. These were the last horses that would go through their hands. The young men watched with critical, callous looks. They were all frightened at the collapse of their lives, and the sense of disaster in which they were in-volved left them no inner freedom.

Yet they were three fine, well-set fellows enough. Joe, the eldest, was a man 5 of thirty-three, broad and handsome in a hot, flushed way. His face was red, he twisted his black mustache over a thick finger, his eyes were shallow and rest-less. He had a sensual way of uncovering his teeth when he laughed, and his bearing was stupid. Now he watched the horses with a glazed look of helpless-ness in his eyes, a certain stupor of downfall.

The great draft-horses swung past. They were tied head to tail, four of them, and they heaved along to where a lane branched off from the high-road, planting their great hoofs floutingly in the fine black mud, swinging their great rounded haunches sumptuously, and trotting a few sudden steps as they were led into the lane, round the corner. Every movement showed a massive, slumbrous strength, and a stupidity which held them in subjection. The groom at the head looked back, jerking the leading rope. And the cavalcade moved out of sight up the lane, the tail of the last horse, bobbed up tight and stiff, held out taut from the swinging great haunches as they rocked behind the hedges in a motionlike sleep.

Joe watched with glazed hopeless eyes. The horses were almost like his own body to him. He felt he was done for now. Luckily he was engaged to a woman as old as himself, and therefore her father, who was steward of a neigh-boring estate, would provide him with a job. He would marry and go into har-ness. His life was over, he would be a subject animal now.

He turned uneasily aside, the retreating steps of the horses echoing in his ears. Then, with foolish restlessness, he reached for the scraps of bacon-rind from the plates, and making a faint whistling sound, flung them to the terrier that lay against the fender. He watched the dog swallow them, and waited till the creature looked into his eyes. Then a faint grin came on his face, and in a high, foolish voice he said:

"You won't get much more bacon, shall you, you little b———?"

The dog faintly and dismally wagged its tail, then lowered its haunches, 10 circled round, and lay down again.

There was another helpless silence at the table. Joe sprawled uneasily in his seat, not willing to go till the family conclave was dissolved. Fred Henry, the second brother, was erect, clean-limbed, alert. He had watched the passing of the horses with more *sang-froid.*° If he was an animal, like Joe, he was an animal which controls, not one which is controlled. He was master of any horse, and he carried himself with a well-tempered air of mastery. But he was not master of the situations of life. He pushed his coarse brown mustache upwards, off his lip, and glanced irritably at his sister, who sat impassive and inscrutable.

"You'll go and stop with Lucy for a bit, shan't you?" he asked. The girl did not answer.

"I don't see what else you can do," persisted Fred Henry.

"Go as a skivvy,"° Joe interpolated laconically.

The girl did not move a muscle.   15

"If I was her, I should go in for training for a nurse," said Malcolm, the youngest of them all. He was the baby of the family, a young man of twenty-two, with a fresh, jaunty *museau.*°

But Mabel did not take any notice of him. They had talked at her and round her for so many years, that she hardly heard them at all.

The marble clock on the mantelpiece softly chimed the half-hour, the dog rose uneasily from the hearth-rug and looked at the party at the breakfast-table. But still they sat on in ineffectual conclave.

"Oh, all right," said Joe suddenly, apropos of nothing. "I'll get a move on."

He pushed back his chair, straddled his knees with a downward jerk, to get 20 them free, in horsey fashion, and went to the fire. Still he did not go out of the room; he was curious to know what the others would do or say. He began to charge his pipe, looking down at the dog and saying in a high, affected voice:

"Going wi' me? Going wi' me are ter? Tha'rt goin' further than tha counts on just now, dost hear?"

The dog faintly wagged its tail, the man stuck out his jaw and covered his pipe with his hands, and puffed intently, losing himself in the tobacco, looking down all the while at the dog with an absent brown eye. The dog looked up at him in mournful distrust. Joe stood with his knees stuck out, in real horsey fashion.

"Have you had a letter from Lucy?" Fred Henry asked of his sister.

"Last week," came the neutral reply.

"And what does she say?"   25

There was no answer.

"Does she *ask* you to go and stop there?" persisted Fred Henry.

"She says I can if I like."

"Well, then, you'd better. Tell her you'll come on Monday."

This was received in silence.   30

sang-froid: Coolness, composure.
skivvy: Domestic worker.
museau: Slang for face.

"That's what you'll do then, is it?" said Fred Henry, in some exasperation.

But she made no answer. There was a silence of futility and irritation in the room. Malcolm grinned fatuously.

"You'll have to make up your mind between now and next Wednesday," said Joe loudly, "or else find yourself lodgings on the curbstone."

The face of the young woman darkened, but she sat on immutable.

"Here's Jack Fergusson!" exclaimed Malcolm, who was looking aimlessly 35 out of the window.

"Where?" exclaimed Joe loudly.

"Just gone past."

"Coming in?"

Malcolm craned his neck to see the gate.

"Yes," he said. 40

There was a silence. Mabel sat on like one condemned, at the head of the table. Then a whistle was heard from the kitchen. The dog got up and barked sharply. Joe opened the door and shouted:

"Come on."

After a moment a young man entered. He was muffled up in overcoat and a purple woolen scarf, and his tweed cap, which he did not remove, was pulled down on his head. He was of medium height, his face was rather long and pale, his eyes looked tired.

"Hello, Jack! Well, Jack!" exclaimed Malcolm and Joe. Fred Henry merely said: "Jack."

"What's doing?" asked the newcomer, evidently addressing Fred Henry. 45

"Same. We've got to be out by Wednesday. Got a cold?"

"I have — got it bad, too."

"Why don't you stop in?"

"*Me* stop in? When I can't stand on my legs, perhaps I shall have a chance," the young man spoke huskily. He had a slight Scotch accent.

"It's a knock-out, isn't it," said Joe, boisterously, "if a doctor goes round 50 croaking with a cold. Looks bad for the patients, doesn't it?"

The young doctor looked at him slowly.

"Anything the matter with *you*, then?" he asked sarcastically.

"Not as I know of. Damn your eyes, hope not. Why?"

"I thought you were very concerned about the patients, wondered if you might be one yourself."

"Damn it, no, I've never been patient to no flaming doctor, and hope I 55 never shall be," returned Joe.

At this point Mabel rose from the table, and they all seemed to become aware of her existence. She began putting the dishes together. The young doctor looked at her, but did not address her. He had not greeted her. She went out of the room with the tray, her face impassive and unchanged.

"When are you off then, all of you?" asked the doctor.

"I'm catching the eleven-forty," replied Malcolm. "Are you goin' down wi' th' trap,° Joe?"

"Yes, I've told you I'm going down wi' th' trap, haven't I?"

"We'd better be getting her in then. So long, Jack, if I don't see you before I 60 go," said Malcolm, shaking hands.

trap: A light two-wheeled carriage.

He went out, followed by Joe, who seemed to have his tail between his legs.
"Well, this is the devil's own," exclaimed the doctor, when he was left alone
with Fred Henry. "Going before Wednesday, are you?"

"That's the orders," replied the other.

"Where, to Northampton?"

"That's it." 65

"The devil!" exclaimed Fergusson, with quiet chagrin.

And there was silence between the two.

"All settled up, are you?" asked Fergusson.

"About."

There was another pause. 70

"Well, I shall miss yer, Freddy, boy," said the young doctor.

"And I shall miss thee, Jack," returned the other.

"Miss you like hell," mused the doctor.

Fred Henry turned aside. There was nothing to say. Mabel came in again,
to finish clearing the table.

"What are *you* going to do, then, Miss Pervin?" asked Fergusson. "Going to 75
your sister's, are you?"

Mabel looked at him with her steady, dangerous eyes, that always made
him uncomfortable, unsettling his superficial ease.

"No," she said.

"Well, what in the name of fortune *are* you going to do? Say what you
mean to do," cried Fred Henry, with futile intensity.

But she only averted her head, and continued her work. She folded the
white table-cloth, and put on the chenille cloth.

"The sulkiest bitch that ever trod!" muttered her brother. 80

But she finished her task with perfectly impassive face, the young doctor
watching her interestedly all the while. Then she went out.

Fred Henry stared after her, clenching his lips, his blue eyes fixing in sharp
antagonism, as he made a grimace of sour exasperation.

"You could bray her into bits, and that's all you'd get out of her," he said,
in a small, narrowed tone.

The doctor smiled faintly.

"What's she *going* to do, then?" he asked. 85

"Strike me if *I* know!" returned the other.

There was a pause. Then the doctor stirred.

"I'll be seeing you tonight, shall I?" he said to his friend.

"Ay—where's it to be? Are we going over to Jessdale?"

"I don't know. I've got such a cold on me. I'll come round to the 'Moon 90
and Stars,' anyway."

"Let Lizzie and May miss their night for once, eh?"

"That's it—if I feel as I do now."

"All's one——"

The two young men went through the passage and down to the back door
together. The house was large, but it was servantless now, and desolate. At the
back was a small bricked houseyard and beyond that a big square, graveled fine
and red, and having stables on two sides. Sloping, dank, winter-dark fields
stretched away on the open sides.

But the stables were empty. Joseph Pervin, the father of the family, had 95
been a man of no education, who had become a fairly large horse dealer. The

stables had been full of horses, there was a great turmoil and come-and-go of horses and of dealers and grooms. Then the kitchen was full of servants. But of late things had declined. The old man had married a second time, to retrieve his fortunes. Now he was dead and everything was gone to the dogs, there was nothing but debt and threatening.

For months, Mabel had been servantless in the big house, keeping the home together in penury for her ineffectual brothers. She had kept house for ten years. But previously it was with unstinted means. Then, however brutal and coarse everything was, the sense of money had kept her proud, confident. The men might be foul-mouthed, the women in the kitchen might have bad reputations, her brothers might have illegitimate children. But so long as there was money, the girl felt herself established, and brutally proud, reserved.

No company came to the house, save dealers and coarse men. Mabel had no associates of her own sex, after her sister went away. But she did not mind. She went regularly to church, she attended to her father. And she lived in the memory of her mother, who had died when she was fourteen, and whom she had loved. She had loved her father, too, in a different way, depending upon him, and feeling secure in him, until at the age of fifty-four he married again. And then she had set hard against him. Now he had died and left them all hopelessly in debt.

She had suffered badly during the period of poverty. Nothing, however, could shake the curious, sullen, animal pride that dominated each member of the family. Now, for Mabel, the end had come. Still she would not cast about her. She would follow her own way just the same. She would always hold the keys of her own situation. Mindless and persistent, she endured from day to day. Why should she think? Why should she answer anybody? It was enough that this was the end, and there was no way out. She need not pass any more darkly along the main street of the small town, avoiding every eye. She need not demean herself any more, going into the shops and buying the cheapest food. This was at an end. She thought of nobody, not even of herself. Mindless and persistent, she seemed in a sort of ecstasy to be coming nearer to her fulfillment, her own glorification, approaching her dead mother, who was glorified.

In the afternoon she took a little bag, with shears and sponge and a small scrubbing-brush, and went out. It was a gray, wintry day, with saddened, dark green fields and an atmosphere blackened by the smoke of foundries not far off. She went quickly, darkly along the causeway, heeding nobody, through the town to the churchyard.

There she always felt secure, as if no one could see her, although as a mat- 100 ter of fact she was exposed to the stare of everyone who passed along under the churchyard wall. Nevertheless, once under the shadow of the great looming church, among the graves, she felt immune from the world, reserved within the thick churchyard wall as in another country.

Carefully she clipped the grass from the grave, and arranged the pinky white, small chrysanthemums in the tin cross. When this was done, she took an empty jar from a neighboring grave, brought water, and carefully, most scrupulously sponged the marble headstone and the coping-stone.

It gave her sincere satisfaction to do this. She felt in immediate contact with the world of her mother. She took minute pains, went through the park in a state bordering on pure happiness, as if in performing this task she came into a subtle, intimate connection with her mother. For the life she followed here in the world was far less real than the world of death she inherited from her mother.

The doctor's house was just by the church. Fergusson, being a mere hired assistant, was slave to the countryside. As he hurried now to attend to the out-patients in the surgery, glancing across the graveyard with his quick eye, he saw the girl at her task at the grave. She seemed so intent and remote, it was like looking into another world. Some mystical element was touched in him. He slowed down as he walked, watching her as if spellbound.

She lifted her eyes, feeling him looking. Their eyes met. And each looked again at once, each feeling, in some way, found out by the other. He lifted his cap and passed on down the road. There remained distinct in his conscious-ness, like a vision, the memory of her face, lifted from the tombstone in the churchyard, and looking at him with slow, large, portentous eyes. It *was* por-tentous, her face. It seemed to mesmerize him. There was a heavy power in her eyes which laid hold of his whole being, as if he had drunk some powerful drug. He had been feeling weak and done before. Now the life came back into him, he felt delivered from his own fretted, daily self.

He finished his duties at the surgery as quickly as might be, hastily filling 105 up the bottles of the waiting people with cheap drugs. Then, in perpetual haste, he set off again to visit several cases in another part of his round, before teatime. At all times he preferred to walk if he could, but particularly when he was not well. He fancied the motion restored him.

The afternoon was falling. It was gray, deadened, and wintry, with a slow, moist, heavy coldness sinking in and deadening all the faculties. But why should he think or notice? He hastily climbed the hill and turned across the dark green fields, following the black cinder-track. In the distance, across a shallow dip in the country, the small town was clustered like smoldering ash, a tower, a spire, a heap of low, raw, extinct houses. And on the nearest fringe of the town, sloping into the dip, was Oldmeadow, the Pervins' house. He could see the stables and the outbuildings distinctly, as they lay towards him on the slope. Well, he would not go there many more times! Another resource would be lost to him, another place gone: the only company he cared for in the alien, ugly little town he was losing. Nothing but work, drudgery, constant hasten-ing from dwelling to dwelling among the colliers and the iron-workers. It wore him out, but at the same time he had a craving for it. It was a stimulant to him to be in the homes of the working people, moving, as it were, through the in-nermost body of their life. His nerves were excited and gratified. He could come so near, into the very lives of the rough, inarticulate, powerful emotional men and women: He grumbled, he said he hated the hellish hole. But as a mat-ter of fact it excited him, the contact with the rough, strongly-feeling people was a stimulant applied direct to his nerves.

Below Oldmeadow, in the green, shallow, soddened hollow of fields, lay a square, deep pond. Roving across the landscape, the doctor's quick eye de-tected a figure in black passing through the gate of the field, down towards the pond. He looked again. It would be Mabel Pervin. His mind suddenly became alive and attentive.

Why was she going down there? He pulled up on the path on the slope above, and stood staring. He could just make sure of the small black figure moving in the hollow of the failing day. He seemed to see her in the midst of such obscurity, that he was like a clairvoyant, seeing rather with the mind's eye than with ordinary sight. Yet he could see her positively enough, whilst he kept his eye attentive. He felt, if he looked away from her, in the thick, ugly falling dusk, he would lose her altogether.

He followed her minutely as she moved, direct and intent, like something transmitted rather than stirring in voluntary activity, straight down from the field towards the pond. There she stood on the bank for a moment. She never raised her head. Then she waded slowly into the water.

He stood motionless as the small black figure walked slowly and deliber- 110 ately towards the center of the pond, very slowly, gradually moving deeper into the motionless water, and still moving forward as the water got up to her breast. Then he could see her no more in the dusk of the dead afternoon.

"There!" he exclaimed. "Would you believe it?"

And he hastened straight down, running over the wet, soddened fields, pushing through the hedges, down into the depression of callous wintry obscurity. It took him several minutes to come to the pond. He stood on the bank, breathing heavily. He could see nothing. His eyes seemed to penetrate the dead water. Yes, perhaps that was the dark shadow of her black clothing beneath the surface of the water.

He slowly ventured into the pond. The bottom was deep, soft clay, he sank in, and the water clasped dead cold round his legs. As he stirred he could smell the cold, rotten clay that fouled up into the water. It was objectionable in his lungs. Still, repelled and yet not heeding, he moved deeper into the pond. The cold water rose over his thighs, over his loins, upon his abdomen. The lower part of his body was all sunk in the hideous cold element. And the bottom was so deeply soft and uncertain, he was afraid of pitching with his mouth underneath. He could not swim, and was afraid.

He crouched a little, spreading his hands under the water and moving them round, trying to feel for her. The dead cold pond swayed upon his chest. He moved again, a little deeper, and again, with his hands underneath, he felt all around under the water. And he touched her clothing. But it evaded his fingers. He made a desperate effort to grasp it.

And so doing he lost his balance and went under, horribly, suffocating in 115 the foul earthy water, struggling madly for a few moments. At last, after what seemed an eternity, he got his footing, rose again into the air, and looked around. He gasped, and knew he was in the world. Then he looked at the water. She had risen near him. He grasped her clothing, and drawing her nearer, turned to take his way to land again.

He went very slowly, carefully, absorbed in the slow progress. He rose higher, climbing out of the pond. The water was now only about his legs; he was thankful, full of relief to be out of the clutches of the pond. He lifted her and staggered on to the bank, out of the horror of wet, gray clay.

He laid her down on the bank. She was quite unconscious and running with water. He made the water come from her mouth, he worked to restore her. He did not have to work very long before he could feel the breathing begin again in her; she was breathing naturally. He worked a little longer. He could feel her live beneath his hands; she was coming back. He wiped her face, wrapped her in his overcoat, looked round into the dim, dark gray world, then lifted her and staggered down the bank and across the fields.

It seemed an unthinkably long way, and his burden so heavy he felt he would never get to the house. But at last he was in the stable-yard, and then in the house-yard. He opened the door and went into the house. In the kitchen he laid her down on the hearth-rug and called. The house was empty. But the fire was burning in the grate.

Then again he kneeled to attend to her. She was breathing regularly, her eyes were wide open and as if conscious, but there seemed something missing in her look. She was conscious in herself, but unconscious of her surroundings.

He ran upstairs, took blankets from a bed, and put them before the fire to 120 warm. Then he removed her saturated, earthy-smelling clothing, rubbed her dry with a towel, and wrapped her naked in the blankets. Then he went into the dining-room, to look for spirits. There was a little whiskey. He drank a gulp himself, and put some into her mouth.

The effect was instantaneous. She looked full into his face, as if she had been seeing him for some time, and yet had only just become conscious of him.

"Dr. Fergusson?" she said.

"What?" he answered.

He was divesting himself of his coat, intending to find some dry clothing upstairs. He could not bear the smell of the dead, clayey water, and he was mortally afraid for his own health.

"What did I do?" she asked. 125

"Walked into the pond," he replied. He had begun to shudder like one sick, and could hardly attend to her. Her eyes remained full on him, he seemed to be going dark in his mind, looking back at her helplessly. The shuddering became quieter in him, his life came back to him, dark and unknowing, but strong again.

"Was I out of my mind?" she asked, while her eyes were fixed on him all the time.

"Maybe, for the moment," he replied. He felt quiet, because his strength had come back. The strange fretful strain had left him.

"Am I out of my mind now?" she asked.

"Are you?" he reflected a moment. "No," he answered truthfully, "I don't 130 see that you are." He turned his face aside. He was afraid now, because he felt dazed, and felt dimly that her power was stronger than his, in this issue. And she continued to look at him fixedly all the time. "Can you tell me where I shall find some dry things to put on?" he asked.

"Did you dive into the pond for me?" she asked.

"No," he answered. "I walked in. But I went in overhead as well."

There was silence for a moment. He hesitated. He very much wanted to go upstairs to get into dry clothing. But there was another desire in him. And she seemed to hold him. His will seemed to have gone to sleep, and left him, standing there slack before her. But he felt warm inside himself. He did not shudder at all, though his clothes were sodden on him.

"Why did you?" she asked.

"Because I didn't want you to do such a foolish thing," he said. 135

"It wasn't foolish," she said, still gazing at him as she lay on the floor, with a sofa cushion under her head. "It was the right thing to do. *I* knew best, then."

"I'll go and shift these wet things," he said. But still he had not the power to move out of her presence, until she sent him. It was as if she had the life of his body in her hands, and he could not extricate himself. Or perhaps he did not want to.

Suddenly she sat up. Then she became aware of her own immediate condition. She felt the blankets about her, she knew her own limbs. For a moment it seemed as if her reason were going. She looked round, with wild eyes, as if seeking something. He stood still with fear. She saw her clothing lying scattered.

"Who undressed me?" she asked, her eyes resting full and inevitable on his face.

"I did," he replied, "to bring you round."   140

For some moments she sat and gazed at him, awfully, her lips parted.

"Do you love me, then?" she asked.

He only stood and stared at her, fascinated. His soul seemed to melt.

She shuffled forward on her knees, and put her arms round him, round his legs, as he stood there, pressing her breasts against his knees and thighs, clutching him with strange, convulsive certainty, pressing his thighs against her, drawing him to her face, her throat, as she looked up at him with flaring, humble eyes of transfiguration, triumphant in first possession.

"You love me," she murmured, in strange transport, yearning and tri-   145
umphant and confident. "You love me. I know you love me, I know."

And she was passionately kissing his knees, through the wet clothing, passionately and indiscriminately kissing his knees, his legs, as if unaware of everything.

He looked down at the tangled wet hair, the wild, bare, animal shoulders. He was amazed, bewildered, and afraid. He had never thought of loving her. He had never wanted to love her. When he rescued her and restored her, he was a doctor, and she was a patient. He had had no single personal thought of her. Nay, this introduction of the personal element was very distasteful to him, a violation of his professional honor. It was horrible to have her there embracing his knees. It was horrible. He revolted from it, violently. And yet—and yet—he had not the power to break away.

She looked at him again, with the same supplication of powerful love, and that same transcendent, frightening light of triumph. In view of the delicate flame which seemed to come from her face like a light, he was powerless. And yet he had never intended to love her. He had never intended. And something stubborn in him could not give way.

"You love me," she repeated, in a murmur of deep, rhapsodic assurance. "You love me."

Her hands were drawing him, drawing him down to her. He was afraid,   150
even a little horrified. For he had, really, no intention of loving her. Yet her hands were drawing him towards her. He put out his hand quickly to steady himself, and grasped her bare shoulder. A flame seemed to burn the hand that grasped her soft shoulder. He had no intention of loving her: his whole will was against his yielding. It was horrible. And yet wonderful was the touch of her shoulders, beautiful the shining of her face. Was she perhaps mad? He had a horror of yielding to her. Yet something in him ached also.

He had been staring away at the door, away from her. But his hand remained on her shoulder. She had gone suddenly very still. He looked down at her. Her eyes were now wide with fear, with doubt, the light was dying from her face, a shadow of terrible grayness was returning. He could not bear the touch of her eyes' question upon him, and the look of death behind the question.

With an inward groan he gave way, and let his heart yield towards her. A sudden gentle smile came on his face. And her eyes, which never left his face, slowly, slowly filled with tears. He watched the strange water rise in her eyes, like some slow fountain coming up. And his heart seemed to burn and melt away in his breast.

He could not bear to look at her any more. He dropped on his knees and caught her head with his arms and pressed her face against his throat. She was very still. His heart, which seemed to have broken, was burning with a kind of agony in his breast. And he felt her slow, hot tears wetting his throat. But he could not move.

He felt the hot tears wet his neck and the hollows of his neck, and he remained motionless, suspended through one of man's eternities. Only now it had become indispensable to him to have her face pressed close to him; he could never let her go again. He could never let her head go away from the close clutch of his arm. He wanted to remain like that for ever, with his heart hurting him in a pain that was also life to him. Without knowing, he was looking down on her damp, soft brown hair.

Then, as it were suddenly, he smelt the horrid stagnant smell of that 155 water. And at the same moment she drew away from him and looked at him. Her eyes were wistful and unfathomable. He was afraid of them, and he fell to kissing her, not knowing what he was doing. He wanted her eyes not to have that terrible, wistful, unfathomable look.

When she turned her face to him again, a faint delicate flush was glowing, and there was again dawning that terrible shining of joy in her eyes, which really terrified him, and yet which he now wanted to see, because he feared the look of doubt still more.

"You love me?" she said, rather faltering.

"Yes." The word cost him a painful effort. Not because it wasn't true. But because it was too newly true, the *saying* seemed to tear open again his newly-torn heart. And he hardly wanted it to be true, even now.

She lifted her face to him, and he bent forward and kissed her on the mouth, gently, with the one kiss that is an eternal pledge. And as he kissed her his heart strained again in his breast. He never intended to love her. But now it was over. He had crossed over the gulf to her, and all that he had left behind had shriveled and become void.

After the kiss, her eyes again slowly filled with tears. She sat still, away 160 from him, with her face drooped aside, and her hands folded in her lap. The tears fell very slowly. There was complete silence. He too sat there motionless and silent on the hearth-rug. The strange pain of his heart that was broken seemed to consume him. That he should love her? That this was love! That he should be ripped open in this way! Him, a doctor! How they would all jeer if they knew! It was agony to him to think they might know.

In the curious naked pain of the thought he looked again to her. She was still sitting there drooped into a muse. He saw a tear fall, and his heart flared hot. He saw for the first time that one of her shoulders was quite uncovered, one arm bare, he could see one of her small breasts; dimly, because it had become almost dark in the room.

"Why are you crying?" he asked, in an altered voice.

She looked up at him, and behind her tears the consciousness of her situation for the first time brought a dark look of shame to her eyes.

"I'm not crying, really," she said, watching him, half frightened.

He reached his hand, and softly closed it on her bare arm. 165

"I love you! I love you!" he said in a soft, low vibrating voice, unlike himself.

She shrank, and dropped her head. The soft, penetrating grip of his hand on her arm distressed her. She looked up at him.

"I want to go," she said. "I want to go and get you some dry things."

"Why?" he said. "I'm all right."

"But I want to go," she said. "And I want you to change your things." 170

He released her arm, and she wrapped herself in the blanket, looking at him rather frightened. And still she did not rise.

"Kiss me," she said wistfully.

He kissed her, but briefly, half in anger.

Then, after a second, she rose nervously, all mixed up in the blanket. He watched her in her confusion as she tried to extricate herself and wrap herself up so that she could walk. He watched her relentlessly, as she knew. And as she went, the blanket trailing, and as he saw a glimpse of her feet and her white leg, he tried to remember her as she was when he had wrapped her in the blanket. But then he didn't want to remember, because she had been nothing to him then, and his nature revolted from remembering her as she was when she was nothing to him.

A tumbling, muffled noise from within the dark house startled him. Then 175
he heard her voice: "There are clothes." He rose and went to the foot of the stairs, and gathered up the garments she had thrown down. Then he came back to the fire, to rub himself down and dress. He grinned at his own appearance when he had finished.

The fire was sinking, so he put on coal. The house was now quite dark, save for the light of a street-lamp that shone in faintly from beyond the holly trees. He lit the gas with matches he found on the mantelpiece. Then he emptied the pockets of his own clothes, and threw all his wet things in a heap into the scullery. After which he gathered up her sodden clothes, gently, and put them in a separate heap on the copper-top in the scullery.

It was six o'clock on the clock. His own watch had stopped. He ought to go back to the surgery. He waited, and still she did not come down. So he went to the foot of the stairs and called:

"I shall have to go."

Almost immediately he heard her coming down. She had on her best dress of black voile, and her hair was tidy, but still damp. She looked at him — and in spite of herself, smiled.

"I don't like you in those clothes," she said. 180

"Do I look a sight?" he answered.

They were shy of one another.

"I'll make you some tea," she said.

"No, I must go."

"Must you?" And she looked at him again with the wide, strained, doubt- 185
ful eyes. And again, from the pain of his breast, he knew how he loved her. He went and bent to kiss her, gently, passionately, with his heart's painful kiss.

"And my hair smells so horrible," she murmured in distraction. "And I'm so awful, I'm so awful! Oh, no, I'm too awful." And she broke into bitter, heart-broken sobbing. "You can't want to love me, I'm horrible."

"Don't be silly, don't be silly," he said, trying to comfort her, kissing her, holding her in his arms. "I want you, I want to marry you, we're going to be married, quickly, quickly — tomorrow if I can."

But she only sobbed terribly, and cried:
"I feel awful. I feel awful. I feel I'm horrible to you."

"No, I want you, I want you," was all he answered, blindly, with that ter- 190
rible intonation which frightened her almost more than her horror lest he
should *not* want her.

EDGAR ALLAN POE (1809–1849)

Edgar Allan Poe grew up in the home of John Allan, in Richmond, Virginia, after his mother died in 1811, and he was educated in Scotland and
England for five years before completing his classical education in Richmond. After a short stint at the University of Virginia, Poe married and
went to Boston, where he began publishing his poetry. His foster father
sent him to West Point Military Academy, but Poe was expelled and moved
on to New York, where he published a book of poems inspired by the romantic movement. Divorced, and moving among editorial jobs in Baltimore, Richmond, and New York, Poe married his thirteen-year-old cousin
Virginia Clemm. Early in his story-writing career, Poe published his only
novel-length piece, *The Narrative of Arthur Gordon Pym* (1938), and the
following year, he began to work in the genre of the supernatural and
horrible, with the stories "William Wilson" and "The Fall of the House of
Usher." He gained publicity with the detective story "The Murders in the
Rue Morgue," became nationally famous with the publication of his poem
"The Raven" in 1845, and died four years later in Baltimore after a drinking
binge. Poe theorized that the short story writer should plan every word toward the achievement of a certain effect, and that stories should be read in
a single sitting. Morbidity and dreamlike flights of fancy, for which Poe is
often recognized, do not detract from his lucid crafting of suspense and
his erudite control of language and symbol.

Web   *Research Edgar Allan Poe with LitLinks at*
http://www.bedfordstmartins.com/meyer/bedintrolit

The Cask of Amontillado   *1846*

The thousand injuries of Fortunato I had borne as I best could; but when he ventured upon insult, I vowed revenge. You, who so well know the nature of my soul,
will not suppose, however, that I gave utterance to a threat. *At length* I would be
avenged; this was a point definitely settled—but the very definitiveness with
which it was resolved precluded the idea of risk. I must not only punish, but
punish with impunity. A wrong is unredressed when retribution overtakes its re-
dresser. It is equally unredressed when the avenger fails to make himself felt as
such to him who has done the wrong.

It must be understood, that neither by word nor deed had I given Fortunato cause to doubt my good-will. I continued, as was my wont, to smile in

his face, and he did not perceive that my smile *now* was at the thought of his immolation.

He had a weak point—this Fortunato—although in other regards he was a man to be respected and even feared. He prided himself on his connoisseurship in wine. Few Italians have the true virtuoso spirit. For the most part their enthusiasm is adopted to suit the time and opportunity—to practise imposture upon the British and Austrian *millionnaires*. In painting and gemmary Fortunato, like his countrymen, was a quack—but in the matter of old wines he was sincere. In this respect I did not differ from him materially: I was skilful in the Italian vintages myself, and bought largely whenever I could.

It was about dusk, one evening during the supreme madness of the carnival season, that I encountered my friend. He accosted me with excessive warmth, for he had been drinking much. The man wore motley. He had on a tight-fitting parti-striped dress, and his head was surmounted by the conical cap and bells. I was so pleased to see him, that I thought I should never have done wringing his hand.

I said to him: "My dear Fortunato, you are luckily met. How remarkably 5 well you are looking to-day! But I have received a pipe° of what passes for Amontillado, and I have my doubts."

"How?" said he. "Amontillado? A pipe? Impossible! And in the middle of the carnival!"

"I have my doubts," I replied; "and I was silly enough to pay the full Amontillado price without consulting you in the matter. You were not to be found, and I was fearful of losing a bargain."

"Amontillado!"

"I have my doubts."

"Amontillado!"

"And I must satisfy them." 10

"Amontillado!"

"As you are engaged, I am on my way to Luchesi. If any one has a critical turn, it is he. He will tell me——"

"Luchesi cannot tell Amontillado from Sherry."

"And yet some fools will have it that his taste is a match for your own." 15

"Come, let us go."

"Whither?"

"To your vaults."

"My friend, no; I will not impose upon your good nature. I perceive you have an engagement. Luchesi——"

"I have no engagement;—come." 20

"My friend, no. It is not the engagement, but the severe cold with which I perceive you are afflicted. The vaults are insufferably damp. They are encrusted with nitre."

"Let us go, nevertheless. The cold is merely nothing. Amontillado! You have been imposed upon. And as for Luchesi, he cannot distinguish Sherry from Amontillado."

Thus speaking, Fortunato possessed himself of my arm. Putting on a mask of black silk, and drawing a *roquelaire*° closely about my person, I suffered him to hurry me to my palazzo.

pipe: A large keg.
roquelaire: A short cloak.

There were no attendants at home; they had absconded to make merry in honor of the time. I had told them that I should not return until the morning, and had given them explicit orders not to stir from the house. These orders were sufficient, I well knew, to insure their immediate disappearance, one and all, as soon as my back was turned.

I took from their sconces two flambeaux, and giving one to Fortunato, 25 bowed him through several suites of rooms to the archway that led into the vaults. I passed down a long and winding staircase, requesting him to be cautious as he followed. We came at length to the foot of the descent, and stood together on the damp ground of the catacombs of the Montresors.

The gait of my friend was unsteady, and the bells upon his cap jingled as he strode.

"The pipe?" said he.

"It is farther on," said I; "but observe the white web-work which gleams from these cavern walls."

He turned toward me, and looked into my eyes with two filmy orbs that distilled the rheum of intoxication.

"Nitre?" he asked, at length.   30

"Nitre," I replied. "How long have you had that cough?"

"Ugh! ugh! ugh! — ugh! ugh! ugh! — ugh! ugh! ugh! — ugh! ugh! ugh! — ugh! ugh! ugh!"

My poor friend found it impossible to reply for many minutes.

"It is nothing," he said, at last.

"Come," I said, with decision, "we will go back; your health is precious. 35 You are rich, respected, admired, beloved; you are happy, as once I was. You are a man to be missed. For me it is no matter. We will go back; you will be ill, and I cannot be responsible. Besides, there is Luchesi —"

"Enough," he said; "the cough is a mere nothing; it will not kill me. I shall not die of a cough."

"True — true," I replied; "and, indeed, I had no intention of alarming you unnecessarily; but you should use all proper caution. A draught of this Medoc will defend us from the damps."

Here I knocked off the neck of a bottle which I drew from a long row of its fellows that lay upon the mould.

"Drink," I said, presenting him the wine.

He raised it to his lips with a leer. He paused and nodded to me familiarly, 40 while his bells jingled.

"I drink," he said, "to the buried that repose around us."

"And I to your long life."

He again took my arm, and we proceeded.

"These vaults," he said, "are extensive."

"The Montresors," I replied, "were a great and numerous family."   45

"I forget your arms."

"A huge human foot d'or,° in a field azure; the foot crushes a serpent rampant whose fangs are imbedded in the heel."

"And the motto?"

"*Nemo me impune lacessit.*"°

"Good!" he said.   50

---

d'or: Of gold.
Nemo . . . lacessit: "No one wounds me with impunity" (Latin).

The wine sparkled in his eyes and the bells jingled. My own fancy grew warm with the Medoc. We had passed through walls of piled bones, with casks and puncheons intermingling into the inmost recesses of the catacombs. I paused again, and this time I made bold to seize Fortunato by an arm above the elbow.

"The nitre!" I said; "see, it increases. It hangs like moss upon the vaults. We are below the river's bed. The drops of moisture trickle among the bones. Come, we will go back ere it is too late. Your cough——"

"It is nothing," he said; "let us go on. But first, another draught of the Medoc."

I broke and reached him a flagon of De Grâve. He emptied it at a breath. His eyes flashed with a fierce light. He laughed and threw the bottle upward with a gesticulation I did not understand.

I looked at him in surprise. He repeated the movement—a grotesque one. 55

"You do not comprehend?" he said.

"Not I," I replied.

"Then you are not of the brotherhood."

"How?"

"You are not of the masons." 60

"Yes, yes," I said; "yes, yes."

"You? Impossible! A mason?"

"A mason," I replied.

"A sign," he said.

"It is this," I answered, producing a trowel from beneath the folds of my 65
roquelaire.

"You jest," he exclaimed, recoiling a few paces. "But let us proceed to the Amontillado."

"Be it so," I said, replacing the tool beneath the cloak, and again offering him my arm. He leaned upon it heavily. We continued our route in search of the Amontillado. We passed through a range of low arches, descended, passed on, and descending again, arrived at a deep crypt, in which the foulness of the air caused our flambeaux rather to glow than flame.

At the most remote end of the crypt there appeared another less spacious. Its walls had been lined with human remains, piled to the vault overhead, in the fashion of the great catacombs of Paris. Three sides of this interior crypt were still ornamented in this manner. From the fourth the bones had been thrown down, and lay promiscuously upon the earth, forming at one point a mound of some size. Within the wall thus exposed by the displacing of the bones, we perceived a still interior recess, in depth about four feet, in width three, in height six or seven. It seemed to have been constructed for no especial use within itself, but formed merely the interval between two of the colossal supports of the roof of the catacombs, and was backed by one of their circumscribing walls of solid granite.

It was in vain that Fortunato, uplifting his dull torch, endeavored to pry into the depth of the recess. Its termination the feeble light did not enable us to see.

"Proceed," I said; "herein is the Amontillado. As for Luchesi——" 70

"He is an ignoramus," interrupted my friend, as he stepped unsteadily forward, while I followed immediately at his heels. In an instant he had reached the extremity of the niche, and finding his progress arrested by the rock, stood stupidly bewildered. A moment more and I had fettered him to the granite. In its surface were two iron staples, distant from each other about two feet, horizontally. From one of these depended a short chain, from the other a padlock. Throwing the links about his waist, it was but the work of a few seconds to secure it. He was too much astounded to resist. Withdrawing the key I stepped back from the recess.

"Pass your hand," I said, "over the wall; you cannot help feeling the nitre. Indeed it is *very* damp. Once more let me *implore* you to return. No? Then I must positively leave you. But I must first render you all the little attentions in my power."

"The Amontillado!" ejaculated my friend, not yet recovered from his astonishment.

"True," I replied; "the Amontillado."

As I said these words I busied myself among the pile of bones of which I have before spoken. Throwing them aside, I soon uncovered a quantity of building stone and mortar. With these materials and with the aid of my trowel, I began vigorously to wall up the entrance of the niche. 75

I had scarcely laid the first tier of the masonry when I discovered that the intoxication of Fortunato had in a great measure worn off. The earliest indication I had of this was a low moaning cry from the depth of the recess. It was *not* the cry of a drunken man. There was then a long and obstinate silence. I laid the second tier, and the third, and the fourth; and then I heard the furious vibrations of the chain. The noise lasted for several minutes, during which, that I might hearken to it with the more satisfaction, I ceased my labors and sat down upon the bones. When at last the clanking subsided, I resumed the trowel, and finished without interruption the fifth, the sixth, and the seventh tier. The wall was now nearly upon a level with my breast. I again paused, and holding the flambeaux over the masonwork, threw a few feeble rays upon the figure within.

A succession of loud and shrill screams, bursting suddenly from the throat of the chained form, seemed to thrust me violently back. For a brief moment I hesitated—I trembled. Unsheathing my rapier, I began to grope with it about the recess; but the thought of an instant reassured me. I placed my hand upon the solid fabric of the catacombs, and felt satisfied. I reapproached the wall. I replied to the yells of him who clamored. I reechoed—I aided—I surpassed them in volume and in strength. I did this, and the clamorer grew still.

It was now midnight, and my task was drawing to a close. I had completed the eighth, the ninth, and the tenth tier. I had finished a portion of the last and the eleventh; there remained but a single stone to be fitted and plastered in. I struggled with its weight; I placed it partially in its destined position. But now there came from out the niche a low laugh that erected the hairs upon my head. It was succeeded by a sad voice, which I had difficulty in recognizing as that of the noble Fortunato. The voice said—

"Ha! ha! ha!—he! he!—a very good joke indeed—an excellent jest. We will have many a rich laugh about it at the palazzo—he! he! he!—over our wine—he! he! he!" 80

"The Amontillado!" I said.

"He! he! he!—he! he! he!—yes, the Amontillado. But is it not getting late? Will not they be awaiting us at the palazzo, the Lady Fortunato and the rest? Let us be gone."

"Yes," I said, "let us be gone."
"For the love of God, Montresor!"
"Yes," I said, "for the love of God!"

But to these words I hearkened in vain for a reply. I grew impatient. I called   85
aloud:

"Fortunato!"

No answer. I called again:

"Fortunato!"

No answer still. I thrust a torch through the remaining aperture and let it fall within. There came forth in return only a jingling of the bells. My heart grew sick — on account of the dampness of the catacombs. I hastened to make an end of my labor. I forced the last stone into its position; I plastered it up. Against the new masonry I re-erected the old rampart of bones. For the half of a century no mortal has disturbed them. *In pace requiescat!*°

In pace requiescat!: In peace may he rest (Latin)!

MARK TWAIN (1835–1910)

Mark Twain is the pen name of Samuel Clemens, born in Missouri in 1835. Twain spent most of his childhood in Hannibal, Missouri, on the Mississippi River, and after the death of his father when he was eleven, he worked at a series of jobs to help the family income. A newspaper job prepared him to wander east working for papers and exploring St. Louis, New York, and Philadelphia. Later he trained as a steamboat pilot on the Mississippi and piloted boats professionally until the onset of the Civil War. Clemens had used a couple of different pseudonyms for minor publications before this point, but in 1863 he signed a travel narrative "Mark Twain," from a boating term that means "two fathoms deep," and the name for the great American humorist was created. Twain gained fame in 1865 with his story "The Celebrated Jumping Frog of Calaveras County," which appeared in New York–based *The Saturday Press*. He then became a traveling correspondent, writing pieces on his travels to Europe and the Middle East, and returned to the United States in 1870, when he married and moved to Connecticut. Twain produced *Roughing It* (1872) and *The Gilded Age* (1873) while he toured the country lecturing, and in 1876 published *The Adventures of Tom Sawyer*, an instant hit. His subsequent publications include *A Tramp Abroad* (1880), *The Prince and the Pauper* (1881), and the masterpiece *The Adventures of Huckleberry Finn* (1884). Often traveling and lecturing, Twain wrote several more books, including story collections, *The Tragedy of Pudd'nhead Wilson* (1894), and *Tom Sawyer, Detective* (1896), before he died in Italy in 1910. His work is noted for the combination of rough humor and vernacular language it often uses to convey keen social insights.

Web   *Research Mark Twain with LitLinks at*
http://www.bedfordstmartins.com/meyer/bedintrolit

The Story of the Good Little Boy   *1870*

Once there was a good little boy by the name of Jacob Blivens. He always obeyed his parents, no matter how absurd and unreasonable their demands were; and he always learned his book, and never was late at Sabbath-school. He would not play hookey, even when his sober judgment told him it was the most profitable thing he could do. None of the other boys could ever make that boy out, he acted so strangely. He wouldn't lie, no matter how convenient it was. He just said it was wrong to lie, and that was sufficient for him. And he was so honest that he was simply ridiculous. The curious ways that that Jacob had, surpassed everything. He wouldn't play marbles on Sunday, he wouldn't rob birds' nests, he wouldn't give hot pennies to organ-grinders' monkeys; he didn't seem to take any interest in any kind of rational amusement. So the other boys used to try to reason it out and come to an understanding of him, but they couldn't arrive at any satisfactory conclusion. As I said before, they could only figure out a sort of vague idea that he was "afflicted," and so they took him under their protection, and never allowed any harm to come to him.

This good little boy read all the Sunday-school books; they were his greatest delight. This was the whole secret of it. He believed in the good little boys they put in the Sunday-school books; he had every confidence in them. He longed to come across one of them alive once; but he never did. They all died before his time, maybe. Whenever he read about a particularly good one he turned over quickly to the end to see what became of him, because he wanted to travel thousands of miles and gaze on him; but it wasn't any use; that good little boy always died in the last chapter, and there was a picture of the funeral, with all his relations and the Sunday-school children standing around the grave in pantaloons that were too short, and bonnets that were too large, and everybody crying into handkerchiefs that had as much as a yard and a half of stuff in them. He was always headed off in this way. He never could see one of those good little boys on account of his always dying in the last chapter.

Jacob had a noble ambition to be put in a Sunday-school book. He wanted to be put in, with pictures representing him gloriously declining to lie to his mother, and her weeping for joy about it; and pictures representing him standing on the doorstep giving a penny to a poor beggar-woman with six children, and telling her to spend it freely, but not to be extravagant, because extravagance is a sin; and pictures of him magnanimously refusing to tell on the bad boy who always lay in wait for him around the corner as he came from school, and welted him over the head with a lath, and then chased him home, saying, "Hi! hi!" as he proceeded. That was the ambition of young Jacob Blivens. He wished to be put in a Sunday-school book. It made him feel a little uncomfortable sometimes when he reflected that the good little boys always died. He loved to live, you know, and this was the most unpleasant feature about being a Sunday-school-book boy. He knew it was not healthy to be good. He knew it was more fatal than consumption to be so supernaturally good as the boys in the books were; he knew that none of them had ever been able to stand it long, and it pained him to think that if they put him in a book he wouldn't ever see it, or even if they did get the book out before he died it wouldn't be popular without any picture of his funeral in the back part of it. It couldn't be much of a Sunday-school book that couldn't tell about the advice he gave to the community when he was dying. So at last, of course, he had to make up his mind to do the best he could under the circumstances — to live right, and, hang on as long as he could, and have his dying speech all ready when his time came.

But somehow nothing ever went right with this good little boy; nothing ever turned out with him the way it turned out with the good little boys in the books. They always had a good time, and the bad boys had the broken legs; but in his case there was a screw loose somewhere, and it all happened just the other way. When he found Jim Blake stealing apples, and went under the tree to read to him about the bad little boy who fell out of a neighbor's apple tree and broke his arm, Jim fell out of the tree, too, but he fell on *him* and broke *his* arm, and Jim wasn't hurt at all. Jacob couldn't understand that. There wasn't anything in the books like it.

And once, when some bad boys pushed a blind man over in the mud, and 5 Jacob ran to help him up and receive his blessing, the blind man did not give him any blessing at all, but whacked him over the head with his stick and said he would like to catch him shoving *him* again, and then pretending to help him up. This was not in accordance with any of the books. Jacob looked them all over to see.

One thing that Jacob wanted to do was to find a lame dog that hadn't any place to stay, and was hungry and persecuted, and bring him home and pet him and have that dog's imperishable gratitude. And at last he found one and was happy; and he brought him home and fed him, but when he was going to pet him the dog flew at him and tore all the clothes off him except those that were in front, and made a spectacle of him that was astonishing. He examined authorities, but he could not understand the matter. It was of the same breed of dogs that was in the books, but it acted very differently. Whatever this boy did he got into trouble. The very things the boys in the books got rewarded for turned out to be about the most unprofitable things he could invest in.

Once, when he was on his way to Sunday-school, he saw some bad boys starting off pleasuring in a sailboat. He was filled with consternation, because he knew from his reading that boys who went sailing on Sunday invariably got drowned. So he ran out on a raft to warn them, but a log turned with him and slid him into the river. A man got him out pretty soon, and the doctor pumped the water out of him, and gave him a fresh start with his bellows, but he caught cold and lay sick abed nine weeks. But the most unaccountable thing about it was that the bad boys in the boat had a good time all day, and then reached home alive and well in the most surprising manner. Jacob Blivens said there was nothing like these things in the books. He was perfectly dumfounded.

When he got well he was a little discouraged, but he resolved to keep on trying anyhow. He knew that so far his experiences wouldn't do to go in a book, but he hadn't yet reached the allotted term of life for good little boys, and he hoped to be able to make a record yet if he could hold on till his time was fully up. If everything else failed he had his dying speech to fall back on.

He examined his authorities, and found that it was now time for him to go to sea as a cabin-boy. He called on a ship-captain and made his application, and when the captain asked for his recommendations he proudly drew out a tract and pointed to the word, "To Jacob Blivens, from his affectionate teacher." But the captain was a coarse, vulgar man, and he said, "Oh, that be blowed! *that* wasn't any proof that he knew how to wash dishes or handle a slush-bucket, and he guessed he didn't want him." This was altogether the most extraordinary thing that ever happened to Jacob in all his life. A compliment from a teacher, on a tract, had never failed to move the tenderest emotions of ship-captains, and open the way to all offices of honor and profit in their gift — it never had in any book that ever *he* had read. He could hardly believe his senses.

This boy always had a hard time of it. Nothing ever came out according to 10 the authorities with him. At last, one day, when he was around hunting up bad little boys to admonish, he found a lot of them in the old iron-foundry fixing up a little joke on fourteen or fifteen dogs, which they had tied together in long procession, and were going to ornament with empty nitroglycerin cans made fast to their tails. Jacob's heart was touched. He sat down on one of those cans (for he never minded grease when duty was before him), and he took hold of the foremost dog by the collar, and turned his reproving eye upon wicked Tom Jones. But just at that moment Alderman McWelter, full of wrath, stepped in. All the bad boys ran away, but Jacob Blivens rose in conscious innocence and began one of those stately little Sunday-school-book speeches which always commence with "Oh, sir!" in dead opposition to the fact that no boy, good or bad, ever starts a remark with "Oh, sir." But the alderman never waited to hear the rest. He took Jacob Blivens by the ear and turned him around, and hit him a whack in the rear with the flat of his hand; and in an instant that good little boy shot out through the roof and soared away toward the sun, with the fragments of those fifteen dogs stringing after him like the tail of a kite. And there wasn't a sign of that alderman or that old iron-foundry left on the face of the earth; and, as for young Jacob Blivens, he never got a chance to make his last dying speech after all his trouble fixing it up, unless he made it to the birds; because, although the bulk of him came down all right in a tree-top in an adjoining county, the rest of him was apportioned around among four townships, and so they had to hold five inquests on him to find out whether he was dead or not, and how it occurred. You never saw a boy scattered so.[1]

Thus perished the good little boy who did the best he could, but didn't come out according to the books. Every boy who ever did as he did prospered except him. His case is truly remarkable. It will probably never be accounted for.

[1] This glycerin catastrophe is borrowed from a floating newspaper item, whose author's name I would give if I knew it. M. T.

JOHN UPDIKE (B. 1932)

John Updike grew up in the small town of Shillington, Pennsylvania, and a family farm nearby. Academic success in school earned him a scholarship to Harvard, where he studied English and graduated in 1954. He soon sold his first story and poem to *The New Yorker*. Also an artist, Updike studied drawing in Oxford, England, and returned to take a position on the staff at

The New Yorker. His first book, a collection of poems titled *The Carpentered Hen and Other Tame Creatures,* appeared in 1958, and the following year he published a book of stories and a novel, *The Poorhouse Fair,* which received the Rosenthal Foundation Award in 1960. Updike produced his second novel, *Rabbit, Run,* in the same year. The prolific Updike, located in Massachusetts for the past forty years, has continued to publish essays and poems and has published a novel or a book of stories nearly every year since 1959, including *The Centaur* (1963), winner of the National Book Award, *Rabbit Is Rich* (1981) and *Rabbit at Rest* (1990), both Pulitzer Prize winners, and *The Witches of Eastwick* (1984), which was made into a major motion picture (Warner Bros., 1987). Updike's fiction is noted for its exemplary use of storytelling conventions, its unique prose style, and its engaging picture of middle-class American life.

Web *Research John Updike with LitLinks at*
http://www.bedfordstmartins.com/meyer/bedintrolit

A & P   1961

In walks these three girls in nothing but bathing suits. I'm in the third checkout slot, with my back to the door, so I don't see them until they're over by the bread. The one that caught my eye first was the one in the plaid green two-piece. She was a chunky kid, with a good tan and a sweet broad soft-looking can with those two crescents of white just under it, where the sun never seems to hit, at the top of the backs of her legs. I stood there with my hand on a box of HiHo crackers trying to remember if I rang it up or not. I ring it up again and the customer starts giving me hell. She's one of these cash-register-watchers, a witch about fifty with rouge on her cheekbones and no eyebrows, and I know it made her day to trip me up. She'd been watching cash registers for fifty years and probably never seen a mistake before.

By the time I got her feathers smoothed and her goodies into a bag—she gives me a little snort in passing, if she'd been born at the right time they would have burned her over in Salem—by the time I get her on her way the girls had circled around the bread and were coming back, without a pushcart, back my way along the counters, in the aisle between the checkouts and the Special bins. They didn't even have shoes on. There was this chunky one, with the two-piece—it was bright green and the seams on the bra were still sharp and her belly was still pretty pale so I guessed she just got it (the suit)—there was this one, with one of those chubby berry-faces, the lips all bunched together under her nose, this one, and a tall one, with black hair that hadn't quite frizzed right, and one of these sunburns right across under the eyes, and a chin that was too long—you know, the kind of girl other girls think is very "striking" and "attractive" but never quite makes it, as they very well know, which is why they like her so much—and then the third one, that wasn't quite so tall. She was the queen. She kind of led them, the other two peeking around and making their shoulders round. She didn't look around, not this queen, she just walked straight on slowly, on these long white prima-donna legs. She came down a little hard on her heels, as if she didn't walk in her bare feet that much, putting down her heels and then letting the weight move along to her toes as if she was testing the floor with every step, putting a little deliberate extra action into it. You never know for sure how girls' minds work (do you really think it's a mind in there or just a little buzz like a bee in a glass jar?) but you got the idea she had talked the other two into coming in here with her, and now she was showing them how to do it, walk slow and hold yourself straight.

She had on a kind of dirty-pink — beige maybe, I don't know — bathing suit with a little nubble all over it and, what got me, the straps were down. They were off her shoulders looped loose around the cool tops of her arms, and I guess as a result the suit had slipped a little on her, so all around the top of the cloth there was this shining rim. If it hadn't been there you wouldn't have known there could have been anything whiter than those shoulders. With the straps pushed off, there was nothing between the top of the suit and the top of her head except just *her,* this clean bare plane of the top of her chest down from the shoulder bones like a dented sheet of metal tilted in the light. I mean, it was more than pretty.

She had sort of oaky hair that the sun and salt had bleached, done up in a bun that was unraveling, and a kind of prim face. Walking into the A & P with your straps down, I suppose it's the only kind of face you *can* have. She held her head so high her neck, coming up out of those white shoulders, looked kind of stretched, but I didn't mind. The longer her neck was, the more of her there was.

She must have felt in the corner of her eye me and over my shoulder Stokesie 5
in the second slot watching, but she didn't tip. Not this queen. She kept her eyes moving across the racks, and stopped, and turned so slow it made my stomach rub the inside of my apron, and buzzed to the other two, who kind of huddled against her for relief, and then they all three of them went up the cat-and-dogfood-breakfast-cereal-macaroni-rice-raisins-seasonings-spreads-spaghetti-soft-drinks-crackers-and-cookies aisle. From the third slot I look straight up this aisle to the meat counter, and I watched them all the way. The fat one with the tan sort of fumbled with the cookies, but on second thought she put the package back. The sheep pushing their carts down the aisle — the girls were walking against the usual traffic (not that we have one-way signs or anything) — were pretty hilarious. You could see them, when Queenie's white shoulders dawned on them, kind of jerk, or hop, or hiccup, but their eyes snapped back to their own baskets and on they pushed. I bet you could set off dynamite in an A & P and the people would by and large keep reaching and checking oatmeal off their lists and muttering "Let me see, there was a third thing, began with A, asparagus, no, ah, yes, applesauce!" or whatever it is they do mutter. But there was no doubt, this jiggled them. A few houseslaves in pin curlers even looked around after pushing their carts past to make sure what they had seen was correct.

You know, it's one thing to have a girl in a bathing suit down on the beach, where what with the glare nobody can look at each other much anyway, and another thing in the cool of the A & P, under the fluorescent lights, against all those stacked packages, with her feet paddling along naked over our checkerboard green-and-cream rubber-tile floor.

"Oh Daddy," Stokesie said beside me. "I feel so faint."

"Darling," I said. "Hold me tight." Stokesie's married, with two babies chalked up on his fuselage already, but as far as I can tell that's the only difference. He's twenty-two, and I was nineteen this April.

"Is it done?" he asks, the responsible married man finding his voice. I forgot to say he thinks he's going to be manager some sunny day, maybe in 1990 when it's called the Great Alexandrov and Petrooshki Tea Company or something.

What he meant was, our town is five miles from a beach, with a big sum- 10 mer colony out on the Point, but we're right in the middle of town, and the women generally put on a shirt or shorts or something before they get out of the car into the street. And anyway these are usually women with six children and varicose veins mapping their legs and nobody, including them, could care less. As I say, we're right in the middle of town, and if you stand at our front doors you can see two banks and the Congregational church and the newspaper store and three real-estate offices and about twenty-seven old freeloaders tearing up Central Street because the sewer broke again. It's not as if we're on the Cape, we're north of Boston and there's people in this town haven't seen the ocean for twenty years.

The girls had reached the meat counter and were asking McMahon something. He pointed, they pointed, and they shuffled out of sight behind a pyramid of Diet Delight peaches. All that was left for us to see was old McMahon patting his mouth and looking after them sizing up their joints. Poor kids, I began to feel sorry for them, they couldn't help it.

Now here comes the sad part of the story, at least my family says it's sad, but I don't think it's so sad myself. The store's pretty empty, it being Thursday afternoon, so there was nothing much to do except lean on the register and wait for the girls to show up again. The whole store was like a pinball machine and I didn't know which tunnel they'd come out of. After a while they come around out of the far aisle, around the light bulbs, records at discount of the Caribbean Six or Tony Martin Sings or some such gunk you wonder they waste the wax on, sixpacks of candy bars, and plastic toys done up in cellophane that fall apart when a kid looks at them anyway. Around they come, Queenie still leading the way, and holding a little gray jar in her hands. Slots Three through Seven are unmanned and I could see her wondering between Stokes and me, but Stokesie with his usual luck draws an old party in baggy gray pants who stumbles up with four giant cans of pineapple juice (what do these bums *do* with all that pineapple juice? I've often asked myself). So the girls come to me. Queenie puts down the jar and I take it into my fingers icy cold. Kingfish Fancy Herring Snacks in Pure Sour Cream: 49¢. Now her hands are empty, not a ring or a bracelet, bare as God made them, and I wonder where the money's coming from. Still with that prim look she lifts a folded dollar bill out of the hollow at the center of her nubbled pink top. The jar went heavy in my hand. Really, I thought that was so cute.

Then everybody's luck begins to run out. Lengel comes in from haggling with a truck full of cabbages on the lot and is about to scuttle into that door marked MANAGER behind which he hides all day when the girls touch his eye. Lengel's pretty dreary, teaches Sunday school and the rest, but he doesn't miss that much. He comes over and says, "Girls, this isn't the beach."

Queenie blushes, though maybe it's just a brush of sunburn I was noticing for the first time, now that she was so close. "My mother asked me to pick up a jar of herring snacks." Her voice kind of startled me, the way voices do when you see the people first, coming out so flat and dumb yet kind of tony, too, the way it ticked over "pick up" and "snacks." All of a sudden I slid right down her voice into the living room. Her father and the other men were standing around in ice-cream coats and bow ties and the women were in sandals picking up herring snacks on toothpicks off a big glass plate and they were all holding drinks the color of water with olives and sprigs of mint in them. When my parents have somebody over they get lemonade and if it's a real racy affair Schlitz in tall glasses with "They'll Do It Every Time" cartoons stenciled on.

"That's all right," Lengel said. "But this isn't the beach." His repeating this 15 struck me as funny, as if it had just occurred to him, and he had been thinking all these years the A & P was a great big dune and he was the head lifeguard. He didn't like my smiling—as I say he doesn't miss much—but he concentrates on giving the girls that sad Sunday-school-superintendent stare.

Queenie's blush is no sunburn now, and the plump one in plaid, that I liked better from the back—a really sweet can—pipes up, "We weren't doing any shopping. We just came in for the one thing."

"That makes no difference," Lengel tells her, and I could see from the way his eyes went that he hadn't noticed she was wearing a two-piece before. "We want you decently dressed when you come in here."

"We *are* decent," Queenie says suddenly, her lower lip pushing, getting sore now that she remembers her place, a place from which the crowd that runs the A & P must look pretty crummy. Fancy Herring Snacks flashed in her very blue eyes.

"Girls, I don't want to argue with you. After this come in here with your shoulders covered. It's our policy." He turns his back. That's policy for you. Policy is what the kingpins want. What the others want is juvenile delinquency.

All this while, the customers had been showing up with their carts but, 20 you know, sheep, seeing a scene, they had all bunched up on Stokesie, who shook open a paper bag as gently as peeling a peach, not wanting to miss a word. I could feel in the silence everybody getting nervous, most of all Lengel, who asks me, "Sammy, have you rung up their purchase?"

I thought and said "No" but it wasn't about that I was thinking. I go through the punches, 4, 9, GROC. TOT—it's more complicated than you think, and after you do it often enough, it begins to make a little song, that you hear words to, in my case "Hello (*bing*) there, you (*gung*) hap-py *pee*-pul (*splat*)!"— the *splat* being the drawer flying out. I uncrease the bill, tenderly as you may imagine, it just having come from between the two smoothest scoops of vanilla I had ever known were there, and pass a half and a penny into her narrow pink palm, and nestle the herrings in a bag and twist its neck and hand it over, all the time thinking.

The girls, and who'd blame them, are in a hurry to get out, so I say "I quit" to Lengel quick enough for them to hear, hoping they'll stop and watch me, their unsuspected hero. They keep right on going, into the electric eye; the door flies open and they flicker across the lot to their car, Queenie and Plaid and Big Tall Goony-Goony (not that as raw material she was so bad), leaving me with Lengel and a kink in his eyebrow.

"Did you say something, Sammy?"

"I said I quit."

"I thought you did." 25

"You didn't have to embarrass them."

"It was they who were embarrassing us."

I started to say something that came out "Fiddle-de-doo." It's a saying of my grandmother's, and I know she would have been pleased.

"I don't think you know what you're saying," Lengel said.

"I know you don't," I said. "But I do." I pull the bow at the back of my 30 apron and start shrugging it off my shoulders. A couple customers that had been heading for my slot begin to knock against each other, like scared pigs in a chute.

Lengel sighs and begins to look very patient and old and gray. He's been a friend of my parents for years. "Sammy, you don't want to do this to your Mom and Dad," he tells me. It's true, I don't. But it seems to me that once you begin a gesture it's fatal not to go through with it. I fold the apron, "Sammy" stitched in red on the pocket, and put it on the counter, and drop the bow tie on top of it. The bow tie is theirs, if you've ever wondered. "You'll feel this for the rest of your life," Lengel says, and I know that's true, too, but remembering how he made the pretty girl blush makes me so scrunchy inside I punch the No Sale tab and the machine whirs "pee-pul" and the drawer splats out. One advantage to this scene taking place in summer, I can follow this up with a clean exit, there's no fumbling around getting your coat and galoshes, I just saunter into the electric eye in my white shirt that my mother ironed the night before, and the door heaves itself open, and outside the sunshine is skating around on the asphalt.

I look around for my girls, but they're gone, of course. There wasn't anybody but some young married screaming with her children about some candy they didn't get by the door of a powder-blue Falcon station wagon. Looking back in the big windows, over the bags of peat moss and aluminum lawn furniture stacked on the pavement, I could see Lengel in my place in the slot, checking the sheep through. His face was dark gray and his back stiff, as if he'd just had an injection of iron, and my stomach kind of fell as I felt how hard the world was going to be to me hereafter.

18

An Album of
World Literature

ISABEL ALLENDE (CHILE / B. 1942)

Isabel Allende was born in Peru to an intensely political family. Her father, a Chilean diplomat, suddenly and mysteriously disappeared when she was very young. After high school she worked as a secretary in the Department of Information of the United Nations Food and Agriculture organization in Chile. She subsequently developed a weekly television program and wrote for magazines. In 1973 her father's first cousin Salvadore Allende, the president of Chile, was assassinated. To escape the repressive political climate, she moved to Venezuela in 1975, where she worked as a journalist, taught school, and began writing her first novel based on her exile. An English translation of *House of Spirits* appeared in 1985 and made her one of the most internationally popular women writers from Latin America. Her two other translated novels, *Of Love and Shadows* (1987) and *Eva Luna* (1989), also center on the political instability in Latin America. Her most recent novel, *The Infinite Plan* (1993), takes place in the United States. Though her characters are often faced with terrible choices generated by repressive social conditions, Allende creates strong characters — particularly women — who take courageous risks.

Veb *Research Isabel Allende with LitLinks at*
http://www.bedfordstmartins.com/meyer/bedintrolit

The Judge's Wife   1989

TRANSLATED BY NICK CAISTOR

Nicolas Vidal always knew he would lose his head over a woman. So it was fore-told on the day of his birth, and later confirmed by the Turkish woman in the corner shop the one time he allowed her to read his fortune in the coffee grounds. Little did he imagine though that it would be on account of Casilda, Judge Hidalgo's wife. It was on her wedding day that he first glimpsed her. He was not impressed, preferring his women dark-haired and brazen. This ethe-real slip of a girl in her wedding gown, eyes filled with wonder, and fingers obviously unskilled in the art of rousing a man to pleasure, seemed to him almost ugly. Mindful of his destiny, he had always been wary of any emotional contact with women, hardening his heart and restricting himself to the briefest of encounters whenever the demands of manhood needed satisfying. Casilda, however, appeared so insubstantial, so distant, that he cast aside all precaution and, when the fateful moment arrived, forgot the prediction that usually weighed in all his decisions. From the roof of the bank, where he was crouching with two of his men, Nicolas Vidal peered down at this young lady from the capital. She had a dozen equally pale and dainty relatives with her, who spent the whole of the ceremony fanning themselves with an air of utter bewilderment, then departed straight away, never to return. Along with every-one else in the town, Vidal was convinced the young bride would not with-stand the climate, and that within a few months the old women would be dressing her up again, this time for her funeral. Even if she did survive the heat and the dust that filtered in through every pore to lodge itself in the soul, she would be bound to succumb to the fussy habits of her confirmed bachelor of a husband. Judge Hidalgo was twice her age, and had slept alone for so many years he didn't have the slightest notion of how to go about pleasing a woman. The severity and stubbornness with which he executed the law even at the ex-pense of justice had made him feared throughout the province. He refused to apply any common sense in the exercise of his profession, and was equally harsh in his condemnation of the theft of a chicken as of a premeditated mur-der. He dressed formally in black, and, despite the all-pervading dust in this godforsaken town, his boots always shone with beeswax. A man such as he was never meant to be a husband, and yet not only did the gloomy wedding-day prophecies remain unfulfilled, but Casilda emerged happy and smiling from three pregnancies in rapid succession. Every Sunday at noon she would go to mass with her husband, cool and collected beneath her Spanish mantilla, seemingly untouched by our pitiless summer, as wan and frail-looking as on the day of her arrival: a perfect example of delicacy and refinement. Her loudest words were a soft-spoken greeting; her most expressive gesture was a graceful nod of the head. She was such an airy, diaphanous creature that a moment's carelessness might mean she disappeared altogether. So slight an impression did she make that the changes noticeable in the Judge were all the more re-markable. Though outwardly he remained the same — he still dressed as black as a crow and was as stiff-necked and brusque as ever — his judgments in court altered dramatically. To general amazement, he found the youngster who robbed the Turkish shopkeeper innocent, on the grounds that she had been selling him short for years, and the money he had taken could therefore be seen as compensation. He also refused to punish an adulterous wife, arguing that since her husband himself kept a mistress he did not have the moral authority to demand fidelity. Word in the town had it that the Judge was transformed the minute he crossed the threshold at home: that he flung off his gloomy apparel, rollicked with his children, chuckled as he sat Casilda on his lap. Though no one ever succeeded in confirming these rumors, his wife got the credit for his newfound kindness, and her reputation grew accordingly. None of this was of the slightest interest to Nicolas Vidal, who as a wanted man was sure there would be no mercy shown him the day he was brought in chains before the Judge. He paid no heed to the talk about Doña Casilda, and the rare occasions he glimpsed her from afar only confirmed his first impression of her as a lifeless ghost.

Born thirty years earlier in a windowless room in the town's only brothel, Vidal was the son of Juana the Forlorn and an unknown father. The world had no place for him. His mother knew it, and so tried to wrench him from her womb with sprigs of parsley, candle butts, douches of ashes, and other violent purgatives, but the child clung to life. Once, years later, Juana was looking at her mysterious son and realized that, while all her infallible methods of aborting might have failed to dislodge him, they had none the less tempered his soul to the hardness of iron. As soon as he came into the world, he was lifted in the air by the midwife who examined him by the light of an oil lamp. She saw he had four nipples.

"Poor creature: he'll lose his head over a woman," she predicted, drawing on her wealth of experience.

Her words rested on the boy like a deformity. Perhaps a woman's love would have made his existence less wretched. To atone for all her attempts to kill him before birth, his mother chose him a beautiful first name, and an imposing family name picked at random. But the lofty name of Nicolas Vidal was no protection against the fateful cast of his destiny. His face was scarred from knife fights before he reached his teens, so it came as no surprise to decent folk that he ended up a bandit. By the age of twenty, he had become the leader of a band of desperadoes. The habit of violence toughened his sinews. The solitude he was condemned to for fear of falling prey to a woman lent his face a doleful expression. As soon as they saw him, everyone in the town knew from his eyes, clouded by tears he would never allow to fall, that he was the son of Juana the Forlorn. Whenever there was an outcry after a crime had been committed in the region, the police set out with dogs to track him down, but after scouring the hills invariably returned empty-handed. In all honesty they preferred it that way, because they could never have fought him. His gang gained such a fearsome reputation that the surrounding villages and estates paid to keep them away. This money would have been plenty for his men, but Nicolas Vidal kept them constantly on horseback in a whirlwind of death and destruction so they would not lose their taste for battle. Nobody dared take them on. More than once, Judge Hidalgo had asked the government to send troops to reinforce the police, but after several useless forays the soldiers returned to their barracks and Nicolas Vidal's gang to their exploits. On one occasion only did Vidal come close to falling into the hands of justice, and then he was saved by his hardened heart.

Weary of seeing the laws flouted, Judge Hidalgo resolved to forget his scruples 5
and set a trap for the outlaw. He realized that to defend justice he was committing

an injustice, but chose the lesser of two evils. The only bait he could find was Juana the Forlorn, as she was Vidal's sole known relative. He had her dragged from the brothel where by now, since no clients were willing to pay for her exhausted charms, she scrubbed floors and cleaned out the lavatories. He put her in a specially made cage which was set up in the middle of the Plaza de Armas, with only a jug of water to meet her needs.

"As soon as the water's finished, she'll start to squawk. Then her son will come running, and I'll be waiting for him with the soldiers," Judge Hidalgo said.

News of this torture, unheard of since the days of slavery, reached Nicolas Vidal's ears shortly before his mother drank the last of the water. His men watched as he received the report in silence, without so much as a flicker of emotion on his blank lone wolf's face, or a pause in the sharpening of his dagger blade on a leather strap. Though for many years he had had no contact with Juana, and retained few happy childhood memories, this was a question of honor. No man can accept such an insult, his gang reasoned as they got guns and horses ready to rush into the ambush and, if need be, lay down their lives. Their chief showed no sign of being in a hurry. As the hours went by tension mounted in the camp. The perspiring, impatient men stared at each other, not daring to speak. Fretful, they caressed the butts of their revolvers and their horses' manes, or busied themselves coiling their lassos. Night fell. Nicolas Vidal was the only one in the camp who slept. At dawn, opinions were divided. Some of the men reckoned he was even more heartless than they had ever imagined, while others maintained their leader was planning a spectacular ruse to free his mother. The one thing that never crossed any of their minds was that his courage might have failed him, for he had always proved he had more than enough to spare. By noon, they could bear the suspense no longer, and went to ask him what he planned to do.

"I'm not going to fall into his trap like an idiot," he said.

"What about your mother?"

"We'll see who's got more balls, the Judge or me," Nicolas Vidal coolly replied. 10

By the third day, Juana the Forlorn's cries for water had ceased. She lay curled on the cage floor, with wildly staring eyes and swollen lips, moaning softly whenever she regained consciousness, and the rest of the time dreaming she was in hell. Four armed guards stood watch to make sure nobody brought her water. Her groans penetrated the entire town, filtering through closed shutters or being carried by the wind through the cracks in doors. They got stuck in corners, where dogs worried at them, and passed them on in their howls to the newly born, so that whoever heard them was driven to distraction. The Judge couldn't prevent a steady stream of people filing through the square to show their sympathy for the old woman, and was powerless to stop the prostitutes going on a sympathy strike just as the miners' fortnight holiday was beginning. That Saturday, the streets were thronged with lusty workmen desperate to unload their savings, who now found nothing in town apart from the spectacle of the cage and this universal wailing carried mouth to mouth down from the river to the coast road. The priest headed a group of Catholic ladies to plead with Judge Hidalgo for Christian mercy and to beg him to spare the poor old innocent woman such a frightful death, but the man of the law bolted his door and refused to listen to them. It was then they decided to turn to Doña Casilda.

The Judge's wife received them in her shady living room. She listened to their pleas looking, as always, bashfully down at the floor. Her husband had not been home for three days, having locked himself in his office to wait for Nicolas Vidal to fall into his trap. Without so much as glancing out of the window, she was aware of what was going on, for Juana's long-drawn-out agony had forced its way even into the vast rooms of her residence. Doña Casilda waited until her visitors had left, dressed her children in their Sunday best, tied a black ribbon round their arms as a token of mourning, then strode out with them in the direction of the square. She carried a food hamper and a bottle of fresh water for Juana the Forlorn. When the guards spotted her turning the corner, they realized what she was up to, but they had strict orders, and barred her way with their rifles. When, watched now by a small crowd, she persisted, they grabbed her by the arms. Her children began to cry.

Judge Hidalgo sat in his office overlooking the square. He was the only person in the town who had not stuffed wax in his ears, because his mind was intent on the ambush and he was straining to catch the sound of horses' hoofs, the signal for action. For three long days and nights he put up with Juana's groans and the insults of the townspeople gathered outside the courtroom, but when he heard his own children start to wail he knew he had reached the bounds of his endurance. Vanquished, he walked out of the office with his three days' beard, his eyes bloodshot from keeping watch, and the weight of a thousand years on his back. He crossed the street, turned into the square and came face to face with his wife. They gazed at each other sadly. In seven years, this was the first time she had gone against him, and she had chosen to do so in front of the whole town. Easing the hamper and the bottle from Casilda's grasp, Judge Hidalgo himself opened the cage to release the prisoner.

"Didn't I tell you he wouldn't have the balls?" laughed Nicolas Vidal when the news reached him.

His laughter turned sour the next day, when he heard that Juana the For- 15 lorn had hanged herself from the chandelier in the brothel where she had spent her life, overwhelmed by the shame of her only son leaving her to fester in a cage in the middle of the Plaza de Armas.

"That Judge's hour has come," said Vidal.

He planned to take the Judge by surprise, put him to a horrible death, then dump him in the accursed cage for all to see. The Turkish shopkeeper sent him word that the Hidalgo family had left that same night for a seaside resort to rid themselves of the bitter taste of defeat.

The Judge learned he was being pursued when he stopped to rest at a wayside inn. There was little protection for him there until an army patrol could arrive, but he had a few hours' start, and his motor car could outrun the gang's horses. He calculated he could make it to the next town and summon help there. He ordered his wife and children into the car, put his foot down on the accelerator, and sped off along the road. He ought to have arrived with time to spare, but it had been ordained that Nicolas Vidal was that day to meet the woman who would lead him to his doom.

Overburdened by the sleepless nights, the townspeople's hostility, the blow to his pride, and the stress of this race to save his family, Judge Hidalgo's heart gave a massive jolt, then split like a pomegranate. The car ran out of control, turned several somersaults and finally came to a halt in the ditch. It took Doña Casilda some minutes to work out what had happened. Her husband's advancing years had often led her to think what it would be like to be left a widow, yet she had never imagined he would leave her at the mercy of his enemies. She wasted little time dwelling on her situation, knowing she must act at once to get her children to safety. When she gazed around her, she almost burst into tears. There was no sign of life in the vast plain baked by a scorching sun, only barren cliffs beneath an unbounded sky bleached colorless by the fierce light. A second look revealed the dark shadow of a passage or cave on a distant slope, so she ran towards it with two children in her arms and the third clutching her skirts.

One by one she carried her children up the cliff. The cave was a natural 20 one, typical of many in the region. She peered inside to be certain it wasn't the den of some wild animal, sat her children against its back wall, then, dry-eyed, kissed them good-bye.

"The troops will come to find you a few hours from now. Until then, don't for any reason whatsoever come out of here, even if you hear me screaming— do you understand?"

Their mother gave one final glance at the terrified children clinging to each other, then clambered back down to the road. She reached the car, closed her husband's eyes, smoothed back her hair and settled down to wait. She had no idea how many men were in Nicolas Vidal's gang, but prayed there were a lot of them so it would take them all the more time to have their way with her. She gathered strength pondering on how long it would take her to die if she determined to do it as slowly as possible. She willed herself to be desirable, luscious, to create more work for them and thus gain time for her children.

Casilda did not have long to wait. She soon saw a cloud of dust on the horizon and heard the gallop of horses' hoofs. She clenched her teeth. Then, to her astonishment, she saw there was only one rider, who stopped a few yards from her, gun at the ready. By the scar on his face she recognized Nicolas Vidal, who had set out all alone in pursuit of Judge Hidalgo, as this was a private matter between the two men. The Judge's wife understood she was going to have to endure something far worse than a lingering death.

A quick glance at her husband was enough to convince Vidal that the Judge was safely out of his reach in the peaceful sleep of death. But there was his wife, a shimmering presence in the plain's glare. He leapt from his horse and strode over to her. She did not flinch or lower her gaze, and to his amazement he realized that for the first time in his life another person was facing him without fear. For several seconds that stretched to eternity, they sized each other up, trying to gauge the other's strength, and their own powers of resistance. It gradually dawned on both of them that they were up against a formidable opponent. He lowered his gun. She smiled.

Casilda won each moment of the ensuing hours. To all the wiles of seduction 25 known since the beginning of time she added new ones born of necessity to bring this man to the heights of rapture. Not only did she work on his body like an artist, stimulating his every fiber to pleasure, but she brought all the delicacy of her spirit into play on her side. Both knew their lives were at stake, and this added a new and terrifying dimension to their meeting. Nicolas Vidal had fled from love since birth, and knew nothing of intimacy, tenderness, secret laughter, the riot of the senses, the joy of shared passion. Each minute brought the detachment of troops and the noose that much nearer, but he gladly accepted this in return for her prodigious gifts. Casilda was a passive, demure, timid woman who had been married to an austere old man in front of whom she had never even dared appear naked. Not once during that unforgettable afternoon did she forget that her aim was to win time for her children, and yet at some point, marveling at her own possibilities, she gave herself completely, and felt something akin to gratitude towards him. That was why, when she heard the soldiers in the distance, she begged him to flee to the hills. Instead, Nicolas Vidal chose to fold her in a last embrace, thus fulfilling the prophecy that had sealed his fate from the start.

CONNECTIONS TO OTHER SELECTIONS

1. Discuss Allende's treatment of justice with that of Andre Dubus in "Killings" (p. 84).
2. Write an essay comparing Allende's use of irony with T. Coraghessan Boyle's in "Carnal Knowledge" (p. 290).

TADEUSZ BOROWSKI (POLAND/1922–1951)

Tadeusz Borowski was born in 1922 in Zytomierz, Ukraine, into a Polish family living in the Soviet Union. Borowski's life was characterized by constant tragedy and loss as a result of political upheaval and oppression. His parents were both arrested during the Soviet purges, though the family managed to reunite and settle in Warsaw in 1932, only seven years before the Nazi occupation. Borowski graduated from high school in 1940 and began to study Polish language and literature at the underground Warsaw University, and wrote poetry while he worked as a night watchman. He published a book of poems in 1942 titled *Wherever the Earth* and was seen as a promising young member of the "war generation" of Polish poets. In 1943, suspecting that his lover Maria had been arrested by the Nazis, he went to a friend's apartment to look for her and was arrested himself by the Gestapo. He was sent to Auschwitz. Both he and Maria survived the concentration camp, and afterward, Borowski abandoned poetry in favor of short stories that tell of his experiences in the Holocaust. Borowski committed suicide using oven gas in 1951.

web *Research Tadeusz Borowski with LitLinks at*
http://www.bedfordstmartins.com/meyer/bedintrolit

This Way for the Gas, Ladies and Gentlemen   *1948*

TRANSLATED BY BARBARA VEDDER

All of us walk around naked. The delousing is finally over, and our striped suits are back from the tanks of Cyclone B solution, an efficient killer of lice in clothing and of men in gas chambers. Only the inmates in the blocks cut off from ours by the "Spanish goats"° still have nothing to wear. But all the same,

---

Spanish goats: Barbed-wire-wrapped wooden barricades.

all of us walk around naked: the heat is unbearable. The camp has been sealed off tight. Not a single prisoner, not one solitary louse, can sneak through the gate. The labor Kommandos have stopped working. All day, thousands of naked men shuffle up and down the roads, cluster around the squares, or lie against the walls and on top of the roofs. We have been sleeping on plain boards, since our mattresses and blankets are still being disinfected. From the rear blockhouses we have a view of the F.K.L.—*Frauen Konzentration Lager;*° there too the delousing is in full swing. Twenty-eight thousand women have been stripped naked and driven out of the barracks. Now they swarm around the large yard between the blockhouses.

The heat rises, the hours are endless. We are without even our usual diversion: the wide roads leading to the crematoria are empty. For several days now, no new transports have come in. Part of "Canada"° has been liquidated and detailed to a labor Kommando—one of the very toughest—at Harmenz. For there exists in the camp a special brand of justice based on envy: when the rich and mighty fall, their friends see to it that they fall to the very bottom. And Canada, our Canada, which smells not of maple forests but of French perfume, has amassed great fortunes in diamonds and currency from all over Europe.

Several of us sit on the top bunk, our legs dangling over the edge. We slice the neat loaves of crisp, crunchy bread. It is a bit coarse to the taste, the kind that stays fresh for days. Sent all the way from Warsaw—only a week ago my mother held this white loaf in her hands...dear Lord, dear Lord...

We unwrap the bacon, the onion, we open a can of evaporated milk. Henri, the fat Frenchman, dreams aloud of the French wine brought by the transports from Strasbourg, Paris, Marseille.... Sweat streams down his body.

"Listen, *mon ami*, next time we go up on the loading ramp, I'll bring you   5 real champagne. You haven't tried it before, eh?"

"No. But you'll never be able to smuggle it through the gate, so stop teasing. Why not try and 'organize' some shoes for me instead—you know, the perforated kind, with a double sole, and what about that shirt you promised me long ago?"

"*Patience, patience.* When the new transports come, I'll bring all you want. We'll be going on the ramp again!"

"And what if there aren't any more 'cremo' transports?" I say spitefully. "Can't you see how much easier life is becoming around here: no limit on packages, no more beatings? You even write letters home.... One hears all kind of talk, and, dammit, they'll run out of people!"

"Stop talking nonsense." Henri's serious fat face moves rhythmically, his mouth is full of sardines. We have been friends for a long time, but I do not even know his last name. "Stop talking nonsense," he repeats, swallowing with effort. "They can't run out of people, or we'll starve to death in this blasted camp. All of us live on what they bring."

"All? We have our packages..."   10

"Sure, you and your friend, and ten other friends of yours. Some of you Poles get packages. But what about us, and the Jews, and the Russkis? And what if we had no food, no 'organization' from the transports, do you think you'd be eating those packages of yours in peace? We wouldn't let you!"

Frauen...Lager: Women's concentration camp.
Canada: A relatively benign part of the camp.

"You would, you'd starve to death like the Greeks. Around here, whoever has grub, has power."

"Anyway, you have enough, we have enough, so why argue?"

Right, why argue? They have enough, I have enough, we eat together and we sleep on the same bunks. Henri slices the bread, he makes a tomato salad. It tastes good with the commissary mustard.

Below us, naked sweat-drenched men crowd the narrow barracks aisles or lie packed in eights and tens in the lower bunks. Their nude, withered bodies stink of sweat and excrement; their cheeks are hollow. Directly beneath me, in the bottom bunk, lies a rabbi. He has covered his head with a piece of rag torn off a blanket and reads from a Hebrew prayer book (there is no shortage of this type of literature at the camp), wailing loudly, monotonously.

"Can't somebody shut him up? He's been raving as if he'd caught God himself by the feet."

"I don't feel like moving. Let him rave. They'll take him to the oven that much sooner."

"Religion is the opium of the people," Henri, who is a Communist and a *rentier,* says sententiously. "If they didn't believe in God and eternal life, they'd have smashed the crematoria long ago."

"Why haven't you done it then?"

The question is rhetorical; the Frenchman ignores it.

"Idiot," he says simply, and stuffs a tomato in his mouth.

Just as we finish our snack, there is a sudden commotion at the door. The Muslims° scurry in fright to the safety of their bunks, a messenger runs into the Block Elder's shack. The Elder, his face solemn, steps out at once.

"Canada! *Antreten!*° But fast! There's a transport coming!"

"Great God!" yells Henri, jumping off the bunk. He swallows the rest of his tomato, snatches his coat, screams *"Raus"*° at the men below, and in a flash is at the door. We can hear a scramble in the other bunks. Canada is leaving for the ramp.

"Henri, the shoes!" I call after him.

"Keine Angst!"° he shouts back, already outside.

I proceed to put away the food. I tie a piece of rope around the suitcase where the onions and the tomatoes from my father's garden in Warsaw mingle with Portuguese sardines, bacon from Lublin (that's from my brother), and authentic sweetmeats from Salonica. I tie it all up, pull on my trousers, and slide off the bunk.

"Platz!"° I yell, pushing my way through the Greeks. They step aside. At the door I bump into Henri.

"Was ist los?"°

"Want to come with us on the ramp?"

"Sure, why not?"

"Come along then, grab your coat! We're short a few men. I've already told the Kapo," and he shoves me out of the barracks door.

Muslims: A camp term for prisoners near death.
Antreten!: "Get going!" (German; all subsequent translations are also from German).
Raus: "Get out."
Keine Angst!: "Don't worry!"
Platz!: "Place!"
Was ist los?: "What's the matter?"

We line up. Someone has marked down our numbers, someone up ahead yells, "March, march," and now we are running towards the gate, accompanied by the shouts of a multilingual throng that is already being pushed back to the barracks. Not everybody is lucky enough to be going on the ramp. . . . We have almost reached the gate. *Links, zwei, drei, vier! Mützen ab!* Erect, arms stretched stiffly along our hips, we march past the gate briskly, smartly, almost gracefully. A sleepy S.S. man with a large pad in his hand checks us off, waving us ahead in groups of five.

"*Hundert!*" he calls after we have all passed.

"*Stimmt!*" comes a hoarse answer from out front.   35

We march fast, almost at a run. There are guards all around, young men with automatics. We pass camp II B, then some deserted barracks and a clump of unfamiliar green — apple and pear trees. We cross the circle of watchtowers and, running, burst on to the highway. We have arrived. Just a few more yards. There, surrounded by trees, is the ramp.

A cheerful little station, very much like any other provincial railway stop: a small square framed by tall chestnuts and paved with yellow gravel. Not far off, beside the road, squats a tiny wooden shed, uglier and more flimsy than the ugliest and flimsiest railway shack; farther along lie stacks of old rails, heaps of wooden beams, barracks parts, bricks, paving stones. This is where they load freight for Birkenau: supplies for the construction of the camp, and people for the gas chambers. Trucks drive around, load up lumber, cement, people — a regular daily routine.

And now the guards are being posted along the rails, across the beams, in the green shade of the Silesian chestnuts, to form a tight circle around the ramp. They wipe the sweat from their faces and sip out of their canteens. It is unbearably hot; the sun stands motionless at its zenith.

"Fall out!"

We sit down in the narrow streaks of shade along the stacked rails. The   40
hungry Greeks (several of them managed to come along, God only knows how) rummage underneath the rails. One of them finds some pieces of mildewed bread, another a few half-rotten sardines. They eat.

"*Schweinedreck,*"° spits a young, tall guard with corn-colored hair and dreamy blue eyes. "For God's sake, any minute you'll have so much food to stuff down your guts, you'll bust!" He adjusts his gun, wipes his face with a handkerchief.

"Hey you, fatso!" His boot lightly touches Henri's shoulder. "*Pass mal auf,*° want a drink?"

"Sure, but I haven't got any marks," replies the Frenchman with a professional air.

"*Schade,* too bad."

"Come, come, Herr Posten, isn't my word good enough any more? Haven't   45
we done business before? How much?"

"One hundred. *Gemacht?*"°

"*Gemacht.*"

We drink the water, lukewarm and tasteless. It will be paid for by the people who have not yet arrived.

Schweinedreck: "Dirty pigs."
Pass mal auf: "Pay attention."
Gemacht: "Done."

"Now you be careful," says Henri, turning to me. He tosses away the empty bottle. It strikes the rails and bursts into tiny fragments. "Don't take any money, they might be checking. Anyway, who the hell needs money? You've got enough to eat. Don't take suits, either, or they'll think you're planning to escape. Just get a shirt, silk only, with a collar. And a vest. And if you find something to drink, don't bother calling me. I know how to shift for myself, but you watch your step or they'll let you have it."

"Do they beat you up here?" 50

"Naturally. You've got to have eyes in your ass. *Arschaugen.*"°

Around us sit the Greeks, their jaws working greedily, like huge human insects. They munch on stale lumps of bread. They are restless, wondering what will happen next. The sight of the large beams and the stacks of rails has them worried. They dislike carrying heavy loads.

"*Was wir arbeiten?*"° they ask.

"*Niks. Transport kommen, alles Krematorium, compris?*"°

"*Alles verstehen,*"° they answer in crematorium Esperanto. All is well — they 55 will not have to move the heavy rails or carry the beams.

In the meantime, the ramp has become increasingly alive with activity, increasingly noisy. The crews are being divided into those who will open and unload the arriving cattle cars and those who will be posted by the wooden steps. They receive instructions on how to proceed most efficiently. Motorcycles drive up, delivering S.S. officers, bemedalled, glittering with brass, beefy men with highly polished boots and shiny, brutal faces. Some have brought their briefcases, others hold thin, flexible whips. This gives them an air of military readiness and agility. They walk in and out of the commissary — for the miserable little shack by the road serves as their commissary, where in the summertime they drink mineral water, *Studentenquelle,* and where in winter they can warm up with a glass of hot wine. They greet each other in the state-approved way, raising an arm Roman fashion, then shake hands cordially, exchange warm smiles, discuss mail from home, their children, their families. Some stroll majestically on the ramp. The silver squares on their collars glitter, the gravel crunches under their boots, their bamboo whips snap impatiently.

We lie against the rails in the narrow streaks of shade, breathe unevenly, occasionally exchange a few words in our various tongues, and gaze listlessly at the majestic men in green uniforms, at the green trees, and at the church steeple of a distant village.

"The transport is coming," somebody says. We spring to our feet, all eyes turn in one direction. Around the bend, one after another, the cattle cars begin rolling in. The train backs into the station, a conductor leans out, waves his hand, blows a whistle. The locomotive whistles back with a shrieking noise, puffs, the train rolls slowly alongside the ramp. In the tiny barred windows appear pale, wilted, exhausted human faces, terror-stricken women with tangled hair, unshaven men. They gaze at the station in silence. And then, suddenly, there is a stir inside the cars and a pounding against the wooden boards.

"Water! Air!" — weary, desperate cries.

Arschaugen: "Ass eyes."
Was wir arbeiten?: "What will we be working on?"
Niks ... compris?: "Nothing. Transport coming, all Crematorium, understand?"
Alles verstehen: "We understand."

Heads push through the windows, mouths gasp frantically for air. They 60
draw a few breaths, then disappear; others come in their place, then also disappear. The cries and moans grow louder.

A man in a green uniform covered with more glitter than any of the others jerks his head impatiently, his lips twist in annoyance. He inhales deeply, then with a rapid gesture throws his cigarette away and signals to the guard. The guard removes the automatic from his shoulder, aims, sends a series of shots along the train. All is quiet now. Meanwhile, the trucks have arrived, steps are being drawn up, and the Canada men stand ready at their posts by the train doors. The S.S. officer with the briefcase raises his hand.

"Whoever takes gold, or anything at all besides food, will be shot for stealing Reich property. Understand? *Verstanden?*"

"*Jawohl!*"° we answer eagerly.

"*Also los!* Begin!*"

The bolts crack, the doors fall open. A wave of fresh air rushes inside the 65 train. People . . . inhumanly crammed, buried under incredible heaps of luggage, suitcases, trunks, packages, crates, bundles of every description (everything that had been their past and was to start their future). Monstrously squeezed together, they have fainted from heat, suffocated, crushed one another. Now they push towards the opened doors, breathing like fish cast out on the sand.

"Attention! Out, and take your luggage with you! Take out everything. Pile all your stuff near the exits. Yes, your coats too. It is summer. March to the left. Understand?"

"Sir, what's going to happen to us?" They jump from the train on to the gravel, anxious, worn-out.

"Where are you people from?"

"Sosnowiec-Będzin. Sir, what's going to happen to us?" They repeat the question stubbornly, gazing into our tired eyes.

"I don't know. I don't understand Polish." 70

It is the camp law: people going to their death must be deceived to the very end. This is the only permissible form of charity. The heat is tremendous. The sun hangs directly over our heads, the white, hot sky quivers, the air vibrates, an occasional breeze feels like a sizzling blast from a furnace. Our lips are parched, the mouth fills with the salty taste of blood, the body is weak and heavy from lying in the sun. Water!

A huge, multicoloured wave of people loaded down with luggage pours from the train like a blind, mad river trying to find a new bed. But before they have a chance to recover, before they can draw a breath of fresh air and look at the sky, bundles are snatched from their hands, coats ripped off their backs, their purses and umbrellas taken away.

"But please, sir, it's for the sun, I cannot . . ."

"*Verboten!*"° one of us barks through clenched teeth. There is an S.S. man standing behind your back, calm, efficient, watchful.

"*Meine Herrschaften,*° this way, ladies and gentlemen, try not to throw your 75 things around, please. Show some goodwill," he says courteously, his restless hands playing with the slender whip.

Jawohl!: "Yes!"
Verboten!: "Forbidden!"
Meine Herrschaften: "Distinguished ladies and gentlemen."

"Of course, of course," they answer as they pass, and now they walk along-side the train somewhat more cheerfully. A woman reaches down quickly to pick up her handbag. The whip flies, the woman screams, stumbles, and falls under the feet of the surging crowd. Behind her, a child cries in a thin little voice "Mamele!" — a very small girl with tangled black curls.

The heaps grow. Suitcases, bundles, blankets, coats, handbags that open as they fall, spilling coins, gold, watches; mountains of bread pile up at the exits, heaps of marmalade, jams, masses of meat, sausages; sugar spills on the gravel. Trucks, loaded with people, start up with a deafening roar and drive off amidst the wailing and screaming of the women separated from their children, and the stupefied silence of the men left behind. They are the ones who had been or-dered to step to the right — the healthy and the young who will go to the camp. In the end, they too will not escape death, but first they must work.

Trucks leave and return, without interruption, as on a monstrous con-veyor belt. A Red Cross van drives back and forth, back and forth, incessantly: it transports the gas that will kill these people. The enormous cross on the hood, red as blood, seems to dissolve in the sun.

The Canada men at the trucks cannot stop for a single moment, even to catch their breath. They shove the people up the steps, pack them in tightly, sixty per truck, more or less. Near by stands a young, cleanshaven "gentleman," an S.S. officer with a notebook in his hand. For each departing truck he enters a mark; sixteen gone means one thousand people, more or less. The gentleman is calm, precise. No truck can leave without a signal from him, or a mark in his notebook: *Ordnung muss sein.*° The marks swell into thousands, the thousands into whole transports, which afterwards we shall simply call "from Salonica," "from Stras-bourg," "from Rotterdam." This one will be called "Sosnowiec-Będzin." The new prisoners from Sosnowiec-Będzin will receive serial numbers 131-2 — thousand, of course, though afterwards we shall simply say 131-2, for short.

The transports swell into weeks, months, years. When the war is over, they 80 will count up the marks in their notebooks — all four and a half million of them. The bloodiest battle of the war, the greatest victory of the strong, united Germany. *Ein Reich, ein Volk, ein Führer*° — and four crematoria.

The train has been emptied. A thin, pock-marked S.S. man peers inside, shakes his head in disgust, and motions to our group, pointing his finger at the door.

"*Rein.* Clean it up!"

We climb inside. In the corners amid human excrement and abandoned wrist-watches lie squashed, trampled infants, naked little monsters with enor-mous heads and bloated bellies. We carry them out like chickens, holding sev-eral in each hand.

"Don't take them to the trucks, pass them on to the women," says the S.S. man, lighting a cigarette. His cigarette lighter is not working properly; he ex-amines it carefully.

"Take them, for God's sake!" I explode as the women run from me in hor- 85 ror, covering their eyes.

The name of God sounds strangely pointless, since the women and the in-fants will go on the trucks, every one of them, without exception. We all know what this means, and we look at each other with hate and horror.

Ordnung muss sein: There must be order.
Ein . . . Führer: One Empire, one People, one Leader.

"What, you don't want to take them?" asks the pock-marked S.S. man with a note of surprise and reproach in his voice, and reaches for his revolver.

"You mustn't shoot, I'll carry them." A tall, grey-haired woman takes the little corpses out of my hands and for an instant gazes straight into my eyes.

"My poor boy," she whispers and smiles at me. Then she walks away, staggering along the path. I lean against the side of the train. I am terribly tired. Someone pulls at my sleeve.

"*En avant*, to the rails, come on!" 90

I look up, but the face swims before my eyes, dissolves, huge and transparent, melts into the motionless trees and the sea of people…I blink rapidly: Henri.

"Listen, Henri, are we good people?"

"That's stupid. Why do you ask?"

"You see, my friend, you see, I don't know why, but I am furious, simply furious with these people — furious because I must be here because of them. I feel no pity. I am not sorry they're going to the gas chamber. Damn them all! I could throw myself at them, beat them with my fists. It must be pathological, I just can't understand…"

"Ah, on the contrary, it is natural, predictable, calculated. The ramp exhausts you, you rebel — and the easiest way to relieve your hate is to turn 95 against someone weaker. Why, I'd even call it healthy. It's simple logic, *compris?*" He props himself up comfortably against the heap of rails. "Look at the Greeks, they know how to make the best of it! They stuff their bellies with anything they find. One of them has just devoured a full jar of marmalade."

"Pigs! Tomorrow half of them will die of the shits."

"Pigs? You've been hungry."

"Pigs!" I repeat furiously. I close my eyes. The air is filled with ghastly cries, the earth trembles beneath me, I can feel sticky moisture on my eyelids. My throat is completely dry.

The morbid procession streams on and on — trucks growl like mad dogs. I shut my eyes tight, but I can still see corpses dragged from the train, trampled infants, cripples piled on top of the dead, wave after wave . . . freight cars roll in, the heaps of clothing, suitcases, and bundles grow, people climb out, look at the sun, take a few breaths, beg for water, get into the trucks, drive away. And again freight cars roll in, again people. . . . The scenes become confused in my mind — I am not sure if all of this is actually happening, or if I am dreaming. There is a humming inside my head; I feel that I must vomit.

Henri tugs at my arm. 100

"Don't sleep, we're off to load up the loot."

All the people are gone. In the distance, the last few trucks roll along the road in clouds of dust, the train has left, several S.S. officers promenade up and down the ramp. The silver glitters on their collars. Their boots shine, their red, beefy faces shine. Among them there is a woman — only now I realize she has been here all along — withered, flat-chested, bony, her thin, colourless hair pulled back and tied in a "Nordic" knot; her hands are in the pockets of her wide skirt. With a rat-like, resolute smile glued on her thin lips she sniffs around the corners of the ramp. She detests feminine beauty with the hatred of a woman who is herself repulsive, and knows it. Yes, I have seen her many times before and I know her well: she is the commandant of the F.K.L. She has come to look over the new crop of women, for some of them, instead of going on the trucks, will go on foot — to the concentration camp. There our boys, the barbers from Zauna, will shave their heads and will have a good laugh at their "outside world" modesty.

We proceed to load the loot. We lift huge trunks, heave them on to the trucks. There they are arranged in stacks, packed tightly. Occasionally somebody slashes one open with a knife, for pleasure or in search of vodka and perfume. One of the crates falls open; suits, shirts, books drop out on the ground. . . . I pick up a small, heavy package. I unwrap it — gold, about two handfuls, bracelets, rings, brooches, diamonds. . . .

"*Gib hier,*"° an S.S. man says calmly, holding up his briefcase already full of gold and colorful foreign currency. He locks the case, hands it to an officer, takes another, an empty one, and stands by the next truck, waiting. The gold will go to the Reich.

It is hot, terribly hot. Our throats are dry, each word hurts. Anything for a   105
sip of water! Faster, faster, so that it is over, so that we may rest. At last we are done, all the trucks have gone. Now we swiftly clean up the remaining dirt: there must be "no trace left of the *Schweinerei.*"° But just as the last truck disappears behind the trees and we walk, finally, to rest in the shade, a shrill whistle sounds around the bend. Slowly, terribly slowly, a train rolls in, the engine whistles back with a deafening shriek. Again weary, pale faces at the windows, flat as though cut out of paper, with huge, feverishly burning eyes. Already trucks are pulling up, already the composed gentleman with the notebook is at his post, and the S.S. men emerge from the commissary carrying briefcases for the gold and money. We unseal the train doors.

It is impossible to control oneself any longer. Brutally we tear suitcases from their hands, impatiently pull off their coats. Go on, go on, vanish! They go, they vanish. Men, women, children. Some of them know.

Here is a woman — she walks quickly, but tries to appear calm. A small child with a pink cherub's face runs after her and, unable to keep up, stretches out his little arms and cries: "Mama! Mama!"

"Pick up your child, woman!"

"It's not mine, sir, not mine!" she shouts hysterically and runs on, covering her face with her hands. She wants to hide, she wants to reach those who will not ride the trucks, those who will go on foot, those who will stay alive. She is young, healthy, good-looking, she wants to live.

But the child runs after her, wailing loudly: "Mama, mama, don't leave me!"   110
"It's not mine, not mine, no!"

Andrei, a sailor from Sevastopol, grabs hold of her. His eyes are glassy from vodka and the heat. With one powerful blow he knocks her off her feet, then, as she falls, takes her by the hair and pulls her up again. His face twitches with rage.

"Ah, you bloody Jewess! So you're running from your own child! I'll show you, you whore!" His huge hand chokes her, he lifts her in the air and heaves her on to the truck like a heavy sack of grain.

"Here! And take this with you, bitch!" and he throws the child at her feet.

Gib hier: "Give it here."
Schweinerei: "Obscenity."

"*Gut gemacht,* good work. That's the way to deal with degenerate mothers," 115
says the S.S. man standing at the foot of the truck. "*Gut, gut, Russki.*"

"Shut your mouth," growls Andrei through clenched teeth, and walks
away. From under a pile of rags he pulls out a canteen, unscrews the cork, takes
a few deep swallows, passes it to me. The strong vodka burns the throat. My
head swims, my legs are shaky, again I feel like throwing up.

And suddenly, above the teeming crowd pushing forward like a river driven
by an unseen power, a girl appears. She descends lightly from the train, hops on
to the gravel, looks around inquiringly, as if somewhat surprised. Her soft,
blonde hair has fallen on her shoulders in a torrent, she throws it back impatiently. With a natural gesture she runs her hands down her blouse, casually
straightens her skirt. She stands like this for an instant, gazing at the crowd,
then turns and with a gliding look examines our faces, as though searching for
someone. Unknowingly, I continue to stare at her, until our eyes meet.

"Listen, tell me, where are they taking us?"

I look at her without saying a word. Here, standing before me, is a girl, a
girl with enchanting blonde hair, with beautiful breasts, wearing a little cotton
blouse, a girl with a wise, mature look in her eyes. Here she stands, gazing
straight into my face, waiting. And over there is the gas chamber: communal
death, disgusting and ugly. And over in the other direction is the concentration camp: the shaved head, the heavy Soviet trousers in sweltering heat, the
sickening, stale odour of dirty, damp female bodies, the animal hunger, the inhuman labor, and later the same gas chamber, only an even more hideous,
more terrible death. . . .

Why did she bring it? I think to myself, noticing a lovely gold watch on her 120
delicate wrist. They'll take it away from her anyway.

"Listen, tell me," she repeats.

I remain silent. Her lips tighten.

"I know," she says with a shade of proud contempt in her voice, tossing
her head. She walks off resolutely in the direction of the trucks. Someone tries
to stop her; she boldly pushes him aside and runs up the steps. In the distance
I can only catch a glimpse of her blonde hair flying in the breeze.

I go back inside the train; I carry out dead infants; I unload luggage. I touch
corpses, but I cannot overcome the mounting, uncontrollable terror. I try to escape from the corpses, but they are everywhere: lined up on the gravel, on the
cement edge of the ramp, inside the cattle cars. Babies, hideous naked women,
men twisted by convulsions. I run off as far as I can go, but immediately a whip
slashes across my back. Out of the corner of my eye I see an S.S. man, swearing
profusely. I stagger forward and run, lose myself in the Canada group. Now, at
last, I can once more rest against the stack of rails. The sun has leaned low over
the horizon and illuminates the ramp with a reddish glow; the shadows of the
trees have become elongated, ghostlike. In the silence that settles over nature at
this time of day, the human cries seem to rise all the way to the sky.

Only from this distance does one have a full view of the inferno on the 125
teeming ramp. I see a pair of human beings who have fallen to the ground
locked in a last desperate embrace. The man has dug his fingers into the
woman's flesh and has caught her clothing with his teeth. She screams hysterically, swears, cries, until at last a large boot comes down over her throat and she
is silent. They are pulled apart and dragged like cattle to the truck. I see four
Canada men lugging a corpse: a huge, swollen female corpse. Cursing, dripping

wet from the strain, they kick out of their way some stray children who have been running all over the ramp, howling like dogs. The men pick them up by the collars, heads, arms, and toss them inside the trucks, on top of the heaps. The four men have trouble lifting the fat corpse on to the car, they call others for help, and all together they hoist up the mound of meat. Big, swollen, puffed-up corpses are being collected from all over the ramp; on top of them are piled the invalids, the smothered, the sick, the unconscious. The heap seethes, howls, groans. The driver starts the motor, the truck begins rolling.

"Halt! Halt!" an S.S. man yells after them. "Stop, damn you!"

They are dragging to the truck an old man wearing tails and a band around his arm. His head knocks against the gravel and pavement; he moans and wails in an uninterrupted monotone: *"Ich will mit dem Herrn Kommandanten sprechen* — I wish to speak with the commandant . . ." With senile stubbornness he keeps repeating these words all the way. Thrown on the truck, trampled by others, choked, he still wails: *"Ich will mit dem . . ."*

"Look here, old man!" a young S.S. man calls, laughing jovially. "In half an hour you'll be talking with the top commandant! Only don't forget to greet him with a *Heil Hitler!*"

Several other men are carrying a small girl with only one leg. They hold her by the arms and the one leg. Tears are running down her face and she whispers faintly: "Sir, it hurts, it hurts . . ." They throw her on the truck on top of the corpses. She will burn alive along with them.

The evening has come, cool and clear. The stars are out. We lie against the 130 rails. It is incredibly quiet. Anaemic bulbs hang from the top of the high lamp-posts; beyond the circle of light stretches an impenetrable darkness. Just one step, and a man could vanish for ever. But the guards are watching, their automatics ready.

"Did you get the shoes?" asks Henri.

"No."

"Why?"

"My God, man, I am finished, absolutely finished!"

"So soon? After only two transports? Just look at me, I . . . since Christ- 135 mas, at least a million people have passed through my hands. The worst of all are the transports from around Paris — one is always bumping into friends."

"And what do you say to them?"

"That first they will have a bath, and later we'll meet at the camp. What would you say?"

I do not answer. We drink coffee with vodka; somebody opens a tin of cocoa and mixes it with sugar. We scoop it up by the handful, the cocoa sticks to the lips. Again coffee, again vodka.

"Henri, what are we waiting for?"

"There'll be another transport." 140

"I'm not going to unload it! I can't take any more."

"So, it's got you down? Canada is nice, eh?" Henri grins indulgently and disappears into the darkness. In a moment he is back again.

"All right. Just sit here quietly and don't let an S.S. man see you. I'll try to find you your shoes."

"Just leave me alone. Never mind the shoes." I want to sleep. It is very late.

Another whistle, another transport. Freight cars emerge out of the dark- 145 ness, pass under the lamp-posts, and again vanish in the night. The ramp is small, but the circle of lights is smaller. The unloading will have to be done gradually. Somewhere the trucks are growling. They back up against the steps, black, ghostlike, their searchlights flash across the trees. *Wasser! Luft!* The same all over again, like a late showing of the same film: a volley of shots, the train falls silent. Only this time a little girl pushes herself halfway through the small window and, losing her balance, falls out on to the gravel. Stunned, she lies still for a moment, then stands up and begins walking around in a circle, faster and faster, waving her rigid arms in the air, breathing loudly and spasmodically, whining in a faint voice. Her mind has given way in the inferno inside the train. The whining is hard on the nerves: an S.S. man approaches calmly, his heavy boot strikes between her shoulders. She falls. Holding her down with his foot, he draws his revolver, fires once, then again. She remains face down, kicking the gravel with her feet, until she stiffens. They proceed to unseal the train.

I am back on the ramp, standing by the doors. A warm, sickening smell gushes from inside. The mountain of people filling the car almost halfway up to the ceiling is motionless, horribly tangled, but still steaming.

"*Ausladen!*"° comes the command. An S.S. man steps out from the darkness. Across his chest hangs a portable searchlight. He throws a stream of light inside.

"Why are you standing about like sheep? Start unloading!" His whip flies and falls across our backs. I seize a corpse by the hand; the fingers close tightly around mine. I pull back with a shriek and stagger away. My heart pounds, jumps up to my throat. I can no longer control the nausea. Hunched under the train I begin to vomit. Then, like a drunk, I weave over to the stack of rails.

I lie against the cool, kind metal and dream about returning to the camp, about my bunk, on which there is no mattress, about sleep among comrades who are not going to the gas tonight. Suddenly I see the camp as a haven of peace. It is true, others may be dying, but one is somehow still alive, one has enough food, enough strength to work. . . .

The lights on the ramp flicker with a spectral glow, the wave of people — feverish, agitated, stupefied people — flows on and on, endlessly. They think that now they will have to face a new life in the camp, and they prepare themselves emotionally for the hard struggle ahead. They do not know that in just a few moments they will die, that the gold, money, and diamonds which they have so prudently hidden in their clothing and on their bodies are now useless to them. Experienced professionals will probe into every recess of their flesh, will pull the gold from under the tongue and the diamonds from the uterus and the colon. They will rip out gold teeth. In tightly sealed crates they will ship them to Berlin. 150

The S.S. men's black figures move about, dignified, businesslike. The gentleman with the notebook puts down his final marks, rounds out the figures: fifteen thousand.

Many, very many, trucks have been driven to the crematoria today.

It is almost over. The dead are being cleared off the ramp and piled into the last truck. The Canada men, weighed down under a load of bread, marmalade, and sugar, and smelling of perfume and fresh linen, line up to go. For several days the entire camp will live off this transport. For several days the entire camp will talk about "Sosnowiec-Będzin." "Sosnowiec-Będzin" was a good, rich transport.

The stars are already beginning to pale as we walk back to the camp. The sky grows translucent and opens high above our heads — it is getting light.

Ausladen!: "Unload!"

Great columns of smoke rise from the crematoria and merge up above into   155
a huge black river which very slowly floats across the sky over Birkenau and disappears beyond the forests in the direction of Trzebinia. The "Sosnowiec-
Będzin" transport is already burning.

We pass a heavily armed S.S. detachment on its way to change guard. The
men march briskly, in step, shoulder to shoulder, one mass, one will.

"*Und morgen die ganze Welt . . .*"° they sing at the top of their lungs.

"*Rechts ran!* To the right march!" snaps a command from up front. We
move out of their way.

Und . . . Welt: "And tomorrow the whole world…"

Connections to Other Selections

1. Consider the nature of what it means to be a prisoner in this story and in
   Bessie Head's "The Prisoner Who Wore Glasses" (below). How do you account for the differences? Are there any significant similarities?

2. Discuss the use of violence in Borowski's story and in Tim O'Brien's "How
   to Tell a True War Story" (p. 548). How does the violence in each story affect
   you? How is it related to the themes of each story?

3. Explain how a reading of this story affects your response to William
   Heyen's poem "The Trains" (p. 850).

BESSIE HEAD (BOTSWANA / 1937–1986)

Born in Pietermaritzburg, South Africa, Bessie Head was the daughter of a
black father and a white mother. After growing up in a foster home and or-
phanage, she taught grammar school and wrote fiction for a local paper. In
her twenties she moved to a farm commune in Botswana to avoid the
apartheid of her homeland. Her first novel, *When Rain Clouds Gather,* was
published in 1969. Her collection of stories, *The Collector of Treasures and
Other Botswana Village Tales* (1977), was followed by two other novels, *Serowe:
Village of the Rain Wind* (1981) and *A Bewitched Crossroad* (1984). Head's familiarity with oppression and the daily difficulties endured by its victims produced in her work a heightened sensitivity to the necessity for human decency. In "The Prisoner Who Wore Glasses," oppression and decency turn
out to be complex matters.

Web *Research Bessie Head with LitLinks at*
http://www.bedfordstmartins.com/meyer/bedintrolit

The Prisoner Who Wore Glasses   1974

Scarcely a breath of wind disturbed the stillness of the day and the long rows
of cabbages were bright green in the sunlight. Large white clouds drifted
slowly across the deep blue sky. Now and then they obscured the sun and
caused a chill on the backs of the prisoners who had to work all day long in the

cabbage field. This trick the clouds were playing with the sun eventually caused one of the prisoners who wore glasses to stop work, straighten up, and peer shortsightedly at them. He was a thin little fellow with a hollowed-out chest and comic knobbly knees. He also had a lot of fanciful ideas because he smiled at the clouds.

"Perhaps they want me to send a message to the children," he thought, tenderly, noting that the clouds were drifting in the direction of his home some hundred miles away. But before he could frame the message, the warder in charge of his work span° shouted: "Hey, what you tink you're doing, Brille?"

The prisoner swung round, blinking rapidly, yet at the same time sizing up the enemy. He was a new warder, named Jacobus Stephanus Hannetjie. His eyes were the color of the sky but they were frightening. A simple, primitive, brutal soul gazed out of them. The prisoner bent down quickly and a message was quietly passed down the line: "We're in for trouble this time, comrades."

"Why?" rippled back up the line.

"Because he's not human," the reply rippled down and yet only the 5 crunching of the spades as they turned over the earth disturbed the stillness.

This particular work span was known as Span One. It was composed of ten men and they were all political prisoners. They were grouped together for convenience as it was one of the prison regulations that no black warder should be in charge of a political prisoner lest this prisoner convert him to his views. It never seemed to occur to the authorities that this very reasoning was the strength of Span One and a clue to the strange terror they aroused in the warders. As political prisoners they were unlike the other prisoners in the sense that they felt no guilt nor were they outcasts of society. All guilty men instinctively cower, which was why it was the kind of prison where men got knocked out cold with a blow at the back of the head from an iron bar. Up until the arrival of Warder Hannetjie, no warder had dared beat any member of Span One and no warder had lasted more than a week with them. The battle was entirely psychological. Span One was assertive and it was beyond the scope of white warders to handle assertive black men. Thus, Span One had got out of control. They were the best thieves and liars in the camp. They lived all day on raw cabbages. They chatted and smoked tobacco. And since they moved, thought, and acted as one, they had perfected every technique of group concealment.

Trouble began that very day between Span One and Warder Hannetjie. It was because of the shortsightedness of Brille. That was the nickname he was given in prison and is the Afrikaans word for someone who wears glasses. Brille could never judge the approach of the prison gates and on several previous occasions he had munched on cabbages and dropped them almost at the feet of the warder and all previous warders had overlooked this. Not so Warder Hannetjie.

"Who dropped that cabbage?" he thundered.

Brille stepped out of line.

"I did," he said meekly.

"Alright," said Hannetjie. "The whole Span goes three meals off." 10

"But I told you I did it," Brille protested.

The blood rushed to Warder Hannetjie's face.

span: Squad.

"Look 'ere," he said. "I don't take orders from a kaffir.° I don't know what kind of kaffir you tink you are. Why don't you say Baas? I'm your Baas. Why don't you say Baas, hey?"

Brille blinked his eyes rapidly but by contrast his voice was strangely calm.   15

"I'm twenty years older than you," he said. It was the first thing that came to mind but the comrades seemed to think it a huge joke. A titter swept up the line. The next thing Warder Hannetjie whipped out a knobkerrie° and gave Brille several blows about the head. What surprised his comrades was the speed with which Brille had removed his glasses or else they would have been smashed to pieces on the ground.

That evening in the cell Brille was very apologetic.

"I'm sorry, comrades," he said. "I've put you into a hell of a mess."

"Never mind, brother," they said. "What happens to one of us, happens to all."

"I'll try to make up for it, comrades," he said. "I'll steal something so that   20 you don't go hungry."

Privately, Brille was very philosophical about his head wounds. It was the first time an act of violence had been perpetrated against him but he had long been a witness of extreme, almost unbelievable human brutality. He had twelve children and his mind traveled back that evening through the sixteen years of bedlam in which he had lived. It had all happened in a small drab little three-bedroomed house in a small drab little street in the Eastern Cape and the children kept coming year after year because neither he nor Martha ever managed the contraceptives the right way and a teacher's salary never allowed moving to a bigger house and he was always taking exams to improve his salary only to have it all eaten up by hungry mouths. Everything was pretty horrible, especially the way the children fought. They'd get hold of each other's heads and give them a good bashing against the wall. Martha gave up somewhere along the line so they worked out a thing between them. The bashings, biting, and blood were to operate in full swing until he came home. He was to be the bogeyman and when it worked he never failed to have a sense of godhead at the way in which his presence could change savages into fairly reasonable human beings.

Yet somehow it was this chaos and mismanagement at the center of his life that drove him into politics. It was really an ordered beautiful world with just a few basic slogans to learn along with the rights of mankind. At one stage, before things became very bad, there were conferences to attend, all very far away from home.

"Let's face it," he thought ruefully. "I'm only learning right now what it means to be a politician. All this while I've been running away from Martha and the kids."

And the pain in his head brought a hard lump to his throat. That was what the children did to each other daily and Martha wasn't managing and if Warder Hannetjie had not interrupted him that morning he would have sent the following message: "Be good comrades, my children. Cooperate, then life will run smoothly."

The next day Warder Hannetjie caught this old man of twelve children   25 stealing grapes from the farm shed. They were an enormous quantity of grapes

kaffir: A black South African; often used as a disparaging term.
knobkerrie: A club.

in a ten-gallon tin and for this misdeed the old man spent a week in the isolation cell. In fact, Span One as a whole was in constant trouble. Warder Hannetjie seemed to have eyes at the back of his head. He uncovered the trick about the cabbages, how they were split in two with the spade and immediately covered with earth and then unearthed again and eaten with split-second timing. He found out how tobacco smoke was beaten into the ground and he found out how conversations were whispered down the wind.

For about two weeks Span One lived in acute misery. The cabbages, tobacco, and conversations had been the pivot of jail life to them. Then one evening they noticed that their good old comrade who wore the glasses was looking rather pleased with himself. He pulled out a four-ounce packet of tobacco by way of explanation and the comrades fell upon it with great greed. Brille merely smiled. After all, he was the father of many children. But when the last shred had disappeared, it occurred to the comrades that they ought to be puzzled. Someone said: "I say, brother. We're watched like hawks these days. Where did you get the tobacco?"

"Hannetjie gave it to me," said Brille.

There was a long silence. Into it dropped a quiet bombshell.

"I saw Hannetjie in the shed today," and the failing eyesight blinked rapidly. "I caught him in the act of stealing five bags of fertilizer and he bribed me to keep my mouth shut."

There was another long silence.   30

"Prison is an evil life," Brille continued, apparently discussing some irrelevant matter. "It makes a man contemplate all kinds of evil deeds."

He held out his hand and closed it.

"You know, comrades," he said. "I've got Hannetjie. I'll betray him tomorrow."

Everyone began talking at once.

"Forget it, brother. You'll get shot."   35

Brille laughed.

"I won't," he said. "That is what I mean about evil. I am a father of children and I saw today that Hannetjie is just a child and stupidly truthful. I'm going to punish him severely because we need a good warder."

The following day, with Brille as witness, Hannetjie confessed to the theft of the fertilizer and was fined a large sum of money. From then on Span One did very much as they pleased while Warder Hannetjie stood by and said nothing. But it was Brille who carried this to extremes. One day, at the close of work Warder Hannetjie said: "Brille, pick up my jacket and carry it back to the camp."

"But nothing in the regulations say I'm your servant, Hannetjie," Brille replied coolly.

"I've told you not to call me Hannetjie. You must say, 'Baas,'" but Warder   40
Hannetjie's voice lacked conviction. In turn, Brille squinted up at him.

"I'll tell you something about this Baas business, Hannetjie," he said. "One of these days we are going to run the country. You are going to clean my car. Now I have a fifteen-year-old son and I'd die of shame if you had to tell him that I ever called you Baas."

Warder Hannetjie went red in the face and picked up his coat.

On another occasion Brille was seen to be walking about the prison yard, openly smoking tobacco. On being taken before the prison commander he claimed to have received the tobacco from Warder Hannetjie. All throughout the tirade from his chief, Warder Hannetjie failed to defend himself but his nerve broke completely. He called Brille to one side.

"Brille," he said. "This thing between you and me must end. You may not know it but I have a wife and children and you're driving me to suicide."

"Why don't you like your own medicine, Hannetjie?" Brille asked quietly.   45

"I can give you anything you want," Warder Hannetjie said in desperation.

"It's not only me but the whole of Span One," said Brille, cunningly. "The whole of Span One wants something from you."

Warder Hannetjie brightened with relief.

"I tink I can manage if it's tobacco you want," he said.

Brille looked at him, for the first time struck with pity, and guilt.   50

He wondered if he had carried the whole business too far. The man was really a child.

"It's not tobacco we want, but you," he said. "We want you on our side. We want a good warder because without a good warder we won't be able to manage the long stretch ahead."

Warder Hannetjie interpreted this request in his own fashion and his interpretation of what was good and human often left the prisoners of Span One speechless with surprise. He had a way of slipping off his revolver and picking up a spade and digging alongside Span One. He had a way of producing unheard-of luxuries like boiled eggs from his farm nearby and things like cigarettes, and Span One responded nobly and got the reputation of being the best work span in the camp. And it wasn't only take from their side. They were awfully good at stealing certain commodities like fertilizer which were needed on the farm of Warder Hannetjie.

CONNECTIONS TO OTHER SELECTIONS

1. Discuss how the issue of race relations is presented in "The Prisoner Who Wore Glasses" and Ralph Ellison's "Battle Royal" (p. 231). Compare Brille's strategy of dealing with racial issues with the strategy suggested by the last words from the grandfather in "Battle Royal" (para. 2).

2. Compare Brille's character with Abner Snopes's in William Faulkner's "Barn Burning" (p. 493). How does each character cope with oppression?

3. Write an essay about the effect of the final sentence in Head's story and in Isabel Allende's "The Judge's Wife" (p. 612). How does the last sentence of each story affect your response to what has come before it?

NAGUIB MAHFOUZ (EGYPT / B. 1911)

Born in Cairo, Egypt, Naguib Mahfouz graduated from Cairo University in 1934 and spent most of his life writing while working as a government employee in the Ministry of Islamic Affairs until his retirement in 1971. He continues to write fiction and has published nearly forty novels along with fourteen collections of short stories. His reputation in the Arab world is secure, and he has been celebrated internationally since 1988, when he was awarded the Nobel Prize in literature. Among his most popular novels translated into English are *Miramar* (1978), *Children of Gebelawi* (1981), and *Sugar Street: The Cairo Trilogy* (1992). "The Answer Is No" is reprinted from *The Time and the Place and Other Stories* (1991).

Web   *Research Naguib Mahfouz with LitLinks at*
http://www.bedfordstmartins.com/meyer/bedintrolit

The Answer Is No

1991

TRANSLATED BY DENYS JOHNSON-DAVIES

The important piece of news that the new headmaster had arrived spread through the school. She heard of it in the women teachers' common room as she was casting a final glance at the day's lessons. There was no getting away from joining the other teachers in congratulating him, and from shaking him by the hand too. A shudder passed through her body, but it was unavoidable.

"They speak highly of his ability," said a colleague of hers. "And they talk too of his strictness."

It had always been a possibility that might occur, and now it had. Her pretty face paled, and a staring look came to her wide black eyes.

When the time came, the teachers went in single file, decorously attired, to his open room. He stood behind his desk as he received the men and women. He was of medium height, with a tendency to portliness, and had a spherical face, hooked nose, and bulging eyes; the first thing that could be seen of him was a thick, puffed-up mustache, arched like a foam-laden wave. She advanced with her eyes fixed on his chest. Avoiding his gaze, she stretched out her hand. What was she to say? Just what the others had said? However, she kept silent, uttered not a word. What, she wondered, did his eyes express? His rough hand shook hers, and he said in a gruff voice, "Thanks." She turned elegantly and moved off.

She forgot her worries through her daily tasks, though she did not look in   5 good shape. Several of the girls remarked, "Miss is in a bad mood." When she returned to her home at the beginning of the Pyramids Road, she changed her clothes and sat down to eat with her mother. "Everything all right?'" inquired her mother, looking her in the face.

"Badran, Badran Badawi," she said briefly. "Do you remember him? He's been appointed our headmaster."

"Really!"

Then, after a moment of silence, she said, "It's of no importance at all — it's an old and long-forgotten story."

After eating, she took herself off to her study to rest for a while before correcting some exercise books. She had forgotten him completely. No, not completely. How could he be forgotten completely? When he had first come to give her a private lesson in mathematics, she was fourteen years of age. In fact not quite fourteen. He had been twenty-five years older, the same age as her father. She had said to her mother, "His appearance is a mess, but he explains things well." And her mother had said, "We're not concerned with what he looks like; what's important is how he explains things."

He was an amusing person, and she got on well with him and benefited 10
from his knowledge. How, then, had it happened? In her innocence she had
not noticed any change in his behavior to put her on her guard. Then one day
he had been left on his own with her, her father having gone to her aunt's
clinic. She had not the slightest doubts about a man she regarded as a second
father. How, then, had it happened? Without love or desire on her part the
thing had happened. She had asked in terror about what had occurred, and he
had told her, "Don't be frightened or sad. Keep it to yourself and I'll come and
propose to you the day you come of age."

And he had kept his promise and had come to ask for her hand. By then
she had attained a degree of maturity that gave her an understanding of the
dimensions of their tragic position. She had found that she had no love or respect for him and that he was as far as he could be from her dreams and from
the ideas she had formed of what constituted an ideal and moral person. But
what was to be done? Her father had passed away two years ago, and her
mother had been taken aback by the forwardness of the man. However, she
had said to her, "I know your attachment to your personal independence, so I
leave the decision to you."

She had been conscious of the critical position she was in. She had either
to accept or to close the door forever. It was the sort of situation that could
force her into something she detested. She was the rich, beautiful girl, a by-
word in Abbasiyya for her nobility of character, and now here she was struggling helplessly in a well-sprung trap, while he looked down at her with rapacious eyes. Just as she had hated his strength, so too did she hate her own
weakness. To have abused her innocence was one thing, but for him to have the
upper hand now that she was fully in possession of her faculties was something else. He had said, "So here I am, making good my promise because I love
you." He had also said, "I know of your love of teaching, and you will complete
your studies at the College of Science."

She had felt such anger as she had never felt before. She had rejected coer-
cion in the same way as she rejected ugliness. It had meant little to her to sacrifice marriage. She had welcomed being on her own, for solitude accompanied
by self-respect was not loneliness. She had also guessed he was after her money.
She had told her mother quite straightforwardly, "No," to which her mother
had replied, "I am astonished you did not make this decision from the first
moment."

The man had blocked her way outside and said, "How can you refuse?
Don't you realize the outcome?" And she had replied with an asperity he had
not expected, "For me any outcome is preferable to being married to you."

After finishing her studies, she had wanted something to do to fill her 15
spare time, so she had worked as a teacher. Chances to marry had come time
after time, but she had turned her back on them all.

"Does no one please you?" her mother asked her.

"I know what I'm doing," she had said gently.

"But time is going by."

"Let it go as it pleases, I am content."

Day by day she becomes older. She avoids love, fears it. With all her strength 20
she hopes that life will pass calmly, peacefully, rather than happily. She goes on
persuading herself that happiness is not confined to love and motherhood.

Never has she regretted her firm decision. Who knows what the morrow holds? But she was certainly unhappy that he should again make his appearance in her life, that she would be making of the past a living and painful present.

Then, the first time he was alone with her in his room, he asked her, "How are you?"

She answered coldly, "I'm fine."

He hesitated slightly before inquiring, "Have you not . . . I mean, did you get married?"

In the tone of someone intent on cutting short a conversation, she said, "I told you, I'm fine."

CONNECTIONS TO OTHER SELECTIONS

1. Discuss the similarities and differences between the older men in "The Answer Is No" and Fay Weldon's "IND AFF, or Out of Love in Sarajevo" (p. 165).

2. In an essay compare the protagonists' decisions not to marry in "The Answer Is No" and James Joyce's "Eveline" (p. 524).

19

An Album of
Contemporary Stories

SHERMAN ALEXIE (B. 1966)

American Indian author Sherman Alexie was born in the reservation town
of Wellpinit, Washington, to a mother of Spokane background and a
Coeur d'Alene father. After attending an all-white high school, Alexie went
to Washington State University intending to prepare for medical school,
but a writing class changed his mind. He began to write and took a degree
in American studies. Alexie is now the author of more than three hundred
essays, reviews, poems, and stories. His poetry volumes include *The Business
of Fancydancing* (1992), *First Indian on the Moon* (1993), *Old Shirts and New Skins*
(1993), and *Water Flowing Home: Poems* (1996); his novels and story collections include *The Lone Ranger and Tonto Fistfight in Heaven* (1993), *Reservation
Blues* (1995), *Indian Killer* (1996), and *The Toughest Indian in the World* (2000).
Alexie's screenplay *Smoke Signals,* produced by Miramax films in 1998, was
the first feature film to be written, produced, and directed by American Indians. Depicting the experience of contemporary American Indians, Alexie's
work tends to include realistic characters in current situations, and his
style is influenced by indigenous oral storytelling.

Web *Research Sherman Alexie with LitLinks at*
     http://www.bedfordstmartins.com/meyer/bedintrolit

Class   2000

She wanted to know if I was Catholic.
     I was completely unprepared to respond with any degree of clarity to such
a dangerous question. After all, we had been talking about the shrimp appetizers (which were covered with an ambitious pesto sauce) and where they fit, in

terms of quality, in our very separate histories of shrimp appetizers in particular and seafood appetizers in general. I'd just been describing to her how cayenne and lobster seemed to be mortal enemies, one of the more secular and inane culinary observations I'd ever made, when she'd focused her blue eyes on me, really looked at me for the first time in the one minute and thirty-five seconds we'd known each other, and asked me if I was Catholic.

How do you answer a question like that, especially when you've just met the woman at one of those house parties where you'd expected to know everybody in attendance but had gradually come to realize that you knew only the host couple, and then only well enough to ask about the welfare of the two kids (a boy and a girl or two boys) you thought they parented? As far as I could tell, there were no priests, ministers, or pastors milling about, so I had no easy visual aids in guessing at the dominant denomination in the room. If there'd been a Jesuit priest, Hasidic rabbi, or Tibetan monk drinking a pale ale over by the saltwater aquarium, I might have known the best response, the clever, scintillating answer that would have compelled her to take me home with her for a long night of safe and casual sex.

"Well," she asked again, with a musical lilt in her voice. "Are you Catholic?"
Her left eye was a significantly darker blue than the right.   5
"Your eyes," I said, trying to change the subject. "They're different."
"I'm blind in this one," she said, pointing to the left eye.
"Oh, I'm sorry," I said, mortified by my lack of decorum.
"Why? It was my big brother who stabbed me with the pencil. He didn't mean it, though."
She told the story as if she'd only skinned a knee or received a slight concussion, as if the injury had been temporary.   10
"He was aiming for my little sister's eye," she added. "But she ducked. She was always more athletic than me."
"Where's your sister now?"
"She's dead. Car wreck. Bang, bang, bang."
So much pain for such a white woman. I wondered how often a man can say the wrong thing during the course of a particular conversation.
"What about your brother?" I asked, praying that he had not been driving   15
the car that killed her sister.
"He's right over there," she said and pointed at a handsome man, taller than everybody else in the room, who was sitting on the carpeted stairs with a woman whose red hair I'd been admiring all evening. Though engaged in what appeared to be a passionate conversation, the brother sensed his sister's attention and looked up. Both of his eyes were the same shade of blue as her good eye.
"He's the one who did it," she said and tapped her blind eye.
In response, the brother smiled and tapped his left eye. He could see perfectly.
"You cruel bastard," she mouthed at him, though she made it sound like an affectionate nickname, like a tender legacy from childhood.
"You cruel bastard," she repeated. Her brother could obviously read her   20
lips because he laughed again, loud enough for me to hear him over the din of the party, and hugged the redhead in a tender but formal way that indicated they'd made love only three or four times in their young relationship.
"Your brother," I said, trying to compliment her by complimenting the family genetics. "He's good-looking."

"He's okay," she said.

"He's got your eyes."

"Only one of them, remember," she said and moved one step closer to me. "Now, quit trying to change the subject. Tell me. Are you Catholic or are you not Catholic?"

"Baptized," I said. "But not confirmed." 25

"That's very ambiguous."

"I read somewhere that many women think ambiguity is sexy."

"Not me. I like men who are very specific."

"You don't like mystery?"

"I always know who did it," she said and moved so close that I could smell 30 the red wine and dinner mints on her breath.

I took a step back.

"Don't be afraid," she said. "I'm not drunk. And I just chewed on a few Altoids because I thought I might be kissing somebody very soon."

She could read minds. She was also drunk enough that her brother had already pocketed the keys to her Lexus.

"Who is this somebody you're going to be kissing?" I asked. "And why just somebody? That sounds very ambiguous to me."

"And very sexy," she said and touched my hand. Blond, maybe thirty-five, 35 and taller than me, she was the tenth most attractive white woman in the room. I always approached the tenth most attractive white woman at any gathering. I didn't have enough looks, charm, intelligence, or money to approach anybody more attractive than that, and I didn't have enough character to approach the less attractive. Crassly speaking, I'd always made sure to play ball only with my equals.

"You're Indian," she said, stretching the word into three syllables and nearly a fourth.

"Do you like that?"

"I like your hair," she said, touching the black braids that hung down past my chest. I'd been growing the braids since I'd graduated from law school. My hair impressed jurors but irritated judges. Perfect.

"I like your hair, too," I said and brushed a pate strand away from her forehead. I counted three blemishes and one mole on her face. I wanted to kiss the tips of her fingers. Women expected kisses on the parts of their bodies hidden by clothes, the private places, but were often surprised when I paid more attention to their public features: hands, hairline, the soft skin around their eyes.

"You're beautiful," I said. 40

"No, I'm not," she said. "I'm just pretty. But pretty is good enough."

I still didn't know her name, but I could have guessed at it. Her generation of white women usually carried two-syllable names, like Becky, Erin, and Wendy, or monosyllabic nicknames that lacked any adornment. Peg, Deb, or Sam. Efficient names, quick-in-the-shower names, just-brush-it-and-go names. Her mother and her mother's friends would be known by more ornate monikers, and if she had daughters, they would be named after their grandmothers. The country was filling up with little white girls named Rebecca, Elizabeth, and Willamena.

"Sara," I guessed. "Your name is Sara."

"With or without an *h*?" she asked.

"Without," I said, pleased with my psychic ability. 45

"Actually, it's neither. My name is Susan. Susan McDermott. Without the *h.*"

"I'm Edgar Eagle Runner," I said, though my driver's license still read Edgar Joseph.

"Eagle Runner," she repeated, feeling the shape of my name fill her mouth, then roll past her tongue, teeth, and lips.

"Susan," I said.

"Eagle Runner," she whispered. "What kind of Indian are you?"   50

"Spokane."

"Never heard of it."

"We're a small tribe. Salmon people."

"The salmon are disappearing," she said.

"Yes," I said. "Yes, they are."   55

Susan McDermott and I were married in a small ceremony seven months later in St. Therese Catholic Church in Madrona, a gentrified neighborhood ten minutes from downtown Seattle. She'd been baptized at St. Therese as a toddler by a Jesuit who many years later went hiking on Mount Rainier and vanished. Father David or Joseph or Father Something Biblical. She didn't remember anything about him, neither the color of his hair nor the exact shape of his theology, but she thought that his disappearance was a metaphor for her love life.

"One day, many years ago," she said, "my heart walked into the snow and vanished. But then you found it and gave it heat."

"Is that a simile or a metaphor?" I asked.

"It might be an analogy," she said.

Our vows were witnessed by three dozen of Susan's best friends, along   60
with most of her coworkers at the architecture firm, but Susan's handsome brother and parents stayed away as a protest against my pigmentation.

"I can understand fucking him," her brother had said upon hearing the news of our engagement. "But why do you want to share a checking account?"

He was so practical.

Half of the partners and all of my fellow associates from the law firm showed up to watch me tie the knot.

Velma, my dark-skinned mother, was overjoyed by my choice of mate. She'd always wanted me to marry a white woman and beget half-breed children who would marry white people who would beget quarter-bloods, and so on and so on, until simple mathematics killed the Indian in us.

When asked, my mother told white people she was Spanish, not Mexican,   65
not Hispanic, not Chicana, and certainly not Spokane Indian with a little bit of Aztec thrown in for spice, even though she was all of these things.

As for me, I'd told any number of white women that I was part Aztec and I'd told a few that I was completely Aztec. That gave me some mystery, some ethnic weight, a history of glorious color and mass executions. Strangely enough, there were aphrodisiacal benefits to claiming to be descended from ritual cannibals. In any event, pretending to be an Aztec warrior was a lot more impressive than revealing I was just some bright kid who'd fought his way off the Spokane Indian Reservation in Washington State and was now a corporate lawyer in Seattle who pretended to have a lot more money than he did.

I'd emptied my meager savings account to pay for the wedding and reception, refusing to allow Susan to help, though she made twice what I did. I was living paycheck to paycheck, a bizarre circumstance for a man whose monthly wage exceeded his mother's yearly income as a social worker in the small city of Spokane, Washington.

My mother was an Indian woman who taught drunk white people not to drink, stoned whites not to smoke, and abusive whites not to throw the punch. A simple and honorable job. She was very good at it and I loved her. She wore a black dress to the wedding, nearly funeral wear, but brightened it with a salmon-colored scarf and matching shoes.

I counted seventeen white women at the wedding. On an average day, Susan would have been the fourth or fifth most attractive. On this, her wedding day, dressed in an ivory gown with plunging neckline, she was easily the most beautiful white woman in the chapel; she was more serene, sexy, and spiritual than the wooden Mary hanging on the west wall or the stained-glassed Mary filling up one of the windows.

Susan's niece, an eighteen-year-old, served as her maid of honor. She modeled teen wear for Nordstrom's. I tried not to stare at her. My best man was one of the partners in the law firm where I worked.   70

"Hey, Runner," he had said just before the ceremony began. "I love you, man."

I'd hugged him, feeling guilty. My friendship with him was strictly professional.

During the ceremony, he cried. I couldn't believe it. I'm not one of those men who believe tears are a sign of weakness. On the contrary, I believe it's entirely appropriate, even attractive, for a man to cry under certain circumstances, but my wedding was not tearworthy. In fact, there was a decided lack of emotion during the ceremony, mostly due to the absence of Susan's immediate family.

My mother was the only member of my family sitting in the pews, but that didn't bother or surprise me. She was the only one I had invited.

The ceremony itself was short and simple, because Susan believed brevity   75
was always more elegant, and more sexy, than excess. I agreed with her.

"I will," she said.

"I will," I said.

We did.

During the first two years of our marriage, we attended thirty-seven cocktail parties, eighteen weddings, one divorce, seven Christmas parties, two New Year's Eve parties, three New Year's Day parties, nine birthday parties — only one of them for a child under the age of eighteen — six opera performances, nine literary readings, twelve museum openings, one museum closing, three ballets, including a revival of *Swan Lake* in New York City, one spouse-swapping party we left before we took off our coats, and thirty-two films, including most of those nominated for Oscars and two or three that had screened at the Sundance Film Festival.

I attended business lunches Monday through Friday, and occasionally on   80
Saturdays, while Susan kept her Friday lunches free so she could carry on an affair with an architect named Harry. She'd begun the affair a few days after our first anniversary and it had gone on for seven months before she'd voluntarily quit him, never having known that I'd known about the tryst, that I'd discovered his love letters hidden in a shoe box at the bottom of her walk-in closet.

I hadn't been snooping on her when I'd found the letters and I didn't bother to read any of them past the salutation that began each. "My love, my love, my love," they'd read, three times, always three times, like a chant, like a prayer. Brokenhearted, betrayed, I'd kept the letters sacred by carefully placing them back, intact and unread, in the shoe box and sliding the box back into its hiding place.

I suppose I could have exacted revenge on her by sleeping with one or more of her friends or coworkers. I'd received any number of subtle offers to do such a thing, but I didn't want to embarrass her. Personal pain should never be made public. Instead, in quiet retaliation, I patronized prostitutes whenever I traveled out of town. Miami, Los Angeles, Boston, Chicago, Minneapolis, Houston.

In San Francisco for a deposition hearing, I called the first service listed in the Yellow Pages.

"A-1 Escorts," said the woman. A husky voice, somehow menacing. I'm sure her children hated the sound of it, even as I found myself aroused by its timbre.

"A-1 Escorts," she said again when I did not speak.   85

"Oh," I said. "Hi. Hello. Uh, I'm looking for some company this evening."

"Where you at?"

"The Prescott."

"Nice place."

"Yeah, they have whirlpool bathtubs."   90

"Water sports will cost you extra."

"Oh, no, no, no. I'm, uh, rather traditional."

"Okay, Mr. Traditional, what are you looking for?"

I'd slept with seventeen prostitutes, all of them blond and blue-eyed. Twelve of them had been busty while the other five had been small-breasted. Eight of them had claimed to be college students; one of them even had a chemistry textbook in her backpack.

"Do you employ any Indian women?" I asked.   95

"Indian? Like with the dot in the forehead?"

"No, no, that's East Indian. From India. I'm looking for American Indian. You know, like Tonto."

"We don't have any boys."

"Oh, no, I mean, I want an Indian woman."

There was a long silence on the other end. Was she looking through some   100
kind of catalogue? Searching her inventory for the perfect woman for me? Was she calling other escort companies, looking for a referral? I wanted to hang up the phone. I'd never had intercourse with an Indian woman.

"Yeah, we got somebody. She's a pro."

"What do you mean by pro?"

"She used to work pornos."

"Pornos?"

"Dirty movies? X-rated? You got them right there on the pay-per-view in   105
your room, buddy."

"What's her name?"

"She calls herself Tawny Feather."

"You're kidding."

"I never kid."

I wondered what kind of Indian woman would call herself Tawny Feather. 110
Sexually speaking, Indian women and men are simultaneously promiscuous
and modest. That's a contradiction, but it also happens to be the truth. I just
couldn't imagine an Indian woman who would star in pornographic movies.

"Well, you want a date or not?" asked the husky-voiced woman.

"How much?"

"How much you got?"

"How much you want?"

"Two hundred." 115

"Sold," I said.

"What room?"

"1216."

"Who should she ask for?"

"Geronimo." 120

"Ha, ha," she said and hung up the phone.

Less than an hour later, there was a knock on the door. I peered through
the peephole and saw her.

Tawny Feather.

She wore a conservative tan suit and a string of fake pearls. Dream-catcher
earrings, turquoise rings, a stainless-steel eagle pinned to her lapel. Good camou-
flage. Professional but eccentric. She looked like a woman on her way to or from
a meeting. She looked like a woman with an Individualized Retirement Account.

She was also a white woman wearing a black wig over her short blond hair. 125

"You're not Indian," I said when I opened the door.

She looked me up and down.

"No, I'm not," she said. "But you are."

"Mostly."

"Well," she said as she stepped into the room and kissed my neck. "Then 130
you can mostly pretend I'm Indian."

She stayed all night, which cost me another five hundred dollars, and ordered eggs and toast for breakfast, which cost me another twenty.

"You're the last one," I said as she prepared to leave.

"The last what?"

"My last prostitute."

"The last one today?" she asked. "Or the last one this month? What kind 135
of time period are we talking about here?"

She swore she was an English major.

"The last one forever," I said.

She smiled, convinced that I was lying and/or fooling myself, having heard
these same words from any number of customers. She knew that she and her
coworkers were drugs for men like me.

"Sure I am," she said.

"No, really," I said. "I promise." 140

She laughed.

"Son," she said, though she was ten years younger than me. "You don't
have to make me any damn promises."

She took off her black wig and handed it to me.

"You keep it," she said and gave me a free good-bye kiss.

Exactly three years after our wedding, Susan gave birth to our first child, a 145
boy. He weighed eight pounds, seven ounces, and was twenty-two inches long.

A big baby. His hair was black and his eyes were a strange gray. He died ten minutes after leaving Susan's body.

After our child died, Susan and I quit having sex. Or rather, she stopped wanting to have sex. I just want to tell the whole story. For months I pressured, coerced, seduced, and emotionally blackmailed her into sleeping with me. At first, I assumed she'd been engaged in another affair with another architect named Harry, but my private detective found only evidence of her grief, crying jags in public rest rooms, aimless wandering in the children's departments of Nordstrom's and the Bon Marche, and visits to a therapist I'd never heard about.

She wasn't touching anybody else but me. Our lives moved on.

After a year of reluctant sex, I believed her orgasms were mostly due to my refusal to quit touching her until she did come, the arduous culmination of my physical endeavors rather than the result of any emotional investment she might have had in fulfillment. And then, one night, while I was still inside her, moving my hips in rhythm with hers, I looked into her eyes, her blue eyes, and saw that her good eye held no more light in it than her dead eye. She wasn't literally blind, of course. She'd just stopped seeing me. I was startled by the sudden epiphany that she'd been faking her orgasms all along, certainly since our child had died, and probably since the first time we'd made love.

"What?" she asked, a huge question to ask and answer at any time in our lives. Her hands never left their usual place at the small of my back.

"I'm sorry," I told her, and I was sorry, and left her naked and alone in bed 150 while I quickly dressed and went out for a drink.

I don't drink alcohol, never have, mostly because I don't want to maintain and confirm any of my ethnic stereotypes, let alone the most prevalent one, but also because my long-lost father, a half-breed, is still missing somewhere in the bottom of a tequila bottle. I had always wondered if he was a drunk because he was Indian or because he was white or because he was both.

Personally, I like bottled water, with gas, as the Europeans like to say. If I drink enough of that bubbly water in the right environment, I can get drunk. After a long night of Perrier or Pellegrino, I can still wake up with a vicious hangover. Obviously, I place entirely too much faith in the power of metaphor.

When I went out carousing with my fellow lawyers, I ended up in fancy hotel lounges, private clubs, and golf course cigar rooms, the places where the alcoholics adhere to a rigid dress code, but after leaving my marriage bed I wanted to drink in a place free from lawyers and their dress codes, from emotional obligations and beautiful white women, even the kind of white woman who might be the tenth most attractive in any room in the world.

I chose Chuck's, a dive near the corner of Virginia and First.

I'd driven by the place any number of times, had seen the Indians who loi- 155 tered outside. I assumed it was an Indian bar, one of those establishments where the clientele, through chance and design, is mostly indigenous. I'd heard about these kinds of places. They are supposed to exist in every city.

"What can I get you?" asked the bartender when I sat on the stool closest to the door. She was an Indian woman with scars on her face and knuckles. A fighter. She was a woman who had once been pretty but had grown up in a place where pretty was punished. Now, twenty pounds overweight, on her way to forty pounds more, she was most likely saving money for a complete move to a city yet to be determined.

"Hey, handsome," she asked again as I stared blankly at her oft-broken nose. I decided that her face resembled most of the furniture in the bar: dark, stained by unknown insults, and in a continual state of repair. "What the fuck would you like to drink?"

"Water," I said, surprised that the word "fuck" could sound so friendly.

"Water?"

"Yeah, water." 160

She filled a glass from the tap behind her and plunked it down in front of me.

"A dollar," she said.

"For tap water?"

"For space rental."

I handed her a five-dollar bill. 165

"Keep the change," I said and took a big drink.

"Cool. Next time, you get a clean glass," she said and waited for my reaction. I swallowed hard, kept my dinner down, and smiled.

"I don't need to know what's coming next," I said. "I like mysteries."

"What kind of mysteries?" 170

"Hard-boiled. The kind where the dog gets run over, the hero gets punched in the head, and the bad guy gets eaten by sharks."

"Not me," she said. "I got too much blood in my life already. I like romances."

I wondered if she wanted to sleep with me.

"You want something else," she said, "just shout it out. I'll hear you.

She moved to the other end of the bar where an old Indian man sipped at 175 a cup of coffee. They talked and laughed. Surprisingly jealous of their camaraderie, I turned away and looked around the bar. It was a small place, maybe fifty feet long by twenty feet wide, with one pinball machine, one pool table, and two bathrooms. I supposed the place would be packed on a weekend.

As it was, on a cold Thursday, there were only five Indians in the bar, other than the bartender, her old friend, and me.

Two obese Indian women shared a table in the back, an Indian couple danced in front of a broken jukebox, and one large and muscular Indian guy played pool by himself. In his white T-shirt, blue-jean jacket, tight jeans, and cowboy boots, he looked like Chief Broom from *One Flew Over the Cuckoo's Nest*. I decided he could have killed me with a flick of one finger.

He looked up from his pool cue when he felt my eyes on him.

"What the fuck are you looking at?" he asked. His eyes were darker than the eight ball. I had no idea that "fuck" could be such a dangerous word.

"Nothing," I said. 180

Still holding his cue stick, he walked a few paces closer to me. I was afraid, very afraid.

"Nothing?" he asked. "Do I look like nothing to you?"

"No, no, that's not what I meant. I mean, I was just watching you play pool. That's all."

He stared at me, studied me like an owl might study a field mouse.

"You just keep your eyes to yourself," he said and turned back to his game. 185

I thought I was safe. I looked down to the bartender, who was shaking her head at me.

"Because I just, I just want to know," sputtered the big Indian. "I just want to know who the hell you think you are."

Furious, he shouted, a primal sort of noise, as he threw the cue stick against the wall. He rushed at me and lifted me by the collar.

"Who are you?" he shouted. "Who the fuck are you?"

"I'm nobody," I said, wet with fear. "Nobody. Nobody."   190

"Put him down, Junior," said the bartender.

Junior and I both turned to look at her. She held a pistol down by her hip, not as a threat, but more like a promise. Junior studied the bartender's face, estimated the level of her commitment, and dropped me back onto the stool.

He took a few steps back, pointed at me.

"I'm sick of little shits like you," he said. "Fucking urban Indians in your fancy fucking clothes. Fuck you. Fuck you."

I looked down and saw my denim jacket and polo shirt, the khakis and   195
brown leather loafers. I looked like a Gap ad.

"I ever see you again," Junior said. "I'm going to dislocate your hips."

I flinched. Junior obviously had some working knowledge of human anatomy and the most effective means of creating pain therein. He saw my fear, examined its corners and edges, and decided it was large enough.

"Jesus," he said. "I don't know why I'm even talking to you. What are you going to do? You fucking wimp. You're not worth my time. Why don't you get the fuck out of here? Why don't you just get in your BMW, that's what you drive, enit? Why don't you get in your fucking BMW and get out of here before I change my mind, before I pop out one of your eyes with a fucking spoon, all right?"

I didn't drive a BMW; I drove a Saab.

"Yeah, fuck you," Junior said, thoroughly enjoying himself now. "Just   200
drive back to your fucking mansion on Mercer Island or Edmonds or whatever white fucking neighborhood you live in. Drive back to your white wife. She's white, enit? Yeah, blond and blue-eyed, I bet. White, white. I bet her pussy hair is blond, too. Isn't it? Isn't it?"

I wanted to hate him.

"Go back to your mansion and read some fucking Teletubbies to your white fucking kids."

"What?" I asked.

"I said, go home to your white fucking kids."

"Fuck you," I said and completely surprised Junior. Good thing. He hesi-   205
tated for a brief moment before he rushed at me again. His hesitation gave the bartender enough time to vault the bar and step in between Junior and me. I couldn't believe how fast she was.

She pressed the pistol tightly against Junior's forehead.

"Let it go, Junior," said the bartender.

"Why are you protecting him?" Junior asked.

"I don't give a shit about him," she said. "But I do care about you. You get into trouble again and you're going to jail forever. You know that."

Junior smiled.   210

"Sissy," he said to the bartender. "In another world, you and I are Romeo and Juliet."

"But we live in this world, Junior."

"Okay," said Sissy. "This is what's going to happen, Junior. You're going to walk over behind the bar, get yourself another Diet Pepsi, and mellow out. And Mr. Tap Water here is going to walk out the front door and never return. How does that sound to the both of you?"

"Make it two Pepsis," said Junior.

"Deal," said Sissy. "How about you, Polo?"   215

"Fuck him," I said.

Junior didn't move anything except his mouth.

"Sissy," he said. "How can you expect me to remain calm, how can you expect me to stay reasonable, when this guy so obviously wants to die?"

"I'll fight you," I said.

"What?" asked Sissy and Junior, both amazed.   220

"I'll fight you," I said again.

"All right, that's what I want to hear," said Junior. "Maybe you do have some balls. There's an alley out back."

"You don't want to do this," Sissy said to me.

"I'll meet you out there, Junior," I said.

Junior laughed and shook his head.   225

"Listen up, Tommy Hilfiger," he said. "I'm not stupid. I go out the back door and you're going to run out the front door. You don't have to make things so complicated. You want to leave, I'll let you leave. Just do it now, man."

"He's giving you a chance," Sissy said to me. "You better take it."

"No," I said. "I want to fight. I'll meet you out there. I promise."

Junior studied my eyes.

"You don't lie, do you?"   230

"I lie all the time," I said. "Most of the time. But I'm not lying now. I want to fight."

"All right, then, bring your best," he said and walked out the back door.

"Are you out of your mind?" Sissy asked. "Have you ever been in a fight?"

"I boxed a little in college."

"You boxed a little in college? You boxed a little in college? I can't believe   235
this. Do you have any idea who Junior is?"

"No, why should I?"

"He's a pro."

"What? You mean, like a professional boxer?"

"No, man. A professional street fighter. No judges, no ring, no rules. The loser is the guy who don't get up."

"Isn't that illegal?"   240

"Illegal? Illegal? What, you think you're a lawyer now?"

"Actually, I am a lawyer."

Sissy laughed until tears ran down her face.

"Sweetheart," she said after she'd finally calmed down. "You need to leave. Please. Junior's got a wicked temper but he'll calm down soon enough. Hell, you come in a week from now and he'll probably buy you some water."

"Really?"   245

"No, not at all. I'm lying. You come in a week from now and Junior will break your thumbs."

She laughed again, laughed until she had to lean against the bar for support.

"Stop it," I said.

She kept laughing.

"Stop it," I shouted. 250

She kept laughing.

"Sweetheart," she said, trying to catch her breath. "I could kick your ass."

I shrugged off my denim jacket and marched for the back door. Sissy tried to stop me, but I pulled away from her and stepped into the alley.

Junior was surprised to see me. I felt a strange sense of pride. Without another word, I rushed at Junior, swinging at him with a wide right hook, with dreams of connecting with his jaw and knocking him out with one punch.

Deep in the heart of the heart of every Indian man's heart, he believes he 255 is Crazy Horse.

My half-closed right hand whizzed over Junior's head as he expertly ducked under my wild punch and then rose, surely and accurately, with a left uppercut that carried with it the moon and half of every star in the universe.

I woke up with my head in Sissy's lap. She was washing my face with a cold towel.

"Where are we?" I asked.

"In the storeroom," she said.

"Where is he?" 260

"Gone."

My face hurt.

"Am I missing any teeth?"

"No," said Sissy. "But your nose is broken."

"Are you sure?" 265

"Trust me."

I looked up at her. I decided she was still pretty and pretty was good enough. I grabbed her breast.

"Shit," she said and shoved me away.

I sprawled on the floor while she scrambled to her feet.

"What's wrong with you?" she asked. "What is wrong with you?" 270

"What do you mean? What?"

"Did you think, did you somehow get it into your crazy head that I was going to fuck you back here? On the goddamn floor in the goddamn dirt?"

I didn't know what to say.

"Jesus Christ, you really thought I was going to fuck you, didn't you?

"Well, I mean, I just . . ." 275

"You just thought because I'm an ugly woman that I'd be easy."

"You're not ugly," I said.

"Do you think I'm impressed by this fighting bullshit? Do you think it makes you some kind of warrior or something?"

She could read minds.

"You did, didn't you? All of you Indian guys think you're Crazy Horse." 280

I struggled to my feet and walked over to the sink. I looked in the mirror and saw a bloody mess. I also noticed that one of my braids was missing.

"Junior cut it off," said Sissy. "And took it with him. You're lucky he liked you. Otherwise, he would have taken a toe. He's done that before."

I couldn't imagine what that would have meant to my life.

"Look at you," she said. "Do you think that's attractive? Is that who you want to be?"

I carefully washed my face. My nose was most certainly broken.   285
"I just want to know, man. What are you doing here? Why'd you come here?"
My left eye was swelling shut. I wouldn't be able to see out of it in the morning.
"I wanted to be with my people," I said.
"Your people?" asked Sissy. "Your people? We're not your people'."
"We're Indians."   290
"Yeah, we're Indians. You, me, Junior. But we live in this world and you live in your world."
"I don't like my world."
"You pathetic bastard," she said, her eyes swelling with tears that had nothing to do with laughter. "You sorry, sorry piece of shit. Do you know how much I want to live in your world? Do you know how much Junior wants to live in your world?"
Of course I knew. For most of my life, I'd dreamed about the world where I currently resided.
"Junior and me," she said. "We have to worry about having enough to eat.   295
What do you have to worry about? That you're lonely? That you have a mortgage? That your wife doesn't love you? Fuck you, fuck you. *I have to worry about having enough to eat.*"
She stormed out of the room, leaving me alone.
I stood there in the dark for a long time. When I walked out, the bar was nearly empty. Another bartender was cleaning glasses. He didn't look at me. Sissy was gone. The front door was wide open. I stepped into the street and saw her sitting at the bus stop.
"I'm sorry," I said.
"Whatever."
"Can I give you a ride somewhere?"   300
"Do you really want to do that?" she asked.
"No," I said.
"Finally, you're being honest."
I stared at her. I wanted to say the exact right thing.
"Go home," she said. "Just go home."   305
I walked away, stopped halfway down the block.
"Do you have any kids?" I shouted back at her.
"Three," she said.

Without changing my clothes, I crawled back into bed with Susan. Her skin was warm to the touch. The house ticked, ticked, ticked. In the morning, my pillow would be soaked with my blood.
"Where did you go?" Susan asked me.   310
"I was gone," I said. "But now I'm back."

CONNECTIONS TO OTHER SELECTIONS

1. Discuss the treatment of class distinctions in Alexie's story and in Langston Hughes's "On the Road" (p. 574).
2. Compare the ending of "Class" with the ending of Ernest Hemingway's "Soldier's Home" (p. 152). Explain whether or not these endings can be considered "happy."

3. Consider the use of obscenities in "Class" and Tim O'Brien's "How to Tell a True War Story" (p. 548), and explain why you think the use of obscenities in each story is justified or not.

AMY BLOOM (B. 1953)

Born and raised in the suburbs of New York City, Amy Bloom "started writing unexpectedly." Bloom reports that before she began writing she had "picked peanuts, scooped felafel, waitressed up and down the East Coast, tended bar, written catalogue copy, and worked as a psychotherapist, for both the worried well and the very ill." Her first book, a collection of short stories, *Come to Me* (1993), was nominated for the National Book Award. It was followed by *Love Invents Us* in 1998 and *A Blind Man Can See How Much I Love You*, published in 2000, from which "Hold Tight" was taken. Currently working as a psychotherapist, Bloom lives in Connecticut and contributes to *The New Yorker, The Atlantic Monthly,* and a variety of other magazines here and abroad.

Web   *Research Amy Bloom with LitLinks at*
http://www.bedfordstmartins.com/meyer/bedintrolit

Hold Tight   2000

My senior year in high school, I was in two car accidents, neither of them my fault, and I was arrested twice, also not my fault. I couldn't keep my hands on the wheel, and the guardrails flew right at me.

I found myself on emergency room examining tables, looking into slow-moving penlights, counting backward from forty to demonstrate consciousness, and calling my mother terrible names. I hate hospitals. The smell makes me sick, and the slick floors trip me up. When I visited my four dying grandparents, who dropped like dominoes the winter I was ten, I had to leave their rooms and go throw up. By February I had a favorite stall. With my mother, I could never get that far; before I even saw her I'd throw up from the thick green smell laid over the pain and stink and helplessness. When there was no reason to keep her, they let her come home.

My mother painted about forty pictures every year, and her hands smelled of turpentine, even when she just got out of the shower. This past year she started five or six paintings but only finished one. She couldn't do the big canvases anymore, couldn't hang off her stepladder to reach the upper corners, and that last one was small enough to sit on a little easel near her bed so she could work on it when she had the strength. After December she didn't leave the bed. My mother, who could stand for hours in her cool white studio, shifting her weight from foot to foot, moving in on the canvas and backing off again, like a smart boxer waiting for the perfect opening. And then, in two months, she shrank down to an ancient little girl, loose skin and bones so light they seemed hollow. A friend suggested scarves for her bald head, but they always slipped down, half covering her eyes and ears, making her look more like a bag lady than a soap opera star. For a while she wore a white fisherman's hat with a button that said "Don't Get Me Mad," and then she just gave up. I got used to the baldness and to the shadowy fuzz that grew back, but the puffiness in her face drove me crazy. Her true face, with cheekbones so high and sharp people didn't think she spoke English, was hidden from me, kidnapped.

When I got too angry at her, I'd leave the house and throw rocks against the neighbors' fences, hoping to hit someone's healthy mother not as smart or as beautiful or as talented as mine. My friends bickered with their mothers over clothes or the phone or Nathan Zigler's parties, and I wanted to stab them to death. I didn't return calls and they all stopped trying, except for Kay, who left a jar of hollyhocks or snapdragons on the front porch every few weeks. When I can talk again, I'll talk to her.

I could hardly see the painting my mother was still working on, since I 5 went blind and deaf as soon as I touched the doorknob. I stared at the dust motes until my vision blurred and I could look toward the bed. My mother held my hand and sighed, and her weakness made me so angry and sick that I'd leave the room, pretending I had homework. And she knew everything, and I couldn't, and cannot, forgive myself for letting her know.

It was June, and everything outside was bright green and pale pink, and our house was dark and thick with dust. My mother used to say that we were messy but clean, and that used to be true. My father hid out in his study, emerging to entertain my mother and then lumbering back to his den. He'd come out, blink in the light, and feel his way to the kitchen, as if he'd never been in our front hall before. We avoided dinner conversation by investing heavily in frozen foods. He'd stay with my mother from five to six, reading to her from the *National Enquirer,* all the Liz Taylor stories, and then I'd take over the chitchat brigade while he drank bourbon and soda and nuked a Healthy Choice. The nurse's aide went home at five, and my father and I agreed we could save money by not getting another aide until the late shift. Six terrifying hours every night. While my mother rested a little, if the pain wasn't too bad, I'd go down to the empty kitchen and toast a couple of apple-cinnamon Pop-Tarts. Sometimes I'd smoke a joint and eat the whole box. If my father's door was open, I'd sit in the hall outside and wait until the sharp, woody smell brought him out shaking his head like a bloodied stag; we didn't have the energy to really fight. More often than not, we'd end up back in the brown fog of his study, me taking a few last puffs with my legs thrown over his big leather armchair, my father sipping his bourbon and staring out at the backyard. I ate Cheez Doodles most of the night, leaving oval orange prints all over the house. We took turns sitting with my mother until eleven. I watched the clock. One night I woke up on the floor of my mother's room, my feet tangled in the dust ruffle. I could see my father's black shoes sticking out on the other side of the bed, gleaming in the moonlight. He'd fallen asleep on the floor too, his arms wrapped around my mother's cross-stitch pillow, the one that said "If you can't say anything nice, come sit by me." I don't know what happened to the aide that night. By morning I was under my father's old wool bathrobe and he was gone.

On her last good days, in March and April, I helped my mother paint a little. She always said I had a great eye but no hand. But my hands were all she had then, and she guided me for the bigger strokes. It was like being a kid again, sitting down at our dining room table covered over with a dozen sheets of slippery tan drawing paper.

And I said, "Mommy, I can't make a fish, not a really *fishy* one." And she told me to see it, to think it, to feel its movements in my hand. In my mind it glistened and flipped its adorable lavender tail through bubbling rainbows (I saw *Fantasia* four times), but on paper all I had were two big purple marks and two small scribbles where I wanted fins. She laid her big, square hand over mine lightly, like a magic cloak, and the crayons glided over the paper and the fish flipped its tail and even blew me a kiss from its hot-pink Betty Boop lips. And I was so happy that her hand could do what my mind could see.

By the end of June, though, she stopped trying to have me do the same for her. We just sat, and I'd bring in paintings from the year before, or even five years before, to give her something new to look at. And we looked hard, for hours, at the last painting she'd done on her own, not a sketch or an exercise, a finished piece called *Lot's Wife*. The sky was grays and blues, beginning to storm, and in the foreground, in the barren landscape, was a shrouded figure. Or it could have been just the upright shroud itself, or a woman in a full-length muslin wrap. But the body was no longer alive; it had set into something dense and immobile. And far off to the right, bright and grim, were the little sticky flames of the destroyed city, nothing, not even rubble, around it.

"It's so sad," I complained to my mother.   10

"Is it?" She hardly talked anymore; she didn't argue; she didn't command. She never said, "Can I make a suggestion?" A few requests for nothing much, mostly silence. She took a deep breath. "Look again. The sky is so full and there is so much happening." She looked cross and disappointed in my perception until she closed her eyes and then she just looked tired.

My graduation was the next day, and it went about the way I expected. I overslept. My father overslept. The aide didn't wake us when she left. I didn't even open my eyes until Kay called me from the pay phone at school. I told her I didn't know if I could get there on time. I didn't know if I wanted to. I asked my father, who shrugged. He was still half asleep on his couch.

"I don't know if you want to go, Della. I suppose you should. I could come if you like."

My father was, and is, a very quiet man, but he wasn't always like *that*. This past year she took the life right out of him. I have spent one whole year of my life with a dying woman and a ghost.

I went, in my boxer shorts and ratty T-shirt, and until I saw all the girls   15 slipping their blue robes down over off-the-shoulder clouds of pink and white, I forgot that we were supposed to look nice. Kay flattened my hair with spit, stuck my mortarboard on my head, and elbowed me into our section (Barstow, Belfer). In our class picture there are five rows of dyed-to-match silk shoes and polished loafers and a few pairs of sneakers and my ten dirty toes. I didn't win any prizes either, which I might have if I hadn't been absent for fifty-seven days my senior year.

Kay's parents, who are extremely normal, dropped me off on their way home to Kay's graduation party. Mrs. Belfer showed me the napkins with Kay's name flowing across in deep blue script, and she reached into the bag on the front seat to show me the blue-and-white-striped plastic glasses and the white Chinet plates.

"Send our. . . . Tell your father we're thinking of you all," Mrs. Belfer said. Kay and I had made sure our parents didn't know each other, and even when my mother was okay, she was not the kind of person to bond with other mothers.

My father made room for me on the porch swing. He ran one finger over the back of my hand, and then he folded his arms around his chest.

"How'd it go?"

"Okay. Mr. Switzer says hi." Mr. Switzer was my ninth-grade algebra teacher. 20 He used to play chess with my father, when we had people over.

"That's nice. You were a hell of a chess player a few years ago. Eight years ago."

I didn't even remember playing chess; my father hadn't taken the set out for ages, and when he did, he didn't ask me to play, he just polished the marble pieces and rubbed a chamois cloth over the board. My mother got him that set in Greece, on their honeymoon.

"Eight years ago I was a chess player?"

My father shut his eyes. "I taught you when you were five. Your mother thought I was crazy, but she was wrong. You were good, you got the structure immediately. We played for a few years, until you were in fourth grade."

"What happened?" I saw him sitting across from me, thinner, with more 25 brown hair. We were on the living room floor, a little bowl of lemon drops between us. My mother was cooking chicken in the big red wok, and the chess pieces were gray-and-white soldiers. My queen was gray with one white stripe for her crown.

"Mommy got sick, the first time. You don't remember?"

I didn't say anything.

"You don't have to remember, Della. We don't even have to talk about this now. Your mother says, your mother used to say, that I don't say what needs to be said."

He put his head back, and I did too. We looked up at the old hornet's nest in the corner of the porch.

"Car accidents or no, she's going to die. She is going to leave us to live this 30 life. Even if I am blind drunk and you are dead in a ditch, she is still going."

The swing creaked, and I watched our feet flip back and forth, long, skinny feet, like our hands.

"The aide's leaving. Let's go upstairs. It'll be a treat for your mother, two for the price of one."

"I'll stay here."

His fingers left five red marks on my arm, which bruises up at nothing.

"Please come." 35

The swing rocked forward, free of us, and I followed him.

When she died that night, I wrapped the painting of Lot's wife in an old sheet and hid it in the closet, behind my winter boots. My father said it was mine. We sprinkled her ashes at the Devil's Hopyard.

My father began tucking me in, for the first time in years. He did it for weeks. We still hadn't really cleaned up, not ourselves, not the house. My father stepped over my CDs and cleared a space for himself on my bed. He said, "It's a little late for bedtime stories, I guess."

"Tell me about Mommy."

"All right," he said. "Ask me something. Ask me anything." 40

"Anything?" I didn't even know how many siblings my father had, and now I could ask him anything?

My father put the bottle of Jack Daniel's on the floor and rubbed my feet. "Cast discretion to the winds, Della."

"Why did Mommy get cancer?"

"I have no idea. I'm sorry. Next?"

"Did Mommy mind your drinking?" 45

"Not very much. I don't think I drank too much when she was well, do you?"

"I don't remember. Next. Were you and Mommy virgins when you got married?"

My father laughed so hard he stamped his feet up and down and wiped his eyes.

"Christ on a crutch, no. Your mother had had a dozen lovers before me — I think a dozen. She may have rounded down to the nearest bearable number. I was a callow youth, you know, I didn't really appreciate that being last was much, much better than being first. And I had slept with two very patient girls when I was at Swarthmore. Slept with. Lain down with for a few afternoons. Sorry. Too much?"

"Was it great, with Mommy?" I said this into my pillow. 50

My father pushed the pillow away from my ears. "It was great. It was not always fireworks, but it was great, and when it was fireworks —"

"She rocked your world."

My father patted my feet again. "That's right. That's a great expression. She rocked my world."

I still don't know where to hang the picture. My father says no room in our house is right for it. We don't want it to be in a museum. I unwrap it at night and prop it up next to my bed and fall asleep with my hand on the clean canvas edge, and I smell the oil and the wood frame, and I smell salt.

CONNECTIONS TO OTHER SELECTIONS

1. Compare the narrator of "Hold Tight" and the narrator of Alice Munro's "An Ounce of Cure" (p. 451). To what extent do you think that their emotional lives are similar despite the obvious differences in their circumstances?

2. How does the significance of the mother's painting, *Lot's Wife*, compare with the meanings associated with that biblical story in Anna Ahkmatova's poem "Lot's Wife" (p. 1198)?

3. Compare Della's relationship with her father in "Hold Tight" with the speaker's relationship with her father in Margaret Atwood's poem "Bored" (p. 735).

JOYCE CAROL OATES (B. 1938)

A biographical note for Joyce Carol Oates appears on page 200, before her story "The Lady with the Pet Dog." In "The Night Nurse" Oates presents a tense encounter during an unexpected medical emergency.

The Night Nurse   1993

Don't doubt there's a future. Rushing toward you.

It was flat pavement, a busy pedestrian mall between downtown streets where she was walking in the tattered sunshine of a moist April morning when without warning the sidewalk tilted to her left, and a sharp pain like a wasp's stinging attacked the calf of her left leg. Wide-eyed and astonished, too surprised at this time to be frightened, she did not scream. She was not the kind of person to scream, especially in a public place.

She fell heavily on her side. Her glasses went flying, her handsome leather handbag dropped from her fingers, the side of her face struck concrete. Her immediate thought was *I've been shot.* The pain was so sudden and so absolute.

Strangers hurried to help. They seemed, to the stricken woman, to be materializing out of the air, with remarkable swiftness and kindness. Afterward she would count herself lucky that she was a well-dressed, well-groomed Caucasian woman stricken in this particular pedestrian mall with its Bonwit's, its Waldenbooks, its gourmet food store and pricey boutiques, and not elsewhere on the fringes of downtown. She was lucky that her handbag wasn't taken from her in the confusion of her fall and that strangers perceived her as one of their kind and not someone diseased, homeless, threatening.

She would remember little of her collapse afterward except its suddenness.   5
And the terrible helplessness of her body fallen to the pavement. An ambulance arrived, its deafening siren translating to her confused brain as a lurid neon-red color. White-clad youngish medics examined her, lifted her onto a stretcher. As in a dream she was being borne aloft. A crowd of curious, snatching eyes parted for her. Alive? Dead? Dying? No one, least of all the stricken woman, seemed to know.

And in the speeding ambulance delirious with pain and mounting terror, an incandescent bulb of pain in her left leg just below the knee but still she did not scream biting her lips to keep from screaming and thinking even at this time *I am behaving well, look how calm and civilized.* Then she was being carried into a room glaring with laser-lights, again the quick purposeful hands of strangers probed her, her blood pressure was taken and blood extracted from her limp arm and her voice faltered trying to explain to someone she could not see what had happened to her, the pain in her leg more terrible than any pain she'd known, and a tightness in her chest and shortness of breath but she did not break down sobbing nor did she ask *Am I dying? Will I die?* nor did she beg *Save me!* Her name was Grace Burkhardt and she was forty-four years old and she was a woman accustomed, as the chief administrator of a state arts council, to exercising authority but she seemed to remember none of these external facts as if they applied not to her but to another person and that person a stranger to her. She wanted to explain *I am in good health, I can't believe this has happened to me* as if to repudiate responsibility but she was fainting and could not speak. They would check her identification, they would contact her nearest-of-kin, they would rush her into surgery and all this would be done apart from her volition and so there was a perverse comfort in that — in knowing that, if she died, now, it would not be her fault.

Of course they saved her. Emergency surgery for a "massive" blood clot in her leg which, had it broken free and been carried to her heart, would have resulted in a pulmonary embolism. Grace Burkhardt, dead at the age of forty-four never regaining consciousness even to realize the future had been condensed into the present tense and all was over.

By degrees she woke moaning in the post-op room not knowing where she was but knowing that this was a place strange and frightening to her. And so cold! — she was shivering, her teeth chattering. She experienced a sensation of utter sick helplessness as if she were paralyzed. She could not recall the surgery, or having collapsed. She could not recall if she had been saved from death or was even now being prepared for death. Her vision was blurred as if she were underwater. A face floated near, a stranger's face that was at the same time familiar as a lost sister's.

Help me! she begged the face. *I'm so cold, I'm so frightened!*

The face was a woman's. The features were indistinct but the skin was 10 strangely flushed and shiny, like something not quite fully hatched. There was a smile, thin-lipped and tentative. No-color eyes. *Don't leave me, help! I'm so frightened!* Grace Burkhardt begged as like a large bubble playful and elusive the face rose, lifted lighter than air to disappear through the invisible ceiling.

Her nearest-of-kin was a married, older sister who drove forty miles from Rochester to be with her, staying through much of the day. As news of her "emergency surgery" spread among friends, acquaintances, colleagues at the arts council, there were telephone calls and the first of the floral deliveries. The public self, the self that was Grace Burkhardt, and not this woman in a hospital bed hooked to an IV gurney, her left leg raised and immobile swathed in bandages, struggled to emerge. You could not have guessed that Grace Burkhardt had survived a life-threatening collapse for, on the phone, she was wry, ironic, slightly embarrassed, determined to minimalize her condition. Her eyes were ringed with fatigue, her skin waxy-white, yet her voice maintained its usual timbre, or almost. Nothing meant more to her than to take back the control she'd lost back there in the pedestrian mall, to tell her story as if it were her own. For it was her own. *You wouldn't believe it! So suddenly. Yes, this morning. Yes, downtown. By ambulance. No, no warning. Yes, vascular surgery. A Dr. Rodman, do you know him? Yes, I'm lucky. I know. If it had to happen at all.*

Her sister finally took the telephone from her. She was protesting but too weak to prevail. Her head rang like the interior of a giant seashell. The pain in her leg was a balloon floating at a little distance from her — recognizable as her own, yet not *her. My name is Grace Burkhardt, my name is Grace Burkhardt* believing that this fact would save her. If anything would save her.

A powerful anti-coagulant drug was dripping into her veins to forestall more blood clots — that would save her.

The telephone messages. Daffodils, hyacinth, narcissus from the arts council staff, a potted pink azalea from a woman friend, another potted azalea so vividly crimson she could not look directly at it — these would save her. And the vascular surgeon who'd operated on her and saved her life, who came by the room to speak with her and with her sister. And her own doctor, an internist associated with the hospital who also dropped by on his rounds. And medical insurance forms, with which her sister helped her, and which, in a frail spidery hand, she signed. *You see? I'm fine, my mind hasn't been affected at all.*

And abruptly then, the day ended. This day that stretched dreamlike behind 15 Grace Burkhardt as if to the very horizon to a region she could not see, nor even recall. It was evening, and she was alone. A nurse came to examine her and to give her a barbiturate, a nurse's aide, a young cocoa-skinned woman, came to take away her bedpan discreetly covered with an aluminum lid, the light in her room was switched off. She called her sister's name not seeming to recall her sister's actual departure. Now alone, with no witness to admire her bravery, she tasted panic. Her left leg was swollen and stiff encased in bandages and elevated above the bed to reduce the condition the surgeon called "thrombophlebitis" which was the way, she understood, that death would enter her. The crepey-soft interior of her right elbow stung with a mysterious IV fluid dripping into a vein. Death would come as a lethal blood clot or death would come as a sudden massive hemorrhage that was the result of anti-coagulant medication. Though the stricken woman had not prayed in more than thirty years her parched lips moved silently *Help me through the night. Help me through the night.*

She felt a moment's rage at the injustice — that she, a good person, a woman known for her intelligence and her graciousness and her dependability in all things, a woman so widely liked, yes and respected, should be in this position, a life-threatening position. And trapped.

Help me through the night dear God, oh please!

As mercifully the contours of the room melted, the floor sank into darkness as into a pit, the powerful sleeping pill took her.

But then she woke, agitated and open-eyed as if she hadn't slept at all.

As if someone had called her name — "Grace Burkhardt."   20

There was a pinching sensation in her bladder, an urgent need to urinate. And such cold, why was the room so cold? — she woke shivering beneath a freezing sheet, a single-ply flannel blanket. The hospital by night was perceptibly cooler than by day. A ventilator rumbled, drafts of cold air passed over her. She'd been dreaming strangely and hadn't there been birds' wings flapping overhead stirring the air against her face . . .

"Grace Burkhardt."

The door had opened, now the door was closed. Someone had been in the room? — Grace tried to sit up, frightened, but was nearly immobilized. A sudden movement awakened pain, her heart's panicked throbbing that was pain, a sharp stinging in her right arm. Her eyes, mildly myopic, dulled with medication, moved blinking in the dark, this was an unfamiliar dark, she understood it was not her bedroom in her home nor any bedroom in her memory. The smell of disinfectant, the ventilator smell. The compression of space that was the size of a cell. She stared at the door a few yards away seeing a rim of light beneath it. For some moments she tried to remember where she was, and why such discomfort and pain, her leg elevated and held fast, her heartbeat so accelerated. As if pulling out of the dark a tangled dream of such complexity, the very effort was exhausting. She heard herself moan but the sound seemed to come from another part of the room. It was self-pity, it was terror and animal pain, it was not *her. I almost died, I'm in the hospital. I'm alone.* Struggling to sit up, to raise her head which swayed dangerously heavy on her shoulders, in a sudden mad terror of choking on her own tears and saliva and the mucus rapidly forming in her sinuses.

She fumbled to switch on her bedside light. Her sister had bought a traveler's digital clock in the gift shop downstairs — it was 2:55 A.M. She would never get through the night.

Yet she tried to calm herself. She was a patient in an excellent suburban   25
hospital, she could not possibly be in danger of dying. *Help me! Help me I'm
alone* but she rang the bedside buzzer because she desperately needed a bedpan. The barbiturate had apparently knocked her out so completely, at 8:30
P.M., she hadn't wakened until the need to urinate was painful. And she needed
an extra blanket. She rang the buzzer as she'd been instructed earlier to ring it
and waited and there was no reply over the intercom so she rang it again and
still there was no reply and so she counted twenty before ringing it again *Where
are you? Isn't anyone there? Please help me* and this time a voice, a female voice,
sounded over the intercom asking curtly what did she want and she explained
her needs as clearly and politely as possible and the voice mumbled what
sounded like *Yes ma'am* and was gone.

And now she waited. Waited and waited. It was three A.M., it was 3:10 A.M.,
it was 3:16 A.M. She could not get a comfortable position in the bed, her bladder
so stricken, her leg at such an angle. Each second was agony. She tried to contract her lower body, her loins, as, as a small child, she'd tried to hold in the
warm pee by pressing her thighs as tightly together as possible and not moving, hardly breathing. If she had an accident, urinating in the bed! — if that
happened! All her life's history, all the striving of her very soul — to come to
that. She felt a helpless child-anxiety she hadn't recalled for nearly forty years.
The child-anxiety deep in the body of the adult. Remembering the agony of
being trapped in some place (in the car, her father driving and unwilling to
stop; in school assembly where she would have had to push her way out over
the legs of her classmates enduring their jeering attention and the annoyance
of her teacher) unable to get to a bathroom. The shame of it. The helplessness.

She rang the buzzer another, protracted time. Just as, thank God, the door
was pushed open, and a nurse entered carrying a bedpan.

The night nurse, so short as to seem almost dwarfish. Hardly five feet tall. But
round-bodied, with a moon face, peculiar flushed skin that was smooth and
shiny as scar tissue; small close-set damp eyes; a thin pursed mouth. At a first
glance the nurse might appear young but closer up she was obviously middle-
aged, her eyes bracketed by fine white creases. "Here, lift up, like this, come
on —" she issued instructions to the patient not so much coldly as mechanically, shoving the enamel bedpan beneath her buttocks, pulling down but not
replacing the covers. Her manner was brisk and on the edge of impatience as if
she and the patient had gone through this routine many times already and
there was no need for coyness.

Grace's teeth were chattering with cold. She whispered, flinching under
the nurse's unsmiling stare, "Thank you — very much." She could not help herself but began urinating immediately, as soon as the receptacle was in place,
while the nurse was still in the room, though on her way out, turning away
from Grace as if in disgust. No further words, no questioning of the patient if
she needed anything else, no backwards glance. But Grace Burkhardt trapped
in the bed was so grateful for this awkward receptacle, this adult-size potty, in
which to empty her bursting bladder, she scarcely noticed the nurse's rudeness. If it was rudeness.

Her eyes smarted with the tears of gratitude and humility. Even the pain   30
in her leg seemed to subside. The panicky numbness in her brain. But how
long she urinated, in a gush of scalding liquid, then a thinning stream, ceasing

and beginning again, she did not know. Minutes? Actual minutes? Looking at the clock finally, when the last of the urine dripped from her, she saw it was 3:38 A.M.

Outside the room's single window it was night. Yet not true night for the room, being lighted now, was reflected in the glass; not as in a mirror but dimly, shapes without substance or color.

I could die here in this room. Others have died here.

She'd had a lover once who had been terrified of hospitals. An intelligent man, a reasonable man, yet, on the subject of hospitals, adamantly irrational. Hospitals are seething with germs, hospitals are where you die. Hospitals are where you have to entrust strangers with your life and you pay for the privilege.

A lover, and not a husband. So many years later, Grace could not clearly remember which of them had loved more deeply, which had been more hurt.

Now they lived a thousand miles apart, and kept in touch by telephone, a few times a year. Thank God they no longer had any mutual friends who might tell him of her collapse, her emergency surgery. *Massive blood clot. Risk of embolism.* He knew her as a healthy, independent woman. Not the kind of woman you feel sorry for. 35

Now Grace was finished with the bedpan, and the sharp smell of urine pinched her nostrils, she waited for the night nurse, or an attendant, to come take it away. Surely they knew, at the nurses' station?—she hesitated to ring the buzzer again.

So she waited. It was 3:40 A.M., it was 3:50 A.M. Finally, shyly, she rang the buzzer. There was no reply over the intercom.

Maybe the night nurse was making rounds. Giving medication, checking patients. Maybe, routinely, she would be back in a few minutes. Maybe she would bring an extra blanket.

At four A.M. Grace rang the buzzer again. There was a sound of static or shrill voices, then silence. "Hello? Hello—" her voice was plaintive, faltering.

Could die here in this room. Others have died here. 40

The enamel bedpan was pressing into the soft flesh of her buttocks. The elevation of her leg, and its stiffness, made the pressure more intense.

And how cold the room was—freezing. A continual draft from the window and another, smelling of something dank, metallic, unclean, from the air vent overhead.

In desperation she wondered if she could remove the damned bedpan herself. But set it where? On the bedside table, only a few inches away? And what if she spilled it, as certainly she would?—it was impossible to lift herself and to remove the bedpan at the same time. And now her leg, the entire left side of her body, was throbbing with pain.

She rang the buzzer again, trying not to panic. Though the intercom was dead she begged for help—"Please, can you come? I need medication, I'm in pain. I need a blanket—"

If the night nurse withheld the painkiller from her, what would she do? 45

Don't be absurd. Why would a complete stranger want to hurt you resolved not to give in to panic though she was trapped in this cell of a room in this bed at the mercy of the nursing staff. Whom she knew it would be a mistake to antagonize, especially so early in her hospitalization—Dr. Rodman had told her she might have to be here a week or more, thrombophlebitis is a serious condition. And her sister, meaning well, had told her alarming tales of negligent and even hostile nurses and attendants at big-city hospitals as a way of assuring Grace that here, by contrast, in this suburban hospital, she would receive better treatment.

At night, the hospital seemed very different than it did by day. It was closed to visitors until 8:30 A.M. In a panicked fantasy, Grace imagined a fire, at once she could smell smoke, and she, here, trapped, crippled with pain, paralyzed. If she wrenched her leg free, would its wound be torn open? — would she begin to bleed? She shuddered, whimpering to herself. Trapped! Trapped on a bedpan! It was ludicrous, it was laughable! Her own urine sloshing beneath her, threatening to spill and soak the bed.

She thought she heard the door being opened, the doorknob turning — but no. If there were footsteps out in the corridor they were gone now.

Strange how the hospital was not much quieter at night. A different and more mysterious kind of sound prevailed — a ceaseless churning like a motor turning over, never quite starting; a deeper throbbing like a jazz downbeat, but arhythmic, irregular. Beyond the vibrating of the ventilator there were distant voices. Pleading, crying. *Help me. Help. Me. Help me.* The voices overlapped, drowning one another out.

When she stopped breathing to listen more closely, the voices faded.   50

Grace did not want to think whose voices these were.

It seemed to her that she could feel tiny blood clots forming in her afflicted leg, like rain at the point at which it turns to sleet. If a single one of these clots broke free into her bloodstream it would be carried to her heart, to her pulmonary artery, and kill her.

What it is, what finality — to fall to the ground, on dirty pavement, at the feet of strangers. Grace Burkhardt now knew.

She pressed the buzzer another time. The intercom remained dead.

"Help me! Where are you!"   55

She was agitated, on the brink of hysteria and yet, somehow, she was falling asleep. The room began to shift and lose its contours; the light rapidly fading as if sucked down a drain. The bedpan filled with cooling piss, *her* piss, began to melt, too, its hard enamel warmed by her body. She'd drawn the inadequate covers up to her chin and her eyes were starkly open waiting for the night nurse to return and suddenly she saw — was it possible? — the night nurse *was* back, had been back for some time, evidently? — standing motionless, watching her, just inside the door.

"Grace Burkhardt."

The nurse enunciated these syllables in a flat, nasal, ironic voice.

"Grace Burkhardt."

Grace whispered, frightened, "Yes? Do you know me?"   60

It was as if she'd never heard her own name before. Never heard its strangeness before.

The nurse's thin lips stretched in a smile. Her small close-set eyes shone with the opacity of glass marbles. "Do you know *me*, Grace Burkhardt?"

Grace stared. Quick as a thread pulled through the eye of a needle and out again she *knew* — knew the woman, or knew the girl the woman had been; but she remembered no name; and did not remember that face. She heard herself saying, quickly, "No. I've never been in this hospital before. I've never —" Her voice trailed off weakly.

There was an awkward pause. The nurse continued to stand motionless, arms folded tight across her breasts. Her peculiar shiny-smooth skin that looked like scar tissue, or like something incompletely hatched, was the color of spoiled cantaloupe. Her lips were bemused, childish in derision. "You wouldn't remember, Grace Burkhardt. No, not *you*."

The stricken woman lay trapped in bed. Her stiff throbbing leg, her arm 65 hooked to an IV apparatus. *She's mad, she's come to injure me* though smiling at the nurse, trying to smile. As if this was an ordinary exchange. Or might become so, if she smiled the right way, if she spoke the right words. "I—can't see very well. My glasses—my eyes—*Do* I know you?"

The nurse made a derisive laughing sound though her eyes showed no mirth. She jerked her chin at the bed—"You're finished there, eh? Grace Burkhardt? So you want *me* to take it away?"

Quickly, apologetically, Grace said, "If you would, please—"

"Registered nurses aren't required to touch bedpans."

"Then—an attendant? Could you call one?"

The nurse shook her head slowly. Bemused, disgusted. Still she stood 70 without moving, arms folded across her breasts. In that face, in those eyes, Grace saw—who? It had been years. Half her lifetime. *No! No I don't know you!* She whispered, pleading, "Please, I'm helpless. I need medication, I'm in pain. And this bedpan—"

"*You're* helpless. *You* need help. So what? 'Grace Burkhardt.'"

"Why do you keep saying my name? Do you know me?"

"Why don't you say *my* name? Don't you know *me*?"

Grace stared, and swallowed hard. *I am a good person, I am well-liked, respected.* Recalling how through the years of her career, in her several administrative positions at Wells College, and at the State University at Buffalo, and more recently on the New York State Council of the Arts, she'd been praised for her industry, her fair-mindedness, her diplomacy; her intelligence, her warmth, her inconspicuous competency. Hadn't she overheard, to her embarrassment, just the other day, two young women staff members at the arts council speaking of Grace Burkhardt warmly, comparing her favorably to her male predecessor. *I am an adult now, I am a professional woman, I am no one you know.* Grace heard herself saying in a voice of forced surprise, with a forced smile, "Harriet—? Is it—Zimmer?"

The nurse said curtly, "*Zink*. Harriet *Zink*." 75

"Of course. Harriet *Zink*."

Grace should have exclaimed what a coincidence, after so many years, twenty-five? twenty-six? so you became a nurse after all, you didn't give up, how wonderful, Harriet, I'm happy for you—remembering vaguely that Harriet Zink, one of her roommates for part of her freshman year at the State University at Albany had been enrolled in nursing school. But when she drew breath to speak a wave of nausea swept over her. She whispered, "—Please, I need help. My leg—the pain. And the bedpan—"

As if aroused by the word *pain*, the night nurse became more animated. She came closer to Grace, peering at her curiously, almost hungrily. Grace had not given Harriet Zink a thought, or hardly a thought, in twenty-six years, and now—what an irony! The mere face of Harriet Zink, with that childish moon face, now middle-aged—how repulsive! Grace recalled her ex-roommate's prominent front teeth, the peculiar blush of her skin, her unnerving manner that was both groveling and insolent—oh, unmistakable.

They'd lived on the fourth, top floor of Ailey Hall, one of the older residences south of campus near the university hospital. Entering freshman, class of 1967. They were of the same generation glancing at the other's third finger, left hand, to see if there was a wedding band. Neither wore one.

Harriet Zink was asking in a bright, mock-earnest voice, "How is Jilly Herman?" and Grace Burkhardt had to stop to think, "—Jilly Herman?" and Harriet Zink said impatiently, "Grace Burkhardt's roomie Jilly Herman—how is *she?*" Grace stared at her, perplexed. *I am dreaming this, am I dreaming this* trying not to show the fear she felt as Harriet Zink went on derisively, "The one with the cute blond curls, Jilly Herman," gesturing at her own steely-gray hair with exaggerated wriggly fingers, "—the one with the cute *ass.*"

Grace said, in a faltering voice, "—I haven't seen or heard from Jill Herman in twenty years." Though this was true it sounded weak, like a lie.

Harriet Zink said suspiciously, "You haven't? You expect me to believe that?" When Grace began to protest she cut her off with childish vehemence, "Oh no! I don't believe that! Gracie Burkhardt and Jilly Herman were *best friends.* I bet you still *are.*"

These words were mocking, singsong. Grace tried to maintain her smile which was strained and ghastly against her bared teeth. She explained that, after freshman year, she and Jill went their separate ways, speaking earnestly as if this exchange in the middle of the night in such circumstances was not at all extraordinary but normal, and no occasion for alarm. But Harriet Zink interrupted, "And what about Linda Mecky, and Sandy McGuire, and Dolly Slosson," spitting out these names Grace scarcely recalled, and had hardly given a thought to since graduation, "—Barbara West, Sue Ferguson—" the names of freshman girls who'd roomed on the fourth floor of the old sandstone residence hall in the fall of 1963.

There had been six rooms on the floor, all doubles except for the largest which was a triple to which Grace Burkhardt and Jill Herman and Harriet Zink were assigned. But Harriet Zink didn't arrive on campus until October, twelve days late; there'd been an "emergency crisis" in her family. (The residence advisor hinted that Harriet's mother had died, and there'd been other trouble besides. She warned the girls not to bring up the subject unless Harriet initiated it herself—which she was never to do.) By the time the mysterious Harriet Zink arrived at Ailey Hall, friendships and alliances had been formed among the fourth-floor girls in that quick, desperate way in which such relationships are formed in new, disorienting surroundings. There had not seemed space enough for another girl. There had not seemed any need for another girl. And there was the problem, too, of Harriet Zink.

I tried to be nice to you. I did what I could. How am I to blame.

Harriet Zink was demanding to know what of these other girls, and Grace Burkhardt was trying to explain she really knew nothing of them, she wasn't in contact with any of them, but Harriet Zink seemed not to believe her, and angry that she should be lying. Grace tried to explain that most of them had only been friends during freshman year and that had been a kind of accident, stuck away on the top floor of Ailey Hall so far from the center of campus life, she tried to evoke the shabby comedy of Ailey Hall with its falling plaster and its leaky windows and its cockroaches, but Harriet Zink kept interrupting, pursuing her own line of inquiry. "Do you remember what you did to me? You, and your friends?" Her face was heated and her small eyes brightly moist. There were half-moons of perspiration beneath the arms of her snug-fitting white nylon uniform and Grace remembered across the abyss of twenty-six years a snug-fitting clumsily homemade red plaid jumper of Harriet Zink's whose underarms were permanently stained. "Don't say you don't remember, Grace Burkhardt!"

Grace frowned, innocently perplexed. She was miserable in her bed, her leg pounding in pain, her head pounding, and, dear God, the sharp smell of urine penetrating the covers, had she spilled some of the urine into the bed, she bit her lip to keep from sobbing *I must not let her see I'm afraid of her, I must stay calm* shaking her head saying, "No, please, Harriet, I don't—" which brought the angry little woman closer to the bed, how like a dwarf she was, so short, and stouter now than she'd been at the age of eighteen, her face rounder, puffier, and that mouth made you think of a slug, always moving, working. Harriet Zink said in a tone of near-dignity, "I remember. I still dream about it sometimes."

Grace said softly, "Harriet, I'm sorry."

"Huh! How can you be sorry, if you don't remember?"

"Please, I'm in pain. If you could help me—"   90

"*I* was in pain. You didn't help *me*."

"—I need medication. Painkiller. Please. And this bedpan—please could you take it away—"

"I told you: registered nurses aren't required to take away bedpans. That's not our job."

You never took showers or baths. You wore your clothes until they were filthy. You smelled. You stank. You cried yourself to sleep every night. How am I to blame! Grace knew, yet didn't know: couldn't quite remember. It was so long ago, it was like a bad dream, not her own dream but another's. What exactly had happened between the time Harriet Zink, who like Grace Burkhardt was from a farming family in the central part of the state, and the weekend before Thanksgiving when she moved out of Ailey Hall, dropped out of nursing school. Disappeared. *I tried to be nice to you. I did what I could. How am I to blame!*

In a lowered, quavering voice Harriet Zink was saying, "You and Jill Her-   95
man, you wouldn't talk to me. I'd be there in the room and you'd send each other signals. Look right through me. Like I was dirt. If I came into the lounge you'd all stop talking and make like there was a bad smell. If I came into the cafeteria where you were all sitting you'd look away and freeze me out. You knew about my mother and how I cried at night and that was funny to you wasn't it. Everything about me was funny to you wasn't it. I was late starting classes and behind on all my work and you could see how scared I was, I couldn't sleep and I couldn't keep food down and all of you knew it, all twelve of you, but it was just a joke to you wasn't it—that I wanted to die."

Grace Burkhardt could not believe what she was hearing. She said, weakly, "Not me, Harriet. Not me. I tried—"

"Oh sure! You'd say to them sometimes, 'Let her alone.' Once in the downstairs lounge when they were laughing together you said to them, 'That's enough, it isn't funny, let her alone.' But you wouldn't say my name. You wouldn't ever say my name. It was like I was *it* to you. You wouldn't look at me even when we were alone together and if I talked to you, you'd just mumble something back and walk away. I could see in your face you felt sorry for me, sure, you pitied me like a leper, you thought you were so much better than me, you, 'Grace Burkhardt'! You tried to stop them from the worst of what they did but you didn't try hard *enough*."

"Harriet, I'm sorry. We were so young, then — so ignorant."

"You weren't ignorant. *You* were a scholarship student."

"We didn't mean to be cruel —"   100

"Yes you did! You meant to be cruel," Harriet Zink said, with angry satisfaction. "It made you happy, all of you, to be cruel."

"Harriet, no —"

Harriet Zink continued speaking in her low, accusing voice, her face now brightly flushed, recounting incidents Grace Burkhardt had long since forgotten, if indeed she'd ever known. She tried to remember how long pathetic Harriet Zink had actually roomed with her and Jill Herman before moving downstairs to a single room near the resident advisor's suite — that room kept in readiness for just such an emergency. *Yes, it's so. It made us happy. Our cruelty. Our loathing for the true freak among us.* After Harriet Zink dropped out of school, having failed more of her midterms, the girls of the fourth floor, including several nursing students to whom she'd been a particular embarrassment, had not missed her. Or, if they missed her, they did not dwell upon her absence. They did not consider its significance. It had nothing to do with them, did it? — *they* were normal, *they* were adjusting to college life. After Harriet Zink moved out of their room Grace and Jill cleaned it as they'd never cleaned it before, exhilarated, singing along with the Kingston Trio whose hit record Jill played repeatedly on her turntable, airing out the room, windows open to a bright dry autumn day, a breeze lifting papers on their desks. Gaily they vacuumed, they scrubbed. Their door was wide open to welcome their friends. *Sad to say, I'm on my way, won't be back for many a day* but their lifted voices, their shining eyes, were anything but sad. The third desk, in the corner, was bare. The third bed, beneath the tilt of the eave, was bare. Later, Grace would cover the bed with a beautiful afghan quilt knitted by her grandmother. The third desk was used by both girls. They were particularly grateful for the extra closet space.

Now Harriet Zink, middle-aged, squat body in her nurse's uniform solid as a little barrel, was leaning over Grace Burkhardt in her bed, saying, in disgust, "'Grace Burkhardt' — you were the evil one among them because you were the one who *knew.* I could see it in your face. And right now! You knew, but you wouldn't help me, you wouldn't be my friend."

Grace said stammering, "Harriet, I'm — I didn't —" her eyes brimming   105
with tears of shame, "— forgive me!" She was so frightened she'd leaned away from the angry woman and caused the IV needle to pop out of her vein.

There was a pause. Harriet Zink stared at Grace, leaning so close over her that Grace could see specks of hazel in the iris of her eyes; a glimmer of gold fillings in her mouth. Harriet was breathing harshly, like an overweight woman who has climbed a stairs too quickly. Yet her expression shifted suddenly, turned unexpectedly thoughtful. She said, with the air of one making a discovery, "Yes, I can forgive you, Grace Burkhardt. I'm a Christian woman. In my heart I'm empowered to forgive." She nodded gravely, as if, not knowing until this instant what she'd intended, what she would do, she was taking pleasure in it. "When I saw you here, Grace Burkhardt, and I thought, 'Am I strong enough to forgive that woman? Even with Jesus' help, am I strong enough?' I didn't know. But now I know. I *am* strong enough, I *can* forgive." She spoke with such sudden pride, it was as if sunshine flooded the room.

In this way, as a terrified Grace Burkhardt would not have anticipated, the siege ended.

* * *

For a long time after the night nurse left the room Grace lay unmoving too shocked to think even *How am I to blame! I tried, I did try* incredulous thinking *Evil—me? Of all people—me? The woman is a religious maniac.* She was too agitated to sleep yet somehow must have slept if only briefly and then waking opening her eyes wide and amazed that it was still night? still night? when in her dream she'd been staring into the sun as if in penance and her eyes were seared and aching.

She struggled to sit up. She could breathe better, sitting up. Her leg throbbed with pain, pain was like a wave that washed over her and through her leaving her exhausted but wakeful. The bedside lamp was still on. She'd thought the night nurse had turned it off. In the room's single window flat, ghostly reflections floated. She could not identify her own among them.

The night nurse, after her mad outburst, had treated Grace Burkhardt kindly. Or, if not kindly, with a brisk businesslike efficiency. She'd replaced the needle in Grace's bruised right arm, and saw that the IV fluid was dripping into her vein. She called an aide, a young black girl, to bring an extra blanket and to carry away, at last, the bedpan. But, as she explained, she could not give Grace any of the painkiller Oxycodone prescribed for her by Dr. Rodman because the next dosage was scheduled for seven A.M. By that time the day staff would be on duty and another nurse would take care of her. Thank you, Grace murmured, thank you so much, Harriet, humbled and grateful as a chastened child but the night nurse merely shrugged as if embarrassed and then she was gone.

It was only 4:54 A.M. The extra blanket seemed not to make much difference—Grace was still shivering, the room was still very cold. There was a smell of something close, damp, unclean like mold. There was a faint smell of urine. *Help me, help* but Grace had already rung the buzzer and she understood that she'd already been helped and that there was no more help. She decided to sit up sleepless through the remainder of this terrible night though believing, with the resigned half-humor of the damned, that it would never end. Never would it be dawn and never the miraculous hour of seven A.M. and a respite from pain. Thinking, *I am not that strong. I am not evil, but I am not that strong. In her place, I could not forgive.* When she looked at the little digital clock her sister had brought her she saw it was 4:56 A.M.

CONNECTIONS TO OTHER SELECTIONS

1. Discuss the effects of the settings in "The Night Nurse" and Hawthorne's "Young Goodman Brown" (p. 331). Pay particular attention to how the night is treated.
2. Write an essay comparing the protagonist's sense of herself as a human being in "The Night Nurse" and in Susan Minot's "Lust" (p. 304).

E. ANNIE PROULX (B. 1935)

Edna Annie Proulx was born in 1935 and did not finish her first book until 1988. She received a B.A. from the University of Vermont in 1969 and a master's degree from Sir George Williams University, both in history, and later became a free-lance writer of articles for magazines in the United States.

She published short stories occasionally until she had enough to make her first collection, *Heart Songs and Other Stories* (1988), which she followed with the novel *Postcards* in 1992. Her breakthrough novel was *The Shipping News* (1993), which won both the Pulitzer Prize and the National Book Award, and she has since produced another novel, *Accordion Crimes* (1996), and a book of short stories, *Close Range: Wyoming Stories*. Setting her works in places as distant as Newfoundland and Wyoming, Proulx conveys her dark, comic stories by creating a strong sense of place, using her talent for keen detail and for reproducing the peculiarities of local speech.

Web   *Research E. Annie Proulx with LitLinks at*
http://www.bedfordstmartins.com/meyer/bedintrolit

55 Miles to the Gas Pump   *1999*

Rancher Croom in handmade boots and filthy hat, that walleyed cattleman, stray hairs like curling fiddle string ends, that warm-handed, quick-foot dancer on splintery boards or down the cellar stairs to a rack of bottles of his own strange beer, yeasty, cloudy, bursting out in garlands of foam, Rancher Croom at night galloping drunk over the dark plain, turning off at a place he knows to arrive at a canyon brink where he dismounts and looks down on tumbled rock, waits, then steps out, parting the air with his last roar, sleeves surging up windmill arms, jeans riding over boot tops, but before he hits he rises again to the top of the cliff like a cork in a bucket of milk.

Mrs. Croom on the roof with a saw cutting a hole into the attic where she has not been for twelve years thanks to old Croom's padlocks and warnings, whets to her desire, and the sweat flies as she exchanges the saw for a chisel and hammer until a ragged slab of peak is free and she can see inside: just as she thought: the corpses of Mr. Croom's paramours — she recognizes them from their photographs in the paper: MISSING WOMAN — some desiccated as jerky and much the same color, some moldy from lying beneath roof leaks, and all of them used hard, covered with tarry handprints, the marks of boot heels, some bright blue with the remnants of paint used on the shutters years ago, one wrapped in newspaper nipple to knee.

When you live a long way out you make your own fun.

CONNECTIONS TO OTHER SELECTIONS

1. Despite their brevity, how do "55 Miles to the Gas Pump" and Raymond Carver's "Popular Mechanics" (p. 286) manage to create compelling fictional worlds?

2. Compare Proulx's treatment of the West to Stephen Crane's in "The Bride Comes to Yellow Sky" (p. 251).

3. Consider the use of irony in Proulx's story and in Mark Twain's "The Story of the Good Little Boy" (p. 603). Explain why you find the endings of the stories similar or different in tone.

POETRY

The Elements of Poetry

20

Reading Poetry

READING POETRY RESPONSIVELY

Perhaps the best way to begin reading poetry responsively is not to allow yourself to be intimidated by it. Come to it, initially at least, the way you might listen to a song on the radio. You probably listen to a song several times before you hear it all, before you have a sense of how it works, where it's going, and how it gets there. You don't worry about analyzing a song when you listen to it, even though after repeated experiences with it you know and anticipate a favorite part and know, on some level, why it works for you. Give yourself a chance to respond to poetry. The hardest work has already been done by the poet, so all you need to do at the start is listen for the pleasure produced by the poet's arrangement of words.

Try reading the following poem aloud. Read it aloud before you read it silently. You may stumble once or twice, but you'll make sense of it if you pay attention to its punctuation and don't stop at the end of every line where there is no punctuation. The title gives you an initial sense of what the poem is about.

MARGE PIERCY (B. 1936)

The Secretary Chant   1973

My hips are a desk.
From my ears hang
chains of paper clips.
Rubber bands form my hair.
My breasts are wells of mimeograph ink.   5
My feet bear casters.
Buzz. Click.
My head is a badly organized file.

My head is a switchboard
where crossed lines crackle.
Press my fingers
and in my eyes appear
credit and debit.
Zing. Tinkle.
My navel is a reject button.
From my mouth issue canceled reams.
Swollen, heavy, rectangular
I am about to be delivered
of a baby
Xerox machine.
File me under W
because I wonce
was
a woman.

What is your response to this secretary's chant? The point is simple enough—she feels dehumanized by her office functions—but the pleasures are manifold. Piercy makes the speaker's voice sound mechanical by using short bursts of sound and by having her make repetitive, flat, matter-of-fact statements ("My breasts . . . My feet . . . My head . . . My navel"). "The Secretary Chant" makes a serious statement about how such women are reduced to functionaries. The point is made, however, with humor since we are asked to visualize the misappropriation of the secretary's body—her identity—as it is transformed into little more than a piece of office equipment, which seems to be breaking down in the final lines, when we learn that she "wonce / was / a woman." Is there the slightest hint of something subversive in this misspelling of "wonce"? Maybe so, but the humor is clear enough, particularly if you try to make a drawing of what this dehumanized secretary has become.

The next poem creates a different kind of mood. Think about the title, "Those Winter Sundays," before you begin reading the poem. What associations do you have with winter Sundays? What emotions does the phrase evoke in you?

ROBERT HAYDEN (1913–1980)

Those Winter Sundays   1962

Sundays too my father got up early
and put his clothes on in the blueblack cold,
then with cracked hands that ached
from labor in the weekday weather made
banked fires blaze. No one ever thanked him.

I'd wake and hear the cold splintering, breaking.
When the rooms were warm, he'd call,
and slowly I would rise and dress,
fearing the chronic angers of that house,

Speaking indifferently to him,   10
who had driven out the cold
and polished my good shoes as well.
What did I know, what did I know
of love's austere and lonely offices?

Does the poem match the feelings you have about winter Sundays? Either way your response can be useful in reading the poem. For most of us Sundays are days at home; they might be cozy and pleasant experiences or they might be dull and depressing. Whatever they are, Sundays are more evocative than, say, Tuesdays. Hayden uses that response to call forth a sense of missed opportunity in the poem. The person who reflects on those winter Sundays didn't know until much later how much he had to thank his father for "love's austere and lonely offices." This is a poem about a cold past and a present reverence for his father — elements brought together by the phrase "Winter Sundays." *His* father? You may have noticed that the poem doesn't use a masculine pronoun; hence the voice could be a woman's. Does the sex of the voice make any difference to your reading? Would it make any difference about which details are included or what language is used?

What is most important about your initial readings of a poem is that you ask questions. If you read responsively, you'll find yourself asking all kinds of questions about the words, descriptions, sounds, and structures of a poem. The specifics of those questions will be generated by the particular poem. We don't, for example, ask how humor is achieved in "Those Winter Sundays" because there is none, but it is worth asking what kind of tone is established by the description of "the chronic angers of that house." The remaining chapters in this part will help you to formulate and answer questions about a variety of specific elements in poetry, such as speaker, image, metaphor, symbol, rhyme, and rhythm. For the moment, however, read the following poem several times and note your response at different points in the poem. Then write down a half dozen or so questions about what produces your response to the poem. To answer questions, it's best to know first what the questions are, and that's what the rest of this chapter is about.

JOHN UPDIKE (B. 1932)

Dog's Death   *1969*

She must have been kicked unseen or brushed by a car.
Too young to know much, she was beginning to learn
To use the newspapers spread on the kitchen floor
And to win, wetting there, the words, "Good dog! Good dog!"

We thought her shy malaise was a shot reaction.   5
The autopsy disclosed a rupture in her liver.
As we teased her with play, blood was filling her skin
And her heart was learning to lie down forever.

Monday morning, as the children were noisily fed
And sent to school, she crawled beneath the youngest's bed.   10
We found her twisted and limp but still alive.
In the car to the vet's, on my lap, she tried

To bite my hand and died. I stroked her warm fur
And my wife called in a voice imperious with tears.
Though surrounded by love that would have upheld her,   15
Nevertheless she sank and, stiffening, disappeared.

Back home, we found that in the night her frame,
Drawing near to dissolution, had endured the shame
Of diarrhoea and had dragged across the floor
To a newspaper carelessly left there. *Good dog.*   20

Here's a simple question to get started with your own questions: what would its effect have been if Updike had titled the poem "Good Dog" instead of "Dog's Death"?

THE PLEASURE OF WORDS

The impulse to create and appreciate poetry is as basic to human experience as language itself. Although no one can point to the precise origins of poetry, it is one of the most ancient of the arts, because it has existed ever since human beings discovered pleasure in language. The tribal ceremonies of peoples without written languages suggest that the earliest primitive cultures incorporated rhythmic patterns of words into their rituals. These chants, very likely accompanied by the music of a simple beat and the dance of a measured step, expressed what people regarded as significant and memorable in their lives. They echoed the concerns of the chanters and the listeners by chronicling acts of bravery, fearsome foes, natural disasters, mysterious events, births, deaths, and whatever else brought people pain or pleasure, bewilderment or revelation. Later cultures, such as the ancient Greeks, made poetry an integral part of religion.

Thus, from its very beginnings, poetry has been associated with what has mattered most to people. These concerns — whether natural or supernatural — can, of course, be expressed without vivid images, rhythmic patterns, and pleasing sounds, but human beings have always sensed a magic in words that goes beyond rational, logical understanding. Poetry is not simply a method of communication; it is a unique experience in itself.

What is special about poetry? What makes it valuable? Why should we read it? How is reading it different from reading prose? To begin with, poetry pervades our world in a variety of forms, ranging from advertising jingles to song lyrics. These may seem to be a long way from the chants heard around a primitive campfire, but they serve some of the same purposes. Like poems printed in a magazine or book, primitive chants, catchy jingles, and popular songs attempt to stir the imagination through the carefully measured use of words.

Although reading poetry usually makes more demands than does the kind of reading used to skim a magazine or newspaper, the appreciation of poetry comes naturally enough to anyone who enjoys playing with words. Play is an important element of poetry. Consider, for example, how the following words appeal to the children who gleefully chant them in playgrounds:

> I scream, you scream
> We all scream
> For ice cream.

These lines are an exuberant evocation of the joy of ice cream. Indeed, chanting the words turns out to be as pleasurable as eating ice cream. In poetry, the expression of the idea is as important as the idea expressed.

But is "I scream . . ." poetry? Some poets and literary critics would say that it certainly is one kind of poem because the children who chant it experience some of the pleasures of poetry in its measured beat and repeated sounds. However, other poets and critics would define poetry more narrowly and insist, for a variety of reasons, that this isn't true poetry but merely **doggerel**, a term used for lines whose subject matter is trite and whose rhythm and sounds are monotonously heavy-handed.

Although probably no one would argue that "I scream . . ." is a great poem, it does contain some poetic elements that appeal, at the very least, to children. Does that make it poetry? The answer depends on one's definition, but poetry has a way of breaking loose from definitions. Because there are nearly as many definitions of poetry as there are poets, Edwin Arlington Robinson's succinct observations are useful: "poetry has two outstanding characteristics. One is that it is undefinable. The other is that it is eventually unmistakable."

This comment places more emphasis on how a poem affects a reader than on how a poem is defined. By characterizing poetry as "undefinable," Robinson acknowledges that it can include many different purposes, subjects, emotions, styles, and forms. What effect does the following poem have on you?

WILLIAM HATHAWAY (B. 1944)

Oh, Oh   *1982*

My girl and I amble a country lane,
moo cows chomping daisies, our own
sweet saliva green with grass stems.
"Look, look," she says at the crossing,
"the choo-choo's light is on." And sure   5
enough, right smack dab in the middle
of maple dappled summer sunlight
is the lit headlight — so funny.
An arm waves to us from the black window.
We wave gaily to the arm. "When I hear   10
trains at night I dream of being president,"

I say dreamily. "And me first lady," she
says loyally. So when the last boxcars,
named after wonderful, faraway places,
and the caboose chuckle by we look   15
eagerly to the road ahead. And there,
poised and growling, are fifty Hell's Angels.

    Hathaway's poem serves as a convenient reminder that poetry can be
full of surprises. Even on a first reading there is no mistaking the emotional
reversal created by the last few words of this poem. With the exception of
the final line, the poem's language conjures up an idyllic picture of a young
couple taking a pleasant walk down a country lane. Contented as "moo
cows," they taste the sweetness of the grass, hear peaceful country sounds,
and are dazzled by "dappled summer sunlight." Their future together seems
to be all optimism as they anticipate "wonderful, faraway places" and the
"road ahead." Full of confidence, this couple, like the reader, is unprepared
for the shock to come. When we see those "fifty Hell's Angels," we are confronted with something like a bucket of cold water in the face.
    But even though our expectations are abruptly and powerfully reversed,
we are finally invited to view the entire episode from a safe distance — the distance provided by the delightful humor in this poem. After all, how seriously
can we take a poem that is titled "Oh, Oh"? The poet has his way with us, but
we are brought in on the joke too. The terror takes on comic proportions as
the innocent couple is confronted by no fewer than *fifty* Hell's Angels. This is
the kind of raucous overkill that informs a short animated film produced
some years ago titled *Bambi Meets Godzilla:* you might not have seen it, but you
know how it ends. The poem's good humor comes through when we realize
how pathetically inadequate the response of "Oh, Oh" is to the circumstances.
    As you can see, reading a description of what happens in a poem is not the
same as experiencing a poem. The exuberance of "I scream . . ." and the surprise of Hathaway's "Oh, Oh" are in the hearing or reading rather than in the
retelling. A *paraphrase* is a prose restatement of the central ideas of a poem in
your own language. Consider the difference between the following poem and
the paraphrase that follows it. What is missing from the paraphrase?

ROBERT FRANCIS (1901–1987)

Catch   1950

Two boys uncoached are tossing a poem together,
Overhand, underhand, backhand, sleight of hand, every hand,
Teasing with attitudes, latitudes, interludes, altitudes,
High, make him fly off the ground for it, low, make him stoop,
Make him scoop it up, make him as-almost-as-possible miss it,   5
Fast, let him sting from it, now, now fool him slowly,
Anything, everything tricky, risky, nonchalant,
Anything under the sun to outwit the prosy,

Over the tree and the long sweet cadence down,
Over his head, make him scramble to pick up the meaning,   10
And now, like a posy, a pretty one plump in his hands.

Paraphrase: A poet's relationship to a reader is similar to a game of catch. The poem, like a ball, should be pitched in a variety of ways to challenge and create interest. Boredom and predictability must be avoided if the game is to be engaging and satisfying.

A paraphrase can help us achieve a clearer understanding of a poem, but, unlike a poem, it misses all the sport and fun. It is the poem that "outwit[s] the prosy" because the poem serves as an example of what it suggests poetry should be. Moreover, the two players — the poet and the reader — are "uncoached." They know how the game is played, but their expectations do not preclude spontaneity and creativity or their ability to surprise and be surprised. The solid pleasure of the workout — of reading poetry — is the satisfaction derived from exercising your imagination and intellect.

That pleasure is worth emphasizing. Poetry uses language to move and delight even when it includes a cast of fifty Hell's Angels. The pleasure is in having the poem work its spell on us. For that to happen, it is best to relax and enjoy poetry rather than worry about definitions of it. Pay attention to what the poet throws you. We read poems for emotional and intellectual discovery — to feel and to experience something about the world and ourselves. The ideas in poetry — what can be paraphrased in prose — are important, but the real value of a poem consists in the words that work their magic by allowing us to feel, see, and be more than we were before. Perhaps the best way to approach a poem is similar to what Francis's "Catch" implies: expect to be surprised; stay on your toes; and concentrate on the delivery.

A SAMPLE ANALYSIS

Tossing Metaphors Together in "Catch"

The following sample paper on Robert Francis's "Catch" was written in response to an assignment that asked students to discuss the use of metaphor in the poem. Notice that Chris Leggett's paper is clearly focused and well organized. His discussion of the use of metaphor in the poem stays on track from beginning to end without any detours concerning unrelated topics (for a definition of *metaphor,* see p. 779). His title draws on the central metaphor of the poem, and he organizes the paper around four key words used in the poem: "attitudes, latitudes, interludes, altitudes." These constitute the heart of the paper's four substantive paragraphs, and they are effectively framed by introductory and concluding paragraphs. Moreover, the transitions between paragraphs clearly indicate that the author was not merely tossing a paper together.

Chris Leggett
Professor Lyles
English 203-1
November 9, 20--

Tossing Metaphors Together in "Catch"

The word "catch" is an attention getter. It usually
means something is about to be hurled at someone and that
he or she is expected to catch it. "Catch" can also signal
a challenge to another player if the toss is purposefully
difficult. Robert Francis, in his poem "Catch," uses the
extended metaphor of two boys playing catch to explore
the considerations a poet makes when "tossing a poem together." Line 3 of "Catch" enumerates these considerations
metaphorically as "attitudes, latitudes, interludes, [and]
altitudes." While regular prose is typically straightforward and easily understood, poetry usually takes great
effort to understand and appreciate. To exemplify this,
Francis presents the reader not with a normal game of
catch with the ball flying back and forth in a repetitive
and predictable fashion, but with a physically challenging
game in which one must concentrate, scramble, and exert
oneself to catch the ball, as one must stretch the intellect to truly grasp a poem.

The first consideration mentioned by Francis is attitude. Attitude, when applied to the game of catch, indicates the ball's pitch in flight, upward, downward, or
straight. It could also describe the players' attitudes
toward each other or toward the game in general. Below
this literal level lies attitude's meaning in relation to
poetry. Attitude in this case represents a poem's tone. A
poet may "teas[e] with attitude" by experimenting with
different tones to achieve the desired mood. The underlying tone of "Catch" is a playful one, set and reinforced

by the use of a game. This playfulness is further reinforced by such words and phrases as "teasing," "outwit,"
and "fool him."

Considered also in the metaphorical game of catch is
latitude, which, when applied to the game, suggests the
range the object may be thrown--how high, how low, or how
far. Poetic latitude, along similar lines, concerns a
poem's breadth, or the scope of topic. Taken one level
further, latitude suggests freedom from normal restraints
or limitations, indicating the ability to go outside the
norm to find originality of expression. The entire game of
catch described in Francis's poem reaches outside the normal expectations of something being merely tossed back and
forth in a predictable manner. The ball is thrown in almost every conceivable fashion, "overhand, underhand . . .
every hand." Other terms describing the throws--such as
"tricky," "risky," "fast," "slowly," and "Anything under
the sun"--express endless latitude for avoiding predictability in Francis's game of catch and metaphorically in
writing poetry.

During a game of catch the ball may be thrown at different intervals, establishing a steady rhythm or a broken, irregular one. Other intervening features, such
as the field being played on or the weather, could also
affect the game. These features of the game are alluded
to in the poem by the use of the word "interludes." "Interlude" in the poetic sense represents the poem's form,
which can similarly establish or diminish rhythm or enhance meaning. Lines 6 and 9 respectively show a broken
and a flowing rhythm. Line 6 begins rapidly as a hard toss
that stings the catcher's hand is described. The rhythm of
the line is immediately slowed, however, by the word "now"
followed by a comma, followed by the rest of the line. In

contrast, line 9 flows smoothly as the reader visualizes the ball flying over the tree and sailing downward. The words chosen for this line function perfectly. The phrase "the long sweet cadence down" establishes a sweet rhythm that reads smoothly and rolls off the tongue easily. The choice of diction not only affects the poem's rhythmic flow but also establishes through connotative language the various levels at which the poem can be understood, represented in "Catch" as altitude.

While "altitudes" when referring to the game of catch means how high an object is thrown, in poetry it could refer to the level of diction, lofty or down-to-earth, formal or informal. It suggests also the levels at which a poem can be comprehended, the literal as well as the interpretive. In Francis's game of catch the ball is thrown either high to make the player reach, low to make him stoop, or over his head to make him scramble, implying that the player should have to exert himself to catch it. So too, then, should the reader of poetry put great effort into understanding the full meaning of a poem. Francis exemplifies this consideration in writing poetry by giving "Catch" not only an enjoyable literal meaning concerning the game of catch but also a rich metaphorical meaning--reflecting the process of writing poetry. Francis uses several phrases and words with multiple meanings. The phrase "tossing a poem together" can be understood as tossing something back and forth or the process of constructing a poem. While "prosy" suggests prose itself, it also means the mundane or the ordinary. In the poem's final line the word "posy" of course represents a flower, while it is also a variant of the word "poesy," meaning poetry, or the practice of composing poetry.

Leggett 4

Francis effectively describes several considerations
to be taken in writing poetry in order to "outwit the
prosy." His use of the extended metaphor in "Catch" shows
that a poem must be unique, able to be comprehended on
multiple levels, and a challenge to the reader. The various rhythms in the lines of "Catch" exemplify the ideas
they express. While achieving an enjoyable poem on the
literal level, Francis has also achieved a rich metaphorical meaning. The poem offers a good workout both physically and intellectually.

Before beginning your own writing assignment on poetry, you should review Chapter 21, "Writing about Poetry," and Chapter 53, "Reading and Writing," which provides a step-by-step overview of how to choose a topic, develop a thesis, and organize various types of writing assignments. If you are using outside sources in your paper, you should make sure that you are familiar with the conventional documentation procedures described in Chapter 54, "The Literary Research Paper."

WOLE SOYINKA (B. 1934)

Telephone Conversation   *1960*

The price seemed reasonable, location
Indifferent. The landlady swore she lived
Off premises. Nothing remained
But self-confession. "Madam," I warned,
"I hate a wasted journey — I am African."   5
Silence. Silenced transmission of
Pressurized good-breeding. Voice, when it came,
Lipstick coated, long gold-rolled
Cigarette-holder pipped. Caught I was, foully.
"HOW DARK?" . . . I had not misheard . . . "ARE YOU LIGHT   10
OR VERY DARK?" Button B. Button A. Stench
Of rancid breath of public hide-and-speak.
Red booth. Red pillar-box. Red double-tiered
Omnibus squelching tar. It *was* real! Shamed

By ill-mannered silence, surrender   15
Pushed dumbfoundment to beg simplification.
Considerate she was, varying the emphasis —
"ARE YOU DARK? OR VERY LIGHT?" Revelation came.
"You mean — like plain or milk chocolate?"
Her assent was clinical, crushing in its light   20
Impersonality. Rapidly, wave-length adjusted,
I chose. "West African sepia" — and as afterthought,
"Down in my passport." Silence for spectroscopic
Flight of fancy, till truthfulness clanged her accent
Hard on the mouthpiece. "WHAT'S THAT?" conceding   25
"DON'T KNOW WHAT THAT IS." "Like brunette."
"THAT'S DARK, ISN'T IT?" "Not altogether.
Facially, I am brunette, but madam, you should see
The rest of me. Palm of my hand, soles of my feet
Are a peroxide blonde. Friction, caused —   30
Foolishly madam — by sitting down, has turned
My bottom raven black — One moment madam!" — sensing
Her receiver rearing on the thunderclap
About my ears — "Madam," I pleaded, "wouldn't you rather
See for yourself?"   35

The conversation that we hear in this traditional English telephone box evokes serious racial tensions as well as a humorous treatment of them; the benighted tradition represented by the landlady seems to be no match for the speaker's satiric wit.

Poets often remind us that beauty can be found in unexpected places. What is it that Elizabeth Bishop finds so beautiful about the "battered" fish she describes in the following poem?

ELIZABETH BISHOP (1911–1979)

The Fish   *1946*

I caught a tremendous fish
and held him beside the boat
half out of water, with my hook
fast in a corner of his mouth.
He didn't fight.   5
He hadn't fought at all.
He hung a grunting weight,
battered and venerable
and homely. Here and there
his brown skin hung in strips   10
like ancient wall-paper,
and its pattern of darker brown
was like wall-paper:
shapes like full-blown roses

stained and lost through age.   15
He was speckled with barnacles,
fine rosettes of lime,
and infested
with tiny white sea-lice,
and underneath two or three   20
rags of green weed hung down.
While his gills were breathing in
the terrible oxygen
— the frightening gills,
fresh and crisp with blood,   25
that can cut so badly —
I thought of the coarse white flesh
packed in like feathers,
the big bones and the little bones,
the dramatic reds and blacks   30
of his shiny entrails,
and the pink swim-bladder
like a big peony.
I looked into his eyes
which were far larger than mine   35
but shallower, and yellowed,
the irises backed and packed
with tarnished tinfoil
seen through the lenses
of old scratched isinglass.   40
They shifted a little, but not
to return my stare.
— It was more like the tipping
of an object toward the light.
I admired his sullen face,   45
the mechanism of his jaw,
and then I saw
that from his lower lip
— if you could call it a lip —
grim, wet, and weapon-like,   50
hung five old pieces of fish-line,
or four and a wire leader
with the swivel still attached,
with all their five big hooks
grown firmly in his mouth.   55
A green line, frayed at the end
where he broke it, two heavier lines,
and a fine black thread
still crimped from the strain and snap
when it broke and he got away.   60
Like medals with their ribbons
frayed and wavering,
a five-haired beard of wisdom
trailing from his aching jaw.

I stared and stared   65
and victory filled up
the little rented boat,
from the pool of bilge
where oil had spread a rainbow
around the rusted engine   70
to the bailer rusted orange,
the sun-cracked thwarts,
the oarlocks on their strings,
the gunnels — until everything
was rainbow, rainbow, rainbow!   75
And I let the fish go.

CONSIDERATIONS FOR CRITICAL THINKING AND WRITING

1. FIRST RESPONSE. Which lines in this poem provide especially vivid details of
   the fish? What makes these descriptions effective?
2. How is the fish characterized? Is it simply a weak victim because it "didn't
   fight"?
3. Comment on lines 65–76. In what sense has "victory filled up" the boat,
   given that the speaker finally lets the fish go?

The speaker in Bishop's "The Fish" ends on a triumphantly joyful
note. The *speaker* is the voice used by the author in the poem; like the narrator in a work of fiction, the speaker is often a created identity rather than
the author's actual self. The two should not automatically be equated.
Contrast the attitude toward life of the speaker in "The Fish" with that of
the speaker in the following poem.

PHILIP LARKIN (1922–1985)

A Study of Reading Habits   1964

When getting my nose in a book
Cured most things short of school,
It was worth ruining my eyes
To know I could still keep cool,
And deal out the old right hook   5
To dirty dogs twice my size.

Later, with inch-thick specs,
Evil was just my lark:
Me and my cloak and fangs
Had ripping times in the dark.
The women I clubbed with sex!   10
I broke them up like meringues.

Don't read much now: the dude
Who lets the girl down before

The hero arrives, the chap   15
Who's yellow and keeps the store,
Seem far too familiar. Get stewed:
Books are a load of crap.

What the speaker sees and describes in "The Fish" is close if not identical to Bishop's own vision and voice. The joyful response to the fish is clearly
shared by the speaker and the poet, between whom there is little or no distance. In "A Study of Reading Habits," however, Larkin distances himself
from a speaker whose sensibilities he does not wholly share. The poet—and
many readers—might identify with the reading habits described by the
speaker in the first twelve lines, but Larkin uses the last six lines to criticize
the speaker's attitude toward life as well as reading. The speaker recalls in
lines 1–6 how as a schoolboy he identified with the hero, whose virtuous
strength always triumphed over "dirty dogs," and in lines 7–12 he recounts
how his schoolboy fantasies were transformed by adolescence into a fascination with violence and sex. This description of early reading habits is pleasantly amusing, because many readers of popular fiction will probably recall
having moved through similar stages, but at the end of the poem the
speaker provides more information about himself than he intends to.

As an adult the speaker has lost interest in reading because it is no
longer an escape from his own disappointed life. Instead of identifying
with heroes or villains, he finds himself identifying with minor characters
who are irresponsible and cowardly. Reading is now a reminder of his failures, so he turns to alcohol. His solution, to "Get stewed" because "Books
are a load of crap," is obviously self-destructive. The speaker is ultimately
exposed by Larkin as someone who never grew beyond fantasies. Getting
drunk is consistent with the speaker's immature reading habits. Unlike the
speaker, the poet understands that life is often distorted by escapist fantasies, whether through a steady diet of popular fiction or through alcohol. The speaker in this poem, then, is not Larkin but a created identity
whose voice is filled with disillusionment and delusion.

The problem with Larkin's speaker is that he misreads books as well as
his own life. Reading means nothing to him unless it serves as an escape
from himself. It is not surprising that Larkin has him read fiction rather
than poetry because poetry places an especially heavy emphasis on language. Fiction, indeed any kind of writing, including essays and drama, relies on carefully chosen and arranged words, but poetry does so to an even
greater extent. Notice, for example, how Larkin's deft use of trite expressions and slang characterizes the speaker so that his language reveals
nearly as much about his dreary life as what he says. Larkin's speaker
would have no use for poetry.

What is "unmistakable" in poetry (to use Robinson's term again) is its
intense, concentrated use of language—its emphasis on individual words
to convey meanings, experiences, emotions, and effects. Poets never simply
process words; they savor them. Words in poems frequently create their

own tastes, textures, scents, sounds, and shapes. They often seem more sensuous than ordinary language, and readers usually sense that a word has been hefted before making its way into a poem. Although poems are crafted differently from the ways a painting, sculpture, or musical composition is created, in each form of art the creator delights in the medium. Poetry is carefully orchestrated so that the words work together as elements in a structure to sustain close, repeated readings. The words are chosen to interact with one another to create the maximum desired effect, whether the purpose is to capture a mood or feeling, create a vivid experience, express a point of view, narrate a story, or portray a character.

Here is a poem that looks quite different from most *verse,* a term used for lines composed in a measured rhythmical pattern, which are often, but not necessarily, rhymed.

ROBERT MORGAN (B. 1944)

Mountain Graveyard   *1979*

for the author of "Slow Owls"

Spore Prose

stone	notes
slate	tales
sacred	cedars
heart	earth
asleep	please
hated	death

Though unconventional in its appearance, this is unmistakably poetry because of its concentrated use of language. The poem demonstrates how serious play with words can lead to some remarkable discoveries. At first glance "Mountain Graveyard" may seem intimidating. What, after all, does this list of words add up to? How is it in any sense a poetic use of language? But if the words are examined closely, it is not difficult to see how they work. The wordplay here is literally in the form of a game. Morgan uses a series of **anagrams** (words made from the letters of other words, such as *read* and *dare*) to evoke feelings about death. "Mountain Graveyard" is one of several poems that Morgan has called "Spore Prose" (another anagram) because he finds in individual words the seeds of poetry. He wrote the poem in honor of the fiftieth birthday of another poet, Jonathan Williams, the author of "Slow Owls," whose title is also an anagram.

The title, "Mountain Graveyard," indicates the poem's setting, which is also the context in which the individual words in the poem interact to provide a larger meaning. Morgan's discovery of the words on the stones of a graveyard is more than just clever. The observations he makes among the silent graves go beyond the curious pleasure a reader experiences in finding the words *sacred cedars,* referring to evergreens common in cemeteries, to consist of the same letters. The surprise and delight of realizing the connection between heart and earth is tempered by the more sober recognition that everyone's story ultimately ends in the ground. The hope that the dead are merely asleep is expressed with a plea that is answered grimly by a hatred of death's finality.

Little is told in this poem. There is no way of knowing who is buried or who is looking at the graves, but the emotions of sadness, hope, and pain are unmistakable — and are conveyed in fewer than half the words of this sentence. Morgan takes words that initially appear to be a dead, prosaic list and energizes their meanings through imaginative juxtapositions.

The following poem also involves a startling discovery about words. With the peculiar title "l(a," the poem cannot be read aloud, so there is no sound, but is there sense, a *theme,* a central idea or meaning, in the poem?

E. E. CUMMINGS (1894–1962)

l(a   *1958*

l(a

le

af

fa

ll

s)

one

l

iness

CONSIDERATIONS FOR CRITICAL THINKING AND WRITING

1. FIRST RESPONSE. Discuss the connection between what appears inside and outside the parentheses in this poem.
2. What does Cummings draw attention to by breaking up the words? How do this strategy and the poem's overall shape contribute to its theme?
3. Which seems more important in this poem — what is expressed, or the way it is expressed?

Although "Mountain Graveyard" and "l(a" do not resemble the kind of verse that readers might recognize immediately as poetry on a page, both are actually a very common type of poem, called the *lyric,* usually a brief poem that expresses the personal emotions and thoughts of a single speaker. Lyrics are often written in the first person but sometimes — as in "Spore Prose" and "l(a" — no speaker is specified. Lyrics present a subjective mood, emotion, or idea. Very often they are about love or death, but almost any subject or experience that evokes some intense emotional response can be found in lyrics. In addition to brevity and emotional intensity, lyrics are also frequently characterized by their musical qualities. The word *lyric* derives from the Greek word *lyre,* meaning a musical instrument that originally accompanied the singing of a lyric. Lyric poems can be organized in a variety of ways, such as the sonnet, elegy, and ode (see Chapter 28), but it is enough to point out here that lyrics are an extremely popular kind of poetry with writers and readers.

The following anonymous lyric was found in a sixteenth-century manuscript.

Anonymous

Western Wind

c. 1500

Western wind, when wilt thou blow,
The small rain down can rain?
Christ, if my love were in my arms,
And I in my bed again!

This speaker's intense longing for his lover is characteristic of lyric poetry. He impatiently addresses the western wind that brings spring to England and could make it possible for him to be reunited with the woman he loves. We do not know the details of these lovers' lives because this poem focuses on the speaker's emotion. We do not learn why the lovers are apart or if they will be together again. We don't even know if the speaker is a man. But those issues are not really important. The poetry gives us a feeling rather than a story.

A poem that tells a story is called a **narrative poem.** Narrative poetry may be short or very long. An **epic,** for example, is a long narrative poem on a serious subject chronicling heroic deeds and important events. Among the most famous epics are Homer's *Iliad* and *Odyssey,* the Old English *Beowulf,* Dante's *Divine Comedy,* and John Milton's *Paradise Lost.* More typically, however, narrative poems are considerably shorter, such as the following poem, which tells the story of a child's memory of her father.

Regina Barreca (b. 1957)

Nighttime Fires

1986

When I was five in Louisville
we drove to see nighttime fires. Piled seven of us,
all pajamas and running noses, into the Olds,
drove fast toward smoke. It was after my father

lost his job, so not getting up in the morning _5_
gave him time: awake past midnight, he read old newspapers
with no news, tried crosswords until he split the pencil
between his teeth, mad. When he heard
the wolf whine of the siren, he woke my mother,
and she pushed and shoved _10_
us all into waking. Once roused we longed for burnt wood
and a smell of flames high into the pines. My old man liked
driving to rich neighborhoods best, swearing in a good mood
as he followed fire engines that snaked like dragons
and split the silent streets. It was festival, carnival. _15_

If there were a Cadillac or any car
in a curved driveway, my father smiled a smile
from a secret, brittle heart.
His face lit up in the heat given off by destruction
like something was being made, or was being set right. _20_
I bent my head back to see where sparks
ate up the sky. My father who never held us
would take my hand and point to falling cinders that
covered the ground like snow, or, excited, show us
the swollen collapse of a staircase. My mother _25_
watched my father, not the house. She was happy
only when we were ready to go, when it was finally over
and nothing else could burn.
Driving home, she would sleep in the front seat
as we huddled behind. I could see his quiet face in the _30_
rearview mirror, eyes like hallways filled with smoke.

This narrative poem could have been a short story if the poet had wanted to say more about the "brittle heart" of this unemployed man whose daughter so vividly remembers the desperate pleasure he took in watching fire consume other people's property. Indeed, a reading of William Faulkner's famous short story "Barn Burning" suggests how such a character can be further developed and how his child responds to him. The similarities between Faulkner's angry character and the poem's father, whose "eyes [are] like hallways filled with smoke," are coincidental, but the characters' sense of "something . . . being set right" by flames is worth comparing. Although we do not know everything about this man and his family, we have a much firmer sense of their story than we do of the story of the couple in "Western Wind."

Although narrative poetry is still written, short stories and novels have largely replaced the long narrative poem. Lyric poems tend to be the predominant type of poetry today. Regardless of whether a poem is a narrative or a lyric, however, the strategies for reading it are somewhat different from those for reading prose. Try these suggestions for approaching poetry.

SUGGESTIONS FOR APPROACHING POETRY

1. Assume that it will be necessary to read a poem more than once. Give yourself a chance to become familiar with what the poem has to offer. Like a piece of music, a poem becomes more pleasurable with each encounter.

2. Pay attention to the title; it will often provide a helpful context for the poem and serve as an introduction to it. Larkin's "A Study of Reading Habits" is precisely what its title describes.

3. As you read the poem for the first time, avoid becoming entangled in words or lines that you don't understand. Instead, give yourself a chance to take in the entire poem before attempting to resolve problems encountered along the way.

4. On a second reading, identify any words or passages that you don't understand. Look up words you don't know; these might include names, places, historical and mythical references, or anything else that is unfamiliar to you.

5. Read the poem aloud (or perhaps have a friend read it to you). You'll probably discover that some puzzling passages suddenly fall into place when you hear them. You'll find that nothing helps, though, if the poem is read in an artificial, exaggerated manner. Read in as natural a voice as possible, with slight pauses at line breaks. Silent reading is preferable to imposing a te-tumpty-te-tum reading on a good poem.

6. Read the punctuation. Poems use punctuation marks — in addition to the space on the page — as signals for readers. Be especially careful not to assume that the end of a line marks the end of a sentence, unless it is concluded by punctuation. Consider, for example, the opening lines of Hathaway's "Oh, Oh":

   > My girl and I amble a country lane,
   > moo cows chomping daisies, our own
   > sweet saliva green with grass stems.

   Line 2 makes little or no sense if a reader stops after "own." Keeping track of the subjects and verbs will help you find your way among the sentences.

7. Paraphrase the poem to determine whether you understand what happens in it. As you work through each line of the poem, a paraphrase will help you to see which words or passages need further attention.

8. Try to get a sense of who is speaking and what the setting or situation is. Don't assume that the speaker is the author; often it is a created character.

9. Assume that each element in the poem has a purpose. Try to explain how the elements of the poem work together.

10. Be generous. Be willing to entertain perspectives, values, experiences, and subjects that you might not agree with or approve. Even if baseball

bores you, you should be able to comprehend its imaginative use in Francis's "Catch."

11. Try developing a coherent approach to the poem that helps you to shape a discussion of the text. See Chapter 52, "Critical Strategies for Reading," to review formalist, biographical, historical, psychological, feminist, and other possible critical approaches.

12. Don't expect to produce a definitive reading. Many poems do not resolve all the ideas, issues, or tensions in them, and so it is not always possible to drive their meaning into an absolute corner. Your reading will explore rather than define the poem. Poems are not trophies to be stuffed and mounted. They're usually more elusive. And don't be afraid that a close reading will damage the poem. Poems aren't hurt when we analyze them; instead, they come alive as we experience them and put into words what we discover through them.

A list of more specific questions using the literary terms and concepts discussed in the following chapters begins on page 709. That list, like the suggestions just made, raises issues and questions that can help you to read just about any poem closely. These strategies should be a useful means for getting inside poems to understand how they work. Furthermore, because reading poetry inevitably increases sensitivity to language, you're likely to find yourself a better reader of words in any form — whether in a novel, a newspaper editorial, an advertisement, a political speech, or a conversation — after having studied poetry. In short, many of the reading skills that make poetry accessible also open up the world you inhabit.

You'll probably find some poems amusing or sad, some fierce or tender, and some fascinating or dull. You may find, too, some poems that will get inside you. Their kinds of insights — the poet's and yours — are what Emily Dickinson had in mind when she defined poetry this way: "If I read a book and it makes my whole body so cold no fire can ever warm me, I know that it is poetry. If I feel physically as if the top of my head were taken off, I know that it is poetry." Dickinson's response may be more intense than most — poetry was, after all, at the center of her life — but you too might find yourself moved by poems in unexpected ways. In any case, as Edwin Arlington Robinson knew, poetry is, to an alert and sensitive reader, "eventually unmistakable."

POETRY IN POPULAR FORMS

Before you try out these strategies for reading on a few more poems, it is worth acknowledging that the verse that enjoys the widest readership appears not in collections, magazines, or even anthologies for students, but in greeting cards. A significant amount of the personal daily mail delivered in the United States consists of greeting cards. That represents millions of lines of verse going by us on the street and in planes over our heads. These verses share some similarities with the poetry included in this anthology, but there are also important differences that indicate the need for reading serious poetry closely rather than casually.

The popularity of greeting cards is easy to explain: just as many of us have neither the time nor the talent to make gifts for birthdays, weddings, anniversaries, graduations, Valentine's Day, Mother's Day, and other holidays, we are unlikely to write personal messages when cards conveniently say them for us. Although impersonal, cards are efficient and convey an important message no matter what the occasion for them: I care. These greetings are rarely serious poetry; they are not written to be. Nevertheless, they demonstrate the impulse in our culture to generate and receive poetry.

In a handbook for greeting-card freelancers, a writer and past editor of such verse began with this advice:

> Once you determine what you want to say—and in this regard it is best to stick to one basic idea—you must choose your words to do several things at the same time:
>
> 1. Your idea must be expressed as a complete idea; it must have a beginning, a middle, and an end.
>
> 2. There must be coherence in your verse. Every line must be linked logically and smoothly with its neighbors.
>
> 3. Your expressions . . . must be conversational. High-flown language rarely comes off successfully in greeting-card writing.
>
> 4. You must write with emphasis—and something else: enthusiasm. It's necessary to create interest in that all-important first line. From that point on, writing your verse is a matter of developing your idea and bringing it to a peak of emphasis in the last line. Occasionally you will find that you have shot your wad too early in the verse, and whatever you say after that point sounds like an afterthought.
>
> 5. You must do all of the above and at the same time make everything come out right in the meter-and-rhyme department.[1]

This advice is followed by a list of approximately fifty of the most frequently used rhyme sounds accompanied by rhyming words, such as *love, of, above* for the sound *uv*. The point of these prescriptions is that the verse must be written so that it is immediately accessible—consumable—by both the buyer and the recipient. Writers of these cards are expected to avoid any complexity.

Compare the following greeting-card verse with the poem that comes after it. "Magic of Love," by Helen Farries, has been a longtime favorite in a major greeting-card company's "wedding line"; with different endings it has been used also in valentines and friendship cards.

---

[1] Chris Fitzgerald, "Conventional Verse: The Sentimental Favorite," *The Greeting Card Writer's Handbook,*" ed. H. Joseph Chadwick (Cincinnati: Writer's Digest, 1975): 13, 17.

Helen Farries

Magic of Love

date unknown

There's a wonderful gift that can give you a lift,
It's a blessing from heaven above!
It can comfort and bless, it can bring happiness —
It's the wonderful MAGIC OF LOVE!

Like a star in the night, it can keep your faith bright,   5
Like the sun, it can warm your hearts, too —
It's a gift you can give every day that you live,
And when given, it comes back to you!

When love lights the way, there is joy in the day
And all troubles are lighter to bear,   10
Love is gentle and kind, and through love you will find
There's an answer to your every prayer!

May it never depart from your two loving hearts,
May you treasure this gift from above —
You will find if you do, all your dreams will come true,   15
In the wonderful MAGIC OF LOVE!

John Frederick Nims (1913–1999)

Love Poem

1947

My clumsiest dear, whose hands shipwreck vases,
At whose quick touch all glasses chip and ring,
Whose palms are bulls in china, burs in linen,
And have no cunning with any soft thing

Except all ill-at-ease fidgeting people: 5
The refugee uncertain at the door
You make at home; deftly you steady
The drunk clambering on his undulant floor.

Unpredictable dear, the taxi drivers' terror,
Shrinking from far headlights pale as a dime   10
Yet leaping before red apoplectic streetcars —
Misfit in any space. And never on time.

A wrench in clocks and the solar system. Only
With words and people and love you move at ease.
In traffic of wit expertly maneuver   15
And keep us, all devotion, at your knees.

Forgetting your coffee spreading on our flannel,
Your lipstick grinning on our coat,
So gaily in love's unbreakable heaven
Our souls on glory of spilt bourbon float.   20

Be with me, darling, early and late. Smash glasses —
I will study wry music for your sake.
For should your hands drop white and empty
All the toys of the world would break.

CONSIDERATIONS FOR CRITICAL THINKING AND WRITING

1. FIRST RESPONSE. Read these two works aloud. How are they different? How the same?
2. To what extent does the advice to would-be greeting-card writers apply to each work?
3. Compare the two speakers. Which do you find more appealing? Why?
4. How does Nims's description of love differ from Farries's?

In contrast to poetry, which transfigures and expresses an emotion or experience through an original use of language, the verse in "Magic of Love" relies on *clichés,* ideas or expressions that have become tired and trite from overuse, such as describing love as "a blessing from heaven above." Clichés anesthetize readers instead of alerting them to the possibility of fresh perceptions. They are used to draw out *stock responses,* predictable, conventional reactions to language, characters, symbols, or situations; God, heaven, the flag, motherhood, hearts, puppies, and peace are some often-used objects of stock responses. Advertisers manufacture careers from this sort of business.

Clichés and stock responses are two of the major ingredients of sentimentality in literature. *Sentimentality* exploits the reader by inducing responses that exceed what the situation warrants. This pejorative term should not be confused with *sentiment,* which is synonymous with *emotion* or *feeling.* Sentimentality cons readers into falling for the mass murderer who is devoted to stray cats, and it requires that we not think twice about what we're feeling because those tears shed for the little old lady, the rage aimed at the vicious enemy soldier, and the longing for the simple virtues of poverty might disappear under the slightest scrutiny. The experience of sentimentality is not unlike biting into a swirl of cotton candy; it's momentarily sweet but wholly insubstantial.

Clichés, stock responses, and sentimentality are generally the hallmarks of weak writing. Poetry — the kind that is unmistakable — achieves freshness, vitality, and genuine emotion that sharpen our perceptions of life.

Although the most widely read verse is found in greeting cards, the most widely *heard* poetry appears in song lyrics. Not all songs are poetic, but a good many share the same effects and qualities as poems. Consider these lyrics by Bruce Springsteen about Philadelphia, the City of Brotherly Love.

BRUCE SPRINGSTEEN (B. 1949)

Streets of Philadelphia

1993

I was bruised and battered and I couldn't tell
What I felt
I was unrecognizable to myself
I saw my reflection in a window I didn't know
My own face   5
Oh brother are you gonna leave me
Wastin' away
On the streets of Philadelphia

I walked the avenue till my legs felt like stone
I heard the voices of friends vanished and gone   10
At night I could hear the blood in my veins
Black and whispering as the rain
On the streets of Philadelphia

Ain't no angel gonna greet me
It's just you and I my friend   15
My clothes don't fit me no more
I walked a thousand miles
Just to slip this skin

The night has fallen, I'm lyin' awake
I can feel myself fading away   20
So receive me brother with your faithless kiss
Or will we leave each other alone like this
On the streets of Philadelphia

CONSIDERATIONS FOR CRITICAL THINKING AND WRITING

1. FIRST RESPONSE. Characterize Philadelphia in this song lyric. What sort of life
   is described by the speaker? Which images seem especially evocative to you?

2. Why is there almost no punctuation in these lines? How do you make sense
   of the lines in the absence of conventional punctuation?

3. What kind of mood is evoked by the language of this song? How does your
   reading of "Streets of Philadelphia" compare with listening to Springsteen
   singing it (available on his *Greatest Hits,* a Columbia CD)?

4. Explain whether you think this song can be accurately called a narrative
   poem.

SAUNDRA SHARP (B. 1942)

It's the Law: A Rap Poem

1991

You can learn about the state of the U.S.A.
By the laws we have on the books today.
The rules we break are the laws we make
The things that we fear, we legislate.

We got laws designed to keep folks in line   5
Laws for what happens when you lose your mind
Laws against stealing, laws against feeling,
The laws we have are a definite sign
That our vision of love is going blind.
(They probably got a law against this rhyme.)   10
Unh-hunh . . . . .

We got laws for cool cats & laws for dirty dogs
Laws about where you can park your hog
Laws against your mama and your papa, too
Even got a law to make the laws come true.   15

It's against the law to hurt an ol' lady,
It's against the law to steal a little baby,
The laws we make are what we do to each other
There is no law to make brother love brother
Hmmm   20

Now this respect thang is hard for some folks to do
They don't respect themselves so they can't respect you
This is the word we should get around —
These are the rules: we gonna run 'em on down.
Listen up!:   25

It ain't enough to be cute,
It ain't enough to be tough
You gotta walk tall
You gotta strut your stuff

You gotta learn to read, you gotta learn to write.   30
Get the tools you need to win this fight
Get your common sense down off the shelf
Start in the mirror . . . . Respect your Self!

When you respect yourself you keep your body clean
You walk tall, walk gentle, don't have to be mean   35
You keep your mind well fed, you keep a clear head
And you think 'bout who you let in your bed —
Unh-hunh . . . . . .

When you respect yourself you come to understand
That your body is a temple for a natural plan,   40
It's against that plan to use drugs or dope —
Use your heart and your mind when you need to cope . . .
It's the law!

We got laws that got started in '86
And laws made back when the Indians got kicked   45
If we want these laws to go out of favor
Then we've got to change our behavior

Change what!? you say, well let's take a look
How did the laws get on the books? Yeah.

I said it up front but let's get tougher 50
The laws we make are what we do to each other

If you never shoot at me then I don't need
A law to keep you from shooting at me, do you see?
There's a universal law that's tried and true
Says Don't do to me — 55
What you don't want done to you
Unh-hunh!
Don't do to me —
What you don't want done to you
It's the law! 60

CONSIDERATIONS FOR CRITICAL THINKING AND WRITING

1. FIRST RESPONSE. According to this rap poem, what do laws reveal "about the state of the U.S.A."?

2. How are the "laws" different from the "rules" prescribed in the middle stanzas of the poem?

3. What is the theme of this rap poem?

PERSPECTIVE

ROBERT FRANCIS (1901–1987)

On "Hard" Poetry 1965

When Robert Frost said he liked poems hard he could scarcely have meant he liked them difficult. If he had meant difficult he would have said he didn't like them easy. What he said was that he didn't like them soft.

Poems can be soft in several ways. They can be soft in form (invertebrate). They can be soft in thought and feeling (sentimental). They can be soft with excess verbiage. Frost used to advise [writers] to squeeze the water out of a poem. He liked poems dry. What is dry tends to be hard, and what is hard is always dry, except perhaps on the outside.

Yet though hardness here does not mean difficulty, some difficulty naturally goes with hardness. A hard poem may not be hard to read but is hard to write. Not too hard, preferably. Not so hard to write that there is no flow in the writer. But hard enough for the growing poem to meet with some healthy resistance. Frost often found this healthy resistance in a tight rhyme scheme and strict meter. There are other ways of getting good resistance, of course.

And in the reader too, a hard poem will bring some difficulty. Preferably not too much. Not enough difficulty to completely baffle him. Ideally a hard poem should not be too hard to make sense of, but hard to exhaust its meaning and its beauty.

"What I care about is the hardness of the poems. I don't like them soft, I want them to be little pebbles, but placed where they won't dislodge easily.

And I'd like them to be little pebbles of precious stone — precious, or semi-precious" (interview with John Ciardi, *Saturday Review*, March 21, 1959).

Here is hard prose talking about hard poetry. Frost was never shrewder or more illuminating. Here, as well as in anything else he ever said, is his flavor.

What contemporary of his can you imagine saying this or anything like it?

In 1843 Emerson jotted in his journal: "Hard clouds and hard expressions, and hard manners, I love."

From *The Satirical Rogue on Poetry*

CONSIDERATIONS FOR CRITICAL THINKING AND WRITING

1. What is the distinction between "hard" and "soft" poetry?
2. Given Francis's brief essay and his poem "Catch" (p. 676), write a review of Helen Farries's "Magic of Love" (p. 693) as you think Francis would.
3. Explain whether you would characterize Bruce Springsteen's "Streets of Philadelphia" (p. 695) as hard or soft.

POEMS FOR FURTHER STUDY

RUDYARD KIPLING (1865–1936)

If—

1910

If you can keep your head when all about you
   Are losing theirs and blaming it on you,
If you can trust yourself when all men doubt you,
   But make allowance for their doubting too;
If you can wait and not be tired by waiting,   5
   Or being lied about, don't deal in lies,
Or being hated, don't give way to hating,
   And yet don't look too good, nor talk too wise:

If you can dream — and not make dreams your master;
   If you can think — and not make thoughts your aim;   10
If you can meet with Triumph and Disaster
   And treat those two impostors just the same;
If you can bear to hear the truth you've spoken
   Twisted by knaves to make a trap for fools,
Or watch the things you gave your life to, broken,   15
   And stoop and build 'em up with worn-out tools:

If you can make one heap of all your winnings
   And risk it in one turn of pitch-and-toss,°   *pitching coins*
And lose, and start again at your beginnings
   And never breathe a word about your loss;   20
If you can force your heart and nerve and sinew
   To serve your turn long after they are gone,

And so hold on when there is nothing in you
   Except the Will which says to them: "Hold on!"

If you can talk with crowds and keep your virtue,   25
   Or walk with Kings — nor lose the common touch,
If neither foes nor loving friends can hurt you,
   If all men count with you, but none too much;
If you can fill the unforgiving minute
   With sixty seconds' worth of distance run,   30
Yours is the Earth and everything that's in it,
   And — which is more — you'll be a Man, my son!

CONSIDERATIONS FOR CRITICAL THINKING AND WRITING

1. FIRST RESPONSE. Though the poem is addressed to the speaker's son, could the speaker's advice apply to a daughter as well? Explain why or why not.

2. What does it mean that Kipling capitalized "Man" in the last line of the poem? Is this speaker defining masculinity or something else? Do these definitions seem dated to you? Why or why not?

3. Read the poem aloud and comment on the effects of the rhymes and rhythms of the lines.

CONNECTION TO ANOTHER SELECTION

1. Discuss Kipling's treatment of what a man is in contrast to Alice Walker's description of what a woman is not in "a woman is not a potted plant," the next poem. What significant differences do you find in their definitions?

ALICE WALKER (B. 1944)

a woman is not a potted plant   *1991*

A WOMAN IS NOT
A POTTED PLANT

   her roots bound
   to the confines
   of her house   5

   a woman is not
   a potted plant
   her leaves trimmed
   to the contours
   of her sex   10

   a woman is not
   a potted plant
   her branches
   espaliered
   against the fences   15
   of her race
   her country

her mother
her man

her trained blossom   20
turning
this way
& that
to follow
the sun   25
of whoever feeds
and waters
her

a woman
is wilderness   30
unbounded
holding the future
between each breath
walking the earth
only because   35
she is free
and not creepervine
or tree.

Nor even honeysuckle
or bee.   40

CONSIDERATIONS FOR CRITICAL THINKING AND WRITING

1. FIRST RESPONSE. According to the speaker, how do the properties of a potted plant inappropriately describe a woman? (Have you ever considered a
   woman to be *like* a potted plant?)

2. What *is* a woman, according to the speaker? What is the effect of defining
   her primarily by what she is not?

3. Describe the meaning and effect of the poem's final two lines.

CONNECTION TO ANOTHER SELECTION

1. Compare Walker's take on female identity in this poem with Piercy's in "The
   Secretary Chant" (p. 671). How are their conceptions similar? Different?

LISA PARKER (B. 1971)
Snapping Beans   *1998*

for Susan Squier

I snapped beans into the silver bowl
that sat on the splintering slats
of the porchswing between my grandma and me.
I was home for the weekend,

from school, from the North,   5
Grandma hummed "What A Friend We Have In Jesus"
as the sun rose, pushing its pink spikes
through the slant of cornstalks,
through the fly-eyed mesh of the screen.
We didn't speak until the sun overcame   10
the feathered tips of the cornfield
and Grandma stopped humming. I could feel
the soft gray of her stare
against the side of my face
when she asked, *How's school a-goin'?*   15
I wanted to tell her about my classes,
the revelations by book and lecture,
as real as any shout of faith
and potent as a swig of strychnine.
She reached the leather of her hand   20
over the bowl and cupped
my quivering chin; the slick smooth of her palm
held my face the way she held tomatoes
under the spigot, careful not to drop them,
and I wanted to tell her   25
about the nights I cried into the familiar
heartsick panels of the quilt she made me,
wishing myself home on the evening star.
I wanted to tell her
the evening star was a planet,   30
that my friends wore noserings and wrote poetry
about sex, about alcoholism, about Buddha.
I wanted to tell her how my stomach burned
acidic holes at the thought of speaking in class,
speaking in an accent, speaking out of turn,   35
how I was tearing, splitting myself apart
with the slow-simmering guilt of being happy
despite it all.
I said, *School's fine.*
We snapped beans into the silver bowl between us   40
and when a hickory leaf, still summer green,
skidded onto the porchfront,
Grandma said,
It's funny how things blow loose like that.

CONSIDERATIONS FOR CRITICAL THINKING AND WRITING

1. FIRST RESPONSE. Describe the speaker's feelings about starting a life at college. How do those feelings compare with your own experiences?

2. How does the grandmother's world differ from the speaker's at school? What details especially reveal those differences?

3. Given that the poem is about how "school['s] a-goin'," why do you think the title is "Snapping Beans"?

4. Discuss the significance of the grandmother's response to the hickory leaf in line 41. How do you read the last line?

CONNECTION TO ANOTHER SELECTION

1. Discuss the treatment of the grandmother in "Snapping Beans" and in "Behind Grandma's House" by Gary Soto (p. 830).

WYATT PRUNTY (B. 1947)

Elderly Lady Crossing on Green   1993

And give her no scouts doing their one good deed
Or sentimental cards to wish her well
During Christmas time or gallstone time —
Because there was a time, she'd like to tell,

She drove a loaded V8 powerglide   5
And would have run you flat as paint
To make the light before it turned on her,
Make it as she watched you faint

When looking up you saw her bearing down
Eyes locking you between the wheel and dash,   10
And you either scrambled back where you belonged
Or jaywalked to eternity, blown out like trash

Behind the grease spot where she braked on you. . . .
Never widow, wife, mother, or a bride,
And nothing up ahead she's looking for   15
But asphalt, the dotted line, the other side,

The way she's done a million times before,
With nothing in her brief to tell you more
Than she's a small tug on the tidal swell
Of her own sustaining notion that she's doing well.   20

CONSIDERATIONS FOR CRITICAL THINKING AND WRITING

1. FIRST RESPONSE. Does the description of the elderly lady in the poem undercut your expectations about her created by the title? Is this poem sentimental, ironic, or something else?

2. In what ways is this elderly woman "doing well" (line 20)? Does the poem suggest any ways in which she's not?

3. Describe the effect produced by the first line's beginning with "And . . . ." Why is this a fitting introduction to this elderly lady?

CONNECTION TO ANOTHER SELECTION

1. Write an essay comparing the humor in this poem with that of Hathaway's "Oh, Oh" (p. 675).

ALBERTO RÍOS (B. 1952)

Seniors   *1985*

William cut a hole in his Levi's pocket
so he could flop himself out in class
behind the girls so the other guys
could see and shit what guts we all said.
All Konga wanted to do over and over   5
was the rubber band trick, but he showed
everyone how, so nobody wanted to see
anymore and one day he cried, just cried
until his parents took him away forever.
Maya had a Hotpoint refrigerator standing   10
in his living room, just for his family to show
anybody who came that they could afford it.

Me, I got a French kiss, finally, in the catholic
darkness, my tongue's farthest half vacationing
loudly in another mouth like a man in Bermudas,   15
and my body jumped against a flagstone wall,
I could feel it through her thin, almost
nonexistent body: I had, at that moment, that moment,
a hot girl on a summer night, the best of all
the things we tried to do. Well, she   20
let me kiss her, anyway, all over.

Or it was just a flagstone wall
with a flaw in the stone, an understanding cavity
for burning young men with smooth dreams—
the true circumstance is gone, the true   25
circumstances about us all then
are gone. But when I kissed her, all water,
she would close her eyes, and they into somewhere
would disappear. Whether she was there
or not, I remember her, clearly, and she moves   30
around the room, sometimes, until I sleep.

I have lain on the desert in watch
low in the back of a pick-up truck
for nothing in particular, for stars, for
the things behind stars, and nothing comes   35
more than the moment: always now, here in a truck,
the moment again to dream of making love and sweat,
this time to a woman, or even to all of them
in some allowable way, to those boys, then,
who couldn't cry, to the girls before they were   40
women, to friends, me on my back, the sky over me
pressing its simple weight into her body
on me, into the bodies of them all, on me.

Considerations for Critical Thinking and Writing

1. FIRST RESPONSE. Comment on the use of slang in the poem. Does it surprise you? How does it characterize the speaker?

2. How does the language of the final stanza differ from that of the first stanza? To what purpose?

3. Write an essay that discusses the speaker's attitudes toward sex and life. How are they related?

Connections to Other Selections

1. Compare the treatment of sex in this poem with that in Sharon Olds's "Sex without Love" (p. 739).

2. Think about "Seniors" as a kind of love poem and compare the speaker's voice here with the one in T. S. Eliot's "The Love Song of J. Alfred Prufrock" (p. 1068). How are these two voices used to evoke different cultures? Of what value is love in these cultures?

JOHN DONNE (1572–1631)

The Sun Rising   *c. 1633*

Busy old fool, unruly sun,
　　Why dost thou thus,
Through windows, and through curtains, call on us?
Must to thy motions lovers' seasons run?
　　Saucy pedantic wretch, go chide   5
　　Late schoolboys, and sour prentices,
　Go tell court-huntsmen that the king will ride,
　Call country ants° to harvest offices;   *farm workers*
Love, all alike, no season knows, nor clime,
Nor hours, days, months, which are the rags of time.   10

　　Thy beams, so reverend and strong
　　Why shouldst thou think?
I could eclipse and cloud them with a wink,
But that I would not lose her sight so long:
　　If her eyes have not blinded thine,   15
　　Look, and tomorrow late, tell me
　Whether both the Indias° of spice and mine   *East and West Indies*
　Be where thou left'st them, or lie here with me.
Ask for those kings whom thou saw'st yesterday,
And thou shalt hear, all here in one bed lay.   20

　　She is all states, and all princes I,
　　Nothing else is.
Princes do but play us; compared to this,
All honor's mimic, all wealth alchemy.
　　Thou, sun, art half as happy as we,   25
　　In that the world's contracted thus;

Thine age asks ease, and since thy duties be
To warm the world, that's done in warming us.
Shine here to us, and thou art every where;
This bed thy center° is, these walls thy sphere.   *of orbit*   30

CONSIDERATIONS FOR CRITICAL THINKING AND WRITING

1. FIRST RESPONSE. What is the situation in this poem? Why is the speaker angry with the sun? What does he urge the sun to do in the first stanza?

2. What claims does the speaker make about the power of love in stanzas 2 and 3? What does he mean when he says, "Shine here to us, and thou art every where"?

3. Are any of the speaker's exaggerations in any sense true? How?

CONNECTION TO ANOTHER SELECTION

1. Compare this lyric poem with Richard Wilbur's "A Late Aubade" (p. 731). What similarities do you find in the ideas and emotions expressed in each?

LI HO (791–817)

A Beautiful Girl Combs Her Hair   *date unknown*

TRANSLATED BY DAVID YOUNG

Awake at dawn
she's dreaming
by cool silk curtains

fragrance of spilling hair
half sandalwood, half aloes   5

windlass creaking at the well
singing jade

the lotus blossom wakes, refreshed

her mirror
two phoenixes   10
a pool of autumn light

standing on the ivory bed
loosening her hair
watching the mirror

one long coil, aromatic silk   15
a cloud down to the floor

drop the jade comb — no sound

delicate fingers
pushing the coils into place
color of raven feathers   20

shining blue-black stuff
the jewelled comb will hardly hold it

spring wind makes me restless
her slovenly beauty upsets me

eighteen and her hair's so thick   25
she wears herself out fixing it!

she's finished now
the whole arrangement in place

in a cloud-patterned skirt
she walks with even steps   30
a wild goose on the sand

turns away without a word
where is she off to?

down the steps to break a spray of
      cherry blossoms   35

CONSIDERATIONS FOR CRITICAL THINKING AND WRITING

1. FIRST RESPONSE. Try to paraphrase the poem. What is lost by rewording?
2. How does the speaker use sensuous language to create a vivid picture of the girl?
3. What are the speaker's feelings toward the girl? Do they remain the same throughout the poem?

CONNECTIONS TO OTHER SELECTIONS

1. Compare the description of hair in this poem with that in Cathy Song's "The White Porch" (p. 773). What significant similarities do you find?
2. Write an essay that explores the differing portraits in this poem and in Sylvia Plath's "Mirror" (p. 789). Which portrait is more interesting to you? Explain why.

ROBERT HASS (B. 1941)

Happiness   1996

Because yesterday morning from the steamy window
we saw a pair of red foxes across the creek
eating the last windfall apples in the rain —
they looked up at us with their green eyes
long enough to symbolize the wakefulness of living things   5
and then went back to eating —

and because this morning
when she went into the gazebo with her black pen and yellow pad
to coax an inquisitive soul
from what she thinks of as the reluctance of matter,   10

I drove into town to drink tea in the cafe
and write notes in a journal — mist rose from the bay
like the luminous and indefinite aspect of intention,
and a small flock of tundra swans
for the second winter in a row were feeding on new grass   15
in the soaked fields; they symbolize mystery, I suppose,
they are also called whistling swans, are very white,
and their eyes are black —

and because the tea steamed in front of me,
and the notebook, turned to a new page,   20
was blank except for a faint blue idea of order,
I wrote: *happiness! it is December, very cold,*
we woke early this morning,
and lay in bed kissing,
our eyes squinched up like bats.   25

CONSIDERATIONS FOR CRITICAL THINKING AND WRITING

1. FIRST RESPONSE. What kinds of experiences contribute to the speaker's happiness? Describe the person speaking.

2. Try writing a paraphrase of "Happiness." What happens to the poem when it's changed to prose? What accounts for these changes?

3. As Hass has done, define happiness or a moment in which you felt that emotion, in poetry or prose.

CONNECTION TO ANOTHER SELECTION

1. Write an essay that compares and contrasts "Happiness" with Emily Dickinson's "I like a look of Agony" (p. 962). Do they both succeed in capturing an emotion? What message do you take away from each?

21

Writing about Poetry

FROM READING TO WRITING

Writing about poetry can be a rigorous means of testing the validity of your own reading of a poem. Anyone who has been asked to write several pages about a fourteen-line poem knows how intellectually challenging this exercise is, because it means paying close attention to language. Such scrutiny of words, however, not only sensitizes you to the poet's use of language, but to your own use of language as well. At first you may feel intimidated by having to compose a paper that is longer than the poem you're writing about, but a careful reading will reveal that there's plenty to write about what the poem says and how it says it. Keep in mind that your job is not to produce a definitive reading of the poem — even Carl Sandburg once confessed that "I've written some poetry I don't understand myself." It is enough to develop an interesting thesis and to present it clearly and persuasively.

An interesting thesis will come to you if you read and reread, take notes, annotate the text, and generate ideas (for a discussion of this process see Chapter 53, "Reading and Writing"). Although it requires energy to read closely and to write convincingly about the charged language found in poetry, there is nothing mysterious about such reading and writing. This chapter provides a set of questions designed to sharpen your reading and writing about poetry. Following these questions is a sample paper that offers a clear and well-developed thesis concerning Elizabeth Bishop's "Manners."

QUESTIONS FOR RESPONSIVE
READING AND WRITING

The following questions can help you respond to important elements that reveal a poem's effects and meanings. The questions are general, so not all of them will necessarily be relevant to a particular poem. Many, however, should prove useful for thinking, talking, and writing about each poem in this collection. If you are uncertain about the meaning of a term used in a question, consult the Glossary of Literary Terms beginning on page 2190.

Before addressing these questions, read the poem you are studying in its entirety. Don't worry about interpretation on a first reading; allow yourself the pleasure of enjoying whatever makes itself apparent to you. Then on subsequent readings, use the questions to understand and appreciate how the poem works.

1. Who is the speaker? Is it possible to determine the speaker's age, sex, sensibilities, level of awareness, and values?
2. Is the speaker addressing anyone in particular?
3. How do you respond to the speaker? Favorably? Negatively? What is the situation? Are there any special circumstances that inform what the speaker says?
4. Is there a specific setting of time and place?
5. Does reading the poem aloud help you to understand it?
6. Does a paraphrase reveal the basic purpose of the poem?
7. What does the title emphasize?
8. Is the theme presented directly or indirectly?
9. Do any allusions enrich the poem's meaning?
10. How does the diction reveal meaning? Are any words repeated? Do any carry evocative connotative meanings? Are there any puns or other forms of verbal wit?
11. Are figures of speech used? How does the figurative language contribute to the poem's vividness and meaning?
12. Do any objects, persons, places, events, or actions have allegorical or symbolic meanings? What other details in the poem support your interpretation?
13. Is irony used? Are there any examples of situational irony, verbal irony, or dramatic irony? Is understatement or paradox used?
14. What is the tone of the poem? Is the tone consistent?
15. Does the poem use onomatopoeia, assonance, consonance, or alliteration? How do these sounds affect you?
16. What sounds are repeated? If there are rhymes, what is their effect? Do they seem forced or natural? Is there a rhyme scheme? Do the rhymes contribute to the poem's meaning?
17. Do the lines have a regular meter? What is the predominant meter? Are there significant variations? Does the rhythm seem appropriate for the tone of the poem?

18. Does the poem's form—its overall structure—follow an established pattern? Do you think the form is a suitable vehicle for the poem's meaning and effects?

19. Is the language of the poem intense and concentrated? Do you think it warrants more than one or two close readings?

20. Did you enjoy the poem? What, specifically, pleased or displeased you about what was expressed and how it was expressed?

21. Is there a particular critical approach that seems especially appropriate for this poem? (See the discussion of critical strategies for reading beginning on p. 2091.)

22. How might biographical information about the author help to determine the central concerns of the poem?

23. How might historical information about the poem provide a useful context for interpretation?

24. To what extent do your own experiences, values, beliefs, and assumptions inform your interpretation?

25. What kinds of evidence from the poem are you focusing on to support your interpretation? Does your interpretation leave out any important elements that might undercut or qualify your interpretation?

26. Given that there are a variety of ways to interpret the poem, which one seems the most useful to you?

A SAMPLE ANALYSIS

Memory in Elizabeth Bishop's "Manners"

The following sample paper on Elizabeth Bishop's "Manners" was written in response to an assignment that called for a 750-word discussion of the ways in which at least five of the following elements work to develop and reinforce the poem's themes:

diction and tone	irony	form
images	sound and rhyme	speaker
figures of speech	rhythm and meter	setting and situation
symbols		

In her paper, Debra Epstein discusses the ways in which a number of these elements contribute to what she sees as a central theme of "Manners": the loss of a way of life that Bishop associates with the end of World War I. Not all of the elements of poetry are covered equally in Epstein's paper because some, such as the speaker and setting, are more important to her argument than others. Notice how rather than merely listing each of the elements, Epstein mentions them in her discussion as she needs to in order to develop the thesis that she clearly and succinctly expresses in her opening paragraph.

ELIZABETH BISHOP (1911–1979)

Manners

1965

for a Child of 1918

My grandfather said to me
as we sat on the wagon seat,
"Be sure to remember to always
speak to everyone you meet."

We met a stranger on foot.   5
My grandfather's whip tapped his hat.
"Good day, sir. Good day. A fine day."
And I said it and bowed where I sat.

Then we overtook a boy we knew
with his big pet crow on his shoulder.   10
"Always offer everyone a ride;
don't forget that when you get older,"

my grandfather said. So Willy
climbed up with us, but the crow
gave a "Caw!" and flew off. I was worried.   15
How would he know where to go?

But he flew a little way at a time
from fence post to fence post, ahead;
and when Willy whistled he answered.
"A fine bird," my grandfather said,   20

"and he's well brought up. See, he answers
nicely when he's spoken to.
Man or beast, that's good manners.
Be sure that you both always do."

When automobiles went by,   25
the dust hid the people's faces,
but we shouted "Good day! Good day!
Fine day!" at the top of our voices.

When we came to Hustler Hill,
he said that the mare was tired,   30
so we all got down and walked,
as our good manners required.

Debra Epstein
Professor Brown
English 210
May 1, 20--

Memory in Elizabeth Bishop's "Manners"

The subject of Elizabeth Bishop's "Manners" has to do
with behaving well, but the theme of the poem has more to
do with a way of life than with etiquette. The poem suggests that modern society has lost something important--
a friendly openness, a generosity of spirit, a sense of
decency and consideration--in its race toward progress.
Although the narrative is simply told, Bishop enriches
this poem about manners by developing an implicit theme
through her subtle use of such elements of poetry as
speaker, setting, rhyme, meter, symbol, and images.

The dedication suggests that the speaker is "a Child
of 1918" who accompanies his or her grandfather on a
wagon ride and who is urged to practice good manners by
greeting people, offering everyone a ride, and speaking
when spoken to by anyone. During the ride they say hello
to a stranger, give a ride to a boy with a pet crow, shout
greetings to a passing automobile, and get down from the
wagon when they reach a hill because the horse is tired.
They walk because "good manners required" (line 32) such
consideration, even for a horse. This summary indicates
what goes on in the poem but not its significance. That
requires a closer look at some of the poem's elements.

Given the speaker's simple language (there are no
metaphors or similes and only a few words out of thirty-
two lines are more than two syllables), it seems likely
that he or she is a fairly young child, rather than an
adult reminiscing. (It is interesting to note that Bishop
herself, though not identical with the speaker, would have

been seven in 1918.) Because the speaker is a young child
who uses simple diction, Bishop has to show us the ride's
significance indirectly rather than having the speaker
explicitly state it.

The setting for the speaker's narrative is important
because 1918 was the year World War I ended, and it marked
the beginning of a new era of technology that was the result of rapid industrialization during the war. Horses and
wagons would soon be put out to pasture. The grandfather's
manners emphasize a time gone by; the child must be told
to "remember" what the grandfather says because he or she
will take that advice into a new and very different world.

The grandfather's world of the horse and wagon is
uncomplicated, and this is reflected in both the simple
quatrains that move predictably along in an abcb rhyme
scheme and the frequent anapestic meter (ăs wĕ sát ŏn tħe
wágŏn [2]) that pulls the lines rapidly and lightly. The
one moment Bishop breaks the set rhyme scheme is in the
seventh stanza when the automobile (the single four-
syllable word in the poem) rushes by in a cloud of dust so
that people cannot see or hear each other. The only off
rhymes in the poem--"faces" (26) and "voices" (28)--are
also in this stanza, which suggests that the automobile
and the people in it are somehow off or out of sync with
what goes on in the other stanzas. The automobile is a
symbol of a way of life in which people--their faces hid-
den--and manners take a back seat to speed and noise. The
people in the car don't wave, don't offer a ride, and
don't speak when spoken to.

Maybe the image of the crow's noisy cawing and flying
from post to post is a foreshadowing that should prepare
readers for the automobile. The speaker feels "worried"
about the crow's apparent directionlessness: "How would

he know where to go?" (16). However, neither the child
nor the grandfather (nor the reader on a first reading)
clearly sees the two worlds that Bishop contrasts in the
final stanza.

"Hustler Hill" is the perfect name for what finally
tires out the mare. There is no hurry for the grandfather
and child, but there is for those people in the car and
the postwar hustle and bustle they represent. The fast-
paced future overtakes the tired symbol of the past in the
poem. The pace slows as the wagon passengers get down to
walk, but the reader recognizes that the grandfather's
way has been lost to a world in which good manners are
not required.

22

Word Choice,
Word Order, and Tone

DICTION

web *For activities on diction, check out the Interactive Poetry Tutorial at*
http://www.bedfordstmartins.com/meyer/bedintrolit

Like all good writers, poets are keenly aware of *diction,* their choice of
words. Poets, however, choose words especially carefully because the words
in poems call attention to themselves. Characters, actions, settings, and
symbols may appear in a poem, but in the foreground, before all else, is the
poem's language. Also, poems are usually briefer than other forms of writing. A few inappropriate words in a 200-page novel (which would have
about 100,000 words) create fewer problems than they would in a 100-word
poem. Functioning in a compressed atmosphere, the words in a poem
must convey meanings gracefully and economically. Readers therefore
have to be alert to the ways in which those meanings are released.

Although poetic language is often more intensely charged than ordinary speech, the words used in poetry are not necessarily different from
everyday speech. Inexperienced readers may sometimes assume that language must be high-flown and out of date to be included in a poem: instead of reading about a boy "enjoying a swim," they expect to read about a
boy "disporting with pliant arm o'er a glassy wave." During the eighteenth
century this kind of *poetic diction* — the use of elevated language over ordinary language — was highly valued in English poetry, but since the nineteenth century poets have generally overridden the distinctions that were
once made between words used in everyday speech and those used in poetry.
Today all levels of diction can be found in poetry.

A poet, like any writer, has several levels of diction from which to choose;
they range from formal to middle to informal. *Formal diction* consists of a

715

dignified, impersonal, and elevated use of language. Notice, for example, the formality of Thomas Hardy's description of the sunken luxury liner *Titanic* in this stanza from "The Convergence of the Twain" (the entire poem appears on p. 736):

> In a solitude of the sea
> Deep from human vanity,
> And the Pride of Life that planned her, stilly couches she.

There is nothing casual or relaxed about these lines. Hardy's use of "stilly," meaning "quietly" or "calmly," is purely literary; the word rarely, if ever, turns up in everyday English.

The language used in Richard Wilbur's "A Late Aubade" (p. 731) represents a less formal level of diction; the speaker uses a *middle diction* spoken by most educated people. Consider how Wilbur's speaker tells his lover what she might be doing instead of being with him:

> You could be sitting now in a carrel
> Turning some liver-spotted page,
> Or rising in an elevator-cage
> Toward Ladies' Apparel.

The speaker elegantly enumerates his lover's unattractive alternatives to being with him — reading old books in a library or shopping in a department store — but the wit of his description lessens its formality.

Informal diction is evident in Larkin's "A Study of Reading Habits" (p. 684). The speaker's account of his early reading is presented *colloquially*, in a conversational manner that in this instance includes slang expressions not used by the culture at large:

> When getting my nose in a book
> Cured most things short of school,
> It was worth ruining my eyes
> To know I could still keep cool,
> And deal out the old right hook
> To dirty dogs twice my size.

This level of diction is clearly not that of Hardy's or Wilbur's speakers.

Poets may also draw on another form of informal diction, called *dialect.* Dialects are spoken by definable groups of people from a particular geographic region, economic group, or social class. New England dialects are often heard in Robert Frost's poems, for example. Gwendolyn Brooks employs a black dialect in "We Real Cool" (p. 744) to characterize a group of pool players. Another form of diction related to particular groups is *jargon,* a category of language defined by a trade or profession. Sociologists, photographers, carpenters, baseball players, and dentists, for example, all use words that are specific to their fields. E. E. Cummings manages to get quite a lot of mileage out of automobile jargon in "she being Brand" (p. 720).

Many levels of diction are available to poets. The variety of diction to be found in poetry is enormous, and that is how it should be. No language is foreign to poetry because it is possible to imagine any human voice as the speaker of a poem. When we say a poem is formal, informal, or somewhere in between, we are making a descriptive statement rather than an evaluative one. What matters in a poem is not only which words are used but how they are used.

DENOTATIONS AND CONNOTATIONS

eb *For activities of denotations and connotations check out the*
Interactive Poetry Tutorial at
http://www.bedfordstmartins.com/meyer/bedintrolit

One important way that the meaning of a word is communicated in a poem is through sound: snakes *hiss*, saws *buzz*. This and other matters related to sound are discussed in Chapter 26. Individual words also convey meanings through denotations and connotations. *Denotations* are the literal, dictionary meanings of a word. For example, *bird* denotes a feathered animal with wings (other denotations for the same word include a shuttlecock, an airplane, or an odd person), but in addition to its denotative meanings, *bird* also carries *connotations,* associations and implications that go beyond a word's literal meanings. Connotations derive from how the word has been used and the associations people make with it. Therefore, the connotations of *bird* might include fragility, vulnerability, altitude, the sky, or freedom, depending on the context in which the word is used. Consider also how different the connotations are for the following types of birds: hawk, dove, penguin, pigeon, chicken, peacock, duck, crow, turkey, gull, owl, goose, coot, and vulture. These words have long been used to refer to types of people as well as birds. They are rich in connotative meanings.

Connotations derive their resonance from a person's experiences with a word. Those experiences may not always be the same, especially when the people having them are in different times and places. *Theater,* for instance, was once associated with depravity, disease, and sin, whereas today the word usually evokes some sense of high culture and perhaps visions of elegant opulence. In several ethnic communities in the United States many people would find *squid* appetizing, but elsewhere the word is likely to produce negative connotations. Readers must recognize, then, that words written in other times and places may have unexpected connotations. Annotations usually help in these matters, which is why it makes sense to pay attention to them when they are available.

Ordinarily, though, the language of poetry is accessible, even when the circumstances of the reader and the poet are different. Although connotative language may be used subtly, it mostly draws on associations experienced by many people. Poets rely on widely shared associations rather than the idiosyncratic response that an individual might have to a word. Someone who has received a severe burn from a fireplace accident may associate the word *hearth* with intense pain instead of home and family life, but that reader must not allow a personal experience to undermine the response the poet intends to evoke. Connotative meanings are usually public meanings.

Perhaps this can be seen most clearly in advertising, where language is also used primarily to convey moods and feelings rather than information. For instance, nearly three decades of increasing interest in nutrition and general fitness have created a collective consciousness that advertisers have capitalized on successfully. Knowing that we want to be slender or lean or slim (not *spare* or *scrawny* and certainly not *gaunt*), advertisers have created a new word to describe beers, wines, sodas, cheeses, canned fruits, and other products that tend to overload what used to be called sweatclothes and sneakers. The word is *lite*. The assumed denotative meaning of *lite* is "low in calories," but as close readers of ingredient labels know, some *lites* are heavier than regularly prepared products. There can be no doubt about the connotative meaning of *lite*, however. Whatever is *lite* cannot hurt you; less is more. Even the word is lighter than *light*; there is no unnecessary droopy *g* or plump *h*. *Lite* is a brilliantly manufactured use of connotation.

Connotative meanings are valuable because they allow poets to be economical and suggestive simultaneously. In this way emotions and attitudes are carefully woven into the texture of the poem's language. Read the following poem and pay close attention to the connotative meanings of its words.

RANDALL JARRELL (1914–1965)

The Death of the Ball Turret Gunner   1945

From my mother's sleep I fell into the State
And I hunched in its belly till my wet fur froze.
Six miles from earth, loosed from its dream of life,
I woke to black flack and the nightmare fighters.
When I died they washed me out of the turret with a hose.

The title of this poem establishes the setting and the speaker's situation. Like the setting of a short story, the setting of a poem is important when the time and place influence what happens. "The Death of the Ball Turret Gunner" is set in the midst of a war and, more specifically, in a ball turret—a Plexiglas sphere housing machine guns on the underside of a bomber. The speaker's situation obviously places him in extreme danger; indeed, his fate is announced in the title.

Although the poem is written in the first-person singular, its speaker is clearly not the poet. Jarrell uses a *persona,* a speaker created by the poet. In this poem the persona is a disembodied voice that makes the gunner's story all the more powerful. What is his story? A paraphrase might read something like this:

After I was born, I grew up to find myself at war, cramped into the turret of a bomber's belly some 31,000 feet above the ground. Below me were exploding shells from antiaircraft guns and attacking fighter planes. I was killed, but the bomber returned to base, where my remains were cleaned out of the turret so the next man could take my place.

This paraphrase is accurate, but its language is much less suggestive than the poem's. The first line of the poem has the speaker emerge from his "mother's sleep," the anesthetized sleep of her giving birth. The phrase also suggests the comfort, warmth, and security he knew as a child. This safety was left behind when he "fell," a verb that evokes the danger and involuntary movement associated with his subsequent "State" (*fell* also echoes, perhaps, the fall from innocence to experience related in the Bible).

Several dictionary definitions appear for the noun *state;* it can denote a territorial unit, the power and authority of a government, a person's social status, or a person's emotional or physical condition. The context provided by the rest of the poem makes clear that "State" has several denotative meanings here: because it is capitalized, it certainly refers to the violent world of a government at war, but it also refers to the gunner's vulnerable status as well as his physical and emotional condition. By having "State" carry more than one meaning, Jarrell has created an intentional ambiguity. *Ambiguity* allows for two or more simultaneous interpretations of a word, phrase, action, or situation, all of which can be supported by the context of a work. Through his ambiguous use of "State," Jarrell connects the horrors of war not just to bombers and gunners but to the governments that control them.

Related to this ambiguity is the connotative meaning of "State" in the poem. The context demands that the word be read with a negative charge. The word is not used with patriotic pride but to suggest an anonymous, impersonal "State" that kills rather than nurtures the life in its "belly." The state's "belly" is a bomber, and the gunner is "hunched" like a fetus in the cramped turret, where, in contrast to the warmth of his mother's womb, everything is frozen, even the "wet fur" of his flight jacket (newborn infants have wet fur too). The gunner is not just 31,000 feet from the ground but "Six miles from earth." *Six miles* has roughly the same denotative meaning as 31,000 feet, but Jarrell knew that the connotative meaning of *six miles* makes the speaker's position seem even more remote and frightening.

When the gunner is born into the violent world of war, he finds himself waking up to a "nightmare" that is all too real. The poem's final line is grimly understated, but it hits the reader with the force of an exploding shell: what the State-bomber-turret gives birth to is a gruesome death that is merely one of an endless series. It may be tempting to reduce the theme of this poem to the idea that "war is hell," but Jarrell's target is more specific. He implicates the "State," which routinely executes such violence, and he does so without preaching or hysterical denunciations. Instead, his use of language conveys his theme subtly and powerfully. Consider how this next poem uses connotative meanings to express its theme.

E. E. CUMMINGS (1894–1962)

she being Brand   1926

she being Brand

-new;and you
know consequently a
little stiff i was
careful of her and(having   5

thoroughly oiled the universal
joint tested my gas felt of
her radiator made sure her springs were O.

K.)i went right to it flooded-the-carburetor cranked her

up,slipped the   10
clutch(and then somehow got into reverse she
kicked what
the hell)next
minute i was back in neutral tried and

again slo-wly;bare,ly nudg. ing (my   15

lev-er Right-
oh and her gears being in
A 1 shape passed
from low through
second-in-to-high like   20
greasedlightning) just as we turned the corner of Divinity

avenue i touched the accelerator and give

her the juice,good

(it
was the first ride and believe i we was   25
happy to see how nice she acted right up to
the last minute coming back down by the Public
Gardens i slammed on

the
internalexpanding   30
&
externalcontracting
brakes Bothatonce and

brought allofher tremB
-ling   35
to a:dead.

stand-
;Still)

CONSIDERATIONS FOR CRITICAL THINKING AND WRITING

1. FIRST RESPONSE. How does Cummings's arrangement of the words on the page help you to read this poem aloud? What does the poem describe?
2. What ambiguities in language does the poem ride on? At what point were you first aware of these double meanings?
3. Explain why you think the poem is primarily serious or humorous.
4. CRITICAL STRATEGIES. Read the section on cultural criticism (pp. 2104–05) in Chapter 52, "Critical Strategies for Reading." Then find some advertisements for convertibles or sports cars in magazines and read them closely. What similarities do you find in the use of connotative language in them and in Cummings's poem? Write a brief essay explaining how language is used to convey the theme of one of the advertisements and the poem.

WORD ORDER

Meanings in poems are conveyed not only by denotations and connotations but also by the poet's arrangement of words into phrases, clauses, and sentences to achieve particular effects. The ordering of words into meaningful verbal patterns is called *syntax.* A poet can manipulate the syntax of a line to place emphasis on a word; this is especially apparent when a poet varies normal word order. In Dickinson's "A narrow Fellow in the Grass" (p. 2), for example, the speaker says about the snake that "His notice sudden is." Ordinarily, that would be expressed as "his notice is sudden." By placing the verb *is* unexpectedly at the end of the line, Dickinson creates the sense of surprise we feel when we suddenly come upon a snake. Dickinson's inversion of the standard word order also makes the final sound of the line a hissing *is.*

Cummings uses one long sentence in "she being Brand" to take the reader on a ride that begins with a false start but accelerates quickly before coming to a halt. The jargon creates an exuberantly humorous mood that is helped along by the poem's syntax. How do Cummings's ordering of words and sentence structure reinforce the meaning of the lines?

TONE

Tone is the writer's attitude toward the subject, the mood created by all the elements in the poem. Writing, like speech, may be characterized as serious or light, sad or happy, private or public, angry or affectionate, bitter or nostalgic, or any other attitudes and feelings that human beings experience. In Jarrell's "The Death of the Ball Turret Gunner," the tone is clearly serious; the voice in the poem even sounds dead. Listen again to the persona's final words: "When I died they washed me out of the turret with a hose." The brutal, restrained matter-of-factness of this line is effective because the reader is called on to supply the appropriate anger and despair, a strategy that makes those emotions all the more convincing.

Consider how tone is used to convey meaning in the next poem, inspired by the poet's contemplation of mortality.

JUDITH ORTIZ COFER (B. 1952)

Common Ground   1987

Blood tells the story of your life
in heartbeats as you live it;
bones speak in the language
of death, and flesh thins
with age when up   5
through your pores rises
the stuff of your origin.

These days,
when I look into the mirror I see
my grandmother's stern lips   10
speaking in parentheses at the corners
of my mouth of pain and deprivation
I have never known. I recognize
my father's brows arching in disdain
over the objects of my vanity, my mother's   15
nervous hands smoothing lines
just appearing on my skin,
like arrows pointing downward
to our common ground.

CONSIDERATIONS FOR CRITICAL THINKING AND WRITING

1. FIRST RESPONSE. How do you interpret the title? How did your idea of its
   meaning change as you read the poem?
2. What is the relationship between the first and second stanzas?
3. How does this poem make you feel? What is its tone? How do the diction
   and imagery create the tone?

ROBIN MORGAN (B. 1941)

Invocation   1999

for Isel Rivero

*Gunmen attacked a school in northwestern Rwanda last Monday, killing seventeen
girls. . . . The attack took place after the Hutu gunmen ordered the girls to separate into
groups of ethnic Hutu and Tutsi, and the students refused to comply.*
                                    —*from* The New York Times, *April 30, 1997*

Insane, sadistic gods to whom I offer
only my denial and disgust,

how do we bear witness to each other
when such defiance gleams beyond our trust?

They stupify us, these small, nameless girls   5
in whose name Love linked arms with her best friend.
Courage skulks shamed before these little skulls
rotting on the grassy school playground.

Let me be worthy of such children, slain
where they stand, who in the face of dying, cling.   10
Let me be equal to my small, sufficient pain
and in the broken teeth of horror, sing.

CONSIDERATIONS FOR CRITICAL THINKING AND WRITING

1. FIRST RESPONSE. How does your own response to the news report of the massacre compare with the poet's?
2. Look up *invocation* in the dictionary. In what sense is this poem an invocation?
3. Describe the tone of each stanza. How does the tone change from stanza to stanza?
4. What do lines 11 and 12 mean? What words and images affect you? How?

CONNECTION TO ANOTHER SELECTION

1. How is the strategy used in the final line of this poem similar to that of the final line in James Merrill's "Casual Wear" (p. 823)? Though the strategy is similar, how is the tone different at the end of each poem?

The next work is a *dramatic monologue,* a type of poem in which a character — the speaker — addresses a silent audience in such a way as to reveal unintentionally some aspect of his or her temperament or personality. What tone is created by Machan's use of a persona?

KATHARYN HOWD MACHAN (B. 1952)

Hazel Tells LaVerne   1976

last night
im cleanin out my
howard johnsons ladies room
when all of a sudden
up pops this frog   5
musta come from the sewer
swimmin aroun an tryin ta
climb up the sida the bowl
so i goes ta flushm down
but sohelpmegod he starts talkin   10
bout a golden ball
an how i can be a princess
me a princess

well my mouth drops
all the way to the floor   15
an he says
kiss me just kiss me
once on the nose
well i screams
ya little green pervert   20
an i hitsm with my mop
an has ta flush
the toilet down three times
me
a princess   25

CONSIDERATIONS FOR CRITICAL THINKING AND WRITING

1. FIRST RESPONSE. What do you imagine the situation and setting are for this poem? Do you like this revision of the fairy tale "The Frog Prince"?

2. What creates the poem's humor? How does Hazel's use of language reveal her personality? Is her treatment of the frog consistent with her character?

3. Although it has no punctuation, this poem is easy to follow. How does the arrangement of the lines organize Hazel's speech for clarity and emphasis?

4. What is the theme? Is it conveyed through denotative or connotative language?

5. Write what you think might be LaVerne's reply to Hazel. First, write LaVerne's response as a series of ordinary sentences, and then try editing and organizing them into poetic lines.

CONNECTION TO ANOTHER SELECTION

1. Although Robert Browning's "My Last Duchess" (p. 827) is a more complex poem than Machan's, both use dramatic monologues to reveal character. How are the strategies in each poem similar?

MARTÍN ESPADA (B. 1957)
Latin Night at the Pawnshop   1987

Chelsea, Massachusetts
Christmas, 1987

The apparition of a salsa band
gleaming in the Liberty Loan
pawnshop window:

Golden trumpet,
silver trombone,
congas, maracas, tambourine,
all with price tags dangling
like the city morgue ticket
on a dead man's toe.

CONSIDERATIONS FOR CRITICAL THINKING AND WRITING

1. FIRST RESPONSE. What is "Latin" about this night at the pawnshop?
2. What kind of tone is created by the poet's word choice and by the rhythm of the poem?
3. Does it matter that this apparition occurs on Christmas night? Why or why not?
4. What do you think is the central point of this poem?

How do the speaker's attitude and tone change during the course of this next poem?

SARAH LINDSAY (B. 1958)

Aluminum Chlorohydrate   1997

Am I then to understand
that with every matins' sociable embalming of the armpit
molecular aluminum insinuates itself, through sheared follicles,
bright fleck by bright invisible fleck, into the tiny tender kinks
of capillaries? slides along their permeable wisps   5
into the jostling rivers of depleted scarlet doughnuts and white ghosts,
into a hectic Amazon, through endlessly wrung chambers,
out the roaring wide aorta, rising blandly through the neck
by ever subtler pulses toward the tingling gray curd
all flushed with its matted electrical storms? and lays   10
a glinting finger on one sparked synaptic mouth
that hushes. Whose voice may never be missed.
A number, a name, the Latin for *greed*,
clopping upstairs that March day in Florence with brand-new clogs,
the blister they raised. But supposing senility   15
takes the brain in its soft retriever's mouth
and carries it to be gutted, supposing all
the recent layers plucked away and memory's microscopic doors flung wide
for the oldest to come forth: Would third-grade Ruth be missing
and unmissed, or Mary or Brenda, with random trivial comrades,   20
or would the whole host stagger out, one missing legs, another clothes,
with synthetic pearls for eyes or carrot noses?
Or would each corridor dead-end on a scaly tinfoil mirror
showing nothing but the scowling smear
of some old unfamiliar woman's face?   25

CONSIDERATIONS FOR CRITICAL THINKING AND WRITING

1. FIRST RESPONSE. What do you make of this poem on the first reading? Carefully read the poem at least three times and record how your understanding develops from reading to reading. How does your third reading differ from your initial response?
2. What is aluminum chlorohydrate? Why is it an appropriate title for this poem? How does it contribute to the poem's tone?

3. Explain how the tone shifts in the second half of the poem beginning with "But supposing . . ." (15)? Pay particular attention to the final image in lines 23 to 25.

4. What is the effect of the speaker asking a series of questions rather than making statements?

CONNECTION TO ANOTHER SELECTION

1. Discuss the ways in which diction helps create tone in "Aluminum Chlorohydrate" and "The Foot" by Alice Jones (p. 870). What does each poem have to say about what it means to be a human being?

DICTION AND TONE IN FOUR LOVE POEMS

The first three of these love poems share the same basic situation and theme: a male speaker addresses a female (in the first poem it is a type of female) urging that love should not be delayed because time is short. This theme is as familiar in poetry as it is in life. In Latin this tradition is known as *carpe diem,* "seize the day." Notice how the poets' diction helps create a distinctive tone in each poem, even though the subject matter and central ideas are similar (although not identical) in all three.

ROBERT HERRICK (1591–1674)

To the Virgins, to Make Much of Time 1648

Gather ye rose-buds while ye may,
  Old Time is still a-flying;
And this same flower that smiles today,
  Tomorrow will be dying.

The glorious lamp of heaven, the sun, 5
  The higher he's a-getting,
The sooner will his race be run,
  And nearer he's to setting.

That age is best which is the first,
  When youth and blood are warmer; 10
But being spent, the worse, and worst
  Times still succeed the former.

Then be not coy, but use your time,
  And while ye may, go marry;
For having lost but once your prime, 15
  You may for ever tarry.

CONSIDERATIONS FOR CRITICAL THINKING AND WRITING

1. FIRST RESPONSE. Would there be any change in meaning if the title of this poem were "To Young Women, to Make Much of Time"? Do you think the poem can apply to young men too?

2. What do the virgins have in common with the flowers (lines 1-4) and the course of the day (5-8)?

3. How does the speaker develop his argument? What will happen to the virgins if they don't "marry"? Paraphrase the poem.

4. What is the tone of the speaker's advice?

The next poem was also written in the seventeenth century, but it includes some words that have changed in usage and meaning over the past three hundred years. The title of Marvell's "To His Coy Mistress" requires some explanation. "Mistress" does not refer to a married man's illicit lover but to a woman who is loved and courted — a sweetheart. Marvell uses "coy" to describe a woman who is reserved and shy rather than coquettish or flirtatious. Often such shifts in meanings over time are explained in the notes that accompany reprintings of poems. You should keep in mind, however, that it is helpful to have a reasonably thick dictionary available when you are reading poetry. The most thorough is the *Oxford English Dictionary (OED)*, which provides histories of words. The *OED* is a multivolume leviathan, but there are other useful unabridged dictionaries and desk dictionaries.

Knowing its original meaning can also enrich your understanding of why a contemporary poet chooses a particular word. Elizabeth Bishop begins "The Fish" (p. 682) this way: "I caught a tremendous fish." We know immediately in this context that "tremendous" means very large. In addition, given that the speaker clearly admires the fish in the lines that follow, we might even understand "tremendous" in the colloquial sense of wonderful and extraordinary. But a dictionary gives us some further relevant insights. Because, by the end of the poem, we see the speaker thoroughly moved as a result of the encounter with the fish ("everything / was rainbow, rainbow, rainbow!"), the dictionary's additional information about the history of *tremendous* shows why it is the perfect adjective to introduce the fish. The word comes from the Latin *tremere* (to tremble) and therefore once meant "such as to make one tremble." That is precisely how the speaker is at the end of the poem: deeply affected and trembling. Knowing the origin of *tremendous* gives us the full heft of the poet's word choice.

Although some of the language in "To His Coy Mistress" requires annotations for the modern reader, this poem continues to serve as a powerful reminder that time is a formidable foe, even for lovers.

ANDREW MARVELL (1621–1678)

To His Coy Mistress   *1681*

Had we but world enough, and time,
This coyness, lady, were no crime.
We would sit down, and think which way
To walk, and pass our long love's day.
Thou by the Indian Ganges'° side   5
Shouldst rubies find; I by the tide
Of Humber° would complain.° I would   *write love songs*
Love you ten years before the Flood,
And you should, if you please, refuse
Till the conversion of the Jews.   10
My vegetable love should grow°
Vaster than empires, and more slow;
An hundred years should go to praise
Thine eyes and on thy forehead gaze,
Two hundred to adore each breast,   15
But thirty thousand to the rest:
An age at least to every part,
And the last age should show your heart.
For, lady, you deserve this state,
Nor would I love at lower rate.   20
    But at my back I always hear
Time's wingèd chariot hurrying near;
And yonder all before us lie
Deserts of vast eternity.
Thy beauty shall no more be found,   25
Nor in thy marble vault shall sound
My echoing song; then worms shall try
That long preserved virginity,
And your quaint honor turn to dust,
And into ashes all my lust.   30
The grave's a fine and private place,
But none, I think, do there embrace.
    Now, therefore, while the youthful hue
Sits on thy skin like morning dew,
And while thy willing soul transpires°   *breathes forth* 35
At every pore with instant fires,
Now let us sport us while we may,
And now, like amorous birds of prey,
Rather at once our time devour
Than languish in his slow-chapped° power.   *slow-jawed* 40
Let us roll all our strength and all

---

5 *Ganges:* A river in India sacred to the Hindus.   7 *Humber:* A river that flows through Marvell's native town, Hull.   11 *My vegetable love . . . grow:* A slow, unconscious growth.

Our sweetness up into one ball,
And tear our pleasures with rough strife
Thorough° the iron gates of life.   *through*
Thus, though we cannot make our sun   45
Stand still, yet we will make him run.

CONSIDERATIONS FOR CRITICAL THINKING AND WRITING

1. FIRST RESPONSE. Do you think this *carpe diem* poem is hopelessly dated or
   does it speak to our contemporary concerns?

2. This poem is divided into a three-part argument. Briefly summarize each
   section: if (lines 1–20), but (21–32), therefore (33–46).

3. What is the speaker's tone in lines 1–20? How much time would he spend
   adoring his mistress? Is he sincere? How does he expect his mistress to respond to these lines?

4. How does the speaker's tone change beginning with line 21? What is his
   view of time in lines 21–32? What does this description do to the lush and
   leisurely sense of time in lines 1–20? How do you think his mistress would
   react to lines 21–32?

5. In the final lines of Herrick's "To the Virgins, to Make Much of Time," the
   speaker urges the virgins to "go marry." What does Marvell's speaker urge
   in lines 33–46? How is the pace of these lines (notice the verbs) different
   from that of the first twenty lines of the poem?

6. This poem is sometimes read as a vigorous but simple celebration of flesh.
   Is there more to the theme than that?

PERSPECTIVE

BERNARD DUYFHUIZEN (B. 1953)

*"To His Coy Mistress": On How a Female
Might Respond*   1988

Clearly a female reader of "To His Coy Mistress" might have trouble identifying
with the poem's speaker; therefore, her first response would be to identify with
the listener-in-the-poem, the eternally silent Coy Mistress. In such a reading she is
likely to recognize that she has heard this kind of line before although maybe not
with the same intensity and insistence. Moreover, she is likely to (re)experience
the unsettling emotions that such an egoistic assault on her virginal autonomy
would provoke. She will also see differently, even by contemporary standards, the
plot beyond closure, the possible consequences—both physical and social—that
the Mistress will encounter. Lastly, she is likely to be angered by this poem, by her
marginalization in an argument that seeks to overpower the core of her being.

From "Textual Harassment of Marvell's Coy Mistress:
The Institutionalization of Masculine Criticism,"
College English, April 1988

CONSIDERATIONS FOR CRITICAL THINKING AND WRITING

1. Explain whether you find convincing Duyfhuizen's description of a female's potential response to the poem. How does his description compare with your own response?

2. Characterize the silent mistress of the poem. How do you think the speaker treats her? What do his language and tone suggest about his relationship to her?

3. Does the fact that this description of a female response is written by a man make any difference in your assessment of it? Explain why or why not.

The third in this series of *carpe diem* poems is a twentieth-century work. The language of Wilbur's "A Late Aubade" is more immediately accessible than that of Marvell's "To His Coy Mistress"; a dictionary will quickly identify any words unfamiliar to a reader, including the allusion to Arnold Schoenberg, the composer, in line 11. An *allusion* is a brief reference to a person, place, thing, event, or idea in history or literature. Allusive words, like connotative words, are both suggestive and economical; poets use allusions to conjure up biblical authority, scenes from Shakespeare's plays, historic figures, wars, great love stories, and anything else that might serve to deepen and enrich their own work. The speaker in "A Late Aubade" makes an allusion that an ordinary dictionary won't explain. He tells his lover: "I need not rehearse / The rosebuds-theme of centuries of verse." True to his word, he says no more about this for her or the reader. The lines refer, of course, to the *carpe diem* theme as found familiarly in Herrick's "To the Virgins, to Make Much of Time." Wilbur assumes that his reader will understand the allusion.

Allusions imply reading and cultural experiences shared by the poet and reader. Literate audiences once had more in common than they do today because more people had similar economic, social, and educational backgrounds. But a judicious use of specialized dictionaries, encyclopedias, and other reference tools can help you decipher allusions that grow out of this body of experience. (See page 2167 for a list of useful reference works for students of literature.) As you read more, you'll be able to make connections based on your own experiences with literature. In a sense, allusions make available what other human beings have deemed worth remembering, and that is certainly an economical way of supplementing and enhancing your own experience.

Wilbur's version of the *carpe diem* theme follows. What strikes you as particularly modern about it?

RICHARD WILBUR (B. 1921)

A Late Aubade   1968

You could be sitting now in a carrel
Turning some liver-spotted page,
Or rising in an elevator-cage
Toward Ladies' Apparel.

You could be planting a raucous bed   5
Of salvia, in rubber gloves,
Or lunching through a screed of someone's loves
With pitying head,

Or making some unhappy setter
Heel, or listening to a bleak   10
Lecture on Schoenberg's serial technique.
Isn't this better?

Think of all the time you are not
Wasting, and would not care to waste,
Such things, thank God, not being to your taste.   15
Think what a lot

Of time, by woman's reckoning,
You've saved, and so may spend on this,
You who had rather lie in bed and kiss
Than anything.   20

It's almost noon, you say? If so,
Time flies, and I need not rehearse
The rosebuds-theme of centuries of verse.
If you *must* go,

Wait for a while, then slip downstairs   25
And bring us up some chilled white wine,
And some blue cheese, and crackers, and some fine
Ruddy-skinned pears.

CONSIDERATIONS FOR CRITICAL THINKING AND WRITING

1. FIRST RESPONSE. Explain whether or not you find the speaker appealing.
2. An *aubade* is a song about lovers parting at dawn, but in this "late aubade," "It's almost noon." Is there another way of reading the adjective *late* in the title?
3. How does the speaker's diction characterize both him and his lover? What sort of lives do they live? What does the casual allusion to Herrick's poem (line 23) reveal about them?
4. What is the effect of using "liver-spotted page," "elevator-cage," "raucous bed," "screed," "unhappy setter," and "bleak / Lecture" to describe the woman's activities?

1. How does the man's argument in "A Late Aubade" differ from the speakers' in Herrick's and Marvell's poems? Which of the three arguments do you find most convincing?
2. Explain how the tone of each poem is suited to its theme.

This fourth love poem is by a woman. Listen to the speaker's voice. Does it sound different from the way the men speak in the previous three poems?

DIANE ACKERMAN (B. 1948)

A Fine, a Private Place   1983

He took her one day
under the blue horizon
where long sea fingers
parted like beads
hitched in the doorway   5
of an opium den,
and canyons mazed the deep
reef with hollows,
cul-de-sacs, and narrow boudoirs,
and had to ask twice   10
before she understood
his stroking her arm
with a marine feather
slobbery as aloe pulp
was wooing, or saw the octopus   15
in his swimsuit
stretch one tentacle
and ripple its silky bag.

While bubbles rose
like globs of mercury,   20
they made love
mask to mask, floating
with oceans of air between them,
she his sea-geisha
in an orange kimono   25
of belts and vests,
her lacquered hair waving,
as Indigo Hamlets
tattooed the vista,
and sunlight   30
cut through the water,
twisting its knives
into corridors of light.

His sandy hair
and sea-blue eyes,   35
his kelp-thin waist
and chest ribbed wider
than a sandbar
where muscles domed
clear and taut as shells   40
(freckled cowries,
flat, brawny scallops
the color of dawn),
his sea-battered hands
gripping her thighs   45
like tawny starfish
and drawing her close
as a pirate vessel
to let her board:
who was this she loved?   50

Overhead, sponges
sweating raw color
jutted from a coral arch,
Clown Wrasses°   *brightly colored tropical fish*
hovered like fireworks,   55
and somewhere an abalone opened
its silver wings.
Part of a lusty dream
under aspic, her hips rolled
like a Spanish galleon,   60
her eyes swam
and chest began to heave.
Gasps melted on the tide.
Knowing she would soon be
breathless as her tank,   65
he pumped his brine
deep within her,
letting sea water drive it
through petals
delicate as anemone veils   70
to the dark purpose
of a conch-shaped womb.
An ear to her loins
would have heard the sea roar.

When panting ebbed,   75
and he signaled *Okay?*
as lovers have asked,
land or waterbound
since time heaved ho,
he led her to safety: 80
shallower realms,
heading back toward

the boat's even keel,
though ocean still petted her
cell by cell, murmuring   85
along her legs and neck,
caressing her
with pale, endless arms.

Later, she thought often
of that blue boudoir,   90
pillow-soft and filled
with cascading light,
where together
they'd made a bell
that dumbly clanged   95
beneath the waves
and minutes lurched
like mountain goats.
She could still see
the quilted mosaics   100
that were fish
twitching spangles overhead,
still feel the ocean
inside and out, turning her
evolution around.   105

She thought of it miles
and fathoms away, often,
at odd moments: watching
the minnow snowflakes
dip against the windowframe,   110
holding a sponge
idly under tap-gush,
sinking her teeth
into the cleft
of a voluptuous peach.   115

CONSIDERATIONS FOR CRITICAL THINKING AND WRITING

1. FIRST RESPONSE. How is your response to this poem affected by the fact that the speaker is female?

2. Read Marvell's "To His Coy Mistress" (p. 728). To what in Marvell's poem does Ackerman's title allude? Explain how the allusion to Marvell is crucial to understanding Ackerman's poem.

3. Comment on the descriptive passages of "A Fine, a Private Place." Which images seem especially vivid to you? How do they contribute to the poem's meanings?

4. What are the speaker's reflections on her experience in lines 106–115? What echoes of Marvell do you hear in these lines?

CONNECTIONS TO OTHER SELECTIONS

1. Write an essay comparing the tone of Ackerman's poem with that of Mar-vell's "To His Coy Mistress" (p. 728). To what extent are the central ideas in the poems similar?

2. Compare the speaker's voice in Ackerman's poem with the voice you imag-ine for the coy mistress in Marvell's poem.

3. CRITICAL STRATEGIES. Read the section on feminist criticism (pp. 0000–00) in Chapter 52, "Critical Strategies for Reading," and compare the themes in Ackerman's and Marvell's poems the way you think a feminist critic might analyze them.

POEMS FOR FURTHER STUDY

MARGARET ATWOOD (B. 1939)

Bored   1995

All those times I was bored
out of my mind. Holding the log
while he sawed it. Holding
the string while he measured, boards,
distances between things, or pounded   5
stakes into the ground for rows and rows
of lettuces and beets, which I then (bored)
weeded. Or sat in the back
of the car, or sat still in boats,
sat, sat, while at the prow, stern, wheel   10
he drove, steered, paddled. It
wasn't even boredom, it was looking,
looking hard and up close at the small
details. Myopia. The worn gunwales,
the intricate twill of the seat   15
cover. The acid crumbs of loam, the granular
pink rock, its igneous veins, the sea-fans
of dry moss, the blackish and then the greying
bristles on the back of his neck.
Sometimes he would whistle, sometimes   20
I would. The boring rhythm of doing
things over and over, carrying
the wood, drying
the dishes. Such minutiae. It's what
the animals spend most of their time at,   25
ferrying the sand, grain by grain, from their tunnels,
shuffling the leaves in their burrows. He pointed
such things out, and I would look
at the whorled texture of his square finger, earth under
the nail. Why do I remember it as sunnier   30

all the time then, although it more often
rained, and more birdsong?
I could hardly wait to get
the hell out of there to
anywhere else. Perhaps though   35
boredom is happier. It is for dogs or
groundhogs. Now I wouldn't be bored.
Now I would know too much.
Now I would know.

CONSIDERATIONS FOR CRITICAL THINKING AND WRITING

1. FIRST RESPONSE. Atwood has described this poem as one of several about her father and his death. Is it possible to determine that "he" is the speaker's father from the details of the poem? Explain whether or not you think it matters who "he" is.

2. Play with the possible meanings of the word "bored" and its variations in the poem. What function does the repetition of the word serve?

3. What does the speaker "know" at the end of the poem that she didn't before?

CONNECTION TO ANOTHER SELECTION

1. Write an essay on the speaker's attitude toward the father in this poem and in Hayden's "Those Winter Sundays" (p. 672).

THOMAS HARDY (1840-1928)

The Convergence of the Twain   *1912*

Lines on the Loss of the "Titanic"°

I

    In a solitude of the sea
    Deep from human vanity,
And the Pride of Life that planned her, stilly couches she.

II

    Steel chambers, late the pyres
    Of her salamandrine fires,°   5
Cold currents thrid,° and turn to rhythmic tidal lyres.   *thread*

Titanic: A luxurious ocean liner, reputed to be unsinkable, which sank after hitting an iceberg on its maiden voyage in 1912. Only a third of the 2,200 passengers survived.   5 *salamandrine fires:* Salamanders were, according to legend, able to survive fire; hence, the ship's fires burned even though under water.

III
      Over the mirrors meant
      To glass the opulent
The sea-worm crawls — grotesque, slimed, dumb, indifferent.

IV
      Jewels in joy designed   10
      To ravish the sensuous mind
Lie lightless, all their sparkles bleared and black and blind.

V
      Dim moon-eyed fishes near
      Gaze at the gilded gear
And query: "What does this vaingloriousness down here?"   15

VI
      Well: while was fashioning
      This creature of cleaving wing,
The Immanent Will that stirs and urges everything

VII
      Prepared a sinister mate
      For her — so gaily great —   20
A Shape of Ice, for the time far and dissociate.

VIII
      And as the smart ship grew
      In stature, grace, and hue,
In shadowy silent distance grew the Iceberg too.

IX
      Alien they seemed to be: 25
      No mortal eye could see
The intimate welding of their later history,

X
      Or sign that they were bent
      By paths coincident
On being anon twin halves of one august event,   30

XI
      Till the Spinner of the Years
      Said "Now!" And each one hears,
And consummation comes, and jars two hemispheres.

Considerations for Critical Thinking and Writing

1. FIRST RESPONSE. Describe a contemporary disaster comparable to the *Titanic.* How was your response to it similar to or different from the speaker's response to the *Titanic?*

2. How do the words used to describe the ship in this poem reveal the speaker's attitude toward the *Titanic?*

3. The diction of the poem suggests that the *Titanic* and the iceberg partici-pate in something like an arranged marriage. What specific words imply this?

4. Who or what causes the disaster? Does the speaker assign responsibility?

DAVID R. SLAVITT (B. 1935)
Titanic   1983

Who does not love the *Titanic?*
If they sold passage tomorrow for that same crossing,
who would not buy?

To go down . . . We all go down, mostly
alone. But with crowds of people, friends, servants,   5
well fed, with music, with lights! Ah!

And the world, shocked, mourns, as it ought to do
and almost never does. There will be the books and movies
to remind our grandchildren who we were
and how we died, and give them a good cry.   10

Not so bad, after all. The cold
water is anesthetic and very quick.
The cries on all sides must be a comfort.

We all go: only a few, first-class.

CONSIDERATIONS FOR CRITICAL THINKING AND WRITING

1. FIRST RESPONSE. What, according to the speaker in this poem, is so com-pelling about the *Titanic?* Do you agree?

2. Discuss the speaker's tone. Why would it be inaccurate to describe it as solemn and mournful?

3. What is the effect of the poem's final line? What emotions does it produce in you?

CONNECTIONS TO OTHER SELECTIONS

1. Which poem, "Titanic" or "The Convergence of the Twain," is more emo-tionally satisfying to you? Explain why.

2. Compare the speakers' tones in "Titanic" and "The Convergence of the Twain."

3. CRITICAL STRATEGIES. Read the section on Marxist criticism (p. 2103) in Chapter 52, "Critical Strategies for Reading," and analyze the attitudes toward opulence that are manifested in the two poems.

4. Hardy wrote his poem in 1912, the year the *Titanic* went down, but Slavitt wrote his more than seventy years later. How do you think Slavitt's poem would have been received if it had been published in 1912? Write an essay ex-plaining why you think what you do.

LIONEL JOHNSON (1867–1902)
A Decadent's Lyric   1897

Sometimes, in very joy of shame,
Our flesh becomes one living flame:
And she and I
Are no more separate, but the same.

Ardour and agony unite;   5
Desire, delirium, delight:
And I and she
Faint in the fierce and fevered night.

Her body music is: and ah,
The accords of lute and viola!   10
When she and I
Play on live limbs love's opera!

CONSIDERATIONS FOR CRITICAL THINKING AND WRITING

1. FIRST RESPONSE. Comment on the title. To what extent do you think the title captures the tone of the poem?
2. What does the speaker mean by using the phrase "joy of shame" to characterize the couple's passion?
3. Read the poem aloud. How do the sounds of the lines contribute to its effects?

CONNECTION TO ANOTHER SELECTION

1. Discuss the views of sexuality presented in this poem and in the following poem, "Sex without Love," by Sharon Olds.

SHARON OLDS (B. 1942)
Sex without Love   1984

How do they do it, the ones who make love
without love? Beautiful as dancers,
gliding over each other like ice skaters
over the ice, fingers hooked
inside each other's bodies, faces   5
red as steak, wine, wet as the
children at birth whose mothers are going to
give them away. How do they come to the
come to the   come to the   God   come to the
still waters, and not love   10
the one who came there with them, light
rising slowly as steam off their joined
skin? These are the true religious,

the purists, the pros, the ones who will not
accept a false Messiah, love the   15
priest instead of the God. They do not
mistake the lover for their own pleasure,
they are like great runners: they know they are alone
with the road surface, the cold, the wind,
the fit of their shoes, their over-all cardio-   20
vascular health — just factors, like the partner
in the bed, and not the truth, which is the
single body alone in the universe
against its own best time.

CONSIDERATIONS FOR CRITICAL THINKING AND WRITING

1. FIRST RESPONSE. What is the nature of the question asked by the speaker in the poem's first two lines? What is being asked here?

2. What is the effect of describing the lovers as athletes? How do these descriptions and phrases reveal the speaker's tone toward the lovers?

3. To what extent does the title suggest the central meaning of this poem? Try to create some alternative titles that are equally descriptive.

CONNECTIONS TO OTHER SELECTIONS

1. How does the treatment of sex and love in Olds's poem compare with that in Cummings's "she being Brand" (p. 720)?

2. Just as Olds describes sex without love, she implies a definition of love in this poem. Consider whether the lovers in Wilbur's "A Late Aubade" (p. 731) fall within Olds's definition.

CATHY SONG (B. 1955)

The Youngest Daughter   *1983*

The sky has been dark
for many years.
My skin has become as damp
and pale as rice paper
and feels the way   5
mother's used to before the drying sun
parched it out there in the fields.

Lately, when I touch myself,
my hands react as if
I had just touched something   10
hot enough to burn.
My skin, aspirin-colored,
tingles with migraine. Mother
has been massaging the left side of my face

especially in the evenings
when it flares up.   15

This morning
her breathing was graveled,
her voice gruff with affection
when I took her into the bath.   20
She was in good humor,
making jokes about her great breasts,
floating in the milky water
like two walruses,
flaccid and whiskered around the nipples.   25
I scrubbed them with a sour taste
in my mouth, thinking:
six children and an old man
have sucked from these brown nipples.

I was almost tender   30
when I came to the blue bruises
that freckle her body,
places where she has been injecting insulin
for thirty years, ever since
I can remember. I soaped her slowly,   35
she sighed deeply, her eyes closed.

In the afternoons
when she has rested,
she prepares our ritual of tea and rice,
garnished with a shred of gingered fish,   40
a slice of pickled turnip
a token for my white body.
We eat in the familiar silence.
She knows I am not to be trusted,
even now planning my escape.   45
As I toast to her health
with the tea she has poured,
a thousand cranes curtain the window,
fly up in a sudden breeze.

CONSIDERATIONS FOR CRITICAL THINKING AND WRITING

1. FIRST RESPONSE. Though the speaker is the youngest daughter in the family, how old do you think she is based on the description of her in the poem? What, specifically, makes you think so?

2. How would you characterize the relationship between mother and daughter? How are lines 44–45 ("She knows I am not to be trusted, / even now planning my escape.") particularly revealing of the nature of the relationship?

3. Interpret the final four lines of the poem. Why do you think it ends with this image?

JOHN KEATS (1795–1821)

Ode on a Grecian Urn

1819

I

Thou still unravished bride of quietness,
    Thou foster-child of silence and slow time,
Sylvan° historian, who canst thus express
    A flowery tale more sweetly than our rhyme:
What leaf-fringed legend haunts about thy shape   5
    Of deities or mortals, or of both,
        In Tempe or the dales of Arcady?°
What men or gods are these? What maidens loath?
What mad pursuit? What struggle to escape?
    What pipes and timbrels? What wild ecstasy?   10

II

Heard melodies are sweet, but those unheard
    Are sweeter; therefore, ye soft pipes, play on;
Not to the sensual ear, but, more endeared,
    Pipe to the spirit ditties of no tone:
Fair youth, beneath the trees, thou canst not leave   15
    Thy song, nor ever can those trees be bare;
        Bold Lover, never, never canst thou kiss,
Though winning near the goal — yet, do not grieve;
    She cannot fade, though thou hast not thy bliss,
        For ever wilt thou love, and she be fair!   20

III

Ah, happy, happy boughs! that cannot shed
    Your leaves, nor ever bid the Spring adieu;
And, happy melodist, unwearièd,
    For ever piping songs for ever new;
More happy love! more happy, happy love!   25
    For ever warm and still to be enjoyed,
        For ever panting, and for ever young;
All breathing human passion far above,
    That leaves a heart high-sorrowful and cloyed,
        A burning forehead, and a parching tongue.   30

IV

Who are these coming to the sacrifice?
    To what green altar, O mysterious priest,
Lead'st thou that heifer lowing at the skies,
    And all her silken flanks with garlands drest?
What little town by river or sea shore,   35
    Or mountain-built with peaceful citadel,
        Is emptied of this folk, this pious morn?

3 *Sylvan:* Rustic. The urn is decorated with a forest scene.   7 *Tempe, Arcady:* Beautiful rural valleys in Greece.

And, little town, thy streets for evermore
  Will silent be; and not a soul to tell
    Why thou art desolate, can e'er return.   40

V
O Attic° shape! Fair attitude! with brede°
  Of marble men and maidens overwrought,
With forest branches and the trodden weed;
  Thou, silent form, dost tease us out of thought
As doth eternity: Cold Pastoral!   45
  When old age shall this generation waste,
    Thou shalt remain, in midst of other woe
Than ours, a friend to man, to whom thou say'st,
  Beauty is truth, truth beauty — that is all
  Ye know on earth, and all ye need to know.   50

41 *Attic:* Possessing classic Athenian simplicity; *brede:* Design.

CONSIDERATIONS FOR CRITICAL THINKING AND WRITING

1. FIRST RESPONSE. What does the speaker's diction reveal about his attitude toward the urn in this ode? Does his view develop or change?

2. How is the happiness in stanza III related to the assertion in lines 11–12 that "Heard melodies are sweet, but those unheard / Are sweeter"?

3. What is the difference between the world depicted on the urn and the speaker's world?

4. What do lines 49 and 50 suggest about the relation of art to life? Why is the urn described as a "Cold Pastoral" (line 45)?

5. Which world does the speaker seem to prefer, the urn's or his own?

6. Describe the overall tone of the poem.

CONNECTIONS TO OTHER SELECTIONS

1. Write an essay comparing the view of time in this ode with that in Marvell's "To His Coy Mistress" (p. 728). Pay particular attention to the connotative language in each poem.

2. Discuss the treatment and meaning of love in this ode and in Richard Wilbur's "Love Calls Us to the Things of This World" (p. 1188).

3. Compare the tone and attitude toward life in this ode with those in John Keats's "To Autumn" (p. 771).

Gwendolyn Brooks (1917–2000)
We Real Cool
1960

The Pool Players.
Seven at the Golden Shovel.

We real cool. We
Left school. We

Lurk late. We
Strike straight. We   5

Sing sin. We
Thin gin. We

Jazz June. We
Die soon.   10

Considerations for Critical Thinking and Writing

1. FIRST RESPONSE. How does the speech of the pool players in this poem help to characterize them? What is the effect of the pronouns coming at the ends of the lines? How would the poem sound if the pronouns came at the beginnings of lines?

2. What is the author's attitude toward the players? Is there a change in tone in the last line?

3. How is the pool hall's name related to the rest of the poem and its theme?

Eric Ormsby (b. 1941)
Nose
1997

The nose is antithetical. It sniffs,
snuffles, wallows in sneezes, then recoils
in Roman nobility, profile-proud;
pampers its fleshy shadow in bas-
reliefs; or is serenely alcoved within   5
rotunda where the chiseled light
dapples its expansive flanges.
                              Nose
is tuberous, rootlike, with subsoil
affinities, has its own mossy   10
aromas, feels bulbous as corms or
crimped as rhizomes but, even so,
stands graced with little wings above
the harbored nostrils.
                       The nose   15
sunders the face in symmetry,
bisects us in hemispheres where selves

negotiate along the boundary lines
of smiles or scowls.
All night,   20
in the snug bed of the face,
the nose exults.

CONSIDERATIONS FOR CRITICAL THINKING AND WRITING

1. FIRST RESPONSE. What do you think is the speaker's attitude toward the nose?

2. In what ways is the nose "antithetical"?

3. Discuss the speaker's diction and its effect on your reading of the poem. What words or phrases are particularly effective? How?

4. Look up *exults* in the dictionary. Why is it just right in the final line?

CONNECTION TO ANOTHER SELECTION

1. Compare the central idea of the "Nose" with "The Larynx," the next poem, by Alice Jones. Which poem do you prefer? Why?

ALICE JONES (B. 1949)

The Larynx   *1993*

Under the epiglottic flap
the long-ringed tube sinks
its shaft down to the bronchial
fork, divides from two
to four then infinite branches,   5
each ending finally in a clump
of transparent sacs knit
with small vessels into a mesh
that sponge-like soaks up breath
and gives it off with a push   10
from the diaphragm's muscular wall,
forces wind out of the lungs'
wide tree, up through this organ's
single pipe, through the puzzle
box of gristle, where resonant   15
plates of cartilage fold
into shield, horns, bows,
bound by odd half-spirals
of muscles that modulate air
as it rises through this empty place   20
at our core, where lip-like
folds stretch across the vestibule,
small and tough, they flutter,
bend like birds' wings finding
just the right angle to stay   25
airborne; here the cords arch

in the hollow of this ancient instrument,
curve and vibrate to make a song.

CONSIDERATIONS FOR CRITICAL THINKING AND WRITING

1. FIRST RESPONSE. What is the effect of having this poem written as one long sentence? How does the length of the sentence contribute to the poem's meaning?

2. Make a list of words and phrases from the poem that strike you as scientific, and compare those with a list of words that seem poetic. How do they compete or complement each other in terms of how they affect your reading?

3. Comment on the final three lines. How would your interpretation of this poem change if it ended before the semicolon in line 26?

CONNECTION TO ANOTHER SELECTION

1. Compare the diction and ending that Jones writes in "The Larynx" with those of "The Foot" (p. 870), another poem by Jones.

OLIVER RICE (B. 1921)

The Doll House   *1998*

Such authenticity may be more than cunning,
all this minuteness more than dear,
itsy highboy and ladderback,
bitsy tea set and banjo clock.
The figure in this teeny afghan,   5
the stick for this weeny candle
may be as credible as Ibsen's inkwell.°

    Stoop and enter this little milieu.
      An alertness hangs on the air.
      An anxiety rustles the light.   10
    Credulities nestle among the cushions.

In these rooms the very mores may lie in wait,
secret necessities and vulgar realities.

Here the rules may discover the game,

the self conceive a grace or splendor,   15

and love make its first mistake,

itty doilies on teensy upholstered arms,
bitty apples in weensy silver bowl.

---

7 *Ibsen's inkwell:* A reference to the Norwegian playwright Henrik Ibsen (1828–1906), who wrote about the tensions of nineteenth-century middle-class marriage in *A Doll House* (1879).

CONSIDERATIONS FOR CRITICAL THINKING AND WRITING

1. FIRST RESPONSE. What do you think is the purpose of the childish diction in this poem?

2. Discuss the significance of the title and the reference to Ibsen. Why is an understanding of the allusion to Ibsen important for developing an interpretation of this poem? Is it possible to make sense of the poem without knowing anything about Ibsen? Explain.

3. Discuss what you take the meaning of line 14 to be: "Here the rules may discover the game."

LOUIS SIMPSON (B. 1923)

In the Suburbs   *1963*

There's no way out.
You were born to waste your life.
You were born to this middleclass life

As others before you
Were born to walk in procession
To the temple, singing.

CONSIDERATIONS FOR CRITICAL THINKING AND WRITING

1. FIRST RESPONSE. Is the title of this poem especially significant? What images does it conjure up for you?

2. What does the repetition in lines 2–3 suggest?

3. Discuss the possible connotative meanings of lines 5 and 6. Who are the "others before you"?

CONNECTION TO ANOTHER SELECTION

1. Write an essay on suburban life based on this poem and John Ciardi's "Suburban" (p. 824).

A NOTE ON READING TRANSLATIONS

Sometimes translation can inadvertently be a comic business. Consider, for example, the discovery made by John Steinbeck's wife, Elaine, when in a Yokohama bookstore she asked for a copy of her husband's famous novel *The Grapes of Wrath* and learned that it had been translated into Japanese as *Angry Raisins*. Close but no cigar (perhaps translated as: Nearby, yet no smoke). As amusing as that *Angry Raisins* title is, it teaches an important lesson about the significance of a poet's or a translator's choices when crafting a poem: a powerful piece moves us through diction and tone, both built word by careful word. Translations are frequently regarded as merely vehicular, a way to arrive at the original work. It is, of course, the original work — its spirit, style, and meaning—that most readers expect to find in a translation. Even so, it is important to understand that a translation is *by nature* different from the original—and that despite that difference, a fine translation can be an important part of the journey and become part of the literary landscape itself. Reading a translation of a poem is not the same as reading the original, but neither is watching two different performances of *Hamlet.* The translator provides a reading of the poem in much the same way that a director shapes the play. Each interprets the text from a unique perspective.

Basically, there are two distinct approaches to translation: literal translations and adaptations. A literal translation sets out to create a word-for-word equivalent that is absolutely faithful to the original. As simple and direct as this method may sound, literal translations are nearly impossible over extended passages because of the structural differences between languages. Moreover, the meaning of a single word in one language may not exist in another language, or it may require a phrase, clause, or entire sentence to capture its implications. Adaptations of works offer broader, more open-ended approaches to translation. Unlike a literal translation, an adaptation moves beyond denotative meanings in an attempt to capture the spirit of a work so that its idioms, dialects, slang, and other conventions are recreated in the language of the translation.

The question we ask of an adaptation should not be "Is this exactly how the original reads?" Instead, we ask "Is this an insightful, graceful rendering worth reading?" To translate poetry it is not enough to know the language of the original; it is also necessary that the translator be a poet. A translated poem is more than a collation of decisions based on dictionaries and grammars; it must also be poetry. However undefinable poetry may be, it is unmistakable in its intense use of language. Poems are not merely translated; they are savored.

Four Translations of a Poem by Sappho

Sappho, born about 630 B.C. and a native of the Greek island of Lesbos, is the author of a hymn to Aphrodite, the goddess of love and beauty in Greek myth. The four translations that follow suggest how widely translations can differ from one another. The first, by Henry T. Wharton, is intended to be a literal prose translation of the original Greek.

SAPPHO (C. 630 B.C.–C. 570 B.C.)

Immortal Aphrodite of the broidered throne   *date unknown*

TRANSLATED BY HENRY T. WHARTON (1885)

Immortal Aphrodite of the broidered throne, daughter of Zeus, weaver of wiles, I pray thee break not my spirit with anguish and distress, O Queen. But come hither, if ever before thou didst hear my voice afar, and listen, and leaving thy father's golden house camest with chariot yoked, and fair fleet sparrows drew thee, flapping fast their wings around the dark earth, from heaven through mid sky. Quickly arrived they; and thou, blessed one, smiling with immortal countenance, didst ask What now is befallen me, and Why now I call, and What I in my mad heart most desire to see. 'What Beauty now wouldst thou draw to love thee? Who wrongs thee, Sappho? For even if she flies she shall soon follow, and if she rejects gifts shall yet give, and if she loves not shall soon love, however loth.' Come, I pray thee, now too, and release me from cruel cares; and all that my heart desires to accomplish, accomplish thou, and be thyself my ally.

Beautiful-throned, immortal Aphrodite

TRANSLATED BY T. W. HIGGINSON (1871)

Beautiful-throned, immortal Aphrodite,
Daughter of Zeus, beguiler, I implore thee,
Weigh me not down with weariness and anguish
    O Thou most holy!

Come to me now, if ever thou in kindness   5
Hearkenedst my words, — and often hast thou
    hearkened —
Heeding, and coming from the mansions golden
    Of thy great Father,

Yoking thy chariot, borne by the most lovely   10
Consecrated birds, with dusky-tinted pinions,
Waving swift wings from utmost heights of
    heaven
    Through the mid-ether;

Swiftly they vanished, leaving thee, O goddess,   15
Smiling, with face immortal in its beauty,
Asking why I grieved, and why in utter longing
    I had dared call thee;

Asking what I sought, thus hopeless in desiring,
Wildered in brain, and spreading nets of   20
    passion —
Alas, for whom? and saidst thou, "Who has
    harmed thee?
    "O my poor Sappho!

"Though now he flies, ere long he shall pursue   25
    thee;
"Fearing thy gifts, he too in turn shall bring
    them;
"Loveless to-day, to-morrow he shall woo thee,
    "Though thou shouldst spurn him."   30

Thus seek me now, O holy Aphrodite!
Save me from anguish; give me all I ask for,
Gifts at thy hand; and thine shall be the glory,
    Sacred protector!

Invocation to Aphrodite

TRANSLATED BY RICHARD LATTIMORE (1955)

Throned in splendor, deathless, O Aphrodite,
child of Zeus, charm-fashioner, I entreat you
not with griefs and bitternesses to break my
    spirit, O goddess;

standing by me rather, if once before now   5
far away you heard, when I called upon you,
left your father's dwelling place and descended,
    yoking the golden

chariot to sparrows, who fairly drew you
down in speed aslant the black world, the bright   10
trembling at the heart to the pulse of countless
    fluttering wingbeats.

Swiftly then they came, and you, blessed lady,
smiling on me out of immortal beauty,
asked me what affliction was on me, why I   15
    called thus upon you,

what beyond all else I would have befall my
tortured heart: "Whom then would you have Per-
    suasion
force to serve desire in your heart? Who is it,   20
    Sappho, that hurt you?

Though she now escape you, she soon will follow;
though she take not gifts from you, she will give
    them:
though she love not, yet she will surely love you   25
    even unwilling."

In such guise come even again and set me
free from doubt and sorrow; accomplish all those
things my heart desires to be done; appear and
    stand at my shoulder.   30

Artfully adorned Aphrodite, deathless

TRANSLATED BY JIM POWELL (1993)

Artfully adorned Aphrodite, deathless
child of Zeus and weaver of wiles I beg you
please don't hurt me, don't overcome my spirit,
    goddess, with longing,

but come here, if ever at other moments   5
hearing these my words from afar you listened
and responded: leaving your father's house, all
    golden, you came then,

hitching up your chariot: lovely sparrows
drew you quickly over the dark earth, whirling   10
on fine beating wings from the heights of heaven
    down through the sky and

instantly arrived — and then O my blessed
goddess with a smile on your deathless face you
asked me what the matter was *this* time, what I   15
    called you for this time,

what I now most wanted to happen in my
raving heart: "Whom *this* time should I persuade to
lead you back again to her love? Who *now*, oh
    Sappho, who wrongs you?   20

If she flees you now, she will soon pursue you;
if she won't accept what you give, she'll give it;
if she doesn't love you, she'll love you soon now,
    even unwilling."

Come to me again, and release me from this   25
want past bearing. All that my heart desires to
happen — make it happen. And stand beside me,
    goddess, my ally.

CONSIDERATIONS FOR CRITICAL THINKING AND WRITING

1. FIRST RESPONSE. Try rewriting Wharton's prose version in contemporary language. How does your prose version differ in tone from Wharton's?

2. Explain which translation seems closest to Wharton's prose version.

3. Discuss the images and metaphors in Higginson's and Lattimore's versions. Which version is more appealing to you? Explain why.

4. How does Powell's use of language clearly make his version the most contemporary of the translations?

23

Images

POETRY'S APPEAL TO THE SENSES

A poet, to borrow a phrase from Henry James, is one of those on whom nothing is lost. Poets take in the world and give us impressions of what they experience through images. An *image* is language that addresses the senses. The most common images in poetry are visual; they provide verbal pictures of the poets' encounters — real or imagined — with the world. But poets also create images that appeal to our other senses. Richard Wilbur arouses several senses when he has the speaker in "A Late Aubade" (p. 731) gently urge his lover to linger in bed with him instead of getting on with her daily routines and obligations:

> Wait for a while, then slip downstairs
> And bring us up some chilled white wine,
> And some blue cheese, and crackers, and some fine
> Ruddy-skinned pears.

These images are simultaneously tempting and satisfying. We don't have to literally touch that cold, clear glass of wine (or will it come in a green bottle beaded with moisture?) or smell the cheese or taste the crackers to appreciate this vivid blend of colors, textures, tastes, and fragrances.

Images give us the physical world to experience in our imaginations. Some poems, like the following one, are written to do just that; they make no comment about what they describe.

WILLIAM CARLOS WILLIAMS (1883–1963)

Poem

1934

As the cat
climbed over
the top of

the jamcloset
first the right   5
forefoot

carefully
then the hind
stepped down

into the pit of   10
the empty
flowerpot

This poem defies paraphrase because it is all an image of agile movement. No statement is made about the movement; the title, "Poem" — really no title — signals Williams's refusal to comment on the movements. To impose a meaning on the poem, we'd probably have to knock over the flowerpot.

We experience the image in Williams's "Poem" more clearly because of how the sentence is organized into lines and groups of lines, or stanzas. Consider how differently the sentence is read if it is arranged as prose:

> As the cat climbed over the top of the jamcloset, first the right forefoot carefully then the hind stepped down into the pit of the empty flowerpot.

The poem's line and stanza division transforms what is essentially an awkward prose sentence into a rhythmic verbal picture. Especially when the poem is read aloud, this line and stanza division allows us to feel the image we see. Even the lack of a period at the end suggests that the cat is only pausing.

Images frequently do more than offer only sensory impressions, however. They also convey emotions and moods, as in the following poem.

JEANNETTE BARNES (B. 1956)

Battle-Piece

1999

Confederate monument, Ocean Pond, Olustee, Florida, 1864

Picknickers sojourn here an hour,
get their fill, get gone.
Seldom, they quickstep as far downhill
as this bivouac; they miss sting, snap,

grit in clenched teeth, carbine, cartridge,   5
cap, *hurrah boys.* Cannon-cracks
the peal, the clap of doom.

Into the billows, white, filthy,
choked by smoke, Clem, Eustace, Willy—
it would be useless to name names or call them all.   10

Anyway, that's done already. Every fall
sons of sons and reverent veterans' wives
lay wreaths, a prize of plastic daisies,

everlasting. Nobody calls this lazy.
It's August, and it's late, it's afternoon,   15
heat-mist glistens on slick granite, sun

fingers through sleek pines, their edges cropped
like the clipped elegant grass. It is a shock
to see a caisson blown

to flinders; a horse shrieks,   20
the mortar-shell zooms, spiral-
ripping tender belly. Oh, yes, here

are raked paths, cindered, sweet trees
and cool water. That whimper
you do not hear now was the doves,   25
spooning. Evening calls you all, eager

as spruce-gum-chewing, apple-filching boys
to pull one long last gulp of switchel
as if, now, somebody's sons had almost done

haying. Keen to victual, nearly home, feature the sharp   30
surprise when, smooth as oiled stone
stroking the clean edge of a scythe, these boys achieved
each his marble pillow, astonished by the sky.

CONSIDERATIONS FOR CRITICAL THINKING AND WRITING

1. FIRST RESPONSE. Contrast the images used to describe the present moment
   at the battle site with the images used to describe the actual battle.

2. Describe the speaker's tone. What do the images reveal about the speaker's
   emotions?

3. Analyze the diction and images of the final stanza. What makes it so powerful?

What mood is established in this next poem's view of Civil War troops
moving across a river?

WALT WHITMAN (1819–1892)

Cavalry Crossing a Ford   *1865*

A line in long array where they wind betwixt green islands,
They take a serpentine course, their arms flash in the sun—hark to the
    musical clank,
Behold the silvery river, in it the splashing horses loitering stop to drink,

Behold the brown-faced men, each group, each person, a picture, the
    negligent rest on the saddles,
Some emerge on the opposite bank, others are just entering the ford — while,
Scarlet and blue and snowy white,
The guidon flags flutter gaily in the wind.

CONSIDERATIONS FOR CRITICAL THINKING AND WRITING

1. FIRST RESPONSE. Do the colors and sounds establish the mood of this poem? What *is* the mood?
2. How would the poem's mood have been changed if Whitman had used "look" or "see" instead of "behold" (lines 3-4)?
3. Where is the speaker as he observes this troop movement?
4. Does "serpentine" in line 2 have an evil connotation in this poem? Explain your answer.

Whitman seems to capture momentarily all the troop's actions, and through carefully chosen, suggestive details — really very few — he succeeds in making "each group, each person, a picture." Specific details, even when few are provided, give us the impression that we see the entire picture; it is as if those are the details we would remember if we had viewed the scene ourselves. Notice too that the movement of the "line in long array" is emphasized by the continuous winding syntax of the poem's lengthy lines.

Movement is also central to the next poem, in which action and motion are created through carefully chosen verbs.

DAVID SOLWAY (B. 1941)

Windsurfing   1993

It rides upon the wrinkled hide
of water, like the upturned hull
of a small canoe or kayak
waiting to be righted — yet its law
is opposite to that of boats,   5
it floats upon its breastbone and
brings whatever spine there is to light.
A thin shaft is slotted into place.
Then a puffed right-angle of wind
pushes it forward, out into the bay,   10
where suddenly it glitters into speed,
tilts, knifes up, and for the moment's
nothing but a slim projectile
of cambered fiberglass,
peeling the crests.   15

        The man's
clamped to the mast, taut as a guywire.
Part of the sleek apparatus

he controls, immaculate nerve
of balance, plunge and curvet,   20
he clinches all component movements
into single motion.
It bucks, stalls, shudders, yaws, and dips
its hissing sides beneath the surface
that sustains it, tensing   25
into muscle that nude ellipse
of lunging appetite and power.

And now the mechanism's wholly
dolphin, springing toward its prey
of spume and beaded sunlight,   30
tossing spray, and hits the vertex
of the wide, salt glare of distance,
and reverses.

          Back it comes through
a screen of particles,   35
scalloped out of water, shimmer
and reflection, the wind snapping
and lashing it homeward,
shearing the curve of the wave,
breaking the spell of the caught breath   40
and articulate play of sinew, to enter
the haven of the breakwater
and settle in a rush of silence.

Now the crossing drifts
in the husk of its wake   45
and nothing's the same again
as, gliding elegantly on a film of water,
the man guides
his brash, obedient legend
into shore.   50

Considerations for Critical Thinking and Writing

1. FIRST RESPONSE. Draw a circle around the verbs that seem especially effective in conveying a strong sense of motion, and explain why they are effective.
2. How is the man made to seem to be one with his board and sail?
3. How does the rhythm of the poem change beginning with line 45?

Connections to Other Selections

1. Consider the effects of the images in "Windsurfing" and Ho's "A Beautiful Girl Combs Her Hair" (p. 705). In an essay explain how these images produce emotional responses in you.
2. Compare the descriptions in "Windsurfing" and Bishop's "The Fish" (p. 682). How does each poet appeal to your senses to describe windsurfing and fishing?

"Windsurfing" is awash with images of speed, fluidity, and power. Even the calming aftermath of the breakwater is described as a "rush of silence," adding to the sense of motion that is detailed and expanded throughout the poem.

Poets choose details the way they choose the words to present those details: only telling ones will do. Consider the images Theodore Roethke uses in "Root Cellar."

THEODORE ROETHKE (1908–1963)

Root Cellar

1948

Nothing would sleep in that cellar, dank as a ditch,
Bulbs broke out of boxes hunting for chinks in the dark,
Shoots dangled and drooped,
Lolling obscenely from mildewed crates,
Hung down long yellow evil necks, like tropical snakes.   5
And what a congress of stinks!
Roots ripe as old bait,
Pulpy stems, rank, silo-rich,
Leaf-mold, manure, lime, piled against slippery planks.
Nothing would give up life: 10
Even the dirt kept breathing a small breath.

CONSIDERATIONS FOR CRITICAL THINKING AND WRITING

1. FIRST RESPONSE. Explain why you think this is a positive or negative rendition of a root cellar.

2. What senses are engaged by the images in this poem? Is the poem simply a series of sensations, or do the detailed images make some kind of point about the root cellar?

3. What controls the choice of details in the poem? Why isn't there, for example, a rusty shovel leaning against a dirt wall or a worn gardener's glove atop one of the crates?

4. Look up *congress* in a dictionary for its denotative meanings. Explain why "congress of stinks" is especially appropriate given the nature of the rest of the poem's imagery.

5. What single line in the poem suggests a theme?

The tone of the images and mood of the speaker are consistent in Roethke's "Root Cellar." In Matthew Arnold's "Dover Beach," however, they shift as the theme is developed.

MATTHEW ARNOLD (1822–1888)

Dover Beach

1867

The sea is calm tonight.
The tide is full, the moon lies fair
Upon the straits; — on the French coast the light
Gleams and is gone; the cliffs of England stand,
Glimmering and vast, out in the tranquil bay.   5
Come to the window, sweet is the night-air!
Only, from the long line of spray
Where the sea meets the moon-blanched land,
Listen! you hear the grating roar
Of pebbles which the waves draw back, and fling,   10
At their return, up the high strand,
Begin, and cease, and then again begin,
With tremulous cadence slow, and bring
The eternal note of sadness in.

Sophocles long ago   15
Heard it on the Aegean, and it brought
Into his mind the turbid ebb and flow
Of human misery;° we
Find also in the sound a thought,
Hearing it by this distant northern sea.   20

The Sea of Faith
Was once, too, at the full, and round earth's shore
Lay like the folds of a bright girdle furled.
But now I only hear
Its melancholy, long, withdrawing roar,   25
Retreating, to the breath
Of the night-wind, down the vast edges drear
And naked shingles° of the world.   *pebble beaches*

Ah, love, let us be true
To one another! for the world, which seems   30
To lie before us like a land of dreams,
So various, so beautiful, so new,
Hath really neither joy, nor love, nor light,
Nor certitude, nor peace, nor help for pain;
And we are here as on a darkling plain   35
Swept with confused alarms of struggle and flight,
Where ignorant armies clash by night.

15–18 *Sophocles... misery:* In *Antigone* (lines 656–677), Sophocles likens the disasters that
beset the house of Oedipus to a "mounting tide."

CONSIDERATIONS FOR CRITICAL THINKING AND WRITING

1. FIRST RESPONSE. Discuss what you consider to be this poem's central point.
   How do the speaker's descriptions of the ocean work toward making that
   point?

2. Contrast the images in lines 4–8 and 9–13. How do they reveal the speaker's mood? To whom is he speaking?

3. What is the cause of the "sadness" in line 14? What is the speaker's response to the ebbing "Sea of Faith"? Is there anything to replace his sense of loss?

4. What details of the beach seem related to the ideas in the poem? How is the sea used differently in lines 1–14 and lines 21–28?

5. Describe the differences in tone between lines 1–8 and 35–37. What has caused the change?

6. CRITICAL STRATEGIES. Read the section on mythological criticism (pp. 2107–09) in Chapter 52, "Critical Strategies for Reading," and discuss how you think a mythological critic might make use of the allusion to Sophocles in this poem.

CONNECTIONS TO OTHER SELECTIONS

1. Explain how the images in Wilfred Owen's "Dulce et Decorum Est" (p. 764) develop further the ideas and sentiments suggested by Arnold's final line concerning "ignorant armies clash[ing] by night."

2. Contrast Arnold's images with those of Anthony Hecht in his parody "The Dover Bitch" (p. 1160). How do Hecht's images create a very different mood from that of "Dover Beach"?

Consider the poetic appetite for images displayed in the celebration of chile peppers in the following passionate poem.

JIMMY SANTIAGO BACA (B. 1952)

Green Chile   1989

I prefer red chile over my eggs
and potatoes for breakfast.
Red chile *ristras*° decorate my door,   *a braided string of peppers*
dry on my roof, and hang from eaves.
They lend open-air vegetable stands   5
historical grandeur, and gently swing
with an air of festive welcome.
I can hear them talking in the wind,
haggard, yellowing, crisp, rasping
tongues of old men, licking the breeze.   10

        But grandmother loves green chile.
When I visit her,
she holds the green chile pepper
in her wrinkled hands.
Ah, voluptuous, masculine,   15
an air of authority and youth simmers
from its swan-neck stem, tapering to a flowery
collar, fermenting resinous spice.
A well-dressed gentleman at the door

my grandmother takes sensuously in her hand,   20
rubbing its firm glossed sides,
caressing the oily rubbery serpent,
with mouth-watering fulfillment,
fondling its curves with gentle fingers.
Its bearing magnificent and taut   25
as flanks of a tiger in mid-leap,
she thrusts her blade into
and cuts it open, with lust
on her hot mouth, sweating over the stove,
bandanna round her forehead,   30
mysterious passion on her face
and she serves me green chile con carne
between soft warm leaves of corn tortillas,
with beans and rice — her sacrifice
to her little prince.   35
I slurp from my plate
with last bit of tortilla, my mouth burns
and I hiss and drink a tall glass of cold water.

All over New Mexico, sunburned men and women
drive rickety trucks stuffed with gunny-sacks   40
of green chile, from Belen, Veguita, Willard, Estancia,
San Antonio y Socorro, from fields
to roadside stands, you see them roasting green chile
in screen-sided homemade barrels, and for a dollar a bag,
we relive this old, beautiful ritual again and again.   45

CONSIDERATIONS FOR CRITICAL THINKING AND WRITING

1. FIRST RESPONSE. What's the difference between red and green chiles in this
   poem? Find the different images the speaker uses to draw a distinction between the two.

2. What kinds of images are used to describe the grandmother's preparation
   of green chile? What is the effect of those images?

3. Try writing a description — in poetry or prose — that uses vivid images to
   evoke a powerful response (either positive or negative) to a particular food.

POEMS FOR FURTHER STUDY

H. D.   (HILDA DOOLITTLE/1886–1961)

Heat   *1916*

O wind, rend open the heat,
cut apart the heat,
rend it to tatters.

Fruit cannot drop
through this thick air —   5

fruit cannot fall into heat
that presses up and blunts
the points of pears
and rounds the grapes.

Cut the heat—   10
plough through it,
turning it on either side
of your path.

CONSIDERATIONS FOR CRITICAL THINKING AND WRITING

1. FIRST RESPONSE. Is this poem more about heat or fruit? Explain your answer.
2. What physical properties are associated with heat in this poem?
3. Explain the effect of the description of fruit in lines 4–9.
4. Why is the image of the cutting plow especially effective in lines 10–13?

MICHAEL COLLIER (B. 1953)

The Barber   1995

Even in death he roams the yard in his boxer shorts,
plowing the push-mower through bermuda grass,
bullying it against the fence and tree trunks,
chipping its twisted blades on the patio's edge.

The chalky flint and orange spark of struck concrete   5
floats in the air, tastes like metal, smells,
like the slow burn of hair on his electric clippers.
And smelling it, I feel the hot shoe of the shaver

as he guided it in a high arc around my ears,
then set the sharp toothy edge against my sideburns   10
to trim them square, and how he used his huge stomach
to butt the chair and his flat hand palming my head

to keep me still, pressing my chin down as he cleaned
the ragged wisps of hair along my neck.
A fat inconsolable man whose skill and pleasure   15
was to clip and shear, to make raw and stubble

all that grew in this world, expose the scalp,
the place of roots and nerves and make vulnerable,
there in the double mirrors of his shop, the long
stem-muscles of our necks. And so we hung below   20

his license in its cheap black frame, above the violet
light of the scissors shed with its glass jars
of germicide and the long tapered combs soaking
in its blue iridescence. Gruff when he wasn't silent,

he was a neighbor to fear, yet we trusted him   25
beyond his anger, beyond his privacy. He was like a father

we could hate, a foil for our unspent vengeance,
though vengeance was always his. He sent us back

into the world burning and itching, alive with the horror
of closing eyes in the pinkish darkness   30
of his shop and having felt the horse-hair brush, talc-filled,
cloying, too sweet for boyhood, whisked across the face.

CONSIDERATIONS FOR CRITICAL THINKING AND WRITING

1. FIRST RESPONSE. How does the speaker feel about the barber?
2. Which images do you think especially reveal the barber's character? How?
   How would *you* describe him?
3. How successful are the poem's images in evoking a sense of the barbershop? What images in particular lend the poem a sense of the shop?
4. Comment on lines 26–27: "He was like a father / we could hate, a foil for our
   unspent vengeance." What is the speaker revealing about himself here?

CONNECTION TO ANOTHER SELECTION

1. Compare the treatment of the barber and barbershop in this poem with
   that of Stephen Perry's "Blue Spruce" (p. 798).

MARY ROBINSON (1758–1800)
London's Summer Morning   *1806*

Who has not wak'd to list° the busy sounds   *listen to*
Of summer's morning, in the sultry smoke
Of noisy London? On the pavement hot
The sooty chimney-boy, with dingy face
And tatter'd covering, shrilly bawls his trade,   5
Rousing the sleepy housemaid. At the door
The milk-pail rattles, and the tinkling bell
Proclaims the dustman's office; while the street
Is lost in clouds impervious. Now begins
The din of hackney-coaches, waggons, carts;   10
While tinmen's shops, and noisy trunk-makers,
Knife-grinders, coopers, squeaking cork-cutters,
Fruit-barrows, and the hunger-giving cries
Of vegetable venders, fill the air.
Now ev'ry shop displays its varied trade,   15
And the fresh-sprinkled pavement cools the feet
Of early walkers. At the private door
The ruddy housemaid twirls the busy mop,
Annoying the smart 'prentice, or neat girl,
Tripping with band-box° lightly. Now the sun   *hat box*   20
Darts burning splendour on the glitt'ring pane,
Save where the canvas awning throws a shade
On the gay merchandize. Now, spruce and trim,

In shops (where beauty smiles with industry,)
Sits the smart damsel; while the passenger   25
Peeps thro' the window, watching ev'ry charm.
Now pastry dainties catch the eye minute
Of humming insects, while the limy snare
Waits to enthral them. Now the lamp-lighter
Mounts the tall ladder, nimbly vent'rous,   30
To trim the half-fill'd lamp; while at his feet
The pot-boy° yells discordant! All along   *drink server*
The sultry pavement, the old-clothes-man cries
In tones monotonous, and side-long views
The area for his traffic: now the bag   35
Is slily open'd, and the half-worn suit
(Sometimes the pilfer'd treasure of the base
Domestic spoiler), for one half its worth,
Sinks in the green abyss. The porter now
Bears his huge load along the burning way;   40
And the poor poet wakes from busy dreams,
To paint the summer morning.

Considerations for Critical Thinking and Writing

1. FIRST RESPONSE. How effective is this picture of a London summer morning in 1806? Which images do you find particularly effective?

2. How does the end of the poem bring us full circle to its beginning? What effect does this structure have on your understanding of the poem?

3. Try writing about the start of your own day — in the dormitory, at home, the start of a class — using a series of images that provide a vivid sense of what happens and how you experience it.

Connection to Another Selection

1. How does Robinson's description of London differ from William Blake's "London," the next poem? What would you say is the essential difference in purpose between the two poems?

William Blake (1757–1827)

London   *1794*

I wander through each chartered° street,   *defined by law*
Near where the chartered Thames does flow,
And mark in every face I meet
Marks of weakness, marks of woe.

In every cry of every man,   5
In every Infant's cry of fear,
In every voice, in every ban,
The mind-forged manacles I hear.

How the Chimney-sweeper's cry
Every black'ning Church appalls;   10

And the hapless Soldier's sigh
Runs in blood down Palace walls.

But most through midnight streets I hear
How the youthful Harlot's curse
Blasts the new-born Infant's tear,   15
And blights with plagues the Marriage hearse.

CONSIDERATIONS FOR CRITICAL THINKING AND WRITING

1. FIRST RESPONSE. What feelings do the visual images in this poem suggest to you?

2. What is the predominant sound heard in the poem?

3. What is the meaning of line 8? What is the cause of the problems that the speaker sees and hears in London? Does the speaker suggest additional causes?

4. The image in lines 11 and 12 cannot be read literally. Comment on its effectiveness.

5. How does Blake's use of denotative and connotative language enrich this poem's meaning?

6. An earlier version of Blake's last stanza appeared this way:

> But most the midnight harlot's curse
> From every dismal street I hear,
> Weaves around the marriage hearse
> And blasts the new-born infant's tear.

Examine carefully the differences between the two versions. How do Blake's revisions affect his picture of London life? Which version do you think is more effective? Why?

WILFRED OWEN (1893–1918)

Dulce et Decorum Est   *1920*

Bent double, like old beggars under sacks,
Knock-kneed, coughing like hags, we cursed through sludge,
Till on the haunting flares we turned our backs,
And towards our distant rest began to trudge.

Men marched asleep. Many had lost their boots,   5
But limped on, blood-shod. All went lame, all blind;
Drunk with fatigue; deaf even to the hoots
Of gas-shells dropping softly behind.

Gas! GAS! Quick, boys! — An ecstasy of fumbling,
Fitting the clumsy helmets just in time,   10
But someone still was yelling out and stumbling
And flound'ring like a man in fire or lime. —
Dim through the misty panes and thick green light,
As under a green sea, I saw him drowning.

In all my dreams before my helpless sight   15
He plunges at me, guttering, choking, drowning.

If in some smothering dreams, you too could pace
Behind the wagon that we flung him in,
And watch the white eyes writhing in his face,
His hanging face, like a devil's sick of sin,   20
If you could hear, at every jolt, the blood
Come gargling from the froth-corrupted lungs
Bitter as the cud
Obscene as cancer,
Of vile, incurable sores on innocent tongues,—   25
My friend, you would not tell with such high zest
To children ardent for some desperate glory,
The old lie: *Dulce et decorum est*
Pro patria mori.

CONSIDERATIONS FOR CRITICAL THINKING AND WRITING

1. FIRST RESPONSE. The Latin quotation in lines 27 and 28 is from Horace: "It
   is sweet and fitting to die for one's country." Owen served as a British soldier during World War I and was killed. Is this poem unpatriotic? What is
   its purpose?

2. Which images in the poem are most vivid? To which senses do they speak?

3. Describe the speaker's tone. What is his relationship to his audience?

4. How are the images of the soldiers in this poem different from the images
   that typically appear in recruiting posters?

5. CRITICAL STRATEGIES. Read the section on biographical criticism (pp. 2097–
   99) in Chapter 52, "Critical Strategies for Reading," and use the library
   to learn about Owen's response to being a soldier during World War I.
   How might a biographical critic use this information to shed light on
   the poem?

SANDRA M. GILBERT (B. 1936)

Mafioso   1979

Frank Costello eating spaghetti in a cell at San Quentin,
Lucky Luciano mixing up a mess of bullets and
calling for parmesan cheese,
Al Capone baking a sawed-off shotgun into a
huge lasagna—   5
               are you my uncles, my
only uncles?

        O Mafiosi,
bad uncles of the barren
cliffs of Sicily—was it only you   10
that they transported in barrels

like pure olive oil
across the Atlantic?
                    Was it only you
who got out at Ellis Island with   15
black scarves on your heads and cheap cigars
and no English and a dozen children?

No carts were waiting, gallant with paint,
no little donkeys plumed like the dreams of peacocks.
Only the evil eyes of a thousand buildings   20
stared across at the echoing debarcation center,
making it seem so much smaller than a piazza,

only a half dozen Puritan millionaires stood on the wharf,
in the wind colder than the impossible snows of the Abruzzi,
ready with country clubs and dynamos   25

to grind the organs out of you.

CONSIDERATIONS FOR CRITICAL THINKING AND WRITING

1. FIRST RESPONSE. In what sense are the gangsters Frank Costello, Lucky Luciano, and Al Capone to be understood as "bad uncles"? How does the
   speaker, in particular, feel about the "uncles"?

2. Explain how nearly all the images in this poem are associated with Italian
   life. Does this poem reinforce stereotypes about Italians or invoke images
   about them for some other purpose? What other purpose?

3. What sort of people are the "Puritan millionaires"? What is their relationship to the "bad uncles"?

CONNECTION TO ANOTHER SELECTION

1. Discuss the ways in which ethnicity is used to create meaning in "Mafioso"
   and in Jimmy Santiago Baca's "Green Chile" (p. 759).

PATRICIA SMITH (B. 1955)

What It's Like to Be a Black Girl
(For Those of You Who Aren't)   1991

First of all, it's being 9 years old and
feeling like you're not finished, like your
edges are wild, like there's something,
everything, wrong. it's dropping food coloring
in your eyes to make them blue and suffering   5
their burn in silence. it's popping a bleached
white mophead over the kinks of your hair and
primping in front of the mirrors that deny your
reflection. it's finding a space between your
legs, a disturbance at your chest, and not knowing   10

what to do with the whistles. it's jumping
double dutch until your legs pop, it's sweat
and vaseline and bullets, it's growing tall and
wearing a lot of white, it's smelling blood in
your breakfast, it's learning to say fuck with   15
grace but learning to fuck without it, it's
flame and fists and life according to motown,
it's finally having a man reach out for you
then caving in
around his fingers.   20

CONSIDERATIONS FOR CRITICAL THINKING AND WRITING

1. FIRST RESPONSE. Describe the speaker's tone. What images in particular
   contribute to it? How do you account for it?

2. How does the speaker characterize her life? What elements of it does she
   focus on?

3. Discuss the poem's final image. What sort of emotions does it evoke
   in you?

JAMES DICKEY (1923–1997)

Deer Among Cattle   1981

Here and there in the searing beam
Of my hand going through the night meadow
They all are grazing

With pins of human light in their eyes.
A wild one also is eating   5
The human grass,

Slender, graceful, domesticated
By darkness, among the bred-
for-slaughter,

Having bounded their paralyzed fence   10
And inclined his branched forehead onto
Their green frosted table,

The only live thing in this flashlight
Who can leave whenever he wishes,
Turn grass into forest,   15

Foreclose inhuman brightness from his eyes
But stands here still, unperturbed,
In their wide-open country,

The sparks from my hand in his pupils
Unmatched anywhere among cattle,   20

Grazing with them the night of the hammer
As one of their own who shall rise.

CONSIDERATIONS FOR CRITICAL THINKING AND WRITING

1. FIRST RESPONSE. What images distinguish the deer from the cattle?
2. Do the words "domesticated" and "human" have positive or negative connotations in this poem? Explain your answer.
3. Discuss the possible implications of the last two lines. You may want to consider the speaker and his role in this tableau.

CONNECTION TO ANOTHER SELECTION

1. Discuss the idea of confinement in "Deer Among Cattle" and Rainer Maria Rilke's "The Panther" (below).

RAINER MARIA RILKE (1875–1926)

The Panther   *1927*

TRANSLATED BY STEPHEN MITCHELL

His vision, from the constantly passing bars,
has grown so weary that it cannot hold
anything else. It seems to him there are
a thousand bars; and behind the bars, no world.

As he paces in cramped circles, over and over,   5
the movement of his powerful soft strides
is like a ritual dance around a center
in which a mighty will stands paralyzed.

Only at times, the curtain of the pupils
lifts, quietly — . An image enters in,   10
rushes down through the tensed, arrested muscles,
plunges into the heart and is gone.

CONSIDERATIONS FOR CRITICAL THINKING AND WRITING

1. FIRST RESPONSE. Why do you think Rilke chooses a panther rather than, say, a lion as the subject of the poem's images?
2. What kind of "image enters in" the heart of the panther in the final stanza?
3. How are images of confinement achieved in the poem? Why doesn't Rilke describe the final image in lines 10–12?

CONNECTION TO ANOTHER SELECTION

1. Write an essay explaining how a sense of movement is achieved by the images and rhythms in this poem and in Dickinson's "A Bird came down the Walk — " (p. 836).

JANE KENYON (1947–1995)
The Blue Bowl

1990

Like primitives we buried the cat
with his bowl. Bare-handed
we scraped sand and gravel
back into the hole.
            They fell with a hiss   5
and thud on his side,
on his long red fur, the white feathers
between his toes, and his
long, not to say aquiline, nose.

We stood and brushed each other off.   10
There are sorrows keener than these.

Silent the rest of the day, we worked,
ate, stared, and slept. It stormed
all night; now it clears, and a robin
burbles from a dripping bush   15
like the neighbor who means well
but always says the wrong thing.

CONSIDERATIONS FOR CRITICAL THINKING AND WRITING

1. FIRST RESPONSE. How do the descriptions of the cat — "the white feathers / between his toes" — affect your reading of the poem?

2. Why do you think Kenyon titles the poem "The Blue Bowl" rather than, perhaps, "The Cat's Bowl"?

3. What is the effect of being reminded that "There are sorrows keener than these"?

4. Why is the robin's song "the wrong thing"?

CONNECTION TO ANOTHER SELECTION

1. Write an essay comparing the death of this cat with the death of the dog in Updike's "Dog's Death" (p. 673). Which poem draws a more powerful response from you? Explain why.

SALLY CROFT (B. 1935)
Home-Baked Bread

1981

Nothing gives a household a greater sense of stability and common comfort than the aroma of cooling bread. Begin, if you like, with a loaf of whole wheat, which requires neither sifting nor kneading, and go on from there to more cunning triumphs.
                                                     — The Joy of Cooking

What is it she is not saying?
Cunning triumphs. It rings
of insinuation. Step into my kitchen,
I have prepared a cunning triumph
for you. Spices and herbs   5
sealed in this porcelain jar,

a treasure of my great-aunt
who sat up past midnight
in her Massachusetts bedroom
when the moon was dark. Come,   10
rest your feet. I'll make
you tea with honey and slices

of warm bread spread with peach butter.
I picked the fruit this morning
still fresh with dew. The fragrance   15
is seductive? I hoped you would say that.
See how the heat rises
when the bread opens. Come,

we'll eat together, the small flakes
have scarcely any flavor. What cunning   20
triumphs we can discover in my upstairs room
where peach trees breathe their sweetness
beside the open window and
sun lies like honey on the floor.

CONSIDERATIONS FOR CRITICAL THINKING AND WRITING

1. FIRST RESPONSE. Why does the speaker in this poem seize on the phrase
   "cunning triumphs" from the *Joy of Cooking* excerpt?
2. Distinguish between the voice we hear in lines 1–3 and the second voice in
   lines 3–24. Who is the "you" in the poem?
3. Why is "insinuation" an especially appropriate word choice in line 3?
4. How do the images in lines 20–24 bring together all the senses evoked in the
   preceding lines?
5. Write a paragraph that describes the sensuous (and perhaps sensual) qualities of a food you enjoy.

ANN CHOI (B. 1969)

The Shower   *1991*

In the sixth grade
your hands were not much smaller
than they are now,
the reach between your thumb
and last finger not quite   5
an octave. You did not complain

and learned to choose
your music carefully.

Sharing noodles after school
in your house full of trophies,   10
we spoke of things expiring
without our knowledge. How time
quickens and wraps around us,
makes us women in bright clothes
caught by the permanence of the ring   15
around your finger.

I am your friend, accustomed
to your diligence.
Soon you will marry and fill
a house with sounds of dishes   20
and of children whose weight
you will gain and lose,
whose small fingers will separate
to play staccato,
one brief note after another.   25

CONSIDERATIONS FOR CRITICAL THINKING AND WRITING

1. FIRST RESPONSE. How does the speaker characterize her friend? Which images seem especially revealing?
2. Discuss the sense of time as it moves through the poem.
3. Do you think this is a sad or a celebratory poem? Explain why.

JOHN KEATS (1795–1821)

To Autumn   *1819*

I
Season of mists and mellow fruitfulness,
   Close bosom-friend of the maturing sun;
Conspiring with him how to load and bless
   With fruit the vines that round the thatch-eves run;
To bend with apples the mossed cottage-trees,   5
   And fill all fruit with ripeness to the core;
      To swell the gourd, and plump the hazel shells
   With a sweet kernel; to set budding more,
And still more, later flowers for the bees,
Until they think warm days will never cease,   10
      For summer has o'er-brimmed their clammy cells.

II
Who hath not seen thee oft amid thy store?
   Sometimes whoever seeks abroad may find
Thee sitting careless on a granary floor,

Thy hair soft-lifted by the winnowing wind;   15
Or on a half-reaped furrow sound asleep,
  Drowsed with the fume of poppies, while thy hook°   *scythe*
    Spares the next swath and all its twinèd flowers:
And sometimes like a gleaner thou dost keep
  Steady thy laden head across a brook;   20
  Or by a cider-press, with patient look,
    Thou watchest the last oozings hours by hours.

III
Where are the songs of spring? Ay, where are they?
  Think not of them, thou hast thy music too,—
While barred clouds bloom the soft-dying day,   25
  And touch the stubble-plains with rosy hue;
Then in a wailful choir the small gnats mourn
  Among the river swallows,° borne aloft   *willows*
    Or sinking as the light wind lives or dies;
And full-grown lambs loud bleat from hilly bourn;°   *territory*   30
  Hedge-crickets sing; and now with treble soft
  The redbreast whistles from a garden-croft,
    And gathering swallows twitter in the skies.

CONSIDERATIONS FOR CRITICAL THINKING AND WRITING

1. FIRST RESPONSE. How is autumn made to seem like a person in each stanza of this ode?
2. Which senses are most emphasized in each stanza?
3. How is the progression of time expressed in the ode?
4. How does the imagery convey tone? Which words have particularly strong connotative values?
5. What is the speaker's view of death?

CONNECTIONS TO OTHER SELECTIONS

1. Compare this poem's tone and its perspective on death with those of Robert Frost's "After Apple-Picking" (p. 1008).
2. Write an essay comparing the significance of the images of "mellow fruit-fulness" (line 1) in "To Autumn" with that of the images of ripeness in Roethke's "Root Cellar" (p. 757). Explain how the images in each poem lead to very different feelings about the same phenomenon.

CHARLES SIMIC (B. 1938)

Filthy Landscape   1999

The season of lurid wildflowers
Strewn on the meadows
Drunk with kissing
The red-hot summer breezes.

A ditch opens its legs   5
In the half-undressed orchard
Teeming with foulmouthed birds
And smutty shadows.

Scandalous view of a hilltop
In pink clouds of debauchery.   10
The sun peeked between them
Now and then like a whoremaster.

CONSIDERATIONS FOR CRITICAL THINKING AND WRITING

1. FIRST RESPONSE. What do you think is the central point of this poem? Were
   you surprised by it? How does it differ from other poems about landscapes
   that you have read?
2. Describe the poem's images. How do they affect your response to this landscape?
3. How would you describe the tone of this description?

CONNECTION TO ANOTHER SELECTION

1. Discuss the use of images to evoke summer in "Filthy Landscape" and in
   "August" by Sophie Cabot Black (p. 788). How do the poems' images create
   very different perceptions of a summer landscape?

EZRA POUND (1885–1972)

In a Station of the Metro°   1913

The apparition of these faces in the crowd;
Petals on a wet, black bough.

Metro: Underground railroad in Paris.

CONSIDERATIONS FOR CRITICAL THINKING AND WRITING

1. FIRST RESPONSE. Why is the title essential for this poem?
2. What kind of mood does the image in the second line convey?
3. Why is "apparition" a better word choice than, say, "appearance" or "sight"?

CATHY SONG (B. 1955)

The White Porch   1983

I wrap the blue towel
after washing,
around the damp
weight of hair, bulky

as a sleeping cat,
and sit out on the porch.
Still dripping water,
it'll be dry by supper,
by the time the dust
settles off your shoes,   10
though it's only five
past noon. Think
of the luxury: how to use
the afternoon like the stretch
of lawn spread before me.   15
There's the laundry,
sun-warm clothes at twilight,
and the mountain of beans
in my lap. Each one,
I'll break and snap   20
thoughtfully in half.

But there is this slow arousal.
The small buttons
of my cotton blouse
are pulling away from my body.   25
I feel the strain of threads,
the swollen magnolias
heavy as a flock of birds
in the tree. Already,
the orange sponge cake   30
is rising in the oven.
I know you'll say it makes
your mouth dry
and I'll watch you
drench your slice of it   35
in canned peaches
and lick the plate clean.

So much hair, my mother
used to say, grabbing
the thick braided rope   40
in her hands while we washed
the breakfast dishes, discussing
dresses and pastries.
My mind often elsewhere
as we did the morning chores together.   45
Sometimes, a few strands
would catch in her gold ring.
I worked hard then,
anticipating the hour
when I would let the rope down   50
at night, strips of sheets,
knotted and tied,
while she slept in tight blankets.

My hair, freshly washed
like a measure of wealth,
like a bridal veil.   55
Crouching in the grass,
you would wait for the signal,
for the movement of curtains
before releasing yourself   60
from the shadow of moths.
Cloth, hair and hands,
smuggling you in.

CONSIDERATIONS FOR CRITICAL THINKING AND WRITING

1. FIRST RESPONSE. How is hair made erotic in this poem? Discuss the images that you deem especially effective.
2. Who is the "you" that the speaker refers to in each stanza?
3. What role does the mother play in this poem about desire?
4. Why do you think the poem is titled "The White Porch"?

CONNECTIONS TO OTHER SELECTIONS

1. Compare the images used to describe the speaker's "slow arousal" (line 22) in this poem with Croft's images in "Home-Baked Bread" (p. 769). What similarities do you see? What makes each description so effective?
2. Write an essay comparing the images of sensuality in this poem with those in Ho's "A Beautiful Girl Combs Her Hair" (p. 705). Which poem seems more erotic to you? Why?

PERSPECTIVE

T. E. HULME (1883–1917)

On the Differences between Poetry and Prose   *1924*

In prose as in algebra concrete things are embodied in signs or counters which are moved about according to rules, without being visualized at all in the process. There are in prose certain type situations and arrangements of words, which move as automatically into certain other arrangements as do functions in algebra. One only changes the X's and the Y's back into physical things at the end of the process. Poetry, in one aspect at any rate, may be considered as an effort to avoid this characteristic of prose. It is not a counter language, but a visual concrete one. It is a compromise for a language of intuition which would hand over sensations bodily. It always endeavors to arrest you, and to make you continuously see a physical thing, to prevent you gliding through an abstract process. It chooses fresh epithets and fresh metaphors, not so much because they are new, and we are tired of the old, but because the old cease to convey a physical thing and become abstract counters. A poet says a ship "coursed the seas" to get a physical image, instead of the counter word "sailed." Visual meanings can only be transferred by the new bowl of metaphor; prose is an old pot that lets them leak out. Images in verse are not mere decoration, but the very essence of an intuitive language. Verse is a pedestrian taking you over the ground, prose — a train which delivers you at a destination.

From "Romanticism and Classicism," in *Speculations*,
edited by Herbert Read

CONSIDERATIONS FOR CRITICAL THINKING AND WRITING

1. What distinctions does Hulme make between poetry and prose? Which seems to be the most important difference?
2. Write an essay that discusses Hulme's claim that poetry "is a compromise for a language of intuition which would hand over sensations bodily."

24

Figures of Speech

Figures of speech are broadly defined as a way of saying one thing in terms of something else. An overeager funeral director might, for example, be described as a vulture. Although figures of speech are indirect, they are designed to clarify, not obscure, our understanding of what they describe. Poets frequently use them because, as Emily Dickinson said, the poet's work is to "Tell all the Truth but tell it slant" to capture the reader's interest and imagination. But figures of speech are not limited to poetry. Hearing them, reading them, or using them is as natural as using language itself.

Suppose that in the middle of a class discussion concerning the economic causes of World War II your history instructor introduces a series of statistics by saying, "Let's get down to brass tacks." Would anyone be likely to expect a display of brass tacks for students to examine? Of course not. To interpret the statement literally would be to wholly misunderstand the instructor's point that the time has come for a close look at the economic circumstances leading to the war. A literal response transforms the statement into the sort of hilariously bizarre material often found in a sketch by Woody Allen.

The class does not look for brass tacks because, to put it in a nutshell, they understand that the instructor is speaking figuratively. They would understand, too, that in the preceding sentence "in a nutshell" refers to brevity and conciseness rather than to the covering of a kernel of a nut. Figurative language makes its way into our everyday speech and writing as well as into literature because it is a means of achieving color, vividness, and intensity.

Consider the difference, for example, between these two statements:

Literal: The diner strongly expressed anger at the waiter.
Figurative: The diner leaped from his table and roared at the waiter.

The second statement is more vivid because it creates a picture of ferocious anger by likening the diner to some kind of wild animal, such as a lion or tiger. By comparison, "strongly expressed anger" is neither especially strong nor especially expressive; it is flat. Not all figurative language avoids this kind of flatness, however. Figures of speech such as "getting down to brass tacks" and "in a nutshell" are clichés because they lack originality and freshness. Still, they suggest how these devices are commonly used to give language some color, even if that color is sometimes a bit faded.

There is nothing weak about William Shakespeare's use of figurative language in the following passage from *Macbeth*. Macbeth has just learned that his wife is dead, and he laments her loss as well as the course of his own life.

WILLIAM SHAKESPEARE (1564–1616)

From Macbeth (Act V, Scene v)   *1605–1606*

Tomorrow, and tomorrow, and tomorrow
Creeps in this petty pace from day to day
To the last syllable of recorded time;
And all our yesterdays have lighted fools
The way to dusty death. Out, out, brief candle!   5
Life's but a walking shadow, a poor player,
That struts and frets his hour upon the stage,
And then is heard no more. It is a tale
Told by an idiot, full of sound and fury,
Signifying nothing.   10

This passage might be summarized as "life has no meaning," but such a brief paraphrase does not take into account the figurative language that reveals the depth of Macbeth's despair and his view of the absolute meaninglessness of life. By comparing life to a "brief candle," Macbeth emphasizes the darkness and death that surround human beings. The light of life is too brief and unpredictable to be of any comfort. Indeed, life for Macbeth is a "walking shadow," futilely playing a role that is more farcical than dramatic, because life is, ultimately, a desperate story filled with pain and devoid of significance. What the figurative language provides, then, is the emotional force of Macbeth's assertion; his comparisons are disturbing because they are so apt.

The remainder of this chapter discusses some of the most important figures of speech used in poetry. A familiarity with them will help you to understand how poetry achieves its effects.

SIMILE AND METAPHOR

Web *For activities on simile and metaphor, check out the Interactive Poetry Tutorial at* http://www.bedfordstmartins.com/meyer/bedintrolit

The two most common figures of speech are simile and metaphor. Both compare things that are ordinarily considered unlike each other. A *simile* makes an explicit comparison between two things by using words such as *like, as, than, appears,* or *seems:* "A sip of Mrs. Cook's coffee is like a punch in the stomach." The force of the simile is created by the differences between the two things compared. There would be no simile if the comparison were stated this way: "Mrs. Cook's coffee is as strong as the cafeteria's coffee." This is a literal comparison because Mrs. Cook's coffee is compared with something like it, another kind of coffee. Consider how simile is used in this poem.

MARGARET ATWOOD (B. 1939)

you fit into me
1971

you fit into me
like a hook into an eye

a fish hook
an open eye

If you blinked on a second reading, you got the point of this poem because you recognized that the simile "like a hook into an eye" gives way to a play on words in the final two lines. There the hook and eye, no longer a pleasant domestic image of fitting closely together, become a literal, sharp fishhook and a human eye. The wordplay qualifies the simile and drastically alters the tone of this poem by creating a strong and unpleasant surprise.

A *metaphor,* like a simile, makes a comparison between two unlike things, but it does so implicitly, without words such as *like* or *as:* "Mrs. Cook's coffee is a punch in the stomach." Metaphor asserts the identity of dissimilar things. Macbeth tells us that life *is* a "brief candle," life *is* "a walking shadow," life *is* "a poor player," life *is* "a tale / Told by an idiot." Metaphor transforms people, places, objects, and ideas into whatever the poet imagines them to be, and if metaphors are effective, the reader's experience, understanding, and appreciation of what is described are enhanced. Metaphors are frequently more demanding than similes because they are not signaled by particular words. They are both subtle and powerful.

Here is a poem about presentiment, a foreboding that something terrible is about to happen.

EMILY DICKINSON (1830–1886)

*Presentiment—is that long Shadow—
on the lawn—*
c. 1863

Presentiment—is that long Shadow—on the lawn—
Indicative that Suns go down—

The notice to the startled Grass
That Darkness—is about to pass—

The metaphors in this poem define the abstraction "Presentiment." The sense of foreboding that Dickinson expresses is identified with a particular moment, the moment when darkness is just about to envelop an otherwise tranquil ordinary scene. The speaker projects that fear onto the "startled Grass," so that it seems any life must be frightened by the approaching "Shadow" and "Darkness" — two richly connotative words associated with death. The metaphors obliquely tell us ("tell it slant" was Dickinson's motto, remember) that presentiment is related to a fear of death, and, more important, the metaphors convey the feelings that attend that idea.

Some metaphors are more subtle than others because their comparison of terms is less explicit. Notice the difference between the following two metaphors, both of which describe a shaggy derelict refusing to leave the warmth of a hotel lobby: "He was a mule standing his ground" is a quite explicit comparison. The man is a mule; X is Y. But this metaphor is much more covert: "He brayed his refusal to leave." This second version is an *implied metaphor* because it does not explicitly identify the man with a mule. Instead, it hints at or alludes to the mule. Braying is associated with mules and is especially appropriate in this context because of those animals' reputation for stubbornness. Implied metaphors can slip by readers, but they offer the alert reader the energy and resonance of carefully chosen, highly concentrated language.

Some poets write extended comparisons in which part or all of the poem consists of a series of related metaphors or similes. Extended metaphors are more common than extended similes. In "Catch" (p. 676), Francis creates an *extended metaphor* that compares poetry to a game of catch. The entire poem is organized around this comparison, just as all of the elements in Cummings's "she being Brand" (p. 720) are clustered around the extended comparison of a car and a woman. Because these comparisons are at work throughout the entire poem, they are called *controlling metaphors.* Extended comparisons can serve as a poem's organizing principle; they are also a reminder that in good poems metaphor and simile are not merely decorative but inseparable from what is expressed.

Notice the controlling metaphor in this poem, published posthumously by a woman whose contemporaries identified her more as a wife and mother than as a poet. Bradstreet's first volume of poetry, *The Tenth Muse,* was published by her brother-in-law in 1650 without her prior knowledge.

ANNE BRADSTREET (c. 1612–1672)

The Author to Her Book 1678

Thou ill-formed offspring of my feeble brain,
Who after birth did'st by my side remain,
Till snatched from thence by friends, less wise than true,
Who thee abroad exposed to public view;
Made thee in rags, halting, to the press to trudge,   5

Where errors were not lessened, all may judge.
At thy return my blushing was not small,
My rambling brat (in print) should mother call;
I cast thee by as one unfit for light,
Thy visage was so irksome in my sight;   10
Yet being mine own, at length affection would
Thy blemishes amend, if so I could:
I washed thy face, but more defects I saw,
And rubbing off a spot, still made a flaw.
I stretched thy joints to make thee even feet,   15
Yet still thou run'st more hobbling than is meet;
In better dress to trim thee was my mind,
But nought save homespun cloth in the house I find.
In this array, 'mongst vulgars may'st thou roam;
In critics' hands beware thou dost not come;   20
And take thy way where yet thou are not known.
If for thy Father asked, say thou had'st none;
And for thy Mother, she alas is poor,
Which caused her thus to send thee out of door.

The extended metaphor likening her book to a child came naturally to
Bradstreet and allowed her to regard her work both critically and affectionately. Her conception of the book as her child creates just the right tone of
amusement, self-deprecation, and concern.

The controlling metaphor in the following poem is identified by the
title. The game of chess these two players are engaged in is simultaneously
literal and metaphoric.

Rosario Castellanos (1925–1974)

Chess   *1988*

TRANSLATED BY MAUREEN AHERN

Because we were friends and sometimes loved each other,
perhaps to add one more tie
to the many that already bound us,
we decided to play games of the mind.

We set up a board between us;   5
equally divided into pieces, values,
and possible moves.
We learned the rules, we swore to respect them,
and the match began.

We've been sitting here for centuries, meditating   10
ferociously
how to deal the one last blow that will finally
annihilate the other one forever.

CONSIDERATIONS FOR CRITICAL THINKING AND WRITING

1. FIRST RESPONSE. Why do the players decide to play chess? Are you surprised by the effect the game has on their relationship?

2. Why is chess a particularly resonant controlling metaphor? Explain why chess is more evocative than, say, cards or checkers?

3. How does the poem's diction suggest tensions between the two players that go beyond a literal game of chess? Which lines are especially suggestive to you?

4. Do you think the players are men, women, or a man and a woman? Explain your response. How does the sex of the players affect your reading of the poem?

OTHER FIGURES

Perhaps the humblest figure of speech — if not one of the most familiar — is the pun. A *pun* is a play on words that relies on a word having more than one meaning or sounding like another word. For example, "A fad is in one era and out the other" is the sort of pun that produces obligatory groans. But most of us find pleasant and interesting surprises in puns. Here's one that has a slight edge to its humor.

EDMUND CONTI (B. 1929)

Pragmatist   1985

Apocalypse soon
Coming our way
Ground zero at noon
Halve a nice day.

Grimly practical under the circumstances, the pragmatist divides the familiar cheerful cliché by half. As simple as this poem is, its tone is mixed because it makes us laugh and wince at the same time.

Puns can be used to achieve serious effects as well as humorous ones. Although we may have learned to underrate puns as figures of speech, it is a mistake to underestimate their power and the frequency with which they appear in poetry. A close examination, for example, of Henry Reed's "Naming of Parts" (p. 823), Robert Frost's "Design" (p. 1018), or almost any lengthy passage from a Shakespeare play will confirm the value of puns.

Synecdoche is a figure of speech in which part of something is used to signify the whole: a neighbor is a "wagging tongue" (a gossip); a criminal is placed "behind bars" (in prison). Less typically, synecdoche refers to the whole used to signify the part: "Germany invaded Poland"; "Princeton won the fencing match." Clearly, certain individuals participated in these activities, not all of Germany or Princeton. Another related figure of speech is *metonymy*, in which something closely associated with a subject is substituted for it: "She preferred the silver screen [motion pictures] to reading." "At precisely ten o'clock the paper shufflers [office workers] stopped for coffee."

Synecdoche and metonymy may overlap and are therefore sometimes difficult to distinguish. Consider this description of a disapproving minister entering a noisy tavern: "As those pursed lips came through the swinging door, the atmosphere was suddenly soured." The pursed lips signal the presence of the minister and are therefore a synecdoche, but they additionally suggest an inhibiting sense of sin and guilt that makes the bar patrons feel uncomfortable. Hence, the pursed lips are also a metonymy, since they are in this context so closely connected with religion. Although the distinction between synecdoche and metonymy can be useful, when a figure of speech overlaps categories, it is usually labeled a metonymy.

Knowing the precise term for a figure of speech is, finally, less important than responding to its use in a poem. Consider how metonymy and synecdoche convey the tone and meaning of the following poem.

DYLAN THOMAS (1914–1953)

The Hand That Signed the Paper   1936

The hand that signed the paper felled a city;
Five sovereign fingers taxed the breath,
Doubled the globe of dead and halved a country;
These five kings did a king to death.

The mighty hand leads to a sloping shoulder,   5
The finger joints are cramped with chalk;
A goose's quill has put an end to murder
That put an end to talk.

The hand that signed the treaty bred a fever,
And famine grew, and locusts came;   10
Great is the hand that holds dominion over
Man by a scribbled name.

The five kings count the dead but do not soften
The crusted wound nor stroke the brow;
A hand rules pity as a hand rules heaven;   15
Hands have no tears to flow.

The "hand" in this poem is a synecdoche for a powerful ruler because it is a part of someone used to signify the entire person. The "goose's quill" is a metonymy that also refers to the power associated with the ruler's hand. By using these figures of speech, Thomas depersonalizes and ultimately dehumanizes the ruler. The final synecdoche tells us that "Hands have no tears to flow." It makes us see the political power behind the hand as remote and inhuman. How is the meaning of the poem enlarged when the speaker says, "A hand rules pity as a hand rules heaven"?

One of the ways writers energize the abstractions, ideas, objects, and animals that constitute their created worlds is through **personification,** the attribution of human characteristics to nonhuman things: temptation pursues the innocent; trees scream in the raging wind; mice conspire in the cupboard. We are not explicitly told that these things are people; instead, we are invited to see that they behave like people. Perhaps it is human vanity that makes personification a frequently used figure of speech. Whatever the reason, personification, a form of metaphor that connects the non-human with the human, makes the world understandable in human terms. Consider this concise example from William Blake's *The Marriage of Heaven and Hell,* a long poem that takes delight in attacking conventional morality: "Prudence is a rich ugly old maid courted by Incapacity." By personifying prudence, Blake transforms what is usually considered a virtue into a comic figure hardly worth emulating.

Often related to personification is another rhetorical figure called **apostrophe,** an address either to someone who is absent and therefore cannot hear the speaker or to something nonhuman that cannot comprehend. Apostrophe provides an opportunity for the speaker of a poem to think aloud, and often the thoughts expressed are in a formal tone. John Keats, for example, begins "Ode on a Grecian Urn" (p. 742) this way: "Thou still unravished bride of quietness." Apostrophe is frequently accompanied by intense emotion that is signaled by phrasing such as "O Life." In the right hands — such as Keats's — apostrophe can provide an intense and immediate voice in a poem, but when it is overdone or extravagant it can be ludicrous. Modern poets are more wary of apostrophe than their predecessors because apostrophizing strikes many self-conscious twentieth-century sensibilities as too theatrical. Thus modern poets tend to avoid exaggerated situations in favor of less charged though equally meditative moments, as in this next poem, with its amusing, half-serious cosmic twist.

JANICE TOWNLEY MOORE (B. 1939)

To a Wasp   1984

You must have chortled
finding that tiny hole
in the kitchen screen. Right
into my cheese cake batter
you dived,   5
no chance to swim ashore,
no saving spoon,
the mixer whirring
your legs, wings, stinger,

churning you into such   10
delicious death.
Never mind the bright April day.
Did you not see
rising out of cumulus clouds
That fist aimed at both of us?   15

Moore's apostrophe "To a Wasp" is based on the simplest of domestic circumstances; there is almost nothing theatrical or exaggerated in the poem's tone until "That fist" in the last line, when exaggeration takes center stage. As a figure of speech exaggeration is known as **overstatement** or **hyperbole** and adds emphasis without intending to be literally true: "The teenage boy ate everything in the house." Notice how the speaker of Marvell's "To His Coy Mistress" (p. 728) exaggerates his devotion in the following overstatement:

> An hundred years should go to praise
> Thine eyes and on thy forehead gaze,
> Two hundred to adore each breast,
> But thirty thousand to the rest:

That comes to 30,500 years. What is expressed here is heightened emotion, not deception.

The speaker also uses the opposite figure of speech, **understatement,** which says less than is intended. In the next section he sums up why he cannot take 30,500 years to express his love:

> The grave's a fine and private place,
> But none, I think, do there embrace.

The speaker is correct, of course, but by deliberately understating — saying "I think" when he is actually certain — he makes his point, that death will overtake their love, all the more emphatic. Another powerful example of understatement appears in the final line of Randall Jarrell's "The Death of the Ball Turret Gunner" (p. 718), when the disembodied voice of the machine-gunner describes his death in a bomber: "When I died they washed me out of the turret with a hose."

Paradox is a statement that initially appears to be self-contradictory but that, on closer inspection, turns out to make sense: "The pen is mightier than the sword." In a fencing match, anyone would prefer the sword, but if the goal is to win the hearts and minds of people, the art of persuasion can be more compelling than swordplay. To resolve the paradox, it is necessary to discover the sense that underlies the statement. If we see that "pen" and "sword" are used as metonymies for writing and violence, then the paradox rings true. **Oxymoron** is a condensed form of paradox in which two contradictory words are used together. Combinations such as "sweet sorrow," "silent scream," "sad joy," and "cold fire" indicate the kinds of startling effects that oxymorons can produce. Paradox is useful in

poetry because it arrests a reader's attention by its seemingly stubborn refusal to make sense, and once a reader has penetrated the paradox, it is difficult to resist a perception so well earned. Good paradoxes are knotty pleasures. Here is a simple but effective one.

J. PATRICK LEWIS (B. 1942)
The Unkindest Cut   1993

Knives can harm you, heaven forbid;
Axes may disarm you, kid;
Guillotines are painful, but
There's nothing like a paper cut!

This quatrain is a humorous version of "the pen is mightier than the
sword." The wounds escalate to the paper cut, which paradoxically is more
damaging than even the broad blade of a guillotine. "The unkindest cut"
of all (an allusion to Shakespeare's *Julius Caesar,* III.ii.188) is produced by
chilling words on a page rather than cold steel, but it is more painfully
fatal nonetheless.

The following poems are rich in figurative language. As you read and
study them, notice how their figures of speech vivify situations, clarify
ideas, intensify emotions, and engage your imagination. Although the
terms for the various figures discussed in this chapter are useful for label-
ing the particular devices used in poetry, they should not be allowed to get
in the way of your response to a poem. Don't worry about rounding up examples of figurative language. First relax and let the figures work their effects on you. Use the terms as a means of taking you further into poetry,
and they will serve your reading well.

POEMS FOR FURTHER STUDY

SUE OWEN (B. 1942)
Zero   1988

This is the story of zero,
born to live a life
of emptiness, only
child of plus and minus.

Its bones invisible   5
so it could be seen through
like an eye.
With that vision, you could

see the past and future
and how they mimic each other.   10
At first, it was thought
the zero was a mouth

and would say something
profound to the numbers.
But added to them, it never   15
amounted to much, and

subtracted, it never wanted
to take anything away.
Zero was a sad case,
only wanted to master emotion   20

and silence like chess.
Each winter, the approaching
degrees never could locate
its cold, missing heart.

CONSIDERATIONS FOR CRITICAL THINKING AND WRITING

1. FIRST RESPONSE. How does the poet's use of personification create a kind of life story of "zero"? What kind of story is it?
2. What is the poem's controlling metaphor?
3. How do the metaphors and similes in this poem enrich its meaning? Which ones seem particularly effective to you?

MARGARET ATWOOD (B. 1939)

February   1995

Winter. Time to eat fat
and watch hockey. In the pewter mornings, the cat,
a black fur sausage with yellow
Houdini eyes, jumps up on the bed and tries
to get onto my head. It's his   5
way of telling whether or not I'm dead.
If I'm not, he wants to be scratched; if I am
he'll think of something. He settles
on my chest, breathing his breath
of burped-up meat and musty sofas,   10
purring like a washboard. Some other tomcat,
not yet a capon, has been spraying our front door,
declaring war. It's all about sex and territory,
which are what will finish us off
in the long run. Some cat owners around here   15
should snip a few testicles. If we wise
hominids were sensible, we'd do that too,
or eat our young, like sharks.

But it's love that does us in. Over and over
again, *He shoots, he scores!* and famine   20
crouches in the bedsheets, ambushing the pulsing
eiderdown, and the windchill factor hits
thirty below, and pollution pours
out of our chimneys to keep us warm.
February, month of despair,   25
with a skewered heart in the centre.
I think dire thoughts, and lust for French fries
with a splash of vinegar.
Cat, enough of your greedy whining
and your small pink bumhole.   30
Off my face! You're the life principle,
more or less, so get going
on a little optimism around here.
Get rid of death. Celebrate increase. Make it be spring.

CONSIDERATIONS FOR CRITICAL THINKING AND WRITING

1. FIRST RESPONSE. How do your own associations with February compare
   with the speaker's?
2. Explain how the poem is organized around an extended metaphor that defines winter as a "Time to eat fat / and watch hockey" (lines 1–2).
3. Explain the paradox in "it's love that does us in" (line 19).
4. What theme(s) do you find in the poem? How is the cat central to them?

SOPHIE CABOT BLACK (B. 1958)

August   *1994*

A doe puts her nose to sky: stark hub
Around which the second cut of hay spins
Into one direction. A man rests
Against the fence, waiting

For the last minute to turn home. By heart   5
He knows the tilt and decline of each field,
His own faulty predictions. The well
Hoards its shadow while a raw haze gluts

With harvest, with guessing rains, presses
At the temple and wrist. The pastures, tired   10
Of abiding, begin to burn. Gold takes over,
Loose, unguarded. Cows stay deep

In the chafe of underbush; reckless leaves shawl
The edges, unaware of the sap that will send them down.

CONSIDERATIONS FOR CRITICAL THINKING AND WRITING

1. FIRST RESPONSE. How does the final line affect your understanding of the
   poem?

2. What tone is created by the poem's images of August?
3. How does Black's use of personification contribute to the tone?
4. Discuss what you think is the poem's theme.

CONNECTION TO ANOTHER SELECTION

1. Discuss the moods created in "August" and Atwood's "February." To what extent do you think each poem is successful in capturing the essence of the title's subject?

2. CRITICAL STRATEGIES. Read the section on mythological criticism (pp. 2107–09) in Chapter 52, "Critical Strategies for Reading." Write a comparison of the two poems from the perspective of a mythological critic.

ERNEST SLYMAN (B. 1946)

Lightning Bugs   1988

In my backyard,
They burn peepholes in the night
And take snapshots of my house.

CONSIDERATIONS FOR CRITICAL THINKING AND WRITING

1. FIRST RESPONSE. Explain why the title is essential to this poem.
2. What makes the description of the lightning bugs effective? How do the second and third lines complement each other?
3. As Slyman has done, take a simple, common fact of nature and make it vivid by using a figure of speech to describe it.

SYLVIA PLATH (1932–1963)

Mirror   1963

I am silver and exact. I have no preconceptions.
Whatever I see I swallow immediately
Just as it is, unmisted by love or dislike.
I am not cruel, only truthful —
The eye of a little god, four-cornered.   5
Most of the time I meditate on the opposite wall.
It is pink, with speckles. I have looked at it so long
I think it is a part of my heart. But it flickers.
Faces and darkness separate us over and over.

Now I am a lake. A woman bends over me,   10
Searching my reaches for what she really is.
Then she turns to those liars, the candles or the moon.
I see her back, and reflect it faithfully.
She rewards me with tears and an agitation of hands.
I am important to her. She comes and goes.   15

Each morning it is her face that replaces the darkness.
In me she has drowned a young girl, and in me an old woman
Rises toward her day after day, like a terrible fish.

CONSIDERATIONS FOR CRITICAL THINKING AND WRITING

1. FIRST RESPONSE. What is the effect of the personification in this poem?
   How would our view of the aging woman be different if she, rather than
   the mirror, told her story?
2. What is the mythical allusion in "Now I am a lake" (line 10)?
3. In what sense can "candles or the moon" be regarded as "liars"? Explain
   this metaphor.
4. Discuss the effectiveness of the simile in the final line of the poem.

SHARON OLDS (B. 1942)

Poem for the Breasts   1999

Like other identical twins, they can be
better told apart in adulthood.
One is fast to wrinkle her brow,
her brain, her quick intelligence. The other
dreams inside a constellation,   5
freckles of Orion. They were born when I was thirteen,
they rose up, half out of my chest,
now they're forty, wise, generous.
I am inside them — in a way, under them,
or I carry them, I was alive so long without them.   10
I can't say I am them, though their feelings are almost
      my feelings,
as with someone one deeply loves. They seem,
to me, like a gift that I have to give.
That boys were said to worship their category of   15
being, almost starve for it,
did not escape me, and some young men
loved them the way one would want, oneself, to be loved.
All year, they have been calling to my husband,
singing to him, like a pair of soaking   20
sirens on a scaled rock.
They cannot believe he could leave them, it isn't
vanity, they themselves
were made of promise and so they believed his word.
Sometimes, now, I hold them a moment,   25
one in each hand, twin widows.
heavy with grief. They were a gift to me,
and then they were ours, like little nurslings
of excitement and plenty. And now it is summer
again, late summer, the very week   30
he moved out. Didn't he whisper to them
wait here for me one year? No.

He said, God be with you, God
by with you, God
by, for the rest   35
of this life and for the long nothing. And they do not
know language, they are waiting for him, my
Christ they are dumb, they do not even
know they are mortal — sweet, I guess,
refreshing to live with, beings without   40
the knowledge of death, creatures of ignorant suffering.

CONSIDERATIONS FOR CRITICAL THINKING AND WRITING

1. FIRST RESPONSE. Personifying breasts and using them as extended metaphors
   and similes may not seem like a promising premise for a poem. As you read the
   poem, did you find that the premise worked for you? Explain why or why not
   by considering the poem's personification, metaphors, and similes.

2. Describe the difference in tone between lines 1–18 and 19–41.

3. Read lines 31–36 aloud. How do you make sense of the fragmented nature
   of these lines?

4. What kinds of emotions does this poem create for you?

CONNECTIONS TO OTHER SELECTIONS

1. Compare and contrast the use of extended metaphor in "Poem for the
   Breasts" and in Anne Bradstreet's "The Author to Her Book" (p. 780).

2. Discuss Olds's strategies for using extended metaphors in "Poem for the
   Breasts" and in two other poems by her: "Sex without Love" (p. 739) and
   "Rite of Passage" (p. 927).

WILLIAM WORDSWORTH (1770–1850)

London, 1802   *1802*

Milton!° thou should'st be living at this hour:
England hath need of thee: she is a fen
Of stagnant waters: altar, sword, and pen,
Fireside, the heroic wealth of hall and bower,
Have forfeited their ancient English dower   5
Of inward happiness. We are selfish men;
Oh! raise us up, return to us again;
And give us manners, virtue, freedom, power.
Thy soul was like a star, and dwelt apart:
Thou hadst a voice whose sound was like the sea: 10
Pure as the naked heavens, majestic, free,
So didst thou travel on life's common way,
In cheerful godliness; and yet thy heart
The lowliest duties on herself did lay.

1 *Milton:* John Milton (1608–1674), poet, famous especially for his religious epic *Paradise Lost*
and his defense of political freedom.

Considerations for Critical Thinking and Writing

1. FIRST RESPONSE. Describe the poem's tone. Is it nostalgic, angry, or something else?

2. Explain the metonymies in lines 3-6 of this poem. What is the speaker's assessment of England?

3. How would the effect of the poem be different if it were in the form of an address to Wordsworth's contemporaries rather than an apostrophe to Milton? What qualities does Wordsworth attribute to Milton by the use of figurative language?

4. CRITICAL STRATEGIES. Read the section on literary history criticism (pp. 2102-03) in Chapter 52, "Critical Strategies for Reading," and use the library to find out about the state of London in 1802. How does the poem reflect or refute the social values of its time?

JIM STEVENS (B. 1922)

Schizophrenia   1992

It was the house that suffered most.

It had begun with slamming doors, angry feet scuffing the carpets,
dishes slammed onto the table,
greasy stains spreading on the cloth.

Certain doors were locked at night,   5
feet stood for hours outside them,
dishes were left unwashed, the cloth
disappeared under a hardened crust.

The house came to miss the shouting voices,
the threats, the half-apologies, noisy   10
reconciliations, the sobbing that followed.

Then lines were drawn, borders established,
some rooms declared their loyalties,
keeping to themselves, keeping out the other.
The house divided against itself.   15

Seeing cracking paint, broken windows,
the front door banging in the wind,
the roof tiles flying off, one by one,
the neighbors said it was a madhouse.

It was the house that suffered most.   20

Considerations for Critical Thinking and Writing

1. FIRST RESPONSE. What is the effect of personifying the house in this poem?

2. How are the people who live in the house characterized? What does their behavior reveal about them? How does the house respond to them?

3. Comment on the title. If the title were missing, what, if anything, would be missing from the poem? Explain your answer.

WALT WHITMAN (1819–1892)

A Noiseless Patient Spider   1868

A noiseless patient spider,
I mark'd where on a little promontory it stood isolated,
Mark'd how to explore the vacant vast surrounding,
It launch'd forth filament, filament, filament, out of itself,
Ever unreeling them, ever tirelessly speeding them.   5

And you O my soul where you stand,
Surrounded, detached, in measureless oceans of space,
Ceaselessly musing, venturing, throwing, seeking the spheres to connect
    them,
Till the bridge you will need be form'd, till the ductile anchor hold,
Till the gossamer thread you fling catch somewhere, O my soul.   10

CONSIDERATIONS FOR CRITICAL THINKING AND WRITING

1. FIRST RESPONSE. Spiders are not usually regarded as pleasant creatures.
Why does the speaker in this poem liken his soul to one? What similarities
are there in the poem between spider and soul? Are there any significant
differences?

2. How do the images of space relate to the connections made between the
speaker's soul and the spider?

JOHN DONNE (1572–1631)

A Valediction: Forbidding Mourning   1611

As virtuous men pass mildly away,
    And whisper to their souls to go,
While some of their sad friends do say,
    The breath goes now, and some say, no:

So let us melt, and make no noise,   5
    No tear-floods, nor sigh-tempests move;
'Twere profanation of our joys
    To tell the laity our love.

Moving of th' earth° brings harms and fears,   *earthquakes*
    Men reckon what it did and meant,   10
But trepidation of the spheres,°
    Though greater far, is innocent.

Dull sublunary° lovers' love
    (Whose soul is sense) cannot admit

11 *trepidation of the spheres:* According to Ptolemaic astronomy, the planets sometimes moved
violently, like earthquakes, but these movements were not felt by people on earth.   13 *sublunary:* Under the moon; hence, mortal and subject to change.

Absence, because it doth remove
    Those things which elemented° it.   *composed*

But we by a love so much refined,
    That ourselves know not what it is,
Inter-assured of the mind,
    Care less, eyes, lips, and hands to miss.   20

Our two souls therefore, which are one,
    Though I must go, endure not yet
A breach, but an expansion,
    Like gold to airy thinness beat.

If they be two, they are two so   25
    As stiff twin compasses are two;
Thy soul the fixed foot, makes no show
    To move, but doth, if th' other do.

And though it in the center sit,
    Yet when the other far doth roam,   30
It leans, and hearkens after it,
    And grows erect, as that comes home.

Such wilt thou be to me, who must
    Like th' other foot, obliquely run;
Thy firmness makes my circle just,°   35
    And makes me end, where I begun.

35 *circle just:* The circle is a traditional symbol of perfection.

CONSIDERATIONS FOR CRITICAL THINKING AND WRITING

1. FIRST RESPONSE. A valediction is a farewell. Donne wrote this poem for his wife before leaving on a trip to France. What kind of "mourning" is the speaker forbidding?
2. Explain how the simile in lines 1–4 is related to the couple in lines 5–8. Who is described as dying?
3. How does the speaker contrast the couple's love to "sublunary lovers' love" (line 13)?
4. Explain the similes in lines 24 and 25–36.

LINDA PASTAN (B. 1932)

Marks   *1978*

My husband gives me an A
for last night's supper,
an incomplete for my ironing,
a B plus in bed.
My son says I am average,   5
an average mother, but if

I put my mind to it
I could improve.
My daughter believes
in Pass/Fail and tells me   10
I pass. Wait 'til they learn
I'm dropping out.

Considerations for Critical Thinking and Writing

1. FIRST RESPONSE. Explain the appropriateness of the controlling metaphor
   in this poem. How does it reveal the woman's relationship to her family?
2. Discuss the meaning of the title.
3. How does the last line serve as both the climax of the woman's story and
   the controlling metaphor of the poem?

Thomas Lynch (b. 1948)

Liberty   1998

Some nights I go out and piss on the front lawn
as a form of freedom — liberty from
porcelain and plumbing and the Great Beyond
beyond the toilet and the sewage works.
Here is the statement I am trying to make: 5
to say I am from a fierce bloodline of men
who made their water in the old way, under stars
that overarched the North Atlantic where
the River Shannon empties into sea.
The ex-wife used to say, "Why can't you pee   10
in concert with the most of humankind
who do their business tidily indoors?"
It was gentility or envy, I suppose,
because I could do it anywhere, and do
whenever I begin to feel encumbered.   15
Still, there is nothing, here in the suburbs,
as dense as the darkness in West Clare
nor any equivalent to the nightlong wind
that rattles in the hedgerow of whitethorn there
on the east side of the cottage yard in Moveen.   20
It was market day in Kilrush, years ago:
my great-great-grandfather bargained with tinkers
who claimed it was whitethorn that Christ's crown was made from.
So he gave them two and six and brought them home —
mere saplings then — as a gift for the missus,   25
who planted them between the house and garden.
For years now, men have slipped out the back door
during wakes or wedding feasts or nights of song

796 | *Figures of Speech*

to pay their homage to the holy trees
and, looking up into that vast firmament,   30
consider liberty in that last townland where
they have no crowns, no crappers and no ex-wives.

CONSIDERATIONS FOR CRITICAL THINKING AND WRITING

1. FIRST RESPONSE. Does "gentility or envy" (13) get in the way of your enjoying and appreciating this poem? Explain why or why not.
2. Characterize the speaker and explain why you find him engaging or not.
3. How does the speaker metaphorically define *liberty*?
4. Discuss the tone of the speaker's definition of freedom. Explain why you
   find the purpose of this poem to be humorous or serious — or both.

CONNECTION TO ANOTHER SELECTION

1. Discuss Lynch's treatment of suburban life and compare it with John
   Ciardi's in "Suburban" (p. 824). What similarities are there in the themes
   and metaphoric strategies of these two poems?

STEPHEN DUNN (B. 1939)

John & Mary   1998

John & Mary had never met. They were like two
hummingbirds who also had never met.
        — from a freshman's short story

They were like gazelles who occupied different
grassy plains, running in opposite directions
from different lions. They were like postal clerks
in different zip codes, with different vacation time,
their bosses adamant and clock-driven.   5
How could they get together?
They were like two people who couldn't get together.
John was a Sufi with a love of the dervish,
Mary of course a Christian with a curfew.
They were like two dolphins in the immensity   10
of the Atlantic, one playful,
the other stuck in a tuna net —
two absolutely different childhoods!
There was simply no hope for them.
They would never speak in person.   15
When they ran across that windswept field
toward each other, they were like two freight trains,
one having left Seattle at 6:36 P.M.
at an unknown speed, the other delayed
in Topeka for repairs.   20

The math indicated that they'd embrace
in another world, if at all, like parallel lines.
Or merely appear kindred and close, like stars.

CONSIDERATIONS FOR CRITICAL THINKING AND WRITING

1. FIRST RESPONSE. Why is the epigraph "from a freshman's short story" crucial for an understanding of this poem?
2. What's the problem with the freshman's simile? How does it serve as an inspiration for the similes in the poem?
3. Discuss the speaker's tone. Did you find it amusing? Explain why you find
it appealing or not. What does the tone contribute to your understanding
of the poem?
4. How do the similes in lines 20–23 differ from those that precede it?

CONNECTION TO ANOTHER SELECTION

1. Compare the speaker's tone in "John & Mary" with that of Mark Halliday's
"Graded Paper" (p. 1110). What significant similarities and differences do
you find in each speaker's attitude toward the student writer?

ELAINE MAGARRELL (B. 1928)

The Joy of Cooking 1988

I have prepared my sister's tongue,
scrubbed and skinned it,
trimmed the roots, small bones, and gristle.
Carved through the hump it slices thin and neat.
Best with horseradish   5
and economical — it probably will grow back.
Next time perhaps a creole sauce
or mold of aspic?

I will have my brother's heart,
which is firm and rather dry,   10
slow cooked. It resembles muscle
more than organ meat
and needs an apple-onion stuffing
to make it interesting at all.
Although beef heart serves six   15
my brother's heart barely feeds two.
I could also have it braised
and served in sour sauce.

CONSIDERATIONS FOR CRITICAL THINKING AND WRITING

1. FIRST RESPONSE. Describe the poem's tone. Do you find it amusing, bitter,
or something else?

2. How are the tongue and heart used to characterize the sister and brother in this poem?

3. Describe the speaker's tone. What effect does the title have on your determining the tone?

CONNECTION TO ANOTHER SELECTION

1. Write an essay that explains how cooking becomes a way of talking about something else in this poem and in Croft's "Home-Baked Bread" (p. 769).

STEPHEN PERRY (B. 1947)

Blue Spruce   *1991*

My grandfather worked in a barbershop
smelling of lotions he'd slap on your face,
hair and talc. The black razor strop

hung like the penis of an ox. He'd draw
the sharp blade in quick strokes over   5
the smooth-rough hide, and then carefully

over your face. The tiny hairs would gather
on the blade, a congregation singing
under blue spruce in winter,

a bandstand in the center of town   10
bright with instruments, alto sax, tenor
sax, tuba or sousaphone — the bright

oompah-pahs shaving the town somehow,
a bright cloth shaking the air
into flakes of silvering hair   15

floating down past the houses, the horses
pulling carriages past the town fountain,
which had frozen into a coiffure

of curly glass. My grandfather had an affair
with the girl who did their nails   20
bright pink, bright red, never blue,

perhaps as the horses clip-clopped on ice
outside his shop, his kisses
smelling of lather and new skin —

when she grew too big and round   25
with his child, with his oompah love,
with his bandstand love, with his brassy love,

and the town dropped its grace notes
of gossip and whispered hiss,
he bundled her out of town   30

with the savings which should have gone
to my mom. But how could you hate him?
My mother did, my father did,

and my grandmother, who bore his neglect.
When she was covered in sheets   35
at her last death,

he flirted with the nurses, bright
as winter birds in spruces
above a bandstand —

I'll always remember him in snow, a deep lather   40
of laughter, the picture
where he took me from my mother

and raised me high, a baby, into the bell
of his sousaphone, as if I were a note
he'd play into light —   45

CONSIDERATIONS FOR CRITICAL THINKING AND WRITING

1. FIRST RESPONSE. The grandfather is presented as an outrageous figure,
   "But how could you hate him?" (line 32). Do you think the speaker is successful in preventing the reader from hating his grandfather? Explain.

2. What are the controlling metaphors in "Blue Spruce"? How do they help to
   characterize the grandfather?

3. Write a paragraph detailing what you think the speaker means by his
   grandfather's "oompah love" (line 26).

PERSPECTIVE

JOHN R. SEARLE (B. 1932)

Figuring Out Metaphors   *1979*

If you hear somebody say, "Sally is a block of ice," or, "Sam is a pig," you are
likely to assume that the speaker does not mean what he says literally, but that
he is speaking metaphorically. Furthermore, you are not likely to have very
much trouble figuring out what he means. If he says, "Sally is a prime number
between 17 and 23," or "Bill is a barn door," you might still assume he is speaking
metaphorically, but it is much harder to figure out what he means. The existence
of such utterances — utterances in which the speaker means metaphorically
something different from what the sentence means literally — poses a series of
questions for any theory of language and communication: What is metaphor,
and how does it differ from both literal and other forms of figurative utterances? Why do we use expressions metaphorically instead of saying exactly and
literally what we mean? How do metaphorical utterances work, that is, how is it

possible for speakers to communicate to hearers when speaking metaphorically inasmuch as they do not say what they mean? And why do some metaphors work and others do not?

From *Expression and Meaning*

CONSIDERATIONS FOR CRITICAL THINKING AND WRITING

1. Searle poses a series of important questions. Write an essay that explores one of these questions, basing your discussion on the poems in this chapter.

2. Try writing a brief poem that provides a context for the line "Sally is a prime number between 17 and 23" or the line "Bill is a barn door." Your task is to create a context so that either one of these metaphoric statements is as readily understandable as "Sally is a block of ice" or "Sam is a pig." Share your poem with your classmates and explain how the line generated the poem you built around it.

25

Symbol, Allegory, and Irony

SYMBOL

Web *For activities on symbol, check out the Interactive Poetry Tutorial at* http://www.bedfordstmartins.com/meyer/bedintrolit

A *symbol* is something that represents something else. An object, person, place, event, or action can suggest more than its literal meaning. A handshake between two world leaders might be simply a greeting, but if it is done ceremoniously before cameras, it could be a symbolic gesture signifying unity, issues resolved, and joint policies that will be followed. We live surrounded by symbols. When an $80,000 Mercedes-Benz comes roaring by in the fast lane, we get a quick glimpse of not only an expensive car but an entire lifestyle that suggests opulence, broad lawns, executive offices, and power. One of the reasons some buyers are willing to spend roughly the cost of five Chevrolets for a single Mercedes-Benz is that they are aware of the car's symbolic value. A symbol is a vehicle for two things at once: it functions as itself, and it implies meanings beyond itself.

The meanings suggested by a symbol are determined by the context in which they appear. The Mercedes could symbolize very different things depending on where it was parked. Would an American political candidate be likely to appear in a Detroit blue-collar neighborhood with such a car? Probably not. Although a candidate might be able to afford the car, it would be an inappropriate symbol for someone seeking votes from all the people. As a symbol, the German-built Mercedes would backfire if voters perceived it as representing an entity partially responsible for layoffs of automobile workers or, worse, as a sign of decadence and corruption. Similarly, a huge portrait of Mao Tse-tung conveys different meanings to residents of Beijing than it would to farmers in Prairie Center, Illinois.

Because symbols depend on contexts for their meaning, literary artists provide those contexts so that the reader has enough information to determine the probable range of meanings suggested by a symbol.

In the following poem the speaker describes walking at night. How is the night used symbolically?

ROBERT FROST (1874–1963)

Acquainted with the Night   1928

I have been one acquainted with the night.
I have walked out in rain — and back in rain.
I have outwalked the furthest city light.

I have looked down the saddest city lane.
I have passed by the watchman on his beat   5
And dropped my eyes, unwilling to explain.

I have stood still and stopped the sound of feet
When far away an interrupted cry
Came over houses from another street,

But not to call me back or say good-by;   10
And further still at an unearthly height
One luminary clock against the sky

Proclaimed the time was neither wrong nor right.
I have been one acquainted with the night.

In approaching this or any poem, you should read for literal meanings first and then allow the elements of the poem to invite you to symbolic readings, if they are appropriate. Here the somber tone suggests that the lines have symbolic meaning too. The flat matter-of-factness created by the repetition of "I have" (lines 1–5, 7, 14) understates the symbolic subject matter of the poem, which is, finally, more about the "night" located in the speaker's mind or soul than it is about walking away from a city and back again. The speaker is "acquainted with the night." The importance of this phrase is emphasized by Frost's title and by the fact that he begins and ends the poem with it. Poets frequently use this kind of repetition to alert readers to details that carry more than literal meanings.

The speaker in this poem has personal knowledge of the night but does not indicate specifically what the night means. To arrive at the potential meanings of the night in this context, it is necessary to look closely at its connotations, along with the images provided in the poem. The connotative meanings of night suggest, for example, darkness, death, and grief. By drawing on these connotations, Frost uses a ***conventional symbol***, something that is recognized by many people to represent certain ideas. Roses conventionally symbolize love or beauty; laurels, fame; spring, growth; the moon, romance. Poets often use conventional symbols to convey tone and meaning.

Frost uses the night as a conventional symbol, but he also develops it into a *literary* or *contextual symbol* that goes beyond traditional, public meanings. A literary symbol cannot be summarized in a word or two. It tends to be as elusive as experience itself. The night cannot be reduced to or equated with darkness or death or grief, but it evokes those associations and more. Frost took what perhaps initially appears to be an overworked, conventional symbol and prevented it from becoming a cliché by deepening and extending its meaning.

The images in "Acquainted with the Night" lead to the poem's symbolic meaning. Unwilling, and perhaps unable, to explain explicitly to the watchman (and to the reader) what the night means, the speaker nevertheless conveys feelings about it. The brief images of darkness, rain, sad city lanes, the necessity for guards, the eerie sound of a distressing cry coming over rooftops, and the "luminary clock against the sky" proclaiming "the time was neither wrong nor right" all help to create a sense of anxiety in this tight-lipped speaker. Although we cannot know what unnamed personal experiences have acquainted the speaker with the night, the images suggest that whatever the night means, it is somehow associated with insomnia, loneliness, isolation, coldness, darkness, death, fear, and a sense of alienation from humanity and even time. Daylight—ordinary daytime thoughts and life itself—seems remote and unavailable in this poem. The night is literally the period from sunset to sunrise, but, more important, it is an internal state of being felt by the speaker and revealed through the images.

Frost used symbols rather than an expository essay that would explain the conditions that cause these feelings because most readers can provide their own list of sorrows and terrors that evoke similar emotions. Through symbol, the speaker's experience is compressed and simultaneously expanded by the personal darkness that each reader brings to the poem. The suggestive nature of symbols makes them valuable for poets and evocative for readers.

ALLEGORY

Web *For activities on allegory, check out the Interactive Poetry Tutorial at*
http://www.bedfordstmartins.com/meyer/bedintrolit

Unlike expansive, suggestive symbols, *allegory* is a narration or description usually restricted to a single meaning because its events, actions, characters, settings, and objects represent specific abstractions or ideas. Although the elements in an allegory may be interesting in themselves, the emphasis tends to be on what they ultimately mean. Characters may be given names such as Hope, Pride, Youth, and Charity; they have few, if any, personal qualities beyond their abstract meanings. These personifications are a form of extended metaphor, but their meanings are severely restricted. They are not symbols because, for instance, the meaning of a character named Charity is precisely that virtue.

There is little or no room for broad speculation and exploration in allegories. If Frost had written "Acquainted with the Night" as an allegory, he might have named his speaker Loneliness and had him leave the City of Despair to walk the Streets of Emptiness, where Crime, Poverty, Fear, and other characters would define the nature of city life. The literal elements in an allegory tend to be de-emphasized in favor of the message. Symbols, however, function both literally and symbolically, so that "Acquainted with the Night" is about both a walk and a sense that something is terribly wrong.

Allegory especially lends itself to **didactic poetry,** which is designed to teach an ethical, moral, or religious lesson. Many stories, poems, and plays are concerned with values, but didactic literature is specifically created to convey a message. "Acquainted with the Night" does not impart advice or offer guidance. If the poem argued that city life is self-destructive or sinful, it would be didactic; instead, it is a lyric poem that expresses the emotions and thoughts of a single speaker.

Although allegory is often enlisted in didactic causes because it can so readily communicate abstract ideas through physical representations, not all allegories teach a lesson. Here is a poem describing a haunted palace while also establishing a consistent pattern that reveals another meaning.

EDGAR ALLAN POE (1809–1849)

The Haunted Palace   *1839*

I
In the greenest of our valleys,
　By good angels tenanted,
Once a fair and stately palace —
　Radiant palace — reared its head.
In the monarch Thought's dominion —   5
　It stood there!
Never seraph spread a pinion
　Over fabric half so fair.

II
Banners yellow, glorious, golden,
　On its roof did float and flow;   10
(This — all this — was in the olden
　Time long ago)
And every gentle air that dallied,
　In that sweet day,
Along the ramparts plumed and pallid,   15
　A wingèd odor went away.

III

Wanderers in that happy valley
  Through two luminous windows saw
Spirits moving musically
  To a lute's well-tunèd law,   20
Round about a throne, where sitting
  (Porphyrogene!)°   *born to purple, royal*
In state his glory well befitting,
  The ruler of the realm was seen.

IV

And all with pearl and ruby glowing   25
  Was the fair palace door,
Through which came flowing, flowing, flowing
  And sparkling evermore,
A troop of Echoes whose sweet duty
  Was but to sing,   30
In voices of surpassing beauty,
  The wit and wisdom of their king.

V

But evil things, in robes of sorrow,
  Assailed the monarch's high estate;
(Ah, let us mourn, for never morrow   35
  Shall dawn upon him, desolate!)
And, round about his home, the glory
  That blushed and bloomed
Is but a dim-remembered story
  Of the old time entombed.   40

VI

And travelers now within that valley,
  Through the red-litten windows see
Vast forms that move fantastically
  To a discordant melody;
While, like a rapid ghastly river,   45
  Through the pale door,
A hideous throng rush out forever,
  And laugh—but smile no more.

On one level this poem describes how a once happy palace is desolated by "evil things" (line 33). If the reader pays close attention to the diction, however, an allegorical meaning becomes apparent on a second reading. A systematic pattern develops in the choice of words used to describe the palace, so that it comes to stand for a human mind. The palace, banners, windows, door, echoes, and throng are equated with a person's head, hair, eyes, mouth, voice, and laughter. That mind, once harmoniously ordered, is overthrown by evil, haunting thoughts that lead to the mad laughter in the poem's final lines. Once the general pattern is seen, the rest of the details fall neatly into place to strengthen the parallels between the surface description of a palace and the allegorical representation of a disordered mind.

Modern writers generally prefer symbol over allegory because they tend to be more interested in opening up the potential meanings of an experience instead of transforming it into a closed pattern of meaning. Perhaps the major difference is that while allegory may delight a reader's imagination, symbol challenges and enriches it.

IRONY

Web *For activities on irony, check out the Interactive Poetry Tutorial at*
http://www.bedfordstmartins.com/meyer/bedintrolit

Another important resource writers use to take readers beyond literal meanings is *irony,* a technique that reveals a discrepancy between what appears to be and what is actually true. Here is a classic example in which appearances give way to the underlying reality.

EDWIN ARLINGTON ROBINSON (1869–1935)
Richard Cory   *1897*

Whenever Richard Cory went down town,
We people on the pavement looked at him:
He was a gentleman from sole to crown,
Clean favored, and imperially slim.

And he was always quietly arrayed,   5
And he was always human when he talked;
But still he fluttered pulses when he said,
"Good-morning," and he glittered when he walked.

And he was rich — yes, richer than a king —
And admirably schooled in every grace: 10
In fine, we thought that he was everything
To make us wish that we were in his place.

So on we worked, and waited for the light,
And went without the meat, and cursed the bread;
And Richard Cory, one calm summer night,   15
Went home and put a bullet through his head.

Richard Cory seems to have it all. Those less fortunate, the "people on the pavement," regard him as well-bred, handsome, tasteful, and richly endowed with both money and grace. Until the final line of the poem, the reader, like the speaker, is charmed by Cory's good fortune, so quietly expressed in his decent, easy manner. That final, shocking line, however, shatters the appearances of Cory's life and reveals him to have been a desperately unhappy man. While everyone else assumes that Cory represented "everything" to which they aspire, the reality is that he could escape his miserable life only as a suicide. This discrepancy between what appears to be true and what actually exists is known as *situational irony:* what happens is entirely different from what is expected. We are not told why Cory shoots himself; instead, the irony in the poem shocks us into the recognition that appearances do not always reflect realities.

Words are also sometimes intended to be taken at other than face value. *Verbal irony* is saying something different from what is meant. After reading "Richard Cory," to say "That rich gentleman sure was happy" is ironic. The tone of voice would indicate that just the opposite was meant; hence, verbal irony is usually easy to detect in spoken language. In literature, however, a reader can sometimes take literally what a writer intends ironically. The remedy for this kind of misreading is to pay close attention to the poem's context. There is no formula that can detect verbal irony, but contradictory actions and statements as well as the use of understatement and overstatement can often be signals that verbal irony is present.

Consider how verbal irony is used in this poem.

KENNETH FEARING (1902–1961)

AD   *1938*

Wanted: Men;
Millions of men are *wanted at once* in a big new field;
New, tremendous, thrilling, great.
If you've ever been a figure in the chamber of horrors,
If you've ever escaped from a psychiatric ward,   5
If you thrill at the thought of throwing poison into wells, have heavenly
      visions of people, by the thousands, dying in flames —
You are the very man we want
We mean business and our business is *you*
Wanted: A race of brand-new men.   10

Apply: Middle Europe;
No skill needed;
No ambition required; no brains wanted and no character allowed;

Take a permanent job in the coming profession
Wages: *Death.*   15

This poem was written as Nazi troops stormed across Europe at the start of World War II. The advertisement suggests on the surface that killing is just an ordinary job, but the speaker indicates through understatement that there is nothing ordinary about the "business" of this "*coming profession.*" Fearing uses verbal irony to indicate how casually and mindlessly people are prepared to accept the horrors of war.

Consider how the next poem, by Janice Mirikitani, a third-generation Japanese American, uses a similar ironic strategy in a different context.

JANICE MIRIKITANI (B. 1942)

Recipe   1987

Round Eyes

Ingredients: scissors, Scotch magic transparent tape,
               eyeliner — water based, black.
               Optional: false eyelashes.

Cleanse face thoroughly.   5

For best results, powder entire face, including eyelids.
    (lighter shades suited to total effect desired)

With scissors, cut magic tape ⅟₁₆" wide, ¾"–½" long —
depending on length of eyelid.

Stick firmly onto mid–upper eyelid area   10
    (looking down into handmirror facilitates finding
    adequate surface)

If using false eyelashes, affix first on lid, folding any
excess lid over the base of eyelash with glue.

Paint black eyeliner on tape and entire lid.   15

Do not cry.

CONSIDERATIONS FOR CRITICAL THINKING AND WRITING

1. FIRST RESPONSE. Discuss your response to the poem's final line.
2. What is the effect of the very specific details of this recipe?
3. Why is "false eyelashes" a particularly resonant phrase in the context of this poem?
4. Try writing your own "recipe" in poetic lines — one that makes a commentary concerning a social issue that you feel strongly about.

CONNECTION TO ANOTHER SELECTION

1. Why are the formulas for an advertisement and a recipe especially suited for Fearing's and Mirikitani's respective purposes? To what extent do the ironic strategies lead to a similar tone and theme?

Like "AD," "Recipe" is a *satire,* an example of the literary art of ridiculing a folly or vice in an effort to expose or correct it. The object of satire is usually some human frailty; people, institutions, ideas, and things are all fair game for satirists. Fearing satirizes the insanity of a world mobilizing itself for war: his irony reveals the speaker's knowledge that there is nothing *"New, tremendous, thrilling,* [or] *great"* about going off to kill and be killed. The implication of the poem is that no one should respond to advertisements for war. The poem serves as a satiric corrective to those who would troop off armed with unrealistic expectations; wage war and the wages consist of death.

Dramatic irony is used when a writer allows a reader to know more about a situation than a character does. This creates a discrepancy between what a character says or thinks and what the reader knows to be true. Dramatic irony is often used to reveal character. In the following poem the speaker delivers a public speech that ironically tells us more about him than it does about the patriotic holiday he is commemorating.

E. E. CUMMINGS (1894–1962)

next to of course god america i   1926

"next to of course god america i
love you land of the pilgrims' and so forth oh
say can you see by the dawn's early my
country 'tis of centuries come and go
and are no more what of it we should worry   5
in every language even deafanddumb
thy sons acclaim your glorious name by gorry
by jingo by gee by gosh by gum
why talk of beauty what could be more beaut-
iful than these heroic happy dead   10
who rushed like lions to the roaring slaughter
they did not stop to think they died instead
then shall the voice of liberty be mute?"

He spoke. And drank rapidly a glass of water

This verbal debauch of chauvinistic clichés (notice the run-on phrases and lines) reveals that the speaker's relationship to God and country is not, as he claims, one of love. His public address suggests a hearty mindlessness that leads to "roaring slaughter" rather than to reverence or patriotism. Cummings allows the reader to see through the speaker's words to their dangerous emptiness. What the speaker means and what Cummings means are entirely different. Like Fearing's "AD," this poem is a satire that invites the reader's laughter and contempt in order to deflate the benighted attitudes expressed in it.

When a writer uses God, destiny, or fate to dash the hopes and expectations of a character or humankind in general, it is called **cosmic irony**. In "The Convergence of the Twain" (p. 736), for example, Hardy describes how "The Immanent Will" brought together the *Titanic* and a deadly iceberg.

Technology and pride are no match for "the Spinner of the Years." Here's a painfully terse version of cosmic irony.

STEPHEN CRANE (1871–1900)

A Man Said to the Universe
1899

A man said to the universe:
"Sir, I exist!"
"However," replied the universe,
"The fact has not created in me
A sense of obligation."

Unlike in "The Convergence of the Twain," there is the slightest bit of humor in Crane's poem, but the joke is on us.

Irony is an important technique that allows a writer to distinguish between appearances and realities. In situational irony a discrepancy exists between what we expect to happen and what actually happens; in verbal irony a discrepancy exists between what is said and what is meant; in dramatic irony a discrepancy exists between what a character believes and what the reader knows to be true; and in cosmic irony a discrepancy exists between what a character aspires to and what universal forces provide. With each form of irony, we are invited to move beyond surface appearances and sentimental assumptions to see the complexity of experience. Irony is often used in literature to reveal a writer's perspective on matters that previously seemed settled.

POEMS FOR FURTHER STUDY

JANE KENYON (1947–1995)

Surprise
1996

He suggests pancakes at the local diner,
followed by a walk in search of mayflowers,
while friends convene at the house
bearing casseroles and a cake, their cars
pulled close along the sandy shoulders   5
of the road, where tender ferns unfurl
in the ditches, and this year's budding leaves
push last year's spectral leaves from the tips
of the twigs of the ash trees. The gathering
itself is not what astounds her, but the casual   10
accomplishment with which he has lied.

CONSIDERATIONS FOR CRITICAL THINKING AND WRITING

1. FIRST RESPONSE. Does it matter that this poem is set in the spring?

2. Consider the connotative meaning of "ash trees." Why are they particularly appropriate?

3. Why do you suppose Kenyon uses "astounds" rather than "surprises" in line 10? Use a dictionary to help you determine the possible reasons for this choice.

4. Discuss the irony in the poem.

CONNECTIONS TO OTHER SELECTIONS

1. Write an essay on the nature of the surprises in Kenyon's poem and in Hathaway's "Oh, Oh" (p. 675). Include in your discussion a comparison of the tone and irony in each poem.

2. Compare and contrast in an essay the irony associated with the birthday parties in "Surprise" and Sharon Olds's "Rite of Passage" (p. 927).

LAURE-ANNE BOSSELAAR (B. 1943)

The Bumper-Sticker   1994

"Yield" says the sign, so you do. The bearded man
nods thank-you, pulls out. "It's never too late
to have a happy childhood" reads his bumper-sticker.
You want to stop him, ask him if he knows how. No one
waits for you at home, so you follow: it could be God   5
in that Buick, leading you to where you change
the past like tires with a bad grip, or get a quick lube,
the old stuff dripping out murky and dark.

You'd get a new mother first. You'd have the pick
of the lot: she'd be a bright color, green maybe, with safety   10
belts and such comfort you'd swear she was custom
made. A good, reliable car, never running on empty,
with enough room for the two of you. You'd leave
the garage smiling, head high, motor humming, gears
changing noiselessly, and never look back at the old jalopy   15
that nearly killed you and broke your back every day.

A new father next. He'd slide into the driver's seat,
teach you the right way to steer, check the rearview often,
stop holding your foot on the brake. He'd pull out
a technicolor map and with a finger like Michael Angelo's   20
"Adam" he'd show you where to go without getting lost.
No dead-ends, no potholes, a smooth ride my baby,
tell me where you're heading and I'll take you there,
no problem.

            The Buick signals left. You follow. You lose   25
him in a tunnel when a sixteen-wheeler reading "Safeway"
passes you and almost sends you to the wall.

CONSIDERATIONS FOR CRITICAL THINKING AND WRITING

1. FIRST RESPONSE. Discuss the use of symbols in each stanza and explain what you think is the central theme of the poem. How do the symbols work together to contribute to the theme?

2. Why do you think the poet chooses a Buick rather than, say, a Honda for her narrator to follow?

3. Describe the speaker's sense of the present as well as of the past.

4. What is the effect of the speaker addressing the reader as "you"?

CONNECTION TO ANOTHER SELECTION

1. Discuss the use of irony in this poem and in Jane Kenyon's "Surprise" (p. 810). How does irony reveal the sensibilities of the speaker in each poem?

RENNIE MCQUILKIN (B. 1936)

The Lighters   *1999*

In her eighty-ninth year, she's reducing
her inventory — china to the children, mementos
to the trash — but in her boudoir
keeps half a dozen square-shouldered Zippos,

her husband's initials on one,   5
the best man's on a second, the rest anyone's guess.
Dry-chambered, their spark wheels rusted shut,
they are lined up gravely on a jewelry chest

full of antique gap-toothed keys,
elaborate scrollwork on their hilts, fit to open   10
high-backed steamer trunks, perhaps the secret entrance
to a sunken garden

where every night the dry-bones assemble
in mothballed flannels and handknit sweaters
to roll their own, light up   15
like fireflies and, sotte voce, remember her.

CONSIDERATIONS FOR CRITICAL THINKING AND WRITING

1. FIRST RESPONSE. How are the lighters more than simply mementos? What meanings are associated with them?

2. Discuss McQuilkin's use of diction. How does it contribute to the poem's mood?

3. How would you describe the physical appearance of this woman?

CONNECTION TO ANOTHER SELECTION

1. Compare the treatment of this elderly woman with that of Wyatt Prunty's "Elderly Lady Crossing on Green" (p. 702). How is aging depicted in each poem?

KATHY MANGAN (B. 1950)

An Arithmetic   1999

Because the world insists on still giving and giving at six,
mastering addition seemed its natural complement,
a kind of cataloguing the earth's surplus.
I loved the fat green pencil
shedding graphite as I pressed rounded   5
threes, looping eights into the speckled
yellow newsprint. Loved, too, the sturdy,
crossed bars of the plus sign, *carrying over*
in stacked columns of double,
triple digits: the plump sums I'd *arrive* at.   10

Subtraction proved another sort
of reckoning. First I had to learn
to *take away* (apples or pennies pictured
in the workbook), then settle
for the solace of a *remainder*.   15
I've never wanted less of anything — money, food
or love — but over time,
have come to understand the process:
like any human calculation,
the *difference* being   20
between what I have wanted
and what I got.

CONSIDERATIONS FOR CRITICAL THINKING AND WRITING

1. FIRST RESPONSE. How do addition and subtraction take on new meanings
   owing to Mangan's treatment of them?
2. Explain the difference in tone between stanzas one and two.
3. Try writing a stanza of your own that describes your take on multiplication
   or division, using Mangan's strategies for diction.

CONNECTION TO ANOTHER SELECTION

1. Compare the memory of childhood and school with that of Judy Page
   Heitzman's "The Schoolroom on the Second Floor of the Knitting Mill"
   (p. 1111). What significant similarities do you find in the two poems?

ROBERT BLY (B. 1926)

Snowbanks North of the House   1975

Those great sweeps of snow that stop suddenly six feet
   from the house . . .
Thoughts that go so far.

The boy gets out of high school and reads no more books;
the son stops calling home.

The mother puts down her rolling pin and makes no more
    bread.   5
And the wife looks at her husband one night at a party
    and loves him no more.
The energy leaves the wine, and the minister falls leaving
    the church.
It will not come closer —
the one inside moves back, and the hands touch nothing,
    and are safe.

And the father grieves for his son, and will not leave the
    room where the coffin stands;   10
he turns away from his wife, and she sleeps alone.

And the sea lifts and falls all night; the moon goes on
    through the unattached heavens alone.
And the toe of the shoe pivots
in the dust. . . .
The man in the black coat turns, and goes back down the
    hill.   15
No one knows why he came, or why he turned away, and
    did not climb the hill.

Considerations for Critical Thinking and Writing

1. FIRST RESPONSE. How can the varying images in the poem be related to one another? What do they have in common?

2. Describe the tone produced by the images. What emotions do you experience after carefully considering the images?

3. What symbolic meanings do you think are associated with the poem's images? Describe in a paragraph what you think the poem's themes are.

Connections to Other Selections

1. "Snowbanks North of the House" is the first poem in Bly's collection titled *The Man in the Black Coat Turns* (1981), a title drawn from line 15 of the poem. In *Selected Poems* (1986) Bly explains that

> I wanted the poems in *The Man in the Black Coat Turns* to rise out of some darkness beneath us, as when the old Norse poets fished with an ox head as bait in the ocean. We know that the poem will break water only for a moment before it sinks again, but just seeing it rise beneath the boat is enough pleasure for one day; and to know that a large thing lives down there puts us in a calm mood, lets us endure our deprived lives with more grace.

How does Bly's observation that such a poem "lets us endure our deprived lives with more grace" shed light on "Snowbanks North of the House" and Bly's "Snowfall in the Afternoon" (p. 1148)? Write an essay that details your response.

2. Compare and contrast the symbolic images in "Snowbanks North of the House" and Robert Frost's "Stopping by Woods on a Snowy Evening" (p. 1015).

PERSPECTIVE

Robert Bly (b. 1926)
On "Snowbanks North of the House"   *1996*

William Stafford has spoken so beautifully about what an assertion means in a poem, and how early you can make one. In one of his books, maybe *Writing the Australian Crawl,* he says if you make strong assertions too early in the poem, you can lose the reader. Readers need to receive a couple of assertions first that they can agree with, such as "It's summer," or "Animals own a fur world," or "Those lines on your palm, they can be read," or "There was a river under First and Main." The reader needs to experience rather mild assertions so that he or she can begin to trust your mind; then when you make a wilder assertion later, the reader is more likely to climb up with you into that intense place from which the assertion came. My first assertion is

> Those great sweeps of snow that stop suddenly six feet from the house.

Some snow blows all the way down from Canada and then stops six feet from the house. For people who've never lived on the prairie and have experienced only gently falling snow or snow interrupted by woods, my first line may seem a risky assertion. So my second line is mild.

> Thoughts that go so far.

I want my poem to continue, but not to ascend, so I need an ordinary event, something we've all known a thousand times:

> The boy gets out of high school and reads no more books.

I can stay with that ordinariness for a little while:

> The son stops calling home.

I experienced that refusal to call home when I lived in New York during my late twenties. Certain ways of living come to an end:

> The mother puts down her rolling pin and makes no more bread.

I was thinking of my grandmother making Norwegian flat bread; readers correctly told me that ordinary bread these days is not made with rolling pins. But the child in me wrote that line. The adult in me wrote the next line:

> And the wife looks at her husband one night at a party and loves him no more.

I'm not conscious that that line happened to me, but it's possible. I do recall seeing both halves of the line at one instant in the wife's glance. It's another sadness. It's just an ordinary sadness. It doesn't happen only to special people.

> The energy leaves the wine, and the minister falls leaving the church.

My father always had a particular tenderness for the old Lutheran minister in our town, and made sure that he received game such as pheasants in the fall, and geese at Christmas; I had some sympathy for the way a minister has to hold himself up and perform his role no matter what is happening in his private life. He has to keep giving the Communion.

A month or two after I wrote the poem, I read it to a friend who was an Episcopal priest of great spirit; he told me that I had described exactly what had happened to him a month before. He couldn't say the Communion words whole-heartedly on that particular Sunday, and he fell on the steps outside. One could say that for many ordinary people — and I am one of those — a fine energy sometimes refuses to become friends with us, or perhaps we refuse to make the courtly gesture that would welcome that energy. When we fall, it's an ordinary sadness.

> It will not come closer —
> the one inside moves back, and the hands touch nothing, and are safe.

I think a lot of my childhood is alive in that last half-sentence. And I spent in my mid-twenties two years alone in New York, talking to people barely once a month. It was all right. I felt safe: "The hands touch nothing, and are safe."

I must have felt that grief during the poem. The poem is moving away from sadness now and toward grief. And I recalled a scene from Abraham Lincoln's life. He loved his son Tad so much, and when the boy was eight, he died of tuberculosis or some such thing. They put the coffin into a room by itself in that kind of home visitation that people did at that time. Lincoln went into the room and didn't come out. He stayed all afternoon, and then he stayed there all night, and then he stayed there the next day. Around noon people started pounding on the door and telling him to come out, but he paid no attention. There was something a little extraordinary in that, but the general situation is not unusual, it's something we've all noticed or heard about many times. Sometimes after the death of a child, the husband and wife never do come back to each other.

> The father grieves for his son, and will not leave the room where the coffin
> stands.
> He turns away from his wife, and she sleeps alone.

Now what to do? Now we've arrived at a really ordinary place, in which life and its motions go on, but the shocked man or woman doesn't pay much informed attention to those motions anymore. Donald Hall has written about this place in his poem called "Mr. Wakeville on Interstate 90":

> I will work forty hours a week clerking at the paintstore. . . .
> I will watch my neighbors' daughters grow up, marry,
> raise children. The joints of my fingers will stiffen.

The way such a life moves mechanically is a form of depression. At the beginning of *A Farewell to Arms*, Hemingway says, "That fall the war was still there, but we didn't go to it anymore."

> And the sea lifts and falls all night; the moon goes on through the unattached
> heavens alone.

I loved that word "unattached" when I saw it on the page. It brought together the son who stops calling home and the man who lives alone in New York for two years.

Then I saw the toe of a black shoe. It seemed like an ordinary shoe, not standing on marble or red carpet, but on ordinary dust. Some elegant movement as of a hinge suddenly arrived, breaking all these long forward motions:

The toe of the shoe pivots
in the dust . . .
and the man in the black coat turns, and goes back down the hill.

The first time I read the poem to an audience, there was some silence afterwards, and a woman asked, "Who is the man in the black coat?" I said, "I don't
know." She said, "That's outrageous; you wrote the poem." I didn't answer. It
was only when I got back to the farm that I thought of the proper answer: "If I
had known who the man in the black coat was, I could have written an essay." I
don't mean to demean essays with such a sentence, but it's good to think
clearly in an essay, which can be a series of really clear and interlocking
thoughts that are luminous. But sometimes a poem amounts to the creation
of some sort of nourishing mud pond in which partly developed tadpoles can
live for a while, and certain images can receive enough sustenance from the
darkness around them to keep breathing without being forced into some early
adulthood or job or retirement. It's possible the man in the black coat is Lincoln. He did turn and go back down the hill, and his face got sadder every year
that the war went on. I also noticed in a family album a photograph of my father about 25 years old, standing by the windmill holding a baby rather awkwardly couched in his right arm; it's possible the baby was myself. He was
wearing a large black coat. I don't know exactly why the last line closes the
poem. I didn't intend it. It just came along. Perhaps it's the most ordinary
thing of all. Our mother, or our grandmother, or grandfather, or our father,
goes through incredible labors, keeping despite turbulent winds and strong
blows the chosen direction forward, following some route. But why? What
was the aim of Lincoln's life? What was the aim of my father's life? Or my life?
We know a little bit of the story—what's the rest of the story? Why don't we
know that?

No one knows why he came, or why he turned away, and did not climb the hill.

From a typed manuscript sent to Michael Meyer, 1997

CONSIDERATIONS FOR CRITICAL THINKING AND WRITING

1. What do you think Bly means when he says he begins with "mild assertions"
   and "ordinariness" to help readers "climb up" to "wilder assertion[s]"? How
   does "Snowbanks North of the House" proceed this way?

2. Why do you think the woman in the audience thinks it "outrageous" that
   the poet doesn't know the identity of "the man in the black coat"? Explain
   why you agree or disagree with her response.

3. Discuss Bly's idea that "sometimes a poem amounts to the creation of
   some sort of nourishing mud pond in which partly developed tadpoles
   can live for a while." What does this description (and the rest of the
   sentence in which it appears) suggest about the nature of meaning in this
   poem?

4. How does Bly's reading and explanation of the poem compare with your
   own experience of it? Do you think his essay limits or expands your interpretation of the poem? Explain your response.

CARL SANDBURG (1878–1967)

Buttons   1905

I have been watching the war map slammed up for advertising in front of the
    newspaper office.
Buttons — red and yellow buttons — blue and black buttons — are shoved back
    and forth across the map.

A laughing young man, sunny with freckles,
Climbs a ladder, yells a joke to somebody in the crowd,
And then fixes a yellow button one inch west   5
And follows the yellow button with a black button one inch west.

(Ten thousand men and boys twist on their bodies in a red soak along a river
    edge,
Gasping of wounds, calling for water, some rattling death in their throats.)
Who would guess what it cost to move two buttons one inch on the war map
    here in front of the newspaper office where the freckle-faced young man
    is laughing to us?

CONSIDERATIONS FOR CRITICAL THINKING AND WRITING

1. FIRST RESPONSE. Why is the date of this poem significant?
2. Discuss the symbolic meaning of the buttons and explain why you think
   the symbolism is too spelled out or not.
3. What purpose does the "laughing young man, sunny with freckles" serve in
   the poem?

CONNECTIONS TO OTHER SELECTIONS

1. Discuss the symbolic treatment of war in this poem, Kenneth Fearing's
   "AD" (p. 807), and Henry Reed's "Naming of Parts" (p. 823).

WILLIAM STAFFORD (B. 1914)

Traveling through the Dark   1962

Traveling through the dark I found a deer
dead on the edge of the Wilson River road.
It is usually best to roll them into the canyon:
that road is narrow; to swerve might make more dead.

By glow of the tail-light I stumbled back of the car   5
and stood by the heap, a doe, a recent killing;
she had stiffened already, almost cold.
I dragged her off; she was large in the belly.

My fingers touching her side brought me the reason —
her side was warm; her fawn lay there waiting,   10

alive, still, never to be born.
Beside that mountain road I hesitated.

The car aimed ahead its lowered parking lights;
under the hood purred the steady engine.
I stood in the glare of the warm exhaust turning red;   15
around our group I could hear the wilderness listen.

I thought hard for us all — my only swerving —
then pushed her over the edge into the river.

CONSIDERATIONS FOR CRITICAL THINKING AND WRITING

1. FIRST RESPONSE. Notice the description of the car in this poem: the "glow of the tail-light," the "lowered parking lights," and how the engine "purred." How do these and other details suggest symbolic meanings for the car and the "recent killing"?

2. Discuss the speaker's tone. Does the speaker seem, for example, tough, callous, kind, sentimental, confused, or confident?

3. What is the effect of the last stanza's having only two lines rather than the established four lines of the previous stanzas?

4. Discuss the appropriateness of this poem's title. In what sense has the speaker "thought hard for us all"? What are those thoughts?

5. Is this a didactic poem?

ANDREW HUDGINS (B. 1951)

Seventeen   *1991*

Ahead of me, the dog reared on its rope,
and swayed. The pickup took a hard left turn,
and the dog tipped off the side. He scrambled, fell,
and scraped along the hot asphalt
before he tumbled back into the air.   5
I pounded on my horn and yelled. The rope
snapped and the brown dog hurtled into the weeds.
I braked, still pounding on my horn. The truck
stopped too.

　　　　　　　We met halfway, and stared   10
down at the shivering dog, which flinched
and moaned and tried to flick its tail.
Most of one haunch was scraped away
and both hind legs were twisted. *You stupid shit!*
I said. He squinted at me. "Well now, bud —   15
you best watch what you say to me."
I'd never cussed a grown-up man before.
I nodded. I figured on a beating. He grinned.
"You so damn worried about that ole dog,

he's yours." He strolled back to his truck,   20
gunned it, and slewed off, spraying gravel.
The dog whined harshly.

                    By the road,
gnats rose waist-high as I waded through
the dry weeds, looking for a rock.   25
I knelt down by the dog — tail flick —
and slammed the rock down twice. The first
blow did the job, but I had planned for two.
My hands swept up and down again. I grabbed
the hind legs, swung twice, and heaved the dog   30
into a clump of butterfly weed and vetch.
But then I didn't know that they had names,
those roadside weeds. His truck was a blue Ford,
the dog a beagle. I was seventeen.
The gnats rose, gathered to one loose cloud,   35
then scattered through coarse orange and purple weeds.

CONSIDERATIONS FOR CRITICAL THINKING AND WRITING

1. FIRST RESPONSE. Hudgins has described "Seventeen" as a "rite of passage."
   How does the title focus this idea?

2. What kind of language does Hudgins use to describe the injured dog (lines
   1–14)? What is its effect?

3. Characterize the speaker and the driver of the pickup. What clues does the
   poem provide to the way each perceives the other?

4. Might killing the dog be understood as a symbolic action? Try to come up
   with more than one interpretation for the speaker's actions.

CONNECTIONS TO OTHER SELECTIONS

1. Write an essay that compares the speakers and themes of "Seventeen" and
   "Traveling through the Dark (p. 818)."

2. In an essay discuss the speakers' attitudes toward dogs in "Seventeen" and
   Ronald Wallace's "Dogs" (p. 1229). What do these attitudes reveal about the
   speakers?

ALDEN NOWLAN (1933–1983)

The Bull Moose   *1962*

Down from the purple mist of trees on the mountain,
lurching through forests of white spruce and cedar,
stumbling through tamarack swamps,
came the bull moose
to be stopped at last by a pole-fenced pasture.   5

Too tired to turn or, perhaps, aware
there was no place left to go, he stood with the cattle.

They, scenting the musk of death, seeing his great head
like the ritual mask of a blood god, moved to the other end
of the field, and waited.   10

The neighbors heard of it, and by afternoon
cars lined the road. The children teased him
with alder switches and he gazed at them
like an old, tolerant collie. The women asked
if he could have escaped from a Fair.   15

The oldest man in the parish remembered seeing
a gelded moose yoked with an ox for plowing.
The young men snickered and tried to pour beer
down his throat, while their girl friends took their pictures.

The bull moose let them stroke his tick-ravaged flanks,   20
let them pry open his jaws with bottles, let a giggling girl
plant a little purple cap
of thistles on his head.

When the wardens came, everyone agreed it was a shame
to shoot anything so shaggy and cuddlesome.   25
He looked like the kind of pet
women put to bed with their sons.

So they held their fire. But just as the sun dropped in the river
the bull moose gathered his strength
like a scaffolded king, straightened and lifted his horns   30
so that even the wardens backed away as they raised their rifles.
When he roared, people ran to their cars. All the young men
leaned on their automobile horns as he toppled.

CONSIDERATIONS FOR CRITICAL THINKING AND WRITING

1. FIRST RESPONSE. How does the speaker present the moose and the townspeople? How are the moose and townspeople contrasted? Discuss specific
lines to support your response.

2. Explain how the symbols in this poem point to a conflict between humanity and nature. What do you think the speaker's attitude toward this conflict is?

3. CRITICAL STRATEGIES. Read the section on mythological criticism
(pp. 2107–09) in Chapter 52, "Critical Strategies for Reading," and write an
essay on "The Bull Moose" that approaches the poem from a mythological
perspective.

CONNECTION TO ANOTHER SELECTION

1. In an essay compare and contrast how the animals portrayed in "The Bull
Moose" and in Stafford's "Traveling through the Dark" (p. 818) are used
as symbols.

JULIO MARZÁN (B. 1946)

Ethnic Poetry

1994

The ethnic poet said: "The earth is maybe
a huge maraca / and the sun a trombone /
and life / is to move your ass / to slow beats."
The ethnic audience roasted a suckling pig.

The ethnic poet said: "Oh thank Goddy, Goddy / 5
I be me, my toenails curled downward /
deep, deep, deep into Mama earth."
The ethnic audience shook strands of sea shells.

The ethnic poet said: "The sun was created black /
so we should imagine light / and also dream / 10
a walrus emerging from the broken ice."
The ethnic audience beat on sealskin drums.

The ethnic poet said: "Reproductive organs /
Eagles nesting California redwoods /
Shut up and listen to my ancestors." 15
The ethnic audience ate fried bread and honey.

The ethnic poet said: "Something there is that
doesn't love a wall / That sends
the frozen-ground-swell under it."
The ethnic audience deeply understood humanity. 20

CONSIDERATIONS FOR CRITICAL THINKING AND WRITING

1. FIRST RESPONSE. What is the implicit definition of ethnic poetry in this poem?

2. The final stanza quotes lines from Robert Frost's "Mending Wall" (p. 1004). Read the entire poem. Why do you think Marzán chooses these lines and this particular poem as one kind of ethnic poetry?

3. What is the poem's central irony? Pay particular attention to the final line. What is being satirized here?

4. CRITICAL STRATEGIES. Read the section on the literary canon (pp. 2093–95) in Chapter 52, "Critical Strategies for Reading," and consider how the formation of the literary canon is related to the theme of "Ethnic Poetry."

CONNECTION TO ANOTHER SELECTION

1. Write an essay that discusses the speaker's ideas about what poetry should be in "Ethnic Poetry" and in Langston Hughes's "Formula" (p. 1044).

James Merrill (1926–1995)

Casual Wear   1984

Your average tourist: Fifty. 2.3
Times married. Dressed, this year, in Ferdi Plinthbower
Originals. Odds 1 to 9
Against her strolling past the Embassy

Today at noon. Your average terrorist: 5
Twenty-five. Celibate. No use for trends,
At least in clothing. Mark, though, where it ends.
People have come forth made of colored mist

Unsmiling on one hundred million screens
To tell of his prompt phone call to the station,   10
"Claiming responsibility" — devastation
Signed with a flourish, like the dead wife's jeans.

CONSIDERATIONS FOR CRITICAL THINKING AND WRITING

1. FIRST RESPONSE. What is the effect of the statistics in this poem?
2. Describe the speaker's tone. Is it appropriate for the subject matter? Explain why or why not.
3. Comment on the ironies that emerge from the final two lines. How are the tourist and terrorist linked by the speaker's description? Explain why you think the speaker sympathizes more with the tourist or the terrorist — or with neither.

CONNECTION TO ANOTHER SELECTION

1. Compare the satire in this poem with that in Peter Meinke's "The ABC of Aerobics" (p. 933). What is satirized in each poem? Which satire is more pointed from your perspective?

Henry Reed (1914–1986)

Naming of Parts   1946

Today we have naming of parts. Yesterday,
We had daily cleaning. And tomorrow morning,
We shall have what to do after firing. But today,
Today we have naming of parts. Japonica
Glistens like coral in all of the neighboring gardens,   5
        And today we have naming of parts.

This is the lower sling swivel. And this
Is the upper sling swivel, whose use you will see,
When you are given your slings. And this is the piling swivel,
Which in your case you have not got. The branches   10

Hold in the gardens their silent, eloquent gestures,
        Which in our case we have not got.

This is the safety-catch, which is always released
With an easy flick of the thumb. And please do not let me
See anyone using his finger. You can do it quite easy   15
If you have any strength in your thumb. The blossoms
Are fragile and motionless, never letting anyone see
        Any of them using their finger.

And this you can see is the bolt. The purpose of this
Is to open the breech, as you see. We can slide it   20
Rapidly backwards and forwards: we call this
Easing the spring. And rapidly backwards and forwards
The early bees are assaulting and fumbling the flowers:
        They call it easing the Spring.

They call it easing the Spring: it is perfectly easy   25
If you have any strength in your thumb: like the bolt,
And the breech, and the cocking-piece, and the point of balance,
Which in our case we have not got; and the almond-blossom
Silent in all of the gardens and the bees going backwards and forwards,
        For today we have naming of parts.   30

CONSIDERATIONS FOR CRITICAL THINKING AND WRITING

1. FIRST RESPONSE. Characterize the two speakers in this poem. Identify the
   lines spoken by each. How do their respective lines differ in tone?

2. What is the effect of the last line of each stanza?

3. How do ambiguities and puns contribute to the poem's meaning?

4. What symbolic contrast is made between the rifle instruction and the gardens? How is this contrast ironic?

JOHN CIARDI (1916–1986)

Suburban   *1978*

Yesterday Mrs. Friar phoned. "Mr. Ciardi,
    how do you do?" she said. "I am sorry to say
this isn't exactly a social call. The fact is
    your dog has just deposited — forgive me —
a large repulsive object in my petunias."   5

I thought to ask, "Have you checked the rectal grooving
    for a positive I.D.?" My dog, as it happened,
was in Vermont with my son, who had gone fishing —
    if that's what one does with a girl, two cases of beer,
and a borrowed camper. I guessed I'd get no trout.   10

But why lose out on organic gold for a wise crack?
    "Yes, Mrs. Friar," I said, "I understand."

"Most kind of you," she said. "Not at all," I said.
  I went with a spade. She pointed, looking away.
"I always have loved dogs," she said, "but really!"   15

I scooped it up and bowed. "The animal of it.
  I hope this hasn't upset you, Mrs. Friar."
"Not really," she said, "but really!" I bore the turd
  across the line to my own petunias
and buried it till the glorious resurrection   20

when even these suburbs shall give up their dead.

CONSIDERATIONS FOR CRITICAL THINKING AND WRITING

1. FIRST RESPONSE. How does the speaker transform Mrs. Friar into a symbolic figure of the suburbs?

2. Why do you suppose Ciardi focuses on this particular incident to make a comment upon the suburbs? What is the speaker's attitude toward suburban life?

3. Write a one-paragraph physical description of Mrs. Friar that captures her character for you.

CONNECTION TO ANOTHER SELECTION

1. Compare the speakers' voices in "Suburban" and in Updike's "Dog's Death" (p. 673).

CHITRA BANERJEE DIVAKARUNI (B. 1956)

Indian Movie, New Jersey   *1990*

Not like the white filmstars, all rib
and gaunt cheekbone, the Indian sex-goddess
smiles plumply from behind a flowery
branch. Below her brief red skirt, her thighs
are satisfying-solid, redeeming   5
as tree trunks. She swings her hips
and the men-viewers whistle. The lover-hero
dances in to a song, his lip-sync
a little off, but no matter, we
know the words already and sing along.   10
It is safe here, the day
golden and cool so no one sweats,
roses on every bush and the Dal Lake
clean again.
                    The sex-goddess switches   15
to thickened English to emphasize
a joke. We laugh and clap. Here
we need not be embarrassed by words
dropping like lead pellets into foreign ears.
The flickering movie-light   20

wipes from our faces years of America, sons
who want mohawks and refuse to run
the family store, daughters who date
on the sly.

         When at the end the hero   25
dies for his friend who also
loves the sex-goddess and now can marry her,
we weep, understanding. Even the men
clear their throats to say, "What *qurbani!*°   *sacrifice*
What *dosti!*"° After, we mill around   *friendship*   30
unwilling to leave, exchange greetings
and good news: a new gold chain, a trip
to India. We do not speak
of motel raids, canceled permits, stones
thrown through glass windows, daughters and sons   35
raped by Dotbusters.°

         In this dim foyer
we can pull around us the faint, comforting smell
of incense and *pakoras,*° can arrange   *fried appetizers*
our children's marriages with hometown boys and girls,   40
open a franchise, win a million
in the mail. We can retire
in India, a yellow two-storied house
with wrought-iron gates, our own
Ambassador car. Or at least   45
move to a rich white suburb, Summerfield
or Fort Lee, with neighbors that will
talk to us. Here while the film-songs still echo
in the corridors and restrooms, we can trust
in movie truths: sacrifice, success, love and luck,   50
the America that was supposed to be.

36 *Dotbusters:* New Jersey gangs that attack Indians.

Considerations for Critical Thinking and Writing

1. FIRST RESPONSE. Why does the speaker feel comfortable at the movies? How is the world inside the theater different from life outside in New Jersey?

2. Explain the differences portrayed by the speaker between life in India and life in New Jersey. What connotative values are associated with each location in the poem?

3. Discuss the irony in the final two lines.

ROBERT BROWNING (1812–1889)

My Last Duchess   1842

Ferrara °

That's my last Duchess painted on the wall,
Looking as if she were alive. I call
That piece a wonder, now: Frà Pandolf's° hands
Worked busily a day, and there she stands.
Will't please you sit and look at her? I said   5
"Frà Pandolf" by design, for never read
Strangers like you that pictured countenance,
The depth and passion of its earnest glance,
But to myself they turned (since none puts by
The curtain I have drawn for you, but I)   10
And seemed as they would ask me, if they durst,
How such a glance came there; so, not the first
Are you to turn and ask thus. Sir, 'twas not
Her husband's presence only, called that spot
Of joy into the Duchess' cheek: perhaps   15
Frà Pandolf chanced to say "Her mantle laps
Over my lady's wrist too much," or "Paint
Must never hope to reproduce the faint
Half-flush that dies along her throat": such stuff
Was courtesy, she thought, and cause enough   20
For calling up that spot of joy. She had
A heart — how shall I say? — too soon made glad,
Too easily impressed; she liked whate'er
She looked on, and her looks went everywhere.
Sir, 'twas all one! My favor at her breast,   25
The dropping of the daylight in the West,
The bough of cherries some officious fool
Broke in the orchard for her, the white mule
She rode with round the terrace — all and each
Would draw from her alike the approving speech,   30
Or blush, at least. She thanked men, — good! but thanked
Somehow — I know not how — as if she ranked
My gift of a nine-hundred-years-old name
With anybody's gift. Who'd stoop to blame
This sort of trifling? Even had you skill   35
In speech — which I have not — to make your will
Quite clear to such an one, and say, "Just this
Or that in you disgusts me; here you miss,
Or there exceed the mark" — and if she let

Ferrara: In the sixteenth century, the duke of this Italian city arranged to marry a second time after the mysterious death of his very young first wife.   3 *Frà Pandolf:* A fictitious artist.

Herself be lessoned so, nor plainly set   40
Her wits to yours, forsooth, and made excuse,
— E'en then would be some stooping; and I choose
Never to stoop. Oh sir, she smiled, no doubt,
Whene'er I passed her; but who passed without
Much the same smile? This grew; I gave commands;   45
Then all smiles stopped together. There she stands
As if alive. Will't please you rise? We'll meet
The company below, then. I repeat,
The Count your master's known munificence
Is ample warrant that no just pretense   50
Of mine for dowry will be disallowed;
Though his fair daughter's self, as I avowed
At starting, is my object. Nay, we'll go
Together down, sir. Notice Neptune, though,
Taming a sea-horse, thought a rarity,   55
Which Claus of Innsbruck° cast in bronze for me!

56 *Claus of Innsbruck:* Also a fictitious artist.

CONSIDERATIONS FOR CRITICAL THINKING AND WRITING

1. FIRST RESPONSE. What do you think happened to the duchess?

2. To whom is the duke addressing his remarks about the duchess in this poem? What is ironic about the situation?

3. Why was the duke unhappy with his first wife? What does this reveal about the duke? What does the poem's title suggest about his attitude toward women in general?

4. What seems to be the visitor's response (lines 53–54) to the duke's account of his first wife?

CONNECTION TO ANOTHER SELECTION

1. Write an essay describing the ways in which the speakers of "My Last Duchess" and "Hazel Tells LaVerne" (p. 723) by Katharyn Howd Machan inadvertently reveal themselves.

WILLIAM BLAKE (1757–1827)

The Chimney Sweeper   1789

When my mother died I was very young,
And my father sold me while yet my tongue
Could scarcely cry "'weep! 'weep! 'weep! 'weep!"
So your chimneys I sweep, and in soot I sleep.

There's little Tom Dacre, who cried when his head,   5
That curled like a lamb's back, was shaved: so I said
"Hush, Tom! never mind it, for when your head's bare
You know that the soot cannot spoil your white hair."

And so he was quiet, and that very night,
As Tom was a-sleeping, he had such a sight!   10
That thousands of sweepers, Dick, Joe, Ned, and Jack,
Were all of them locked up in coffins of black.

And by came an Angel who had a bright key,
And he opened the coffins and set them all free;
Then down a green plain leaping, laughing, they run,   15
And wash in a river, and shine in the sun.

Then naked and white, all their bags left behind,
They rise upon clouds and sport in the wind;
And the Angel told Tom, if he'd be a good boy,
He'd have God for his father, and never want joy.   20

And so Tom awoke; and we rose in the dark,
And got with our bags and our brushes to work.
Though the morning was cold, Tom was happy and warm;
So if all do their duty they need not fear harm.

CONSIDERATIONS FOR CRITICAL THINKING AND WRITING

1. FIRST RESPONSE. Discuss the validity of this statement: "'The Chimney Sweeper' is a sentimental poem about a shameful eighteenth-century social problem; such a treatment of child abuse cannot be taken seriously."

2. Characterize the speaker in this poem, and describe his tone. Is his tone the same as the poet's? Consider especially lines 7, 8, and 24.

3. What is the symbolic value of the dream in lines 11 to 20?

4. Why is irony central to the meaning of this poem?

DIANE THIEL (B. 1967)

The Minefield   *2000*

He was running with his friend from town to town.
They were somewhere between Prague and Dresden.
He was fourteen. His friend was faster
and knew a shortcut through the fields they could take.
He said there was lettuce growing in one of them,   5
and they hadn't eaten all day. His friend ran a few lengths ahead,
like a wild rabbit across the grass,
turned his head, looked back once,
and his body was scattered across the field.

My father told us this, one night,   10
and then continued eating dinner.

He brought them with him — the minefields.
He carried them underneath his good intentions.
He gave them to us — in the volume of his anger,
in the bruises we covered up with sleeves,   15

In the way he threw anything against the wall —
a radio, that wasn't even ours,
a melon, once, opened like a head.
In the way we still expect, years later and continents away,
that anything might explode at any time,   20
and we would have to run on alone
with a vision like that
only seconds behind.

CONSIDERATIONS FOR CRITICAL THINKING AND WRITING

1. FIRST RESPONSE. What are the effects of the minefields on the father — and on the speaker?

2. How does the speaker feel about the father? How does this poem make you feel about the father?

3. Discuss the significance of the title. How can it read symbolically in more than one way?

CONNECTION TO ANOTHER SELECTION

1. Discuss the treatment of fathers in "The Minefield" and in Regina Barreca's "Nighttime Fires" (p. 688). Compare how the memory of the father affects the speaker in each poem.

GARY SOTO (B. 1952)

Behind Grandma's House   *1985*

At ten I wanted fame. I had a comb
And two Coke bottles, a tube of Bryl-creem.
I borrowed a dog, one with
Mismatched eyes and a happy tongue,
And wanted to prove I was tough   5
In the alley, kicking over trash cans,
A dull chime of tuna cans falling.
I hurled light bulbs like grenades
And men teachers held their heads,
Fingers of blood lengthening   10
On the ground. I flicked rocks at cats,
Their goofy faces spurred with foxtails.
I kicked fences. I shooed pigeons.
I broke a branch from a flowering peach
And frightened ants with a stream of spit.   15
I said "*Chale*," "In your face," and "No way
Daddy-O" to an imaginary priest
Until grandma came into the alley,
Her apron flapping in a breeze,
Her hair mussed, and said, "Let me help you,"   20
And punched me between the eyes.

CONSIDERATIONS FOR CRITICAL THINKING AND WRITING

1. FIRST RESPONSE. What is the central irony of this poem?

2. How does the speaker characterize himself at ten?

3. Though the "grandma" appears only briefly, she seems, in a sense, fully characterized. How would you describe her? Why do you think she says, "Let me help you"?

CONNECTION TO ANOTHER SELECTION

1. Write an essay comparing the themes of "Behind Grandma's House" and Sharon Olds's "Rite of Passage" (p. 927).

PERSPECTIVE

EZRA POUND (1885–1972)

On Symbols   1912

I believe that the proper and perfect symbol is the natural object, that if a man uses "symbols" he must so use them that their symbolic function does not obtrude; so that *a* sense, and the poetic quality of the passage, is not lost to those who do not understand the symbol as such, to whom, for instance, a hawk is a hawk.

From "Prolegomena," *Poetry Review,* February 1912

CONSIDERATIONS FOR CRITICAL THINKING AND WRITING

1. Discuss whether you agree with Pound that the "perfect symbol" is a "natural object" that does not insist on being read as a symbol.

2. Write an essay in which you discuss Alden Nowlan's "The Bull Moose" (p. 820) as an example of the "perfect symbol" Pound proposes.

26

Sounds

Web *For activities on the sounds of poetry, check out the Interactive Poetry Tutorial at* http://www.bedfordstmartins.com/meyer/bedintrolit

Poems yearn to be read aloud. Much of their energy, charm, and beauty comes to life only when they are heard. Poets choose and arrange words for their sounds as well as for their meanings. Most poetry is best read with your lips, teeth, and tongue because they serve to articulate the effects that sound may have in a poem. When a voice is breathed into a good poem, there is pleasure in the reading, the saying, and the hearing.

LISTENING TO POETRY

The earliest poetry—before writing and painting—was chanted or sung. The rhythmic quality of such oral performances served two purposes: it helped the chanting bard remember the lines, and it entertained audiences with patterned sounds of language, which were sometimes accompanied by musical instruments. Poetry has always been closely related to music. Indeed, as the word suggests, lyric poetry evolved from songs. "Western Wind" (p. 688), an anonymous Middle English lyric, survived as song long before it was written down. Had Robert Frost lived in a nonliterate society, he probably would have sung some version—a very different version to be sure—of "Acquainted with the Night" (p. 802) instead of writing it down. Even though Frost creates a speaking rather than a singing voice, the speaker's anxious tone is distinctly heard in any careful reading of the poem.

Like lyrics, early narrative poems were originally part of an anonymous oral folk tradition. A **ballad** such as "Bonny Barbara Allan" (p. 1146) told a story that was sung from one generation to the next until it was finally transcribed. Since the eighteenth century, this narrative form has sometimes been imitated by poets who write **literary ballads.** John Keats's "La Belle Dame sans Merci" (p. 1166) is, for example, a more complex and sophisticated nineteenth-century reflection of the original ballad traditions that developed in the fifteenth century and earlier. In considering poetry as sound, we should not forget that poetry traces its beginnings to song.

These next lines exemplify poetry's continuing relation to song. What poetic elements can you find in this ballad, which was adapted by Simon and Garfunkel and became a popular antiwar song in the 1960s?

ANONYMOUS

Scarborough Fair   *date unknown*

Where are you going? To Scarborough Fair?
Parsley, sage, rosemary, and thyme,
Remember me to a bonny lass there,
For once she was a true lover of mine.

Tell her to make me a cambric shirt,   5
Parsley, sage, rosemary, and thyme,
Without any needle or thread work'd in it,
And she shall be a true lover of mine.

Tell her to wash it in yonder well,
Parsley, sage, rosemary, and thyme,   10
Where water ne'er sprung nor a drop of rain fell,
And she shall be a true lover of mine.

Tell her to plough me an acre of land,
Parsley, sage, rosemary, and thyme,
Between the sea and the salt sea strand,   15
And she shall be a true lover of mine.

Tell her to plough it with one ram's horn,
Parsley, sage, rosemary, and thyme,
And sow it all over with one peppercorn,
And she shall be a true lover of mine.   20

Tell her to reap it with a sickle of leather,
Parsley, sage, rosemary, and thyme,
And tie it all up with a tom tit's feather,
And she shall be a true lover of mine.

Tell her to gather it all in a sack,   25
Parsley, sage, rosemary, and thyme,
And carry it home on a butterfly's back,
And then she shall be a true lover of mine.

CONSIDERATIONS FOR CRITICAL THINKING AND WRITING

1. FIRST RESPONSE. What do you associate with "Parsley, sage, rosemary, and thyme"? What images does this poem evoke? How?
2. What kinds of demands does the speaker make on his former lover? What do these demands have in common?
3. What is the tone of this ballad?
4. Choose a contemporary song that you especially like and examine the lyrics. Write an essay explaining whether or not you consider the lyrics poetic.

Of course, reading "Scarborough Fair" is not the same as hearing it. Like the lyrics of a song, many poems must be heard — or at least read with listening eyes — before they can be fully understood and enjoyed. The sounds of words are a universal source of music for human beings. This has been so from ancient tribes to bards to the two-year-old child in a bakery gleefully chanting "Cuppitycake, cuppitycake!"

Listen to the sound of this poem as you read it aloud. How do the words provide, in a sense, their own musical accompaniment?

JOHN UPDIKE (B. 1932)

Player Piano   1958

My stick fingers click with a snicker
And, chuckling, they knuckle the keys;
Light-footed, my steel feelers flicker
And pluck from these keys melodies.

My paper can caper; abandon   5
Is broadcast by dint of my din,
And no man or band has a hand in
The tones I turn on from within.

At times I'm a jumble of rumbles,
At others I'm light like the moon,   10
But never my numb plunker fumbles,
Misstrums me, or tries a new tune.

The speaker in this poem is a piano that can play automatically by means of a mechanism that depresses keys in response to signals on a perforated roll. Notice how the speaker's voice approximates the sounds of a piano. In each stanza a predominant sound emerges from the carefully chosen words. How is the sound of each stanza tuned to its sense?

Like Updike's "Player Piano," this next poem is also primarily about sounds.

MAY SWENSON (B. 1919)

A Nosty Fright   1984

The roldengod and the soneyhuckle,
the sack eyed blusan and the wistle theed
are all tangled with the oison pivy,
the fallen nine peedles and the wumbleteed.

A mipchunk caught in a wobceb tried   5
to hip and skide in a dandy sune
but a stobler put up a EEP KOFF sign.
Then the unfucky lellow met a phytoon

and was sept out to swea. He difted for drays
till a hassgropper flying happened to spot   10
the boolish feast all debraggled and wet,
covered with snears and tot.

Loonmight shone through the winey poods
where rushmooms grew among risted twoots.
Back blats flew betreen the twees   15
and orned howls hounded their soots.

A kumkpin stood with tooked creeth
on the sindow will of a house
where a icked wold itch lived all alone
except for her stoombrick, a mitten and a kouse.   20

"Here we part," said hassgropper.
"Pere we hart," said mipchunk, too.
They purried away on opposite haths,
both scared of some "Bat!" or "Scoo!"

October was ending on a nosty fright   25
with scroans and greeches and chanking clains,
with oblins and gelfs, coaths and urses,
skinning grulls and stoodblains.

Will it ever be morning, Nofember virst,
skue bly and the sappy hun, our friend?   30
With light breaves of wall by the fayside?
I sope ho, so that this oem can pend.

At just the right moments Swenson transposes letters to create amusing
sound effects and wild wordplays. Although there is a story lurking in "A
Nosty Fright," any serious attempt to interpret its meaning is confronted
with "a EEP KOFF sign." Instead, we are invited to enjoy the delicious
sounds the poet has cooked up.

Few poems revel in sound so completely. More typically, the sounds of
a poem contribute to its meaning rather than become its meaning. Consider how sound is used in the next poem.

Emily Dickinson (1830–1886)
A Bird came down the Walk —

c. 1862

A Bird came down the Walk —
He did not know I saw —
He bit an Angleworm in halves
And ate the fellow, raw,

And then he drank a Dew
From a convenient Grass —
And then hopped sidewise to the Wall
To let a Beetle pass —

He glanced with rapid eyes
That hurried all around —
They looked like frightened Beads, I thought —
He stirred his Velvet Head

Like one in danger, Cautious,
I offered him a Crumb
And he unrolled his feathers
And rowed him softer home —

Than Oars divide the Ocean,
Too silver for a seam —
Or Butterflies, off Banks of Noon
Leap, plashless as they swim.

5

10

15

20

This description of a bird offers a close look at how differently a bird moves when it hops on the ground than when it flies in the air. On the ground the bird moves quickly, awkwardly, and irregularly as it plucks up a worm, washes it down with dew, and then hops aside to avoid a passing beetle. The speaker recounts the bird's rapid, abrupt actions from a somewhat superior, amused perspective. By describing the bird in human terms (as if, for example, it chose to eat the worm "raw"), the speaker is almost condescending. But when the attempt to offer a crumb fails and the frightened bird flies off, the speaker is left looking up instead of down at the bird.

With that shift in perspective the tone shifts from amusement to awe in response to the bird's graceful flight. The jerky movements of lines 1 to 13 give way to the smooth motion of lines 15 to 20. The pace of the first three stanzas is fast and discontinuous. We tend to pause at the end of each line, and this reinforces a sense of disconnected movements. In contrast, the final six lines are to be read as a single sentence in one flowing movement, lubricated by various sounds.

Read again the description of the bird flying away. Several *o*-sounds contribute to the image of the serene, expansive, confident flight, just as the *s*-sounds serve as smooth transitions from one line to the next. Notice how these sounds are grouped in the following vertical columns:

unrolled	softer	*too*	his	Ocean	Banks
rowed	Oars	Noon	feathers	silver	plashless
home	Or		softer	seam	as
Ocean	off		Oars	Butterflies	swim

This blending of sounds (notice how "Leap, plashless" brings together the *p*- and *l*-sounds without a ripple) helps convey the bird's smooth grace in the air. Like a feathered oar, the bird moves seamlessly in its element.

The repetition of sounds in poetry is similar to the function of the tones and melodies that are repeated, with variations, in music. Just as the patterned sounds in music unify a work, so do the words in poems, which have been carefully chosen for the combinations of sounds they create. These sounds are produced in a number of ways.

The most direct way in which the sound of a word suggests its meaning is through **onomatopoeia,** which is the use of a word that resembles the sound it denotes: *quack, buzz, rattle, bang, squeak, bowwow, burp, choo-choo, ding-a-ling, sizzle.* The sound and sense of these words are closely related, but they represent a very small percentage of the words available to us. Poets usually employ more subtle means for echoing meanings.

Onomatopoeia can consist of more than just single words. In its broadest meaning the term refers to lines or passages in which sounds help to convey meanings, as in these lines from Updike's "Player Piano":

> My stick fingers click with a snicker
> And, chuckling, they knuckle the keys.

The sharp, crisp sounds of these two lines approximate the sounds of a piano; the syllables seem to "click" against one another. Contrast Updike's rendition with the following lines:

> My long fingers play with abandon
> And, laughing, they cover the keys.

The original version is more interesting and alive because the sounds of the words are pleasurable and they reinforce the meaning through a careful blending of consonants and vowels.

Alliteration is the repetition of the same consonant sounds at the beginnings of nearby words: "*d*escending *d*ewdrops"; "*l*uscious *l*emons." Sometimes the term is also used to describe the consonant sounds within words: "tres*p*asser's re*p*roach"; "we*dd*ed la*d*y." Alliteration is based on sound rather than spelling. "*K*een" and "*c*ar" alliterate, but "*c*ar" does not alliterate with "*c*ite." Rarely is heavy-handed alliteration effective. Used too self-consciously, it can be distracting instead of strengthening meaning or emphasizing a relation between words. Consider the relentless *h*s in this line: "Horrendous horrors haunted Helen's happiness." Those *h*s certainly suggest that Helen is being pursued, but they have a more comic than serious effect because they are overdone.

Assonance is the repetition of the same vowel sound in nearby words: "asl*ee*p under a tr*ee*"; "t*i*me and t*i*de"; "h*au*nt" and "*aw*esome"; "*ea*ch *e*vening." Both alliteration and assonance help to establish relations among words in a line or a series of lines. Whether the effect is **euphony** (lines that are musically pleasant to the ear and smooth, like the final lines of Dickinson's "A Bird came down the Walk—") or the effect is **cacophony** (lines that are discordant and difficult to pronounce, like the claim that "never my numb plunker fumbles" in Updike's "Player Piano"), the sounds of words in poetry can be as significant as the words' denotative or connotative meanings.

This next poem provides a feast of sounds. Read the poem aloud and try to determine the effects of its sounds.

GALWAY KINNELL (B. 1927)

Blackberry Eating   *1980*

I love to go out in late September
among the fat, overripe, icy, black blackberries
to eat blackberries for breakfast,
the stalks very prickly, a penalty
they earn for knowing the black art   5
of blackberry-making; and as I stand among them
lifting the stalks to my mouth, the ripest berries
fall almost unbidden to my tongue,
as words sometimes do, certain peculiar words
like *strengths* or *squinched*,   10
many-lettered, one-syllabled lumps,
which I squeeze, squinch open, and splurge well
in the silent, startled, icy, black language
of blackberry-eating in late September.

CONSIDERATIONS FOR CRITICAL THINKING AND WRITING

1. FIRST RESPONSE. What types of sounds does Kinnell use throughout this poem? What categories can you place them in? What is the effect of these sounds?

2. How do lines 4–6 fit into the poem? What does this prickly image add to the poem?

3. Explain what you think the poem's theme is.

4. Write an essay that considers the speaker's love of blackberry eating along with the speaker's appetite for words. How are the two blended in the poem?

RHYME

Web *For activities on rhyme, check out the Interactive Poetry Tutorial at*
http://www.bedfordstmartins.com/meyer/bedintrolit

Like alliteration and assonance, *rhyme* is a way of creating sound patterns. Rhyme, broadly defined, consists of two or more words or phrases that repeat the same sounds: *happy* and *snappy*. Rhyme words often have similar spellings, but that is not a requirement of rhyme; what matters is that the words sound alike: *vain* rhymes with *reign* as well as *rain*. Moreover, words may look alike but not rhyme at all. In *eye rhyme* the spellings are similar, but the pronunciations are not, as with *bough* and *cough*, or *brow* and *blow*.

Not all poems employ rhyme. Many great poems have no rhymes, and many weak verses use rhyme as a substitute for poetry. These are especially apparent in commercial messages and greeting-card lines. At its worst, rhyme is merely a distracting decoration that can lead to dullness and predictability. But used skillfully, rhyme creates lines that are memorable and musical.

Following is a poem using rhyme that you might remember the next time you are in a restaurant.

RICHARD ARMOUR (1906–1989)

Going to Extremes   1954

Shake and shake
    The catsup bottle
None'll come —
    And then a lot'll.

The experience recounted in Armour's poem is common enough, but the rhyme's humor is special. The final line clicks the poem shut, an effect that is often achieved by the use of rhyme. That click provides a sense of a satisfying and fulfilled form. Rhymes have a number of uses: they can emphasize words, direct a reader's attention to relations between words, and provide an overall structure for a poem.

Rhyme is used in the following poem to imitate the sound of cascading water.

ROBERT SOUTHEY (1774–1843)

From "The Cataract of Lodore"   1820

    "How does the water

        Come down at Lodore?"
    . . . .
    From its sources which well

                In the tarn on the fell;
                    From its fountains   5
                    In the mountains,
                Its rills and its gills;
            Through moss and through brake,
                It runs and it creeps
                For awhile, till it sleeps   10
                    In its own little lake.
            And thence at departing,
            Awakening and starting,
                It runs through the reeds
                And away it proceeds,   15
            Through meadow and glade,
                In sun and in shade,
            And through the wood-shelter,
                Among crags in its flurry,
                    Helter-skelter,   20
                    Hurry-scurry.
                Here it comes sparkling,
            And there it lies darkling;
            Now smoking and frothing
                Its tumult and wrath in,   25
                Till in this rapid race
                    On which it is bent,
                    It reaches the place
                    Of its steep descent.

                The cataract strong   30
                Then plunges along,
                Striking and raging
                As if a war waging
            Its caverns and rocks among:
                Rising and leaping,   35
                Sinking and creeping,
                Swelling and sweeping,
            Showering and springing,
                    Flying and flinging,
                    Writhing and ringing,   40
            Eddying and whisking,
            Spouting and frisking,
            Turning and twisting,
                    Around and around
                    With endless rebound!   45
                Smiting and fighting,
                    A sight to delight in;
                Confounding, astounding,
            Dizzying and deafening the ear with its sound.
. . . .

            Dividing and gliding and sliding,   50
            And falling and brawling and spawling,
            And driving and riving and striving,

And sprinkling and twinkling and wrinkling,
And sounding and bounding and rounding,
And bubbling and troubling and doubling,   55
And grumbling and rumbling and tumbling,
And clattering and battering and shattering;
Retreating and beating and meeting and sheeting,
Delaying and straying and playing and spraying,
Advancing and prancing and glancing and dancing,   60
Recoiling, turmoiling and toiling and boiling,
And gleaming and streaming and steaming and beaming,
And rushing and flushing and brushing and gushing,
And flapping and rapping and clapping and slapping,
And curling and whirling and purling and twirling,   65
And thumping and plumping and bumping and jumping,
And dashing and flashing and splashing and clashing;
And so never ending, but always descending,
Sounds and motions forever and ever are blending,
All at once and all o'er, with a mighty uproar;   70
And this way the water comes down at Lodore.

This deluge of rhymes consists of "Sounds and motions forever and ever . . . blending" (line 69). The pace quickens as the water creeps from its mountain source and then descends in rushing cataracts. As the speed of the water increases, so do the number of rhymes, until they run in fours: "dashing and flashing and splashing and clashing" (67). Most rhymes meander through poems instead of flooding them; nevertheless, Southey's use of rhyme suggests how sounds can flow with meanings. "The Cataract of Lodore" has been criticized, however, for overusing onomatopoeia. Some readers find the poem silly; others regard it as a brilliant example of sound effects. What do you think?

A variety of types of rhyme is available to poets. The most common form, **end rhyme,** comes at the ends of lines (14–17).

> It runs through the reeds
>   And away it proceeds,
> Through meadow and glade,
>   In sun and in shade.

Internal rhyme places at least one of the rhymed words within the line, as in "Dividing and gliding and sliding" (50) or, more subtly, in the fourth and final words of "In mist or cloud, on mast or shroud."

The rhyming of single-syllable words such as *glade* and *shade* is known as **masculine rhyme:**

> Loveliest of trees, the cherry now
> Is hung with bloom along the bough.
> —A. E. Housman

Rhymes using words of more than one syllable are also called masculine when the same sound occurs in a final stressed syllable, as in *defend, contend;*

betray, away. A *feminine rhyme* consists of a rhymed stressed syllable followed by one or more rhymed unstressed syllables, as in *butter, clutter; gratitude, attitude; quivering, shivering:*

> Lord confound this surly sister,
> Blight her brow and blotch and blister.
> —John Millington Synge

All the examples so far have been **exact rhymes** because they share the same stressed vowel sounds as well as any sounds that follow the vowel. In **near rhyme** (also called **off rhyme, slant rhyme,** and **approximate rhyme**), the sounds are almost but not exactly alike. There are several kinds of near rhyme. One of the most common is **consonance,** an identical consonant sound preceded by a different vowel sound: *home, same; worth, breath; trophy, daffy.* Near rhyme can also be achieved by using different vowel sounds with identical consonant sounds: *sound, sand; kind, conned; fellow, fallow.* The dissonance of *blade* and *blood* in the following lines helps to reinforce their grim tone:

> Let the boy try along this bayonet-blade
> How cold steel is, and keen with hunger of blood.
> —Wilfred Owen

Near rhymes greatly broaden the possibility for musical effects in English, a language that, compared with Spanish or Italian, contains few exact rhymes. Do not assume, however, that a near rhyme represents a failed attempt at exact rhyme. Near rhymes allow a musical subtlety and variety and can avoid the sometimes overpowering jingling effects that exact rhymes may create.

These basic terms hardly exhaust the ways in which the sounds in poems can be labeled and discussed, but the terms can help you to describe how poets manipulate sounds for effect. Read "God's Grandeur" (p. 843) aloud and try to determine how the sounds of the lines contribute to their sense.

PERSPECTIVE

DAVID LENSON (B. 1945)

On the Contemporary Use of Rhyme   1988

One impediment to a respectable return to rhyme is the popular survival of "functional" verse: greeting cards, pedagogical and mnemonic devices ("Thirty days hath September"), nursery rhymes, advertising jingles, and of course song lyrics. Pentameters, irregular rhymes, and free verse aren't much use in songwriting, where the meter has to be governed by the time signature of the music.

Far from universities, there has been a revival of rhymed couplets in rap music, in which, to the accompaniment of synthesizers, vocalists deliver lengthy first-person narratives in tetrameter. While most writing teachers would dismiss such lyrics as doggerel, the aim of the songs is really not so far from that of Alexander Pope: to use rhyme to sharpen social insight, in the hope that the world may be reordered.

From *The Chronicle of Higher Education*, February 24, 1988

CONSIDERATIONS FOR CRITICAL THINKING AND WRITING

1. Read some contemporary song lyrics from a wide range of groups or vocalists. Is Lenson correct in his assessment that irregular rhyme is not much use in songwriting?

2. Examine the rhymed couplets of some rap music. Discuss whether they are used "to sharpen social insight." What is the effect of using rhymes in rap music?

3. What is your own response to rhymed poetry? Do you like yours with or without? What do you think informs your preference?

SOUND AND MEANING

GERARD MANLEY HOPKINS (1844–1889)
God's Grandeur   1877

The world is charged with the grandeur of God
   It will flame out, like shining from shook foil;°   *shaken gold foil*
   It gathers to a greatness, like the ooze of oil
Crushed.° Why do men then now not reck his rod?°
Generations have trod, have trod, have trod;   5
   And all is seared with trade; bleared, smeared with toil;
   And wears man's smudge and shares man's smell: the soil
Is bare now, nor can foot feel, being shod.
And for all this, nature is never spent;
   There lives the dearest freshness deep down things;   10
And though the last lights off the black West went
   Oh, morning, at the brown brink eastward, springs —
Because the Holy Ghost over the bent
   World broods with warm breast and with ah! bright wings.

The subject of this poem is announced in the title and the first line: "The world is charged with the grandeur of God." The poem is a celebration of the power and greatness of God's presence in the world, but the speaker is also perplexed and dismayed by people who refuse to recognize God's authority and grandeur as they are manifested in the creation.

4 *Crushed:* Olives crushed in their oil;   *reck his rod:* Obey God.

Instead of glorifying God, "men" have degraded the earth through meaningless toil and cut themselves off from the spiritual renewal inherent in the beauty of nature. The relentless demands of commerce and industry have blinded people to the earth's natural and spiritual resources. In spite of this abuse and insensitivity to God's grandeur, however, "nature is never spent"; the morning light that "springs" in the east redeems the "black West" of the night and is a sign that the spirit of the Holy Ghost is ever present in the world. This summary of the poem sketches some of the thematic significance of the lines, but it does not do justice to how they are organized around the use of sound. Hopkins's poem, unlike Southey's "The Cataract of Lodore," employs sounds in a subtle and complex way.

In the opening line Hopkins uses alliteration — a device apparent in almost every line of the poem — to connect "God" to the "world," which is "charged" with his "grandeur." These consonants unify the line as well. The alliteration in lines 2 and 3 suggests a harmony in the creation: the *f*'s in "*f*lame" and "*f*oil," the *sh*'s in "*sh*ining" and "*sh*ook," the *g*'s in "*g*athers" and "*g*reatness," and the visual (not alliterative) similarities of "*oo*ze of *oi*l" emphasize a world that is held together by God's will.

That harmony is abruptly interrupted by the speaker's angry question in line 4: "Why do men then now not reck his rod?" The question is as painful to the speaker as it is difficult to pronounce. The arrangement of the alliteration ("*n*ow," "*n*ot"; "*r*eck," "*r*od"), the assonance ("n*o*t," "r*o*d"; "m*e*n," "th*e*n," "r*e*ck"), and the internal rhyme ("m*en*," "th*en*") contribute to the difficulty in saying the line, a difficulty associated with human behavior. That behavior is introduced in line 5 by the repetition of "have trod" to emphasize the repeated mistakes — sins — committed by human beings. The tone is dirgelike because humanity persists in its mistaken path rather than progressing. The speaker's horror at humanity is evident in the cacophonous sounds of lines 6 to 8. Here the alliteration of "*sm*eared," "*sm*udge," and "*sm*ell" along with the internal rhymes of "s*eared*," "bl*eared*," and "sm*eared*" echo the disgust with which the speaker views humanity's "toil" with the "soil," an end rhyme that calls attention to our mistaken equation of nature with production rather than with spirituality.

In contrast to this cacophony, the final six lines build toward the joyful recognition of the new possibilities that accompany the rising sun. This recognition leads to the euphonic description of the "H*o*ly Gh*o*st *o*ver" (notice the reassuring consistency of the assonance) the world. Traditionally represented as a dove, the Holy Ghost brings love and peace to the "*w*orld," and "*b*roods *w*ith *w*arm *b*reast and *w*ith ah! *b*right *w*ings." The effect of this alliteration is mellifluous: the sound bespeaks the harmony that prevails at the end of the poem resulting from the speaker's recognition that "nature is never spent" because God loves and protects the world.

The sounds of "God's Grandeur" enhance the poem's theme; more can be said about its sounds, but it is enough to point out here that for this poem the sound strongly echoes the theme in nearly every line. Here are some more poems in which sound plays a significant role.

POEMS FOR FURTHER STUDY

EDGAR ALLAN POE (1809–1849)

The Bells   1849

I

Hear the sledges with the bells —
    Silver bells!
What a world of merriment their melody foretells!
How they tinkle, tinkle, tinkle,
    In the icy air of night!   5
While the stars that oversprinkle
All the heavens, seem to twinkle
    With a crystalline delight;
      Keeping time, time, time,
    In a sort of Runic rhyme,   10
To the tintinnabulation that so musically wells
    From the bells, bells, bells, bells,
      Bells, bells, bells —
From the jingling and the tinkling of the bells

II

Hear the mellow wedding bells —   15
    Golden bells!
What a world of happiness their harmony foretells!
    Through the balmy air of night
    How they ring out their delight! —
      From the molten-golden notes,   20
      And all in tune,
      What a liquid ditty floats
To the turtle-dove that listens, while she gloats
        On the moon!
      Oh, from out the sounding cells,   25
What a gush of euphony voluminously wells!
      How it swells!
      How it dwells
      On the Future! — how it tells
      Of the rapture that impels   30
      To the swinging and the ringing
      Of the bells, bells, bells —
Of the bells, bells, bells, bells,
      Bells, bells, bells —
To the rhyming and the chiming of the bells!   35

III

Hear the loud alarum bells —
    Brazen bells!
What a tale of terror, now, their turbulency tells!
    In the startled ear of night
    How they scream out their affright!   40

Too much horrified to speak,
They can only shriek, shriek,
    Out of tune,
In a clamorous appealing to the mercy of the fire,
In a mad expostulation with the deaf and frantic fire,   45
    Leaping higher, higher, higher,
  With a desperate desire,
  And a resolute endeavor
  Now — now to sit, or never,
By the side of the pale-faced moon.   50
    Oh, the bells, bells, bells!
  What a tale their terror tells
    Of Despair!
How they clang, and clash, and roar!
  What a horror they outpour   55
On the bosom of the palpitating air!
    Yet the ear, it fully knows,
    By the twanging
    And the clanging,
    How the danger ebbs and flows;   60
  Yet the ear distinctly tells,
    In the jangling
    And the wrangling,
  How the danger sinks and swells,
By the sinking or the swelling in the anger of the bells —   65
    Of the bells, —
  Of the bells, bells, bells, bells,
    Bells, bells, bells —
In the clamor and the clangor of the bells!

       IV

  Hear the tolling of the bells —   70
    Iron bells!
What a world of solemn thought their monody compels!
  In the silence of the night,
  How we shiver with affright
At the melancholy menace of their tone!   75
  For every sound that floats
From the rust within their throats
    Is a groan.
    And the people — ah, the people —
    They that dwell up in the steeple,
    All alone,   80
And who tolling, tolling, tolling,
  In that muffled monotone,
Feel a glory in so rolling
    On the human heart a stone —   85
They are neither man nor woman —
They are neither brute nor human —
    They are Ghouls: —
  And their king it is who tolls: —

And he rolls, rolls, rolls,   90
            Rolls
        A pæan from the bells!
And his merry bosom swells
        With the pæan of the bells!
And he dances, and he yells;   95
Keeping time, time, time,
In a sort of Runic rhyme,
        To the pæan of the bells —
            Of the bells:
Keeping time, time, time,   100
In a sort of Runic rhyme,
        To the throbbing of the bells —
    Of the bells, bells, bells —
        To the sobbing of the bells;
Keeping time, time, time,   105
        As he knells, knells, knells.
In a happy Runic rhyme,
        To the rolling of the bells —
Of the bells, bells, bells: —
        To the tolling of the bells —   110
Of the bells, bells, bells, bells,
        Bells, bells, bells —
To the moaning and the groaning of the bells.

CONSIDERATIONS FOR CRITICAL THINKING AND WRITING

1. FIRST RESPONSE. How does Poe create the sounds of each kind of bell in each of the poem's four sections?
2. How is onomatopoeia used in each section to echo meanings?
3. What is the effect of the many repetitions of the word "bells"?
4. How do the length of the lines in the poem create musical rhythms?
5. What kinds of rhymes are used to achieve sound effects?
6. What do you think is the theme of "The Bells"?

CONNECTION TO ANOTHER SELECTION

1. Compare Poe's sound effects with Southey's in "The Cataract of Lodore" (p. 839). Which poem do you find more effective in its use of sound? Explain why.

PAULA GUNN ALLEN (B. 1939)

Hoop Dancer   *1982*

It's hard to enter
circling clockwise and counter
clockwise moving no
regard for time, metrics

irrelevant to this dance where pain   5
is the prime counter and soft
stepping feet praise water from the skies:
I have seen the face of triumph
the winding line stare down all moves to desecration
guts not cut from arms, fingers joined to minds,   10
together Sky and Water one dancing one
circle of a thousand turning lines beyond the march of years —
out of time, out of
time, out
of time.   15

CONSIDERATIONS FOR CRITICAL THINKING AND WRITING

1. FIRST RESPONSE. How does the sound of this Indian dance reflect its movement?

2. Discuss the images of circling in the poem. How are they related to the poem's theme?

LEWIS CARROLL (CHARLES LUTWIDGE DODGSON/1832–1898)

Jabberwocky   *1871*

'Twas brillig, and the slithy toves
    Did gyre and gimble in the wabe:
All mimsy were the borogoves,
    And the mome raths outgrabe.

"Beware the Jabberwock, my son!   5
    The jaws that bite, the claws that catch!
Beware the Jubjub bird, and shun
    The frumious Bandersnatch!"

He took his vorpal sword in hand;
    Long time the manxome foe he sought —   10
So rested he by the Tumtum tree,
    And stood awhile in thought.

And, as in uffish thought he stood,
    The Jabberwock, with eyes of flame,
Came whiffling through the tulgey wood,   15
    And burbled as it came!

One, two! One, two! And through and through
    The vorpal blade went snicker-snack!
He left it dead, and with its head
    He went galumphing back.   20

"And hast thou slain the Jabberwock?
    Come to my arms, my beamish boy!

O frabjous day! Callooh, Callay!"
  He chortled in his joy.

'Twas brillig, and the slithy toves   25
  Did gyre and gimble in the wabe:
All mimsy were the borogoves,
  And the mome raths outgrabe.

CONSIDERATIONS FOR CRITICAL THINKING AND WRITING

1. FIRST RESPONSE. What happens in this poem? Does it have any meaning?
2. Not all the words used in this poem appear in dictionaries. In *Through the Looking Glass,* Humpty Dumpty explains to Alice that "'slithy' means 'lithe and slimy.' 'Lithe' is the same as 'active.' You see it's like a portmanteau — there are two meanings packed up into one word." Are there any other portmanteau words in the poem?
3. Which words in the poem sound especially meaningful, even if they are devoid of any denotative meanings?

CONNECTION TO ANOTHER SELECTION

1. Compare Carroll's strategies for creating sound and meaning with those used by Swenson in "A Nosty Fright" (p. 835).

SYLVIA PLATH (1932–1963)

Mushrooms   *1960*

Overnight, very
Whitely, discreetly,
Very quietly

Our toes, our noses   5
Take hold on the loam,
Acquire the air.

Nobody sees us,
Stops us, betrays us;
The small grains make room.

Soft fists insist on   10
Heaving the needles,
The leafy bedding,

Even the paving.
Our hammers, our rams,
Earless and eyeless,   15

Perfectly voiceless,
Widen the crannies,
Shoulder through holes. We

Diet on water,
On crumbs of shadow,   20
Bland-mannered, asking

Little or nothing.
So many of us!
So many of us!

We are shelves, we are   25
Tables, we are meek,
We are edible,

Nudgers and shovers
In spite of ourselves.
Our kind multiplies: 30

We shall by morning
Inherit the earth.
Our foot's in the door.

CONSIDERATIONS FOR CRITICAL THINKING AND WRITING

1. FIRST RESPONSE. Is the tone of this poem serious or comic? What effects do alliteration and assonance have on your reading of the tone?
2. How important is the title?
3. Discuss what you take to be the poem's theme.

WILLIAM HEYEN (B. 1940)

The Trains   *1984*

Signed by Franz Paul Stangl, Commandant,
there is in Berlin a document,
an order of transmittal from Treblinka:

248 freight cars of clothing,
400,000 gold watches,   5
25 freight cars of women's hair.

Some clothing was kept, some pulped for paper.
The finest watches were never melted down.
All the women's hair was used for mattresses, or dolls.

Would these words like to use some of that same paper?   10
One of those watches may pulse in your own wrist.
Does someone you know collect dolls, or sleep on human hair?

He is dead at last, Commandant Stangl of Treblinka,
but the camp's three syllables still sound like freight cars
straining around a curve, Treblinka,   15

Treblinka. Clothing, time in gold watches,
women's hair for mattresses and dolls' heads.
Treblinka. The trains from Treblinka.

CONSIDERATIONS FOR CRITICAL THINKING AND WRITING

1. FIRST RESPONSE. How does the sound of the word *Treblinka* inform your understanding of the poem?

2. Why does the place name of Treblinka continue to resonate over time? If you don't know why Treblinka is infamous, use the library to find out.

3. Why do you suppose Heyen uses the word *in* instead of *on* in line 11?

4. Why is sound so important for establishing the tone of this poem? In what sense do the "camp's three syllables still sound like freight cars"?

5. CRITICAL STRATEGIES. Read the section on reader-response criticism (pp. 2109–11) in Chapter 52, "Critical Strategies for Reading." How does this poem make you feel? Why?

VIRGINIA HAMILTON ADAIR (B. 1913)

Dirty Old Man   *1998*

A few beers make his mood pugnacious,
his jokes and stories more salacious,
his eye for nymphets more rapacious,
with older women most ungracious;
his appetite for fat, voracious,   5
swells his manly gut capacious.
With piety somewhat audacious
he calls upon his saint, Ignatius,
"Save me a bed in Heaven so spacious
that it will hold a hundred geishas."   10

CONSIDERATIONS FOR CRITICAL THINKING AND WRITING

1. FIRST RESPONSE. What kind of tone does this series of rhymes create?

2. Is the poet cheating a bit with the final "geishas" rhyme, or can its two syllables be justified, given all the three syllable rhymes that precede it?

3. Try writing a brief poem that characterizes someone by using a series of rhymes.

JOHN DONNE (1572–1631)

Song   *1633*

Go and catch a falling star
    Get with child a mandrake root,°
Tell me where all past years are,
    Or who cleft the Devil's foot,
Teach me to hear mermaids singing,   5
    Or to keep off envy's stinging,

2 *mandrake root:* This V-shaped root resembles the lower half of the human body.

And find
What wind
Serves to advance an honest mind.

If thou be'st borne to strange sights,   10
    Things invisible to see,
Ride ten thousand days and nights,
    Till age snow white hairs on thee,
Thou, when thou return'st, wilt tell me
    All strange wonders that befell thee,   15
        And swear
        Nowhere
Lives a woman true, and fair.

If thou findst one, let me know,
    Such a pilgrimage were sweet —   20
Yet do not, I would not go,
    Though at next door we might meet;
Though she were true, when you met her,
    And last, till you write your letter,
        Yet she   25
        Will be
False, ere I come, to two or three.

CONSIDERATIONS FOR CRITICAL THINKING AND WRITING

1. FIRST RESPONSE. What is the speaker's tone in this poem? What is his view
   of a woman's love? What does the speaker's use of hyperbole reveal about
   his emotional state?

2. Do you think Donne wants the speaker's argument to be taken seriously?
   Is there any humor in the poem?

3. Most of these lines end with masculine rhymes. What other kinds of
   rhymes are used for end rhymes?

MONA VAN DUYN (B. 1921)

What the Motorcycle Said   1973

Br-r-r-am-m-m, rackety-am-m, OM, *Am:*
All — r-r-room, r-r-ram, ala-bas-ter —
Am, the world's my oyster.

I hate plastic, wear it black and slick,
hate hardhats, wear one on my head,   5
that's what the motorcycle said.

Passed phonies in Fords, knocked down billboards, landed
on the other side of The Gap, and Whee,
bypassed history.

When I was born (The Past), baby knew best.   10
They shook when I bawled, took Freud's path,
threw away their wrath.

R-r-rackety-am-m. *Am*. War, rhyme,
soap, meat, marriage, the Phantom Jet
are shit, and like that.   15

Hate pompousness, punishment, patience, am into Love,
hate middle-class moneymakers, live on Dad,
that's what the motorcycle said.

Br-r-r-am-m-m. It's Nowsville, man. Passed Oldies, Uglies,
Straighties, Honkies. I'll never be   20
mean, tired or unsexy.

Passed cigarette suckers, souses, mother-fuckers,
losers, went back to Nature and found
how to get VD, stoned.

Passed a cow, too fast to hear her moo, "*I* rolled   25
our leaves of grass into one ball.
I am the grassy All."

Br-r-r-am-m-m, rackety-am-m, OM, *Am:*
All — gr-r-rin, oooohgah, gl-l-lutton —
Am, the world's my smilebutton.   30

CONSIDERATIONS FOR CRITICAL THINKING AND WRITING

1. FIRST RESPONSE. Write a paraphrase of the poem, paying particular attention to how you can paraphrase the *sounds* of the motorcycle.

2. What kind of personality emerges from the motorcycle? Explain which
   lines seem especially revealing to you.

CONNECTION TO ANOTHER SELECTION

1. Compare the theme and tone of "What the Motorcycle Said" with the excerpt from Walt Whitman's "Song of the Open Road" (p. 864).

ALEXANDER POPE (1688–1774)
From An Essay on Criticism   *1711*

But most by numbers° judge a poet's song;   *versification*
And smooth or rough, with them, is right or wrong;
In the bright muse though thousand charms conspire,
Her voice is all these tuneful fools admire;
Who haunt Parnassus° but to please their ear,   5
Not mend their minds; as some to church repair,
Not for the doctrine, but the music there.
These equal syllables alone require,
Though oft the ear the open vowels tire;
While expletives° their feeble aid do join;   10

5 *Parnassus:* A Greek mountain sacred to the Muses.   10 *expletives:* Unnecessary words
used to fill a line, as the *do* in this line.

And ten low words oft creep in one dull line;
While they ring round the same unvaried chimes,
With sure returns of still expected rhymes;
Where'er you find "the cooling western breeze,"
In the next line, it "whispers through the trees":   15
If crystal streams "with pleasing murmurs creep,"
The reader's threatened (not in vain) with "sleep":
Then, at the last and only couplet fraught
With some unmeaning thing they call a thought,
A needless Alexandrine° ends the song,   20
That, like a wounded snake, drags its slow length along.
Leave such to tune their own dull rhymes, and know
What's roundly smooth, or languishingly slow;
And praise the easy vigor of a line,
Where Denham's strength, and Waller's° sweetness join.   25
True ease in writing comes from art, not chance,
As those move easiest who have learned to dance.
'Tis not enough no harshness gives offense,
The sound must seem an echo to the sense:
Soft is the strain when Zephyr° gently blows,   *the west wind*   30
And the smooth stream in smoother numbers flows;
But when loud surges lash the sounding shore,
The hoarse, rough verse should like the torrent roar:
When Ajax° strives some rock's vast weight to throw,
The line too labors, and the words move slow;   35
Not so, when swift Camilla° scours the plain,
Flies o'er th' unbending corn, and skims along the main.

20 *Alexandrine:* A twelve-syllable line, as line 21.   25 *Denham's . . . Waller's:* Sir John Denham (1615–1669) and Edmund Waller (1606–1687) were poets who used heroic couplets.
34 *Ajax:* A Greek warrior famous for his strength in the Trojan War.   36 *Camilla:* A goddess famous for her delicate speed.

Considerations for Critical Thinking and Writing

1. First response. In these lines Pope describes some faults he finds in
    poems and illustrates those faults within the lines that describe them. How
    do the sounds in lines 4, 9, 10, 11, and 21 illustrate what they describe?

2. What is the objection to the "expected rhymes" in lines 12–17? How do they
    differ from Pope's end rhymes?

3. Some lines discuss how to write successful poetry. How do lines 23, 24,
    32–33, 35, 36, and 37 illustrate what they describe?

4. Do you agree that in a good poem "The sound must seem an echo to the
    sense"?

GWENDOLYN BROOKS (1917–2000)

Sadie and Maud

1945

Maud went to college.
Sadie stayed at home.
Sadie scraped life
With a fine-tooth comb.

She didn't leave a tangle in.   5
Her comb found every strand.
Sadie was one of the livingest chits°   *pert girls*
In all the land.

Sadie bore two babies
Under her maiden name.   10
Maud and Ma and Papa
Nearly died of shame.

When Sadie said her last so-long
Her girls struck out from home.
(Sadie had left as heritage   15
Her fine-tooth comb.)

Maud, who went to college,
Is a thin brown mouse.
She is living all alone
In this old house.   20

CONSIDERATIONS FOR CRITICAL THINKING AND WRITING

1. FIRST RESPONSE. Read this poem aloud and describe the pattern and effect
   of the rhymes.
2. How does the speaker compare Sadie's and Maud's lives? With whom do
   you sympathize more?
3. How does this poem compare to any jump rope songs you remember from
   childhood?

MAXINE HONG KINGSTON (B. 1940)

Restaurant

1981

for Lilah Kan

The main cook lies sick on a banquette, and his assistant
has cut his thumb. So the quiche cook takes
their places at the eight-burner range, and you and I
get to roll out twenty-three rounds of pie
dough and break a hundred eggs, four at a crack,   5
and sift out shell with a China cap, pack
spinach in the steel sink, squish and squeeze
the water out, and grate a full moon of cheese.

Pam, the pastry chef, who is baking Choco-
late Globs (once called Mulattos) complains about the disco,   10
which Lewis, the salad man, turns up louder out of spite.
"Black so-called musician," "Broads. Whites."
The porters, who speak French, from the Ivory Coast,
sweep up droppings and wash the pans without soap.
We won't be out of here until three A.M. In this basement,   15
I lose my size. I am a bent-over
child, Gretel or Jill, and I can
lift a pot as big as a tub with both hands.
Using a pitchfork, you stoke the broccoli and bacon.
Then I find you in the freezer, taking   20
a nibble of a slab of chocolate as big as a table.
We put the quiches in the oven, then we are able
to stick our heads up out of the sidewalk into the night
and wonder at the clean diners behind glass in candlelight.

CONSIDERATIONS FOR CRITICAL THINKING AND WRITING

1. FIRST RESPONSE. How do the sounds of this poem contribute to the descriptions of what goes on in the restaurant kitchen? How do they contribute to the diners?
2. In what sense does the speaker "lose [her] size" in the kitchen? How would
   you describe her?
3. Examine the poem's rhymes. What effect do they have on your reading?
4. Describe the tone of the final line. How does it differ from the rest of the
   poem?

CONNECTION TO ANOTHER SELECTION

1. Write an essay analyzing how the kitchen activities described in "Restaurant" and Magarrell's "The Joy of Cooking" (p. 797) are used to convey the
   themes of these poems.

PAUL HUMPHREY (B. 1915)

Blow   *1983*

Her skirt was lofted by the gale;
When I, with gesture deft,
Essayed to stay her frisky sail
She luffed, and laughed, and left.

CONSIDERATIONS FOR CRITICAL THINKING AND WRITING

1. FIRST RESPONSE. How do alliteration and assonance contribute to the euphonic effects in this poem?
2. What is the poem's controlling metaphor? Why is it especially appropriate?
3. Explain the ambiguity of the title.

ROBERT FRANCIS (1901–1987)

The Pitcher   *1953*

His art is eccentricity, his aim
How not to hit the mark he seems to aim at,

His passion how to avoid the obvious,
His technique how to vary the avoidance.

The others throw to be comprehended. He   5
Throws to be a moment misunderstood.

Yet not too much. Not errant, arrant, wild,
But every seeming aberration willed.

Not to, yet still, still to communicate
Making the batter understand too late.   10

CONSIDERATIONS FOR CRITICAL THINKING AND WRITING

1. FIRST RESPONSE. Explain how each pair of lines in this poem works together to describe the pitcher's art.
2. Consider how the poem itself works the way a good pitcher does. Which
   lines illustrate what they describe?
3. Comment on the effects of the poem's rhymes. How are the final two lines
   different in their rhyme from the previous lines? How does sound echo
   sense in lines 9–10?
4. Write an essay that considers "The Pitcher" as an extended metaphor for
   talking about poetry. How well does the poem characterize strategies for
   writing poetry as well as pitching?
5. Write an essay that develops an extended comparison between writing or
   reading poetry and playing or watching another sport.

CONNECTIONS TO OTHER SELECTIONS

1. Compare this poem with Robert Wallace's "The Double-Play" (p. 1187), another poem that explores the relation of baseball to poetry.
2. Write an essay comparing "The Pitcher" with Francis's "Catch" (p. 676).
   One poem defines poetry implicitly, the other defines it explicitly. Which
   poem do you prefer? Why?

HELEN CHASIN (B. 1938)

The Word Plum   *1968*

The word *plum* is delicious

pout and push, luxury of
self-love, and savoring murmur
full in the mouth and falling
like fruit   5

taut skin
pierced, bitten, provoked into
juice, and tart flesh

question
and reply, lip and tongue   10
of pleasure.

CONSIDERATIONS FOR CRITICAL THINKING AND WRITING

1. FIRST RESPONSE. What is the effect of the repetitions of the alliteration and assonance throughout the poem? How does it contribute to the poem's meaning?

2. Which sounds in the poem are like the sounds one makes while eating a plum?

3. Discuss the title. Explain whether you think this poem is more about the word *plum* or about the plum itself. Consider whether the two can be separated in the poem.

4. CRITICAL STRATEGIES. Read the section on deconstructionist criticism (pp. 2111–13) in Chapter 52, "Critical Strategies for Reading." How does meaning break down or deconstruct itself in this poem?

CONNECTION TO ANOTHER SELECTION

1. How is Kinnell's "Blackberry Eating" (p. 838) similar in technique to Chasin's poem? Try writing such a poem yourself: choose a food to describe that allows you to evoke its sensuousness in sounds.

JOHN KEATS (1795–1821)

Ode to a Nightingale   *1819*

I
My heart aches, and a drowsy numbness pains
　My sense, as though of hemlock° I had drunk,   *a poison*
Or emptied some dull opiate to the drains
　One minute past, and Lethe-wards° had sunk:
'Tis not through envy of thy happy lot,   5
　But being too happy in thine happiness —
　　That thou, light-wingèd Dryad° of the trees,   *wood nymph*
　　　In some melodious plot
　Of beechen green, and shadows numberless,
　　Singest of summer in full-throated ease.   10

II
O, for a draught of vintage! that hath been
　Cooled a long age in the deep-delved earth,

4 *Lethe-wards:* Toward Lethe, the river of forgetfulness in the Hades of Greek mythology.

Tasting of Flora° and the country green,   *goddess of flowers*
   Dance, and Provençal song,° and sunburnt mirth!
O for a beaker full of the warm South,   15
   Full of the true, the blushful Hippocrene,°
     With beaded bubbles winking at the brim,
      And purple-stainèd mouth;
   That I might drink, and leave the world unseen,
     And with thee fade away into the forest dim.   20

III
Fade far away, dissolve, and quite forget
   What thou among the leaves hast never known,
The weariness, the fever, and the fret
   Here, where men sit and hear each other groan;
Where palsy shakes a few, sad, last gray hairs,   25
   Where youth grows pale, and specter-thin, and dies,
     Where but to think is to be full of sorrow
      And leaden-eyed despairs,
   Where Beauty cannot keep her lustrous eyes;
     Or new Love pine at them beyond tomorrow.   30

IV
Away! away! for I will fly to thee,
   Not charioted by Bacchus and his pards,°
But on the viewless wings of Poesy,
   Though the dull brain perplexes and retards:
Already with thee! tender is the night,   35
   And haply the Queen-Moon is on her throne,
     Clustered around by all her starry Fays;
      But here there is no light,
   Save what from heaven is with the breezes blown
     Through verdurous glooms and winding mossy ways.   40

V
I cannot see what flowers are at my feet,
   Nor what soft incense hangs upon the boughs,
But, in embalmèd° darkness, guess each sweet   *perfumed*
   Wherewith the seasonable month endows
The grass, the thicket, and the fruit-tree wild;   45
   What hawthorn, and the pastoral eglantine;
     Fast fading violets covered up in leaves;
      And mid-May's eldest child,
   The coming musk-rose, full of dewy wine,
     The murmurous haunt of flies on summer eves.   50

14 *Provençal song:* The medieval troubadours of Provence, France, were known for their
singing.   16 *Hippocrene:* The fountain of the Muses in Greek mythology.   32 *Bacchus and
his pards:* The Greek god of wine traveled in a chariot drawn by leopards.

VI

Darkling° I listen; and for many a time *in the dark*
    I have been half in love with easeful Death,
Called him soft names in many a musèd rhyme,
    To take into the air my quiet breath;
Now more than ever seems it rich to die, 55
    To cease upon the midnight with no pain,
        While thou art pouring forth thy soul abroad
            In such an ecstasy!
        Still wouldst thou sing, and I have ears in vain—
            To thy high requiem become a sod. 60

VII

Thou wast not born for death, immortal Bird!
    No hungry generations tread thee down;
The voice I hear this passing night was heard
    In ancient days by emperor and clown:
Perhaps the selfsame song that found a path 65
    Through the sad heart of Ruth,° when, sick for home,
        She stood in tears amid the alien corn:
            The same that oft-times hath
        Charmed magic casements, opening on the foam
            Of perilous seas, in faery lands forlorn. 70

VIII

Forlorn! the very word is like a bell
    To toll me back from thee to my sole self!
Adieu! the fancy cannot cheat so well
    As she is famed to do, deceiving elf.
Adieu! adieu! thy plaintive anthem fades 75
    Past the near meadows, over the still stream,
        Up the hill side; and now 'tis buried deep
            In the next valley-glades:
        Was it a vision, or a waking dream?
            Fled is that music:— Do I wake or sleep? 80

66 *Ruth:* A young widow in the Bible (see the Book of Ruth).

CONSIDERATIONS FOR CRITICAL THINKING AND WRITING

1. FIRST RESPONSE. Why does the speaker in this ode want to leave his world for the nightingale's? What might the nightingale symbolize?
2. How does the speaker attempt to escape his world? Is he successful?
3. What changes the speaker's view of death at the end of stanza VI?
4. What does the allusion to Ruth (line 66) contribute to the ode's meaning?
5. In which lines is the imagery especially sensuous? How does this effect add to the conflict presented?
6. What calls the speaker back to himself at the end of stanza VII and the beginning of stanza VIII?
7. Choose a stanza and explain how sound is related to its meaning.
8. How regular is the stanza form of this ode?

PERSPECTIVE

DYLAN THOMAS (1914–1953)
On the Words in Poetry   1961

You want to know why and how I just began to write poetry. . . .

To answer . . . this question, I should say I wanted to write poetry in the beginning because I had fallen in love with words. The first poems I knew were nursery rhymes, and before I could read them for myself I had come to love just the words of them, the words alone. What the words stood for, symbolized, or meant, was of very secondary importance. What mattered was the *sound* of them as I heard them for the first time on the lips of the remote and incomprehensible grown-ups who seemed, for some reason, to be living in my world. And these words were, to me, as the notes of bells, the sounds of musical instruments, the noises of wind, sea, and rain, the rattle of milkcarts, the clopping of hooves on cobbles, the fingering of branches on a window pane, might be to someone, deaf from birth, who has miraculously found his hearing. I did not care what the words said, overmuch, not what happened to Jack and Jill and the Mother Goose rest of them; I cared for the shapes of sound that their names, and the words describing their actions, made in my ears; I cared for the colors the words cast on my eyes. I realize that I may be, as I think back all that way, romanticizing my reactions to the simple and beautiful words of those pure poems; but that is all I can honestly remember, however much time might have falsified my memory. I fell in love — that is the only expression I can think of, at once, and am still at the mercy of words, though sometimes now, knowing a little of their behavior very well, I think I can influence them slightly and have even learned to beat them now and then, which they appear to enjoy. I tumbled for words at once. And, when I began to read the nursery rhymes for myself, and, later, to read other verses and ballads, I knew that I had discovered the most important things, to me, that could be ever. There they were, seemingly lifeless, made only of black and white, but out of them, out of their own being, came love and terror and pity and pain and wonder and all the other vague abstractions that make our ephemeral lives dangerous, great, and bearable. Out of them came the gusts and grunts and hiccups and heehaws of the common fun of the earth; and though what the words meant was, in its own way, often deliciously funny enough, so much funnier seemed to me, at that almost forgotten time, the shape and shade and size and noise of the words as they hummed, strummed, jugged, and galloped along. That was the time of innocence; words burst upon me, unencumbered by trivial or portentous association; words were their springlike selves, fresh with Eden's dew, as they flew out of the air. They made their own original associations as they sprang and shone. The words "Ride a cock-horse to Banbury Cross" were as haunting to me, who did not know then what a cock-horse was nor cared a damn where Banbury Cross might be, as, much later, were such lines as John Donne's "Go and catch a falling star, Get with child a mandrake root," which also I could not understand when I first read them. And as I read more and more, and it was not all verse, by any means, my love for the real life of words increased until I knew that I must live *with* them and *in* them always.

I knew, in fact, that I must be a writer of words, and nothing else. The first thing was to feel and know their sound and substance; what I was going to do with those words, what use I was going to make of them, what I was going to *say* through them, would come later. I knew I had to know them most intimately in all their forms and moods, their ups and downs, their chops and changes, their needs and demands. (Here, I am afraid, I am beginning to talk too vaguely. I do not like writing *about* words, because then I often use bad and wrong and stale and wooly words. What I like to do is treat words as a craftsman does his wood or stone or what-have-you, to hew, carve, mold, coil, polish, and plane them into patterns, sequences, sculptures, fugues of sound expressing some lyrical impulse, some spiritual doubt or conviction, some dimly-realized truth I must try to reach and realize.)

From *Early Prose Writings*

CONSIDERATIONS FOR CRITICAL THINKING AND WRITING

1. Why does Thomas value nursery rhymes so highly? What nursery rhyme was your favorite as a child? Why were you enchanted by it?

2. Explain what you think Thomas would have to say about Carroll's "Jabberwocky" (p. 848) or Swenson's "A Nosty Fright" (p. 835).

3. Consider Thomas's comparison at the end of this passage, in which he likens a poet's work to a craftsman's. In what sense is making poetry similar to sculpting, painting, or composing music? What are some of the significant differences?

27

Patterns of Rhythm

The rhythms of everyday life surround us in regularly recurring movements and sounds. As you read these words, your heart pulsates while somewhere else a clock ticks, a cradle rocks, a drum beats, a dancer sways, a foghorn blasts, a wave recedes, or a child skips. We may tend to overlook rhythm since it is so tightly woven into the fabric of our experience, but it is there nonetheless, one of the conditions of life. Rhythm is also one of the conditions of speech because the voice alternately rises and falls as words are stressed or unstressed and as the pace quickens or slackens. In poetry *rhythm* refers to the recurrence of stressed and unstressed sounds. Depending on how the sounds are arranged, this can result in a pace that is fast or slow, choppy or smooth.

SOME PRINCIPLES OF METER

Web *For activities on meter, check out the Interactive Poetry Tutorial at*
http://www.bedfordstmartins.com/meyer/bedintrolit

Poets use rhythm to create pleasurable sound patterns and to reinforce meanings. "Rhythm," Edith Sitwell once observed, "might be described as, to the world of sound, what light is to the world of sight. It shapes and gives new meaning." Prose can use rhythm effectively too, but prose that does so tends to be an exception. The following exceptional lines are from a speech by Winston Churchill to the House of Commons after Allied forces lost a great battle to German forces at Dunkirk during World War II:

> We shall not flag or fail. We shall go on to the end. We shall fight in France, we
> shall fight on the seas and oceans, we shall fight with growing confidence and

growing strength in the air, we shall defend our island, whatever the cost may be, we shall fight on the beaches, we shall fight on the landing grounds, we shall fight in the fields and in the streets, we shall fight in the hills; we shall never surrender.

The stressed repetition of "we shall" bespeaks the resolute singleness of purpose that Churchill had to convey to the British people if they were to win the war. Repetition is also one of the devices used in poetry to create rhythmic effects. In the following excerpt from "Song of the Open Road," Walt Whitman urges the pleasures of limitless freedom on his reader:

> Allons!° the road is before us!   *Let's go!*
> It is safe — I have tried it — my own feet have tried it well — be not detain'd!
> Let the paper remain on the desk unwritten, and the book on the
>   shelf unopen'd!
> Let the tools remain in the workshop! Let the money remain unearn'd!
> Let the school stand! mind not the cry of the teacher!   5
> Let the preacher preach in his pulpit! Let the lawyer plead in the
>   court, and the judge expound the law.
> Camerado,° I give you my hand!   *friend*
> I give you my love more precious than money,
> I give you myself before preaching or law;
> Will you give me yourself? will you come travel with me?   10
> Shall we stick by each other as long as we live?

These rhythmic lines quickly move away from conventional values to the open road of shared experiences. Their recurring sounds are not created by rhyme or alliteration and assonance (see Chapter 26) but by the repetition of words and phrases.

Although the repetition of words and phrases can be an effective means of creating rhythm in poetry, the more typical method consists of patterns of accented or unaccented syllables. Words contain syllables that are either stressed or unstressed. A **stress** (or **accent**) places more emphasis on one syllable than on another. We say "*syl*lable" not "syl*la*ble," "*em*phasis" not "em*pha*sis." We routinely stress syllables when we speak: "*Is* she con*tent* with the *con*tents of the *yel*low *pack*age?" To distinguish between two people we might say "Is *she* content. . . ?" In this way stress can be used to emphasize a particular word in a sentence. Poets often arrange words so that the desired meaning is suggested by the rhythm; hence, emphasis is controlled by the poet rather than left entirely to the reader.

When a rhythmic pattern of stresses recurs in a poem, the result is **meter**. Taken together, all the metrical elements in a poem make up what is called the poem's **prosody**. **Scansion** consists of measuring the stresses in a line to determine its metrical pattern. Several methods can be used to mark lines. One widely used system employs ´ for a stressed syllable and ˘ for an unstressed syllable. In a sense, the stress mark represents the equivalent of tapping one's foot to a beat:

Hickory, dickory, dock,
The mouse ran up the clock.
The clock struck one,
And down he run,
Hickory, dickory, dock.

In the first two lines and the final line of this familiar nursery rhyme we hear three stressed syllables. In lines 3 and 4, where the meter changes for variety, we hear just two stressed syllables. The combination of stresses provides the pleasure of the rhythm we hear.

To hear the rhythms of "Hickory, dickory, dock" does not require a formal study of meter. Nevertheless, an awareness of the basic kinds of meter that appear in English poetry can enhance your understanding of how a poem achieves its effects. Understanding the sound effects of a poem and having a vocabulary with which to discuss those effects can intensify your pleasure in poetry. Although the study of meter can be extremely technical, the terms used to describe the basic meters of English poetry are relatively easy to comprehend.

The *foot* is the metrical unit by which a line of poetry is measured. A foot usually consists of one stressed and one or two unstressed syllables. A vertical line is used to separate the feet: "The clock | struck one" consists of two feet. A foot of poetry can be arranged in a variety of patterns; here are five of the chief ones:

Foot	Pattern	Example
iamb	˘ ´	away
trochee	´ ˘	Lovely
anapest	˘ ˘ ´	understand
dactyl	´ ˘ ˘	desperate
spondee	´ ´	dead set

The most common lines in English poetry contain meters based on iambic feet. However, even lines that are predominantly iambic will often include variations to create particular effects. Other important patterns include trochaic, anapestic, and dactylic feet. The spondee is not a sustained meter but occurs for variety or emphasis.

Iambic
What kept | his eyes | from giv | ing back | the gaze
Trochaic
He was | louder | than the | preacher
Anapestic
I am called | to the front | of the room
Dactylic
Sing it all | merrily

These meters have different rhythms and can create different effects. Iambic and anapestic are known as *rising meters* because they move from unstressed to stressed sounds, while trochaic and dactylic are known as *falling meters.* Anapests and dactyls tend to move more lightly and rapidly than iambs or trochees. Although no single kind of meter can be considered always better than another for a given subject, it is possible to determine whether the meter of a specific poem is appropriate for its subject. A serious poem about a tragic death would most likely not be well served by lilting rhythms. Keep in mind too that though one or another of these four basic meters might constitute the predominant rhythm of a poem, variations can occur within lines to change the pace or call attention to a particular word.

A *line* is measured by the number of feet it contains. Here, for example, is an iambic line with three feet: "If she | should write | a note." These are the names for line lengths:

monometer: one foot	pentameter: five feet
dimeter: two feet	hexameter: six feet
trimeter: three feet	heptameter: seven feet
tetrameter: four feet	octameter: eight feet

By combining the name of a line length with the name of a foot, we can describe the metrical qualities of a line concisely. Consider, for example, the pattern of feet and length of this line:

I didn't want the boy to hit the dog.

The iambic rhythm of this line falls into five feet; hence it is called *iambic pentameter.* Iambic is the most common pattern in English poetry because its rhythm appears so naturally in English speech and writing. Unrhymed iambic pentameter is called *blank verse;* Shakespeare's plays are built on such lines.

Less common than the iamb, trochee, anapest, or dactyl is the *spondee,* a two-syllable foot in which both syllables are stressed (′ ′). Note the effect of the spondaic foot at the beginning of this line:

Dead set | against | the plan | he went | away.

Spondees can slow a rhythm and provide variety and emphasis, particularly in iambic and trochaic lines. A line that ends with a stressed syllable is said to have a *masculine ending,* whereas a line that ends with an extra unstressed syllable is said to have a *feminine ending.* Consider, for example, these two lines from Timothy Steele's "Waiting for the Storm" (the entire poem appears on p. 868):

feminine: The sand | at my feet | grow cold | er,
masculine: The damp | air chill | and spread.

The effects of English meters are easily seen in the following lines by Samuel Taylor Coleridge, in which the rhythm of each line illustrates the meter described in it:

Trochee trips from long to short;
From long to long in solemn sort
Slow Spondee stalks; strong foot yet ill able
Ever to come up with Dactylic trisyllable.
Iambics march from short to long—
With a leap and a bound the swift Anapests throng.

The speed of a line is also affected by the number of pauses in it. A pause within a line is called a *caesura* and is indicated by a double vertical line (‖). A caesura can occur anywhere within a line and need not be indicated by punctuation:

Camerado, ‖ I give you my hand!
I give you my love ‖ more precious than money.

A slight pause occurs within each of these lines and at its end. Both kinds of pauses contribute to the lines' rhythm.

When a line has a pause at its end, it is called an *end-stopped line.* Such pauses reflect normal speech patterns and are often marked by punctuation. A line that ends without a pause and continues into the next line for its meaning is called a *run-on line.* Running over from one line to another is also called *enjambment.* The first and eighth lines of the following poem are run-on lines; the rest are end-stopped.

WILLIAM WORDSWORTH (1770–1850)

My Heart Leaps Up   *1807*

My heart leaps up when I behold
     A rainbow in the sky:
So was it when my life began;
So is it now I am a man;
So be it when I shall grow old,
     Or let me die!
The child is father of the Man;
And I could wish my days to be
Bound each to each by natural piety.

Run-on lines have a different rhythm from end-stopped lines. Lines 3 and 4 and lines 8 and 9 are iambic, but the effect of their two rhythms is very different when we read these lines aloud. The enjambment of lines 8 and 9 reinforces their meaning; just as the "days" are bound together, so are the lines.

The rhythm of a poem can be affected by several devices: the kind and number of stresses within lines, the length of lines, and the kinds of pauses that appear within lines or at their ends. In addition, as we saw in Chapter 26, the sound of a poem is affected by alliteration, assonance, rhyme, and consonance. These sounds help to create rhythms by controlling our pronunciations, as in the following lines by Alexander Pope:

Soft is the strain when Zephyr gently blows,
And the smooth stream in smoother numbers flows;
But when loud surges lash the sounding shore,
The hoarse, rough verse should like the torrent roar.

These lines are effective because their rhythm and sound work with their meaning.

SUGGESTIONS FOR SCANNING A POEM

These suggestions should help you in talking about a poem's meter.

1. After reading the poem through, read it aloud and mark the stressed syllables in each line. Then mark the unstressed syllables.
2. From your markings, identify what kind of foot is dominant (iambic, trochaic, dactylic, or anapestic) and divide the lines into feet, keeping in mind that the vertical line marking a foot may come in the middle of a word as well as at its beginning or end.
3. Determine the number of feet in each line. Remember that there may be variations; some lines may be shorter or longer than the predominant meter. What is important is the overall pattern. Do not assume that variations represent the poet's inability to fulfill the overall pattern. Notice the effects of variations and whether they emphasize words and phrases or disrupt your expectation for some other purpose.
4. Listen for pauses within lines and mark the caesuras; many times there will be no punctuation to indicate them.
5. Recognize that scansion does not always yield a definitive measurement of a line. Even experienced readers may differ over the scansion of a given line. What is important is not a precise description of the line but an awareness of how a poem's rhythms contribute to its effects.

The following poem demonstrates how you can use an understanding of meter and rhythm to gain a greater appreciation for what a poem is saying.

TIMOTHY STEELE (B. 1948)

Waiting for the Storm 1986

Breeze sent | ă wrink | lĭng dark | ness
Across | the bay. ‖ Ĭ knelt
Beneath | ăn up | turned boat,
And, mo | ment by mo | ment, felt
The sand | ăt my feet | grow cold | er,

The damp | air chill | and spread.
Then the | first rain | drops sound | ed
On the hull | above | my head.

The predominant meter of this poem is iambic trimeter, but there is plenty of variation as the storm rapidly approaches and finally begins to pelt the sheltered speaker. The emphatic spondee ("Breeze sent") pushes the darkness quickly across the bay while the caesura at the end of the sentence in line 2 creates a pause that sets up a feeling of suspense and expectation that is measured in the ticking rhythm of line 4, a run-on line that brings us into the chilly sand and air of the second stanza. Perhaps the most impressive sound effect used in the poem appears in the second syllable of "sounded" in line 7. That "ed" precedes the sound of the poem's final word "head" just as if it were the first drop of rain hitting the hull above the speaker. The visual, tactile, and auditory images make "Waiting for the Storm" an intense sensory experience.

This next poem also reinforces meanings through its use of meter and rhythm.

WILLIAM BUTLER YEATS (1865–1939)

That the Night Come   *1912*

She lived | in storm | and strife,
Her soul | had such | desire
For what | proud death | may bring
That it | could not | endure
The com | mon good | of life,   5
But lived | as 'twere | a king
That packed | his mar | riage day
With ban | neret | and pen | non,
Trumpet | and ket | tledrum,
And the | outrag | eous can | non,   10
To bun | dle time | away
That the | night come.

Scansion reveals that the predominant meter here is iambic trimeter. Each line contains three stressed and unstressed syllables that form a regular, predictable rhythm through line 7. That rhythm is disrupted, however, when the speaker compares the woman's longing for what death brings to a king's eager anticipation of his wedding night. The king packs the day with noisy fanfares and celebrations to fill up time and distract himself. Unable to accept "The common good of life," the woman fills her days with "storm and strife." In a determined effort "To bundle time away," she, like the king, impatiently awaits the night.

Lines 8–10 break the regular pattern established in the first seven lines. The extra unstressed syllable in lines 8 and 10 along with the trochaic feet in lines 9 ("trumpet") and 10 ("And the") interrupt the basic iambic trimeter and parallel the woman's and the king's frenetic activity. These lines thus echo the inability of the woman and king to "endure" regular or normal time. The last line is the most irregular in the poem. The final two accented syllables sound like the deep resonant beats of a kettledrum or a cannon firing. The words "night come" dramatically remind us that what the woman anticipates is not a lover but the mysterious finality of death. The meter serves, then, in both its regularity and variations to reinforce the poem's meaning and tone.

The following poems are especially rich in their rhythms and sounds. As you read and study them, notice how patterns of rhythm and the sounds of words reinforce meanings and contribute to the poems' effects. And, perhaps most important, read the poems aloud so that you can hear them.

POEMS FOR FURTHER STUDY

ALICE JONES (B. 1949)

The Foot   *1993*

Our improbable support, erected
on the osseous architecture
of the calcaneus, talus, cuboid,
navicular, cuneiforms, metatarsals,
phalanges, a plethora of hinges,   5

all strung together by gliding
tendons, covered by the pearly
plantar fascia, then fat-padded
to form the sole, humble surface
of our contact with earth.   10

Here the body's broadest tendon
anchors the heel's fleshy base,
the finely wrinkled skin stretches
forward across the capillaried arch,
to the ball, a balance point.   15

A wide web of flexor tendons
and branched veins maps the dorsum,
fades into the stub-laden bone

splay, the stuffed sausage sacks
of toes, each with a tuft   20

of proximal hairs to introduce
the distal nail, whose useless
curve remembers an ancestor,
the vanished creature's wild
and necessary claw.   25

CONSIDERATIONS FOR CRITICAL THINKING AND WRITING

1. FIRST RESPONSE. What is the effect of the diction? What sort of tone is established by the use of anatomical terms? How do the terms affect the rhythm?

2. Alice Jones has described the form of "The Foot" as "five stubby stanzas."
Explain why the lines of this poem may or may not warrant this description of the stanzas.

3. CRITICAL STRATEGIES. Read the section on formalist criticism (pp. 2095–97)
in Chapter 52, "Critical Strategies for Reading." Describe the effect of the
final stanza. How would your reading be affected if the poem ended after
the comma in the middle of line 22?

A. E. HOUSMAN (1859–1936)

When I was one-and-twenty   *1896*

When I was one-and-twenty
    I heard a wise man say,
"Give crowns and pounds and guineas
    But not your heart away;
Give pearls away and rubies   5
    But keep your fancy free."
But I was one-and-twenty,
    No use to talk to me.

When I was one-and-twenty
    I heard him say again,   10
"The heart out of the bosom
    Was never given in vain;
'Tis paid with sighs a plenty
    And sold for endless rue."
And I am two-and-twenty,   15
    And oh, 'tis true, 'tis true.

CONSIDERATIONS FOR CRITICAL THINKING AND WRITING

1. FIRST RESPONSE. How does the basic metrical pattern affect your understanding of the speaker?

2. How do lines 1–8 parallel lines 9–16 in their use of rhyme and metaphor?
Are there any significant differences between the stanzas?

3. What do you think has happened to change the speaker's attitude toward love?

4. Explain why you agree or disagree with the advice given by the "wise man."

5. What is the effect of the repetition in line 16?

NIKKI GIOVANNI (B. 1943)

Clouds   1999

I want to swim with hippos
    jump with salmon
        fly with geese
    land with robins
        walk with turtles   5
    sleep with possum
    dress with penguins
    preen with peacocks
        fish with grizzlies
        hunt with lions   10
forage with pigs for truffles
eat nuts with the squirrels
plant seeds with the wind
and ride on off with the clouds
        at the end   15

CONSIDERATIONS FOR CRITICAL THINKING AND WRITING

1. FIRST RESPONSE. Explain how the rhythms of the lines render punctuation unnecessary in this poem.

2. Why do you suppose Giovanni begins to use longer lines with line 11?

3. What effect does the different metrical scheme have on your understanding of the poem? Comment on the appropriateness of the oxymoronic phrase "ride on off" in line 14.

RACHEL HADAS (B. 1948)

The Red Hat   1995

It started before Christmas. Now our son
officially walks to school alone.
Semi-alone, it's accurate to say:
I or his father track him on the way.
He walks up on the east side of West End,   5
we on the west side. Glances can extend
(and do) across the street; not eye contact.
Already ties are feeling and not fact.
Straus Park is where these parallel paths part;

he goes alone from there. The watcher's heart   10
stretches, elastic in its love and fear,
toward him as we see him disappear,
striding briskly. Where two weeks ago,
holding a hand, he'd dawdle, dreamy, slow,
he now is hustled forward by the pull   15
of something far more powerful than school.

The mornings we turn back to are no more
than forty minutes longer than before,
but they feel vastly different — flimsy, strange,
wavering in the eddies of this change,   20
empty, unanchored, perilously light
since the red hat vanished from our sight.

CONSIDERATIONS FOR CRITICAL THINKING AND WRITING

1. FIRST RESPONSE. What emotions do the parents experience throughout the poem? How do you think the boy feels? Does the metrical pattern affect your understanding of the parents or the boy?

2. What prevents the rhymed couplets in this poem from sounding sing-songy? What is the predominant meter?

3. What is it that "pull[s]" the boy along in lines 15–16?

4. Why do you think Hadas titled the poem "The Red Hat" rather than, for example, "Paths Part" (line 9)?

5. CRITICAL STRATEGIES. Read the section on psychological criticism (pp. 2099–2101) in Chapter 52, "Critical Strategies for Reading." How does the speaker reveal her personal psychology in this poem?

CONNECTION TO ANOTHER SELECTION

1. In an essay discuss the themes of "The Red Hat" and Bosselaar's "The Bumper-Sticker" (p. 811). Pay particular attention to the way parents are presented in each poem.

ROBERT HERRICK (1591–1674)
Delight in Disorder   1648

A sweet disorder in the dress
Kindles in clothes a wantonness.
A lawn° about the shoulders thrown   *linen scarf*
Into a fine distraction;
An erring lace, which here and there   5
Enthralls the crimson stomacher,
A cuff neglectful, and thereby
Ribbons to flow confusedly;
A winning wave, deserving note,
In the tempestuous petticoat;   10

A careless shoestring, in whose tie
I see a wild civility;
Do more bewitch me than when art
Is too precise in every part.

CONSIDERATIONS FOR CRITICAL THINKING AND WRITING

1. FIRST RESPONSE. Why does the speaker in this poem value "disorder" so highly? How do the poem's organization and rhythmic order relate to its theme? Are they "precise in every part"?

2. Which words in the poem indicate disorder? Which words indicate the speaker's response to that disorder? What are the connotative meanings of each set of words? Why are they appropriate? What do they suggest about the woman and the speaker?

3. Write a short essay in which you agree or disagree with the speaker's views on dress.

BEN JONSON (1573–1637)
Still to Be Neat   1609

Still° to be neat, still to be dressed,   *continually*
As you were going to a feast;
Still to be powdered, still perfumed;
Lady, it is to be presumed,
Though art's hid causes are not found,   5
All is not sweet, all is not sound.

Give me a look, give me a face
That makes simplicity a grace;
Robes loosely flowing, hair as free;
Such sweet neglect more taketh me   10
Then all th' adulteries of art.
They strike mine eyes, but not my heart.

CONSIDERATIONS FOR CRITICAL THINKING AND WRITING

1. FIRST RESPONSE. What are the speaker's reservations about the lady in the first stanza? What do you think "sweet" means in line 6?

2. What does the speaker want from the lady in the second stanza? How has the meaning of "sweet" shifted from line 6 to line 10? What other words in the poem are especially charged with connotative meanings?

3. How do the rhythms of Jonson's lines help to reinforce meanings? Pay particular attention to lines 6 and 12.

CONNECTIONS TO OTHER SELECTIONS

1. Write an essay comparing the themes of "Still to Be Neat" and Herrick's preceding poem, "Delight in Disorder." How do the speakers make similar points but from different perspectives?

2. How does the rhythm of "Still to Be Neat" compare with that of "Delight in Disorder"? Which do you find more effective? Explain why.

DIANE BURNS (B. 1950)

Sure You Can Ask Me a Personal Question 1981

How do you do?
   No, I am not Chinese.
No, not Spanish.
   No, I am American Indi — uh, Native American.
No, not from India.   5
   No, not Apache.
No, not Navajo.
   No, not Sioux.
No, we are not extinct.
   Yes, Indin.   10
Oh?
   So that's where you got those high cheekbones.
Your great grandmother, huh?
   An Indian Princess, huh?
Hair down to there?   15
   Let me guess. Cherokee?
Oh, so you've had an Indian friend?
   That close?
Oh, so you've had an Indian lover?
   That tight?   20
Oh, so you've had an Indian servant?
   That much?
Yeah, it was awful what you guys did to us.
   It's real decent of you to apologize.
No. I don't know where you can get peyote.   25
   No, I don't know where you can get Navajo rugs real cheap.
No, I didn't make this. I bought it at Bloomingdales.
   Thank you. I like your hair too.
I don't know if anyone knows whether or not Cher is really Indian.
   No, I didn't make it rain tonight.   30
Yeah. Uh-huh. Spirituality.
   Uh-huh. Yeah. Spirituality. Uh-huh. Mother
Earth. Yeah. Uh-huh. Uh-huh. Spirituality.
   No. I didn't major in archery.
Yeah, a lot of us drink too much.   35
   Some of us can't drink enough.
This ain't no stoic look.
   This is my face.

CONSIDERATIONS FOR CRITICAL THINKING AND WRITING

1. FIRST RESPONSE. What sort of person do you imagine the speaker is addressing?

2. Discuss the poem's humor. Does it also have a serious theme? Explain.

3. What is the effect of the repeated phrases throughout the poem?

WILLIAM BLAKE (1757–1827)

The Lamb   1789

    Little Lamb, who made thee?
    Dost thou know who made thee?
Gave thee life, and bid thee feed
By the stream and o'er the mead;
Gave thee clothing of delight,   5
Softest clothing, wooly, bright;
Gave thee such a tender voice,
Making all the vales rejoice?
    Little Lamb, who made thee?
    Dost thou know who made thee?   10

    Little Lamb, I'll tell thee,
    Little Lamb, I'll tell thee:
He is callèd by thy name,
For he calls himself a Lamb.
He is meek, and he is mild;   15
He became a little child.
I a child, and thou a lamb,
We are callèd by his name.
    Little Lamb, God bless thee!
    Little Lamb, God bless thee!   20

CONSIDERATIONS FOR CRITICAL THINKING AND WRITING

1. FIRST RESPONSE. This poem is from Blake's *Songs of Innocence*. Describe its tone. How do the meter, rhyme, and repetition help to characterize the speaker's voice?

2. Why is it significant that the animal addressed by the speaker is a lamb? What symbolic value would be lost if the animal were, for example, a doe?

3. How does the second stanza answer the question raised in the first? What is the speaker's view of the creation?

WILLIAM BLAKE (1757–1827)

The Tyger   1794

Tyger! Tyger! burning bright
In the forests of the night,
What immortal hand or eye
Could frame thy fearful symmetry?

In what distant deeps or skies   5
Burnt the fire of thine eyes?
On what wings dare he aspire?
What the hand dare seize the fire?

And what shoulder, and what art,
Could twist the sinews of thy heart?   10
And when thy heart began to beat,
What dread hand? and what dread feet?

What the hammer? what the chain?
In what furnace was thy brain?
What the anvil? what dread grasp   15
Dare its deadly terrors clasp?

When the stars threw down their spears,
And watered heaven with their tears,
Did he smile his work to see?
Did he who made the Lamb make thee?   20

Tyger! Tyger! burning bright
In the forests of the night,
What immortal hand or eye
Dare frame thy fearful symmetry?

CONSIDERATIONS FOR CRITICAL THINKING AND WRITING

1. FIRST RESPONSE. This poem from Blake's *Songs of Experience* is often paired
   with "The Lamb." Describe the poem's tone. Is the speaker's voice the same
   here as in "The Lamb"? Which words are repeated, and how do they contribute to the tone?

2. What is revealed about the nature of the tiger by the words used to describe
   its creation? What do you think the tiger symbolizes?

3. Unlike in "The Lamb," more than one question is raised in "The Tyger."
   What are these questions? Are they answered?

4. Compare the rhythms in "The Lamb" and "The Tyger." Each basically uses
   a seven-syllable line, but the effects are very different. Why?

5. Using these two poems as the basis of your discussion, describe what distinguishes innocence from experience.

ANNA LAETITIA BARBAULD (1743–1825)

On a Lady's Writing   1773

Her even lines her steady temper show,
Neat as her dress, and polished as her brow;
Strong as her judgment, easy as her air;
Correct though free, and regular though fair:
And the same graces o'er her pen preside,
That form her manners and her footsteps guide.

CONSIDERATIONS FOR CRITICAL THINKING AND WRITING

1. FIRST RESPONSE. How does the date of this poem affect your reading of it? Would your response be any different if you had come across it in a magazine last week?
2. How is the style of this poem related to its meaning? More specifically, how do "Her even lines her steady temper show"?
3. Why is "On a Lady's Writing" a more appropriate title than, say, "On a Woman's Writing"?

CONNECTION TO ANOTHER SELECTION

1. Discuss the idea of order in "On a Lady's Writing" and in Robert Herrick's "Delight in Disorder" (p. 873). How does each poem implicitly—though coincidentally—comment on the other?

ALFRED, LORD TENNYSON (1809–1892)
The Charge of the Light Brigade   *1855*

1

Half a league, half a league,
  Half a league onward,
All in the valley of Death
  Rode the six hundred.
"Forward, the Light Brigade!   5
Charge for the guns!" he said:
Into the valley of Death
  Rode the six hundred.

2

"Forward, the Light Brigade!"
Was there a man dismayed?   10
Not though the soldier knew
  Some one had blundered:
Their's not to make reply,
Their's not to reason why,
Their's but to do and die: 15
Into the valley of Death
  Rode the six hundred.

3

Cannon to right of them,
Cannon to left of them,
Cannon in front of them   20
  Volleyed and thundered;
Stormed at with shot and shell,
Boldly they rode and well,
Into the jaws of Death,
Into the mouth of Hell   25
  Rode the six hundred.

4

Flashed all their sabers bare,
Flashed as they turned in air
Sabring the gunners there,
Charging an army, while   30
    All the world wondered:
Plunged in the battery-smoke
Right through the line they broke;
Cossack and Russian
Reeled from the saber-stroke   35
    Shattered and sundered.
Then they rode back, but not
    Not the six hundred.

5

Cannon to right of them,
Cannon to left of them,
Cannon behind them   40
    Volleyed and thundered;
Stormed at with shot and shell,
While horse and hero fell,
They that had fought so well   45
Came through the jaws of Death,
Back from the mouth of Hell,
All that was left of them,
    Left of six hundred.

6

When can their glory fade?   50
O the wild charge they made!
    All the world wondered.
Honor the charge they made!
Honor the Light Brigade,
    Noble six hundred!   55

CONSIDERATIONS FOR CRITICAL THINKING AND WRITING

1. FIRST RESPONSE. How do the meter and rhyme contribute to the meaning of this poem's lines?

2. What is the speaker's attitude toward war?

3. Describe the tone, paying particular attention to stanza 2.

CONNECTION TO ANOTHER SELECTION

1. Compare the theme of "The Charge of the Light Brigade" with Owen's "Dulce et Decorum Est" (p. 764).

THEODORE ROETHKE (1908–1963)

My Papa's Waltz

1948

The whiskey on your breath
Could make a small boy dizzy;
But I hung on like death:
Such waltzing was not easy.

We romped until the pans   5
Slid from the kitchen shelf;
My mother's countenance
Could not unfrown itself.

The hand that held my wrist
Was battered on one knuckle;   10
At every step you missed
My right ear scraped a buckle.

You beat time on my head
With a palm caked hard by dirt,
Then waltzed me off to bed   15
Still clinging to your shirt.

CONSIDERATIONS FOR CRITICAL THINKING AND WRITING

1. FIRST RESPONSE. What details characterize the father in this poem? How
   does the speaker's choice of words reveal his feeling about his father? Is the
   remembering speaker still a boy?
2. Characterize the rhythm of the poem. Does it move "like death," or is it more
   like a waltz? Is the rhythm regular throughout the poem? What is its effect?
3. Comment on the appropriateness of the title. Why do you suppose
   Roethke didn't use "My Father's Waltz"?

ARON KEESBURY (B. 1971)

Song to a Waitress

1997

Yes. I want a big fat cup of coffee and
I want it hot. I want a big hot cup
of coffee in a big fat mug. And bring
it here and put it down and get the hell

away from me. And I want sugar in   5
a jar. A glass jar. Big, fat, glass jar with
a metal top and none of them pink, pansy
sugar packs in dainty little cups.

And come back every now and then and fill
my big fat mug and keep it hot and full.   10

And I don't want to hear your waitress talk
and I don't want to see you smile. So fill

my big fat mug and get the hell away.
I don't want to see your face today.

CONSIDERATIONS FOR CRITICAL THINKING AND WRITING

1. FIRST RESPONSE. What does this speaker want?
2. What is the predominant metrical pattern in the poem? Where does the poem deviate from that pattern? How do these deviations affect the speaker's tone?
3. In what ways does this poem resemble a sonnet? How does it differ? (See p. 888 for a description of a sonnet.) What do the similarities and differences to the form add to your understanding of the speaker's intent?
4. What is the effect of the repetition of "big," "fat," and "mug" throughout the poem? What other patterns of repetition can you find? Why does the speaker repeat those specific words when he does?

CONNECTION TO ANOTHER SELECTION

1. Write a reply to the speaker in "Song to a Waitress" from the point of view of the waitress. You might begin by writing a prose paragraph and then try organizing it into lines of poetry. Read Machan's "Hazel Tells LaVerne" (p. 723) for a source of inspiration.

EDWARD HIRSCH (B. 1950)
Fast Break   1985

(In Memory of Dennis Turner, 1946–1984)

A hook shot kisses the rim and
hangs there, helplessly, but doesn't drop

and for once our gangly starting center
boxes out his man and times his jump

perfectly, gathering the orange leather   5
from the air like a cherished possession

and spinning around to throw a strike
to the outlet who is already shoveling

an underhand pass toward the other guard
scissoring past a flat-footed defender   10

who looks stunned and nailed to the floor
in the wrong direction, turning to catch sight

of a high, gliding dribble and a man
letting the play develop in front of him

in slow motion, almost exactly   15
like a coach's drawing on the blackboard,

both forwards racing down the court
the way that forwards should, fanning out

and filling the lanes in tandem, moving
together as brothers passing the ball   20

between them without a dribble, without
a single bounce hitting the hardwood

until the guard finally lunges out
and commits to the wrong man

while the power-forward explodes past them   25
in a fury, taking the ball into the air

by himself now and laying it gently
against the glass for a layup,

but losing his balance in the process,
inexplicably falling, hitting the floor   30

with a wild, headlong motion
for the game he loved like a country

and swiveling back to see an orange blur
floating perfectly through the net.

CONSIDERATIONS FOR CRITICAL THINKING AND WRITING

1. FIRST RESPONSE. How might this poem — to borrow a phrase from Robert
   Frost — represent a "momentary stay against confusion"?
2. Why are run-on lines especially appropriate for this poem? How do they
   affect its sound and sense? Do the lines have a regular meter? What is the
   effect of the poem being one long sentence?
3. In addition to accurately describing a fast break, this poem is a tribute to a
   dead friend. How are the two purposes related in the poem?
4. CRITICAL STRATEGIES. Read the section on cultural criticism (pp. 2104–05) in
   Chapter 52, "Critical Strategies for Reading." How are contemporary
   attitudes and values associated with basketball incorporated into the poem?

DAVID BARBER (B. 1960)

A Colonial Epitaph Annotated   *1999*

Here lies as silent clay
Miss Arabella Young
Who on the 21st of May, 1771
Began to hold her tongue

Here rests as circumspect dust   5
A maid who spoke her mind

Without the ghost of a blush
Or a nod to her prim kind.

Here silt her tart remarks
And her spirited retorts,   10
Her mordant takes on politics
And the sermon's finer points.

Here chafes in stony hush
An erstwhile spitfire.
Finally they can rest in peace,   15
The fools she wouldn't suffer!

Here in her boneyard bower
Look sharp for the shards of a quip.
The lady was no flower.
She'd cut you to the quick.   20

Here beneath this slate
You can sense her mute dismay,
Who was the soul of wit
And revelled in repartee.

Here lies as silent clay   25
Miss Arabella Young.
Be that as it may,
Here's to the sting in her tongue.

CONSIDERATIONS FOR CRITICAL THINKING AND WRITING

1. FIRST RESPONSE. Based on just the first four lines, the original epitaph, what sort of person do you think Arabella Young was thought to be by her contemporaries?

2. How does the rest of the poem serve as a spirited toast to Arabella Young from the perspective of more than two hundred years later?

3. Comment on rhymes in stanzas three and four. How are they different from the other stanzas?

4. Try writing an additional stanza for the original epitaph as you think it would have been written in 1771.

CONNECTION TO ANOTHER SELECTION

1. Compare the rhythms and themes of this poem with those of "On a Lady's Writing" by Anna Laetitia Barbauld (p. 877).

PERSPECTIVE

LOUISE BOGAN (1897–1970)

On Formal Poetry   *1953*

What is formal poetry? It is poetry written in form. And what is *form?* The elements of form, so far as poetry is concerned, are meter and rhyme. Are these elements merely mold and ornaments that have been impressed upon poetry from without? Are they indeed restrictions which bind and fetter language and the thought and emotion behind, under, within language in a repressive way? Are they arbitrary rules which have lost all validity since they have been broken to good purpose by "experimental poets," ancient and modern? Does the breaking up of form, or its total elimination, always result in an increase of power and of effect; and is any return to form a sort of relinquishment of freedom, or retreat to old fogeyism?

From *A Poet's Alphabet*

CONSIDERATIONS FOR CRITICAL THINKING AND WRITING

1. Choose one of the questions Bogan raises and write an essay in response to it using two or three poems from this chapter to illustrate your answer.

2. Try writing a poem in meter and rhyme. Does the experience make your writing feel limited or not?

28

Poetic Forms

Poems come in a variety of shapes. Although the best poems always have their own unique qualities, many of them also conform to traditional patterns. Frequently the *form* of a poem — its overall structure or shape — follows an already established design. A poem that can be categorized by the patterns of its lines, meter, rhymes, and stanzas is considered a *fixed form* because it follows a prescribed model such as a sonnet. However, poems written in a fixed form do not always fit models precisely; writers sometimes work variations on traditional forms to create innovative effects.

Not all poets are content with variations on traditional forms. Some prefer to create their own structures and shapes. Poems that do not conform to established patterns of meter, rhyme, and stanza are called *free verse* or *open form* poetry. (See Chapter 29 for further discussion of open forms.) This kind of poetry creates its own ordering principles through the careful arrangement of words and phrases in line lengths that embody rhythms appropriate to the meaning. Modern and contemporary poets in particular have learned to use the blank space on the page as a significant functional element (for a striking example, see Cummings's "in Just-" (p. 913). Good poetry of this kind is structured in ways that can be as demanding, interesting, and satisfying as fixed forms. Open and fixed forms represent different poetic styles, but they are identical in the sense that both use language in concentrated ways to convey meanings, experiences, emotions, and effects.

SOME COMMON POETIC FORMS

A familiarity with some of the most frequently used fixed forms of poetry is useful because it allows for a better understanding of how a poem works. Classifying patterns allows us to talk about the effects of established rhythm and rhyme and recognize how significant variations from them affect the pace and meaning of the lines. An awareness of form also allows us to anticipate how a poem is likely to proceed. As we shall see, a sonnet creates a different set of expectations in a reader from those of, say, a limerick. A reader isn't likely to find in limericks the kind of serious themes that often make their way into sonnets. The discussion that follows identifies some of the important poetic forms frequently encountered in English poetry.

The shape of a fixed form poem is often determined by the way in which the lines are organized into stanzas. A *stanza* consists of a grouping of lines, set off by a space, that usually has a set pattern of meter and rhyme. This pattern is ordinarily repeated in other stanzas throughout the poem. What is usual is not obligatory, however; some poems may use a different pattern for each stanza, somewhat like paragraphs in prose.

Traditionally, though, stanzas do share a common *rhyme scheme,* the pattern of end rhymes. We can map out rhyme schemes by noting patterns of rhyme with lowercase letters: the first rhyme sound is designated *a,* the second becomes *b,* the third *c,* and so on. Using this system, we can describe the rhyme scheme in the following poem this way: *aabb, ccdd, eeff.*

A. E. HOUSMAN (1859–1936)

Loveliest of trees, the cherry now   *1896*

Loveliest of trees, the cherry now	*a*
Is hung with bloom along the bough,	*a*
And stands about the woodland ride	*b*
Wearing white for Eastertide.	*b*
Now, of my threescore years and ten,	*c* 5
Twenty will not come again,	*c*
And take from seventy springs a score,	*d*
It only leaves me fifty more.	*d*
And since to look at things in bloom	*e*
Fifty springs are little room,	*e* 10
About the woodlands I will go	*f*
To see the cherry hung with snow.	*f*

CONSIDERATIONS FOR CRITICAL THINKING AND WRITING

1. FIRST RESPONSE. What is the speaker's attitude in this poem toward time and life?

2. Why is spring an appropriate season for the setting rather than, say, winter?

3. Paraphrase each stanza. How do the images in each reinforce the poem's themes?

4. Lines 1 and 12 are not intended to rhyme, but they are close. What is the effect of the near rhyme of "now" and "snow"? How does the rhyme enhance the theme?

Poets often create their own stanzaic patterns; hence there is an infinite number of kinds of stanzas. One way of talking about stanzaic forms is to describe a given stanza by how many lines it contains.

A *couplet* consists of two lines that usually rhyme and have the same meter; couplets are frequently not separated from each other by space on the page. A *heroic couplet* consists of rhymed iambic pentameter. Here is an example from Pope's "An Essay on Criticism":

One science only will one genius fit;	*a*
So vast is art, so narrow human wit:	*a*
Not only bounded to peculiar arts,	*b*
But oft in those confined to single parts.	*b*

A *tercet* is a three-line stanza. When all three lines rhyme they are called a *triplet.* Two triplets make up this captivating poem.

ROBERT HERRICK (1591–1674)

Upon Julia's Clothes 1648

Whenas in silks my Julia goes,	*a*
Then, then, methinks, how sweetly flows	*a*
That liquefaction of her clothes.	*a*
Next, when I cast mine eyes, and see	*b*
That brave vibration, each way free,	*b*
O, how that glittering taketh me!	*b*

CONSIDERATIONS FOR CRITICAL THINKING AND WRITING

1. FIRST RESPONSE. What purpose does alliteration serve in this poem?
2. Comment on the effect of the meter. How is it related to the speaker's description of Julia's clothes?
3. Look up the word *brave* in the *Oxford English Dictionary*. Which of its meanings is appropriate to describe Julia's movement? Some readers interpret lines 4–6 to mean that Julia has no clothes on. What do you think?

CONNECTION TO ANOTHER SELECTION

1. Compare the tone of this poem with that of Humphrey's "Blow" (p. 856). Are the situations and speakers similar? Is there any difference in tone between these two poems?

Terza rima consists of an interlocking three-line rhyme scheme: *aba, bcb, cdc, ded,* and so on. Dante's *The Divine Comedy* uses this pattern, as does Frost's "Acquainted with the Night" (p. 802) and Percy Bysshe Shelley's "Ode to the West Wind" (p. 905).

A *quatrain,* or four-line stanza, is the most common stanzaic form in the English language and can have various meters and rhyme schemes (if any). The most common rhyme schemes are *aabb, abba, aaba,* and *abcb.* This last pattern is especially characteristic of the popular **ballad stanza,** which consists of alternating eight- and six-syllable lines. Samuel Taylor Coleridge adopted this pattern in "The Rime of the Ancient Mariner"; here is one representative stanza:

> All in a hot and copper sky
> The bloody Sun, at noon,
> Right up above the mast did stand,
> No bigger than the Moon.

There are a number of longer stanzaic forms and the list of types of stanzas could be extended considerably, but knowing these three most basic patterns should prove helpful to you in talking about the form of a great many poems. In addition to stanzaic forms, there are fixed forms that characterize entire poems. Lyric poems can be, for example, sonnets, villanelles, sestinas, or epigrams.

Sonnet

The **sonnet** has been a popular literary form in English since the sixteenth century, when it was adopted from the Italian *sonnetto,* meaning "little song." A sonnet consists of fourteen lines, usually written in iambic pentameter. Because the sonnet has been such a favorite form, writers have experimented with many variations on its essential structure. Nevertheless, there are two basic types of sonnets: the Italian and the English.

The **Italian sonnet** (also known as the **Petrarchan sonnet,** from the fourteenth-century Italian poet Petrarch) divides into two parts. The first eight lines (the **octave**) typically rhyme *abbaabba.* The final six lines (the **sestet**) may vary; common patterns are *cdecde, cdcdcd,* and *cdccdc.* Very often the octave presents a situation, attitude, or problem that the sestet comments upon or resolves, as in John Keats's "On First Looking into Chapman's Homer."

JOHN KEATS (1795–1821)

On First Looking into Chapman's Homer°   *1816*

> Much have I traveled in the realms of gold,
>   And many goodly states and kingdoms seen;
>   Round many western islands have I been
> Which bards in fealty to Apollo° hold.
> Oft of one wide expanse had I been told   5
>   That deep-browed Homer ruled as his demesne;

Chapman's Homer: Before reading George Chapman's (c. 1560–1634) poetic Elizabethan translations of Homer's *Iliad* and *Odyssey,* Keats had known only stilted and pedestrian eighteenth-century translations.   4 *Apollo:* Greek god of poetry.

Yet did I never breathe its pure serene°   *atmosphere*
Till I heard Chapman speak out loud and bold:
Then felt I like some watcher of the skies
    When a new planet swims into his ken;   10
Or like stout Cortez° when with eagle eyes
    He stared at the Pacific — and all his men
Looked at each other with a wild surmise —
    Silent, upon a peak in Darien.

11 *Cortez:* Vasco Núñez de Balboa, not Hernando Cortés, was the first European to sight the Pacific from Darien, a peak in Panama.

CONSIDERATIONS FOR CRITICAL THINKING AND WRITING

1. FIRST RESPONSE. How do the images shift from the octave to the sestet? How does the tone change? Does the meaning?
2. What is the controlling metaphor of this poem?
3. What is it that the speaker discovers?
4. How does the rhythm of the lines change between the octave and the sestet? How does that change reflect the tones of both the octave and the sestet?
5. Does Keats's mistake concerning Cortés and Balboa affect your reading of the poem? Explain why or why not.

The Italian sonnet pattern is also used in the next sonnet, but notice that the thematic break between octave and sestet comes within line 9 rather than between lines 8 and 9. This unconventional break helps to reinforce the speaker's impatience with the conventional attitudes he describes.

WILLIAM WORDSWORTH (1770–1850)
The World Is Too Much with Us   *1807*

The world is too much with us; late and soon,
Getting and spending, we lay waste our powers;
Little we see in Nature that is ours;
We have given our hearts away, a sordid boon!
This Sea that bares her bosom to the moon;   5
The winds that will be howling at all hours,
And are up-gathered now like sleeping flowers;
For this, for everything, we are out of tune;
It moves us not. — Great God! I'd rather be
A Pagan suckled in a creed outworn;   10
So might I, standing on this pleasant lea,
Have glimpses that would make me less forlorn;
Have sight of Proteus rising from the sea;
Or hear old Triton blow his wreathèd horn.

CONSIDERATIONS FOR CRITICAL THINKING AND WRITING

1. FIRST RESPONSE. What is the speaker's complaint in this sonnet? How do the conditions described affect him?

2. Look up "Proteus" and "Triton." What do these mythological allusions contribute to the sonnet's tone?

3. What is the effect of the personification of the sea and wind in the octave?

CONNECTION TO ANOTHER SELECTION

1. Compare the theme of this sonnet with that of Hopkins's "God's Grandeur" (p. 843).

The *English sonnet,* more commonly known as the *Shakespearean sonnet,* is organized into three quatrains and a couplet, which typically rhyme *abab cdcd efef gg.* This rhyme scheme is more suited to English poetry because English has fewer rhyming words than Italian. English sonnets, because of their four-part organization, also have more flexibility about where thematic breaks can occur. Frequently, however, the most pronounced break or turn comes with the concluding couplet.

In the following Shakespearean sonnet, the three quatrains compare the speaker's loved one to a summer's day and explain why the loved one is even more lovely. The couplet bestows eternal beauty and love upon both the loved one and the sonnet.

WILLIAM SHAKESPEARE (1564–1616)

Shall I compare thee to a summer's day?   1609

Shall I compare thee to a summer's day?
Thou art more lovely and more temperate:
Rough winds do shake the darling buds of May,
And summer's lease hath all too short a date.
Sometime too hot the eye of heaven shines,   5
And often is his gold complexion dimmed;
And every fair from fair sometime declines,
By chance, or nature's changing course, untrimmed.
But thy eternal summer shall not fade,
Nor lose possession of that fair thou ow'st°   *possess* 10
Nor shall death brag thou wand'rest in his shade,
When in eternal lines to time thou grow'st.
    So long as men can breathe or eyes can see,
    So long lives this, and this gives life to thee.

CONSIDERATIONS FOR CRITICAL THINKING AND WRITING

1. FIRST RESPONSE. Describe the shift in tone and subject matter that begins in line 9.

2. Why is the speaker's loved one more lovely than a summer's day? What qualities does he admire in the loved one?

3. What does the couplet say about the relation between art and love?
4. Which syllables are stressed in the final line? How do these syllables relate to the meaning of the line?

Sonnets have been the vehicles for all kinds of subjects, including love, death, politics, and cosmic questions. Although most sonnets tend to treat their subjects seriously, this fixed form does not mean a fixed expression; humor is also possible in it. Compare this next Shakespearean sonnet with "Shall I compare thee to a summer's day?" They are, finally, both love poems, but their tones are markedly different.

WILLIAM SHAKESPEARE (1564–1616)

My mistress' eyes are nothing like the sun   1609

My mistress' eyes are nothing like the sun;
Coral is far more red than her lips' red;
If snow be white, why then her breasts are dun;
If hairs be wires, black wires grow on her head.
I have seen roses damasked red and white,   5
But no such roses see I in her cheeks;
And in some perfumes is there more delight
Than in the breath that from my mistress reeks.
I love to hear her speak, yet well I know
That music hath a far more pleasing sound;   10
I grant I never saw a goddess go:
My mistress, when she walks, treads on the ground.
    And yet, by heaven, I think my love as rare
    As any she,° belied with false compare.   *lady*

CONSIDERATIONS FOR CRITICAL THINKING AND WRITING

1. FIRST RESPONSE. What does "mistress" mean in this sonnet? Write a description of this particular mistress based on the images used in the sonnet.
2. What sort of person is the speaker? Does he truly love the woman he describes?
3. In what sense are this sonnet and "Shall I compare thee to a summer's day" about poetry as well as love?

EDNA ST. VINCENT MILLAY (1892–1950)

I will put Chaos into fourteen lines   1954

I will put Chaos into fourteen lines
And keep him there; and let him thence escape
If he be lucky; let him twist, and ape
Flood, fire, and demon — his adroit designs
Will strain to nothing in the strict confines   5

Of this sweet Order, where, in pious rape,
I hold his essence and amorphous shape,
Till he with Order mingles and combines.
Past are the hours, the years, of our duress,
His arrogance, our awful servitude: 10
I have him. He is nothing more nor less
Than something simple not yet understood;
I shall not even force him to confess;
Or answer. I will only make him good.

CONSIDERATIONS FOR CRITICAL THINKING AND WRITING

1. FIRST RESPONSE. Does the poem contain "Chaos"? If so, how? If not, why not?

2. What properties of a sonnet does this poem possess?

3. What do you think is meant by the phrase "pious rape" in line 6?

4. What is the effect of the personification in the poem?

5. CRITICAL STRATEGIES. Read the section on formalist criticism (pp. 2095–97) in Chapter 52, "Critical Strategies for Reading." How does the work's structure resolve the issues raised in the poem?

CONNECTION TO ANOTHER SELECTION

1. Compare the theme of this poem with that of Robert Frost's "Design" (p. 1018).

MARK DOTY (B. 1953)

Golden Retrievals   *1998*

Fetch? Balls and sticks capture my attention
seconds at a time. Catch? I don't think so.
Bunny, tumbling leaf, a squirrel who's — oh
joy — actually scared. Sniff the wind, then

I'm off again: muck, pond, ditch, residue   5
of any thrillingly dead thing. And you?
Either you're sunk in the past, half our walk,
thinking of what you never can bring back,

or else you're off in some fog concerning
— tomorrow, is that what you call it? My work: 10
to unsnare time's warp (and woof!), retrieving,
my haze-headed friend, you. This shining bark,

a Zen master's bronzy gong, calls you here,
entirely, now: bow-wow, bow-wow, bow-wow.

CONSIDERATIONS FOR CRITICAL THINKING AND WRITING

1. FIRST RESPONSE. In what sense is the purpose (and voice) of this sonnet a golden retrieval?

2. How does the dog differ from the master? And what does the master need to learn from the dog?

3. As simple as the final line is, how and why does it work so well as the conclusion to this poem?

CONNECTION TO ANOTHER SELECTION

1. Compare the relationship between dog and master in this poem and horse and owner in Robert Frost's "Stopping by Woods on a Snowy Evening" (p. 1015). Though these poems are quite different in tone, what similarities do you find in their themes?

MOLLY PEACOCK (B. 1947)

Desire   1984

It doesn't speak and it isn't schooled,
like a small foetal animal with wettened fur.
It is the blind instinct for life unruled,
visceral frankincense and animal myrrh.
It is what babies bring to kings,   5
an eyes-shut, ears-shut medicine of the heart
that smells and touches endings and beginnings
without the details of time's experienced *part-
fit-into-part-fit-into-part*. Like a paw,
it is blunt; like a pet who knows you   10
and nudges your knee with its snout—but more raw
and blinder and younger and more divine, too,
than the tamed wild—it's the drive for what is real,
deeper than the brain's detail: the drive to feel.

CONSIDERATIONS FOR CRITICAL THINKING AND WRITING

1. FIRST RESPONSE. Taken together, what do all the metaphors that appear in this poem reveal about the speaker's conception of desire?

2. What is the "it" being described in lines 3–5? How do the allusions to the three wise men relate to the other metaphors used to define desire?

3. How is this English sonnet structured? What is the effect of its irregular meter?

CONNECTION TO ANOTHER SELECTION

1. Compare the treatment of desire in this poem with that of Ackerman's "A Fine, a Private Place" (p. 732). In an essay, identify the theme of each poem and compare their conceptions of desire. How alike are these two poems?

MARK JARMAN (B. 1952)

Unholy Sonnet   1993

After the praying, after the hymn-singing,
After the sermon's trenchant commentary
On the world's ills, which make ours secondary,
After communion, after the hand-wringing,
And after peace descends upon us, bringing   5
Our eyes up to regard the sanctuary
And how the light swords through it, and how, scary
In their sheer numbers, motes of dust ride, clinging—
There is, as doctors say about some pain,
Discomfort knowing that despite your prayers,   10
Your listening and rejoicing, your small part
In this communal stab at coming clean,
There is one stubborn remnant of your cares
Intact. There is still murder in your heart.

CONSIDERATIONS FOR CRITICAL THINKING AND WRITING

1. FIRST RESPONSE. Describe the rhyme scheme and structure of this sonnet. Explain why it is an English or Italian sonnet.

2. What are the effects of the use of "after" in lines 1, 2, 4, and 5 and "there" in lines 9, 13, and 14?

3. In what sense might this poem be summed up as a "communal stab" (line 12)? Discuss the accuracy of this assessment.

4. Try writing a reply to the theme of Jarman's poem using the same sonnet form that he uses.

CONNECTIONS TO OTHER SELECTIONS

1. Jarman has said that his "Unholy Sonnets" (there are about twenty of them) are modeled after John Donne's *Holy Sonnets* but that he does not share the same Christian assumptions about faith and mercy that inform Donne's sonnets. Instead, Jarman says, he "work[s] against any assumption or shared expression of faith, to write a devotional poetry against the grain." Keeping this statement in mind, write an essay comparing and contrasting the tone and theme of Jarman's sonnet with John Donne's "Batter My Heart" (p. 1155) or "Death Be Not Proud" (p. 938).

Villanelle

The *villanelle* is a fixed form consisting of nineteen lines of any length divided into six stanzas: five tercets and a concluding quatrain. The first and third lines of the initial tercet rhyme; these rhymes are repeated in each subsequent tercet (*aba*) and in the final two lines of the quatrain (*abaa*). Moreover, line 1 appears in its entirety as lines 6, 12, and 18, while line 3 appears as lines 9, 15, and 19. This form may seem to risk monotony, but in

competent hands a villanelle can create haunting echoes, as in Dylan
Thomas's "Do not go gentle into that good night."

DYLAN THOMAS (1914–1953)

Do not go gentle into that good night   *1952*

Do not go gentle into that good night,
Old age should burn and rave at close of day;
Rage, rage against the dying of the light.

Though wise men at their end know dark is right,
Because their words had forked no lightning they   5
Do not go gentle into that good night.

Good men, the last wave by, crying how bright
Their frail deeds might have danced in a green bay,
Rage, rage against the dying of the light.

Wild men who caught and sang the sun in flight,   10
And learn, too late, they grieved it on its way,
Do not go gentle into that good night.

Grave men, near death, who see with blinding sight
Blind eyes could blaze like meteors and be gay,
Rage, rage against the dying of the light.   15

And you, my father, there on the sad height,
Curse, bless, me now with your fierce tears, I pray.
Do not go gentle into that good night.
Rage, rage against the dying of the light.

CONSIDERATIONS FOR CRITICAL THINKING AND WRITING

1. FIRST RESPONSE. How does Thomas vary the meanings of the poem's two
   refrains: "Do not go gentle into that good night," and "Rage, rage against
   the dying of the light"?
2. Thomas's father was close to death when this poem was written. How does
   the tone contribute to the poem's theme?
3. How is "good" used in line 1?
4. Characterize the men who are "wise" (line 4), "Good" (7), "Wild" (10), and
   "Grave" (13).
5. What do figures of speech contribute to this poem?
6. Discuss this villanelle's sound effects.

CONNECTION TO ANOTHER SELECTION

1. In Thomas's poem we experience "rage against the dying of the light." Contrast this with the rage you find in Sylvia Plath's "Daddy" (p. 1177). What
   produces the emotion in Plath's poem?

ROBYN SARAH (B. 1949)

Villanelle for a Cool April 1998

I like a leafing-out by increments,
— not bolting bloom, in sudden heat begun.
Life's sweetest savoured in the present tense.

I like to watch the shadows pack their tents
before the creep of the advancing sun. 5
I like a leafing-out by increments:

to watch the tendrils inch along the fence,
to take my pleasures slow and one by one.
Life's sweetest savoured in the present tense.

Oh, leave tomorrow's fruit to providence 10
and dote upon the bud — from which is spun
a leafing-out to love in increments,

a greening in the cool of swooning sense,
a feathered touch, a button just undone.
Life's sweetest savoured in the present tense, 15

as love when it withholds and then relents,
as a cool April lets each moment stun.
I like a leafing-out by increments;
life's sweetest savoured in the present tense.

CONSIDERATIONS FOR CRITICAL THINKING AND WRITING

1. FIRST RESPONSE. How is "a cool April" compared to a love relationship?
2. Examine the poem carefully to determine if its structure is that of a conventional villanelle. Are there any significant variations?
3. Discuss how the images serve to reinforce the idea that life can be "savoured" best when it's "a leafing-out by increments."

CONNECTIONS TO OTHER SELECTIONS

1. Compare this description of April with Margaret Atwood's "February" (p. 787) and Sophie Cabot Black's "August" (p. 788). Which poem did you find to be the most effective description of a month? Explain why.

Sestina

Although the *sestina* usually does not rhyme, it is perhaps an even more demanding fixed form than the villanelle. A sestina consists of thirty-nine lines of any length divided into six, six-line stanzas and a three-line concluding stanza called an *envoy*. The difficulty is in repeating the six words at the ends of the first stanza's lines at the ends of the lines in the other five, six-line stanzas as well. Those words must also appear in the final three lines, where they often resonate important themes. The sestina originated in the Middle Ages, but contemporary poets continue to find it a fascinating and challenging form.

Elizabeth Bishop (1911–1979)

Sestina   1965

September rain falls on the house.
In the failing light, the old grandmother
sits in the kitchen with the child
beside the Little Marvel Stove,
reading the jokes from the almanac,   5
laughing and talking to hide her tears.

She thinks that her equinoctial tears
and the rain that beats on the roof of the house
were both foretold by the almanac,
but only known to a grandmother.   10
The iron kettle sings on the stove.
She cuts some bread and says to the child,

It's time for tea now; but the child
is watching the teakettle's small hard tears
dance like mad on the hot black stove,   15
the way the rain must dance on the house.
Tidying up, the old grandmother
hangs up the clever almanac

on its string. Birdlike, the almanac
hovers half open above the child,   20
hovers above the old grandmother
and her teacup full of dark brown tears.
She shivers and says she thinks the house
feels chilly, and puts more wood in the stove.

It was to be, says the Marvel Stove.   25
I know what I know, says the almanac.
With crayons the child draws a rigid house
and a winding pathway. Then the child
puts in a man with buttons like tears
and shows it proudly to the grandmother.   30

But secretly, while the grandmother
busies herself about the stove,
the little moons fall down like tears
from between the pages of the almanac
into the flower bed the child   35
has carefully placed in the front of the house.

Time to plant tears, says the almanac.
The grandmother sings to the marvelous stove
and the child draws another inscrutable house.

CONSIDERATIONS FOR CRITICAL THINKING AND WRITING

1. FIRST RESPONSE. How are the six end words — "house," "grandmother," "child," "stove," "almanac," and "tears" — central to the sestina's meaning?

2. Number the end words of the first stanza 1, 2, 3, 4, 5, and 6, and then use those numbers for the corresponding end words in the remaining five stanzas to see how the pattern of the line-end words is worked out in this sestina. Also locate the six end words in the envoy.

3. What happens in this sestina? Why is the grandmother "laughing and talking to hide her tears" (line 6)?

4. Underline the images that seem especially vivid to you. What effects do they create? What is the tone of the sestina?

5. How is the almanac used symbolically? Does Bishop use any other symbols to convey meanings?

6. CRITICAL STRATEGIES. Read the section on psychological criticism (pp. 2099–2101) in Chapter 52, "Critical Strategies for Reading." Write a brief essay explaining why you think a poet might derive pleasure from writing in a fixed form such as a villanelle or sestina. Can you think of similar activities outside the field of writing in which discipline and restraint give pleasure? How might this reflect an author's personal psychology?

FLORENCE CASSEN MAYERS (B. 1940)

All-American Sestina   1996

One nation, indivisible
two-car garage
three strikes you're out
four-minute mile
five-cent cigar   5
six-string guitar

six-pack Bud
one-day sale
five-year warranty
two-way street   10
fourscore and seven years ago
three cheers

three-star restaurant
sixty-
four-dollar question   15
one-night stand
two-pound lobster
five-star general

five-course meal
three sheets to the wind   20
two bits
six-shooter
one-armed bandit
four-poster

four-wheel drive   25
five-and-dime
hole in one
three-alarm fire
sweet sixteen
two-wheeler   30

two-tone Chevy
four rms, hi flr, w/vu
six-footer
high five
three-ring circus   35
one-room schoolhouse

two thumbs up, five-karat diamond
Fourth of July, three-piece suit
six feet under, one-horse town

CONSIDERATIONS FOR CRITICAL THINKING AND WRITING

1. FIRST RESPONSE. Discuss the significance of the title; what is "All-American"? Why a sestina?

2. How is the structure of this poem different from a conventional sestina? (What structural requirement does Mayers add for this sestina?)

3. Do you think important themes are raised by this poem, as is traditional for a sestina? If so, what are they? If not, what is being played with by using this convention?

4. CRITICAL STRATEGIES. Read the section on cultural criticism (pp. 2104–05) in Chapter 52, "Critical Strategies for Reading," and discuss how this poem incorporates aspects of American culture and how it makes an implicit comment upon that culture.

CONNECTION TO ANOTHER SELECTION

1. Describe and compare the strategy used to create meaning in "All-American Sestina" with that used by Cummings in "next to of course god america i" (p. 809).

Epigram

An *epigram* is a brief, pointed, and witty poem. Although most rhyme and often are written in couplets, epigrams take no prescribed form. Instead, they are typically polished bits of compressed irony, satire, or paradox. Here is an epigram that defines itself.

SAMUEL TAYLOR COLERIDGE (1772–1834)

What Is an Epigram?   1802

What is an epigram? A dwarfish whole;
Its body brevity, and wit its soul.

These additional examples by A. R. Ammons, David McCord, and Paul Laurence Dunbar satisfy Coleridge's definition.

A. R. AMMONS (1926–2001)

Coward   1975

Bravery runs in my family.

DAVID McCORD (1897–1997)

Epitaph on a Waiter   1954

By and by
God caught his eye.

PAUL LAURENCE DUNBAR (1872–1906)

Theology   1896

There is a heaven, for ever, day by day,
The upward longing of my soul doth tell me so.
There is a hell, I'm quite as sure; for pray,
If there were not, where would my neighbors go?

CONSIDERATIONS FOR CRITICAL THINKING AND WRITING

1. FIRST RESPONSE. In what sense is each of these epigrams, as Coleridge puts it, a "dwarfish whole"?
2. Explain which of these epigrams, in addition to being witty, makes a serious point.
3. Try writing a few epigrams that say something memorable about whatever you choose to focus upon.

Limerick

The *limerick* is always light and humorous. Its usual form consists of five predominantly anapestic lines rhyming *aabba;* lines 1, 2, and 5 contain three feet, while lines 3 and 4 contain two. Limericks have delighted everyone from schoolchildren to sophisticated adults, and they range in subject matter from the simply innocent and silly to the satiric or obscene. The sexual humor helps to explain why so many limericks are written anonymously. Here is one that is anonymous but more concerned with physics than physiology:

There was a young lady named Bright,
Who traveled much faster than light,
    She started one day
    In a relative way,
And returned on the previous night.

This next one is a particularly clever definition of a limerick.

LAURENCE PERRINE (B. 1915)

The limerick's never averse   1982

The limerick's never averse
To expressing itself in a terse
    Economical style,
    And yet, all the while,
The limerick's *always* a verse.

CONSIDERATIONS FOR CRITICAL THINKING AND WRITING

1. FIRST RESPONSE. How does this limerick differ from others you know? How is it similar?

2. Scan Perrine's limerick. How do the lines measure up to the traditional fixed metrical pattern?

3. Try writing a limerick. Use the following basic pattern.

    ˘ ˘ ´   ˘ ˘ ´   ˘ ˘ ´
    ˘ ˘ ´   ˘ ˘ ´   ˘ ˘ ´
        ˘ ˘ ´   ˘ ˘ ´
        ˘ ˘ ´   ˘ ˘ ´
    ˘ ˘ ´   ˘ ˘ ´   ˘ ˘ ´

You might begin with a friend's name or the name of your school or town. Your instructor is, of course, fair game, too, provided your tact matches your wit.

And here's a real tongue twister:

KEITH CASTO

She Don't Bop   1987

A nervous young woman named Trudy
Was at odds with a horn player, Rudy.
His horn so annoyed her
The neighbors would loiter
To watch Rudy toot Trudy fruity.

Haiku

Another brief fixed poetic form, borrowed from the Japanese, is the *haiku*. A haiku is usually described as consisting of seventeen syllables organized into three unrhymed lines of five, seven, and five syllables. Owing to language difference, however, English translations of haiku are often only approximated, because a Japanese haiku exists in time (Japanese syllables have duration). The number of syllables in our sense is not as significant as the duration. These poems typically present an intense emotion or vivid image of nature, which, in the Japanese, are also designed to lead to a spiritual insight.

MATSUO BASHŌ (1644–1694)

Under cherry trees   *date unknown*

Under cherry trees
Soup, the salad, fish and all . . .
Seasoned with petals.

CAROLYN KIZER (B. 1925)

After Bashō   *1984*

Tentatively, you
slip onstage this evening,
pallid, famous moon.

CONSIDERATIONS FOR CRITICAL THINKING AND WRITING

1. FIRST RESPONSE. What different emotions do these two haiku evoke?
2. What differences and similarities are there between the effects of a haiku and those of an epigram?
3. Compose a haiku. Try to make it as allusive and suggestive as possible.

Elegy

An elegy in classical Greek and Roman literature was written in alternating hexameter and pentameter lines. Since the seventeenth century, however, the term *elegy* has been used to describe a lyric poem written to commemorate someone who is dead. The word is also used to refer to a serious meditative poem produced to express the speaker's melancholy thoughts. Elegies no longer conform to a fixed pattern of lines and stanzas, but their characteristic subject is related to death and their tone is mournfully contemplative.

SEAMUS HEANEY (B. 1939)

Mid-term Break   *1966*

I sat all morning in the college sick bay
Counting bells knelling classes to a close.
At two o'clock our neighbors drove me home.

In the porch I met my father crying —
He had always taken funerals in his stride —   5
And Big Jim Evans saying it was a hard blow.

The baby cooed and laughed and rocked the pram
When I came in, and I was embarrassed
By old men standing up to shake my hand

And tell me they were "sorry for my trouble,"   10
Whispers informed strangers I was the eldest,
Away at school, as my mother held my hand

In hers and coughed out angry tearless sighs.
At ten o'clock the ambulance arrived
With the corpse, stanched and bandaged by the nurses.   15

Next morning I went up into the room. Snowdrops
And candles soothed the bedside; I saw him
For the first time in six weeks. Paler now,

Wearing a poppy bruise on his left temple,
He lay in the four foot box as in his cot.   20
No gaudy scars, the bumper knocked him clear.

A four foot box, a foot for every year.

CONSIDERATIONS FOR CRITICAL THINKING AND WRITING

1. FIRST RESPONSE. What effect does the title have on your understanding of
   the speaker? What else does the title imply?

2. How do simple details contribute to the effects of this elegy?

3. Does this elegy use any kind of formal pattern for its structure? What is the
   effect of the last line standing by itself?

4. Another spelling for *stanched* (line 15) is *staunched*. Usage is about evenly divided between the two in the United States. What is the effect of Heaney's
   choosing the former spelling rather than the latter?

CONNECTIONS TO OTHER SELECTIONS

1. Compare Heaney's elegy with A. E. Housman's "To an Athlete Dying
   Young" (p. 1164). Which do you find more moving? Explain why.

2. Write an essay comparing this story of a boy's death with Updike's "Dog's
   Death" (p. 673). Do you think either of the poems is sentimental? Explain
   why or why not.

ANDREW HUDGINS (B. 1951)

Elegy for My Father, Who Is Not Dead 1991

One day I'll lift the telephone
and be told my father's dead. He's ready.
In the sureness of his faith, he talks
about the world beyond this world
as though his reservations have 5
been made. I think he wants to go,
a little bit — a new desire
to travel building up, an itch
to see fresh worlds. Or older ones.
He thinks that when I follow him 10
he'll wrap me in his arms and laugh,
the way he did when I arrived
on earth. I do not think he's right.
He's ready. I am not. I can't
just say good-bye as cheerfully 15
as if he were embarking on a trip
to make my later trip go well.
I see myself on deck, convinced
his ship's gone down, while he's convinced
I'll see him standing on the dock 20
and waving, shouting, Welcome back.

CONSIDERATIONS FOR CRITICAL THINKING AND WRITING

1. FIRST RESPONSE. Why does this speaker elegize his father if the father "is not dead"?

2. How does the speaker's view of immortality differ from his father's?

3. Explain why you think this is an optimistic or pessimistic poem — or explain why these two categories fail to describe the poem.

4. In what sense can this poem be regarded as an elegy?

CONNECTION TO ANOTHER SELECTION

1. Write an essay comparing attitudes toward death in this poem and in Thomas's "Do not go gentle into that good night" (p. 895). Both speakers invoke their fathers, nearer to death than they are; what impact does this have?

Ode

An *ode* is characterized by a serious topic and formal tone, but no prescribed formal pattern describes all odes. In some odes the pattern of each stanza is repeated throughout, while in others each stanza introduces a new pattern. Odes are lengthy lyrics that often include lofty emotions conveyed by a dignified style. Typical topics include truth, art, freedom, justice, and the meaning of life. Frequently such lyrics tend to be more public than private, and their speakers often employ apostrophe.

PERCY BYSSHE SHELLEY (1792–1822)

Ode to the West Wind   1820

I

O wild West Wind, thou breath of Autumn's being,
Thou, from whose unseen presence the leaves dead
Are driven, like ghosts from an enchanter fleeing,

Yellow, and black, and pale, and hectic red,
Pestilence-stricken multitudes: O thou,   5
Who chariotest to their dark wintry bed

The wingèd seeds, where they lie cold and low,
Each like a corpse within its grave, until
Thine azure sister of the Spring shall blow

Her clarion o'er the dreaming earth, and fill   10
(Driving sweet buds like flocks to feed in air)
With living hues and odors plain and hill:

Wild Spirit, which art moving everywhere;
Destroyer and preserver; hear, oh, hear!

II

Thou on whose stream, mid the steep sky's commotion,   15
Loose clouds like earth's decaying leaves are shed,
Shook from the tangled boughs of Heaven and Ocean,

Angels° of rain and lightning: there are spread   *messengers*
On the blue surface of thine airy surge,
Like the bright hair uplifted from the head   20

Of some fierce Maenad,° even from the dim verge
Of the horizon to the zenith's height,
The locks of the approaching storm. Thou dirge

Of the dying year, to which this closing night
Will be the dome of a vast sepulcher,   25
Vaulted with all thy congregated might

Of vapors, from whose solid atmosphere
Black rain, and fire, and hail will burst: oh, hear!

III

Thou who didst waken from his summer dreams
The blue Mediterranean, where he lay,   30
Lulled by the coil of his crystálline streams,

---

21 *Maenad:* In Greek mythology, a frenzied worshiper of Dionysus, god of wine and fertility.

Beside a pumice isle in Baiae's bay,°
And saw in sleep old palaces and towers
Quivering within the wave's intenser day,

All overgrown with azure moss and flowers   35
So sweet, the sense faints picturing them! Thou
For whose path the Atlantic's level powers

Cleave themselves into chasms, while far below
The sea-blooms and the oozy woods which wear
The sapless foliage of the ocean, know   40

Thy voice, and suddenly grow gray with fear,
And tremble and despoil themselves: oh, hear!

IV
If I were a dead leaf thou mightest bear;
If I were a swift cloud to fly with thee;
A wave to pant beneath thy power, and share   45

The impulse of thy strength, only less free
Than thou, O uncontrollable! If even
I were as in my boyhood, and could be

The comrade by thy wanderings over Heaven,
As then, when to outstrip thy skyey speed   50
Scarce seemed a vision; I would ne'er have striven

As thus with thee in prayer in my sore need.
Oh, lift me as a wave, a leaf, a cloud!
I fall upon the thorns of life! I bleed!

A heavy weight of hours has chained and bowed   55
One too like thee: tameless, and swift, and proud.

V
Make me thy lyre,° even as the forest is:
What if my leaves are falling like its own!
The tumult of thy mighty harmonies

Will take from both a deep, autumnal tone,   60
Sweet though in sadness. Be thou, Spirit fierce,
My spirit! Be thou me, impetuous one!

Drive my dead thoughts over the universe
Like withered leaves to quicken a new birth!
And, by the incantation of this verse,   65

Scatter, as from an unextinguished hearth
Ashes and sparks, my words among mankind!
Be through my lips to unawakened earth

The trumpet of a prophecy! O Wind,
If Winter comes, can Spring be far behind?   70

---

32 *Baiae's bay:* A bay in the Mediterranean Sea.   57 *Make me thy lyre:* Sound is produced
on an Aeolian lyre, or wind harp, by wind blowing across its strings.

CONSIDERATIONS FOR CRITICAL THINKING AND WRITING

1. FIRST RESPONSE. Write a summary of each of this ode's five sections.

2. What is the speaker's situation? What is his "sore need" (line 52)? What does the speaker ask of the wind in lines 57–70?

3. What does the wind signify in this ode? How is it used symbolically?

4. Determine the meter and rhyme of the first five stanzas. How do these elements contribute to the ode's movement? Is this pattern continued in the other four sections?

Picture Poem

By arranging lines into particular shapes, poets can sometimes organize typography into *picture poems* of what they describe. Words have been arranged into all kinds of shapes, from apples to light bulbs. Notice how the shape of this next poem embodies its meaning.

MICHAEL MCFEE (B. 1954)

In Medias Res°   *1985*

His waist
like the plot
thickens, wedding
pants now breathtaking,
belt no longer the cinch   5
it once was, belly's cambium
expanding to match each birthday,
his body a wad of anonymous tissue
swung in the same centrifuge of years
that separates a house from its foundation,   10
undermining sidewalks grim with joggers
and loose-filled graves and families
and stars collapsing on themselves,
no preservation society capable
of plugging entropy's dike,   15
under his zipper's sneer
a belly hibernation-
soft, ready for
the kill.

In Medias Res: A Latin term for a story that begins "in the middle of things."

CONSIDERATIONS FOR CRITICAL THINKING AND WRITING

1. FIRST RESPONSE. Explain how the title is related to this poem's shape. How is the meaning related?

2. Identify the puns. How do they work in the poem?

3. What is "cambium" (line 6)? Why is the phrase "belly's cambium" especially appropriate?
4. What is the tone of this poem? Is it consistent throughout?

Parody

A *parody* is a humorous imitation of another, usually serious, work. It can take any fixed or open form because parodists imitate the tone, language, and shape of the original. While a parody may be teasingly close to a work's style, it typically deflates the subject matter to make the original seem absurd. Parody can be used as a kind of literary criticism to expose the defects in a work, but it is also very often an affectionate acknowledgment that a well-known work has become both institutionalized in our culture and fair game for some fun. Read Marvell's "To His Coy Mistress" (p. 728) and then study this parody.

PETER DE VRIES (B. 1910)

To His Importunate Mistress

1986

Andrew Marvell Updated

Had we but world enough, and time,
My coyness, lady, were a crime,
But at my back I always hear
Time's wingèd chariot, striking fear
The hour is nigh when creditors   5
Will prove to be my predators.
As wages of our picaresque,
Bag lunches bolted at my desk
Must stand as fealty to you
For each expensive rendezvous.   10
Obeisance at your marble feet
Deserves the best-appointed suite,
And would have, lacked I not the pelf
To pleasure also thus myself;
But aptly sumptuous amorous scenes   15
Rule out the rake of modest means.

Since mistress presupposes wife,
It means a doubly costly life;
For fools by second passion fired
A second income is required,   20
The earning which consumes the hours
They'd hoped to spend in rented bowers.
To hostelries the worst of fates
That weekly raise their daily rates!

I gather, lady, from your scoffing 25
A bloke more solvent in the offing.
So revels thus to rivals go
For want of monetary flow.
How vexing that inconstant cash
The constant suitor must abash, 30
Who with excuses vainly pled
Must rue the undisheveled bed,
And that for paltry reasons given
His conscience may remain unriven.

CONSIDERATIONS FOR CRITICAL THINKING AND WRITING

1. FIRST RESPONSE. To what extent does this poem duplicate Marvell's style? How does it differ?

2. How is De Vries's use of "mistress" different from Marvell's? How does the speaker's complaint in this poem differ from that in "To His Coy Mistress"?

3. Explain how "picaresque" is used in line 7.

4. Choose a poet whose work you know reasonably well or would like to know better and determine what is characteristic about his or her style. Then choose a poem to parody. It's probably best to attempt a short poem or a section of a long work. If you have difficulty selecting an author, you might consider Herrick, Blake, Keats, Dickinson, Whitman, or Frost, since a number of their works are included in this book.

CONNECTIONS TO OTHER SELECTIONS

1. Read Anthony Hecht's "The Dover Bitch" (p. 1160), a parody of Arnold's "Dover Beach" (p. 758). Write an essay comparing the effectiveness of Hecht's parody with that of De Vries's "To His Importunate Mistress." Which parody do you prefer? Explain why.

Here's a parody for all seasons—not just Christmas—that brings together two popular icons of our culture.

X. J. KENNEDY (B. 1929)

A Visit from St. Sigmund   1993

Freud is just an old Santa Claus.
    —*Margaret Mead°*

'Twas the night before Christmas, when all through each kid
Not an Ego was stirring, not even an Id.
The hangups were hung by the chimney with care
In hopes that St. Sigmund Freud soon would be there.

Margaret Mead (1901-1978): Noted American anthropologist.

The children in scream class had knocked off their screams,   5
Letting Jungian archetypes dance through their dreams,
And Mamma with her bra off and I on her lap
Had just snuggled down when a vast thunderclap
Boomed and from my unconscious arose such a chatter
As Baptist John's teeth made on Salome's platter.   10
Away from my darling I flew like a flash,
Tore straight to the bathroom and threw up, and — *smash!*
Through the windowpane hurtled and bounced on the floor
A big brick — holy smoke, it was hard to ignore.
As I heard further thunderclaps — lo and behold —   15
Came a little psychiatrist eighty years old.
He drove a wheeled couch pulled by five fat psychoses
And the gleam in his eye might induce a hypnosis.
Like subliminal meanings his coursers they came
And, consulting his notebook, he called them by name: 20
"Now Schizo, now Fetish, now Fear of Castration!
On Paranoia! on Penis-fixation!
Ach, yes, that big brick through your glass I should mention:
Just a simple device to compel your attention.
You need, boy, to be in an analyst's power: 25
You talk, I take notes — fifty schillings an hour."
A bag full of symbols he'd slung on his back;
He looked smug as a junk-peddler laden with smack
Or a shrewd politician soliciting votes
And his chinbeard was stiff as a starched billygoat's.   30
Then laying one finger aside of his nose,
He chortled, "What means this? Mein Gott, I suppose
There's a meaning in fingers, in candles und wicks,
In mouseholes und doughnut holes, steeples und sticks.
You see, it's the imminent prospect of sex   35
That makes all us humans run round till we're wrecks,
Und each innocent infant since people began
Wants to bed with his momma und kill his old man;
So never you fear that you're sick as a swine —
Your hangups are every sane person's und mine.   40
Even Hamlet was hot for his mom — there's the rub;
Even Oedipus Clubfoot was one of the club.
Hmmm, that's humor unconscious." He gave me rib-pokes
And for almost two hours explained phallic jokes.
Then he sprang to his couch, to his crew gave a nod,   45
And away they all flew like the concept of God.
In the worst of my dreams I can hear him shout still,
"Merry Christmas to all! In the mail comes my bill."

CONSIDERATIONS FOR CRITICAL THINKING AND WRITING

1. FIRST RESPONSE. What makes Freud a particularly appropriate substitute for Santa Claus? How does this substitute facilitate the poem's humor?
2. What is the tone of this parody? How does the quotation from Margaret Mead help to establish the poem's tone?

3. What do you think is the poet's attitude toward Freud? Cite specific lines to support your point.

4. Is the focus of this parody the Christmas story or Freud? Explain your response.

PERSPECTIVES

ROBERT MORGAN (B. 1944)

On the Shape of a Poem

1983

In the body of the poem, lineation is part flesh and part skeleton, as form is the towpath along which the burden of content, floating on the formless, is pulled. All language is both mental and sacramental, is not "real" but is the working of lip and tongue to subvert the "real." Poems empearl irritating facts until they become opalescent spheres of moment, not so much résumés of history as of human faculties working with pain. Every poem is necessarily a fragment empowered by its implicitness. We sing to charm the snake in our spines, to make it sway with the pulse of the world, balancing the weight of consciousness on the topmost vertebra.

From *Epoch,* Fall/Winter 1983

CONSIDERATIONS FOR CRITICAL THINKING AND WRITING

1. Explain Morgan's metaphors for describing lineation and form in a poem. Why are these metaphors useful?

2. Choose one of the poems in this chapter that makes use of a particular form and explain how it is "a fragment empowered by its implicitness."

ELAINE MITCHELL (B. 1924)

Form

1994

Is it a corset
or primal wave?
Don't try to force it.

Even endorse it
to shape and deceive.   5
Ouch, too tight a corset.

Take it off. No remorse. It
's an ace up your sleeve.
No need to force it.

Can you make a horse knit?   10
Who would believe?
Consider. Of course, it

might be a resource. Wit,
your grateful slave.
Form. Sometimes you force it,   15

sometimes divorce it
to make it behave.
So don't try to force it.
Respect a good corset.

Considerations for Critical Thinking and Writing

1. FIRST RESPONSE. What is the speaker's attitude toward form?

2. Explain why you think the form of this poem does or does not conform to the advice of the speaker.

3. Why is the metaphor of a corset a particularly apt image for this poem?

29

Open Form

Many poems, especially those written in the twentieth century, are composed of lines that cannot be scanned for a fixed or predominant meter.
Moreover, very often these poems do not rhyme. Known as *free verse* (from
the French, *vers libre*), such lines can derive their rhythmic qualities from
the repetition of words, phrases, or grammatical structures; the arrangement of words on the printed page; or some other means. In recent years
the term **open form** has been used in place of *free verse* to avoid the erroneous suggestion that this kind of poetry lacks all discipline and shape.

Although the following two poems do not use measurable meters, they
do have rhythm.

E. E. CUMMINGS (1894–1962)

in Just-   *1923*

in Just-
spring   when the world is mud-
luscious the little
lame balloonman

whistles   far   and wee   5

and eddieandbill come
running from marbles and
piracies and it's
spring

when the world is puddle-wonderful   10

the queer
old balloonman whistles
far   and   wee
and bettyandisbel come dancing

from hop-scotch and jump-rope and   15

it's
spring
and
  the

     goat-footed   20

balloonMan   whistles
far
and
wee

CONSIDERATIONS FOR CRITICAL THINKING AND WRITING

1. FIRST RESPONSE. What is the effect of this poem's arrangement of words
   and use of space on the page? How would the effect differ if it was written
   out in prose?
2. What is the effect of Cummings's combining the names "eddieandbill" and
   "bettyandisbel"?
3. The allusion in line 20 refers to Pan, a Greek god associated with nature.
   How does this allusion add to the meaning of the poem?

WALT WHITMAN (1819–1892)
From "I Sing the Body Electric"   *1855*

O my body! I dare not desert the likes of you in other men and women,
    nor the likes of the parts of you,
I believe the likes of you are to stand or fall with the likes of the soul, (and
    that they are the soul,)
I believe the likes of you shall stand or fall with my poems, and that they
    are my poems.
Man's, woman's, child's, youth's, wife's, husband's, mother's, father's,
    young man's, young woman's poems.
Head, neck, hair, ears, drop and tympan of the ears.   5
Eyes, eye-fringes, iris of the eye, eyebrows, and the waking or sleeping of
    the lids,
Mouth, tongue, lips, teeth, roof of the mouth, jaws, and the jaw-hinges,
Nose, nostrils of the nose, and the partition,
Cheeks, temples, forehead, chin, throat, back of the neck, neck-slue,
Strong shoulders, manly beard, scapula, hind-shoulders, and the ample
    side-round of the chest,   10
Upper-arm, armpit, elbow-socket, lower-arm, arm-sinews, arm-bones,
Wrist and wrist-joints, hand, palm, knuckles, thumb, forefinger, finger-
    joints, finger-nails,
Broad breast-front, curling hair of the breast, breast-bone, breast-side,
Ribs, belly, backbone, joints of the backbone,
Hips, hip-sockets, hip-strength, inward and outward round, man-balls,
    man-root,   15

Strong set of thighs, well carrying the trunk above,
Leg-fibers, knee, knee-pan, upper-leg, under-leg,
Ankles, instep, foot-ball, toes, toe-joints, the heel;
All attitudes, all the shapeliness, all the belongings of my or your body or
    of any one's body, male or female,
The lung-sponges, the stomach-sac, the bowels sweet and clean,   20
The brain in its folds inside the skull-frame,
Sympathies, heart-valves, palate-valves, sexuality, maternity,
Womanhood, and all that is a woman, and the man that comes from woman,
The womb, the teats, nipples, breast-milk, tears, laughter, weeping, love-
    looks, love-perturbations and risings,
The voice, articulation, language, whispering, shouting aloud,   25
Food, drink, pulse, digestion, sweat, sleep, walking, swimming,
Poise on the hips, leaping, reclining, embracing, arm-curving and tightening,
The continual changes of the flex of the mouth, and around the eyes,
The skin, the sunburnt shade, freckles, hair,
The curious sympathy one feels when feeling with the hand the naked
    meat of the body,   30
The circling rivers the breath, and breathing it in and out,
The beauty of the waist, and thence of the hips, and thence downward
    toward the knees,
The thin red jellies within you or within me, the bones and the marrow
    in the bones,
The exquisite realization of health;
O I say these are not the parts and poems of the body only, but of the soul, 35
O I say now these are the soul!

CONSIDERATIONS FOR CRITICAL THINKING AND WRITING

1. FIRST RESPONSE. What informs this speaker's attitude toward the human body?

2. Read the poem aloud. Is it simply a tedious enumeration of body parts, or do the lines achieve some kind of rhythmic cadence?

PERSPECTIVE

WALT WHITMAN (1819–1892)

On Rhyme and Meter   *1855*

The poetic quality is not marshaled in rhyme or uniformity or abstract addresses to things nor in melancholy complaints or good precepts, but is the life of these and much else and is in the soul. The profit of rhyme is that it drops seeds of a sweeter and more luxuriant rhyme, and of uniformity that it conveys itself into its own roots in the ground out of sight. The rhyme and uniformity of perfect poems show the free growth of metrical laws and bud from them as unerringly and loosely as lilacs or roses on a bush, and take shapes as compact as the shapes of chestnuts and oranges and melons and pears, and shed the perfume impalpable to form. The fluency and ornaments of the finest poems or music or orations or recitations are not independent but dependent. All beauty comes from beautiful blood and a beautiful brain. If the greatnesses are in conjunction in a man or woman it is enough . . . the fact will prevail through the universe . . . but the gaggery and gilt of a million years will not prevail. Who troubles himself about his ornaments or fluency is lost.

From the preface to the 1855 edition of *Leaves of Grass*

CONSIDERATIONS FOR CRITICAL THINKING AND WRITING

1. According to Whitman, what determines the shape of a poem?
2. Why does Whitman prefer open forms over fixed forms such as the sonnet?
3. Is Whitman's poetry devoid of any structure or shape? Choose one of his poems (listed in the index) to illustrate your answer.

Open form poetry is sometimes regarded as formless because it is unlike the strict fixed forms of a sonnet, villanelle, or sestina. But even though open form poems may not employ traditional meters and rhymes, they still rely on an intense use of language to establish rhythms and relations between meaning and form. Open form poems use the arrangement of words and phrases on the printed page, pauses, line lengths, and other means to create unique forms that express their particular meaning and tone.

Cummings's "in Just-" and the excerpt from Whitman's "I Sing the Body Electric" demonstrate how the white space on a page and rhythmic cadences can be aligned with meaning, but there is one kind of open form poetry that doesn't even look like poetry on a page. A *prose poem* is printed as prose and represents, perhaps, the most clear opposite of fixed forms. Here is a brief example.

JAY MEEK (B. 1937)

Swimmers   1994

Coming out of the theater, in the light of the marquee, I can see there is something on my clothing and my hands. When I look back I can see it on the others too, the light off the screen on their faces during the film, or the grey illuminations made at night by summer lightning. It doesn't go away. We are covered with it, like grease, and when by accident we touch each other, we feel it on our bodies. It is not sensual, not exciting. It is slippery, this film over our lives, so that when we come up against one another and slide away, it is as if nothing has happened: we go on, as though swimming the channel at night, lights on the water, hundreds of us rising up on the beach on the far side.

CONSIDERATIONS FOR CRITICAL THINKING AND WRITING

1. FIRST RESPONSE. What is the effect of this prose poem? Does it have a theme?

2. What, if anything, is poetic in this work?

3. Arrange the lines so that they look like poetry on a page. What determines where you break the lines?

Much of the poetry published today is written in open form; however, many poets continue to take pleasure in the requirements imposed by fixed forms. Some write both fixed form and open form poetry. Each kind offers rewards to careful readers as well. Here are several more open form poems that establish their own unique patterns.

GALWAY KINNELL (B. 1927)

After Making Love We Hear Footsteps   *1980*

For I can snore like a bullhorn
or play loud music
or sit up talking with any reasonably sober Irishman
and Fergus will only sink deeper
into his dreamless sleep, which goes by all in one flash,   5
but let there be that heavy breathing
or a stifled come-cry anywhere in the house
and he will wrench himself awake
and make for it on the run — as now, we lie together,
after making love, quiet, touching along the length of our bodies,   10
familiar touch of the long-married,
and he appears — in his baseball pajamas, it happens,
the neck opening so small
he has to screw them on, which one day may make him wonder
about the mental capacity of baseball players —   15
and says, "Are you loving and snuggling? May I join?"
He flops down between us and hugs us and snuggles himself to sleep,
his face gleaming with satisfaction at being this very child.

In the half darkness we look at each other
and smile
and touch arms across his little, startlingly muscled body —   20
this one whom habit of memory propels to the ground of his making,
sleeper only the mortal sounds can sing awake,
this blessing love gives again into our arms.

CONSIDERATIONS FOR CRITICAL THINKING AND WRITING

1. FIRST RESPONSE. Explore Kinnell's line endings. Why does he break the lines where he does?

2. How does the speaker's language reveal his character?

3. Describe the shift in tone between lines 18 and 19 with the shift in focus from child to adult. How does the use of space here emphasize this shift?

4. Do you think this poem is sentimental? Explain why or why not.

CONNECTION TO ANOTHER SELECTION

1. Discuss how this poem helps to bring into focus the sense of loss Robert Frost evokes in "Home Burial" (p. 1005).

KELLY CHERRY (B. 1940)

Alzheimer's 1990

He stands at the door, a crazy old man
Back from the hospital, his mind rattling
Like the suitcase, swinging from his hand,
That contains shaving cream, a piggy bank,
A book he sometimes pretends to read, 5
His clothes. On the brick wall beside him
Roses and columbine slug it out for space, claw the mortar.
The sun is shining, as it does late in the afternoon
In England, after rain.
Sun hardens the house, reifies it, 10
Strikes the iron grillwork like a smithy
And sparks fly off, burning in the bushes —
The rosebushes —
While the white wood trim defines solidity in space.
This is his house. He remembers it as his, 15
Remembers the walkway he built between the front room
And the garage, the rhododendron he planted in back,
The car he used to drive. He remembers himself,
A younger man, in a tweed hat, a man who loved
Music. There is no time for that now. No time for music, 20
The peculiar screeching of strings, the luxurious
Fiddling with emotion.
Other things have become more urgent.
Other matters are now of greater import, have more
Consequence, must be attended to. The first 25
Thing he must do, now that he is home, is decide who
This woman is, this old, white-haired woman
Standing here in the doorway,
Welcoming him in.

CONSIDERATIONS FOR CRITICAL THINKING AND WRITING

1. FIRST RESPONSE. Why is it impossible to dismiss the character in this poem as merely "a crazy old man"?

2. Discuss the effect of the line breaks in lines 1–6 of the first complete sentence of the poem. How do the line breaks contribute to the meaning of these lines?

3. What do the images in lines 6–20 indicate about the nature of the man's memory?

4. Why is the final image of the "white-haired woman" especially effective? How does the final line serve as the emotional climax of the poem?

CONNECTION TO ANOTHER SELECTION

1. Compare the treatment of remembering and forgetting in "Alzheimer's" and in Sarah Lindsay's "Aluminum Chlorohydrate" (p. 725). How does the final image of an old woman in each poem affect your understanding of the poem's thematics?

WILLIAM CARLOS WILLIAMS (1883–1963)

The Red Wheelbarrow   1923

so much depends
upon

a red wheel
barrow

glazed with rain
water

beside the white
chickens.

CONSIDERATIONS FOR CRITICAL THINKING AND WRITING

1. FIRST RESPONSE. What "depends upon" the things mentioned in the poem? What is the effect of these images? Do they have a particular meaning?

2. Do these lines have any kind of rhythm?

3. How does this poem resemble a haiku? How is it different?

KATE RUSHIN (B. 1951)

The Black Back-Ups   1993

This is dedicated to Merry Clayton, Fontella Bass, Vonetta
Washington, Carolyn Franklin, Yolanda McCullough,
Carolyn Willis, Gwen Guthrie, Helaine Harris, and Darlene
Love. This is for all of the Black women who sang back-up for
Elvis Presley, John Denver, James Taylor, Lou Reed.   5
Etc. Etc. Etc.

I said Hey Babe
Take a Walk on the Wild Side
I said Hey Babe
Take a Walk on the Wild Side   10

And the colored girls say
Do dodo do do dodododo
Do dodo do do dodododo
Do dodo do do dodododo ooooo

This is for my Great-Grandmother Esther, my Grandmother   15
Addie, my grandmother called Sister, my Great-Aunt
Rachel, my Aunt Hilda, my Aunt Tine, my Aunt Breda,
my Aunt Gladys, my Aunt Helen, my Aunt Ellie,
my Cousin Barbara, my Cousin Dottie and my Great-Great-
Aunt Vene.   20

This is dedicated to all the Black women riding on buses
and subways back and forth to the Main Line, Haddonfield,
Cherry Hill and Chevy Chase. This is for the women who
spend their summers in Rockport, Newport, Cape Cod and
Camden, Maine. This is for the women who open those   25
bundles of dirty laundry sent home from those ivy-covered
campuses.

My Great-Aunt Rachel worked for the Carters
Ever since I can remember
There was *The Boy*   30
Whose name I never knew
And there was *The Girl*
Whose name was Jane

Great-Aunt Rachel brought Jane's dresses for me to wear
Perfectly Good Clothes   35
And I should've been glad to get them
Perfectly Good Clothes
No matter they didn't fit quite right
Perfectly Good Clothes
Brought home in a brown paper bag   40
With an air of accomplishment and excitement
Perfectly Good Clothes
Which I hated

At school
In Ohio   45
I swear to Gawd
There was always somebody
Telling me that the only person
In their whole house
Who listened and understood them   50
Despite the money and the lessons
Was the housekeeper

And I knew it was true
But what was I supposed to say

I know it's true   55
I watch her getting off the train
Moving slowly toward the Country Squire
With her uniform in her shopping bag
And the closer she gets to the car
The more the two little kids jump and laugh   60
And even the dog is about to
Turn inside out
Because they just can't wait until she gets there
Edna Edna   Wonderful Edna

But Aunt Edna to me, or Gram, or Miz Johnson, or   65
Sister Johnson on Sundays

And the colored girls say
Do dodo do do dodododo
Do dodo do do dodododo
Do dodo do do dodododo ooooo   70

This is for Hattie McDaniels, Butterfly McQueen
Ethel Waters
Sapphire
Saphronia
Ruby Begonia   75
Aunt Jemima
Aunt Jemima on the Pancake Box
Aunt Jemima on the Pancake Box?
AuntJemimaonthepancakebox?
Ainchamamaonthepancakebox?   80
Ain't chure Mama on the pancake box?

Mama Mama
Get off that box
And come home to me
And my Mama leaps off that box   85
She swoops down in her nurse's cape
Which she wears on Sunday
And for Wednesday night prayer meeting
And she wipes my forehead
And she fans my face   90
And she makes me a cup of tea
And it don't do a thing for my real pain
Except she is my mama

Mama Mommy Mammy
Mam-mee Mam-mee   95
I'd Walk a Mill-yon Miles
For one of your smiles

This is for the Black Back-Ups
This is for my mama and your mama
My grandma and your grandma   100
This is for the thousand thousand Black Back-Ups

And the colored girls say
Do   dodo   do do   dododo
do   dodo
*   dodo*   105
*   do*
*   do*

CONSIDERATIONS FOR CRITICAL THINKING AND WRITING

1. FIRST RESPONSE. What do you think is the point of the many dedications
   to various black women throughout the poem? In what sense are they all
   "Black Back-Ups"?

2. There are many allusions to popular culture that echo in the poem. Which
   can you identify, and how are they relevant to this tribute to black women?

3. What is the speaker's attitude toward the "Perfectly Good Clothes" in lines
   34–45?

4. Explain the significance of lines 67–70. How do they reveal important class
   differences among whites and blacks?

5. Read lines 77–81 aloud, and explain how meaning evolves in these lines.

6. What is the effect of the use of repetition in the poem? Why would a paraphrase of this poem be particularly unsatisfying in capturing its meaning?

CONNECTION TO ANOTHER SELECTION

1. Compare Rushin's strategy for creating lists in this poem with Walt Whitman's in the excerpt from "I Sing the Body Electric" (p. 914). How do you
   respond to the lists in each poem?

JONATHAN HOLDEN (B. 1941)

Cutting Loose on an August Night   1985

Roll the windows all
the way down and keep it
floored until you can hear the doors
between the corn-rows bursting
open with the August hay   5
and the full force of the packed earth
being unpacked and shredded
up with speed as the center line
pours tracer bullets
at the bug-spattered windshield   10
and the night's rush outshouts
static on the radio

where New York trails Cincinnati
and Oklahoma City's
cutting in to say high   15
tomorrow in the mid to upper
90s, low, and a full slate
of night action out there
like dusty fairgrounds
fierce under arc light roars   20
no runs, no hits, no errors, one
man left, and the entire north
winces, takes the snap-
shot of a cloud
formed like a horse's head,   25
and you are fixed firmly
in the cool pressure of the night,
the glare of the Philadelphia
and Boston games as sure
as constellations,   30
you're weightless
in the thick of speed, going
nowhere in all directions
at once, nothing but the pennant
race at stake.   35

CONSIDERATIONS FOR CRITICAL THINKING AND WRITING

1. FIRST RESPONSE. Discuss how Holden punctuates this poem and describe
   how punctuation (or the lack of it) affects your reading.
2. Does the title adequately express the poem's central meaning, or is there
   more to be said about the theme?
3. How do the images produce a sensation of speed? How do the line breaks
   produce a sensation of speed? Explain which images and line breaks seem
   most effective to you.

CONNECTION TO ANOTHER SELECTION

1. Compare the sense of freedom expressed in this poem with that offered by
   Thomas Lynch in "Liberty" (p. 795). What significant similarities and differences do you find in the poems' themes and the manner in which they
   are presented?

MARILYN NELSON WANIEK (B. 1946)
Emily Dickinson's Defunct   1978

She used to
pack poems
in her hip pocket.
Under all the

gray old lady 5
clothes she was
dressed for action.
She had hair,
imagine,
in certain places, and 10
believe me
she smelled human
on a hot summer day.
Stalking snakes
or counting 15
the thousand motes
in sunlight
she walked just
like an Indian.
She was New England's 20
favorite daughter,
she could pray
like the devil.
She was a
two-fisted woman, 25
this babe.
All the flies
just stood around
and buzzed
when she died. 30

CONSIDERATIONS FOR CRITICAL THINKING AND WRITING

1. FIRST RESPONSE. How does the speaker characterize Dickinson? Explain why this characterization is different from the popular view of Dickinson.

2. How does the diction of the poem serve to characterize the speaker?

3. Discuss the function of the poem's title.

4. CRITICAL STRATEGIES. Read the section on biographical criticism (pp. 2097–99) in Chapter 52, "Critical Strategies for Reading," and the biographical overview of Dickinson in Chapter 31 (pp. 949–51). How is the speaker's characterization of Dickinson different from the biographical facts of her life? How does this perspective affect your reading of the poem?

CONNECTIONS TO OTHER SELECTIONS

1. Waniek alludes to at least two other poems in "Emily Dickinson's Defunct." The title refers to E. E. Cummings's "Buffalo Bill 's" (p. 1154), and the final lines (27–30) refer to Dickinson's "I heard a Fly buzz—when I died—" (p. 969). Read those poems and write an essay discussing how they affect your reading of Waniek's poem.

JEFFREY HARRISON (B. 1957)

Horseshoe Contest   *1999*

East Woodstock, Connecticut
Fourth of July

After the parade
of tractors and fire trucks,
old cars and makeshift floats,
after speeches by
the minister and selectman,   5
after the cakewalk and hayrides
and children's games
are over and the cornet band
has packed up its instruments
and left the gazebo,   10
the crowd on the town
green begins to gather
around the horseshoe pit
where a tournament
has been going on all day   15
and is now down
to the four or five
best players — the same ones
every year, these old guys
who, beneath their feigned   20
insouciance, care about this
more than anything.
The stakes are high:
their names on a plaque,
their pride, their whole idea   25
of who they are,
held onto since high school
when they played football
or ran track — something
unchanging at their core,   30
small but of a certain heft.
Limber as gunslingers
preparing for a showdown,
they step up in pairs
to take their turns   35
pitching the iron shoes,
lofting these emblems
of luck with a skill
both deliberate and
offhand, landing ringer   40
after ringer, metal
clashing against metal,
while the others, those

who entered the contest
just for the hell of it   45
and who dropped out
hours ago, their throws
going wild or just
not good enough, stand
quietly at the sidelines,   50
watching with something close
to awe as their elders
stride with the casual
self-consciousness of heroes,
becoming young again   55
in the crowd's hush
and the flush of suspense,
elevated for these moments
like a horseshoe hanging
in the sunlit air   60
above them, above their lives
as dairymen and farmers,
their bodies moving
with a kind of knowledge
unknown to most of us   65
and too late for most of us
to learn — though I'd give
almost anything
to be able to do anything
that well.   70

CONSIDERATIONS FOR CRITICAL THINKING AND WRITING

1. FIRST RESPONSE. How does Harrison economically create a picture of a July 4th celebration in lines 1–10?

2. In what sense are the "stakes . . . high" for the horseshoe tournament players? Why is the tournament important to the speaker?

3. Type out this poem as a prose paragraph. How is the experience of reading the poem different from reading the paragraph? What do the line breaks of the poem contribute to your reading experience?

CONNECTION TO ANOTHER SELECTION

1. Consider the contest described by Harrison along with Edward Hirsch's "Fast Break" (p. 881). What similarities and differences are there in the theme?

ROBERT HASS (B. 1941)

A Story about the Body   1989

The young composer, working that summer at an artists' colony, had watched her for a week. She was Japanese, a painter, almost sixty, and he thought he was in love with her. He loved her work, and her work was like the way she moved her body, used her hands, looked at him directly when she made amused and considered answers to his questions. One night, walking back from a concert, they came to her door and she turned to him and said, "I think you would like to have me. I would like that too, but I must tell you that I have had a double mastectomy," and when he didn't understand, "I've lost both my breasts." The radiance that he had carried around in his belly and chest cavity—like music—withered very quickly, and he made himself look at her when he said, "I'm sorry. I don't think I could." He walked back to his own cabin through the pines, and in the morning he found a small blue bowl on the porch outside his door. It looked to be full of rose petals, but he found when he picked it up that the rose petals were on top; the rest of the bowl—she must have swept them from the corners of her studio—was full of dead bees.

CONSIDERATIONS FOR CRITICAL THINKING AND WRITING

1. FIRST RESPONSE. Why this title? What other potential titles can you come up with that evoke your reading of the poem?

2. What impression about the "young composer" do you derive from the poem?

3. Why are bees very appropriate in the final line rather than, for example, moths?

CONNECTIONS TO OTHER SELECTIONS

1. Discuss the treatments of love in "A Story about the Body" and Nims's "Love Poem" (p. 693).

2. Read Hulme's "On the Differences between Poetry and Prose" (p. 775) and write an essay on what you think Hulme would have to say about "A Story about the Body."

SHARON OLDS (B. 1942)

Rite of Passage   1983

As the guests arrive at my son's party
they gather in the living room —
short men, men in first grade
with smooth jaws and chins.
Hands in pockets, they stand around   5
jostling, jockeying for place, small fights
breaking out and calming. One says to another
How old are you? Six. I'm seven. So?
They eye each other, seeing themselves
tiny in the other's pupils. They clear their   10
throats a lot, a room of small bankers,
they fold their arms and frown. *I could beat you
up*, a seven says to a six,
the dark cake, round and heavy as a
turret, behind them on the table. My son,   15
freckles like specks of nutmeg on his cheeks,
chest narrow as the balsa keel of a

model boat, long hands
cool and thin as the day they guided him
out of me, speaks up as a host   20
for the sake of the group.
We could easily kill a two-year-old,
he says in his clear voice. The other
men agree, they clear their throats
like Generals, they relax and get down to   25
playing war, celebrating my son's life.

CONSIDERATIONS FOR CRITICAL THINKING AND WRITING

1. FIRST RESPONSE. In what sense is this birthday party a "Rite of Passage"?
2. How does the speaker transform these six- and seven-year-old boys into men? What is the point of doing so?
3. Comment on the appropriateness of the image of the cake in lines 14–15.
4. Why does the son's claim that "We could easily kill a two-year-old" (line 22) come as such a shock at that point in the poem?

CONNECTION TO ANOTHER SELECTION

1. Discuss the use of irony in "Rite of Passage" and Owen's "Dulce et Decorum Est" (p. 764). Which do you think is a more effective antiwar poem? Explain why.

JULIO MARZÁN (B. 1946)

The Translator at the Reception for Latin American Writers   *1997*

Air-conditioned introductions,
then breezy Spanish conversation
fan his curiosity to know
what country I come from.
"Puerto Rico and the Bronx."   5

Spectacled downward eyes
translate disappointment
like a poison mushroom
puffed in his thoughts as if,
after investing a sizable   10
intellectual budget, transporting
a huge cast and camera crew
to film on location
Mayan pyramid grandeur,
indigenes whose ancient gods   15
and comet-tail plumage
inspire a glorious epic
of revolution across a continent,
he received a lurid script

for a social documentary   20
rife with dreary streets
and pathetic human interest,
meager in the profits of high culture.

Understandably he turns,
catches up with the hostess,   25
praising the uncommon quality
of her offerings of cheese.

CONSIDERATIONS FOR CRITICAL THINKING AND WRITING

1. FIRST RESPONSE. What is the speaker's attitude toward the person he meets at the reception? What lines in particular lead you to that conclusion?
2. Why is that person so disappointed about "Puerto Rico and the Bronx"?
3. Explain lines 6–23. How do they reveal both the speaker and the person encountered at the reception?
4. Why is the setting of this poem significant?

CAROLYNN HOY (B. 1947)

In the Summer Kitchen   *1993*

We speared long wooden spoons
into steaming galvanized tubs
churning and scooping the checked cotton
to feed back and forth
through a wringer   5
from her hand to mine.

And there, on that Monday,
she mentioned Harry, her first born,
my uncle, who died at three months.
That was all,   10
a slip of the tongue
as she hastily turned away.

On the stoop by the clothesline
beyond the screen door,
she snapped our flattened   15
shirts to attention,
shoulders as straight and squared
as her chiselled headstone
I now visit.
That silence.   20

The dignity of it all.

CONSIDERATIONS FOR CRITICAL THINKING AND WRITING

1. FIRST RESPONSE. Explain how the details about doing the wash take on more than a literal significance.

2. How do the grouping of stanzas and the spacing of lines affect your reading?

3. How do you think the speaker feels about her grandmother?

4. How might the poem be regarded as a kind of elegy for the grandmother?

CONNECTION TO ANOTHER SELECTION

1. Compare the tone of this poem with that of Emily Dickinson's "The Bustle in a House" (p. 975).

ALLEN GINSBERG (1926–1997)

First Party at Ken Kesey's with Hell's Angels   1965

Cool black night thru the redwoods
cars parked outside in shade
behind the gate, stars dim above
the ravine, a fire burning by the side
porch and a few tired souls hunched over   5
in black leather jackets. In the huge
wooden house, a yellow chandelier
at 3 A.M. the blast of loudspeakers
hi-fi Rolling Stones Ray Charles Beatles
Jumping Joe Jackson and twenty youths   10
dancing to the vibration thru the floor,
a little weed in the bathroom, girls in scarlet
tights, one muscular smooth skinned man
sweating dancing for hours, beer cans
bent littering the yard, a hanged man   15
sculpture dangling from a high creek branch,
children sleeping softly in their bedroom bunks.
And 4 police cars parked outside the painted
gate, red lights revolving in the leaves.

CONSIDERATIONS FOR CRITICAL THINKING AND WRITING

1. FIRST RESPONSE. How does the list of images help to set the poem's scene? What is the effect of the poem's last two lines (18–19) on the overall tone?

2. Who is Ken Kesey? Use the library to find out the kinds of books he writes. How does his name help to establish the poem's setting?

3. How does the absence of commas in lines 8–10 indicate how to read these lines aloud?

CONNECTION TO ANOTHER SELECTION

1. Write an essay that compares the impact of this poem's ending with that of Hathaway's "Oh, Oh" (p. 675).

ANONYMOUS
The Frog
date unknown

What a wonderful bird the frog are!
When he stand he sit almost;
When he hop he fly almost.
He ain't got no sense hardly;
He ain't got no tail hardly either.
When he sit, he sit on what he ain't got almost.

CONSIDERATIONS FOR CRITICAL THINKING AND WRITING

1. FIRST RESPONSE. How is the poem a description of the speaker as well as of a frog?
2. Though this poem is ungrammatical, it does have a patterned structure. How does the pattern of sentences create a formal structure?

TATO LAVIERA (B. 1951)
AmeRícan
1985

we gave birth to a new generation,
AmeRícan, broader than lost gold
never touched, hidden inside the
puerto rican mountains.

we gave birth to a new generation,   5
AmeRícan, it includes everything
imaginable you-name-it-we-got-it
society.

we gave birth to a new generation,
AmeRícan salutes all folklores,   10
european, indian, black, spanish,
and anything else compatible:

AmeRícan,   singing to composer pedro flores'° palm
            trees high up in the universal sky!

AmeRícan,   sweet soft spanish danzas gypsies   15
            moving lyrics la *española*° cascabelling   *Spanish*
            presence always singing at our side!

AmeRícan,   beating jíbaro° modern troubadours
            crying guitars romantic continental
            bolero love songs!   20

AmeRícan,   across forth and across back
            back across and forth back

13 *Pedro Flores:* Puerto Rican composer of popular romantic songs.   18 *jíbaro:* A particular style of music played by Puerto Rican mountain farmers.

                    forth across and back and forth
                    our trips are walking bridges!

                    it all dissolved into itself, the attempt   25
                    was truly made, the attempt was truly
                    absorbed, digested, we spit out
                    the poison, we spit out the malice,
                    we stand, affirmative in action,
                    to reproduce a broader answer to the   30
                    marginality that gobbled us up abruptly!

AmeRícan,   walking plena- rhythms° in new york,
                    strutting beautifully alert, alive,
                    many turning eyes wondering,
                    admiring!   35

AmeRícan,   defining myself my own way any way many
                    ways Am e Rícan, with the big R and the
                    accent on the í!

AmeRícan,   like the soul gliding talk of gospel
                    boogie music!   40

AmeRícan,   speaking new words in spanglish tenements,
                    fast tongue moving street corner *"que
                    corta"*° talk being invented at the insistence   *that cuts*
                    of a smile!

AmeRícan,   abounding inside so many ethnic english   45
                    people, and out of humanity, we blend
                    and mix all that is good!

AmeRícan,   integrating in new york and defining our
                    own *destino,*° our own way of life,   *destiny*

AmeRícan,   defining the new america, humane america,   50
                    admired america, loved america, harmonious
                    america, the world in peace, our energies
                    collectively invested to find other civili-
                    zations, to touch God, further and further,
                    to dwell in the spirit of divinity!   55

AmeRícan,   yes, for now, for i love this, my second
                    land, and i dream to take the accent from
                    the altercation, and be proud to call
                    myself american, in the u.s. sense of the
                    word, AmeRícan, America!   60

32 *plena-rhythms:* African–Puerto Rican folklore, music, and dance.

Considerations for Critical Thinking and Writing

1. **First response.** How does the arrangement of lines communicate a sense of energy and vitality?

2. How does the speaker portray Puerto Ricans living in the United States?

3. How does the poet describe the United States?

PETER MEINKE (B. 1932)

The ABC of Aerobics   *1983*

Air seeps through alleys and our diaphragms
balloon blackly with this mix of
carbon monoxide and the thousand corrosives a city
doles out free to its constituents;
everyone's jogging through Edgemont Park,   5
frightened by death and fatty tissue,
gasping at the maximal heart rate,
hoping to outlive all the others streaming
in the lanes like lemmings lurching toward their last
jump. I join in despair   10
knowing my arteries jammed with
lint and tobacco, lard and bourbon — my
medical history a noxious marsh:
newts and moles slink through the sodden veins,
owls hoot in the lungs' dark branches;   15
probably I shall keel off the john like
queer Uncle George and lie on the bathroom floor
raging about Shirley Clark, my true love in
seventh grade, God bless her wherever she lives
tied to that turkey who hugely   20
undervalues the beauty of her tiny earlobes, one
view of which (either one: they are both perfect)
would add years to my life and I could skip these
x-rays, turn in my insurance card, and trade
yoga and treadmills and jogging and zen and   25
zucchini for drinking and dreaming of her, breathing hard.

CONSIDERATIONS FOR CRITICAL THINKING AND WRITING

1. FIRST RESPONSE. How does the title help to establish a pattern throughout
   the poem? How does the pattern contribute to the poem's meaning?

2. How does the speaker feel about exercise? How do his descriptions of his
   physical condition serve to characterize him?

3. A primer is a book that teaches children to read or introduces them, in an
   elementary way, to the basics of a subject. The title "The ABC of Aerobics"
   indicates that this poem is meant to be a primer. What is it trying to teach
   us? Is its final lesson serious or ironic?

4. Discuss Meinke's use of humor. Is it effective?

1. Write an essay comparing the way Olds connects sex and exercise in "Sex without Love" (p. 739) with Meinke's treatment here.

2. Compare the voice in this poem with that in Kinnell's "After Making Love We Hear Footsteps" (p. 917). Which do you find more appealing? Why?

GARY SOTO (B. 1952)

Mexicans Begin Jogging   *1995*

At the factory I worked
In the fleck of rubber, under the press
Of an oven yellow with flame,
Until the border patrol opened
Their vans and my boss waved for us to run.   5
"Over the fence, Soto," he shouted,
And I shouted that I was American.
"No time for lies," he said, and pressed
A dollar in my palm, hurrying me
Through the back door.   10

Since I was on his time, I ran
And became the wag to a short tail of Mexicans—
Ran past the amazed crowds that lined
The street and blurred like photographs, in rain.
I ran from that industrial road to the soft   15
Houses where people paled at the turn of an autumn sky.
What could I do but yell *vivas*
To baseball, milkshakes, and those sociologists
Who would clock me
As I jog into the next century   20
On the power of a great, silly grin.

1. FIRST RESPONSE. What ironies are present in this poem?

2. Soto was born and raised in Fresno, California. How does this fact affect your reading of the first stanza?

3. In what different ways does the speaker become "the wag" (line 12) in this poem? (You may want to look up the word to consider all possible meanings.)

4. Explain lines 17-21. What serious point is being made in these humorous lines?

1. Compare the speakers' ironic attitudes toward exercise in this poem and in Meinke's "The ABC of Aerobics" (p. 933).

Found Poem

This next poem is a *found poem,* an unintentional poem discovered in a nonpoetic context, such as a conversation, news story, or an advertisement. Found poems are playful reminders that the words in poems are very often the language we use every day. Whether such found language should be regarded as a poem is an issue left for you to consider.

DONALD JUSTICE (B. 1925)

Order in the Streets   *1969*

(From instructions printed on a child's toy, Christmas 1968, as reported in the New York Times)

1. 2. 3.
Switch on.

Jeep rushes
to the scene
of riot   5

Jeep goes
in all directions
by mystery action.

Jeep stops periodically
to turn hood over   10

machine gun appears
with realistic
shooting noise.

After putting down riot,
jeep goes   15
back to the headquarters.

CONSIDERATIONS FOR CRITICAL THINKING AND WRITING

1. FIRST RESPONSE. What is the effect of arranging these instructions in lines? How are the language and meaning enhanced by this arrangement?

2. Look for phrases or sentences in ads, textbooks, labels, or directions — in anything that might inadvertently contain provocative material that would be revealed by arranging the words in lines. You may even discover some patterns of rhyme and rhythm. After arranging the lines, explain why you organized them as you did.

30

Combining the Elements
of Poetry

THE ELEMENTS TOGETHER

The elements of poetry that you have studied in the first ten chapters of
this section offer a vocabulary and series of perspectives that open up avenues of inquiry into a poem. As you have learned, there are many potential routes that you can take. By asking questions, for example, about the
speaker, diction, figurative language, sounds, rhythm, tone, or theme, you
clarify your understanding while simultaneously sensitizing yourself to
elements and issues especially relevant to the poem under consideration.
This process of careful, informed reading allows you to see how the various
elements of the poem reinforce its meanings.

A poem's elements do not exist in isolation, however. They work together to create a complete experience for the reader. Knowing how the elements combine helps you understand the poem's structure and to appreciate it as a whole. Robert Herrick's "Delight in Disorder," (p. 873), for
example, is more easily understood (and the humor of the poem is better
appreciated) when meter and rhyme are considered together with the
poem's meaning. Musing about how he is more charmed by a naturally disheveled appearance than by those whose appearance seems contrived, the
speaker lists several attributes of dishevelment and concludes that they

> Do more bewitch me than when art
> Is too precise in every part.

Noticing how the couplet's precise and sing-songy rhythm combines
with the solid, obvious, and final rhyme of art / part helps in understanding
what the speaker means by "too precise," since the lines are a little too precise themselves. Noticing this, you may even want to chart out how rhythm
and rhyme work together throughout the early (more disheveled) lines of

936

the poem. Finding a pattern in the ways the elements work together throughout the poem will help you understand how the poem works.

MAPPING THE POEM

When you write about a poem, you are, in some ways, providing a guide for a place that might otherwise seem unfamiliar and remote. Put simply, writing enables you to chart a work so that you can comfortably move around in it to discuss or write about what interests you. Your paper represents a record and a map of your intellectual journey through the poem, pointing out the things worth noting and your impressions about them. Your role as writer is to offer insights into the challenges, pleasures, and discoveries that the poem harbors. These insights are a kind of sightseeing, as you navigate the various elements of the poem to make some overall point about it.

This chapter shows you how one student, Rose Bostwick, moves through the stages of writing about how a poem's elements combine for a final effect. Included here are Rose's first response, her informal outline, and the final draft of an explication of a poem by John Donne, "Death Be Not Proud." A detailed explanation of what is implicit in a poem, an explication requires a line-by-line examination of the poem. (For more on explication, see page 2147 in Chapter 53, "Reading and Writing.") After reviewing the elements of poetry covered in the preceding chapters, Rose read the poem (which follows) several times, paying careful attention to diction, figurative language, irony, symbol, rhythm, sound, and so on. Because her final paper is more concerned with the overall effect of the combination of elements than with a line-by-line breakdown, her early notes are not included here. As you read and reread "Death Be Not Proud," however, keep notes on how *you* think the elements of this poem work together and to what overall effect.

JOHN DONNE (1572–1631)

John Donne, now regarded as a major poet of the early seventeenth century, wrote love poems at the beginning of his career but shifted to religious themes after converting from Catholicism to Anglicanism in the early 1590s. Although trained in law, he was also

John Donne (1572–1631), the English metaphysical poet and writer of sermons, as depicted in an engraving by W. Skelton Sculp.

ordained a priest and became dean of St. Paul's Cathedral in London in 1621. The following poem, from "Holy Sonnets," reflects both his religious faith and his ability to create elegant arguments in verse.

JOHN DONNE (1572–1631)

Death Be Not Proud 1611

Death be not proud, though some have callèd thee
Mighty and dreadful, for thou art not so;
For those whom thou think'st thou dost overthrow
Die not, poor Death, nor yet canst thou kill me.
From rest and sleep, which but thy pictures° be,   *images* 5
Much pleasure; then from thee much more must flow,
And soonest our best men with thee do go,
Rest of their bones, and soul's delivery.°   *deliverance*
Thou art slave to Fate, Chance, kings, and desperate men,
And dost with Poison, War, and Sickness dwell;   10
And poppy or charms can make us sleep as well,
And better than thy stroke; why swell'st° thou then?   *swell with pride*
One short sleep past, we wake eternally
And death shall be no more; Death, thou shalt die.

CONSIDERATIONS FOR CRITICAL THINKING AND WRITING

1. FIRST RESPONSE. Why doesn't the speaker fear death? Explain why you find the argument convincing or not.

2. How does the speaker compare death with rest and sleep in lines 5–8? What is the point of this comparison?

3. Discuss the poem's rhythm by examining the breaks and end-stopped lines. How does the poem's rhythm contribute to its meaning?

4. What are the signs that this poem is structured as a sonnet?

ASKING QUESTIONS ABOUT THE ELEMENTS

After reading a poem, use the "Questions for Responsive Reading and Writing" (p. 709) to help you think, talk, and write about any poem. Before you do, though, be sure that you have read the poem several times without worrying actively about interpretation. With poetry, as with all literature, it's important to allow yourself the pleasure of enjoying whatever makes itself apparent to you. On subsequent readings, use the questions to understand and appreciate how the poem works; remember to keep in mind that not all questions will necessarily be relevant to a particular poem. A good starting point is to ask yourself what elements are exemplified in the parts of the poem that particularly interest you. Then ask the questions for responsive reading and writing that relate to those elements. Finally, as you begin to get a sense of what elements are important to the poem and how those elements fit together, it often helps to put your impressions on paper.

A SAMPLE FIRST RESPONSE

After Rose has carefully read "Death Be Not Proud" and has a sense of how the elements work, she takes the first step toward a formal explication by writing informally about the relevant elements and addressing the question *Why doesn't the speaker fear death? Explain why you find the argument convincing or not.* Note that at this point, she is not as concerned with textual evidence and detail as she will need to be in her final paper.

> I've read the poem "Death Be Not Proud" by John Donne a few times now, and I have a sense of how it works. The poem is a sonnet, and each of the three quatrains presents a piece of the argument that Death should not be proud, because it is not really all-powerful, and may even be a source of pleasure. As a reader, I resist this seeming paradox at first, but I know it must be a trick, a riddle of some sort that the poem will proceed to untangle. I think one of the reasons the poem comes off as such a powerful statement is that Donne at first seems to be playful and paradoxical in his characterizations of Death. He's almost teasing Death. But beneath the teasing tone you feel the strong foundation of the real reason Death should not be proud--Donne's faith in the immortality of the soul. The poem begins to feel more solemn as it progresses, as the hints at the idea of immortality become more clearly articulated.
>
> Donne utilizes two literary conventions to increase the effect of this poem: he uses the convention of personifying death, so that he can address it directly, and he uses the metaphor of death as a kind of sleep. These two things determine the tone and the progression from playful to solemn in the poem.
>
> The last clause of the poem (line 14) plays with the paradoxical-seeming character of what he's been declaring.

Ironically, it seems the only thing susceptible to death is death itself. Or, when death becomes powerless is when it only has power over itself.

ORGANIZING YOUR THOUGHTS

Showing in a paper how different elements of a particular poem work together is often quite challenging. While you may have a clear intuitive sense of what elements are important to the poem and how they complement each other, it is important to organize your thoughts in such a way as to make the relationships clear to your audience. The simplest way is to go line by line, but that can quickly become rote for writer and reader. Because you will want to organize your paper in the way that best serves your thesis, it may help to write an informal outline that charts how you think the argument moves. You may find, for example, that the argument is not persuasive if you start with the final lines and go back to the beginning of the poem or passage. However you decide to organize your argument, keep in mind that a single idea, or thesis, will have to run throughout the entire paper.

A SAMPLE INFORMAL OUTLINE

In her informal outline (below), Rose discovers that her argument works best if she begins at the beginning. Note how, though her later paper concerns itself with how several elements of poetry contribute to the poem's theme and message, her informal outline concerns itself much more with what that message is and how it develops as the poem progresses. She will fill in the details later.

Thesis: *From the very first word, addressing "Death" directly, Donne uses the literary conventions of personifying death and comparing it to sleep to begin an argument that Death should not be proud of its might or dreadfulness. But these two elements of his argument come to be seen as the superficial points when the true reason for death's powerlessness becomes clear. The Christian belief in the immortality of the soul is the reason for death's powerlessness and likeness to sleep.*

Body of essay: *Show how argument proceeds by quatrains from playful address to Death, and statement that Death is much like sleep, its "picture," to statement that Death is "slave" to other forces (and so should not be proud of being the mightiest), to the couplet, which articulates clearly the idea of immortality and gives the final paradox, "Death, thou shalt die."*

Conclusion: *Donne's faith in the immortality of the soul enables him to "prove" in this argument that Death is truly like its metaphorical representation, sleep. Faith allows him to derive a source for this conventional trope, and it allows him to state his truth in paradoxes. He relies on the conventional idea that death is an end, and a conqueror, and the only all-powerful force, to make the paradoxes that lend his argument the force of mystery — the mystery of faith.*

THE ELEMENTS AND THEME

As you create an informal outline, your understanding of the poem will grow, change, and finally, solidify. You will develop a much clearer sense of what the poem's elements combine to create, and you will have chosen a scheme for organizing your argument. The next step before drafting is to determine the paper's thesis, which will not only keep your paper focused but will help you center your thoughts. For papers that discuss how the elements of poetry come together, the thesis is a single and concise statement of what the elements combine to create — the idea around which all the elements revolve. In the earlier discussion of Robert Herrick's "Delight in Disorder," for example, the two elements, rhythm and rhyme, work together to create the speaker's self-directed irony. To state this as a thesis, we might say that by making his own rhythm and rhyme "too precise," Herrick's speaker is making fun of himself while complimenting a certain type of woman. (You may ask yourself if he's doing a little flirting.)

Once you understand how all the elements of the poem fit together and have articulated your understanding in the thesis statement, the next step is to flesh out your argument. By including quotations from the poem to illustrate the points you will be making, you will better explain exactly how each element relates to the others and, more specifically, to your thesis, and you will have created a finished paper that helps readers navigate the poem's geography.

A SAMPLE EXPLICATION

In Rose's final draft, she focuses on the use of metaphor in "Death Be Not Proud." Her essay provides a coherent reading that relates each line of the poem to the speaker's intense awareness of death. Although the essay discusses each stanza in order, the introductory paragraph provides a brief overview explaining how the poem's metaphor and arguments contribute to its total meaning. In addition, Rose does not hesitate to discuss a line out of sequence when it can be usefully connected to another phrase. She also works quotations into her sentences to support her points. When she adds something to a quotation to clarify it, she encloses her words in brackets so that they will not be mistaken for the poet's, and she uses a slash to indicate line divisions: "soonest . . . with thee do go, / [for] Rest of their bones, and soul's delivery." Finally, because the essay focuses on a short poem, it is not necessary to include line numbers, though they would be required in a study of a longer work. As you read through her final draft, remember that the word *explication* comes from the Latin *explicare*, "to unfold." How successful do you think Rose is at unfolding this poem to reveal how its elements — here ranging from metaphor, structure, meter, personification, paradox, and irony to theme — contribute to its meaning?

Rose Bostwick

English 101

Prof. Hart

February 14, 20--

The Use of Conventional Metaphors for Death

in John Donne's "Death Be Not Proud"

In the sonnet which begins "Death be not proud . . ."
John Donne argues that death is not "mighty and dreadful,"
but is more like its metaphorical representation, sleep,
and is even a source of pleasure and rest. Donne builds
this argument on two foundations. One is made up of the
metaphors and literary conventions for death: death is
compared with sleep and is often personified, so that
it can be addressed directly. The poem is an address to
death that at first seems paradoxical and somewhat playful, but which then rises in all the emotion of faith as
it reveals the second foundation of the argument--the
Christian belief in the immortality of the soul. Seen
against the backdrop of this belief, death loses its powerful threat and comes to be seen as only a metaphorical
sleep, or rest.

The poem is an ironic argument that proceeds according to the structure of the sonnet form. Each quatrain
contains a new development or aspect of the argument, and
the final couplet serves as a conclusion. The metrical
scheme is mainly iambic pentameter, but in several places
in the poem, the stress pattern is altered for emphasis.
For example, the first foot of the poem is inverted, so
that "Death," the first word, receives the stress. This
announces to us right away that Death is being personified
and addressed. This inversion also serves to begin the
poem energetically and forcefully. The second line behaves
in the same way. The first syllable of "Mighty" receives

the stress, emphasizing the meaning of the word and its assumed relation to Death.

This first quatrain offers the first paradox and sets up the argument that death has been conventionally personified with the wrong attributes, might and dreadfulness. The poet tells death not to be proud, "though some have called thee / Mighty and dreadful," because, he says, death is not so. Donne will turn this conventional characterization of death on its head with the paradox of the third and fourth lines: he says the people overthrown by death (as if by a conqueror) "Die not, poor death, nor yet canst thou kill me." These lines establish the paradox of death not being able to cause death.

The next quatrain will not begin to answer the question of why this paradox is so, but will posit another slight paradox--the idea of death as pleasurable. In lines 5-8, Donne uses the literary convention of describing death as a metaphorical sleep, or rest, to construct the argument that death must give pleasure: "From rest and sleep, which but thy pictures be, / Much pleasure, then from thee much more must flow." At this point, the argument seems almost playful, but is carefully hinting at the solemnity of the deeper foundation of the belief in immortality. The metaphor of sleep for death includes the idea of waking; one doesn't sleep forever. The next two lines put forth the idea that death is pleasurable enough to be desired by "our best men" who "soonest . . . with thee do go, / [for] Rest of their bones, and soul's delivery." This last line comes closer to announcing the true reason for death's powerlessness and pleasure: it is the way to the "soul's delivery" from the body and life on earth, and implicitly, into another, better realm.

A new reason for death's powerlessness arises in the next four lines. The poet says to death:

> Thou art slave to Fate, Chance, kings, and
> desperate men,
> And dost with Poison, War, and Sickness dwell;
> And poppy or charms can make us sleep as well,
> And better than thy stroke; why swell'st thou then?

Donne argues here that there are forces more powerful than death that actually control it. Fate and chance determine when death occurs, and to whom it comes. Kings, with the powers of law and war, can summon death and throw it on whom they wish. And desperate men, murderers or suicides, can also summon death with the strength of their emotions. In lines 11 and 12, Donne again uses the metaphor of death as a kind of sleep, but says that drugs or "charms" give one a better sleep than death. And he asks playfully why death should be so proud, after all these illustrations of its weakness have been given: "why swell'st thou then?"

Finally, with the last couplet, Donne reveals the true, deeper reason behind his argument that death should not be proud of its power. These lines also offer an explanation of the metaphor for death of sleep, or rest:

> One short sleep past, we wake eternally
> And death shall be no more; Death, thou shalt die.

After death, the soul lives on, according to Christian theology and belief. In the Christian heaven, where the soul is immortal, death will no longer exist, and so this last paradox, "Death, thou shalt die," becomes true. Again in this line, a significant inversion of metrical stress

occurs. "Death," in the second clause, receives the
stress, recalling the first line, emphasizing that it is
an address and giving the clause a forceful sense of finality. His belief in the immortality of the soul enables
Donne to "prove" in this argument that death is in actuality like its metaphorical representation, sleep. His faith
allows him to derive a source for this conventional
metaphor and to "disprove" the metaphor of death as an
all-powerful conqueror. His Christian beliefs also allow
him to state his truth in paradoxes, the mysteries which
are justified by the mystery of faith.

Before you begin writing your own paper on poetry, review the Suggestions for Approaching Poetry (pp. 690–91) and Chapter 21, "Writing About Poetry," particularly the Questions for Responsive Reading and Writing (pp. 709–10). These suggestions and questions will help you to focus and sharpen your critical thinking and writing. You'll also find help in Chapter 53, "Reading and Writing," which offers a systematic overview of choosing a topic, developing a thesis, and organizing various types of assignments. If you use outside sources for the paper, be sure to acknowledge them adequately by using the conventional documentation procedures detailed in Chapter 54, "The Literary Research Paper."

Approaches
to Poetry

A Study of Emily Dickinson

This chapter includes a variety of poems by Emily Dickinson in order to provide an opportunity to study her work in some depth. While this collection is not wholly representative of her work, it does offer enough poems to suggest some of the techniques and concerns that characterize her writings. The poems speak not only to readers but also to one another. That's natural enough: the more familiar you are with a writer's work, the easier it is to perceive and enjoy the strategies and themes the poet employs. If you are asked to write about a number of poems by the same author, you may find useful the Questions for Writing about an Author in Depth (p. 988) and the sample paper on Emily Dickinson's attitudes toward religious faith in four of her poems (pp. 991–94).

A BRIEF BIOGRAPHY

Emily Dickinson (1830–1886) grew up in a prominent and prosperous household in Amherst, Massachusetts. Along with her younger sister Lavinia and older brother Austin, she experienced a quiet and reserved family life headed by her father, Edward Dickinson. In a letter to Austin at law school, she once described the atmosphere in her father's house as "pretty much all sobriety." Her mother, Emily Norcross Dickinson, was not as powerful a presence in her life; she seems not

PHOTO ABOVE: *Daguerreotype of Emily Dickinson at seventeen, the only authenticated likeness of the poet. Reprinted by permission of the Amherst College Library.*

to have been as emotionally accessible as Dickinson would have liked. Her daughter is said to have characterized her as not the sort of mother "to whom you hurry when you are troubled." Both parents raised Dickinson to be a cultured Christian woman who would one day be responsible for a family of her own. Her father attempted to protect her from reading books that might "joggle" her mind, particularly her religious faith, but Dickinson's individualistic instincts and irreverent sensibilities created conflicts that did not allow her to fall into step with the conventional piety, domesticity, and social duty prescribed by her father and the orthodox Congregationalism of Amherst.

The Dickinsons were well known in Massachusetts. Her father was a lawyer and served as the treasurer of Amherst College (a position Austin eventually took up as well), and her grandfather was one of the college's founders. Although nineteenth-century politics, economics, and social issues do not appear in the foreground of her poetry, Dickinson lived in a family environment that was steeped in them: her father was an active town official and served in the General Court of Massachusetts, the state senate, and the United States House of Representatives.

Dickinson, however, withdrew not only from her father's public world but also from almost all social life in Amherst. She refused to see most people, and aside from a single year at South Hadley Female Seminary (now Mount Holyoke College), one excursion to Philadelphia and Washington, and several brief trips to Boston to see a doctor about eye problems, she lived all her life in her father's house. She dressed only in white and developed a reputation as a reclusive eccentric. Dickinson selected her own society carefully and frugally. Like her poetry, her relationship to the world was intensely reticent. Indeed, during the last twenty years of her life she rarely left the house.

Though Dickinson never married, she had significant relationships with several men who were friends, confidants, and mentors. She also enjoyed an intimate relationship with her friend Susan Huntington Gilbert, who became her sister-in-law by marrying Austin. Susan and her husband lived next door and were extremely close with Dickinson. Biographers have attempted to find in a number of her relationships the source for the passion of some of her love poems and letters. Several possibilities have been put forward as the person she addressed in three letters as "Dear Master": Benjamin Newton, a clerk in her father's office who talked about books with her; Samuel Bowles, editor of the *Springfield Republican* and friend of the family; the Reverend Charles Wadsworth, a Presbyterian preacher with a reputation for powerful sermons; and an old friend and widower, Judge Otis P. Lord. Despite these speculations, no biographer has been able to identify definitively the object of Dickinson's love. What matters, of course, is not with whom she was in love — if, in fact, there was any single person — but that she wrote about such passions so intensely and convincingly in her poetry.

Choosing to live life internally within the confines of her home, Dickinson brought her life into sharp focus. For she also chose to live within the limitless expanses of her imagination, a choice she was keenly aware of and which she described in one of her poems this way: "I dwell in Possibility—" (p. 967). Her small circle of domestic life did not impinge on her creative sensibilities. Like Henry David Thoreau, she simplified her life so that doing without was a means of being within. In a sense she redefined the meaning of deprivation because being denied something—whether it was faith, love, literary recognition, or some other desire—provided a sharper, more intense understanding than she would have experienced had she achieved what she wanted: "'Heaven,'" she wrote, "is what I cannot reach!" This poem (p. 961), along with many others, such as "Water, is taught by thirst" (p. 958) and "Success is counted sweetest / By those who ne'er succeed" (p. 957), suggests just how persistently she saw deprivation as a way of sensitizing herself to the value of what she was missing. For Dickinson hopeful expectation was always more satisfying than achieving a golden moment. Perhaps that's one reason she was so attracted to John Keats's poetry (see, for example, his "Ode on a Grecian Urn," p. 742).

Dickinson enjoyed reading Keats as well as Emily and Charlotte Brontë; Robert and Elizabeth Barrett Browning; Alfred, Lord Tennyson; and George Eliot. Even so, these writers had little or no effect on the style of her writing. In her own work she was original and innovative, but she did draw on her knowledge of the Bible, classical myths, and Shakespeare for allusions and references in her poetry. She also used contemporary popular church hymns, transforming their standard rhythms into freeform hymn meters. Among American writers she appreciated Ralph Waldo Emerson and Thoreau, but she apparently felt Walt Whitman was better left unread. She once mentioned to Thomas Wentworth Higginson, a leading critic with whom she corresponded about her poetry, that as for Whitman "I never read his Book—but was told that he was disgraceful" (for the kind of Whitman poetry she had been warned against, see his "I Sing the Body Electric," p. 914). Nathaniel Hawthorne, however, intrigued her with his faith in the imagination and his dark themes: "Hawthorne appals—entices," a remark that might be used to describe her own themes and techniques.

AN INTRODUCTION TO HER WORK

Today, Dickinson is regarded as one of America's greatest poets, but when she died at the age of fifty-six after devoting most of her life to writing poetry, her nearly two thousand poems—only a dozen of which were published, anonymously, during her lifetime—were unknown except to a small number of friends and relatives. Dickinson was not recognized as a major poet until the twentieth century, when modern readers ranked her as a major new voice whose literary innovations were unmatched by any other nineteenth-century poet in the United States.

Manuscript page for "What Soft—Cherubic Creatures—" (p. 965), taken from one of Dickinson's forty fascicles—small booklets hand-sewn with white string that contained her poetry as well as other miscellaneous writings. These fascicles are important for Dickinson scholars, as this manuscript page makes clear: her style to some extent resists translation into the conventions of print. Courtesy of the Amherst College Library.

Dickinson neither completed many poems nor prepared them for publication. She wrote her drafts on scraps of paper, grocery lists, and the backs of recipes and used envelopes. Early editors of her poems took the liberty of making them more accessible to nineteenth-century readers when several volumes of selected poems were published in the 1890s. The poems were made to appear like traditional nineteenth-century verse by assigning them titles, rearranging their syntax, normalizing their grammar, and regularizing their capitalizations. Instead of dashes editors used standard punctuation; instead of the highly elliptical telegraphic lines so characteristic of her poems editors added articles, conjunctions, and prepositions to make them more readable and in line with conventional expectations. In addition, the poems were made more predictable by organizing them into categories such as friendship, nature, love, and death. Not until 1955, when Thomas Johnson published Dickinson's complete works in a form that attempted to be true to her manuscript versions, did readers have the opportunity to see the full range of her style and themes.

Like that of Robert Frost, Dickinson's popular reputation has sometimes relegated her to the role of a New England regionalist who writes quaint uplifting verses that touch the heart. In 1971 that image was mailed first class all over the country by the United States Postal Service. In addition to issuing a commemorative stamp featuring a portrait of Dickinson, the Postal Service affixed the stamp to a first-day-of-issue envelope that included an engraved rose and one of her poems. Here's the poem chosen from among the nearly two thousand she wrote:

If I can stop one Heart from breaking   *c. 1864*

If I can stop one Heart from breaking
I shall not live in vain
If I can ease one Life the Aching
or cool one Pain

Or help one fainting Robin
Unto his Nest again
I shall not live in Vain.

This is typical not only of many nineteenth-century popular poems but of the kind of verse that can be found in contemporary greeting cards. The speaker tells us what we imagine we should think about and makes the point simply with a sentimental image of a "fainting Robin." To point out that robins don't faint or that altruism isn't necessarily the only rule of conduct by which one should live one's life is to make trouble for this poem. Moreover, its use of language is unexceptional; the metaphors used, like that robin, are a bit weary. If this poem were characteristic of Dickinson's poetry, the U.S. Postal Service probably would not have been urged to issue a stamp in her honor, nor would you be reading her poems in this anthology or many others. Here's a poem by Dickinson that is more typical of her writing:

If I shouldn't be alive   c. 1860

If I shouldn't be alive
When the Robins come,
Give the one in Red Cravat,
A Memorial crumb.

If I couldn't thank you,
Being fast asleep,
You will know I'm trying
With my Granite lip!

This poem is more representative of Dickinson's sensibilities and techniques. Although the first stanza sets up a rather mild concern that the
speaker might not survive the winter (a not uncommon fear for those who
fell prey to pneumonia, for example, during Dickinson's time), the concern
can't be taken too seriously—a gentle humor lightens the poem when we realize that all robins have red cravats and are therefore the speaker's favorite.
Furthermore, the euphemism that describes the speaker "Being fast asleep"
in line 6 makes death seem not so threatening after all. But the sentimental
expectations of the first six lines—lines that could have been written by any
number of popular nineteenth-century writers—are dashed by the penultimate word of the last line. "Granite" is the perfect word here because it
forces us to reread the poem and to recognize that it's not about feeding
robins or offering a cosmetic treatment of death; rather, it's a bone-chilling
description of a corpse's lip that evokes the cold, hard texture and grayish
color of tombstones. These lips will never say "thank you" or anything else.

Instead of the predictable rhymes and sentiments of "If I can stop
one Heart from breaking," this poem is unnervingly precise in its use of language and tidily points out how much emphasis Dickinson places on an individual word. Her use of near rhyme with "asleep" and "lip" brilliantly
mocks a euphemistic approach to death by its jarring dissonance. This is a
better poem, not because it's grim or about death, but because it demonstrates Dickinson's skillful use of language to produce a shocking irony.

Dickinson found irony, ambiguity, and paradox lurking in the simplest and commonest experiences. The materials and subject matter of her
poetry are quite conventional. Her poems are filled with robins, bees, winter light, household items, and domestic duties. These materials represent
the range of what she experienced in and around her father's house. She
used them because they constituted so much of her life and, more important, because she found meanings latent in them. Though her world was
simple, it was also complex in its beauties and its terrors. Her lyric poems
capture impressions of particular moments, scenes, or moods, and she
characteristically focuses on topics such as nature, love, immortality, death,
faith, doubt, pain, and the self.

Though her materials were conventional, her treatment of them was
innovative because she was willing to break whatever poetic conventions

stood in the way of the intensity of her thought and images. Her conciseness, brevity, and wit are tightly packed. Typically she offers her observations via one or two images that reveal her thought in a powerful manner.
She once characterized her literary art by writing "My business is circumference." Her method is to reveal the inadequacy of declarative statements
by evoking qualifications and questions with images that complicate firm
assertions and affirmations. In one of her poems she describes her strategies this way: "Tell all the Truth but tell it slant — / Success in Circuit lies."
This might well stand as a working definition of Dickinson's aesthetics
and is embodied in the following poem:

The Thought beneath so slight a film —   *c. 1860*

The Thought beneath so slight a film —
Is more distinctly seen —
As laces just reveal the surge —
Or Mists — the Apennine°   *Italian mountain range*

    Paradoxically, "Thought" is more clearly understood precisely because
a slight "film" — in this case language — covers it. Language, like lace, enhances what it covers and reveals it all the more — just as a mountain range
is more engaging to the imagination if it is covered in mists rather than
starkly presenting itself. Poetry for Dickinson intensifies, clarifies, and organizes experience.

    Dickinson's poetry is challenging because it is radical and original in its
rejection of most traditional nineteenth-century themes and techniques. Her
poems require active engagement from the reader because she seems to leave
out so much with her elliptical style and remarkable contracting metaphors.
But these apparent gaps are filled with meaning if we are sensitive to her use
of devices such as personification, allusion, symbolism, and startling syntax
and grammar. Since her use of dashes is sometimes puzzling, it helps to read
her poems aloud to hear how carefully the words are arranged. What might
initially seem intimidating on a silent page can surprise the reader with
meaning when heard. It's also worth keeping in mind that Dickinson was
not always consistent in her views and that they can change from poem to
poem, depending on how she felt at a given moment. For example, her definition of religious belief in " 'Faith' is a fine invention" (p. 989) reflects an ironically detached wariness in contrast to the faith embraced in "I never saw a
Moor—" (p. 990). Dickinson was less interested in absolute answers to questions than she was in examining and exploring their "circumference."

    Because Dickinson's poems are all relatively brief (none is longer than
fifty lines), they invite browsing and sampling, but perhaps a useful way
into their highly metaphoric and witty world is through this "how to"
poem that reads almost like a recipe:

To make a prairie it takes a clover and one bee   date unknown

To make a prairie it takes a clover and one bee,
One clover, and a bee,
And revery.
The revery alone will do,
If bees are few.

This quiet but infinite claim for a writer's imagination brings together the range of ingredients in Dickinson's world of domestic and ordinary natural details. Not surprisingly, she deletes rather than adds to the recipe, because the one essential ingredient is the writer's creative imagination. *Bon appétit.*

CHRONOLOGY

1830	Born December 10 in Amherst, Massachusetts.
1840	Starts her first year at Amherst Academy.
1847–48	Graduates from Amherst Academy and enters South Hadley Female Seminary (now Mount Holyoke College).
1855	Visits Philadelphia and Washington, D.C.
1857	Emerson lectures in Amherst.
1862	Starts corresponding with Thomas Wentworth Higginson, asking for advice about her poems.
1864	Visits Boston for eye treatments.
1870	Higginson visits her in Amherst.
1873	Higginson visits her for a second and final time.
1874	Her father dies in Boston.
1875	Her mother suffers from paralysis.
1882	Her mother dies.
1886	Dies on May 15 in Amherst, Massachusetts.
1890	First edition of her poetry, edited by Mabel Loomis Todd and Thomas Wentworth Higginson, is published.
1955	Thomas H. Johnson publishes *The Poems of Emily Dickinson* in three volumes, thereby making available her poetry known to that date.

Web *Research Emily Dickinson with LitLinks at*
http://www.bedfordstmartins.com/meyer/bedintrolit

Success is counted sweetest   *c. 1859*

Success is counted sweetest
By those who ne'er succeed.
To comprehend a nectar
Requires sorest need.

Not one of all the purple Host   5
Who took the Flag today
Can tell the definition
So clear of Victory

As he defeated — dying —
On whose forbidden ear   10
The distant strains of triumph
Burst agonized and clear!

CONSIDERATIONS FOR CRITICAL THINKING AND WRITING

1. FIRST RESPONSE. How is "success" defined in this poem? To what extent does that definition agree with your own understanding of the word?

2. What do you think is meant by the use of "comprehend" in line 3? How can a nectar be comprehended?

3. Why do the defeated understand victory better than the victorious?

4. Discuss the effect of the poem's final line.

CONNECTION TO ANOTHER SELECTION

1. In an essay compare the themes of this poem with those of John Keats's "Ode on a Grecian Urn" (p. 742).

These are the days when Birds come back—   *c. 1859*

These are the days when Birds come back —
A very few — a Bird or two —
To take a backward look.

These are the days when skies resume
The old — old sophistries   of June —   5
A blue and gold mistake.

Oh fraud that cannot cheat the Bee —
Almost thy plausibility
Induces my belief.

Till ranks of seeds their witness bear —   10
And softly thro' the altered air
Hurries a timid leaf.

Of Sacrament of summer days,
Oh Last Communion   in the Haze —
Permit a child to join.   15

The sacred emblems to partake —
Thy consecrated bread to take
And thine immortal wine!

CONSIDERATIONS FOR CRITICAL THINKING AND WRITING

1. FIRST RESPONSE. This poem was long known by the title "Indian Summer" (supplied by an unauthorized editor). How does an awareness of this bit of information affect your reading of the poem?

2. In what sense are "These . . . days" regarded as a "fraud" by the speaker?

3. Discuss the significance of the religious allusions in stanzas five and six. What, finally, do you think is the speaker's attitude toward Indian summer?

Water, is taught by thirst   c. 1859

Water, is taught by thirst.
Land — by the Oceans passed.
Transport — by throe —
Peace — by its battles told —
Love, by Memorial Mold —
Birds, by the Snow.

CONSIDERATIONS FOR CRITICAL THINKING AND WRITING

1. FIRST RESPONSE. Which image do you find most powerful? Explain why.

2. How is the paradox of each line of the poem resolved? How is the first word of each line "taught" by the phrase that follows it?

3. Try your hand at writing similar lines in which something is "taught."

CONNECTIONS TO OTHER SELECTIONS

1. What does this poem have in common with "Success is counted sweetest" (p. 957)? Which poem do you think is more effective? Explain why.

2. How is the crucial point of this poem related to "I like a look of Agony" (p. 962)?

Safe in their Alabaster Chambers —   1859 version

Safe in their Alabaster Chambers —
Untouched by Morning
And untouched by Noon —
Sleep the meek members of the Resurrection —

Rafter of satin,   5
And Roof of stone.

Light laughs the breeze
In her Castle above them —
Babbles the Bee in a stolid Ear,
Pipe the Sweet Birds in ignorant cadence —   10
Ah, what sagacity perished here!

Safe in their Alabaster Chambers —   *1861 version*

Safe in their Alabaster Chambers —
Untouched by Morning —
And untouched by Noon —
Lie the meek members of the Resurrection —
Rafter of Satin — and Roof of Stone!   5

Grand go the Years — in the Crescent — above them —
Worlds scoop their arcs —
And Firmaments — row —
Diadems — drop — and Doges° — surrender —
Soundless as dots — on a Disc of Snow —   10

9 *Doges:* Chief magistrates of Venice from the twelfth to the sixteenth centuries.

CONSIDERATIONS FOR CRITICAL THINKING AND WRITING

1. FIRST RESPONSE. Dickinson permitted the 1859 version of this poem, entitled "The Sleeping," to be printed in the *Springfield Republican*. The second version she sent privately to Thomas Wentworth Higginson. Why do you suppose she would agree to publish the first but not the second version?

2. Are there any significant changes in the first stanzas of the two versions? If you answered yes, explain the significance of the changes.

3. Describe the different kinds of images used in the two second stanzas. How do those images affect the tones and meanings of those stanzas?

4. Discuss why you prefer one version of the poem to the other.

CONNECTIONS TO OTHER SELECTIONS

1. Compare the theme in the 1861 version with the theme of Robert Frost's "Design" (p. 1018).

2. In an essay discuss the attitude toward death in the 1859 version and in "Apparently with no surprise" (p. 990).

How many times these low feet staggered — c. 1860

How many times these low feet staggered —
Only the soldered mouth can tell —
Try — can you stir the awful rivet —
Try — can you lift the hasps of steel!

Stroke the cool forehead — hot so often — 5
Lift — if you care — the listless hair —
Handle the adamantine fingers
Never a thimble — more — shall wear —

Buzz the dull flies — on the chamber window —
Brave — shines the sun through the freckled pane — 10
Fearless — the cobweb swings from the ceiling —
Indolent Housewife — in Daisies — lain!

CONSIDERATIONS FOR CRITICAL THINKING AND WRITING

1. FIRST RESPONSE. List the images of death in this poem and discuss their effects.

2. How is the housewife's life characterized? How is her death different from her life?

3. Look up the definitions and origin of "indolent." Why is this an especially appropriate word for discussing the housewife?

CONNECTION TO ANOTHER SELECTION

1. Discuss Dickinson's treatment of the fly in this poem and in "I heard a Fly buzz — when I died —" (p. 969). How is the fly in each poem a significant element of the poems' themes?

Portraits are to daily faces c. 1860

Portraits are to daily faces
As an Evening West,
To a fine, pedantic sunshine —
In a satin Vest!

CONSIDERATIONS FOR CRITICAL THINKING AND WRITING

1. FIRST RESPONSE. Dickinson once described her literary art this way: "My business is circumference." Does this poem fit her characterization of her poetry?

2. How is the basic strategy of this poem similar to the following statement: "Doorknob is to door as button is to sweater"?

3. Identify the four metonymies in the poem. Pay close attention to their connotative meanings.

4. If you don't know the meaning of "pedantic," look it up in a dictionary. How does its meaning affect your reading of "fine"?

1. Compare Dickinson's view of poetry in this poem with Francis's perspective in "Catch" (p. 676). What important similarities and differences do you find?

2. Write an essay describing Robert Frost's strategy in "Mending Wall" (p. 1004) or "Birches" (p. 1009) as the business of circumference.

3. How is the theme of this poem related to the central idea in "The Thought beneath so slight a film—" (p. 955)?

4. Compare the use of the word "fine" here with its use in "'Faith' is a fine invention" (p. 989).

Some keep the Sabbath going to Church—   *c. 1860*

Some keep the Sabbath going to Church —
I keep it, staying at Home —
With a Bobolink for a Chorister —
And an Orchard, for a Dome —

Some keep the Sabbath in Surplice°   *holy robes*   5
I just wear my Wings —
And instead of tolling the Bell, for Church,
Our little Sexton — sings.

God preaches, a noted Clergyman —
And the sermon is never long,   10
So instead of getting to Heaven, at last —
I'm going, all along.

Considerations for Critical Thinking and Writing

1. FIRST RESPONSE. What is the effect of referring to "Some" people?

2. Characterize the speaker's tone.

3. How does the speaker distinguish himself or herself from those who go to church?

4. How might "Surplice" be read as a pun?

5. According to the speaker, how should the Sabbath be observed?

Connection to Another Selection

1. Write an essay that discusses nature in this poem and in Walt Whitman's "When I Heard the Learn'd Astronomer" (p. 1188).

"Heaven" — is what I cannot reach!   *c. 1861*

"Heaven" — is what I cannot reach!
The Apple on the Tree —
Provided it do hopeless — hang —
That — "Heaven" is — to Me!

The Color, on the Cruising Cloud —   5
The interdicted Land —
Behind the Hill — the House behind —
There — Paradise — is found!

Her teasing Purples — Afternoons —
The credulous — decoy —   10
Enamored — of the Conjuror —
That spurned us — Yesterday!

CONSIDERATIONS FOR CRITICAL THINKING AND WRITING

1. FIRST RESPONSE. How does the speaker define heaven? How does that definition compare with conventional views of heaven?
2. Look up the myth of Tantalus and explain the allusion in line 3.
3. Given the speaker's definition of heaven, how do you think the speaker would describe hell?

CONNECTIONS TO OTHER SELECTIONS

1. Write an essay that discusses desire in this poem and in "Water, is taught by thirst" (p. 958).
2. Discuss the speakers' attitudes toward pleasure in this poem and in Ackerman's "A Fine, a Private Place" (p. 732).

I like a look of Agony   *c. 1861*

I like a look of Agony,
Because I know it's true —
Men do not sham Convulsion,
Nor simulate, a Throe —

The Eyes glaze once — and that is Death —
Impossible to feign
The Beads upon the Forehead
By homely Anguish strung.

CONSIDERATIONS FOR CRITICAL THINKING AND WRITING

1. FIRST RESPONSE. Why does the speaker "like a look of Agony"? How do you respond to her appreciation of "Convulsion"?
2. Discuss the image of "The Eyes glaze once —." Why is that a particularly effective metaphor for death?
3. Characterize the speaker. One critic once described the voice in this poem as "almost a hysterical shriek." Explain why you agree or disagree.

CONNECTION TO ANOTHER SELECTION

1. Write an essay on Dickinson's attitudes toward pain and deprivation, using this poem and "'Heaven' — is what I cannot reach!" (p. 961).

Wild Nights—Wild Nights! c. 1861

Wild Nights—Wild Nights!
Were I with thee
Wild Nights should be
Our luxury!

Futile—the Winds—
To a Heart in port—
Done with the Compass—
Done with the Chart!

Rowing in Eden—
Ah, the Sea!
Might I but moor—Tonight—
In Thee!

5

10

CONSIDERATIONS FOR CRITICAL THINKING AND WRITING

1. FIRST RESPONSE. Thomas Wentworth Higginson, Dickinson's mentor, once said he was afraid that some "malignant" readers might "read into [a poem like this] more than that virgin recluse ever dreamed of putting there." What do you think?
2. Look up the meaning of "luxury" in a dictionary. Why does this word work especially well here?
3. Given the imagery of the final stanza, do you think the speaker is a man or a woman? Explain why.
4. CRITICAL STRATEGIES. Read the section on psychological criticism (pp. 2099–2101) in Chapter 52, "Critical Strategies for Reading." What do you think this poem reveals about the author's personal psychology?

CONNECTION TO ANOTHER SELECTION

1. Write an essay that compares the voice, figures of speech, and theme of this poem with those of Atwood's "you fit into me" (p. 779).

Nature—sometimes sears a Sapling— c. 1862

Nature—sometimes sears a Sapling—
Sometimes—scalps a Tree—
Her Green People recollect it
When they do not die—

Fainter Leaves—to Further Seasons—
Dumbly testify—
We—who have the Souls—
Die oftener—Not so vitally—

CONSIDERATIONS FOR CRITICAL THINKING AND WRITING

1. FIRST RESPONSE. How is nature presented in this poem? How is it compared with human nature?

2. Why do you suppose Dickinson uses "sometimes" twice? What does this repetition suggest about the nature of nature?

3. What sort of observation do you think Dickinson is making about what it means to be a human being in the final two lines?

CONNECTION TO ANOTHER SELECTION

1. Discuss the treatment of nature in this poem and in "Apparently with no surprise" (p. 990), paying particular attention to the verbs associated with nature in each poem.

I would not paint — a picture —   *c. 1862*

I would not paint — a picture —
I'd rather be the One
It's bright impossibility
To dwell — delicious — on —
And wonder how the fingers feel   5
Whose rare — celestial — stir —
Evokes so sweet a Torment —
Such sumptuous — Despair —

I would not talk, like Cornets —
I'd rather be the One   10
Raised softly to the Ceilings —
And out, and easy on —
Through Villages of Ether —
Myself endued Balloon
By but a lip of Metal —   15
The pier to my Pontoon —

Nor would I be a Poet —
It's finer — own the Ear —
Enamored — impotent — content —
The License to revere,   20
A privilege so awful
What would the Dower be,
Had I the Art to stun myself
With Bolts of Melody!

CONSIDERATIONS FOR CRITICAL THINKING AND WRITING

1. FIRST RESPONSE. Paraphrase each stanza and explain how they are thematically related to each other.

2. What is the speaker's attitude toward creativity and art?

3. What do the final two lines suggest about how the speaker thinks about the art of poetry?

CONNECTIONS TO OTHER SELECTIONS

1. Discuss Dickinson's attitude toward poetry in this poem, "I dwell in Possibility—" (p. 967), and "This was a Poet—It is That" (p. 967).

What Soft—Cherubic Creatures— 1862

What Soft—Cherubic Creatures—
These Gentlewomen are—
One would as soon assault a Plush—
Or violate a Star—

Such Dimity° Convictions— *sheer cotton fabric* 5
A Horror so refined
Of freckled Human Nature—
Of Deity—ashamed—

It's such a common—Glory—
A Fisherman's—Degree— 10
Redemption—Brittle Lady—
Be so—ashamed of Thee—

CONSIDERATIONS FOR CRITICAL THINKING AND WRITING

1. FIRST RESPONSE. Characterize the "Gentlewomen" in this poem.
2. How do the sounds produced in the first line help to reinforce their meaning?
3. What are "Dimity Convictions," and what do they make "Of freckled Human Nature"?
4. Discuss the irony in the final stanza.

CONNECTION TO ANOTHER SELECTION

1. How are the "Gentlewomen" in this poem similar to the "Gentlemen" in "'Faith' is a fine invention" (p. 989)?

The Soul selects her own Society— c. 1862

The Soul selects her own Society—
Then—shuts the Door—
To her divine Majority—
Present no more—

Unmoved—she notes the Chariots—pausing— 5
At her low Gate—

Unmoved — an Emperor be kneeling
Upon her Mat —

I've known her — from an ample nation —
Choose One —   10
Then — close the Valves of her attention —
Like Stone —

Considerations for Critical Thinking and Writing

1. FIRST RESPONSE. Characterize the speaker. Is she self-reliant and self-sufficient? Cold? Angry?

2. Why do you suppose the "Soul" in this poem is female? Would it make any difference if it were male?

3. Discuss the effect of the images in the final two lines. Pay particular attention to the meanings of "Valves" in line 11.

Much Madness is divinest Sense —   *c. 1862*

Much Madness is divinest Sense —
To a discerning Eye —
Much Sense — the starkest Madness —
'Tis the Majority
In this, as All, prevail —
Assent — and you are sane —
Demur — you're straightway dangerous —
And handled with a Chain —

Considerations for Critical Thinking and Writing

1. FIRST RESPONSE. Thomas Wentworth Higginson's wife once referred to Dickinson as the "partially cracked poetess of Amherst." Assuming that Dickinson had some idea of how she was regarded by the "Majority," how might this poem be seen as an insight into her life?

2. Discuss the conflict between the individual and society in this poem. Which images are used to describe each? How do these images affect your attitudes about them?

3. Comment on the effectiveness of the poem's final line.

Connection to Another Selection

1. Discuss the theme of self-reliance in this poem and in "The Soul selects her own Society —" (p. 965).

I dwell in Possibility—   *c. 1862*

I dwell in Possibility—
A fairer House than Prose—
More numerous of Windows—
Superior—for Doors—

Of Chambers as the Cedars—   5
Impregnable of Eye—
And for an Everlasting Roof
The Gambrels° of the Sky—   *angled roofs*

Of Visitors—the fairest—
For Occupation—This—   10
The spreading wide my narrow Hands
To gather Paradise—

CONSIDERATIONS FOR CRITICAL THINKING AND WRITING

1. FIRST RESPONSE. What distinction is made between poetry and prose in this poem? Explain why you agree or disagree with the speaker's distinctions.

2. What is the poem's central metaphor in the second and third stanzas?

3. How does the use of metaphor in this poem become a means for the speaker to envision and create a world beyond the circumstances of the speaker's actual life?

CONNECTIONS TO OTHER SELECTIONS

1. Compare what this poem says about poetry and prose with Hulme's comments in the perspective "On the Differences between Poetry and Prose" (p. 775).

2. How can the speaker's sense of expansiveness in this poem be reconciled with the speaker's insistence on contraction in "The Soul selects her own Society—" (p. 965)? Are these poems contradictory? Explain why or why not.

This was a Poet—It is That   *c. 1862*

This was a Poet—It is That
Distills amazing sense
From ordinary Meanings—
And Attar so immense

From the familiar species   5
That perished by the Door—
We wonder it was not Ourselves
Arrested it—before—

Of Pictures, the Discloser—
The Poet—it is He—   10

Entitles Us — by Contrast —
To ceaseless Poverty —

Of Portion — so unconscious —
The Robbing — could not harm —
Himself — to Him — a Fortune —   15
Exterior — to Time —

CONSIDERATIONS FOR CRITICAL THINKING AND WRITING

1. FIRST RESPONSE. According to the speaker, what powers does a poet have? Why are these powers important?

2. Explain the metaphors of "Poverty" (line 12) and "Fortune" (15) and how they contribute to the poem's theme.

CONNECTIONS TO OTHER SELECTIONS

1. Write an essay about a life lived in imagination as depicted in this poem and in "I dwell in Possibility —" (p. 967).

2. Discuss "A Bird came down the Walk —" (p. 836) as an example of a poem that "Distills amazing sense / From ordinary Meanings —" (2–3).

I read my sentence — steadily —   *c. 1862*

I read my sentence — steadily —
Reviewed it with my eyes,
To see that I made no mistake
In its extremest clause —
The Date, and manner, of the shame —   5
And then the Pious Form
That "God have mercy" on the Soul
The Jury voted Him —
I made my soul familiar — with her extremity —
That at the last, it should not be a novel Agony —   10
But she, and Death, acquainted —
Meet tranquilly, as friends —
Salute, and pass, without a Hint —
And there, the Matter ends —

CONSIDERATIONS FOR CRITICAL THINKING AND WRITING

1. FIRST RESPONSE. What is the speaker's "sentence"? What do you think of the tone of the poem, considering its subject?

2. What is the central metaphor? Why is it appropriate for this poem's subject matter?

3. How does the speaker regard death in lines 9–14?

1. Compare the treatment of death in this poem and in "Because I could not stop for Death —" (p. 971).
2. In an essay discuss the "Agony" in this poem and in "I like a look of Agony" (p. 962).

After great pain, a formal feeling comes —   *c. 1862*

After great pain, a formal feeling comes —
The Nerves sit ceremonious, like Tombs —
The stiff Heart questions was it He, that bore,
And Yesterday, or Centuries before?

The Feet, mechanical, go round —   5
Of Ground, or Air, or Ought —
A Wooden way
Regardless grown,
A Quartz contentment, like a stone —

This is the Hour of Lead —   10
Remembered, if outlived,
As Freezing persons, recollect the Snow —
First — Chill — then Stupor — then the letting go —

CONSIDERATIONS FOR CRITICAL THINKING AND WRITING

1. FIRST RESPONSE. What do you think has caused the speaker's pain?
2. How does the rhythm of the lines create a slow, somber pace?
3. Discuss why "the Hour of Lead" (line 10) could serve as a useful title for this poem.

CONNECTIONS TO OTHER SELECTIONS

1. How might this poem be read as a kind of sequel to "The Bustle in a House" (p. 975).
2. Write an essay that discusses this poem in relation to Robert Frost's "Home Burial" (p. 1005).

I heard a Fly buzz — when I died —   *c. 1862*

I heard a Fly buzz — when I died —
The Stillness in the Room
Was like the Stillness in the Air —
Between the Heaves of Storm —

The Eyes around — had wrung them dry —   5
And Breaths were gathering firm

For that last Onset — when the King
Be witnessed — in the Room —

I willed my Keepsakes — Signed away
What portion of me be   10
Assignable — and then it was
There interposed a Fly —

With Blue — uncertain stumbling Buzz —
Between the light — and me —
And then the Windows failed — and then   15
I could not see to see —

CONSIDERATIONS FOR CRITICAL THINKING AND WRITING

1. FIRST RESPONSE. What was expected to happen "when the King" was "witnessed"? What happened instead?
2. Why do you think Dickinson chooses a fly rather than perhaps a bee or gnat?
3. What is the effect of the last line? Why not end the poem with "I could not
   see" instead of the additional "to see"?
4. Discuss the sounds in the poem. Are there any instances of onomatopoeia?

CONNECTIONS TO OTHER SELECTIONS

1. Contrast the symbolic significance of the fly with the spider in Whitman's
   "A Noiseless Patient Spider" (p. 793).
2. Consider the meaning of "light" in this poem and in "There's a certain
   Slant of light" (p. 2148).

One need not be a Chamber — to be Haunted —   *c. 1863*

One need not be a Chamber — to be Haunted —
One need not be a House —
The Brain has Corridors — surpassing
Material Place —

Far safer, of a Midnight Meeting   5
External Ghost
Than its interior Confronting —
That Cooler Host.

Far safer, through an Abbey gallop,
The Stones a'chase —   10
Than Unarmed, one's a'self encounter —
In lonesome Place —

Ourself behind ourself, concealed —
Should startle most —
Assassin hid in our Apartment   15
Be Horror's least.

The Body — borrows a Revolver —
He bolts the Door —
O'erlooking a superior spectre —
Or More —   20

CONSIDERATIONS FOR CRITICAL THINKING AND WRITING

1. FIRST RESPONSE. Paraphrase the poem. Which stanza is most difficult to
   paraphrase? Why?
2. What is the controlling metaphor? Explain why you think it is effective or not.
3. What is the "superior spectre" in line 19?

CONNECTIONS TO OTHER SELECTIONS

1. Compare and contrast this poem with Poe's "The Haunted Palace" (p. 804)
   and Stevens's "Schizophrenia" (p. 792). In an essay explain which poem you
   find the most frightening.

Because I could not stop for Death —   *c. 1863*

Because I could not stop for Death —
He kindly stopped for me —
The Carriage held but just Ourselves —
And Immortality.

We slowly drove — He knew no haste   5
And I had put away
My labor and my leisure too,
For His Civility —

We passed the School, where Children strove
At Recess — in the Ring —   10
We passed the Fields of Gazing Grain —
We passed the Setting Sun —

Or rather — He passed Us —
The Dews drew quivering and chill —
For only Gossamer, my Gown —   15
My Tippet° — only Tulle —   *shawl*

We paused before a House that seemed
A Swelling of the Ground —
The Roof was scarcely visible —
The Cornice — in the Ground —   20

Since then — 'tis Centuries — and yet
Feels shorter than the Day
I first surmised the Horses' Heads
Were toward Eternity —

CONSIDERATIONS FOR CRITICAL THINKING AND WRITING

1. FIRST RESPONSE. Why couldn't the speaker "stop for Death"?
2. How is death personified in this poem? How does the speaker respond to him? Why are they accompanied by immortality?
3. What is the significance of the things they "passed" in the third stanza?
4. What is the "House" in lines 17–20?
5. Discuss the rhythm of the lines. How, for example, is the rhythm of line 14 related to its meaning?

CONNECTIONS TO OTHER SELECTIONS

1. Compare the tone of this poem with that of Dickinson's "Apparently with no surprise" (p. 990).
2. Write an essay comparing Dickinson's view of death in this poem and in "If I shouldn't be alive" (p. 954). Which poem is more powerful for you? Explain why.

I felt a Cleaving in my Mind — c. 1864

I felt a Cleaving in my Mind —
As if my Brain had split —
I tried to match it — Seam by Seam —
But could not make them fit.

The thought behind, I strove to join
Unto the thought before —
But Sequence ravelled out of Sound
Like Balls — upon a Floor.

CONSIDERATIONS FOR CRITICAL THINKING AND WRITING

1. FIRST RESPONSE. What is going on in the speaker's mind?
2. What is the poem's controlling metaphor? Describe the simile in lines 7 and 8. How does it clarify further the first stanza?
3. Discuss the rhymes. How do they reinforce meaning?

CONNECTION TO ANOTHER SELECTION

1. Compare the power of the speaker's mind described here with the power of imagination described in "To make a prairie it takes a clover and one bee" (p. 956).

The Wind begun to knead the Grass —   *c. 1864*

The Wind begun to knead the Grass —
As Women do a Dough —
He flung a Hand full at the Plain —
A Hand full at the Sky —
The Leaves unhooked themselves from Trees —   5
And started all abroad —
The Dust did scoop itself like Hands —
And throw away the Road —
The Wagons quickened on the Street —
The Thunders gossiped low —   10
The Lightning showed a Yellow Head —
And then a livid Toe —
The Birds put up the Bars to Nests —
The Cattle flung to Barns —
Then came one drop of Giant Rain —   15
And then, as if the Hands
That held the Dams — had parted hold —
The Waters Wrecked the Sky —
But overlooked my Father's House —
Just Quartering a Tree —   20

CONSIDERATIONS FOR CRITICAL THINKING AND WRITING

1. FIRST RESPONSE. How successfully do you think this poem captures the excitement of a violent storm?

2. What sort of tone is created by the use of personification to describe the storm?

3. How do you read the poem's last two lines? Explain why you think the tone is (or isn't) consistent with the rest of the poem.

CONNECTION TO ANOTHER SELECTION

1. Discuss the themes of this poem and "Nature — sometimes sears a Sapling —" (p. 963).

A loss of something ever felt I —   *c. 1864*

A loss of something ever felt I —
The first that I could recollect
Bereft I was — of what I knew not
Too young that any should suspect

A Mourner walked among the children   5
I notwithstanding went about
As one bemoaning a Dominion
Itself the only Prince cast out —

Elder, Today, a session wiser
And fainter, too, as Wiseness is —   10
I find myself still softly searching
For my Delinquent Palaces —

And a Suspicion, like a Finger
Touches my Forehead now and then
That I am looking oppositely   15
For the site of the Kingdom of Heaven —

CONSIDERATIONS FOR CRITICAL THINKING AND WRITING

1. FIRST RESPONSE. How does the sense of loss affect the speaker's life?
2. Is it possible to know specifically what is mourned in this poem? Explain why or why not.
3. What distinction is made between the speaker's identity as a youth and the speaker's adult identity?
4. Discuss the final stanza. Do you think this is a hopeful or despairing poem? Explain.

CONNECTION TO ANOTHER SELECTION

1. To what extent are the "Delinquent Palaces" in this poem present in "I felt a Cleaving in my Mind —" (p. 972)? How are the themes in each poem related?

Oh Sumptuous moment   *c. 1868*

Oh Sumptuous moment
Slower go
That I may gloat on thee —
'Twill never be the same to starve
Now I abundance see —

Which was to famish, then or now —
The difference of Day
Ask him unto the Gallows led —
With morning in the sky

CONSIDERATIONS FOR CRITICAL THINKING AND WRITING

1. FIRST RESPONSE. How do the sounds of the first stanza contribute to its meaning?
2. What kind of moment do you imagine the speaker is describing?
3. How do the final three lines shed light on the meaning of lines 1–6?

CONNECTIONS TO OTHER SELECTIONS

1. Compare and contrast the themes of this poem, "Water, is taught by thirst," (p. 958), and "'Heaven' — is what I cannot reach!" (p. 961).

The Bustle in a House

c. 1866

The Bustle in a House
The Morning after Death
Is solemnest of industries
Enacted upon Earth —

The Sweeping up the Heart
And putting Love away
We shall not want to use again
Until Eternity.

CONSIDERATIONS FOR CRITICAL THINKING AND WRITING

1. FIRST RESPONSE. What is the relationship between love and death in this poem?

2. Why do you think mourning (notice the pun in line 2) is described as industry?

3. Discuss the tone of the ending of the poem. Consider whether you think it is hopeful, sad, resigned, or some other mood.

CONNECTIONS TO OTHER SELECTIONS

1. Compare this poem with "After great pain, a formal feeling comes—" (p. 969). Which poem is, for you, a more powerful treatment of mourning?

2. How does this poem qualify "I like a look of Agony" (p. 962)? Does it contradict the latter poem? Explain why or why not.

Tell all the Truth but tell it slant—

c. 1868

Tell all the Truth but tell it slant —
Success in Circuit lies
Too bright for our infirm Delight
The Truth's superb surprise

As Lightning to the Children eased
With explanation kind
The Truth must dazzle gradually
Or every man be blind —

CONSIDERATIONS FOR CRITICAL THINKING AND WRITING

1. FIRST RESPONSE. What do you think the first line means? Why should truth be told "slant" and circuitously?

2. How does the second stanza explain the first?

3. How is this poem an example of its own theme?

CONNECTIONS TO OTHER SELECTIONS

1. How does the first stanza of "I know that He exists" (p. 990) suggest an idea similar to this poem's? Why do you think the last eight lines of the former aren't similar in theme to this poem?

2. Write an essay on Dickinson's attitudes about the purpose and strategies of poetry by considering this poem as well as "The Thought beneath so slight a film—" (p. 955) and "Portraits are to daily faces" (p. 960).

PERSPECTIVES ON DICKINSON

Dickinson's Description of Herself   1862

Mr Higginson,
    Your kindness claimed earlier gratitude — but I was ill — and write today, from my pillow.
    Thank you for the surgery — it was not so painful as I supposed. I bring you others° — as you ask — though they might not differ —
    While my thought is undressed — I can make the distinction, but when I put them in the Gown — they look alike, and numb.
    You asked how old I was? I made no verse — but one or two° — until this winter — Sir —
    I had a terror — since September — I could tell to none — and so I sing, as the Boy does by the Burying Ground — because I am afraid — You inquire my Books — For Poets — I have Keats — and Mr and Mrs Browning. For Prose — Mr Ruskin — Sir Thomas Browne — and the Revelations. I went to school — but in your manner of the phrase — had no education. When a little Girl, I had a friend, who taught me Immortality — but venturing too near, himself — he never returned — Soon after, my Tutor, died — and for several years, my Lexicon — was my only companion — Then I found one more — but he was not contented I be his scholar — so he left the Land.
    You ask of my Companions Hills — Sir — and the Sundown — and a Dog — large as myself, that my Father bought me — They are better than Beings — because they know — but do not tell — and the noise in the Pool, at Noon — excels my Piano. I have a Brother and Sister — My Mother does not care for thought — and Father, too busy with his Briefs — to notice what we do — He buys me many Books — but begs me not to read them — because he fears they joggle the Mind. They are religious — except me — and address an Eclipse, every morning — whom they call their "Father." But I fear my story fatigues you — I would like to learn — Could you tell me how to grow — or is it unconveyed — like Melody — or Witchcraft?
                    From a letter to Thomas Wentworth Higginson, April 25, 1862

others: Dickinson had sent poems to Higginson for his opinions and enclosed more with this letter. *one or two:* Actually she had written almost three hundred poems.

Considerations for Critical Thinking and Writing

1. What impression does this letter give you of Dickinson?
2. What kinds of thoughts are there in the foreground of her thinking?
3. To what extent is the style of her letter writing like that of her poetry?

THOMAS WENTWORTH HIGGINSON (1823-1911)

On Meeting Dickinson for the First Time   1870

A large county lawyer's house, brown brick, with great trees & a garden—I sent up my card. A parlor dark & cool & stiffish, a few books & engravings & an open piano. . . .
    A step like a pattering child's in entry & in glided a little plain woman with two smooth bands of reddish hair & a face a little like Belle Dove's; not plainer—with no good feature—in a very plain & exquisitely clean white pique & a blue net worsted shawl. She came to me with two day lilies which she put in a sort of childlike way into my hand & said "These are my introduction" in a soft frightened breathless childlike voice—& added under her breath Forgive me if I am frightened; I never see strangers & hardly know what I say—but she talked soon & thenceforward continuously—& deferentially—sometimes stopping to ask me to talk instead of her—but readily recommencing . . . thoroughly ingenuous & simple . . . & saying many things which you would have thought foolish & I wise—& some things you wd. hv. liked. I add a few over the page. . . .

    "Women talk; men are silent; that is why I dread women."
    "My father only reads on Sunday—he reads *lonely* & *rigorous* books."
    "If I read a book [and] it makes my whole body so cold no fire ever can warm me I know *that* is poetry. If I feel physically as if the top of my head were taken off, I know *that* is poetry. These are the only ways I know it. Is there any other way."
    "How do most people live without any thoughts. There are many people in the world (you must have noticed them in the street) How do they live. How do they get strength to put on their clothes in the morning"
    "When I lost the use of my Eyes it was a comfort to think there were so few real *books* that I could easily find some one to read me all of them"
    "Truth is such a *rare* thing it is delightful to tell it."
    "I find ecstasy in living—the mere sense of living is joy enough"
    I asked if she never felt want of employment, never going off the place & never seeing any visitor "I never thought of conceiving that I could ever have the slightest approach to such a want in all future time" (& added) "I feel that I have not expressed myself strongly enough."

From a letter to his wife, August 16, 1870

CONSIDERATIONS FOR CRITICAL THINKING AND WRITING

1. How old is Dickinson when Higginson meets her? Does this description seem commensurate with her age? Explain why or why not.

2. Choose one of the quotations from Dickinson that Higginson includes and write an essay about what it reveals about her.

MABEL LOOMIS TODD (1856–1932)

The Character *of Amherst*   *1881*

I must tell you about the *character* of Amherst. It is a lady whom the people call the *Myth*. She is a sister of Mr. Dickinson, & seems to be the climax of all the family oddity. She has not been outside of her own house in fifteen years, except once to see a new church, when she crept out at night, & viewed it by moonlight. No one who calls upon her mother & sister ever see her, but she allows little children once in a great while, & one at a time, to come in, when she gives them cake or candy, or some nicety, for she is very fond of little ones. But more often she lets down the sweetmeat by a string, out of a window, to them. She dresses wholly in white, & her mind is said to be perfectly wonderful. She writes finely, but no one *ever* sees her. Her sister, who was at Mrs. Dickinson's party, invited me to come & sing to her mother sometime. . . . People tell me the *myth* will hear every note — she will be near, but unseen. . . . Isn't that like a book? So interesting.

From a letter to her parents, November 6, 1881

CONSIDERATIONS FOR CRITICAL THINKING AND WRITING

1. Todd, who in the 1890s would edit Dickinson's poems and letters, had known her for only two months when she wrote this letter. How does Todd characterize Dickinson?

2. Does this description seem positive or negative to you? Explain your answer.

3. A few of Dickinson's poems, such as "Much Madness is divinest Sense—" (p. 966) suggest that she was aware of this perception of her. Refer to her poems in discussing Dickinson's response to this perception.

RICHARD WILBUR (B. 1921)

On Dickinson's Sense of Privation   *1960*

What did Emily Dickinson do, as a poet, with her sense of privation? One thing she quite often did was to pose as the laureate and attorney of the empty-handed, and question God about the economy of His creation. Why, she asked, is a fatherly God so sparing of His presence? Why is there never a sign that prayers are heard? Why does Nature tell us no comforting news of its Maker? Why do some receive a whole loaf, while others must starve on a crumb? Where is the benevolence in shipwreck and earthquake? By asking such questions as these, she turned complaint into critique, and used her own sufferings as experiential evidence about the nature of the deity. The God who emerges from these poems is a God who does not answer, an unrevealed God whom one cannot confidently approach through Nature or through doctrine.

But there was another way in which Emily Dickinson dealt with her sentiment of lack — another emotional strategy which was both more frequent and more fruitful. I refer to her repeated assertion of the paradox that privation is more plentiful than plenty; that to renounce is to possess the more; that "The Banquet of abstemiousness / Defaces that of wine." We all know how the poet illustrated this ascetic paradox in her behavior—how in her latter years she chose to live in relative retirement, keeping the world, even in its dearest aspects, at a physical remove. She would write her friends, telling them how she missed them, then flee upstairs when they came to see her; afterward, she might send a note of apology, offering the odd explanation that "We shun because we prize." Any reader of Dickinson biographies can furnish other examples, dramatic or homely, of this prizing and shunning, this yearning and renouncing: in my own mind's eye is a picture of Emily Dickinson watching a gay circus caravan from the distance of her chamber window.

From "Sumptuous Destitution" in *Emily Dickinson: Three Views,* by Richard Wilbur, Louise Bogan, and Archibald MacLeish

CONSIDERATIONS FOR CRITICAL THINKING AND WRITING

1. Which poems by Dickinson reprinted in this anthology suggest that she was "the laureate and attorney of the empty-handed"?
2. Which poems suggest that "privation is more plentiful"?
3. Of these two types of poems, which do you prefer? Write an essay that explains your preference.

SANDRA M. GILBERT (B. 1936) AND
SUSAN GUBAR (B. 1944)
On Dickinson's White Dress   *1979*

Today a dress that the Amherst Historical Society assures us is *the* white dress Dickinson wore—or at least one of her "Uniforms of Snow"—hangs in a drycleaner's plastic bag in the closet of the Dickinson homestead. Perfectly preserved, beautifully flounced and tucked, it is larger than most readers would have expected this self-consciously small poet's dress to be, and thus reminds visiting scholars of the enduring enigma of Dickinson's central metaphor, even while it draws gasps from more practical visitors, who reflect with awe upon the difficulties of maintaining such a costume. But what exactly did the literal and figurative whiteness of this costume represent? What rewards did it offer that would cause an intelligent woman to overlook those practical difficulties? Comparing Dickinson's obsession with whiteness to Melville's, William R. Sherwood suggests that "it reflected in her case the Christian mystery and not a Christian enigma . . . a decision to announce . . . the assumption of a worldly death that paradoxically involved regeneration." This, he adds, her gown—"a typically slant demonstration of truth"—should have revealed "to anyone with the wit to catch on."[1]

We might reasonably wonder, however, if Dickinson herself consciously intended her wardrobe to convey any one message. The range of associations her white poems imply suggests, on the contrary, that for her, as for Melville, white is the ultimate symbol of enigma, paradox, and irony, "not so much a

[1] *Circumference and Circumstance: Stages in the Mind and Art of Emily Dickinson* (New York: Columbia UP, 1968) 152, 231.

color as the visible absence of color, and at the same time the concrete of all colors." Melville's question [in *Moby-Dick*] might, therefore, also be hers: "is it for these reasons that there is such a dumb blankness, full of meaning, in a wide landscape of snows—a colorless, all-color of atheism from which we shrink?" And his concluding speculation might be hers too, his remark "that the mystical cosmetic which produces every one of [Nature's] hues, the great principle of light, for ever remains white or colorless in itself, and if operating without medium upon matter, would touch all objects . . . with its own blank tinge." For white, in Dickinson's poetry, frequently represents both the energy (the white heat) of Romantic creativity, and the loneliness (the polar cold) of the renunciation or tribulation Romantic creativity may demand, both the white radiance of eternity—or Revelation—and the white terror of a shroud.

From *The Madwoman in the Attic: The Woman Writer and the Nineteenth-Century Literary Imagination*

Considerations for Critical Thinking and Writing

1. What meanings do Gilbert and Gubar attribute to Dickinson's white dress?

2. Discuss the meaning of the implicit whiteness in "Safe in their Alabaster Chambers—" (p. 958) and "After great pain, a formal feeling comes—" (p. 969). To what extent do these poems incorporate the meanings of whiteness that Gilbert and Gubar suggest?

3. What other possible reasons can you think of that would account for Dickinson's wearing only white?

Karl Keller (b. 1933)

Robert Frost on Dickinson   1979

Frost lived in Amherst for quite a number of years—1917–20, 1923–25, 1926–38, and then intermittently in the late 1940s and throughout the 1950s when he taught regularly at Amherst College. He often recited her poems from memory, and he conversed with students, friends, and townspeople about her poetry; his concern was almost always over her ability to contain/limit an open-ended universe. He felt this was "what Emily Dickinson surely intends," as he put it, "when she contends: 'In insecurity to lie / Is Joy's insuring quality.'"

It appears that Frost had a one-track mind about Emily Dickinson—her doggedness. For him she was an example of the poet "whose 'state,'" as he put it himself, "never gets sidetracked."

> Since she wrote without thought of publication and was not under the necessity of revamping and polishing, it was easy for her to go right to the point and say precisely what she thought and felt. Her technical irregularities give her poems strength as if she were saying, "Look out, Rhyme and Meter, here I come."

Frost apparently liked this willfulness, the unmanageability of the thought by the poetic form, and yet he thought she arrived at it a little too easily and that it was therefore sometimes indistinguishable from carelessness. He felt she had given up the technical struggle too easily. For Frost, to use a general statement of his about poetic rhythm, she was a little too "easy in [her] harness."[1]

Emily Dickinson succeeded, Frost was forced to admit, by flouting poetic systems, by playing freely with the form.

> I try to make good sentences fit the meter. That is important. Good grammar. I don't like to twist the order around in order to fit a form. I try to keep to regular structure and good rhymes. Though I admit that Emily Dickinson, for one, didn't do this always. When she started a poem, it was "Here I come!" and she came plunging through. The meter and rhyme often had to take care of itself.[2]

Though envious of this carefree energy, Frost was also critical of her when she did not achieve regular forms.

> Emily Dickinson didn't study technique. But she should have been more careful. She was more interested in getting the poem down and writing a new one. I feel that she left some to be revised later, and she never revised them. And those two ladies at Amherst printed a lot of her slipshod work which she might not have liked to see printed. She has all kinds of off rhymes. Some that do not rhyme. Her meter does not always go together.[3]

She was therefore substantially different from him; her ability to be conscious of poetic conventions and yet to rise above them surprised him. He generously yielded her his highest admiration for the heresy.

> One of the great things in life is being true within the conventions. I deny in a good poem or a good life that there is compromise. When there is, it is an attempt to so flex the lines that no suspicion can be cast upon what the poet does. Emily Dickinson's poems are examples of this. When the rhyme begins to bother, she says, "Here I come with my truth. Let the rhyme take care of itself." This makes me feel her strength.[4]

For him the large strain of poetry was "a little shifted from the straight-out, a little curved from the straight." Emily Dickinson's poems were, for him, the best examples of this liberty, this flawing. "Can you imagine some people taking that? Can't you imagine some people not accepting that kind of play at all?"[5]

It was this factor of play in Emily Dickinson's poetry that consistently attracted Frost. "Rime reminds you that poetry is play," he said on one occasion, after reciting a Dickinson poem ("The Mountains — grow unnoticed") and calling it "particularly fine," "and that is one of its chief importances. You shouldn't be too sincere to play or you'll be a fraud."[6] Her mischief with poetic form was an indication to him that she was serious about what she was saying and would bend conventions to get it said, and also that she was having a good time trying to say it, but more important than that, that with her poetry (and her ideas) she was *at play*. He appears to have marveled at that in her. "Poetry," Frost used to exclaim to his friends, "is fooling."[7]

From *The Only Kangaroo Among the Beauty: Emily Dickinson in America*

[1] Robert Francis, *Frost: A Time to Talk* (Amherst, 1972) 53–54.
[2] Daniel Smythe, *Robert Frost Speaks* (New York, np, 1964) 140.
[3] Smythe, 140.
[4] Reginald Lansing Cook, *The Dimensions of Robert Frost* (New York: Barnes and Noble, 1968) 57–58.
[5] Cook, 99.
[6] Cook, 180.
[7] Cook, 181.

CONSIDERATIONS FOR CRITICAL THINKING AND WRITING

1. According to Keller, how did Frost respond to Dickinson's "poetic systems" of rhyme and meter?

2. Explain why you agree or disagree with Frost's assessment of Dickinson's poetry as being "slipshod."

3. Choose a poem from each poet and demonstrate how both are versions of "play."

CYNTHIA GRIFFIN WOLFF (B. 1935)

On the Many Voices in Dickinson's Poetry   1986

There were many "Voices." This fact has sometimes puzzled Dickinson's readers. One poem may be delivered in a child's Voice; another in the Voice of a young woman scrutinizing nature and the society in which she makes her place. Sometimes the Voice is that of a woman self-confidently addressing her lover in a language of passion and sexual desire. At still other times, the Voice of the verse seems so precariously balanced at the edge of hysteria that even its calmest observations grate like the shriek of dementia. There is the Voice of the housewife and the Voice that has recourse to the occasionally agonizing, occasionally regal language of the conversion experience of latter-day New England Puritanism. In some poems the Voice is distinctive principally because it speaks in the aftermath of wounding and can comprehend extremities of pain. Moreover, these Voices are not always entirely distinct from one another: the child's Voice that opens a poem may yield to the Voice of a young woman speaking the idiom of ardent love; in a different poem, the speaker may fall into a mood of almost religious contemplation in an attempt to analyze or define such abstract entities as loneliness or madness or eternity; the diction of the housewife may be conflated with the sovereign language of the New Jerusalem, and taken together, they may render some aspect of the wordsmith's labor. No manageable set of discrete categories suffices to capture the diversity of discourse, and any attempt to simplify Dickinson's methods does violence to the verse.

Yet there is a paradox here. This is, by no stretch of the imagination, a body of poetry that might be construed as a series of lyrics spoken by many different people. Disparate as these many Voices are, somehow they all appear to issue from the same "self." . . . It is the enigmatic "Emily Dickinson" readers suppose themselves to have found in this poetry, even in the extreme case when Dickinson's supposed speaker is male. One explanation for this sense of intrinsic unity in the midst of diversity is the persistence with which Dickinson addresses the same set of problems, using a remarkably durable repertoire of linguistic modes. Evocations of injury and wounding—threats to the coherence of the self—appear in the earliest poems and continue until the end; ways of rendering face-to-face encounters change, but this preoccupation with "interview" is sustained by metaphors of "confrontation" that weave throughout. The summoning of one or another Voice in a given poem, then, is not an unselfconscious emotive reflection of Emily Dickinson's mood at the moment of creation. Rather, each different Voice is a calculated tactic, an attempt to touch her readers and engage them intimately with the poetry. Each Voice had its unique advantages; each its limitations. A poet self-conscious in her craft, she calculated this element as carefully as every other.

From *Emily Dickinson*

CONSIDERATIONS FOR CRITICAL THINKING AND WRITING

1. From the poems in this anthology, try adding to the list of voices Wolff cites.

2. Despite the many voices in Dickinson's poetry, why, according to Wolff, is there still a "sense of intrinsic unity" in her poetry?

3. Choose a Dickinson poem and describe how the choice of voice is a "calculated tactic."

PAULA BENNETT (B. 1936)

On "I heard a Fly buzz — when I died —" 1990

Dickinson's rage against death, a rage that led her at times to hate both life and death, might have been alleviated, had she been able to gather hard evidence about an afterlife. But, of course, she could not. "The *Bareheaded life* — under the grass —," she wrote to Samuel Bowles in c. 1860, "worries one like a Wasp." If death was the gate to a better life in "the childhood of the kingdom of Heaven," as the sentimentalists — and Christ — claimed, then, perhaps, there was compensation and healing for life's woes. . . . But how do we know? What can we know? In "I heard a Fly buzz — when I died," Dickinson concludes that we do not know much. . . .

Like many people in her period, Dickinson was fascinated by death-bed scenes. How, she asked various correspondents, did this or that person die? In particular, she wanted to know if their deaths revealed any information about the nature of the afterlife. In this poem, however, she imagines her own death-bed scene, and the answer she provides is grim, as grim (and, at the same time, as ironically mocking), as anything she ever wrote.

In the narrowing focus of death, the fly's insignificant buzz, magnified tenfold by the stillness in the room, is all that the speaker hears. This kind of distortion in scale is common. It is one of the "illusions" of perception. But here it is horrifying because it defeats every expectation we have. Death is supposed to be an experience of awe. It is the moment when the soul, departing the body, is taken up by God. Hence the watchers at the bedside wait for the moment when the "King" (whether God or death) "be witnessed" in the room. And hence the speaker assigns away everything but that which she expects God (her soul) or death (her body) to take.

What arrives instead, however, is neither God nor death but a fly, "[w]ith Blue — uncertain — stumbling Buzz," a fly, that is, no more secure, no more sure, than we are. Dickinson had associated flies with death once before in the exquisite lament, "How many times these low feet / staggered." In this poem, they buzz "on the / chamber window," and speckle it with dirt, reminding us that the housewife, who once protected us from such intrusions, will protect us no longer. Their presence is threatening but only in a minor way, "dull" like themselves. They are a background noise we do not have to deal with yet.

In "I heard a Fly buzz," on the other hand, there is only one fly and its buzz is not only foregrounded. Before the poem is over, the buzz takes up the entire field of perception, coming between the speaker and the "light" (of day, of life, of knowledge). It is then that the "Windows" (the eyes that are the windows of the soul as well as, metonymically, the light that passes through the panes of glass) "fail" and the speaker is left in darkness—in death, in ignorance. She cannot "see" to "see" (understand).

Given that the only sure thing we know about "life after death" is that flies—in their adult form and more particularly, as maggots—devour us, the poem is at the very least a grim joke. In projecting her death-bed scene, Dickinson confronts her ignorance and gives back the only answer human knowledge can with any certainty give. While we may hope for an afterlife, no one, not even the dying, can prove it exists.

From *Emily Dickinson: Woman Poet*

CONSIDERATIONS FOR CRITICAL THINKING AND WRITING

1. According to Bennett, what is the symbolic value of the fly?
2. Does Bennett leave out any significant elements of the poem in her analysis? Explain why you think she did or did not.
3. Choose a Dickinson poem and write a detailed analysis that attempts to account for all its major elements.

GALWAY KINNELL (B. 1927)

The Deconstruction of Emily Dickinson   1994

The lecture had ended when I came in,
and the professor was answering questions.
I do not know what he had been doing with her
poetry, but now he was speaking of her
as a victim of reluctant male publishers.   5
When the questions dwindled, I put up my hand.
I said the ignorant meddling of the Springfield *Daily Republican*
and the hidebound response of literary men,
and the gulf between the poetic wishfulness
then admired and her own harsh knowledge,   10
had let her see that her poems
would not be understood in her time;
and therefore, passionate to publish,
she vowed not to publish again. I said
I would recite a version of her vow,   15

      Publication—is the Auction
      Of the mind of Man—

But before I could, the professor broke in.
"Yes," he said, "'the Auction'—'auction,' from *augere, auctum,* to augment,
      to author . . ."

"Let's hear the poem!" "The poem!" several women,   20
who at such a moment are more outspoken than men, shouted,
but I kept still and he kept going.
"In *auctum* the economy of the signifier is split, revealing an unconscious
    collusion in the bourgeois commodification of consciousness. While
    our author says 'no,' the unreified text says 'yes,' yes?"
He kissed his lips together and turned to me
saying, "Now, may we hear the poem?"   25
I waited a moment for full effect.
Without rising to my feet, I said,
"Professor, to understand Dickinson
it may not always be necessary to uproot her words.
Why not, first, try *listening* to her?   30
Loyalty forbids me to recite her poem now."
No, I didn't say that — I realized
she would want me to finish him off with one wallop.
So I said, "Professor, I thought you
would welcome the words of your author.   35
I see you prefer to hear yourself speak."
No, I held back — for I could hear her
urging me to put outrage into my voice
and substance into my argument.
I stood up so that everyone might see   40
the derision in my smile. "Professor," I said,
"you live in Amherst at the end of the twentieth century.
For you 'auction' means a quaint event
where somebody coaxes out the bids
on butter churns on a summer Saturday.   45
Forget etymology, this is history.
In Amherst in 1860 'auction' meant
the slave auction, you dope!"
Well, I didn't say that either,
although I have said them all,   50
many times, in the middle of the night.
In reality, I stood up and recited
like a schoolboy called upon in class.
My voice gradually weakened, and the women
who had called out for the poem   55
now looked as though they were thinking
of errands to be done on the way home.
When I finished, the professor smiled.
"Thank you. So, what at first some of us may have taken as a simple outcry,
    we all now see is an ambivalent, self-subversive text."
As people got up to go, I moved   60
into that sanctum within me where Emily
sometimes speaks a verse, and listened
for a sign of how she felt, such as,
"Thanks — Sweet — countryman —
for wanting — to Sing out — of Me —   65
after all that Humbug." But she was silent.

CONSIDERATIONS FOR CRITICAL THINKING AND WRITING

1. Describe the professor's critical approach to Dickinson's poetry (for information about deconstructionist criticism, see pp. 2111–13). How does it compare to the speaker's approach? What does he value in Dickinson's poetry?

2. Discuss the use of irony in the poem.

3. Do you think it inevitable that a poet's response to poetry will be different from a critic's? Explain your answer.

TWO COMPLEMENTARY
CRITICAL READINGS

CHARLES R. ANDERSON (B. 1902)

Eroticism in "Wild Nights — Wild Nights!"   *1960*

The frank eroticism of this poem might puzzle the biographer of a spinster, but the critic can only be concerned with its effectiveness as a poem. Unless one insists on taking the "I" to mean Emily Dickinson, there is not even any reversal of the lovers' roles (which has been charged, curiously enough, as a fault in this poem). The opening declaration — "Wild Nights should be / Our luxury!" — sets the key of her song, for *luxuria* included the meaning of lust as well as lavishness of sensuous enjoyment, as she was Latinist enough to know. This is echoed at the end in "Eden," her recurring image, in letters and poems, for the paradise of earthly love. The theme here is that of sexual passion which is lawless, outside the rule of "Chart" and "Compass." But it lives by a law of its own, the law of Eden, which protects it from mundane wind and wave.

This is what gives the magic to her climactic vision, "Rowing in Eden," sheltered luxuriously in those paradisiac waters while the wild storms of this world break about them. Such love was only possible before the Fall. Since then the bower of bliss is frugal of her leases, limiting each occupant to "an instant" she says in another poem, for "Adam taught her Thrift / Bankrupt once through his excesses." In the present poem she limits her yearning to the mortal term, just "Tonight." But this echoes the surge of ecstasy that initiated her song and gives the reiterated "Wild Nights!" a double reference, to the passionate experience in Eden as well as to the tumult of the world shut out by it. So she avoids the chief pitfall of the love lyric, the tendency to exploit emotion for its own sake. Instead she generates out of the conflicting aspects of love, its ecstasy and its brevity, the symbol that contains the poem's meaning.

From *Emily Dickinson's Poetry: Stairway of Surprise*

CONSIDERATIONS FOR CRITICAL THINKING AND WRITING

1. According to Anderson what is the theme of "Wild Nights — Wild Nights!"?

2. How does Anderson discuss the "frank eroticism" of the poem? How detailed is his discussion?

3. If there is a "reversal of the lovers' roles" in this poem, do you think it represents, as some critics have charged, "a fault in this poem"? Explain why or why not.

4. Compare Anderson's treatment of this poem with David S. Reynolds's reading that follows. Discuss which one you find more useful and explain why.

DAVID S. REYNOLDS (B. 1949)
Popular Literature and "Wild Nights—Wild Nights!"   1988

It is not known whether Dickinson had read any of the erotic literature of the day or if she knew of the stereotype of the sensual woman. Given her fascination with sensational journalism and with popular literature in general, it is hard to believe she would not have had at least some exposure to erotic literature. At any rate, her treatment of the daring theme of woman's sexual fantasy in this deservedly famous poem bears comparison with erotic themes as they appeared in popular sensational writings. The first stanza of the poem provides an uplifting or purification of sexual fantasy not distant from the effect of Whitman's cleansing rhetoric, which, as we have seen, was consciously designed to counteract the prurience of the popular "love plot." Dickinson's repeated phrase "Wild Nights" is a simple but dazzling metaphor that communicates wild passion—even lust—but simultaneously lifts sexual desire out of the scabrous by fusing it with the natural image of the night. The second verse introduces a second nature image, the turbulent sea and the contrasting quiet port, which at once universalizes the passion and purifies it further by distancing it through a more abstract metaphor. Also, the second verse makes clear that this is not a poem of sexual consummation but rather of pure fantasy and sexual impossibility. Unlike popular erotic literature, the poem portrays neither a consummated seduction nor the heartless deception that it involves. There is instead a pure, fervent fantasy whose frustration is figured forth in the contrasting images of the ocean (the longed-for-but-never-achieved consummation) and the port (the reality of the poet's isolation). The third verse begins with an image, "Rowing in Eden," that further uplifts sexual passion by yoking it with a religious archetype. Here as elsewhere, Dickinson capitalizes nicely on the new religious style, which made possible such fusions of the divine and the earthly. The persona's concluding wish to "moor" in the sea expresses the sustained intense sexual longing and the simultaneous frustration of that longing. In the course of the poem, Dickinson has communicated great erotic passion, and yet, by effectively projecting this passion through unusual nature and religious images, has rid it of even the tiniest residue of sensationalism.

From *Beneath the American Renaissance: The Subversive Imagination*
in the Age of Emerson and Melville

CONSIDERATIONS FOR CRITICAL THINKING AND WRITING

1. According to Reynolds, how do Dickinson's images provide a "cleansing" effect in the poem?
2. Explain whether you agree that the poem portrays a "pure, fervent fantasy" or something else.
3. Does Reynolds's reading of the poem compete with Anderson's or complement it? Explain your answer.
4. Given the types of critical strategies described in Chapter 52, how would you characterize Anderson's and Reynolds's approaches?

QUESTIONS FOR WRITING ABOUT AN AUTHOR IN DEPTH

This section includes four poems by Emily Dickinson as the subject of a sample in-depth study of her poetry. The following questions can help you to respond to multiple works by the same author. You're likely to be struck by the similarities and differences in works by the same author. Previous knowledge of a writer's work can set up useful expectations in a reader. By being familiar with a number of works by the same writer you can begin to discern particular kinds of concerns and techniques that characterize and help to shed light on a writer's work.

As you read multiple works by the same author you'll begin to recognize situations, events, characters, issues, perspectives, styles, and strategies — even recurring words or phrases — that provide a kind of signature, making the poem in some way identifiable with that particular writer. In the case of the four Dickinson poems included in this section, religion emerges as a central topic linked to a number of issues including faith, immortality, skepticism, and the nature of God. The student selected these poems because he noticed Dickinson's intense interest in religious faith owing to the many poems that explore a variety of religious attitudes in her work. He chose these four because they were closely related, but he also might have found equally useful clusters of poems about love, nature, domestic life, or writing as well as other topics. What especially intrigued him was some of the information he read about Dickinson's sternly religious father and the orthodox nature of the religious values of her hometown of Amherst, Massachusetts. Since this paper was not a research paper, he did not pursue these issues beyond the level of the general remarks provided in an introduction to her poetry (though he might have). He did, however, use this biographical and historical information as a means of framing his search for poems that were related to one another. In doing so he discovered consistent concerns along with contradictory themes that became the basis of his paper.

The questions provided below should help you to listen to how a writer's works can speak to each other and to you. Additional useful questions will be found in other chapters of this book. See Writing about Poetry (p. 708) and Arguing about Literature (p. 2137).

1. What topics reappear in the writer's work? What seem to be the major concerns of the author?
2. Does the author have a definable world view that can be discerned from work to work? Is, for example, the writer liberal, conservative, apolitical, or religious?
3. What social values come through in the author's work? Does he or she seem to identify with a particular group or social class?
4. Is there a consistent voice or point of view from work to work? Is it a persona or the author's actual self?

5. How much of the author's own life experiences and historical moment make their way into the works?

6. Does the author experiment with style from work to work, or are the works mostly consistent with one another?

7. Can the author's work be identified with a literary tradition, such as *carpe diem* poetry, that aligns his or her work with that of other writers?

8. What is distinctive about the author's writing? Is the language innovative? Are the themes challenging? Are the voices conventional? Is the tone characteristic?

9. Could you identify another work by the same author without a name being attached to it? What are the distinctive features that allow you to do so?

10. Do any of the writer's works seem *not* to be by that writer? Why?

11. What other writers are most like this author in style and content? Why?

12. Has the writer's work evolved over time? Are there significant changes or developments? Are there new ideas and styles, or do the works remain largely the same?

13. How would you characterize the writing habits of the writer? Is it possible to anticipate what goes on in different works, or are you surprised by their content or style?

14. Can difficult or ambiguous passages in a work be resolved by referring to a similar passage in another work?

15. What does the writer say about his or her own work? Do you trust the teller or the tale? Which do you think is more reliable?

A SAMPLE IN-DEPTH STUDY

Religious Faith in Four Poems by Emily Dickinson

The following paper was written for an assignment that called for an analysis (about 750 words) on any topic that could be traced in three or four poems by Dickinson. The student chose "'Faith' is a fine invention," "I know that He exists," "I never saw a Moor —," and "Apparently with no surprise."

"Faith" is a fine invention   c. 1860

"Faith" is a fine invention
When Gentlemen can *see* —
But *Microscopes* are prudent
In an Emergency.

I know that He exists

c. 1862

I know that He exists.
Somewhere — in Silence —
He has hid his rare life
From our gross eyes.

'Tis an instant's play.   5
'Tis a fond Ambush —
Just to make Bliss
Earn her own surprise!

But — should the play
Prove piercing earnest —   10
Should the glee-glaze —
In Death's — stiff — stare —

Would not the fun
Look too expensive!
Would not the jest —   15
Have crawled too far!

I never saw a Moor —

c. 1865

I never saw a Moor —
I never saw the Sea —
Yet know I how the Heather looks
And what a Billow be.

I never spoke with God
Nor visited in Heaven —
Yet certain am I of the spot
As if the Checks were given —

Apparently with no surprise

c. 1884

Apparently with no surprise
To any happy Flower
The Frost beheads it at its play —
In accidental power —
The blond Assassin passes on —
The Sun proceeds unmoved
To measure off another Day
For an Approving God.

Michael Weitz

Professor Pearl

English 270

May 5, 20--

Religious Faith in Four Poems by Emily Dickinson

Throughout much of her poetry, Emily Dickinson wrestles with complex notions of God, faith, and religious devotion. She adheres to no consistent view of religion; rather, her poetry reveals a vision of God and faith that is constantly evolving. Dickinson's gods range from the strict and powerful Old Testament father to a loving spiritual guide to an irrational and ridiculous imaginary figure. Through these varying images of God, Dickinson portrays contrasting images of the meaning and validity of religious faith. Her work reveals competing attitudes toward religious devotion as conventional religious piety struggles with a more cynical perception of God and religious worship.

Dickinson's "I never saw a Moor--" reveals a vision of traditional religious sensibilities. Although the speaker readily admits that "I never spoke with God / Nor visited in Heaven," her devout faith in a supreme being does not waver. The poem appears to be a straightforward profession of true faith stemming from the argument that the proof of God's existence is the universe's existence. Dickinson's imagery therefore evolves from the natural to the supernatural, first establishing her convictions that Moors and Seas exist, in spite of her lack of personal contact with either. This leads to the foundation of her religious faith, again based not on physical experience but on intellectual convictions. The speaker professes that she believes in the existence of Heaven even without conclusive evidence: "Yet certain am I of the spot / As if the

Checks were given--" But the appearance of such idealistic
views of God and faith in "I never saw a Moor--" are
transformed in Dickinson's other poems into a much more
skeptical vision of the validity of religious piety.

While faith is portrayed as an authentic and deeply
important quality in "I never saw a Moor--," Dickinson's
"'Faith' is a fine invention" portrays faith as much less
essential. Faith is defined in the poem as "a fine invention" suggesting that it is created by man for man and
therefore is not a crucial aspect of the natural universe.
Thus the strong idealistic faith of "I never saw a Moor--"
becomes discredited in the face of scientific rationalism.
The speaker compares religious faith with actual microscopes, both of which are meant to enhance one's vision in
some way. But "Faith" is useful only "When Gentlemen can
see--" already; "In an Emergency," when one ostensibly
cannot see, "Microscopes are prudent." Dickinson pits religion against science, suggesting that science, with its
tangible evidence and rational attitude, is a more reliable lens through which to view the world. Faith is irreverently reduced to a mere invention and one that is
ultimately less useful than microscopes or other scientific instruments.

Rational, scientific observations are not the only
contributing factor to the portrayal of religious skepticism in Dickinson's poems; nature itself is seen to be
incompatible in some ways with conventional religious ideology. In "Apparently with no surprise," the speaker recognizes the inexorable cycle of natural life and death as
a morning frost kills a flower. But the tension in this
poem stems not from the "happy Flower" struck down by the
frost's "accidental power" but from the apparent indifference of the "Approving God" who condones this seemingly

cruel and unnecessary death. God is seen as remote and uncompromising, and it is this perceived distance between the speaker and God that reveals the increasing absurdity of traditional religious faith. The speaker understands that praying to God or believing in religion cannot change the course of nature, and as a result feels so helplessly distanced from God that religious faith becomes virtually meaningless.

Dickinson's religious skepticism becomes even more explicit in "I know that He exists," in which the speaker attempts to understand the connection between seeing God and facing death. In this poem Dickinson characterizes God as a remote and mysterious figure; the speaker mockingly asserts, "I know that He exists," even though "He has hid his rare life / From our gross eyes." The skepticism toward religious faith revealed in this poem stems from the speaker's recognition of the paradoxical quest that people undertake to know and to see God. A successful attempt to see God, to win the game of hide-and-seek that He apparently is orchestrating, results inevitably in death. With this recognition the speaker comes to view religion as an absurd and reckless game in which the prize may be "Bliss" but more likely is "Death's--stiff--stare--." For to see God and to meet one's death as a result certainly suggests that the game of trying to see God (the so-called "fun") is much "too expensive" and that religion itself is a "jest" that, like the serpent in Genesis, has "crawled too far."

Ultimately, the vision of religious faith that Dickinson describes in her poems is one of suspicion and cynicism. She cannot reconcile the physical world to the spiritual existence that Christian doctrine teaches, and as a result the traditional perception of God becomes ludicrous. "I never saw a Moor--" does attempt to sustain a conventional vision of religious devotion, but Dickinson's poems overall are far more likely to suggest that God is elusive, indifferent, and often cruel, thus undermining the traditional vision of God as a loving father worthy of devout worship. Thus, not only religious faith but also those who are religiously faithful become targets for Dickinson's irreverent criticism of conventional belief.

SUGGESTED TOPICS FOR LONGER PAPERS

1. Irony is abundant in Dickinson's poetry. Choose five poems from this chapter that strike you as especially ironic and discuss her use of irony in each. Taken individually and collectively, what do these poems suggest to you about the poet's sensibilities and her ways of looking at the world?

2. Readers have often noted that Dickinson's poetry does not reflect very much of the social, political, economic, religious, and historical events of her lifetime. Using the poems in this chapter as the basis of your discussion, what can you say about the contexts in which Dickinson wrote? What kind of world do you think she inhabited, and how did she respond to it?

3. MULTIMEDIA PROJECT. Use the library and the Internet to find poems published by women during the 1860s in American newspapers and magazines. How do these poems compare in style, tone, content, and theme to Dickinson's?

Web *For help with this project, use the Multimedia Project Guides Online at* http://www.bedfordstmartins.com/meyer/bedintrolit

32

A Study of Robert Frost

Though all poets' works are undoubtedly affected by the facts of their biographies, Robert Frost's poems are especially known for their reflection of New England life. Although the poems included in this chapter evoke the landscapes of Frost's life and work, the depth and range of those landscapes are far more complicated than his popular reputation typically acknowledges. He was an enormously private man and a much more subtle poet than many of his readers have expected him to be. His poems warrant careful, close readings. As you explore his poetry, you may find useful the Questions for Writing about an Author in Depth (p. 988) as a means of stimulating your thinking about his life and work.

A BRIEF BIOGRAPHY

Few poets have enjoyed the popular success that Robert Frost (1874–1963) achieved during his lifetime, and no twentieth-century American poet has had his or her work as widely read and honored. Frost is as much associated with New England as the stone walls that help define its landscape; his reputation, however, transcends regional boundaries. Although he was named poet laureate of Vermont only two years before his death, he was for many years the nation's unofficial poet laureate. Frost collected honors the way some people pick up burrs on country walks. Among his awards were four Pulitzer Prizes, the Bollingen Prize, a Congressional Medal, and dozens of honorary degrees. Perhaps his most moving appearance was his recitation of "The Gift Outright" for millions of Americans at the inauguration of John F. Kennedy in 1961.

Robert Frost at his writing desk in Franconia, New Hampshire, 1915. Courtesy of the Jones Library, Inc., Amherst, Mass. Reprinted by permission of the Robert Frost Estate.

Frost's recognition as a poet is especially remarkable because his career as a writer did not attract any significant attention until he was nearly forty years old. He taught himself to write while he labored at odd jobs, taught school, or farmed.

Frost's early identity seems very remote from the New England soil. Although his parents were descended from generations of New Englanders, he was born in San Francisco and was named Robert Lee Frost after the Confederate general. After his father died in 1885, his mother moved the family back to Massachusetts to live with relatives. Frost graduated from high school sharing valedictorian honors with the classmate who would become his wife three years later. Between high school and marriage, he attended Dartmouth College for a few months and then taught. His teaching prompted him to enroll in Harvard in 1897, but after less than two years he withdrew without a degree (though Harvard would eventually award him an honorary doctorate in 1937, four years after Dartmouth conferred its honorary degree on him). For the next decade, Frost read and wrote poems when he was not chicken farming or teaching. In 1912, he sold his farm and moved his family to England, where he hoped to find the audience that his poetry did not have in America.

Three years in England made it possible for Frost to return home as a poet. His first two volumes of poetry, *A Boy's Will* (1913) and *North of Boston*

(1914), were published in England. During the next twenty years, honors and awards were conferred on collections such as *Mountain Interval* (1916), *New Hampshire* (1923), *West-Running Brook* (1928), and *A Further Range* (1936). These are the volumes on which most of Frost's popular and critical reputation rests. Later collections include *A Witness Tree* (1942), *A Masque of Reason* (1945), *Steeple Bush* (1947), *A Masque of Mercy* (1947), *Complete Poems* (1949), and *In the Clearing* (1962). In addition to publishing his works, Frost endeared himself to audiences throughout the country by presenting his poetry almost as conversations. He also taught at a number of schools, including Amherst College, the University of Michigan, Harvard University, Dartmouth College, and Middlebury College.

Frost's countless poetry readings generated wide audiences eager to claim him as their poet. The image he cultivated resembled closely what the public likes to think a poet should be. Frost was seen as a lovable, wise old man; his simple wisdom and cracker-barrel sayings appeared comforting and homey. From this Yankee rustic, audiences learned that "There's a lot yet that isn't understood" or "We love the things we love for what they are" or "Good fences make good neighbors."

In a sense, Frost packaged himself for public consumption. "I am . . . my own salesman," he said. When asked direct questions about the meanings of his poems, he often winked or scratched his head to give the impression that the customer was always right. To be sure, there is a simplicity in Frost's language, but that simplicity does not fully reflect the depth of the man, the complexity of his themes, or the richness of his art.

The folksy optimist behind the public lectern did not reveal his private troubles to his audiences, although he did address those problems at his writing desk. Frost suffered from professional jealousies, anger, and depression. His family life was especially painful. Three of his four children died: a son at the age of four, a daughter in her late twenties from tuberculosis, and another son by suicide. His marriage was filled with tension. Although Frost's work is landscaped with sunlight, snow, birches, birds, blueberries, and squirrels, it is important to recognize that he was also intimately "acquainted with the night," a phrase that serves as the haunting title of one of his poems (see p. 802).

As a corrective to Frost's popular reputation, one critic, Lionel Trilling, described the world Frost creates in his poems as a "terrifying universe," characterized by loneliness, anguish, frustration, doubts, disappointment, and despair (see p. 1024 for an excerpt from this essay). To point this out is not to annihilate the pleasantness and even good-natured cheerfulness that can be enjoyed in Frost's poetry, but it is to say that Frost is not so one-dimensional as he is sometimes assumed to be. Frost's poetry requires readers who are alert and willing to penetrate the simplicity of its language to see the elusive and ambiguous meanings that lie below the surface.

Neither Out Far nor In Deep

The people along the sand
All turn and look one way.
They turn their backs on the land;
They look at the sea all day.

As long as it takes to pass
A ship keeps raising its hull.
The wetter ground like glass
Reflects a standing gull.

The land may vary more,
But wherever the truth may be —
The water comes ashore
And the people look at the sea.

They cannot look out far;
They cannot look in deep;
But when was that ever a bar
To any watch they keep.

                              Robert Frost

With the permission of The Yale Review.

Manuscript page for Robert Frost's "Neither Out Far nor In Deep" (p. 1018), which was first published in The Yale Review in 1934 and later, with a few punctuation changes, in A Further Range in 1936. Courtesy of the Amherst College Library. Reprinted by permission of the Robert Frost Estate.

AN INTRODUCTION TO HIS WORK

Frost's treatment of nature helps to explain the various levels of meaning in his poetry. The familiar natural world his poems evoke is sharply detailed. We hear icy branches clicking against themselves, we see the snow-white trunks of birches, we feel the smarting pain of a twig lashing across a face. The aspects of the natural world Frost describes are designated to give pleasure, but they are also frequently calculated to provoke thought. His use of nature tends to be symbolic. Complex meanings are derived from simple facts, such as a spider killing a moth or the difference between fire and ice (see "Design," p. 1018, and "Fire and Ice," p. 1015). Although Frost's strategy is to talk about particular events and individual experiences, his poems evoke universal issues.

Frost's poetry has strong regional roots and is "versed in country things," but it flourishes in any receptive imagination because, in the final analysis, it is concerned with human beings. Frost's New England landscapes are the occasion rather than the ultimate focus of his poems. Like the rural voices he creates in his poems, Frost typically approaches his themes indirectly. He explained the reason for this in a talk titled "Education by Poetry":

> Poetry provides the one permissible way of saying one thing and meaning another. People say, "Why don't you say what you mean?" We never do that, do we, being all of us too much poets. We like to talk in parables and in hints and in indirections — whether from diffidence or some other instinct.

The result is that the settings, characters, and situations that make up the subject matter of Frost's poems are vehicles for his perceptions about life.

In "Stopping by Woods on a Snowy Evening" (p. 1015), for example, Frost uses the kind of familiar New England details that constitute his poetry for more than descriptive purposes. He shapes them into a meditation on the tension we sometimes feel between life's responsibilities and the "lovely, dark, and deep" attraction that death offers. When the speaker's horse "gives his harness bells a shake," we are reminded that we are confronting a universal theme as well as a quiet moment of natural beauty.

Among the major concerns that appear in Frost's poetry are the fragility of life, the consequences of rejecting or accepting the conditions of one's life, the passion of inconsolable grief, the difficulty of sustaining intimacy, the fear of loneliness and isolation, the inevitability of change, the tensions between the individual and society, and the place of tradition and custom.

Whatever theme is encountered in a poem by Frost, a reader is likely to agree with him that "the initial delight is in the surprise of remembering something I didn't know." To achieve that fresh sense of discovery, Frost allowed himself to follow his instincts; his poetry

> inclines to the impulse, it assumes direction with the first line laid down, it runs a course of lucky events, and ends in a clarification of life — not necessarily a great clarification, such as sects and cults are founded on, but in a momentary stay against confusion.

This description from "The Figure a Poem Makes" (see p. 1021 for the complete essay), Frost's brief introduction to *Complete Poems,* may sound as if his poetry is formless and merely "lucky," but his poems tend to be more conventional than experimental: "The artist in me," as he put the matter in one of his poems, "cries out for design."

From Frost's perspective, "free verse is like playing tennis with the net down." He exercised his own freedom in meeting the challenges of rhyme and meter. His use of fixed forms such as couplets, tercets, quatrains, blank verse, and sonnets was not slavish because he enjoyed working them into the natural English speech patterns — especially the rhythms, idioms, and tones of speakers living north of Boston — that give voice to his themes. Frost often liked to use "Stopping by Woods on a Snowy Evening" as an example of his graceful way of making conventions appear natural and inevitable. He explored "the old ways to be new."

Frost's eye for strong, telling details was matched by his ear for natural speech rhythms. His flexible use of what he called "iambic and loose iambic" enabled him to create moving lyric poems that reveal the personal thoughts of a speaker and dramatic poems that convincingly characterize people caught in intense emotional situations. The language in his poems appears to be little more than a transcription of casual and even rambling speech, but it is in actuality Frost's poetic creation, carefully crafted to reveal the joys and sorrows that are woven into people's daily lives. What is missing from Frost's poems is artificiality, not art. Consider this poem.

The Road Not Taken   1916

Two roads diverged in a yellow wood,
And sorry I could not travel both
And be one traveler, long I stood
And looked down one as far as I could
To where it bent in the undergrowth;   5

Then took the other, as just as fair,
And having perhaps the better claim,
Because it was grassy and wanted wear;
Though as for that the passing there
Had worn them really about the same,   10

And both that morning equally lay
In leaves no step had trodden black.
Oh, I kept the first for another day!
Yet knowing how way leads on to way,
I doubted if I should ever come back.   15

I shall be telling this with a sigh
Somewhere ages and ages hence:
Two roads diverged in a wood, and I —
I took the one less traveled by,
And that has made all the difference.   20

This poem intrigues readers because it is at once so simple and so deeply resonant. Recalling a walk in the woods, the speaker describes how he came to a fork in the road, which forced him to choose one path over another. Though "sorry" that he "could not travel both," he made a choice after carefully weighing his two options. This, essentially, is what happens in the poem; there is no other action. However, the incident is charged with symbolic significance by the speaker's reflections on the necessity and consequences of his decision.

The final stanza indicates that the choice concerns more than simply walking down a road, for the speaker says that choosing the "less traveled" path has affected his entire life — that "that has made all the difference." Frost draws on a familiar enough metaphor when he compares life to a journey, but he is also calling attention to a less commonly noted problem: despite our expectations, aspirations, appetites, hopes, and desires, we can't have it all. Making one choice precludes another. It is impossible to determine what particular decision the speaker refers to: perhaps he had to choose a college, a career, a spouse; perhaps he was confronted with mutually exclusive ideas, beliefs, or values. There is no way to know because Frost wisely creates a symbolic choice and implicitly invites us to supply our own circumstances.

The speaker's reflections about his choice are as central to an understanding of the poem as the choice itself; indeed, they may be more central. He describes the road taken as "having perhaps the better claim, / Because it was grassy and wanted wear"; he prefers the "less traveled" path. This seems to be an expression of individualism, which would account for "the difference" his choice made in his life. But Frost complicates matters by having the speaker also acknowledge that there was no significant difference between the two roads; one was "just as fair" as the other; each was "worn . . . really about the same"; and "both that morning equally lay / In leaves no step had trodden black."

The speaker imagines that in the future, "ages and ages hence," he will recount his choice with "a sigh" that will satisfactorily explain the course of his life, but Frost seems to be having a little fun here by showing us how the speaker will embellish his past decision to make it appear more dramatic. What we hear is someone trying to convince himself that the choice he made significantly changed his life. When he recalls what happened in the "yellow wood," a color that gives a glow to that irretrievable moment when his life seemed to be on verge of a momentous change, he appears more concerned with the path he did not choose than with the one he took. Frost shrewdly titles the poem to suggest the speaker's sense of loss at not being able to "travel both" roads. When the speaker's reflections about his choice are examined, the poem reveals his nostalgia instead of affirming his decision to travel a self-reliant path in life.

The rhymed stanzas of "The Road Not Taken" follow a pattern established in the first five lines (*abaab*). This rhyme scheme reflects, perhaps, the speaker's efforts to shape his life into a pleasing and coherent form. The natural speech rhythms Frost uses allow him to integrate the rhymes unobtrusively, but there is a slight shift in lines 19 and 20, when the speaker asserts self-consciously that the "less traveled" road — which we already know to be basically the same as the other road — "made all the difference." Unlike all the other rhymes in the poem, "difference" does not rhyme precisely with "hence." The emphasis that must be placed on "diffe*rence*" to make it rhyme perfectly with "hence" may suggest that the speaker is trying just a little too hard to pattern his life on his earlier choice in the woods.

Perhaps the best way to begin reading Frost's poetry is to accept the invitation he placed at the beginning of many volumes of his poems. "The Pasture" means what it says of course; it is about taking care of some farm chores, but it is also a means of "saying one thing in terms of another."

The Pasture   1913

I'm going out to clean the pasture spring;
I'll only stop to rake the leaves away
(And wait to watch the water clear, I may):
I shan't be gone long. — You come too.

I'm going out to fetch the little calf
That's standing by the mother. It's so young
It totters when she licks it with her tongue.
I shan't be gone long. — You come too.

"The Pasture" is a simple but irresistible songlike invitation to the pleasure of looking at the world through the eyes of a poet.

CHRONOLOGY

1874	Born on March 26 in San Francisco, California.
1885	Father dies and family moves to Lawrence, Massachusetts.
1892	Graduates from Lawrence High School.
1893–94	Studies at Dartmouth College.
1895	Marries his high school sweetheart, Elinor White.
1897–99	Studies at Harvard College.
1900	Moves to a farm in West Derry, New Hampshire.
1912	Moves to England, where he farms and writes.
1913	*A Boy's Will* is published in London.
1914	*North of Boston* is published in London.
1915	Moves to a farm near Franconia, New Hampshire.
1916	Elected to National Institute of Letters.
1917–20	Teaches at Amherst College.

1919	Moves to South Shaftsbury, Vermont.
1921–23	Teaches at the University of Michigan.
1923	*Selected Poems* and *New Hampshire* are published; the latter is awarded a Pulitzer Prize.
1928	*West-Running Brook* is published.
1930	*Collected Poems* is published.
1936	*A Further Range* is published; teaches at Harvard.
1938	Wife dies.
1939–42	Teaches at Harvard.
1942	*A Witness Tree*, which is awarded a Pulitzer Prize, is published.
1943–49	Teaches at Dartmouth.
1945	*A Masque of Reason* is published.
1947	*Steeple Bush* and *A Masque of Mercy* are published.
1949	*Complete Poems* (enlarged) is published.
1961	Reads "The Gift Outright" at President John F. Kennedy's inauguration.
1963	Dies on January 29 in Boston.

eb *Research Robert Frost with LitLinks at*
http://www.bedfordstmartins.com/meyer/bedintrolit

Mowing   1913

There was never a sound beside the wood but one,
And that was my long scythe whispering to the ground.
What was it it whispered? I knew not well myself;
Perhaps it was something about the heat of the sun,
Something, perhaps, about the lack of sound —   5
And that was why it whispered and did not speak.
It was no dream of the gift of idle hours,
Or easy gold at the hand of fay or elf:
Anything more than the truth would have seemed too weak
To the earnest love that laid the swale in rows,   10
Not without feeble-pointed spikes of flowers
(Pale orchises), and scared a bright green snake.
The fact is the sweetest dream that labour knows.
My long scythe whispered and left the hay to make.

CONSIDERATIONS FOR CRITICAL THINKING AND WRITING

1. FIRST RESPONSE. Describe the tone of "Mowing." How does reading it aloud affect your understanding of it?

2. Discuss the image of the scythe. Do you think it has any symbolic value? Explain why or why not.

3. Paraphrase the poem. What do you think its thematic significance is?

4. Describe the type of sonnet Frost uses in "Mowing."

Mending Wall 1914

Something there is that doesn't love a wall,
That sends the frozen-ground-swell under it,
And spills the upper boulders in the sun;
And makes gaps even two can pass abreast.
The work of hunters is another thing: 5
I have come after them and made repair
Where they have left not one stone on a stone,
But they would have the rabbit out of hiding,
To please the yelping dogs. The gaps I mean,
No one has seen them made or heard them made, 10
But at spring mending-time we find them there.
I let my neighbor know beyond the hill;
And on a day we meet to walk the line
And set the wall between us once again.
We keep the wall between us as we go. 15
To each the boulders that have fallen to each.
And some are loaves and some so nearly balls
We have to use a spell to make them balance:
"Stay where you are until our backs are turned!"
We wear our fingers rough with handling them. 20
Oh, just another kind of outdoor game,
One on a side. It comes to little more:
There where it is we do not need the wall:
He is all pine and I am apple orchard.
My apple trees will never get across 25
And eat the cones under his pines, I tell him.
He only says, "Good fences make good neighbors."
Spring is the mischief in me, and I wonder
If I could put a notion in his head:
"*Why* do they make good neighbors? Isn't it 30
Where there are cows? But here there are no cows.
Before I built a wall I'd ask to know
What I was walling in or walling out,
And to whom I was like to give offense.
Something there is that doesn't love a wall, 35
That wants it down." I could say "Elves" to him,
But it's not elves exactly, and I'd rather
He said it for himself. I see him there
Bringing a stone grasped firmly by the top
In each hand, like an old-stone savage armed. 40

He moves in darkness as it seems to me,
Not of woods only and the shade of trees.
He will not go behind his father's saying,
And he likes having thought of it so well
He says again, "Good fences make good neighbors."　　45

CONSIDERATIONS FOR CRITICAL THINKING AND WRITING

1. FIRST RESPONSE. What might the "Something" be that "doesn't love a wall"? Why does the speaker remind his neighbor each spring that the wall needs to be repaired? Is it ironic that the *speaker* initiates the mending? Is there anything good about the wall?

2. How do the speaker and his neighbor in this poem differ in sensibilities? What is suggested about the neighbor in lines 41 and 42?

3. The neighbor likes the saying "Good fences make good neighbors" so well that he repeats it (lines 27, 45). Does the speaker also say something twice? What else suggests that the speaker's attitude toward the wall is not necessarily Frost's?

4. Although the speaker's language is colloquial, what is poetic about the sounds and rhythms he uses?

5. This poem was first published in 1914; Frost read it to an audience when he visited Russia in 1962. What do these facts suggest about the symbolic value of "Mending Wall"?

CONNECTIONS TO OTHER SELECTIONS

1. How do you think the neighbor in this poem would respond to Dickinson's idea of imagination in "To make a prairie it takes a clover and one bee" (p. 956)?

2. What similarities and differences does the neighbor have with the people Frost describes in "Neither Out Far nor In Deep" (p. 1018)?

Home Burial　　　　　　　　　　　　　　　　　　　　1914

He saw her from the bottom of the stairs
Before she saw him. She was starting down,
Looking back over her shoulder at some fear.
She took a doubtful step and then undid it
To raise herself and look again. He spoke　　　　5
Advancing toward her: "What is it you see
From up there always—for I want to know."
She turned and sank upon her skirts at that,
And her face changed from terrified to dull.
He said to gain time: "What is it you see,"　　　　10
Mounting until she cowered under him.
"I will find out now—you must tell me, dear."
She, in her place, refused him any help
With the least stiffening of her neck and silence.

She let him look, sure that he wouldn't see,   15
Blind creature; and awhile he didn't see.
But at last he murmured, "Oh," and again, "Oh."

"What is it — what?" she said.

                                "Just that I see."

"You don't," she challenged. "Tell me what it is."   20

"The wonder is I didn't see at once.
I never noticed it from here before.
I must be wonted° to it — that's the reason.
The little graveyard where my people are!
So small the window frames the whole of it.   25
Not so much larger than a bedroom, is it?
There are three stones of slate and one of marble,
Broad-shouldered little slabs there in the sunlight
On the sidehill. We haven't to mind *those*.
But I understand: it is not the stones,   30
But the child's mound —"

                                "Don't, don't, don't, don't," she cried.

She withdrew, shrinking from beneath his arm
That rested on the banister, and slid downstairs;
And turned on him with such a daunting look,   35
He said twice over before he knew himself:
"Can't a man speak of his own child he's lost?"

"Not you! — Oh, where's my hat? Oh, I don't need it!
I must get out of here. I must get air.
I don't know rightly whether any man can."   40

"Amy! Don't go to someone else this time.
Listen to me. I won't come down the stairs."
He sat and fixed his chin between his fists.
"There's something I should like to ask you, dear."

"You don't know how to ask it."   45

                                "Help me, then."
Her fingers moved the latch for all reply.

"My words are nearly always an offense.
I don't know how to speak of anything
So as to please you. But I might be taught,   50
I should suppose. I can't say I see how.
A man must partly give up being a man
With women-folk. We could have some arrangement
By which I'd bind myself to keep hands off
Anything special you're a-mind to name.   55
Though I don't like such things 'twixt those that love.
Two that don't love can't live together without them.

23 *wonted:* Accustomed.

But two that do can't live together with them."
She moved the latch a little. "Don't—don't go.
Don't carry it to someone else this time.   60
Tell me about it if it's something human.
Let me into your grief. I'm not so much
Unlike other folks as your standing there
Apart would make me out. Give me my chance.
I do think, though, you overdo it a little.   65
What was it brought you up to think it the thing
To take your mother-loss of a first child
So inconsolably—in the face of love.
You'd think his memory might be satisfied—"

"There you go sneering now!"   70

                "I'm not, I'm not!
You make me angry. I'll come down to you.
God, what a woman! And it's come to this,
A man can't speak of his own child that's dead."

"You can't because you don't know how to speak.   75
If you had any feelings, you that dug
With your own hand—how could you?—his little grave;
I saw you from that very window there,
Making the gravel leap and leap in air,
Leap up, like that, like that, and land so lightly   80
And roll back down the mound beside the hole.
I thought, Who is that man? I didn't know you.
And I crept down the stairs and up the stairs
To look again, and still your spade kept lifting.
Then you came in. I heard your rumbling voice   85
Out in the kitchen, and I don't know why,
But I went near to see with my own eyes.
You could sit there with the stains on your shoes
Of the fresh earth from your own baby's grave
And talk about your everyday concerns.   90
You had stood the spade up against the wall
Outside there in the entry, for I saw it."

"I shall laugh the worst laugh I ever laughed.
I'm cursed. God, if I don't believe I'm cursed."

"I can repeat the very words you were saying.   95
'Three foggy mornings and one rainy day
Will rot the best birch fence a man can build.'
Think of it, talk like that at such a time!
What had how long it takes a birch to rot
To do with what was in the darkened parlor   100
You *couldn't* care! The nearest friends can go
With anyone to death, comes so far short
They might as well not try to go at all.
No, from the time when one is sick to death,

One is alone, and he dies more alone. 105
Friends make pretense of following to the grave.
But before one is in it, their minds are turned
And making the best of their way back to life
And living people, and things they understand.
But the world's evil. I won't have grief so 110
If I can change it. Oh, I won't, I won't!"

"There, you have said it all and you feel better.
You won't go now. You're crying. Close the door.
The heart's gone out of it: why keep it up.
Amy! There's someone coming down the road!" 115

"*You*—oh, you think the talk is all. I must go—
Somewhere out of this house. How can I make you—"

"If—you—do!" She was opening the door wider.
"Where do you mean to go? First tell me that.
I'll follow and bring you back by force. I *will!*—" 120

CONSIDERATIONS FOR CRITICAL THINKING AND WRITING

1. FIRST RESPONSE. This poem tells a story of a relationship. Is the husband insensitive and indifferent to his wife's grief? Characterize the wife. Has Frost invited us to sympathize with one character more than with the other?

2. How has the burial of the child within sight of the stairway window affected the relationship of the couple in this poem? Is the child's grave a symptom or a cause of the conflict between them?

3. What is the effect of splitting the iambic pentameter pattern in lines 18 and 19, 31 and 32, 45 and 46, and 70 and 71?

4. Is the conflict resolved at the conclusion of the poem? Do you think the husband and wife will overcome their differences?

After Apple-Picking 1914

My long two-pointed ladder's sticking through a tree
Toward heaven still,
And there's a barrel that I didn't fill
Beside it, and there may be two or three
Apples I didn't pick upon some bough. 5
But I am done with apple-picking now.
Essence of winter sleep is on the night,
The scent of apples: I am drowsing off.
I cannot rub the strangeness from my sight
I got from looking through a pane of glass 10
I skimmed this morning from the drinking trough
And held against the world of hoary grass.
It melted, and I let it fall and break.
But I was well
Upon my way to sleep before it fell, 15

And I could tell
What form my dreaming was about to take.
Magnified apples appear and disappear,
Stem end and blossom end,
And every fleck of russet showing clear.   20
My instep arch not only keeps the ache,
It keeps the pressure of a ladder-round.
I feel the ladder sway as the boughs bend.
And I keep hearing from the cellar bin
The rumbling sound   25
Of load on load of apples coming in.
For I have had too much
Of apple-picking: I am overtired
Of the great harvest I myself desired.
There were ten thousand thousand fruit to touch,   30
Cherish in hand, lift down, and not let fall.
For all
That struck the earth,
No matter if not bruised or spiked with stubble,
Went surely to the cider-apple heap   35
As of no worth.
One can see what will trouble
This sleep of mine, whatever sleep it is.
Were he not gone,
The woodchuck could say whether it's like his   40
Long sleep, as I describe its coming on,
Or just some human sleep.

CONSIDERATIONS FOR CRITICAL THINKING AND WRITING

1. FIRST RESPONSE. How does this poem illustrate Frost's view that "Poetry
   provides the one permissible way of saying one thing and meaning another"? When do you first sense that the detailed description of apple picking is being used that way?

2. What comes after apple picking? What does the speaker worry about in the
   dream beginning in line 18?

3. Why do you suppose Frost uses apples rather than, say, pears or squash?

Birches   1916

When I see birches bend to left and right
Across the lines of straighter darker trees,
I like to think some boy's been swinging them.
But swinging doesn't bend them down to stay
As ice-storms do. Often you must have seen them   5
Loaded with ice a sunny winter morning
After a rain. They click upon themselves
As the breeze rises, and turn many-colored

As the stir cracks and crazes their enamel.
Soon the sun's warmth makes them shed crystal shells   10
Shattering and avalanching on the snow-crust—
Such heaps of broken glass to sweep away
You'd think the inner dome of heaven had fallen.
They are dragged to the withered bracken by the load,
And they seem not to break; though once they are bowed   15
So low for long, they never right themselves:
You may see their trunks arching in the woods
Years afterwards, trailing their leaves on the ground
Like girls on hands and knees that throw their hair
Before them over their heads to dry in the sun.   20
But I was going to say when Truth broke in
With all her matter-of-fact about the ice-storm,
I should prefer to have some boy bend them
As he went out and in to fetch the cows—
Some boy too far from town to learn baseball,   25
Whose only play was what he found himself,
Summer or winter, and could play alone.
One by one he subdued his father's trees
By riding them down over and over again
Until he took the stiffness out of them,   30
And not one but hung limp, not one was left
For him to conquer. He learned all there was
To learn about not launching out too soon
And so not carrying the tree away
Clear to the ground. He always kept his poise   35
To the top branches, climbing carefully
With the same pains you use to fill a cup
Up to the brim, and even above the brim.
Then he flung outward, feet first, with a swish,
Kicking his way down through the air to the ground.   40
So was I once myself a swinger of birches.
And so I dream of going back to be.
It's when I'm weary of considerations,
And life is too much like a pathless wood
Where your face burns and tickles with the cobwebs   45
Broken across it, and one eye is weeping
From a twig's having lashed across it open.
I'd like to get away from earth awhile
And then come back to it and begin over.
May no fate willfully misunderstand me   50
And half grant what I wish and snatch me away
Not to return. Earth's the right place for love:
I don't know where it's likely to go better.
I'd like to go by climbing a birch tree,
And climb black branches up a snow-white trunk,   55
Toward heaven, till the tree could bear no more,
But dipped its top and set me down again.
That would be good both going and coming back.
One could do worse than be a swinger of birches.

CONSIDERATIONS FOR CRITICAL THINKING AND WRITING

1. FIRST RESPONSE. What do you think the swinging of birches symbolizes?

2. Why does the speaker in this poem prefer the birches to have been bent by boys instead of ice storms?

3. How is "earth" (line 52) described in the poem? Why does the speaker choose it over "heaven" (line 56)?

4. How might the effect of this poem be changed if it were written in heroic couplets instead of blank verse?

5. CRITICAL STRATEGIES. Read the section on reader-response criticism (pp. 2109–11) in Chapter 52, "Critical Strategies for Reading." Trace your response to this poem over three successive careful readings. How does your understanding of the poem change or develop?

A Girl's Garden   1916

A neighbor of mine in the village
   Likes to tell how one spring
When she was a girl on the farm, she did
   A childlike thing.

One day she asked her father   5
   To give her a garden plot
To plant and tend and reap herself,
   And he said, "Why not?"

In casting about for a corner
   He thought of an idle bit   10
Of walled-off ground where a shop had stood,
   And he said, "Just it."

And he said, "That ought to make you
   An ideal one-girl farm,
And give you a chance to put some strength   15
   On your slim-jim arm."

It was not enough of a garden,
   Her father said, to plow;
So she had to work it all by hand,
   But she don't mind now.   20

She wheeled the dung in the wheelbarrow
   Along a stretch of road;
But she always ran away and left
   Her not-nice load,

And hid from anyone passing.   25
   And then she begged the seed.
She says she thinks she planted one
   Of all things but weed.

A hill each of potatoes,
   Radishes, lettuce, peas,   30

Tomatoes, beets, beans, pumpkins, corn
    And even fruit trees.

And yes, she has long mistrusted
    That a cider apple tree
In bearing there today is hers,   35
    Or at least may be.

Her crop was a miscellany
    When all was said and done,
A little bit of everything,
    A great deal of none.   40

Now when she sees in the village
    How village things go,
Just when it seems to come in right,
    She says, "*I* know!"

"It's as when I was a farmer —"   45
    Oh, never by way of advice!
And she never sins by telling the tale
    To the same person twice.

CONSIDERATIONS FOR CRITICAL THINKING AND WRITING

1. FIRST RESPONSE. Write a paraphrase of the poem. What do you think it is about?

2. Why do you suppose Frost uses a narrator to tell the story about the girl instead of having her tell the story herself?

3. What purpose does the father's character serve in the poem?

4. Discuss the distinction that is made between the "ideal one-girl farm" (line 14) and "How village things go" (42).

CONNECTIONS TO OTHER SELECTIONS

1. Compare the narrator in this poem to the narrator in "Stopping by Woods on a Snowy Evening" (p. 1015). How, in each poem, do simple activities reveal something about the narrator?

2. Discuss the narrator's treatment of the neighbor in this poem and in "Mending Wall" (p. 1004).

"Out, Out —"°   1916

The buzz-saw snarled and rattled in the yard
And made dust and dropped stove-length sticks of wood,
Sweet-scented stuff when the breeze drew across it.
And from there those that lifted eyes could count
Five mountain ranges one behind the other   5
Under the sunset far into Vermont.

"Out, Out—": From Act V, Scene v, of Shakespeare's *Macbeth*.

And the saw snarled and rattled, snarled and rattled,
As it ran light, or had to bear a load.
And nothing happened: day was all but done.
Call it a day, I wish they might have said   10
To please the boy by giving him the half hour
That a boy counts so much when saved from work.
His sister stood beside them in her apron
To tell them "Supper." At the word, the saw,
As if to prove saws knew what supper meant,   15
Leaped out at the boy's hand, or seemed to leap—
He must have given the hand. However it was,
Neither refused the meeting. But the hand!
The boy's first outcry was a rueful laugh,
As he swung toward them holding up the hand   20
Half in appeal, but half as if to keep
The life from spilling. Then the boy saw all—
Since he was old enough to know, big boy
Doing a man's work, though a child at heart—
He saw all spoiled. "Don't let him cut my hand off—   25
The doctor, when he comes. Don't let him, sister!"
So. But the hand was gone already.
The doctor put him in the dark of ether.
He lay and puffed his lips out with his breath.
And then—the watcher at his pulse took fright.   30
No one believed. They listened at his heart.
Little—less—nothing!—and that ended it.
No more to build on there. And they, since they
Were not the one dead, turned to their affairs.

CONSIDERATIONS FOR CRITICAL THINKING AND WRITING

1. FIRST RESPONSE. This narrative poem is about the accidental death of a Vermont boy. What is the purpose of the story? Some readers have argued that the final lines reveal the speaker's callousness and indifference. What do you think?

2. How does Frost's allusion to *Macbeth* contribute to the meaning of this poem? Does the speaker seem to agree with the view of life expressed in Macbeth's lines?

3. CRITICAL STRATEGIES. Read the section on Marxist criticism (p. 2103) in Chapter 52, "Critical Strategies for Reading." How do you think a Marxist critic would interpret the family and events described in this poem?

CONNECTIONS TO OTHER SELECTIONS

1. What are the similarities and differences in theme between this poem and Frost's "Nothing Gold Can Stay" (p. 1016)?

2. Write an essay comparing how grief is handled by the boy's family in this poem and the couple in "Home Burial" (p. 1005).

3. Compare the tone and theme of "'Out, Out—'" and those of Crane's "A Man Said to the Universe" (p. 810).

A Boundless Moment

1923

He halted in the wind, and—what was that
Far in the maples, pale, but not a ghost?
He stood there bringing March against his thought,
And yet too ready to believe the most.

"Oh, that's the Paradise-in-Bloom," I said;   5
And truly it was fair enough for flowers
Had we but in us to assume in March
Such white luxuriance of May for ours.

We stood a moment so, in a strange world,
Myself as one his own pretense deceives;   10
And then I said the truth (and we moved on).
A young beech clinging to its last year's leaves.

Considerations for Critical Thinking and Writing

1. FIRST RESPONSE. Describe the speaker's temperament. How does his differ from his companion's?

2. How does the diction of the final line create a particular tone?

3. Discuss the significance of the title. How can the action in the poem be taken as boundless? What would be the effect of replacing the title with "A Mistaken Moment"? How would that change your reading of the poem?

Connection to Another Selection

1. Discuss the tone and theme of "A Boundless Moment" and "Nothing Gold Can Stay" (p. 1016).

The Investment

1923

Over back where they speak of life as staying
(You couldn't call it living, for it ain't),
There was an old, old house renewed with paint,
And in it a piano loudly playing.

Out in the plowed ground in the cold a digger,   5
Among unearthed potatoes standing still,
Was counting winter dinners, one a hill,
With half an ear to the piano's vigor.

All that piano and new paint back there,
Was it some money suddenly come into?   10
Or some extravagance young love had been to?
Or old love on an impulse not to care—

Not to sink under being man and wife,
But get some color and music out of life?

CONSIDERATIONS FOR CRITICAL THINKING AND WRITING

1. FIRST RESPONSE. In what sense does the idea of "Over back where" or "back there" serve as more than a physical setting in the poem? What do these phrases imply about the poem's meaning?

2. Discuss the symbolic significance of the "piano and new paint" in contrast to the potato digger.

3. What kind of sonnet is this poem? Why is the concluding couplet an especially appropriate way to end the poem?

CONNECTION TO ANOTHER SELECTION

1. Compare the relationship of the man and wife in "The Investment" with that of "Home Burial" (p. 1005).

Fire and Ice   1923

Some say the world will end in fire,
Some say in ice.
From what I've tasted of desire
I hold with those who favor fire.
But if it had to perish twice,
I think I know enough of hate
To say that for destruction ice
Is also great
And would suffice.

CONSIDERATIONS FOR CRITICAL THINKING AND WRITING

1. FIRST RESPONSE. What characteristics of human behavior does the speaker associate with fire and ice?

2. What theories about the end of the world are alluded to in lines 1 and 2?

3. How does the speaker's use of understatement and rhyme affect the tone of this poem?

Stopping by Woods on a Snowy Evening   1923

Whose woods these are I think I know.
His house is in the village, though;
He will not see me stopping here
To watch his woods fill up with snow.

My little horse must think it queer   5
To stop without a farmhouse near
Between the woods and frozen lake
The darkest evening of the year.

He gives his harness bells a shake
To ask if there is some mistake.   10
The only other sound's the sweep
Of easy wind and downy flake.

The woods are lovely, dark and deep,
But I have promises to keep,
And miles to go before I sleep,   15
And miles to go before I sleep.

CONSIDERATIONS FOR CRITICAL THINKING AND WRITING

1. FIRST RESPONSE. What is the significance of the setting in this poem? How
   is tone conveyed by the images?
2. What does the speaker find appealing about the woods? What is the purpose of the horse in the poem?
3. Although the last two lines are identical, they are not read at the same
   speed. Why the difference? What is achieved by the repetition?
4. What is the rhyme scheme of this poem? What is the effect of the rhyme in
   the final stanza?

Nothing Gold Can Stay   *1923*

Nature's first green is gold,
Her hardest hue to hold.
Her early leaf's a flower;
But only so an hour.
The leaf subsides to leaf.
So Eden sank to grief.
So dawn goes down to day.
Nothing gold can stay.

CONSIDERATIONS FOR CRITICAL THINKING AND WRITING

1. FIRST RESPONSE. What is meant by "gold" in the poem? Why can't it "stay"?
2. What do the leaf, humanity, and a day have in common?

CONNECTION TO ANOTHER SELECTION

1. Write an essay comparing the tone and theme of "Nothing Gold Can Stay"
   with Herrick's "To the Virgins, to Make Much of Time" (p. 726).

The Armful   *1928*

For every parcel I stoop down to seize
I lose some other off my arms and knees,
And the whole pile is slipping, bottles, buns —
Extremes too hard to comprehend at once,

Yet nothing I should care to leave behind.   5
With all I have to hold with, hand and mind
And heart, if need be, I will do my best
To keep their building balanced at my breast.
I crouch down to prevent them as they fall;
Then sit down in the middle of them all.   10
I had to drop the armful in the road.
And try to stack them in a better load.

CONSIDERATIONS FOR CRITICAL THINKING AND WRITING

1. FIRST RESPONSE. How does this poem add up to more than a simple vignette
   of dropping things? What words, in particular, suggest other interpretations?
2. Discuss the effects of the rhymes and meter. In what ways does the poem
   do with words what the speaker does with packages? How do you think this
   poem would read differently if it were written in free verse?

CONNECTION TO ANOTHER SELECTION

1. Compare the central metaphor and theme of "The Armful" with those of
   Emily Dickinson's "I felt a Cleaving in my Mind—" (p. 972).

Spring Pools   1928

These pools that, though in forests, still reflect
The total sky almost without defect,
And like the flowers beside them, chill and shiver,
Will like the flowers beside them soon be gone,
And yet not out by any brook or river,   5
But up by roots to bring dark foliage on.

The trees that have it in their pent-up buds
To darken nature and be summer woods—
Let them think twice before they use their powers
To blot out and drink up and sweep away   10
These flowery waters and these watery flowers
From snow that melted only yesterday.

CONSIDERATIONS FOR CRITICAL THINKING AND WRITING

1. FIRST RESPONSE. In what sense is this poem more than just a detailed picture of nature?
2. How does the speaker create tension between the pools, flowers, and trees?
   What do you see as the central conflict in the poem?
3. Comment on the rhythm and rhyme of lines 7 and 8. How do they differ
   from the other lines of the poem? How is their placement unique?

CONNECTION TO ANOTHER SELECTION

1. Compare the speaker's reaction to nature in this poem and in "Design," the
   next poem.

Design   *1936*

I found a dimpled spider, fat and white,
On a white heal-all,° holding up a moth
Like a white piece of rigid satin cloth —
Assorted characters of death and blight
Mixed ready to begin the morning right,   5
Like the ingredients of a witches' broth —
A snow-drop spider, a flower like a froth,
And dead wings carried like a paper kite.

What had the flower to do with being white,
The wayside blue and innocent heal-all?
What brought the kindred spider to that height,   10
Then steered the white moth thither in the night?
What but design of darkness to appall? —
If design govern in a thing so small.

2 *heal-all:* A common flower, usually blue, once used for medicinal purposes.

CONSIDERATIONS FOR CRITICAL THINKING AND WRITING

1. FIRST RESPONSE. What kinds of speculations are raised in the final two lines? Consider the meaning of the title. Is there more than one way to read it?

2. How does the division of the octave and sestet in this sonnet serve to organize the speaker's thoughts and feelings? What is the predominant rhyme? How does that rhyme relate to the poem's meaning?

3. CRITICAL STRATEGIES. Read the section on formalist criticism (pp. 2095– 97) in Chapter 52, "Critical Strategies for Reading." Which words seem especially rich in connotative meanings? Explain how they function in the sonnet.

CONNECTIONS TO OTHER SELECTIONS

1. Compare the ironic tone of "Design" with the tone of Hathaway's "Oh, Oh" (p. 675). What would you have to change in Hathaway's poem to make it more like Frost's?

2. In an essay discuss Frost's view of God in this poem and Dickinson's perspective in "I know that He exists" (p. 990).

3. Compare "Design" with "In White," Frost's early version of it (p. 1020).

Neither Out Far nor In Deep   *1936*

The people along the sand
All turn and look one way.
They turn their back on the land.
They look at the sea all day.

As long as it takes to pass   5
A ship keeps raising its hull;

The wetter ground like glass
Reflects a standing gull.

The land may vary more;
But wherever the truth may be —   10
The water comes ashore,
And the people look at the sea.

They cannot look out far.
They cannot look in deep.
But when was that ever a bar   15
To any watch they keep?

CONSIDERATIONS FOR CRITICAL THINKING AND WRITING

1. FIRST RESPONSE. Frost built this poem around a simple observation that raises some questions. Why do people at the beach almost always face the ocean? What feelings and thoughts are evoked by looking at the ocean?

2. Notice how the verb "look" takes on added meaning as the poem progresses. What are the people looking for?

3. How does the final stanza extend the poem's significance?

4. Does the speaker identify with the people described, or does he ironically distance himself from them?

The Silken Tent   *1942*

She is as in a field a silken tent
At midday when a sunny summer breeze
Has dried the dew and all its ropes relent,
So that in guys° it gently sways at ease,   *ropes that steady a tent*
And its supporting central cedar pole,   5
That is its pinnacle to heavenward
And signifies the sureness of the soul,
Seems to owe naught to any single cord,
But strictly held by none, is loosely bound
By countless silken ties of love and thought   10
To everything on earth the compass round,
And only by one's going slightly taut
In the capriciousness of summer air
Is of the slightest bondage made aware.

CONSIDERATIONS FOR CRITICAL THINKING AND WRITING

1. FIRST RESPONSE. What is being compared in this sonnet? How does the detail accurately describe both elements of the comparison?

2. How does the form of this one-sentence sonnet help to express its theme? Pay particular attention to the final three lines.

3. How do the sonnet's sounds contribute to its meaning?

PERSPECTIVES ON FROST

"In White": Frost's Early Version of "Design"   1912

A dented spider like a snow drop white
On a white Heal-all, holding up a moth
Like a white piece of lifeless satin cloth —
Saw ever curious eye so strange a sight? —
Portent in little, assorted death and blight   5
Like the ingredients of a witches' broth? —
The beady spider, the flower like a froth,
And the moth carried like a paper kite.

What had that flower to do with being white,
The blue prunella every child's delight.   10
What brought the kindred spider to that height?
(Make we no thesis of the miller's° plight.)   *miller moth*
What but design of darkness and of night?
Design, design! Do I use the word aright?

CONSIDERATIONS FOR CRITICAL THINKING AND WRITING

1. Read "In White" and "Design" (p. 1018) aloud. Which version sounds better to you? Why?

2. Compare these versions line for line, paying particular attention to word choice. List the differences, and try to explain why you think Frost revised the lines.

3. How does the change in titles reflect a shift in emphasis in the poem?

Frost on the Living Part of a Poem   1914

The living part of a poem is the intonation entangled somehow in the syntax, idiom, and meaning of a sentence. It is only there for those who have heard it previously in conversation. . . . It is the most volatile and at the same time important part of poetry. It goes and the language becomes dead language, the poetry dead poetry. With it go the accents, the stresses, the delays that are not the property of vowels and syllables but that are shifted at will with the sense. Vowels have length there is no denying. But the accent of sense supersedes all other accent, overrides it and sweeps it away. I will find you the word *come* variously used in various passages, a whole, half, third, fourth, fifth, and sixth note. It is as long as the sense makes it. When men no longer know the intonations on which we string our words they will fall back on what I may call the absolute length of our syllables, which is the length we would give them in passages that meant nothing. . . . I say you can't read a single good sentence with the salt in it unless you have previously heard it spoken. Neither can you with the help of all the characters and diacritical marks pronounce a single word unless you have previously heard it actually pronounced. Words exist in the mouth not books.

From a letter to Sidney Cox in *A Swinger of Birches: A Portrait of Robert Frost*

CONSIDERATIONS FOR CRITICAL THINKING AND WRITING

1. Why does Frost place so much emphasis on hearing poetry spoken?

2. Choose a passage from "Home Burial" (p. 1005) or "After Apple-Picking" (p. 1008) and read it aloud. How does Frost's description of his emphasis on intonation help explain the effects he achieves in the passage you have selected?

3. Do you think it is true that all poetry must be heard? Do "Words exist in the mouth not books"?

AMY LOWELL (1874–1925)

On Frost's Realistic Technique   1915

I have said that Mr. Frost's work is almost photographic. The qualification was unnecessary, it is photographic. The pictures, the characters, are reproduced directly from life, they are burnt into his mind as though it were a sensitive plate. He gives out what has been put in unchanged by any personal mental process. His imagination is bounded by what he has seen, he is confined within the limits of his experience (or at least what might have been his experience) and bent all one way like the windblown trees of New England hillsides.

From a review of *North of Boston*, *The New Republic*, February 20, 1915

CONSIDERATIONS FOR CRITICAL THINKING AND WRITING

1. Consider the "photographic" qualities of Frost's poetry by discussing particular passages that strike you as having been "reproduced directly from life."

2. Write an essay that supports or refutes Lowell's assertion that "He gives out what has been put in unchanged by any personal mental process."

Frost on the Figure a Poem Makes   1939

Abstraction is an old story with the philosophers, but it has been like a new toy in the hands of the artists of our day. Why can't we have any one quality of poetry we choose by itself? We can have in thought. Then it will go hard if we can't in practice. Our lives for it.

Granted no one but a humanist much cares how sound a poem is if it is only *a* sound. The sound is the gold in the ore. Then we will have the sound out alone and dispense with the inessential. We do till we make the discovery that the object in writing poetry is to make all poems sound as different as possible from each other, and the resources for that of vowels, consonants, punctuation, syntax, words, sentences, meter are not enough. We need the help of context — meaning — subject matter. That is the greatest help towards variety. All that can be done with words is soon told. So also with meters — particularly in our language where there are virtually but two, strict iambic and loose iambic. The ancients with many were still poor if they depended on meters for all tune. It is painful to watch our sprung-rhythmists straining at the point of omitting one short from a foot for relief from monotony. The possibilities for tune from the dramatic tones of meaning struck across the rigidity of a limited meter are endless. And we are back in poetry as merely one more art of having something to say, sound or unsound. Probably better if sound, because deeper and from wider experience.

Then there is this wildness whereof it is spoken. Granted again that it has an equal claim with sound to being a poem's better half. If it is a wild tune, it is a poem. Our problem then is, as modern abstractionists, to have the wildness pure; to be wild with nothing to be wild about. We bring up as aberrationists, giving way to undirected associations and kicking ourselves from one chance suggestion to another in all directions as of a hot afternoon in the life of a grasshopper. Theme alone can steady us down. Just as the first mystery was how a poem could have a tune in such a straightness as meter, so the second mystery is how a poem can have wildness and at the same time a subject that shall be fulfilled.

It should be of the pleasure of a poem itself to tell how it can. The figure a poem makes. It begins in delight and ends in wisdom. The figure is the same as for love. No one can really hold that the ecstasy should be static and stand still in one place. It begins in delight, it inclines to the impulse, it assumes direction with the first line laid down, it runs a course of lucky events, and ends in a clarification of life — not necessarily a great clarification, such as sects and cults are founded on, but in a momentary stay against confusion. It has denouement. It has an outcome that though unforeseen was predestined from the first image of the original mood — and indeed from the very mood. It is but a trick poem and no poem at all if the best of it was thought of first and saved for the last. It finds its own name as it goes and discovers the best waiting for it in some final phrase at once wise and sad — the happy-sad blend of the drinking song.

No tears in the writer, no tears in the reader. No surprise for the writer, no surprise for the reader. For me the initial delight is in the surprise of remembering something I didn't know I knew. I am in a place, in a situation, as if I had materialized from cloud or risen out of the ground. There is a glad recognition of the long lost and the rest follows. Step by step the wonder of unexpected supply keeps going. The impressions most useful to my purpose seem always those I was unaware of and so made no note of at the time when taken, and the conclusion is come to that like giants we are always hurling experience ahead of us to pave the future with against the day when we may want to strike a line of purpose across it for somewhere. The line will have the more charm for not being mechanically straight. We enjoy the straight crookedness of a good walking stick. Modern instruments of precision are being used to make things crooked as if by eye and hand in the old days.

I tell how there may be a better wildness of logic than of inconsequence. But the logic is backward, in retrospect, after the act. It must be more felt than seen ahead like prophecy. It must be a revelation, or a series of revelations, as much for the poet as for the reader. For it to be that there must have been the greatest freedom of the material to move about in it and to establish relations in it regardless of time and space, previous relation, and everything but affinity. We prate of freedom. We call our schools free because we are not free to stay away from them till we are sixteen years of age. I have given up my democratic prejudices and now willingly set the lower classes free to be completely taken care of by the upper classes. Political freedom is nothing to me. I bestow it right and left. All I would keep for myself is the freedom of my material — the condition of body and mind now and then to summons aptly from the vast chaos of all I have lived through.

Scholars and artists thrown together are often annoyed at the puzzle of where they differ. Both work for knowledge; but I suspect they differ most importantly in the way their knowledge is come by. Scholars get theirs with conscientious thoroughness along projected lines of logic; poets theirs cavalierly and as it happens in and out of books. They stick to nothing deliberately, but let what will stick to them like burrs where they walk in the fields. No acquirement is on assignment, or even self-assignment. Knowledge of the second kind is much more available in the wild free ways of wit and art. A school boy may be defined as one who can tell you what he knows in the order in which he learned it. The artist must value himself as he snatches a thing from some previous order in time and space into a new order with not so much as a ligature clinging to it of the old place where it was organic.

More than once I should have lost my soul to radicalism if it had been the originality it was mistaken for by its young converts. Originality and initiative are what I ask for my country. For myself the originality need be no more than the freshness of a poem run in the way I have described: from delight to wisdom. The figure is the same as for love. Like a piece of ice on a hot stove the poem must ride on its own melting. A poem may be worked over once it is in being, but may not be worried into being. Its most precious quality will remain its having run itself and carried away the poet with it. Read it a hundred times: it will forever keep its freshness as a metal keeps its fragrance. It can never lose its sense of a meaning that once unfolded by surprise as it went.

From *Complete Poems of Robert Frost*

CONSIDERATIONS FOR CRITICAL THINKING AND WRITING

1. Frost places a high premium on sound in his poetry because it "is the gold in the ore." Choose one of Frost's poems in this book and explain the effects of its sounds and how they contribute to its meaning.

2. Discuss Frost's explanation of how his poems are written. In what sense is the process both spontaneous and "predestined"?

3. What do you think Frost means when he says he's given up his "democratic prejudices"? Why is "political freedom" nothing to him?

4. Write an essay that examines in more detail the ways scholars and artists "come by" knowledge.

5. Explain what you think Frost means when he writes that "Like a piece of ice on a hot stove the poem must ride on its own melting."

Frost on the Way to Read a Poem   1951

The way to read a poem in prose or verse is in the light of all the other poems ever written. We may begin anywhere. We *duff* into our first. We read that imperfectly (thoroughness with it would be fatal), but the better to read the second. We read the second the better to read the third, the third the better to read the fourth, the fourth better to read the fifth, the fifth the better to read the first again, or the second if it so happens. For poems are not meant to be read in course any more than they are to be made a study of. I once made a resolve never to put any book to any use it wasn't intended for by its author. Improvement will not be a progression but a widening circulation. Our instinct is to settle down like a revolving dog and make ourselves at home among the poems, completely at our ease as to how they should be taken. The same people will be apt to take poems right as know how to take a hint when there is one and not to take a hint when none is intended. Theirs is the ultimate refinement.

From "Poetry and School," Atlantic Monthly, June 1951

CONSIDERATIONS FOR CRITICAL THINKING AND WRITING

1. Given your own experience, how good is Frost's advice about reading in general and his poems in particular?

2. In what sense is a good reader like a "revolving dog" and a person who knows "how to take a hint"?

3. Frost elsewhere in this piece writes, "One of the dangers of college to anyone who wants to stay a human reader (that is to say a humanist) is that he will become a specialist and lose his sensitive fear of landing on the lovely too hard. (With beak and talon.)" Write an essay in response to this concern. Do you agree with Frost's distinction between a "human reader" and a "specialist"?

LIONEL TRILLING (1905–1975)

On Frost as a Terrifying Poet   1959

I have to say that my Frost — *my Frost:* what airs we give ourselves when once we believe that we have come into possession of a poet! — I have to say that my Frost is not the Frost I seem to perceive existing in the minds of so many of his admirers. He is not the Frost who confounds the characteristically modern practice of poetry by his notable democratic simplicity of utterance: on the contrary. He is not the Frost who controverts the bitter modern astonishment at the nature of human life: the opposite is so. He is not the Frost who reassures us by his affirmation of old virtues, simplicities, pieties, and ways of feeling: anything but. I will not go so far as to say that my Frost is not essentially an American poet at all: I believe that he is quite as American as everyone thinks he is, but not in the way that everyone thinks he is.

In the matter of the Americanism of American literature one of my chief guides is that very remarkable critic, D. H. Lawrence. Here are the opening sentences of Lawrence's great outrageous book about classic American literature. "We like to think of the old fashioned American classics as children's books. Just childishness on our part. The old American art speech contains an alien quality which belongs to the American continent and to nowhere else." And this unique alien quality, Lawrence goes on to say, the world has missed. "It is hard to hear a new voice," he says, "as hard as to listen to an unknown language. . . . Why? Out of fear. The world fears a new experience more than it fears anything. It can pigeonhole any idea. But it can't pigeonhole a real new experience. It can only dodge. The world is a great dodger, and the Americans the greatest. Because they dodge their own very selves." I should like to pick up a few more of Lawrence's sentences, feeling the freer to do so because they have an affinity to Mr. Frost's prose manner and substance: "An artist is usually a damned liar, but his art, if it be art, will tell you the truth of his day. And that is all that matters. Away with eternal truth. Truth lives from day to day. . . . The old American artists were hopeless liars. . . . Never trust the artist. Trust the tale. The proper function of the critic is to save the tale from the artist who created it. . . . Now listen to me, don't listen to him. He'll tell you the lie you expect, which is partly your fault for expecting it."

Now in point of fact Robert Frost is *not* a liar. I would not hesitate to say that he was if I thought he was. But no, he is not. In certain of his poems—I shall mention one or two in a moment—he makes it perfectly plain what he is doing; and if we are not aware of what he is doing in other of his poems, where he is not quite so plain, that is not his fault but our own. It is not from him that the tale needs to be saved.

I conceive that Robert Frost is doing in his poems what Lawrence says the great writers of the classic American tradition did. That enterprise of theirs was of an ultimate radicalism. It consisted, Lawrence says, of two things: a disintegration and sloughing off of the old consciousness, by which Lawrence means the old European consciousness, and the forming of a new consciousness underneath.

So radical a work, I need scarcely say, is not carried out by reassurance, nor by the affirmation of old virtues and pieties. It is carried out by the representation of the terrible actualities of life in a new way. I think of Robert Frost as a terrifying poet. Call him, if it makes things any easier, a tragic poet, but it might be useful every now and then to come out from under the shelter of that literary word. The universe that he conceives is a terrifying universe. Read the poem called "Design" and see if you sleep the better for it. Read "Neither Out Far nor In Deep," which often seems to me the most perfect poem of our time, and see if you are warmed by anything in it except the energy with which emptiness is perceived.

But the *people*, it will be objected, the *people* who inhabit this possibly terrifying universe! About them there is nothing that can terrify; surely the people in Mr. Frost's poems can only reassure us by their integrity and solidity. Perhaps so. But I cannot make the disjunction. It may well be that ultimately they reassure us in some sense, but first they terrify us, or should. We must not be misled about them by the curious tenderness with which they are represented, a tenderness which extends to a recognition of the tenderness which they themselves can often give. But when ever have people been so isolated, so lightning-blasted, so tied down and calcined by life, so reduced, each in his own way, to some last irreducible core of being. Talk of the disintegration and sloughing off of the old consciousness! The people of Robert Frost's poems have done that with a vengeance. Lawrence says that what the Americans refused to accept was "the post-Renaissance humanism of Europe," "the old European spontaneity," "the flowing easy humor of Europe" and that seems to me a good way to describe the people who inhabit Robert Frost's America. In the interests of what great other thing these people have made this rejection we cannot know for certain. But we can guess that it was in the interest of truth, of some truth of the self. This is what they all affirm by their humor (which is so *not* "the easy flowing humor of Europe"), by their irony, by their separateness and isolateness. They affirm *this* of themselves: that they are what they are, that this is their truth, and that if the truth be bare, as the truth often is, it is far better than a lie. For me the process by which they arrive at that truth is always terrifying. The manifest America of Mr. Frost's poems may be pastoral; the actual America is tragic.

From "A Speech on Robert Frost: A Cultural Episode,"
Partisan Review, Summer 1959

CONSIDERATIONS FOR CRITICAL THINKING AND WRITING

1. How does Trilling distinguish *"my Frost"* from other readers'?

2. Read the section on biographical criticism in Chapter 52 (pp. 2097–99) and familiarize yourself with Frost's life. How does a knowledge of Frost's biography influence your reading of his poems?

3. Write an essay indicating whether you agree or disagree with Trilling's assessment of Frost "as a Terrifying Poet." Use evidence from the poems to support your view.

HERBERT R. COURSEN JR. (B. 1932)

A Parodic Interpretation of "Stopping by Woods on a Snowy Evening"   1962

Much ink has spilled on many pages in exegesis of this little poem. Actually, critical jottings have only obscured what has lain beneath critical noses all these years. To say that the poem means merely that a man stops one night to observe a snowfall, or that the poem contrasts the mundane desire for creature comfort with the sweep of aesthetic appreciation, or that it renders worldly responsibilities paramount, or that it reveals the speaker's latent death-wish is to miss the point rather badly. Lacking has been that mind simple enough to see what is *really* there. . . .

The "darkest evening of the year" in New England is December 21st, a date near that on which the western world celebrates Christmas. It may be that December 21st *is* the date of the poem, or (and with poets this seems more likely) that this is the closest the poet can come to Christmas without giving it all away. Who has "promises to keep" at or near this date, and who must traverse much territory to fulfill these promises? Yes, and who but St. Nick would know the location of *each* home? Only he would know who had "just settled down for a long winter's nap" (the poem's third line—"He will not see me stopping here"—is clearly a veiled allusion) and would not be out inspecting his acreage this night. The unusual phrase "fill up with snow," in the poem's fourth line, is a transfer of Santa's occupational preoccupation to the countryside; he is mulling the filling of countless stockings hung above countless fireplaces by countless careful children. "Harness bells," of course, allude to "Sleighing Song," a popular Christmas tune of the time the poem was written in which the refrain "Jingle Bells! Jingle Bells!" appears; thus again are we put on the Christmas track. The "little horse," like the date, is another attempt at poetic obfuscation. Although the "rein-reindeer" ambiguity has been eliminated from the poem's final version,[1] probably because too obvious, we may speculate that the

---

[1] The original draft contained the following line: "That bid me give the reins a shake" (Stageberg-Anderson, *Poetry as Experience* [New York, 1952], p. 457). [Coursen's note.]

animal is really a reindeer disguised as a horse by the poet's desire for obscurity, a desire which we must concede has been fulfilled up to now.

The animal is clearly concerned, like the faithful Rudolph — another possible allusion (post facto, hence unconscious) — lest his master fail to complete his mission. Seeing no farmhouse in the second quatrain, but pulling a load of presents, no wonder the little beast wonders! It takes him a full two quatrains to rouse his driver to remember all the empty stockings which hang ahead. And Santa does so reluctantly at that, poor soul, as he ponders the myriad farmhouses and villages which spread between him and his own "winter's nap." The modern St. Nick, lonely and overworked, tosses no "Happy Christmas to all and to all a good night!" into the precipitation. He merely shrugs his shoulders and resignedly plods away.

From "The Ghost of Christmas Past: 'Stopping by Woods on a Snowy Evening,'" *College English,* December 1962

CONSIDERATIONS FOR CRITICAL THINKING AND WRITING

1. Is this critical spoof at all credible? Does the interpretation hold any water? Is the evidence reasonable? Why or why not? Which of the poem's details are accounted for and which are ignored?

2. Choose a Frost poem and try writing a parodic interpretation of it.

3. What criteria do you use to distinguish between a sensible interpretation of a poem and an absurd one? In an essay compare and contrast your criteria with the criteria suggested by Peter Rabinowitz in his perspective "On Close Readings" (pp. 2122–24).

BLANCHE FARLEY (B. 1937)

The Lover Not Taken   *1984*

Committed to one, she wanted both
And, mulling it over, long she stood,
Alone on the road, loath
To leave, wanting to hide in the undergrowth.
This new guy, smooth as a yellow wood   5

Really turned her on. She liked his hair,
His smile. But the other, Jack, had a claim
On her already and she had to admit, he did wear
Well. In fact, to be perfectly fair,
He understood her. His long, lithe frame   10

Beside hers in the evening tenderly lay.
Still, if this blond guy dropped by someday,
Couldn't way just lead on to way?
No. For if way led on and Jack
Found out, she doubted if he would ever come back.   15

Oh, she turned with a sigh.
Somewhere ages and ages hence,
She might be telling this. "And I —"

She would say, "stood faithfully by."
But by then who would know the difference?   20

With that in mind, she took the fast way home,
The road by the pond, and phoned the blond.

CONSIDERATIONS FOR CRITICAL THINKING AND WRITING

1. Which Frost poem is the object of this parody?
2. Describe how the stylistic elements mirror Frost's poem.
3. Does this parody seem successful to you? Explain what makes a successful parody.
4. Choose a Frost poem — or a portion of one if it is long — and try writing a parody of it.

DEREK WALCOTT (B. 1930)

The Road Taken   1996

Robert Frost: the icon of Yankee values, the smell of wood smoke, the sparkle of dew, the reality of farmhouse dung, the jocular honesty of an uncle.

Why is the favorite figure of American patriotism not paternal but avuncular? Because uncles are wiser than fathers. They have humor, they keep their distance, they are bachelors, they can't be fooled by rhetoric. Frost loved playing the uncle, relishing the dry enchantment of his own voice, the homely gravel in the throat, the keep-your-distance pseudo-rusticity that suspected every stranger, meaning every reader. The voice is like its weather. It tells you to stay away until you are invited. Its first lines, in the epigraph to Frost's 1949 *Complete Poems*, are not so much invitations as warnings.

> I'm going out to clean the pasture spring;
> I'll only stop to rake the leaves away
> (And wait to watch the water clear, I may):
> I sha'n't be gone long. — You come too.

From the very epigraph, then, the surly ambiguities slide in. Why "I may"? Not for the rhyme, the desperation of doggerel, but because of this truth: that it would take too long to watch the agitated clouded water settle, that is, for as long as patience allows the poet to proceed to the next line. (Note that the parentheses function as a kind of container, or bank, or vessel, of the churned spring.) The refrain, "You come too." An invitation? An order? And how sincere is either? That is the point of Frost's tone, the authoritative but ambiguous distance of a master ironist.

Frost is an autocratic poet rather than a democratic poet. His invitations are close-lipped, wry, quiet; neither the voice nor the metrical line has the open-armed municipal mural expansion of the other democratic poet, Whitman. The people in Frost's dramas occupy a tight and taciturn locale. They are not part of Whitman's parade of blacksmiths, wheelwrights made communal by work. Besieged and threatened, their virtues are as cautious and measured as the scansion by which they are portrayed.

From Joseph Brodsky, Seamus Heaney, and Derek Walcott,
Homage to Robert Frost

CONSIDERATIONS FOR CRITICAL THINKING AND WRITING

1. Why does Walcott characterize Frost as more an uncle than a father? Explain why you agree or disagree.

2. Choose one of Frost's poems in this anthology and use it to demonstrate that he is a "master ironist."

3. Write an essay that fleshes out Walcott's observation that the people in Frost's poems are "Besieged and threatened, their virtues . . . as cautious and measured as the scansion by which they are portrayed."

TWO COMPLEMENTARY
CRITICAL READINGS

RICHARD POIRIER (B. 1925)

On Emotional Suffocation in "Home Burial"   1977

Frost's poetry recurrently dramatizes the discovery that the sharing of a "home" can produce imaginations of uncontrollable threat inside or outside. "Home" can become the source of those fears from which it is supposed to protect us; it can become the habitation of that death whose anguish it is supposed to ameliorate. And this brings us to one of Frost's greatest poetic dramatizations of the theme, "Home Burial." [T]he pressure is shared by a husband and wife, but . . . the role of the husband is ambiguous. Though he does his best to comprehend the wife's difficulties, he is only partly able to do so. The very title of the poem means something about the couple as well as about the dead child buried in back of the house. It is as if "home" were a burial plot for all of them.

The opening lines of Frost's dramatic narratives are usually wonderfully deft in suggesting the metaphoric nature of "home," the human opportunities or imperatives which certain details represent for a husband or a wife. . . . [I]n "Home Burial," the couple are trapped inside the house, which is described as a kind of prison, or perhaps more aptly, a mental hospital. Even the wife's glance out the window can suggest to the husband the desperation she feels within the confines of what has always been his family's "home"; it looks directly on the family graveyard which now holds the body of their recently dead child: [lines 1–30 of "Home Burial" are quoted here].

The remarkable achievement here is that the husband and wife have become so nearly inarticulate in their animosities that the feelings have been transferred to a vision of household arrangements and to their own bodily movements. They and the house conspire together to create an aura of suffocation. . . . Frost's special genius is in the placement of words. The first line poses the husband as a kind of spy; the opening of the second line suggests a habituated wariness on her part, but from that point to line 5 we are shifted back to his glimpse of her as she moves obsessively again, as yet unaware of being watched, to the window. Suggestions of alienation, secretiveness, male intimidation ("advancing toward her") within a situation of mutual distrust, a miasmic fear inside as well as outside the house — we are made to sense this before anyone speaks. Initially the fault seems to lie mostly with the husband.

But as soon as she catches him watching her, and as soon as he begins to talk, it is the grim mutuality of their dilemma and the shared responsibilities for it that sustain the dramatic intelligence and power of the poem.

From *Robert Frost: The Work of Knowing*

Considerations for Critical Thinking and Writing

1. According to Poirier, how can the couple's home be regarded as a kind of "mental hospital"? Compare Poirier's view with Kearns's description in the following perspective on the house as a "marital asylum."

2. Explain why you agree or disagree that the husband's behavior is a form of "male intimidation."

3. Write an essay that discusses the "grim mutuality" of the couple's "dilemma."

Katherine Kearns (b. 1949)
On the Symbolic Setting of "Home Burial"   1987

"Home Burial" may be used to clarify Frost's intimate relationships between sex, death, and madness. The physical iconography is familiar—a stairwell, a window, a doorway, and a grave—elements which Frost reiterates throughout his poetry. The marriage in "Home Burial" has been destroyed by the death of a first and only son. The wife is in the process of leaving the house, crossing the threshold from marital asylum into freedom. The house is suffocating her. Her window view of the graveyard is not enough and is, in fact, a maddening reminder that she could not enter the earth with her son. With its transparent barrier, the window is a mockery of a widened vision throughout Frost's poetry and seems to incite escape rather than quelling it; in "Home Burial" the woman can "see" through the window and into the grave in a way her husband cannot, and the fear is driving her down the steps toward the door—"She was starting down—/Looking back over her shoulder at some fear"—even before she sees her husband. He threatens to follow his wife and bring her back by force, as if he is the cause of her leaving, but his gesture will be futile because it is based on the mistaken assumption that she is escaping him. Pathetically, he is merely an obstacle toward which she reacts at first dully and then with angry impatience. He is an inanimate part of the embattled household, her real impetus for movement comes from the grave.

The house itself, reduced symbolically and literally to a womblike passageway between the bedroom and the threshold, is a correlative for the sexual tension generated by the man's insistence on his marital rights. He offers to "give up being a man" by binding himself "to keep hands off," but their marriage is already sexually damaged and empty. The man and woman move in an intricate dance, she coming downward and then retracing a step, he "Mounting until she cower[s] under him," she "shrinking from beneath his arm" to slide downstairs. Randall Jarrell examines the image of the woman sinking into "a modest, compact, feminine bundle" upon her skirts;[1] it might be further observed that this childlike posture is also very much a gesture of sexual denial,

---

[1] "Robert Frost's 'Home Burial,'" in *The Moment of Poetry*, ed. Don Cameron Allen (Baltimore: Johns Hopkins UP, 1962), p. 104.

body bent, knees drawn up protectively against the breasts, all encompassed by voluminous skirts. The two are in profound imbalance, and Frost makes the wife's speech and movements the poetic equivalent of stumbling and resistance; her lines are frequently eleven syllables, and often are punctuated by spondees whose forceful but awkward slowness embodies the woman's vacillations "from terrified to dull," and from frozen and silent immobility to anger. Her egress from the house will be symbolic verification of her husband's impotence, and if she leaves it and does not come back, the house will rot as the best birch fence will rot. Unfilled, without a woman with child, it will fall into itself, an image that recurs throughout Frost's poetry. Thus the child's grave predicts the dissolution of household, . . . almost a literal "home burial."

From "'The Place Is the Asylum': Women and Nature in
Robert Frost's Poetry," *American Literature*, May 1987

CONSIDERATIONS FOR CRITICAL THINKING AND WRITING

1. How does Kearns's discussion of the stairwell, window, doorway, and grave shed light on your reading of "Home Burial"?

2. Discuss whether Kearns sympathizes more with the wife or the husband. Which character do you feel more sympathetic toward? Do you think Frost sides with one or the other? Explain your response.

3. Write an essay in which you agree or disagree with Kearns's assessment that "The wife is in the process of crossing the threshold from marital asylum into freedom."

SUGGESTED TOPICS FOR LONGER PAPERS

1. Research Frost's popular reputation and compare that with recent biographical accounts of his personal life. How does knowledge of his personal life affect your reading of his poetry?

2. Frost has been described as a cheerful poet of New England who creates pleasant images of the region as well as a poet who creates a troubling, frightening world bordered by anxiety, anguish, doubts, and darkness. How do the poems in this chapter support both of these readings of Frost's poetry?

3. MULTIMEDIA PROJECT. There are many books of photographs and paintings of stone walls, pastures, and so on, used to illustrate Frost's New England settings in his poems. Drawing upon whatever sources you deem useful, put together a collection of images that you think illustrate the people to be found in the Frost poems reprinted in this chapter. Provide a one-paragraph caption for each image that explains your choice.

Web *For help with this project, use the Multimedia Project Guides Online at*
http://www.bedfordstmartins.com/meyer/bedintrolit

33

A Study of Langston Hughes

The poetry of Langston Hughes represents a significant chapter in twentieth-century American literature. The poetry included here both chronicles and evokes African American life during the middle decades of the last century. Moreover, it celebrates the culture and heritage of what is called the "Harlem Renaissance" of the 1920s, which has continued to be a vital tradition and presence in American life. As you introduce yourself to Hughes's innovative techniques and the cultural life embedded in his poetry, keep in mind the Questions for Writing about an Author in Depth (p. 988), which can serve as a guide in your explorations.

A BRIEF BIOGRAPHY

Even as a child, Langston Hughes (1902–1967) was wrapped in an important African American legacy. He was raised by his maternal grandmother, who was the widow of Lewis Sheridan Leary, one of the band of men who participated in John Brown's raid on the federal arsenal at Harpers Ferry in 1859. The raid was a desperate attempt to

Photo Above: *Langston Hughes testifying before the Senate Investigations Subcommittee — Senator Joseph McCarthy's subcommittee on subversive activities — on March 27, 1953. (See "Un-American Investigators," p. 1054.) Reprinted by permission of UPI/Corbis-Bettmann.*

ignite an insurrection that would ultimately liberate slaves in the South. It was a failure. Leary was killed, but the shawl he wore, which was returned to his wife bloodstained and riddled with bullet holes, was proudly worn by Hughes's grandmother fifty years after the raid, and she used it to cover her grandson at night when he was a young boy.

Throughout his long career as a professional writer, Hughes remained true to the African American heritage he celebrated in his writings, which were frankly "racial in theme and treatment, derived from the life I know." In an influential essay published in *The Nation,* "The Negro Artist and the Racial Mountain" (1926), he insisted on the need for black artists to draw on their heritage rather than "to run away spiritually from . . . race":

> We younger Negro artists who create now intend to express our individual dark-skinned selves without fear or shame. If white people are pleased, we are glad. If they are not, it doesn't matter. We know we are beautiful. And ugly too. The tom-tom cries and the tom-tom laughs. If colored people are pleased we are glad. If they are not, their displeasure doesn't matter either. We build our temples for tomorrow, strong as we know how, and we stand on top of the mountain, free within ourselves.

That freedom was hard won for Hughes. His father, James Nathaniel Hughes, could not accommodate the racial prejudice and economic frustration that were the result of James's black and white racial ancestry. James abandoned his wife, Carrie Langston Hughes, only one year after their son was born in Joplin, Missouri, and went to find work in Mexico, where he hoped the color of his skin would be less of an issue than in the United States. During the periods when Hughes's mother shuttled from city to city in the Midwest looking for work, she sent her son to live with his grandmother.

Hughes's spotty relationship with his father — a connection he developed in his late teens and maintained only sporadically thereafter — consisted mostly of arguments about his becoming a writer rather than an engineer and businessman as his father wished. Hughes's father could not appreciate or even tolerate his son's ambition to write about the black experience, and Hughes (whose given name was also James but who refused to be identified by it) could not abide his father's contempt for blacks. Consequently, his determination, as he put it in "The Negro Artist," "to express our individual dark-skinned selves without fear or shame" was not only a profound response to African American culture but also an intensely personal commitment that made a relationship with his own father impossible. Though Hughes had been abandoned by his father, he nevertheless felt an early and deep connection to his ancestors, as he reveals in the following poem, written while crossing over the Mississippi River by train as he traveled to visit his father in Mexico, just a month after his high-school graduation.

The Negro Speaks of Rivers

1921

I've known rivers:
I've known rivers ancient as the world and older than the
　　flow of human blood in human veins.

My soul has grown deep like the rivers.

I bathed in Euphrates when dawns were young.   5
I built my hut near the Congo and it lulled me to sleep.
I looked upon the Nile and raised the pyramids above it.
I heard the singing of the Mississippi when Abe Lincoln
　　went down to New Orleans, and I've seen its muddy
　　bosom turn all golden in the sunset.   10

I've known rivers:
Ancient, dusky rivers.

My soul has grown deep like the rivers.

    This poem appeared in *The Crisis,* the official publication of the National
Association for the Advancement of Colored People, which eventually published more of Hughes's poems than any other magazine or journal. This famous poem's simple and direct free verse makes clear that Africa's "dusky
rivers" run concurrently with the poet's soul as he draws spiritual strength as
well as individual identity from the collective experience of his ancestors.
The themes of racial pride and personal dignity work their way through
some forty books that Hughes wrote, edited, or compiled during his forty-
five years of writing.

AN INTRODUCTION TO HIS WORK

His works include volumes of poetry, novels, short stories, essays, plays,
opera librettos, histories, documentaries, autobiographies, biographies, anthologies, children's books, and translations, as well as radio and television
scripts. This impressive body of work makes him an important literary
artist and a leading African American voice of the twentieth century. First
and foremost, he considered himself a poet. He set out to be a poet who
could address himself to the concerns of his people in poems that could be
read with no formal training or extensive literary background. He wanted
his poetry to be "direct, comprehensible, and the epitome of simplicity."
    His poetry echoes the voices of ordinary African Americans and the
rhythms of their music. Hughes drew on an oral tradition of working-class
folk poetry that embraced black vernacular language at a time when some
middle-class blacks of the 1920s felt that the use of the vernacular was an
embarrassing handicap and an impediment to social progress. Hughes's
response to such concerns was unequivocal; at his readings, some of which
were accompanied by jazz musicians or singers, his innovative voice found

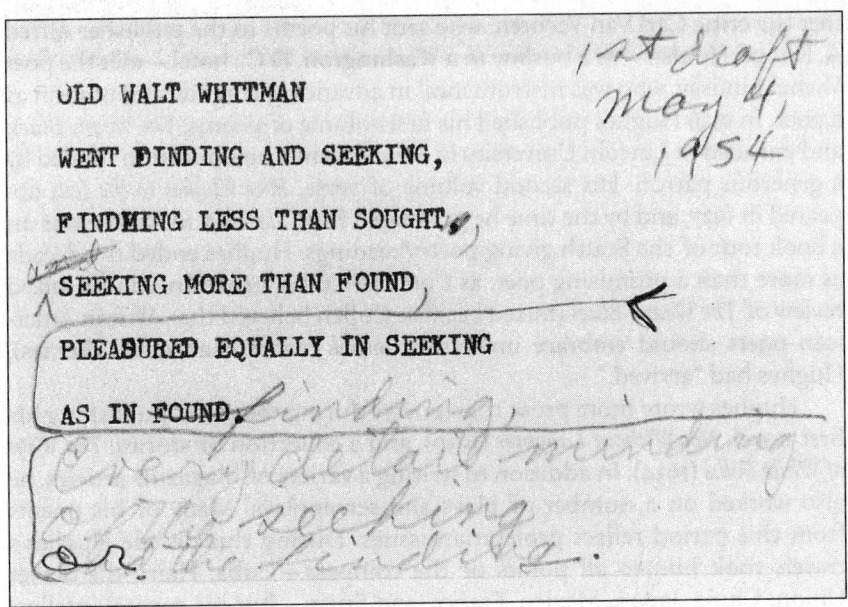

Manuscript page for "Old Walt" (1954) showing an earlier stage of the poem than the one published here (p. 1055) and Hughes's revisions.

an appreciative audience. As Hughes very well knew, much of the pleasure associated with his poetry comes from reading it aloud; his many recorded readings give testimony to that pleasure.

The blues can be heard moving through Hughes's poetry as well as in the works of many of his contemporaries associated with the Harlem Renaissance, a movement of African American artists—writers, painters, sculptors, actors, and musicians—who were active in New York City's Harlem of the 1920s. Hughes's introduction to the "laughter and pain, hunger and heartache" of blues music began the year he spent at Columbia University. He dropped out after only two semesters because he preferred the night life and culture of Harlem to academic life. The sweet, sad blues songs captured for Hughes the intense pain and yearning that he saw around him and that he incorporated into poems such as "The Weary Blues" (p. 1043). He also reveled in the jazz music of Harlem and discovered in its open forms and improvisations an energy and freedom that significantly influenced the style of his poetry.

Hughes's life, like the jazz music that influenced his work, was characterized by improvisation and openness. After leaving Columbia, he worked a series of odd jobs and then traveled as a merchant seaman to Africa and Europe from 1923 to 1924. He jumped ship to work for several months in the kitchen of a Paris nightclub. As he broadened his experience through travel, he continued to write poetry. After his return to the United States in 1925 he published poems in two black magazines, *The Crisis* and *Opportunity*, and met the critic Carl Van Vechten, who sent his poems to the publisher Alfred A. Knopf. He also — as a busboy in a Washington, D.C., hotel — met the poet Vachel Lindsay, who was instrumental in advancing Hughes's reputation as a poet. In 1926 Hughes published his first volume of poems, *The Weary Blues*, and enrolled in Lincoln University in Pennsylvania, his education funded by a generous patron. His second volume of verse, *Fine Clothes to the Jew*, appeared in 1927, and by the time he graduated from Lincoln in 1929 he was on a book tour of the South giving poetry readings. Hughes ended the decade as more than a promising poet; as Countee Cullen pronounced in a mixed review of *The Weary Blues* (mixed because Cullen believed that African American poets should embrace universal themes rather than racial themes), Hughes had "arrived."

Hughes wrote more prose than poetry during the 1930s, publishing his first novel, *Not Without Laughter* (1930), and a collection of stories, *The Ways of White Folks* (1934). In addition to writing a variety of magazine articles, he also worked on a number of plays and screenplays. Many of his poems from this period reflect proletarian issues. During this decade Hughes's travels took him to all points of the compass — Cuba, Haiti, the Soviet Union, China, Japan, Mexico, France, and Spain — but his general intellectual movement was decidedly toward the left. Hughes was attracted to the American Communist Party, owing to its insistence on equality for all working-class people regardless of race. Like many other Americans of the thirties, he turned his attention away from the exotic twenties and focused on the economic and political issues attending the Great Depression that challenged the freedom and dignity of common humanity.

During World War II, Hughes helped the war effort by writing jingles and catchy verses to sell war bonds and to bolster morale. His protest poems of the thirties were largely replaced by poems that returned to earlier themes centered on the everyday lives of African Americans. In 1942 Hughes described his new collection of poems, *Shakespeare in Harlem*, as "light verse. Afro-American in the blues mood . . . to be read aloud, crooned, shouted, recited, and sung. Some with gestures, some not — as you like." Soon after this collection appeared, the character of Jesse B. Simple emerged from Hughes's 1943 newspaper column for the Chicago *Defender.* Hughes developed this popular urban African American character in five humorous books published over a fifteen-year period: *Simple Speaks His Mind* (1950), *Simple Takes a Wife* (1953), *Simple Stakes a Claim* (1957), *The Best of Simple* (1961), and *Simple's Uncle Sam* (1965). Two more poetry collections appeared in the forties: *Fields of Wonder* (1947) and *One-Way Ticket* (1949).

In the 1950s and 1960s Hughes's poetry again revealed the strong influence of black music, especially in the rhythms of *Montage of a Dream Deferred* (1951) and *Ask Your Mama: 12 Moods for Jazz* (1961). From the poem "Harlem" (p. 1053) in *Montage of a Dream Deferred*, Lorraine Hansberry derived the title of her 1959 play *A Raisin in the Sun*. This is only a small measure of Hughes's influence on his fellow African American writers, but it is suggestive nonetheless. For some in the 1950s, however, Hughes and his influence occasioned suspicion. He was watched closely by the FBI and the Special Committee on Un-American Activities of the House of Representatives because of his alleged communist activities in the 1930s. Hughes denied that he was ever a member of the Communist Party, but he and others, including Albert Einstein and Paul Robeson, were characterized as "dupes and fellow travelers" by *Life* magazine in 1949. Hughes was subpoenaed to appear before Senator Joseph McCarthy's subcommittee on subversive activities in 1953 and listed by the FBI as a security risk until 1959. His anger and indignation over these attacks from the right can be seen in his poem "Un-American Investigators" (p. 1054), published posthumously in *The Panther and the Lash* (1967).

Despite the tremendous amount that Hughes published, including two autobiographies, *The Big Sea* (1940) and *I Wonder as I Wander* (1956), he remains somewhat elusive. He never married or had friends who can lay claim to truly knowing him beyond what he wanted them to know (even though there are several biographies). And yet Hughes is well known — not for his personal life but for his treatment of the possibilities of African American experiences and identities. Like Walt Whitman, one of his favorite writers, Hughes created a persona that spoke for more than himself. Consider Hughes's voice in the following poem.

I, Too   1925

I, too, sing America.

I am the darker brother.
They send me to eat in the kitchen
When company comes,
But I laugh,   5
And eat well,
And grow strong.

Tomorrow,
I'll be at the table
When company comes.   10
Nobody'll dare
Say to me,
"Eat in the kitchen,"
Then.

Besides,   15
They'll see how beautiful I am
And be ashamed —

I, too, am America.

The "darker brother" who celebrates America is certain of a better future when he will no longer be shunted aside by "company." The poem is characteristic of Hughes's faith in the racial consciousness of African Americans, a consciousness that reflects their integrity and beauty while simultaneously demanding respect and acceptance from others: "Nobody'll dare / Say to me, / 'Eat in the kitchen,' / Then."

Hughes's poetry reveals his hearty appetite for all humanity, his insistence on justice for all, and his faith in the transcendent possibilities of joy and hope that make room for everyone at America's table.

CHRONOLOGY

1902	Born on February 1, in Joplin, Missouri.
1903–14	Lives primarily with his grandmother in Lawrence, Kansas.
1920	Graduates from high school in Cleveland, Ohio.
1921–22	Attends Columbia University for one year but then drops out to work odd jobs and discover Harlem.
1923–24	Travels to Africa and Europe while working on a merchant ship.
1926	Publishes his first collection of poems, *The Weary Blues,* and enters Lincoln University in Pennsylvania.
1929	Graduates from Lincoln University.
1930	Publishes his first novel, *Not Without Laughter.*
1932	Travels to the Soviet Union.
1934	Publishes his first collection of short stories, *The Ways of White Folks.*
1935	His play *Mulatto* is produced on Broadway.
1937	Covers the Spanish Civil War for the Baltimore *Afro-American.*
1938–39	Founds African American theaters in Harlem and Los Angeles.
1940	Publishes his first autobiography, *The Big Sea.*
1943	Creates the character of Simple in columns for the Chicago *Defender.*
1947	Is poet-in-residence at Atlanta University.
1949	Teaches at University of Chicago's Laboratory School.
1950	Publishes his first volume of Simple sketches, *Simple Speaks His Mind.*
1951	Publishes a translation of Federico García Lorca's *Gypsy Ballads.*
1953	Is subpoenaed to appear before Senator Joseph McCarthy's subcommittee on subversive activities in Washington, D.C.
1954–55	Publishes a number of books for young readers including *The First Book of Jazz* and *Famous American Negroes.*
1956	Publishes his second autobiography, *I Wonder as I Wander.*
1958	Publishes *The Langston Hughes Reader.*
1960	Publishes *An African Treasury: Articles, Essays, Stories, Poems by Black Africans.*
1961	Is inducted into the National Institute of Arts and Letters.

Web   *Research Langston Hughes with LitLinks at*
http://www.bedfordstmartins.com/meyer/bedintrolit

Negro   1922

I am a Negro:
  Black as the night is black,
  Black like the depths of my Africa.

I've been a slave:
  Caesar told me to keep his door-steps clean.   5
  I brushed the boots of Washington.

I've been a worker:
  Under my hand the pyramids arose.
  I made mortar for the Woolworth Building.

I've been a singer: 10
  All the way from Africa to Georgia
  I carried my sorrow songs.
  I made ragtime.

I've been a victim:
  The Belgians cut off my hands in the Congo.   15
  They lynch me still in Mississippi.

I am a Negro:
  Black as the night is black,
  Black like the depths of my Africa.

CONSIDERATIONS FOR CRITICAL THINKING AND WRITING

1. FIRST RESPONSE. What sort of identity does the speaker claim for the "Negro"? What is the effect of the litany of roles?

2. What is the effect of the repetition of the first and last stanzas?

3. What kind of history of black people does the speaker describe?

CONNECTIONS TO OTHER SELECTIONS

1. How does Hughes's use of night and blackness in "Negro" help to explain their meaning in the poem "Dream Variations" (p. 1042)?

2. Write an essay comparing the treatment of oppression in "Negro" with that in Blake's "The Chimney Sweeper" (p. 828).

Danse Africaine   1922

The low beating of the tom-toms,
The slow beating of the tom-toms,
    Low . . . slow
    Slow . . . low—
    Stirs your blood.
       Dance!   5
A night-veiled girl
    Whirls softly into a
    Circle of light.
    Whirls softly . . . slowly,   10
Like a wisp of smoke around the fire—
    And the tom-toms beat,
    And the tom-toms beat,
And the low beating of the tom-toms
    Stirs your blood.   15

CONSIDERATIONS FOR CRITICAL THINKING AND WRITING

1. FIRST RESPONSE. How do the sounds of this poem build its meaning? (What *is* its meaning?)

2. What effect do the repeated rhythms have? You may need to read the poem aloud to answer.

CONNECTION TO ANOTHER SELECTION

1. Try rewriting this poem based on the prescription for poetry in "Formula" (p. 1044).

Mother to Son   1922

Well, son, I'll tell you:
Life for me ain't been no crystal stair.
It's had tacks in it,
And splinters,
And boards torn up,   5

And places with no carpet on the floor —
Bar.
But all the time
I'se been a-climbin' on,
And reachin' landin's,   10
And turnin' corners,
And sometimes goin' in the dark
Where there ain't been no light.
So boy, don't you turn back.
Don't you set down on the steps   15
'Cause you finds it's kinder hard.
Don't you fall now —
For I'se still goin', honey,
I'se still climbin',
And life for me ain't been no crystal stair.   20

CONSIDERATIONS FOR CRITICAL THINKING AND WRITING

1. FIRST RESPONSE. How is the central metaphor of climbing stairs a particularly appropriate idea for conveying this poem's theme?
2. Try rewriting the dialect of this poem in formal diction. How does this change your response to the poem?
3. What does it imply that the stairs are crystal rather than, say, carpeted?

Jazzonia   *1923*

Oh, silver tree!
Oh, shining rivers of the soul!

In a Harlem cabaret
Six long-headed jazzers play.
A dancing girl whose eyes are bold   5
Lifts high a dress of silken gold.

Oh, singing tree!
Oh, shining rivers of the soul!

Were Eve's eyes
In the first garden   10
Just a bit too bold?
Was Cleopatra gorgeous
In a gown of gold?

Oh, shining tree!
Oh, silver rivers of the soul!   15

In a whirling cabaret
Six long-headed jazzers play.

1. FIRST RESPONSE. Does "Jazzonia" capture what you imagine a Harlem cabaret to have been like? Discuss the importance of the setting.

2. What is the effect of the variations in lines 1–2, 7–8, and 14–15?

3. What do the allusions to Eve and Cleopatra add to the poem's meaning? Are the questions raised about them answered?

Connection to Another Selection

1. Compare in an essay the rhythms of "Jazzonia" and "Danse Africaine" (p. 1040).

Dream Variations   1924

To fling my arms wide
In some place of the sun,
To whirl and to dance
Till the white day is done.
Then rest at cool evening   5
Beneath a tall tree
While night comes on gently,
    Dark like me —
That is my dream!

To fling my arms wide   10
In the face of the sun,
Dance! Whirl! Whirl!
Till the quick day is done.
Rest at pale evening . . .
A tall, slim tree . . .   15
Night coming tenderly
    Black like me.

Considerations for Critical Thinking and Writing

1. FIRST RESPONSE. What distinctions are made in the poem between night and day? Which is the dream?

2. Describe the speaker's "Dream." How might the dream be understood metaphorically?

3. How do the rhythms of the lines contribute to the effects of the poem?

Connections to Other Selections

1. In an essay compare and contrast the meanings of darkness and the night in this poem and in Stafford's "Traveling through the Dark" (p. 818).

2. Discuss the significance of the dream in this poem and in "Dream Boogie" (p. 1052).

The Weary Blues   *1925*

Droning a drowsy syncopated tune,
Rocking back and forth to a mellow croon,
   I heard a Negro play.
Down on Lenox Avenue° the other night   *street in Harlem*
By the pale dull pallor of an old gas light   5
   He did a lazy sway. . . .
   He did a lazy sway. . . .
To the tune o' those Weary Blues.
With his ebony hands on each ivory key
He made that poor piano moan with melody.   10
   O Blues!
Swaying to and fro on his rickety stool
He played that sad raggy tune like a musical fool.
   Sweet Blues!
Coming from a black man's soul.   15
   O Blues!
In a deep song voice with a melancholy tone
I heard that Negro sing, that old piano moan —
   "Ain't got nobody in all this world,
      Ain't got nobody but ma self.   20
      I's gwine to quit ma frownin'
      And put ma troubles on the shelf."

Thump, thump, thump, went his foot on the floor.
He played a few chords then he sang some more —
   "I got the Weary Blues   25
      And I can't be satisfied.
      Got the Weary Blues
      And can't be satisfied —
      I ain't happy no mo'
      And I wish that I had died."   30
And far into the night he crooned that tune.
The stars went out and so did the moon.
The singer stopped playing and went to bed
While the Weary Blues echoed through his head.
He slept like a rock or a man that's dead.   35

Considerations for Critical Thinking and Writing

1. FIRST RESPONSE. Write a one-paragraph description of the blues based on how the poem presents blues music.

2. How does the speaker's voice compare with the singer's?

3. Comment on the effects of the rhymes.

4. CRITICAL STRATEGIES. Read the section on formalist criticism (pp. 2095–97) in Chapter 52, "Critical Strategies for Reading," and explain how the rhythm of the lines reflects their meaning.

CONNECTION TO ANOTHER SELECTION

1. Discuss "The Weary Blues" and "Lenox Avenue: Midnight" (p. 1045) as vignettes of urban life in America. Do you think that, though written more than seventy years ago, they are still credible descriptions of city life? Explain why or why not.

Cross   1925

My old man's a white old man
And my old mother's black.
If ever I cursed my white old man
I take my curses back.

If ever I cursed my black old mother   5
And wished she were in hell,
I'm sorry for that evil wish
And now I wish her well.

My old man died in a fine big house.
My ma died in a shack.   10
I wonder where I'm gonna die,
Being neither white nor black?

CONSIDERATIONS FOR CRITICAL THINKING AND WRITING

1. FIRST RESPONSE. What do you think has caused the speaker to retract his or her hard feelings about his or her parents?
2. Discuss the possible meaning of the title.
3. Why do you think the speaker regrets having "cursed" his or her father and mother? Is it possible to determine if the speaker is male or female? Why or why not?
4. What informs the speaker's attitude toward life?

CONNECTION TO ANOTHER SELECTION

1. Read the perspective by Francis, "On 'Hard' Poetry" (p. 697), and write an essay explaining why you would characterize "Cross" as "hard" or "soft" poetry.

Formula   1926

Poetry should treat
    Of lofty things
Soaring thoughts
    And birds with wings.

The Muse of Poetry   5
    Should not know

That roses
    In manure grow.
The Muse of Poetry
    Should not care   10
That earthly pain
    Is everywhere.

Poetry!
    Treats of lofty things:
Soaring thoughts   15
    And birds with wings.

CONSIDERATIONS FOR CRITICAL THINKING AND WRITING

1. FIRST RESPONSE. What makes this poem a parody? What assumptions about poetry are being made fun of in the poem?

2. How does "Formula" fit the prescriptions offered in the advice to greeting-card freelancers (p. 692)?

3. CRITICAL STRATEGIES. Read the section on deconstructionist criticism (pp. 2111–13) in Chapter 52, "Critical Strategies for Reading," and discuss how contradictory and opposing meanings in this poem reveal implicit ideological values.

CONNECTIONS TO OTHER SELECTIONS

1. Choose any two poems by Hughes in this collection and explain why they do not fit the "Formula."

2. Write an essay that explains how Farries's "Magic of Love" (p. 693) conforms to the ideas about poetry presented in "Formula."

Lenox Avenue: Midnight   *1926*

The rhythm of life
Is a jazz rhythm,
Honey.
The gods are laughing at us.

The broken heart of love,   5
The weary, weary heart of pain,—
    Overtones,
    Undertones,
To the rumble of street cars,
To the swish of rain.   10

Lenox Avenue,
Honey.
Midnight,
And the gods are laughing at us.

CONSIDERATIONS FOR CRITICAL THINKING AND WRITING

1. FIRST RESPONSE. What, in your own experience, is the equivalent of Lenox Avenue for the speaker?

2. For so brief a poem there are many sounds in these fourteen lines. What are they? How do they reinforce the poem's meanings?

3. What do you think is the poem's theme?

CONNECTIONS TO OTHER SELECTIONS

1. In an essay compare the theme of this poem with that of Emily Dickinson's "I know that He exists" (p. 990).

2. Compare and contrast the speaker's tone in this poem with the tone of the speaker in Thomas Hardy's "Hap" (p. 1157).

Song for a Dark Girl   1927

Way Down South in Dixie
  (Break the heart of me)
They hung my black young lover
  To a cross roads tree.

Way Down South in Dixie   5
  (Bruised body high in air)
I asked the white Lord Jesus
  What was the use of prayer.

Way down South in Dixie
  (Break the heart of me)   10
Love is a naked shadow
  On a gnarled and naked tree.

CONSIDERATIONS FOR CRITICAL THINKING AND WRITING

1. FIRST RESPONSE. What allusion is made in the first line of each stanza? How is that allusion ironic?

2. What *is* "the use of prayer" in this poem? Is the question answered? What, in particular, leads you to your conclusion?

3. Discuss the relationship between love and hatred in the poem.

CONNECTION TO ANOTHER SELECTION

1. Compare the speaker's sensibilities in this poem and in Emily Dickinson's "If I can stop one Heart from breaking" (p. 953). What kinds of cultural assumptions are implicit in each speaker's voice?

Red Silk Stockings 1927

Put on yo' red silk stockings,
Black gal.
Go out an' let de white boys
Look at yo' legs.

Ain't nothin' to do for you, nohow, 5
Round this town, —
You's too pretty.

Put on yo' red silk stockings, gal,
An' tomorrow's chile'll
Be a high yaller. 10

Go out an' let de white boys
Look at yo' legs.

CONSIDERATIONS FOR CRITICAL THINKING AND WRITING

1. FIRST RESPONSE. Who do you think is speaking? Describe his or her tone.
2. Discuss the racial dimensions of this poem.
3. Write a response from the girl — does she put on the red silk stockings? Explain why you imagine her reacting in a certain way.

CONNECTION TO ANOTHER SELECTION

1. Write an essay that compares relations between whites and blacks in this poem and in "Dinner Guest: Me" (p. 1057).

Bad Man 1927

I'm a bad, bad man
Cause everbody tells me so.
I'm a bad, bad man.
Everbody tells me so.
I takes ma meanness and ma licker 5
Everwhere I go.

I beats ma wife an'
I beats ma side gal too.
Beats ma wife an'
Beats ma side gal too. 10
Don't know why I do it but
It keeps me from feelin' blue.

I'm so bad I
Don't even want to be good.
So bad, bad I 15
Don't even want to be good.

I'm goin' to de devil an'
I wouldn't go to heaben if I could.

1. FIRST RESPONSE. What, if anything, do you find redeeming about this "bad, bad man"?

2. How would you describe the effects of the repetition in this poem? How does the repetition affect your understanding of the character and the meaning of the poem?

Rent-Party° Shout: For a Lady Dancer   1930

Whip it to a jelly!
Too bad Jim!
Mamie's got ma man —
An' I can't find him.
Shake that thing! O!   5
Shake it slow!
That man I love is
Mean an' low.
Pistol an' razor!
Razor an' gun!   10
If I sees ma man he'd
Better run —
For I'll shoot him in de shoulder,
Else I'll cut him down,
Cause I knows I can find him   15
When he's in de ground —
Then can't no other women
Have him layin' round.
So play it, Mr. Nappy!
Yo' music's fine!   20
I'm gonna kill that
Man o' mine!

Rent-Party: In Harlem during the 1920s, parties were given that charged admission to raise money for rent.

1. FIRST RESPONSE. Describe the type of music you think might be played at this party today.

2. In what sense is this poem a kind of "Shout"?

3. How is the speaker's personality characterized by her use of language?

4. How does Hughes's use of short lines affect your reading of the poem?

Drum 1931

Bear in mind
That death is a drum
Beating forever
Till the last worms come
To answer its call, 5
Till the last stars fall,
Until the last atom
Is no atom at all,
Until time is lost
And there is no air 10
And space itself
Is nothing nowhere,
Death is a drum,
A signal drum,
Calling life 15
To come!
Come!
Come!

CONSIDERATIONS FOR CRITICAL THINKING AND WRITING

1. FIRST RESPONSE. How would you read the poem differently if it had ended
   at line 14? Why are lines 15-18 so surprising?
2. Comment on the effects of the rhythm and rhymes.
3. Would the poem be better titled "Death" rather than "Drum"? Why or
   why not?

CONNECTION TO ANOTHER SELECTION

1. Discuss the definition of death in "Drum" and in Emily Dickinson's "If I
   shouldn't be alive" (p. 954).

Ballad of the Landlord 1940

Landlord, landlord,
My roof has sprung a leak.
Don't you 'member I told you about it
Way last week?

Landlord, landlord, 5
These steps is broken down.
When you come up yourself
It's a wonder you don't fall down.

Ten Bucks you say I owe you?
Ten Bucks you say is due? 10
Well, that's Ten Bucks more'n I'll pay you
Till you fix this house up new.

What? You gonna get eviction orders?
You gonna cut off my heat?
You gonna take my furniture and   15
Throw it in the street?

Um-huh! You talking high and mighty.
Talk on — till you get through.
You ain't gonna be able to say a word
If I land my fist on you.   20

Police! Police!
Come and get this man!
He's trying to ruin the government
And overturn the land!

Copper's whistle!   25
Patrol bell!
Arrest.

Precinct Station.
Iron cell.
Headlines in press: 30

MAN THREATENS LANDLORD

TENANT HELD NO BAIL

JUDGE GIVES NEGRO 90 DAYS IN COUNTY JAIL

CONSIDERATIONS FOR CRITICAL THINKING AND WRITING

1. FIRST RESPONSE. The poem incorporates both humor and serious social commentary. Which do you think is dominant? Explain.

2. Why is the literary ballad an especially appropriate form for the content of this poem?

3. How does the speaker's language simultaneously characterize him and the landlord?

CONNECTION TO ANOTHER SELECTION

1. Write an essay on landlords based on this poem and Soyinka's "Telephone Conversation" (p. 681).

Uncle Tom   *1944*

Within—
The beaten pride.
Without—
The grinning face,
The low, obsequious,   5
Double bow,
The sly and servile grace

Of one the white folks
Long ago
Taught well   10
To know his
Place.

CONSIDERATIONS FOR CRITICAL THINKING AND WRITING

1. FIRST RESPONSE. Explain whether or not you think the cultural evidence for this poem draws more on a stereotype or an archetype.

2. Why do you suppose Hughes devotes only one line to what is "Within" Uncle Tom compared to nine lines devoted to what is "Without"?

3. What is, finally, the speaker's attitude toward Uncle Tom?

CONNECTION TO ANOTHER SELECTION

1. Compare the treatment of Uncle Tom here with that of "Frederick Douglass: 1817–1895" (p. 1058). How do these two figures represent polar opposites in the culture of African American manhood?

Madam and the Census Man   *1949*

The census man,
The day he came round,
Wanted my name
To put it down.

I said JOHNSON,   5
ALBERTA K.
But he hated to write
The K that way.

He said, What
Does K stand for?   10
I said K —
And nothing more.

He said, I'm gonna put it
K-A-Y.
I said, If you do,   15
You lie.

My mother christened me
ALBERTA K.
You leave my name
Just that way!   20

He said, Mrs.,
(With a snort)
Just a K
Makes your name too short.

I said, I don't   25
Give a damn!
Leave me and my name
Just like I am!

Furthermore, rub out
that MRS., too —   30
I'll have you know
I'm *Madam* to you!

CONSIDERATIONS FOR CRITICAL THINKING AND WRITING

1. FIRST RESPONSE. How are Madam and the census man characterized in the poem? Try writing a physical description of each of them that captures their personalities for you.
2. Although an amusing conflict is presented in the poem, why is it also a serious issue?

CONNECTION TO ANOTHER SELECTION

1. Contrast Madam's demeanor with that of the subject of "Uncle Tom" (p. 1050). How might the poems be read as companion pieces?

Dream Boogie   1951

Good morning, daddy!
Ain't you heard
The boogie-woogie rumble
Of a dream deferred?
Listen closely: 5
You'll hear their feet
Beating out and beating out a —

  *You think
  It's a happy beat?*

Listen to it closely: 10
Ain't you heard
something underneath
like a —

  What did I say?

Sure,   15
I'm happy!
Take it away!

  *Hey, pop!
  Re-bop!
  Mop!*   20

  Y-e-a-h!

CONSIDERATIONS FOR CRITICAL THINKING AND WRITING

1. FIRST RESPONSE. Answer the question, *"You think / It's a happy beat?"*
2. Discuss the poem's musical qualities. Which lines are most musical?
3. Describe the competing tones in the poem. Which do you think is predominant?

CONNECTIONS TO OTHER SELECTIONS

1. In an essay compare and contrast the thematic tensions in this poem and in "Harlem," the next poem.
2. How are the "dreams" different in "Dream Boogie" and "Dream Variations" (p. 1042)?

Harlem   1951

What happens to a dream deferred?

Does it dry up
like a raisin in the sun?
Or fester like a sore —
And then run?   5
Does it stink like rotten meat?
Or crust and sugar over —
like a syrupy sweet?

Maybe it just sags
like a heavy load.   10

Or does it explode?

CONSIDERATIONS FOR CRITICAL THINKING AND WRITING

1. How might the question asked in this poem be raised by any individual or group whose dreams and aspirations are thwarted?
2. In some editions of Hughes's poetry the title of this poem is "Dream Deferred." What would the effect of this change be on your reading of the poem's symbolic significance?
3. How might the final line be completed as a simile? What is the effect of the speaker not completing the simile? Why is this an especially useful strategy?

CONNECTION TO ANOTHER SELECTION

1. Write an essay on the themes of "Harlem" and Merrill's "Casual Wear" (p. 823).

Democracy

1949

Democracy will not come
Today, this year
     Nor ever
Through compromise and fear.

I have as much right   5
As the other fellow has
     To stand
On my two feet
And own the land.

I tire so of hearing people say,   10
Let things take their course.
Tomorrow is another day.
I do not need my freedom when I'm dead.
I cannot live on tomorrow's bread.

     Freedom   15
     Is a strong seed
     Planted
     In a great need.

     I live here, too.
     I want freedom   20
     Just as you.

CONSIDERATIONS FOR CRITICAL THINKING AND WRITING

1. FIRST RESPONSE. Comment on the way in which the lines are arranged. Explain what purpose the arrangement might serve. How?
2. Describe the speaker's tone. Is it too strong, too weak, or just right? Why?
3. "Tomorrow is another day" is a line spoken by Scarlett O'Hara at the end of Margaret Mitchell's novel *Gone with the Wind* (1936) about the Civil War (the line appears in the film version, too). Consider the appropriateness of this allusion.

Un-American Investigators

1953

The committee's fat,
Smug, almost secure
Co-religionists
Shiver with delight
In warm manure   5
As those investigated—
Too brave to name a name—
Have pseudonyms revealed
In Gentile game

Of who,   10
Born Jew,
Is who?
Is not your name Lipshitz?
Yes.
Did you not change it   15
For subversive purposes?
No.
For nefarious gain?
Not so.
Are you sure?   20
The committee shivers
With delight in
Its manure.

CONSIDERATIONS FOR CRITICAL THINKING AND WRITING

1. FIRST RESPONSE. What are the politics of the speaker, do you think? What in the poem suggests this?
2. How does the speaker characterize the investigators?
3. Given the images in the poem, what might serve as a substitute for its ironic title?
4. CRITICAL STRATEGIES. Read the section on new historicist criticism (pp. 2103–04) in Chapter 52, "Critical Strategies for Reading." Research in the library the hearings and investigations of the House of Representatives' Special Committee on Un-American Activities. How is this background information relevant to an understanding of this poem?

CONNECTION TO ANOTHER SELECTION

1. Write an essay that connects the committee described in this poem with the speaker in E. E. Cummings's "next to of course god america i" (p. 809). What do they have in common?

Old Walt   *1954*

Old Walt Whitman
Went finding and seeking,
Finding less than sought
Seeking more than found,
Every detail minding   5
Of the seeking or the finding.

Pleasured equally
In seeking as in finding,
Each detail minding,
Old Walt went seeking   10
And finding.

CONSIDERATIONS FOR CRITICAL THINKING AND WRITING

1. FIRST RESPONSE. Read any poem by Whitman in this book. Do you agree with the speaker's take on Whitman's poetry?

2. Write an explication of "Old Walt." (For a discussion of how to explicate a poem, see the sample explication on pp. 2147–48.)

3. What is the effect of the poem's repeated sounds?

4. To what extent do you think lines 3 and 4 could be used to describe Hughes's poetry as well as Whitman's?

CONNECTION TO ANOTHER SELECTION

1. How does Hughes's tribute to Whitman compare with his tribute to Frederick Douglass (p. 1058)?

doorknobs   1961

The simple silly terror
of a doorknob on a door
that turns to let in life
on two feet standing,
walking, talking,   5
wearing dress or trousers,
maybe drunk or maybe sober,
maybe smiling, laughing, happy,
maybe tangled in the terror
of a yesterday past grandpa   10
when the door from out there opened
into here where I, antenna,
recipient of your coming,
received the talking image
of the simple silly terror   15
of a door that opens
at the turning of a knob
to let in life
walking, talking, standing
wearing dress or trousers,   20
drunk or maybe sober,
smiling, laughing, happy,
or tangled in the terror
of a yesterday past grandpa
not of our own doing.   25

CONSIDERATIONS FOR CRITICAL THINKING AND WRITING

1. FIRST RESPONSE. Why is the doorknob associated with "terror"? Does it have any symbolic value or should it be read literally?

2. How do the style and content of this poem differ from those of the other poems by Hughes in this anthology?

3. The final eight lines repeat much of the first part of the poem. What is repeated and what is changed? What is the effect of this repetition?

CONNECTION TO ANOTHER SELECTION

1. Write an essay comparing the theme of this poem with that of Stevens's "Schizophrenia" (p. 792).

Dinner Guest: Me   *1965*

I know I am
The Negro Problem
Being wined and dined,
Answering the usual questions
That come to white mind   5
Which seeks demurely
To probe in polite way
The why and wherewithal
Of darkness U.S.A.—
Wondering how things got this way   10
In current democratic night,
Murmuring gently
Over *fraises du bois*,
"I'm so ashamed of being white."

The lobster is delicious,   15
The wine divine,
And center of attention
At the damask table, mine.
To be a Problem on
Park Avenue at eight   20
Is not so bad.
Solutions to the Problem,
Of course, wait.

CONSIDERATIONS FOR CRITICAL THINKING AND WRITING

1. FIRST RESPONSE. What does the speaker satirize in this description of a dinner party? Do you think this "Problem" exists today?
2. Why is line 9, "Of darkness U.S.A.—," especially resonant?
3. What effects are created by the speaker's diction?
4. Discuss the effects of the rhymes in lines 15-23.

CONNECTION TO ANOTHER SELECTION

1. Write an essay on the speaker's treatment of the diners in this poem and in Kingston's "Restaurant" (p. 855).

Frederick Douglass: 1817–1895°   *1966*

Douglass was someone who,
Had he walked with wary foot
And frightened tread,
From very indecision
Might be dead,   5
Might have lost his soul,
But instead decided to be bold
And capture every street
On which he set his feet,
To route each path   10
Toward freedom's goal,
To make each highway
Choose *his* compass' choice,
To all the world cried,
Hear my voice! . . .   15
Oh, to be a beast, a bird,
Anything but a slave! he said.

Who would be free
Themselves must strike
The first blow, he said.   20

    He died in 1895.
    He is not dead.

1817–1895: Douglass was actually born in 1818; as a slave, he did not know his true birth date.

CONSIDERATIONS FOR CRITICAL THINKING AND WRITING

1. FIRST RESPONSE. This poem was published when the civil rights movement was very active in America. Does that information affect your reading of it?
2. What does Hughes celebrate about the life of Douglass, author of *Narrative of the Life of Frederick Douglass, an American Slave, Written by Himself* (1845)?

CONNECTION TO ANOTHER SELECTION

1. How is the speaker's attitude toward violence in this poem similar to that of the speaker in "Harlem" (p. 1053)?

PERSPECTIVES ON HUGHES

Hughes on Racial Shame and Pride   *1926*

[J]azz to me is one of the inherent expressions of Negro life in America: the eternal tom-tom beating in the Negro soul — the tom-tom of revolt against weariness in a white world, a world of subway trains, and work, work, work; the tom-tom of joy and laughter, and pain swallowed in a smile. Yet the Philadelphia clubwoman is ashamed to say that her race created it and she does not like me to write about it. The old subconscious "white is best" runs through her mind. Years of study under white teachers, a lifetime of white books, pictures, and papers, and white manners, morals, and Puritan standards made her dislike the spirituals. And now she turns up her nose at jazz and all its manifestations—likewise almost everything else distinctly racial. She doesn't care for the Winold Reiss° portraits of Negroes because they are "too Negro." She does not want a true picture of herself from anybody. She wants the artist to flatter her, to make the white world believe that all Negroes are as smug and as near white in soul as she wants to be. But, to my mind, it is the duty of the younger Negro artist, if he accepts any duties at all from outsiders, to change through the force of his art that old whispering "I want to be white," hidden in the aspirations of his people, to "Why should I want to be white? I am a Negro—and beautiful!"

From "The Negro Artist and the Racial Mountain,"
The Nation, June 23, 1926

Winold Reiss (1887–1953): A white painter whose work emphasized the individuality of blacks.

CONSIDERATIONS FOR CRITICAL THINKING AND WRITING

1. Why does the Philadelphia clubwoman refuse to accept jazz as part of her heritage?

2. Compare and contrast Hughes's description of the Philadelphia clubwoman with M. Carl Holman's "Mr. Z" (p. 1162). In what sense are these two characters made for each other?

Hughes on Harlem Rent Parties   *1940*

Then [in the late twenties and early thirties] it was that house-rent parties began to flourish—and not always to raise the rent either. But, as often as not, to have a get-together of one's own, where you could do the black-bottom with no stranger behind you trying to do it, too. Non-theatrical, non-intellectual Harlem was an unwilling victim of its own vogue. It didn't like to be stared at by white folks. But perhaps the downtowners never knew this—for the cabaret owners, the entertainers, and the speakeasy proprietors treated them fine—as long as they paid.

The Saturday night rent parties that I attended were often more amusing than any night club, in small apartments where God knows who lived—because the guests seldom did—but where the piano would often be augmented by a guitar, or an odd cornet, or somebody with a pair of drums walking in off the street. And where awful bootleg whiskey and good fried fish or steaming chitterling were sold at very low prices. And the dancing and singing and impromptu entertaining went on until dawn came in at the windows.

These parties, often termed whist parties or dances, were usually announced by brightly colored cards stuck in the grille of apartment house elevators. Some of the cards were highly entertaining in themselves:

> We got yellow girls, we've got black and tan
> Will you have a good time? - YEAH MAN !
>
> ## A Social Whist Party
> —GIVEN BY—
> MARY WINSTON
> 147 West 145th Street   Apt. 5
>
> ### SATURDAY EVE., MARCH 19th, 1932
>
> GOOD MUSIC   REFRESHMENTS

Almost every Saturday night when I was in Harlem I went to a house-rent party. I wrote lots of poems about house-rent parties, and ate thereat many a fried fish and pig's foot — with liquid refreshments on the side. I met ladies' maids and truck drivers, laundry workers and shoe shine boys, seamstresses and porters. I can still hear their laughter in my ears, hear the soft slow music, and feel the floor shaking as the dancers danced.

> From "When the Negro Was in Vogue," in *The Big Sea*

CONSIDERATIONS FOR CRITICAL THINKING AND WRITING

1. What, according to Hughes, was the appeal of the rent parties in contrast to the nightclubs?

2. Describe the tone in which Hughes recounts his memory of these parties.

DONALD B. GIBSON (B. 1933)

The Essential Optimism of Hughes and Whitman   1971

As optimists generally do, Langston Hughes and Walt Whitman lacked a sense of evil. This (and all it implies) puts Hughes in a tradition with other American writers. He stands with Whitman, Emerson, Thoreau, and later Sandburg, Lindsay, and Steinbeck, as opposed to Hawthorne, Poe, Melville, James, Faulkner, and Eliot. This is not to say that he did not recognize the existence of evil, but, as Yeats says of Emerson and Whitman, he lacked the "Vision of Evil." He did not see evil as inherent in the character of nature and man, hence he felt that the evil (small *e*) about which he wrote so frequently in his poems (lynchings, segregation, discrimination of all kinds) would be eradicated with the passage of time. Of course the Hughes of *The Panther and the Lash* (1967) is not as easily optimistic as the poet was twenty or twenty-five years before. Hughes could not have written "I, Too," or even "The Negro Speaks of Rivers" in the sixties. But the evidence as I see it has it that though he does not speak so readily about the fulfillment of the American ideal for black people, and though something of the spirit of having waited too long prevails, still the optimism remains. . . .

Montage of a Dream Deferred (1951), included in Selected Poems, describes the dream as deferred, not dead nor incapable of fulfillment. There is a certain grimness in the poem, for example in its most famous section, "Harlem," which begins, "What happens to a dream deferred? / Does it dry up / like a raisin in the sun?" but the grimness is by no means unrelieved. There is, as a matter of fact, a lightness of tone throughout the poem which could not exist did the poet see the ravages of racial discrimination as manifestations of Evil. . . . The whole tone of Montage of a Dream Deferred is characterized by the well-known "Ballad of the Landlord." There the bitter-sweet quality of Hughes's attitude toward his subject is clear.

From "The Good Black Poet and the Good Grey Poet: The Poetry of Hughes and Whitman," in *Langston Hughes: Black Genius: A Critical Evaluation*, edited by Therman B. O'Daniel

CONSIDERATIONS FOR CRITICAL THINKING AND WRITING

1. What distinction does Gibson make between "Evil" and "evil"?
2. Discuss whether you agree or disagree that Hughes lacked a "Vision of Evil."
3. Why do you think Gibson writes that Hughes couldn't have written "The Negro Speaks of Rivers" (p. 1034) or "I, Too" (p. 1037) in the 1960s?
4. What aspects of Whitman does Hughes seem to admire in "Old Walt" (p. 1055)?

JAMES A. EMANUEL (B. 1921)

Hughes's Attitudes toward Religion   1973

Religion, because of its historical importance during and after slavery, is an undeniably useful theme in the work of any major black writer. In a writer whose special province for almost forty-five years was more recent black experience, the theme is doubly vital. Hughes's personal religious orientation is pertinent. Asked about it by the Reverend Dana F. Kennedy of the "Viewpoint" radio and television show (on December 10, 1960), the poet responded:

> I grew up in a not very religious family, but I had a foster aunt who saw that I
> went to church and Sunday school . . . and I was very much moved, always, by
> the, shall I say, the rhythms of the Negro church . . . of the spirituals, . . . of
> those wonderful old-time sermons. . . . There's great beauty in the mysticism
> of much religious writing, and great help there — but I also think that we live
> in a world . . . of solid earth and vegetables and a need for jobs and a need for
> housing. . . .

Two years earlier, the poet had told John Kirkwood of British Columbia's *Vancouver Sun* (December 3, 1958): "I'm not anti-Christian. I'm not against anyone's religion. Religion is one of the innate needs of mankind. What I am against is the misuse of religion. But I won't ridicule it. . . . Whatever part of God is in anybody is not to be played with, and everybody has got a part of God in them."

These typical public protestations by Hughes boil down to his insistence that religion is naturally sacred and beautiful, and that its needed sustenance must not be exploited.

From "Christ in Alabama: Religion in the Poetry of Langston Hughes,"
in *Modern Black Poets*, edited by Donald B. Gibson

CONSIDERATIONS FOR CRITICAL THINKING AND WRITING

1. Why do you think Emanuel asserts that, owing to slavery, religion "is an undeniably useful theme in the work of any major Black writer"?

2. How does Hughes's concern for the "solid earth and vegetables and a need for jobs and a need for housing" qualify his attitudes toward religion?

RICHARD K. BARKSDALE (B. 1915)

On Censoring "Ballad of the Landlord"   1977

In 1940, ["Ballad of the Landlord"] was a rather innocuous rendering of an imaginary dialogue between a disgruntled tenant and a tight-fisted landlord. In creating a poem about two such social archetypes, the poet was by no means taking any new steps in dramatic poetry. The literature of most capitalist and noncapitalist societies often pits the haves against the have-nots, and not infrequently the haves are wealthy men of property who "lord" it over improvident men who own nothing. So the confrontation between tenant and landlord was in 1940 just another instance of the social malevolence of a system that punished the powerless and excused the powerful. In fact, Hughes's tone of dry irony throughout the poem leads one to suspect that the poet deliberately overstated a situation and that some sardonic humor was supposed to be squeezed out of the incident. . . .

Ironically, this poem, which in 1940 depicted a highly probable incident in American urban life and was certainly not written to incite an economic revolt or promote social unrest, became, by the mid-1960s, a verboten assignment in a literature class in a Boston high school. In his Langston Hughes headnote in *Black Voices* (1967), Abraham Chapman reported that a Boston high school English teacher named Jonathan Kozol was fired for assigning it to his students. By the mid-sixties, Boston and many other American cities had become riot-torn, racial tinderboxes, and their ghettos seethed with tenant anger and discontent. So the poem gathered new meanings reflecting the times, and the word of its tenant persona bespoke the collective anger of thousands of black have-nots.

From *Langston Hughes: The Poet and His Critics*

CONSIDERATIONS FOR CRITICAL THINKING AND WRITING

1. Why do you think the Boston School Committee believed the "Ballad of the Landlord" (p. 1049) should be censored?

2. Do you agree with Barksdale that the poem is a "rather innocuous rendering" of economic and social issues? Explain your answer.

3. How did the poem acquire "new meanings reflecting the times" between the 1940s and 1960s? What new meanings might it have for readers today?

DAVID CHINITZ (B. 1962)

The Romanticization of Africa in the 1920s   1997

In Europe black culture was an exotic import; in America it was domestic and increasingly mass-produced. If postwar [World War I] disillusionment judged the majority culture mannered, neurotic, and repressive, Americans had an easily accessible alternative. The need for such an Other produced a discourse in which black Americans figured as barely civilized exiles from the jungle, with — so the clichés ran — tom-toms beating in their blood and dark laughter in their souls. The African American became a model of "natural" human behavior to contrast with the falsified, constrained and impotent modes of the "civilized."

Far from being immune to the lure of this discourse, for the better part of the 1920s Hughes asserted an open pride in the supposed primitive qualities of his race, the atavistic legacy of the African motherland. Unlike most of those who romanticized Africa, Hughes had at least some firsthand experience of the continent; yet he processed what he saw there in images conditioned by European primitivism, rendering "[the land] wild and lovely, the people dark and beautiful, the palm trees tall, the sun bright, and the rivers deep."[1] His short story "Luani of the Jungle," in attempting to glorify aboriginal African vigor as against European anemia, shows how predictable and unextraordinary even Hughes's primitivism could be. To discover in the descendents of idealized Africans the same qualities of innate health, spontaneity, and naturalness requires no great leap; one has only to identify the African American as a displaced primitive, as Hughes does repeatedly in his first book, *The Weary Blues:*

> They drove me out of the forest.
> They took me away from the jungles.
> I lost my trees.
> I lost my silver moons.
>
> Now they've caged me
> In the circus of civilization.[2]

Hughes depicts black atavism vividly and often gracefully, yet in a way that is entirely consistent with the popular iconography of the time. His African Americans retain "among the skyscrapers" the primal fears and instincts of their ancestors "among the palms in Africa."[3] The scion of Africa is still more than half primitive: "All the tom-toms of the jungles beat in my blood, / And all the wild hot moons of the jungles shine in my soul."[4]

From "Rejuvenation through Joy: Langston Hughes, Primitivism and Jazz," in *American Literary History,* Spring 1997

[1] *The Big Sea.* 1940. N.Y.: Thunder's Mouth, 1986, 11.
[2] *The Weary Blues.* N.Y.: Knopf, 1926, 100.
[3] *Ibid.* 101.
[4] *Ibid.* 102.

CONSIDERATIONS FOR CRITICAL THINKING AND WRITING

1. According to Chinitz, why did Europeans and Americans romanticize African culture?

2. Consider the poems published by Hughes in the 1920s reprinted in this anthology. Explain whether you find any "primitivism" in these poems.

3. Later in this essay, Chinitz points out that Hughes eventually rejected the "reductive mischaracterizations of black culture, the commercialism, the sham sociology, and the downright silliness of the primitivist fad." Choose and discuss a poem from this anthology that you think reflects Hughes's later views of primitivism.

TWO COMPLEMENTARY CRITICAL READINGS

COUNTEE CULLEN (1903–1946)

On Racial Poetry   1926

Here is a poet with whom to reckon, to experience, and here and there, with that apologetic feeling of presumption that should companion all criticism, to quarrel.

What has always struck me most forcibly in reading Mr. Hughes' poems has been their utter spontaneity and expression of a unique personality. . . . This poet represents a transcendently emancipated spirit among a class of young writers whose particular battle-cry is freedom. With the enthusiasm of a zealot, he pursues his way, scornful, in subject matter, in photography, and rhythmical treatment, of whatever obstructions time and tradition have placed before him. To him it is essential that he be himself. Essential and commendable surely; yet the thought persists that some of these poems would have been better had Mr. Hughes held himself a bit in check. . . .

If I have the least powers of prediction, the first section of this book, *The Weary Blues,* will be most admired, even if less from intrinsic poetical worth than because of its dissociation from the traditionally poetic. Never having been one to think all subjects and forms proper for poetic consideration, I regard these jazz poems as interlopers in the company of the truly beautiful poems in other sections of the book. They move along with the frenzy and electric heat of a Methodist or Baptist revival meeting, and affect me in much the same manner. The revival meeting excites me, cooling and flushing me with alternate chills and fevers of emotion; so do these poems. But when the storm is over, I wonder if the quiet way of communing is not more spiritual for the God-seeking heart; and in the light of reflection I wonder if jazz poems really belong to that dignified company, that select and austere circle of high literary expression which we call poetry. . . .

Taken as a group the selections in this book seem one-sided to me. They tend to hurl this poet into the gaping pit that lies before all Negro writers, in the confines of which they become racial artists instead of artists pure and simple. There is too much emphasis here on strictly Negro themes; and this is probably an added reason for my coldness toward the jazz poems — they seem to set a too definite limit upon an already limited field.

From *Opportunity: A Journal of Negro Life*

CONSIDERATIONS FOR CRITICAL THINKING AND WRITING

1. In Cullen's review of *The Weary Blues,* what is his "quarrel" (para. 1) with Hughes?

2. Given the tenor of Hughes's comments on racial pride in the excerpt from "The Negro Artist and the Racial Mountain" (p. 1058), what do you think his response to Cullen would be?

3. Explain why you agree or disagree with Cullen's view that Hughes's poems are "one-sided" (para. 4).

4. Do you think his argument is dated, or is it relevant to today's social climate?

ONWUCHEKWA JEMIE (B. 1940)

On Universal Poetry   1976

Hughes entertained no doubts as to the sufficiency and greatness of the molds provided by black music, nor of black life as subject matter. On the question of whether such black matter and manner could attain "universality," Hughes in his Spingarn Speech issued a definitive answer:

> There is so much richness in Negro humor, so much beauty in black dreams, so much dignity in our struggle, and so much universality in our problems, in us— in each living human being of color—that I do not understand the tendency today that some American Negro artists have of seeking to run away from themselves, of running away from us, of being afraid to sing our own songs, paint our own pictures, write about ourselves—when it is our music that has given America its greatest music, our humor that has enriched its entertainment media, our rhythm that has guided its dancing feet from plantation days to the Charleston, the Lindy Hop, and currently the Madison....
>
> Could you possibly be afraid that the rest of the world will not accept it? Our spirituals are sung and loved in the great concert halls of the whole world. Our blues are played from Topeka to Tokyo. Harlem's jive talk delights Hong Kong. Those of our writers who have concerned themselves with our very special problems are translated and read around the world. The local, the regional can—and does—become universal. Sean O'Casey's Irishmen are an example. So I would say to young Negro writers, do not be afraid of yourselves. You are the world.[1]

Hughes's confidence in blackness is a major part of his legacy, for the questions he had to answer have had to be answered over again by subsequent generations of black artists. Black culture is still embattled; and Hughes provides a model for answering the questions and making the choices. Whether they say so or not, those who, like Cullen, ... plead the need to be "universal" as an excuse for avoiding racial material, or for treating such material from perspectives rooted in alien sensibilities, invariably equate "white" or "Western" with "universal," and "black" or "non-Western" with its opposite, forgetting that the truly universal—that is, the foundation elements of human experience, the circumstances attending birth, growth, decline, and death, the emotions of joy and grief, love and hate, fear and guilt, anger and pain—are common to all humanity. The multiplicity of nations and cultures in the world makes it inevitable

[1] See Hughes, Letter to the Editor, *The Crisis,* 35:9 (September 1928), 302.

that the details and particulars of human experience will vary according to time, place, and circumstance, and it follows that the majority of writers will dramatize and interpret human life according to the usages of their particular nation and epoch. Indeed, the question whether a writer's work is universal or not rarely arises when that writer is European or white American. It arises so frequently in discussions of black writers for no other reason than that the long-standing myth of white superiority and black inferiority has led so many to believe that in literature, and in other areas of life as well, the black particular of universal human experience is less appropriate than the white particular.

From *Langston Hughes: An Introduction to Poetry*

CONSIDERATIONS FOR CRITICAL THINKING AND WRITING

1. How does Jemie go beyond Hughes's own argument to make a case for the universality of poetry about black experience?

2. How might Jemie's argument be extended to other minority groups or to women?

3. Do you think that Jemie's or Cullen's argument is more persuasive? Explain.

SUGGESTED TOPICS FOR LONGER PAPERS

1. Discuss Hughes's use of rhyme, meter, and sounds in five poems of your choice. How do these elements contribute to the poems' meanings?

2. Taken together, how do Hughes's poems provide a critique of relations between blacks and whites in America?

3. MULTIMEDIA PROJECT. Do some exploratory reading, viewing, and listening about life in Harlem from about 1920 to the 1950s. Based on your research, how effectively do you think Hughes's poetry evokes Harlem life?

Web *For help with this project, use the Multimedia Project Guides Online at* http://www.bedfordstmartins.com/meyer/bedintrolit

34

A Critical Case Study:
T. S. Eliot's "The Love Song
of J. Alfred Prufrock"

This chapter provides several critical approaches to a challenging but highly rewarding poem by T. S. Eliot. After studying this poem, you're likely to find yourself quoting bits of its striking imagery. At the very least, you'll recognize the lines when you hear other people fold them into their own conversations. There have been numerous critical approaches to this poem because it raises so many issues relating to matters such as history and biography as well as imagery, symbolism, irony, and myth. The following critical excerpts offer a small and partial sample of the possible formalist, biographical, historical, mythological, psychological, sociological, and other perspectives that have attempted to shed light on the poem (see Chapter 52, "Critical Strategies for Reading," for a discussion of a variety of critical methods). They should help you to enjoy the poem more by raising questions, providing insights, and inviting you further into the text.

T. S. ELIOT (1888–1965)

Born into a prominent New England family that had moved to St. Louis, Missouri, Thomas Stearns Eliot was a major figure in English literature between the two world wars. He studied literature and philosophy at Harvard and on the Continent, subsequently choosing to live in England for most of his life and becoming a citizen of that country in 1927. His allusive and challenging poetry had a powerful influence on other writers, particularly his treatment of postwar life in *The Waste Land* (1922) and his exploration of religious questions in *The Four Quartets* (1943). In addition, he wrote plays, including *Murder in the Cathedral* (1935) and *The Cocktail Party* (1950). He was

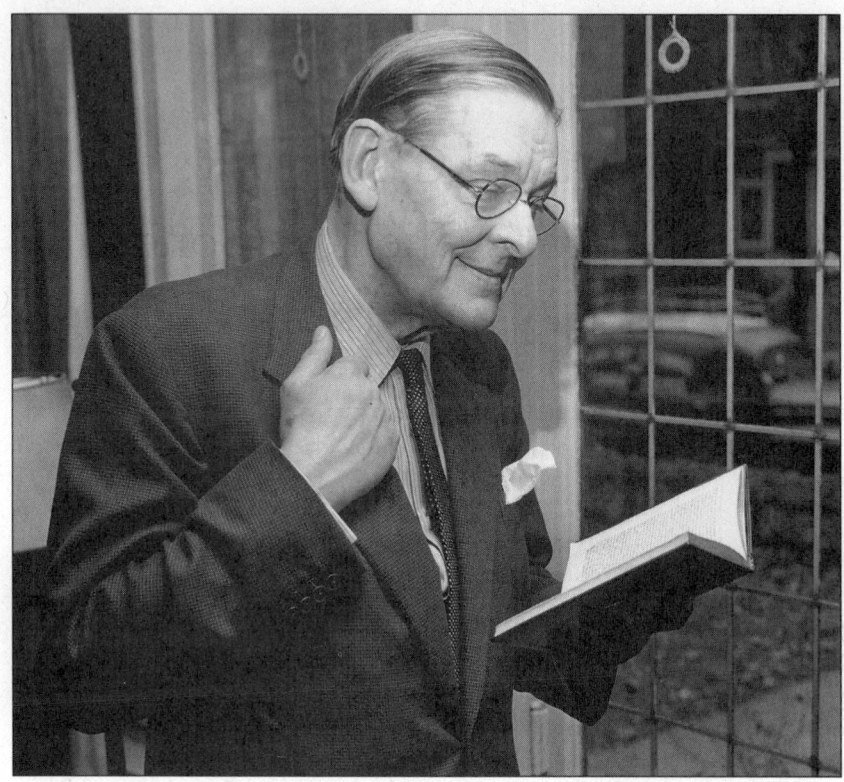

T. S. Eliot (November 10, 1959), in a pose that suggests the Prufrock persona, holding a book containing some of his earlier work during a press conference at the University of Chicago. Reprinted by permission of Corbis-Bettmann.

awarded the Nobel Prize for literature in 1948. In "The Love Song of J. Alfred Prufrock," Eliot presents a comic but serious figure who expresses through a series of fragmented images the futility, boredom, and meaninglessness associated with much of modern life.

Web *Research T. S. Eliot with LitLinks at*
http://www.bedfordstmartins.com/meyer/bedintrolit

The Love Song of J. Alfred Prufrock   1917

S'io credesse che mia risposta fosse
A persona che mai tornasse al mondo,
Questa fiamma staria senza più scosse.
Ma perciocchè giammai di questo fondo

Non tornò vivo alcun, s'i'odo il vero,
Senza tema d'infamia ti rispondo.°

    Let us go then, you and I,
When the evening is spread out against the sky
Like a patient etherized upon a table;
Let us go, through certain half-deserted streets,
The muttering retreats   5
Of restless nights in one-night cheap hotels
And sawdust restaurants with oyster-shells:
Streets that follow like a tedious argument
Of insidious intent
To lead you to an overwhelming question . . .   10
Oh, do not ask, "What is it?"
Let us go and make our visit.

In the room the women come and go
Talking of Michelangelo.

    The yellow fog that rubs its back upon the window panes,   15
The yellow smoke that rubs its muzzle on the window panes
Licked its tongue into the corners of the evening,
Lingered upon the pools that stand in drains,
Let fall upon its back the soot that falls from chimneys,
Slipped by the terrace, made a sudden leap,   20
And seeing that it was a soft October night,
Curled once about the house, and fell asleep.

    And indeed there will be time°
For the yellow smoke that slides along the street,
Rubbing its back upon the window panes;   25
There will be time, there will be time
To prepare a face to meet the faces that you meet;
There will be time to murder and create,
And time for all the works and days° of hands
That lift and drop a question on your plate: 30
Time for you and time for me,
And time yet for a hundred indecisions,
And for a hundred visions and revisions,
Before the taking of a toast and tea.

Epigraph: *S'io credesse . . . rispondo:* Dante's *Inferno,* XXVII, 58–63. In the Eighth Chasm of the Inferno, Dante and Virgil meet Guido da Montefeltro, one of the False Counselors, who is punished by being enveloped in an eternal flame. When Dante asks Guido to tell his life story, the spirit replies: "If I thought that my answer were to one who might ever return to the world, this flame would shake no more; but since from this depth none ever returned alive, if what I hear is true, I answer you without fear of infamy." 23 *there will be time:* An allusion to Ecclesiastes 3:1–8: "To everything there is a season, and a time to every purpose under heaven. . . ." 29 *works and days:* Hesiod's eighth-century B.C. poem *Works and Days* gave practical advice on how to conduct one's life in accordance with the seasons.

In the room the women come and go   35
Talking of Michelangelo.

    And indeed there will be time
To wonder, "Do I dare?" and, "Do I dare?" —
Time to turn back and descend the stair,
With a bald spot in the middle of my hair —   40
(They will say: "How his hair is growing thin!")
My morning coat, my collar mounting firmly to the chin,
My necktie rich and modest, but asserted by a simple pin —
(They will say: "But how his arms and legs are thin!")
Do I dare   45
Disturb the universe?
In a minute there is time
For decisions and revisions which a minute will reverse.

    For I have known them all already, known them all:
Have known the evenings, mornings, afternoons,   50
I have measured out my life with coffee spoons;
I know the voices dying with a dying fall
Beneath the music from a farther room.
      So how should I presume?

    And I have known the eyes already, known them all —   55
The eyes that fix you in a formulated phrase.
And when I am formulated, sprawling on a pin,
When I am pinned and wriggling on the wall,
Then how should I begin
To spit out all the butt-ends of my days and ways?   60
      And how should I presume?

    And I have known the arms already, known them all —
Arms that are braceleted and white and bare
(But in the lamplight, downed with light brown hair!)
      Is it perfume from a dress   65
      That makes me so digress?
Arms that lie along a table, or wrap about a shawl.
      And should I then presume?
      And how should I begin?

      Shall I say, I have gone at dusk through narrow streets,   70
And watched the smoke that rises from the pipes
Of lonely men in shirtsleeves, leaning out of windows? . . .

I should have been a pair of ragged claws
Scuttling across the floors of silent seas.

      And the afternoon, the evening, sleeps so peacefully!   75
Smoothed by long fingers,
Asleep . . . tired . . . or it malingers,
Stretched on the floor, here beside you and me.
Should I, after tea and cakes and ices,
Have the strength to force the moment to its crisis?   80

But though I have wept and fasted, wept and prayed,
Though I have seen my head (grown slightly bald) brought in upon a platter,°
I am no prophet — and here's no great matter;
I have seen the moment of my greatness flicker,
And I have seen the eternal Footman hold my coat, and snicker,   85
And in short, I was afraid.

And would it have been worth it, after all,
After the cups, the marmalade, the tea,
Among the porcelain, among some talk of you and me,
Would it have been worth while   90
To have bitten off the matter with a smile,
To have squeezed the universe into a ball°
To roll it toward some overwhelming question,
To say: "I am Lazarus,° come from the dead,
Come back to tell you all, I shall tell you all" —   95
If one, settling a pillow by her head,
     Should say: "That is not what I meant at all;
     That is not it, at all."

And would it have been worth it, after all,
Would it have been worth while,   100
After the sunsets and the dooryards and the sprinkled streets,
After the novels, after the teacups, after the skirts that trail along the floor —
And this, and so much more? —
It is impossible to say just what I mean!
But as if a magic lantern threw the nerves in patterns on a screen: 105
Would it have been worth while
If one, settling a pillow or throwing off a shawl,
And turning toward the window, should say:
     "That is not it at all,
     That is not what I meant, at all."   110

No! I am not Prince Hamlet, nor was meant to be;
Am an attendant lord,° one that will do
To swell a progress,° start a scene or two   *state procession*
Advise the prince: withal, an easy tool,
Deferential, glad to be of use,   115
Politic, cautious, and meticulous;
Full of high sentence, but a bit obtuse;
At times, indeed, almost ridiculous —
Almost, at times, the Fool.
I grow old . . . I grow old . . .   120
I shall wear the bottoms of my trowsers rolled.

82 *head . . . upon a platter:* At Salome's request, Herod had John the Baptist decapitated and
had the severed head delivered to her on a platter (see Matt. 14:1–12 and Mark 6:17–29).   92
squeezed the universe into a ball: See Marvell's "To His Coy Mistress" (p. 728), lines 41–42: "Let
us roll all our strength and all / Our sweetness up into one ball."   94 *Lazarus:* The brother
of Mary and Martha who was raised from the dead by Jesus (John 11:1–44). In Luke 16:19–31, a
rich man asks that another Lazarus return from the dead to warn the living about their
treatment of the poor.   112 *attendant lord:* Like Polonius in Shakespeare's *Hamlet.*

Shall I part my hair behind? Do I dare to eat a peach?
I shall wear white flannel trowsers, and walk upon the beach.
I have heard the mermaids singing, each to each.

I do not think that they will sing to me.   125

I have seen them riding seaward on the waves,
Combing the white hair of the waves blown back
When the wind blows the water white and black.

We have lingered in the chambers of the sea
By seagirls wreathed with seaweed red and brown,   130
Till human voices wake us, and we drown.

CONSIDERATIONS FOR CRITICAL THINKING AND WRITING

1. What does J. Alfred Prufrock's name connote? How would you characterize
   him?
2. What do you think is the purpose of the epigraph from Dante's *Inferno*?
3. What is it that Prufrock wants to do? How does he behave? What does he
   think of himself? Which parts of the poem answer these questions?
4. Who is the "you" of line 1 and the "we" in the final lines?
5. Discuss the imagery in the poem. How does the imagery reveal Prufrock's
   character? Which images seem especially striking to you?

CONNECTIONS TO OTHER SELECTIONS

1. Write an essay comparing Prufrock's sense of himself as an individual with
   that of Walt Whitman's speaker in "One's-Self I Sing" (p. 1188).
2. Discuss in an essay the tone of "The Love Song of J. Alfred Prufrock" and
   Frost's "Acquainted with the Night" (p. 802).

PERSPECTIVES ON ELIOT

ELISABETH SCHNEIDER (1897–1984)

Schneider uses a biographical approach to the poem to suggest that part
of what went into the characterization of Prufrock were some of Eliot's
own sensibilities.

Hints of Eliot in Prufrock   1952

Perhaps never again did Eliot find an epigraph quite so happily suited to his
use as the passage from the *Inferno* which sets the underlying serious tone for
Prufrock and conveys more than one level of its meaning: "S'io credesse che mia
risposta . . . ," lines in which Guido da Montefeltro consents to tell his story to

Dante only because he believes that none ever returns to the world of the living from his depth. One in Hell can bear to expose his shame only to another of the damned; Prufrock speaks to, will be understood only by, other Prufrocks (the "you and I" of the opening, perhaps), and, I imagine the epigraph also hints, Eliot himself is speaking to those who know this kind of hell. The poem, I need hardly say, is not in a literal sense autobiographical: for one thing, though it is clear that Prufrock will never marry, the poem was published in the year of Eliot's own first marriage. Nevertheless, friends who knew the young Eliot almost all describe him, retrospectively but convincingly, in Prufrockian terms; and Eliot himself once said of dramatic monologue in general that what we normally hear in it "is the voice of the poet, who has put on the costume and make-up either of some historical character, or of one out of fiction." . . . I suppose it to be one of the many indirect clues to his own poetry planted with evident deliberation throughout his prose. "What every poet starts from," he also once said, "is his own emotions," and, writing of Dante, he asserted that the *Vita nuova* "could only have been written around a personal experience," a statement that, under the circumstances, must be equally applicable to Prufrock; Prufrock was Eliot, though Eliot was much more than Prufrock. We miss the whole tone of the poem, however, if we read it as social satire only. Eliot was not either the dedicated apostle in theory, or the great exemplar in practice, of complete "depersonalization" in poetry that one influential early essay of his for a time led readers to suppose.

From "Prufrock and After: The Theme of Change," *PMLA*, October 1952

CONSIDERATIONS FOR CRITICAL THINKING AND WRITING

1. Though Schneider concedes that the poem is not literally autobiographical, she does assert that "Prufrock was Eliot." How does she argue this point? Explain why you find her argument convincing or unconvincing.
2. Find information in the library about Eliot's early career when he was writing this poem. To what extent does the poem reveal his circumstances and concerns at that point in his life?

BARBARA EVERETT

Everett's discussion of tone is used to make a distinction between Eliot and his characterization of Prufrock.

The Problem of Tone in Prufrock   1974

Eliot's poetry presents a peculiar problem as far as tone is concerned. *Tone* really means the way the attitude of a speaker is manifested by the inflections of his speaking voice. Many critics have already recognized that for a mixture of reasons it is difficult, sometimes almost impossible, to ascertain Eliot's tone in this way. It is not that the poetry lacks "voice," for in fact Eliot has an extraordinarily recognizable poetic voice, often imitated and justifying his own comment in the . . . *Paris Review* that "in a poem you're writing for your own voice, which is very important. You're thinking in terms of your own voice." It is this authoritative, idiosyncratic, and exact voice that holds our complete attention in poem after poem, however uninterested we are in what opinions it may seem or happen to be expressing. But Eliot too seems uninterested in what opinions it may happen to be expressing, for he invariably dissociates himself from his poems before they are even finished — before they are hardly begun — by balancing a derisory name or title against an "I," by reminding us that there is always going to be a moment at which detachment will take place or has taken place, a retrospective angle from which, far in the future, critical judgment alters the scene, and the speaking voice of the past has fallen silent. "I have known them all already, known them all." Thus whatever started to take place in the beginning of a poem by Eliot cannot truly be said to be Eliot's opinion because at some extremely early stage he began that process of dissociation to be loosely called "dramatization," a process reflected in the peculiar distances of the tone, as though everything spoken was in inverted commas.

From "In Search of Prufrock," *Critical Quarterly,* Summer 1974

CONSIDERATIONS FOR CRITICAL THINKING AND WRITING

1. According to Everett, why is it difficult to describe Eliot's tone in his poetry?
2. How does Eliot's tone make it difficult to make an autobiographical connection between Prufrock and Eliot?
3. How does Everett's reading of the relationship between Prufrock and Eliot differ from Schneider's in the preceding perspective?

MICHAEL L. BAUMANN (B. 1926)

Baumann takes a close look at the poem's images in his formalist efforts to make a point about Prufrock's character.

The "Overwhelming Question" for Prufrock   *1981*

Most critics . . . have seen the overwhelming question related to sex. . . . They have implicitly assumed — and given their readers to understand — that Prufrock's is the male's basic question: Can I?

Delmore Schwartz once said that "J. Alfred Prufrock is unable to make love to women of his own class and kind because of shyness, self-consciousness, and fear of rejection."[1] This is undoubtedly true, but Prufrock's inability to *feel* love has something to do with his inability to *make* love, too. . . . A simple desire, lust, is more than honest Prufrock can cope with as he mounts the stairs.

[1] "T. S. Eliot as the International Hero," *Partisan Review,* 12 (1945), 202; rpt in *T. S. Eliot: A Selected Critique,* ed. Leonard Unger (New York: Rinehart & Company, Inc., 1948), 46.

But Prufrock is coping with another, less simple desire as well. . . . If birth, copulation, and death is all there is, then, once we are born, once we have copulated, only death remains (for the male of the species, at least). Prufrock, having "known them all already, known them all," having "known the evenings, mornings, afternoons," having "measured out" his life "with coffee spoons," desires death. The "overwhelming question" that assails him would no longer be the romantic rhetorical "Is life worth living?" (to which the answer is obviously No), but the more immediate shocker: "Should one commit suicide?" which is to say: "Should I?" . . .

. . . The poem makes clear that Prufrock wants more than the "entire destruction of consciousness as we understand it," a notion Prufrock expresses by wishing he were "a pair of ragged claws, / Scuttling across the floors of silent seas." Prufrock wants death itself, physical death, and the poem, I believe, is explicit about this desire.

Not only does Prufrock seem to be tired of time—"time yet for a hundred indecisions"—a tiredness that goes far beyond the acedia Prufrock is generally credited with feeling, if only because "there will be time to murder and create," time, in other words (in one sense at least) to copulate, but Prufrock is also tired of his own endless vanities, from feeling he must "prepare a face to meet the faces that you meet," to having to summon up those ironies with which to contemplate his own thin arms and legs, and, indeed, to asking if, in the rather tedious enterprise of preparing for copulation, the moment is worth "forcing to its crisis." No wonder Prufrock compares himself to John the Baptist and, in conjuring up this first concrete image of his own death, sees his head brought in upon a platter. That would be the easy way out. He had, after all, "wept and fasted, wept and prayed," but he realizes he is no prophet—and no Salome will burst into passion, will ignite for him. When the eternal Footman, Death, who holds his coat, snickers, he does so because Prufrock has let "the moment" of his "greatness" flicker, because Prufrock was unable to comply with the one imperative greatness would have thrust upon him: to kill himself. Prufrock explains: "I was afraid." Yet the achievement of his vision at the end of the poem, his being able to linger "in the chambers of the sea / By sea-girls wreathed with seaweed red and brown," is an act of the imagination that only physical death can complete, unless Prufrock wants human voices to wake him, and drown him. His romantic vision demands the voluntary act: suicide. It is to be expected that he will fail in this too, as he has failed in everything else.

From "Let Us Ask 'What Is It,'" *Arizona Quarterly,* Spring 1981

Considerations for Critical Thinking and Writing

1. Describe the evidence used by Baumann to argue that Prufrock contemplates suicide.

2. Explain in an essay why you do or do not find Baumann's argument convincing.

3. Later in his essay Baumann connects Prufrock's insistence that "No, I am not Prince Hamlet" with Hamlet's "To be or not to be" speech. How do you think this reference might be used to support Baumann's argument?

FREDERIK L. RUSCH (B. 1938)

Rusch makes use of the insights developed by Erich Fromm, a social psychologist who believed "psychic forces [are] a process of constant interaction between man's needs and the social and historical reality in which he participates."

Society and Character in "The Love Song of J. Alfred Prufrock" 1984

In looking at fiction, drama, and poetry from the Frommian point of view, the critic understands literature to be social portrayal as well as character portrayal or personal statement. Society and character are inextricably joined. The Frommian approach opens up the study of literary work, giving a social context to its characters, which suggests why those characters behave as they do. The Frommian approach recognizes human beings for what they are — basically gregarious individuals who are interdependent upon each other, in need of each other, and thus, to a certain degree, products of their social environments, although those environments may be inimical to their mental well-being. That is, as stated earlier, the individual's needs and drives have a social component and are not purely biological. The Frommian approach to literature assumes that a writer is — at least by implication — analyzing society and its setting as well as character. . . .

In T. S. Eliot's "The Love Song of J. Alfred Prufrock," Prufrock is talking to himself, expressing a fantasy or daydream. In his monologue, Prufrock, as noted by Grover Smith, "is addressing, as if looking into a mirror, his whole public personality."[1] Throughout the poem, Prufrock is extremely self-conscious, believing that the people in his imaginary drawing room will examine him as a specimen insect, "sprawling on a pin, / . . . pinned and wriggling on the wall. . . ." Of course, self-consciousness — being conscious of one's self — is not necessarily neurotic. Indeed, it is part of being a human being. It is only when self-consciousness, which has always led man to feel a separation from nature, becomes obsessive that we have a problem. Prufrock is certainly obsessed with his self-consciousness, convinced that everyone notices his balding head, his clothes (his prudent frocks), his thin arms and legs.

On one level, however, Prufrock is merely expressing the pain that all human beings must feel. Although his problem is extreme, he is quite representative of the human race:

Self-awareness, reason, and imagination have disrupted the "harmony" that characterizes animal existence. Their emergence has made man into an anomaly, the freak of the universe. He is part of nature, subject to her physical laws and unable to change them, yet he transcends nature. He is set apart while being a part; he is homeless, yet chained to the home he shares with all creatures. . . . Being aware of himself, he realizes his powerlessness and the limita-

[1] Grover Smith, *T. S. Eliot's Poetry and Plays: A Study in Sources and Meaning* (Chicago: U of Chicago P, 1962), 16.

tions of his existence. He is never free from the dichotomy of his existence: he cannot rid himself of his mind, even if he would want to; he cannot rid himself of his body as long as he is alive — and his body makes him want to be alive.[2]

This is the predicament of the human being. His self-awareness has made him feel separate from nature. This causes pain and sorrow. What, then, is the solution to the predicament? Fromm believed that mankind filled the void of alienation from nature with the creation of a culture, a society: "Man's existential, and hence unavoidable disequilibrium can be relatively stable when he has found, with the support of his culture, a more or less adequate way of coping with his existential problems" (*Destructiveness* 225). But, unfortunately for Prufrock, his culture and society do not allow him to overcome his existential predicament. The fact is, he is bored by his modern, urban society.

In image after image, Prufrock's mind projects boredom:

> For I have known them all already, known them all:
> Have known the evenings, mornings, afternoons,
> I have measured out my life with coffee spoons. . . .
> . . . .
> And I have known the eyes already, known them all —
> . . . .
> Then how should I begin
> To spit out all the butt-ends of my days and ways?
> . . . .
> And I have known the arms already, known them all — . . . .

Prufrock is completely unstimulated by his social environment, to the point of near death. The evening in which he proposes to himself to make a social visit is "etherized upon a table." The fog, as a cat, falls asleep; it is "tired . . . or it malingers, / Stretched on the floor. . . ."

Prufrock, living in a city of "half-deserted streets, / . . . one-night cheap hotels / And sawdust restaurants with oyster-shells," gets no comfort, no nurturing from his environment. He is, in the words of Erich Fromm, a "modern mass man . . . isolated and lonely" (*Destructiveness* 107). He lives in a destructive environment. Instead of providing communion with fellow human beings, it alienates him through boredom. Such boredom leads to "a state of chronic depression" that can cause the pathology of "insufficient inner productivity" in the individual (*Destructiveness* 243). Such a lack of productivity is voiced by Prufrock when he confesses that he is neither Hamlet nor John the Baptist.

An interesting tension in "The Love Song of J. Alfred Prufrock" is caused by the reader's knowledge that Prufrock understands his own predicament quite well. Although he calls himself a fool, he has wisdom about himself and his predicament. This, however, only reinforces his depression and frustration. In his daydream, he is able to reveal truths about himself that, while they lead to self-understanding, apparently cannot alleviate his problems in his waking life. The poem suggests no positive movement out of the predicament. Prufrock is like a patient cited by Fromm, who under hypnosis envisioned "a

---

[2] Erich Fromm, *The Anatomy of Human Destructiveness* (New York: Holt, Rinehart & Winston, 1973), 225.

black barren place with many masks," and when asked what the vision meant said "that everything was dull, dull, dull; that the masks represent the different roles he takes to fool people into thinking he is feeling well" (*Destructiveness* 246). Likewise, Prufrock understands that "There will be time, there will be time / To prepare a face to meet the faces that you meet. . . ." But despite his understanding of the nature of his existence, he cannot attain a more productive life.

It was Fromm's belief that with boredom "the decisive conditions are to be found in the overall environmental situation. . . . It is highly probable that even cases of severe depression-boredom would be less frequent and less intense . . . in a society where a mood of hope and love of life predominated. But in recent decades the opposite is increasingly the case, and thus a fertile soil for the development of individual depressive states is provided" (*Destructiveness* 251). There is no "mood of hope and love of life" in Prufrock's society. Prufrock is a lonely man, as lonely as "the lonely men in shirt-sleeves, leaning out of windows" of his fantasy. His only solution is to return to the animal state that his race was in before evolving into human beings.

Animals are one with nature, not alienated from their environments. They *are* nature, unselfconscious. Prufrock would return to a preconscious existence in the extreme: "I should have been a pair of ragged claws / Scuttling across the floors of silent seas." Claws *without a head* surely would not be alienated, bored, or depressed. They would seek and would need no psychological nurturing from their environment. And in the end Prufrock's fantasy of becoming claws is definitely more positive for him than his life as a human being. He completes his monologue with depressing irony, to say the least: it is with human voices waking us, bringing us back to human society, that we drown.

From "Approaching Literature through the Social Psychology of
Erich Fromm," in *Psychological Perspectives on Literature:
Freudian Dissidents and Non-Freudians*, edited by Joseph Natoli

CONSIDERATIONS FOR CRITICAL THINKING AND WRITING

1. According to Rusch, why is Fromm's approach useful for understanding Prufrock's character as well as his social context?

2. In what ways is Prufrock "representative of the human race" (para. 3)? Is he like any other characters you have read about in this anthology? Explain your response.

3. In an essay consider how Rusch's analysis of Prufrock might be used to support Baumann's argument that Prufrock's "overwhelming question" is whether or not he should kill himself (p. 1074).

ROBERT SWARD (B. 1933)

Sward, a poet, provides a detailed explication, framed by his own personal experiences during the war in Korea.

A Personal Analysis of
"The Love Song of J. Alfred Prufrock"   1996

In 1952, sailing to Korea as a U.S. Navy librarian for Landing Ship Tank 914, I read T. S. Eliot's "The Love Song of J. Alfred Prufrock." Ill-educated, a product of Chicago's public-school system, I was nineteen-years-old and, awakened by Whitman, Eliot, and Williams, had just begun writing poetry. I was also reading all the books I could get my hands on.

Eliot had won the Nobel Prize in 1948 and, curious, I was trying to make sense of poems like "Prufrock" and "The Waste Land."

"What do you know about T. S. Eliot?" I asked a young officer who'd been to college and studied English literature. I knew from earlier conversations that we shared an interest in what he called "modern poetry." A yeoman third class, two weeks at sea and bored, I longed for someone to talk to. "T. S. Eliot was born in St. Louis, Missouri, but he lives now in England and is studying to become an Englishman," the officer said, tapping tobacco into his pipe. "The 'T. S.' stands for 'tough shit.' You read Eliot's 'Love Song of J. Alfred Prufrock,' what one English prof called 'the first poem of the modern movement,' and if you don't understand it, 'tough shit.' All I can say is that's some love song."

An anthology of poetry open before us, we were sitting in the ship's all-metal, eight by eight-foot library eating bologna sandwiches and drinking coffee. Fortunately, the captain kept out of sight and life on the slow-moving (eight to ten knots), flat-bottomed amphibious ship was unhurried and anything but formal.

"Then why does Eliot bother calling it a love song?" I asked, as the ship rolled and the coffee sloshed onto a steel table. The tight metal room smelled like a cross between a diesel engine and a New York deli.

"Eliot's being ironic, sailor. 'Prufrock' is the love song of a sexually repressed and horny man who has no one but himself to sing to." Drawing on his pipe, the officer scratched his head. "Like you and I, Mr. Prufrock is a lonely man on his way to a war zone. We're sailing to Korea and we know the truth, don't we? We may never make it back. Prufrock marches like a brave soldier to a British drawing room that, he tells us, may be the death of him. He's a mock heroic figure who sings of mermaids and peaches and drowning."

Pointing to lines 129–31, the officer read aloud:

We have lingered in the chambers of the sea
By sea-girls wreathed with seaweed red and brown
Till human voices wake us and we drown.

"Prufrock is also singing because he's a poet. Prufrock *is* T. S. Eliot and, the truth is, Eliot is so much like Prufrock that he has to distance himself from his creation. That's why he gives the man that pompous name. Did you know 'Tough Shit,' as a young man, sometimes signed himself 'T. Stearns Eliot'? You have to see the humor — the irony — in 'Prufrock' to understand the poem."

"I read it, I hear it in my head, but I still don't get it," I confessed. "What is 'Prufrock' about?"

"'Birth, death and copulation, that's all there is.' That's what Eliot himself says. Of course the poem also touches on aging, social status, and fashion."

"Aging and fashion?" I asked.

The officer threw back his head and recited:

(They will say: "How his hair is growing thin!")
My morning coat, my collar mounting firmly to the chin,
My necktie rich and modest, but asserted by a simple pin.

He paused, then went on:

I grow old . . . I grow old . . .
I shall wear the bottoms of my trousers rolled.

"At the time the poem was written it was fashionable for young men to roll their trousers. In lines 120–21, Thomas Stearns Prufrock is laughing at himself for being middle-aged and vain.

"Anyway, 'The Love Song of J. Alfred Prufrock' is an interior monologue," said the officer, finishing his bologna sandwich and washing it down with dark rum. Wiping mustard from his mouth, he continued. "The whole thing takes place in J. Alfred Prufrock's head. That's clear, isn't it?"

I had read Browning's "My Last Duchess" and understood about interior monologues.

"Listen, sailor: Prufrock thinks about drawing rooms, but he never actually sets foot in one. Am I right?"

"Yeah," I said after rereading the first ten lines. "I think so."

"The poem is about what goes through Prufrock's mind on his way to some upper-class drawing room. It's a foggy evening in October, and what Mr. Prufrock really needs is a drink. He's a tightass Victorian, a lonely teetotaling intellectual. Anyone else would forget the toast and marmalade and step into a pub and ask for a pint of beer."

Setting down his pipe, the naval officer opened the flask and refilled our coffee mugs.

"Every time I think I know what 'Prufrock' means it turns out to mean something else," I said. "Eliot uses too many symbols. Why doesn't he just say what he means?"

"The city — 'the lonely men in shirt-sleeves' and the 'one-night cheap hotels' — are masculine," said the officer. "That's what cities are like, aren't they: ugly and oppressive. What's symbolic — or should I say, what's obscure — about that?"

"Nothing," I said. "That's the easy part — Prufrock walking along like that."

"Okay," said the officer. "And in contrast to city streets, you've got the oppressive drawing room that, in Prufrock's mind, is feminine — 'Arms that are braceleted and white and bare' and 'the marmalade, the tea, / Among the porcelain, among some talk of you and me.'" Using a pencil, the officer underlined those images in the paperback anthology.

"You ever been to a tea party, Sward?"

"No, sir, I haven't. Not like Prufrock's."

"Well," said the officer, "I have and I have a theory about that 'overwhelming question' Prufrock wants to ask in line 10 — and again in line 93. Twice in the poem we hear about an 'overwhelming question.' What do you think he's getting at with that 'overwhelming question,' sailor?"

"Prufrock wants to ask the women what they're doing with their lives, but he's afraid they'll laugh at him," I said.

"Guess again, Sward," he said leaning back in his chair, stretching his arms.

"What's your theory, sir?"

"Sex," said the officer. "On the one hand, it's true, he wants to fit in and play the game because, after all, he's privileged. He belongs in the drawing room with the clever Englishwomen. At the same time he fantasizes. If he could, I think he'd like to shock them. Prufrock longs to put down his dainty porcelain teacup and shout, 'I am Lazarus, come from the dead, / Come back to tell you all, I shall tell you all.'"

"Why doesn't he do it?" I asked.

"Because Prufrock is convinced no matter what he says he won't reach them. He feels the English gentlewomen he's dealing with are unreachable. He believes his situation is as hopeless as theirs. He's dead and they're dead, too. That's why the poem begins with an image of sickness, 'a patient etherized upon a table,' and ends with people drowning. Prufrock is tough shit, man."

"You said you think there's a connection between Eliot the poet and J. Alfred Prufrock," I said.

"Of course there's a connection. Tommy Eliot from St. Louis, Missouri," said the officer. "Try as he will, he doesn't fit in. His English friends call him 'The American' and laugh. Tom Eliot the outsider with his rolled umbrella. T. S. Eliot is a self-conscious, make-believe Englishman and you have to understand that to understand 'Prufrock.'

"The poem is dark and funny at the same time. It's filled with humor and Prufrock is capable of laughing at himself. Just read those lines, 'Is it perfume from a dress / That makes me so digress?'"

"You were talking about Prufrock being sexually attracted to the women. How could that be if he is, as you say, 'dead.'" I asked.

"By 'dead' I mean desolate, inwardly barren, godforsaken. Inwardly, spiritually, Prufrock is a desolate creature. He's a moral man, he's a civilized man, but he's also hollow. But there's hope for him. In spite of himself, Prufrock is drawn to women.

"Look at line 64. He's attracted and repelled. Prufrock attends these teas, notices the women's arms 'downed with light brown hair!' and it scares the hell out of him because what he longs to do is to get them onto a drawing-room floor or a beach somewhere and bury his face in that same wonderfully tantalizing 'light brown hair.' What do you think of that, sailor?"

"I think you're right, sir."

"Then tell me this, Mr. Sward: Why doesn't he ask the overwhelming question? Hell, man, maybe it's not sexual. Maybe I'm wrong. Maybe what he wants to do is to ask some question like what you yourself suggested: 'What's the point in going on living when, in some sense, we're all already dead?'"

"I think he doesn't ask the question because he's so repressed, sir. He longs for physical contact, like you say, but he also wants another kind of intimacy, and he's afraid to ask for it and it's making him crazy."

"That's right, sailor. He's afraid. Eliot wrote the poem in 1911 when women were beginning to break free."

"Break free of what?" I asked.

"Of the prim and proper Victorian ideal. Suffragettes, feminists they called themselves. At the time Eliot wrote 'Prufrock,' women in England and America were catching on to the fact that they were disfranchised and had begun fighting for the right to vote, among other things, and for liberation, equality with men.

"Of course Prufrock is more prim and proper than the bored, overcivilized women in the poem. And it's ironic, isn't it, that he doesn't understand that the women are one step ahead of him. What you have in Prufrock is a man who tries to reconcile the image of real women with 'light brown hair' on their arms with some ideal, women who are a cross between the goddess Juno and a sweet Victorian maiden."

"Prufrock seems to know pretty well what he's feeling," I said. "He's not a liar and he's not a coward. To be honest, sir, I identify with Prufrock. He may try on one mask or another, but he ends up removing the mask and exposing himself."

"Now, about interior monologues: to understand 'Prufrock' you have to understand that most poems have one or more speakers and an audience, implied or otherwise. Let's go back to line 1. Who is this 'you and I' Eliot writes about?"

"Prufrock is talking to both his inner self and the reader," I said.

"How do you interpret the first ten lines?" the officer asked, pointing with his pencil.

"'Let us go then, you and I,' he's saying, let us stroll, somnolent and numb as a sedated patient, through these seedy 'half-deserted streets, / The muttering retreats / Of restless nights in one-night cheap hotels.'"

"That's it, sailor. And while one might argue that Prufrock 'wakes' at the end of the poem, he is for the most part a ghostly inhabitant of a world that is, for him, a sort of hell. He is like the speaker in the Italian epigraph from Dante's *Inferno,* who says, essentially, 'Like you, reader, I'm in purgatory and there is no way out. Nobody ever escapes from this pit and, for that reason, I can speak the truth without fear of ill fame.'

"Despairing and sick of heart, Prufrock is a prisoner. Trapped in himself and trapped in society, he attends another and another in an endless series of effete, decorous teas.

> In the room the women come and go
> Talking of Michelangelo.

"Do you get it now? Do you see what I mean when I say 'tough shit'?" said the officer.

"Yeah, I'm beginning to," I said.

"T. S. Eliot's 'Prufrock' has become so much a part of the English language that people who have never read the poem are familiar with phrases like 'I have measured out my life with coffee spoons' and 'I grow old . . . I grow old . . . / I shall wear the bottoms of my trousers rolled' and 'Do I dare to eat a peach?' and 'In the room the women come and go.'

"Do you get it now? Eliot's irregularly rhymed, 131-line interior monologue has become part of the monologue all of us carry on in our heads. We are all of us, whether we know it or not, love-hungry, sex-crazed soldiers and sailors, brave, bored and lonely. At some level in our hearts, we are all J. Alfred Prufrock, every one of us, and we are all sailing into a war zone from which, as the last line of the poem implies, we may never return."

From "T. S. Eliot's 'Love Song of J. Alfred Prufrock'" in *Touchstones: American Poets on a Favorite Poem,* edited by Robert Pack and Jay Parini

CONSIDERATIONS FOR CRITICAL THINKING AND WRITING

1. How satisfactory is this reading of the poem? Are any significant portions of the poem left out of this reading?

2. Compare the tone of this critical approach to any other in this chapter. Explain why you prefer one over another.

3. Using Sward's personal approach, write an analysis of a poem of your choice in this anthology.

SUGGESTED TOPICS FOR LONGER PAPERS

1. "The Love Song of J. Alfred Prufrock" has proved to be popular among generations of college students who are fond of quoting bits of the poem. What do you think accounts for that popularity among your own generation of students? Alternatively, why doesn't this poem speak to your concerns or your generation's?

2. Of the five critical perspectives on the poem provided in this chapter, which did you find to be the most satisfying reading? Explain your response by describing how your choice opened up the poem more than the other four perspectives.

3. MULTIMEDIA PROJECT. Use the library and the Internet to develop a sense of the social context for the year 1917 in England or the United States. How is the speaker's class made a significant issue in the poem?

Web   *For help with this project, use the Multimedia Project Guides Online at* http://www.bedfordstmartins.com/meyer/bedintrolit

35

A Cultural Case Study: Julia Alvarez's "Queens, 1963"

Close readings allow us to appreciate and understand the literary art of a text. These formalist approaches to literature study the intrinsic elements of a work to determine how it is constructed, emphasizing how various elements such as diction, image, figures of speech, tone, symbol, irony, sound, rhythm, and other literary techniques provide patterns related to the work's meaning. Instead of examining extrinsic matters such as social, political, and economic contexts related to a poem, formalist critics focus on the intrinsic qualities of the text itself. A formalist might, for example, approach Thomas Hardy's 1912 poem "The Convergence of the Twain" (p. 736) by placing significant emphasis on the form of this poem — its rhyming three-line stanzas — rather than the historical contexts around the sinking of the *Titanic*. A formalist would be more concerned with the effects produced by these triplets rather than the identities of some of the enormously wealthy people who went down with the ship. In more recent literary criticism, however, there has been a renewed interest in the historical and cultural contexts of works that go beyond close readings of the text.

Cultural critics pay close attention to the historical contexts of a work, but unlike literary historians, they do not limit themselves to major historical events or famous people. A cultural critic might, for example, approach "The Convergence of the Twain" not only as an opportunity to examine the "vaingloriousness" of the rich who put their faith in the technology that produced the *Titanic*, but also as an occasion to investigate how poor people made jokes about the sinking to deflate the pretensions of the rich. The ironies that go unsuspected by "human vanity" can be seen to go even deeper in the nervous jokes that infiltrate popular culture when such a catastrophe occurs. Hardy's dignified, if pessimistic, poetic response can be illuminated in radically different ways such as by advertising before the voyage or the jokes and sentimental poetic eulogies published after the disaster. Cultural critics study material drawn from a broad spectrum that includes "high" culture and popular culture. A cultural critic's approach to Hardy's treatment of the *Titanic*'s fate—captained by what Hardy calls the "Spinner of the Years"—might include discussions of everything from the actual construction plans of the ship, to passenger cabin accommodations, to manuals for lifeboat drills, as well as connections to Hardy's contemporaries, who also wrote about the *Titanic*.

The documents that follow Alvarez's "Queens, 1963" are provided to suggest how cultural criticism can be used to contextualize a literary work historically. The documents include an excerpt from an interview with Alvarez on growing up as an immigrant in New York City; an advertisement showing typical row houses; a newspaper article that summarizes the Chamber of Commerce's perspective of Queens in 1963; an excerpt from a television script for *All in the Family* (set in Queens); and a photograph of a civil rights demonstration at a Queens construction site. These documents offer some possible approaches to understanding the culture contemporary to "Queens, 1963." A variety of such approaches can create a wider and more informed understanding of the poem while deepening one's appreciation of Alvarez's achievement in writing it.

JULIA ALVAREZ (B. 1950)

Although Julia Alvarez was born in New York City, she lived in the Dominican Republic until she was ten years old. She returned to New York after her father, a physician, was connected to a plot to overthrow the dictatorship of Rafael Trujillo, and the family had to flee. Growing up in Queens was radically different from the Latino Caribbean world she experienced during her early childhood. A new culture and new language sensitized Alvarez to her surroundings and her use of language so that emigration from the Dominican Republic to Queens was the beginning of her movement toward becoming a writer. Alvarez quotes the Polish poet Czeslow Milosz's assertion that "Language is the only homeland" to explain her own sense that what she really settled into was not so much the United States as the English language.

Her fascination with English continued into high school and took shape in college as she became a serious writer—first at Connecticut College from 1967 to 1969 and then at Middlebury College, where she earned her B.A. in 1971. At Syracuse University she was awarded the American Academy of Poetry Prize and, in 1975, earned an M.A. in creative writing. Since then she has worked as a writer-in-residence for the Kentucky Arts Commission, the Delaware Arts Council, and the Arts Council of Fayetteville, North

Carolina, working in schools and community organizations. She has taught at California State College, College of Sequoias, Phillips Andover Academy, the University of Vermont, George Washington University, the University of Illinois, and, since 1988, at Middlebury College where she is a professor of literature and creative writing.

Alvarez's poetry has been widely published in journals and magazines ranging from *The New Yorker* to *Mirabella* to *The Kenyon Review*. Her book of poems, *Homecoming* (1984; second edition, 1986), uses simple — yet incisive — language to explore issues related to love, domestic life, and work. Her second book of poetry, *The Other Side/El Otro Lado* (1995), is a bilingual collection of meditations on her childhood memories of immigrant life that served to shape her adult identity and sensibilities.

In addition to her two volumes of poetry, Alvarez has also published three novels. The first, *How the García Girls Lost Their Accents* (1991), is a collection of fifteen separate but interrelated stories that cover thirty years of the lives of the García sisters from the late 1950s to the late 1980s. Drawing upon her own experiences, Alvarez describes the sisters fleeing the Dominican Republic and growing up as Latinas in the United States as well as their relationship to the country they left behind. Alvarez's second novel, *In the Time of the Butterflies* (1994), is a fictional account of a true story concerning four sisters who opposed Trujillo's dictatorship. Three of the sisters were murdered in 1960 by the government, and the fourth surviving sister recounts the events of their personal and political lives that led up to her sisters' deaths. Shaped by the history of Dominican freedom and tyranny, the novel also explores the sisters' relationships to each other and their country.

In *¡Yo!* (1997), her third novel, Alvarez focuses on Yolanda, one of the García sisters from her first novel, who is now a writer. Written in the different voices of Yo's friends and family members, this fractured narrative constructs a complete picture of a woman who uses her relationships as fodder for fiction; a woman who is selfish, aggravating, and finally lovable — and who is deeply embedded in American culture while remaining aware of her Dominican roots. Alvarez's book, *Something to Declare* (1998), is a collection of essays that describes her abiding concerns about how to respond to competing cultures. Her most recent books include the novel, *In the Name of Salome,* and the illustrated poetry collection, *The Secret Footprints.*

In "Queens, 1963" Alvarez remembers the neighborhood she lived in when she was thirteen years old and how "Everyone seemed more American / than we, newly arrived." The tensions that arose when new immigrants and ethnic groups moved onto the block were mirrored in many American neighborhoods in 1963. Indeed, the entire nation was made keenly aware of such issues as antisegregation when demonstrations were organized across the South and a massive march on Washington in support of civil rights for African Americans drew hundreds of thousands of demonstrators who listened to Martin Luther King deliver his electrifying "I have a dream" speech. But the issues were hardly resolved, as evidenced by 1963's two best-selling books: *Happiness Is a Warm Puppy* and *Security Is a Thumb and a Blanket,* by Charles M. Schulz of "Peanuts" cartoon fame.

The popularity of these books is, perhaps, understandable given the tensions that moved across the country and which seemed to culminate on November 22, 1963, when President Kennedy was assassinated in Dallas, Texas. These events are not mentioned in "Queens, 1963," but they are certainly part of the context that helps us to understand Alvarez's particular neighborhood.

CHRONOLOGY

1950	Born on March 27 in New York City.
1950–60	Raised in the Dominican Republic.
1960	Alvarez family flees the Dominican Republic for New York City after her father joins efforts to overthrow the dictatorship of Rafael Trujillo.
1961	Rafael Trujillo is assassinated.
1967–69	Attends Connecticut College.
1971	Graduates from Middlebury College with a B.A.
1975	Graduates from Syracuse University with an M.A.
1979–80	Attends Bread Loaf School of English.
1979–81	Instructor at Phillips Andover Academy.
1981–83	Visiting assistant professor at University of Vermont.
1984	Publishes *Homecoming,* a volume of poems.
1984–85	Visiting writer-in-residence at George Washington University.
1985–88	Assistant professor of English at University of Illinois.
1987–88	Awarded a National Endowment for the Arts fellowship.
1988– Present	Professor of English at Middlebury College.
1991	Publishes *How the García Girls Lost Their Accents,* a novel.
1994	Publishes *In the Time of the Butterflies,* a novel.
1995	Publishes *The Other Side/El Otro Lado,* a volume of poems.
1997	Publishes *¡Yo!,* a novel.
1998	Publishes *Something to Declare,* essays.

Web *Research Julia Alvarez with LitLinks at*
http://www.bedfordstmartins.com/meyer/bedintrolit

Queens, 1963   *1995*

Everyone seemed more American
than we, newly arrived,
foreign dirt still on our soles.
By year's end, a sprinkler waving

like a flag on our mowed lawn,   5
we were melted into the block,
owned our own mock Tudor house.
Then the house across the street
sold to a black family.
Cop cars patrolled our block   10
from the Castellucci's at one end
to the Balakian's on the other.
We heard rumors of bomb threats,
a burning cross on their lawn.
(It turned out to be a sprinkler.)   15
Still the neighborhood buzzed.
The barber's family, Haralambides,
our left side neighbors, didn't want trouble.
They'd come a long way to be free!
Mr. Scott, the retired plumber,   20
and his plump midwestern wife,
considered moving back home
where white and black got along
by staying where they belonged.
They had cultivated our street   25
like the garden she'd given up
on account of her ailing back,
bad knees, poor eyes, arthritic hands.
She went through her litany daily.
Politely, my mother listened —   30
¡Ay, Mrs. Scott, qué pena!°
— her Dominican good manners
still running on automatic.
The Jewish counselor next door,
had a practice in her house;   35
clients hurried up her walk
ashamed to be seen needing.
(I watched from my upstairs window,
gloomy with adolescence,
and guessed how they too must have   40
hypocritical old world parents.)
Mrs. Bernstein said it was time
the neighborhood opened up.
As the first Jew on the block,
she remembered the snubbing she got   45
a few years back from Mrs. Scott.
But real estate worried her,
our houses' plummeting value.
She shook her head as she might
at a client's grim disclosures.   50
Too bad the world works this way.
The German girl playing the piano

31 *qué pena!:* What a shame!

down the street abruptly stopped
in the middle of a note.
I completed the tune in my head   55
as I watched *their* front door open.
A dark man in a suit
with a girl about my age
walked quickly into a car.
My hand lifted but fell   60
before I made a welcoming gesture.
On her face I had seen a look
from the days before we had melted
into the United States of America.
It was hardness mixed with hurt.   65
It was knowing she never could be
the right kind of American.
A police car followed their car.
Down the street, curtains fell back.
Mrs. Scott swept her walk   70
as if it had just been dirtied.
Then the German piano commenced
downward scales as if tracking
the plummeting real estate.
One by one I imagined the houses   75
sinking into their lawns,
the grass grown wild and tall
in the past tense of this continent
before the first foreigners owned
any of this free country.   80

CONSIDERATIONS FOR CRITICAL THINKING AND WRITING

1. FIRST RESPONSE. What nationalities live in this neighborhood in the New
   York City Borough of Queens? Are they neighborly to each other?

2. In line 3, why do you suppose Alvarez writes "foreign dirt still on our soles"
   rather than "foreign soil still on our shoes"? What does Alvarez's particular
   word choice suggest about her feelings for her native country?

3. Characterize the speaker. How old is she? How does she feel about having
   come from the Dominican Republic? About living in the United States?

4. Do you think this poem is optimistic or pessimistic about racial relations
   in the United States? Explain your answer by referring to specific details in
   the poem.

CONNECTIONS TO OTHER SELECTIONS

1. Compare the use of irony in "Queens, 1963" with that in John Ciardi's
   "Suburban" (p. 824). How does irony contribute to each poem?

2. Discuss the problems immigrants encounter in this poem and in Chitra
   Banerjee Divakaruni's "Indian Movie, New Jersey" (p. 825).

3. Write an essay comparing and contrasting the tone and theme in "Queens,
   1963" and in Tato Laviera's "AmeRícan" (p. 931).

DOCUMENTS

Marny Requa (b. 1971)

From an Interview with Julia Alvarez   1997

M.R.   What was it like when you came to the United States?

J.A. When we got to Queens, it was really a shock to go from a totally Latino, *familia* Caribbean world into this very cold and kind of forbidding one in which we didn't speak the language. I didn't grow up with a tradition of writing or reading books at all. People were always telling stories but it wasn't a tradition of literary . . . reading a book or doing something solitary like that. Coming to this country I discovered books, I discovered that it was a way to enter into a portable homeland that you could carry around in your head. You didn't have to suffer what was going on around you. I found in books a place to go. I became interested in language because I was learning a language intentionally at the age of ten. I was wondering, "Why is it that word and not another?" which any writer has to do with their language. I always say I came to English late but to the profession early. By high school I was pretty set: that's what I want to do, be a writer.

M.R.   Did you have culture shock returning to the Dominican Republic as you were growing up?

J.A. The culture here had an effect on me — at the time this country was coming undone with protests and flower children and drugs. Here I was back in the Dominican Republic and I wouldn't keep my mouth shut. I had my own ideas and I had my own politics, and it, I just didn't gel anymore with the family. I didn't quite feel I ever belonged in this North American culture and I always had this nostalgia that when I went back I'd belong, and then I found out I didn't belong there either.

M.R.   Was it a source of inspiration to have a foot in both cultures?

J.A. I only came to that later. [Then], it was a burden because I felt torn. I wanted to be part of one culture and then part of the other. It was a time when the model for the immigrant was that you came and you became an American and you cut off your ties and that was that. My parents had that frame of mind, because they were so afraid, and they were "Learn your English" and "Become one of them," and that left out so much. Now I see the richness. Part of what I want to do with my work is that complexity, that richness. I don't want it to be simplistic and either/or.

From "The Politics of Fiction," *Frontera* magazine 5 (1997)

Considerations for Critical Thinking and Writing

1. What do you think Alvarez means when she describes books as "a portable homeland that you could carry around in your head"?

2. Why is it difficult for Alvarez to feel that she belongs in either the Dominican or the North American culture?

3. Alvarez says that in the 1960s "the model for the immigrant was that you came and you became an American and you cut off your ties and that was

that." Do you think this model has changed in the United States since then? Explain your response.

4. How might this interview alter your understanding of "Queens, 1963"? What light is shed, for example, on the speaker's feeling that her family "melted into the block" in line 6?

An Advertisement for Tudor Row Houses   *1920*

NEW YORK CITY   209

AT ELMHURST MANOR
WITH AUTO DRIVEWAYS

The Perfect Low Priced American Home
Designed and constructed for the Homeseeker
who desires the best at the least cost

The Ideal Home Place for the Children
Well Drained, Sewered, Convenient to Schools
Churches, Stores and Amusements

W. R. GIBSON
BUILDER AND DEVELOPER
OFFICE AND BUILDINGS
Burnside Avenue and Thirty-Seventh Street
Elmhurst Manor, L. I.
PHONE NEWTOWN 2073

From *Queen's Borough New York City, 1910–1920*

CONSIDERATIONS FOR CRITICAL THINKING AND WRITING

1. This advertisement from a publication of the Queens Chamber of Commerce shows row houses as the "Ideal Home Place." Write a paragraph describing how the details in the photograph make you feel about living there.

2. Compare the neighborhood in this picture with the neighborhood Alvarez describes in "Queens, 1963." How might the physical characteristics of such a neighborhood have changed between 1920 and 1963? What factors might have influenced such a change?

3. How does this advertisement shed light on "Queens, 1963"?

Queens: "The 'Fair' Borough"   1963

This newspaper account anticipates the opening of the 1964 World's Fair in Queens.

Cariello Glorifies Queens as Example of Gracious Living

The borough of Queens "truly represents the full flowering of advanced urban living," Borough President Mario J. Cariello says.

His encomium is in a brightly colored eight-page brochure entitled "The 'Fair' Borough." Mr. Cariello's foreword says the brochure was prepared "to reacquaint our residents" with the borough's history and present stature when they play host to "millions of visitors to the World's Fair."

Twenty-five thousand copies have been printed by photo-offset at a competitive bid cost of $1,600. The money came from the Borough President's special expense fund for proclamations, certificates and the like, a spokesman said yesterday.

A section on current "Data about Queens," compiled by the Queens Chamber of Commerce, says the borough has "such beautiful rural home communities as Forest Hills, Jamaica Estates, Kew Gardens, Jackson Heights, Flushing and Douglaston."

The booklet includes a map of 44 communities, a list of bus routes, a description of the Borough President's functions, the text of the 1657 Flushing Remonstrance as "the first declaration of religious freedom by a group of free citizens in America," a picture of the borough flag, and a brief history.

From the *New York Times*, July 18, 1963

CONSIDERATIONS FOR CRITICAL THINKING AND WRITING

1. Based on the newspaper article, how would you describe the probable tone of the eight-page brochure about Queens?

2. After reading Alvarez's poem about Queens, do you see any irony in the title of the brochure, "The 'Fair' Borough"? Explain why or why not.

3. What is left out of Borough President Cariello's account of Queens? Why do you suppose its focus is very different from that of "Queens, 1963"?

4. Try writing a dialogue between the Borough President and Alvarez on the subject of Queens as a representation of "the full flowering of advanced urban living." If you prefer, write an essay on this topic instead.

"Talkin' about Prejudice" in Queens

All in the Family, created by Norman Lear, was produced for nine seasons from 1971 to 1979, and at the height of its popularity, an estimated one-third of all Americans regularly viewed the program. Although this famous series has ceased production, reruns have preserved its popularity. The show's main character, Archie Bunker — a resident of a row house in a working-class Queens neighborhood — is so well known that his name has been used to describe anyone who is loud, stubborn, and blindly prejudiced. The basic conflict of the series centers on the verbal skirmishes that occur when Archie's middle-aged, working-class biases are challenged by his son-in-law Mike's liberal views. One reason for the show's popularity during its original run was that it mirrored so many issues of its time, such as racism, sexism, politics, religion, and alternative lifestyles. The following excerpt is from the first episode of *All in the Family*.

NORMAN LEAR (B. 1922)

Meet the Bunkers   *1971*

CHARACTERS

Archie Bunker
Edith Bunker, Archie's wife
Michael Stivic, the Bunkers' son-in-law
Gloria Stivic, the Bunkers' daughter
Lionel, a neighbor

In this scene, Lionel, a black neighbor of the Bunkers, appears at the door on the heels of a dinner conversation in which Archie has fervently denied but amply demonstrated his prejudices. Earlier we learn from Lionel that Archie likes to ask him what he wants to study when he goes to college so that Lionel will say, "Ahm gwana be a 'lectical ingineer." Lionel obliges Archie because he believes that by giving "people what they want," he indeed can become an electrical engineer. He also enjoys watching Archie fall for his put-ons.

Mike: Hey, Lionel. How you doin'? Come on in. You know, in a way we were just talking about you.
Gloria: Michael!
Archie: Talkin' about prejudice, I'm glad you're here Lionel. (*Gets up and goes to living room.*)
Lionel: Yes, sir. Mr. Bunker, sir. (*Hands flowers to Edith.*) These are for you, Mrs. Bunker. A present from an admirer.
Edith (overwhelmed): For me? Oh my goodness, I ain't had a present for ten years.
Gloria: I wonder who it's from.
Archie (coming back to table): There's something I want to ask you, Lionel.
Gloria: Wait a minute, Daddy. Let her open her gift first.
Archie: She waited ten years; another minute ain't gonna kill her! (*Puts gift on table, takes Lionel to living room.*) Come here, Lionel. Let me ask your opinion

of somethin' there, Lionel. When you started doin' odd jobs in the neighborhood, wasn't I one of the first guys to throw a little work your way — by the way, didya fix the TV up in the bedroom?

Lionel: Sure did, Mr. Bunker. *(Lionel nods. Archie slips him some change.)*

Archie: Swell. Good boy . . . Here, put this in your pocket.

Edith: Cheaper than a repairman, believe me.

Archie: Is anybody talkin' to you . . . Now, Lionel you could say by throwin' you these little jobs, in a way I was helpin' you get some money so you can get through college so's you can become . . .

Lionel: A 'lectical ingineer.

Archie (loves it): Yeah. Ya hear that?

Mike (impatient): Archie, ask your question already!

Archie: Will you keep your drawers on? Hey, by the way, that's a pretty nice looking suit you got on there. I mean it's classy, it's quiet. Where'd you get it?

Lionel: Up in Harlem.

Archie (looks): Nah.

Lionel: Now I got two more, but one's in yellow with stripes, the other one's in purple with checks. You know, for when I'm with *my* people.

Archie: Well, anyway Lionel, I'd say you know me pretty good, wouldn't you?

Lionel: Oh, yes, sir. I got a bead on you, all right. I know you real good.

Archie: Good, good.

Mike (crossing to living room): Alright, alright, let's get to the point. Lionel, what he wants to know, is if you think he's prejudiced.

Lionel (feigning innocence): Prejudiced?

Archie: Yeah.

Lionel: Prejudiced against who?

Mike: Against Black People.

Lionel: Against Black People! Mr. Bunker! That's the most ridiculous thing I ever heard!

Archie turns proudly to the others.

Archie: There, you see that, wise guy. *(Turns to Mike.)* You thought you knew him. You thought you knew me. Oh these liberals — they're supposed to be so sensitive, ya know. I'll tell you where this guy's sensitive, Lionel — right in his tochas. *(Archie goes to dining room table.)*

Lionel (surprise): Where?

Mike: It's a Yiddish word. It means — *(points to buttocks)*.

Lionel: Oh, I know where it's at. I was just wonderin', Mr. Bunker — what's with the Jewish word?

Archie: I hear them. We got a couple of Hebes working down the building.

Lionel: Does he use words like that very often?

Mike: Now and then.

Archie: I told ya, I work with a couple of Jews.

Lionel: Beggin' your pardon, Mr. Bunker, but you wouldn't happen to be one of them, would you?

Archie (no humor about this): What??

Lionel: I mean people don't use Jewish words just like that, do they, Mike?

Mike (crossing to table, sits): No, not in my experience.

Archie: Maybe people don't but *I* do! And I ain't no Yid!

Mike: Come to think of it . . . when your father was visiting last year . . . wasn't his name Davie, or somethin'?

Archie: David, my father's name is David.

Mike: Yeah, David. And your mother's name . . . uh . . . Sarah, wasn't it?

Archie (to Lionel): Sarah, my mother's name is Sarah — So what?

Lionel: David and Sarah, two Jewish names.

Archie: David and Sarah. Two names right out of the Bible — which is got nothin' to do with the Jews.

Lionel: You don't wanna get up tight about it, Mr. Bunker. There's nothing to be ashamed of being Jewish.

Archie: But I ain't Jewish!

Mike: Look at that — see the way he uses his hands when he argues. A very Semitic gesture.

Archie: What do you know about it, you dumb Polack.

Mike: All right, I'm a Polack.

Archie: You sure are! You're a Polack Joke!

Mike: Okay, I don't mind, so I'm Polish. I don't mind. I'm proud of it!

Lionel: There you are, Mr. Bunker. Now you oughta be proud that you're Jewish.

Archie (whining): But I ain't Jewish.

Edith: I didn't know you was Jewish.

Archie: What the hell are you talking about? You, of all people, should *know* that I ain't Jewish.

Edith: You *are* talking with your hands.

Lionel: See, the Jews tend to be emotional.

Archie (blowing): Now listen to me, Lionel. I'm going to give it to you just once more and that's all. I am not Jewish.

Lionel: Yes, Sir, Mr. Bunker. But even if you are, it doesn't change things between you and me. I mean I'm not gonna throw away nine years of friendship over a little thing like that. So long, everybody. *(He exits.)*

All: Bye, Lionel!

Archie watches him go and turns to others. They resume eating quickly.

Archie: Well, I hate a smart aleck kid, and I don't care what color he is!

Applause. Fade to black.

CONSIDERATIONS FOR CRITICAL THINKING AND WRITING

1. What kinds of assumptions does Archie make about Lionel because he is black? How does Lionel use Archie's prejudices to satirize him?

2. Some critics have insisted that *All in the Family* negatively affected society because the series presents a bigot who is likable, thereby characterizing his racial prejudices as funny and acceptable rather than harmful and repugnant. Do you think Archie is a dangerous character because his prejudices are presented humorously? Explain why or why not.

3. Compare and contrast how racial prejudice is treated in this script and in "Queens, 1963." Which treatment do you find more effective? Explain why.

4. How do the script and the poem suggest what it was like to be Jewish in Queens in the 1960s? Write an essay that explores how each work treats Jewishness. Consider whether these treatments are simplistic and reductive or complex and subtle.

A Civil Rights Demonstration 1963

In this photograph police remove a Congress of Racial Equality (CORE) demonstrator from a Queens construction site. Demonstrators blocked the delivery entrance to the site because they wanted more African Americans and Puerto Ricans hired in the building-trade industry. Reprinted by permission of AP/Wide World Photos.

CONSIDERATIONS FOR CRITICAL THINKING AND WRITING

1. Discuss the role played by the police in this photograph and in "Queens, 1963." What attitudes toward the police do the photograph and the poem display?

2. How do you think the Scotts and Mrs. Bernstein would have responded to this photograph in 1963?

3. Compare the tensions in "Queens, 1963" to those depicted in this picture. How do the speaker's private reflections relate to this public protest?

——— SUGGESTED TOPICS FOR LONGER PAPERS ———

1. Describe how various elements of this poem—diction, image, tone, metaphor, irony, theme, symbol—constitute a meditation on immigration, assimilation into a culture, and racism.

2. Use the library or the Internet to supplement the documents provided in this chapter that help to characterize Queens in 1963. Search for and comment on additional material that provides relevant contexts for the poem.

3. **MULTIMEDIA PROJECT.** Choose another poem from this textbook—on any subject that interests you—and put together a multimedia cultural portfolio that reveals whatever you think is central to an understanding of the poem, and write a commentary that explains your choices.

Web *For help with this project, use the Multimedia Project Guides Online at*
http://www.bedfordstmartins.com/meyer/bedintrolit

36

Two Thematic Case Studies: The Love Poem and Teaching and Learning

Behind all the elements that make up a poem, and even behind its cultural contexts and critical reception, lies its theme. Its idea and the point around which the entire poem revolves, the theme is ultimately what we respond to — or fail to respond to. All the other elements, in fact, are typically there to contribute to the theme, whether or not that theme is explicitly stated. Reading thematically means extending what you have learned about the analysis of individual elements at work in the poem to make connections between the text and the world we inhabit.

This chapter focuses on single themes as they reappear throughout various parts of poetic history. The poems here are organized into two case studies. The first consists of love poems and the second consists of poems about teaching and learning. These poems have much to say about human experience — experience that is contradictory, confusing, complicated, and fascinating. You'll find diverse perspectives in each case study from different historical, cultural, generational, or political moments in time. You'll also discover writers who aim to entertain, to describe, to convince, to teach, and to complain. After reading these poems in the context of one another, you're likely to come away with a richer understanding of how the themes of love and of learning and teaching play out in your own life.

POEMS ABOUT LOVE

Poems about love have probably enchanted and intrigued their hearers since people began making poetry. Like poetry itself, love is, after all, about intensity, acute impressions, and powerful responsibilities. The emotional dimensions of love do not lend themselves to analytic expository essays.

Although such writing can be satisfying intellectually, it is most inadequate for evoking and capturing the thick excitement and swooning reveries that love engenders. The poems in this section include spiritual as well as physical explorations of love that range over four centuries. As you'll see, poetic responses to love by men and women can be quite similar as well as different from one another, just as poems from different periods can reflect a variety of values and attitudes toward love. It is indeed an engaging theme — but as you read, don't forget to pay attention to the formal elements of each of these selections and how they work together to create the particular points about love each poem makes. Also, remember to read not only for the presence of love; many other themes can be found in these works, and many other connections can be made to the literature elsewhere in this anthology.

The oldest love poem in this case study, Christopher Marlowe's "The Passionate Shepherd to His Love," opens with the line, "Come live with me and be my love." This famous pastoral lyric set a tone for love poetry that has been replicated since its publication. Before concluding with "Then live with me and be my love," Marlowe embraces the kinds of generous pleasure that readers have traditionally and happily received for centuries. The feelings, if not the particular images, are likely to be quite familiar to you.

CHRISTOPHER MARLOWE (1564–1593)
The Passionate Shepherd to His Love   *1599?*

Come live with me and be my love,
And we will all the pleasure prove
That valleys, groves, hills, and fields,
Woods, or steepy mountain yields.

And we will sit upon the rocks,   5
Seeing the shepherds feed their flocks,
By shallow rivers to whose falls
Melodious birds sing madrigals.

And I will make thee beds of roses
And a thousand fragrant posies,   10
A cap of flowers, and a kirtle°   *Dress or skirt*
Embroidered all with leaves of myrtle;

A gown made of the finest wool
Which from our pretty lambs we pull;
Fair lined slippers for the cold,   15
With buckles of the purest gold;

A belt of straw and ivy buds,
With coral clasps and amber studs:

And if these pleasures may thee move,
Come live with me, and be my love.   20

The shepherd swains shall dance and sing
For thy delight each May morning:
If these delights thy mind may move,
Then live with me and be my love.

CONSIDERATIONS FOR CRITICAL THINKING AND WRITING

1. FIRST RESPONSE. How persuasive do you find the shepherd's arguments to his potential lover?

2. What do you think might be the equivalent of the shepherd's arguments in the twenty-first century? What kinds of appeals and images of love would be made by a contemporary lover?

3. Try writing a response to the shepherd from the female's point of view using the rhythms, rhyme scheme, and quatrains employed by Marlowe.

CONNECTION TO ANOTHER SELECTION

1. Read Sir Walter Ralegh's "The Nymph's Reply to the Shepherd" (p. 1179). How does the nymph's response compare with your imagined reply?

While Marlow's shepherd focuses his energies on convincing his potential love to join him (in the delights associated with love), the speaker in the following sonnet by William Shakespeare demonstrates his love for poetry as well and focuses on the beauty of the object of the poem. In doing so, he introduces a theme that has become a perennial challenge to love — the corrosive, destructive nature of what Shakespeare shockingly calls "sluttish time." His resolution of this issue is intriguing: see if you agree with it.

WILLIAM SHAKESPEARE (1564–1616)

Not marble, nor the gilded monuments   1609

Not marble, nor the gilded monuments
Of princes, shall outlive this powerful rhyme;
But you shall shine more bright in these conténts
Than unswept stone, besmeared with sluttish time.
When wasteful war shall statues overturn,   5
And broils root out the work of masonry,
Nor Mars his° swords nor war's quick fire shall burn   possessive of Mars
The living record of your memory.
'Gainst death and all-oblivious enmity
Shall you pace forth; your praise shall still find room   10
Even in the eyes of all posterity
That wear this world out to the ending doom.
   So, till the judgment that yourself arise,
   You live in this, and dwell in lovers' eyes.

CONSIDERATIONS FOR CRITICAL THINKING AND WRITING

1. FIRST RESPONSE. What do you think is the central point of this poem? Explain whether you agree or disagree with its theme.

2. How does "sluttish time" represent the poem's major conflict?

3. Consider whether this poem is more about the poet's loved one or the poet's love of his own poetry.

CONNECTIONS TO OTHER SELECTIONS

1. Compare the theme of this poem with that of Marvell's "To His Coy Mistress" (p. 728), paying particular attention to the speaker's beliefs about how time affects love.

2. Discuss whether you find this love poem more or less appealing than Marlowe's "The Passionate Shepherd to His Love." As you make this comparison, consider what the criteria for an appealing love poem should be.

As Shakespeare's speaker presents a love that will withstand the destruction of time, Anne Bradstreet's "To My Dear and Loving Husband" evokes a marital love that confirms a connection that transcends space and matter as well as time. Although Bradstreet wrote more than three centuries ago, such devotion remains undated for many (but, of course, not all) readers of love poetry. She begins, naturally enough, with the pleasure and paradox of how two people can be one.

ANNE BRADSTREET (c. 1612–1672)

To My Dear and Loving Husband   *1678*

If ever two were one, then surely we.
If ever man were loved by wife, then thee;
If ever wife was happy in a man,
Compare with me, ye women, if you can.
I prize thy love more than whole mines of gold   5
Or all the riches that the East doth hold.
My love is such that rivers cannot quench,
Nor ought but love from thee, give recompense.
Thy love is such I can no way repay,
The heavens reward thee manifold, I pray.   10
Then while we live, in love let's so persevere
That when we live no more, we may live ever.

CONSIDERATIONS FOR CRITICAL THINKING AND WRITING

1. FIRST RESPONSE. Describe the poem's tone. Is it what you'd expect from a seventeenth-century Puritan? Why or why not?

2. Consider whether Bradstreet's devotion is directed more toward her husband here on earth or toward the eternal rewards of heaven.

3. What is the paradox of the final line? How is it resolved?

CONNECTIONS TO OTHER SELECTIONS

1. How does the theme of this poem compare with that of Bradstreet's "Before the Birth of One of Her Children" (p. 1149)? Explain why you find the poems consistent or contradictory.

2. Discuss the relation between love and the contemplation of death in this poem and the relation between love and the reality of death in Donald Hall's "Letter with No Address" (p. 1217).

The remaining poems in this case study are modern and contemporary pieces that both maintain and revise the perspectives on love provided by Marlowe, Shakespeare, and Bradstreet. As you read them, consider what each adds to your understanding of the others and of love in general.

ELIZABETH BARRETT BROWNING (1806–1861)

How Do I Love Thee?
Let Me Count the Ways   1850

How do I love thee? Let me count the ways.
I love thee to the depth and breadth and height
My soul can reach, when feeling out of sight
For the ends of being and ideal grace.
I love thee to the level of every day's   5
Most quiet need, by sun and candle-light.
I love thee freely, as men strive for right.
I love thee purely, as they turn from praise.
I love thee with the passion put to use
In my old griefs, and with my childhood's faith.   10
I love thee with a love I seemed to lose
With my lost saints. I love thee with the breath,
Smiles, tears, of all my life; and, if God choose,
I shall but love thee better after death.

CONSIDERATIONS FOR CRITICAL THINKING AND WRITING

1. FIRST RESPONSE. This poem has remained extraordinarily popular for more than 150 years. Why do you think it has been so often included in collections of love poems? What is its appeal? Does it speak to a contemporary reader? To you?

2. Comment on the effect of the diction. What kind of tone does it create?

3. Would you characterize this poem as having a religious theme—or is it a substitute for religion?

CONNECTION TO ANOTHER SELECTION

1. Compare and contrast the images, tone, and theme of this poem with those of Christina Rossetti's "Promises Like Pie-Crust" (p. 1180). Explain why you find one poem more promising than the other.

E. E. CUMMINGS (1894–1962)

since feeling is first 1926

since feeling is first
who pays any attention
to the syntax of things
will never wholly kiss you;

wholly to be a fool 5
while Spring is in the world

my blood approves,
and kisses are a better fate
than wisdom
lady i swear by all flowers. Don't cry 10
— the best gesture of my brain is less than
your eyelids' flutter which says

we are for each other: then
laugh, leaning back in my arms
for life's not a paragraph 15

And death i think is no parenthesis

CONSIDERATIONS FOR CRITICAL THINKING AND WRITING

1. FIRST RESPONSE. What is the speaker's initial premise? Why is it crucial to his argument? What is his argument?

2. Does this poem fit into the *carpe diem* tradition? How?

3. How are nature and society presented in the conflict? Why is this relevant to the speaker's argument?

4. List and describe the grammatical metaphors in the poem. How do they further the speaker's argument?

CONNECTIONS TO OTHER SELECTIONS

1. Contrast the theme of this poem with that of Marlowe's "The Passionate Shepherd to His Love" (p. 1099). How do you account for the differences, in both style and content, between the two love poems?

2. Discuss attitudes toward "feeling" in this poem and in Molly Peacock's "Desire" (p. 893).

JANE KENYON (1947–1995)

The Shirt 1978

The shirt touches his neck
and smooths over his back.
It slides down his sides.
It even goes down below his belt —

down into his pants.
Lucky shirt.

Considerations for Critical Thinking and Writing

1. FIRST RESPONSE. Chart your emotions as you experienced this poem. Were you surprised? Explain why you were delighted or offended by this poem.
2. Discuss whether you consider this to be a love poem or something else.
3. Why is the title, "The Shirt," a much better title than, for example, "Below His Belt"?

Connections to Other Selections

1. What does a comparison of "The Shirt" with Bradstreet's "To My Dear and Loving Husband" (p. 1101) and Browning's "How Do I Love Thee? Let Me Count the Ways" (p. 1102) suggest to you about the history of women writing love poems?

Timothy Steele (b. 1948)

An Aubade   1986

As she is showering, I wake to see
A shine of earrings on the bedside stand,
A single yellow sheet which, over me,
Has folds as intricate as drapery
In paintings from some fine old master's hand.   5

The pillow which, in dozing, I embraced
Retains the salty sweetness of her skin;
I sense her smooth back, buttocks, belly, waist,
The leggy warmth which spread and gently laced
Around my legs and loins, and drew me in.   10

I stretch and curl about a bit and hear her
Singing among the water's hiss and race.
Gradually the early light makes clearer
The perfume bottles by the dresser's mirror,
The silver flashlight, standing on its face,   15

Which shares the corner of the dresser with
An ivy spilling tendrils from a cup.
And so content am I, I can forgive
Pleasure for being brief and fugitive.
I'll stretch some more, but postpone getting up   20

Until she finishes her shower and dries
(Now this and now that foot placed on a chair)
Her fineboned ankles, and her calves and thighs,
The pink full nipples of her breasts, and ties
Her towel up, turban-style, about her hair.   25

CONSIDERATIONS FOR CRITICAL THINKING AND WRITING

1. FIRST RESPONSE. Characterize the poem's speaker. What does his language reveal about him?
2. How does this poem fit the definition of an aubade?
3. What do you think is the central point of this poem?
4. Is this a *carpe diem* poem? Explain why or why not.

CONNECTIONS TO OTHER SELECTIONS

1. How does the tone of Steele's poem compare with Wilbur's "A Late Aubade" (p. 731)? Explain why you prefer one over the other.
2. Write an essay that compares and contrasts the speaker/observer in "An Aubade" with that of Joan Murray's in "Play-By-Play" (p. 1227) or Jane Kenyon's "The Shirt" (p. 1103).

RON KOERTGE (B. 1940)

1989   1999

Because AIDS was slaughtering people left and right,
    I went to a lot of memorial services that year.
There were so many, I'd pencil them in between
    a movie or a sale at Macy's. The other thing that
made them tolerable was the funny stories people   5
    got up and told about the deceased: the time he
hurled a mushroom frittata across a crowded room,
    those green huaraches he refused to throw away,
the joke about the flight attendant and the banana
    that cracked him up every time.   10

But this funeral was for a blind friend of my wife's
    who'd merely died. And the interesting thing
about it was the guide dogs; with all the harness
    and the sniffing around, the vestibule of the church
looked like the starting line of the Iditarod. But   15
    nobody got up to talk. We just sat there
and the pastor read the King James version. Then he
    said someday we would see Robert and he us.

Throughout the service, the dogs slumped beside their
    masters. But when the soloist stood and launched   20
into a screechy rendition of "Abide with Me," they sank
    into the carpet. A few put their paws over their ears.
Someone whispered to one of the blind guys; he told
    another, and the laughter started to spread. People
in the back looked around, startled and embarrassed,   25
    until they spotted all those chunky Labradors
flattened out like animals in a cartoon about
    steamrollers. Then they started, too.

That was more like it. That was what I was used to —
a roomful of people laughing and crying, taking off   30
their sunglasses to blot their inconsolable eyes.

CONSIDERATIONS FOR CRITICAL THINKING AND WRITING

1. FIRST RESPONSE. In what sense can "1989" be read as a love poem? Explain why it does or doesn't fit your definition of a love poem.

2. Describe the tone of each of the stanzas and trace your emotional response to them as you move through the poem. What is your emotional reaction to the entire poem?

3. Describe the relation between death and love in the poem. How is that relation central to the theme?

CONNECTION TO ANOTHER SELECTION

1. Discuss the connection between love and death in "1989" and in "Thinking about Bill, Dead of AIDS" (p. 1189), by Miller Williams.

POEMS ABOUT TEACHING AND LEARNING

You've spent a significant portion of your life in school learning and being taught, and as you well know, the lessons come in many forms and sometimes at unexpected moments. The poems included in this section all depict a lesson of sorts — even if what has been taught and what has been learned are not always clear (and they are not always the same thing). With the exception of Emily Dickinson's "From all the Jails the Boys and Girls," all the poetry included here was written within the last fifty years or so, and most of it is quite recent. The contemporary nature of these poems should allow you to make some vivid and striking connections to your own experience — and it may make you grind your teeth a bit, too. As you read, think about who is learning what, how you might link each reading with another, and how you personally respond to the work in question. The lessons discovered in this poetry will undoubtedly add to your understanding that learning is a complicated matter that goes well beyond anyone's lesson plans.

In the first poem here, Emily Dickinson's description of the "Jails" inhabited by children is a metaphor that nearly every child has learned the truth of firsthand. The sense of relief and escape expressed in this poem is, however, as complicated as it is welcomed.

EMILY DICKINSON (1830–1886)

From all the Jails the Boys and Girls

c. 1881

From all the Jails the Boys and Girls
Ecstatically leap —
Beloved only Afternoon
That Prison doesn't keep

They storm the Earth and stun the Air,
A Mob of solid Bliss —
Alas — that Frowns should lie in wait
For such a Foe as this —

CONSIDERATIONS FOR CRITICAL THINKING AND WRITING

1. FIRST RESPONSE. What are the "Jails"? How are children characterized in this poem?
2. Comment on the effectiveness of the description in lines 5 and 6.
3. How might "Frowns" be read symbolically?

CONNECTION TO ANOTHER SELECTION

1. In an essay discuss the treatment of childhood in this poem and in Robert Frost's "Out, Out—" (p. 1012).

As Emily Dickinson's idea of school is complicated in her poem, the writing assignment in Langston Hughes's "Theme for English B" is more problematic than it seems — especially for the African American student who must complete it for a white teacher. There are themes within themes in this poem.

LANGSTON HUGHES (1902–1967)

Theme for English B

1949

The instructor said,

> Go home and write
> a page tonight.
> And let that page come out of you —
> Then, it will be true.   5

I wonder if it's that simple?
I am twenty-two, colored, born in Winston-Salem.
I went to school there, then Durham, then here
to this college on the hill above Harlem.
I am the only colored student in my class.   10
The steps from the hill lead down into Harlem,
through a park, then I cross St. Nicholas,
Eighth Avenue, Seventh, and I come to the Y,

the Harlem Branch Y, where I take the elevator
up to my room, sit down, and write this page: 15

It's not easy to know what is true for you or me
at twenty-two, my age. But I guess I'm what
I feel and see and hear, Harlem, I hear you:
hear you, hear me — we two — you, me, talk on this page.
(I hear New York, too.) Me — who?   20
Well, I like to eat, sleep, drink, and be in love.
I like to work, read, learn, and understand life.
I like a pipe for a Christmas present,
or records — Bessie,° bop, or Bach.
I guess being colored doesn't make me *not* like   25
the same things other folks like who are other races.
So will my page be colored that I write?
Being me, it will not be white.
But it will be
a part of you, instructor.   30
You are white —
yet a part of me, as I am part of you.
That's American.
Sometimes perhaps you don't want to be a part of me.
Nor do I often want to be a part of you.   35
But we are, that's true!
As I learn from you,
I guess you learn from me —
although you're older — and white —
and somewhat more free.   40

This is my page for English B.

24 *Bessie:* Bessie Smith (1898?–1937), a famous blues singer.

Considerations for Critical Thinking and Writing

1. FIRST RESPONSE. Try to write "a page" in response to the instructor that, like the speaker's, captures who you are.

2. What complicates the writing assignment for the speaker? Does he fulfill the assignment? Explain why or why not.

3. What are the circumstances of the speaker's life? How does the speaker respond to the question "So will my page be colored that I write?" (line 27). Discuss the tone of lines 27–40.

4. Write a one-paragraph response to this poem as you think the speaker's instructor would in grading it.

Connection to Another Selection

1. Discuss the attitudes expressed toward the United States in this poem and in Divakaruni's "Indian Movie, New Jersey" (p. 825).

While the speaker in "Theme for English B" wrote a poem as a student in a composition class, the next poem features a speaker from the other side of the assignments in a poetry class. If you've ever been in a creative writing class or simply been asked to write a poem in an English course, you may have experienced some version of what's going on in this classroom. The picture may not be pretty, but it is brilliantly drawn in Marilyn Hacker's "Groves of Academe."

MARILYN HACKER (B. 1942)

Groves of Academe   *1984*

The hour dragged on, and I was badly needing
coffee; that encouraged my perversity.
I asked the students of Poetry Writing,
"Tell me about the poetry you're reading."
There was some hair chewing and some nail biting.   5
Snowdrifts piled up around the university.
"I've really gotten into science fiction."
"I don't read much — it breaks my concentration.
I wouldn't want to influence my style."
"We taped some Sound Poems for the college station."   10
"When *I* give readings, should I work on diction?"
"Is it true that no really worthwhile
contemporary poets write in rhyme?"
"Do you think it would be a waste of time
to send my poems to *Vanity Fair*?   15
I mean — could they relate to my work there?"

CONSIDERATIONS FOR CRITICAL THINKING AND WRITING

1. FIRST RESPONSE. Characterize the speaker. How do the students compare?
2. What do the students' comments and questions in response to the teacher's request (line 4) reveal about themselves?
3. How does the speaker implicitly answer the question about poetic rhy lines 12 and 13?

CONNECTION TO ANOTHER SELECTION

1. Write an essay that compares the teachers in "Groves of Mark Halliday's "Graded Paper" (p. 1110). Which teach have teach you? Explain why.

The next four poems in this case study dep learning situations as well as various teaching As you read them, consider how much div proach can be represented, all within the c

MARK HALLIDAY (B. 1949)

Graded Paper

1991

On the whole this is quite successful work:
your main argument about the poet's ambivalence —
how he loves the very things he attacks —
is mostly persuasive and always engaging.

At the same time,   5
               there are spots
where your thinking becomes, for me,
alarmingly opaque, and your syntax seems to jump
backwards through unnecessary hoops,
as on p. 2 where you speak of "precognitive awareness   10
not yet disestablished by the shell that encrusts
each thing that a person actually says"
or at the top of p. 5 where your discussion of
"subverbal undertow miming the subversion of self-belief
woven counter to desire's outreach"   15
leaves me groping for firmer footholds.
(I'd have said it differently,
or rather, said something else.)
And when you say that women "could not fulfill themselves" (p. 6)
"in that era" (only forty years ago, after all!)   20
are you so sure that the situation is so different today?
Also, how does Whitman bluff his way into
your penultimate paragraph? He is the *last* poet
I would have quoted in this context!
What plausible way of behaving   25
does the passage you quote represent? Don't you think
literature should ultimately reveal possibilities for *action*?

Please notice how I've repaired your use of semicolons.

And yet, despite what may seem my cranky response,
I do admire the freshness of   30
  ur thinking and your style; there is
    tality here; your sentences thrust themselves forward
     a confidence as impressive as it is cheeky. . . .
     not
     me, finally,   35
     h this is an awkward problem, involving
     it ble fact that you are so young, so young
     ightful provocation.

(A-)

1.
NS FOR CRITICAL THINKING AND WRITING

How do you characterize the grader of this paper based
of the paper?

2. Is the speaker a man or a woman? What makes you think so? Does the sex of the speaker affect your reading of the poem? How?

3. Explain whether or not you think the teacher's comments on the paper are consistent with the grade awarded it. How do you account for the grade?

CONNECTION TO ANOTHER SELECTION

1. Compare the ways in which Halliday reveals the speaker's character in this poem with the strategies used by Browning in "My Last Duchess" (p. 827).

JUDY PAGE HEITZMAN (B. 1952)

The Schoolroom on the Second Floor of the Knitting Mill   *1991*

While most of us copied letters out of books,
Mrs. Lawrence carved and cleaned her nails.
Now the red and buff cardinals at my back-room window
make me miss her, her room, her hallway,
even the chimney outside   5
that broke up the sky.

In my memory it is afternoon.
Sun streams in through the door
next to the fire escape where we are lined up
getting our coats on to go out to the playground,   10
the tether ball, its towering height, the swings.
She tells me to make sure the line
does not move up over the threshold.
That would be dangerous.
So I stand guard at the door.   15
Somehow it happens
the way things seem to happen when we're not really looking,
or we are looking, just not the right way.
Kids crush up like cattle, pushing me over the line.

Judy is not a good leader is all Mrs. Lawrence says.   20
She says it quietly. Still, everybody hears.
Her arms hang down like sausages.
I hear her every time I fail.

CONSIDERATIONS FOR CRITICAL THINKING AND WRITING

1. FIRST RESPONSE. Does your impression of Mrs. Lawrence change from the beginning to the end of the poem? How?

2. How can line 2 be read as an implied metaphor?

3. Discuss the use of similes in the poem. How do they contribute to the poem's meaning?

CONNECTIONS TO OTHER SELECTIONS

1. Compare the representations and meanings of being a schoolchild in this poem with those in Dickinson's "From all the Jails the Boys and Girls" (p. 1107).

2. Discuss how the past impinges on the present in Heitzman's poem and in Larkin's "This Be the Verse" (p. 1170).

R. S. GWYNN (B. 1948)

The Classroom at the Mall

1993

Our Dean of Something thought it would be good
For Learning (even better for P.R.)
To make the school "accessible to all"
And leased the bankrupt bookstore at the Mall
A few steps from Poquito's Mexican Food   5
And Chocolate Chips Aweigh. So here we are —

Four housewives, several solemn student nurses,
Ms. Light — serious, heavy, and very dark —
Pete Fontenot, who teaches high-school shop
And is besides a part-time private cop   10
Who leaves his .38 among the purses,
And I, not quite as thin as Chaucer's Clerk —

Met for our final class while Season's Greetings
Echo subliminally with calls to buy
Whatever this year's ads deem necessary   15
For Happiness and Joy. The Virgin Mary,
Set up outside to audit our last meetings,
Adores her infant with a glassy eye.

Descend, O Musak! Hail to thee, World Lit!
Hail, Epic ("most of which was wrote in Greek")   20
And hail three hours deep in Dante's Hell
(The occupants of which no one could spell) —
As much as our tight schedule might admit
Of the Great Thoughts of Man — one thought per week.

I've lectured facing towards "The Esplanade"   25
Through plate-glass windows. Ah, what do I see?
Is that the face "that launched a thousand ships"
Awash with pimples? Oh, those chocolate chips!
Ms. Light breaks in: "Will this be for a grade?"
It's a good thing the students all face *me*.   30

One night near Halloween I filled the board
With notes on FAUST. A Pentacostal hair-
Do with a woman underneath looked in,
Copying down my scrawl with a tight grin

That threatened she'd be back with flaming sword   35
To corner me and Satan in our lair.

Tonight, though, all is calm. They take their quiz
While I sit calculating if I've made
Enough to shop for presents. From my chair
I watch the Christmas window-shoppers stare   40
At what must seem a novelty, and is,
The Church of Reason in the Stalls of Trade —

Like the blond twins who press against the door,
Accompanied by footsore, pregnant Mummy,
Who tiredly spells out for them the reason   45
I am not price-tagged as befits the season,
Explaining what is sold in such a store
With nothing but this animated dummy

Who rises, takes the papers one by one
With warm assurances that all shall pass   50
Because "requirements have been met," because
I am an academic Santa Claus,
Because mild-mannered Pete's strapped on his gun.
Ms. Light declares she has enjoyed the class:

"They sure had thoughts, those old guys," she begins,   55
Then falters for the rest. And I agree
Because, for once, I've nothing left to say
And couldn't put it better anyway.
I pack the tests, gather my grading pens,
And fumble in my jacket for the key,   60

With time to spend and promises to keep
And not one "hidden meaning" to the tale,
Among these drifting schools of moon-eyed teens,
License and credit pulsing in their jeans,
Who circle, hungry for the choice and cheap —   65
Something of value, soon to go on sale.

CONSIDERATIONS FOR CRITICAL THINKING AND WRITING

1. FIRST RESPONSE. What expectations does the title of the poem set up for you? What values are juxtaposed between the classroom and the mall?

2. How does the first stanza characterize both the speaker and the school?

3. Discuss the poem's humor. Locate and analyze specific lines that strike you as especially amusing. What is the point of this humor?

4. What is the theme? Can you find the theme summed up or alluded to in a specific passage, or is the theme implicit? Explain.

CONNECTION TO ANOTHER SELECTION

1. How do the students in this poem compare with those in Marilyn Hacker's "Groves of Academe" (p. 1109)? Where would you rather be a student? Why?

RICHARD WAKEFIELD (B. 1952)

In a Poetry Workshop

1999

Let us begin with the basics of modern verse.
Meter, of course, is forbidden, and lines must be,
like life, broken arbitrarily
lest anyone mistake us for budding Wordsworths
(don't be alarmed if you've never heard of him).   5
Rhyme is allowed, but only in moderation
and preferably very slant. Alliteration
and assonance must only be used at whim
so the reader doesn't think we're playing God
by sneaking in a pattern of sounds and echoes.   10
As for subjects, the modern poet knows
that modern readers prefer the decidedly odd,
so flowers, except for weeds, are out, and love,
except the very weed-like, is also out.
So thistles and incest are fine to write about   15
but roses and happy marriage get the shove
into the editor's outbox with hardly a glance.
Now note that language matters, so "I" must be
in lower case, thus "i," to show that we
don't put on airs despite our government grants.   20
This also shows we've read our Marx and know
the self is a bourgeois fiction. We understand
the common speech, and so the ampersand,
pronounced "uhn," replaces "and," although
judicious use of allusions to classical thought   25
will keep the great unwashed from getting our drift,
while those outside of Plato's cave will lift
a knowing eyebrow, declaring our work "well-wrought."
And speaking of work, this is not a "class":
We modern poets roll up our sleeves and write   30
our verse in "workshops," no place for sissies, we fight
to find "a voice," and only the fittest pass.
I've summarized these rules in a convenient list,
it's wallet-sized, laminated, so keep
it handy, use it, recite it in your sleep.   35
First poems are due tomorrow. You're dismissed.

CONSIDERATIONS FOR CRITICAL THINKING AND WRITING

1. FIRST RESPONSE. What are the speaker's attitudes toward modern poetry?
   How does this parallel the speaker's attitudes toward students?

2. How accurate do you think the speaker's assessment of modern poetry is?
   Explain why you agree or disagree.

3. What about that list of rules on the "wallet-sized, laminated" card? How
   does this reveal the speaker to you?

4. Write a character sketch of a teacher who reminds you of this kind of instructor. No names, please.

CONNECTION TO ANOTHER SELECTION

1. How does the speaker's use of language in this poem suggest a very different sort of teacher than Mark Halliday's in "Graded Paper" (p. 1110)?

SUGGESTED TOPICS FOR LONGER PAPERS

1. Choose one of the love poems in this chapter and compare its themes with the lyrics of a contemporary love song in terms of poetic elements such as diction, tone, images, figures of speech, sounds, and rhythms.

2. Which one of the poems about teaching and learning most speaks to your own experiences as a student? As you discuss the thematics of the poem, fold in your own personal response and experience using Robert Sward's essay "A Personal Analysis of 'The Love Song of J. Alfred Prufrock'" (p. 1079) as a model.

3. **MULTIMEDIA PROJECT.** Put together a portfolio of popular songs about school (ask around—nearly everyone can recall at least one example—or use the Internet), and analyze them in terms of their style, themes, historical context, or whatever interests you most about them.

Web *For help with this project, use the Multimedia Project Guides Online at*
http://www.bedfordstmartins.com/meyer/bedintrolit

Brief Biographies of Selected Poets

The following biographical notes for selected poets represented in this book briefly describe their writings and lives in order to provide contexts that will enhance your readings of their poems. Poets who are in some way connected to one another and referred to in a biographical note are cross-referenced to their own entry by way of small capital letters. For example, in the entry for Gwendolyn Brooks, cross-references appear for Langston Hughes, T. S. Eliot, Ezra Pound, E. E. Cummings, and Carl Sandburg. In addition, at the end of many of the entries, you'll also find a revealing or provocative quotation from the poet to stimulate your reading and thinking about the poetry.

A. R. AMMONS (AMERICAN, 1926–2001). Born on a farm outside Whiteville, North Carolina, Archie Randolph Ammons was educated at Wake Forest College, where he earned his bachelor of science degree in 1949. He wrote his first poetry aboard a U.S. Navy destroyer in the South Pacific. After a two-year at the University of California, Berkeley, Ammons became an executive of a New Jersey glass-making firm. In 1964, he took a teaching position at Cornell University and remained there until his death. His first book, *Doxology, Ommateum, Expressions of a major; a second book combines, essays, compiled observations, his first book suggests the eye of an ins skepticism; many or light through syn ... some measure ... have been

several editions, among them *Collected Poems: 1951–1971* (1972), *The Selected Poems: 1951–1977* (1977), and *Selected Longer Poems* (1980). His poetry received many awards, including the Lannan Poetry Award (1992), the National Book Critics Circle Award (1981), the Bollingen Prize (1975), and the National Book Award (1973). One of the first recipients of a MacArthur Fellowship, he received other fellowships from the Guggenheim Foundation and the American Academy of Arts and Letters.

MATTHEW ARNOLD (ENGLISH, 1822–1888). Matthew Arnold was born in Middlesex and educated at Winchester, Rugby, and Balliol College, Oxford. While at Oxford, he won the Newdigate Prize for poetry with his poem "Cromwell." He traveled abroad in the late 1840s, and by 1851 he was working as an inspector of schools, a position that brought him financial security enough ... marry Frances Lucy Wightman. He held ... post until 1886, working tirelessly to ... ve English education. What Arnold's poetic career lacked in longevity, it compensated for in variety. There are lyrics — the "Marguerite" poems (based on a Swiss girl he met in the 1840s) and "Dover Beach" — as well as poetic drama, narrative poems, and elegies. After the 1867 volume *New Poems,* he wrote prose for the rest of his life, becoming one of the most influential literary and cultural critics of his age. Like many Victorian thinkers, he was absorbed with the theological controversies of the time, the rise of Darwinism, and the loss of faith, and he writes movingly of intellectuals "wandering between two worlds, / One dead, the other powerless to be born." His prose volumes *Essays in Criticism* and *Culture and Anarchy* are valuable for their pioneering and synthetic approach to a kind of total culture, "the pursuit of total perfection by means of getting to know, on all the matters which most concern us, the best which has been thought and said in the world."

Quotable: "Poetry is simply the most beautiful, impressive and wisely effective mode of saying things, and hence its importance." — *Essays in Criticism*

MARGARET ATWOOD (CANADIAN, B. 1939). As does much of her work, Margaret Atwood's retelling of how she became a poet blurs the line between the poetic and prosaic, the mundane and the marvelous: "The day I became a poet was a sunny day of no particular ominousness. I was walking across the football field . . . scuttling along in my usual furtive way, suspecting no ill, when a large invisible thumb descended from the sky and pressed down on the top of my head. A poem formed." This "gift from an anonymous donor," she recall was "both exciting and sinister at the time." Born in 1939 in Ottawa, Ontario wood has become one of the noted writers of her time, as well known for of fiction as for her poetry. After first at Victoria College, *Game,* appeared in Toronto, and Harvard she has produced collection of poems, novels, children's books in many genres — for the screen and re-duced a novel, *The Handmaid's* television T

leased as a film in 1990. Her poetry collections include *Selected Poems* (1976), *Selected Poems II* (1986), and *Eating Fire: Selected Poems 1965–1995*. She has been the recipient of numerous literary awards; from 1981 to 1982 she served as president of the Writers' Union of Canada and from 1984 to 1986 as president of International P.E.N., Canadian Centre. She lives in Toronto.

W. H. AUDEN (ENGLISH, 1907–1973). The most influential English poet of the generation immediately following that of YEATS and ELIOT, Wystan Hugh Auden was born in 1907 in York. He was educated at St. Edmund's preparatory school (where his future collaborator Christopher Isherwood was a pupil) and later at Christ Church, Oxford. While at Oxford, he met Stephen Spender, C. Day-Lewis, and Louis MacNeice, all of whom would, with Auden, soon announce a new voice in English letters. After graduation, Auden took a post as a schoolmaster and worked on film documentaries for the English Postal Service. His early books, beginning with *Poems* (1930), and especially *Look Stranger!* (1936), quickly established him as a leading poet. He wrote plays with Isherwood during the 1930s and spent time in Spain as an ambulance driver for the Republicans in the Spanish Civil War. He emigrated to the United States in 1939 and became an American citizen in 1946. Before this time, Auden's work showed strong leftist and materialistic sympathies. Marx and reveal a deep interest read poems are influenced by his in psychology. Following his move to America, Auden converted to the Anglican Church. While his interest in Freud continued, many of his earlier political sympathies fell away; Anglicanism informs a large part of his later poetry. He became professor of poetry at Oxford in 1956 and returned to live there in 1972. Much of his later life was spent in Austria; he died there, at Kirchstetten, in 1973.

Quotable: "Speaking for myself, the questions which interest me most when reading a poem are two. The first is technical: 'Here is a verbal contraption. How does it work?' The second is, in the broadest sense, moral: 'What kind of guy inhabits this poem? What is his notion of the good life or the good place? His notion of the Evil One?

What does he conceal from the reader? What does he conceal even from himself?'"
— *The Dyer's Hand*

ELIZABETH BISHOP (AMERICAN, 1911–1979). Elizabeth Bishop was born in Worcester, Massachusetts in 1911. Following the death of her father and her mother's mental illness, Bishop was raised by her grandparents in Nova Scotia and in Worcester. She was educated at Vassar and lived after that in New York, France, Mexico, Key West, and, for sixteen years, Brazil. These varied landscapes and experiences inform her 1965 volume of poems, *Questions of Travel,* and much of her later work. Her *Poems: North and South a Cold Spring* (1955) won the Pulitzer Prize; *Complete Poems* (1969) won the National Book Award. Her poetry, like that of her longtime friend MARIANNE MOORE, is admired for its fastidious attention to the natural world, as well as for its muted irony and humor. ROBERT LOWELL and RANDALL JARRELL thought her work exquisite; Lowell modeled his "Skunk Hour" after Bishop, to whom the poem is dedicated. *Collected Prose,* published in 1984, includes autobiographical sketches, travel accounts, a memoir of Marianne Moore, and short stories. She lived in Cambridge, Massachusetts, during the last years of her life, teaching at Harvard.

WILLIAM BLAKE (ENGLISH, 1757–1827). Poet, mystic, engraver, painter, William Blake remains one of the most ʼilliam Blake popular figures of English matic, and was born in London in 1757 ancure. He to school. Educated at home, went widely in Milton, Shakespeare, ʰad Bible, and somehow picked up a know of French, Italian, Latin, Greek, and brew. At fourteen, Blake was apprenticed an engraver. His talent for art flourished and he was eventually made a member of London's Royal Academy. In 1782 he married Catherine Boucher, and the two would work together for the rest of their lives developing colored engravings of Blake's poems. His first book, *Poetical Sketches* (1783), was printed by friends. In 1789 he published *Songs of Innocence,* followed in 1794 by *Songs of Experience.* At times deceptively simple, at others most profound, these lyrics express Blake's ardent belief in

the freedom of the imagination and his scorn of rationalism and materialism. Also issued during this time were his mystical and prophetic works, *The Book of Thel* (1789) and his principle prose work, *The Marriage of Heaven and Hell* (1791). In 1793 the Blakes moved to Lambeth, south of London, and here Blake began work on *The Book of Job,* arguably his finest illustrations, completed when he was nearly seventy. Largely dismissed in his time as eccentric, even mad, his books attracted no more than a circle of readers. At his death in 1827 he was buried in an unmarked grave.

Quotable: "If the doors of perception were cleansed every thing would appear to man as it is: infinite."
— *The Marriage of Heaven and Hell*

ROBERT BLY (AMERICAN, B. 1926). Of Norwegian descent, Robert Bly was born in Madison, Minnesota, in 1926. Following naval service in World War II, he attended St. Olaf College before transferring to Harvard, where he earned his degree in 1950. While at Harvard, and during several years' residence in New York, he wrote the poems that form his first book, *The Lute of Three Loudnesses.* Of them he has said, "The early poems I wrote were musical, but the 'I' in them had no weight. I lived for several years in various parts of New York City, longing for 'the depths,' by which I meant the fruitful depths. I was already underground, but in a solitary dry well, not a depth." In his later poems, especially in their exploration of the unconscious, of myth, and of psychological landscapes, he was to discover a fruitful depth that has informed most of his work since. His poems, along with those of JAMES WRIGHT and W. S. MERWIN, have been called poems of "the deep image," full of quiet archetypal resonance culled from natural world. His work also has a political dimension; during the Vietnam War oled American Writers against the for ʳ and was an ardent supporter ously He has also been responsible Americ into English many previ- PABLO NE European and South farm in Mi gene Montale and *Quotable:* hem. He lives on a go from somewhere else. The ʲourneys. They ʳe else. The best poems take long journeys. I like poetry best that journeys — while remaining in the human scale — to the other world, which may be a place as easily overlooked as a bee's wing. . . . The old people say that each object in the universe — seashell, bat's wing, pine cone, patch of lichen — contains some fragment of our missing soul, and so our soul is thin. Making journeys of this sort could be called thickening the soul."

— Selected Poems

ANNE BRADSTREET (AMERICAN, 1612–1672). The first American poet to be published in America, Anne Bradstreet was born in England in 1612, the daughter of Thomas Dudley, former steward to the earl of London. At sixteen she married Simon Bradstreet and sailed two years later for America with her husband and father, both of whom eventually became governors of Massachusetts. She lived in Ipswich, then in Andover, and had eight children. Her first collection of poems, *The Tenth Muse*, was published without her knowledge in 1650 by her brother-in-law in London. The book concerns itself with historical, cosmological, and metaphysical matters; it is conventional in style, and shows the influence of Spenser, SIDNEY, and Raleigh. Along with the familiar preoccupations of the age — time and mutability — it contains elegies on Sidney and on Queen Elizabeth. A second edition, with corrections and additions, appeared in Boston six years after the poet's death. In this group, Bradstreet turns more frequently towards the personal, often addressing domestic topics from a religious point of view. This latter group contains elegies on her children and the poems to her beloved husband.

GWENDOLYN BROOKS (AMERICAN, 1917–2000). Though born in Topeka, Kansas, Gwendolyn Brooks is most closely associated with Chicago, particularly with the city's South Side, where her family moved shortly after her birth and where she lived until her death. She was educated at Wilson Junior College and taught at Columbia College (Chicago), Northeastern Illinois University, Columbia University, and the University of Wisconsin, to name a few. Early in her writing career, she met LANGSTON HUGHES, who encouraged her to read the poetry of T. S. ELIOT, EZRA POUND, and E. E. CUMMINGS — all of whom had some impact on her development. In the 1960s her work took a turning point, influenced by the politically and socially radical Black Arts Movement. Her poetry has been distinguished by its variety of voices and styles — traditional and experimental — and Brooks herself by her consummate command of technique. She authored more than twenty books of poetry, beginning with *A Street in Bronzeville* (1945), followed by *Annie Allen* (1949), for which she received the Pulitzer Prize (the first time that honor had been conveyed to a black poet). Her *Selected Poems* appeared in 1982. In 1986 she was named poetry consultant to the Library of Congress, and she succeeded CARL SANDBURG in 1968 as poet laureate of Illinois. She was also the author of a novel, an autobiography, and critical prose.

ELIZABETH BARRETT BROWNING (ENGLISH, 1806–1861). The eldest of twelve children, Elizabeth Barrett Browning was born at Coxhoe Hall, near Durham, in 1806. She spent most of her childhood and youth at the family estate of Hope End, near Malvern. She was an avid learner and began to write verse at an early age. Her first volume, *The Battle of Marathon,* was privately printed in 1820, and a second book followed in 1826. In 1832 the family moved to London, where Elizabeth began to associate with literary circles. Her volume *The Seraphim and Other Poems* (1838) was well received, and *Poems* (1844) attracted considerable acclaim. One of its admirers, ROBERT BROWNING, initiated a correspondence; the two met in 1843 and fell in love. Seeking to avoid her father's suspected prohibitions, they eloped in 1846 and left for Italy. There, in Florence, their son Robert was born in 1849. In 1850, Elizabeth published a further volume of poems, among them the *Sonnets from the Portuguese,* which had been composed during her and Robert's courtship ("Portuguese" being his pet name for her). Her fame continued to grow; she was the foremost woman poet of her time, and at WORDSWORTH's death there was talk of making her poet laureate. She died in Florence in 1861. Her husband prepared her posthumous *Last Poems* for publication later that year.

ROBERT BROWNING (ENGLISH, 1812–1889).
One of the most famous poets of the Victorian age, Robert Browning was the son of a bank clerk. He received little formal education, though he read voraciously from his father's library. He wrote poems from an early age, taking as his model SHELLEY, under whose influence he briefly became a vegetarian and touted atheistic principles. Until the publication of *Paracelsus* (1835) and *Bells and Pomegranates* (1841–1846), his poetry attracted little attention. His first volume, *Pauline: A Fragment of a Confession,* published anonymously in 1833, prompted a strong reaction from John Stuart Mill: in these poems the philosopher noted "a more intense and morbid self-consciousness than I ever knew in any sane human being." Such censure may have been responsible for Browning's subsequent turning to the creation of dramatic characters and his development of the dramatic monologue, a form now associated almost exclusively with him. In 1846 he married Elizabeth Barrett and the two moved to Florence, where he composed *Men and Women* (1855) and *Dramatis Personae* (1864). After the death of his wife, he returned to London, where he wrote his masterpiece, *The Ring and the Book* (1869). He died in 1889 while visiting his son in Venice. His request for burial in Florence being impossible to fulfill, his body was returned to England and buried in Westminster Abbey. His work, especially the dramatic monologues, had great influence on writers in the early twentieth century, notably EZRA POUND.

GEORGE GORDON, LORD BYRON (ENGLISH, 1788–1824). Lord Byron — poet, celebrity, and father of the "Byronic hero" — was born in London. Descended from James I, his mother was a Scottish heiress. His father, "Mad Jack" Byron, was a captain notorious for squandering the family's money. Wishing to avoid creditors, his father fled to France, where he died when his son was three. Byron's mother returned to Scotland, and the boy was educated at home and at Aberdeen Grammar School. He went on to study at Cambridge, where he published a small volume of verse, *Fugitive Pieces* (1807), followed by *Hours of Idleness* in the same year. The second volume was attacked for its pretension in the *Edinburgh Review;*

Byron responded with his satirical *English Bards and Scotch Reviewers* (1809). Soon after taking his seat in the House of Lords, Byron left on a tour of the Mediterranean, an experience that informed the first two cantos of *Childe Harold's Pilgrimage* (1812), completed after his return. Of its publication and immediate success, Byron later wrote, "I awoke one morning and found myself famous." Following his brief marriage to Annabella Milbanke and the ensuing scandal over their separation, Byron left England for Switzerland and never returned. He met the poet SHELLEY and lived for two years in Venice, where he completed the first cantos of *Don Juan* (1819–1824) and other important works. Ever a man of action, he was an ardent supporter of the Italian revolutionaries. He died in 1824 assisting the Greek war for independence.

LEWIS CARROLL (ENGLISH, 1832–1898).
Charles Lutwidge Dodgson was born in Cheshire, the son of a scholarly country parson. He was educated at Yorkshire Grammar School, at Rugby, and at Christ Church, Oxford, where he studied mathematics. Following graduation, he took a university teaching post and was ordained to the ministry in 1861. He taught and preached only rarely, however, due to his shyness and a bad stammer. He published mathematical textbooks and occasional comic writing, but it was in 1865, with the publication of *Alice's Adventures under Ground* (now generally known as *Alice in Wonderland*), that he became immediately established as a children's writer of the first order. Indeed, the book was revolutionary in its time for its absence of educational or religious pieties, seeking instead to amuse for amusement's sake. His later successes include *Through the Looking-Glass and What Alice Found There* (1871) and nonsense poems such as *The Hunting of the Snark* (1876) and "Jabberwocky."

JOHN CIARDI (AMERICAN, 1916–1986). John Ciardi — poet, critic, translator, and editor — was born in Boston and grew up in the nearby suburb of Medford. He studied at Tufts University and at the University of Michigan before serving as an aerial gunner aboard B-29 bombers in World War II. Among his nearly forty volumes of poetry are *Homeward to America* (1940); *Other Skies* (1947), a collection of war poems; *In the Stoneworks* (1961); and *Manner of Speaking* (1972). His *Selected Poems* was published in 1984. He is widely known for his translation of Dante's *Divine Comedy* (1954–1970) into colloquial American verse. His works of criticism include *How Does a Poem Mean?* (1950) and *Dialogue with an Audience* (1963). From 1956 to 1972 he was poetry editor of *Saturday Review/World;* he taught at the University of Kansas and at Harvard and Rutgers Universities and lectured at the annual Bread Loaf Writers' Conference at Middlebury College in Vermont. From 1980 on, Ciardi broadcast a popular weekly program on etymology titled "A Word in Your Ear."

Quotable: "What has any poet to trust more than the feel of the thing? Theory concerns him only until he picks up his pen, and it begins to concern him again as soon as he lays it down." — *New York Times*

SAMUEL TAYLOR COLERIDGE (ENGLISH, 1772–1834). The poet, philosopher, and critic Samuel Taylor Coleridge was born at Ottery St. Mary, Devon, where his father was vicar. He entered Jesus College, Cambridge, in 1791, intending a profession in the church, but abandoned his studies in 1793 to enlist in the Light Dragoons. His first poems were published in 1794, but it was in 1798, in *Lyrical Ballads,* that his mature writing appeared. The book was a collaborative venture between Coleridge and WILLIAM WORDSWORTH. In that work, and in their later poems, the two not only laid the foundations of English Romanticism but also expanded the contours of poetic form. One of Coleridge's most important developments was the conversation poem, which was influential on later forms such as the dramatic monologue and the confessional poem. He also experimented with preexisting forms, ranging from the ballad (*Lyrical Ballads* included his *Rime of the Ancient Mariner*) to the ode. His visionary fragment, "Kubla Khan," was written in 1797. Despite his break with Wordsworth after 1810 and the decline of his poetic powers (due in part to a long-term opium addiction), Coleridge continued to write philosophical and social tracts, as well as sermons and literary criticism. His magnum

opus, *Biographia Literaria,* belongs to this later period. Revolutionary in thought, catholic in work and taste, Coleridge has continued to inspire generations of writers since his death in 1834.

Quotable: "The poet, described in *ideal* perfection, brings the whole soul of man into activity, with the subordination of its faculties to each other, according to their relative worth and dignity. He diffuses a tone and spirit of unity, that blends, and (as it were) *fuses,* each into each, by that synthetic and magical power . . . imagination." — *Biographia Literaria,* Chapter 14

COUNTEE CULLEN (AMERICAN, 1903–1946). A leading poet of the Harlem Renaissance, Countee Cullen was born in New York and was brought up by foster parents there. He attended New York University and Harvard. His first book, *Color* (1925), showed a poet highly adept at traditional forms. Later volumes include *Copper Sun* (1927) and *The Ballad of the Brown Girl: An Old Ballad Retold* (1927). Cullen received a Guggenheim fellowship and went to France; while there, he wrote *The Black Christ and Other Poems* (1929). He authored one novel, *One Way to Heaven* (1932), and collaborated with Arna Bontemps on the play *St. Louis Woman* (1946). His 1935 collection, *The Medea and Some Poems,* combines sonnets and other lyrics with a translation of Euripides' tragedy. He edited the magazine *Opportunity* and an anthology of black poetry, *Caroling Dusk* (1927).

E. E. CUMMINGS (AMERICAN, 1894–1962). One of the more eccentric poets of the twentieth century, Edward Estlin Cummings was born in 1894 in Cambridge, Massachusetts. His father was a Unitarian minister who also taught sociology at Harvard. Cummings attended Harvard, taking his B.A. in 1915 and his M.A. in 1916. Following graduation, he volunteered to go to France and serve in the ambulance corps. After the war he lived in Paris, where he took up painting as well as writing. His first book of poems, *Tulips and Chimneys,* was published in 1923, followed by *XLI Poems* in 1925. But it is in *&* and *is 5* (both published 1925) that his innovative style begins to appear. Influenced by jazz rhythms and slang, and marked by idiosyncratic use of syntax, punctuation, and typography, Cummings's poetry is antiestablishment. It bridles at rules, regulations, and restrictions, which he thought corroded the fluid life of the soul. Against science, mechanism, and the collective tyranny of "manunkind" he holds the spontaneous, childlike "is"-ness of the individual. His heroes are typically the poor, the misfits, the lovers, those who dare to be themselves. He is best known for his satires and love poems. He died in Conway, New Hampshire, in 1962 and is buried in the Forest Hills Cemetery in Boston.

JAMES DICKEY (AMERICAN, 1923–1997). "Gothic," "surreal," "morbid," "grotesque"—such are the terms some critics use to describe the poetry of James Dickey. Born in Atlanta, Georgia, as a boy Dickey was inspired by the poetry of LORD BYRON. He also loved athletics and was a high school football star. These interests combine in his ideal of the poet as a man of action, as one who walks "the razor's edge between sublimity and absurdity." Dickey entered Clemson College in 1942, but left after a year to serve in the air force in World War II. He completed his undergraduate education at Vanderbilt University following the war, and went on for graduate study there and later at Rice University. His first book of poems, *Into the Stone and Other Poems,* was published in 1960, but his reputation was secured by *Drowning with Others* (1962) and *Helmets* (1964), both drawing on his experiences as a pilot. Most of his work has been gathered in *Whole Motion: Collected Poems 1948–1992* (1992). Dickey traveled widely and taught at a variety of universities besides working for a number of years as a writer of advertisements. Between 1966 and 1968 he was poetry consultant to the Library of Congress. In addition to his poems, he is best known for his novel *Deliverance* (1970), for which he also wrote the screenplay.

JOHN DONNE (ENGLISH, 1572–1631). John Donne was born in London. Though educated at Oxford and Cambridge, he left without taking any degrees. During the 1590s he traveled widely, read voraciously, and lived the mayfly life of a courtier in Queen Elizabeth's court. In 1601 he married Ann Moore, still a minor, an offense for which he was briefly imprisoned and left unemployed. Ann died in 1617, leaving him with seven children. In 1621, however, Donne's prospects turned: King James, convinced of his promise as a preacher, made Donne the dean of St. Paul's Cathedral, a position he held until his death in 1631. Donne's metaphysical poetry is characterized by passionate thought and intellectual play; it delights in puns, paradox, poses, and conceits. In love poems such as "The Good Morrow" and "Go and Catch a Falling Star," Donne injected life into the tired Petrarchan conventions of the 1590s. Similarly, in his *Holy Sonnets* he infused English religious verse with sinewy toughness. Though his poetry fell out of favor in the seventeenth and eighteenth centuries, it has since been reclaimed as one of the treasures of English Renaissance literature.

HILDA DOOLITTLE (AMERICAN, 1886–1961). Also known by her pseudonym, H. D., Hilda Doolittle was born in Bethlehem, Pennsylvania, in 1886. In 1911 she went to London, where she married the poet Richard Aldingham in 1913. She became associated with EZRA POUND (to whom she had been briefly engaged) and with him developed the literary form Imagism, which seeks among other things concrete expression of a particular experience. Pound arranged for her early work to be published in *Poetry* magazine and in the anthology *Des Imagistes* (1914). Her first collection of poems, *Sea Garden,* appeared in 1916, followed by *Hymen* (1921), *Heliodora and Other Poems* (1924), and *Red Roses for Bronze* (1929). Her work is heavily informed by the classical Greek tradition; indeed she produced numerous translations of Sappho, Meleager, Euripides, and others. Her fiction includes *Palimpsest* and *Hedylus* (both published 1928); three additional works, *Pilate's Wife, Asphodel,* and *Her,* were published posthumously as *Hermione* in 1981. After her divorce in 1937, she settled near Lake Geneva and continued a stream of literary output: *Trilogy* (1944–1946), a description of London during the blitz of World War II; *By Avon River* (1949), a tribute to SHAKESPEARE and other Elizabethans; *Bid Me to Live* (1960), which treats London during World War I; and *Helen in Egypt* (1961), a long poem about Helen of Troy. A final set of poetic sequences was published in 1972.

PAUL LAURENCE DUNBAR (AMERICAN, 1872–1906). Paul Laurence Dunbar was born in Dayton, Ohio, the son of former slaves. His first collection of poems, *Oak and Ivy*, was printed privately in 1893. A second collection, *Majors and Minors*, appeared in 1895. William Dean Howells, influential novelist and journalist, took an interest in Dunbar's work and wrote the preface to his third volume, *Lyrics of Lowly Life* (1896). His later collections of poetry include *Lyrics of the Hearthside* (1899), *Lyrics of Love and Laughter* (1903), and *Lyrics of Sunshine and Shadow* (1905). Dunbar achieved national recognition in his time, conducted numerous lecture tours, and was known primarily as a writer of dialect verse. Since then, his poems have fallen under criticism for their alleged sentimental treatment of black life in the South. In addition to poetry, he wrote four novels: *The Uncalled* (1898), *The Love of Landry* (1900), *The Fanatics* (1901), and *The Sport of the Gods* (1902).

MARTÍN ESPADA (AMERICAN, B. 1957). Hailed as "well on his way to becoming the Latino poet of his generation," Martín Espada writes a primarily political poetry that seeks to combine politics with art, to find what he calls the "political imagination [which] goes beyond protest to articulate an artistry of dissent." Claiming WALT WHITMAN and PABLO NERUDA as precursors, Espada has allied himself with poets who, against the suffering and injustice of the world, sing "defiant, extravagant hope." Born in Brooklyn in 1957, Espada was early immersed in the climate of political activism by his father, a leader in the Puerto Rican community. "Long Island was tough when you were the only Puerto Rican in town. I needed a way to respond. I think writing poetry is a great way to assert your humanity. So I started to do that, and I never looked back." His 1996 collection *Imagine the Angels of Bread* won the American Book Award. Other books of poetry include *Rebellion Is the Circle of a Lover's Hand* (1990) and *City of Coughing and Dead Radiators* (1993); a collection of essays, *Zapata's Disciple*, appeared in 1998. The recipient of a Massachusetts Artists' Fellowship, a PEN/Revson Fellowship, and the Paterson Poetry Prize, he teaches at the University of Massachusetts in Amherst.

Quotable: "Poetry of the political imagination is a matter of both vision and language. Any progressive social change must be imagined first, and that vision must find its most eloquent possible expression to move from vision to reality."
— *Zapata's Disciple*

ALLEN GINSBERG (AMERICAN, 1926–1997). Leading Beat poet Allen Ginsberg was born in Newark, New Jersey. His father was a high school teacher, his mother a Communist who may have encouraged her son's radical views. Ginsberg grew up in Paterson, New Jersey, where he fell under the tutelage of WILLIAM CARLOS WILLIAMS. He attended Columbia, where he met fellow writers Jack Kerouac and William Burroughs. He completed his B.A. in 1948, after a temporary suspension, and in 1953 left for San Francisco, where he joined Kerouac, Burroughs, Lawrence Ferlinghetti, and others associated with the newly emerging Beat movement. In 1956 his first collection, *Howl and Other Poems,* appeared. Numerous collections followed, significantly *Kaddish and Other Poems* (1961), *Reality Sandwiches* (1963), and *Poems All Over the Place: Mostly Seventies* (1978). His *Collected Poems* appeared in 1984. In addition to poems, he wrote two plays and several volumes of prose. Ginsberg's style is, like that of his predecessor WALT WHITMAN, open, expansive, at times journalistic, always improvisatory. Apart from Whitman, he claimed WILLIAM BLAKE as an influence, and he shares with both the vision of poet as prophet. Over the course of his career, his work continued to open American poetry to a new range of styles and subjects.
Quotable: "[I see myself] as someone in the tradition of the oldtime American transcendentalist individualism . . . Thoreau, Emerson . . . Whitman . . . just carrying it on into the 20th century." — *Interview*

THOMAS HARDY (ENGLISH, 1840–1928). Thomas Hardy was born in Higher Brockhampton near Dorchester, a town that would become the center of his fictional Wessex. He attended a village school in Dorchester, where he studied to be an architect. At twenty-two he moved to London and began to write his first verses. Unable to publish his poetry, however, Hardy turned to fiction. His first successful novel, *Far from the Madding Crowd*, appeared in 1874 and allowed him to marry Emma Gifford. Hardy took up writing as a profession and produced a stream of remarkable novels, notably *The Return of the Native* (1878), *The Mayor of Casterbridge* (1886), *Tess of the D'Urbervilles* (1891), and *Jude the Obscure* (1896). Following the cold reception of *Jude*, Hardy turned again to poetry, of which he published a vast amount during the remaining thirty years of his life. Collections such as *Wessex Poems and Other Verses* (1898), *Poems of the Past and Present* (1902), and *Satires of Circumstance, Lyrics and Reveries* (1914) contain sardonic lyrics (Hardy had long been known as a pessimist) as well as moving elegies to his wife, who died in 1912. In addition to poems and novels, he wrote two plays, *The Dynasts* (1903–1908) and *The Famous Tragedy of the Queen of Cornwall* (1923). Technically and metrically adroit, Hardy's work strongly influenced later poets such as W. H. AUDEN, PHILIP LARKIN, and DYLAN THOMAS.

ROBERT HASS (AMERICAN, B. 1941). Born in San Francisco of German and Irish parents, Robert Hass was educated at St. Mary's College and at Stanford University. His first book of poems, *Field Guide* (1973), was selected by the poet Stanley Kunitz as a winner of the prestigious Yale Series of Younger Poets Award. Other collections include *Praise* (1979), *Human Wishes* (1989), *Sun under Wood: New Poems* (1996), and a volume of criticism, *Twentieth Century Pleasures: Prose on Poetry* (1984); the latter two won National Book Critics Circle Awards. Hass has also published translations from the Japanese of Bashō, Buson, and Issa (*The Essential Haiku*, 1994) and has collaborated with the Polish poet Czeslaw Milosz on *Unattainable Earth* (1986), *Provinces* (1993), and *Facing the River* (1995); with Robert Pinsky he has translated Milosz's *The Separate Notebooks* (1983). From 1995 to 1997 he served as poet laureate of the United States. He has taught at the State University of New York, Buffalo, and at St. Mary's College, California; since 1987 he has been a professor of English at the University of California, Berkeley.

ROBERT HAYDEN (AMERICAN, 1913–1980). Robert Hayden once described himself as "a

romantic forced to be realistic." Hayden was raised by a foster family in the Detroit ghetto sardonically nicknamed "Paradise Valley." After a traumatic childhood in a house fraught with "chronic angers," Hayden attended Detroit City College (later Wayne State University) and worked for the Federal Writers' Project, where he was chief researcher on negro history and folklore. His first book, *Heart-Shape in the Dust* (1940), showed Hayden's awareness of Harlem Renaissance writers such as LANGSTON HUGHES and COUNTEE CULLEN. Later collections would continue to explore the complexities of African American life. In 1941 Hayden enrolled in the graduate program at the University of Michigan. There he studied under W. H. AUDEN, who turned his attention to matters of poetic technique and form. He won the Jule and Avery Hopwood Prize for Poetry in 1942 and in 1944. After graduation, he taught for several years at Michigan, then took a post at Fisk University. In 1969 he returned to Michigan to complete his teaching career. During the 1960s Hayden's poetry received international attention; his book *The Ballad of Remembrance* (1966) won the grand prize at the First World Festival of Negro Arts in Dakar, Senegal. In 1976 he became the first black American to be appointed poetry consultant to the Library of Congress.

Quotable: "There is no such thing as Black literature. There's good literature and bad. That's all."

—*Dictionary of Literary Biography*

SEAMUS HEANEY (IRISH, B. 1939). Of Seamus Heaney's poetry, fellow poet and former classmate Seamus Deane has said, "At the root of every word there is a tentacular handshake between the speaker and the thing spoken of." Indeed, it is this tactile correspondence between things and their representations that has attracted readers to Heaney's work since his first volume of poetry appeared in 1966. He was born in Mossbawn, County Derry, into a Roman Catholic farming family. The landscape of rural Mossbawn figures prominently in his early poetry, particularly in his first two books, *Death of a Naturalist* (1966) and *Door into the Dark* (1969), as do the memories of childhood. In later works, particularly in his acclaimed collection *North* (1975), he turns to confront the greater political and historical matters of Ireland. He was educated at St. Columb's College and at Queen's University, Belfast. After a stint as a lecturer at the University of California, Berkeley, he left Northern Ireland, moving first to County Wicklow and then to Dublin. In 1984 he was appointed Boylston Professor of Rhetoric at Harvard and in 1989 professor of poetry at Oxford. He won the Nobel Prize for Literature in 1995, the third Irish writer after YEATS to achieve that honor. Recently, his poetry has lightened in tone, though not in expressive vigor: his latest books, *Seeing Things* (1991) and *The Spirit Level* (1996), aim "to credit marvels." Apart from poetry, he has published three volumes of criticism and one play. He divides his time between Dublin and Cambridge, Massachusetts.

Quotable: "I have always listened for poems, they come sometimes like bodies come out of a bog, almost complete, seeming to have been laid down a long time ago, surfacing with a touch of mystery. They certainly involve craft and determination, but chance and instinct have a role in the thing too." —*Preoccupations*

GEORGE HERBERT (ENGLISH, 1593–1633). A member of the noble family that included the earldoms of Pembroke and Montgomery, George Herbert was born in Montgomery Castle, Powys. He studied at Westminster and at Trinity College, Cambridge; upon graduation he became a fellow and was public orator to the university from 1619 to 1627. Though he seems to have entertained aspirations for public advancement, Herbert became a deacon in 1626, a position that barred him from civil office. His mother, who was a patron of JOHN DONNE, died in 1627, and Herbert married Jane Danvers in 1629. During this period, Herbert was working on the poems that would form his collection *The Temple* (published after his death). He became a priest in 1630, but soon after his health began to decline; he died in 1633. By 1680 his poems had gone through thirteen editions. Celebrated for their craft as well as their quiet yet passionate devotion, Herbert's poems rank among the finest of English religious verse. The ingenuity of their imagery, tight logic, and meticulous attention to shape

situate them in the metaphysical tradition of poets like Donne. COLERIDGE greatly admired them; they have been influential on poets as different as T. S. ELIOT and DYLAN THOMAS.

ROBERT HERRICK (ENGLISH, 1591–1674). Extremely prolific (throughout his life he was responsible for 2,000 compositions), Robert Herrick was born in London. On taking his M.A. from Cambridge in 1620, he returned to London, where he began to mix with literary circles. There he met BEN JONSON, the poet with whom he is now most closely associated. In 1623, he took holy orders and in 1629 was appointed by Charles I to the living of Dean Prior in Exeter. Herrick enjoyed the quiet country life that the parish afforded but was ejected under the Commonwealth for his royalist sympathies. (He was reinstated in 1662 after the Restoration.) Just before leaving, he had published his major collection of verse, *Hesperides* (1648), which contains epigrams, epigraphs, elegies, hymns, songs, as well as imitations of the Roman writers Horace and Catullus. He is best known, however, for his love lyrics, of which the *carpe diem* poem "To the Virgins, to Make Much of Time" is a classic example. He died a bachelor, in his own parish, in 1674 at the age of eighty-three. The nineteenth-century poet Charles Swinburne would praise him as "the greatest songwriter ever born of English race."

GERARD MANLEY HOPKINS (ENGLISH, 1844–1889). Of the expansive verbal range and variety of Gerard Manley Hopkins's work, the poet and critic Donald Davie has said, "One feels [he] could have found a place for every word in the language if only he could have written enough poems. One feels the same about Shakespeare." Born in Stratford, Essex, Hopkins was educated at Highgate School, where he won the poetry prize, and at Balliol College, Oxford. In 1866 he shocked his family by converting to Roman Catholicism, and in 1868 he became a Jesuit priest. Doubting his ability to combine poetry with his vocation, he burned most of his early work and vowed to write "no more . . . unless by the wish of my superiors." He remained silent until 1875. In that year, encouraged by a rector to compose some verses on the sinking of the *Deutsch-*

land, in which five Franciscan nuns had been drowned, he wrote *The Wreck of the Deutschland,* a splendid ode in thirty-five stanzas. The editor of the Jesuit paper, however, refused to print it. Hopkins continued to write, composing "God's Grandeur," "The Windhover," and "Pied Beauty" before his ordination; his poetic career ended in his last post, in Dublin, where he wrote his "terrible sonnets" before his death from typhoid fever in 1889. None of his poems were published in his lifetime. Despite the brevity of his career and his small literary output, his poems, and particularly his metrical innovations, had — and continue to have — enormous influence on later writers.

Quotable: "The poetical language of an age should be the current language heightened, to any degree heightened and unlike itself, but not . . . an obsolete one."
— *Letters*

A. E. HOUSMAN (ENGLISH, 1859–1936). The poet and classics scholar Alfred Edward Housman attended St. John's College, Oxford. After graduation he worked as a clerk in the London Patent Office, publishing his work on Propertius, Ovid, and Juvenal in his spare time. The quality of his scholarship earned him the post of professor of Latin at London University in 1892. He later became professor of Latin at Cambridge and was made a fellow of Trinity College, Oxford, in 1911. Chiefly known for his collection *A Shropshire Lad,* which he published in 1896 at his own expense, Housman was an accomplished lyricist who celebrated the English countryside and the "golden" lads and lasses who inhabited it. A healthy dose of pessimism keeps many of his poems free of sentimentality, and lyrics like "To an Athlete Dying Young," and "Is My Team Ploughing," continue to delight readers. His "Loveliest of trees, the cherry now" is a fine example of the *carpe diem* poem in English. Despite the success of his first book, Housman wrote little poetry after it, though in 1922 he issued his collection *Last Poems.* A further collection, *More Poems,* was published by his brother Laurence after his death in 1936.

Quotable: "Good literature continually read for pleasure must, let us hope, do some good to the reader: must quicken his

perception though dull, and sharpen his discrimination though blunt, and mellow the rawness of his personal opinions."
— *The Name and Nature of Poetry*

ANDREW HUDGINS (AMERICAN, B. 1951). Called "the most readable poet of his generation," Andrew Hudgins is the author of five books of poems. He was born in Killeen, Texas, into a military family and raised in Alabama, an experience vividly, humorously, and poignantly described in his collection *The Glass Hammer: A Southern Childhood* (1994). Other books of poetry are *Saints and Sinners* (1985), runner-up for the Pulitzer Prize; *After the Lost War* (1988), a narrative based on the life of the early American poet Sidney Lanier; *The Never-Ending: New Poems* (1991), finalist for the National Book Award; and most recently *Babylon in a Jar* (1998). Largely autobiographical, ironically yet sensitively attuned to history and religion, Hudgins's work is at home inside contemporary American life. In "Compost: An Ode," he celebrates its indiscriminate variety and improbable regeneration: "The compost heap is both — life, death — a slow / simmer, / a leisurely collapsing of / the thing / into its possibilities . . . the opulence / of everything that rots." Winner of the Poet's Prize and numerous fellowships, he has taught at Princeton and at the University of Cincinnati, where he is currently professor of English. His collection of essays, *The Glass Anvil,* was published in 1997.

RANDALL JARRELL (AMERICAN, 1914–1965). A poet as well as an influential critic of poetry, Randall Jarrell was born in Nashville, Tennessee. Following his education at Vanderbilt, he joined the army and served in the air corps from 1942 to 1946. Two volumes of poetry, *Blood for a Stranger* (1942) and *Little Friend, Little Friend* (1945), were issued during this time. The poet Robert Fitzgerald has described Jarrell as "practically the only American poet able to cope with the Second Great War"; the experience of war and its grotesque realities form an important feature of much of his work. His *Selected Poems* was issued in 1955 (again in 1964), and in 1961 he won the National Book Award. His *Complete Poems* was published posthumously in 1969. Jarrell worked in various editorial positions at *The Nation,*

Partisan Review, the *Yale Review,* and *American Scholar.* He taught English literature and creative writing at Kenyon College (where he was friends with ROBERT LOWELL and John Crowe Ransom), Sarah Lawrence College, and, from 1947 until his death in 1965, at the Women's College of the University of North Carolina, Greensboro.

Quotable: "Poetry does not need to be defended, any more than air or food needs to be defended."   — *Poetry and the Age*

ALICE JONES (AMERICAN, B. 1949). Alice Jones is a graduate of Goddard College and New York Medical College. After several years of practice in internal medicine, she completed a second residency in psychiatry, which she now practices in California. Her work, then, uniquely combines the vocations of the poet and the psychoanalyst. Jones's first collection of poetry, *The Knot* (1992), won the 1992 Beatrice Hawley Award from Alice James Books and was praised as an "extraordinary combination of lyricism, mythmaking, and an informed use of the language of medicine." She is the author of two chapbooks of poems, *Anatomy* (1997), published in letter press edition by Bullnettle Press, San Francisco, and *Isthmus* (1999) from Alice James Books and winner of the Jane Kenyon Award. Jones has been awarded fellowships in poetry from the Bread Loaf Writers' Conference and from the National Endowment for the Arts; her poems have appeared in *Ploughshares, Poetry, Kenyon Review,* and *The Best American Poetry: 1994.* She lives in Oakland, California, and is a member of the San Francisco Psychoanalytic Institute.

BEN JONSON (ENGLISH, 1572–1637). Born in Westminster and educated at Westminster School, Ben Jonson is probably the best-known Elizabethan playwright next to SHAKESPEARE. Though an accomplished lyric poet and scholar, it is on the strength of his comedies that his reputation primarily rests: *Every Man in His Humour* (1598) made Jonson a celebrity; it was followed by the great comedies *Volpone* (1605), *The Alchemist* (1610), and *Bartholomew Fair* (1614). He was rewarded with a royal pension and was made England's first poet laureate. Heavily influenced by classical Roman literature, particularly Horace, whose *Ars Poetica*

(The Art of Poetry) he translated, Jonson embodies the urbanity and broad learning that are characteristic of the Renaissance. In 1678 he was appointed city chronologer of London; in that same year he suffered a debilitating stroke. His friends remained loyal to him in his final years, and he was honored with a collection of memorial elegies, *Jonsonus virbius,* at his death in 1637. He is buried in Westminster Abbey; his stone in Poet's Corner reads simply, "O rare Ben Jonson."

JOHN KEATS (ENGLISH, 1795–1821). John Keats was born in London, the eldest of four children. After his father's death in 1804, Keats's mother moved the family to Edmonton; she died of tuberculosis in 1810. Keats studied medicine at Guy's Hospital, intending to become a surgeon, but gave up that field in 1816 for a life of writing. His first poems were composed in 1814. In 1816 *The Examiner* printed his sonnet "On First Looking into Chapman's Homer" and hailed Keats, alongside SHELLEY, as one of the most promising writers of his generation. His *Poems* (1817), however, appeared to little applause. Keats began work on his long poem *Endymion,* published in 1818, but by then his brother Tom had become ill with tuberculosis, and Keats devoted much time to nursing him. In 1818, after Tom's death, he moved to Hampstead, where he fell in love with Fanny Brawne, the subject of some of his poems. He finished *Hyperion,* wrote lyrics such as "La Belle Dame sans Merci," and completed the great odes of 1819, for which he is chiefly remembered. In the winter of 1820 he fell seriously ill with tuberculosis and sailed for Italy. He died in Rome that summer, aged twenty-five. Despite doubts over the permanence of his achievement, Keats exerted enormous influence on later poets, notably TENNYSON and ARNOLD, and remains one of the best-loved poets of the later Romantic period.

Quotable: "Poetry should surprise by a fine excess, and not by singularity. It should strike the reader as a wording of his own highest thoughts, and appear almost as a remembrance."   — *Letters*

JANE KENYON (AMERICAN, 1947–1995). Born in Ann Arbor, Michigan, Jane Kenyon received her M.A. in English language and iterature from the University of Michigan. Her first book, *From Room to Room,* was published in 1978; of it one critic was to remark, "Rarely does one encounter a first book which gives so much, so economically; and it is also rare that a first book leaves the reader with so rich a sense of reward, for the poet's careful labors are in the interest of the Mystery lying beneath everyday circumstances." Indeed, it was Kenyon's gift to see, as WORDSWORTH said, "into the mystery of things." She published four other volumes: *The Boat of Quiet Hours* (1986), *Let Evening Come* (1990), *Constance* (1993), and *Otherwise: New and Selected Poems* (published posthumously in 1996). Apart from her poetry she translated *Twenty Poems of Anna Akhmatova.* The recipient of a Guggenheim fellowship, the PEN/Voelcker Award, and a creative writing fellowship from the National Endowment for the Arts, she lived with her husband, the poet DONALD HALL, on Eagle Pond Farm in New Hampshire. She died there of leukemia in 1995.

MAXINE HONG KINGSTON (AMERICAN, B. 1940). Born in Stockton, California, to Chinese emigrants, Maxine Hong Kingston attended both American and Chinese schools while working with her parents in the family laundry. She has described her childhood as rich in story, with her mother the dominant storyteller. Her first book, *The Woman Warrior: Memoir of a Girlhood Among Ghosts* (1976), a partly fictionalized memoir of her childhood with her Chinese ancestors, explores bicultural identity, myth, and memory and was an immediate critical success. It won the 1976 National Book Critics Circle Award for nonfiction and was named one of the top ten nonfiction works of the decade by *Time* magazine. Following her graduation from the University of California, Berkeley, Kingston taught high school English in Hayward, California, then moved to Hawaii, where she worked as a schoolteacher. She currently lives in Oakland, California, and teaches at her alma mater. Apart from her novels and nonfiction, Kingston has published poems, short stories, and articles. Her collection of twelve prose sketches, *Hawaii One Summer,* was published in a limited edition with original woodblock print and calligraphy. She is currently working on what she calls "The Global Novel."

Quotable: "I learned to make my mind large, as the universe is large, so that there is room for paradoxes."
— *The Woman Warrior*

GALWAY KINNELL (AMERICAN, B. 1927). Galway Kinnell was born in Providence, Rhode Island, and attended Princeton and the University of Rochester. He served in the navy in World War II. His first three books, *What a Kingdom It Was* (1960), *Flower Herding on Mount Monadnock* (1964), and *Body Rags* (1968), established him as an accomplished writer of free verse. His ten-part poem, *The Book of Nightmares* (1971), is a sustained exploration of human finitude and loss, leading the reader to the point where "one / and zero / walk off together, / walk off the end of these pages together, / one creature / walking away side by side with the emptiness." His *Selected Poems* won the Pulitzer Prize and the American Book Award in 1982. Later collections include *When One Has Lived a Long Time Alone* (1990) and *Imperfect Thirst* (1994). Apart from his own poems, he has published translations of François Villon and RAINER MARIA RILKE, among others. His prose includes one novel, *Black Light* (1966), and a collection of interviews, *Walking Down the Stairs* (1978). A former MacArthur fellow and state poet of Vermont, he teaches creative writing at New York University. He lives in New York and Vermont.

Quotable: "The death of the self I seek, in poetry and out of poetry, is not a drying up or withering. It is a death, yes, but a death out of which one might hope to be reborn more giving, more alive, more open, more related to the natural life."
— *Walking Down the Stairs*

PHILIP LARKIN (ENGLISH, 1922–1985). Philip Larkin was born in Coventry, Warwickshire. After graduation from St. John's College, Oxford, he moved to Shropshire to take a library position. He remained a librarian throughout his life, working at universities in Leicester and Belfast before settling at the University of Hull in 1955. As an undergraduate at Oxford, Larkin belonged to a group of poets that came to be known as the Movement. The Movement Poets (of whom Donald Davie and Thom Gunn were two) sought an evenness of expression, a conversational, plain idiom opposed to the rhetorical excess and apocalyptic urgency of poets such as DYLAN THOMAS and George Barker. Peter Levi has said of the poems in Larkin's last two books that Larkin's reputation rests on "85 perfect poems" in which he treats, with characteristic wryness, compassionate generosity, and consummate craftsmanship, the England of his time. In 1973 he edited *The Oxford Book of Twentieth-Century English Verse,* and he was a strong candidate for the post of poet laureate of England in 1984. His death in December of 1985 intervened.

Quotable: "The poetry I've enjoyed has been the kind of poetry you'd associate with me [. . .] on the whole, people to whom technique seems to matter less than content, people who accept the forms they have inherited but use them to express their own content."   — *Four Conversations*

HENRY WADSWORTH LONGFELLOW (AMERICAN, 1807–1882). Henry Wadsworth Longfellow was born in Portland, Maine, and attended Bowdoin College, where he was later a professor of languages. Following a tour of Europe from 1826 to 1829 he married Mary Potter who then died during a second journey abroad in 1835. In 1836 he took a post as professor at Harvard and moved to Cambridge, Massachusetts, where he became a prominent figure in literary circles. His first collection of poems, *Voices in the Night* (1839), was followed by *Ballads and Other Poems* (1842). He was married again, to Frances Appleton, but she died in 1861. His remaining years were overshadowed by her death. Longfellow remained until recent years one of the most popular of American poets. His work, at times sentimental or didactic, was well suited to the tastes of its time. Such poems as "A Psalm of Life," "The Village Blacksmith," and "Paul Revere's Ride" have been cherished as much for their narrative delight as for their moral edification and expression of communally accepted values. In later works such as *The Song of Hiawatha* (1855) and *The Courtship of Miles Standish* (1858) he attempted the creation of an American mythology drawn from native lore. Apart from his poetry, he published a prose romance, *Hyperion* (1839),

and a translation of Dante's *Divine Comedy* in 1867. He died in 1882.

ROBERT LOWELL (AMERICAN, 1917–1977). A descendant of the Fireside Poet James Russell Lowell and distant cousin of the modern experimental poet AMY LOWELL, Robert Lowell was born in Boston. He attended Harvard before transferring to Kenyon College to study under John Crowe Ransom. Following graduation, Lowell married the novelist Jean Stafford and the two moved to Louisiana, were Lowell attended Louisiana State University. In 1948 the couple divorced, and in 1949 Lowell married Elizabeth Hardwick. At LSU, under the tutelage of Robert Penn Warren and Allen Tate, Lowell composed much of his early work; its style, formally rigorous, dense in imagery and symbolism, was informed as well by his conversion to Catholicism. His first book, *Land of Unlikeness,* appeared in 1944, followed by the Pulitzer Prize–winning *Lord Weary's Castle* in 1946. In 1959 he published *Life Studies;* its looser style and personal subject matter had a great effect on the emerging confessional verse. During World War II, Lowell was arrested for his role as a conscientious objector and was held six months. During the Vietnam War, which he also opposed, his work exhibited a political dimension. Later collections, *Notebooks* (1970), *History* (1973), and *Day by Day* (1977), continued to explore the nexus of private life and public events. In 1970 Lowell withdrew from the political scene and moved to England, where he married Caroline Blackwood. He was on his way back to his second wife in 1977 when he died in a New York City taxicab.

ARCHIBALD MACLEISH (AMERICAN, 1892–1982). The poet and playwright Archibald MacLeish was born in Glencoe, Illinois. Following his graduation from Yale University in 1915, he served as an ambulance driver and captain of field artillery in World War I. His first collection of poems, *Tower of Ivory,* appeared in 1917. After the war he attended Harvard Law School and practiced briefly in Boston before moving to Paris, where he published four books of poetry. On returning to America, he wrote *New Found Land* (1930) and *Conquistador* (1932), winner of the Pulitzer Prize. A second

Pulitzer was awarded him in 1953 for his *Collected Poems* (1952). Aside from poetry, he wrote verse-plays and radio plays; his best-known work for the stage is *J. B.* (1958), a modern retelling of the story of Job that won him yet another Pulitzer in 1959. MacLeish played an active role in politics and the academy as well as being a distinguished man of letters. He was librarian of Congress from 1939 to 1944, assistant secretary of state from 1944 to 1945, and a U.S. representative at the first UNESCO conference in Paris in 1946. From 1949 to 1962 he was Boylston Professor of Rhetoric and Oratory at Harvard University; his lectures on poetry were published as *Poetry and Experience* (1961). He died in 1982.

Quotable: "A book of poems is not a bouquet from which to pick a choice of posies. A book of poems is an attempt to come to terms with the experiences of a mortal life and it is almost always a whole thing—as whole in its way as a well-made novel."
— Foreword to *Selected Poems 1926–1972*

CHRISTOPHER MARLOWE (ENGLISH, 1564–1593). Little is known about the short life and violent death of Christopher Marlowe. He was born two months before SHAKESPEARE in 1564, the son of a Canterbury shoemaker. He attended King's School in Canterbury and then Corpus Christi College, Cambridge, taking his B.A. in 1583. By the time he received his M.A. from Cambridge in 1587 he had certainly written his first successful work for the London stage, the first part of *Tamburlaine the Great* (1587). The second part of *Tamburlaine* soon followed, rivaling the first in popularity; English theatergoers thrilled as much to the hero's energy and overreaching ambition as to his language, "Threatening the world in high astounding terms." Other dramatic successes followed in the six short years left to him: *The Jew of Malta* (1590), *Edward II* (c. 1592), and his best-known work, *The Tragical History of Doctor Faustus* (1604, 1616). In these plays Marlowe laid the foundations for the English chronicle play and the new English tragedy. In the last few months of his life he worked in plague-ridden London completing his long narrative poem, *Hero and Leander* (1598), which, with "The Passionate Shepherd to His Love," stands as his poetic achievement. He was stabbed in a Deptford tavern in 1593 and, as a contemporary wrote, "dyed swearing."

ANDREW MARVELL (ENGLISH, 1621–1678). Into the century that included writers as disparate as DONNE, SHAKESPEARE, and MILTON, Andrew Marvell was born in 1621 in Yorkshire, the son of a vicar. He was educated at Trinity College, Cambridge, where he read Juvenal and Horace, Roman satirists who were to influence his own poetry. From 1642 to 1647 Marvell traveled widely in Europe. He was greatly influenced by John Donne, whose metaphysical conceit became more supple in Marvell's hands. He was a friend of John Milton, by whom he was recommended in 1653 for the post of assistant Latin secretary to the Council of State, a position he finally secured in 1657. Throughout the 1660s and 1670s he was embroiled in political matters and wrote many of his best satires. But Marvell is perhaps best remembered for his lyrics, especially "To His Coy Mistress" and "The Garden." In these and like poems, Marvell's chief ability lies in his minute attention to the physical world and human perception of that world. He also wrote political verse—"An Horatian Ode upon Cromwell's Return from Ireland" being his best-known poem of this kind—and highly wrought, elaborately sustained pastoral poems such as "Upon Appleton House." Little of his poetry appeared before 1681, when *Miscellaneous Poems* was published. His work was rediscovered in the nineteenth century, and was highly influential on TENNYSON.

JULIO MARZÁN (AMERICAN, B. 1946). The poet and fiction writer Julio Marzán has published a variety of works in English and in Spanish. His poetry, deeply immersed in Latino culture, has appeared in *Parnassus: Poetry in Review* and *Harper's* magazine. His most recent books of nonfiction are *The Spanish American Roots of William Carlos Williams* (1994) and *The Numinous Site: The Poetry of Luis Palés Matos* (1995); he has also edited *Luna, Luna: Creative Writing Ideas from Spanish & Latino Literature* (1997). He has been an artist-in-residence at the Millay Colony and has taught at William Paterson University. He is presently a professor at Nassau Community College. A book of poetry in Spanish, *Puerta de Tierra*, is forthcoming.

JAMES MERRILL (AMERICAN, 1926–1995). Born in New York City, James Merrill was educated at Amherst College, where he received his B.A. in 1947 following brief service in World War II. His earliest volume, *Jim's Book: A Collection of Poems and Short Stories* (1942), appeared when he was still in his teens, but it was his second, *First Poems* (1951), that gained him the attention of poetry readers. His reputation as an exquisite craftsman and elegant lyric poet was established in succeeding volumes such as *The Country of a Thousand Years of Peace and Other Poems* (1959, revised in 1970), *Selected Poems* (1961), and *Water Street* (1962). Later works such as *The Divine Comedies* (1976), *Metamorphosis of 741* (1977), and *Mirabell: Books of Numbers* (1978) turned toward the esoteric and the metaphysical, culminating in his epic *The Changing Light at Sandhover* (1982), which uses a Ouija board and a host of personages (many of them dead) to assemble a poetic galaxy in the tradition of WILLLIAM BLAKE's prophetic books. His most recent volumes include *Marbled Paper* (1982), *Santorini: Stopping the Leak* (1982), *Souvenirs* (1984), *Bronze* (1984), *Late Settings* (1985), and *The Inner Room* (1988). His *New Selected Poems* appeared in 1993. A winner of the National Book Award, the Bollingen Prize, and a Pulitzer, he also authored two novels, *The Seraglio* (1957) and *The (Diblos) Notebook* (1965), and a collection of essays, *Recitative* (1986). He was elected to the American Academy of Poets in 1971 and served there until his death in 1995.

EDNA ST. VINCENT MILLAY (AMERICAN, 1892–1950). Edna St. Vincent Millay was born in Rockport, Maine. With her mother's encouragement, she developed her literary interests and wrote her first poem at the age of five. She attended Vassar College, and her first collection, *Renascence and Other Poems* (1917), contained much she had written as an undergraduate. It was followed by *A Few Figs from Thistles* (1920), which established her as one of the more popular poets of her time. She moved to Greenwich Village and immersed herself in the Bohemian lifestyle, developing the literary personality of one hungry for experience, at odds with conventional morality, haunted by the brevity of life. Her third volume, *The Harp-Weaver and Other Poems* (1923), won the Pulitzer Prize in 1923. A member of the Provincetown Players, she was the author of *Three Plays* (1926); a libretto, *The King's Henchman* (1927); and a sonnet sequence, *Fatal Interview* (1928). Though her literary output slowed with the years, she still continued to publish poetry collections; later volumes include *Wine from These Grapes* (1934), *Conversation at Midnight* (1937), *Huntsman, What Quarry?* (1939), and *Make Bright the Arrows* (1940), a book dealing with the experience of World War II. Her reputation dimmed considerably during her life, but she is still admired for her graceful work within traditional lyric forms, particularly the sonnet.

JOHN MILTON (ENGLISH, 1608–1674). John Milton was born in London's Cheapside district, the son of a businessman. He was educated at St. Paul's, where he showed great aptitude with languages. Following his graduation from Christ's College, Cambridge, where he earned his B.A. in 1629 and his M.A. in 1632, Milton returned to his father's house in Buckinghamshire and continued his education, reading day and night for six years. In 1634 he wrote his masque, *Comus,* and in 1637 the great elegy *Lycidas* for a college classmate who had been drowned. From 1640 to 1660, he was embroiled in the political-religious controversies of the time, publishing tract after tract in what are known as the pamphlet wars. In 1663, following marriage to his third wife, blind and impoverished, Milton began work on his masterpiece, a long poem aimed at "justifying the ways of God to men." *Paradise Lost* was published in 1667 and was at once recognized as a supreme epic achievement. It was followed by *Paradise Regained* in 1671 and *Samson Agonistes,* a tragedy, in 1674. He died that year from complications arising from gout. Combining Renaissance learning and Latinate style with a staunchly Reformation temperament, Milton's work continues to inspire and challenge readers three centuries after his death.

Quotable: "By labor and intent study (which I take to be my portion in this life), joined with the strong propensity of nature, I might perhaps leave something so written to aftertimes, as they should not willingly let it die."

— *The Reason of Church Government*

MARIANNE MOORE (AMERICAN, 1887–1972). Marianne Moore was born in St. Louis, Missouri. Her father left the family when she was an infant, and Moore grew up with her mother in the home of her grandfather, a Presbyterian minister. In 1894, the family moved to Carlisle, Pennsylvania, where Moore attended the Metzger Institute before going to Bryn Mawr. In 1918 she moved to New York City where she attended literary functions at which she met other young poets, WALLACE STEVENS and WILLIAM CARLOS WILLIAMS among them. In 1921 her first book, *Poems*, was published by friends without her knowledge. A second volume, *Marriage*, appeared in 1923. Her *Observations* (1924) won *Dial* magazine's award for "distinguished service to American letters." *Selected Poems* appeared in 1935; of it T. S. ELIOT remarked, "Miss Moore's poems form part of the small body of durable poetry written in our time." In 1947 Moore became a member of the National Institute of Arts and Letters. In 1951 her *Collected Poems* received Bollingen and Pulitzer Prizes as well as the National Book Award. In 1955 she was elected to the American Academy. Her poems reveal the quiet, restrained passion of the details of this world. Writers as diverse as ROBERT LOWELL, ELIZABETH BISHOP, and DONALD HALL have paid tribute to her unerring vision in their works.

SHARON OLDS (AMERICAN, B. 1942). With the publication of her first book, *Satan Says* (1980), Sharon Olds established herself as a breaker of restrictive social norms. In ensuing collections, she has explored domestic and political violence, sexuality, and the body. Though her concentration on pain and suffering has been called a "dark witness-bearing," she is also seen as a poet of purification and redemption. Her confessional style situates her in a line of American poetry descending from Anne Sexton and SYLVIA PLATH; one critic allies her with WALT WHITMAN: "Like Whitman, Ms. Olds sings the body in celebration of a power stronger than political oppression." A native of San Francisco, Olds was educated at Stanford and then at Columbia, where she received her Ph.D. Her first collection appeared when she was thirty-seven. Her second book, *The Dead and the Living* (1984), won the Lamont Poetry Prize and the National Book Critics Circle Award. *The Gold Cell* (1987) and *The Father* (1992) were followed by *The Wellspring* (1996) and, most recently, *Blood, Tin, Straw* (1999). A popular reader of her work and a leader of workshops across the country, she currently teaches at the Writing Program at Goldwater Hospital for the severely physically disabled and chairs the creative writing program at New York University.

Quotable: "There are some things that have to do with art that we can't control. This creature of the poem may assemble itself into a being with its own centrifugal force. That's what I'm thinking about when I'm trying to get out of art's way. Not trying to look good, if a poem's about me. Not trying to look bad. Not asking a poem to carry a lot of rocks in its pockets. But just being an ordinary observer and liver and feeler and letting the experience get through you onto the notebook with the pen, through the arm, out of the body, onto the page, without distortion."

— *Interview*

WILFRED OWEN (ENGLISH, 1893–1918). "My subject is War, and the pity of War," wrote Wilfred Owen in a draft preface to his poems. "The Poetry is in the pity." And in works such as "Dulce et Decorum Est" he records with slant rhyme and steady eye the horror and the pity of his subject. Born in Plas Wilmot, Oswestry, in 1893, Owen graduated from Shrewsbury Technical College in 1911, though without the honors necessary to enter university. He left England in 1913 for France, where he taught at the Berlitz School of Languages at Bordeaux. At the outbreak of World War I, Owen returned to England to enlist. On the Western Front in January 1917, he endured the worst winter of the war. In May 1917, he was diagnosed with shell-shock and sent to Craiglockhart Hospital in Edinburgh, where he met the poet Siegfried Sassoon, whose poems Owen admired. Sassoon encouraged Owen in his writing. Discharged in late October, Owen returned to the front and was killed on November 4, 1918, one week before the armistice. Only four of his poems were published during his lifetime. Enlarged editions began to appear, first in 1920 (edited by Sassoon), and then in 1931 and 1963. *The Complete Poems and Fragments* was published in 1983, edited by John Stallworthy.

SYLVIA PLATH (AMERICAN, 1932–1963). Born in Boston, Sylvia Plath was educated at Smith College. Her father, Otto Plath, was a German emigrant who taught biology and German at Boston University. In 1957, while on a Fulbright Fellowship at Cambridge, Plath met the poet Ted Hughes, whom she married that year. She returned to Boston to study at Boston University with ROBERT LOWELL; the painful personal element in her work aligns her with confessional poets like him and Anne Sexton. Her work is laced with archetypal resonance, fired by what Ted Hughes called a "crackling verbal energy." It is also laced with terror. While at Smith she had suffered a breakdown, and over the years, despite congenial outward appearances, she made numerous attempts at suicide. She spent the last part of her life living in London with her two children. Her collection, *The Colossus and Other Poems* (1960), was the only one of her books of poetry to be published in her lifetime. Posthumous collections include *Ariel* (1965), *Crossing the Water* (1971), and *Winter Trees* (1971). She wrote one autobiographical novel, *The Bell Jar* (1963); *The Journals of Sylvia Plath* appeared in 1982. Her posthumous *Collected Poems* was awarded the Pulitzer Prize in 1982. She took her own life in 1963.

Quotable: "What I fear most, I think, is the death of the imagination. When the sky outside is merely pink, and the rooftops merely black: that photographic mind which paradoxically tells the truth, but the worthless truth, about the world. It is that synthesizing spirit, that 'shaping' force, which prolifically sprouts and makes up its own worlds with more inventiveness than God which I desire." —*Journals*

EDGAR ALLAN POE (AMERICAN, 1809–1849). Edgar Allan Poe, author of "The Tell-Tale Heart," was born in Boston in 1809. Following his parents' early death, he was adopted by a merchant, John Allan, and spent most of his childhood in England. In 1826, he entered the University of Virginia, but left soon after to pursue a literary career. His first book, *Tamerlane and Other Poems* (1827), was published anonymously and at his own expense; another volume of poems, *Al Araaf*, followed in 1829. In 1830, he entered West Point, but was dismissed for neglect of duty the next year. Having settled briefly in New York, where he published his third volume, *Poems* (1831), Poe moved to Baltimore and began to write stories for magazines. In 1836, he married his thirteen-year-old cousin, Virginia Clemm. The two moved to Richmond, Virginia. The next few years were marked by more moves—New York, Philadelphia—until, at his wife's death in 1847, he returned to Richmond. He died in Baltimore in 1849, in poverty and under mysterious circumstances. Despite his itinerant and brief career, Poe produced a varied and admirable body of work, ranging from reviews and literary criticism to poems, short stories, and one novel. The title piece of *The Raven and Other Poems* (1845) is perhaps his best-known work and provided him with considerable popular success. His obsession with darkness, with psychological terror and the macabre, influenced later French Symbolist poets, notably Charles Baudelaire.

Quotable: "With me poetry has been not a purpose, but a passion; and the passions should be held in reverence: they must not—they cannot at will be excited, with an eye to the paltry compensations, or the more paltry commendations, of mankind." —*The Raven and Other Poems*, Preface

ALEXANDER POPE (ENGLISH, 1688–1744). A brilliant satirist in an age of satire, Alexander Pope was born in London to a Roman Catholic family in 1688, the year of the Protestant Revolution. Debarred from university education because of his religion, Pope was largely self-taught. As a child he suffered from tuberculosis and asthma. He also had a curvature of the spine, resulting in his diminutive stature (four feet, six inches), a condition that later became a target for critics in the literary vendettas of the time. In 1711 he moved to London and wrote his *Essay on Criticism*. In this and other works, notably *The Rape of the Lock* (1712–1720), he showed himself a master of the heroic couplet; its concision and balance made it a fit form for the play of wit, for logical or philosophical meditation, and of course for the whip and sting of satire. The success of his translation of Homer's *Iliad* (1715–1720) allowed him to set up a home in Twickenham after he had been forced to leave London following the Jacobite rebellion of 1715. There he wrote his major poem, *The Dunciad* (1728, continued in 1742), the *Epistle to Doctor Arbuthnot* (1734), and the philosophical *Essay on Man* (1733–1734). Though his reputation suffered later due to vast changes in taste, he was influential among many mid-twentieth-century poets, notably Allen Tate and ROBERT LOWELL.

EZRA POUND (AMERICAN, 1885–1972). There is virtually no modern poet whose work Ezra Pound's influence has not touched. His dictum, "Make it New!," along with his tireless promotion of others, left an indelible mark on English letters. Born in Hailey, Idaho, in 1885, he was educated at the University of Pennsylvania and Hamilton College. In 1908 he sailed for Venice, where he published his first book of poems, *A Lume Spento* (1908). Later volumes, especially *Personae* (1910), showed the influence of ROBERT BROWNING's dramatic monologues. In 1908 Pound moved to London, where he began to promote the work of new writers like T. S. ELIOT, HILDA DOOLITTLE, WILLIAM CARLOS WILLIAMS, and ROBERT FROST. During World War I, he continued to write. His *Hugh Selwyn Mauberly* (1920) records his disillusionment with modern civilization. In 1924 Pound returned to Italy and began work on his major poem, an epic conceived in his school days. *A Draft of XVI Cantos* was published in 1925; he continued to work on *The Cantos* for the rest of his life. During World War II, Pound remained in Italy, making pro-Axis broadcasts in Rome. Following the war, he was turned over to American authorities and imprisoned near Pisa. On return to the United States, he was charged with treason but declared insane and unfit to stand trial. He was confined at St. Elizabeth's Hospital, where he spent the next thirteen years. On his release in 1958 (which was partially negotiated by Robert Frost), he returned to Italy, where he lived until his death in 1972.

Quotable: "Poetry must be *as well written as prose* [. . . .] There must be no book words,

no periphrases, no inversions [. . . .] no hindside-beforeness, no straddled adjectives (as 'addled mosses dank), no Tennysonianness of speech; nothing — nothing that you couldn't, in some circumstance, in the stress of some emotion, actually say."

— *Letters*

RAINER MARIA RILKE (GERMAN, 1875–1926). Rainer Maria Rilke was born in Prague, the son of an army officer. After attending military school, he studied philosophy, history, literature, and art in Prague, Munich, and Berlin. He wrote verses from a very early age. In 1899 he traveled to Russia (one of his two visits there) and, returning, married Clara Westhoff in 1901. Following the birth of their daughter, Ruth, the two moved to Paris, where Clara worked for the sculptor Rodin (Rilke was writing a monograph on the artist). During the next twelve years, Rilke traveled widely, using Paris as his base. He composed much of his major work during this time: *Stundenbuch* (*The Book of Objects*), *Neue Gedichte* (*New Poems*), and his autobiographical prose work, *The Notebooks of Malte Laurids Brigge*. The *Book of Objects* was particularly influential in its invention of a new form of lyric poetry, the object poem, which attempts to capture the essence of a physical thing. After the outbreak of World War I he lived mostly in Munich, and in 1919 moved to Switzerland. There he was to write his masterworks, the *Duineser Elegien* (*Duino Elegies*) and *Sonette an Orpheus* (*Sonnets to Orpheus*). The former stands as his supreme testament of spiritual experience. He died at Valmont near Glion in 1926.

Quotable: "Works of art are indeed always products of having been in danger, of having gone to the very end in an experience, to where man can go no further."

— *Letters*

EDWIN ARLINGTON ROBINSON (AMERICAN, 1869–1935). Born in Head Tide, Maine, Edwin Arlington Robinson was educated at Harvard University from 1891 to 1893. His early poetry was deeply influenced by such Romantic and Victorian giants as WILLIAM WORDSWORTH and Rudyard Kipling. Despite his denial of ROBERT BROWNING's influence, many have felt a likeness in Robinson's creation of character sketches and particularly in his use of dramatic monologues. His treatment of the New England landscape also invites comparison with Robert Frost, five years his junior. In 1896 he published his first collection, *The Torrent and the Night Before,* expanded and reissued in 1897 as *The Children of the Night.* His mature style dates from 1916 with *The Man against the Sky* and *Collected Poems* (1921). Though his predilection for formal poetry and traditional forms situated him against the rising tide of modernism, he enjoyed popularity throughout his career and was three times awarded the Pulitzer Prize. His many later volumes include a trilogy based on Arthurian romance, *Merlin* (1917), *Lancelot* (1920), and *Tristam* (1927), and *The Man Who Died Twice* (1924). He is best known, however, for his shorter lyrics, particularly his Tilbury poems, which include such wry, ironic works as "Richard Cory."

THEODORE ROETHKE (AMERICAN, 1908–1963). Theodore Roethke was born in Saginaw, Michigan, and educated at the University of Michigan and at Harvard. He taught at several universities, his last and longest appointment at the University of Washington. In his first book, *Open House* (1941), he treats the themes of childhood and nature; "I have a genuine love of nature," he was later to say. Later collections include *The Lost Son and Other Poems* (1948), *Praise to the End!* (1951), and the posthumously published *The Far Field* (1964). In 1953 he received the Pulitzer Prize for his collection *The Waking: Poems, 1933–1953.* His *Words for the Wind: The Collected Verse of Theodore Roethke* (1957) won the 1958 Bollingen Prize and the 1959 National Book Award. A tormented man, a victim of breakdowns and alcoholism, he nonetheless achieved a kind of transcendence in his work; he traced his lineage along the line of visionaries that includes Emerson, Thoreau, WHITMAN, BLAKE, WORDSWORTH, and YEATS. A new edition of *Collected Poems* was issued in 1975.

CHRISTINA GEORGINA ROSSETTI (ENGLISH, 1830–1894). The daughter of a Neapolitan political exile and sister of Dante Gabriel Rossetti, Christina Rossetti was born in London in 1830. She was educated at home

by her mother. While still a youth she showed so much poetic promise that her grandfather had small collections of her poems published when she was twelve and fifteen. Her first mature volume of verse, *Goblin Market and Other Poems,* was published in 1862. Before that, lyrics such as "An End" and "Dream Lane" had found publication in magazines under her pseudonym, Ellen Alleyne. *Goblin Market* was followed by *The Prince's Progress and Other Poems* (1866) and *Sing Song: A Nursery Rhyme Book* (1872). By the 1880s, ill health had made her an invalid, but she continued to write poetry. *A Pageant and Other Poems* was published in 1881; it contains her sonnet sequence "Monna Innominata." It was followed by *Time Flies: A Reading Diary* (1885) and *The Face of the Deep: A Devotional Commentary on the Apocalypse* (1892), her last published work. Highly accomplished in its verbal precision and metrical invention, her verse bears the influence of the pre-Raphaelite movement, which her brother Dante Gabriel helped to found. Her brother William edited her complete works (1904) after her death in 1894.

CARL SANDBURG (AMERICAN, 1878–1967). Born in Galesburg, Illinois, to Swedish immigrant parents, Carl Sandburg left school at the age of thirteen. He worked as an itinerant laborer and served in the Spanish-American War before becoming a journalist and advertising copywriter. In 1904 he published his first book of poems, *Reckless Ecstasy.* In 1916, with the publication of *Chicago Poems,* he was firmly established as a major poet of the American Midwest. His poetry, like WALT WHITMAN's, takes America as its subject matter; it champions the underdog and extols the enduring qualities of ordinary, working-class Americans. Though labeled "artless" by some of his contemporaries (ROBERT FROST called him a fraud), he was widely read and admired during his lifetime. His *Complete Poems* (1950) won the Pulitzer Prize. The governor of Illinois proclaimed his seventy-fifth birthday "Carl Sandburg Day," he was decorated by the king of Sweden, and in 1964, he received the Presidential Medal of Freedom from Lyndon B. Johnson. In addition to his poetry, he is known for his four-volume biography of Abraham Lincoln.

WILLIAM SHAKESPEARE (ENGLISH, 1564–1616). The Bard of Avon was born in 1564 in Stratford-upon-Avon, the eldest son of a glover and wool dealer. The young Shakespeare probably went to Stratford Grammar School, where he established his wide knowledge of classical literature, on which he would draw continually in his plays. In 1582, he married Anne Hathaway, with whom he fathered three children. Not much is known of Shakespeare's life after he came to London, but by 1594 he was a presence on the English stage. In that decade he composed at least some of his sonnets, published together in folio edition in 1609. Throughout the 1590s Shakespeare continued to write plays, averaging about two a year. In 1603 the new monarch, James, honored his troupe with royal patronage; now a member of The King's Men, Shakespeare launched into his great period, following his earlier *Julius Caesar* and *Hamlet* with such masterpieces as *Macbeth, King Lear,* and *Antony and Cleopatra.* After 1613 Shakespeare returned to Stratford, where he lived the rest of his life. After his death appeared the folio edition (1623), containing high tributes from fellow writers, among them Ben Jonson's "He was not of an age, but for all time!"

PERCY BYSSHE SHELLEY (ENGLISH, 1792–1822). Belonging to the generation of later Romantic poets including BYRON and KEATS, Percy Bysshe Shelley was born at Field Place, near Horsham, West Sussex, in 1792. He attended Oxford but was expelled after he published his pamphlet *The Necessity of Atheism* (1811). He eloped to Scotland with Harriet Westbrook, a move that, combined with his refusal to retract his pamphlet, caused a permanent break with his family. While in Scotland, Shelley corresponded with the radical thinker William Godwin, published a series of political works, and composed his poem *Queen Mab* (1813). Having moved to London, Shelley joined Godwin and fell in love with his sixteen-year-old daughter, Mary (later the author of *Frankenstein*). The two eloped to the Continent in 1814, despite the birth of a daughter by Harriet. Harriet drowned herself that autumn, and Shelley immediately married Mary. In 1818, they left England permanently and settled in Italy. Shelley completed his long poem *Prometheus Unbound* in 1819; that year and the next comprised his most productive period. *The Cenci* and *Ode to the West Wind*, as well as many important lyrics, belong to this time. At twenty-nine he was drowned when his boat went down in a tempest in the Gulf of Spezia. Grudgingly admired in his own day, his poetry was a dominant influence on later nineteenth-century poets, such as TENNYSON and BROWNING. Mary Shelley collected his *Poetical Works* in 1839.

Quotable: "All high poetry is infinite; it is as the first acorn, which contained all oaks potentially. Veil after veil may be undrawn, and the inmost naked beauty of the meaning never exposed. A great poem is a fountain for ever overflowing with the waters of wisdom and delight; and after one person and one age has exhausted all its divine effluence which their peculiar relations enable them to share, another and yet another succeeds, and new relations are ever developed, the source of an unforeseen and an unconceived delight." — *A Defence of Poetry*

CHARLES SIMIC (AMERICAN, B. 1938). Charles Simic was born in Belgrade, Yugoslavia. He emigrated to the United States with his family in 1949, settled in Chicago, and began attending the University of Chicago. He served briefly in the army before completing his B.A. at New York University. Since 1974 he has taught at the University of New Hampshire. His first book of poems, *What the Grass Says*, was published in 1967; *Selected Poems: Nineteen Sixty-Three to Nineteen Eighty-Five* appeared in 1985. In the many books written between those dates, and in the poems since published, Simic is continually drawn to the surreal and the strange, the dream image, the archetypal form. He places his readers in a world where, as he says, "magic is possible, where chance reigns, where metaphors have their supreme logic." Besides work on his own poetry, he has devoted much time to translations of other Yugoslav poets, contained in *Four Modern Yugoslav Poets* (1970) and *Horse Has Six Legs: Contemporary Serbian Poetry* (1992). He has translated and co-edited with Mark Strand *Another Republic: 17 European and South American Writers* (1976). The recipient of numerous awards, including a MacArthur Foundation Fellowship and a

Pulitzer Prize (1990), he currently resides in New Hampshire.

CATHY SONG (AMERICAN, B. 1955). Cathy Song's work explores the world of family and ancestry, the complications of one's moving through life, sensing all that lies behind. Of Chinese and Korean descent, she was born in Honolulu. Her first book, *Picture Bride* (1983), takes its title from the "mail order" brides that were sent from Asia to Hawaii, in the hope of being accepted on the strength of the photograph. (Song's grandmother was one of these.) The book won the Yale Series of Younger Poets Award in 1983. Her later collections, *Frameless Windows, Squares of Light* (1988), and *School Figures* (1994), have continued to probe the knowns and unknowns of bloodline and descent. Song received her B.A. from Wellesley College before pursuing an M.A. in creative writing at Boston University. The recipient of a number of grants and awards, including the Shelley Memorial Award from the Poetry Society of America and the Hawaii Award for Literature, she has taught creative writing at various universities. She currently serves as consulting editor for Bamboo Ridge Press in Honolulu, where she resides.

GARY SOTO (AMERICAN, B. 1952). Chicano life and the world of the San Joaquin Valley worker comprise much of the work of Gary Soto. He was born in Fresno, California, in 1952 to a family of field and factory workers. When Soto was five, his father died in an industrial accident. Soto took up writing poetry at an early age. In 1974 he earned his B.A. from California State University and his M.F.A. at the University of California, Irvine, in 1976. His first collections of poems, *The Element of San Joaquin* (1977) and *The Tale of Sunlight* (1978), document a journey from his own beginnings to the town of Taxco, in central Mexico, where, as his narrator says, "we all begin." Along the way, Soto treats the experience of the migrant worker in the San Joaquin Valley (work that Soto himself has done), where, as a custom, "The skin of my belly will tighten like a belt / And there will be no reason for pockets." Since then he has authored eight other books of poetry and three short story collections; his *New and Selected Poems* ap-

peared in 1995 and was a finalist for both the Los Angeles Times Book Prize and the National Book Award. He has taught Chicano studies and English at the University of California, Berkeley; recently he was appointed distinguished professor of creative writing at the University of California, Riverside.

WOLE SOYINKA (NIGERIAN, B. 1934). Wole Soyinka, the popular name of Akinwande Oluwole Soyinka, was born in Nigeria, near Abeokuta. He studied at Ibadan and Leeds. While in England he was a play reader for the Royal Court Theatre. His first play, *The Invention*, was performed there in 1955. In 1959 he returned to Ibaban, where he founded two theaters for the establishment of a Nigerian drama. During the Nigerian Civil War he was imprisoned (1967–1969), an experience he has written about in *Poems from Prison* (1969) and *A Shuttle in the Crypt* (1972). His first novel, *The Interpreters* (1965), has been called the first modern African novel. He became professor of comparative literature at Obafemi Awolowo University (formerly the University of Ife) and was professor of African studies and theater at Cornell University in 1988. Deeply engaged with the politics of his country, especially in the tensions between an old and new Africa, Soyinka has been praised for his work's verbal inventiveness and imaginative power. His plays draw on traditional African myths; these include *The Swamp Dwellers* and *The Strong Breed* (both in *Three Plays*, 1963), *The Road* (1965), and *Death and the King's Horseman* (1975). He has adapted Euripides in *The Bacchae* (1973), and Gay and Brecht in *Opera Wonyosi* (1981). He has edited *Poems from Black Africa* (1975); many of his essays have been collected in *Art, Dialogue and Outrage: Essays on Literature and Culture* (1988). In 1986 he was awarded the Nobel Prize for Literature.

WILLIAM STAFFORD (AMERICAN, 1914–1993). William Stafford was born in Hutchinson, Kansas. He was educated at the University of Kansas and at the University of Iowa, where he earned his Ph.D. An extremely prolific writer—he has published thirty-four volumes of poetry alone—Stafford began his lifelong habit of writing before dawn each day. His first book, *Poems*, was not published until he was forty-five; it was followed by *West of the City* (1960) and *Traveling through the Dark* (1962), winner of the National Book Award. *The Way It Is: New and Selected Poems* was published in 1998. Stafford's work is distinguished by its evenness of tone and its conversational idiom: he likes his poetry, as he has said, "much like talk, with some enhancement." His favored landscapes, mental and physical, are planes: "In scenery I like flat country. / In life I don't like much to happen," he wrote in "Passing Remark." Apart from poems, he has published critical prose, including *Writing the Australian Crawl: Views on the Writer's Vocation* (1978), *You Must Revise Your Life* (1986), and the posthumous *Crossing Unmarked Snow.* For thirty years he taught at Lewis and Clarke College in Portland, Oregon, and in 1970 he served as poetry consultant to the Library of Congress. He was named Oregon's poet laureate in 1975 and was honored in 1992 with a Western States Book Award for lifetime achievement in poetry. He died in his home in Oregon in 1993.

WALLACE STEVENS (AMERICAN, 1879–1955). The facts of Wallace Stevens's professional life are perhaps different from what one would expect of a poet one critic has named the twentieth century's "third great imaginative force" along with YEATS and ELIOT. Born in Reading, Pennsylvania, in 1879 and educated at Harvard, Stevens worked first as a journalist with the *New York Herald Tribune.* He was, however, unhappy, and at his father's suggestion entered New York Law School and was admitted to the New York Bar in 1904. In 1916 he joined the legal staff of Hartford Accident and Indemnity Company and remained with the firm all his life, becoming vice president in 1934. Stevens's early verse had been published in *Poetry* magazine. His first collection, *Harmonium,* appeared in 1923 and, though it sold little, was well received by reviewers such as MARIANNE MOORE. His second volume, *Ideas of Order,* appeared in 1935. In these and other collections — *The Man with the Blue Guitar and Other Poems* (1937), *Parts of a World,* and *Notes toward a Supreme Fiction* (both published 1942) — Stevens puts forth his views on reality, art, and the imagination. He combines his Romantic heritage with a distinctly modern sensibility, aiming to capture a "physical poetry" of the world while placing poetry against religion as "the

supreme fiction." He was awarded the Bollingen Prize in 1950, and his *Collected Poems* (1954) won the Pulitzer Prize. *Opus Posthumous* (1957) contains poems, essays, and plays, many previously unpublished.

Quotable: "There is, in fact, a world of poetry indistinguishable from the world in which we live, or, I ought to say, no doubt, from the world in which we shall come to live, since what makes the poet the potent figure that he is, or was, or ought to be, is that he creates the world to which we turn incessantly and without knowing it and that he gives to life the supreme fictions without which we are unable to conceive it."
— *The Necessary Angel*

MAY SWENSON (AMERICAN, 1919–1989). May Swenson was born in Logan, Utah, and earned her bachelor's degree from Utah State University in 1939. Her first book of poems, *Another Animal,* appeared in 1954, followed by *A Cage of Spines* (1958) and *To Mix with Time: New and Selected Poems* (1963). From 1959 to 1966, she served as editor at New Directions publishers; she taught poetry at Bryn Mawr, the University of North Carolina, the University of California, Riverside, Purdue University, and Utah State University. Though much of her later poetry is devoted to children, she also published translations of contemporary Swedish poets, including the collection *Iconographs* (1970) and the selected poems of Tomas Tranströmer (*Windows and Stones,* 1972). A recipient of numerous grants and fellowships — among them a Guggenheim, a Ford Foundation Poet-Playwright Grant, an Amy Lowell Poetry Traveling Scholarship, and a Robert Frost Fellowship — she was a member of the National Institute of Arts and Letters and served as chancellor of The Academy of American Poets from 1980 until her death in 1989. Experimental yet formally sound, her work delights in artistic arrangement and visual placement, in the shape of a poem on the page. According to the critic Harold Bloom, she ranks with MARIANNE MOORE and ELIZABETH BISHOP as one of the three best women poets of the twentieth century.

ALFRED, LORD TENNYSON (ENGLISH, 1809–1892). Born in Somersby, Lincolnshire, Alfred, Lord Tennyson was educated at Trinity

College, Cambridge but left without taking a degree. His early collection, *Poems, Chiefly Lyrical*, was published in 1830 but was not well received. Following ten years' silence, during which his friend from Cambridge, Arthur Henry Hallam, died, Tennyson published a revised edition of *Poems* (1842), including such major works as "The Lady of Shallott," "Ulysses," and "The Lotos-Eaters." He had begun his long elegy for Hallam as early as 1834, published in 1850 as *In Memoriam*. In that year he succeeded WORDSWORTH as poet laureate. In 1855 he published *Maud and Other Poems*, including the monodrama of the title and "The Charge of the Light Brigade," and from 1859 to 1885 he issued his series of Arthurian poems, *The Idylls of the King*. He continued to write poems and plays until his death in 1892. A meticulous craftsman with an exquisite ear for the music of verse and the fluctuations of thought, Tennyson stands with ROBERT BROWNING as creator of the Victorian dramatic monologue. His variety of verse forms extended the range of metrical poetry in English. Though his reputation has wavered somewhat since his death, his work has deeply influenced poets of the twentieth century, particularly T. S. ELIOT. Of Tennyson's technical accomplishment in *In Memoriam*, Eliot wrote: "I do not think any poet in English has ever had a finer ear for vowel sound, as well as a subtler feeling for some moods of anguish."

DYLAN THOMAS (WELSH, 1914–1953). Dylan Marlais Thomas was born in what he later remembered as the "ugly lovely town" of Swansea, Wales. His father taught English at Swansea Grammar School, and Thomas was educated there. He left school in 1931 and worked for a time as a reporter. In 1934 he moved to London and published his first book, *18 Poems*. A second collection, *Twenty-five Poems* (1936), attracted the attention of distinguished literary figures, among them Dame Edith Sitwell. During World War I, Thomas worked as a scriptwriter and broadcaster for the BBC. His volumes of stories, *The Map of Love* (1939) and *Portrait of the Artist as a Young Dog* (1940), as well as his *New Poems* (1943), established his reputation. Following the publication of *Collected Poems* (1953), Thomas embarked on a number of reading tours in the United States, where his charismatic and ebullient personality and rich intoning of his work drew large audiences. His play for voices, *Under Milk Wood*, was written in 1952. In 1953, while in New York, he died of alcohol poisoning. His poems revel in rhetorical exuberance and formal limitation: they seem, like his speaker in "Fern Hill," to "[sing] in [their] chains like the sea." Their linguistic richness and clotted texture at times recall the poetry of GERARD MANLEY HOPKINS, while their networks of religious, archetypal, and biological imagery and wealth of paradox resemble the poetry of the metaphysical and symbolist traditions.

Quotable: "Poetry is the rhythmic, inevitably narrative, movement from an over-clothed blindness to a naked vision that depends in its intensity on the strength of the labour put into the creation of the poetry. My poetry is, or should be, useful to me for one reason: it is the record of my individual struggle from darkness towards some measure of light." — *Reply to a Questionnaire*

JOHN UPDIKE (AMERICAN, B. 1932). Born in Shillington, Pennsylvania, John Updike has authored numerous works of prose fiction, poetry, and literary criticism. His mother was a writer, his father a high school mathematics teacher. He graduated *summa cum laude* from Harvard in 1954 and left for England, where he spent a year on fellowship at the Ruskin School of Drawing and Fine Art in Oxford. Following his return to the United States, Updike took a position on the staff of *The New Yorker*, to which he has contributed short stories, poems, humor, and book reviews since 1960. In 1958 he published his first collection of verse, *The Carpentered Hen* (issued in Britain as *Hoping for a Hoopoe*). His novels, beginning with *The Poorhouse Fair* (1959), established him as a keen observer of American life; his tetralogy *Rabbit, Run* (1960), *Rabbit Redux* (1971), *Rabbit Is Rich* (1981), and *Rabbit at Rest* (1990), won two Pulitzer Prizes and secured his reputation. *The Centaur* won the National Book Award; other novels, notably *The Witches of Eastwick* (1982) and *Roger's Version* (1986), have turned to metaphysical matters. His prose has been collected in *Forty Stories* (1987) and the autobiographical *Self-Consciousness* (1989), while his book reviews and essays for *The New Yorker* and *The New York Review of Books* may be found in *Assorted Prose* (1965), *Picked-Up Pieces* (1978), *Hugging the Shore* (1983), and *Odd Jobs* (1991). Of his life in letters he has written, "We walk through volumes of the unexpressed and like snails leave behind a faint thread excreted out of ourselves."

ALICE WALKER (AMERICAN, B. 1944). The eighth child of Southern sharecroppers, Alice Walker was born in Eatonton, Georgia. A gunshot accident at the age of eight left her permanently blind in one eye. Of that time she has written, "I no longer felt like the little girl I was . . . I retreated into solitude, and read stories and began to write poems." In 1961, Walker received a scholarship to attend Spelman College in Atlanta; she was dismissed for her involvement in civil rights demonstrations. She transferred to Sarah Lawrence College in 1963 and received her B.A. in 1965. She was awarded a writing fellowship after graduation, with which she planned to return to Africa, where she had been an exchange student. She decided, however, to spend the time as a volunteer in the voter registration drive in Mississippi in the summer of 1966, later claiming that she "could never live happily in Africa — or anywhere else — until [she] could live freely in Mississippi." Her first book of poetry, *Once,* appeared in 1968, followed by *Revolutionary Petunias and Other Poems* in 1973. In 1982, her novel *The Color Purple* was published; it won the Pulitzer Prize and was adapted into a film in 1985. Since that time, she has continued to write poetry and fiction, as well as critical essays. In all of her work, she treats with insight and clarity the experience of African Americans in the twentieth century.

Quotable: "No one could wish for a more advantageous heritage than that bequeathed to the black writer in the South: a compassion for the earth, a trust in humanity beyond our knowledge of evil, and abiding love of justice. We inherit a great responsibility . . . for we must give voice to centuries not only of silent bitterness and hate but also of neighborly kindness and sustaining love." — *Everyday Use*

WALT WHITMAN (AMERICAN, 1819–1892). Born on Long Island, Walt Whitman left school in 1830 to become a printer's apprentice. Through the mid-1840s he worked as an editor for newspapers in Brooklyn and Long Island. During this time he also began to write poetry and short stories. In 1855, he published his first book of poems, *Leaves of Grass.* The book made little impression, though Whitman did receive a letter of praise from Ralph Waldo Emerson, which was printed in the second edition (1856). *Leaves of Grass,* Whitman's chief work, contains such major poems as *Song of Myself, Crossing Brooklyn Ferry,* and *When Lilacs Last in the Dooryard Bloom'd* — Whitman's elegy for Abraham Lincoln. *Drum Taps,* the sequence inspired by his experience in the Civil War (he served as a nurse), was included in the 1867 edition. Whitman's verse represents a turning point in American poetry. In form, in subject matter, it was revolutionary; its scope seemed determined to include everything. Nothing human was to be alien, and if such inclusiveness disturbed the reader, it did not bother Whitman: "Do I contradict myself?" he asks famously in *Song of Myself.* "Very well then I contradict myself. / (I am large, I contain multitudes.)" Barbaric, profane, crude — all charges to which Whitman was subjected in his career (and which he welcomed) — he has continued to influence American poets.

Quotable: "Every really new person (poet or other,) *makes* his style — sometimes a little removed from the previous models — sometimes very far removed." — *Letters*

RICHARD WILBUR (AMERICAN, B. 1921). Of the distinguished generation of American poets that included A. R. AMMONS, ROBERT BLY, JAMES DICKEY, GALWAY KINNELL, Adrienne Rich, and W. D. Snodgrass, Richard Wilbur was born in New York City in 1921, the son of a portrait painter. He attended Amherst College and served in World War II. Following the war, he completed his education at Harvard and then taught, first there, then at Wellesley College, Wesleyan University, and Smith College. He has since retired to write. His first volume of poems, *The Beautiful Changes* (1947), established him as an already adroit practitioner in traditional verse forms; it was followed by *Ceremony and Other Poems* (1950). His *Things of This World* (1956), achieved the rare distinction of winning both the Pulitzer Prize and the National Book Award for poetry. Numerous collections have followed; his *New and Collected Poems* was issued in 1988, earning him another Pulitzer. Apart from his own poetry he has shown himself an accomplished translator of the plays of Racine and Molière (for which he won the Bollingen Prize in 1963) and the poetry of Jorge Luis Borges. In 1987 he was named poet laureate of the United States. Witty, urbane, yet passionately attached to the world, his poems at their best clarify and sharpen consciousness, record "The Beautiful Changes" subtly, gracefully, "as a forest is changed / By a chameleon's tuning his skin to it."

Quotable: "In general, I would say that [poetic] limitation makes for power: the strength of the genie comes of his being confined in a bottle."
— *Mid-Century American Poets*

WILLIAM CARLOS WILLIAMS (AMERICAN, 1883–1963). William Carlos Williams was born in Rutherford, New Jersey, the son of an English father and a Puerto Rican mother. He attended French and Swiss schools before entering the University of Pennsylvania, where he studied medicine. While there, he became acquainted with EZRA POUND and HILDA DOOLITTLE, figures who perhaps inspired his conviction that poetry must occupy itself with the objective and concrete treatment of things ("No ideas but in things," he was later to write). Following further medical study in New York and Leipzig, Williams returned to Rutherford in 1909 and began to practice medicine there. His first volume, *Poems,* had appeared in 1900; it was followed by *The Tempers* (1913), *Al Que Quiere!* (1917), *Kora in Hell: Improvisations* (1920), *Sour Grapes* (1921), and *Spring and All* (1923). In these and later works Williams established himself as one of the more innovative and original poets of his day. His poetry was extremely influential in its casting off of traditional verse structures and in its forging of a colloquial language for poetry "in the American grain." For Williams, the ordinary provided world enough for poems; the treatment was all. His *Pictures from Brueghel and Other Poems* (1962) was awarded the Pulitzer Prize in 1963. His *Collected Poems* appeared posthumously in two volumes from 1986 to 1988.

Quotable: "I propose sweeping changes from top to bottom of the poetic structure.... I say we are *through* with the iambic pentameter as presently conceived, at least for dramatic verse; through with the measured quatrain, the staid concatenations of sounds in the usual stanza, the sonnet."
— *Selected Essays*

WILLIAM WORDSWORTH (ENGLISH, 1770–1850). William Wordsworth was born in Cockermouth, Cumberland. He was educated at Hawkshead in the Lake District and at St. John's College, Cambridge. In 1790 he embarked on a walking tour through France and Switzerland, commemorated in his early collection, *Descriptive Sketches* (1793). While in France, Wordsworth became devoted to the ideals of the French Revolution. On returning to England, Wordsworth lived with his sister, Dorothy, who was to have a profound effect on his early poetry. Settling at Somerset, he developed a friendship with SAMUEL TAYLOR COLERIDGE, and the two began to compose the poems that would appear in *Lyrical Ballads* (1798), issued with a preface by Wordsworth that was effectively a manifesto for early English Romanticism. Following a year in Germany with Coleridge and Dorothy, Wordsworth married Mary Hutchinson in 1802 and began work on *The Prelude,* in which he traces the growth of a poet's mind. The first thirteen books were published in 1805; a revised edition appeared posthumously in 1850. In 1843 he was made poet laureate. In later life Wordsworth became a kind of institution, receiving visits from admirers and political sympathizers at his home in Rydal Mount. Though his poetic powers waned in old age, and though his conservatism fell under criticism by the younger generation of Romantic poets, his revolutionary early work, his experiment with new verse forms, and his opening of new territory for poetry remained a deep and enduring legacy.

Quotable: "I have said that poetry is the spontaneous overflow of powerful feelings; it takes its origin from emotion recollected in tranquillity: the emotion is contemplated till, by a species of reaction, the tranquillity gradually disappears, and an emotion, kindred to that which was before the subject of contemplation, is gradually produced, and does itself exist in the mind. In this mood successful composition generally begins, and in a mood similar to this it is carried on." — *Preface to Lyrical Ballads*

WILLIAM BUTLER YEATS (IRISH, 1865–1939). Born near Dublin, William Butler Yeats remains one of the most influential and widely studied poets of the twentieth century. His early work is immersed in the mythology and folktales of his native Ireland, combined with an interest in mysticism and the occult. His childhood was divided between London and Sligo, in the west of Ireland, where his mother's family lived. He was involved in Ireland's struggle for independence, concentrating his energies in the creation of a national literature and culture rather than in the political insurgence of many nationalists of the time. One of these, the beautiful Maud Gonne, remained his love throughout his life, and he composed a number of love poems to and about her. Yeats was also an accomplished playwright, and he helped to found the Abbey, Ireland's national theater, in 1904. In 1922 he became senator of the Irish Free State and in 1923 was awarded the Nobel Prize for Literature. His poems, plays, essays, memoirs, and correspondence have appeared in numerous editions; they include *The Collected Poems of W. B. Yeats* (1989), *Collected Plays* (1953), *Essays and Introductions* (1961), *Explorations* (1962), *Autobiographies* (1955), and *Collected Letters* (1986). He died in France in 1939; his coffin was disinterred in 1948 and taken to Sligo to be buried, as one of his last poems dictates, "Under Ben Bulben."

Quotable: "We make out of the quarrel with others, rhetoric, but of the quarrel with ourselves, poetry." — *Mythologies*

A Collection
of Poems

38

Poems for Further Reading

MAYA ANGELOU (B. 1924)

Africa   1975

Thus she had lain
sugar cane sweet
deserts her hair
golden her feet
mountains her breasts   5
two Niles her tears
Thus she has lain
Black through the years.

Over the white seas
rime white and cold   10
brigands ungentled
icicle bold
took her young daughters
sold her strong sons
churched her with Jesus   15
bled her with guns.
Thus she has lain.

Now she is rising
remember her pain
remember the losses   20
her screams loud and vain
remember her riches
her history slain
now she is striding
although she had lain.   25

ANONYMOUS (TRADITIONAL SCOTTISH BALLAD)

Bonny Barbara Allan

date unknown

It was in and about the Martinmas° time,
    When the green leaves were afalling,
That Sir John Graeme, in the West Country,
    Fell in love with Barbara Allan.

He sent his men down through the town,   5
    To the place where she was dwelling:
"Oh haste and come to my master dear,
    Gin° ye be Barbara Allan."   *if*

O hooly,° hooly rose she up,   *slowly*
    To the place where he was lying,   10
And when she drew the curtain by:
    "Young man, I think you're dying."

"O it's I'm sick, and very, very sick,
    And 'tis a' for Barbara Allan." —
"O the better for me ye's never be,   15
    Tho your heart's blood were aspilling."

"O dinna ye mind,° young man," she said,   *don't you remember*
    "When ye was in the tavern adrinking,
That ye made the health° gae round and round,   *toasts*
    And slighted Barbara Allan?"   20

He turned his face unto the wall,
    And death was with him dealing:
"Adieu, adieu, my dear friends all,
    And be kind to Barbara Allan."

And slowly, slowly raise her up,   25
    And slowly, slowly left him,
And sighing said she could not stay,
    Since death of life had reft him.

She had not gane a mile but twa,
    When she heard the dead-bell ringing,   30
And every jow° that the dead-bell geid,   *stroke*
    It cried, "Woe to Barbara Allan!"

"O mother, mother, make my bed!
    O make it saft and narrow!
Since my love died for me today,   35
    I'll die for him tomorrow."

1 *Martinmas:* St. Martin's Day, November 11.

W. H. AUDEN (1907–1973)

The Unknown Citizen   1940

(To JS/07/M/378
This Marble Monument
Is Erected by the State)

He was found by the Bureau of Statistics to be
One against whom there was no official complaint,
And all the reports on his conduct agree
That, in the modern sense of an old-fashioned word, he was a saint,
For in everything he did he served the Greater Community.   5
Except for the War till the day he retired
He worked in a factory and never got fired,
But satisfied his employers, Fudge Motors Inc.
Yet he wasn't a scab or odd in his views,
For his Union reports that he paid his dues,   10
(Our report on his Union shows it was sound)
And our Social Psychology workers found
That he was popular with his mates and liked a drink.
The Press are convinced that he bought a paper every day
And that his reactions to advertisements were normal in every way.   15
Policies taken out in his name prove that he was fully insured,
And his Health-card shows he was once in hospital but left it cured.
Both Producers Research and High-Grade Living declare
He was fully sensible to the advantages of the Installment Plan
And had everything necessary to the Modern Man,   20
A phonograph, radio, car and a frigidaire.
Our researchers into Public Opinion are content
That he held the proper opinions for the time of year;
When there was peace, he was for peace; when there was war, he went.
He was married and added five children to the population,   25
Which our Eugenist says was the right number for a parent of his generation,
And our teachers report that he never interfered with their education.
Was he free? Was he happy? The question is absurd:
Had anything been wrong, we should certainly have heard.

WILLIAM BLAKE (1757–1827)

The Garden of Love   1794

I went to the Garden of Love,
And saw what I never had seen:
A Chapel was built in the midst,
Where I used to play on the green.

And the gates of this Chapel were shut,   5
And "Thou shalt not" writ over the door;

So I turned to the Garden of Love
That so many sweet flowers bore;

And I saw it was filled with graves,
And tomb-stones where flowers should be;   10
And Priests in black gowns were walking their rounds,
And binding with briars my joys and desires.

WILLIAM BLAKE (1757–1827)

Infant Sorrow   1792

My mother groand! my father wept.
Into the dangerous world I leapt:
Helpless naked piping loud:
Like a fiend hid in a cloud.

Struggling in my fathers hands:
Striving against my swadling bands
Bound and weary I thought best
To sulk upon my mothers breast.

ROBERT BLY (B. 1926)

Snowfall in the Afternoon   1962

1
The grass is half-covered with snow.
It was the sort of snowfall that starts in late afternoon.
And now the little houses of the grass are growing dark.

2
If I reached my hands down, near the earth,
I could take handfuls of darkness!   5
A darkness was always there, which we never noticed.

3
As the snow grows heavier, the cornstalks fade farther away,
And the barn moves nearer to the house.
The barn moves all alone in the growing storm.

4
The barn is full of corn, and moving toward us now,   10
Like a hulk blown toward us in a storm at sea;
All the sailors on deck have been blind for many years.

ANNE BRADSTREET (C. 1612–1672)

Before the Birth of One of Her Children   1678

All things within this fading world hath end,
Adversity doth still our joys attend;
No ties so strong, no friends so dear and sweet,
But with death's parting blow is sure to meet.
The sentence past is most irrevocable,   5
A common thing, yet oh, inevitable.
How soon, my Dear, death may my steps attend,
How soon't may be thy lot to lose thy friend,
We both are ignorant, yet love bids me
These farewell lines to recommend to thee,   10
That when that knot's untied that made us one,
I may seem thine, who is effect am none.
And if I see not half my days that's due,
What nature would, God grant to yours and you;
The many faults that well you know I have   15
Let be interred in my oblivious grave;
If any worth or virtue were in me,
Let that live freshly in thy memory
And when thou feel'st no grief, as I no harms,
Yet love thy dead, who long lay in thine arms,   20
And when thy loss shall be repaid with gains
Look to my little babes, my dear remains.
And if thou love thyself, or loved'st me,
These O protect from stepdame's° injury.   *stepmother's*
And if chance to thine eyes shall bring this verse,   25
With some sad sighs honor my absent hearse;
And kiss this paper for thy love's dear sake,
Who with salt tears this last farewell did take.

GWENDOLYN BROOKS (1917–2000)

The Mother   1945

Abortions will not let you forget.
You remember the children you got that you did not get,
The damp small pulps with a little or with no hair,
The singers and workers that never handled the air.
You will never neglect or beat   5
Them, or silence or buy with a sweet.
You will never wind up the sucking-thumb
Or scuttle off ghosts that come.
You will never leave them, controlling your luscious sigh,
Return for a snack of them, with gobbling mother-eye.   10

I have heard in the voices of the wind the voices of my dim
          killed children
I have contracted. I have eased

My dim dears at the breasts they could never suck.
I have said, Sweets, if I sinned, if I seized
Your luck   15
And your lives from your unfinished reach,
If I stole your births and your names,
Your straight baby tears and your games,
Your stilted or lovely loves, your tumults, your marriages, aches,
        and your deaths,
If I poisoned the beginnings of your breaths,   20
Believe that even in my deliberateness I was not deliberate.
Though why should I whine,
Whine that the crime was other than mine? —
Since anyhow you are dead.
Or rather, or instead,   25
You were never made.

But that too, I am afraid,
Is faulty: oh, what shall I say, how is the truth to be said?
You were born, you had body, you died.
It is just that you never giggled or planned or cried.   30

Believe me, I loved you all.
Believe me, I knew you, though faintly, and I loved, I loved you
All.

ROBERT BROWNING (1812–1889)

Meeting at Night   1845

The gray sea and the long black land;
And the yellow half-moon large and low;
And the startled little waves that leap
In firey ringlets from their sleep,
As I gain the cove with pushing prow,   5
And quench its speed i' the slushy sand.

Then a mile of warm sea-scented beach;
Three fields to cross till a farm appears;
A tap at the pane, the quick sharp scratch
And blue spurt of a lighted match,   10
And a voice less loud, through its joys and fears,
Than the two hearts beating each to each!

ROBERT BROWNING (1812–1889)

Parting at Morning   1845

Round the cape of a sudden came the sea,
And the sun looked over the mountain's rim:
And straight was a path of gold for him,
And the need of a world of men for me.

GEORGE GORDON, LORD BYRON (1788–1824)

She Walks in Beauty   1814

From Hebrew Melodies

I
She walks in Beauty, like the night
  Of cloudless climes and starry skies;
And all that's best of dark and bright
  Meet in her aspect and her eyes:
Thus mellowed to that tender light   5
  Which Heaven to gaudy day denies.

II
One shade the more, one ray the less,
  Had half impaired the nameless grace
Which waves in every raven tress,
  Or softly lightens o'er her face;   10
Where thoughts serenely sweet express,
  How pure, how dear their dwelling-place.

III
And on that cheek, and o'er that brow,
  So soft, so calm, yet eloquent,
The smiles that win, the tints that glow,   15
  But tell of days in goodness spent,
A mind at peace with all below,
  A heart whose love is innocent!

SAMUEL TAYLOR COLERIDGE (1772–1834)

Kubla Khan: or, a Vision in a Dream°   1798

In Xanadu did Kubla Khan°
  A stately pleasure-dome decree:
Where Alph, the sacred river, ran
Through caverns measureless to man
  Down to a sunless sea.   5

So twice five miles of fertile ground
With walls and towers were girdled round:
And here were gardens bright with sinuous rills
Where blossomed many an incense-bearing tree;
And there were forests ancient as the hills,   10
Enfolding sunny spots of greenery.

Vision in a Dream: This poem came to Coleridge in an opium-induced dream, but he was interrupted by a visitor while writing it down. He was later unable to remember the rest of the poem. 1 *Kubla Khan:* The historical Kublai Khan (1216–1294, grandson of Genghis Khan) was the founder of the Mongol dynasty in China.

But oh! that deep romantic chasm which slanted
Down the green hill athwart a cedarn cover!°
A savage place! as holy and enchanted
As e'er beneath a waning moon was haunted   15
By woman wailing for her demon-lover!
And from this chasm, with ceaseless turmoil seething,
As if this earth in fast thick pants were breathing,
A mighty fountain momently was forced,
Amid whose swift half-intermitted burst   20
Huge fragments vaulted like rebounding hail,
Of chaffy grain beneath the thresher's flail:
And 'mid these dancing rocks at once and ever
It flung up momently the sacred river.
Five miles meandering with a mazy motion   25
Through wood and dale the sacred river ran,
Then reached the caverns measureless to man,
And sank in tumult to a lifeless ocean:
And 'mid this tumult Kubla heard from far
Ancestral voices prophesying war!   30
    The shadow of the dome of pleasure
    Floated midway on the waves;
    Where was heard the mingled measure
    From the fountain and the caves.
It was a miracle of rare device,   35
A sunny pleasure-dome with caves of ice!

    A damsel with a dulcimer
    In a vision once I saw:
    It was an Abyssinian maid,
    And on her dulcimer she played,   40
    Singing of Mount Abora.
    Could I revive within me
    Her symphony and song,
    To such a deep delight 'twould win me,
That with music loud and long,   45
I would build that dome in air,
That sunny dome! those caves of ice!
And all who heard should see them there,
And all should cry, Beware! Beware!
His flashing eyes, his floating hair!   50
Weave a circle round him thrice,
And close your eyes with holy dread,
For he on honey-dew hath fed,
And drunk the milk of Paradise.

13 *athwart . . . cover:* Spanning a grove of cedar trees.

SAMUEL TAYLOR COLERIDGE (1772–1834)

Sonnet to the River Otter   *1797*

Dear native brook! wild streamlet of the West!
    How many various-fated years have past,
    What happy, and what mournful hours, since last
I skimmed the smooth thin stone along thy breast,
Numbering its light leaps! yet so deep imprest   5
Sink the sweet scenes of childhood, that mine eyes
    I never shut amid the sunny ray,
But straight with all their tints thy waters rise,
    Thy crossing plank, thy marge with willows gray,
And bedded sand that, veined with various dyes,   10
Gleamed through thy bright transparence! On my way,
    Visions of childhood! oft have ye beguiled
Lone manhood's cares, yet waking fondest sighs:
    Ah! that once more I were a careless child!

VICTOR HERNÁNDEZ CRUZ (B. 1949)

Anonymous   *1982*

And if I lived in those olden times
With a funny name like Choicer or
Henry Howard, Earl of Surrey, what chimes!
I would spend my time in search of rhymes
Make sure the measurement termination surprise   5
In the court of kings snapping till woo sunrise
Plus always be using the words *alas* and *hath*
And not even knowing that that was my path
Just think on the Lower East Side of Manhattan
It would have been like living in satin   10
Alas! The projects hath not covered the river
Thou see-est vision to make thee quiver
Hath I been delivered to that "wildernesse"
So past
I would have been the last one in the   15
Dance to go
Taking note the minuet so slow
All admire my taste
Within thou *mambo* of much more haste.

COUNTEE CULLEN (1903–1946)

Yet Do I Marvel   *1925*

I doubt not God is good, well-meaning, kind,
And did He stoop to quibble could tell why
The little buried mole continues blind,

Why flesh that mirrors Him must some day die,
Make plain the reason tortured Tantalus   5
Is baited by the fickle fruit, declare
If merely brute caprice dooms Sisyphus
To struggle up a never-ending stair.
Inscrutable His ways are, and immune
To catechism by a mind too strewn   10
With petty cares to slightly understand
What awful brain compels His awful hand.
Yet do I marvel at this curious thing:
To make a poet black, and bid him sing!

E. E. Cummings (1894–1962)

Buffalo Bill's°   1923

Buffalo Bill's
defunct
            who used to
            ride a watersmooth-silver
                                        stallion   5
and break onetwothreefourfive pigeonsjustlikethat
                                        Jesus
he was a handsome man
                        and what i want to know is
how do you like your blueeyed boy   10
Mister Death

Buffalo Bill: William Frederick Cody (1846–1917) was an American frontier scout and Indian killer turned international circus showman with his Wild West show, which employed Sitting Bull and Annie Oakley.

Gregory Djanikian (b. 1949)

When I First Saw Snow   1989

Tarrytown, N.Y.

Bing Crosby was singing "White Christmas"
        on the radio, we were staying at my aunt's house
        waiting for papers, my father was looking for a job.
We had trimmed the tree the night before,
        sap had run on my fingers and for the first time   5
        I was smelling pine wherever I went.
Anais, my cousin, was upstairs in her room
        listening to Danny and the Juniors.
Haigo was playing Monopoly with Lucy, his sister,
        Buzzy, the boy next door, had eyes for her   10

and there was a rattle of dice, a shuffling
of Boardwalk, Park Place, Marvin Gardens.
There were red bows on the Christmas tree.
It had snowed all night.
My boot buckles were clinking like small bells   15
    as I thumped to the door and out
    onto the gray planks of the porch dusted with snow.
The world was immaculate, new,
    even the trees had changed color,
    and when I touched the snow on the railing   20
    I didn't know what I had touched, ice or fire.
I heard, "I'm dreaming . . ."
I heard, "At the hop, hop, hop . . . oh, baby."
I heard "B & O" and the train in my imagination
    was whistling through the great plains.   25
And I was stepping off,
I was falling deeply into America.

JOHN DONNE (1572–1631)

Batter My Heart   *1610*

Batter my heart, three-personed God; for You
As yet but knock, breathe, shine, and seek to mend;
That I may rise and stand, o'erthrow me, and bend
Your force, to break, blow, burn, and make me new.
I, like an usurped town, to another due,   5
Labor to admit You, but Oh, to no end!
Reason, Your viceroy in me, me should defend,
But is captived, and proves weak or untrue.
Yet dearly I love You, and would be loved fain.
But am betrothed unto Your enemy: 10
Divorce me, untie, or break that knot again,
Take me to You, imprison me, for I,
Except You enthrall me, never shall be free,
Nor ever chaste, except You ravish me.

JOHN DONNE (1572–1631)

The Flea   *1633*

Mark but this flea, and mark in this°
How little that which thou deny'st me is;
It sucked me first, and now sucks thee,
And in this flea our two bloods mingled be;
Thou know'st that this cannot be said   5

---

1 *mark in this:* Take note of the moral lesson in this object.

A sin, nor shame, nor loss of maidenhead,
   Yet this enjoys before it woo,
   And pampered swells with one blood made of two,
   And this, alas, is more than we would do.°

Oh stay, three lives in one flea spare,   10
Where we almost, yea more than, married are.
This flea is you and I, and this
Our marriage bed, and marriage temple is;
Though parents grudge, and you, we're met
And cloistered in these living walls of jet.   15
   Though use° make you apt to kill me,   *habit*
   Let not to that, self-murder added be,
   And sacrilege, three sins in killing three.

Cruel and sudden, hast thou since
Purpled thy nail in blood of innocence?
Wherein could this flea guilty be,   20
Except in that drop which it sucked from thee?
Yet thou triumph'st, and say'st that thou
Find'st not thyself, nor me, the weaker now;
   'Tis true; then learn how false, fears be;   25
   Just so much honor, when thou yield'st to me,
   Will waste, as this flea's death took life from thee.

9 *more than we would do:* That is, if we do not join our blood in conceiving a child.

GEORGE ELIOT (MARY ANN EVANS / 1819–1880)

In a London Drawingroom   *1865*

The sky is cloudy, yellowed by the smoke.
For view there are the houses opposite,
Cutting the sky with one long line of wall
Like solid fog: far as the eye can stretch
Monotony of surface and of form   5
Without a break to hang a guess upon.
No bird can make a shadow as it flies,
For all its shadow, as in ways o'erhung
By thickest canvas, where the golden rays
Are clothed in hemp. No figure lingering   10
Pauses to feed the hunger of the eye
Or rest a little on the lap of life.
All hurry on and look upon the ground
Or glance unmarking at the passersby.
The wheels are hurrying, too, cabs, carriages   15
All closed, in multiplied identity.
The world seems one huge prison-house and court
Where men are punished at the slightest cost,
With lowest rate of color, warmth, and joy.

THOMAS HARDY (1840–1928)

Hap   *1866*

If but some vengeful god would call to me
From up the sky, and laugh: "Thou suffering thing,
Know that thy sorrow is my ecstasy,
That thy love's loss is my hate's profiting!"

Then would I bear it, clench myself, and die,   5
Steeled by the sense of ire unmerited;
Half-eased in that a Powerfuller than I
Had willed and meted me the tears I shed.

But not so. How arrives it joy lies slain,
And why unblooms the best hope ever sown?   10
— Crass Casualty obstructs the sun and rain,
And dicing Time for gladness casts a moan. . . .
These purblind Doomsters had as readily strown
Blisses about my pilgrimage as pain.

THOMAS HARDY (1840–1928)

In Time of "The Breaking of Nations"°   *1915*

1
Only a man harrowing clods
    In a slow silent walk
With an old horse that stumbles and nods
    Half asleep as they stalk.

2
Only thin smoke without flame   5
    From the heaps of couch-grass;
Yet this will go onward the same
    Though Dynasties pass.

3
Yonder a maid and her wight°   *man*
    Come whispering by: 10
War's annals will cloud into night
    Ere their story die.

The Breaking of Nations: See Jeremiah 51:20: "Thou art my battle axe and weapons of war: for
with thee will I break in pieces the nations, and with thee will I destroy kingdoms."

JOY HARJO (B. 1951)

Fishing

1991

This is the longest day of the year, on the Illinois River or a similar river in
the same place. Cicadas are part of the song as they praise their invisible
ancestors while fish blinking back the relentless sun in Oklahoma circle in
the muggy river of life. They dare the fisher to come and get them. Fish too
anticipate the game of fishing. Their ancestors perfected the moves, sent   5
down stories that appear as electrical impulse when sunlight hits water.
The hook carries great symbology in the coming of age, and is crucial to
the making of warriors. The greatest warriors are those who dangle a
human for hours on a string, break sacred water for the profanity of air
then snap fiercely back into pearly molecules that describe fishness. They   10
smell me as I walk the banks with fishing pole, nightcrawlers and a
promise I made to that old friend Louis to fish with him this summer. This
is the only place I can keep that promise, inside a poem as familiar to him
as the banks of his favorite fishing place. I try not to let the fish see me see
them as they look for his tracks on the soft earth made of fossils and ashes.   15
I hear the burble of fish talk: When is that old Creek coming back? He
was the one we loved to tease most, we liked his songs and once in awhile
he gave us a good run. Last night I dreamed I tried to die, I was going to
look for Louis. It was rather comical. I worked hard to muster my last
breath, then lay down in the summer, along the banks of the last mythic   20
river, my pole and tackle box next to me. What I thought was my last
breath floated off as a cloud making an umbrella of grief over my relatives.
How embarrassing when the next breath came, and then the next. I reeled
in one after another, as if I'd caught a bucket of suckers instead of bass. I
guess it wasn't my time, I explained, and went fishing anyway as a liar   25
and I know most fishers to be liars most of the time. Even Louis when it
came to fishing, or even dying. The leap between the sacred and profane is
as thin as a fishing line, and is part of the mystery on this river of life, as is
the way our people continue to make warriors in the strangest of times. I
save this part of the poem for the fish camp next to the oldest spirits whose   30
dogs bark to greet visitors. It's near Louis's favorite spot where the
wisest and fattest fish laze. I'll meet him there.

FRANCES E. W. HARPER (1825-1911)

Learning to Read

1872

Very soon the Yankee teachers
    Came down and set up school;
But oh! how the Rebs did hate it, —
    It was agin' their rule

Our masters always tried to hide   5
    Book learning from our eyes;

Knowledge didn't agree with slavery —
'Twould make us all too wise.

But some of us would try to steal
    A little from the book,
And put the words together,
    And learn by hook or crook.   10

I remember Uncle Caldwell,
    Who took pot-liquor fat
And greased the pages of his book,   15
    And hid it in his hat.

And had his master ever seen
    The leaves upon his head,
He'd have thought them greasy papers,
    But nothing to be read.   20

And there was Mr. Turner's Ben
    Who heard the children spell,
And picked the words right up by heart,
    And learned to read 'em well.

Well the Northern folks kept sending   25
    The Yankee teachers down
And they stood right up and helped us,
    Though Rebs did sneer and frown,

And, I longed to read my Bible,
    For precious words it said;   30
But when I begun to learn it,
    Folks just shook their heads,

And said there is no use trying,
    Oh! Chloe, you're too late;
But as I was rising sixty,   35
    I had no time to wait.

So I got a pair of glasses,
    And straight to work I went,
And never stopped till I could read
    The hymns and Testament.   40

Then I got a little cabin —
    A place to call my own —
And I felt as independent
    As the queen upon her throne.

ANTHONY HECHT (B. 1923)

The Dover Bitch°

1968

A Criticism of Life

So there stood Matthew Arnold and this girl
With the cliffs of England crumbling away behind them,
And he said to her, "Try to be true to me,
And I'll do the same for you, for things are bad
All over, etc., etc."   5
Well now, I knew this girl. It's true she had read
Sophocles in a fairly good translation
And caught that bitter allusion to the sea,°
But all the time he was talking she had in mind
The notion of what his whiskers would feel like   10
On the back of her neck. She told me later on
That after a while she got to looking out
At the lights across the channel, and really felt sad,
Thinking of all the wine and enormous beds
And blandishments in French and the perfumes.   15
And then she got really angry. To have been brought
All the way down from London, and then be addressed
As a sort of mournful cosmic last resort
Is really tough on a girl, and she was pretty.
Anyway, she watched him pace the room   20
And finger his watch-chain and seem to sweat a bit,
And then she said one or two unprintable things.
But you mustn't judge her by that. What I mean to say is,
She's really all right. I still see her once in a while
And she always treats me right. We have a drink   25
And I give her a good time, and perhaps it's a year
Before I see her again, but there she is,
Running to fat, but dependable as they come.
And sometimes I bring her a bottle of *Nuit d'Amour.*

The Dover Bitch: A parody of Arnold's poem "Dover Beach" (see p. 758).   8 *allusion to the sea:*
Lines 9–18 in "Dover Beach" refer to Sophocles' *Antigone,* lines 583–591.

GEORGE HERBERT (1593–1633)

The Collar

1633

I struck the board° and cried, "No more;   table
        I will abroad!
What? shall I ever sigh and pine?
My lines and life are free, free as the road,
        Loose as the wind, as large as store.°   5

5 *store:* A storehouse or warehouse.

Shall I be still in suit?° serving another
Have I no harvest but a thorn
To let me blood, and not restore
What I have lost with cordial° fruit? restorative
Sure there was wine 10
Before my sighs did dry it; there was corn
Before my tears did drown it.
Is the year only lost to me?
Have I no bays° to crown it, triumphal wreaths
No flowers, no garlands gay? All blasted? 15
All wasted?
Not so, my heart; but there is fruit,
And thou hast hands.
Recover all thy sigh-blown age
On double pleasures: leave thy cold dispute 20
Of what is fit, and not. Forsake thy cage,
Thy rope of sands,
Which petty thoughts have made, and made to thee
Good cable, to enforce and draw,
And be thy law, 25
While thou didst wink and wouldst not see.
Away! take heed;
I will abroad.
Call in thy death's-head° there; tie up thy fears.
He that forbears 30
To suit and serve his need,
Deserves his load."
But as I raved and grew more fierce and wild
At every word,
Methought I heard one calling, *Child!* 35
And I replied, *My Lord.*

29 *death's-head:* A skull, reminder of mortality.

LINDA HOGAN (B. 1947)

Song for My Name 1979

Before sunrise
think of brushing out an old woman's
dark braids.
Think of your hands,
fingertips on the soft hair. 5

If you have this name,
your grandfather's dark hands
lead horses toward the wagon
and a cloud of dust follows,
ghost of silence. 10

That name is full of women
with black hair

and men with eyes like night.
It means no money
tomorrow.   15

Such a name my mother loves
while she works gently
in the small house.
She is a white dove
and in her own land   20
the mornings are pale,
birds sing into the white curtains
and show off their soft breasts.

If you have a name like this,
there's never enough water.   25
There is too much heat.
When lightning strikes, rain
refuses to follow.
It's my name,
that of a woman living   30
between the white moon
and the red sun, waiting to leave.
It's the name that goes with me
back to earth
no one else can touch.   35

M. CARL HOLMAN (1919–1988)

Mr. Z   *1967*

Taught early that his mother's skin was the sign of error,
He dressed and spoke the perfect part of honor;
Won scholarships, attended the best schools,
Disclaimed kinship with jazz and spirituals;
Chose prudent, raceless views for each situation,   5
Or when he could not cleanly skirt dissension,
Faced up to the dilemma, firmly seized
Whatever ground was Anglo-Saxonized.

In diet, too, his practice was exemplary:
Of pork in its profane forms he was wary;   10
Expert in vintage wines, sauces and salads,
His palate shrank from cornbread, yams and collards.

He was as careful whom he chose to kiss:
His bride had somewhere lost her Jewishness,
But kept her blue eyes; an Episcopalian   15
Prelate proclaimed them matched chameleon.
Choosing the right addresses, here, abroad,
They shunned those places where they might be barred;

Even less anxious to be asked to dine
Where hosts catered to kosher accent or exotic skin.   20

And so he climbed, unclogged by ethnic weights,
An airborne plant, flourishing without roots.
Not one false note was struck — until he died:
His subtly grieving widow could have flayed
The obit writers, ringing crude changes on a clumsy phrase: 25
"One of the most distinguished members of his race."

GERARD MANLEY HOPKINS (1844–1889)

Hurrahing in Harvest   *1877*

Summer ends now; now, barbarous in beauty, the stooks° arise   *sheaves*
    Around; up above, what wind walks! what lovely behaviour
    Of silk-sack clouds! has wilder, wilful-wavier
Meal-drift moulded ever and melted across skies?

I walk, I lift up, I lift up heart, eyes,   5
    Down all that glory in the heavens to glean our Saviour;
    And, eyes, heart, what looks, what lips yet gave you a
Rapturous love's greeting of realer, of rounder replies?

And the azurous hung hills are his world-wielding shoulder
    Majestic — as a stallion stalwart, very-violet-sweet! —   10
These things, these things were here and but the beholder
    Wanting; which two when they once meet,
The heart rears wings bold and bolder
    And hurls for him, O half furls earth for him off under his feet.

GERARD MANLEY HOPKINS (1844–1889)

Pied Beauty   *1877*

Glory be to God for dappled things —
    For skies of couple-color as a brinded cow;
        For rose-moles all in stipple upon trout that swim;
Fresh-firecoal chestnut-falls;° finches' wings;   *fallen chestnut*
    Landscape plotted and pieced — fold, fallow, and plow;   5
        And all trades, their gear and tackle and trim.

All things counter, original, spare, strange;
    Whatever is fickle, freckled (who knows how?)
        With swift, slow; sweet, sour; adazzle, dim;
He fathers-forth whose beauty is past change: 10
                Praise him.

GERARD MANLEY HOPKINS (1844–1889)
The Windhover°   *1877*

To Christ Our Lord

I caught this morning morning's minion,° king-   *favorite*
   dom of daylight's dauphin, dapple-dawn-drawn Falcon, in his riding
   Of the rolling level underneath him steady air, and striding
High there, how he rung upon the rein of a wimpling wing
In his ecstasy! then off, off forth on swing,   5
   As a skate's heel sweeps smooth on a bow-bend: the hurl and gliding
   Rebuffed the big wind. My heart in hiding
Stirred for a bird, — the achieve of, the mastery of the thing!

Brute beauty and valour and act, oh, air, pride, plume, here
   Buckle!° AND the fire that breaks from thee then, a billion   10
Times told lovelier, more dangerous, O my chevalier!

   No wonder of it: shéer plód makes plough down sillion°   *furrow*
Shine, and blue-bleak embers, ah my dear,
   Fall, gall themselves, and gash gold-vermilion.

The Windhover: "A name for the kestrel [a kind of small hawk], from its habit of hovering or hanging with its head to the wind" [*OED*]. 10 *Buckle:* To join, to equip for battle, to crumple.

A. E. HOUSMAN (1859–1936)
To an Athlete Dying Young   *1896*

The time you won your town the race
We chaired° you through the marketplace;
Man and boy stood cheering by,
And home we brought you shoulder-high.

Today, the road all runners come,   5
Shoulder-high we bring you home,
And set you at your threshold down,
Townsman of a stiller town.

Smart lad, to slip betimes away
From fields where glory does not stay,   10
And early though the laurel° grows
It withers quicker than the rose.

Eyes the shady night has shut
Cannot see the record cut,

2 *chaired:* Carried on the shoulders in triumphal parade. 11 *laurel:* Flowering shrub traditionally used to fashion wreaths of honor.

And silence sounds no worse than cheers   15
After earth has stopped the ears:

Now you will not swell the rout
Of lads that wore their honors out,
Runners whom renown outran
And the name died before the man.   20

To set, before its echoes fade,
The fleet foot on the sill of shade,
And hold to the low lintel up
The still-defended challenge-cup.

And round that early-laureled head   25
Will flock to gaze the strengthless dead,
And find unwithered on its curls
The garland briefer than a girl's.

BEN JONSON (1573–1637)

On My First Son   *1603*

Farewell, thou child of my right hand,° and joy.
My sin was too much hope of thee, loved boy;
Seven years thou wert lent to me, and I thee pay,
Exacted by thy fate, on the just day.°   *his birthday*
Oh, could I lose all father° now. For why   *fatherhood* 5
Will man lament the state he should envy? —
To have so soon 'scaped world's and flesh's rage,
And, if no other misery, yet age.
Rest in soft peace, and asked, say, "Here doth lie
Ben Jonson his best piece of poetry,"   10
For whose sake henceforth all his vows be such
As what he loves may never like too much.

1 *child of my right hand:* This phrase translates the Hebrew name "Benjamin," Jonson's son.

BEN JONSON (1573–1637)

To Celia   *1616*

Drink to me only with thine eyes,
    And I will pledge with mine;
Or leave a kiss but in the cup,
    And I'll not ask for wine.
The thirst that from the soul doth rise   5
    Doth ask a drink divine;
But might I of Jove's nectar sup,
    I would not change for thine.

I sent thee late a rosy wreath,
    Not so much honoring thee   10
As giving it a hope that there
    It could not withered be.
But thou thereon didst only breathe,
    And sent'st it back to me;
Since when it grows, and smells, I swear,   15
    Not of itself but thee.

JOHN KEATS (1795–1821)

La Belle Dame sans Merci °   1819

O what can ail thee, knight-at-arms,
    Alone and palely loitering?
The sedge has withered from the lake,
    And no birds sing.

O what can ail thee, knight-at-arms,   5
    So haggard and so woe-begone?
The squirrel's granary is full,
    And the harvest's done.

I see a lily on thy brow,
    With anguish moist and fever dew,   10
And on thy cheeks a fading rose
    Fast withereth too.

I met a lady in the meads,
    Full beautiful — a faery's child,
Her hair was long, her foot was light,   15
    And her eyes were wild.

I made a garland for her head,
    And bracelets too, and fragrant zone;°   *belt*
She looked at me as she did love,
    And made sweet moan.   20

I set her on my pacing steed,
    And nothing else saw all day long,
For sidelong would she bend, and sing
    A faery's song.

She found me roots of relish sweet,   25
    And honey wild, and manna dew,
And sure in language strange she said,
    "I love thee true."

She took me to her elfin grot,
    And there she wept, and sighed full sore,   30

La Belle Dame sans Merci: This title is borrowed from a medieval poem and means "The Beautiful Lady without Mercy."

And there I shut her wild wild eyes
    With kisses four.

And there she lullèd me asleep,
    And there I dreamed — Ah! woe betide!
The latest° dream I ever dreamed   *last*   35
    On the cold hill side.

I saw pale kings and princes too,
    Pale warriors, death-pale were they all;
They cried — "La Belle Dame sans Merci
    Hath thee in thrall!"   40

I saw their starved lips in the gloam,
    With horrid warning gapèd wide,
And I awoke and found me here,
    On the cold hill's side.

And this is why I sojourn here,   45
    Alone and palely loitering,
Though the sedge has withered from the lake,
    And no birds sing.

JOHN KEATS (1795–1821)

To One Who Has Been Long in City Pent   *1816*

To one who has been long in city pent,
    'Tis very sweet to look into the fair
    And open face of heaven, — to breathe a prayer
Full in the smile of the blue firmament.
Who is more happy, when, with heart's content,   5
    Fatigued he sinks into some pleasant lair
    Of wavy grass, and reads a debonair
And gentle tale of love and languishment?

Returning home at evening, with an ear
    Catching the notes of Philomel,° — an eye   *a nightingale*   10
Watching the sailing cloudlet's bright career,
    He mourns that day so soon has glided by:
    E'en like the passage of an angel's tear
That falls through the clear ether silently.

JOHN KEATS (1795–1821)

When I have fears that I may cease to be   *1818*

When I have fears that I may cease to be
    Before my pen has gleaned my teeming brain,
Before high-piled books, in charactery,°   *print*
    Hold like rich garners the full ripened grain;

When I behold, upon the night's starred face,   5
    Huge cloudy symbols of a high romance,
And think that I may never live to trace
    Their shadows, with the magic hand of chance;
And when I feel, fair creature of an hour,
    That I shall never look upon thee more,   10
Never have relish in the faery° power   *magic*
    Of unreflecting love;—then on the shore
Of the wide world I stand alone, and think
Till love and fame to nothingness do sink.

JOHN KEATS (1795–1821)

Written in Disgust of Vulgar Superstition   *1816*

The church bells toll a melancholy round,
    Calling the people to some other prayers,
    Some other gloominess, more dreadful cares,
More hearkening to the sermon's horrid sound:
Surely the mind of man is closely bound   5
    In some black spell; seeing that each one tears
    Himself from fireside joys, and Lydian airs,
And converse high of those with glory crown'd.
Still, still they toll, and I should feel a damp—
    A chill as from a tomb, did I not know   10
That they are going like an outburnt lamp;
    That 'tis their sighing, wailing ere they go
    Into oblivion;—that fresh flowers will grow,
And many glories of immortal stamp.

WILLYCE KIM (B. 1946)

In This Heat   *1986*

In this heat
we gather ourselves
and hold together
day folding into night
we press for darkness   5
as if the heat
would steal away
like some errant ship,
vanquished by moon
and stars,   10
we close our eyes
the night half-swollen
with the whispers
of the day.

Out, across the way   15
a dog barks.
Yesterday,
a Chinese girl
with skin the color
of dragon's eyes   20
and hair as fine
as my beloved's
killed herself.
She answered an ad
in one of the dailies   25
and was raped
during the long interview.
No one believed her.
You know the old story.
Tonight I hold your   30
hands between my palms.
Afraid of yesterday.
Uncertain of tomorrow.
Outside the moon pales
against the window   35
as shadows lap across
the sky.
Sleep flutters
like burning incense.
We curl into darkness   40
and are gone.

ETHERIDGE KNIGHT (B. 1931)

A Watts Mother Mourns while Boiling Beans   1973

The blooming flower of my life is roaming
in the night, and I think surely
that never since he was born
have I been free from fright.
My boy is bold, and his blood   5
grows quickly hot even now
he could be crawling in the street
bleeding out his life, likely as not.
Come home, my bold and restless son. — Stop
my heart's yearning! But I must quit   10
this thinking — my husband is coming
and the beans are burning.

PHILIP LARKIN (1922–1985)

This Be the Verse   1974

They fuck you up, your mum and dad.
    They may not mean to, but they do.
They fill you with the faults they had
    And add some extras, just for you.

But they were fucked up in their turn   5
    By fools in old-style hats and coats,
Who half the time were soppy-stern
    And half at one another's throats.

Man hands on misery to man.
    It deepens like a coastal shelf.   10
Get out as early as you can,
    And don't have any kids yourself.

LI-YOUNG LEE (B. 1957)

Eating Together   1986

In the steamer is the trout
seasoned with slivers of ginger,
two sprigs of green onion, and sesame oil.
We shall eat it with rice for lunch,
brothers, sister, my mother who will   5
taste the sweetest meat of the head,
holding it between her fingers
deftly, the way my father did
weeks ago. Then he lay down
to sleep like a snow-covered road   10
winding through pines older than him,
without any travelers, and lonely for no one.

RACHEL LODEN (B. 1948)

We Are Sorry to Say   1999

that the decision has gone against
these poems. It just up and went

against them, like an enormous rearing
horse, a careening locomotive, and we

tried to get out of the way. We still   5
wake up screaming. Frankly

the decision scares us
more than a little. We think it wears

a muscle shirt and is named Bluto,
but who really knows? All we want   10

is peace and quiet, maybe a cottage
in the Hamptons, some sort of tonic

for our splintered nerves. That's what
we want, but there are sparrows

on the roof. And white roiling seas   15
of manuscripts that curse

and shriek, and tender envelopes
that bleed hysterically when opened.

AUDRE LORDE (1934–1992)

Hanging Fire   *1978*

I am fourteen
and my skin has betrayed me
the boy I cannot live without
still sucks his thumb
in secret   5
how come my knees are
always so ashy
what if I die
before morning
and momma's in the bedroom   10
with the door closed.

I have to learn how to dance
in time for the next party
my room is too small for me
suppose I die before graduation   15
they will sing sad melodies
but finally
tell the truth about me
There is nothing I want to do
and too much   20
that has to be done
and momma's in the bedroom
with the door closed.

Nobody even stops to think
about my side of it   25
I should have been on Math Team
my marks were better than his
why do I have to be
the one
wearing braces   30
I have nothing to wear tomorrow

will I live long enough
to grow up
and momma's in the bedroom
with the door closed.   35

ROBERT LOWELL (1917–1977)

For Sale   *1959*

Poor sheepish plaything,
organized with prodigal animosity,
lived in just a year —
my Father's cottage at Beverly Farms
was on the market the month he died.   5
Empty, open, intimate,
its town-house furniture
had an on tiptoe air
of waiting for the mover
on the heels of the undertaker.   10
Ready, afraid
of living alone till eighty,
Mother mooned in a window,
as if she had stayed on a train
one stop past her destination.   15

ARCHIBALD MACLEISH (1892–1982)

Ars Poetica   *1926*

A poem should be palpable and mute
As a globed fruit,

Dumb
As old medallions to the thumb,

Silent as the sleeve-worn stone   5
Of casement ledges where the moss has grown —

A poem should be wordless
As the flight of birds.

A poem should be motionless in time
As the moon climbs,   10

Leaving, as the moon releases
Twig by twig the night-entangled trees,

Leaving, as the moon behind the winter leaves,
Memory by memory the mind —

A poem should be motionless in time   15
As the moon climbs.

A poem should be equal to:
Not true.

For all the history of grief
An empty doorway and a maple leaf.   20

For love
The leaning grasses and two lights above the sea —

A poem should not mean
But be.

W. S. MERWIN (B. 1927)
For the Anniversary of My Death   1967

Every year without knowing it I have passed the day
When the last fires will wave to me
And the silence will set out
Tireless traveller
Like the beam of a lightless star   5

Then I will no longer
Find myself in life as in a strange garment
Surprised at the earth
And the love of one woman
And the shamelessness of men   10
As today writing after three days of rain
Hearing the wren sing and the falling cease
And bowing not knowing to what

EDNA ST. VINCENT MILLAY (1892–1950)
I, Being Born a Woman and Distressed   1923

I, being born a woman and distressed
By all the needs and notions of my kind,
Am urged by your propinquity to find
Your person fair, and feel a certain zest
To bear your body's weight upon my breast: 5
So subtly is the fume of life designed,
To clarify the pulse and cloud the mind,
And leave me once again undone, possessed.
Think not for this, however, the poor treason
Of my stout blood against my staggering brain,   10
I shall remember you with love, or season
My scorn with pity, — let me make it plain:
I find this frenzy insufficient reason
For conversation when we meet again.

JOHN MILTON (1608–1674)

On the Late Massacre in Piedmont°   1655

Avenge, O Lord, thy slaughtered saints, whose bones
   Lie scattered on the Alpine mountains cold;
   Even them who kept thy truth so pure of old,
When all our fathers worshiped stocks and stones,°
Forget not: in thy book record their groans   5
   Who were thy sheep, and in their ancient fold
   Slain by the bloody Piedmontese, that rolled
Mother with infant down the rocks.° Their moans
The vales redoubled to the hills, and they
   To heaven. Their martyred blood and ashes sow   10
O'er all the Italian fields, where still doth sway
   The triple Tyrant;° that from these may grow
A hundredfold, who, having learnt thy way,
   Early may fly the Babylonian woe.°

On the Late Massacre . . . : Milton's protest against the treatment of the Waldenses, members
of a Puritan sect living in the Piedmont region of northwest Italy, was not limited to this
sonnet. It is thought that he wrote Cromwell's appeals to the duke of Savoy and to others to
end the persecution.   4 *When . . . stones:* In Milton's Protestant view, English Catholics had
worshiped their stone and wooden statues in the twelfth century, when the Waldensian sect
was formed.   5–8 *in thy book . . . rocks:* On Easter Day, 1655, 1,700 members of the Waldensian sect were massacred in Piedmont by the duke of Savoy's forces.   12 *triple Tyrant:* The
Pope, with his three-crowned tiara, has authority on earth and in Heaven and Hell.
14 *Babylonian woe:* The destruction of Babylon, symbol of vice and corruption, at the end of
the world (see Rev. 17–18). Protestants interpreted the "Whore of Babylon" as the Roman
Catholic Church.

JOHN MILTON (1608–1674)

When I consider how my light is spent   c. 1655

When I consider how my light is spent,°
   Ere half my days in this dark world and wide,
   And that one talent° which is death to hide
Lodged with me useless, though my soul more bent
To serve therewith my Maker, and present   5
   My true account, lest He returning chide;
   "Doth God exact day-labor, light denied?"
I fondly° ask. But Patience, to prevent   *foolishly*
That murmur, soon replies, "God doth not need
   Either man's work or His own gifts. Who best   10
   Bear His mild yoke, they serve Him best. His state
Is kingly: thousands at His bidding speed,
   And post o'er land and ocean without rest;
   They also serve who only stand and wait."

1 *how my light is spent:* Milton had been totally blind since 1651.   3 *that one talent:* Refers to
Jesus' parable of the talents (units of money), in which a servant entrusted with a talent
buries it rather than invests it and is punished on his master's return (Matt. 25:14–30).

N. Scott Momaday (b. 1934)

Crows in a Winter Composition   *1976*

This morning the snow,
The soft distances
Beyond the trees
In which nothing appeared —
Nothing appeared.   5
The several silences,
Imposed one upon another,
Were unintelligible.

I was therefore ill at ease
When the crows came down,   10
Whirling down and calling,
Into the yard below
And stood in a mindless manner
On the gray, luminous crust,
Altogether definite, composed,   15
In the bright enmity of my regard,
In the hard nature of crows.

Marianne Moore (1887–1972)

Poetry   *1921*

I, too, dislike it: there are things that are important beyond all this fiddle.
    Reading it, however, with a perfect contempt for it, one discovers in it
    after all, a place for the genuine.
        Hands that can grasp, eyes
        that can dilate, hair that can rise   5
            if it must, these things are important not because a

high-sounding interpretation can be put upon them but because they are
    useful. When they become so derivative as to become unintelligible,
    the same thing may be said for all of us, that we
        do not admire what   10
        we cannot understand: the bat
            holding on upside down or in quest of something to

eat, elephants pushing, a wild horse taking a roll, a tireless wolf under
    a tree, the immovable critic twitching his skin like a horse that feels a
    flea, the base-   15
        ball fan, the statistician —
        nor is it valid
            to discriminate against "business documents and

school-books"; all these phenomena are important. One must make a
        distinction
however: when dragged into prominence by half poets, the result is
        not poetry,

nor till the poets among us can be 20
   "literalists of
      the imagination" — above
         insolence and triviality and can present

for inspection, "imaginary gardens with real toads in them," shall we have
   it. In the meantime, if you demand on the one hand, 25
      the raw material of poetry in
         all its rawness and
         that which is on the other hand
            genuine, you are interested in poetry.

PAT MORA (B. 1942)

Another Brown Man 1995

Startling as blood
from a pinprick,
my tears, pull
me to him, away from hipsway,
drumbeats, música cubana. 5

His hands, like yours,
the color of tobacco
he smooths, cuts, rolls,
another brown man,
hands and humor busy. Like yours. 10

His chuckles curl with his cigar smoke,
he teases to girls in nearby shops,
"Oye, linda,"
banter familiar as the work,
rhythm I remember. 15

        You stopped breathing
        once this year. Your body,
        solid as an álamo,
        we can never trust again.
        It practiced stillness. 20

I stare at him, hover
near music I once knew,
listen, hear you
whose voice alone
pricks my tears. 25

I turn, and he's gone,
light off, cigar rolling done for the day,
his spot bare under the palm trees,
only a shadow.
Like yours. 30

SARAH MORGAN BRYAN PIATT (1836–1919)

A New Thanksgiving   1910

For war, plague, pestilence, flood, famine, fire,
  For Christ discrowned, for false gods set on high;
For fools, whose hands must have their hearts' desire,
  We thank Thee — in the darkness — and so die.

For shipwreck: Oh, the sob of strangling seas! —   5
  No matter. For the snake that charms the dove;
And (is it not the bitterest of all these?)
  We thank Thee — in our blind faith — even for Love.

For breaking hearts; for all that breaks the heart;
  For Death, the one thing after all the rest,   10
We thank Thee, O our Father! Thou who art,
  And wast, and shalt be — knowing these are best.

SYLVIA PLATH (1932–1963)

Daddy   1962

You do not do, you do not do
Any more, black shoe
In which I have lived like a foot
For thirty years, poor and white,
Barely daring to breathe or Achoo.   5

Daddy, I have had to kill you.
You died before I had time —
Marble-heavy, a bag full of God,
Ghastly statue with one gray toe
Big as a Frisco seal   10

And a head in the freakish Atlantic
Where it pours bean green over blue
In the waters off beautiful Nauset.°   *Cape Cod inlet*
I used to pray to recover you.
Ach, du.°   *Oh, you*   15

In the German tongue, in the Polish Town°
Scraped flat by the roller
Of wars, wars, wars.
But the name of the town is common.
My Polack friend   20

Says there are a dozen or two.
So I never could tell where you
Put your foot, your root,

---

16 *Polish Town:* Refers to Otto Plath's birthplace, Granbow.

I never could talk to you.
The tongue stuck in my jaw.   25

It stuck in a barb wire snare.
Ich, ich, ich, ich,°   *I, I, I, I,*
I could hardly speak.
I thought every German was you.
And the language obscene   30

An engine, an engine
Chuffing me off like a Jew.
A Jew to Dachau, Auschwitz, Belsen.°
I began to talk like a Jew.
I think I may well be a Jew.   35

The snows of the Tyrol, the clear beer of Vienna
Are not very pure or true.
With my gypsy-ancestress and my weird luck
And my Taroc° pack and my Taroc pack
I may be a bit of a Jew.   40

I have always been scared of *you*,
With your Luftwaffe,° your gobbledygoo.
And your neat mustache
And your Aryan eye, bright blue.
Panzer-man, panzer-man,° O You —   45

Not God but a swastika
So black no sky could squeak through.
Every woman adores a Fascist,
The boot in the face, the brute
Brute heart of a brute like you.   50

You stand at the blackboard, daddy,
In the picture I have of you,
A cleft in your chin instead of your foot
But no less a devil for that, no not
Any less the black man who   55

Bit my pretty red heart in two.
I was ten when they buried you.
At twenty I tried to die
And get back, back, back to you.
I thought even the bones would do   60

But they pulled me out of the sack,
And they stuck me together with glue.
And then I knew what to do.

---

33 *Dachau . . . Belsen:* Nazi death camps in World War II.   39 *Taroc:* Or *Tarot,* a pack of cards
used to tell fortunes. It is said to have originated among the early Jewish Cabalists and to have
been transmitted to European Gypsies during the Middle Ages.   42 *Luftwaffe:* World War II
German air force.   45 *panzer-man:* A member of the panzer division of the German army in
World War II, which used armored vehicles and was organized for rapid attack.

I made a model of you,
A man in black with a Meinkampf° look   65

And a love of the rack and the screw.
And I said I do, I do.
So daddy, I'm finally through.
The black telephone's off at the root,
The voices just can't worm through.   70

If I've killed one man, I've killed two —
The vampire who said he was you
And drank my blood for a year,
Seven years, if you want to know.
Daddy, you can lie back now.   75

There's a stake in your fat black heart
And the villagers never liked you.
They are dancing and stamping on you.
They always *knew* it was you.
Daddy, daddy, you bastard, I'm through.   80

65 *Meinkampf:* An allusion to Hitler's autobiography (*My Struggle*).

SIR WALTER RALEGH (1554–1618)

The Nymph's Reply to the Shepherd   1600

If all the world and love were young,
And truth in every shepherd's tongue,
These pretty pleasures might me move
To live with thee and be thy love.

Time drives the flocks from field to fold,   5
When rivers rage and rocks grow cold,
And Philomel° becometh dumb;   *nightingale*
The rest complains of cares to come.

The flowers do fade, and wanton fields
To wayward winter reckoning yields;   10
A honey tongue, a heart of gall,
Is fancy's spring, but sorrow's fall.

Thy gowns, thy shoes, thy beds of roses,
Thy cap, thy kirtle, and thy posies
Soon break, soon wither, soon forgotten —   15
In folly ripe, in reason rotten.

Thy belt of straw and ivy buds,
Thy coral clasps and amber studs,
All these in me no means can move
To come to thee and be thy love.   20

But could youth last and love still breed,
Had joys no date° nor age no need,   *end*

Then these delights my mind might move
To live with thee and be thy love.

ADRIENNE RICH (B. 1929)

Living in Sin   1955

She had thought the studio would keep itself;
no dust upon the furniture of love.
Half heresy, to wish the taps less vocal,
the panes relieved of grime. A plate of pears,
a piano with a Persian shawl, a cat   5
stalking the picturesque amusing mouse
had risen at his urging.
Not that at five each separate stair would writhe
under the milkman's tramp; that morning light
so coldly would delineate the scraps   10
of last night's cheese and three sepulchral bottles;
that on the kitchen shelf among the saucers
a pair of beetle-eyes would fix her own—
envoy from some black village in the mouldings . . .
Meanwhile, he, with a yawn,   15
sounded a dozen notes upon the keyboard,
declared it out of tune, shrugged at the mirror,
rubbed at his beard, went out for cigarettes;
while she, jeered by the minor demons,
pulled back the sheets and made the bed and found   20
a towel to dust the table-top,
and let the coffee-pot boil over on the stove.
By evening she was back in love again,
though not so wholly but throughout the night
she woke sometimes to feel the daylight coming   25
like a relentless milkman up the stairs.

CHRISTINA GEORGINA ROSSETTI (1830–1894)

Promises Like Pie-Crust°   1896

Promise me no promises,
    So will I not promise you;
Keep we both our liberties,
    Never false and never true:
Let us hold the die uncast,   5
    Free to come as free to go;
For I cannot know your past,
    And of mine what can you know?

Pie-Crust: An old English proverb: "Promises are like pie-crust, made to be broken."

You, so warm, may once have been
    Warmer towards another one;   10
I, so cold, may once have seen
    Sunlight, once have felt the sun:
Who shall show us if it was
    Thus indeed in time of old?
Fades the image from the glass   15
And the fortune is not told.

If you promised, you might grieve
    For lost liberty again;
If I promised, I believe
    I should fret to break the chain: 20
Let us be the friends we were,
    Nothing more but nothing less;
Many thrive on frugal fare
    Who would perish of excess.

WILLIAM SHAKESPEARE (1564–1616)

That time of year thou mayst in me behold   *1609*

That time of year thou mayst in me behold
When yellow leaves, or none, or few, do hang
Upon those boughs which shake against the cold,
Bare ruined choirs, where late the sweet birds sang.
In me thou see'st the twilight of such day   5
As after sunset fadeth in the west;
Which by and by black night doth take away,
Death's second self,° that seals up all in rest.   *sleep*
In me thou see'st the glowing of such fire,
That on the ashes of his youth doth lie,   10
As the deathbed whereon it must expire,
Consumed with that which it was nourished by.
    This thou perceiv'st, which makes thy love more strong,
    To love that well which thou must leave ere long.

WILLIAM SHAKESPEARE (1564–1616)

When forty winters shall besiege thy brow   *1609*

When forty winters shall besiege thy brow
And dig deep trenches in thy beauty's field,
Thy youth's proud livery, so gazed on now,
Will be a tattered weed,° of small worth held.   *garment*
Then being asked where all thy beauty lies,   5
Where all the treasure of thy lusty days,
To say within thine own deep-sunken eyes

Were an all-eating shame and thriftless praise.
How much more praise deserved thy beauty's use
If thou couldst answer, "This fair child of mine   10
Shall sum my count and make my old excuse,"
Proving his beauty by succession thine.
    This were to be new made when thou art old,
    And see thy blood warm when thou feel'st it cold.

WILLIAM SHAKESPEARE (1564–1616)

When, in disgrace with Fortune and men's eyes   *1609*

When, in disgrace with Fortune and men's eyes,
I all alone beweep my outcast state,
And trouble deaf heaven with my bootless cries,
And look upon myself and curse my fate,
Wishing me like to one more rich in hope,   5
Featured like him, like him with friends possessed,
Desiring this man's art, and that man's scope,
With what I most enjoy contented least,
Yet in these thoughts myself almost despising,
Haply I think on thee, and then my state,   10
Like to the lark at break of day arising
From sullen earth, sings hymns at heaven's gate;
    For thy sweet love remembered such wealth brings
    That then I scorn to change my state with kings.

PERCY BYSSHE SHELLEY (1792–1822)

Ozymandias°   *1818*

I met a traveler from an antique land
Who said: Two vast and trunkless legs of stone
Stand in the desert. . . . Near them, on the sand,
Half sunk, a shattered visage lies, whose frown,
And wrinkled lip, and sneer of cold command,   5
Tell that its sculptor well those passions read
Which yet survive, stamped on these lifeless things,
The hand that mocked them, and the heart that fed:
And on the pedestal these words appear:
"My name is Ozymandias, King of Kings: 10
Look on my works, ye Mighty, and despair!"
Nothing beside remains. Round the decay

Ozymandias: Greek name for Ramses II, pharaoh of Egypt for sixty-seven years during the thirteenth century B.C. His colossal statue lies prostrate in the sands of Luxor. Napoleon's soldiers measured it (56 feet long, ear 3½ feet long, weight 1,000 tons). Its inscription, according to the Greek historian Diodorus Siculus, was "I am Ozymandias, King of Kings; if anyone wishes to know what I am and where I lie, let him surpass me in some of my exploits."

Of that colossal wreck, boundless and bare
The lone and level sands stretch far away.

PERCY BYSSHE SHELLEY (1792–1822)

Sonnet: Lift not the painted veil   *1818*

Lift not the painted veil which those who live
Call Life: though unreal shapes be pictured there,
And it but mimic all we would believe
With colours idly spread,— behind, lurk Fear
And Hope, twin Destinies; who ever weave   5
Their shadows, o'er the chasm, sightless and drear.
I knew one who had lifted it— he sought,
For his lost heart was tender, things to love,
But found them not, alas! nor was there aught
The world contains, the which he could approve.   10
Through the unheeding many he did move,
A splendour among shadows, a bright blot
Upon this gloomy scene, a Spirit that strove
For truth, and like the Preacher° found it not.

14 *Preacher:* The preacher of Ecclesiastes who insists that "all is vanity."

GARY SOTO (B. 1952)

Black Hair   *1985*

At eight I was brilliant with my body.
In July, that ring of heat
We all jumped through, I sat in the bleachers
Of Romain Playground, in the lengthening
Shade that rose from our dirty feet.   5
The game before us was more than baseball.
It was a figure— Hector Moreno
Quick and hard with turned muscles,
His crouch the one I assumed before an altar
Of worn baseball cards, in my room.   10
I came here because I was Mexican, a stick
Of brown light in love with those
Who could do it— the triple and hard slide,
The gloves eating balls into double plays.
What could I do with 50 pounds, my shyness,   15
My black torch of hair, about to go out?
Father was dead, his face no longer
Hanging over the table or our sleep,
And mother was the terror of mouths
Twisting hurt by butter knives.   20

In the bleachers I was brilliant with my body,
Waving players in and stomping my feet,
Growing sweaty in the presence of white shirts.
I chewed sunflower seeds. I drank water
And bit my arm through the late innings.　　25
When Hector lined balls into deep
Center, in my mind I rounded the bases
With him, my face flared, my hair lifting
Beautifully, because we were coming home
To the arms of brown people.　　30

WALLACE STEVENS (1879–1955)

The Emperor of Ice-Cream　　1923

Call the roller of big cigars,
The muscular one, and bid him whip
In kitchen cups concupiscent curds.°
Let the wenches dawdle in such dress
As they are used to wear, and let the boys　　5
Bring flowers in last month's newspapers.
Let be be finale of seem.°
The only emperor is the emperor of ice-cream.

Take from the dresser of deal,
Lacking the three glass knobs, that sheet　　10
On which she embroidered fantails once
And spread it so as to cover her face.
If her horny feet protrude, they come
To show how cold she is, and dumb.
Let the lamp affix its beam.　　15
The only emperor is the emperor of ice-cream.

3 *concupiscent curds:* "The words 'concupiscent curds' have no genealogy; they are merely expressive: at least, I hope they are expressive. They express the concupiscence of life, but, by contrast with the things in relation in the poem, they express or accentuate life's destitution, and it is this that gives them something more than a cheap lustre" (Wallace Stevens, *Letters* [New York: Knopf, 1960], p. 500). 7 *Let . . . seem:* "The true sense of 'Let be be finale of seem' is let being become the conclusion or denouement of appearing to be: in short, ice cream is an absolute good. The poem is obviously not about ice cream, but about being as distinguished from seeming to be" (*Letters*, p. 341).

ALFRED, LORD TENNYSON (1809–1892)

Tears, Idle Tears　　1847

Tears, idle tears, I know not what they mean,
Tears from the depth of some divine despair
Rise in the heart, and gather to the eyes,
In looking on the happy Autumn-fields,
And thinking of the days that are no more.　　5

Fresh as the first beam glittering on a sail,
That brings our friends up from the underworld,
Sad as the last which reddens over one
That sinks with all we love below the verge;
So sad, so fresh, the days that are no more.   10

Ah, sad and strange as in dark summer dawns
The earliest pipe of half-awaken'd birds
To dying ears, when unto dying eyes
The casement° slowly grows a glimmering square;   *window*
So sad, so strange, the days that are no more.   15

Dear as remember'd kisses after death,
And sweet as those by hopeless fancy feign'd
On lips that are for others; deep as love,
Deep as first love, and wild with all regret;
O Death in Life, the days that are no more.   20

ALFRED, LORD TENNYSON (1809–1892)

Ulysses°   *1833*

It little profits that an idle king,
By this still hearth, among these barren crags,
Matched with an agèd wife,° I mete and dole   *Penelope*
Unequal laws unto a savage race,
That hoard, and sleep, and feed, and know not me.   5
     I cannot rest from travel; I will drink
Life to the lees. All times I have enjoyed
Greatly, have suffered greatly, both with those
That loved me, and alone; on shore, and when
Through scudding drifts the rainy Hyades°   10
Vexed the dim sea. I am become a name;
For always roaming with a hungry heart
Much have I seen and known — cities of men
And manners, climates, councils, governments,
Myself not least, but honored of them all —   15
And drunk delight of battle with my peers,
Far on the ringing plains of windy Troy.
I am a part of all that I have met;
Yet all experience is an arch wherethrough
Gleams that untraveled world, whose margin fades   20
For ever and for ever when I move.
How dull it is to pause, to make an end,
To rust unburnished, not to shine in use!
As though to breathe were life. Life piled on life
Were all too little, and of one to me   25

Ulysses: Ulysses, the hero of Homer's epic poem the *Odyssey,* is presented by Dante in *The Inferno,* XXVI, as restless after his return to Ithaca, and eager for new adventures. 10 *Hyades:* Five stars in the constellation Taurus, supposed by the ancients to predict rain when they rose with the sun.

Little remains; but every hour is saved
From that eternal silence, something more,
A bringer of new things; and vile it were
For some three suns to store and hoard myself,
And this gray spirit yearning in desire   30
To follow knowledge like a sinking star,
Beyond the utmost bound of human thought.

    This is my son, mine own Telemachus,
To whom I leave the scepter and the isle —
Well-loved of me, discerning to fulfill   35
This labor, by slow prudence to make mild
A rugged people, and through soft degrees
Subdue them to the useful and the good.
Most blameless is he, centered in the sphere
Of common duties, decent not to fail   40
In offices of tenderness, and pay
Meet adoration to my household gods,
When I am gone. He works his work, I mine.

    There lies the port; the vessel puffs her sail:
There gloom the dark, broad seas. My mariners,   45
Souls that have toiled, and wrought, and thought with me —
That ever with a frolic welcome took
The thunder and the sunshine, and opposed
Free hearts, free foreheads — you and I are old;
Old age hath yet his honor and his toil.   50
Death closes all; but something ere the end,
Some work of noble note, may yet be done,
Not unbecoming men that strove with Gods.
The lights begin to twinkle from the rocks;
The long day wanes; the slow moon climbs; the deep   55
Moans round with many voices. Come, my friends.
'Tis not too late to seek a newer world.
Push off, and sitting well in order smite
The sounding furrows; for my purpose holds
To sail beyond the sunset, and the baths   60
Of all the western stars, until I die.
It may be that the gulfs will wash us down;
It may be we shall touch the Happy Isles,°
And see the great Achilles,° whom we knew.
Though much is taken, much abides; and though   65
We are not now that strength which in old days
Moved earth and heaven, that which we are, we are:
One equal temper of heroic hearts,
Made weak by time and fate, but strong in will
To strive, to seek, to find, and not to yield.   70

---

63 *Happy Isles:* Elysium, the home after death of heroes and others favored by the gods. It
was thought by the ancients to lie beyond the sunset in the uncharted Atlantic.   64 *Achilles:*
The hero of Homer's *Iliad.*

ROBERT WALLACE (B. 1932)

The Double-Play   1961

In his sea lit
distance, the pitcher winding
like a clock about to chime comes down with

the ball, hit
sharply, under the artificial   5
banks of arc-lights, bounds like a vanishing string

over the green
to the shortstop magically
scoops to his right whirling above his invisible

shadows   10
in the dust redirects
its flight to the running poised second baseman

pirouettes
leaping, above the slide, to throw
from mid-air, across the colored tightened interval,   15

to the leaning-
out first baseman ends the dance
drawing it disappearing into his long brown glove

stretches. What
is too swift for deception   20
is final, lost, among the loosened figures

jogging off the field
(the pitcher walks), casual
in the space where the poem has happened.

PHILLIS WHEATLEY (1753?–1784)

On Being Brought from Africa to America   1773

'Twas mercy brought me from my pagan land,
Taught my benighted soul to understand
That there's a God — that there's a Saviour too;
Once I redemption neither sought nor knew.
Some view our sable race with scornful eye —
'Their color is a diabolic dye.'
Remember, Christians, Negroes black as Cain
May be refined, and join the angelic train.

WALT WHITMAN (1819–1892)

One's-Self I Sing   *1867*

One's-Self I sing, a simple separate person,
Yet utter the word Democratic, the word En-Masse.

Of physiology from top to toe I sing,
Not physiognomy alone nor brain alone is worthy for the Muse, I say the
    Form complete is worthier far,
The Female equally with the Male I sing.

Of Life immense in passion, pulse, and power,
Cheerful, for freest action formed under the laws divine,
The Modern Man I sing.

WALT WHITMAN (1819–1892)

When I Heard the Learn'd Astronomer   *1865*

When I heard the learn'd astronomer,
When the proofs, the figures, were ranged in columns before me,
When I was shown the charts and diagrams, to add, divide, and measure them,
When I sitting heard the astronomer where he lectured with much applause
    in the lecture-room,
How soon unaccountable I became tired and sick,
Till rising and gliding out I wandered off by myself,
In the mystical moist night-air, and from time to time,
Looked up in perfect silence at the stars.

RICHARD WILBUR (B. 1921)

Love Calls Us to the Things of This World°   *1956*

        The eyes open to a cry of pulleys,°
And spirited from sleep, the astounded soul
Hangs for a moment bodiless and simple
As false dawn.
                Outside the open window   5
The morning air is all awash with angels.
Some are in bed-sheets, some are in blouses,
Some are in smocks: but truly there they are.
Now they are rising together in calm swells
Of halcyon feeling, filling whatever they wear
With the deep joy of their impersonal breathing;   10
Now they are flying in place, conveying

Loves Calls Us . . . : From St. Augustine's *Commentary on the Psalms.* 1 *pulleys:* Grooved wheels
at each end of a laundry line; clothes are hung on the line and advance as the line is moved.

The terrible speed of their omnipresence, moving
And staying like white water; and now of a sudden
They swoon down into so rapt a quiet   15
That nobody seems to be there.
                                  The soul shrinks

                                  From all that it is about to remember,
From the punctual rape of every blessèd day,
And cries,   20
          "Oh, let there be nothing on earth but laundry,
Nothing but rosy hands in the rising steam
And clear dances done in the sight of heaven."

Yet, as the sun acknowledges
With a warm look the world's hunks and colors,   25
The soul descends once more in bitter love
To accept the waking body, saying now
In a changed voice as the man yawns and rises,

"Bring them down from their ruddy gallows;
Let there be clean linen for the backs of thieves;   30
Let lovers go fresh and sweet to be undone,
And the heaviest nuns walk in a pure floating
Of dark habits,
                keeping their difficult balance."

MILLER WILLIAMS (B. 1930)

Thinking about Bill, Dead of AIDS   *1989*

We did not know the first thing about
how blood surrenders to even the smallest threat
when old allergies turn inside out,

the body rescinding all its normal orders
to all defenders of flesh, betraying the head,   5
pulling its guards back from all its borders.

Thinking of friends afraid to shake your hand,
we think of your hand shaking, your mouth set,
your eyes drained of any reprimand.

Loving, we kissed you, partly to persuade   10
both you and us, seeing what eyes had said,
that we were loving and we were not afraid.

If we had had more, we would have given more.
As it was we stood next to your bed,
stopping, though, to set our smiles at the door.   15

Not because we were less sure at the last.
Only because, not knowing anything yet,
we didn't know what look would hurt you least.

WILLIAM CARLOS WILLIAMS (1883–1963)

Spring and All

1923

By the road to the contagious hospital
under the surge of the blue
mottled clouds driven from the
northeast—a cold wind. Beyond, the
waste of broad, muddy fields   5
brown with dried weeds, standing and fallen

patches of standing water
and scattering of tall trees

All along the road the reddish
purplish, forked, upstanding, twiggy   10
stuff of bushes and small trees
with dead, brown leaves under them
leafless vines—

Lifeless in appearance, sluggish
dazed spring approaches—   15

They enter the new world naked,
cold, uncertain of all
save that they enter. All about them
the cold, familiar wind—

Now the grass, tomorrow   20
the stiff curl of wildcarrot leaf
One by one objects are defined—
It quickens: clarity, outline of leaf

But now the stark dignity of
entrance—Still, the profound change   25
has come upon them: rooted, they
grip down and begin to awaken

WILLIAM CARLOS WILLIAMS (1883–1963)

This Is Just to Say

1934

I have eaten
the plums
that were in
the icebox

and which   5
you were probably
saving
for breakfast

Forgive me
they were delicious   10

so sweet
and so cold

WILLIAM WORDSWORTH (1770–1850)

I Wandered Lonely as a Cloud   1807

I wandered lonely as a cloud
That floats on high o'er vales and hills,
When all at once I saw a crowd,
A host, of golden daffodils,
Beside the lake, beneath the trees,   5
Fluttering and dancing in the breeze.

Continuous as the stars that shine
And twinkle on the milky way,
They stretched in never-ending line
Along the margin of a bay;   10
Ten thousand saw I at a glance,
Tossing their heads in sprightly dance.

The waves beside them danced, but they
Outdid the sparkling waves in glee;
A poet could not but be gay,   15
In such a jocund company;
I gazed — and gazed — but little thought
What wealth the show to me had brought:

For oft, when on my couch I lie
In vacant or in pensive mood,   20
They flash upon that inward eye
Which is the bliss of solitude;
And then my heart with pleasure fills,
And dances with the daffodils.

WILLIAM WORDSWORTH (1770–1850)

Lines Written in Early Spring   1798

I heard a thousand blended notes,
While in a grove I sate reclined,
In that sweet mood when pleasant thoughts
Bring sad thoughts to the mind.

To her fair works did nature link   5
The human soul that through me ran;
And much it griev'd my heart to think
What man has made of man.

Through primrose-tufts, in that sweet bower,
The periwinkle trail'd its wreathes;   10

And 'tis my faith that every flower
Enjoys the air it breathes.

The birds around me hopp'd and play'd:
Their thoughts I cannot measure,
But the least motion which they made,   15
It seem'd a thrill of pleasure.

The budding twigs spread out their fan,
To catch the breezy air;
And I must think, do all I can,
That there was pleasure there.   20

If I these thoughts may not prevent,
If such be of my creed the plan,
Have I not reason to lament
What man has made of man?

WILLIAM WORDSWORTH (1770–1850)

Mutability   *1822*

From low to high doth dissolution climb,
And sink from high to low, along a scale
Of awful° notes, whose concord shall not fail;   *awe-filled*
A muscial but melancholy chime,
Which they can hear who meddle not with crime,   5
Nor avarice, nor over-anxious care.
Truth fails not; but her outward forms that bear
The longest date do melt like frosty rime,
That in the morning whitened hill and plain
And is no more; drop like the tower sublime   10
Of yesterday, which royally did wear
His crown of weeds, but could not even sustain
Some casual shout that broke the silent air,
Or the unimaginable touch of Time.

WILLIAM WORDSWORTH (1770–1850)

A Slumber Did My Spirit Seal   *1800*

A slumber did my spirit seal;
   I had no human fears—
She seemed a thing that could not feel
   The touch of earthly years.

No motion has she now, no force;
   She neither hears nor sees;
Rolled round in earth's diurnal course.
   With rocks, and stones, and trees.

MITSUYE YAMADA (B. 1923)

A Bedtime Story

1976

Once upon a time,
an old Japanese legend
goes as told
by Papa,
an old woman traveled through   5
many small villages
seeking refuge
for the night.

Each door opened
a sliver   10
in answer to her knock
then closed.
Unable to walk
any further
she wearily climbed a hill   15
found a clearing
and there lay down to rest
a few moments to catch
her breath.

The village town below   20
lay asleep except
for a few starlike lights.
Suddenly the clouds opened
and a full moon came into view
over the town.   25

The old woman sat up
turned toward
the village town
and in supplication
called out   30
Thank you people
of the village,
If it had not been for your
kindness
in refusing me a bed   35
for the night
these humble eyes would never
have seen this
memorable sight.

Papa paused, I waited.   40
In the comfort of our
hilltop home in Seattle
overlooking the valley,
I shouted
"That's the *end?*"   45

WILLIAM BUTLER YEATS (1865–1939)
Crazy Jane Talks with the Bishop   1933

I met the Bishop on the road
And much said he and I.
"Those breasts are flat and fallen now,
Those veins must soon be dry;
Live in a heavenly mansion,   5
Not in some foul sty."

"Fair and foul are near of kin,
And fair needs foul," I cried.
"My friends are gone, but that's a truth
Nor grave nor bed denied,   10
Learned in bodily lowliness
And in the heart's pride.

"A woman can be proud and stiff
When on love intent;
But Love has pitched his mansion in   15
The place of excrement;
For nothing can be sole or whole
That has not been rent."

WILLIAM BUTLER YEATS (1865–1939)
Leda and the Swan°   1924

A sudden blow: the great wings beating still
Above the staggering girl, her thighs caressed
By the dark webs, her nape caught in his bill,
He holds her helpless breast upon his breast.

How can those terrified vague fingers push   5
The feathered glory from her loosening thighs?
And how can body, laid in that white rush,
But feel the strange heart beating where it lies?

A shudder in the loins engenders there
The broken wall, the burning roof and tower   10
And Agamemnon dead.
                    Being so caught up,
So mastered by the brute blood of the air,
Did she put on his knowledge with his power
Before the indifferent beak could let her drop?   15

Leda and the Swan: In Greek myth, Zeus in the form of a swan seduced Leda and fathered Helen of Troy (whose abduction started the Trojan War) and Clytemnestra, Agamemnon's wife and murderer. Yeats thought of Zeus's appearance to Leda as a type of annunciation, like the angel appearing to Mary.

WILLIAM BUTLER YEATS (1865–1939)

Sailing to Byzantium°   1927

I

That is no country for old men.° The young
In one another's arms, birds in the trees
— Those dying generations — at their song,
The salmon-falls, the mackerel-crowded seas
Fish, flesh, or fowl, commend all summer long   5
Whatever is begotten, born and dies.
Caught in that sensual music all neglect
Monuments of unaging intellect.

II

An aged man is but a paltry thing,
A tattered coat upon a stick, unless   10
Soul clap its hands and sing, and louder sing
For every tatter in its mortal dress,
Nor is there singing school but studying
Monuments of its own magnificence;
And therefore I have sailed the seas and come   15
To the holy city of Byzantium.

III

O sages standing in God's holy fire
As in the gold mosaic of a wall,
Come from the holy fire, perne in a gyre,°
And be the singing-masters of my soul.   20
Consume my heart away; sick with desire
And fastened to a dying animal
It knows not what it is; and gather me
Into the artifice of eternity.

IV

Once out of nature I shall never take   25
My bodily form from any natural thing,
But such a form as Grecian goldsmiths make
Of hammered gold and gold enameling
To keep a drowsy Emperor awake;°
Or set upon a golden bough° to sing   30
To lords and ladies of Byzantium
Of what is past, or passing, or to come.

Byzantium: Old name for the modern city of Istanbul, capital of the Eastern Roman Empire, ancient artistic and intellectual center. Yeats uses Byzantium as a symbol for "artificial" (and therefore, deathless) art and beauty, as opposed to the beauty of the natural world, which is bound to time and death. 1 *That . . . men:* Ireland, part of the time-bound world. 19 *perne in a gyre:* Bobbin making a spiral pattern. 27–29 *such . . . awake:* "I have read somewhere that in the Emperor's palace at Byzantium was a tree made of gold and silver, and artificial birds that sang." [Yeats's note.] 30 *golden bough:* In Greek legend, Aeneas had to pluck a golden bough from a tree in order to descend into Hades. As soon as the bough was plucked, another grew in its place.

WILLIAM BUTLER YEATS (1865–1939)

The Second Coming°   *1921*

Turning and turning in the widening gyre°
The falcon cannot hear the falconer;
Things fall apart; the center cannot hold;
Mere anarchy is loosed upon the world,
The blood-dimmed tide is loosed, and everywhere   5
The ceremony of innocence is drowned;
The best lack all conviction, while the worst
Are full of passionate intensity.

Surely some revelation is at hand;
Surely the Second Coming is at hand.   10
The Second Coming! Hardly are those words out
When a vast image out of *Spiritus Mundi*°   *Soul of the world*
Troubles my sight: somewhere in sands of the desert
A shape with lion body and the head of a man,
A gaze blank and pitiless as the sun,   15
Is moving its slow thighs, while all about it
Reel shadows of the indignant desert birds.
The darkness drops again; but now I know
That twenty centuries of stony sleep
Were vexed to nightmare by a rocking cradle,   20
And what rough beast, its hour come round at last,
Slouches towards Bethlehem to be born?

The Second Coming: According to Matthew 24:29–44, Christ will return to earth after a time
of tribulation to reward the righteous and establish the millennium of heaven on earth.
Yeats saw his troubled time as the end of the Christian era and feared the portents of the
new cycle.   1 *gyre:* Widening spiral of a falcon's flight, used by Yeats to describe the cycling
of history.

WILLIAM BUTLER YEATS (1865–1939)

The Wild Swans at Coole   *1916*

The trees are in their autumn beauty,
The woodland paths are dry,
Under the October twilight the water
Mirrors a still sky;
Upon the brimming water among the stones   5
Are nine-and-fifty swans.

The nineteenth autumn has come upon me
Since I first made my count;
I saw, before I had well finished,
All suddenly mount   10
And scatter wheeling in great broken rings
Upon their clamorous wings.

I have looked upon those brilliant creatures,
And now my heart is sore.
All's changed since I, hearing at twilight,   15
The first time on this shore,
The bell-beat of their wings above my head,
Trod with a lighter tread.

Unwearied still, lover by lover,
They paddle in the cold   20
Companionable streams or climb the air;
Their hearts have not grown old;
Passion or conquest, wander where they will,
Attend upon them still.

But now they drift on the still water,   25
Mysterious, beautiful;
Among what rushes will they build,
By what lake's edge or pool
Delight men's eyes when I awake some day
To find they have flown away?   30

39

An Album of World Literature

ANNA AKHMATOVA (RUSSIA / 1889–1966)

Born in Russia, Anna Akhmatova was a poet and translator who was regarded as a major modern poet in Russia. Although she was expelled from
the Union of Soviet Writers during Stalin's rule, she was reclaimed by her
country in the 1960s. Her poetry is characterized by its clarity, precision, and
simplicity. Her work is translated in *Complete Poems of Anna Akhmatova* (1990).

Lot's Wife   *1922*

TRANSLATED BY RICHARD WILBUR

The just man followed then his angel guide
Where he strode on the black highway, hulking and bright;
But a wild grief in his wife's bosom cried,
Look back, it is not too late for a last sight

Of the red towers of your native Sodom, the square   5
Where once you sang, the gardens you shall mourn,
And the tall house with empty windows where
You loved your husband and your babes were born.

She turned, and looking on the bitter view
Her eyes were welded shut by mortal pain;   10
Into transparent salt her body grew,
And her quick feet were rooted in the plain.

Who would waste tears upon her? Is she not
The least of our losses, this unhappy wife?
Yet in my heart she will not be forgot   15
Who, for a single glance, gave up her life.

CONNECTIONS TO OTHER SELECTIONS

1. Discuss the use of Biblical allusions in "Lot's Wife" and in William Butler Yeats's "The Second Coming" (p. 1196). How is an understanding of the allusions crucial to interpreting each poem?
2. Consider the "unhappy wife" in this poem and in Linda Pastan's "Marks" (p. 794). Discuss how you regard the wife in each poem.

CLARIBEL ALEGRÍA (EL SALVADOR / B. 1924)

Born in Estelí, Nicaragua, Claribel Alegría moved with her family to El Salvador within a year of her birth. A 1948 graduate of George Washington University, she considers herself a Salvadoran, and much of her writing reflects the political upheaval of recent Latin American history. In 1978 she was awarded the Casa de las Americas Prize for her book *I Survive*. A bilingual edition of her major works, *Flowers from the Volcano*, was published in 1982.

I Am Mirror   *1978*

TRANSLATED BY ELECTA ARENAL AND MARSHA GABRIELA DREYER

Water sparkles
on my skin
and I don't feel it
water streams
down my back   5
I don't feel it
I rub myself with a towel
I pinch myself in the arm
I don't feel
frightened I look at myself in the mirror   10
she also pricks herself
I begin to get dressed
stumbling
from the corners
shouts like lightning bolts   15
tortured eyes
scurrying rats
and teeth shoot forth
although I feel nothing
I wander through the streets: 20
children with dirty faces
ask me for charity
child prostitutes
who are not yet fifteen
the streets are paved with pain   25
tanks that approach
raised bayonets

bodies that fall
weeping
finally I feel my arm   30
I am no longer a phantom
I hurt
therefore I exist
I return to watch the scene:
children who run   35
bleeding
women with panic
in their faces
this time it hurts me less
I pinch myself again   40
and already I feel nothing
I simply reflect
what happens at my side
the tanks
are not tanks   45
nor are the shouts
shouts
I am a blank mirror
that nothing penetrates
my surface   50
is hard
is brilliant
is polished
I became a mirror
and I am fleshless   55
scarcely preserving
a vague memory
of pain.

CONNECTIONS TO OTHER SELECTIONS

1. Compare the ways Alegría uses mirror images to reflect life in El Salvador
   with Plath's concerns in "Mirror" (p. 789).
2. Write an essay comparing the speaker's voice in this poem and that in
   Blake's "London" (p. 763). How do the speakers evoke emotional responses
   to what they describe?

YEHUDA AMICHAI (ISRAEL / B. 1924)

A leading contemporary Hebrew poet, Yehuda Amichai was born in Germany in 1924 and later moved with his family to Jerusalem. Amichai fought
with the Jewish Brigade of the British Army during World War II and in
the War of Independence. After the war, he attended Hebrew University.
His first volume of poetry, *Achshav Uve-Yamin HaAharim* ("Now and in
Other Days") appeared in 1955 and immediately attracted the interest of

the poetry-reading public. Widely read and admired outside his country, his works have been translated into thirty-three languages. His *Collected Poems* appeared in 1963; he is also the author of two novels and a book of short stories. *The Selected Poems of Yehuda Amichai* was published in 1996.

Jerusalem, 1985   *1985*

TRANSLATED BY CHANA BLOCH

Scribbled wishes stuck between the stones
of the Wailing Wall:
bits of crumpled, wadded paper.

And across the way, stuck in an old iron gate
half-hidden by jasmine:
"Couldn't make it,
I hope you'll understand."

CONNECTIONS TO OTHER SELECTIONS

1. Consider the use of irony in this poem and in Emily Dickinson's "I know that He exists" (p. 990).
2. Based on the content and style of "Jerusalem, 1985" and Wislawa Szymborska's "Maybe All This" (p. 1208), characterize the speaker in each poem. Explain why you think they are more alike or different.

FAIZ AHMED FAIZ (PAKISTAN / 1911–1984)

Born in Pakistan, Faiz Ahmed Faiz served in the British Indian Army during World War II. After the war he became a spokesman for Pakistani and Indian rights by editing the *Pakistani Times* and writing poetry in Urdu. Faiz served several jail sentences for his political activism, spending a considerable amount of time in solitary confinement. His poetry is widely known in India and the subcontinent; a translation of some is available as *Poems by Faiz* (1971).

If You Look at the City from Here   *1971*

TRANSLATED BY NAOMI LAZARD

If you look at the city from here
you see it is laid out in concentric circles,
each circle surrounded by a wall
            exactly like a prison.

Each street is a dog-run for prisoners, 5
no milestones, no destinations, no way out.

If anyone moves too quickly you wonder
why he hasn't been stopped by a shout.
If someone raises his arm
you expect to hear the jangling of chains. 10

If you look at the city from here
there is no one with dignity,
no one fully in control of his senses.
Every young man bears the brand of a criminal,
every young woman the emblem of a slave. 15

You cannot tell whether you see
        a group of revelers or mourners
in the shadows dancing around the distant lamps,
and from here you cannot tell
whether the color streaming down the walls 20
is that of blood or roses.

CONNECTIONS TO OTHER SELECTIONS

1. Compare the treatment of the city in this poem and in Blake's "London" (p. 763).
2. Write an essay on the meaning of confinement in Faiz's poem and in Rilke's "The Panther" (p. 768).

XU GANG (CHINA / B. 1945)

Born in Shanghai, China, Xu Gang served in the army after being drafted in 1962 and began writing poetry in support of the Cultural Revolution. However, after graduating from Beijing University in 1974, he questioned the principles and brutally disruptive consequences of the Cultural Revolution, a disillusionment suggested by "Red Azalea on the Cliff." His collections of poems include *The Flower of Rain*, *Songs for the Far Away*, and *One Hundred Lyrics*.

Red Azalea on the Cliff   1982

TRANSLATED BY FANG DAI, DENNIS DING, AND EDWARD MORIN

Red azalea, smiling
From the cliffside at me,
You make my heart shudder with fear!
A body could smash and bones splinter in the canyon —
Beauty, always looking on at disaster. 5

But red azalea on the cliff,
That you comb your twigs even in a mountain gale

Calms me down a bit.
Of course you're not wilfully courting danger,
Nor are you at ease with whatever happens to you. 10
You're merely telling me: beauty is nature.

Would anyone like to pick a flower
To give to his love
Or pin to his own lapel?
On the cliff there is no road 15
And no azalea grows where there is a road.
If someone actually reached that azalea,
Then an azalea would surely bloom in his heart.

Red azalea on the cliff,
You smile like the Yellow Mountains, 20
Whose sweetness encloses slyness,
Whose intimacy embraces distance.
You remind us all of our first love.
Sometimes the past years look
Just like the azalea on the cliff. 25

MAY 1982
Yellow Mountain
Revised at Hangzhou

CONNECTION TO ANOTHER SELECTION

1. In an essay explain how beauty is associated with danger in Xu Gang's
poem and in Keats's "La Belle Dame sans Merci" (p. 1166).

PABLO NERUDA (CHILE / 1904–1973)

Born in Chile, Pablo Neruda insisted all his life on the connection between
poetry and politics. He was an activist and a Chilean diplomat in a number of
countries during the 1920s and 1930s and remained politically active until his
death. Neruda was regarded as a great and influential poet (he was awarded
the Nobel Prize in 1971) whose poetry ranged from specific political issues to
the yearnings of romantic love. Among his many works are *Twenty Love Poems
and a Song of Despair* (1924), *Residence on Earth* (three series, 1925–45), *Spain in the
Heart* (1937), *The Captain's Verses* (1952), and *Memorial of Isla Negra* (1964).

Sweetness, Always 1958

TRANSLATED BY ALASTAIR REID

Why such harsh machinery?
Why, to write down the stuff
and people of every day,
must poems be dressed up in gold,

in old and fearful stone?
I want verses of felt or feather
which scarcely weigh, mild verses
with the intimacy of beds
where people have loved and dreamed.
I want poems stained
by hands and everydayness.

Verses of pastry which melt
into milk and sugar in the mouth,
air and water to drink,
the bites and kisses of love.
I long for eatable sonnets,
poems of honey and flour.

Vanity keeps prodding us
to lift ourselves skyward
or to make deep and useless
tunnels underground.
So we forget the joyous
love-needs of our bodies.
We forget about pastries.
We are not feeding the world.

In Madras a long time since,
I saw a sugary pyramid,
a tower of confectionery—
one level after another,
and in the construction, rubies,
and other blushing delights,
medieval and yellow.

Someone dirtied his hands
to cook up so much sweetness.

Brother poets from here
and there, from earth and sky,
from Medellín, from Veracruz,
Abyssinia, Antofagasta,
do you know the recipe for honeycombs?

Let's forget all about that stone.

Let your poetry fill up
the equinoctial pastry shop
our mouths long to devour—
all the children's mouths
and the poor adults' also.
Don't go on without seeing,
relishing, understanding
all these hearts of sugar.

Don't be afraid of sweetness.

With us or without us,
sweetness will go on living

and is infinitely alive,
forever being revived,
for it's in a man's mouth,
whether he's eating or singing,   55
that sweetness has its place.

CONNECTIONS TO OTHER SELECTIONS

1. Compare the view of life offered in this poem with that in Frost's "Birches" (p. 1009).

2. Write an essay that discusses Kinnell's "Blackberry Eating" (p. 838) and Chasin's "The Word *Plum*" (p. 857) as the sort of "eatable" poetry the speaker calls for in this poem.

OCTAVIO PAZ (MEXICO / 1914–1998)

Born in Mexico City, Octavio Paz studied at the National Autonomous University and in 1943 helped found one of Mexico's most important literary reviews, the *Prodigal Son*. He served in the Mexican diplomatic corps in Paris, New Delhi, and New York. Much of Paz's poetry reflects Hispanic traditions and European modernism as well as Buddhism. In 1990 he received the Nobel Prize for Literature. Paz's major works include *Sun Stone* (1958), *The Violent Season* (1958), *Salamander* (1962), *Blanco* (1966), *Eastern Rampart* (1968), *Renga* (1971), and *Collected Poems, 1957–1987* (1987).

The Street   1963

A long silent street.
I walk in blackness and I stumble and fall
and rise, and I walk blind, my feet
stepping on silent stones and dry leaves.
Someone behind me also stepping on stones, leaves: 5
if I slow down, he slows;
if I run, he runs. I turn: nobody.
Everything dark and doorless.
Turning and turning among these corners
which lead forever to the street   10
where nobody waits for, nobody follows me,
where I pursue a man who stumbles
and rises and says when he sees me: nobody.

CONNECTIONS TO OTHER SELECTIONS

1. How does the speaker's anxiety in this poem compare with that in Frost's "Acquainted with the Night" (p. 802)?

2. Write an essay comparing the tone of this poem and that of Hughes's "Lenox Avenue: Midnight" (p. 1045).

INDIRA SANT (INDIA / B. 1914)

Born in Pune in the state of Maharashtra, India, Indira Sant began her career as a teacher and a writer of children's fiction. In the 1950s she focused her talent on writing feminist poetry that sympathetically described the hardships endured by Indian mothers, wives, and daughters. Her work has not been widely translated, but the following poem appeared in the journal *Daedalus*.

Household Fires   *1989*

TRANSLATED BY VINAY DHARWADKER

The daughter's job: without a murmur
to do the chores piling up around the house
until she leaves for work,
to pay her younger brother's fees,
to buy her sister ribbons,   5
to get her father's spectacles changed.
To take the others to the movies on holidays,
to keep back a little and hand over the rest
on payday.

The son's job: fresh savory snacks   10
for the whole household to eat:
to bring back the clothes from the washerman,
to clean and put away the bicycle,
to sing out of key while packing his father's lunch
at the stroke of the hour,   15
to open the door sulkily
whenever someone comes home from the movies,
to wrinkle his brow
when he puts out his hand for money
and is asked instead, "How much? For what?"   20

The younger daughter's job:
to savor the joys of shyness,
to shrink back minute by minute.
The younger son's job:
to choke all the while, grow up slowly   25
in states of wet and dry.

Four children learning in her fold,
her body drained by hardship,
what's left of her? A mass of tatters,
five tongues of flame   30
licking and licking at her on every side,
fanning and fanning the fire in her eyes
till her mind boils over,
gets burned.

1. Implicit in this poem is the father's presence. Compare the treatment of the father in "Household Fires" and Plath's "Daddy" (p. 1177).

2. Write an essay that compares the life described in this poem with Divakaruni's "Indian Movie, New Jersey" (p. 825).

WOLE SOYINKA (NIGERIA / B. 1934)

Born Oluwole Akinwande Soyinka, in the western Nigerian town of Akinwande, Wole Soyinka has embodied in his life and art the contradictions and tensions that can often seem inevitable for the European-educated, English-speaking African writers. Although he has written and published novels and poetry (the following poem is from *A Shuttle in the Crypt* [1972]), Soyinka is most renowned as a playwright whose work embodies his concerns as a political reformer and social critic. His many plays include *The Lion and the Jewel* (1959), *The Strong Bond* (1963), and *Death of the King's Horseman* (1976). His autobiography *The Man Died* (1973) records his experiences as a political prisoner in Nigeria. In 1986 he was awarded the Nobel Prize for Literature.

Future Plans   *1972*

The meeting is called
To odium: Forgers, framers
Fabricators Inter-
national. Chairman,
A dark horse, a circus nag turned blinkered sprinter   5

Mach Three°
We rate him — one for the Knife°
Two for 'iavelli,° Three —
Breaking speed
Of the truth barrier by a swooping detention decree   10
Projects in view:
Mao Tse Tung° in league
With Chiang Kai. Nkrumah°
Makes a secret

---

6 *Mach Three:* An air speed of three times the speed of sound.   7 *Knife:* Mack the Knife, an unsavory character from *The Threepenny Opera* (1933), by Bertolt Brecht and Kurt Weill. 8 *'iavelli:* Niccolò Machiavelli (1469-1527), an Italian political theorist who described ruthless strategies for gaining power in *The Prince* (1532).   12 *Mao Tse Tung:* Mao Tse-tung (1893-1975), Chinese Communist leader.   13 *Chiang Kai, Nkrumah:* Chiang Kai-shek (1887-1975), Chinese Nationalist leader exiled in Taiwan by Mao Tse-tung; Kwame Nkrumah (1909-1972), first president of Ghana.

Pact with Verwood, sworn by Hastings Banda.°   15
Proven: Arafat°
In flagrante cum
Golda Meir. Castro° drunk
With Richard Nixon°
Contraceptives stacked beneath the papal bunk . . .   20
              . . . and more to come

15 *Verwood, Hastings Banda:* Hendrick Verwoerd (1901–1966), former prime minister of South
Africa, assassinated in 1966; Hastings Banda (b. 1905), African political leader and first president of Malawi.   16 *Arafat:* Yasir Arafat (b. 1929), Palestinian leader.   18 *Golda Meir, Castro:*
Golda Meir (1898–1978), former prime minister of Israel; Fidel Castro (b. 1927), Cuban pre-
mier since 1959.   19 *Richard Nixon* (1913–1994): Former U.S. president forced to resign in
1974 due to political scandal.

CONNECTIONS TO OTHER SELECTIONS

1. Discuss the political satire in "Future Plans" and in Fearing's "AD" (p. 807).

2. Write an essay on whether the leaders alluded to in "Future Plans" are man-
    ifestations of the type of leader described in Thomas's "The Hand That
    Signed the Paper" (p. 783).

WISLAWA SZYMBORSKA (POLAND / B. 1923)

Born in Poland, Wislawa Szymborska has lived in Cracow since the age of
eight. She steadfastly refuses to reveal biographical details of her life, insisting that her poems should speak for themselves. With the exception of
Sounds, Feelings, Thoughts: Seventy Poems by Wislawa Szymborska (1981), translated and introduced by Magnus J. Krynski and Robert A. Maguire, and
View with a Grain of Sand: Selected Poems (1995), translated by Stanislaw
Barańczak and Clare Cavanagh, only some of Szymborska's poems have
been translated into English. Three of her later poetry collections — as
yet untranslated — are *There But for the Grace* (1972), *A Great Number* (1976),
and *The People of the Bridge* (1986). She was awarded the Nobel Prize in Literature in 1996.

Maybe All This   *1993*

TRANSLATED BY STANISLAW BARAŃCZAK AND CLARE CAVANAGH

Maybe all this
is happening in some lab?
Under one lamp by day
and billions by night?

Maybe we're experimental generations?   5
Poured from one vial to the next,

shaken in test tubes,
not scrutinized by eyes alone,
each of us separately
plucked up by tweezers in the end?   10

Or maybe it's more like this:
No interference?
The changes occur on their own
according to plan?
The graph's needle slowly etches   15
its predictable zigzags?

Maybe thus far we aren't of much interest?
The control monitors aren't usually plugged in?
Only for wars, perferably large ones,
for the odd ascent above our clump of Earth,   20
for major migrations from point A to B?

Maybe just the opposite:
They've got a taste for trivia up there?
Look! on the big screen a little girl
is sewing a button on her sleeve.   25
The radar shrieks,
the staff comes at a run.
What a darling little being
with its tiny heart beating inside it!
How sweet, its solemn   30
threading of the needle!
Someone cries enraptured:
Get the Boss,
tell him he's got to see this for himself!

Connections to Other Selections

1. Discuss the themes of "Maybe All This" and Dickinson's "Apparently with no surprise" (p. 990).
2. Write an essay on the tone of "Maybe All This" and Robert Frost's "Design" (p. 1018).

Tomas Transtromer (Sweden / b. 1931)

Born in Stockholm, Sweden, Tomas Transtromer's work is translated more than any other contemporary Scandinavian poet's. He has worked as a psychologist with juvenile offenders and handicapped persons. His collections of poetry include *Night Vision* (1971), *Windows and Stones: Selected Poems* (1972), *Truth Barriers* (1978), and *Selected Poems* (1981). Among his awards are the Petrarch Prize (1981) and a lifetime subsidy from the government of Sweden.

April and Silence   *1991*

TRANSLATED BY ROBIN FULTON

Spring lies desolate.
The velvet-dark ditch
crawls by my side
without reflections.

The only thing that shines   5
is yellow flowers.

I am carried in my shadow
like a violin
in its black box.

The only thing I want to say   10
glitters out of reach
like the silver
in a pawnbroker's.

CONNECTIONS TO OTHER SELECTIONS

1. Discuss the description of spring in this poem and in William Carlos Williams's "Spring and All" (p. 1190).

2. In an essay explain how the dictions used in "April and Silence" and Espada's "Latin Night at the Pawnshop" (p. 724) contribute to the poems' meanings and tone.

40

An Album of
Contemporary Poems

BILLY COLLINS (B. 1941)

Since the publication of his first book, *The Apple That Astonished Paris* (1988), Billy Collins (born in New York City in 1941) has established himself as a prominent voice in contemporary American poetry. His recent books include *Picnic, Lightning* (1998), *The Art of Drowning* (1995) — a finalist for the Lenore Marshall Prize — and *Questions about Angels* (1991), selected for the National Poetry Series and reissued in 1999.

Marginalia   *1998*

Sometimes the notes are ferocious,
skirmishes against the author
raging along the borders of every page
in tiny black script.
If I could just get my hands on you,   5
Kierkegaard,° or Conor Cruise O'Brien,°
they seem to say,
I would bolt the door and beat some logic into your head.

Other comments are more offhand, dismissive —
"Nonsense." "Please!" "HA!!" —   10
that kind of thing.
I remember once looking up from my reading,
my thumb as a bookmark,
trying to imagine what the person must look like

6 *Kierkegaard:* Sören Aaby Kierkegaard (1813–1855), Danish philosopher and theologian. *Conor Cruise O'Brien* (b. 1917): Irish historian, critic, and statesman.

who wrote "Don't be a ninny"   15
alongside a paragraph in *The Life of Emily Dickinson.*

Students are more modest
needing to leave only their splayed footprints
along the shore of the page.
One scrawls "Metaphor" next to a stanza of Eliot's.°   20
Another notes the presence of "Irony"
fifty times outside the paragraphs of *A Modest Proposal.*°

Or they are fans who cheer from the empty bleachers,
hands cupped around their mouths.
"Absolutely," they shout   25
to Duns Scotus° and James Baldwin.°
"Yes." "Bull's-eye." "My man!"
Check marks, asterisks, and exclamation points
rain down along the sidelines.

And if you have managed to graduate from college   30
without ever having written "Man vs. Nature"
in a margin, perhaps now
is the time to take one step forward.

We have all seized the white perimeter as our own
and reached for a pen if only to show   35
we did not just laze in an armchair turning pages;
we pressed a thought into the wayside,
planted an impression along the verge.

Even Irish monks in their cold scriptoria°
jotted along the borders of the Gospels   40
brief asides about the pains of copying,
a bird singing near their window,
or the sunlight that illuminated their page —
anonymous men catching a ride into the future
on a vessel more lasting than themselves.   45

And you have not read Joshua Reynolds,°
they say, until you have read him
enwreathed with Blake's° furious scribbling.

Yet the one I think of most often,
the one that dangles from me like a locket,   50
was written in the copy of *Catcher in the Rye*°
I borrowed from the local library
one slow, hot summer.
I was just beginning high school then,

---

20 *Eliot's:* Thomas Stearns Eliot (1888–1965), American-born English poet and critic.   22 *A Modest Proposal:* An essay by English satirist Jonathan Swift (1667–1745).   26 *Duns Scotus* (1265?–1308): Scottish theologian.   *James Baldwin* (1924–1987): African American essayist and novelist.   39 *scriptoria:* Rooms in a monastery used for writing and copying.   46 *Joshua Reynolds* (1723–1792): English portrait artist who entertained many of the important writers of his time.   48 *Blake's:* William Blake (1757–1827), English mystic and poet.   51 *Catcher in the Rye:* A novel (1951) about adolescence by American author J. D. Salinger (b. 1919).

reading books on a davenport in my parents' living room, 55
and I cannot tell you
how vastly my loneliness was deepened,
how poignant and amplified the world before me seemed,
when I found on one page

a few greasy looking smears 60
and next to them, written in soft pencil —
by a beautiful girl, I could tell,
whom I would never meet —
"Pardon the egg salad stains, but I'm in love."

CONNECTIONS TO OTHER SELECTIONS

1. Discuss the speaker's response to reading in "Marginalia" and in Philip Larkin's "A Study of Reading Habits" (p. 684). How is reading used as a measure of each speaker's character?

2. Describe the impact made on the speaker's imagination by what is contemplated in "Marginalia" and in Joan Murray's "Play-By-Play" (p. 1227).

CORNELIUS EADY (B. 1954)

Cornelius Eady, born in Rochester, New York, has taught poetry at several colleges and universities; he is currently director of the Poetry Center at the State University of New York at Stony Brook. The recipient of many fellowships and awards, he has published five books of poetry including *Victims of the Latest Dance Craze* (1986) and *The Gathering of My Name* (1991).

The Supremes   *1991*

We were born to be gray. We went to school,
Sat in rows, ate white bread,
Looked at the floor a lot. In the back
Of our small heads

A long scream. We did what we could, 5
And all we could do was
Turn on each other. How the fat kids suffered!
Not even being jolly could save them.

And then there were the anal retentives,
The terrified brown-noses, the desperately 10
Athletic or popular. This, of course,
Was training. At home

Our parents shook their heads and waited.
We learned of the industrial revolution,
The sectioning of the clock into pie slices. 15

We drank cokes and twiddled our thumbs. In the
Back of our minds

A long scream. We snapped butts in the showers,
Froze out shy girls on the dance floor,
Pin-pointed flaws like radar.   20
Slowly we understood: this was to be the world.

We were born insurance salesmen and secretaries,
Housewives and short order cooks,
Stock room boys and repairmen,
And it wouldn't be a bad life, they promised,   25
In a tone of voice that would force some of us
To reach in self-defense for wigs,
Lipstick,

Sequins.

CONNECTIONS TO OTHER SELECTIONS

1. Discuss the speakers' memories of school in "The Supremes" and in Judy
    Page Heitzman's "The Schoolroom on the Second Floor of the Knitting
    Mill" (p. 1111).
2. In an essay compare the themes of "The Supremes" and Dickinson's "From
    all the Jails the Boys and Girls" (p. 1107).

MARTÍN ESPADA (B. 1957)

Martín Espada was born in Brooklyn, New York. He has worked as a tenant
lawyer in Boston and now teaches in the English Department at the University of Massachusetts at Amherst. He has been awarded several fellowships including two from the National Endowment for the Arts. His books
of poetry include *Rebellion Is the Circle of a Lover's Hand* (1990), *City of Coughing and Dead Radiators* (1993), and *Imagine the Angels of Bread* (1996).

Coca-Cola and Coco Frío   1993

On his first visit to Puerto Rico,
island of family folklore,
the fat boy wandered
from table to table
with his mouth open.   5
At every table, some great-aunt
would steer him with cool spotted hands
to a glass of Coca-Cola.
One even sang to him, in all the English
she could remember, a Coca-Cola jingle   10

from the forties. He drank obediently, though
he was bored with this potion, familiar
from soda fountains in Brooklyn.

Then, at a roadside stand off the beach, the fat boy
opened his mouth to coco frío, a coconut   15
chilled, then scalped by a machete
so that a straw could inhale the clear milk.
The boy tilted the green shell overhead
and drooled coconut milk down his chin;
suddenly, Puerto Rico was not Coca-Cola   20
or Brooklyn, and neither was he.

For years afterward, the boy marveled at an island
where the people drank Coca-Cola
and sang jingles from World War II
in a language they did not speak,   25
while so many coconuts in the trees
sagged heavy with milk, swollen
and unsuckled.

CONNECTIONS TO OTHER SELECTIONS

1. Compare what the boy in this poem discovers about Puerto Rico with what
   the speaker learns in Hughes's "Theme for English B" (p. 1107).

2. Write an essay discussing the images used to describe Puerto Rico and the
   United States in this poem and in Laviera's "AmeRícan" (p. 931).

DEBORAH GARRISON (B. 1965)

Raised in Ann Arbor, Michigan, Deborah Garrison graduated from Brown
University and works on the editorial staff of *The New Yorker*. She published a collection of poems, *A Working Girl Can't Win*, in 1998. Her poetry
appears regularly in *The New Yorker*.

The Boss   *1998*

A firecracker, even after middle age
set in, a prince of repression
in his coat and tie, with cynical words

for everything dear to him.
Once I saw a snapshot of the house   5
he lives in, its fence painted

white, the flowers a wife
had planted leaning into the frame
on skinny stalks, shaking little pom-poms

of color, the dazzle all   10
accidental, and I felt
a hot, corrective

sting: our lives would never
intersect. At some point
he got older, trimmer, became   15

the formidable man around the office.
His bearing upright, what hair he has
silver and smooth, he shadows my doorway,

jostling the change in his pocket —
milder now, and mildly vexed.   20
The other day he asked what on earth

was wrong with me, and sat me down
on his big couch, where I cried
for twenty minutes straight,

snuffling, my eyeliner   25
betraying itself in the stained
tears. Impossible to say I was crying

because he had asked. He passed
tissues, at ease with the fearsome
womanly squall that made me alien   30

even to myself. No, it didn't make him
squirm. Across his seventy years,
over his glasses, he eyed me kindly,

and I thought what countless scenes
of tears, of love revealed,   35
he must have known.

CONNECTIONS TO OTHER SELECTIONS

1. Compare and contrast the tone and theme of "The Boss" with those of
   Marge Piercy's "The Secretary Chant" (p. 671).
2. Discuss the author's use of metaphors in "The Boss" and in Alice Walker's
   "a woman is not a potted plant" (p. 699).

DONALD HALL (B. 1928)

Born in New Haven, Connecticut, Donald Hall taught at the University of
Michigan and for years has made his living in New Hampshire as a free-
lance writer of numerous books of poetry as well as literary criticism, essays, and children's books. His collections of poems include *The One Day*
(1988), winner of the National Book Critics Award, *The Museum of Clear
Ideas* (1993), and *Without* (1998).

Letter with No Address   *1996*

Your daffodils rose up
and collapsed in their yellow
bodies on the hillside
garden above the bricks
you laid out in sand, squatting   5
with pants pegged and face
masked like a beekeeper's
against the black flies.
Buttercups circle the planks
of the old wellhead   10
this May while your silken
gardener's body withers or moulds
in the Proctor graveyard.
I drive and talk to you crying
and come back to this house   15
to talk to your photographs.

There's news to tell you:
Maggie Fisher's pregnant.
I carried myself like an egg
at Abigail's birthday party   20
a week after you died,
as three-year-olds bounced
uproarious on a mattress.
Joyce and I met for lunch
at the mall and strolled weepily   25
through Sears and B. Dalton.

Today it's four weeks
since you lay on our painted bed
and I closed your eyes.
Yesterday I cut irises to set   30
in a pitcher on your grave;
today I brought a carafe
to fill it with fresh water.
I remember the bone-pain,
vomiting, and delirium. I remember   35
the pond afternoons.

                    My routine
is established: coffee;
the *Globe*; breakfast;
writing you this letter   40
at my desk. When I go to bed
to sleep after baseball,
Gus follows me into the bedroom
as he used to follow us.
Most of the time he flops   45

down in the parlor
with his head on his paws.

Once a week I drive to Tilton
to see Dick and Nan.
Nan doesn't understand much
but she knows you're dead;   50
I feel her fretting. The tune
of Dick and me talking
seems to console her.

               You know now
whether the soul survives death.   55
Or you don't. When you were dying
you said you didn't fear
punishment. We never dared
to speak of Paradise.   60

At five a.m., when I walk outside,
mist lies thick on hayfields.
By eight, the air is clear,
cool, sunny with the pale yellow
light of mid-May. Kearsarge   65
rises huge and distinct,
each birch and balsam visible.
To the west the waters
of Eagle Pond waver
and flash through popples just   70
leafing out.

              Always the weather,
writing its book of the world,
returns you to me.
Ordinary days were best,   75
when we worked over poems
in our separate rooms.
I remember watching you gaze
out the January window
into the garden of snow   80
and ice, your face rapt
as you imagined burgundy lilies.

Your presence in this house
is almost as enormous
and painful as your absence.   85
Driving home from Tilton,
I remember how you cherished
that vista with its center
the red door of a farmhouse
against green fields.   90
Are you past pity?
If you have consciousness now,
if something I can call

"you" has something
like "consciousness," I doubt   95
you remember the last days.
I play them over and over:
I lift your wasted body
onto the commode, your arms
looped around my neck, aiming   100
your bony bottom so that
it will not bruise on a rail.
Faintly you repeat,
"Momma, Momma."

           You lay   105
astonishing in the long box
while Alice Ling prayed
and sang "Amazing Grace"
a capella. Three times today
I drove to your grave.   110
Sometimes, coming back home
to our circular driveway,
I imagine you've returned
before me, bags of groceries upright
in the back of the Saab,   115
its trunklid delicately raised
as if proposing an encounter,
dog-fashion, with the Honda.

CONNECTIONS TO OTHER SELECTIONS

1. Compare how the speaker copes with grief in "Letter with No Address" with the speaker in Dickinson's "The Bustle in a House" (p. 975).

2. Write an essay on the tone of this poem and Frost's "Home Burial" (p. 1005).

JANE HIRSHFIELD (B. 1953)

Born in New York City, Jane Hirshfield is the author of four books of poetry, most recently *The Lives of the Heart* (1997), and a collection of essays, *Nine Gates: Entering the Mind of Poetry* (1997). She has also edited and co-translated two collections of poetry by women from the past, *Women in Praise of the Sacred: Forty-three Centuries of Spiritual Poetry by Women* (1995) and *The Ink Dark Moon: Poems by Ono no Komachi and Izumi Shikibu, Women of the Ancient Court of Japan* (1990). Hirshfield's awards include the Poetry Center Book Award, the Bay Area Book Reviewers Award, Columbia University's Translation Center Award, and fellowships from the Guggenheim and Rockefeller Foundations.

The Lives of the Heart   *1997*

Are ligneous, muscular, chemical.
Wear birch-colored feathers,
green tunnels of horse-tail reed.
Wear calcified spirals, Fibonnacian° spheres.
Are edible; are glassy; are clay; blue schist.   5
Can be burned as tallow, as coal,
can be skinned for garnets, for shoes.
Cast shadows or light;
shuffle; snort; cry out in passion.
Are salt, are bitter,   10
tear sweet grass with their teeth.
Step silently into blue needle-fall at dawn.
Thrash in the net until hit.
Rise up as cities, as serpentined magma, as maples,
hiss lava-red into the sea.   15
Leave the strange kiss of their bodies
in Burgess Shale. Can be found, can be lost,
can be carried, broken, sung.
Lie dormant until they are opened by ice,
by drought. Go blind in the service of lace.   20
Are starving, are sated, indifferent, curious, mad.
Are stamped out in plastic, in tin.
Are stubborn, are careful, are slipshod,
are strung on the blue backs of flies
on the black backs of cows.   25
Wander the vacant whale-roads, the white thickets
heavy with slaughter.
Wander the fragrant carpets of alpine flowers.
Not one is not held in the arms of the rest, to blossom.
Not one is not given to ecstasy's lions.   30
Not one does not grieve.
Each of them opens and closes, closes and opens
the heavy gate — violent, serene, consenting, suffering it all.

4 *Fibonnacian:* An apparent reference to Leonardo Fibonacci (1170-1240), a famous Italian mathematician.

CONNECTIONS TO OTHER SELECTIONS

1. Discuss the use of personification in this poem and Stevens's "Schizophrenia" (p. 792).

2. Write an essay that compares the diction and images of "The Lives of the Heart" and Alice Jones's "The Foot" (p. 870).

LINDA HOGAN (B. 1947)

Born in Denver, Colorado, and raised in Oklahoma, Linda Hogan is a member of the Chickasaw tribe. She was educated at the University of Colorado, where she now teaches creative writing. She has been awarded fellowships from the Guggenheim Foundation and the National Endowment for the Arts and has received an American Book Award. In addition to publishing fiction — her novel *Mean Spirit* appeared in 1989 — she has published several volumes of poetry including *Eclipse* (1985), *Seeing through the Sun* (1985), *Savings* (1988), and *The Book of Medicines* (1993).

Hunger   *1993*

Hunger crosses oceans.
It loses its milk teeth.
It sits on the ship and cries.

Thin, afraid,
it fashioned hooks to catch   5
the passing songs of whales so large
the men grew small
as distant, shrinking lands.
They sat on the ship and cried.

Hunger was the fisherman   10
who said dolphins are like women,
we took them from the sea
and had our way
with them.

Hunger knows we have not yet reached   15
the black and raging depths of anything.

It is the old man
who comes in the night
to cast a line
and wait at the luminous shore.   20
He knows the sea is pregnant
with clear fish
and their shallow pools of eggs
and that the ocean has hidden
signs of its own hunger,   25
lost men and boats
and squid that flew
toward churning light.

Hunger lives in the town
whose walls are made of shells   30

white and shining in the moon,
where people live surrounded
by what they've eaten
to forget that hunger
sits on a ship and cries.   35

And it is a kind of hunger
that brings us to love,
to rocking currents of a secret wave
and the body that wants to live beyond itself
like the destitute men   40
who took the shining dolphins from the sea.
They were like women,
they said,
and had their way
with them,   45
wanting to be inside,
to drink
and be held in
the thin, clear milk of the gods.

CONNECTIONS TO OTHER SELECTIONS

1. Write an essay comparing Hogan's definition of hunger with Dickinson's definition of heaven in "'Heaven'—is what I cannot reach!" (p. 961). Which definition do you find more complete and satisfying? Explain why.

2. Discuss the relation between love and hunger in this poem and in Croft's "Home-Baked Bread" (p. 769).

PHILIP LEVINE (B. 1928)

Immersed in the working-class milieu of Detroit, where he was born in 1928, Philip Levine's work records an America where the "time will never come / nor the ripeness be all." Nonetheless his poems celebrate—quietly, with irony and humor—the stoicism of the human spirit. Levine attended Wayne State University and while there studied with the poet John Berryman. In 1958 he was awarded the prestigious Fellowship in Poetry at Stanford University. Since 1969 he has taught English at California State University in Fresno and now divides his time between Fresno and New York University. His most recent collections include *What Work Is* (1991), *The Simple Truth* (1994), *Unselected Poems* (1997), *The Return* (1999), and an autobiography, *The Bread of Time* (1994). *Selected Poems* appeared in 1984. He has received two Pulitzer Prizes, two National Book Awards, two National Book Critics Circle Awards, the Lenore Marshall Award, and the Ruth Lilly Award.

Reinventing America   *1999*

The city was huge. A boy of twelve could walk
for hours while the closed houses stared down at him
from early morning to dusk, and he'd get nowhere.
Oh no, I was not that boy. Even at twelve I knew
enough to stay in my own neighborhood,   5
I knew anyone who left might not return.
Boys were animals with animal hungers
I learned early. Better to stay close to home.
I'd try to bum cigarettes from the night workers
as they left the bars in the heavy light of noon   10
or I'd hang around the grocery hoping
one of the beautiful young wives would ask me
to help her carry her shopping bags home.
You're wondering what I was up to. Not much.
The sun rose late in November and set early.   15
At times I thought life was rushing by too fast.
Before I knew it I'd be my half-blind uncle
married to a woman who cried all day long
while in the basement he passed his time working
on short-wave radio calls to anywhere.   20
I'd sneak down and talk to him, Uncle Nathan,
wiry in his boxer's shorts and high-topped boots,
chewing on a cigar, the one dead eye catching
the overhead light while he mused on his life
on the road or at sea. How he loved the whores   25
in the little Western towns or the Latin ports!
He'd hold his hands out to approximate
their perfect breasts. The months in jail had taught him
a man had only his honor and his ass
to protect. "You turn your fist this way," he said,   30
taking my small hand in both of his, "and fire
from the shoulder, so," and he'd extend it out
to the face of an imaginary foe.
Why he'd returned to this I never figured out,
though life was ample here, a grid of crowded blocks   35
of Germans, Wops, Polacks, Jews, wild Irish,
plus some square heads from the Upper Peninsula.
Six bakeries, four barber shops, a five and dime,
twenty beer gardens, a Catholic church with a *shul*
next door where we studied the Talmud-Torah.   40
Wonderful how all the old hatreds bubbled
so quietly on the back burner you could
forget until one day they tore through the pool halls,
the bowling alley, the high school athletic fields
leaving an eye gone, a long fresh, livid scar   45
running to touch a mouth, young hands raw or broken,
boys and girls ashamed of what they were, ashamed

of what they were not. It was merely village life,
exactly what our parents left in Europe
brought to America with pure fidelity.   50

CONNECTIONS TO OTHER SELECTIONS

1. Compare the description of immigrant life in "Reinventing America" with
   that in Tato Laviera's "AmeRícan" (p. 931).
2. What kind of values are associated with village life in Europe in Levine's
   poem? How do those values compare with the values associated with Indian life depicted in the movies in Chitra Banerjee Divakaruni's "Indian
   Movie, New Jersey" (p. 825)?

GAIL MAZUR (B. 1937)

Gail Mazur was born in Cambridge, Massachusetts, and grew up there in
the nearby town of Newton. Her three collections of poetry are *Nightfire*
(1978), *The Pose of Happiness* (1986), and *The Common* (1995). A fourth, titled
They Can't Take That Away From Me, is due in 2001. She has been visiting
professor at the University of Houston and is currently writer-in-residence
at Emerson College in Boston. From 1996 to 1997, she was the Fellow in Poetry at the Bunting Institute at Radcliffe College. Mazur founded and has
for many years directed the Blacksmith House Poetry Center in Cambridge, an organization committed to the support of contemporary American poets. She lives in Cambridge and in Provincetown, Massachusetts,
where, with her husband Michael Mazur, she is involved with the Provincetown Fine Arts Work Center.

Snake in the Grass   *1995*

—I'd screamed when it slithered under my hand
as I leaned to pick the first ripe blueberry.
It was noon, a Monday in late July. The sun,
as always, was hot on my shoulders, hot
on the back of my blouse. I'd forgotten   5
the universe wasn't all dead pines and Indian
graves and boarded-up houses, that I wasn't
the only creature left alive in it, that I'd
never found my comfortable place inside it.
I wanted to be someone who doesn't scare,   10
who can't be shaken, so I wanted no witnesses
to this paradigm in the Garden. Then, the snake
slid noiselessly under the rotting porch
of our family cottage. The reduced summer woods,
the wide sky, were stunned and silent. Imagine   15

a silence, all you hear your own scream vanishing.
A second before, you'd knelt to the ground,
humming, and something writhed at your left hand,
wild as migraine, while your right reached
through transparent air to the first sweet berry,   20
treasure of asthmatic childhood's summers.
It isn't death you fear now, or years ago,
it's the sneak attack, the large hand clapped
over your mouth, bad moments that suddenly
come back when you think you're at home   25
in the frayed landcape you've already lost,
and a snake, a *not-you*, invisible, camouflaged
in the famished grass, jolts you out of your dream.
Try being rational and patient:
get into your car, drive down the old road   30
to Dunroamin' Campgrounds. You've got a quarter—
telephone a friend, he'll probably be in
his amber-lit air-conditioned office, reading
student papers. He might say postmodernism's
days are numbered, but he'd like to get away.   35
Tell him not to come down to the Cape.
Tell him about the harmless snake, give him
the scream, how you blushed that one of nature's
creatures should think you're a silly woman.
Embellish a little, laugh at yourself in the hot   40
glass booth. There'll be kids playing volleyball
on the parched field, mosquitoes, mothers
spreading mustard on baloney sandwiches.
—Wouldn't anyone have screamed at the chill
reptilian underhand move of that snake?   45
Wasn't that scream waiting for years?
Can't you relent, can't you love yet
your small bewildering part in this world?

CONNECTIONS TO OTHER SELECTIONS

1. How does this speaker's response to being surprised by a snake compare with the speaker's response in Emily Dickinson's "A narrow Fellow in the Grass" (p. 2).
2. Compare the theme of this poem with that of Ronald Wallace's "Dogs" (p. 1229).

ROBERT MORGAN (B. 1944)

Robert Morgan is a poet and novelist who has been widely praised as the poet laureate of Appalachia. Morgan was born and raised in North Carolina in a small and isolated valley in the Blue Ridge Mountains. He earned his B.A. from the University of North Carolina at Chapel Hill and attended the University of North Carolina at Greensboro, where he earned his M.F.A. Morgan has published four books of fiction since 1969, including *The Hinterlands* (1994) and *The Truest Pleasure* (1995). He has been widely published in magazines including *The Atlantic Monthly, The New Republic, Poetry, The Southern Review, The Yale Review, The Carolina Quarterly,* and *The New England Review.* Morgan has also published nine volumes of poetry. In 1971 Morgan began teaching at Cornell University where, since 1992, he has been Kappa Alpha Professor of English. He has won several awards, including four National Endowment for the Art Fellowships, a Guggenheim Fellowship, and has been included in *New Stories from the South* and *Prize Stories: The O. Henry Awards.* His most recent novel, *Gap Creek* (1999), was selected for Oprah's Book Club.

Time's Music   1996

Insects in an August field seem
to register the background noise
of space and amplify the twitch
of partners in atoms. The click
of little timepieces, chirp of   5
tiny chisels, as grasshoppers
and crickets effervesce and spread
in the weeds ahead, then wash back
in a wake of crackling music
that sparkles through grass, ticking   10
away the summer, whispering of
frost and stars overhead and chatter
of memory in every bit
of matter, of half-life in
the thick and flick of creation.   15

CONNECTIONS TO OTHER SELECTIONS

1. Discuss the treatment of time in Morgan's poem and in Sophie Cabot Black's "August" (p. 788).
2. Consider Morgan's use of sounds and their effects along with Galway Kinnell's in "Blackberry Eating" (p. 838).

JOAN MURRAY (B. 1945)

Born and raised in New York City, Joan Murray was educated at Hunter College and New York University. She has taught at Lehman College of the City University of New York. Among her awards for poetry are the National Endowment for the Arts and a Pushcart Prize. Her published volumes of poetry include *Egg Tooth* (1975) and *The Same Water* (1990).

Play-By-Play   *1997*

Yaddo °

Would it surprise the young men
playing softball on the hill to hear the women
on the terrace admiring their bodies:
the slim waist of the pitcher, the strength
of the runner's legs, the torso of the catcher   5
rising off his knees to toss the ball back to the mound?
Would it embarrass them
to hear two women, sitting together after dinner,
praising even their futile motions:
the flex of a batter's hips   10
before his missed swing, the wide-spread stride
of a man picked off his base, the intensity
on the new man's face
as he waits on deck and fans the air?

Would it annoy them, the way some women   15
take offense when men caress them with their eyes?
And why should it surprise me that these women,
well past sixty, haven't put aside desire
but sit at ease and in pleasure,
watching the young men move above the rose garden   20
where the marble Naiads
pose and yawn in their fountain?
Who better than these women, with their sweaters
draped across their shoulders, their perspectives
honed from years of lovers, to recognize   25
the beauty that would otherwise
go unnoticed on this hill?
And will it compromise their pleasure
if I sit down at their table to listen
to the play-by-play and see it through their eyes?   30

Would it distract the young men if they realized
that three women laughing softly on the terrace
above closed books and half-filled wineglasses
are moving beside them on the field?
Would they want to know how they've been   35
held to the light till some motion or expression
showed the unsuspected loveliness
in a common shape or face?
Wouldn't they have liked to see how they looked
down there, as they stood for a moment at the plate,   40
bathed in the light of perfect expectation,
before their shadows lengthened, before they

Yaddo: An artist's colony in Saratoga Springs, New York.

walked together up the darkened hill,
so beautiful they would not have
recognized themselves?

45

CONNECTIONS TO OTHER SELECTIONS

1. Compare the voice of the speaker in "Play-By-Play" with that of Acker-man's "A Fine, a Private Place" (p. 732).

2. Write an essay on the speaker's gaze in this poem and in Steele's "An Aubade" (p. 1104).

MARY OLIVER (B. 1935)

Mary Oliver taps the resplendent depths of the natural world and brings brightness back to share. Born in Cleveland, Ohio, in 1935, Oliver attended Vassar College. Since then she has taught and been poet-in-residence at several colleges. Her early collection, *American Primitive* (1983), won the Pulitzer Prize; other collections include *No Voyage and Other Poems* (1965), *The River Styx, Ohio and Other Poems* (1972), *Twelve Moons* (1979), and *Dream Work* (1986). Her *New and Selected Poems* won the National Book Award. She currently teaches at Bennington College and lives in Provincetown, Massa-chusetts, and in Bennington, Vermont.

Seven White Butterflies　　　　　　　　　　　　1995

Seven white butterflies
delicate in a hurry look
how they bang the pages
    of their wings as they fly

to the fields of mustard yellow　　　　　　　　5
and orange and plain
gold all eternity
    is in the moment this is what

Blake said Whitman said such
wisdom in the agitated　　　　　　　　　　　10
motions of the mind seven
    dancers floating

even as worms toward
paradise see how they banter
and riot and rise　　　　　　　　　　　　　15
    to the trees flutter

lob their white bodies into
the invisible wind weightless

lacy willing
   to deliver themselves unto   20

the universe now each settles
down on a yellow thumb on a
brassy stem now
   all seven are rapidly sipping

from the golden towers who   25
would have thought it could be so easy?

CONNECTIONS TO OTHER SELECTIONS

1. Compare the sounds and rhythms used to describe the movement of butterflies in Oliver's poem with Emily Dickinson's use of sound and rhythm
   in "A Bird came down the Walk —" (p. 836).
2. Discuss the theme of this poem and of Robert Frost's "Nothing Gold Can
   Stay" (p. 1016).

RONALD WALLACE (B. 1945)

Born in Cedar Rapids, Iowa, Ronald Wallace earned a B.A. at the College of
Wooster, and an M.A. and a Ph.D. at the University of Michigan. He has
taught in the Department of English at the University of Wisconsin,
Madison, since 1972. Among his awards are a Rackham Prize Fellowship
and several American Council of Learned Society fellowships. His collections of poems include *People and Dog in the Sun* (1987), *The Makings of Happiness* (1991), and *Time's Fancy* (1994).

Dogs   *1997*

When I was six years old I hit one with
a baseball bat. An accident, of course,
and broke his jaw. They put that dog to sleep,
a euphemism even then I knew
could not excuse me from the lasting wrath   5
of memory's flagellation. My remorse
could dog me as it would, it wouldn't keep
me from the life sentence that I drew:

For I've been barked at, bitten, nipped, knocked flat,
slobbered over, humped, sprayed, beshat,   10
by spaniel, terrier, retriever, bull, and Dane.
But through the years what's given me most pain
of all the dogs I've been the victim of
are those whose slow eyes gazed at me, in love.

CONNECTIONS TO OTHER SELECTIONS

1. Compare this poem's theme with Updike's "Dog's Death" (p. 673).
2. In an essay discuss the strategies used in this sonnet and Shakespeare's "My mistress' eyes are nothing like the sun" (p. 891) to create emotion in the reader.

DRAMA

The Study
of Drama

41

Reading Drama

READING DRAMA RESPONSIVELY

The publication of a short story, novel, or poem represents for most writers the final step in a long creative process that might have begun with an idea, issue, emotion, or question that demanded expression. *Playwrights* — writers who make plays — may begin a work in the same way as other writers, but rarely are they satisfied with only its publication because most dramatic literature — what we call *plays* — is written to be performed by actors on a stage before an audience. Playwrights typically create a play keeping in mind not only readers but also actors, producers, directors, costumers, designers, technicians, and a theater full of other support staff who have a hand in presenting the play to a live audience.

Drama is literature equipped with arms, legs, tears, laughs, whispers, shouts, and gestures that are alive and immediate. Indeed, the word *drama* derives from the Greek word *dran*, meaning "to do" or "to perform." The text of many plays — the *script* — may come to life fully only when the written words are transformed into a performance. Although there are plays that do not invite production, they are relatively few. Such plays, written to be read rather than performed, are called *closet dramas.* In this kind of work (primarily associated with nineteenth-century English literature), literary art outweighs all other considerations. The majority of playwrights, however, view the written word as the beginning of a larger creation and hope that a producer will deem their scripts worthy of production.

Given that most playwrights intend their works to be performed, it might be argued that reading a play is a poor substitute for seeing it acted on a stage — perhaps something like reading a recipe without having access to the ingredients and a kitchen. This analogy is tempting, but it overlooks the literary dimensions of a script; the words we hear on a stage were written first. Read from a page, these words can feed an imagination in ways that a recipe cannot satisfy a hungry cook. We can fill in a play's missing faces, voices, actions, and settings in much the same way that we imagine these elements in a short story or novel. Like any play director, we are free to include as many ingredients as we have an appetite for.

This imaginative collaboration with the playwright creates a mental world that can be nearly as real and vivid as a live performance. Sometimes readers find that they prefer their own reading of a play to a director's interpretation. Shakespeare's Hamlet, for instance, has been presented as a whining son, but you may read him as a strong prince. Rich plays often accommodate a wide range of imaginative responses to their texts. Reading, then, is an excellent way to appreciate and evaluate a production of a play. Moreover, reading is valuable in its own right because it allows us to enter the playwright's created world even when a theatrical production is unavailable.

Reading a play, however, requires more creative imagining than sitting in an audience watching actors on a stage presenting lines and actions before you. As a reader you become the play's director; you construct an interpretation based on the playwright's use of language, development of character, arrangement of incidents, description of settings, and directions for staging. Keeping track of the playwright's handling of these elements will help you to organize your response to the play. You may experience suspense, fear, horror, sympathy, or humor, but whatever experience a play evokes, ask yourself why you respond to it as you do. You may discover that your assessment of Hamlet's character is different from someone else's, but whether you find him heroic, indecisive, neurotic, or a complex of competing qualities, you'll be better equipped to articulate your interpretation of him if you pay attention to your responses and ask yourself questions as you read. Consider, for example, how his reactions might be similar to or different from your own. How does his language reveal his character? Does his behavior seem justified? How would you play the role yourself? What actor do you think might best play the Hamlet that you have created in your imagination? Why would he or she (women have also played Hamlet onstage) fill the role best?

These kinds of questions (see Questions for Responsive Reading and Writing, p. 1276) can help you to think and talk about your responses to a play. Happily, such questions needn't — and often can't — be fully answered as you read the play. Frequently you must experience the entire play before you can determine how its elements work together. That's why reading a play can be such a satisfying experience. You wouldn't think of asking a live actor onstage to repeat her lines because you didn't quite comprehend their significance, but you can certainly reread a page in a book. Rereading allows you to replay language, characters, and incidents carefully and thoroughly to your own satisfaction.

Trifles

In the following play, Susan Glaspell skillfully draws on many dramatic elements and creates an intense story that is as effective on the page as it is in the theater. Glaspell wrote *Trifles* in 1916 for the Provincetown Players on Cape Cod, in Massachusetts. Their performance of the work helped her develop a reputation as a writer sensitive to feminist issues. The year after *Trifles* was produced, Glaspell transformed the play into a short story titled "A Jury of Her Peers." (A passage from the story appears on p. 1248 for comparison.)

Glaspell's life in the Midwest provided her with the setting for *Trifles*. Born and raised in Davenport, Iowa, she graduated from Drake University in 1899 and then worked for a short time as a reporter on the *Des Moines News*, until her short stories were accepted in magazines such as *Harper's* and *Ladies' Home Journal*. Glaspell moved to the Northeast when she was in her early thirties to continue writing fiction and drama. She published some twenty plays, novels, and more than forty short stories. *Alison's House*, based on Emily Dickinson's life, earned her a Pulitzer Prize for drama in 1931. *Trifles* and "A Jury of Her Peers" remain, however, Glaspell's best-known works.

Glaspell wrote *Trifles* to complete a bill that was to feature several one-act plays by Eugene O'Neill. In *The Road to the Temple* (1926) she recalls how the play came to her as she sat in the theater looking at a bare stage. First, "the stage became a kitchen. . . . Then the door at the back opened, and people all bundled up came in — two or three men. I wasn't sure which, but sure enough about the two women, who hung back, reluctant to enter that kitchen. When I was a newspaper reporter out in Iowa, I was sent down-state to do a murder trial, and I never forgot going to the kitchen of a woman who had been locked up in town."

Trifles is about a murder committed in a midwestern farmhouse, but the play goes beyond the kinds of questions raised by most whodunit stories. The murder is the occasion instead of the focus. The play's major concerns are the moral, social, and psychological aspects of the assumptions and perceptions of the men and women who search for the murderer's motive. Glaspell is finally more interested in the meaning of Mrs. Wright's life than in the details of Mr. Wright's death.

As you read the play keep track of your responses to the characters and note in the margin the moments when Glaspell reveals how men and women respond differently to the evidence before them. What do those moments suggest about the kinds of assumptions these men and women make about themselves and each other? How do their assumptions compare with your own?

Research Susan Glaspell with LitLinks at
http://www.bedfordstmartins.com/meyer/bedintrolit

Trifles 1916

CHARACTERS

George Henderson, county attorney
Henry Peters, sheriff
Lewis Hale, a neighboring farmer
Mrs. Peters
Mrs. Hale

SCENE: *The kitchen in the now abandoned farmhouse of John Wright, a gloomy kitchen, and left without having been put in order—unwashed pans under the sink, a loaf of bread outside the breadbox, a dish towel on the table—other signs of incompleted work. At the rear the outer door opens and the Sheriff comes in followed by the County Attorney and Hale. The Sheriff and Hale are men in middle life, the County Attorney is a young man; all are much bundled up and go at once to the stove. They are followed by the two women—the Sheriff's wife first; she is a slight wiry woman, a thin nervous face. Mrs. Hale is larger and would ordinarily be called more comfortable looking, but she is disturbed now and looks fearfully about as she enters. The women have come in slowly, and stand close together near the door.*

County Attorney (rubbing his hands): This feels good. Come up to the fire, ladies.
Mrs. Peters (after taking a step forward): I'm not—cold.
Sheriff (unbuttoning his overcoat and stepping away from the stove as if to mark the beginning of official business): Now, Mr. Hale, before we move things about, you explain to Mr. Henderson just what you saw when you came here yesterday morning.
County Attorney: By the way, has anything been moved? Are things just as you left them yesterday?
Sheriff (looking about): It's just about the same. When it dropped below zero last night I thought I'd better send Frank out this morning to make a fire for us—no use getting pneumonia with a big case on, but I told him not to touch anything except the stove—and you know Frank.
County Attorney: Somebody should have been left here yesterday.
Sheriff: Oh—yesterday. When I had to send Frank to Morris Center for that man who went crazy—I want you to know I had my hands full yesterday. I knew you could get back from Omaha by today and as long as I went over everything here myself—
County Attorney: Well, Mr. Hale, tell just what happened when you came here yesterday morning.
Hale: Harry and I had started to town with a load of potatoes. We came along the road from my place and as I got here I said, "I'm going to see if I can't get John Wright to go in with me on a party telephone." I spoke to Wright about it once before and he put me off, saying folks talked too much anyway, and all he asked was peace and quiet—I guess you know about how much he talked himself; but I thought maybe if I went to the house and talked about it before his wife, though I said to Harry that I didn't know as what his wife wanted made much difference to John—
County Attorney: Let's talk about that later, Mr. Hale. I do want to talk about that, but tell now just what happened when you got to the house.

Hale: I didn't hear or see anything; I knocked at the door, and still it was all quiet inside. I knew they must be up, it was past eight o'clock. So I knocked again, and I thought I heard somebody say, "Come in." I wasn't sure, I'm not sure yet, but I opened the door — this door *(indicating the door by which the two women are still standing)* and there in that rocker — *(pointing to it)* sat Mrs. Wright. *(They all look at the rocker.)*

County Attorney: What — was she doing?

Hale: She was rockin' back and forth. She had her apron in her hand and was kind of — pleating it.

County Attorney: And how did she — look?

Hale: Well, she looked queer.

County Attorney: How do you mean — queer?

Hale: Well, as if she didn't know what she was going to do next. And kind of done up.

County Attorney: How did she seem to feel about your coming?

Hale: Why, I don't think she minded — one way or other. She didn't pay much attention. I said, "How do, Mrs. Wright, it's cold, ain't it?" And she said, "Is it?" — and went on kind of pleating at her apron. Well, I was surprised; she didn't ask me to come up to the stove, or to set down, but just sat there, not even looking at me, so I said, "I want to see John." And then she — laughed. I guess you would call it a laugh. I thought of Harry and the team outside, so I said a little sharp: "Can't I see John?" "No," she says, kind o' dull like. "Ain't he home?" says I. "Yes," says she, "he's home." "Then why can't I see him?" I asked her, out of patience. "'Cause he's dead," says she. *"Dead?"* says I. She just nodded her head, not getting a bit excited, but rockin' back and forth. "Why — where is he?" says I, not knowing what to say. She just pointed upstairs — like that *(himself pointing to the room above)*. I started for the stairs, with the idea of going up there. I walked from there to here — then I says, "Why, what did he die of?" "He died of a rope round his neck," says she, and just went on pleatin' at her apron. Well, I went out and called Harry. I thought I might — need help. We went upstairs and there he was lyin' —

County Attorney: I think I'd rather have you go into that upstairs, where you can point it all out. Just go on now with the rest of the story.

Hale: Well, my first thought was to get that rope off. It looked . . . *(stops; his face twitches)* . . . but Harry, he went up to him, and he said, "No, he's dead all right, and we'd better not touch anything." So we went back downstairs. She was still sitting that same way. "Has anybody been notified?" I asked. "No," says she, unconcerned. "Who did this, Mrs. Wright?" said Harry. He said it businesslike — and she stopped pleatin' of her apron. "I don't know," she says. "You don't *know?*" says Harry. "No," says she. "Weren't you sleepin' in the bed with him?" says Harry. "Yes," says she, "but I was on the inside." "Somebody slipped a rope round his neck and strangled him and you didn't wake up?" says Harry. "I didn't wake up," she said after him. We must 'a' looked as if we didn't see how that could be, for after a minute she said, "I sleep sound." Harry was going to ask her more questions but I said maybe we ought to let her tell her story first to the coroner, or the sheriff, so Harry went fast as he could to Rivers' place, where there's a telephone.

County Attorney: And what did Mrs. Wright do when she knew that you had gone for the coroner?

Hale: She moved from the rocker to that chair over there *(pointing to a small chair in the corner)* and just sat there with her hands held together and looking down. I got a feeling that I ought to make some conversation, so I said I had come in to see if John wanted to put in a telephone, and at that she started to laugh, and then she stopped and looked at me — scared. *(The County Attorney, who has had his notebook out, makes a note.)* I dunno, maybe it wasn't scared. I wouldn't like to say it was. Soon Harry got back, and then Dr. Lloyd came and you, Mr. Peters, and so I guess that's all I know that you don't.

County Attorney (looking around): I guess we'll go upstairs first — and then out to the barn and around there. *(To the Sheriff.)* You're convinced that there was nothing important here — nothing that would point to any motive?

Sheriff: Nothing here but kitchen things. *(The County Attorney, after again looking around the kitchen, opens the door of a cupboard closet. He gets up on a chair and looks on a shelf. Pulls his hand away, sticky.)*

County Attorney: Here's a nice mess. *(The women draw nearer.)*

Mrs. Peters (to the other woman): Oh, her fruit; it did freeze. *(To the Lawyer.)* She worried about that when it turned so cold. She said the fire'd go out and her jars would break.

Sheriff (rises): Well, can you beat the woman! Held for murder and worryin' about her preserves.

County Attorney: I guess before we're through she may have something more serious than preserves to worry about.

Hale: Well, women are used to worrying over trifles. *(The two women move a little closer together.)*

County Attorney (with the gallantry of a young politician): And yet, for all their worries, what would we do without the ladies? *(The women do not unbend. He goes to the sink, takes a dipperful of water from the pail, and pouring it into a basin, washes his hands. Starts to wipe them on the roller towel, turns it for a cleaner place.)* Dirty towels! *(Kicks his foot against the pans under the sink.)* Not much of a housekeeper, would you say, ladies?

Mrs. Hale (stiffly): There's a great deal of work to be done on a farm.

County Attorney: To be sure. And yet *(with a little bow to her)* I know there are some Dickson county farmhouses which do not have such roller towels. *(He gives it a pull to expose its full length again.)*

Mrs. Hale: Those towels get dirty awful quick. Men's hands aren't always as clean as they might be.

County Attorney: Ah, loyal to your sex, I see. But you and Mrs. Wright were neighbors. I suppose you were friends, too.

Mrs. Hale (shaking her head): I've not seen much of her of late years. I've not been in this house — it's more than a year.

County Attorney: And why was that? You didn't like her?

Mrs. Hale: I liked her all well enough. Farmers' wives have their hands full, Mr. Henderson. And then —

County Attorney: Yes — ?

Mrs. Hale (looking about): It never seemed a very cheerful place.

County Attorney: No — it's not cheerful. I shouldn't say she had the homemaking instinct.

Mrs. Hale: Well, I don't know as Wright had, either.

County Attorney: You mean that they didn't get on very well?

Mrs. Hale: No, I don't mean anything. But I don't think a place'd be any cheerfuller for John Wright's being in it.

County Attorney: I'd like to talk more of that a little later. I want to get the lay of things upstairs now. *(He goes to the left where three steps lead to a stair door.)*

Sheriff: I suppose anything Mrs. Peters does'll be all right. She was to take in some clothes for her, you know, and a few little things. We left in such a hurry yesterday.

County Attorney: Yes, but I would like to see what you take, Mrs. Peters, and keep an eye out for anything that might be of use to us.

Mrs. Peters: Yes, Mr. Henderson. *(The women listen to the men's steps on the stairs, then look about the kitchen.)*

Mrs. Hale: I'd hate to have men coming into my kitchen, snooping around and criticizing. *(She arranges the pans under sink which the lawyer had shoved out of place.)*

Mrs. Peters: Of course it's no more than their duty.

Mrs. Hale: Duty's all right, but I guess that deputy sheriff that came out to make the fire might have got a little of this on. *(Gives the roller towel a pull.)* Wish I'd thought of that sooner. Seems mean to talk about her for not having things slicked up when she had to come away in such a hurry.

Mrs. Peters (who has gone to a small table in the left rear corner of the room, and lifted one end of a towel that covers a pan): She had bread set. *(Stands still.)*

Mrs. Hale (eyes fixed on a loaf of bread beside the breadbox, which is on a low shelf at the other side of the room. Moves slowly toward it.): She was going to put this in there. *(Picks up loaf, then abruptly drops it. In a manner of returning to familiar things.)* It's a shame about her fruit. I wonder if it's all gone. *(Gets up on the chair and looks.)* I think there's some here that's all right, Mrs. Peters. Yes — here; *(holding it toward the window)* this is cherries, too. *(Looking again.)* I declare I believe that's the only one. *(Gets down, bottle in her hand. Goes to the sink and wipes it off on the outside.)* She'll feel awful bad after all her hard work in the hot weather. I remember the afternoon I put up my cherries last summer. *(She puts the bottle on the big kitchen table, center of the room. With a sigh, is about to sit down in the rocking-chair. Before she is seated realizes what chair it is; with a slow look at it, steps back. The chair which she has touched rocks back and forth.)*

Mrs. Peters: Well, I must get those things from the front room closet. *(She goes to the door at the right, but after looking into the other room, steps back.)* You coming with me, Mrs. Hale? You could help me carry them. *(They go in the other room; reappear, Mrs. Peters carrying a dress and skirt, Mrs. Hale following with a pair of shoes.)* My, it's cold in there. *(She puts the clothes on the big table, and hurries to the stove.)*

Mrs. Hale (examining the skirt): Wright was close. I think maybe that's why she kept so much to herself. She didn't even belong to the Ladies' Aid. I suppose she felt she couldn't do her part, and then you don't enjoy things when you feel shabby. I heard she used to wear pretty clothes and be lively, when she was Minnie Foster, one of the town girls singing in the choir. But that — oh, that was thirty years ago. This all you want to take in?

Mrs. Peters: She said she wanted an apron. Funny thing to want, for there isn't much to get you dirty in jail, goodness knows. But I suppose just to make her feel more natural. She said they was in the top drawer in this cupboard. Yes, here. And then her little shawl that always hung behind the door. (*Opens stair door and looks.*) Yes, here it is. (*Quickly shuts door leading upstairs.*)

Mrs. Hale (abruptly moving toward her): Mrs. Peters?

Mrs. Peters: Yes, Mrs. Hale?

Mrs. Hale: Do you think she did it?

Mrs. Peters (in a frightened voice): Oh, I don't know.

Mrs. Hale: Well, I don't think she did. Asking for an apron and her little shawl. Worrying about her fruit.

Mrs. Peters (starts to speak, glances up, where footsteps are heard in the room above. In a low voice): Mr. Peters says it looks bad for her. Mr. Henderson is awful sarcastic in a speech and he'll make fun of her sayin' she didn't wake up.

Mrs. Hale: Well, I guess John Wright didn't wake when they was slipping that rope under his neck.

Mrs. Peters: No, it's strange. It must have been done awful crafty and still. They say it was such a — funny way to kill a man, rigging it all up like that.

Mrs. Hale: That's just what Mr. Hale said. There was a gun in the house. He says that's what he can't understand.

Mrs. Peters: Mr. Henderson said coming out that what was needed for the case was a motive; something to show anger, or — sudden feeling.

Mrs. Hale (who is standing by the table): Well, I don't see any signs of anger around here. (*She puts her hand on the dish towel which lies on the table, stands looking down at table, one-half of which is clean, the other half messy.*) It's wiped to here. (*Makes a move as if to finish work, then turns and looks at loaf of bread outside the breadbox. Drops towel. In that voice of coming back to familiar things.*) Wonder how they are finding things upstairs. I hope she had it a little more red-up up there. You know, it seems kind of *sneaking*. Locking her up in town and then coming out here and trying to get her own house to turn against her!

Mrs. Peters: But, Mrs. Hale, the law is the law.

Mrs. Hale: I s'pose 'tis. (*Unbuttoning her coat.*) Better loosen up your things, Mrs. Peters. You won't feel them when you go out. (*Mrs. Peters takes off her fur tippet, goes to hang it on hook at back of room, stands looking at the under part of the small corner table.*)

Mrs. Peters: She was piecing a quilt. (*She brings the large sewing basket and they look at the bright pieces.*)

Mrs. Hale: It's a log cabin pattern. Pretty, isn't it? I wonder if she was goin' to quilt it or just knot it? (*Footsteps have been heard coming down the stairs. The Sheriff enters followed by Hale and the County Attorney.*)

Sheriff: They wonder if she was going to quilt it or just knot it! (*The men laugh, the women look abashed.*)

County Attorney (rubbing his hands over the stove): Frank's fire didn't do much up there, did it? Well, let's go out to the barn and get that cleared up. (*The men go outside.*)

Mrs. Hale (resentfully): I don't know as there's anything so strange, our takin' up our time with little things while we're waiting for them to get the evidence. (*She sits down at the big table smoothing out a block with decision.*) I don't see as it's anything to laugh about.

Mrs. Peters (apologetically): Of course they've got awful important things on their minds. *(Pulls up a chair and joins Mrs. Hale at the table.)*

Mrs. Hale (examining another block): Mrs. Peters, look at this one. Here, this is the one she was working on, and look at the sewing! All the rest of it has been so nice and even. And look at this! It's all over the place! Why, it looks as if she didn't know what she was about! *(After she has said this they look at each other, then start to glance back at the door. After an instant Mrs. Hale has pulled at a knot and ripped the sewing.)*

Mrs. Peters: Oh, what are you doing, Mrs. Hale?

Mrs. Hale (mildly): Just pulling out a stitch or two that's not sewed very good. *(Threading a needle.)* Bad sewing always made me fidgety.

Mrs. Peters (nervously): I don't think we ought to touch things.

Mrs. Hale: I'll just finish up this end. *(Suddenly stopping and leaning forward.)* Mrs. Peters?

Mrs. Peters: Yes, Mrs. Hale?

Mrs. Hale: What do you suppose she was so nervous about?

Mrs. Peters: Oh—I don't know. I don't know as she was nervous. I sometimes sew awful queer when I'm just tired. *(Mrs. Hale starts to say something, looks at Mrs. Peters, then goes on sewing.)* Well, I must get these things wrapped up. They may be through sooner than we think. *(Putting apron and other things together.)* I wonder where I can find a piece of paper, and string. *(Rises.)*

Mrs. Hale: In that cupboard, maybe.

Mrs. Peters (looking in cupboard): Why, here's a bird-cage. *(Holds it up.)* Did she have a bird, Mrs. Hale?

Mrs. Hale: Why, I don't know whether she did or not—I've not been here for so long. There was a man around last year selling canaries cheap, but I don't know as she took one; maybe she did. She used to sing real pretty herself.

Mrs. Peters (glancing around): Seems funny to think of a bird here. But she must have had one, or why would she have a cage? I wonder what happened to it?

Mrs. Hale: I s'pose maybe the cat got it.

Mrs. Peters: No, she didn't have a cat. She's got that feeling some people have about cats—being afraid of them. My cat got in her room and she was real upset and asked me to take it out.

Mrs. Hale: My sister Bessie was like that. Queer, ain't it?

Mrs. Peters (examining the cage): Why, look at this door. It's broke. One hinge is pulled apart.

Mrs. Hale (looking too): Looks as if someone must have been rough with it.

Mrs. Peters: Why, yes. *(She brings the cage forward and puts it on the table.)*

Mrs. Hale: I wish if they're going to find any evidence they'd be about it. I don't like this place.

Mrs. Peters: But I'm awful glad you came with me, Mrs. Hale. It would be lonesome for me sitting here alone.

Mrs. Hale: It would, wouldn't it? *(Dropping her sewing.)* But I tell you what I do wish, Mrs. Peters. I wish I had come over sometimes when *she* was here. I—*(looking around the room)*—wish I had.

Mrs. Peters: But of course you were awful busy, Mrs. Hale—your house and your children.

Mrs. Hale: I could've come. I stayed away because it weren't cheerful—and that's why I ought to have come. I—I've never liked this place. Maybe because it's down in a hollow and you don't see the road. I dunno what it is, but it's a lonesome place and always was. I wish I had come over to see Minnie Foster sometimes. I can see now—*(Shakes her head.)*

Mrs. Peters: Well, you mustn't reproach yourself, Mrs. Hale. Somehow we just don't see how it is with other folks until—something turns up.

Mrs. Hale: Not having children makes less work—but it makes a quiet house, and Wright out to work all day, and no company when he did come in. Did you know John Wright, Mrs. Peters?

Mrs. Peters: Not to know him; I've seen him in town. They say he was a good man.

Mrs. Hale: Yes—good; he didn't drink, and kept his word as well as most, I guess, and paid his debts. But he was a hard man, Mrs. Peters. Just to pass the time of day with him—*(Shivers.)* Like a raw wind that gets to the bone. *(Pauses, her eye falling on the cage.)* I should think she would 'a' wanted a bird. But what do you suppose went with it?

Mrs. Peters: I don't know, unless it got sick and died. *(She reaches over and swings the broken door, swings it again, both women watch it.)*

Mrs. Hale: You weren't raised round here, were you? *(Mrs. Peters shakes her head.)* You didn't know—her?

Mrs. Peters: Not till they brought her yesterday.

Mrs. Hale: She—come to think of it, she was kind of like a bird herself—real sweet and pretty, but kind of timid and—fluttery. How—she—did—change. *(Silence: then as if struck by a happy thought and relieved to get back to everyday things.)* Tell you what, Mrs. Peters, why don't you take the quilt in with you? It might take up her mind.

Mrs. Peters: Why, I think that's a real nice idea, Mrs. Hale. There couldn't possibly be any objection to it could there? Now, just what would I take? I wonder if her patches are in here—and her things. *(They look in the sewing basket.)*

Mrs. Hale: Here's some red. I expect this has got sewing things in it. *(Brings out a fancy box.)* What a pretty box. Looks like something somebody would give you. Maybe her scissors are in here. *(Opens box. Suddenly puts her hand to her nose.)* Why—*(Mrs. Peters bends nearer, then turns her face away.)* There's something wrapped up in this piece of silk.

Mrs. Peters: Why, this isn't her scissors.

Mrs. Hale (lifting the silk): Oh, Mrs. Peters—it's—*(Mrs. Peters bends closer.)*

Mrs. Peters: It's the bird.

Mrs. Hale (jumping up): But, Mrs. Peters—look at it! Its neck! Look at its neck! It's all—other side *to.*

Mrs. Peters: Somebody—wrung—its—neck. *(Their eyes meet. A look of growing comprehension, of horror. Steps are heard outside. Mrs. Hale slips box under quilt pieces, and sinks into her chair. Enter Sheriff and County Attorney. Mrs. Peters rises.)*

County Attorney (as one turning from serious things to little pleasantries): Well, ladies, have you decided whether she was going to quilt it or knot it?

Mrs. Peters: We think she was going to—knot it.

County Attorney: Well, that's interesting, I'm sure. *(Seeing the bird-cage.)* Has the bird flown?

Mrs. Hale (putting more quilt pieces over the box): We think the — cat got it.

County Attorney (preoccupied): Is there a cat? *(Mrs. Hale glances in a quick covert way at Mrs. Peters.)*

Mrs. Peters: Well, not *now.* They're superstitious, you know. They leave.

County Attorney (to Sheriff Peters, continuing an interrupted conversation): No sign at all of anyone having come from the outside. Their own rope. Now let's go up again and go over it piece by piece. *(They start upstairs.)* It would have to have been someone who knew just the — *(Mrs. Peters sits down. The two women sit there not looking at one another, but as if peering into something and at the same time holding back. When they talk now it is in the manner of feeling their way over strange ground, as if afraid of what they are saying, but as if they cannot help saying it.)*

Mrs. Hale: She liked the bird. She was going to bury it in that pretty box.

Mrs. Peters (in a whisper): When I was a girl — my kitten — there was a boy took a hatchet, and before my eyes — and before I could get there — *(Covers her face an instant.)* If they hadn't held me back I would have — *(catches herself, looks upstairs where steps are heard, falters weakly)* — hurt him.

Mrs. Hale (with a slow look around her): I wonder how it would seem never to have had any children around. *(Pause.)* No, Wright wouldn't like the bird — a thing that sang. She used to sing. He killed that, too.

Mrs. Peters (moving uneasily): We don't know who killed the bird.

Mrs. Hale: I knew John Wright.

Mrs. Peters: It was an awful thing was done in this house that night, Mrs. Hale. Killing a man while he slept, slipping a rope around his neck that choked the life out of him.

Mrs. Hale: His neck. Choked the life out of him. *(Her hand goes out and rests on the bird-cage.)*

Mrs. Peters (with rising voice): We don't know who killed him. We don't *know.*

Mrs. Hale (her own feeling not interrupted): If there'd been years and years of nothing, then a bird to sing to you, it would be awful — still, after the bird was still.

Mrs. Peters (something within her speaking): I know what stillness is. When we homesteaded in Dakota, and my first baby died — after he was two years old, and me with no other then —

Mrs. Hale (moving): How soon do you suppose they'll be through looking for the evidence?

Mrs. Peters: I know what stillness is. *(Pulling herself back.)* The law has got to punish crime, Mrs. Hale.

Mrs. Hale (not as if answering that): I wish you'd seen Minnie Foster when she wore a white dress with blue ribbons and stood up there in the choir and sang. *(A look around the room.)* Oh, I *wish* I'd come over here once in a while! That was a crime! That was a crime! Who's going to punish that?

Mrs. Peters (looking upstairs): We mustn't — take on.

Mrs. Hale: I might have known she needed help! I know how things can be — for women. I tell you, it's queer, Mrs. Peters. We live close together and we live far apart. We all go through the same things — it's all just a different kind of the same thing. *(Brushes her eyes, noticing the bottle of fruit, reaches out for it.)* If I was you I wouldn't tell her her fruit was gone. Tell her it *ain't.* Tell her it's all right. Take this in to prove it to her. She — she may never know whether it was broke or not.

Mrs. Peters (takes the bottle, looks about for something to wrap it in; takes petticoat from the clothes brought from the other room, very nervously begins winding this around the bottle. In a false voice): My, it's a good thing the men couldn't hear us. Wouldn't they just laugh! Getting all stirred up over a little thing like a — dead canary. As if that could have anything to do with — with — wouldn't they *laugh! (The men are heard coming down stairs.)*

Mrs. Hale (under her breath): Maybe they would — maybe they wouldn't.

County Attorney: No, Peters, it's all perfectly clear except a reason for doing it. But you know juries when it comes to women. If there was some definite thing. Something to show — something to make a story about — a thing that would connect up with this strange way of doing it — *(The women's eyes meet for an instant. Enter Hale from outer door.)*

Hale: Well, I've got the team around. Pretty cold out there.

County Attorney: I'm going to stay here a while by myself. *(To the Sheriff.)* You can send Frank out for me, can't you? I want to go over everything. I'm not satisfied that we can't do better.

Sheriff: Do you want to see what Mrs. Peters is going to take in? *(The Lawyer goes to the table, picks up the apron, laughs.)*

County Attorney: Oh, I guess they're not very dangerous things the ladies have picked out. *(Moves a few things about, disturbing the quilt pieces which cover the box. Steps back.)* No, Mrs. Peters doesn't need supervising. For that matter a sheriff's wife is married to the law. Ever think of it that way, Mrs. Peters?

Mrs. Peters: Not — just that way.

Sheriff (chuckling): Married to the law. *(Moves toward the other room.)* I just want you to come in here a minute, George. We ought to take a look at these windows.

County Attorney (scoffingly): Oh, windows!

Sheriff: We'll be right out, Mr. Hale. *(Hale goes outside. The Sheriff follows the County Attorney into the other room. Then Mrs. Hale rises, hands tight together, looking intensely at Mrs. Peters, whose eyes make a slow turn, finally meeting Mrs. Hale's. A moment Mrs. Hale holds her, then her own eyes point the way to where the box is concealed. Suddenly Mrs. Peters throws back quilt pieces and tries to put the box in the bag she is wearing. It is too big. She opens box, starts to take bird out, cannot touch it, goes to pieces, stands there helpless. Sound of a knob turning in the other room. Mrs. Hale snatches the box and puts it in the pocket of her big coat. Enter County Attorney and Sheriff.)*

County Attorney (facetiously): Well, Henry, at least we found out that she was not going to quilt it. She was going to — what is it you call it, ladies?

Mrs. Hale (her hand against her pocket): We call it — knot it, Mr. Henderson.

Curtain.

CONSIDERATIONS FOR CRITICAL THINKING AND WRITING

1. FIRST RESPONSE. Describe the setting of this play. What kind of atmosphere is established by the details in the opening scene? Does the atmosphere change through the course of the play?

2. Where are Mrs. Hale and Mrs. Peters while Mr. Hale explains to the county attorney how the murder was discovered? How does their location suggest the relationship between the men and the women in the play?

3. What kind of person was Minnie Foster before she married? How do you think her marriage affected her?

4. Characterize John Wright. Why did his wife kill him?

5. Why do the men fail to see the clues that Mrs. Hale and Mrs. Peters discover?

6. What is the significance of the birdcage and the dead bird? Why do Mrs. Hale and Mrs. Peters respond so strongly to them? How do you respond?

7. Why don't Mrs. Hale and Mrs. Peters reveal the evidence they have uncovered? What would you have done?

8. How do the men's conversations and actions reveal their attitudes toward women?

9. Why do you think Glaspell allows us only to hear about Mr. and Mrs. Wright? What is the effect of their never appearing on stage?

10. Does your impression of Mrs. Wright change during the course of the play? If so, what changes it?

11. What is the significance of the play's last line, spoken by Mrs. Hale: "We call it — knot it, Mr. Henderson"? Explain what you think the tone of Mrs. Hale's voice is when she says this line. What is she feeling? What are you feeling?

12. Explain the significance of the play's title. Do you think *Trifles* or "A Jury of Her Peers," Glaspell's title for the short story version of the play, is more appropriate? Can you think of other titles that capture the play's central concerns?

13. If possible, find a copy of "A Jury of Her Peers" in the library (reprinted in *The Best Short Stories of 1917*, ed. E. J. O'Brien [Boston: Small, Maynard, 1918], pp. 256–282), and write an essay that explores the differences between the play and the short story. (An alternative is to work with the excerpt on p. 1248.)

14. CRITICAL STRATEGIES. Read the section on formalist criticism (pp. 2095–97) in Chapter 52, "Critical Strategies for Reading." Several times the characters say things that they don't mean, and this creates a discrepancy between what appears to be and what is actually true. Point to instances of irony in the play and explain how they contribute to its effects and meanings. (For discussions of irony elsewhere in this book, see the Index of Terms.)

Connections to Other Selections

1. Compare and contrast how Glaspell provides background information in *Trifles* with how Sophocles does so in *Oedipus the King* (p. 1289).

2. Write an essay comparing the views of marriage in *Trifles* and in Kate Chopin's short story "The Story of an Hour" (p. 12). What similarities do you find in the themes of these two works? Are there any significant differences between the works?

3. In an essay compare Mrs. Wright's motivation for committing murder with that of Matt Fowler, the central character from Andre Dubus's short story "Killings" (p. 84). To what extent do you think they are responsible for and guilty of these crimes?

PERSPECTIVE

SUSAN GLASPELL (1882–1948)

From the Short Story Version of Trifles   1917

When Martha Hale opened the storm-door and got a cut of the north wind, she ran back for her big woolen scarf. As she hurriedly wound that round her head her eye made a scandalized sweep of her kitchen. It was no ordinary thing that called her away — it was probably farther from ordinary than anything that had ever happened in Dickson County. But what her eye took in was that her kitchen was in no shape for leaving: her bread all ready for mixing, half the flour sifted and half unsifted.

She hated to see things half done; but she had been at that when the team from town stopped to get Mr. Hale, and then the sheriff came running in to say his wife wished Mrs. Hale would come too — adding, with a grin, that he guessed she was getting scarey and wanted another woman along. So she had dropped everything right where it was.

"Martha!" now came her husband's impatient voice. "Don't keep folks waiting out here in the cold."

She again opened the storm-door, and this time joined the three men and the one woman waiting for her in the big two-seated buggy.

After she had the robes tucked around her she took another look at the woman who sat beside her on the back seat. She had met Mrs. Peters the year before at the county fair, and the thing she remembered about her was that she didn't seem like a sheriff's wife. She was small and thin and didn't have a strong voice. Mrs. Gorman, sheriff's wife before Gorman went out and Peters came in, had a voice that somehow seemed to be backing up the law with every word. But if Mrs. Peters didn't look like a sheriff's wife, Peters made it up in looking like a sheriff. He was to a dot the kind of man who could get himself elected sheriff — a heavy man with a big voice, who was particularly genial with the law-abiding, as if to make it plain that he knew the difference between criminals and noncriminals. And right there it came into Mrs. Hale's mind, with a stab, that this man who was so pleasant and lively with all of them was going to the Wrights' now as a sheriff.

"The country's not very pleasant this time of year," Mrs. Peters at last ventured, as if she felt they ought to be talking as well as the men.

Mrs. Hale scarcely finished her reply, for they had gone up a little hill and could see the Wright place now, and seeing it did not make her feel like talking. It looked very lonesome this cold March morning. It had always been a lonesome-looking place. It was down in a hollow, and the poplar trees around it were lonesome-looking trees. The men were looking at it and talking about what had happened. The county attorney was bending to one side of the buggy, and kept looking steadily at the place as they drew up to it.

"I'm glad you came with me," Mrs. Peters said nervously, as the two women were about to follow the men in through the kitchen door.

Even after she had her foot on the door-step, her hand on the knob, Martha Hale had a moment of feeling she could not cross that threshold. And the reason it seemed she couldn't cross it now was simply because she hadn't crossed it before. Time and time again it had been in her mind, "I ought to go over and see Minnie Foster"—she still thought of her as Minnie Foster, though for twenty years she had been Mrs. Wright. And then there was always something to do and Minnie Foster would go from her mind. But *now* she could come.

The men went over to the stove. The women stood close together by the door. Young Henderson, the county attorney, turned around and said, "Come up to the fire, ladies."

Mrs. Peters took a step forward, then stopped. "I'm not—cold," she said.

And so the two women stood by the door, at first not even so much as looking around the kitchen.

The men talked for a minute about what a good thing it was the sheriff had sent his deputy out that morning to make a fire for them, and then Sheriff Peters stepped back from the stove, unbuttoned his outer coat, and leaned his hands on the kitchen table in a way that seemed to mark the beginning of official business. "Now, Mr. Hale," he said in a sort of semiofficial voice, "before we move things about, you tell Mr. Henderson just what it was you saw when you came here yesterday morning."

The county attorney was looking around the kitchen.

"By the way," he said, "has anything been moved?" He turned to the sheriff. "Are things just as you left them yesterday?"

Peters looked from cupboard to sink; from that to a small worn rocker a little to one side of the kitchen table.

"It's just the same."

"Somebody should have been left here yesterday," said the county attorney.

"Oh—yesterday," returned the sheriff, with a little gesture as of yesterday having been more than he could bear to think of. "When I had to send Frank to Morris Center for that man who went crazy—let me tell you, I had my hands full *yesterday*. I knew you could get back from Omaha by to-day, George, and as long as I went over everything here myself—"

"Well, Mr. Hale," said the county attorney, in a way of letting what was past and gone go, "tell just what happened when you came here yesterday morning."

Mrs. Hale, still leaning against the door, had that sinking feeling of the mother whose child is about to speak a piece. Lewis often wandered along and got things mixed up in a story. She hoped he would tell this straight and plain, and not say unnecessary things that would just make things harder for Minnie Foster. He didn't begin at once, and she noticed that he looked queer—as if standing in that kitchen and having to tell what he had seen there yesterday morning made him almost sick.

"Yes, Mr. Hale?" the county attorney reminded.

"Harry and I had started to town with a load of potatoes," Mrs. Hale's husband began.

Harry was Mrs. Hale's oldest boy. He wasn't with them now, for the very good reason that those potatoes never got to town yesterday and he was taking them this morning, so he hadn't been home when the sheriff stopped to say he wanted Mr. Hale to come over to the Wright place and tell the county attorney his story there, where he could point it all out. With all Mrs. Hale's other emotions came the fear that maybe Harry wasn't dressed warm enough—they hadn't any of them realized how that north wind did bite.

"We come along this road," Hale was going on, with a motion of his hand to the road over which they had just come, "and as we got in sight of the house I says to Harry, 'I'm goin' to see if I can't get John Wright to take a telephone.' You see," he explained to Henderson, "unless I can get somebody to go in with me they won't come out this branch road except for a price *I* can't pay. I'd spoke to Wright about it once before; but he put me off, saying folks talked too much anyway, and all he asked was peace and quiet — guess you know about how much he talked himself. But I thought maybe if I went to the house and talked about it before his wife, and said all the women-folks liked the telephones, and that in this lonesome stretch of road it would be a good thing — well, I said to Harry that that was what I was going to say — though I said at the same time that I didn't know as what his wife wanted made much difference to John —"

Now, there he was! — saying things he didn't need to say. Mrs. Hale tried to catch her husband's eye, but fortunately the county attorney interrupted with:

"Let's talk about that a little later, Mr. Hale. I do want to talk about that, but I'm anxious now to get along to just what happened when you got here."

From "A Jury of Her Peers"

CONSIDERATIONS FOR CRITICAL THINKING AND WRITING

1. In this opening scene from the story, how is the setting established differently from the way it is in the play (p. 1238)?

2. What kind of information is provided in the opening paragraphs of the story that is missing from the play's initial scene? What is emphasized early in the story but not in the play?

3. Which version brings us into more intimate contact with the characters? How is that achieved?

4. Does the short story's title, "A Jury of Her Peers," suggest any shift in emphasis from the play's title, *Trifles*?

5. Explain why you prefer one version over the other.

ELEMENTS OF DRAMA

Trifles is a **one-act play;** in other words, the entire play takes place in a single location and unfolds as one continuous action. As in a short story, the characters in a one-act play are presented economically, and the action is sharply focused. In contrast, full-length plays can include many characters as well as different settings in place and time. The main divisions of a full-length play are typically **acts;** their ends are indicated by lowering a curtain or turning up the houselights. Playwrights frequently employ acts to accommodate changes in time, setting, characters on stage, or mood. In many full-length plays, such as Shakespeare's *Hamlet,* acts are further divided into **scenes;** according to tradition a scene changes when the location of the action changes or when a new character enters. Acts and scenes are **conventions** that are understood and accepted by audiences because they have come, through usage and time, to be recognized as familiar techniques. The major convention of a one-act play is that it typically consists of only a single scene; nevertheless, one-act plays contain many of the elements of drama that characterize their full-length counterparts.

One-act plays create their effects through compression. They especially lend themselves to modestly budgeted productions with limited stage facilities, such as those put on by little theater groups. However, the potential of a one-act play to move audiences and readers is not related to its length. As *Trifles* shows, one-acts represent a powerful form of dramatic literature.

The single location that comprises the **setting** for *Trifles* is described at the very beginning of the play; it establishes an atmosphere that will later influence our judgment of Mrs. Wright. The kitchen, "gloomy" and with walls "covered with a faded wall paper," is disordered, bare, and sparsely equipped with a stove, sink, and rocker—each of them "old"—an unpainted table, some chairs, three doors, and an uncurtained window. The only color mentioned is, appropriately, black. These details are just enough to allow us to imagine the stark, uninviting place where Mrs. Wright spent most of her time. Moreover, "signs of incompleted work," coupled with the presence of the sheriff and county attorney, create an immediate tension by suggesting that something is terribly wrong. Before a single word is spoken, **suspense** is created as the characters enter. This suspenseful situation causes an anxious uncertainty about what will happen next.

The setting is further developed through the use of **exposition,** a device that provides the necessary background information about the characters and their circumstances. For example, we immediately learn through **dialogue**—the verbal exchanges between characters—that Mr. Henderson, the county attorney, is just back from Omaha. This establishes the setting as somewhere in the Midwest, where winters can be brutally cold and barren. We also find out that John Wright has been murdered and that his wife has been arrested for the crime.

Even more important, Glaspell deftly characterizes the Wrights through exposition alone. Mr. Hale's conversation with Mr. Henderson explains how Mr. Wright's body was discovered, but it also reveals that Wright was a noncommunicative man, who refused to share a "party telephone" and who did not consider "what his wife wanted." Later Mrs. Hale adds to this characterization when she tells Mrs. Peters that though Mr. Wright was an honest, good man who paid his bills and did not drink, he was a "hard man" and "Like a raw wind that gets to the bone." Mr. Hale's description of Mrs. Wright sitting in the kitchen dazed and disoriented gives us a picture of a shattered, exhausted woman. But it is Mrs. Hale who again offers further insights when she describes how Minnie Foster, a sweet, pretty, timid young woman who sang in the choir, was changed by her marriage to Mr. Wright and by her childless, isolated life on the farm.

This information about Mr. and Mrs. Wright is worked into the dialogue throughout the play in order to suggest the nature of the **conflict** or struggle between them, a motive, and, ultimately, a justification for the murder. In the hands of a skillful playwright, exposition is not merely a mechanical device; it can provide important information while simultaneously developing characterizations and moving the action forward.

The action is shaped by the *plot,* the author's arrangement of incidents in the play that gives the story a particular focus and emphasis. Plot involves more than simply what happens; it involves how and why things happen. Glaspell begins with a discussion of the murder. Why? She could have begun with the murder itself: the distraught Mrs. Wright looping the rope around her husband's neck. The moment would be dramatic and horribly vivid. We neither see the body nor hear very much about it. When Mr. Hale describes finding Mr. Wright's body, Glaspell has the county attorney cut him off by saying, "I think I'd rather have you go into that upstairs, where you can point it all out. Just go on now with the rest of the story." It is precisely the "rest of the story" that interests Glaspell. Her arrangement of incidents prevents us from sympathizing with Mr. Wright. We are, finally, invited to see Mrs. Wright instead of her husband as the victim.

Mr. Henderson's efforts to discover a motive for the murder appear initially to be the play's focus, but the real conflicts are explored in what seems to be a *subplot,* a secondary action that reinforces or contrasts with the main plot. The discussions between Mrs. Hale and Mrs. Peters and the tensions between the men and the women turn out to be the main plot because they address the issues that Glaspell chooses to explore. Those issues are not about murder but about marriage and how men and women relate to each other.

The *protagonist* of *Trifles,* the central character with whom we tend to identify, is Mrs. Hale. The *antagonist,* the character who is in some kind of opposition to the central character, is the county attorney, Mr. Henderson. These two characters embody the major conflicts presented in the play because each speaks for a different set of characters who represent disparate values. Mrs. Hale and Mr. Henderson are developed less individually than as representative types.

Mrs. Hale articulates a sensitivity to Mrs. Wright's miserable life as well as an awareness of how women are repressed in general by men; she also helps Mrs. Peters to arrive at a similar understanding. When Mrs. Hale defends Mrs. Wright's soiled towels from Mr. Henderson's criticism, Glaspell has her say more than the county attorney is capable of hearing. The *stage directions,* the playwright's instructions about how the actors are to move and behave, indicate that Mrs. Hale responds "stiffly" to Mr. Henderson's disparagements: "Men's hands aren't always as clean as they might be." Mrs. Hale eventually comes to see that the men are, in a sense, complicit because it was insensitivity like theirs that drove Mrs. Wright to murder.

Mr. Henderson, on the other hand, represents the law in a patriarchal, conventional society that blithely places a minimal value on the concerns of women. In his attempt to gather evidence against Mrs. Wright, he implicitly defends men's severe dominance over women. He also patronizes Mrs. Hale and Mrs. Peters. Like Sheriff Peters and Mr. Hale, he regards the women's world as nothing more than "kitchen things" and "trifles." Glaspell, however, patterns the plot so that the women see more about Mrs. Wright's motives than the men do and shows that the women have a deeper understanding of justice.

Many plays are plotted in what has come to be called a *pyramidal pattern,* because the plot is divided into three essential parts. Such plays begin with a *rising action,* in which complication creates conflict for the protagonist. The resulting tension builds to the second major division, known as the *climax,* when the action reaches a final *crisis,* a turning point that has a powerful effect on the protagonist. The third part consists of *falling action;* here the tensions are diminished in the *resolution* of the plot's conflicts and complications (the resolution is also referred to as the *conclusion* or *dénouement,* a French word meaning "unknotting"). These divisions may occur at different times. There are many variations to this pattern. The terms are helpful for identifying various moments and movements within a given plot, but they are less useful if seen as a means of reducing dramatic art to a formula.

Because *Trifles* is a one-act play, this pyramidal pattern is less elaborately worked out than it might be in a full-length play, but the basic elements of the pattern can still be discerned. The complication consists mostly of Mrs. Hale's refusal to assign moral or legal guilt to Mrs. Wright's murder of her husband. Mrs. Hale is able to discover the motive in the domestic details that are beneath the men's consideration. The men fail to see the significance of the fruit jars, messy kitchen, and badly sewn quilt.

At first Mrs. Peters seems to voice the attitudes associated with the men. Unlike Mrs. Hale, who is "more comfortable looking," Mrs. Peters is "a slight wiry woman" with "a thin nervous face" who sounds like her husband, the sheriff, when she insists, "the law is the law." She also defends the men's patronizing attitudes, because "they've got awful important things on their minds." But Mrs. Peters is a *foil*—a character whose behavior and values contrast with the protagonist's—only up to a point. When the most telling clue is discovered, Mrs. Peters suddenly understands, along with Mrs. Hale, the motive for the killing. Mrs. Wright's caged life was no longer tolerable to her after her husband had killed the bird (which was the one bright spot in her life and which represents her early life as the young Minnie Foster). This revelation brings about the climax, when the two women must decide whether to tell the men what they have discovered. Both women empathize with Mrs. Wright as they confront this crisis, and their sense of common experience leads them to withhold the evidence.

This resolution ends the play's immediate conflicts and complications. Presumably, without a motive the county attorney will have difficulty prosecuting Mrs. Wright—at least to the fullest extent of the law. However, the larger issues related to the *theme,* the central idea or meaning of the play, are left unresolved. The men have both missed the clues and failed to perceive the suffering that acquits Mrs. Wright in the minds of the two women. The play ends with Mrs. Hale's ironic answer to Mr. Henderson's question about quilting. When she says "knot it," she gives him part of the evidence he needs to connect Mrs. Wright's quilting with the knot used to strangle her husband. Mrs. Hale knows — and we know — that Mr. Henderson will miss the clue she offers because he is blinded by his own self-importance and assumptions.

Though brief, *Trifles* is a masterful representation of dramatic elements working together to keep both audiences and readers absorbed in its characters and situations.

Sure Thing

Sure Thing is a one-act play that's even briefer than *Trifles* but that manages to include a variety of characters and a wide range of emotions despite the fact that all the action takes place between two characters sitting in a city café. How, you might ask, can there be a "variety of characters" in a two-character play? The answer is found in the play's premise, which experiments with the intriguing question of what life would be like if we could instantly replay moments in our lives that do not go our way. Imagine how interesting an encounter with someone might be if we could immediately revise what we said until we got the response we desired and thus script our own lives. David Ives plays with this fantasy in *Sure Thing* with insight and wicked wit.

Born in Chicago and educated at Northwestern University and the Yale Drama School, David Ives writes for television, film, and opera and has created a number of one-act plays for the annual comedy festival of Manhattan Punch Line, where *Sure Thing* was first produced in 1988. As you read, notice how many elements of drama Ives works into the play, with comic effect.

Web   *Research David Ives with LitLinks at*
http://www.bedfordstmartins.com/meyer/bedintrolit

DAVID IVES (B. 1950)

Sure Thing   *1988*

CHARACTERS

Bill and *Betty,* both in their late twenties

SETTING: *A café table, with a couple of chairs*
Betty, reading at the table. An empty chair opposite her. Bill enters.

Bill: Excuse me. Is this chair taken?

Betty: Excuse me?

Bill: Is this taken?

Betty: Yes it is.

Bill: Oh. Sorry.

Betty: Sure thing. *(A bell rings softly.)*

Bill: Excuse me. Is this chair taken?

Betty: Excuse me?

Bill: Is this taken?

Betty: No, but I'm expecting somebody in a minute.

Bill: Oh. Thanks anyway.

Betty: Sure thing. *(A bell rings softly.)*

Bill: Excuse me. Is this chair taken?

Betty: No, but I'm expecting somebody very shortly.

Bill: Would you mind if I sit here till he or she or it comes?

Betty (glances at her watch): They seem to be pretty late. . . .

Bill: You never know who you might be turning down.

Betty: Sorry. Nice try, though.

Bill: Sure thing. *(Bell.)* Is this seat taken?

Betty: No it's not.

Bill: Would you mind if I sit here?

Betty: Yes I would.

Bill: Oh. *(Bell.)* Is this chair taken?

Betty: No it's not.

Bill: Would you mind if I sit here?

Betty: No. Go ahead.

Bill: Thanks. *(He sits. She continues reading.)* Everyplace else seems to be taken.

Betty: Mm-hm.

Bill: Great place.

Betty: Mm-hm.

Bill: What's the book?

Betty: I just wanted to read in quiet, if you don't mind.

Bill: No. Sure thing. *(Bell.)*

Bill: Everyplace else seems to be taken.

Betty: Mm-hm.

Bill: Great place for reading.

Betty: Yes, I like it.

Bill: What's the book?

Betty: *The Sound and the Fury.*

Bill: Oh. Hemingway. *(Bell.)* What's the book?

Betty: *The Sound and the Fury.*

Bill: Oh. Faulkner.

Betty: Have you read it?

Bill: Not . . . actually. I've sure read *about* . . . it, though. It's supposed to be great.

Betty: It is great.

Bill: I hear it's great. *(Small pause.)* Waiter? *(Bell.)* What's the book?

Betty: *The Sound and the Fury.*

Bill: Oh. Faulkner.

Betty: Have you read it?

Bill: I'm a Mets fan, myself. *(Bell.)*

Betty: Have you read it?

Bill: Yeah, I read it in college.

Betty: Where was college?

Bill: I went to Oral Roberts University. *(Bell.)*

Betty: Where was college?

Bill: I was lying. I never really went to college. I just like to party. *(Bell.)*

Betty: Where was college?

Bill: Harvard.

Betty: Do you like Faulkner?

Bill: I love Faulkner. I spent a whole winter reading him once.

Betty: I've just started.

Bill: I was so excited after ten pages that I went out and bought everything else
 he wrote. One of the greatest reading experiences of my life. I mean, all
 that incredible psychological understanding. Page after page of gorgeous
 prose. His profound grasp of the mystery of time and human existence.
 The smells of the earth . . . What do you think?

Betty: I think it's pretty boring. *(Bell.)*

Bill: What's the book?

Betty: The Sound and the Fury.

Bill: Oh! Faulkner!

Betty: Do you like Faulkner?

Bill: I love Faulkner.

Betty: He's incredible.

Bill: I spent a whole winter reading him once.

Betty: I was so excited after ten pages that I went out and bought everything
 else he wrote.

Bill: All that incredible psychological understanding.

Betty: And the prose is so gorgeous.

Bill: And the way he's grasped the mystery of time —

Betty: — and human existence. I can't believe I've waited this long to read him.

Bill: You never know. You might not have liked him before.

Betty: That's true.

Bill: You might not have been ready for him. You have to hit these things at the
 right moment or it's no good.

Betty: That's happening to me.

Bill: It's all in the timing. *(Small pause.)* My name's Bill, by the way.

Betty: I'm Betty.

Bill: Hi.

Betty: Hi. *(Small pause.)*

Bill: Yes I thought reading Faulkner was . . . a great experience.

Betty: Yes. *(Small pause.)*

Bill: The Sound and the Fury . . . *(Another small pause.)*

Betty: Well. Onwards and upwards. *(She goes back to her book.)*

Bill: Waiter — ? *(Bell.)* You have to hit these things at the right moment or it's
 no good.

Betty: That's happened to me.

Bill: It's all in the timing. My name's Bill, by the way.

Betty: I'm Betty.

Bill: Hi.

Betty: Hi.

Bill: Do you come in here a lot?

Betty: Actually I'm just in town for two days from Pakistan.

Bill: Oh. Pakistan. *(Bell.)* My name's Bill, by the way.

Betty: I'm Betty.

Bill: Hi.

Betty: Hi.

Bill: Do you come here a lot?

Betty: Every once in a while. Do you?

Bill: Not much anymore. Not as much as I used to. Before my nervous break-down. *(Bell.)* Do you come in here a lot?

Betty: Why are you asking?

Bill: Just interested.

Betty: Are you really interested, or do you just want to pick me up?

Bill: No, I'm really interested.

Betty: Why would you be interested in whether I come in here a lot?

Bill: Just . . . getting acquainted.

Betty: Maybe you're only interested for the sake of making small talk long enough to ask me back to your place to listen to some music, or because you've just rented some great tape for your VCR, or because you've got some terrific unknown Django Reinhardt record, only all you'll really want to do is fuck—which you won't do very well—after which you'll go into the bathroom and pee very loudly, then pad into the kitchen and get yourself a beer from the refrigerator without asking me whether I'd like anything, and then you'll proceed to lie back down beside me and confess that you've got a girlfriend named Stephanie who's away at medical school in Belgium for a year, and that you've been involved with her—*off and on*—in what you'll call a very "intricate" relationship, for about *seven YEARS*. None of which *interests* me, mister!

Bill: Okay. *(Bell.)* Do you come in here a lot?

Betty: Every other day, I think.

Bill: I come in here quite a lot and I don't remember seeing you.

Betty: I guess we must be on different schedules.

Bill: Missed connections.

Betty: Yes. Different time zones.

Bill: Amazing how you can live right next door to somebody in this town and never even know it.

Betty: I know.

Bill: City life.

Betty: It's crazy.

Bill: We probably pass each other in the street every day. Right in front of this place, probably.

Betty: Yep.

Bill (looks around): Well, the waiters here sure seem to be in some different time zone. I can't seem to locate one anywhere . . . Waiter! *(He looks back.)* So what do you— *(He sees that she's gone back to her book.)*

Betty: I beg pardon?

Bill: Nothing. Sorry. *(Bell.)*

Betty: I guess we must be on different schedules.

Bill: Missed connections.

Betty: Yes. Different time zones.

Bill: Amazing how you can live right next door to somebody in this town and never even know it.

Betty: I know.

Bill: City life.

Betty: It's crazy.

Bill: You weren't waiting for somebody when I came in, were you?

Betty: Actually, I was.

Bill: Oh. Boyfriend?

Betty: Sort of.

Bill: What's a sort-of boyfriend?

Betty: My husband.

Bill: Ah-ha. *(Bell.)* You weren't waiting for somebody when I came in, were you?

Betty: Actually I was.

Bill: Oh. Boyfriend?

Betty: Sort of.

Bill: What's a sort-of boyfriend?

Betty: We were meeting here to break up.

Bill: Mm-hm . . . *(Bell.)* What's a sort-of boyfriend?

Betty: My lover. Here she comes right now! *(Bell.)*

Bill: You weren't waiting for somebody when I came in, were you?

Betty: No, just reading.

Bill: Sort of a sad occupation for a Friday night, isn't it? Reading here, all by yourself?

Betty: Do you think so?

Bill: Well sure. I mean, what's a good-looking woman like you doing out alone on a Friday night?

Betty: Trying to keep away from lines like that.

Bill: No, listen — *(Bell.)* You weren't waiting for somebody when I came in, were you?

Betty: No, just reading.

Bill: Sort of a sad occupation for a Friday night, isn't it? Reading here all by yourself?

Betty: I guess it is, in a way.

Bill: What's a good-looking woman like you doing out alone on a Friday night anyway? No offense, but . . .

Betty: I'm out alone on a Friday night for the first time in a very long time.

Bill: Oh.

Betty: You see, I just recently ended a relationship.

Bill: Oh.

Betty: Of rather long standing.

Bill: I'm sorry. *(Small pause.)* Well listen, since reading by yourself *is* such a sad occupation for a Friday night, would you like to go elsewhere?

Betty: No . . .

Bill: Do something else?

Betty: No thanks.

Bill: I was headed out to the movies in a while anyway.

Betty: I don't think so.

Bill: Big chance to let Faulkner catch his breath. All those long sentences get him pretty tired.

Betty: Thanks anyway.

Bill: Okay.

Betty: I appreciate the invitation.

Bill: Sure thing. *(Bell.)* You weren't waiting for somebody when I came in, were you?

Betty: No, just reading.

Bill: Sort of a sad occupation for a Friday night, isn't it? Reading here all by yourself?

Betty: I guess I was trying to think of it as existentially romantic. You know— cappuccino, great literature, rainy night . . .

Bill: That only works in Paris. We *could* hop the late plane to Paris. Get on a Concorde. Find a café . . .

Betty: I'm a little short on plane fare tonight.

Bill: Darn it, so am I.

Betty: To tell you the truth, I was headed to the movies after I finished this section. Would you like to come along? Since you can't locate a waiter?

Bill: That's a very nice offer, but . . .

Betty: Uh-huh. Girlfriend?

Bill: Two, actually. One of them's pregnant, and Stephanie— *(Bell.)*

Betty: Girlfriend?

Bill: No, I don't have a girlfriend. Not if you mean the castrating bitch I dumped last night. *(Bell.)*

Betty: Girlfriend?

Bill: Sort of. Sort of.

Betty: What's a sort-of girlfriend?

Bill: My mother. *(Bell.)* I just ended a relationship, actually.

Betty: Oh.

Bill: Of rather long standing.

Betty: I'm sorry to hear it.

Bill: This is my first night out alone in a long time. I feel a little bit at sea, to tell you the truth.

Betty: So you didn't stop to talk because you're a Moonie, or you have some weird political affiliation—?

Bill: Nope. Straight-down-the-ticket Republican. *(Bell.)* Straight-down-the-ticket Democrat. *(Bell.)* Can I tell you something about politics? *(Bell.)* I like to think of myself as a citizen of the universe. *(Bell.)* I'm unaffiliated.

Betty: That's a relief. So am I.

Bill: I vote my beliefs.

Betty: Labels are not important.

Bill: Labels are not important, exactly. Like me, for example. I mean, what does it matter if I had a two-point at— *(bell)*—three-point at *(bell)*—four-point at college, or if I did come from Pittsburgh— *(bell)*—Cleveland— *(bell)*— Westchester County?

Betty: Sure.

Bill: I believe that a man is what he is. *(Bell.)* A person is what he is. *(Bell.)* A person is . . . what they are.

Betty: I think so too.

Bill: So what if I admire Trotsky? *(Bell.)* So what if I once had a total-body liposuction? *(Bell.)* So what if I don't have a penis? *(Bell.)* So what if I once spent a year in the Peace Corps? I was acting on my convictions.

Betty: Sure.

Bill: You can't just hang a sign on a person.

Betty: Absolutely. I'll bet you're a Scorpio. *(Many bells ring.)* Listen, I was headed to the movies after I finished this section. Would you like to come along?

Bill: That sounds like fun. What's playing?

Betty: A couple of the really early Woody Allen movies.

Bill: Oh.

Betty: Don't you like Woody Allen?

Bill: Sure. I like Woody Allen.

Betty: But you're not crazy about Woody Allen.

Bill: Those early ones kind of get on my nerves.

Betty: Uh-huh. *(Bell.)*

Bill: Y'know I was   — *(simultaneously)* —   *Betty:* I was thinking
headed to the —   about —

Bill: I'm sorry.

Betty: No, go ahead.

Bill: I was going to say that I was headed to the movies in a little while, and . . .

Betty: So was I.

Bill: The Woody Allen festival?

Betty: Just up the street.

Bill: Do you like the early ones?

Betty: I think anybody who doesn't ought to be run off the planet.

Bill: How many times have you seen *Bananas?*

Betty: Eight times.

Bill: Twelve. So are you still interested? *(Long pause.)*

Betty: Do you like Entenmann's crumb cake . . . ?

Bill: Last night I went out at two in the morning to get one. *(Small pause.)* Did you have an Etch-a-Sketch as a child?

Betty: Yes! And do you like Brussels sprouts? *(Small pause.)*

Bill: I think they're gross.

Betty: They *are* gross!

Bill: Do you still believe in marriage in spite of current sentiments against it?

Betty: Yes.

Bill: And children?

Betty: Three of them.

Bill: Two girls and a boy.

Betty: Harvard, Vassar, and Brown.

Bill: And will you love me?

Betty: Yes.

Bill: And cherish me forever?

Betty: Yes.

Bill: Do you still want to go to the movies?

Betty: Sure thing.

Bill and Betty (together): Waiter!

(Blackout.)

CONSIDERATIONS FOR CRITICAL THINKING AND WRITING

1. FIRST RESPONSE. Very little information is provided about the play's setting. How do you envision the café? What does the setting suggest to you about the characters?

2. What is the purpose of the ringing bell?

3. Which character would you describe as the antagonist? What do you think is the play's central conflict?

4. How is the formulaic plot of "boy meets girl" complicated and made suspenseful in this play? Where would you say that the climax occurs? What is the plot's resolution?

5. How would you describe the play's theme?

6. Discuss the significance of the title. How is it related to your understanding of the play's theme?

7. At one point Bill says, "You have to hit these things at the right moment or it's no good" (p. 1256). How might this line be used to describe Ives's strategy for writing this play?

8. Try your hand at writing another scene between Betty and Bill that takes place after they come out of the movies. Write a comic scene the way you think Ives might create it.

CONNECTIONS TO OTHER SELECTIONS

1. Choose what you think is an appropriate moment in Susan Glaspell's *Trifles* (p. 1238) and rewrite the scene using Ives's ringing bell.

2. Compare and contrast Ives's treatment of romance and love with their treatment in Shakespeare's *A Midsummer Night's Dream* (p. 1394).

DRAMA IN POPULAR FORMS

Audiences for live performances of plays have been thinned by high ticket prices but perhaps even more significantly by the impact of motion pictures and television. Motion pictures, the original threat to live theater, have in turn been superseded by television (along with videocassettes), now the most popular form of entertainment in America. Television audiences are measured in the millions. Probably more people have seen a single weekly episode of a top-rated prime-time program such as *ER* in one evening than have viewed a live performance of *Hamlet* in nearly four hundred years.

Though most of us are seated more often before a television than before live actors, our limited experience with the theater presents relatively few obstacles to appreciation because many of the basic elements of drama are similar whether the performance is on videotape or on a stage. Television has undoubtedly seduced audiences that otherwise might have been attracted to the theater, but television obviously satisfies some aspects of our desire for drama and can be seen as a potential introduction to live theater rather than as its irresistible rival.

Significant differences do, of course, exist between television and theater productions. Most obviously, television's special camera effects can capture phenomena such as earthquakes, raging fires, car chases, and space travel that cannot be realistically rendered on a live stage. The presentation of characters and the plotting of action are also handled differently owing to both the possibilities and limitations of television and the theater. Television's multiple camera angles and close-ups provide a degree of intimacy that cannot be duplicated by actors on stage, yet this intimacy does not achieve the immediacy that live actors create. On commercial television the plot must accommodate itself to breaks in the action so that advertisements can be aired at regular intervals. Beyond these and many other differences, however, there are enough important similarities that the experience of watching television shows can enhance our understanding of a theater production.

Seinfeld

Seinfeld, which aired on NBC, was first produced during the summer of 1989. Although the series ended in the spring of 1998, it remains popular in syndicated reruns. No one expected the half-hour situation comedy that evolved from the pilot to draw some twenty-seven million viewers per week who avidly watched Jerry Seinfeld playing himself as a standup comic. Nominated for numerous Emmys, the show became one of the most popular programs of the 1990s. Although *Seinfeld* portrays a relatively narrow band of contemporary urban life concerning four thirty-something characters living in New York City's Upper West Side, its quirky humor and engaging characters have attracted vast numbers of devoted fans who have conferred on it a kind of cult status. If you haven't watched an episode on television, noticed the T-shirts and posters, or read *Seinlanguage* (a bestselling collection of Seinfeld's monologues), you can catch up on the Internet, where fans discuss the popularity and merits of the show.

The setting for *Seinfeld* is determined by its subject matter, which is everyday life in Manhattan. Most of the action alternates between two principal locations: Jerry's modest one-bedroom apartment on West 81st Street and the characters' favorite restaurant in the neighborhood. Viewers are often surprised to learn that the show is filmed on a soundstage before a live audience in Studio City, California, because the sights, sounds, and seemingly unmistakable texture of Manhattan appear in background shots so that the city functions almost as a major character in many episodes. If you ever find yourself on the corner of Broadway and 112th Street, you'll recognize the facade of Jerry's favorite restaurant; but don't bother to look for the building that matches the exterior shot of his apartment building because it is in Los Angeles, as are the scenes in which the characters actually appear on the street. The care with which the sets are created suggests how important the illusion of the New York City environment is to the show.

As the central character, Jerry begins and ends each episode with a standup comedy act delivered before a club audience. These monologues (played down in later episodes) are connected to the events in the episodes and demonstrate with humor and insight that ordinary experience — such as standing in line at a supermarket or getting something caught in your teeth — can be a source of genuine humor. For Jerry, life is filled with daily annoyances that he copes with by making sharp humorous observations. Here's a brief instance from "The Pitch" (not reprinted in the excerpt on p. 1264) in which Jerry is in the middle of a conversation with friends when he is interrupted by a phone call.

> *Jerry (into phone):* Hello?
> *Man (v[oice] o[ver]):* Hi, would you be interested in switching over to T.M.I. long distance service?
> *Jerry:* Oh gee, I can't talk right now, why don't you give me your home number and I'll call you later?
> *Man (v[oice] o[ver]):* Uh, well I'm sorry, we're not allowed to do that.
> *Jerry:* Oh, I guess you don't want people calling you at home.
> *Man (v[oice] o[ver]):* No.
> *Jerry:* Well now you know how I feel.
> *Hangs up.*

This combination of polite self-assertion and humor is Jerry's first line of defense in his ongoing skirmishes with the irritations of daily life. Unthreatening in his Nikes and neatly pressed jeans, Jerry nonetheless knows how to give it back when he is annoyed. Seinfeld has described his fictional character as a "nice, New York Jewish boy," but his character's bemused and pointed observations reveal a tough-mindedness that is often wittily on target.

Jerry's life and apartment are continually invaded by his three closest friends: George, Kramer, and Elaine. His refrigerator is the rallying point from which they feed each other lines over cardboard takeout cartons and containers of juice. Jerry's success as a standup comic is their cue to enjoy his groceries as well as his company, but they know their intrusions are welcome because the refrigerator is always restocked.

Jerry's closest friend is George Costanza (played by Jason Alexander), a frequently unemployed, balding, pudgy schlemiel. Any straightforward description of his behavior and sensibilities makes him sound starkly unappealing: he is hypochondriacal, usually upset and depressed, inept with women, embarrassingly stingy, and persistently demanding while simultaneously displaying a vain and cocky nature. As intolerable as he can be, he is nonetheless endearing. The pleasure of his character is in observing how he talks his way into trouble and then attempts to talk his way out of it to Jerry's amazement and amusement.

Across the hall from Jerry's apartment lives Kramer (played by Michael Richards), who is strategically located so as to be the mooch in Jerry's life.

Known only as Kramer (until an episode later than "The Pitch" revealed his first name to be Cosmo), his slapstick twitching, tripping, and falling serve as a visual contrast to all the talking that goes on. His bizarre schemes and eccentric behavior have their physical counterpart in his vertical hair and his outrageous thrift-shop shirts from the 1960s.

Elaine Benes (played by Julia Louis-Dreyfus), on the other hand, is a sharp-tongued, smart, sexy woman who can hold her own and is very definitely a female member of this boy's club. As Jerry's ex-girlfriend, she provides some interesting romantic tension while serving as a sounding board for the relationship issues that George and Jerry obsess about. Employed at a book company at the time of the episode reprinted here, she, like George and Kramer, is also in the business of publishing her daily problems in Jerry's apartment.

The plots of most *Seinfeld* episodes are generated by the comical situations that Jerry and his friends encounter during the course of their daily lives. Minor irritations develop into huge conflicts that are offbeat, irreverent, or even absurd. The characters have plenty of time to create conflicts in their lives over such everyday situations as dealing with parents, finding an apartment, getting a date, riding the subway, ordering a meal, and losing a car in a mall parking garage. The show's screwball plots involve freewheeling misadventures that are played out in unremarkable but hilarious conversations.

The following scenes from *Seinfeld* are from a script titled "The Pitch" that concerns Jerry's and George's efforts to develop a television show for NBC. The script is loosely based on events that actually occurred when Jerry Seinfeld and his real-life friend Larry David (the author of "The Pitch") sat down to discuss ideas for the pilot NBC produced in 1989. As brief as these scenes are, they contain some of the dramatic elements found in a play.

LARRY DAVID (B. 1947)

Seinfeld

1992

"THE PITCH"

[The following excerpted scenes do not appear one after the other in the original script but are interspersed through several subplots involving Kramer and Elaine.]

ACT ONE

SCENE A: *Int[erior] comedy club bar—night*

> *Jerry and George are talking. Suits enter, Stu and Jay.*

Stu: Excuse me, Jerry? I'm Stu Chermak. I'm with NBC.
Jerry: Hi.

Stu: Could we speak for a few moments?

Jerry: Sure, sure.

Jay: Hi, Jay Crespi.

Jerry: Hello.

George: C-R-E-S-P-I?

Jay: That's right.

George: I'm unbelievable at spelling last names. Give me a last name.

Jay: Mm, I'm not—

Jerry: George.

George (backing off): Huh? All right, fine.

Stu: First of all, that was a terrific show.

Jerry: Oh thank you very much.

Stu: And basically, I just wanted to let you know that we've been discussing you at some of our meetings and we'd be very interested in doing something.

Jerry: Really? Wow.

Stu: So, if you have an idea for like a TV show for yourself, well, we'd just love to talk about it.

Jerry: I'd be very interested in something like that.

Stu: Well, here, why don't you give us a call and maybe we can develop a series.

They start to exit.

Jerry: Okay. Great. Thanks.

Stu: It was very nice meeting you.

Jerry: Thank you.

Jay: Nice meeting you.

Jerry: Nice meeting you.

George returns.

George: What was that all about?

Jerry: They said they were interested in me.

George: For what?

Jerry: You know, a TV show.

George: Your own show?

Jerry: Yeah, I guess so.

George: They want you to do a TV show?

Jerry: Well, they want me to come up with an idea. I mean, I don't have any ideas.

George: Come on, how hard is that? Look at all the junk that's on TV. You want an idea? Here's an idea. You coach a gymnastics team in high school. And you're married. And your son's not interested in gymnastics and you're pushing him into gymnastics.

Jerry: Why should I care if my son's into gymnastics?

George: Because you're a gymnastics teacher. It's only natural.

Jerry: But gymnastics is not for everybody.

George: I know, but he's your son.

Jerry: So what?

George: All right, forget that idea, it's not for you. . . . Okay, okay, I got it, I got it. You run an antique store.

Jerry: Yeah and . . . ?

George: And people come in the store and you get involved in their lives.

Jerry: What person who runs an antique store gets involved in people's lives?

George: Why not?

Jerry: So someone comes in to buy an old lamp and all of a sudden I'm getting them out of a jam? I could see if I was a pharmacist because a pharmacist knows what's wrong with everybody that comes in.

George: I know, but antiques are very popular right now.

Jerry: No they're not, they used to be.

George: Oh yeah, like you know.

Jerry: Oh like you do.

    Cut to:

ACT ONE

SCENE B: *Int[erior] Jerry's apartment—day*

    Jerry and Kramer.

Kramer: . . . And you're the manager of the circus.

Jerry: A circus?

Kramer: Come on, this is a great idea. Look at the characters. You've got all these freaks on the show. A woman with a moustache? I mean, who wouldn't tune in to see a woman with a moustache? You've got the tallest man in the world; the guy who's just a head.

Jerry: I don't think so.

Kramer: Look Jerry, the show isn't about the circus, it's about watching freaks.

Jerry: I don't think the network will go for it.

Kramer: Why not?

Jerry: Look, I'm not pitching a show about freaks.

Kramer: Oh come on Jerry, you're wrong. People they want to watch freaks. This is a "can't miss."

ACT ONE

SCENE C: *Int[erior] coffee shop—lunchtime—day*

    Jerry and George enter.

George: So, what's happening with the TV show? You come up with anything?

Jerry: No, nothing.

George: Why don't they have salsa on the table?

Jerry: What do you need salsa for?

George: Salsa is now the number one condiment in America.

Jerry: You know why? Because people like to say "salsa." "Excuse me, do you have salsa?" "We need more salsa." "Where is the salsa? No salsa?"

George: You know it must be impossible for a Spanish person to order seltzer and not get salsa. *(Angry.)* "I wanted seltzer, not salsa."

Jerry: "Don't you know the difference between seltzer and salsa? You have the seltzer after the salsa!"

George: See, this should be the show. This is the show.
Jerry: What?
George: This. Just talking.
Jerry (dismissing): Yeah, right.
George: I'm really serious. I think that's a good idea.
Jerry: Just talking? What's the show about?
George: It's about nothing.
Jerry: No story?
George: No, forget the story.
Jerry: You've got to have a story.
George: Who says you gotta have a story? Remember when we were waiting for that table in that Chinese restaurant that time? That could be a TV show.
Jerry: And who is on the show? Who are the characters?
George: I could be a character.
Jerry: You?
George: You could base a character on me.
Jerry: So on the show there's a character named George Costanza?
George: Yeah. There's something wrong with that? I'm a character. People are always saying to me, "You know you're quite a character."
Jerry: And who else is on the show?
George: Elaine could be a character. Kramer.
Jerry: Now he's a character. . . . So, everyone I know is a character on the show.
George: Right.
Jerry: And it's about nothing?
George: Absolutely nothing.
Jerry: So you're saying, I go in to NBC and tell them I got this idea for a show about nothing.
George: *We* go into NBC.
Jerry: We? Since when are you a writer?
George: Writer. We're talking about a sit-com.
Jerry: You want to go with me to NBC?
George: Yeah, I think we really got something here.
Jerry: What do we got?
George: An idea.
Jerry: What idea?
George: An idea for the show.
Jerry: I still don't know what the idea is.
George: It's about nothing.
Jerry: Right.
George: Everybody's doing something, we'll do nothing.
Jerry: So we go into NBC, we tell them we've got an idea for a show about nothing.
George: Exactly.
Jerry: They say, "What's your show about?" I say, "Nothing."
George: There you go.

   A beat.

Jerry: I think you may have something there.

   Cut to:

ACT ONE

SCENE D: *Int[erior] Jerry's apartment—day*

Jerry and Kramer.

Jerry: So it would be about my real life. And one of the characters would be based on you.

Kramer (thinks): No. I don't think so.

Jerry: What do you mean you don't think so?

Kramer: I don't like it.

Jerry: I don't understand. What don't you like about it?

Kramer: I don't like the idea of a character based on me.

Jerry: Why not?

Kramer: Doesn't sit well.

Jerry: You're my neighbor. There's got to be a character based on you.

Kramer: That's your problem, buddy.

Jerry: I don't understand what the big deal is.

Kramer: Hey I'll tell you what, you can do it on one condition.

Jerry: Whatever you want.

Kramer: I get to play Kramer.

Jerry: You can't play Kramer.

Kramer: I am Kramer.

Jerry: But you can't act.

ACT ONE

SCENE G: *Int[erior] NBC reception area—day*

Jerry and George.

Jerry (to himself): Salsa, seltzer. Hey excuse me, you got any salsa? No not seltzer, salsa. *(George doesn't react.)* What's the matter?

George (nervous): Nothing.

Jerry: You sure? You look a little pale.

George: No, I'm fine. I'm good. I'm fine. I'm very good.

Jerry: What are you, nervous?

George: No, not nervous. I'm good, very good. *(A beat, then: explodes.)* I can't do this! Can't do this!

Jerry: What?

George: I can't do this! I can't do it. I have tried. I'm here. It's impossible.

Jerry: This was your idea.

George: What idea? I just said something. I didn't know you'd listen to me.

Jerry: Don't worry about it. They're just TV executives.

George: They're men with jobs, Jerry! They wear suits and ties. They're married, they have secretaries.

Jerry: I told you not to come.

George: I need some water. I gotta get some water.

Jerry: They'll give us water inside.

George: Really? That's pretty good. . . .

> *Receptionist enters.*

Receptionist: They're ready for you.
George: Okay, okay, look, you do all the talking, okay?
Jerry: Relax. Who are they?
George: Yeah, they're not better than me.
Jerry: Course not.
George: Who are they?
Jerry: They're nobody.
George: What about me?
Jerry: What about you?
George: Why them? Why not me?
Jerry: Why not you?
George: I'm as good as them.
Jerry: Better.
George: You really think so?
Jerry: No.

> *Door opens, Jerry and George P.O.V., the four execs stand up.*

> *Fade out.*

ACT TWO

Scene G: *Int[erior] NBC president's office—day*

> The mood is jovial. Stu Chermak is there—along with Susan Ross, Jay Crespi, and Russell Dalrymple, the head of the network.

Stu (to Jerry): The bit, the bit I really liked was where the parakeet flew into the mirror. Now that's funny.
George: The parakeet in the mirror. That is a good one, Stu.
Jerry: Yeah, it's one of my favorites.
Russell: What about you George, have you written anything we might know?
George: Well, possibly. I wrote an off-Broadway show, "La Cocina". . . . Actually it was off-off-Broadway. It was a comedy about a Mexican chef.
Jerry: Oh it was very funny. There was one great scene with the chef—what was his name?
George: Pepe.
Jerry: Oh Pepe, yeah Pepe. And, uh, he was making tamales.
Susan: Oh, he actually cooked on the stage?
George: No, no, he mimed it. That's what was so funny about it.
Russell: So what have you two come up with?
Jerry: Well we've thought about this in a variety of ways. But the basic idea is I will play myself.
George (interrupting, to Jerry): May I?
Jerry: Go ahead.
George: I think I can sum up the show for you with one word. NOTHING.
Russell: Nothing?
George: Nothing.

Russell: What does that mean?

George: The show is about nothing.

Jerry (to George): Well, it's not about nothing.

George (to Jerry): No, it's about nothing.

Jerry: Well, maybe in philosophy. But even nothing is something.

Jerry and George glare at each other. Receptionist sticks her head in.

Receptionist: Mr. Dalrymple, your niece is on the phone.

Russell: I'll call back.

George: D-A-L-R-I-M-P-E-L.

Russell: Not even close.

George: Is it with a "y"?

Russell: No.

Susan: What's the premise?

Jerry: . . . Well, as I was saying, I would play myself. And as a comedian, living in New York, and I have a friend and a neighbor and an ex-girlfriend, which is all true.

George: Yeah, but nothing happens on the show. You see, it's just like life. You know, you eat, you go shopping, you read. You eat, you read, you go shopping.

Russell: You read? You read on the show?

Jerry: Well I don't know about the reading. We didn't discuss the reading.

Russell: All right, tell me, tell me about the stories. What kind of stories?

George: Oh no, no stories.

Russell: No stories? So what is it?

George: What'd you do today?

Russell: I got up and came to work.

George: There's a show. That's a show.

Russell (confused): How is that a show?

Jerry: Well, uh, maybe something happens on the way to work.

George: No, no, no. Nothing happens.

Jerry: Well, something happens.

Russell: Well why am I watching it?

George: Because it's on TV.

Russell: Not yet.

George: Okay, uh, look, if you want to just keep on doing the same old thing, then maybe this idea is not for you. I for one will not compromise my artistic integrity. And I'll tell you something else. This is the show and we're not going to change it. *(To Jerry.)* Right?

Jerry: How about this? I manage a circus . . .

CONSIDERATIONS FOR CRITICAL THINKING AND WRITING

1. FIRST RESPONSE. What does George mean when he says the proposed show should be about "nothing"? Why is George's idea both a comic and a serious proposal?

2. How does the stage direction "Suits enter" serve to characterize Stu and Jay? Write a description of how you think they would look.

3. What is revealed about George's character when he spells Crespi's and Dalrymple's names?

4. Discuss Kramer's assertion that people "want to watch freaks." Do you think this line could be used to sum up accurately audience responses to *Seinfeld*?

5. Choose a scene, and explain how humor is worked into it. What other emotions are evoked in the scene?

6. View an episode of *Seinfeld*. How does reading a script compare with watching the show? Which do you prefer? Why?

7. CRITICAL STRATEGIES. Read the section on reader-response criticism (pp. 2109–11) in Chapter 52, "Critical Strategies for Reading," and discuss why you like or dislike "The Pitch" and *Seinfeld* in general. Try to account for your personal response to the script and the show.

CONNECTION TO ANOTHER SELECTION

1. In an essay explain whether or not you think David Ives's play *Sure Thing* (p. 1254) fills George's prescription that a story should be about "nothing."

Like those of many plays, the settings for these scenes are not detailed. Jerry's apartment and the coffee shop are, to cite only two examples, not described at all. We are told only that it is lunchtime in the coffee shop. Even without a set designer's version of these scenes, we readily create a mental picture of these places that provides a background for the characters. In the coffee shop scene we can assume that Jerry and George are having lunch, but we must supply the food, the plates and cutlery, the tables and chairs, and the other customers. For the television show sets were used that replicated the details of a Manhattan coffee shop, right down to the menus and cash register. If the scene were presented on a stage, a set designer might use minimal sets and props to suggest the specific location. The director of such a production would rely on the viewers' imagination to create the details of the setting.

As brief as they are, these scenes include some exposition to provide the necessary background about the characters and their circumstances. We learn through dialogue, for example, that George is not a writer and that he doesn't think it takes very much talent to write a sit-com even though he's unemployed. These bits of information help to characterize George and allow an audience to place his attitudes and comments in a larger context that will be useful for understanding how other characters read them. Rather than dramatizing background information, the scriptwriter arranges incidents to create a particular focus and effect while working in the necessary exposition through dialogue.

The plot in these scenes shapes the conflicts to emphasize humor. As in any good play, incidents are carefully arranged to achieve a particular effect. In the first scene we learn that NBC executives are interested in having Jerry do his own television show. We also learn, through his habit of spelling people's last names when he meets them, that George is a potential embarrassment. The dialogue between Jerry and George quickly establishes the conflict. The NBC executives would like to produce a TV show with Jerry provided that he can come up with an idea for the series; Jerry, however, has no ideas (here's the complication of the pyramidal plot pattern discussed in Elements of Drama, p. 1250). This complication sets up a conflict for Jerry because George assumes that he can help Jerry develop an idea for the show, which, after all, shouldn't be any more difficult than spelling a stranger's name. As George says, "How hard is that? Look at all the junk that's on TV."

All of a sudden everyone is an expert on scriptwriting. George's off-the-wall suggestions that the premise for the show be Jerry's running an antique shop or teaching gymnastics are complemented by Kramer's idea that Jerry be "the manager of the circus" because "people they want to watch freaks." As unhelpful as Kramer's suggestion is, there is some truth here as well as humor, given his own freakish behavior. However, it is George who comes through with the most intriguing suggestion. As a result of the exuberantly funny riff he and Jerry do on "the difference between seltzer and salsa," George suddenly realizes that the show should be "about nothing"—that it should consist of nothing more than Jerry talking and hanging out with his friends George, Elaine, and Kramer. Jerry's initial skepticism gives way as he seriously considers George's proposal and is intrigued enough to bring George with him to the NBC offices to make the pitch. His decision to bring George to the meeting can only, of course, complicate matters further.

Before the meeting with the NBC executives, George is stricken with one of his crises of confidence when he compares himself to the "men with jobs" who are married and have secretaries. Characteristically, George's temporary lack of confidence shifts to an equally ill-timed arrogance once the meeting begins. He usurps Jerry's role and makes the pitch himself: "Nothing happens on the show. You see, it's just like life. You know, you eat, you go shopping, you read. You eat, you read, you go shopping." The climax occurs when George refuses even to consider any of the reservations the executives have about "nothing" happening on the show. George's insistence that he not compromise his "artistic integrity" creates a crisis for Jerry, a turning point that makes him realize that George's ridiculous arrogance might cost him his opportunity to have a TV show. Jerry's final lines to the executives—"How about this? I manage a circus . . ."—work two ways: he resignedly acknowledges that something—not "nothing"—has just happened and that George is, indeed, something of a freak.

The falling action and resolution typical of a pyramidal plot are not present in "The Pitch" because the main plot is not resolved until a later episode. "The Pitch" also contains several subplots not included in the scenes excerpted in this book. Like the main plot, these subplots involving Elaine, Kramer, and a few minor characters are not resolved until later episodes. Self-contained series episodes are increasingly rare on television, as programmers attempt to hook viewers week after week by creating suspense once associated with serialized stories that appeared weekly or monthly in magazines.

The theme of "The Pitch" is especially interesting because it self-reflexively comments on the basic premise of *Seinfeld* scripts: they are all essentially about "nothing" in that they focus on the seemingly trivial details of the four main characters' lives. The unspoken irony of this theme is that such details are in fact significant because it is just such small, everyday activities that constitute most people's lives.

PERSPECTIVE

GEOFFREY O'BRIEN (B. 1948)

On Seinfeld *as Sitcom Moneymaker*   1997

If *Seinfeld* is indeed, in the words of *Entertainment Weekly*, "the defining sitcom of our age" (one wonders how many such ages, each defined by its own sitcom, have already elapsed), the question remains what exactly it defines. Deliberate satire is alien to the spirit of the enterprise. *Seinfeld* has perfected a form in which anything can be invoked—masturbation, Jon Voight, death, kasha, deafness, faked orgasms, Salman Rushdie, Pez dispensers—without assuming the burden of saying anything about it (thereby avoiding the "social message" trap of programs like Norman Lear's *All in the Family* or *Maude*).

The show does not comment on anything except, famously, itself, in the series of episodes where Jerry and George create a pilot for a sitcom "about nothing," a sitcom identical to the one we are watching. This ploy—which ultimately necessitates a whole set of look-alikes to impersonate the cast of the show-within-a-show *Jerry*—ties in with the recursive, alternate-universe mode of such comedies as *The Purple Rose of Cairo* and *Groundhog Day,* while holding back just this side of the paranormal. If conspiracy theories surface from time to time, it is purely for amusement value, as in the episode where a spitting incident at the ballpark becomes the occasion for an elaborate parody—complete with Zapruder-like home movie°—of the Single Bullet Theory (figuring in this context as the ultimate joke on the idea of explanation).

The result is a vastly entertaining mosaic of observed bits and traits and frames. Imagine some future researcher trying to annotate any one of these episodes, like a Shakespearean scholar dutifully noting that "tapsters were proverbially poor at arithmetic." It would not merely be a matter of explaining jokes and cultural references and curt showbiz locutions—"He does fifteen minutes on Ovaltine" or "They cancelled Rick James"—but of explicating (always assuming that they were detected in the first place) each shrug and curtailed expostulation and deftly averted glance.

Where it might once have been asked if *Seinfeld* was a commentary on society, the question now should probably be whether society has not been reconfigured as a milieu for commenting on *Seinfeld.* If the craziness enacted on the show is nothing more than the usual business of comedy, the craziness that

---

Zapruder-like home movie: A reference to the Dallas bystander who captured John F. Kennedy's assassination on film.

swirls around it in the outside world is of a less hilarious order. Comedy and money have always been around, but not always in such intimate linkage, and certainly not on so grandiose a scale. In the fifteenth century, the fate of Tudor commerce was not perceived to hinge on the traveling English players who wowed foreign audiences as far afield as Denmark.

The information-age money culture for which *Seinfeld* is only another, fatter, bargaining chip clearly lost its sense of humor a long time ago, a fact that becomes ever more apparent as we move into an economy where sit-coms replace iron and steel as principal products and where fun is not merely big business but seemingly the only business. The once-endearing razzmatazz of showbiz hype warps into a perceptible desperation that registers all too plainly how much is at stake for the merchandisers. One becomes uncomfortably aware of them looming behind the audience, running electronic analyses of the giggles, and nervously watching for the dreaded moment when the laughter begins to dry up. It all begins to seem too much like work even for the audience, who may well begin to wonder why they should be expected to care about precisely how much their amusement is worth to the ticket-sellers.

As for the actual creators of the fun, I would imagine that—allowing for difference of scale and pressure—they go about their work pretty much the same way regardless of the going price for a good laugh. Some years ago, in a dusty corner of Languedoc,° I watched a dented circus truck pull up unannounced along the roadside. The family of performers who clambered out proceeded to set up a makeshift stage, which in a few hours time was ready for their show: a display of tumbling and magic that could have been presented without significant difference in the fifteenth century. After two hours of sublime entertainment, they passed the hat around and drove away toward the next bend in the road. It is strange to think of the fate of empires, even entertainment empires, hinging on such things.

From the *New York Review of Books*, August 14, 1997

Languedoc: A region in southern France.

CONSIDERATIONS FOR CRITICAL THINKING AND WRITING

1. In what sense might *Seinfeld* be described as "the defining sitcom of our age"? Do you think this is an accurate description of the show? Why or why not?

2. Explain why you agree or disagree with O'Brien's assertion that *Seinfeld* "does not comment on anything except, famously, itself."

3. Comment on O'Brien's idea that "Comedy and money have always been around, but not always in such intimate linkage." How does *Seinfeld* fit into an "information-age money culture"?

42

Writing about Drama

FROM READING TO WRITING

Because dramatic literature is written to be performed, writing about reading a play may seem twice removed from what playwrights intend the experience of drama to be: a live audience responding to live actors. Although reading a play creates distance between yourself and a performance of it, reading a play can actually bring you closer to understanding that what supports a stage production of any play is the literary dimension of a script. Writing about that script — examining carefully how the language of the stage directions, setting, exposition, dialogue, plot, and other dramatic elements serve to produce effects and meanings — can enhance an imaginative re-creation of a performance. In a sense, writing about a play gauges your own interpretative response as an audience member — the difference, of course, is that instead of applauding, you are typing.

"There's the rub," as Hamlet might say, because you're working with the precision of your fingertips rather than with the hearty response of your palms. Composing an essay about drama records more than your response to a play; writing also helps you explore, clarify, and discover dimensions of the play you may not have perceived by simply watching a performance of it. Writing is work, of course, but it's the kind of work that brings you closer to your own imagination as well as to the play. That process is more accessible if you read carefully, take notes, and annotate the text to generate ideas (for a discussion of this process see Chapter 53, "Reading and Writing"). This chapter offers a set of questions to help you read and write about drama and includes a sample paper that argues for a feminist reading of Susan Glaspell's *Trifles*.

QUESTIONS FOR RESPONSIVE READING AND WRITING

The questions in this chapter can help you consider important elements that reveal a play's effects and meanings. These questions are general and will not, therefore, always be relevant to a particular play. Many of them, however, should prove to be useful for thinking, talking, and writing about drama. If you are uncertain about the meaning of a term used in a question, consult the Glossary of Literary Terms beginning on page 2190.

1. Did you enjoy the play? What, specifically, pleased or displeased you about what was expressed and how it was expressed?

2. What is the significance of the play's title? How does it suggest the author's overall emphasis?

3. What information do the stage directions provide about the characters, action, and setting? Are these directions primarily descriptive, or are they also interpretive?

4. How is the exposition presented? What does it reveal? How does the playwright's choice *not* to dramatize certain events on stage help to determine what the focus of the play is?

5. In what ways is the setting important? Would the play be altered significantly if the setting were changed?

6. Are foreshadowings used to suggest what is to come? Are flashbacks used to dramatize what has already happened?

7. What is the major conflict the protagonist faces? What complications constitute the rising action? Where is the climax? Is the conflict resolved?

8. Are one or more subplots used to qualify or complicate the main plot? Is the plot unified so that each incident somehow has a function that relates it to some other element in the play?

9. Does the author purposely avoid a pyramidal plot structure of rising action, climax, and falling action? Is the plot experimental? Is the plot logically and chronologically organized, or is it fantastical or absurd? What effects are produced by the plot? How does it reflect the author's view of life?

10. Who is the protagonist? Who (or what) is the antagonist?

11. By what means does the playwright reveal character? What do the characters' names, physical qualities, actions, and words convey about them? What do the characters reveal about each other?

12. What is the purpose of the minor characters? Are they individualized, or do they primarily represent ideas or attitudes? Are any character foils used?

13. Do the characters all use the same kind of language, or is their speech differentiated? Is it formal or informal? How do the characters' diction and manner of speaking serve to characterize them?

14. Does your response to the characters change in the course of the play? What causes the change?

15. Are words and images repeated in the play so that they take on special meanings? Which speeches seem particularly important? Why?

16. How does the playwright's use of language contribute to the tone of the play? Is the dialogue, for example, predominantly light, humorous, relaxed, sentimental, sad, angry, intense, or violent?

17. Are any symbols used in the play? Which actions, characters, settings, objects, or words convey more than their literal meanings?

18. Are any unfamiliar theatrical conventions used that present problems in understanding the play? How does knowing more about the nature of the theater from which the play originated help to resolve these problems?

19. Is the theme stated directly, or is it developed implicitly through the plot, characters, or some other element? Does the theme confirm or challenge most people's values?

20. How does the play reflect the values of the society in which it is set and in which it was written?

21. How does the play reflect or challenge your own values?

22. Is there a recording, film, or videocassette of the play available in your library or media center? How does this version compare with your own reading?

23. How would you produce the play on a stage? Consider scenery, costumes, casting, and characterizations. What would you emphasize most in your production?

24. Is there a particular critical approach that seems especially appropriate for this play? (See Chapter 52, "Critical Strategies for Reading," which begins on p. 2091.)

25. How might biographical information about the author help the reader to grasp the central concerns of the play?

26. How might historical information about the play provide a useful context for interpretation?

27. To what extent do your own experiences, values, beliefs, and assumptions inform your interpretation?

28. What kinds of evidence from the play are you focusing on to support your interpretation? Does your interpretation leave out any important elements that might undercut or qualify your interpretation?

29. Given that there are a variety of ways to interpret the play, which one seems the most useful to you?

A SAMPLE PAPER

The Feminist Evidence in **Trifles**

The following paper was written in response to an assignment that required an analysis — about 750 words — of an assigned play. Chris Duffy's paper argues that although *Trifles* was written close to eighty years ago, it should be seen as a feminist play because its treatment of the tensions between men and women deliberately reveals the oppressiveness that women have had to cope with in their everyday lives. The paper discusses a number of the play's elements, but the discussion is unified through its focus on how the women characters are bound together by a set of common concerns. Notice that page numbers are provided to document quoted passages but no separate list for the work cited is included because the play appears in the anthology assigned for the course.

Chris Duffy
Professor Barrina-Barrou
English 109-2
October 6, 20--

The Feminist Evidence in Trifles

Despite its early publication date, Susan Glaspell's Trifles (1916) can be regarded as a work of feminist literature. The play depicts the life of a woman who has been suppressed, oppressed, and subjugated by a patronizing, patriarchal husband. Mrs. Wright is eventually driven to kill her "hard" (1244) husband who has stifled every last twitch of her identity. Trifles dramatizes the hypocrisy and ingrained discrimination of male-dominated society while simultaneously speaking to the dangers for women who succumb to such hierarchies. Because Mrs. Wright follows the role mapped by her husband and is directed by society's patriarchal expectations, her identity is lost somewhere along the way. However, Mrs. Hale and Mrs. Peters quietly insist on preserving their own identities by protecting Mrs. Wright from the men who seek to convict her of murder.

Mrs. Wright is described as someone who used to have a flair for life. Her neighbor, Mrs. Hale, comments that the last time Mrs. Wright appeared happy and vivacious was before she was married or, more important, when she was

Minnie Foster and not Mrs. Wright. Mrs. Hale laments, "I heard she used to wear pretty clothes and be lively, when she was Minnie Foster, one of the town girls singing in the choir" (1241). But after thirty years of marriage, Mrs. Wright is now worried about her canned preserves freezing and being without an apron while she is in jail. This subservient image was so accepted in society that Mrs. Peters, the sheriff's wife, speculates that Mrs. Wright must want her apron in order to "feel more natural" (1242). Any other roles would be considered uncharacteristic.

This wifely role is predicated on the supposition that women have no ability to make complicated decisions, to think critically, or to rely on themselves. As the title suggests, the men in this story think of homemaking as much less important than a husband's breadwinning role. Mr. Hale remarks, "Well, women are used to worrying over trifles" (1240), and Sheriff Peters assumes the insignificance of "kitchen things" (1240). Hence, women are forced into a domestic, secondary role, like it or not, and are not even respected for that. Mr. Hale, Sheriff Peters, and the county attorney all dismiss the dialogue between Mrs. Peters and Mrs. Hale as feminine chitchat. Further, the county attorney allows the women to leave the Wrights' house unsupervised because he sees Mrs. Peters as merely an extension of her husband.

Even so, the domestic system the men have set up for their wives and their disregard for them after the rules and boundaries have been laid down prove to be the men's downfall. The evidence that Mrs. Wright killed her husband is woven into Mrs. Hale's and Mrs. Peters's conversations about Mrs. Wright's sewing and her pet bird. The knots in her quilt match those in the rope used to strangle Mr.

Wright, and the bird, the last symbol of Mrs. Wright's
vitality to be taken by her husband, is found dead. Unable
to play the role of subservient wife anymore, Mrs. Wright
is foreign to herself and therefore lives a lie. As Mrs.
Hale proclaims, "Why, it looks as if she didn't know what
she was about!" (1243).

    Mrs. Hale, however, does ultimately understand what
Mrs. Wright is about. She comprehends the desperation,
loneliness, and pain that Mrs. Wright experienced, and she
instinctively knows that the roles Mrs. Wright played--
even that of murderer--are scripted by the male-dominated
circumstances of her life. As Mrs. Hale shrewdly and
covertly observes in the context of a discussion about
housecleaning with the county attorney: "Men's hands
aren't always as clean as they might be" (1240). In fact,
even Mrs. Hale feels some guilt for not having made an
effort to visit Mrs. Wright over the years to help relieve
the monotony of Mrs. Wright's life with her husband:

> I might have known she needed help! I know how
> things can be--for women. I tell you, it's
> queer, Mrs. Peters. We live close together
> and we live far apart. We all go through the
> same things--it's all just a different kind of
> the same thing. (1245)

Mrs. Hale cannot help identifying with her neighbor.

    In contrast, Mrs. Peters is initially reluctant to
support Mrs. Wright. Not only is she married to the sheriff, but, as the county attorney puts it, "a sheriff's
wife is married to the law" (1246) as well. She reminds
Mrs. Hale that "the law has got to punish crime" (1245),
even if it means revealing the existence of the dead bird
and exposing the motive that could convict Mrs. Wright
of murdering her husband. But finally Mrs. Peters also

becomes complicit in keeping information from her husband
and other men. She too--owing to the loss of her first
child--understands what loss means and what Mrs. Hale
means when she says that women "all go through the same
things" (1245).

The women in Trifles cannot, as the play reveals, be
trifled with. Although Glaspell wrote the play close to
eighty years ago, it continues to be relevant to contemporary relationships between men and women because its essentially feminist perspective provides a convincing case
for the necessity of women to move beyond destructive
stereotypes and oppressive assumptions in order to be true
to their own significant--not trifling--experiences.

43

A Study of Sophocles

Sophocles lived a long, productive life (496?–406 B.C.) in Athens. During his life Athens became a dominant political and cultural power after the Persian Wars, but before he died Sophocles witnessed the decline of Athens as a result of the Peloponnesian Wars and the city's subsequent surrender to Sparta. He saw Athenian culture reach remarkable heights as well as collapse under enormous pressures.

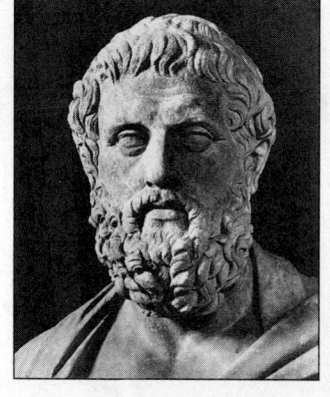

Sophocles embodied much of the best of Athenian culture; he enjoyed success as a statesman, general, treasurer, priest, and, of course, prize-winning dramatist. Although surviving fragments indicate that he wrote over 120 plays, only a handful remain intact. Those that survive consist of the three plays he wrote about Oedipus and his children — *Oedipus the King, Oedipus at Colonus,* and *Antigone* — and four additional tragedies: *Philoctetes, Ajax, Maidens of Trachis,* and *Electra.*

His plays won numerous prizes at festival competitions because of his careful, subtle plotting and the sense of inevitability with which their action is charged. Moreover, his development of character is richly complex. Instead of relying on the extreme situations and exaggerated actions that earlier tragedians used, Sophocles created powerfully motivated characters who even today fascinate audiences with their psychological depth.

In addition to crafting sophisticated tragedies for the Greek theater, Sophocles introduced several important innovations to the stage. Most important, he broke the tradition of using only two actors; adding a third resulted in more complicated relationships and intricate dialogue among characters. As individual actors took center stage more often, Sophocles reduced the role of the chorus (discussed on p. 1284). This shift placed even more emphasis on the actors, although the chorus remained important as a means of commenting on the action and establishing its tone. Sophocles was also the first dramatist to write plays with specific actors in mind, a development that many later playwrights, including Shakespeare, exploited usefully. But without question Sophocles' greatest contribution to drama was *Oedipus the King,* which, it has been argued, is the most influential drama ever written.

CHRONOLOGY

c. 496 B.C. Born at Colonus.

480 Athenian victory over the Persians at Salamis. (Sophocles participates as a musician in the victory celebration.)

468 Sophocles' first triumph (over Aeschylus) in the drama competition at the Festival of Dionysus.

443–42 Serves as one of the treasurers of the league against Persia.

c. 441 Writes *Antigone.*

431 The Peloponnesian War begins. This conflict among the Greek states (including Athens and Sparta) lasts nearly thirty years.

c. 430 Writes *Oedipus the King.*

413 Athenian force defeated in Sicily. Sophocles is chosen as one of the leaders to deal with the Sicilian crisis.

406 Sophocles dies.

404 Athens capitulates to Sparta.

401 *Oedipus at Colonus* produced posthumously.

Research Sophocles with LitLinks at
http://www.bedfordstmartins.com/meyer/bedintrolit

THEATRICAL CONVENTIONS OF GREEK DRAMA

More than twenty-four hundred years have passed since 430 B.C., when Sophocles' *Oedipus the King* was probably first produced on a Greek stage. We inhabit a vastly different planet than Sophocles' audience did, yet concerns about what it means to be human in a world that frequently runs counter to our desires and aspirations have remained relatively constant. The ancient Greeks continue to speak to us. But inexperienced readers or viewers may have some initial difficulty understanding the theatrical conventions used in classical Greek tragedies such as *Oedipus the King* and *Antigone*. If Sophocles were alive today, he would very likely need some sort of assistance with the conventions of an Arthur Miller play or a television production of *Seinfeld*.

Classical Greek drama developed from religious festivals that paid homage to Dionysus, the god of wine and fertility. Most of the details of these festivals have been lost, but we do know that they included dancing and singing that celebrated legends about Dionysus. From these choral songs developed stories of both Dionysus and mortal culture-heroes. These heroes became the subject of playwrights whose works were produced in contests at the festivals. The Dionysian festivals lasted more than five hundred years, but relatively few of their plays have survived. Among the works of the three great writers of tragedy, only seven plays each by Sophocles and Aeschylus (525?–456 B.C.) and nineteen plays by Euripides (480?–406 B.C.) survive.

Plays were such important events in Greek society that they were partially funded by the state. The Greeks associated drama with religious and community values as well as entertainment. In a sense, their plays celebrate their civilization; in approving the plays, audiences applauded their own culture. The enormous popularity of the plays is indicated by the size of surviving amphitheaters. Although information about these theaters is sketchy, we do know that most of them shared a common form. They were built into hillsides with rising rows of seats accommodating more than fourteen thousand people. These seats partially encircled an *orchestra* or "dancing place," where the *chorus* of a dozen or so men chanted lines and danced.

Tradition credits the Greek poet Thespis with adding an actor who was separate from the choral singing and dancing of early performances. A second actor was subsequently included by Aeschylus and a third, as noted earlier, by Sophocles. These additions made possible the conflicts and complicated relationships that evolved into the dramatic art we know today. The two or three male actors who played all the roles appeared behind the orchestra in front of the *skene,* a stage building that served as dressing rooms. As Greek theater evolved, a wall of the skene came to be painted to suggest a palace or some other setting, and the roof was employed to indicate, for instance, a mountain location. Sometimes gods were lowered from the roof by mechanical devices to set matters right among the mortals below. This method of rescuing characters from complications beyond their abilities to resolve was known in Latin as *deus ex machina* ("god from the machine"), a term now used to describe any improbable means by which an author provides a too-easy resolution for a story.

Inevitably, the conventions of the Greek theaters affected how plays were presented. Few if any scene changes occurred because the amphitheater stage was set primarily for one location. If an important event happened somewhere else, it was reported by a minor character, such as a messenger. The chorus also provided necessary background information.

Based on scholarly sources, this drawing represents the features typical of a classical Greek theater. (Drawing by Gerda Becker. From Kenneth Macgowan and William Melnitz, The Living Stage, © 1990 by Prentice Hall/A Division of Simon & Schuster.)

In *Oedipus the King* and *Antigone,* the choruses, acting as townspeople, also assess the characters' strengths and weaknesses, praising them for their virtues, chiding them for their rashness, and giving them advice. The reactions of the chorus provide a connection between the actors and audience because the chorus is at once a participant in and an observer of the action. In addition, the chorus helps structure the action by indicating changes in scene or mood. Thus the chorus could be used in a variety of ways to shape the audience's response to the play's action and characters.

Actors in classical Greek amphitheaters faced considerable challenges. An intimate relationship with the audience was impossible because many spectators would have been too far away to see a facial expression or subtle gesture. Indeed, some in the audience would have had difficulty even hearing the voices of individual actors. To compensate for these disadvantages, actors wore large masks that extravagantly expressed the major characters' emotions or identified the roles of minor characters. The masks also allowed the two or three actors in a performance to play all the characters without confusing the audience. Each mask was fitted so that the mouthpiece amplified the actor's voice. The actors were further equipped with padded costumes and elevated shoes (**cothurni** or **buskins**) that made them appear larger than life.

As a result of these adaptive conventions, Greek plays tend to emphasize words—formal, impassioned speeches—more than physical action. We are invited to ponder actions and events rather than to see all of them enacted. Although the stark simplicity of Greek theater does not offer an audience realistic detail, the classical tragedies that have survived present characters in dramatic situations that transcend theatrical conventions. Tragedy, it seems, has always been compelling for human beings, regardless of the theatrical forms it has taken.

A Greek tragedy is typically divided into five parts: prologue, parodos, episodia, stasimon, and exodus. In some translations these terms appear as headings, but in more recent translations, as those by Robert Fagles included here, the headings do not appear. Still, understanding these terms provides a sense of the overall rhythm of a Greek play. The opening speech or dialogue is known as the *prologue* and usually gives the exposition necessary to follow the subsequent action. In the *parodos* the chorus makes its first entrance and gives its perspective on what the audience has learned in the prologue. Several *episodia,* or episodes, follow, in which characters engage in dialogue that frequently consists of heated debates dramatizing the play's conflicts. Following each episode is a choral ode or *stasimon,* in which the chorus responds to and interprets the preceding dialogue. The *exodus,* or last scene, follows the final episode and stasimon; in it the resolution occurs and the characters leave the stage.

The effect of alternating dialogues and choral odes has sometimes been likened to that of opera. Greek tragedies were written in verse, and the stasima were chanted or sung as the chorus moved rhythmically, so the plays have a strong musical element that is not always apparent on the printed page. If we remember their musical qualities we are less likely to forget that no matter how terrifying or horrific the conflicts they describe, these plays are stately, measured, and dignified works that reflect a classical Greek sense of order and proportion.

TRAGEDY

Newspapers are filled with daily reports of tragedies: a child is struck and crippled by a car; an airplane plunges into a suburban neighborhood; a volcano erupts and kills thousands. These unexpected instances of suffering are commonly and accurately described as tragic, but they are not tragedies in the literary sense of the term. A literary *tragedy* presents courageous individuals who confront powerful forces within or outside themselves with a dignity that reveals the breadth and depth of the human spirit in the face of failure, defeat, and even death.

Aristotle (384–322 B.C.), in his *Poetics,* defined *tragedy* on the basis of the plays contemporary to him. His definition has generated countless variations, qualifications, and interpretations, but we still derive our literary understanding of this term from Aristotle.

The protagonist of a Greek tragedy is someone regarded as extraordinary rather than typical: a great man or woman brought from happiness to agony. The character's stature is important because it makes his or her fall all the more terrifying. The protagonist also carries mythic significance for the audience. Oedipus and Antigone, for example, are not only human beings but legendary figures from a distant, revered past. Although the gods do not appear onstage in either *Oedipus the King* or *Antigone,* their power is ever present as the characters invoke their help or attempt to defy them. In addition, Greek tragedy tends to be public rather than private. The fate of the community — the state — is often linked with that of the protagonist, as when Thebes suffers a plague as a result of Oedipus's mistaken actions.

The protagonists of classical Greek tragedies (and of those of Shakespeare) are often rulers of noble birth who represent the monarchical values of their periods, but in modern tragedies the protagonists are more likely to reflect democratic values that make it possible for anyone to be a suitable subject. What is finally important is not so much the protagonist's social stature as a greatness of character that steadfastly confronts suffering, whether it comes from supernatural, social, or psychological forces. Although Greek tragic heroes were aristocrats, the nobility of their characters was more significant than their inherited titles and privileges.

The protagonist's eminence and determination to complete some task or goal make him or her admirable in Greek tragedy, but that does not free the protagonist from what Aristotle described as "some error or frailty" that brings about his or her misfortune. The term Aristotle used for this weakness is *hamartia.* This word has frequently been interpreted to mean that the protagonist's fall is the result of an internal *tragic flaw,* such as an excess of pride, ambition, passion, or some other character trait that leads directly to disaster.

Sometimes, however, misfortunes are not the result of a character flaw but of misunderstood events that overtake and thwart the protagonist's best intentions. Thus, virtue can lead to tragedy too. *Hamártia* has also been interpreted to mean "wrong act" — a mistake based not on a personal failure but on circumstances outside the protagonist's personality and control. Many readers find that a combination of these two interpretations sheds the most light on the causes of the tragic protagonist's fall. Both internal and external forces can lead to downfall because the protagonist's personality may determine crucial judgments that result in mistaken actions.

However the idea of tragic flaw is understood, it is best not to use it as a means of reducing the qualities of a complex character to an adjective or two that labels Oedipus as guilty of "overweening pride" (the Greek term for which is *hubris* or *hybris*) or Antigone as "fated." The protagonists of tragedies require more careful characterization than a simplistic label can provide.

Whatever the causes of the tragic protagonist's downfall, he or she accepts responsibility for it. Hence, even in his or her encounter with failure (and possibly death) the tragic protagonist displays greatness of character. Perhaps it is the witnessing of this greatness, which seems both to accept and to transcend human limitations, that makes audiences feel relief rather than hopelessness at the end of a tragedy. Aristotle described this response as a **catharsis,** or purgation of the emotions of "pity and fear." We are faced with the protagonist's misfortune, which often seems out of proportion to his or her actions, and so we are likely to feel compassionate pity. Simultaneously, we may experience fear because the failure of the protagonist, who is so great in stature and power, is a frightening reminder of our own vulnerabilities. Ultimately, however, both these negative emotions are purged because the tragic protagonist's suffering is an affirmation of human values — even if they are not always triumphant — rather than a despairing denial of them.

Nevertheless, tragedies are disturbing. Instead of coming away with the reassurance of a happy ending, we must take solace in the insight produced by the hero's suffering. And just as our expectations are changed, so are the protagonist's. Aristotle described the moment in the plot when this change occurs as a **reversal** (*peripeteia*), the point when the hero's fortunes turn in an unexpected direction. He more specifically defined this term as meaning an action performed by a character that has the opposite of its intended effect. An example cited by Aristotle is the messenger's attempts to relieve Oedipus's anxieties about his relationship to his father and mother. Instead, the messenger reveals previously unknown information that eventually results in a **recognition** (*anagnorisis*); Oedipus discovers the terrible truth that he has killed his father and married his mother.

Tragedy is typically filled with ironies because there are so many moments in the plot when what seems to be turns out to be radically different from what actually is. Because of this, a particular form of irony called **dramatic irony** is also known as **tragic irony.** In dramatic irony, the meaning of a character's words or actions is understood by the audience but not by the character. Audiences of Greek tragedy shared with the playwrights a knowledge of the stories on which many tragic plots were based. Consequently, they frequently were aware of what was going to happen before the characters were. When Oedipus declares that he will seek out the person responsible for the plague that ravishes his city, the audience already knows that the person Oedipus pursues is himself.

Oedipus the King

A familiarity with the Oedipus legend allows modern readers to appreciate the series of ironies that unfolds in Sophocles' *Oedipus the King*. In the opening scene, Oedipus appears with a "telltale limp." As an infant, he had been abandoned by his parents, Laius and Jocasta, the king and queen of

Thebes, because a prophecy warned that their son would kill his father and marry his mother. They instructed a servant to leave him on a mountain to die. The infant's feet were pierced and pinned together, but he was not left on the mountain; instead the servant, out of pity, gave him to a shepherd, who in turn presented him to the king and queen of Corinth. They named him Oedipus (for "swollen foot") and raised him as their own son.

On reaching manhood, Oedipus learned from an oracle that he would kill his father and marry his mother; to avoid this horrendous fate, he left Corinth forever. In his travels, Oedipus found his way blocked by a chariot at a crossroads; in a fit of anger, he killed the servants and their passenger. That passenger, unknown to Oedipus, was his real father. In Thebes, Oedipus successfully answered the riddle of the Sphinx, a winged lion with a woman's head. The reward for defeating this dreaded monster was both the crown and the dead king's wife. Oedipus and Jocasta had four children and prospered. But when the play begins, Oedipus's rule is troubled by a plague that threatens to destroy Thebes, and he is determined to find the cause of the plague in order to save the city again.

Oedipus the King is widely recognized as the greatest of the surviving Greek tragedies. Numerous translations are available (Robert Fagles's recent highly regarded translations of *Oedipus the King* and *Antigone,* the choice here, are especially accessible to modern readers. For an excerpt from another version of *Oedipus the King,* see Perspectives on Sophocles, p. 1372). The play has absorbed readers for centuries because Oedipus's character — his intelligence, confidence, rashness, and suffering — represents powers and limitations that are both exhilarating and chastening. Although no reader or viewer is likely to identify with Oedipus's extreme circumstances, anyone can appreciate his heroic efforts to find the truth about himself. In that sense, he is one of us — at our best.

SOPHOCLES (496?–406 B.C.)

Oedipus the King   *c. 430 B.C.*

TRANSLATED BY ROBERT FAGLES

CHARACTERS

Oedipus, king of Thebes
A Priest of Zeus
Creon, brother of Jocasta
A Chorus of Theban citizens and their *Leader*
Tiresias, a blind prophet
Jocasta, the queen, wife of Oedipus
A Messenger from Corinth
A Shepherd
A Messenger from inside the palace
Antigone, Ismene, daughters of Oedipus and Jocasta

Guards and attendants
Priests of Thebes

TIME AND SCENE: *The royal house of Thebes. Double doors dominate the facade; a stone altar stands at the center of the stage.*

    Many years have passed since Oedipus solved the riddle of the Sphinx and ascended the throne of Thebes, and now a plague has struck the city. A procession of priests enters; suppliants, broken and despondent, they carry branches wound in wool and lay them on the altar.

    The doors open. Guards assemble. Oedipus comes forward, majestic but for a telltale limp, and slowly views the condition of his people.

Oedipus: Oh my children, the new blood of ancient Thebes,
    why are you here? Huddling at my altar,
    praying before me, your branches wound in wool.°
    Our city reeks with the smoke of burning incense,
    rings with cries for the Healer and wailing for the dead.   5
    I thought it wrong, my children, to hear the truth
    from others, messengers. Here I am myself —
    you all know me, the world knows my fame:
    I am Oedipus.

    Helping a Priest to his feet.

                       Speak up, old man. Your years,
    your dignity — you should speak for the others.   10
    Why here and kneeling, what preys upon you so?
    Some sudden fear? some strong desire?
    You can trust me; I am ready to help,
    I'll do anything. I would be blind to misery
    not to pity my people kneeling at my feet.   15
Priest: Oh Oedipus, king of the land, our greatest power!
    You see us before you, men of all ages
    clinging to your altars. Here are boys,
    still too weak to fly from the nest,
    and here the old, bowed down with the years,   20
    the holy ones — a priest of Zeus° myself — and here
    the picked, unmarried men, the young hope of Thebes.
    And all the rest, your great family gathers now,
    branches wreathed, massing in the squares,
    kneeling before the two temples of queen Athena°   25
    or the river-shrine where the embers glow and die
    and Apollo sees the future in the ashes.
                               Our city —
    look around you, see with your own eyes —
    our ship pitches wildly, cannot lift her head
    from the depths, the red waves of death . . .   30
    Thebes is dying. A blight on the fresh crops
    and the rich pastures, cattle sicken and die,

---

3 *wool:* Wool was used in offerings to Apollo, god of poetry, the sun, prophecy, and healing.
21 *Zeus:* The highest Olympian deity and father of Apollo.   25 *Athena:* Goddess of wisdom and protector of Greek cities.

and the women die in labor, children stillborn,
and the plague, the fiery god of fever hurls down
on the city, his lightning slashing through us — 35
raging plague in all its vengeance, devastating
the house of Cadmus!° And Black Death luxuriates
in the raw, wailing miseries of Thebes.

Now we pray to you. You cannot equal the gods,
your children know that, bending at your altar. 40
But we do rate you first of men,
both in the common crises of our lives
and face-to-face encounters with the gods.
You freed us from the Sphinx; you came to Thebes
and cut us loose from the bloody tribute we had paid 45
that harsh, brutal singer. We taught you nothing,
no skill, no extra knowledge, still you triumphed.
A god was with you, so they say, and we believe it —
you lifted up our lives.
                        So now again,
Oedipus, king, we bend to you, your power — 50
we implore you, all of us on our knees:
find us strength, rescue! Perhaps you've heard
the voice of a god or something from other men,
Oedipus . . . what do you know?
The man of experience — you see it every day — 55
his plans will work in a crisis, his first of all.
Act now — we beg you, best of men, raise up our city!
Act, defend yourself, your former glory!
Your country calls you savior now
for your zeal, your action years ago. 60
Never let us remember of your reign:
you helped us stand, only to fall once more.
Oh raise up our city, set us on our feet.
The omens were good that day you brought us joy —
be the same man today! 65
Rule our land, you know you have the power,
but rule a land of the living, not a wasteland.
Ship and towered city are nothing, stripped of men
alive within it, living all as one.

Oedipus: My children,
I pity you. I see — how could I fail to see 70
what longings bring you here? Well I know
you are sick to death, all of you,
but sick as you are, not one is sick as I.
Your pain strikes each of you alone, each
in the confines of himself, no other. But my spirit 75
grieves for the city, for myself and all of you.
I wasn't asleep, dreaming. You haven't wakened me —

---

37 *Cadmus:* The legendary founder of Thebes.

I've wept through the nights, you must know that,
groping, laboring over many paths of thought.
After a painful search I found one cure: 80
I acted at once. I sent Creon,
my wife's own brother, to Delphi° —
Apollo the Prophet's oracle — to learn
what I might do or say to save our city.

Today's the day. When I count the days gone by 85
it torments me . . . what is he doing?
Strange, he's late, he's gone too long.
But once he returns, then, then I'll be a traitor
if I do not do all the god makes clear.

Priest: Timely words. The men over there 90
are signaling — Creon's just arriving.
Oedipus:

Sighting Creon, then turning to the altar.

Lord Apollo,
let him come with a lucky word of rescue,
shining like his eyes!
Priest: Welcome news, I think — he's crowned, look,
and the laurel wreath is bright with berries. 95
Oedipus: We'll soon see. He's close enough to hear —

Enter Creon from the side; his face is shaded with a wreath.

Creon, prince, my kinsman, what do you bring us?
What message from the god?
Creon: Good news.
I tell you even the hardest things to bear,
if they should turn out well, all would be well.
Oedipus: Of course, but what were the god's *words*? There's no hope 100
and nothing to fear in what you've said so far.
Creon: If you want my report in the presence of these . . .

Pointing to the priests while drawing Oedipus toward the palace.

I'm ready now, or we might go inside.
Oedipus: Speak out,
speak to us all. I grieve for these, my people, 105
far more than I fear for my own life.
Creon: Very well,
I will tell you what I heard from the god.
Apollo commands us — he was quite clear —
"Drive the corruption from the land,
don't harbor it any longer, past all cure, 110
don't nurse it in your soil — root it out!"
Oedipus: How can we cleanse ourselves — what rites?
What's the source of the trouble?

82 *Delphi:* The shrine where the oracle of Apollo held forth.

Creon: Banish the man, or pay back blood with blood.
　　Murder sets the plague-storm on the city.
Oedipus:　　　　　　　　　　　　　Whose murder?　　　　115
　　Whose fate does Apollo bring to light?
Creon:　　　　　　　　　　　Our leader,
　　my lord, was once a man named Laius,
　　before you came and put us straight on course.
Oedipus:　　　　　　　　　　　　　I know—
　　or so I've heard. I never saw the man myself.
Creon: Well, he was killed, and Apollo commands us now—　　　120
　　he could not be more clear,
　　"Pay the killers back—whoever is responsible."
Oedipus: Where on earth are they? Where to find it now,
　　the trail of the ancient guilt so hard to trace?
Creon: "Here in Thebes," he said.　　　　　　　　　　125
　　Whatever is sought for can be caught, you know,
　　whatever is neglected slips away.
Oedipus:　　　　　　　　　But where,
　　in the palace, the fields or foreign soil,
　　where did Laius meet his bloody death?
Creon: He went to consult an oracle, he said,　　　　　　　130
　　and he set out and never came home again.
Oedipus: No messenger, no fellow-traveler saw what happened?
　　Someone to cross-examine?
Creon:　　　　　　　　No,
　　they were all killed but one. He escaped,
　　terrified, he could tell us nothing clearly,　　　　　　　135
　　nothing of what he saw—just one thing.
Oedipus:　　　　　　　　　　　What's that?
　　One thing could hold the key to it all,
　　a small beginning gives us grounds for hope.
Creon: He said thieves attacked them—a whole band,
　　not single-handed, cut King Laius down.
Oedipus:　　　　　　　　　　A thief,　　　　140
　　so daring, wild, he'd kill a king? Impossible,
　　unless conspirators paid him off in Thebes.
Creon: We suspected as much. But with Laius dead
　　no leader appeared to help us in our troubles.
Oedipus: Trouble? Your *king* was murdered—royal blood!　　　145
　　What stopped you from tracking down the killer
　　then and there?
Creon:　　　　　　　The singing, riddling Sphinx.
　　She . . . persuaded us to let the mystery go
　　and concentrate on what lay at our feet.
Oedipus:　　　　　　　　　　No,
　　I'll start again—I'll bring it all to light myself!　　　150
　　Apollo is right, and so are you, Creon,
　　to turn our attention back to the murdered man.
　　Now you have *me* to fight for you, you'll see:

I am the land's avenger by all rights
and Apollo's champion too.   155
But not to assist some distant kinsman, no,
for my own sake I'll rid us of this corruption.
Whoever killed the king may decide to kill me too,
with the same violent hand — by avenging Laius
I defend myself.

To the priests.

                      Quickly, my children.   160
Up from the steps, take up your branches now.

To the guards.

One of you summon the city here before us,
tell them I'll do everything. God help us,
we will see our triumph — or our fall.

Oedipus and Creon enter the palace, followed by the guards.

Priest: Rise, my sons. The kindness we came for   165
Oedipus volunteers himself.
Apollo has sent his word, his oracle —
Come down, Apollo, save us, stop the plague.

*The priests rise, remove their branches, and exit to the side. Enter a Chorus, the
citizens of Thebes, who have not heard the news that Creon brings. They march
around the altar, chanting.*

Chorus: Zeus!
Great welcome voice of Zeus, what do you bring?
What word from the gold vaults of Delphi   170
comes to brilliant Thebes? I'm racked with terror —
                    terror shakes my heart
and I cry your wild cries, Apollo, Healer of Delos°
I worship you in dread . . . what now, what is your price?
some new sacrifice? some ancient rite from the past   175
come round again each spring? —
                  what will you bring to birth?
Tell me, child of golden Hope
        warm voice that never dies!

You are the first I call, daughter of Zeus   180
deathless Athena — I call your sister Artemis,°
heart of the market place enthroned in glory,
                  guardian of our earth —
I call Apollo astride the thunderheads of heaven —
O triple shield against death, shine before me now!   185
If ever, once in the past, you stopped some ruin
launched against our walls
               you hurled the flame of pain

---

173 *Delos:* Apollo was born on this sacred island.   181 *Artemis:* Apollo's sister, goddess of
hunting, the moon, and chastity.

far, far from Thebes—you gods
　　come now, come down once more!

　　　　　　　　　　　No, no　　　　　　　　190
the miseries numberless, grief on grief, no end—
too much to bear, we are all dying
O my people . . .
　　　　Thebes like a great army dying
and there is no sword of thought to save us, no　　195
and the fruits of our famous earth, they will not ripen
no and the women cannot scream their pangs to birth—
screams for the Healer, children dead in the womb
　　　　　　and life on life goes down
　　　　　　　　　　you can watch them go　　200
　　like seabirds winging west, outracing the day's fire
down the horizon, irresistibly
　　　　　　streaking on to the shores of Evening
　　　　　　　　　　　　　　　　Death
so many deaths, numberless deaths on deaths, no end—
Thebes is dying, look, her children　　　　　　205
stripped of pity . . .
　　　　generations strewn on the ground
unburied, unwept, the dead spreading death
and the young wives and gray-haired mothers with them
cling to the altars, trailing in from all over the city—　　210
Thebes, city of death, one long cortege
　　　　and the suffering rises
　　　　　　wails for mercy rise
　　and the wild hymn for the Healer blazes out
clashing with our sobs our cries of mourning—　　215
　　O golden daughter of god, send rescue
　　radiant as the kindness in your eyes!
Drive him back!—the fever, the god of death
　　　　　　that raging god of war
not armored in bronze, not shielded now, he burns me,　　220
battle cries in the onslaught burning on—
O rout him from our borders!
Sail him, blast him out to the Sea-queen's chamber
　　　　　　the black Atlantic gulfs
　　or the northern harbor, death to all　　225
where the Thracian surf comes crashing.
Now what the night spares he comes by day and kills—
the god of death.

　　　　　O lord of the stormcloud,
you who twirl the lightning, Zeus, Father,
thunder Death to nothing!　　　　　　230

Apollo, lord of the light, I beg you—
　　whip your longbow's golden cord

showering arrows on our enemies — shafts of power
champions strong before us rushing on!

Artemis, Huntress,   235
torches flaring over the eastern ridges —
                    ride Death down in pain!

God of the headdress gleaming gold, I cry to you —
your name and ours are one, Dionysus° —
                    come with your face aflame with wine   240
                              your raving women's cries°
              your army on the march! Come with the lightning
come with torches blazing, eyes ablaze with glory!
Burn that god of death that all gods hate!

*Oedipus enters from the palace to address the Chorus, as if addressing the entire
city of Thebes.*

Oedipus: You pray to the gods? Let me grant your prayers.   245
              Come, listen to me — do what the plague demands:
              you'll find relief and lift your head from the depths.

              I will speak out now as a stranger to the story,
              a stranger to the crime. If I'd been present then,
              there would have been no mystery, no long hunt   250
              without a clue in hand. So now, counted
              a native Theban years after the murder,
              to all of Thebes I make this proclamation:
              if any one of you knows who murdered Laius,
              the son of Labdacus, I order him to reveal   255
              the whole truth to me. Nothing to fear,
              even if he must denounce himself,
              let him speak up
              and so escape the brunt of the charge —
              he will suffer no unbearable punishment,   260
              nothing worse than exile, totally unharmed.

              Oedipus pauses, waiting for a reply.

                                                    Next,
              if anyone knows the murderer is a stranger,
              a man from alien soil, come, speak up.
              I will give him a handsome reward, and lay up
              gratitude in my heart for him besides.   265

              Silence again, no reply.

              But if you keep silent, if anyone panicking,
              trying to shield himself or friend or kin,
              rejects my offer, then hear what I will do.
              I order you, every citizen of the state
              where I hold throne and power: banish this man —   270

239 *Dionysus:* God of fertility and wine.   241 *your . . . cries:* Dionysus was attended by female celebrants.

whoever he may be — never shelter him, never
speak a word to him, never make him partner
to your prayers, your victims burned to the gods.
Never let the holy water touch his hands.
Drive him out, each of you, from every home.   275
He is the plague, the heart of our corruption,
as Apollo's oracle has revealed to me
just now. So I honor my obligations:
I fight for the god and for the murdered man.

Now my curse on the murderer. Whoever he is,   280
a lone man unknown in his crime
or one among many, let that man drag out
his life in agony, step by painful step —
I curse myself as well . . . if by any chance
he proves to be an intimate of our house,   285
here at my hearth, with my full knowledge,
may the curse I just called down on him strike me!

These are your orders: perform them to the last.
I command you, for my sake, for Apollo's, for this country
blasted root and branch by the angry heavens.   290
Even if god had never urged you on to act,
how could you leave the crime uncleansed so long?
A man so noble — your king, brought down in blood —
you should have searched. But I am the king now,
I hold the throne that he held then, possess his bed   295
and a wife who shares our seed . . . why, our seed
might be the same, children born of the same mother
might have created blood-bonds between us
if his hope of offspring hadn't met disaster —
but fate swooped at his head and cut him short.   300
So I will fight for him as if he were my father,
stop at nothing, search the world
to lay my hands on the man who shed his blood,
the son of Labdacus descended of Polydorus,
Cadmus of old and Agenor, founder of the line: 305
their power and mine are one.
                              Oh dear gods,
my curse on those who disobey these orders!
Let no crops grow out of the earth for them —
shrivel their women, kill their sons,
burn them to nothing in this plague   310
that hits us now, or something even worse.
But you, loyal men of Thebes who approve my actions,
may our champion, Justice, may all the gods
be with us, fight beside us to the end!

Leader: In the grip of your curse, my king, I swear   315
I'm not the murderer, cannot point him out.
As for the search, Apollo pressed it on us —
he should name the killer.

Oedipus: Quite right,
but to force the gods to act against their will—
no man has the power.
Leader: Then if I might mention
the next best thing . . .
Oedipus: The third best too—
don't hold back, say it.
Leader: I still believe . . .
Lord Tiresias sees with the eyes of Lord Apollo.
Anyone searching for the truth, my king,
might learn it from the prophet, clear as day.
Oedipus: I've not been slow with that. On Creon's cue
I sent the escorts, twice, within the hour.
I'm surprised he isn't here.
Leader: We need him—
without him we have nothing but old, useless rumors.
Oedipus: Which rumors? I'll search out every word.
Leader: Laius was killed, they say, by certain travelers.
Oedipus: I know—but no one can find the murderer.
Leader: If the man has a trace of fear in him
he won't stay silent long,
not with your curses ringing in his ears.
Oedipus: He didn't flinch at murder,
he'll never flinch at words.

Enter Tiresias, the blind prophet, led by a boy with escorts in attendance. He remains at a distance.

Leader: Here is the one who will convict him, look,
they bring him on at last, the seer, the man of god.
The truth lives inside him, him alone.
Oedipus: O Tiresias,
master of all the mysteries of our life,
all you teach and all you dare not tell,
signs in the heavens, signs that walk the earth!
Blind as you are, you can feel all the more
what sickness haunts our city. You, my lord,
are the one shield, the one savior we can find.

We asked Apollo—perhaps the messengers
haven't told you—he sent his answer back:
"Relief from the plague can only come one way.
Uncover the murderers of Laius,
put them to death or drive them into exile."
So I beg you, grudge us nothing now, no voice,
no message plucked from the birds, the embers
or the other mantic ways within your grasp.
Rescue yourself, your city, rescue me—
rescue everything infected by the dead.
We are in your hands. For a man to help others
with all his gifts and native strength:
that is the noblest work.

320

325

330

335

340

345

350

355

Tiresias: How terrible — to see the truth
    when the truth is only pain to him who sees!   360
    I knew it well, but I put it from my mind,
    else I never would have come.
Oedipus: What's this? Why so grim, so dire?
Tiresias: Just send me home. You bear your burdens,
    I'll bear mine. It's better that way,   365
    please believe me.
Oedipus: Strange response — unlawful,
    unfriendly too to the state that bred and raised you;
    you're withholding the word of god.
Tiresias: I fail to see
    that your own words are so well-timed.
    I'd rather not have the same thing said of me . . .   370
Oedipus: For the love of god, don't turn away,
    not if you know something. We beg you,
    all of us on our knees.
Tiresias: None of you knows —
    and I will never reveal my dreadful secrets,
    not to say your own.   375
Oedipus: What? You know and you won't tell?
    You're bent on betraying us, destroying Thebes?
Tiresias: I'd rather not cause pain for you or me.
    So why this . . . useless interrogation?
    You'll get nothing from me.
Oedipus: Nothing! You,   380
    you scum of the earth, you'd enrage a heart of stone!
    You won't talk? Nothing moves you?
    Out with it, once and for all!
Tiresias: You criticize my temper . . . unaware
    of the one *you* live with, you revile me.   385
Oedipus: Who could restrain his anger hearing you?
    What outrage — you spurn the city!
Tiresias: What will come will come.
    Even if I shroud it all in silence.
Oedipus: What will come? You're bound to *tell* me that.   390
Tiresias: I'll say no more. Do as you like, build your anger
    to whatever pitch you please, rage your worst —
Oedipus: Oh I'll let loose, I have such fury in me —
    now I see it all. You helped hatch the plot,
    you did the work, yes, short of killing him   395
    with your own hands — and given eyes I'd say
    you did the killing single-handed!
Tiresias: Is that so!
    I charge you, then, submit to that decree
    you just laid down: from this day onward
    speak to no one, not these citizens, not myself.   400
    You are the curse, the corruption of the land!
Oedipus: You, shameless —
    aren't you appalled to start up such a story?
    You think you can get away with this?

Tiresias: I have already.
    The truth with all its power lives inside me.   405
Oedipus: Who primed you for this? Not your prophet's trade.
Tiresias: You did, you forced me, twisted it out of me.
Oedipus: What? Say it again—I'll understand it better.
Tiresias: Didn't you understand, just now?
    Or are you tempting me to talk?   410
Oedipus: No, I can't say I grasped your meaning.
    Out with it, again!
Tiresias: I say you are the murderer you hunt.
Oedipus: That obscenity, twice—by god, you'll pay.
Tiresias: Shall I say more, so you can really rage?   415
Oedipus: Much as you want. Your words are nothing—futile.
Tiresias: You cannot imagine . . . I tell you,
    you and your loved ones live together in infamy,
    you cannot see how far you've gone in guilt.
Oedipus: You think you can keep this up and never suffer?   420
Tiresias: Indeed, if the truth has any power.
Oedipus: It does
    but not for you, old man. You've lost your power,
    stone-blind, stone-deaf—senses, eyes blind as stone!
Tiresias: I pity you, flinging at me the very insults
    each man here will fling at you so soon.
Oedipus: Blind,   425
    lost in the night, endless night that nursed you!
    You can't hurt me or anyone else who sees the light—
    you can never touch me.
Tiresias: True, it is not your fate
    to fall at my hands. Apollo is quite enough,
    and he will take some pains to work this out.   430
Oedipus: Creon! Is this conspiracy his or yours?
Tiresias: Creon is not your downfall, no, you are your own.
Oedipus: O power—
    wealth and empire, skill outstripping skill
    in the heady rivalries of life,
    what envy lurks inside you! Just for this,   435
    the crown the city gave me—I never sought it,
    they laid it in my hands—for this alone, Creon,
    the soul of trust, my loyal friend from the start
    steals against me . . . so hungry to overthrow me
    he sets this wizard on me, this scheming quack,   440
    this fortune-teller peddling lies, eyes peeled
    for his own profit—seer blind in his craft!

    Come here, you pious fraud. Tell me,
    when did you ever prove yourself a prophet?
    When the Sphinx, that chanting Fury kept her deathwatch here,   445
    why silent then, not a word to set our people free?
    There was a riddle, not for some passer-by to solve—
    it cried out for a prophet. Where were you?

Did you rise to the crisis? Not a word,
you and your birds, your gods—nothing.   450
No, but I came by, Oedipus the ignorant,
I stopped the Sphinx! With no help from the birds,
the flight of my own intelligence hit the mark.

And this is the man you'd try to overthrow?
You think you'll stand by Creon when he's king?   455
You and the great mastermind—
you'll pay in tears, I promise you, for this,
this witch-hunt. If you didn't look so senile
the lash would teach you what your scheming means!

Leader: I'd suggest his words were spoken in anger,   460
Oedipus . . . yours too, and it isn't what we need.
The best solution to the oracle, the riddle
posed by god—we should look for that.

Tiresias: You are the king no doubt, but in one respect,
at least, I am your equal: the right to reply.   465
I claim that privilege too.
I am not your slave. I serve Apollo.
I don't need Creon to speak for me in public.
           So,
you mock my blindness? Let me tell you this.
You with your precious eyes,   470
you're blind to the corruption of your life,
to the house you live in, those you live with—
who *are* your parents? Do you know? All unknowing
you are the scourge of your own flesh and blood,
the dead below the earth and the living here above,   475
and the double lash of your mother and your father's curse
will whip you from this land one day, their footfall
treading you down in terror, darkness shrouding
your eyes that now can see the light!
           Soon, soon
you'll scream aloud—what haven won't reverberate?   480
What rock of Cithaeron° won't scream back in echo?
That day you learn the truth about your marriage,
the wedding-march that sang you into your halls,
the lusty voyage home to the fatal harbor!
And a load of other horrors you'd never dream   485
will level you with yourself and all your children.

There. Now smear us with insults—Creon, myself
and every word I've said. No man will ever
be rooted from the earth as brutally as you.

Oedipus: Enough! Such filth from him? Insufferable—   490
what, still alive? Get out—
faster, back where you came from—vanish!

481 *Cithaeron:* The mountains where Oedipus was abandoned as an infant.

Tiresias: I'd never have come if you hadn't called me here.
Oedipus: If I thought you'd blurt out such absurdities,
    you'd have died waiting before I'd had you summoned.   495
Tiresias: Absurd, am I? To you, not to your parents:
    the ones who bore you found me sane enough.
Oedipus: Parents—who? Wait . . . who is my father?
Tiresias: This day will bring your birth and your destruction.
Oedipus: Riddles—all you can say are riddles, murk and darkness.   500
Tiresias: Ah, but aren't you the best man alive at solving riddles?
Oedipus: Mock me for that, go on, and you'll reveal my greatness.
Tiresias: Your great good fortune, true, it was your ruin.
Oedipus: Not if I saved the city—what do I care?
Tiresias: Well then, I'll be going.

    To his attendant.

                                      Take me home, boy.   505
Oedipus: Yes, take him away. You're a nuisance here.
    Out of the way, the irritation's gone.

    Turning his back on Tiresias, moving toward the palace.

Tiresias: I will go,
    once I have said what I came here to say.
    I'll never shrink from the anger in your eyes—
    you can't destroy me. Listen to me closely: 510
    the man you've sought so long, proclaiming,
    cursing up and down, the murderer of Laius—
    he is here. A stranger,
    you may think, who lives among you,
    he soon will be revealed a native Theban   515
    but he will take no joy in the revelation.
    Blind who now has eyes, beggar who now is rich,
    he will grope his way toward a foreign soil,
    a stick tapping before him step by step.

    Oedipus enters the palace.

    Revealed at last, brother and father both   520
    to the children he embraces, to his mother
    son and husband both—he sowed the loins
    his father sowed, he spilled his father's blood!

    Go in and reflect on that, solve that.
    And if you find I've lied   525
    from this day onward call the prophet blind.

    Tiresias and the boy exit to the side.

Chorus: Who—
    who is the man the voice of god denounces
    resounding out of the rocky gorge of Delphi?
        The horror too dark to tell,
    whose ruthless bloody hands have done the work?   530
    His time has come to fly

to outrace the stallions of the storm
                his feet a streak of speed —
Cased in armor, Apollo son of the Father
lunges on him, lightning-bolts afire!   535
And the grim unerring Furies°
                closing for the kill.
                                Look,
the word of god has just come blazing
flashing off Parnassus'° snowy heights!
        That man who left no trace —   540
after him, hunt him down with all our strength!
Now under bristling timber
        up through rocks and caves he stalks
                like the wild mountain bull —
cut off from men, each step an agony, frenzied, racing blind   545
but he cannot outrace the dread voices of Delphi
ringing out of the heart of Earth,
        the dark wings beating around him shrieking doom
                the doom that never dies, the terror —

The skilled prophet scans the birds and shatters me with terror! 550
I can't accept him, can't deny him, don't know what to say,
I'm lost, and the wings of dark foreboding beating —
I cannot see what's come, what's still to come . . .
and what could breed a blood feud between
        Laius' house and the son of Polybus?°   555
I know of nothing, not in the past and not now,
no charge to bring against our king, no cause
to attack his fame that rings throughout Thebes —
        not without proof — not for the ghost of Laius,
                not to avenge a murder gone without a trace.   560

Zeus and Apollo know, they know, the great masters
                of all the dark and depth of human life.
But whether a mere man can know the truth,
whether a seer can fathom more than I —
there is no test, no certain proof   565
                though matching skill for skill
a man can outstrip a rival. No, not till I see
these charges proved will I side with his accusers.
We saw him then, when the she-hawk° swept against him,
saw with our own eyes his skill, his brilliant triumph —   570
        there was the test — he was the joy of Thebes!
        Never will I convict my king, never in my heart.

Enter Creon from the side.

---

536 *Furies:* Three spirits who avenged evildoers.   539 *Parnassus:* A mountain in Greece associated with Apollo.   555 *Polybus:* The King of Corinth, who is thought to be Oedipus's father.   569 *she-hawk:* The Sphinx.

Creon: My fellow-citizens, I hear King Oedipus
  levels terrible charges at me. I had to come.
  I resent it deeply. If, in the present crisis,   575
  he thinks he suffers any abuse from me,
  anything I've done or said that offers him
  the slightest injury, why, I've no desire
  to linger out this life, my reputation a shambles.
  The damage I'd face from such an accusation   580
  is nothing simple. No, there's nothing worse:
  branded a traitor in the city, a traitor
  to all of you and my good friends.
Leader: True,
  but a slur might have been forced out of him,
  by anger perhaps, not any firm conviction.   585
Creon: The charge was made in public, wasn't it?
  I put the prophet up to spreading lies?
Leader: Such things were said . . .
  I don't know with what intent, if any.
Creon: Was his glance steady, his mind right   590
  when the charge was brought against me?
Leader: I really couldn't say. I never look
  to judge the ones in power.

  The doors open. Oedipus enters.

          Wait,
  here's Oedipus now.
Oedipus: You — here? You have the gall
  to show your face before the palace gates?
  You, plotting to kill me, kill the king —   595
  I see it all, the marauding thief himself
  scheming to steal my crown and power!
            Tell me,
  in god's name, what did you take me for,
  coward or fool, when you spun out your plot?   600
  Your treachery — you think I'd never detect it
  creeping against me in the dark? Or sensing it,
  not defend myself? Aren't you the fool,
  you and your high adventure. Lacking numbers,
  powerful friends, out for the big game of empire —   605
  you need riches, armies to bring that quarry down!
Creon: Are you quite finished? It's your turn to listen
  for just as long as you've . . . instructed me.
  Hear me out, then judge me on the facts.
Oedipus: You've a wicked way with words, Creon,   610
  but I'll be slow to learn — from you.
  I find you a menace, a great burden to me.
Creon: Just one thing, hear me out in this.
Oedipus: Just one thing,
  don't tell me you're not the enemy, the traitor.

Creon: Look, if you think crude, mindless stubbornness   615
    such a gift, you've lost your sense of balance.
Oedipus: If you think you can abuse a kinsman,
    then escape the penalty, you're insane.
Creon: Fair enough, I grant you. But this injury
    you say I've done you, what is it?   620
Oedipus: Did you induce me, yes or no,
    to send for that sanctimonious prophet?
Creon: I did. And I'd do the same again.
Oedipus: All right then, tell me, how long is it now
    since Laius . . .
Creon: Laius — what did *he* do?
Oedipus: Vanished,   625
    swept from sight, murdered in his tracks.
Creon: The count of the years would run you far back . . .
Oedipus: And that far back, was the prophet at his trade?
Creon: Skilled as he is today, and just as honored.
Oedipus: Did he ever refer to me then, at that time?
Creon: No,   630
    never, at least, when I was in his presence.
Oedipus: But you did investigate the murder, didn't you?
Creon: We did our best, of course, discovered nothing.
Oedipus: But the great seer never accused me then — why not?
Creon: I don't know. And when I don't, *I* keep quiet.   635
Oedipus: You do know this, you'd tell it too —
    if you had a shred of decency.
Creon: What?
    If I know, I won't hold back.
Oedipus: Simply this:
    if the two of you had never put heads together,
    we'd never have heard about *my* killing Laius.   640
Creon: If that's what he says . . . well, you know best.
    But now I have a right to learn from you
    as you just learned from me.
Oedipus: Learn your fill,
    you never will convict me of the murder.
Creon: Tell me, you're married to my sister, aren't you?   645
Oedipus: A genuine discovery — there's no denying that.
Creon: And you rule the land with her, with equal power?
Oedipus: She receives from me whatever she desires.
Creon: And I am the third, all of us are equals?
Oedipus: Yes, and it's there you show your stripes —   650
    you betray a kinsman.
Creon: Not at all.
    Not if you see things calmly, rationally,
    as I do. Look at it this way first:
    who in his right mind would rather rule
    and live in anxiety than sleep in peace?   655
    Particularly if he enjoys the same authority.

Not I, I'm not the man to yearn for kingship,
not with a king's power in my hands. Who would?
No one with any sense of self-control.
Now, as it is, you offer me all I need,   660
not a fear in the world. But if I wore the crown . . .
there'd be many painful duties to perform,
hardly to my taste.
                   How could kingship
please me more than influence, power
without a qualm? I'm not that deluded yet,   665
to reach for anything but privilege outright,
profit free and clear.
Now all men sing my praises, all salute me,
now all who request your favors curry mine.
I'm their best hope: success rests in me.   670
Why give up that, I ask you, and borrow trouble?
A man of sense, someone who sees things clearly
would never resort to treason.
No, I've no lust for conspiracy in me,
nor could I ever suffer one who does.   675

Do you want proof? Go to Delphi yourself,
examine the oracle and see if I've reported
the message word-for-word. This too:
if you detect that I and the clairvoyant
have plotted anything in common, arrest me,   680
execute me. Not on the strength of one vote,
two in this case, mine as well as yours.
But don't convict me on sheer unverified surmise.

How wrong it is to take the good for bad,
purely at random, or take the bad for good.   685
But reject a friend, a kinsman? I would as soon
tear out the life within us, priceless life itself.
You'll learn this well, without fail, in time.
Time alone can bring the just man to light;
the criminal you can spot in one short day.

Leader: Good advice,   690
my lord, for anyone who wants to avoid disaster.
Those who jump to conclusions may be wrong.
Oedipus: When my enemy moves against me quickly,
plots in secret, I move quickly too, I must,
I plot and pay him back. Relax my guard a moment,   695
waiting his next move — he wins his objective,
I lose mine.
Creon: What do you want?
You want me banished?
Oedipus: No, I want you dead.
Creon: Just to show how ugly a grudge can . . .
Oedipus: So,
still stubborn? you don't think I'm serious?   700

Creon: I think you're insane.
Oedipus: Quite sane — in my behalf.
Creon: Not just as much in mine?
Oedipus: You — my mortal enemy?
Creon: What if you're wholly wrong?
Oedipus: No matter — I must rule.
Creon: Not if you rule unjustly.
Oedipus: Hear him, Thebes, my city!
Creon: My city too, not yours alone!   705
Leader: Please, my lords.

    Enter Jocasta from the palace.

               Look, Jocasta's coming,
and just in time too. With her help
you must put this fighting of yours to rest.
Jocasta: Have you no sense? Poor misguided men,
such shouting — why this public outburst?   710
Aren't you ashamed, with the land so sick,
to stir up private quarrels?

    To Oedipus.

Into the palace now. And Creon, you go home.
Why make such a furor over nothing?
Creon: My sister, it's dreadful . . . Oedipus, your husband,   715
he's bent on a choice of punishments for me,
banishment from the fatherland or death.
Oedipus: Precisely. I caught him in the act, Jocasta,
plotting, about to stab me in the back.
Creon: Never — curse me, let me die and be damned   720
if I've done you any wrong you charge me with.
Jocasta: Oh god, believe it, Oedipus,
honor the solemn oath he swears to heaven.
Do it for me, for the sake of all your people.

    The Chorus begins to chant.

Chorus: Believe it, be sensible   725
             give way, my king, I beg you!
Oedipus: What do you want from me, concessions?
Chorus: Respect him — he's been no fool in the past
and now he's strong with the oath he swears to god.
Oedipus: You know what you're asking?
Chorus: I do.
Oedipus: Then out with it!   730
Chorus: The man's your friend, your kin, he's under oath —
don't cast him out, disgraced
branded with guilt on the strength of hearsay only.
Oedipus: Know full well, if that's what you want
you want me dead or banished from the land.
Chorus: Never —   735
no, by the blazing Sun, first god of the heavens!
    Stripped of the gods, stripped of loved ones,

let me die by inches if that ever crossed my mind.
But the heart inside me sickens, dies as the land dies
and now on top of the old griefs you pile this,   740
your fury—both of you!

Oedipus: Then let him go,
even if it does lead to my ruin, my death
or my disgrace, driven from Thebes for life.
It's you, not him I pity—your words move me.
He, wherever he goes, my hate goes with him.   745

Creon: Look at you, sullen in yielding, brutal in your rage—
you'll go too far. It's perfect justice:
natures like yours are hardest on themselves.

Oedipus: Then leave me alone—get out!

Creon: I'm going.
You're wrong, so wrong. These men know I'm right.   750

Exit to the side. The Chorus turns to Jocasta.

Chorus: Why do you hesitate, my lady
       why not help him in?

Jocasta: Tell me what's happened first.

Chorus: Loose, ignorant talk started dark suspicions
and a sense of injustice cut deeply too.   755

Jocasta: On both sides?

Chorus: Oh yes.

Jocasta: What did they say?

Chorus: Enough, please, enough! The land's so racked already
or so it seems to me . . .
End the trouble here, just where they left it.

Oedipus: You see what comes of your good intentions now?   760
And all because you tried to blunt my anger.

Chorus: My king,
I've said it once, I'll say it time and again—
   I'd be insane, you know it,
senseless, ever to turn my back on you.
You who set our beloved land—storm-tossed, shattered—   765
straight on course. Now again, good helmsman,
steer us through the storm!

The Chorus draws away, leaving Oedipus and Jocasta side by side.

Jocasta: For the love of god,
Oedipus, tell me too, what is it?
Why this rage? You're so unbending.

Oedipus: I will tell you. I respect you, Jocasta,   770
much more than these . . .

Glancing at the Chorus.

Creon's to blame, Creon schemes against me.

Jocasta: Tell me clearly, how did the quarrel start?

Oedipus: He says *I* murdered Laius—I am guilty.

Jocasta: How does he know? Some secret knowledge 775
    or simple hearsay?
Oedipus: Oh, he sent his prophet in
    to do his dirty work. You know Creon,
    Creon keeps his own lips clean.
Jocasta: A prophet?
    Well then, free yourself of every charge!
    Listen to me and learn some peace of mind: 780
    no skill in the world,
    nothing human can penetrate the future.
    Here is proof, quick and to the point.
    An oracle came to Laius one fine day
    (I won't say from Apollo himself 785
    but his underlings, his priests) and it said
    that doom would strike him down at the hands of a son,
    our son, to be born of our own flesh and blood. But Laius,
    so the report goes at least, was killed by strangers,
    thieves, at a place where three roads meet . . . my son — 790
    he wasn't three days old and the boy's father
    fastened his ankles, had a henchman fling him away
    on a barren, trackless mountain.
                     There, you see?
    Apollo brought neither thing to pass. My baby
    no more murdered his father than Laius suffered — 795
    his wildest fear — death at his own son's hands.
    That's how the seers and their revelations
    mapped out the future. Brush them from your mind.
    Whatever the god needs and seeks
    he'll bring to light himself, with ease.
Oedipus: Strange, 800
    hearing you just now . . . my mind wandered,
    my thoughts racing back and forth.
Jocasta: What do you mean? Why so anxious, startled?
Oedipus: I thought I heard you say that Laius
    was cut down at a place where three roads meet. 805
Jocasta: That was the story. It hasn't died out yet.
Oedipus: Where did this thing happen? Be precise.
Jocasta: A place called Phocis, where two branching roads,
    one from Daulia, one from Delphi,
    come together — a crossroads. 810
Oedipus: When? How long ago?
Jocasta: The heralds no sooner reported Laius dead
    than you appeared and they hailed you king of Thebes.
Oedipus: My god, my god — what have you planned to do to me?
Jocasta: What, Oedipus? What haunts you so?
Oedipus: Not yet. 815
    Laius — how did he look? Describe him.
    Had he reached his prime?
Jocasta: He was swarthy,
    and the gray had just begun to streak his temples,
    and his build . . . wasn't far from yours.

Oedipus: Oh no no,
    I think I've just called down a dreadful curse   820
    upon myself — I simply didn't know!
Jocasta: What are you saying? I shudder to look at you.
Oedipus: I have a terrible fear the blind seer can see.
    I'll know in a moment. One thing more —
Jocasta: Anything,
    afraid as I am — ask, I'll answer, all I can.   825
Oedipus: Did he go with a light or heavy escort,
    several men-at-arms, like a lord, a king?
Jocasta: There were five in the party, a herald among them,
    and a single wagon carrying Laius.
Oedipus: Ai —
    now I can see it all, clear as day.   830
    Who told you all this at the time, Jocasta?
Jocasta: A servant who reached home, the lone survivor.
Oedipus: So, could he still be in the palace — even now?
Jocasta: No indeed. Soon as he returned from the scene
    and saw you on the throne with Laius dead and gone,   835
    he knelt and clutched my hand, pleading with me
    to send him into the hinterlands, to pasture,
    far as possible, out of sight of Thebes.
    I sent him away. Slave though he was,
    he'd earned that favor — and much more.   840
Oedipus: Can we bring him back, quickly?
Jocasta: Easily. Why do you want him so?
Oedipus: I'm afraid,
    Jocasta, I have said too much already.
    That man — I've got to see him.
Jocasta: Then he'll come.
    But even I have a right, I'd like to think,   845
    to know what's torturing you, my lord.
Oedipus: And so you shall — I can hold nothing back from you,
    now I've reached this pitch of dark foreboding.
    Who means more to me than you? Tell me,
    whom would I turn toward but you   850
    as I go through all this?

    My father was Polybus, king of Corinth.
    My mother, a Dorian, Merope. And I was held
    the prince of the realm among the people there,
    till something struck me out of nowhere,   855
    something strange . . . worth remarking perhaps,
    hardly worth the anxiety I gave it.
    Some man at a banquet who had drunk too much
    shouted out — he was far gone, mind you —
    that I am not my father's son. Fighting words!   860
    I barely restrained myself that day
    but early the next I went to mother and father,
    questioned them closely, and they were enraged

at the accusation and the fool who let it fly.
So as for my parents I was satisfied,   865
but still this thing kept gnawing at me,
the slander spread — I had to make my move.
                                        And so,
unknown to mother and father I set out for Delphi,
and the god Apollo spurned me, sent me away
denied the facts I came for,   870
but first he flashed before my eyes a future
great with pain, terror, disaster — I can hear him cry,
"You are fated to couple with your mother, you will bring
a breed of children into the light no man can bear to see —
you will kill your father, the one who gave you life!"   875
I heard all that and ran. I abandoned Corinth,
from that day on I gauged its landfall only
by the stars, running, always running
toward some place where I would never see
the shame of all those oracles come true.   880
And as I fled I reached that very spot
where the great king, you say, met his death.
Now, Jocasta, I will tell you all.
Making my way toward this triple crossroad
I began to see a herald, then a brace of colts   885
drawing a wagon, and mounted on the bench . . . a man,
just as you've described him, coming face-to-face,
and the one in the lead and the old man himself
were about to thrust me off the road — brute force —
and the one shouldering me aside, the driver,   890
I strike him in anger! — and the old man, watching me
coming up along his wheels — he brings down
his prod, two prongs straight at my head!
I paid him back with interest!
Short work, by god — with one blow of the staff   895
in this right hand I knock him out of his high seat,
roll him out of the wagon, sprawling headlong —
I killed them all — every mother's son!

Oh, but if there is any blood-tie
between Laius and this stranger . . .   900
what man alive more miserable than I?
More hated by the gods? *I* am the man
no alien, no citizen welcomes to his house,
law forbids it — not a word to me in public,
driven out of every hearth and home.   905
And all these curses I — no one but I
brought down these piling curses on myself!
And you, his wife, I've touched your body with these,
the hands that killed your husband cover you with blood.

Wasn't I born for torment? Look me in the eyes!   910
I am abomination — heart and soul!

I must be exiled, and even in exile
never see my parents, never set foot
on native earth again. Else I'm doomed
to couple with my mother and cut my father down . . .   915
Polybus who reared me, gave me life.

                                      But why, why?
Wouldn't a man of judgment say — and wouldn't he be right —
some savage power has brought this down upon my head?

Oh no, not that, you pure and awesome gods,
never let me see that day! Let me slip   920
from the world of men, vanish without a trace
before I see myself stained with such corruption,
stained to the heart.

Leader: My lord, you fill our hearts with fear.
But at least until you question the witness,   925
do take hope.

Oedipus: Exactly. He is my last hope —
I'm waiting for the shepherd. He is crucial.

Jocasta: And once he appears, what then? Why so urgent?

Oedipus: I'll tell you. If it turns out that his story
matches yours, I've escaped the worst.   930

Jocasta: What did I say? What struck you so?

Oedipus: You said *thieves* —
he told you a whole band of them murdered Laius.
So, if he still holds to the same number,
I cannot be the killer. One can't equal many.
But if he refers to one man, one alone,   935
clearly the scales come down on me:
I am guilty.

Jocasta: Impossible. Trust me,
I told you precisely what he said,
and he can't retract it now;
the whole city heard it, not just I.   940
And even if he should vary his first report
by one man more or less, still, my lord,
he could never make the murder of Laius
truly fit the prophecy. Apollo was explicit:
my son was doomed to kill my husband . . . my son,   945
poor defenseless thing, he never had a chance
to kill his father. They destroyed him first.

So much for prophecy. It's neither here nor there.
From this day on, I wouldn't look right or left.

Oedipus: True, true. Still, that shepherd,   950
someone fetch him — now!

Jocasta: I'll send at once. But do let's go inside.
I'd never displease you, least of all in this.

    Oedipus and Jocasta enter the palace.

Chorus: Destiny guide me always
       Destiny find me filled with reverence   955

pure in word and deed.
Great laws tower above us, reared on high
born for the brilliant vault of heaven —
    Olympian sky their only father,
nothing mortal, no man gave them birth,   960
their memory deathless, never lost in sleep:
within them lives a mighty god, the god does not grow old.

Pride breeds the tyrant
violent pride, gorging, crammed to bursting
    with all that is overripe and rich with ruin —   965
clawing up to the heights, headlong pride
crashes down the abyss — sheer doom!
    No footing helps, all foothold lost and gone,
But the healthy strife that makes the city strong —
I pray that god will never end that wrestling: 970
god, my champion, I will never let you go.

But if any man comes striding, high and mighty
    in all he says and does,
no fear of justice, no reverence
for the temples of the gods —   975
    let a rough doom tear him down,
repay his pride, breakneck, ruinous pride!
If he cannot reap his profits fairly
    cannot restrain himself from outrage —
mad, laying hands on the holy things untouchable!   980

        Can such a man, so desperate, still boast
        he can save his life from the flashing bolts of god?
        If all such violence goes with honor now
          why join the sacred dance?

Never again will I go reverent to Delphi,   985
    the inviolate heart of Earth
or Apollo's ancient oracle at Abae
or Olympia of the fires —
    unless these prophecies all come true
for all mankind to point toward in wonder.   990
King of kings, if you deserve your titles
    Zeus, remember, never forget!
You and your deathless, everlasting reign.

        They are dying, the old oracles sent to Laius,
        now our masters strike them off the rolls.   995
        Nowhere Apollo's golden glory now —
          the gods, the gods go down.

Enter Jocasta from the palace, carrying a suppliant's branch wound in wool.

Jocasta: Lords of the realm, it occurred to me,
just now, to visit the temples of the gods,
so I have my branch in hand and incense too.   1000

Oedipus is beside himself. Racked with anguish,
no longer a man of sense, he won't admit
the latest prophecies are hollow as the old—
he's at the mercy of every passing voice
if the voice tells of terror.   1005
I urge him gently, nothing seems to help,
so I turn to you, Apollo, you are nearest.

*Placing her branch on the altar, while an old herdsman enters from the side, not
the one just summoned by the king but an unexpected messenger from Corinth.*

I come with prayers and offerings . . . I beg you,
cleanse us, set us free of defilement!
Look at us, passengers in the grip of fear,   1010
watching the pilot of the vessel go to pieces.

Messenger:

Approaching Jocasta and the Chorus.

Strangers, please, I wonder if you could lead us
to the palace of the king . . . I think it's Oedipus.
Better, the man himself—you know where he is?
Leader: This is his palace, stranger. He's inside.   1015
But here is his queen, his wife and mother
of his children.
Messenger: Blessings on you, noble queen,
queen of Oedipus crowned with all your family—
blessings on you always!
Jocasta: And the same to you, stranger, you deserve it . . .   1020
such a greeting. But what have you come for?
Have you brought us news?
Messenger: Wonderful news—
for the house, my lady, for your husband too.
Jocasta: Really, what? Who sent you?
Messenger: Corinth.
I'll give you the message in a moment.   1025
You'll be glad of it—how could you help it?—
though it costs a little sorrow in the bargain.
Jocasta: What can it be, with such a double edge?
Messenger: The people there, they want to make your Oedipus
king of Corinth, so they're saying now.   1030
Jocasta: Why? Isn't old Polybus still in power?
Messenger: No more. Death has got him in the tomb.
Jocasta: What are you saying? Polybus, dead?—dead?
Messenger: If not,
if I'm not telling the truth, strike me dead too.
Jocasta:

To a servant.

Quickly, go to your master, tell him this!   1035

You prophecies of the gods, where are you now?
This is the man that Oedipus feared for years,

he fled him, not to kill him—and now he's dead,
quite by chance, a normal, natural death,
not murdered by his son.

Oedipus:

Emerging from the palace.

                        Dearest,   1040
what now? Why call me from the palace?

Jocasta:

Bringing the Messenger closer.

Listen to *him,* see for yourself what all
those awful prophecies of god have come to.

Oedipus: And who is he? What can he have for me?

Jocasta: He's from Corinth, he's come to tell you   1045
your father is no more—Polybus—he's dead!

Oedipus:

Wheeling on the Messenger.

What? Let me have it from your lips.

Messenger: Well,
if that's what you want first, then here it is:
make no mistake, Polybus is dead and gone.

Oedipus: How—murder? sickness?—what? what killed him? 1050

Messenger: A light tip of the scales can put old bones to rest.

Oedipus: Sickness then—poor man, it wore him down.

Messenger: That,
and the long count of years he'd measured out.

Oedipus: So!
Jocasta, why, why look to the Prophet's hearth,
the fires of the future? Why scan the birds   1055
that scream above our heads? They winged me on
to the murder of my father, did they? That was my doom?
Well look, he's dead and buried, hidden under the earth,
and here I am in Thebes, I never put hand to sword—
unless some longing for me wasted him away,   1060
then in a sense you'd say I caused his death.
But now, all those prophecies I feared—Polybus
packs them off to sleep with him in hell!
They're nothing, worthless.

Jocasta: There.
Didn't I tell you from the start?   1065

Oedipus: So you did. I was lost in fear.

Jocasta: No more, sweep it from your mind forever.

Oedipus: But my mother's bed, surely I must fear—

Jocasta: Fear?
What should a man fear? It's all chance,
chance rules our lives. Not a man on earth   1070
can see a day ahead, groping through the dark.
Better to live at random, best we can.
And as for this marriage with your mother—

have no fear. Many a man before you,
in his dreams, has shared his mother's bed.   1075
Take such things for shadows, nothing at all —
Live, Oedipus,
as if there's no tomorrow!

Oedipus: Brave words,
and you'd persuade me if mother weren't alive.
But mother lives, so for all your reassurances   1080
I live in fear, I must.

Jocasta: But your father's death,
that, at least, is a great blessing, joy to the eyes!

Oedipus: Great, I know . . . but I fear *her* — she's still alive.

Messenger: Wait, who is this woman, makes you so afraid?

Oedipus: Merope, old man. The wife of Polybus.   1085

Messenger: The queen? What's there to fear in her?

Oedipus: A dreadful prophecy, stranger, sent by the gods.

Messenger: Tell me, could you? Unless it's forbidden
other ears to hear.

Oedipus: Not at all.
Apollo told me once — it is my fate —   1090
I must make love with my own mother,
shed my father's blood with my own hands.
So for years I've given Corinth a wide berth,
and it's been my good fortune too. But still,
to see one's parents and look into their eyes   1095
is the greatest joy I know.

Messenger: You're afraid of that?
That kept you out of Corinth?

Oedipus: My *father*, old man —
so I wouldn't kill my father.

Messenger: So that's it.
Well then, seeing I came with such good will, my king,
why don't I rid you of that old worry now?   1100

Oedipus: What a rich reward you'd have for that.

Messenger: What do you think I came for, majesty?
So you'd come home and I'd be better off.

Oedipus: Never, I will never go near my parents.

Messenger: My boy, it's clear, you don't know what you're doing.   1105

Oedipus: What do you mean, old man? For god's sake, explain.

Messenger: If you ran from *them*, always dodging home . . .

Oedipus: Always, terrified Apollo's oracle might come true —

Messenger: And you'd be covered with guilt, from both your parents.

Oedipus: That's right, old man, that fear is always with me.   1110

Messenger: Don't you know? You've really nothing to fear.

Oedipus: But why? If I'm their son — Merope, Polybus?

Messenger: Polybus was nothing to you, that's why, not in blood.

Oedipus: What are you saying — Polybus was not my father?

Messenger: No more than I am. He and I are equals.

Oedipus: My father —   1115
how can my father equal nothing? You're nothing to me!

Messenger: Neither was he, no more your father than I am.
Oedipus: Then why did he call me his son?
Messenger: You were a gift,
    years ago — know for a fact he took you
    from my hands.
Oedipus: No, from another's hands?   1120
    Then how could he love me so? He loved me, deeply . . .
Messenger: True, and his early years without a child
    made him love you all the more.
Oedipus: And you, did you . . .
    buy me? find me by accident?
Messenger: I stumbled on you,
    down the woody flanks of Mount Cithaeron.
Oedipus: So close,   1125
    what were you doing here, just passing through?
Messenger: Watching over my flocks, grazing them on the slopes.
Oedipus: A herdsman, were you? A vagabond, scraping for wages?
Messenger: Your savior too, my son, in your worst hour.
Oedipus: Oh —
    when you picked me up, was I in pain? What exactly?   1130
Messenger: Your ankles . . . they tell the story. Look at them.
Oedipus: Why remind me of that, that old affliction?
Messenger: Your ankles were pinned together; I set you free.
Oedipus: That dreadful mark — I've had it from the cradle.
Messenger: And you got your name from that misfortune too,   1135
    the name's still with you.
Oedipus: Dear god, who did it? —
    mother? father? Tell me.
Messenger: I don't know.
    The one who gave you to me, he'd know more.
Oedipus: What? You took me from someone else?
    You didn't find me yourself?
Messenger: No sir,   1140
    another shepherd passed you on to me.
Oedipus: Who? Do you know? Describe him.
Messenger: He called himself a servant of . . .
    if I remember rightly — Laius.

    Jocasta turns sharply.

Oedipus: The king of the land who ruled here long ago?   1145
Messenger: That's the one. That herdsman was *his* man.
Oedipus: Is he still alive? Can I see him?
Messenger: They'd know best, the people of these parts.

    Oedipus and the Messenger turn to the Chorus.

Oedipus: Does anyone know that herdsman,
    the one he mentioned? Anyone seen him   1150
    in the fields, in town? Out with it!
    The time has come to reveal this once for all.
Leader: I think he's the very shepherd you wanted to see,

a moment ago. But the queen, Jocasta,
she's the one to say.

Oedipus: Jocasta,   1155
you remember the man we just sent for?
Is *that* the one he means?

Jocasta: That man . . .
why ask? Old shepherd, talk, empty nonsense,
don't give it another thought, don't even think —

Oedipus: What — give up now, with a clue like this?   1160
Fail to solve the mystery of my birth?
Not for all the world!

Jocasta: Stop — in the name of god,
if you love your own life, call off this search!
My suffering is enough.

Oedipus: Courage!
Even if my mother turns out to be a slave,   1165
and I a slave, three generations back,
you would not seem common.

Jocasta: Oh no,
listen to me, I beg you, don't do this.

Oedipus: Listen to you? No more. I must know it all,
see the truth at last.

Jocasta: No, please —   1170
for your sake — I want the best for you!

Oedipus: Your best is more than I can bear.

Jocasta: You're doomed —
may you never fathom who you are!

Oedipus:

To a servant.

Hurry, fetch me the herdsman, now!
Leave her to glory in her royal birth.   1175

Jocasta: Aieeeeee —
         man of agony —
that is the only name I have for you,
that, no other — ever, ever, ever!

Flinging [herself] through the palace doors. A long, tense silence follows.

Leader: Where's she gone, Oedipus?
Rushing off, such wild grief . . .   1180
I'm afraid that from this silence
something monstrous may come bursting forth.

Oedipus: Let it burst! Whatever will, whatever must!
I must know my birth, no matter how common
it may be — must see my origins face-to-face.   1185
She perhaps, she with her woman's pride
may well be mortified by my birth,
but I, I count myself the son of Chance,
the great goddess, giver of all good things —
I'll never see myself disgraced. She is my mother!   1190
And the moons have marked me out, my blood-brothers,

one moon on the wane, the next moon great with power.
That is my blood, my nature — I will never betray it,
never fail to search and learn my birth!
Chorus: Yes — if I am a true prophet   1195
        if I can grasp the truth,
    by the boundless skies of Olympus,
at the full moon of tomorrow, Mount Cithaeron
you will know how Oedipus glories in you —
you, his birthplace, nurse, his mountain-mother!   1200
And we will sing you, dancing out your praise —
you lift our monarch's heart!
    Apollo, Apollo, god of the wild cry
            may our dancing please you!
                                        Oedipus —
            son, dear child, who bore you?   1205
Who of the nymphs who seem to live forever
mated with Pan,° the mountain-striding Father?
Who was your mother? who, some bride of Apollo
the god who loves the pastures spreading toward the sun?
        Or was it Hermes, king of the lightning ridges?   1210
Or Dionysus, lord of frenzy, lord of the barren peaks —
did he seize you in his hands, dearest of all his lucky finds? —
        found by the nymphs, their warm eyes dancing, gift
to the lord who loves them dancing out his joy!

Oedipus strains to see a figure coming from the distance. Attended by palace
guards, an old Shepherd enters slowly, reluctant to approach the king.

Oedipus: I never met the man, my friends . . . still,   1215
if I had to guess, I'd say that's the shepherd,
the very one we've looked for all along.
Brothers in old age, two of a kind,
he and our guest here. At any rate
the ones who bring him in are my own men,   1220
I recognize them.

Turning to the Leader.

                    But you know more than I,
you should, you've seen the man before.
Leader: I know him, definitely. One of Laius' men,
a trusty shepherd, if there ever was one.
Oedipus: You, I ask you first, stranger,   1225
you from Corinth — is this the one you mean?
Messenger: You're looking at him. He's your man.
Oedipus:

To the Shepherd.

You, old man, come over here —

1207 *Pan:* God of shepherds, who was, like Hermes and Dionysus, associated with the
wilderness.

look at me. Answer all my questions.
Did you ever serve King Laius?
Shepherd: So I did . . .   1230
a slave, not bought on the block though,
born and reared in the palace.
Oedipus: Your duties, your kind of work?
Shepherd: Herding the flocks, the better part of my life.
Oedipus: Where, mostly? Where did you do your grazing?
Shepherd: Well,   1235
Cithaeron sometimes, or the foothills round about.
Oedipus: This man—you know him? ever see him there?
Shepherd:

Confused, glancing from the Messenger to the King.

Doing what—what man do you mean?
Oedipus:

Pointing to the Messenger.

This one here—ever have dealings with him?
Shepherd: Not so I could say, but give me a chance,   1240
my memory's bad . . .
Messenger: No wonder he doesn't know me, master.
But let me refresh his memory for him.
I'm sure he recalls old times we had
on the slopes of Mount Cithaeron;   1245
he and I, grazing our flocks, he with two
and I with one—we both struck up together,
three whole seasons, six months at a stretch
from spring to the rising of Arcturus° in the fall,
then with winter coming on I'd drive my herds   1250
to my own pens, and back he'd go with his
to Laius' folds.

To the Shepherd.

                        Now that's how it was,
wasn't it—yes or no?
Shepherd: Yes, I suppose . . .
it's all so long ago.
Messenger: Come, tell me,
you gave me a child back then, a boy, remember?   1255
A little fellow to rear, my very own.
Shepherd: What? Why rake up that again?
Messenger: Look, here he is, my fine old friend—
the same man who was just a baby then.
Shepherd: Damn you, shut your mouth—quiet!   1260
Oedipus: Don't lash out at him, old man—
you need lashing more than he does.
Shepherd: Why,
master, majesty—what have I done wrong?

1249 *Arcturus:* A star whose rising marked the end of summer.

Oedipus: You won't answer his question about the boy.
Shepherd: He's talking nonsense, wasting his breath.   1265
Oedipus: So, you won't talk willingly—
    then you'll talk with pain.

The guards seize the Shepherd.

Shepherd: No, dear god, don't torture an old man!
Oedipus: Twist his arms back, quickly!
Shepherd: God help us, why?—
    what more do you need to know?   1270
Oedipus: Did you give him that child? He's asking.
Shepherd: I did . . . I wish to god I'd died that day.
Oedipus: You've got your wish if you don't tell the truth.
Shepherd: The more I tell, the worse the death I'll die.
Oedipus: Our friend here wants to stretch things out, does he?   1275

Motioning to his men for torture.

Shepherd: No, no, I gave it to him—I just said so.
Oedipus: Where did you get it? Your house? Someone else's?
Shepherd: It wasn't mine, no, I got it from . . . someone.
Oedipus: Which one of them?

Looking at the citizens.

                              Whose house?
Shepherd: No—
    god's sake, master, no more questions!   1280
Oedipus: You're a dead man if I have to ask again.
Shepherd: Then—the child came from the house . . .
    of Laius.
Oedipus: A slave? or born of his own blood?
Shepherd: Oh no,
    I'm right at the edge, the horrible truth—I've got to say it!   1285
Oedipus: And I'm at the edge of hearing horrors, yes, but I must hear!
Shepherd: All right! His son, they said it was—his son!
    But the one inside, your wife,
    she'd tell it best.
Oedipus: My wife—   1290
    she gave it to you?
Shepherd: Yes, yes, my king.
Oedipus: Why, what for?
Shepherd: To kill it.
Oedipus: Her own child,   1295
    how could she?
Shepherd: She was afraid—
    frightening prophecies.
Oedipus: What?
Shepherd: They said—
    he'd kill his parents.   1300
Oedipus: But you gave him to this old man—why?
Shepherd: I pitied the little baby, master,

hoped he'd take him off to his own country,
far away, but he saved him for this, this fate.
If you are the man he says you are, believe me, 1305
you were born for pain.

Oedipus: O god —
all come true, all burst to light!
O light — now let me look my last on you!
I stand revealed at last —
cursed in my birth, cursed in marriage, 1310
cursed in the lives I cut down with these hands!

*Rushing through the doors with a great cry. The Corinthian Messenger, the
Shepherd, and attendants exit slowly to the side.*

Chorus: O the generations of men
the dying generations — adding the total
of all your lives I find they come to nothing . . .
       does there exist, is there a man on earth 1315
who seizes more joy than just a dream, a vision?
And the vision no sooner dawns than dies
blazing into oblivion.

You are my great example, you, your life,
your destiny, Oedipus, man of misery — 1320
I count no man blest.

           You outranged all men!
       Bending your bow to the breaking-point
you captured priceless glory, O dear god,
and the Sphinx came crashing down,
        the virgin, claws hooked 1325
like a bird of omen singing, shrieking death —
like a fortress reared in the face of death
you rose and saved our land.

From that day on we called you king
we crowned you with honors, Oedipus, towering over all — 1330
mighty king of the seven gates of Thebes.

But now to hear your story — is there a man more agonized?
More wed to pain and frenzy? Not a man on earth,
the joy of your life ground down to nothing
O Oedipus, name for the ages — 1335
     one and the same wide harbor served you
           son and father both
son and father came to rest in the same bridal chamber.
How, how could the furrows your father plowed
bear you, your agony, harrowing on 1340
in silence O so long?
         But now for all your power
Time, all-seeing Time has dragged you to the light,
judged your marriage monstrous from the start —

the son and the father tangling, both one —
O child of Laius, would to god   1345
    I'd never seen you, never never!
        Now I weep like a man who wails the dead
and the dirge comes pouring forth with all my heart!
I tell you the truth, you gave me life
my breath leapt up in you   1350
and now you bring down night upon my eyes.

Enter a Messenger from the palace.

Messenger: Men of Thebes, always the first in honor,
    what horrors you will hear, what you will see,
    what a heavy weight of sorrow you will shoulder . . .
    if you are true to your birth, if you still have   1355
    some feeling for the royal house of Thebes.
    I tell you neither the waters of the Danube
    nor the Nile can wash this palace clean.
    Such things it hides, it soon will bring to light —
    terrible things, and none done blindly now,   1360
    all done with a will. The pains
    we inflict upon ourselves hurt most of all.
Leader: God knows we have pains enough already.
    What can you add to them?
Messenger: The queen is dead.
Leader: Poor lady — how?   1365
Messenger: By her own hand. But you are spared the worst,
    you never had to watch . . . I saw it all,
    and with all the memory that's in me
    you will learn what that poor woman suffered.

    Once she'd broken in through the gates,   1370
    dashing past us, frantic, whipped to fury,
    ripping her hair out with both hands —
    straight to her rooms she rushed, flinging herself
    across the bridal-bed, doors slamming behind her —
    once inside, she wailed for Laius, dead so long,   1375
    remembering how she bore his child long ago,
    the life that rose up to destroy him, leaving
    its mother to mother living creatures
    with the very son she'd borne.
    Oh how she wept, mourning the marriage-bed   1380
    where she let loose that double brood — monsters —
    husband by her husband, children by her child.
                                And then —
    but how she died is more than I can say. Suddenly
    Oedipus burst in, screaming, he stunned us so
    we couldn't watch her agony to the end,   1385
    our eyes were fixed on him. Circling
    like a maddened beast, stalking, here, there

crying out to us —
                    Give him a sword! His wife,
no wife, his mother, where can he find the mother earth
that cropped two crops at once, himself and all his children?   1390
He was raging — one of the dark powers pointing the way,
none of us mortals crowding around him, no,
with a great shattering cry — someone, something leading him on —
he hurled at the twin doors and bending the bolts back
out of their sockets, crashed through the chamber.   1395
And there we saw the woman hanging by the neck,
cradled high in a woven noose, spinning,
swinging back and forth. And when he saw her,
giving a low, wrenching sob that broke our hearts,
slipping the halter from her throat, he eased her down,   1400
in a slow embrace he laid her down, poor thing . . .
then, what came next, what horror we beheld!

He rips off her brooches, the long gold pins
holding her robes — and lifting them high,
looking straight up into the points,   1405
he digs them down the sockets of his eyes, crying, "You,
you'll see no more the pain I suffered, all the pain I caused!
Too long you looked on the ones you never should have seen,
blind to the ones you longed to see, to know! Blind
from this hour on! Blind in the darkness — blind!"   1410
His voice like a dirge, rising, over and over
raising the pins, raking them down his eyes.
And at each stroke blood spurts from the roots,
splashing his beard, a swirl of it, nerves and clots —
black hail of blood pulsing, gushing down.   1415

These are the griefs that burst upon them both,
coupling man and woman. The joy they had so lately,
the fortune of their old ancestral house
was deep joy indeed. Now, in this one day,
wailing, madness and doom, death, disgrace,   1420
all the griefs in the world that you can name,
all are theirs forever.

Leader: Oh poor man, the misery —
has he any rest from pain now?

A voice within, in torment.

Messenger: He's shouting,
"Loose the bolts, someone, show me to all of Thebes!
My father's murderer, my mother's —"   1425
No, I can't repeat it, it's unholy.
Now he'll tear himself from his native earth,
not linger, curse the house with his own curse.
But he needs strength, and a guide to lead him on.
This is sickness more than he can bear.

The palace doors open.

Look,   1430
he'll show you himself. The great doors are opening —
you are about to see a sight, a horror
even his mortal enemy would pity.

*Enter Oedipus, blinded, led by a boy. He stands at the palace steps, as if
surveying his people once again.*

Chorus: O the terror —
the suffering, for all the world to see,
the worst terror that ever met my eyes.   1435
What madness swept over you? What god,
what dark power leapt beyond all bounds,
beyond belief, to crush your wretched life? —
godforsaken, cursed by the gods!
I pity you but I can't bear to look.   1440
I've much to ask, so much to learn,
so much fascinates my eyes,
but you . . . I shudder at the sight.

Oedipus: Oh, Ohhh —
the agony! I am agony —
where am I going? where on earth?   1445
        where does all this agony hurl me?
where's my voice? —
        winging, swept away on a dark tide —
My destiny, my dark power, what a leap you made!

Chorus: To the depths of terror, too dark to hear, to see.   1450

Oedipus: Dark, horror of darkness
    my darkness, drowning, swirling around me
    crashing wave on wave — unspeakable, irresistible
                headwind, fatal harbor! Oh again,
    the misery, all at once, over and over   1455
    the stabbing daggers, stab of memory
raking me insane.

Chorus: No wonder you suffer
twice over, the pain of your wounds,
the lasting grief of pain.

Oedipus: Dear friend, still here?
    Standing by me, still with a care for me,   1460
    the blind man? Such compassion,
                loyal to the last. Oh it's you,
    I know you're here, dark as it is
    I'd know you anywhere, your voice —
it's yours, clearly yours.

Chorus: Dreadful, what you've done . . .   1465
how could you bear it, gouging out your eyes?
What superhuman power drove you on?

Oedipus: Apollo, friends, Apollo —
he ordained my agonies — these, my pains on pains!

But the hand that struck my eyes was mine,   1470
  mine alone — no one else —
         I did it all myself!
What good were eyes to me?
Nothing I could see could bring me joy.
Chorus: No, no, exactly as you say.
Oedipus: What can I ever see?   1475
     What love, what call of the heart
     can touch my ears with joy? Nothing, friends.
       Take me away, far, far from Thebes,
       quickly, cast me away, my friends —
this great murderous ruin, this man cursed to heaven,   1480
  the man the deathless gods hate most of all!
Chorus: Pitiful, you suffer so, you understand so much . . .
  I wish you'd never known.
Oedipus: Die, die —
  whoever he was that day in the wilds
who cut my ankles free of the ruthless pins,   1485
  he pulled me clear of death, he saved my life
  for this, this kindness —
              Curse him, kill him!
If I'd died then, I'd never have dragged myself,
  my loved ones through such hell.   1490
Chorus: Oh if only . . . would to god.
Oedipus: I'd never have come to this,
  my father's murderer — never been branded
mother's husband, all men see me now! Now,
  loathed by the gods, son of the mother I defiled
    coupling in my father's bed, spawning lives in the loins   1495
that spawned my wretched life. What grief can crown this grief?
             It's mine alone, my destiny — I am Oedipus!
Chorus: How can I say you've chosen for the best?
  Better to die than be alive and blind.
Oedipus: What I did was best — don't lecture me,   1500
  no more advice. I, with *my* eyes,
  how could I look my father in the eyes
  when I go down to death? Or mother, so abused . . .
  I've done such things to the two of them,
  crimes too huge for hanging.
                Worse yet,   1505
the sight of my children, born as they were born,
how could I long to look into their eyes?
No, not with these eyes of mine, never.
Not this city either, her high towers,
the sacred glittering images of her gods —   1510
I am misery! I, her best son, reared
as no other son of Thebes was ever reared,
I've stripped myself, I gave the command myself.
All men must cast away the great blasphemer,

the curse now brought to light by the gods,   1515
the son of Laius — I, my father's son!

Now I've exposed my guilt, horrendous guilt,
could I train a level glance on you, my countrymen?
Impossible! No, if I could just block off my ears,
the springs of hearing, I would stop at nothing —   1520
I'd wall up my loathsome body like a prison,
blind to the sound of life, not just the sight.
Oblivion — what a blessing . . .
for the mind to dwell a world away from pain.

O Cithaeron, why did you give me shelter?   1525
Why didn't you take me, crush my life out on the spot?
I'd never have revealed my birth to all mankind.

O Polybus, Corinth, the old house of my fathers,
so I believed — what a handsome prince you raised —
under the skin, what sickness to the core.   1530
Look at me! Born of outrage, outrage to the core.

O triple roads — it all comes back, the secret,
dark ravine, and the oaks closing in
where the three roads join . . .
You drank my father's blood, my own blood   1535
spilled by my own hands — you still remember me?
What things you saw me do? Then I came here
and did them all once more!
                   Marriages! O marriage,
you gave me birth, and once you brought me into the world
you brought my sperm rising back, springing to light   1540
fathers, brothers, sons — one deadly breed —
brides, wives, mothers. The blackest things
a man can do, I have done them all!
                   No more —
it's wrong to name what's wrong to do. Quickly,
for the love of god, hide me somewhere,   1545
kill me, hurl me into the sea
where you can never look on me again.

Beckoning to the Chorus as they shrink away.

                   Closer,
it's all right. Touch the man of sorrow.
Do. Don't be afraid. My troubles are mine
and I am the only man alive who can sustain them.   1550

Enter Creon from the palace, attended by palace guards.

Leader: Put your requests to Creon. Here he is,
    just when we need him. He'll have a plan, he'll act.
    Now that he's the sole defense of the country
    in your place.

Oedipus: Oh no, what can I say to him?
    How can I ever hope to win his trust?
    I wronged him so, just now, in every way.   1555
    You must see that — I was so wrong, so wrong.
Creon: I haven't come to mock you, Oedipus,
    or to criticize your former failings.

    Turning to the guards.

                     You there,
    have you lost all respect for human feeling?   1560
    At least revere the Sun, the holy fire
    that keeps us all alive. Never expose a thing
    of guilt and holy dread so great it appalls
    the earth, the rain from heaven, the light of day!
    Get him into the halls — quickly as you can.   1565
    Piety demands no less. Kindred alone
    should see a kinsman's shame. This is obscene.
Oedipus: Please, in god's name . . . you wipe my fears away,
    coming so generously to me, the worst of men.
    Do one thing more, for your sake, not mine.   1570
Creon: What do you want? Why so insistent?
Oedipus: Drive me out of the land at once, far from sight,
    where I can never hear a human voice.
Creon: I'd have done that already, I promise you.
    First I wanted the god to clarify my duties.   1575
Oedipus: The god? His command was clear, every word:
    death for the father-killer, the curse —
    he said destroy me!
Creon: So he did. Still, in such a crisis
    it's better to ask precisely what to do.   1580
Oedipus: You'd ask the oracle about a man like me?
Creon: By all means. And this time, I assume,
    even you will obey the god's decrees.
Oedipus: I will,
    I will. And you, I command you — I beg you . . .
    the woman inside, bury her as you see fit.   1585
    It's the only decent thing,
    to give your own the last rites. As for me,
    never condemn the city of my fathers
    to house my body, not while I'm alive, no,
    let me live on the mountains, on Cithaeron,   1590
    my favorite haunt, I have made it famous.
    Mother and father marked out that rock
    to be my everlasting tomb — buried alive.
    Let me die there, where they tried to kill me.
    Oh but this I know: no sickness can destroy me,   1595
    nothing can. I would never have been saved
    from death — I have been saved
    for something great and terrible, something strange.
    Well let my destiny come and take me on its way!

About my children, Creon, the boys at least,   1600
don't burden yourself. They're men;
wherever they go, they'll find the means to live.
But my two daughters, my poor helpless girls,
clustering at our table, never without me
hovering near them ... whatever I touched,   1605
they always had their share. Take care of them,
I beg you. Wait, better — permit me, would you?
Just to touch them with my hands and take
our fill of tears. Please ... my king.
Grant it, with all your noble heart.   1610
If I could hold them, just once, I'd think
I had them with me, like the early days
when I could see their eyes.

Antigone and Ismene, two small children, are led in from the palace by a nurse.

                      What's that?
O god! Do I really hear you sobbing? —
my two children. Creon, you've pitied me?   1615
Sent me my darling girls, my own flesh and blood!
Am I right?

Creon: Yes, it's my doing.
I know the joy they gave you all these years,
the joy you must feel now.

Oedipus: Bless you, Creon!
May god watch over you for this kindness,   1620
better than he ever guarded me.
                    Children, where are you?
Here, come quickly —

Groping for Antigone and Ismene, who approach their father cautiously, then embrace him.

                Come to these hands of mine,
your brother's hands, your own father's hands
that served his once bright eyes so well —
that made them blind. Seeing nothing, children,   1625
knowing nothing, I became your father,
I fathered you in the soil that gave me life.

How I weep for you — I cannot see you now ...
just thinking of all your days to come, the bitterness,
the life that rough mankind will thrust upon you.   1630
Where are the public gatherings you can join,
the banquets of the clans? Home you'll come,
in tears, cut off from the sight of it all,
the brilliant rites unfinished.
And when you reach perfection, ripe for marriage,   1635
who will he be, my dear ones? Risking all
to shoulder the curse that weighs down my parents,
yes and you too — that wounds us all together.
What more misery could you want?

Your father killed his father, sowed his mother,   1640
one, one and the selfsame womb sprang you—
he cropped the very roots of his existence.
Such disgrace, and you must bear it all!
Who will marry you then? Not a man on earth.
Your doom is clear: you'll wither away to nothing,   1645
single, without a child.

Turning to Creon.

                          Oh Creon,
you are the only father they have now . . .
we who brought them into the world
are gone, both gone at a stroke—
Don't let them go begging, abandoned,   1650
women without men. Your own flesh and blood!
Never bring them down to the level of my pains.
Pity them. Look at them, so young, so vulnerable,
shorn of everything—you're their only hope.
Promise me, noble Creon, touch my hand.   1655

Reaching toward Creon, who draws back.

You, little ones, if you were old enough
to understand, there is much I'd tell you.
Now, as it is, I'd have you say a prayer.
Pray for life, my children,
live where you are free to grow and season.   1660
Pray god you find a better life than mine,
the father who begot you.
Creon: Enough.
You've wept enough. Into the palace now.
Oedipus: I must, but I find it very hard.
Creon: Time is the great healer, you will see.   1665
Oedipus: I am going—you know on what condition?
Creon: Tell me. I'm listening.
Oedipus: Drive me out of Thebes, in exile.
Creon: Not I. Only the gods can give you that.
Oedipus: Surely the gods hate me so much—   1670
Creon: You'll get your wish at once.
Oedipus: You consent?
Creon: I try to say what I mean; it's my habit.
Oedipus: Then take me away. It's time.
Creon: Come along, let go of the children.
Oedipus: No—
don't take them away from me, not now! No no no!   1675

*Clutching his daughters as the guards wrench them loose and take them
through the palace doors.*

Creon: Still the king, the master of all things?
No more: here your power ends.
None of your power follows you through life.

Exit Oedipus and Creon to the palace. The Chorus comes forward to address the audience directly.

Chorus: People of Thebes, my countrymen, look on Oedipus.
He solved the famous riddle with his brilliance,   1680
he rose to power, a man beyond all power.
Who could behold his greatness without envy?
Now what a black sea of terror has overwhelmed him.
Now as we keep our watch and wait the final day,
count no man happy till he dies, free of pain at last.   1685

Exit in procession.

CONSIDERATIONS FOR CRITICAL THINKING AND WRITING

1. FIRST RESPONSE. Is it possible for a twentieth-century reader to identify with Oedipus's plight? What philosophic issues does he confront?

2. In the opening scene what does the priest's speech reveal about how Oedipus has been regarded as a ruler of Thebes?

3. What do Oedipus's confrontations with Tiresias and Creon indicate about his character?

4. Aristotle defined a tragic flaw as consisting of "error and frailties." What errors does Oedipus make? What are his frailties?

5. What causes Oedipus's downfall? Is he simply a pawn in a predetermined game played by the gods? Can he be regarded as responsible for the suffering and death in the play?

6. Locate instances of dramatic irony in the play. How do they serve as foreshadowings?

7. Describe the function of the Chorus. How does the Chorus's view of life and the gods differ from Jocasta's?

8. Trace the images of vision and blindness throughout the play. How are they related to the theme? Why does Oedipus blind himself instead of joining Jocasta in suicide?

9. What is your assessment of Oedipus at the end of the play? Was he foolish? Heroic? Fated? To what extent can your emotions concerning him be described as "pity and fear"?

10. CRITICAL STRATEGIES. Read the section on psychological criticism (pp. 2099–101) in Chapter 52, "Critical Strategies for Reading," and Sigmund Freud "On the Oedipus Complex" (p. 1371). Given that the *Oedipus complex* is a well-known term used in psychoanalysis, what does it mean? Does the concept offer any insights into the conflicts dramatized in the play?

CONNECTIONS TO OTHER SELECTIONS

1. Consider the endings of *Oedipus the King* and Shakespeare's *Hamlet* (p. 1450). What feelings do you have about these endings? Are they irredeemably unhappy? Is there anything that suggests hope for the future at the ends of these plays?

2. Sophocles does not include violence in his plays; any bloodshed occurs offstage. Compare and contrast the effects of this strategy with the use of violence in *Hamlet* (p. 1450).

3. Write an essay explaining why *Oedipus the King* cannot be considered a realistic play in the way that Henrik Ibsen's *A Doll House* (p. 1568) can be.

Antigone

Antigone was actually written before Sophocles' other two plays about Oedipus and his family. *Oedipus the King* ends with Oedipus, the king of Thebes, blinding himself because he has unknowingly murdered his father and married his mother, Jocasta. Creon, his brother-in-law, becomes the ruler of Thebes and is entrusted with caring for Oedipus's two daughters, Antigone and Ismene. *Oedipus at Colonus* continues the story some twenty years later. Oedipus has been rejected by his two sons, Polynices and Eteocles, and wanders in exile, cared for by Antigone. Meanwhile, his sons struggle for power in Thebes. Polynices travels to Argos to gather a force to attack his brother as Oedipus arrives in Colonus, near Athens. There Oedipus curses his sons for their ruthless selfishness and predicts their violent deaths. Oedipus, however, dies in peace, with dignity, and bestows a blessing on Athens.

Antigone begins after the two brothers have killed each other in battle. The throne of Thebes subsequently returns to Creon, who decrees that Polynices was traitorous and therefore must not be buried. As the play opens, Antigone tells her sister that she will defy Creon's ruling, even though the penalty for disobedience is death.

Antigone's insistence on obeying the law of the gods instead of civil laws dramatizes a conflict that continues to move audiences and readers who ponder the relation of the individual's conscience to the demands of the state. One manifestation of this concern in the twentieth century is Jean Anouilh's 1944 production of *Antigone* in Paris, when that city was occupied by German troops during World War II. Anouilh's Antigone reflects the French resistance movement, and his Creon is a representative of German authority who must preserve order in the face of unyielding opposition. (A brief excerpt of this play appears on p. 1376.) Sophocles' play — as does Anouilh's — presents an agonizing dilemma. Neither Antigone nor Creon is wholly virtuous or blameless, so the complexities they embody remain a moral and intellectual challenge.

SOPHOCLES (496?–406 B.C.)

Antigone

c. 441 B.C.

TRANSLATED BY ROBERT FAGLES

CHARACTERS

Antigone, daughter of Oedipus and Jocasta
Ismene, sister of Antigone
A *Chorus* of old Theban citizens and their *Leader*
Creon, king of Thebes, uncle of Antigone and Ismene
A *Sentry*
Haemon, son of Creon and Eurydice
Tiresias, a blind prophet
A *Messenger*
Eurydice, wife of Creon
Guards, attendants, and a boy

TIME AND SCENE: *The royal house of Thebes. It is still night, and the invading armies of Argos have just been driven from the city. Fighting on opposite sides, the sons of Oedipus, Eteocles and Polynices, have killed each other in combat. Their uncle, Creon, is now king of Thebes.*

Enter Antigone, slipping through the central doors of the palace. She motions to her sister, Ismene, who follows her cautiously toward an altar at the center of the stage.

Antigone: My own flesh and blood—dear sister, dear Ismene,
how many griefs our father Oedipus handed down!
Do you know one, I ask you, one grief
that Zeus° will not perfect for the two of us
while we still live and breathe? There's nothing,   5
no pain—our lives are pain—no private shame,
no public disgrace, nothing I haven't seen
in your griefs and mine. And now this:
an emergency decree, they say, the Commander
has just declared for all of Thebes.   10
What, haven't you heard? Don't you see?
The doom reserved for enemies
marches on the ones we love the most.
Ismene: Not I, I haven't heard a word, Antigone.
Nothing of loved ones,   15
no joy or pain has come my way, not since
the two of us were robbed of our two brothers,
both gone in a day, a double blow—
not since the armies of Argos vanished,
just this very night. I know nothing more,   20
whether our luck's improved or ruin's still to come.

4 *Zeus:* The highest Olympian deity.

Antigone: I thought so. That's why I brought you out here,
  past the gates, so you could hear in private.
Ismene: What's the matter? Trouble, clearly . . .
  you sound so dark, so grim. 25
Antigone: Why not? Our own brothers' burial!
  Hasn't Creon graced one with all the rites,
  disgraced the other? Eteocles, they say,
  has been given full military honors,
  rightly so — Creon's laid him in the earth 30
  and he goes with glory down among the dead.
  But the body of Polynices, who died miserably —
  why, a city-wide proclamation, rumor has it,
  forbids anyone to bury him, even mourn him.
  He's to be left unwept, unburied, a lovely treasure 35
  for birds that scan the field and feast to their heart's content.

  Such, I hear, is the martial law our good Creon
  lays down for you and me — yes, me, I tell you —
  and he's coming here to alert the uninformed
  in no uncertain terms, 40
  and he won't treat the matter lightly. Whoever
  disobeys in the least will die, his doom is sealed:
  stoning to death inside the city walls!

  There you have it. You'll soon show what you are,
  worth your breeding, Ismene, or a coward — 45
  for all your royal blood.
Ismene: My poor sister, if things have come to this,
  who am I to make or mend them, tell me,
  what good am I to you?
Antigone: Decide.
  Will you share the labor, share the work? 50
Ismene: What work, what's the risk? What do you mean?
Antigone:

  Raising her hands.

  Will you lift up his body with these bare hands
  and lower it with me?
Ismene: What? You'd bury him —
  when a law forbids the city?
Antigone: Yes!
  He is my brother and — deny it as you will — 55
  your brother too.
  No one will ever convict me for a traitor.
Ismene: So desperate, and Creon has expressly —
Antigone: No,
  he has no right to keep me from my own.
Ismene: Oh my sister, think — 60
  think how our own father died, hated,
  his reputation in ruins, driven on
  by the crimes he brought to light himself

to gouge out his eyes with his own hands —
then mother . . . his mother and wife, both in one,   65
mutilating her life in the twisted noose —
and last, our two brothers dead in a single day,
both shedding their own blood, poor suffering boys,
battling out their common destiny hand-to-hand.

Now look at the two of us, left so alone . . .   70
think what a death we'll die, the worst of all
if we violate the laws and override
the fixed decree of the throne, its power —
we must be sensible. Remember we are women,
we're not born to contend with men. Then too,   75
we're underlings, ruled by much stronger hands,
so we must submit in this, and things still worse.

I, for one, I'll beg the dead to forgive me —
I'm forced, I have no choice — I must obey
the ones who stand in power. Why rush to extremes?   80
It's madness, madness.

Antigone: I won't insist,
no, even if you should have a change of heart,
I'd never welcome you in the labor, not with me.
So, do as you like, whatever suits you best —
I'll bury him myself.   85
And even if I die in the act, that death will be a glory.
I'll lie with the one I love and loved by him —
an outrage sacred to the gods! I have longer
to please the dead than please the living here:
in the kingdom down below I'll lie forever.   90
Do as you like, dishonor the laws
the gods hold in honor.

Ismene: I'd do them no dishonor . . .
but defy the city? I have no strength for that.

Antigone: You have your excuses. I am on my way,
I'll raise a mound for him, for my dear brother.   95

Ismene: Oh Antigone, you're so rash — I'm so afraid for you!

Antigone: Don't fear for me. Set your own life in order.

Ismene: Then don't, at least, blurt this out to anyone.
Keep it a secret. I'll join you in that, I promise.

Antigone: Dear god, shout it from the rooftops. I'll hate you   100
all the more for silence — tell the world!

Ismene: So fiery — and it ought to chill your heart.

Antigone: I know I please where I must please the most.

Ismene: Yes, if you can, but you're in love with impossibility.

Antigone: Very well then, once my strength gives out   105
I will be done at last.

Ismene: You're wrong from the start,
you're off on a hopeless quest.

Antigone: If you say so, you will make me hate you,
and the hatred of the dead, by all rights,

will haunt you night and day.   110
But leave me to my own absurdity, leave me
to suffer this — dreadful thing. I'll suffer
nothing as great as death without glory.

Exit to the side.

Ismene: Then go if you must, but rest assured,
wild, irrational as you are, my sister,   115
you are truly dear to the ones who love you.

*Withdrawing to the palace. Enter a Chorus, the old citizens of Thebes,
chanting as the sun begins to rise.*

Chorus: Glory! — great beam of sun, brightest of all
that ever rose on the seven gates of Thebes,
     you burn through night at last!
        Great eye of the golden day,   120
mounting the Dirce's° banks you throw him back —
the enemy out of Argos, the white shield, the man of bronze —
he's flying headlong now
        the bridle of fate stampeding him with pain!

    And he had driven against our borders,   125
    launched by the warring claims of Polynices —
    like an eagle screaming, winging havoc
    over the land, wings of armor
    shielded white as snow,
    a huge army massing,   130
    crested helmets bristling for assault.

He hovered above our roofs, his vast maw gaping
closing down around our seven gates,
     his spears thirsting for the kill
             but now he's gone, look,   135
before he could glut his jaws with Theban blood
or the god of fire put our crown of towers to the torch.
He grappled the Dragon none can master — Thebes —
     the clang of our arms like thunder at his back!

    Zeus hates with a vengeance all bravado,   140
    the mighty boasts of men. He watched them
    coming on in a rising flood, the pride
    of their golden armor ringing shrill —
    and brandishing his lightning
    blasted the fighter just at the goal,   145
    rushing to shout his triumph from our walls.

Down from the heights he crashed, pounding down on the earth!
And a moment ago, blazing torch in hand —
     mad for attack, ecstatic
    he breathed his rage, the storm   150

121 *the Dirce:* A river near Thebes.

of his fury hurling at our heads!
But now his high hopes have laid him low
and down the enemy ranks the iron god of war
    deals his rewards, his stunning blows — Ares°
    rapture of battle, our right arm in the crisis.   155

    Seven captains marshaled at seven gates
    seven against their equals, gave
    their brazen trophies up to Zeus,
    god of the breaking rout of battle,
    all but two: those blood brothers,   160
    one father, one mother — matched in rage,
    spears matched for the twin conquest —
    clashed and won the common prize of death.

But now for Victory! Glorious in the morning,
joy in her eyes to meet our joy   165
    she is winging down to Thebes,
our fleets of chariots wheeling in her wake —
    Now let us win oblivion from the wars,
thronging the temples of the gods
in singing, dancing choirs through the night!   170
    Lord Dionysus,° god of the dance
    that shakes the land of Thebes, now lead the way!

Enter Creon from the palace, attended by his guard.

    But look, the king of the realm is coming,
    Creon, the new man for the new day,
    whatever the gods are sending now . . .   175
    what new plan will he launch?
    Why this, this special session?
    Why this sudden call to the old men
    summoned at one command?

Creon: My countrymen,
the ship of state is safe. The gods who rocked her,   180
after a long, merciless pounding in the storm,
have righted her once more.
                         Out of the whole city
I have called you here alone. Well I know,
first, your undeviating respect
for the throne and royal power of King Laius.   185
Next, while Oedipus steered the land of Thebes,
and even after he died, your loyalty was unshakable,
you still stood by their children. Now then,
since the two sons are dead — two blows of fate
in the same day, cut down by each other's hands,   190
both killers, both brothers stained with blood —

---

154 *Ares:* God of war.   171 *Dionysus:* God of fertility and wine.

as I am next in kin to the dead,
I now possess the throne and all its powers.

Of course you cannot know a man completely,
his character, his principles, sense of judgment,   195
not till he's shown his colors, ruling the people,
making laws. Experience, there's the test.
As I see it, whoever assumes the task,
the awesome task of setting the city's course,
and refuses to adopt the soundest policies   200
but fearing someone, keeps his lips locked tight,
he's utterly worthless. So I rate him now,
I always have. And whoever places a friend
above the good of his own country, he is nothing:
I have no use for him. Zeus my witness,   205
Zeus who sees all things, always—
I could never stand by silent, watching destruction
march against our city, putting safety to rout,
nor could I ever make that man a friend of mine
who menaces our country. Remember this: 210
our country *is* our safety.
Only while she voyages true on course
can we establish friendships, truer than blood itself.
Such are my standards. They make our city great.

Closely akin to them I have proclaimed,   215
just now, the following decree to our people
concerning the two sons of Oedipus.
Eteocles, who died fighting for Thebes,
excelling all in arms: he shall be buried,
crowned with a hero's honors, the cups we pour   220
to soak the earth and reach the famous dead.

But as for his blood brother, Polynices,
who returned from exile, home to his father-city
and the gods of his race, consumed with one desire—
to burn them roof to roots—who thirsted to drink   225
his kinsmen's blood and sell the rest to slavery:
that man—a proclamation has forbidden the city
to dignify him with burial, mourn him at all.
No, he must be left unburied, his corpse
carrion for the birds and dogs to tear,   230
an obscenity for the citizens to behold!

These are my principles. Never at my hands
will the traitor be honored above the patriot.
But whoever proves his loyalty to the state:
I'll prize that man in death as well as life.   235
Leader: If this is your pleasure, Creon, treating
   our city's enemy and our friend this way . . .
   The power is yours, I suppose, to enforce it

with the laws, both for the dead and all of us,
  the living.

Creon: Follow my orders closely then,   240
  be on your guard.

Leader: We're too old.
  Lay that burden on younger shoulders.

Creon: No, no,
  I don't mean the body—I've posted guards already.

Leader: What commands for us then? What other service?

Creon: See that you never side with those who break my orders.   245

Leader: Never. Only a fool could be in love with death.

Creon: Death is the price—you're right. But all too often
  the mere hope of money has ruined many men.

A Sentry enters from the side.

Sentry: My lord,
  I can't say I'm winded from running, or set out
  with any spring in my legs either—no sir,   250
  I was lost in thought, and it made me stop, often,
  dead in my tracks, wheeling, turning back,
  and all the time a voice inside me muttering,
  "Idiot, why? You're going straight to your death."
  Then muttering, "Stopped again, poor fool?   255
  If somebody gets the news to Creon first,
  what's to save your neck?"
                   And so,
  mulling it over, on I trudged, dragging my feet,
  you can make a short road take forever . . .
  but at last, look, common sense won out,   260
  I'm here, and I'm all yours,
  and even though I come empty-handed
  I'll tell my story just the same, because
  I've come with a good grip on one hope,
  what will come will come, whatever fate—   265

Creon: Come to the point!
  What's wrong—why so afraid?

Sentry: First, myself, I've got to tell you,
  I didn't do it, didn't see who did—
  Be fair, don't take it out on me.   270

Creon: You're playing it safe, soldier,
  barricading yourself from any trouble.
  It's obvious, you've something strange to tell.

Sentry: Dangerous too, and danger makes you delay
  for all you're worth.   275

Creon: Out with it—then dismiss!

Sentry: All right, here it comes. The body—
  someone's just buried it, then run off . . .
  sprinkled some dry dust on the flesh,
  given it proper rites.

Creon: What?   280

     What man alive would dare —

Sentry: I've no idea, I swear it.

     There was no mark of a spade, no pickaxe there,
     no earth turned up, the ground packed hard and dry,
     unbroken, no tracks, no wheelruts, nothing,
     the workman left no trace. Just at sunup   285
     the first watch of the day points it out —
     it was a wonder! We were stunned . . .
     a terrific burden too, for all of us, listen:
     you can't see the corpse, not that it's buried,
     really, just a light cover of road-dust on it,   290
     as if someone meant to lay the dead to rest
     and keep from getting cursed.
     Not a sign in sight that dogs or wild beasts
     had worried the body, even torn the skin.

     But what came next! Rough talk flew thick and fast,   295
     guard grilling guard — we'd have come to blows
     at last, nothing to stop it; each man for himself
     and each the culprit, no one caught red-handed,
     all of us pleading ignorance, dodging the charges,
     ready to take up red-hot iron in our fists,   300
     go through fire, swear oaths to the gods —
     "I didn't do it, I had no hand in it either,
     not in the plotting, not in the work itself!"

     Finally, after all this wrangling came to nothing,
     one man spoke out and made us stare at the ground,   305
     hanging our heads in fear. No way to counter him,
     no way to take his advice and come through
     safe and sound. Here's what he said:
     "Look, we've got to report the facts to Creon,
     we can't keep this hidden." Well, that won out,   310
     and the lot fell on me, condemned me,
     unlucky as ever, I got the prize. So here I am,
     against my will and yours too, well I know —
     no one wants the man who brings bad news.

Leader: My king,
     ever since he began I've been debating in my mind,   315
     could this possibly be the work of the gods?

Creon: Stop —
     before you make me choke with anger — the gods!
     You, you're senile, must you be insane?
     You say — why it's intolerable — say the gods
     could have the slightest concern for that corpse?   320
     Tell me, was it for meritorious service
     they proceeded to bury him, prized him so? The hero
     who came to burn their temples ringed with pillars,
     their golden treasures — scorch their hallowed earth
     and fling their laws to the winds.   325

Exactly when did you last see the gods
celebrating traitors? Inconceivable!

No, from the first there were certain citizens
who could hardly stand the spirit of my regime,
grumbling against me in the dark, heads together,   330
tossing wildly, never keeping their necks beneath
the yoke, loyally submitting to their king.
These are the instigators, I'm convinced —
they've perverted my own guard, bribed them
to do their work.
                    Money! Nothing worse   335
in our lives, so current, rampant, so corrupting.
Money — you demolish cities, root men from their homes,
you train and twist good minds and set them on
to the most atrocious schemes. No limit,
you make them adept at every kind of outrage,   340
every godless crime — money!
                    Everyone —
the whole crew bribed to commit this crime,
they've made one thing sure at least:
sooner or later they will pay the price.

Wheeling on the Sentry.

You —   345
I swear to Zeus as I still believe in Zeus,
if you don't find the man who buried that corpse,
the very man, and produce him before my eyes,
simple death won't be enough for you,
not till we string you up alive   350
and wring the immorality out of you.
Then you can steal the rest of your days,
better informed about where to make a killing.
You'll have learned, at last, it doesn't pay
to itch for rewards from every hand that beckons.   355
Filthy profits wreck most men, you'll see —
they'll never save your life.
Sentry: Please,
     may I say a word or two, or just turn and go?
Creon: Can't you tell? Everything you say offends me.
Sentry: Where does it hurt you, in the ears or in the heart?   360
Creon: And who are you to pinpoint my displeasure?
Sentry: The culprit grates on your feelings,
     I just annoy your ears.
Creon: Still talking?
     You talk too much! A born nuisance —
Sentry: Maybe so,
     but I never did this thing, so help me!
Creon: Yes you did —   365
     what's more, you squandered your life for silver!

Sentry: Oh it's terrible when the one who does the judging
    judges things all wrong.
Creon: Well now,
    you just be clever about your judgments—
    if you fail to produce the criminals for me,   370
    you'll swear your dirty money brought you pain.

Turning sharply, reentering the palace.

Sentry: I hope he's found. Best thing by far.
    But caught or not, that's in the lap of fortune;
    I'll never come back, you've seen the last of me.
    I'm saved, even now, and I never thought,   375
    I never hoped—
    dear gods, I owe you all my thanks!

Rushing out.

Chorus: Numberless wonders
    terrible wonders walk the world but none the match for man—
    that great wonder crossing the heaving gray sea,
               driven on by the blasts of winter   380
    on through breakers crashing left and right,
        holds his steady course
    and the oldest of the gods he wears away—
    the Earth, the immortal, the inexhaustible—
    as his plows go back and forth, year in, year out   385
        with the breed of stallions turning up the furrows.

    And the blithe, lightheaded race of birds he snares,
    the tribes of savage beasts, the life that swarms the depths—
               with one fling of his nets
    woven and coiled tight, he takes them all,   390
        man the skilled, the brilliant!
    He conquers all, taming with his techniques
    the prey that roams the cliffs and wild lairs,
    training the stallion, clamping the yoke across
        his shaggy neck, and the tireless mountain bull.   395

    And speech and thought, quick as the wind
    and the mood and mind for law that rules the city—
        all these he has taught himself
    and shelter from the arrows of the frost
    when there's rough lodging under the cold clear sky   400
    and the shafts of lashing rain—
            ready, resourceful man!
                  Never without resources
    never an impasse as he marches on the future—
    only Death, from Death alone he will find no rescue   405
    but from desperate plagues he has plotted his escapes.

    Man the master, ingenious past all measure
    past all dreams, the skills within his grasp—
        he forges on, now to destruction

now again to greatness. When he weaves in   410
the laws of the land, and the justice of the gods
that binds his oaths together
                he and his city rise high—
                        but the city casts out
that man who weds himself to inhumanity   415
thanks to reckless daring. Never share my hearth
never think my thoughts, whoever does such things.

Enter Antigone from the side, accompanied by the Sentry.

        Here is a dark sign from the gods—
        what to make of this? I know her,
        how can I deny it? That young girl's Antigone!   420
        Wretched, child of a wretched father,
        Oedipus. Look, is it possible?
        They bring you in like a prisoner—
        why? did you break the king's laws?
        Did they take you in some act of mad defiance?   425

Sentry: She's the one, she did it single-handed—
        we caught her burying the body. Where's Creon?

    Enter Creon from the palace.

Leader: Back again, just in time when you need him.
Creon: In time for what? What is it?
Sentry: My king,
        there's nothing you can swear you'll never do—   430
        second thoughts make liars of us all.
        I could have sworn I wouldn't hurry back
        (what with your threats, the buffeting I just took),
        but a stroke of luck beyond our wildest hopes,
        what a joy, there's nothing like it. So,   435
        back I've come, breaking my oath, who cares?
        I'm bringing in our prisoner—this young girl—
        we took her giving the dead the last rites.
        But no casting lots this time; this is *my* luck,
        my prize, no one else's.
                        Now, my lord,   440
        here she is. Take her, question her,
        cross-examine her to your heart's content.
        But set me free, it's only right—
        I'm rid of this dreadful business once for all.
Creon: Prisoner! Her? You took her—where, doing what?   445
Sentry: Burying the man. That's the whole story.
Creon: What?
        You mean what you say, you're telling me the truth?
Sentry: She's the one. With my own eyes I saw her
        bury the body, just what you've forbidden.
        There. Is that plain and clear?   450
Creon: What did you see? Did you catch her in the act?
Sentry: Here's what happened. We went back to our post,
        those threats of yours breathing down our necks—

we brushed the corpse clean of the dust that covered it,
stripped it bare . . . it was slimy, going soft,   455
and we took to high ground, backs to the wind
so the stink of him couldn't hit us;
jostling, baiting each other to keep awake,
shouting back and forth—no napping on the job,
not this time. And so the hours dragged by   460
until the sun stood dead above our heads,
a huge white ball in the noon sky, beating,
blazing down, and then it happened—
suddenly, a whirlwind!
Twisting a great dust-storm up from the earth,   465
a black plague of the heavens, filling the plain,
ripping the leaves off every tree in sight,
choking the air and sky. We squinted hard
and took our whipping from the gods.

And after the storm passed—it seemed endless—   470
there, we saw the girl!
And she cried out a sharp, piercing cry,
like a bird come back to an empty nest,
peering into its bed, and all the babies gone . . .
Just so, when she sees the corpse bare   475
she bursts into a long, shattering wail
and calls down withering curses on the heads
of all who did the work. And she scoops up dry dust,
handfuls, quickly, and lifting a fine bronze urn,
lifting it high and pouring, she crowns the dead   480
with three full libations.
                                        Soon as we saw
we rushed her, closed on the kill like hunters,
and she, she didn't flinch. We interrogated her,
charging her with offenses past and present—
she stood up to it all, denied nothing. I tell you,   485
it made me ache and laugh in the same breath.
It's pure joy to escape the worst yourself,
it hurts a man to bring down his friends.
But all that, I'm afraid, means less to me
than my own skin. That's the way I'm made.

Creon:

    Wheeling on Antigone.

                                  You,   490
with your eyes fixed on the ground—speak up.
Do you deny you did this, yes or no?

Antigone: I did it. I don't deny a thing.

Creon:

    To the Sentry.

    You, get out, wherever you please—
    you're clear of a very heavy charge.   495

He leaves; Creon turns back to Antigone.

You, tell me briefly, no long speeches—
were you aware a decree had forbidden this?
Antigone: Well aware. How could I avoid it? It was public.
Creon: And still you had the gall to break this law?
Antigone: Of course I did. It wasn't Zeus, not in the least,   500
who made this proclamation—not to me.
Nor did that Justice, dwelling with the gods
beneath the earth, ordain such laws for men.
Nor did I think your edict had such force
that you, a mere mortal, could override the gods,   505
the great unwritten, unshakeable traditions.
They are alive, not just today or yesterday:
they live forever, from the first of time,
and no one knows when they first saw the light.

These laws—I was not about to break them,   510
not out of fear of some man's wounded pride,
and face the retribution of the gods.
Die I must, I've known it all my life—
how could I keep from knowing?—even without
your death-sentence ringing in my ears.   515
And if I am to die before my time
I consider that a gain. Who on earth,
alive in the midst of so much grief as I,
could fail to find his death a rich reward?
So for me, at least, to meet this doom of yours   520
is precious little pain. But if I had allowed
my own mother's son to rot, an unburied corpse—
that would have been an agony! This is nothing.
And if my present actions strike you as foolish,
let's just say I've been accused of folly   525
by a fool.
Leader: Like father like daughter,
passionate, wild . . .
she hasn't learned to bend before adversity.
Creon: No? Believe me, the stiffest stubborn wills
fall the hardest; the toughest iron,   530
tempered strong in the white-hot fire,
you'll see it crack and shatter first of all.
And I've known spirited horses you can break
with a light bit—proud, rebellious horses.
There's no room for pride, not in a slave,   535
not with the lord and master standing by.

This girl was an old hand at insolence
when she overrode the edicts we made public.
But once she'd done it—the insolence,
twice over—to glory in it, laughing,   540
mocking us to our face with what she'd done.

I'm not the man, not now: she is the man
if this victory goes to her and she goes free.

Never! Sister's child or closer in blood
than all my family clustered at my altar   545
worshiping Guardian Zeus — she'll never escape,
she and her blood sister, the most barbaric death.
Yes, I accuse her sister of an equal part
in scheming this, this burial.

To his attendants.

                      Bring her here!
I just saw her inside, hysterical, gone to pieces.   550
It never fails: the mind convicts itself
in advance, when scoundrels are up to no good,
plotting in the dark. Oh but I hate it more
when a traitor, caught red-handed,
tries to glorify his crimes.   555
Antigone: Creon, what more do you want
    than my arrest and execution?
Creon: Nothing. Then I have it all.
Antigone: Then why delay? Your moralizing repels me,
    every word you say — pray god it always will.   560
    So naturally all I say repels you too.
                     Enough.
    Give me glory! What greater glory could I win
    than to give my own brother decent burial?
    These citizens here would all agree,

To the Chorus.

    they'd praise me too   565
    if their lips weren't locked in fear.

Pointing to Creon.

    Lucky tyrants — the perquisites of power!
    Ruthless power to do and say whatever pleases *them*.
Creon: You alone, of all the people in Thebes,
    see things that way.
Antigone: They see it just that way   570
    but defer to you and keep their tongues in leash.
Creon: And you, aren't you ashamed to differ so from them?
    So disloyal!
Antigone: Not ashamed for a moment,
    not to honor my brother, my own flesh and blood.
Creon: Wasn't Eteocles a brother too — cut down, facing him?   575
Antigone: Brother, yes, by the same mother, the same father.
Creon: Then how can you render his enemy such honors,
    such impieties in his eyes?
Antigone: He'll never testify to that,
    Eteocles dead and buried.

Creon: He will—   580
   if you honor the traitor just as much as him.
Antigone: But it was his brother, not some slave that died—
Creon: Ravaging our country!—
   but Eteocles died fighting in our behalf.
Antigone: No matter—Death longs for the same rites for all.   585
Creon: Never the same for the patriot and the traitor.
Antigone: Who, Creon, who on earth can say the ones below
   don't find this pure and uncorrupt?
Creon: Never. Once an enemy, never a friend,
   not even after death.   590
Antigone: I was born to join in love, not hate—
   that is my nature.
Creon: Go down below and love,
   if love you must—love the dead! While I'm alive,
   no woman is going to lord it over me.

   Enter Ismene from the palace, under guard.

Chorus: Look,
   Ismene's coming, weeping a sister's tears,   595
   loving sister, under a cloud . . .
   her face is flushed, her cheeks streaming.
   Sorrow puts her lovely radiance in the dark.
Creon: You—
   in my house, you viper, slinking undetected,
   sucking my life-blood! I never knew   600
   I was breeding twin disasters, the two of you
   rising up against my throne. Come, tell me,
   will you confess your part in the crime or not?
   Answer me. Swear to me.
Ismene: I did it, yes—
   if only she consents—I share the guilt,   605
   the consequences too.
Antigone: No,
   Justice will never suffer that—not you,
   you were unwilling. I never brought you in.
Ismene: But now you face such dangers . . . I'm not ashamed
   to sail through trouble with you,   610
   make your troubles mine.
Antigone: Who did the work?
   Let the dead and the god of death bear witness!
   I've no love for a friend who loves in words alone.
Ismene: Oh no, my sister, don't reject me, please,
   let me die beside you, consecrating   615
   the dead together.
Antigone: Never share my dying,
   don't lay claim to what you never touched.
   My death will be enough.
Ismene: What do I care for life, cut off from you?

Antigone: Ask Creon. Your concern is all for him.   620
Ismene: Why abuse me so? It doesn't help you now.
Antigone: You're right—
    if I mock you, I get no pleasure from it,
    only pain.
Ismene: Tell me, dear one,
    what can I do to help you, even now?
Antigone: Save yourself. I don't grudge you your survival.   625
Ismene: Oh no, no, denied my portion in your death?
Antigone: You chose to live, I chose to die.
Ismene: Not, at least,
    without every kind of caution I could voice.
Antigone: Your wisdom appealed to one world—mine, another.
Ismene: But look, we're both guilty, both condemned to death.   630
Antigone: Courage! Live your life. I gave myself to death,
    long ago, so I might serve the dead.
Creon: They're both mad, I tell you, the two of them.
    One's just shown it, the other's been that way
    since she was born.
Ismene: True, my king,   635
    the sense we were born with cannot last forever . . .
    commit cruelty on a person long enough
    and the mind begins to go.
Creon: Yours did,
    when you chose to commit your crimes with her.
Ismene: How can I live alone, without her?
Creon: Her?   640
    Don't even mention her—she no longer exists.
Ismene: What? You'd kill your own son's bride?
Creon: Absolutely:
    there are other fields for him to plow.
Ismene: Perhaps,
    but never as true, as close a bond as theirs.
Creon: A worthless woman for my son? It repels me.   645
Ismene: Dearest Haemon, your father wrongs you so!
Creon: Enough, enough—you and your talk of marriage!
Ismene: Creon—you're really going to rob your son of Antigone?
Creon: Death will do it for me—break their marriage off.
Leader: So, it's settled then? Antigone must die?   650
Creon: Settled, yes—we both know that.

    To the guards.

    Stop wasting time. Take them in.
    From now on they'll act like women.
    Tie them up, no more running loose;
    even the bravest will cut and run,   655
    once they see Death coming for their lives.

    *The guards escort Antigone and Ismene into the palace. Creon remains while
    the old citizens form their chorus.*

Chorus:　Blest, they are the truly blest who all their lives
　　　have never tasted devastation. For others, once
　　　the gods have rocked a house to its foundations
　　　　　the ruin will never cease, cresting on and on　　　660
　　　from one generation on throughout the race—
　　　like a great mounting tide
　　　driven on by savage northern gales,
　　　　　　surging over the dead black depths
　　　roiling up from the bottom dark heaves of sand　　　665
　　　and the headlands, taking the storm's onslaught full-force,
　　　roar, and the low moaning
　　　　　　　　　echoes on and on
　　　　　　　　　　　and now
　　　as in ancient times I see the sorrows of the house,
　　　the living heirs of the old ancestral kings,
　　　piling on the sorrows of the dead　　　670
　　　　　and one generation cannot free the next—
　　　some god will bring them crashing down,
　　　the race finds no release.
　　　And now the light, the hope
　　　　　　springing up from the late last root　　　675
　　　in the house of Oedipus, that hope's cut down in turn
　　　by the long, bloody knife swung by the gods of death
　　　by a senseless word
　　　　　　　by fury at the heart.
　　　　　　　　　　Zeus,
　　　yours is the power, Zeus, what man on earth
　　　can override it, who can hold it back?　　　680
　　　Power that neither Sleep, the all-ensnaring
　　　　　no, nor the tireless months of heaven
　　　can ever overmaster—young through all time,
　　　mighty lord of power, you hold fast
　　　　　the dazzling crystal mansions of Olympus.　　　685
　　　And throughout the future, late and soon
　　　as through the past, your law prevails:
　　　no towering form of greatness
　　　　　enters into the lives of mortals
　　　　　　　free and clear of ruin.
　　　　　　　　　　True,　　　690
　　　our dreams, our high hopes voyaging far and wide
　　　bring sheer delight to many, to many others
　　　　　delusion, blithe, mindless lusts
　　　and the fraud steals on one slowly . . . unaware
　　　till he trips and puts his foot into the fire.　　　695
　　　　　He was a wise old man who coined
　　　the famous saying: "Sooner or later
　　　foul is fair, fair is foul
　　　to the man the gods will ruin"—
　　　　　He goes his way for a moment only　　　700
　　　　　　　free of blinding ruin.

Enter Haemon from the palace.

Here's Haemon now, the last of all your sons.
Does he come in tears for his bride,
his doomed bride, Antigone —
bitter at being cheated of their marriage?   705

Creon: We'll soon know, better than seers could tell us.

Turning to Haemon.

Son, you've heard the final verdict on your bride?
Are you coming now, raving against your father?
Or do you love me, no matter what I do?

Haemon: Father, I'm your *son* . . . you in your wisdom   710
set my bearings for me — I obey you.
No marriage could ever mean more to me than you,
whatever good direction you may offer.

Creon: Fine, Haemon.
That's how you ought to feel within your heart,
subordinate to your father's will in every way.   715
That's what a man prays for: to produce good sons —
households full of them, dutiful and attentive,
so they can pay his enemy back with interest
and match the respect their father shows his friend.
But the man who rears a brood of useless children,   720
what has he brought into the world, I ask you?
Nothing but trouble for himself, and mockery
from his enemies laughing in his face.
                                        Oh Haemon,
never lose your sense of judgment over a woman.
The warmth, the rush of pleasure, it all goes cold   725
in your arms, I warn you . . . a worthless woman
in your house, a misery in your bed.
What wound cuts deeper than a loved one
turned against you? Spit her out,
like a mortal enemy — let the girl go.   730
Let her find a husband down among the dead.

Imagine it: I caught her in naked rebellion,
the traitor, the only one in the whole city.
I'm not about to prove myself a liar,
not to my people, no, I'm going to kill her!   735
That's right — so let her cry for mercy, sing her hymns
to Zeus who defends all bonds of kindred blood.
Why, if I bring up my own kin to be rebels,
think what I'd suffer from the world at large.
Show me the man who rules his household well: 740
I'll show you someone fit to rule the state.
That good man, my son,
I have every confidence he and he alone
can give commands and take them too. Staunch
in the storm of spears he'll stand his ground,   745
a loyal, unflinching comrade at your side.

But whoever steps out of line, violates the laws
or presumes to hand out orders to his superiors,
he'll win no praise from me. But that man
the city places in authority, his orders   750
must be obeyed, large and small,
right and wrong.
                    Anarchy—
show me a greater crime in all the earth!
She, she destroys cities, rips up houses,
breaks the ranks of spearmen into headlong rout.   755
But the ones who last it out, the great mass of them
owe their lives to discipline. Therefore
we must defend the men who live by law,
never let some woman triumph over us.
Better to fall from power, if fall we must,   760
at the hands of a man—never be rated
inferior to a woman, never.

Leader: To us,
    unless old age has robbed us of our wits,
    you seem to say what you have to say with sense.

Haemon: Father, only the gods endow a man with reason,   765
    the finest of all their gifts, a treasure.
    Far be it from me—I haven't the skill,
    and certainly no desire, to tell you when,
    if ever, you make a slip in speech . . . though
    someone else might have a good suggestion.   770

    Of course it's not for you,
    in the normal run of things, to watch
    whatever men say or do, or find to criticize.
    The man in the street, you know, dreads your glance,
    he'd never say anything displeasing to your face.   775
    But it's for me to catch the murmurs in the dark,
    the way the city mourns for this young girl.
    "No woman," they say, "ever deserved death less,
    and such a brutal death for such a glorious action.
    She, with her own dear brother lying in his blood—   780
    she couldn't bear to leave him dead, unburied,
    food for the wild dogs or wheeling vultures.
    Death? She deserves a glowing crown of gold!"
    So they say, and the rumor spreads in secret,
    darkly . . .
                    I rejoice in your success, father—   785
    nothing more precious to me in the world.
    What medal of honor brighter to his children
    than a father's growing glory? Or a child's
    to his proud father? Now don't, please,
    be quite so single-minded, self-involved,   790
    or assume the world is wrong and you are right.
    Whoever thinks that he alone possesses intelligence,
    the gift of eloquence, he and no one else,

and character too . . . such men, I tell you,
spread them open — you will find them empty.

                                                No,   795
it's no disgrace for a man, even a wise man,
to learn many things and not to be too rigid.
You've seen trees by a raging winter torrent,
how many sway with the flood and salvage every twig,
but not the stubborn — they're ripped out, roots and all.   800
Bend or break. The same when a man is sailing:
haul your sheets too taut, never give an inch,
you'll capsize, go the rest of the voyage
keel up and the rowing-benches under.

Oh give way. Relax your anger — change!   805
I'm young, I know, but let me offer this:
it would be best by far, I admit,
if a man were born infallible, right by nature.
If not — and things don't often go that way,
it's best to learn from those with good advice.   810

Leader: You'd do well, my lord, if he's speaking to the point,
to learn from him,

    Turning to Haemon.

                    and you, my boy, from him.
You both are talking sense.

Creon: So,
men our age, we're to be lectured, are we? —
schooled by a boy his age?   815

Haemon: Only in what is right. But if I seem young,
look less to my years and more to what I do.

Creon: Do? Is admiring rebels an achievement?

Haemon: I'd never suggest that you admire treason.

Creon: Oh? —
isn't that just the sickness that's attacked her?   820

Haemon: The whole city of Thebes denies it, to a man.

Creon: And is Thebes about to tell me how to rule?

Haemon: Now, you see? Who's talking like a child?

Creon: Am I to rule this land for others — or myself?

Haemon: It's no city at all, owned by one man alone.   825

Creon: What? The city *is* the king's — that's the law!

Haemon: What a splendid king you'd make of a desert island —
you and you alone.

Creon:

    To the Chorus.

                    This boy, I do believe,
is fighting on her side, the woman's side.

Haemon: If you are a woman, yes;   830
my concern is all for you.

Creon: Why, you degenerate — bandying accusations,
threatening me with justice, your own father!

Haemon: I see my father offending justice — wrong.
Creon: Wrong?
    To protect my royal rights?
Haemon: Protect your rights?   835
    When you trample down the honors of the gods?
Creon: You, you soul of corruption, rotten through —
    woman's accomplice!
Haemon: That may be,
    but you'll never find me accomplice to a criminal.
Creon: That's what *she* is,   840
    and every word you say is a blatant appeal for her —
Haemon: And you, and me, and the gods beneath the earth.
Creon: You'll never marry her, not while she's alive.
Haemon: Then she'll die . . . but her death will kill another.
Creon: What, brazen threats? You go too far!
Haemon: What threat?   845
    Combating your empty, mindless judgments with a word?
Creon: You'll suffer for your sermons, you and your empty wisdom!
Haemon: If you weren't my father, I'd say you were insane.
Creon: Don't flatter me with Father — you woman's slave!
Haemon: You really expect to fling abuse at me   850
    and not receive the same?
Creon: Is that so!
    Now, by heaven, I promise you, you'll pay —
    taunting, insulting me! Bring her out,
    that hateful — she'll die now, here,
    in front of his eyes, beside her groom!   855
Haemon: No, no, she will never die beside me —
    don't delude yourself. And you will never
    see me, never set eyes on my face again.
    Rage your heart out, rage with friends
    who can stand the sight of you.   860

    Rushing out.

Leader: Gone, my king, in a burst of anger.
    A temper young as his . . . hurt him once,
    he may do something violent.
Creon: Let him do —
    dream up something desperate, past all human limit!
    Good riddance. Rest assured,   865
    he'll never save those two young girls from death.
Leader: Both of them, you really intend to kill them both?
Creon: No, not her, the one whose hands are clean;
    you're quite right.
Leader: But Antigone —
    what sort of death do you have in mind for her?   870
Creon: I'll take her down some wild, desolate path
    never trod by men, and wall her up alive
    in a rocky vault, and set out short rations,
    just a gesture of piety

to keep the entire city free of defilement.   875
There let her pray to the one god she worships:
Death — who knows? — may just reprieve her from death.
Or she may learn at last, better late than never,
what a waste of breath it is to worship Death.

Exit to the palace.

Chorus: Love, never conquered in battle   880
    Love the plunderer laying waste the rich!
    Love standing the night-watch
             guarding a girl's soft cheek,
you range the seas, the shepherds' steadings off in the wilds —
not even the deathless gods can flee your onset,   885
nothing human born for a day —
whoever feels your grip is driven mad.
                         Love
you wrench the minds of the righteous into outrage,
swerve them to their ruin — you have ignited this,
this kindred strife, father and son at war   890
                and Love alone the victor —
warm glance of the bride triumphant, burning with desire!
Throned in power, side-by-side with the mighty laws!
Irresistible Aphrodite,° never conquered —
Love, you mock us for your sport.   895

Antigone is brought from the palace under guard.

    But now, even I'd rebel against the king,
    I'd break all bounds when I see this —
    I fill with tears, can't hold them back,
    not any more . . . I see Antigone make her way
    to the bridal vault where all are laid to rest.   900
Antigone: Look at me, men of my fatherland,
      setting out on the last road
    looking into the last light of day
    the last I'll ever see . . .
    the god of death who puts us all to bed   905
    takes me down to the banks of Acheron° alive —
      denied my part in the wedding-songs,
    no wedding-song in the dusk has crowned my marriage —
    I go to wed the lord of the dark waters.
Chorus: Not crowned with glory, crowned with a dirge,   910
      you leave for the deep pit of the dead.
    No withering illness laid you low,
    no strokes of the sword — a law to yourself,
    alone, no mortal like you, ever, you go down
    to the halls of Death alive and breathing.   915

894 *Aphrodite:* Goddess of love.   906 *Acheron:* A river in the underworld, to which the
dead go.

Antigone: But think of Niobe°—well I know her story—
        think what a living death she died,
    Tantalus' daughter, stranger queen from the east:
    there on the mountain heights, growing stone
    binding as ivy, slowly walled her round   920
    and the rains will never cease, the legends say
    the snows will never leave her . . .
        wasting away, under her brows the tears
    showering down her breasting ridge and slopes—
    a rocky death like hers puts me to sleep.   925
Chorus: But she was a god, born of gods,
        and we are only mortals born to die.
        And yet, of course, it's a great thing
        for a dying girl to hear, just hear
        she shares a destiny equal to the gods,   930
        during life and later, once she's dead.
Antigone: O you mock me!
    Why, in the name of all my fathers' gods
    why can't you wait till I am gone—
        must you abuse me to my face?
    O my city, all your fine rich sons!   935
    And you, you springs of the Dirce,
    holy grove of Thebes where the chariots gather,
            you at least, you'll bear me witness, look,
    unmourned by friends and forced by such crude laws
    I go to my rockbound prison, strange new tomb—   940
        always a stranger, O dear god,
        I have no home on earth and none below,
            not with the living, not with the breathless dead.
Chorus: You went too far, the last limits of daring—
        smashing against the high throne of Justice!   945
            Your life's in ruins, child—I wonder . . .
        do you pay for your father's terrible ordeal?
Antigone: There—at last you've touched it, the worst pain
    the worst anguish! Raking up the grief for father
        three times over, for all the doom   950
    that's struck us down, the brilliant house of Laius.
    O mother, your marriage-bed
    the coiling horrors, the coupling there—
    you with your own son, my father—doomstruck mother!
    Such, such were my parents, and I their wretched child.   955
    I go to them now, cursed, unwed, to share their home—
        I am a stranger! O dear brother, doomed
        in your marriage—your marriage murders mine,
            your dying drags me down to death alive!

    Enter Creon.

916 *Niobe:* A queen of Thebes who was punished by the gods for her pride and was turned
into stone.

Chorus: Reverence asks some reverence in return — 960
               but attacks on power never go unchecked,
                   not by the man who holds the reins of power.
               Your own blind will, your passion has destroyed you.

Antigone: No one to weep for me, my friends,
               no wedding-song — they take me away 965
               in all my pain . . . the road lies open, waiting.
               Never again, the law forbids me to see
               the sacred eye of day. I am agony!
               No tears for the destiny that's mine,
               no loved one mourns my death.

Creon: Can't you see? 970
     If a man could wail his own dirge *before* he dies,
     he'd never finish.

     To the guards.

                      Take her away, quickly!
     Wall her up in the tomb, you have your orders.
     Abandon her there, alone, and let her choose —
     death or a buried life with a good roof for shelter. 975
     As for myself, my hands are clean. This young girl —
     dead or alive, she will be stripped of her rights,
     her stranger's rights, here in the world above.

Antigone: O tomb, my bridal-bed — my house, my prison
     cut in the hollow rock, my everlasting watch! 980
     I'll soon be there, soon embrace my own,
     the great growing family of our dead
     Persephone° has received among her ghosts.
                                  I,
     the last of them all, the most reviled by far,
     go down before my destined time's run out. 985
     But still I go, cherishing one good hope:
     my arrival may be dear to father,
     dear to you, my mother,
     dear to you, my loving brother, Eteocles —
     When you died I washed you with my hands, 990
     I dressed you all, I poured the cups
     across your tombs. But now, Polynices,
     because I laid your body out as well,
     this, this is my reward. Nevertheless
     I honored you — the decent will admit it — 995
     well and wisely too.
                   Never, I tell you,
     if I had been the mother of children
     or if my husband died, exposed and rotting —
     I'd never have taken this ordeal upon myself,
     never defied our people's will. What law, 1000
     you ask, do I satisfy with what I say?

983 *Persephone:* Queen of the underworld.

A husband dead, there might have been another.
A child by another too, if I had lost the first.
But mother and father both lost in the halls of Death,
no brother could ever spring to light again.   1005

For this law alone I held you first in honor.
For this, Creon, the king, judges me a criminal
guilty of dreadful outrage, my dear brother!
And now he leads me off, a captive in his hands,
with no part in the bridal-song, the bridal-bed,   1010
denied all joy of marriage, raising children —
deserted so by loved ones, struck by fate,
I descend alive to the caverns of the dead.

What law of the mighty gods have I transgressed?
Why look to the heavens any more, tormented as I am?   1015
Whom to call, what comrades now? Just think,
my reverence only brands me for irreverence!
Very well: if this is the pleasure of the gods,
once I suffer I will know that I was wrong.
But if these men are wrong, let them suffer   1020
nothing worse than they mete out to me —
these masters of injustice!

Leader: Still the same rough winds, the wild passion
raging through the girl.

Creon:

To the guards.

                Take her away.
You're wasting time — you'll pay for it too.   1025

Antigone: Oh god, the voice of death. It's come, it's here.

Creon: True. Not a word of hope — your doom is sealed.

Antigone: Land of Thebes, city of all my fathers —
    O you gods, the first gods of the race!
    They drag me away, now, no more delay.   1030
    Look on me, you noble sons of Thebes —
    the last of a great line of kings,
    I alone, see what I suffer now
    at the hands of what breed of men —
    all for reverence, my reverence for the gods!   1035

She leaves under guard; the Chorus gathers.

Chorus: Danaë, Danaë° —
   even she endured a fate like yours,
     in all her lovely strength she traded
   the light of day for the bolted brazen vault —
   buried within her tomb, her bridal-chamber,   1040
   wed to the yoke and broken.
     But she was of glorious birth

1036 *Danaë:* Locked in a cell by her father because it was prophesied that her son would kill
him, but visited by Zeus in the form of a shower of gold. Their son was Perseus.

           my child, my child
and treasured the seed of Zeus within her womb,
the cloudburst streaming gold!   1045
      The power of fate is a wonder,
      dark, terrible wonder—
      neither wealth nor armies
      towered walls nor ships
      black hulls lashed by the salt   1050
      can save us from that force.

The yoke tamed him too
      young Lycurgus° flaming in anger
king of Edonia, all for his mad taunts
Dionysus clamped him down, encased   1055
in the chain-mail of rock
      and there his rage
                  his terrible flowering rage burst—
sobbing, dying away . . . at last that madman
came to know his god—   1060
the power he mocked, the power
      he taunted in all his frenzy
      trying to stamp out
      the women strong with the god—
      the torch, the raving sacred cries— 1065
      enraging the Muses° who adore the flute.

And far north where the Black Rocks
      cut the sea in half
and murderous straits
split the coast of Thrace   1070
      a forbidding city stands
where once, hard by the walls
the savage Ares thrilled to watch
a king's new queen, a Fury rearing in rage
      against his two royal sons—   1075
      her bloody hands, her dagger-shuttle
stabbing out their eyes—cursed, blinding wounds—
their eyes blind sockets screaming for revenge!

They wailed in agony, cries echoing cries
      the princes doomed at birth . . .   1080
and their mother doomed to chains,
walled off in a tomb of stone—
      but she traced her own birth back
to a proud Athenian line and the high gods
and off in caverns half the world away,   1085
born of the wild North Wind
      she sprang on her father's gales,
        racing stallions up the leaping cliffs—

1053 *Lycurgus:* Punished by Dionysus because he would not worship him.   1066 *Muses:*
Goddesses of the arts.

child of the heavens. But even on her the Fates
the gray everlasting Fates rode hard   1090
my child, my child.

Enter Tiresias, the blind prophet, led by a boy.

Tiresias: Lords of Thebes,
  I and the boy have come together,
  hand in hand. Two see with the eyes of one . . .
  so the blind must go, with a guide to lead the way.
Creon: What is it, old Tiresias? What news now?   1095
Tiresias: I will teach you. And you obey the seer.
Creon: I will,
  I've never wavered from your advice before.
Tiresias: And so you kept the city straight on course.
Creon: I owe you a great deal, I swear to that.
Tiresias: Then reflect, my son: you are poised,   1100
  once more, on the razor-edge of fate.
Creon: What is it? I shudder to hear you.
Tiresias: You will learn
  when you listen to the warnings of my craft.
  As I sat on the ancient seat of augury,°
  in the sanctuary where every bird I know   1105
  will hover at my hands — suddenly I heard it,
  a strange voice in the wingbeats, unintelligible,
  barbaric, a mad scream! Talons flashing, ripping,
  they were killing each other — that much I knew —
  the murderous fury whirring in those wings   1110
  made that much clear!
               I was afraid,
  I turned quickly, tested the burnt-sacrifice,
  ignited the altar at all points — but no fire,
  the god in the fire never blazed.
  Not from those offerings . . . over the embers   1115
  slid a heavy ooze from the long thighbones,
  smoking, sputtering out, and the bladder
  puffed and burst — spraying gall into the air —
  and the fat wrapping the bones slithered off
  and left them glistening white. No fire!   1120
  The rites failed that might have blazed the future
  with a sign. So I learned from the boy here;
  he is my guide, as I am guide to others.
              And it's you —
  your high resolve that sets this plague on Thebes.
  The public altars and sacred hearths are fouled,   1125
  one and all, by the birds and dogs with carrion
  torn from the corpse, the doomstruck son of Oedipus!
  And so the gods are deaf to our prayers, they spurn
  the offerings in our hands, the flame of holy flesh.

1104 *seat of augury:* Where Tiresias looked for omens among birds.

No birds cry out an omen clear and true—   1130
they're gorged with the murdered victim's blood and fat.
Take these things to heart, my son, I warn you.
All men make mistakes, it is only human.
But once the wrong is done, a man
can turn his back on folly, misfortune too,   1135
if he tries to make amends, however low he's fallen,
and stops his bullnecked ways. Stubbornness
brands you for stupidity—pride is a crime.
No, yield to the dead!
Never stab the fighter when he's down.   1140
Where's the glory, killing the dead twice over?

I mean you well. I give you sound advice.
It's best to learn from a good adviser
when he speaks for your own good:
it's pure gain.
Creon: Old man—all of you! So,   1145
you shoot your arrows at my head like archers at the target—
I even have *him* loosed on me, this fortune-teller.
Oh his ilk has tried to sell me short
and ship me off for years. Well,
drive your bargains, traffic—much as you like—   1150
in the gold of India, silver-gold of Sardis.
You'll never bury that body in the grave,
not even if Zeus's eagles rip the corpse
and wing their rotten pickings off to the throne of god!
Never, not even in fear of such defilement   1155
will I tolerate his burial, that traitor.
Well I know, we can't defile the gods—
no mortal has the power.
               No,
reverend old Tiresias, all men fall,
it's only human, but the wisest fall obscenely   1160
when they glorify obscene advice with rhetoric—
all for their own gain.
Tiresias: Oh god, is there a man alive
who knows, who actually believes . . .
Creon: What now?
What earth-shattering truth are you about to utter?   1165
Tiresias: . . . just how much a sense of judgment, wisdom
is the greatest gift we have?
Creon: Just as much, I'd say,
as a twisted mind is the worst affliction going.
Tiresias: You are the one who's sick, Creon, sick to death.
Creon: I am in no mood to trade insults with a seer.   1170
Tiresias: You have already, calling my prophecies a lie.
Creon: Why not?
You and the whole breed of seers are mad for money!
Tiresias: And the whole race of tyrants lusts to rake it in.
Creon: This slander of yours—
are you aware you're speaking to the king?   1175

Tiresias: Well aware. Who helped you save the city?
Creon: You—
     you have your skills, old seer, but you lust for injustice!
Tiresias: You will drive me to utter the dreadful secret in my heart.
Creon: Spit it out! Just don't speak it out for profit.
Tiresias: Profit? No, not a bit of profit, not for you.   1180
Creon: Know full well, you'll never buy off my resolve.
Tiresias: Then know this too, learn this by heart!
     The chariot of the sun will not race through
     so many circuits more, before you have surrendered
     one born of your own loins, your own flesh and blood,   1185
     a corpse for corpses given in return, since you have thrust
     to the world below a child sprung for the world above,
     ruthlessly lodged a living soul within the grave—
     then you've robbed the gods below the earth,
     keeping a dead body here in the bright air,   1190
     unburied, unsung, unhallowed by the rites.

     You, you have no business with the dead,
     nor do the gods above—this is violence
     you have forced upon the heavens.
     And so the avengers, the dark destroyers late   1195
     but true to the mark, now lie in wait for you,
     the Furies sent by the gods and the god of death
     to strike you down with the pains that you perfected!

     There. Reflect on that, tell me I've been bribed.
     The day comes soon, no long test of time, not now,   1200
     that wakes the wails for men and women in your halls.
     Great hatred rises against you—
     cities in tumult, all whose mutilated sons
     the dogs have graced with burial, or the wild beasts,
     some wheeling crow that wings the ungodly stench of carrion   1205
     back to each city, each warrior's hearth and home.

     These arrows for your heart! Since you've raked me
     I loose them like an archer in my anger,
     arrows deadly true. You'll never escape
     their burning, searing force.   1210

Motioning to his escort.

     Come, boy, take me home.
     So he can vent his rage on younger men,
     and learn to keep a gentler tongue in his head
     and better sense than what he carries now.

Exit to the side.

Leader: The old man's gone, my king—   1215
     terrible prophecies. Well I know,
     since the hair on this old head went gray,
     he's never lied to Thebes.
Creon: I know it myself—I'm shaken, torn.
     It's a dreadful thing to yield . . . but resist now?   1220

Lay my pride bare to the blows of ruin?
That's dreadful too.

Leader: But good advice,
Creon, take it now, you must.

Creon: What should I do? Tell me . . . I'll obey.

Leader: Go! Free the girl from the rocky vault   1225
and raise a mound for the body you exposed.

Creon: That's your advice? You think I should give in?

Leader: Yes, my king, quickly. Disasters sent by the gods
cut short our follies in a flash.

Creon: Oh it's hard.
giving up the heart's desire . . . but I will do it—   1230
no more fighting a losing battle with necessity.

Leader: Do it now, go, don't leave it to others.

Creon: Now—I'm on my way! Come, each of you,
take up axes, make for the high ground,
over there, quickly! I and my better judgment   1235
have come round to this—I shackled her,
I'll set her free myself. I am afraid . . .
it's best to keep the established laws
to the very day we die.

Rushing out, followed by his entourage. The Chorus clusters around the altar.

Chorus: God of a hundred names!

           Great Dionysus—   1240
Son and glory of Semele! Pride of Thebes—
Child of Zeus whose thunder rocks the clouds—
Lord of the famous lands of evening—
King of the Mysteries!

         King of Eleusis, Demeter's plain°
her breasting hills that welcome in the world—   1245
Great Dionysus!

        Bacchus,° living in Thebes
the mother-city of all your frenzied women—

             Bacchus
living along the Ismenus'° rippling waters
standing over the field sown with the Dragon's teeth!

You—we have seen you through the flaring smoky fires,   1250
   your torches blazing over the twin peaks
where nymphs of the hallowed cave climb onward
        fired with you, your sacred rage—
we have seen you at Castalia's running spring°
and down from the heights of Nysa° crowned with ivy   1255
the greening shore rioting vines and grapes
     down you come in your storm of wild women
        ecstatic, mystic cries—

1244 *Demeter's plain:* The goddess of grain was worshiped at Eleusis, near Athens.
1246 *Bacchus:* Another name for Dionysus.   1248 *Ismenus:* A river near Thebes where the
founders of the city were said to have sprung from a dragon's teeth.   1254 *Castalia's running spring:* The sacred spring of Apollo's oracle at Delphi.   1255 *Nysa:* A mountain
where Dionysus was worshiped.

Dionysus—
down to watch and ward the roads of Thebes!

First of all cities, Thebes you honor first   1260
you and your mother, bride of the lightning—
come, Dionysus! now your people lie
in the iron grip of plague,
come in your racing, healing stride
                    down Parnassus'° slopes   1265
or across the moaning straits.
                    Lord of the dancing—
dance, dance the constellations breathing fire!
Great master of the voices of the night!
Child of Zeus, God's offspring, come, come forth!
Lord, king, dance with your nymphs, swirling, raving   1270
arm-in-arm in frenzy through the night
          they dance you, Iacchus°—
                    Dance, Dionysus
giver of all good things!

Enter a Messenger from the side.

Messenger: Neighbors,
friends of the house of Cadmus° and the kings,
there's not a thing in this life of ours   1275
I'd praise or blame as settled once for all.
Fortune lifts and Fortune fells the lucky
and unlucky every day. No prophet on earth
can tell a man his fate. Take Creon:
there was a man to rouse your envy once,   1280
as I see it. He saved the realm from enemies;
taking power, he alone, the lord of the fatherland,
he set us true on course—flourished like a tree
with the noble line of sons he bred and reared . . .
and now it's lost, all gone.
                    Believe me,   1285
when a man has squandered his true joys,
he's good as dead, I tell you, a living corpse.
Pile up riches in your house, as much as you like—
live like a king with a huge show of pomp,
but if real delight is missing from the lot,   1290
I wouldn't give you a wisp of smoke for it,
not compared with joy.
Leader: What now?
What new grief do you bring the house of kings?
Messenger: Dead, dead—and the living are guilty of their death!
Leader: Who's the murderer? Who is dead? Tell us.   1295
Messenger: Haemon's gone, his blood spilled by the very hand—
Leader: His father's or his own?

1265 *Parnassus:* A mountain in Greece that was sacred to Dionysus as well as other gods and goddesses.   1272 *Iacchus:* Dionysus.   1274 *Cadmus:* The legendary founder of Thebes.

Messenger: His own . . .
raging mad with his father for the death —
Leader: Oh great seer,
you saw it all, you brought your word to birth!
Messenger: Those are the facts. Deal with them as you will. 1300

As he turns to go, Eurydice enters from the palace.

Leader: Look, Eurydice. Poor woman, Creon's wife,
so close at hand. By chance perhaps,
unless she's heard the news about her son.
Eurydice: My countrymen,
all of you — I caught the sound of your words
as I was leaving to do my part, 1305
to appeal to queen Athena° with my prayers.
I was just loosing the bolts, opening the doors,
when a voice filled with sorrow, family sorrow,
struck my ears, and I fell back, terrified,
into the women's arms — everything went black. 1310
Tell me the news, again, whatever it is . . .
sorrow and I are hardly strangers;
I can bear the worst.
Messenger: I — dear lady,
I'll speak as an eye-witness. I was there.
And I won't pass over one word of the truth. 1315
Why should I try to soothe you with a story,
only to prove a liar in a moment?
Truth is always best.
So,
I escorted your lord, I guided him
to the edge of the plain where the body lay, 1320
Polynices, torn by the dogs and still unmourned.
And saying a prayer to Hecate of the Crossroads,
Pluto° too, to hold their anger and be kind,
we washed the dead in a bath of holy water
and plucking some fresh branches, gathering . . . 1325
what was left of him, we burned them all together
and raised a high mound of native earth, and then
we turned and made for that rocky vault of hers,
the hollow, empty bed of the bride of Death.
And far off, one of us heard a voice, 1330
a long wail rising, echoing
out of that unhallowed wedding-chamber;
he ran to alert the master and Creon pressed on,
closer — the strange, inscrutable cry came sharper,
throbbing around him now, and he let loose 1335
a cry of his own, enough to wrench the heart,
"Oh god, am I the prophet now? going down
the darkest road I've ever gone? My son —

1306 *Athena:* Goddess of wisdom and protector of Greek cities. 1322–1323 *Hecate, Pluto:* Gods of the underworld.

it's *his* dear voice, he greets me! Go, men,
closer, quickly! Go through the gap,   1340
the rocks are dragged back —
right to the tomb's very mouth — and look,
see if it's Haemon's voice I think I hear,
or the gods have robbed me of my senses."

The king was shattered. We took his orders,   1345
went and searched, and there in the deepest,
dark recesses of the tomb we found her . . .
hanged by the neck in a fine linen noose,
strangled in her veils — and the boy,
his arms flung around her waist,   1350
clinging to her, wailing for his bride,
dead and down below, for his father's crimes
and the bed of his marriage blighted by misfortune.
When Creon saw him, he gave a deep sob,
he ran in, shouting, crying out to him,   1355
"Oh my child — what have you done? what seized you,
what insanity? what disaster drove you mad?
Come out, my son! I beg you on my knees!"
But the boy gave him a wild burning glance,
spat in his face, not a word in reply,   1360
he drew his sword — his father rushed out,
running as Haemon lunged and missed! —
and then, doomed, desperate with himself,
suddenly leaning his full weight on the blade,
he buried it in his body, halfway to the hilt.   1365
And still in his senses, pouring his arms around her,
he embraced the girl and breathing hard,
released a quick rush of blood,
bright red on her cheek glistening white.
And there he lies, body enfolding body . . .   1370
he has won his bride at last, poor boy,
not here but in the houses of the dead.

Creon shows the world that of all the ills
afflicting men the worst is lack of judgment.

Eurydice turns and reenters the palace.

Leader: What do you make of that? The lady's gone,   1375
    without a word, good or bad.
Messenger: I'm alarmed too
    but here's my hope — faced with her son's death,
    she finds it unbecoming to mourn in public.
    Inside, under her roof, she'll set her women
    to the task and wail the sorrow of the house.   1380
    She's too discreet. She won't do something rash.
Leader: I'm not so sure. To me, at least,
    a long heavy silence promises danger,
    just as much as a lot of empty outcries.

Messenger: We'll see if she's holding something back,   1385
          hiding some passion in her heart.
          I'm going in. You may be right—who knows?
          Even too much silence has its dangers.

*Exit to the palace. Enter Creon from the side, escorted by attendants carrying
Haemon's body on a bier.*

Leader: The king himself! Coming toward us,
          look, holding the boy's head in his hands.   1390
          Clear, damning proof, if it's right to say so—
          proof of his own madness, no one else's,
                    no, his own blind wrongs.
Creon: Ohhh,
          so senseless, so insane . . . my crimes,
          my stubborn, deadly—   1395
          Look at us, the killer, the killed,
          father and son, the same blood—the misery!
          My plans, my mad fanatic heart,
          my son, cut off so young!
          Ai, dead, lost to the world,   1400
          not through your stupidity, no, my own.
Leader: Too late,
          too late, you see what justice means.
Creon: Oh I've learned
          through blood and tears! Then, it was then,
          when the god came down and struck me—a great weight
          shattering, driving me down that wild savage path,   1405
          ruining, trampling down my joy. Oh the agony,
                    the heartbreaking agonies of our lives.

Enter the Messenger from the palace.

Messenger: Master,
          what a hoard of grief you have, and you'll have more.
          The grief that lies to hand you've brought yourself—

Pointing to Haemon's body.

          the rest, in the house, you'll see it all too soon.   1410
Creon: What now? What's worse than this?
Messenger: The queen is dead.
          The mother of this dead boy . . . mother to the end—
          poor thing, her wounds are fresh.
Creon: No, no,
          harbor of Death, so choked, so hard to cleanse!—
          why me? why are you killing me?   1415
          Herald of pain, more words, more grief?
          I died once, you kill me again and again!
          What's the report, boy . . . some news for me?
          My wife dead? O dear god!
          Slaughter heaped on slaughter?

The doors open; the body of Eurydice is brought out on her bier.

Messenger:　　　　　　　　　　　　　　See for yourself:　　　　1420
　　now they bring her body from the palace.
Creon:　　　　　　　　　　　　　　　　　　Oh no,
　　　　another, a second loss to break the heart.
　　　　What next, what fate still waits for me?
　　　　I just held my son in my arms and now,
　　　　look, a new corpse rising before my eyes—　　　　1425
　　　　　　wretched, helpless mother—O my son!
Messenger: She stabbed herself at the altar,
　　　　then her eyes went dark, after she'd raised
　　　　a cry for the noble fate of Megareus,° the hero
　　　　killed in the first assault, then for Haemon,　　　　1430
　　　　then with her dying breath she called down
　　　　torments on your head—you killed her sons.
Creon:　　　　　　　　　　　　　　　　Oh the dread,
　　　　I shudder with dread! Why not kill me too?—
　　　　run me through with a good sharp sword?
　　　　Oh god, the misery, anguish—　　　　1435
　　　　I, I'm churning with it, going under.
Messenger: Yes, and the dead, the woman lying there,
　　　　piles the guilt of all their deaths on you.
Creon: How did she end her life, what bloody stroke?
Messenger: She drove home to the heart with her own hand,　　　　1440
　　　　once she learned her son was dead . . . that agony.
Creon: And the guilt is all mine—
　　　　can never be fixed on another man,
　　　　no escape for me. I killed you,
　　　　I, god help me, I admit it all!　　　　1445

　　To his attendants.

　　　　Take me away, quickly, out of sight.
　　　　I don't even exist—I'm no one. Nothing.
Leader: Good advice, if there's any good in suffering.
　　Quickest is best when troubles block the way.
Creon:

　　Kneeling in prayer.

　　　　Come, let it come!—that best of fates for me　　　　1450
　　　　that brings the final day, best fate of all.
　　　　Oh quickly, now—
　　　　so I never have to see another sunrise.
Leader: That will come when it comes;
　　we must deal with all that lies before us.　　　　1455
　　The future rests with the ones who tend the future.
Creon: That prayer—I poured my heart into that prayer!
Leader: No more prayers now. For mortal men
　　there is no escape from the doom we must endure.
Creon: Take me away, I beg you, out of sight.　　　　1460
　　　　A rash, indiscriminate fool!
　　　　I murdered you, my son, against my will—

1429 *Megareus:* A son of Creon and Eurydice; he died when Thebes was attacked.

you too, my wife . . .
                    Wailing wreck of a man,
whom to look to? where to lean for support?

Desperately turning from Haemon to Eurydice on their biers.

Whatever I touch goes wrong — once more   1465
a crushing fate's come down upon my head.

The Messenger and attendants lead Creon into the palace.

Chorus: Wisdom is by far the greatest part of joy,
            and reverence toward the gods must be safeguarded.
            The mighty words of the proud are paid in full
            with mighty blows of fate, and at long last   1470
                those blows will teach us wisdom.

The old citizens exit to the side.

CONSIDERATIONS FOR CRITICAL THINKING AND WRITING

1. FIRST RESPONSE. What are Creon's reasons for issuing the decree forbidding Polynices' burial? What are Antigone's reasons for rejecting Creon's order? Whose arguments are more convincing?

2. What is the Chorus's position on Creon's decree? Does the Chorus see the conflict between Antigone and Creon as simply a collision between two strong-willed individuals, or does it see a larger issue at stake?

3. How does Ismene serve as a foil to Antigone? Does Ismene seem weak, or is she reasonable? Why does Antigone reject her sister's offer to martyr herself?

4. How does Haemon serve as a foil to Creon? Is Haemon's decision to commit suicide plausible?

5. What is Creon's attitude toward women? How does this affect his reaction to Antigone's disobedience to the state?

6. Who is responsible for what happens? Does Sophocles suggest that the tragedy could have been avoided if Creon or Antigone had behaved differently? Do Creon and Antigone share any similar characteristics?

7. Describe what you think Sophocles' attitudes were concerning the competing claims for the authority of the state over the individual. Explain how those views are indicated in the play and whether you agree or disagree with them.

8. How might the emphasis of the play have been changed if Sophocles had included the scene in the tomb between Haemon and Antigone? Why do you think he left out such a potentially affecting scene?

9. If you were to stage this play in a contemporary setting, describe what kinds of sets you would use and how you would costume the players.

CONNECTIONS TO OTHER SELECTIONS

1. How is Creon's reaction to Haemon's and Tiresias's pleas that he rescind the decree similar to Oedipus's reaction to Creon and Tiresias in *Oedipus the King*?

2. What similarities and differences are there in Sophocles' characterization of Creon in *Antigone* and in *Oedipus the King*?

3. Consider this assessment of Antigone by the leader of the Chorus (lines 526–528):

> Like father like daughter,
> passionate, wild . . .
> she hasn't learned to bend before adversity.

Does this accurately characterize Antigone? What similarities are there between Oedipus and his daughter? Could these lines also be used to describe Haemon and Ismene?

PERSPECTIVES ON SOPHOCLES

ARISTOTLE (384–322 B.C.)

On Tragic Character

c. 340 B.C.

Now since in the finest kind of tragedy the structure should be complex and not simple, and since it should also be a representation of terrible and piteous events (that being the special mark of this type of imitation), in the first place, it is evident that good men ought not to be shown passing from happiness to misfortune, for this does not inspire either pity or fear, but only revulsion; nor evil men rising from ill fortune to prosperity, for this is the most untragic plot of all — it lacks every requirement, in that it neither elicits human sympathy nor stirs pity or fear. And again, neither should an extremely wicked man be seen falling from prosperity into misfortune, for a plot so constructed might indeed call forth human sympathy, but would not excite pity or fear, since the first is felt for a person whose misfortune is undeserved and the second for someone like ourselves — pity for the man suffering undeservedly, fear for the man like ourselves — and hence neither pity nor fear would be aroused in this case. We are left with the man whose place is between these extremes. Such is the man who on the one hand is not preeminent in virtue and justice, and yet on the other hand does not fall into misfortune through vice or depravity, but falls because of some mistake; one among the number of the highly renowned and prosperous, such as Oedipus . . . and other famous men from families like [his].

It follows that the plot which achieves excellence will necessarily be single in outcome and not, as some say, double, and will consist in a change of fortune, not to prosperity from misfortune, but the opposite, from prosperity to misfortune, occasioned not by depravity, but by some great mistake on the part of one who is either such as I have described or better than this rather than worse. What actually has taken place has confirmed this; for though at first the poets accepted whatever myths came to hand, today the finest tragedies are founded upon the stories of only a few houses . . . and such . . . as have chanced to suffer terrible things or to do them. So then, tragedy having this construction is the finest kind of tragedy from an artistic point of view. And consequently those persons fall into the same error who bring it as a charge against Euripides° that this is what he does in his tragedies and that most of his plays have unhappy endings. For this is in fact the right procedure,

---

Euripides: Fifth century B.C. Greek playwright whose tragedies include Electra, Medea, and Alcestis.

as I have said; and the best proof is that on the stage and in the dramatic contests, plays of this kind seem the most tragic, provided they are successfully worked out, and Euripides, even if in everything else his management is faulty, seems at any rate to be the most tragic of the poets.

Second to this is the kind of plot that some persons place first, that which like the *Odyssey*° has a double structure and ends in opposite ways for the better characters and the worse. If it seems to be first, that is attributable to the weakness of the audience, since the poets only follow their lead and compose the kind of plays the spectators want. The pleasure it gives, however, is not that which comes from tragedy, but is rather the pleasure proper to comedy; for in comedy those who in the legend are the worst of enemies . . . end by leaving the scene as friends, and nobody is killed by anybody. . . .

With regard to the characters there are four things to aim at. First and foremost is that the characters be good. The personages will have character if, as aforesaid, they reveal in speech or in action what their moral choices are, and a good character will be one whose choices are good. It is possible to portray goodness in every class of persons; a woman may be good and a slave may be good, though perhaps as a class women are inferior and slaves utterly base. The second requisite is to make the character appropriate. Thus it is possible to portray any character as manly, but inappropriate for a female character to be manly or formidable in the way I mean. Third is to make the characters lifelike, which is something different from making them good and appropriate as described above. Fourth is to make them consistent. Even if the person being imitated is inconsistent and this is what the character is supposed to be, he should nevertheless be portrayed as consistently inconsistent. . . .

In the characters and in the plot-construction alike, one must strive for that which is either necessary or probable, so that whatever a character of any kind says or does may be the sort of thing such a character will inevitably or probably say or do and the events of the plot may follow one after another either inevitably or with probability. (Obviously, then, the *dénouement* of the plot should arise from the plot itself and not be brought about "from the machine." . . . The machine is to be used for matters lying outside the drama, either antecedents of the action which a human being cannot know, or things subsequent to the action that have to be prophesied and announced; for we accept it that the gods see everything. Within the events of the plot itself, however, there should be nothing unreasonable, or if there is, it should be kept outside the play proper as is done in the *Oedipus* of Sophocles.)

Inasmuch as tragedy is an imitation of persons who are better than the average, the example of good portrait-painters should be followed. These, while reproducing the distinctive appearance of their subjects in a recognizable likeness, make them handsomer in the picture than they are in reality. Similarly the poet when he comes to imitate men who are irascible or easygoing or have other defects of character should depict them as such and yet as good men at the same time.

From Poetics, translated by James Hutton

Odyssey: The epic by the ancient Greek poet Homer that chronicles the voyage home from the Trojan War of Odysseus (also known as Ulysses).

CONSIDERATIONS FOR CRITICAL THINKING AND WRITING

1. Why does Aristotle insist that both virtuous and depraved characters are unsuitable as tragic figures? What kind of person constitutes a tragic character according to him?

2. Aristotle argues that it is "inappropriate for a female character to be manly or formidable" (para. 4). Do you think Antigone fits this negative description? Does she seem "inferior" to the men in the play?

3. Aristotle says that characters should be "lifelike" (para. 4), but he also points out that characters should be made "handsomer . . . than they are in reality" (para. 6). Is this a contradiction? Explain why or why not.

SIGMUND FREUD (1856–1939)

On the Oedipus Complex   1900

If *Oedipus Rex* moves a modern audience no less than it did the contemporary Greek one, the explanation can only be that its effect does not lie in the contrast between destiny and human will, but is to be looked for in the particular nature of the material on which that contrast is exemplified. There must be something which makes a voice within us ready to recognize the compelling force of destiny in the *Oedipus*. . . . His destiny moves us only because it might have been ours—because the oracle laid the same curse upon us before our birth as upon him. It is the fate of all of us, perhaps, to direct our first sexual impulse toward our mother and our first hatred and our first murderous wish against our father. Our dreams convince us that this is so. King Oedipus, who slew his father Laïus and married his mother Jocasta, merely shows us the fulfillment of our own childhood wishes. But, more fortunate than he, we have meanwhile succeeded, in so far as we have not become psychoneurotics, in detaching our sexual impulses from our mothers and in forgetting our jealousy of our fathers. Here is one in whom these primeval wishes of our childhood have been fulfilled, and we shrink back from him with the whole force of the repression by which those wishes have since that time been held down within us. While the poet, as he unravels the past, brings to light the guilt of Oedipus, he is at the same time compelling us to recognize our own inner minds, in which those same impulses, though suppressed, are still to be found. The contrast with which the closing Chorus leaves us confronted—

> . . . Fix on Oedipus your eyes,
> Who resolved the dark enigma, noblest champion and most wise.
> Like a star his envied fortune mounted beaming far and wide:
> Now he sinks in seas of anguish, whelmed beneath a raging tide . . .[1]

—strikes as a warning at ourselves and our pride, at us who since our childhood have grown so wise and so mighty in our own eyes. Like Oedipus, we live in ignorance of these wishes, repugnant to morality, which have been forced upon us by Nature, and after their revelation we may all of us well seek to close our eyes to the scenes of our childhood.

[1]Lewis Campbell's translation, lines 1524ff [in *The Bedford Introduction to Literature*, lines 1678-1682].

There is an unmistakable indication in the text of Sophocles' tragedy itself that the legend of Oedipus sprang from some primeval dream material which had as its content the distressing disturbance of a child's relation to his parents owing to the first stirrings of sexuality. At a point when Oedipus, though he is not yet enlightened, has begun to feel troubled by his recollection of the oracle, Jocasta consoles him by referring to a dream which many people dream, though, as she thinks, it has no meaning:

> Many a man ere now in dreams hath lain
> With her who bare him. He hath least annoy
> Who with such omens troubleth not his mind.[2]

Today, just as then, many men dream of having sexual relations with their mothers, and speak of the fact with indignation and astonishment. It is clearly the key to the tragedy and the complement to the dream of the dreamer's father being dead. The story of Oedipus is the reaction of the imagination to these two typical dreams. And just as these dreams, when dreamt by adults, are accompanied by feelings of repulsion, so too the legend must include horror and self-punishment. Its further modification originates once again in a misconceived secondary revision of the material, which has sought to exploit it for theological purposes. . . . The attempt to harmonize divine omnipotence with human responsibility must naturally fail in connection with this subject matter just as with any other.

From Interpretation of Dreams, translated by James Strachey

[2]Lewis Campbell's translation, lines 982ff [in *The Bedford Introduction to Literature*, lines 1074–1076].

CONSIDERATIONS FOR CRITICAL THINKING AND WRITING

1. Read the section on psychological criticism in Chapter 52, "Critical Strategies for Reading" (pp. 2099–101) for additional information about Freud's theory concerning the Oedipus complex. Explain whether you agree or disagree that Freud's approach offers the "key to the tragedy" of *Oedipus the King.*

2. How does Freud's view of tragic character differ from Aristotle's (p. 1369)?

SOPHOCLES (496?–406 B.C.)

Another Translation of a Scene from Oedipus the King   *1920*

Enter Oedipus, blind.

Chorus: O sight for all the world to see
    Most terrible! O suffering
    Of all mine eyes have seen most terrible!
    Alas! What Fury came on thee?
    What evil Spirit, from afar,
    O Oedipus! O Wretched!
        Leapt on thee, to destroy?
    I cannot even Alas! look

Upon thy face, though much I have
To ask of thee, and much to hear,
Aye, and to see — I cannot!
Such terror is in thee!

Oedipus: Alas! O Wretched! Whither go
My steps? My voice? It seems to float
Far, far away from me.
Alas! Curse of my Life, how far
Thy leap hath carried thee!

Chorus: To sorrows none can bear to see or hear.

Oedipus: Ah! The cloud!
Visitor unspeakable! Darkness upon me horrible!
Unconquerable! Cloud that may not ever pass away!
Alas!
And yet again, alas! How deep they stab —
These throbbing pains, and all those memories.

Chorus: Where such afflictions are, I marvel not,
If soul and body made one doubled woe.

Oedipus: Ah! My friend!
Still remains thy friendship. Still thine is the help that comforts me,
And kindness, that can look upon these dreadful eyes unchanged.
Ah me!
My friend, I feel thy presence. Though mine eyes
Be darkened, yet I hear thy voice, and know.

Chorus: Oh, dreadful deed! How wert thou steeled to quench
Thy vision thus? What Spirit came on thee?

Oedipus: Apollo! 'Twas Apollo, friends,
Willed the evil, willed, and brought the agony to pass!
And yet the hand that struck was mine, mine only, wretched.
Why should I see, whose eyes
Had no more any good to look upon?

Chorus: 'Twas even as thou sayest.

Oedipus: Aye. For me . . . Nothing is left for sight.
Nor anything to love:
Nor shall the sound of greetings any more
Fall pleasant on my ear.
Away! Away! Out of the land, away!
Banishment, Banishment! Fatal am I, accursed,
And the hate on me, as on no man else, of the gods!

Chorus: Unhappy in thy fortune and the wit
That shows it thee. Would thou hadst never known.

Oedipus: A curse upon the hand that loosed
In the wilderness the cruel fetters of my feet,
Rescued me, gave me life! Ah! Cruel was his pity,
Since, had I died, so much
I had not harmed myself and all I love.

Chorus: Aye, even so 'twere better.

Oedipus: Aye, for life never had led me then
To shed my father's blood;

Men had not called me husband of the wife
That bore me in the womb.
But now—but now—Godless am I, the son
Born of impurity, mate of my father's bed,
And if worse there be, I am Oedipus! It is mine!

Chorus: In this I know not how to call thee wise,
For better wert thou dead than living—blind.

Oedipus: Nay, give me no more counsel. Bid me not
Believe my deed, thus done, is not well done.
I know 'tis well. When I had passed the grave,
How could those eyes have met my father's gaze,
Or my unhappy mother's—since on both
I have done wrongs beyond all other wrong?
Or live and see my children?—Children born
As they were born! What pleasure in that sight?
None for these eyes of mine, for ever, none.
Nor in the sight of Thebes, her castles, shrines
And images of the gods, whereof, alas!
I robbed myself—myself, I spoke that word,
I that she bred and nurtured, I her prince,
And bade her thrust the sinner out, the man
Proved of the gods polluted—Laïus' son.
When such a stain by my own evidence
Was on me, could I raise my eyes to them?
No! Had I means to stop my ears, and choke
The wells of sound, I had not held my hand,
But closed my body like a prison-house
To hearing as to sight. Sweet for the mind
To dwell withdrawn, where troubles could not come.
Cithaeron! Ah, why didst thou welcome me?
Why, when thou hadst me there, didst thou not kill,
Never to show the world myself—my birth!
O Polybus, and Corinth, and the home
Men called my father's ancient house, what sores
Festered beneath that beauty that ye reared,
Discovered now, sin out of sin begot.
O ye three roads, O secret mountain-glen,
Trees, and a pathway narrowed to the place
Where met the three, do you remember me?
I gave you blood to drink, my father's blood,
And so my own! Do you remember that?
The deed I wrought for you? Then, how I passed
Hither to other deeds?
O Marriage-bed
That gave me birth, and, having borne me, gave
Fresh children to your seed, and showed the world
Father, son, brother, mingled and confused,
Bride, mother, wife in one, and all the shame
Of deeds the foulest ever known to man.

No. Silence for a deed so ill to do
Is better. Therefore lead me hence, away!
To hide me or to kill. Or to the sea
Cast me, where you shall look on me no more.
Come! Deign to touch me, though I am a man
Accursèd. Yield! Fear nothing! Mine are woes
That no man else, but I alone, must bear.

Translated by J. T. Sheppard

CONSIDERATIONS FOR CRITICAL THINKING AND WRITING

1. This excerpt from Sheppard's translation corresponds to lines 1433–1550 in Robert Fagles's translation (p. 1289). Examine both versions of the scene and describe the diction and tone of each. If you find one of the translations more effective than the other, indicate why.

2. Explain whether the different translations affect your understanding or interpretation of the scene.

MURIEL RUKEYSER (1913–1980)

On Oedipus the King   1973

Myth

Long afterward, Oedipus, old and blinded, walked the
roads.   He smelled a familiar smell.   It was
the Sphinx.   Oedipus said, "I want to ask one question.
Why didn't I recognize my mother?"   "You gave the
wrong answer," said the Sphinx.   "But that was what   5
made everything possible," said Oedipus.   "No," she said.
"When I asked, What walks on four legs in the morning,
two at noon, and three in the evening, you answered,
Man.   You didn't say anything about woman."
"When you say Man," said Oedipus, "you include women   10
too. Everyone knows that." She said, "That's what
you think."

CONSIDERATIONS FOR CRITICAL THINKING AND WRITING

1. What elements of the Oedipus story does Rukeyser allude to in the poem?

2. To what does the title of Rukeyser's poem, "Myth," refer? How does the word *myth* carry more than one meaning?

3. This poem is amusing, but its ironic ending points to a serious theme. What is it? Does Sophocles' play address any of the issues raised in the poem?

Jean Anouilh (1910–1987)

A Scene from Antigone   1944

Creon: I shall save you yet. *(He goes below the table to the chair at end of table, takes off his coat, and places it on the chair.)* God knows, I have things enough to do today without wasting my time on an insect like you. There's plenty to do, I assure you, when you've just put down a revolution. But urgent things can wait. I am not going to let politics be the cause of your death. For it is a fact that this whole business is nothing but politics: the mournful shade of Polynices, the decomposing corpse, the sentimental weeping, and the hysteria that you mistake for heroism — nothing but politics.

Look here. I may not be soft, but I'm fastidious. I like things clean, ship-shape, well scrubbed. Don't think that I am not just as offended as you are by the thought of that meat rotting in the sun. In the evening, when the breeze comes in off the sea, you can smell it in the palace, and it nauseates me. But I refuse even to shut my window. It's vile; and I can tell you what I wouldn't tell anybody else: it's stupid, monstrously stupid. But the people of Thebes have got to have their noses rubbed into it a little longer. My God! If it was up to me, I should have had them bury your brother long ago as a mere matter of public hygiene. I admit that what I am doing is childish. But if the featherheaded rabble I govern are to understand what's what, that stench has got to fill the town for a month!

Antigone (turns to him): You are a loathsome man!

Creon: I agree. My trade forces me to be. We could argue whether I ought or ought not to follow my trade; but once I take on the job, I must do it properly.

Antigone: Why do you do it at all?

Creon: My dear, I woke up one morning and found myself King of Thebes. God knows, there were other things I loved in life more than power.

Antigone: Then you should have said no.

Creon: Yes, I could have done that. Only, I felt that it would have been cowardly. I should have been like a workman who turns down a job that has to be done. So I said yes.

Antigone: So much the worse for you, then. I didn't say yes. I can say no to anything I think vile, and I don't have to count the cost. But because you said yes, all that you can do, for all your crown and your trappings, and your guards — all that you can do is to have me killed.

Creon: Listen to me.

Antigone: If I want to. I don't have to listen to you if I don't want to. You've said your *yes*. There is nothing more you can tell me that I don't know. You stand there, drinking in my words. *(She moves behind chair.)* Why is it that you don't call your guards? I'll tell you why. You want to hear me out to the end; that's why.

Creon: You amuse me.

Antigone: Oh, no, I don't. I frighten you. That is why you talk about saving me. Everything would be so much easier if you had a docile, tongue-tied little Antigone living in the palace. I'll tell you something, Uncle Creon: I'll give you back one of your own words. You are too fastidious to make a good tyrant. But you are going to have to put me to death today, and you know it. And that's what frightens you. God! Is there anything uglier than a frightened man!

Creon: Very well. I am afraid, then. Does that satisfy you? I am afraid that if you insist upon it, I shall have to have you killed. And I don't want to.

Antigone: I don't have to do things that I think are wrong. If it comes to that, you didn't really want to leave my brother's body unburied, did you? Say it! Admit that you didn't.

Creon: I have said it already.

Antigone: But you did it just the same. And now, though you don't want to do it, you are going to have me killed. And you call that being a king!

Creon: Yes, I call that being a king.

Antigone: Poor Creon! My nails are broken, my fingers are bleeding, my arms are covered with the welts left by the paws of your guards—but I am a queen!

Creon: Then why not have pity on me, and live? Isn't your brother's corpse, rotting there under my windows, payment enough for peace and order in Thebes? My son loves you. Don't make me add your life to the payment. I've paid enough.

Antigone: No, Creon! You said yes, and made yourself king. Now you will never stop paying.

Creon: But God in heaven! Won't you try to understand me! I'm trying hard enough to understand you! There had to be one man who said yes. Somebody had to agree to captain the ship. She had sprung a hundred leaks; she was loaded to the water line with crime, ignorance, poverty. The wheel was swinging with the wind. The crew refused to work and were looting the cargo. The officers were building a raft, ready to slip overboard and desert the ship. The mast was splitting, the wind was howling, the sails were beginning to rip. Every man jack on board was about to drown—and only because the only thing they thought of was their own skins and their cheap little day-to-day traffic. Was that a time, do you think, for playing with words like yes and no? Was that a time for a man to be weighing the pros and cons, wondering if he wasn't going to pay too dearly later on; if he wasn't going to lose his life, or his family, or his touch with other men? You grab the wheel, you right the ship in the face of a mountain of water. You shout an order, and if one man refuses to obey, you shoot straight into the mob. Into the mob, I say! The beast as nameless as the wave that crashes down upon your deck; as nameless as the whipping wind. The thing that drops when you shoot may be someone who poured you a drink the night before; but it has no name. And you, braced at the wheel, you have no name, either. Nothing has a name—except the ship, and the storm. *(A pause as he looks at her.)* Now do you understand?

Antigone: I am not here to understand. That's all very well for you. I am here to say no to you, and die.

Creon: It is easy to say no.

Antigone: Not always.

Creon: It is easy to say no. To say yes, you have to sweat and roll up your sleeves and plunge both hands into life up to the elbows. It is easy to say no, even if saying no means death. All you have to do is to sit still and wait. Wait to go on living; wait to be killed. That is the coward's part. *No* is one of your man-made words. Can you imagine a world in which trees say *no* to the sap? In which beasts say *no* to hunger or to propagation? Animals are good, simple, tough. They move in droves, nudging one another onwards, all traveling the same road. Some of them keel over, but the rest go on; and no matter how many may fall by the wayside, there are always those few left that go on bringing their young into the world, traveling the same road with the same obstinate will, unchanged from those who went before.

Antigone: Animals, eh, Creon! What a king you could be if only men were animals!

Translated by Lewis Galantière

CONSIDERATIONS FOR CRITICAL THINKING AND WRITING

1. What are Creon's reasons for not burying Polynices? How does he defend his actions as a ruler?
2. In what sense is Antigone correct when she describes Creon as "too fastidious to make a good tyrant"?
3. Do you agree with Creon that Antigone takes "the coward's part" by saying no rather than yes? With which character do you sympathize more? How might Creon's position be related to the fact that France was occupied by German troops during World War II, when Anouilh wrote this play?
4. How does Anouilh's treatment of Creon compare with Sophocles'?

MAURICE SAGOFF

A Humorous Distillation of Antigone   *1980*

Tyrant Creon's stern advice is
"Do not bury Polynices!
Thebes' defenders had to squash him —
Now we'll let the buzzards nosh him!"
But Antigone, the brave,   5
Dared to dig her brother's grave:
"Man-made laws my soul defies —
Live by laws divine!" she cries.

Creon locks her up, the demon!
Though she's pledged to marry Haemon   10
(That's his son). Now comes a seer
Prophesying woes severe:
If her brother's not entombed
And she dies, then Haemon's doomed!

Creon seeing things go screwy,   15
Wilts, and tries to bang a U-ee,
But the Gods who drive the hearse
Seldom shove it in reverse . . .
Carnage follows, sure as Fate;
Here's the body-count to date —   20
1. Antigone 2. her brother

3. young Haemon   4. his mother
(If more bodies fail to fall,
It's because the cast is small).

Strung-out Creon takes the blame.   25
Exits, croaking "Rotten shame!"
From *Shrinklits: Seventy of the World's Towering Classics Cut Down to Size*

CONSIDERATIONS FOR CRITICAL THINKING AND WRITING

1. Sagoff writes in his tongue-in-cheek introduction to *Shrinklits* that "inside every fat book is a skinny book trying to get out, struggling to cut through the mummylike wrappings of long-winded descriptions, superfluous characters, endless conversations, and turgid style." How successful is this poem in summarizing the plot of *Antigone*? What is left out of Sagoff's account?

2. Using Sagoff's version of *Antigone* as your inspiration, choose another play in the text and try writing a shrinklit that does it humorous justice.

BERNARD KNOX (B. 1914)

On Oedipus and Human Freedom   *1982*

Oedipus did have one freedom: he was free to find out or not find out the truth. This was the element of Sophoclean sleight-of-hand that enabled him to make a drama out of the situation which the philosophers used as the classic demonstration of man's subjection to fate. But it is more than a solution to an apparently insoluble dramatic problem; it is the key to the play's tragic theme and the protagonist's heroic stature. One freedom is allowed him: the freedom to search for the truth, the truth about the prophecies, about the gods, about himself. And of this freedom he makes full use. Against the advice and appeals of others, he pushes on, searching for the truth, the whole truth, and nothing but the truth. And in this search he shows all those great qualities that we admire in him — courage, intelligence, perseverance, the qualities that make human beings great. This freedom to search, and the heroic way in which Oedipus uses it, makes the play not a picture of man's utter feebleness caught in the toils of fate, but on the contrary, a heroic example of man's dedication to the search for truth, the truth about himself. This is perhaps the only human freedom, the play seems to say, but there could be none more noble.

From the Introduction to *Three Theban Plays*, translated by Robert Fagles

CONSIDERATIONS FOR CRITICAL THINKING AND WRITING

1. Do you agree with Knox that Oedipus's "freedom to search for the truth" represents a genuine kind of freedom, despite the outcome of his search?

2. What other qualities do you find in Oedipus besides "courage, intelligence," and "perseverance"?

3. Write an essay that considers whether Oedipus should be regarded as a "classic demonstration of man's subjection to fate."

TWO COMPLEMENTARY CRITICAL READINGS

R. G. A. BUXTON (B. 1948)

The Major Critical Issue in Antigone   *1984*

It seems agreed that the main critical issue is: how do we evaluate the respective moral positions of Antigone and Creon. Provided this is not asked in order to achieve "that nice apportionment of blame to which critics are so much more prone than dramatists,"[1] but rather with the aim of teasing out just what is at stake between the two principal figures, the question is worthwhile.

Defenders of Creon appear from time to time. There is no doubt that some of the sentiments he expresses, particularly in his opening program-matic speech, are laudable in themselves; nor should there be any doubt that Creon receives some measure of sympathy as he carries his son's body on stage at the end. But is his original proclamation (it is not a law) morally acceptable? Tiresias' dire warnings strongly suggest it is not. There has been much argu-ment about how Creon's edict related to Athenian law, but certain points are clear: although there was apparently nothing abnormal in the denial of burial in his homeland to a traitor, not only was there a custom, specifically associ-ated with Athens, according to which one should not pass a corpse by without placing some dust upon it, but also, in forbidding Polynices burial *anywhere,* in actively ensuring that his body be torn apart by dogs and birds, Creon plainly went too far.

Most critics accept the moral impropriety of Creon's proclamation and disagree only in the degree (or absence) of qualification which they allow in their approval of Antigone. For some the approval is absolute; others, believ-ing gray to be a more interesting color than black and white, stress problem-atic aspects of her behavior — harshness towards Ismene, relentless concern with honor, etc. A beneficial corollary of the latter approach is that, by em-phasizing the particularity of Antigone's character, it makes us less likely to reduce the play to an opposition between principles — city *versus* kin-bond, state *versus* individual, or whatever. Neither Creon nor Antigone is the vehicle for a simple idea: "the theme of ... *Antigone* ... [is] the tragedy of two human downfalls, separate in nature, ... following one another as contrasting patterns."[2]

From Sophocles

[1] R. P. Winnington-Ingram, *Sophocles: Art Interpretation* (Cambridge, England: Cambridge UP, 1980), 75.
[2] Reinhardt, *Sophocles* (Oxford, England: Oxford UP, 1979), 65. For *Antigone* as comprising two interdependent and equally important downfalls, see J. C. Hogan, "The Protagonists of the *Antigone,*" *Arethusa* 5 (1972), 93–100.

CONSIDERATIONS FOR CRITICAL THINKING AND WRITING

1. How do you think "the particularity of Antigone's character . . . makes us less likely to reduce the play to an opposition between principles" (para. 3)? How does Sophocles' characterization of her make the play more complex?

2. Write an essay in which you agree or disagree that the theme of *Antigone* is "the tragedy of two human downfalls, separate in nature . . . following one another as contrasting patterns" (para. 3). Do you think this theme is a means of resolving critical debate about the play or a way to evade having to choose between Antigone and Creon?

CYNTHIA P. GARDINER (B. 1942)
The Function of the Chorus in Antigone   *1987*

[*Antigone* is] concerned with the topic of political morality, with philosophies of governance and the conflict of religion and law. Yet despite the immensity of these abstractions, the immediate dramatic intent of the poet is not the subject of critical dispute, in that critics do not tend to hold violently contradictory opinions about the poet's own views. Nearly everyone agrees that Sophocles intended to portray Antigone's burial of Polynices as "right" — sanctioned by the gods according to Tiresias' revelations — and Creon's opposition to the burial as "wrong," insofar as his opposition arises from tyrannical behavior. It then becomes merely a question of the degree to which one condemns Creon or approves Antigone; the latter course usually involves an appraisal of Antigone's motives and of her behavior as a woman.

The lengthy and frequent lyrics have exerted considerable influence upon the interpretation of the play's symbolism and judgment. Some of the odes are apparently so loosely connected to the action that they can be readily lifted out of context to function as independent poems. Or, when left in the play, they seem sometimes so ambiguous that their relevance to the plot is perceptible only through the most detailed and subtle analysis. It is generally agreed nowadays that the most productive approach to interpreting the choral lyrics is to assume that they arise from a distinct and consistent persona. This being accepted, it is again a question of the degree to which one believes that the chorus support either Creon or Antigone. Some say that the chorus are utterly devoted to Creon throughout the play, or right up to the last possible moment at line 1272; some, that they begin by supporting the king but change their minds at one earlier point or another during the action. Others see the chorus as vacillating between viewpoints until a decision is forced upon them by Tiresias; still others see them as Antigone's partisans, though necessarily secret ones, from the very beginning.

From *The Sophoclean Chorus: A Study of Character and Function*

CONSIDERATIONS FOR CRITICAL THINKING AND WRITING

1. Do you agree with Gardiner that Antigone was "right" and Creon "wrong" (para. 1)? Explain why. How is this issue made complicated by Antigone's character?

2. Of the various interpretations Gardiner summarizes concerning the chorus's loyalty to Creon or Antigone, which do you think is most accurate? In an essay explain why.

—————— SUGGESTED TOPICS FOR LONGER PAPERS ——————

1. In *Oedipus the King* and in *Antigone,* private and public worlds collide and produce overwhelming conflicts for the protagonists. In your essay, explore how the plays' conflicts can be framed by a consideration of the private and public identities of the major characters.

2. Individual responses to authority loom large in each play. Use the library to determine how Sophocles' contemporaries regarded individuals' responsibility to their kings and their kings' obligations to them. Given this context, how do you judge the behavior of Oedipus and Creon as kings in their respective societies?

3. **MULTIMEDIA PROJECT.** Many performances of *Oedipus the King* and *Antigone* are available on video. Find at least two videotapes or clips of either one of the plays and view the same scene of your choice for each. Write an analysis of the scene that compares the performance of each version. Which do you prefer? Explain why.

Web   *For help with this project, use the Multimedia Project Guides Online at* http://www.bedfordstmartins.com/meyer/bedintrolit

44

A Study of William Shakespeare

Although relatively little is known about William Shakespeare's life, his writings reveal him to have been an extraordinary man. His vitality, compassion, and insights are evident in his broad range of characters, who have fascinated generations of audiences, and his powerful use of the English language, which has been celebrated since his death nearly four centuries ago. Ben Jonson, his contemporary, rightly claimed that "he was not of an age, but for all time!" Shakespeare's plays have been produced so often and his writings read so widely that quota-

tions from them have woven their way into our everyday conversations. If you have ever experienced "fear and trembling" because there was "something in the wind" or discovered that it was "a foregone conclusion" that you would "make a virtue of necessity," then it wouldn't be quite accurate for you to say that Shakespeare "was Greek to me" because these phrases come, respectively, from his plays *Much Ado about Nothing*, *Comedy of Errors*, *Othello*, *The Two Gentlemen of Verona*, and *Julius Caesar*. Many more examples could be cited, but it is enough to say that Shakespeare's art endures. His words may give us only an oblique glimpse of his life, but they continue to give us back the experience of our own lives.

Shakespeare was born in Stratford-on-Avon on or about April 23, 1564. His father, an important citizen who held several town offices, married a

PHOTO ABOVE: *Image of William Shakespeare included on the First Folio, a collected edition of Shakespeare plays published seven years after his death. Reprinted by permission of The Folger Shakespeare Library.*

woman from a prominent family; however, when their son was only a teenager, the family's financial situation became precarious. Shakespeare probably attended the Stratford grammar school, but no records of either his schooling or his early youth exist. As limited as his education was, it is clear that he was for his time a learned man. At the age of eighteen, he struck out on his own and married the twenty-six-year-old Anne Hathaway, who bore him a daughter in 1583 and twins, a boy and a girl, in 1585. Before he was twenty-one, Shakespeare had a wife and three children to support.

What his life was like for the next seven years is not known, but there is firm evidence that by 1592 he was in London enjoying some success as both an actor and a playwright. By 1594 he had also established himself as a poet with two lengthy poems, *Venus and Adonis* and *The Rape of Lucrece*. But it was in the theater that he made his living and his strongest reputation. He was well connected with a successful troupe first known as the Lord Chamberlain's Men; they built the famous Globe Theatre in 1599. Later this company, because of the patronage of King James, came to be known as the King's Men. Writing plays for this company throughout his career, Shakespeare also became one of its principal shareholders, an arrangement that allowed him to prosper in London as well as in his native Stratford, where in 1597 he bought a fine house called New Place. About 1611 he retired there with his family, although he continued writing plays. He died on April 23, 1616, and was buried at Holy Trinity Church in Stratford.

The documented details of Shakespeare's life provide barely enough information for a newspaper obituary. But if his activities remain largely unknown, his writings — among them thirty-seven plays and 154 sonnets — more than compensate for that loss. Plenty of authors have produced more work, but no writer has created so much literature that has been so universally admired. Within twenty-five years Shakespeare's dramatic works included *Hamlet, Macbeth, King Lear, Othello, Julius Caesar, Richard III, 1 Henry IV, Romeo and Juliet, Love's Labour's Lost, A Midsummer Night's Dream, The Tempest, Twelfth Night,* and *Measure for Measure*. These plays represent a broad range of characters and actions conveyed in poetic language that reveals human nature as well as the author's genius.

CHRONOLOGY

1564	Born in April in Stratford-on-Avon. Shakespeare's birthday is traditionally observed on April 23.
1568	Shakespeare's father becomes bailiff (comparable to mayor).
1582	Marries Anne Hathaway.
1583	Daughter Susanna is born.
1585	Twins, Hamnet and Judith, are born.

1585–92	The "lost years." There are many myths about how Shakespeare spent this time before he became known as a playwright in London, but none can be proven and nothing definite is known.
1592	Works as an actor and playwright in London.
1592–93	Writes *Richard III,* among other plays.
1593	Narrative poem *Venus and Adonis* is published.
1594	Works as actor and playwright with the Lord Chamberlain's Company of players, a company that performs at the Globe Theatre.
c. 1594–96	Writes *Romeo and Juliet, Richard II,* and *A Midsummer Night's Dream,* among other plays.
1596	Hamnet (Shakespeare's son) dies.
1596–98	Writes *1 Henry IV* and *2 Henry IV.*
1599	Writes *Julius Caesar.*
c. 1600	Writes *Hamlet.*
1601	Shakespeare's father dies.
1603	Queen Elizabeth I of England dies.
1603–04	Writes *Othello.*
1604	King James I of England is coronated. (James patronizes Shakespeare's company, so they become known as the King's Men.)
1605–07	Writes *King Lear, Macbeth,* and *Antony and Cleopatra.*
c. 1610–11	Writes *The Tempest.*
1616	Dies on April 23.
1623	First Folio edition of Shakespeare's plays is published.

Research William Shakespeare with LitLinks at
http://www.bedfordstmartins.com/meyer/bedintrolit

SHAKESPEARE'S THEATER

Drama languished in Europe after the fall of Rome during the fifth and sixth centuries. From about A.D. 400 to 900 almost no record of dramatic productions exists except for those of minstrels and other entertainers, such as acrobats and jugglers, who traveled through the countryside. The Catholic church was instrumental in suppressing drama because the theater — represented by the excesses of Roman productions — was seen as subversive. No state-sponsored festivals brought people together in huge theaters the way they had in Greek and Roman times.

In the tenth century, however, the church helped revive theater by incorporating dialogues into the Mass as a means of dramatizing portions of the

Gospels. These brief dialogues developed into more elaborate mystery plays, miracle plays, and morality plays, anonymous works that were created primarily to inculcate religious principles rather than to entertain. But these works also marked the reemergence of relatively large dramatic productions.

Mystery plays dramatize stories from the Bible, such as the Creation, the Fall of Adam and Eve, or the Crucifixion. The most highly regarded surviving example is *The Second Shepherd's Play* (c. 1400), which dramatizes Christ's nativity. *Miracle plays* are based on the lives of saints. An extant play of the late fifteenth century, for example, is titled *Saint Mary Magdalene*. *Morality plays* present allegorical stories in which virtues and vices are personified to teach humanity how to achieve salvation. *Everyman* (c. 1500), the most famous example, has as its central conflict every person's struggle to avoid the sins that lead to hell and practice the virtues that are rewarded in heaven.

The clergy who performed these plays gave way to trade guilds that presented them outside the church on stages featuring scenery and costumed characters. The plays' didactic content was gradually abandoned in favor of broad humor and worldly concerns. Thus by the sixteenth century religious drama had been replaced largely by secular drama.

Because theatrical productions were no longer sponsored and financed by the church or trade guilds during Shakespeare's lifetime, playwrights had to figure out ways to draw audiences willing to pay for entertainment. This necessitated some simple but important changes. Somehow, people had to be prevented from seeing a production unless they paid. Hence an enclosed space with controlled access was created. In addition, the plays had to change frequently enough to keep audiences returning, and this resulted in more experienced actors and playwrights sensitive to their audiences' tastes and interests. Plays compelling enough to attract audiences had to employ a powerful writing brought to life by convincing actors in entertaining productions. Shakespeare always wrote his dramas for the stage — for audiences who would see and hear the characters. The conventions of the theater for which he wrote are important, then, for appreciating and understanding his plays. Detailed information about Elizabethan theater (theater during the reign of Elizabeth I, from 1558 to 1603) is less than abundant, but historians have been able to piece together a good sense of what theaters were like from sources such as drawings, building contracts, and stage directions.

Early performances of various kinds took place in the courtyards of inns and taverns. These secular entertainments attracted people of all classes. To the dismay of London officials, such gatherings were also settings for the illegal activities of brawlers, thieves, and prostitutes. To avoid licensing regulations, some theaters were constructed outside the city's limits. The Globe, for instance, built by the Lord Chamberlain's Company, with which Shakespeare was closely associated, was located on the south bank of the Thames River. Regardless of the play, an Elizabethan theatergoer was likely to have an exciting time. Playwrights understood the varied nature of their audiences, so the plays appealed to a broad range of sensibilities and tastes. Philosophy and poetry rubbed shoulders with violence and sexual jokes, and somehow all were made compatible.

Physically, Elizabethan theaters resembled the courtyards where they originated, but the theaters could accommodate more people — perhaps as many as twenty-five hundred. The exterior of a theater building was many-sided or round and enclosed a yard that was only partially roofed over, to take advantage of natural light. The interior walls consisted of three galleries of seats looking onto a platform stage that extended from the rear wall. These seats were sheltered from the weather and more comfortable than the area in front of the stage, which was known as the *pit*. Here "groundlings" paid a penny to stand and watch the performance. Despite the large number of spectators, the theater created an intimate atmosphere because the audience closely surrounded the stage on three sides.

This arrangement produced two theatrical conventions: asides and soliloquies. An *aside* is a speech directed only to the audience. It makes the audience privy to a character's thoughts, allowing them to perceive ironies and intrigues that other characters know nothing about. In a large performing space, such as a Greek amphitheater, asides would be unconvincing because they would have to be declaimed loudly to be heard, but they were well suited to Elizabethan theaters. A *soliloquy* is a speech delivered while an actor is alone on the stage; like an aside, it reveals a character's state of mind. Hamlet's "To be or not to be" speech is the most famous example of a soliloquy.

The Elizabethan platform stage was large enough — approximately 25 feet deep and 40 feet wide — to allow a wide variety of actions, ranging from festive banquets to bloody battles. Sections of the floor could be opened or removed to create, for instance, the gravediggers' scene in *Hamlet* or to allow characters to exit through trapdoors. At the rear of the platform an inner stage was covered by curtains that could be drawn to reveal an interior setting, such as a bedroom or tomb. The curtains were also a natural location for a character to hide in order to overhear conversations. On each side of the curtains were doors through which characters entered and exited. An upper stage could be used as a watchtower, a castle wall, or a balcony. Although most of the action occurred on the main platform stage, there were opportunities for fluid movements from one acting area to another, providing a variety of settings.

These settings were not, however, elaborately indicated by scenery or props. A scene might change when one group of characters left the stage and another entered. A table and some chairs could be carried on quickly to suggest a tavern. But the action was not interrupted for set changes. Instead, the characters' speeches often identify the location of a scene. (In modern editions of Shakespeare's plays, editors indicate in brackets the scene breaks, settings, and movements of actors not identified in the original manuscripts to help readers keep track of things.) Today's performances of the plays frequently use more elaborate settings and props. But

A	Main entrance
B	The yard
C	Entrances to lowest gallery
D	Position of entrances to staircase and upper galleries
E	Corridor serving the different sections of the middle gallery
F	Middle gallery ("Twopenny Rooms")
G	Position of "Gentlemen's Rooms" or "Lords' Rooms"
H	The stage
J	The hanging being put up round the stage
K	The "hell" under the stage

L	The stage trap leading down to the hell
M	Stage doors
N	Curtained "place behind the stage"
O	Gallery above the stage, used as required sometimes by musicians, sometimes by spectators, and often as part of the play
P	Backstage area (the tiring-house)
Q	Tiring-house door
R	Dressing-rooms
S	Wardrobe and storage
T	The hut housing the machine for lowering enthroned gods, etc., to the stage
U	The "heavens"
W	Hoisting the playhouse flag

A conjectural reconstruction of the Globe Theatre, 1599–1613. (Drawing by C. Walter Hodges from his The Globe Restored, *published by Oxford University Press. © 1968 C. Walter Hodges. Reprinted by permission of Oxford University Press.)*

Shakespeare's need to paint his scenery with words resulted in many poetic descriptions. Here is one of moonlight from *Merchant of Venice:*

> How sweet the moonlight sleeps upon this bank!
> Here will we sit and let the sounds of music
> Creep in our ears. Soft stillness and the night
> Become the touches of sweet harmony.

Although the settings were scant and the props mostly limited to what an actor carried onto the stage (a sword, a document, a shovel), Elizabethan costuming was an elaborate visual treat that identified the characters. Moreover, because women were not permitted to act in the theater, their roles were played by young boys dressed in female costumes. In addition, elaborate sound effects were used to create atmosphere. A flourish of trumpets might accompany the entrance of a king; small cannons might be heard during a battle; thunder might punctuate a storm. In short, Elizabethan theater was alive with sights and sounds, but at the center of the stage was the playwright's language; that's where the magic began.

THE RANGE OF SHAKESPEARE'S DRAMA: HISTORY, COMEDY, AND TRAGEDY

Shakespeare's plays fall into three basic categories: histories, comedies, and tragedies. Broadly speaking, a history play is any drama based on historical materials. In this case, Shakespeare's *Antony and Cleopatra* and *Julius Caesar* would fit the definition, since they feature historical figures. More specifically, though, a **history play** is a British play based primarily on Raphael Holinshed's *Chronicles of England, Scotland, and Ireland* (1578). This account of British history was popular toward the end of the sixteenth century because of the patriotic pride that was produced by the British defeat of the Spanish Armada in 1588, and it was an important source for a series of plays Shakespeare wrote treating the reigns of British kings from Richard II to Henry VIII. The political subject matter of these plays both entertained audiences and instructed them in virtues and vices involved in England's past efforts to overcome civil war and disorder. Ambition, deception, and treason were of more than historical interest. Shakespeare's audiences saw these plays about the fifteenth century as ways of sorting through the meanings of both the calamities of the past and the uncertainties of the present.

Although Shakespeare used Holinshed's *Chronicles* as a source, he did not hesitate to make changes for dramatic purposes. In *1 Henry IV,* for example, he ages Henry IV to contrast him with the youthful Prince Hal, and he makes Hotspur younger than he actually was to have him serve as a foil to the prince. The serious theme of Hal's growth into the kind of man who would make an ideal king is counterweighted by Shakespeare's comic creation of Falstaff, that good-humored "huge hill of flesh" filled with delightful contradictions. Falstaff had historic antecedents, but the true source of his identity is the imagination of Shakespeare, a writer who was, after all, a dramatist first.

Comedy is a strong element in *1 Henry IV*, but the play's overall tone is serious. Falstaff's behavior ultimately gives way to the measured march of English history. While Shakespeare encourages us to laugh at some of the participants, we are not invited to laugh at the history of English monarchies. Comedy even appears in Shakespeare's tragedies, as in Hamlet's jests with the gravediggers or in Emilia's biting remarks in *Othello*. This use of comedy is called **comic relief,** a humorous scene or incident that alleviates tension in an otherwise serious work. In many instances these moments enhance the thematic significance of the story in addition to providing laughter. When Hamlet jokes with the gravediggers, we laugh, but something hauntingly serious about the humor also intensifies our more serious emotions.

A true comedy, however, lacks a tragedy's sense that some great disaster will finally descend on the protagonist. There are conflicts and obstacles that must be confronted, but in comedy the characters delight us by overcoming whatever initially thwarts them. We can laugh at their misfortunes because we are confident that everything will turn out fine in the end. Shakespearean comedy tends to follow this general principle; it begins with problems and ends with their resolution.

Shakespeare's comedies are called **romantic comedies** because they typically involve lovers whose hearts are set on each other but whose lives are complicated by disapproving parents, deceptions, jealousies, illusions, confused identities, disguises, or other misunderstandings. Conflicts are present, but they are more amusing than threatening. This lightness is apparent in some of the comedies' titles: the conflict in a play such as *A Midsummer Night's Dream* is, in a sense, *Much Ado about Nothing—As You Like It* in a comedy. Shakespeare orchestrates the problems and confusion that typify the initial plotting of a romantic comedy into harmonious wedding arrangements in the final scenes. In these comedies life is a celebration, a feast that always satisfies, because the generosity of the humor leaves us with a revived appetite for life's surprising possibilities. Discord and misunderstanding give way to concord and love. Marriage symbolizes a pledge that life itself is renewable, so we are left with a sense of new beginnings.

Although a celebration of life, comedy is also frequently used as a vehicle for criticizing human affairs. **Satire** casts a critical eye on vices and follies by holding them up to ridicule—usually to point out an absurdity so that it can be avoided or corrected. In *Twelfth Night* Malvolio is satirized for his priggishness and pomposity. He thinks himself better than almost everyone around him, but Shakespeare reveals him to be comic as well as pathetic. We come to understand what Malvolio will apparently never comprehend: that no one can take him as seriously as he takes himself. Polonius is subjected to a similar kind of scrutiny in *Hamlet*.

Malvolio's ambitious efforts to attract Olivia's affections are rendered absurd by Shakespeare's use of both high and low comedy. **High comedy** consists of verbal wit, while **low comedy** is generally associated with physical action and is less intellectual. Through puns and witty exchanges, Shakespeare's high comedy displays Malvolio's inconsistencies of character. His self-importance is deflated by low comedy. We are treated to a *farce*, a form of humor based on exaggerated, improbable incongruities, when the staid Malvolio is tricked into wearing bizarre clothing and behaving like a fool to win Olivia. Our laughter is Malvolio's pain, but though he has been "notoriously abus'd" and he vows in the final scene to be "reveng'd on the whole pack" of laughing conspirators who have tricked him, the play ends on a light note. Indeed, it concludes with a song, the last line of which reminds us of the predominant tone of the play as well as the nature of comedy: "And we'll strive to please you every day."

Tragedy, in contrast, does not promise peace and contentment. The basic characteristics of tragedy have already been outlined in the context of Greek drama (see Chapter 43). Like Greek tragic heroes, Shakespeare's protagonists are exceptional human beings whose stature makes their misfortune all the more dramatic. These characters pay a high price for their actions. Oedipus's search for the killer of Laius, Antigone's and Creon's refusal to compromise their principles, Hamlet's agonized conviction that "The time is out of joint," and Othello's willingness to doubt his wife's fidelity all lead to irreversible results. Comic plots are largely free of this sense of inevitability. Instead of the festive mood that prevails once the characters in a comedy recognize their true connection to each other, tragedy gives us dark reflections that emanate from suffering. The laughter of comedy is a shared experience, a recognition of human likeness, but suffering estranges tragic heroes from the world around them.

Some of the wrenching differences between comedy and tragedy can be experienced in *Othello.* Although this play is a tragedy, Shakespeare includes in its plot many of the ingredients associated with comedy. For a time it seems possible that Othello and Desdemona will overcome the complications of a disapproving father, along with the seemingly minor deceptions, awkward misperceptions, and tender illusions that hover around them. But in *Othello* marriage is not a sign of concord displacing discord; instead, love and marriage mark the beginning of the tragic action.

Another important difference between tragedy and comedy is the way characters are presented. The tragic protagonist is portrayed as a remarkable individual whose unique qualities compel us with their power and complexity. Macbeth is not simply a murderer nor is Othello merely a jealous husband. But despite their extreme passions, behavior, and even crimes, we identify with tragic heroes in ways that we do not with comic characters. We can laugh at pretentious fools, smug hypocrites, clumsy oafs, and thwarted lovers because we see them from a distance. They are amusing precisely because their problems are not ours; we recognize them as types instead of as ourselves (or so we think). No reader of *Twelfth Night* worries about Sir Toby Belch's excessive drinking; he is a cheerful "sot" whose passion for ale is cause for celebration rather than concern. Shakespeare's comedy is sometimes disturbing—Malvolio's character certainly is—but it is never devastating. Tragic heroes do confront devastation; they command our respect and compassion because they act in spite of terrifying risks. Their triumph is not measured by the attainment of what they seek but by the wisdom that defeat imposes on them.

A NOTE ON READING SHAKESPEARE

Readers who have had no previous experience with Shakespeare's language may find it initially daunting. They might well ask whether people ever talked the way, for example, Hamlet does in his most famous soliloquy:

> To be, or not to be: that is the question:
> Whether 'tis nobler in the mind to suffer
> The slings and arrows of outrageous fortune,
> Or to take arms against a sea of troubles,
> And by opposing end them?

People did not talk like this in Elizabethan times. Hamlet speaks poetry. Shakespeare might have had him say something like this: "The most important issue one must confront is whether the pain that life inevitably creates should be passively accepted or resisted." But Shakespeare chose poetry to reveal the depth and complexity of Hamlet's experience. This heightened language is used to clarify rather than obscure his characters' thoughts. Shakespeare has Hamlet, as well as many other characters, speak in prose too, but in general his plays are written in poetry. If you keep in mind that Shakespeare's dialogue is not typically intended to imitate everyday speech, it should be easier to understand that his language is more than simply a vehicle for expressing the action of the play.

Here are a few practical suggestions to enhance your understanding of and pleasure in reading Shakespeare's plays.

1. Keep track of the characters by referring to the *dramatis personae* (characters) listed and briefly described at the beginning of each play.
2. Remember that poetic language deserves to be read slowly and carefully. A difficult passage can sometimes be better understood if it's read aloud. Don't worry if every line isn't absolutely clear to you.
3. Pay attention to the annotations, which explain unfamiliar words, phrases, and allusions in the text. These can be distracting, but they are sometimes necessary to determine the basic meaning of a passage.
4. As you read each scene, try to imagine how it would be played on a stage.
5. If you find the reading especially difficult, try listening to a recording of the play. (Most college libraries have records and tapes of Shake-

speare's plays.) Allowing professional actors to do the reading aloud for you can enrich your imaginative reconstruction of the action and characters. Hearing a play can help you with subsequent readings of it.

6. After reading the play, view a film or videocassette recording of a performance. It is important to view the performance *after* your reading, though, so that your own mental re-creation of the play is not short-circuited by a director's production.

And finally, to quote Hamlet, "Be not too tame . . . let your own discretion be your tutor." Read Shakespeare's work as best you can; it warrants such careful attention not because the language and characters are difficult to understand but because they offer so much to enjoy.

A Midsummer Night's Dream

A Midsummer Night's Dream, one of Shakespeare's most popular plays with readers and audiences, is a romantic comedy about the complex nature of love and marriage. Though some serious points about law and social order are made along the way, the action is propelled by the powers of youth, romance, love, passion, and the hilarious pursuits of characters turned about by fairies, illusions, and their own misunderstandings.

Shakespeare uses several sets of couples to dramatize love's tribulations and triumphs. The play opens with Theseus, Duke of Athens, making arrangements to wed Hippolyta, queen of the Amazons. Once enemies, they now seek love and peace in the harmony of marriage. Their union represents the happy necessity of order in the state and suggests a model of behavior that the other characters struggle to achieve.

In contrast to the serene plans for the royal wedding is the conflict produced by four Athenian youths who are thwarted in love: Helena loves Demetrius, but Demetrius loves Hermia, who wants to marry Lysander. This collision of passions is further complicated by Hermia's father, who insists in the Duke's presence that if she doesn't marry Demetrius, she must die or spend her life in a nunnery. Much of the play's conflict concerns how these two young couples align their love for one another so that each desires and is desired by the right person. When Hermia defies her father and refuses to marry Demetrius, she flees to the woods, followed by Lysander and Demetrius as well as Helena, who is in pursuit of Demetrius.

Once in the woods, the lovers find themselves in a supernatural world, the unpredictable kingdom of Oberon and Titania, the king and queen of the fairies. The fourth couple creates even more confusion through Oberon's impatience with Titania. Their quarrel results in Oberon ordering his servant, Puck, to cast magical spells on the lovers as well as on Titania. This gives Puck the license to reveal their foolishness while eventually saving them from their own confused passions. Their reconciliations and reunions are not achieved, however, until Puck puts them through a series of comic encounters based on their illusions and vulnerabilities.

The final act includes the play within the play, "the most lamentable comedy" of two more lovers, Pyramus and Thisbe, who misunderstand one another. This travesty of a tragedy is put on by Athenian craftsmen — who are clearly better laborers than they are actors — at the Duke's request for a wedding entertainment. This play within the play reinforces the larger play's concerns about the nature of love and, indeed, of reality itself, because it raises questions about the fluid, complex relationship between art and reality. Ultimately, however, questions, issues, and conflicts give way to a generous sense of everything working out for the best as the play ends with Puck's warm assurances to the audience and his gentle urging to "Give me your hands."

WILLIAM SHAKESPEARE (1564–1616)

A Midsummer Night's Dream   *c. 1595*

[DRAMATIS PERSONAE

Theseus, Duke of Athens
Hippolyta, Queen of the Amazons, betrothed to Theseus
Philostrate, Master of the Revels
Egeus, father of Hermia

Hermia, daughter of Egeus, in love with Lysander
Lysander, in love with Hermia
Demetrius, in love with Hermia and favored by Egeus
Helena, in love with Demetrius

Oberon, King of the Fairies
Titania, Queen of the Fairies
Puck, or *Robin Goodfellow*
Peaseblossom,
Cobweb,
Mote,   } fairies attending Titania
Mustardseed
Other Fairies attending

Peter Quince, a carpenter,		*Prologue*
Nick Bottom, a weaver,		*Pyramus*
Francis Flute, a bellows mender,	representing	*Thisbe*
Tom Snout, a tinker,		*Wall*
Snug, a joiner,		*Lion*
Robin Starveling, a tailor,		*Moonshine*

Lords and Attendants on Theseus and Hippolyta

SCENE: *Athens, and a wood near it.*]

[ACT I

SCENE I: *Athens. Theseus' court.*]

Enter Theseus, Hippolyta, [and Philostrate,] with others.

Theseus: Now, fair Hippolyta, our nuptial hour
Draws on apace. Four happy days bring in
Another moon; but, O, methinks, how slow
This old moon wanes! She lingers° my desires,
Like to a stepdame° or a dowager°   5
Long withering out° a young man's revenue.

Hippolyta: Four days will quickly steep themselves° in night;
Four nights will quickly dream away the time;
And then the moon, like to a silver bow
New bent in heaven, shall behold the night   10
Of our solemnities.°

Theseus: Go Philostrate,
Stir up the Athenian youth to merriments.
Awake the pert and nimble spirit of mirth.
Turn melancholy forth to funerals;
The pale companion° is not for our pomp.°   *[Exit Philostrate.]*   15
Hippolyta, I wooed thee with my sword°
And won thy love doing thee injuries;
But I will wed thee in another key,
With pomp, with triumph,° and with reveling.

Enter Egeus and his daughter Hermia, and Lysander, and Demetrius.

Egeus: Happy be Theseus, our renownèd duke!   20
Theseus: Thanks, good Egeus. What's the news with thee?
Egeus: Full of vexation come I, with complaint
Against my child, my daughter Hermia.—
Stand forth, Demetrius.—My noble lord,
This man hath my consent to marry her.—   25
Stand forth, Lysander.—And, my gracious Duke,
This man hath bewitched the bosom of my child.
Thou, thou Lysander, thou hast given her rhymes
And interchanged love tokens with my child.
Thou hast by moonlight at her window sung   30
With feigning° voice verses of feigning° love,
And stol'n the impression of her fantasy°
With bracelets of thy hair, rings, gauds,° conceits,°
Knacks,° trifles, nosegays, sweetmeats — messengers

Act I, Scene I. 4 *lingers:* Postpones, delays the fulfillment of.   5 *stepdame:* Step-mother; *a dowager:* I.e., a widow (whose right of inheritance from her dead husband is eating into her son's estate).   6 *withering out:* Causing to dwindle.   7 *steep themselves:* Saturate themselves, to be absorbed in.   11 *solemnities:* Festive ceremonies of marriage.   15 *companion:* Fellow; *pomp:* Ceremonial magnificence.   16 *with my sword:* In a military engagement against the Amazons, when Hippolyta was taken captive.   19 *triumph:* Public festivity.   31 *feigning:* (1) Counterfeiting (2) faining, desirous.   32 *And...fantasy:* And made her fall in love with you (imprinting your image on her imagination) by stealthy and dishonest means.   33 *gauds:* Playthings; *conceits:* Fanciful trifles.   34 *Knacks:* Knickknacks.

Of strong prevailment in° unhardened youth.   35
With cunning hast thou filched my daughter's heart,
Turned her obedience, which is due to me,
To stubborn harshness. And, my gracious Duke,
Be it so° she will not here before Your Grace
Consent to marry with Demetrius,   40
I beg the ancient privilege of Athens:
As she is mine, I may dispose of her,
Which shall be either to this gentleman
Or to her death, according to our law
Immediately° provided in that case.   45

Theseus: What say you, Hermia? Be advised, fair maid.
To you your father should be as a god—
One that composed your beauties, yea, and one
To whom you are but as a form in wax
By him imprinted, and within his power   50
To leave° the figure or disfigure° it.
Demetrius is a worthy gentleman.

Hermia: So is Lysander.

Theseus: In himself he is;
But in this kind,° wanting° your father's voice,°
The other must be held the worthier.   55

Hermia: I would my father looked but with my eyes.

Theseus: Rather your eyes must with his judgment look.

Hermia: I do entreat Your Grace to pardon me.
I know not by what power I am made bold,
Nor how it may concern° my modesty   60
In such a presence here to plead my thoughts;
But I beseech Your Grace that I may know
The worst that may befall me in this case
If I refuse to wed Demetrius.

Theseus: Either to die the death° or to abjure   65
Forever the society of men.
Therefore, fair Hermia, question your desires,
Know of your youth, examine well your blood,°
Whether, if you yield not to your father's choice,
You can endure the livery° of a nun,   70
For aye° to be in shady cloister mewed,°
To live a barren sister all your life,
Chanting faint hymns to the cold fruitless moon.
Thrice blessèd they that master so their blood
To undergo such maiden pilgrimage;   75
But earthlier happy° is the rose distilled°

---

35 *prevailment in:* Influence on.   39 *Be it so:* If.   45 *Immediately:* Directly, with nothing intervening.   51 *leave:* Leave unaltered; *disfigure:* Obliterate.   54 *kind:* Respect; *wanting:* Lacking; *voice:* Approval.   60 *concern:* Befit.   65 *die the death:* Be executed by legal process.   68 *blood:* Passions.   70 *livery:* Habit, costume.   71 *aye:* Ever; *mewed:* Shut in (said of a hawk, poultry, etc.).   76 *earthlier happy:* Happier as respects this world; *distilled:* Separated to make perfume.

Than that which, withering on the virgin thorn,
Grows, lives, and dies in single blessedness.
Hermia: So will I grow, so live, so die, my lord,
  Ere I will yield my virgin patent° up   80
  Unto his lordship, whose unwishèd yoke
  My soul consents not to give sovereignty.
Theseus: Take time to pause, and by the next new moon—
  The sealing day betwixt my love and me
  For everlasting bond of fellowship—   85
  Upon that day either prepare to die
  For disobedience to your father's will,
  Or° else to wed Demetrius, as he would,
  Or on Diana's altar to protest°
  For aye austerity and single life.   90
Demetrius: Relent, sweet Hermia, and, Lysander, yield
  Thy crazèd° title to my certain right.
Lysander: You have her father's love, Demetrius;
  Let me have Hermia's. Do you marry him.
Egeus: Scornful Lysander! True, he hath my love,   95
  And what is mine my love shall render him.
  And she is mine, and all my right of her
  I do estate unto° Demetrius.
Lysander: I am, my lord, as well derived° as he,
  As well possessed;° my love is more than his;   100
  My fortunes every way as fairly° ranked,
  If not with vantage,° as Demetrius';
  And, which is more than all these boasts can be,
  I am beloved of beauteous Hermia.
  Why should not I then prosecute my right?   105
  Demetrius, I'll avouch it to his head,°
  Made love to Nedar's daughter, Helena,
  And won her soul; and she, sweet lady, dotes,
  Devoutly dotes, dotes in idolatry
  Upon this spotted° and inconstant man.   110
Theseus: I must confess that I have heard so much,
  And with Demetrius thought to have spoke thereof;
  But, being overfull of self-affairs,°
  My mind did lose it. But, Demetrius, come,
  And come, Egeus, you shall go with me;   115
  I have some private schooling° for you both.
  For you, fair Hermia, look you arm° yourself
  To fit your fancies° to your father's will,
  Or else the law of Athens yields you up—
  Which by no means we may extenuate°—   120

---

80 *patent:* Privilege.   88 *Or:* Either.   89 *protest:* Vow.   92 *crazèd:* Cracked, unsound.
98 *estate unto:* Settle or bestow upon.   99 *as well derived:* As well born and descended.
100 *possessed:* Endowed with wealth.   101 *fairly:* Handsomely.   102 *vantage:* Superiority.   106 *head:* I.e., face.   110 *spotted:* I.e., morally stained.   113 *self-affairs:* My own concerns.   116 *schooling:* Admonition.   117 *look you arm:* Take care you prepare.   118 *fancies:*
Likings, thoughts of love.   120 *extenuate:* Mitigate, relax.

To death or to a vow of single life.
Come, my Hippolyta. What cheer, my love?
Demetrius and Egeus, go° along.
I must employ you in some business
Against° our nuptial, and confer with you   125
Of something nearly that° concerns yourselves.

Egeus: With duty and desire we follow you.

Exeunt [all but Lysander and Hermia].

Lysander: How now, my love, why is your cheek so pale?
How chance the roses there do fade so fast?

Hermia: Belike° for want of rain, which I could well   130
Beteem° them from the tempest of my eyes.

Lysander: Ay me! For aught that I could ever read,
Could ever hear by tale or history,
The course of true love never did run smooth;
But either it was different in blood°—   135

Hermia: O cross!° Too high to be enthralled to low.

Lysander: Or else misgrafted° in respect of years—

Hermia: O spite! Too old to be engaged to young.

Lysander: Or else it stood upon the choice of friends°—

Hermia: O hell, to choose love by another's eyes!   140

Lysander: Or if there were a sympathy° in choice,
War, death, or sickness did lay siege to it,
Making it momentany° as a sound,
Swift as a shadow, short as any dream,
Brief as the lightning in the collied° night   145
That in a spleen° unfolds° both heaven and earth,
And ere a man hath power to say "Behold!"
The jaws of darkness do devour it up.
So quick° bright things come to confusion.°

Hermia: If then true lovers have been ever crossed,°   150
It stands as an edict in destiny.
Then let us teach our trial patience,°
Because it is a customary cross,
As due to love as thoughts, and dreams, and sighs,
Wishes, and tears, poor fancy's° followers.   155

Lysander: A good persuasion.° Therefore, hear me, Hermia:
I have a widow aunt, a dowager
Of great revenue, and she hath no child.
From Athens is her house remote seven leagues;
And she respects° me as her only son.   160
There, gentle Hermia, may I marry thee,

---

123 *go:* I.e., come.   125 *Against:* In preparation for.   126 *nearly that:* That closely.
130 *Belike:* Very likely.   131 *Beteem:* Grant, afford.   135 *blood:* Hereditary station.
136 *cross:* Vexation.   137 *misgrafted:* Ill grafted, badly matched.   139 *friends:* Relatives.
141 *sympathy:* Agreement.   143 *momentany:* Lasting but a moment.   145 *collied:* Blackened (as with coal dust), darkened.   146 *in a spleen:* In a swift impulse, in a violent flash;
unfolds: Reveals.   149 *quick:* Quickly; also, living, alive; *confusion:* Ruin.   150 *ever crossed:*
Always thwarted.   152 *teach...patience:* I.e., teach ourselves patience in this trial.
155 *fancy's:* Amorous passion's.   156 *persuasion:* Doctrine.   160 *respects:* Regards.

And to that place the sharp Athenian law
Cannot pursue us. If thou lovest me, then,
Steal forth thy father's house tomorrow night;
And in the wood, a league without° the town,   165
Where I did meet thee once with Helena
To do observance to a morn of May,°
There will I stay for thee.

Hermia: My good Lysander!
I swear to thee, by Cupid's strongest bow,
By his best arrow° with the golden head,   170
By the simplicity° of Venus' doves,°
By that which knitteth souls and prospers loves,
And by that fire which burned the Carthage queen°
When the false Trojan° under sail was seen,
By all the vows that ever men have broke,   175
In number more than ever women spoke,
In that same place thou hast appointed me
Tomorrow truly will I meet with thee.

Lysander: Keep promise, love. Look, here comes Helena.

Enter Helena.

Hermia: God speed, fair° Helena! Whither away?   180
Helena: Call you me fair? That "fair" again unsay.
Demetrius loves your fair.° O happy fair!°
Your eyes are lodestars,° and your tongue's sweet air°
More tunable° than lark to shepherd's ear
When wheat is green, when hawthorn buds appear.   185
Sickness is catching. O, were favor° so,
Yours would I catch, fair Hermia, ere I go;
My ear should catch your voice, my eye your eye,
My tongue should catch your tongue's sweet melody.
Were the world mine, Demetrius being bated,°   190
The rest I'd give to be to you translated.°
O, teach me how you look and with what art
You sway the motion° of Demetrius' heart.

Hermia: I frown upon him, yet he loves me still.
Helena: O, that your frowns would teach my smiles such skill! 195
Hermia: I give him curses, yet he gives me love.
Helena: O, that my prayers could such affection° move!°
Hermia: The more I hate, the more he follows me.
Helena: The more I love, the more he hateth me.

---

165 *without:* Outside.   167 *do… May:* Perform the ceremonies of May Day.   170 *best arrow:* Cupid's best gold-pointed arrows were supposed to induce love; his blunt leaden arrows, aversion.   171 *simplicity:* Innocence; *Venus's doves:* Doves that drew Venus's chariot.   173, 174 *Carthage queen, false Trojan:* (Dido, Queen of Carthage, immolated herself on a funeral pyre after having been deserted by the Trojan hero Aeneas.)   180 *fair:* Fair-complexioned (generally regarded by the Elizabethans as more beautiful than a dark complexion).   182 *your fair:* Your beauty (even though Hermia is dark-complexioned); *happy fair:* Lucky fair one.   183 *lodestars:* Guiding stars; *air:* Music.   184 *tunable:* Tuneful, melodious.   186 *favor:* Appearance, looks.   190 *bated:* Excepted.   191 *translated:* Transformed.   193 *sway the motion:* Control the impulse.   197 *affection:* Passion; *move:* Arouse.

Hermia: His folly, Helena, is no fault of mine.   200
Helena: None, but your beauty. Would that fault were mine!
Hermia: Take comfort. He no more shall see my face.
    Lysander and myself will fly this place.
    Before the time I did Lysander see
    Seemed Athens as a paradise to me.°   205
    O, then, what graces in my love do dwell,
    That he hath turned a heaven unto a hell?
Lysander: Helen, to you our minds we will unfold.
    Tomorrow night, when Phoebe° doth behold
    Her silver visage in the watery glass,°   210
    Decking with liquid pearl the bladed grass,
    A time that lovers' flights doth still° conceal,
    Through Athens' gates have we devised to steal.
Hermia: And in the wood, where often you and I
    Upon faint° primrose beds were wont to lie,   215
    Emptying our bosoms of their counsel° sweet,
    There my Lysander and myself shall meet,
    And thence from Athens turn away our eyes
    To seek new friends and stranger companies.°
    Farewell, sweet playfellow. Pray thou for us,   220
    And good luck grant thee thy Demetrius!
    Keep word, Lysander. We must starve our sight
    From lovers' food till morrow deep midnight.
Lysander: I will, my Hermia. *(Exit Hermia.)* Helena, adieu.
    As you on him, Demetrius dote on you!   *Exit Lysander.* 225
Helena: How happy some o'er other some can be!°
    Through Athens I am thought as fair as she.
    But what of that? Demetrius thinks not so;
    He will not know what all but he do know.
    And as he errs, doting on Hermia's eyes,   230
    So I, admiring of° his qualities,
    Things base and vile, holding no quantity,°
    Love can transpose to form and dignity.
    Love looks not with the eyes, but with the mind,
    And therefore is winged Cupid painted blind.   235
    Nor hath Love's mind of any judgment taste;°
    Wings and no eyes figure° unheedy haste.
    And therefore is Love said to be a child,
    Because in choice° he is so oft beguiled.°
    As waggish° boys in game° themselves forswear,   240

204–205 *Before . . . to me:* (Hermia seemingly means that love has led to complications and jealousies, making Athens hell for her.)   209 *Phoebe:* Diana, the moon.   210 *glass:* Mirror.   212 *still:* Always.   215 *faint:* Pale.   216 *counsel:* Secret thought.   219 *stranger companies:* The company of strangers.   226 *o'er . . . can be:* Can be in comparison to some others.   231 *admiring of:* Wondering at.   232 *holding no quantity:* I.e., unsubstantial, unshapely.   236 *Nor . . . taste:* I.e., nor has Love, which dwells in the fancy or imagination, any *taste* or least bit of judgment or reason.   237 *figure:* Are a symbol of.   239 *in choice:* In choosing; *beguiled:* Self-deluded, making unaccountable choices.   240 *waggish:* Playful, mischievous; *game:* Sport, jest.

So the boy Love is perjured everywhere.
For ere Demetrius looked on Hermia's eyne,°
He hailed down oaths that he was only mine;
And when this hail some heat from Hermia felt,
So he dissolved, and showers of oaths did melt.   245
I will go tell him of fair Hermia's flight.
Then to the wood will he tomorrow night
Pursue her; and for this intelligence°
If I have thanks, it is a dear° expense.°
But herein mean I to enrich my pain,   250
To have his sight thither and back again.   *Exit.*

[SCENE II: *Athens.*]

*Enter Quince the carpenter, and Snug the joiner, and Bottom the weaver, and Flute
the bellows mender, and Snout the tinker, and Starveling the tailor.*

Quince: Is all our company here?
Bottom: You were best to call them generally,° man by man, according to
        the scrip.°
Quince: Here is the scroll of every man's name which is thought fit,
        through all Athens, to play in our interlude° before the Duke and the   5
        Duchess on his wedding day at night.
Bottom: First, good Peter Quince, say what the play treats on, then read
        the names of the actors, and so grow to° a point.
Quince: Marry,° our play is "The most lamentable comedy and most cruel
        death of Pyramus and Thisbe."   10
Bottom: A very good piece of work, I assure you, and a merry. Now, good
        Peter Quince, call forth your actors by the scroll. Masters, spread
        yourselves.
Quince: Answer as I call you. Nick Bottom,° the weaver.
Bottom: Ready. Name what part I am for, and proceed.   15
Quince: You, Nick Bottom, are set down for Pyramus.
Bottom: What is Pyramus? A lover or a tyrant?
Quince: A lover, that kills himself most gallant for love.
Bottom: That will ask some tears in the true performing of it. If I do it, let
        the audience look to their eyes. I will move storms; I will condole° in   20
        some measure. To the rest—yet my chief humor° is for a tyrant. I
        could play Ercles° rarely, or a part to tear a cat° in, to make all split.°
                "The raging rocks
                And shivering shocks
                Shall break the locks   25
                        Of prison gates;

---

242 *eyne:* Eyes (old form of plural).   248 *intelligence:* Information.   249 *a dear expense:*
I.e., a trouble worth taking on my part, or a begrudging effort on his part; *dear:* Costly.
Scene II.   2 *generally:* (Bottom's blunder for "individually.")   3 *scrip:* Scrap (Bottom's
error for "script").   5 *interlude:* Play.   8 *grow to:* Come to.   9 *Marry:* (A mild oath;
originally the name of the Virgin Mary.)   14 *Bottom:* Object around which weavers wound
thread.   20 *condole:* Lament, arouse pity.   21 *humor:* Inclination, whim.   22 *Ercles:*
Hercules (the tradition of ranting came from Seneca's *Hercules Furens*); *tear a cat:* I.e., rant;
make all split: I.e., cause a stir, bring the house down.

> And Phibbus' car°
> Shall shine from far
> And make and mar
>   The foolish Fates." 30

This was lofty! Now name the rest of the players. This is Ercles' vein, a tyrant's vein. A lover is more condoling.

Quince: Francis Flute, the bellows mender.

Flute: Here, Peter Quince.

Quince: Flute, you must take Thisbe on you. 35

Flute: What is Thisbe? A wandering knight?

Quince: It is the lady that Pyramus must love.

Flute: Nay, faith, let not me play a woman. I have a beard coming.

Quince: That's all one.° You shall play it in a mask, and you may speak as small° as you will. 40

Bottom: An° I may hide my face, let me play Thisbe too. I'll speak in a monstrous little voice: "Thisne, Thisne!" "Ah, Pyramus, my lover dear! Thy Thisbe dear, and lady dear!"

Quince: No, no, you must play Pyramus, and Flute, you Thisbe.

Bottom: Well, proceed. 45

Quince: Robin Starveling, the tailor.

Starveling: Here, Peter Quince.

Quince: Robin Starveling, you must play Thisbe's mother. Tom Snout, the tinker.

Snout: Here, Peter Quince. 50

Quince: You, Pyramus' father; myself, Thisbe's father; Snug, the joiner, you, the lion's part; and I hope here is a play fitted.

Snug: Have you the lion's part written? Pray you, if it be, give it me, for I am slow of study.

Quince: You may do it extempore, for it is nothing but roaring. 55

Bottom: Let me play the lion too. I will roar that I will do any man's heart good to hear me. I will roar that I will make the Duke say, "Let him roar again, let him roar again."

Quince: An you should do it too terribly, you would fright the Duchess and the ladies, that they would shriek; and that were enough to hang 60 us all.

All: That would hang us, every mother's son.

Bottom: I grant you, friends, if you should fright the ladies out of their wits, they would have no more discretion but to hang us; but I will aggravate° my voice so that I will roar you° as gently as any sucking 65 dove;° I will roar you an 'twere° any nightingale.

Quince: You can play no part but Pyramus; for Pyramus is a sweet-faced man, a proper° man as one shall see in a summer's day, a most lovely gentlemanlike man. Therefore you must needs play Pyramus.

Bottom: Well, I will undertake it. What beard were I best to play it in? 70

Quince: Why, what you will.

---

27 *Phibbus' car:* Phoebus', the sun god's, chariot.   39 *That's all one:* It makes no difference.
40 *small:* High-pitched.   41 *An:* If (also at line 59).   65 *aggravate:* (Bottom's blunder for "moderate.")*; roar you:* I.e., roar for you.   66 *sucking dove:* (Bottom conflates *sitting dove* and *sucking lamb,* two proverbial images of innocence.)*; an 'twere:* As if it were.   68 *proper:* Handsome.

Bottom: I will discharge° it in either your° straw-color beard, your orange-tawny beard, your purple-in-grain° beard, or your French-crown-color° beard, your perfect yellow.

Quince: Some of your French crowns° have no hair at all, and then you   75
will play barefaced. But, masters, here are your parts. *[He distributes parts.]* And I am to entreat you, request you, and desire you to con° them by tomorrow night, and meet me in the palace wood, a mile without the town, by moonlight. There will we rehearse; for if we meet in the city, we shall be dogged with company, and our devices°   80
known. In the meantime I will draw a bill° of properties, such as our play wants. I pray you, fail me not.

Bottom: We will meet, and there we may rehearse most obscenely° and courageously. Take pains, be perfect.° Adieu.

Quince: At the Duke's oak we meet.   85

Bottom: Enough. Hold, or cut bowstrings.°   *Exeunt.*

[ACT II

SCENE I: *A wood near Athens.*]

Enter a Fairy at one door, and Robin Goodfellow [Puck] at another.

Puck: How now, spirit, whither wander you?

Fairy: Over hill, over dale,
    Thorough° bush, thorough brier,
  Over park, over pale,°
    Thorough flood, thorough fire,   5
I do wander everywhere,
Swifter than the moon's sphere;°
And I serve the Fairy Queen,
To dew° her orbs° upon the green.
The cowslips tall her pensioners° be.   10
In their gold coats spots you see;
Those be rubies, fairy favors;°
In those freckles live their savors.°
I must go seek some dewdrops here
And hang a pearl in every cowslip's ear.   15
Farewell, thou lob° of spirits; I'll be gone.

---

72 *discharge:* Perform; *your:* I.e., you know the kind I mean.   73 *purple-in-grain:* Dyed a very deep red (from *grain,* the name applied to the dried insect used to make the dye).   74 *French-crown-color:* I.e., color of a French crown, a gold coin.   75 *crowns:* Heads bald from syphilis, the "French disease."   77 *con:* Learn by heart.   80 *devices:* Plans.   81 *draw a bill:* Draw up a list.   83 *obscenely:* (An unintentionally funny blunder, whatever Bottom meant to say.)   84 *perfect:* I.e., letter-perfect in memorizing your parts.   86 *Hold...bowstrings:* (An archer's expression, not definitely explained, but probably meaning here "keep your promises, or give up the play.")   **Act II, Scene I.**   3 *Thorough:* Through.   4 *pale:* Enclosure.   7 *sphere:* Orbit.   9 *dew:* Sprinkle with dew; *orbs:* Circles, i.e., fairy rings (circular bands of grass, darker than the surrounding area, caused by fungi enriching the soil).   10 *pensioners:* Retainers, members of the royal bodyguard.   12 *favors:* Love tokens.   13 *savors:* Sweet smells.   16 *lob:* Country bumpkin.

     Our Queen and all her elves come here anon.°
Puck: The King doth keep his revels here tonight.
     Take heed the Queen come not within his sight.
     For Oberon is passing fell° and wrath,°   20
     Because that she as her attendant hath
     A lovely boy, stolen from an Indian king;
     She ne'er had so sweet a changeling.°
     And jealous Oberon would have the child
     Knight of his train, to trace° the forests wild.   25
     But she perforce° withholds the lovèd boy,
     Crowns him with flowers, and makes him all her joy.
     And now they never meet in grove or green,
     By fountain° clear, or spangled starlight sheen,°
     But they do square,° that all their elves for fear   30
     Creep into acorn cups and hide them there.
Fairy: Either I mistake your shape and making quite,
     Or else you are that shrewd° and knavish sprite°
     Called Robin Goodfellow. Are not you he
     That frights the maidens of the villagery,°   35
     Skim milk,° and sometimes labor in the quern,°
     And bootless° make the breathless huswife° churn,
     And sometimes make the drink to bear no barm,°
     Mislead night wanderers,° laughing at their harm?
     Those that "Hobgoblin" call you, and "Sweet Puck,"°   40
     You do their work, and they shall have good luck.
     Are you not he?
Puck: Thou speakest aright;
     I am that merry wanderer of the night.
     I jest to Oberon and make him smile
     When I a fat and bean-fed° horse beguile,   45
     Neighing in likeness of a filly foal;
     And sometimes lurk I in a gossip's° bowl
     In very likeness of a roasted crab,°
     And when she drinks, against her lips I bob
     And on her withered dewlap° pour the ale.   50
     The wisest aunt,° telling the saddest° tale,
     Sometimes for three-foot stool mistaketh me;
     Then slip I from her bum, down topples she,

---

17 *anon:* At once.   20 *passing fell:* Exceedingly angry; *wrath:* Wrathful.   23 *changeling:*
Child exchanged for another by the fairies.   25 *trace:* Range through.   26 *perforce:*
Forcibly.   29 *fountain:* Spring; *starlight sheen:* Shining starlight.   30 *square:* Quarrel.
33 *shrewd:* Mischievous; *sprite:* Spirit.   35 *villagery:* Village population.   36 *Skim milk:*
I.e., steal the cream; *quern:* Hand mill (where Puck presumably hampers the grinding of
grain).   37 *bootless:* In vain (Puck prevents the cream from turning to butter); *huswife:*
Housewife.   38 *barm:* Head on the ale (Puck prevents the barm or yeast from producing
fermentation).   39 *Mislead night wanderers:* I.e., mislead with false fire those who walk
abroad at night (hence earning Puck his other names of Jack o' Lantern and Will o' the
Wisp).   40 *Those . . . Puck:* I.e., those who call you by the names you favor rather than
those denoting the mischief you do.   45 *bean-fed:* Well fed on field beans.   47 *gossip's:*
Old woman's.   48 *crab:* Crab apple.   50 *dewlap:* Loose skin on neck.   51 *aunt:* Old
woman; *saddest:* Most serious.

And "Tailor"° cries, and falls into a cough;
And then the whole choir° hold their hips and laugh,　　55
And waxen° in their mirth, and neeze,° and swear
A merrier hour was never wasted° there.
But, room,° fairy! Here comes Oberon.

Fairy: And here my mistress. Would that he were gone!

*Enter [Oberon] the King of Fairies at one door, with his train, and [Titania] the
Queen at another, with hers.*

Oberon: Ill met by moonlight, proud Titania.　　60

Titania: What, jealous Oberon? Fairies, skip hence.
I have forsworn his bed and company.

Oberon: Tarry, rash wanton.° Am not I thy lord?

Titania: Then I must be thy lady; but I know
When thou hast stolen away from Fairyland　　65
And in the shape of Corin° sat all day,
Playing on the pipes of corn° and versing love
To amorous Phillida.° Why art thou here
Come from the farthest step° of India,
But that, forsooth, the bouncing Amazon,　　70
Your buskined° mistress and your warrior love,
To Theseus must be wedded, and you come
To give their bed joy and prosperity.

Oberon: How canst thou thus for shame, Titania,
Glance at my credit with Hippolyta,°　　75
Knowing I know thy love to Theseus?
Didst not thou lead him through the glimmering night
From Perigenia,° whom he ravishèd?
And make him with fair Aegles° break his faith,
With Ariadne° and Antiopa?°　　80

Titania: These are the forgeries of jealousy;
And never, since the middle summer's spring,°
Met we on hill, in dale, forest, or mead,°
By pavèd° fountain or by rushy° brook,
Or in° the beachèd margent° of the sea,　　85
To dance our ringlets to° the whistling wind,

54 *Tailor:* (Possibly because she ends up sitting cross-legged on the floor, looking like a tailor, or else referring to the *tail* or buttocks.)　55 *choir:* Company.　56 *waxen:* Increase;
neeze: Sneeze.　57 *wasted:* Spent.　58 *room:* Stand aside, make room.　63 *wanton:*
Headstrong creature.　66, 68 *Corin, Phillida:* (Conventional names of pastoral lovers).
67 *corn:* (Here, oat stalks.)　69 *step:* Farthest limit of travel, or, perhaps, *steep,* "mountain
range."　71 *buskined:* Wearing half-boots called buskins.　75 *Glance . . . Hippolyta:* Make
insinuations about my favored relationship with Hippolyta.　78 *Perigenia:* I.e., Perigouna,
one of Theseus' conquests. (This and the following women are named in Thomas North's
translation of Plutarch's "Life of Theseus.")　79 *Aegles:* I.e., Aegle, for whom Theseus deserted Ariadne according to some accounts.　80 *Ariadne:* The daughter of Minos, King of
Crete, who helped Theseus to escape the labyrinth after killing the Minotaur; later she was
abandoned by Theseus; *Antiopa:* Queen of the Amazons and wife of Theseus, elsewhere
identified with Hippolyta, but here thought of as a separate woman.　82 *middle summer's
spring:* Beginning of midsummer.　83 *mead:* Meadow.　84 *pavèd:* With pebbled bottom; *rushy:* Bordered with rushes.　85 *in:* On; *margent:* Edge, border.　86 *ringlets to:*
Dances in a ring (see *orbs* in II.i.9) to the sound of.

But with thy brawls thou hast disturbed our sport.
Therefore the winds, piping to us in vain,
As in revenge, have sucked up from the sea
Contagious° fogs which, falling in the land,   90
Hath every pelting° river made so proud
That they have overborne their continents.°
The ox hath therefore stretched his yoke° in vain,
The plowman lost his sweat, and the green corn°
Hath rotted ere his youth attained a beard;   95
The fold° stands empty in the drownèd field,
And crows are fatted with the murrain° flock;
The nine-men's morris° is filled up with mud,
And the quaint mazes° in the wanton° green
For lack of tread are indistinguishable.   100
The human mortals want° their winter° here;
No night is now with hymn or carol blessed.
Therefore° the moon, the governess of floods,
Pale in her anger, washes° all the air,
That rheumatic diseases° do abound.   105
And thorough this distemperature° we see
The seasons alter: hoary-headed frosts
Fall in the fresh lap of the crimson rose,
And on old Hiems'° thin and icy crown
An odorous chaplet of sweet summer buds   110
Is, as in mockery, set. The spring, the summer,
The childing° autumn, angry winter, change
Their wonted liveries,° and the mazèd° world
By their increase° now knows not which is which.
And this same progeny of evils comes   115
From our debate,° from our dissension.
We are their parents and original.°
Oberon: Do you amend it, then. It lies in you.
  Why should Titania cross her Oberon?
  I do but beg a little changeling boy   120
  To be my henchman.°
Titania: Set your heart at rest.
  The fairy land buys not the child of me.
  His mother was a vot'ress of my order,°

90 *Contagious:* Noxious.   91 *pelting:* Paltry.   92 *continents:* Banks that contain them.
93 *stretched his yoke:* I.e., pulled at his yoke in plowing.   94 *corn:* Grain of any kind.
96 *fold:* Pen for sheep or cattle.   97 *murrain:* Having died of the plague.   98 *nine-men's morris:* I.e., portion of the village green marked out in a square for a game played with nine pebbles or pegs.   99 *quaint mazes:* I.e., intricate paths marked out on the village green to be followed rapidly on foot as a kind of contest; *wanton:* Luxuriant.   101 *want:* Lack; *winter:* I.e., regular winter season; or, proper observances of winter, such as the *hymn* or *carol* in the next line (?).   103 *Therefore:* I.e., as a result of our quarrel.   104 *washes:* Saturates with moisture.   105 *rheumatic diseases:* Colds, flu, and other respiratory infections.   106 *distemperature:* Disturbance in nature.   109 *Hiems':* The winter god's.   112 *childing:* Fruitful, pregnant.   113 *wonted liveries:* Usual apparel; *mazèd:* Bewildered.   114 *their increase:* Their yield, what they produce.   116 *debate:* Quarrel.   117 *original:* Origin.   121 *henchman:* Attendant, page.   123 *was . . . order:* Had taken a vow to serve me.

And in the spicèd Indian air by night
Full often hath she gossiped by my side   125
And sat with me on Neptune's yellow sands,
Marking th' embarkèd traders° on the flood,°
When we have laughed to see the sails conceive
And grow big-bellied with the wanton° wind;
Which she, with pretty and with swimming° gait,   130
Following—her womb then rich with my young squire—
Would imitate, and sail upon the land
To fetch me trifles, and return again
As from a voyage, rich with merchandise.
But she, being mortal, of that boy did die;   135
And for her sake do I rear up her boy,
And for her sake I will not part with him.

Oberon: How long within this wood intend you stay?

Titania: Perchance till after Theseus' wedding day.
If you will patiently dance in our round°   140
And see our moonlight revels, go with us;
If not, shun me, and I will spare° your haunts.

Oberon: Give me that boy, and I will go with thee.

Titania: Not for thy fairy kingdom. Fairies, away!
We shall chide downright, if I longer stay.   145

Exeunt [Titania with her train].

Oberon: Well, go thy way. Thou shalt not from° this grove
Till I torment thee for this injury.
My gentle Puck, come hither. Thou rememb'rest
Since° once I sat upon a promontory,
And heard a mermaid on a dolphin's back   150
Uttering such dulcet° and harmonious breath°
That the rude° sea grew civil at her song,
And certain stars shot madly from their spheres
To hear the sea-maid's music?

Puck: I remember.

Oberon: That very time I saw, but thou couldst not,   155
Flying between the cold moon and the earth
Cupid, all° armed. A certain° aim he took
At a fair vestal° thronèd by° the west,
And loosed° his love shaft smartly from his bow
As° it should pierce a hundred thousand hearts;   160
But I might° see young Cupid's fiery shaft
Quenched in the chaste beams of the watery moon,
And the imperial vot'ress passèd on,
In maiden meditation, fancy-free.°

---

127 *traders:* Trading vessels; *flood:* Flood tide.   129 *wanton:* (1) Playful (2) amorous.
130 *swimming:* Smooth, gliding.   140 *round:* Circular dance.   142 *spare:* Shun.
146 *from:* Go from.   149 *Since:* When.   151 *dulcet:* Sweet;   *breath:* Voice,   song.
152 *rude:* Rough.   157 *all:* Fully;   *certain:* Sure.   158 *vestal:* Vestal virgin (contains a complimentary allusion to Queen Elizabeth as a votaress of Diana and probably refers to an actual entertainment in her honor at Elvetham in 1591); *by:* In the region of.   159 *loosed:* Released.   160 *As:* As if.   161 *might:* Could.   164 *fancy-free:* Free of love's spell.

Yet marked I where the bolt° of Cupid fell: 165
It fell upon a little western flower,
Before milk-white, now purple with love's wound,
And maidens call it love-in-idleness.°
Fetch me that flower; the herb I showed thee once.
The juice of it on sleeping eyelids laid 170
Will make or man or° woman madly dote
Upon the next live creature that it sees.
Fetch me this herb, and be thou here again
Ere the leviathan° can swim a league.

Puck: I'll put a girdle round about the earth 175
In forty° minutes. *[Exit.]*

Oberon: Having once this juice,
I'll watch Titania when she is asleep
And drop the liquor of it in her eyes.
The next thing then she waking looks upon,
Be it on lion, bear, or wolf, or bull, 180
On meddling monkey, or on busy ape,
She shall pursue it with the soul of love.
And ere I take this charm from off her sight,
As I can take it with another herb,
I'll make her render up her page to me. 185
But who comes here? I am invisible,
And I will overhear their conference.

Enter Demetrius, Helena following him.

Demetrius: I love thee not; therefore pursue me not.
Where is Lysander and fair Hermia?
The one I'll slay; the other slayeth me. 190
Thou toldst me they were stol'n unto this wood;
And here am I, and wood° within this wood
Because I cannot meet my Hermia.
Hence, get thee gone, and follow me no more.

Helena: You draw me, you hardhearted adamant!° 195
But yet you draw not iron, for my heart
Is true as steel. Leave you° your power to draw,
And I shall have no power to follow you.

Demetrius: Do I entice you? Do I speak you fair?°
Or rather do I not in plainest truth 200
Tell you I do not nor I cannot love you?

Helena: And even for that do I love you the more.
I am your spaniel; and, Demetrius,
The more you beat me I will fawn on you.
Use me but as your spaniel, spurn me, strike me, 205

---

165 *bolt:* Arrow.   168 *love-in-idleness:* Pansy, heartsease.   171 *or . . . or:* Either . . . or. 174 *leviathan:* Sea monster, whale.   176 *forty:* (Used indefinitely.)   192 *and wood:* And mad, frantic (with an obvious wordplay on *wood*, meaning "woods").   195 *adamant:* Lodestone, magnet (with pun on *hardhearted*, since adamant was also thought to be the hardest of all stones and was confused with the diamond).   197 *Leave you:* Give up.   199 *speak you fair:* Speak courteously to you.

Neglect me, lose me; only give me leave,
Unworthy as I am, to follow you.
What worser place can I beg in your love—
And yet a place of high respect with me—
Than to be usèd as you use your dog?   210
Demetrius: Tempt not too much the hatred of my spirit,
For I am sick when I do look on thee.
Helena: And I am sick when I look not on you.
Demetrius: You do impeach° your modesty too much
To leave° the city and commit yourself   215
Into the hands of one that loves you not,
To trust the opportunity of night
And the ill counsel of a desert° place
With the rich worth of your virginity.
Helena: Your virtue° is my privilege.° For that°   220
It is not night when I do see your face,
Therefore I think I am not in the night;
Nor doth this wood lack worlds of company,
For you, in my respect,° are all the world.
Then how can it be said I am alone   225
When all the world is here to look on me?
Demetrius: I'll run from thee and hide me in the brakes,°
And leave thee to the mercy of wild beasts.
Helena: The wildest hath not such a heart as you.
Run when you will. The story shall be changed:
Apollo flies and Daphne holds the chase,°   230
The dove pursues the griffin,° the mild hind°
Makes speed to catch the tiger—bootless° speed,
When cowardice pursues and valor flies!
Demetrius: I will not stay thy questions.° Let me go!   235
Or if thou follow me, do not believe
But I shall do thee mischief in the wood.
Helena: Ay, in the temple, in the town, the field,
You do me mischief. Fie, Demetrius!
Your wrongs do set a scandal on my sex.°   240
We cannot fight for love, as men may do;
We should be wooed and were not made to woo.   *[Exit Demetrius.]*
I'll follow thee and make a heaven of hell,
To die upon° the hand I love so well.   *[Exit.]*
Oberon: Fare thee well, nymph. Ere he do leave this grove   245
Thou shalt fly him, and he shall seek thy love.

---

214 *impeach:* Call into question.   215 *To leave:* By leaving.   218 *desert:* Deserted.
220 *virtue:* Goodness or power to attract; *privilege:* Safeguard, warrant; *For that:* Because.
224 *in my respect:* As far as I am concerned, in my esteem.   227 *brakes:* Thickets.   231
Apollo...chase: (In the ancient myth, Daphne fled from Apollo and was saved from rape by
being transformed into a laurel tree; here it is the female who *holds the chase,* or pursues, instead of the male.)   232 *griffin:* A fabulous monster with the head and wings of an eagle
and the body of a lion; *hind:* Female deer.   233 *bootless:* Fruitless.   235 *stay thy questions:*
Wait for or put up with your talk or argument.   240 *Your...sex:* I.e., the wrongs that you
do me cause me to act in a manner that disgraces my sex.   244 *upon:* By.

Enter Puck.

Has thou the flower there? Welcome, wanderer.

Puck: Aye, there it is.   *[He offers the flower.]*

Oberon: I pray thee, give it to me.
    I know a bank where the wild thyme blows,°
    Where oxlips° and the nodding violet grows,   250
    Quite overcanopied with luscious woodbine,°
    With sweet muskroses° and with eglantine.°
    There sleeps Titania sometime of° the night,
    Lulled in these flowers with dances and delight;
    And there the snake throws° her enameled skin,   255
    Weed° wide enough to wrap a fairy in.
    And with the juice of this I'll streak° her eyes
    And make her full of hateful fantasies.
    Take thou some of it, and seek through this grove.

                                [He gives some love juice.]

    A sweet Athenian lady is in love   260
    With a disdainful youth. Anoint his eyes,
    But do it when the next thing he espies
    May be the lady. Thou shalt know the man
    By the Athenian garments he hath on.
    Effect it with some care, that he may prove   265
    More fond on° her than she upon her love;
    And look thou meet me ere the first cock crow.

Puck: Fear not, my lord, your servant shall do so.   *Exeunt [separately].*

[SCENE II: *The wood.*]

Enter Titania, Queen of Fairies, with her train.

Titania: Come, now a roundel° and a fairy song;
    Then, for the third part of a minute,° hence —
    Some to kill cankers° in the muskrose buds,
    Some war with reremice° for their leathern wings
    To make my small elves coats, and some keep back   5
    The clamorous owl, that nightly hoots and wonders
    At our quaint° spirits. Sing me now asleep.
    Then to your offices, and let me rest.

Fairies sing.

First Fairy: You spotted snakes with double° tongue,
        Thorny hedgehogs, be not seen;   10

---

249 *blows:* Blooms.   250 *oxlips:* Flowers resembling cowslip and primrose.   251 *woodbine:* Honeysuckle.   252 *muskroses:* A kind of large, sweet-scented rose; *eglantine:* Sweetbrier, another kind of rose.   253 *sometime of:* For part of.   255 *throws:* Sloughs off, sheds. 256 *Weed:* Garment.   257 *streak:* Anoint, touch gently.   266 *fond on:* Doting on. **Scene II.**   1 *roundel:* Dance in a ring.   2 *the third . . . minute:* (Indicative of the fairies' quickness.)   3 *cankers:* Cankerworms (i.e., caterpillars or grubs).   4 *reremice:* Bats. 7 *quaint:* Dainty.   9 *double:* Forked.

Newts° and blindworms, do no wrong;
  Come not near our Fairy Queen.
Chorus [dancing]: Philomel,° with melody
  Sing in our sweet lullaby;
  Lulla, lulla, lullaby, lulla, lulla, lullaby.   15
    Never harm
    Nor spell nor charm
  Come our lovely lady nigh.
  So good night, with lullaby.
First Fairy: Weaving spiders, come not here;   20
  Hence, you long-legged spinners, hence!
  Beetles black, approach not near;
  Worm nor snail, do no offense.°
Chorus [dancing]: Philomel, with melody
  Sing in our sweet lullaby;   25
  Lulla, lulla, lullaby, lulla, lulla, lullaby.
    Never harm
    Nor spell nor charm
  Come our lovely lady nigh.
  So good night, with lullaby.   *[Titania sleeps.]*   30
Second Fairy: Hence, away! Now all is well.
  One aloof stand sentinel.°   *[Exeunt Fairies, leaving one sentinel.]*

Enter Oberon [and squeezes the flower on Titania's eyelids].

Oberon: What thou seest when thou dost wake,
  Do it for thy true love take;
  Love and languish for his sake.   35
  Be it ounce,° or cat, or bear,
  Pard,° or boar with bristled hair,
  In thy eye that shall appear
  When thou wak'st, it is thy dear.
  Wake when some vile thing is near.   *[Exit.]* 40

Enter Lysander and Hermia.

Lysander: Fair love, you faint with wandering in the wood;
  And to speak truth, I have forgot our way.
  We'll rest us, Hermia, if you think it good,
  And tarry for the comfort of the day.
Hermia: Be it so, Lysander. Find you out a bed,   45
  For I upon this bank will rest my head.
Lysander: One turf shall serve as pillow for us both;
  One heart, one bed, two bosoms, and one troth.°

---

11 *Newts:* Water lizards (considered poisonous, as were *blindworms* — small snakes with tiny eyes — and spiders).   13 *Philomel:* The nightingale. (Philomela, daughter of King Pandion, was transformed into a nightingale, according to Ovid's *Metamorphoses* 6, after she had been raped by her sister Procne's husband, Tereus.)   23 *offense:* Harm.   32 *sentinel:* (Presumably Oberon is able to outwit or intimidate this guard.)   36 *ounce:* Lynx.   37 *Pard:* Leopard.   48 *troth:* Faith, trothplight.

Hermia: Nay, good Lysander, for my sake, my dear,
       Lie further off yet. Do not lie so near.   50
Lysander: O, take the sense, sweet, of my innocence!°
       Love takes the meaning in love's conference.°
       I mean that my heart unto yours is knit,
       So that but one heart we can make of it;
       Two bosoms interchainèd with an oath—   55
       So then two bosoms and a single troth.
       Then by your side no bed-room me deny,
       For lying so, Hermia, I do not lie.°
Hermia: Lysander riddles very prettily.
       Now much beshrew° my manners and my pride   60
       If Hermia meant to say Lysander lied.
       But, gentle friend, for love and courtesy
       Lie further off, in human° modesty.
       Such separation as may well be said
       Becomes a virtuous bachelor and a maid,   65
       So far be distant; and, good night, sweet friend.
       Thy love ne'er alter till thy sweet life end!
Lysander: Amen, amen, to that fair prayer, say I,
       And then end life when I end loyalty!
       Here is my bed. Sleep give thee all his rest!   70
Hermia: With half that wish the wisher's eyes be pressed!°
                    [They sleep, separated by a short distance.]

       Enter Puck.

Puck: Through the forest have I gone,
       But Athenian found I none
       On whose eyes I might approve°
       This flower's force in stirring love.   75
       Night and silence.—Who is here?
       Weeds of Athens he doth wear.
       This is he, my master said,
       Despisèd the Athenian maid;
       And here the maiden, sleeping sound,   80
       On the dank and dirty ground.
       Pretty soul, she durst not lie
       Near this lack-love, this kill-courtesy.
       Churl, upon thy eyes I throw
       All the power this charm doth owe.°   *[He applies the love juice.]*   85
       When thou wak'st, let love forbid
       Sleep his seat on thy eyelid.
       So awake when I am gone,
       For I must now to Oberon.   *Exit.*

---

51 *take . . . innocence:* I.e., interpret my intention as innocent.   52 *Love . . . conference:* I.e.,
when lovers confer, love teaches each lover to interpret the other's meaning lovingly.
58 *lie:* Tell a falsehood (with a riddling pun on *lie,* "recline").   60 *beshrew:* Curse (but
mildly meant).   63 *human:* Courteous (and perhaps suggesting "humane").   71 *With . . .
pressed:* I.e., may we share your wish, so that your eyes too are *pressed,* closed, in sleep.
74 *approve:* Test.   85 *owe:* Own.

Enter Demetrius and Helena, running.

Helena: Stay, though thou kill me, sweet Demetrius!   90
Demetrius: I charge thee, hence, and do not haunt me thus.
Helena: O, wilt thou darkling° leave me? Do not so.
Demetrius: Stay, on thy peril!° I alone will go.   *[Exit.]*
Helena: O, I am out of breath in this fond° chase!
        The more my prayer, the lesser is my grace.°   95
        Happy is Hermia, wheresoe'er she lies,°
        For she hath blessèd and attractive eyes.
        How came her eyes so bright? Not with salt tears;
        If so, my eyes are oftener washed than hers.
        No, no, I am as ugly as a bear,   100
        For beasts that meet me run away for fear.
        Therefore no marvel though Demetrius
        Do, as a monster, fly my presence thus.°
        What wicked and dissembling glass of mine
        Made me compare° with Hermia's sphery eyne?°   105
        But who is here? Lysander, on the ground?
        Dead, or asleep? I see no blood, no wound.
        Lysander, if you live, good sir, awake.
Lysander [awaking]: And run through fire I will for thy sweet sake.
        Transparent° Helena! Nature shows art,°   110
        That through thy bosom makes me see thy heart.
        Where is Demetrius? O, how fit a word
        Is that vile name to perish on my sword!
Helena: Do not say so, Lysander; say not so.
        What though he love your Hermia? Lord, what though?   115
        Yet Hermia still loves you. Then be content.
Lysander: Content with Hermia? No! I do repent
        The tedious minutes I with her have spent.
        Not Hermia but Helena I love.
        Who will not change a raven for a dove?   120
        The will° of man is by his reason swayed,
        And reason says you are the worthier maid.
        Things growing are not ripe until their season;
        So I, being young, till now ripe not° to reason.
        And, touching° now the point° of human skill,°   125
        Reason becomes the marshal to my will
        And leads me to your eyes, where I o'erlook°
        Love's stories written in love's richest book.
Helena: Wherefore° was I to this keen mockery born?
        When at your hands did I deserve this scorn?   130
        Is't not enough, is't not enough, young man,

92 *darkling:* In the dark.   93 *on thy peril:* I.e., on pain of danger to you if you don't obey me and stay.   94 *fond:* Doting.   95 *my grace:* The favor I obtain.   96 *lies:* Dwells. 102–103 *no marvel . . . thus:* I.e., no wonder that Demetrius flies from me as from a monster. 105 *compare:* Vie; *sphery eyne:* Eyes as bright as stars in their spheres.   110 *Transparent:* (1) Radiant (2) able to be seen through, lacking in deceit; *art:* Skill, magic power.   121 *will:* Desire.   124 *ripe not:* (Am) not ripened.   125 *touching:* Reaching; *point:* Summit; *skill:* Judgment.   127 *o'erlook:* Read.   129 *Wherefore:* Why.

That I did never — no, nor never can —
Deserve a sweet look from Demetrius' eye,
But you must flout my insufficiency?
Good troth,° you do me wrong, good sooth,° you do,   135
In such disdainful manner me to woo.
But fare you well. Perforce I must confess
I thought you lord of° more true gentleness.°
O, that a lady, of° one man refused,
Should of another therefore be abused!°   *Exit.* 140

Lysander: She sees not Hermia. Hermia, sleep thou there,
And never mayst thou come Lysander near!
For as a surfeit of the sweetest things
The deepest loathing to the stomach brings,
Or as the heresies that men do leave   145
Are hated most of those they did deceive,°
So thou, my surfeit and my heresy,
Of all be hated, but the most of° me!
And, all my powers, address° your love and might
To honor Helen and to be her knight!   *Exit.* 150

Hermia [awaking]: Help me, Lysander, help me! Do thy best
To pluck this crawling serpent from my breast!
Ay me, for pity! What a dream was here!
Lysander, look how I do quake with fear.
Methought a serpent ate my heart away,   155
And you sat smiling at his cruel prey.°
Lysander! What, removed? Lysander! Lord!
What, out of hearing? Gone? No sound, no word?
Alack, where are you? Speak, an if° you hear;
Speak, of all loves!° I swoon almost with fear.   160
No? Then I well perceive you are not nigh.
Either death, or you, I'll find immediately.

                                    Exit. [The sleeping Titania remains.]

[ACT III

SCENE I: *The wood.*]

Enter the clowns° [*Quince, Snug, Bottom, Flute, Snout, and Starveling*].

Bottom: Are we all met?

Quince: Pat, pat,° and here's a marvelous convenient place for our rehearsal. This green plot shall be our stage, this hawthorn brake° our
tiring-house,° and we will do it in action as we will do it before
the Duke.   5

---

135 *Good troth, good sooth:* I.e., indeed, truly.   138 *lord of:* I.e., possessor of; *gentleness:* Courtesy.   139 *of:* By.   140 *abused:* Ill treated.   145–146 *as . . . deceive:* As renounced heresies
are hated most by those persons who formerly were deceived by them.   148 *Of . . . of:*
By . . . by.   149 *address:* Direct, apply.   156 *prey:* Act of preying.   159 *an if:* If.
160 *of all loves:* For love's sake.   **Act III, Scene I.**   *clowns:* Rustics.   2 *Pat:* On the
dot, punctually.   3 *brake:* Thicket.   4 *tiring-house:* Attiring area, hence backstage.

Bottom: Peter Quince?

Quince: What sayest thou, bully° Bottom?

Bottom: There are things in this comedy of Pyramus and Thisbe that will
never please. First, Pyramus must draw a sword to kill himself, which
the ladies cannot abide. How answer you that?   10

Snout: By 'r lakin,° a parlous° fear.

Starveling: I believe we must leave the killing out, when all is done.°

Bottom: Not a whit. I have a device to make all well. Write me° a prologue,
and let the prologue seem to say, we will do no harm with our swords,
and that Pyramus is not killed indeed; and for the more better   15
assurance, tell them that I, Pyramus, am not Pyramus but Bottom the
weaver. This will put them out of fear.

Quince: Well, we will have such a prologue, and it shall be written in eight
and six.°

Bottom: No, make it two more: let it be written in eight and eight.   20

Snout: Will not the ladies be afeard of the lion?

Starveling: I fear it, I promise you.

Bottom: Masters, you ought to consider with yourself, to bring in — God
shield us! — a lion among ladies° is a most dreadful thing. For there is
not a more fearful° wildfowl than your lion living, and we ought to   25
look to 't.

Snout: Therefore another prologue must tell he is not a lion.

Bottom: Nay, you must name his name, and half his face must be seen
through the lion's neck, and he himself must speak through, saying
thus or to the same defect:° "Ladies," or "Fair ladies, I would wish   30
you," or "I would request you," or "I would entreat you, not to fear,
not to tremble; my life for yours.° If you think I come hither as a lion,
it were pity of my life.° No, I am no such thing; I am a man as other
men are." And there indeed let him name his name, and tell them
plainly he is Snug the joiner.   35

Quince: Well, it shall be so. But there is two hard things: that is, to bring
the moonlight into a chamber; for, you know, Pyramus and Thisbe
meet by moonlight.

Snout: Doth the moon shine that night we play our play?

Bottom: A calendar, a calendar! Look in the almanac. Find out moon-   40
shine, find out moonshine.   *[They consult an almanac.]*

Quince: Yes, it doth shine that night.

Bottom: Why then may you leave a casement of the great chamber window where we play open, and the moon may shine in at the case-
ment.   45

---

7 *bully:* I.e., worthy, jolly, fine fellow.   11 *By 'r lakin:* By our ladykin, i.e., the Virgin Mary;
parlous: Perilous, alarming.   12 *when all is done:* I.e., when all is said and done.   13 *Write
me:* I.e., write at my suggestion (*me* is used colloquially).   19 *eight and six:* Alternate lines
of eight and six syllables, a common ballad measure.   24 *lion among ladies:* (A contemporary pamphlet tells how, at the christening in 1594 of Prince Henry, eldest son of King James
VI of Scotland, later James I of England, a "blackamoor" instead of a lion drew the triumphal chariot, since the lion's presence might have "brought some fear to the nearest.")
25 *fearful:* Fear-inspiring.   30 *defect:* (Bottom's blunder for "effect.")   32 *my life for
yours:* I.e., I pledge my life to make your lives safe.   33 *it were . . . life:* I.e., I should be sorry,
by my life; or, my life would be endangered.

Quince: Ay; or else one must come in with a bush of thorns° and a
lantern and say he comes to disfigure,° or to present,° the person of
Moonshine. Then there is another thing: we must have a wall in
the great chamber; for Pyramus and Thisbe, says the story, did talk
through the chink of a wall.   50
Snout: You can never bring in a wall. What say you, Bottom?
Bottom: Some man or other must present Wall. And let him have some
plaster, or some loam, or some roughcast° about him, to signify wall;
or let him hold his fingers thus, and through that cranny shall
Pyramus and Thisbe whisper.   55
Quince: If that may be, then all is well. Come, sit down, every mother's
son, and rehearse your parts. Pyramus, you begin. When you have spoken your speech, enter into that brake, and so everyone according to
his cue.

   Enter Robin [Puck].

Puck [aside]: What hempen homespuns° have we swaggering here   60
   So near the cradle° of the Fairy Queen?
   What, a play toward?° I'll be an auditor;
   An actor, too, perhaps, if I see cause.
Quince: Speak, Pyramus. Thisbe, stand forth.
Bottom [as Pyramus]: "Thisbe, the flowers of odious savors sweet—"   65
Quince: Odors, odors.
Bottom: "—Odors savors sweet;
   So hath thy breath, my dearest Thisbe dear.
   But hark, a voice! Stay thou but here awhile,
   And by and by I will to thee appear."   *Exit.* 70
Puck: A stranger Pyramus than e'er played here.°   *[Exit.]*
Flute: Must I speak now?
Quince: Ay, marry, must you; for you must understand he goes but to see a
   noise that he heard, and is to come again.
Flute [as Thisbe]: "Most radiant Pyramus, most lily-white of hue,   75
   Of color like the red rose on triumphant° brier,
   Most brisky juvenal° and eke° most lovely Jew,°
   As true as truest horse that yet would never tire.
   I'll meet thee, Pyramus, at Ninny's tomb."
Quince: "Ninus'° tomb," man. Why, you must not speak that yet. That you 80
   answer to Pyramus. You speak all your part° at once, cues and all.
   Pyramus, enter. Your cue is past; it is "never tire."

46 *bush of thorns:* Bundle of thornbush fagots (part of the accoutrements of the man in the
moon, according to the popular notions of the time, along with his lantern and his dog).
47 *disfigure:* (Quince's blunder for "figure"); *present:* Represent.   53 *roughcast:* A mixture
of lime and gravel used to plaster the outside of buildings.   60 *hempen homespuns:* I.e.,
rustics dressed in clothes woven of coarse, homespun fabric made from hemp.   61 *cradle:*
I.e., Titania's bower.   62 *toward:* About to take place.   71 *A stranger . . . here:* (Either Puck
refers to an earlier dramatic version played in the same theater, or he has conceived of a plan
to present a "stranger" Pyramus than ever seen before.)   76 *triumphant:* Magnificent.
77 *brisky juvenal:* Lively youth; *eke:* Also; *Jew:* (An absurd repetition of the first syllable of *juvenal* and an indication of how desperately Quince searches for his rhymes.)   80 *Ninus':*
Mythical founder of Nineveh (whose wife, Semiramis, was supposed to have built the walls of
Babylon where the story of Pyramus and Thisbe takes place).   81 *part:* (An actor's *part* was
a script consisting only of his speeches and their cues.)

Flute: O — "As true as truest horse, that yet would never tire."

[Enter Puck, and Bottom as Pyramus with the ass head.°]

Bottom: "If I were fair,° Thisbe, I were° only thine."

Quince: O, monstrous! O, strange! We are haunted. Pray, masters! Fly, mas-   85
    ters! Help!   *[Exeunt Quince, Snug, Flute, Snout, and Starveling.]*

Puck: I'll follow you, I'll lead you about a round,°
    Thorough bog, thorough bush, thorough brake, thorough brier.
    Sometimes a horse I'll be, sometimes a hound,
       A hog, a headless bear, sometimes a fire;°   90
    And neigh, and bark, and grunt, and roar, and burn,
    Like horse, hound, hog, bear, fire, at every turn.   *Exit.*

Bottom: Why do they run away? This is a knavery of them to make me
    afeard.

    Enter Snout.

Snout: O Bottom, thou art changed! What do I see on thee?   95

Bottom: What do you see? You see an ass head of your own, do you?
                                                          [Exit Snout.]

    Enter Quince.

Quince: Bless thee, Bottom, bless thee! Thou art translated.°   *Exit.*

Bottom: I see their knavery. This is to make an ass of me, to fright me, if
    they could. But I will not stir from this place, do what they can. I will
    walk up and down here, and will sing, that they shall hear I am not   100
    afraid.   *[He sings.]*
       The ouzel cock° so black of hue,
          With orange-tawny bill,
       The throstle° with his note so true,
          The wren with little quill° —   105

Titania [awaking]: What angel wakes me from my flowery bed?

Bottom [sings]:
       The finch, the sparrow, and the lark,
          The plainsong° cuckoo gray,
       Whose note full many a man doth mark,
          And dares not answer nay° —   110
    For indeed, who would set his wit to° so foolish a bird? Who would give a
    bird the lie,° though he cry "cuckoo" never so?°

Titania: I pray thee, gentle mortal, sing again.
    Mine ear is much enamored of thy note;
    So is mine eye enthrallèd to thy shape;   115
    And thy fair virtue's force° perforce doth move me
    On the first view to say, to swear, I love thee.

---

with the ass head: (This stage direction presumably refers to a standard stage property.)
84 *fair:* Handsome; *were:* Would be.   87 *about a round:* Roundabout.   90 *fire:* Will-o'-
the-wisp.   97 *translated:* Transformed.   102 *ouzel cock:* Male blackbird.   104 *throstle:*
Song thrush.   105 *quill:* (Literally, a reed pipe; hence, the bird's piping song.)   108 *plainsong:* Singing a melody without variations.   110 *dares . . . nay:* I.e., cannot deny that he is
a cuckold.   111 *set his wit to:* Employ his intelligence to answer.   112 *give . . . lie:* Call the
bird a liar; *never so:* Ever so much.   116 *thy . . . force:* The power of your unblemished
excellence.

Bottom: Methinks, mistress, you should have little reason for that. And
yet, to say the truth, reason and love keep little company together
nowadays — the more the pity that some honest neighbors will not   120
make them friends. Nay, I can gleek° upon occasion.
Titania: Thou art as wise as thou art beautiful.
Bottom: Not so, neither. But if I had wit enough to get out of this wood,
I have enough to serve mine own turn.°
Titania: Out of this wood do not desire to go.   125
Thou shalt remain here, whether thou wilt or no.
I am a spirit of no common rate.°
The summer still doth tend upon my state,°
And I do love thee. Therefore, go with me.
I'll give thee fairies to attend on thee,   130
And they shall fetch thee jewels from the deep,
And sing while thou on pressèd flowers dost sleep.
And I will purge thy mortal grossness° so
That thou shalt like an airy spirit go.
Peaseblossom, Cobweb, Mote,° and Mustardseed!   135

Enter four Fairies [Peaseblossom, Cobweb, Mote, and Mustardseed].

Peaseblossom: Ready.
Cobweb: And I.
Mote: And I.
Mustardseed: And I.
All: Where shall we go?
Titania: Be kind and courteous to this gentleman.
Hop in his walks and gambol in his eyes;°
Feed him with apricots and dewberries,°   140
With purple grapes, green figs, and mulberries;
The honey bags steal from the humble-bees,
And for night tapers crop their waxen thighs
And light them at the fiery glowworms' eyes,
To have my love to bed and to arise;   145
And pluck the wings from painted butterflies
To fan the moonbeams from his sleeping eyes.
Nod to him, elves, and do him courtesies.
Peaseblossom: Hail, mortal!
Cobweb: Hail!   150
Mote: Hail!
Mustardseed: Hail!
Bottom: I cry your worships mercy,° heartily. I beseech your worship's name.
Cobweb: Cobweb.

121 *gleek:* Jest.   124 *serve … turn:* Answer my purpose.   127 *rate:* Rank, value.   128 *still …
state:* Always waits upon me as a part of my royal retinue.   133 *mortal grossness:* Materiality
(i.e., the corporeal nature of a mortal being).   135 *Mote:* I.e., speck. (The two words *moth*
and *mote* were pronounced alike, and both meanings may be present.)   139 *in his eyes:* In his
sight (i.e., before him).   140 *dewberries:* Blackberries.   153 *I cry … mercy:* I beg pardon of
your worships (for presuming to ask a question).

Bottom: I shall desire you of more acquaintance,° good Master Cobweb.   155
    If I cut my finger, I shall make bold with you.°—Your name, honest
    gentleman?
Peaseblossom: Peaseblossom.
Bottom: I pray you, commend me to Mistress Squash,° your mother,
    and to Master Peascod,° your father. Good Master Peaseblossom, I   160
    shall desire you of more acquaintance too.—Your name, I beseech
    you, sir?
Mustardseed: Mustardseed.
Bottom: Good Master Mustardseed, I know your patience° well. That same
    cowardly, giantlike ox-beef hath devoured many a gentleman of your   165
    house. I promise you, your kindred hath made my eyes water° ere now.
    I desire you of more acquaintance, good Master Mustardseed.
Titania: Come wait upon him; lead him to my bower.
     The moon methinks looks with a watery eye;
    And when she weeps,° weeps every little flower,   170
      Lamenting some enforcèd° chastity.
      Tie up my lover's tongue;° bring him silently.   *Exeunt.*

[SCENE II: *The wood.*]

    Enter [Oberon,] King of Fairies.

Oberon: I wonder if Titania be awaked;
    Then, what it was that next came in her eye,
    Which she must dote on in extremity.

    [Enter] Robin Goodfellow [Puck].

    Here comes my messenger. How now, mad spirit?
    What night-rule° now about this haunted° grove?   5
Puck: My mistress with a monster is in love.
    Near to her close° and consecrated bower,
    While she was in her dull° and sleeping hour,
    A crew of patches,° rude mechanicals,°
    That work for bread upon Athenian stalls,°   10
    Were met together to rehearse a play
    Intended for great Theseus' nuptial day.
    The shallowest thickskin of that barren sort,°
    Who Pyramus presented,° in their sport
    Forsook his scene° and entered in a brake.   15
    When I did him at this advantage take,

---

155 *I . . . acquaintance:* I crave to be better acquainted with you.   155–156 *If . . . you:* (Cobwebs were used to stanch bleeding.)   159 *Squash:* Unripe pea pod.   160 *Peascod:* Ripe pea pod.   164 *your patience:* What you have endured (mustard is eaten with beef).   166 *water:* (1) Weep for sympathy (2) smart, sting.   170 *she weeps:* I.e., she causes dew.   171 *enforcèd:* Forced, violated; or, possibly, constrained (since Titania at this moment is hardly concerned about chastity).   172 *Tie . . . tongue:* (Presumably Bottom is braying like an ass.) **Scene II.**   5 *night-rule:* Diversion or misrule for the night; *haunted:* Much frequented. 7 *close:* Secret, private.   8 *dull:* Drowsy.   9 *patches:* Clowns, fools; *rude mechanicals:* Ignorant artisans.   10 *stalls:* Market booths.   13 *barren sort:* Stupid company or crew. 14 *presented:* Acted.   15 *scene:* Playing area.

An ass's noll° I fixèd on his head.
Anon his Thisbe must be answerèd,
And forth my mimic° comes. When they him spy,
As wild geese that the creeping fowler° eye,   20
Or russet-pated choughs,° many in sort,°
Rising and cawing at the gun's report,
Sever° themselves and madly sweep the sky,
So, at his sight, away his fellows fly;
And, at our stamp, here o'er and o'er one falls;   25
He "Murder!" cries and help from Athens calls.
Their sense thus weak, lost with their fears thus strong,
Made senseless things begin to do them wrong,
For briers and thorns at their apparel snatch;
Some, sleeves — some, hats; from yielders all things catch.°   30
I led them on in this distracted fear
And left sweet Pyramus translated there,
When in that moment, so it came to pass,
Titania waked and straightway loved an ass.

Oberon: This falls out better than I could devise.   35
But hast thou yet latched° the Athenian's eyes
With the love juice, as I did bid thee do?

Puck: I took him sleeping — that is finished too —
And the Athenian woman by his side,
That, when he waked, of force° she must be eyed.   40

Enter Demetrius and Hermia.

Oberon: Stand close. This is the same Athenian.

Puck: This is the woman, but not this the man.   *[They stand aside.]*

Demetrius: O, why rebuke you him that loves you so?
Lay breath so bitter on your bitter foe.

Hermia: Now I but chide; but I should use thee worse,   45
For thou, I fear, hast given me cause to curse.
If thou hast slain Lysander in his sleep,
Being o'er shoes° in blood, plunge in the deep,
And kill me too.
The sun was not so true unto the day   50
As he to me. Would he have stolen away
From sleeping Hermia? I'll believe as soon
This whole° earth may be bored, and that the moon
May through the center creep, and so displease
Her brother's° noontide with th' Antipodes.°   55
It cannot be but thou hast murdered him;
So should a murderer look, so dead,° so grim.

---

17 *noll:* Noddle, head.   19 *mimic:* Burlesque actor.   20 *fowler:* Hunter of game birds.
21 *russet-pated choughs:* Reddish brown or gray-headed jackdaws; *in sort:* In a flock.
23 *Sever:* I.e., scatter.   30 *from . . . catch:* I.e., everything preys on those who yield to fear.
36 *latched:* Fastened, snared.   40 *of force:* Perforce.   48 *Being o'er shoes:* Having waded
in so far.   53 *whole:* Solid.   55 *Her brother's:* I.e., the sun's; *th' Antipodes:* The people on
the opposite side of the earth (where the moon is imagined bringing night to noontime).
57 *dead:* Deadly, or deathly pale.

Demetrius: So should the murdered look, and so should I,
    Pierced through the heart with your stern cruelty.
    Yet you, the murderer, look as bright, as clear   60
    As yonder Venus in her glimmering sphere.
Hermia: What's this to° my Lysander? Where is he?
    Ah, good Demetrius, wilt thou give him me?
Demetrius: I had rather give his carcass to my hounds.
Hermia: Out, dog! Out, cur! Thou driv'st me past the bounds   65
    Of maiden's patience. Hast thou slain him, then?
    Henceforth be never numbered among men.
    O, once° tell true, tell true, even for my sake:
    Durst thou have looked upon him being awake?
    And hast thou killed him sleeping? O brave touch!°   70
    Could not a worm,° an adder, do so much?
    An adder did it; for with doubler° tongue
    Than thine, thou serpent, never adder stung.
Demetrius: You spend your passion° on a misprised mood.°
    I am not guilty of Lysander's blood,   75
    Nor is he dead, for aught that I can tell.
Hermia: I pray thee, tell me then that he is well.
Demetrius: And if I could, what should I get therefor?°
Hermia: A privilege never to see me more.
    And from thy hated presence part I so.   80
    See me no more, whether he be dead or no.   *Exit.*
Demetrius: There is no following her in this fierce vein.
    Here therefore for a while I will remain.
    So sorrow's heaviness doth heavier° grow
    For debt that bankrupt° sleep doth sorrow owe,   85
    Which now in some slight measure it will pay,
    If for his tender here I make some stay.°   *[He] lie[s] down [and sleeps].*
Oberon: What hast thou done? Thou hast mistaken quite
    And laid the love juice on some true love's sight.
    Of thy misprision° must perforce ensue   90
    Some true love turned, and not a false turned true.
Puck: Then fate o'errules, that, one man holding troth,°
    A million fail, confounding oath on oath.°
Oberon: About the wood go swifter than the wind,
    And Helena of Athens look° thou find.   95
    All fancy-sick° she is and pale of cheer°
    With sighs of love, that cost the fresh blood° dear.

---

62 *to:* To do with.   68 *once:* Once and for all.   70 *brave touch!:* Fine stroke! (said ironically).   71 *worm:* Serpent.   72 *doubler:* (1) More forked (2) more deceitful.   74 *passion:* Violent feelings; *misprised mood:* Anger based on misconception.   78 *therefor:* In return for that.   84 *heavier:* (1) Harder to bear (2) more drowsy.   85 *bankrupt:* (Demetrius
is saying that his sleepiness adds to the weariness caused by sorrow.)   86–87 *Which . . . stay:*
I.e., to a small extent, I will be able to "pay back" and hence find some relief from sorrow, if I
pause here awhile (*make some stay*) while sleep "tenders" or offers itself by way of paying the
debt owed to sorrow.   90 *misprision:* Mistake.   92 *that . . . troth:* In that, for each man
keeping true faith in love.   93 *confounding . . . oath:* I.e., breaking oath after oath.
95 *look:* I.e., be sure.   96 *fancy-sick:* Lovesick; *cheer:* Face.   97 *sighs . . . blood:* (An allusion to the physiological theory that each sigh costs the heart a drop of blood.)

By some illusion see thou bring her here.
I'll charm his eyes against she do appear.°

Puck: I go, I go, look how I go,
        Swifter than arrow from the Tartar's bow.°   [*Exit.*]   100

Oberon [applying love juice to Demetrius' eyes]: Flower of this purple dye,
        Hit with Cupid's archery,
        Sink in apple° of his eye.
        When his love he doth espy,   105
        Let her shine as gloriously
        As the Venus of the sky.
        When thou wak'st, if she be by,
        Beg of her for remedy.

        Enter Puck.

Puck: Captain of our fairy band,   110
        Helena is here at hand,
        And the youth, mistook by me,
        Pleading for a lover's fee.°
        Shall we their fond pageant° see?
        Lord, what fools these mortals be!   115

Oberon: Stand aside. The noise they make
        Will cause Demetrius to awake.

Puck: Then will two at once woo one;
        That must needs be sport alone.°
        And those things do best please me   120
        That befall preposterously.°   [*They stand aside.*]

        Enter Lysander and Helena.

Lysander: Why should you think that I should woo in scorn?
        Scorn and derision never come in tears.
        Look when° I vow, I weep; and vows so born,
        In their nativity all truth appears.°   125
        How can these things in me seem scorn to you,
        Bearing the badge° of faith to prove them true?

Helena: You do advance° your cunning more and more.
        When truth kills truth,° O, devilish-holy fray!
        These vows are Hermia's. Will you give her o'er?   130
        Weigh oath with oath, and you will nothing weigh.
        Your vows to her and me, put in two scales,
        Will even weigh, and both as light as tales.°

Lysander: I had no judgment when to her I swore.

Helena: Nor none, in my mind, now you give her o'er.   135

Lysander: Demetrius loves her, and he loves not you.

---

99 *against . . . appear:* In anticipation of her coming.   101 *Tartar's bow:* (Tartars were famed
for their skill with the bow.)   104 *apple:* Pupil.   113 *fee:* Privilege, reward.   114 *fond
pageant:* Foolish spectacle.   119 *alone:* Unequaled.   121 *preposterously:* Out of the natural order.   124 *Look when:* Whenever.   124–125 *vows . . . appears:* I.e., vows made by one
who is weeping give evidence thereby of their sincerity.   127 *badge:* Identifying device
such as that worn on the servants' livery (here, his tears).   128 *advance:* Carry forward, display.   129 *truth kills truth:* I.e., one of Lysander's vows must invalidate the other.
133 *tales:* Lies.

Demetrius [awaking]: O Helen, goddess, nymph, perfect, divine!
　　　To what, my love, shall I compare thine eyne?
　　　Crystal is muddy. O, how ripe in show°
　　　Thy lips, those kissing cherries, tempting grow! 　　　140
　　　That pure congealèd white, high Taurus'° snow,
　　　Fanned with the eastern wind, turns to a crow°
　　　When thou hold'st up thy hand. O, let me kiss
　　　This princess of pure white, this seal° of bliss!
Helena: O spite! O hell! I see you all are bent 　　　145
　　　To set against° me for your merriment.
　　　If you were civil and knew courtesy,
　　　You would not do me thus much injury.
　　　Can you not hate me, as I know you do,
　　　But you must join in souls° to mock me too? 　　　150
　　　If you were men, as men you are in show,
　　　You would not use a gentle lady so —
　　　To vow, and swear, and superpraise° my parts,°
　　　When I am sure you hate me with your hearts.
　　　You both are rivals, and love Hermia, 　　　155
　　　And now both rivals to mock Helena.
　　　A trim° exploit, a manly enterprise,
　　　To conjure tears up in a poor maid's eyes
　　　With your derision! None of noble sort°
　　　Would so offend a virgin and extort° 　　　160
　　　A poor soul's patience, all to make you sport.
Lysander: You are unkind, Demetrius. Be not so.
　　　For you love Hermia; this you know I know.
　　　And here, with all good will, with all my heart,
　　　In Hermia's love I yield you up my part; 　　　165
　　　And yours of Helena to me bequeath,
　　　Whom I do love, and will do till my death.
Helena: Never did mockers waste more idle breath.
Demetrius: Lysander, keep thy Hermia; I will none.°
　　　If e'er I loved her, all that love is gone. 　　　170
　　　My heart to her but as guestwise sojourned,°
　　　And now to Helen is it home returned,
　　　There to remain.
Lysander:　　　　　　　Helen, it is not so.
Demetrius: Disparage not the faith thou dost not know,
　　　Lest, to thy peril, thou aby° it dear. 　　　175
　　　Look where thy love comes; yonder is thy dear.

　　　Enter Hermia.

---

139 *show:* Appearance. 　　141 *Taurus:* A lofty mountain range in Asia Minor. 　　142 *turns
to a crow:* I.e., seems black by contrast. 　　144 *seal:* Pledge. 　　146 *set against:* Attack.
150 *in souls:* I.e., heart and soul. 　　153 *superpraise:* Overpraise; *parts:* Qualities. 　　157 *trim:*
Pretty, fine (said ironically). 　　159 *sort:* Character, quality. 　　160 *extort:* Twist, torture.
169 *will none:* I.e., want no part of her. 　　171 *to . . . sojourned:* Only visited with her.
175 *aby:* Pay for.

Hermia: Dark night, that from the eye his° function takes,
    The ear more quick of apprehension makes;
    Wherein it doth impair the seeing sense,
    It pays the hearing double recompense.   180
    Thou art not by mine eye, Lysander, found;
    Mine ear, I thank it, brought me to thy sound.
    But why unkindly didst thou leave me so?
Lysander: Why should he stay, whom love doth press to go?
Hermia: What love could press Lysander from my side?   185
Lysander: Lysander's love, that would not let him bide —
    Fair Helena, who more engilds° the night
    Than all yon fiery oes° and eyes of light.
    Why seek'st thou me? Could not this make thee know
    The hate I bear thee made me leave thee so?   190
Hermia: You speak not as you think. It cannot be.
Helena: Lo, she is one of this confederacy!
    Now I perceive they have conjoined all three
    To fashion this false sport, in spite of me.°
    Injurious Hermia, most ungrateful maid!   195
    Have you conspired, have you with these contrived°
    To bait° me with this foul derision?
    Is all the counsel° that we two have shared —
    The sisters' vows, the hours that we have spent
    When we have chid the hasty-footed time   200
    For parting us — O, is all forgot?
    All schooldays' friendship, childhood innocence?
    We, Hermia, like two artificial° gods
    Have with our needles created both one flower,
    Both on one sampler, sitting on one cushion,   205
    Both warbling of one song, both in one key,
    As if our hands, our sides, voices, and minds
    Had been incorporate.° So we grew together,
    Like to a double cherry, seeming parted,
    But yet an union in partition,   210
    Two lovely° berries molded on one stem;
    So, with two seeming bodies but one heart,
    Two of the first, like coats in heraldry,
    Due but to one and crownèd with one crest.°
    And will you rend our ancient love asunder,   215
    To join with men in scorning your poor friend?
    It is not friendly, 'tis not maidenly.
    Our sex, as well as I, may chide you for it,
    Though I alone do feel the injury.
Hermia: I am amazèd at your passionate words.   220
    I scorn you not. It seems that you scorn me.

---

177 *his:* Its.   187 *engilds:* Gilds, brightens with a golden light.   188 *oes:* Spangles (here, stars).   194 *in spite of me:* To vex me.   196 *contrived:* Plotted.   197 *bait:* Torment, as one sets on dogs to bait a bear.   198 *counsel:* Confidential talk.   203 *artificial:* Skilled in art or creation.   208 *incorporate:* Of one body.   211 *lovely:* Loving.   213-214 *Two . . . crest:* I.e., we have two separate bodies, just as a coat of arms in heraldry can be represented twice on a shield but surmounted by a single crest.

Helena: Have you not set Lysander, as in scorn,
　　　To follow me and praise my eyes and face?
　　　And made your other love, Demetrius,
　　　Who even but now did spurn me with his foot,   225
　　　To call me goddess, nymph, divine, and rare,
　　　Precious, celestial? Wherefore speaks he this
　　　To her he hates? And wherefore doth Lysander
　　　Deny your love, so rich within his soul,
　　　And tender° me, forsooth, affection,   230
　　　But by your setting on, by your consent?
　　　What though I be not so in grace° as you,
　　　So hung upon with love, so fortunate,
　　　But miserable most, to love unloved?
　　　This you should pity rather than despise.   235
Hermia: I understand not what you mean by this.
Helena: Ay, do! Persever, counterfeit sad° looks,
　　　Make mouths° upon° me when I turn my back,
　　　Wink each at other, hold the sweet jest up.°
　　　This sport, well carried,° shall be chronicled.   240
　　　If you have any pity, grace, or manners,
　　　You would not make me such an argument.°
　　　But fare ye well. 'Tis partly my own fault,
　　　Which death, or absence, soon shall remedy.
Lysander: Stay, gentle Helena; hear my excuse,   245
　　　My love, my life, my soul, fair Helena!
Helena: O excellent!
Hermia [to Lysander]: Sweet, do not scorn her so.
Demetrius [to Lysander]: If she cannot entreat,° I can compel.
Lysander: Thou canst compel no more than she entreat.   250
　　　Thy threats have no more strength than her weak prayers.
　　　Helen, I love thee, by my life, I do!
　　　I swear by that which I will lose for thee,
　　　To prove him false that says I love thee not.
Demetrius [to Helena]: I say I love thee more than he can do.   255
Lysander: If thou say so, withdraw, and prove it too.°
Demetrius: Quick, come!
Hermia: Lysander, whereto tends all this?
Lysander: Away, you Ethiope!°   *[He tries to break away from Hermia.]*
Demetrius: No, no; he'll
　　　Seem to break loose; take on as° you would follow,
　　　But yet come not. You are a tame man. Go!   260
Lysander [to Hermia]: Hang off,° thou cat, thou burr! Vile thing, let loose,
　　　Or I will shake thee from me like a serpent!
Hermia: Why are you grown so rude? What change is this,
　　　Sweet love?

---

230 *tender:* Offer.   232 *grace:* Favor.   237 *sad:* Grave, serious.   238 *mouths:* I.e., mows, faces, grimaces; *upon:* At.   239 *hold...up:* Keep up the joke.   240 *carried:* Managed.
242 *argument:* Subject for a jest.   249 *entreat:* I.e., succeed by entreaty.   256 *withdraw... too:* I.e., withdraw with me and prove your claim in a duel (the two gentlemen are armed).
258 *Ethiope:* (Referring to Hermia's relatively dark hair and complexion; see also *tawny Tartar* six lines later.)   259 *take on as:* Act as if, make a fuss as if.   261 *Hang off:* Let go.

Lysander: Thy love? Out, tawny Tartar, out!
     Out, loathèd med'cine!° O hated potion, hence!   265
Hermia: Do you not jest?
Helena: Yes, sooth,° and so do you.
Lysander: Demetrius, I will keep my word with thee.
Demetrius: I would I had your bond, for I perceive
     A weak bond° holds you. I'll not trust your word.
Lysander: What, should I hurt her, strike her, kill her dead?   270
     Although I hate her, I'll not harm her so.
Hermia: What, can you do me greater harm than hate?
     Hate me? Wherefore? O me, what news,° my love?
     Am not I Hermia? Are not you Lysander?
     I am as fair now as I was erewhile.°   275
     Since night you loved me; yet since night you left me.
     Why, then you left me — O, the gods forbid! —
     In earnest, shall I say?
Lysander: Ay, by my life!
     And never did desire to see thee more.
     Therefore be out of hope, of question, of doubt;   280
     Be certain, nothing truer. 'Tis no jest
     That I do hate thee and love Helena.
Hermia [to Helena]: O me! You juggler! You cankerblossom!°
     You thief of love! What, have you come by night
     And stol'n my love's heart from him?
Helena: Fine, i' faith!   285
     Have you no modesty, no maiden shame,
     No touch of bashfulness? What, will you tear
     Impatient answers from my gentle tongue?
     Fie, fie! You counterfeit, you puppet,° you!
Hermia: "Puppet"? Why, so!° Ay, that way goes the game.   290
     Now I perceive that she hath made compare
     Between our statures; she hath urged her height,
     And with her personage, her tall personage,
     Her height, forsooth, she hath prevailed with him.
     And are you grown so high in his esteem   295
     Because I am so dwarfish and so low?
     How low am I, thou painted maypole? Speak!
     How low am I? I am not yet so low
     But that my nails can reach unto thine eyes.
                         [She flails at Helena but is restrained.]
Helena: I pray you, though you mock me, gentlemen,   300
     Let her not hurt me. I was never curst;°
     I have no gift at all in shrewishness;
     I am a right° maid for my cowardice.
     Let her not strike me. You perhaps may think,

---

265 *med'cine:* I.e., poison.   266 *sooth:* Truly.   269 *weak bond:* I.e., Hermia's arm (with a pun on *bond,* "oath," in the previous line).   273 *what news:* What is the matter.   275 *erewhile:* Just now.   283 *cankerblossom:* Worm that destroys the flower bud, or wild rose. 289 *puppet:* (1) Counterfeit (2) dwarfish woman (in reference to Hermia's smaller stature). 290 *Why, so:* I.e., Oh, so that's how it is.   301 *curst:* Shrewish.   303 *right:* True.

Because she is something° lower than myself,   305
  That I can match her.
Hermia: Lower? Hark, again!
Helena: Good Hermia, do not be so bitter with me.
  I evermore did love you, Hermia,
  Did ever keep your counsels, never wronged you,
  Save that, in love unto Demetrius,   310
  I told him of your stealth° unto this wood.
  He followed you; for love I followed him.
  But he hath chid me hence° and threatened me
  To strike me, spurn me, nay, to kill me too.
  And now, so° you will let me quiet go,   315
  To Athens will I bear my folly back
  And follow you no further. Let me go.
  You see how simple and how fond° I am.
Hermia: Why, get you gone. Who is't that hinders you?
Helena: A foolish heart, that I leave here behind.   320
Hermia: What, with Lysander?
Helena: With Demetrius.
Lysander: Be not afraid; she shall not harm thee, Helena.
Demetrius: No, sir, she shall not, though you take her part.
Helena: O, when she is angry, she is keen° and shrewd.°
  She was a vixen when she went to school;   325
  And though she be but little, she is fierce.
Hermia: "Little" again? Nothing but "low" and "little"?
  Why will you suffer her to flout me thus?
  Let me come to her.
Lysander: Get you gone, you dwarf!
  You minimus,° of hindering knotgrass° made!   330
  You bead, you acorn!
Demetrius: You are too officious
  In her behalf that scorns your services.
  Let her alone. Speak not of Helena;
  Take not her part. For, if thou dost intend°
  Never so little show of love to her,   335
  Thou shalt aby° it.
Lysander: Now she holds me not.
  Now follow, if thou dar'st, to try whose right,
  Of thine or mine, is most in Helena.   *[Exit.]*
Demetrius: Follow? Nay, I'll go with thee, cheek by jowl.°
                              [Exit, following Lysander.]
Hermia: You, mistress, all this coil° is 'long of° you.   340
  Nay, go not back.°
Helena: I will not trust you, I,

---

305 *something:* Somewhat.   311 *stealth:* Stealing away.   313 *chid me hence:* Driven me away with his scolding.   315 *so:* If only.   318 *fond:* Foolish.   324 *keen:* Fierce, cruel; *shrewd:* Shrewish.   330 *minimus:* Diminutive creature; *knotgrass:* A weed, an infusion of which was thought to stunt the growth.   334 *intend:* Give sign of.   336 *aby:* Pay for. 339 *cheek by jowl:* I.e., side by side.   340 *coil:* Turmoil, dissension; *'long of:* On account of. 341 *go not back:* I.e., don't retreat (Hermia is again proposing a flight).

Nor longer stay in your curst company.
Your hands than mine are quicker for a fray;
My legs are longer, though, to run away.   *[Exit.]*
Hermia: I am amazed and know not what to say.   *Exit.* 345

[Oberon and Puck come forward.]

Oberon: This is thy negligence. Still thou mistak'st,
Or else committ'st thy knaveries willfully.
Puck: Believe me, king of shadows, I mistook.
Did not you tell me I should know the man
By the Athenian garments he had on?   350
And so far blameless proves my enterprise
That I have 'nointed an Athenian's eyes;
And so far° am I glad it so did sort,°
As° this their jangling I esteem a sport.
Oberon: Thou seest these lovers seek a place to fight.   355
Hie° therefore, Robin, overcast the night;
The starry welkin° cover thou anon
With drooping fog as black as Acheron,°
And lead these testy rivals so astray
As° one come not within another's way.   360
Like to Lysander sometimes frame thy tongue,
Then stir Demetrius up with bitter wrong;°
And sometimes rail thou like Demetrius.
And from each other look thou lead them thus,
Till o'er their brows death-counterfeiting sleep   365
With leaden legs and batty° wings doth creep.
Then crush this herb° into Lysander's eye,   *[giving herb]*
Whose liquor hath this virtuous° property,
To take from thence all error with his° might
And make his eyeballs roll with wonted° sight.   370
When they next wake, all this derision°
Shall seem a dream and fruitless vision,
And back to Athens shall the lovers wend
With league whose date° till death shall never end.
Whiles I in this affair do thee employ,   375
I'll to my queen and beg her Indian boy;
And then I will her charmèd eye release
From monster's view, and all things shall be peace.
Puck: My fairy lord, this must be done with haste,
For night's swift dragons° cut the clouds full fast,   380
And yonder shines Aurora's harbinger,°
At whose approach ghosts, wand'ring here and there,
Troop home to churchyards. Damnèd spirits all,

353 *so far:* At least to this extent; *sort:* Turn out.   354 *As:* In that.   356 *Hie:* Hasten.
357 *welkin:* Sky.   358 *Acheron:* River of Hades (here representing Hades itself).   360 *As:*
That.   362 *wrong:* Insults.   366 *batty:* Batlike.   367 *this herb:* I.e., the antidote
(mentioned in II.i.184) to love-in-idleness.   368 *virtuous:* Efficacious.   369 *his:* Its.
370 *wonted:* Accustomed.   371 *derision:* Laughable business.   374 *date:* Term of existence.   380 *dragons:* (Supposed by Shakespeare to be yoked to the car of the goddess of
night or the moon.)   381 *Aurora's harbinger:* The morning star, precursor of dawn.

That in crossways and floods have burial,°
Already to their wormy beds are gone.   385
For fear lest day should look their shames upon,
They willfully themselves exile from light
And must for aye° consort with black-browed night.

Oberon: But we are spirits of another sort.
    I with the Morning's love° have oft made sport,   390
    And, like a forester,° the groves may tread
    Even till the eastern gate, all fiery red,
    Opening on Neptune with fair blessèd beams,
    Turns into yellow gold his salt green streams.
    But notwithstanding, haste, make no delay.   395
    We may effect this business yet ere day.   *[Exit.]*

Puck: Up and down, up and down,
    I will lead them up and down.
    I am feared in field and town.
    Goblin,° lead them up and down.   400
    Here comes one.

    Enter Lysander.

Lysander: Where art thou, proud Demetrius? Speak thou now.
Puck [mimicking Demetrius]: Here, villain, drawn° and ready. Where art
    thou?
Lysander: I will be with thee straight.°
Puck: Follow me, then,
    To plainer° ground.   *[Lysander wanders about,° following the voice.]*

    Enter Demetrius.

Demetrius: Lysander! Speak again!   405
    Thou runaway, thou coward, art thou fled?
    Speak! In some bush? Where dost thou hide thy head?
Puck [mimicking Lysander]: Thou coward, art thou bragging to the stars,
    Telling the bushes that thou look'st for wars,
    And wilt not come? Come, recreant;° come, thou child,   410
    I'll whip thee with a rod. He is defiled
    That draws a sword on thee.
Demetrius: Yea, art thou there?
Puck: Follow my voice. We'll try° no manhood here.   *Exeunt.*

    [Lysander returns.]

Lysander: He goes before me and still dares me on.
    When I come where he calls, then he is gone.   415

---

384 *crossways . . . burial:* (Those who had committed suicide were buried at crossways, with a
stake driven through them; those who intentionally or accidentally drowned [in *floods* or
deep water] would be condemned to wander disconsolately for lack of burial rights.)
388 *for aye:* Forever.   390 *the Morning's love:* Cephalus, a beautiful youth beloved by Aurora; or perhaps the goddess of the dawn herself.   391 *forester:* Keeper of a royal forest.
400 *Goblin:* Hobgoblin (Puck refers to himself).   403 *drawn:* With drawn sword.
404 *straight:* Immediately.   405 *plainer:* More open.   *Lysander wanders about:* (Lysander
may exit here, but perhaps not; neither exit nor reentrance is indicated in the early texts.)
410 *recreant:* Cowardly wretch.   413 *try:* Test.

The villain is much lighter-heeled than I.
I followed fast, but faster he did fly,
That fallen am I in dark uneven way,
And here will rest me. *[He lies down.]* Come, thou gentle day!
For if but once thou show me thy gray light,   420
I'll find Demetrius and revenge this spite. *[He sleeps.]*

[Enter] Robin [Puck] and Demetrius.

Puck: Ho, ho, ho! Coward, why com'st thou not?
Demetrius: Abide° me, if thou dar'st; for well I wot°
     Thou runn'st before me, shifting every place,
     And dar'st not stand nor look me in the face.   425
     Where art thou now?
Puck: Come hither. I am here.
Demetrius: Nay, then, thou mock'st me. Thou shalt buy° this dear,°
     If ever I thy face by daylight see.
     Now go thy way. Faintness constraineth me
     To measure out my length on this cold bed.
     By day's approach look to be visited.   *[He lies down and sleeps.]*   430

Enter Helena.

Helena: O weary night, O long and tedious night,
     Abate° thy hours! Shine comforts from the east,
     That I may back to Athens by daylight
       From these that my poor company detest;   435
     And sleep, that sometimes shuts up sorrow's eye,
     Steal me awhile from mine own company.   *[She lies down and] sleep[s].*
Puck: Yet but three? Come one more;
     Two of both kinds makes up four.
     Here she comes, curst° and sad.   440
     Cupid is a knavish lad,
     Thus to make poor females mad.

[Enter Hermia.]

Hermia: Never so weary, never so in woe,
       Bedabbled with the dew and torn with briers,
     I can no further crawl, no further go;
       My legs can keep no pace with my desires.   445
     Here will I rest me till the break of day.
     Heavens shield Lysander, if they mean a fray! *[She lies down and sleeps.]*
Puck: On the ground
     Sleep sound.
     I'll apply   450
     To your eye,
     Gentle lover, remedy.   *[He squeezes the juice on Lysander's eyes.]*
     When thou wak'st,
     Thou tak'st   455
     True delight

---

423 *Abide:* Confront, face; *wot:* know.   427 *buy:* Aby, pay for; *dear:* Dearly.   433 *Abate:* Lessen, shorten.   440 *curst:* Ill-tempered.

In the sight
Of thy former lady's eye;
And the country proverb known,
That every man should take his own,   460
In your waking shall be shown:
    Jack shall have Jill;°
    Naught shall go ill;
The man shall have his mare again, and all shall be well.

> *[Exit. The four sleeping lovers remain.]*

[ACT IV

SCENE I: *The wood. The lovers are still asleep onstage.*]

Enter [Titania,] Queen of Fairies, and [Bottom the] clown, and Fairies; and [Oberon,] the King, behind them.

Titania: Come, sit thee down upon this flowery bed,
    While I thy amiable° cheeks do coy,°
    And stick muskroses in thy sleek smooth head,
        And kiss thy fair large ears, my gentle joy.   *[They recline.]*
Bottom: Where's Peaseblossom?   5
Peaseblossom: Ready.
Bottom: Scratch my head, Peaseblossom. Where's Monsieur Cobweb?
Cobweb: Ready.
Bottom: Monsieur Cobweb, good monsieur, get you your weapons in your
    hand, and kill me a red-hipped humble-bee on the top of a thistle;   10
    and, good monsieur, bring me the honey bag. Do not fret yourself too
    much in the action, monsieur; and, good monsieur, have a care the
    honey bag break not. I would be loath to have you overflown with a
    honey bag, signor. *[Exit Cobweb.]* Where's Monsieur Mustardseed?
Mustardseed: Ready.   15
Bottom: Give me your neaf,° Monsieur Mustardseed. Pray you, leave your
    courtesy,° good monsieur.
Mustardseed: What's your will?
Bottom: Nothing, good monsieur, but to help Cavalery° Cobweb° to
    scratch. I must to the barber's, monsieur, for methinks I am mar-   20
    velous hairy about the face; and I am such a tender ass, if my hair do
    but tickle me I must scratch.
Titania: What, wilt thou hear some music, my sweet love?
Bottom: I have a reasonable good ear in music. Let's have the tongs and
    the bones.°   *[Music: tongs, rural music.°]*   25

---

462 *Jack shall have Jill:* (Proverbial for "boy gets girl.")   **Act IV, Scene I.**   2 *amiable:*
Lovely; *coy:* Caress.   16 *neaf:* Fist.   16–17 *leave your courtesy:* I.e., stop bowing, or put on
your hat.   19 *Cavalery:* Cavalier (form of address for a gentleman); *Cobweb:* (Seemingly an
error, since Cobweb has been sent to bring honey, while Peaseblossom has been asked to
scratch.)   24–25 *tongs . . . bones:* Instruments for rustic music (the tongs were played like a
triangle, whereas the bones were held between the fingers and used as clappers).   *Music . . .*
music: (This stage direction is added from the Folio.)

Titania: Or say, sweet love, what thou desirest to eat.

Bottom: Truly, a peck of provender.° I could munch your good dry oats.
     Methinks I have a great desire to a bottle° of hay. Good hay, sweet hay,
     hath no fellow.°

Titania: I have a venturous fairy that shall seek   30
     The squirrel's hoard, and fetch thee new nuts.

Bottom: I had rather have a handful or two of dried peas. But, I pray you,
     let none of your people stir° me. I have an exposition of° sleep come
     upon me.

Titania: Sleep thou, and I will wind thee in my arms.   35
     Fairies, begone, and be all ways° away.   *[Exeunt Fairies.]*
     So doth the woodbine° the sweet honeysuckle
     Gently entwist; the female ivy so
     Enrings the barky fingers of the elm.
     O, how I love thee! How I dote on thee!   *[They sleep.]*   40

Enter Robin Goodfellow [Puck].

Oberon [coming forward]:   Welcome, good Robin. Seest thou this sweet sight?
     Her dotage now I do begin to pity.
     For, meeting her of late behind the wood
     Seeking sweet favors° for this hateful fool,
     I did upbraid her and fall out with her.   45
     For she his hairy temples then had rounded
     With coronet of fresh and fragrant flowers;
     And that same dew, which sometime° on the buds
     Was wont to swell like round and orient pearls,°
     Stood now within the pretty flowerets' eyes   50
     Like tears that did their own disgrace bewail.
     When I had at my pleasure taunted her,
     And she in mild terms begged my patience,
     I then did ask of her her changeling child,
     Which straight she gave me, and her fairy sent   55
     To bear him to my bower in Fairyland.
     And, now I have the boy, I will undo
     This hateful imperfection of her eyes.
     And, gentle Puck, take this transformèd scalp
     From off the head of this Athenian swain,   60
     That he, awaking when the other° do,
     May all to Athens back again repair,°
     And think no more of this night's accidents
     But as the fierce vexation of a dream.
     But first I will release the Fairy Queen.   65

                         [He squeezes an herb on her eyes.]

---

27 *peck of provender:* One-quarter bushel of grain.   28 *bottle:* Bundle.   29 *fellow:* Equal.
33 *stir:* Disturb; *exposition of:* (Bottom's phrase for "disposition to.")   36 *all ways:* In all directions.   37 *woodbine:* Bindweed, a climbing plant that twines in the opposite direction from that of honeysuckle.   44 *favors:* I.e., gifts of flowers.   48 *sometime:* Formerly.
49 *orient pearls:* I.e., the most beautiful of all pearls, those coming from the Orient.
61 *other:* Others.   62 *repair:* Return.

                    Be as thou wast wont to be;
                    See as thou wast wont to see.
                    Dian's bud° o'er Cupid's flower
                    Hath such force and blessèd power.
                    Now, my Titania, wake you, my sweet queen.   70
Titania [awaking]: My Oberon! What visions have I seen!
                    Methought I was enamored of an ass.
Oberon: There lies your love.
Titania: How came these things to pass?
                    O, how mine eyes do loathe his visage now!
Oberon: Silence awhile. Robin, take off this head.   75
                    Titania, music call, and strike more dead
                    Than common sleep of all these five° the sense.
Titania: Music, ho! Music, such as charmeth° sleep!   *[Music.]*
Puck [removing the ass head]: Now, when thou wak'st, with thine own fool's
                    eyes peep.
Oberon: Sound, music! Come, my queen, take hands with me,   80
                    And rock the ground whereon these sleepers be.   *[They dance.]*
                    Now thou and I are new in amity,
                    And will tomorrow midnight solemnly°
                    Dance in Duke Theseus' house triumphantly,
                    And bless it to all fair prosperity.   85
                    There shall the pairs of faithful lovers be
                    Wedded, with Theseus, all in jollity.
Puck: Fairy King, attend, and mark:
                    I do hear the morning lark.
Oberon: Then, my queen, in silence sad,°   90
                    Trip we after night's shade.
                    We the globe can compass soon,
                    Swifter than the wandering moon.
Titania: Come, my lord, and in our flight
                    Tell me how it came this night   95
                    That I sleeping here was found
                    With these mortals on the ground.
                    Exeunt [Oberon, Titania, and Puck]. Wind horn [within].

          Enter Theseus and all his train; [Hippolyta, Egeus].

Theseus: Go, one of you, find out the forester,
                    For now our observation° is performed;
                    And since we have the vaward° of the day,   100
                    My love shall hear the music of my hounds.
                    Uncouple° in the western valley; let them go.
                    Dispatch, I say, and find the forester.   *[Exit an Attendant.]*
                    We will, fair queen, up to the mountain's top

---

68 *Dian's bud:* (Perhaps the flower of the *agnus castus* or chaste-tree, supposed to preserve chastity; or perhaps referring simply to Oberon's herb by which he can undo the effects of "Cupid's flower," the love-in-idleness of II.i.166–168.)   77 *these five:* I.e., the four lovers and Bottom.   78 *charmeth:* Brings about, as though by a charm.   83 *solemnly:* Ceremoniously.   90 *sad:* Sober.   99 *observation:* I.e., observance to a morn of May (I.i.167). 100 *vaward:* Vanguard, i.e., earliest part.   102 *Uncouple:* Set free for the hunt.

And mark the musical confusion   105
Of hounds and echo in conjunction.
Hippolyta: I was with Hercules and Cadmus° once
When in a wood of Crete they bayed° the bear
With hounds of Sparta.° Never did I hear
Such gallant chiding;° for, besides the groves,   110
The skies, the fountains, every region near
Seemed all one mutual cry. I never heard
So musical a discord, such sweet thunder.
Theseus: My hounds are bred out of the Spartan kind,°
So flewed,° so sanded,° and their heads are hung   115
With ears that sweep away the morning dew;
Crook-kneed, and dewlapped° like Thessalian bulls;
Slow in pursuit, but matched in mouth like bells,
Each under each.° A cry° more tunable°
Was never holloed to nor cheered° with horn   120
In Crete, in Sparta, nor in Thessaly.
Judge when you hear. *[He sees the sleepers.]* But soft!° What nymphs
are these?
Egeus: My lord, this is my daughter here asleep,
And this Lysander; this Demetrius is;
This Helena, old Nedar's Helena.   125
I wonder of° their being here together.
Theseus: No doubt they rose up early to observe
The rite of May, and hearing our intent,
Came here in grace of our solemnity.°
But speak, Egeus. Is not this the day   130
That Hermia should give answer of her choice?
Egeus: It is, my lord.
Theseus: Go bid the huntsmen wake them with their horns.

                                             [Exit an Attendant.]

Shout within. Wind horns. They all start up.

Good morrow, friends. Saint Valentine° is past.
Begin these woodbirds but to couple now?   135
Lysander: Pardon, my lord.   *[They kneel.]*
Theseus: I pray you all, stand up. *[They stand.]*
I know you two are rival enemies;
How comes this gentle concord in the world,
That hatred is so far from jealousy°
To sleep by hate and fear no enmity?   140

---

107 *Cadmus:* Mythical founder of Thebes. (This story about him is unknown.)   108 *bayed:*
Brought to bay.   109 *hounds of Sparta:* (A breed famous in antiquity for their hunting skill.)
110 *chiding:* I.e., yelping.   114 *kind:* Strain, breed.   115 *So flewed:* Similarly having large
hanging chaps or fleshy covering of the jaw; *sanded:* Of sandy color.   117 *dewlapped:* Having
pendulous folds of skin under the neck.   118–119 *matched . . . each:* I.e., harmoniously
matched in their various cries like a set of bells, from treble down to bass; *cry:* Pack of
hounds; *tunable:* Well tuned, melodious.   120 *cheered:* Encouraged.   122 *soft:* I.e., gently, wait a minute.   126 *wonder of:* Wonder at.   129 *in . . . solemnity:* In honor of our
wedding ceremony.   134 *Saint Valentine:* (Birds were supposed to choose their mates on
Saint Valentine's Day.)   139 *jealousy:* Suspicion.

Lysander: My lord, I shall reply amazedly,
    Half sleep, half waking; but as yet, I swear,
    I cannot truly say how I came here.
    But, as I think — for truly would I speak,
    And now I do bethink me, so it is —   145
    I came with Hermia hither. Our intent
    Was to be gone from Athens, where° we might,
    Without° the peril of the Athenian law —
Egeus: Enough, enough, my lord; you have enough.
    I beg the law, the law, upon his head.   150
    They would have stol'n away; they would, Demetrius,
    Thereby to have defeated° you and me,
    You of your wife and me of my consent,
    Of my consent that she should be your wife.
Demetrius: My lord, fair Helen told me of their stealth,   155
    Of this their purpose hither° to this wood,
    And I in fury hither followed them,
    Fair Helena in fancy° following me.
    But, my good lord, I wot not by what power —
    But by some power it is — my love to Hermia,   160
    Melted as the snow, seems to me now
    As the remembrance of an idle gaud°
    Which in my childhood I did dote upon;
    And all the faith, the virtue of my heart,
    The object and the pleasure of mine eye,   165
    Is only Helena. To her, my lord,
    Was I betrothed ere I saw Hermia,
    But like a sickness did I loathe this food;
    But, as in health, come to my natural taste,
    Now I do wish it, love it, long for it,   170
    And will forevermore be true to it.
Theseus: Fair lovers, you are fortunately met.
    Of this discourse we more will hear anon.
    Egeus, I will overbear your will;
    For in the temple, by and by, with us   175
    These couples shall eternally be knit.
    And, for° the morning now is something° worn,
    Our purposed hunting shall be set aside.
    Away with us to Athens. Three and three,
    We'll hold a feast in great solemnity.°   180
    Come Hippolyta.   *[Exeunt Theseus, Hippolyta, Egeus, and train.]*
Demetrius: These things seem small and undistinguishable,
    Like far-off mountains turnèd into clouds.
Hermia: Methinks I see these things with parted° eye,
    When everything seems double.

---

147 *where:* Wherever; or, to where.   148 *Without:* Outside of, beyond.   152 *defeated:* Defrauded.   156 *hither:* In coming hither.   158 *in fancy:* Driven by love.   162 *idle gaud:* Worthless trinket.   177 *for:* Since; *something:* Somewhat.   180 *in great solemnity:* With great ceremony.   184 *parted:* I.e., improperly focused.

Helena: So methinks;   185
And I have found Demetrius like a jewel,
Mine own, and not mine own.°
Demetrius: Are you sure
That we are awake? It seems to me
That yet we sleep, we dream. Do not you think
The Duke was here, and bid us follow him?   190
Hermia: Yea, and my father.
Helena: And Hippolyta.
Lysander: And he did bid us follow to the temple.
Demetrius: Why, then, we are awake. Let's follow him,
And by the way let us recount our dreams.   *[Exeunt the lovers.]*
Bottom [awaking]: When my cue comes, call me, and I will answer. My   195
next is "Most fair Pyramus." Heigh-ho! Peter Quince! Flute, the bellows mender! Snout, the tinker! Starveling! God's° my life, stolen
hence and left me asleep! I have had a most rare vision. I have had a
dream, past the wit of man to say what dream it was. Man is but an
ass if he go about° to expound this dream. Methought I was — there is   200
no man can tell what. Methought I was — and methought I had — but
man is but a patched° fool if he will offer° to say what methought I
had. The eye of man hath not heard, the ear of man hath not seen,
man's hand is not able to taste, his tongue to conceive, nor his heart
to report° what my dream was. I will get Peter Quince to write a bal-   205
lad° of this dream. It shall be called "Bottom's Dream," because it
hath no bottom;° and I will sing it in the latter end of a play, before
the Duke. Peradventure, to make it the more gracious, I shall sing it
at her° death.   *[Exit.]*

[Scene II: *Athens.*]

Enter Quince, Flute, [Snout, and Starveling].

Quince: Have you sent to Bottom's house? Is he come home yet?
Starveling: He cannot be heard of. Out of doubt he is transported.°
Flute: If he come not, then the play is marred. It goes not forward. Doth it?
Quince: It is not possible. You have not a man in all Athens able to dis-
charge° Pyramus but he.   5
Flute: No, he hath simply the best wit° of any handicraft man in Athens.
Quince: Yea, and the best person° too, and he is a very paramour for a
sweet voice.
Flute: You must say "paragon." A paramour is, God bless us, a thing of
naught.°   10

Enter Snug the joiner.

186-187 *like . . . mine own:* I.e., like a jewel that one finds by chance and therefore possesses
but cannot certainly consider one's own property.   197 *God's:* May God save.   200 *go
about:* Attempt.   202 *patched:* Wearing motley, i.e., a dress of various colors; *offer:*
Venture.   203-205 *The eye . . . report:* (Bottom garbles the terms of 1 Corinthians 2:9.)
206 *ballad:* (The proper medium for relating sensational stories and preposterous events.)
207 *hath no bottom:* Is unfathomable.   209 *her:* Thisbe's (?).   **Scene II.**   2 *transported:*
Carried off by fairies; or, possibly, transformed.   5 *discharge:* Perform.   6 *wit:* Intellect.
7 *person:* Appearance.   9-10 *a . . . naught:* A shameful thing.

Snug: Masters, the Duke is coming from the temple, and there is two or
three lords and ladies more married. If our sport had gone forward,
we had all been made men.°

Flute: O sweet bully Bottom! Thus hath he lost sixpence a day° during his   15
life; he could not have scaped sixpence a day. An the Duke had not
given him sixpence a day for playing Pyramus, I'll be hanged. He
would have deserved it. Sixpence a day in Pyramus, or nothing.

Enter Bottom.

Bottom: Where are these lads? Where are these hearts?°

Quince: Bottom! O most courageous day! O most happy hour!

Bottom: Masters, I am to discourse wonders.° But ask me not what; for if I   20
tell you, I am no true Athenian. I will tell you everything, right as it fell
out.

Quince: Let us hear, sweet Bottom.

Bottom: Not a word of° me. All that I will tell you is that the Duke hath
dined. Get your apparel together, good strings° to your beards, new   25
ribbons to your pumps;° meet presently° at the palace; every man
look o'er his part; for the short and the long is, our play is preferred.°
In any case, let Thisbe have clean linen; and let not him that plays the
lion pare his nails, for they shall hang out for the lion's claws. And,
most dear actors, eat no onions nor garlic, for we are to utter sweet   30
breath; and I do not doubt but to hear them say it is a sweet comedy.
No more words. Away! Go, away!   *[Exeunt.]*

[ACT V

SCENE I: *Athens. The palace of Theseus.*]

Enter Theseus, Hippolyta, and Philostrate, [lords, and attendants].

Hippolyta: 'Tis strange, my Theseus, that° these lovers speak of.

Theseus: More strange than true. I never may° believe
These antique° fables nor these fairy toys.°
Lovers and madmen have such seething brains,
Such shaping fantasies,° that apprehend°   5
More than cool reason ever comprehends.°
The lunatic, the lover, and the poet
Are of imagination all compact.°
One sees more devils than vast hell can hold;
That is the madman. The lover, all as frantic,   10

---

13 *we . . . men:* I.e., we would have had our fortunes made.   14 *sixpence a day:* I.e., as a royal
pension.   18 *hearts:* Good fellows.   20 *am . . . wonders:* Have wonders to relate.   24 *of:*
Out of.   25 *strings:* (To attach the beards.)   26 *pumps:* Light shoes or slippers; *presently:*
Immediately.   27 *preferred:* Selected for consideration.   **Act V, Scene I.**   1 *that:* That
which.   2 *may:* Can.   3 *antique:* Old-fashioned (punning, too, on *antic,* "strange,"
"grotesque"); *fairy toys:* Trifling stories about fairies.   5 *fantasies:* Imaginations; *apprehend:*
Conceive, imagine.   6 *comprehends:* Understands.   8 *compact:* Formed, composed.

Sees Helen's° beauty in a brow of Egypt.°
The poet's eye, in a fine frenzy rolling,
Doth glance from heaven to earth, from earth to heaven;
And as imagination bodies forth
The forms of things unknown, the poet's pen   15
Turns them to shapes and gives to airy nothing
A local habitation and a name.
Such tricks hath strong imagination
That, if it would but apprehend some joy,
It comprehends some bringer° of that joy;   20
Or in the night, imagining some fear,°
How easy is a bush supposed a bear!

Hippolyta: But all the story of the night told over,
And all their minds transfigured so together,
More witnesseth than fancy's images°   25
And grows to something of great constancy;°
But, howsoever,° strange and admirable.°

Enter lovers: Lysander, Demetrius, Hermia, and Helena.

Theseus: Here come the lovers, full of joy and mirth.
Joy, gentle friends! Joy and fresh days of love
Accompany your hearts!

Lysander: More than to us   30
Wait in your royal walks, your board, your bed!

Theseus: Come now, what masques,° what dances shall we have,
To wear away this long age of three hours
Between our after-supper and bedtime?
Where is our usual manager of mirth?   35
What revels are in hand? Is there no play
To ease the anguish of a torturing hour?
Call Philostrate.

Philostrate: Here, mighty Theseus.

Theseus: Say, what abridgment° have you for this evening?
What masque? What music? How shall we beguile   40
The lazy time, if not with some delight?

Philostrate [giving him a paper]: There is a brief° how many sports are ripe.
Make choice of which Your Highness will see first.

Theseus [reads.]: "The battle with the Centaurs,° to be sung
By an Athenian eunuch to the harp"?   45
We'll none of that. That have I told my love,
In glory of my kinsman° Hercules.

---

11 *Helen's:* I.e., of Helen of Troy, pattern of beauty; *brow of Egypt:* I.e., face of a gypsy.
20 *bringer:* I.e., source. 21 *fear:* Object of fear. 25 *More . . . images:* Testifies to something
more substantial than mere imaginings. 26 *constancy:* Certainty. 27 *howsoever:* In any
case; *admirable:* A source of wonder. 32 *masques:* Courtly entertainments. 39 *abridg-
ment:* Pastime (to abridge or shorten the evening). 42 *brief:* Short written statement,
summary. 44 *battle . . . Centaurs:* (Probably refers to the battle of the Centaurs and the
Lapithae, when the Centaurs attempted to carry off Hippodamia, bride of Theseus' friend
Pirothous. The story is told in Ovid's *Metamorphoses* 12.) 47 *kinsman:* (Plutarch's "Life of
Theseus" states that Hercules and Theseus were near kinsmen. Theseus is referring to a version of the battle of the Centaurs in which Hercules was said to be present.)

[He reads.] "The riot of the tipsy Bacchanals,
Tearing the Thracian singer in their rage"?°
That is an old device;° and it was played   50
When I from Thebes came last a conqueror.
[He reads.] "The thrice three Muses mourning for the death
Of Learning, late deceased in beggary"?°
That is some satire, keen and critical,
Not sorting with° a nuptial ceremony.   55
[He reads.] "A tedious brief scene of young Pyramus
And his love Thisbe; very tragical mirth"?
Merry and tragical? Tedious and brief?
That is, hot ice and wondrous strange° snow.
How shall we find the concord of this discord?   60
Philostrate: A play there is, my lord, some ten words long,
  Which is as brief as I have known a play;
  But by ten words, my lord, it is too long,
  Which makes it tedious. For in all the play
  There is not one word apt, one player fitted.   65
  And tragical, my noble lord, it is,
  For Pyramus therein doth kill himself.
  Which, when I saw rehearsed, I must confess,
  Made mine eyes water; but more merry tears
  The passion of loud laughter never shed.   70
Theseus: What are they that do play it?
Philostrate: Hardhanded men that work in Athens here,
  Which never labored in their minds till now,
  And now have toiled° their unbreathed° memories
  With this same play, against° your nuptial.   75
Theseus: And we will hear it.
Philostrate: No, my noble lord,
  It is not for you. I have heard it over,
  And it is nothing, nothing in the world;
  Unless you can find sport in their intents,
  Extremely stretched° and conned° with cruel pain   80
  To do you service.
Theseus: I will hear that play;
  For never anything can be amiss
  When simpleness° and duty tender it.
  Go, bring them in; and take your places, ladies.
                       [Philostrate goes to summon the players.]
Hippolyta: I love not to see wretchedness o'ercharged,°   85
  And duty in his service° perishing.

48–49 *The riot . . . rage:* (This was the story of the death of Orpheus, as told in *Metamorphoses* 11.)   50 *device:* Show, performance.   52–53 *The thrice . . . beggary:* (Possibly an allusion to Spenser's *Teares of the Muses,* 1591, though "satires" deploring the neglect of learning and the creative arts were commonplace.)   55 *sorting with:* Befitting.   59 *strange:* (Sometimes emended to an adjective that would contrast with *snow,* just as *hot* contrasts with *ice.*)   74 *toiled:* Taxed; *unbreathed:* Unexercised.   75 *against:* In preparation for.   80 *stretched:* Strained; *conned:* Memorized.   83 *simpleness:* Simplicity.   85 *wretchedness o'ercharged:* Social or intellectual inferiors overburdened.   86 *his service:* Its attempt to serve.

Theseus: Why, gentle sweet, you shall see no such thing.

Hippolyta: He says they can do nothing in this kind.°

Theseus: The kinder we, to give them thanks for nothing.

    Our sport shall be to take what they mistake;   90

    And what poor duty cannot do, noble respect°

    Takes it in might, not merit.°

    Where I have come, great clerks° have purposèd

    To greet me with premeditated welcomes;

    Where I have seen them shiver and look pale,   95

    Make periods in the midst of sentences,

    Throttle their practiced accent° in their fears,

    And in conclusion dumbly have broke off,

    Not paying me a welcome. Trust me, sweet,

    Out of this silence yet I picked a welcome;   100

    And in the modesty of fearful duty

    I read as much as from the rattling tongue

    Of saucy and audacious eloquence.

    Love, therefore, and tongue-tied simplicity

    In least° speak most, to my capacity.°   105

[Philostrate returns.]

Philostrate: So please Your Grace, the Prologue° is addressed.°

Theseus: Let him approach.   *[A flourish of trumpets.]*

    Enter the Prologue [Quince].

Prologue: If we offend, it is with our good will.

    That you should think, we come not to offend,

    But with good will. To show our simple skill,   110

    That is the true beginning of our end.

    Consider, then, we come but in despite.

    We do not come, as minding° to content you,

    Our true intent is. All for your delight

    We are not here. That you should here repent you,   115

    The actors are at hand; and, by their show,

    You shall know all that you are like to know.

Theseus: This fellow doth not stand upon points.°

Lysander: He hath rid° his prologue like a rough° colt; he knows not the stop.° A good moral, my lord: it is not enough to speak, but to speak   120 true.

Hippolyta: Indeed, he hath played on his prologue like a child on a recorder:° a sound, but not in government.°

---

88 *kind:* Kind of thing.   91 *respect:* Evaluation, consideration.   92 *Takes ... merit:* Values it for the effort made rather than for the excellence achieved.   93 *clerks:* Learned men. 97 *practiced accent:* I.e., rehearsed speech; or, usual way of speaking.   105 *least:* I.e., saying least; *to my capacity:* In my judgment and understanding.   106 *Prologue:* Speaker of the prologue; *addressed:* Ready.   113 *minding:* Intending.   118 *stand upon points:* (1) Heed niceties or small points (2) pay attention to punctuation in his reading. (The humor of Quince's speech is in the blunders of its punctuation.)   119 *rid:* Ridden; *rough:* unbroken. 120 *stop:* (1) Stopping of a colt by reining it in (2) punctuation mark.   123 *recorder:* Wind instrument like a flute; *government:* Control.

Theseus: His speech was like a tangled chain: nothing° impaired, but all
    disordered. Who is next?   125

    Enter Pyramus [Bottom], and Thisbe [Flute], and Wall [Snout], and
    Moonshine [Starveling], and Lion [Snug].

Prologue: Gentles, perchance you wonder at this show;
    But wonder on, till truth make all things plain.
    This man is Pyramus, if you would know;
       This beauteous lady Thisbe is, certain.
    This man with lime and roughcast doth present   130
       Wall, that vile wall which did these lovers sunder;
    And through Wall's chink, poor souls, they are content
       To whisper. At the which let no man wonder.
    This man, with lantern, dog, and bush of thorn,
       Presenteth Moonshine; for, if you will know,   135
    By moonshine did these lovers think no scorn°
       To meet at Ninus' tomb, there, there to woo.
    This grisly beast, which Lion hight° by name,
       The trusty Thisbe coming first by night
    Did scare away, or rather did affright;   140
       And as she fled, her mantle she did fall,°
       Which Lion vile with bloody mouth did stain.
    Anon comes Pyramus, sweet youth and tall,°
       And finds his trusty Thisbe's mantle slain;
    Whereat, with blade, with bloody, blameful blade,   145
       He bravely broached° his boiling bloody breast.
    And Thisbe, tarrying in mulberry shade,
       His dagger drew, and died. For all the rest,
    Let Lion, Moonshine, Wall, and lovers twain
    At large° discourse, while here they do remain.   150
                                   Exeunt Lion, Thisbe, and Moonshine.

Theseus: I wonder if the lion be to speak.
Demetrius: No wonder, my lord. One lion may, when many asses do.
Wall: In this same interlude° it doth befall
    That I, one Snout by name, present a wall;
    And such a wall as I would have you think   155
    That had in it a crannied hole or chink,
    Through which the lovers, Pyramus and Thisbe,
    Did whisper often, very secretly.
    This loam, this roughcast, and this stone doth show
    That I am that same wall; the truth is so.   160
    And this the cranny is, right and sinister,°
    Through which the fearful lovers are to whisper.
Theseus: Would you desire lime and hair to speak better?
Demetrius: It is the wittiest partition° that ever I heard discourse, my lord.

---

124 *nothing:* Not at all.   136 *think no scorn:* Think it no disgraceful matter.   138 *hight:* Is
called.   141 *fall:* Let fall.   143 *tall:* Courageous.   146 *broached:* Stabbed.   150 *At
large:* In full, at length.   153 *interlude:* Play.   161 *right and sinister:* I.e., the right side of it
and the left; or, running from right to left, horizontally.   164 *partition:* (1) Wall (2) section
of a learned treatise or oration.

[Pyramus comes forward.]

Theseus: Pyramus draws near the wall. Silence!   165

Pyramus: O grim-looked° night! O night with hue so black!
   O night, which ever art when day is not!
   O night, O night! Alack, alack, alack,
     I fear my Thisbe's promise is forgot.
   And thou, O wall, O sweet, O lovely wall,   170
     That stand'st between her father's ground and mine,
   Thou wall, O wall, O sweet and lovely wall,
     Show me thy chink, to blink through with mine eyne.
   Thanks, courteous wall. Jove shield thee well for this.
     But what see I? No Thisbe do I see.   175
   O wicked wall, through whom I see no bliss!
     Cursed be thy stones for thus deceiving me!

Theseus: The wall, methinks, being sensible,° should curse again.°

Pyramus: No, in truth, sir, he should not. "Deceiving me" is Thisbe's cue:
she is to enter now, and I am to spy her through the wall. You shall see,   180
it will fall pat° as I told you. Yonder she comes.

Enter Thisbe.

Thisbe: O wall, full often hast thou heard my moans
     For parting my fair Pyramus and me.
   My cherry lips have often kissed thy stones,
     Thy stones with lime and hair knit up in thee.   185

Pyramus: I see a voice. Now will I to the chink,
     To spy an° I can hear my Thisbe's face.
   Thisbe!

Thisbe: My love! Thou art my love, I think.

Pyramus: Think what thou wilt, I am thy lover's grace,°   190
   And like Limander° am I trusty still.

Thisbe: And I like Helen,° till the Fates me kill.

Pyramus: Not Shafalus to Procrus° was so true.

Thisbe: As Shafalus to Procrus, I to you.

Pyramus: O, kiss me through the hole of this vile wall!   195

Thisbe: I kiss the wall's hole, not your lips at all.

Pyramus: Wilt thou at Ninny's tomb meet me straightway?

Thisbe: 'Tide life, 'tide° death, I come without delay.

                [Exeunt Pyramus and Thisbe.]

Wall: Thus have I, Wall, my part dischargèd so;
   And, being done, thus Wall away doth go.   *[Exit.]* 200

Theseus: Now is the mural down between the two neighbors.

Demetrius: No remedy, my lord, when walls are so willful° to hear without
warning.°

Hippolyta: This is the silliest stuff that ever I heard.

---

166 *grim-looked:* Grim-looking.   178 *sensible:* Capable of feeling; *again:* In return.   181 *pat:*
Exactly.   187 *an:* If.   190 *lover's grace:* I.e., gracious lover.   191-192 *Limander, Helen:*
(Blunders for "Leander" and "Hero").   193 *Shafalus, Procrus:* (Blunders for "Cephalus"
and "Procris," also famous lovers.)   198 *'tide:* Betide, come.   202 *willful:* Willing.
202-203 *without warning:* I.e., without warning the parents. (Demetrius makes a joke on the
proverb "Walls have ears.")

Theseus: The best in this kind° are but shadows,° and the worst are no   205
worse, if imagination amend them.
Hippolyta: It must be your imagination then, and not theirs.
Theseus: If we imagine no worse of them than they of themselves, they
may pass for excellent men. Here come two noble beasts in, a man
and a lion.   210

Enter Lion and Moonshine.

Lion: You, ladies, you, whose gentle hearts do fear
       The smallest monstrous mouse that creeps on floor,
    May now perchance both quake and tremble here,
       When lion rough in wildest rage doth roar.
    Then know that I, as Snug the joiner, am   215
    A lion fell,° nor else no lion's dam;
    For, if I should as lion come in strife
    Into this place, 'twere pity on my life.
Theseus: A very gentle beast, and of a good conscience.
Demetrius: The very best at a beast, my lord, that e'er I saw.   220
Lysander: This lion is a very fox for his valor.°
Theseus: True; and a goose for his discretion.°
Demetrius: Not so, my lord, for his valor cannot carry his discretion, and
the fox carries the goose.
Theseus: His discretion, I am sure, cannot carry his valor; for the goose car- 225
ries not the fox. It is well. Leave it to his discretion, and let us listen
to the moon.
Moon: This lanthorn° doth the hornèd moon present—
Demetrius: He should have worn the horns on his head.°
Theseus: He is no crescent,° and his horns are invisible within the cir-   230
cumference.
Moon: This lanthorn doth the hornèd moon present;
    Myself the man i' the moon do seem to be.
Theseus: This is the greatest error of all the rest. The man should be put
into the lanthorn. How is it else the man i' the moon?   235
Demetrius: He dares not come there for° the candle, for you see it is already
in snuff.°
Hippolyta: I am weary of this moon. Would he would change!
Theseus: It appears, by his small light of discretion, that he is in the wane;
but yet, in courtesy, in all reason, we must stay the time.   240
Lysander: Proceed, Moon.
Moon: All that I have to say is to tell you that the lanthorn is the moon, I,
the man i' the moon, this thornbush my thornbush, and this dog my
dog.

205 *in this kind:* Of this sort; *shadows:* Likenesses, representations.   216 *lion fell:* Fierce lion
(with a play on the idea of "lion skin").   221 *is . . . valor:* I.e., his valor consists of craftiness
and discretion.   222 *a goose . . . discretion:* I.e., as discreet as a goose, that is, more foolish
than discreet.   228 *lanthorn:* (This original spelling, *lanthorn,* may suggest a play on the
horn of which lanterns were made and also on a cuckold's horns; however, the spelling *lanthorn* is not used consistently for comic effect in this play or elsewhere. At Act V, Scene I, line
134, for example, the word is *lantern* in the original.)   229 *on his head:* (As a sign of cuckoldry.)   230 *crescent:* A waxing moon.   236 *for:* Because of, for fear of.   237 *in snuff:* (1)
Offended (2) in need of snuffing or trimming.

Demetrius: Why, all these should be in the lanthorn, for all these are in   245
   the moon. But silence! Here comes Thisbe.

   Enter Thisbe.

Thisbe: This is old Ninny's tomb. Where is my love?
Lion [roaring]: O!
Demetrius: Well roared, Lion.   *[Thisbe runs off, dropping her mantle.]*
Theseus: Well run, Thisbe.   250
Hippolyta: Well shone, Moon. Truly, the moon shines with a good grace.
                                              [The Lion worries Thisbe's mantle.]
Theseus: Well moused,° Lion.

   [Enter Pyramus; exit Lion.]

Demetrius: And then came Pyramus.
Lysander: And so the Lion vanished.
Pyramus: Sweet Moon, I thank thee for thy sunny beams;   255
      I thank thee, Moon, for shining now so bright;
   For, by thy gracious, golden, glittering gleams,
      I trust to take of truest Thisbe sight.
         But stay, O spite!
         But mark, poor knight,   260
      What dreadful dole° is here?
         Eyes, do you see?
         How can it be?
      O dainty duck! O dear!
         Thy mantle good,   265
      What, stained with blood?
      Approach, ye Furies° fell!°
         O Fates,° come, come,
      Cut thread and thrum;°
      Quail,° crush, conclude, and quell!°   270
Theseus: This passion, and the death of a dear friend, would go near to
   make a man look sad.°
Hippolyta: Beshrew my heart, but I pity the man.
Pyramus: O, wherefore, Nature, didst thou lions frame?
      Since lion vile hath here deflowered my dear,   275
      Which is — no, no, which was — the fairest dame
      That lived, that loved, that liked, that looked with cheer.°
         Come, tears, confound,
         Out, sword, and wound
      The pap° of Pyramus;   280
         Ay, that left pap,
         Where heart doth hop.   *[He stabs himself.]*
      Thus die I, thus, thus, thus.

252 *moused:* Shaken, torn, bitten.   261 *dole:* Grievous event.   267 *Furies:* Avenging goddesses of Greek myth; *fell:* Fierce.   268 *Fates:* The three goddesses (Clotho, Lachesis, Atro-
pos) of Greek myth who spun, drew, and cut the thread of human life.   269 *thread and
thrum:* I.e., everything — the good and bad alike; literally, the warp in weaving and the loose
end of the warp.   270 *Quail:* Overpower; *quell:* Kill, destroy.   271-272 *This . . . sad:* I.e., if
one had other reason to grieve, one might be sad, but not from this absurd portrayal of passion.   277 *cheer:* Countenance.   280 *pap:* Breast.

Now am I dead,
Now am I fled;   285
My soul is in the sky.
Tongue, lose thy light;
Moon, take thy flight.   *[Exit Moonshine.]*
Now die, die, die, die, die.   *[Pyramus dies.]*

Demetrius: No die, but an ace,° for him; for he is but one.°   290
Lysander: Less than an ace, man; for he is dead, he is nothing.
Theseus: With the help of a surgeon he might yet recover, and yet prove
     an ass.°
Hippolyta: How chance Moonshine is gone before Thisbe comes back and
     finds her lover?   295
Theseus: She will find him by starlight.

     [Enter Thisbe.]

     Here she comes; and her passion ends the play.
Hippolyta: Methinks she should not use a long one for such a Pyramus. I
     hope she will be brief.
Demetrius: A mote° will turn the balance, which Pyramus, which° Thisbe, 300
     is the better: he for a man, God warrant us; she for a woman, God
     bless us.
Lysander: She hath spied him already with those sweet eyes.
Demetrius: And thus she means,° videlicet:°
Thisbe: Asleep, my love?   305
     What, dead, my dove?
     O Pyramus, arise!
     Speak, speak. Quite dumb?
     Dead, dead? A tomb
     Must cover thy sweet eyes.   310
     These lily lips,
     This cherry nose,
     These yellow cowslip cheeks,
     Are gone, are gone!
     Lovers, make moan.   315
     His eyes were green as leeks.
     O Sisters Three,°
     Come, come to me,
     With hands as pale as milk;
     Lay them in gore,   320
     Since you have shore°
     With shears his thread of silk.
     Tongue, not a word.
     Come, trusty sword,
     Come, blade, my breast imbrue!°   *[She stabs herself.]* 325

---

290 *ace:* The side of the die featuring the single pip, or spot (the pun is on *die* as a singular of
dice; Bottom's performance is not worth a whole *die* but rather one single face of it, one small
portion); *one:* (1) An individual person (2) unique.   293 *ass:* (With a pun on *ace.*)   300 *mote:*
Small particle; *which . . . which:* Whether . . . or.   304 *means:* Moans, laments (with a pun on
the meaning "lodge a formal complaint"); *videlicet:* To wit.   317 *Sisters Three:* The Fates.
321 *shore:* Shorn.   325 *imbrue:* Stain with blood.

> And farewell, friends.
> Thus Thisbe ends.
> Adieu, adieu, adieu.   *[She dies.]*

Theseus: Moonshine and Lion are left to bury the dead.

Demetrius: Ay, and Wall too.   330

Bottom [starting up, as Flute does also]: No, I assure you, the wall is down
    that parted their fathers. Will it please you to see the epilogue, or to
    hear a Bergomask dance° between two of our company?

[The other players enter.]

Theseus: No epilogue, I pray you; for your play needs no excuse. Never
    excuse; for when the players are all dead, there need none to be   335
    blamed. Marry, if he that writ it had played Pyramus and hanged him-
    self in Thisbe's garter, it would have been a fine tragedy; and so it
    is, truly, and very notably discharged. But, come, your Bergomask.
    Let your epilogue alone.   *[A dance.]*
    The iron tongue° of midnight hath told° twelve.   340
    Lovers, to bed, 'tis almost fairy time.
    I fear we shall outsleep the coming morn
    As much as we this night have overwatched.°
    This palpable-gross° play hath well beguiled
    The heavy° gait of night. Sweet friends, to bed.   345
    A fortnight hold we this solemnity,
    In nightly revels and new jollity.   *Exeunt.*

Enter Puck [carrying a broom].

Puck: Now the hungry lion roars,
    And the wolf behowls the moon,
    Whilst the heavy° plowman snores,   350
       All with weary task fordone.°
    Now the wasted brands° do glow,
       Whilst the screech owl, screeching loud,
    Puts the wretch that lies in woe
       In remembrance of a shroud.   355
    Now it is the time of night
       That the graves, all gaping wide,
    Every one lets forth his sprite,°
       In the church-way paths to glide.
    And we fairies, that do run   360
       By the triple Hecate's° team
    From the presence of the sun,
       Following darkness like a dream,
    Now are frolic.° Not a mouse

---

333 *Bergomask dance:* A rustic dance named from Bergamo, a province in the state of Venice.
340 *iron tongue:* Clapper of a bell; *told:* Counted, struck ("tolled").   343 *overwatched:*
Stayed up too late.   344 *palpable-gross:* Palpably gross, obviously crude.   345 *heavy:*
Drowsy, dull.   350 *heavy:* Tired.   351 *fordone:* Exhausted.   352 *wasted brands:* Burned-
out logs.   358 *Every . . . sprite:* Every grave lets forth its ghost.   361 *triple Hecate's:* (Hecate
ruled in three capacities: as Luna or Cynthia in heaven, as Diana on earth, and as Proserpina
in hell.)   364 *frolic:* Merry.

    Shall disturb this hallowed house.   365
  I am sent with broom before,
  To sweep the dust behind° the door.

Enter [Oberon and Titania,] King and Queen of Fairies, with all their train.

Oberon: Through the house give glimmering light,
    By the dead and drowsy fire;
  Every elf and fairy sprite   370
    Hop as light as bird from brier;
  And this ditty, after me,
  Sing, and dance it trippingly.
Titania: First, rehearse° your song by rote,
  To each word a warbling note.   375
  Hand in hand, with fairy grace,
  Will we sing, and bless this place.   *[Song and dance.]*
Oberon: Now, until the break of day,
  Through this house each fairy stray.
  To the best bride-bed will we,   380
  Which by us shall blessèd be;
  And the issue there create°
  Ever shall be fortunate.
  So shall all the couples three
  Ever true in loving be;   385
  And the blots of Nature's hand
  Shall not in their issue stand;
  Never mole, harelip, nor scar,
  Nor mark prodigious,° such as are
  Despisèd in nativity,   390
  Shall upon their children be.
  With this field dew consecrate,°
  Every fairy take his gait,°
  And each several° chamber bless,
  Through this palace, with sweet peace;   395
  And the owner of it blest
  Ever shall in safety rest.
  Trip away; make no stay;
  Meet me all by break of day.   *Exeunt [Oberon, Titania, and train].*
Puck [to the audience]: If we shadows have offended,   400
  Think but this, and all is mended,
  That you have but slumbered here°
  While these visions did appear.
  And this weak and idle theme,
  No more yielding but° a dream,   405

---

367 *behind:* From behind, or else like sweeping the dirt under the carpet (Robin Goodfellow was a household spirit who helped good housemaids and punished lazy ones, but he could, of course, be mischievous).   374 *rehearse:* Recite.   382 *create:* Created.   389 *prodigious:* Monstrous, unnatural.   392 *consecrate:* Consecrated.   393 *take his gait:* Go his way. 394 *several:* Separate.   402 *That . . . here:* I.e., that it is a "midsummer night's dream." 405 *No . . . but:* Yielding no more than.

Gentles, do not reprehend.
If you pardon, we will mend.°
And, as I am an honest Puck,
If we have unearnèd luck
Now to scape the serpent's tongue,°   410
We will make amends ere long;
Else the Puck a liar call.
So, good night unto you all.
Give me your hands,° if we be friends,
And Robin shall restore amends.°   [*Exit.*]   415

407 *mend:* Improve.   410 *serpent's tongue:* I.e., hissing.   414 *Give...hands:* Applaud.
415 *restore amends:* Give satisfaction in return.

CONSIDERATIONS FOR CRITICAL THINKING AND WRITING

1. FIRST RESPONSE. Discuss the significance of the play's title. What expectations does it create for you?

2. Describe how the two settings, Athens and the nearby woods, reflect different social and physical environments as well as different types of behavior among the characters.

3. What is the symbolic function of the marriage of Theseus and Hippolyta? How is that function revealed in the scenes in which they appear?

4. Characterize the four young lovers. How individualized are their personalities? How does the extent of their characterizations suggest their function in the play?

5. What makes Bottom such a comic figure? How does his behavior shed light on the behavior of the other characters?

6. Consider how women — Hippolyta, Titania, Hermia, and Helena — are presented in the play. What characteristics do they have in common? How do they relate to the men in their lives?

7. Why does Puck describe "mortals" as "fools" (III.ii.115)? To what degree does this description fit the fairies as well?

8. How might Puck be regarded as the play's director as well as a central character?

9. How does the plot bring together the four groups of characters — Theseus and Hippolyta, the four lovers, the craftsmen, and the fairies — into a unified whole? Write a plot summary of the play that connects these four groups of characters. How does this summary resemble popular situation comedies that you've seen on television?

10. Choose a scene that you find particularly funny, and analyze how the humor is created. Describe how the scene contributes to the rest of the play.

11. What is the relationship between the play within the play, "Pyramus and Thisbe," and *A Midsummer Night's Dream*? How do the plot and theme of each serve as commentaries on each other?

12. Despite its comic scenes and happy ending, at various moments this play does raise the specter of potential tragedy. How seriously do you think we are meant to worry about the characters? What are your emotions about the young lovers as they struggle to sort things out in the woods? Discuss how this play might be transformed into a tragedy.

CONNECTIONS TO OTHER SELECTIONS

1. Write an essay concerning the problematic nature of love in *A Midsummer Night's Dream* and David Ives's *Sure Thing* (p. 1254). How is the depiction of love in each play used to create conflict?

2. Discuss Shakespeare's use of the play within the play in *A Midsummer Night's Dream* and *Hamlet*. What emotions does each produce? What conflicts and themes do they emphasize? What attitudes do they suggest about the nature of drama?

3. In an essay discuss the significance of marriage in *A Midsummer Night's Dream* and Henrik Ibsen's *A Doll House* (p. 1568).

4. Write an essay that explores the difficulty of distinguishing between reality and illusion in *A Midsummer Night's Dream* and a very different work, Tim O'Brien's short story "How to Tell a True War Story" (p. 548). What are the similarities and differences in their perspectives on the actual and imaginary?

Hamlet, Prince of Denmark

Hamlet, the most famous play in English literature, continues to fascinate and challenge both readers and audiences. Interpretations of Hamlet's character and actions abound, because the play has produced so many intense and varied responses. No small indication of the tragedy's power is that actors long to play its title role.

A brief summary can suggest the movement of the plot but not the depth of Hamlet's character. After learning of his father's death, Prince Hamlet returns to the Danish court from his university studies to find Claudius, the dead king's brother, ruling Denmark and married to Hamlet's mother, Gertrude. Her remarriage within two months of his father's death has left Hamlet disillusioned, confused, and suspicious of Claudius. When his father's ghost appears before Hamlet to reveal that Claudius murdered the king, Hamlet is confronted with having to avenge his father's death.

Hamlet's efforts to carry out this obligation would have been a familiar kind of plot to Elizabethan audiences. **Revenge tragedy** was a well-established type of drama that traced its antecedents to Greek and Roman plays, particularly through the Roman playwright Seneca (c. 3 B.C.–A.D. 65), whose plays were translated and produced in English in the late sixteenth century. Shakespeare's audiences knew its conventions, particularly from Thomas Kyd's popular *Spanish Tragedy* (c. 1587). Basically, this type of play consists of a murder that has to be avenged by a relative of the victim. Typically, the victim's ghost appears to demand revenge, and invariably madness of some sort is worked into subsequent events, which ultimately result in the deaths of the murderer, the avenger, and a number of other characters. Crime, madness, ghostly anguish, poison, overheard conversations, conspiracies, and a final scene littered with corpses: *Hamlet* subscribes to the basic ingredients of the formula, but it also transcends the conventions of revenge tragedy because Hamlet contemplates not merely revenge but suicide and the meaning of life itself.

Hamlet must face not only a diseased social order but also conflicts within himself when his indecisiveness becomes as agonizing as the corruption surrounding him. However, Hamlet is also a forceful and attractive character. His intelligence is repeatedly revealed in his penetrating use of language; through images and metaphors he creates a perspective on his world that is at once satiric and profoundly painful. His astonishing and sometimes shocking wit is leveled at his mother, his beloved Ophelia, and Claudius as well as himself. Nothing escapes his critical eye and divided imagination. Hamlet, no less than the people around him, is perplexed by his alienation from life.

Hamlet's limitations as well as his virtues make him one of Shakespeare's most complex characters. His keen self-awareness is both agonizing and liberating. Although he struggles throughout the play with painful issues ranging from family loyalties to matters of state, he retains his dignity as a tragic hero, whom generations of audiences have found compelling.

WILLIAM SHAKESPEARE (1564–1616)

Hamlet, Prince of Denmark   1600

[DRAMATIS PERSONAE

Claudius, King of Denmark
Hamlet, son to the late and nephew to the present king
Polonius, lord chamberlain
Horatio, friend to Hamlet
Laertes, son to Polonius
Voltimand
Cornelius
Rosencrantz   } courtiers
Guildenstern
Osric
A Gentleman
A Priest
Marcellus } officers
Bernardo
Francisco, a soldier
Reynaldo, servant to Polonius
Players
Two Clowns, grave-diggers
Fortinbras, Prince of Norway
A Captain
English Ambassadors

Gertrude, Queen of Denmark, and mother to Hamlet
Ophelia, daughter to Polonius
Lords, Ladies, Officers, Soldiers, Sailors, Messengers, and other Attendants
Ghost of Hamlet's Father

SCENE: *Denmark.*]

[ACT I

SCENE I: *Elsinore. A platform° before the castle.*]

    Enter Bernardo and Francisco, two sentinels.

Bernardo: Who's there?
Francisco: Nay, answer me:° stand, and unfold yourself.
Bernardo: Long live the king!°
Francisco: Bernardo?
Bernardo: He.   5
Francisco: You come most carefully upon your hour.
Bernardo: 'Tis now struck twelve; get thee to bed, Francisco.
Francisco: For this relief much thanks: 'tis bitter cold,
    And I am sick at heart.
Bernardo: Have you had quiet guard?
Francisco: Not a mouse stirring.   10
Bernardo: Well, good night.
    If you do meet Horatio and Marcellus,
    The rivals° of my watch, bid them make haste.

    Enter Horatio and Marcellus.

Francisco: I think I hear them. Stand, ho! Who is there?
Horatio: Friends to this ground.
Marcellus: And liegemen to the Dane.   15
Francisco: Give you° good night.
Marcellus: O, farewell, honest soldier:
    Who hath reliev'd you?
Francisco: Bernardo hath my place.
    Give you good night.   *Exit Francisco.*
Marcellus: Holla! Bernardo!
Bernardo: Say,
    What, is Horatio there?
Horatio: A piece of him.
Bernardo: Welcome, Horatio: welcome, good Marcellus.   20
Marcellus: What, has this thing appear'd again to-night?
Bernardo: I have seen nothing.
Marcellus: Horatio says 'tis but our fantasy,

Act I, Scene I.   *platform:* A level space on the battlements of the royal castle at Elsinore, a Danish seaport; now Helsingör.   2 *me:* This is emphatic, since Francisco is the sentry. 3 *Long live the king:* Either a password or greeting; Horatio and Marcellus use a different one in line 15.   13 *rivals:* Partners.   16 *Give you:* God give you.

And will not let belief take hold of him
Touching this dreaded sight, twice seen of us: 25
Therefore I have entreated him along
With us to watch the minutes of this night;
That if again this apparition come,
He may approve° our eyes and speak to it.

Horatio: Tush, tush, 'twill not appear.

Bernardo: Sit down awhile;   30
And let us once again assail your ears,
That are so fortified against our story
What we have two nights seen.

Horatio: Well, sit we down,
And let us hear Bernardo speak of this.

Bernardo: Last night of all,   35
When yond same star that's westward from the pole°
Had made his course t' illume that part of heaven
Where now it burns, Marcellus and myself,
The bell then beating one, —

     Enter Ghost.

Marcellus: Peace, break thee off; look, where it comes again!   40
Bernardo: In the same figure, like the king that's dead.
Marcellus: Thou art a scholar;° speak to it, Horatio.
Bernardo: Looks 'a not like the king? mark it, Horatio.
Horatio: Most like: it harrows° me with fear and wonder.
Bernardo: It would be spoke to.°
Marcellus: Speak to it, Horatio.   45
Horatio: What art thou that usurp'st this time of night,
Together with that fair and warlike form
In which the majesty of buried Denmark°
Did sometimes march? by heaven I charge thee, speak!
Marcellus: It is offended.
Bernardo: See it stalks away!   50
Horatio: Stay! speak, speak! I charge thee, speak!   *Exit Ghost.*
Marcellus: 'Tis gone, and will not answer.
Bernardo: How now, Horatio! you tremble and look pale:
Is not this something more than fantasy?
What think you on 't?   55
Horatio: Before my God, I might not this believe
Without the sensible and true avouch
Of mine own eyes.
Marcellus: Is it not like the king?
Horatio: As thou art to thyself:
Such was the very armour he had on   60
When he the ambitious Norway combated;

---

29 *approve:* Corroborate.   36 *pole:* Polestar.   42 *scholar:* Exorcisms were performed in Latin, which Horatio as an educated man would be able to speak.   44 *harrows:* Lacerates the feelings.   45 *It . . . to:* A ghost could not speak until spoken to.   48 *buried Denmark:* The buried king of Denmark.

So frown'd he once, when, in an angry parle,
He smote° the sledded Polacks° on the ice.
'Tis strange.

Marcellus: Thus twice before, and jump° at this dead hour,   65
With martial stalk hath he gone by our watch.

Horatio: In what particular thought to work I know not;
But in the gross and scope° of my opinion,
This bodes some strange eruption to our state.

Marcellus: Good now,° sit down, and tell me, he that knows,   70
Why this same strict and most observant watch
So nightly toils° the subject° of the land,
And why such daily cast° of brazen cannon,
And foreign mart° for implements of war;
Why such impress° of shipwrights, whose sore task   75
Does not divide the Sunday from the week;
What might be toward, that this sweaty haste
Doth make the night joint-labourer with the day:
Who is't that can inform me?

Horatio: That can I;   80
At least, the whisper goes so. Our last king,
Whose image even but now appear'd to us,
Was, as you know, by Fortinbras of Norway,
Thereto prick'd on° by a most emulate° pride,
Dar'd to the combat; in which our valiant Hamlet—
For so this side of our known world esteem'd him—   85
Did slay this Fortinbras; who, by a seal'd compact,
Well ratified by law and heraldry,°
Did forfeit, with his life, all those his lands
Which he stood seiz'd° of, to the conqueror:
Against the which, a moiety competent°   90
Was gaged by our king; which had return'd
To the inheritance of Fortinbras,
Had he been vanquisher; as, by the same comart,°
And carriage° of the article design'd,
His fell to Hamlet. Now, sir, young Fortinbras,   95
Of unimproved° mettle hot and full,°
Hath in the skirts of Norway here and there
Shark'd up° a list of lawless resolutes,°
For food and diet,° to some enterprise
That hath a stomach in't; which is no other—   100
As it doth well appear unto our state—

---

63 *smote:* Defeated; *sledded Polacks:* Polanders using sledges.   65 *jump:* Exactly.   68 *gross and scope:* General drift.   70 *Good now:* An expression denoting entreaty or expostulation. 72 *toils:* Causes or makes to toil; *subject:* People, subjects.   73 *cast:* Casting, founding. 74 *mart:* Buying and selling, traffic.   75 *impress:* Impressment.   83 *prick'd on:* Incited; *emulate:* Rivaling.   87 *law and heraldry:* Heraldic law, governing combat.   89 *seiz'd:* Possessed.   90 *moiety competent:* Adequate or sufficient portion.   93 *comart:* Joint bargain.   94 *carriage:* Import, bearing.   96 *unimproved:* Not turned to account; *hot and full:* Full of fight.   98 *Shark'd up:* Got together in haphazard fashion; *resolutes:* Desperadoes.   99 *food and diet:* No pay but their keep.

But to recover of us, by strong hand
And terms compulsatory, those foresaid lands
So by his father lost: and this, I take it,
Is the main motive of our preparations,   105
The source of this our watch and the chief head
Of this post-haste and romage° in the land.

Bernardo: I think it be no other but e'en so:
   Well may it sort° that this portentous figure
   Comes armed through our watch; so like the king   110
   That was and is the question of these wars.

Horatio: A mote° it is to trouble the mind's eye.
   In the most high and palmy state° of Rome,
   A little ere the mightiest Julius fell,
   The graves stood tenantless and the sheeted dead   115
   Did squeak and gibber in the Roman streets:
   As stars with trains of fire° and dews of blood,
   Disasters° in the sun; and the moist star°
   Upon whose influence Neptune's empire° stands
   Was sick almost to doomsday with eclipse: 120
   And even the like precurse° of fear'd events,
   As harbingers preceding still the fates
   And prologue to the omen coming on,
   Have heaven and earth together demonstrated
   Unto our climatures and countrymen. —   125

Enter Ghost.

   But soft, behold! lo, where it comes again!
   I'll cross° it, though it blast me. Stay, illusion!
   If thou hast any sound, or use of voice,
   Speak to me!   *It° spreads his arms.*
   If there be any good thing to be done,   130
   That may to thee do ease and grace to me,
   Speak to me!
   If thou art privy to thy country's fate,
   Which, happily, foreknowing may avoid,
   O, speak!   135
   Or if thou hast uphoarded in thy life
   Extorted treasure in the womb of earth,
   For which, they say, you spirits oft walk in death,   *The cock crows.*
   Speak of it:° stay, and speak! Stop it, Marcellus.

Marcellus: Shall I strike at it with my partisan?°   140
Horatio: Do, if it will not stand.
Bernardo: 'Tis here!

---

107 *romage:* Bustle, commotion.   109 *sort:* Suit.   112 *mote:* Speck of dust.   113 *palmy state:* Triumphant sovereignty.   117 *stars . . . fire:* I.e., comets.   118 *Disasters:* Unfavorable aspects; *moist star:* The moon, governing tides.   119 *Neptune's empire:* The sea. 121 *precurse:* Heralding.   127 *cross:* Meet, face, thus bringing down the evil influence on the person who crosses it.   129 *It:* The Ghost, or perhaps Horatio.   133–139 *If . . . it:* Horatio recites the traditional reasons why ghosts might walk.   140 *partisan:* Long-handled spear with a blade having lateral projections.

Horatio: 'Tis here!
Marcellus: 'Tis gone!   *[Exit Ghost.]*
    We do it wrong, being so majestical,
    To offer it the show of violence;
    For it is, as the air, invulnerable,   145
    And our vain blows malicious mockery.
Bernardo: It was about to speak, when the cock crew.°
Horatio: And then it started like a guilty thing
    Upon a fearful summons. I have heard,
    The cock, that is the trumpet to the morn,   150
    Doth with his lofty and shrill-sounding throat
    Awake the god of day; and, at his warning,
    Whether in sea or fire, in earth or air,
    Th' extravagant and erring° spirit hies
    To his confine:° and of the truth herein   155
    This present object made probation.°
Marcellus: It faded on the crowing of the cock.
    Some say that ever 'gainst° that season comes
    Wherein our Saviour's birth is celebrated,
    The bird of dawning singeth all night long: 160
    And then, they say, no spirit dare stir abroad;
    The nights are wholesome; then no planets strike,°
    No fairy takes, nor witch hath power to charm,
    So hallow'd and so gracious° is that time.
Horatio: So have I heard and do in part believe it.   165
    But, look, the morn, in russet mantle clad,
    Walks o'er the dew of yon high eastward hill:
    Break we our watch up; and by my advice,
    Let us impart what we have seen to-night
    Unto young Hamlet; for, upon my life,   170
    This spirit, dumb to us, will speak to him.
    Do you consent we shall acquaint him with it,
    As needful in our loves, fitting our duty?
Marcellus: Let's do 't, I pray; and I this morning know
    Where we shall find him most conveniently.   *Exeunt.* 175

[SCENE II: *A room of state in the castle.*]

Flourish. Enter Claudius, King of Denmark, Gertrude the Queen, Councilors,
Polonius and his Son Laertes, Hamlet, cum aliis° [including Voltimand and
Cornelius].

King: Though yet of Hamlet our dear brother's death
    The memory be green, and that it us befitted
    To bear our hearts in grief and our whole kingdom

---

147 *cock crew:* According to traditional ghost lore, spirits returned to their confines at cock-crow.   154 *extravagant and erring:* Wandering. Both words mean the same thing.   155 *confine:* Place of confinement.   156 *probation:* Proof, trial.   158 *'gainst:* Just before.   162 *planets strike:* It was thought that planets were malignant and might strike travelers by night. 164 *gracious:* Full of goodness.   **Scene II.**   *cum aliis:* With others.

To be contracted in one brow of woe,
Yet so far hath discretion fought with nature   5
That we with wisest sorrow think on him,
Together with remembrance of ourselves.
Therefore our sometime sister, now our queen,
Th' imperial jointress° to this warlike state,
Have we, as 'twere with a defeated joy, —   10
With an auspicious and a dropping eye,
With mirth in funeral and with dirge in marriage,
In equal scale weighing delight and dole, —
Taken to wife: nor have we herein barr'd
Your better wisdoms, which have freely gone   15
With this affair along. For all, our thanks.
Now follows, that° you know, young Fortinbras,
Holding a weak supposal° of our worth,
Or thinking by our late dear brother's death
Our state to be disjoint° and out of frame,°   20
Colleagued° with this dream of his advantage,°
He hath not fail'd to pester us with message,
Importing° the surrender of those lands
Lost by his father, with all bands of law,
To our most valiant brother. So much for him.   25
Now for ourself and for this time of meeting:
Thus much the business is: we have here writ
To Norway, uncle of young Fortinbras, —
Who, impotent and bed-rid, scarcely hears
Of this his nephew's purpose, — to suppress   30
His further gait° herein; in that the levies,
The lists and full proportions, are all made
Out of his subject:° and we here dispatch
You, good Cornelius, and you, Voltimand,
For bearers of this greeting to old Norway;   35
Giving to you no further personal power
To business with the king, more than the scope
Of these delated° articles allow.
Farewell, and let your haste commend your duty.

Cornelius: } In that and all things will we show our duty.
Voltimand: }   40
King: We doubt it nothing: heartily farewell.

                              [Exeunt Voltimand and Cornelius.]
And now, Laertes, what's the news with you?
You told us of some suit; what is't, Laertes?
You cannot speak of reason to the Dane,°
And lose your voice:° what wouldst thou beg, Laertes,   45

---

9 *jointress:* Woman possessed of a jointure, or, joint tenancy of an estate.   17 *that:* That which.   18 *weak supposal:* Low estimate.   20 *disjoint:* Distracted, out of joint; *frame:* Order.   21 *Colleagued:* added to; *dream . . . advantage:* Visionary hope of success.   23 *Importing:* Purporting, pertaining to.   31 *gait:* Proceeding.   33 *Out of his subject:* At the expense of Norway's subjects (collectively).   38 *delated:* Expressly stated.   44 *the Dane:* Danish king.   45 *lose your voice:* Speak in vain.

That shall not be my offer, not thy asking?
The head is not more native° to the heart,
The hand more instrumental° to the mouth,
Than is the throne of Denmark to thy father.
What wouldst thou have, Laertes?

Laertes: My dread lord,   50
Your leave and favour to return to France;
From whence though willingly I came to Denmark,
To show my duty in your coronation,
Yet now, I must confess, that duty done,
My thoughts and wishes bend again toward France   55
And bow them to your gracious leave and pardon.°

King: Have you your father's leave? What says Polonius?

Polonius: He hath, my lord, wrung from me my slow leave
By laboursome petition, and at last
Upon his will I seal'd my hard consent: 60
I do beseech you, give him leave to go.

King: Take thy fair hour, Laertes; time be thine,
And thy best graces spend it at thy will!
But now, my cousin° Hamlet, and my son, —

Hamlet [aside]: A little more than kin, and less than kind!°   65

King: How is it that the clouds still hang on you?

Hamlet: Not so, my lord; I am too much in the sun.°

Queen: Good Hamlet, cast thy nighted colour off,
And let thine eye look like a friend on Denmark.
Do not for ever with thy vailed lids   70
Seek for thy noble father in the dust:
Thou know'st 'tis common; all that lives must die,
Passing through nature to eternity.

Hamlet: Ay, madam, it is common.°

Queen: If it be,
Why seems it so particular with thee?   75

Hamlet: Seems, madam! nay, it is; I know not "seems."
'Tis not alone my inky cloak, good mother,
Nor customary suits° of solemn black,
Nor windy suspiration° of forc'd breath,
No, nor the fruitful river in the eye,   80
Nor the dejected 'haviour of the visage,
Together with all forms, moods, shapes of grief,
That can denote me truly: these indeed seem,
For they are actions that a man might play:

47 *native:* Closely connected, related.   48 *instrumental:* Serviceable.   56 *leave and pardon:* Permission to depart.   64 *cousin:* Any kin not of the immediate family.   65 *A little ... kind:* My relation to you has become more than kinship warrants; it has also become unnatural.   67 *I am ... sun:* (1) I am too much out of doors, (2) I am too much in the sun of your grace (ironical), (3) I am too much of a son to you. Possibly an allusion to the proverb "Out of heaven's blessing into the warm sun"; i.e., Hamlet is out of house and home in being deprived of the kingship.   74 *Ay ... common:* It is common, but it hurts nevertheless; possibly a reference to the commonplace quality of the queen's remark.   78 *customary suits:* Suits prescribed by custom for mourning.   79 *windy suspiration:* Heavy sighing.

But I have that within which passeth show;   85
These but the trappings and the suits of woe.

King: 'Tis sweet and commendable in your nature, Hamlet,
To give these mourning duties to your father:
But, you must know, your father lost a father;
That father lost, lost his, and the survivor bound   90
In filial obligation for some term
To do obsequious° sorrow: but to persever
In obstinate condolement° is a course
Of impious stubbornness; 'tis unmanly grief;
It shows a will most incorrect° to heaven,   95
A heart unfortified, a mind impatient,
An understanding simple and unschool'd:
For what we know must be and is as common
As any the most vulgar thing° to sense,
Why should we in our peevish opposition   100
Take it to heart? Fie! 'tis a fault to heaven,
A fault against the dead, a fault to nature,
To reason most absurd; whose common theme
Is death of fathers, and who still hath cried,
From the first corse till he that died to-day,   105
"This must be so." We pray you, throw to earth
This unprevailing° woe, and think of us
As of a father: for let the world take note,
You are the most immediate° to our throne;
And with no less nobility° of love   110
Than that which dearest father bears his son,
Do I impart° toward you. For your intent
In going back to school in Wittenberg,°
It is most retrograde° to our desire:
And we beseech you, bend you° to remain   115
Here, in the cheer and comfort of our eye,
Our chiefest courtier, cousin, and our son.

Queen: Let not thy mother lose her prayers, Hamlet:
I pray thee, stay with us; go not to Wittenberg.

Hamlet: I shall in all my best obey you, madam.   120

King: Why, 'tis a loving and a fair reply:
Be as ourself in Denmark. Madam, come;
This gentle and unforc'd accord of Hamlet
Sits smiling to my heart: in grace whereof,
No jocund health that Denmark drinks to-day,   125
But the great cannon to the clouds shall tell,
And the king's rouse° the heaven shall bruit again,°
Re-speaking earthly thunder. Come away.

---

92 *obsequious:* Dutiful.   93 *condolement:* Sorrowing.   95 *incorrect:* Untrained, uncor-
rected.   99 *vulgar thing:* Common experience.   107 *unprevailing:* Unavailing.   109 *most
immediate:* Next in succession.   110 *nobility:* High degree.   112 *impart:* The object is
apparently *love* (l. 110).   113 *Wittenberg:* Famous German university founded in 1502.
114 *retrograde:* Contrary.   115 *bend you:* Incline yourself; imperative.   127 *rouse:* Draft
of liquor; *bruit again:* Echo.

Flourish. Exeunt all but Hamlet.

Hamlet: O, that this too too sullied flesh would melt,
    Thaw and resolve itself into a dew!   130
    Or that the Everlasting had not fix'd
    His canon 'gainst self-slaughter! O God! God!
    How weary, stale, flat and unprofitable,
    Seem to me all the uses of this world!
    Fie on't! ah fie! 'tis an unweeded garden,   135
    That grows to seed; things rank and gross in nature
    Possess it merely.° That it should come to this!
    But two months dead: nay, not so much, not two:
    So excellent a king; that was, to this,
    Hyperion° to a satyr; so loving to my mother   140
    That he might not beteem° the winds of heaven
    Visit her face too roughly. Heaven and earth!
    Must I remember? why, she would hang on him,
    As if increase of appetite had grown
    By what it fed on: and yet, within a month —   145
    Let me not think on't — Frailty, thy name is woman! —
    A little month, or ere those shoes were old
    With which she followed my poor father's body,
    Like Niobe,° all tears: — why she, even she —
    O God! a beast, that wants discourse of reason,°   150
    Would have mourn'd longer — married with my uncle,
    My father's brother, but no more like my father
    Than I to Hercules: within a month:
    Ere yet the salt of most unrighteous tears
    Had left the flushing in her galled° eyes,   155
    She married. O, most wicked speed, to post
    With such dexterity° to incestuous sheets!
    It is not nor it cannot come to good:
    But break, my heart; for I must hold my tongue.

Enter Horatio, Marcellus, and Bernardo.

Horatio: Hail to your lordship!
Hamlet: I am glad to see you well: 160
    Horatio! — or I do forget myself.
Horatio: The same, my lord, and your poor servant ever.
Hamlet: Sir, my good friend; I'll change that name with you:°
    And what make you from Wittenberg, Horatio?
    Marcellus?   165
Marcellus: My good lord —
Hamlet: I am very glad to see you. Good even, sir.
    But what, in faith, make you from Wittenberg?

---

137 *merely:* Completely, entirely.   140 *Hyperion:* God of the sun in the older regime of ancient gods.   141 *beteem:* Allow.   149 *Niobe:* Tantalus's daughter, who boasted that she
had more sons and daughters than Leto; for this Apollo and Artemis slew her children. She
was turned into stone by Zeus on Mount Sipylus.   150 *discourse of reason:* Process or faculty
of reason.   155 *galled:* Irritated.   157 *dexterity:* Facility.   163 *I'll . . . you:* I'll be your servant, you shall be my friend; also explained as "I'll exchange the name of friend with you."

Horatio: A truant disposition, good my lord.

Hamlet: I would not hear your enemy say so,   170
   Nor shall you do my ear that violence,
   To make it truster of your own report
   Against yourself: I know you are no truant.
   But what is your affair in Elsinore?
   We'll teach you to drink deep ere you depart.   175

Horatio: My lord, I came to see your father's funeral.

Hamlet: I prithee, do not mock me, fellow-student;
   I think it was to see my mother's wedding.

Horatio: Indeed, my lord, it follow'd hard° upon.

Hamlet: Thrift, thrift, Horatio! the funeral bak'd meats°   180
   Did coldly furnish forth the marriage tables.
   Would I had met my dearest° foe in heaven
   Or ever I had seen that day, Horatio!
   My father! — methinks I see my father.

Horatio: Where, my lord!

Hamlet: In my mind's eye, Horatio.   185

Horatio: I saw him once; 'a° was a goodly king.

Hamlet: 'A was a man, take him for all in all,
   I shall not look upon his like again.

Horatio: My lord, I think I saw him yesternight.

Hamlet: Saw? who?   190

Horatio: My lord, the king your father.

Hamlet: The king my father!

Horatio: Season your admiration° for a while
   With an attent ear, till I may deliver,
   Upon the witness of these gentlemen,
   This marvel to you.

Hamlet: For God's love, let me hear.   195

Horatio: Two nights together had these gentlemen,
   Marcellus and Bernardo, on their watch,
   In the dead waste and middle of the night,
   Been thus encount'red. A figure like your father,
   Armed at point exactly, cap-a-pe,°   200
   Appears before them, and with solemn march
   Goes slow and stately by them: thrice he walk'd
   By their oppress'd° and fear-surprised eyes,
   Within his truncheon's° length; whilst they, distill'd°
   Almost to jelly with the act° of fear,   205
   Stand dumb and speak not to him. This to me
   In dreadful secrecy impart they did;
   And I with them the third night kept the watch:
   Where, as they had deliver'd, both in time,
   Form of the thing, each word made true and good,   210

179 *hard:* Close.   180 *bak'd meats:* Meat pies.   182 *dearest:* Direst. The adjective *dear* in Shakespeare has two different origins: O.E. *deore,* "beloved," and O.E. *deor,* "fierce." *Dearest* is the superlative of the second.   186 *'a:* He.   192 *Season your admiration:* Restrain your astonishment.   200 *cap-a-pe:* From head to foot.   203 *oppress'd:* Distressed.   204 *truncheon:* Officer's staff; *distill'd:* Softened, weakened.   205 *act:* Action.

The apparition comes: I knew your father;
These hands are not more like.
Hamlet: But where was this?
Marcellus: My lord, upon the platform where we watch'd.
Hamlet: Did you not speak to it?
Horatio: My lord, I did;
  But answer made it none: yet once methought   215
  It lifted up it° head and did address
  Itself to motion, like as it would speak;
  But even then the morning cock crew loud,
  And at the sound it shrunk in haste away,
  And vanish'd from our sight.
Hamlet: 'Tis very strange.   220
Horatio: As I do live, my honour'd lord, 'tis true;
  And we did think it writ down in our duty
  To let you know of it.
Hamlet: Indeed, indeed, sirs, but this troubles me.
  Hold you the watch to-night?
Marcellus: ⎱
Bernardo: ⎰   We do, my lord.   225
Hamlet: Arm'd, say you?
Marcellus: ⎱
Bernardo: ⎰   Arm'd, my lord.
Hamlet: From top to toe?
Marcellus: ⎱
Bernardo: ⎰   My lord, from head to foot.
Hamlet: Then saw you not his face?
Horatio: O, yes, my lord; he wore his beaver° up.
Hamlet: What, look'd he frowningly?
Horatio: A countenance more   230
  In sorrow than in anger.
Hamlet: Pale or red?
Horatio: Nay, very pale.
Hamlet: And fix'd his eyes upon you?
Horatio: Most constantly.
Hamlet: I would I had been there.
Horatio: It would have much amaz'd you.
Hamlet: Very like, very like. Stay'd it long?   235
Horatio: While one with moderate haste might tell a hundred.
Marcellus: ⎱
Bernardo: ⎰   Longer, longer.
Horatio: Not when I saw't.
Hamlet: His beard was grizzled,—no?
Horatio: It was, as I have seen it in his life,
  A sable° silver'd.
Hamlet: I will watch to-night;   240
  Perchance 'twill walk again.
Horatio: I warr'nt it will.

---

216 *it:* Its.   229 *beaver:* Visor on the helmet.   240 *sable:* Black color.

Hamlet: If it assume my noble father's person,
    I'll speak to it, though hell itself should gape
    And bid me hold my peace. I pray you all,
    If you have hitherto conceal'd this sight,   245
    Let it be tenable in your silence still;
    And whatsoever else shall hap to-night,
    Give it an understanding, but no tongue:
    I will requite your loves. So, fare you well:
    Upon the platform, 'twixt eleven and twelve,   250
    I'll visit you.
All: Our duty to your honour.
Hamlet: Your loves, as mine to you: farewell.   *Exeunt [all but Hamlet].*
    My father's spirit in arms! all is not well;
    I doubt° some foul play: would the night were come!
    Till then sit still, my soul: foul deeds will rise,   255
    Though all the earth o'erwhelm them, to men's eyes.   *Exit.*

[SCENE III: *A room in Polonius's house.*]

    Enter Laertes and Ophelia, his Sister.

Laertes: My necessaries are embark'd: farewell:
    And, sister, as the winds give benefit
    And convoy is assistant,° do not sleep,
    But let me hear from you.
Ophelia: Do you doubt that?
Laertes: For Hamlet and the trifling of his favour,   5
    Hold it a fashion° and a toy in blood,°
    A violet in the youth of primy° nature,
    Forward,° not permanent, sweet, not lasting,
    The perfume and suppliance of a minute;°
    No more.
Ophelia: No more but so?
Laertes: Think it no more: 10
    For nature, crescent,° does not grow alone
    In thews° and bulk, but, as this temple° waxes,
    The inward service of the mind and soul
    Grows wide withal. Perhaps he loves you now,
    And now no soil° nor cautel° doth besmirch   15
    The virtue of his will: but you must fear,
    His greatness weigh'd,° his will is not his own;
    For he himself is subject to his birth:
    He may not, as unvalued persons do,
    Carve for himself; for on his choice depends   20

---

254 *doubt:* Fear.   **Scene III.**   3 *convoy is assistant:* Means of conveyance are available.
6 *fashion:* Custom, prevailing usage; *toy in blood:* Passing amorous fancy.   7 *primy:* In its
prime.   8 *Forward:* Precocious.   9 *suppliance of a minute:* Diversion to fill up a minute.
11 *crescent:* Growing, waxing.   12 *thews:* Bodily strength; *temple:* Body.   15 *soil:* Blemish; *cautel:* Crafty device.   17 *greatness weigh'd:* High position considered.

The safety and health of this whole state;
And therefore must his choice be circumscrib'd
Unto the voice and yielding° of that body
Whereof he is the head. Then if he says he loves you,
It fits your wisdom so far to believe it   25
As he in his particular act and place
May give his saying deed;° which is no further
Than the main voice of Denmark goes withal.
Then weigh what loss your honour may sustain,
If with too credent° ear you list his songs,   30
Or lose your heart, or your chaste treasure open
To his unmast'red° importunity.
Fear it, Ophelia, fear it, my dear sister,
And keep you in the rear of your affection,
Out of the shot and danger of desire.   35
The chariest° maid is prodigal enough,
If she unmask her beauty to the moon:
Virtue itself 'scapes not calumnious strokes:
The canker galls the infants of the spring,°
Too oft before their buttons° be disclos'd,°   40
And in the morn and liquid dew° of youth
Contagious blastments° are most imminent.
Be wary then; best safety lies in fear:
Youth to itself rebels, though none else near.

Ophelia: I shall the effect of this good lesson keep,   45
As watchman to my heart. But, good my brother,
Do not, as some ungracious° pastors do,
Show me the steep and thorny way to heaven;
Whiles, like a puff'd° and reckless libertine,
Himself the primrose path of dalliance treads,   50
And recks° not his own rede.°

Enter Polonius.

Laertes: O, fear me not.
I stay too long: but here my father comes.
A double° blessing is a double grace;
Occasion° smiles upon a second leave.

Polonius: Yet here, Laertes? aboard, aboard, for shame!   55
The wind sits in the shoulder of your sail,
And you are stay'd for. There; my blessing with thee!
And these few precepts° in thy memory
Look thou character.° Give thy thoughts no tongue,

23 *voice and yielding:* Assent, approval.   27 *deed:* Effect.   30 *credent:* Credulous.   32 *unmast'red:* Unrestrained.   36 *chariest:* Most scrupulously modest.   39 *The canker . . . spring:* The cankerworm destroys the young plants of spring.   40 *buttons:* Buds; *disclos'd:* Opened. 41 *liquid dew:* I.e., time when dew is fresh.   42 *blastments:* Blights.   47 *ungracious:* Graceless.   49 *puff'd:* Bloated.   51 *recks:* Heeds; *rede:* Counsel.   53 *double:* I.e., Laertes has already bade his father good-by.   54 *Occasion:* Opportunity.   58 *precepts:* Many parallels have been found to the series of maxims which follows, one of the closer being that in Lyly's *Euphues.*   59 *character:* Inscribe.

Nor any unproportion'd° thought his act.   60
Be thou familiar, but by no means vulgar.°
Those friends thou hast, and their adoption tried,
Grapple them to thy soul with hoops of steel;
But do not dull thy palm with entertainment
Of each new-hatch'd, unfledg'd° comrade. Beware   65
Of entrance to a quarrel, but being in,
Bear't that th' opposed may beware of thee.
Give every man thy ear, but few thy voice;
Take each man's censure, but reserve thy judgement.
Costly thy habit as thy purse can buy,   70
But not express'd in fancy;° rich, not gaudy;
For the apparel oft proclaims the man,
And they in France of the best rank and station
Are of a most select and generous chief in that.°
Neither a borrower nor a lender be;   75
For loan oft loses both itself and friend,
And borrowing dulleth edge of husbandry.°
This above all: to thine own self be true,
And it must follow, as the night the day,
Thou canst not then be false to any man.   80
Farewell: my blessing season° this in thee!
Laertes: Most humbly do I take my leave, my lord.
Polonius: The time invites you; go; your servants tend.
Laertes: Farewell, Ophelia; and remember well
    What I have said to you.
Ophelia: 'Tis in my memory lock'd,   85
    And you yourself shall keep the key of it.
Laertes: Farewell.   *Exit Laertes.*
Polonius: What is 't, Ophelia, he hath said to you?
Ophelia: So please you, something touching the Lord Hamlet.
Polonius: Marry, well bethought: 90
    'Tis told me, he hath very oft of late
    Given private time to you; and you yourself
    Have of your audience been most free and bounteous:
    If it be so, as so't is put on° me,
    And that in way of caution, I must tell you,   95
    You do not understand yourself so clearly
    As it behooves my daughter and your honour.
    What is between you? give me up the truth.
Ophelia: He hath, my lord, of late made many tenders°
    Of his affection to me.   100
Polonius: Affection! pooh! you speak like a green girl,
    Unsifted° in such perilous circumstance.
    Do you believe his tenders,° as you call them?

---

60 *unproportion'd:* Inordinate.   61 *vulgar:* Common.   65 *unfledg'd:* Immature.
71 *express'd in fancy:* Fantastical in design.   74 *Are . . . that: Chief* is usually taken as a substantive meaning "head," "eminence."   77 *husbandry:* Thrift.   81 *season:* Mature.
94 *put on:* Impressed on.   99, 103 *tenders:* Offers.   102 *Unsifted:* Untried.

Ophelia: I do not know, my lord, what I should think.

Polonius: Marry, I will teach you: think yourself a baby;   105
    That you have ta'en these tenders° for true pay,
    Which are not sterling.° Tender° yourself more dearly;
    Or—not to crack the wind° of the poor phrase,
    Running it thus—you'll tender me a fool.°

Ophelia: My lord, he hath importun'd me with love   110
    In honourable fashion.

Polonius: Ay, fashion° you may call it; go to, go to.

Ophelia: And hath given countenance° to his speech, my lord,
    With almost all the holy vows of heaven.

Polonius: Ay, springes° to catch woodcocks.° I do know,   115
    When the blood burns, how prodigal the soul
    Lends the tongue vows: these blazes, daughter,
    Giving more light than heat, extinct in both,
    Even in their promise, as it is a-making,
    You must not take for fire. From this time   120
    Be somewhat scanter of your maiden presence;
    Set your entreatments° at a higher rate
    Than a command to parley.° For Lord Hamlet,
    Believe so much in him,° that he is young,
    And with a larger tether may he walk   125
    Than may be given you: in few,° Ophelia,
    Do not believe his vows; for they are brokers;°
    Not of that dye° which their investments° show,
    But mere implorators of° unholy suits,
    Breathing° like sanctified and pious bawds,   130
    The better to beguile. This is for all:
    I would not, in plain terms, from this time forth,
    Have you so slander° any moment leisure,
    As to give words or talk with the Lord Hamlet.
    Look to 't, I charge you: come your ways.   135

Ophelia: I shall obey, my lord.   *Exeunt.*

[SCENE IV: *The platform.*]

Enter Hamlet, Horatio, and Marcellus.

Hamlet: The air bites shrewdly; it is very cold.

Horatio: It is a nipping and an eager air.

Hamlet: What hour now?

Horatio: I think it lacks of twelve.

Marcellus: No, it is struck.

---

106 *tenders:* Promises to pay.   107 *sterling:* Legal currency; *Tender:* Hold.   108 *crack the wind:* I.e., run it until it is broken-winded.   109 *tender ... fool:* Show me a fool (for a daughter).   112 *fashion:* Mere form, pretense.   113 *countenance:* Credit, support.   115 *springes:* Snares; *woodcocks:* Birds easily caught, type of stupidity.   122 *entreatments:* Conversations, interviews.   123 *command to parley:* Mere invitation to talk.   124 *so ... him:* This much concerning him.   126 *in few:* Briefly.   127 *brokers:* Go-betweens, procurers.   128 *dye:* Color or sort; *investments:* Clothes.   129 *implorators of:* Solicitors of.   130 *Breathing:* Speaking.   133 *slander:* Bring disgrace or reproach upon.

Horatio: Indeed? I heard it not: then it draws near the season   5
    Wherein the spirit held his wont to walk.

    A flourish of trumpets, and two pieces go off.

    What does this mean, my lord?

Hamlet: The king doth wake° to-night and takes his rouse,°
    Keeps wassail,° and the swagg'ring up-spring° reels;°
    And, as he drains his draughts of Rhenish° down,   10
    The kettle-drum and trumpet thus bray out
    The triumph of his pledge.°

Horatio: Is it a custom?

Hamlet: Ay, marry, is 't:
    But to my mind, though I am native here
    And to the manner born,° it is a custom   15
    More honour'd in the breach than the observance.
    This heavy-headed revel east and west
    Makes us traduc'd and tax'd of other nations:
    They clepe° us drunkards, and with swinish phrase°
    Soil our addition;° and indeed it takes   20
    From our achievements, though perform'd at height,
    The pith and marrow of our attribute.°
    So, oft it chances in particular men,
    That for some vicious mole of nature° in them,
    As, in their birth—wherein they are not guilty,   25
    Since nature cannot choose his origin—
    By the o'ergrowth of some complexion,
    Oft breaking down the pales° and forts of reason,
    Or by some habit that too much o'er-leavens°
    The form of plausive° manners, that these men,   30
    Carrying, I say, the stamp of one defect,
    Being nature's livery,° or fortune's star,° —
    Their virtues else—be they as pure as grace,
    As infinite as man may undergo—
    Shall in the general censure take corruption   35
    From that particular fault: the dram of eale°
    Doth all the noble substance of a doubt
    To his own scandal.°

    Enter Ghost.

Horatio: Look, my lord, it comes!

Scene IV.   8 *wake:* Stay awake, hold revel; *rouse:* Carouse, drinking bout.   9 *wassail:* Carousal; *up-spring:* Last and wildest dance at German merry-makings; *reels:* Reels through. 10 *Rhenish:* Rhine wine.   12 *triumph...pledge:* His glorious achievement as a drinker. 15 *to...born:* Destined by birth to be subject to the custom in question.   19 *clepe:* Call; *with swinish phrase:* By calling us swine.   20 *addition:* Reputation.   22 *attribute:* Reputation.   24 *mole of nature:* Natural blemish in one's constitution.   28 *pales:* Palings (as of a fortification).   29 *o'er-leavens:* Induces a change throughout (as yeast works in bread). 30 *plausive:* Pleasing.   32 *nature's livery:* Endowment from nature; *fortune's star:* The position in which one is placed by fortune, a reference to astrology. The two phrases are aspects of the same thing.   36–38 *the dram...scandal:* A famous crux: *dram of eale* has had various interpretations, the preferred one being probably, "a dram of evil."

Hamlet: Angels and ministers of grace° defend us!
    Be thou a spirit of health or goblin damn'd,   40
    Bring with thee airs from heaven or blasts from hell,
    Be thy intents wicked or charitable,
    Thou com'st in such a questionable° shape
    That I will speak to thee: I'll call thee Hamlet,
    King, father, royal Dane: O, answer me!   45
    Let me not burst in ignorance; but tell
    Why thy canoniz'd° bones, hearsed° in death,
    Have burst their cerements;° why the sepulchre,
    Wherein we saw thee quietly interr'd,
    Hath op'd his ponderous and marble jaws,   50
    To cast thee up again. What may this mean,
    That thou, dead corse, again in complete steel
    Revisits thus the glimpses of the moon,°
    Making night hideous; and we fools of nature°
    So horridly to shake our disposition   55
    With thoughts beyond the reaches of our souls?
    Say, why is this? wherefore? what should we do?

    [Ghost] beckons [Hamlet].

Horatio: It beckons you to go away with it,
    As if it some impartment° did desire
    To you alone.
Marcellus: Look, with what courteous action   60
    It waves you to a more removed° ground:
    But do not go with it.
Horatio: No, by no means.
Hamlet: It will not speak; then I will follow it.
Horatio: Do not, my lord!
Hamlet: Why, what should be the fear?
    I do not set my life at a pin's fee;   65
    And for my soul, what can it do to that,
    Being a thing immortal as itself?
    It waves me forth again: I'll follow it.
Horatio: What if it tempt you toward the flood, my lord,
    Or to the dreadful summit of the cliff   70
    That beetles o'er° his base into the sea,
    And there assume some other horrible form,
    Which might deprive your sovereignty of reason°
    And draw you into madness? think of it:
    The very place puts toys of desperation,°   75

---

39 *ministers of grace:* Messengers of God.   43 *questionable:* Inviting question or conversation.   47 *canoniz'd:* Buried according to the canons of the church; *hearsed:* Coffined. 48 *cerements:* Grave-clothes.   53 *glimpses of the moon:* The earth by night.   54 *fools of nature:* Mere men, limited to natural knowledge.   59 *impartment:* Communication. 61 *removed:* Remote.   71 *beetles o'er:* Overhangs threateningly.   73 *deprive ... reason:* Take away the sovereignty of your reason. It was thought that evil spirits would sometimes assume the form of departed spirits in order to work madness in a human creature. 75 *toys of desperation:* Freakish notions of suicide.

Without more motive, into every brain
That looks so many fathoms to the sea
And hears it roar beneath.
Hamlet: It waves me still.
    Go on; I'll follow thee.
Marcellus: You shall not go, my lord.
Hamlet: Hold off your hands!   80
Horatio: Be rul'd; you shall not go.
Hamlet: My fate cries out,
    And makes each petty artere° in this body
    As hardy as the Nemean lion's° nerve.°
    Still am I call'd. Unhand me, gentlemen.
    By heaven, I'll make a ghost of him that lets° me!   85
    I say, away! Go on; I'll follow thee.   *Exeunt Ghost and Hamlet.*
Horatio: He waxes desperate with imagination.
Marcellus: Let's follow; 'tis not fit thus to obey him.
Horatio: Have after. To what issue° will this come?
Marcellus: Something is rotten in the state of Denmark.   90
Horatio: Heaven will direct it.°
Marcellus: Nay, let's follow him.   *Exeunt.*

[SCENE V: *Another part of the platform.*]

    Enter Ghost and Hamlet.

Hamlet: Whither wilt thou lead me? speak; I'll go no further.
Ghost: Mark me.
Hamlet: I will.
Ghost: My hour is almost come,
    When I to sulphurous and tormenting flames
    Must render up myself.
Hamlet: Alas, poor ghost!
Ghost: Pity me not, but lend thy serious hearing   5
    To what I shall unfold.
Hamlet: Speak; I am bound to hear.
Ghost: So art thou to revenge, when thou shalt hear.
Hamlet: What?
Ghost: I am thy father's spirit,
    Doom'd for a certain term to walk the night,   10
    And for the day confin'd to fast° in fires,
    Till the foul crimes done in my days of nature
    Are burnt and purg'd away. But that I am forbid
    To tell the secrets of my prison-house,
    I could a tale unfold whose lightest word   15

82 *artere:* Artery.   83 *Nemean lion's:* The Nemean lion was one of the monsters slain by Hercules; *nerve:* Sinew, tendon. The point is that the arteries which were carrying the spirits out into the body were functioning and were as stiff and hard as the sinews of the lion.   85 *lets:* Hinders.   89 *issue:* Outcome.   91 *it:* I.e., the outcome. **Scene V.** 11 *fast:* Probably, do without food. It has been sometimes taken in the sense of doing general penance.

Would harrow up thy soul, freeze thy young blood,
Make thy two eyes, like stars, start from their spheres,°
Thy knotted° and combined° locks to part
And each particular hair to stand an end,
Like quills upon the fretful porpentine:°   20
But this eternal blazon° must not be
To ears of flesh and blood. List, list, O, list!
If thou didst ever thy dear father love —
Hamlet: O God!
Ghost: Revenge his foul and most unnatural° murder.   25
Hamlet: Murder!
Ghost: Murder most foul, as in the best it is;
But this most foul, strange and unnatural.
Hamlet: Haste me to know't, that I, with wings as swift
As meditation or the thoughts of love,   30
May sweep to my revenge.
Ghost: I find thee apt;
And duller shouldst thou be than the fat weed°
That roots itself in ease on Lethe wharf,°
Wouldst thou not stir in this. Now, Hamlet, hear:
'Tis given out that, sleeping in my orchard,   35
A serpent stung me; so the whole ear of Denmark
Is by a forged process of my death
Rankly abus'd: but know, thou noble youth,
The serpent that did sting thy father's life
Now wears his crown.
Hamlet: O my prophetic soul!   40
My uncle!
Ghost: Ay, that incestuous, that adulterate° beast,
With witchcraft of his wit, with traitorous gifts, —
O wicked wit and gifts, that have the power
So to seduce! — won to his shameful lust   45
The will of my most seeming-virtuous queen:
O Hamlet, what a falling-off was there!
From me, whose love was of that dignity
That it went hand in hand even with the vow
I made to her in marriage, and to decline   50
Upon a wretch whose natural gifts were poor
To those of mine!
But virtue, as it never will be moved,
Though lewdness court it in a shape of heaven,
So lust, though to a radiant angel link'd,   55
Will sate itself in a celestial bed,
And prey on garbage.

17 *spheres:* Orbits.   18 *knotted:* Perhaps intricately arranged; *combined:* Tied, bound.
20 *porpentine:* Porcupine.   21 *eternal blazon:* Promulgation or proclamation of eternity,
revelation of the hereafter.   25 *unnatural:* I.e., pertaining to fratricide.   32 *fat weed:*
Many suggestions have been offered as to the particular plant intended, including asphodel;
probably a general figure for plants growing along rotting wharves and piles.   33 *Lethe*
wharf: Bank of the river of forgetfulness in Hades.   42 *adulterate:* Adulterous.

But, soft! methinks I scent the morning air;
Brief let me be. Sleeping within my orchard,
My custom always of the afternoon,   60
Upon my secure° hour thy uncle stole,
With juice of cursed hebona° in a vial,
And in the porches of my ears did pour
The leperous° distilment; whose effect
Holds such an enmity with blood of man   65
That swift as quicksilver it courses through
The natural gates and alleys of the body,
And with a sudden vigour it doth posset°
And curd, like eager° droppings into milk,
The thin and wholesome blood: so did it mine;   70
And a most instant tetter bark'd about,
Most lazar-like,° with vile and loathsome crust,
All my smooth body.
Thus was I, sleeping, by a brother's hand
Of life, of crown, of queen, at once dispatch'd:°   75
Cut off even in the blossoms of my sin,
Unhous'led,° disappointed,° unanel'd,°
No reck'ning made, but sent to my account
With all my imperfections on my head:
O, horrible! O, horrible! most horrible!°   80
If thou hast nature in thee, bear it not;
Let not the royal bed of Denmark be
A couch for luxury° and damned incest.
But, howsomever thou pursues this act,
Taint not thy mind,° nor let thy soul contrive   85
Against thy mother aught: leave her to heaven
And to those thorns that in her bosom lodge,
To prick and sting her. Fare thee well at once!
The glow-worm shows the matin° to be near,
And 'gins to pale his uneffectual fire:°   90
Adieu, adieu, adieu! remember me.   [*Exit.*]
Hamlet: O all you host of heaven! O earth! what else?
And shall I couple° hell? O, fie! Hold, hold, my heart;
And you, my sinews, grow not instant old,
But bear me stiffly up. Remember thee!   95
Ay, thou poor ghost, whiles memory holds a seat
In this distracted globe.° Remember thee!
Yea, from the table of my memory

---

61 *secure:* Confident, unsuspicious.   62 *hebona:* Generally supposed to mean henbane, conjectured *hemlock; ebenus,* meaning "yew."   64 *leperous:* Causing leprosy.   68 *posset:* Coagulate, curdle.   69 *eager:* Sour, acid.   72 *lazar-like:* Leperlike.   75 *dispatch'd:* Suddenly bereft.   77 *Unhous'led:* Without having received the sacrament; *disappointed:* Unready, without equipment for the last journey; *unanel'd:* Without having received extreme unction.   80 *O . . . horrible:* Many editors give this line to Hamlet; Garrick and Sir Henry Irving spoke it in that part.   83 *luxury:* Lechery.   85 *Taint . . . mind:* Probably, deprave not thy character, do nothing except in the pursuit of a natural revenge.   89 *matin:* Morning.   90 *uneffectual fire:* Cold light.   93 *couple:* Add.   97 *distracted globe:* Confused head.

I'll wipe away all trivial fond records,
All saws° of books, all forms, all pressures° past,   100
That youth and observation copied there;
And thy commandment all alone shall live
Within the book and volume of my brain,
Unmix'd with baser matter: yes, by heaven!
O most pernicious woman!   105
O villain, villain, smiling, damned villain!
My tables,° — meet it is I set it down,
That one may smile, and smile, and be a villain;
At least I am sure it may be so in Denmark: *[Writing.]*
So, uncle, there you are. Now to my word;°   110
It is "Adieu, adieu! remember me,"
I have sworn't.

Enter Horatio and Marcellus.

Horatio: My lord, my lord —
Marcellus: Lord Hamlet, —
Horatio: Heavens secure him!
Hamlet: So be it!
Marcellus: Hillo, ho, ho,° my lord!   115
Hamlet: Hillo, ho, ho, boy! come, bird, come.
Marcellus: How is't, my noble lord?
Horatio: What news, my lord?
Hamlet: O, wonderful!
Horatio: Good my lord, tell it.
Hamlet: No; you will reveal it.
Horatio: Not I, my lord, by heaven.
Marcellus: Nor I, my lord.   120
Hamlet: How say you, then; would heart of man once think it?
    But you'll be secret?
Horatio: ⎫
Marcellus: ⎬   Ay, by heaven, my lord.
Hamlet: There's ne'er a villain dwelling in all Denmark
    But he's an arrant° knave.
Horatio: There needs no ghost, my lord, come from the grave   125
    To tell us this.
Hamlet: Why, right; you are in the right;
    And so, without more circumstance at all,
    I hold it fit that we shake hands and part:
    You, as your business and desire shall point you;
    For every man has business and desire,   130
    Such as it is; and for my own poor part,
    Look you, I'll go pray.
Horatio: These are but wild and whirling words, my lord.
Hamlet: I am sorry they offend you, heartily;
    Yes, 'faith, heartily.

---

100 *saws:* Wise sayings; *pressures:* Impressions stamped.   107 *tables:* Probably a small portable writing-tablet carried at the belt.   110 *word:* Watchword.   115 *Hillo, ho, ho:* A falconer's call to a hawk in air.   124 *arrant:* Thoroughgoing.

Horatio: There's no offence, my lord.   135
Hamlet: Yes, by Saint Patrick,° but there is, Horatio,
    And much offence too. Touching this vision here,
    It is an honest° ghost, that let me tell you:
    For your desire to know what is between us,
    O'ermaster 't as you may. And now, good friends,   140
    As you are friends, scholars and soldiers,
    Give me one poor request.
Horatio: What is 't, my lord? we will.
Hamlet: Never make known what you have seen to-night.
Horatio: ⎫
Marcellus: ⎬ My lord, we will not.
       ⎭
Hamlet: Nay, but swear 't.
Horatio: In faith,   145
    My lord, not I.
Marcellus: Nor I, my lord, in faith.
Hamlet: Upon my sword.°
Marcellus: We have sworn, my lord, already.
Hamlet: Indeed, upon my sword, indeed.   *Ghost cries under the stage.*
Ghost: Swear.
Hamlet: Ah, ha, boy! say'st thou so? art thou there, truepenny?°   150
    Come on — you hear this fellow in the cellarage —
    Consent to swear.
Horatio: Propose the oath, my lord.
Hamlet: Never to speak of this that you have seen,
    Swear by my sword.
Ghost [beneath]: Swear.   155
Hamlet: Hic et ubique?° then we'll shift our ground.
    Come hither, gentlemen,
    And lay your hands again upon my sword:
    Swear by my sword,
    Never to speak of this that you have heard.   160
Ghost [beneath]: Swear by his sword.
Hamlet: Well said, old mole! canst work i' th' earth so fast?
    A worthy pioner!° Once more remove, good friends.
Horatio: O day and night, but this is wondrous strange!
Hamlet: And therefore as a stranger give it welcome.   165
    There are more things in heaven and earth, Horatio,
    Than are dreamt of in your philosophy.
    But come;
    Here, as before, never, so help you mercy,
    How strange or odd soe'er I bear myself,   170
    As I perchance hereafter shall think meet
    To put an antic° disposition on,
    That you, at such times seeing me, never shall,
    With arms encumb'red° thus, or this head-shake,

---

136 *Saint Patrick:* St. Patrick was keeper of Purgatory and patron saint of all blunders and confusion.   **138** *honest:* I.e., a real ghost and not an evil spirit.   **147** *sword:* I.e., the hilt in the form of a cross.   **150** *truepenny:* Good old boy, or the like.   **156** *Hic et ubique?:* Here and everywhere?   **163** *pioner:* Digger, miner.   **172** *antic:* Fantastic.   **174** *encumb'red:* Folded or entwined.

Or by pronouncing of some doubtful phrase,   175
As "Well, well, we know," or "We could, an if we would,"
Or "If we list to speak," or "There be, an if they might,"
Or such ambiguous giving out,° to note°
That you know aught of me: this not to do,
So grace and mercy at your most need help you,   180
Swear.
Ghost [beneath]: Swear.
Hamlet: Rest, rest, perturbed spirit! *[They swear.]* So, gentlemen,
With all my love I do commend me to you:
And what so poor a man as Hamlet is   185
May do, t' express his love and friending° to you,
God willing, shall not lack. Let us go in together;
And still your fingers on your lips, I pray.
The time is out of joint: O cursed spite,
That ever I was born to set it right!   190
Nay, come, let's go together.   *Exeunt.*

[ACT II

SCENE I: *A room in Polonius's house.*]

Enter old Polonius with his man [Reynaldo].

Polonius: Give him this money and these notes, Reynaldo.
Reynaldo: I will, my lord.
Polonius: You shall do marvellous wisely, good Reynaldo,
Before you visit him, to make inquire
Of his behaviour.
Reynaldo: My lord, I did intend it.   5
Polonius: Marry, well said; very well said. Look you, sir,
Inquire me first what Danskers° are in Paris;
And how, and who, what means, and where they keep,°
What company, at what expense; and finding
By this encompassment° and drift° of question   10
That they do know my son, come you more nearer
Than your particular demands will touch it:°
Take° you as 'twere, some distant knowledge of him;
As thus, "I know his father and his friends,
And in part him": do you mark this, Reynaldo?   15
Reynaldo: Ay, very well, my lord.
Polonius: "And in part him; but" you may say "not well:
But, if 't be he I mean, he's very wild;
Addicted so and so": and there put on° him

---

178 *giving out:* Profession of knowledge; *to note:* To give a sign.   186 *friending:* Friendliness.   **Act II, Scene I.**   7 *Danskers:* Danke was a common variant for "Denmark"; hence "Dane."   8 *keep:* Dwell.   10 *encompassment:* Roundabout talking; *drift:* Gradual approach or course.   11–12 *come . . . it:* I.e., you will find out more this way than by asking pointed questions.   13 *Take:* Assume, pretend.   19 *put on:* Impute to.

What forgeries° you please; marry, none so rank   20
As may dishonour him; take heed of that;
But, sir, such wanton,° wild and usual slips
As are companions noted and most known
To youth and liberty.
Reynaldo: As gaming, my lord.
Polonius: Ay, or drinking, fencing,° swearing, quarrelling,   25
    Drabbing;° you may go so far.
Reynaldo: My lord, that would dishonour him.
Polonius: 'Faith, no; as you may season it in the charge.
    You must not put another scandal on him,
    That he is open to incontinency;°   30
    That's not my meaning: but breathe his faults so quaintly°
    That they may seem the taints of liberty,°
    The flash and outbreak of a fiery mind,
    A savageness in unreclaimed° blood,
    Of general assault.°
Reynaldo: But, my good lord, —   35
Polonius: Wherefore should you do this?
Reynaldo: Ay, my lord,
    I would know that.
Polonius: Marry, sir, here's my drift;
    And, I believe, it is a fetch of wit:°
    You laying these slight sullies on my son,
    As 'twere a thing a little soil'd i' th' working,   40
    Mark you,
    Your party in converse, him you would sound,
    Having ever° seen in the prenominate° crimes
    The youth you breathe of guilty, be assur'd
    He closes with you in this consequence;°   45
    "Good sir," or so, or "friend," or "gentleman,"
    According to the phrase or the addition
    Of man and country.
Reynaldo: Very good, my lord.
Polonius: And then, sir, does 'a this — 'a does — what was I about to say? By
    the mass, I was about to say something: where did I leave?   50
Reynaldo: At "closes in the consequence," at "friend or so," and "gentle-
    man."
Polonius: At "closes in the consequence," ay, marry;
    He closes thus: "I know the gentleman;
    I saw him yesterday, or t' other day,   55
    Or then, or then; with such, or such; and, as you say,

---

20 *forgeries:* Invented tales.   22 *wanton:* Sportive, unrestrained.   25 *fencing:* Indicative
of the ill repute of professional fencers and fencing schools in Elizabethan times.
26 *Drabbing:* Associating with immoral women.   30 *incontinency:* Habitual loose behavior.   31 *quaintly:* Delicately, ingeniously.   32 *taints of liberty:* Blemishes due to freedom.
34 *unreclaimed:* Untamed.   35 *general assault:* Tendency that assails all untrained youth.
38 *fetch of wit:* Clever trick.   43 *ever:* At any time; *prenominate:* Before-mentioned.
45 *closes . . . consequence:* Agrees with you in this conclusion.

There was 'a gaming; there o'ertook in 's rouse;°
There falling out at tennis": or perchance,
"I saw him enter such a house of sale,"
Videlicet,° a brothel, or so forth.   60
See you now;
Your bait of falsehood takes this carp of truth:
And thus do we of wisdom and of reach,°
With windlasses° and with assays of bias,°
By indirections° find directions° out: 65
So by my former lecture° and advice,
Shall you my son. You have me, have you not?

Reynaldo: My lord, I have.

Polonius: God bye ye;° fare ye well.

Reynaldo: Good my lord!

Polonius: Observe his inclination in yourself.°   70

Reynaldo: I shall, my lord.

Polonius: And let him ply his music.°

Reynaldo: Well, my lord.

Polonius: Farewell!   *Exit Reynaldo.*

     Enter Ophelia.

           How now, Ophelia! what's the matter?

Ophelia: O, my lord, my lord, I have been so affrighted!

Polonius: With what, i' th' name of God?   75

Ophelia: My lord, as I was sewing in my closet,°
Lord Hamlet, with his doublet° all unbrac'd;°
No hat upon his head; his stockings foul'd,
Ungart'red, and down-gyved° to his ankle;
Pale as his shirt; his knees knocking each other;   80
And with a look so piteous in purport
As if he had been loosed out of hell
To speak of horrors, — he comes before me.

Polonius: Mad for thy love?

Ophelia: My lord, I do not know;
But truly, I do fear it.

Polonius: What said he?   85

Ophelia: He took me by the wrist and held me hard;
Then goes he to the length of all his arm;
And, with his other hand thus o'er his brow,
He falls to such perusal of my face
As 'a would draw it. Long stay'd he so;   90
At last, a little shaking of mine arm

---

57 *o'ertook in 's rouse:* Overcome by drink.   60 *Videlicet:* Namely.   63 *reach:* Capacity, ability.   64 *windlasses:* I.e., circuitous paths; *assays of bias:* Attempts that resemble the course of the bowl, which, being weighted on one side, has a curving motion.   65 *indirections:* Devious courses; *directions:* Straight courses, i.e., the truth.   66 *lecture:* Admonition. 68 *bye ye:* Be with you.   70 *Observe . . . yourself:* In your own person, not by spies; or conform your own conduct to his inclination; or test him by studying yourself.   72 *ply his music:* Probably to be taken literally.   76 *closet:* Private chamber.   77 *doublet:* Close-fitting coat; *unbrac'd:* Unfastened.   79 *down-gyved:* Fallen to the ankles (like gyves or fetters).

And thrice his head thus waving up and down,
He rais'd a sigh so piteous and profound
As it did seem to shatter all his bulk°
And end his being: that done, he lets me go: 95
And, with his head over his shoulder turn'd,
He seem'd to find his way without his eyes;
For out o' doors he went without their helps,
And, to the last, bended their light on me.

Polonius: Come, go with me: I will go seek the king.   100
This is the very ecstasy of love,
Whose violent property° fordoes° itself
And leads the will to desperate undertakings
As oft as any passion under heaven
That does afflict our natures. I am sorry.   105
What, have you given him any hard words of late?

Ophelia: No, my good lord, but, as you did command,
I did repel his letters and denied
His access to me.

Polonius: That hath made him mad.
I am sorry that with better heed and judgement   110
I had not quoted° him: I fear'd he did but trifle,
And meant to wrack thee; but, beshrew my jealousy!°
By heaven, it is as proper to our age
To cast beyond° ourselves in our opinions
As it is common for the younger sort   115
To lack discretion. Come, go we to the king:
This must be known; which, being kept close, might move
More grief to hide than hate to utter love.°
Come.   *Exeunt.*

[SCENE II: *A room in the castle.*]

Flourish. Enter King and Queen, Rosencrantz, and Guildenstern [with others].

King: Welcome, dear Rosencrantz and Guildenstern!
Moreover that° we much did long to see you,
The need we have to use you did provoke
Our hasty sending. Something have you heard
Of Hamlet's transformation; so call it,   5
Sith° nor th' exterior nor the inward man
Resembles that it was. What it should be,
More than his father's death, that thus hath put him
So much from th' understanding of himself,
I cannot dream of: I entreat you both,   10
That, being of so young days° brought up with him,

94 *bulk:* Body.   102 *property:* Nature; *fordoes:* Destroys.   111 *quoted:* Observed.   112 *beshrew my jealousy:* Curse my suspicions.   114 *cast beyond:* Overshoot, miscalculate. 117–118 *might . . . love:* I.e., I might cause more grief to others by hiding the knowledge of Hamlet's love to Ophelia than hatred to me and mine by telling of it. **Scene II.** 2 *Moreover that:* Besides the fact that.   6 *Sith:* Since.   11 *of . . . days:* From such early youth.

And sith so neighbour'd to his youth and haviour,
That you vouchsafe your rest° here in our court
Some little time: so by your companies
To draw him on to pleasures, and to gather,   15
So much as from occasion you may glean,
Whether aught, to us unknown, afflicts him thus,
That, open'd, lies within our remedy.

Queen: Good gentlemen, he hath much talk'd of you;
And sure I am two men there are not living   20
To whom he more adheres. If it will please you
To show us so much gentry° and good will
As to expend your time with us awhile,
For the supply and profit° of our hope,
Your visitation shall receive such thanks   25
As fits a king's remembrance.

Rosencrantz: Both your majesties
Might, by the sovereign power you have of us,
Put your dread pleasures more into command
Than to entreaty.

Guildenstern: But we both obey,
And here give up ourselves, in the full bent°   30
To lay our service freely at your feet,
To be commanded.

King: Thanks, Rosencrantz and gentle Guildenstern.

Queen: Thanks, Guildenstern and gentle Rosencrantz:
And I beseech you instantly to visit   35
My too much changed son. Go, some of you,
And bring these gentlemen where Hamlet is.

Guildenstern: Heavens make our presence and our practices
Pleasant and helpful to him!

Queen: Ay, amen!

        Exeunt Rosencrantz and Guildenstern [with some Attendants].

    Enter Polonius.

Polonius: Th' ambassadors from Norway, my good lord,   40
Are joyfully return'd.

King: Thou still hast been the father of good news.

Polonius: Have I, my lord? I assure my good liege,
I hold my duty, as I hold my soul,
Both to my God and to my gracious king: 45
And I do think, or else this brain of mine
Hunts not the trail of policy so sure
As it hath us'd to do, that I have found
The very cause of Hamlet's lunacy.

King: O, speak of that; that do I long to hear.   50

Polonius: Give first admittance to th' ambassadors;
My news shall be the fruit to that great feast.

---

13 *vouchsafe your rest*: Please to stay.   22 *gentry*: Courtesy.   24 *supply and profit*: Aid and
successful outcome.   30 *in ... bent*: To the utmost degree of our mental capacity.

King: Thyself do grace to them, and bring them in.   *[Exit Polonius.]*
    He tells me, my dear Gertrude, he hath found
    The head and source of all your son's distemper.   55
Queen: I doubt° it is no other but the main;°
    His father's death, and our o'erhasty marriage.
King: Well, we shall sift him.

    Enter Ambassadors [Voltimand and Cornelius, with Polonius.]
                    Welcome, my good friends!
    Say, Voltimand, what from our brother Norway?
Voltimand: Most fair return of greetings and desires.   60
    Upon our first, he sent out to suppress
    His nephew's levies; which to him appear'd
    To be a preparation 'gainst the Polack;
    But, better look'd into, he truly found
    It was against your highness: whereat griev'd,   65
    That so his sickness, age and impotence
    Was falsely borne in hand,° sends out arrests
    On Fortinbras; which he, in brief, obeys;
    Receives rebuke from Norway, and in fine°
    Makes vow before his uncle never more   70
    To give th' assay° of arms against your majesty.
    Whereon old Norway, overcome with joy,
    Gives him three score thousand crowns in annual fee,
    And his commission to employ those soldiers,
    So levied as before, against the Polack: 75
    With an entreaty, herein further shown,   *[Giving a paper.]*
    That it might please you to give quiet pass
    Through your dominions for this enterprise,
    On such regards of safety and allowance°
    As therein are set down.
King: It likes° us well;   80
    And at our more consider'd° time we'll read,
    Answer, and think upon this business.
    Meantime we thank you for your well-took labour:
    Go to your rest; at night we'll feast together:
    Most welcome home!   *Exeunt Ambassadors.*
Polonius: This business is well ended.   85
    My liege, and madam, to expostulate
    What majesty should be, what duty is,
    Why day is day, night night, and time is time,
    Were nothing but to waste night, day and time.
    Therefore, since brevity is the soul of wit,°   90
    And tediousness the limbs and outward flourishes,°
    I will be brief: your noble son is mad:
    Mad call I it; for, to define true madness

---

56 *doubt:* Fear; *main:* Chief point, principal concern.   67 *borne in hand:* Deluded.
69 *in fine:* In the end.   71 *assay:* Assault, trial (of arms).   79 *safety and allowance:*
Pledges of safety to the country and terms of permission for the troops to pass.   80 *likes:*
Pleases.   81 *consider'd:* Suitable for deliberation.   90 *wit:* Sound sense or judgment.
91 *flourishes:* Ostentation, embellishments.

What is 't but to be nothing else but mad?
But let that go.
Queen: More matter, with less art.   95
Polonius: Madam, I swear I use no art at all.
That he is mad, 'tis true: 'tis true 'tis pity;
And pity 'tis 'tis true: a foolish figure;°
But farewell it, for I will use no art.
Mad let us grant him, then: and now remains   100
That we find out the cause of this effect,
Or rather say, the cause of this defect,
For this effect defective comes by cause:
Thus it remains, and the remainder thus.
Perpend.°   105
I have a daughter — have while she is mine —
Who, in her duty and obedience, mark,
Hath given me this: now gather, and surmise. *[Reads the letter.]* "To the
celestial and my soul's idol,
the most beautified Ophelia," —   110
That's an ill phrase, a vile phrase; "beautified" is a vile phrase: but you
shall hear. Thus: *[Reads.]*
"In her excellent white bosom, these, & c."
Queen: Came this from Hamlet to her?
Polonius: Good madam, stay awhile; I will be faithful.   *[Reads.]*   115
            "Doubt thou the stars are fire;
                Doubt that the sun doth move;
                Doubt truth to be a liar;
                But never doubt I love.
"O dear Ophelia, I am ill at these numbers;° I have not art to reckon°   120
my groans: but that I love thee best, O most best, believe it. Adieu.
    "Thine evermore, most dear lady, whilst this machine° is to him,
                                                         HAMLET."
This, in obedience, hath my daughter shown me,
And more above,° hath his solicitings,   125
As they fell out° by time, by means° and place,
All given to mine ear.
King: But how hath she
Receiv'd his love?
Polonius: What do you think of me?
King: As of a man faithful and honourable.
Polonius: I would fain prove so. But what might you think,   130
When I had seen this hot love on the wing —
As I perceiv'd it, I must tell you that,
Before my daughter told me — what might you,
Or my dear majesty your queen here, think,
If I had play'd the desk or table-book,°   135
Or given my heart a winking,° mute and dumb,

---

98 *figure:* Figure of speech.   105 *Perpend:* Consider.   120 *ill . . . numbers:* Unskilled at
writing verses; *reckon:* Number metrically, scan.   122 *machine:* Bodily frame.   125 *more
above:* Moreover.   126 *fell out:* Occurred; *means:* Opportunities (of access).   135 *play'd . . .
table-book:* I.e., remained shut up, concealed this information.   136 *given . . . winking:*
Given my heart a signal to keep silent.

Or look'd upon this love with idle sight;
What might you think? No, I went round to work,
And my young mistress thus I did bespeak:°
"Lord Hamlet is a prince, out of thy star;°   140
This must not be": and then I prescripts gave her,
That she should lock herself from his resort,
Admit no messengers, receive no tokens.
Which done, she took the fruits of my advice;
And he, repelled — a short tale to make —   145
Fell into a sadness, then into a fast,
Thence to a watch,° thence into a weakness,
Thence to a lightness,° and, by this declension,°
Into the madness wherein now he raves,
And all we mourn for.

King: Do you think 'tis this?   150
Queen: It may be, very like.
Polonius: Hath there been such a time — I would fain know that —
    That I have positively said "'Tis so,"
    When it prov'd otherwise?
King: Not that I know.
Polonius [pointing to his head and shoulder]: Take this from this, if this be
        otherwise: 155
    If circumstances lead me, I will find
    Where truth is hid, though it were hid indeed
    Within the centre.°
King: How may we try it further?
Polonius: You know, sometimes he walks four hours together
    Here in the lobby.
Queen: So he does indeed.   160
Polonius: At such a time I'll loose my daughter to him:
    Be you and I behind an arras° then;
    Mark the encounter: if he love her not
    And be not from his reason fall'n thereon,°
    Let me be no assistant for a state,   165
    But keep a farm and carters.
King: We will try it.

    Enter Hamlet [reading on a book].

Queen: But, look, where sadly the poor wretch comes reading.
Polonius: Away, I do beseech you both, away:
                          Exeunt King and Queen [with Attendants].
    I'll board° him presently. O, give me leave.
    How does my good Lord Hamlet?   170
Hamlet: Well, God-a-mercy.
Polonius: Do you know me, my lord?
Hamlet: Excellent well; you are a fishmonger.°

---

139 *bespeak:* Address.   140 *out...star:* Above thee in position.   147 *watch:* State of sleeplessness.   148 *lightness:* Lightheadedness; *declension:* Decline, deterioration.   158 *centre:* Middle point of the earth.   162 *arras:* Hanging, tapestry.   164 *thereon:* On that account.   169 *board:* Accost.   173 *fishmonger:* An opprobrious expression meaning "bawd," "procurer."

Polonius: Not I, my lord.

Hamlet: Then I would you were so honest a man.   175

Polonius: Honest, my lord!

Hamlet: Ay, sir; to be honest, as this world goes, is to be one man picked
out of ten thousand.

Polonius: That's very true, my lord.

Hamlet: For if the sun breed maggots in a dead dog, being a good kissing   180
carrion,° — Have you a daughter?

Polonius: I have, my lord.

Hamlet: Let her not walk i' the sun:° conception° is a blessing: but as your
daughter may conceive — Friend, look to 't.

Polonius [aside]: How say you by° that? Still harping on my daughter: yet   185
he knew me not at first; 'a said I was a fishmonger: 'a is far gone, far
gone: and truly in my youth I suffered much extremity for love; very
near this. I'll speak to him again. What do you read, my lord?

Hamlet: Words, words, words.

Polonius: What is the matter,° my lord?   190

Hamlet: Between who?°

Polonius: I mean, the matter that you read, my lord.

Hamlet: Slanders, sir: for the satirical rogue says here that old men have
grey beards, that their faces are wrinkled, their eyes purging° thick
amber and plum-tree gum and that they have a plentiful lack of wit,   195
together with most weak hams: all which, sir, though I most powerfully and potently believe, yet I hold it not honesty° to have it thus set
down, for yourself, sir, should be old as I am, if like a crab you could
go backward.

Polonius [aside]: Though this be madness, yet there is method in 't. — Will   200
you walk out of the air, my lord?

Hamlet: Into my grave.

Polonius: Indeed, that's out of the air. *(Aside.)* How pregnant sometimes
his replies are! a happiness° that often madness hits on, which reason
and sanity could not so prosperously° be delivered of. I will leave   205
him, and suddenly contrive the means of meeting between him and
my daughter. — My honourable lord, I will most humbly take my
leave of you.

Hamlet: You cannot, sir, take from me any thing that I will more willingly
part withal: except my life, except my life, except my life.   210

Enter Guildenstern and Rosencrantz.

Polonius: Fare you well, my lord.

Hamlet: These tedious old fools!

Polonius: You go to seek the Lord Hamlet; there he is.

Rosencrantz [to Polonius]: God save you, sir!   *[Exit Polonius.]*

Guildenstern: My honoured lord!   215

Rosencrantz: My most dear lord!

180-181 *good kissing carrion:* I.e., a good piece of flesh for kissing (?).   183 *i' the sun:* In the
sunshine of princely favors; *conception:* Quibble on "understanding" and "pregnancy."
185 *by:* Concerning.   190 *matter:* Substance.   191 *Between who:* Hamlet deliberately
takes *matter* as meaning "basis of dispute."   194 *purging:* discharging.   197 *honesty:* Decency.   204 *happiness:* Felicity of expression.   205 *prosperously:* Successfully.

Hamlet: My excellent good friends! How dost thou, Guildenstern? Ah, Rosencrantz! Good lads, how do ye both?

Rosencrantz: As the indifferent° children of the earth.

Guildenstern: Happy, in that we are not over-happy; 220
On Fortune's cap we are not the very button.

Hamlet: Nor the soles of her shoe?

Rosencrantz: Neither, my lord.

Hamlet: Then you live about her waist, or in the middle of her favours?

Guildenstern: 'Faith, her privates° we. 225

Hamlet: In the secret parts of Fortune? O, most true; she is a strumpet. What's the news?

Rosencrantz: None, my lord, but that the world's grown honest.

Hamlet: Then is doomsday near: but your news is not true. Let me question more in particular: what have you, my good friends, deserved at 230 the hands of Fortune, that she sends you to prison hither?

Guildenstern: Prison, my lord!

Hamlet: Denmark's a prison.

Rosencrantz: Then is the world one.

Hamlet: A goodly one; in which there are many confines,° wards and 235 dungeons, Denmark being one o' the worst.

Rosencrantz: We think not so, my lord.

Hamlet: Why, then, 'tis none to you; for there is nothing either good or bad, but thinking makes it so: to me it is a prison.

Rosencrantz: Why then, your ambition makes it one; 'tis too narrow for 240 your mind.

Hamlet: O God, I could be bounded in a nutshell and count myself a king of infinite space, were it not that I have bad dreams.

Guildenstern: Which dreams indeed are ambition, for the very substance of the ambitious° is merely the shadow of a dream. 245

Hamlet: A dream itself is but a shadow.

Rosencrantz: Truly, and I hold ambition of so airy and light a quality that it is but a shadow's shadow.

Hamlet: Then are our beggars bodies, and our monarchs and outstretched heroes the beggars' shadows. Shall we to the court? for, by 250 my fay,° I cannot reason.°

Rosencrantz: ⎫
⎬ We'll wait upon you.°
Guildenstern: ⎭

Hamlet: No such matter: I will not sort° you with the rest of my servants, for, to speak to you like an honest man, I am most dreadfully attended.° But, in the beaten way of friendship,° what make you at 255 Elsinore?

Rosencrantz: To visit you, my lord: no other occasion.

Hamlet: Beggar that I am, I am ever poor in thanks; but I thank you: and sure, dear friends, my thanks are too dear a° halfpenny. Were you not sent for? Is it your own inclining? Is it a free visitation? Come, come, 260 deal justly with me: come, come; nay, speak.

---

219 *indifferent:* Ordinary.   225 *privates:* I.e., ordinary men (sexual pun on *private parts*). 235 *confines:* Places of confinement.   244–245 *very...ambitious:* That seemingly most substantial thing which the ambitious pursue.   251 *fay:* Faith; *reason:* Argue.   252 *wait upon:* Accompany.   253 *sort:* Class.   254–255 *dreadfully attended:* Poorly provided with servants.   255 *in the...friendship:* As a matter of course among friends.   259 *a:* I.e., at a.

Guildenstern: What should we say, my lord?

Hamlet: Why, any thing, but to the purpose. You were sent for; and there
    is a kind of confession in your looks which your modesties have not
    craft enough to colour: I know the good king and queen have sent for 265
    you.

Rosencrantz: To what end, my lord?

Hamlet: That you must teach me. But let me conjure° you, by the rights of
    our fellowship, by the consonancy of our youth,° by the obligation of
    our ever-preserved love, and by what more dear a better proposer° 270
    could charge you withal, be even and direct with me, whether you
    were sent for, or no?

Rosencrantz [aside to Guildenstern]: What say you?

Hamlet [aside]: Nay, then, I have an eye of you.—If you love me, hold not
    off. 275

Guildenstern: My lord, we were sent for.

Hamlet: I will tell you why; so shall my anticipation prevent your discov-
    ery,° and your secrecy to the king and queen moult no feather. I have
    of late—but wherefore I know not—lost all my mirth, forgone all
    custom of exercises; and indeed it goes so heavily with my disposition 280
    that this goodly frame, the earth, seems to me a sterile promontory,
    this most excellent canopy, the air, look you, this brave o'erhanging
    firmament, this majestical roof fretted° with golden fire, why, it
    appeareth nothing to me but a foul and pestilent congregation of
    vapours. What a piece of work is a man! how noble in reason! how 285
    infinite in faculties!° in form and moving how express° and ad-
    mirable! in action how like an angel! in apprehension° how like a
    god! the beauty of the world! the paragon of animals! And yet, to me,
    what is this quintessence° of dust? man delights not me: no, nor
    woman neither, though by your smiling you seem to say so. 290

Rosencrantz: My lord, there was no such stuff in my thoughts.

Hamlet: Why did you laugh then, when I said "man delights not me"?

Rosencrantz: To think, my lord, if you delight not in man, what lenten° en-
    tertainment the players shall receive from you: we coted° them on
    the way; and hither are they coming, to offer you service. 295

Hamlet: He that plays the king shall be welcome; his majesty shall have
    tribute of me; the adventurous knight shall use his foil and target;°
    the lover shall not sigh gratis; the humorous man° shall end his part
    in peace; the clown shall make those laugh whose lungs are tickle o'
    the sere;° and the lady shall say her mind freely, or the blank verse 300
    shall halt for 't.° What players are they?

Rosencrantz: Even those you were wont to take delight in, the tragedians
    of the city.

---

268 *conjure:* Adjure, entreat.   269 *consonancy of our youth:* The fact that we are of the same
age.   270 *better proposer:* One more skillful in finding proposals.   277–278 *prevent your
discovery:* Forestall your disclosure.   283 *fretted:* Adorned.   286 *faculties:* Capacity; *express:* Well-framed (?), exact (?).   287 *apprehension:* Understanding.   289 *quintessence:*
The fifth essence of ancient philosophy, supposed to be the substance of the heavenly bodies
and to be latent in all things.   293 *lenten:* Meager.   294 *coted:* Overtook and passed
beyond.   297 *foil and target:* Sword and shield.   298 *humorous man:* Actor who takes
the part of the humor characters.   299–300 *tickle o' the sere:* Easy on the trigger.
300–301 *the lady . . . for 't:* The lady (fond of talking) shall have opportunity to talk, blank
verse or no blank verse.

Hamlet: How chances it they travel? their residence,° both in reputation
and profit, was better both ways. 305

Rosencrantz: I think their inhibition° comes by the means of the late
innovation.°

Hamlet: Do they hold the same estimation they did when I was in the city?
are they so followed?

Rosencrantz: No, indeed, are they not. 310

Hamlet: How° comes it? do they grow rusty?

Rosencrantz: Nay, their endeavour keeps in the wonted pace: but there is,
sir, an aery° of children, little eyases,° that cry out on the top of question,° and are most tyrannically° clapped for 't: these are now the
fashion, and so berattle° the common stages° — so they call them — 315
that many wearing rapiers° are afraid of goose-quills° and dare scarce
come thither.

Hamlet: What, are they children? who maintains 'em? how are they escoted?° Will they pursue the quality° no longer than they can sing?°
will they not say afterwards, if they should grow themselves to com- 320
mon° players — as it is most like, if their means are no better — their
writers do them wrong, to make them exclaim against their own
succession?°

Rosencrantz: 'Faith, there has been much to do on both sides; and the nation holds it no sin to tarre° them to controversy: there was, for a 325
while, no money bid for argument,° unless the poet and the player
went to cuffs° in the question.°

Hamlet: Is't possible?

Guildenstern: O, there has been much throwing about of brains.

Hamlet: Do the boys carry it away?° 330

Rosencrantz: Ay, that they do, my lord; Hercules and his load° too.

Hamlet: It is not very strange; for my uncle is king of Denmark, and those
that would make mows° at him while my father lived, give twenty,
forty, fifty, a hundred ducats° a-piece for his picture in little.° 'Sblood,
there is something in this more than natural, if philosophy could find 335
it out. *A flourish [of trumpets within].*

Guildenstern: There are the players.

---

304 *residence:* Remaining in one place.   306 *inhibition:* Formal prohibition (from acting
plays in the city or, possibly, at court).   307 *innovation:* The new fashion in satirical plays
performed by boy actors in the "private" theaters.   311–331 *How . . . load:* The passage is
the famous one dealing with the War of the Theatres (1599–1602); namely, the rivalry between
the children's companies and the adult actors.   313 *aery:* Nest; *eyases:* Young hawks.
313–314 *cry . . . question:* Speak in a high key dominating conversation; clamor forth the
height of controversy; probably "excel"; perhaps intended to decry leaders of the dramatic
profession.   314 *tyrannically:* Outrageously.   315 *berattle:* Berate; *common stages:* Public
theaters.   316 *many wearing rapiers:* Many men of fashion, who were afraid to patronize the
common players for fear of being satirized by the poets who wrote for the children; *goose-quills:*
I.e., pens of satirists.   318–319 *escoted:* Maintained;   319 *quality:* Acting profession; *no
longer . . . sing:* I.e., until their voices change.   320–321 *common:* Regular, adult.   323 *succession:* Future careers.   325 *tarre:* Set on (as dogs).   326 *argument:* Probably, plot for a play.
327 *went to cuffs:* Came to blows; *question:* Controversy.   330 *carry it away:* Win the day.
331 *Hercules . . . load:* Regarded as an allusion to the sign of the Globe Theatre, which was Hercules bearing the world on his shoulder.   333 *mows:* Grimaces.   334 *ducats:* Gold coins
worth 9s. 4d; *in little:* In miniature.

Hamlet: Gentlemen, you are welcome to Elsinore. Your hands, come then: the appurtenance of welcome is fashion and ceremony: let me comply° with you in this garb,° lest my extent° to the players, which, I tell 340 you, must show fairly outwards, should more appear like entertainment than yours. You are welcome: but my uncle-father and aunt-mother are deceived.

Guildenstern: In what, my dear lord?

Hamlet: I am but mad north-north-west:° when the wind is southerly I 345 know a hawk from a handsaw.°

Enter Polonius.

Polonius: Well be with you, gentlemen!

Hamlet: Hark you, Guildenstern; and you too: at each ear a hearer: that great baby you see there is not yet out of his swaddling-clouts.°

Rosencrantz: Happily he is the second time come to them; for they say an 350 old man is twice a child.

Hamlet: I will prophesy he comes to tell me of the players; mark it. — You say right, sir: o' Monday morning;° 'twas then indeed.

Polonius: My lord, I have news to tell you.

Hamlet: My lord, I have news to tell you. When Roscius° was an actor in 355 Rome, —

Polonius: The actors are come hither, my lord.

Hamlet: Buz, buz!°

Polonius: Upon my honour, —

Hamlet: Then came each actor on his ass, — 360

Polonius: The best actors in the world, either for tragedy, comedy, history, pastoral, pastoral-comical, historical-pastoral, tragical-historical, tragical-comical-historical-pastoral, scene individable,° or poem unlimited:° Seneca° cannot be too heavy, nor Plautus° too light. For the law of writ and the liberty,° these are the only men. 365

Hamlet: O Jephthah, judge of Israel,° what a treasure hadst thou!

Polonius: What a treasure had he, my lord?

Hamlet: Why,
"One fair daughter, and no more,
    The which he loved passing well." 370

Polonius [aside]: Still on my daughter.

Hamlet: Am I not i' the right, old Jephthah?

339–340 *comply:* Observe the formalities of courtesy.   340 *garb:* Manner; *extent:* Showing of kindness.   345 *I am . . . north-north-west:* I am only partly mad, i.e., in only one point of the compass.   346 *handsaw:* A proposed reading of *hernshaw* would mean "heron"; *handsaw* may be an early corruption of *hernshaw.* Another view regards *hawk* as the variant of *hack,* a tool of the pickax type, and *handsaw* as a saw operated by hand.   349 *swaddling-clouts:* Cloths in which to wrap a newborn baby.   353 *o' Monday morning:* Said to mislead Polonius.   355 *Roscius:* A famous Roman actor.   358 *Buz, buz:* An interjection used at Oxford to denote stale news.   363 *scene individable:* A play observing the unity of place. 364 *poem unlimited:* A play disregarding the unities of time and place; *Seneca:* Writer of Latin tragedies, model of early Elizabethan writers of tragedy; *Plautus:* Writer of Latin comedy.   365 *law . . . liberty:* Pieces written according to rules and without rules, i.e., "classical" and "romantic" dramas.   366 *Jephthah . . . Israel:* Jephthah had to sacrifice his daughter; see Judges 11.

Polonius: If you call me Jephthah, my lord, I have a daughter that I love
passing° well.

Hamlet: Nay, that follows not. 375

Polonius: What follows, then, my lord?

Hamlet: Why,

"As by lot, God wot,"

and then, you know,

"It came to pass, as most like° it was," — 380

the first row° of the pious chanson° will show you more; for look,
where my abridgement comes.°

Enter the Players.

You are welcome, masters; welcome, all. I am glad to see thee well.
Welcome, good friends. O, old friend! why, thy face is valanced° since
I saw thee last: comest thou to beard me in Denmark? What, my 385
young lady and mistress! By'r lady, your ladyship is nearer to heaven
than when I saw you last, by the altitude of a chopine.° Pray God,
your voice, like a piece of uncurrent° gold, be not cracked within the
ring.° Masters, you are all welcome. We'll e'en to 't like French falcon-
ers, fly at any thing we see: we'll have a speech straight: come, give us 390
a taste of your quality; come, a passionate speech.

First Player: What speech, my good lord?

Hamlet: I heard thee speak me a speech once, but it was never acted; or, if
it was, not above once; for the play, I remember, pleased not the million; 'twas caviary to the general:° but it was — as I received it, and 395
others, whose judgements in such matters cried in the top of°
mine — an excellent play, well digested in the scenes, set down with as
much modesty as cunning.° I remember, one said there were no sal-
lets° in the lines to make the matter savoury, nor no matter in the
phrase that might indict° the author of affectation; but called it an 400
honest method, as wholesome as sweet, and by very much more handsome than fine.° One speech in 't I chiefly loved: 'twas Æneas' tale to
Dido;° and thereabout of it especially, where he speaks of Priam's
slaughter: if it live in your memory, begin at this line: let me
see, let me see — 405

"The rugged Pyrrhus,° like th' Hyrcanian beast,"° —

'tis not so: — it begins with Pyrrhus: —

374 *passing:* Surpassingly.   380 *like:* Probable.   381 *row:* Stanza; *chanson:* Ballad.
382 *abridgement comes:* Opportunity comes for cutting short the conversation.   384 *valanced:*
Fringed (with a beard).   387 *chopine:* Kind of shoe raised by the thickness of the heel;
worn in Italy, particularly at Venice.   388 *uncurrent:* Not passable as lawful coinage.
388-389 *cracked within the ring:* In the center of coins were rings enclosing the sovereign's
head; if the coin was cracked within this ring, it was unfit for currency.   395 *caviary to the
general:* Not relished by the multitude.   396 *cried in the top of:* Spoke with greater authority
than.   398 *cunning:* Skill.   398-399 *sallets:* Salads: here, spicy improprieties.   400 *indict:*
Convict.   401-402 *as wholesome . . . fine:* Its beauty was not that of elaborate ornament, but
that of order and proportion.   402-403 *Æneas' tale to Dido:* The lines recited by the player
are imitated from Marlowe and Nashe's *Dido Queen of Carthage* (II.i.214 ff.). They are written
in such a way that the conventionality of the play within a play is raised above that of ordinary drama.   406 *Pyrrhus:* A Greek hero in the Trojan War; *Hyrcanian beast:* The tiger; see
Virgil, *Aeneid,* IV.266.

> "The rugged Pyrrhus, he whose sable arms,
> Black as his purpose, did the night resemble
> When he lay couched in the ominous horse,°   410
> Hath now this dread and black complexion smear'd
> With heraldry more dismal; head to foot
> Now is he total gules;° horridly trick'd°
> With blood of fathers, mothers, daughters, sons,
> Bak'd and impasted° with the parching streets,   415
> That lend a tyrannous and a damned light
> To their lord's murder: roasted in wrath and fire,
> And thus o'er-sized° with coagulate gore,
> With eyes like carbuncles, the hellish Pyrrhus
> Old grandsire Priam seeks."   420
> So, proceed you.

Polonius: 'Fore God, my lord, well spoken, with good accent and good discretion.

First Player: "Anon he finds him
> Striking too short at Greeks; his antique sword,   425
> Rebellious to his arm, lies where it falls,
> Repugnant° to command: unequal match'd,
> Pyrrhus at Priam drives; in rage strikes wide;
> But with the whiff and wind of his fell sword
> Th' unnerved father falls. Then senseless Ilium,°   430
> Seeming to feel this blow, with flaming top
> Stoops to his base, and with a hideous crash
> Takes prisoner Pyrrhus' ear: for, lo! his sword
> Which was declining on the milky head
> Of reverend Priam, seem'd i' th' air to stick: 435
> So, as a painted tyrant,° Pyrrhus stood,
> And like a neutral to his will and matter,°
> Did nothing.
> But, as we often see, against° some storm,
> A silence in the heavens, the rack° stand still,   440
> The bold winds speechless and the orb below
> As hush as death, anon the dreadful thunder
> Doth rend the region,° so, after Pyrrhus' pause,
> Aroused vengeance sets him new a-work;
> And never did the Cyclops' hammers fall   445
> On Mars's armour forg'd for proof eterne°
> With less remorse than Pyrrhus' bleeding sword
> Now falls on Priam.
> Out, out, thou strumpet, Fortune! All you gods,
> In general synod,° take away her power;   450
> Break all the spokes and fellies° from her wheel,

---

410 *ominous horse:* Trojan horse.   413 *gules:* Red, a heraldic term; *trick'd:* Spotted, smeared.   415 *impasted:* Made into a paste.   418 *o'er-sized:* Covered as with size or glue. 427 *Repugnant:* Disobedient.   430 *Then senseless Ilium:* Insensate Troy.   436 *painted tyrant:* Tyrant in a picture.   437 *matter:* Task.   439 *against:* Before.   440 *rack:* Mass of clouds.   443 *region:* Assembly.   446 *proof eterne:* External resistance to assault. 450 *synod:* Assembly.   451 *fellies:* Pieces of wood forming the rim of a wheel.

And bowl the round nave° down the hill of heaven,
As low as to the fiends!"
Polonius: This is too long.
Hamlet: It shall to the barber's, with your beard. Prithee, say on: he's for a   455
jig° or a tale of bawdry,° or he sleeps: say on: come to Hecuba.°
First Player: "But who, ah woe! had seen the mobled° queen —"
Hamlet: "The mobled queen?"
Polonius: That's good; "mobled queen" is good.
First Player: "Run barefoot up and down, threat'ning the flames   460
With bisson rheum;° a clout° upon that head
Where late the diadem stood, and for a robe,
About her lank and all o'er-teemed° loins,
A blanket, in the alarm of fear caught up;
Who this had seen, with tongue in venom steep'd,   465
'Gainst Fortune's state would treason have pronounc'd:°
But if the gods themselves did see her then
When she saw Pyrrhus make malicious sport
In mincing with his sword her husband's limbs,
The instant burst of clamour that she made,   470
Unless things mortal move them not at all,
Would have made milch° the burning eyes of heaven,
And passion in the gods."
Polonius: Look, whe'r he has not turned° his colour and has tears in 's
eyes. Prithee, no more.   475
Hamlet: 'Tis well; I'll have thee speak out the rest soon. Good my lord, will
you see the players well bestowed? Do you hear, let them be well used;
for they are the abstract° and brief chronicles of the time: after
your death you were better have a bad epitaph than their ill report
while you live.   480
Polonius: My lord, I will use them according to their desert.
Hamlet: God's bodykins,° man, much better: use every man after his
desert, and who shall 'scape whipping? Use them after your own honour and dignity: the less they deserve, the more merit is in your
bounty. Take them in.   485
Polonius: Come, sirs.
Hamlet: Follow him, friends: we'll hear a play tomorrow. [*Aside to First
Player.*] Dost thou hear me, old friend; can you play the Murder of
Gonzago?
First Player: Ay, my lord.   490
Hamlet: We'll ha 't to-morrow night. You could, for a need, study a speech
of some dozen or sixteen lines,° which I would set down and insert
in 't, could you not?

452 *nave:* Hub.   456 *jig:* Comic performance given at the end or in an interval of a play;
bawdry: Indecency; *Hecuba:* Wife of Priam, king of Troy.   457 *mobled:* Muffled.   461 *bisson rheum:* Blinding tears; *clout:* Piece of cloth.   463 *o'er-teemed:* Worn out with bearing
children.   466 *pronounc'd:* Proclaimed.   472 *milch:* Moist with tears.   474 *turned:*
Changed.   478 *abstract:* Summary account.   482 *bodykins:* Diminutive form of the
oath "by God's body."   492 *dozen or sixteen lines:* Critics have amused themselves by trying
to locate Hamlet's lines. Lucianus's speech III.ii.229-234 is the best guess.

First Player: Ay, my lord.

Hamlet: Very well. Follow that lord; and look you mock him not. — My   495
good friends, I'll leave you till night: you are welcome to Elsinore.

                              Exeunt Polonius and Players.

Rosencrantz: Good my lord!   *Exeunt [Rosencrantz and Guildenstern.]*

Hamlet: Ay, so, God bye to you. — Now I am alone.

 O, what a rogue and peasant° slave am I!
 Is it not monstrous that this player here,   500
 But in a fiction, in a dream of passion,
 Could force his soul so to his own conceit
 That from her working all his visage wann'd,°
 Tears in his eyes, distraction in 's aspect,
 A broken voice, and his whole function suiting   505
 With forms to his conceit?° and all for nothing!
 For Hecuba!
 What's Hecuba to him, or he to Hecuba,
 That he should weep for her? What would he do,
 Had he the motive and the cue for passion   510
 That I have? He would drown the stage with tears
 And cleave the general ear with horrid speech,
 Make mad the guilty and appall the free,
 Confound the ignorant, and amaze indeed
 The very faculties of eyes and ears.   515
 Yet I,
 A dull and muddy-mettled° rascal, peak,°
 Like John-a-dreams,° unpregnant of° my cause,
 And can say nothing; no, not for a king.
 Upon whose property° and most dear life   520
 A damn'd defeat was made. Am I a coward?
 Who calls me villain? breaks my pate across?
 Plucks off my beard, and blows it in my face?
 Tweaks me by the nose? gives me the lie i' th' throat,
 As deep as to the lungs? who does me this?   525
 Ha!
 'Swounds, I should take it: for it cannot be
 But I am pigeon-liver'd° and lack gall
 To make oppression bitter, or ere this
 I should have fatted all the region kites°   530
 With this slave's offal: bloody, bawdy villain!
 Remorseless, treacherous, lecherous, kindless° villain!
 O, vengeance!
 Why, what an ass am I! This is most brave,

---

499 *peasant:* Base. 503 *wann'd:* Grew pale. 505–506 *his whole…conceit:* His whole
being responded with forms to suit his thought. 517 *muddy-mettled:* Dull-spirited; *peak:*
Mope, pine. 518 *John-a-dreams:* An expression occurring elsewhere in Elizabethan literature to indicate a dreamer; *unpregnant of:* Not quickened by. 520 *property:* Proprietorship
(of crown and life). 528 *pigeon-liver'd:* The pigeon was supposed to secrete no gall; if
Hamlet, so he says, had had gall, he would have felt the bitterness of oppression, and
avenged it. 530 *region kites:* Kites of the air. 532 *kindless:* Unnatural.

That I, the son of a dear father murder'd,   535
Prompted to my revenge by heaven and hell,
Must, like a whore, unpack my heart with words,
And fall a-cursing, like a very drab,°
A stallion!°
Fie upon 't! foh! About,° my brains! Hum, I have heard   540
That guilty creatures sitting at a play
Have by the very cunning of the scene
Been struck so to the soul that presently
They have proclaim'd their malefactions;
For murder, though it have no tongue, will speak   545
With most miraculous organ. I'll have these players
Play something like the murder of my father
Before mine uncle: I'll observe his looks:
I'll tent° him to the quick: if 'a do blench,°
I know my course. The spirit that I have seen   550
May be the devil:° and the devil hath power
T' assume a pleasing shape; yea, and perhaps
Out of my weakness and my melancholy,
As he is very potent with such spirits,°
Abuses me to damn me: I'll have grounds   555
More relative° than this:° the play's the thing
Wherein I'll catch the conscience of the king.   *Exit.*

[ACT III

SCENE I: *A room in the castle.*]

Enter King, Queen, Polonius, Ophelia, Rosencrantz, Guildenstern, Lords.

King: And can you, by no drift of conference,°
    Get from him why he puts on this confusion,
    Grating so harshly all his days of quiet
    With turbulent and dangerous lunacy?
Rosencrantz: He does confess he feels himself distracted;   5
    But from what cause 'a will by no means speak.
Guildenstern: Nor do we find him forward° to be sounded,
    But, with a crafty madness, keeps aloof,
    When we would bring him on to some confession
    Of his true state.
Queen: Did he receive you well?   10
Rosencrantz: Most like a gentleman.
Guildenstern: But with much forcing of his disposition.°

---

538 *drab:* Prostitute.   539 *stallion:* Prostitute (male or female).   540 *About:* About it, or turn thou right about.   549 *tent:* Probe; *blench:* Quail, flinch.   551 *May be the devil:* Hamlet's suspicion is properly grounded in the belief of the time.   554 *spirits:* Humors.   556 *relative:* Closely related, definite; *this:* I.e., the ghost's story. **Act III, Scene I.**   1 *drift of conference:* Device of conversation.   7 *forward:* Willing.   12 *forcing of his disposition:* I.e., against his will.

Rosencrantz: Niggard of question;° but, of our demands,
    Most free in his reply.
Queen: Did you assay° him
    To any pastime?   15
Rosencrantz: Madam, it so fell out, that certain players
    We o'er-raught° on the way: of these we told him;
    And there did seem in him a kind of joy
    To hear of it: they are here about the court,
    And, as I think, they have already order   20
    This night to play before him.
Polonius: 'Tis most true:
    And he beseech'd me to entreat your majesties
    To hear and see the matter.
King: With all my heart; and it doth much content me
    To hear him so inclin'd.   25
    Good gentlemen, give him a further edge,°
    And drive his purpose into these delights.
Rosencrantz: We shall, my lord.   *Exeunt Rosencrantz and Guildenstern.*
King: Sweet Gertrude, leave us too;
    For we have closely° sent for Hamlet hither,
    That he, as 'twere by accident, may here   30
    Affront° Ophelia:
    Her father and myself, lawful espials,°
    Will so bestow ourselves that, seeing, unseen,
    We may of their encounter frankly judge,
    And gather by him, as he is behav'd,   35
    If 't be th' affliction of his love or no
    That thus he suffers for.
Queen: I shall obey you.
    And for your part, Ophelia, I do wish
    That your good beauties be the happy cause
    Of Hamlet's wildness:° so shall I hope your virtues   40
    Will bring him to his wonted way again,
    To both your honours.
Ophelia: Madam, I wish it may.   *[Exit Queen.]*
Polonius: Ophelia, walk you here. Gracious,° so please you,
    We will bestow ourselves. *[To Ophelia.]* Read on this book;
    That show of such an exercise° may colour°   45
    Your loneliness. We are oft to blame in this, —
    'Tis too much prov'd — that with devotion's visage
    And pious action we do sugar o'er
    The devil himself.
King: *[aside]* O, 'tis too true!
    How smart a lash that speech doth give my conscience!   50

---

13 *Niggard of question:* Sparing of conversation.   14 *assay:* Try to win.   17 *o'er-raught:* Overtook.   26 *edge:* Incitement.   29 *closely:* Secretly.   31 *Affront:* Confront.   32 *lawful espials:* Legitimate spies.   40 *wildness:* Madness.   43 *Gracious:* Your grace (addressed to the king).   45 *exercise:* Act of devotion (the book she reads is one of devotion); *colour:* Give a plausible appearance to.

The harlot's cheek, beautied with plast'ring art,
Is not more ugly to° the thing° that helps it
Than is my deed to my most painted word:
O heavy burthen!

Polonius: I hear him coming: let's withdraw, my lord.   55

[Exeunt King and Polonius.]

Enter Hamlet.

Hamlet: To be, or not to be: that is the question:
Whether 'tis nobler in the mind to suffer
The slings and arrows of outrageous fortune,
Or to take arms against a sea° of troubles,
And by opposing end them? To die: to sleep;   60
No more; and by a sleep to say we end
The heart-ache and the thousand natural shocks
That flesh is heir to, 'tis a consummation
Devoutly to be wish'd. To die, to sleep;
To sleep: perchance to dream: ay, there's the rub;   65
For in that sleep of death what dreams may come
When we have shuffled° off this mortal coil,°
Must give us pause: there's the respect°
That makes calamity of so long life;°
For who would bear the whips and scorns of time,°   70
Th' oppressor's wrong, the proud man's contumely,
The pangs of despis'd° love, the law's delay,
The insolence of office° and the spurns°
That patient merit of th' unworthy takes,
When he himself might his quietus° make   75
With a bare bodkin?° who would fardels° bear,
To grunt and sweat under a weary life,
But that the dread of something after death,
The undiscover'd country from whose bourn°
No traveller returns, puzzles the will   80
And makes us rather bear those ills we have
Than fly to others that we know not of?
Thus conscience° does make cowards of us all;
And thus the native hue° of resolution
Is sicklied o'er° with the pale cast° of thought,   85
And enterprises of great pitch° and moment°

---

52 *to:* Compared to; *thing:* I.e., the cosmetic.   59 *sea:* The mixed metaphor of this speech
has often been commented on; a later emendation *siege* has sometimes been spoken on
the stage.   67 *shuffled:* Sloughed, cast; *coil:* Usually means "turmoil"; here, possibly
"body" (conceived of as wound about the soul like rope); *clay, soil, veil,* have been suggested as
emendations.   68 *respect:* Consideration.   69 *of . . . life:* So long-lived.   70 *time:* The
world.   72 *despis'd:* Rejected.   73 *office:* Office-holders; *spurns:* Insults.   75 *quietus:*
Acquittance; here, death.   76 *bare bodkin:* Mere dagger; *bare* is sometimes understood as
"unsheathed"; *fardels:* Burdens.   79 *bourn:* Boundary.   83 *conscience:* Probably, inhibition by the faculty of reason restraining the will from doing wrong.   84 *native hue:* Natural color; metaphor derived from the color of the face.   85 *sicklied o'er:* Given a sickly
tinge; *cast:* Shade of color.   86 *pitch:* Height (as of a falcon's flight); *moment:* Importance.

With this regard° their currents° turn awry,
And lose the name of action — Soft you now!
The fair Ophelia! Nymph, in thy orisons°
Be all my sins rememb'red.

Ophelia: Good my lord, 90
How does your honour for this many a day?

Hamlet: I humbly thank you; well, well, well.

Ophelia: My lord, I have remembrances of yours,
That I have longed long to re-deliver;
I pray you, now receive them.

Hamlet: No, not I; 95
I never gave you aught.

Ophelia: My honour'd lord, you know right well you did;
And, with them, words of so sweet breath compos'd
As made the things more rich: their perfume lost,
Take these again; for to the noble mind 100
Rich gifts wax poor when givers prove unkind.
There, my lord.

Hamlet: Ha, ha! are you honest?°

Ophelia: My lord?

Hamlet: Are you fair? 105

Ophelia: What means your lordship?

Hamlet: That if you be honest and fair, your honesty° should admit no
discourse to° your beauty.

Ophelia: Could beauty, my lord, have better commerce° than with honesty?

Hamlet: Ay, truly; for the power of beauty will sooner transform honesty 110
from what it is to a bawd than the force of honesty can translate beauty into his likeness: this was sometime a paradox, but now
the time° gives it proof. I did love you once.

Ophelia: Indeed, my lord, you made me believe so.

Hamlet: You should not have believed me; for virtue cannot so inoculate° 115
our old stock but we shall relish of it:° I loved you not.

Ophelia: I was the more deceived.

Hamlet: Get thee to a nunnery: why wouldst thou be a breeder of sinners?
I am myself indifferent honest;° but yet I could accuse me of such
things that it were better my mother had not borne me: I am very 120
proud, revengeful, ambitious, with more offences at my beck° than I
have thoughts to put them in, imagination to give them shape, or
time to act them in. What should such fellows as I do crawling between earth and heaven? We are arrant knaves, all; believe none of us.
Go thy ways to a nunnery. Where's your father? 125

---

87 *regard:* Respect, consideration; *currents:* Courses. 89 *orisons:* Prayers. 103–108 *are
you honest . . . beauty: Honest* meaning "truthful" and "chaste" and *fair* meaning "just, honorable" (line 105) and "beautiful" (line 107) are not mere quibbles; the speech has the irony of a
double entendre. 107 *your honesty:* Your chastity. 108 *discourse to:* Familiar intercourse
with. 109 *commerce:* Intercourse. 113 *the time:* The present age. 115 *inoculate:* Graft
(metaphorical). 116 *but . . . it:* I.e., that we do not still have about us a taste of the old
stock; i.e., retain our sinfulness. 119 *indifferent honest:* Moderately virtuous. 121 *beck:*
Command.

Ophelia: At home, my lord.

Hamlet: Let the doors be shut upon him, that he may play the fool no where but in 's own house. Farewell.

Ophelia: O, help him, you sweet heavens!

Hamlet: If thou dost marry, I'll give thee this plague for thy dowry: be 130
thou as chaste as ice, as pure as snow, thou shalt not escape calumny.
Get thee to a nunnery, go: farewell. Or, if thou wilt needs marry,
marry a fool; for wise men know well enough what monsters° you
make of them. To a nunnery, go, and quickly too. Farewell.

Ophelia: O heavenly powers, restore him!   135

Hamlet: I have heard of your° paintings too, well enough; God hath given
you one face, and you make yourselves another: you jig,° you amble,
and you lisp; you nick-name God's creatures, and make your wantonness your ignorance.° Go to, I'll no more on 't; it hath made me mad. I
say, we will have no moe marriage: those that are married already, all 140
but one,° shall live; the rest shall keep as they are. To a nunnery, go.

Exit.

Ophelia: O, what a noble mind is here o'er-thrown!
The courtier's, soldier's, scholar's, eye, tongue, sword;
Th' expectancy and rose° of the fair state,
The glass of fashion and the mould of form,°   145
Th' observ'd of all observers,° quite, quite down!
And I, of ladies most deject and wretched,
That suck'd the honey of his music vows,
Now see that noble and most sovereign reason,
Like sweet bells jangled, out of time and harsh;   150
That unmatch'd form and feature of blown° youth
Blasted with ecstasy:° O, woe is me,
T' have seen what I have seen, see what I see!

Enter King and Polonius.

King: Love! his affections do not that way tend;
Nor what he spake, though it lack'd form a little,   155
Was not like madness. There's something in his soul,
O'er which his melancholy sits on brood;
And I do doubt° the hatch and the disclose°
Will be some danger: which for to prevent,
I have in quick determination   160
Thus set it down: he shall with speed to England,
For the demand of our neglected tribute:
Haply the seas and countries different
With variable° objects shall expel

---

133 *monsters:* An allusion to the horns of a cuckold.   136 *your:* Indefinite use.   137 *jig:*
Move with jerky motion; probably allusion to the *jig,* or song and dance, of the current stage.
138–139 *make . . . ignorance:* I.e., excuse your wantonness on the ground of your ignorance.
141 *one:* I.e., the king.   144 *expectancy and rose:* Source of hope.   145 *The glass . . . form:*
The mirror of fashion and the pattern of courtly behavior.   146 *observ'd . . . observers:* I.e.,
the center of attention in the court.   151 *blown:* Blooming.   152 *ecstasy:* Madness.
158 *doubt:* Fear; *disclose:* Disclosure or revelation (by chipping of the shell).   164 *variable:*
Various.

This something-settled° matter in his heart,   165
Whereon his brains still beating puts him thus
From fashion of himself.° What think you on 't?

Polonius: It shall do well: but yet do I believe
The origin and commencement of his grief
Sprung from neglected love. How now, Ophelia!   170
You need not tell us what Lord Hamlet said;
We heard it all. My lord, do as you please;
But, if you hold it fit, after the play
Let his queen mother all alone entreat him
To show his grief: let her be round° with him;   175
And I'll be plac'd, so please you, in the ear
Of all their conference. If she find him not,
To England send him, or confine him where
Your wisdom best shall think.

King: It shall be so: 180
Madness in great ones must not unwatch'd go.   *Exeunt.*

[SCENE II: *A hall in the castle.*]

Enter Hamlet and three of the Players.

Hamlet: Speak the speech, I pray you, as I pronounced it to you, trippingly on the tongue: but if you mouth it, as many of your° players do, I had as lief the town-crier spoke my lines. Nor do not saw the
air too much with your hand, thus, but use all gently; for in the very
torrent, tempest, and, as I may say, whirlwind of your passion, you   5
must acquire and beget a temperance that may give it smoothness.
O, it offends me to the soul to hear a robustious° periwig-pated° fellow tear a passion to tatters, to very rags, to split the ears of the
groundlings,° who for the most part are capable of° nothing but
inexplicable° dumb-shows and noise: I would have such a fellow   10
whipped for o'er-doing Termagant;° it out-herods Herod:° pray you,
avoid it.

First Player: I warrant your honour.

Hamlet: Be not too tame neither, but let your own discretion be your
tutor: suit the action to the word, the word to the action; with this   15
special observance, that you o'er-step not the modesty of nature: for
any thing so overdone is from the purpose of playing, whose end,
both at the first and now, was and is, to hold, as 't were, the mirror up
to nature; to show virtue her own feature, scorn her own image, and
the very age and body of the time his form and pressure.° Now this   20

---

165 *something-settled:* Somewhat settled.   167 *From . . . himself:* Out of his natural manner.
175 *round:* Blunt.   **Scene II.**   2 *your:* Indefinite use.   7 *robustious:* Violent, boisterous; *periwig-pated:* Wearing a wig.   9 *groundlings:* Those who stood in the yard of the theater; *capable of:* Susceptible of being influenced by.   10 *inexplicable:* Of no significance
worth explaining.   11 *Termagant:* A god of the Saracens; a character in the St. Nicholas
play, where one of his worshipers, leaving him in charge of goods, returns to find them
stolen; whereupon he beats the god (or idol), which howls vociferously; *Herod:* Herod of
Jewry; a character in *The Slaughter of the Innocents* and other cycle plays. The part was played
with great noise and fury.   20 *pressure:* Stamp, impressed character.

overdone, or come tardy off,° though it make the unskilful laugh,
cannot but make the judicious grieve; the censure of the which one°
must in your allowance o'erweigh a whole theatre of others. O, there
be players that I have seen play, and heard others praise, and that
highly, not to speak it profanely, that, neither having the accent of   25
Christians nor the gait of Christian, pagan, nor man, have so strut-
ted and bellowed that I have thought some of nature's journeymen°
had made men and not made them well, they imitated humanity so
abominably.

First Player: I hope we have reformed that indifferently° with us, sir.   30

Hamlet: O, reform it altogether. And let those that play your clowns speak
no more than is set down for them; for there be of° them that will
themselves laugh, to set on some quantity of barren° spectators to
laugh too; though, in the mean time, some necessary question of the
play be then to be considered: that's villanous, and shows a most   35
pitiful ambition in the fool that uses it. Go, make you ready.

[Exeunt Players.]

Enter Polonius, Guildenstern, and Rosencrantz.

How now, my lord! will the king hear this piece of work?

Polonius: And the queen too, and that presently.

Hamlet: Bid the players make haste.   *[Exit Polonius.]*
Will you two help to hasten them?   40

Rosencrantz:
Guildenstern: } We will, my lord.   *Exeunt they two.*

Hamlet: What ho! Horatio!

Enter Horatio.

Horatio: Here, sweet lord, at your service.

Hamlet: Horatio, thou art e'en as just° a man
As e'er my conversation cop'd withal.

Horatio: O, my dear lord, —

Hamlet: Nay, do not think I flatter;   45
For what advancement may I hope from thee
That no revenue hast but thy good spirits,
To feed and clothe thee? Why should the poor be flatter'd?
No, let the candied tongue lick absurd pomp,
And crook the pregnant° hinges of the knee   50
Where thrift° may follow fawning. Dost thou hear?
Since my dear soul was mistress of her choice
And could of men distinguish her election,
S' hath seal'd thee for herself; for thou hast been
As one, in suff'ring all, that suffers nothing,   55
A man that fortune's buffets and rewards
Hast ta'en with equal thanks: and blest are those
Whose blood and judgement are so well commeddled,

---

21 *come tardy off:* Inadequately done.   22 *the censure . . . one:* The judgment of even one of
whom.   27 *journeymen:* Laborers not yet masters in their trade.   30 *indifferently:* Fairly,
tolerably.   32 *of:* I.e., some among them.   33 *barren:* I.e., of wit.   43 *just:* Honest,
honorable.   50 *pregnant:* Pliant.   51 *thrift:* Profit.

That they are not a pipe for fortune's finger
To sound what stop° she please. Give me that man   60
That is not passion's slave, and I will wear him
In my heart's core, ay, in my heart of heart,
As I do thee. — Something too much of this. —
There is a play to-night before the king;
One scene of it comes near the circumstance   65
Which I have told thee of my father's death:
I prithee, when thou seest that act afoot,
Even with the very comment of thy soul°
Observe my uncle: if his occulted° guilt
Do not itself unkennel in one speech,   70
It is a damned° ghost that we have seen,
And my imaginations are as foul
As Vulcan's stithy.° Give him heedful note;
For I mine eyes will rivet to his face,
And after we will both our judgements join   75
In censure of his seeming.°

Horatio: Well, my lord:
If 'a steal aught the whilst this play is playing,
And 'scape detecting, I will pay the theft.

*Enter trumpets and kettledrums, King, Queen, Polonius, Ophelia,
[Rosencrantz, Guildenstern, and others].*

Hamlet: They are coming to the play; I must be idle:° Get you a place.
King: How fares our cousin Hamlet?   80
Hamlet: Excellent, i' faith; of the chameleon's dish:° I eat the air, promise-
crammed: you cannot feed capons so.
King: I have nothing with° this answer, Hamlet; these words are not
mine.°
Hamlet: No, nor mine now. *[To Polonius.]* My lord, you played once i' the   85
university, you say?
Polonius: That did I, my lord; and was accounted a good actor.
Hamlet: What did you enact?
Polonius: I did enact Julius Cæsar: I was killed i' the Capitol; Brutus
killed me.   90
Hamlet: It was a brute part of him to kill so capital a calf there. Be the
players ready?
Rosencrantz: Ay, my lord; they stay upon your patience.
Queen: Come hither, my dear Hamlet, sit by me.
Hamlet: No, good mother, here's metal more attractive.   95
Polonius [to the king]: O, ho! do you mark that?
Hamlet: Lady, shall I lie in your lap?   *[Lying down at Ophelia's feet.]*

---

60 *stop:* Hole in a wind instrument for controlling the sound.   68 *very . . . soul:* Inward
and sagacious criticism.   69 *occulted:* Hidden.   71 *damned:* In league with Satan.
73 *stithy:* Smithy, place of *stiths* (anvils).   76 *censure . . . seeming:* Judgment of his appearance or behavior.   79 *idle:* Crazy, or not attending to anything serious.   81 *chameleon's
dish:* Chameleons were supposed to feed on air. (Hamlet deliberately misinterprets the king's
"fares" as "feeds.")   83 *have . . . with:* Make nothing of.   83–84 *are not mine:* Do not respond to what I ask.

Ophelia: No, my lord.
Hamlet: I mean, my head upon your lap?
Ophelia: Ay, my lord.   100
Hamlet: Do you think I meant country° matters?
Ophelia: I think nothing, my lord.
Hamlet: That's a fair thought to lie between maids' legs.
Ophelia: What is, my lord?
Hamlet: Nothing.   105
Ophelia: You are merry, my lord.
Hamlet: Who, I?
Ophelia: Ay, my lord.
Hamlet: O God, your only° jig-maker.° What should a man do but be
merry? for, look you, how cheerfully my mother looks, and my father   110
died within's two hours.
Ophelia: Nay, 'tis twice two months, my lord.
Hamlet: So long? Nay then, let the devil wear black, for I'll have a suit of
sables.° O heavens! die two months ago, and not forgotten yet? Then
there's hope a great man's memory may outlive his life half a year: 115
but, by 'r lady, 'a must build churches, then; or else shall 'a suffer not
thinking on,° with the hobbyhorse, whose epitaph is "For, O, for, O,
the hobbyhorse is forgot."°

The trumpets sound. Dumb show follows.

*Enter a King and a Queen [very lovingly]; the Queen embracing him,
and he her. [She kneels, and makes show of protestation unto him.] He takes
her up, and declines his head upon her neck: he lies him down upon a bank of
flowers: she, seeing him asleep, leaves him. Anon comes in another man, takes
off his crown, kisses it, pours poison in the sleeper's ears, and leaves him. The
Queen returns; finds the King dead, makes passionate action. The Poisoner,
with some three or four come in again, seem to condole with her. The dead
body is carried away. The Poisoner woos the Queen with gifts: she seems harsh
awhile, but in the end accepts love. [Exeunt.]*

Ophelia: What means this, my lord?
Hamlet: Marry, this is miching mallecho;° it means mischief.   120
Ophelia: Belike this show imports the argument of the play.

Enter Prologue.

Hamlet: We shall know by this fellow: the players cannot keep counsel;
they'll tell all.
Ophelia: Will 'a tell us what this show meant?
Hamlet: Ay, or any show that you'll show him: be not you ashamed to   125
show, he'll not shame to tell you what it means.
Ophelia: You are naught, you are naught:° I'll mark the play.
Prologue: For us, and for our tragedy,

---

101 *country:* With a bawdy pun.   109 *your only:* Only your; *jig-maker:* Composer of jigs
(song and dance).   113-114 *suit of sables:* Garments trimmed with the fur of the sable, with
a quibble on *sable* meaning "black."   116-117 *suffer...on:* Undergo oblivion.
117-118 *"For...forgot":* Verse of a song occurring also in *Love's Labour's Lost*, III.i.30. The
hobbyhorse was a character in the Morris Dance.   120 *miching mallecho:* Sneaking mischief.   127 *naught:* Indecent.

                    Here stooping° to your clemency,
                    We beg your hearing patiently.   *[Exit.]*   130
Hamlet: Is this a prologue, or the posy° of a ring?
Ophelia: 'Tis brief, my lord.
Hamlet: As woman's love.

         Enter [two Players as] King and Queen.

Player King: Full thirty times hath Phoebus' cart gone round
                Neptune's salt wash° and Tellus'° orbed ground,   135
                And thirty dozen moons with borrowed° sheen
                About the world have times twelve thirties been,
                Since love our hearts and Hymen° did our hands
                Unite commutual° in most sacred bands.
Player Queen: So many journeys may the sun and moon   140
                Make us again count o'er ere love be done!
                But, woe is me, you are so sick of late,
                So far from cheer and from your former state,
                That I distrust° you. Yet, though I distrust,
                Discomfort you, my lord, it nothing must: 145
                For women's fear and love holds quantity;°
                In neither aught, or in extremity.
                Now, what my love is, proof hath made you know;
                And as my love is siz'd, my fear is so:
                Where love is great, the littlest doubts are fear;   150
                Where little fears grow great, great love grows there.
Player King: 'Faith, I must leave thee, love, and shortly too;
                My operant° powers their functions leave° to do:
                And thou shalt live in this fair world behind,
                Honour'd, belov'd; and haply one as kind   155
                For husband shalt thou—
Player Queen: O, confound the rest!
                Such love must needs be treason in my breast:
                In second husband let me be accurst!
                None wed the second but who kill'd the first.
Hamlet (aside): Wormwood, wormwood.   160
Player Queen: The instances that second marriage move
                Are base respects of thrift, but none of love:
                A second time I kill my husband dead,
                When second husband kisses me in bed.
Player King: I do believe you think what now you speak;   165
                But what we do determine oft we break.
                Purpose is but the slave to memory,
                Of violent birth, but poor validity:
                Which now, like fruit unripe, sticks on the tree;
                But fall, unshaken, when they mellow be.   170
                Most necessary 'tis that we forget

---

129 *stooping:* Bowing.   131 *posy:* Motto.   135 *salt wash:* The sea; *Tellus:* Goddess of the
earth *(orbed ground).*   136 *borrowed:* I.e., reflected.   138 *Hymen:* God of matrimony.
139 *commutual:* Mutually.   144 *distrust:* Am anxious about.   146 *holds quantity:* Keeps
proportion between.   153 *operant:* Active; *leave:* Cease.

To pay ourselves what to ourselves is debt:
What to ourselves in passion we propose,
The passion ending, doth the purpose lose.
The violence of either grief or joy   175
Their own enactures° with themselves destroy:
Where joy most revels, grief doth most lament;
Grief joys, joy grieves, on slender accident.
This world is not for aye,° nor 'tis not strange
That even our loves should with our fortunes change;   180
For 'tis a question left us yet to prove,
Whether love lead fortune, or else fortune love.
The great man down, you mark his favourite flies;
The poor advanc'd makes friends of enemies.
And hitherto doth love on fortune tend;   185
For who° not needs shall never lack a friend,
And who in want a hollow friend doth try,
Directly seasons° him his enemy.
But, orderly to end where I begun,
Our wills and fates do so contrary run   190
That our devices still are overthrown;
Our thoughts are ours, their ends° none of our own:
So think thou wilt no second husband wed;
But die thy thoughts when thy first lord is dead.

Player Queen: Nor earth to me give food, nor heaven light!   195
Sport and repose lock from me day and night!
To desperation turn my trust and hope!
An anchor's° cheer° in prison be my scope!
Each opposite° that blanks° the face of joy
Meet what I would have well and it destroy!   200
Both here and hence pursue me lasting strife,
If, once a widow, ever I be wife!

Hamlet: If she should break it now!

Player King: 'Tis deeply sworn. Sweet, leave me here awhile;
My spirits grow dull, and fain I would beguile   205
The tedious day with sleep.   *[Sleeps.]*

Player Queen: Sleep rock thy brain;
And never come mischance between us twain!   *Exit.*

Hamlet: Madam, how like you this play?

Queen: The lady doth protest too much, methinks.

Hamlet: O, but she'll keep her word.   210

King: Have you heard the argument? Is there no offence in 't?

Hamlet: No, no, they do but jest, poison in jest; no offence i' the world.

King: What do you call the play?

Hamlet: The Mouse-trap. Marry, how? Tropically.° This play is the image
of a murder done in Vienna: Gonzago° is the duke's name; his wife,   215

---

176 *enactures:* Fulfillments.   179 *aye:* Ever.   186 *who:* Whoever.   188 *seasons:* Matures, ripens.   192 *ends:* Results.   198 *An anchor's:* An anchorite's; *cheer:* Fare; sometimes printed as *chair.*   199 *opposite:* Adverse thing; *blanks:* Causes to *blanch* or grow pale.
214 *Tropically:* Figuratively, *trapically* suggests a pun on *trap* in *Mouse-trap* (l. 214).   215 *Gonzago:* In 1538 Luigi Gonzago murdered the Duke of Urbano by pouring poisoned lotion in his ears.

Baptista: you shall see anon; 't is a knavish piece of work: but what o'
that? your majesty and we that have free souls, it touches us not: let
the galled jade° winch,° our withers° are unwrung.°

Enter Lucianus.

This is one Lucianus, nephew to the king.

Ophelia: You are as good as a chorus,° my lord.   220

Hamlet: I could interpret between you and your love, if I could see the
    puppets dallying.°

Ophelia: You are keen, my lord, you are keen.

Hamlet: It would cost you a groaning to take off my edge.

Ophelia: Still better, and worse.°   225

Hamlet: So you mistake° your husbands. Begin, murderer; pox,° leave thy
    damnable faces, and begin. Come: the croaking raven doth bellow for
    revenge.

Lucianus: Thoughts black, hands apt, drugs fit, and time agreeing;
    Confederate° season, else no creature seeing;   230
    Thou mixture rank, of midnight weeds collected,
    With Hecate's° ban° thrice blasted, thrice infected,
    Thy natural magic and dire property,
    On wholesome life usurp immediately.

                        [Pours the poison into the sleeper's ears.]

Hamlet: 'A poisons him i' the garden for his estate. His name's Gonzago: 235
    the story is extant, and written in very choice Italian: you shall see
    anon how the murderer gets the love of Gonzago's wife.

Ophelia: The king rises.

Hamlet: What, frighted with false fire!°

Queen: How fares my lord?   240

Polonius: Give o'er the play.

King: Give me some light: away!

Polonius: Lights, lights, lights!   *Exeunt all but Hamlet and Horatio.*

Hamlet: Why, let the strucken deer go weep,
    The hart ungalled play;   245
  For some must watch, while some must sleep:
    Thus runs the world away.°
  Would not this,° sir, and a forest of feathers° — if the rest of my fortunes turn Turk with° me — with two Provincial roses° on my razed°
  shoes, get me a fellowship in a cry° of players,° sir?   250

218 *galled jade:* Horse whose hide is rubbed by saddle or harness; *winch:* Wince; *withers:* The
part between the horse's shoulder blades; *unwrung:* Not wrung or twisted.   220 *chorus:* In
many Elizabethan plays the action was explained by an actor known as the "chorus"; at a puppet show the actor who explained the action was known as an "interpreter," as indicated by
the lines following.   222 *dallying:* With sexual suggestion, continued in *keen* (sexually
aroused), *groaning* (i.e., in pregnancy), and *edge* (i.e., sexual desire or impetuosity).
225 *Still . . . worse:* More keen, less decorous.   226 *mistake:* Err in taking; *pox:* An impreca-
tion.   230 *Confederate:* Conspiring (to assist the murderer).   232 *Hecate:* The goddess of
witchcraft; *ban:* Curse.   239 *false fire:* Fireworks, or a blank discharge.   244–247 *Why . . .
away:* Probably from an old ballad, with allusion to the popular belief that a wounded deer
retires to weep and die. Cf. *As You Like It*, II.i.66.   248 *this:* I.e., the play; *feathers:* Allusion to
the plumes which Elizabethan actors were fond of wearing.   249 *turn Turk with:* Go back
on; *two Provincial roses:* Rosettes of ribbon like the roses of Provins near Paris, or else the
roses of Provence; *razed:* Cut, slashed (by way of ornament).   250 *cry:* Pack (as of
hounds); *fellowship . . . players:* Partnership in a theatrical company.

Horatio: Half a share.°
Hamlet: A whole one, I.
    For thou dost know, O Damon dear,
      This realm dismantled° was
    Of Jove himself; and now reigns here   255
      A very, very° — pajock.°
Horatio: You might have rhymed.
Hamlet: O good Horatio, I'll take the ghost's word for a thousand pound.
    Didst perceive?
Horatio: Very well, my lord.   260
Hamlet: Upon the talk of the poisoning?
Horatio: I did very well note him.
Hamlet: Ah, ha! Come, some music! come, the recorders!°
    For if the king like not the comedy,
    Why then, belike, he likes it not, perdy.°   265
    Come, some music!

    Enter Rosencrantz and Guildenstern.

Guildenstern: Good my lord, vouchsafe me a word with you.
Hamlet: Sir, a whole history.
Guildenstern: The king, sir, —
Hamlet: Ay, sir, what of him?   270
Guildenstern: Is in his retirement marvellous distempered.
Hamlet: With drink, sir?
Guildenstern: No, my lord, rather with choler.°
Hamlet: Your wisdom should show itself more richer to signify this to
    his doctor; for, for me to put him to his purgation would perhaps 275
    plunge him into far more choler.
Guildenstern: Good my lord, put your discourse into some frame° and
    start not so wildly from my affair.
Hamlet: I am tame, sir: pronounce.
Guildenstern: The queen, your mother, in most great affliction of spirit, 280
    hath sent me to you.
Hamlet: You are welcome.
Guildenstern: Nay, good my lord, this courtesy is not of the right breed. If
    it shall please you to make me a wholesome° answer, I will do your
    mother's commandment; if not, your pardon and my return shall be 285
    the end of my business.
Hamlet: Sir, I cannot.
Guildenstern: What, my lord?
Hamlet: Make you a wholesome answer; my wit's diseased: but, sir, such
    answer as I can make, you shall command; or, rather, as you say, my 290
    mother: therefore no more, but to the matter:° my mother, you say, —

---

251 *Half a share:* Allusion to the custom in dramatic companies of dividing the ownership into a number of shares among the householders.   254 *dismantled:* Stripped, divested. 253-256 *For... very:* Probably from an old ballad having to do with Damon and Pythias. 256 *pajock:* Peacock (a bird with a bad reputation). Possibly the word was *patchock,* diminutive of *patch,* clown.   263 *recorders:* Wind instruments of the flute kind.   265 *perdy:* Corruption of *par dieu.*   273 *choler:* Bilious disorder, with quibble on the sense "anger." 277 *frame:* Order.   284 *wholesome:* Sensible.   291 *matter:* Matter in hand.

Rosencrantz: Then thus she says; your behaviour hath struck her into amazement and admiration.

Hamlet: O wonderful son, that can so 'stonish a mother! But is there no sequel at the heels of this mother's admiration? Impart.   295

Rosencrantz: She desires to speak with you in her closet, ere you go to bed.

Hamlet: We shall obey, were she ten times our mother. Have you any further trade with us?

Rosencrantz: My lord, you once did love me.

Hamlet: And do still, by these pickers and stealers.°   300

Rosencrantz: Good my lord, what is your cause of distemper? you do, surely, bar the door upon your own liberty, if you deny your griefs to your friend.

Hamlet: Sir, I lack advancement.

Rosencrantz: How can that be, when you have the voice° of the king himself for your succession in Denmark?   305

Hamlet: Ay, sir, but "While the grass grows,"° — the proverb is something musty.

Enter the Players with recorders.

O, the recorders! let me see one. To withdraw° with you: — why do you go about to recover the wind° of me, as if you would drive me into a toil?°   310

Guildenstern: O, my lord, if my duty be too bold, my love is too unmannerly.°

Hamlet: I do not well understand that. Will you play upon this pipe?

Guildenstern: My lord, I cannot.   315

Hamlet: I pray you.

Guildenstern: Believe me, I cannot.

Hamlet: I beseech you.

Guildenstern: I know no touch of it, my lord.

Hamlet: 'Tis as easy as lying: govern these ventages° with your fingers and thumb, give it breath with your mouth, and it will discourse most eloquent music. Look you, these are the stops.   320

Guildenstern: But these cannot I command to any utterance of harmony; I have not the skill.

Hamlet: Why, look you now, how unworthy a thing you make of me! You would play upon me; you would seem to know my stops; you would pluck out the heart of my mystery; you would sound me from my lowest note to the top of my compass:° and there is much music, excellent voice, in this little organ;° yet cannot you make it speak. 'Sblood, do you think I am easier to be played on than a pipe? Call me what instrument you will, though you can fret° me, you cannot play upon me.   325   330

300 *pickers and stealers:* Hands, so called from the catechism "to keep my hands from picking and stealing."   305 *voice:* Support.   307 *"While...grows":* The rest of the proverb is "the silly horse starves." Hamlet may be destroyed while he is waiting for the succession to the kingdom.   309 *withdraw:* Speak in private.   310 *recover the wind:* Get to the windward side.   311 *toil:* Snare.   312–313 *if...unmannerly:* If I am using an unmannerly boldness, it is my love which occasions it.   320 *ventages:* Stops of the recorders.   328 *compass:* Range of voice.   329 *organ:* Musical instrument, i.e., the pipe.   331 *fret:* Quibble on meaning "irritate" and the piece of wood, gut, or metal which regulates the fingering.

Enter Polonius.

God bless you, sir!

Polonius: My lord, the queen would speak with you, and presently.

Hamlet: Do you see yonder cloud that 's almost in shape of a camel? 335

Polonius: By the mass, and 'tis like a camel, indeed.

Hamlet: Methinks it is like a weasel.

Polonius: It is backed like a weasel.

Hamlet: Or like a whale?

Polonius: Very like a whale. 340

Hamlet: Then I will come to my mother by and by. *[Aside.]* They fool me to
    the top of my bent.° — I will come by and by.°

Polonius: I will say so. *[Exit.]*

Hamlet: By and by is easily said.

    Leave me, friends. *[Exeunt all but Hamlet.]* 345

    'Tis now the very witching time° of night,

    When churchyards yawn and hell itself breathes out

    Contagion to this world: now could I drink hot blood,

    And do such bitter business as the day

    Would quake to look on. Soft! now to my mother. 350

    O heart, lose not thy nature; let not ever

    The soul of Nero° enter this firm bosom:

    Let me be cruel, not unnatural:

    I will speak daggers to her, but use none;

    My tongue and soul in this be hypocrites; 355

    How in my words somever she be shent,°

    To give them seals° never, my soul, consent! *Exit.*

[SCENE III: *A room in the castle.*]

Enter King, Rosencrantz, and Guildenstern.

King: I like him not, nor stands it safe with us

    To let his madness range. Therefore prepare you;

    I your commission will forthwith dispatch,°

    And he to England shall along with you:

    The terms° of our estate° may not endure 5

    Hazard so near us as doth hourly grow

    Out of his brows.°

Guildenstern: We will ourselves provide:

    Most holy and religious fear it is

    To keep those many many bodies safe

    That live and feed upon your majesty. 10

Rosencrantz: The single and peculiar° life is bound,

    With all the strength and armour of the mind,

342 *top of my bent:* Limit of endurance, i.e., extent to which a bow may be bent; *by and by:* Immediately.   346 *witching time:* I.e., time when spells are cast.   352 *Nero:* Murderer of his mother, Agrippina.   356 *shent:* Rebuked.   357 *give them seals:* Confirm with deeds.   **Scene III.**   3 *dispatch:* Prepare.   5 *terms:* Condition, circumstances; *estate:* State.   7 *brows:* Effronteries.   11 *single and peculiar:* Individual and private.

To keep itself from noyance;° but much more
That spirit upon whose weal depend and rest
The lives of many. The cess° of majesty　　　　　　　15
Dies not alone; but, like a gulf,° doth draw
What's near it with it: it is a massy wheel,
Fix'd on the summit of the highest mount,
To whose huge spokes ten thousand lesser things
Are mortis'd and adjoin'd; which, when it falls,　　　20
Each small annexment, petty consequence,
Attends° the boist'rous ruin. Never alone
Did the king sigh, but with a general groan.

King: Arm° you, I pray you, to this speedy voyage;
For we will fetters put about this fear,　　　　　　25
Which now goes too free-footed.

Rosencrantz: 　　　　　　　　　　We will haste us.
　　　　　　　Exeunt Gentlemen [Rosencrantz and Guildenstern].

　　　Enter Polonius.

Polonius: My lord, he's going to his mother's closet:
Behind the arras° I'll convey° myself,
To hear the process;° I'll warrant she'll tax him home:°
And, as you said, and wisely was it said,　　　　　30
'Tis meet that some more audience than a mother,
Since nature makes them partial, should o'erhear
The speech, of vantage.° Fare you well, my liege:
I'll call upon you ere you go to bed,
And tell you what I know.

King: 　　　　　　　Thanks, dear my lord.　　*Exit [Polonius].*　35
O, my offence is rank, it smells to heaven;
It hath the primal eldest curse° upon't,
A brother's murder. Pray can I not,
Though inclination be as sharp as will:°
My stronger guilt defeats my strong intent;　　　40
And, like a man to double business bound,
I stand in pause where I shall first begin,
And both neglect. What if this cursed hand
Were thicker than itself with brother's blood,
Is there not rain enough in the sweet heavens　　45
To wash it white as snow? Whereto serves mercy
But to confront° the visage of offence?
And what's in prayer but this two-fold force,
To be forestalled° ere we come to fall,
Or pardon'd being down? Then I'll look up;　　　50

---

13 *noyance:* Harm.　15 *cess:* Decease.　16 *gulf:* Whirlpool.　22 *Attends:* Participates in.　24 *Arm:* Prepare.　28 *arras:* Screen of tapestry placed around the walls of household apartments; *convey:* Implication of secrecy, *convey* was often used to mean "steal."　29 *process:* Proceedings; *tax him home:* Reprove him severely.　33 *of vantage:* From an advantageous place.　37 *primal eldest curse:* The curse of Cain, the first to kill his brother.　39 *sharp as will:* I.e., his desire is as strong as his determination.　47 *confront:* Oppose directly.　49 *forestalled:* Prevented.

My fault is past. But, O, what form of prayer
Can serve my turn? "Forgive me my foul murder"?
That cannot be: since I am still possess'd
Of those effects for which I did the murder,
My crown, mine own ambition° and my queen. 55
May one be pardon'd and retain th' offence?°
In the corrupted currents° of this world
Offence's gilded hand° may shove by justice,
And oft 'tis seen the wicked prize° itself
Buys out the law: but 'tis not so above; 60
There is no shuffling,° there the action lies°
In his true nature; and we ourselves compell'd,
Even to the teeth and forehead° of our faults,
To give in evidence. What then? what rests?°
Try what repentance can: what can it not? 65
Yet what can it when one can not repent?
O wretched state! O bosom black as death!
O limed° soul, that, struggling to be free,
Art more engag'd!° Help, angels! Make assay!°
Bow, stubborn knees; and, heart with strings of steel, 70
Be soft as sinews of the new-born babe!
All may be well. *[He kneels.]*

Enter Hamlet.

Hamlet: Now might I do it pat,° now he is praying;
And now I'll do't. And so 'a goes to heaven;
And so am I reveng'd. That would be scann'd:° 75
A villain kills my father; and for that,
I, his sole son, do this same villain send
To heaven.
Why, this is hire and salary, not revenge.
'A took my father grossly, full of bread;° 80
With all his crimes broad blown,° as flush° as May;
And how his audit stands who knows save heaven?
But in our circumstance and course° of thought,
'Tis heavy with him: and am I then reveng'd,
To take him in the purging of his soul, 85
When he is fit and season'd for his passage?°
No!
Up, sword; and know thou a more horrid hent:°
When he is drunk asleep,° or in his rage,
Or in th' incestuous pleasure of his bed; 90

---

55 *ambition:* I.e., realization of ambition.   56 *offence:* Benefit accruing from offense.
57 *currents:* Courses.   58 *gilded hand:* Hand offering gold as a bribe.   59 *wicked prize:*
Prize won by wickedness.   61 *shuffling:* Escape by trickery; *lies:* Is sustainable.   63 *teeth
and forehead:* Very face.   64 *rests:* Remains.   68 *limed:* Caught as with birdlime.
69 *engag'd:* Embedded; *assay:* Trial.   73 *pat:* Opportunely.   75 *would be scann'd:* Needs
to be looked into.   80 *full of bread:* Enjoying his worldly pleasures (see Ezekiel 16:49).
81 *broad blown:* In full bloom; *flush:* Lusty.   83 *in ... course:* As we see it in our mortal situation.   86 *fit ... passage:* I.e., reconciled to heaven by forgiveness of his sins.   88 *hent:*
Seizing; or more probably, occasion of seizure.   89 *drunk asleep:* In a drunken sleep.

At game, a-swearing, or about some act
That has no relish of salvation in't;
Then trip him, that his heels may kick at heaven,
And that his soul may be as damn'd and black
As hell, whereto it goes. My mother stays: 95
This physic° but prolongs thy sickly days.   *Exit.*
King: [*Rising*] My words fly up, my thoughts remain below:
        Words without thoughts never to heaven go.   *Exit.*

[SCENE IV: *The Queen's closet.*]

        Enter [Queen] Gertrude and Polonius.

Polonius: 'A will come straight. Look you lay° home to him:
        Tell him his pranks have been too broad° to bear with,
        And that your grace hath screen'd and stood between
        Much heat° and him. I'll sconce° me even here.
        Pray you, be round° with him.   5
Hamlet (within): Mother, mother, mother!
Queen: I'll warrant you,
        Fear me not: withdraw, I hear him coming.
                                        [*Polonius hides behind the arras.*]

        Enter Hamlet.

Hamlet: Now, mother, what's the matter?
Queen: Hamlet, thou hast thy father much offended.
Hamlet: Mother, you have my father° much offended.   10
Queen: Come, come, you answer with an idle tongue.
Hamlet: Go, go, you question with a wicked tongue.
Queen: Why, how now, Hamlet!
Hamlet: What's the matter now?
Queen: Have you forgot me?
Hamlet: No, by the rood,° not so:
        You are the queen, your husband's brother's wife;   15
        And—would it were not so!—you are my mother.
Queen: Nay, then, I'll set those to you that can speak.
Hamlet: Come, come, and sit you down; you shall not budge;
        You go not till I set you up a glass
        Where you may see the inmost part of you.   20
Queen: What wilt thou do? thou wilt not murder me?
        Help, help, ho!
Polonius [*behind*]: What, ho! help, help; help!
Hamlet [*drawing*]: How now! a rat? Dead, for a ducat, dead!
                                        [*Makes a pass through the arras.*]
Polonius [*behind*]: O, I am slain!   [*Falls and dies.*] 25
Queen: O me, what hast thou done?

---

96 *physic:* Purging (by prayer).   **Scene IV.**   1 *lay:* Thrust.   2 *broad:* Unrestrained.
4 *Much heat:* I.e., the king's anger; *sconce:* Hide.   5 *round:* Blunt.   9–10 *thy father, my fa-*
ther: I.e., Claudius, the elder Hamlet.   14 *rood:* Cross.

Hamlet: Nay, I know not:
    Is it the king?
Queen: O, what a rash and bloody deed is this!
Hamlet: A bloody deed! almost as bad, good mother,
    As kill a king, and marry with his brother.   30
Queen: As kill a king!
Hamlet: Ay, lady, it was my word.
                    [*Lifts up the arras and discovers Polonius.*]
    Thou wretched, rash, intruding fool, farewell!
    I took thee for thy better: take thy fortune;
    Thou find'st to be too busy is some danger.
    Leave wringing of your hands: peace! sit you down,   35
    And let me wring your heart; for so I shall,
    If it be made of penetrable stuff,
    If damned custom have not braz'd° it so
    That it be proof and bulwark against sense.
Queen: What have I done, that thou dar'st wag thy tongue   40
    In noise so rude against me?
Hamlet: Such an act
    That blurs the grace and blush of modesty,
    Calls virtue hypocrite, takes off the rose
    From the fair forehead of an innocent love
    And sets a blister° there, makes marriage-vows   45
    As false as dicers' oaths: O, such a deed
    As from the body of contraction° plucks
    The very soul, and sweet religion° makes
    A rhapsody° of words: heaven's face does glow
    O'er this solidity and compound mass   50
    With heated visage, as against the doom
    Is thought-sick at the act.°
Queen: Ay me, what act,
    That roars so loud, and thunders in the index?°
Hamlet: Look here, upon this picture, and on this.
    The counterfeit presentment° of two brothers.   55
    See, what a grace was seated on this brow;
    Hyperion's° curls; the front° of Jove himself;
    An eye like Mars, to threaten and command;
    A station° like the herald Mercury
    New-lighted on a heaven-kissing hill;   60
    A combination and a form indeed,
    Where every god did seem to set his seal,
    To give the world assurance° of a man:
    This was your husband. Look you now, what follows:

---

38 *braz'd:* Brazened, hardened.   45 *sets a blister:* Brands as a harlot.   47 *contraction:*
The marriage contract.   48 *religion:* Religious vows.   49 *rhapsody:* Senseless string.
49–52 *heaven's . . . act:* Heaven's face blushes to look down on this world, and Gertrude's
marriage makes heaven feel as sick as though the day of doom were near.   53 *index:* Prelude or preface.   55 *counterfeit presentment:* Portrayed representation.   57 *Hyperion's:*
The sun god's; *front:* Brow.   59 *station:* Manner of standing.   63 *assurance:* Pledge,
guarantee.

Here is your husband; like a mildew'd ear,°   65
Blasting his wholesome brother. Have you eyes?
Could you on this fair mountain leave to feed,
And batten° on this moor?° Ha! have you eyes?
You cannot call it love; for at your age
The hey-day° in the blood is tame, it's humble,   70
And waits upon the judgement: and what judgement
Would step from this to this? Sense, sure, you have,
Else could you not have motion;° but sure, that sense
Is apoplex'd;° for madness would not err,
Nor sense to ecstasy was ne'er so thrall'd°   75
But it reserv'd some quantity of choice,°
To serve in such a difference. What devil was't
That thus hath cozen'd° you at hoodman-blind?°
Eyes without feeling, feeling without sight,
Ears without hands or eyes, smelling sans° all,   80
Or but a sickly part of one true sense
Could not so mope.°
O shame! where is thy blush? Rebellious hell,
If thou canst mutine° in a matron's bones,
To flaming youth let virtue be as wax,   85
And melt in her own fire: proclaim no shame
When the compulsive ardour gives the charge,°
Since frost itself as actively doth burn
And reason pandars will.°
Queen: O Hamlet, speak no more:
Thou turn'st mine eyes into my very soul;   90
And there I see such black and grained° spots
As will not leave their tinct.
Hamlet: Nay, but to live
In the rank sweat of an enseamed° bed,
Stew'd in corruption, honeying and making love
Over the nasty sty,—
Queen: O, speak to me no more;   95
These words, like daggers, enter in mine ears;
No more, sweet Hamlet!
Hamlet: A murderer and a villain;
A slave that is not twentieth part the tithe
Of your precedent lord;° a vice of kings;°

---

65 *mildew'd ear:* See Genesis 41:5-7.   68 *batten:* Grow fat; *moor:* Barren upland.   70 *hey-day:* State of excitement.   72-73 *Sense . . . motion:* Sense and motion are functions of the middle or sensible soul, the possession of sense being the basis of motion.   74 *apoplex'd:* Paralyzed. Mental derangement was thus of three sorts: apoplexy, ecstasy, and diabolic possession.   75 *thrall'd:* Enslaved.   76 *quantity of choice:* Fragment of the power to choose. 78 *cozen'd:* Tricked, cheated;   *hoodman-blind:* Blindman's buff.   80 *sans:* Without. 82 *mope:* Be in a depressed, spiritless state, act aimlessly.   84 *mutine:* Mutiny, rebel. 87 *gives the charge:* Delivers the attack.   89 *reason pandars will:* The normal and proper situation was one in which reason guided the will in the direction of good; here, reason is perverted and leads in the direction of evil.   91 *grained:* Dyed in grain.   93 *enseamed:* Loaded with grease, greased.   99 *precedent lord:* I.e., the elder Hamlet; *vice of kings:* Buffoon of kings; a reference to the Vice, or clown, of the morality plays and interludes.

A cutpurse of the empire and the rule,   100
That from a shelf the precious diadem stole,
And put it in his pocket!
Queen: No more!

Enter Ghost.

Hamlet: A king of shreds and patches,° —
Save me, and hover o'er me with your wings,
You heavenly guards! What would your gracious figure?   105
Queen: Alas, he's mad!
Hamlet: Do you not come your tardy son to chide,
That, laps'd in time and passion,° lets go by
Th' important° acting of your dread command?
O, say!   110
Ghost: Do not forget: this visitation
Is but to whet thy almost blunted purpose.
But, look, amazement° on thy mother sits:
O, step between her and her fighting soul:
Conceit in weakest bodies strongest works: 115
Speak to her, Hamlet.
Hamlet: How is it with you, lady?
Queen: Alas, how is 't with you,
That you do bend your eye on vacancy
And with th' incorporal° air do hold discourse?
Forth at your eyes your spirits wildly peep;   120
And, as the sleeping soldiers in th' alarm,
Your bedded° hair, like life in excrements,°
Start up, and stand an° end. O gentle son,
Upon the heat and flame of thy distemper
Sprinkle cool patience. Whereon do you look?   125
Hamlet: On him, on him! Look you, how pale he glares!
His form and cause conjoin'd,° preaching to stones,
Would make them capable. — Do not look upon me;
Lest with this piteous action you convert
My stern effects:° then what I have to do   130
Will want true colour;° tears perchance for blood.
Queen: To whom do you speak this?
Hamlet: Do you see nothing there?
Queen: Nothing at all; yet all that is I see.
Hamlet: Nor did you nothing hear?
Queen: No, nothing but ourselves.
Hamlet: Why, look you there! look, how it steals away!   135

---

103 *shreds and patches:* I.e., motley, the traditional costume of the Vice.   108 *laps'd . . . passion:*
Having suffered time to slip and passion to cool; also explained as "engrossed in casual events
and lapsed into mere fruitless passion, so that he no longer entertains a rational purpose."
109 *important:* Urgent.   113 *amazement:* Frenzy, distraction.   119 *incorporal:* Immaterial.
122 *bedded:* Laid in smooth layers; *excrements:* The hair was considered an excrement or voided
part of the body.   123 *an:* On.   127 *conjoin'd:* United.   129–130 *convert . . . effects:* Divert
me from my stern duty. For *effects,* possibly *affects* (affections of the mind).   131 *want true
colour:* Lack good reason so that (with a play on the normal sense of *colour*) I shall shed tears
instead of blood.

My father, in his habit as he liv'd!
Look, where he goes, even now, out at the portal!   *Exit Ghost.*
Queen: This is the very coinage of your brain:
This bodiless creation ecstasy
Is very cunning in.
Hamlet: Ecstasy!   140
My pulse, as yours, doth temperately keep time,
And makes as healthful music: it is not madness
That I have utt'red: bring me to the test,
And I the matter will re-word,° which madness
Would gambol° from. Mother, for love of grace,   145
Lay not that flattering unction° to your soul,
That not your trespass, but my madness speaks:
It will but skin and film the ulcerous place,
Whiles rank corruption, mining° all within,
Infects unseen. Confess yourself to heaven;   150
Repent what's past; avoid what is to come;°
And do not spread the compost° on the weeds,
To make them ranker. Forgive me this my virtue;°
For in the fatness° of these pursy° times
Virtue itself of vice must pardon beg,   155
Yea, curb° and woo for leave to do him good.
Queen: O Hamlet, thou hast cleft my heart in twain.
Hamlet: O, throw away the worser part of it,
And live the purer with the other half.
Good night: but go not to my uncle's bed;   160
Assume a virtue, if you have it not.
That monster, custom, who all sense doth eat,
Of habits devil, is angel yet in this,
That to the use of actions fair and good
He likewise gives a frock or livery,   165
That aptly is put on. Refrain to-night,
And that shall lend a kind of easiness
To the next abstinence: the next more easy;
For use almost can change the stamp of nature,
And either . . . the devil, or throw him out°   170
With wondrous potency. Once more, good night:
And when you are desirous to be bless'd,°
I'll blessing beg of you. For this same lord,   *[Pointing to Polonius.]*
I do repent: but heaven hath pleas'd it so,
To punish me with this and this with me,   175
That I must be their scourge and minister.
I will bestow him, and will answer well

---

144 *re-word:* Repeat in words.   145 *gambol:* Skip away.   146 *unction:* Ointment used medicinally or as a rite; suggestion that forgiveness for sin may not be so easily achieved.
149 *mining:* Working under the surface.   151 *what is to come:* I.e., the sins of the future.
152 *compost:* Manure.   153 *this my virtue:* My virtuous talk in reproving you.   154 *fatness:* Grossness; *pursy:* Short-winded, corpulent.   156 *curb:* Bow, bend the knee.   170 Defective line usually emended by inserting *master* after *either.*   172 *be bless'd:* Become blessed, i.e., repentant.

The death I gave him. So, again, good night.
I must be cruel, only to be kind:
Thus bad begins and worse remains behind. 180
One word more, good lady.
Queen: What shall I do?
Hamlet: Not this, by no means, that I bid you do:
Let the bloat° king tempt you again to bed;
Pinch wanton on your cheek; call you his mouse;
And let him, for a pair of reechy° kisses, 185
Or paddling in your neck with his damn'd fingers,
Make you to ravel all this matter out,
That I essentially° am not in madness,
But mad in craft. 'Twere good you let him know;
For who, that's but a queen, fair, sober, wise, 190
Would from a paddock,° from a bat, a gib,°
Such dear concernings° hide? who would do so?
No, in despite of sense and secrecy,
Unpeg the basket on the house's top,
Let the birds fly, and, like the famous ape,° 195
To try conclusions,° in the basket creep,
And break your own neck down.
Queen: Be thou assur'd, if words be made of breath,
And breath of life, I have no life to breathe
What thou hast said to me. 200
Hamlet: I must to England; you know that?
Queen: Alack,
I had forgot: 'tis so concluded on.
Hamlet: There's letters seal'd: and my two schoolfellows,
Whom I will trust as I will adders fang'd,
They bear the mandate; they must sweep my way,° 205
And marshal me to knavery. Let it work;
For 'tis the sport to have the enginer°
Hoist° with his own petar:° and 't shall go hard
But I will delve one yard below their mines,
And blow them at the moon: O, 'tis most sweet, 210
When in one line two crafts° directly meet.
This man shall set me packing:°
I'll lug the guts into the neighbour room.
Mother, good night. Indeed this counsellor
Is now most still, most secret and most grave, 215

183 *bloat:* Bloated.   185 *reechy:* Dirty, filthy.   188 *essentially:* In my essential nature.
191 *paddock:* Toad; *gib:* Tomcat.   192 *dear concernings:* Important affairs.   195 *the famous ape:* A letter from Sir John Suckling seems to supply other details of the story, otherwise not identified: "It is the story of the jackanapes and the partridges; thou starest after a beauty till it be lost to thee, then let'st out another, and starest after that till it is gone too."
196 *conclusions:* Experiments.   205 *sweep my way:* Clear my path.   207 *enginer:* Constructor of military works, or possibly, artilleryman.   208 *Hoist:* Blown up; *petar:* Defined as a small engine of war used to blow in a door or make a breach, and as a case filled with explosive materials.   211 *two crafts:* Two acts of guile, with quibble on the sense of "two ships."   212 *set me packing:* Set me to making schemes, and set me to lugging (him), and, also, send me off in a hurry.

Who was in life a foolish prating knave.
Come, sir, to draw° toward an end with you.
Good night, mother.   *Exeunt [severally; Hamlet dragging in Polonius.]*

[ACT IV

SCENE I: *A room in the castle.]*

Enter King and Queen, with Rosencrantz and Guildenstern.

King: There's matter in these sighs, these profound heaves:
    You must translate: 'tis fit we understand them.
    Where is your son?
Queen: Bestow this place on us a little while.
                     [Exeunt Rosencrantz and Guildenstern.]
    Ah, mine own lord, what have I seen to-night!   5
King: What, Gertrude? How does Hamlet?
Queen: Mad as the sea and wind, when both contend
    Which is the mightier: in his lawless fit,
    Behind the arras hearing something stir,
    Whips out his rapier, cries, "A rat, a rat!"   10
    And, in this brainish° apprehension,° kills
    The unseen good old man.
King: O heavy deed!
    It had been so with us, had we been there:
    His liberty is full of threats to all;
    To you yourself, to us, to every one.   15
    Alas, how shall this bloody deed be answer'd?
    It will be laid to us, whose providence°
    Should have kept short,° restrain'd and out of haunt,°
    This mad young man: but so much was our love,
    We would not understand what was most fit;   20
    But, like the owner of a foul disease,
    To keep it from divulging,° let it feed
    Even on the pith of life. Where is he gone?
Queen: To draw apart the body he hath kill'd:
    O'er whom his very madness, like some ore   25
    Among a mineral° of metals base,
    Shows itself pure; 'a weeps for what is done.
King: O Gertrude, come away!
    The sun no sooner shall the mountains touch,
    But we will ship him hence: and this vile deed   30
    We must, with all our majesty and skill,
    Both countenance and excuse. Ho, Guildenstern!

---

217 *draw:* Come, with quibble on literal sense.   **Act IV, Scene I.**   11 *brainish:* Headstrong, passionate; *apprehension:* Conception, imagination.   17 *providence:* Foresight.
18 *short:* I.e., on a short tether; *out of haunt:* Secluded.   22 *divulging:* Becoming evident.
26 *mineral:* Mine.

Enter Rosencrantz and Guildenstern.

Friends both, go join you with some further aid:
Hamlet in madness hath Polonius slain,
And from his mother's closet hath he dragg'd him:
Go seek him out; speak fair, and bring the body   35
Into the chapel. I pray you, haste in this.
                    [Exeunt Rosencrantz and Guildenstern.]
Come, Gertrude, we'll call up our wisest friends;
And let them know, both what we mean to do,
And what's untimely done . . .°   40
Whose whisper o'er the world's diameter,°
As level° as the cannon to his blank,°
Transports his pois'ned shot, may miss our name,
And hit the woundless° air. O, come away!
My soul is full of discord and dismay.   *Exeunt.* 45

[SCENE II: *Another room in the castle.*]

Enter Hamlet.

Hamlet: Safely stowed.
Rosencrantz: ⎫
Guildenstern: ⎬ *(within)* Hamlet! Lord Hamlet!
Hamlet: But soft, what noise? who calls on Hamlet? O, here they come.

Enter Rosencrantz and Guildenstern.

Rosencrantz: What have you done, my lord, with the dead body?
Hamlet: Compounded it with dust, whereto 'tis kin.
Rosencrantz: Tell us where 'tis, that we may take it thence   5
    And bear it to the chapel.
Hamlet: Do not believe it.
Rosencrantz: Believe what?
Hamlet: That I can keep your counsel° and not mine own. Besides, to be
    demanded of a sponge! what replication° should be made by the son   10
    of a king?
Rosencrantz: Take you me for a sponge, my lord?
Hamlet: Ay, sir, that soaks up the king's countenance, his rewards, his
    authorities.° But such officers do the king best service in the end: he
    keeps them, like an ape an apple, in the corner of his jaw; first   15
    mouthed, to be last swallowed: when he needs what you have gleaned,
    it is but squeezing you, and, sponge, you shall be dry again.
Rosencrantz: I understand you not, my lord.
Hamlet: I am glad of it: a knavish speech sleeps in a foolish ear.
Rosencrantz: My lord, you must tell us where the body is, and go with us   20
    to the king.

---

40 Defective line; some editors add: *so, haply, slander;* others add: *for, haply, slander;* other
conjectures.   41 *diameter:* Extent from side to side.   42 *level:* Straight; *blank:* White
spot in the center of a target.   44 *woundless:* Invulnerable.   **Scene II.**   9 *keep your
counsel:* Hamlet is aware of their treachery but says nothing about it.   10 *replication:*
Reply.   14 *authorities:* Authoritative backing.

Hamlet: The body is with the king, but the king is not with the body.° The
    king is a thing—
Guildenstern: A thing, my lord!
Hamlet: Of nothing: bring me to him. Hide fox, and all after.°   *Exeunt.*   25

[SCENE III: *Another room in the castle.*]

    Enter King, and two or three.

King: I have sent to seek him, and to find the body.
    How dangerous is it that this man goes loose!
    Yet must not we put the strong law on him:
    He's lov'd of the distracted° multitude,
    Who like not in their judgement, but their eyes;   5
    And where 'tis so, th' offender's scourge° is weigh'd,°
    But never the offence. To bear all smooth and even,
    This sudden sending him away must seem
    Deliberate pause:° diseases desperate grown
    By desperate appliance are reliev'd,   10
    Or not at all.

    Enter Rosencrantz, [Guildenstern,] and all the rest.

               How now! what hath befall'n?
Rosencrantz: Where the dead body is bestow'd, my lord,
    We cannot get from him.
King: But where is he?
Rosencrantz: Without, my lord; guarded, to know your pleasure.
King: Bring him before us.   15
Rosencrantz: Ho! bring in the lord.

    They enter [with Hamlet].

King: Now, Hamlet, where's Polonius?
Hamlet: At supper.
King: At supper! where?
Hamlet: Not where he eats, but where 'a is eaten: a certain convocation of   20
    politic° worms° are e'en at him. Your worm is your only emperor for
    diet: we fat all creatures else to fat us, and we fat ourselves for mag-
    gots: your fat king and your lean beggar is but variable service,° two
    dishes, but to one table: that's the end.
King: Alas, alas!   25
Hamlet: A man may fish with the worm that hath eat of a king, and eat of
    the fish that hath fed of that worm.

22 *The body . . . body:* There are many interpretations; possibly, "The body lies in death with
the king, my father; but my father walks disembodied"; or "Claudius has the bodily possession of kingship, but kingliness, or justice of inheritance, is not with him."   25 *Hide . . .
after:* An old signal cry in the game of hide-and-seek.   **Scene III.**   4 *distracted:* I.e., without power of forming logical judgments.   6 *scourge:* Punishment; *weigh'd:* Taken into
consideration.   9 *Deliberate pause:* Considered action.   20–21 *convocation . . . worms:* Allusion to the Diet of Worms (1521).   21 *politic:* Crafty.   23 *variable service:* A variety of
dishes.

King: What dost thou mean by this?

Hamlet: Nothing but to show you how a king may go a progress° through
    the guts of a beggar.   30

King: Where is Polonius?

Hamlet: In heaven; send thither to see: if your messenger find him not
    there, seek him i' the other place yourself. But if indeed you find him
    not within this month, you shall nose him as you go up the stairs
    into the lobby.   35

King [to some Attendants]: Go seek him there.

Hamlet: 'A will stay till you come.   *[Exeunt Attendants.]*

King: Hamlet, this deed, for thine especial safety, —
    Which we do tender,° as we dearly grieve
    For that which thou hast done, — must send thee hence   40
    With fiery quickness: therefore prepare thyself;
    The bark is ready, and the wind at help,
    Th' associates tend, and everything is bent
    For England.

Hamlet: For England!

King: Ay, Hamlet.

Hamlet: Good.

King: So is it, if thou knew'st our purposes.   45

Hamlet: I see a cherub° that sees them. But, come; for England! Farewell,
    dear mother.

King: Thy loving father, Hamlet.

Hamlet: My mother: father and mother is man and wife; man and wife is
    one flesh; and so, my mother. Come, for England!   *Exit.* 50

King: Follow him at foot;° tempt him with speed aboard;
    Delay it not; I'll have him hence to-night:
    Away! for every thing is seal'd and done
    That else leans on th' affair: pray you, make haste.
                      [Exeunt all but the King.]
    And, England, if my love thou hold'st at aught —   55
    As my great power thereof may give thee sense,
    Since yet thy cicatrice° looks raw and red
    After the Danish sword, and thy free awe°
    Pays homage to us — thou mayst not coldly set
    Our sovereign process; which imports at full,   60
    By letters congruing to that effect,
    The present death of Hamlet. Do it, England;
    For like the hectic° in my blood he rages,
    And thou must cure me: till I know 'tis done,
    Howe'er my haps,° my joys were ne'er begun.   *Exit.* 65

---

29 *progress:* Royal journey of state.   39 *tender:* Regard, hold dear.   46 *cherub:* Cheru-
bim are angels of knowledge.   51 *at foot:* Close behind, at heel.   57 *cicatrice:* Scar.
58 *free awe:* Voluntary show of respect.   63 *hectic:* Fever.   65 *haps:* Fortunes.

[SCENE IV: *A plain in Denmark.*]

    Enter Fortinbras with his Army over the stage.

Fortinbras: Go, captain, from me greet the Danish king;
    Tell him that, by his license,° Fortinbras
    Craves the conveyance° of a promis'd march
    Over his kingdom. You know the rendezvous.
    If that his majesty would aught with us,   5
    We shall express our duty in his eye;°
    And let him know so.
Captain: I will do't, my lord.
Fortinbras: Go softly° on.   *[Exeunt all but Captain.]*

    Enter Hamlet, Rosencrantz, [Guildenstern,] &c.

Hamlet: Good sir, whose powers are these?
Captain: They are of Norway, sir.   10
Hamlet: How purpos'd, sir, I pray you?
Captain: Against some part of Poland.
Hamlet: Who commands them, sir?
Captain: The nephew to old Norway, Fortinbras.
Hamlet: Goes it against the main° of Poland, sir,   15
    Or for some frontier?
Captain: Truly to speak, and with no addition,
    We go to gain a little patch of ground
    That hath in it no profit but the name.
    To pay five ducats, five, I would not farm it;°   20
    Nor will it yield to Norway or the Pole
    A ranker rate, should it be sold in fee.°
Hamlet: Why, then the Polack never will defend it.
Captain: Yes, it is already garrison'd.
Hamlet: Two thousand souls and twenty thousand ducats   25
    Will not debate the question of this straw:°
    This is th' imposthume° of much wealth and peace,
    That inward breaks, and shows no cause without
    Why the man dies. I humbly thank you, sir.
Captain: God be wi' you, sir.   *[Exit.]*
Rosencrantz: Will 't please you go, my lord?   30
Hamlet: I'll be with you straight. Go a little before.
                  [Exeunt all except Hamlet.]
    How all occasions° do inform against° me,
    And spur my dull revenge! What is a man,
    If his chief good and market of his time°

Scene IV.   2 *license:* Leave.   3 *conveyance:* Escort, convoy.   6 *in his eye:* In his presence.   8 *softly:* Slowly.   15 *main:* Country itself.   20 *farm it:* Take a lease of it.   22 *fee:* Fee simple.   26 *debate . . . straw:* Settle this trifling matter.   27 *imposthume:* Purulent abscess or swelling.   32 *occasions:* Incidents, events; *inform against:* Generally defined as "show," "betray" (i.e., his tardiness); more probably *inform* means "take shape," as in *Macbeth,* II.i.48.   34 *market of his time:* The best use he makes of his time, or, that for which he sells his time.

Be but to sleep and feed? a beast, no more.   35
Sure, he that made us with such large discourse,
Looking before and after, gave us not
That capability and god-like reason
To fust° in us unus'd. Now, whether it be
Bestial oblivion, or some craven scruple   40
Of thinking too precisely on th' event,
A thought which, quarter'd, hath but one part wisdom
And ever three parts coward, I do not know
Why yet I live to say "This thing 's to do";
Sith I have cause and will and strength and means   45
To do 't. Examples gross as earth exhort me:
Witness this army of such mass and charge
Led by a delicate and tender prince,
Whose spirit with divine ambition puff'd
Makes mouths at the invisible event,   50
Exposing what is mortal and unsure
To all that fortune, death and danger dare,
Even for an egg-shell. Rightly to be great
Is not to stir without great argument,
But greatly to find quarrel in a straw   55
When honour's at the stake. How stand I then,
That have a father kill'd, a mother stain'd,
Excitements of° my reason and my blood,
And let all sleep? while, to my shame, I see
The imminent death of twenty thousand men,   60
That, for a fantasy and trick° of fame,
Go to their graves like beds, fight for a plot°
Whereon the numbers cannot try the cause,
Which is not tomb enough and continent
To hide the slain? O, from this time forth,   65
My thoughts be bloody, or be nothing worth!   *Exit.*

[SCENE V: *Elsinore. A room in the castle.*]

Enter Horatio, [Queen] Gertrude, and a Gentleman.

Queen: I will not speak with her.
Gentleman: She is importunate, indeed distract:
   Her mood will needs be pitied.
Queen: What would she have?
Gentleman: She speaks much of her father; says she hears
   There's tricks° i' th' world; and hems, and beats her heart;°   5
   Spurns enviously at straws;° speaks things in doubt,
   That carry but half sense: her speech is nothing,
   Yet the unshaped° use of it doth move

39 *fust:* Grow moldy. 58 *Excitements of:* Incentives to. 61 *trick:* Toy, trifle. 62 *plot:* Piece of ground. **Scene V.** 5 *tricks:* Deceptions; *heart:* I.e., breast. 6 *Spurns... straws:* Kicks spitefully at small objects in her path. 8 *unshaped:* Unformed, artless.

The hearers to collection;° they yawn° at it,
And botch° the words up fit to their own thoughts;   10
Which, as her winks, and nods, and gestures yield° them,
Indeed would make one think there might be thought,
Though nothing sure, yet much unhappily.°

Horatio: 'Twere good she were spoken with: for she may strew
    Dangerous conjectures in ill-breeding minds.°   15

Queen: Let her come in.   *[Exit Gentleman.]*

    [Aside.] To my sick soul, as sin's true nature is,
    Each toy seems prologue to some great amiss:°
    So full of artless jealousy is guilt,
    It spills itself in fearing to be spilt.°   20

    Enter Ophelia [distracted].

Ophelia: Where is the beauteous majesty of Denmark?

Queen: How now, Ophelia!

Ophelia (she sings): How should I your true love know
       From another one?
By his cockle hat° and staff,   25
       And his sandal shoon.°

Queen: Alas, sweet lady, what imports this song?

Ophelia: Say you? nay, pray you mark.
    (Song) He is dead and gone, lady,
       He is dead and gone;   30
    At his head a grass-green turf,
       At his heels a stone.
    O, ho!

Queen: Nay, but, Ophelia—

Ophelia: Pray you, mark   35
    [Sings.] White his shroud as the mountain snow,—

    Enter King.

Queen: Alas, look here, my lord.

Ophelia (Song): Larded° all with flowers;
       Which bewept to the grave did not go
       With true-love showers.   40

King: How do you, pretty lady?

Ophelia: Well, God 'ild° you! They say the owl° was a baker's daughter.
    Lord, we know what we are, but know not what we may be. God be at
    your table!

---

9 *collection:* Inference, a guess at some sort of meaning; *yawn:* Wonder.   10 *botch:* Patch.
11 *yield:* Deliver, bring forth (her words).   13 *much unhappily:* Expressive of much unhappiness.   15 *ill-breeding minds:* Minds bent on mischief.   18 *great amiss:* Calamity, disaster.   19-20 *So . . . spilt:* Guilt is so full of suspicion that it unskillfully betrays itself in fearing to be betrayed.   25 *cockle hat:* Hat with cockleshell stuck in it as a sign that the wearer
has been a pilgrim to the shrine of St. James of Compostella. The pilgrim's garb was a conventional disguise for lovers.   26 *shoon:* Shoes.   38 *Larded:* Decorated.   42 *God 'ild:*
God yield or reward; *owl:* Reference to a monkish legend that a baker's daughter was turned
into an owl for refusing bread to the Savior.

King: Conceit upon her father.   45
Ophelia: Pray let's have no words of this; but when they ask you what it
    means, say you this:
    (Song) To-morrow is Saint Valentine's day,
        All in the morning betime,
    And I a maid at your window,   50
        To be your Valentine.°
    Then up he rose, and donn'd his clothes,
        And dupp'd° the chamber-door;
    Let in the maid, that out a maid
        Never departed more.   55
King: Pretty Ophelia!
Ophelia: Indeed, la, without an oath, I'll make an end on 't:
    [Sings.] By Gis° and by Saint Charity,
        Alack, and fie for shame!
    Young men will do 't, if they come to 't;   60
        By cock,° they are to blame.
    Quoth she, before you tumbled me,
        You promis'd me to wed.
    So would I ha' done, by yonder sun,
        An thou hadst not come to my bed.   65
King: How long hath she been thus?
Ophelia: I hope all will be well. We must be patient: but I cannot choose
    but weep, to think they would lay him i' the cold ground. My brother
    shall know of it: and so I thank you for your good counsel. Come, my
    coach! Good night, ladies; good night, sweet ladies; good night, good   70
    night.   *[Exit.]*
King: Follow her close; give her good watch, I pray you.   *[Exit Horatio.]*
    O, this is the poison of deep grief; it springs
    All from her father's death. O Gertrude, Gertrude,
    When sorrows come, they come not single spies,   75
    But in battalions. First, her father slain:
    Next your son gone; and he most violent author
    Of his own just remove: the people muddied,
    Thick and unwholesome in their thoughts and whispers,
    For good Polonius' death; and we have done but greenly,°   80
    In hugger-mugger° to inter him: poor Ophelia
    Divided from herself and her fair judgement,
    Without the which we are pictures, or mere beasts:
    Last, and as much containing as all these,
    Her brother is in secret come from France;   85
    Feeds on his wonder, keeps himself in clouds,°
    And wants not buzzers° to infect his ear
    With pestilent speeches of his father's death;
    Wherein necessity, of matter beggar'd,°
    Will nothing stick° our person to arraign   90

---

51 *Valentine:* This song alludes to the belief that the first girl seen by a man on the morning
of this day was his valentine or true love.   53 *dupp'd:* Opened.   58 *Gis:* Jesus.
61 *cock:* Perversion of "God" in oaths.   80 *greenly:* Foolishly.   81 *hugger-mugger:* Secret
haste.   86 *in clouds:* Invisible.   87 *buzzers:* Gossipers.   89 *of matter beggar'd:* Unprovided with facts.   90 *nothing stick:* Not hesitate.

In ear and ear.° O my dear Gertrude, this,
Like to a murd'ring-piece,° in many places
Gives me superfluous death.   *A noise within.*
Queen: Alack, what noise is this?
King: Where are my Switzers?° Let them guard the door.

Enter a Messenger.

What is the matter?
Messenger: Save yourself, my lord: 95
The ocean, overpeering° of his list,°
Eats not the flats with more impiteous haste
Than young Laertes, in a riotous head,
O'erbears your officers. The rabble call him lord;
And, as the world were now but to begin,   100
Antiquity forgot, custom not known,
The ratifiers and props of every word,°
They cry "Choose we: Laertes shall be king":
Caps, hands, and tongues, applaud it to the clouds:
"Laertes shall be king, Laertes king!"   *A noise within.* 105
Queen: How cheerfully on the false trail they cry!
O, this is counter,° you false Danish dogs!
King: The doors are broke.

Enter Laertes with others.

Laertes: Where is this king? Sirs, stand you all without.
Danes: No, let's come in.
Laertes: I pray you, give me leave.   110
Danes: We will, we will.   *[They retire without the door.]*
Laertes: I thank you: keep the door. O thou vile king,
Give me my father!
Queen: Calmly, good Laertes.
Laertes: That drop of blood that's calm proclaims me bastard,
Cries cuckold to my father, brands the harlot   115
Even here, between the chaste unsmirched brow
Of my true mother.
King: What is the cause, Laertes,
That thy rebellion looks so giant-like?
Let him go, Gertrude; do not fear our person:
There's such divinity doth hedge a king,   120
That treason can but peep to° what it would,°
Acts little of his will. Tell me, Laertes,
Why thou art thus incens'd. Let him go, Gertrude.
Speak, man.
Laertes: Where is my father?
King: Dead.
Queen: But not by him.   125
King: Let him demand his fill.

91 *In ear and ear:* In everybody's ears.   92 *murd'ring-piece:* Small cannon or mortar; suggestion of numerous missiles fired.   94 *Switzers:* Swiss guards, mercenaries.   96 *overpeering:* Overflowing; *list:* Shore.   102 *word:* Promise.   107 *counter:* A hunting term meaning to follow the trail in a direction opposite to that which the game has taken.   121 *peep to:* I.e., look at from afar off; *would:* Wishes to do.

Laertes: How came he dead? I'll not be juggled with:
    To hell, allegiance! vows, to the blackest devil!
    Conscience and grace, to the profoundest pit!
    I dare damnation. To this point I stand,   130
    That both the worlds I give to negligence,°
    Let come what comes; only I'll be reveng'd
    Most throughly° for my father.
King: Who shall stay you?
Laertes: My will,° not all the world's:
    And for my means, I'll husband them so well,   135
    They shall go far with little.
King: Good Laertes,
    If you desire to know the certainty
    Of your dear father, is 't writ in your revenge,
    That, swoopstake,° you will draw both friend and foe,
    Winner and loser?   140
Laertes: None but his enemies.
King: Will you know them then?
Laertes: To his good friends thus wide I'll ope my arms;
    And like the kind life-rend'ring pelican,°
    Repast° them with my blood.
King: Why, now you speak
    Like a good child and a true gentleman.   145
    That I am guiltless of your father's death,
    And am most sensibly in grief for it,
    It shall as level to your judgement 'pear
    As day does to your eye.   *A noise within:* "Let her come in."
Laertes: How now! what noise is that?   150

    Enter Ophelia.

    O heat,° dry up my brains! tears seven times salt,
    Burn out the sense and virtue of mine eye!
    By heaven, thy madness shall be paid with weight,
    Till our scale turn the beam. O rose of May!
    Dear maid, kind sister, sweet Ophelia!   155
    O heavens! is 't possible, a young maid's wits
    Should be as mortal as an old man's life?
    Nature is fine in love, and where 'tis fine,
    It sends some precious instance of itself
    After the thing it loves.   160
Ophelia (Song): They bore him barefac'd on the bier;
    Hey non nonny, nonny, hey nonny;
    And in his grave rain'd many a tear: —
    Fare you well, my dove!

---

131 *give to negligence:* He despises both the here and the hereafter.   133 *throughly:* thoroughly.   134 *My will:* He will not be stopped except by his own will.   139 *swoopstake:* Literally, drawing the whole stake at once, i.e., indiscriminately.   143 *pelican:* Reference to the belief that the pelican feeds its young with its own blood.   144 *Repast:* Feed. 151 *heat:* Probably the heat generated by the passion of grief.

Laertes: Hadst thou thy wits, and didst persuade revenge,   165
  It could not move thus.
Ophelia [sings]: You must sing a-down a-down,
  An you call him a-down-a.
  O, how the wheel° becomes it! It is the false steward,° that stole his
  master's daughter.   170
Laertes: This nothing's more than matter.
Ophelia: There's rosemary,° that's for remembrance; pray you, love, re-
  member: and there is pansies,° that's for thoughts.
Laertes: A document° in madness, thoughts and remembrance fitted.
Ophelia: There's fennel° for you, and columbines:° there's rue° for you;   175
  and here's some for me: we may call it herb of grace° o' Sundays: O,
  you must wear your rue with a difference. There's a daisy:° I would
  give you some violets,° but they withered all when my father died:
  they say 'a made a good end,—
  [Sings.] For bonny sweet Robin is all my joy.°   180
Laertes: Thought° and affliction, passion, hell itself,
  She turns to favour and to prettiness.
Ophelia (Song): And will 'a not come again?°
  And will 'a not come again?
    No, no, he is dead: 185
    Go to thy death-bed:
  He never will come again.

  His beard was as white as snow,
  All flaxen was his poll:°
    He is gone, he is gone,   190
    And we cast away° moan:
  God ha' mercy on his soul!
  And of all Christian souls, I pray God. God be wi' you.   *[Exit.]*
Laertes: Do you see this, O God?
King: Laertes, I must commune with your grief,   195
  Or you deny me right.° Go but apart,
  Make choice of whom your wisest friends you will,
  And they shall hear and judge 'twixt you and me:
  If by direct or by collateral° hand
  They find us touch'd,° we will our kingdom give,   200
  Our crown, our life, and all that we call ours,
  To you in satisfaction; but if not,

---

169 *wheel:* Spinning wheel as accompaniment to the song refrain; *false steward:* The story is unknown.   172 *rosemary:* Used as a symbol of remembrance both at weddings and at funerals.
173 *pansies:* Emblems of love and courtship (from the French *pensée*).   174 *document:* Piece
of instruction or lesson.   175, 176 *fennel:* Emblem of flattery; *columbines:* Emblem of un-
chastity (?) or ingratitude (?); *rue:* Emblem of repentance. It was usually mingled with holy
water and then known as *herb of grace*. Ophelia is probably playing on the two meanings of *rue*,
"repentant" and "even for ruth (pity)"; the former signification is for the queen, the latter for
herself.   177 *daisy:* Emblem of dissembling, faithlessness.   178 *violets:* Emblems of faith-
fulness.   180 *For...joy:* Probably a line from a Robin Hood ballad.   181 *Thought:* Melancholy thought.   183 *And...again:* This song appeared in the songbooks as "The Merry
Milkmaids' Dumps."   189 *poll:* Head.   191 *cast away:* Shipwrecked.   196 *right:* My
rights.   199 *collateral:* Indirect.   200 *touch'd:* Implicated.

Be you content to lend your patience to us,
And we shall jointly labour with your soul
To give it due content.

Laertes: Let this be so;   205
His means of death, his obscure funeral—
No trophy, sword, nor hatchment° o'er his bones,
No noble rite nor formal ostentation—
Cry to be heard, as 'twere from heaven to earth,
That I must call 't in question.

King: So you shall;   210
And where th' offence is let the great axe fall.
I pray you, go with me.   *Exeunt.*

[SCENE VI: *Another room in the castle.*]

Enter Horatio and others.

Horatio: What are they that would speak with me?
Gentleman: Sea-faring men, sir: they say they have letters for you.
Horatio: Let them come in.   *[Exit Gentleman.]*
I do not know from what part of the world
I should be greeted, if not from lord Hamlet.   5

Enter Sailors.

First Sailor: God bless you, sir.
Horatio: Let him bless thee too.
First Sailor: 'A shall sir, an 't please him. There's a letter for you, sir; it comes from the ambassador that was bound for England; if your name be Horatio, as I am let to know it is.   10
Horatio [reads]: "Horatio, when thou shalt have overlooked this, give these fellows some means° to the king: they have letters for him. Ere we were two days old at sea, a pirate of very warlike appointment gave us chase. Finding ourselves too slow of sail, we put on a compelled valour, and in the grapple I boarded them: on the instant they got   15
clear of our ship; so I alone became their prisoner. They have dealt with me like thieves of mercy:° but they knew what they did; I am to do a good turn for them. Let the king have the letters I have sent; and repair thou to me with as much speed as thou wouldest fly death. I have words to speak in thine ear will make thee dumb; yet are they   20
much too light for the bore° of the matter. These good fellows will bring thee where I am. Rosencrantz and Guildenstern hold their course for England: of them I have much to tell thee. Farewell.
                          "He that thou knowest thine, HAMLET."
Come, I will give you way for these your letters;   25
And do 't the speedier, that you may direct me
To him from whom you brought them.   *Exeunt.*

---

207 *hatchment:* Tablet displaying the armorial bearings of a deceased person.   **Scene VI.**
12 *means:* Means of access.   17 *thieves of mercy:* Merciful thieves.   21 *bore:* Caliber, importance.

[SCENE VII: *Another room in the castle.*]

Enter King and Laertes.

King: Now must your conscience° my acquittance seal,
And you must put me in your heart for friend,
Sith you have heard, and with a knowing ear,
That he which hath your noble father slain
Pursued my life.

Laertes: It well appears: but tell me   5
Why you proceeded not against these feats,
So criminal and so capital° in nature,
As by your safety, wisdom, all things else,
You mainly° were stirr'd up.

King: O, for two special reasons;
Which may to you, perhaps, seem much unsinew'd,°   10
But yet to me th' are strong. The queen his mother
Lives almost by his looks; and for myself—
My virtue or my plague, be it either which—
She's so conjunctive° to my life and soul,
That, as the star moves not but in his sphere,°   15
I could not but by her. The other motive,
Why to a public count° I might not go,
Is the great love the general gender° bear him;
Who, dipping all his faults in their affection,
Would, like the spring° that turneth wood to stone,   20
Convert his gyves° to graces; so that my arrows,
Too slightly timber'd° for so loud° a wind,
Would have reverted to my bow again,
And not where I had aim'd them.

Laertes: And so have I a noble father lost;   25
A sister driven into desp'rate terms,°
Whose worth, if praises may go back° again,
Stood challenger on mount° of all the age°
For her perfections: but my revenge will come.

King: Break not your sleeps for that: you must not think   30
That we are made of stuff so flat and dull
That we can let our beard be shook with danger
And think it pastime. You shortly shall hear more:
I lov'd your father, and we love ourself;
And that, I hope, will teach you to imagine—   35

Scene VII.   1 *conscience:* Knowledge that this is true.   7 *capital:* Punishable by death.
9 *mainly:* Greatly.   10 *unsinew'd:* Weak.   14 *conjunctive:* Conformable (the next line suggesting planetary conjunction).   15 *sphere:* The hollow sphere in which, according to Ptolemaic astronomy, the planets were supposed to move.   17 *count:* Account, reckoning.
18 *general gender:* Common people.   20 *spring:* I.e., one heavily charged with lime.
21 *gyves:* Fetters; here, faults, or possibly, punishments inflicted (on him).   22 *slightly timber'd:* Light; *loud:* Strong.   26 *terms:* State, condition.   27 *go back:* Return to Ophelia's former virtues.   28 *on mount:* Set up on high, *mounted* (on horseback); *of all the age:* Qualifies *challenger* and not *mount.*

Enter a Messenger with letters.

How now! what news?

Messenger: Letters, my lord, from Hamlet:
These to your majesty; this to the queen.°

King: From Hamlet! who brought them?

Messenger: Sailors, my lord, they say; I saw them not:
They were given me by Claudio;° he receiv'd them   40
Of him that brought them.

King: Laertes, you shall hear them.
Leave us.   *[Exit Messenger.]*

[Reads.] "High and mighty, You shall know I am set naked° on your
kingdom. To-morrow shall I beg leave to see your kingly eyes: when I
shall, first asking your pardon thereunto, recount the occasion of my   45
sudden and more strange return.   "HAMLET."
What should this mean? Are all the rest come back?
Or is it some abuse, and no such thing?

Laertes: Know you the hand?

King: 'Tis Hamlet's character. "Naked!"
And in a postscript here, he says "alone."   50
Can you devise° me?

Laertes: I'm lost in it, my lord. But let him come;
It warms the very sickness in my heart,
That I shall live and tell him to his teeth,
"Thus didst thou."

King: If it be so, Laertes —   55
As how should it be so? how otherwise?° —
Will you be rul'd by me?

Laertes: Ay, my lord;
So you will not o'errule me to a peace.

King: To thine own peace. If he be now return'd,
As checking at° his voyage, and that he means   60
No more to undertake it, I will work him
To an exploit, now ripe in my device,
Under the which he shall not choose but fall:
And for his death no wind of blame shall breathe,
But even his mother shall uncharge the practice°   65
And call it accident.

Laertes: My lord, I will be rul'd;
The rather, if you could devise it so
That I might be the organ.°

King: It falls right.
You have been talk'd of since your travel much,

---

37 *to the queen:* One hears no more of the letter to the queen.   40 *Claudio:* This character
does not appear in the play.   43 *naked:* Unprovided (with retinue).   51 *devise:* Explain
to.   56 *As . . . otherwise?* How can this (Hamlet's return) be true? (yet) how otherwise than
true (since we have the evidence of his letter)? Some editors read *How should it not be so,* etc.,
making the words refer to Laertes's desire to meet with Hamlet.   60 *checking at:* Used in
falconry of a hawk's leaving the quarry to fly at a chance bird; turn aside.   65 *uncharge the
practice:* Acquit the stratagem of being a plot.   68 *organ:* Agent, instrument.

And that in Hamlet's hearing, for a quality   70
Wherein, they say, you shine: your sum of parts
Did not together pluck such envy from him
As did that one, and that, in my regard,
Of the unworthiest siege.°

Laertes: What part is that, my lord?
King: A very riband in the cap of youth,   75
Yet needful too; for youth no less becomes
The light and careless livery that it wears
Than settled age his sables° and his weeds,
Importing health and graveness. Two months since,
Here was a gentleman of Normandy: —   80
I have seen myself, and serv'd against, the French,
And they can well° on horseback: but this gallant
Had witchcraft in 't; he grew unto his seat;
And to such wondrous doing brought his horse,
As had he been incorps'd and demi-natur'd°   85
With the brave beast: so far he topp'd° my thought,
That I, in forgery° of shapes and tricks,
Come short of what he did.

Laertes: A Norman was 't?
King: A Norman.
Laertes: Upon my life, Lamord.°
King: The very same.   90
Laertes: I know him well: he is the brooch indeed
And gem of all the nation.
King: He made confession° of you,
And gave you such a masterly report
For art and exercise° in your defence°   95
And for your rapier most especial,
That he cried out, 'twould be a sight indeed,
If one could match you: the scrimers° of their nation,
He swore, had neither motion, guard, nor eye,
If you oppos'd them. Sir, this report of his   100
Did Hamlet so envenom with his envy
That he could nothing do but wish and beg
Your sudden coming o'er, to play° with you.
Now, out of this, —

Laertes: What out of this, my lord?
King: Laertes, was your father dear to you?   105
Or are you like the painting of a sorrow,
A face without a heart?

---

74 *siege:* Rank.   78 *sables:* Rich garments.   82 *can well:* Are skilled.   85 *incorps'd and demi-natur'd:* Of one body and nearly of one nature (like the centaur).   86 *topp'd:* Surpassed.   87 *forgery:* Invention.   90 *Lamord:* This refers possibly to Pietro Monte, instructor to Louis XII's master of the horse.   93 *confession:* Grudging admission of superiority.   95 *art and exercise:* Skillful exercise; *defence:* Science of defense in sword practice. 98 *scrimers:* Fencers.   103 *play:* Fence.

Laertes: Why ask you this?
King: Not that I think you did not love your father;
     But that I know love is begun by time;
     And that I see, in passages of proof,°   110
     Time qualifies the spark and fire of it.
     There lives within the very flame of love
     A kind of wick or snuff that will abate it;
     And nothing is at a like goodness still;
     For goodness, growing to a plurisy,°   115
     Dies in his own too much:° that we would do,
     We should do when we would; for this "would" changes
     And hath abatements° and delays as many
     As there are tongues, are hands, are accidents;°
     And then this "should" is like a spendthrift° sigh,   120
     That hurts by easing. But, to the quick o' th' ulcer:° —
     Hamlet comes back: what would you undertake,
     To show yourself your father's son in deed
     More than in words?
Laertes: To cut his throat i' th' church.
King: No place, indeed, should murder sanctuarize;°   125
     Revenge should have no bounds. But, good Laertes,
     Will you do this, keep close within your chamber.
     Hamlet return'd shall know you are come home:
     We'll put on those shall praise your excellence
     And set a double varnish on the fame   130
     The Frenchman gave you, bring you in fine together
     And wager on your heads: he, being remiss,
     Most generous and free from all contriving,
     Will not peruse the foils; so that, with ease,
     Or with a little shuffling, you may choose   135
     A sword unbated,° and in a pass of practice°
     Requite him for your father.
Laertes: I will do 't:
     And, for that purpose, I'll anoint my sword.
     I bought an unction of a mountebank,°
     So mortal that, but dip a knife in it,   140
     Where it draws blood no cataplasm° so rare,
     Collected from all simples° that have virtue
     Under the moon,° can save the thing from death
     That is but scratch'd withal: I'll touch my point

---

110 *passages of proof:* Proved instances.   115 *plurisy:* Excess, plethora.   116 *in his own too much:* Of its own excess.   118 *abatements:* Diminutions.   119 *accidents:* Occurrences, incidents.   120 *spendthrift:* An allusion to the belief that each sigh cost the heart a drop of blood.   121 *quick o' th' ulcer:* Heart of the difficulty.   125 *sanctuarize:* Protect from punishment; allusion to the right of sanctuary with which certain religious places were invested.   136 *unbated:* Not blunted, having no button; *pass of practice:* Treacherous thrust.   139 *mountebank:* Quack doctor.   141 *cataplasm:* Plaster or poultice.   142 *simples:* Herbs.   143 *Under the moon:* I.e., when collected by moonlight to add to their medicinal value.

With this contagion, that, if I gall° him slightly,   145
It may be death.

King: Let's further think of this;
Weigh what convenience both of time and means
May fit us to our shape:° if this should fail,
And that our drift look through our bad performance,°
'Twere better not assay'd: therefore this project   150
Should have a back or second, that might hold,
If this should blast in proof.° Soft! let me see:
We'll make a solemn wager on your cunnings:°
I ha 't:
When in your motion you are hot and dry—   155
As make your bouts more violent to that end—
And that he calls for drink, I'll have prepar'd him
A chalice° for the nonce, whereon but sipping,
If he by chance escape your venom'd stuck,°
Our purpose may hold there. But stay, what noise?   160

Enter Queen.

Queen: One woe doth tread upon another's heel,
So fast they follow: your sister's drown'd, Laertes.
Laertes: Drown'd! O, where?
Queen: There is a willow° grows askant° the brook,
That shows his hoar° leaves in the glassy stream;   165
There with fantastic garlands did she make
Of crow-flowers,° nettles, daisies, and long purples°
That liberal° shepherds give a grosser name,
But our cold maids do dead men's fingers call them:
There, on the pendent boughs her crownet° weeds   170
Clamb'ring to hang, an envious sliver° broke;
When down her weedy° trophies and herself
Fell in the weeping brook. Her clothes spread wide;
And, mermaid-like, awhile they bore her up:
Which time she chanted snatches of old lauds;°   175
As one incapable° of her own distress,
Or like a creature native and indued°
Upon that element: but long it could not be
Till that her garments, heavy with their drink,
Pull'd the poor wretch from her melodious lay   180
To muddy death.
Laertes: Alas, then, she is drown'd?

---

145 *gall:* Graze, wound.   148 *shape:* Part we propose to act.   149 *drift . . . performance:*
Intention be disclosed by our bungling.   152 *blast in proof:* Burst in the test (like a cannon).
153 *cunnings:* Skills.   158 *chalice:* Cup.   159 *stuck:* Thrust (from *stoccado*).   164 *willow:*
For its significance of forsaken love; *askant:* Aslant.   165 *hoar:* White (i.e., on the underside).   167 *crow-flowers:* Buttercups; *long purples:* Early purple orchids.   168 *liberal:*
Probably, free-spoken.   170 *crownet:* Coronet; made into a chaplet.   171 *sliver:* Branch.
172 *weedy:* I.e., of plants.   175 *lauds:* Hymns.   176 *incapable:* Lacking capacity to apprehend.   177 *indued:* Endowed with qualities fitting her for living in water.

Queen: Drown'd, drown'd.
Laertes: Too much of water hast thou, poor Ophelia,
    And therefore I forbid my tears: but yet
    It is our trick;° nature her custom holds,   185
    Let shame say what it will: when these are gone,
    The woman will be out.° Adieu, my lord:
    I have a speech of fire, that fain would blaze,
    But that this folly drowns it.   *Exit.*
King: Let's follow, Gertrude:
    How much I had to do to calm his rage!   190
    Now fear I this will give it start again;
    Therefore let's follow.   *Exeunt.*

[ACT V

Scene I: *A churchyard.*]

    Enter two Clowns° [with spades, &c.].

First Clown: Is she to be buried in Christian burial when she wilfully seeks
    her own salvation?
Second Clown: I tell thee she is; therefore make her grave straight:° the
    crowner° hath sat on her, and finds it Christian burial.
First Clown: How can that be, unless she drowned herself in her own   5
    defence?
Second Clown: Why, 'tis found so.
First Clown: It must be "se offendendo";° it cannot be else. For here lies
    the point: if I drown myself wittingly,° it argues an act: and an act
    hath three branches;° it is, to act, to do, and to perform: argal,° she   10
    drowned herself wittingly.
Second Clown: Nay, but hear you, goodman delver,°—
First Clown: Give me leave. Here lies the water; good: here stands the man;
    good: if the man go to this water, and drown himself, it is, will he,
    nill he, he goes,—mark you that; but if the water come to him and   15
    drown him, he drowns not himself: argal, he that is not guilty of his
    own death shortens not his own life.
Second Clown: But is this law?
First Clown: Ay, marry, is 't; crowner's quest° law.
Second Clown: Will you ha' the truth on 't? If this had not been a gentle-   20
    woman, she should have been buried out o' Christian burial.
First Clown: Why, there thou say'st:° and the more pity that great folk

---

185 *trick:* Way.   186–187 *when . . . out:* When my tears are all shed, the woman in me will be
satisfied.   **Act V, Scene I.**   *Clowns:* The word *clown* was used to denote peasants as well
as humorous characters; here applied to the rustic type of clown.   3 *straight:* Straightway,
immediately; some interpret "from east to west in a direct line, parallel with the church."
4 *crowner:* Coroner.   8 *"se offendendo":* For *se defendendo,* term used in verdicts of justifiable homicide.   9 *wittingly:* Intentionally.   10 *three branches:* Parody of legal phraseol-
ogy;   *argal:* Corruption of *ergo,* therefore.   12 *delver:* Digger.   19 *quest:* Inquest.
22 *there thou say'st:* That's right.

should have countenance° in this world to drown or hang themselves, more than their even° Christian. Come, my spade. There is no
ancient gentlemen but gardeners, ditchers, and grave-makers: they   25
hold up° Adam's profession.

Second Clown: Was he a gentleman?

First Clown: 'A was the first that ever bore arms.

Second Clown: Why, he had none.

First Clown: What, art a heathen? How dost thou understand the Scrip-   30
ture? The Scripture says "Adam digged": could he dig without arms?
I'll put another question to thee: if thou answerest me not to the
purpose, confess thyself°—

Second Clown: Go to.°

First Clown: What is he that builds stronger than either the mason, the   35
shipwright, or the carpenter?

Second Clown: The gallows-maker; for that frame outlives a thousand
tenants.

First Clown: I like thy wit well, in good faith: the gallows does well; but
how does it well? it does well to those that do ill: now thou dost ill to   40
say the gallows is built stronger than the church: argal, the gallows
may do well to thee. To 't again, come.

Second Clown: "Who builds stronger than a mason, a shipwright, or a carpenter?"

First Clown: Ay, tell me that, and unyoke.°   45

Second Clown: Marry, now I can tell.

First Clown: To 't.

Second Clown: Mass,° I cannot tell.

Enter Hamlet and Horatio [at a distance].

First Clown: Cudgel thy brains no more about it, for your dull ass will not
mend his pace with beating; and, when you are asked this question   50
next, say "a grave-maker": the houses he makes lasts till doomsday.
Go, get thee in, and fetch me a stoup° of liquor.
                              [Exit Second Clown.] Song. [He digs.]
     In youth, when I did love, did love,
          Methought it was very sweet,
     To contract — O — the time, for — a — my behove,°   55
          O, methought, there — a — was nothing — a — meet.

Hamlet: Has this fellow no feeling of his business, that 'a sings at grave-
making?

Horatio: Custom hath made it in him a property of easiness.°

Hamlet: 'Tis e'en so: the hand of little employment hath the daintier   60
sense.

First Clown: (*Song.*) But age, with his stealing steps,
          Hath claw'd me in his clutch,

---

23 *countenance:* Privilege.   24 *even:* Fellow.   26 *hold up:* Maintain, continue.   33 *confess thyself:* "And be hanged" completes the proverb.   34 *Go to:* Perhaps, "begin," or some
other form of concession.   45 *unyoke:* After this great effort you may unharness the team
of your wits.   48 *Mass:* By the Mass.   52 *stoup:* Two-quart measure.   55 *behove:* Benefit.   59 *property of easiness:* A peculiarity that now is easy.

And hath shipped me into the land
　　As if I had never been such.　　　　　　　　　　*[Throws up a skull.]*　65
Hamlet:　That skull had a tongue in it, and could sing once: how the knave
　　jowls° it to the ground, as if 'twere Cain's jaw-bone,° that did the first
　　murder! This might be the pate of a politician,° which this ass now
　　o'er-reaches;° one that would circumvent God, might it not?
Horatio:　It might, my lord.　　　　　　　　　　　　　　　　　　　　70
Hamlet:　Or of a courtier; which could say "Good morrow, sweet lord! How
　　dost thou, sweet lord?" This might be my lord such-a-one, that
　　praised my lord such-a-one's horse, when he meant to beg it; might it
　　not?
Horatio:　Ay, my lord.　　　　　　　　　　　　　　　　　　　　　75
Hamlet:　Why, e'en so: and now my Lady Worm's; chapless,° and knocked
　　about the mazzard° with a sexton's spade: here's fine revolution, an
　　we had the trick to see 't. Did these bones cost no more the breeding,
　　but to play at loggats° with 'em? mine ache to think on 't.
First Clown:　*(Song.)* A pick-axe, and a spade, a spade,　　　　　　80
　　　　For and° a shrouding sheet:
　　　　O, a pit of clay for to be made
　　　　For such a guest is meet.　　　　　　　　　*[Throws up another skull.]*
Hamlet:　There's another: why may not that be the skull of a lawyer?
　　Where be his quiddities° now, his quillities,° his cases, his tenures,°　85
　　and his tricks? why does he suffer this mad knave now to knock him
　　about the sconce° with a dirty shovel, and will not tell him of his ac-
　　tion of battery? Hum! This fellow might be in 's time a great buyer
　　of land, with his statutes, his recognizances,° his fines, his double
　　vouchers,° his recoveries:° is this the fine° of his fines, and the re-　90
　　covery of his recoveries, to have his fine pate full of fine dirt? will
　　his vouchers vouch him no more of his purchases, and double ones
　　too, than the length and breadth of a pair of indentures?° The very
　　conveyances of his lands will scarcely lie in this box; and must the
　　inheritor° himself have no more, ha?　　　　　　　　　　　　95
Horatio:　Not a jot more, my lord.
Hamlet:　Is not parchment made of sheep-skins?
Horatio:　Ay, my lord, and of calf-skins° too.
Hamlet:　They are sheep and calves which seek out assurance in that.°
　　I will speak to this fellow. Whose grave's this, sirrah?　　　　100
First Clown:　Mine, sir.
　　[Sings.] O, a pit of clay for to be made
　　　　For such a guest is meet.

---

67 *jowls:* Dashes; *Cain's jaw-bone:* Allusion to the old tradition that Cain slew Abel with the
jawbone of an ass.　68 *politician:* Schemer, plotter.　69 *o'er-reaches:* Quibble on the literal sense and the sense "circumvent."　76 *chapless:* Having no lower jaw.　77 *mazzard:*
Head.　79 *loggats:* A game in which six sticks are thrown to lie as near as possible to a stake
fixed in the ground, or block of wood on a floor.　81 *For and:* And moreover.　85 *quiddi-
ties:* Subtleties, quibbles; *quillities:* Verbal niceties, subtle distinctions; *tenures:* The holding of
a piece of property or office or the conditions or period of such holding.　87 *sconce:*
Head.　89 *statutes, recognizances:* Legal terms connected with the transfer of land.
90 *vouchers:* Persons called on to warrant a tenant's title; *recoveries:* Process for transfer of
entailed estate; *fine:* The four uses of this word are as follows: (1) end, (2) legal process, (3) elegant, (4) small.　93 *indentures:* Conveyances or contracts.　95 *inheritor:* Possessor,
owner.　98 *calf-skins:* Parchments.　99 *assurance in that:* Safety in legal parchments.

Hamlet: I think it be thine, indeed; for thou liest in 't.

First Clown: You lie out on 't, sir, and therefore 't is not yours: for my part, 105
I do not lie in 't, yet it is mine.

Hamlet: Thou dost lie in 't, to be in 't and say it is thine: 'tis for the dead,
not for the quick; therefore thou liest.

First Clown: 'Tis a quick lie, sir; 'twill away again, from me to you.

Hamlet: What man dost thou dig it for?   110

First Clown: For no man, sir.

Hamlet: What woman, then?

First Clown: For none, neither.

Hamlet: Who is to be buried in 't?

First Clown: One that was a woman, sir; but, rest her soul, she's dead.   115

Hamlet: How absolute° the knave is! we must speak by the card,° or
equivocation° will undo us. By the Lord, Horatio, these three years I
have taken note of it; the age is grown so picked° that the toe of the
peasant comes so near the heel of the courtier, he galls° his kibe.°
How long hast thou been a grave-maker?   120

First Clown: Of all the day i' the year, I came to 't that day that our last
king Hamlet overcame Fortinbras.

Hamlet: How long is that since?

First Clown: Cannot you tell that? every fool can tell that: it was the very
day that young Hamlet was born; he that is mad, and sent into   125
England.

Hamlet: Ay, marry, why was he sent into England?

First Clown: Why, because 'a was mad: 'a shall recover his wits there; or, if
'a do not, 'tis no great matter there.

Hamlet: Why?   130

First Clown: 'Twill not be seen in him there; there the men are as mad
as he.

Hamlet: How came he mad?

First Clown: Very strangely, they say.

Hamlet: How strangely?   135

First Clown: Faith, e'en with losing his wits.

Hamlet: Upon what ground?

First Clown: Why, here in Denmark: I have been sexton here, man and boy,
thirty years.°

Hamlet: How long will a man lie i' the earth ere he rot?   140

First Clown: Faith, if 'a be not rotten before 'a die—as we have many
pocky° corses now-a-days, that will scarce hold the laying in—'a will
last you some eight year or nine year: a tanner will last you nine year.

Hamlet: Why he more than another?

First Clown: Why, sir, his hide is so tanned with his trade, that 'a will keep   145
out water a great while; and your water is a sore decayer of your
whoreson dead body. Here's a skull now hath lain you i' th' earth
three and twenty years.

Hamlet: Whose was it?

---

116 *absolute:* Positive, decided; *by the card:* With precision, i.e., by the mariner's card on
which the points of the compass were marked.   117 *equivocation:* Ambiguity in the use of
terms.   118 *picked:* Refined, fastidious.   119 *galls:* Chafes; *kibe:* Chilblain.   139 *thirty
years:* This statement with that in line 125 shows Hamlet's age to be thirty years.
142 *pocky:* Rotten, diseased.

First Clown: A whoreson mad fellow's it was: whose do you think it was?   150
Hamlet: Nay, I know not.
First Clown: A pestilence on him for a mad rogue! 'a poured a flagon of
    Rhenish on my head once. This same skull, sir, was Yorick's skull, the
    king's jester.
Hamlet: This?   155
First Clown: E'en that.
Hamlet: Let me see. *[Takes the skull.]* Alas, poor Yorick! I knew him, Hora-
    tio: a fellow of infinite jest, of most excellent fancy: he hath borne me
    on his back a thousand times; and now, how abhorred in my imagi-
    nation it is! my gorge rises at it. Here hung those lips that I have   160
    kissed I know not how oft. Where be your gibes now? your gam-
    bols? your songs? your flashes of merriment, that were wont to set the
    table on a roar? Not one now, to mock your own grinning? quite
    chap-fallen? Now get you to my lady's chamber, and tell her, let her
    paint an inch thick, to this favour she must come; make her laugh at   165
    that. Prithee, Horatio, tell me one thing.
Horatio: What's that, my lord?
Hamlet: Dost thou think Alexander looked o' this fashion i' the earth?
Horatio: E'en so.
Hamlet: And smelt so? pah!   *[Puts down the skull.]*   170
Horatio: E'en so, my lord.
Hamlet: To what base uses we may return, Horatio! Why may not imagi-
    nation trace the noble dust of Alexander, till 'a find it stopping a
    bung-hole?
Horatio: 'Twere to consider too curiously,° to consider so.   175
Hamlet: No, faith, not a jot; but to follow him thither with modesty
    enough, and likelihood to lead it: as thus: Alexander died, Alexander
    was buried, Alexander returneth into dust; the dust is earth; of earth
    we make loam;° and why of that loam, whereto he was converted,
    might they not stop a beer-barrel?   180
         Imperious° Cæsar, dead and turn'd to clay,
         Might stop a hole to keep the wind away:
         O, that that earth, which kept the world in awe,
         Should patch a wall t'expel the winter's flaw!°
    But soft! but soft awhile! here comes the king,   185

*Enter King, Queen, Laertes, and the Corse of [Ophelia, in procession, with
Priest, Lords, etc.].*

    The queen, the courtiers: who is this they follow?
    And with such maimed rites? This doth betoken
    The corse they follow did with desp'rate hand
    Fordo° it° own life: 'twas of some estate.
    Couch° we awhile, and mark.   *[Retiring with Horatio.]*   190
Laertes: What ceremony else?
Hamlet: That is Laertes,
    A very noble youth: mark.

---

175 *curiously:* Minutely.   179 *loam:* Clay paste for brickmaking.   181 *Imperious:* Imperial.   184 *flaw:* Gust of wind.   189 *Fordo:* Destroy; *it:* Its.   190 *Couch:* Hide, lurk.

Laertes: What ceremony else?

First Priest: Her obsequies have been as far enlarg'd°
  As we have warranty: her death was doubtful;   195
  And, but that great command o'ersways the order,
  She should in ground unsanctified have lodg'd
  Till the last trumpet; for charitable prayers,
  Shards,° flints and pebbles should be thrown on her:
  Yet here she is allow'd her virgin crants,°   200
  Her maiden strewments° and the bringing home
  Of bell and burial.°

Laertes: Must there no more be done?

First Priest: No more be done:
  We should profane the service of the dead
  To sing a requiem and such rest to her   205
  As to peace-parted° souls.

Laertes: Lay her i' th' earth:
  And from her fair and unpolluted flesh
  May violets spring! I tell thee, churlish priest,
  A minist'ring angel shall my sister be,
  When thou liest howling.°

Hamlet: What, the fair Ophelia!   210

Queen: Sweets to the sweet: farewell!   *[Scattering flowers.]*
  I hop'd thou shouldst have been my Hamlet's wife;
  I thought thy bride-bed to have deck'd, sweet maid,
  And not have strew'd thy grave.

Laertes: O, treble woe
  Fall ten times treble on that cursed head,   215
  Whose wicked deed thy most ingenious sense°
  Depriv'd thee of! Hold off the earth awhile,
  Till I have caught her once more in mine arms: *[Leaps into the grave.]*
  Now pile your dust upon the quick and dead,
  Till of this flat a mountain you have made,   220
  T' o'ertop old Pelion,° or the skyish head
  Of blue Olympus.

Hamlet: *[Advancing]* What is he whose grief
  Bears such an emphasis? whose phrase of sorrow
  Conjures the wand'ring stars,° and makes them stand
  Like wonder-wounded hearers? This is I,   225
  Hamlet the Dane.   *[Leaps into the grave.]*

Laertes: The devil take thy soul!   *[Grappling with him.]*

Hamlet: Thou pray'st not well.
  I prithee, take thy fingers from my throat;

---

194 *enlarg'd:* Extended, referring to the fact that suicides are not given full burial rites. 199 *Shards:* Broken bits of pottery.   200 *crants:* Garlands customarily hung upon the biers of unmarried women.   201 *strewments:* Traditional strewing of flowers.   201-202 *bringing...burial:* The laying to rest of the body, to the sound of the bell.   206 *peace-parted:* Allusion to the text "Lord, now lettest thou thy servant depart in peace."   210 *howling:* I.e., in hell.   216 *ingenious sense:* Mind endowed with finest qualities.   221 *Pelion:* Olympus, Pelion, and Ossa are mountains in the north of Thessaly.   224 *wand'ring stars:* Planets.

For, though I am not splenitive° and rash,
Yet have I in me something dangerous,
Which let thy wisdom fear: hold off thy hand.   230
King: Pluck them asunder.
Queen: Hamlet, Hamlet!
All: Gentlemen, —
Horatio: Good my lord, be quiet.

[The Attendants part them, and they come out of the grave.]

Hamlet: Why, I will fight with him upon this theme
Until my eyelids will no longer wag.°   235
Queen: O my son, what theme?
Hamlet: I lov'd Ophelia: forty thousand brothers
Could not, with all their quantity° of love,
Make up my sum. What wilt thou do for her?
King: O, he is mad, Laertes.   240
Queen: For love of God, forbear° him.
Hamlet: 'Swounds,° show me what thou 'lt do:
Woo 't° weep? woo 't fight? woo 't fast? woo 't tear thyself?
Woo 't drink up eisel?° eat a crocodile?
I'll do 't. Dost thou come here to whine?   245
To outface me with leaping in her grave?
Be buried quick with her, and so will I:
And, if thou prate of mountains, let them throw
Millions of acres on us, till our ground,
Singeing his pate against the burning zone,°   250
Make Ossa like a wart! Nay, an thou 'lt mouth,
I'll rant as well as thou.
Queen: This is mere madness:
And thus awhile the fit will work on him;
Anon, as patient as the female dove.
When that her golden couplets° are disclos'd,   255
His silence will sit drooping.
Hamlet: Hear you, sir;
What is the reason that you use me thus?
I lov'd you ever: but it is no matter;
Let Hercules himself do what he may,
The cat will mew and dog will have his day.   260
King: I pray thee, good Horatio, wait upon him.   *Exit Hamlet and Horatio.*
[To Laertes.] Strengthen your patience in° our last night's speech;
We'll put the matter to the present push.°
Good Gertrude, set some watch over your son.

---

229 *splenitive:* Quick-tempered.   235 *wag:* Move (not used ludicrously).   238 *quantity:*
Some suggest that the word is used in a deprecatory sense (little bits, fragments).   241 *for-
bear:* Leave alone.   242 *'Swounds:* Oath, "God's wounds."   243 *Woo 't:* Wilt thou.
244 *eisel:* Vinegar. Some editors have taken this to be the name of a river, such as the Yssel,
the Weissel, and the Nile.   250 *burning zone:* Sun's orbit.   255 *golden couplets:* The pigeon lays two eggs; the young when hatched are covered with golden down.   262 *in:* By recalling.   263 *present push:* Immediate test.

This grave shall have a living° monument: 265
An hour of quiet shortly shall we see;
Till then, in patience our proceeding be.   *Exeunt.*

[SCENE II: *A hall in the castle.*]

Enter Hamlet and Horatio.

Hamlet: So much for this, sir: now shall you see the other;
        You do remember all the circumstance?
Horatio: Remember it, my lord!
Hamlet: Sir, in my heart there was a kind of fighting,
        That would not let me sleep: methought I lay   5
        Worse than the mutines in the bilboes.° Rashly,°
        And prais'd be rashness for it, let us know,
        Our indiscretion sometime serves us well,
        When our deep plots do pall:° and that should learn us
        There's a divinity that shapes our ends,   10
        Rough-hew° them how we will, —
Horatio: That is most certain.
Hamlet: Up from my cabin,
        My sea-gown° scarf'd about me, in the dark
        Grop'd I to find out them; had my desire,
        Finger'd° their packet, and in fine° withdrew   15
        To mine own room again; making so bold,
        My fears forgetting manners, to unseal
        Their grand commission; where I found, Horatio, —
        O royal knavery! — an exact command,
        Larded° with many several sorts of reasons   20
        Importing Denmark's health and England's too,
        With, ho! such bugs° and goblins in my life,°
        That, on the supervise,° no leisure bated,°
        No, not to stay the grinding of the axe,
        My head should be struck off.
Horatio: Is 't possible?   25
Hamlet: Here's the commission: read it at more leisure.
        But wilt thou hear me how I did proceed?
Horatio: I beseech you.
Hamlet: Being thus be-netted round with villanies, —
        Ere I could make a prologue to my brains,   30
        They had begun the play° — I sat me down,

---

265 *living:* Lasting; also refers (for Laertes's benefit) to the plot against Hamlet.   **Scene II.**
6 *mutines in the bilboes:* Mutineers in shackles; *Rashly:* Goes with line 12.   9 *pall:* Fail.
11 *Rough-hew:* Shape roughly; it may mean "bungle."   13 *sea-gown:* "A sea-gown, or a
coarse, high-collered, and short-sleeved gowne, reaching down to the mid-leg, and used most
by seamen and saylors" (Cotgrave, quoted by Singer).   15 *Finger'd:* Pilfered, filched; *in fine:*
Finally.   20 *Larded:* Enriched.   22 *bugs:* Bugbears; *such...life:* Such imaginary dangers if I
were allowed to live.   23 *supervise:* Perusal; *leisure bated:* Delay allowed.   30–31 *prologue...
play:* I.e., before I could begin to think, my mind had made its decision.

Devis'd a new commission, wrote it fair:
I once did hold it, as our statists° do,
A baseness to write fair° and labour'd much
How to forget that learning, but, sir, now   35
It did me yeoman's° service: wilt thou know
Th' effect of what I wrote?

Horatio: Ay, good my lord.

Hamlet: An earnest conjuration from the king,
As England was his faithful tributary,
As love between them like the palm might flourish,   40
As peace should still her wheaten garland° wear
And stand a comma° 'tween their amities,
And many such-like 'As'es° of great charge,°
That, on the view and knowing of these contents,
Without debatement further, more or less,   45
He should the bearers put to sudden death,
Not shriving-time° allow'd.

Horatio: How was this seal'd?

Hamlet: Why, even in that was heaven ordinant.°
I had my father's signet in my purse,
Which was the model of that Danish seal;   50
Folded the writ up in the form of th' other,
Subscrib'd it, gave 't th' impression, plac'd it safely,
The changeling never known. Now, the next day
Was our sea-fight; and what to this was sequent°
Thou know'st already.   55

Horatio: So Guildenstern and Rosencrantz go to 't.

Hamlet: Why, man, they did make love to this employment;
They are not near my conscience; their defeat
Does by their own insinuation° grow:
'Tis dangerous when the baser nature comes   60
Between the pass° and fell incensed° points
Of mighty opposites.

Horatio: Why, what a king is this!

Hamlet: Does it not, think thee, stand° me now upon —
He that hath kill'd my king and whor'd my mother,
Popp'd in between th' election° and my hopes,   65
Thrown out his angle° for my proper life,
And with such coz'nage° — is 't not perfect conscience,
To quit° him with this arm? and is 't not to be damn'd,

---

33 *statists:* Statesmen.   34 *fair:* In a clear hand.   36 *yeoman's:* I.e., faithful.   41 *wheaten garland:* Symbol of peace.   42 *comma:* Smallest break or separation. Here *amity* begins and *amity* ends the period, and *peace* stands between like a dependent clause. The comma indicates continuity, link.   43 *'As'es:* The "whereases" of a formal document, with play on the word *ass; charge:* Import, and burden.   47 *shriving-time:* Time for absolution.   48 *ordinant:* Directing.   54 *sequent:* Subsequent.   59 *insinuation:* Interference.   61 *pass:* Thrust; *fell incensed:* Fiercely angered.   63 *stand:* Become incumbent.   65 *election:* The Danish throne was filled by election.   66 *angle:* Fishing line.   67 *coz'nage:* Trickery.   68 *quit:* Repay.

To let this canker° of our nature come
In further evil?   70
Horatio: It must be shortly known to him from England
        What is the issue of the business there.
Hamlet: It will be short: the interim is mine;
        And a man's life's no more than to say "One."
        But I am very sorry, good Horatio,   75
        That to Laertes I forgot myself;
        For, by the image of my cause, I see
        The portraiture of his: I'll court his favours:
        But, sure, the bravery° of his grief did put me
        Into a tow'ring passion.
Horatio: Peace! who comes here?   80

        Enter a Courtier [Osric].

Osric: Your lordship is right welcome back to Denmark.
Hamlet: I humbly thank you, sir. *[To Horatio.]* Dost know this water-fly?°
Horatio: No, my good lord.
Hamlet: Thy state is the more gracious; for 'tis a vice to know him. He
        hath much land, and fertile: let a beast be lord of beasts,° and his crib   85
        shall stand at the king's mess:° 'tis a chough;° but, as I say, spacious
        in the possession of dirt.
Osric: Sweet lord, if your lordship were at leisure, I should impart a thing
        to you from his majesty.
Hamlet: I will receive it, sir, with all diligence of spirit. Put your bonnet to   90
        his right use; 'tis for the head.
Osric: I thank your lordship, it is very hot.
Hamlet: No, believe me, 'tis very cold; the wind is northerly.
Osric: It is indifferent° cold, my lord, indeed.
Hamlet: But yet methinks it is very sultry and hot for my complexion.   95
Osric: Exceedingly, my lord; it is very sultry,—as 'twere,—I cannot tell
        how. But, my lord, his majesty bade me signify to you that 'a has laid a
        great wager on your head: sir, this is the matter,—
Hamlet: I beseech you, remember°—

                              [Hamlet moves him to put on his hat.]
Osric: Nay, good my lord; for mine ease,° in good faith. Sir, here is newly   100
        come to court Laertes; believe me, an absolute gentleman, full of
        most excellent differences, of very soft° society and great showing:°
        indeed, to speak feelingly° of him, he is the card° or calendar of gen-
        try,° for you shall find in him the continent of what part a gentleman
        would see.   105

---

69 *canker:* Ulcer, or possibly the worm which destroys buds and leaves.   79 *bravery:*
Bravado.   82 *water-fly:* Vain or busily idle person.   85 *lord of beasts:* See Genesis 1:26, 28.
85–86 *his crib … mess:* He shall eat at the king's table and be one of the group of persons
(usually four) constituting a *mess* at a banquet.   86 *chough:* Probably, chattering jackdaw;
also explained as *chuff,* provincial boor or churl.   94 *indifferent:* Somewhat.   99 *remem-*
ber: I.e., remember thy courtesy; conventional phrase for "Be covered."   100 *mine ease:*
Conventional reply declining the invitation of "Remember thy courtesy."   102 *soft:* Gentle; *showing:* Distinguished appearance.   103 *feelingly:* With just perception; *card:* Chart,
map.   103–104 *gentry:* Good breeding.

Hamlet: Sir, his definement° suffers no perdition° in you; though, I know, to divide him inventorially° would dozy° the arithmetic of memory, and yet but yaw° neither, in respect of his quick sail. But, in the verity of extolment, I take him to be a soul of great article;° and his infusion° of such dearth and rareness,° as, to make true diction of him, 110 his semblable° is his mirror; and who else would trace° him, his umbrage,° nothing more.

Osric: Your lordship speaks most infallibly of him.

Hamlet: The concernancy,° sir? why do we wrap the gentleman in our more rawer breath?° 115

Osric: Sir?

Horatio [aside to Hamlet]: Is 't not possible to understand in another tongue?° You will do 't, sir, really.

Hamlet: What imports the nomination° of this gentleman?

Osric: Of Laertes? 120

Horatio [aside to Hamlet]: His purse is empty already; all 's golden words are spent.

Hamlet: Of him, sir.

Osric: I know you are not ignorant—

Hamlet: I would you did, sir; yet, in faith, if you did, it would not much 125 approve° me. Well, sir?

Osric: You are not ignorant of what excellence Laertes is—

Hamlet: I dare not confess that, lest I should compare with him in excellence; but, to know a man well, were to know himself.°

Osric: I mean, sir, for his weapon; but in the imputation° laid on him by 130 them, in his meed° he's unfellowed.

Hamlet: What's his weapon?

Osric: Rapier and dagger.

Hamlet: That's two of his weapons: but, well.

Osric: The king, sir, hath wagered with him six Barbary horses: against 135 the which he has impawned,° as I take it, six French rapiers and poniards, with their assigns, as girdle, hangers,° and so: three of the carriages, in faith, are very dear to fancy,° very responsive° to the hilts, most delicate° carriages, and of very liberal conceit.°

Hamlet: What call you the carriages? 140

Horatio [aside to Hamlet]: I knew you must be edified by the margent° ere you had done.

Osric: The carriages, sir, are the hangers.

---

106 *definement:* Definition; *perdition:* Loss, diminution.   107 *divide him inventorially:* I.e., enumerate his graces; *dozy:* Dizzy.   108 *yaw:* To move unsteadily (of a ship).   109 *article:* Moment or importance.   109–110 *infusion:* Infused temperament, character imparted by nature. 110 *dearth and rareness:* Rarity.   111 *semblable:* True likeness; *trace:* Follow.   111–112 *umbrage:* Shadow.   114 *concernancy:* Import.   115 *breath:* Speech.   117–118 *Is 't...tongue?:* I.e., can one converse with Osric only in this outlandish jargon?   119 *nomination:* Naming. 126 *approve:* Command.   129 *but...himself:* But to know a man as excellent were to know Laertes.   130 *imputation:* Reputation.   131 *meed:* Merit.   136 *he has impawned:* He has wagered.   137 *hangers:* Straps on the sword belt from which the sword hung.   138 *dear to fancy:* Fancifully made; *responsive:* Probably, well balanced, corresponding closely. 139 *delicate:* Fine in workmanship; *liberal conceit:* Elaborate design.   141 *margent:* Margin of a book, place for explanatory notes.

Hamlet: The phrase would be more german° to the matter, if we could
carry cannon by our sides: I would it might be hangers till then. But,   145
on: six Barbary horses against six French swords, their assigns, and
three liberal-conceited carriages; that's the French bet against the
Danish. Why is this "impawned," as you call it?

Osric: The king, sir, hath laid, that in a dozen passes between yourself
and him, he shall not exceed you three hits: he hath laid on twelve for   150
nine; and it would come to immediate trial, if your lordship would
vouchsafe the answer.

Hamlet: How if I answer "no"?

Osric: I mean, my lord, the opposition of your person in trial.

Hamlet: Sir, I will walk here in the hall: if it please his majesty, it is the   155
breathing time° of day with me; let the foils be brought, the gentle-
man willing, and the king hold his purpose, I will win for him as I
can; if not, I will gain nothing but my shame and the odd hits.

Osric: Shall I re-deliver you e'en so?

Hamlet: To this effect, sir; after what flourish your nature will.   160

Osric: I commend my duty to your lordship.

Hamlet: Yours, yours. *[Exit Osric.]* He does well to commend it himself;
there are no tongues else for 's turn.

Horatio: This lapwing° runs away with the shell on his head.

Hamlet: 'A did comply, sir, with his dug,° before 'a sucked it. Thus has   165
he — and many more of the same breed that I know the drossy° age
dotes on — only got the tune° of the time and out of an habit of encounter;° a kind of yesty° collection, which carries them through and
through the most fann'd and winnowed° opinions; and do but
blow them to their trial, the bubbles are out.°   170

Enter a Lord.

Lord: My lord, his majesty commended him to you by young Osric, who
brings back to him, that you attend him in the hall: he sends to know
if your pleasure hold to play with Laertes, or that you will take longer
time.

Hamlet: I am constant to my purposes; they follow the king's pleasure: if   175
his fitness speaks, mine is ready; now or whensoever, provided I be so
able as now.

Lord: The king and queen and all are coming down.

Hamlet: In happy time.°

Lord: The queen desires you to use some gentle entertainment to Laertes   180
before you fall to play.

Hamlet: She well instructs me.   *[Exit Lord.]*

Horatio: You will lose this wager, my lord.

---

144 *german:* Germane, appropriate.   156 *breathing time:* Exercise period.   164 *lapwing:*
Peewit; noted for its wiliness in drawing a visitor away from its nest and its supposed habit of
running about when newly hatched with its head in the shell; possibly an allusion to Osric's
hat.   165 *did comply . . . dug:* Paid compliments to his mother's breast.   166 *drossy:* Frivolous.   167 *tune:* Temper, mood.   167–168 *habit of encounter:* Demeanor of social intercourse.   168 *yesty:* Frothy.   169 *fann'd and winnowed:* Select and refined.   170 *blow . . .
out:* I.e., put them to the test, and their ignorance is exposed.   179 *In happy time:* A phrase
of courtesy.

Hamlet: I do not think so; since he went into France, I have been in continual practice; I shall win at the odds. But thou wouldst not think   185
how ill all 's here about my heart: but it is no matter.

Horatio: Nay, good my lord, —

Hamlet: It is but foolery; but it is such a kind of gain-giving,° as would
perhaps trouble a woman.

Horatio: If your mind dislike any thing, obey it: I will forestall their repair   190
hither, and say you are not fit.

Hamlet: Not a whit, we defy augury: there's a special providence in the
fall of a sparrow. If it be now, 'tis not to come; if it be not to come,
it will be now; if it be not now, yet it will come: the readiness is all:°
since no man of aught he leaves knows, what is 't to leave betimes?   195
Let be.

*A table prepared. [Enter] Trumpets, Drums, and Officers with cushions; King,
Queen, [Osric,] and all the State; foils, daggers, [and wine borne in;] and Laertes.*

King: Come, Hamlet, come, and take this hand from me.

[The King puts Laertes's hand into Hamlet's.]

Hamlet: Give me your pardon, sir: I have done you wrong;
But pardon 't as you are a gentleman.
This presence° knows,   200
And you must needs have heard, how I am punish'd
With a sore distraction. What I have done,
That might your nature, honour and exception°
Roughly awake, I here proclaim was madness.
Was 't Hamlet wrong'd Laertes? Never Hamlet: 205
If Hamlet from himself be ta'en away,
And when he's not himself does wrong Laertes,
Then Hamlet does it not, Hamlet denies it.
Who does it, then? His madness: if 't be so,
Hamlet is of the faction that is wrong'd;   210
His madness is poor Hamlet's enemy.
Sir, in this audience,
Let my disclaiming from a purpos'd evil
Free me so far in your most generous thoughts,
That I have shot mine arrow o'er the house,   215
And hurt my brother.

Laertes: I am satisfied in nature,°
Whose motive, in this case, should stir me most
To my revenge: but in my terms of honour
I stand aloof; and will no reconcilement,
Till by some elder masters, of known honour,   220
I have a voice° and precedent of peace,
To keep my name ungor'd. But till that time,
I do receive your offer'd love like love,
And will not wrong it.

188 *gain-giving:* Misgiving.   194 *all:* All that matters.   200 *presence:* Royal assembly.
203 *exception:* Disapproval.   216 *nature:* I.e., he is personally satisfied, but his honor must
be satisfied by the rules of the code of honor.   221 *voice:* Authoritative pronouncement.

Hamlet: I embrace it freely;
     And will this brother's wager frankly play.   225
     Give us the foils. Come on.
Laertes: Come, one for me.
Hamlet: I'll be your foil,° Laertes: in mine ignorance
     Your skill shall, like a star i' th' darkest night,
     Stick fiery off° indeed.
Laertes: You mock me, sir.
Hamlet: No, by this hand.   230
King: Give them the foils, young Osric. Cousin Hamlet,
     You know the wager?
Hamlet: Very well, my lord;
     Your grace has laid the odds o' th' weaker side.
King: I do not fear it; I have seen you both:
     But since he is better'd, we have therefore odds.   235
Laertes: This is too heavy, let me see another.
Hamlet: This likes me well. These foils have all a length?

     [They prepare to play.]

Osric: Ay, my good lord.
King: Set me the stoups of wine upon that table.
     If Hamlet give the first or second hit,   240
     Or quit in answer of the third exchange,
     Let all the battlements their ordnance fire;
     The king shall drink to Hamlet's better breath;
     And in the cup an union° shall he throw,
     Richer than that which four successive kings   245
     In Denmark's crown have worn. Give me the cups;
     And let the kettle° to the trumpet speak,
     The trumpet to the cannoneer without,
     The cannons to the heavens, the heavens to earth,
     "Now the king drinks to Hamlet." Come begin: *Trumpets the while.*   250
     And you, the judges, bear a wary eye.
Hamlet: Come on, sir.
Laertes: Come, my lord.   *[They play.]*
Hamlet: One.
Laertes: No.
Hamlet: Judgement.
Osric: A hit, a very palpable hit.

     Drum, trumpets, and shot. Flourish. A piece goes off.

Laertes: Well; again.
King: Stay; give me drink. Hamlet, this pearl° is thine;
     Here's to thy health. Give him the cup.   255
Hamlet: I'll play this bout first; set it by awhile.
     Come. *[They play.]* Another hit; what say you?
Laertes: A touch, a touch, I do confess 't.

---

227 *foil:* Quibble on the two senses: "background which sets something off," and
"blunted rapier for fencing."   229 *Stick fiery off:* Stand out brilliantly.   244 *union:* Pearl.
247 *kettle:* Kettledrum.   254 *pearl:* I.e., the poison.

King: Our son shall win.

Queen: He's fat,° and scant of breath.

       Here, Hamlet, take my napkin, rub thy brows: 260

       The queen carouses° to thy fortune, Hamlet.

Hamlet: Good madam!

King: Gertrude, do not drink.

Queen: I will, my lord; I pray you, pardon me.   *[Drinks.]*

King [aside]: It is the poison'd cup: it is too late.

Hamlet: I dare not drink yet, madam; by and by.   265

Queen: Come, let me wipe thy face.

Laertes: My lord, I'll hit him now.

King: I do not think 't.

Laertes [aside]: And yet 'tis almost 'gainst my conscience.

Hamlet: Come, for the third, Laertes: you but dally;

       I pray you, pass with your best violence;   270

       I am afeard you make a wanton° of me.

Laertes: Say you so? come on.   *[They play.]*

Osric: Nothing, neither way.

Laertes: Have at you now!

[Laertes wounds Hamlet; then, in scuffling, they change rapiers,° and Hamlet wounds Laertes.]

King: Part them; they are incens'd.

Hamlet: Nay, come again.   *[The Queen falls.]*

Osric: Look to the queen there, ho!   275

Horatio: They bleed on both sides. How is it, my lord?

Osric: How is 't, Laertes?

Laertes: Why, as a woodcock° to mine own springe,° Osric;

       I am justly kill'd with mine own treachery.

Hamlet: How does the queen?

King: She swounds° to see them bleed.   280

Queen: No, no, the drink, the drink, — O my dear Hamlet, —

       The drink, the drink! I am poison'd.   *[Dies.]*

Hamlet: O villany! Ho! let the door be lock'd:

       Treachery! Seek it out.   *[Laertes falls.]*

Laertes: It is here, Hamlet: Hamlet, thou art slain;   285

       No med'cine in the world can do thee good;

       In thee there is not half an hour of life;

       The treacherous instrument is in thy hand,

       Unbated° and envenom'd: the foul practice

       Hath turn'd itself on me; lo, here I lie,   290

       Never to rise again: thy mother's poison'd:

       I can no more: the king, the king's to blame.

---

259 *fat:* Not physically fit, out of training. Some earlier editors speculated that the term applied to the corpulence of Richard Burbage, who originally played the part, but the allusion now appears unlikely. *Fat* may also suggest "sweaty."   261 *carouses:* Drinks a toast. 271 *wanton:* Spoiled child.   *in scuffling, they change rapiers:* According to a widespread stage tradition, Hamlet receives a scratch, realizes that Laertes's sword is unbated, and accordingly forces an exchange.   278 *woodcock:* As type of stupidity or as decoy; *springe:* Trap, snare. 280 *swounds:* Swoons.   289 *Unbated:* Not blunted with a button.

Hamlet: The point envenom'd too!
          Then, venom, to thy work.   *[Stabs the King.]*
All: Treason! treason!   295
King: O, yet defend me, friends; I am but hurt.
Hamlet: Here, thou incestuous, murd'rous, damned Dane,
          Drink off this potion. Is thy union here?
          Follow my mother.   *[King dies.]*
Laertes: He is justly serv'd;
          It is a poison temper'd° by himself.   300
          Exchange forgiveness with me, noble Hamlet:
          Mine and my father's death come not upon thee,
          Nor thine on me!   *[Dies.]*
Hamlet: Heaven make thee free of it! I follow thee.
          I am dead, Horatio. Wretched queen, adieu!   305
          You that look pale and tremble at this chance,
          That are but mutes° or audience to this act,
          Had I but time — as this fell sergeant,° Death,
          Is strict in his arrest — O, I could tell you —
          But let it be. Horatio, I am dead;   310
          Thou livest; report me and my cause aright
          To the unsatisfied.
Horatio: Never believe it:
          I am more an antique Roman° than a Dane:
          Here 's yet some liquor left.
Hamlet: As th' art a man,
          Give me the cup: let go, by heaven, I'll ha 't.   315
          O God! Horatio, what a wounded name,
          Things standing thus unknown, shall live behind me!
          If thou didst ever hold me in thy heart,
          Absent thee from felicity awhile,
          And in this harsh world draw thy breath in pain,   320
          To tell my story.   *A march afar off.*
                   What warlike noise is this?
Osric: Young Fortinbras, with conquest come from Poland,
          To the ambassadors of England gives
          This warlike volley.
Hamlet: O, I die, Horatio;
          The potent poison quite o'er-crows° my spirit: 325
          I cannot live to hear the news from England;
          But I do prophesy th' election lights
          On Fortinbras: he has my dying voice;
          So tell him, with th' occurrents,° more and less,
          Which have solicited.° The rest is silence.   *[Dies.]* 330
Horatio: Now cracks a noble heart. Good night, sweet prince;
          And flights of angels sing thee to thy rest!
          Why does the drum come hither?   *[March within.]*

---

300 *temper'd:* Mixed.   307 *mutes:* Performers in a play who speak no words.   308 *sergeant:* Sheriff's officer.   313 *Roman:* It was the Roman custom to follow masters in death.
325 *o'er-crows:* Triumphs over.   329 *occurrents:* Events, incidents.   330 *solicited:* Moved, urged.

Enter Fortinbras, with the [English] Ambassadors [and others].

Fortinbras: Where is this sight?
Horatio: What is it you would see?
      If aught of woe or wonder, cease your search.   335
Fortinbras: This quarry° cries on havoc.° O proud Death,
      What feast is toward in thine eternal cell,
      That thou so many princes at a shot
      So bloodily hast struck?
First Ambassador: The sight is dismal;
      And our affairs from England come too late: 340
      The ears are senseless that should give us hearing,
      To tell him his commandment is fulfill'd,
      That Rosencrantz and Guildenstern are dead:
      Where should we have our thanks?
Horatio: Not from his mouth,°
      Had it th' ability of life to thank you: 345
      He never gave commandment for their death.
      But since, so jump° upon this bloody question,°
      You from the Polack wars, and you from England,
      Are here arriv'd, give order that these bodies
      High on a stage° be placed to the view;   350
      And let me speak to th' yet unknowing world
      How these things came about: so shall you hear
      Of carnal, bloody, and unnatural acts,
      Of accidental judgements, casual slaughters,
      Of deaths put on by cunning and forc'd cause,   355
      And, in this upshot, purposes mistook
      Fall'n on th' inventors' heads: all this can I
      Truly deliver.
Fortinbras: Let us haste to hear it,
      And call the noblest to the audience.
      For me, with sorrow I embrace my fortune: 360
      I have some rights of memory° in this kingdom,
      Which now to claim my vantage doth invite me.
Horatio: Of that I shall have also cause to speak,
      And from his mouth whose voice will draw on more:°
      But let this same be presently perform'd,   365
      Even while men's minds are wild; lest more mischance,
      On° plots and errors, happen.
Fortinbras: Let four captains
      Bear Hamlet, like a soldier, to the stage;
      For he was likely, had he been put on,
      To have prov'd most royal: and, for his passage,°   370

336 *quarry:* Heap of dead; *cries on havoc:* Proclaims a general slaughter.   344 *his mouth:*
I.e., the king's.   347 *jump:* Precisely; *question:* Dispute.   350 *stage:* Platform.   361 *of
memory:* Traditional, remembered.   364 *voice . . . more:* Vote will influence still others.
367 *On:* On account of, or possibly, on top of, in addition to.   370 *passage:* Death.

The soldiers' music and the rites of war
Speak loudly for him.
Take up the bodies: such a sight as this
Becomes the field,° but here shows much amiss.
Go, bid the soldiers shoot.   375

Exeunt [marching, bearing off the dead bodies; after which a peal of ordnance is shot off].

---

374 *field:* I.e., of battle.

CONSIDERATIONS FOR CRITICAL THINKING AND WRITING

1. FIRST RESPONSE. Why does Hamlet find avenging his father's death so difficult? Why doesn't he take decisive action as soon as he seems convinced of Claudius's guilt?

2. Claudius urges Hamlet to leave behind his "obstinate condolement" and give up grieving for his dead father because it represents "impious stubbornness" (I.ii.93-94). Consider Claudius's advice in this speech (lines 87-117). Is it sensible? Why won't Hamlet heed this advice?

3. Are Polonius's admonitions to Laertes and Ophelia good advice (I.iii.55-81, 115-135)? What does his advice suggest about life at court, given that he is the chief counselor to the king?

4. When the ghost tells Hamlet that Claudius murdered him, Hamlet cries out, "O my prophetic soul!" (I.v.40). Why? What does the ghost demand of Hamlet?

5. What is known about the kind of person Hamlet was before his father's death? Does he have the stature of a tragic hero such as Oedipus? How does news of the murder and his mother's remarriage affect his behavior and view of life? Is he mad, as Polonius assumes, or is he pretending to be mad? Is there a "method in 't" (II.ii.200)? What do we learn from Hamlet's soliloquies?

6. What is the purpose of the play within the play? How does it provide a commentary on the action of the larger play?

7. Is Ophelia connected in any way with the crime Hamlet seeks to avenge? Why is he so brutal to Ophelia in Act III, Scene i? Why does she go mad?

8. Does Hamlet think Gertrude is as guilty as Claudius? Why is Hamlet so thoroughly disgusted by her in Act III, Scene iv?

9. Why doesn't Hamlet kill Claudius as he prays (III.iii)? Do you feel any sympathy for Claudius in this scene, or is he presented as a callous murderer?

10. If Hamlet had killed Claudius in Act III and the play had ended there, what would be missing in Hamlet's perceptions of himself and the world? How does his character develop in Acts IV and V? What softens our realization that Hamlet is in various degrees responsible for the deaths of Polonius, Ophelia, Laertes, Rosencrantz, Guildenstern, Claudius, and Gertrude?

11. What purpose does Fortinbras serve in the action? Would anything be lost if he were edited out of the play?

12. Despite its tragic dimensions, *Hamlet* includes humorous scenes and many witty lines delivered by the title character himself. Locate those scenes and lines, and then determine the tone and purpose of the play's humor.

13. CRITICAL STRATEGIES. Read the section on formalist criticism (pp. 2095–97) in Chapter 52, "Applying a Critical Strategy." Choose a soliloquy by Hamlet and write an analysis of its images so that you reveal some significant portion of his character.

CONNECTIONS TO OTHER SELECTIONS

1. Compare in an essay Hamlet's attitudes about revenge with Matt Fowler's in Andre Dubus's short story "Killings" (p. 84).

2. What kind of king is Claudius? How does he compare with Creon in Sophocles' *Antigone* (p. 1333)? How are matters of state and the political atmosphere in the world of each play affected by the rules of Claudius and Creon?

3. Here's a long reach but a potentially interesting one: write an essay that considers Gertrude as a wife and mother alongside Nora in Henrik Ibsen's *A Doll House* (p. 1568). How responsible are they to themselves and to others? Can they be discussed in the same breath, or are they from such different worlds that nothing useful can be said about comparing them? Either way, explain your response.

PERSPECTIVES ON SHAKESPEARE

Objections to the Elizabethan Theater *by the Mayor of London*   1597

The inconueniences that grow by Stage playes abowt the Citie of London.

1. They are a speaciall cause of corrupting their Youth, conteninge nothinge but vnchast matters, lascivious devices, shiftes of Coozenage,° & other lewd & vngodly practizes, being so as that they impresse the very qualitie & corruption of manners which they represent, Contrary to the rules & art prescribed for the makinge of Comedies eaven amonge the Heathen, who vsd them seldom & at certen sett tymes, and not all the year longe as our manner is. Whearby such as frequent them, beinge of the base & refuze sort of people or such young gentlemen as have small regard of credit or conscience, drawe the same into imitacion and not to the avoidinge the like vices which they represent.

2. They are the ordinary places for vagrant persons, Maisterles men, thieves, horse stealers, whoremongers, Coozeners, Conycatchers,° contrivers of treason, and other idele and daungerous persons to meet together & to make theire matches to the great displeasure of Almightie God & the hurt & annoyance of her Maiesties people, which cannot be prevented nor discovered

---

shiftes of Coozenage: Perverse behavior.   *Conycatchers:* Tricksters.

by the Gouernours of the Citie for that they are owt of the Citiees iuris-
diction.

3. They maintaine idlenes in such persons as haue no vocation & draw ap-
prentices and other seruantes from theire ordinary workes and all sortes
of people from the resort vnto sermons and other Christian exercises, to
the great hinderance of traides & prophanation of religion established by
her highnes within this Realm.

4. In the time of sickness it is fownd by experience, that many hauing sores
and yet not hart sicke take occasion hearby to walk abroad & to recreat
themselves by heareinge a play Whearby others are infected, and them
selves also many things miscarry.

From Edmund K. Chambers, The Elizabethan Stage

CONSIDERATIONS FOR CRITICAL THINKING AND WRITING

1. Summarize the mayor's objections to the theater. Do any of his reasons
for protesting theatrical productions seem reasonable to you? Why or why
not?

2. Are any of these concerns reflected in attitudes about the theater today?
Why or why not?

3. How would you defend *Hamlet* or *A Midsummer Night's Dream* against
charges that they draw some people into "imitacion and not to the
avoidinge the like vices which they represent"?

LISA JARDINE (B. 1944)

On Boy Actors in Female Roles   *1989*

Every schoolchild knows that there were no women actors on the Elizabethan
stage; the female parts were taken by young male actors. But every schoolchild
also learns that this fact is of little consequence for the twentieth-century
reader of Shakespeare's plays. Because the taking of female parts by boys was
universal and commonplace, we are told, it was accepted as "verisimilitude" by
the Elizabethan audience, who simply disregarded it, as we would disregard
the creaking of stage scenery and accept the backcloth forest as "real" for the
duration of the play.

Conventional or no, the taking of female parts by boy players actually occasioned a good deal of contemporary comment and created considerable moral
uneasiness, even amongst those who patronized and supported the theaters.
Amongst those who opposed them, transvestism on stage was a main plank in
the anti-stage polemic. "The appareil of wemen is a great provocation of men to
lust and leacherie," wrote Dr. John Rainoldes, a leading Oxford divine (quoting
the Bishop of Paris), in *Th' Overthrow of Stage-Playes* (Middleburgh, 1599). And he
continues with an unhealthy interest which infuses the entire pamphlet: "A
womans garment beeing put on a man doeth vehemently touch and moue him
with the remembrance and imagination of a woman; and the imagination of a
thing desirable doth stirr up the desire."

According to Rainoldes, and the authorities with whose independent testimony he lards his polemic, the wearing of female dress by boy players "is an occasion of wantonnes and lust." Sexuality, misdirected toward the boy masquerading in female dress, is "stirred" by attire and gesture; male prostitution and perverted sexual activity is the inevitable accompaniment of female impersonation.

From *Still Harping on Daughters*, Second Edition

CONSIDERATIONS FOR CRITICAL THINKING AND WRITING

1. How does Jardine complicate the Elizabethan convention of boy actors assuming female roles? To what extent does it add to the representation of Elizabethan theater put forward by the Mayor of London?

2. What do you think would be your own response to a boy actor playing a female role? Consider, for example, Hippolyta in *A Midsummer Night's Dream* or Ophelia in *Hamlet*.

SAMUEL JOHNSON (1709–1784)

On Shakespeare's Characters   1765

Shakespeare is above all writers, at least above all modern writers, the poet of nature: the poet that holds up to his readers a faithful mirror of manners and life. His characters are not modified by the customs of particular places, unpracticed by the rest of the world; by the peculiarities of studies or professions, which can operate but upon small numbers; or by the accidents of transient fashions or temporary opinions: they are the genuine progeny of common humanity, such as the world will always supply, and observation will always find. His persons act and speak by the influence of those general passions and principles by which all minds are agitated, and the whole system of life is continued in motion. In the writings of other poets a character is too often an individual; in those of Shakespeare it is commonly a species.

From the preface to Johnson's edition of Shakespeare's works

CONSIDERATIONS FOR CRITICAL THINKING AND WRITING

1. Johnson made this famous assessment of Shakespeare's ability to portray "common humanity" in the eighteenth century. As a twentieth-century reader, explain why you agree or disagree with Johnson's view that Shakespeare's characters have universal appeal.

2. Write an essay discussing whether you think it is desirable or necessary for characters to be "a faithful mirror of manners and life." Along the way consider whether you encountered any characters in *Hamlet* or *A Midsummer Night's Dream* that do not provide what you consider to be an accurate mirror of human life.

SIGMUND FREUD (1856–1939)

On Repression in Hamlet   1900

Another of the great creations of tragic poetry, Shakespeare's *Hamlet,* has its roots in the same soil as *Oedipus Rex.* But the changed treatment of the same material reveals the whole difference in the mental life of these two widely separated epochs of civilization: the secular advance of repression in the emotional life of mankind. In the *Oedipus* the child's wishful fantasy that underlies it is brought into the open and realized as it would be in a dream. In *Hamlet* it remains repressed; and—just as in the case of a neurosis—we only learn of its existence from its inhibiting consequences. Strangely enough, the overwhelming effect produced by the more modern tragedy has turned out to be compatible with the fact that people have remained completely in the dark as to the hero's character. The play is built up on Hamlet's hesitations over fulfilling the task of revenge that is assigned to him; but its text offers no reasons or motives for these hesitations and an immense variety of attempts at interpreting them have failed to produce a result. According to the view which was originated by Goethe and is still the prevailing one today, Hamlet represents the type of man whose power of direct action is paralyzed by an excessive development of his intellect. (He is "sicklied o'er with the pale cast of thought.") According to another view, the dramatist has tried to portray a pathologically irresolute character which might be classed as neurasthenic. The plot of the drama shows us, however, that Hamlet is far from being represented as a person incapable of taking any action. We see him doing so on two occasions: first in a sudden outburst of temper, when he runs his sword through the eavesdropper behind the arras, and secondly, in a premeditated and even crafty fashion, when, with all the callousness of a Renaissance prince, he sends the two courtiers to the death that had been planned for himself. What is it, then, that inhibits him in fulfilling the task set him by his father's ghost? The answer, once again, is that it is the peculiar nature of the task. Hamlet is able to do anything—except take vengeance on the man who did away with his father and took that father's place with his mother, the man who shows him the repressed wishes of his own childhood realized. Thus the loathing which should drive him on to revenge is replaced in him by self-reproaches, by scruples of conscience, which remind him that he himself is literally no better than the sinner whom he is to punish. Here I have translated into conscious terms what was bound to remain unconscious in Hamlet's mind; and if anyone is inclined to call him a hysteric, I can only accept the fact as one that is implied by my interpretation. The distaste for sexuality expressed by Hamlet in his conversation with Ophelia fits in very well with this: the same distaste which was destined to take possession of the poet's mind more and more during the years that followed, and which reached its extreme expression in *Timon of Athens.* For it can of course only be the poet's own mind which confronts us in Hamlet. I observe in a book on Shakespeare by Georg Brandes (1896) a statement that *Hamlet* was written immediately after the death of Shakespeare's father (in 1601), that is, under the immediate impact of his bereavement and, as we may well assume, while his childhood feelings about his father had been freshly revived. It is known, too, that Shakespeare's own son who died at an early age bore the name "Hamnet," which is identical with "Hamlet." Just as *Hamlet* deals with the relation of a son to his parents, so *Macbeth* (written at approximately the same period) is concerned with the subject of childlessness. But just as all neurotic symptoms, and, for that matter, dreams, are capable of being "overinterpreted" and indeed need to be, if they are to be fully understood, so all genuinely creative writings are the product of more than a single motive and more than a single impulse in the poet's mind, and are open to more than a single interpretation. In what I have written I have only attempted to interpret the deepest layer of impulses in the mind of the creative writer.

From *The Interpretation of Dreams*, translated by James Strachey

CONSIDERATIONS FOR CRITICAL THINKING AND WRITING

1. What reason does Freud offer for Hamlet's inability to avenge his father's death? Explain whether you find Freud's reasoning convincing.

2. Read the section on psychological criticism (p. 2099) in Chapter 52, "Critical Strategies for Reading," and then discuss Freud's assertion that "it can of course only be the poet's mind which confronts us in Hamlet." Explain why you agree or disagree.

3. Write an essay discussing whether you think Freud's approach to *Hamlet* opens up perspectives on the play or narrowly limits them.

JAN KOTT (B. 1914)
On Producing Hamlet   *1964*

No Dane of flesh and blood has been written about so extensively as Hamlet. Shakespeare's prince is certainly the best known representative of his nation. Innumerable glossaries and commentaries have grown round Hamlet, and he is one of the few literary heroes who live apart from the text, apart from the theater. His name means something even to those who have never seen or read Shakespeare's play. In this respect he is rather like Leonardo's Mona Lisa. We know she is smiling even before we have seen the picture, as it were. It contains not only what Leonardo expressed in it but also everything that has been written about it. Too many people — girls, women, poets, painters — have tried to solve the mystery of that smile. It is not just Mona Lisa that is smiling at us now, but all those who have tried to analyze, or imitate, that smile.

This is also the case with *Hamlet,* or rather — with *Hamlet* in the theater. For we have been separated from the text not only by Hamlet's "independent life" in our culture, but simply by the size of the play. *Hamlet* cannot be performed in its entirety, because the performance would last nearly six hours. One has to select, curtail, and cut. One can perform only one of several *Hamlet*s potentially existing in this arch-play. It will always be a poorer *Hamlet* than Shakespeare's *Hamlet* is; but it may also be a *Hamlet* enriched by being of our time. It may, but I would rather say — it must be so.

For *Hamlet* cannot be played simply. This may be the reason why it is so tempting to producers and actors. Many generations have seen their own reflections in this play. The genius of *Hamlet* consists, perhaps, in the fact that the play can serve as a mirror. An ideal *Hamlet* would be one most true to Shakespeare and most modern at the same time. Is this possible? I do not know. But we can only appraise any Shakespearean production by asking how much there is of Shakespeare in it, and how much of us.

What I have in mind is not a forced topicality, a *Hamlet* that would be set in a cellar of young existentialists. *Hamlet* has been performed for that matter in evening dress and in circus tights; in medieval armor and in Renaissance costume. Costumes do not matter. What matters is that through Shakespeare's text we ought to get at our modern experience, anxiety, and sensibility. There are many subjects in *Hamlet*. There is politics, force opposed to morality; there is discussion of the divergence between the theory and practice, of the ultimate purpose of life; there is tragedy of love, as well as family drama, political, eschatological, and metaphysical problems are considered. There is everything you want, including deep psychological analysis, a bloody story, a duel, and general slaughter. One can select at will. But one must know what one selects, and why.

From "*Hamlet* of the Mid-Century" in *Shakespeare Our Contemporary*,
translated by Boleslaw Taborski

CONSIDERATIONS FOR CRITICAL THINKING AND WRITING

1. "Many generations have seen their own reflections in this play." Use this statement as a basis for researching productions of *Hamlet*. How have events contemporary to the play's performances influenced the ways it has been presented?

2. Explain why you think it is good or bad for a producer to interpret a play in light of events contemporary to it.

3. If you were to produce *Hamlet* today, what would you emphasize? Consider how you would handle the setting, costuming, casting, and theme.

4. What do you think a reader-response critic would have to say about Kott's comments on producing *Hamlet*? Base your answer on the discussion of reader-response criticism (p. 2109) in Chapter 52, "Critical Strategies for Reading."

COPPÉLIA KAHN (B. 1939)

On Cuckoldry in Hamlet   *1981*

The Ghost in *Hamlet* is so poignantly powerful in his injured majesty that it seems ungracious to remember that he is also a cuckold. He himself obliquely notes it when he calls Claudius "that incestuous, that adulterate beast," distinguishing incest, the fact of his brother's sexual liaison with Gertrude, from its timing, which made it adultery (I.v.42). Hamlet's awareness of this ignominious aspect of his father's grievance, though only indirectly revealed to us, shapes his attitude toward the great task of revenge by complicating his identification with his father.[1] A

---

[1]Cf. Avi Erlich's interesting argument in *Hamlet's Absent Father* (Princeton: Princeton UP, 1978). He contends that Hamlet delays his revenge because he is waiting for his absent, ghostly father to prove his strength by returning to kill Claudius himself. The source of Hamlet's perception of his father as weak and absent, Erlich holds, is his unconscious fantasy that his father was castrated by Gertrude in a primal scene. I see evidence of a different kind of castration, in the fact rather than the fantasy of King Hamlet's cuckoldry.

mighty wrong has been done to a noble king; as he is noble, so must his anger and his cause be great. But insofar as part of that wrong is cuckoldry, his nobility is diminished, his anger impotent, and his cause an embarrassment. Viewed in this context, Hamlet's well-known misogyny and preoccupation with Gertrude's faults are an outlet for the rage mingled with shame he feels at his father's situation. He must bury or disguise his awareness of it, because to admit it would damage severely his idealized image of that father. So long as he can blame a woman's frailty for the indignity his father suffers, as the conventions of cuckoldry enable him to do, that image can be saved. But at the same time, his concern with his mother's crime diverts him from revenge and inevitably reminds him of his father's weakness: King Hamlet, like the most ordinary cuckold, was hoodwinked by his own wife. Thus to the extent that Hamlet sees his father as a cuckold, his anxiety and propensity to delay revenge are increased by a paralyzing ambivalence.[2]

... I do not suggest that cuckoldry is a major issue in *Hamlet*, or for Hamlet himself. Rather, I merely wish to show that it is one aspect of Hamlet's dilemma, largely ignored by critics, and that if taken into account it deepens the tragic complications of his task. Much of the evidence I offer for the importance of cuckoldry has been presented before as evidence of the oedipal situation in the play.[3] In a longer study, it could be shown how cuckoldry participates in that situation, but here I am only concerned with isolating cuckoldry somewhat artificially from the play's other concerns so as to demonstrate its presence and its importance.

From *Man's Estate: Masculine Identity in Shakespeare*

[2] Richard Flatter, in his *Hamlet's Father* (New Haven: Yale UP, 1949), argues that Hamlet's delay is largely caused by the Ghost's prohibition against harming his mother, for Hamlet cannot properly revenge his father's murder until he discovers whether his mother was complicit in it. Flatter dismisses the question of Gertrude's adultery, saying that it has been partly absolved by time and her subsequent marriage, and stresses the problem of her complicity. But he does show, in a penetrating analysis of the closet scene, how obsessed Hamlet is with the connection between the adultery and the murder, and how the purposes of the father, to conceal this connection, and of the son, to discover it, diverge.

[3] Ernest Jones's *Hamlet and Oedipus* (Garden City, NY: Doubleday Anchor, 1955) remains the classic oedipal interpretation. For a useful review of similar interpretations from Freud to 1965, see Norman Holland, *Psychoanalysis and Shakespeare* (New York: McGraw-Hill, 1964), especially pp. 164–178 and pp. 180–184. In the oedipal situation, the son's feelings toward his mother are at least as complicated and ambivalent as those toward his father. Not only does he desire her, he also feels that she has betrayed him, because he once thought her the virginal object solely of his affections — a feeling that would powerfully reinforce Hamlet's resentment at Gertrude's betrayal of his father. Incestuous desire also goes hand in hand with matricidal impulses, as Frederic C. Wertham believes, in "The Matricidal Impulse: Critique of Freud's Interpretation of *Hamlet*," in *The Design Within: Psychoanalytic Approaches to Shakespeare,* ed. Melvin D. Faber (New York: Science House, 1970), pp. 113–120, arguing that "The basis of Hamlet's hostility against his mother is his overattachment to her," a reaction-formation sparked by fear of the castrating father. Hamlet's sexual disgust at Gertrude and women in general can be read both in oedipal terms and in terms of cuckoldry without conflict. In both contexts, Hamlet as son shares his father's sense of shame at having been sexually betrayed by a woman he loved.

CONSIDERATIONS FOR CRITICAL THINKING AND WRITING

1. According to Kahn, why is cuckoldry important for understanding Hamlet's "propensity to delay revenge"?

2. In an essay compare Sigmund Freud's analysis (p. 1551) of why Hamlet delays his revenge with Kahn's analysis.

RUSSELL JACKSON (B. 1949)

A Film Diary of the Shooting of Kenneth Branagh's Hamlet

1996

Wednesday 3 January
Rehearsals Begin

First morning in Shepperton. This may be one of the major British studios but it's not, on first sight, impressive. Located in a semi-suburban hinterland southwest of London, it seems at first like an industrial estate, a jumble of sheds, hangars, workshops, and what look like builders' yards, with a mansion trapped in the middle of it all like a genteel hostage from Edwardian England. . . .

We're in the elegant boardroom of the old house, round a long green-baize covered table. First session is with Derek Jacobi (Claudius) and Julie Christie (Gertrude), plus Ken, Orlando Seale (his "acting double"), Annie Wotton (Script Supervisor), Simon Mosley (First A.D.), and Hugh Cruttwell.

Ken distributes phials [vials] of a herbal "Rescue Remedy" (only half a joke, admitting nervous apprehension). Everyone has read the screenplay, and the actors have already had some discussion of their roles with Ken, but these days of rehearsal before we begin shooting will give everyone time for reappraisal, adjustments, and (most important) finding out how the story will be told by *this* company of actors, in *these* circumstances. We won't start with a read-through: better to edge toward the play. We discuss royal families (including the current one), privacy, politics, and draw toward a reading of the scenes when Claudius and Gertrude are together. There's talk about the issue of complicity between them (not at all, so far as murder is concerned) and the "essential" Claudius, which she took (and part of him still takes) as loving, kind, a "good" man. Derek goes along with this, though he and Hugh Cruttwell remind us of Hamlet's very different point of view. Gertrude and Claudius feel responsible for Hamlet but Claudius has another agenda she knows nothing about — concerning the potential threat posed by her son.

After lunch the Polonius family join us, with Horatio. By now we feel able to discuss frankly and simply (and off the record) our own experiences of family, bereavement, grief. (This is not just to canvass ideas about the emotions of the play to draw on them in performance: it also establishes common ground among us.) Then we try to imagine an "ideal" family, successful and well-balanced according to current middle-class notions, professional but not competitive, materially well-off but not showy — which (we agree) turns out quite repulsive. Then on to the Polonius family.

Polonius (Richard Briers) was promoted by new king. Laertes (Michael Maloney) is in Paris getting the gentlemanly accomplishments (N.B. not at Wittenberg). Ophelia (Kate Winslett) and Hamlet have been having an affair (yes, they have been to bed together, because we want this relationship to be as serious as possible) since the death of Hamlet senior. (Effect of a surge of feeling in time of bereavement and crisis?)

Thursday 4 — Monday 8 January

We work through scenes, trying various approaches, finding snags, problems, opportunities. Ophelia's motivations in returning Hamlet's love tokens are considered: she is going further than Polonius suggested in any instructions we have heard, and whatever her father and the king expect from this confrontation, she has her own agenda (perhaps to find out why Hamlet is behaving this way to her, to put him on the spot?). The kinder and more circumspect Polonius seems, the harder it will be for her to betray him — hence her lying to Hamlet ("Where's your father? — At home, my lord"). In "To be or not to be" Ken wants to show Hamlet alone with his mirror image(s) in the vast space of the mirrored hall. He has to be careful not to give the soliloquy an energy or momentum that it does not need — those qualities are coming soon enough in what follows when he encounters Ophelia. Ken steers Derek toward seeming even more vulnerable as Claudius, "quietly anxious" about Hamlet after "nunnery" scene, rarely openly angry, even when Rosencrantz and Guildenstern have screwed up. So, when he does flare up, becomes desperate, it will be more shocking.

On 8 January we go over each actor's list of their character's priorities. Claudius has specific aims: inspiring confidence and trust in himself; loving Gertrude; making Hamlet look indulgent and neurotic (and thus defusing him); creating a new, strong, triumphalist Denmark (a military regime). Gertrude's aims are more general: decorum, sense of behaving properly in public; *noblesse oblige,* etiquette; sense of culture, confidence; loving Hamlet. Old Hamlet (Brian Blessed) points out that when he was alive he never let Claudius see how little he mattered — there has to be an underlying bitterness in what Claudius has done to get the crown as well as intense love for Gertrude. We consider different ways of showing these relationships in a short flashback — perhaps Old Hamlet and his son playing chess while Gertrude and Claudius watch, or some other activity (perhaps outdoors) that will focus their various feelings for each other.

From *Hamlet.* Screenplay and Introduction by
Kenneth Branagh. Film diary by Russell Jackson

Considerations for Critical Thinking and Writing

1. In what sense can the actors' discussions of character motivation and background be considered an interpretation of *Hamlet*? Why do you suppose the actors find these kinds of discussions useful?

2. Create a list of "priorities" for characters *not* already discussed by the actors on Branagh's set. Consider, for example, Horatio, Laertes, Rosencrantz, Guildenstern, Marcellus, or Bernardo.

3. How does Jackson's comment that it was essential for the actors to determine "how the story will be told by *this* company of actors, in *these* circumstances" compare with Jan Kott's observations on producing *Hamlet* (p. 1552)?

4. Rent a videotape of Branagh's *Hamlet* and write an essay that focuses on a single character or scene that you find especially effective (or not).

Louis Adrian Montrose (b. 1946)

On Amazonian Mythology
in A Midsummer Night's Dream   1983

The beginning of *A Midsummer Night's Dream* coincides with the end of a struggle in which Theseus has been victorious over the Amazon warrior:

> Hippolyta, I woo'd thee with my sword,
> And won thy love doing thee injuries;
> But I will wed thee in another key,
> With pomp, with triumph, and with revelling.
>   (I.i.16–19)

Descriptions of the Amazons are ubiquitous in Elizabethan texts. . . .

Sixteenth-century travel narratives often recreate the ancient Amazons of Scythia in South America or in Africa. Invariably, the Amazons are relocated just beyond the receding boundary of *terra incognita*.° Thus, in Sierra Leone in 1582, the chaplain of an English expedition to the Spice Islands recorded the report of a Portuguese trader that "near the mountains of the moon there is a queen, empress of all these Amazons, a witch and a cannibal who daily feeds on the flesh of boys. She ever remains unmarried, but she has intercourse with a great number of men by whom she begets offspring. The kingdom, however, remains hereditary to the daughters, not to the sons."[1] This cultural fantasy assimilates Amazonian myth, witchcraft, and cannibalism into an anticulture which precisely inverts European norms of political authority, sexual license, marriage practices, and inheritance rules.[2] The attitude toward the Amazons expressed in such Renaissance texts is a mixture of fascination and horror. Amazonian mythology seems symbolically to embody and to control a collective anxiety about the power of the female not only to dominate or reject the male but to create and destroy him. It is an ironic acknowledgment by an androcentric° culture of the degree to which men are in fact dependent upon women: upon mothers and nurses, for their birth and nurture; upon mistresses and wives, for the validation of their manhood.

Shakespeare engages his wedding play in a dialectic with this mythological formation. The Amazons have been defeated before the play begins; and nuptial rites are to be celebrated when it ends. *A Midsummer Night's Dream* focuses upon different crucial transitions in the male and female life cycles: the fairy plot, upon taking "a little changeling boy" from childhood into youth,

---

terra incognita: Unknown land   *androcentric*: Male-centered.

[1] *An Elizabethan in 1582: The Diary of Richard Madox, Fellow of All Souls,* ed. Elizabeth Story Donno, Hakluyt Society, second ser., no. 47 (London, 1977), p. 183. I owe this reference to Stephen Greenblatt, *Renaissance Self-Fashioning: From More to Shakespeare* (Chicago, 1980), p. 181.
[2] The linkage of Amazon, witch, and cannibal exemplifies a logic of inversion ingrained in European categories of thought. It has been suggested recently that sixteenth- and seventeenth-century witchcraft beliefs were a coherent, meaningful, and indeed necessary component of a larger intellectual system based upon principles of hierarchy, opposition, and inversion. This system linked together demonism, political sedition and rebellion, and female misrule as inversions of the divinely sanctioned order in the cosmos, state, and family. See Stuart Clark, "Inversion, Misrule and the Meaning of Witchcraft," *Past & Present,* no. 87 (May 1980), 98–127. . . .

from the world of the mother into the world of the father; the Athenian plot, upon taking a maiden from youth into maturity, from the world of the father into the world of the husband. The pairing of the four Athenian lovers is made possible by the magical powers of Oberon and made lawful by the political authority of Theseus. Each of these rulers is preoccupied with the fulfillment of his own desires in the possession or repossession of a wife. Only after Hippolyta has been mastered by Theseus may marriage seal them "in everlasting bond of fellowship" (I.i.85). And only after "proud Titania" has been degraded by "jealous Oberon" (II.i.60, 61), has "in mild terms begg'd" (IV.i.53) his patience, and has readily yielded the changeling boy to him, may they be "new in amity" (IV.i.82).

The . . . structure of *A Midsummer Night's Dream* eventually restores the inverted Amazonian system of gender and nurture to a patriarchal norm.

> From "'Shaping Fantasies': Figurations of Gender and Power
> in Elizabethan Culture," *Representations*, Spring 1983

CONSIDERATIONS FOR CRITICAL THINKING AND WRITING

1. How does Montrose use "Amazonian mythology" to account for the plot elements in the play?
2. In an essay use the insights provided in Montrose's perspective to explore how order is associated with masculinity and rebellion is associated with femininity in *A Midsummer Night's Dream*.

JAMES KINCAID (B. 1937)
On the Value of Comedy in the Face of Tragedy   1991

[O]ur current hierarchical arrangement (tragedy high—comedy low) betrays an acquiescence in the most smothering of political conservatisms. Put another way, by coupling tragedy with the sublime, the ineffable, the metaphysical and by aligning comedy with the mundane, the quotidian, and the material we manage to muffle, even to erase, the most powerful narratives of illumination and liberation we have. . . .

The point is comic relief, the *concept* of comic relief and who it relieves. Now we usually refer to comic relief in the same tone we use for academic deans, other people's children, Melanie Griffith, the new criticism, jogging, Big Macs, the *New York Times Book Review*, leisure suits, people who go on cruises, realtors, and the MLA: bemused contempt. (Which is what we think about comic relief.) Comedy is that which attends on, offers relaxation from, prepares us for more of—something else, something serious and demanding. Comedy is not demanding—it does not demand or take, it gives. And we know that any agency which gives cannot be worth much. Tragedy's seriousness is guaranteed by its bullying greed, its insistence on having things its own way and pulling from us not only our tears, which we value little, but our attention, which we hate to give. Comedy, on the other hand, doesn't care if we attend closely. Tragedy is sleek and single-minded, comedy rumpled and hospitable to any idea or agency. Tragedy stares us out of countenance; comedy winks and leers and drools. Tragedy is all dressed up; comedy is always taking things off, mooning us. We find it inevitable that we associate tragedy with the high, comedy with the low. What is at issue here is the nature of that inevitability, our willingness to conspire in a discourse which pays homage to tragic grandeur and reduces comedy to release, authorized license, periodic relief—like a sneeze or yawn or belch. By allowing such discourse to flow through us, we add our bit of cement to the cultural edifice that sits on top of comedy, mashes it down into a mere adjunct to tragedy, its reverse and inferior half, its silly little carnival. By cooperating in this move, we relieve orthodox and conservative power structures of any pressure that might be exercised against them. Comic relief relieves the status quo, in other words, contains the power of comedy. . . .

Let's put it this way, comedy is not a mode that stands in opposition to tragedy. Comedy is the *whole* story, the narrative which refuses to leave things out. Tragedy insists on a formal structure that is unified and coherent, formally balanced and elegantly tight. Only that which is coordinate is allowed to adorn the tragic body. With comedy, nothing is sacrificed, nothing lost; the discoordinate and the discontinuous are especially welcome. Tragedy protects itself by its linearity, its tight conclusiveness; comedy's generosity and ability never to end make it gloriously vulnerable. Pitting tragedy against comedy is running up algebra against recess. . . .

From a paper read at the 1991 meeting of the Modern Language Association, "Who Is Relieved by the Idea of Comic Relief?"

Considerations for Critical Thinking and Writing

1. What distinctions does Kincaid make between comedy and tragedy? How does his description of tragedy compare with Aristotle's (see p. 1369)?

2. How does Kincaid's description of comedy fit *A Midsummer Night's Dream*?

3. According to Kincaid, why is the denigration of comedy a conservative impulse? In an essay explain why you agree or disagree with the argument.

TWO COMPLEMENTARY CRITICAL READINGS

Joan Montgomery Byles (b. 1939)

Ophelia's Desperation   1989

Critics from Bradley on have been perplexed by Ophelia. Bradley found "slight psychological incongruity" in Hamlet's treatment of Ophelia as a wanton, for "there is nothing in the least wanton about Ophelia." Traversi saw Hamlet as "shattering Ophelia's spirit." Dover Wilson thought Hamlet's attitude towards Ophelia the "greatest puzzle" in the play, and Wilson-Knight saw Ophelia as Hamlet's "only hope." Francis Fergusson viewed Ophelia's death as a "maimed rite" where instead of a marraige we have a funeral. Linda Bamber suggests that Ophelia has no choices in the play, and as a consequence we are not very interested in her. Leverenz suggests that rather than "get mad, Ophelia goes mad."[1]

Ophelia is anxious; her alertness to disapproval encourages her to be uncertain in expression. At four different times she says, "I do not know what to think, my lord," twice to her father and twice to Hamlet. Ophelia is frightened of her father and dare not disobey him. She is not allowed to have, much less declare an emotional world of her own. Her sense of self seems very much defined and controlled by the men in her life: her father, her brother, and her lover. She exists in a world created by their need, in which she is an object at all times conformable to their egos — at least until she goes mad. . . .

Ophelia has been unable to establish a real dialogue with anyone in the play, now she establishes one with herself but — the listeners, who really listen to her for the first time, are no longer necessary. She needs no reply. She has discovered her own voice, her inner self. Her speech confers a spoken meaning on her frustration and suffering, her uncertain sense of self, her anger and dismay, and gives her an impressive independence for the first and last time in the play. Her death is the ultimate expression of her repressed anger and aggression turned inwards. Unable not to love, cruelly denied her desperate need to be loved, unable to displace her repressed anger and aggression directly onto Hamlet, her father, or her brother, she turns it against herself. Whose fault is this? Hers? Her father's? Hamlet's? Where does the problem in Ophelia's subjective identity and its inability to adequately express itself come from? Why is her only way out of her predicament madness and suicide? Shakespeare shows that Ophelia's destiny is the result of her position within her family circle, which is embedded in Elizabethan sexist society. The structure of Elizabethan family life, the objective conditions of women, and the role men played as fathers, brothers, and lovers, caused many women to live attached, dependent lives, with weak self-images. Shakespeare is well aware that his society and audience is a sexist one. Only exceptional women were educated sufficiently to be independent, socially, economically, and intellectually. There were precious few divorces and such divorces could leave a woman in a penurious or "beggarly" condition. . . . For some women one sort of release from the stranglehold family life could have on them was madness and even suicide.

From "The Problem of the Self and the Other in the Language of Ophelia, Desdemona and Cordelia," *American Imago,* Spring 1989

[1] A. C. Bradley, *Shakespearean Tragedy* (London: Macmillan, 1960); Derek Traversi, *An Approach to Shakespeare* (New York: Doubleday, 1956); J. Dover Wilson, *What Happens in Hamlet* (Cambridge: England, Cambridge Univ. Press, 1956); G. Wilson-Knight, *The Imperial Theme* (London: Methuen, 1970); Francis Fergusson, *The Idea of a Theater* (New York: Doubleday, 1972); Linda Bamber, *Comic Women, Tragic Men* (Stamford: Univ. of California, Stamford, 1982); David Leverenz, "The Woman in Hamlet: An Interpersonal View," in *Representing Shakespeare: New Psychoanalytic Essays,* ed. Murray M. Schwartz and Coppélia Kahn (Baltimore: Johns Hopkins UP, 1980).

CONSIDERATIONS FOR CRITICAL THINKING AND WRITING

1. Of the competing readings of Ophelia cited by Byles in her first paragraph, which do you find most compelling?

2. How is Ophelia's "sense of self . . . defined and controlled by the men in her life"? What kind of evidence does Byles use to support this claim?

3. Explain why you agree or disagree that Ophelia's final speech "gives her an impressive independence for the first and last time in the play."

SANDRA K. FISCHER (B. 1950)

Ophelia's Mad Speeches   1990

Critical opinion about the function of Ophelia's mad rhetoric differs widely. Placing Ophelia in a dramatic context of madwomen and their talk, the Charneys find that "Madness enables her to assert her being; she is no longer enforced to keep silent" and that through madness she can "suddenly make a forceful assertion of . . . being. The lyric form and broken syntax and unbridled imagination all show ways of breaking through unbearable social restraints."[1] Certainly Ophelia's mad speeches rivet the attention, but they seem to point to a loss rather than an assertion of self: a theme of the songs is the inability to choose among a socially-circumscribed series of insufficient options. The voice of madness is indeed louder than her earlier rhetoric, yet it fails to break through or change the constraints. It manages to articulate them only indirectly, and her meaning remains unheard. R. S. White makes her allusiveness more mystical than insane: "By a kind of sympathetic magic, the conditions which face Ophelia find their way into her songs, in oblique and confused fashion."[2] David Leverenz, in applying gender theory to both Hamlet and Ophelia and their language, offers a perceptive summary of the pastiche of meanings embedded in Ophelia's final appearance:

> . . . contemporary work with schizophrenics reveals the tragic variety of people whose voices are only amalgams of other people's voices, with caustic self-observation or a still more terrifying vacuum as their incessant inward reality. This is Hamlet to a degree, as it is Ophelia completely. . . . [T]here are many voices in Ophelia's madness speaking through her, all making sense, and none of them her own. She becomes the mirror for a madness-inducing world. . . . Through her impossible attempt to obey contradictory voices, Ophelia mirrors in her madness the tensions that Hamlet perceives. . . . Her history is another instance of how someone can be driven mad by having her inner feelings misrepresented, not responded to, or acknowledged only through chastisement and repression.[3]

The ambiguity of the voices in Ophelia's songs and mad commentary is complex and fascinating. Nearly every reference has multiple signification, as if she attempts to squeeze and condense all the censored feelings and observations of the play into a compact logic of expression — hence, her admonitions to "mark," that is, to hear and understand. For example, "He is dead and gone" is actually the center of the play, referring to Hamlet, Sr., Polonius, and, if Claudius's order were carried out, to Hamlet himself. As Hamlet must try to connect past, present, and future, so Ophelia becomes a repository

---

[1]Maurice Charney and Hanna Charney, "The Language of Madwomen in Shakespeare and His Fellow Dramatists," *Signs* 3 (1977), 456, 459.
[2]"The Tragedy of Ophelia," *Ariel*, 9, 2 (1978), 49.
[3]David Leverenz, "The Woman in Hamlet: An Interpersonal View," in *Representing Shakespeare: New Psychoanalytic Essays*, ed. Murray M. Schwartz and Coppélia Kahn (Baltimore: Johns Hopkins UP, 1980), 112, 117.

of memory, of events unconnected but through destiny linked in fatal concatenation.

From "Hearing Ophelia: Gender and Tragic Discourse in *Hamlet*,"
From *Renaissance and Reformation,* Winter 1990

CONSIDERATIONS FOR CRITICAL THINKING AND WRITING

1. Do you think Ophelia finds herself or loses herself in her speeches? Explain.

2. Discuss Leverenz's observation that "Ophelia mirrors in her madness the tensions that Hamlet perceives."

3. Compare Fisher's view of Ophelia's madness with Byles's treatment in the preceding perspective. Explain why you think they complement or contradict one another.

SUGGESTED TOPICS FOR LONGER PAPERS

1. Discuss Shakespeare's use of humor in *A Midsummer Night's Dream* and in *Hamlet*. Focus on at least one humorous scene in each play as the basis of your discussion and characterize the tone of the humor. What generalizations can you make about the tone and purpose of the humor in the plays?

2. Research how marriage was regarded in Elizabethan times and compare those attitudes and values with the treatment of marriage in *A Midsummer Night's Dream* or *Hamlet*.

3. MULTIMEDIA PROJECT. Use the Internet and the library to gather drawings and photographs of actors playing the roles of Hamlet since the nineteenth century. Organize the images chronologically, and write an essay that connects those images to the historical moment in which the role of Hamlet was played by the actors. How do you account for the changes?

Web   *For help with this project, use the Multimedia Project Guides Online at*
http://www.bedfordstmartins.com/meyer/bedintrolit

45

Modern Drama

REALISM

Realism is a literary technique that attempts to create the appearance of life as it is actually experienced. Characters in modern realistic plays (written during and after the last quarter of the nineteenth century) speak dialogue that we might hear in our daily lives. These characters are not larger than life but representative of it; they seem to speak the way we do rather than in highly poetic language, formal declarations, asides, or soliloquies. It is impossible to imagine a heroic figure such as Oedipus inhabiting a comfortably furnished living room and chatting about his wife's household budget the way Torvald Helmer does in Henrik Ibsen's *A Doll House*. Realism brings into focus commonplace, everyday life rather than the extraordinary kinds of events that make up Sophocles' *Oedipus the King* or Shakespeare's *Hamlet*.

Realistic characters can certainly be heroic, but like Nora Helmer, they find that their strength and courage are tested in the context of events ordinary people might experience. Work, love, marriage, children, and death are often the focus of realistic dramas. These subjects can also constitute much of the material in nonrealistic plays, but modern realistic dramas present such material in the realm of the probable. Conflicts in realistic plays are likely to reflect problems in our own lives. Hence, making ends meet takes precedence over saving a kingdom; middle- and lower-class individuals take center stage as primary characters in main plots rather than being secondary characters in subplots. Thus we can see why the nineteenth-century movement toward realism paralleled the rise of a middle class eagerly seeking representations of its concerns in the theater.

Before the end of the nineteenth century, however, few attempts were made in the theater to present life as it is actually lived. The chorus's role in Sophocles' *Oedipus the King*, the allegorical figures in morality plays, the remarkable mistaken identities in Shakespeare's comedies, or the rhymed couplets spoken in seventeenth-century plays such as Molière's *Tartuffe* represent theatrical conventions rather than life. Theatergoers have understood and appreciated these conventions for centuries — and still do — but in the nineteenth century social, political, and industrial revolutions helped create an atmosphere in which some playwrights found it necessary to create works that more directly reflected their audiences' lives.

Playwrights such as Henrik Ibsen and Anton Chekhov refused to join the ranks of their romantic contemporaries, who they felt falsely idealized life. The most popular plays immediately preceding the works of these realistic writers consisted primarily of love stories and action-packed plots. Such **melodramas** offer audiences thrills and chills as well as happy endings. They typically include a virtuous individual struggling under the tyranny of a wicked oppressor, who is defeated only at the last moment. Suspense is reinforced by a series of pursuits, captures, and escapes that move the plot quickly and de-emphasize character or theme. These representations of extreme conflicts enjoyed wide popularity in the nineteenth century — indeed, they still do — because their formula was varied enough to be entertaining yet their outcomes were always comforting to the audience's sense of justice. From the realists' perspective, melodramas were merely escape fantasies that distorted life by refusing to examine the real world closely and objectively. But an indication of the popularity of such happy endings can be seen in Chekhov's farcical comedies, such as *The Proposal,* a one-act play filled with exaggerated characters and action. Despite his realist's values, Chekhov was also sometimes eager to please audiences.

Realists attempted to open their audiences' eyes; to their minds, the only genuine comfort was in knowing the truth. Many of their plays concern controversial issues of the day and focus on people who fall prey to indifferent societal institutions. English dramatist John Galsworthy (1867–1933) examined social values in *Strife* (1909) and *Justice* (1910), two plays whose titles broadly suggest the nature of his concerns. British playwright George Bernard Shaw (1856–1950) often used comedy and irony as means of awakening his audiences to contemporary problems: *Arms and the Man* (1894) satirizes romantic attitudes toward war, and *Mrs. Warren's Profession* (1898) indicts a social and economic system that drives a woman to prostitution. Chekhov's major plays are populated by characters frustrated by their social situations and their own sensibilities; they are ordinary people who long for happiness but become entangled in everyday circumstances that limit their lives. Ibsen also took a close look at his characters' daily lives. His plays attack social conventions and challenge popular attitudes toward marriage; he stunned audiences by dramatizing the suffering of a man dying of syphilis.

With these kinds of materials, Ibsen and his contemporaries popularized the **problem play,** a drama that represents a social issue in order to awaken the audience to it. These plays usually reject romantic plots in favor of holding up a mirror that reflects not simply what audiences want to see but what the playwright sees in them. Nineteenth-century realistic theater was no refuge from the social, economic, and psychological problems that melodrama ignored or sentimentalized.

NATURALISM

Related to realism is another movement, called **naturalism.** Essentially more of a philosophical attitude than a literary technique, naturalism derives its name from the idea that human beings are part of nature and subject to its laws. According to naturalists, heredity and environment shape and control people's lives; their behavior is determined more by instinct than by reason. This deterministic view argues that human beings have no transcendent identity because there is no soul or spiritual world that ultimately distinguishes humanity from any other form of life. Characters in naturalistic plays are generally portrayed as victims overwhelmed by internal and external forces. Thus literary naturalism tends to include not only the commonplace but the sordid, destructive, and chaotic aspects of life. Naturalism, then, is an extreme form of realism.

The earliest and most articulate voice of naturalism was that of French author Émile Zola (1840–1902), who urged artists to draw their characters from life and present their histories as faithfully as scientists report laboratory findings. Zola's best-known naturalistic play, *Thérèse Raquin* (1873), is a dramatization of an earlier novel involving a woman whose passion causes her to take a lover and plot with him to kill her husband. In his preface to the novel, Zola explains that his purpose is to take "a strong man and unsatisfied woman," "throw them into a violent drama and note scrupulously the sensations and acts of these creatures." The diction of Zola's statement reveals his nearly clinical approach, which becomes even more explicit when Zola likens his method of revealing character to that of an autopsy: "I have simply done on two living bodies the work which surgeons do on corpses."

Although some naturalistic plays have been successfully produced and admired (notably Maxim Gorky's *The Lower Depths* [1902], set in a grim boardinghouse occupied by characters who suffer poverty, crime, betrayal, disease, and suicide), few important dramatists fully subscribed to naturalism's extreme methods and values. Nevertheless, the movement significantly influenced playwrights. Because of its insistence on the necessity of closely observing characters' environment, playwrights placed a new emphasis on detailed settings and natural acting. This verisimilitude became a significant feature of realistic drama.

THEATRICAL CONVENTIONS
OF MODERN DRAMA

The picture-frame stage that is often used for realistic plays typically reproduces the setting of a room in some detail. Within the stage, framed by a proscenium arch (from which the curtain hangs), scenery and props are used to create an illusion of reality. Whether the "small bookcase with richly bound books" described in the opening scene of Ibsen's *A Doll House* is only painted scenery or an actual case with books, it will probably look real to the audience. Removing the fourth wall of a room so that an audience can look in fosters the illusion that the actions onstage are real events happening before unseen spectators. The texture of Nora's life is communicated by the set as well as by what she says and does. That doesn't happen in a play like Sophocles' *Oedipus the King*. Technical effects can make us believe there is wood burning in a fireplace or snow falling outside a window. Outdoor settings are made similarly realistic by props and painted sets. In one of Chekhov's full-length plays, for example, the second act opens in a meadow with the faint outline of a city on the horizon.

In addition to lifelike sets, a particular method of acting is used to create a realistic atmosphere. Actors address each other instead of directing formal speeches toward the audience; they act within the setting, not merely before it. At the beginning of the twentieth century Konstantin Stanislavsky (1863–1938), a Russian director, teacher, and actor, developed a system of acting that was an important influence in realistic theater. He trained actors to identify with the inner emotions of the characters they played. They were encouraged to recall from their own lives emotional responses similar to those they were portraying. The goal was to present a role truthfully by first feeling and then projecting the character's situation. Among Stanislavsky's early successes in this method were the plays of Chekhov.

There are, however, degrees of realism on the stage. Tennessee Williams's *The Glass Menagerie* (p. 1893), for example, is a partially realistic portrayal of characters whose fragile lives are founded on illusions. Williams's dialogue rings true, and individual scenes resemble the kind of real-life action we would imagine such vulnerable characters engaging in, but other elements of the play are nonrealistic. For instance, Williams uses Tom as a major character in the play as well as narrator and stage manager. Here is part of Williams's stage directions: "The narrator is an undisguised convention of the play. He takes whatever license with dramatic convention as is convenient to his purposes." Although this play can be accurately described as including realistic elements, Williams, like many other contemporary playwrights, does not attempt an absolute fidelity to reality. He uses flashbacks — as does Arthur Miller in *Death of a Salesman* (p. 1824) — to present incidents that occurred before the opening scene because the past impinges so heavily on the present. Most playwrights don't attempt to duplicate reality, since that can now be done so well by motion pictures.

Realism needn't lock a playwright into a futile attempt to make everything appear as it is in life. There is no way to avoid theatrical conventions: actors impersonate characters in a setting that is, after all, a stage. Indeed, even the dialogue in a realistic play is quite different from the pauses, sentence fragments, repetitions, silences, and incoherencies that characterize the way people usually speak. Realistic dialogue may seem like ordinary speech, but it, like Shakespeare's poetic language, is constructed. If we remember that realistic drama represents only the appearance of reality and that what we read on a page or see and hear onstage is the result of careful selecting, editing, and even distortion, then we are more likely to appreciate the playwright's art.

A Doll House

Henrik Ibsen was born in Skien, Norway, to wealthy parents, who lost their money while he was a young boy. His early experiences with small-town life and genteel poverty sensitized him to the problems that he subsequently dramatized in a number of his plays. At age sixteen he was apprenticed to a druggist; he later thought about studying medicine, but by his early twenties he was earning a living writing and directing plays in various Norwegian cities. By the time of his death he enjoyed an international reputation for his treatment of social issues related to middle-class life.

Ibsen's earliest dramatic works were historical and romantic plays, some in verse. His first truly realistic work was *The Pillars of Society* (1877), whose title ironically hints at the corruption and hypocrisy exposed in it. The realistic social-problem plays for which he is best known followed. These dramas at once fascinated and shocked international audiences. Among his most produced and admired works are *A Doll House* (1879), *Ghosts* (1881), *An Enemy of the People* (1882), *The Wild Duck* (1884), and *Hedda Gabler* (1890). The common denominator in many of Ibsen's dramas is his interest in individuals struggling for an authentic identity in the face of tyrannical social conventions. This conflict often results in his characters' being divided between a sense of duty to themselves and their responsibility to others.

Ibsen used such external and internal conflicts to propel his plays' action. Like many of his contemporaries who wrote realistic plays, he adopted the form of the well-made play. A dramatic structure popularized in France by Eugène Scribe (1791–1861) and Victorien Sardou (1831–1908), the **well-made play** employs conventions including plenty of suspense created by meticulous plotting. Extensive exposition explains past events that ultimately lead to an inevitable climax. Tension is released when a secret that reverses the protagonist's fortunes is revealed. Ibsen, having directed a number of Scribe's plays in Norway, knew their cause-to-effect plot arrangements and used them for his own purposes in his problem plays.

A Doll House dramatizes the tensions of a nineteenth-century middle-class marriage in which a wife struggles to step beyond the limited identity imposed on her by her husband and society. Although the Helmers' pleasant apartment seems an unlikely setting for the fierce conflicts that develop, the issues raised in the play are unmistakably real. *A Doll House* affirms the necessity to reject hypocrisy, complacency, cowardice, and stifling conventions if life is to have dignity and meaning. Several critical approaches to the play can be found in Chapter 46, "A Critical Case Study: Henrik Ibsen's *A Doll House*."

Web *Research Henrik Ibsen with LitLinks at*
http://www.bedfordstmartins.com/meyer/bedintrolit

HENRIK IBSEN (1828–1906)

A Doll House   1879

TRANSLATED BY ROLF FJELDE

THE CHARACTERS

Torvald Helmer, a lawyer
Nora, his wife
Dr. Rank
Mrs. Linde
Nils Krogstad, a bank clerk
The Helmers' three small children
Anne-Marie, their nurse
Helene, a maid
A Delivery Boy

SCENE: *The action takes place in Helmer's residence.*

ACT I

A comfortable room, tastefully but not expensively furnished. A door to the right in the back wall leads to the entryway; another to the left leads to Helmer's study. Between these doors, a piano. Midway in the left-hand wall a door, and further back a window. Near the window a round table with an armchair and a small sofa. In the right-hand wall, toward the rear, a door, and nearer the foreground a porcelain stove with two armchairs and a rocking chair beside it. Between the stove and the side door, a small table. Engravings on the walls. An etagère with china figures and other small art objects; a small bookcase with richly bound books; the floor carpeted; a fire burning in the stove. It is a winter day.

A bell rings in the entryway; shortly after we hear the door being unlocked. Nora comes into the room, humming happily to herself; she is wearing street clothes and carries an armload of packages, which she puts down on the table to the right. She has left the hall door open; and through it a Delivery Boy *is seen, holding a Christmas tree and a basket, which he gives to the* Maid *who let them in.*

Nora: Hide the tree well, Helene. The children mustn't get a glimpse of it till this evening, after it's trimmed. *(To the* Delivery Boy, *taking out her purse.)* How much?

Delivery Boy: Fifty, ma'am.

Nora: There's a crown. No, keep the change. *(The* Boy *thanks her and leaves.* Nora *shuts the door. She laughs softly to herself while taking off her street things. Drawing a bag of macaroons from her pocket, she eats a couple, then steals over and listens at her husband's study door.)* Yes, he's home. *(Hums again as she moves to the table right.)*

Helmer (from the study): Is that my little lark twittering out there?

Nora (busy opening some packages): Yes, it is.

Helmer: Is that my squirrel rummaging around?

Nora: Yes!

Helmer: When did my squirrel get in?

Nora: Just now. *(Putting the macaroon bag in her pocket and wiping her mouth.)* Do come in, Torvald, and see what I've bought.

Helmer: Can't be disturbed. *(After a moment he opens the door and peers in, pen in hand.)* Bought, you say? All that there? Has the little spendthrift been out throwing money around again?

Nora: Oh, but Torvald, this year we really should let ourselves go a bit. It's the first Christmas we haven't had to economize.

Helmer: But you know we can't go squandering.

Nora: Oh yes, Torvald, we can squander a little now. Can't we? Just a tiny, wee bit. Now that you've got a big salary and are going to make piles and piles of money.

Helmer: Yes—starting New Year's. But then it's a full three months till the raise comes through.

Nora: Pooh! We can borrow that long.

Helmer: Nora! *(Goes over and playfully takes her by the ear.)* Are your scatterbrains off again? What if today I borrowed a thousand crowns, and you squandered them over Christmas week, and then on New Year's Eve a roof tile fell on my head and I lay there—

Nora (putting her hand on his mouth): Oh! Don't say such things!

Helmer: Yes, but what if it happened—then what?

Nora: If anything so awful happened, then it just wouldn't matter if I had debts or not.

Helmer: Well, but the people I'd borrowed from?

Nora: Them? Who cares about them! They're strangers.

Helmer: Nora, Nora, how like a woman! No, but seriously, Nora, you know what I think about that. No debts! Never borrow! Something of freedom's lost—and something of beauty, too—from a home that's founded on borrowing and debt. We've made a brave stand up to now, the two of us; and we'll go right on like that the little while we have to.

Nora (going toward the stove): Yes, whatever you say, Torvald.

Helmer (following her): Now, now, the little lark's wings mustn't droop. Come on, don't be a sulky squirrel. *(Taking out his wallet.)* Nora, guess what I have here.

Nora (turning quickly): Money!

Helmer: There, see. *(Hands her some notes.)* Good grief, I know how costs go up in a house at Christmastime.

Nora: Ten — twenty — thirty — forty. Oh, thank you, Torvald; I can manage no end on this.

Helmer: You really will have to.

Nora: Oh yes, I promise I will! But come here so I can show you everything I bought. And so cheap! Look, new clothes for Ivar here — and a sword. Here a horse and a trumpet for Bob. And a doll and a doll's bed here for Emmy; they're nothing much, but she'll tear them to bits in no time anyway. And here I have dress material and handkerchiefs for the maids. Old Anne-Marie really deserves something more.

Helmer: And what's in that package there?

Nora (with a cry): Torvald, no! You can't see that till tonight!

Helmer: I see. But tell me now, you little prodigal, what have you thought of for yourself?

Nora: For myself? Oh, I don't want anything at all.

Helmer: Of course you do. Tell me just what — within reason — you'd most like to have.

Nora: I honestly don't know. Oh, listen, Torvald —

Helmer: Well?

Nora (fumbling at his coat buttons, without looking at him): If you want to give me something, then maybe you could — you could —

Helmer: Come on, out with it.

Nora (hurriedly): You could give me money, Torvald. No more than you think you can spare; then one of these days I'll buy something with it.

Helmer: But Nora —

Nora: Oh please, Torvald darling, do that! I beg you, please. Then I could hang the bills in pretty gilt paper on the Christmas tree. Wouldn't that be fun?

Helmer: What are those little birds called that always fly through their fortunes?

Nora: Oh yes, spendthrifts: I know all that. But let's do as I say, Torvald; then I'll have time to decide what I really need most. That's very sensible, isn't it?

Helmer (smiling): Yes, very — that is, if you actually hung onto the money I give you, and you actually used it to buy yourself something. But it goes for the house and for all sorts of foolish things, and then I only have to lay out some more.

Nora: Oh, but Torvald —

Helmer: Don't deny it, my dear little Nora. *(Putting his arm around her waist.)* Spendthrifts are sweet, but they use up a frightful amount of money. It's incredible what it costs a man to feed such birds.

Nora: Oh, how can you say that! Really, I save everything I can.

Helmer (laughing): Yes, that's the truth. Everything you can. But that's nothing at all.

Nora (humming, with a smile of quiet satisfaction): Hm, if you only knew what expenses we larks and squirrels have, Torvald.

Helmer: You're an odd little one. Exactly the way your father was. You're never at a loss for scaring up money; but the moment you have it, it runs right out through your fingers; you never know what you've done with it. Well, one takes you as you are. It's deep in your blood. Yes, these things are hereditary, Nora.

Nora: Ah, I could wish I'd inherited many of Papa's qualities.

Helmer: And I couldn't wish you anything but just what you are, my sweet little lark. But wait; it seems to me you have a very—what should I call it?—a very suspicious look today—

Nora: I do?

Helmer: You certainly do. Look me straight in the eye.

Nora (looking at him): Well?

Helmer (shaking an admonitory finger): Surely my sweet tooth hasn't been running riot in town today, has she?

Nora: No. Why do you imagine that?

Helmer: My sweet tooth really didn't make a little detour through the confectioner's?

Nora: No, I assure you, Torvald—

Helmer: Hasn't nibbled some pastry?

Nora: No, not at all.

Helmer: Not even munched a macaroon or two?

Nora: No, Torvald, I assure you, really—

Helmer: There, there now. Of course I'm only joking.

Nora (going to the table, right): You know I could never think of going against you.

Helmer: No, I understand that; and you *have* given me your word. *(Going over to her.)* Well, you keep your little Christmas secrets to yourself, Nora darling. I expect they'll come to light this evening, when the tree is lit.

Nora: Did you remember to ask Dr. Rank?

Helmer: No. But there's no need for that: it's assumed he'll be dining with us. All the same, I'll ask him when he stops by here this morning. I've ordered some fine wine. Nora, you can't imagine how I'm looking forward to this evening.

Nora: So am I. And what fun for the children, Torvald!

Helmer: Ah, it's so gratifying to know that one's gotten a safe, secure job, and with a comfortable salary. It's a great satisfaction, isn't it?

Nora: Oh, it's wonderful!

Helmer: Remember last Christmas? Three whole weeks before, you shut yourself in every evening till long after midnight, making flowers for the Christmas tree, and all the other decorations to surprise us. Ugh, that was the dullest time I've ever lived through.

Nora: It wasn't at all dull for me.

Helmer (smiling): But the outcome *was* pretty sorry, Nora.

Nora: Oh, don't tease me with that again. How could I help it that the cat came in and tore everything to shreds.

Helmer: No, poor thing, you certainly couldn't. You wanted so much to please us all, and that's what counts. But it's just as well that the hard times are past.

Nora: Yes, it's really wonderful.

Helmer: Now I don't have to sit here alone, boring myself, and you don't have to tire your precious eyes and your fair little delicate hands—

Nora (clapping her hands): No, is it really true, Torvald, I don't have to? Oh, how wonderfully lovely to hear! *(Taking his arm.)* Now I'll tell you just how I've thought we should plan things. Right after Christmas — *(The doorbell rings.)* Oh, the bell. *(Straightening the room up a bit.)* Somebody would have to come. What a bore!

Helmer: I'm not home to visitors, don't forget.

Maid (from the hall doorway): Ma'am, a lady to see you —

Nora: All right, let her come in.

Maid (to Helmer): And the doctor's just come too.

Helmer: Did he go right to my study?

Maid: Yes, he did.

Helmer goes into his room. The Maid shows in Mrs. Linde, dressed in traveling clothes, and shuts the door after her.

Mrs. Linde (in a dispirited and somewhat hesitant voice): Hello, Nora.

Nora (uncertain): Hello —

Mrs. Linde: You don't recognize me.

Nora: No, I don't know — but wait, I think — *(Exclaiming.)* What! Kristine! Is it really you?

Mrs. Linde: Yes, it's me.

Nora: Kristine! To think I didn't recognize you. But then, how could I? *(More quietly.)* How you've changed, Kristine!

Mrs. Linde: Yes, no doubt I have. In nine — ten long years.

Nora: Is it so long since we met! Yes, it's all of that. Oh, these last eight years have been a happy time, believe me. And so now you've come in to town, too. Made the long trip in the winter. That took courage.

Mrs. Linde: I just got here by ship this morning.

Nora: To enjoy yourself over Christmas, of course. Oh, how lovely! Yes, enjoy ourselves, we'll do that. But take your coat off. You're not still cold? *(Helping her.)* There now, let's get cozy here by the stove. No, the easy chair there! I'll take the rocker here. *(Seizing her hands.)* Yes, now you have your old look again; it was only in that first moment. You're a bit more pale, Kristine — and maybe a bit thinner.

Mrs. Linde: And much, much older, Nora.

Nora: Yes, perhaps a bit older: a tiny, tiny bit; not much at all. *(Stopping short, suddenly serious.)* Oh, but thoughtless me, to sit here, chattering away. Sweet, good Kristine, can you forgive me?

Mrs. Linde: What do you mean, Nora?

Nora (softly): Poor Kristine, you've become a widow.

Mrs. Linde: Yes, three years ago.

Nora: Oh, I knew it, of course; I read it in the papers. Oh, Kristine, you must believe me; I often thought of writing you then, but I kept postponing it, and something always interfered.

Mrs. Linde: Nora dear, I understand completely.

Nora: No, it was awful of me, Kristine. You poor thing, how much you must have gone through. And he left you nothing?

Mrs. Linde: No.

Nora: And no children?

Mrs. Linde: No.

Nora: Nothing at all, then?

Mrs. Linde: Not even a sense of loss to feed on.

Nora (looking incredulously at her): But Kristine, how could that be?

Mrs. Linde (smiling wearily and smoothing her hair): Oh, sometimes it happens, Nora.

Nora: So completely alone. How terribly hard that must be for you. I have three lovely children. You can't see them now; they're out with the maid. But now you must tell me everything —

Mrs. Linde: No, no, no, tell me about yourself.

Nora: No, you begin. Today I don't want to be selfish. I want to think only of you today. But there *is* something I must tell you. Did you hear of the wonderful luck we had recently?

Mrs. Linde: No, what's that?

Nora: My husband's been made manager in the bank, just think!

Mrs. Linde: Your husband? How marvelous!

Nora: Isn't it? Being a lawyer is such an uncertain living, you know, especially if one won't touch any cases that aren't clean and decent. And of course Torvald would never do that, and I'm with him completely there. Oh, we're simply delighted, believe me! He'll join the bank right after New Year's and start getting a huge salary and lots of commissions. From now on we can live quite differently — just as we want. Oh, Kristine, I feel so light and happy! Won't it be lovely to have stacks of money and not a care in the world?

Mrs. Linde: Well, anyway, it would be lovely to have enough for necessities.

Nora: No, not just for necessities, but stacks and stacks of money!

Mrs. Linde (smiling): Nora, Nora, aren't you sensible yet? Back in school you were such a free spender.

Nora (with a quiet laugh): Yes, that's what Torvald still says. *(Shaking her finger.)* But "Nora, Nora" isn't as silly as you all think. Really, we've been in no position for me to go squandering. We've had to work, both of us.

Mrs. Linde: You too?

Nora: Yes, at odd jobs — needlework, crocheting, embroidery, and such — *(Casually.)* and other things too. You remember that Torvald left the department when we were married? There was no chance of promotion in his office, and of course he needed to earn more money. But that first year he drove himself terribly. He took on all kinds of extra work that kept him going morning and night. It wore him down, and then he fell deathly ill. The doctors said it was essential for him to travel south.

Mrs. Linde: Yes, didn't you spend a whole year in Italy?

Nora: That's right. It wasn't easy to get away, you know. Ivar had just been born. But of course we had to go. Oh, that was a beautiful trip, and it saved Torvald's life. But it cost a frightful sum, Kristine.

Mrs. Linde: I can well imagine.

Nora: Four thousand, eight hundred crowns it cost. That's really a lot of money.

Mrs. Linde: But it's lucky you had it when you needed it.

Nora: Well, as it was, we got it from Papa.

Mrs. Linde: I see. It was just about the time your father died.

Nora: Yes, just about then. And, you know, I couldn't make that trip out to nurse him. I had to stay here, expecting Ivar any moment, and with my poor sick Torvald to care for. Dearest Papa, I never saw him again, Kristine. Oh, that was the worst time I've known in all my marriage.

Mrs. Linde: I know how you loved him. And then you went off to Italy?

Nora: Yes. We had the means now, and the doctors urged us. So we left a month after.

Mrs. Linde: And your husband came back completely cured?

Nora: Sound as a drum!

Mrs. Linde: But — the doctor?

Nora: Who?

Mrs. Linde: I thought the maid said he was a doctor, the man who came in with me.

Nora: Yes, that was Dr. Rank — but he's not making a sick call. He's our closest friend, and he stops by at least once a day. No, Torvald hasn't had a sick moment since, and the children are fit and strong, and I am, too. *(Jumping up and clapping her hands.)* Oh, dear God, Kristine, what a lovely thing to live and be happy! But how disgusting of me — I'm talking of nothing but my own affairs. *(Sits on a stool close by Kristine, arms resting across her knees.)* Oh, don't be angry with me! Tell me, is it really true that you weren't in love with your husband? Why did you marry him, then?

Mrs. Linde: My mother was still alive, but bedridden and helpless — and I had my two younger brothers to look after. In all conscience, I didn't think I could turn him down.

Nora: No, you were right there. But was he rich at the time?

Mrs. Linde: He was very well off, I'd say. But the business was shaky, Nora. When he died, it all fell apart, and nothing was left.

Nora: And then — ?

Mrs. Linde: Yes, so I had to scrape up a living with a little shop and a little teaching and whatever else I could find. The last three years have been like one endless workday without a rest for me. Now it's over, Nora. My poor mother doesn't need me, for she's passed on. Nor the boys, either; they're working now and can take care of themselves.

Nora: How free you must feel —

Mrs. Linde: No — only unspeakably empty. Nothing to live for now. *(Standing up anxiously.)* That's why I couldn't take it any longer out in that desolate hole. Maybe here it'll be easier to find something to do and keep my mind occupied. If I could only be lucky enough to get a steady job, some office work —

Nora: Oh, but Kristine, that's so dreadfully tiring, and you already look so tired. It would be much better for you if you could go off to a bathing resort.

Mrs. Linde (going toward the window): I have no father to give me travel money, Nora.

Nora (rising): Oh, don't be angry with me.

Mrs. Linde (going to her): Nora dear, don't you be angry with me. The worst of my kind of situation is all the bitterness that's stored away. No one to work for, and yet you're always having to snap up your opportunities. You have to live; and so you grow selfish. When you told me the happy change in your lot, do you know I was delighted less for your sakes than for mine?

Nora: How so? Oh, I see. You think maybe Torvald could do something for you.

Mrs. Linde: Yes, that's what I thought.

Nora: And he will, Kristine! Just leave it to me; I'll bring it up so delicately — find something attractive to humor him with. Oh, I'm so eager to help you.

Mrs. Linde: How very kind of you, Nora, to be so concerned over me — doubly kind, considering you really know so little of life's burdens yourself.

Nora: I — ? I know so little — ?

Mrs. Linde (smiling): Well, my heavens — a little needlework and such — Nora, you're just a child.

Nora (tossing her head and pacing the floor): You don't have to act so superior.

Mrs. Linde: Oh?

Nora: You're just like the others. You all think I'm incapable of anything serious —

Mrs. Linde: Come now —

Nora: That I've never had to face the raw world.

Mrs. Linde: Nora dear, you've just been telling me all your troubles.

Nora: Hm! Trivia! *(Quietly.)* I haven't told you the big thing.

Mrs. Linde: Big thing? What do you mean?

Nora: You look down on me so, Kristine, but you shouldn't. You're proud that you worked so long and hard for your mother.

Mrs. Linde: I don't look down on a soul. But it *is* true: I'm proud — and happy, too — to think it was given to me to make my mother's last days almost free of care.

Nora: And you're also proud thinking of what you've done for your brothers.

Mrs. Linde: I feel I've a right to be.

Nora: I agree. But listen to this, Kristine — I've also got something to be proud and happy for.

Mrs. Linde: I don't doubt it. But whatever do you mean?

Nora: Not so loud. What if Torvald heard! He mustn't, not for anything in the world. Nobody must know, Kristine. No one but you.

Mrs. Linde: But what is it, then?

Nora: Come here. *(Drawing her down beside her on the sofa.)* It's true — I've also got something to be proud and happy for. I'm the one who saved Torvald's life.

Mrs. Linde: Saved — ? Saved how?

Nora: I told you about the trip to Italy. Torvald never would have lived if he hadn't gone south —

Mrs. Linde: Of course; your father gave you the means —

Nora (smiling): That's what Torvald and all the rest think, but —

Mrs. Linde: But — ?

Nora: Papa didn't give us a pin. I was the one who raised the money.

Mrs. Linde: You? That whole amount?

Nora: Four thousand, eight hundred crowns. What do you say to that?

Mrs. Linde: But Nora, how was it possible? Did you win the lottery?

Nora (disdainfully): The lottery? Pooh! No art to that.

Mrs. Linde: But where did you get it from then?

Nora (humming, with a mysterious smile): Hmm, tra-la-la-la.

Mrs. Linde: Because you couldn't have borrowed it.

Nora: No? Why not?

Mrs. Linde: A wife can't borrow without her husband's consent.

Nora (tossing her head): Oh, but a wife with a little business sense, a wife who knows how to manage —

Mrs. Linde: Nora, I simply don't understand —

Nora: You don't have to. Whoever said I *borrowed* the money? I could have gotten it other ways. *(Throwing herself back on the sofa.)* I could have gotten it from some admirer or other. After all, a girl with my ravishing appeal —

Mrs. Linde: You lunatic.

Nora: I'll bet you're eaten up with curiosity, Kristine.

Mrs. Linde: Now listen here, Nora — you haven't done something indiscreet?

Nora (sitting up again): Is it indiscreet to save your husband's life?

Mrs. Linde: I think it's indiscreet that without his knowledge you —

Nora: But that's the point: he mustn't know! My Lord, can't you understand? He mustn't ever know the close call he had. It was to *me* the doctors came to say his life was in danger — that nothing could save him but a stay in the south. Didn't I try strategy then! I began talking about how lovely it would be for me to travel abroad like other young wives; I begged and I cried; I told him please to remember my condition, to be kind and indulge me; and then I dropped a hint that he could easily take out a loan. But at that, Kristine, he nearly exploded. He said I was frivolous, and it was his duty as man of the house not to indulge me in whims and fancies — as I think he called them. Aha, I thought, now you'll just have to be saved — and that's when I saw my chance.

Mrs. Linde: And your father never told Torvald the money wasn't from him?

Nora: No, never. Papa died right about then. I'd considered bringing him into my secret and begging him never to tell. But he was too sick at the time — and then, sadly, it didn't matter.

Mrs. Linde: And you've never confided in your husband since?

Nora: For heaven's sake, no! Are you serious? He's so strict on that subject. Besides — Torvald, with all his masculine pride — how painfully humiliating for him if he ever found out he was in debt to me. That would just ruin our relationship. Our beautiful, happy home would never be the same.

Mrs. Linde: Won't you ever tell him?

Nora (thoughtfully, half smiling): Yes — maybe sometime, years from now, when I'm no longer so attractive. Don't laugh! I only mean when Torvald loves me less than now, when he stops enjoying my dancing and dressing up and reciting for him. Then it might be wise to have something in reserve — *(Breaking off.)* How ridiculous! That'll never happen — Well, Kristine, what do you think of my big secret? I'm capable of something too, hm? You can imagine, of course, how this thing hangs over me. It really hasn't been easy meeting the payments on time. In the business world there's what they call quarterly interest and what they call amortization, and these are always so terribly hard to manage. I've had to skimp a little here and there, wherever I could, you know. I could hardly spare anything from my house allowance, because Torvald has to live well. I couldn't let the children go poorly dressed; whatever I got for them, I felt I had to use up completely — the darlings!

Mrs. Linde: Poor Nora, so it had to come out of your own budget, then?

Nora: Yes, of course. But I was the one most responsible, too. Every time Torvald gave me money for new clothes and such, I never used more than half; always bought the simplest, cheapest outfits. It was a godsend that everything looks so well on me that Torvald never noticed. But it did weigh me down at times, Kristine. It *is* such a joy to wear fine things. You understand.

Mrs. Linde: Oh, of course.

Nora: And then I found other ways of making money. Last winter I was lucky
enough to get a lot of copying to do. I locked myself in and sat writing
every evening till late in the night. Ah, I was tired so often, dead tired. But
still it was wonderful fun, sitting and working like that, earning money. It
was almost like being a man.

Mrs. Linde: But how much have you paid off this way so far?

Nora: That's hard to say, exactly. These accounts, you know, aren't easy to figure. I only know that I've paid out all I could scrape together. Time and
again I haven't known where to turn. *(Smiling.)* Then I'd sit here dreaming
of a rich old gentleman who had fallen in love with me —

Mrs. Linde: What! Who is he?

Nora: Oh, really! And that he'd died, and when his will was opened, there in
big letters it said, "All my fortune shall be paid over in cash, immediately,
to that enchanting Mrs. Nora Helmer."

Mrs. Linde: But Nora dear — who *was* this gentleman?

Nora: Good grief, can't you understand? The old man never existed; that was
only something I'd dream up time and again whenever I was at my wits'
end for money. But it makes no difference now; the old fossil can go where
he pleases for all I care; I don't need him or his will — because now I'm free.
(Jumping up.) Oh, how lovely to think of that, Kristine! Carefree! To know
you're carefree, utterly carefree; to be able to romp and play with the children, and to keep up a beautiful, charming home — everything just the
way Torvald likes it! And think, spring is coming, with big blue skies.
Maybe we can travel a little then. Maybe I'll see the ocean again. Oh yes, it
is so marvelous to live and be happy!

The front doorbell rings.

Mrs. Linde (rising): There's the bell. It's probably best that I go.

Nora: No, stay. No one's expected. It must be for Torvald.

Maid (from the hall doorway): Excuse me, ma'am — there's a gentleman here to
see Mr. Helmer, but I didn't know — since the doctor's with him —

Nora: Who is the gentleman?

Krogstad (from the doorway): It's me, Mrs. Helmer.

Mrs. Linde starts and turns away toward the window.

Nora (stepping toward him, tense, her voice a whisper): You? What is it? Why do you
want to speak to my husband?

Krogstad: Bank business — after a fashion. I have a small job in the investment
bank, and I hear now your husband is going to be our chief —

Nora: In other words, it's —

Krogstad: Just dry business, Mrs. Helmer. Nothing but that.

Nora: Yes, then please be good enough to step into the study. *(She nods indifferently as she sees him out by the hall door, then returns and begins stirring up the
stove.)*

Mrs. Linde: Nora — who was that man?

Nora: That was a Mr. Krogstad — a lawyer.

Mrs. Linde: Then it really was him.

Nora: Do you know that person?

Mrs. Linde: I did once — many years ago. For a time he was a law clerk in our
town.

Nora: Yes, he's been that.

Mrs. Linde: How he's changed.

Nora: I understand he had a very unhappy marriage.

Mrs. Linde: He's a widower now.

Nora: With a number of children. There now, it's burning. *(She closes the stove door and moves the rocker a bit to one side.)*

Mrs. Linde: They say he has a hand in all kinds of business.

Nora: Oh? That may be true; I wouldn't know. But let's not think about business. It's so dull.

Dr. Rank enters from Helmer's study.

Rank (still in the doorway): No, no really — I don't want to intrude, I'd just as soon talk a little while with your wife. *(Shuts the door, then notices Mrs. Linde.)* Oh, beg pardon. I'm intruding here too.

Nora: No, not at all. *(Introducing him.)* Dr. Rank, Mrs. Linde.

Rank: Well now, that's a name much heard in this house. I believe I passed the lady on the stairs as I came.

Mrs. Linde: Yes, I take the stairs very slowly. They're rather hard on me.

Rank: Uh-hm, some touch of internal weakness?

Mrs. Linde: More overexertion, I'd say.

Rank: Nothing else? Then you're probably here in town to rest up in a round of parties?

Mrs. Linde: I'm here to look for work.

Rank: Is that the best cure for overexertion?

Mrs. Linde: One has to live, Doctor.

Rank: Yes, there's a common prejudice to that effect.

Nora: Oh, come on, Dr. Rank — you really do want to live yourself.

Rank: Yes, I really do. Wretched as I am, I'll gladly prolong my torment indefinitely. All my patients feel like that. And it's quite the same, too, with the morally sick. Right at this moment there's one of those moral invalids in there with Helmer —

Mrs. Linde (softly): Ah!

Nora: Who do you mean?

Rank: Oh, it's a lawyer, Krogstad, a type you wouldn't know. His character is rotten to the root — but even he began chattering all-importantly about how he had to *live.*

Nora: Oh? What did he want to talk to Torvald about?

Rank: I really don't know. I only heard something about the bank.

Nora: I didn't know that Krog — that this man Krogstad had anything to do with the bank.

Rank: Yes, he's gotten some kind of berth down there. *(To Mrs. Linde.)* I don't know if you also have, in your neck of the woods, a type of person who scuttles about breathlessly, sniffing out hints of moral corruption, and then maneuvers his victim into some sort of key position where he can keep an eye on him. It's the healthy these days that are out in the cold.

Mrs. Linde: All the same, it's the sick who most need to be taken in.

Rank (with a shrug): Yes, there we have it. That's the concept that's turning society into a sanatorium.

Nora, lost in her thoughts, breaks out into quiet laughter and claps her hands.

Rank: Why do you laugh at that? Do you have any real idea of what society is?

Nora: What do I care about dreary old society? I was laughing at something quite different — something terribly funny. Tell me, Doctor — is everyone who works in the bank dependent now on Torvald?

Rank: Is that what you find so terribly funny?

Nora (smiling and humming): Never mind, never mind! *(Pacing the floor.)* Yes, that's really immensely amusing: that we — that Torvald has so much power now over all those people. *(Taking the bag out of her pocket.)* Dr. Rank, a little macaroon on that?

Rank: See here, macaroons! I thought they were contraband here.

Nora: Yes, but these are some that Kristine gave me.

Mrs. Linde: What? I —?

Nora: Now, now, don't be afraid. You couldn't possibly know that Torvald had forbidden them. You see, he's worried they'll ruin my teeth. But hmp! Just this once! Isn't that so, Dr. Rank? Help yourself! *(Puts a macaroon in his mouth.)* And you too, Kristine. And I'll also have one, only a little one — or two, at the most. *(Walking about again.)* Now I'm really tremendously happy. Now there's just one last thing in the world that I have an enormous desire to do.

Rank: Well! And what's that?

Nora: It's something I have such a consuming desire to say so Torvald could hear.

Rank: And why can't you say it?

Nora: I don't dare. It's quite shocking.

Mrs. Linde: Shocking?

Rank: Well, then it isn't advisable. But in front of us you certainly can. What do you have such a desire to say so Torvald could hear?

Nora: I have such a huge desire to say — to hell and be damned!

Rank: Are you crazy?

Mrs. Linde: My goodness, Nora!

Rank: Go on, say it. Here he is.

Nora (hiding the macaroon bag): Shh, shh, shh!

Helmer comes in from his study, hat in hand, overcoat over his arm.

Nora (going toward him): Well, Torvald dear, are you through with him?

Helmer: Yes, he just left.

Nora: Let me introduce you — this is Kristine, who's arrived here in town.

Helmer: Kristine —? I'm sorry, but I don't know —

Nora: Mrs. Linde, Torvald dear. Mrs. Kristine Linde.

Helmer: Of course. A childhood friend of my wife's, no doubt?

Mrs. Linde: Yes, we knew each other in those days.

Nora: And just think, she made the long trip down here in order to talk with you.

Helmer: What's this?

Mrs. Linde: Well, not exactly —

Nora: You see, Kristine is remarkably clever in office work, and so she's terribly eager to come under a capable man's supervision and add more to what she already knows —

Helmer: Very wise, Mrs. Linde.

Nora: And then when she heard that you'd become a bank manager — the story was wired out to the papers — then she came in as fast as she could and — Really, Torvald, for my sake you can do a little something for Kristine, can't you?

Helmer: Yes, it's not at all impossible. Mrs. Linde, I suppose you're a widow?

Mrs. Linde: Yes.

Helmer: Any experience in office work?

Mrs. Linde: Yes, a good deal.

Helmer: Well, it's quite likely that I can make an opening for you —

Nora (clapping her hands): You see, you see!

Helmer: You've come at a lucky moment, Mrs. Linde.

Mrs. Linde: Oh, how can I thank you?

Helmer: Not necessary. *(Putting his overcoat on.)* But today you'll have to excuse me —

Rank: Wait, I'll go with you. *(He fetches his coat from the hall and warms it at the stove.)*

Nora: Don't stay out long, dear.

Helmer: An hour; no more.

Nora: Are you going too, Kristine?

Mrs. Linde (putting on her winter garments): Yes, I have to see about a room now.

Helmer: Then perhaps we can all walk together.

Nora (helping her): What a shame we're so cramped here, but it's quite impossible for us to —

Mrs. Linde: Oh, don't even think of it! Good-bye, Nora dear, and thanks for everything.

Nora: Good-bye for now. Of course you'll be back this evening. And you too, Dr. Rank. What? If you're well enough? Oh, you've got to be! Wrap up tight now.

In a ripple of small talk the company moves out into the hall; children's voices are heard outside on the steps.

Nora: There they are! There they are! *(She runs to open the door. The children come in with their nurse, Anne-Marie.)* Come in, come in! *(Bends down and kisses them.)* Oh, you darlings — ! Look at them, Kristine. Aren't they lovely!

Rank: No loitering in the draft here.

Helmer: Come, Mrs. Linde — this place is unbearable now for anyone but mothers.

Dr. Rank, Helmer, and Mrs. Linde go down the stairs. Anne-Marie goes into the living room with the children. Nora follows, after closing the hall door.

Nora: How fresh and strong you look. Oh, such red cheeks you have! Like apples and roses. *(The children interrupt her throughout the following.)* And it was so much fun? That's wonderful. Really? You pulled both Emmy and Bob on the sled? Imagine, all together! Yes, you're a clever boy, Ivar. Oh, let me hold her a bit, Anne-Marie. My sweet little doll baby! *(Takes the smallest from the nurse and dances with her.)* Yes, yes, Mama will dance with Bob as well. What? Did you throw snowballs? Oh, if I'd only been there! No, don't bother, Anne-Marie — I'll undress them myself. Oh yes, let me. It's such fun. Go in and rest; you look half frozen. There's hot coffee waiting for you on the stove. *(The nurse goes into the room to the left. Nora takes the chil-*

dren's winter things off, throwing them about, while the children talk to her all at once.) Is that so? A big dog chased you? But it didn't bite? No, dogs never bite little, lovely doll babies. Don't peek in the packages, Ivar! What is it? Yes, wouldn't you like to know. No, no, it's an ugly something. Well? Shall we play? What shall we play? Hide-and-seek? Yes, let's play hide-and-seek. Bob must hide first. I must? Yes, let me hide first. *(Laughing and shouting, she and the children play in and out of the living room and the adjoining room to the right. At last Nora hides under the table. The children come storming in, search, but cannot find her, then hear her muffled laughter, dash over to the table, lift the cloth up and find her. Wild shouting. She creeps forward as if to scare them. More shouts. Meanwhile, a knock at the hall door; no one has noticed it. Now the door half opens, and Krogstad appears. He waits a moment; the game goes on.)*

Krogstad: Beg pardon, Mrs. Helmer—

Nora (with a strangled cry, turning and scrambling to her knees): Oh! What do you want?

Krogstad: Excuse me. The outer door was ajar; it must be someone forgot to shut it—

Nora (rising): My husband isn't home, Mr. Krogstad.

Krogstad: I know that.

Nora: Yes—then what do you want here?

Krogstad: A word with you.

Nora: With—? *(To the children, quietly.)* Go in to Anne-Marie. What? No, the strange man won't hurt Mama. When he's gone, we'll play some more. *(She leads the children into the room to the left and shuts the door after them. Then, tense and nervous:)* You want to speak to me?

Krogstad: Yes, I want to.

Nora: Today? But it's not yet the first of the month—

Krogstad: No, it's Christmas Eve. It's going to be up to you how merry a Christmas you have.

Nora: What is it you want? Today I absolutely can't—

Krogstad: We won't talk about that till later. This is something else. You do have a moment to spare, I suppose?

Nora: Oh yes, of course—I do, except—

Krogstad: Good. I was sitting over at Olsen's Restaurant when I saw your husband go down the street—

Nora: Yes?

Krogstad: With a lady.

Nora: Yes. So?

Krogstad: If you'll pardon my asking: wasn't that lady a Mrs. Linde?

Nora: Yes.

Krogstad: Just now come into town?

Nora: Yes, today.

Krogstad: She's a good friend of yours?

Nora: Yes, she is. But I don't see—

Krogstad: I also knew her once.

Nora: I'm aware of that.

Krogstad: Oh? You know all about it. I thought so. Well, then let me ask you short and sweet: is Mrs. Linde getting a job in the bank?

Nora: What makes you think you can cross-examine me, Mr. Krogstad—you, one of my husband's employees? But since you ask, you might as well know—yes, Mrs. Linde's going to be taken on at the bank. And I'm the one who spoke for her, Mr. Krogstad. Now you know.

Krogstad: So I guessed right.

Nora (pacing up and down): Oh, one does have a tiny bit of influence, I should hope. Just because I am a woman, don't think it means that—When one has a subordinate position, Mr. Krogstad, one really ought to be careful about pushing somebody who—hm—

Krogstad: Who has influence?

Nora: That's right.

Krogstad (in a different tone): Mrs. Helmer, would you be good enough to use your influence on my behalf?

Nora: What? What do you mean?

Krogstad: Would you please make sure that I keep my subordinate position in the bank?

Nora: What does that mean? Who's thinking of taking away your position?

Krogstad: Oh, don't play the innocent with me. I'm quite aware that your friend would hardly relish the chance of running into me again; and I'm also aware now whom I can thank for being turned out.

Nora: But I promise you—

Krogstad: Yes, yes, yes, to the point: there's still time, and I'm advising you to use your influence to prevent it.

Nora: But Mr. Krogstad, I have absolutely no influence.

Krogstad: You haven't? I thought you were just saying—

Nora: You shouldn't take me so literally. I! How can you believe that I have any such influence over my husband?

Krogstad: Oh, I've known your husband from our student days. I don't think the great bank manager's more steadfast than any other married man.

Nora: You speak insolently about my husband, and I'll show you the door.

Krogstad: The lady has spirit.

Nora: I'm not afraid of you any longer. After New Year's, I'll soon be done with the whole business.

Krogstad (restraining himself): Now listen to me, Mrs. Helmer. If necessary, I'll fight for my little job in the bank as if it were life itself.

Nora: Yes, so it seems.

Krogstad: It's not just a matter of income; that's the least of it. It's something else—All right, out with it! Look, this is the thing. You know, just like all the others, of course, that once, a good many years ago, I did something rather rash.

Nora: I've heard rumors to that effect.

Krogstad: The case never got into court; but all the same, every door was closed in my face from then on. So I took up those various activities you know about. I had to grab hold somewhere; and I dare say I haven't been among the worst. But now I want to drop all that. My boys are growing up. For their sakes, I'll have to win back as much respect as possible here in town. That job in the bank was like the first rung in my ladder. And now your husband wants to kick me right back down in the mud again.

Nora: But for heaven's sake, Mr. Krogstad, it's simply not in my power to help you.

Krogstad: That's because you haven't the will to—but I have the means to make you.

Nora: You certainly won't tell my husband that I owe you money?

Krogstad: Hm — what if I told him that?

Nora: That would be shameful of you. *(Nearly in tears.)* This secret — my joy and my pride — that he should learn it in such a crude and disgusting way — learn it from you. You'd expose me to the most horrible unpleasantness —

Krogstad: Only unpleasantness?

Nora (vehemently): But go on and try. It'll turn out the worse for you, because then my husband will really see what a crook you are, and then you'll *never* be able to hold your job.

Krogstad: I asked if it was just domestic unpleasantness you were afraid of?

Nora: If my husband finds out, then of course he'll pay what I owe at once, and then we'd be through with you for good.

Krogstad (a step closer): Listen, Mrs. Helmer — you've either got a very bad memory, or else no head at all for business. I'd better put you a little more in touch with the facts.

Nora: What do you mean?

Krogstad: When your husband was sick, you came to me for a loan of four thousand, eight hundred crowns.

Nora: Where else could I go?

Krogstad: I promised to get you that sum —

Nora: And you got it.

Krogstad: I promised to get you that sum, on certain conditions. You were so involved in your husband's illness, and so eager to finance your trip, that I guess you didn't think out all the details. It might just be a good idea to remind you. I promised you the money on the strength of a note I drew up.

Nora: Yes, and that I signed.

Krogstad: Right. But at the bottom I added some lines for your father to guarantee the loan. He was supposed to sign down there.

Nora: Supposed to? He did sign.

Krogstad: I left the date blank. In other words, your father would have dated his signature himself. Do you remember that?

Nora: Yes, I think —

Krogstad: Then I gave you the note for you to mail to your father. Isn't that so?

Nora: Yes.

Krogstad: And naturally you sent it at once — because only some five, six days later you brought me the note, properly signed. And with that, the money was yours.

Nora: Well, then; I've made my payments regularly, haven't I?

Krogstad: More or less. But — getting back to the point — those were hard times for you then, Mrs. Helmer.

Nora: Yes, they were.

Krogstad: Your father was very ill, I believe.

Nora: He was near the end.

Krogstad: He died soon after?

Nora: Yes.

Krogstad: Tell me, Mrs. Helmer, do you happen to recall the date of your father's death? The day of the month, I mean.

Nora: Papa died the twenty-ninth of September.

Krogstad: That's quite correct; I've already looked into that. And now we come to a curious thing — *(Taking out a paper.)* which I simply cannot comprehend.

Nora: Curious thing? I don't know —

Krogstad: This is the curious thing: that your father co-signed the note for your loan three days after his death.

Nora: How — ? I don't understand.

Krogstad: Your father died the twenty-ninth of September. But look. Here your father dated his signature October second. Isn't that curious, Mrs. Helmer? (*Nora is silent.*) Can you explain it to me? (*Nora remains silent.*) It's also remarkable that the words "October second" and the year aren't written in your father's hand, but rather in one that I think I know. Well, it's easy to understand. Your father forgot perhaps to date his signature, and then someone or other added it, a bit sloppily, before anyone knew of his death. There's nothing wrong in that. It all comes down to the signature. And there's no question about *that*, Mrs. Helmer. It really *was* your father who signed his own name here, wasn't it?

Nora (after a short silence, throwing her head back and looking squarely at him): No, it wasn't. *I* signed Papa's name.

Krogstad: Wait, now — are you fully aware that this is a dangerous confession?

Nora: Why? You'll soon get your money.

Krogstad: Let me ask you a question — why didn't you send the paper to your father?

Nora: That was impossible. Papa was so sick. If I'd asked him for his signature, I also would have had to tell him what the money was for. But I couldn't tell him, sick as he was, that my husband's life was in danger. That was just impossible.

Krogstad: Then it would have been better if you'd given up the trip abroad.

Nora: I couldn't possibly. The trip was to save my husband's life. I couldn't give that up.

Krogstad: But didn't you ever consider that this was a fraud against me?

Nora: I couldn't let myself be bothered by that. You weren't any concern of mine. I couldn't stand you, with all those cold complications you made, even though you knew how badly off my husband was.

Krogstad: Mrs. Helmer, obviously you haven't the vaguest idea of what you've involved yourself in. But I can tell you this: it was nothing more and nothing worse that I once did — and it wrecked my whole reputation.

Nora: You? Do you expect me to believe that you ever acted bravely to save your wife's life?

Krogstad: Laws don't inquire into motives.

Nora: Then they must be very poor laws.

Krogstad: Poor or not — if I introduce this paper in court, you'll be judged according to law.

Nora: This I refuse to believe. A daughter hasn't a right to protect her dying father from anxiety and care? A wife hasn't a right to save her husband's life? I don't know much about laws, but I'm sure that somewhere in the books these things are allowed. And you don't know anything about it — you who practice the law? You must be an awful lawyer, Mr. Krogstad.

Krogstad: Could be. But business — the kind of business we two are mixed up in — don't you think I know about that? All right. Do what you want now. But I'm telling you *this*: if I get shoved down a second time, you're going to keep me company. (*He bows and goes out through the hall.*)

Nora (pensive for a moment, then tossing her head): Oh, really! Trying to frighten me! I'm not so silly as all that. *(Begins gathering up the children's clothes, but soon stops.)* But —? No, but that's impossible! I did it out of love.

The Children (in the doorway, left): Mama, that strange man's gone out the door.

Nora: Yes, yes, I know it. But don't tell anyone about the strange man. Do you hear? Not even Papa!

The Children: No, Mama. But now will you play again?

Nora: No, not now.

The Children: Oh, but Mama, you promised.

Nora: Yes, but I can't now. Go inside; I have too much to do. Go in, go in, my sweet darlings. *(She herds them gently back in the room and shuts the door after them. Settling on the sofa, she takes up a piece of embroidery and makes some stitches, but soon stops abruptly.)* No! *(Throws the work aside, rises, goes to the hall door and calls out.)* Helene! Let me have the tree in here. *(Goes to the table, left, opens the table drawer, and stops again.)* No, but that's utterly impossible!

Maid (with the Christmas tree): Where should I put it, ma'am?

Nora: There. The middle of the floor.

Maid: Should I bring anything else?

Nora: No, thanks. I have what I need.

> *The Maid, who has set the tree down, goes out.*

Nora (absorbed in trimming the tree): Candles here — and flowers here. That terrible creature! Talk, talk, talk! There's nothing to it at all. The tree's going to be lovely. I'll do anything to please you, Torvald. I'll sing for you, dance for you —

> *Helmer comes in from the hall, with a sheaf of papers under his arm.*

Nora: Oh! You're back so soon?

Helmer: Yes. Has anyone been here?

Nora: Here? No.

Helmer: That's odd. I saw Krogstad leaving the front door.

Nora: So? Oh yes, that's true. Krogstad was here a moment.

Helmer: Nora, I can see by your face that he's been here, begging you to put in a good word for him.

Nora: Yes.

Helmer: And it was supposed to seem like your own idea? You were to hide it from me that he'd been here. He asked you that, too, didn't he?

Nora: Yes, Torvald, but —

Helmer: Nora, Nora, and you could fall for that? Talk with that sort of person and promise him anything? And then in the bargain, tell me an untruth.

Nora: An untruth —?

Helmer: Didn't you say that no one had been here? *(Wagging his finger.)* My little songbird must never do that again. A songbird needs a clean beak to warble with. No false notes. *(Putting his arm about her waist.)* That's the way it should be, isn't it? Yes, I'm sure of it. *(Releasing her.)* And so, enough of that. *(Sitting by the stove.)* Ah, how snug and cozy it is here. *(Leafing among his papers.)*

Nora (busy with the tree, after a short pause): Torvald!

Helmer: Yes.

Nora: I'm so much looking forward to the Stenborgs' costume party, day after tomorrow.

Helmer: And I can't wait to see what you'll surprise me with.

Nora: Oh, that stupid business!

Helmer: What?

Nora: I can't find anything that's right. Everything seems so ridiculous, so inane.

Helmer: So my little Nora's come to *that* recognition?

Nora (going behind his chair, her arms resting on its back): Are you very busy, Torvald?

Helmer: Oh —

Nora: What papers are those?

Helmer: Bank matters.

Nora: Already?

Helmer: I've gotten full authority from the retiring management to make all necessary changes in personnel and procedure. I'll need Christmas week for that. I want to have everything in order by New Year's.

Nora: So that was the reason this poor Krogstad —

Helmer: Hm.

Nora (still leaning on the chair and slowly stroking the nape of his neck): If you weren't so very busy, I would have asked you an enormous favor, Torvald.

Helmer: Let's hear. What is it?

Nora: You know, there isn't anyone who has your good taste — and I want so much to look well at the costume party. Torvald, couldn't you take over and decide what I should be and plan my costume?

Helmer: Ah, is my stubborn little creature calling for a lifeguard?

Nora: Yes, Torvald, I can't get anywhere without your help.

Helmer: All right — I'll think it over. We'll hit on something.

Nora: Oh, how sweet of you. *(Goes to the tree again. Pause.)* Aren't the red flowers pretty —? But tell me, was it really such a crime that this Krogstad committed?

Helmer: Forgery. Do you have any idea what that means?

Nora: Couldn't he have done it out of need?

Helmer: Yes, or thoughtlessness, like so many others. I'm not so heartless that I'd condemn a man categorically for just one mistake.

Nora: No, of course not, Torvald!

Helmer: Plenty of men have redeemed themselves by openly confessing their crimes and taking their punishment.

Nora: Punishment —?

Helmer: But now Krogstad didn't go that way. He got himself out by sharp practices, and that's the real cause of his moral breakdown.

Nora: Do you really think that would —?

Helmer: Just imagine how a man with that sort of guilt in him has to lie and cheat and deceive on all sides, has to wear a mask even with the nearest and dearest he has, even with his own wife and children. And with the children, Nora — that's where it's most horrible.

Nora: Why?

Helmer: Because that kind of atmosphere of lies infects the whole life of a home. Every breath the children take in is filled with the germs of something degenerate.

Nora (coming closer behind him): Are you sure of that?

Helmer: Oh, I've seen it often enough as a lawyer. Almost everyone who goes bad early in life has a mother who's a chronic liar.

Nora: Why just — the mother?

Helmer: It's usually the mother's influence that's dominant, but the father's works in the same way, of course. Every lawyer is quite familiar with it. And still this Krogstad's been going home year in, year out, poisoning his own children with lies and pretense; that's why I call him morally lost. *(Reaching his hands out toward her.)* So my sweet little Nora must promise me never to plead his cause. Your hand on it. Come, come, what's this? Give me your hand. There, now. All settled. I can tell you it'd be impossible for me to work alongside of him. I literally feel physically revolted when I'm anywhere near such a person.

Nora (withdraws her hand and goes to the other side of the Christmas tree): How hot it is here! And I've got so much to do.

Helmer (getting up and gathering his papers): Yes, and I have to think about getting some of these read through before dinner. I'll think about your costume, too. And something to hang on the tree in gilt paper, I may even see about that. *(Putting his hand on her head.)* Oh you, my darling little songbird. *(He goes into his study and closes the door after him.)*

Nora (softly, after a silence): Oh, really! It isn't so. It's impossible. It must be impossible.

Anne-Marie (in the doorway, left): The children are begging so hard to come in to Mama.

Nora: No, no, no, don't let them in to me! You stay with them, Anne-Marie.

Anne-Marie: Of course, ma'am. *(Closes the door.)*

Nora (pale with terror): Hurt my children —! Poison my home? *(A moment's pause; then she tosses her head.)* That's not true. Never. Never in all the world.

ACT II

Same room. Beside the piano the Christmas tree now stands stripped of ornament, burned-down candle stubs on its ragged branches. Nora's street clothes lie on the sofa. Nora, alone in the room, moves restlessly about; at last she stops at the sofa and picks up her coat.

Nora (dropping the coat again): Someone's coming! *(Goes toward the door, listens.)* No — there's no one. Of course — nobody's coming today, Christmas Day — or tomorrow, either. But maybe — *(Opens the door and looks out.)* No, nothing in the mailbox. Quite empty. *(Coming forward.)* What nonsense! He won't do anything serious. Nothing terrible could happen. It's impossible. Why, I have three small children.

Anne-Marie, with a large carton, comes in from the room to the left.

Anne-Marie: Well, at last I found the box with the masquerade clothes.

Nora: Thanks. Put it on the table.

Anne-Marie (does so): But they're all pretty much of a mess.

Nora: Ahh! I'd love to rip them in a million pieces!

Anne-Marie: Oh, mercy, they can be fixed right up. Just a little patience.

Nora: Yes, I'll go get Mrs. Linde to help me.

Anne-Marie: Out again now? In this nasty weather? Miss Nora will catch cold — get sick.

Nora: Oh, worse things could happen. How are the children?

Anne-Marie: The poor mites are playing with their Christmas presents, but —

Nora: Do they ask for me much?

Anne-Marie: They're so used to having Mama around, you know.

Nora: Yes, but Anne-Marie, I *can't* be together with them as much as I was.

Anne-Marie: Well, small children get used to anything.

Nora: You think so? Do you think they'd forget their mother if she was gone for good?

Anne-Marie: Oh, mercy — gone for good!

Nora: Wait, tell me, Anne-Marie — I've wondered so often — how could you ever have the heart to give your child over to strangers?

Anne-Marie: But I had to, you know, to become little Nora's nurse.

Nora: Yes, but how could you *do* it?

Anne-Marie: When I could get such a good place? A girl who's poor and who's gotten in trouble is glad enough for that. Because that slippery fish, he didn't do a thing for me, you know.

Nora: But your daughter's surely forgotten you.

Anne-Marie: Oh, she certainly has not. She's written to me, both when she was confirmed and when she was married.

Nora (clasping her about the neck): You old Anne-Marie, you were a good mother for me when I was little.

Anne-Marie: Poor little Nora, with no other mother but me.

Nora: And if the babies didn't have one, then I know that you'd — What silly talk! *(Opening the carton.)* Go in to them. Now I'll have to — Tomorrow you can see how lovely I'll look.

Anne-Marie: Oh, there won't be anyone at the party as lovely as Miss Nora. *(She goes off into the room, left.)*

Nora (begins unpacking the box, but soon throws it aside): Oh, if I dared to go out. If only nobody would come. If only nothing would happen here while I'm out. What craziness — nobody's coming. Just don't think. This muff — needs a brushing. Beautiful gloves, beautiful gloves. Let it go. Let it go! One, two, three, four, five, six — *(With a cry.)* Oh, there they are! *(Poises to move toward the door, but remains irresolutely standing. Mrs. Linde enters from the hall, where she has removed her street clothes.)*

Nora: Oh, it's you, Kristine. There's no one else out there? How good that you've come.

Mrs. Linde: I hear you were up asking for me.

Nora: Yes, I just stopped by. There's something you really can help me with. Let's get settled on the sofa. Look, there's going to be a costume party tomorrow evening at the Stenborgs' right above us, and now Torvald wants me to go as a Neapolitan peasant girl and dance the tarantella that I learned in Capri.

Mrs. Linde: Really, are you giving a whole performance?

Nora: Torvald says yes, I should. See, here's the dress. Torvald had it made for me down there; but now it's all so tattered that I just don't know —

Mrs. Linde: Oh, we'll fix that up in no time. It's nothing more than the trimmings — they're a bit loose here and there. Needle and thread? Good, now we have what we need.

Nora: Oh, how sweet of you!

Mrs. Linde (sewing): So you'll be in disguise tomorrow, Nora. You know what? I'll stop by then for a moment and have a look at you all dressed up. But listen, I've absolutely forgotten to thank you for that pleasant evening yesterday.

Nora (getting up and walking about): I don't think it was as pleasant as usual yesterday. You should have come to town a bit sooner, Kristine — Yes, Torvald really knows how to give a home elegance and charm.

Mrs. Linde: And you do, too, if you ask me. You're not your father's daughter for nothing. But tell me, is Dr. Rank always so down in the mouth as yesterday?

Nora: No, that was quite an exception. But he goes around critically ill all the time — tuberculosis of the spine, poor man. You know, his father was a disgusting thing who kept mistresses and so on — and that's why the son's been sickly from birth.

Mrs. Linde (lets her sewing fall to her lap): But my dearest Nora, how do you know about such things?

Nora (walking more jauntily): Hmp! When you've had three children, then you've had a few visits from — from women who know something of medicine, and they tell you this and that.

Mrs. Linde (resumes sewing; a short pause): Does Dr. Rank come here every day?

Nora: Every blessed day. He's Torvald's best friend from childhood, and *my* good friend, too. Dr. Rank almost belongs to this house.

Mrs. Linde: But tell me — is he quite sincere? I mean, doesn't he rather enjoy flattering people?

Nora: Just the opposite. Why do you think that?

Mrs. Linde: When you introduced us yesterday, he was proclaiming that he'd often heard my name in this house; but later I noticed that your husband hadn't the slightest idea who I really was. So how could Dr. Rank — ?

Nora: But it's all true, Kristine. You see, Torvald loves me beyond words, and, as he puts it, he'd like to keep me all to himself. For a long time he'd almost be jealous if I even mentioned any of my old friends back home. So of course I dropped that. But with Dr. Rank I talk a lot about such things, because he likes hearing about them.

Mrs. Linde: Now listen, Nora; in many ways you're still like a child. I'm a good deal older than you, with a little more experience. I'll tell you something: you ought to put an end to all this with Dr. Rank.

Nora: What should I put an end to?

Mrs. Linde: Both parts of it, I think. Yesterday you said something about a rich admirer who'd provide you with money —

Nora: Yes, one who doesn't exist — worse luck. So?

Mrs. Linde: Is Dr. Rank well off?

Nora: Yes, he is.

Mrs. Linde: With no dependents?

Nora: No, no one. But —

Mrs. Linde: And he's over here every day?

Nora: Yes, I told you that.

Mrs. Linde: How can a man of such refinement be so grasping?

Nora: I don't follow you at all.

Mrs. Linde: Now don't try to hide it, Nora. You think I can't guess who loaned you the forty-eight hundred crowns?

Nora: Are you out of your mind? How could you think such a thing! A friend of ours, who comes here every single day. What an intolerable situation that would have been!

Mrs. Linde: Then it really wasn't him.

Nora: No, absolutely not. It never even crossed my mind for a moment—And he had nothing to lend in those days; his inheritance came later.

Mrs. Linde: Well, I think that was a stroke of luck for you, Nora dear.

Nora: No, it never would have occurred to me to ask Dr. Rank—Still, I'm quite sure that if I had asked him—

Mrs. Linde: Which you won't, of course.

Nora: No, of course not. I can't see that I'd ever need to. But I'm quite positive that if I talked to Dr. Rank—

Mrs. Linde: Behind your husband's back?

Nora: I've got to clear up this other thing; *that's* also behind his back. I've *got* to clear it all up.

Mrs. Linde: Yes, I was saying that yesterday, but—

Nora (pacing up and down): A man handles these problems so much better than a woman—

Mrs. Linde: One's husband does, yes.

Nora: Nonsense. *(Stopping.)* When you pay everything you owe, then you get your note back, right?

Mrs. Linde: Yes, naturally.

Nora: And can rip it into a million pieces and burn it up—that filthy scrap of paper!

Mrs. Linde (looking hard at her, laying her sewing aside, and rising slowly): Nora, you're hiding something from me.

Nora: You can see it in my face?

Mrs. Linde: Something's happened to you since yesterday morning. Nora, what is it?

Nora (hurrying toward her): Kristine! *(Listening.)* Shh! Torvald's home. Look, go in with the children a while. Torvald can't bear all this snipping and stitching. Let Anne-Marie help you.

Mrs. Linde (gathering up some of the things): All right, but I'm not leaving here until we've talked this out. *(She disappears into the room, left, as Torvald enters from the hall.)*

Nora: Oh, how I've been waiting for you, Torvald dear.

Helmer: Was that the dressmaker?

Nora: No, that was Kristine. She's helping me fix up my costume. You know, it's going to be quite attractive.

Helmer: Yes, wasn't that a bright idea I had?

Nora: Brilliant! But then wasn't I good as well to give in to you?

Helmer: Good—because you give in to your husband's judgment? All right, you little goose, I know you didn't mean it like that. But I won't disturb you. You'll want to have a fitting, I suppose.

Nora: And you'll be working?

Helmer: Yes. *(Indicating a bundle of papers.)* See. I've been down to the bank.
 (Starts toward his study.)
Nora: Torvald.
Helmer (stops): Yes.
Nora: If your little squirrel begged you, with all her heart and soul, for some-
 thing—?
Helmer: What's that?
Nora: Then would you do it?
Helmer: First, naturally, I'd have to know what it was.
Nora: Your squirrel would scamper about and do tricks, if you'd only be sweet
 and give in.
Helmer: Out with it.
Nora: Your lark would be singing high and low in every room—
Helmer: Come on, she does that anyway.
Nora: I'd be a wood nymph and dance for you in the moonlight.
Helmer: Nora—don't tell me it's that same business from this morning?
Nora (coming closer): Yes, Torvald, I beg you, please!
Helmer: And you actually have the nerve to drag that up again?
Nora: Yes, yes, you've got to give in to me; you *have* to let Krogstad keep his job
 in the bank.
Helmer: My dear Nora, I've slated his job for Mrs. Linde.
Nora: That's awfully kind of you. But you could just fire another clerk instead
 of Krogstad.
Helmer: This is the most incredible stubbornness! Because you go and give an
 impulsive promise to speak up for him, I'm expected to—
Nora: That's not the reason, Torvald. It's for your own sake. That man does
 writing for the worst papers; you said it yourself. He could do you any
 amount of harm. I'm scared to death of him—
Helmer: Ah, I understand. It's the old memories haunting you.
Nora: What do you mean by that?
Helmer: Of course, you're thinking about your father.
Nora: Yes, all right. Just remember how those nasty gossips wrote in the papers
 about Papa and slandered him so cruelly. I think they'd have had him dismissed if the department hadn't sent you up to investigate, and if you
 hadn't been so kind and open-minded toward him.
Helmer: My dear Nora, there's a notable difference between your father and
 me. Your father's official career was hardly above reproach. But mine is;
 and I hope it'll stay that way as long as I hold my position.
Nora: Oh, who can ever tell what vicious minds can invent? We could be so
 snug and happy now in our quiet, carefree home—you and I and the children, Torvald! That's why I'm pleading with you so—
Helmer: And just by pleading for him you make it impossible for me to keep
 him on. It's already known at the bank that I'm firing Krogstad. What if
 it's rumored around now that the new bank manager was vetoed by his
 wife—
Nora: Yes, what then—?
Helmer: Oh yes—as long as our little bundle of stubbornness gets her way—!
 I should go and make myself ridiculous in front of the whole office—
 give people the idea I can be swayed by all kinds of outside pressure. Oh,
 you can bet I'd feel the effects of that soon enough! Besides—there's

something that rules Krogstad right out at the bank as long as I'm the manager.

Nora: What's that?

Helmer: His moral failings I could maybe overlook if I had to —

Nora: Yes, Torvald, why not?

Helmer: And I hear he's quite efficient on the job. But he was a crony of mine back in my teens — one of those rash friendships that crop up again and again to embarrass you later in life. Well, I might as well say it straight out: we're on a first-name basis. And that tactless fool makes no effort at all to hide it in front of others. Quite the contrary — he thinks that entitles him to take a familiar air around me, and so every other second he comes booming out with his "Yes, Torvald!" and "Sure thing, Torvald!" I tell you, it's been excruciating for me. He's out to make my place in the bank unbearable.

Nora: Torvald, you can't be serious about all this.

Helmer: Oh no? Why not?

Nora: Because these are such petty considerations.

Helmer: What are you saying? Petty? You think I'm petty!

Nora: No, just the opposite, Torvald dear. That's exactly why —

Helmer: Never mind. You call my motives petty; then I might as well be just that. Petty! All right! We'll put a stop to this for good. *(Goes to the hall door and calls.)* Helene!

Nora: What do you want?

Helmer (searching among his papers): A decision. *(The maid comes in.)* Look here; take this letter; go out with it at once. Get hold of a messenger and have him deliver it. Quick now. It's already addressed. Wait, here's some money.

Maid: Yes, sir. *(She leaves with the letter.)*

Helmer (straightening his papers): There, now, little Miss Willful.

Nora (breathlessly): Torvald, what was that letter?

Helmer: Krogstad's notice.

Nora: Call it back, Torvald! There's still time. Oh, Torvald, call it back! Do it for my sake — for your sake, for the children's sake! Do you hear, Torvald; do it! You don't know how this can harm us.

Helmer: Too late.

Nora: Yes, too late.

Helmer: Nora dear, I can forgive you this panic, even though basically you're insulting me. Yes, you are! Or isn't it an insult to think that *I* should be afraid of a courtroom hack's revenge? But I forgive you anyway, because this shows so beautifully how much you love me. *(Takes her in his arms.)* This is the way it should be, my darling Nora. Whatever comes, you'll see; when it really counts, I have strength and courage enough as a man to take on the whole weight myself.

Nora (terrified): What do you mean by that?

Helmer: The whole weight, I said.

Nora (resolutely): No, never in all the world.

Helmer: Good. So we'll share it, Nora, as man and wife. That's as it should be. *(Fondling her.)* Are you happy now? There, there, there — not these frightened dove's eyes. It's nothing at all but empty fantasies — Now you should run through your tarantella and practice your tambourine. I'll go to the inner office and shut both doors, so I won't hear a thing; you can make all the noise you like. *(Turning in the doorway.)* And when Rank comes, just tell him where he can find me. *(He nods to her and goes with his papers into the study, closing the door.)*

Nora (standing as though rooted, dazed with fright, in a whisper): He really could do it. He will do it. He'll do it in spite of everything. No, not that, never, never! Anything but that! Escape! A way out — *(The doorbell rings.)* Dr. Rank! Anything but that! *Anything*, whatever it is! *(Her hands pass over her face, smoothing it; she pulls herself together, goes over and opens the hall door. Dr. Rank stands outside, hanging his fur coat up. During the following scene, it begins getting dark.)*

Nora: Hello, Dr. Rank. I recognized your ring. But you mustn't go in to Torvald yet; I believe he's working.

Rank: And you?

Nora: For you, I always have an hour to spare — you know that. *(He has entered, and she shuts the door after him.)*

Rank: Many thanks. I'll make use of these hours while I can.

Nora: What do you mean by that? While you can?

Rank: Does that disturb you?

Nora: Well, it's such an odd phrase. Is anything going to happen?

Rank: What's going to happen is what I've been expecting so long — but I honestly didn't think it would come so soon.

Nora (gripping his arm): What is it you've found out? Dr. Rank, you have to tell me!

Rank (sitting by the stove): It's all over for me. There's nothing to be done about it.

Nora (breathing easier): Is it you — then — ?

Rank: Who else? There's no point in lying to one's self. I'm the most miserable of all my patients, Mrs. Helmer. These past few days I've been auditing my internal accounts. Bankrupt! Within a month I'll probably be laid out and rotting in the churchyard.

Nora: Oh, what a horrible thing to say.

Rank: The thing itself is horrible. But the worst of it is all the other horror before it's over. There's only one final examination left; when I'm finished with that, I'll know about when my disintegration will begin. There's something I want to say. Helmer with his sensitivity has such a sharp distaste for anything ugly. I don't want him near my sickroom.

Nora: Oh, but Dr. Rank —

Rank: I won't have him in there. Under no condition. I'll lock my door to him — As soon as I'm completely sure of the worst, I'll send you my calling card marked with a black cross, and you'll know then the wreck has started to come apart.

Nora: No, today you're completely unreasonable. And I wanted you so much to be in a really good humor.

Rank: With death up my sleeve? And then to suffer this way for somebody else's sins. Is there any justice in that? And in every single family, in some way or another, this inevitable retribution of nature goes on —

Nora (her hands pressed over her ears): Oh, stuff! Cheer up! Please — be gay!

Rank: Yes, I'd just as soon laugh at it all. My poor, innocent spine, serving time for my father's gay army days.

Nora (by the table, left): He was so infatuated with asparagus tips and pâté de foie gras, wasn't that it?

Rank: Yes — and with truffles.

Nora: Truffles, yes. And then with oysters, I suppose?

Rank: Yes, tons of oysters, naturally.

Nora: And then the port and champagne to go with it. It's so sad that all these delectable things have to strike at our bones.

Rank: Especially when they strike at the unhappy bones that never shared in the fun.

Nora: Ah, that's the saddest of all.

Rank (looks searchingly at her): Hm.

Nora (after a moment): Why did you smile?

Rank: No, it was you who laughed.

Nora: No, it was you who smiled, Dr. Rank!

Rank (getting up): You're even a bigger tease than I'd thought.

Nora: I'm full of wild ideas today.

Rank: That's obvious.

Nora (putting both hands on his shoulders): Dear, dear Dr. Rank, you'll never die for Torvald and me.

Rank: Oh, that loss you'll easily get over. Those who go away are soon forgotten.

Nora (looks fearfully at him): You believe that?

Rank: One makes new connections, and then —

Nora: Who makes new connections?

Rank: Both you and Torvald will when I'm gone. I'd say you're well under way already. What was that Mrs. Linde doing here last evening?

Nora: Oh, come — you can't be jealous of poor Kristine?

Rank: Oh yes, I am. She'll be my successor here in the house. When I'm down under, that woman will probably —

Nora: Shh! Not so loud. She's right in there.

Rank: Today as well. So you see.

Nora: Only to sew on my dress. Good gracious, how unreasonable you are. *(Sitting on the sofa.)* Be nice now, Dr. Rank. Tomorrow you'll see how beautifully I'll dance; and you can imagine then that I'm dancing only for you — yes, and of course for Torvald, too — that's understood. *(Takes various items out of the carton.)* Dr. Rank, sit over here and I'll show you something.

Rank (sitting): What's that?

Nora: Look here. Look.

Rank: Silk stockings.

Nora: Flesh-colored. Aren't they lovely? Now it's so dark here, but tomorrow — No, no, no, just look at the feet. Oh well, you might as well look at the rest.

Rank: Hm —

Nora: Why do you look so critical? Don't you believe they'll fit?

Rank: I've never had any chance to form an opinion on that.

Nora (glancing at him a moment): Shame on you. *(Hits him lightly on the ear with the stockings.)* That's for you. *(Puts them away again.)*

Rank: And what other splendors am I going to see now?

Nora: Not the least bit more, because you've been naughty. *(She hums a little and rummages among her things.)*

Rank (after a short silence): When I sit here together with you like this, completely easy and open, then I don't know — I simply can't imagine — whatever would have become of me if I'd never come into this house.

Nora (smiling): Yes, I really think you feel completely at ease with us.

Rank (more quietly, staring straight ahead): And then to have to go away from it all —

Nora: Nonsense, you're not going away.

Rank (his voice unchanged): — and not even be able to leave some poor show of gratitude behind, scarcely a fleeting regret — no more than a vacant place that anyone can fill.

Nora: And if I asked you now for — ? No —

Rank: For what?

Nora: For a great proof of your friendship —

Rank: Yes, yes?

Nora: No, I mean — for an exceptionally big favor —

Rank: Would you really, for once, make me so happy?

Nora: Oh, you haven't the vaguest idea what it is.

Rank: All right, then tell me.

Nora: No, but I can't, Dr. Rank — it's all out of reason. It's advice and help, too — and a favor —

Rank: So much the better. I can't fathom what you're hinting at. Just speak out. Don't you trust me?

Nora: Of course. More than anyone else. You're my best and truest friend, I'm sure. That's why I want to talk to you. All right, then, Dr. Rank: there's something you can help me prevent. You know how deeply, how inexpressibly dearly Torvald loves me; he'd never hesitate a second to give up his life for me.

Rank (leaning close to her): Nora — do you think he's the only one —

Nora (with a slight start): Who — ?

Rank: Who'd gladly give up his life for you.

Nora (heavily): I see.

Rank: I swore to myself you should know this before I'm gone. I'll never find a better chance. Yes, Nora, now you know. And also you know now that you can trust me beyond anyone else.

Nora (rising, natural and calm): Let me by.

Rank (making room for her, but still sitting): Nora —

Nora (in the hall doorway): Helene, bring the lamp in. *(Goes over to the stove.)* Ah, dear Dr. Rank, that was really mean of you.

Rank (getting up): That I've loved you just as deeply as somebody else? Was *that* mean?

Nora: No, but that you came out and told me. That was quite unnecessary —

Rank: What do you mean? Have you known — ?

The Maid comes in with the lamp, sets it on the table, and goes out again.

Rank: Nora — Mrs. Helmer — I'm asking you: have you known about it?

Nora: Oh, how can I tell what I know or don't know? Really, I don't know what to say — Why did you have to be so clumsy, Dr. Rank! Everything was so good.

Rank: Well, in any case, you now have the knowledge that my body and soul are at your command. So won't you speak out?

Nora (looking at him): After that?

Rank: Please, just let me know what it is.

Nora: You can't know anything now.

Rank: I have to. You mustn't punish me like this. Give me the chance to do whatever is humanly possible for you.

Nora: Now there's nothing you can do for me. Besides, actually, I don't need any help. You'll see — it's only my fantasies. That's what it is. Of course! *(Sits in the rocker, looks at him, and smiles.)* What a nice one you are, Dr. Rank. Aren't you a little bit ashamed, now that the lamp is here?

Rank: No, not exactly. But perhaps I'd better go — for good?

Nora: No, you certainly can't do that. You must come here just as you always have. You know Torvald can't do without you.

Rank: Yes, but *you?*

Nora: You know how much I enjoy it when you're here.

Rank: That's precisely what threw me off. You're a mystery to me. So many times I've felt you'd almost rather be with me than with Helmer.

Nora: Yes — you see, there are some people that one loves most and other people that one would almost prefer being with.

Rank: Yes, there's something to that.

Nora: When I was back home, of course I loved Papa most. But I always thought it was so much fun when I could sneak down to the maids' quarters, because they never tried to improve me, and it was always so amusing, the way they talked to each other.

Rank: Aha, so it's *their* place that I've filled.

Nora (jumping up and going to him): Oh, dear, sweet Dr. Rank, that's not what I meant at all. But you can understand that with Torvald it's just the same as with Papa —

The Maid enters from the hall.

Maid: Ma'am — please! *(She whispers to Nora and hands her a calling card.)*

Nora (glancing at the card): Ah! *(Slips it into her pocket.)*

Rank: Anything wrong?

Nora: No, no, not at all. It's only some — it's my new dress —

Rank: Really? But — there's your dress.

Nora: Oh, that. But this is another one — I ordered it — Torvald mustn't know —

Rank: Ah, now we have the big secret.

Nora: That's right. Just go in with him — he's back in the inner study. Keep him there as long as —

Rank: Don't worry. He won't get away. *(Goes into the study.)*

Nora (to the Maid): And he's standing waiting in the kitchen?

Maid: Yes, he came up by the back stairs.

Nora: But didn't you tell him somebody was here?

Maid: Yes, but that didn't do any good.

Nora: He won't leave?

Maid: No, he won't go till he's talked with you, ma'am.

Nora: Let him come in, then — but quietly. Helene, don't breathe a word about this. It's a surprise for my husband.

Maid: Yes, yes, I understand — *(Goes out.)*

Nora: This horror — it's going to happen. No, no, no, it can't happen, it mustn't. *(She goes and bolts Helmer's door. The Maid opens the hall door for Krogstad and shuts it behind him. He is dressed for travel in a fur coat, boots, and a fur cap.)*

Nora (going toward him): Talk softly. My husband's home.

Krogstad: Well, good for him.

Nora: What do you want?

Krogstad: Some information.

Nora: Hurry up, then. What is it?

Krogstad: You know, of course, that I got my notice.

Nora: I couldn't prevent it, Mr. Krogstad. I fought for you to the bitter end, but nothing worked.

Krogstad: Does your husband's love for you run so thin? He knows everything I can expose you to, and all the same he dares to —

Nora: How can you imagine he knows anything about this?

Krogstad: Ah, no — I can't imagine it either, now. It's not at all like my fine Torvald Helmer to have so much guts —

Nora: Mr. Krogstad, I demand respect for my husband!

Krogstad: Why, of course — all due respect. But since the lady's keeping it so carefully hidden, may I presume to ask if you're also a bit better informed than yesterday about what you've actually done?

Nora: More than you could ever teach me.

Krogstad: Yes, I *am* such an awful lawyer.

Nora: What is it you want from me?

Krogstad: Just a glimpse of how you are, Mrs. Helmer. I've been thinking about you all day long. A cashier, a night-court scribbler, a — well, a type like me also has a little of what they call a heart, you know.

Nora: Then show it. Think of my children.

Krogstad: Did you or your husband ever think of mine? But never mind. I simply wanted to tell you that you don't need to take this thing too seriously. For the present, I'm not proceeding with any action.

Nora: Oh no, really! Well — I knew that.

Krogstad: Everything can be settled in a friendly spirit. It doesn't have to get around town at all; it can stay just among us three.

Nora: My husband must never know anything of this.

Krogstad: How can you manage that? Perhaps you can pay me the balance?

Nora: No, not right now.

Krogstad: Or you know some way of raising the money in a day or two?

Nora: No way that I'm willing to use.

Krogstad: Well, it wouldn't have done you any good, anyway. If you stood in front of me with a fistful of bills, you still couldn't buy your signature back.

Nora: Then tell me what you're going to do with it.

Krogstad: I'll just hold onto it — keep it on file. There's no outsider who'll even get wind of it. So if you've been thinking of taking some desperate step —

Nora: I have.

Krogstad: Been thinking of running away from home —

Nora: I have!

Krogstad: Or even of something worse —

Nora: How could you guess that?

Krogstad: You can drop those thoughts.

Nora: How could you guess I was thinking of *that*?

Krogstad: Most of us think about *that* at first. I thought about it too, but I discovered I hadn't the courage —

Nora (lifelessly): I don't either.

Krogstad (relieved): That's true, you haven't the courage? You too?

Nora: I don't have it—I don't have it.

Krogstad: It would be terribly stupid, anyway. After that first storm at home blows out, why, then—I have here in my pocket a letter for your husband—

Nora: Telling everything?

Krogstad: As charitably as possible.

Nora (quickly): He mustn't ever get that letter. Tear it up. I'll find some way to get money.

Krogstad: Beg pardon, Mrs. Helmer, but I think I just told you—

Nora: Oh, I don't mean the money I owe you. Let me know how much you want from my husband, and I'll manage it.

Krogstad: I don't want money from your husband.

Nora: What do you want, then?

Krogstad: I'll tell you what. I want to recoup, Mrs. Helmer; I want to get on in the world—and there's where your husband can help me. For a year and a half I've kept myself clean of anything disreputable—all that time struggling with the worst conditions; but I was satisfied, working my way up step by step. Now I've been written right off, and I'm just not in the mood to come crawling back. I tell you, I want to move on. I want to get back in the bank—in a better position. Your husband can set up a job for me—

Nora: He'll never do that!

Krogstad: He'll do it. I know him. He won't dare breathe a word of protest. And once I'm in there together with him, you just wait and see! Inside of a year, I'll be the manager's right-hand man. It'll be Nils Krogstad, not Torvald Helmer, who runs the bank.

Nora: You'll never see the day!

Krogstad: Maybe you think you can—

Nora: I have the courage now—for *that*.

Krogstad: Oh, you don't scare me. A smart, spoiled lady like you—

Nora: You'll see; you'll see!

Krogstad: Under the ice, maybe? Down in the freezing coal-black water? There, till you float up in the spring, ugly, unrecognizable, with your hair falling out—

Nora: You don't frighten me.

Krogstad: Nor do you frighten me. One doesn't do these things, Mrs. Helmer. Besides, what good would it be? I'd still have him safe in my pocket.

Nora: Afterwards? When I'm no longer—?

Krogstad: Are you forgetting that *I'll* be in control then over your final reputation? *(Nora stands speechless, staring at him.)* Good; now I've warned you. Don't do anything stupid. When Helmer's read my letter, I'll be waiting for his reply. And bear in mind that it's your husband himself who's forced me back to my old ways. I'll never forgive him for that. Good-bye, Mrs. Helmer. *(He goes out through the hall.)*

Nora (goes to the hall door, opens it a crack, and listens): He's gone. Didn't leave the letter. Oh no, no, that's impossible too! *(Opening the door more and more.)* What's that? He's standing outside—not going downstairs. He's thinking it over? Maybe he'll—? *(A letter falls in the mailbox; then Krogstad's footsteps are heard, dying away down a flight of stairs. Nora gives a muffled cry and runs over toward the sofa table. A short pause.)* In the mailbox. *(Slips warily over to the hall door.)* It's lying there. Torvald, Torvald — now we're lost!

Mrs. Linde (entering with costume from the room, left): There now, I can't see anything else to mend. Perhaps you'd like to try —

Nora (in a hoarse whisper): Kristine, come here.

Mrs. Linde (tossing the dress on the sofa): What's wrong? You look upset.

Nora: Come here. See that letter? *There!* Look — through the glass in the mailbox.

Mrs. Linde: Yes, yes, I see it.

Nora: That letter's from Krogstad —

Mrs. Linde: Nora — it's Krogstad who loaned you the money!

Nora: Yes, and now Torvald will find out everything.

Mrs. Linde: Believe me, Nora, it's best for both of you.

Nora: There's more you don't know. I forged a name.

Mrs. Linde: But for heaven's sake — ?

Nora: I only want to tell you that, Kristine, so that you can be my witness.

Mrs. Linde: Witness? Why should I — ?

Nora: If I should go out of my mind — it could easily happen —

Mrs. Linde: Nora!

Nora: Or anything else occurred — so I couldn't be present here —

Mrs. Linde: Nora, Nora, you aren't yourself at all!

Nora: And someone should try to take on the whole weight, all of the guilt, you follow me —

Mrs. Linde: Yes, of course, but why do you think — ?

Nora: Then you're the witness that it isn't true, Kristine. I'm very much myself; my mind right now is perfectly clear; and I'm telling you: nobody else has known about this; I alone did everything. Remember that.

Mrs. Linde: I will. But I don't understand all this.

Nora: Oh, how could you ever understand it? It's the miracle now that's going to take place.

Mrs. Linde: The miracle?

Nora: Yes, the miracle. But it's so awful, Kristine. It mustn't take place, not for anything in the world.

Mrs. Linde: I'm going right over and talk with Krogstad.

Nora: Don't go near him; he'll do you some terrible harm!

Mrs. Linde: There was a time once when he'd gladly have done anything for me.

Nora: He?

Mrs. Linde: Where does he live?

Nora: Oh, how do I know? Yes. *(Searches in her pocket.)* Here's his card. But the letter, the letter — !

Helmer (from the study, knocking on the door): Nora!

Nora (with a cry of fear): Oh! What is it? What do you want?

Helmer: Now, now, don't be so frightened. We're not coming in. You locked the door — are you trying on the dress?

Nora: Yes, I'm trying it. I'll look just beautiful, Torvald.

Mrs. Linde (who has read the card): He's living right around the corner.

Nora: Yes, but what's the use? We're lost. The letter's in the box.

Mrs. Linde: And your husband has the key?

Nora: Yes, always.

Mrs. Linde: Krogstad can ask for his letter back unread; he can find some excuse—

Nora: But it's just this time that Torvald usually—

Mrs. Linde: Stall him. Keep him in there. I'll be back as quick as I can. *(She hurries out through the hall entrance.)*

Nora (goes to Helmer's door, opens it, and peers in): Torvald!

Helmer (from the inner study): Well—does one dare set foot in one's own living room at last? Come on, Rank, now we'll get a look—*(In the doorway.)* But what's this?

Nora: What, Torvald dear?

Helmer: Rank had me expecting some grand masquerade.

Rank (in the doorway): That was my impression, but I must have been wrong.

Nora: No one can admire me in my splendor—not till tomorrow.

Helmer: But Nora dear, you look so exhausted. Have you practiced too hard?

Nora: No, I haven't practiced at all yet.

Helmer: You know, it's necessary—

Nora: Oh, it's absolutely necessary, Torvald. But I can't get anywhere without your help. I've forgotten the whole thing completely.

Helmer: Ah, we'll soon take care of that.

Nora: Yes, take care of me, Torvald, please! Promise me that? Oh, I'm so nervous. That big party—You must give up everything this evening for me. No business—don't even touch your pen. Yes? Dear Torvald, promise?

Helmer: It's a promise. Tonight I'm totally at your service—you little helpless thing. Hm—but first there's one thing I want to—*(Goes toward the hall door.)*

Nora: What are you looking for?

Helmer: Just to see if there's any mail.

Nora: No, no, don't do that, Torvald!

Helmer: Now what?

Nora: Torvald, please. There isn't any.

Helmer: Let me look, though. *(Starts out. Nora, at the piano, strikes the first notes of the tarantella. Helmer, at the door, stops.)* Aha!

Nora: I can't dance tomorrow if I don't practice with you.

Helmer (going over to her): Nora dear, are you really so frightened?

Nora: Yes, so terribly frightened. Let me practice right now; there's still time before dinner. Oh, sit down and play for me, Torvald. Direct me. Teach me, the way you always have.

Helmer: Gladly, if it's what you want. *(Sits at the piano.)*

Nora (snatches the tambourine up from the box, then a long, varicolored shawl, which she throws around herself, whereupon she springs forward and cries out): Play for me now! Now I'll dance!

Helmer plays and Nora dances. Rank stands behind Helmer at the piano and looks on.

Helmer (as he plays): Slower. Slow down.

Nora: Can't change it.

Helmer: Not so violent, Nora!

Nora: Has to be just like this.

Helmer (stopping): No, no, that won't do at all.

Nora (laughing and swinging her tambourine): Isn't that what I told you?

Rank: Let me play for her.

Helmer (getting up): Yes, go on. I can teach her more easily then.

> *Rank sits at the piano and plays; Nora dances more and more wildly. Helmer has stationed himself by the stove and repeatedly gives her directions; she seems not to hear them; her hair loosens and falls over her shoulders; she does not notice, but goes on dancing. Mrs. Linde enters.*

Mrs. Linde (standing dumbfounded at the door): Ah —!

Nora (still dancing): See what fun, Kristine!

Helmer: But Nora darling, you dance as if your life were at stake.

Nora: And it is.

Helmer: Rank, stop! This is pure madness. Stop it, I say!

> *Rank breaks off playing, and Nora halts abruptly.*

Helmer (going over to her): I never would have believed it. You've forgotten everything I taught you.

Nora (throwing away the tambourine): You see for yourself.

Helmer: Well, there's certainly room for instruction here.

Nora: Yes, you see how important it is. You've got to teach me to the very last minute. Promise me that, Torvald?

Helmer: You can bet on it.

Nora: You mustn't, either today or tomorrow, think about anything else but me; you mustn't open any letters — or the mailbox —

Helmer: Ah, it's still the fear of that man —

Nora: Oh yes, yes, that too.

Helmer: Nora, it's written all over you — there's already a letter from him out there.

Nora: I don't know. I guess so. But you mustn't read such things now; there mustn't be anything ugly between us before it's all over.

Rank (quietly to Helmer): You shouldn't deny her.

Helmer (putting his arms around her): The child can have her way. But tomorrow night, after you've danced —

Nora: Then you'll be free.

Maid (in the doorway, right): Ma'am, dinner is served.

Nora: We'll be wanting champagne, Helene.

Maid: Very good, ma'am. *(Goes out.)*

Helmer: So — a regular banquet, hm?

Nora: Yes, a banquet — champagne till daybreak! *(Calling out.)* And some macaroons, Helene. Heaps of them — just this once.

Helmer (taking her hands): Now, now, now — no hysterics. Be my own little lark again.

Nora: Oh, I will soon enough. But go on in — and you, Dr. Rank. Kristine, help me put up my hair.

Rank (whispering, as they go): There's nothing wrong — really wrong, is there?

Helmer: Oh, of course not. It's nothing more than this childish anxiety I was telling you about. *(They go out, right.)*

Nora: Well?

Mrs. Linde: Left town.

Nora: I could see by your face.

Mrs. Linde: He'll be home tomorrow evening. I wrote him a note.

Nora: You shouldn't have. Don't try to stop anything now. After all, it's a wonderful joy, this waiting here for the miracle.

Mrs. Linde: What is it you're waiting for?

Nora: Oh, you can't understand that. Go in to them; I'll be along in a moment.

> *Mrs. Linde goes into the dining room. Nora stands a short while as if composing herself, then she looks at her watch.*

Nora: Five. Seven hours to midnight. Twenty-four hours to the midnight after, and then the tarantella's done. Seven and twenty-four? Thirty-one hours to live.

Helmer (in the doorway, right): What's become of the little lark?

Nora (going toward him with open arms): Here's your lark!

ACT III

> *Same scene. The table, with chairs around it, has been moved to the center of the room. A lamp on the table is lit. The hall door stands open. Dance music drifts down from the floor above. Mrs. Linde sits at the table, absently paging through a book, trying to read, but apparently unable to focus her thoughts. Once or twice she pauses, tensely listening for a sound at the outer entrance.*

Mrs. Linde (glancing at her watch): Not yet — and there's hardly any time left. If only he's not — (*Listening again.*) Ah, there he is. (*She goes out in the hall and cautiously opens the outer door. Quiet footsteps are heard on the stairs. She whispers:*) Come in. Nobody's here.

Krogstad (in the doorway): I found a note from you at home. What's back of all this?

Mrs. Linde: I just *had* to talk to you.

Krogstad: Oh? And it just *had* to be here in this house?

Mrs. Linde: At my place it was impossible; my room hasn't a private entrance. Come in; we're all alone. The maid's asleep, and the Helmers are at the dance upstairs.

Krogstad (entering the room): Well, well, the Helmers are dancing tonight? Really?

Mrs. Linde: Yes, why not?

Krogstad: How true — why not?

Mrs. Linde: All right, Krogstad, let's talk.

Krogstad: Do we two have anything more to talk about?

Mrs. Linde: We have a great deal to talk about.

Krogstad: I wouldn't have thought so.

Mrs. Linde: No, because you've never understood me, really.

Krogstad: Was there anything more to understand — except what's all too common in life? A calculating woman throws over a man the moment a better catch comes by.

Mrs. Linde: You think I'm so thoroughly calculating? You think I broke it off lightly?

Krogstad: Didn't you?

Mrs. Linde: Nils — is that what you really thought?

Krogstad: If you cared, then why did you write me the way you did?

Mrs. Linde: What else could I do? If I had to break off with you, then it was my job as well to root out everything you felt for me.

Krogstad (wringing his hands): So that was it. And this — all this, simply for money!

Mrs. Linde: Don't forget I had a helpless mother and two small brothers. We couldn't wait for you, Nils; you had such a long road ahead of you then.

Krogstad: That may be; but you still hadn't the right to abandon me for somebody else's sake.

Mrs. Linde: Yes — I don't know. So many, many times I've asked myself if I did have that right.

Krogstad (more softly): When I lost you, it was as if all the solid ground dissolved from under my feet. Look at me; I'm a half-drowned man now, hanging onto a wreck.

Mrs. Linde: Help may be near.

Krogstad: It was near — but then you came and blocked it off.

Mrs. Linde: Without my knowing it, Nils. Today for the first time I learned that it's you I'm replacing at the bank.

Krogstad: All right — I believe you. But now that you know, will you step aside?

Mrs. Linde: No, because that wouldn't benefit you in the slightest.

Krogstad: Not "benefit" me, hm! I'd step aside anyway.

Mrs. Linde: I've learned to be realistic. Life and hard, bitter necessity have taught me that.

Krogstad: And life's taught me never to trust fine phrases.

Mrs. Linde: Then life's taught you a very sound thing. But you do have to trust in actions, don't you?

Krogstad: What does that mean?

Mrs. Linde: You said you were hanging on like a half-drowned man to a wreck.

Krogstad: I've good reason to say that.

Mrs. Linde: I'm also like a half-drowned woman on a wreck. No one to suffer with; no one to care for.

Krogstad: You made your choice.

Mrs. Linde: There wasn't any choice then.

Krogstad: So — what of it?

Mrs. Linde: Nils, if only we two shipwrecked people could reach across to each other.

Krogstad: What are you saying?

Mrs. Linde: Two on one wreck are at least better off than each on his own.

Krogstad: Kristine!

Mrs. Linde: Why do you think I came into town?

Krogstad: Did you really have some thought of me?

Mrs. Linde: I have to work to go on living. All my born days, as long as I can remember, I've worked, and it's been my best and my only joy. But now I'm completely alone in the world; it frightens me to be so empty and lost. To work for yourself — there's no joy in that. Nils, give me something — someone to work for.

Krogstad: I don't believe all this. It's just some hysterical feminine urge to go out and make a noble sacrifice.

Mrs. Linde: Have you ever found me to be hysterical?

Krogstad: Can you honestly mean this? Tell me — do you know everything about my past?

Mrs. Linde: Yes.

Krogstad: And you know what they think I'm worth around here.

Mrs. Linde: From what you were saying before, it would seem that with me you could have been another person.

Krogstad: I'm positive of that.

Mrs. Linde: Couldn't it happen still?

Krogstad: Kristine — you're saying this in all seriousness? Yes, you are! I can see it in you. And do you really have the courage, then — ?

Mrs. Linde: I need to have someone to care for; and your children need a mother. We both need each other. Nils, I have faith that you're good at heart — I'll risk everything together with you.

Krogstad (gripping her hands): Kristine, thank you, thank you — Now I know I can win back a place in their eyes. Yes — but I forgot —

Mrs. Linde (listening): Shh! The tarantella. Go now! Go on!

Krogstad: Why? What is it?

Mrs. Linde: Hear the dance up there? When that's over, they'll be coming down.

Krogstad: Oh, then I'll go. But — it's all pointless. Of course, you don't know the move I made against the Helmers.

Mrs. Linde: Yes, Nils, I know.

Krogstad: And all the same, you have the courage to — ?

Mrs. Linde: I know how far despair can drive a man like you.

Krogstad: Oh, if I only could take it all back.

Mrs. Linde: You easily could — your letter's still lying in the mailbox.

Krogstad: Are you sure of that?

Mrs. Linde: Positive. But —

Krogstad (looks at her searchingly): Is that the meaning of it, then? You'll save your friend at any price. Tell me straight out. Is that it?

Mrs. Linde: Nils — anyone who's sold herself for somebody else once isn't going to do it again.

Krogstad: I'll demand my letter back.

Mrs. Linde: No, no.

Krogstad: Yes, of course. I'll stay here till Helmer comes down; I'll tell him to give me my letter again — that it only involves my dismissal — that he shouldn't read it —

Mrs. Linde: No, Nils, don't call the letter back.

Krogstad: But wasn't that exactly why you wrote me to come here?

Mrs. Linde: Yes, in that first panic. But it's been a whole day and night since then, and in that time I've seen such incredible things in this house. Helmer's got to learn everything; this dreadful secret has to be aired; those two have to come to a full understanding; all these lies and evasions can't go on.

Krogstad: Well, then, if you want to chance it. But at least there's one thing I can do, and do right away —

Mrs. Linde (listening): Go now, go quick! The dance is over. We're not safe another second.

Krogstad: I'll wait for you downstairs.

Mrs. Linde: Yes, please do; take me home.

Krogstad: I can't believe it; I've never been so happy. (*He leaves by way of the outer door; the door between the room and the hall stays open.*)

Mrs. Linde (*straightening up a bit and getting together her street clothes*): How different now! How different! Someone to work for, to live for—a home to build. Well, it is worth the try! Oh, if they'd only come! (*Listening.*) Ah, there they are. Bundle up. (*She picks up her hat and coat. Nora's and Helmer's voices can be heard outside; a key turns in the lock, and Helmer brings Nora into the hall almost by force. She is wearing the Italian costume with a large black shawl about her; he has on evening dress, with a black domino open over it.*)

Nora (*struggling in the doorway*): No, no, no, not inside! I'm going up again. I don't want to leave so soon.

Helmer: But Nora dear—

Nora: Oh, I beg you, please, Torvald. From the bottom of my heart, *please*—only an hour more!

Helmer: Not a single minute, Nora darling. You know our agreement. Come on, in we go; you'll catch cold out here. (*In spite of her resistance, he gently draws her into the room.*)

Mrs. Linde: Good evening.

Nora: Kristine!

Helmer: Why, Mrs. Linde—are you here so late?

Mrs. Linde: Yes, I'm sorry, but I did want to see Nora in costume.

Nora: Have you been sitting here, waiting for me?

Mrs. Linde: Yes. I didn't come early enough; you were all upstairs; and then I thought I really couldn't leave without seeing you.

Helmer (*removing Nora's shawl*): Yes, take a good look. She's worth looking at, I can tell you that, Mrs. Linde. Isn't she lovely?

Mrs. Linde: Yes, I should say—

Helmer: A dream of loveliness, isn't she? That's what everyone thought at the party, too. But she's horribly stubborn—this sweet little thing. What's to be done with her? Can you imagine, I almost had to use force to pry her away.

Nora: Oh, Torvald, you're going to regret you didn't indulge me, even for just a half hour more.

Helmer: There, you see. She danced her tarantella and got a tumultuous hand—which was well earned, although the performance may have been a bit too naturalistic—I mean it rather overstepped the proprieties of art. But never mind—what's important is, she made a success, an overwhelming success. You think I could let her stay on after that and spoil the effect? Oh no; I took my lovely little Capri girl—my capricious little Capri girl, I should say—took her under my arm; one quick tour of the ballroom, a curtsy to every side, and then—as they say in novels—the beautiful vision disappeared. An exit should always be effective, Mrs. Linde, but that's what I can't get Nora to grasp. Phew, it's hot in here. (*Flings the domino on a chair and opens the door to his room.*) Why's it dark in here? Oh yes, of course. Excuse me. (*He goes in and lights a couple of candles.*)

Nora (*in a sharp, breathless whisper*): So?

Mrs. Linde (*quietly*): I talked with him.

Nora: And—?

Mrs. Linde: Nora—you must tell your husband everything.

Nora (*dully*): I knew it.

Mrs. Linde: You've got nothing to fear from Krogstad, but you have to speak out.

Nora: I won't tell.

Mrs. Linde: Then the letter will.

Nora: Thanks, Kristine. I know now what's to be done. Shh!

Helmer (reentering): Well, then, Mrs. Linde — have you admired her?

Mrs. Linde: Yes, and now I'll say good night.

Helmer: Oh, come, so soon? Is this yours, this knitting?

Mrs. Linde: Yes, thanks. I nearly forgot it.

Helmer: Do you knit, then?

Mrs. Linde: Oh yes.

Helmer: You know what? You should embroider instead.

Mrs. Linde: Really? Why?

Helmer: Yes, because it's a lot prettier. See here, one holds the embroidery so, in the left hand, and then one guides the needle with the right — so — in an easy, sweeping curve — right?

Mrs. Linde: Yes, I guess that's —

Helmer: But, on the other hand, knitting — it can never be anything but ugly. Look, see here, the arms tucked in, the knitting needles going up and down — there's something Chinese about it. Ah, that was really a glorious champagne they served.

Mrs. Linde: Yes, good night, Nora, and don't be stubborn anymore.

Helmer: Well put, Mrs. Linde!

Mrs. Linde: Good night, Mr. Helmer.

Helmer (accompanying her to the door): Good night, good night. I hope you get home all right. I'd be very happy to — but you don't have far to go. Good night, good night. *(She leaves. He shuts the door after her and returns.)* There, now, at last we got her out the door. She's a deadly bore, that creature.

Nora: Aren't you pretty tired, Torvald?

Helmer: No, not a bit.

Nora: You're not sleepy?

Helmer: Not at all. On the contrary, I'm feeling quite exhilarated. But you? Yes, you really look tired and sleepy.

Nora: Yes, I'm very tired. Soon now I'll sleep.

Helmer: See! You see! I was right all along that we shouldn't stay longer.

Nora: Whatever you do is always right.

Helmer (kissing her brow): Now my little lark talks sense. Say, did you notice what a time Rank was having tonight?

Nora: Oh, was he? I didn't get to speak with him.

Helmer: I scarcely did either, but it's a long time since I've seen him in such high spirits. *(Gazes at her a moment, then comes nearer her.)* Hm — it's marvelous, though, to be back home again — to be completely alone with you. Oh, you bewitchingly lovely young woman!

Nora: Torvald, don't look at me like that!

Helmer: Can't I look at my richest treasure? At all that beauty that's mine, mine alone — completely and utterly.

Nora (moving around to the other side of the table): You mustn't talk to me that way tonight.

Helmer (following her): The tarantella is still in your blood, I can see — and it makes you even more enticing. Listen. The guests are beginning to go. *(Dropping his voice.)* Nora—it'll soon be quiet through this whole house.

Nora: Yes, I hope so.

Helmer: You do, don't you, my love? Do you realize—when I'm out at a party like this with you—do you know why I talk to you so little, and keep such a distance away; just send you a stolen look now and then—you know why I do it? It's because I'm imagining then that you're my secret darling, my secret bride-to-be, and that no one suspects there's anything between us.

Nora: Yes, yes; oh, yes, I know you're always thinking of me.

Helmer: And then when we leave and I place the shawl over those fine young rounded shoulders—over that wonderful curving neck—then I pretend that you're my young bride, that we're just coming from the wedding, that for the first time I'm bringing you into my house—that for the first time I'm alone with you—completely alone with you, your trembling young beauty! All this evening I've longed for nothing but you. When I saw you turn and sway in the tarantella—my blood was pounding till I couldn't stand it—that's why I brought you down here so early—

Nora: Go away, Torvald! Leave me alone. I don't want all this.

Helmer: What do you mean? Nora, you're teasing me. You will, won't you? Aren't I your husband—?

A knock at the outside door.

Nora (startled): What's that?

Helmer (going toward the hall): Who is it?

Rank (outside): It's me. May I come in a moment?

Helmer (with quiet irritation): Oh, what does he want now? *(Aloud.)* Hold on. *(Goes and opens the door.)* Oh, how nice that you didn't just pass us by!

Rank: I thought I heard your voice, and then I wanted so badly to have a look in. *(Lightly glancing about.)* Ah, me, these old familiar haunts. You have it snug and cozy in here, you two.

Helmer: You seemed to be having it pretty cozy upstairs, too.

Rank: Absolutely. Why shouldn't I? Why not take in everything in life? As much as you can, anyway, and as long as you can. The wine was superb—

Helmer: The champagne especially.

Rank: You noticed that too? It's amazing how much I could guzzle down.

Nora: Torvald also drank a lot of champagne this evening.

Rank: Oh?

Nora: Yes, and that always makes him so entertaining.

Rank: Well, why shouldn't one have a pleasant evening after a well-spent day?

Helmer: Well spent? I'm afraid I can't claim that.

Rank (slapping him on the back): But I can, you see!

Nora: Dr. Rank, you must have done some scientific research today.

Rank: Quite so.

Helmer: Come now—little Nora talking about scientific research!

Nora: And can I congratulate you on the results?

Rank: Indeed you may.

Nora: Then they were good?

Rank: The best possible for both doctor and patient—certainty.

Nora (quickly and searchingly): Certainty?

Rank: Complete certainty. So don't I owe myself a gay evening afterwards?

Nora: Yes, you're right, Dr. Rank.

Helmer: I'm with you — just so long as you don't have to suffer for it in the morning.

Rank: Well, one never gets something for nothing in life.

Nora: Dr. Rank — are you very fond of masquerade parties?

Rank: Yes, if there's a good array of odd disguises —

Nora: Tell me, what should we two go as at the next masquerade?

Helmer: You little featherhead — already thinking of the next!

Rank: We two? I'll tell you what: you must go as Charmed Life —

Helmer: Yes, but find a costume for *that!*

Rank: Your wife can appear just as she looks every day.

Helmer: That was nicely put. But don't you know what you're going to be?

Rank: Yes, Helmer, I've made up my mind.

Helmer: Well?

Rank: At the next masquerade I'm going to be invisible.

Helmer: That's a funny idea.

Rank: They say there's a hat — black, huge — have you never heard of the hat that makes you invisible? You put it on, and then no one on earth can see you.

Helmer (suppressing a smile): Ah, of course.

Rank: But I'm quite forgetting what I came for. Helmer, give me a cigar, one of the dark Havanas.

Helmer: With the greatest pleasure. *(Holds out his case.)*

Rank: Thanks. *(Takes one and cuts off the tip.)*

Nora (striking a match): Let me give you a light.

Rank: Thank you. *(She holds the match for him; he lights the cigar.)* And now good-bye.

Helmer: Good-bye, good-bye, old friend.

Nora: Sleep well, Doctor.

Rank: Thanks for that wish.

Nora: Wish me the same.

Rank: You? All right, if you like — Sleep well. And thanks for the light. *(He nods to them both and leaves.)*

Helmer (his voice subdued): He's been drinking heavily.

Nora (absently): Could be. *(Helmer takes his keys from his pocket and goes out in the hall.)* Torvald — what are you after?

Helmer: Got to empty the mailbox; it's nearly full. There won't be room for the morning papers.

Nora: Are you working tonight?

Helmer: You know I'm not. Why — what's this? Someone's been at the lock.

Nora: At the lock — ?

Helmer: Yes, I'm positive. What do you suppose — ? I can't imagine one of the maids — ? Here's a broken hairpin. Nora, it's yours —

Nora (quickly): Then it must be the children —

Helmer: You'd better break them of that. Hm, hm — well, opened it after all. *(Takes the contents out and calls into the kitchen.)* Helene! Helene, would you put out the lamp in the hall. *(He returns to the room shutting the hall door, then displays the handful of mail.)* Look how it's piled up. *(Sorting through them.)* Now what's this?

Nora (at the window): The letter! Oh, Torvald, no!

Helmer: Two calling cards — from Rank.

Nora: From Dr. Rank?

Helmer (examining them): "Dr. Rank, Consulting Physician." They were on top. He must have dropped them in as he left.

Nora: Is there anything on them?

Helmer: There's a black cross over the name. See? That's a gruesome notion. He could almost be announcing his own death.

Nora: That's just what he's doing.

Helmer: What! You've heard something? Something he's told you?

Nora: Yes. That when those cards came, he'd be taking his leave of us. He'll shut himself in now and die.

Helmer: Ah, my poor friend! Of course I knew he wouldn't be here much longer. But so soon — And then to hide himself away like a wounded animal.

Nora: If it has to happen, then it's best it happens in silence — don't you think so, Torvald?

Helmer (pacing up and down): He'd grown right into our lives. I simply can't imagine him gone. He with his suffering and loneliness — like a dark cloud setting off our sunlit happiness. Well, maybe it's best this way. For him, at least. *(Standing still.)* And maybe for us too, Nora. Now we're thrown back on each other, completely. *(Embracing her.)* Oh you, my darling wife, how can I hold you close enough? You know what, Nora — time and again I've wished you were in some terrible danger, just so I could stake my life and soul and everything, for your sake.

Nora (tearing herself away, her voice firm and decisive): Now you must read your mail, Torvald.

Helmer: No, no, not tonight. I want to stay with you, dearest.

Nora: With a dying friend on your mind?

Helmer: You're right. We've both had a shock. There's ugliness between us — these thoughts of death and corruption. We'll have to get free of them first. Until then — we'll stay apart.

Nora (clinging about his neck): Torvald — good night! Good night!

Helmer (kissing her on the cheek): Good night, little songbird. Sleep well, Nora. I'll be reading my mail now. *(He takes the letters into his room and shuts the door after him.)*

Nora (with bewildered glances, groping about, seizing Helmer's domino, throwing it around her, and speaking in short, hoarse, broken whispers): Never see him again. Never, never. *(Putting her shawl over her head.)* Never see the children either — them, too. Never, never. Oh, the freezing black water! The depths — down — Oh, I wish it were over — He has it now; he's reading it — now. Oh no, no, not yet. Torvald, good-bye, you and the children — *(She starts for the hall; as she does, Helmer throws open his door and stands with an open letter in his hand.)*

Helmer: Nora!

Nora (screams): Oh — !

Helmer: What is this? You know what's in this letter?

Nora: Yes, I know. Let me go! Let me out!

Helmer (holding her back): Where are you going?

Nora (struggling to break loose): You can't save me, Torvald!

Helmer (slumping back): True! Then it's true what he writes? How horrible! No, no, it's impossible — it can't be true.

Nora: It *is* true. I've loved you more than all this world.

Helmer: Ah, none of your slippery tricks.

Nora (taking one step toward him): Torvald — !

Helmer: What *is* this you've blundered into!

Nora: Just let me loose. You're not going to suffer for my sake. You're not going to take on my guilt.

Helmer: No more play-acting. *(Locks the hall door.)* You stay right here and give me a reckoning. You understand what you've done? Answer! You understand?

Nora (looking squarely at him, her face hardening): Yes. I'm beginning to understand everything now.

Helmer (striding about): Oh, what an awful awakening! In all these eight years — she who was my pride and joy — a hypocrite, a liar — worse, worse — a criminal! How infinitely disgusting it all is! The shame! *(Nora says nothing and goes on looking straight at him. He stops in front of her.)* I should have suspected something of the kind. I should have known. All your father's flimsy values — Be still! All your father's flimsy values have come out in you. No religion, no morals, no sense of duty — Oh, how I'm punished for letting him off! I did it for your sake, and you repay me like this.

Nora: Yes, like this.

Helmer: Now you've wrecked all my happiness — ruined my whole future. Oh, it's awful to think of. I'm in a cheap little grafter's hands; he can do anything he wants with me, ask for anything, play with me like a puppet — and I can't breathe a word. I'll be swept down miserably into the depths on account of a featherbrained woman.

Nora: When I'm gone from this world, you'll be free.

Helmer: Oh, quit posing. Your father had a mess of those speeches too. What good would that ever do me if you were gone from this world, as you say? Not the slightest. He can still make the whole thing known; and if he does, I could be falsely suspected as your accomplice. They might even think that I was behind it — that I put you up to it. And all that I can thank you for — you that I've coddled the whole of our marriage. Can you see now what you've done to me?

Nora (icily calm): Yes.

Helmer: It's so incredible, I just can't grasp it. But we'll have to patch up whatever we can. Take off the shawl. I said, take if off! I've got to appease him somehow or other. The thing has to be hushed up at any cost. And as for you and me, it's got to seem like everything between us is just as it was — to the outside world, that is. You'll go right on living in this house, of course. But you can't be allowed to bring up the children; I don't dare trust you with them — Oh, to have to say this to someone I've loved so much! Well, that's done with. From now on happiness doesn't matter; all that matters is saving the bits and pieces, the appearance — *(The doorbell rings. Helmer starts.)* What's that? And so late. Maybe the worst — ? You think he'd — ?

Hide, Nora! Say you're sick. *(Nora remains standing motionless. Helmer goes and opens the door.)*

Maid (half dressed, in the hall): A letter for Mrs. Helmer.

Helmer: I'll take it. *(Snatches the letter and shuts the door.)* Yes, it's from him. You don't get it; I'm reading it myself.

Nora: Then read it.

Helmer (by the lamp): I hardly dare. We may be ruined, you and I. But — I've got to know. *(Rips open the letter, skims through a few lines, glances at an enclosure, then cries out joyfully.)* Nora! *(Nora looks inquiringly at him.)* Nora! Wait — better check it again — Yes, yes, it's true. I'm saved. Nora, I'm saved!

Nora: And I?

Helmer: You too, of course. We're both saved, both of us. Look. He's sent back your note. He says he's sorry and ashamed — that a happy development in his life — oh, who cares what he says! Nora, we're saved! No one can hurt you. Oh, Nora, Nora — but first, this ugliness all has to go. Let me see — *(Takes a look at the note.)* No, I don't want to see it; I want the whole thing to fade like a dream. *(Tears the note and both letters to pieces, throws them into the stove and watches them burn.)* There — now there's nothing left — He wrote that since Christmas Eve you — Oh, they must have been three terrible days for you, Nora.

Nora: I fought a hard fight.

Helmer: And suffered pain and saw no escape but — No, we're not going to dwell on anything unpleasant. We'll just be grateful and keep on repeating: it's over now, it's over! You hear me, Nora? You don't seem to realize — it's over. What's it mean — that frozen look? Oh, poor little Nora, I understand. You can't believe I've forgiven you. But I have, Nora; I swear I have. I know that what you did, you did out of love for me.

Nora: That's true.

Helmer: You loved me the way a wife ought to love her husband. It's simply the means that you couldn't judge. But you think I love you any the less for not knowing how to handle your affairs? No, no — just lean on me; I'll guide you and teach you. I wouldn't be a man if this feminine helplessness didn't make you twice as attractive to me. You mustn't mind those sharp words I said — that was all in the first confusion of thinking my world had collapsed. I've forgiven you, Nora; I swear I've forgiven you.

Nora: My thanks for your forgiveness. *(She goes out through the door, right.)*

Helmer: No, wait — *(Peers in.)* What are you doing in there?

Nora (inside): Getting out of my costume.

Helmer (by the open door): Yes, do that. Try to calm yourself and collect your thoughts again, my frightened little songbird. You can rest easy now; I've got wide wings to shelter you with. *(Walking about close by the door.)* How snug and nice our home is, Nora. You're safe here; I'll keep you like a hunted dove I've rescued out of a hawk's claws. I'll bring peace to your poor, shuddering heart. Gradually it'll happen, Nora; you'll see. Tomorrow all this will look different to you; then everything will be as it was. I won't have to go on repeating I forgive you; you'll feel it for yourself. How can you imagine I'd ever conceivably want to disown you — or even blame you in any way? Ah, you don't know a man's heart, Nora. For a man there's something indescribably sweet and satisfying in knowing he's forgiven his wife—and forgiven her out of a full and open heart. It's as if she belongs to him in two ways now: in a sense he's given her fresh into the world again, and she's become his wife and his child as well. From now on that's what you'll be to me—you little, bewildered, helpless thing. Don't be afraid of anything, Nora; just open your heart to me, and I'll be conscience and will to you both — *(Nora enters in her regular clothes.)* What's this? Not in bed? You've changed your dress?

Nora: Yes, Torvald, I've changed my dress.

Helmer: But why now, so late?

Nora: Tonight I'm not sleeping.

Helmer: But Nora dear—

Nora (looking at her watch): It's still not so very late. Sit down, Torvald; we have a lot to talk over. *(She sits at one side of the table.)*

Helmer: Nora—what is this? That hard expression—

Nora: Sit down. This'll take some time. I have a lot to say.

Helmer (sitting at the table directly opposite her): You worry me, Nora. And I don't understand you.

Nora: No, that's exactly it. You don't understand me. And I've never understood you either—until tonight. No, don't interrupt. You can just listen to what I say. We're closing out accounts, Torvald.

Helmer: How do you mean that?

Nora (after a short pause): Doesn't anything strike you about our sitting here like this?

Helmer: What's that?

Nora: We've been married now eight years. Doesn't it occur to you that this is the first time we two, you and I, man and wife, have ever talked seriously together?

Helmer: What do you mean—seriously?

Nora: In eight whole years—longer even—right from our first acquaintance, we've never exchanged a serious word on any serious thing.

Helmer: You mean I should constantly go and involve you in problems you couldn't possibly help me with?

Nora: I'm not talking of problems. I'm saying that we've never sat down seriously together and tried to get to the bottom of anything.

Helmer: But dearest, what good would that ever do you?

Nora: That's the point right there: you've never understood me. I've been wronged greatly, Torvald—first by Papa, and then by you.

Helmer: What! By us—the two people who've loved you more than anyone else?

Nora (shaking her head): You never loved me. You've thought it fun to be in love with me, that's all.

Helmer: Nora, what a thing to say!

Nora: Yes, it's true now, Torvald. When I lived at home with Papa, he told me all his opinions, so I had the same ones too; or if they were different I hid them, since he wouldn't have cared for that. He used to call me his doll-child, and he played with me the way I played with my dolls. Then I came into your house—

Helmer: How can you speak of our marriage like that?

Nora (unperturbed): I mean, then I went from Papa's hands into yours. You arranged everything to your own taste, and so I got the same taste as you—

or I pretended to; I can't remember. I guess a little of both, first one, then the other. Now when I look back, it seems as if I'd lived here like a beggar—just from hand to mouth. I've lived by doing tricks for you, Torvald. But that's the way you wanted it. It's a great sin what you and Papa did to me. You're to blame that nothing's become of me.

Helmer: Nora, how unfair and ungrateful you are! Haven't you been happy here?

Nora: No, never. I thought so—but I never have.

Helmer: Not—not happy!

Nora: No, only lighthearted. And you've always been so kind to me. But our home's been nothing but a playpen. I've been your doll-wife here, just as at home I was Papa's doll-child. And in turn the children have been my dolls. I thought it was fun when you played with me, just as they thought it fun when I played with them. That's been our marriage, Torvald.

Helmer: There's some truth in what you're saying—under all the raving exaggeration. But it'll all be different after this. Playtime's over; now for the schooling.

Nora: Whose schooling—mine or the children's?

Helmer: Both yours and the children's, dearest.

Nora: Oh, Torvald, you're not the man to teach me to be a good wife to you.

Helmer: And you can say that?

Nora: And I—how am I equipped to bring up children?

Helmer: Nora!

Nora: Didn't you say a moment ago that that was no job to trust me with?

Helmer: In a flare of temper! Why fasten on that?

Nora: Yes, but you were so very right. I'm not up to the job. There's another job I have to do first. I have to try to educate myself. You can't help me with that. I've got to do it alone. And that's why I'm leaving you now.

Helmer (jumping up): What's that?

Nora: I have to stand completely alone, if I'm ever going to discover myself and the world out there. So I can't go on living with you.

Helmer: Nora, Nora!

Nora: I want to leave right away. Kristine should put me up for the night—

Helmer: You're insane! You've no right! I forbid you!

Nora: From here on, there's no use forbidding me anything. I'll take with me whatever is mine. I don't want a thing from you, either now or later.

Helmer: What kind of madness is this!

Nora: Tomorrow I'm going home—I mean, home where I came from. It'll be easier up there to find something to do.

Helmer: Oh, you blind, incompetent child!

Nora: I must learn to be competent, Torvald.

Helmer: Abandon your home, your husband, your children! And you're not even thinking what people will say.

Nora: I can't be concerned about that. I only know how essential this is.

Helmer: Oh, it's outrageous. So you'll run out like this on your most sacred vows.

Nora: What do you think are my most sacred vows?

Helmer: And I have to tell you that! Aren't they your duties to your husband and children?

Nora: I have other duties equally sacred.

Helmer: That isn't true. What duties are they?

Nora: Duties to myself.

Helmer: Before all else, you're a wife and mother.

Nora: I don't believe in that anymore. I believe that, before all else, I'm a human being, no less than you — or anyway, I ought to try to become one. I know the majority thinks you're right, Torvald, and plenty of books agree with you, too. But I can't go on believing what the majority says, or what's written in books. I have to think over these things myself and try to understand them.

Helmer: Why can't you understand your place in your own home? On a point like that, isn't there one everlasting guide you can turn to? Where's your religion?

Nora: Oh, Torvald, I'm really not sure what religion is.

Helmer: What — ?

Nora: I only know what the minister said when I was confirmed. He told me religion was this thing and that. When I get clear and away by myself, I'll go into that problem too. I'll see if what the minister said was right, or, in any case, if it's right for me.

Helmer: A young woman your age shouldn't talk like that. If religion can't move you, I can try to rouse your conscience. You do have some moral feeling? Or, tell me — has that gone too?

Nora: It's not easy to answer that, Torvald. I simply don't know. I'm all confused about these things. I just know I see them so differently from you. I find out, for one thing, that the law's not at all what I'd thought — but I can't get it through my head that the law is fair. A woman hasn't a right to protect her dying father or save her husband's life! I can't believe that.

Helmer: You talk like a child. You don't know anything of the world you live in.

Nora: No, I don't. But now I'll begin to learn for myself. I'll try to discover who's right, the world or I.

Helmer: Nora, you're sick; you've got a fever. I almost think you're out of your head.

Nora: I've never felt more clearheaded and sure in my life.

Helmer: And — clearheaded and sure — you're leaving your husband and children?

Nora: Yes.

Helmer: Then there's only one possible reason.

Nora: What?

Helmer: You no longer love me.

Nora: No. That's exactly it.

Helmer: Nora! You can't be serious!

Nora: Oh, this is so hard, Torvald — you've been so kind to me always. But I can't help it. I don't love you anymore.

Helmer (struggling for composure): Are you also clearheaded and sure about that?

Nora: Yes, completely. That's why I can't go on staying here.

Helmer: Can you tell me what I did to lose your love?

Nora: Yes, I can tell you. It was this evening when the miraculous thing didn't come — then I knew you weren't the man I'd imagined.

Helmer: Be more explicit; I don't follow you.

Nora: I've waited now so patiently eight long years — for, my Lord, I know miracles don't come every day. Then this crisis broke over me, and such a certainty filled me: *now* the miraculous event would occur. While Krogstad's letter was lying out there, I never for an instant dreamed that you could give in to his terms. I was so utterly sure you'd say to him: go on, tell your tale to the whole wide world. And when he'd done that —

Helmer: Yes, what then? When I'd delivered my own wife into shame and disgrace —

Nora: When he'd done that, I was so utterly sure that you'd step forward, take the blame on yourself and say: I am the guilty one.

Helmer: Nora —!

Nora: You're thinking I'd never accept such a sacrifice from you? No, of course not. But what good would my protests be against you? That was the miracle I was waiting for, in terror and hope. And to stave that off, I would have taken my life.

Helmer: I'd gladly work for you day and night, Nora — and take on pain and deprivation. But there's no one who gives up honor for love.

Nora: Millions of women have done just that.

Helmer: Oh, you think and talk like a silly child.

Nora: Perhaps. But you neither think nor talk like the man I could join myself to. When your big fright was over — and it wasn't from any threat against me, only for what might damage you — when all the danger was past, for you it was just as if nothing had happened. I was exactly the same, your little lark, your doll, that you'd have to handle with double care now that I'd turned out so brittle and frail. *(Gets up.)* Torvald — in that instant it dawned on me that for eight years I've been living here with a stranger, and that I've even conceived three children — oh, I can't stand the thought of it! I could tear myself to bits.

Helmer (heavily): I see. There's a gulf that's opened between us — that's clear. Oh, but Nora, can't we bridge it somehow?

Nora: The way I am now, I'm no wife for you.

Helmer: I have the strength to make myself over.

Nora: Maybe — if your doll gets taken away.

Helmer: But to part! To part from you! No, Nora no — I can't imagine it.

Nora (going out, right): All the more reason why it has to be. *(She reenters with her coat and a small overnight bag, which she puts on a chair by the table.)*

Helmer: Nora, Nora, not now! Wait till tomorrow.

Nora: I can't spend the night in a strange man's room.

Helmer: But couldn't we live here like brother and sister —

Nora: You know very well how long that would last. *(Throws her shawl about her.)* Good-bye, Torvald. I won't look in on the children. I know they're in better hands than mine. The way I am now, I'm no use to them.

Helmer: But someday, Nora — someday —?

Nora: How can I tell? I haven't the least idea what'll become of me.

Helmer: But you're my wife, now and wherever you go.

Nora: Listen, Torvald — I've heard that when a wife deserts her husband's house just as I'm doing, then the law frees him from all responsibility. In any case, I'm freeing you from being responsible. Don't feel yourself bound, any more than I will. There has to be absolute freedom for us both. Here, take your ring back. Give me mine.

Helmer: That too?

Nora: That too.

Helmer: There it is.

Nora: Good. Well, now it's all over. I'm putting the keys here. The maids know all about keeping up the house — better than I do. Tomorrow, after I've left town, Kristine will stop by to pack up everything that's mine from home. I'd like those things shipped up to me.

Helmer: Over! All over! Nora, won't you ever think about me?

Nora: I'm sure I'll think of you often, and about the children and the house here.

Helmer: May I write you?

Nora: No — never. You're not to do that.

Helmer: Oh, but let me send you —

Nora: Nothing. Nothing.

Helmer: Or help you if you need it.

Nora: No. I accept nothing from strangers.

Helmer: Nora — can I never be more than a stranger to you?

Nora (picking up her overnight bag): Ah, Torvald — it would take the greatest miracle of all —

Helmer: Tell me the greatest miracle!

Nora: You and I both would have to transform ourselves to the point that — Oh, Torvald, I've stopped believing in miracles.

Helmer: But I'll believe. Tell me! Transform ourselves to the point that — ?

Nora: That our living together could be a true marriage. *(She goes out down the hall.)*

Helmer (sinks down on a chair by the door, face buried in his hands): Nora! Nora! *(Looking about and rising.)* Empty. She's gone. *(A sudden hope leaps in him.)* The greatest miracle — ?

From below, the sound of a door slamming shut.

CONSIDERATIONS FOR CRITICAL THINKING AND WRITING

1. FIRST RESPONSE. What is the significance of the play's title?

2. Nora lies several times during the play. What kinds of lies are they? Do her lies indicate that she is not to be trusted, or are they a sign of something else about her personality?

3. What kind of wife does Helmer want Nora to be? He affectionately calls her names such as "lark" and "squirrel." What does this reveal about his attitude toward her?

4. Why is Nora "pale with terror" at the end of Act I? What is the significance of the description of the Christmas tree now "stripped of ornament, [with] burned-down candle stubs on its ragged branches" that opens Act II? What other symbols are used in the play?

5. What is Dr. Rank's purpose in the play?

6. How does the relationship between Krogstad and Mrs. Linde serve to emphasize certain qualities in the Helmers' marriage?

7. Is Krogstad's decision not to expose Nora's secret convincing? Does his shift from villainy to generosity seem adequately motivated?

8. Why does Nora reject Helmer's efforts to smooth things over between them and start again? Do you have any sympathy for Helmer?

9. Would you describe the ending as essentially happy or unhappy? Is the play more like a comedy or a tragedy?

10. Ibsen believed that a "dramatist's business is not to answer questions, but only to ask them." What questions are raised in the play? Does Ibsen propose any specific answers?

11. What makes this play a work of realism? Are there any elements that seem not to be realistic?

12. CRITICAL STRATEGIES. Read the section on new historicist criticism (pp. 2103–04) in Chapter 52, "Critical Strategies for Reading," and consider the following: Ibsen once wrote a different ending for the play to head off producers who might have been tempted to change the final scene to placate the public's sense of morality. In the second conclusion, Helmer forces Nora to look in on their sleeping children. This causes her to realize that she cannot leave her family even though it means sacrificing herself. Ibsen called this version of the ending a "barbaric outrage" and didn't use it. How do you think the play reflects or refutes social values contemporary to it?

CONNECTIONS TO OTHER SELECTIONS

1. What does Nora have in common with the protagonist in Gail Godwin's "A Sorrowful Woman" (p. 35)? What significant differences are there between them?

2. Explain how Torvald's attitude toward Nora is similar to the men's attitudes toward women in Susan Glaspell's *Trifles* (p. 1238). Write an essay exploring how the assumptions the men make about women in both plays contribute to the plays' conflicts.

3. Write an essay that compares and contrasts Nora's response to the social and legal expectations of her society with Antigone's in Sophocles' play (p. 1333). To what values does each character pledge her allegiance?

PERSPECTIVE

HENRIK IBSEN (1828–1906)

Notes for A Doll House   1878

There are two kinds of spiritual law, two kinds of conscience, one in man and another, altogether different, in woman. They do not understand each other; but in practical life the woman is judged by man's law, as though she were not a woman but a man.

The wife in the play ends by having no idea of what is right or wrong; natural feeling on the one hand and belief in authority on the other have altogether bewildered her.

A woman cannot be herself in the society of the present day, which is an exclusively masculine society, with laws framed by men and with a judicial system that judges feminine conduct from a masculine point of view.

She has committed forgery, and she is proud of it; for she did it out of love for her husband, to save his life. But this husband with his commonplace principles of honor is on the side of the law and looks at the question from the masculine point of view.

Spiritual conflicts. Oppressed and bewildered by the belief in authority, she loses faith in her moral right and ability to bring up her children. Bitterness. A mother in modern society, like certain insects who go away and die when she has done her duty in the propagation of the race. Love of life, of home, of husband and children and family. Now and then a womanly shaking off of her thoughts. Sudden return of anxiety and terror. She must bear it all alone. The catastrophe approaches, inexorably, inevitably. Despair, conflict, and destruction.

From *From Ibsen's Workshop,* translated by A. G. Chater

CONSIDERATIONS FOR CRITICAL THINKING AND WRITING

1. Given the ending of *A Doll House,* what do you think of Ibsen's early view in his notes that "the wife in the play ends by having no idea of what is right or wrong" (para. 2)? Would you describe Nora as "altogether bewildered" (2)? Why or why not?

2. "A woman cannot be herself in the society of the present day, which is an exclusively masculine society" (3). Why is this statement true of Nora? Explain why you agree or disagree that this observation is accurate today.

3. How does oppressive "authority" (5) loom large for Nora? What kind of authority creates "spiritual conflicts" for her?

More perspectives appear in the next chapter, "A Critical Case Study: Henrik Ibsen's *A Doll House,*" page 1626.

A Reluctant Tragic Hero

Anton Chekhov, grandson of a serf and son of an unsuccessful grocer, was born in Taganrog, a small town in southern Russia. He studied medicine at Moscow University and began practicing in 1884. During his medical training, he wrote short stories to support himself and his family (one of the stories, "The Lady with the Pet Dog," appears on p. 187). Within a few years Chekhov had published two well-received collections of short stories. After this he practiced medicine only occasionally, continuing to treat his poor neighbors without charge. His compassion and generosity are also reflected in his ability to create sympathetic, convincing characters in his literary works.

Chekhov's first significant success in the theater was *The Seagull* (1896), which was produced by the Moscow Art Theater under the direction of Konstantin Stanislavsky, a champion of realistic methods of acting. *The Seagull* and Chekhov's three other major plays, *Uncle Vanya* (1899), *The Three Sisters* (1901), and *The Cherry Orchard* (1903), are studies of the changing texture of Russian life at the turn of the century. His characters come from a cross-section of society, ranging from valiant but ineffectual aristocrats to noble peasants. The future seems bleak for everyone because there is no energy or direction: civil government is merely officious, intellectuals are too self-absorbed, and the church has retreated to backward-looking tradition.

In contrast to Ibsen's plays, little appears to happen in Chekhov's major dramas. They lack the sense of inevitable direction intrinsic to the well-made play. Although Ibsen's characters are typically riddled with uncertainties, they take decisive actions or are forcefully acted upon. But in a Chekhov play changes, if any, are measured in small, seemingly inconsequential actions. He creates a slice of life onstage, in which characters frequently talk around issues or past each other so that direct confrontations — the makings of dramatic moments — are relatively rare. Therefore, we must listen carefully to the characters' small talk if we are to follow their deepest concerns. Chekhov uses this method intentionally to mirror the circumstances of most people's lives. He avoids heroics and extreme actions in favor of daily lives. Chekhov does incorporate some melodramatic elements in his plays, but they occur offstage and are subordinated to his interest in subtleties of character.

Before he wrote his major works of tragicomic realism, Chekhov also wrote brief farces, or "jests," as he called them. The following play, *A Reluctant Tragic Hero*, is a one-act comedy filled with the kind of humor associated with the incongruities of farce, in which character and actions are exaggerated. The play's protagonist is a married man who attempts to juggle his life between his job and the summer home where his wife and children are vacationing.

Research Anton Chekhov with LitLinks at
http://www.bedfordstmartins.com/meyer/bedintrolit

ANTON CHEKHOV (1860–1904)

A Reluctant Tragic Hero   1889
(A Scene from Country Life)

TRANSLATED BY PAUL SCHMIDT

CHARACTERS
Iván Ivánovich Tolkachóv, a family man
Alexéy Alexéyevich Muráshkin, his friend

The action takes place in St. Petersburg, in Muráshkin's apartment.

A room. Muráshkin alone. Enter Tolkachóv.

Muráshkin: Iván Ivánich! Good to see you! What brings you here?
Tolkachóv (Breathing heavily): Favor. Please! You're my friend, you have to . . . Favor. I'm in trouble, real trouble; I need your help. Can you lend me a gun? Please! Just till tomorrow. Be a friend. Do me a favor.
Muráshkin: What do you need a gun for?
Tolkachóv: What do I need a gun for . . . ? Oh, boy. Oh boy oh boy oh boy. Give me a drink. Have to have something to drink. Fast. A glass of water, have to have water . . . See, I . . . Well, the fact is, I'm going to be spending the night out in the woods alone, way out in the woods, so I . . . You know. Just in case anything happens. So can you lend me a gun? Please! Do me a favor!

Muráshkin: Iván Ivánich, you're not making any sense! What's all this woods business? You sound like Little Red Riding Hood. Are you in trouble? You're involved in something illegal, right? What's happened? What's the matter with you? You look sick.

Tolkachóv: Wait a minute. Give me a minute. I have to catch my breath. Oh, my God! I'm a wreck! My head, my whole body . . . I feel like a shish kebab. I can't stand it anymore. This is the end! Listen, don't ask questions, don't ask me for details — just be a real friend and give me a gun. Please!

Muráshkin: Now that's enough! You're acting like a crybaby! Listen to yourself! A man like you, a married man, with a good steady job . . . You ought to be ashamed of yourself.

Tolkachóv: A married man! That's the whole problem! You know what it means, being a married man? It means I suffer. It means I am a pack animal, a garbage collector. I am a slave, a serf; I am a coward who sits quietly waiting for the next disaster and hasn't got the brains to blow his brains out. I am a fool and an idiot. Why am I still alive? *(Jumps to his feet)* Well? Tell me, why am I alive! Oh, what is the point of it all, this uninterrupted concatenation of mental and physical punishments? Hm? Look, I can understand sacrifice, I could suffer for ideas, or ideals, but to suffer for ladies' dresses and lightbulbs, no! A thousand times, no! No, no, and no! This is the end! It's all over! I can't stand it anymore!

Muráshkin: Stop shouting! The neighbors will hear.

Tolkachóv: Let the neighbors hear. I don't care! You won't give me a gun, someone else will, no problem, and then everything will be over and done with. At last. I've made up my mind, do you hear? I've made up my mind!

Muráshkin: Stop that! You've just ripped off one of my buttons! Get a hold of yourself, man! Now! Now, just what's so bad about your life? I don't understand any of this.

Tolkachóv: What's so bad? You want to know what's so bad? All right, I'll tell you. I'll lay it all out for you in detail, in black and white, and then you'll know. And then maybe I'll feel better. Let's sit down, shall we? Good. Now. Just listen. *(Beat)* My God. I'm always so short of breath. Now. Suppose we consider, just for example, today. Take today. All right? Now. As you know, I go to the office by nine and I stay until four, taking care of business. Now, it is hot in the office, and it is stuffy, and there are flies all over the place, and it is, as you very well know, a bottomless and never-to-be-enlightened outpost of chaos. My secretary is on vacation, my assistant, Krápov, has gone off somewhere to get married, and what is laughingly referred to as "the staff" is preoccupied with the joys of summer: weekends in the country, the possibility of illicit love affairs, and probably, for all I know, amateur theatricals. They're always asleep, or exhausted, or hungover, and you can't get a lick of work out of them. I have a temporary replacement of a secretary who is deaf in one ear — the left ear — and hopelessly in love. The clients haven't got a brain in their heads; you can't get them to sit still: they run, they jump, they get mad, they shout. The whole thing is beyond bedlam. It leaves you screaming for help. It is a disaster area, it is a nest of vipers, it is a zoo for incurables. And the work! Well, it's the same thing over and over again: issue a certificate, write up a memo, issue a certificate, write up a memo. Monotonous. Like waves. Have you ever watched waves? Little ones? Very monotonous, waves. No variety. You know what I mean? Give me another drink of water. . . . So. Finally you leave the office. You are beaten into little bits. All you want is a drink and some dinner and a good night's sleep, but no! Because it dawns on you that it is summertime, and you have rented a place in the country for the summer, and that means you are an insignificant cog in the greater scheme of things, a niggling nothing, and now—do you follow me?—now you are about to flap around like a chicken with its head chopped off, because you have errands to run!

You see, we have a little custom out where we rent for the summer: if anybody is going into town, then any little sonofabitch whatsoever—and this is without even counting his own wife—has a perfectly natural, God-given right to give him a huge list of errands to run. My wife, for instance, wants me to go by the dress shop and tell them in no uncertain terms that the blouse is much too big . . . except the shoulders, which are much too small. Sónya wants me to return her slippers, and my sister-in-law needs two-thirds of a yard of crimson silk to match this sample here and six yards of braid. . . . No, wait a minute—I can read you the whole thing. *(Takes a list from his pocket and reads)* A globe for the lamp. One pound of smoked sausage. Cloves and cinnamon. Some castor oil for Mísha. Ten pounds of powdered sugar. Get the copper washtub and the sugar tongs from the house. Mothballs and bleach. Twenty bottles of beer. Smelling salts and a size eighty-two corset for Mademoiselle Chanceau. Oof! And bring out Mísha's galoshes and his fall jacket. *That* is my wife's list, and the family's. Now, *here's* the list from all my dear friends and gentle neighbors, goddamn every one of them to hell. Tomorrow is Volódya Vlásin's birthday, so I'm supposed to buy him a bicycle. Colonel Víkhrin's wife is in what they call an interesting condition, so I have to go by the doctor's every other day and remind her to show up for the blessed event. And so on and so forth. I've got four different lists in my pocket and knots tied in my handkerchief for the rest of it. So there you are. Between the time you leave the office and the time your train leaves, you have to run all over town like a dog with its tongue in the mud, run run run run run, and curse the day you were born. The department store to the drugstore, the drugstore to the dress shop, the dress shop to the delicatessen, the delicatessen back to the drugstore. You're soaked in sweat, you keep dropping your money, the third stop you forget to pay and they carry on like you tried to rob them, the fourth stop a lady is wearing a long skirt and you step on it. . . . Oof! And what happens is, all this running around makes you crazy and turns you into a physical wreck, to the point where your bones crack all night long and you dream about crocodiles. So anyway, you finally get all your errands done, you've bought everything you're supposed to buy.

Now. Has it occurred to you that you might have a slight problem carting all this stuff out to the country with you? How, for example, do you pack a heavy copper washtub and a plunger and a lamp globe? And have you ever tried to make a single package out of twenty bottles of beer and a bicycle? You address the problem, you work at it like a Chinese puzzle, you try this way and that way, you wear out your ingenuity and your time trying to come up with something that will hold together, and of course something always falls out or rolls off at the last minute, no matter what you do, and when you get to the train station you have to stand there with your arms spread and your legs bowed, using your chin to hold on to a bundle held together with wire and tape and God knows what all. Finally the train arrives, and the crowd starts shoving and knocking your packages all over the place—you've got *your* things in *their* seats. They all start shouting, they get the conductor, they threaten to kick you off the train, and what can I do? I just stand there rolling my eyes, like a donkey with a stick in its mouth and a carrot up its ass.

So. Now comes the next round. I finally arrive at the cottage. And naturally what I'd like is what I'm entitled to: a couple of good stiff drinks and a little something to eat, and finally a little rest from the labors of the just. A little visit from Mr. Sandman! And I have a perfectly natural, God-given right to it, no? No! That's *not* what happens. What happens is, my wife has been waiting for this moment all day long. So you barely get started on your soup, and all of a sudden—wham, bam, thank you very much—wouldn't it be lovely to go out this evening, the drama group is putting on a show, or there's a dance at the club. . . . And that's that. You can protest and protest, and it doesn't mean a thing. You are a married man, and the words "married man" in the summertime mean a dumb beast of burden; you can load him down with anything you want, and nobody even mentions animal rights. So you go, and start losing your eyesight watching *The Duke's Decadent Daughter* or something with a short French name, and you clap your hands whenever your wife pokes you, and you sit there fading faster and faster until you start hoping an early emphysema will carry you off. Or suppose you go to the dance at the club. Then you have to work fast and try to round up enough suckers for your wife to dance with, and if you can't find enough suckers, you wind up dancing with her yourself. Dancing dance after dance with her! You get home from the show or the dance and it's after midnight and you're no longer a human being, you're a piece of dead meat. But at least you have attained your goal, the summit of your day is at hand, you proceed to divest yourself of your garments, and you get into bed. Unbelievable luxury! You close your eyes, and you are about to sleep. . . . Everything is suddenly wonderful and comfortable; it is positively poetry. The children aren't crying or fussing in the next room, your wife is still out, your conscience is clear, you cannot imagine anything better anywhere ever. You begin to drift off . . . you are falling asleep . . . And suddenly—suddenly you hear a tiny noise! Mosquitos! *(Leaps to his feet)* Mosquitos! Goddamn mosquitos! Damn damn damn damn damn! Mosquitos! *(Shakes his fist heavenward)* The ninth plague of Egypt! They bzzz and bzzz, and it is such a sorry sound, such a sad, depressing sound, you almost feel sorry for them, but since *you* are the poor sonofabitch they are biting, you begin to itch. Then you scratch. For a whole hour you scratch. Then you light a cigarette and blow smoke at them and you swat at them and you put your head under the covers, and nothing works. Finally you say the hell with it and you just lie back and let them destroy you: Eat me, you monsters, eat me! Finally you begin getting used to the mosquitos. And then suddenly the tenth plague of Egypt strikes! Your wife has come home; she is in the living room, and she has brought along her tenors, and they begin rehearsing show tunes for their next show. You see, they spend their days sleeping, these tenors, and their nights rehearsing show tunes. And tenors, by Christ, are a torment beside which mosquitos are positively benign. *(Sings)* "Never say thy youth was wasted . . ." Or this: "Once more, love, before you, enchanted I stand . . ." Oh, I tell you, tenors are mean and vicious. They attack the central nervous system, they pull your nerves shrieking from your body. . . . But I have discovered this little trick, you understand, and I use it against them, and it really seems to help. What I do is, I tap like this with my finger right here on my temple, right next to my ear. And I just go on tapping right here like this for the next four hours or so, until they all go away. . . . Water, please, water, I need a glass of water—I can't go on. . . .

Well, finally, there you are. It's morning, you haven't slept, and now you have to get up! And march on down to the station! And get on the train! And you run, because you're afraid you'll miss the train, and it is not a pleasant day; it is a miserable day! It's cold and rainy and you're freezing and the train is filthy! And then you get to town, and you go to the office, and the whole merry-go-round starts all over again. There. I've told you the whole thing, exactly as it happens. *That* is *life*. And that life, believe me, I can say in all seriousness, I would not wish on my worst enemy. It has made a wreck of me! I am ill, do you understand, physically ill! I suffer from shortness of breath. I have heartburn, my digestion is not functioning, my vision is blurred, and I am in constant fear of something. . . . You may not believe this, but I have become a psychopath. *(Glances quickly around him)* You understand this is strictly between you and me. I'm even thinking of going to see one of those doctors, you know, a psych . . . psychi . . . Psychic! No, no, I mean a psychiatrist. I can feel myself coming down with something, friend, and it's not going to be very pretty. You see, in these moments of aggravation, of stupefaction, when the mosquitos are biting and the tenors are singing, I suddenly get this blur in my eyes, and what happens is, I leap up and run all over the house, screaming, "Blood! Blood, Iago, blood!"° And the funny thing is, I really do get the urge to stick a knife into somebody or break a chair over their heads. So . . . you see what summertime can drive you to. And the worst of it is, nobody feels sorry for you, nobody knows how you feel, they all act as if it was perfectly normal. They even laugh. But I am a human being—you have to understand that—and I *want to live!* This isn't a comedy—it's a tragedy. Look, if you haven't got a gun you can lend me, at least tell me you know how I feel.

Muráshkin: Believe me, I know how you feel.

Tolkachóv: I know. I can see that you know how I feel. *(Beat)* Goodbye. I've got to pick up the sardines and the sausage, and then there's the toothpaste, and then I catch my train.

Muráshkin: Where exactly is it you're spending the summer?

Tolkachóv: At Rotten River.

Muráshkin (Overjoyed): No! Rotten River! I don't believe it! Do you happen to know Ólga Fineberg? She's spending the summer there too!

Tolkachóv: Do I know her? Of course I know her.

Muráshkin: Oh, I can hardly believe this! What a surprise! What a coincidence! Listen, this is really wonderful of you—

Tolkachóv: What is?

"Blood . . . blood!": A reference to Shakespeare's tragic hero Othello, who murders his wife, because he is deceived by Iago, a false friend.

Muráshkin: You've got to do me a little favor. You won't mind — I know you're a friend! You will, won't you? Promise me you will!

Tolkachóv: Will what?

Muráshkin: Be a friend! Oh, promise me you will! First of all, say hello to Ólga and tell her you saw me and that everything's fine, just fine, give her my best, and second of all, just take this one little thing with you when you go: she asked me to buy her a sewing machine, which of course I did, but of course there was no way to get it out to her, but now you can take it with you! And also there's this little cage with this little canary in it that has to go too, only you have to be very careful because the little door of the little cage is awfully loose and . . . What's the matter? Why are you looking at me like that?

Tolkachóv: A sewing machine . . . A little cage with a little canary . . . A little birdie . . . a little yellow birdie . . .

Muráshkin: Iván Ivánich, what's the matter with you? Why are you getting so red?

Tolkachóv (Stamps his foot): Give me the goddamn machine! Give me the goddamn cage! Here! You want to ride me out there yourself? You want to play horsie? Go on, kick the horsie! Kill him! *(Makes two fists)* Blood! Blood, Iago, blood!

Muráshkin: You're going crazy!

Tolkachóv (Jumps him): Blood! Blood, Iago, blood!

Muráshkin (Horrified): He's gone crazy! *(Shouts)* Help! Help! Somebody help! Help!

Tolkachóv (Chases him around the room): Blood! Blood, Iago, blood!

CURTAIN.

CONSIDERATIONS FOR CRITICAL THINKING AND WRITING

1. FIRST RESPONSE. What do you think is this play's theme? Is the theme the play's most interesting feature, or does the central interest of the play lie elsewhere?

2. How is Tolkachóv's emotional state indicated in his initial encounter with Muráshkin? Why does he want a gun? How do you know that he is not a tragic but a comic character?

3. Why is Tolkachóv's marriage such a problem for him?

4. How does Tolkachóv describe the routine of his life? What effect does it have on the reader for Tolkachóv to supply so many details about the errands he must run? What do you think of his life?

5. Comment on the play's humor. How does its tone serve to characterize Tolkachóv?

6. What do you think is Muráshkin's purpose in the play? How would the play be different if it consisted only of Tolkachóv's long monologue?

7. How do you think this play could be turned into a tragedy instead of a comedy?

CONNECTIONS TO OTHER SELECTIONS

1. Discuss the different ways Tolkachóv and Big Eight in Jane Martin's *Rodeo* (p. 1656) reveal themselves. What kinds of conflicts are presented in each play?

2. Discuss the treatment of husbands in *A Reluctant Tragic Hero* and in Ibsen's *A Doll House* (p. 1568).

PERSPECTIVE

Anton Chekhov (1860–1904)
On What Artists Do Best 1888

In conversation with my literary colleagues I always insist that it is not the artist's business to solve problems that require a specialist's knowledge. It is a bad thing if a writer tackles a subject he does not understand. We have specialists for dealing with special questions: it is their business to judge of the commune, of the future, of capitalism, of the evils of drunkenness, of boots, of the diseases of women. An artist must judge only of what he understands, his field is just as limited as that of any other specialist — I repeat this and insist on it always. That in his sphere there are no questions, but only answers, can be maintained only by those who have never written and have had no experience of thinking in images. An artist observes, selects, guesses, combines — and this in itself presupposes a problem: unless he had set himself a problem from the very first there would be nothing to conjecture and nothing to select. To put it briefly, I will end by using the language of psychiatry: if one denies that creative work involves problems and purposes, one must admit that an artist creates without premeditation or intention, in a state of abberation; therefore, if an author boasted to me of having written a novel without a preconceived design, under a sudden inspiration, I should call him mad.

You are right in demanding that an artist should take an intelligent attitude to his work, but you confuse two things: *solving a problem and stating a problem correctly.* It is only the second that is obligatory for the artist. . . . It is the business of the judge to put the right questions, but the answers must be given by the jury according to their own lights.

From a letter to A. S. Souvorin, October 27, 1888,
in *Letters of Anton Tchekhov to His Family and Friends,*
translated by Constance Garnett

Considerations for Critical Thinking and Writing

1. Explain whether you agree with Chekhov that an artist's "field is just as limited as that of any other specialist" (para. 1). Write an essay on Chekhov's assertion that "it is not the artist's business to solve problems" (1).

2. How does the humor in *A Reluctant Tragic Hero* reflect Chekhov's insistence that his job is to "put the right questions" (2) rather than to answer them?

46

A Critical Case Study:
Henrik Ibsen's
A Doll House

This chapter provides several critical approaches to Henrik Ibsen's *A Doll House*, which appears in Chapter 45, page 1568. There have been numerous critical approaches to this play because it raises so many issues relating to matters such as relationships between men and women, history, and biography, as well as imagery, symbolism, and irony. The following critical excerpts offer a small and partial sample of the possible biographical, historical, mythological, psychological, sociological, and other perspectives that have attempted to shed light on the play (see Chapter 52, "Critical Strategies for Reading," for a discussion of a variety of critical methods). They should help you to enjoy the play more by raising questions, providing insights, and inviting you to delve further into the text.

The following letter offers a revealing vignette of the historical contexts for *A Doll House*. Professor Richard Panofsky of the University of Massachusetts–Dartmouth has provided the letter and this background information: "The translated letter was written in 1844 by Marcus (1807–1865) to his wife Ulrike (1816–1888), after six children had been born. This upper-middle-class Jewish family lived in Hamburg, Germany, where Marcus was a doctor. As the letter implies, Ulrike had left home and children: the letter establishes conditions for her to return. A woman in upper-class society of the time had few choices in an unhappy marriage. Divorce or separation meant ostracism; as Marcus writes, 'your husband, children, and the entire city threaten indifference or even contempt.' And she could not take a job, as she would have no profession to step into. In any case, Ulrike did return home. Between 1846 and 1857 the marriage produced eight more children. Beyond what the letter shows, we do not know the reasons for the separation or what the later marriage relationship was like."

PERSPECTIVES

A Nineteenth-Century Husband's Letter to His Wife   1844

Dear Wife,   June 23, 1844

You have sinned greatly — and maybe I too; but this much is certain: Adam sinned after Eve had already sinned. So it is with us; you, alone, carry the guilt of all the misfortune which, however, I helped to enlarge later by my behavior. Listen now, since I still believe certain things to be necessary in order that we may have a peaceful life. If we want not only to be content for a day but forever, you will have to follow my wishes. So examine yourself and determine if you are strong enough to conquer your false ambitions and your stubbornness to submit to all the conditions, the fulfillment of which I cannot ignore. Every sensible person will tell you that all I ask of you is what is easily understood. If you insist on remaining stubborn, then do not return to my house, for you will never be happy with me; your husband, children, and the entire city threaten indifference or even contempt.

But if you decide to act *sensibly* and *correctly*, that is *justly* and *kindly*, then be certain that many in the world will envy you.

I am including here the paper which I read to you in front of the rabbi; ask anyone in your residence if the wishes expressed by me are not quite reasonable, and are of a kind to which every wife can agree for the welfare of domestic happiness. In any case, act in a way you think best.

When you decide to return, write to tell me on which day and hour you depart from Berlin and give me your itinerary whether by way of Kuestrin and Pinne or by way of Wollstein. I will then meet you at Wollstein or Pinne. I expect you will bring Solomon with you.

Don't travel unprepared. If you need money, ask your father.

May God enlighten your heart and mind

                              I remain your so far unhappy,   [Marcus]

Greetings to my parents, brothers, and sisters; also your brother. Show them what you wish, this letter, the enclosure, whatever you want. The children are fortunately healthy.

If you want to return with joy and peace, write me by return mail. In that case, I would rather send you a carriage. Maybe Madam Fraenkel will come along. . . .

[*Enclosure*]

My wife promises — for which every wife is obligated to her husband — to follow my wishes in everything and to strictly obey my orders. It is already self-evident that our marital relations have often been disturbed by the fact that my wife does not follow my wishes but believes herself to be entitled to act on her own, even if this is totally against my orders. In order not to have to remind my wife every second what my wishes are regarding homemaking and public conduct — wishes which I have often expressed — I want to make here a few rules which shall serve as a code of conduct. A home is best run if the work for each hour is planned ahead of time, if possible.

Servants get up no later than 5:00 A.M. in summer and 6:00 A.M. in winter, the children an hour later. The cook prepares breakfast. The nursemaid puts out clothes for every child, prepares water and sponge, cleans the combs, etc. The cook should stay in the kitchen unless there is time to clean the rooms. At least once a week the rooms should be cleaned whenever possible, but not all on the same day.

Every Wednesday, the people in the house should do a laundry. Every last Wednesday in the month, there shall be a large laundry with an outside washerwoman. At least every Monday, the seamstress shall come into the house to fix what is necessary.

Every Thursday or Friday, bread is baked for the week; I think it is best to buy grain and have it ground, but to knead it at home.

Every Friday special bread (Barches) should be bought for the evening meal.

The kitchen list will be prepared and discussed every Thursday evening, jointly, by me and my wife; but my wish is to be decisive.

After this, provisions are to be bought every Friday at the market. For this purpose, my wife, herself, will go to the market on Fridays, accompanied by a servant; she can substitute a special woman who does errands (*Faktorfrau*) if she wishes, but not a servant.

All expenditures have to be written down daily and punctually.

The children receive a bath every Thursday evening. The children's clothes must be kept in a specially appointed chest, with a separate compartment for each child with the child's name upon it. The boys' suits and girls' dresses are to be kept separately. To keep used laundry, there must be a hamper easily accessible. Equally important is the food storage box in which provisions are kept in order, locked and safe from vermin.

The kitchen should be kept in order. Once a week all woodwork and copper must be scoured. The lights and lamps have to be cleaned daily. Toward servants, one has to be strict and just. Therefore, one should not call them names which aren't suitable for a decent wife. One should give them enough nourishing food. Disobedience and obstinacy are to be referred to me.

My wife will never make visits in my absence. However, she should visit the synagogue every Saturday — at least once a month; also she should go for a walk with the children at least once a week.

CONSIDERATIONS FOR CRITICAL THINKING AND WRITING

1. Describe the tone of Marcus's letter to his wife. To what extent does he accept responsibility for their separation? What significant similarities and differences do you find between Marcus and Torvald Helmer?

2. Read the discussion on historical criticism in Chapter 52, "Critical Strategies for Reading" (p. 2101). How do you think a new historicist would use this letter to shed light on *A Doll House*?

3. Write a response to the letter from what you imagine the wife's point of view to be.

4. No information is available about this couple's marriage after Ulrike returned home. In an essay, speculate on what you think their relationship was like later in their marriage.

BARRY WITHAM (B. 1939) AND
JOHN LUTTERBIE (B. 1948)

Witham and Lutterbie describe how they use a Marxist approach to teach *A Doll House* in their drama class, in which they teach plays from a variety of critical perspectives.

A Marxist Approach to A Doll House   *1985*

A principal tenet of Marxist criticism is that human consciousness is a product of social conditions and that human relationships are often subverted by and through economic considerations. Mrs. Linde has sacrificed a genuine love to provide for her brothers, and Krogstad has committed a crime to support his children. Anne-Marie, the maid, has also been the victim of her economic background. Because she's "a girl who's poor and gotten in trouble," her relationship with her child has been interrupted and virtually destroyed. In each instance the need for money is linked with the ability to exist. But while the characters accept the social realities of their misfortunes, they do not appear to question how their human attitudes have been thoroughly shaped by socioeconomic considerations.

Once students begin to perceive how consciousness is affected by economics, a Marxist reading of Ibsen's play can illuminate a number of areas. Krogstad, for example, becomes less of a traditional villain when we realize that he is fighting for his job at the bank "as if it were life itself." And his realization of the senselessness of their lives is poignantly revealed when he reflects on Mrs. Linde's past, "all this simply for money." Even Dr. Rank speaks about his failing health and imminent death in entirely financial terms. "These past few days I've been auditing my internal accounts. Bankrupt! Within a month I'll probably be laid out and rotting in the churchyard."

All these characters, however, serve as foils for the central struggle between Nora and Torvald and highlight the pilgrimage that Nora makes in the play. At the outset two things are clear: (1) Nora is enslaved by Torvald in economic terms, and (2) she equates personal freedom with the acquisition of wealth. The play begins joyfully not only because it is the holiday season but also because Torvald's promotion to bank manager will ensure "a safe, secure job with a comfortable salary." Nora is happy because she sees the future in wholly economic terms. "Won't it be lovely to have stacks of money and not a care in the world?"

What she learns, however, is that financial enslavement is symptomatic of other forms of enslavement—master-slave, male-female, sexual objectification, all of which characterize her relationship with Torvald — and that money is no guarantee of happiness. At the end of the play she renounces not only her marital vows but also her financial dependence because she has discovered that personal and human freedom are not measured in economic terms.

This discovery also prompts her to reexamine the society of which she is a part and leads us into a consideration of the ideology in the play. In what sense has Nora committed a criminal offense in forging her father's name? Is it indeed just that she should be punished for an altruistic act, one that cost her dearly both in terms of self-denial and the destruction of her family? Ibsen's defense of Nora is clear, of course, and his implicit indictment of a society that encourages this kind of injustice stimulates a discussion of the assumptions that created the law.

One of the striking things about *A Doll House* is how Anne-Marie accepts her alienation from her child as if it were natural, given the circumstances of class and money. It does not occur to her that laws were framed by other people and thus are capable of imperfection and susceptible to change. Nora broke a law that not only tries to stop thievery (the appropriation of capital) by outlawing forgery but also discriminates against anyone deemed a bad risk. Question leads to question as the class investigates why women were bad risks and why they had difficulty finding employment. It becomes obvious that the function of women in this society was not "natural" but artificial, a role created by their relationship to the family and by their subservience to men. In the marketplace they were a labor force expecting subsistence wages and providing an income to supplement that earned by their husbands or fathers.

An even clearer picture of Nora's society emerges when the Marxist critic examines those features or elements that are not in the play. These "absences" become valuable clues in understanding the ideology in the text. In the words of Fredric Jameson, absences are

> terms or nodal points implicit in the ideological system which have, however, remained unrealized in surface of the text, which have failed to become manifest in the logic of the narrative, and which we can therefore read as what the text represses.[1]

The notion of absences is particularly intriguing for students, who learn quickly to apply it to such popular media as films and television (what can we learn about the experience of urban black Americans from sitcoms like *Julia* and *The Jeffersons*?). Absent from *A Doll House* is Nora's mother, an omission that ties her more firmly to a male-dominated world and the bank owners who promoted Torvald. These absences shape our view because they form a layer of reality that is repressed in the play. And an examination of this "repressed" material leads us to our final topic of discussion: What is the relation between this play and the society in which it was created and produced?

Most Marxist critics believe that there are only three possible answers: the play supports the status quo, argues for reforms in an essentially sound system, or advocates a radical restructuring. Though these options are seemingly reductive, discussion reveals the complexities of reaching any unanimous agreement, and students frequently disagree about Ibsen's intentions regarding reform or revolution. Nora's leaving is obviously a call for change, but

---

[1] Fredric Jameson, *The Political Unconscious: Narrative as a Socially Symbolic Act* (Ithaca: Cornell UP, 1981), p. 48.

many students are not sure whether this leave-taking is a way forward or a cul-de-sac for a system that is thoroughly controlled by the prevailing power structure. . . .

Viewing the play through the lens of Marxist atheists does make one thing clear. Nora's departure had ramifications for her society that went beyond the marriage bed. By studying the play within the context of its socioeconomic structure, we can see how the ideology in the text affects the characters and how they perpetuate the ideology. The conclusion of *A Doll House* was a challenge to the economic superstructures that had controlled and excluded the Noras of the world by manipulating their economic status and, by extension, their conscious estimation of themselves and their place in society.

From "A Marxist Approach to *A Doll House*"
in *Approaches to Teaching Ibsen's* A Doll House

CONSIDERATIONS FOR CRITICAL THINKING AND WRITING

1. To what extent do you agree or disagree with the Marxist "tenet" (para. 1) that "consciousness is affected by economics" (2)?

2. Do you think that Nora's "leave-taking is a way forward or a cul-de-sac for a system that is thoroughly controlled by the prevailing power structure"? Explain your response.

3. Consider whether "A Nineteenth-Century Husband's Letter to His Wife" (p. 1627) supports or challenges Witham and Lutterbie's Marxist reading of *A Doll House*.

CAROL STRONGIN TUFTS (B. 1947)
A Psychoanalytic Reading of Nora   1986

I am not a member of the Women's Rights League. Whatever I have written has been without any conscious thought of making propaganda. I have been more the poet and less the social philosopher than people generally seem inclined to believe. . . . To me it has seemed a problem of mankind in general. And if you read my books carefully you will understand this. . . . My task has been the *description of humanity*. To be sure, whenever such a description is felt to be reasonably true, the reader will read his own feelings and sentiments into the work of the poet. These are then attributed to the poet; but incorrectly so. Every reader remolds the work beautifully and neatly, each according to his own personality. Not only those who write but also those who read are poets. They are collaborators.[1]

To look again at Ibsen's famous and often-quoted words — his assertion that *A Doll House* was not intended as propaganda to promote the cause of women's rights — is to realize the sarcasm aimed by the playwright at those nineteenth-century "collaborators" who insisted on viewing his play as a treatise and Nora, his heroine, as the romantic standard-bearer for the feminist cause. Yet there is also a certain irony implicit in such a realization, for directors,

---

[1] Speech delivered at the Banquet of the Norwegian League for Women's Rights, Christiana, 26 May 1898, in *Ibsen: Letters and Speeches,* ed. Evert Sprinchorn (New York: Hill and Wang, 1964), p. 337.

actors, audiences, and critics turning to this play a little over one hundred years after its first performance bring with them the historical, cultural, and psychological experience which itself places them in the role of Ibsen's collaborators. Because it is a theatrical inevitability that each dramatic work which survives its time and place of first performance does so to be recast in productions mounted in succeeding times and different places, *A Doll House* can never so much be simply reproduced as it must always be re-envisioned. And if the spectacle of a woman walking out on her husband and children in order to fulfill her "duties to (her)self" is no longer the shock for us today that it was for audiences at the end of the nineteenth century, a production of *A Doll House* which resonates with as much immediacy and power for us as it did for its first audiences may do so through the discovery within Ibsen's text of something of our own time and place. For in *A Doll House*, as Rolf Fjelde has written, "(i)t is the entire house . . . which is on trial, the total complex of relationships, including husband, wife, children, servants, upstairs and downstairs, that is tested by the visitors that come and go, embodying aspects of the inescapable reality outside."[2] And a production which approaches that reality through the experience of Western culture in the last quarter of the twentieth century may not only discover how uneasy was Ibsen's relationship to certain aspects of the forces of Romanticism at work in his own society, but, in so doing, may also come to fashion *A Doll House* which shifts emphasis away from the celebration of the Romantic belief in the sovereignty of the individual to the revelation of an isolating narcissism—a narcissism that has become all too familiar to us today.[3]

The characters of *A Doll House* are, to be sure, not alone in dramatic literature in being self-preoccupied, for self-preoccupation is a quality shared by characters from Oedipus to Hamlet and on into modern drama. Yet if a contemporary production is to suggest the narcissistic self-absorption of Ibsen's characters, it must do so in such a way as to imply motivations for their actions and delineate their relationships with one another. Thus it is important to establish a conceptual framework which will provide a degree of precision for the use of the term "narcissism" in this discussion so as to distinguish it from the kind of self-absorption which is an inherent quality necessarily shared by all dramatic characters. For that purpose, it is useful to turn to the criteria established by the Task Force on Nomenclature and Statistics of the American Psychiatric Association for diagnosing the narcissistic personality:

A. Grandiose sense of self-importance and uniqueness, e.g., exaggerates achievements and talents, focuses on how special one's problems are.
B. Preoccupation with fantasies of unlimited success, power, brilliance, beauty, or ideal love.
C. Exhibitionistic: requires constant attention and admiration.

[2] Rolf Fjelde, Introduction to *A Doll House,* in Henrik Ibsen, *The Complete Major Prose Plays* (New York: Farrar, Straus, Giroux, 1978), p. 121.
[3] For studies of the prevalence of the narcissistic personality disorder in contemporary psychoanalytic literature, see Otto F. Kernberg, *Borderline Conditions and Pathological Narcissism* (New York: J. Aronson, 1975); Heinz Kohut, *The Analysis of the Self* (New York: International Universities Press, 1971); and Peter L. Giovachinni, *Psychoanalysis of Character Disorders* (New York: J. Aronson, 1975). See also Christopher Lasch, *The Culture of Narcissism* (New York: Norton, 1979), for a discussion of narcissism as the defining characteristic of contemporary American society.

D. Responds to criticism, indifference of others, or defeat with either cool indifference, or with marked feelings of rage, inferiority, shame, humiliation, or emptiness.

E. At least two of the following are characteristics of disturbances in interpersonal relationships:

1. Lack of empathy: inability to recognize how others feel, e.g., unable to appreciate the distress of someone who is seriously ill.

2. Entitlement: expectation of special favors without assuming reciprocal responsibilities, e.g., surprise and anger that people won't do what he wants.

3. Interpersonal exploitiveness: takes advantage of others to indulge own desires for self-aggrandizement, with disregard for the personal integrity and rights of others.

4. Relationships characteristically vacillate between the extremes of over-idealization and devaluation.[4]

These criteria, as they provide a background against which to consider Nora's relationship with both Kristine Linde and Dr. Rank, will serve to illuminate not only those relationships themselves, but also the relationship of Nora and her husband which is at the center of the play. Moreover, if these criteria are viewed as outlines for characterization — but not as reductive psychoanalytic constructs leading to "case studies" — it becomes possible to discover a Nora of greater complexity than the totally sympathetic victim turned romantic heroine who has inhabited most productions of the play. And, most important of all, as Nora and her relationships within the walls of her "doll house" come to imply a paradigm of the dilemma of all human relationships in the greater society outside, the famous sound of the slamming door may come to resonate even more loudly for us than it did for the audiences of the nineteenth century with a profound and immediate sense of irony and ambiguity, an irony and ambiguity which could not have escaped Ibsen himself.

From "Recasting *A Doll House:* Narcissism as Character Motivation in Ibsen's Play," *Comparative Drama,* Summer 1986

[4] Task Force on Nomenclature and Statistics, American Psychiatric Association, *DSM-III: Diagnostic Criteria Draft* (New York, 1978), pp. 103–04.

CONSIDERATIONS FOR CRITICAL THINKING AND WRITING

1. What is Tufts's purpose in arguing that Nora be seen as narcissistic?

2. Using the criteria of the American Psychiatric Association, consider Nora's personality. Write an essay either refuting the assertion that she has a narcissistic personality or supporting it.

3. How does Tufts's reading compare with Joan Templeton's feminist reading of Nora in the perspective that follows? Which do you find more convincing? Why?

JOAN TEMPLETON (B. 1940)

This feminist perspective summarizes the arguments against reading the play as a dramatization of a feminist heroine.

Is A Doll House *a Feminist Text?* 1989

A Doll House is no more about women's rights than Shakespeare's Richard II *is about the divine right of kings, or* Ghosts *about syphilis. . . . Its theme is the need of every individual to find out the kind of person he or she is and to strive to become that person.*[1]

Ibsen has been resoundingly saved from feminism, or, as it was called in his day, "the woman question." His rescuers customarily cite a statement the dramatist made on 26 May 1898 at a seventieth-birthday banquet given in his honor by the Norwegian Women's Rights League:

> I thank you for the toast, but must disclaim the honor of having consciously worked for the women's rights movement. . . . True enough, it is desirable to solve the woman problem, along with all the others; but that has not been the whole purpose. My task has been the description of humanity.[2]

Ibsen's champions like to take this disavowal as a precise reference to his purpose in writing *A Doll House* twenty years earlier, his "original intention," according to Maurice Valency.[3] Ibsen's biographer Michael Meyer urges all reviewers of *Doll House* revivals to learn Ibsen's speech by heart,[4] and James McFarlane, editor of *The Oxford Ibsen,* includes it in his explanatory material on *A Doll House,* under "Some Pronouncements of the Author," as though Ibsen had been speaking of the play.[5] Whatever propaganda feminists may have made of *A Doll House,* Ibsen, it is argued, never meant to write a play about the highly topical subject of women's rights; Nora's conflict represents something other than, or something more than, woman's. In an article commemorating the half century of Ibsen's death, R. M. Adams explains, "*A Doll House* represents a woman imbued with the idea of becoming a person, but it proposes nothing categorical about women becoming people; in fact, its real theme has nothing to do with the sexes."[6] Over twenty years later, after feminism had resurfaced as an international movement, Einar Haugen, the doyen of American Scandinavian studies, insisted that "Ibsen's Nora is not just a woman arguing for female liberation; she is much more. She embodies the comedy as well as the tragedy of modern life."[7] In the Modern Language Association's *Approaches to Teaching* A Doll House, the editor speaks disparagingly of "reductionist views of *(A Doll House)* as a feminist drama." Summarizing a "major theme" in the volume as "the need for a broad view of the play and a condemnation of a static approach," she warns that discussions of the play's "connection with feminism" have value only if they are monitored, "properly channeled and kept firmly linked to Ibsen's text."[8]

Removing the woman question from *A Doll House* is presented as part of a corrective effort to free Ibsen from his erroneous reputation as a writer of thesis plays, a wrongheaded notion usually blamed on Shaw, who, it is claimed,

---

[1] Michael Meyer, *Ibsen* (Garden City: Doubleday, 1971), 457. [This is not the Michael Meyer who is editor of *The Bedford Introduction to Literature.*]

[2] Henrik Ibsen, *Letter and Speeches,* ed. and trans. Evert Sprinchorn (New York: Hill, 1964), 337.

[3] Maurice Valency, *The Flower and the Castle: An Introduction to Modern Drama* (New York: Schocken, 1982), 151.

[4] Meyer, 774.

[5] James McFarlane, "*A Doll's House:* Commentary" in *The Oxford Ibsen,* ed. McFarlane (Oxford UP, 1961), V, 456.

[6] R. M. Adams, "The Fifty-First Anniversary," *Hudson Review* 10 (1957), 416.

[7] Einar Haugen, *Ibsen's Drama: Author to Audience* (Minneapolis: U of Minnesota P, 1979), vii.

[8] Yvonne Shafer, ed., *Approaches to Teaching Ibsen's* A Doll House (New York: MLA, 1985), 32.

mistakenly saw Ibsen as the nineteenth century's greatest iconoclast and offered that misreading to the public as *The Quintessence of Ibsenism*. Ibsen, it is
now de rigueur to explain, did not stoop to "issues." He was a poet of the truth
of the human soul. That Nora's exit from her dollhouse has long been the
principal international symbol for women's issues, including many that far exceed the confines of her small world, is irrelevant to the essential meaning of
A Doll House, a play, in Richard Gilman's phrase, "pitched beyond sexual difference."[9] Ibsen, explains Robert Brustein, "was completely indifferent to (the
woman question) except as a metaphor for individual freedom."[10] Discussing
the relation of *A Doll House* to feminism, Halvdan Koht, author of the definitive Norwegian Ibsen life, says in summary, "Little by little the topical controversy died away; what remained was the work of art, with its demand for truth
in every human relation."[11]

Thus, it turns out, the *Uncle Tom's Cabin* of the women's rights movement
is not really about women at all. "Fiddle-faddle," pronounced R. M. Adams,
dismissing feminist claims for the play.[12] Like angels, Nora has no sex. Ibsen
meant her to be Everyman.

From "The *Doll House* Backlash: Criticism, Feminism, and Ibsen,"
PMLA, January, 1989

[9] Richard Gilman, *The Making of Modern Drama* (New York: Farrar, 1972), 65.
[10] Robert Brustein, *The Theatre of Revolt* (New York: Little, 1962), 105.
[11] Halvdan Koht, *Life of Ibsen* (New York: Blom, 1971), 323.
[12] Adams, 416.

CONSIDERATIONS FOR CRITICAL THINKING AND WRITING

1. According to Templeton, what kinds of arguments are used to reject *A Doll House* as a feminist text?
2. From the tone of the summaries provided, what would you say is Temple-
   ton's attitude toward these arguments?
3. Read the section on feminist criticism in "Critical Strategies for Reading"
   (p. 2106), and write an essay addressing the summarized arguments as you
   think a feminist critic might respond.

QUESTIONS FOR WRITING
Applying a Critical Strategy

This section offers advice about developing an argument that draws on the
different strategies, or schools of literary theory, covered in Chapter 52.
The following list of questions and suggestions will help you to apply one
or more of these critical strategies to a work in order to shed light on it.
Following the questions is a sample paper based on *A Doll House* (p. 1567).

There are many possible lenses through which to read a literary work.
The Perspectives, Complementary Critical Readings, and Critical Case
Studies in this anthology suggest a variety of approaches — including
formalist, biographical, psychological, Marxist, new historicist, feminist,
mythological, reader-response, and deconstructionist strategies — that can

be used to explore the effects, meanings, and significances of a poem, short story, or play (see Chapter 52 for a discussion of these strategies).

Once you have generated a central idea about a work, you will need to choose the critical approach(es) that will allow you to develop your argument. In the following sample paper, the writer chose a new historicist approach because she was interested in speculating about what Nora faced after she left her husband on the other side of the slammed door in *A Doll House.* By using evidence external to the play, from a letter written by a nineteenth-century husband to his wife, the writer was able to recreate some of the historical context for *A Doll House* in order to argue that Nora's leaving home is a more risky, problematic action than her simple declaration of freedom from her husband. This historical approach allowed the writer to offer a substantive argument about what Nora might have faced beyond the slammed door.

Regardless of the approach — or combination of approaches — you find helpful, it is essential that you be thoroughly familiar with the text of the literary work before examining it through the lens of a particular critical strategy. Without a strong familiarity with the literary work you will not be able to judge the accuracy and validity of a critic's arguments, and you might find your own insights immediately superseded by those of the first critic you read. For additional advice on how to incorporate material from critical essays into your writing without losing track of your own argument about a work, see Questions for Writing: Incorporating the Critics (p. 513).

1. Which of the critical strategies discussed in Chapter 52 seems the most appropriate to the literary work under consideration? Why do you prefer one particular approach over another? Do any critical strategies seem especially inappropriate? Why?

2. Does the historical context of a literary work suggest that certain critical strategies, such as Marxism or feminism, might be particularly productive?

3. Does the literary work reflect or challenge the cultural assumptions contemporary to it in such a way as to suggest a critical approach for your paper?

4. Does the author comment on his or her own literary work in letters, interviews, or lectures? If so, how might these comments help you to develop an approach for your paper?

5. Are you able to formulate an interpretation of the work you want to discuss before reading the critics extensively? If so, how might the critics' discussions help you to develop, enhance, or qualify your argument about how to interpret the work?

6. If you haven't developed an argument before reading the critics, how might some exploratory reading lead you into significant questions and controversial issues that would offer topics that could be developed into a thesis?

7. If you are drawing on the work of a number of critics, how are their critical strategies — whether formalist, biographical, psychological, his-

torical, or other — relevant to your own? How can you use their insights to support your own argument?

8. Is it possible and desirable to combine approaches — such as psychological and historical or biographical and feminist — so that multiple perspectives can be used to support your argument?

9. If the strategies or approaches the critics use to interpret the literary work tend to be similar, are there questions and issues that have been neglected or ignored that can become the focus of your argument about the literary work?

10. If the critics' approaches are very different from one another, is there a way to use those differences to argue your own critical approach that allows you to support one critic rather than another or to resolve a controversy among the critics?

11. Is your argument adequately supported with specific evidence from the literary text? Have you been careful not to avoid discussing parts of the text that do not seem to support your argument?

12. Is your own discussion of the literary text free of simple plot summary? Does each paragraph include a thesis statement that advances your argument rather than merely consisting of facts and plot summary?

13. Have you accurately and fairly represented the critics' arguments?

14. Have you made your own contributions, qualifications, or disagreements with the critics clear to your reader?

A SAMPLE PAPER

On the Other Side of the Slammed Door in A Doll House

The following sample paper focuses on the magnitude of Nora Helmer's decision to leave her husband in *A Doll House*. Kathy Atner uses a new historicist perspective to show just how difficult Nora's decision would have been in the context of nineteenth-century attitudes toward marriage and women. The paper develops an argument primarily from evidence supplied by "A Nineteenth-Century Husband's Letter to His Wife" (p. 1627). By drawing on a source that ordinarily might have been ignored by literary critics, Atner is able to suggest how difficult Nora's life would have been after abandoning her husband and family. This historical strategy is combined with a feminist perspective that gives the modern reader a greater understanding of the issues Nora must inevitably confront once she slams the door shut on her conventional and accepted life as devoted wife and mother. By using both New Historicist and feminist perspectives, Atner suggests that twentieth-century readers should be sensitive to the tragic as well as the heroic dimension of Nora's life.

Kathy Atner

Professor Porter

English 216

April 8, 20--

On the Other Side of the Slammed Door

in A Doll House

Nora Helmer's decision to leave her family in Henrik Ibsen's 1879 play A Doll House reflects the dilemma faced by many nineteenth-century women who were forced either to conform to highly restrictive gender roles or to abandon these roles in order to realize their value as individuals. Although Ibsen brings his audience to the moment that Nora chooses to disregard her social role and opt for her "freedom," his play does not clearly reveal the true fate of women who followed Nora's path in the nineteenth century. Historically, most women who chose not to acquiesce to the socially prescribed roles of marriage were treated as unnatural creatures and shunned by the respectable public. An actual letter, written in 1844 by Marcus to his estranged wife, Ulrike, reveals the effects of this severe social condemnation (1627). His letter implies the desperate fate that inevitably befalls women who reject their prescribed duties as wives and mothers. Through Marcus's letter to his wife, the painful ramifications of Nora's decision to accommodate her own personal desires instead of those of her family become even more poignant, courageous, and tragic.

In the nineteenth century, women had few alternatives to marriage, and women who "failed" at marriage were thought to have failed in their most important duty. In his letter, Marcus articulates society's deep disgust for women who reject what it believes is the sacred female role of homemaker. His letter, while on one level an angry

condemnation of his wife's "stubbornness" (1627) and a
cruelly condescending list of conditions to be met on her
return, is on another level a plea for her to accept again
the role that society has assigned her. He is clearly
shaken by his wife's abandonment and interprets it as a
betrayal of a social "law" or tradition, which, to Marcus's mind, ought to be carved in stone. He responds to
this betrayal by demanding complete obedience from his
wife in the form of a promise "to follow in my wishes in
everything and to strictly obey my orders" (1627). Only
when she acquiesces to his conditions and returns to her
role as docile and obedient wife will Marcus in turn be
able to resume the comfortably familiar, socially sanctioned role of dominant, morally superior husband.

Like Ulrike, Nora decides to leave the security and
comfort of her restrictive domestic life to try to become
a human being. Ibsen neglects, however, to show his audience the actual result of that decision. At the conclusion
of A Doll House, Nora slams the door on her past life,
hoping to begin a new life that will somehow be more satisfying. Yet the modern audience has no genuine sense of
what she may have found beyond that door, and perhaps neither did Nora. Through Ulrike's story, however, the reader
understands the historical truth that the world awaiting
Nora was hostile and unsympathetic. Marcus warns his wife
that "your husband, your children, and the entire city
threaten indifference or even contempt" (1627) if she refuses to return immediately to her socially acceptable
domestic role. This pressure to conform, combined with the
bleak prospects of a single woman, results in Ulrike's
ultimate choice to keep up "appearances" rather than further subject herself to a contemptuous world that neither
wants nor understands her. Although we cannot know Nora's

fate after she leaves Torvald, we may assume that her future would be as bleak as Ulrike's and that the pressure
to return to her domestic life would be equally strong.

When A Doll House was first produced in 1879, audiences had no more sympathy for Nora's predicament than
they did for the real-life stories of women such as
Ulrike. As Errol Durbach points out, in the nineteenth
century, Ibsen's play "did not precipitate heated debate about feminism, women's rights, or male domination.
The sound and the fury were addressed to the very question . . . What credible wife and mother would ever walk out
this way on her family?" (14). A great many readers and
audience members tended to side with Torvald, who seemed,
to them, the innocent victim of Nora's consuming selfishness. The audience's repulsion toward Nora's apparently
"unnatural" action of abandoning her family mirrors the
responses of Marcus and Torvald Helmer, the bereft, perplexed, and angry husbands. Nora and Ulrike radically disrupt their husbands' perceptions of family relationships
by walking out of their lives, preferring to recognize
their own needs before any others. These women suggest
that Torvald's claim that "before all else, you're a wife
and mother" (1614) may not necessarily be true for all
women, but their brave rejections of domestic life cannot
force society to condone their behavior.

Ibsen maintains that A Doll House is not about
women's rights specifically but encompasses a more universal "description of humanity" (Letters 337). In showing a
human being trying to create a new identity for herself,
however, Ibsen reveals the extent to which people are
trapped in societal norms and expectations. Nora's
acknowledgment that she "can't go on believing what the
majority says, or what's written in books" (1614) suggests

a profound social upheaval that has the potential to subvert long-established gender roles. If Nora and Ulrike relinquish the role of the subservient and helpless wife, then Torvald and Marcus can no longer play the role of the dominating, protective husband. Without this role, the men are as helpless as they want their wives to be, and the traditional gender expectations are no longer beyond question. Yet the historical reality is that in spite of Nora's daring escape from her oppressive family, the world was not ready to accommodate women who rejected their feminine duties. Ulrike was thwarted in her attempt to free herself from her family; history suggests that Nora may have met a similar fate.

Modern audiences tend to see Nora as a strong, admirable woman who is courageous enough to sacrifice everything in order to fulfill her own needs as an individual and as a woman. She shatters gender stereotypes through her defiant disregard for all that society demands of her. Yet, taken in the context of nineteenth-century life, perhaps Nora's story is more tragic than we might initially like to believe. Ulrike's story, told through her husband's letter, suggests that in a time of turbulent social upheaval, what was interpreted as a collapse of what we now call "family values" was shocking, scandalous, and deeply frightening to many. In the nineteenth century, Nora was not the sympathetic character that she is today; instead, she symbolized many negative attributes--what Marcus calls "false ambitions" and "stubbornness" (1627)--that were often ascribed to women. Ulrike's forced return to her role as dutiful wife and mother suggests that society was quick to punish disobedient women and that the slamming door at the end of <u>A Doll House</u> was not necessarily the sound of freedom for Nora.

Atner 5

Works Cited

Durbach, Errol. A Doll's House: Ibsen's Myth of Transformation. Boston: Twayne, 1991.

Ibsen, Henrik. A Doll House. Trans. Rolf Fjelde. Meyer
   1567-616.

---. Letters and Speeches. Ed. and trans. Evert
   Sprinchorn. New York: Hill, 1964. 337.

Meyer, Michael, ed. The Bedford Introduction to Literature. 6th ed. Boston: Bedford/St. Martin's, 2001.

"A Nineteenth-Century Husband's Letter to His Wife." Meyer
   1627-28.

──── SUGGESTED TOPICS FOR LONGER PAPERS ────

1. In an essay, discuss whether you think *A Doll House* challenges or affirms the social order it describes. Pay particular attention to the ending of the play by providing a close reading of it.

2. Research marriage laws in the United States for the late nineteenth century. To what extent is Ibsen's 1879 Norwegian play relevant to American laws and attitudes toward marriage? Do you think any significant changes would have had to be made if the play had been set in the United States rather than Norway? Explain why or why not.

3. **MULTIMEDIA PROJECT.** Using newspapers and the Internet for your sources, read reviews and gather images of productions of *A Doll House* during the past thirty years. Select two or three productions that you find interesting from each decade, and organize your essay around how the productions shift emphases over time.

Web *For help with this project, use the Multimedia Project Guides Online at*
   http://www.bedfordstmartins.com/meyer/bedintrolit

47

Experimental Trends
in Drama

BEYOND REALISM

Realistic drama has remained popular throughout the twentieth century, but from its beginnings it has been continually challenged by nonrealistic modes of theater. By the end of the nineteenth century, playwrights reacting against realism began to develop a variety of new approaches to setting, action, and character. Instead of creating a slice of life onstage, modern experimental playwrights drew on purely theatrical devices, ranging from stark sets and ritualistic actions to symbolic characterizations and audience participation. In general, such devices were designed to jar audiences' expectations and to heighten their awareness that what appeared before them was indeed a theatrical production. A glimpse of some of the nonrealistic movements in drama suggests how the possibilities for affecting audiences have been broadened by experimental theater.

Symbolist drama rejected the realists' assumption that life can be understood objectively and scientifically. The symbolists emphasized a subjective, emotional response to life because they believed that ultimate realities can be recognized only intuitively. Since absolute truth cannot be directly perceived, symbolists such as the Belgian playwright Maurice Maeterlinck (1862-1949) sought to express spiritual truth through settings, characters, and actions that suggest a transcendent reality. Maeterlinck's most famous symbolist play, *Pelléas and Mélisande* (1892), is a story of love and vengeance that includes mysterious forebodings, symbolic objects, and unexplained powerful forces. The elements of the play make no attempt to create the texture of ordinary life.

Other playwrights — such as William Butler Yeats (1865-1939) in Ireland, Paul Claudel (1868-1955) in France, Leonid Andreyev (1871-1919) in Russia, and Federico García Lorca (1898-1936) in Spain — also used some of the techniques associated with symbolist plays, but the movement never enjoyed wide popularity because audiences often found the plays' action too vague and their language too cryptic. Nevertheless, symbolist drama had an important influence on the work of subsequent playwrights, such as Tennessee Williams's *The Glass Menagerie* (p. 1893) and Arthur Miller's *Death of a Salesman* (p. 1824); these dramatists effectively used symbols in plays that contain both realistic and nonrealistic qualities.

Another nonrealistic movement, known as *expressionism,* was popular from the end of World War I until the mid-1920s. Expressionist playwrights emphasized the internal lives of their characters and deliberately distorted reality by creating an outward manifestation of an inner state of being. The late plays of Swedish dramatist August Strindberg (1849–1912) anticipate expressionistic techniques. Strindberg's preface to *A Dream Play* (1902) reflects the impact that Freudian psychology would eventually have on the theater:

> The author has tried to imitate the disconnected but seemingly logical form of the dream. Anything may happen; everything is possible and probable. Time and space do not exist. On an insignificant background of reality, imagination designs and embroiders novel patterns: a medley of memories, experiences, free fancies, absurdities, and improvisations.

In such nonrealistic drama the action does not have to proceed chronologically because the playwright dramatizes the emotional life of the characters, which blends the past with the present rather than moving in a fixed, linear way. This fluidity of development can be seen in the *flashbacks* of Williams's *The Glass Menagerie* and Miller's *Death of a Salesman.*

The *epic theater* of Bertolt Brecht (1898–1956) is, like symbolism and expressionism, a long way from the realistic elements in Ibsen's *A Doll House.* Brecht kept a distance between his characters and the audience. This strategy of alienation was designed to alert audiences to important social problems that might be overlooked if an individual's struggles became too emotionally absorbing. Brecht's drama, by casting new light on chronic human problems such as poverty, injustice, and war, was a means to convey hope and evidence that society could be changed for the better. Brecht called his drama "epic" to distinguish it from Aristotle's notion of drama. The episodic structure was designed to prevent the audience from being swept up in the action or losing themselves in an inevitable tragedy. Instead, Brecht wanted the audience to analyze the action and realize that certain consequences weren't inevitable but could be avoided. This distancing, the dramatization of societal issues, and the use of loosely connected scenes sometimes narrated by a kind of stage manager are the hallmarks of "epic" drama.

Epic theater revels in stylized theatricality. The major action in *The Caucasian Chalk Circle,* for example, consists of a play within a play. Brecht's dramas use suggestive rather than detailed settings, and their scenery and props are frequently changed as the audience watches. His actors make clear that they are pretending to be characters. They may speak or sing in verse, address the audience, or comment on issues with other characters who are not participants in the immediate action. In brief, Brecht's theater is keenly conscious of itself as theater.

In contrast to this didactic theater, the ***theater of the absurd*** was a response to the twentieth century's loss of faith in reason, religion, and life itself. These doubts produced an approach to drama that emphasizes chaotic, irrational forces and portrays human beings as more the victims than the makers of their world.

Absurdists such as Samuel Beckett (1906–1989), French dramatist Eugène Ionesco (1912–1994), English playwright Harold Pinter (B. 1930), and American writer Edward Albee (B. 1928) employ a variety of approaches to drama, but they share some assumptions about what subjects are important. Absurdism challenges the belief that life is ordered and meaningful. Instead of positing traditional values that give human beings a sense of purpose in life, absurdists dramatize our inability to comprehend fully our identities and destinies. Unlike heroic characters such as Oedipus or Hamlet, who retain their dignity despite their defeats, the characters in absurdist dramas frequently seem pathetically comic as they drift from one destructive moment to the next. These ***antiheroes*** are often bewildered, ineffectual, deluded, and lost. If they learn anything, it is that the world isolates them in an existence devoid of God and absolute values.

The basic premise of absurdism — that life is meaningless — is often presented in a nonrealistic manner to disrupt our expectations. In a realistic play such as Ibsen's *A Doll House,* characters act pretty much the way we believe people behave. The motivation of these characters and the plausibility of their actions are comprehensible, but in an absurdist drama we are confronted with characters who appear in a series of disconnected incidents that lead to deeper confusion. What would we make of Nora if Ibsen had her appear in the final act costumed as a doll? This would be not only bizarre but unacceptable in a realistic play. However, it could make dramatic sense in an absurdist adaptation that sought to dramatize Nora's loss of identity and dehumanization as a result of her marriage.

Nora's appearance as a doll would, of course, be laughably inconsistent with what we judge to be real or reasonable. And yet we might find ourselves sympathizing with her situation. Suppose that instead of slamming the door and leaving her husband in the final scene, Nora moved stiffly about the room costumed as a doll while Helmer complacently sipped sherry and read the evening paper. Such an ending would suggest that she had been defeated by the circumstances in her life. Her condition — being nothing more than someone's toy — would be both absurd and pathetic. If we laughed at this scene, we would do so because Nora's situation is grotesquely humorous, a parody of her assumptions, hopes, and expectations. This is the world of ***tragicomedy,*** where laughter and pain coexist and where there is neither the happy resolution that typifies comic plots nor the transformational suffering that brings clarification to the tragic hero. It is the world dramatized, for example, in the opening scene of Harold Pinter's *The Dumb Waiter* when Ben tells Gus about an item he's read in the paper.

> *Ben:* A man of eighty-seven wanted to cross the road. But there was a lot of traffic, see? He couldn't see how he was going to squeeze through. So he crawled under a lorry [truck].
> *Gus:* He what?
> *Ben:* He crawled under a lorry. A stationary lorry.
> *Gus:* No?
> *Ben:* The lorry started and ran over him.
> *Gus:* Go on!
> *Ben:* That's what it says here.
> *Gus:* Get away.
> *Ben:* It's enough to make you want to puke, isn't it?
> *Gus:* Who advised him to do a thing like that?
> *Ben:* A man of eighty-seven crawling under a lorry!
> *Gus:* It's unbelievable.
> *Ben:* It's down here in black and white.
> *Gus:* Incredible.

As much as Gus finds the story difficult to believe and Ben is sickened by it, it is a fact that the old man was crushed under ridiculous circumstances. His death is unexpected, accidental, incomprehensible, and meaningless — except that what happened to the old man is, from an absurdist's perspective, really no different from what life has in store for all of us one way or the other.

An absurdist playwright may, as Pinter does, employ realistic settings and speech, but he or she goes beyond realistic conventions to challenge the rational assumptions we make about our lives. Pinter insists that "a play is not an essay." Background information, character motivation, action — nothing presented on an absurdist's stage is governed by the conventions of realism. The absurdists typically refuse to create the illusion of reality because there is, finally, no reality to imitate. If conversations in their plays are sometimes fragmented and seemingly inconsequential, the reason is that absurdists dramatize people's combined inability and unwillingness to communicate with one another. Indeed, Samuel Beckett's *Act without Words* contains no dialogue, and in his *Krapp's Last Tape* a single character addresses only his own tape-recorded voice. To some extent we must suspend common sense and logic if we are to appreciate the visions and voices in an absurdist play.

Although many other nonrealistic movements developed in the twentieth century, these four — symbolism, expressionism, epic theater, and the theater of the absurd — embrace the major differences between nonrealistic and realistic drama. The theater continually tests its own possibilities. In the 1960s and 1970s, for example, some acting companies in New York completely collapsed the usual distinctions between audience and actors. The Living Theater went even further by moving into the streets, where the actors and audiences engaged in dramatic political statements aimed at raising the social consciousness of people wherever they were. Some critics argued that this was not really theater but merely an exuberant kind of political rally. However, proponents of these productions — known as ***guerrilla theater*** — argued that protest drama is both politically and artistically valid. In any case, although today's playwrights seem considerably less inclined to take to the streets, there is a tolerance for a wide range of possible relationships between actors and audiences. Audiences (and readers) can expect symbolic characters, expressionistic settings, poetic language, monologues, and extreme actions in productions that also contain realistic elements. In *Route 1 & 9* (1981), a piece created by an experimental theater company called The Wooster Group, for example, audiences found themselves confronted with passages from Thornton Wilder's idealized version of America in *Our Town* that were coupled with a pornographic film and a black vaudeville act. This unlikely combination was used to comment on Wilder's conception of America in which issues of sex and race are largely ignored. Increasingly, experimental theater has cultivated an eclectic approach to drama, using a variety of media, cultures, playwrights, and even languages to enrich an audience's experience. Parts of Robert Wilson's *CIVIL warS* (1984) — a work never staged in its entirety in any one place — were performed in several countries, including France, Italy, and the United States, and drew on different languages as well as cultures to evoke a wide range of experiences from history, literature, myths, and even dreams. Chapter 51, "An Album of Contemporary Plays," attests to the traditions and innovations that contemporary dramatists have incorporated into their dramatic art.

Krapp's Last Tape

Samuel Beckett was born near Dublin to a middle-class Irish-Protestant family. After graduating from Trinity College, Dublin, in 1927, he studied in Paris, where he met James Joyce and was influenced by Joyce's innovative use of language. There Beckett began his own experiments in poetry and fiction. He returned to Ireland to teach at Trinity College and earned an M.A. in 1931, but he left teaching the following year to travel in Europe. He permanently settled in Paris in the late 1930s. During this period his publications included two volumes of poetry, *Whoroscope* (1930) and *Echo's Bones* (1935); a collection of stories, *More Pricks Than Kicks* (1934); and a novel, *Murphy* (1938).

During World War II, Beckett's work for the French resistance made it necessary for him to flee German-occupied France, but he returned to Paris at the end of the war and began writing the works that would earn him the Nobel Prize for Literature in 1969. Writing mostly in French and translating his work into English later, Beckett produced both novels — *Molloy* (1951), *Malone Dies* (1951), *Watt* (1953), *The Unnamable* (1953), and *How*

It Is (1961) — and plays — *Waiting for Godot* (1952), *Endgame* (1957), *Krapp's Last Tape* (1958, first written in English), and *Happy Days* (1961).

These works are populated by characters who live meager, isolated existences that sometimes seem barely human. Yet their aspirations and desires are expressed in simple activities that are attempts to transcend the endless meaningless routines that make up their lives. In an illogical and absurdly comic world stripped of any lasting meaning, these characters appear in minimal settings, having little to say and even less to do.

Waiting for Godot, Beckett's most famous play, brought absurdist principles to popular audiences. Its seemingly pointless dialogue is spoken by two clownish vagabonds while they wait for a mysterious Mr. Godot, who never appears. The play has no clearly identifiable conflict; instead, the action tends to be random and repetitive. Nothing much happens, but there is tension nonetheless among strange characters who hope in an apparently hopeless world.

In *Krapp's Last Tape,* Beckett uses only one character onstage. The play is more than a monologue, however, because the protagonist engages in a kind of conversation with his own tape-recorded voice. Every year on his birthday Krapp has recorded his impressions of that year's events and methodically cataloged and indexed them. Krapp observes his sixty-ninth birthday by listening to portions of a tape he recorded thirty years earlier. Hence, there are two Krapps in the play: an elderly man and his younger self on tape. This device allows Beckett to present Krapp's relation to his past in an intriguing, complex manner; we witness a character thinking aloud with a part of himself he no longer knows. If the older Krapp appears strange to us, we should not overlook the fact that he is even stranger to himself.

Web   *Research Samuel Beckett with LitLinks at*
       http://www.bedfordstmartins.com/meyer/bedintrolit

Samuel Beckett (1906–1989)
Krapp's Last Tape   *1958*

A PLAY IN ONE ACT

SCENE: *A late evening in the future.*

> *Krapp's den. Front center a small table, the two drawers of which open towards*
> *audience. Sitting at the table, facing front, i.e. across from the drawers, a wearish°*
> *old man: Krapp.*
>   *Rusty black narrow trousers too short for him. Rusty black sleeveless waist-*
> *coat, four capacious pockets. Heavy silver watch and chain. Grimy white shirt open*

wearish: Withered.

at neck, no collar. Surprising pair of dirty white boots, size ten at least, very narrow and pointed.

White face. Purple nose. Disordered gray hair. Unshaven.

Very near-sighted (but unspectacled). Hard of hearing.

Cracked voice. Distinctive intonation.

Laborious walk.

On the table a tape-recorder with microphone and a number of cardboard boxes containing reels of recorded tapes.

Table and immediately adjacent area in strong white light. Rest of stage in darkness.

Krapp remains a moment motionless, heaves a great sigh, looks at his watch, fumbles in his pockets, takes out an envelope, puts it back, fumbles, takes out a small bunch of keys, raises it to his eyes, chooses a key, gets up and moves to front of table. He stoops, unlocks first drawer, peers into it, feels about inside it, takes out a reel of tape, peers at it, puts it back, locks drawer, unlocks second drawer, peers into it, feels about inside it, takes out a large banana, peers at it, locks drawer, puts keys back in his pocket. He turns, advances to edge of stage, halts, strokes banana, peels it, drops skin at his feet, puts end of banana in his mouth and remains motionless, staring vacuously before him. Finally he bites off the end, turns aside, and begins pacing to and fro at edge of stage, in the light, i.e. not more than four or five paces either way, meditatively eating banana. He treads on skin, slips, nearly falls, recovers himself, stoops and peers at skin and finally pushes it, still stooping, with his foot over the edge of stage into pit. He resumes his pacing, finishes banana, returns to table, sits down, remains a moment motionless, heaves a great sigh, takes keys from his pockets, raises them to his eyes, chooses key, gets up and moves to front of table, unlocks second drawer, takes out a second large banana, peers at it, locks drawer, puts back keys in his pocket, turns, advances to edge of stage, halts, strokes banana, peels it, tosses skin into pit, puts end of banana in his mouth, and remains motionless, staring vacuously before him. Finally he has an idea, puts banana in his waistcoat pocket, the end emerging, and goes with all the speed he can muster backstage into darkness. Ten seconds. Loud pop of cork. Fifteen seconds. He comes back into light carrying an old ledger and sits down at table. He lays ledger on table, wipes his mouth, wipes his hands on the front of his waistcoat, brings them smartly together and rubs them.

Krapp (briskly): Ah! *(He bends over ledger, turns the pages, finds the entry he wants, reads.)* Box . . . thrree . . . spool . . . five. *(He raises his head and stares front. With relish.)* Spool! *(Pause.)* Spooool! *(Happy smile. Pause. He bends over table, starts peering and poking at the boxes.)* Box . . . thrree . . . thrree . . . four . . . two . . . *(with surprise)* nine! good God! . . . seven . . . ah! the little rascal! *(He takes up box, peers at it.)* Box thrree. *(He lays it on table, opens it, and peers at spools inside.)* Spool . . . *(he peers at ledger)* . . . five *(he peers at spools)* . . . five . . . five! . . . ah! the little scoundrel! *(He takes out a spool, peers at it.)* Spool five. *(He lays it on table, closes box three, puts it back with the others, takes up the spool.)* Box thrree, spool five. *(He bends over the machine, looks up. With relish.)* Spooool! *(Happy smile. He bends, loads spool on machine, rubs his hands.)* Ah! *(He peers at ledger, reads entry at foot of page.)* Mother at rest at last . . . Hm . . . The black ball . . . *(He raises his head, stares blankly front. Puzzled.)* Black ball? . . . *(He peers again at ledger, reads.)* The dark nurse . . . *(He raises his head, broods, peers again at ledger, reads.)* Slight improvement in bowel condition . . . Hm . . . Memorable . . . what? *(He peers closer.)* Equinox, memorable equinox. *(He raises his head, stares blankly front. Puzzled.)* Memorable equinox? . . . *(Pause. He shrugs his shoulders, peers again at ledger, reads.)* Farewell to — *(he turns the page)* — love.

He raises his head, broods, bends over machine, switches on, and assumes listening posture; i.e. leaning forward, elbows on table, hand cupping ear towards machine, face front.

Tape *(strong voice, rather pompous, clearly Krapp's at a much earlier time):* Thirty-nine today, sound as a — *(Settling himself more comfortably he knocks one of the boxes off the table, curses, switches off, sweeps boxes and ledger violently to the ground, winds tape back to beginning, switches on, resumes posture.)* Thirty-nine today, sound as a bell, apart from my old weakness, and intellectually I have now every reason to suspect at the . . . *(hesitates)* . . . crest of the wave — or thereabouts. Celebrated the awful occasion, as in recent years, quietly at the Winehouse. Not a soul. Sat before the fire with closed eyes, separating the grain from the husks. Jotted down a few notes, on the back of an envelope. Good to be back in my den, in my old rags. Have just eaten I regret to say three bananas and only with difficulty refrained from a fourth. Fatal things for a man with my condition. *(Vehemently.)* Cut 'em out! *(Pause.)* The new light above my table is a great improvement. With all this darkness round me I feel less alone. *(Pause.)* In a way. *(Pause.)* I love to get up and move about in it, then back here to . . . *(hesitates)* . . . me. *(Pause.)* Krapp.

Pause.

The grain, now what I wonder do I mean by that, I mean . . . *(hesitates)* . . . I suppose I mean those things worth having when all the dust has — when all *my* dust has settled. I close my eyes and try and imagine them.

Pause. Krapp closes his eyes briefly.

Extraordinary silence this evening, I strain my ears and do not hear a sound. Old Miss McGlome always sings at this hour. But not tonight. Songs of her girlhood, she says. Hard to think of her as a girl. Wonderful woman though. Connaught, I fancy. *(Pause.)* Shall I sing when I am her age, if I ever am? No. *(Pause.)* Did I sing as a boy? No. *(Pause.)* Did I ever sing? No.

Pause.

Just been listening to an old year, passages at random. I did not check in the book, but it must be at least ten or twelve years ago. At that time I think I was still living on and off with Bianca in Kedar Street. Well out of that, Jesus yes! Hopeless business. *(Pause.)* Not much about her, apart from a tribute to her eyes. Very warm. I suddenly saw them again. *(Pause.)* Incomparable! *(Pause.)* Ah well . . . *(Pause.)* These old P.M.s are gruesome, but I often find them — *(Krapp switches off, broods, switches on)* — a help before embarking on a new . . . *(hesitates)* . . . retrospect. Hard to believe I was ever that young whelp. The voice! Jesus! And the aspirations! *(Brief laugh in which Krapp joins.)* And the resolutions! *(Brief laugh in which Krapp joins.)* To drink less, in particular. *(Brief laugh of Krapp alone.)* Statistics. Seventeen hundred hours, out of the preceding eight thousand odd, consumed on licensed premises alone. More than 20%, say 40% of his waking life. *(Pause.)* Plans for a less ... *(hesitates)* ... engrossing sexual life. Last illness of his father. Flagging pursuit of happiness. Unattainable laxation. Sneers at what he calls his youth and thanks to God that it's over. *(Pause.)* False ring there. *(Pause.)* Shadows of the opus ... magnum. Closing with a — *(brief laugh)* — yelp to Providence. *(Prolonged laugh in which Krapp joins.)* What remains of all that misery? A girl in a shabby green coat, on a railway-station platform? No?

Pause.

When I look —

Krapp switches off, broods, looks at his watch, gets up, goes backstage into darkness. Ten seconds. Pop of cork. Ten seconds. Second cork. Ten seconds. Third cork. Ten seconds. Brief burst of quavering song.

Krapp *(sings):*   Now the day is over,
                     Night is drawing nigh-igh,
                     Shadows — °

Fit of coughing. He comes back into light, sits down, wipes his mouth, switches on, resumes his listening posture.

Tape: — back on the year that is gone, with what I hope is perhaps a glint of the old eye to come, there is of course the house on the canal where mother lay a-dying, in the late autumn, after her long viduity° *(Krapp gives a start),* and the — *(Krapp switches off, winds back tape a little, bends his ear closer to machine, switches on)* — a-dying, after her long viduity, and the —

Krapp switches off, raises his head, stares blankly before him. His lips move in the syllables of "viduity." No sound. He gets up, goes backstage into darkness, comes back with an enormous dictionary, lays it on table, sits down and looks up the word.

Krapp *(reading from dictionary):* "State — or condition of being — or remaining — a widow — or widower." *(Looks up. Puzzled.)* Being — or remaining? ... *(Pause. He peers again at dictionary. Reading.)* "Deep weeds of viduity... Also of an animal, especially a bird ... the vidua or weaver-bird ... Black plumage of male ..." *(He looks up. With relish.)* The vidua-bird!

Pause. He closes dictionary, switches on, resumes listening posture.

Tape: — bench by the weir from where I could see her window. There I sat, in the biting wind, wishing she were gone. *(Pause.)* Hardly a soul, just a few regulars, nursemaids, infants, old men, dogs. I got to know them quite well — oh by appearance of course I mean! One dark young beauty I recollect particularly, all white and starch, incomparable bosom, with a big black hooded perambulator, most funereal thing. Whenever I looked in her direction she had her eyes on me. And yet when I was bold enough to speak to her — not having been introduced — she threatened to call a policeman. As if I had designs on her virtue! *(Laugh. Pause.)* The face she had! The eyes! Like ... *(hesitates)* ... chrysolite! *(Pause.)* Ah well ... *(Pause.)* I

Now ... Shadows: From the hymn "Now the Day Is Over" by Sabine Baring-Gould (1834–1924), author of "Onward, Christian Soldiers."
viduity: Widowhood.

was there when — *(Krapp switches off, broods, switches on again)* — the blind went down, one of those dirty brown roller affairs, throwing a ball for a little white dog, as chance would have it. I happened to look up and there it was. All over and done with, at last. I sat on for a few moments with the ball in my hand and the dog yelping and pawing at me. *(Pause.)* Moments. Her moments, my moments. *(Pause.)* The dog's moments. *(Pause.)* In the end I held it out to him and he took it in his mouth, gently, gently. A small, old, black, hard, solid rubber ball. *(Pause.)* I shall feel it, in my hand, until my dying day. *(Pause.)* I might have kept it. *(Pause.)* But I gave it to the dog.

Pause.

Ah well . . .

Pause.

Spiritually a year of profound gloom and indigence until that memorable night in March, at the end of the jetty, in the howling wind, never to be forgotten, when suddenly I saw the whole thing. The vision, at last. This fancy is what I have chiefly to record this evening, against the day when my work will be done and perhaps no place left in my memory, warm or cold, for the miracle that . . . *(hesitates)* . . . for the fire that set it alight. What I suddenly saw then was this, that the belief I had been going on all my life, namely — *(Krapp switches off impatiently, winds tape forward, switches on again)* — great granite rocks the foam flying up in the light of the light-house and the wind-gauge spinning like a propeller, clear to me at last that the dark I have always struggled to keep under is in reality my most — *(Krapp curses, switches off, winds tape forward, switches on again)* — unshatterable association until my dissolution of storm and night with the light of the understanding and the fire — *(Krapp curses louder, switches off, winds tape forward, switches on again)* — my face in her breasts and my hand on her. We lay there without moving. But under us all moved, and moved us, gently, up and down, and from side to side.

Pause.

Past midnight. Never knew such silence. The earth might be uninhabited.

Pause.

Here I end —

Krapp switches off, winds tape back, switches on again.

— upper lake, with the punt, bathed off the bank, then pushed out into the stream and drifted. She lay stretched out on the floorboards with her hands under her head and her eyes closed. Sun blazing down, bit of a breeze, water nice and lively. I noticed a scratch on her thigh and asked her how she came by it. Picking gooseberries, she said. I said again I thought it was hopeless and no good going on, and she agreed, without opening her eyes. *(Pause.)* I asked her to look at me and after a few moments — *(pause)* — after a few moments she did, but the eyes just slits, because of the glare. I bent over her to get them in the shadow and they opened. *(Pause. Low.)* Let me in. *(Pause.)* We drifted in among the flags and stuck. The way they went down, sighing, before the stem! *(Pause.)* I lay down across her with my face in her breasts and my hand on her. We lay there without moving. But under us all moved, and moved us, gently, up and down, and from side to side.

Pause.

Past midnight. Never knew—

Krapp switches off, broods. Finally he fumbles in his pockets, encounters the banana, takes it out, peers at it, puts it back, fumbles, brings out the envelope, fumbles, puts back envelope, looks at his watch, gets up and goes backstage into darkness. Ten seconds. Sound of bottle against glass, then brief siphon. Ten seconds. Bottle against glass alone. Ten seconds. He comes back a little unsteadily into light, goes to front of table, takes out keys, raises them to his eyes, chooses key, unlocks first drawer, peers into it, feels about inside, takes out reel, peers at it, locks drawer, puts keys back in his pocket, goes and sits down, takes reel off machine, lays it on dictionary, loads virgin reel on machine, takes envelope from his pocket, consults back of it, lays it on table, switches on, clears his throat, and begins to record.

Krapp: Just been listening to that stupid bastard I took myself for thirty years ago, hard to believe I was ever as bad as that. Thank God that's all done with anyway. *(Pause.)* The eyes she had! *(Broods, realizes he is recording silence, switches off, broods. Finally.)* Everything there, everything, all the — *(Realizes this is not being recorded, switches on.)* Everything there, everything on this old muckball, all the light and dark and famine and feasting of . . . *(hesitates)* . . . the ages! *(In a shout.)* Yes! *(Pause.)* Let that go! Jesus! Take his mind off his homework! Jesus! *(Pause. Weary.)* Ah well, maybe he was right. *(Pause.)* Maybe he was right. *(Broods. Realizes. Switches off. Consults envelope.)* Pah! *(Crumples it and throws it away. Broods. Switches on.)* Nothing to say, not a squeak. What's a year now? The sour cud and the iron stool. *(Pause.)* Revelled in the word spool. *(With relish.)* Spooool! Happiest moment of the past half million. *(Pause.)* Seventeen copies sold, of which eleven at trade price to free circulating libraries beyond the seas. Getting known. *(Pause.)* One pound six and something, eight I have little doubt. *(Pause.)* Crawled out once or twice, before the summer was cold. Sat shivering in the park, drowned in dreams and burning to be gone. Not a soul. *(Pause.)* Last fancies. *(Vehemently.)* Keep 'em under! *(Pause.)* Scalded the eyes out of me reading *Effie* again, a page a day, with tears again. Effie . . . *(Pause.)* Could have been happy with her, up there on the Baltic, and the pines, and the dunes. *(Pause.)* Could I? *(Pause.)* And she? *(Pause.)* Pah! *(Pause.)* Fanny came in a couple of times. Bony old ghost of a whore. Couldn't do much, but I suppose better than a kick in the crutch. The last time wasn't so bad. How do you manage it, she said, at your age? I told her I'd been saving up for her all my life. *(Pause.)* Went to Vespers once, like when I was in short trousers. *(Pause. Sings.)*

Now the day is over,
Night is drawing nigh-igh,
Shadows — *(coughing, then almost inaudible)* — of the evening
Steal across the sky.

(Gasping.) Went to sleep and fell off the pew. *(Pause.)* Sometimes wondered in the night if a last effort mightn't — *(Pause.)* Ah finish your booze now and get to your bed. Go on with this drivel in the morning. Or leave it at

that. *(Pause.)* Leave it at that. *(Pause.)* Lie propped up in the dark – and wander. Be again in the dingle on a Christmas Eve, gathering holly, the red-berried. *(Pause.)* Be again on Croghan on a Sunday morning, in the haze, with the bitch, stop and listen to the bells. *(Pause.)* And so on. *(Pause.)* Be again, be again. *(Pause.)* All that old misery. *(Pause.)* Once wasn't enough for you. *(Pause.)* Lie down across her.

Long pause. He suddenly bends over machine, switches off, wrenches off tape, throws it away, puts on the other, winds it forward to the passage he wants, switches on, listens staring front.

Tape: — gooseberries, she said. I said again I thought it was hopeless and no good going on, and she agreed, without opening her eyes. *(Pause.)* I asked her to look at me and after a few moments – *(pause)* – after a few moments she did, but the eyes just slits, because of the glare. I bent over her to get them in the shadow and they opened. *(Pause. Low.)* Let me in. *(Pause.)* We drifted in among the flags and stuck. The way they went down, sighing, before the stem! *(Pause.)* I lay down across her with my face in her breasts and my hand on her. We lay there without moving. But under us all moved, and moved us, gently, up and down, and from side to side.

Pause. Krapp's lips move. No sound.

Past midnight. Never knew such silence. The earth might be uninhabited.

Pause.

Here I end this reel. Box – *(pause)* – three, spool – *(pause)* – five. *(Pause.)* Perhaps my best years are gone. When there was a chance of happiness. But I wouldn't want them back. Not with the fire in me now. No, I wouldn't want them back.

Krapp motionless staring before him. The tape runs on in silence.

Curtain

CONSIDERATIONS FOR CRITICAL THINKING AND WRITING

1. FIRST RESPONSE. Why do you think the play is set in "a late evening in the future" rather than the present?

2. What does Krapp's physical description reveal about him?

3. Why does Krapp make tape recordings? How does he use them?

4. What is the effect of the many pauses in the play?

5. What are Krapp's attitudes toward his earlier perceptions about life? Compare and contrast the sixty-nine-year-old Krapp with the thirty-nine-year-old on the tape.

6. What career hopes did the younger Krapp have? How do you know whether he was successful?

7. How does Krapp, in retrospect, seem to feel about his life?

8. Although Krapp is obviously not a conventional dramatic hero, is there anything heroic about what he says or does? How do you respond to him?

9. What do you make of the play's title? A student once suggested that if the play were to have a subtitle, Beckett could have used the heading of one of Krapp's ledger entries: "Farewell to love." Explain whether this proposed subtitle reflects the play's major concerns.

10. Do you think the sixty-nine-year-old Krapp changes or develops during the play? In the final scene, how does he act differently from the way he behaved in the opening scene?

CONNECTIONS TO OTHER SELECTIONS

1. Write an essay in which you explore some important similarities or differences between Krapp and Willy Loman in Arthur Miller's *Death of a Salesman* (p. 1824) or the narrator in Robert Frost's "The Road Not Taken" (p. 1000).

2. Compare and contrast the use of tape recorders in *Krapp's Last Tape* and David Henry Hwang's *M. Butterfly* (p. 1672). Do you think the tape recorders heighten or lessen the dramatic effects of each play?

PERSPECTIVE

MARTIN ESSLIN (B. 1918)

On the Theater of the Absurd 1961

Concerned as it is with the ultimate realities of the human condition, the relatively few fundamental problems of life and death, isolation and communication, the Theater of the Absurd, however grotesque, frivolous, and irreverent it may appear, represents a return to the original, religious function of the theater — the confrontation of man with the spheres of myth and religious reality. Like ancient Greek tragedy and the medieval mystery plays and baroque allegories, the Theater of the Absurd is intent on making its audience aware of man's precarious and mysterious position in the universe.

The difference is merely that in ancient Greek tragedy — and comedy — as well as in the medieval mystery play and the baroque *auto sacramental,* the ultimate realities concerned were generally known and universally accepted metaphysical systems, while the Theater of the Absurd expresses the absence of any such generally accepted cosmic system of values. Hence, much more modestly, the Theater of the Absurd makes no pretense at explaining the ways of God to man. It can merely present, in anxiety or with derision, an individual human being's intuition of the ultimate realities as he experiences them; the fruits of one man's descent into the depths of his personality, his dreams, fantasies, and nightmares.

While former attempts at confronting man with the ultimate realities of his condition projected a coherent and generally recognized version of the truth, the Theater of the Absurd merely communicates one poet's most intimate and personal intuition of the human situation, his own *sense of being,* his individual vision of the world. This is the *subject matter* of the Theater of the Absurd, and it determines its *form,* which must, of necessity, represent a convention of the stage basically different from the "realistic" theater of our time.

As the Theater of the Absurd is not concerned with conveying information or presenting the problems or destinies of characters that exist outside the author's inner world, as it does not expound a thesis or debate ideological propositions, it is not concerned with the representation of events, the narration of the fate or the adventures of characters, but instead with the presentation of one individual's basic situation. It is a theater of situation as against a theater of events in sequence, and therefore it uses a language based on patterns of concrete images rather than argument and discursive speech. And since it is trying to present a sense of being, it can neither investigate nor solve problems of conduct or morals.

From *The Theater of the Absurd*

CONSIDERATIONS FOR CRITICAL THINKING AND WRITING

1. What does Esslin see as the essential difference between the theater of the absurd and Greek or medieval theaters in terms of their treatment of "ultimate realities" (para. 1)?

2. To what extent does Esslin's description of the theater of the absurd apply to *Krapp's Last Tape*?

3. Here's one to stretch your imagination: take Krapp's "situation" and write a summary of how you think Sophocles, Shakespeare, or Ibsen might have developed it into a play. Consider, for example, what the focus of the conflict would be and how the story would end.

Rodeo

Jane Martin is a pseudonym. The author's identity is known only to a handful of administrators at the Actors Theatre of Louisville who handle permissions for productions and reprints of the play. *Rodeo* is one of eleven monologues in *Talking With. . . .* Martin has also published other plays including *Coup/Clucks* (1982), *What Mama Don't Know* (1988), and *Cementville* (1991).

Although only one character appears in *Rodeo,* the monologue is surprisingly moving as she describes what the rodeo once was, how it has changed, and what it means to her. At first glance the subject matter may not seem very promising for drama, but the character's energy, forthrightness, and colorful language transform seemingly trivial details into significant meanings.

JANE MARTIN

Rodeo   *1981*

A young woman in her late twenties sits working on a piece of tack. Beside her is a Lone Star beer in the can. As the lights come up we hear the last verse of a Tanya Tucker song or some other female country-western vocalist. She is wearing old worn jeans and boots plus a long-sleeved workshirt with the sleeves rolled up. She works until the song is over and then speaks.

Big Eight: Shoot — Rodeo's just goin' to hell in a handbasket. Rodeo used to be somethin'. I loved it. I did. Once Daddy an' a bunch of 'em was foolin' around with some old bronc over to our place and this ol' red nose named Cinch got bucked off and my Daddy hooted and said he had him a nine-year-old girl, namely me, wouldn't have no damn trouble cowboyin' that horse. Well, he put me on up there, stuck that ridin' rein in my hand, gimme a kiss, and said, "Now there's only one thing t' remember Honey Love, if ya fall off you jest don't come home." Well I stayed up. You gotta stay on a bronc eight seconds. Otherwise the ride don't count. So from that day on my daddy called me Big Eight. Heck! That's all the name I got anymore . . . Big Eight.

Used to be fer cowboys, the rodeo did. Do it in some open field, folks would pull their cars and pick-ups round it, sit on the hoods, some ranch hand'd bulldog him some rank steer and everybody'd wave their hats and call him by name. Ride us some buckin' stock, rope a few calves, git throwed off a bull, and then we'd jest git us to a bar and tell each other lies about how good we were.

Used to be a family thing. Wooly Billy Tilson and Tammy Lee had them five kids on the circuit. Three boys, two girls and Wooly and Tammy. Wasn't no two-beer rodeo in Oklahoma didn't have a Tilson entered. Used to call the oldest girl Tits. Tits Tilson. Never seen a girl that top-heavy could ride so well. Said she only fell off when the gravity got her. Cowboys used to say if she landed face down you could plant two young trees in the holes she'd leave. Ha! Tits Tilson.

Used to be people came to a rodeo had a horse of their own back home. Farm people, ranch people — lord, they *knew* what they were lookin' at. Knew a good ride from a bad ride, knew hard from easy. You broke some bones er spent the day eatin' dirt, at least ya got appreciated.

Now they bought the rodeo. Them. Coca-Cola, Pepsi Cola, Marlboro damn cigarettes. You know the ones I mean. Them. Hire some New York faggot t' sit on some ol' stuffed horse in front of a sagebrush photo n' smoke that junk. Hell, tobacco wasn't made to smoke, honey, it was made to chew. Lord wanted ya filled up with smoke he would've set ya on fire. Damn it gets me!

There's some guy in a banker's suit runs the rodeo now. Got him a pinky ring and a digital watch, honey. Told us we oughta have a watchamacallit, choriographus or somethin', some ol' ballbuster used to be with the Ice damn Capades. Wants us to ride around dressed up like Mickey Mouse, Pluto, crap like that. Told me I had to haul my butt through the barrel race done up like Minnie damn Mouse in a tu-tu. Huh uh, honey! Them people is so screwed-up they probably eat what they run over in the road.

Listen, they got the clowns wearin' Astronaut suits! I ain't lyin'. You know what a rodeo clown does! You go down, fall off whatever — the clown runs in front of the bull so's ya don't git stomped. Pin-stripes, he got 'em in space suits tellin' jokes on a microphone. First horse see 'em, done up like the Star Wars went crazy. Best buckin' horse on the circuit, name of Piss 'N' Vinegar, took one look at them clowns, had him a heart attack and died. Cowboy was ridin' him got hisself squashed. Twelve hundred pounds of coronary arrest jes fell right through 'em. Blam! Vio con dios. Crowd thought that was funnier than the astronauts. I swear it won't be long before they're strappin' ice-skates on the ponies. Big crowds now.

Ain't hardly no ranch people, no farm people, nobody I know. Buncha disco babies and dee-vorce lawyers — designer jeans and day-glo Stetsons. Hell, the whole bunch of 'em wears French perfume. Oh it smells like money now! Got it on the cable T and V — hey, you know what, when ya rodeo yer just bound to kick yerself up some dust — well now, seems like that fogs up the ol' TV camera, so they told us a while back that from now on we was gonna ride on some new stuff called Astro-dirt. Dust free. Artificial damn dirt, honey. Lord have mercy.

Banker Suit called me in the other day said "Lurlene . . ." "Hold it," I said, "Who's this Lurlene? Round here they call me Big Eight." "Well, Big Eight," he said, "My name's Wallace." "Well that's a real surprise t' me," I said, "Cause aroun' here everybody jes calls you Dumb-ass." My, he laughed real big, slapped his big ol' desk, an' then he said I wasn't suitable for the rodeo no more. Said they was lookin' fer another type, somethin' a little more in the showgirl line, like the Dallas Cowgirls maybe. Said the ridin' and ropin' wasn't the thing no more. Talked on about floats, costumes, dancin' choreog-aphy. If I was a man I woulda pissed on his shoe. Said he'd give me a lifetime pass though. Said I could come to his rodeo any time I wanted.

Rodeo used to be people ridin' horses for the pleasure of people who rode horses — made you feel good about what you could do. Rodeo wasn't worth no money to nobody. Money didn't have nothing to do with it! Used to be seven Tilsons riding in the rodeo. Wouldn't none of 'em dress up like Donald damn Duck so they quit. That there's the law of gravity!

There's a bunch of assholes in this country sneak around until they see ya havin' fun and then they buy the fun and start in sellin' it. See, they figure if ya love it, they can sell it. Well you look out, honey! They want to make them a dollar out of what you love. Dress *you* up like Minnie Mouse. Sell your rodeo. Turn *yer* pleasure into Ice damn Capades. You hear what I'm sayin'? You're jus' merchandise to them, sweetie. You're jus' merchandise to them.

Blackout.

CONSIDERATIONS FOR CRITICAL THINKING AND WRITING

1. FIRST RESPONSE. Big Eight is presented as an old-fashioned rodeo type. What associations or stereotypes do you have about such people? What assumptions do you make about them? How does the author use those expectations to heighten your understanding of Big Eight's character?

2. How has the rodeo changed from how it "used to be"? How do you account for those changes?

3. Comment on Big Eight's use of language. Why is it appropriate for her character?

4. How would you describe Big Eight's brand of humor? How does it affect your understanding of her?

5. How do your feelings about Big Eight develop during the course of the monologue?

6. What does the rodeo mean to Big Eight?

CONNECTIONS TO OTHER SELECTIONS

1. Compare and contrast a Shakespeare monologue from either *Hamlet* (p. 1450) or *A Midsummer Night's Dream* (p. 1394) with the style and content of *Rodeo*.

2. In an essay discuss the nostalgic tone in *Rodeo* and Stephen Crane's short story "The Bride Comes to Yellow Sky" (p. 251). In your response consider each work's treatment of the West.

3. Compare the attitudes expressed about merchandising in *Rodeo* with those expressed in Arthur Miller's *Death of a Salesman* (p. 1824).

Los Vendidos

Born in Delano, California, in 1940, Luis Valdez grew up in a family of migrant farm workers. After graduating as a literature major in 1964 from San Jose State College, he became an actor with the San Francisco Mime Troupe. In 1965, he founded El Teatro Campesino (The Farmworkers Theater), which performed brief satirical plays in public spaces in support of oppressed farm workers. These plays incorporated the exaggerated humor of mime plays in order to make serious political points about Chicano experiences. Among his plays focusing on Chicano life are *The Shrunken Head of Pancho Villa* (1968), *Dark Root of a Scream* (1971), *Zoot Suit* (1978), and *I Don't Have to Show You No Stinking Badges* (1986). In 1987 he wrote and directed *La Bamba* (1986), a film biography of the 1950s rock singer Ritchie Valens.

Los Vendidos was first performed in 1967 for El Teatro Campesino and was awarded an Emmy in 1972. In this brief play Valdez deftly explores whites' stereotypical images of Mexicans while also exposing those who willingly play stereotypical roles.

Research Luis Valdez with LitLinks at
http://www.bedfordstmartins.com/meyer/bedintrolit

LUIS VALDEZ (B. 1940)
Los Vendidos°   1967

CHARACTERS

Honest Sancho	*Johnny [Pachuco]*
Secretary	*Revolucionario*
Farm Worker	*Mexican American*

SCENE: *Honest Sancho's Used Mexican Lot and Mexican Curio Shop. Three models are on display in Honest Sancho's shop. To the right, there is a Revolucionario, complete with*

Los Vendidos: The Sellouts.

sombrero, carrilleras,° *and carabina 30-30.*° *At center, on the floor, there is the Farm Worker,*
under a broad straw sombrero. At stage left is the Pachuco, filero° *in hand. Honest Sancho is*
moving among his models, dusting them off and preparing for another day of business.

Sancho: Bueno, bueno, mis monos, vamos a ver a quién vendemos ahora, ¿no?°
  (To audience.) ¡Quihubo!° I'm Honest Sancho and this is my shop. Antes
  fui contratista, pero ahora logré mi negocito.° All I need now is a customer.
  (A bell rings offstage.) Ay, a customer!

Secretary (entering): Good morning, I'm Miss Jimenez from . . .

Sancho: Ah, una chicana! Welcome, welcome Señorita Jiménez.

Secretary (Anglo pronunciation): JIM-enez.

Sancho: ¿Qué?°

Secretary: My name is Miss JIM-enez. Don't you speak English? What's wrong
  with you?

Sancho: Oh, nothing, Señorita JIM-enez. I'm here to help you.

Secretary: That's better. As I was starting to say, I'm a secretary from Governor
  Reagan's office, and we're looking for a Mexican type for the administration.

Sancho: Well, you come to the right place, lady. This is Honest Sancho's Used
  Mexican Lot, and we got all types here. Any particular type you want?

Secretary: Yes, we were looking for somebody suave . . .

Sancho: Suave.

Secretary: Debonair.

Sancho: De buen aire.

Secretary: Dark.

Sancho: Prieto.

Secretary: But of course, not too dark.

Sancho: No muy prieto.

Secretary: Perhaps, beige.

Sancho: Beige, just the tone. Asi como cafecito con leche,° ¿no?

Secretary: One more thing. He must be hardworking.

Sancho: That could only be one model. Step right over here to the center of the
  shop, lady. *(They cross to the Farm Worker.)* This is our standard farm worker
  model. As you can see, in the words of our beloved Senator George Murphy, he is "built close to the ground." Also, take special notice of his 4-ply
  Goodyear huaraches,° made from the rain tire. This wide-brimmed sombrero is an extra added feature; keeps off the sun, rain, and dust.

Secretary: Yes, it does look durable.

Sancho: And our farm worker model is friendly. Muy amable.° Watch. *(Snaps*
  his fingers.)

Farm Worker (lifts up head): Buenos días, señorita. *(His head drops.)*

Secretary: My, he is friendly.

Sancho: Didn't I tell you? Loves his patrones!° But his most attractive feature is
  that he's hard-working. Let me show you. *(Snaps fingers. Farm Worker stands.)*

Farm Worker: ¡El jale!° *(He begins to work.)*

---

carrilleras . . . 30-30: Cartridge belts and 30-30 rifle. *filero:* Knife. *Bueno . . . Quihubo!:*
Good, good, my cuties, let's see who we can sell now. Hey! *Antes fui . . . negocito:* I used to
be a contractor, but now I run my own little business. *¿Qué?:* What? *Asi . . . leche:* Like
coffee with milk. *huaraches:* Sandals. *Muy amable:* Very friendly. *patrones:* Bosses.
¡El jale!: The job.

Sancho: As you can see he is cutting grapes.

Secretary: Oh, I wouldn't know.

Sancho: He also picks cotton. *(Snaps. Farm Worker begins to pick cotton.)*

Secretary: Versatile, isn't he?

Sancho: He also picks melons. *(Snaps. Farm Worker picks melons.)* That's his slow speed for late in the season. Here's his fast speed. *(Snap. Farm Worker picks faster.)*

Secretary: Chihuahua° . . . I mean, goodness, he sure is a hard worker.

Sancho (pulls the Farm Worker to his feet): And that isn't the half of it. Do you see these little holes on his arms that appear to be pores? During those hot sluggish days in the field when the vines or the branches get so entangled, it's almost impossible to move, these holes emit a certain grease that allows our model to slip and slide right through the crop with no trouble at all.

Secretary: Wonderful. But is he economical?

Sancho: Economical? Señorita, you are looking at the Volkswagen of Mexicans. Pennies a day is all it takes. One plate of beans and tortillas will keep him going all day. That, and chile. Plenty of chile. Chile jalapeños, chile verde, chile colorado. But, of course, if you do give him chile *(Snap. Farm Worker turns left face. Snap. Farm Worker bends over.),* then you have to change his oil filter once a week.

Secretary: What about storage?

Sancho: No problem. You know these new farm labor camps our Honorable Governor Reagan has built out by Parlier or Raisin City? They were designed with our model in mind. Five, six, seven, even ten in one of those shacks will give you no trouble at all. You can also put him in old barns, old cars, riverbanks. You can even leave him out in the field overnight with no worry!

Secretary: Remarkable.

Sancho: And here's an added feature: every year at the end of the season, this model goes back to Mexico and doesn't return, automatically, until next spring.

Secretary: How about that. But tell me, does he speak English?

Sancho: Another outstanding feature is that last year this model was programmed to go out on STRIKE! *(Snap.)*

Farm Worker: ¡Huelga! ¡Huelga! Hermanos, sálganse de esos files.° *(Snap. He stops.)*

Secretary: No! Oh no, we can't strike in the State Capitol.

Sancho: Well, he also scabs. *(Snap.)*

Farm Worker: Me vendo barato, ¿y qué?° *(Snap.)*

Secretary: That's much better, but you didn't answer my question. Does he speak English?

Sancho: Bueno . . . no, pero° he has other . . .

Secretary: No.

Sancho: Other features.

Secretary: No! He just won't do!

Sancho: Okay, okay, pues.° We have other models.

Secretary: I hope so. What we need is something a little more sophisticated.

Chihuahua: Hot damn!   *¡Huelga! . . . files:* Strike! strike! Brothers, leave those rows.   *Me vendo . . . qué?:* I come cheap, so what?   *Bueno . . . pero:* Well . . . no, but.   *pues:* Then.

Sancho: Sophisti-qué?

Secretary: An urban model.

Sancho: Ah, from the city! Step right back. Over here in this corner of the shop is exactly what you're looking for. Introducing our new 1969 JOHNNY PACHUCO° model! This is our fast-back model. Streamlined. Built for speed, low-riding, city life. Take a look at some of these features. Mag shoes, dual exhausts, green chartreuse paint-job, dark-tint windshield, a little poof on top. Let me just turn him on. (*Snap. Johnny walks to stage center with a Pachuco bounce.*)

Secretary: What was that?

Sancho: That, señorita, was the Chicano shuffle.

Secretary: Okay, what does he do?

Sancho: Anything and everything necessary for city life. For instance, survival: he knife fights. (*Snaps. Johnny pulls out switchblade and swings at Secretary. Secretary screams.*) He dances. (*Snap.*)

Johnny (singing): "Angel Baby, my Angel Baby . . ." (*Snap.*)

Sancho: And here's a feature no city model can be without. He gets arrested, but not without resisting, of course. (*Snap.*)

Johnny: En la madre, la placa.° I didn't do it! I didn't do it!

> (*Johnny turns and stands up against an imaginary wall, legs spread out, arms behind his back.*)

Secretary: Oh no, we can't have arrests! We must maintain law and order.

Sancho: But he's bilingual.

Secretary: Bilingual?

Sancho: Simón que yes. He speaks English! Johnny, give us some English. (*Snap.*)

Johnny (comes downstage): Fuck-you!

Secretary (gasps): Oh! I've never been so insulted in my whole life!

Sancho: Well, he learned it in your school.

Secretary: I don't care where he learned it.

Sancho: But he's economical.

Secretary: Economical?

Sancho: Nickels and dimes. You can keep Johnny running on hamburgers, Taco Bell tacos, Lucky Lager beer, Thunderbird wine, yesca . . .

Secretary: Yesca?

Sancho: Mota.

Secretary: Mota?

Sancho: Leños . . . marijuana. (*Snap. Johnny inhales on an imaginary joint.*)

Secretary: That's against the law!

Johnny (big smile, holding his breath): Yeah.

Sancho: He also sniffs glue. (*Snap. Johnny inhales glue, big smile.*)

Johnny: Tha's too much, man, ése.°

Secretary: No, Mr. Sancho, I don't think this . . .

Sancho: Wait a minute, he has other qualities I know you'll love. For example, an inferiority complex. (*Snap.*)

Pachuco: Slang for an urban tough.   *En la . . . placa:* Uh, oh, the cops.   *Ése:* Buddy, dude.

Johnny (to Sancho): You think you're better than me, huh, ése? *(Swings switch-blade.)*

Sancho: He can also be beaten and he bruises. Cut him and he bleeds, kick him and he . . . *(He beats, bruises and kicks Pachuco.)* Would you like to try it?

Secretary: Oh, I couldn't.

Sancho: Be my guest. He's a great scapegoat.

Secretary: No really.

Sancho: Please.

Secretary: Well, all right. Just once. *(She kicks Pachuco.)* Oh, he's so soft.

Sancho: Wasn't that good? Try again.

Secretary (kicks Pachuco): Oh, he's wonderful! *(She kicks him again.)*

Sancho: Okay, that's enough, lady. You'll ruin the merchandise. Yes, our Johnny Pachuco model can give you many hours of pleasure. Why, the LAPD just bought twenty of these to train their rookie cops on. And talk about maintenance. Señorita, you are looking at an entirely self-supporting machine. You're never going to find our Johnny Pachuco model on the relief rolls. No, sir, this model knows how to liberate.

Secretary: Liberate?

Sancho: He steals. *(Snap. Johnny rushes to Secretary and steals her purse.)*

Johnny: ¡Dame esa bolsa, vieja!° *(He grabs the purse and runs. Snap by Sancho, he stops. Secretary runs after Johnny and grabs purse away from him, kicking him as she goes.)*

Secretary: No, no, no! We can't have any more thieves in the State Administration. Put him back.

Sancho: Okay, we still got other models. Come on, Johnny, we'll sell you to some old lady. *(Sancho takes Johnny back to his place.)*

Secretary: Mr. Sancho, I don't think you quite understand what we need. What we need is something that will attract the women voters. Something more traditional, more romantic.

Sancho: Ah, a lover. *(He smiles meaningfully.)* Step right over here, señorita. Introducing our standard Revolucionario and/or Early California Bandit type. As you can see, he is well-built, sturdy, durable. This is the International Harvester of Mexicans.

Secretary: What does he do?

Sancho: You name it, he does it. He rides horses, stays in the mountains, crosses deserts, plains, rivers, leads revolutions, follows revolutions, kills, can be killed, serves as a martyr, hero, movie star. Did I say movie star? Did you ever see *Viva Zapata? Viva Villa, Villa Rides, Pancho Villa Returns, Pancho Villa Goes Back, Pancho Villa Meets Abbott and Costello?*

Secretary: I've never seen any of those.

Sancho: Well, he was in all of them. Listen to this. *(Snap.)*

Revolucionario (scream): ¡Viva Villaaaaa!

Secretary: That's awfully loud.

Sancho: He has a volume control. *(He adjusts volume. Snap.)*

Revolucionario (mousey voice): Viva Villa.

Secretary: That's better.

¡Dame . . . vieja!: Give me that bag, old lady!

Sancho: And even if you didn't see him in the movies, perhaps you saw him on TV. He makes commercials. (*Snap.*)

Revolucionario: Is there a Frito Bandito in your house?

Secretary: Oh, yes, I've seen that one!

Sancho: Another feature about this one is that he is economical. He runs on raw horsemeat and tequila!

Secretary: Isn't that rather savage?

Sancho: Al contrario,° it makes him a lover. (*Snap.*)

Revolucionario (to Secretary): Ay, mamasota, cochota, ven pa 'ca!° (*He grabs Secretary and folds her back, Latin-lover style.*)

Sancho (Snap. Revolucionario goes back upright.): Now wasn't that nice?

Secretary: Well, it was rather nice.

Sancho: And finally, there is one outstanding feature about this model I know the ladies are going to love: he's a genuine antique! He was made in Mexico in 1910!

Secretary: Made in Mexico?

Sancho: That's right. Once in Tijuana, twice in Guadalajara, three times in Cuernavaca.

Secretary: Mr. Sancho, I thought he was an American product.

Sancho: No, but . . .

Secretary: No, I'm sorry. We can't buy anything but American made products. He just won't do.

Sancho: But he's an antique!

Secretary: I don't care. You still don't understand what we need. It's true we need Mexican models, such as these, but it's more important that he be American.

Sancho: American?

Secretary: That's right, and judging from what you've shown me, I don't think you have what we want. Well, my lunch hour's almost over, I better . . .

Sancho: Wait a minute! Mexican but American?

Secretary: That's correct.

Sancho: Mexican but . . . (*A sudden flash.*) American! Yeah, I think we've got exactly what you want. He just came in today! Give me a minute. (*He exits. Talks from backstage.*) Here he is in the shop. Let me just get some papers off. There. Introducing our new 1970 Mexican American! Ta-ra-ra-raaaa! (*Sancho brings out the Mexican American model, a clean-shaven middle class type in a business suit, with glasses.*)

Secretary (impressed): Where have you been hiding this one?

Sancho: He just came in this morning. Ain't he a beauty? Feast your eyes on him! Sturdy U.S. Steel frame, streamlined, modern. As a matter of fact, he is built exactly like our Anglo models, except that he comes in a variety of darker shades: naugahyde, leather, or leatherette.

Secretary: Naugahyde.

Sancho: Well, we'll just write that down. Yes, señorita, this model represents the apex of American engineering! He is bilingual, college educated, ambitious! Say the word "acculturate" and he accelerates. He is intelligent, well-mannered, clean. Did I say clean? (*Snap. Mexican American raises his arm.*) Smell.

Al contrario: On the contrary.   *Ay . . . pa 'ca!:* Hey, c'mere, big mama!

Secretary (smells): Old Sobaco,° my favorite.

Sancho (Snap. Mexican American turns toward Sancho.): Eric? *(To Secretary.)* We call him Eric García. *(To Eric.)* I want you to meet Miss JIM-enez, Eric.

Mexican American: Miss JIM-enez, I am delighted to make your acquaintance. *(He kisses her hand.)*

Secretary: Oh, my, how charming!

Sancho: Did you feel the suction? He has seven especially engineered suction cups right behind his lips. He's a charmer all right!

Secretary: How about boards, does he function on boards?

Sancho: You name them, he is on them. Parole boards, draft boards, school boards, taco quality control boards, surf boards, two by fours.

Secretary: Does he function in politics?

Sancho: Señorita, you are looking at a political machine. Have you ever heard of the OEO, EOC, COD, WAR ON POVERTY? That's our model! Not only that, he makes political speeches.

Secretary: May I hear one?

Sancho: With pleasure. *(Snap.)* Eric, give us a speech.

Mexican American: Mr. Congressman, Mr. Chairman, members of the board, honored guests, ladies and gentlemen. *(Sancho and Secretary applaud.)* Please, please. I come before you as a Mexican American to tell you about the problems of the Mexican. The problems of the Mexican stem from one thing and one thing only: he's stupid. He's uneducated. He needs to stay in school. He needs to be ambitious, forward-looking, harder-working. He needs to think American, American, American, American, American! God bless America! God bless America! God bless America! *(He goes out of control. Sancho snaps frantically and the Mexican American finally slumps forward, bending at the waist.)*

Secretary: Oh my, he's patriotic too!

Sancho: Sí, señorita, he loves his country. Let me just make a little adjustment here. *(Stands Mexican American up.)*

Secretary: What about upkeep? Is he economical?

Sancho: Well, no, I won't lie to you. The Mexican American costs a little bit more, but you get what you pay for. He's worth every extra cent. You can keep him running on dry Martinis, Langendorf bread . . .

Secretary: Apple pie?

Sancho: Only Mom's. Of course, he's also programmed to eat Mexican food on ceremonial functions, but I must warn you, an overdose of beans will plug up his exhaust.

Secretary: Fine! There's just one more question: How much do you want for him?

Sancho: Well, I tell you what I'm gonna do. Today and today only, because you've been so sweet, I'm gonna let you steal this model from me! I'm gonna let you drive him off the lot for the simple price of, let's see, taxes and license included, $15,000.

Secretary: Fifteen thousand dollars? For a Mexican!!!!

Sancho: Mexican? What are you talking about? This is a Mexican American! We had to melt down two pachucos, a farm worker and three gabachos° to make this model! You want quality, but you gotta pay for it! This is no cheap run-about. He's got class!

Sobaco: Armpit.   *Gabachos:* whites.

Secretary: Okay, I'll take him.

Sancho: You will?

Secretary: Here's your money.

Sancho: You mind if I count it?

Secretary: Go right ahead.

Sancho: Well, you'll get your pink slip in the mail. Oh, do you want me to wrap him up for you? We have a box in the back.

Secretary: No, thank you. The Governor is having a luncheon this afternoon, and we need a brown face in the crowd. How do I drive him?

Sancho: Just snap your fingers. He'll do anything you want. *(Secretary snaps. Mexican American steps forward.)*

Mexican American: ¡Raza querida, vamos levantando armas para liberarnos de estos desgraciados gabachos que nos explotan! Vamos . . .°

Secretary: What did he say?

Sancho: Something about taking up arms, killing white people, etc.

Secretary: But he's not supposed to say that!

Sancho: Look, lady, don't blame me for bugs from the factory. He's your Mexican American, you bought him, now drive him off the lot!

Secretary: But he's broken!

Sancho: Try snapping another finger. *(Secretary snaps. Mexican American comes to life again.)*

Mexican American: Esta gran humanidad ha dicho basta! ¡Y se ha puesto en marcha! ¡Basta! ¡Basta! ¡Viva la raza! ¡Viva la causa! ¡Viva la huelga! ¡Vivan los brown berets! ¡Vivan los estudiantes!° ¡Chicano power! *(The Mexican American turns toward the Secretary, who gasps and backs up. He keeps turning toward the Pachuco, Farm Worker, and Revolucionario, snapping his fingers and turning each of them on, one by one.)*

Pachuco (Snap. To Secretary.): I'm going to get you, baby! ¡Viva la raza!

Farm Worker (Snap. To Secretary.): ¡Viva la huelga! ¡Viva la huelga! ¡Viva la huelga!

Revolucionario (Snap. To Secretary.): ¡Viva la revolución! *(The three models join together and advance toward the Secretary, who backs up and runs out of the shop screaming. Sancho is at the other end of the shop holding his money in his hand. All freeze. After a few seconds of silence, the Pachuco moves and stretches, shaking his arms and loosening up. The Farm Worker and Revolucionario do the same. Sancho stays where he is, frozen to his spot.)*

Johnny: Man, that was a long one, ése. *(Others agree with him.)*

Farm Worker: How did we do?

Johnny: Pretty good, look at all that lana,° man! *(He goes over to Sancho and removes the money from his hand. Sancho stays where he is.)*

Revolucionario: En la madre, look at all the money.

Johnny: We keep this up, we're going to be rich.

Farm Worker: They think we're machines.

Revolucionario: Burros.

Johnny: Puppets.

¡Raza querida . . . Vamos: Beloved members of our Mexican race, let's take up arms to free ourselves from those damned whites who exploit us! Let's go!   Esta . . . estudiantes!: This great mass of humanity has had enough! And it has begun to march! Enough! Enough! Long live our race! Long live our cause! Long live the strike! Long live the brown berets! Long live the students!   lana: Money.

Mexican American: The only thing I don't like is how come I always get to play the goddamn Mexican American?
Johnny: That's what you get for finishing high school.
Farm Worker: How about our wages, ése?
Johnny: Here it comes right now, $3,000 for you, $3,000 for you, $3,000 for you and $3,000 for me. The rest we put back into the business.
Mexican American: Too much, man. Hey, where you vatos° going tonight?
Farm Worker: I'm going over to Concha's. There's a party.
Johnny: Wait a minute, vatos. What about our salesman? I think he needs an oil job.
Revolucionario: Leave him to me. *(The Pachuco, Farm Worker, and Mexican American exit, talking loudly about their plans for the night. The Revolucionario goes over to Sancho, removes his derby hat and cigar, lifts him up and throws him over his shoulder. Sancho hangs loose, lifeless. To audience.)* He's the best model we got! ¡Ajúa!° *(Exit.)*

vatos: Guys.   ¡*Ajúa!*: A jubilant exclamation.

CONSIDERATIONS FOR CRITICAL THINKING AND WRITING

1. FIRST RESPONSE. How do you respond to the ending of the play? Were you surprised? How does the ending contribute to the play's themes?
2. What kind of racial stereotypes are represented by the play's six characters? How are the characters differentiated from each other?
3. Consider whether or not the racial stereotypes in *Los Vendidos* remain relevant as social issues decades after its first production in 1967.
4. Do you identify with any of the characters? Explain why or why not.
5. Why can't this play be accurately described as a work of realism?
6. Comment on the significance of the title.
7. CRITICAL STRATEGIES. Read the section on historical criticism (pp. 2101–05) in Chapter 52, "Critical Strategies for Reading," and research the politics of Governor Ronald Reagan and Senator George Murphy when they served in California during the 1960s. How do the allusions to Reagan and Murphy provide a political context for the conflicts in the plot?

CONNECTIONS TO OTHER SELECTIONS

1. Discuss the themes in *Los Vendidos* and M. Carl Holman's poem "Mr. Z" (p. 1162).
2. How is merchandising made an important issue in this play and in Jane Martin's *Rodeo* (p. 1656)?

48

A Cultural Case Study:
David Henry Hwang's
M. Butterfly

Formalist readings of plays examine how various elements — such as setting, exposition, dialogue, characterization, conflict, subplot, climax, resolution, and other literary techniques — create patterns that contribute to the play's meanings or themes. This kind of close reading emphasizes the intrinsic elements of a work to describe and appreciate how it is artistically unified. Rather than taking the social, political, and economic contexts of a play into account, formalist critics focus on how literary elements within the play interact to produce a coherent and carefully made work of art. A formalist, for example, might approach Susan Glaspell's *Trifles* (p. 1238) by discussing how its opening setting establishes the play's tone. More than a whodunit, *Trifles* examines the nature of Mrs. Wright's married life rather than her guilt or innocence concerning the death of her husband. In the opening scene, the stage directions make clear the stark, gloomy kitchen that evokes the hard life Mr. Wright imposed on his wife. Through this cold environment, the Wrights' difficult relationship is subtly recapitulated by the dark, disordered setting. A formalist's analysis would be concerned with how the setting frames the theme rather than with the actual conditions of living on a midwestern farm in the early twentieth century. Recently, however, there has been an increased interest among literary critics in the historical and cultural contexts of texts.

Like literary historians, cultural critics examine the historical circumstances relevant to a work, but they do not emphasize only major events or famous historical figures. A literary historian would be intrigued by the fact that Glaspell's *Trifles* was written to complete a theater bill that featured several one-act plays by Eugene O'Neill produced by the Provincetown Players on Cape Cod, Massachusetts, in 1916. Glaspell's relationship to O'Neill, generally regarded as one of America's greatest dramatists, certainly would not escape the interest of a cultural critic, but such a critic might find even more revealing Glaspell's experiences as a newspaper reporter covering a murder trial in Iowa. She recalls that she "never forgot going to the kitchen of a woman who had been locked up [for murder] in town." The interests of cultural critics embrace popular culture as well as "high culture." A cultural critic is likely to find more relevant to *Trifles* the Federal Farm Loan Bank Act passed in 1916 than O'Neill's *Bound East for Cardiff,* one of the 1916 one-act plays written for the Provincetown Players.

The documents that follow Hwang's *M. Butterfly* in this chapter suggest how cultural criticism can be used to ask new questions of a literary work. They include a plot synopsis of Giacomo Puccini's opera *Madame Butterfly,* the newspaper source for *M. Butterfly,* a photograph of Shi Pei Pu (model for Hwang's Song Liling) dressed in the costume of a Chinese opera star, a review of a performance of *M. Butterfly,* and an interview with Hwang. These documents provide a glimpse of some approaches that a cultural critic might use to contextualize *M. Butterfly* historically in order to offer a wider and deeper understanding of the play.

DAVID HENRY HWANG
(B. 1957)

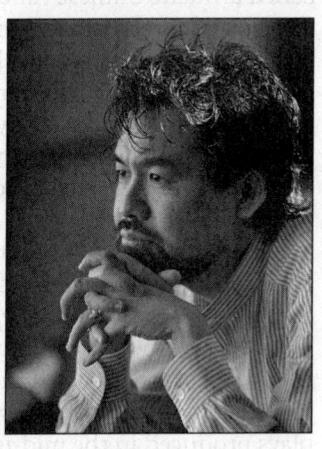

Born in Los Angeles, David Henry Hwang is the son of immigrant Chinese American parents; his father worked as a banker, and his mother was a professor of piano. Educated at Stanford University, from which he earned his B.A. in English in 1979, he became interested in theater after attending plays at the American Conservatory in San Francisco. His marginal interest in a law career quickly gave way to his involvement in the engaging world of live theater. By his senior year, he had written and produced his first play, *FOB* (an acronym for "fresh off the boat"), which marked the beginning of a meteoric rise as a playwright. After a brief stint as a writing teacher at a Menlo Park high school, Hwang attended the Yale University School of Drama from 1980 to 1981. Although he didn't stay to complete a degree, he studied theater history before leaving for New York City, where he thought the professional theater would provide a richer education than the student workshops at Yale.

In New York Hwang's work received a warm reception. In 1980 an off-Broadway production of *FOB* won an Obie Award for the best new play of the season. The play incorporates many of Hwang's characteristic concerns as a playwright. Growing up in California as a Chinese American made him politically conscious during his college years in the late 1970s; this interest in his Chinese roots is evident in the central conflicts of *FOB*, which focuses on a Chinese immigrant's relationship with two Chinese American students he meets in Los Angeles. The immigrant quickly learns that he is expected to abandon much of his Chinese identity if he is to fit into mainstream American culture. The issues that arise between East and West are played out with comic effect in a Western theater but enriched and complicated by Hwang's innovative use of a Chinese theatrical tradition that portrays major characters as figures from Chinese mythology.

Chinese American life is also the focus of *The Dance and the Railroad* and *Family Devotions,* both produced off-Broadway in 1981. *The Dance and the Railroad,* set in the nineteenth century, focuses on two immigrant Chinese men working on the transcontinental railroad and attempting to sort out their pasts while confronting new identities and uncertain futures in America. Hwang mirrors the characters' conflicts in the play's form by creating a mixture of Eastern and Western theater and incorporating the nonrealistic modes of Chinese opera. *Family Devotions* examines an established affluent Chinese American family in the twentieth century through the lens of a television sitcom. The problems faced by immigrants living hyphenated lives are comically played out through the interaction of a visiting Communist uncle from China and his great-nephew, who struggles to find an authentic identity amid his family's materialism and Christianity. Hwang's early plays are populated with Chinese Americans attempting to find the center of their own lives as they seesaw between the conventions, traditions, and values of East and West.

Hwang's next two dramas, produced in 1983, consist of two one-act plays set in Japan. Together they are titled *Sound and Beauty,* but each has its own title — *The House of Sleeping Beauties* and *The Sound of a Voice.* In these plays Hwang moves away from tales of Chinese American immigrants and themes of race and assimilation to stories about tragic love based on Japanese materials. Although Hwang was successful in having additional plays produced in the mid-1980s and won prestigious fellowships from the Guggenheim Foundation and the National Endowment for the Arts, it was not until 1988, when *M. Butterfly* was produced on Broadway, that he achieved astonishing commercial success as well as widespread acclaim. His awards for this play include the Outer Critics Circle Award for best Broadway play, the Drama Desk Award for best new play, the John Gassner Award for best American play, and the Tony Award for best play of the year. By the end of 1988, Hwang was regarded by many critics as the most talented young playwright in the United States, and since then *M. Butterfly* has been staged in theaters around the world.

According to Hwang, *M. Butterfly* was inspired by newspaper accounts of an espionage trial. In his "Playwright's Notes" he cites an excerpt from the *New York Times* for May 11, 1986 (see p. 1719 for the entire news report). Hwang takes this fascinating true story of espionage and astonishing sexual misidentification and transforms it into a complex treatment of social, political, racial, cultural, and sexual issues that has dazzled both audiences and readers with its remarkable eroticism, insights, and beauty.

CHRONOLOGY

1957	Born on August 11 in Los Angeles, California.
1957–1979	Attends Stanford University, graduates with a B.A. in English.
1978	First play, *FOB*, produced at Stanford.
1979	Teaches at a high school in Menlo Park, California.
1980–81	Attends Yale University School of Drama.
1980	Wins Obie Award for *FOB*.
1981	*The Dance and the Railroad* and *Family Devotions* produced in New York City.
1983	*The House of Sleeping Beauties* and *The Sound of a Voice* produced off-Broadway; publishes *Broken Promises: Four Plays;* awarded Rockefeller Fellowship.
1984	Awarded a Guggenheim Fellowship.
1985	Awarded a National Endowment for the Arts Fellowship.
1986	*Rich Relations* produced off-Broadway; *As the Crow Flies* produced in Los Angeles.
1987	*My American Son*, a television drama, airs on Home Box Office.
1988	*M. Butterfly* produced on Broadway and wins the Outer Critics Circle Award, Drama Desk Award, John Gassner Award, and Tony Award; establishes the American Playwrights Project; *1000 Airplanes on the Roof* produced in Vienna, Austria.
1989	Publishes *1000 Airplanes on the Roof.*
1990	Publishes *FOB and Other Plays.*
1991	*Bondage* produced.
1992	*Face Value* and *The Voyage* (libretto for opera) produced.
1997	*Seven Years in Tibet* (screenplay for film).

Research David Henry Hwang with LitLinks at
http://www.bedfordstmartins.com/meyer/bedintrolit

DAVID HENRY HWANG (B. 1957)

M. Butterfly

1988

THE CHARACTERS

Rene Gallimard
Song Liling
Marc/Man No. 2/Consul Sharpless
Renee/Woman at Party/Pinup Girl
Comrade Chin/Suzuki/Shu-Fang
Helga
Toulon/Man No. 1/Judge
Dancers

TIME AND PLACE

The action of the play takes place in a Paris prison in the present, and, in recall, during the decade 1960–1970 in Beijing, and from 1966 to the present in Paris.

PLAYWRIGHT'S NOTES

A former French diplomat and a Chinese opera singer have been sentenced to six years in jail for spying for China after a two-day trial that traced a story of clandestine love and mistaken sexual identity....

Mr. Boursicot was accused of passing information to China after he fell in love with Mr. Shi, whom he believed for twenty years to be a woman.

— The New York Times, May 11, 1986

This play was suggested by international newspaper accounts of a recent espionage trial. For purposes of dramatization, names have been changed, characters created, and incidents devised or altered, and this play does not purport to be a factual record of real events or real people.

> I could escape this feeling
> With my China girl ...
> — David Bowie & Iggy Pop

ACT I

SCENE I

M. Gallimard's prison cell. Paris. 1988.

Lights fade up to reveal Rene Gallimard, sixty-five, in a prison cell. He wears a comfortable bathrobe and looks old and tired. The sparsely furnished cell contains a wooden crate, upon which sits a hot plate with a kettle and a portable tape recorder. Gallimard sits on the crate staring at the recorder, a sad smile on his face.

Upstage Song, who appears as a beautiful woman in traditional Chinese garb, dances a traditional piece from the Peking Opera, surrounded by the percussive clatter of Chinese music.

Then, slowly, lights and sound cross-fade; the Chinese opera music dissolves into a Western opera, the "Love Duet" from Puccini's Madame Butterfly. *Song continues dancing, now to the Western accompaniment. Though her movements are the same, the difference in music now gives them a balletic quality.*

Gallimard rises, and turns upstage towards the figure of Song, who dances without acknowledging him.

Gallimard: Butterfly, Butterfly . . .

He forces himself to turn away, as the image of Song fades out, and talks to us.

Gallimard: The limits of my cell are as such: four-and-a-half meters by five. There's one window against the far wall; a door, very strong, to protect me from autograph hounds. I'm responsible for the tape recorder, the hot plate, and this charming coffee table.

When I want to eat, I'm marched off to the dining room — hot, steaming slop appears on my plate. When I want to sleep, the light bulb turns itself off — the work of fairies. It's an enchanted space I occupy. The French — we know how to run a prison.

But, to be honest, I'm not treated like an ordinary prisoner. Why? Because I'm a celebrity. You see, I make people laugh.

I never dreamed this day would arrive. I've never been considered witty or clever. In fact, as a young boy, in an informal poll among my grammar school classmates, I was voted "least likely to be invited to a party." It's a title I managed to hold on to for many years. Despite some stiff competition.

But now, how the tables turn! Look at me: the life of every social function in Paris. Paris? Why be modest: My fame has spread to Amsterdam, London, New York. Listen to them! In the world's smartest parlors. I'm the one who lifts their spirits!

With a flourish, Gallimard directs our attention to another part of the stage.

Scene II

A party. 1988.

Lights go up on a chic-looking parlor, where a well-dressed trio, two men and one woman, make conversation. Gallimard also remains lit; he observes them from his cell.

Woman: And what of Gallimard?

Man 1: Gallimard?

Man 2: Gallimard!

Gallimard (to us): You see? They're all determined to say my name, as if it were some new dance.

Woman: He still claims not to believe the truth.

Man 1: What? Still? Even since the trial?

Woman: Yes. Isn't it mad?

Man 2 (laughing): He says . . . it was dark . . . and she was very modest!

The trio break into laughter.

Man 1: So — what? He never touched her with his hands?

Man 2: Perhaps he did, and simply misidentified the equipment. A compelling case for sex education in the schools.

Woman: To protect the National Security — the Church can't argue with that.
Man 1: That's impossible! How could he not know?
Man 2: Simple ignorance.
Man 1: For twenty years?
Man 2: Time flies when you're being stupid.
Woman: Well, I thought the French were ladies' men.
Man 2: It seems Monsieur Gallimard was overly anxious to live up to his national reputation.
Woman: Well, he's not very good-looking.
Man 1: No, he's not.
Man 2: Certainly not.
Woman: Actually, I feel sorry for him.
Man 2: A toast! To Monsieur Gallimard!
Woman: Yes! To Gallimard!
Man 1: To Gallimard!
Man 2: *Vive la différence!*

They toast, laughing. Lights down on them.

SCENE III

M. Gallimard's cell.

Gallimard (smiling): You see? They toast me. I've become a patron saint of the socially inept. Can they really be so foolish? Men like that — they should be scratching at my door, begging to learn my secrets! For I, Rene Gallimard, you see, I have known, and been loved by . . . the Perfect Woman.

Alone in this cell, I sit night after night, watching our story play through my head, always searching for a new ending, one which redeems my honor, where she returns at last to my arms. And I imagine you — my ideal audience — who come to understand and even, perhaps just a little, to envy me.

He turns on his tape recorder. Over the house speakers, we hear the opening phrases of Madame Butterfly.

Gallimard: In order for you to understand what I did and why, I must introduce you to my favorite opera: *Madame Butterfly.* By Giacomo Puccini. First produced at La Scala, Milan, in 1904, it is now beloved throughout the Western world.

As Gallimard describes the opera, the tape segues in and out to sections he may be describing.

Gallimard: And why not? Its heroine, Cio-Cio-San, also known as Butterfly, is a feminine ideal, beautiful and brave. And its hero, the man for whom she gives up everything, is — *(He pulls out a naval officer's cap from under his crate, pops it on his head, and struts about.)* — not very good-looking, not too bright, and pretty much a wimp: Benjamin Franklin Pinkerton of the U.S. Navy. As the curtain rises, he's just closed on two great bargains: one on a house, the other on a woman — call it a package deal.

Pinkerton purchased the rights to Butterfly for one hundred yen — in modern currency, equivalent to about . . . sixty-six cents. So, he's feeling pretty pleased with himself as Sharpless, the American consul, arrives to witness the marriage.

Marc, wearing an official cap to designate Sharpless, enters and plays the character.

Sharpless/Marc: Pinkerton!

Pinkerton/Gallimard: Sharpless! How's it hangin'? It's a great day, just great. Between my house, my wife, and the rickshaw ride in from town, I've saved nineteen cents just this morning.

Sharpless: Wonderful. I can see the inscription on your tombstone already: "I saved a dollar, here I lie." *(He looks around.)* Nice house.

Pinkerton: It's artistic. Artistic, don't you think? Like the way the shoji screens slide open to reveal the wet bar and disco mirror ball? Classy, huh? Great for impressing the chicks.

Sharpless: "Chicks"? Pinkerton, you're going to be a married man!

Pinkerton: Well, sort of.

Sharpless: What do you mean?

Pinkerton: This country—Sharpless, it is okay. You got all these geisha girls running around—

Sharpless: I know! I live here!

Pinkerton: Then, you know the marriage laws, right? I split for one month, it's annulled!

Sharpless: Leave it to you to read the fine print. Who's the lucky girl?

Pinkerton: Cio-Cio-San. Her friends call her Butterfly. Sharpless, she eats out of my hand!

Sharpless: She's probably very hungry.

Pinkerton: Not like American girls. It's true what they say about Oriental girls. They want to be treated bad!

Sharpless: Oh, please!

Pinkerton: It's true!

Sharpless: Are you serious about this girl?

Pinkerton: I'm marrying her, aren't I?

Sharpless: Yes—with generous trade-in terms.

Pinkerton: When I leave, she'll know what it's like to have loved a real man. And I'll even buy her a few nylons.

Sharpless: You aren't planning to take her with you?

Pinkerton: Huh? Where?

Sharpless: Home!

Pinkerton: You mean, America? Are you crazy? Can you see her trying to buy rice in St. Louis?

Sharpless: So, you're not serious.

   Pause.

Pinkerton/Gallimard (as Pinkerton): Consul, I am a sailor in port. *(As Gallimard.)* They then proceed to sing the famous duet, "The Whole World Over."

   The duet plays on the speakers. Gallimard, as Pinkerton, lip-syncs his lines from the opera.

Gallimard: To give a rough translation: "The whole world over, the Yankee travels, casting his anchor wherever he wants. Life's not worth living unless he can win the hearts of the fairest maidens, then hotfoot it off the premises ASAP." *(He turns towards Marc.)* In the preceding scene, I played Pinkerton, the womanizing cad, and my friend Marc from school . . . *(Marc bows grandly for our benefit.)* played Sharpless, the sensitive soul of reason. In life, however, our positions were usually — no, always — reversed.

SCENE IV

École Nationale.° Aix-en-Provence. 1947.

Gallimard: No, Marc, I think I'd rather stay home.

Marc: Are you crazy?! We are going to Dad's condo in Marseilles! You know what happened last time?

Gallimard: Of course I do.

Marc: Of course you don't! You never know. . . . They stripped, Rene!

Gallimard: Who stripped?

Marc: The girls!

Gallimard: Girls? Who said anything about girls?

Marc: Rene, we're a buncha university guys goin' up to the woods. What are we gonna do — talk philosophy?

Gallimard: What girls? Where do you get them?

Marc: Who cares? The point is, they come. On trucks. Packed in like sardines. The back flips open, babes hop out, we're ready to roll.

Gallimard: You mean, they just — ?

Marc: Before you know it, every last one of them — they're stripped and splashing around my pool. There's no moon out, they can't see what's going on, their boobs are flapping, right? You close your eyes, reach out — it's grab bag, get it? Doesn't matter whose ass is between whose legs, whose teeth are sinking into who. You're just in there, going at it, eyes closed, on and on for as long as you can stand. *(Pause.)* Some fun, huh?

Gallimard: What happens in the morning?

Marc: In the morning, you're ready to talk some philosophy. *(Beat.)* So how 'bout it?

Gallimard: Marc, I can't . . . I'm afraid they'll say no — the girls. So I never ask.

Marc: You don't have to ask! That's the beauty — don't you see? They don't have to say yes. It's perfect for a guy like you, really.

Gallimard: You go ahead . . . I may come later.

Marc: Hey, Rene — it doesn't matter that you're clumsy and got zits — they're not looking!

Gallimard: Thank you very much.

Marc: Wimp.

Marc walks over to the other side of the stage, and starts waving and smiling at women in the audience.

Gallimard (to us): We now return to my version of *Madame Butterfly* and the events leading to my recent conviction for treason.

Gallimard notices Marc making lewd gestures.

Gallimard: Marc, what are you doing?

Marc: Huh? *(Sotto voce.)* Rene, there're a lotta great babes out there. They're probably lookin' at me and thinking, "What a dangerous guy."

Gallimard: Yes — how could they help but be impressed by your cool sophistication?

École Nationale: National School.

Gallimard pops the Sharpless cap on Marc's head, and points him offstage. Marc exits, leering.

SCENE V

M. Gallimard's cell.

Gallimard: Next, Butterfly makes her entrance. We learn her age—fifteen . . . but very mature for her years.

Lights come up on the area where we saw Song dancing at the top of the play. She appears there again, now dressed as Madame Butterfly, moving to the "Love Duet." Gallimard turns upstage slightly to watch, transfixed.

Gallimard: But as she glides past him, beautiful, laughing softly behind her fan, don't we who are men sigh with hope? We, who are not handsome, nor brave, nor powerful, yet somehow believe, like Pinkerton, that we de-serve a Butterfly. She arrives with all her possessions in the folds of her sleeves, lays them all out, for her man to do with as he pleases. Even her life itself—she bows her head as she whispers that she's not even worth the hundred yen he paid for her. He's already given too much, when we know he's really had to give nothing at all.

Music and lights on Song out. Gallimard sits at his crate.

Gallimard: In real life, women who put their total worth at less than sixty-six cents are quite hard to find. The closest we come is in the pages of these magazines. (*He reaches into his crate, pulls out a stack of girlie magazines, and be-gins flipping through them.*) Quite a necessity in prison. For three or four dol-lars, you get seven or eight women.

I first discovered these magazines at my uncle's house. One day, as a boy of twelve. The first time I saw them in his closet . . . all lined up—my body shook. Not with lust—no, with power. Here were women—a shelfful—who would do exactly as I wanted.

The "Love Duet" creeps in over the speakers. Special comes up, revealing, not Song this time, but a pinup girl in a sexy negligee, her back to us. Gallimard turns up-stage and looks at her.

Girl: I know you're watching me.
Gallimard: My throat . . . it's dry.
Girl: I leave my blinds open every night before I go to bed.
Gallimard: I can't move.
Girl: I leave my blinds open and the lights on.
Gallimard: I'm shaking. My skin is hot, but my penis is soft. Why?
Girl: I stand in front of the window.
Gallimard: What is she going to do?
Girl: I toss my hair, and I let my lips part . . . barely.
Gallimard: I shouldn't be seeing this. It's so dirty. I'm so bad.
Girl: Then, slowly, I lift off my nightdress.
Gallimard: Oh, god. I can't believe it. I can't—
Girl: I toss it to the ground.
Gallimard: Now, she's going to walk away. She's going to—

Girl: I stand there, in the light, displaying myself.

Gallimard: No. She's — why is she naked?

Girl: To you.

Gallimard: In front of a window? This is wrong. No —

Girl: Without shame.

Gallimard: No, she must . . . like it.

Girl: I like it.

Gallimard: She . . . she wants me to see.

Girl: I want you to see.

Gallimard: I can't believe it! She's getting excited!

Girl: I can't see you. You can do whatever you want.

Gallimard: I can't do a thing. Why?

Girl: What would you like me to do . . . next?

Lights go down on her. Music off. Silence, as Gallimard puts away his magazines. Then he resumes talking to us.

Gallimard: Act Two begins with Butterfly staring at the ocean. Pinkerton's been called back to the U.S., and he's given his wife a detailed schedule of his plans. In the column marked "return date," he's written "when the robins nest." This failed to ignite her suspicions. Now, three years have passed without a peep from him. Which brings a response from her faithful servant, Suzuki.

Comrade Chin enters, playing Suzuki.

Suzuki: Girl, he's a loser. What'd he ever give you? Nineteen cents and those ugly Day-Glo stockings? Look, it's finished! Kaput! Done! And you should be glad! I mean, the guy was a woofer! He tried before, you know — before he met you, he went down to geisha central and plunked down his spare change in front of the usual candidates — everyone else gagged! These are hungry prostitutes, and they were not interested, get the picture? Now, stop slathering when an American ship sails in, and let's make some bucks — I mean, yen! We are broke!

Now, what about Yamadori? Hey, hey — don't look away — the man is a prince — figuratively, and, what's even better, literally. He's rich, he's handsome, he says he'll die if you don't marry him — and he's even willing to overlook the little fact that you've been deflowered all over the place by a foreign devil. What do you mean, "But he's Japanese"? What do you think you are? You think you've been touched by the whitey god? He was a sailor with dirty hands!

Suzuki stalks offstage.

Gallimard: She's also visited by Consul Sharpless, sent by Pinkerton on a minor errand.

Marc enters, as Sharpless.

Sharpless: I hate this job.

Gallimard: This Pinkerton — he doesn't show up personally to tell his wife he's abandoning her. No, he sends a government diplomat . . . at taxpayers' expense.

Sharpless: Butterfly? Butterfly? I have some bad — I'm going to be ill. Butterfly, I came to tell you —

Gallimard: Butterfly says she knows he'll return and if he doesn't she'll kill herself rather than go back to her own people. *(Beat.)* This causes a lull in the conversation.

Sharpless: Let's put it this way . . .

Gallimard: Butterfly runs into the next room, and returns holding —

Sound cue: a baby crying. Sharpless, "seeing" this, backs away.

Sharpless: Well, good. Happy to see things going so well. I suppose I'll be going now. Ta ta. Ciao. *(He turns away. Sound cue out.)* I hate this job. *(He exits.)*

Gallimard: At that moment, Butterfly spots in the harbor an American ship — the *Abramo Lincoln!*

Music cue: "The Flower Duet." Song, still dressed as Butterfly, changes into a wedding kimono, moving to the music.

Gallimard: This is the moment that redeems her years of waiting. With Suzuki's help, they cover the room with flowers —

Chin, as Suzuki, trudges onstage and drops a lone flower without much enthusiasm.

Gallimard: — and she changes into her wedding dress to prepare for Pinkerton's arrival.

Suzuki helps Butterfly change. Helga enters, and helps Gallimard change into a tuxedo.

Gallimard: I married a woman older than myself — Helga.

Helga: My father was ambassador to Australia. I grew up among criminals and kangaroos.

Gallimard: Hearing that brought me to the altar —

Helga exits.

Gallimard: — where I took a vow renouncing love. No fantasy woman would ever want me, so, yes, I would settle for a quick leap up the career ladder. Passion, I banish, and in its place — practicality!

But my vows had long since lost their charm by the time we arrived in China. The sad truth is that all men want a beautiful woman, and the uglier the man, the greater the want.

Suzuki makes final adjustments of Butterfly's costume, as does Gallimard of his tuxedo.

Gallimard: I married late, at age thirty-one. I was faithful to my marriage for eight years. Until the day when, as a junior-level diplomat in puritanical Peking, in a parlor at the German ambassador's house, during the "Reign of a Hundred Flowers,"° I first saw her . . . singing the death scene from *Madame Butterfly.*

Suzuki runs offstage.

Scene VI

German ambassador's house. Beijing. 1960.

The upstage special area now becomes a stage. Several chairs face upstage, representing seating for some twenty guests in the parlor. A few "diplomats" — Renee, Marc, Toulon — in formal dress enter and take seats.

Reign of a Hundred Flowers: A brief period in 1957 when freedom of expression was allowed in China.

> *Gallimard also sits down, but turns towards us and continues to talk. Orchestral accompaniment on the tape is now replaced by a simple piano. Song picks up the death scene from the point where Butterfly uncovers the hara-kiri knife.*

Gallimard: The ending is pitiful. Pinkerton, in an act of great courage, stays home and sends his American wife to pick up Butterfly's child. The truth, long deferred, has come up to her door.

> *Song, playing Butterfly, sings the lines from the opera in her own voice—which, though not classical, should be decent.*

Song: "Con onor muore / chi non puo serbar / vita con onore."

Gallimard (simultaneously): "Death with honor / Is better than life / Life with dishonor."

> *The stage is illuminated; we are now completely within an elegant diplomat's residence. Song proceeds to play out an abbreviated death scene. Everyone in the room applauds. Song, shyly, takes her bows. Others in the room rush to congratulate her. Gallimard remains with us.*

Gallimard: They say in opera the voice is everything. That's probably why I'd never before enjoyed opera. Here . . . here was a Butterfly with little or no voice—but she had the grace, the delicacy . . . I believed this girl. I believed her suffering. I wanted to take her in my arms—so delicate, even I could protect her, take her home, pamper her until she smiled.

> *Over the course of the preceding speech, Song has broken from the upstage crowd and moved directly upstage of Gallimard.*

Song: Excuse me. Monsieur . . . ?

> *Gallimard turns upstage, shocked.*

Gallimard: Oh! Gallimard. Mademoiselle . . . ? A beautiful . . .
Song: Song Liling.
Gallimard: A beautiful performance.
Song: Oh, please.
Gallimard: I usually—
Song: You make me blush. I'm no opera singer at all.
Gallimard: I usually don't like *Butterfly*.
Song: I can't blame you in the least.
Gallimard: I mean, the story—
Song: Ridiculous.
Gallimard: I like the story, but . . . what?
Song: Oh, you like it?
Gallimard: I . . . what I mean is, I've always seen it played by huge women in so much bad makeup.
Song: Bad makeup is not unique to the West.
Gallimard: But, who can believe them?
Song: And you believe me?
Gallimard: Absolutely. You were utterly convincing. It's the first time—
Song: Convincing? As a Japanese woman? The Japanese used hundreds of our people for medical experiments during the war, you know. But I gather such an irony is lost on you.
Gallimard: No! I was about to say, it's the first time I've seen the beauty of the story.

Song: Really?

Gallimard: Of her death. It's a . . . a pure sacrifice. He's unworthy, but what can she do? She loves him . . . so much. It's a very beautiful story.

Song: Well, yes, to a Westerner.

Gallimard: Excuse me?

Song: It's one of your favorite fantasies, isn't it? The submissive Oriental woman and the cruel white man.

Gallimard: Well, I didn't quite mean . . .

Song: Consider it this way: what would you say if a blonde homecoming queen fell in love with a short Japanese businessman? He treats her cruelly, then goes home for three years, during which time she prays to his picture and turns down marriage from a young Kennedy. Then, when she learns he has remarried, she kills herself. Now, I believe you would consider this girl to be a deranged idiot, correct? But because it's an Oriental who kills herself for a Westerner—ah!—you find it beautiful.

Silence.

Gallimard: Yes . . . well . . . I see your point . . .

Song: I will never do Butterfly again, Monsieur Gallimard. If you wish to see some real theater, come to the Peking Opera sometime. Expand your mind.

Song walks offstage. Other guests exit with her.

Gallimard (to us): So much for protecting her in my big Western arms.

Scene VII

M. Gallimard's apartment. Beijing. 1960.
    Gallimard changes from his tux into a casual suit. Helga enters.

Gallimard: The Chinese are an incredibly arrogant people.

Helga: They warned us about that in Paris, remember?

Gallimard: Even Parisians consider them arrogant. That's a switch.

Helga: What is it that Madame Su says? "We are a very old civilization." I never know if she's talking about her country or herself.

Gallimard: I walk around here, all I hear every day, everywhere is how *old* this culture is. The fact that "old" may be synonymous with "senile" doesn't occur to them.

Helga: You're not going to change them. "East is east, west is west, and . . ." whatever that guy said.

Gallimard: It's just that—silly. I met . . . at Ambassador Koening's tonight—you should've been there.

Helga: Koening? Oh god, no. Did he enchant you all again with the history of Bavaria?

Gallimard: No. I met, I suppose, the Chinese equivalent of a diva. She's a singer in the Chinese opera.

Helga: They have an opera, too? Do they sing in Chinese? Or maybe—in Italian?

Gallimard: Tonight, she did sing in Italian.

Helga: How'd she manage that?

Gallimard: She must've been educated in the West before the Revolution. Her French is very good also. Anyway, she sang the death scene from *Madame Butterfly.*

Helga: Madame Butterfly! Then I should have come. *(She begins humming, floating around the room as if dragging long kimono sleeves.)* Did she have a nice costume? I think it's a classic piece of music.

Gallimard: That's what *I* thought, too. Don't let her hear you say that.

Helga: What's wrong?

Gallimard: Evidently the Chinese hate it.

Helga: She hated it, but she performed it anyway? Is she perverse?

Gallimard: They hate it because the white man gets the girl. Sour grapes if you ask me.

Helga: Politics again? Why can't they just hear it as a piece of beautiful music? So, what's in their opera?

Gallimard: I don't know. But, whatever it is, I'm sure it must be *old*.

Helga exits.

Scene VIII

Chinese opera house and the streets of Beijing. 1960.
The sound of gongs clanging fills the stage.

Gallimard: My wife's innocent question kept ringing in my ears. I asked around, but no one knew anything about the Chinese opera. It took four weeks, but my curiosity overcame my cowardice. This Chinese diva—this unwilling Butterfly—what did she do to make her so proud?

The room was hot, and full of smoke. Wrinkled faces, old women, teeth missing—a man with a growth on his neck, like a human toad. All smiling, pipes falling from their mouths, cracking nuts between their teeth, a live chicken pecking at my foot—all looking, screaming, gawking . . . at her.

The upstage area is suddenly hit with a harsh white light. It has become the stage for the Chinese opera performance. Two dancers enter, along with Song. Gallimard stands apart, watching. Song glides gracefully amidst the two dancers. Drums suddenly slam to a halt. Song strikes a pose, looking straight at Gallimard. Dancers exit. Light change. Pause, then Song walks right off the stage and straight up to Gallimard.

Song: Yes. You. White man. I'm looking straight at you.

Gallimard: Me?

Song: You see any other white men? It was too easy to spot you. How often does a man in my audience come in a tie?

Song starts to remove her costume. Underneath, she wears simple baggy clothes. They are now backstage. The show is over.

Song: So, you are an adventurous imperialist?

Gallimard: I . . . thought it would further my education.

Song: It took you four weeks. Why?

Gallimard: I've been busy.

Song: Well, education has always been undervalued in the West, hasn't it?

Gallimard (laughing): I don't think that's true.

Song: No, you wouldn't. You're a Westerner. How can you objectively judge your own values?

Gallimard: I think it's possible to achieve some distance.

Song: Do you? *(Pause.)* It stinks in here. Let's go.

Gallimard: These are the smells of your loyal fans.

Song: I love them for being my fans, I hate the smell they leave behind. I too can distance myself from my people. *(She looks around, then whispers in his ear.)* "Art for the masses" is a shitty excuse to keep artists poor. *(She pops a cigarette in her mouth.)* Be a gentleman, will you? And light my cigarette.

Gallimard fumbles for a match.

Gallimard: I don't . . . smoke.

Song (lighting her own): Your loss. Had you lit my cigarette, I might have blown a puff of smoke right between your eyes. Come.

They start to walk about the stage. It is a summer night on the Beijing streets. Sounds of the city play on the house speakers.

Song: How I wish there were even a tiny café to sit in. With cappuccinos, and men in tuxedos and bad expatriate jazz.

Gallimard: If my history serves me correctly, you weren't even allowed into the clubs in Shanghai before the Revolution.

Song: Your history serves you poorly, Monsieur Gallimard. True, there were signs reading "No dogs and Chinamen." But a woman, especially a delicate Oriental woman — we always go where we please. Could you imagine it otherwise? Clubs in China filled with pasty, big-thighed white women, while thousands of slender lotus blossoms wait just outside the door? Never. The clubs would be empty. *(Beat.)* We have always held a certain fascination for you Caucasian men, have we not?

Gallimard: But . . . that fascination is imperialist, or so you tell me.

Song: Do you believe everything I tell you? Yes. It is always imperialist. But sometimes . . . sometimes, it is also mutual. Oh — this is my flat.

Gallimard: I didn't even —

Song: Thank you. Come another time and we will further expand your mind.

Song exits. Gallimard continues roaming the streets as he speaks to us.

Gallimard: What was that? What did she mean, "Sometimes . . . it is mutual"? Women do not flirt with me. And I normally can't talk to them. But tonight, I held up my end of the conversation.

Scene IX

Gallimard's bedroom. Beijing. 1960.
Helga enters.

Helga: You didn't tell me you'd be home late.

Gallimard: I didn't intend to. Something came up.

Helga: Oh? Like what?

Gallimard: I went to the . . . to the Dutch ambassador's home.

Helga: Again?

Gallimard: There was a reception for a visiting scholar. He's writing a six-volume treatise on the Chinese revolution. We all gathered that meant he'd have to live here long enough to actually write six volumes, and we all expressed our deepest sympathies.

Helga: Well, I had a good night too. I went with the ladies to a martial arts demonstration. Some of those men—when they break those thick boards—(*she mimes fanning herself*) whoo-whoo!

Helga exits. Lights dim.

Gallimard: I lied to my wife. Why? I've never had any reason to lie before. But what reason did I have tonight? I didn't do anything wrong. That night, I had a dream. Other people, I've been told, have dreams when angels appear. Or dragons, or Sophia Loren in a towel. In my dream, Marc from school appeared.

Marc enters, in a nightshirt and cap.

Marc: Rene! You met a girl!

Gallimard and Marc stumble down the Beijing streets. Night sounds over the speakers.

Gallimard: It's not that amazing, thank you.

Marc: No! It's so monumental, I heard about it halfway around the world in my sleep!

Gallimard: I've met girls before, you know.

Marc: Name one. I've come across time and space to congratulate you. (*He hands Gallimard a bottle of wine.*)

Gallimard: Marc, this is expensive.

Marc: On those rare occasions when you become a formless spirit, why not steal the best?

Marc pops open the bottle, begins to share it with Gallimard.

Gallimard: You embarrass me. She . . . there's no reason to think she likes me.

Marc: "Sometimes, it is mutual"?

Gallimard: Oh.

Marc: "Mutual"? "Mutual"? What does that mean?

Gallimard: You heard?

Marc: It means the money is in the bank, you only have to write the check!

Gallimard: I am a married man!

Marc: And an excellent one too. I cheated after . . . six months. Then again and again, until now—three hundred girls in twelve years.

Gallimard: I don't think we should hold that up as a model.

Marc: Of course not! My life—it is disgusting! Phooey! Phooey! But, you— you are the model husband.

Gallimard: Anyway, it's impossible. I'm a foreigner.

Marc: Ah, yes. She cannot love you, it is taboo, but something deep inside her heart . . . she cannot help herself . . . she must surrender to you. It is her destiny.

Gallimard: How do you imagine all this?

Marc: The same way you do. It's an old story. It's in our blood. They fear us, Rene. Their women fear us. And their men—their men hate us. And, you know something? They are all correct.

They spot a light in a window.

Marc: There! There, Rene!

Gallimard: It's her window.

Marc: Late at night—it burns. The light—it burns for you.

Gallimard: I won't look. It's not respectful.
Marc: We don't have to be respectful. We're foreign devils.

> *Enter Song, in a sheer robe, her face completely swathed in black cloth. The "One Fine Day" aria creeps in over the speakers. With her back to us, Song mimes attending to her toilette. Her robe comes loose, revealing her white shoulders.*

Marc: All your life you've waited for a beautiful girl who would lay down for you. All your life you've smiled like a saint when it's happened to every other man you know. And you see them in magazines and you see them in movies. And you wonder, what's wrong with me? Will anyone beautiful ever want me? As the years pass, your hair thins and you struggle to hold on to even your hopes. Stop struggling, Rene. The wait is over. *(He exits.)*
Gallimard: Marc? Marc?

> *At that moment, Song, her back still towards us, drops her robe. A second of her naked back, then a sound cue: a phone ringing, very loud. Blackout, followed in the next beat by a special up on the bedroom area, where a phone now sits. Gallimard stumbles across the stage and picks up the phone. Sound cue out. Over the course of his conversation, area lights fill in the vicinity of his bed. It is the following morning.*

Gallimard: Yes? Hello?
Song (offstage): Is it very early?
Gallimard: Why, yes.
Song (offstage): How early?
Gallimard: It's . . . it's 5:30. Why are you—?
Song (offstage): But it's light outside. Already.
Gallimard: It is. The sun must be in confusion today.

> *Over the course of Song's next speech, her upstage special comes up again. She sits in a chair, legs crossed, in a robe, telephone to her ear.*

Song: I waited until I saw the sun. That was as much discipline as I could manage for one night. Do you forgive me?
Gallimard: Of course . . . for what?
Song: Then I'll ask you quickly. Are you really interested in the opera?
Gallimard: Why, yes. Yes I am.
Song: Then come again next Thursday. I am playing *The Drunken Beauty*. May I count on you?
Gallimard: Yes. You may.
Song: Perfect. Well, I must be getting to bed. I'm exhausted. It's been a very long night for me.

> *Song hangs up; special on her goes off. Gallimard begins to dress for work.*

SCENE X

> *Song Liling's apartment. Beijing. 1960.*

Gallimard: I returned to the opera that next week, and the week after that . . . she keeps our meetings so short—perhaps fifteen, twenty minutes at most. So I am left each week with a thirst which is intensified. In this way, fifteen weeks have gone by. I am starting to doubt the words of my friend Marc. But no, not really. In my heart, I know she has . . . an interest in me. I suspect this is her way. She is outwardly bold and outspoken, yet her heart is shy and afraid. It is the Oriental in her at war with her Western education.

Song (offstage): I will be out in an instant. Ask the servant for anything you want.

Gallimard: Tonight, I have finally been invited to enter her apartment. Though the idea is almost beyond belief, I believe she is afraid of me.

Gallimard looks around the room. He picks up a picture in a frame, studies it. Without his noticing, Song enters, dressed elegantly in a black gown from the twenties. She stands in the doorway looking like Anna May Wong.°

Song: That is my father.

Gallimard (surprised): Mademoiselle Song . . .

She glides up to him, snatches away the picture.

Song: It is very good that he did not live to see the Revolution. They would, no doubt, have made him kneel on broken glass. Not that he didn't deserve such a punishment. But he is my father. I would've hated to see it happen.

Gallimard: I'm very honored that you've allowed me to visit your home.

Song curtseys.

Song: Thank you. Oh! Haven't you been poured any tea?

Gallimard: I'm really not —

Song (to her offstage servant): Shu-Fang! Cha! Kwai-lah! *(To Gallimard.)* I'm sorry. You want everything to be perfect —

Gallimard: Please.

Song: — and before the evening even begins —

Gallimard: I'm really not thirsty.

Song: — it's ruined.

Gallimard (sharply): Mademoiselle Song!

Song sits down.

Song: I'm sorry.

Gallimard: What are you apologizing for now?

Pause; Song starts to giggle.

Song: I don't know!

Gallimard laughs.

Gallimard: Exactly my point.

Song: Oh, I am silly. Light-headed. I promise not to apologize for anything else tonight, do you hear me?

Gallimard: That's a good girl.

Shu-Fang, a servant girl, comes out with a tea tray and starts to pour.

Song (to Shu-Fang): No! I'll pour myself for the gentleman!

Shu-Fang, staring at Gallimard, exits.

Gallimard: You have a beautiful home.

Song: No, I . . . I don't even know why I invited you up.

Anna May Wong (1905–1961): Chinese American actor known for her exotic beauty and most often cast as a villain.

Gallimard: Well, I'm glad you did.

    Song looks around the room.

Song: There is an element of danger to your presence.

Gallimard: Oh?

Song: You must know.

Gallimard: It doesn't concern me. We both know why I'm here.

Song: It doesn't concern me either. No . . . well perhaps . . .

Gallimard: What?

Song: Perhaps I am slightly afraid of scandal.

Gallimard: What are we doing?

Song: I'm entertaining you. In my parlor.

Gallimard: In France, that would hardly —

Song: France. France is a country living in the modern era. Perhaps even ahead of it. China is a nation whose soul is firmly rooted two thousand years in the past. What I do, even pouring the tea for you now . . . it has . . . implications. The walls and windows say so. Even my own heart, strapped inside this Western dress . . . even it says things — things I don't care to hear.

    Song hands Gallimard a cup of tea. Gallimard puts his hand over both the teacup and Song's hand.

Gallimard: This is a beautiful dress.

Song: Don't.

Gallimard: What?

Song: I don't even know if it looks right on me.

Gallimard: Believe me —

Song: You are from France. You see so many beautiful women.

Gallimard: France? Since when are the European women — ?

Song: Oh! What am I trying to do, anyway?!

    Song runs to the door, composes herself, then turns towards Gallimard.

Song: Monsieur Gallimard, perhaps you should go.

Gallimard: But . . . why?

Song: There's something wrong about this.

Gallimard: I don't see what.

Song: I feel . . . I am not myself.

Gallimard: No. You're nervous.

Song: Please. Hard as I try to be modern, to speak like a man, to hold a Western woman's strong face up to my own . . . in the end, I fail. A small, frightened heart beats too quickly and gives me away. Monsieur Gallimard, I'm a Chinese girl. I've never . . . never invited a man up to my flat before. The forwardness of my actions makes my skin burn.

Gallimard: What are you afraid of? Certainly not me, I hope.

Song: I'm a modest girl.

Gallimard: I know. And very beautiful. *(He touches her hair.)*

Song: Please — go now. The next time you see me, I shall again be myself.

Gallimard: I like you the way you are right now.

Song: You are a cad.

Gallimard: What do you expect? I'm a foreign devil.

    Gallimard walks downstage. Song exits.

Gallimard (to us): Did you hear the way she talked about Western women? Much differently than the first night. She does — she feels inferior to them — and to me.

SCENE XI

The French embassy. Beijing. 1960.
Gallimard moves towards a desk.

Gallimard: I determined to try an experiment. In *Madame Butterfly*, Cio-Cio-San fears that the Western man who catches a butterfly will pierce its heart with a needle, then leave it to perish. I began to wonder: had I, too, caught a butterfly who would writhe on a needle?

Marc enters, dressed as a bureaucrat, holding a stack of papers. As Gallimard speaks, Marc hands papers to him. He peruses, then signs, stamps, or rejects them.

Gallimard: Over the next five weeks, I worked like a dynamo. I stopped going to the opera, I didn't phone or write her. I knew this little flower was waiting for me to call, and, as I wickedly refused to do so, I felt for the first time that rush of power — the absolute power of a man.

Marc continues acting as the bureaucrat, but he now speaks as himself.

Marc: Rene! It's me.

Gallimard: Marc — I hear your voice everywhere now. Even in the midst of work.

Marc: That's because I'm watching you — all the time.

Gallimard: You were always the most popular guy in school.

Marc: Well, there's no guarantee of failure in life like happiness in high school. Somehow I knew I'd end up in the suburbs working for Renault and you'd be in the Orient picking exotic women off the trees. And they say there's no justice.

Gallimard: That's why you were my friend?

Marc: I gave you a little of my life, so that now you can give me some of yours. *(Pause.)* Remember Isabelle?

Gallimard: Of course I remember! She was my first experience.

Marc: We all wanted to ball her. But she only wanted me.

Gallimard: I had her.

Marc: Right. You balled her.

Gallimard: You were the only one who ever believed me.

Marc: Well, there's a good reason for that. *(Beat.)* C'mon. You must've guessed.

Gallimard: You told me to wait in the bushes by the cafeteria that night. The next thing I knew, she was on me. Dress up in the air.

Marc: She never wore underwear.

Gallimard: My arms were pinned to the dirt.

Marc: She loved the superior position. A girl ahead of her time.

Gallimard: I looked up, and there was this woman . . . bouncing up and down on my loins.

Marc: Screaming, right?

Gallimard: Screaming, and breaking off the branches all around me, and pounding my butt up and down into the dirt.

Marc: Huffing and puffing like a locomotive.

Gallimard: And in the middle of all this, the leaves were getting into my mouth, my legs were losing circulation, I thought, "God. So this is *it?*"

Marc: You thought that?

Gallimard: Well, I was worried about my legs falling off.

Marc: You didn't have a good time?

Gallimard: No, that's not what I—I had a great time!

Marc: You're sure?

Gallimard: Yeah. Really.

Marc: 'Cuz I wanted you to have a good time.

Gallimard: I did.

    Pause.

Marc: Shit. (*Pause.*) When all is said and done, she was kind of a lousy lay, wasn't she? I mean, there was a lot of energy there, but you never knew what she was doing with it. Like when she yelled "I'm coming!"—hell, it was so loud, you wanted to go, "Look, it's not that big a deal."

Gallimard: I got scared. I thought she meant someone was actually coming. (*Pause.*) But, Marc?

Marc: What?

Gallimard: Thanks.

Marc: Oh, don't mention it.

Gallimard: It was my first experience.

Marc: Yeah. You got her.

Gallimard: I got her.

Marc: Wait! Look at that letter again!

    Gallimard picks up one of the papers he's been stamping, and rereads it.

Gallimard (to us): After six weeks, they began to arrive. The letters.

    Upstage special on Song, as Madame Butterfly. The scene is underscored by the "Love Duet."

Song: Did we fight? I do not know. Is the opera no longer of interest to you? Please come—my audiences miss the white devil in their midst.

    Gallimard looks up from the letter, towards us.

Gallimard (to us): A concession, but much too dignified. (*Beat; he discards the letter.*) I skipped the opera again that week to complete a position paper on trade.

    The bureaucrat hands him another letter.

Song: Six weeks have passed since last we met. Is this your practice—to leave friends in the lurch? Sometimes I hate you, sometimes I hate myself, but always I miss you.

Gallimard (to us): Better, but I don't like the way she calls me "friend." When a woman calls a man her "friend," she's calling him a eunuch or a homosexual. (*Beat; he discards the letter.*) I was absent from the opera for the seventh week, feeling a sudden urge to clean out my files.

    Bureaucrat hands him another letter.

Song: Your rudeness is beyond belief. I don't deserve this cruelty. Don't bother to call. I'll have you turned away at the door.

Gallimard (to us): I didn't. *(He discards the letter; bureaucrat hands him another.)* And then finally, the letter that concluded my experiment.

Song: I am out of words. I can hide behind dignity no longer. What do you want? I have already given you my shame.

Gallimard gives the letter back to Marc, slowly. Special on Song fades out.

Gallimard (to us): Reading it, I became suddenly ashamed. Yes, my experiment had been a success. She was turning on my needle. But the victory seemed hollow.

Marc: Hollow?! Are you crazy?

Gallimard: Nothing, Marc. Please go away.

Marc (exiting, with papers): Haven't I taught you anything?

Gallimard: "I have already given you my shame." I had to attend a reception that evening. On the way, I felt sick. If there is a God, surely he would punish me now. I had finally gained power over a beautiful woman, only to abuse it cruelly. There must be justice in the world. I had the strange feeling that the ax would fall this very evening.

Scene XII

Ambassador Toulon's residence. Beijing. 1960.
    Sound cue: party noises. Light change. We are now in a spacious residence.
Toulon, the French ambassador, enters and taps Gallimard on the shoulder.

Toulon: Gallimard? Can I have a word? Over here.

Gallimard (to us): Manuel Toulon. French ambassador to China. He likes to think of us all as his children. Rather like God.

Toulon: Look, Gallimard, there's not much to say. I've liked you. From the day you walked in. You were no leader, but you were tidy and efficient.

Gallimard: Thank you, sir.

Toulon: Don't jump the gun. Okay, our needs in China are changing. It's embarrassing that we lost Indochina. Someone just wasn't on the ball there. I don't mean you personally, of course.

Gallimard: Thank you, sir.

Toulon: We're going to be doing a lot more information-gathering in the future. The nature of our work here is changing. Some people are just going to have to go. It's nothing personal.

Gallimard: Oh.

Toulon: Want to know a secret? Vice-Consul LeBon is being transferred.

Gallimard (to us): My immediate superior!

Toulon: And most of his department.

Gallimard (to us): Just as I feared! God has seen my evil heart—

Toulon: But not you.

Gallimard (to us): —and he's taking her away just as . . . *(To Toulon.)* Excuse me, sir?

Toulon: Scare you? I think I did. Cheer up, Gallimard. I want you to replace LeBon as vice-consul.

Gallimard: You—? Yes, well, thank you, sir.

Toulon: Anytime.

Gallimard: I . . . accept with great humility.

Toulon: Humility won't be part of the job. You're going to coordinate the revamped intelligence division. Want to know a secret? A year ago, you
would've been out. But the past few months, I don't know how it happened, you've become this new aggressive confident . . . thing. And they
also tell me you get along with the Chinese. So I think you're a lucky man,
Gallimard. Congratulations.

*They shake hands. Toulon exits. Party noises out. Gallimard stumbles across a
darkened stage.*

Gallimard: Vice-consul? Impossible! As I stumbled out of the party, I saw it
written across the sky: There is no God. Or, no — say that there is a God.
But that God . . . understands. Of course! God who creates Eve to serve
Adam, who blesses Solomon with his harem but ties Jezebel to a burning
bed° — that God is a man. And he understands! At age thirty-nine, I was
suddenly initiated into the way of the world.

Scene XIII

Song Liling's apartment. Beijing. 1960.
  Song enters, in a sheer dressing gown.

Song: Are you crazy?
Gallimard: Mademoiselle Song —
Song: To come here — at this hour? After . . . after eight weeks?
Gallimard: It's the most amazing —
Song: You bang on my door? Scare my servants, scandalize the neighbors?
Gallimard: I've been promoted. To vice-consul.

  Pause.

Song: And what is that supposed to mean to me?
Gallimard: Are you my Butterfly?
Song: What are you saying?
Gallimard: I've come tonight for an answer: are you my Butterfly?
Song: Don't you know already?
Gallimard: I want you to say it.
Song: I don't want to say it.
Gallimard: So, that is your answer?
Song: You know how I feel about —
Gallimard: I do remember one thing.
Song: What?
Gallimard: In the letter I received today.
Song: Don't.
Gallimard: "I have already given you my shame."
Song: It's enough that I even wrote it.
Gallimard: Well, then —
Song: I shouldn't have it splashed across my face.
Gallimard: — if that's all true —
Song: Stop!
Gallimard: Then what is one more short answer?

God who creates Eve . . . burning bed: Eve, Adam, Solomon, and Jezebel are biblical characters.
See Gen. 2:18–25; I Kings 11:1–8; and II Kings 9:11–37.

Song: I don't want to!

Gallimard: Are you my Butterfly? *(Silence; he crosses the room and begins to touch her hair.)* I want from you honesty. There should be nothing false between us. No false pride.

Pause.

Song: Yes, I am. I am your Butterfly.

Gallimard: Then let me be honest with you. It is because of you that I was promoted tonight. You have changed my life forever. My little Butterfly, there should be no more secrets: I love you.

He starts to kiss her roughly. She resists slightly.

Song: No . . . no . . . gently . . . please, I've never . . .

Gallimard: No?

Song: I've tried to appear experienced, but . . . the truth is . . . no.

Gallimard: Are you cold?

Song: Yes. Cold.

Gallimard: Then we will go very, very slowly.

He starts to caress her; her gown begins to open.

Song: No . . . let me . . . keep my clothes . . .

Gallimard: But . . .

Song: Please . . . it all frightens me. I'm a modest Chinese girl.

Gallimard: My poor little treasure.

Song: I am your treasure. Though inexperienced, I am not . . . ignorant. They teach us things, our mothers, about pleasing a man.

Gallimard: Yes?

Song: I'll do my best to make you happy. Turn off the lights.

Gallimard gets up and heads for a lamp. Song, propped up on one elbow, tosses her hair back and smiles.

Song: Monsieur Gallimard?

Gallimard: Yes, Butterfly?

Song: "Vieni, vieni!"

Gallimard: "Come, darling."

Song: "Ah! Dolce notte!"

Gallimard: "Beautiful night."

Song: "Tutto estatico d'amor ride il ciel!"

Gallimard: "All ecstatic with love, the heavens are filled with laughter."

He turns off the lamp. Blackout.

ACT II

SCENE I

M. Gallimard's cell. Paris. 1988.
    Lights up on Gallimard. He sits in his cell, reading from a leaflet.

Gallimard: This, from a contemporary critic's commentary on *Madame Butterfly:* "Pinkerton suffers from . . . being an obnoxious bounder whom every man in the audience itches to kick." Bully for us men in the audience! Then, in the same note: "Butterfly is the most irresistibly appealing of Puccini's 'Little Women.' Watching the succession of her humiliations is like watching a child under torture." *(He tosses the pamphlet over his shoulder.)* I suggest that, while we men may all want to kick Pinkerton, very few of us would pass up the opportunity to *be* Pinkerton.

Gallimard moves out of his cell.

SCENE II

Gallimard and Butterfly's flat. Beijing. 1960.
    We are in a simple but well-decorated parlor. Gallimard moves to sit on a sofa, while Song, dressed in a cheongsam,° enters and curls up at his feet.

Gallimard (to us): We secured a flat on the outskirts of Peking. Butterfly, as I was calling her now, decorated our "home" with Western furniture and Chinese antiques. And there, on a few stolen afternoons or evenings each week, Butterfly commenced her education.
Song: The Chinese men — they keep us down.
Gallimard: Even in the "New Society"?
Song: In the "New Society," we are all kept ignorant equally. That's one of the exciting things about loving a Western man. I know you are not threatened by a woman's education.
Gallimard: I'm no saint, Butterfly.
Song: But you come from a progressive society.
Gallimard: We're not always reminding each other how "old" we are, if that's what you mean.
Song: Exactly. We Chinese — once, I suppose, it is true, we ruled the world. But so what? How much more exciting to be part of the society ruling the world today. Tell me — what's happening in Vietnam?
Gallimard: Oh, Butterfly — you want me to bring my work home?
Song: I want to know what you know. To be impressed by my man. It's not the particulars so much as the fact that you're making decisions which change the shape of the world.
Gallimard: Not the world. At best, a small corner.

Toulon enters, and sits at a desk upstage.

SCENE III

French embassy. Beijing. 1961.
    Gallimard moves downstage, to Toulon's desk. Song remains upstage, watching.

Toulon: And a more troublesome corner is hard to imagine.
Gallimard: So, the Americans plan to begin bombing?
Toulon: This is very secret, Gallimard: yes. The Americans don't have an embassy here. They're asking us to be their eyes and ears. Say Jack Kennedy signed an order to bomb North Vietnam, Laos. How would the Chinese react?
Gallimard: I think the Chinese will squawk —

cheongsam: A fitted dress with side slits in the skirt.

Toulon: Uh-huh.

Gallimard: — but, in their hearts, they don't even like Ho Chi Minh.°

   Pause.

Toulon: What a bunch of jerks. Vietnam was *our* colony. Not only didn't the Americans help us fight to keep them, but now, seven years later, they've come back to grab the territory for themselves. It's very irritating.

Gallimard: With all due respect, sir, why should the Americans have won our war for us back in fifty-four if we didn't have the will to win it ourselves?

Toulon: You're kidding, aren't you?

   Pause.

Gallimard: The Orientals simply want to be associated with whoever shows the most strength and power. You live with the Chinese, sir. Do you think they like Communism?

Toulon: I live in China. Not with the Chinese.

Gallimard: Well, I—

Toulon: *You* live with the Chinese.

Gallimard: Excuse me?

Toulon: I can't keep a secret.

Gallimard: What are you saying?

Toulon: Only that I'm not immune to gossip. So, you're keeping a native mistress? Don't answer. It's none of my business. *(Pause.)* I'm sure she must be gorgeous.

Gallimard: Well . . .

Toulon: I'm impressed. You had the stamina to go out into the streets and hunt one down. Some of us have to be content with the wives of the expatriate community.

Gallimard: I do feel . . . fortunate.

Toulon: So, Gallimard, you've got the inside knowledge — what *do* the Chinese think?

Gallimard: Deep down, they miss the old days. You know, cappuccinos, men in tuxedos —

Toulon: So what do we tell the Americans about Vietnam?

Gallimard: Tell them there's a natural affinity between the West and the Orient.

Toulon: And that you speak from experience?

Gallimard: The Orientals are people too. They want the good things we can give them. If the Americans demonstrate the will to win, the Vietnamese will welcome them into a mutually beneficial union.

Toulon: I don't see how the Vietnamese can stand up to American firepower.

Gallimard: Orientals will always submit to a greater force.

Toulon: I'll note your opinions in my report. The Americans always love to hear how "welcome" they'll be. *(He starts to exit.)*

Gallimard: Sir?

Toulon: Mmmm?

Gallimard: This . . . rumor you've heard.

Toulon: Uh-huh?

Gallimard: How . . . widespread do you think it is?

Ho Chi Minh (1890–1969): First president of North Vietnam (1945–1969).

Toulon: It's only widespread within this embassy. Where nobody talks because everybody is guilty. We were worried about you, Gallimard. We thought you were the only one here without a secret. Now you go and find a lotus blossom . . . and top us all. *(He exits.)*

Gallimard (to us): Toulon knows! And he approves! I was learning the benefits of being a man. We form our own clubs, sit behind thick doors, smoke — and celebrate the fact that we're still boys. *(He starts to move downstage, towards Song.)* So, over the —

Suddenly Comrade Chin enters. Gallimard backs away.

Gallimard (to Song): No! Why does she have to come in?

Song: Rene, be sensible. How can they understand the story without her? Now, don't embarrass yourself.

Gallimard moves down center.

Gallimard (to us): Now, you will see why my story is so amusing to so many people. Why they snicker at parties in disbelief. Please — try to understand it from my point of view. We are all prisoners of our time and place. *(He exits.)*

SCENE IV

Gallimard and Butterfly's flat. Beijing. 1961.

Song (to us): 1961. The flat Monsieur Gallimard rented for us. An evening after he has gone.

Chin: Okay, see if you can find out when the Americans plan to start bombing Vietnam. If you can find out what cities, even better.

Song: I'll do my best, but I don't want to arouse his suspicions.

Chin: Yeah, sure, of course. So, what else?

Song: The Americans will increase troops in Vietnam to 170,000 soldiers with 120,000 militia and 11,000 American advisors.

Chin (writing): Wait, wait, 120,000 militia and —

Song: — 11,000 American —

Chin: — American advisors. *(Beat.)* How do you remember so much?

Song: I'm an actor.

Chin: Yeah. *(Beat.)* Is that how come you dress like that?

Song: Like what, Miss Chin?

Chin: Like that dress! You're wearing a dress. And every time I come here, you're wearing a dress. Is that because you're an actor? Or what?

Song: It's a . . . disguise, Miss Chin.

Chin: Actors, I think they're all weirdos. My mother tells me actors are like gamblers or prostitutes or —

Song: It helps me in my assignment.

Pause.

Chin: You're not gathering information in any way that violates Communist Party principles, are you?

Song: Why would I do that?

Chin: Just checking. Remember: when working for the Great Proletarian State, you represent our Chairman Mao in every position you take.

Song: I'll try to imagine the Chairman taking my positions.

Chin: We all think of him this way. Good-bye, comrade. *(She starts to exit.)* Comrade?

Song: Yes?

Chin: Don't forget: there is no homosexuality in China!

Song: Yes, I've heard.

Chin: Just checking. *(She exits.)*

Song (to us): What passes for a woman in modern China.

Gallimard sticks his head out from the wings.

Gallimard: Is she gone?

Song: Yes, Rene. Please continue in your own fashion.

SCENE V

Beijing. 1961–1963.
Gallimard moves to the couch where Song still sits. He lies down in her lap, and she strokes his forehead.

Gallimard (to us): And so, over the years 1961, '62, '63, we settled into our routine, Butterfly and I. She would always have prepared a light snack and then, ever so delicately, and only if I agreed, she would start to pleasure me. With her hands, her mouth . . . too many ways to explain, and too sad, given my present situation. But mostly we would talk. About my life. Perhaps there is nothing more rare than to find a woman who passionately listens.

Song remains upstage, listening, as Helga enters and plays a scene downstage with Gallimard.

Helga: Rene, I visited Dr. Bolleart this morning.

Gallimard: Why? Are you ill?

Helga: No, no. You see, I wanted to ask him . . . that question we've been discussing.

Gallimard: And I told you, it's only a matter of time. Why did you bring a doctor into this? We just have to keep trying—like a crapshoot, actually.

Helga: I went, I'm sorry. But listen: he says there's nothing wrong with me.

Gallimard: You see? Now, will you stop—?

Helga: Rene, he says he'd like you to go in and take some tests.

Gallimard: Why? So he can find there's nothing wrong with both of us?

Helga: Rene, I don't ask for much. One trip! One visit! And then, whatever you want to do about it—you decide.

Gallimard: You're assuming he'll find something defective!

Helga: No! Of course not! Whatever he finds—if he finds nothing, we decide what to do about nothing! But go!

Gallimard: If he finds nothing, we keep trying. Just like we do now.

Helga: But at least we'll know! *(Pause.)* I'm sorry. *(She starts to exit.)*

Gallimard: Do you really want me to see Dr. Bolleart?

Helga: Only if you want a child, Rene. We have to face the fact that time is running out. Only if you want a child. *(She exits.)*

Gallimard (to Song): I'm a modern man, Butterfly. And yet, I don't want to go. It's the same old voodoo. I feel like God himself is laughing at me if I can't produce a child.

Song: You men of the West—you're obsessed by your odd desire for equality. Your wife can't give you a child, and *you're* going to the doctor?

Gallimard: Well, you see, she's already gone.

Song: And because this incompetent can't find the defect, you now have to subject yourself to him? It's unnatural.

Gallimard: Well, what is the "natural" solution?

Song: In Imperial China, when a man found that one wife was inadequate, he turned to another — to give him his son.

Gallimard: What do you —? I can't . . . marry you, yet.

Song: Please. I'm not asking you to be my husband. But I am already your wife.

Gallimard: Do you want to . . . have my child?

Song: I thought you'd never ask.

Gallimard: But, your career . . . your —

Song: Phooey on my career! That's your Western mind, twisting itself into strange shapes again. Of course I love my career. But what would I love most of all? To feel something inside me — day and night — something I know is yours. *(Pause.)* Promise me . . . you won't go to this doctor. Who is this Western quack to set himself as judge over the man I love? I know who is a man, and who is not. *(She exits.)*

Gallimard (to us): Dr. Bolleart? Of course I didn't go. What man would?

SCENE VI

Beijing. 1963.
    Party noises over the house speakers. Renee enters, wearing a revealing gown.

Gallimard: 1963. A party at the Austrian embassy. None of us could remember the Austrian ambassador's name, which seemed somehow appropriate. *(To Renee.)* So, I tell the Americans, Diem° must go. The U.S. wants to be respected by the Vietnamese, and yet they're propping up this no-body seminarian as her president. A man whose claim to fame is his sister-in-law imposing fanatic "moral order" campaigns? Oriental women — when they're good, they're very good, but when they're bad, they're Christians.

Renee: Yeah.

Gallimard: And what do you do?

Renee: I'm a student. My father exports a lot of useless stuff to the Third World.

Gallimard: How useless?

Renee: You know. Squirt guns, confectioner's sugar, Hula Hoops . . .

Gallimard: I'm sure they appreciate the sugar.

Renee: I'm here for two years to study Chinese.

Gallimard: Two years!

Renee: That's what everybody says.

Gallimard: When did you arrive?

Renee: Three weeks ago.

Gallimard: And?

Renee: I like it. It's primitive, but . . . well, this is the place to learn Chinese, so here I am.

Gallimard: Why Chinese?

Diem: Ngo Dinh Diem (1901-1963), president of South Vietnam (1955-1963), assassinated in a coup d'etat supported by the United States.

Renee: I think it'll be important someday.
Gallimard: You do?
Renee: Don't ask me when, but . . . that's what I think.
Gallimard: Well, I agree with you. One hundred percent. That's very farsighted.
Renee: Yeah. Well of course, my father thinks I'm a complete weirdo.
Gallimard: He'll thank you someday.
Renee: Like when the Chinese start buying Hula Hoops?
Gallimard: There're a billion bellies out there.
Renee: And if they end up taking over the world—well, then I'll be lucky to know Chinese too, right?

> *Pause.*

Gallimard: At this point, I don't see how the Chinese can possibly take—
Renee: You know what I *don't* like about China?
Gallimard: Excuse me? No—what?
Renee: Nothing to do at night.
Gallimard: You come to parties at embassies like everyone else.
Renee: Yeah, but they get out at ten. And then what?
Gallimard: I'm afraid the Chinese idea of a dance hall is a dirt floor and a man with a flute.
Renee: Are you married?
Gallimard: Yes. Why?
Renee: You wanna . . . fool around?

> *Pause.*

Gallimard: Sure.
Renee: I'll wait for you outside. What's your name?
Gallimard: Gallimard. Rene.
Renee: Weird. I'm Renee too. *(She exits.)*
Gallimard (to us): And so, I embarked on my first extra-extramarital affair. Renee was picture perfect. With a body like those girls in the magazines. If I put a tissue paper over my eyes, I wouldn't have been able to tell the difference. And it was exciting to be with someone who wasn't afraid to be seen completely naked. But is it possible for a woman to be *too* uninhibited, *too* willing, so as to seem almost too . . . masculine?

> *Chuck Berry*° *blares from the house speakers, then comes down in volume as Renee enters, toweling her hair.*

Renee: You have a nice weenie.
Gallimard: What?
Renee: Penis. You have a nice penis.
Gallimard: Oh. Well, thank you. That's very . . .
Renee: What—can't take a compliment?
Gallimard: No, it's very . . . reassuring.
Renee: But most girls don't come out and say it, huh?
Gallimard: And also . . . what did you call it?
Renee: Oh. Most girls don't call it a "weenie," huh?
Gallimard: It sounds very—
Renee: Small, I know.

Chuck Berry: Influential American rock 'n' roll musician whose first recording came out in 1955.

Gallimard: I was going to say, "young."

Renee: Yeah. Young, small, same thing. Most guys are pretty, uh, sensitive about that. Like, you know, I had a boyfriend back home in Denmark. I got mad at him once and called him a little weeniehead. He got so mad! He said at least I should call him a great big weeniehead.

Gallimard: I suppose I just say "penis."

Renee: Yeah. That's pretty clinical. There's "cock," but that sounds like a chicken. And "prick" is painful, and "dick" is like you're talking about someone who's not in the room.

Gallimard: Yes. It's a . . . bigger problem than I imagined.

Renee: I—I think maybe it's because I really don't know what to do with them—that's why I call them "weenies."

Gallimard: Well, you did quite well with . . . mine.

Renee: Thanks, but I mean, really *do* with them. Like, okay, have you ever looked at one? I mean, really?

Gallimard: No, I suppose when it's part of you, you sort of take it for granted.

Renee: I guess. But, like, it just hangs there. This little . . . flap of flesh. And there's so much fuss that we make about it. Like, I think the reason we fight wars is because we wear clothes. Because no one knows—between the men, I mean—who has the biggest . . . weenie. So, if I'm a guy with a small one, I'm going to build a really big building or take over a really big piece of land or write a really long book so the other men don't know, right? But, see, it never really works, that's the problem. I mean, you conquer the country, or whatever, but you're still wearing clothes, so there's no way to prove absolutely whose is bigger or smaller. And that's what we call a civilized society. The whole world run by a bunch of men with pricks the size of pins. *(She exits.)*

Gallimard (to us): This was simply not acceptable.

A high-pitched chime rings through the air. Song, dressed as Butterfly, appears in the upstage special. She is obviously distressed. Her body swoons as she attempts to clip the stems of flowers she's arranging in a vase.

Gallimard: But I kept up our affair, wildly, for several months. Why? I believe because of Butterfly. She knew the secret I was trying to hide. But, unlike a Western woman, she didn't confront me, threaten, even pout. I remembered the words of Puccini's *Butterfly:*

Song: *"Noi siamo gente avvezza / alle piccole cose / umili e silenziose."*

Gallimard: "I come from a people / Who are accustomed to little / Humble and silent." I saw Pinkerton and Butterfly, and what she would say if he were unfaithful . . . nothing. She would cry, alone, into those wildly soft sleeves, once full of possessions, now empty to collect her tears. It was her tears and her silence that excited me, every time I visited Renee.

Toulon (offstage): Gallimard!

Toulon enters. Gallimard turns towards him. During the next section, Song, up center, begins to dance with the flowers. It is a drunken, reckless dance, where she breaks small pieces off the stems.

Toulon: They're killing him.

Gallimard: Who? I'm sorry? What?

Toulon: Bother you to come over at this late hour?

Gallimard: No . . . of course not.

Toulon: Not after you hear my secret. Champagne?

Gallimard: Um . . . thank you.

Toulon: You're surprised. There's something that you've wanted, Gallimard. No, not a promotion. Next time. Something in the world. You're not aware of this, but there's an informal gossip circle among intelligence agents. And some of ours heard from some of the Americans —

Gallimard: Yes?

Toulon: That the U.S. will allow the Vietnamese generals to stage a coup . . . and assassinate President Diem.

The chime rings again. Toulon freezes. Gallimard turns upstage and looks at Butterfly, who slowly and deliberately clips a flower off its stem. Gallimard turns back towards Toulon.

Gallimard: I think . . . that's a very wise move!

Toulon unfreezes.

Toulon: It's what you've been advocating. A toast?

Gallimard: Sure. I consider this a vindication.

Toulon: Not exactly. "To the test. Let's hope you pass."

They drink. The chime rings again. Toulon freezes. Gallimard turns upstage, and Song clips another flower.

Gallimard (to Toulon): The test?

Toulon (unfreezing): It's a test of everything you've been saying. I personally think the generals probably will stop the Communists. And you'll be a hero. But if anything goes wrong, then your opinions won't be worth a pig's ear. I'm sure that won't happen. But sometimes it's easier when they don't listen to you.

Gallimard: They're your opinions too, aren't they?

Toulon: Personally, yes.

Gallimard: So we agree.

Toulon: But my opinions aren't on that report. Yours are. Cheers.

Toulon turns away from Gallimard and raises his glass. At that instant Song picks up the vase and hurls it to the ground. It shatters. Song sinks down amidst the shards of the vase, in a calm, childlike trance. She sings softly, as if reciting a child's nursery rhyme.

Song (repeat as necessary): "The whole world over, the white man travels, setting anchor, wherever he likes. Life's not worth living, unless he finds, the finest maidens, of every land . . . "

Gallimard turns downstage towards us. Song continues singing.

Gallimard: I shook as I left his house. That coward! That worm! To put the burden for his decisions on my shoulders!

   I started for Renee's. But no, that was all I needed. A schoolgirl who would question the role of the penis in modern society. What I wanted was revenge. A vessel to contain my humiliation. Though I hadn't seen her in several weeks, I headed for Butterfly's.

Gallimard enters Song's apartment.

Song: Oh! Rene . . . I was dreaming!

Gallimard: You've been drinking?

Song: If I can't sleep, then yes, I drink. But then, it gives me these dreams which—Rene, it's been almost three weeks since you visited me last.

Gallimard: I know. There's been a lot going on in the world.

Song: Fortunately I am drunk. So I can speak freely. It's not the world, it's you and me. And an old problem. Even the softest skin becomes like leather to a man who's touched it too often. I confess I don't know how to stop it. I don't know how to become another woman.

Gallimard: I have a request.

Song: Is this a solution? Or are you ready to give up the flat?

Gallimard: It may be a solution. But I'm sure you won't like it.

Song: Oh well, that's very important. "Like it?" Do you think I "like" lying here alone, waiting, always waiting for your return? Please—don't worry about what I may not "like."

Gallimard: I want to see you . . . naked.

> *Silence.*

Song: I thought you understood my modesty. So you want me to—what— strip? Like a big cowboy girl? Shiny pasties on my breasts? Shall I fling my kimono over my head and yell "ya-hoo" in the process? I thought you respected my shame!

Gallimard: I believe you gave me your shame many years ago.

Song: Yes—and it is just like a white devil to use it against me. I can't believe it. I thought myself so repulsed by the passive Oriental and the cruel white man. Now I see—we are always most revolted by the things hidden within us.

Gallimard: I just mean—

Song: Yes?

Gallimard: —that it will remove the only barrier left between us.

Song: No, Rene. Don't couch your request in sweet words. Be yourself—a cad—and know that my love is enough, that I submit—submit to the worst you can give me. *(Pause.)* Well, come. Strip me. Whatever happens, know that you have willed it. Our love, in your hands. I'm helpless before my man.

> *Gallimard starts to cross the room.*

Gallimard: Did I not undress her because I knew, somewhere deep down, what I would find? Perhaps. Happiness is so rare that our mind can turn somersaults to protect it.

At the time, I only knew that I was seeing Pinkerton stalking towards his Butterfly, ready to reward her love with his lecherous hands. The image sickened me, pulled me to my knees, so I was crawling towards her like a worm. By the time I reached her, Pinkerton . . . had vanished from my heart. To be replaced by something new, something unnatural, that flew in the face of all I'd learned in the world—something very close to love.

> *He grabs her around the waist; she strokes his hair.*

Gallimard: Butterfly, forgive me.

Song: Rene . . .

Gallimard: For everything. From the start.

Song: I'm . . .

Gallimard: I want to —

Song: I'm pregnant. (*Beat.*) I'm pregnant. (*Beat.*) I'm pregnant.

> *Beat.*

Gallimard: I want to marry you!

SCENE VII

> *Gallimard and Butterfly's flat. Beijing. 1963.*
>   *Downstage, Song paces as Comrade Chin reads from her notepad. Upstage, Gallimard is still kneeling. He remains on his knees throughout the scene, watching it.*

Song: I need a baby.

Chin (from pad): He's been spotted going to a dorm.

Song: I need a baby.

Chin: At the Foreign Language Institute.

Song: I need a baby.

Chin: The room of a Danish girl. . . . What do you mean, you need a baby?!

Song: Tell Comrade Kang — last night, the entire mission, it could've ended.

Chin: What do you mean?

Song: Tell Kang — he told me to strip.

Chin: Strip?!

Song: Write!

Chin: I tell you, I don't understand nothing about this case anymore. Nothing.

Song: He told me to strip, and I took a chance. Oh, we Chinese, we know how to gamble.

Chin (writing): ". . . told him to strip."

Song: My palms were wet, I had to make a split-second decision.

Chin: Hey! Can you slow down?!

> *Pause.*

Song: You write faster, I'm the artist here. Suddenly, it hit me — "All he wants is for her to submit. Once a woman submits, a man is always ready to become 'generous.'"

Chin: You're just gonna end up with rough notes.

Song: And it worked! He gave in! Now, if I can just present him with a baby. A Chinese baby with blond hair — he'll be mine for life!

Chin: Kang will never agree! The trading of babies has to be a counterrevolutionary act!

Song: Sometimes, a counterrevolutionary act is necessary to counter a counterrevolutionary act.

> *Pause.*

Chin: Wait.

Song: I need one . . . in seven months. Make sure it's a boy.

Chin: This doesn't sound like something the Chairman would do. Maybe you'd better talk to Comrade Kang yourself.

Song: Good. I will.

> *Chin gets up to leave.*

Song: Miss Chin? Why, in the Peking Opera, are women's roles played by men?
Chin: I don't know. Maybe, a reactionary remnant of male —
Song: No. *(Beat.)* Because only a man knows how a woman is supposed to act.

> *Chin exits. Song turns upstage, towards Gallimard.*

Gallimard (calling after Chin): Good riddance! *(To Song.)* I could forget all that betrayal in an instant, you know. If you'd just come back and become Butterfly again.
Song: Fat chance. You're here in prison, rotting in a cell. And I'm on a plane, winging my way back to China. Your President pardoned me of our treason, you know.
Gallimard: Yes, I read about that.
Song: Must make you feel . . . lower than shit.
Gallimard: But don't you, even a little bit, wish you were here with me?
Song: I'm an artist, Rene. You were my greatest . . . acting challenge. *(She laughs.)* It doesn't matter how rotten I answer, does it? You still adore me. That's why I love you, Rene. *(She points to us.)* So — you were telling your audience about the night I announced I was pregnant.

> *Gallimard puts his arms around Song's waist. He and Song are in the positions they were in at the end of Scene VI.*

Scene VIII

> *Same.*

Gallimard: I'll divorce my wife. We'll live together here, and then later in France.
Song: I feel so . . . ashamed.
Gallimard: Why?
Song: I had begun to lose faith. And now, you shame me with your generosity.
Gallimard: Generosity? No, I'm proposing for very selfish reasons.
Song: Your apologies only make me feel more ashamed. My outburst a moment ago!
Gallimard: Your outburst? What about my request?!
Song: You've been very patient dealing with my . . . eccentricities. A Western man, used to women freer with their bodies —
Gallimard: It was sick! Don't make excuses for me.
Song: I have to. You don't seem willing to make them for yourself.

> *Pause.*

Gallimard: You're crazy.
Song: I'm happy. Which often looks like crazy.
Gallimard: Then make me crazy. Marry me.

> *Pause.*

Song: No.
Gallimard: What?
Song: Do I sound silly, a slave, if I say I'm not worthy?
Gallimard: Yes. In fact you do. No one has loved me like you.
Song: Thank you. And no one ever will. I'll see to that.

Gallimard: So what is the problem?

Song: Rene, we Chinese are realists. We understand rice, gold, and guns. You are a diplomat. Your career is skyrocketing. Now, what would happen if you divorced your wife to marry a Communist Chinese actress?

Gallimard: That's not being realistic. That's defeating yourself before you begin.

Song: We conserve our strength for the battles we can win.

Gallimard: That sounds like a fortune cookie!

Song: Where do you think fortune cookies come from!

Gallimard: I don't care.

Song: You do. So do I. And we should. That is why I say I'm not worthy. I'm worthy to love and even to be loved by you. But I am not worthy to end the career of one of the West's most promising diplomats.

Gallimard: It's not that great a career! I made it sound like more than it is!

Song: Modesty will get you nowhere. Flatter yourself, and you flatter me. I'm flattered to decline your offer. *(She exits.)*

Gallimard (to us): Butterfly and I argued all night. And, in the end, I left, knowing I would never be her husband. She went away for several months — to the countryside, like a small animal. Until the night I received her call.

A baby's cry from offstage. Song enters, carrying a child.

Song: He looks like you.

Gallimard: Oh! *(Beat; he approaches the baby.)* Well, babies are never very attractive at birth.

Song: Stop!

Gallimard: I'm sure he'll grow more beautiful with age. More like his mother.

Song: *"Chi vide mai / a bimbo del Giappon . . ."*

Gallimard: "What baby, I wonder, was ever born in Japan" — or China, for that matter —

Song: *". . . occhi azzurrini?"*

Gallimard: "With azure eyes" — they're actually sort of brown, wouldn't you say?

Song: *"E il labbro."*

Gallimard: "And such lips!" *(He kisses Song.)* And such lips.

Song: *"E i ricciolini d'oro schietto?"*

Gallimard: "And such a head of golden" — if slightly patchy — "curls?"

Song: I'm going to call him "Peepee."

Gallimard: Darling, could you repeat that because I'm sure a rickshaw just flew by overhead.

Song: You heard me.

Gallimard: "Song Peepee"? May I suggest Michael, or Stephan, or Adolph?

Song: You may, but I won't listen.

Gallimard: You can't be serious. Can you imagine the time this child will have in school?

Song: In the West, yes.

Gallimard: It's worse than naming him Ping Pong or Long Dong or —

Song: But he's never going to live in the West, is he?

Pause.

Gallimard: That wasn't my choice.

Song: It is mine. And this is my promise to you: I will raise him, he will be our child, but he will never burden you outside of China.
Gallimard: Why do you make these promises? I want to be burdened! I want a scandal to cover the papers!
Song (to us): Prophetic.
Gallimard: I'm serious.
Song: So am I. His name is as I registered it. And he will never live in the West.

> *Song exits with the child.*

Gallimard (to us): Is it possible that her stubbornness only made me want her more? That drawing back at the moment of my capitulation was the most brilliant strategy she could have chosen? It is possible. But it is also possible that by this point she could have said, could have done . . . anything, and I would have adored her still.

Scene IX

> *Beijing. 1966.*
> *A driving rhythm of Chinese percussion fills the stage.*

Gallimard: And then, China began to change. Mao became very old, and his cult became very strong. And, like many old men, he entered his second childhood. So he handed over the reins of state to those with minds like his own. And children ruled the Middle Kingdom° with complete caprice. The doctrine of the Cultural Revolution° implied continuous anarchy. Contact between Chinese and foreigners became impossible. Our flat was confiscated. Her fame and my money now counted against us.

> *Two dancers in Mao suits and red-starred caps enter, and begin crudely mimicking revolutionary violence, in an agitprop fashion.*

Gallimard: And somehow the American war went wrong too. Four hundred thousand dollars were being spent for every Viet Cong° killed; so General Westmoreland's° remark that the Oriental does not value life the way Americans do was oddly accurate. Why weren't the Vietnamese people giving in? Why were they content instead to die and die and die again?

> *Toulon enters. Percussion and dancers continue upstage.*

Toulon: Congratulations, Gallimard.
Gallimard: Excuse me, sir?
Toulon: Not a promotion. That was last time. You're going home.
Gallimard: What?
Toulon: Don't say I didn't warn you.

Middle Kingdom: The royal domain of China during its feudal period.   *Cultural Revolution:* The reform campaign of 1965–1967 to purge counterrevolutionary thought in China that challenged Mao Zedong.   *Viet Cong:* Member of the National Liberation Front of South Vietnam, against which U.S. forces were fighting.   *General Westmoreland:* William Westmoreland (b. 1914), commander of American troops in Vietnam from 1964 to 1968.

Gallimard: I'm being transferred ... because I was wrong about the American war?

Toulon: Of course not. We don't care about the Americans. We care about your mind. The quality of your analysis. In general, everything you've predicted here in the Orient ... just hasn't happened.

Gallimard: I think that's premature.

Toulon: Don't force me to be blunt. Okay, you said China was ready to open to Western trade. The only thing they're trading out there are Western heads. And, yes, you said the Americans would succeed in Indochina. You were kidding, right?

Gallimard: I think the end is in sight.

Toulon: Don't be pathetic. And don't take this personally. You were wrong. It's not your fault.

Gallimard: But I'm going home.

Toulon: Right. Could I have the number of your mistress? *(Beat.)* Joke! Joke! Eat a croissant for me.

Toulon exits. Song, wearing a Mao suit, is dragged in from the wings as part of the upstage dance. They "beat" her, then lampoon the acrobatics of the Chinese opera, as she is made to kneel onstage.

Gallimard (simultaneously): I don't care to recall how Butterfly and I said our hurried farewell. Perhaps it was better to end our affair before it killed her.

Gallimard exits. Percussion rises in volume. The lampooning becomes faster, more frenetic. At its height, Comrade Chin walks across the stage with a banner reading: "The Actor Renounces His Decadent Profession!" She reaches the kneeling Song. At the moment Chin touches Song's chin, percussion stops with a thud. Dancers strike poses.

Chin: Actor-oppressor, for years you have lived above the common people and looked down on their labor. While the farmer ate millet—

Song: I ate pastries from France and sweetmeats from silver trays.

Chin: And how did you come to live in such an exalted position?

Song: I was a plaything for the imperialists!

Chin: What did you do?

Song: I shamed China by allowing myself to be corrupted by a foreigner ...

Chin: What does this mean? The People demand a full confession!

Song: I engaged in the lowest perversions with China's enemies!

Chin: What perversions? Be more clear!

Song: I let him put it up my ass!

Dancers look over, disgusted.

Chin: Aaaa-ya! How can you use such sickening language?!

Song: My language ... is only as foul as the crimes I committed ...

Chin: Yeah. That's better. So—what do you want to do ... now?

Song: I want to serve the people!

Percussion starts up, with Chinese strings.

Chin: What?

Song: I want to serve the people!

Dancers regain their revolutionary smiles, and begin a dance of victory.

Chin: What?!

Song: I want to serve the people!!

Dancers unveil a banner: "The Actor Is Re-Habilitated!" Song remains kneeling before Chin, as the dancers bounce around them, then exit. Music out.

Scene X

A commune. Hunan Province. 1970.

Chin: How you planning to do that?

Song: I've already worked four years in the fields of Hunan, Comrade Chin.

Chin: So? Farmers work all their lives. Let me see your hands.

Song holds them out for her inspection.

Chin: Goddamn! Still so smooth! How long does it take to turn you actors into good anythings? Hunh. You've just spent too many years in luxury to be any good to the Revolution.

Song: I served the Revolution.

Chin: Serve the Revolution? Bullshit! You wore dresses! Don't tell me — I was there. I saw you! You and your white vice-consul! Stuck up there in your flat, living off the People's Treasury! Yeah, I knew what was going on! You two . . . homos! Homos! Homos! *(Pause; she composes herself.)* Ah! Well . . . you will serve the people, all right. But not with the Revolution's money. This time, you use your own money.

Song: I have no money.

Chin: Shut up! And you won't stink up China anymore with your pervert stuff. You'll pollute the place where pollution begins — the West.

Song: What do you mean?

Chin: Shut up! You're going to France. Without a cent in your pocket. You find your consul's house, you make him pay your expenses —

Song: No.

Chin: And you give us weekly reports! Useful information!

Song: That's crazy. It's been four years.

Chin: Either that, or back to rehabilitation center!

Song: Comrade Chin, he's not going to support me! Not in France! He's a white man! I was just his plaything —

Chin: Oh yuck! Again with the sickening language? Where's my stick?

Song: You don't understand the mind of a man.

Pause.

Chin: Oh no? No I don't? Then how come I'm married, huh? How come I got a man? Five, six years ago, you always tell me those kind of things, I felt very bad. But not now! Because what does the Chairman say? He tells us *I'm* now the smart one, you're now the nincompoop! *You're* the blockhead, the harebrain, the nitwit! You think you're so smart? You understand "The Mind of a Man"? Good! Then *you* go to France and be a pervert for Chairman Mao!

Chin and Song exit in opposite directions.

SCENE XI

> *Paris. 1968–1970.*
> *Gallimard enters.*

Gallimard: And what was waiting for me back in Paris? Well, better Chinese food than I'd eaten in China. Friends and relatives. A little accounting, regular schedule, keeping track of traffic violations in the suburbs. . . . And the indignity of students shouting the slogans of Chairman Mao at me — in French.

Helga: Rene? Rene? *(She enters, soaking wet.)* I've had a . . . problem.

> *(She sneezes.)*

Gallimard: You're wet.

Helga: Yes, I . . . coming back from the grocer's. A group of students, waving red flags, they —

> *Gallimard fetches a towel.*

Helga: — they ran by, I was caught up along with them. Before I knew what was happening —

> *Gallimard gives her the towel.*

Helga: Thank you. The police started firing water cannons at us. I tried to shout, to tell them I was the wife of a diplomat, but — you know how it is . . . *(Pause.)* Needless to say, I lost the groceries. Rene, what's happening to France?

Gallimard: What's — ? Well, nothing, really.

Helga: Nothing?! The storefronts are in flames, there's glass in the streets, buildings are toppling — and I'm wet!

Gallimard: Nothing! . . . that I care to think about.

Helga: And is that why you stay in this room?

Gallimard: Yes, in fact.

Helga: With the incense burning? You know something? I hate incense. It smells so sickly sweet.

Gallimard: Well, I hate the French. Who just smell — period!

Helga: And the Chinese were better?

Gallimard: Please — don't start.

Helga: When we left, this exact same thing, the riots —

Gallimard: No, no . . .

Helga: Students screaming slogans, smashing down doors —

Gallimard: Helga —

Helga: It was all going on in China, too. Don't you remember?!

Gallimard: Helga! Please! *(Pause.)* You have never understood China, have you? You walk in here with these ridiculous ideas, that the West is falling apart, that China was spitting in our faces. You come in, dripping of the streets, and you leave water all over my floor. *(He grabs Helga's towel, begins mopping up the floor.)*

Helga: But it's the truth!

Gallimard: Helga, I want a divorce.

> *Pause; Gallimard continues mopping the floor.*

Helga: I take it back. China is . . . beautiful. Incense, I like incense.

Gallimard: I've had a mistress.

Helga: So?

Gallimard: For eight years.

Helga: I knew you would. I knew you would the day I married you. And now what? You want to marry her?

Gallimard: I can't. She's in China.

Helga: I see. You know that no one else is ever going to marry me, right?

Gallimard: I'm sorry.

Helga: And you want to leave. For someone who's not here, is that right?

Gallimard: That's right.

Helga: You can't live with her, but still you don't want to live with me.

Gallimard: That's right.

> *Pause.*

Helga: Shit. How terrible that I can figure that out. *(Pause.)* I never thought I'd say it. But, in China, I was happy. I knew, in my own way, I knew that you were not everything you pretended to be. But the pretense — going on your arm to the embassy ball, visiting your office and the guards saying, "Good morning, good morning, Madame Gallimard" — the pretense . . . was very good indeed. *(Pause.)* I hope everyone is mean to you for the rest of your life. *(She exits.)*

Gallimard (to us): Prophetic.

> *Marc enters with two drinks.*

Gallimard (to Marc): In China, I was different from all other men.

Marc: Sure. You were white. Here's your drink.

Gallimard: I felt . . . touched.

Marc: In the head? Rene, I don't want to hear about the Oriental love goddess. Okay? One night — can we just drink and throw up without a lot of conversation?

Gallimard: You still don't believe me, do you?

Marc: Sure I do. She was the most beautiful, et cetera, et cetera, blasé, blasé.

> *Pause.*

Gallimard: My life in the West has been such a disappointment.

Marc: Life in the West is like that. You'll get used to it. Look, you're driving me away. I'm leaving. Happy, now? *(He exits, then returns.)* Look, I have a date tomorrow night. You wanna come? I can fix you up with —

Gallimard: Of course. I would love to come.

> *Pause.*

Marc: Uh — on second thought, no. You'd better get ahold of yourself first.

> *He exits; Gallimard nurses his drink.*

Gallimard (to us): This is the ultimate cruelty, isn't it? That I can talk and talk and to anyone listening, it's only air — too rich a diet to be swallowed by a mundane world. Why can't anyone understand? That in China, I once loved, and was loved by, very simply, the Perfect Woman.

> *Song enters, dressed as Butterfly in wedding dress.*

Gallimard (to Song): Not again. My imagination is hell. Am I asleep this time? Or did I drink too much?

Song: Rene!

Gallimard: God, it's too painful! That you speak?

Song: What are you talking about? Rene — touch me.

Gallimard: Why?

Song: I'm real. Take my hand.

Gallimard: Why? So you can disappear again and leave me clutching at the air? For the entertainment of my neighbors who — ?

> *Song touches Gallimard.*

Song: Rene?

> *Gallimard takes Song's hand. Silence.*

Gallimard: Butterfly? I never doubted you'd return.

Song: You hadn't . . . forgotten — ?

Gallimard: Yes, actually, I've forgotten everything. My mind, you see — there wasn't enough room in this hard head — not for the world *and* for you. No, there was only room for one. *(Beat.)* Come, look. See? Your bed has been waiting, with the Klimt° poster you like, and — see? The *xiang lu°* you gave me?

Song: I . . . I don't know what to say.

Gallimard: There's nothing to say. Not at the end of a long trip. Can I make you some tea?

Song: But where's your wife?

Gallimard: She's by my side. She's by my side at last.

> *Gallimard reaches to embrace Song. Song sidesteps, dodging him.*

Gallimard: Why?!

Song (to us): So I did return to Rene in Paris. Where I found —

Gallimard: Why do you run away? Can't we show them how we embraced that evening?

Song: Please. I'm talking.

Gallimard: You have to do what I say! I'm conjuring you up in *my* mind!

Song: Rene, I've never done what you've said. Why should it be any different in your mind? Now split — the story moves on, and I must change.

Gallimard: I welcomed you into my home! I didn't have to, you know! I could've left you penniless on the streets of Paris! But I took you in!

Song: Thank you.

Gallimard: So . . . please . . . don't change.

Song: You know I have to. You know I will. And anyway, what difference does it make? No matter what your eyes tell you, you can't ignore the truth. You already know too much.

> *Gallimard exits. Song turns to us.*

Song: The change I'm going to make requires about five minutes. So I thought you might want to take this opportunity to stretch your legs, enjoy a drink, or listen to the musicians. I'll be here, when you return, right where you left me.

Klimt: Gustav Klimt (1863–1918), Austrian painter in the art nouveau style, whose most famous painting is *The Kiss.*   *xiang lu:* Incense burner.

> *Song goes to a mirror in front of which is a wash basin of water. She starts to remove her makeup as stagelights go to half and houselights come up.*

ACT III

SCENE I

> *A courthouse in Paris. 1986.*
>   *As he promised, Song has completed the bulk of his transformation onstage by the time the houselights go down and the stagelights come up full. As he speaks to us, he removes his wig and kimono, leaving them on the floor. Underneath, he wears a well-cut suit.*

Song: So I'd done my job better than I had a right to expect. Well, give him some credit, too. He's right — I was in a fix when I arrived in Paris. I walked from the airport into town, then I located, by blind groping, the Chinatown district. Let me make one thing clear: whatever else may be said about the Chinese, they are stingy! I slept in doorways three days until I could find a tailor who would make me this kimono on credit. As it turns out, maybe I didn't even need it. Maybe he would've been happy to see me in a simple shift and mascara. But . . . better safe than sorry.

That was 1970, when I arrived in Paris. For the next fifteen years, yes, I lived a very comfy life. Some relief, believe me, after four years on a fucking commune in Nowheresville, China. Rene supported the boy and me, and I did some demonstrations around the country as part of my "cultural exchange" cover. And then there was the spying.

> *Song moves upstage, to a chair. Toulon enters as a judge, wearing the appropriate wig and robes. He sits near Song. It's 1986, and Song is testifying in a courtroom.*

Song: Not much at first. Rene had lost all his high-level contacts. Comrade Chin wasn't very interested in parking-ticket statistics. But finally, at my urging, Rene got a job as a courier, handling sensitive documents. He'd photograph them for me, and I'd pass them on to the Chinese embassy.

Judge: Did he understand the extent of his activity?

Song: He didn't ask. He knew that I needed those documents, and that was enough.

Judge: But he must've known he was passing classified information.

Song: I can't say.

Judge: He never asked what you were going to do with them?

Song: Nope.

> *Pause.*

Judge: There is one thing that the court — indeed, that all of France — would like to know.

Song: Fire away.

Judge: Did Monsieur Gallimard know you were a man?

Song: Well, he never saw me completely naked. Ever.

Judge: But surely, he must've . . . how can I put this?

Song: Put it however you like. I'm not shy. He must've felt around?

Judge: Mmmmm.

Song: Not really. I did all the work. He just laid back. Of course we did enjoy more . . . complete union, and I suppose he *might* have wondered why I was always on my stomach, but. . . . But what you're thinking is, "Of course a wrist must've brushed . . . a hand hit . . . over twenty years!" Yeah. Well, Your Honor, it was my job to make him think I was a woman. And chew on this: it wasn't all that hard. See, my mother was a prostitute along the Bundt before the Revolution. And, uh, I think it's fair to say she learned a few things about Western men. So I borrowed her knowledge. In service to my country.

Judge: Would you care to enlighten the court with this secret knowledge? I'm sure we're all very curious.

Song: I'm sure you are. *(Pause.)* Okay, Rule One is: Men always believe what they want to hear. So a girl can tell the most obnoxious lies and the guys will believe them every time — "This is my first time" — "That's the biggest I've ever seen" — or *both,* which, if you really think about it, is not possible in a single lifetime. You've maybe heard those phrases a few times in your own life, yes, Your Honor?

Judge: It's not my life, Monsieur Song, which is on trial today.

Song: Okay, okay, just trying to lighten up the proceedings. Tough room.

Judge: Go on.

Song: Rule Two: As soon as a Western man comes into contact with the East — he's already confused. The West has sort of an international rape mentality towards the East. Do you know rape mentality?

Judge: Give us your definition, please.

Song: Basically, "Her mouth says no, but her eyes say yes."

    The West thinks of itself as masculine — big guns, big industry, big money — so the East is feminine — weak, delicate, poor . . . but good at art, and full of inscrutable wisdom — the feminine mystique.

    Her mouth says no, but her eyes say yes. The West believes the East, deep down, *wants* to be dominated — because a woman can't think for herself.

Judge: What does this have to do with my question?

Song: You expect Oriental countries to submit to your guns, and you expect Oriental women to be submissive to your men. That's why you say they make the best wives.

Judge: But why would that make it possible for you to fool Monsieur Gallimard? Please — get to the point.

Song: One, because when he finally met his fantasy woman, he wanted more than anything to believe that she was, in fact, a woman. And second, I am an Oriental. And being an Oriental, I could never be completely a man.

    Pause.

Judge: Your armchair political theory is tenuous, Monsieur Song.

Song: You think so? That's why you'll lose in all your dealings with the East.

Judge: Just answer my question: did he know you were a man?

    Pause.

Song: You know, Your Honor, I never asked.

SCENE II

Same.

> *Music from the "Death Scene" from Butterfly blares over the house speakers. It is the loudest thing we've heard in this play.*
> *Gallimard enters, crawling towards Song's wig and kimono.*

Gallimard: Butterfly? Butterfly?

> *Song remains a man, in the witness box, delivering a testimony we do not hear.*

Gallimard (to us): In my moment of greatest shame, here, in this courtroom —with that . . . person up there, telling the world. . . . What strikes me especially is how shallow he is, how glib and obsequious . . . completely . . . without substance! The type that prowls around discos with a gold medallion stinking of garlic. So little like my Butterfly.

Yet even in this moment my mind remains agile, flip-flopping like a man on a trampoline. Even now, my picture dissolves, and I see that . . . witness . . . talking to me.

> *Song suddenly stands straight up in his witness box, and looks at Gallimard.*

Song: Yes. You. White man.

> *Song steps out of the witness box, and moves downstage towards Gallimard. Light change.*

Gallimard (to Song): Who? Me?

Song: Do you see any other white men?

Gallimard: Yes. There're white men all around. This is a French courtroom.

Song: So you are an adventurous imperialist. Tell me, why did it take you so long? To come back to this place?

Gallimard: What place?

Song: This theater in China. Where we met many years ago.

Gallimard (to us): And once again, against my will, I am transported.

> *Chinese opera music comes up on the speakers. Song begins to do opera moves, as he did the night they met.*

Song: Do you remember? The night you gave your heart?

Gallimard: It was a long time ago.

Song: Not long enough. A night that turned your world upside down.

Gallimard: Perhaps.

Song: Oh, be honest with me. What's another bit of flattery when you've already given me twenty years' worth? It's a wonder my head hasn't swollen to the size of China.

Gallimard: Who's to say it hasn't?

Song: Who's to say? And what's the shame? In pride? You think I could've pulled this off if I wasn't already full of pride when we met? No, not just pride. Arrogance. It takes arrogance, really — to believe you can will, with your eyes and your lips, the destiny of another. *(He dances.)* C'mon. Admit it. You still want me. Even in slacks and a button-down collar.

Gallimard: I don't see what the point of —

Song: You don't? Well maybe, Rene, just maybe — I want you.

Gallimard: You do?

Song: Then again, maybe I'm just playing with you. How can you tell? *(Repris-ing his feminine character, he sidles up to Gallimard.)* "How I wish there were even a small café to sit in. With men in tuxedos, and cappuccinos, and bad expatriate jazz." Now you want to kiss me, don't you?

Gallimard (pulling away): What makes you —?

Song: — so sure? See? I take the words from your mouth. Then I wait for you to come and retrieve them. *(He reclines on the floor.)*

Gallimard: Why?! Why do you treat me so cruelly?

Song: Perhaps I *was* treating you cruelly. But now — I'm being nice. Come here, my little one.

Gallimard: I'm not your little one!

Song: My mistake. It's I who am *your* little one, right?

Gallimard: Yes, I —

Song: So come get your little one. If you like, I may even let you strip me.

Gallimard: I mean, you were! Before . . . but not like this!

Song: I was? Then perhaps I still am. If you look hard enough. *(He starts to re-move his clothes.)*

Gallimard: What — what are you doing?

Song: Helping you to see through my act.

Gallimard: Stop that! I don't want to! I don't —

Song: Oh, but you asked me to strip, remember?

Gallimard: What? That was years ago! And I took it back!

Song: No. You postponed it. Postponed the inevitable. Today, the inevitable has come calling.

> *From the speakers, cacophony: Butterfly mixed in with Chinese gongs.*

Gallimard: No! Stop! I don't want to see!

Song: Then look away.

Gallimard: You're only in my mind! All this is in my mind! I order you! To stop!

Song: To what? To strip? That's just what I'm —

Gallimard: No! Stop! I want you —!

Song: You want me?

Gallimard: To stop!

Song: You know something, Rene? Your mouth says no, but your eyes say yes. Turn them away. I dare you.

Gallimard: I don't have to! Every night, you say you're going to strip, but then I beg you and you stop!

Song: I guess tonight is different.

Gallimard: Why? Why should that be?

Song: Maybe I've become frustrated. Maybe I'm saying "Look at me, you fool!" Or maybe I'm just feeling . . . sexy. *(He is down to his briefs.)*

Gallimard: Please. This is unnecessary. I know what you are.

Song: You do? What am I?

Gallimard: A — a man.

Song: You don't really believe that.

Gallimard: Yes I do! I knew all the time somewhere that my happiness was tem-porary, my love a deception. But my mind kept the knowledge at bay. To make the wait bearable.

Song: Monsieur Gallimard — the wait is over.

Song drops his briefs. He is naked. Sound cue out. Slowly, we and Song come to the realization that what we had thought to be Gallimard's sobbing is actually his laughter.

Gallimard: Oh god! What an idiot! Of course!

Song: Rene—what?

Gallimard: Look at you! You're a man! *(He bursts into laughter again.)*

Song: I fail to see what's so funny!

Gallimard: "You fail to see—!" I mean, you never did have much of a sense of humor, did you? I just think it's ridiculously funny that I've wasted so much time on just a man!

Song: Wait. I'm not "just a man."

Gallimard: No? Isn't that what you've been trying to convince me of?

Song: Yes, but what I mean—

Gallimard: And now, I finally believe you, and you tell me it's not true? I think you must have some kind of identity problem.

Song: Will you listen to me?

Gallimard: Why?! I've been listening to you for twenty years. Don't I deserve a vacation?

Song: I'm not just any man!

Gallimard: Then, what exactly are you?

Song: Rene, how can you ask—? Okay, what about this?

He picks up Butterfly's robes, starts to dance around. No music.

Gallimard: Yes, that's very nice. I have to admit.

Song holds out his arm to Gallimard.

Song: It's the same skin you've worshipped for years. Touch it.

Gallimard: Yes, it does feel the same.

Song: Now—close your eyes.

Song covers Gallimard's eyes with one hand. With the other, Song draws Gallimard's hand up to his face. Gallimard, like a blind man, lets his hands run over Song's face.

Gallimard: This skin, I remember. The curve of her face, the softness of her cheek, her hair against the back of my hand . . .

Song: I'm your Butterfly. Under the robes, beneath everything, it was always me. Now, open your eyes and admit it—you adore me. *(He removes his hand from Gallimard's eyes.)*

Gallimard: You, who knew every inch of my desires—how could you, of all people, have made such a mistake?

Song: What?

Gallimard: You showed me your true self. When all I loved was the lie. A perfect lie, which you let fall to the ground—and now, it's old and soiled.

Song: So—you never really loved me? Only when I was playing a part?

Gallimard: I'm a man who loved a woman created by a man. Everything else— simply falls short.

Pause.

Song: What am I supposed to do now?

Gallimard: You were a fine spy, Monsieur Song, with an even finer accomplice. But now I believe you should go. Get out of my life!

Song: Go where? Rene, you can't live without me. Not after twenty years.

Gallimard: I certainly can't live with you — not after twenty years of betrayal.

Song: Don't be stubborn! Where will you go?

Gallimard: I have a date . . . with my Butterfly.

Song: So, throw away your pride. And come . . .

Gallimard: Get away from me! Tonight, I've finally learned to tell fantasy from reality. And, knowing the difference, I choose fantasy.

Song: I'm your fantasy!

Gallimard: You? You're as real as hamburger. Now get out! I have a date with my Butterfly and I don't want your body polluting the room! *(He tosses Song's suit at him.)* Look at these — you dress like a pimp.

Song: Hey! These are Armani slacks and—! *(He puts on his briefs and slacks.)* Let's just say . . . I'm disappointed in you, Rene. In the crush of your adoration, I thought you'd become something more. More like . . . a woman.

But no. Men. You're like the rest of them. It's all in the way we dress, and make up our faces, and bat our eyelashes. You really have so little imagination!

Gallimard: You, Monsieur Song? Accuse me of too little imagination? You, if anyone, should know — I am pure imagination. And in imagination I will remain. Now get out!

Gallimard bodily removes Song from the stage, taking his kimono.

Song: Rene! I'll never put on those robes again! You'll be sorry!

Gallimard (to Song): I'm already sorry! *(Looking at the kimono in his hands.)* Exactly as sorry . . . as a Butterfly.

SCENE III

M. Gallimard's prison cell. Paris. 1988.

Gallimard: I've played out the events of my life night after night, always searching for a new ending to my story, one where I leave this cell and return forever to my Butterfly's arms.

Tonight I realize my search is over. That I've looked all along in the wrong place. And now, to you, I will prove that my love was not in vain — by returning to the world of fantasy where I first met her.

He picks up the kimono; dancers enter.

Gallimard: There is a vision of the Orient that I have. Of slender women in cheongsams and kimonos who die for the love of unworthy foreign devils. Who are born and raised to be the perfect women. Who take whatever punishment we give them, and bounce back, strengthened by love, unconditionally. It is a vision that has become my life.

Dancers bring the washbasin to him and help him make up his face.

Gallimard: In public, I have continued to deny that Song Liling is a man. This brings me headlines, and is a source of great embarrassment to my French colleagues, who can now be sent into a coughing fit by the mere mention of Chinese food. But alone, in my cell, I have long since faced the truth.

And the truth demands a sacrifice. For mistakes made over the course of a lifetime. My mistakes were simple and absolute — the man I loved was a cad, a bounder. He deserved nothing but a kick in the behind, and instead I gave him . . . all my love.

Yes — love. Why not admit it all? That was my undoing, wasn't it? Love warped my judgment, blinded my eyes, rearranged the very lines on my face . . . until I could look in the mirror and see nothing but . . . a woman.

Dancers help him put on the Butterfly wig.

Gallimard: I have a vision. Of the Orient. That, deep within its almond eyes, there are still women. Women willing to sacrifice themselves for the love of a man. Even a man whose love is completely without worth.

Dancers assist Gallimard in donning the kimono. They hand him a knife.

Gallimard: Death with honor is better than life . . . life with dishonor. *(He sets himself center stage, in a seppuku position.)* The love of a Butterfly can withstand many things — unfaithfulness, loss, even abandonment. But how can it face the one sin that implies all others? The devastating knowledge that, underneath it all, the object of her love was nothing more, nothing less than . . . a man. *(He sets the tip of the knife against his body.)* It is 1988. And I have found her at last. In a prison on the outskirts of Paris. My name is Rene Gallimard — also known as Madame Butterfly.

Gallimard turns upstage and plunges the knife into his body, as music from the "Love Duet" blares over the speakers. He collapses into the arms of the dancers, who lay him reverently on the floor. The image holds for several beats. Then a tight special up on Song, who stands as a man, staring at the dead Gallimard. He smokes a cigarette; the smoke filters up through the lights. Two words leave his lips.

Song: Butterfly? Butterfly?

Smoke rises as lights fade slowly to black.

CONSIDERATIONS FOR CRITICAL THINKING AND WRITING

1. FIRST RESPONSE. Do you think Gallimard is a sympathetic or despicable character? Does he have any redeeming qualities? Explain why or why not.

2. In addition to Gallimard, which other characters in the play reveal prejudices of one kind or another? What is the nature of these prejudices?

3. How does Gallimard's response to Song's letters reveal his attitudes toward her?

4. What purpose do Marc and Helga serve in the play?

5. What are some of the explanations for Gallimard's belief that Song is a woman? Which is the most plausible?

6. Why does Gallimard link magazine centerfold models with Asian women?

7. How does the structure of the play help to reinforce its themes?

8. Discuss the role reversal that takes place in the final scene.

9. Is *M. Butterfly* a comedy or a tragedy or something else?

10. Some critics have faulted *M. Butterfly* for the heavy-handed way in which Hwang links Western sexism to the events in Vietnam rather than letting the audience draw its own conclusions. In what ways do you think the play too polemical, and how do you feel the story carries its themes effectively?

11. CRITICAL STRATEGIES. Read the section on gender criticism (pp. 2105–07) in Chapter 52, "Critical Strategies for Reading," and discuss how the characters' ideas about gender — and, in particular, their ideas about what

constitutes masculine and feminine behavior — are created by cultural institutions and conditioning.

CONNECTIONS TO OTHER SELECTIONS

1. At first glance Rene Gallimard and Sophocles' Oedipus in *Oedipus the King* (p. 1289) are very different kinds of characters, but how might their situations — particularly their discoveries about themselves — be compared? What significant similarities do you find in these two characters? Explain whether you think Gallimard can be seen as a tragic character.

2. Compare the function of Puccini's *Madame Butterfly* in *M. Butterfly* with that of the play within the play in Shakespeare's *Hamlet* (p. 1450). How are these internal dramatic actions used to comment on the events of each larger play? How is role-playing relevant to the theme of each play?

3. Write an essay comparing Gallimard's illusions with those of Amanda in Tennessee Williams's *The Glass Menagerie* (p. 1893).

DOCUMENTS

A Plot Synopsis of Madame Butterfly   *1964*

Madama Butterfly

Opera in 2 acts by Puccini; text by Giacosa and Illica, after David Belasco's drama (1900) on the story by John Luther Long, possibly based on a real event. Prod. Milan, Sc., 17 Feb. 1904, with Storchio, Zenatello, De Luca, when it was a fiasco. New version (three acts) prod. Brescia, Grande, 28 May 1904, with Krusceniski, cond. Toscanini; London, C.G., 10 July 1905 with Destinn, Caruso, Scotti; Washington, D.C., Belasco Theatre, 15 Oct. 1906, by Savage Company.

Act I. Goro (tenor), the Japanese marriage broker, is showing Pinkerton (tenor), lieutenant of the U.S. Navy, the little house he has leased for him and his Japanese child-bride, Cio-Cio-San (Madama Butterfly). The American Consul Sharpless (baritone) comes to see Pinkerton who tells him jokingly that he is going to marry in Japanese fashion for 999 years; and he drinks to the day he will marry an American girl. Sharpless warns Pinkerton that Butterfly really loves him and has renounced her religion to marry him. Butterfly (soprano) and her friends appear and the wedding ceremony takes place. In the midst of the celebrations the Bonze, a Japanese priest and her uncle, arrives and denounces her for giving up her religion. Pinkerton comforts the weeping Butterfly, and the act ends with an extended love duet.

Act II. Scene I. Three years have passed, and the faithful Butterfly still awaits Pinkerton. She tries to convince her servant Suzuki (mezzo) in the famous aria "Un bel dì vedremo" that he will return. Sharpless now comes to see Butterfly with a letter from Pinkerton telling him that he is indeed returning. She is so thrilled with the prospect of seeing Pinkerton again that Sharpless is unable to tell her that Pinkerton will be bringing his new American wife. Goro appears with

Prince Yamadori, a wealthy suitor. Sharpless tries to persuade her to accept Yamadori's proposal. He asks Butterfly what she would do if Pinkerton was never to return. She replies that she would kill herself, and then brings in the child she has borne Pinkerton. The harbor cannon announces the arrival of a ship—it is Pinkerton's. Butterfly, with Suzuki, decks the house with flowers; she then puts on her wedding dress, and they watch for Pinkerton's arrival. Night falls.

Act II. Scene II. After an intermezzo, the curtain rises to show Suzuki and the baby asleep, with Butterfly still waiting. Suzuki awakens and persuades her to rest. Pinkerton now arrives, and when Suzuki sees the American woman with him she guesses the truth. He sings a farewell to the little dwelling he had loved so well, and thrusting some money into Sharpless's hand leaves him to resolve the situation as best he can. Butterfly enters, and seeing Suzuki in tears, and then Kate Pinkerton, realizes what has happened. Kate begs her to let them have the child, and Butterfly agrees on condition that Pinkerton comes to collect him. Butterfly bids him a tearful farewell and then stabs herself. As she falls dying to the floor, Pinkerton's voice is heard calling her name. He enters the house to fetch his son just as Butterfly expires.

From Harold Rosenthal and John Warrack,
Concise Oxford Dictionary of Opera

CONSIDERATIONS FOR CRITICAL THINKING AND WRITING

1. In Act I, Scene III, Gallimard sits alone in his prison cell and directly tells the audience that "In order for you to understand what I did and why, I must introduce you to my favorite opera: *Madame Butterfly*. By Giacomo Puccini." Why is the opera so central to telling Gallimard's story?

2. What does Gallimard's account of the opera emphasize? What details are foregrounded? Are any significant elements of the plot left out?

3. Is Gallimard to be more identified with Pinkerton or Butterfly? Explain your response.

4. Listen to a recording of *Madame Butterfly*. How does the music affect your understanding of the play?

RICHARD BERNSTEIN (B. 1944)
The News Source for M. Butterfly   1986

France Jails Two in Odd Case of Espionage

Paris, May 10. A former French diplomat and a Chinese opera singer have been sentenced to six years in jail for spying for China after a two-day trial that traced a story of clandestine love and mistaken sexual identity.

A member of the French counterespionage service said at the trial, which ended Tuesday, that the operation to collect information on France was carried out by a Chinese Communist Party intelligence unit that no longer exists.

The Chinese government has denied any involvement in the case.

The case has been the talk of Paris lately, not so much because of the charge of spying itself as because of the circumstances. The case centered on a love affair between a young French diplomat, Bernard Boursicot, now forty-one years old, who was stationed in Peking two decades ago, and a popular Chinese opera singer, Shi Pei Pu, forty-six.

Mr. Boursicot was accused of passing information to China after he fell in love with Mr. Shi, whom he believed for twenty years to be a woman.

Testimony in the trial indicated that the affair began in 1964 when Mr. Boursicot, then twenty years old, was posted at the French Embassy in Peking as an accountant. There he met Mr. Shi, a celebrated singer at the Peking Opera, where female roles have, according to tradition, often been played by men.

Mr. Shi was a well-known cultural figure in Peking and one of the few individuals allowed by the Chinese authorities to have contacts with foreigners.

According to testimony, Mr. Shi told Mr. Boursicot at a reception in the French Embassy in Peking that he was actually a woman.

A love affair between the two ensued to the point where, after several months, Mr. Shi told Mr. Boursicot that he was pregnant; later he announced to the apparently credulous Mr. Boursicot that he had had a son, Shi Dudu, that the diplomat had fathered.

Asked by the trial judge how he could have been so completely taken in, Mr. Boursicot said: "I was shattered to learn that he is a man, but my conviction remains unshakable that for me at that time he was really a woman and was the first love of my life. And then, there was the child that I saw, Shi Dudu. He looked like me."

Further explaining his sexual misidentification of Mr. Shi, Mr. Boursicot said their meetings had been hasty affairs that always took place in the dark.

"He was very shy," Mr. Boursicot said. "I thought it was a Chinese custom."

Mr. Boursicot's espionage activities began in 1969, when he returned to Peking after a three-year absence. By then, China was at the height of the Cultural Revolution, and it was virtually impossible for foreigners to have personal relations with Chinese citizens.

Mr. Boursicot testified that a member of the Chinese secret service, whom he said he knew only as "Kang," approached him and said he could continue to see Mr. Shi if he provided intelligence information from the French Embassy. Mr. Boursicot apparently believed that if he refused to comply, Mr. Shi would be persecuted.

Mr. Boursicot was accused of having turned over some 150 documents to Shi Peipu, who passed them on to "Kang." Mr. Boursicot said at the trial that the materials were generally not sensitive and were publicly available.

Later, from 1977 to 1979, Mr. Boursicot was posted at the French Embassy in Ulan Bator in Mongolia, where one of his duties was to make a weekly trip to Peking with the diplomatic pouch. He said he made photocopies of the documents in the diplomatic pouch and turned them over to Mr. Shi.

The case was uncovered in 1983 when Mr. Shi, accompanied by his putative son, Shi Dudu, was allowed to leave China. He lived in Paris with Mr. Boursicot, who said he continued to believe that Mr. Shi was a woman.

The arrival of a Chinese citizen in the home of a former French diplomat attracted the attention of the French counterespionage service. When the French police questioned Mr. Boursicot about his relations with Mr. Shi, he disclosed his spying activities.

From the *New York Times,* May 11, 1986

CONSIDERATIONS FOR CRITICAL THINKING AND WRITING

1. What details of the news story does Hwang use? Which does he ignore?

2. Explain whether your knowledge of its source has any effect on your understanding or enjoyment of *M. Butterfly*.

3. Write a response to this explanation of the relationship: Mr. Shi "was very shy," Mr. Boursicot said. "I thought it was a Chinese custom" (para. 12).

Shi Pei Pu *in* The Story of the Butterfly

CONSIDERATIONS FOR CRITICAL THINKING AND WRITING

1. Shi Pei Pu plays a central role as a source for Song Liling's character in *M. Butterfly* (see "The News Source for *M. Butterfly*"). This photograph shows him as he appeared in the opera production of *The Story of the Butterfly*, in which he played the role of a girl who dresses up as a boy and falls in love with another boy. Does this photograph confirm or damage Boursicot's/Gallimard's credibility when he says he believed his object of love to be a woman?

2. How does this image of Shi Pei Pu evoke ideas, feelings, and attitudes about the East? Does Song Liling's character confirm or refute the image presented in the photograph? Explain your response.

FRANK RICH (B. 1949)

A Theater Review of M. Butterfly   1988

M. Butterfly, A Story of a Strange Love, Conflict, and Betrayal

It didn't require genius for David Henry Hwang to see that there were the makings of a compelling play in the 1986 newspaper story that prompted him to write M. Butterfly. Here was the incredible true-life tale of a career French foreign service officer brought to ruin — conviction for espionage — by a bizarre 20-year affair with a Beijing Opera diva. Not only had the French diplomat failed to recognize that his lover was a spy; he'd also failed to figure out that "she" was a he in drag. "It was dark, and she was very modest," says Gallimard (John Lithgow), Mr. Hwang's fictionalized protagonist, by half-joking way of explanation. When we meet him in the prison cell where he reviews his life, Gallimard has become, according to his own understatement, "the patron saint of the socially inept."

But if this story is a corker, what is it about, exactly? That's where Mr. Hwang's imagination, one of the most striking to emerge in the American theater in this decade, comes in, and his answer has nothing to do with journalism. This playwright, the author of *The Dance and the Railroad* and *Family Devotions,* does not tease us with obvious questions such as is she or isn't she?, or does he know or doesn't he? Mr. Hwang isn't overly concerned with how the opera singer, named Song Liling (B. D. Wong), pulled his hocus-pocus in the boudoir, and he refuses to explain away Gallimard by making him a closeted, self-denying homosexual. An inversion of Puccini's *Madama Butterfly, M. Butterfly* is also the inverse of most American plays. Instead of reducing the world to an easily digested cluster of sexual or familial relationships, Mr. Hwang cracks open a liaison to reveal a sweeping, universal meditation on two of the most heated conflicts — men versus women, East versus West — of this or any other time.

The play's form — whether the clashing and blending of Western and Eastern cultures or of male and female characters — is wedded to its content. It's Mr. Hwang's starting-off point that a cultural icon like *Madama Butterfly* bequeaths the sexist and racist roles that burden Western men: Gallimard believes he can become "a real man" only if he can exercise power over a beautiful and submissive woman, which is why he's so ripe to be duped by Song Liling's impersonation of a shrinking butterfly. Mr. Hwang broadens his message by making Gallimard an architect of the Western foreign policy in Vietnam. The diplomat disastrously reasons that a manly display of American might can bring the Viet Cong to submission as easily as he or Puccini's Pinkerton can overpower a Madama Butterfly.

Lest that ideological leap seem too didactic, the playwright shuffles the deck still more, suggesting that the roles played by Gallimard and Song Liling run so deep that they cross the boundaries of nations, cultures, revolutions, and sexual orientations. That Gallimard was fated to love "a woman created by a man" proves to be figuratively as well as literally true: we see that the male culture that inspired his "perfect woman" is so entrenched that the attitudes of *Madama Butterfly* survive in his cherished present-day porno magazines. Nor is the third world, in Mr. Hwang's view, immune from adopting the roles it condemns in foreign devils. We're sarcastically told that men continue to play women in Chinese opera because "only a man knows how a woman is supposed to act." When Song Liling reassumes his male "true self," he still must play a submissive Butterfly to Gallimard—whatever his or Gallimard's actual sexual persuasions—unless he chooses to play the role of aggressor to a Butterfly of his own.

Mr. Hwang's play is not without its repetitions and its overly explicit bouts of thesis mongering. When the playwright stops trusting his own instinct for the mysterious, the staging often helps out. Using Eiko Ishioka's towering, blood-red Oriental variant on the abstract sets Mr. Dexter has employed in *Equus* and the Metropolitan Opera *Dialogues of the Carmelites,* the director stirs together Mr. Hwang's dramatic modes and settings until one floats to a purely theatrical imaginative space suspended in time and place. That same disorienting quality can be found in Mr. Wong's Song Liling—a performance that, like John Lone's in the early Hwang plays, finds even more surprises in the straddling of cultures than in the blurring of genders.

From the *New York Times,* March 21, 1988

CONSIDERATIONS FOR CRITICAL THINKING AND WRITING

1. What do you think Rich means when he says that "The play's form . . . is wedded to its content" (para. 3)?
2. Why doesn't Rich judge the play to be "too didactic" (4)? What saves the play from excessive didacticism?
3. Explain why you agree or disagree that the play "is overly explicit" and indulges in "bouts of thesis mongering" (5).
4. See the film version of *M. Butterfly* (on videotape), and write a review of it.

DAVID SAVRAN (B. 1950)
An Interview with David Henry Hwang   *1988*

Savran: You strongly historicize the personal story [in *M. Butterfly*], comparing various imperialist ventures, like Vietnam, with Boursicot's sexual imperialism.

Hwang: What I was trying to do in *Butterfly*—I didn't really know this except in retrospect—was to link imperialism, racism, and sexism. It necessitates a certain historical perspective.

Savran: And a look at the mythologies created to justify them.

Hwang: Particularly Puccini's *Madame Butterfly*.

Savran: So the play is really focused on two systems of domination, the cultural and the sexual.

Hwang: Cultural superiority is essentially economic. Whatever country dominates the world economically determines what culture is, for a while.

There's a lag, because the country gets to determine the culture even after somebody else takes over economically. It still has the mystique of being the old culture, whether it's Britain or the United States. Probably the next world power is going to be Japan. You can't deal with cultural mystique unless you deal with political mystique, political power.

Savran: I was interested in how you handled the fact that Boursicot's mistress, Shi Peipu, is really a man. That makes for the reversal at the end, the fact that Shi turns out to be Pinkerton.

Hwang: That's the axis on which the play turns. Insofar as this is possible, I would like to seduce the audience during the first act into believing that Shi is a woman. We're so conditioned to think in certain ways about Oriental women and the relationship of the West to the East, that I think it would be fun to get into the audience's head in the first act, in a very reactionary way, and then blow it out later. I don't know to what degree that's possible because anyone who goes to see this play, especially if it runs any length of time, will probably know what it's about. But I still think it can work on some level.

Savran: So you want Shi played by a man?

Hwang: Definitely. You have to create the illusion for the audience, you have to trick them. It's dirty pool if you give them a woman and say, this is a woman, and later, when he appears as a man, you give them a man. You have to play by the rules. If you're saying that Boursicot was seduced by a man, then you have to seduce the audience with a man. *Butterfly* runs the risk of indulging the sin it condemns, like violent movies that are supposedly antiviolence. If you cast a woman in that role, you'd condemn the oppression of women by oppressing a woman in a very attractive way on the stage. If you oppress a woman who actually is a man, it's much more interesting.

From *In Their Own Voices*

CONSIDERATIONS FOR CRITICAL THINKING AND WRITING

1. Why does Hwang think it is essential that Shi/Song be played by a man? Discuss whether you agree or disagree with his assessment of who should play the role.
2. Consider your response to Song as you read the play. How does knowing that Song is actually a man rather than a woman affect your response to him and to Gallimard?
3. Write an essay that discusses the ways in which Hwang weaves his concerns about imperialism, racism, and sexism into the play.

SUGGESTED TOPICS FOR LONGER PAPERS

1. How is exposition presented in *M. Butterfly*? What does it reveal? How does Hwang's choice not to dramatize certain events onstage help determine the focus of the play?

2. Research the 1986 news stories that reported the relationship and trial of the French diplomat and the Chinese opera singer who were the source for *M. Butterfly*. How does Hwang develop these facts into a powerful human drama?

3. **MULTIMEDIA PROJECT.** Consider recent Western images of Asians that you can find in advertising, film, television, and the Internet. How do these cultural constructions compare with Gallimard's assumptions, desires, and fears concerning Song Liling?

Web *For help with this project, use the Multimedia Project Guides Online at* http://www.bedfordstmartins.com/meyer/bedintrolit

A Collection
of Plays

PLAYS IN PERFORMANCE

TOP: *At center stage is Jocasta (Ching Valdes/Aran) in a scene from the 1993 production of* Oedipus the King *(p. 1289) at Philadelphia's Wilma Theater, directed by Blanka Zizka and Jiri Zizka. Copyright © T. Charles Erikson.*
BOTTOM: *Martha Henry as Antigone (p. 1333) in a scene from the 1971 production at the Repertory Theatre of Lincoln Center. Martha Swope © Time Inc.*

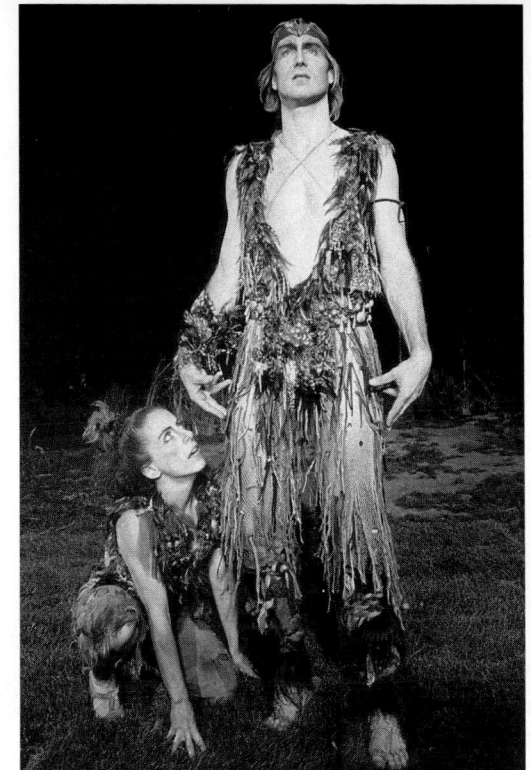

RIGHT: *Oberon, King of the Fairies (William Hurt), and Puck (Marcell Rosenblatt) in a scene from the 1982 New York Shakespeare Festival Central Park production of* A Midsummer Night's Dream *(p. 1394). Martha Swope © Time Inc.*
BELOW: *The "play within the play" scene from* Hamlet *(p. 1450). N. R. Farbman, Life Magazine © Time Inc.*

ABOVE: *Owen Teale and Janet McTeer in two scenes from the 1997 Bill Kenwright London production of* A Doll House *(p. 1568) performed at New York's Belasco Theater—winner of the 1997 Tony Award for Best Revival of a Play.*

ABOVE: *Hume Cronyn as Krapp in the 1972 Repertory Theatre of Lincoln Center production of* Krapp's Last Tape *(p. 1648). Martha Swope © Time Inc.*
LEFT: *Margo Martindale in* Rodeo *(p. 1656), during the Sixth Annual Humana Festival of New American Plays, at the Actor's Theatre of Louisville, Kentucky, in 1982. Katherine Wisniewski, photographer.*

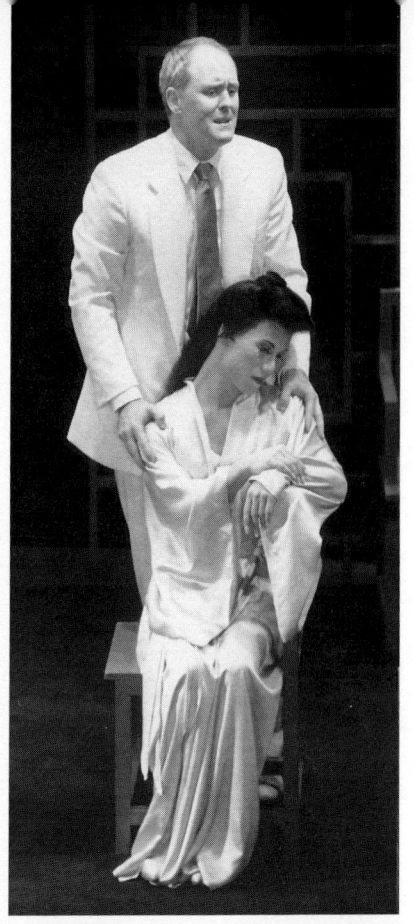

LEFT: *John Lithgow and B. D. Wong in* M. Butterfly *(p. 1672). This award-winning play opened on Broadway at the Eugene O'Neill Theatre in 1988. Joan Marcus, photographer.*
BELOW: *Sydney Poitier and Ruby Dee (and unknown actor, on the left) in a March 1959 performance of* A Raisin in the Sun *(p. 1731). Gordon Parks, Life Magazine © Time Inc.*

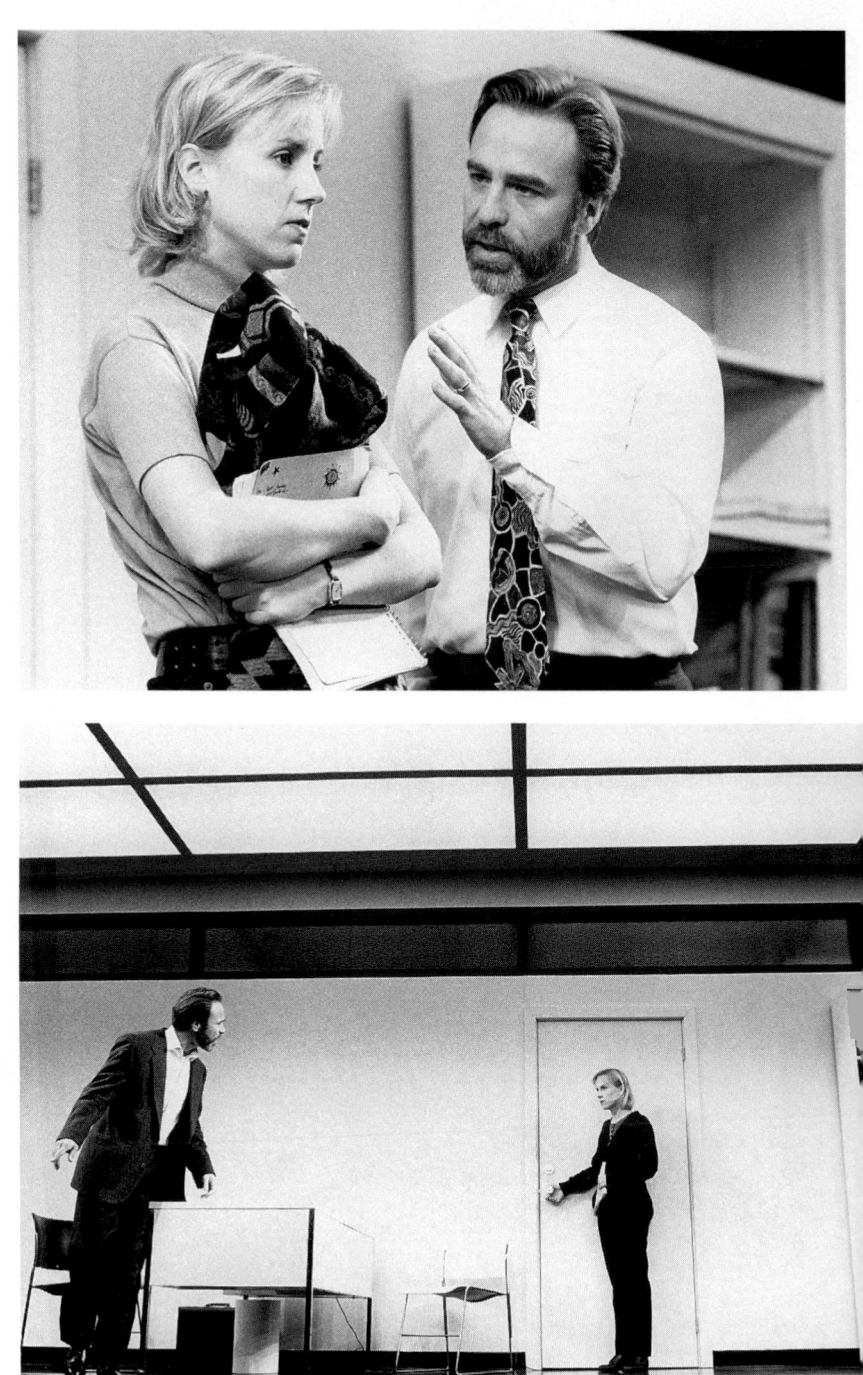

ABOVE: *Welker White as Carol and Casey Biggs as John in two scenes from the Yale Repertory Theatre's 1993 production of* Oleanna *(p. 1795) in New Haven, Connecticut, directed by Stan Wojewodski, Jr. Copyright © T. Charles Erickson*

ABOVE: *Willy (Lee J. Cobb) with sons Hap (Cameron Mitchell) and Biff (Arthur Kennedy) in* Death of a Salesman *(p. 1824). W. Eugene Smith,* Life Magazine © 1949 Time Inc.

RIGHT: *Amanda (Ruby Dee) and Tom (Jonathan Earl Peck) in the 1989 Arena Stage production of* The Glass Menagerie *(p. 1893).*

TOP: *Callie (Jessica Hecht), Sara (Sandra Oh), and George (Kevin Carroll) share a moment together in the 1998 Public Theater/NYSF production of* Stop Kiss *(p. 1982), directed by Jo Bonney.*
BOTTOM: *Charles Dutton in* The Piano Lesson *(p. 2031), at a 1989 performance at the Kennedy Center, Washington D.C.*

49

Plays for Further Reading

A Raisin in the Sun

Lorraine Hansberry, the youngest of four children raised by African American parents who migrated from the South, was born in Chicago, Illinois. Her father was a successful businessman who provided the family with a comfortable middle-class home where distinguished blacks such as W. E. B. Du Bois, Langston Hughes, Duke Ellington, and Paul Robeson visited. Her mother was politically active and served as a ward commissioner for the Republican Party. When Hansberry was eight years old, the family bought a house in a white neighborhood, challenging segregationist real estate practices that excluded blacks. The Hansberrys endured violent hostility while fighting a lower court eviction and with the support from the National Association for the Advancement of Colored People won a victory in the U.S. Supreme Court.

After graduating from the segregated public schools of Chicago, Hansberry studied at the University of Wisconsin for two years but in 1950 moved to New York City. There she attended classes at the New School for Social Research and wrote for *Freedom,* a radical Harlem periodical published by Paul Robeson. During the course of her brief career, ended by cancer when she was only thirty-four years old, Hansberry remained a committed civil rights activist.

She began writing *A Raisin in the Sun* in 1956. It was produced on Broadway in 1959, bringing her international recognition. At the age of twenty-eight, Hansberry was the first black female playwright to be produced on Broadway, and the play was awarded the New York Drama Critics Circle Award for Best Play of the Year in competition with such successful dramatists as Eugene O'Neill and Tennessee Williams. *A Raisin in the Sun* has been translated into more than thirty languages and produced around the world. Among Hansberry's other writings are *The Movement: Documentary of a Struggle for Equality* (1964); *The Sign in Sidney Brustein's Window* (1965), a play in production at the time of her death; *To Be Young, Gifted and Black* (1969), a play published posthumously; and *Lorraine Hansberry: The Collected Last Plays* (1983).

In *A Raisin in the Sun,* Hansberry does not flinch from the tough realities that confronted African Americans contemporary to her. Racism, segregation, and a lack of economic opportunities seem to brutally mock the aspirations of her characters. Yet Hansberry sustained a sense of optimism owing to the growing activism of the civil rights movement during the 1950s. The play explores the difficulties of a black working-class family's struggle to overcome the racism and poverty in their lives and makes a connection between their efforts and the struggles of African countries to become free from colonialism. Her characters retain their humanity and dignity in the face of fierce social pressures and individual crises. Her realistic portrayal of racial issues, family conflicts, and relations between men and women presents a hostile world but also one that is capable of change. Her work, she once wrote, was about "not only what *is* but what is *possible.*"

The following poem by Langston Hughes (1902–1967) is the source for the play's title and serves as a fitting introduction to many of the issues dramatized in *A Raisin in the Sun.*

Web *Research Lorraine Hansberry with LitLinks at*
http://www.bedfordstmartins.com/meyer/bedintrolit

Harlem (A Dream Deferred)

What happens to a dream deferred?

Does it dry up
Like a raisin in the sun?
Or fester like a sore —
And then run?
Does it stink like rotten meat?
Or crust and sugar over —
Like a syrupy sweet?

Maybe it just sags
Like a heavy load.

Or does it explode?

     — Langston Hughes

LORRAINE HANSBERRY (1930–1965)

A Raisin in the Sun   1959

CHARACTERS (in order of appearance)

Ruth Younger
Travis Younger
Walter Lee Younger, brother
Beneatha Younger
Lena Younger, Mama
Joseph Asagai
George Murchison
Mrs. Johnson
Karl Lindner
Bobo
Moving Men

> The action of the play is set in Chicago's Southside, sometime between World War II
> and the present.

ACT I

SCENE I. *[Friday morning.]*

> The Younger living room would be a comfortable and well-ordered room if it were
> not for a number of indestructible contradictions to this state of being. Its furnish-
> ings are typical and undistinguished and their primary feature now is that they
> have clearly had to accommodate the living of too many people for too many
> years—and they are tired. Still, we can see that at some time, a time probably no
> longer remembered by the family (except perhaps for Mama), the furnishings of
> this room were actually selected with care and love and even hope—and brought to
> this apartment and arranged with taste and pride.
>
>   That was a long time ago. Now the once loved pattern of the couch upholstery
> has to fight to show itself from under acres of crocheted doilies and couch covers
> which have themselves finally come to be more important than the upholstery. And
> here a table or a chair has been moved to disguise the worn places in the carpet; but
> the carpet has fought back by showing its weariness, with depressing uniformity,
> elsewhere on its surface.
>
>   Weariness has, in fact, won in this room. Everything has been polished,
> washed, sat on, used, scrubbed too often. All pretenses but living itself have long
> since vanished from the very atmosphere of this room.
>
>   Moreover, a section of this room, for it is not really a room unto itself, though
> the landlord's lease would make it seem so, slopes backward to provide a small
> kitchen area, where the family prepares the meals that are eaten in the living room
> proper, which must also serve as dining room. The single window that has been
> provided for these "two" rooms is located in this kitchen area. The sole natural light

the family may enjoy in the course of a day is only that which fights its way through this little window.

At left, a door leads to a bedroom which is shared by Mama and her daughter, Beneatha. At right, opposite, is a second room (which in the beginning of the life of this apartment was probably a breakfast room) which serves as a bedroom for Walter and his wife, Ruth.

Time: Sometime between World War II and the present.

Place: Chicago's Southside.

At Rise: It is morning dark in the living room. Travis is asleep on the make-down bed at center. An alarm clock sounds from within the bedroom at right, and presently Ruth enters from that room and closes the door behind her. She crosses sleepily toward the window. As she passes her sleeping son she reaches down and shakes him a little. At the window she raises the shade and a dusky Southside morning light comes in feebly. She fills a pot with water and puts it on to boil. She calls to the boy, between yawns, in a slightly muffled voice.

Ruth is about thirty. We can see that she was a pretty girl, even exceptionally so, but now it is apparent that life has been little that she expected, and disappointment has already begun to hang in her face. In a few years, before thirty-five even, she will be known among her people as a "settled woman."

She crosses to her son and gives him a good, final, rousing shake.

Ruth: Come on now, boy, it's seven thirty! *(Her son sits up at last, in a stupor of sleepiness.)* I say hurry up, Travis! You ain't the only person in the world got to use a bathroom! *(The child, a sturdy, handsome little boy of ten or eleven, drags himself out of the bed and almost blindly takes his towels and "today's clothes" from drawers and a closet and goes out to the bathroom, which is in an outside hall and which is shared by another family or families on the same floor. Ruth crosses to the bedroom door at right and opens it and calls in to her husband.)* Walter Lee! . . . It's after seven thirty! Lemme see you do some waking up in there now! *(She waits.)* You better get up from there, man! It's after seven thirty I tell you. *(She waits again.)* All right, you just go ahead and lay there and next thing you know Travis be finished and Mr. Johnson'll be in there and you'll be fussing and cussing round here like a madman! And be late too! *(She waits, at the end of patience.)* Walter Lee — it's time for you to GET UP!

She waits another second and then starts to go into the bedroom, but is apparently satisfied that her husband has begun to get up. She stops, pulls the door to, and returns to the kitchen area. She wipes her face with a moist cloth and runs her fingers through her sleep-disheveled hair in a vain effort and ties an apron around her housecoat. The bedroom door at right opens and her husband stands in the doorway in his pajamas, which are rumpled and mismated. He is a lean, intense young man in his middle thirties, inclined to quick nervous movements and erratic speech habits — and always in his voice there is a quality of indictment.

Walter: Is he out yet?

Ruth: What you mean *out?* He ain't hardly got in there good yet.

Walter (wandering in, still more oriented to sleep than to a new day): Well, what was you doing all that yelling for if I can't even get in there yet? *(Stopping and thinking.)* Check coming today?

Ruth: They *said* Saturday and this is just Friday and I hopes to God you ain't going to get up here first thing this morning and start talking to me 'bout no money — 'cause I 'bout don't want to hear it.

Walter: Something the matter with you this morning?

Ruth: No — I'm just sleepy as the devil. What kind of eggs you want?

Walter: Not scrambled. *(Ruth starts to scramble eggs.)* Paper come? *(Ruth points impatiently to the rolled up* Tribune *on the table, and he gets it and spreads it out and vaguely reads the front page.)* Set off another bomb yesterday.

Ruth (maximum indifference): Did they?

Walter (looking up): What's the matter with you?

Ruth: Ain't nothing the matter with me. And don't keep asking me that this morning.

Walter: Ain't nobody bothering you. *(Reading the news of the day absently again.)* Say Colonel McCormick is sick.

Ruth (affecting tea-party interest): Is he now? Poor thing.

Walter (sighing and looking at his watch): Oh, me. *(He waits.)* Now what is that boy doing in that bathroom all this time? He just going to have to start getting up earlier. I can't be being late to work on account of him fooling around in there.

Ruth (turning on him): Oh, no he ain't going to be getting up no earlier no such thing! It ain't his fault that he can't get to bed no earlier nights 'cause he got a bunch of crazy good-for-nothing clowns sitting up running their mouths in what is supposed to be his bedroom after ten o'clock at night . . .

Walter: That's what you mad about, ain't it? The things I want to talk about with my friends just couldn't be important in your mind, could they?

He rises and finds a cigarette in her handbag on the table and crosses to the little window and looks out, smoking and deeply enjoying this first one.

Ruth (almost matter of factly, a complaint too automatic to deserve emphasis): Why you always got to smoke before you eat in the morning?

Walter (at the window): Just look at 'em down there . . . Running and racing to work . . . *(He turns and faces his wife and watches her a moment at the stove, and then, suddenly.)* You look young this morning, baby.

Ruth (indifferently): Yeah?

Walter: Just for a second — stirring them eggs. Just for a second it was — you looked real young again. *(He reaches for her; she crosses away. Then, drily.)* It's gone now — you look like yourself again!

Ruth: Man, if you don't shut up and leave me alone.

Walter (looking out to the street again): First thing a man ought to learn in life is not to make love to no colored woman first thing in the morning. You all some eeeevil people at eight o'clock in the morning.

Travis appears in the hall doorway, almost fully dressed and quite wide awake now, his towels and pajamas across his shoulders. He opens the door and signals for his father to make the bathroom in a hurry.

Travis (watching the bathroom): Daddy, come on!

Walter gets his bathroom utensils and flies out to the bathroom.

Ruth: Sit down and have your breakfast, Travis.

Travis: Mama, this is Friday. *(Gleefully.)* Check coming tomorrow, huh?

Ruth: You get your mind off money and eat your breakfast.

Travis (eating): This is the morning we supposed to bring the fifty cents to school.

Ruth: Well, I ain't got no fifty cents this morning.

Travis: Teacher say we have to.

Ruth: I don't care what teacher say. I ain't got it. Eat your breakfast, Travis.

Travis: I *am* eating.

Ruth: Hush up now and just eat!

> *The boy gives her an exasperated look for her lack of understanding, and eats grudgingly.*

Travis: You think Grandmama would have it?

Ruth: No! And I want you to stop asking your grandmother for money, you hear me?

Travis (outraged): Gaaaleee! I don't ask her, she just gimme it sometimes!

Ruth: Travis Willard Younger — I got too much on me this morning to be —

Travis: Maybe Daddy —

Ruth: Travis!

> *The boy hushes abruptly. They are both quiet and tense for several seconds.*

Travis (presently): Could I maybe go carry some groceries in front of the super-market for a little while after school then?

Ruth: Just hush, I said. *(Travis jabs his spoon into his cereal bowl viciously, and rests his head in anger upon his fists.)* If you through eating, you can get over there and make up your bed.

> *The boy obeys stiffly and crosses the room, almost mechanically, to the bed and more or less folds the bedding into a heap, then angrily gets his books and cap.*

Travis (sulking and standing apart from her unnaturally): I'm gone.

Ruth (looking up from the stove to inspect him automatically): Come here. *(He crosses to her and she studies his head.)* If you don't take this comb and fix this here head, you better! *(Travis puts down his books with a great sigh of oppression, and crosses to the mirror. His mother mutters under her breath about his "slubborn-ness.")* 'Bout to march out of here with that head looking just like chickens slept in it! I just don't know where you get your slubborn ways . . . And get your jacket, too. Looks chilly out this morning.

Travis (with conspicuously brushed hair and jacket): I'm gone.

Ruth: Get carfare and milk money — *(Waving one finger.)* — and not a single penny for no caps, you hear me?

Travis (with sullen politeness): Yes'm.

> *He turns in outrage to leave. His mother watches after him as in his frustration he approaches the door almost comically. When she speaks to him, her voice has become a very gentle tease.*

Ruth (mocking; as she thinks he would say it): Oh, Mama makes me so mad some-times, I don't know what to do! *(She waits and continues to his back as he stands stock-still in front of the door.)* I wouldn't kiss that woman good-bye for nothing in this world this morning! *(The boy finally turns around and rolls his eyes at her, knowing the mood has changed and he is vindicated; he does not, how-ever, move toward her yet.)* Not for nothing in this world! *(She finally laughs aloud at him and holds out her arms to him and we see that it is a way between them, very old and practiced. He crosses to her and allows her to embrace him warmly but keeps his face fixed with masculine rigidity. She holds him back from her presently and looks at him and runs her fingers over the features of his face. With utter gentleness—.)* Now—whose little old angry man are you?

Travis (the masculinity and gruffness start to fade at last): Aw gaalee—Mama . . .

Ruth (mimicking): Aw—gaaaaalleeeee, Mama! *(She pushes him, with rough playfulness and finality, toward the door.)* Get on out of here or you going to be late.

Travis (in the face of love, new aggressiveness): Mama, could I *please* go carry groceries?

Ruth: Honey, it's starting to get so cold evenings.

Walter (coming in from the bathroom and drawing a make-believe gun from a make-believe holster and shooting at his son): What is it he wants to do?

Ruth: Go carry groceries after school at the supermarket.

Walter: Well, let him go . . .

Travis (quickly, to the ally): I *have* to—she won't gimme the fifty cents . . .

Walter (to his wife only): Why not?

Ruth (simply, and with flavor): 'Cause we don't have it.

Walter (to Ruth only): What you tell the boy things like that for? *(Reaching down into his pants with a rather important gesture.)* Here, son—

He hands the boy the coin, but his eyes are directed to his wife's. Travis takes the money happily.

Travis: Thanks, Daddy.

He starts out. Ruth watches both of them with murder in her eyes. Walter stands and stares back at her with defiance, and suddenly reaches into his pocket again on an afterthought.

Walter (without even looking at his son, still staring hard at his wife): In fact, here's another fifty cents . . . Buy yourself some fruit today—or take a taxicab to school or something!

Travis: Whoopee—

He leaps up and clasps his father around the middle with his legs, and they face each other in mutual appreciation; slowly Walter Lee peeks around the boy to catch the violent rays from his wife's eyes and draws his head back as if shot.

Walter: You better get down now—and get to school, man.

Travis (at the door): O.K. Good-bye.

He exits.

Walter (after him, pointing with pride): That's *my* boy. *(She looks at him in disgust and turns back to her work.)* You know what I was thinking 'bout in the bathroom this morning?

Ruth: No.

Walter: How come you always try to be so pleasant!

Ruth: What is there to be pleasant 'bout!

Walter: You want to know what I was thinking 'bout in the bathroom or not!

Ruth: I know what you thinking 'bout.

Walter (ignoring her): 'Bout what me and Willy Harris was talking about last night.

Ruth (immediately—a refrain): Willy Harris is a good-for-nothing loudmouth.

Walter: Anybody who talks to me has got to be a good-for-nothing loudmouth, ain't he? And what you know about who is just a good-for-nothing loudmouth? Charlie Atkins was just a "good-for-nothing loudmouth" too, wasn't he! When he wanted me to go in the dry-cleaning business with him. And now — he's grossing a hundred thousand a year. A hundred thousand dollars a year! You still call *him* a loudmouth!

Ruth (bitterly): Oh, Walter Lee . . .

She folds her head on her arms over the table.

Walter (rising and coming to her and standing over her): You tired, ain't you? Tired of everything. Me, the boy, the way we live — this beat-up hole — everything. Ain't you? *(She doesn't look up, doesn't answer.)* So tired — moaning and groaning all the time, but you wouldn't do nothing to help, would you? You couldn't be on my side that long for nothing, could you?

Ruth: Walter, please leave me alone.

Walter: A man needs for a woman to back him up . . .

Ruth: Walter —

Walter: Mama would listen to you. You know she listen to you more than she do me and Bennie. She think more of you. All you have to do is just sit down with her when you drinking your coffee one morning and talking 'bout things like you do and — *(He sits down beside her and demonstrates graphically what he thinks her methods and tone should be.)* — you just sip your coffee, see, and say easy like that you been thinking 'bout that deal Walter Lee is so interested in, 'bout the store and all, and sip some more coffee, like what you saying ain't really that important to you — And the next thing you know, she be listening good and asking you questions and when I come home — I can tell her the details. This ain't no fly-by-night proposition, baby. I mean we figured it out, me and Willy and Bobo.

Ruth (with a frown): Bobo?

Walter: Yeah. You see, this little liquor store we got in mind cost seventy-five thousand and we figured the initial investment on the place be 'bout thirty thousand, see. That be ten thousand each. Course, there's a couple of hundred you got to pay so's you don't spend your life just waiting for them clowns to let your license get approved —

Ruth: You mean graft?

Walter (frowning impatiently): Don't call it that. See there, that just goes to show you what women understand about the world. Baby, don't *nothing* happen for you in the world 'less you pay *somebody* off!

Ruth: Walter, leave me alone! *(She raises her head and stares at him vigorously — then says, more quietly.)* Eat your eggs, they gonna be cold.

Walter (straightening up from her and looking off): That's it. There you are. Man say to his woman: I got me a dream. His woman say: Eat your eggs. *(Sadly, but gaining in power.)* Man say: I got to take hold of this here world, baby! And a woman will say: Eat your eggs and go to work. *(Passionately now.)* Man say: I got to change my life, I'm choking to death, baby! And his woman say — *(In utter anguish as he brings his fists down on his thighs.)* — Your eggs is getting cold!

Ruth (softly): Walter, that ain't none of our money.

Walter (not listening at all or even looking at her): This morning, I was lookin' in the mirror and thinking about it . . . I'm thirty-five years old; I been married eleven years and I got a boy who sleeps in the living room — *(Very, very quietly.)* — and all I got to give him is stories about how rich white people live . . .

Ruth: Eat your eggs, Walter.

Walter (slams the table and jumps up): — DAMN MY EGGS — DAMN ALL THE EGGS THAT EVER WAS!

Ruth: Then go to work.

Walter (looking up at her): See — I'm trying to talk to you 'bout myself — *(Shaking his head with the repetition.)* — and all you can say is eat them eggs and go to work.

Ruth (wearily): Honey, you never say nothing new. I listen to you every day, every night and every morning, and you never say nothing new. *(Shrugging.)* So you would rather *be* Mr. Arnold than be his chauffeur. So — I would *rather* be living in Buckingham Palace.

Walter: That is just what is wrong with the colored woman in this world . . . Don't understand about building their men up and making 'em feel like they somebody. Like they can do something.

Ruth (drily, but to hurt): There *are* colored men who do things.

Walter: No thanks to the colored woman.

Ruth: Well, being a colored woman, I guess I can't help myself none.

She rises and gets the ironing board and sets it up and attacks a huge pile of rough-dried clothes, sprinkling them in preparation for the ironing and then rolling them into tight fat balls.

Walter (mumbling): We one group of men tied to a race of women with small minds!

His sister Beneatha enters. She is about twenty, as slim and intense as her brother. She is not as pretty as her sister-in-law, but her lean, almost intellectual face has a handsomeness of its own. She wears a bright-red flannel nightie, and her thick hair stands wildly about her head. Her speech is a mixture of many things; it is different from the rest of the family's insofar as education has permeated her sense of English — and perhaps the Midwest rather than the South has finally — at last — won out in her inflection; but not altogether, because over all of it is a soft slurring and transformed use of vowels which is the decided influence of the Southside. She passes through the room without looking at either Ruth or Walter and goes to the outside door and looks, a little blindly, out to the bathroom. She sees that it has been lost to the Johnsons. She closes the door with a sleepy vengeance and crosses to the table and sits down a little defeated.

Beneatha: I am going to start timing those people.

Walter: You should get up earlier.

Beneatha (her face in her hands. She is still fighting the urge to go back to bed): Really — would you suggest dawn? Where's the paper?

Walter (pushing the paper across the table to her as he studies her almost clinically, as though he has never seen her before): You a horrible-looking chick at this hour.

Beneatha (drily): Good morning, everybody.

Walter (senselessly): How is school coming?

Beneatha (in the same spirit): Lovely. Lovely. And you know, biology is the greatest. *(Looking up at him.)* I dissected something that looked just like you yesterday.

Walter: I just wondered if you've made up your mind and everything.

Beneatha (gaining in sharpness and impatience): And what did I answer yesterday morning — and the day before that?

Ruth (from the ironing board, like someone disinterested and old): Don't be so nasty, Bennie.

Beneatha (still to her brother): And the day before that and the day before that!

Walter (defensively): I'm interested in you. Something wrong with that? Ain't many girls who decide—

Walter and Beneatha (in unison):   —"to be a doctor."

   Silence.

Walter: Have we figured out yet just exactly how much medical school is going to cost?

Ruth: Walter Lee, why don't you leave that girl alone and get out of here to work?

Beneatha (exits to the bathroom and bangs on the door): Come on out of there, please!

   She comes back into the room.

Walter (looking at his sister intently): You know the check is coming tomorrow.

Beneatha (turning on him with a sharpness all her own): That money belongs to Mama, Walter, and it's for her to decide how she wants to use it. I don't care if she wants to buy a house or a rocket ship or just nail it up somewhere and look at it. It's hers. Not ours — *hers.*

Walter (bitterly): Now ain't that fine! You just got your mother's interest at heart, ain't you, girl? You such a nice girl — but if Mama got that money she can always take a few thousand and help you through school too — can't she?

Beneatha: I have never asked anyone around here to do anything for me!

Walter: No! And the line between asking and just accepting when the time comes is big and wide — ain't it!

Beneatha (with fury): What do you want from me, Brother — that I quit school or just drop dead, which!

Walter: I don't want nothing but for you to stop acting holy 'round here. Me and Ruth done made some sacrifices for you — why can't you do something for the family?

Ruth: Walter, don't be dragging me in it.

Walter: You are in it — Don't you get up and go work in somebody's kitchen for the last three years to help put clothes on her back?

Ruth: Oh, Walter — that's not fair . . .

Walter: It ain't that nobody expects you to get on your knees and say thank you, Brother; thank you, Ruth; thank you, Mama — and thank you, Travis, for wearing the same pair of shoes for two semesters —

Beneatha (dropping to her knees): Well — I *do* — all right? — thank everybody! And forgive me for ever wanting to be anything at all! *(Pursuing him on her knees across the floor.)* FORGIVE ME, FORGIVE ME, FORGIVE ME!

Ruth: Please stop it! Your mama'll hear you.

Walter: Who the hell told you you had to be a doctor? If you so crazy 'bout messing 'round with sick people — then go be a nurse like other women — or just get married and be quiet . . .

Beneatha: Well — you finally got it said . . . It took you three years but you finally got it said. Walter, give up; leave me alone — it's Mama's money.

Walter: He *was* my father, too!

Beneatha: So what? He was mine, too—and Travis' grandfather—but the insurance money belongs to Mama. Picking on me is not going to make her give it to you to invest in any liquor stores—*(Under breath, dropping into a chair.)*—and I for one say, God bless Mama for that!

Walter (to Ruth): See—did you hear? Did you hear!

Ruth: Honey, please go to work.

Walter: Nobody in this house is ever going to understand me.

Beneatha: Because you're a nut.

Walter: Who's a nut?

Beneatha: You—you are a nut. Thee is mad, boy.

Walter (looking at his wife and his sister from the door, very sadly): The world's most backward race of people, and that's a fact.

Beneatha (turning slowly in her chair): And then there are all those prophets who would lead us out of the wilderness—*(Walter slams out of the house.)*—into the swamps!

Ruth: Bennie, why you always gotta be pickin' on your brother? Can't you be a little sweeter sometimes? *(Door opens. Walter walks in. He fumbles with his cap, starts to speak, clears throat, looks everywhere but at Ruth. Finally:)*

Walter (to Ruth): I need some money for carfare.

Ruth (looks at him, then warms; teasing, but tenderly): Fifty cents? *(She goes to her bag and gets money.)* Here—take a taxi!

> *Walter exits. Mama enters. She is a woman in her early sixties, full-bodied and strong. She is one of those women of a certain grace and beauty who wear it so unobtrusively that it takes a while to notice. Her dark-brown face is surrounded by the total whiteness of her hair, and, being a woman who has adjusted to many things in life and overcome many more, her face is full of strength. She has, we can see, wit and faith of a kind that keep her eyes lit and full of interest and expectancy. She is, in a word, a beautiful woman. Her bearing is perhaps most like the noble bearing of the women of the Hereros of Southwest Africa—rather as if she imagines that as she walks she still bears a basket or a vessel upon her head. Her speech, on the other hand, is as careless as her carriage is precise—she is inclined to slur everything—but her voice is perhaps not so much quiet as simply soft.*

Mama: Who that 'round here slamming doors at this hour?

> *She crosses through the room, goes to the window, opens it, and brings in a feeble little plant growing doggedly in a small pot on the window sill. She feels the dirt and puts it back out.*

Ruth: That was Walter Lee. He and Bennie was at it again.

Mama: My children and they tempers. Lord, if this little old plant don't get more sun than it's been getting it ain't never going to see spring again. *(She turns from the window.)* What's the matter with you this morning, Ruth? You looks right peaked. You aiming to iron all them things? Leave some for me. I'll get to 'em this afternoon. Bennie honey, it's too drafty for you to be sitting 'round half dressed. Where's your robe?

Beneatha: In the cleaners.

Mama: Well, go get mine and put it on.

Beneatha: I'm not cold, Mama, honest.

Mama: I know—but you so thin . . .

Beneatha (irritably): Mama, I'm not cold.

Mama (seeing the make-down bed as Travis has left it): Lord have mercy, look at that poor bed. Bless his heart—he tries, don't he?

She moves to the bed Travis has sloppily made up.

Ruth: No—he don't half try at all 'cause he knows you going to come along behind him and fix everything. That's just how come he don't know how to do nothing right now—you done spoiled that boy so.

Mama (folding bedding): Well—he's a little boy. Ain't supposed to know 'bout housekeeping. My baby, that's what he is. What you fix for his breakfast this morning?

Ruth (angrily): I feed my son, Lena!

Mama: I ain't meddling—*(Under breath; busy-bodyish.)* I just noticed all last week he had cold cereal, and when it starts getting this chilly in the fall a child ought to have some hot grits or something when he goes out in the cold—

Ruth (furious): I gave him hot oats—is that all right!

Mama: I ain't meddling. *(Pause.)* Put a lot of nice butter on it? *(Ruth shoots her an angry look and does not reply.)* He likes lots of butter.

Ruth (exasperated): Lena—

Mama (to Beneatha. Mama is inclined to wander conversationally sometimes): What was you and your brother fussing 'bout this morning?

Beneatha: It's not important, Mama.

She gets up and goes to look out at the bathroom, which is apparently free, and she picks up her towels and rushes out.

Mama: What was they fighting about?

Ruth: Now you know as well as I do.

Mama (shaking her head): Brother still worrying hisself sick about that money?

Ruth: You know he is.

Mama: You had breakfast?

Ruth: Some coffee.

Mama: Girl, you better start eating and looking after yourself better. You almost thin as Travis.

Ruth: Lena—

Mama: Un-hunh?

Ruth: What are you going to do with it?

Mama: Now don't you start, child. It's too early in the morning to be talking about money. It ain't Christian.

Ruth: It's just that he got his heart set on that store—

Mama: You mean that liquor store that Willy Harris want him to invest in?

Ruth: Yes—

Mama: We ain't no business people, Ruth. We just plain working folks.

Ruth: Ain't nobody business people till they go into business. Walter Lee say colored people ain't never going to start getting ahead till they start gambling on some different kinds of things in the world—investments and things.

Mama: What done got into you, girl? Walter Lee done finally sold you on investing.

Ruth: No. Mama, something is happening between Walter and me. I don't know what it is—but he needs something—something I can't give him any more. He needs this chance, Lena.

Mama (frowning deeply): But liquor, honey—

Ruth: Well—like Walter say—I spec people going to always be drinking themselves some liquor.

Mama: Well—whether they drinks it or not ain't none of my business. But whether I go into business selling it to 'em *is*, and I don't want that on my ledger this late in life. *(Stopping suddenly and studying her daughter-in-law.)* Ruth Younger, what's the matter with you today? You look like you could fall over right there.

Ruth: I'm tired.

Mama: Then you better stay home from work today.

Ruth: I can't stay home. She'd be calling up the agency and screaming at them, "My girl didn't come in today—send me somebody! My girl didn't come in!" Oh, she just have a fit . . .

Mama: Well, let her have it. I'll just call her up and say you got the flu—

Ruth (laughing): Why the flu?

Mama: 'Cause it sounds respectable to 'em. Something white people get, too. They know 'bout the flu. Otherwise they think you been cut up or something when you tell 'em you sick.

Ruth: I got to go in. We need the money.

Mama: Somebody would of thought my children done all but starved to death the way they talk about money here late. Child, we got a great big old check coming tomorrow.

Ruth (sincerely, but also self-righteously): Now that's your money. It ain't got nothing to do with me. We all feel like that—Walter and Bennie and me—even Travis.

Mama (thoughtfully, and suddenly very far away): Ten thousand dollars—

Ruth: Sure is wonderful.

Mama: Ten thousand dollars.

Ruth: You know what you should do, Miss Lena? You should take yourself a trip somewhere. To Europe or South America or someplace—

Mama (throwing up her hands at the thought): Oh, child!

Ruth: I'm serious. Just pack up and leave! Go on away and enjoy yourself some. Forget about the family and have yourself a ball for once in your life—

Mama (drily): You sound like I'm just about ready to die. Who'd go with me? What I look like wandering 'round Europe by myself?

Ruth: Shoot—these here rich white women do it all the time. They don't think nothing of packing up they suitcases and piling on one of them big steamships and—swoosh!—they gone, child.

Mama: Something always told me I wasn't no rich white woman.

Ruth: Well—what are you going to do with it then?

Mama: I ain't rightly decided. *(Thinking. She speaks now with emphasis.)* Some of it got to be put away for Beneatha and her schoolin'—and ain't nothing going to touch that part of it. Nothing. *(She waits several seconds, trying to make up her mind about something, and looks at Ruth a little tentatively before going on.)* Been thinking that we maybe could meet the notes on a little old two-story somewhere, with a yard where Travis could play in the summertime, if we use part of the insurance for a down payment and everybody kind of pitch in. I could maybe take on a little day work again, few days a week—

Ruth (studying her mother-in-law furtively and concentrating on her ironing, anxious to encourage without seeming to): Well, Lord knows, we've put enough rent into this here rat trap to pay for four houses by now . . .

Mama *(looking up at the words "rat trap" and then looking around and leaning back and sighing—in a suddenly reflective mood—):* "Rat trap"—yes, that's all it is. *(Smiling.)* I remember just as well the day me and Big Walter moved in here. Hadn't been married but two weeks and wasn't planning on living here no more than a year. *(She shakes her head at the dissolved dream.)* We was going to set away, little by little, don't you know, and buy a little place out in Morgan Park. We had even picked out the house. *(Chuckling a little.)* Looks right dumpy today. But Lord, child, you should know all the dreams I had 'bout buying that house and fixing it up and making me a little garden in the back — *(She waits and stops smiling.)* And didn't none of it happen.

Dropping her hands in a futile gesture.

Ruth *(keeps her head down, ironing):* Yes, life can be a barrel of disappointments, sometimes.

Mama: Honey, Big Walter would come in here some nights back then and slump down on that couch there and just look at the rug, and look at me and look at the rug and then back at me—and I'd know he was down then . . . really down. *(After a second very long and thoughtful pause; she is seeing back to times that only she can see.)* And then, Lord, when I lost that baby—little Claude—I almost thought I was going to lose Big Walter too. Oh, that man grieved hisself! He was one man to love his children.

Ruth: Ain't nothin' can tear at you like losin' your baby.

Mama: I guess that's how come that man finally worked hisself to death like he done. Like he was fighting his own war with this here world that took his baby from him.

Ruth: He sure was a fine man, all right. I always liked Mr. Younger.

Mama: Crazy 'bout his children! God knows there was plenty wrong with Walter Younger—hard-headed, mean, kind of wild with women—plenty wrong with him. But he sure loved his children. Always wanted them to have something—be something. That's where Brother gets all these notions, I reckon. Big Walter used to say, he'd get right wet in the eyes sometimes, lean his head back with the water standing in his eyes and say, "Seem like God didn't see fit to give the black man nothing but dreams—but He did give us children to make them dreams seem worthwhile." *(She smiles.)* He could talk like that, don't you know.

Ruth: Yes, he sure could. He was a good man, Mr. Younger.

Mama: Yes, a fine man—just couldn't never catch up with his dreams, that's all.

Beneatha comes in, brushing her hair and looking up to the ceiling, where the sound of a vacuum cleaner has started up.

Beneatha: What could be so dirty on that woman's rugs that she has to vacuum them every single day?

Ruth: I wish certain young women 'round here who I could name would take inspiration about certain rugs in a certain apartment I could also mention.

Beneatha *(shrugging):* How much cleaning can a house need, for Christ's sakes.

Mama *(not liking the Lord's name used thus):* Bennie!

Ruth: Just listen to her—just listen!

Beneatha: Oh, God!

Mama: If you use the Lord's name just one more time—

Beneatha *(a bit of a whine):* Oh, Mama—

Ruth: Fresh — just fresh as salt, this girl!

Beneatha (drily): Well — if the salt loses its savor —

Mama: Now that will do. I just ain't going to have you 'round here reciting the scriptures in vain — you hear me?

Beneatha: How did I manage to get on everybody's wrong side by just walking into a room?

Ruth: If you weren't so fresh —

Beneatha: Ruth, I'm twenty years old.

Mama: What time you be home from school today?

Beneatha: Kind of late. *(With enthusiasm.)* Madeline is going to start my guitar lessons today.

Mama and Ruth look up with the same expression.

Mama: Your *what* kind of lessons?

Beneatha: Guitar.

Ruth: Oh, Father!

Mama: How come you done taken it in your mind to learn to play the guitar?

Beneatha: I just want to, that's all.

Mama (smiling): Lord, child, don't you know what to do with yourself? How long it going to be before you get tired of this now — like you got tired of that little play-acting group you joined last year? *(Looking at Ruth.)* And what was it the year before that?

Ruth: The horseback-riding club for which she bought that fifty-five-dollar riding habit that's been hanging in the closet ever since!

Mama (to Beneatha): Why you got to flit so from one thing to another, baby?

Beneatha (sharply): I just want to learn to play the guitar. Is there anything wrong with that?

Mama: Ain't nobody trying to stop you. I just wonders sometimes why you has to flit so from one thing to another all the time. You ain't never done nothing with all that camera equipment you brought home —

Beneatha: I don't flit! I — I experiment with different forms of expression —

Ruth: Like riding a horse?

Beneatha: — People have to express themselves one way or another.

Mama: What is it you want to express?

Beneatha (angrily): Me! *(Mama and Ruth look at each other and burst into raucous laughter.)* Don't worry — I don't expect you to understand.

Mama (to change the subject): Who you going out with tomorrow night?

Beneatha (with displeasure): George Murchison again.

Mama (pleased): Oh — you getting a little sweet on him?

Ruth: You ask me, this child ain't sweet on nobody but herself — *(Under breath.)* Express herself!

They laugh.

Beneatha: Oh — I like George all right, Mama. I mean I like him enough to go out with him and stuff, but —

Ruth (for devilment): What does *and stuff* mean?

Beneatha: Mind your own business.

Mama: Stop picking at her now, Ruth. *(She chuckles — then a suspicious sudden look at her daughter as she turns in her chair for emphasis.)* What DOES it mean?

Beneatha (wearily): Oh, I just mean I couldn't ever really be serious about George. He's — he's so shallow.

Ruth: Shallow—what do you mean he's shallow? He's *rich!*

Mama: Hush, Ruth.

Beneatha: I know he's rich. He knows he's rich, too.

Ruth: Well—what other qualities a man got to have to satisfy you, little girl?

Beneatha: You wouldn't even begin to understand. Anybody who married Walter could not possibly understand.

Mama (outraged): What kind of way is that to talk about your brother?

Beneatha: Brother is a flip—let's face it.

Mama (to Ruth, helplessly): What's a flip?

Ruth (glad to add kindling): She's saying he's crazy.

Beneatha: Not crazy. Brother isn't really crazy yet—he—he's an elaborate neurotic.

Mama: Hush your mouth!

Beneatha: As for George. Well. George looks good—he's got a beautiful car and he takes me to nice places and, as my sister-in-law says, he is probably the richest boy I will ever get to know and I even like him sometimes—but if the Youngers are sitting around waiting to see if their little Bennie is going to tie up the family with the Murchisons, they are wasting their time.

Ruth: You mean you wouldn't marry George Murchison if he asked you someday? That pretty, rich thing? Honey, I knew you was odd—

Beneatha: No I would not marry him if all I felt for him was what I feel now. Besides, George's family wouldn't really like it.

Mama: Why not?

Beneatha: Oh, Mama—The Murchisons are honest-to-God-real-*live*-rich colored people, and the only people in the world who are more snobbish than rich white people are rich colored people. I thought everybody knew that. I've met Mrs. Murchison. She's a scene!

Mama: You must not dislike people 'cause they well off, honey.

Beneatha: Why not? It makes just as much sense as disliking people 'cause they are poor, and lots of people do that.

Ruth (a wisdom-of-the-ages manner. To Mama): Well, she'll get over some of this—

Beneatha: Get over it? What are you talking about, Ruth? Listen, I'm going to be a doctor. I'm not worried about who I'm going to marry yet—if I ever get married.

Mama and Ruth: If!

Mama: Now, Bennie—

Beneatha: Oh, I probably will . . . but first I'm going to be a doctor, and George, for one, still thinks that's pretty funny. I couldn't be bothered with that. I am going to be a doctor and everybody around here better understand that!

Mama (kindly): 'Course you going to be a doctor, honey, God willing.

Beneatha (drily): God hasn't got a thing to do with it.

Mama: Beneatha—that just wasn't necessary.

Beneatha: Well—neither is God. I get sick of hearing about God.

Mama: Beneatha!

Beneatha: I mean it! I'm just tired of hearing about God all the time. What has He got to do with anything? Does He pay tuition?

Mama: You 'bout to get your fresh little jaw slapped!

Ruth: That's just what she needs, all right!

Beneatha: Why? Why can't I say what I want to around here, like everybody else?

Mama: It don't sound nice for a young girl to say things like that—you wasn't brought up that way. Me and your father went to trouble to get you and Brother to church every Sunday.

Beneatha: Mama, you don't understand. It's all a matter of ideas, and God is just one idea I don't accept. It's not important. I am not going out and be immoral or commit crimes because I don't believe in God. I don't even think about it. It's just that I get tired of Him getting credit for all the things the human race achieves through its own stubborn effort. There simply is no blasted God—there is only man and it is *He* who makes miracles!

Mama absorbs this speech, studies her daughter, and rises slowly and crosses to Beneatha and slaps her powerfully across the face. After, there is only silence and the daughter drops her eyes from her mother's face, and Mama is very tall before her.

Mama: Now—you say after me, in my mother's house there is still God. *(There is a long pause and Beneatha stares at the floor wordlessly. Mama repeats the phrase with precision and cool emotion.)* In my mother's house there is still God.

Beneatha: In my mother's house there is still God.

A long pause.

Mama (walking away from Beneatha, too disturbed for triumphant posture. Stopping and turning back to her daughter): There are some ideas we ain't going to have in this house. Not long as I am at the head of this family.

Beneatha: Yes, ma'am.

Mama walks out of the room.

Ruth (almost gently, with profound understanding): You think you a woman, Bennie—but you still a little girl. What you did was childish—so you got treated like a child.

Beneatha: I see. *(Quietly.)* I also see that everybody thinks it's all right for Mama to be a tyrant. But all the tyranny in the world will never put a God in the heavens!

She picks up her books and goes out. Pause.

Ruth (goes to Mama's door): She said she was sorry.

Mama (coming out, going to her plant): They frightens me, Ruth. My children.

Ruth: You got good children, Lena. They just a little off sometimes—but they're good.

Mama: No—there's something come down between me and them that don't let us understand each other and I don't know what it is. One done almost lost his mind thinking 'bout money all the time and the other done commence to talk about things I can't seem to understand in no form or fashion. What is it that's changing, Ruth.

Ruth (soothingly, older than her years): Now . . . you taking it all too seriously. You just got strong-willed children and it takes a strong woman like you to keep 'em in hand.

Mama (looking at her plant and sprinkling a little water on it): They spirited all right, my children. Got to admit they got spirit—Bennie and Walter. Like this little old plant that ain't never had enough sunshine or nothing—and look at it . . .

She has her back to Ruth, who has had to stop ironing and lean against something and put the back of her hand to her forehead.

Ruth (trying to keep Mama from noticing): You ... sure ... loves that little old thing, don't you? ...

Mama: Well, I always wanted me a garden like I used to see sometimes at the back of the houses down home. This plant is close as I ever got to having one. *(She looks out of the window as she replaces the plant.)* Lord, ain't nothing as dreary as the view from this window on a dreary day, is there? Why ain't you singing this morning, Ruth? Sing that "No Ways Tired." That song always lifts me up so — *(She turns at last to see that Ruth has slipped quietly to the floor, in a state of semiconsciousness.)* Ruth! Ruth honey— what's the matter with you ... Ruth!

Curtain.

SCENE II. *[The following morning.]*

It is the following morning; a Saturday morning, and house cleaning is in progress at the Youngers'. Furniture has been shoved hither and yon and Mama is giving the kitchen-area walls a washing down. Beneatha, in dungarees, with a handkerchief tied around her face, is spraying insecticide into the cracks in the walls. As they work, the radio is on and a Southside disk-jockey program is inappropriately filling the house with a rather exotic saxophone blues. Travis, the sole idle one, is leaning on his arms, looking out of the window.

Travis: Grandmama, that stuff Bennie is using smells awful. Can I go downstairs, please?

Mama: Did you get all them chores done already? I ain't seen you doing much.

Travis: Yes'm — finished early. Where did Mama go this morning?

Mama (looking at Beneatha): She had to go on a little errand.

The phone rings. Beneatha runs to answer it and reaches it before Walter, who has entered from bedroom.

Travis: Where?

Mama: To tend to her business.

Beneatha: Haylo ... *(Disappointed.)* Yes, he is. *(She tosses the phone to Walter, who barely catches it.)* It's Willie Harris again.

Walter (as privately as possible under Mama's gaze): Hello, Willie. Did you get the papers from the lawyer? ... No, not yet. I told you the mailman doesn't get here till ten-thirty ... No, I'll come there ... Yeah! Right away. *(He hangs up and goes for his coat.)*

Beneatha: Brother, where did Ruth go?

Walter (as he exits): How should I know!

Travis: Aw come on, Grandma. Can I go outside?

Mama: Oh, I guess so. You stay right in front of the house, though, and keep a good lookout for the postman.

Travis: Yes'm. *(He darts into bedroom for stickball and bat, reenters, and sees Beneatha on her knees spraying under sofa with behind upraised. He edges closer to the target, takes aim, and lets her have it. She screams.)* Leave them poor little cockroaches alone, they ain't bothering you none! *(He runs as she swings the spraygun at him viciously and playfully.)* Grandma! Grandma!

Mama: Look out there, girl, before you be spilling some of that stuff on that child!

Travis (safely behind the bastion of Mama): That's right—look out, now! *(He exits.)*

Beneatha (drily): I can't imagine that it would hurt him—it has never hurt the roaches.

Mama: Well, little boys' hides ain't as tough as Southside roaches. You better get over there behind the bureau. I seen one marching out of there like Napoleon yesterday.

Beneatha: There's really only one way to get rid of them, Mama—

Mama: How?

Beneatha: Set fire to this building! Mama, where did Ruth go?

Mama (looking at her with meaning): To the doctor, I think.

Beneatha: The doctor? What's the matter? *(They exchange glances.)* You don't think—

Mama (with her sense of drama): Now I ain't saying what I think. But I ain't never been wrong 'bout a woman neither.

The phone rings.

Beneatha (at the phone): Hay-lo . . . *(Pause, and a moment of recognition.)* Well— when did you get back! . . . And how was it? . . . Of course I've missed you—in my way . . . This morning? No . . . house cleaning and all that and Mama hates it if I let people come over when the house is like this . . . You *have?* Well, that's different . . . What is it—Oh, what the hell, come on over . . . Right, see you then. *Arrivederci.*

She hangs up.

Mama (who has listened vigorously, as is her habit): Who is that you inviting over here with this house looking like this? You ain't got the pride you was born with!

Beneatha: Asagai doesn't care how houses look, Mama—he's an intellectual.

Mama: Who?

Beneatha: Asagai—Joseph Asagai. He's an African boy I met on campus. He's been studying in Canada all summer.

Mama: What's his name?

Beneatha: Asagai, Joseph. Ah-sah-guy . . . He's from Nigeria.

Mama: Oh, that's the little country that was founded by slaves way back . . .

Beneatha: No, Mama—that's Liberia.

Mama: I don't think I never met no African before.

Beneatha: Well, do me a favor and don't ask him a whole lot of ignorant questions about Africans. I mean, do they wear clothes and all that—

Mama: Well, now, I guess if you think we so ignorant 'round here maybe you shouldn't bring your friends here—

Beneatha: It's just that people ask such crazy things. All anyone seems to know about when it comes to Africa is Tarzan—

Mama (indignantly): Why should I know anything about Africa?

Beneatha: Why do you give money at church for the missionary work?

Mama: Well, that's to help save people.

Beneatha: You mean save them from *heathenism*—

Mama (innocently): Yes.

Beneatha: I'm afraid they need more salvation from the British and the French.

Ruth comes in forlornly and pulls off her coat with dejection. They both turn to look at her.

Ruth (*dispiritedly*): Well, I guess from all the happy faces—everybody knows.

Beneatha: You pregnant?

Mama: Lord have mercy, I sure hope it's a little old girl. Travis ought to have a sister.

Beneatha and Ruth give her a hopeless look for this grandmotherly enthusiasm.

Beneatha: How far along are you?

Ruth: Two months.

Beneatha: Did you mean to? I mean did you plan it or was it an accident?

Mama: What do you know about planning or not planning?

Beneatha: Oh, Mama.

Ruth (*wearily*): She's twenty years old, Lena.

Beneatha: Did you plan it, Ruth?

Ruth: Mind your own business.

Beneatha: It is my business—where is he going to live, on the *roof*? (*There is silence following the remark as the three women react to the sense of it.*) Gee—I didn't mean that, Ruth, honest. Gee, I don't feel like that at all. I—I think it is wonderful.

Ruth (*dully*): Wonderful.

Beneatha: Yes—really.

Mama (*looking at Ruth, worried*): Doctor say everything going to be all right?

Ruth (*far away*): Yes—she says everything is going to be fine . . .

Mama (*immediately suspicious*): "She"—What doctor you went to?

Ruth folds over, near hysteria.

Mama (*worriedly hovering over Ruth*): Ruth honey—what's the matter with you—you sick?

Ruth has her fists clenched on her thighs and is fighting hard to suppress a scream that seems to be rising in her.

Beneatha: What's the matter with her, Mama?

Mama (*working her fingers in Ruth's shoulders to relax her*): She be all right. Women gets right depressed sometimes when they get her way. (*Speaking softly, expertly, rapidly.*) Now you just relax. That's right . . . just lean back, don't think 'bout nothing at all . . . nothing at all—

Ruth: I'm all right . . .

The glassy-eyed look melts and then she collapses into a fit of heavy sobbing. The bell rings.

Beneatha: Oh, my God—that must be Asagai.

Mama (*to Ruth*): Come on now, honey. You need to lie down and rest awhile . . . then have some nice hot food.

They exit, Ruth's weight on her mother-in-law. Beneatha, herself profoundly disturbed, opens the door to admit a rather dramatic-looking young man with a large package.

Asagai: Hello, Alaiyo—

Beneatha (*holding the door open and regarding him with pleasure*): Hello . . . (*Long pause.*) Well—come in. And please excuse everything. My mother was very upset about my letting anyone come here with the place like this.

Asagai (coming into the room): You look disturbed too . . . Is something wrong?

Beneatha (still at the door, absently): Yes . . . we've all got acute ghetto-itus. *(She smiles and comes toward him, finding a cigarette and sitting.)* So — sit down! No! Wait! *(She whips the spraygun off sofa where she had left it and puts the cushions back. At last perches on arm of sofa. He sits.)* So, how was Canada?

Asagai (a sophisticate): Canadian.

Beneatha (looking at him): Asagai, I'm very glad you are back.

Asagai (looking back at her in turn): Are you really?

Beneatha: Yes — very.

Asagai: Why? — you were quite glad when I went away. What happened?

Beneatha: You went away.

Asagai: Ahhhhhhhh.

Beneatha: Before — you wanted to be so serious before there was time.

Asagai: How much time must there be before one knows what one feels?

Beneatha (stalling this particular conversation. Her hands pressed together, in a deliberately childish gesture): What did you bring me?

Asagai (handing her the package): Open it and see.

Beneatha (eagerly opening the package and drawing out some records and the colorful robes of a Nigerian woman): Oh Asagai! . . . You got them for me! . . . How beautiful . . . and the records too! *(She lifts out the robes and runs to the mirror with them and holds the drapery up in front of herself.)*

Asagai (coming to her at the mirror): I shall have to teach you how to drape it properly. *(He flings the material about her for the moment and stands back to look at her.)* Ah — Oh-pay-gay-day, oh-gbah-mu-shay. *(A Yoruba exclamation for admiration.)* You wear it well . . . very well . . . mutilated hair and all.

Beneatha (turning suddenly): My hair — what's wrong with my hair?

Asagai (shrugging): Were you born with it like that?

Beneatha (reaching up to touch it): No . . . of course not.

She looks back to the mirror, disturbed.

Asagai (smiling): How then?

Beneatha: You know perfectly well how . . . as crinkly as yours . . . that's how.

Asagai: And it is ugly to you that way?

Beneatha (quickly): Oh, no — not ugly . . . *(More slowly, apologetically.)* But it's so hard to manage when it's, well — raw.

Asagai: And so to accommodate that — you mutilate it every week?

Beneatha: It's not mutilation!

Asagai (laughing aloud at her seriousness): Oh . . . please! I am only teasing you because you are so very serious about these things. *(He stands back from her and folds his arms across his chest as he watches her pulling at her hair and frowning in the mirror.)* Do you remember the first time you met me at school? . . . *(He laughs.)* You came up to me and you said — and I thought you were the most serious little thing I had ever seen — you said: *(He imitates her.)* "Mr. Asagai — I want very much to talk with you. About Africa. You see, Mr. Asagai, I am looking for my *identity!*"

He laughs.

Beneatha (turning to him, not laughing): Yes —

Her face is quizzical, profoundly disturbed.

Asagai (still teasing and reaching out and taking her face in his hands and turning her profile to him): Well . . . it is true that this is not so much a profile of a

Hollywood queen as perhaps a queen of the Nile — *(A mock dismissal of the importance of the question.)* But what does it matter? Assimilationism is so popular in your country.

Beneatha (wheeling, passionately, sharply): I am not an assimilationist!

Asagai (the protest hangs in the room for a moment and Asagai studies her, his laughter fading): Such a serious one. *(There is a pause.)* So — you like the robes? You must take excellent care of them — they are from my sister's personal wardrobe.

Beneatha (with incredulity): You — you sent all the way home — for me?

Asagai (with charm): For you — I would do much more . . . Well, that is what I came for. I must go.

Beneatha: Will you call me Monday?

Asagai: Yes . . . We have a great deal to talk about. I mean about identity and time and all that.

Beneatha: Time?

Asagai: Yes. About how much time one needs to know what one feels.

Beneatha: You see! You never understood that there is more than one kind of feeling which can exist between a man and a woman — or, at least, there should be.

Asagai (shaking his head negatively but gently): No. Between a man and a woman there need be only one kind of feeling. I have that for you . . . Now even . . . right this moment . . .

Beneatha: I know — and by itself — it won't do. I can find that anywhere.

Asagai: For a woman it should be enough.

Beneatha: I know — because that's what it says in all the novels that men write. But it isn't. Go ahead and laugh — but I'm not interested in being someone's little episode in America or — *(With feminine vengeance.)* — one of them! *(Asagai has burst into laughter again.)* That's funny as hell, huh!

Asagai: It's just that every American girl I have known has said that to me. White — black — in this you are all the same. And the same speech, too!

Beneatha (angrily): Yuk, yuk, yuk!

Asagai: It's how you can be sure that the world's most liberated women are not liberated at all. You all talk about it too much!

Mama enters and is immediately all social charm because of the presence of a guest.

Beneatha: Oh — Mama — this is Mr. Asagai.

Mama: How do you do?

Asagai (total politeness to an elder): How do you do, Mrs. Younger. Please forgive me for coming at such an outrageous hour on a Saturday.

Mama: Well, you are quite welcome. I just hope you understand that our house don't always look like this. *(Chatterish.)* You must come again. I would love to hear all about — *(Not sure of the name.)* — your country. I think it's so sad the way our American Negroes don't know nothing about Africa 'cept Tarzan and all that. And all that money they pour into these churches when they ought to be helping you people over there drive out them French and Englishmen done taken away your land.

The mother flashes a slightly superior look at her daughter upon completion of the recitation.

Asagai (taken aback by this sudden and acutely unrelated expression of sympathy): Yes . . . yes . . .

Mama (smiling at him suddenly and relaxing and looking him over): How many
     miles is it from here to where you come from?
Asagai: Many thousands.
Mama (looking at him as she would Walter): I bet you don't half look after your-
     self, being away from your mama either. I spec you better come 'round
     here from time to time to get yourself some decent homecooked meals . . .
Asagai (moved): Thank you. Thank you very much. *(They are all quiet, then —)*
     Well . . . I must go. I will call you Monday, Alaiyo.
Mama: What's that he call you?
Asagai: Oh — "Alaiyo." I hope you don't mind. It is what you would call a nick-
     name, I think. It is a Yoruba word. I am a Yoruba.
Mama (looking at Beneatha): I — I thought he was from — *(Uncertain.)*
Asagai (understanding): Nigeria is my country. Yoruba is my tribal origin —
Beneatha: You didn't tell us what Alaiyo means . . . for all I know, you might be
     calling me Little Idiot or something . . .
Asagai: Well . . . let me see . . . I do not know how just to explain it . . . The
     sense of a thing can be so different when it changes languages.
Beneatha: You're evading.
Asagai: No — really it is difficult . . . *(Thinking.)* It means . . . it means One for
     Whom Bread — Food — Is Not Enough. *(He looks at her.)* Is that all right?
Beneatha (understanding, softly): Thank you.
Mama (looking from one to the other and not understanding any of it): Well . . . that's
     nice . . . You must come see us again — Mr. —
Asagai: Ah-sah-guy . . .
Mama: Yes . . . Do come again.
Asagai: Good-bye.

     He exits.

Mama (after him): Lord, that's a pretty thing just went out here! *(Insinuatingly,
     to her daughter.)* Yes, I guess I see why we done commence to get so inter-
     ested in Africa 'round here. Missionaries my aunt Jenny!

     She exits.

Beneatha: Oh, Mama! . . .

     *She picks up the Nigerian dress and holds it up to her in front of the mirror again.
     She sets the headdress on haphazardly and then notices her hair again and clutches
     at it and then replaces the headdress and frowns at herself. Then she starts to
     wriggle in front of the mirror as she thinks a Nigerian woman might. Travis enters
     and stands regarding her.*

Travis: What's the matter, girl, you cracking up?
Beneatha: Shut up.

     *She pulls the headdress off and looks at herself in the mirror and clutches at her
     hair again and squinches her eyes as if trying to imagine something. Then, sud-
     denly, she gets her raincoat and kerchief and hurriedly prepares for going out.*

Mama (coming back into the room): She's resting now. Travis, baby, run next
     door and ask Miss Johnson to please let me have a little kitchen cleanser.
     This here can is empty as Jacob's kettle.
Travis: I just came in.
Mama: Do as you told. *(He exits and she looks at her daughter.)* Where you going?

Beneatha (halting at the door): To become a queen of the Nile!

> *She exits in a breathless blaze of glory. Ruth appears in the bedroom doorway.*

Mama: Who told you to get up?

Ruth: Ain't nothing wrong with me to be lying in no bed for. Where did Bennie go?

Mama (drumming her fingers): Far as I could make out—to Egypt. *(Ruth just looks at her.)* What time is it getting to?

Ruth: Ten twenty. And the mailman going to ring that bell this morning just like he done every morning for the last umpteen years.

> *Travis comes in with the cleanser can.*

Travis: She say to tell you that she don't have much.

Mama (angrily): Lord, some people I could name sure is tight-fisted! *(Directing her grandson.)* Mark two cans of cleanser on the list there. If she that hard up for kitchen cleanser, I sure don't want to forget to get her none!

Ruth: Lena—maybe the woman is just short on cleanser—

Mama (not listening): —Much baking powder as she done borrowed from me all these years, she could of done gone into the baking business!

> *The bell sounds suddenly and sharply and all three are stunned—serious and silent—midspeech. In spite of all the other conversations and distractions of the morning, this is what they have been waiting for, even Travis, who looks helplessly from his mother to his grandmother. Ruth is the first to come to life again.*

Ruth (to Travis): Get down them steps, boy!

> *Travis snaps to life and flies out to get the mail.*

Mama (her eyes wide, her hand to her breast): You mean it done really come?

Ruth (excited): Oh, Miss Lena!

Mama (collecting herself): Well . . . I don't know what we all so excited about 'round here for. We known it was coming for months.

Ruth: That's a whole lot different from having it come and being able to hold it in your hands . . . a piece of paper worth ten thousand dollars . . . *(Travis bursts back into the room. He holds the envelope high above his head, like a little dancer, his face is radiant and he is breathless. He moves to his grandmother with sudden slow ceremony and puts the envelope into her hands. She accepts it, and then merely holds it and looks at it.)* Come on! Open it . . . Lord have mercy, I wish Walter Lee was here!

Travis: Open it, Grandmama!

Mama (staring at it): Now you all be quiet. It's just a check.

Ruth: Open it . . .

Mama (still staring at it): Now don't act silly . . . We ain't never been no people to act silly 'bout no money—

Ruth (swiftly): We ain't never had none before—OPEN IT!

> *Mama finally makes a good strong tear and pulls out the thin blue slice of paper and inspects it closely. The boy and his mother study it raptly over Mama's shoulders.*

Mama: Travis! *(She is counting off with doubt.)* Is that the right number of zeros?

Travis: Yes'm . . . ten thousand dollars. Gaalee, grandmama, you rich.

Mama (She holds the check away from her, still looking at it. Slowly her face sobers into a mask of unhappiness): Ten thousand dollars. *(She hands it to Ruth.)* Put it away somewhere, Ruth. *(She does not look at Ruth; her eyes seem to be seeing something somewhere very far off.)* Ten thousand dollars they give you. Ten thousand dollars.

Travis *(to his mother, sincerely):* What's the matter with Grandmama — don't she want to be rich?

Ruth *(distractedly):* You go on out and play now, baby. *(Travis exits. Mama starts wiping dishes absently, humming intently to herself. Ruth turns to her, with kind exasperation.)* You've gone and got yourself upset.

Mama *(not looking at her):* I spec if it wasn't for you all . . . I would just put that money away or give it to the church or something.

Ruth: Now what kind of talk is that. Mr. Younger would just be plain mad if he could hear you talking foolish like that.

Mama *(stopping and staring off):* Yes . . . he sure would. *(Sighing.)* We got enough to do with that money, all right. *(She halts then, and turns and looks at her daughter-in-law hard; Ruth avoids her eyes and Mama wipes her hands with finality and starts to speak firmly to Ruth.)* Where did you go today, girl?

Ruth: To the doctor.

Mama *(impatiently):* Now, Ruth . . . you know better than that. Old Doctor Jones is strange enough in his way but there ain't nothing 'bout him make somebody slip and call him "she" — like you done this morning.

Ruth: Well, that's what happened — my tongue slipped.

Mama: You went to see that woman, didn't you?

Ruth *(defensively, giving herself away):* What woman you talking about?

Mama *(angrily):* That woman who —

Walter enters in great excitement.

Walter: Did it come?

Mama *(quietly):* Can't you give people a Christian greeting before you start asking about money?

Walter *(to Ruth):* Did it come? *(Ruth unfolds the check and lays it quietly before him, watching him intently with thoughts of her own. Walter sits down and grasps it close and counts off the zeros.)* Ten thousand dollars — *(He turns suddenly, frantically to his mother and draws some papers out of his breast pocket.)* Mama — look. Old Willy Harris put everything on paper —

Mama: Son — I think you ought to talk to your wife . . . I'll go on out and leave you alone if you want —

Walter: I can talk to her later — Mama, look —

Mama: Son —

Walter: WILL SOMEBODY PLEASE LISTEN TO ME TODAY!

Mama *(quietly):* I don't 'low no yellin' in this house, Walter Lee, and you know it — *(Walter stares at them in frustration and starts to speak several times.)* And there ain't going to be no investing in no liquor stores.

Walter: But, Mama, you ain't even looked at it.

Mama: I don't aim to have to speak on that again.

A long pause.

Walter: You ain't looked at it and you don't aim to have to speak on that again? You ain't even looked at it and *you* have decided — *(Crumpling his papers.)* Well, *you* tell that to my boy tonight when you put him to sleep on the living-room couch . . . *(Turning to Mama and speaking directly to her.)*

Yeah — and tell it to my wife, Mama, tomorrow when she has to go out of
here to look after somebody else's kids. And tell it to *me,* Mama, every time
we need a new pair of curtains and I have to watch *you* go out and work in
somebody's kitchen. Yeah, you tell me then!

Walter starts out.

Ruth: Where you going?

Walter: I'm going out!

Ruth: Where?

Walter: Just out of this house somewhere —

Ruth (getting her coat): I'll come too.

Walter: I don't want you to come!

Ruth: I got something to talk to you about, Walter.

Walter: That's too bad.

Mama (still quietly): Walter Lee — *(She waits and he finally turns and looks at her.)*
Sit down.

Walter: I'm a grown man, Mama.

Mama: Ain't nobody said you wasn't grown. But you still in my house and my
presence. And as long as you are — you'll talk to your wife civil. Now sit
down.

Ruth (suddenly): Oh, let him go on out and drink himself to death! He makes
me sick to my stomach! *(She flings her coat against him and exits to bedroom.)*

Walter (violently flinging the coat after her): And you turn mine too, baby! *(The
door slams behind her.)* That was my biggest mistake —

Mama (still quietly): Walter, what is the matter with you?

Walter: Matter with me? Ain't nothing the matter with *me!*

Mama: Yes there is. Something eating you up like a crazy man. Something
more than me not giving you this money. The past few years I been watching it happen to you. You get all nervous acting and kind of wild in the
eyes — *(Walter jumps up impatiently at her words.)* I said sit there now, I'm
talking to you!

Walter: Mama — I don't need no nagging at me today.

Mama: Seem like you getting to a place where you always tied up in some kind
of knot about something. But if anybody ask you 'bout it you just yell at
'em and bust out the house and go out and drink somewheres. Walter Lee,
people can't live with that. Ruth's a good, patient girl in her way — but you
getting to be too much. Boy, don't make the mistake of driving that girl
away from you.

Walter: Why — what she do for me?

Mama: She loves you.

Walter: Mama — I'm going out. I want to go off somewhere and be by myself
for a while.

Mama: I'm sorry 'bout your liquor store, son. It just wasn't the thing for us to
do. That's what I want to tell you about —

Walter: I got to go out, Mama —

He rises.

Mama: It's dangerous, son.

Walter: What's dangerous?

Mama: When a man goes outside his home to look for peace.

Walter (beseechingly): Then why can't there never be no peace in this house then?

Mama: You done found it in some other house?

Walter: No — there ain't no woman! Why do women always think there's a woman somewhere when a man gets restless. *(Picks up the check.)* Do you know what this money means to me? Do you know what this money can do for us? *(Puts it back.)* Mama — Mama — I want so many things . . .

Mama: Yes, son —

Walter: I want so many things that they are driving me kind of crazy . . . Mama — look at me.

Mama: I'm looking at you. You a good-looking boy. You got a job, a nice wife, a fine boy, and —

Walter: A job. *(Looks at her.)* Mama, a job? I open and close car doors all day long. I drive a man around in his limousine and I say, "Yes, sir; no, sir; very good, sir; shall I take the Drive, sir?" Mama, that ain't no kind of job . . . that ain't nothing at all. *(Very quietly.)* Mama, I don't know if I can make you understand.

Mama: Understand what, baby?

Walter (quietly): Sometimes it's like I can see the future stretched out in front of me — just plain as day. The future, Mama. Hanging over there at the edge of my days. Just waiting for me — a big, looming blank space — full of *nothing*. Just waiting for *me*. But it don't have to be. *(Pause. Kneeling beside her chair.)* Mama — sometimes when I'm downtown and I pass them cool, quiet-looking restaurants where them white boys are sitting back and talking 'bout things . . . sitting there turning deals worth millions of dollars . . . sometimes I see guys don't look much older than me —

Mama: Son — how come you talk so much 'bout money?

Walter (with immense passion): Because it is life, Mama!

Mama (quietly): Oh — *(Very quietly.)* So now it's life. Money is life. Once upon a time freedom used to be life — now it's money. I guess the world really do change . . .

Walter: No — it was always money, Mama. We just didn't know about it.

Mama: No . . . something has changed. *(She looks at him.)* You something new, boy. In my time we was worried about not being lynched and getting to the North if we could and how to stay alive and still have a pinch of dignity too . . . Now here come you and Beneatha — talking 'bout things we ain't never even thought about hardly, me and your daddy. You ain't satisfied or proud of nothing we done. I mean that you had a home; that we kept you out of trouble till you was grown; that you don't have to ride to work on the back of nobody's streetcar — You my children — but how different we done become.

Walter (a long beat. He pats her hand and gets up): You just don't understand, Mama, you just don't understand.

Mama: Son — do you know your wife is expecting another baby? *(Walter stands, stunned, and absorbs what his mother has said.)* That's what she wanted to talk to you about. *(Walter sinks down into a chair.)* This ain't for me to be telling — but you ought to know. *(She waits.)* I think Ruth is thinking 'bout getting rid of that child.

Walter (slowly understanding): — No — no — Ruth wouldn't do that.

Mama: When the world gets ugly enough — a woman will do anything for her family. *The part that's already living.*

Walter: You don't know Ruth, Mama, if you think she would do that.

Ruth opens the bedroom door and stands there a little limp.

Ruth (beaten): Yes I would too, Walter. *(Pause.)* I gave her a five-dollar down payment.

There is total silence as the man stares at his wife and the mother stares at her son.

Mama (presently): Well — *(Tightly.)* Well — son, I'm waiting to hear you say something . . . *(She waits.)* I'm waiting to hear how you be your father's son. Be the man he was . . . *(Pause. The silence shouts.)* Your wife say she going to destroy your child. And I'm waiting to hear you talk like him and say we a people who give children life, not who destroys them — *(She rises.)* I'm waiting to see you stand up and look like your daddy and say we done give up one baby to poverty and that we ain't going to give up nary another one . . . I'm waiting.

Walter: Ruth — *(He can say nothing.)*

Mama: If you a son of mine, tell her! *(Walter picks up his keys and his coat and walks out. She continues, bitterly.)* You . . . you are a disgrace to your father's memory. Somebody get me my hat!

Curtain.

ACT II

Scene I

TIME: *Later the same day.*

At rise: Ruth is ironing again. She has the radio going. Presently Beneatha's bedroom door opens and Ruth's mouth falls and she puts down the iron in fascination.

Ruth: What have we got on tonight!

Beneatha (emerging grandly from the doorway so that we can see her thoroughly robed in the costume Asagai brought): You are looking at what a well-dressed Nigerian woman wears — *(She parades for Ruth, her hair completely hidden by the headdress; she is coquettishly fanning herself with an ornate oriental fan, mistakenly more like Butterfly than any Nigerian that ever was.)* Isn't it beautiful? *(She promenades to the radio and, with an arrogant flourish, turns off the good loud blues that is playing.)* Enough of this assimilationist junk! *(Ruth follows her with her eyes as she goes to the phonograph and puts on a record and turns and waits ceremoniously for the music to come up. Then, with a shout —)* OCOMOGOSIAY!

Ruth jumps. The music comes up, a lovely Nigerian melody. Beneatha listens, enraptured, her eyes far way — "back to the past." She begins to dance. Ruth is dumfounded.

Ruth: What kind of dance is that?

Beneatha: A folk dance.

Ruth (Pearl Bailey): What kind of folks do that, honey?

Beneatha: It's from Nigeria. It's a dance of welcome.

Ruth: Who you welcoming?

Beneatha: The men back to the village.

Ruth: Where they been?

Beneatha: How should I know — out hunting or something. Anyway, they are coming back now . . .

Ruth: Well, that's good.

Beneatha (with the record):

> Alundi, alundi
> Alundi alunya
> Jop pu a jeepua
> Ang gu soooooooooo
> Ai yai yae . . .
> Ayehaye — alundi . . .

Walter comes in during this performance; he has obviously been drinking. He leans against the door heavily and watches his sister, at first with distaste. Then his eyes look off — "back to the past" — as he lifts both his fists to the roof, screaming.

Walter: YEAH . . . AND ETHIOPIA STRETCH FORTH HER HANDS AGAIN! . . .

Ruth (drily, looking at him): Yes — and Africa sure is claiming her own tonight. *(She gives them both up and starts ironing again.)*

Walter (all in a drunken, dramatic shout): Shut up! . . . I'm diggin them drums . . . them drums move me! . . . *(He makes his weaving way to his wife's face and leans in close to her.)* In my *heart of hearts* — *(He thumps his chest.)* — I am much warrior!

Ruth (without even looking up): In your heart of hearts you are much drunkard.

Walter (coming away from her and starting to wander around the room, shouting): Me and Jomo . . . *(Intently, in his sister's face. She has stopped dancing to watch him in this unknown mood.)* That's my man, Kenyatta. *(Shouting and thumping his chest.)* FLAMING SPEAR! HOT DAMN! *(He is suddenly in possession of an imaginary spear and actively spearing enemies all over the room.)* OCO-MOGOSIAY . . .

Beneatha (to encourage Walter, thoroughly caught up with this side of him): OCO-MOGOSIAY, FLAMING SPEAR!

Walter: THE LION IS WAKING . . . OWIMOWEH!

He pulls his shirt open and leaps up on the table and gestures with his spear.

Beneatha: OWIMOWEH!

Walter (on the table, very far gone, his eyes pure glass sheets. He sees what we cannot, that he is a leader of his people, a great chief, a descendant of Chaka, and that the hour to march has come): Listen, my black brothers —

Beneatha: OCOMOGOSIAY!

Walter: — Do you hear the waters rushing against the shores of the coastlands —

Beneatha: OCOMOGOSIAY!

Walter: — Do you hear the screeching of the cocks in yonder hills beyond where the chiefs meet in council for the coming of the mighty war —

Beneatha: OCOMOGOSIAY!

And now the lighting shifts subtly to suggest the world of Walter's imagination, and the mood shifts from pure comedy. It is the inner Walter speaking: the Southside chauffeur has assumed an unexpected majesty.

Walter: — Do you hear the beating of the wings of the birds flying low over the mountains and the low places of our land —

Beneatha: OCOMOGOSIAY!

Walter: — Do you hear the singing of the women, singing the war songs of our fathers to the babies in the great houses? Singing the sweet war songs! *(The doorbell rings.)* OH, DO YOU HEAR, MY *BLACK* BROTHERS!

Beneatha (completely gone): We hear you, Flaming Spear —

> *Ruth shuts off the phonograph and opens the door. George Murchison enters.*

Walter: Telling us to prepare for the GREATNESS OF THE TIME! *(Lights back to normal. He turns and sees George.)* Black Brother!

> *He extends his hand for the fraternal clasp.*

George: Black Brother, hell!

Ruth (having had enough, and embarrassed for the family): Beneatha, you got company — what's the matter with you? Walter Lee Younger, get down off that table and stop acting like a fool . . .

> *Walter comes down off the table suddenly and makes a quick exit to the bathroom.*

Ruth: He's had a little to drink . . . I don't know what her excuse is.

George (to Beneatha): Look honey, we're going to the theater — we're not going to be *in* it . . . so go change, huh?

> *Beneatha looks at him and slowly, ceremoniously, lifts her hands and pulls off the headdress. Her hair is close-cropped and unstraightened. George freezes mid-sentence and Ruth's eyes all but fall out of her head.*

George: What in the name of —

Ruth (touching Beneatha's hair): Girl, you done lost your natural mind? Look at your head!

George: What have you done to your head — I mean your hair!

Beneatha: Nothing — except cut it off.

Ruth: Now that's the truth — it's what ain't been done to it! You expect this boy to go out with you with your head all nappy like that?

Beneatha (looking at George): That's up to George. If he's ashamed of his heritage —

George: Oh, don't be so proud of yourself, Bennie — just because you look eccentric.

Beneatha: How can something that's natural be eccentric?

George: That's what being eccentric means — being natural. Get dressed.

Beneatha: I don't like that, George.

Ruth: Why must you and your brother make an argument out of everything people say?

Beneatha: Because I hate assimilationist Negroes!

Ruth: Will somebody please tell me what assimila-whoever means!

George: Oh, it's just a college girl's way of calling people Uncle Toms — but that isn't what it means at all.

Ruth: Well, what does it mean?

Beneatha (cutting George off and staring at him as she replies to Ruth): It means someone who is willing to give up his own culture and submerge himself completely in the dominant, and in this case *oppressive* culture!

George: Oh, dear, dear, dear! Here we go! A lecture on the African past! On our Great West African Heritage! In one second we will hear all about the great Ashanti empires; the great Songhay civilizations; and the great sculpture of

Bénin—and then some poetry in the Bantu—and the whole monologue will end with the word *heritage! (Nastily.)* Let's face it, baby, your heritage is nothing but a bunch of raggedy-assed spirituals and some grass huts!

Beneatha: GRASS HUTS! *(Ruth crosses to her and forcibly pushes her toward the bedroom.)* See there . . . you are standing there in your splendid ignorance talking about people who were the first to smelt iron on the face of the earth! *(Ruth is pushing her through the door.)* The Ashanti were performing surgical operations when the English — *(Ruth pulls the door to, with Beneatha on the other side, and smiles graciously at George. Beneatha opens the door and shouts the end of the sentence defiantly at George.)* — were still tatooing themselves with blue dragons! *(She goes back inside.)*

Ruth: Have a seat, George. *(They both sit. Ruth folds her hands rather primly on her lap, determined to demonstrate the civilization of the family.)* Warm, ain't it? I mean for September. *(Pause.)* Just like they always say about Chicago weather: if it's too hot or cold for you, just wait a minute and it'll change. *(She smiles happily at this cliché of clichés.)* Everybody say it's got to do with them bombs and things they keep setting off. *(Pause.)* Would you like a nice cold beer?

George: No, thank you. I don't care for beer. *(He looks at his watch.)* I hope she hurries up.

Ruth: What time is the show?

George: It's an eight-thirty curtain. That's just Chicago, though. In New York standard curtain time is eight forty.

He is rather proud of this knowledge.

Ruth (properly appreciating it): You get to New York a lot?

George (offhand): Few times a year.

Ruth: Oh—that's nice. I've never been to New York.

Walter enters. We feel he has relieved himself, but the edge of unreality is still with him.

Walter: New York ain't got nothing Chicago ain't. Just a bunch of hustling people all squeezed up together—being "Eastern."

He turns his face into a screw of displeasure.

George: Oh—you've been?

Walter: Plenty of times.

Ruth (shocked at the lie): Walter Lee Younger!

Walter (staring her down): Plenty! *(Pause.)* What we got to drink in this house? Why don't you offer this man some refreshment. *(To George.)* They don't know how to entertain people in this house, man.

George: Thank you—I don't really care for anything.

Walter (feeling his head; sobriety coming): Where's Mama?

Ruth: She ain't come back yet.

Walter (looking Murchison over from head to toe, scrutinizing his carefully casual tweed sports jacket over cashmere V-neck sweater over soft eyelet shirt and tie, and soft slacks, finished off with white buckskin shoes): Why all you college boys wear them faggoty-looking white shoes?

Ruth: Walter Lee!

George Murchison ignores the remark.

Walter (to Ruth): Well, they look crazy as hell—white shoes, cold as it is.

Ruth (crushed): You have to excuse him —

Walter: No he don't! Excuse me for what? What you always excusing me for! I'll excuse myself when I needs to be excused! *(A pause.)* They look as funny as them black knee socks Beneatha wears out of here all the time.

Ruth: It's the college *style*, Walter.

Walter: Style, hell. She looks like she got burnt legs or something!

Ruth: Oh, Walter —

Walter (an irritable mimic): Oh, Walter! Oh, Walter! *(To Murchison.)* How's your old man making out? I understand you all going to buy that big hotel on the Drive? *(He finds a beer in the refrigerator, wanders over to Murchison, sipping and wiping his lips with the back of his hand, and straddling a chair backwards to talk to the other man.)* Shrewd move. Your old man is all right, man. *(Tapping his head and half winking for emphasis.)* I mean he knows how to operate. I mean he thinks *big*, you know what I mean, I mean for a *home*, you know? But I think he's kind of running out of ideas now. I'd like to talk to him. Listen, man, I got some plans that could turn this city upside down. I mean think like he does. *Big.* Invest big, gamble big, hell, lose *big* if you have to, you know what I mean. It's hard to find a man on this whole Southside who understands my kind of thinking — you dig? *(He scrutinizes Murchison again, drinks his beer, squints his eyes and leans in close, confidential, man to man.)* Me and you ought to sit down and talk sometimes, man. Man, I got me some ideas . . .

Murchison (with boredom): Yeah — sometimes we'll have to do that, Walter.

Walter (understanding the indifference, and offended): Yeah — well, when you get the time, man. I know you a busy little boy.

Ruth: Walter, please —

Walter (bitterly, hurt): I know ain't nothing in this world as busy as you colored college boys with your fraternity pins and white shoes . . .

Ruth (covering her face with humiliation): Oh, Walter Lee —

Walter: I see you all all the time — with the books tucked under your arms — going to your *(British A — a mimic.)* "clahsses." And for what! What the hell you learning over there? Filling up your heads — *(Counting off on his fingers.)* — with the sociology and the psychology — but they teaching you how to be a man? How to take over and run the world? They teaching you how to run a rubber plantation or a steel mill? Naw — just to talk proper and read books and wear them faggoty-looking white shoes . . .

George (looking at him with distaste, a little above it all): You're all wacked up with bitterness, man.

Walter (intently, almost quietly, between the teeth, glaring at the boy): And you — ain't you bitter, man? Ain't you just about had it yet? Don't you see no stars gleaming that you can't reach out and grab? You happy? — You contented son-of-a-bitch — you happy? You got it made? Bitter? Man, I'm a volcano. Bitter? Here I am a giant — surrounded by ants! Ants who can't even understand what it is the giant is talking about.

Ruth (passionately and suddenly): Oh, Walter — ain't you with nobody!

Walter (violently): No! 'Cause ain't nobody with me! Not even my own mother!

Ruth: Walter, that's a terrible thing to say!

Beneatha enters, dressed for the evening in a cocktail dress and earrings, hair natural.

George: Well — hey — *(Crosses to Beneatha; thoughtful, with emphasis, since this is a reversal.)* You look great!

Walter (seeing his sister's hair for the first time): What's the matter with your head?

Beneatha (tired of the jokes now): I cut it off, Brother.

Walter (coming close to inspect it and walking around her): Well, I'll be damned. So that's what they mean by the African bush . . .

Beneatha: Ha ha. Let's go, George.

George (looking at her): You know something? I like it. It's sharp. I mean it really is. *(Helps her into her wrap.)*

Ruth: Yes — I think so, too. *(She goes to the mirror and starts to clutch at her hair.)*

Walter: Oh no! You leave yours alone, baby. You might turn out to have a pin-shaped head or something!

Beneatha: See you all later.

Ruth: Have a nice time.

George: Thanks. Good night. *(Half out the door, he reopens it. To Walter.)* Good night, Prometheus!

   Beneatha and George exit.

Walter (to Ruth): Who is Prometheus?

Ruth: I don't know. Don't worry about it.

Walter (in fury, pointing after George): See there — they get to a point where they can't insult you man to man — they got to go talk about something ain't nobody never heard of!

Ruth: How do you know it was an insult? *(To humor him.)* Maybe Prometheus is a nice fellow.

Walter: Prometheus! I bet there ain't even no such thing! I bet that simple-minded clown —

Ruth: Walter —

   She stops what she is doing and looks at him.

Walter (yelling): Don't start!

Ruth: Start what?

Walter: Your nagging! Where was I? Who was I with? How much money did I spend?

Ruth (plaintively): Walter Lee — why don't we just try to talk about it . . .

Walter (not listening): I been out talking with people who understand me. People who care about the things I got on my mind.

Ruth (wearily): I guess that means people like Willy Harris.

Walter: Yes, people like Willy Harris.

Ruth (with a sudden flash of impatience): Why don't you all just hurry up and go into the banking business and stop talking about it!

Walter: Why? You want to know why? 'Cause we all tied up in a race of people that don't know how to do nothing but moan, pray and have babies!

   The line is too bitter even for him and he looks at her and sits down.

Ruth: Oh, Walter . . . *(Softly.)* Honey, why can't you stop fighting me?

Walter (without thinking): Who's fighting you? Who even cares about you?

   This line begins the retardation of his mood.

Ruth: Well — *(She waits a long time, and then with resignation starts to put away her things.)* I guess I might as well go on to bed . . . *(More or less to herself.)* I don't know where we lost it . . . but we have . . . *(Then, to him.)* I — I'm sorry about this new baby, Walter. I guess maybe I better go on and do what I started . . . I guess I just didn't realize how bad things was with us . . . I guess I just didn't really realize — (*She starts out to the bedroom and stops.*) You want some hot milk?

Walter: Hot milk?

Ruth: Yes — hot milk.

Walter: Why hot milk?

Ruth: 'Cause after all that liquor you come home with you ought to have something hot in your stomach.

Walter: I don't want no milk.

Ruth: You want some coffee then?

Walter: No, I don't want no coffee. I don't want nothing hot to drink. (*Almost plaintively.*) Why you always trying to give me something to eat?

Ruth (standing and looking at him helplessly): What else can I give you, Walter Lee Younger?

> She stands and looks at him and presently turns to go out again. He lifts his head and watches her going away from him in a new mood which began to emerge when he asked her "Who cares about you?"

Walter: It's been rough, ain't it, baby? (*She hears and stops but does not turn around and he continues to her back.*) I guess between two people there ain't never as much understood as folks generally thinks there is. I mean like between me and you — (*She turns to face him.*) How we gets to the place where we scared to talk softness to each other. (*He waits, thinking hard himself.*) Why you think it got to be like that? (*He is thoughtful, almost as a child would be.*) Ruth, what is it gets into people ought to be close?

Ruth: I don't know, honey. I think about it a lot.

Walter: On account of you and me, you mean? The way things are with us. The way something done come down between us.

Ruth: There ain't so much between us, Walter . . . Not when you come to me and try to talk to me. Try to be with me . . . a little even.

Walter (total honesty): Sometimes . . . sometimes . . . I don't even know how to try.

Ruth: Walter —

Walter: Yes?

Ruth (coming to him, gently and with misgiving, but coming to him): Honey . . . life don't have to be like this. I mean sometimes people can do things so that things are better . . . You remember how we used to talk when Travis was born . . . about the way we were going to live . . . the kind of house . . . (*She is stroking his head.*) Well, it's all starting to slip away from us . . .

> He turns her to him and they look at each other and kiss, tenderly and hungrily. The door opens and Mama enters — Walter breaks away and jumps up. A beat.

Walter: Mama, where have you been?

Mama: My — them steps is longer than they used to be. Whew! (*She sits down and ignores him.*) How you feeling this evening, Ruth?

> Ruth shrugs, disturbed at having been interrupted and watching her husband knowingly.

Walter: Mama, where have you been all day?

Mama (still ignoring him and leaning on the table and changing to more comfortable shoes): Where's Travis?

Ruth: I let him go out earlier and he ain't come back yet. Boy, is he going to get it!

Walter: Mama!

Mama (as if she has heard him for the first time): Yes, son?

Walter: Where did you go this afternoon?

Mama: I went downtown to tend to some business that I had to tend to.

Walter: What kind of business?

Mama: You know better than to question me like a child, Brother.

Walter (rising and bending over the table): Where were you, Mama? *(Bringing his fists down and shouting.)* Mama, you didn't go do something with that insurance money, something crazy?

The front door opens slowly, interrupting him, and Travis peeks his head in, less than hopefully.

Travis (to his mother): Mama, I—

Ruth: "Mama I" nothing! You're going to get it, boy! Get on in that bedroom and get yourself ready!

Travis: But I—

Mama: Why don't you all never let the child explain hisself.

Ruth: Keep out of it now, Lena.

Mama clamps her lips together, and Ruth advances toward her son menacingly.

Ruth: A thousand times I have told you not to go off like that—

Mama (holding out her arms to her grandson): Well—at least let me tell him something. I want him to be the first one to hear . . . Come here, Travis. *(The boy obeys, gladly.)* Travis—*(She takes him by the shoulder and looks into his face.)*—you know that money we got in the mail this morning?

Travis: Yes'm—

Mama: Well—what you think your grandmama gone and done with that money?

Travis: I don't know, Grandmama.

Mama (putting her finger on his nose for emphasis): She went out and she bought you a house! *(The explosion comes from Walter at the end of the revelation and he jumps up and turns away from all of them in a fury. Mama continues, to Travis.)* You glad about the house? It's going to be yours when you get to be a man.

Travis: Yeah—I always wanted to live in a house.

Mama: All right, gimme some sugar then—*(Travis puts his arms around her neck as she watches her son over the boy's shoulder. Then, to Travis, after the embrace.)* Now when you say your prayers tonight, you thank God and your grandfather—'cause it was him who give you the house—in his way.

Ruth (taking the boy from Mama and pushing him toward the bedroom): Now you get out of here and get ready for your beating.

Travis: Aw, Mama—

Ruth: Get on in there—*(Closing the door behind him and turning radiantly to her mother-in-law.)* So you went and did it!

Mama (quietly, looking at her son with pain): Yes, I did.

Ruth (raising both arms classically): PRAISE GOD! *(Looks at Walter a moment, who says nothing. She crosses rapidly to her husband.)* Please, honey—let me be glad . . . you be glad too. *(She has laid her hands on his shoulders, but he shakes himself free of her roughly, without turning to face her.)* Oh, Walter . . . a home . . . *a home. (She comes back to Mama.)* Well — where is it? How big is it? How much it going to cost?

Mama: Well —

Ruth: When we moving?

Mama (smiling at her): First of the month.

Ruth (throwing back her head with jubilance): Praise God!

Mama (tentatively, still looking at her son's back turned against her and Ruth): It's — it's a nice house too . . . *(She cannot help speaking directly to him. An imploring quality in her voice, her manner, makes her almost like a girl now.)* Three bedrooms — nice big one for you and Ruth . . . Me and Beneatha still have to share our room, but Travis have one of his own — and *(With difficulty.)* I figure if the — new baby — is a boy, we could get one of them double-decker outfits . . . And there's a yard with a little patch of dirt where I could maybe get to grow me a few flowers . . . And a nice big basement . . .

Ruth: Walter honey, be glad —

Mama (still to his back, fingering things on the table): 'Course I don't want to make it sound fancier than it is . . . It's just a plain little old house — but it's made good and solid — and it will be *ours*. Walter Lee — it makes a difference in a man when he can walk on floors that belong to *him* . . .

Ruth: Where is it?

Mama (frightened at this telling): Well — well — it's out there in Clybourne Park —

Ruth's radiance fades abruptly, and Walter finally turns slowly to face his mother with incredulity and hostility.

Ruth: Where?

Mama (matter-of-factly): Four o six Clybourne Street, Clybourne Park.

Ruth: Clybourne Park? Mama, there ain't no colored people living in Clybourne Park.

Mama (almost idiotically): Well, I guess there's going to be some now.

Walter (bitterly): So that's the peace and comfort you went out and bought for us today!

Mama (raising her eyes to meet his finally): Son — I just tried to find the nicest place for the least amount of money for my family.

Ruth (trying to recover from the shock): Well — well — 'course I ain't one never been 'fraid of no crackers, mind you — but — well, wasn't there no other houses nowhere?

Mama: Them houses they put up for colored in them areas way out all seem to cost twice as much as other houses. I did the best I could.

Ruth (struck senseless with the news, in its various degrees of goodness and trouble, she sits a moment, her fists propping her chin in thought, and then she starts to rise, bringing her fists down with vigor, the radiance spreading from cheek to cheek again): Well — well — All I can say is — if this is my time in life — MY TIME — to say good-bye — *(And she builds with momentum as she starts to circle the room with an exuberant, almost tearfully happy release.)* — to these Goddamned cracking walls! — *(She pounds the walls.)* — and these marching roaches! — *(She wipes at an imaginary army of marching roaches.)* — and this cramped little closet which ain't now or never was no kitchen! . . . then I say it loud and good, HALLELUJAH! AND GOOD-BYE MISERY . . . I DON'T NEVER WANT TO SEE YOUR UGLY FACE AGAIN! *(She laughs joyously, having practically destroyed the apartment, and flings her arms up and lets them come down happily, slowly, reflectively, over her abdomen, aware for the first time perhaps that the life therein pulses with happiness and not despair.)* Lena?

Mama (moved, watching her happiness): Yes, honey?

Ruth (looking off): Is there — is there a whole lot of sunlight?

Mama (understanding): Yes, child, there's a whole lot of sunlight.

Long pause.

Ruth (collecting herself and going to the door of the room Travis is in): Well — I guess I better see 'bout Travis. *(To Mama.)* Lord, I sure don't feel like whipping nobody today!

She exits.

Mama (the mother and son are left alone now and the mother waits a long time, considering deeply, before she speaks): Son — you — you understand what I done, don't you? *(Walter is silent and sullen.)* I — I just seen my family falling apart today . . . just falling to pieces in front of my eyes . . . We couldn't of gone on like we was today. We was going backwards 'stead of forwards — talking 'bout killing babies and wishing each other was dead . . . When it gets like that in life — you just got to do something different, push on out and do something bigger . . . *(She waits.)* I wish you say something, son . . . I wish you'd say how deep inside you you think I done the right thing —

Walter (crossing slowly to his bedroom door and finally turning there and speaking measuredly): What you need me to say you done right for? *You* the head of this family. You run our lives like you want to. It was your money and you did what you wanted with it. So what you need for me to say it was all right for? *(Bitterly, to hurt her as deeply as he knows is possible.)* So you butchered up a dream of mine — you — who always talking 'bout your children's dreams . . .

Mama: Walter Lee —

He just closes the door behind him. Mama sits alone, thinking heavily.

Curtain.

SCENE II

TIME: *Friday night, a few weeks later.*

At rise: *Packing crates mark the intention of the family to move. Beneatha and George come in, presumably from an evening out again.*

George: O.K. . . . O.K., whatever you say . . . *(They both sit on the couch. He tries to kiss her. She moves away.)* Look, we've had a nice evening; let's not spoil it, huh? . . .

He again turns her head and tries to nuzzle in and she turns away from him, not with distaste but with momentary lack of interest; in a mood to pursue what they were talking about.

Beneatha: I'm *trying* to talk to you.

George: We always talk.

Beneatha: Yes — and I love to talk.

George (exasperated; rising): I know it and I don't mind it sometimes . . . I want you to cut it out, see — The moody stuff, I mean. I don't like it. You're a nice-looking girl . . . all over. That's all you need, honey, forget the atmos-phere. Guys aren't going to go for the atmosphere — they're going to go for what they see. Be glad for that. Drop the Garbo routine. It doesn't go with you. As for myself, I want a nice — *(Groping.)* — simple *(Thoughtfully.)* — so-phisticated girl . . . not a poet — O.K.?

He starts to kiss her, she rebuffs him again and he jumps up.

Beneatha: Why are you angry, George?

George: Because this is stupid! I don't go out with you to discuss the nature of "quiet desperation" or to hear all about your thoughts — because the world will go on thinking what it thinks regardless —

Beneatha: Then why read books? Why go to school?

George *(with artificial patience, counting on his fingers)*: It's simple. You read books — to learn facts — to get grades — to pass the course — to get a de-gree. That's all — it has nothing to do with thoughts.

A long pause.

Beneatha: I see. *(He starts to sit.)* Good night, George.

George looks at her a little oddly, and starts to exit. He meets Mama coming in.

George: Oh — hello, Mrs. Younger.

Mama: Hello, George, how you feeling?

George: Fine — fine, how are you?

Mama: Oh, a little tired. You know them steps can get you after a day's work. You all have a nice time tonight?

George: Yes — a fine time. A fine time.

Mama: Well, good night.

George: Good night. *(He exits. Mama closes the door behind her.)* Hello, honey. What you sitting like that for?

Beneatha: I'm just sitting.

Mama: Didn't you have a nice time?

Beneatha: No.

Mama: No? What's the matter?

Beneatha: Mama, George is a fool — honest. *(She rises.)*

Mama *(hustling around unloading the packages she has entered with. She stops.)*: Is he, baby?

Beneatha: Yes.

Beneatha makes up Travis's bed as she talks.

Mama: You sure?

Beneatha: Yes.

Mama: Well — I guess you better not waste your time with no fools.

Beneatha looks up at her mother, watching her put groceries in the refrigerator. Finally she gathers up her things and starts into the bedroom. At the door she stops and looks back at her mother.

Beneatha: Mama —

Mama: Yes, baby —

Beneatha: Thank you.

Mama: For what?

Beneatha: For understanding me this time.

She exits quickly and the mother stands, smiling a little, looking at the place where Beneatha just stood. Ruth enters.

Ruth: Now don't you fool with any of this stuff, Lena—

Mama: Oh, I just thought I'd sort a few things out. Is Brother here?

Ruth: Yes.

Mama (with concern): Is he—

Ruth (reading her eyes): Yes.

Mama is silent and someone knocks on the door. Mama and Ruth exchange weary and knowing glances and Ruth opens it to admit the neighbor, Mrs. Johnson,[1] who is a rather squeaky wide-eyed lady of no particular age, with a newspaper under her arm.

Mama (changing her expression to acute delight and a ringing cheerful greeting): Oh— hello there, Johnson.

Johnson (this is a woman who decided long ago to be enthusiastic about EVERYTHING in life and she is inclined to wave her wrist vigorously at the height of her exclamatory comments): Hello there, yourself! H'you this evening, Ruth?

Ruth (not much of a deceptive type): Fine, Mis' Johnson, h'you?

Johnson: Fine. *(Reaching out quickly, playfully, and patting Ruth's stomach.)* Ain't you starting to poke out none yet! *(She mugs with delight at the over familiar remark and her eyes dart around looking at the crates and packing preparation; Mama's face is a cold sheet of endurance.)* Oh, ain't we getting ready round here, though! Yessir! Lookathere! I'm telling you the Youngers is really getting ready to "move on up a little higher!"—Bless God!

Mama (a little drily, doubting the total sincerity of the Blesser): Bless God.

Johnson: He's good, ain't He?

Mama: Oh yes, He's good.

Johnson: I mean sometimes He works in mysterious ways . . . but He works, don't He!

Mama (the same): Yes, he does.

Johnson: I'm just soooooo happy for y'all. And this here child—*(About Ruth.)* looks like she could just pop open with happiness, don't she. Where's all the rest of the family?

Mama: Bennie's gone to bed—

Johnson: Ain't no . . . *(The implication is pregnancy.)* sickness done hit you—I hope . . . ?

Mama: No—she just tired. She was out this evening.

Johnson (all is a coo, an emphatic coo): Aw—ain't that lovely. She still going out with the little Murchison boy?

Mama (drily): Ummmm huh.

Johnson: That's lovely. You sure got lovely children, Younger. Me and Isaiah talks all the time 'bout what fine children you was blessed with. We sure do.

Mama: Ruth, give Mis' Johnson a piece of sweet potato pie and some milk.

Johnson: Oh honey, I can't stay hardly a minute—I just dropped in to see if there was anything I could do. *(Accepting the food easily.)* I guess y'all seen the news what's all over the colored paper this week . . .

Mama: No—didn't get mine yet this week.

---

[1]This character and the scene of her visit were cut from the original production and early editions of the play.

Johnson (lifting her head and blinking with the spirit of catastrophe): You mean you
ain't read 'bout them colored people that was bombed out their place out
there?

*Ruth straightens with concern and takes the paper and reads it. Johnson notices her
and feeds commentary.*

Johnson: Ain't it something how bad these here white folks is getting here in
Chicago! Lord, getting so you think you right down in Mississippi! *(With a
tremendous and rather insincere sense of melodrama.)* 'Course I thinks it's wonderful how our folk keeps on pushing out. You hear some of these Negroes round here talking 'bout how they don't go where they ain't wanted
and all that — but not me, honey! *(This is a lie.)* Wilhemenia Othella Johnson goes anywhere, any time she feels like it! *(With head movement for emphasis.)* Yes I do! Why if we left it up to these here crackers, the poor niggers wouldn't have nothing — *(She clasps her hand over her mouth.)* Oh, I
always forgets you don't 'low that word in your house.

Mama (quietly, looking at her): No — I don't 'low it.

Johnson (vigorously again): Me neither! I was just telling Isaiah yesterday when
he come using it in front of me — I said, "Isaiah, it's just like Mis' Younger
says all the time —"

Mama: Don't you want some more pie?

Johnson: No — no thank you; this was lovely. I got to get on over home and have
my midnight coffee. I hear some people say it don't let them sleep but I
finds I can't close my eyes right lessen I done had that laaaast cup of coffee . . . *(She waits. A beat. Undaunted.)* My Goodnight coffee, I calls it!

Mama (with much eye-rolling and communication between herself and Ruth): Ruth,
why don't you give Mis' Johnson some coffee.

Ruth gives Mama an unpleasant look for her kindness.

Johnson (accepting the coffee): Where's Brother tonight?

Mama: He's lying down.

Johnson: MMmmmmm, he sure gets his beauty rest, don't he? Good-looking
man. Sure is a good-looking man! *(Reaching out to pat Ruth's stomach again.)*
I guess that's how come we keep on having babies around here. *(She winks
at Mama.)* One thing 'bout Brother, he always know how to have a *good*
time. And soooooo ambitious! I bet it was his idea y'all moving out to
Clybourne Park. Lord — I bet this time next month y'all's names will have
been in the papers plenty — *(Holding up her hands to mark off each word of the
headline she can see in front of her.)* "NEGROES INVADE CLYBOURNE
PARK — BOMBED!"

Mama (she and Ruth look at the woman in amazement): We ain't exactly moving
out there to get bombed.

Johnson: Oh honey — you know I'm praying to God every day that don't nothing like that happen! But you have to think of life like it is — and these
here Chicago peckerwoods is some baaaad peckerwoods.

Mama (wearily): We done thought about all that Mis' Johnson.

*Beneatha comes out of the bedroom in her robe and passes through to the bath-
room. Mrs. Johnson turns.*

Johnson: Hello there, Bennie!

Beneatha (crisply): Hello, Mrs. Johnson.

Johnson: How is school?

Beneatha (crisply): Fine, thank you. *(She goes out.)*

Johnson (insulted): Getting so she don't have much to say to nobody.

Mama: The child was on her way to the bathroom.

Johnson: I know—but sometimes she act like ain't got time to pass the time of day with nobody ain't been to college. Oh—I ain't criticizing her none. It's just—you know how some of our young people gets when they get a little education. *(Mama and Ruth say nothing, just look at her.)* Yes—well. Well, I guess I better get on home. *(Unmoving.)* 'Course I can understand how she must be proud and everything—being the only one in the family to make something of herself. I know just being a chauffeur ain't never satisfied Brother none. He shouldn't feel like that, though. Ain't nothing wrong with being a chauffeur.

Mama: There's plenty wrong with it.

Johnson: What?

Mama: Plenty. My husband always said being any kind of a servant wasn't a fit thing for a man to have to be. He always said a man's hands was made to make things, or to turn the earth with—not to drive nobody's car for 'em—or—*(She looks at her own hands.)* carry they slop jars. And my boy is just like him—he wasn't meant to wait on nobody.

Johnson (rising, somewhat offended): Mmmmmmmmm. The Youngers is too much for me! *(She looks around.)* You sure one proud-acting bunch of colored folks. Well—I always thinks like Booker T. Washington said that time—"Education has spoiled many a good plow hand"—

Mama: Is that what old Booker T. said?

Johnson: He sure did.

Mama: Well, it sounds just like him. The fool.

Johnson (indignantly): Well—he was one of our great men.

Mama: Who said so?

Johnson (nonplussed): You know, me and you ain't never agreed about some things, Lena Younger. I guess I better be going—

Ruth (quickly): Good night.

Johnson: Good night. Oh—*(Thrusting it at her.)* You can keep the paper! *(With a trill.)* 'Night.

Mama: Good night, Mis' Johnson.

   Mrs. Johnson exits.

Ruth: If ignorance was gold . . .

Mama: Shush. Don't talk about folks behind their backs.

Ruth: You do.

Mama: I'm old and corrupted. *(Beneatha enters.)* You was rude to Mis' Johnson, Beneatha, and I don't like it at all.

Beneatha (at her door): Mama, if there are two things we, as a people, have got to overcome, one is the Klu Klux Klan—and the other is Mrs. Johnson. *(She exits.)*

Mama: Smart aleck.

   The phone rings.

Ruth: I'll get it.

Mama: Lord, ain't this a popular place tonight.

Ruth (at the phone): Hello—Just a minute. *(Goes to door.)* Walter, it's Mrs. Arnold. *(Waits. Goes back to the phone. Tense.)* Hello. Yes, this is his wife speaking . . . He's lying down now. Yes . . . well, he'll be in tomorrow. He's been very sick. Yes—I know we should have called, but we were so sure he'd be able to come in today. Yes—yes, I'm very sorry. Yes . . . Thank you very much. *(She hangs up. Walter is standing in the doorway of the bedroom behind her.)* That was Mrs. Arnold.

Walter (indifferently): Was it?

Ruth: She said if you don't come in tomorrow that they are getting a new man . . .

Walter: Ain't that sad—ain't that crying sad.

Ruth: She said Mr. Arnold has had to take a cab for three days . . . Walter, you ain't been to work for three days! *(This is a revelation to her.)* Where you been, Walter Lee Younger? *(Walter looks at her and starts to laugh.)* You're going to lose your job.

Walter: That's right . . . *(He turns on the radio.)*

Ruth: Oh, Walter, and with your mother working like a dog every day—

A steamy, deep blues pours into the room.

Walter: That's sad too—Everything is sad.

Mama: What you been doing for these three days, son?

Walter: Mama—you don't know all the things a man what got leisure can find to do in this city . . . What's this—Friday night? Well—Wednesday I borrowed Willy Harris' car and I went for a drive . . . just me and myself and I drove and drove . . . Way out . . . way past South Chicago, and I parked the car and I sat and looked at the steel mills all day long. I just sat in the car and looked at them big black chimneys for hours. Then I drove back and I went to the Green Hat. *(Pause.)* And Thursday—Thursday I borrowed the car again and I got in it and I pointed it the other way and I drove the other way—for hours—way, way up to Wisconsin, and I looked at the farms. I just drove and looked at the farms. Then I drove back and I went to the Green Hat. *(Pause.)* And today—today I didn't get the car. Today I just walked. All over the Southside. And I looked at the Negroes and they looked at me and finally I just sat down on the curb at Thirty-ninth and South Parkway and I just sat there and watched the Negroes go by. And then I went to the Green Hat. You all sad? You all depressed? And you know where I am going right now—

Ruth goes out quietly.

Mama: Oh, Big Walter, is this the harvest of our days?

Walter: You know what I like about the Green Hat? I like this little cat they got there who blows a sax . . . He blows. He talks to me. He ain't but 'bout five feet tall and he's got a conked head and his eyes is always closed and he's all music—

Mama (rising and getting some papers out of her handbag): Walter—

Walter: And there's this other guy who plays the piano . . . and they got a sound. I mean they can work on some music . . . They got the best little combo in the world in the Green Hat . . . You can just sit there and drink and listen to them three men play and you realize that don't nothing matter worth a damn, but just being there—

Mama: I've helped do it to you, haven't I, son? Walter I been wrong.

Walter: Naw — you ain't never been wrong about nothing, Mama.

Mama: Listen to me, now. I say I been wrong, son. That I been doing to you what the rest of the world been doing to you. *(She turns off the radio.)* Walter — *(She stops and he looks up slowly at her and she meets his eyes pleadingly.)* What you ain't never understood is that I ain't got nothing, don't own nothing, ain't never really wanted nothing that wasn't for you. There ain't nothing as precious to me . . . There ain't nothing worth holding on to, money, dreams, nothing else — if it means — if it means it's going to destroy my boy. *(She takes an envelope out of her handbag and puts it in front of him and he watches her without speaking or moving.)* I paid the man thirty-five hundred dollars down on the house. That leaves sixty-five hundred dollars. Monday morning I want you to take this money and take three thousand dollars and put it in a savings account for Beneatha's medical schooling. The rest you put in a checking account — with your name on it. And from now on any penny that come out of it or that go in it is for you to look after. For you to decide. *(She drops her hands a little helplessly.)* It ain't much, but it's all I got in the world and I'm putting it in your hands. I'm telling you to be the head of this family from now on like you supposed to be.

Walter (stares at the money): You trust me like that, Mama?

Mama: I ain't never stop trusting you. Like I ain't never stop loving you.

She goes out, and Walter sits looking at the money on the table. Finally, in a decisive gesture, he gets up, and, in mingled joy and desperation, picks up the money. At the same moment, Travis enters for bed.

Travis: What's the matter, Daddy? You drunk?

Walter (sweetly, more sweetly than we have ever known him): No, Daddy ain't drunk. Daddy ain't going to never be drunk again . . .

Travis: Well, good night, Daddy.

The father has come from behind the couch and leans over, embracing his son.

Walter: Son, I feel like talking to you tonight.

Travis: About what?

Walter: Oh, about a lot of things. About you and what kind of man you going to be when you grow up . . . Son — son, what do you want to be when you grow up?

Travis: A bus driver.

Walter (laughing a little): A what? Man, that ain't nothing to want to be!

Travis: Why not?

Walter: 'Cause, man — it ain't big enough — you know what I mean.

Travis: I don't know then. I can't make up my mind. Sometimes Mama asks me that too. And sometimes when I tell her I just want to be like you — she says she don't want me to be like that and sometimes she says she does. . . .

Walter (gathering him up in his arms): You know what, Travis? In seven years you going to be seventeen years old. And things is going to be very different with us in seven years, Travis. . . . One day when you are seventeen I'll come home — home from my office downtown somewhere —

Travis: You don't work in no office, Daddy.

Walter: No — but after tonight. After what your daddy gonna do tonight, there's going to be offices — a whole lot of offices. . . .

Travis: What you gonna do tonight, Daddy?

Walter: You wouldn't understand yet, son, but your daddy's gonna make a transaction . . . a business transaction that's going to change our lives. . . . That's how come one day when you 'bout seventeen years old I'll come home and I'll be pretty tired, you know what I mean, after a day of conferences and secretaries getting things wrong the way they do . . . 'cause an executive's life is hell, man — *(The more he talks the farther away he gets.)* And I'll pull the car up on the driveway . . . just a plain black Chrysler, I think, with white walls — no — black tires. More elegant. Rich people don't have to be flashy . . . though I'll have to get something a little sportier for Ruth — maybe a Cadillac convertible to do her shopping in. . . . And I'll come up the steps to the house and the gardener will be clipping away at the hedges and he'll say, "Good evening, Mr. Younger." And I'll say, "Hello, Jefferson, how are you this evening?" And I'll go inside and Ruth will come downstairs and meet me at the door and we'll kiss each other and she'll take my arm and we'll go up to your room to see you sitting on the floor with the catalogues of all the great schools in America around you. . . . All the great schools in the world! And — and I'll say, all right son — it's your seventeenth birthday, what is it you've decided? . . . Just tell me where you want to go to school and you'll *go.* Just tell me, what it is you want to be — and you'll *be* it. . . . Whatever you want to be — Yessir! *(He holds his arms open for Travis.)* You just name it, son . . . *(Travis leaps into them.)* and I hand you the world!

Walter's voice has risen in pitch and hysterical promise and on the last line he lifts Travis high.

Blackout.

Scene III

TIME: *Saturday, moving day, one week later.*

Before the curtain rises, Ruth's voice, a strident, dramatic church alto, cuts through the silence.

It is, in the darkness, a triumphant surge, a penetrating statement of expectation: "Oh, Lord, I don't feel no ways tired! Children, oh, glory hallelujah!"

As the curtain rises we see that Ruth is alone in the living room, finishing up the family's packing. It is moving day. She is nailing crates and tying cartons. Beneatha enters, carrying a guitar case, and watches her exuberant sister-in-law.

Ruth: Hey!

Beneatha (putting away the case): Hi.

Ruth (pointing at a package): Honey — look in that package there and see what I found on sale this morning at the South Center. *(Ruth gets up and moves to the package and draws out some curtains.)* Lookahere — hand-turned hems!

Beneatha: How do you know the window size out there?

Ruth (who hadn't thought of that): Oh — Well, they bound to fit something in the whole house. Anyhow, they was too good a bargain to pass up. *(Ruth slaps her head, suddenly remembering something.)* Oh, Bennie — I meant to put a special note on that carton over there. That's your mama's good china and she wants 'em to be very careful with it.

Beneatha: I'll do it.

Beneatha finds a piece of paper and starts to draw large letters on it.

Ruth: You know what I'm going to do soon as I get in that new house?

Beneatha: What?

Ruth: Honey—I'm going to run me a tub of water up to here . . . *(With her fingers practically up to her nostrils.)* And I'm going to get in it—and I am going to sit . . . and sit . . . and sit in that hot water and the first person who knocks to tell *me* to hurry up and come out—

Beneatha: Gets shot at sunrise.

Ruth *(laughing happily)*: You said it, sister! *(Noticing how large Beneatha is absentmindedly making the note)*: Honey, they ain't going to read that from no airplane.

Beneatha *(laughing herself)*: I guess I always think things have more emphasis if they are big, somehow.

Ruth *(looking up at her and smiling)*: You and your brother seem to have that as a philosophy of life. Lord, that man—done changed so 'round here. You know—you know what we did last night? Me and Walter Lee?

Beneatha: What?

Ruth *(smiling to herself)*: We went to the movies. *(Looking at Beneatha to see if she understands.)* We went to the movies. You know the last time me and Walter went to the movies together?

Beneatha: No.

Ruth: Me neither. That's how long it been. *(Smiling again.)* But we went last night. The picture wasn't much good, but that didn't seem to matter. We went—and we held hands.

Beneatha: Oh, Lord!

Ruth: We held hands—and you know what?

Beneatha: What?

Ruth: When we come out of the show it was late and dark and all the stores and things was closed up . . . and it was kind of chilly and there wasn't many people on the streets . . . and we was still holding hands, me and Walter.

Beneatha: You're killing me.

Walter enters with a large package. His happiness is deep in him; he cannot keep still with his newfound exuberance. He is singing and wiggling and snapping his fingers. He puts his package in a corner and puts a phonograph record, which he has brought in with him, on the record player. As the music, soulful and sensuous, comes up he dances over to Ruth and tries to get her to dance with him. She gives in at last to his raunchiness and in a fit of giggling allows herself to be drawn into his mood. They dip and she melts into his arms in a classic, body-melting "slow drag."

Beneatha *(regarding them a long time as they dance, then drawing in her breath for a deeply exaggerated comment which she does not particularly mean)*: Talk about—olddddddddddd-fashionedddddddd—Negroes!

Walter *(stopping momentarily)*: What kind of Negroes?

He says this in fun. He is not angry with her today, nor with anyone. He starts to dance with his wife again.

Beneatha: Old-fashioned.

Walter *(as he dances with Ruth)*: You know, when these *New Negroes* have their convention—*(Pointing at his sister.)*—that is going to be the chairman of the Committee on Unending Agitation. *(He goes on dancing, then stops.)* Race, race, race! . . . Girl, I do believe you are the first person in the history of the entire human race to successfully brainwash yourself. *(Beneatha breaks up and he goes on dancing. He stops again, enjoying his tease.)* Damn, even the N double A C P takes a holiday sometimes! *(Beneatha and Ruth laugh. He dances with Ruth some more and starts to laugh and stops and pantomimes someone over an operating table.)* I can just see that chick someday looking down at some poor cat on an operating table and before she starts to slice him, she says . . . *(Pulling his sleeves back maliciously.)* "By the way, what are your views on civil rights down there? . . ."

He laughs at her again and starts to dance happily. The bell sounds.

Beneatha: Sticks and stones may break my bones but . . . words will never hurt me!

Beneatha goes to the door and opens it as Walter and Ruth go on with the clowning. Beneatha is somewhat surprised to see a quiet-looking middle-aged white man in a business suit holding his hat and a briefcase in his hand and consulting a small piece of paper.

Man: Uh — how do you do, miss. I am looking for a Mrs. — *(He looks at the slip of paper.)* Mrs. Lena Younger? *(He stops short, struck dumb at the sight of the oblivious Walter and Ruth.)*

Beneatha *(smoothing her hair with slight embarrassment)*: Oh — yes, that's my mother. Excuse me. *(She closes the door and turns to quiet the other two.)* Ruth! Brother! *(Enunciating precisely but soundlessly: "There's a white man at the door!" They stop dancing, Ruth cuts off the phonograph, Beneatha opens the door. The man casts a curious quick glance at all of them.)* Uh — come in please.

Man *(coming in)*: Thank you.

Beneatha: My mother isn't here just now. Is it business?

Man: Yes . . . well, of a sort.

Walter *(freely, the Man of the House)*: Have a seat. I'm Mrs. Younger's son. I look after most of her business matters.

Ruth and Beneatha exchange amused glances.

Man *(regarding Walter, and sitting)*: Well — My name is Karl Lindner . . .

Walter *(stretching out his hand)*: Walter Younger. This is my wife — *(Ruth nods politely.)* — and my sister.

Lindner: How do you do.

Walter *(amiably, as he sits himself easily on a chair, leaning forward on his knees with interest and looking expectantly into the newcomer's face)*: What can we do for you, Mr. Lindner!

Lindner *(some minor shuffling of the hat and briefcase on his knees)*: Well — I am a representative of the Clybourne Park Improvement Association —

Walter *(pointing)*: Why don't you sit your things on the floor?

Lindner: Oh — yes. Thank you. *(He slides the briefcase and hat under the chair.)* And as I was saying — I am from the Clybourne Park Improvement Association and we have had it brought to our attention at the last meeting that you people — or at least your mother — has bought a piece of residential property at — *(He digs for the slip of paper again.)* — four o six Clybourne Street . . .

Walter: That's right. Care for something to drink? Ruth, get Mr. Lindner a beer.

Lindner (upset for some reason): Oh — no, really. I mean thank you very much, but no thank you.
Ruth (innocently): Some coffee?
Lindner: Thank you, nothing at all.

    Beneatha is watching the man carefully.

Lindner: Well, I don't know how much you folks know about our organization. *(He is a gentle man; thoughtful and somewhat labored in his manner.)* It is one of these community organizations set up to look after — oh, you know, things like block upkeep and special projects and we also have what we call our New Neighbors Orientation Committee . . .
Beneatha (drily): Yes — and what do they do?
Lindner (turning a little to her and then returning the main force to Walter): Well — it's what you might call a sort of welcoming committee, I guess. I mean they, we — I'm the chairman of the committee — go around and see the new people who move into the neighborhood and sort of give them the low-down on the way we do things out in Clybourne Park.
Beneatha (with appreciation of the two meanings, which escape Ruth and Walter): Un-huh.
Lindner: And we also have the category of what the association calls — *(He looks elsewhere.)* — uh — special community problems . . .
Beneatha: Yes — and what are some of those?
Walter: Girl, let the man talk.
Lindner (with understated relief): Thank you. I would sort of like to explain this thing in my own way. I mean I want to explain to you in a certain way.
Walter: Go ahead.
Lindner: Yes. Well. I'm going to try to get right to the point. I'm sure we'll all appreciate that in the long run.
Beneatha: Yes.
Walter: Be still now!
Lindner: Well —
Ruth (still innocently): Would you like another chair — you don't look comfortable.
Lindner (more frustrated than annoyed): No, thank you very much. Please. Well — to get right to the point, I — *(A great breath, and he is off at last.)* I am sure you people must be aware of some of the incidents which have happened in various parts of the city when colored people have moved into certain areas — *(Beneatha exhales heavily and starts tossing a piece of fruit up and down in the air.)* Well — because we have what I think is going to be a unique type of organization in American community life — not only do we deplore that kind of thing — but we are trying to do something about it. *(Beneatha stops tossing and turns with a new and quizzical interest to the man.)* We feel — *(gaining confidence in his mission because of the interest in the faces of the people he is talking to.)* — we feel that most of the trouble in this world, when you come right down to it — *(He hits his knee for emphasis.)* — most of the trouble exists because people just don't sit down and talk to each other.
Ruth (nodding as she might in church, pleased with the remark): You can say that again, mister.
Lindner (more encouraged by such affirmation): That we don't try hard enough in this world to understand the other fellow's problem. The other guy's point of view.

Ruth: Now that's right.

Beneatha and Walter merely watch and listen with genuine interest.

Lindner: Yes—that's the way we feel out in Clybourne Park. And that's why I was elected to come here this afternoon and talk to you people. Friendly like, you know, the way people should talk to each other and see if we couldn't find some way to work this thing out. As I say, the whole business is a matter of *caring* about the other fellow. Anybody can see that you are a nice family of folks, hard working and honest I'm sure. *(Beneatha frowns slightly, quizzically, her head tilted regarding him.)* Today everybody knows what it means to be on the outside of *something.* And of course, there is always somebody who is out to take advantage of people who don't always understand.

Walter: What do you mean?

Lindner: Well—you see our community is made up of people who've worked hard as the dickens for years to build up that little community. They're not rich and fancy people; just hard-working, honest people who don't really have much but those little homes and a dream of the kind of community they want to raise their children in. Now, I don't say we are perfect and there is a lot wrong in some of the things they want. But you've got to admit that a man, right or wrong, has the right to want to have the neighborhood he lives in a certain kind of way. And at the moment the overwhelming majority of our people out there feel that people get along better, take more of a common interest in the life of the community, when they share a common background. I want you to believe me when I tell you that race prejudice simply doesn't enter into it. It is a matter of the people of Clybourne Park believing, rightly or wrongly, as I say, that for the happiness of all concerned that our Negro families are happier when they live in their *own* communities.

Beneatha (with a grand and bitter gesture): This, friends, is the Welcoming Committee!

Walter (dumfounded, looking at Lindner): Is this what you came marching all the way over here to tell us?

Lindner: Well, now we've been having a fine conversation. I hope you'll hear me all the way through.

Walter (tightly): Go ahead, man.

Lindner: You see—in the face of all the things I have said, we are prepared to make your family a very generous offer . . .

Beneatha: Thirty pieces and not a coin less!

Walter: Yeah?

Lindner (putting on his glasses drawing a form out of the briefcase): Our association is prepared, through the collective effort of our people, to buy the house from you at a financial gain to your family.

Ruth: Lord have mercy, ain't this the living gall!

Walter: All right, you through?

Lindner: Well, I want to give you the exact terms of the financial arrangement—

Walter: We don't want to hear no exact terms of no arrangements. I want to know if you got any more to tell us 'bout getting together?

Lindner (taking off his glasses): Well—I don't suppose that you feel . . .

Walter: Never mind how I feel—you got any more to say 'bout how people ought to sit down and talk each other? . . . Get out of my house, man.

    He turns his back and walks to the door.

Lindner (looking around at the hostile faces and reaching and assembling his hat and briefcase): Well—I don't understand why you people are reacting this way. What do you think you are going to gain by moving into a neighborhood where you just aren't wanted and where some elements—well—people can get awful worked up when they feel that their whole way of life and everything they've ever worked for is threatened.

Walter: Get out.

Lindner (at the door, holding a small card): Well—I'm sorry it went like this.

Walter: Get out.

Lindner (almost sadly regarding Walter): You just can't force people to change their hearts, son.

    He turns and puts his card on a table and exits. Walter pushes the door to with stinging hatred, and stands looking at it. Ruth just sits and Beneatha just stands. They say nothing. Mama and Travis enter.

Mama: Well—this all the packing got done since I left out of here this morning. I testify before God that my children got all the energy of the *dead!* What time the moving men due?

Beneatha: Four o'clock. You had a caller, Mama.

    She is smiling, teasingly.

Mama: Sure enough—who?

Beneatha (her arms folded saucily): The Welcoming Committee.

    Walter and Ruth giggle.

Mama (innocently): Who?

Beneatha: The Welcoming Committee. They said they're sure going to be glad to see you when you get there.

Walter (devilishly): Yeah, they said they can't hardly wait to see your face.

    Laughter.

Mama (sensing their facetiousness): What's the matter with you all?

Walter: Ain't nothing the matter with us. We just telling you 'bout the gentleman who came to see you this afternoon. From the Clybourne Park Improvement Association.

Mama: What he want?

Ruth (in the same mood as Beneatha and Walter): To welcome you, honey.

Walter: He said they can't hardly wait. He said the one thing they don't have, that they just *dying* to have out there is a fine family of fine colored people! *(To Ruth and Beneatha.)* Ain't that right!

Ruth (mockingly): Yeah! He left his card—

Beneatha (handing card to Mama): In case.

    Mama reads and throws it on the floor—understanding and looking off as she draws her chair up to the table on which she has put her plant and some sticks and some cord.

Mama: Father, give us strength. *(Knowingly—and without fun.)* Did he threaten us?

Beneatha: Oh — Mama — they don't do it like that any more. He talked Brotherhood. He said everybody ought to learn how to sit down and hate each other with good Christian fellowship.

> *She and Walter shake hands to ridicule the remark.*

Mama (sadly): Lord, protect us . . .

Ruth: You should hear the money those folks raised to buy the house from us. All we paid and then some.

Beneatha: What they think we going to do — eat 'em?

Ruth: No, honey, marry 'em.

Mama (shaking her head): Lord, Lord, Lord . . .

Ruth: Well — that's the way the crackers crumble. *(A beat.)* Joke.

Beneatha (laughingly noticing what her mother is doing): Mama, what are you doing?

Mama: Fixing my plant so it won't get hurt none on the way . . .

Beneatha: Mama, you going to take *that* to the new house?

Mama: Un-huh —

Beneatha: That raggedy-looking old thing?

Mama (stopping and looking at her): It expresses ME!

Ruth (with delight, to Beneatha): So there, Miss Thing!

> *Walter comes to Mama suddenly and bends down behind her and squeezes her in his arms with all his strength. She is overwhelmed by the suddenness of it and, though delighted, her manner is like that of Ruth and Travis.*

Mama: Look out now, boy! You make me mess up my thing here!

Walter (his face lit, he slips down on his knees beside her, his arms still about her): Mama . . . you know what it means to climb up in the chariot?

Mama (gruffly, very happy): Get on away from me now . . .

Ruth (near the gift-wrapped package, trying to catch Walter's eye): Psst —

Walter: What the old song say, Mama . . .

Ruth: Walter — Now?

> *She is pointing at the package.*

Walter (speaking the lines, sweetly, playfully, in his mother's face):
I got wings . . . you got wings . . .
All God's Children got wings . . .

Mama: Boy — get out of my face and do some work . . .

Walter:
When I get to heaven gonna put on my wings,
Gonna fly all over God's heaven . . .

Beneatha (teasingly, from across the room): Everybody talking 'bout heaven ain't going there!

Walter (to Ruth, who is carrying the box across to them): I don't know, you think we ought to give her that . . . Seems to me she ain't been very appreciative around here.

Mama (eying the box, which is obviously a gift): What is that?

Walter (taking it from Ruth and putting it on the table in front of Mama): Well — what you all think? Should we give it to her?

Ruth: Oh — she was pretty good today.

Mama: I'll good you —

She turns her eyes to the box again.

Beneatha: Open it, Mama.

She stands up, looks at it, turns and looks at all of them, and then presses her hands together and does not open the package.

Walter (*sweetly*): Open it, Mama. It's for you. (*Mama looks in his eyes. It is the first present in her life without its being Christmas. Slowly she opens her package and lifts out, one by one, a brand-new sparkling set of gardening tools. Walter continues, prodding.*) Ruth made up the note — read it . . .

Mama (*picking up the card and adjusting her glasses*): "To our own Mrs. Miniver — Love from Brother, Ruth, and Beneatha." Ain't that lovely . . .

Travis (*tugging at his father's sleeve*): Daddy, can I give her mine now?

Walter: All right, son. (*Travis flies to get his gift.*)

Mama: Now I don't have to use my knives and forks no more . . .

Walter: Travis didn't want to go in with the rest of us, Mama. He got his own. (*Somewhat amused.*) We don't know what it is . . .

Travis (*racing back in the room with a large hatbox and putting it in front of his grandmother*): Here!

Mama: Lord have mercy, baby. You done gone and bought your grandmother a hat?

Travis (*very proud*): Open it!

She does and lifts out an elaborate, but very elaborate, wide gardening hat, and all the adults break up at the sight of it.

Ruth: Travis, honey, what is that?

Travis (*who thinks it is beautiful and appropriate*): It's a gardening hat! Like the ladies always have on in the magazines when they work in their gardens.

Beneatha (*giggling fiercely*): Travis — we were trying to make Mama Mrs. Miniver — not Scarlett O'Hara!

Mama (*indignantly*): What's the matter with you all! This here is a beautiful hat! (*Absurdly.*) I always wanted me one just like it!

She pops it on her head to prove it to her grandson, and the hat is ludicrous and considerably oversized.

Ruth: Hot dog! Go, Mama!

Walter (*doubled over with laughter*): I'm sorry, Mama — but you look like you ready to go out and chop you some cotton sure enough!

They all laugh except Mama, out of deference to Travis's feelings.

Mama (*gathering the boy up to her*): Bless your heart — this is the prettiest hat I ever owned — (*Walter, Ruth, and Beneatha chime in — noisily, festively, and insincerely congratulating Travis on his gift.*) What are we all standing around here for? We ain't finished packin' yet. Bennie, you ain't packed one book.

The bell rings.

Beneatha: That couldn't be the movers . . . it's not hardly two good yet —

Beneatha goes into her room. Mama starts for door.

Walter (*turning, stiffening*): Wait — wait — I'll get it.

He stands and looks at the door.

Mama: You expecting company, son?

Walter (just looking at the door): Yeah—yeah . . .

> *Mama looks at Ruth, and they exchange innocent and unfrightened glances.*

Mama (not understanding): Well, let them in, son.

Beneatha (from her room): We need some more string.

Mama: Travis—you run to the hardware and get me some string cord.

> *Mama goes out and Walter turns and looks at Ruth. Travis goes to a dish for money.*

Ruth: Why don't you answer the door, man?

Walter (suddenly bounding across the floor to embrace her): 'Cause sometimes it hard to let the future begin! *(Stooping down in her face.)*

> I got wings! You got wings!
> All God's children got wings!

> *He crosses to the door and throws it open. Standing there is a very slight little man in a not-too-prosperous business suit and with haunted frightened eyes and a hat pulled down tightly, brim up, around his forehead. Travis passes between the men and exits. Walter leans deep in the man's face, still in his jubilance.*

> When I get to heaven gonna put on my wings,
> Gonna fly all over God's heaven . . .

> *The little man just stares at him.*

> Heaven—

> *Suddenly he stops and looks past the little man into the empty hallway.*

Where's Willy, man?

Bobo: He ain't with me.

Walter (not disturbed): Oh—come on in. You know my wife.

Bobo (dumbly, taking off his hat): Yes—h'you, Miss Ruth.

Ruth (quietly, a mood apart from her husband already, seeing Bobo): Hello, Bobo.

Walter: You right on time today . . . Right on time. That's the way! *(He slaps Bobo on his back.)* Sit down . . . lemme hear.

> *Ruth stands stiffly and quietly in back of them, as though somehow she senses death, her eyes fixed on her husband.*

Bobo (his frightened eyes on the floor, his hat in his hands): Could I please get a drink of water, before I tell you about it, Walter Lee?

> *Walter does not take his eyes off the man. Ruth goes blindly to the tap and gets a glass of water and brings it to Bobo.*

Walter: There ain't nothing wrong, is there?

Bobo: Lemme tell you—

Walter: Man—didn't nothing go wrong?

Bobo: Lemme tell you—Walter Lee. *(Looking at Ruth and talking to her more than to Walter.)* You know how it was. I got to tell you how it was. I mean first I got to tell you how it was all the way . . . I mean about the money I put in, Walter Lee . . .

Walter (with taut agitation now): What about the money you put in?

Bobo: Well—it wasn't much as we told you—me and Willy—*(He stops.)* I'm sorry, Walter. I got a bad feeling about it. I got a real bad feeling about it . . .

Walter: Man, what you telling me about all this for? . . . Tell me what happened in Springfield . . .

Bobo: Springfield.

Ruth (like a dead woman): What was supposed to happen in Springfield?

Bobo (to her): This deal that me and Walter went into with Willy — Me and
Willy was going to go down to Springfield and spread some money 'round
so's we wouldn't have to wait so long for the liquor license . . . That's what
we were going to do. Everybody said that was the way you had to do, you
understand, Miss Ruth?

Walter: Man — what happened down there?

Bobo (a pitiful man, near tears): I'm trying to tell you, Walter.

Walter (screaming at him suddenly): THEN TELL ME, GODDAMMIT . . .
WHAT'S THE MATTER WITH YOU?

Bobo: Man . . . I didn't go to no Springfield, yesterday.

Walter (halted, life hanging in the moment): Why not?

Bobo (the long way, the hard way to tell): 'Cause I didn't have no reasons to . . .

Walter: Man, what are you talking about!

Bobo: I'm talking about the fact that when I got to the train station yesterday
morning — eight o'clock like we planned . . . Man — *Willy didn't never show up.*

Walter: Why . . . where was he . . . where is he?

Bobo: That's what I'm trying to tell you . . . I don't know . . . I waited six
hours . . . I called his house . . . and I waited . . . six hours . . . I waited in
that train station six hours . . . *(Breaking into tears.)* That was all the extra
money I had in the world . . . *(Looking up at Walter with the tears running
down his face.)* Man, *Willy is gone.*

Walter: Gone, what you mean Willy is gone? Gone where? You mean he went
by himself. You mean he went off to Springfield by himself — to take care
of getting the license — *(Turns and looks anxiously at Ruth.)* You mean maybe
he didn't want too many people in on the business down there? *(Looks to
Ruth again, as before.)* You know Willy got his own ways. *(Looks back to Bobo.)*
Maybe you was late yesterday and he just went on down there without you.
Maybe — maybe — he's been callin' you at home tryin' to tell you what happened or something. Maybe — maybe — he just got sick. He's somewhere —
he's got to be somewhere. We just got to find him — me and you got
to find him. *(Grabs Bobo senselessly by the collar and starts to shake him.)* We
got to!

Bobo (in sudden angry, frightened agony): What's the matter with you, Walter!
When a cat take off with your money he don't leave you no road maps!

Walter (turning madly, as though he is looking for Willy in the very room): Willy! . . .
Willy . . . don't do it . . . Please don't do it . . . Man, not with that
money . . . Man, please, not with that money . . . Oh, God . . . Don't let it
be true . . . *(He is wandering around, crying out for Willy and looking for him or
perhaps for help from God.)* Man . . . I trusted you . . . Man, I put my life in
your hands . . . *(He starts to crumple down on the floor as Ruth just covers her
face in horror. Mama opens the door and comes into the room, with Beneatha behind her.)* Man . . . *(He starts to pound the floor with his fists, sobbing wildly.)*
THAT MONEY IS MADE OUT OF MY FATHER'S FLESH —

Bobo (standing over him helplessly): I'm sorry, Walter . . . *(only Walter's sobs reply.
Bobo puts on his hat.)* I had my life staked on this deal, too . . .

He exits.

Mama (to Walter): Son—*(She goes to him, bends down to him, talks to his bent head.)* Son . . . Is it gone? Son, I gave you sixty-five hundred dollars. Is it gone? All of it? Beneatha's money too?

Walter (lifting his head slowly): Mama . . . I never . . . went to the bank at all . . .

Mama (not wanting to believe him): You mean . . . your sister's school money . . . you used that too . . . Walter? . . .

Walter: Yessss! All of it . . . It's all gone . . .

> *There is total silence. Ruth stands with her face covered with her hands; Beneatha leans forlornly against a wall, fingering a piece of red ribbon from the mother's gift. Mama stops and looks at her son without recognition and then, quite without thinking about it, starts to beat him senselessly in the face. Beneatha goes to them and stops it.*

Beneatha: Mama!

> *Mama stops and looks at both of her children and rises slowly and wanders vaguely, aimlessly away from them.*

Mama: I seen . . . him . . . night after night . . . come in . . . and look at that rug . . . and then look at me . . . the red showing in his eyes . . . the veins moving in his head . . . I seen him grow thin and old before he was forty . . . working and working and working like somebody's old horse . . . killing himself . . . and you—you give it all away in a day—*(She raises her arms to strike him again.)*

Beneatha: Mama—

Mama: Oh, God . . . *(She looks up to Him.)* Look down here—and show me the strength.

Beneatha: Mama—

Mama (folding over): Strength . . .

Beneatha (plaintively): Mama . . .

Mama: Strength!

> *Curtain.*

ACT III

TIME: *An hour later.*

> *At curtain, there is a sullen light of gloom in the living room, gray light not unlike that which began the first scene of Act I. At left we can see Walter within his room, alone with himself. He is stretched out on the bed, his shirt out and open, his arms under his head. He does not smoke, he does not cry out, he merely lies there, looking up at the ceiling, much as if he were alone in the world.*
>
> *In the living room Beneatha sits at the table, still surrounded by the now almost ominous packing crates. She sits looking off. We feel that this is a mood struck perhaps an hour before, and it lingers now, full of the empty sound of profound disappointment. We see on a line from her brother's bedroom the sameness of their attitudes. Presently the bell rings and Beneatha rises without ambition or interest in answering. It is Asagai, smiling broadly, striding into the room with energy and happy expectation and conversation.*

Asagai: I came over . . . I had some free time. I thought I might help with the packing. Ah, I like the look of packing crates! A household in preparation for a journey! It depresses some people . . . but for me . . . it is another feeling. Something full of the flow of life, do you understand? Movement, progress . . . It makes me think of Africa.

Beneatha: Africa!

Asagai: What kind of a mood is this? Have I told you how deeply you move me?

Beneatha: He gave away the money, Asagai . . .

Asagai: Who gave away what money?

Beneatha: The insurance money. My brother gave it away.

Asagai: Gave it away?

Beneatha: He made an investment! With a man even Travis wouldn't have trusted with his most worn-out marbles.

Asagai: And it's gone?

Beneatha: Gone!

Asagai: I'm very sorry . . . And you, now?

Beneatha: Me? . . . Me? . . . Me, I'm nothing . . . Me. When I was very small . . . we used to take our sleds out in the wintertime and the only hills we had were the ice-covered stone steps of some houses down the street. And we used to fill them in with snow and make them smooth and slide down them all day . . . and it was very dangerous, you know . . . far too steep . . . and sure enough one day a kid named Rufus came down too fast and hit the sidewalk and we saw his face just split open right there in front of us . . . And I remember standing there looking at his bloody open face thinking that was the end of Rufus. But the ambulance came and they took him to the hospital and they fixed the broken bones and they sewed it all up . . . and the next time I saw Rufus he just had a little line down the middle of his face . . . I never got over that . . .

Asagai: What?

Beneatha: That that was what one person could do for another, fix him up — sew up the problem, make him all right again. That was the most marvelous thing in the world . . . I wanted to do that. I always thought it was the one concrete thing in the world that a human being could do. Fix up the sick, you know — and make them whole again. This was truly being God . . .

Asagai: You wanted to be God?

Beneatha: No — I wanted to cure. It used to be so important to me. I wanted to cure. It used to matter. I used to care. I mean about people and how their bodies hurt . . .

Asagai: And you've stopped caring?

Beneatha: Yes — I think so.

Asagai: Why?

Beneatha (bitterly): Because it doesn't seem deep enough, close enough to what ails mankind! It was a child's way of seeing things — or an idealist's.

Asagai: Children see things very well sometimes — and idealists even better.

Beneatha: I know that's what you think. Because you are still where I left off. You with all your talk and dreams about Africa! You still think you can patch up the world. Cure the Great Sore of Colonialism — *(Loftily, mocking it.)* with the Penicillin of Independence — !

Asagai: Yes!

Beneatha: Independence *and then what?* What about all the crooks and thieves and just plain idiots who will come into power and steal and plunder the same as before—only now they will be black and do it in the name of the new Independence—WHAT ABOUT THEM?!

Asagai: That will be the problem for another time. First we must get there.

Beneatha: And where does it end?

Asagai: End? Who even spoke of an end? To life? To living?

Beneatha: An end to misery! To stupidity! Don't you see there isn't any real progress, Asagai, there is only one large circle that we march in, around and around, each of us with our own little picture in front of us—our own little mirage that we think is the future.

Asagai: That is the mistake.

Beneatha: What?

Asagai: What you just said—about the circle. It isn't a circle—it is simply a long line—as in geometry, you know, one that reaches into infinity. And because we cannot see the end—we also cannot see how it changes. And it is very odd but those who see the changes—who dream, who will not give up—are called idealists . . . and those who see only the circle—we call *them* the "realists"!

Beneatha: Asagai, while I was sleeping in that bed in there, people went out and took the future right out of my hands! And nobody asked me, nobody consulted me—they just went out and changed my life!

Asagai: Was it your money?

Beneatha: What?

Asagai: Was it your money he gave away?

Beneatha: It belonged to all of us.

Asagai: But did you earn it? Would you have had it at all if your father had not died?

Beneatha: No.

Asagai: Then isn't there something wrong in a house—in a world—where all dreams, good or bad, must depend on the death of a man? I never thought to see *you* like this, Alaiyo. You! Your brother made a mistake and you are grateful to him so that now you can give up the ailing human race on account of it! You talk about what good is struggle, what good is anything! Where are we all going and why are we bothering!

Beneatha: AND YOU CANNOT ANSWER IT!

Asagai (shouting over her): I LIVE THE ANSWER! (Pause.) In my village at home it is the exceptional man who can even read a newspaper . . . or who ever sees a book at all. I will go home and much of what I will have to say will seem strange to the people of my village. But I will teach and work and things will happen, slowly and swiftly. At times it will seem that nothing changes at all . . . and then again the sudden dramatic events which make history leap into the future. And then quiet again. Retrogression even. Guns, murder, revolution. And I even will have moments when I wonder if the quiet was not better than all that death and hatred. But I will look about my village at the illiteracy and disease and ignorance and I will not wonder long. And perhaps . . . perhaps I will be a great man . . . I mean perhaps I will hold on to the substance of truth and find my way always with the right course . . . and perhaps for it I will be butchered in my bed some night by the servants of empire . . .

Beneatha: The martyr!

Asagai (he smiles): ... or perhaps I shall live to be a very old man, respected and esteemed in my new nation ... And perhaps I shall hold office and this is what I'm trying to tell you, Alaiyo: perhaps the things I believe now for my country will be wrong and outmoded, and I will not understand and do terrible things to have things my way or merely to keep my power. Don't you see that there will be young men and women — not British soldiers then, but my own black countrymen — to step out of the shadows some evening and slit my then useless throat? Don't you see they have always been there ... that they always will be. And that such a thing as my own death will be an advance? They who might kill me even ... actually replenish all that I was.

Beneatha: Oh, Asagai, I know all that.

Asagai: Good! Then stop moaning and groaning and tell me what you plan to do.

Beneatha: Do?

Asagai: I have a bit of a suggestion.

Beneatha: What?

Asagai (rather quietly for him): That when it is all over — that you come home with me —

Beneatha (staring at him and crossing away with exasperation): Oh — Asagai — at this moment you decide to be romantic!

Asagai (quickly understanding the misunderstanding): My dear, young creature of the New World — I do not mean across the city — I mean across the ocean: home — to Africa.

Beneatha (slowly understanding and turning to him with murmured amazement): To Africa?

Asagai: Yes! ... *(smiling and lifting his arms playfully.)* Three hundred years later the African Prince rose up out of the seas and swept the maiden back across the middle passage over which her ancestors had come —

Beneatha (unable to play): To — to Nigeria?

Asagai: Nigeria. Home. *(Coming to her with genuine romantic flippancy.)* I will show you our mountains and our stars; and give you cool drinks from gourds and teach you the old songs and the ways of our people — and, in time, we will pretend that — *(Very softly.)* — you have only been away for a day. Say that you'll come — *(He swings her around and takes her full in his arms in a kiss which proceeds to passion.)*

Beneatha (pulling away suddenly): You're getting me all mixed up —

Asagai: Why?

Beneatha: Too many things — too many things have happened today. I must sit down and think. I don't know what I feel about anything right this minute.

She promptly sits down and props her chin on her fist.

Asagai (charmed): All right, I shall leave you. No — don't get up. *(Touching her, gently, sweetly.)* Just sit awhile and think ... Never be afraid to sit awhile and think. *(He goes to door and looks at her.)* How often I have looked at you and said, "Ah — so this is what the New World hath finally wrought ..."

He exits. Beneatha sits on alone. Presently Walter enters from his room and starts to rummage through things, feverishly looking for something. She looks up and turns in her seat.

Beneatha (hissingly): Yes — just look at what the New World hath wrought! . . . Just look! (*She gestures with bitter disgust.*) There he is! *Monsieur le petit bourgeois noir°* — himself! There he is — Symbol of a Rising Class! Entrepreneur! Titan of the system! (*Walter ignores her completely and continues frantically and destructively looking for something and hurling things to floor and tearing things out of their place in his search. Beneatha ignores the eccentricity of his actions and goes on with the monologue of insult.*) Did you dream of yachts on Lake Michigan, Brother? Did you see yourself on that Great Day sitting down at the Conference Table, surrounded by all the mighty bald-headed men in America? All halted, waiting, breathless, waiting for your pronouncements on industry? Waiting for you — Chairman of the Board! (*Walter finds what he is looking for — a small piece of white paper — and pushes it in his pocket and puts on his coat and rushes out without ever having looked at her. She shouts after him.*) I look at you and I see the final triumph of stupidity in the world!

The door slams and she returns to just sitting again. Ruth comes quickly out of Mama's room.

Ruth: Who was that?

Beneatha: Your husband.

Ruth: Where did he go?

Beneatha: Who knows — maybe he has an appointment at U.S. Steel.

Ruth (anxiously, with frightened eyes): You didn't say nothing bad to him, did you?

Beneatha: Bad? Say anything bad to him? No — I told him he was a sweet boy and full of dreams and everything is strictly peachy keen, as the ofay kids say!

Mama enters from her bedroom. She is lost, vague, trying to catch hold, to make some sense of her former command of the world, but it still eludes her. A sense of waste overwhelms her gait; a measure of apology rides on her shoulders. She goes to her plant, which has remained on the table, looks at it, picks it up and takes it to the window sill and sits it outside, and she stands and looks at it a long moment. Then she closes the window, straightens her body with effort and turns around to her children.

Mama: Well — ain't it a mess in here, though? (*A false cheerfulness, a beginning of something.*) I guess we all better stop moping around and get some work done. All this unpacking and everything we got to do. (*Ruth raises her head slowly in response to the sense of the line; and Beneatha in similar manner turns very slowly to look at her mother.*) One of you all better call the moving people and tell 'em not to come.

Ruth: Tell 'em not to come?

Mama: Of course, baby. Ain't no need in 'em coming all the way here and having to go back. They charges for that too. (*She sits down, fingers to her brow, thinking.*) Lord, ever since I was a little girl, I always remembers people saying, "Lena — Lena Eggleston, you aims too high all the time. You needs to slow down and see life a little more like it is. Just slow down some." That's what they always used to say down home — "Lord, that Lena Eggleston is a high-minded thing. She'll get her due one day!"

Monsieur le petit bourgeois noir: Mr. Black Bourgoisie (French).

Ruth: No, Lena . . .

Mama: Me and Big Walter just didn't never learn right.

Ruth: Lena, no! We gotta go. Bennie — tell her . . .

She rises and crosses to Beneatha with her arms outstretched. Beneatha doesn't respond.

Tell her we can still move . . . the notes ain't but a hundred and twenty-five a month. We got four grown people in this house — we can work . . .

Mama (to herself): Just aimed too high all the time —

Ruth (turning and going to Mama fast — the words pouring out with urgency and desperation): Lena — I'll work . . . I'll work twenty hours a day in all the kitchens in Chicago . . . I'll strap my baby on my back if I have to and scrub all the floors in America and wash all the sheets in America if I have to — but we got to MOVE! We got to get OUT OF HERE!!

Mama reaches out absently and pats Ruth's hand.

Mama: No — I sees things differently now. Been thinking 'bout some of the things we could do to fix this place up some. I seen a second-hand bureau over on Maxwell Street just the other day that could fit right there. *(She points to where the new furniture might go. Ruth wanders away from her.)* Would need some new handles on it and then a little varnish and it look like something brand-new. And — we can put up them new curtains in the kitchen . . . Why this place be looking fine. Cheer us all up so that we forget trouble ever come . . . *(To Ruth.)* And you could get some nice screens to put up in your room round the baby's bassinet . . . *(She looks at both of them pleadingly.)* Sometimes you just got to know when to give up some things . . . and hold on to what you got . . .

Walter enters from the outside, looking spent and leaning against the door, his coat hanging from him.

Mama: Where you been, son?

Walter (breathing hard): Made a call.

Mama: To who, son?

Walter: To The Man. *(He heads for his room.)*

Mama: What man, baby?

Walter (stops in the door): The Man, Mama. Don't you know who The Man is?

Ruth: Walter Lee?

Walter: The Man. Like the guys in the streets say — The Man. Captain Boss — Mistuh Charley . . . Old Cap'n Please Mr. Bossman . . .

Beneatha (suddenly): Lindner!

Walter: That's right! That's good. I told him to come right over.

Beneatha (fiercely, understanding): For what? What do you want to see him for!

Walter (looking at his sister): We going to do business with him.

Mama: What you talking 'bout, son?

Walter: Talking 'bout life, Mama. You all always telling me to see life like it is. Well — I laid in there on my back today . . . and I figured it out. Life just like it is. Who gets and who don't get. *(He sits down with his coat on and laughs.)* Mama, you know it's all divided up. Life is. Sure enough. Between the takers and the "tooken." *(He laughs.)* I've figured it out finally. *(He looks around at them.)* Yeah. Some of us always getting "tooken." *(He laughs.)* People like Willy Harris, they don't never get "tooken." And you know why the rest of us do? 'Cause we all mixed up. Mixed up bad. We get to looking 'round for the right and the wrong; and we worry about it and cry about it and stay up nights trying to figure out 'bout the wrong and the right of things all the time . . . And all the time, man, them takers is out there operating, just taking and taking. Willy Harris? Shoot — Willy Harris don't even count. He don't even count in the big scheme of things. But I'll say one thing for old Willy Harris . . . he's taught me something. He's taught me to keep my eye on what counts in this world. Yeah — *(Shouting out a little.)* Thanks, Willy!

Ruth: What did you call that man for, Walter Lee?

Walter: Called him to tell him to come on over to the show. Gonna put on a show for the man. Just what he wants to see. You see, Mama, the man came here today and he told us that them people out there where you want us to move — well they so upset they willing to pay us *not* to move! *(He laughs again.)* And — and oh, Mama — you would of been proud of the way me and Ruth and Bennie acted. We told him to get out . . . Lord have mercy! We told the man to get out! Oh, we was some proud folks this afternoon, yeah. *(He lights a cigarette.)* We were still full of that old-time stuff . . .

Ruth (coming toward him slowly): You talking 'bout taking them people's money to keep us from moving in that house?

Walter: I ain't just talking 'bout it, baby — I'm telling you that's what's going to happen!

Beneatha: Oh, God! Where is the bottom! Where is the real honest-to-God bottom so he can't go any farther!

Walter: See — that's the old stuff. You and that boy that was here today. You all want everybody to carry a flag and a spear and sing some marching songs, huh? You wanna spend your life looking into things and trying to find the right and the wrong part, huh? Yeah. You know what's going to happen to that boy someday — he'll find himself sitting in a dungeon, locked in forever — and the takers will have the key! Forget it, baby! There ain't no causes — there ain't nothing but taking in this world, and he who takes most is smartest — and it don't make a damn bit of difference *how*.

Mama: You making something inside me cry, son. Some awful pain inside me.

Walter: Don't cry, Mama. Understand. That white man is going to walk in that door able to write checks for more money than we ever had. It's important to him and I'm going to help him . . . I'm going to put on the show, Mama.

Mama: Son — I come from five generations of people who was slaves and sharecroppers — but ain't nobody in my family never let nobody pay 'em no money that was a way of telling us we wasn't fit to walk the earth. We ain't never been that poor. *(Raising her eyes and looking at him.)* We ain't never been that — dead inside.

Beneatha: Well — we are dead now. All the talk about dreams and sunlight that goes on in this house. It's all dead now.

Walter: What's the matter with you all! I didn't make this world! It was give to me this way! Hell, yes, I want me some yachts someday! Yes, I want to hang some real pearls 'round my wife's neck. Ain't she supposed to wear no pearls? Somebody tell me — tell me, who decides which women is suppose to wear pearls in this world. I tell you I am a *man* — and I think my wife should wear some pearls in this world!

This last line hangs a good while and Walter begins to move about the room. The word "Man" has penetrated his consciousness; he mumbles it to himself repeatedly between strange agitated pauses as he moves about.

Mama: Baby, how you going to feel on the inside?

Walter: Fine! . . . Going to feel fine . . . a man . . .

Mama: You won't have nothing left then, Walter Lee.

Walter (coming to her): I'm going to feel fine, Mama. I'm going to look that son-of-a-bitch in the eyes and say — *(He falters.)* — and say, "All right, Mr. Lindner — *(He falters even more.)* — that's *your* neighborhood out there! You got the right to keep it like you want! You got the right to have it like you want! Just write the check and — the house is yours." And — and I am going to say — *(His voice almost breaks.)* "And you — you people just put the money in my hand and you won't have to live next to this bunch of stinking niggers! . . ." *(He straightens up and moves away from his mother, walking around the room.)* And maybe — maybe I'll just get down on my black knees . . . *(He does so; Ruth and Bennie and Mama watch him in frozen horror.)* "Captain, Mistuh, Bossman — *(Groveling and grinning and wringing his hands in profoundly anguished imitation of the slow-witted movie stereotype.)* A-hee-hee-hee! Oh, yassuh boss! Yasssssuh! Great white — *(Voice breaking, he forces himself to go on.)* — Father, just gi' ussen de money, fo' God's sake, and we's — we's ain't gwine come out deh and dirty up yo' white folks neighborhood . . ." *(He breaks down completely.)* And I'll feel fine! Fine! FINE! *(He gets up and goes into the bedroom.)*

Beneatha: That is not a man. That is nothing but a toothless rat.

Mama: Yes — death done come in this here house. *(She is nodding, slowly, reflectively.)* Done come walking in my house on the lips of my children. You what supposed to be my beginning again. You — what supposed to be my harvest. *(To Beneatha.)* You — you mourning your brother?

Beneatha: He's no brother of mine.

Mama: What you say?

Beneatha: I said that that individual in that room is no brother of mine.

Mama: That's what I thought you said. You feeling like you better than he is today? *(Beneatha does not answer.)* Yes? What you tell him a minute ago? That he wasn't a man? Yes? You give him up for me? You done wrote his epitaph too — like the rest of the world? Well, who give you the privilege?

Beneatha: Be on my side for once! You saw what he just did, Mama! You saw him — down on his knees. Wasn't it you who taught me to despise any man who would do that? Do what he's going to do?

Mama: Yes — I taught you that. Me and your daddy. But I thought I taught you something else too . . . I thought I taught you to love him.

Beneatha: Love him? There is nothing left to love.

Mama: There is *always* something left to love. And if you ain't learned that, you ain't learned nothing. *(Looking at her.)* Have you cried for that boy today? I don't mean for yourself and for the family 'cause we lost the money. I mean for him: what he been through and what it done to him. Child, when do you think is the time to love somebody the most? When they done good and made things easy for everybody? Well then, you ain't through learning—because that ain't the time at all. It's when he's at his lowest and can't believe in hisself 'cause the world done whipped him so! When you starts measuring somebody, measure him right, child, measure him right. Make sure you done taken into account what hills and valleys he come through before he got to wherever he is.

Travis bursts into the room at the end of the speech, leaving the door open.

Travis: Grandmama—the moving men are downstairs! The truck just pulled up.

Mama (turning and looking at him): Are they, baby? They downstairs?

She sighs and sits. Lindner appears in the doorway. He peers in and knocks lightly, to gain attention, and comes in. All turn to look at him.

Lindner (hat and briefcase in hand): Uh—hello . . .

Ruth crosses mechanically to the bedroom door and opens it and lets it swing open freely and slowly as the lights come up on Walter within, still in his coat, sitting at the far corner of the room. He looks up and out through the room to Lindner.

Ruth: He's here.

A long minute passes and Walter slowly gets up.

Lindner (coming to the table with efficiency, putting his briefcase on the table and starting to unfold papers and unscrew fountain pens): Well, I certainly was glad to hear from you people. *(Walter has begun the trek out of the room, slowly and awkwardly, rather like a small boy, passing the back of his sleeve across his mouth from time to time.)* Life can really be so much simpler than people let it be most of the time. Well—with whom do I negotiate? You, Mrs. Younger, or your son here? *(Mama sits with her hands folded on her lap and her eyes closed as Walter advances. Travis goes closer to Lindner and looks at the papers curiously.)* Just some official papers, sonny.

Ruth: Travis, you go downstairs—

Mama (opening her eyes and looking into Walter's): No. Travis, you stay right here. And you make him understand what you doing, Walter Lee. You teach him good. Like Willy Harris taught you. You show where our five generations done come to. *(Walter looks from her to the boy, who grins at him innocently.)* Go ahead, son—*(She folds her hands and closes her eyes.)* Go ahead.

Walter (at last crosses to Lindner, who is reviewing the contract): Well, Mr. Lindner. *(Beneatha turns away.)* We called you—*(There is a profound, simple groping quality in his speech.)*—because, well, me and my family *(He looks around and shifts from one foot to the other.)* Well—we are very plain people . . .

Lindner: Yes—

Walter: I mean—I have worked as a chauffeur most of my life—and my wife here, she does domestic work in people's kitchens. So does my mother. I mean—we are plain people . . .

Lindner: Yes, Mr. Younger—

Walter (really like a small boy, looking down at his shoes and then up at the man): And—uh—well, my father, well, he was a laborer most of his life. . . .

Lindner (absolutely confused): Uh, yes—yes, I understand. *(He turns back to the contract.)*

Walter (a beat; staring at him): And my father—*(With sudden intensity.)* My father almost *beat a man to death* once because this man called him a bad name or something, you know what I mean?

Lindner (looking up, frozen): No, no, I'm afraid I don't —

Walter (a beat. The tension hangs; then Walter steps back from it): Yeah. Well — what I mean is that we come from people who had a lot of *pride.* I mean — we are very proud people. And that's my sister over there and she's going to be a doctor — and we are very proud —

Lindner: Well — I am sure that is very nice, but —

Walter: What I am telling you is that we called you over here to tell you that we are very proud and that this — *(Signaling to Travis.)* Travis, come here. *(Travis crosses and Walter draws him before him facing the man.)* This is my son, and he makes the sixth generation our family in this country. And we have all thought about your offer —

Lindner: Well, good . . . good —

Walter: And we have decided to move into our house because my father — my father — he earned it for us brick by brick. *(Mama has her eyes closed and is rocking back and forth as though she were in church, with her head nodding the Amen yes.)* We don't want to make no trouble for nobody or fight no causes, and we will try to be good neighbors. And that's *all* we got to say about that. *(He looks the man absolutely in the eyes.)* We don't want your money. *(He turns and walks away.)*

Lindner (looking around at all of them): I take it then — that you have decided to occupy . . .

Beneatha: That's what the man said.

Lindner (to Mama in her reverie): Then I would like to appeal to you, Mrs. Younger. You are older and wiser and understand things better I am sure . . .

Mama: I am afraid you don't understand. My son said we was going to move and there ain't nothing left for me to say. *(Briskly.)* You know how these young folks is nowadays, mister. Can't do a thing with 'em! *(As he opens his mouth, she rises.)* Good-bye.

Lindner (folding up his materials): Well — if you are that final about it . . . there is nothing left for me to say. *(He finishes, almost ignored by the family, who are concentrating on Walter Lee. At the door Lindner halts and looks around.)* I sure hope you people know what you're getting into.

   He shakes his head and exits.

Ruth (looking around and coming to life): Well, for God's sake — if the moving men are here — LET'S GET THE HELL OUT OF HERE!

Mama (into action): Ain't it the truth! Look at all this here mess. Ruth, put Travis' good jacket on him . . . Walter Lee, fix your tie and tuck your shirt in, you look like somebody's hoodlum! Lord have mercy, where is my plant? *(She flies to get it amid the general bustling of the family, who are deliberately trying to ignore the nobility of the past moment.)* You all start on down . . . Travis child, don't go empty-handed . . . Ruth, where did I put that box with my skillets in it? I want to be in charge of it myself . . . I'm going to make us the biggest dinner we ever ate tonight . . . Beneatha, what's the matter with them stockings? Pull them things up, girl . . .

   The family starts to file out as two moving men appear and begin to carry out the heavier pieces of furniture, bumping into the family as they move about.

Beneatha: Mama, Asagai asked me to marry him today and go to Africa —

Mama (in the middle of her getting-ready activity): He did? You ain't old enough to marry nobody — *(Seeing the moving men lifting one of her chairs precariously.)*

Darling, that ain't no bale of cotton, please handle it so we can sit in it again! I had that chair twenty-five years . . .

The movers sigh with exasperation and go on with their work.

Beneatha (girlishly and unreasonably trying to pursue the conversation): To go to Africa, Mama — be a doctor in Africa . . .

Mama (distracted): Yes, baby —

Walter: Africa! What he want you to go to Africa for?

Beneatha: To practice there . . .

Walter: Girl, if you don't get all them silly ideas out your head! You better marry yourself a man with some loot . . .

Beneatha (angrily, precisely as in the first scene of the play): What have you got to do with who I marry!

Walter: Plenty. Now I think George Murchison —

Beneatha: George Murchison! I wouldn't marry him if he was Adam and I was Eve!

Walter and Beneatha go out yelling at each other vigorously and the anger is loud and real till their voices diminish. Ruth stands at the door and turns to Mama and smiles knowingly.

Mama (fixing her hat at last): Yeah — they something all right, my children . . .

Ruth: Yeah — they're something. Let's go, Lena.

Mama (stalling, starting to look around at the house): Yes — I'm coming. Ruth —

Ruth: Yes?

Mama (quietly, woman to woman): He finally come into his manhood today, didn't he? Kind of like a rainbow after the rain . . .

Ruth (biting her lip lest her own pride explode in front of Mama): Yes, Lena.

Walter's voice calls for them raucously.

Walter (off stage): Y'all come on! These people charges by the hour, you know!

Mama (waving Ruth out vaguely): All right, honey — go on down. I be down directly.

Ruth hesitates, then exits. Mama stands, at last alone in the living room, her plant on the table before her as the lights start to come down. She looks around at all the walls and ceilings and suddenly, despite herself, while the children call below, a great heaving thing rises in her and she puts her fist to her mouth to stifle it, takes a final desperate look, pulls her coat about her, pats her hat, and goes out. The lights dim down. The door opens and she comes back in, grabs her plant, and goes out for the last time.

Curtain.

CONNECTIONS TO OTHER SELECTIONS

1. The play's title is a line from the Langston Hughes poem that introduces the play (p. 1730). Explain how the context of the entire poem helps to explain the play's title and its major concerns.

2. Consider Lena Younger's role as a mother in *A Raisin in the Sun*. Explain why you think she is nurturing or overbearing. Compare her character with Amanda Wingfield's in Tennessee Williams's *The Glass Menagerie* (p. 1893).

3. Write an essay that compares the dreams the Youngers struggle to realize with those of the Lomans in Arthur Miller's *Death of a Salesman* (p. 1824).

What similarities and differences about the nature of each family's dreams do you find in the plays?

4. In an essay compare the economic, social, and moral pressures on the families in *A Raisin in the Sun* and August Wilson's *The Piano Lesson* (p. 2031). How does each family cope with these pressures? Discuss which family you think is more successful in confronting them.

PERSPECTIVE

Thomas P. Adler (b. 1943)
The Political Basis of Lorraine Hansberry's Art   1994

During Lorraine's high school years, the Hansberry home welcomed such luminaries in the black movement as W. E. B. Du Bois, the sociologist and author of the classic *Souls of Black Folk* (1903), under whom Lorraine would study African history; Paul Robeson, the prominent Shakespearean actor and activist with whom she would work on the journal *Freedom* in the early 1950s; Langston Hughes, the leading poet and playwright of the Harlem Renaissance and author of the poem, "A Dream Deferred," a line from which would provide the title for *A Raisin in the Sun;* and her uncle, William Leon Hansberry, an early professor of African studies who became Lorraine's mentor after her father's death. She always subscribed to the Pan-Africanist notion that the destinies of the African and African-American peoples are intertwined. Throughout her brief life she affirmed the responsibility of the writer to speak for those without public voice who share in one or another aspect of her "otherness" — biological, racial, sociocultural — and face oppression because of it.

"The Negro Writer and His Roots: Toward a New Romanticism," written in 1959, contains Lorraine Hansberry's aesthetic credo, outlining facets of her dramatic theory and analyzing the sources of her political radicalism. For her the writer's vocation is ordinarily inseparable from a political agenda. She asserts the duty of black authors to dispel a number of myths or "illusions rampant in contemporary American culture," challenging first "the notion put forth that art is not, and *should* not and, when it is at its best, CANNOT possibly be 'social.'" Ibsen's well-made problem plays exemplify Hansberry's dictum, following Arthur Miller, "that there are *no* plays which are not social and no plays that do not have a thesis." She singles out three additional destructive illusions subverting the American mindset: that somehow people can "exist independent of the world around them"; that the homogeneity in American society allows "one huge sprawling middle class" to be regarded as universally representative of what is a pluralistic and diverse culture and world; and, finally "that there exists an inexhaustible period of time" during which this "nation may leisurely resurrect the promise of our Constitution and begin to institute the equality of man."

Hansberry professes a balanced perspective on the topic of race, rejecting destructive stereotypes on both sides. Blacks as well as whites can be slaves to "ridiculous money values," to a perverted notion of "acquisition for the sake of acquisition" that elevates materialism over the possession of self and personal freedom. Blacks as well as whites can romanticize "the black bourgeoisie" and "Negro urban life," idealizing as eccentric and attractive what is actually evil and diseased. Blacks as well as whites can be politically naive, turning over their cause to those ambitious for power. Finally, well-meaning blacks might try to deny their "slave past or . . . sharecropper and ghetto present [as] an affront to every Negro who wears a shirt and tie" rather than analyze their history of oppression as a step toward overcoming it. Hansberry's analysis reveals a society in need of radical transformation, one still deficient in guaranteeing voting rights to all its citizens, one without equal job opportunities, one where lynchings still occur (she mentions Emmett Till, kidnapped and murdered in 1955), and one committed to racial genocide, since "the social and economic havoc wreaked on the American Negro takes some ten to fifteen years off the life-expectancy of our people." For these reasons, "the Negro writer has a role to play in shaming, if you will, the conscience of the people and the present national government."

From *American Drama, 1940–1960: A Critical History*

CONSIDERATIONS FOR CRITICAL THINKING AND WRITING

1. To what extent does *A Raisin in the Sun* reveal Hansberry's concern about the three "destructive illusions" that Adler quotes in the second paragraph?
2. How does *A Raisin in the Sun* reflect Hansberry's belief that "the Negro writer has a role to play in shaming . . . the conscience of the people and the present national government" (para. 3)?
3. In an essay discuss whether you agree or disagree that Ibsen's *A Doll House* (p. 1568) and Miller's *Death of a Salesman* (p.1824) "exemplify" Hansberry's assertion that "there are *no* plays which are not social and no plays that do not have a thesis" (2).

Oleanna

David Mamet, popular for both his award-winning plays and his numerous screenplay credits, was born in Chicago, Illinois in 1947. He studied at Goddard College in Vermont and the Neighborhood Playhouse School of Theater in New York. Mamet began his career as an actor and director before his first three acclaimed Off-Off Broadway plays were produced, *The Duck Variations* (1972), *Sexual Perversity in Chicago* (1974), and *American Buffalo* (1976), which was later made into a movie starring Dustin Hoffman and Dennis Franz. Known for his forceful, realistic, and sometimes controversial dialogue, Mamet has made a career of writing about the undersides of American business practices, from real estate in *Glengarry Glen Ross* (1992) to the Hollywood film industry in *Speed the Plow* (1988). Mamet also wrote the screenplay for *The Untouchables* (1987), adapted from the popular television show, and translated Anton Chekhov's *Uncle Vanya*, which was turned into the film *Vanya on 42nd Street*.

In addition to his prolific talents as a playwright and screenwriter, Mamet has also enjoyed success as a film director, directing the acclaimed films *The Spanish Prisoner* (1998) and *State and Main* (2001). A common theme of Mamet's is the confidence game, with the American individual as capital to be bought and sold. Concerning this stark depiction of American life, Mamet comments that "all of life is [a con game]. In the United States, it's our pleasure and joy to consider life as a commercial enterprise. That's our national character."

Oleanna, which was also adapted into a movie starring William H. Macy in 1994, takes a different look at this traditional theme: it reflects the gender politics that emerged in the early 1990s on campuses across the country, as people took on a heightened sensitivity to language. The play documents the struggle between a female student and her professor when the potential meanings in their everyday encounters are examined more closely. Mamet's theme of the con game emerges as the audience struggles to decide who is right and who is wrong, if there is a right and wrong.

When not working on a play or screenplay, Mamet has taught at several schools, including Goddard College, the Yale Drama School, New York University, and the Atlantic Theater Company, for which he was a founding member. He lives in eastern Massachusetts and Vermont.

Research David Mamet with LitLinks at
http://www.bedfordstmartins.com/meyer/bedintrolit

DAVID MAMET (B. 1947)

Oleanna   1992

The want of fresh air does not seem much to affect the happiness of children in a London alley: the greater part of them sing and play as though they were on a moor in Scotland. So the absence of a genial mental atmosphere is not commonly recognized by children who have never known it. Young people have a marvelous faculty of either dying or adapting themselves to circumstances. Even if they are unhappy—very unhappy—it is astonishing how easily they can be prevented from finding it out, or at any rate from attributing it to any other cause than their own sinfulness.

— The Way of All Flesh,
Samuel Butler

"Oh, to be in Oleanna,
That's where I would rather be
Than be bound in Norway
And drag the chains of slavery."
—*folk song*

CHARACTERS

Carol, a woman of twenty
John, a man in his forties

The play takes place in John's office.

ACT I

(John is talking on the phone. Carol is seated across the desk from him.)

John *(on phone):* And what about the land. *(Pause.)* The land. And what about the land? *(Pause.)* What about it? *(Pause.)* No. I don't understand. Well, yes, I'm I'm . . . no, I'm *sure* it's signif . . . I'm sure it's significant. *(Pause.)* Because it's significant to mmmmmm . . . did you call Jerry? *(Pause.)* Because . . . no, no, no, no, no. What did they say . . . ? Did you speak to the *real* estate . . . where *is* she . . . ? Well, well, all right. Where are her notes? Where are the notes we took with her. *(Pause.)* I thought you were? No. No, I'm sorry, I didn't mean that, I just thought that I saw you, when we were there . . . what . . . ? I thought I saw you with a *pencil.* WHY NOW? is what I'm say . . . well, that's why I say "call Jerry." Well, I can't right now, be . . . no, I *didn't* schedule any . . . Grace: I *didn't* . . . I'm well aware . . . Look: Look. Did you call Jerry? Will you call Jerry . . . ? Because I can't now. I'll be there, I'm sure I'll be there in fifteen, in twenty. I intend to. No, we aren't *going* to lose the, we aren't *going* to lose the house. Look: Look, I'm not minimizing it. The "easement." Did she say "easement"? *(Pause.)* What did she *say; is* it a "term of art," are we *bound* by it . . . I'm sorry . . . *(Pause.)* are: we: yes. *Bound* by . . . Look: *(he checks his watch)* before the other side *goes home,* all right? "a term of art." Because: that's right *(Pause.)* The yard for the boy. Well, that's the whole . . . Look: I'm going to meet you there . . . *(He checks his watch.)* Is the realtor there? All right, tell her to show you the basement again. Look at the *this* because . . . Bec . . . I'm leaving in, I'm leaving in ten or fifteen . . . Yes. No, no, I'll meet you at the new . . . That's a good. If he thinks it's necc . . . you tell Jerry to meet . . . All right? We *aren't* going to lose the deposit. All right? I'm sure it's going to be . . . *(Pause.)* I hope so. *(Pause.)* I love you, too. *(Pause.)* I love you, too. As soon as . . . I will. *(He hangs up.)* *(He bends over the desk and makes a note.)* *(He looks up.)* *(To Carol:)* I'm sorry . . .

Carol *(pause):* What is a "term of art"?

John *(pause):* I'm sorry . . . ?

Carol *(pause):* What is a "term of art"?

John: Is that what you want to talk about?

Carol: . . . to talk about . . . ?

John: Let's take the mysticism out of it, shall we? Carol? *(Pause.)* Don't you think? I'll tell you: when you have some "thing." Which must be broached. *(Pause.)* Don't you think . . . ? *(Pause.)*

Carol: . . . don't I think . . . ?

John: Mmm?

Carol: . . . did I . . . ?

John: . . . what?

Carol: Did . . . did I . . . did I say something wr . . .

John *(pause):* No. I'm sorry. No. You're right. I'm very sorry. I'm somewhat rushed. As you see. I'm sorry. You're right. *(Pause.)* What is a "term of art"? It seems to mean a *term,* which has come, through its use, to mean something *more specific* than the words would, to someone *not acquainted* with them . . . indicate. That, I believe, is what a "term of art," would mean. *(Pause.)*

Carol: You don't know what it means . . . ?

John: I'm not sure that I know what it means. It's one of those things, perhaps you've had them, that, you look them up, or have someone explain them to you, and you say "aha," and, you immediately *forget* what . . .

Carol: You don't do that.

John: . . . I . . . ?

Carol: You don't do . . .

John: . . . I don't, what . . . ?

Carol: . . . for . . .

John: . . . I don't for . . .

Carol: . . . no . . .

John: . . . forget things? Everybody does that.

Carol: No, they don't.

John: They don't . . .

Carol: No.

John (pause): No. Everybody does that.

Carol: Why would they do that . . . ?

John: Because. I don't know. Because it doesn't interest them.

Carol: No.

John: I think so, though. *(Pause.)* I'm sorry that I was distracted.

Carol: You don't have to say that to me.

John: You paid me the compliment, or the "obeisance" — all right — of coming in here . . . All right. *Carol.* I find that I am at a *standstill.* I find that I . . .

Carol: . . . what . . .

John: . . . one moment. In regard to your . . . to your . . .

Carol: Oh, oh. You're buying a new house!

John: No, let's get on with it.

Carol: "get on"? *(Pause.)*

John: I know how . . . *believe* me. I know how . . . potentially *humiliating* these . . . I have no desire to . . . I have no desire other than to help you. But *(he picks up some papers on his desk)* I won't even say "but." I'll say that as I go back over the . . .

Carol: I'm just, I'm just trying to . . .

John: . . . no, it will not do.

Carol: . . . what? What will . . . ?

John: No. I see, I see what you, it . . . *(He gestures to the papers.)* but your work . . .

Carol: I'm just: I sit in class I . . . *(She holds up her notebook.)* I take notes . . .

John (simultaneously with "notes"*):* Yes. I understand. What I am trying to *tell* you is that some, some basic . . .

Carol: . . . I . . .

John: . . . one moment: some basic missed communi . . .

Carol: I'm doing what I'm told. I bought your book, I read your . . .

John: No, I'm sure you . . .

Carol: No, no, no. I'm doing what I'm told. It's *difficult* for me. It's *difficult* . . .

John: . . . but . . .

Carol: I don't . . . lots of the *language* . . .

John: . . . please . . .

Carol: The *language,* the "things" that you say . . .

John: I'm sorry. No. I don't think that that's true.

Carol: It *is* true. I . . .

John: I think . . .

Carol: It *is* true.

John: . . . I . . .

Carol: Why would I . . . ?

John: I'll tell you why: you're an incredibly bright girl.

Carol: . . . I . . .

John: You're an incredibly . . . you have no problem with the . . . Who's kidding who?

Carol: . . . I . . .

John: No. No. I'll tell you why. I'll tell. . . . I think you're *angry*, I . . .

Carol: . . . why would I . . .

John: . . . wait one moment. I . . .

Carol: It is true. I have *problems* . . .

John: . . . every . . .

Carol: . . . I come from a different *social* . . .

John: . . . ev . . .

Carol: a different economic . . .

John: . . . Look:

Carol: No. I: when I *came* to this school:

John: Yes. Quite . . . *(Pause.)*

Carol: . . . does that mean nothing . . . ?

John: . . . but look: look . . .

Carol: . . . I . . .

John (picks up paper): Here: Please: Sit down. *(Pause.)* Sit down. *(Reads from her paper.)* "I think that the ideas contained in this work express the author's feelings in a way that he intended, based on his results." What can that mean? Do you see? What . . .

Carol: I, the best that I . . .

John: I'm saying, that perhaps this course . . .

Carol: No, no, no, you can't, you can't . . . I have to . . .

John: . . . how . . .

Carol: . . . I have to pass it . . .

John: Carol, I:

Carol: I *have* to pass this course, I . . .

John: Well.

Carol: . . . don't you . . .

John: Either the . . .

Carol: . . . I . . .

John: . . . either the, I . . . either the *criteria* for judging progress in the class are . . .

Carol: No, no, no, no, I have to pass it.

John: Now, look: I'm a human being, I . . .

Carol: I did what you told me. I did, I did everything that, I read your *book,* you told me to buy your book and read it. Everything you *say* I . . . *(She gestures to her notebook.)* *(The phone rings.)* I do. . . . Ev . . .

John: . . . look:

Carol: . . . everything I'm told . . .

John: Look. Look. I'm not your *father.* *(Pause.)*

Carol: What?

John: I'm.

Carol: Did I say you were my father?

John: . . . no . . .

Carol: Why did you say that . . . ?

John: I . . .

Carol: . . . why . . . ?

John: . . . in class I . . . *(He picks up the phone.) (Into phone:)* Hello. I can't talk now. Jerry? Yes? I underst . . . I can't talk now. I know . . . I know . . . Jerry. I can't *talk* now. Yes, I. Call me back in . . . Thank you. *(He hangs up.) (To Carol.)* What do you want me to do? We are two people, all right? Both of whom have subscribed to . . .

Carol: No, no . . .

John: . . . certain arbitrary . . .

Carol: No. You have to help me.

John: Certain institutional . . . you tell me what you want me to do. . . . You tell me what you want me to . . .

Carol: How can I go back and tell them the *grades* that I . . .

John: . . . what can I do . . . ?

Carol: *Teach* me. *Teach* me.

John: . . . I'm trying to teach you.

Carol: I read your book. I read it. I don't under . . .

John: . . . you don't understand it.

Carol: No.

John: Well, perhaps it's not well *written* . . .

Carol *(simultaneously with* "written"): No. No. No. I want to *understand* it.

John: What don't you understand? *(Pause.)*

Carol: *Any* of it. What you're trying to say. When you talk about . . .

John: . . . yes . . . ? *(She consults her notes.)*

Carol: "Virtual warehousing of the young" . . .

John: "Virtual warehousing of the young." If we artificially prolong adolescence . . .

Carol: . . . and about "The Curse of Modern Education."

John: . . . well . . .

Carol: I don't . . .

John: Look. It's just a *course,* it's just a *book,* it's just a . . .

Carol: No. No. There are *people* out there. People who came *here.* To know something they didn't *know.* Who *came* here. To be *helped.* To be *helped.* So someone would *help* them. To *do* something. To *know* something. To get, what do they say? "To get on in the world." How can I do that if I don't, if I fail? But I don't *understand.* I don't *understand.* I don't understand what anything means . . . and I walk around. From morning 'til night: with this one thought in my head. I'm *stupid.*

John: No one thinks you're stupid.

Carol: No? What am I . . . ?

John: I . . .

Carol: . . . what am I, then?

John: I think you're angry. Many people are. I have a *telephone* call that I have to make. And an *appointment,* which is rather *pressing;* though I sympathize with your concerns, and though I wish I had the time, this was not a previously scheduled meeting and I . . .

Carol: . . . you think I'm nothing . . .

John: . . . have an appointment with a *realtor,* and with my wife and . . .

Carol: You think that I'm stupid.

John: No. I certainly don't.

Carol: You said it.

John: No. I did not.

Carol: You did.

John: When?

Carol: . . . you . . .

John: No. I never did, or never would say that to a student, and . . .

Carol: You said, "What can that mean?" *(Pause.)* "What can that mean?" . . . *(Pause.)*

John: . . . and what did that mean to you . . . ?

Carol: That meant I'm stupid. And I'll never learn. That's what that meant. And you're right.

John: . . . I . . .

Carol: But then. But then, what am I doing here . . . ?

John: . . . if you thought that I . . .

Carol: . . . when nobody wants me, and . . .

John: . . . if you interpreted . . .

Carol: Nobody *tells* me anything. And I *sit* there . . . in the *corner.* In the *back.* And everybody's talking about "this" all the time. And "concepts," and "precepts" and, and, and, and, and, WHAT IN THE WORLD ARE YOU *TALKING* ABOUT? And I read your book. And they said, "Fine, go in that class." Because you talked about responsibility to the young. I DON'T KNOW WHAT IT MEANS AND I'M *FAILING* . . .

John: May . . .

Carol: No, you're right. "Oh, hell." I failed. Flunk me out of it. It's garbage. Everything I do. "The ideas contained in this work express the author's feelings." That's right. That's right. I know I'm stupid. I know what I am. *(Pause.)* I know what I am, Professor. You don't have to tell me. *(Pause.)* It's pathetic. Isn't it?

John: . . . Aha . . . *(Pause.)* Sit down. Sit down. Please. *(Pause.)* Please sit down.

Carol: Why?

John: I want to talk to you.

Carol: Why?

John: Just sit down. *(Pause.)* Please. Sit down. Will you, please . . . ?

(Pause. She does so.)

Thank you.

Carol: What?

John: I want to tell you something.

Carol (pause): What?

John: Well, I know what you're talking about.

Carol: No. You don't.

John: I think I do. *(Pause.)*

Carol: How can you?

John: I'll tell you a story about myself. *(Pause.)* Do you mind? *(Pause.)* I was raised to think myself stupid. That's what I want to tell you. *(Pause.)*

Carol: What do you mean?

John: Just what I said. I was brought up, and my earliest, and most persistent memories are of being told that I was stupid. "You have such *intelligence.* Why must you behave so *stupidly*?" Or, "Can't you *understand*? Can't you *understand*?" And I could *not* understand. I could *not* understand.

Carol: What?

John: The simplest problem. Was beyond me. It was a mystery.

Carol: What was a mystery?

John: How people learn. How *I* could learn. Which is what I've been speaking of in class. And of *course* you can't hear it. Carol. Of *course* you can't. *(Pause.)* I used to speak of "real people," and wonder what the *real* people did. The *real* people. Who were they? *They* were the people other than myself. The *good* people. The *capable* people. The people who could do the things, *I* could not do: learn, study, retain . . . all that *garbage* — which is what I have been talking of in class, and that's *exactly* what I have been talking of — If you are told. . . . Listen to this. If the young child is told he cannot understand. Then he takes it as a *description* of himself. What am I? I am *that which can not understand.* And I saw you out there, when we were speaking of the concepts of . . .

Carol: I can't understand any of them.

John: Well, then, that's *my* fault. That's not your fault. And that is not verbiage. That's what I firmly hold to be the truth. And I am sorry, and I owe you an apology.

Carol: Why?

John: And I suppose that I have had some *things* on my mind. . . . We're buying a *house*, and . . .

Carol: People said that you were stupid . . . ?

John: Yes.

Carol: When?

John: I'll tell you when. Through my life. In my childhood; and, perhaps, they stopped. But I heard them continue.

Carol: And what did they say?

John: They said I was incompetent. Do you see? And when I'm tested the, the, the *feelings* of my youth about the *very subject of learning* come up. And I . . . I become, I feel "unworthy," and "unprepared." . . .

Carol: . . . yes.

John: . . . eh?

Carol: . . . yes.

John: And I feel that I must fail. *(Pause.)*

Carol: . . . but then you *do* fail. *(Pause.)* You have to. *(Pause.)* Don't you?

John: A *pilot.* Flying a plane. The pilot is flying the plane. He thinks: Oh, my *God*, my mind's been drifting! Oh, my God! What kind of a cursed imbecile am I, that I, with this so precious cargo of *Life* in my charge, would allow my attention to wander. Why was I born? How deluded are those who put their trust in me, . . . et cetera, so on, and he crashes the plane.

Carol (pause): He could just . . .

John: That's right.

Carol: He could say:

John: My attention *wandered* for a moment . . .

Carol: . . . uh huh . . .

John: I had a *thought* I did not like . . . but now:

Carol: . . . but now it's . . .

John: That's what I'm telling you. It's time to put my attention . . . see: it is not: this is what I learned. It is Not Magic. Yes. Yes. *You.* You are going to be frightened. When faced with what may or may not be but which you are going to perceive as a test. You will become frightened. And you will say: "I am incapable of . . ." and everything *in* you will think these two things. "I must. But I can't." And you will think: Why was I born to be the laughing-stock of a world in which everyone is better than I? In which I am entitled to nothing. Where I can not learn. *(Pause.)*

Carol: Is that . . . *(Pause.)* Is that what I have . . . ?

John: Well. I don't know if I'd put it that way. Listen: I'm talking to you as I'd talk to my son. Because that's what I'd like him to have that I never had. I'm talking to you the way I wish that someone had talked to me. I don't know how to do it, other than to be *personal,* . . . but . . .

Carol: Why would you want to be personal with me?

John: Well, you see? That's what I'm saying. We can only interpret the behavior of others through the screen we . . . *(The phone rings.)* Through . . . *(To phone.)* Hello . . . ? *(To Carol.)* Through the screen we create. *(To phone.)* Hello. *(To Carol.)* Excuse me a moment. *(To phone.)* Hello? No, I can't talk nnn . . . I know I did. In a few . . . I'm . . . is he coming to the . . . yes. I talked to him. We'll meet you at the No, because I'm with a *student.* It's going to be fff . . . This is important, too. I'm with a *student,* Jerry's going to . . . Listen: the sooner I get off, the sooner I'll be down, all right. I love you. Listen, listen, I said "I love you," it's going to work *out* with the, because I feel that it is, I'll be right down. All right? Well, then it's going to take as long as it takes. *(He hangs up.)* *(To Carol.)* I'm sorry.

Carol: What was that?

John: There are some problems, as there usually are, about the final agreements for the new house.

Carol: You're buying a new house.

John: That's right.

Carol: Because of your promotion.

John: Well, I suppose that that's right.

Carol: Why did you stay here with me?

John: Stay here.

Carol: Yes. When you should have gone.

John: Because I like you.

Carol: You like me.

John: Yes.

Carol: Why?

John: Why? Well? Perhaps we're similar. *(Pause.)* Yes. *(Pause.)*

Carol: You said "everyone has problems."

John: Everyone has problems.

Carol: Do they?

John: Certainly.

Carol: You do?

John: Yes.

Carol: What are they?

John: Well. *(Pause.)* Well, you're perfectly right. *(Pause.)* If we're going to take off the Artificial *Stricture,* of "Teacher," and "Student," why should *my* problems be any more a mystery than your own? Of *course* I have problems. As you saw.

Carol: . . . with what?

John: With my *wife* . . . with *work* . . .

Carol: With work?

John: Yes. And, and, perhaps my problems are, do you see? *Similar* to yours.

Carol: Would you tell me?

John: All right. *(Pause.)* I came *late* to teaching. And I found it Artificial. The notion of "I know and you do not"; and I saw an *exploitation* in the education process. I told you. I hated school, I hated teachers. I hated everyone who was in the position of a "boss" because I *knew* — I didn't *think,* mind you, I *knew* I was going to fail. Because I was a fuckup. I was just no goddamned good. When I . . . late in life . . . *(Pause.)* When I *got out from under* . . . when I worked my way out of the need to fail. When I . . .

Carol: How do you do that? *(Pause.)*

John: You have to look at what you are, and what you feel, and how you act. And, finally, you have to look at how you act. And say: If that's what I *did,* that must be how I think of myself.

Carol: I don't understand.

John: If I fail all the time, it must be that I think of myself as a failure. If I do not want to think of myself as a failure, perhaps I should begin by *succeeding* now and again. Look. The tests, you see, which you encounter, in school, in college, in life, were designed, in the most part, for idiots. *By* idiots. There is no need to fail at them. They are not a test of your worth. They are a test of your ability to retain and spout back misinformation. Of *course* you fail them. They're *nonsense.* And I . . .

Carol: . . . no . . .

John: Yes. They're *garbage.* They're a *joke.* Look at me. Look at me. The Tenure Committee. The Tenure Committee. Come to judge me. The Bad Tenure Committee.

     The "Test." Do you see? They put me to the test. Why, they had people voting on me I wouldn't employ to wax my car. And yet, I go before the Great Tenure Committee, and I have an urge, to *vomit,* to, to, to puke my *badness* on the table, to show them: "I'm no good. Why would you pick *me?*"

Carol: They granted you tenure.

John: Oh no, they announced it, but they haven't *signed.* Do you see? "At any moment . . ."

Carol: . . . mmm . . .

John: "They might not *sign*" . . . I might not . . . the *house* might not go through . . . Eh? Eh? They'll find out my "dark secret." *(Pause.)*

Carol: . . . what is it . . . ?

John: There *isn't* one. But *they* will find an index of my badness . . .

Carol: Index?

John: A ". . . pointer." A "Pointer." You see? Do you see? I *understand* you. I. Know. That. Feeling. Am I entitled to my job, and my nice *home,* and my *wife,* and my *family,* and so on. This is what I'm saying: That theory of education which, that *theory:*

Carol: I . . . I . . . *(Pause.)*

John: What?

Carol: I . . .

John: What?

Carol: I want to know about my grade. *(Long pause.)*

John: Of course you do.

Carol: Is that bad?

John: No.

Carol: Is it bad that I asked you that?

John: No.

Carol: Did I upset you?

John: No. And I apologize. Of *course* you want to know about your grade. And, of course, you can't concentrate on anyth . . . *(The telephone starts to ring.)* Wait a moment.

Carol: I should go.

John: I'll make you a deal.

Carol: No, you have to . . .

John: Let it ring. I'll make you a deal. You stay here. We'll start the whole course over. I'm going to say it was not you, it was I who was not paying attention. We'll start the whole course over. Your grade is an "A." Your final grade is an "A." *(The phone stops ringing.)*

Carol: But the class is only half over . . .

John (simultaneously with "over"): Your grade for the whole term is an "A." If you will come back and meet with me. A few more times. Your grade's an "A." Forget about the paper. You didn't like it, you didn't like writing it. It's not important. What's important is that I awake your interest, if I can, and that I answer your questions. Let's start over. *(Pause.)*

Carol: Over. With what?

John: Say this is the beginning.

Carol: The beginning.

John: Yes.

Carol: Of what?

John: Of the class.

Carol: But we can't start over.

John: I say we can. *(Pause.)* I say we can.

Carol: But I don't believe it.

John: Yes, I know that. But it's true. What is The Class but you and me? *(Pause.)*

Carol: There are rules.

John: Well. We'll break them.

Carol: How can we?

John: We won't tell anybody.

Carol: Is that all right?

John: I say that it's fine.

Carol: Why would you do this for me?

John: I like you. Is that so difficult for you to . . .

Carol: Um . . .

John: There's no one here but you and me. *(Pause.)*

Carol: All right. I did not understand. When you referred . . .

John: All right, yes?

Carol: When you referred to hazing.

John: Hazing.

Carol: You wrote, in your book. About the comparative . . . the comparative . . .
(*She checks her notes.*)

John: Are you checking your notes . . . ?

Carol: Yes.

John: Tell me in your own . . .

Carol: I want to make sure that I have it right.

John: No. Of course. You want to be exact.

Carol: I want to know everything that went on.

John: . . . that's good.

Carol: . . . so I . . .

John: That's very good. But I was suggesting, many times, that that which we
wish to retain is retained oftentimes, I think, *better* with less expenditure
of effort.

Carol (*of notes*)**:** Here it is: you wrote of *hazing*.

John: . . . that's correct. Now: I said "hazing." It means ritualized annoyance.
We shove this book at you, we say read it. Now, you say you've read it? I
think that you're *lying*. I'll *grill* you, and when I find you've lied, you'll be
disgraced, and your life will be ruined. It's a sick game. Why do we do it?
Does it educate? In no sense. Well, then, what is higher education? It is
something-other-than-useful.

Carol: What is "something-other-than-useful"?

John: It has become a ritual, it has become an article of faith. That all must be
subjected to, or to put it differently, that all are entitled to Higher Education. And my point . . .

Carol: You disagree with that?

John: Well, let's address that. What do you think?

Carol: I don't know.

John: What do you think, though? (*Pause.*)

Carol: I don't know.

John: I spoke of it in class. Do you remember my example?

Carol: Justice.

John: Yes. Can you repeat it to me?

(*She looks down at her notebook.*)

Without your notes? I ask you as a favor to me, so that I can see if my idea
was interesting.

Carol: You said "justice" . . .

John: Yes?

Carol: . . . that all are entitled . . . (*Pause.*) I . . . I . . . I . . .

John: Yes. To a speedy trial. To a fair trial. But they needn't be given a trial *at all*
unless they stand accused. Eh? Justice is their right, should they choose to
avail themselves of it, they should have a fair trial. It does not follow, of
necessity, a person's life is incomplete without a trial in it. Do you see?
My point is a confusion between equity and *utility* arose. So we confound the *usefulness* of higher education with our, granted, right to equal
access to the same. We, in effect, create a *prejudice* toward it, completely independent of . . .

Carol: . . . that it is prejudice that we should go to school?

John: Exactly. (*Pause.*)

Carol: How can you say that? How . . .

John: Good. Good. *Good.* That's right! Speak up! What is a prejudice? An unreasoned belief. We are all subject to it. None of us is not. When it is threatened, or opposed, we feel anger, and feel, do we not? As you do now. Do you not? Good.

Carol: . . . but how can you . . .

John: . . . let us examine. Good.

Carol: How . . .

John: Good. Good. When . . .

Carol: I'M SPEAKING . . . *(Pause.)*

John: I'm sorry.

Carol: How can you . . .

John: . . . I beg your pardon.

Carol: That's all right.

John: I beg your pardon.

Carol: That's all right.

John: I'm sorry I interrupted you.

Carol: That's all right.

John: You were saying?

Carol: I was saying . . . I was saying . . . *(She checks her notes.)* How can you say in a class. Say in a college class, that college education is prejudice?

John: I said that our predilection for it . . .

Carol: Predilection . . .

John: . . . you know what that means.

Carol: Does it mean "liking"?

John: Yes.

Carol: But how can you say that? That College . . .

John: . . . that's my *job,* don't you know.

Carol: What is?

John: To provoke you.

Carol: No.

John: Oh. Yes, though.

Carol: To provoke me?

John: That's right.

Carol: To make me mad?

John: That's right. To force you . . .

Carol: . . . to make me mad is your job?

John: To force you to . . . listen *(Pause.)* Ah. *(Pause.)* When I was young somebody told me, are you ready, the rich copulate less often than the poor. But when they do, they take more of their clothes off. Years. Years, mind you, I would compare experiences of my own to this dictum, saying, aha, this fits the norm, or ah, this is a variation from it. What did it mean? Nothing. It was some jerk thing, some school kid told me that took up room inside my head. *(Pause.)*

Somebody told *you,* and you hold it as an article of faith, that higher education is an unassailable good. This notion is so dear to you that when I question it you become angry. Good. Good, I say. Are not those the very things which we should question? I say college education, since the war, has become so a matter of course, and such a fashionable necessity, for those either of or aspiring *to* to the new vast middle class, that we *espouse* it, as a matter of right, and have ceased to ask, "What is it good for?" *(Pause.)*

What might be some reasons for pursuit of higher education?
One: A love of learning.
Two: The wish for mastery of a skill.
Three: For economic betterment.

(Stops. Makes a note.)

Carol: I'm keeping you.
John: One moment. I have to make a note . . .
Carol: It's something that I said?
John: No, we're buying a house.
Carol: You're buying the new house.
John: To go with the tenure. That's right. Nice *house,* close to the *private school* . . . *(He continues making his note.)* . . . We were talking of economic betterment . . .

(Carol writes in her notebook.)

I was thinking of the School Tax. *(He continues writing.) (To himself.)* . . . *where is it written* that I have to send my child to public school. . . . Is it a law that I have to improve the City Schools at the expense of my own interest? And, is this not simply *The White Man's Burden?* Good. And *(looks up to Carol)* . . . does this interest you?
Carol: No. I'm taking notes . . .
John: You don't have to take notes, you know, you can just listen.
Carol: I want to make sure I remember it. *(Pause.)*
John: I'm not lecturing you, I'm just trying to tell you some things I think.
Carol: What do you think?
John: Should all kids go to college? Why . . .
Carol (pause): To learn.
John: But if he does not learn.
Carol: If the child does not learn?
John: Then why is he in college? Because he was told it was his "right"?
Carol: Some might find college instructive.
John: I would hope so.
Carol: But how do they feel? Being told they are wasting their time?
John: I don't think I'm telling them that.
Carol: You said that education was "prolonged and systematic hazing."
John: Yes. It can be so.
Carol: . . . if education is so *bad,* why do you do it?
John: I do it because I love it. *(Pause.)* Let's. . . . I suggest you look at the demographics, wage-earning capacity, college- and noncollege-educated men and women, 1855 to 1980, and let's see if we can wring some worth from the statistics. Eh? And . . .
Carol: No.
John: What?
Carol: I can't understand them.
John: . . . you . . . ?
Carol: . . . the "charts." The *Concepts,* the . . .
John: "Charts" are simply . . .
Carol: When I leave here . . .
John: Charts, do you see . . .

Carol: No, I can't . . .

John: You can, though.

Carol: NO, NO — I DON'T UNDERSTAND. DO YOU SEE??? I DON'T *UNDER-STAND* . . .

John: What?

Carol: *Any* of it. *Any* of it. I'm *smiling* in class, I'm *smiling,* the whole time. What are you *talking* about? What is everyone *talking* about? I don't *understand.* I don't know what it *means.* I don't know what it means to *be* here . . . you tell me I'm intelligent, and then you tell me I should not be *here,* what do you *want* with me? What does it *mean?* Who should I *listen* to . . . I . . .

(He goes over to her and puts his arm around her shoulder.)

NO!

(She walks away from him.)

John: Sshhhh.

Carol: No, I don't under . . .

John: Sshhhhh.

Carol: I don't know what you're *saying* . . .

John: Sshhhhh. It's all right.

Carol: . . . I have no . . .

John: Sshhhhh. Sshhhhh. Let it go a moment. *(Pause.)* Sshhhhh . . . let it go. *(Pause.)* Just let it go. *(Pause.)* Just let it go. It's all right. *(Pause.)* Sshhhhh. *(Pause.)* I understand . . . *(Pause.)* What do you feel?

Carol: I feel bad.

John: I know. It's all right.

Carol: I . . . *(Pause.)*

John: What?

Carol: I . . .

John: What? Tell me.

Carol: I don't understand you.

John: I know. It's all right.

Carol: I . . .

John: What? *(Pause.)* What? *Tell* me.

Carol: I can't tell you.

John: No, you must.

Carol: I can't.

John: No. Tell me. *(Pause.)*

Carol: I'm bad. *(Pause.)* Oh, God. *(Pause.)*

John: It's all right.

Carol: I'm . . .

John: It's all right.

Carol: I can't talk about this.

John: It's all right. Tell me.

Carol: Why do you want to know this?

John: I don't want to know. I want to know whatever you . . .

Carol: I always . . .

John: . . . good . . .

Carol: I always . . . all my life . . . I have never told anyone this . . .

John: Yes. Go on. *(Pause.)* Go on.

Carol: All of my life . . . *(The phone rings.)*

   (Pause. John goes to the phone and picks it up.)

John (into phone): I can't talk now. *(Pause.)* What? *(Pause.)* Hmm. *(Pause.)* All right, I . . . I. Can't. Talk. Now. No, no, no, I *Know* I did, but . . . What? Hello. What? She *what?* She *can't,* she said the agreement is void? How, how is the agreement *void? That's Our House.*

    I have the *paper;* when we come down, next week, with the payment, and the paper, that house is . . . wait, wait, wait, wait, wait, wait, wait: Did Jerry . . . is Jerry there? *(Pause.)* Is *she* there . . . ? Does she have a *lawyer* . . . ? How the *hell,* how the *Hell.* That is . . . it's a question, you said, of the *easement.* I don't underst . . . it's not the *whole agreement.* It's just the *easement,* why would she? Put, put, put, *Jerry* on. *(Pause.)* Jer, *Jerry:* What the *Hell* . . . that's my *house.* That's . . . Well, I'm, no, no, no, I'm *not* coming ddd . . . List, *Listen, screw* her. You *tell* her. You, listen: I want you to take *Grace,* you take Grace, and get out of that house. You *leave* her there. Her and her lawyer, and you *tell* them, we'll see them in court next . . . no. No. Leave her there, leave her to *stew* in it: You tell her, we're *getting* that house, and we are going to . . . No. I'm *not* coming down. I'll be damned if I'll sit in the same rrr . . . the next, you tell her the next time I *see* her is in court . . . I . . . *(Pause.)* What? *(Pause.)* What? I don't understand. *(Pause.)* Well, what about the house? *(Pause.)* There isn't any problem with the hhh . . . *(Pause.)* No, no, no, that's all right. All ri . . . All right . . . *(Pause.)* Of course. Tha . . . Thank you. No, I will. Right away. *(He hangs up.) (Pause.)*

Carol: What is it? *(Pause.)*

John: It's a surprise party.

Carol: It is.

John: Yes.

Carol: A party for you.

John: Yes.

Carol: Is it your birthday?

John: No.

Carol: What is it?

John: The tenure announcement.

Carol: The tenure announcement.

John: They're throwing a party for us in our new house.

Carol: Your new house.

John: The house that we're buying.

Carol: You have to go.

John: It seems that I do.

Carol (pause): They're proud of you.

John: Well, there are those who would say it's a form of aggression.

Carol: What is?

John: A surprise.

ACT 2

(John and Carol seated across the desk from each other.)

John: You see, *(pause)* I love to teach. And flatter myself I am *skilled* at it. And I love the, the aspect of *performance*. I think I must confess that.

When I found I loved to teach I swore that I would not become that cold, rigid automaton of an instructor which I had encountered as a child.

Now, I was not unconscious that it was given me to err upon the other side. And, so, I asked and *ask* myself if I engaged in heterodoxy, I will not say "gratuitously" for I do not care to posit orthodoxy as a given good — but, "to the detriment of, of my students." *(Pause.)*

As I said. When the possibility of tenure opened, and, of course, I'd long pursued it, I was, of course *happy*, and *covetous* of it.

I asked myself if I was wrong to covet it. And thought about it long, and, I hope, truthfully, and saw in myself several things in, I think, no particular order. *(Pause.)*

That I *would* pursue it. That I *desired* it, that I was not pure of longing for security, and that that, perhaps, was not reprehensible in me. That I had duties *beyond* the school, and that my duty to my home, for instance, was, or should be, if it were not, of an equal weight. That tenure, and security, and yes, and *comfort*, were not, of themselves, to be scorned; and were even worthy of honorable pursuit. And that it was given me. Here, in this place, which I enjoy, and in which I find comfort, to assure myself of — as far as it rests in The Material — a continuation of that joy and comfort. In exchange for what? Teaching. Which I love.

What was the price of this security? To obtain *tenure*. Which tenure the committee is in the process of granting me. And on the basis of which I contracted to purchase a house. Now, as you don't have your own family, at this point, you may not know what that means. But to me it is important. A home. A Good Home. To raise my family. Now: The Tenure Committee will meet. This is the process, and a *good* process. Under which the school has functioned for quite a long time. They will meet, and hear your complaint — which you have the right to make; and they will dismiss it. They will *dismiss* your complaint; and, in the intervening period, I will lose my house. I will not be able to close on my house. I will lose my *deposit*, and the home I'd picked out for my wife and son will go by the boards. Now: I see I have angered you. I understand your anger at teachers. I was angry with mine. I felt hurt and humiliated by them. Which is one of the reasons that I went into education.

Carol: What do you want of me?

John *(pause):* I was hurt. When I received the report. Of the tenure committee. I was shocked. And I was hurt. No, I don't mean to subject you to my weak sensibilities. All right. Finally, I didn't understand. Then I thought: Is it not always at those points at which we reckon ourselves unassailable that we are most vulnerable and . . . *(Pause.)* Yes. All right. You find me pedantic. Yes. I am. By nature, by *birth*, by profession, I don't know . . . I'm always looking for a *paradigm* for . . .

Carol: I don't know what a paradigm is.

John: It's a model.

Carol: Then why can't you use that word? *(Pause.)*

John: If it is important to you. Yes, all right. I was looking for a model. To continue: I feel that one point . . .

Carol: I . . .

John: One second . . . upon which I am unassailable is my unflinching concern for my students' dignity. I asked you here to . . . in the spirit of *investigation,* to ask you . . . to ask . . . *(Pause.)* What have I done to you? *(Pause.)* And, and, I suppose, how I can make amends. Can we not settle this now? It's pointless, really, and I want to know.

Carol: What you can do to force me to retract?

John: That is not what I meant at all.

Carol: To bribe me, to convince me . . .

John: . . . No.

Carol: To retract . . .

John: That is not what I meant at all. I think that you know it is not.

Carol: That is not what I know. I *wish* I . . .

John: I do not want to . . . you wish what?

Carol: No, you said what amends can you make. To force me to retract.

John: That is not what I said.

Carol: I have my notes.

John: Look. Look. The Stoics say . . .

Carol: The Stoics?

John: The Stoical Philosophers say if you remove the phrase "I have been injured," you have removed the injury. Now: Think: I know that you're upset. Just tell me. Literally. Literally: what wrong have I done you?

Carol: Whatever you have done to me — to the extent that you've done it to *me,* do you know, rather than to me as a *student,* and, so, to the student body, is contained in my report. To the tenure committee.

John: Well, all right. *(Pause.)* Let's see. *(He reads.)* I find that I am sexist. That I am *elitist.* I'm not sure I know what that means, other than it's a derogatory word, meaning "bad." That I . . . That I insist on wasting time, in nonprescribed, in self-aggrandizing and theatrical *diversions* from the prescribed *text* . . . that these have taken both sexist and pornographic forms . . . here we find listed . . . *(Pause.)* Here we find listed . . . instances ". . . closeted with a student" . . . "Told a rambling, sexually explicit story, in which the frequency and attitudes of fornication of the poor and rich are, it would seem, the central point . . . moved to *embrace* said student and . . . all part of a pattern . . ." *(Pause.)*

    (He reads.) That I used the phrase "The White Man's Burden" . . . that I told you how I'd asked you to my room because I quote like you. *(Pause.)*

    (He reads.) "He said he 'liked' me. That he 'liked being with me.' He'd let me write my examination paper over, if I could come back oftener to see him in his office." *(Pause.)* *(To Carol.)* It's *ludicrous.* Don't you know that? It's not *necessary.* It's going to *humiliate* you, and it's going to cost me my *house,* and . . .

Carol: It's "*ludicrous* . . ."?

(John picks up the report and reads again.)

John: "He told me he had problems with his wife; and that he wanted to take off the artificial stricture of Teacher and Student. He put his arm around me . . ."

Carol: Do you deny it? Can you deny it . . . ? Do you see? *(Pause.)* Don't you see? You don't see, do you?

John: I don't see . . .

Carol: You think, you think you can deny that these things happened; or, if they *did,* if they *did,* that they meant what you *said* they meant. Don't you see? You drag me in here, you drag us, to listen to you "go on"; and "go on" about this, or that, or we don't "express" ourselves very well. We don't say what we mean. Don't we? Don't we? We *do* say what we mean. And you say that "I don't understand you . . .": Then *you* . . . *(Points.)*

John: "Consult the Report"?

Carol: . . . that's right.

John: You see. You see. Can't you. . . . You see what I'm saying? Can't you tell me in your own words?

Carol: Those are my own words. *(Pause.)*

John (he reads): "He told me that if I would stay alone with him in his office, he would change my grade to an A." *(To Carol.)* What have I done to you? Oh. My God, are you so hurt?

Carol: What I "feel" is irrelevant. *(Pause.)*

John: Do you know that I tried to help you?

Carol: What I know I have reported.

John: I would like to help you now. I would. Before this escalates.

Carol (simultaneously with "escalates"*):* You see. I don't think that I need your help. I don't think I need anything you have.

John: I feel . . .

Carol: I don't *care* what you feel. Do you see? DO YOU SEE? You can't *do* that anymore. You. Do. Not. Have. The. Power. Did you misuse it? *Someone* did. Are you part of that group? *Yes. Yes.* You Are. You've *done* these things. And to say, and to say, "Oh. Let me help you with your problem . . ."

John: Yes. I understand. I understand. You're *hurt.* You're *angry.* Yes. I think your *anger* is *betraying* you. Down a path which helps no one.

Carol: I don't *care* what you think.

John: You don't? *(Pause.)* But you talk of *rights.* Don't you see? *I* have rights too. Do you see? I have a *house* . . . part of the *real* world; and The Tenure Committee, Good Men and True . . .

Carol: . . . Professor . . .

John: . . . Please: *Also* part of that world: you understand? This is my *life.* I'm not a *bogeyman.* I don't "stand" for something, I . . .

Carol: . . . Professor . . .

John: . . . I . . .

Carol: Professor. I came here as a *favor.* At your personal request. Perhaps I should not have done so. But I did. On my behalf, and on behalf of my group. And you speak of the tenure committee, one of whose members is a woman, as you know. And though you might call it Good Fun, or An Historical Phrase, or An Oversight, or, All of the Above, to refer to the committee as Good Men and True, it is a demeaning remark. It is a sexist remark, and to overlook it is to countenance continuation of that method of thought. It's a remark . . .

John: OH COME ON. Come on. . . . Sufficient to deprive a family of . . .

Carol: Sufficient? Sufficient? Sufficient? Yes. It is a *fact* . . . and that story, which I quote, is *vile* and *classist,* and *manipulative* and *pornographic.* It . . .

John: . . . it's pornographic . . . ?

Carol: What gives you the *right*. Yes. To speak to a *woman* in your private . . . Yes. Yes. I'm sorry. I'm sorry. You feel yourself empowered . . . you say so yourself. To *strut*. To *posture*. To "perform." To "Call me in here . . ." Eh? You say that higher education is a joke. And treat it as such, you *treat* it as such. And *confess* to a taste to play the *Patriarch* in your class. To grant *this*. To deny *that*. To embrace your students.

John: How can you assert. How can you stand there and . . .

Carol: How can you *deny* it. You did it to me. *Here*. You *did*. . . . You *confess*. You love the Power. To *deviate*. To *invent*, to transgress . . . to *transgress* whatever norms have been established for us. And you think it's charming to "question" in yourself this taste to mock and destroy. But you should question it, Professor. And you pick those things which you feel *advance* you: publication, *tenure*, and the steps to get them you call "harmless rituals." And you perform those steps. Although you say it is hypocrisy. But to the aspirations of your students. Of *hardworking students*, who come here, who *slave* to come here — you have no idea what it cost me to come to this school — you *mock* us. You call education "hazing," and from your so-protected, so-elitist seat you hold our confusion as a *joke*, and our hopes and efforts with it. Then you sit there and say "what have I done?" And ask me to understand that *you* have aspirations too. But I tell you. I tell you. That you are vile. And that you are exploitative. And if you possess one ounce of that inner honesty you describe in your book, you can look in yourself and see those things that I see. And you can find revulsion equal to my own. Good day. *(She prepares to leave the room.)*

John: Wait a second, will you, just one moment. *(Pause.)* Nice day today.

Carol: What?

John: You said "Good day." I think that it is a nice day today.

Carol: *Is* it?

John: Yes, I think it is.

Carol: And why is that important?

John: Because it is the essence of all human communication. I say something conventional, you respond, and the information we exchange is not about the "weather," but that we both agree to converse. In effect, we agree that we are both human. *(Pause.)*

     I'm not a . . . "exploiter," and you're not a . . . "deranged," what? *Revolutionary* . . . that we may, that we may have . . . positions, and that we may have . . . desires, which are in *conflict*, but that we're just human. *(Pause.)* That means that sometimes we're *imperfect*. *(Pause.)* Often we're in conflict . . . *(Pause.)* *Much* of what we do, you're right, in the name of "principles" is *self-serving* . . . much of what we do is *conventional*. *(Pause.)* You're right. *(Pause.)* You said you came in the class because you wanted to learn about *education*. I don't know what I can teach you about education. But I know that I can tell you what I *think* about education, and then *you* decide. And you don't have to fight with me. *I'm* not the subject. *(Pause.)* And where I'm *wrong* . . . perhaps it's not your job to "fix" me. I don't want to fix *you*. I would like to tell you what I *think*, because that *is* my job, conventional as it is, and flawed as I may be. And then, if you can show me some better *form*, then we can proceed from there. But, just like "nice day, isn't it . . . ?" I don't think we can proceed until we accept that each of us is human. *(Pause.)* And we still can have difficulties. We *will* have them . . . that's all right too. *(Pause.)* Now:

Carol: . . . wait . . .

John: Yes. I want to hear it.

Carol: . . . the . . .

John: Yes. Tell me frankly.

Carol: . . . my position . . .

John: I want to hear it. In your own words. What you want. And what you feel.

Carol: . . . I . . .

John: . . . yes . . .

Carol: My Group.

John: Your "Group" . . . ? *(Pause.)*

Carol: The people I've been talking to . . .

John: There's no shame in that. Everybody needs advisers. Everyone needs to expose themselves. To various points of view. It's not wrong. It's essential. Good. Good. Now: You and I . . .

(The phone rings.)

You and I . . .

(He hesitates for a moment, and then picks it up.)

(Into phone.) Hello. *(Pause.)* Um . . . no, I know they do. *(Pause.)* I know she does. Tell her that I . . . can I call you back? . . . Then tell her that I think it's going to be fine. *(Pause.)* Tell her just, just hold on, I'll . . . can I get back to you? . . . Well . . . no, no, no, we're *taking* the house . . . we're . . . no, no, nn . . . no, she will nnn, it's not a *question* of refunding the dep . . . no . . . it's not a *question* of the deposit . . . will you call Jerry? Babe, baby, will you just call Jerry? Tell him, nnn . . . tell him they, well, they're to keep the deposit, because the deal, be . . . because the deal is going to go *through* . . . because I know . . . be . . . will you please? Just *trust* me. Be . . . well, I'm dealing with the complaint. Yes. Right *Now*. Which is why I . . . yes, no, no, it's really, I can't *talk* about it now. Call Jerry, and I can't talk now. Ff . . . fine. Gg . . . good-bye. *(Hangs up.)* *(Pause.)* I'm sorry we were interrupted.

Carol: No . . .

John: I . . . I was saying:

Carol: You said that we should agree to talk about my complaint.

John: That's correct.

Carol: But we *are* talking about it.

John: Well, that's correct too. You see? This is the *gist* of education.

Carol: No, no. I mean, we're talking about it at the Tenure Committee Hearing. *(Pause.)*

John: Yes, but I'm saying: we can talk about it *now*, as easily as . . .

Carol: No. I think that we should stick to the process . . .

John: . . . wait a . . .

Carol: . . . the "conventional" process. As you said. *(She gets up.)* And you're right, I'm sorry if I was, um, if I was "discourteous" to you. You're right.

John: Wait, wait a . . .

Carol: I really should go.

John: Now, look, granted. I have an interest. In the status quo. All right? Everyone does. But what I'm saying is that the *committee* . . .

Carol: Professor, you're right. Just don't impinge on me. We'll take our differences, and . . .

John: You're going to make a . . . look, look, look, you're going to . . .

Carol: I shouldn't have come here. They told me . . .

John: One moment. No. No. There are *norms,* here, and there's no reason. Look: I'm trying to *save* you . . .

Carol: No one *asked* you to . . . you're trying to save *me?* Do me the courtesy to . . .

John: I *am* doing you the courtesy. I'm talking *straight* to you. We can settle this *now.* And I want you to sit *down* and . . .

Carol: You must excuse me . . . *(She starts to leave the room.)*

John: Sit down, it seems we each have a. . . . Wait one moment. Wait one moment . . . just do me the courtesy to . . .

(He restrains her from leaving.)

Carol: LET ME GO.

John: I have no desire to *hold* you, I just want to *talk* to you . . .

Carol: LET ME GO. LET ME GO. WOULD SOMEBODY *HELP* ME? WOULD SOMEBODY *HELP* ME PLEASE . . . ?

ACT 3

(At rise, Carol and John are seated.)

John: I have asked you here. *(Pause.)* I have asked you here against, against my . . .

Carol: I was most surprised you asked me.

John: . . . against my better *judgment,* against . . .

Carol: I was most surprised . . .

John: . . . against the . . . yes. I'm sure.

Carol: . . . If you would like me to leave, I'll leave. I'll go right now . . . *(She rises.)*

John: Let us begin *correctly,* may we? I feel . . .

Carol: That is what I wished to do. That's why I came here, but now . . .

John: . . . I feel . . .

Carol: But now perhaps you'd like me to leave . . .

John: I don't want you to leave. I asked you to come . . .

Carol: I didn't have to come here.

John: No. *(Pause.)* Thank you.

Carol: All right. *(Pause.)* *(She sits down.)*

John: Although I feel that it *profits,* it would *profit* you something, to . . .

Carol: . . . what I . . .

John: If you would hear me out, if you would hear me out.

Carol: I came here to, the court officers told me not to come.

John: . . . the "court" officers . . . ?

Carol: I was shocked that you asked.

John: . . . wait . . .

Carol: Yes. But I did *not* come here to hear what it "profits" me.

John: The "court" officers . . .

Carol: . . . no, no, perhaps I should leave . . . *(She gets up.)*

John: Wait.

Carol: No. I shouldn't have . . .

John: . . . wait. Wait. Wait a moment.

Carol: Yes? What is it you want? *(Pause.)* What is it you want?

John: I'd like you to stay.

Carol: You want me to stay.

John: Yes.

Carol: You do.

John: Yes. *(Pause.)* Yes. I would like to have you hear me out. If you would. *(Pause.)* Would you please? If you would do that I would be in your debt. *(Pause.)* *(She sits.)* Thank you. *(Pause.)*

Carol: What is it you wish to tell me?

John: All right. I cannot . . . *(Pause.)* I cannot help but feel you are owed an apology. *(Pause.)* *(Of papers in his hands.)* I have read. *(Pause.)* And reread these accusations.

Carol: What "accusations"?

John: The, the tenure comm . . . what other accusations . . . ?

Carol: The tenure committee . . . ?

John: Yes.

Carol: Excuse me, but those are not accusations. They have been *proved*. They are facts.

John: . . . I . . .

Carol: No. Those are not "accusations."

John: . . . those?

Carol: . . . the committee *(The phone starts to ring.)* the committee has . . .

John: . . . All right . . .

Carol: . . . those are not accusations. The Tenure Committee.

John: ALL RIGHT. ALL RIGHT. ALL RIGHT. *(He picks up the phone.)* Hello. Yes. No. I'm here. Tell Mister . . . No, I can't talk to him now . . . I'm sure he has, but I'm fff . . . I know . . . No, I have no time t . . . tell Mister . . . tell Mist . . . tell Jerry that I'm *fine* and that I'll call him right aw . . . *(Pause.)* My wife . . . Yes. I'm sure she has. Yes, thank you. Yes, I'll call her too. I cannot talk to you now. *(He hangs up.)* *(Pause.)* All right. It was good of you to come. Thank you. I have studied. I have spent some time studying the indictment.

Carol: You will have to explain that word to me.

John: An "indictment" . . .

Carol: Yes.

John: Is a "bill of particulars." A . . .

Carol: All right. Yes.

John: In which is alleged . . .

Carol: No. I cannot allow that. I cannot allow that. Nothing is alleged. Everything is proved . . .

John: Please, wait a sec . . .

Carol: I cannot *come* to allow . . .

John: If I may . . . If I may, from whatever you feel is "established," by . . .

Carol: The issue here is not what I "feel." It is not my "feelings," but the feelings of women. And men. Your superiors, who've been "polled," do you see? To whom *evidence* has been presented, who have *ruled*, do you see?

Who have weighed the testimony and the evidence, and have *ruled*, do you
see? That you are *negligent*. That you are *guilty*, that you are found *wanting*,
and in *error*; and are *not*, for the reasons so-told, to be given tenure. That
you are to be disciplined. For facts. For *facts*. Not "alleged," what is the
word? But *proved*. Do you see? *By your own actions*.

   That is what the tenure committee has said. That is what my lawyer
said. For what you did in class. For what you did *in this office*.

John: They're going to discharge me.

Carol: As full well they should. You don't understand? You're angry? What has
   led you to this place? Not your sex. Not your race. Not your class. YOUR
   OWN ACTIONS. And you're *angry*. You *ask* me here. What *do* you want?
   You want to "charm" me. You want to "convince" me. You want me to recant. I will *not* recant. Why should I . . . ? What I say is right. You tell me,
   you are going to tell me that you have a wife and child. You are going to say
   that you have a career and that you've worked for twenty years for this. Do
   you know what you've *worked* for? *Power*. For *power*. Do you understand?
   And you sit there, and you tell me *stories*. About your *house*, about all the
   private *schools*, and about *privilege*, and how you are entitled. To *buy*, to
   spend, to *mock*, to *summon*. All your stories. All your silly weak *guilt*, it's all
   about *privilege*; and you won't know it. Don't you see? You worked twenty
   years for the right to *insult* me. And you feel entitled to be *paid* for it. Your
   Home. Your Wife . . . Your sweet "deposit" on your house.

John: Don't you have feelings?

Carol: That's my point. You see? Don't you have feelings? Your final argument.
   What is it that has no feelings. *Animals*. I don't take your side, you question if I'm Human.

John: Don't you have feelings?

Carol: I have a responsibility. I . . .

John: . . . to . . . ?

Carol: To? This institution. To the *students*. To my *group*.

John: . . . your "group." . . .

Carol: Because I speak, yes, not for myself. But for the group; for those who
   suffer what I suffer. On behalf of whom, even if I, were, inclined, to what,
   forgive? Forget? What? Overlook your . . .

John: . . . my behavior?

Carol: . . . it would be wrong.

John: Even if you were inclined to "forgive" me.

Carol: It would be wrong.

John: And what would transpire.

Carol: Transpire?

John: Yes.

Carol: "Happen?"

John: Yes.

Carol: Then *say* it. For Christ's sake. Who the *hell* do you think that you are?
   You want a post. You want unlimited power. To do and to say what you
   want. As it pleases you — Testing, Questioning, Flirting . . .

John: I never . . .

Carol: Excuse me, one moment, will you?

(She reads from her notes.)

The twelfth: "Have a good day, dear."

The fifteenth: "Now, don't *you* look fetching . . ."

April seventeenth: "If you girls would come over here . . ." I saw you. I saw you, Professor. For two semesters sit there, stand there and exploit our, as you thought, "paternal prerogative," and what is that but rape; I swear to God. You asked me in here to explain something to me, as a child, that I did not understand. But I came to explain something to you. You Are Not God. You ask me why I came? I came here to instruct you.

(She produces his book.)

And your book? You think you're going to show me some "light"? You *"maverick."* Outside of tradition. No, no, *(She reads from the book's liner notes.)* "of that fine tradition of *inquiry.* Of Polite *skepticism"* . . . and you say you believe in free intellectual discourse. YOU BELIEVE IN NOTHING. YOU BELIEVE IN NOTHING AT ALL.

John: I believe in freedom of thought.

Carol: Isn't that fine. *Do* you?

John: Yes. I do.

Carol: Then why do you question, for one moment, the committee's decision refusing your tenure? Why do you question your suspension? You believe in what *you* call freedom of thought. Then, fine. *You* believe in freedom-of-thought *and* a home, and, *and* prerogatives for your kid, *and* tenure. And I'm going to tell you. You believe *not* in "freedom of thought," but in an elitist, in, in a protected hierarchy which rewards you. And for whom you are the clown. And you mock and exploit the system which pays your rent. You're wrong. I'm not wrong. You're wrong. You think that I'm full of hatred. I know what you think I am.

John: Do you?

Carol: You think I'm a, of course I do. You think I am a frightened, repressed, confused, I don't know, abandoned young thing of some doubtful sexuality, who wants, power and revenge. *(Pause.)* Don't you? *(Pause.)*

John: Yes. I do. *(Pause.)*

Carol: Isn't that better? And I feel that that is the first moment which you've treated me with respect. For you told me the truth. *(Pause.)* I did not come here, as you are assured, to gloat. Why would I want to gloat? I've profited nothing from your, your, as you say, your "misfortune." I came here, as you did me the honor to *ask* me here, I came here to *tell* you something. *(Pause.)*

That I think . . . that I think you've been wrong. That I think you've been terribly wrong. Do you hate me now? *(Pause.)*

John: Yes.

Carol: Why do you hate me? Because you think me wrong? No. Because I have, you think, *power* over you. Listen to me. Listen to me, Professor. *(Pause.)* It is the power that you hate. So deeply that, that any atmosphere of free discussion is impossible. It's not "unlikely." It's *impossible.* Isn't it?

John: Yes.

Carol: Isn't it . . . ?

John: Yes. I suppose.

Carol: Now. The thing which you find so cruel is the selfsame process of selection I, and my group, go through *every day of our lives.* In admittance to school. In our tests, in our class rankings. . . . Is it unfair? I can't tell you.

But, if it is fair. Or even if it is "unfortunate but necessary" for us, then, by God, so must it be for you. *(Pause.)* You write of your "responsibility to the young." Treat us with respect, and that will *show* you your responsibility. You write that education is just hazing. *(Pause.)* But we worked to get to this school. *(Pause.)* And some of us. *(Pause.)* Overcame prejudices. Economic, sexual, you cannot begin to imagine. And endured humiliations I *pray* that you and those you love never will encounter. *(Pause.)* To gain admittance here. To pursue that same dream of security *you* pursue. We, who, who are, at any moment, in danger of being deprived of it. By . . .

John: . . . by . . . ?

Carol: By the administration. By the teachers. By *you*. By, say, one low grade, that keeps us out of graduate school; by one, say, one capricious or inventive answer on our parts, which, perhaps, you don't find amusing. Now you *know*, do you see? What it is to be subject to that power. *(Pause.)*

John: I don't understand. *(Pause.)*

Carol: My charges are not trivial. You see that in the haste, I think, with which they were accepted. A *joke* you have told, with a sexist tinge. The language you use, a verbal or physical caress, yes, yes, I know, you say that it is meaningless. I understand. I differ from you. To lay a hand on someone's shoulder.

John: It was devoid of sexual content.

Carol: I say it was not. I SAY IT WAS NOT. Don't you begin to *see* . . . ? Don't you begin to understand? IT'S NOT FOR YOU TO SAY.

John: I take your point, and I see there is much good in what you refer to.

Carol: . . . do you think so . . . ?

John: . . . but, and this is not to say that I cannot change, in those things in which I am deficient . . . But, the . . .

Carol: Do you hold yourself harmless from the charge of sexual exploitativeness . . . ? *(Pause.)*

John: Well, I . . . I . . . I . . . You know I, as I said. I . . . think I am not too old to *learn*, and I *can* learn, I . . .

Carol: Do you hold yourself innocent of the charge of . . .

John: . . . wait, wait, wait . . . All right, let's go back to . . .

Carol: YOU FOOL. Who do you think I am? To come here and be taken in by a *smile*. You little yapping fool. You think I want "revenge." I don't want revenge. I WANT UNDERSTANDING.

John: . . . *do* you?

Carol: I do. *(Pause.)*

John: What's the use. It's over.

Carol: Is it? What is?

John: My job.

Carol: Oh. Your job. That's what you want to talk about. *(Pause.)* *(She starts to leave the room. She steps and turns back to him.)* All right. *(Pause.)* What if it were possible that my Group withdraws its complaint. *(Pause.)*

John: What?

Carol: That's right. *(Pause.)*

John: Why.

Carol: Well, let's say as an act of friendship.

John: An act of friendship.

Carol: Yes. *(Pause.)*

John: In exchange for what.

Carol: Yes. But I don't think, "exchange." Not "in exchange." For what do we derive from it? *(Pause.)*

John: "Derive."

Carol: Yes.

John (pause): Nothing. *(Pause.)*

Carol: That's right. We derive nothing. *(Pause.)* Do you see that?

John: Yes.

Carol: That is a little word, Professor. "Yes." "I see that." But you will.

John: And you might speak to the committee . . . ?

Carol: To the committee?

John: Yes.

Carol: Well. Of course. That's on your mind. We might.

John: "If" what?

Carol: "Given" what. Perhaps. I think that that is more friendly.

John: GIVEN WHAT?

Carol: And, believe me, I understand your rage. It is not that I don't feel it. But I do not see that it is deserved, so I do not resent it. . . . All right. I have a list.

John: . . . a list.

Carol: Here is a list of books, which we . . .

John: . . . a list of books . . . ?

Carol: That's right. Which we find questionable.

John: What?

Carol: Is this so bizarre . . . ?

John: I can't believe . . .

Carol: It's not necessary you believe it.

John: Academic freedom . . .

Carol: Someone chooses the books. If you can choose them, others can. What are you, "God"?

John: . . . no, no, the "dangerous." . . .

Carol: You have an agenda, we have an agenda. I am not interested in your feelings or your motivation, but your actions. If you would like me to speak to the Tenure Committee, here is my list. You are a Free Person, you decide. *(Pause.)*

John: Give me the list.

(She does so. He reads.)

Carol: I think you'll find . . .

John: I'm capable of reading it. Thank you.

Carol: We have a number of *texts* we need re . . .

John: I see that.

Carol: We're amenable to . . .

John: Aha. Well, let me look over the . . . *(He reads.)*

Carol: I think that . . .

John: LOOK. I'm reading your demands. All right?! *(He reads.) (Pause.)* You want to ban my book?

Carol: We do not . . .

John (of list): It says here . . .

Carol: . . . We want it removed from inclusion as a representative example of the university.

John: Get out of here.

Carol: If you put aside the issues of personalities.

John: Get the fuck out of my office.

Carol: No, I think I would reconsider.

John: . . . you think you can.

Carol: We can and we *will.* Do you want our support? That is the only quest . . .

John: . . . to ban my *book* . . . ?

Carol: . . . that is correct . . .

John: . . . this . . . this is a *university* . . . we . . .

Carol: . . . and we have a statement . . . which we need you to . . . *(She hands him a sheet of paper.)*

John: No, no. It's out of the question. I'm sorry. I don't know what I was thinking of. I want to tell you something. I'm a teacher. I am a teacher. Eh? It's my *name* on the door, and *I* teach the class, and that's what I do. I've got a book with my name on it. And my son will *see* that *book* someday. And I have a respon . . . No, I'm sorry I have a *responsibility* . . . to *myself,* to my *son,* to my *profession.* . . . I haven't been *home* for two days, do you know that? Thinking this out.

Carol: . . . you haven't?

John: I've been, no. If it's of interest to you. I've been in a *hotel. Thinking. (The phone starts ringing.) Thinking* . . .

Carol: . . . you haven't been home?

John: . . . *thinking,* do you see.

Carol: Oh.

John: And, and, I owe you a debt, I see that now. *(Pause.)* You're *dangerous,* you're *wrong* and it's my *job* . . . to say no to you. That's my job. You are absolutely right. You want to ban my book? Go to *hell,* and they can do whatever they want to me.

Carol: . . . you haven't been home in two days . . .

John: I think I told you that.

Carol: . . . you'd better get that phone. *(Pause.)* I think that you should pick up the phone. *(Pause.)*

(John picks up the phone.)

John (on phone): Yes. *(Pause.)* Yes. Wh . . . I. I. I had to be away. All ri . . . did they wor . . . did they worry ab . . . No. I'm all right, now, Jerry. I'm f . . . I got a little turned *around,* but I'm *sitting* here and . . . I've got it figured out. I'm fine. I'm fine don't worry about me. I got a little bit mixed up. But I am not sure that it's not a blessing. It cost me my job? Fine. Then the job was not worth having. Tell Grace that I'm coming home and everything is fff . . . *(Pause.)* What? *(Pause.)* What? *(Pause.)* What do you *mean?* WHAT? Jerry . . . Jerry. They . . . Who, who, what can they do . . . ? *(Pause.)* NO. *(Pause.)* NO. They can't do th . . . What do you mean? *(Pause.)* But how . . . *(Pause.)* She's, she's, she's *here* with me. To . . . Jerry. I don't underst . . . *(Pause.) (He hangs up.) (To Carol.)* What does this mean?

Carol: I thought you knew.

John: What. *(Pause.)* What does it mean. *(Pause.)*

Carol: You tried to rape me. *(Pause.)* According to the law. *(Pause.)*

John: ... what ... ?

Carol: You tried to rape me. I was leaving this office, you "pressed" yourself into me. You "pressed" your body into me.

John: ... I ...

Carol: My Group has told your lawyer that we may pursue criminal charges.

John: ... no ...

Carol: ... under the statute. I am told. It was battery.

John: ... no ...

Carol: Yes. And attempted rape. That's right. *(Pause.)*

John: I think that you should go.

Carol: Of course. I thought you knew.

John: I have to talk to my lawyer.

Carol: Yes. Perhaps you should.

> *(The phone rings again.) (Pause.)*

John (picks up phone, into phone): Hello? I ... Hello...? I ... Yes, he just called. No ... I. I can't talk to you now, Baby. *(To Carol.)* Get out.

Carol: ... your wife ... ?

John: ... who it is is no concern of yours. Get out. *(To phone.)* No, no, it's going to be all right. I. I can't talk now, Baby. *(To Carol.)* Get out of here.

Carol: I'm going.

John: Good.

Carol (exiting): ... and don't call your wife "baby."

John: What?

Carol: Don't call your wife baby. You heard what I said.

> *(Carol starts to leave the room. John grabs her and begins to beat her.)*

John: You vicious little bitch. You think you can come in here with your political correctness and destroy my life?

> *(He knocks her to the floor.)*

After how I treated you ... ? You should be ... *Rape you* ... ? Are you kidding me ... ?

> *(He picks up a chair, raises it above his head, and advances on her.)*

I wouldn't touch you with a ten-foot pole. You little *cunt* ...

> *(She cowers on the floor below him. Pause. He looks down at her. He lowers the chair. He moves to his desk, and arranges the papers on it. Pause. He looks over at her.)*

... well ...

> *(Pause. She looks at him.)*

Carol: Yes. That's right.

> *(She looks away from him, and lowers her head. To herself:)* ... yes. That's right.

CONNECTIONS TO OTHER SELECTIONS

1. Discuss the importance of the political atmospheres implicit in *Oleanna* and in Václav Havel's *Unveiling* (p. 1941). How does an awareness of the political background in each play help you to understand the play's respective conflicts?

2. Consider the endings of *Oleanna* and Diana Son's *Stop Kiss* (p. 1982), and explain why you do or do not find the endings appropriate for the plot and tone of each play.

3. Imagine that you are the student whose paper is evaluated in Mark Halliday's poem "Graded Paper" (p. 1110), and write a response to the instructor's evaluation from the point of view of Carol in *Oleanna*.

Death of a Salesman

Arthur Miller was born in New York City to middle-class Jewish parents. His mother was a teacher and his father a clothing manufacturer. In 1938 he graduated from the University of Michigan, where he had begun writing plays. Six years later his first Broadway play, *The Man Who Had All the Luck,* closed after only a few performances, but *All My Sons* (1947) earned the admiration of both critics and audiences. This drama of family life launched his career, and his next play was even more successful. *Death of a Salesman* (1949) won a Pulitzer Prize and established his international reputation so that Miller, along with Tennessee Williams, became one of the most successful American playwrights of the 1940s and 1950s. During this period, his plays included an adaptation of Henrik Ibsen's *Enemy of the People* (1951), *The Crucible* (1953), and *A View from the Bridge* (1955). Among his later works are *The Misfits* (1961, a screenplay), *After the Fall* (1964), *Incident at Vichy* (1964), *The Price* (1968), *The Creation of the World and Other Business* (1972), *The Archbishop's Ceiling* (1976), *The American Clock* (1980), *Time Bends* (1987, essays), *The Ride Down Mt. Morgan* (1991), and *Broken Glass* (1994).

In *Death of a Salesman* Miller's concerns and techniques are similar to those of social realism. His characters' dialogue sounds much like ordinary speech and deals with recognizable family problems ranging from feelings about one another to personal aspirations. Like Ibsen and Chekhov, Miller places his characters in a social context so that their behavior within the family suggests larger implications: the death of this salesman raises issues concerning the significance and value of the American dream of success.

Although such qualities resemble some of the techniques and concerns of realistic drama, Miller also uses other techniques to express Willy Loman's thoughts. In a sense, the play allows the audience to observe what goes on inside the protagonist's head. (At one point Miller was going to title the play *The Inside of His Head.*) When Willy thinks of the past, we see those events reenacted on stage in the midst of present events. This reenactment is achieved through the use of symbolic nonrealistic sets that appear or disappear as the stage lighting changes to reveal Willy's state of mind.

Willy Loman is in many ways an ordinary human being—indeed, painfully so. He is neither brilliant nor heroic, and his life is made up of unfulfilled dreams and self-deceptions. Yet Miller conceived of him as a tragic figure because, as he wrote in "Tragedy and the Common Man" (see p. 1889), "the common man is as apt a subject for tragedy . . . as kings." Willy's circumstances are radically different from those of Oedipus or Hamlet, but Miller manages to create a character whose human dignity evokes tragic feelings for many readers and viewers.

Web   *Research Arthur Miller with LitLinks at*
http://www.bedfordstmartins.com/meyer/bedintrolit

ARTHUR MILLER (B. 1915)

Death of a Salesman   *1949*

Certain private conversations in two acts and a requiem

CAST

Willy Loman	Uncle Ben
Linda	Howard Wagner
Biff	Jenny
Happy	Stanley
Bernard	Miss Forsythe
The Woman	Letta
Charley	

SCENE: *The action takes place in Willy Loman's house and yard and in various places he visits in the New York and Boston of today.*

Throughout the play, in the stage directions, left and right mean stage left and stage right.

ACT I

A melody is heard, played upon a flute. It is small and fine, telling of grass and trees and the horizon. The curtain rises.

Before us is the Salesman's house. We are aware of towering, angular shapes behind it, surrounding it on all sides. Only the blue light of the sky falls upon the house and forestage; the surrounding area shows an angry glow of orange. As more light appears, we see a solid vault of apartment houses around the small, fragile-seeming home. An air of the dream clings to the place, a dream rising out of reality. The kitchen at center seems actual enough, for there is a kitchen table with three chairs, and a refrigerator. But no other fixtures are seen. At the back of the kitchen there is a draped entrance, which leads to the living-room. To the right of the kitchen, on a level raised two feet, is a bedroom furnished only with a brass bedstead and a straight chair. On a shelf over the bed a silver athletic trophy stands. A window opens onto the apartment house at the side.

Behind the kitchen, on a level raised six and a half feet, is the boys' bedroom, at present barely visible. Two beds are dimly seen, and at the back of the room a

*dormer window. (This bedroom is above the unseen living-room.) At the left a
stairway curves up to it from the kitchen.*

    *The entire setting is wholly or, in some places, partially transparent. The roof-
line of the house is one-dimensional; under and over it we see the apartment buildings. Before the house lies an apron, curving beyond the forestage into the orchestra.
This forward area serves as the back yard as well as the locale of all Willy's imaginings and of his city scenes. Whenever the action is in the present the actors observe
the imaginary wall-lines, entering the house only through its door at the left. But in
the scenes of the past these boundaries are broken, and characters enter or leave a
room by stepping "through" a wall onto the forestage.*

    *From the right, Willy Loman, the Salesman, enters, carrying two large sample
cases. The flute plays on. He hears but is not aware of it. He is past sixty years of
age, dressed quietly. Even as he crosses the stage to the doorway of the house, his
exhaustion is apparent. He unlocks the door, comes into the kitchen, and thankfully
lets his burden down, feeling the soreness of his palms. A word-sigh escapes his lips—
it might be "Oh, boy, oh, boy." He closes the door, then carries his cases out into the
living-room, through the draped kitchen doorway.*

    *Linda, his wife, has stirred in her bed at the right. She gets out and puts on a
robe, listening. Most often jovial, she has developed an iron repression of her exceptions to Willy's behavior—she more than loves him, she admires him, as though his
mercurial nature, his temper, his massive dreams and little cruelties, served her
only as sharp reminders of the turbulent longings within him, longings which she
shares but lacks the temperament to utter and follow to their end.*

Linda (hearing Willy outside the bedroom, calls with some trepidation): Willy!
Willy: It's all right. I came back.
Linda: Why? What happened? *(Slight pause.)* Did something happen, Willy?
Willy: No, nothing happened.
Linda: You didn't smash the car, did you?
Willy (with casual irritation): I said nothing happened. Didn't you hear me?
Linda: Don't you feel well?
Willy: I'm tired to the death. *(The flute has faded away. He sits on the bed beside her,
    a little numb.)* I couldn't make it. I just couldn't make it, Linda.
Linda (very carefully, delicately): Where were you all day? You look terrible.
Willy: I got as far as a little above Yonkers. I stopped for a cup of coffee. Maybe
    it was the coffee.
Linda: What?
Willy (after a pause): I suddenly couldn't drive any more. The car kept going off
    onto the shoulder, y'know?
Linda (helpfully): Oh. Maybe it was the steering again. I don't think Angelo
    knows the Studebaker.
Willy: No, it's me, it's me. Suddenly I realize I'm goin' sixty miles an hour and I
    don't remember the last five minutes. I'm—I can't seem to—keep my
    mind to it.
Linda: Maybe it's your glasses. You never went for your new glasses.
Willy: No, I see everything. I came back ten miles an hour. It took me nearly
    four hours from Yonkers.
Linda (resigned): Well, you'll just have to take a rest, Willy, you can't continue
    this way.
Willy: I just got back from Florida.

Linda: But you didn't rest your mind. Your mind is overactive, and the mind is what counts, dear.

Willy: I'll start out in the morning. Maybe I'll feel better in the morning. *(She is taking off his shoes.)* These goddam arch supports are killing me.

Linda: Take an aspirin. Should I get you an aspirin? It'll soothe you.

Willy (with wonder): I was driving along, you understand? And I was fine. I was even observing the scenery. You can imagine, me looking at scenery, on the road every week of my life. But it's so beautiful up there, Linda, the trees are so thick, and the sun is warm. I opened the windshield and just let the warm air bathe over me. And then all of a sudden I'm goin' off the road! I'm tellin' ya, I absolutely forgot I was driving. If I'd've gone the other way over the white line I might've killed somebody. So I went on again — and five minutes later I'm dreamin' again, and I nearly — *(He presses two fingers against his eyes.)* I have such thoughts, I have such strange thoughts.

Linda: Willy, dear. Talk to them again. There's no reason why you can't work in New York.

Willy: They don't need me in New York. I'm the New England man. I'm vital in New England.

Linda: But you're sixty years old. They can't expect you to keep traveling every week.

Willy: I'll have to send a wire to Portland. I'm supposed to see Brown and Morrison tomorrow morning at ten o'clock to show the line. Goddammit, I could sell them! *(He starts putting on his jacket.)*

Linda (taking the jacket from him): Why don't you go down to the place tomorrow and tell Howard you've simply got to work in New York? You're too accommodating, dear.

Willy: If old man Wagner was alive I'd a been in charge of New York now! That man was a prince, he was a masterful man. But that boy of his, that Howard, he don't appreciate. When I went north the first time, the Wagner Company didn't know where New England was!

Linda: Why don't you tell those things to Howard, dear?

Willy (encouraged): I will, I definitely will. Is there any cheese?

Linda: I'll make you a sandwich.

Willy: No, go to sleep. I'll take some milk. I'll be up right away. The boys in?

Linda: They're sleeping. Happy took Biff on a date tonight.

Willy (interested): That so?

Linda: It was so nice to see them shaving together, one behind the other, in the bathroom. And going out together. You notice? The whole house smells of shaving lotion.

Willy: Figure it out. Work a lifetime to pay off a house. You finally own it, and there's nobody to live in it.

Linda: Well, dear, life is a casting off. It's always that way.

Willy: No, no, some people — some people accomplish something. Did Biff say anything after I went this morning?

Linda: You shouldn't have criticized him, Willy, especially after he just got off the train. You mustn't lose your temper with him.

Willy: When the hell did I lose my temper? I simply asked him if he was making any money. Is that a criticism?

Linda: But, dear, how could he make any money?

Willy (worried and angered): There's such an undercurrent in him. He became a moody man. Did he apologize when I left this morning?

Linda: He was crestfallen, Willy. You know how he admires you. I think if he finds himself, then you'll both be happier and not fight any more.

Willy: How can he find himself on a farm? Is that a life? A farmhand? In the beginning, when he was young, I thought, well, a young man, it's good for him to tramp around, take a lot of different jobs. But it's more than ten years now and he has yet to make thirty-five dollars a week!

Linda: He's finding himself, Willy.

Willy: Not finding yourself at the age of thirty-four is a disgrace!

Linda: Shh!

Willy: The trouble is he's lazy, goddammit!

Linda: Willy, please!

Willy: Biff is a lazy bum!

Linda: They're sleeping. Get something to eat. Go on down.

Willy: Why did he come home? I would like to know what brought him home.

Linda: I don't know. I think he's still lost, Willy. I think he's very lost.

Willy: Biff Loman is lost. In the greatest country in the world a young man with such — personal attractiveness, gets lost. And such a hard worker. There's one thing about Biff — he's not lazy.

Linda: Never.

Willy (with pity and resolve): I'll see him in the morning; I'll have a nice talk with him. I'll get him a job selling. He could be big in no time. My God! Remember how they used to follow him around in high school? When he smiled at one of them their faces lit up. When he walked down the street . . . *(He loses himself in reminiscences.)*

Linda (trying to bring him out of it): Willy, dear, I got a new kind of American-type cheese today. It's whipped.

Willy: Why do you get American when I like Swiss?

Linda: I just thought you'd like a change —

Willy: I don't want a change! I want Swiss cheese. Why am I always being contradicted?

Linda (with a covering laugh): I thought it would be a surprise.

Willy: Why don't you open a window in here, for God's sake?

Linda (with infinite patience): They're all open, dear.

Willy: The way they boxed us in here. Bricks and windows, windows and bricks.

Linda: We should've bought the land next door.

Willy: The street is lined with cars. There's not a breath of fresh air in the neighborhood. The grass don't grow any more, you can't raise a carrot in the back yard. They should've had a law against apartment houses. Remember those two beautiful elm trees out there? When I and Biff hung the swing between them?

Linda: Yeah, like being a million miles from the city.

Willy: They should've arrested the builder for cutting those down. They massacred the neighborhood. *(Lost.)* More and more I think of those days, Linda. This time of year it was lilac and wisteria. And then the peonies would come out, and the daffodils. What fragrance in this room!

Linda: Well, after all, people had to move somewhere.

Willy: No, there's more people now.

Linda: I don't think there's more people. I think —

Willy: There's more people! That's what's ruining this country! Population is getting out of control. The competition is maddening! Smell the stink from that apartment house! And another one on the other side . . . How can they whip cheese?

On Willy's last line, Biff and Happy raise themselves up in their beds, listening.

Linda: Go down, try it. And be quiet.

Willy (turning to Linda, guiltily): You're not worried about me, are you, sweetheart?

Biff: What's the matter?

Happy: Listen!

Linda: You've got too much on the ball to worry about.

Willy: You're my foundation and my support, Linda.

Linda: Just try to relax, dear. You make mountains out of molehills.

Willy: I won't fight with him any more. If he wants to go back to Texas, let him go.

Linda: He'll find his way.

Willy: Sure. Certain men just don't get started till later in life. Like Thomas Edison, I think. Or B. F. Goodrich. One of them was deaf. *(He starts for the bedroom doorway.)* I'll put my money on Biff.

Linda: And Willy — if it's warm Sunday we'll drive in the country. And we'll open the windshield, and take lunch.

Willy: No, the windshields don't open on the new cars.

Linda: But you opened it today.

Willy: Me? I didn't. *(He stops.)* Now isn't that peculiar! Isn't that a remarkable — *(He breaks off in amazement and fright as the flute is heard distantly.)*

Linda: What, darling?

Willy: That is the most remarkable thing.

Linda: What, dear?

Willy: I was thinking of the Chevy. *(Slight pause.)* Nineteen twenty-eight . . . when I had that red Chevy — *(Breaks off.)* That funny? I coulda sworn I was driving that Chevy today.

Linda: Well, that's nothing. Something must've reminded you.

Willy: Remarkable. Ts. Remember those days? The way Biff used to simonize that car? The dealer refused to believe there was eighty thousand miles on it. *(He shakes his head.)* Heh! *(To Linda.)* Close your eyes, I'll be right up. *(He walks out of the bedroom.)*

Happy (to Biff): Jesus, maybe he smashed up the car again!

Linda (calling after Willy): Be careful on the stairs, dear! The cheese is on the middle shelf! *(She turns, goes over to the bed, takes his jacket, and goes out of the bedroom.)*

Light has risen on the boys' room. Unseen, Willy is heard talking to himself, "Eighty thousand miles," and a little laugh. Biff gets out of bed, comes downstage a bit, and stands attentively. Biff is two years older than his brother Happy, well built, but in these days bears a worn air and seems less self-assured. He has succeeded less, and his dreams are stronger and less acceptable than Happy's. Happy is tall, powerfully made. Sexuality is like a visible color on him, or a scent that many women have discovered. He, like his brother, is lost, but in a different way, for he has never al-

lowed himself to turn his face toward defeat and is thus more confused and hard-skinned, although seemingly more content.

Happy (getting out of bed): He's going to get his license taken away if he keeps that up. I'm getting nervous about him, y'know, Biff?

Biff: His eyes are going.

Happy: No, I've driven with him. He sees all right. He just doesn't keep his mind on it. I drove into the city with him last week. He stops at a green light and then it turns red and he goes. *(He laughs.)*

Biff: Maybe he's color-blind.

Happy: Pop? Why he's got the finest eye for color in the business. You know that.

Biff (sitting down on his bed): I'm going to sleep.

Happy: You're not still sour on Dad, are you, Biff?

Biff: He's all right, I guess.

Willy (underneath them, in the living-room): Yes, sir, eighty thousand miles — eighty-two thousand!

Biff: You smoking?

Happy (holding out a pack of cigarettes): Want one?

Biff (taking a cigarette): I can never sleep when I smell it.

Willy: What a simonizing job, heh!

Happy (with deep sentiment): Funny, Biff, y'know? Us sleeping in here again? The old beds. *(He pats his bed affectionately.)* All the talk that went across those two beds, huh? Our whole lives.

Biff: Yeah. Lotta dreams and plans.

Happy (with a deep and masculine laugh): About five hundred women would like to know what was said in this room.

They share a soft laugh.

Biff: Remember that big Betsy something — what the hell was her name — over on Bushwick Avenue?

Happy (combing his hair): With the collie dog!

Biff: That's the one. I got you in there, remember?

Happy: Yeah, that was my first time — I think. Boy, there was a pig! *(They laugh, almost crudely.)* You taught me everything I know about women. Don't forget that.

Biff: I bet you forgot how bashful you used to be. Especially with girls.

Happy: Oh, I still am, Biff.

Biff: Oh, go on.

Happy: I just control it, that's all. I think I got less bashful and you got more so. What happened, Biff? Where's the old humor, the old confidence? *(He shakes Biff's knee. Biff gets up and moves restlessly about the room.)* What's the matter?

Biff: Why does Dad mock me all the time?

Happy: He's not mocking you, he —

Biff: Everything I say there's a twist of mockery on his face. I can't get near him.

Happy: He just wants you to make good, that's all. I wanted to talk to you about Dad for a long time, Biff. Something's — happening to him. He — talks to himself.

Biff: I noticed that this morning. But he always mumbled.

Happy: But not so noticeable. It got so embarrassing I sent him to Florida. And you know something? Most of the time he's talking to you.

Biff: What's he say about me?

Happy: I can't make it out.

Biff: What's he say about me?

Happy: I think the fact that you're not settled, that you're still kind of up in the air . . .

Biff: There's one or two other things depressing him, Happy.

Happy: What do you mean?

Biff: Never mind. Just don't lay it all to me.

Happy: But I think if you just got started—I mean—is there any future for you out there?

Biff: I tell ya, Hap, I don't know what the future is. I don't know—what I'm supposed to want.

Happy: What do you mean?

Biff: Well, I spent six or seven years after high school trying to work myself up. Shipping clerk, salesman, business of one kind or another. And it's a measly manner of existence. To get on that subway on the hot mornings in summer. To devote your whole life to keeping stock, or making phone calls, or selling or buying. To suffer fifty weeks of the year for the sake of a two-week vacation, when all you really desire is to be outdoors, with your shirt off. And always to have to get ahead of the next fella. And still— that's how you build a future.

Happy: Well, you really enjoy it on a farm? Are you content out there?

Biff (with rising agitation): Hap, I've had twenty or thirty different kinds of jobs since I left home before the war, and it always turns out the same. I just realized it lately. In Nebraska when I herded cattle, and the Dakotas, and Arizona, and now in Texas. It's why I came home now, I guess, because I realized it. This farm I work on, it's spring there now, see? And they've got about fifteen new colts. There's nothing more inspiring or—beautiful than the sight of a mare and a new colt. And it's cool there now, see? Texas is cool now, and it's spring. And whenever spring comes to where I am, I suddenly get the feeling, my God, I'm not gettin' anywhere! What the hell am I doing, playing around with horses, twenty-eight dollars a week! I'm thirty-four years old, I oughta be makin' my future. That's when I come running home. And now, I get here, and I don't know what to do with myself. *(After a pause.)* I've always made a point of not wasting my life, and everytime I come back here I know that all I've done is to waste my life.

Happy: You're a poet, you know that, Biff? You're a—you're an idealist!

Biff: No, I'm mixed up very bad. Maybe I oughta get married. Maybe I oughta get stuck into something. Maybe that's my trouble. I'm like a boy. I'm not married. I'm not in business, I just—I'm like a boy. Are you content, Hap? You're a success, aren't you? Are you content?

Happy: Hell, no!

Biff: Why? You're making money, aren't you?

Happy (moving about with energy, expressiveness): All I can do now is wait for the merchandise manager to die. And suppose I get to be merchandise manager? He's a good friend of mine, and he just built a terrific estate on Long

Island. And he lived there about two months and sold it, and now he's building another one. He can't enjoy it once it's finished. And I know that's just what I would do. I don't know what the hell I'm workin' for. Sometimes I sit in my apartment — all alone. And I think of the rent I'm paying. And it's crazy. But then, it's what I always wanted. My own apartment, a car, and plenty of women. And still, goddammit, I'm lonely.

Biff (with enthusiasm): Listen, why don't you come out West with me?

Happy: You and I, heh?

Biff: Sure, maybe we could buy a ranch. Raise cattle, use our muscles. Men built like we are should be working out in the open.

Happy (avidly): The Loman Brothers, heh?

Biff (with vast affection): Sure, we'd be known all over the counties!

Happy (enthralled): That's what I dream about, Biff. Sometimes I want to just rip my clothes off in the middle of the store and outbox that goddam merchandise manager. I mean I can outbox, outrun, and outlift anybody in that store, and I have to take orders from those common, petty sons-of-bitches till I can't stand it any more.

Biff: I'm tellin' you, kid, if you were with me I'd be happy out there.

Happy (enthused): See, Biff, everybody around me is so false that I'm constantly lowering my ideals . . .

Biff: Baby, together we'd stand up for one another, we'd have someone to trust.

Happy: If I were around you —

Biff: Hap, the trouble is we weren't brought up to grub for money. I don't know how to do it.

Happy: Neither can I!

Biff: Then let's go!

Happy: The only thing is — what can you make out there?

Biff: But look at your friend. Builds an estate and then hasn't the peace of mind to live in it.

Happy: Yeah, but when he walks into the store the waves part in front of him. That's fifty-two thousand dollars a year coming through the revolving door, and I got more in my pinky finger than he's got in his head.

Biff: Yeah, but you just said —

Happy: I gotta show some of those pompous, self-important executives over there that Hap Loman can make the grade. I want to walk into the store the way he walks in. Then I'll go with you, Biff. We'll be together yet, I swear. But take those two we had tonight. Now weren't they gorgeous creatures?

Biff: Yeah, yeah, most gorgeous I've had in years.

Happy: I get that any time I want, Biff. Whenever I feel disgusted. The trouble is, it gets like bowling or something. I just keep knockin' them over and it doesn't mean anything. You still run around a lot?

Biff: Naa. I'd like to find a girl — steady, somebody with substance.

Happy: That's what I long for.

Biff: Go on! You'd never come home.

Happy: I would! Somebody with character, with resistance! Like Mom, y'know? You're gonna call me a bastard when I tell you this. That girl Charlotte I was with tonight is engaged to be married in five weeks. *(He tries on his new hat.)*

Biff: No kiddin'!

Happy: Sure, the guy's in line for the vice-presidency of the store. I don't know what gets into me, maybe I just have an overdeveloped sense of competition or something, but I went and ruined her, and furthermore I can't get rid of her. And he's the third executive I've done that to. Isn't that a crummy characteristic? And to top it all, I go to their weddings! (*Indignantly, but laughing.*) Like I'm not supposed to take bribes. Manufacturers offer me a hundred-dollar bill now and then to throw an order their way. You know how honest I am, but it's like this girl, see. I hate myself for it. Because I don't want the girl, and, still, I take it and — I love it!

Biff: Let's go to sleep.

Happy: I guess we didn't settle anything, heh?

Biff: I just got one idea that I think I'm going to try.

Happy: What's that?

Biff: Remember Bill Oliver?

Happy: Sure, Oliver is very big now. You want to work for him again?

Biff: No, but when I quit he said something to me. He put his arm on my shoulder, and he said, "Biff, if you ever need anything, come to me."

Happy: I remember that. That sounds good.

Biff: I think I'll go to see him. If I could get ten thousand or even seven or eight thousand dollars I could buy a beautiful ranch.

Happy: I bet he'd back you. 'Cause he thought highly of you, Biff. I mean, they all do. You're well liked, Biff. That's why I say to come back here, and we both have the apartment. And I'm tellin' you, Biff, any babe you want . . .

Biff: No, with a ranch I could do the work I like and still be something. I just wonder though. I wonder if Oliver still thinks I stole that carton of basketballs.

Happy: Oh, he probably forgot that long ago. It's almost ten years. You're too sensitive. Anyway, he didn't really fire you.

Biff: Well, I think he was going to. I think that's why I quit. I was never sure whether he knew or not. I know he thought the world of me, though. I was the only one he'd let lock up the place.

Willy (below): You gonna wash the engine, Biff?

Happy: Shh!

Biff looks at Happy, who is gazing down, listening. Willy is mumbling in the parlor.

Happy: You hear that?

They listen. Willy laughs warmly.

Biff (growing angry): Doesn't he know Mom can hear that?

Willy: Don't get your sweater dirty, Biff!

A look of pain crosses Biff's face.

Happy: Isn't that terrible? Don't leave again, will you? You'll find a job here. You gotta stick around. I don't know what to do about him, it's getting embarrassing.

Willy: What a simonizing job!

Biff: Mom's hearing that!

Willy: No kiddin', Biff, you got a date? Wonderful!

Happy: Go on to sleep. But talk to him in the morning, will you?

Biff (reluctantly getting into bed): With her in the house. Brother!

Happy (getting into bed): I wish you'd have a good talk with him.

The light on their room begins to fade.

Biff (to himself in bed): That selfish, stupid . . .
Happy: Sh . . . Sleep, Biff.

Their light is out. Well before they have finished speaking, Willy's form is dimly seen below in the darkened kitchen. He opens the refrigerator, searches in there, and takes out a bottle of milk. The apartment houses are fading out, and the entire house and surroundings become covered with leaves. Music insinuates itself as the leaves appear.

Willy: Just wanna be careful with those girls, Biff, that's all. Don't make any promises. No promises of any kind. Because a girl, y'know, they always believe what you tell 'em, and you're very young, Biff, you're too young to be talking seriously to girls.

Light rises on the kitchen. Willy, talking, shuts the refrigerator door and comes downstage to the kitchen table. He pours milk into a glass. He is totally immersed in himself, smiling faintly.

Willy: Too young entirely, Biff. You want to watch your schooling first. Then when you're all set, there'll be plenty of girls for a boy like you. *(He smiles broadly at a kitchen chair.)* That so? The girls pay for you? *(He laughs.)* Boy, you must really be makin' a hit.

Willy is gradually addressing—physically—a point offstage, speaking through the wall of the kitchen, and his voice has been rising in volume to that of a normal conversation.

Willy: I been wondering why you polish the car so careful. Ha! Don't leave the hubcaps, boys. Get the chamois to the hubcaps. Happy, use newspaper on the windows, it's the easiest thing. Show him how to do it, Biff! You see, Happy? Pad it up, use it like a pad. That's it, that's it, good work. You're doin' all right, Hap. *(He pauses, then nods in approbation for a few seconds, then looks upward.)* Biff, first thing we gotta do when we get time is clip that big branch over the house. Afraid it's gonna fall in a storm and hit the roof. Tell you what. We get a rope and sling her around, and then we climb up there with a couple of saws and take her down. Soon as you finish the car, boys, I wanna see ya. I got a surprise for you, boys.
Biff (offstage): Whatta ya got, Dad?
Willy: No, you finish first. Never leave a job till you're finished—remember that. *(Looking toward the "big trees.")* Biff, up in Albany I saw a beautiful hammock. I think I'll buy it next trip, and we'll hang it right between those two elms. Wouldn't that be something? Just swingin' there under those branches. Boy, that would be . . .

Young Biff and Young Happy appear from the direction Willy was addressing. Happy carries rags and a pail of water. Biff, wearing a sweater with a block "S," carries a football.

Biff (pointing in the direction of the car offstage): How's that, Pop, professional?
Willy: Terrific. Terrific job, boys. Good work, Biff.
Happy: Where's the surprise, Pop?
Willy: In the back seat of the car.
Happy: Boy! *(He runs off.)*

Biff: What is it, Dad? Tell me, what'd you buy?

Willy (laughing, cuffs him): Never mind, something I want you to have.

Biff (turns and starts off): What is it, Hap?

Happy (offstage): It's a punching bag!

Biff: Oh, Pop!

Willy: It's got Gene Tunney's signature on it!

 Happy runs onstage with a punching bag.

Biff: Gee, how'd you know we wanted a punching bag?

Willy: Well, it's the finest thing for the timing.

Happy (lies down on his back and pedals with his feet): I'm losing weight, you notice, Pop?

Willy (to Happy): Jumping rope is good too.

Biff: Did you see the new football I got?

Willy (examining the ball): Where'd you get a new ball?

Biff: The coach told me to practice my passing.

Willy: That so? And he gave you the ball, heh?

Biff: Well, I borrowed it from the locker room. (*He laughs confidentially.*)

Willy (laughing with him at the theft): I want you to return that.

Happy: I told you he wouldn't like it!

Biff (angrily): Well, I'm bringing it back!

Willy (stopping the incipient argument, to Happy): Sure, he's gotta practice with a regulation ball, doesn't he? (*To Biff.*) Coach'll probably congratulate you on your initiative!

Biff: Oh, he keeps congratulating my initiative all the time, Pop.

Willy: That's because he likes you. If somebody else took that ball there'd be an uproar. So what's the report, boys, what's the report?

Biff: Where'd you go this time, Dad? Gee we were lonesome for you.

Willy (pleased, puts an arm around each boy and they come down to the apron): Lonesome, heh?

Biff: Missed you every minute.

Willy: Don't say? Tell you a secret, boys. Don't breathe it to a soul. Someday I'll have my own business, and I'll never have to leave home any more.

Happy: Like Uncle Charley, heh?

Willy: Bigger than Uncle Charley! Because Charley is not — liked. He's liked, but he's not — well liked.

Biff: Where'd you go this time, Dad?

Willy: Well, I got on the road, and I went north to Providence. Met the Mayor.

Biff: The Mayor of Providence!

Willy: He was sitting in the hotel lobby.

Biff: What'd he say?

Willy: He said, "Morning!" And I said, "You got a fine city here, Mayor." And then he had coffee with me. And then I went to Waterbury. Waterbury is a fine city. Big clock city, the famous Waterbury clock. Sold a nice bill there. And then Boston — Boston is the cradle of the Revolution. A fine city. And a couple of other towns in Mass., and on to Portland and Bangor and straight home!

Biff: Gee, I'd love to go with you sometime, Dad.

Willy: Soon as summer comes.

Happy: Promise?

Willy: You and Hap and I, and I'll show you all the towns. America is full of beautiful towns and fine, upstanding people. And they know me, boys, they know me up and down New England. The finest people. And when I bring you fellas up, there'll be open sesame for all of us, 'cause one thing, boys: I have friends. I can park my car in any street in New England, and the cops protect it like their own. This summer, heh?

Biff and Happy (together): Yeah! You bet!

Willy: We'll take our bathing suits.

Happy: We'll carry your bags, Pop!

Willy: Oh, won't that be something! Me comin' into the Boston stores with you boys carryin' my bags. What a sensation!

> *Biff is prancing around, practicing passing the ball.*

Willy: You nervous, Biff, about the game?

Biff: Not if you're gonna be there.

Willy: What do they say about you in school, now that they made you captain?

Happy: There's a crowd of girls behind him everytime the classes change.

Biff (taking Willy's hand): This Saturday, Pop, this Saturday—just for you, I'm going to break through for a touchdown.

Happy: You're supposed to pass.

Biff: I'm takin' one play for Pop. You watch me, Pop, and when I take off my helmet, that means I'm breakin' out. Then you watch me crash through that line!

Willy (kisses Biff): Oh, wait'll I tell this in Boston!

> *Bernard enters in knickers. He is younger than Biff, earnest and loyal, a worried boy.*

Bernard: Biff, where are you? You're supposed to study with me today.

Willy: Hey, looka Bernard. What're you lookin' so anemic about, Bernard?

Bernard: He's gotta study, Uncle Willy. He's got Regents next week.

Happy (tauntingly, spinning Bernard around): Let's box, Bernard!

Bernard: Biff! *(He gets away from Happy.)* Listen, Biff, I heard Mr. Birnbaum say that if you don't start studyin' math, he's gonna flunk you, and you won't graduate. I heard him!

Willy: You better study with him, Biff. Go ahead now.

Bernard: I heard him!

Biff: Oh, Pop, you didn't see my sneakers! *(He holds up a foot for Willy to look at.)*

Willy: Hey, that's a beautiful job of printing!

Bernard (wiping his glasses): Just because he printed University of Virginia on his sneakers doesn't mean they've got to graduate him, Uncle Willy!

Willy (angrily): What're you talking about? With scholarships to three universities they're gonna flunk him?

Bernard: But I heard Mr. Birnbaum say—

Willy: Don't be a pest, Bernard! *(To his boys.)* What an anemic!

Bernard: Okay, I'm waiting for you in my house, Biff.

> *Bernard goes off. The Lomans laugh.*

Willy: Bernard is not well liked, is he?

Biff: He's liked, but he's not well liked.

Happy: That's right, Pop.

Willy: That's just what I mean. Bernard can get the best marks in school, y'understand, but when he gets out in the business world, y'understand, you are going to be five times ahead of him. That's why I thank Almighty God you're both built like Adonises.° Because the man who makes an appearance in the business world, the man who creates personal interest, is the man who gets ahead. Be liked and you will never want. You take me, for instance. I never have to wait in line to see a buyer. "Willy Loman is here!" That's all they have to know, and I go right through.

Biff: Did you knock them dead, Pop?

Willy: Knocked 'em cold in Providence, slaughtered 'em in Boston.

Happy (on his back, pedaling again): I'm losing weight, you notice, Pop?

Linda enters, as of old, a ribbon in her hair, carrying a basket of washing.

Linda (with youthful energy): Hello, dear!

Willy: Sweetheart!

Linda: How'd the Chevy run?

Willy: Chevrolet, Linda, is the greatest car ever built. *(To the boys.)* Since when do you let your mother carry wash up the stairs?

Biff: Grab hold there, boy!

Happy: Where to, Mom?

Linda: Hang them up on the line. And you better go down to your friends, Biff. The cellar is full of boys. They don't know what to do with themselves.

Biff: Ah, when Pop comes home they can wait!

Willy (laughs appreciatively): You better go down and tell them what to do, Biff.

Biff: I think I'll have them sweep out the furnace room.

Willy: Good work, Biff.

Biff (goes through wall-line of kitchen to doorway at back and calls down): Fellas! Everybody sweep out the furnace room! I'll be right down!

Voices: All right! Okay, Biff.

Biff: George and Sam and Frank, come out back! We're hangin' up the wash! Come on, Hap, on the double! *(He and Happy carry out the basket.)*

Linda: The way they obey him!

Willy: Well, that's training, the training. I'm tellin' you, I was sellin' thousands and thousands, but I had to come home.

Linda: Oh, the whole block'll be at that game. Did you sell anything?

Willy: I did five hundred gross in Providence and seven hundred gross in Boston.

Linda: No! Wait a minute, I've got a pencil. *(She pulls pencil and paper out of her apron pocket.)* That makes your commission . . . Two hundred — my God! Two hundred and twelve dollars!

Willy: Well, I didn't figure it yet, but . . .

Linda: How much did you do?

Willy: Well, I — I did — about a hundred and eighty gross in Providence. Well, no — it came to — roughly two hundred gross on the whole trip.

Linda (without hesitation): Two hundred gross. That's . . . *(She figures.)*

Adonis: In Greek mythology a young man known for his good looks and favored by Aphrodite, goddess of love and beauty.

Willy: The trouble was that three of the stores were half closed for inventory in Boston. Otherwise I woulda broke records.

Linda: Well, it makes seventy dollars and some pennies. That's very good.

Willy: What do we owe?

Linda: Well, on the first there's sixteen dollars on the refrigerator—

Willy: Why sixteen?

Linda: Well, the fan belt broke, so it was a dollar eighty.

Willy: But it's brand new.

Linda: Well, the man said that's the way it is. Till they work themselves in, y'know.

> *They move through the wall-line into the kitchen.*

Willy: I hope we didn't get stuck on that machine.

Linda: They got the biggest ads of any of them!

Willy: I know, it's a fine machine. What else?

Linda: Well, there's nine-sixty for the washing machine. And for the vacuum cleaner there's three and a half due on the fifteenth. Then the roof, you got twenty-one dollars remaining.

Willy: It don't leak, does it?

Linda: No, they did a wonderful job. Then you owe Frank for the carburetor.

Willy: I'm not going to pay that man! That goddam Chevrolet, they ought to prohibit the manufacture of that car!

Linda: Well, you owe him three and a half. And odds and ends, comes to around a hundred and twenty dollars by the fifteenth.

Willy: A hundred and twenty dollars! My God, if business don't pick up I don't know what I'm gonna do!

Linda: Well, next week you'll do better.

Willy: Oh, I'll knock 'em dead next week. I'll go to Hartford. I'm very well liked in Hartford. You know, the trouble is, Linda, people don't seem to take to me.

> *They move onto the forestage.*

Linda: Oh, don't be foolish.

Willy: I know it when I walk in. They seem to laugh at me.

Linda: Why? Why would they laugh at you? Don't talk that way, Willy.

> *Willy moves to the edge of the stage. Linda goes into the kitchen and starts to darn stockings.*

Willy: I don't know the reason for it, but they just pass me by. I'm not noticed.

Linda: But you're doing wonderful, dear. You're making seventy to a hundred dollars a week.

Willy: But I gotta be at it ten, twelve hours a day. Other men—I don't know— they do it easier. I don't know why—I can't stop myself—I talk too much. A man oughta come in with a few words. One thing about Charley. He's a man of few words, and they respect him.

Linda: You don't talk too much, you're just lively.

Willy (smiling): Well, I figure, what the hell, life is short, a couple of jokes. *(To himself.)* I joke too much! *(The smile goes.)*

Linda: Why? You're—

Willy: I'm fat. I'm very—foolish to look at, Linda. I didn't tell you, but Christmas time I happened to be calling on F. H. Stewarts, and a salesman I know, as I was going in to see the buyer I heard him say something

about—walrus. And I—I cracked him right across the face. I won't take
that. I simply will not take that. But they do laugh at me. I know that.

Linda: Darling . . .

Willy: I gotta overcome it. I know I gotta overcome it. I'm not dressing to advantage, maybe.

Linda: Willy, darling, you're the handsomest man in the world—

Willy: Oh, no, Linda.

Linda: To me you are. *(Slight pause.)* The handsomest.

*From the darkness is heard the laughter of a woman. Willy doesn't turn to it, but it
continues through Linda's lines.*

Linda: And the boys, Willy. Few men are idolized by their children the way you are.

*Music is heard as behind a scrim, to the left of the house, The Woman, dimly seen, is
dressing.*

Willy (with great feeling): You're the best there is, Linda, you're a pal, you know
that? On the road—on the road I want to grab you sometimes and just
kiss the life outa you.

*The laughter is loud now, and he moves into a brightening area at the left, where
The Woman has come from behind the scrim and is standing, putting on her hat,
looking into a "mirror" and laughing.*

Willy: 'Cause I get so lonely—especially when business is bad and there's nobody to talk to. I get the feeling that I'll never sell anything again, that I
won't make a living for you, or a business, a business for the boys. *(He talks
through The Woman's subsiding laughter; The Woman primps at the "mirror.")*
There's so much I want to make for—

The Woman: Me? You didn't make me, Willy. I picked you.

Willy (pleased): You picked me?

The Woman (who is quite proper-looking, Willy's age): I did. I've been sitting at that
desk watching all the salesmen go by, day in, day out. But you've got such a
sense of humor, and we do have such a good time together, don't we?

Willy: Sure, sure. *(He takes her in his arms.)* Why do you have to go now?

The Woman: It's two o'clock . . .

Willy: No, come on in! *(He pulls her.)*

The Woman: . . . my sisters'll be scandalized. When'll you be back?

Willy: Oh, two weeks about. Will you come up again?

The Woman: Sure thing. You do make me laugh. It's good for me. *(She squeezes
his arm, kisses him.)* And I think you're a wonderful man.

Willy: You picked me, heh?

The Woman: Sure. Because you're so sweet. And such a kidder.

Willy: Well, I'll see you next time I'm in Boston.

The Woman: I'll put you right through to the buyers.

Willy (slapping her bottom): Right. Well, bottoms up!

The Woman (slaps him gently and laughs): You just kill me, Willy. *(He suddenly
grabs her and kisses her roughly.)* You kill me. And thanks for the stockings. I
love a lot of stockings. Well, good night.

Willy: Good night. And keep your pores open!

The Woman: Oh, Willy!

*The Woman bursts out laughing, and Linda's laughter blends in. The Woman
disappears into the dark. Now the area at the kitchen table brightens. Linda is*

sitting where she was at the kitchen table, but now is mending a pair of her silk stockings.

Linda: You are, Willy. The handsomest man. You've got no reason to feel that—

Willy (coming out of The Woman's dimming area and going over to Linda): I'll make it all up to you, Linda, I'll—

Linda: There's nothing to make up, dear. You're doing fine, better than—

Willy (noticing her mending): What's that?

Linda: Just mending my stockings. They're so expensive—

Willy (angrily, taking them from her): I won't have you mending stockings in this house! Now throw them out!

Linda puts the stockings in her pocket.

Bernard (entering on the run): Where is he? If he doesn't study!

Willy (moving to the forestage, with great agitation): You'll give him the answers!

Bernard: I do, but I can't on a Regents! That's a state exam! They're liable to arrest me!

Willy: Where is he? I'll whip him, I'll whip him!

Linda: And he'd better give back that football, Willy, it's not nice.

Willy: Biff! Where is he? Why is he taking everything?

Linda: He's too rough with the girls, Willy. All the mothers are afraid of him!

Willy: I'll whip him!

Bernard: He's driving the car without a license!

The Woman's laugh is heard.

Willy: Shut up!

Linda: All the mothers—

Willy: Shut up!

Bernard (backing quietly away and out): Mr. Birnbaum says he's stuck up.

Willy: Get outa here!

Bernard: If he doesn't buckle down he'll flunk math! *(He goes off.)*

Linda: He's right, Willy, you've gotta—

Willy (exploding at her): There's nothing the matter with him! You want him to be a worm like Bernard? He's got spirit, personality . . .

As he speaks, Linda, almost in tears, exits into the living-room. Willy is alone in the kitchen, wilting and staring. The leaves are gone. It is night again, and the apartment houses look down from behind.

Willy: Loaded with it. Loaded! What is he stealing? He's giving it back, isn't he? Why is he stealing? What did I tell him? I never in my life told him anything but decent things.

Happy in pajamas has come down the stairs; Willy suddenly becomes aware of Happy's presence.

Happy: Let's go now, come on.

Willy (sitting down at the kitchen table): Huh! Why did she have to wax the floors herself? Everytime she waxes the floors she keels over. She knows that!

Happy: Shh! Take it easy. What brought you back tonight?

Willy: I got an awful scare. Nearly hit a kid in Yonkers. God! Why didn't I go to Alaska with my brother Ben that time! Ben! That man was a genius, that man was success incarnate! What a mistake! He begged me to go.

Happy: Well, there's no use in—

Willy: You guys! There was a man started with the clothes on his back and ended up with diamond mines!

Happy: Boy, someday I'd like to know how he did it.

Willy: What's the mystery? The man knew what he wanted and went out and got it! Walked into a jungle, and comes out, the age of twenty-one, and he's rich! The world is an oyster, but you don't crack it open on a mattress!

Happy: Pop, I told you I'm gonna retire you for life.

Willy: You'll retire me for life on seventy goddam dollars a week? And your women and your car and your apartment, and you'll retire me for life! Christ's sake, I couldn't get past Yonkers today! Where are you guys, where are you? The woods are burning! I can't drive a car!

Charley has appeared in the doorway. He is a large man, slow of speech, laconic, immovable. In all he says, despite what he says, there is pity, and, now, trepidation. He has a robe over pajamas, slippers on his feet. He enters the kitchen.

Charley: Everything all right?

Happy: Yeah, Charley, everything's . . .

Willy: What's the matter?

Charley: I heard some noise. I thought something happened. Can't we do something about the walls? You sneeze in here, and in my house hats blow off.

Happy: Let's go to bed, Dad. Come on.

Charley signals to Happy to go.

Willy: You go ahead, I'm not tired at the moment.

Happy (to Willy): Take it easy, huh? *(He exits.)*

Willy: What're you doin' up?

Charley (sitting down at the kitchen table opposite Willy): Couldn't sleep good. I had a heartburn.

Willy: Well, you don't know how to eat.

Charley: I eat with my mouth.

Willy: No, you're ignorant. You gotta know about vitamins and things like that.

Charley: Come on, let's shoot. Tire you out a little.

Willy (hesitantly): All right. You got cards?

Charley (taking a deck from his pocket): Yeah, I got them. Someplace. What is it with those vitamins?

Willy (dealing): They build up your bones. Chemistry.

Charley: Yeah, but there's no bones in a heartburn.

Willy: What are you talkin' about? Do you know the first thing about it?

Charley: Don't get insulted.

Willy: Don't talk about something you don't know anything about.

They are playing. Pause.

Charley: What're you doin' home?

Willy: A little trouble with the car.

Charley: Oh. *(Pause.)* I'd like to take a trip to California.

Willy: Don't say.

Charley: You want a job?

Willy: I got a job, I told you that. *(After a slight pause.)* What the hell are you offering me a job for?

Charley: Don't get insulted.

Willy: Don't insult me.

Charley: I don't see no sense in it. You don't have to go on this way.

Willy: I got a good job. *(Slight pause.)* What do you keep comin' in here for?

Charley: You want me to go?

Willy (after a pause, withering): I can't understand it. He's going back to Texas again. What the hell is that?

Charley: Let him go.

Willy: I got nothin' to give him, Charley, I'm clean, I'm clean.

Charley: He won't starve. None a them starve. Forget about him.

Willy: Then what have I got to remember?

Charley: You take it too hard. To hell with it. When a deposit bottle is broken you don't get your nickel back.

Willy: That's easy enough for you to say.

Charley: That ain't easy for me to say.

Willy: Did you see the ceiling I put up in the living-room?

Charley: Yeah, that's a piece of work. To put up a ceiling is a mystery to me. How do you do it?

Willy: What's the difference?

Charley: Well, talk about it.

Willy: You gonna put up a ceiling?

Charley: How could I put up a ceiling?

Willy: Then what the hell are you bothering me for?

Charley: You're insulted again.

Willy: A man who can't handle tools is not a man. You're disgusting.

Charley: Don't call me disgusting, Willy.

> *Uncle Ben, carrying a valise and an umbrella, enters the forestage from around the right corner of the house. He is a stolid man, in his sixties, with a mustache and an authoritative air. He is utterly certain of his destiny, and there is an aura of far places about him. He enters exactly as Willy speaks.*

Willy: I'm getting awfully tired, Ben.

> *Ben's music is heard. Ben looks around at everything.*

Charley: Good, keep playing; you'll sleep better. Did you call me Ben?

> *Ben looks at his watch.*

Willy: That's funny. For a second there you reminded me of my brother Ben.

Ben: I only have a few minutes. *(He strolls, inspecting the place. Willy and Charley continue playing.)*

Charley: You never heard from him again, heh? Since that time?

Willy: Didn't Linda tell you? Couple of weeks ago we got a letter from his wife in Africa. He died.

Charley: That so.

Ben (chuckling): So this is Brooklyn, eh?

Charley: Maybe you're in for some of his money.

Willy: Naa, he had seven sons. There's just one opportunity I had with that man . . .

Ben: I must make a train, William. There are several properties I'm looking at in Alaska.

Willy: Sure, sure! If I'd gone with him to Alaska that time, everything would've been totally different.

Charley: Go on, you'd froze to death up there.

Willy: What're you talking about?

Ben: Opportunity is tremendous in Alaska, William. Surprised you're not up there.

Willy: Sure, tremendous.

Charley: Heh?

Willy: There was the only man I ever met who knew the answers.

Charley: Who?

Ben: How are you all?

Willy (taking a pot, smiling): Fine, fine.

Charley: Pretty sharp tonight.

Ben: Is mother living with you?

Willy: No, she died a long time ago.

Charley: Who?

Ben: That's too bad. Fine specimen of a lady, Mother.

Willy (to Charley): Heh?

Ben: I'd hoped to see the old girl.

Charley: Who died?

Ben: Heard anything from Father, have you?

Willy (unnerved): What do you mean, who died?

Charley (taking a pot): What're you talkin' about?

Ben (looking at his watch): William, it's half-past eight!

Willy (as though to dispel his confusion he angrily stops Charley's hand): That's my build!

Charley: I put the ace—

Willy: If you don't know how to play the game I'm not gonna throw my money away on you!

Charley (rising): It was my ace, for God's sake!

Willy: I'm through, I'm through!

Ben: When did Mother die?

Willy: Long ago. Since the beginning you never knew how to play cards.

Charley (picks up the cards and goes to the door): All right! Next time I'll bring a deck with five aces.

Willy: I don't play that kind of game!

Charley (turning to him): You ought to be ashamed of yourself!

Willy: Yeah?

Charley: Yeah! (He goes out.)

Willy (slamming the door after him): Ignoramus!

Ben (as Willy comes toward him through the wall-line of the kitchen): So you're William.

Willy (shaking Ben's hand): Ben! I've been waiting for you so long! What's the answer? How did you do it?

Ben: Oh, there's a story in that.

Linda enters the forestage, as of old, carrying the wash basket.

Linda: Is this Ben?

Ben (gallantly): How do you do, my dear.

Linda: Where've you been all these years? Willy's always wondered why you—

Willy (pulling Ben away from her impatiently): Where is Dad? Didn't you follow him? How did you get started?

Ben: Well, I don't know how much you remember.

Willy: Well, I was just a baby, of course, only three or four years old —

Ben: Three years and eleven months.

Willy: What a memory, Ben!

Ben: I have many enterprises, William, and I have never kept books.

Willy: I remember I was sitting under the wagon in — was it Nebraska?

Ben: It was South Dakota, and I gave you a bunch of wild flowers.

Willy: I remember you walking away down some open road.

Ben (laughing): I was going to find Father in Alaska.

Willy: Where is he?

Ben: At that age I had a very faulty view of geography, William. I discovered after a few days that I was heading due south, so instead of Alaska, I ended up in Africa.

Linda: Africa!

Willy: The Gold Coast!

Ben: Principally diamond mines.

Linda: Diamond mines!

Ben: Yes, my dear. But I've only a few minutes —

Willy: No! Boys! Boys! *(Young Biff and Happy appear.)* Listen to this. This is your Uncle Ben, a great man! Tell my boys, Ben!

Ben: Why, boys, when I was seventeen I walked into the jungle, and when I was twenty-one I walked out. *(He laughs.)* And by God I was rich.

Willy (to the boys): You see what I been talking about? The greatest things can happen!

Ben (glancing at his watch): I have an appointment in Ketchikan Tuesday week.

Willy: No, Ben! Please tell about Dad. I want my boys to hear. I want them to know the kind of stock they spring from. All I remember is a man with a big beard, and I was in Mamma's lap, sitting around a fire, and some kind of high music.

Ben: His flute. He played the flute.

Willy: Sure, the flute, that's right!

New music is heard, a high, rollicking tune.

Ben: Father was a very great and a very wild-hearted man. We would start in Boston, and he'd toss the whole family into the wagon, and then he'd drive the team right across the country; through Ohio, and Indiana, Michigan, Illinois, and all the Western states. And we'd stop in the towns and sell the flutes that he'd made on the way. Great inventor, Father. With one gadget he made more in a week than a man like you could make in a lifetime.

Willy: That's just the way I'm bringing them up, Ben — rugged, well liked, all-around.

Ben: Yeah? *(To Biff.)* Hit that, boy — hard as you can. *(He pounds his stomach.)*

Biff: Oh, no, sir!

Ben (taking boxing stance): Come on, get to me. *(He laughs.)*

Willy: Go to it, Biff! Go ahead, show him!

Biff: Okay! *(He cocks his fists and starts in.)*

Linda (to Willy): Why must he fight, dear?

Ben (sparring with Biff): Good boy! Good boy!

Willy: How's that, Ben, heh?

Happy: Give him the left, Biff!

Linda: Why are you fighting?

Ben: Good boy! *(Suddenly comes in, trips Biff, and stands over him, the point of his umbrella poised over Biff's eye.)*

Linda: Look out, Biff!

Biff: Gee!

Ben (patting Biff's knee): Never fight fair with a stranger, boy. You'll never get out of the jungle that way. *(Taking Linda's hand and bowing):* It was an honor and a pleasure to meet you, Linda.

Linda (withdrawing her hand coldly, frightened): Have a nice — trip.

Ben (to Willy): And good luck with your — what do you do?

Willy: Selling.

Ben: Yes. Well . . . *(He raises his hand in farewell to all.)*

Willy: No, Ben, I don't want you to think . . . *(He takes Ben's arm to show him.)* It's Brooklyn, I know, but we hunt too.

Ben: Really, now.

Willy: Oh, sure, there's snakes and rabbits and — that's why I moved out here. Why, Biff can fell any one of these trees in no time! Boys! Go right over to where they're building the apartment house and get some sand. We're gonna rebuild the entire front stoop now! Watch this, Ben!

Biff: Yes, sir! On the double, Hap!

Happy (as he and Biff run off): I lost weight, Pop, you notice?

Charley enters in knickers, even before the boys are gone.

Charley: Listen, if they steal any more from that building the watchman'll put the cops on them!

Linda (to Willy): Don't let Biff . . .

Ben laughs lustily.

Willy: You shoulda seen the lumber they brought home last week. At least a dozen six-by-tens worth all kinds a money.

Charley: Listen, if that watchman —

Willy: I gave them hell, understand. But I got a couple of fearless characters there.

Charley: Willy, the jails are full of fearless characters.

Ben (clapping Willy on the back, with a laugh at Charley): And the stock exchange, friend!

Willy (joining in Ben's laughter): Where are the rest of your pants?

Charley: My wife bought them.

Willy: Now all you need is a golf club and you can go upstairs and go to sleep. *(To Ben).* Great athlete! Between him and his son Bernard they can't hammer a nail!

Bernard (rushing in): The watchman's chasing Biff!

Willy (angrily): Shut up! He's not stealing anything!

Linda (alarmed, hurrying off left): Where is he? Biff, dear! *(She exits.)*

Willy (moving toward the left, away from Ben): There's nothing wrong. What's the matter with you?

Ben: Nervy boy. Good!

Willy (laughing): Oh, nerves of iron, that Biff!

Charley: Don't know what it is. My New England man comes back and he's bleedin', they murdered him up there.

Willy: It's contacts, Charley, I got important contacts!

Charley (sarcastically): Glad to hear it, Willy. Come in later, we'll shoot a little casino. I'll take some of your Portland money. *(He laughs at Willy and exits.)*

Willy (turning to Ben): Business is bad, it's murderous. But not for me, of course.

Ben: I'll stop by on my way back to Africa.

Willy (longingly): Can't you stay a few days? You're just what I need, Ben, because I — I have a fine position here, but I — well, Dad left when I was such a baby and I never had a chance to talk to him and I still feel — kind of temporary about myself.

Ben: I'll be late for my train.

> *They are at opposite ends of the stage.*

Willy: Ben, my boys — can't we talk? They'd go into the jaws of hell for me, see, but I —

Ben: William, you're being first-rate with your boys. Outstanding, manly chaps!

Willy (hanging on to his words): Oh, Ben, that's good to hear! Because sometimes I'm afraid that I'm not teaching them the right kind of — Ben, how should I teach them?

Ben (giving great weight to each word, and with a certain vicious audacity): William, when I walked into the jungle, I was seventeen. When I walked out I was twenty-one. And, by God, I was rich! *(He goes off into darkness around the right corner of the house.)*

Willy: . . . was rich! That's just the spirit I want to imbue them with! To walk into a jungle! I was right! I was right! I was right!

> *Ben is gone, but Willy is still speaking to him as Linda, in nightgown and robe, enters the kitchen, glances around for Willy, then goes to the door of the house, looks out, and sees him. Comes down to his left. He looks at her.*

Linda: Willy, dear? Willy?

Willy: I was right!

Linda: Did you have some cheese? *(He can't answer.)* It's very late, darling. Come to bed, heh?

Willy (looking straight up): Gotta break your neck to see a star in this yard.

Linda: You coming in?

Willy: Whatever happened to that diamond watch fob? Remember? When Ben came from Africa that time? Didn't he give me a watch fob with a diamond in it?

Linda: You pawned it, dear. Twelve, thirteen years ago. For Biff's radio correspondence course.

Willy: Gee, that was a beautiful thing. I'll take a walk.

Linda: But you're in your slippers.

Willy (starting to go around the house at the left): I was right! I was! *(Half to Linda, as he goes, shaking his head.)* What a man! There was a man worth talking to. I was right!

Linda (calling after Willy): But in your slippers, Willy!

Willy is almost gone when Biff, in his pajamas, comes down the stairs and enters the kitchen.

Biff: What is he doing out there?
Linda: Sh!
Biff: God Almighty, Mom, how long has he been doing this?
Linda: Don't, he'll hear you.
Biff: What the hell is the matter with him?
Linda: It'll pass by morning.
Biff: Shouldn't we do anything?
Linda: Oh, my dear, you should do a lot of things, but there's nothing to do, so go to sleep.

Happy comes down the stairs and sits on the steps.

Happy: I never heard him so loud, Mom.
Linda: Well, come around more often; you'll hear him. *(She sits down at the table and mends the lining of Willy's jacket.)*
Biff: Why didn't you ever write me about this, Mom?
Linda: How would I write to you? For over three months you had no address.
Biff: I was on the move. But you know I thought of you all the time. You know that, don't you, pal?
Linda: I know, dear, I know. But he likes to have a letter. Just to know that there's still a possibility for better things.
Biff: He's not like this all the time, is he?
Linda: It's when you come home he's always the worst.
Biff: When I come home?
Linda: When you write you're coming, he's all smiles, and talks about the future, and—he's just wonderful. And then the closer you seem to come, the more shaky he gets, and then, by the time you get here, he's arguing, and he seems angry at you. I think it's just that maybe he can't bring himself to—to open up to you. Why are you so hateful to each other? Why is that?
Biff (evasively): I'm not hateful, Mom.
Linda: But you no sooner come in the door than you're fighting!
Biff: I don't know why. I mean to change. I'm tryin', Mom, you understand?
Linda: Are you home to stay now?
Biff: I don't know. I want to look around, see what's doin'.
Linda: Biff, you can't look around all your life, can you?
Biff: I just can't take hold, Mom. I can't take hold of some kind of a life.
Linda: Biff, a man is not a bird, to come and go with the springtime.
Biff: Your hair . . . *(He touches her hair.)* Your hair got so gray.
Linda: Oh, it's been gray since you were in high school. I just stopped dyeing it, that's all.
Biff: Dye it again, will ya? I don't want my pal looking old. *(He smiles.)*
Linda: You're such a boy! You think you can go away for a year and . . . You've got to get it into your head now that one day you'll knock on this door and there'll be strange people here—
Biff: What are you talking about? You're not even sixty, Mom.
Linda: But what about your father?
Biff (lamely): Well, I meant him too.
Happy: He admires Pop.

Linda: Biff, dear, if you don't have any feeling for him, then you can't have any feeling for me.

Biff: Sure I can, Mom.

Linda: No. You can't just come to see me, because I love him. *(With a threat, but only a threat, of tears.)* He's the dearest man in the world to me, and I won't have anyone making him feel unwanted and low and blue. You've got to make up your mind now, darling, there's no leeway any more. Either he's your father and you pay him that respect, or else you're not to come here. I know he's not easy to get along with—nobody knows that better than me—but . . .

Willy (from the left, with a laugh): Hey, hey, Biffo!

Biff (starting to go out after Willy): What the hell is the matter with him? *(Happy stops him.)*

Linda: Don't—don't go near him!

Biff: Stop making excuses for him! He always, always wiped the floor with you. Never had an ounce of respect for you.

Happy: He's always had respect for—

Biff: What the hell do you know about it?

Happy (surlily): Just don't call him crazy!

Biff: He's got no character—Charley wouldn't do this. Not in his own house—spewing out that vomit from his mind.

Happy: Charley never had to cope with what he's got to.

Biff: People are worse off than Willy Loman. Believe me, I've seen them!

Linda: Then make Charley your father, Biff. You can't do that, can you? I don't say he's a great man. Willy Loman never made a lot of money. His name was never in the paper. He's not the finest character that ever lived. But he's a human being, and a terrible thing is happening to him. So attention must be paid. He's not to be allowed to fall into his grave like an old dog. Attention, attention must be finally paid to such a person. You called him crazy—

Biff: I didn't mean—

Linda: No, a lot of people think he's lost his—balance. But you don't have to be very smart to know what his trouble is. The man is exhausted.

Happy: Sure!

Linda: A small man can be just as exhausted as a great man. He works for a company thirty-six years this March, opens up unheard-of territories to their trademark, and now in his old age they take his salary away.

Happy (indignantly): I didn't know that, Mom.

Linda: You never asked, my dear! Now that you get your spending money someplace else you don't trouble your mind with him.

Happy: But I gave you money last—

Linda: Christmas time, fifty dollars! To fix the hot water it cost ninety-seven fifty! For five weeks he's been on straight commission, like a beginner, an unknown!

Biff: Those ungrateful bastards!

Linda: Are they any worse than his sons? When he brought them business, when he was young, they were glad to see him. But now his old friends, the old buyers that loved him so and always found some order to hand him in a pinch—they're all dead, retired. He used to be able to make six, seven calls a day in Boston. Now he takes his valises out of the car and puts them back and takes them out again and he's exhausted. Instead of walking he talks now. He drives seven hundred miles, and when he gets there no one knows him any more, no one welcomes him. And what goes through a man's mind, driving seven hundred miles home without having earned a cent? Why shouldn't he talk to himself? Why? When he has to go to Charley and borrow fifty dollars a week and pretend to me that it's his pay? How long can that go on? How long? You see what I'm sitting here and waiting for? And you tell me he has no character? The man who never worked a day but for your benefit? When does he get the medal for that? Is this his reward — to turn around at the age of sixty-three and find his sons, who he loved better than his life, one a philandering bum —

Happy: Mom!

Linda: That's all you are, my baby! *(To Biff.)* And you! What happened to the love you had for him? You were such pals! How you used to talk to him on the phone every night! How lonely he was till he could come home to you!

Biff: All right, Mom. I'll live here in my room, and I'll get a job. I'll keep away from him, that's all.

Linda: No, Biff. You can't stay here and fight all the time.

Biff: He threw me out of this house, remember that.

Linda: Why did he do that? I never knew why.

Biff: Because I know he's a fake and he doesn't like anybody around who knows!

Linda: Why a fake? In what way? What do you mean?

Biff: Just don't lay it all at my feet. It's between me and him — that's all I have to say. I'll chip in from now on. He'll settle for half my pay check. He'll be all right. I'm going to bed. *(He starts for the stairs.)*

Linda: He won't be all right.

Biff (turning on the stairs, furiously): I hate this city and I'll stay here. Now what do you want?

Linda: He's dying, Biff.

Happy turns quickly to her, shocked.

Biff (after a pause): Why is he dying?

Linda: He's been trying to kill himself.

Biff (with great horror): How?

Linda: I live from day to day.

Biff: What're you talking about?

Linda: Remember I wrote you that he smashed up the car again? In February?

Biff: Well?

Linda: The insurance inspector came. He said that they have evidence. That all these accidents in the last year — weren't — weren't — accidents.

Happy: How can they tell that? That's a lie.

Linda: It seems there's a woman . . . *(She takes a breath as):*

   { *Biff (sharply but contained):* What woman?

   { *Linda (simultaneously):* . . . and this woman . . .

Linda: What?

Biff: Nothing. Go ahead.

Linda: What did you say?

Biff: Nothing. I just said what woman?

Happy: What about her?

Linda: Well, it seems she was walking down the road and saw his car. She says that he wasn't driving fast at all, and that he didn't skid. She says he came to that little bridge, and then deliberately smashed into the railing, and it was only the shallowness of the water that saved him.

Biff: Oh, no, he probably just fell asleep again.

Linda: I don't think he fell asleep.

Biff: Why not?

Linda: Last month . . . *(With great difficulty.)* Oh, boys, it's so hard to say a thing like this! He's just a big stupid man to you, but I tell you there's more good in him than in many other people. *(She chokes, wipes her eyes.)* I was looking for a fuse. The lights blew out, and I went down the cellar. And behind the fuse box — it happened to fall out — was a length of rubber pipe — just short.

Happy: No kidding?

Linda: There's a little attachment on the end of it. I knew right away. And sure enough, on the bottom of the water heater there's a new little nipple on the gas pipe.

Happy (angrily): That — jerk.

Biff: Did you have it taken off?

Linda: I'm — I'm ashamed to. How can I mention it to him? Every day I go down and take away that little rubber pipe. But, when he comes home, I put it back where it was. How can I insult him that way? I don't know what to do. I live from day to day, boys. I tell you, I know every thought in his mind. It sounds so old-fashioned and silly, but I tell you he put his whole life into you and you've turned your backs on him. *(She is bent over in chair, weeping, her face in her hands.)* Biff, I swear to God! Biff, his life is in your hands!

Happy (to Biff): How do you like that damned fool!

Biff (kissing her): All right, pal, all right. It's all settled now. I've been remiss. I know that, Mom. But now I'll stay, and I swear to you, I'll apply myself. *(Kneeling in front of her, in a fever of self-reproach.)* It's just — you see, Mom, I don't fit in business. Not that I won't try. I'll try, and I'll make good.

Happy: Sure you will. The trouble with you in business was you never tried to please people.

Biff: I know, I —

Happy: Like when you worked for Harrison's. Bob Harrison said you were tops, and then you go and do some damn fool thing like whistling whole songs in the elevator like a comedian.

Biff (against Happy): So what? I like to whistle sometimes.

Happy: You don't raise a guy to a responsible job who whistles in the elevator!

Linda: Well, don't argue about it now.

Happy: Like when you'd go off and swim in the middle of the day instead of taking the line around.

Biff (his resentment rising): Well, don't you run off? You take off sometimes, don't you? On a nice summer day?

Happy: Yeah, but I cover myself!

Linda: Boys!

Happy: If I'm going to take a fade the boss can call any number where I'm supposed to be and they'll swear to him that I just left. I'll tell you something that I hate to say, Biff, but in the business world some of them think you're crazy.

Biff (angered): Screw the business world!

Happy: All right, screw it! Great, but cover yourself!

Linda: Hap, Hap!

Biff: I don't care what they think! They've laughed at Dad for years, and you know why? Because we don't belong in this nuthouse of a city! We should be mixing cement on some open plain, or — or carpenters. A carpenter is allowed to whistle!

Willy walks in from the entrance of the house, at left.

Willy: Even your grandfather was better than a carpenter. *(Pause. They watch him.)* You never grew up. Bernard does not whistle in the elevator, I assure you.

Biff (as though to laugh Willy out of it): Yeah, but you do, Pop.

Willy: I never in my life whistled in an elevator! And who in the business world thinks I'm crazy?

Biff: I didn't mean it like that, Pop. Now don't make a whole thing out of it, will ya?

Willy: Go back to the West! Be a carpenter, a cowboy, enjoy yourself!

Linda: Willy, he was just saying —

Willy: I heard what he said!

Happy (trying to quiet Willy): Hey, Pop, come on now . . .

Willy (continuing over Happy's line): They laugh at me, heh? Go to Filene's, go to the Hub, go to Slattery's, Boston. Call out the name Willy Loman and see what happens! Big shot!

Biff: All right, Pop.

Willy: Big!

Biff: All right!

Willy: Why do you always insult me?

Biff: I didn't say a word. *(To Linda.)* Did I say a word?

Linda: He didn't say anything, Willy.

Willy (going to the doorway of the living-room): All right, good night, good night.

Linda: Willy, dear, he just decided . . .

Willy (to Biff): If you get tired hanging around tomorrow, paint the ceiling I put up in the living-room.

Biff: I'm leaving early tomorrow.

Happy: He's going to see Bill Oliver, Pop.

Willy (interestedly): Oliver? For what?

Biff (with reserve, but trying, trying): He always said he'd stake me. I'd like to go into business, so maybe I can take him up on it.

Linda: Isn't that wonderful?

Willy: Don't interrupt. What's wonderful about it? There's fifty men in the City of New York who'd stake him. *(To Biff.)* Sporting goods?

Biff: I guess so. I know something about it and —

Willy: He knows something about it! You know sporting goods better than Spalding, for God's sake! How much is he giving you?

Biff: I don't know, I didn't even see him yet, but —

Willy: Then what're you talkin' about?

Biff (getting angry): Well, all I said was I'm gonna see him, that's all!

Willy (turning away): Ah, you're counting your chickens again.

Biff (starting left for the stairs): Oh, Jesus, I'm going to sleep!

Willy (calling after him): Don't curse in this house!

Biff (turning): Since when did you get so clean?

Happy (trying to stop them): Wait a . . .

Willy: Don't use that language to me! I won't have it!

Happy (grabbing Biff, shouts): Wait a minute! I got an idea. I got a feasible idea. Come here, Biff, let's talk this over now, let's talk some sense here. When I was down in Florida last time, I thought of a great idea to sell sporting goods. It just came back to me. You and I, Biff—we have a line, the Loman Line. We train a couple of weeks, and put on a couple of exhibitions, see?

Willy: That's an idea!

Happy: Wait! We form two basketball teams, see? Two water-polo teams. We play each other. It's a million dollars' worth of publicity. Two brothers, see? The Loman Brothers. Displays in the Royal Palms—all the hotels. And banners over the ring and the basketball court: "Loman Brothers." Baby, we could sell sporting goods!

Willy: That is a one-million-dollar idea!

Linda: Marvelous!

Biff: I'm in great shape as far as that's concerned.

Happy: And the beauty of it is, Biff, it wouldn't be like a business. We'd be out playin' ball again . . .

Biff (enthused): Yeah, that's . . .

Willy: Million-dollar . . .

Happy: And you wouldn't get fed up with it, Biff. It'd be the family again. There'd be the old honor, and comradeship, and if you wanted to go off for a swim or somethin'—well, you'd do it! Without some smart cooky gettin' up ahead of you!

Willy: Lick the world! You guys together could absolutely lick the civilized world.

Biff: I'll see Oliver tomorrow. Hap, if we could work that out . . .

Linda: Maybe things are beginning to—

Willy (wildly enthused, to Linda): Stop interrupting! *(To Biff.)* But don't wear sport jacket and slacks when you see Oliver.

Biff: No, I'll—

Willy: A business suit, and talk as little as possible, and don't crack any jokes.

Biff: He did like me. Always liked me.

Linda: He loved you!

Willy (to Linda): Will you stop! *(To Biff.)* Walk in very serious. You are not applying for a boy's job. Money is to pass. Be quiet, fine, and serious. Everybody likes a kidder, but nobody lends him money.

Happy: I'll try to get some myself, Biff. I'm sure I can.

Willy: I see great things for you kids, I think your troubles are over. But remember, start big and you'll end big. Ask for fifteen. How much you gonna ask for?

Biff: Gee, I don't know—

Willy: And don't say "Gee." "Gee" is a boy's word. A man walking in for fifteen thousand dollars does not say "Gee!"

Biff: Ten, I think, would be top though.

Willy: Don't be so modest. You always started too low. Walk in with a big laugh. Don't look worried. Start off with a couple of your good stories to lighten things up. It's not what you say, it's how you say it — because personality always wins the day.

Linda: Oliver always thought the highest of him —

Willy: Will you let me talk?

Biff: Don't yell at her, Pop, will ya?

Willy (angrily): I was talking, wasn't I?

Biff: I don't like you yelling at her all the time, and I'm tellin' you, that's all.

Willy: What're you, takin' over this house?

Linda: Willy —

Willy (turning on her): Don't take his side all the time, goddammit!

Biff (furiously): Stop yelling at her!

Willy (suddenly pulling on his cheek, beaten down, guilt ridden): Give my best to Bill Oliver — he may remember me. *(He exits through the living-room doorway.)*

Linda (her voice subdued): What'd you have to start that for? *(Biff turns away.)* You see how sweet he was as soon as you talked hopefully? *(She goes over to Biff.)* Come up and say good night to him. Don't let him go to bed that way.

Happy: Come on, Biff, let's buck him up.

Linda: Please, dear. Just say good night. It takes so little to make him happy. Come. *(She goes through the living-room doorway, calling upstairs from within the living-room.)* Your pajamas are hanging in the bathroom, Willy!

Happy (looking toward where Linda went out): What a woman! They broke the mold when they made her. You know that, Biff?

Biff: He's off salary. My God, working on commission!

Happy: Well, let's face it: he's no hot-shot selling man. Except that sometimes, you have to admit, he's a sweet personality.

Biff (deciding): Lend me ten bucks, will ya? I want to buy some new ties.

Happy: I'll take you to a place I know. Beautiful stuff. Wear one of my striped shirts tomorrow.

Biff: She got gray. Mom got awful old. Gee, I'm gonna go in to Oliver tomorrow and knock him for a —

Happy: Come on up. Tell that to Dad. Let's give him a whirl. Come on.

Biff (steamed up): You know, with ten thousand bucks, boy!

Happy (as they go into the living-room): That's the talk, Biff, that's the first time I've heard the old confidence out of you! *(From within the living-room, fading off.)* You're gonna live with me, kid, and any babe you want just say the word . . . *(The last lines are hardly heard. They are mounting the stairs to their parents' bedroom.)*

Linda (entering her bedroom and addressing Willy, who is in the bathroom. She is straightening the bed for him): Can you do anything about the shower? It drips.

Willy (from the bathroom): All of a sudden everything falls to pieces! Goddam plumbing, oughta be sued, those people. I hardly finished putting it in and the thing . . . *(His words rumble off.)*

Linda: I'm just wondering if Oliver will remember him. You think he might?

Willy (coming out of the bathroom in his pajamas): Remember him? What's the matter with you, you crazy? If he'd've stayed with Oliver he'd be on top by now! Wait'll Oliver gets a look at him. You don't know the average caliber any more. The average young man today — *(he is getting into bed)* — is got a caliber of zero. Greatest thing in the world for him was to bum around.

Biff and Happy enter the bedroom. Slight pause.

Willy (stops short, looking at Biff): Glad to hear it, boy.

Happy: He wanted to say good night to you, sport.

Willy (to Biff): Yeah. Knock him dead, boy. What'd you want to tell me?

Biff: Just take it easy, Pop. Good night. *(He turns to go.)*

Willy (unable to resist): And if anything falls off the desk while you're talking to him — like a package or something — don't you pick it up. They have office boys for that.

Linda: I'll make a big breakfast —

Willy: Will you let me finish? *(To Biff.)* Tell him you were in the business in the West. Not farm work.

Biff: All right, Dad.

Linda: I think everything —

Willy (going right through her speech): And don't undersell yourself. No less than fifteen thousand dollars.

Biff (unable to bear him): Okay. Good night, Mom. *(He starts moving.)*

Willy: Because you got a greatness in you, Biff, remember that. You got all kinds a greatness . . . *(He lies back, exhausted. Biff walks out.)*

Linda (calling after Biff): Sleep well, darling!

Happy: I'm gonna get married, Mom. I wanted to tell you.

Linda: Go to sleep, dear.

Happy (going): I just wanted to tell you.

Willy: Keep up the good work. *(Happy exits.)* God . . . remember that Ebbets Field game? The championship of the city?

Linda: Just rest. Should I sing to you?

Willy: Yeah. Sing to me. *(Linda hums a soft lullaby.)* When that team came out — he was the tallest, remember?

Linda: Oh, yes. And in gold.

Biff enters the darkened kitchen, takes a cigarette, and leaves the house. He comes downstage into a golden pool of light. He smokes, staring at the night.

Willy: Like a young god. Hercules — something like that. And the sun, the sun all around him. Remember how he waved to me? Right up from the field, with the representatives of three colleges standing by? And the buyers I brought, and the cheers when he came out — Loman, Loman, Loman! God Almighty, he'll be great yet. A star like that, magnificent, can never really fade away!

The light on Willy is fading. The gas heater begins to glow through the kitchen wall, near the stairs, a blue flame beneath red coils.

Linda (timidly): Willy dear, what has he got against you?

Willy: I'm so tired. Don't talk any more.

Biff slowly returns to the kitchen. He stops, stares toward the heater.

Linda: Will you ask Howard to let you work in New York?

Willy: First thing in the morning. Everything'll be all right.

Biff reaches behind the heater and draws out a length of rubber tubing. He is horrified and turns his head toward Willy's room, still dimly lit, from which the strains of Linda's desperate but monotonous humming rise.

Willy (staring through the window into the moonlight): Gee, look at the moon moving between the buildings!

Biff wraps the tubing around his hand and quickly goes up the stairs.

Curtain

ACT II

Music is heard, gay and bright. The curtain rises as the music fades away. Willy, in shirt sleeves, is sitting at the kitchen table, sipping coffee, his hat in his lap. Linda is filling his cup when she can.

Willy: Wonderful coffee. Meal in itself.

Linda: Can I make you some eggs?

Willy: No. Take a breath.

Linda: You look so rested, dear.

Willy: I slept like a dead one. First time in months. Imagine, sleeping till ten on a Tuesday morning. Boys left nice and early, heh?

Linda: They were out of here by eight o'clock.

Willy: Good work!

Linda: It was so thrilling to see them leaving together. I can't get over the shaving lotion in this house!

Willy (smiling): Mmm —

Linda: Biff was very changed this morning. His whole attitude seemed to be hopeful. He couldn't wait to get downtown to see Oliver.

Willy: He's heading for a change. There's no question, there simply are certain men that take longer to get — solidified. How did he dress?

Linda: His blue suit. He's so handsome in that suit. He could be a — anything in that suit!

Willy gets up from the table. Linda holds his jacket for him.

Willy: There's no question, no question at all. Gee, on the way home tonight I'd like to buy some seeds.

Linda (laughing): That'd be wonderful. But not enough sun gets back there. Nothing'll grow any more.

Willy: You wait, kid, before it's all over we're gonna get a little place out in the country, and I'll raise some vegetables, a couple of chickens . . .

Linda: You'll do it yet, dear.

Willy walks out of his jacket. Linda follows him.

Willy: And they'll get married, and come for a weekend. I'd build a little guest house. 'Cause I got so many fine tools, all I'd need would be a little lumber and some peace of mind.

Linda (joyfully): I sewed the lining . . .

Willy: I could build two guest houses, so they'd both come. Did he decide how much he's going to ask Oliver for?

Linda (getting him into the jacket): He didn't mention it, but I imagine ten or fifteen thousand. You going to talk to Howard today?

Willy: Yeah. I'll put it to him straight and simple. He'll just have to take me off the road.

Linda: And Willy, don't forget to ask for a little advance, because we've got the insurance premium. It's the grace period now.

Willy: That's a hundred . . . ?

Linda: A hundred and eight, sixty-eight. Because we're a little short again.

Willy: Why are we short?

Linda: Well, you had the motor job on the car . . .

Willy: That goddam Studebaker!

Linda: And you got one more payment on the refrigerator . . .

Willy: But it just broke again!

Linda: Well, it's old, dear.

Willy: I told you we should've bought a well-advertised machine. Charley bought a General Electric and it's twenty years old and it's still good, that son-of-a-bitch.

Linda: But, Willy—

Willy: Whoever heard of a Hastings refrigerator? Once in my life I would like to own something outright before it's broken! I'm always in a race with the junkyard! I just finished paying for the car and it's on its last legs. The refrigerator consumes belts like a goddam maniac. They time those things. They time them so when you finally paid for them, they're used up.

Linda (buttoning up his jacket as he unbuttons it): All told, about two hundred dollars would carry us, dear. But that includes the last payment on the mortgage. After this payment, Willy, the house belongs to us.

Willy: It's twenty-five years!

Linda: Biff was nine years old when we bought it.

Willy: Well, that's a great thing. To weather a twenty-five year mortgage is—

Linda: It's an accomplishment.

Willy: All the cement, the lumber, the reconstruction I put in this house! There ain't a crack to be found in it any more.

Linda: Well, it served its purpose.

Willy: What purpose? Some stranger'll come along, move in, and that's that. If only Biff would take this house, and raise a family . . . *(He starts to go.)* Good-by, I'm late.

Linda (suddenly remembering): Oh, I forgot! You're supposed to meet them for dinner.

Willy: Me?

Linda: At Frank's Chop House on Forty-eighth near Sixth Avenue.

Willy: Is that so! How about you?

Linda: No, just the three of you. They're gonna blow you to a big meal!

Willy: Don't say! Who thought of that?

Linda: Biff came to me this morning, Willy, and he said, "Tell Dad, we want to blow him to a big meal." Be there six o'clock. You and your two boys are going to have dinner.

Willy: Gee whiz! That's really somethin'. I'm gonna knock Howard for a loop, kid. I'll get an advance, and I'll come home with a New York job. Goddammit, now I'm gonna do it!

Linda: Oh, that's the spirit, Willy!

Willy: I will never get behind a wheel the rest of my life!

Linda: It's changing, Willy, I can feel it changing!

Willy: Beyond a question. G'by, I'm late. *(He starts to go again.)*

Linda (calling after him as she runs to the kitchen table for a handkerchief): You got your glasses?

Willy (feels for them, then comes back in): Yeah, yeah, got my glasses.

Linda (giving him the handkerchief): And a handkerchief.

Willy: Yeah, handkerchief.

Linda: And your saccharine?

Willy: Yeah, my saccharine.

Linda: Be careful on the subway stairs.

> *She kisses him, and a silk stocking is seen hanging from her hand. Willy notices it.*

Willy: Will you stop mending stockings? At least while I'm in the house. It gets me nervous. I can't tell you. Please.

> *Linda hides the stocking in her hand as she follows Willy across the forestage in front of the house.*

Linda: Remember, Frank's Chop House.

Willy (passing the apron): Maybe beets would grow out there.

Linda (laughing): But you tried so many times.

Willy: Yeah. Well, don't work hard today. *(He disappears around the right corner of the house.)*

Linda: Be careful!

> *As Willy vanishes, Linda waves to him. Suddenly the phone rings. She runs across the stage and into the kitchen and lifts it.*

Linda: Hello? Oh, Biff! I'm so glad you called, I just . . . Yes, sure, I just told him. Yes, he'll be there for dinner at six o'clock, I didn't forget. Listen, I was just dying to tell you. You know that little rubber pipe I told you about? That he connected to the gas heater? I finally decided to go down the cellar this morning and take it away and destroy it. But it's gone! Imagine? He took it away himself, it isn't there! *(She listens.)* When? Oh, then you took it. Oh — nothing, it's just that I'd hoped he'd taken it away himself. Oh, I'm not worried, darling, because this morning he left in such high spirits, it was like the old days! I'm not afraid any more. Did Mr. Oliver see you? . . . Well, you wait there then. And make a nice impression on him, darling. Just don't perspire too much before you see him. And have a nice time with Dad. He may have big news too! . . . That's right, a New York job. And be sweet to him tonight, dear. Be loving to him. Because he's only a little boat looking for a harbor. *(She is trembling with sorrow and joy.)* Oh, that's wonderful, Biff, you'll save his life. Thanks, darling. Just put your arm around him when he comes into the restaurant. Give him a smile. That's the boy . . . Good-by, dear. . . . You got your comb? . . . That's fine. Good-by, Biff dear.

> *In the middle of her speech, Howard Wagner, thirty-six, wheels in a small type-writer table on which is a wire-recording machine and proceeds to plug it in. This is on the left forestage. Light slowly fades on Linda as it rises on Howard. Howard is intent on threading the machine and only glances over his shoulder as Willy appears.*

Willy: Pst! Pst!

Howard: Hello, Willy, come in.

Willy: Like to have a little talk with you, Howard.

Howard: Sorry to keep you waiting. I'll be with you in a minute.

Willy: What's that, Howard?

Howard: Didn't you ever see one of these? Wire recorder.

Willy: Oh. Can we talk a minute?

Howard: Records things. Just got delivery yesterday. Been driving me crazy, the most terrific machine I ever saw in my life. I was up all night with it.

Willy: What do you do with it?

Howard: I bought it for dictation, but you can do anything with it. Listen to this. I had it home last night. Listen to what I picked up. The first one is my daughter. Get this. *(He flicks the switch and "Roll Out the Barrel" is heard being whistled.)* Listen to that kid whistle.

Willy: That is lifelike, isn't it?

Howard: Seven years old. Get that tone.

Willy: Ts, ts. Like to ask a little favor if you . . .

> *The whistling breaks off, and the voice of Howard's daughter is heard.*

His Daughter: "Now you, Daddy."

Howard: She's crazy for me! *(Again the same song is whistled.)* That's me! Ha! *(He winks.)*

Willy: You're very good!

> *The whistling breaks off again. The machine runs silent for a moment.*

Howard: Sh! Get this now, this is my son.

His Son: "The capital of Alabama is Montgomery; the capital of Arizona is Phoenix; the capital of Arkansas is Little Rock; the capital of California is Sacramento . . . " *(and on, and on).*

Howard (holding up five fingers): Five years old, Willy!

Willy: He'll make an announcer some day!

His Son (continuing): "The capital . . . "

Howard: Get that—alphabetical order! *(The machine breaks off suddenly.)* Wait a minute. The maid kicked the plug out.

Willy: It certainly is a—

Howard: Sh, for God's sake!

His Son: "It's nine o'clock, Bulova watch time. So I have to go to sleep."

Willy: That really is—

Howard: Wait a minute! The next is my wife.

> *They wait.*

Howard's Voice: "Go on, say something." *(Pause.)* "Well, you gonna talk?"

His Wife: "I can't think of anything."

Howard's Voice: "Well, talk—it's turning."

His Wife (shyly, beaten): "Hello." *(Silence.)* "Oh, Howard, I can't talk into this . . ."

Howard (snapping the machine off): That was my wife.

Willy: That is a wonderful machine. Can we—

Howard: I tell you, Willy, I'm gonna take my camera, and my bandsaw, and all my hobbies, and out they go. This is the most fascinating relaxation I ever found.

Willy: I think I'll get one myself.

Howard: Sure, they're only a hundred and a half. You can't do without it. Supposing you wanna hear Jack Benny, see? But you can't be at home at that hour. So you tell the maid to turn the radio on when Jack Benny comes on, and this automatically goes on with the radio . . .

Willy: And when you come home you . . .

Howard: You can come home twelve o'clock, one o'clock, any time you like, and you get yourself a Coke and sit yourself down, throw the switch, and there's Jack Benny's program in the middle of the night!

Willy: I'm definitely going to get one. Because lots of time I'm on the road, and I think to myself, what I must be missing on the radio!

Howard: Don't you have a radio in the car?

Willy: Well, yeah, but who ever thinks of turning it on?

Howard: Say, aren't you supposed to be in Boston?

Willy: That's what I want to talk to you about, Howard. You got a minute? *(He draws a chair in from the wing.)*

Howard: What happened? What're you doing here?

Willy: Well . . .

Howard: You didn't crack up again, did you?

Willy: Oh, no. No . . .

Howard: Geez, you had me worried there for a minute. What's the trouble?

Willy: Well, tell you the truth, Howard. I've come to the decision that I'd rather not travel any more.

Howard: Not travel! Well, what'll you do?

Willy: Remember, Christmas time, when you had the party here? You said you'd try to think of some spot for me here in town.

Howard: With us?

Willy: Well, sure.

Howard: Oh, yeah, yeah. I remember. Well, I couldn't think of anything for you, Willy.

Willy: I tell ya, Howard. The kids are all grown up, y'know. I don't need much any more. If I could take home—well, sixty-five dollars a week, I could swing it.

Howard: Yeah, but Willy, see I—

Willy: I tell ya why, Howard. Speaking frankly and between the two of us, y'know—I'm just a little tired.

Howard: Oh, I could understand that, Willy. But you're a road man, Willy, and we do a road business. We've only got a half-dozen salesmen on the floor here.

Willy: God knows, Howard, I never asked a favor of any man. But I was with the firm when your father used to carry you in here in his arms.

Howard: I know that, Willy, but—

Willy: Your father came to me the day you were born and asked me what I thought of the name of Howard, may he rest in peace.

Howard: I appreciate that, Willy, but there just is no spot here for you. If I had a spot I'd slam you right in, but I just don't have a single solitary spot.

He looks for his lighter. Willy has picked it up and gives it to him. Pause.

Willy (with increasing anger): Howard, all I need to set my table is fifty dollars a week.

Howard: But where am I going to put you, kid?

Willy: Look, it isn't a question of whether I can sell merchandise, is it?

Howard: No, but it's a business, kid, and everybody's gotta pull his own weight.

Willy (desperately): Just let me tell you a story, Howard —

Howard: 'Cause you gotta admit, business is business.

Willy (angrily): Business is definitely business, but just listen for a minute. You don't understand this. When I was a boy — eighteen, nineteen — I was already on the road. And there was a question in my mind as to whether selling had a future for me. Because in those days I had a yearning to go to Alaska. See, there were three gold strikes in one month in Alaska, and I felt like going out. Just for the ride, you might say.

Howard (barely interested): Don't say.

Willy: Oh, yeah, my father lived many years in Alaska. He was an adventurous man. We've got quite a little streak of self-reliance in our family. I thought I'd go out with my older brother and try to locate him, and maybe settle in the North with the old man. And I was almost decided to go, when I met a salesman in the Parker House. His name was Dave Singleman. And he was eighty-four years old, and he'd drummed merchandise in thirty-one states. And old Dave, he'd go up to his room, y'understand, put on his green velvet slippers — I'll never forget — and pick up his phone and call the buyers, and without ever leaving his room, at the age of eighty-four, he made his living. And when I saw that, I realized that selling was the greatest career a man could want. 'Cause what could be more satisfying than to be able to go, at the age of eighty-four, into twenty or thirty different cities, and pick up a phone, and be remembered and loved and helped by so many different people? Do you know? when he died — and by the way he died the death of a salesman, in his green velvet slippers in the smoker of the New York, New Haven, and Hartford, going into Boston — when he died, hundreds of salesmen and buyers were at his funeral. Things were sad on a lotta trains for months after that. *(He stands up. Howard has not looked at him.)* In those days there was personality in it, Howard. There was respect, and comradeship, and gratitude in it. Today, it's all cut and dried, and there's no chance for bringing friendship to bear — or personality. You see what I mean? They don't know me any more.

Howard (moving away, to the right): That's just the thing, Willy.

Willy: If I had forty dollars a week — that's all I'd need. Forty dollars, Howard.

Howard: Kid, I can't take blood from a stone, I —

Willy (desperation is on him now): Howard, the year Al Smith° was nominated, your father came to me and —

Howard (starting to go off): I've got to see some people, kid.

Willy (stopping him): I'm talking about your father! There were promises made across this desk! You mustn't tell me you've got people to see — I put thirty-four years into this firm, Howard, and now I can't pay my insurance! You can't eat the orange and throw the peel away — a man is not a piece of fruit! *(After a pause.)* Now pay attention. Your father — in 1928 I had a big year. I averaged a hundred and seventy dollars a week in commissions.

Howard (impatiently): Now, Willy, you never averaged —

Willy (banging his hand on the desk): I averaged a hundred and seventy dollars a week in the year of 1928! And your father came to me — or rather, I was in

---

Al Smith: Democratic candidate for president of the United States in 1928 who lost the election to Herbert Hoover.

the office here — it was right over this desk — and he put his hand on my shoulder —

Howard (getting up): You'll have to excuse me, Willy, I gotta see some people. Pull yourself together. *(Going out.)* I'll be back in a little while.

On Howard's exit, the light on his chair grows very bright and strange.

Willy: Pull myself together! What the hell did I say to him? My God, I was yelling at him! How could I! *(Willy breaks off, staring at the light, which occupies the chair, animating it. He approaches this chair, standing across the desk from it.)* Frank, Frank, don't you remember what you told me that time? How you put your hand on my shoulder, and Frank . . . *(He leans on the desk and as he speaks the dead man's name he accidentally switches on the recorder, and instantly:)*

Howard's Son: ". . . of New York is Albany. The capital of Ohio is Cincinnati, the capital of Rhode Island is . . . " *(The recitation continues.)*

Willy (leaping away with fright, shouting): Ha! Howard! Howard! Howard!

Howard (rushing in): What happened?

Willy (pointing at the machine, which continues nasally, childishly, with the capital cities): Shut it off! Shut it off!

Howard (pulling the plug out): Look, Willy . . .

Willy (pressing his hands to his eyes): I gotta get myself some coffee. I'll get some coffee . . .

Willy starts to walk out. Howard stops him.

Howard (rolling up the cord): Willy, look . . .

Willy: I'll go to Boston.

Howard: Willy, you can't go to Boston for us.

Willy: Why can't I go?

Howard: I don't want you to represent us. I've been meaning to tell you for a long time now.

Willy: Howard, are you firing me?

Howard: I think you need a good long rest, Willy.

Willy: Howard —

Howard: And when you feel better, come back, and we'll see if we can work something out.

Willy: But I gotta earn money, Howard. I'm in no position to —

Howard: Where are your sons? Why don't your sons give you a hand?

Willy: They're working on a very big deal.

Howard: This is no time for false pride, Willy. You go to your sons and you tell them that you're tired. You've got two great boys, haven't you?

Willy: Oh, no question, no question, but in the meantime . . .

Howard: Then that's that, heh?

Willy: All right, I'll go to Boston tomorrow.

Howard: No, no.

Willy: I can't throw myself on my sons. I'm not a cripple!

Howard: Look, kid, I'm busy this morning.

Willy (grasping Howard's arm): Howard, you've got to let me go to Boston!

Howard (hard, keeping himself under control): I've got a line of people to see this morning. Sit down, take five minutes, and pull yourself together, and then go home, will ya? I need the office, Willy. *(He starts to go, turns, remembering the recorder, starts to push off the table holding the recorder.)* Oh, yeah. Whenever you can this week, stop by and drop off the samples. You'll feel better, Willy, and then come back and we'll talk. Pull yourself together, kid, there's people outside.

Howard exits, pushing the table off left. Willy stares into space, exhausted. Now the music is heard—Ben's music—first distantly, then closer, closer. As Willy speaks, Ben enters from the right. He carries valise and umbrella.

Willy: Oh, Ben, how did you do it? What is the answer? Did you wind up the Alaska deal already?

Ben: Doesn't take much time if you know what you're doing. Just a short business trip. Boarding ship in an hour. Wanted to say good-by.

Willy: Ben, I've got to talk to you.

Ben (glancing at his watch): Haven't the time, William.

Willy (crossing the apron to Ben): Ben, nothing's working out. I don't know what to do.

Ben: Now, look here, William. I've bought timberland in Alaska and I need a man to look after things for me.

Willy: God, timberland! Me and my boys in those grand outdoors!

Ben: You've a new continent at your doorstep, William. Get out of these cities, they're full of talk and time payments and courts of law. Screw on your fists and you can fight for a fortune up there.

Willy: Yes, yes! Linda, Linda!

Linda enters as of old, with the wash.

Linda: Oh, you're back?

Ben: I haven't much time.

Willy: No, wait! Linda, he's got a proposition for me in Alaska.

Linda: But you've got — *(To Ben.)* He's got a beautiful job here.

Willy: But in Alaska, kid, I could —

Linda: You're doing well enough, Willy!

Ben (to Linda): Enough for what, my dear?

Linda (frightened of Ben and angry at him): Don't say those things to him! Enough to be happy right here, right now. *(To Willy, while Ben laughs.)* Why must everybody conquer the world? You're well liked, and the boys love you, and someday — *(to Ben)* — why, old man Wagner told him just the other day that if he keeps it up he'll be a member of the firm, didn't he, Willy?

Willy: Sure, sure. I am building something with this firm, Ben, and if a man is building something he must be on the right track, mustn't he?

Ben: What are you building? Lay your hand on it. Where is it?

Willy (hesitantly): That's true, Linda, there's nothing.

Linda: Why? *(To Ben.)* There's a man eighty-four years old —

Willy: That's right, Ben, that's right. When I look at that man I say, what is there to worry about?

Ben: Bah!

Willy: It's true, Ben. All he has to do is go into any city, pick up the phone, and he's making his living and you know why?

Ben (picking up his valise): I've got to go.

Willy (holding Ben back): Look at this boy!

Biff, in his high school sweater, enters carrying suitcase. Happy carries Biff's shoul-der guards, gold helmet, and football pants.

Willy: Without a penny to his name, three great universities are begging for him, and from there the sky's the limit, because it's not what you do, Ben. It's who you know and the smile on your face! It's contacts, Ben, contacts! The whole wealth of Alaska passes over the lunch table at the Com-modore Hotel, and that's the wonder, the wonder of this country, that a man can end with diamonds here on the basis of being liked! *(He turns to Biff.)* And that's why when you get out on that field today it's important. Because thousands of people will be rooting for you and loving you. *(To Ben, who has again begun to leave.)* And Ben! when he walks into a business office his name will sound out like a bell and all the doors will open to him! I've seen it, Ben, I've seen it a thousand times! You can't feel it with your hand like timber, but it's there!

Ben: Good-by, William.

Willy: Ben, am I right? Don't you think I'm right? I value your advice.

Ben: There's a new continent at your doorstep, William. You could walk out rich. Rich! *(He is gone.)*

Willy: We'll do it here, Ben! You hear me? We're gonna do it here!

Young Bernard rushes in. The gay music of the Boys is heard.

Bernard: Oh, gee, I was afraid you left already!

Willy: Why? What time is it?

Bernard: It's half-past one!

Willy: Well, come on, everybody! Ebbets Field next stop! Where's the pennants? *(He rushes through the wall-line of the kitchen and out into the living-room.)*

Linda *(to Biff)*: Did you pack fresh underwear?

Biff *(who has been limbering up)*: I want to go!

Bernard: Biff, I'm carrying your helmet, ain't I?

Happy: I'm carrying the helmet.

Bernard: How am I going to get in the locker room?

Linda: Let him carry the shoulder guards. *(She puts her coat and hat on in the kitchen.)*

Bernard: Can I, Biff? 'Cause I told everybody I'm going to be in the locker room.

Happy: In Ebbets Field it's the clubhouse.

Bernard: I meant the clubhouse. Biff!

Happy: Biff!

Biff *(grandly, after a slight pause)*: Let him carry the shoulder guards.

Happy *(as he gives Bernard the shoulder guards)*: Stay close to us now.

Willy rushes in with the pennants.

Willy *(handing them out)*: Everybody wave when Biff comes out on the field. *(Happy and Bernard run off.)* You set now, boy?

The music has died away.

Biff: Ready to go, Pop. Every muscle is ready.

Willy *(at the edge of the apron)*: You realize what this means?

Biff: That's right, Pop.

Willy *(feeling Biff's muscles)*: You're comin' home this afternoon captain of the All-Scholastic Championship Team of the City of New York.

Biff: I got it, Pop. And remember, pal, when I take off my helmet, that touchdown is for you.

Willy: Let's go! *(He is starting out, with his arm around Biff, when Charley enters, as of old, in knickers.)* I got no room for you, Charley.

Charley: Room? For what?

Willy: In the car.

Charley: You goin' for a ride? I wanted to shoot some casino.

Willy (furiously): Casino! *(Incredulously.)* Don't you realize what today is?

Linda: Oh, he knows, Willy. He's just kidding you.

Willy: That's nothing to kid about!

Charley: No, Linda, what's goin' on?

Linda: He's playing in Ebbets Field.

Charley: Baseball in this weather?

Willy: Don't talk to him. Come on, come on! *(He is pushing them out.)*

Charley: Wait a minute, didn't you hear the news?

Willy: What?

Charley: Don't you listen to the radio? Ebbets Field just blew up.

Willy: You go to hell! *(Charley laughs. Pushing them out.)* Come on, come on! We're late.

Charley (as they go): Knock a homer, Biff, knock a homer!

Willy (the last to leave, turning to Charley): I don't think that was funny, Charley. This is the greatest day of his life.

Charley: Willy, when are you going to grow up?

Willy: Yeah, heh? When this game is over, Charley, you'll be laughing out of the other side of your face. They'll be calling him another Red Grange. Twenty-five thousand a year.

Charley (kidding): Is that so?

Willy: Yeah, that's so.

Charley: Well, then, I'm sorry, Willy. But tell me something.

Willy: What?

Charley: Who is Red Grange?

Willy: Put up your hands. Goddam you, put up your hands!

Charley, chuckling, shakes his head and walks away, around the left corner of the stage. Willy follows him. The music rises to a mocking frenzy.

Willy: Who the hell do you think you are, better than everybody else? You don't know everything, you big, ignorant, stupid . . . Put up your hands!

Light rises, on the right side of the forestage, on a small table in the reception room of Charley's office. Traffic sounds are heard. Bernard, now mature, sits whistling to himself. A pair of tennis rackets and an overnight bag are on the floor beside him.

Willy (offstage): What are you walking away for? Don't walk away! If you're going to say something say it to my face! I know you laugh at me behind my back. You'll laugh out of the other side of your goddam face after this game. Touchdown! Touchdown! Eighty thousand people! Touchdown! Right between the goal posts.

Bernard is a quiet, earnest, but self-assured young man. Willy's voice is coming from right upstage now. Bernard lowers his feet off the table and listens. Jenny, his father's secretary, enters.

Jenny (distressed): Say, Bernard, will you go out in the hall?

Bernard: What is that noise? Who is it?

Jenny: Mr. Loman. He just got off the elevator.

Bernard (getting up): Who's he arguing with?

Jenny: Nobody. There's nobody with him. I can't deal with him any more, and your father gets all upset everytime he comes. I've got a lot of typing to do, and your father's waiting to sign it. Will you see him?

Willy (entering): Touchdown! Touch — *(He sees Jenny.)* Jenny, Jenny, good to see you. How're ya? Workin'? Or still honest?

Jenny: Fine. How've you been feeling?

Willy: Not much any more, Jenny. Ha, ha! *(He is surprised to see the rackets.)*

Bernard: Hello, Uncle Willy.

Willy (almost shocked): Bernard! Well, look who's here! *(He comes quickly, guiltily, to Bernard and warmly shakes his hand.)*

Bernard: How are you? Good to see you.

Willy: What are you doing here?

Bernard: Oh, just stopped by to see Pop. Get off my feet till my train leaves. I'm going to Washington in a few minutes.

Willy: Is he in?

Bernard: Yes, he's in his office with the accountant. Sit down.

Willy (sitting down): What're you going to do in Washington?

Bernard: Oh, just a case I've got there, Willy.

Willy: That so? *(Indicating the rackets.)* You going to play tennis there?

Bernard: I'm staying with a friend who's got a court.

Willy: Don't say. His own tennis court. Must be fine people, I bet.

Bernard: They are, very nice. Dad tells me Biff's in town.

Willy (with a big smile): Yeah, Biff's in. Working on a very big deal, Bernard.

Bernard: What's Biff doing?

Willy: Well, he's been doing very big things in the West. But he decided to establish himself here. Very big. We're having dinner. Did I hear your wife had a boy?

Bernard: That's right. Our second.

Willy: Two boys! What do you know!

Bernard: What kind of a deal has Biff got?

Willy: Well, Bill Oliver — very big sporting-goods man — he wants Biff very badly. Called him in from the West. Long distance, carte blanche, special deliveries. Your friends have their own private tennis court?

Bernard: You still with the old firm, Willy?

Willy (after a pause): I'm — I'm overjoyed to see how you made the grade, Bernard, overjoyed. It's an encouraging thing to see a young man really — really — Looks very good for Biff — very — *(He breaks off, then.)* Bernard — *(He is so full of emotion, he breaks off again.)*

Bernard: What is it, Willy?

Willy (small and alone): What — what's the secret?

Bernard: What secret?

Willy: How — how did you? Why didn't he ever catch on?

Bernard: I wouldn't know that, Willy.

Willy (confidentially, desperately): You were his friend, his boyhood friend. There's something I don't understand about it. His life ended after that

Ebbets Field game. From the age of seventeen nothing good ever happened to him.

Bernard: He never trained himself for anything.

Willy: But he did, he did. After high school he took so many correspondence courses. Radio mechanics; television; God knows what, and never made the slightest mark.

Bernard (taking off his glasses): Willy, do you want to talk candidly?

Willy (rising, faces Bernard): I regard you as a very brilliant man, Bernard. I value your advice.

Bernard: Oh, the hell with the advice, Willy. I couldn't advise you. There's just one thing I've always wanted to ask you. When he was supposed to graduate, and the math teacher flunked him —

Willy: Oh, that son-of-a-bitch ruined his life.

Bernard: Yeah, but, Willy, all he had to do was go to summer school and make up that subject.

Willy: That's right, that's right.

Bernard: Did you tell him not to go to summer school?

Willy: Me? I begged him to go. I ordered him to go!

Bernard: Then why wouldn't he go?

Willy: Why? Why! Bernard, that question has been trailing me like a ghost for the last fifteen years. He flunked the subject, and laid down and died like a hammer hit him!

Bernard: Take it easy, kid.

Willy: Let me talk to you — I got nobody to talk to. Bernard, Bernard, was it my fault? Y'see? It keeps going around in my mind, maybe I did something to him. I got nothing to give him.

Bernard: Don't take it so hard.

Willy: Why did he lay down? What is the story there? You were his friend!

Bernard: Willy, I remember, it was June, and our grades came out. And he'd flunked math.

Willy: That son-of-a-bitch!

Bernard: No, it wasn't right then. Biff just got very angry, I remember, and he was ready to enroll in summer school.

Willy (surprised): He was?

Bernard: He wasn't beaten by it at all. But then, Willy, he disappeared from the block for almost a month. And I got the idea that he'd gone up to New England to see you. Did he have a talk with you then?

Willy stares in silence.

Bernard: Willy?

Willy (with a strong edge of resentment in his voice): Yeah, he came to Boston. What about it?

Bernard: Well, just that when he came back — I'll never forget this, it always mystifies me. Because I'd thought so well of Biff, even though he'd always taken advantage of me. I loved him, Willy, y'know? And he came back after that month and took his sneakers — remember those sneakers with "University of Virginia" printed on them? He was so proud of those, wore them every day. And he took them down in the cellar, and burned them up in the furnace. We had a fist fight. It lasted at least half an hour. Just the two of us, punching each other down the cellar, and crying right through it. I've often thought of how strange it was that I knew he'd given up his life. What happened in Boston, Willy?

Willy looks at him as at an intruder.

Bernard: I just bring it up because you asked me.

Willy (angrily): Nothing. What do you mean, "What happened?" What's that got to do with anything?

Bernard: Well, don't get sore.

Willy: What are you trying to do, blame it on me? If a boy lays down is that my fault?

Bernard: Now, Willy, don't get —

Willy: Well, don't — don't talk to me that way! What does that mean, "What happened?"

Charley enters. He is in his vest, and he carries a bottle of bourbon.

Charley: Hey, you're going to miss that train. (He waves the bottle.)

Bernard: Yeah, I'm going. (He takes the bottle.) Thanks, Pop. (He picks up his rackets and bag.) Good-by, Willy, and don't worry about it. You know. "If at first you don't succeed . . ."

Willy: Yes, I believe in that.

Bernard: But sometimes, Willy, it's better for a man just to walk away.

Willy: Walk away?

Bernard: That's right.

Willy: But if you can't walk away?

Bernard (after a slight pause): I guess that's when it's tough. (Extending his hand.) Good-by, Willy.

Willy (shaking Bernard's hand): Good-by, boy.

Charley (an arm on Bernard's shoulder): How do you like this kid? Gonna argue a case in front of the Supreme Court.

Bernard (protesting): Pop!

Willy (genuinely shocked, pained, and happy): No! The Supreme Court!

Bernard: I gotta run. 'By, Dad!

Charley: Knock 'em dead, Bernard!

Bernard goes off.

Willy (as Charley takes out his wallet): The Supreme Court! And he didn't even mention it!

Charley (counting out money on the desk): He don't have to — he's gonna do it.

Willy: And you never told him what to do, did you? You never took any interest in him.

Charley: My salvation is that I never took any interest in any thing. There's some money — fifty dollars. I got an accountant inside.

Willy: Charley, look . . . (With difficulty.) I got my insurance to pay. If you can manage it — I need a hundred and ten dollars.

Charley doesn't reply for a moment; merely stops moving.

Willy: I'd draw it from my bank but Linda would know, and I . . .

Charley: Sit down, Willy.

Willy (moving toward the chair): I'm keeping an account of everything, remember. I'll pay every penny back. (He sits.)

Charley: Now listen to me, Willy.

Willy: I want you to know I appreciate . . .

Charley (sitting down on the table): Willy, what're you doin'? What the hell is goin' on in your head?

Willy: Why? I'm simply . . .

Charley: I offered you a job. You can make fifty dollars a week. And I won't send you on the road.

Willy: I've got a job.

Charley: Without pay? What kind of a job is a job without pay? *(He rises.)* Now, look, kid, enough is enough. I'm no genius but I know when I'm being insulted.

Willy: Insulted!

Charley: Why don't you want to work for me?

Willy: What's the matter with you? I've got a job.

Charley: Then what're you walkin' in here every week for?

Willy (getting up): Well, if you don't want me to walk in here —

Charley: I am offering you a job.

Willy: I don't want your goddam job!

Charley: When the hell are you going to grow up?

Willy (furiously): You big ignoramus, if you say that to me again I'll rap you one! I don't care how big you are! *(He's ready to fight.)*

    Pause.

Charley (kindly, going to him): How much do you need, Willy?

Willy: Charley, I'm strapped. I'm strapped. I don't know what to do. I was just fired.

Charley: Howard fired you?

Willy: That snotnose. Imagine that? I named him. I named him Howard.

Charley: Willy, when're you gonna realize that them things don't mean anything? You named him Howard, but you can't sell that. The only thing you got in this world is what you can sell. And the funny thing is that you're a salesman, and you don't know that.

Willy: I've always tried to think otherwise, I guess. I always felt that if a man was impressive, and well liked, that nothing —

Charley: Why must everybody like you? Who liked J. P. Morgan? Was he impressive? In a Turkish bath he'd look like a butcher. But with his pockets on he was very well liked. Now listen, Willy, I know you don't like me, and nobody can say I'm in love with you, but I'll give you a job because — just for the hell of it, put it that way. Now what do you say?

Willy: I — I just can't work for you, Charley.

Charley: What're you, jealous of me?

Willy: I can't work for you, that's all, don't ask me why.

Charley (angered, takes out more bills): You been jealous of me all your life, you damned fool! Here, pay your insurance. *(He puts the money in Willy's hand.)*

Willy: I'm keeping strict accounts.

Charley: I've got some work to do. Take care of yourself. And pay your insurance.

Willy (moving to the right): Funny, y'know? After all the highways, and the trains, and the appointments, and the years, you end up worth more dead than alive.

Charley: Willy, nobody's worth nothin' dead. (*After a slight pause.*) Did you hear what I said?

Willy stands still, dreaming.

Charley: Willy!

Willy: Apologize to Bernard for me when you see him. I didn't mean to argue with him. He's a fine boy. They're all fine boys, and they'll end up big—all of them. Someday they'll all play tennis together. Wish me luck, Charley. He saw Bill Oliver today.

Charley: Good luck.

Willy (on the verge of tears): Charley, you're the only friend I got. Isn't that a remarkable thing? (*He goes out.*)

Charley: Jesus!

Charley stares after him a moment and follows. All light blacks out. Suddenly raucous music is heard, and a red glow rises behind the screen at right. Stanley, a young waiter, appears, carrying a table, followed by Happy, who is carrying two chairs.

Stanley (putting the table down): That's all right, Mr. Loman, I can handle it myself. (*He turns and takes the chairs from Happy and places them at the table.*)

Happy (glancing around): Oh, this is better.

Stanley: Sure, in the front there you're in the middle of all kinds a noise. Whenever you got a party, Mr. Loman, you just tell me and I'll put you back here. Y'know, there's a lotta people they don't like it private, because when they go out they like to see a lotta action around them because they're sick and tired to stay in the house by theirself. But I know you, you ain't from Hackensack. You know what I mean?

Happy (sitting down): So how's it coming, Stanley?

Stanley: Ah, it's a dog's life. I only wish during the war they'd a took me in the Army. I coulda been dead by now.

Happy: My brother's back, Stanley.

Stanley: Oh, he come back, heh? From the Far West.

Happy: Yeah, big cattle man, my brother, so treat him right. And my father's coming too.

Stanley: Oh, your father too!

Happy: You got a couple of nice lobsters?

Stanley: Hundred per cent, big.

Happy: I want them with the claws.

Stanley: Don't worry, I don't give you no mice. (*Happy laughs.*) How about some wine? It'll put a head on the meal.

Happy: No. You remember, Stanley, that recipe I brought you from overseas? With the champagne in it?

Stanley: Oh, yeah, sure. I still got it tacked up yet in the kitchen. But that'll have to cost a buck apiece anyways.

Happy: That's all right.

Stanley: What'd you, hit a number or somethin'?

Happy: No, it's a little celebration. My brother is—I think he pulled off a big deal today. I think we're going into business together.

Stanley: Great! That's the best for you. Because a family business, you know what I mean?—that's the best.

Happy: That's what I think.

Stanley: 'Cause what's the difference? Somebody steals? It's in the family. Know what I mean? *(Sotto voce.°)* Like this bartender here. The boss is goin' crazy what kinda leak he's got in the cash register. You put it in but it don't come out.

Happy (raising his head): Sh!

Stanley: What?

Happy: You notice I wasn't lookin' right or left, was I?

Stanley: No.

Happy: And my eyes are closed.

Stanley: So what's the — ?

Happy: Strudel's comin'.

Stanley (catching on, looks around): Ah, no, there's no —

> He breaks off as a furred, lavishly dressed girl enters and sits at the next table. Both follow her with their eyes.

Stanley: Geez, how'd ya know?

Happy: I got radar or something. *(Staring directly at her profile.)* Oooooooo . . . Stanley.

Stanley: I think that's for you, Mr. Loman.

Happy: Look at that mouth. Oh, God. And the binoculars.

Stanley: Geez, you got a life, Mr. Loman.

Happy: Wait on her.

Stanley (going to the girl's table): Would you like a menu, ma'am?

Girl: I'm expecting someone, but I'd like a —

Happy: Why don't you bring her — excuse me, miss, do you mind? I sell champagne, and I'd like you to try my brand. Bring her a champagne, Stanley.

Girl: That's awfully nice of you.

Happy: Don't mention it. It's all company money. *(He laughs.)*

Girl: That's a charming product to be selling, isn't it?

Happy: Oh, gets to be like everything else. Selling is selling, y'know.

Girl: I suppose.

Happy: You don't happen to sell, do you?

Girl: No, I don't sell.

Happy: Would you object to a compliment from a stranger? You ought to be on a magazine cover.

Girl (looking at him a little archly): I have been.

> Stanley comes in with a glass of champagne.

Happy: What'd I say before, Stanley? You see? She's a cover girl.

Stanley: Oh, I could see, I could see.

Happy (to the Girl): What magazine?

Girl: Oh, a lot of them. *(She takes the drink.)* Thank you.

Happy: You know what they say in France, don't you? "Champagne is the drink of the complexion" — Hya, Biff!

> Biff has entered and sits with Happy.

Biff: Hello, kid. Sorry I'm late.

Sotto voce: Softly, "under the breath" (Italian).

Happy: I just got here. Uh, Miss—?

Girl: Forsythe.

Happy: Miss Forsythe, this is my brother.

Biff: Is Dad here?

Happy: His name is Biff. You might've heard of him. Great football player.

Girl: Really? What team?

Happy: Are you familiar with football?

Girl: No, I'm afraid I'm not.

Happy: Biff is quarterback with the New York Giants.

Girl: Well, that is nice, isn't it? *(She drinks.)*

Happy: Good health.

Girl: I'm happy to meet you.

Happy: That's my name. Hap. It's really Harold, but at West Point they called me Happy.

Girl (now really impressed): Oh, I see. How do you do? *(She turns her profile.)*

Biff: Isn't Dad coming?

Happy: You want her?

Biff: Oh, I could never make that.

Happy: I remember the time that idea would never come into your head. Where's the old confidence, Biff?

Biff: I just saw Oliver—

Happy: Wait a minute. I've got to see that old confidence again. Do you want her? She's on call.

Biff: Oh, no. *(He turns to look at the Girl.)*

Happy: I'm telling you. Watch this. *(Turning to the Girl.)* Honey? *(She turns to him.)* Are you busy?

Girl: Well, I am . . . but I could make a phone call.

Happy: Do that, will you, honey? And see if you can get a friend. We'll be here for a while. Biff is one of the greatest football players in the country.

Girl (standing up): Well, I'm certainly happy to meet you.

Happy: Come back soon.

Girl: I'll try.

Happy: Don't try, honey, try hard.

The Girl exits. Stanley follows, shaking his head in bewildered admiration.

Happy: Isn't that a shame now? A beautiful girl like that? That's why I can't get married. There's not a good woman in a thousand. New York is loaded with them, kid!

Biff: Hap, look—

Happy: I told you she was on call!

Biff (strangely unnerved): Cut it out, will ya? I want to say something to you.

Happy: Did you see Oliver?

Biff: I saw him all right. Now look, I want to tell Dad a couple of things and I want you to help me.

Happy: What? Is he going to back you?

Biff: Are you crazy? You're out of your goddam head, you know that?

Happy: Why? What happened?

Biff (breathlessly): I did a terrible thing today, Hap. It's been the strangest day I ever went through. I'm all numb, I swear.

Happy: You mean he wouldn't see you?

Biff: Well, I waited six hours for him, see? All day. Kept sending my name in. Even tried to date his secretary so she'd get me to him, but no soap.

Happy: Because you're not showin' the old confidence, Biff. He remembered you, didn't he?

Biff (stopping Happy with a gesture): Finally, about five o'clock, he comes out. Didn't remember who I was or anything. I felt like such an idiot, Hap.

Happy: Did you tell him my Florida idea?

Biff: He walked away. I saw him for one minute. I got so mad I could've torn the walls down! How the hell did I ever get the idea I was a salesman there? I even believed myself that I'd been a salesman for him! And then he gave me one look and — I realized what a ridiculous lie my whole life has been! We've been talking in a dream for fifteen years. I was a shipping clerk.

Happy: What'd you do?

Biff (with great tension and wonder): Well, he left, see. And the secretary went out. I was all alone in the waiting-room. I don't know what came over me, Hap. The next thing I know I'm in his office — paneled walls, everything. I can't explain it. I — Hap, I took his fountain pen.

Happy: Geez, did he catch you?

Biff: I ran out. I ran down all eleven flights. I ran and ran and ran.

Happy: That was an awful dumb — what'd you do that for?

Biff (agonized): I don't know, I just — wanted to take something, I don't know. You gotta help me, Hap, I'm gonna tell Pop.

Happy: You crazy? What for?

Biff: Hap, he's got to understand that I'm not the man somebody lends that kind of money to. He thinks I've been spiting him all these years and it's eating him up.

Happy: That's just it. You tell him something nice.

Biff: I can't.

Happy: Say you got a lunch date with Oliver tomorrow.

Biff: So what do I do tomorrow?

Happy: You leave the house tomorrow and come back at night and say Oliver is thinking it over. And he thinks it over for a couple of weeks, and gradually it fades away and nobody's the worse.

Biff: But it'll go on forever!

Happy: Dad is never so happy as when he's looking forward to something!

    Willy enters.

Happy: Hello, scout!

Willy: Gee, I haven't been here in years!

    Stanley has followed Willy in and sets a chair for him. Stanley starts off but Happy stops him.

Happy: Stanley!

    Stanley stands by, waiting for an order.

Biff (going to Willy with guilt, as to an invalid): Sit down, Pop. You want a drink?

Willy: Sure, I don't mind.

Biff: Let's get a load on.

Willy: You look worried.

Biff: N-no. *(To Stanley.)* Scotch all around. Make it doubles.

Stanley: Doubles, right. *(He goes.)*

Willy: You had a couple already, didn't you?

Biff: Just a couple, yeah.

Willy: Well, what happened, boy? *(Nodding affirmatively, with a smile.)* Everything go all right?

Biff (takes a breath, then reaches out and grasps Willy's hand): Pal . . . *(He is smiling bravely, and Willy is smiling too.)* I had an experience today.

Happy: Terrific, Pop.

Willy: That so? What happened?

Biff (high, slightly alcoholic, above the earth): I'm going to tell you everything from first to last. It's been a strange day. *(Silence. He looks around, composes himself as best he can, but his breath keeps breaking the rhythm of his voice.)* I had to wait quite a while for him, and —

Willy: Oliver.

Biff: Yeah, Oliver. All day, as a matter of cold fact. And a lot of — instances — facts, Pop, facts about my life came back to me. Who was it, Pop? Who ever said I was a salesman with Oliver?

Willy: Well, you were.

Biff: No, Dad, I was a shipping clerk.

Willy: But you were practically —

Biff (with determination): Dad, I don't know who said it first, but I was never a salesman for Bill Oliver.

Willy: What're you talking about?

Biff: Let's hold on to the facts tonight, Pop. We're not going to get anywhere bullin' around. I was a shipping clerk.

Willy (angrily): All right, now listen to me —

Biff: Why don't you let me finish?

Willy: I'm not interested in stories about the past or any crap of that kind because the woods are burning, boys, you understand? There's a big blaze going on all around. I was fired today.

Biff (shocked): How could you be?

Willy: I was fired, and I'm looking for a little good news to tell your mother, because the woman has waited and the woman has suffered. The gist of it is that I haven't got a story left in my head, Biff. So don't give me a lecture about facts and aspects. I am not interested. Now what've you got to say to me?

Stanley enters with three drinks. They wait until he leaves.

Willy: Did you see Oliver?

Biff: Jesus, Dad!

Willy: You mean you didn't go up there?

Happy: Sure he went up there.

Biff: I did. I — saw him. How could they fire you?

Willy (on the edge of his chair): What kind of a welcome did he give you?

Biff: He won't even let you work on commission?

Willy: I'm out! *(Driving.)* So tell me, he gave you a warm welcome?

Happy: Sure, Pop, sure!

Biff (driven): Well, it was kind of —

Willy: I was wondering if he'd remember you. *(To Happy.)* Imagine, man doesn't see him for ten, twelve years and gives him that kind of a welcome!

Happy: Damn right!

Biff (trying to return to the offensive): Pop, look —

Willy: You know why he remembered you, don't you? Because you impressed him in those days.

Biff: Let's talk quietly and get this down to the facts, huh?

Willy (as though Biff had been interrupting): Well, what happened? It's great news, Biff. Did he take you into his office or'd you talk in the waiting-room?

Biff: Well, he came in, see, and —

Willy (with a big smile): What'd he say? Betcha he threw his arm around you.

Biff: Well, he kinda —

Willy: He's a fine man. *(To Happy.)* Very hard man to see, y'know.

Happy (agreeing): Oh, I know.

Willy (to Biff): Is that where you had the drinks?

Biff: Yeah, he gave me a couple of — no, no!

Happy (cutting in): He told him my Florida idea.

Willy: Don't interrupt. *(To Biff.)* How'd he react to the Florida idea?

Biff: Dad, will you give me a minute to explain?

Willy: I've been waiting for you to explain since I sat down here! What happened? He took you into his office and what?

Biff: Well — I talked. And — and he listened, see.

Willy: Famous for the way he listens, y'know. What was his answer?

Biff: His answer was — *(He breaks off, suddenly angry.)* Dad, you're not letting me tell you what I want to tell you!

Willy (accusing, angered): You didn't see him, did you?

Biff: I did see him!

Willy: What'd you insult him or something? You insulted him, didn't you?

Biff: Listen, will you let me out of it, will you just let me out of it!

Happy: What the hell!

Willy: Tell me what happened!

Biff (to Happy): I can't talk to him!

A single trumpet note jars the ear. The light of green leaves stains the house, which holds the air of night and a dream. Young Bernard enters and knocks on the door of the house.

Young Bernard (frantically): Mrs. Loman, Mrs. Loman!

Happy: Tell him what happened!

Biff (to Happy): Shut up and leave me alone!

Willy: No, no! You had to go and flunk math!

Biff: What math? What're you talking about?

Young Bernard: Mrs. Loman, Mrs. Loman!

Linda appears in the house, as of old.

Willy (wildly): Math, math, math!

Biff: Take it easy, Pop!

Young Bernard: Mrs. Loman!

Willy (furiously): If you hadn't flunked you'd've been set by now!

Biff: Now, look, I'm gonna tell you what happened, and you're going to listen to me.

Young Bernard: Mrs. Loman!

Biff: I waited six hours —

Happy: What the hell are you saying?

Biff: I kept sending in my name but he wouldn't see me. So finally he . . . *(He continues unheard as light fades low on the restaurant.)*

Young Bernard: Biff flunked math!

Linda: No!

Young Bernard: Birnbaum flunked him! They won't graduate him!

Linda: But they have to. He's gotta go to the university. Where is he? Biff! Biff!

Young Bernard: No, he left. He went to Grand Central.

Linda: Grand — You mean he went to Boston!

Young Bernard: Is Uncle Willy in Boston?

Linda: Oh, maybe Willy can talk to the teacher. Oh, the poor, poor boy!

> *Light on house area snaps out.*

Biff (at the table, now audible, holding up a gold fountain pen): . . . so I'm washed up with Oliver, you understand? Are you listening to me?

Willy (at a loss): Yeah, sure. If you hadn't flunked —

Biff: Flunked what? What're you talking about?

Willy: Don't blame everything on me! I didn't flunk math — you did! What pen?

Happy: That was awful dumb, Biff, a pen like that is worth —

Willy (seeing the pen for the first time): You took Oliver's pen?

Biff (weakening): Dad, I just explained it to you.

Willy: You stole Bill Oliver's fountain pen!

Biff: I didn't exactly steal it! That's just what I've been explaining to you!

Happy: He had it in his hand and just then Oliver walked in, so he got nervous and stuck it in his pocket!

Willy: My God, Biff!

Biff: I never intended to do it, Dad!

Operator's Voice: Standish Arms, good evening!

Willy (shouting): I'm not in my room!

Biff (frightened): Dad, what's the matter? *(He and Happy stand up.)*

Operator: Ringing Mr. Loman for you!

Willy: I'm not there, stop it!

Biff (horrified, gets down on one knee before Willy): Dad, I'll make good, I'll make good. *(Willy tries to get to his feet. Biff holds him down.)* Sit down now.

Willy: No, you're no good, you're no good for anything.

Biff: I am, Dad, I'll find something else, you understand? Now don't worry about anything. *(He holds up Willy's face.)* Talk to me, Dad.

Operator: Mr. Loman does not answer. Shall I page him?

Willy (attempting to stand, as though to rush and silence the Operator): No, no, no!

Happy: He'll strike something, Pop.

Willy: No, no . . .

Biff (desperately, standing over Willy): Pop, listen! Listen to me! I'm telling you something good. Oliver talked to his partner about the Florida idea. You listening? He — he talked to his partner, and he came to me . . . I'm going to be all right, you hear? Dad, listen to me, he said it was just a question of the amount!

Willy: Then you . . . got it?

Happy: He's gonna be terrific, Pop!

Willy (trying to stand): Then you got it, haven't you? You got it! You got it!

Biff (agonized, holds Willy down): No, no. Look, Pop. I'm supposed to have lunch with them tomorrow. I'm just telling you this so you'll know that I can still make an impression, Pop. And I'll make good somewhere, but I can't go tomorrow, see?

Willy: Why not? You simply —

Biff: But the pen, Pop!

Willy: You give it to him and tell him it was an oversight!

Happy: Sure, have lunch tomorrow!

Biff: I can't say that —

Willy: You were doing a crossword puzzle and accidentally used his pen!

Biff: Listen, kid, I took those balls years ago, now I walk in with his fountain pen? That clinches it, don't you see? I can't face him like that! I'll try elsewhere.

Page's Voice: Paging Mr. Loman!

Willy: Don't you want to be anything?

Biff: Pop, how can I go back?

Willy: You don't want to be anything, is that what's behind it?

Biff (now angry at Willy for not crediting his sympathy): Don't take it that way! You think it was easy walking into that office after what I'd done to him? A team of horses couldn't have dragged me back to Bill Oliver!

Willy: Then why'd you go?

Biff: Why did I go? Why did I go! Look at you! Look at what's become of you!

Off left, The Woman laughs.

Willy: Biff, you're going to lunch tomorrow, or —

Biff: I can't go. I've got no appointment!

Happy: Biff, for . . . !

Willy: Are you spiting me?

Biff: Don't take it that way! Goddammit!

Willy (strikes Biff and falters away from the table): You rotten little louse! Are you spiting me?

The Woman: Someone's at the door, Willy!

Biff: I'm no good, can't you see what I am?

Happy (separating them): Hey, you're in a restaurant! Now cut it out, both of you! *(The girls enter.)* Hello, girls, sit down.

The Woman laughs, off left.

Miss Forsythe: I guess we might as well. This is Letta.

The Woman: Willy, are you going to wake up?

Biff (ignoring Willy): How're ya, miss, sit down. What do you drink?

Miss Forsythe: Letta might not be able to stay long.

Letta: I gotta get up very early tomorrow. I got jury duty. I'm so excited! Were you fellows ever on a jury?

Biff: No, but I been in front of them! *(The girls laugh.)* This is my father.

Letta: Isn't he cute? Sit down with us, Pop.

Happy: Sit him down, Biff!

Biff (going to him): Come on, slugger, drink us under the table. To hell with it! Come on, sit down, pal.

On Biff's last insistence, Willy is about to sit.

The Woman (now urgently): Willy, are you going to answer the door!

The Woman's call pulls Willy back. He starts right, befuddled.

Biff: Hey, where are you going?

Willy: Open the door.

Biff: The door?

Willy: The washroom . . . the door . . . where's the door?

Biff (*leading Willy to the left*): Just go straight down.

> *Willy moves left.*

The Woman: Willy, Willy, are you going to get up, get up, get up, get up?

> *Willy exits left.*

Letta: I think it's sweet you bring your daddy along.

Miss Forsythe: Oh, he isn't really your father!

Biff (*at left, turning to her resentfully*): Miss Forsythe, you've just seen a prince walk by. A fine, troubled prince. A hard-working, unappreciated prince. A pal, you understand? A good companion. Always for his boys.

Letta: That's so sweet.

Happy: Well, girls, what's the program? We're wasting time. Come on, Biff. Gather round. Where would you like to go?

Biff: Why don't you do something for him?

Happy: Me!

Biff: Don't you give a damn for him, Hap?

Happy: What're you talking about? I'm the one who —

Biff: I sense it, you don't give a good goddamn about him. (*He takes the rolled-up hose from his pocket and puts it on the table in front of Happy.*) Look what I found in the cellar, for Christ's sake. How can you bear to let it go on?

Happy: Me? Who goes away? Who runs off and —

Biff: Yeah, but he doesn't mean anything to you. You could help him — I can't! Don't you understand what I'm talking about? He's going to kill himself, don't you know that?

Happy: Don't I know it! Me!

Biff: Hap, help him! Jesus . . . help him . . . Help me, help me, I can't bear to look at his face! (*Ready to weep, he hurries out, up right.*)

Happy (*starting after him*): Where are you going?

Miss Forsythe: What's he so mad about?

Happy: Come on, girls, we'll catch up with him.

Miss Forsythe (*as Happy pushes her out*): Say, I don't like that temper of his!

Happy: He's just a little overstrung, he'll be all right!

Willy (*off left, as The Woman laughs*): Don't answer! Don't answer!

Letta: Don't you want to tell your father —

Happy: No, that's not my father. He's just a guy. Come on, we'll catch Biff, and, honey, we're going to paint this town! Stanley, where's the check! Hey, Stanley!

> *They exit. Stanley looks toward left.*

Stanley (*calling to Happy indignantly*): Mr. Loman! Mr. Loman!

> *Stanley picks up a chair and follows them off. Knocking is heard off left. The Woman enters, laughing. Willy follows her. She is in a black slip; he is buttoning his shirt. Raw, sensuous music accompanies their speech.*

Willy: Will you stop laughing? Will you stop?

The Woman: Aren't you going to answer the door? He'll wake the whole hotel.

Willy: I'm not expecting anybody.

The Woman: Whyn't you have another drink, honey, and stop being so damn self-centered?

Willy: I'm so lonely.

The Woman: You know you ruined me, Willy? From now on, whenever you come to the office, I'll see that you go right through to the buyers. No waiting at my desk any more, Willy. You ruined me.

Willy: That's nice of you to say that.

The Woman: Gee, you are self-centered! Why so sad? You are the saddest, self-centeredest soul I ever did see-saw. *(She laughs. He kisses her.)* Come on inside, drummer boy. It's silly to be dressing in the middle of the night. *(As knocking is heard.)* Aren't you going to answer the door?

Willy: They're knocking on the wrong door.

The Woman: But I felt the knocking. And he heard us talking in here. Maybe the hotel's on fire!

Willy (his terror rising): It's a mistake.

The Woman: Then tell him to go away!

Willy: There's nobody there.

The Woman: It's getting on my nerves, Willy. There's somebody standing out there and it's getting on my nerves!

Willy (pushing her away from him): All right, stay in the bathroom here, and don't come out. I think there's a law in Massachusetts about it, so don't come out. It may be that new room clerk. He looked very mean. So don't come out. It's a mistake, there's no fire.

The knocking is heard again. He takes a few steps away from her, and she vanishes into the wing. The light follows him, and now he is facing Young Biff, who carries a suitcase. Biff steps toward him. The music is gone.

Biff: Why didn't you answer?

Willy: Biff! What are you doing in Boston?

Biff: Why didn't you answer? I've been knocking for five minutes, I called you on the phone—

Willy: I just heard you. I was in the bathroom and had the door shut. Did anything happen home?

Biff: Dad—I let you down.

Willy: What do you mean?

Biff: Dad . . .

Willy: Biffo, what's this about? *(Putting his arm around Biff.)* Come on, let's go downstairs and get you a malted.

Biff: Dad, I flunked math.

Willy: Not for the term?

Biff: The term. I haven't got enough credits to graduate.

Willy: You mean to say Bernard wouldn't give you the answers?

Biff: He did, he tried, but I only got a sixty-one.

Willy: And they wouldn't give you four points?

Biff: Birnbaum refused absolutely. I begged him, Pop, but he won't give me those points. You gotta talk to him before they close the school. Because if he saw the kind of man you are, and you just talked to him in your way, I'm sure he'd come through for me. The class came right before practice, see, and I didn't go enough. Would you talk to him? He'd like you, Pop. You know the way you could talk.

Willy: You're on. We'll drive right back.

Biff: Oh, Dad, good work! I'm sure he'll change it for you!

Willy: Go downstairs and tell the clerk I'm checkin' out. Go right down.

Biff: Yes, sir! See, the reason he hates me, Pop — one day he was late for class so I got up at the blackboard and imitated him. I crossed my eyes and talked with a lithp.

Willy (laughing): You did? The kids like it?

Biff: They nearly died laughing!

Willy: Yeah? What'd you do?

Biff: The thquare root of thixthy twee is . . . (*Willy bursts out laughing; Biff joins him.*) And in the middle of it he walked in!

Willy laughs and The Woman joins in offstage.

Willy (without hesitation): Hurry downstairs and —

Biff: Somebody in there?

Willy: No, that was next door.

The Woman laughs offstage.

Biff: Somebody got in your bathroom!

Willy: No, it's the next room, there's a party —

The Woman (enters, laughing. She lisps this): Can I come in? There's something in the bathtub, Willy, and it's moving!

Willy looks at Biff, who is staring open-mouthed and horrified at The Woman.

Willy: Ah — you better go back to your room. They must be finished painting by now. They're painting her room so I let her take a shower here. Go back, go back . . . (*He pushes her.*)

The Woman (resisting): But I've got to get dressed, Willy, I can't —

Willy: Get out of here! Go back, go back . . . (*Suddenly striving for the ordinary*): This is Miss Francis, Biff, she's a buyer. They're painting her room. Go back, Miss Francis, go back . . .

The Woman: But my clothes, I can't go out naked in the hall!

Willy (pushing her offstage): Get outa here! Go back, go back!

Biff slowly sits down on his suitcase as the argument continues offstage.

The Woman: Where's my stockings? You promised me stockings, Willy!

Willy: I have no stockings here!

The Woman: You had two boxes of size nine sheers for me, and I want them!

Willy: Here, for God's sake, will you get outa here!

The Woman (enters holding a box of stockings): I just hope there's nobody in the hall. That's all I hope. (*To Biff.*) Are you football or baseball?

Biff: Football.

The Woman (angry, humiliated): That's me too. G'night. (*She snatches her clothes from Willy, and walks out.*)

Willy (after a pause): Well, better get going. I want to get to the school first thing in the morning. Get my suits out of the closet. I'll get my valise. (*Biff doesn't move.*) What's the matter? (*Biff remains motionless, tears falling.*) She's a buyer. Buys for J. H. Simmons. She lives down the hall — they're painting. You don't imagine — *(He breaks off. After a pause.)* Now listen, pal, she's just a buyer. She sees merchandise in her room and they have to keep it looking just so . . . *(Pause. Assuming command.)* All right, get my suits. *(Biff doesn't move.)* Now stop crying and do as I say. I gave you an order. Biff, I gave you an order! Is that what you do when I give you an order? How dare you cry! *(Putting his arm around Biff.)* Now look, Biff, when you grow up you'll understand about these things. You mustn't — you mustn't overemphasize a thing like this. I'll see Birnbaum first thing in the morning.

Biff: Never mind.

Willy (getting down beside Biff): Never mind! He's going to give you those points. I'll see to it.

Biff: He wouldn't listen to you.

Willy: He certainly will listen to me. You need those points for the U. of Virginia.

Biff: I'm not going there.

Willy: Heh? If I can't get him to change that mark you'll make it up in summer school. You've got all summer to —

Biff (his weeping breaking from him): Dad . . .

Willy (infected by it): Oh, my boy . . .

Biff: Dad . . .

Willy: She's nothing to me, Biff. I was lonely, I was terribly lonely.

Biff: You — you gave her Mama's stockings! *(His tears break through and he rises to go.)*

Willy (grabbing for Biff): I gave you an order!

Biff: Don't touch me, you — liar!

Willy: Apologize for that!

Biff: You fake! You phony little fake! You fake! *(Overcome, he turns quickly and weeping fully goes out with his suitcase. Willy is left on the floor on his knees.)*

Willy: I gave you an order! Biff, come back here or I'll beat you! Come back here! I'll whip you!

     Stanley comes quickly in from the right and stands in front of Willy.

Willy (shouts at Stanley): I gave you an order . . .

Stanley: Hey, let's pick it up, pick it up, Mr. Loman. *(He helps Willy to his feet.)* Your boys left with the chippies. They said they'll see you home.

     A second waiter watches some distance away.

Willy: But we were supposed to have dinner together.

     Music is heard, Willy's theme.

Stanley: Can you make it?

Willy: I'll — sure, I can make it. *(Suddenly concerned about his clothes.)* Do I — I look all right?

Stanley: Sure, you look all right. *(He flicks a speck off Willy's lapel.)*

Willy: Here — here's a dollar.

Stanley: Oh, your son paid me. It's all right.

Willy (putting it in Stanley's hand): No, take it. You're a good boy.

Stanley: Oh, no, you don't have to . . .

Willy: Here — here's some more, I don't need it any more. *(After a slight pause.)* Tell me — is there a seed store in the neighborhood?

Stanley: Seeds? You mean like to plant?

As Willy turns, Stanley slips the money back into his jacket pocket.

Willy: Yes. Carrots, peas . . .

Stanley: Well, there's hardware stores on Sixth Avenue, but it may be too late now.

Willy (anxiously): Oh, I'd better hurry. I've got to get some seeds. *(He starts off to the right.)* I've got to get some seeds, right away. Nothing's planted. I don't have a thing in the ground.

Willy hurries out as the light goes down. Stanley moves over to the right after him, watches him off. The other waiter has been staring at Willy.

Stanley (to the waiter): Well, whatta you looking at?

The waiter picks up the chairs and moves off right. Stanley takes the table and follows him. The light fades on this area. There is a long pause, the sound of the flute coming over. The light gradually rises on the kitchen, which is empty. Happy appears at the door of the house, followed by Biff. Happy is carrying a large bunch of long-stemmed roses. He enters the kitchen, looks around for Linda. Not seeing her, he turns to Biff, who is just outside the house door, and makes a gesture with his hands, indicating "Not here, I guess." He looks into the living-room and freezes. Inside, Linda, unseen, is seated, Willy's coat on her lap. She rises ominously and quietly and moves toward Happy, who backs up into the kitchen, afraid.

Happy: Hey, what're you doing up? *(Linda says nothing but moves toward him implacably.)* Where's Pop? *(He keeps backing to the right, and now Linda is in full view in the doorway to the living-room.)* Is he sleeping?

Linda: Where were you?

Happy (trying to laugh it off): We met two girls, Mom, very fine types. Here, we brought you some flowers. *(Offering them to her.)* Put them in your room, Ma.

She knocks them to the floor at Biff's feet. He has now come inside and closed the door behind him. She stares at Biff, silent.

Happy: Now what'd you do that for? Mom, I want you to have some flowers—

Linda (cutting Happy off, violently to Biff): Don't you care whether he lives or dies?

Happy (going to the stairs): Come upstairs, Biff.

Biff (with a flare of disgust, to Happy): Go away from me! *(To Linda.)* What do you mean, lives or dies? Nobody's dying around here, pal.

Linda: Get out of my sight! Get out of here!

Biff: I wanna see the boss.

Linda: You're not going near him!

Biff: Where is he? *(He moves into the living-room and Linda follows.)*

Linda (shouting after Biff): You invite him for dinner. He looks forward to it all day— *(Biff appears in his parents' bedroom, looks around, and exits.)*—and then you desert him there. There's no stranger you'd do that to!

Happy: Why? He had a swell time with us. Listen, when I—*(Linda comes back into the kitchen)*—desert him I hope I don't outlive the day!

Linda: Get out of here!

Happy: Now look, Mom . . .

Linda: Did you have to go to women tonight? You and your lousy rotten whores!

Biff re-enters the kitchen.

Happy: Mom, all we did was follow Biff around trying to cheer him up! *(To Biff.)* Boy, what a night you gave me!

Linda: Get out of here, both of you, and don't come back! I don't want you tormenting him any more. Go on now, get your things together! *(To Biff.)* You can sleep in his apartment. *(She starts to pick up the flowers and stops herself.)* Pick up this stuff, I'm not your maid any more. Pick it up, you bum, you!

Happy turns his back to her in refusal. Biff slowly moves over and gets down on his knees, picking up the flowers.

Linda: You're a pair of animals! Not one, not another living soul would have had the cruelty to walk out on that man in a restaurant!

Biff (not looking at her): Is that what he said?

Linda: He didn't have to say anything. He was so humiliated he nearly limped when he came in.

Happy: But, Mom, he had a great time with us —

Biff (cutting him off violently): Shut up!

Without another word, Happy goes upstairs.

Linda: You! You didn't even go in to see if he was all right!

Biff (still on the floor in front of Linda, the flowers in his hand; with self-loathing): No. Didn't. Didn't do a damned thing. How do you like that, heh? Left him babbling in a toilet.

Linda: You louse. You . . .

Biff: Now you hit it on the nose! *(He gets up, throws the flowers in the wastebasket.)* The scum of the earth, and you're looking at him!

Linda: Get out of here!

Biff: I gotta talk to the boss, Mom. Where is he?

Linda: You're not going near him. Get out of this house!

Biff (with absolute assurance, determination): No. We're gonna have an abrupt conversation, him and me.

Linda: You're not talking to him!

Hammering is heard from outside the house, off right. Biff turns toward the noise.

Linda (suddenly pleading): Will you please leave him alone?

Biff: What's he doing out there?

Linda: He's planting the garden!

Biff (quietly): Now? Oh, my God!

Biff moves outside, Linda following. The light dies down on them and comes up on the center of the apron as Willy walks into it. He is carrying a flashlight, a hoe, and handful of seed packets. He raps the top of the hoe sharply to fix it firmly, and then moves to the left, measuring off the distance with his foot. He holds the flashlight to look at the seed packets, reading off the instructions. He is in the blue of night.

Willy: Carrots . . . quarter-inch apart. Rows . . . one-foot rows. *(He measures it off.)* One foot. *(He puts down a package and measures off.)* Beets. *(He puts down another package and measures again.)* Lettuce. *(He reads the package, puts it down.)* One foot — *(He breaks off as Ben appears at the right and moves slowly down to him.)* What a proposition, ts, ts. Terrific, terrific. 'Cause she's suffered, Ben, the woman has suffered. You understand me? A man can't go out the way he came in, Ben, a man has got to add up to something. You can't, you can't — *(Ben moves toward him as though to interrupt.)* You gotta consider, now. Don't answer so quick. Remember, it's a guaranteed twenty-thousand-dollar proposition. Now look, Ben, I want you to go through the ins and outs of this thing with me. I've got nobody to talk to, Ben, and the woman has suffered, you hear me?

Ben *(standing still, considering)*: What's the proposition?

Willy: It's twenty thousand dollars on the barrelhead. Guaranteed, gilt-edged, you understand?

Ben: You don't want to make a fool of yourself. They might not honor the policy.

Willy: How can they dare refuse? Didn't I work like a coolie to meet every premium on the nose? And now they don't pay off? Impossible!

Ben: It's called a cowardly thing, William.

Willy: Why? Does it take more guts to stand here the rest of my life ringing up a zero?

Ben *(yielding)*: That's a point, William. *(He moves, thinking, turns.)* And twenty thousand — that *is* something one can feel with the hand, it is there.

Willy *(now assured, with rising power)*: Oh, Ben, that's the whole beauty of it! I see it like a diamond, shining in the dark, hard and rough, that I can pick up and touch in my hand. Not like — like an appointment! This would not be another damned-fool appointment, Ben, and it changes all the aspects. Because he thinks I'm nothing, see, and so he spites me. But the funeral — *(Straightening up.)* Ben, that funeral will be massive! They'll come from Maine, Massachusetts, Vermont, New Hampshire! All the old-timers with the strange license plates — that boy will be thunder-struck, Ben, because he never realized — I am known! Rhode Island, New York, New Jersey — I am known, Ben, and he'll see it with his eyes once and for all. He'll see what I am, Ben! He's in for a shock, that boy!

Ben *(coming to the edge of the garden)*: He'll call you a coward.

Willy *(suddenly fearful)*: No, that would be terrible.

Ben: Yes. And a damned fool.

Willy: No, no, he mustn't, I won't have that! *(He is broken and desperate.)*

Ben: He'll hate you William.

The gay music of the Boys is heard.

Willy: Oh, Ben, how do we get back to all the great times? Used to be so full of light, and comradeship, the sleigh-riding in winter, and the ruddiness on his cheeks. And always some kind of good news coming up, always something nice coming up ahead. And never even let me carry the valises in the house, and simonizing, simonizing that little red car! Why, why can't I give him something and not have him hate me?

Ben: Let me think about it. *(He glances at his watch.)* I still have a little time. Remarkable proposition, but you've got to be sure you're not making a fool of yourself.

Ben drifts off upstage and goes out of sight. Biff comes down from the left.

Willy *(suddenly conscious of Biff, turns and looks up at him, then begins picking up the packages of seeds in confusion)*: Where the hell is that seed? *(Indignantly.)* You can't see nothing out here! They boxed in the whole goddamn neighborhood!

Biff: There are people all around here. Don't you realize that?

Willy: I'm busy. Don't bother me.

Biff (taking the hoe from Willy): I'm saying good-by to you, Pop. *(Willy looks at him, silent, unable to move.)* I'm not coming back any more.

Willy: You're not going to see Oliver tomorrow?

Biff: I've got no appointment, Dad.

Willy: He put his arm around you, and you've got no appointment?

Biff: Pop, get this now, will you? Everytime I've left it's been a fight that sent me out of here. Today I realized something about myself and I tried to explain it to you and I—I think I'm just not smart enough to make any sense out of it for you. To hell with whose fault it is or anything like that. *(He takes Willy's arm.)* Let's just wrap it up, heh? Come on in, we'll tell Mom. *(He gently tries to pull Willy to left.)*

Willy (frozen, immobile, with guilt in his voice): No, I don't want to see her.

Biff: Come on! *(He pulls again, and Willy tries to pull away.)*

Willy (highly nervous): No, no, I don't want to see her.

Biff (tries to look into Willy's face, as if to find the answer there): Why don't you want to see her?

Willy (more harshly now): Don't bother me, will you?

Biff: What do you mean, you don't want to see her? You don't want them calling you yellow, do you? This isn't your fault; it's me, I'm a bum. Now come inside! *(Willy strains to get away.)* Did you hear what I said to you?

Willy pulls away and quickly goes by himself into the house. Biff follows.

Linda (to Willy): Did you plant, dear?

Biff (at the door, to Linda): All right, we had it out. I'm going and I'm not writing any more.

Linda (going to Willy in the kitchen): I think that's the best way, dear. 'Cause there's no use drawing it out, you'll just never get along.

Willy doesn't respond.

Biff: People ask where I am and what I'm doing, you don't know, and you don't care. That way it'll be off your mind and you can start brightening up again. All right? That clears it, doesn't it? *(Willy is silent, and Biff goes to him.)* You gonna wish me luck, scout? *(He extends his hand.)* What do you say?

Linda: Shake his hand, Willy.

Willy (turning to her, seething with hurt): There's no necessity to mention the pen at all, y'know.

Biff (gently): I've got no appointment, Dad.

Willy (erupting fiercely): He put his arm around . . . ?

Biff: Dad, you're never going to see what I am, so what's the use of arguing? If I strike oil I'll send you a check. Meantime forget I'm alive.

Willy (to Linda): Spite, see?

Biff: Shake hands, Dad.

Willy: Not my hand.

Biff: I was hoping not to go this way.

Willy: Well, this is the way you're going. Good-by.

Biff looks at him a moment, then turns sharply and goes to the stairs.

Willy (stops him with): May you rot in hell if you leave this house!

Biff (turning): Exactly what is it that you want from me?

Willy: I want you to know, on the train, in the mountains, in the valleys, wherever you go, that you cut down your life for spite!

Biff: No, no.

Willy: Spite, spite, is the word of your undoing! And when you're down and out, remember what did it. When you're rotting somewhere beside the railroad tracks, remember, and don't you dare blame it on me!

Biff: I'm not blaming it on you!

Willy: I won't take the rap for this, you hear?

Happy comes down the stairs and stands on the bottom step, watching.

Biff: That's just what I'm telling you!

Willy (sinking into a chair at the table, with full accusation): You're trying to put a knife in me — don't think I don't know what you're doing!

Biff: All right, phony! Then let's lay it on the line. *(He whips the rubber tube out of his pocket and puts it on the table.)*

Happy: You crazy —

Linda: Biff! *(She moves to grab the hose, but Biff holds it down with his hand.)*

Biff: Leave it there! Don't move it!

Willy (not looking at it): What is that?

Biff: You know goddam well what that is.

Willy (caged, wanting to escape): I never saw that.

Biff: You saw it. The mice didn't bring it into the cellar! What is this supposed to do, make a hero out of you? This supposed to make me sorry for you?

Willy: Never heard of it.

Biff: There'll be no pity for you, you hear it? No pity!

Willy (to Linda): You hear the spite!

Biff: No, you're going to hear the truth — what you are and what I am!

Linda: Stop it!

Willy: Spite!

Happy (coming down toward Biff): You cut it now!

Biff (to Happy): The man don't know who we are! The man is gonna know! *(To Willy.)* We never told the truth for ten minutes in this house!

Happy: We always told the truth!

Biff (turning on him): You big blow, are you the assistant buyer? You're one of the two assistants to the assistant, aren't you?

Happy: Well, I'm practically —

Biff: You're practically full of it! We all are! And I'm through with it. *(To Willy.)* Now hear this, Willy, this is me.

Willy: I know you!

Biff: You know why I had no address for three months? I stole a suit in Kansas City and I was in jail. *(To Linda, who is sobbing.)* Stop crying. I'm through with it.

Linda turns away from them, her hands covering her face.

Willy: I suppose that's my fault!

Biff: I stole myself out of every good job since high school!

Willy: And whose fault is that?

Biff: And I never got anywhere because you blew me so full of hot air I could never stand taking orders from anybody! That's whose fault it is!

Willy: I hear that!

Linda: Don't, Biff!

Biff: It's goddam time you heard that! I had to be boss big shot in two weeks, and I'm through with it!

Willy: Then hang yourself! For spite, hang yourself!

Biff: No! Nobody's hanging himself, Willy! I ran down eleven flights with a pen in my hand today. And suddenly I stopped, you hear me? And in the middle of that office building, do you hear this? I stopped in the middle of that building and I saw — the sky. I saw the things that I love in this world. The work and the food and time to sit and smoke. And I looked at the pen and said to myself, what the hell am I grabbing this for? Why am I trying to become what I don't want to be? What am I doing in an office, making a contemptuous, begging fool of myself, when all I want is out there, waiting for me the minute I say I know who I am! Why can't I say that, Willy? *(He tries to make Willy face him, but Willy pulls away and moves to the left.)*

Willy (with hatred, threateningly): The door of your life is wide open!

Biff: Pop! I'm a dime a dozen, and so are you!

Willy (turning on him now in an uncontrolled outburst): I am not a dime a dozen! I am Willy Loman, and you are Biff Loman!

Biff starts for Willy, but is blocked by Happy. In his fury, Biff seems on the verge of attacking his father.

Biff: I am not a leader of men, Willy, and neither are you. You were never anything but a hard-working drummer who landed in the ash can like all the rest of them! I'm one dollar an hour, Willy! I tried seven states and couldn't raise it. A buck an hour! Do you gather my meaning? I'm not bringing home any prizes any more, and you're going to stop waiting for me to bring them home!

Willy (directly to Biff): You vengeful, spiteful mut!

Biff breaks from Happy. Willy, in fright, starts up the stairs. Biff grabs him.

Biff (at the peak of his fury): Pop, I'm nothing! I'm nothing, Pop. Can't you understand that? There's no spite in it any more. I'm just what I am, that's all.

Biff's fury has spent itself, and he breaks down, sobbing, holding on to Willy, who dumbly fumbles for Biff's face.

Willy (astonished): What're you doing? What're you doing? *(To Linda.)* Why is he crying?

Biff (crying, broken): Will you let me go, for Christ's sake? Will you take that phony dream and burn it before something happens? *(Struggling to contain himself, he pulls away and moves to the stairs.)* I'll go in the morning. Put him — put him to bed. *(Exhausted, Biff moves up the stairs to his room.)*

Willy (after a long pause, astonished, elevated): Isn't that — isn't that remarkable? Biff — he likes me!

Linda: He loves you, Willy!

Happy (deeply moved): Always did, Pop.

Willy: Oh, Biff! *(Staring wildly.)* He cried! Cried to me. *(He is choking with his love, and now cries out his promise.)* That boy — that boy is going to be magnificent!

Ben appears in the light just outside the kitchen.

Ben: Yes, outstanding, with twenty thousand behind him.

Linda (sensing the racing of his mind, fearfully, carefully): Now come to bed, Willy. It's all settled now.

Willy (finding it difficult not to rush out of the house): Yes, we'll sleep. Come on. Go to sleep, Hap.

Ben: And it does take a great kind of a man to crack the jungle.

> *In accents of dread, Ben's idyllic music starts up.*

Happy (his arm around Linda): I'm getting married, Pop, don't forget it. I'm changing everything. I'm gonna run that department before the year is up. You'll see, Mom. *(He kisses her.)*

Ben: The jungle is dark but full of diamonds, Willy.

> *Willy turns, moves, listening to Ben.*

Linda: Be good. You're both good boys, just act that way, that's all.

Happy: 'Night, Pop. *(He goes upstairs.)*

Linda (to Willy): Come, dear.

Ben (with greater force): One must go in to fetch a diamond out.

Willy (to Linda, as he moves slowly along the edge of the kitchen, toward the door): I just want to get settled down, Linda. Let me sit alone for a little.

Linda (almost uttering her fear): I want you upstairs.

Willy (taking her in his arms): In a few minutes, Linda. I couldn't sleep right now. Go on, you look awful tired. *(He kisses her.)*

Ben: Not like an appointment at all. A diamond is rough and hard to the touch.

Willy: Go on now. I'll be right up.

Linda: I think this is the only way, Willy.

Willy: Sure, it's the best thing.

Ben: Best thing!

Willy: The only way. Everything is gonna be — go on, kid, get to bed. You look so tired.

Linda: Come right up.

Willy: Two minutes.

> *Linda goes into the living-room, then reappears in her bedroom. Willy moves just outside the kitchen door.*

Willy: Loves me. *(Wonderingly.)* Always loved me. Isn't that a remarkable thing? Ben, he'll worship me for it!

Ben (with promise): It's dark there, but full of diamonds.

Willy: Can you imagine that magnificence with twenty thousand dollars in his pocket?

Linda (calling from her room): Willy! Come up!

Willy (calling into the kitchen): Yes! Yes. Coming! It's very smart, you realize that, don't you, sweetheart? Even Ben sees it. I gotta go, baby. 'By! 'By! *(Going over to Ben, almost dancing.)* Imagine? When the mail comes he'll be ahead of Bernard again!

Ben: A perfect proposition all around.

Willy: Did you see how he cried to me? Oh, if I could kiss him, Ben!

Ben: Time, William, time!

Willy: Oh, Ben, I always knew one way or another we were gonna make it, Biff and I!

Ben (looking at his watch): The boat. We'll be late. *(He moves slowly off into the darkness.)*

Willy (elegiacally, turning to the house): Now when you kick off, boy, I want a seventy-yard boot, and get right down the field under the ball, and when you hit, hit low and hit hard, because it's important, boy. *(He swings around and faces the audience.)* There's all kinds of important people in the stands, and the first thing you know . . . *(Suddenly realizing he is alone.)* Ben! Ben, where do I . . . ? *(He makes a sudden movement of search.)* Ben, how do I . . . ?

Linda (calling): Willy, you coming up?

Willy (uttering a gasp of fear, whirling about as if to quiet her): Sh! *(He turns around as if to find his way; sounds, faces, voices, seem to be swarming in upon him and he flicks at them, crying.)* Sh! Sh! *(Suddenly music, faint and high, stops him. It rises in intensity, almost to an unbearable scream. He goes up and down on his toes, and rushes off around the house.)* Shhh!

Linda: Willy?

> *There is no answer. Linda waits. Biff gets up off his bed. He is still in his clothes. Happy sits up. Biff stands listening.*

Linda (with real fear): Willy, answer me! Willy!

> *There is the sound of a car starting and moving away at full speed.*

Linda: No!

Biff (rushing down the stairs): Pop!

> *As the car speeds off, the music crashes down in a frenzy of sound, which becomes the soft pulsation of a single cello string. Biff slowly returns to his bedroom. He and Happy gravely don their jackets. Linda slowly walks out of her room. The music has developed into a dead march. The leaves of day are appearing over everything. Charley and Bernard, somberly dressed, appear and knock on the kitchen door. Biff and Happy slowly descend the stairs to the kitchen as Charley and Bernard enter. All stop a moment when Linda, in clothes of mourning, bearing a little bunch of roses, comes through the draped doorway into the kitchen. She goes to Charley and takes his arm. Now all move toward the audience, through the wall-line of the kitchen. At the limit of the apron, Linda lays down the flowers, kneels, and sits back on her heels. All stare down at the grave.*

REQUIEM

Charley: It's getting dark, Linda.

> *Linda doesn't react. She stares at the grave.*

Biff: How about it, Mom? Better get some rest, heh? They'll be closing the gate soon.

> *Linda makes no move. Pause.*

Happy (deeply angered): He had no right to do that. There was no necessity for it. We would've helped him.

Charley (grunting): Hmmm.

Biff: Come along, Mom.

Linda: Why didn't anybody come?

Charley: It was a very nice funeral.

Linda: But where are all the people he knew? Maybe they blame him.

Charley: Naa. It's a rough world, Linda. They wouldn't blame him.

Linda: I can't understand it. At this time especially. First time in thirty-five years we were just about free and clear. He only needed a little salary. He was even finished with the dentist.

Charley: No man only needs a little salary.

Linda: I can't understand it.

Biff: There were a lot of nice days. When he'd come home from a trip; or on Sundays, making the stoop; finishing the cellar; putting on the new porch; when he built the extra bathroom; and put up the garage. You know something, Charley, there's more of him in that front stoop than in all the sales he ever made.

Charley: Yeah. He was a happy man with a batch of cement.

Linda: He was so wonderful with his hands.

Biff: He had the wrong dreams. All, all, wrong.

Happy (almost ready to fight Biff): Don't say that!

Biff: He never knew who he was.

Charley (stopping Happy's movement and reply. To Biff): Nobody dast blame this man. You don't understand: Willy was a salesman. And for a salesman, there is no rock bottom to the life. He don't put a bolt to a nut, he don't tell you the law or give you medicine. He's a man way out there in the blue, riding on a smile and a shoeshine. And when they start not smiling back — that's an earthquake. And then you get yourself a couple of spots on your hat, and you're finished. Nobody dast blame this man. A salesman is got to dream, boy. It comes with the territory.

Biff: Charley, the man didn't know who he was.

Happy (infuriated): Don't say that!

Biff: Why don't you come with me, Happy?

Happy: I'm not licked that easily. I'm staying right in this city, and I'm gonna beat this racket! *(He looks at Biff, his chin set.)* The Loman Brothers!

Biff: I know who I am, kid.

Happy: All right, boy. I'm gonna show you and everybody else that Willy Loman did not die in vain. He had a good dream. It's the only dream you can have — to come out number-one man. He fought it out here, and this is where I'm gonna win it for him.

Biff (with a hopeless glance at Happy, bends toward his mother): Let's go, Mom.

Linda: I'll be with you in a minute. Go on, Charley. *(He hesitates.)* I want to, just for a minute. I never had a chance to say good-by.

Charley moves away, followed by Happy. Biff remains a slight distance up and left of Linda. She sits there, summoning herself. The flute begins, not far away, playing behind her speech.

Linda: Forgive me, dear. I can't cry. I don't know what it is, but I can't cry. I don't understand it. Why did you ever do that? Help me, Willy, I can't cry. It seems to me that you're just on another trip. I keep expecting you. Willy, dear, I can't cry. Why did you do it? I search and search and I search, and I can't understand it, Willy. I made the last payment on the house today. Today, dear. And there'll be nobody home. *(A sob rises in her throat.)* We're free and clear. *(Sobbing more fully, released.)* We're free. *(Biff comes slowly toward her.)* We're free . . . We're free . . .

Biff lifts her to her feet and moves out up right with her in his arms. Linda sobs quietly. Bernard and Charley come together and follow them, followed by Happy. Only the music of the flute is left on the darkening stage as over the house the hard towers of the apartment buildings rise into sharp focus, and

The Curtain Falls

CONNECTIONS TO OTHER SELECTIONS

1. Compare and contrast Willy Loman with Polonius in Shakespeare's *Hamlet* (p. 1450). To what extent is each character wise, foolish, deluded, and hypocritical? Explain why Loman can be seen as a tragic character while Polonius cannot be.

2. Read Tato Laviera's poem "AmeRícan" (p. 931), and compare its treatment of the American dream with the one in *Death of a Salesman*. How do the tones of the two works differ?

3. What similarities do you find between the endings of *Death of a Salesman* and August Wilson's *The Piano Lesson* (p. 2031)? Are the endings happy, unhappy, or something else?

PERSPECTIVES

ARTHUR MILLER (B. 1915)
Tragedy and the Common Man   1949

In this age few tragedies are written. It has often been held that the lack is due to a paucity of heroes among us, or else that modern man has had the blood drawn out of his organs of belief by the skepticism of science, and the heroic attack on life cannot feed on an attitude of reserve and circumspection. For one reason or another, we are often held to be below tragedy — or tragedy above us. The inevitable conclusion is, of course, that the tragic mode is archaic, fit only for the very highly placed, the kings or the kingly, and where this admission is not made in so many words it is most often implied.

I believe that the common man is as apt a subject for tragedy in its highest sense as kings were. On the face of it this ought to be obvious in the light of modern psychiatry, which bases its analysis upon classic formulations, such as the Oedipus and Orestes complexes, for instance, which were enacted by royal beings, but which apply to everyone in similar emotional situations.

More simply, when the question of tragedy in art is not at issue, we never hesitate to attribute to the well-placed and the exalted the very same mental processes as the lowly. And finally, if the exaltation of tragic action were truly a property of the high-bred character alone, it is inconceivable that the mass of mankind should cherish tragedy above all other forms, let alone be capable of understanding it.

As a general rule, to which there may be exceptions unknown to me, I think the tragic feeling is evoked in us when we are in the presence of a character who is ready to lay down his life, if need be, to secure one thing — his sense of personal dignity. From Orestes to Hamlet, Medea to Macbeth, the underlying struggle is that of the individual attempting to gain his "rightful" position in his society.

Sometimes he is one who has been displaced from it, sometimes one who seeks to attain it for the first time, but the fateful wound from which the inevitable events spiral is the wound of indignity, and its dominant force is indignation. Tragedy, then, is the consequence of a man's total compulsion to evaluate himself justly.

In the sense of having been initiated by the hero himself, the tale always reveals what has been called his "tragic flaw," a failing that is not peculiar to grand or elevated characters. Nor is it necessarily a weakness. The flaw, or crack in the character, is really nothing—and need be nothing—but his inherent unwillingness to remain passive in the face of what he conceives to be a challenge to his dignity, his image of his rightful status. Only the passive, only those who accept their lot without active retaliation, are "flawless." Most of us are in that category.

But there are among us today, as there always have been, those who act against the scheme of things that degrades them, and in the process of action, everything we have accepted out of fear or insensitivity or ignorance is shaken before us and examined, and from this total onslaught by an individual against the seemingly stable cosmos surrounding us—from this total examination of the "unchangeable" environment—comes the terror and the fear that is classically associated with tragedy.

More important, from this total questioning of what has been previously unquestioned, we learn. And such a process is not beyond the common man. In revolutions around the world, these past thirty years, he has demonstrated again and again this inner dynamic of all tragedy.

Insistence upon the rank of the tragic hero, or the so-called nobility of his character, is really but a clinging to the outward forms of tragedy. If rank or nobility of character was indispensable, then it would follow that the problems of those with rank were the particular problems of tragedy. But surely the right of one monarch to capture the domain from another no longer raises our passions, nor are our concepts of justice what they were to the mind of an Elizabethan king.

The quality in such plays that does shake us, however, derives from the underlying fear of being displaced, the disaster inherent in being torn away from our chosen image of what and who we are in this world. Among us today this fear is as strong, and perhaps stronger, than it ever was. In fact, it is the common man who knows this fear best.

Now, if it is true that tragedy is the consequence of a man's total compulsion to evaluate himself justly, his destruction in the attempt posits a wrong or an evil in his environment. And this is precisely the morality of tragedy and its lesson. The discovery of the moral law, which is what the enlightenment of tragedy consists of, is not the discovery of some abstract or metaphysical quantity.

The tragic right is a condition of life, a condition in which the human personality is able to flower and realize itself. The wrong is the condition which suppresses man, perverts the flowing out of his love and creative instinct. Tragedy enlightens—and it must, in that it points the heroic finger at the enemy of man's freedom. The thrust for freedom is the quality in tragedy which exalts. The revolutionary questioning of the stable environment is what terrifies. In no way is the common man debarred from such thoughts or such actions.

Seen in this light, our lack of tragedy may be partially accounted for by the turn which modern literature has taken toward the purely psychiatric view of life, or the purely sociological. If all our miseries, our indignities, are born and bred within our minds, then all action, let alone the heroic action, is obviously impossible.

And if society alone is responsible for the cramping of our lives, then the protagonist must needs be so pure and faultless as to force us to deny his validity as a character. From neither of these views can tragedy derive, simply because neither represents a balanced concept of life. Above all else, tragedy requires the finest appreciation by the writer of cause and effect.

No tragedy can therefore come about when its author fears to question absolutely everything, when he regards any institution, habit, or custom as being either everlasting, immutable, or inevitable. In the tragic view the need of man to wholly realize himself is the only fixed star, and whatever it is that hedges his nature and lowers it is ripe for attack and examination. Which is not to say that tragedy must preach revolution.

The Greeks could probe the very heavenly origin of their ways and return to confirm the rightness of laws. And Job could face God in anger, demanding his right, and end in submission. But for a moment everything is in suspension, nothing is accepted, and in this stretching and tearing apart of the cosmos, in the very action of so doing, the character gains "size," the tragic stature which is spuriously attached to the royal or the high born in our minds. The commonest of men may take on that stature to the extent of his willingness to throw all he has into the contest, the battle to secure his rightful place in his world.

There is a misconception of tragedy with which I have been struck in review after review, and in many conversations with writers and readers alike. It is the idea that tragedy is of necessity allied to pessimism. Even the dictionary says nothing more about the word than that it means a story with a sad or unhappy ending. This impression is so firmly fixed that I almost hesitate to claim that in truth tragedy implies more optimism in its author than does comedy, and that its final result ought to be the reinforcement of the onlooker's brightest opinions of the human animal.

For, if it is true to say that in essence the tragic hero is intent upon claiming his whole due as a personality, and if this struggle must be total and without reservation, then it automatically demonstrates the indestructible will of man to achieve his humanity.

The possibility of victory must be there in tragedy. Where pathos rules, where pathos is finally derived, a character has fought a battle he could not possibly have won. The pathetic is achieved when the protagonist is, by virtue of his witlessness, his insensitivity, or the very air he gives off, incapable of grappling with a much superior force.

Pathos truly is the mode for the pessimist. But tragedy requires a nicer balance between what is possible and what is impossible. And it is curious, although edifying, that the plays we revere, century after century, are the tragedies. In them, and in them alone, lies the belief—optimistic, if you will—in the perfectibility of man.

It is time, I think, that we who are without kings, took up this bright thread of our history and followed it to the only place it can possibly lead in our time—the heart and spirit of the average man.

From *Theater Essays of Arthur Miller*

CONSIDERATIONS FOR CRITICAL THINKING AND WRITING

1. According to Miller, why is there a "lack" (para. 1) of tragedy in modern literature? Why do psychological and sociological accounts of human behavior limit the possibilities for tragedy?

2. Why is the "common man" (para. 2) a suitable subject for tragedy? How does Miller's view of tragedy compare with Aristotle's (p. 1369)?

3. What distinction does Miller make between tragedy and pathos? Which term best characterizes Willy Loman in *Death of a Salesman*? Explain why.

ARTHUR MILLER (B. 1915)

On Biff and Willy Loman — 1950

A serious theme is entertaining to the extent that it is not trifled with, not cleverly angled, but met in head-on collision. [The audience] will not consent to suffer while the creators stand by with tongue in cheek. They have a way of knowing. Nobody can blame them.

And there have been certain disappointments, one above all. I am sorry the self-realization of the older son, Biff, is not a weightier counterbalance to Willy's disaster in the audience's mind.

And certain things are more clearly known, or so it seems now. We want to give of ourselves, and yet all we train for is to take, as though nothing less will keep the world at a safe distance. Every day we contradict our will to create, which is to give. The end of man is not security, but without security we are without the elementary condition of humaneness.

To me the tragedy of Willy Loman is that he gave his life, or sold it, in order to justify the waste of it. It is the tragedy of a man who did believe that he alone was not meeting the qualifications laid down for mankind by those clean-shaven frontiersmen who inhabit the peaks of broadcasting and advertising offices. From those forests of canned goods high up near the sky, he heard the thundering command to succeed as it ricocheted down the newspaper-lined canyons of his city, heard not a human voice, but a wind of a voice to which no human can reply in kind, except to stare into the mirror at a failure.

From the *New York Times,* February 5, 1950

CONSIDERATIONS FOR CRITICAL THINKING AND WRITING

1. Discuss what you think Miller has in mind when he refers to Biff's "self-realization" (para. 2).
2. According to Miller, what influences Willy to make him feel like a failure?
3. How is Miller's description of "the tragedy of Willy Loman" (para. 4) dramatized in the play?

The Glass Menagerie

Thomas Lanier Williams, who kept his college nickname, Tennessee, was born in Columbus, Mississippi, the son of a traveling salesman. In 1918 the family moved to St. Louis, Missouri, where his father became the sales manager of a shoe company. Williams's mother, the daughter of an Episcopal clergyman, was withdrawn and genteel in contrast to his aggressive father, who contemptuously called him "Miss Nancy" as a way of mocking his weak physical condition and his literary pursuits. This family atmosphere of repression and anger makes its way into many of Williams's works through characterizations of domineering men and psychologically vulnerable women.

Williams began writing in high school and at the age of seventeen published his first short story in *Weird Tales*. His education at the University of Missouri was interrupted when he had to go to work in a shoe factory. This "living death," as he put it, led to a nervous breakdown, but he eventually resumed his studies at Washington University and finally graduated from the University of Iowa in 1938. During his college years, Williams wrote one-act plays; in 1940 his first full-length play, *Battle of Angels*, opened in Boston, but none of these early plays achieved commercial success. In 1945, however, *The Glass Menagerie* won large, enthusiastic audiences as well as the Drama Critics' Circle Award, which marked the beginning of a series of theatrical triumphs for Williams including *Streetcar Named Desire* (1947), *The Rose Tattoo* (1950), *Cat on a Hot Tin Roof* (1955), *Suddenly Last Summer* (1958), and *The Night of the Iguana* (1961).

The Glass Menagerie reflects Williams's fascination with characters who face lonely struggles in emotionally and financially starved environments. Although Williams's use of colloquial southern speech is realistic, the play also employs nonrealistic techniques, such as shifts in time, projections on screens, music, and lighting effects, to express his characters' thoughts and inner lives. (Williams describes these devices in his production notes to the play; see p. 1938.) As much as these techniques are unconventional, Williams believed that they represented "a more penetrating and vivid expression of things as they are." The lasting popularity of *The Glass Menagerie* indicates that his assessment was correct.

Research Tennessee Williams with LitLinks at
http://www.bedfordstmartins.com/meyer/bedintrolit

TENNESSEE WILLIAMS (1911–1983)
The Glass Menagerie   1945

nobody,not even the rain,has such small hands
           —E. E. Cummings

LIST OF CHARACTERS

Amanda Wingfield, the mother. A little woman of great but confused vitality clinging frantically to another time and place. Her characterization must be carefully created, not copied from type. She is not paranoiac, but her life is paranoia. There is much to admire in Amanda, and as much to love and pity as there is to laugh at. Certainly she has endurance and a kind of heroism, and though her foolishness makes her unwittingly cruel at times, there is tenderness in her slight person.

Laura Wingfield, her daughter. Amanda, having failed to establish contact with reality, continues to live vitally in her illusions, but Laura's situation is even graver. A childhood illness has left her crippled, one leg slightly shorter than the other, and held in a brace. This defect need not be more than suggested on the stage. Stemming from this, Laura's separation increases till she is like a piece of her own glass collection, too exquisitely fragile to move from the shelf.

Tom Wingfield, her son. And the narrator of the play. A poet with a job in a warehouse. His nature is not remorseless, but to escape from a trap he has to act without pity.

Jim O'Connor, the gentleman caller. A nice, ordinary, young man.

SCENE: *An alley in St. Louis.*
PART I: *Preparation for a Gentleman Caller.*
PART II: *The Gentleman Calls.*
TIME: *Now and the Past.*

SCENE I

The Wingfield apartment is in the rear of the building, one of those vast hivelike conglomerations of cellular living-units that flower as warty growths in overcrowded urban centers of lower middle-class population and are symptomatic of the impulse of this largest and fundamentally enslaved section of American society to avoid fluidity and differentiation and to exist and function as one interfused mass of automatism.

The apartment faces an alley and is entered by a fire-escape, a structure whose name is a touch of accidental poetic truth, for all of these huge buildings are always burning with the slow and implacable fires of human desperation. The fire-escape is included in the set—that is, the landing of it and steps descending from it.

The scene is memory and is therefore nonrealistic. Memory takes a lot of poetic license. It omits some details; others are exaggerated, according to the emotional value of the articles it touches, for memory is seated predominantly in the heart. The interior is therefore rather dim and poetic.

At the rise of the curtain, the audience is faced with the dark, grim rear wall of the Wingfield tenement. This building, which runs parallel to the footlights, is flanked on both sides by dark, narrow alleys which run into murky canyons of tangled clotheslines, garbage cans, and the sinister latticework of neighboring fire-escapes. It is up and down these side alleys that exterior entrances and exits are made, during the play. At the end of Tom's opening commentary, the dark tenement wall slowly reveals (by means of a transparency) the interior of the ground floor Wingfield apartment.

Downstage is the living room, which also serves as a sleeping room for Laura, the sofa unfolding to make her bed. Upstage, center, and divided by a wide arch or second proscenium with transparent faded portieres (or second curtain), is the dining room. In an old-fashioned what-not in the living room are seen scores of transparent glass animals. A blown-up photograph of the father hangs on the wall of the living room, facing the audience, to the left of the archway. It is the face of a very handsome young man in a doughboy's First World War cap. He is gallantly smiling, ineluctably smiling, as if to say, "I will be smiling forever."

The audience hears and sees the opening scene in the dining room through both the transparent fourth wall of the building and the transparent gauze portieres of the dining-room arch. It is during this revealing scene that the fourth wall slowly ascends, out of sight. This transparent exterior wall is not brought down again until the very end of the play, during Tom's final speech.

The narrator is an undisguised convention of the play. He takes whatever license with dramatic convention as is convenient to his purposes.

Tom enters dressed as a merchant sailor from alley, stage left, and strolls across the front of the stage to the fire-escape. There he stops and lights a cigarette. He addresses the audience.

Tom: Yes, I have tricks in my pocket, I have things up my sleeve. But I am the opposite of a stage magician. He gives you illusion that has the appearance of truth. I give you truth in the pleasant disguise of illusion. To begin with, I turn back time. I reverse it to that quaint period, the thirties, when the huge middle class of America was matriculating in a school for the blind. Their eyes had failed them, or they had failed their eyes, and so they were having their fingers pressed forcibly down on the fiery Braille alphabet of a dissolving economy. In Spain there was revolution. Here there was only shouting and confusion. In Spain there was Guernica.° Here there were disturbances of labor, sometimes pretty violent, in otherwise peaceful cities such as Chicago, Cleveland, Saint Louis. . . . This is the social background of the play.

(Music.)

The play is memory. Being a memory play, it is dimly lighted, it is sentimental, it is not realistic. In memory everything seems to happen to music. That explains the fiddle in the wings. I am the narrator of the play, and also a character in it. The other characters are my mother, Amanda, my sister, Laura, and a gentleman caller who appears in the final scenes. He is the most realistic character in the play, being an emissary from a world of reality that we were somehow set apart from. But since I have a poet's weakness for symbols, I am using this character also as a symbol; he is the long delayed but always expected something that we live for. There is a fifth character in the play who doesn't appear except in this larger-than-life photograph over the mantel. This is our father who left us a long time ago. He was a telephone man who fell in love with long distances; he gave up his job with the telephone company and skipped the light fantastic out of town. . . . The last we heard of him was a picture post-card from Mazatlán, on the Pacific coast of Mexico, containing a message of two words — "Hello — Good-bye!" and no address. I think the rest of the play will explain itself. . . .

Amanda's voice becomes audible through the portieres.

(Legend on screen: "Où sont les neiges."°)
  He divides the portieres and enters the upstage area.

Guernica: A town in northern Spain destroyed by German bombers in 1937 during the Spanish Civil War.
Où sont les neiges: Part of a line from a poem by the French medieval writer François Villon; the full line translates, "Where are the snows of yesteryear?"

Amanda and Laura are seated at a drop-leaf table. Eating is indicated by gestures without food or utensils. Amanda faces the audience.

Tom and Laura are seated in profile.

The interior has lit up softly and through the scrim we see Amanda and Laura seated at the table in the upstage area.

Amanda *(calling):* Tom?

Tom: Yes, Mother.

Amanda: We can't say grace until you come to the table!

Tom: Coming, Mother. *(He bows slightly and withdraws, reappearing a few moments later in his place at the table.)*

Amanda *(to her son):* Honey, don't *push* with your *fingers.* If you have to push with something, the thing to push with is a crust of bread. And chew — chew! Animals have sections in their stomachs which enable them to digest food without mastication, but human beings are supposed to chew their food before they swallow it down. Eat food leisurely, son, and really enjoy it. A well-cooked meal has lots of delicate flavors that have to be held in the mouth for appreciation. So chew your food and give your salivary glands a chance to function!

Tom deliberately lays his imaginary fork down and pushes his chair back from the table.

Tom: I haven't enjoyed one bite of this dinner because of your constant directions on how to eat it. It's you that makes me rush through meals with your hawklike attention to every bite I take. Sickening — spoils my appetite — all this discussion of animals' secretion — salivary glands — mastication!

Amanda *(lightly):* Temperament like a Metropolitan star! *(He rises and crosses downstage.)* You're not excused from the table.

Tom: I am getting a cigarette.

Amanda: You smoke too much.

Laura rises.

Laura: I'll bring in the blanc mange.

He remains standing with his cigarette by the portieres during the following.

Amanda *(rising):* No, sister, no, sister — you be the lady this time and I'll be the darky.

Laura: I'm already up.

Amanda: Resume your seat, little sister — I want you to stay fresh and pretty — for gentlemen callers!

Laura: I'm not expecting any gentlemen callers.

Amanda *(crossing out to kitchenette. Airily):* Sometimes they come when they are least expected! Why, I remember one Sunday afternoon in Blue Mountain — *(Enters kitchenette.)*

Tom: I know what's coming!

Laura: Yes. But let her tell it.

Tom: Again?

Laura: She loves to tell it.

Amanda returns with bowl of dessert.

Amanda: One Sunday afternoon in Blue Mountain—your mother received—
  seventeen!—gentlemen callers! Why, sometimes there weren't chairs enough
  to accommodate them all. We had to send the nigger over to bring in folding chairs from the parish house.

Tom (remaining at portieres): How did you entertain those gentlemen callers?

Amanda: I understood the art of conversation!

Tom: I bet you could talk.

Amanda: Girls in those days *knew* how to talk, I can tell you.

Tom: Yes?

  (Image: Amanda as a girl on a porch greeting callers.)

Amanda: They knew how to entertain their gentlemen callers. It wasn't
  enough for a girl to be possessed of a pretty face and a graceful figure—
  although I wasn't slighted in either respect. She also needed to have a
  nimble wit and a tongue to meet all occasions.

Tom: What did you talk about?

Amanda: Things of importance going on in the world! Never anything coarse
  or common or vulgar. *(She addresses Tom as though he were seated in the vacant
  chair at the table though he remains by portieres. He plays this scene as though he
  held the book.)* My callers were gentlemen—all! Among my callers were
  some of the most prominent young planters of the Mississippi Delta—
  planters and sons of planters!

  Tom motions for music and a spot of light on Amanda.
    Her eyes lift, her face glows, her voice becomes rich and elegiac.
    (Screen legend: "Où sont les neiges.")

There was young Champ Laughlin who later became vice-president of the
Delta Planters Bank. Hadley Stevenson who was drowned in Moon Lake
and left his widow one hundred and fifty thousand in Government bonds.
There were the Cutrere brothers, Wesley and Bates. Bates was one of my
bright particular beaux! He got in a quarrel with that wild Wainright boy.
They shot it out on the floor of Moon Lake Casino. Bates was shot
through the stomach. Died in the ambulance on his way to Memphis. His
widow was also well-provided for, came into eight or ten thousand acres,
that's all. She married him on the rebound—never loved her—carried my
picture on him the night he died! And there was that boy that every girl in
the Delta had set her cap for! That beautiful, brilliant young Fitzhugh boy
from Green County!

Tom: What did he leave his widow?

Amanda: He never married! Gracious, you talk as though all of my old admirers had turned up their toes to the daisies!

Tom: Isn't this the first you mentioned that still survives?

Amanda: That Fitzhugh boy went North and made a fortune—came to be
  known as the Wolf of Wall Street! He had the Midas touch, whatever he
  touched turned to gold! And I could have been Mrs. Duncan J. Fitzhugh,
  mind you! But—I picked your *father!*

Laura (rising): Mother, let me clear the table.

Amanda: No dear, you go in front and study your typewriter chart. Or practice
  your shorthand a little. Stay fresh and pretty!—It's almost time for our

gentlemen callers to start arriving. (*She flounces girlishly toward the kitchenette.*) How many do you suppose we're going to entertain this afternoon?

Tom throws down the paper and jumps up with a groan.

Laura (*alone in the dining room*): I don't believe we're going to receive any, Mother.

Amanda (*reappearing, airily*): What? No one—not one? You must be joking! (*Laura nervously echoes her laugh. She slips in a fugitive manner through the half-open portieres and draws them gently behind her. A shaft of very clear light is thrown on her face against the faded tapestry of the curtains.*) (*Music: "The Glass Menagerie" under faintly.*) (*Lightly.*) Not one gentleman caller? It can't be true! There must be a flood, there must have been a tornado!

Laura: It isn't a flood, it's not a tornado, Mother. I'm just not popular like you were in Blue Mountain. . . . (*Tom utters another groan. Laura glances at him with a faint, apologetic smile. Her voice catching a little.*) Mother's afraid I'm going to be an old maid.

(*The scene dims out with "Glass Menagerie" music.*)

SCENE II

"Laura, Haven't You Ever Liked Some Boy?"

On the dark stage the screen is lighted with the image of blue roses.
Gradually Laura's figure becomes apparent and the screen goes out.
The music subsides.
Laura is seated in the delicate ivory chair at the small clawfoot table.
She wears a dress of soft violet material for a kimono—her hair tied back from her forehead with a ribbon.
She is washing and polishing her collection of glass.
Amanda appears on the fire-escape steps. At the sound of her ascent, Laura catches her breath, thrusts the bowl of ornaments away, and seats herself stiffly before the diagram of the typewriter keyboard as though it held her spellbound. Something has happened to Amanda. It is written in her face as she climbs to the landing: a look that is grim and hopeless and a little absurd.
She has on one of those cheap or imitation velvety-looking cloth coats with imitation fur collar. Her hat is five or six years old, one of those dreadful cloche hats that were worn in the late twenties, and she is clasping an enormous black patent-leather pocketbook with nickel clasp and initials. This is her full-dress outfit, the one she usually wears to the D.A.R. °
Before entering she looks through the door.
She purses her lips, opens her eyes wide, rolls them upward, and shakes her head.
Then she slowly lets herself in the door. Seeing her mother's expression Laura touches her lips with a nervous gesture.

D.A.R.: Daughters of the American Revolution; members must document that they have ancestors who served the patriots' cause in the Revolutionary War.

Laura: Hello, Mother, I was — *(She makes a nervous gesture toward the chart on the wall. Amanda leans against the shut door and stares at Laura with a martyred look.)*

Amanda: Deception? Deception? *(She slowly removes her hat and gloves, continuing the swift suffering stare. She lets the hat and gloves fall on the floor — a bit of acting.)*

Laura (shakily): How was the D.A.R. meeting? *(Amanda slowly opens her purse and removes a dainty white handkerchief, which she shakes out delicately and delicately touches to her lips and nostrils.)* Didn't you go to the D.A.R. meeting, Mother?

Amanda (faintly, almost inaudibly): — No. — No. *(Then more forcibly.)* I did not have the strength — to go to the D.A.R. In fact, I did not have the courage! I wanted to find a hole in the ground and hide myself in it forever! *(She crosses slowly to the wall and removes the diagram of the typewriter keyboard. She holds it in front of her for a second, staring at it sweetly and sorrowfully — then bites her lips and tears it in two pieces.)*

Laura (faintly): Why did you do that, Mother? *(Amanda repeats the same procedure with the chart of the Gregg Alphabet.°)* Why are you —

Amanda: Why? Why? How old are you, Laura?

Laura: Mother, you know my age.

Amanda: I thought that you were an adult; it seems that I was mistaken. *(She crosses slowly to the sofa and sinks down and stares at Laura.)*

Laura: Please don't stare at me, Mother.

Amanda closes her eyes and lowers her head. Count ten.

Amanda: What are we going to do, what is going to become of us, what is the future?

Count ten.

Laura: Has something happened, Mother? *(Amanda draws a long breath and takes out the handkerchief again. Dabbing process.)* Mother, has — something happened?

Amanda: I'll be all right in a minute. I'm just bewildered — *(count five)* — by life. . . .

Laura: Mother, I wish that you would tell me what's happened.

Amanda: As you know, I was supposed to be inducted into my office at the D.A.R. this afternoon. *(Image: A swarm of typewriters.)* But I stopped off at Rubicam's Business College to speak to your teachers about your having a cold and ask them what progress they thought you were making down there.

Laura: Oh. . . .

Amanda: I went to the typing instructor and introduced myself as your mother. She didn't know who you were. Wingfield, she said. We don't have any such student enrolled at the school! I assured her she did, that you had been going to classes since early in January. "I wonder," she said, "if you could be talking about that terribly shy little girl who dropped out of school after only a few days' attendance?" "No," I said, "Laura, my daughter, has been going to school every day for the past six weeks!" "Excuse me," she said. She took the attendance book out and there was your name,

---

Gregg Alphabet: System of shorthand symbols invented by John Robert Gregg.

unmistakably printed, and all the dates you were absent until they decided that you had dropped out of school. I still said, "No, there must have been some mistake! There must have been some mix-up in the records!" And she said, "No — I remember her perfectly now. Her hand shook so that she couldn't hit the right keys! The first time we gave a speed-test, she broke down completely — was sick at the stomach and almost had to be carried into the wash-room! After that morning she never showed up any more. We phoned the house but never got any answer" — while I was working at Famous and Barr, I suppose, demonstrating those — Oh! I felt so weak I could barely keep on my feet. I had to sit down while they got me a glass of water! Fifty dollars' tuition, all of our plans — my hopes and ambitions for you — just gone up the spout, just gone up the spout like that. *(Laura draws a long breath and gets awkwardly to her feet. She crosses to the Victrola, and winds it up.)* What are you doing?

Laura: Oh! *(She releases the handle and returns to her seat.)*

Amanda: Laura, where have you been going when you've gone out pretending that you were going to business college?

Laura: I've just been going out walking.

Amanda: That's not true.

Laura: It is. I just went walking.

Amanda: Walking? Walking? In winter? Deliberately courting pneumonia in that light coat? Where did you walk to, Laura?

Laura: It was the lesser of two evils, Mother. *(Image: Winter scene in park.)* I couldn't go back up. I — threw up — on the floor!

Amanda: From half past seven till after five every day you mean to tell me you walked around in the park, because you wanted to make me think that you were still going to Rubicam's Business College?

Laura: It wasn't as bad as it sounds. I went inside places to get warmed up.

Amanda: Inside where?

Laura: I went in the art museum and the bird-houses at the Zoo. I visited the penguins every day! Sometimes I did without lunch and went to the movies. Lately I've been spending most of my afternoons in the Jewel-box, that big glass house where they raise the tropical flowers.

Amanda: You did all this to deceive me, just for the deception? *(Laura looks down.)* Why?

Laura: Mother, when you're disappointed, you get that awful suffering look on your face, like the picture of Jesus' mother in the museum!

Amanda: Hush!

Laura: I couldn't face it.

Pause. A whisper of strings.
(Legend: "The Crust of Humility.")

Amanda (hopelessly fingering the huge pocketbook): So what are we going to do the rest of our lives? Stay home and watch the parades go by? Amuse ourselves with the glass menagerie, darling? Eternally play those worn-out phonograph records your father left as a painful reminder of him? We won't have a business career — we've given that up because it gave us nervous indigestion! *(Laughs wearily.)* What is there left but dependency all our lives? I know so well what becomes of unmarried women who aren't prepared to occupy a position. I've seen such pitiful cases in the South — barely tolerated spinsters living upon the grudging patronage of sister's husband or brother's wife! — stuck away in some little mousetrap of a room — encouraged by one in-law to visit another — little birdlike women without any nest — eating the crust of humility all their life! Is that the future that we've mapped out for ourselves? I swear it's the only alternative I can think of! It isn't a very pleasant alternative, is it? Of course — some girls *do* marry. *(Laura twists her hands nervously.)* Haven't you ever liked some boy?

Laura: Yes. I liked one once. *(Rises.)* I came across his picture a while ago.

Amanda (with some interest): He gave you his picture?

Laura: No, it's in the year-book.

Amanda (disappointed): Oh — a high-school boy.

(Screen image: Jim as a high-school hero bearing a silver cup.)

Laura: Yes. His name was Jim. *(Laura lifts the heavy annual from the clawfoot table.)* Here he is in *The Pirates of Penzance.*

Amanda (absently): The what?

Laura: The operetta the senior class put on. He had a wonderful voice and we sat across the aisle from each other Mondays, Wednesdays, and Fridays in the Aud. Here he is with the silver cup for debating! See his grin?

Amanda (absently): He must have had a jolly disposition.

Laura: He used to call me — Blue Roses.

(Image: Blue roses.)

Amanda: Why did he call you such a name as that?

Laura: When I had that attack of pleurosis — he asked me what was the matter when I came back. I said pleurosis — he thought that I said Blue Roses! So that's what he always called me after that. Whenever he saw me, he'd holler, "Hello, Blue Roses!" I didn't care for the girl that he went out with. Emily Meisenbach. Emily was the best-dressed girl at Soldan. She never struck me, though, as being sincere. . . . It says in the Personal Section — they're engaged. That's — six years ago! They must be married by now.

Amanda: Girls that aren't cut out for business careers usually wind up married to some nice man. *(Gets up with a spark of revival.)* Sister, that's what you'll do!

Laura utters a startled, doubtful laugh. She reaches quickly for a piece of glass.

Laura: But, Mother —

Amanda: Yes? *(Crossing to photograph.)*

Laura (in a tone of frightened apology): I'm — crippled!

(Image: Screen.)

Amanda: Nonsense! Laura, I've told you never, never to use that word. Why, you're not crippled, you just have a little defect — hardly noticeable, even! When people have some slight disadvantage like that, they cultivate other things to make up for it — develop charm — and vivacity — and — *charm!* That's all you have to do! *(She turns again to the photograph.)* One thing your father had *plenty of* — was *charm!*

Tom motions to the fiddle in the wings.
(The scene fades out with music.)

SCENE III

(Legend on the screen: "After the Fiasco—")
Tom speaks from the fire-escape landing.

Tom: After the fiasco at Rubicam's Business College, the idea of getting a gentleman caller for Laura began to play a more important part in Mother's calculations. It became an obsession. Like some archetype of the universal unconscious, the image of the gentleman caller haunted our small apartment. . . . *(Image: Young man at door with flowers.)* An evening at home rarely passed without some allusion to this image, this specter, this hope. . . . Even when he wasn't mentioned, his presence hung in Mother's preoccupied look and in my sister's frightened, apologetic manner—hung like a sentence passed upon the Wingfields! Mother was a woman of action as well as words. She began to take logical steps in the planned direction. Late that winter and in the early spring—realizing that extra money would be needed to properly feather the nest and plume the bird—she conducted a vigorous campaign on the telephone, roping in subscribers to one of those magazines for matrons called *The Home-maker's Companion*, the type of journal that features the serialized sublimations of ladies of letters who think in terms of delicate cuplike breasts, slim, tapering waists, rich, creamy thighs, eyes like wood-smoke in autumn, fingers that soothe and caress like strains of music, bodies as powerful as Etruscan sculpture.

(Screen image: Glamour magazine cover.)
Amanda enters with phone on long extension cord. She is spotted in the dim stage.

Amanda: Ida Scott? This is Amanda Wingfield! We *missed* you at the D.A.R. last Monday! I said to myself: She's probably suffering with that sinus condition! How is that sinus condition? Horrors! Heaven have mercy!—You're a Christian martyr, yes, that's what you are, a Christian martyr! Well, I just now happened to notice that your subscription to the *Companion's* about to expire! Yes, it expires with the next issue, honey!—just when that wonderful new serial by Bessie Mae Hopper is getting off to such an exciting start. Oh, honey, it's something that you can't miss! You remember how *Gone with the Wind* took everybody by storm? You simply couldn't go out if you hadn't read it. All everybody *talked* was Scarlett O'Hara. Well, this is a book that critics already compare to *Gone with the Wind*. It's the *Gone with the Wind* of the post–World War generation!—What?—Burning?—Oh, honey, don't let them burn, go take a look in the oven and I'll hold the wire! Heavens—I think she's hung up!

(Dim out.)
(Legend on screen: "You think I'm in love with Continental Shoemakers?")
Before the stage is lighted, the violent voices of Tom and Amanda are heard. They are quarreling behind the portieres. In front of them stands Laura with clenched hands and panicky expression.
A clear pool of light on her figure throughout this scene.

Tom: What in Christ's name am I—

Amanda (shrilly): Don't you use that—
Tom: Supposed to do!
Amanda: Expression! Not in my—
Tom: Ohhh!
Amanda: Presence! Have you gone out of your senses?
Tom: I have, that's true, *driven* out!
Amanda: What is the matter with you, you—big—big—IDIOT!
Tom: Look—I've got *no thing,* no single thing—
Amanda: Lower your voice!
Tom: In my life here that I can call my own! Everything is—
Amanda: Stop that shouting!
Tom: Yesterday you confiscated my books! You had the nerve to—
Amanda: I took that horrible novel back to the library—yes! That hideous
    book by that insane Mr. Lawrence.° *(Tom laughs wildly.)* I cannot control
    the output of diseased minds or people who cater to them—*(Tom laughs
    still more wildly.)* BUT I WON'T ALLOW SUCH FILTH BROUGHT INTO MY HOUSE!
    No, no, no, no, no!
Tom: House, house! Who pays rent on it, who makes a slave of himself to—
Amanda (fairly screeching): Don't you DARE to—
Tom: No, no, I mustn't say things! *I've* got to just—
Amanda: Let me tell you—
Tom: I don't want to hear any more! *(He tears the portieres open. The upstage area
    is lit with a turgid smoky red glow.)*

> *Amanda's hair is in metal curlers and she wears a very old bathrobe, much too
> large for her slight figure, a relic of the faithless Mr. Wingfield.*
>   *An upright typewriter and a wild disarray of manuscripts are on the drop-leaf
> table. The quarrel was probably precipitated by Amanda's interruption of his
> creative labor. A chair lying overthrown on the floor.*
>   *Their gesticulating shadows are cast on the ceiling by the fiery glow.*

Amanda: You *will* hear more, you—
Tom: No, I won't hear more, I'm going out!
Amanda: You come right back in—
Tom: Out, out, out! Because I'm—
Amanda: Come back here, Tom Wingfield! I'm not through talking to you!
Tom: Oh, go—
Laura (desperately): Tom!
Amanda: You're going to listen, and no more insolence from you! I'm at the
    end of my patience! *(He comes back toward her.)*
Tom: What do you think I'm at? Aren't I supposed to have any patience to
    reach the end of, Mother? I know, I know. It seems unimportant to you,
    what I'm *doing*—what I *want* to do—having a little *difference* between
    them! You don't think that—
Amanda: I think you've been doing things that you're ashamed of. That's why
    you act like this. I don't believe that you go every night to the movies. No-
    body goes to the movies night after night. Nobody in their right minds
    goes to the movies as often as you pretend to. People don't go to the

---

Mr. Lawrence: D. H. Lawrence (1885-1930), English poet and novelist who advocated sexual
freedom.

movies at nearly midnight, and movies don't let out at two A.M. Come in stumbling. Muttering to yourself like a maniac! You get three hours' sleep and then go to work. Oh, I can picture the way you're doing down there. Moping, doping, because you're in no condition.

Tom (wildly): No, I'm in no condition!

Amanda: What right have you got to jeopardize your job? Jeopardize the security of us all? How do you think we'd manage if you were —

Tom: Listen! You think I'm crazy *about* the *warehouse*! *(He bends fiercely toward her slight figure.)* You think I'm in love with the Continental Shoemakers? You think I want to spend fifty-five *years* down there in that — *celotex interior!* with — *fluorescent — tubes!* Look! I'd rather somebody picked up a crowbar and battered out my brains — than go back mornings! I *go!* Every time you come in yelling that God damn *"Rise and Shine!" "Rise and Shine!"* I say to myself "How *lucky dead* people are!" But I get up. I *go!* For sixty-five dollars a month I give up all that I dream of doing and being *ever!* And you say self — *self's* all I ever think of. Why, listen, if self is what I thought of, Mother, I'd be where he is — ! *(Pointing to father's picture.)* As far as the system of transportation reaches! *(He starts past her. She grabs his arm.)* Don't grab at me, Mother!

Amanda: Where are you going?

Tom: I'm going to the *movies!*

Amanda: I don't believe that lie!

Tom (crouching toward her, overtowering her tiny figure. She backs away, gasping): I'm going to opium dens! Yes, opium dens, dens of vice and criminals' hangouts, Mother. I've joined the Hogan gang, I'm a hired assassin, I carry a tommy-gun in a violin case! I run a string of cat-houses in the Valley! They call me Killer, Killer Wingfield, I'm leading a double-life, a simple, honest warehouse worker by day, by night a dynamic *czar* of the *underworld,* Mother. I go to gambling casinos, I spin away fortunes on the roulette table! I wear a patch over one eye and a false mustache, sometimes I put on green whiskers. On those occasions they call me — *El Diablo!* ° Oh, I could tell you things to make you sleepless! My enemies plan to dynamite this place. They're going to blow us all sky-high some night! I'll be glad, very happy, and so will you! You'll go up, up on a broomstick, over Blue Mountain with seventeen gentlemen callers! You ugly — babbling old — *witch.* . . . *(He goes through a series of violent, clumsy movements, seizing his overcoat, lunging to the door, pulling it fiercely open. The women watch him, aghast. His arm catches in the sleeve of the coat as he struggles to pull it on. For a moment he is pinioned by the bulky garment. With an outraged groan he tears the coat off again, splitting the shoulders of it, and hurls it across the room. It strikes against the shelf of Laura's glass collection, there is a tinkle of shattering glass. Laura cries out as if wounded.)*

(Music legend: "The Glass Menagerie.")

Laura (shrilly): My glass! — menagerie. . . . *(She covers her face and turns away.)*

But Amanda is still stunned and stupefied by the "ugly witch" so that she barely notices this occurrence. Now she recovers her speech.

El Diablo: The devil (Spanish).

Amanda (in an awful voice): I won't speak to you — until you apologize! *(She crosses through portieres and draws them together behind her. Tom is left with Laura. Laura clings weakly to the mantel with her face averted. Tom stares at her stupidly for a moment. Then he crosses to shelf. Drops awkwardly to his knees to collect the fallen glass, glancing at Laura as if he would speak but couldn't.)*

"The Glass Menagerie" steals in as

    (The scene dims out.)

SCENE IV

The interior is dark. Faint light in the alley.
    A deep-voiced bell in a church is tolling the hour of five as the scene commences.
    Tom appears at the top of the alley. After each solemn boom of the bell in the tower, he shakes a little noise-maker or rattle as if to express the tiny spasm of man in contrast to the sustained power and dignity of the Almighty. This and the unsteadiness of his advance make it evident that he has been drinking.
    As he climbs the few steps to the fire-escape landing light steals up inside. Laura appears in night-dress, observing Tom's empty bed in the front room.
    Tom fishes in his pockets for the door-key, removing a motley assortment of articles in the search, including a perfect shower of movie-ticket stubs and an empty bottle. At last he finds the key, but just as he is about to insert it, it slips from his fingers. He strikes a match and crouches below the door.

Tom (bitterly): One crack — and it falls through!

    Laura opens the door.

Laura: Tom! Tom, what are you doing?
Tom: Looking for a door-key.
Laura: Where have you been all this time?
Tom: I have been to the movies.
Laura: All this time at the movies?
Tom: There was a very long program. There was a Garbo picture and a Mickey Mouse and a travelogue and a newsreel and a preview of coming attractions. And there was an organ solo and a collection for the milk-fund — simultaneously — which ended up in a terrible fight between a fat lady and an usher!
Laura (innocently): Did you have to stay through everything?
Tom: Of course! And, oh, I forgot! There was a big stage show! The headliner on this stage show was Malvolio the Magician. He performed wonderful tricks, many of them, such as pouring water back and forth between pitchers. First it turned to wine and then it turned to beer and then it turned to whiskey. I know it was whiskey it finally turned into because he needed somebody to come up out of the audience to help him, and I came up — both shows! It was Kentucky Straight Bourbon. A very generous fellow, he gave souvenirs. *(He pulls from his back pocket a shimmering rainbow-colored scarf.)* He gave me this. This is his magic scarf. You can have it, Laura. You wave it over a canary cage and you get a bowl of gold-fish. You

wave it over the gold-fish bowl and they fly away canaries. . . . But the won-derfullest trick of all was the coffin trick. We nailed him into a coffin and he got out of the coffin without removing one nail. *(He has come inside.)* There is a trick that would come in handy for me — get me out of this 2 by 4 situation! *(Flops onto bed and starts removing shoes.)*

Laura: Tom — Shhh!

Tom: What you shushing me for?

Laura: You'll wake up Mother.

Tom: Goody, goody! Pay 'er back for all those "Rise an' Shines." *(Lies down, groaning.)* You know it don't take much intelligence to get yourself into a nailed-up coffin, Laura. But who in hell ever got himself out of one with-out removing one nail?

> *As if in answer, the father's grinning photograph lights up.*
> *(Scene dims out.)*
> *Immediately following: The church bell is heard striking six. At the sixth stroke the alarm clock goes off in Amanda's room, and after a few moments we hear her calling: "Rise and Shine! Rise and Shine! Laura, go tell your brother to rise and shine!"*

Tom (sitting up slowly): I'll rise — but I won't shine.

> *The light increases.*

Amanda: Laura, tell your brother his coffee is ready.

> *Laura slips into front room.*

Laura: Tom! It's nearly seven. Don't make Mother nervous. *(He stares at her stu-pidly. Beseechingly.)* Tom, speak to Mother this morning. Make up with her, apologize, speak to her!

Tom: She won't to me. It's her that started not speaking.

Laura: If you just say you're sorry she'll start speaking.

Tom: Her not speaking — is that such a tragedy?

Laura: Please — please!

Amanda (calling from kitchenette): Laura, are you going to do what I asked you to do, or do I have to get dressed and go out myself?

Laura: Going, going — soon as I get on my coat! *(She pulls on a shapeless felt hat with nervous, jerky movement, pleadingly glancing at Tom. Rushes awkwardly for coat. The coat is one of Amanda's, inaccurately made-over, the sleeves too short for Laura.)* Butter and what else?

Amanda (entering upstage): Just butter. Tell them to charge it.

Laura: Mother, they make such faces when I do that.

Amanda: Sticks and stones may break my bones, but the expression on Mr. Garfinkel's face won't harm us! Tell your brother his coffee is getting cold.

Laura (at door): Do what I asked you, will you, will you, Tom?

> *He looks sullenly away.*

Amanda: Laura, go now or just don't go at all!

Laura (rushing out): Going — going! *(A second later she cries out. Tom springs up and crosses to the door. Amanda rushes anxiously in. Tom opens the door.)*

Tom: Laura?

Laura: I'm all right. I slipped, but I'm all right.

Amanda (peering anxiously after her): If anyone breaks a leg on those fire-escape steps, the landlord ought to be sued for every cent he possesses! *(She shuts door. Remembers she isn't speaking and returns to other room.)*

> *As Tom enters listlessly for his coffee, she turns her back to him and stands rigidly facing the window on the gloomy gray vault of the areaway. Its light on her face with its aged but childish features is cruelly sharp, satirical as a Daumier° print.*
> *(Music under: "Ave Maria.")*
> *Tom glances sheepishly but sullenly at her averted figure and slumps at the table. The coffee is scalding hot; he sips it and gasps and spits it back in the cup. At his gasp, Amanda catches her breath and half turns. Then catches herself and turns back to window.*
> *Tom blows on his coffee, glancing sidewise at his mother. She clears her throat. Tom clears his. He starts to rise. Sinks back down again, scratches his head, clears his throat again. Amanda coughs. Tom raises his cup in both hands to blow on it, his eyes staring over the rim of it at his mother for several moments. Then he slowly sets the cup down and awkwardly and hesitantly rises from the chair.*

Tom (hoarsely): Mother. I—I apologize. Mother. *(Amanda draws a quick, shuddering breath. Her face works grotesquely. She breaks into childlike tears.)* I'm sorry for what I said, for everything that I said, I didn't mean it.

Amanda (sobbingly): My devotion has made me a witch and so I make myself hateful to my children!

Tom: No, you *don't*.

Amanda: I worry so much, don't sleep, it makes me nervous!

Tom (gently): I understand that.

Amanda: I've had to put up a solitary battle all these years. But you're my right-hand bower! Don't fall down, don't fail!

Tom (gently): I try, Mother.

Amanda (with great enthusiasm): Try and you will SUCCEED! *(The notion makes her breathless.)* Why, you—you're just *full* of natural endowments! Both of my children—they're *unusual* children! Don't you think I know it? I'm so—proud! Happy and—feel I've—so much to be thankful for but—Promise me one thing, son!

Tom: What, Mother?

Amanda: Promise, son, you'll—never be a drunkard!

Tom (turns to her grinning): I will never be a drunkard, Mother.

Amanda: That's what frightened me so, that you'd be drinking! Eat a bowl of Purina!

Tom: Just coffee, Mother.

Amanda: Shredded wheat biscuit?

Tom: No. No, Mother, just coffee.

Amanda: You can't put in a day's work on an empty stomach. You've got ten minutes—don't gulp! Drinking too-hot liquids makes cancer of the stomach. . . . Put cream in.

Tom: No, thank you.

Amanda: To cool it.

Daumier: Honoré Daumier (1808–1879), French caricaturist, lithographer, and painter who mercilessly satirized bourgeois society.

Tom: No! No, thank you, I want it black.

Amanda: I know, but it's not good for you. We have to do all that we can to build ourselves up. In these trying times we live in, all that we have to cling to is — each other. . . . That's why it's so important to — Tom, I — I sent out your sister so I could discuss something with you. If you hadn't spoken I would have spoken to you. *(Sits down.)*

Tom (gently): What is it, Mother, that you want to discuss?

Amanda: Laura!

> *Tom puts his cup down slowly.*
> *(Legend on screen: "Laura.")*
> *(Music: "The Glass Menagerie.")*

Tom: — Oh. — Laura . . .

Amanda (touching his sleeve): You know how Laura is. So quiet but — still water runs deep! She notices things and I think she — broods about them. *(Tom looks up.)* A few days ago I came in and she was crying.

Tom: What about?

Amanda: You.

Tom: Me?

Amanda: She has an idea that you're not happy here.

Tom: What gave her that idea?

Amanda: What gives her any idea? However, you do act strangely. I — I'm not criticizing, understand *that!* I know your ambitions do not lie in the warehouse, that like everybody in the whole wide world — you've had to — make sacrifices, but — Tom — Tom — life's not easy, it calls for — Spartan endurance! There's so many things in my heart that I cannot describe to you! I've never told you but I — *loved* your father. . . .

Tom (gently): I know that, Mother.

Amanda: And you — when I see you taking after his ways! Staying out late — and — well, you *had* been drinking the night you were in that — terrifying condition! Laura says that you hate the apartment and that you go out nights to get away from it! Is that true, Tom?

Tom: No. You say there's so much in your heart that you can't describe to me. That's true of me, too. There's so much in my heart that I can't describe to *you!* So let's respect each other's —

Amanda: But, why — *why,* Tom — are you always so *restless?* Where do you go to, nights?

Tom: I — go to the movies.

Amanda: Why do you go to the movies so much, Tom?

Tom: I go to the movies because — I like adventure. Adventure is something I don't have much of at work, so I go to the movies.

Amanda: But, Tom, you go to the movies *entirely too much!*

Tom: I like a lot of adventure.

> *Amanda looks baffled, then hurt. As the familiar inquisition resumes he becomes hard and impatient again. Amanda slips back into her querulous attitude toward him.*
> *(Image on screen: Sailing vessel with Jolly Roger.)*

Amanda: Most young men find adventure in their careers.

Tom: Then most young men are not employed in a warehouse.

Amanda: The world is full of young men employed in warehouses and offices and factories.

Tom: Do all of them find adventure in their careers?

Amanda: They do or they do without it! Not everybody has a craze for adventure.

Tom: Man is by instinct a lover, a hunter, a fighter, and none of those instincts are given much play at the warehouse!

Amanda: Man is by instinct! Don't quote instinct to me! Instinct is something that people have got away from! It belongs to animals! Christian adults don't want it!

Tom: What do Christian adults want, then, Mother?

Amanda: Superior things! Things of the mind and the spirit! Only animals have to satisfy instincts! Surely your aims are somewhat higher than theirs! Than monkeys — pigs —

Tom: I reckon they're not.

Amanda: You're joking. However, that isn't what I wanted to discuss.

Tom (rising): I haven't much time.

Amanda (pushing his shoulders): Sit down.

Tom: You want me to punch in red° at the warehouse, Mother?

Amanda: You have five minutes. I want to talk about Laura.

(Legend: "Plans and Provisions.")

Tom: All right! What about Laura?

Amanda: We have to be making plans and provisions for her. She's older than you, two years, and nothing has happened. She just drifts along doing nothing. It frightens me terribly how she just drifts along.

Tom: I guess she's the type that people call home girls.

Amanda: There's no such type, and if there is, it's a pity! That is unless the home is hers, with a husband!

Tom: What?

Amanda: Oh, I can see the handwriting on the wall as plain as I see the nose in front of my face! It's terrifying! More and more you remind me of your father! He was out all hours without explanation — Then *left! Good-bye!* And me with the bag to hold. I saw that letter you got from the Merchant Marine. I know what you're dreaming of. I'm not standing here blindfolded. Very well, then. Then *do* it! But not till there's somebody to take your place.

Tom: What do you mean?

Amanda: I mean that as soon as Laura has got somebody to take care of her, married, a home of her own, independent — why, then you'll be free to go wherever you please, on land, on sea, whichever way the wind blows! But until that time you've got to look out for your sister. I don't say me because I'm old and don't matter! I say for your sister because she's young and dependent. I put her in business college — a dismal failure! Frightened her so it made her sick to her stomach. I took her over to the Young People's League at the church. Another fiasco. She spoke to nobody, nobody spoke to her. Now all she does is fool with those pieces of glass and play those worn-out records. What kind of a life is that for a girl to lead!

Tom: What can I do about it?

Amanda: Overcome selfishness! Self, self, self is all that you ever think of! *(Tom springs up and crosses to get his coat. It is ugly and bulky. He pulls on a cap*

punch in red: Be late for work.

with earmuffs.) Where is your muffler? Put your wool muffler on! *(He snatches it angrily from the closet and tosses it around his neck and pulls both ends tight.)* Tom! I haven't said what I had in mind to ask you.

Tom: I'm too late to —

Amanda (catching his arms — very importunately. Then shyly.): Down at the warehouse, aren't there some — nice young men?

Tom: No!

Amanda: There *must* be — *some.*

Tom: Mother —

Gesture.

Amanda: Find out one that's clean-living — doesn't drink and — ask him out for sister!

Tom: What?

Amanda: For *sister!* To *meet!* Get *acquainted!*

Tom (stamping to door): Oh, my go-osh!

Amanda: Will you? *(He opens door. Imploringly.)* Will you? *(He starts down.)* Will you? *Will* you, dear?

Tom (calling back): YES!

> Amanda closes the door hesitantly and with a troubled but faintly hopeful expression.
> *(Screen image:* Glamour *magazine cover.)*
> Spot Amanda at phone.

Amanda: Ella Cartwright? This is Amanda Wingfield! How are you, honey? How is that kidney condition? *(Count five.)* Horrors! *(Count five.)* You're a Christian martyr, yes, honey, that's what you are, a Christian martyr! Well, I just happened to notice in my little red book that your subscription to the *Companion* has just run out! I knew that you wouldn't want to miss out on the wonderful serial starting in this new issue. It's by Bessie Mae Hopper, the first thing she's written since *Honeymoon for Three.* Wasn't that a strange and interesting story? Well, this one is even lovelier, I believe. It has a sophisticated society background. It's all about the horsey set on Long Island!

(Fade out.)

SCENE V

(Legend on screen: "Annunciation.") Fade with music.

> It is early dusk of a spring evening. Supper has just been finished in the Wingfield apartment. Amanda and Laura in light-colored dresses are removing dishes from the table, in the upstage area, which is shadowy, their movements formalized almost as a dance or ritual, their moving forms as pale and silent as moths.
>
> Tom, in white shirt and trousers, rises from the table and crosses toward the fire-escape.

Amanda (as he passes her): Son, will you do me a favor?

Tom: What?

Amanda: Comb your hair! You look so pretty when your hair is combed! *(Tom slouches on sofa with evening paper. Enormous caption "Franco Triumphs."*°*)* There is only one respect in which I would like you to emulate your father.

Tom: What respect is that?

Amanda: The care he always took of his appearance. He never allowed himself to look untidy. *(He throws down the paper and crosses to fire-escape.)* Where are you going?

Tom: I'm going out to smoke.

Amanda: You smoke too much. A pack a day at fifteen cents a pack. How much would that amount to in a month? Thirty times fifteen is how much, Tom? Figure it out and you will be astounded at what you could save. Enough to give you a night-school course in accounting at Washington U! Just think what a wonderful thing that would be for you, son!

Tom is unmoved by the thought.

Tom: I'd rather smoke. *(He steps out on landing, letting the screen door slam.)*

Amanda (sharply): I know! That's the tragedy of it. . . . *(Alone, she turns to look at her husband's picture.)*

(Dance music: "All the World Is Waiting for the Sunrise!")

Tom (to the audience): Across the alley from us was the Paradise Dance Hall. On evenings in spring the windows and doors were open and the music came outdoors. Sometimes the lights were turned out except for a large glass sphere that hung from the ceiling. It would turn slowly about and filter the dusk with delicate rainbow colors. Then the orchestra played a waltz or a tango, something that had a slow and sensuous rhythm. Couples would come outside, to the relative privacy of the alley. You could see them kissing behind ash-pits and telephone poles. This was the compensation for lives that passed like mine, without any change or adventure. Adventure and change were imminent in this year. They were waiting around the corner for all these kids. Suspended in the mist over the Berchtesgaden,° caught in the folds of Chamberlain's° umbrella — In Spain there was Guernica! But here there was only hot swing music and liquor, dance halls, bars, and movies, and sex that hung in the gloom like a chandelier and flooded the world with brief, deceptive rainbows. . . . All the world was waiting for bombardments!

Amanda turns from the picture and comes outside.

Amanda (sighing): A fire-escape landing's a poor excuse for a porch. *(She spreads a newspaper on a step and sits down, gracefully and demurely as if she were settling into a swing on a Mississippi veranda.)* What are you looking at?

Tom: The moon.

Amanda: Is there a moon this evening?

Tom: It's rising over Garfinkel's Delicatessen.

Amanda: So it is! A little silver slipper of a moon. Have you made a wish on it yet?

"Franco Triumphs": In January 1939 the Republican forces of Francisco Franco (1892–1975) defeated the Loyalists, ending the Spanish Civil War.
Berchtesgaden: A resort in the German Alps where Adolf Hitler had a heavily protected villa.
Chamberlain: Neville Chamberlain (1869–1940), British prime minister who sought to avoid war with Hitler through a policy of appeasement.

Tom: Um-hum.

Amanda: What did you wish for?

Tom: That's a secret.

Amanda: A secret, huh? Well, I won't tell mine either. I will be just as mysterious as you.

Tom: I bet I can guess what yours is.

Amanda: Is my head so transparent?

Tom: You're not a sphinx.

Amanda: No, I don't have secrets. I'll tell you what I wished for on the moon. Success and happiness for my precious children! I wish for that whenever there's a moon, and when there isn't a moon, I wish for it, too.

Tom: I thought perhaps you wished for a gentleman caller.

Amanda: Why do you say that?

Tom: Don't you remember asking me to fetch one?

Amanda: I remember suggesting that it would be nice for your sister if you brought home some nice young man from the warehouse. I think I've made that suggestion more than once.

Tom: Yes, you have made it repeatedly.

Amanda: Well?

Tom: We are going to have one.

Amanda: What?

Tom: A gentleman caller!

> (*The Annunciation is celebrated with music.*)
> Amanda rises.
> (*Image on screen: Caller with bouquet.*)

Amanda: You mean you have asked some nice young man to come over?

Tom: Yep. I've asked him to dinner.

Amanda: You really did?

Tom: I did!

Amanda: You did, and did he — *accept?*

Tom: He did!

Amanda: Well, well — well, well! That's — lovely!

Tom: I thought that you would be pleased.

Amanda: It's definite, then?

Tom: Very definite.

Amanda: Soon?

Tom: Very soon.

Amanda: For heaven's sake, stop putting on and tell me some things, will you?

Tom: What things do you want me to tell you?

Amanda: Naturally I would like to know when he's *coming!*

Tom: He's coming tomorrow.

Amanda: *Tomorrow?*

Tom: Yep. Tomorrow.

Amanda: But, Tom!

Tom: Yes, Mother?

Amanda: Tomorrow gives me no time!

Tom: Time for what?

Amanda: Preparations! Why didn't you phone me at once, as soon as you asked him, the minute that he accepted? Then, don't you see, I could have been getting ready!

Tom: You don't have to make any fuss.

Amanda: Oh, Tom, Tom, Tom, of course I have to make a fuss! I want things nice, not sloppy! Not thrown together. I'll certainly have to do some fast thinking, won't I?

Tom: I don't see why you have to think at all.

Amanda: You just don't know. We can't have a gentleman caller in a pig-sty! All my wedding silver has to be polished, the monogrammed table linen ought to be laundered! The windows have to be washed and fresh curtains put up. And how about clothes? We have to *wear* something, don't we?

Tom: Mother, this boy is no one to make a fuss over!

Amanda: Do you realize he's the first young man we've introduced to your sister? It's terrible, dreadful, disgraceful that poor little sister has never received a single gentleman caller! Tom, come inside! *(She opens the screen door.)*

Tom: What for?

Amanda: I want to ask you some things.

Tom: If you're going to make such a fuss, I'll call it off, I'll tell him not to come.

Amanda: You certainly won't do anything of the kind. Nothing offends people worse than broken engagements. It simply means I'll have to work like a Turk! We won't be brilliant, but we'll pass inspection. Come on inside. *(Tom follows, groaning.)* Sit down.

Tom: Any particular place you would like me to sit?

Amanda: Thank heavens I've got that new sofa! I'm also making payments on a floor lamp I'll have sent out! And put the chintz covers on, they'll brighten things up! Of course I'd hoped to have these walls re-papered. . . . What is the young man's name?

Tom: His name is O'Connor.

Amanda: That, of course, means fish—tomorrow is Friday! I'll have that salmon loaf—with Durkee's dressing! What does he do? He works at the warehouse?

Tom: Of course! How else would I—

Amanda: Tom, he—doesn't drink?

Tom: Why do you ask me that?

Amanda: Your father *did*!

Tom: Don't get started on that!

Amanda: He *does* drink, then?

Tom: Not that I know of!

Amanda: Make sure, be certain! The last thing I want for my daughter's a boy who drinks!

Tom: Aren't you being a little premature? Mr. O'Connor has not yet appeared on the scene!

Amanda: But will tomorrow. To meet your sister, and what do I know about his character? Nothing! Old maids are better off than wives of drunkards!

Tom: Oh, my God!

Amanda: Be still!

Tom (leaning forward to whisper): Lots of fellows meet girls whom they don't marry!

Amanda: Oh, talk sensibly, Tom—and don't be sarcastic! *(She has gotten a hair-brush.)*

Tom: What are you doing?

Amanda: I'm brushing that cow-lick down! What is this young man's position at the warehouse?

Tom (submitting grimly to the brush and the interrogation): This young man's position is that of a shipping clerk, Mother.

Amanda: Sounds to me like a fairly responsible job, the sort of a job *you* would be in if you just had more *get-up*. What is his salary? Have you got any idea?

Tom: I would judge it to be approximately eighty-five dollars a month.

Amanda: Well—not princely, but—

Tom: Twenty more than I make.

Amanda: Yes, how well I know! But for a family man, eighty-five dollars a month is not much more than you can just get by on. . . .

Tom: Yes, but Mr. O'Connor is not a family man.

Amanda: He might be, mightn't he? Some time in the future?

Tom: I see. Plans and provisions.

Amanda: You are the only young man that I know of who ignores the fact that the future becomes the present, the present the past, and the past turns into everlasting regret if you don't plan for it!

Tom: I will think that over and see what I can make of it.

Amanda: Don't be supercilious with your mother! Tell me some more about this—what do you call him?

Tom: James D. O'Connor. The D. is for Delaney.

Amanda: Irish on *both* sides! *Gracious!* And doesn't drink?

Tom: Shall I call him up and ask him right this minute?

Amanda: The only way to find out about those things is to make discreet inquiries at the proper moment. When I was a girl in Blue Mountain and it was suspected that a young man drank, the girl whose attentions he had been receiving, if any girl *was,* would sometimes speak to the minister of his church, or rather her father would if her father was living, and sort of feel him out on the young man's character. That is the way such things are discreetly handled to keep a young woman from making a tragic mistake!

Tom: Then how did you happen to make a tragic mistake?

Amanda: That innocent look of your father's had everyone fooled! He *smiled*—the world was *enchanted!* No girl can do worse than put herself at the mercy of a handsome appearance! I hope that Mr. O'Connor is not too good-looking.

Tom: No, he's not too good-looking. He's covered with freckles and hasn't too much of a nose.

Amanda: He's not right-down homely, though?

Tom: Not right-down homely. Just medium homely, I'd say.

Amanda: Character's what to look for in a man.

Tom: That's what I've always said, Mother.

Amanda: You've never said anything of the kind and I suspect you would never give it a thought.

Tom: Don't be suspicious of me.

Amanda: At least I hope he's the type that's up and coming.

Tom: I think he really goes in for self-improvement.

Amanda: What reason have you to think so?

Tom: He goes to night school.

Amanda (beaming): Splendid! What does he do, I mean study?

Tom: Radio engineering and public speaking!

Amanda: Then he has visions of being advanced in the world! Any young man who studies public speaking is aiming to have an executive job some day! And radio engineering? A thing for the future! Both of these facts are very illuminating. Those are the sort of things that a mother should know concerning any young man who comes to call on her daughter. Seriously or—not.

Tom: One little warning. He doesn't know about Laura. I didn't let on that we had dark ulterior motives. I just said, why don't you come have dinner with us? He said okay and that was the whole conversation.

Amanda: I bet it was! You're eloquent as an oyster. However, he'll know about Laura when he gets here. When he sees how lovely and sweet and pretty she is, he'll thank his lucky stars he was asked to dinner.

Tom: Mother, you mustn't expect too much of Laura.

Amanda: What do you mean?

Tom: Laura seems all those things to you and me because she's ours and we love her. We don't even notice she's crippled any more.

Amanda: Don't say crippled! You know that I never allow that word to be used!

Tom: But face facts, Mother. She is and—that's not all—

Amanda: What do you mean "not all"?

Tom: Laura is very different from other girls.

Amanda: I think the difference is all to her advantage.

Tom: Not quite all—in the eyes of others—strangers—she's terribly shy and lives in a world of her own and those things make her seem a little peculiar to people outside the house.

Amanda: Don't say peculiar.

Tom: Face the facts. She is.

(The dance-hall music changes to a tango that has a minor and somewhat ominous tone.)

Amanda: In what way is she peculiar—may I ask?

Tom (gently): She lives in a world of her own—a world of—little glass ornaments, Mother. . . . *(Gets up. Amanda remains holding brush, looking at him, troubled.)* She plays old phonograph records and—that's about all—*(He glances at himself in the mirror and crosses to door.)*

Amanda (sharply): Where are you going?

Tom: I'm going to the movies. *(Out screen door.)*

Amanda: Not to the movies, every night to the movies! *(Follows quickly to screen door.)* I don't believe you always go to the movies! *(He is gone. Amanda looks worriedly after him for a moment. Then vitality and optimism return and she turns from the door. Crossing to portieres.)* Laura! Laura! *(Laura answers from kitchenette.)*

Laura: Yes, Mother.

Amanda: Let those dishes go and come in front! *(Laura appears with dish towel. Gaily.)* Laura, come here and make a wish on the moon!

Laura (entering): Moon—moon?

Amanda: A little silver slipper of a moon. Look over your left shoulder, Laura, and make a wish! *(Laura looks faintly puzzled as if called out of sleep. Amanda seizes her shoulders and turns her at angle by the door.)* Now! Now, darling, *wish!*

Laura: What shall I wish for, Mother?

Amanda (*her voice trembling and her eyes suddenly filling with tears*): Happiness! Good Fortune!

The violin rises and the stage dims out.

SCENE VI

(*Image: High-school hero.*)

Tom: And so the following evening I brought Jim home to dinner. I had known Jim slightly in high school. In high school Jim was a hero. He had tremendous Irish good nature and vitality with the scrubbed and polished look of white chinaware. He seemed to move in a continual spotlight. He was a star in basketball, captain of the debating club, president of the senior class and the glee club and he sang the male lead in the annual light operas. He was always running or bounding, never just walking. He seemed always at the point of defeating the law of gravity. He was shooting with such velocity through his adolescence that you would logically expect him to arrive at nothing short of the White House by the time he was thirty. But Jim apparently ran into more interference after his graduation from Soldan. His speed had definitely slowed. Six years after he left high school he was holding a job that wasn't much better than mine.

(*Image: Clerk.*)

He was the only one at the warehouse with whom I was on friendly terms. I was valuable to him as someone who could remember his former glory, who had seen him win basketball games and the silver cup in debating. He knew of my secret practice of retiring to a cabinet of the washroom to work on poems when business was slack in the warehouse. He called me Shakespeare. And while the other boys in the warehouse regarded me with suspicious hostility, Jim took a humorous attitude toward me. Gradually his attitude affected the others, their hostility wore off, and they also began to smile at me as people smile at an oddly fashioned dog who trots across their paths at some distance.

I knew that Jim and Laura had known each other at Soldan, and I had heard Laura speak admiringly of his voice. I didn't know if Jim remembered her or not. In high school Laura had been as unobtrusive as Jim had been astonishing. If he did remember Laura, it was not as my sister, for when I asked him to dinner, he grinned and said, "You know, Shakespeare, I never thought of you as having folks!"

He was about to discover that I did. . . .

(*Light upstage.*)

(*Legend on screen: "The Accent of a Coming Foot."*)

Friday evening. It is about five o'clock of a late spring evening which comes "scattering poems in the sky."

A delicate lemony light is in the Wingfield apartment.

Amanda has worked like a Turk in preparation for the gentleman caller. The results are astonishing. The new floor lamp with its rose-silk shade is in place, a colored paper lantern conceals the broken light fixture in the ceiling, new billowing white curtains are at the windows, chintz covers are on chairs and sofa, a pair of new sofa pillows make their initial appearance.

Open boxes and tissue paper are scattered on the floor.

Laura stands in the middle with lifted arms while Amanda crouches before her, adjusting the hem of the new dress, devout and ritualistic. The dress is colored and designed by memory. The arrangement of Laura's hair is changed; it is softer and more becoming. A fragile, unearthly prettiness has come out in Laura: she is like a piece of translucent glass touched by light, given a momentary radiance, not actual, not lasting.

Amanda (impatiently): Why are you trembling?
Laura: Mother, you've made me so nervous!
Amanda: How have I made you nervous?
Laura: By all this fuss! You make it seem so important!
Amanda: I don't understand you, Laura. You couldn't be satisfied with just sitting home, and yet whenever I try to arrange something for you, you seem to resist it. *(She gets up.)* Now take a look at yourself. No, wait! Wait just a moment — I have an idea!
Laura: What is it now?

Amanda produces two powder puffs which she wraps in handkerchiefs and stuffs in Laura's bosom.

Laura: Mother, what are you doing?
Amanda: They call them "Gay Deceivers"!
Laura: I won't wear them!
Amanda: You will!
Laura: Why should I?
Amanda: Because, to be painfully honest, your chest is flat.
Laura: You make it seem like we were setting a trap.
Amanda: All pretty girls are a trap, a pretty trap, and men expect them to be. *(Legend: "A Pretty Trap.")* Now look at yourself, young lady. This is the prettiest you will ever be! I've got to fix myself now! You're going to be surprised by your mother's appearance! *(She crosses through portieres, humming gaily.)*

Laura moves slowly to the long mirror and stares solemnly at herself.

A wind blows the white curtains inward in a slow, graceful motion and with a faint, sorrowful sighing.

Amanda (off stage): It isn't dark enough yet. *(She turns slowly before the mirror with a troubled look).*

(Legend on screen: "This Is My Sister: Celebrate Her with Strings!" Music.)

Amanda (laughing, off): I'm going to show you something. I'm going to make a spectacular appearance!
Laura: What is it, Mother?
Amanda: Possess your soul in patience — you will see! Something I've resurrected from that old trunk! Styles haven't changed so terribly much after all. . . . *(She parts the portieres.)* Now just look at your mother! *(She wears a girlish frock of yellowed voile with a blue silk sash. She carries a bunch of jonquils — the legend of her youth is nearly revived. Feverishly.)* This is the dress in which I

led the cotillion. Won the cakewalk twice at Sunset Hill, wore one spring
to the Governor's ball in Jackson! See how I sashayed around the ballroom, Laura? *(She raises her skirt and does a mincing step around the room.)* I
wore it on Sundays for my gentlemen callers! I had it on the day I met your
father — I had malaria fever all that spring. The change of climate from
East Tennessee to the Delta — weakened resistance — I had a little temperature all the time — not enough to be serious — just enough to make me
restless and giddy! Invitations poured in — parties all over the Delta! "Stay
in bed," said Mother, "you have fever!" — but I just wouldn't. — I took qui-
nine but kept on going, going! — Evenings, dances! — Afternoons, long,
long rides! Picnics — lovely! — So lovely, that country in May. — All lacy
with dogwood, literally flooded with jonquils! — That was the spring I had
the craze for jonquils. Jonquils became an absolute obsession. Mother
said, "Honey, there's no more room for jonquils." And still I kept bringing
in more jonquils. Whenever, wherever I saw them, I'd say, "Stop! Stop! I see
jonquils!" I made the young men help me gather the jonquils! It was a
joke, Amanda and her jonquils! Finally there were no more vases to hold
them, every available space was filled with jonquils. No vases to hold
them? All right, I'll hold them myself! And then I — *(She stops in front of the
picture.) (Music.)* met your father! Malaria fever and jonquils and then —
this — boy. . . . *(She switches on the rose-colored lamp.)* I hope they get here before it starts to rain. *(She crosses upstage and places the jonquils in bowl on
table.)* I gave your brother a little extra change so he and Mr. O'Connor
could take the service car home.

Laura (with altered look): What did you say his name was?
Amanda: O'Connor.
Laura: What is his first name?
Amanda: I don't remember. Oh, yes, I do. It was — Jim!

> *Laura sways slightly and catches hold of a chair.*
>   *(Legend on screen: "Not Jim!")*

Laura (faintly): Not — Jim!
Amanda: Yes, that was it, it was Jim! I've never known a Jim that wasn't nice!

> *(Music: Ominous.)*

Laura: Are you sure his name is Jim O'Connor?
Amanda: Yes. Why?
Laura: Is he the one that Tom used to know in high school?
Amanda: He didn't say so. I think he just got to know him at the warehouse.
Laura: There was a Jim O'Connor we both knew in high school — *(Then, with ef-
fort.)* If that is the one that Tom is bringing to dinner — you'll have to ex-
cuse me, I won't come to the table.
Amanda: What sort of nonsense is this?
Laura: You asked me once if I'd ever liked a boy. Don't you remember I showed
you this boy's picture?
Amanda: You mean the boy you showed me in the year-book?
Laura: Yes, that boy.
Amanda: Laura, Laura, were you in love with that boy?
Laura: I don't know, Mother. All I know is I couldn't sit at the table if it was
him!

Amanda: It won't be him! It isn't the least bit likely. But whether it is or not, you will come to the table. You will not be excused.

Laura: I'll have to be, Mother.

Amanda: I don't intend to humor your silliness, Laura. I've had too much from you and your brother, both! So just sit down and compose yourself till they come. Tom has forgotten his key so you'll have to let them in, when they arrive.

Laura (panicky): Oh, Mother—*you* answer the door!

Amanda (lightly): I'll be in the kitchen—busy!

Laura: Oh, Mother, please answer the door, don't make me do it!

Amanda (crossing into kitchenette): I've got to fix the dressing for the salmon. Fuss, fuss—silliness!—over a gentleman caller!

> *Door swings shut. Laura is left alone.*
>   *(Legend: "Terror!")*
>   *She utters a low moan and turns off the lamp—sits stiffly on the edge of the sofa, knotting her fingers together.*
>   *(Legend on screen: "The Opening of a Door!")*
>   *Tom and Jim appear on the fire-escape steps and climb to landing. Hearing their approach, Laura rises with a panicky gesture. She retreats to the portieres. The doorbell. Laura catches her breath and touches her throat. Low drums.*

Amanda (calling): Laura, sweetheart! The door!

> *Laura stares at it without moving.*

Jim: I think we just beat the rain.

Tom: Uh-huh. *(He rings again, nervously. Jim whistles and fishes for a cigarette.)*

Amanda (very, very gaily): Laura, that is your brother and Mr. O'Connor! Will you let them in, darling?

> *Laura crosses toward kitchenette door.*

Laura (breathlessly): Mother—you go to the door!

> *Amanda steps out of kitchenette and stares furiously at Laura. She points imperiously at the door.*

Laura: Please, please!

Amanda (in a fierce whisper): What is the matter with you, you silly thing?

Laura (desperately): Please, you answer it, *please!*

Amanda: I told you I wasn't going to humor you, Laura. Why have you chosen this moment to lose your mind?

Laura: Please, please, please, you go!

Amanda: You'll have to go to the door because I can't!

Laura (despairingly): I can't either!

Amanda: Why?

Laura: I'm *sick!*

Amanda: I'm sick, too—of your nonsense! Why can't you and your brother be normal people? Fantastic whims and behavior! *(Tom gives a long ring.)* Preposterous goings on! Can you give me one reason—*(Calls out lyrically.)* COMING! JUST ONE SECOND!—why should you be afraid to open a door? Now you answer it, Laura!

Laura: Oh, oh, oh . . . *(She returns through the portieres. Darts to the Victrola and winds it frantically and turns it on.)*

Amanda: Laura Wingfield, you march right to that door!

Laura: Yes—yes, Mother!

> *A faraway, scratchy rendition of "Dardanella" softens the air and gives her strength to move through it. She slips to the door and draws it cautiously open.*
> *Tom enters with the caller, Jim O'Connor.*

Tom: Laura, this is Jim. Jim, this is my sister, Laura.

Jim (stepping inside): I didn't know that Shakespeare had a sister!

Laura (retreating stiff and trembling from the door): How—how do you do?

Jim (heartily extending his hand): Okay!

> *Laura touches it hesitantly with hers.*

Jim: Your hand's *cold*, Laura!

Laura: Yes, well—I've been playing the Victrola . . .

Jim: Must have been playing classical music on it! You ought to play a little hot swing music to warm you up!

Laura: Excuse me—I haven't finished playing the Victrola . . .

> *She turns awkwardly and hurries into the front room. She pauses a second by the Victrola. Then catches her breath and darts through the portieres like a frightened deer.*

Jim (grinning): What was the matter?

Tom: Oh—with Laura? Laura is—terribly shy.

Jim: Shy, huh? It's unusual to meet a shy girl nowadays. I don't believe you ever mentioned you had a sister.

Tom: Well, now you know. I have one. Here is the *Post Dispatch.* You want a piece of it?

Jim: Uh-huh.

Tom: What piece? The comics?

Jim: Sports! *(Glances at it.)* Ole Dizzy Dean is on his bad behavior.

Tom (disinterest): Yeah? *(Lights cigarette and crosses back to fire-escape door.)*

Jim: Where are *you* going?

Tom: I'm going out on the terrace.

Jim (goes after him): You know, Shakespeare—I'm going to sell you a bill of goods!

Tom: What goods?

Jim: A course I'm taking.

Tom: Huh?

Jim: In public speaking! You and me, we're not the warehouse type.

Tom: Thanks—that's good news. But what has public speaking got to do with it?

Jim: It fits you for—executive positions!

Tom: Awww.

Jim: I tell you it's done a helluva lot for me.

> *(Image: Executive at desk.)*

Tom: In what respect?

Jim: In every! Ask yourself what is the difference between you an' me and men in the office down front? Brains?—No!—Ability?—No! Then what? Just one little thing—

Tom: What is that one little thing?

Jim: Primarily it amounts to — social poise! Being able to square up to people and hold your own on any social level!

Amanda (off stage): Tom?

Tom: Yes, Mother?

Amanda: Is that you and Mr. O'Connor?

Tom: Yes, Mother.

Amanda: Well, you just make yourselves comfortable in there.

Tom: Yes, Mother.

Amanda: Ask Mr. O'Connor if he would like to wash his hands.

Jim: Aw — no — no — thank you — I took care of that at the warehouse. Tom —

Tom: Yes?

Jim: Mr. Mendoza was speaking to me about you.

Tom: Favorably?

Jim: What do you think?

Tom: Well —

Jim: You're going to be out of a job if you don't wake up.

Tom: I am waking up —

Jim: You show no signs.

Tom: The signs are interior.

(*Image on screen: The sailing vessel with Jolly Roger again.*)

Tom: I'm planning to change. (*He leans over the rail speaking with quiet exhilaration. The incandescent marquees and signs of the first-run movie houses light his face from across the alley. He looks like a voyager.*) I'm right at the point of committing myself to a future that doesn't include the warehouse and Mr. Mendoza or even a night-school course in public speaking.

Jim: What are you gassing about?

Tom: I'm tired of the movies.

Jim: Movies!

Tom: Yes, movies! Look at them — (*A wave toward the marvels of Grand Avenue.*) All of those glamorous people — having adventures — hogging it all, gobbling the whole thing up! You know what happens? People go to the *movies* instead of *moving!* Hollywood characters are supposed to have all the adventures for everybody in America, while everybody in America sits in a dark room and watches them have them! Yes, until there's a war. That's when adventure becomes available to the masses! *Everyone's* dish, not only Gable's! Then the people in the dark room come out of the dark room to have some adventures themselves — Goody, goody — It's our turn now, to go to the South Sea Island — to make a safari — to be exotic, far-off — But I'm not patient. I don't want to wait till then. I'm tired of the *movies* and I am *about* to *move!*

Jim (incredulously): Move?

Tom: Yes.

Jim: When?

Tom: Soon!

Jim: Where? Where?

(*Theme three: Music seems to answer the question, while Tom thinks it over. He searches among his pockets.*)

Tom: I'm starting to boil inside. I know I seem dreamy, but inside—well, I'm boiling! Whenever I pick up a shoe, I shudder a little thinking how short life is and what I am doing!—Whatever that means. I know it doesn't mean shoes—except as something to wear on a traveler's feet! *(Finds paper.)* Look—

Jim: What?

Tom: I'm a member.

Jim (reading): The Union of Merchant Seamen.

Tom: I paid my dues this month, instead of the light bill.

Jim: You will regret it when they turn the lights off.

Tom: I won't be here.

Jim: How about your mother?

Tom: I'm like my father. The bastard son of a bastard! See how he grins? And he's been absent going on sixteen years!

Jim: You're just talking, you drip. How does your mother feel about it?

Tom: Shhh—Here comes Mother! Mother is not acquainted with my plans!

Amanda (enters portieres): Where are you all?

Tom: On the terrace, Mother.

> *They start inside. She advances to them. Tom is distinctly shocked at her appearance. Even Jim blinks a little. He is making his first contact with girlish Southern vivacity and in spite of the night-school course in public speaking is somewhat thrown off the beam by the unexpected outlay of social charm.*
>
> *Certain responses are attempted by Jim but are swept aside by Amanda's gay laughter and chatter. Tom is embarrassed but after the first shock Jim reacts very warmly. Grins and chuckles, is altogether won over.*
>
> *(Image: Amanda as a girl.)*

Amanda (coyly smiling, shaking her girlish ringlets): Well, well, well, so this is Mr. O'Connor. Introductions entirely unnecessary. I've heard so much about you from my boy. I finally said to him, Tom—good gracious!—why don't you bring this paragon to supper? I'd like to meet this nice young man at the warehouse!—Instead of just hearing him sing your praises so much! I don't know why my son is so stand-offish—that's not Southern behavior! Let's sit down and—I think we could stand a little more air in here! Tom, leave the door open. I felt a nice fresh breeze a moment ago. Where has it gone? Mmm, so warm already! And not quite summer, even. We're going to burn up when summer really gets started. However, we're having—we're having a very light supper. I think light things are better fo' this time of year. The same as light clothes are. Light clothes an' light food are what warm weather calls fo'. You know our blood gets so thick during th' winter—it takes a while fo' us to *adjust* ou'selves!—when the season changes. . . . It's come so quick this year. I wasn't prepared. All of a sudden—heavens! Already summer!—I ran to the trunk an' pulled out this light dress—Terribly old! Historical almost! But feels so good—so good an' co-ol, y'know. . . .

Tom: Mother—

Amanda: Yes, honey?

Tom: How about—supper?

Amanda: Honey, you go ask Sister if supper is ready! You know that Sister is in full charge of supper! Tell her you hungry boys are waiting for it. *(To Jim.)* Have you met Laura?

Jim: She —

Amanda: Let you in? Oh, good, you've met already! It's rare for a girl as sweet an' pretty as Laura to be domestic! But Laura is, thank heavens, not only pretty but also very domestic. I'm not at all. I never was a bit. I never could make a thing but angel-food cake. Well, in the South we had so many servants. Gone, gone, gone. All vestiges of gracious living! Gone completely! I wasn't prepared for what the future brought me. All of my gentlemen callers were sons of planters and so of course I assumed that I would be married to one and raise my family on a large piece of land with plenty of servants. But man proposes — and woman accepts the proposal! — To vary that old, old saying a little bit — I married no planter! I married a man who worked for the telephone company! — that gallantly smiling gentleman over there! *(Points to the picture.)* A telephone man who — fell in love with long distance! — Now he travels and I don't even know where! — But what am I going on for about my — tribulations! Tell me yours — I hope you don't have any! Tom?

Tom (returning): Yes, Mother?

Amanda: Is supper nearly ready?

Tom: It looks to me like supper is on the table.

Amanda: Let me look — *(She rises prettily and looks through portieres.)* Oh, lovely — But where is Sister?

Tom: Laura is not feeling well and she says that she thinks she'd better not come to the table.

Amanda: What? — Nonsense! — Laura? Oh, Laura!

Laura (off stage, faintly): Yes, Mother.

Amanda: You really must come to the table. We won't be seated until you come to the table! Come in, Mr. O'Connor. You sit over there and I'll — Laura? Laura Wingfield! You're keeping us waiting, honey! We can't say grace until you come to the table!

> *The back door is pushed weakly open and Laura comes in. She is obviously quite faint, her lips trembling, her eyes wide and staring. She moves unsteadily toward the table.*
>
> *(Legend: "Terror!")*
>
> *Outside a summer storm is coming abruptly. The white curtains billow inward at the windows and there is a sorrowful murmur and deep blue dusk.*
>
> *Laura suddenly stumbles — She catches at a chair with a faint moan.*

Tom: Laura!

Amanda: Laura! *(There is a clap of thunder.)* *(Legend: "Ah!")* *(Despairingly.)* Why, Laura, you *are* sick, darling! Tom, help your sister into the living room, dear! Sit in the living room, Laura — rest on the sofa. Well! *(To the gentleman caller.)* Standing over the hot stove made her ill! — I told her that it was just too warm this evening, but — *(Tom comes back in. Laura is on the sofa.)* Is Laura all right now?

Tom: Yes.

Amanda: What *is* that? Rain? A nice cool rain has come up! *(She gives the gentleman caller a frightened look.)* I think we may — have grace — now . . . *(Tom looks at her stupidly.)* Tom, honey — you say grace!

Tom: Oh . . . "For these and all thy mercies —" *(They bow their heads, Amanda stealing a nervous glance at Jim. In the living room Laura, stretched on the sofa, clenches her hand to her lips, to hold back a shuddering sob.)* God's Holy Name be praised —

(The scene dims out.)

SCENE VII

A Souvenir

Half an hour later. Dinner is just being finished in the upstage area, which is concealed by the drawn portieres.

    As the curtain rises Laura is still huddled upon the sofa, her feet drawn under her, her head resting on a pale blue pillow, her eyes wide and mysteriously watchful. The new floor lamp with its shade of rose-colored silk gives a soft, becoming light to her face, bringing out the fragile, unearthly prettiness which usually escapes attention. There is a steady murmur of rain, but it is slackening and stops soon after the scene begins; the air outside becomes pale and luminous as the moon breaks out.

    A moment after the curtain rises, the lights in both rooms flicker and go out.

Jim: Hey, there, Mr. Light Bulb!

    Amanda laughs nervously.
    (Legend: "Suspension of a Public Service.") ˙

Amanda: Where was Moses when the lights went out? Ha-ha. Do you know the answer to that one, Mr. O'Connor?

Jim: No, Ma'am, what's the answer?

Amanda: In the dark! *(Jim laughs appreciatively.)* Everybody sit still. I'll light the candles. Isn't it lucky we have them on the table? Where's a match? Which of you gentlemen can provide a match?

Jim: Here.

Amanda: Thank you, sir.

Jim: Not at all, Ma'am!

Amanda: I guess the fuse has burnt out. Mr. O'Connor, can you tell a burnt-out fuse? I know I can't and Tom is a total loss when it comes to mechanics. *(Sound: Getting up: Voices recede a little to kitchenette.)* Oh, be careful you don't bump into something. We don't want our gentleman caller to break his neck. Now wouldn't that be a fine howdy-do?

Jim: Ha-ha! Where is the fuse-box?

Amanda: Right here next to the stove. Can you see anything?

Jim: Just a minute.

Amanda: Isn't electricity a mysterious thing? Wasn't it Benjamin Franklin who tied a key to a kite? We live in such a mysterious universe, don't we? Some people say that science clears up all the mysteries for us. In my opinion it only creates more! Have you found it yet?

Jim: No, Ma'am. All these fuses look okay to me.

Amanda: Tom!

Tom: Yes, Mother?

Amanda: That light bill I gave you several days ago. The one I told you we got the notices about?

Tom: Oh.—Yeah.

(*Legend: "Ha!"*)

Amanda: You didn't neglect to pay it by any chance?

Tom: Why, I—

Amanda: Didn't! I might have known it!

Jim: Shakespeare probably wrote a poem on that light bill, Mrs. Wingfield.

Amanda: I might have known better than to trust him with it! There's such a high price for negligence in this world!

Jim: Maybe the poem will win a ten-dollar prize.

Amanda: We'll just have to spend the remainder of the evening in the nineteenth century, before Mr. Edison made the Mazda lamp!

Jim: Candlelight is my favorite kind of light.

Amanda: That shows you're romantic! But that's no excuse for Tom. Well, we got through dinner. Very considerate of them to let us get through dinner before they plunged us into everlasting darkness, wasn't it, Mr. O'Connor?

Jim: Ha-ha!

Amanda: Tom, as a penalty for your carelessness you can help me with the dishes.

Jim: Let me give you a hand.

Amanda: Indeed you will not!

Jim: I ought to be good for something.

Amanda: Good for something? (*Her tone is rhapsodic.*) You? Why, Mr. O'Connor, nobody, *nobody's* given me this much entertainment in years—as you have!

Jim: Aw, now, Mrs. Wingfield!

Amanda: I'm not exaggerating, not one bit! But Sister is all by her lonesome. You go keep her company in the parlor! I'll give you this lovely old candelabrum that used to be on the altar at the church of the Heavenly Rest. It was melted a little out of shape when the church burnt down. Lightning struck it one spring. Gypsy Jones was holding a revival at the time and he intimated that the church was destroyed because the Episcopalians gave card parties.

Jim: Ha-ha.

Amanda: And how about coaxing Sister to drink a little wine? I think it would be good for her! Can you carry both at once?

Jim: Sure. I'm Superman!

Amanda: Now, Thomas, get into this apron!

The door of kitchenette swings closed on Amanda's gay laughter; the flickering light approaches the portieres.

Laura sits up nervously as he enters. Her speech at first is low and breathless from the almost intolerable strain of being alone with a stranger.

(*Legend: "I Don't Suppose You Remember Me at All!"*)

In her first speeches in this scene, before Jim's warmth overcomes her paralyzing shyness, Laura's voice is thin and breathless as though she has run up a steep flight of stairs.

Jim's attitude is gently humorous. In playing this scene it should be stressed that while the incident is apparently unimportant, it is to Laura the climax of her secret life.

Jim: Hello, there, Laura.

Laura (faintly): Hello. (*She clears her throat.*)

Jim: How are you feeling now? Better?

Laura: Yes. Yes, thank you.

Jim: This is for you. A little dandelion wine. *(He extends it toward her with extravagant gallantry.)*

Laura: Thank you.

Jim: Drink it—but don't get drunk! *(He laughs heartily. Laura takes the glass uncertainly; laughs shyly.)* Where shall I set the candles?

Laura: Oh—oh, anywhere . . .

Jim: How about here on the floor? Any objections?

Laura: No.

Jim: I'll spread a newspaper under to catch the drippings. I like to sit on the floor. Mind if I do?

Laura: Oh, no.

Jim: Give me a pillow?

Laura: What?

Jim: A pillow!

Laura: Oh . . . *(Hands him one quickly.)*

Jim: How about you? Don't you like to sit on the floor?

Laura: Oh—yes.

Jim: Why don't you, then?

Laura: I—will.

Jim: Take a pillow! *(Laura does. Sits on the other side of the candelabrum. Jim crosses his legs and smiles engagingly at her.)* I can't hardly see you sitting way over there.

Laura: I can—see you.

Jim: I know, but that's not fair, I'm in the limelight. *(Laura moves her pillow closer.)* Good! Now I can see you! Comfortable?

Laura: Yes.

Jim: So am I. Comfortable as a cow. Will you have some gum?

Laura: No, thank you.

Jim: I think that I will indulge, with your permission. *(Musingly unwraps it and holds it up.)* Think of the fortune made by the guy that invented the first piece of chewing gum. Amazing, huh? The Wrigley Building is one of the sights of Chicago.—I saw it summer before last when I went up to the Century of Progress. Did you take in the Century of Progress?

Laura: No, I didn't.

Jim: Well, it was quite a wonderful exposition. What impressed me most was the Hall of Science. Gives you an idea of what the future will be in America, even more wonderful than the present time is! *(Pause. Smiling at her.)* Your brother tells me you're shy. Is that right, Laura?

Laura: I—don't know.

Jim: I judge you to be an old-fashioned type of girl. Well, I think that's a pretty good type to be. Hope you don't think I'm being too personal—do you?

Laura (hastily, out of embarrassment): I believe I *will* take a piece of gum, if you—don't mind. *(Clearing her throat.)* Mr. O'Connor, have you—kept up with your singing?

Jim: Singing? Me?

Laura: Yes. I remember what a beautiful voice you had.

Jim: When did you hear me sing?

(Voice offstage in the pause.)

Voice (offstage): O blow, ye winds, heigh-ho,
                          A-roving I will go!
                          I'm off to my love
                          With a boxing glove —
                          Ten thousand miles away!

Jim: You say you've heard me sing?

Laura: Oh, yes! Yes, very often . . . I — don't suppose you remember me — at all?

Jim (smiling doubtfully): You know I have an idea I've seen you before. I had that idea soon as you opened the door. It seemed almost like I was about to remember your name. But the name that I started to call you — wasn't a name! And so I stopped myself before I said it.

Laura: Wasn't it — Blue Roses?

Jim (springs up, grinning): Blue Roses! My gosh, yes — Blue Roses! That's what I had on my tongue when you opened the door! Isn't it funny what tricks your memory plays? I didn't connect you with the high school somehow or other. But that's where it was; it was high school. I didn't even know you were Shakespeare's sister! Gosh, I'm sorry.

Laura: I didn't expect you to. You — barely knew me!

Jim: But we did have a speaking acquaintance, huh?

Laura: Yes, we — spoke to each other.

Jim: When did you recognize me?

Laura: Oh, right away!

Jim: Soon as I came in the door?

Laura: When I heard your name I thought it was probably you. I knew that Tom used to know you a little in high school. So when you came in the door — Well, then I was — sure.

Jim: Why didn't you *say* something, then?

Laura (breathlessly): I didn't know what to say, I was — too surprised!

Jim: For goodness' sakes! You know, this sure is funny!

Laura: Yes! Yes, isn't it, though . . .

Jim: Didn't we have a class in something together?

Laura: Yes, we did.

Jim: What class was that?

Laura: It was — singing — Chorus!

Jim: Aw!

Laura: I sat across the aisle from you in the Aud.

Jim: Aw.

Laura: Mondays, Wednesdays, and Fridays.

Jim: Now I remember — you always came in late.

Laura: Yes, it was so hard for me, getting upstairs. I had that brace on my leg — it clumped so loud!

Jim: I never heard any clumping.

Laura (wincing in the recollection): To me it sounded like — thunder!

Jim: Well, well, well. I never even noticed.

Laura: And everybody was seated before I came in. I had to walk in front of all those people. My seat was in the back row. I had to go clumping all the way up the aisle with everyone watching!

Jim: You shouldn't have been self-conscious.

Laura: I know, but I was. It was always such a relief when the singing started.

Jim: Aw, yes, I've placed you now! I used to call you Blue Roses. How was it that I got started calling you that?

Laura: I was out of school a little while with pleurosis. When I came back you asked me what was the matter. I said I had pleurosis — you thought I said Blue Roses. That's what you always called me after that!

Jim: I hope you didn't mind.

Laura: Oh, no — I liked it. You see, I wasn't acquainted with many — people. . . .

Jim: As I remember you sort of stuck by yourself.

Laura: I — I — never had much luck at — making friends.

Jim: I don't see why you wouldn't.

Laura: Well, I — started out badly.

Jim: You mean being —

Laura: Yes, it sort of — stood between me —

Jim: You shouldn't have let it!

Laura: I know, but it did, and —

Jim: You were shy with people!

Laura: I tried not to be but never could —

Jim: Overcome it?

Laura: No, I — I never could!

Jim: I guess being shy is something you have to work out of kind of gradually.

Laura (sorrowfully): Yes — I guess it —

Jim: Takes time!

Laura: Yes —

Jim: People are not so dreadful when you know them. That's what you have to remember! And everybody has problems, not just you, but practically everybody has got some problems. You think of yourself as having the only problems, as being the only one who is disappointed. But just look around you and you will see lots of people as disappointed as you are. For instance, I hoped when I was going to high school that I would be further along at this time, six years later, than I am now — You remember that wonderful write-up I had in *The Torch?*

Laura: Yes! *(She rises and crosses to table.)*

Jim: It said I was bound to succeed in anything I went into! *(Laura returns with the annual.)* Holy Jeez! *The Torch!* (He accepts it reverently. They smile across it with mutual wonder. Laura crouches beside him and they begin to turn through it. Laura's shyness is dissolving in his warmth.)*

Laura: Here you are in *Pirates of Penzance!*

Jim (wistfully): I sang the baritone lead in that operetta.

Laura (rapidly): So — *beautifully!*

Jim (protesting): Aw —

Laura: Yes, yes — beautifully — beautifully!

Jim: You heard me?

Laura: All three times!

Jim: No!

Laura: Yes!

Jim: All three performances?

Laura (looking down): Yes.

Jim: Why?

Laura: I — wanted to ask you to — autograph my program.

Jim: Why didn't you ask me to?

Laura: You were always surrounded by your own friends so much that I never had a chance to.

Jim: You should have just —

Laura: Well, I — thought you might think I was —

Jim: Thought I might think you was — what?

Laura: Oh —

Jim (with reflective relish): I was beleaguered by females in those days.

Laura: You were terribly popular!

Jim: Yeah —

Laura: You had such a — friendly way —

Jim: I was spoiled in high school.

Laura: Everybody — liked you!

Jim: Including you?

Laura: I — yes, I — I did, too — *(She gently closes the book in her lap.)*

Jim: Well, well, well! — Give me that program, Laura. *(She hands it to him. He signs it with a flourish.)* There you are — better late than never!

Laura: Oh, I — what a — surprise!

Jim: My signature isn't worth very much right now. But some day — maybe — it will increase in value! Being disappointed is one thing and being discouraged is something else. I am disappointed but I'm not discouraged. I'm twenty-three years old. How old are you?

Laura: I'll be twenty-four in June.

Jim: That's not old age.

Laura: No, but —

Jim: You finished high school?

Laura (with difficulty): I didn't go back.

Jim: You mean you dropped out?

Laura: I made bad grades in my final examinations. *(She rises and replaces the book and the program. Her voice strained.)* How is — Emily Meisenbach getting along?

Jim: Oh, that kraut-head!

Laura: Why do you call her that?

Jim: That's what she was.

Laura: You're not still — going with her?

Jim: I never see her.

Laura: It said in the Personal Section that you were — engaged!

Jim: I know, but I wasn't impressed by that — propaganda!

Laura: It wasn't — the truth?

Jim: Only in Emily's optimistic opinion!

Laura: Oh —

> *(Legend: "What Have You Done since High School?")*
>   *Jim lights a cigarette and leans indolently back on his elbows smiling at Laura with a warmth and charm which light her inwardly with altar candles. She remains by the table and turns in her hands a piece of glass to cover her tumult.*

Jim (after several reflective puffs on a cigarette): What have you done since high school? *(She seems not to hear him.)* Huh? *(Laura looks up.)* I said what have you done since high school, Laura?

Laura: Nothing much.

Jim: You must have been doing something these six long years.

Laura: Yes.

Jim: Well, then, such as what?

Laura: I took a business course at business college—

Jim: How did that work out?

Laura: Well, not very—well—I had to drop out, it gave me—indigestion—

Jim laughs gently.

Jim: What are you doing now?

Laura: I don't do anything—much. Oh, please don't think I sit around doing nothing! My glass collection takes up a good deal of my time. Glass is something you have to take good care of.

Jim: What did you say—about glass?

Laura: Collection I said—I have one—(*She clears her throat and turns away again, acutely shy.*)

Jim (*abruptly*): You know what I judge to be the trouble with you? Inferiority complex! Know what that is? That's what they call it when someone low-rates himself! I understand it because I had it, too. Although my case was not so aggravated as yours seems to be. I had it until I took up public speaking, developed my voice, and learned that I had an aptitude for science. Before that time I never thought of myself as being outstanding in any way whatsoever! Now I've never made a regular study of it, but I have a friend who says I can analyze people better than doctors that make a profession of it. I don't claim that to be necessarily true, but I can sure guess a person's psychology, Laura! (*Takes out his gum.*) Excuse me, Laura. I always take it out when the flavor is gone. I'll use this scrap of paper to wrap it in. I know how it is to get it stuck on a shoe. Yep—that's what I judge to be your principal trouble. A lack of confidence in yourself as a person. You don't have the proper amount of faith in yourself. I'm basing that fact on a number of your remarks and also on certain observations I've made. For instance that clumping you thought was so awful in high school. You say that you even dreaded to walk into class. You see what you did? You dropped out of school, you gave up an education because of a clump, which as far as I know was practically nonexistent! A little physical defect is what you have. Hardly noticeable even! Magnified thousands of times by imagination! You know what my strong advice to you is? Think of yourself as *superior* in some way!

Laura: In what way would I think?

Jim: Why, man alive, Laura! Just look about you a little. What do you see? A world full of common people! All of 'em born and all of 'em going to die! Which of them has one-tenth of your good points! Or mine! Or anyone else's, as far as that goes—Gosh! Everybody excels in some one thing. Some in many! (*Unconsciously glances at himself in the mirror.*) All you've got to do is discover in *what!* Take me, for instance. (*He adjusts his tie at the mirror.*) My interest happened to lie in electrodynamics. I'm taking a course in radio engineering at night school, Laura, on top of a fairly responsible job at the warehouse. I'm taking that course and studying public speaking.

Laura: Ohhhh.

Jim: Because I believe in the future of television! (*Turning back to her.*) I wish to be ready to go up right along with it. Therefore I'm planning to get in on the ground floor. In fact, I've already made the right connections and all that remains is for the industry itself to get under way! Full steam — *(His eyes are starry.) Knowledge* — Zzzzzp! *Money* — Zzzzzzp! — *Power!* That's the cycle democracy is built on! *(His attitude is convincingly dynamic. Laura stares at him, even her shyness eclipsed in her absolute wonder. He suddenly grins.)* I guess you think I think a lot of myself!

Laura: No — o-o-o, I —

Jim: Now how about you? Isn't there something you take more interest in than anything else?

Laura: Well, I do — as I said — have my — glass collection —

A peal of girlish laughter from the kitchen.

Jim: I'm not right sure I know what you're talking about. What kind of glass is it?

Laura: Little articles of it, they're ornaments mostly! Most of them are little animals made out of glass, the tiniest little animals in the world. Mother calls them a glass menagerie! Here's an example of one, if you'd like to see it! This one is one of the oldest. It's nearly thirteen. *(He stretches out his hand.) (Music: "The Glass Menagerie.")* Oh, be careful — if you breathe, it breaks!

Jim: I'd better not take it. I'm pretty clumsy with things.

Laura: Go on, I trust you with him! *(Places it in his palm.)* There now — you're holding him gently! Hold him over the light, he loves the light! You see how the light shines through him?

Jim: It sure does shine!

Laura: I shouldn't be partial, but he is my favorite one.

Jim: What kind of thing is this one supposed to be?

Laura: Haven't you noticed the single horn on his forehead?

Jim: A unicorn, huh?

Laura: Mmm-hmmm!

Jim: Unicorns, aren't they extinct in the modern world?

Laura: I know!

Jim: Poor little fellow, he must feel sort of lonesome.

Laura (smiling): Well, if he does he doesn't complain about it. He stays on a shelf with some horses that don't have horns and all of them seem to get along nicely together.

Jim: How do you know?

Laura (lightly): I haven't heard any arguments among them!

Jim (grinning): No arguments, huh? Well, that's a pretty good sign! Where shall I set him?

Laura: Put him on the table. They all like a change of scenery once in a while!

Jim (stretching): Well, well, well, well — Look how big my shadow is when I stretch!

Laura: Oh, oh, yes — it stretches across the ceiling!

Jim (crossing to door): I think it's stopped raining. *(Opens fire-escape door.)* Where does the music come from?

Laura: From the Paradise Dance Hall across the alley.

Jim: How about cutting the rug a little, Miss Wingfield?

Laura: Oh, I —

Jim: Or is your program filled up? Let me have a look at it. *(Grasps imaginary card.)* Why, every dance is taken! I'll have to scratch some out. *(Waltz music:*

"*La Golondrina.*") Ahhh, a waltz! *(He executes some sweeping turns by himself then holds his arms toward Laura.)*

Laura (breathlessly): I — can't dance!

Jim: There you go, that inferiority stuff!

Laura: I've never danced in my life!

Jim: Come on, try!

Laura: Oh, but I'd step on you!

Jim: I'm not made out of glass.

Laura: How — how — how do we start?

Jim: Just leave it to me. You hold your arms out a little.

Laura: Like this?

Jim: A little bit higher. Right. Now don't tighten up, that's the main thing about it — relax.

Laura (laughing breathlessly): It's hard not to.

Jim: Okay.

Laura: I'm afraid you can't budge me.

Jim: What do you bet I can't? *(He swings her into motion.)*

Laura: Goodness, yes, you can!

Jim: Let yourself go, now, Laura, just let yourself go.

Laura: I'm —

Jim: Come on!

Laura: Trying.

Jim: Not so stiff — Easy does it!

Laura: I know but I'm —

Jim: Loosen th' backbone! There now, that's a lot better.

Laura: Am I?

Jim: Lots, lots better! *(He moves her about the room in a clumsy waltz.)*

Laura: Oh, my!

Jim: Ha-ha!

Laura: Goodness, yes you can!

Jim: Ha-ha-ha! *(They suddenly bump into the table. Jim stops.)* What did we hit on?

Laura: Table.

Jim: Did something fall off it? I think —

Laura: Yes.

Jim: I hope it wasn't the little glass horse with the horn!

Laura: Yes.

Jim: Aw, aw, aw. Is it broken?

Laura: Now it is just like all the other horses.

Jim: It's lost its —

Laura: Horn! It doesn't matter. Maybe it's a blessing in disguise.

Jim: You'll never forgive me. I bet that that was your favorite piece of glass.

Laura: I don't have favorites much. It's no tragedy, Freckles. Glass breaks so easily. No matter how careful you are. The traffic jars the shelves and things fall off them.

Jim: Still I'm awfully sorry that I was the cause.

Laura (smiling): I'll just imagine he had an operation. The horn was removed to make him feel less — freakish! *(They both laugh.)* Now he will feel more at home with the other horses, the ones that don't have horns . . .

Jim: Ha-ha, that's very funny! *(Suddenly serious.)* I'm glad to see that you have a sense of humor. You know — you're — well — very different! Surprisingly different from anyone else I know! *(His voice becomes soft and hesitant with a genuine feeling.)* Do you mind me telling you that? *(Laura is abashed beyond speech.)* You make me feel sort of — I don't know how to put it! I'm usually pretty good at expressing things, but — This is something that I don't know how to say! *(Laura touches her throat and clears it — turns the broken unicorn in her hands.)* *(Even softer.)* Has anyone ever told you that you were pretty?

Pause: Music.

(Laura looks up slowly, with wonder, and shakes her head.) Well, you are! In a very different way from anyone else. And all the nicer because of the difference, too. *(His voice becomes low and husky. Laura turns away, nearly faint with the novelty of her emotions.)* I wish that you were my sister. I'd teach you to have some confidence in yourself. The different people are not like other people, but being different is nothing to be ashamed of. Because other people are not such wonderful people. They're one hundred times one thousand. You're one times one! They walk all over the earth. You just stay here. They're common as — weeds, but — you — well, you're — *Blue Roses!*

(Image on screen: Blue Roses.)
    (Music changes.)

Laura: But blue is wrong for — roses . . .
Jim: It's right for you — You're — pretty!
Laura: In what respect am I pretty?
Jim: In all respects — believe me! Your eyes — your hair — are pretty! Your hands are pretty! *(He catches hold of her hand.)* You think I'm making this up because I'm invited to dinner and have to be nice. Oh, I could do that! I could put on an act for you, Laura, and say lots of things without being very sincere. But this time I am. I'm talking to you sincerely. I happened to notice you had this inferiority complex that keeps you from feeling comfortable with people. Somebody needs to build your confidence up and make you proud instead of shy and turning away and — blushing — Somebody ought to — ought to — *kiss* you, Laura! *(His hand slips slowly up her arm to her shoulder.)* *(Music swells tumultuously.)* *(He suddenly turns her about and kisses her on the lips. When he releases her Laura sinks on the sofa with a bright, dazed look. Jim backs away and fishes in his pocket for a cigarette.)* *(Legend on screen: "Souvenir.")* Stumble-john! *(He lights the cigarette, avoiding her look. There is a peal of girlish laughter from Amanda in the kitchen. Laura slowly raises and opens her hand. It still contains the little broken glass animal. She looks at it with a tender, bewildered expression.)* Stumble-john! I shouldn't have done that — That was way off the beam. You don't smoke, do you? *(She looks up, smiling, not hearing the question. He sits beside her a little gingerly. She looks at him speechlessly — waiting. He coughs decorously and moves a little farther aside as he considers the situation and senses her feelings, dimly, with perturbation. Gently.)* Would you — care for a — mint? *(She doesn't seem to hear him but her look grows brighter even.)* Peppermint — Life Saver? My pocket's a regular drug store — wherever I go . . . *(He pops a mint in his mouth. Then gulps and decides to make a clean breast of it. He speaks slowly and gingerly.)* Laura, you know, if I had a sister like you, I'd do the same thing as Tom. I'd bring out fellows — introduce her to them. The right type of boys of a type to — appreciate her.

Only—well—he made a mistake about me. Maybe I've got no call to be saying this. That may not have been the idea in having me over. But what if it was? There's nothing wrong about that. The only trouble is that in my case—I'm not in a situation to—do the right thing. I can't take down your number and say I'll phone. I can't call up next week and—ask for a date. I thought I had better explain the situation in case you misunderstood it and—hurt your feelings. . . . *(Pause. Slowly, very slowly, Laura's look changes, her eyes returning slowly from his to the ornament in her palm.)*

Amanda utters another gay laugh in the kitchen.

Laura (faintly): You—won't—call again?

Jim: No, Laura, I can't. *(He rises from the sofa.)* As I was just explaining, I've—got strings on me, Laura, I've—been going steady! I go out all the time with a girl named Betty. She's a home-girl like you, and Catholic, and Irish, and in a great many ways we—get along fine. I met her last summer on a moonlight boat trip up the river to Alton, on the *Majestic.* Well—right away from the start it was—love! *(Legend: Love!)* *(Laura sways slightly forward and grips the arm of the sofa. He fails to notice, now enrapt in his own comfortable being.)* Being in love has made a new man of me! *(Leaning stiffly forward, clutching the arm of the sofa, Laura struggles visibly with her storm. But Jim is oblivious, she is a long way off.)* The power of love is really pretty tremendous! Love is something that—changes the whole world, Laura! *(The storm abates a little and Laura leans back. He notices her again.)* It happened that Betty's aunt took sick, she got a wire and had to go to Centralia. So Tom—when he asked me to dinner—I naturally just accepted the invitation, not knowing that you—that he—that I—*(He stops awkwardly.)* Huh—I'm a stumble-john! *(He flops back on the sofa. The holy candles in the altar of Laura's face have been snuffed out! There is a look of almost infinite desolation. Jim glances at her uneasily.)* I wish that you would—say something. *(She bites her lip which was trembling and then bravely smiles. She opens her hand again on the broken glass ornament. Then she gently takes his hand and raises it level with her own. She carefully places the unicorn in the palm of his hand, then pushes his fingers closed upon it.)* What are you—doing that for? You want me to have him?—Laura? *(She nods.)* What for?

Laura: A—souvenir . . .

She rises unsteadily and crouches beside the Victrola to wind it up.
    (Legend on screen: "Things Have a Way of Turning Out So Badly.")
    (Or image: "Gentleman caller waving good-bye!—Gaily.")
    At this moment Amanda rushes brightly back in the front room. She bears a pitcher of fruit punch in an old-fashioned cut-glass pitcher and a plate of macaroons. The plate has a gold border and poppies painted on it.

Amanda: Well, well, well! Isn't the air delightful after the shower? I've made you children a little liquid refreshment. *(Turns gaily to the gentleman caller.)* Jim, do you know that song about lemonade?
"Lemonade, lemonade
Made in the shade and stirred with a spade—
Good enough for any old maid!"

Jim (uneasily): Ha-ha! No—I never heard it.

Amanda: Why, Laura! You look so serious!

Jim: We were having a serious conversation.

Amanda: Good! Now you're better acquainted!

Jim (uncertainly): Ha-ha! Yes.

Amanda: You modern young people are much more serious-minded than my generation. I was so gay as a girl!

Jim: You haven't changed, Mrs. Wingfield.

Amanda: Tonight I'm rejuvenated! The gaiety of the occasion, Mr. O'Connor! *(She tosses her head with a peal of laughter. Spills lemonade.)* Oooo! I'm baptizing myself!

Jim: Here — let me —

Amanda (setting the pitcher down): There now. I discovered we had some maraschino cherries. I dumped them in, juice and all!

Jim: You shouldn't have gone to that trouble, Mrs. Wingfield.

Amanda: Trouble, trouble? Why it was loads of fun! Didn't you hear me cutting up in the kitchen? I bet your ears were burning! I told Tom how outdone with him I was for keeping you to himself so long a time! He should have brought you over much, much sooner! Well, now that you've found your way, I want you to be a very frequent caller! Not just occasional but all the time. Oh, we're going to have a lot of gay times together! I see them coming! Mmm, just breathe that air! So fresh, and the moon's so pretty! I'll skip back out — I know where my place is when young folks are having a — serious conversation!

Jim: Oh, don't go out, Mrs. Wingfield. The fact of the matter is I've got to be going.

Amanda: Going, now? You're joking! Why, it's only the shank of the evening, Mr. O'Connor!

Jim: Well, you know how it is.

Amanda: You mean you're a young workingman and have to keep workingmen's hours. We'll let you off early tonight. But only on the condition that next time you stay later. What's the best night for you? Isn't Saturday night the best night for you workingmen?

Jim: I have a couple of time-clocks to punch, Mrs. Wingfield. One at morning, another one at night!

Amanda: My, but you *are* ambitious! You work at night, too?

Jim: No, Ma'am, not work but — Betty! *(He crosses deliberately to pick up his hat. The band at the Paradise Dance Hall goes into a tender waltz.)*

Amanda: Betty? Betty? Who's — Betty! *(There is an ominous cracking sound in the sky.)*

Jim: Oh, just a girl. The girl I go steady with! *(He smiles charmingly. The sky falls.)*

(Legend: "The Sky Falls.")

Amanda (a long-drawn exhalation): Ohhhh . . . Is it a serious romance, Mr. O'Connor?

Jim: We're going to be married the second Sunday in June.

Amanda: Ohhhh — how nice! Tom didn't mention that you were engaged to be married.

Jim: The cat's not out of the bag at the warehouse yet. You know how they are. They call you Romeo and stuff like that. *(He stops at the oval mirror to put on his hat. He carefully shapes the brim and the crown to give a discreetly dashing effect.)* It's been a wonderful evening, Mrs. Wingfield. I guess this is what they mean by Southern hospitality.

Amanda: It really wasn't anything at all.

Jim: I hope it don't seem like I'm rushing off. But I promised Betty I'd pick her up at the Wabash depot, an' by the time I get my jalopy down there her train'll be in. Some women are pretty upset if you keep 'em waiting.

Amanda: Yes, I know — The tyranny of women! *(Extends her hand.)* Good-bye, Mr. O'Connor. I wish you luck — and happiness — and success! All three of them, and so does Laura — Don't you, Laura?

Laura: Yes!

Jim (taking her hand): Good-bye, Laura. I'm certainly going to treasure that souvenir. And don't you forget the good advice I gave you. *(Raises his voice to a cheery shout.)* So long, Shakespeare! Thanks again, ladies — Good night!

He grins and ducks jauntily out.

Still bravely grimacing, Amanda closes the door on the gentleman caller. Then she turns back to the room with a puzzled expression. She and Laura don't dare to face each other. Laura crouches beside the Victrola to wind it.

Amanda (faintly): Things have a way of turning out so badly. I don't believe that I would play the Victrola. Well, well — well — Our gentleman caller was engaged to be married! Tom!

Tom (from back): Yes, Mother?

Amanda: Come in here a minute. I want to tell you something awfully funny.

Tom (enters with macaroon and a glass of the lemonade): Has the gentleman caller gotten away already?

Amanda: The gentleman caller has made an early departure. What a wonderful joke you played on us!

Tom: How do you mean?

Amanda: You didn't mention that he was engaged to be married.

Tom: Jim? Engaged?

Amanda: That's what he just informed us.

Tom: I'll be jiggered! I didn't know about that.

Amanda: That seems very peculiar.

Tom: What's peculiar about it?

Amanda: Didn't you call him your best friend down at the warehouse?

Tom: He is, but how did I know?

Amanda: It seems extremely peculiar that you wouldn't know your best friend was going to be married!

Tom: The warehouse is where I work, not where I know things about people!

Amanda: You don't know things anywhere! You live in a dream; you manufacture illusions! *(He crosses to door.)* Where are you going?

Tom: I'm going to the movies.

Amanda: That's right, now that you've had us make such fools of ourselves. The effort, the preparations, all the expense! The new floor lamp, the rug, the clothes for Laura! All for what? To entertain some other girl's fiancé! Go to the movies, go! Don't think about us, a mother deserted, an unmarried sister who's crippled and has no job! Don't let anything interfere with your selfish pleasure! Just go, go, go — to the movies!

Tom: All right, I will! The more you shout about my selfishness to me the quicker I'll go, and I won't go to the movies!

Amanda: Go, then! Then go to the moon — you selfish dreamer!

Tom smashes his glass on the floor. He plunges out on the fire-escape, slamming the door. Laura screams—cut by door.

Dance-hall music up. Tom goes to the rail and grips it desperately, lifting his face in the chill white moonlight penetrating the narrow abyss of the alley.

(Legend on screen: "And So Good-Bye . . .")

Tom's closing speech is timed with the interior pantomime. The interior scene is played as though viewed through sound-proof glass. Amanda appears to be making a comforting speech to Laura who is huddled upon the sofa. Now that we cannot hear the mother's speech, her silliness is gone and she has dignity and tragic beauty. Laura's dark hair hides her face until at the end of the speech she lifts it to smile at her mother. Amanda's gestures are slow and graceful, almost dancelike, as she comforts the daughter. At the end of her speech she glances a moment at the father's picture—then withdraws through the portieres. At close of Tom's speech, Laura blows out the candles, ending the play.

Tom: I didn't go to the moon, I went much further—for time is the longest distance between two places—Not long after that I was fired for writing a poem on the lid of a shoe-box. I left Saint Louis. I descended the steps of this fire-escape for a last time and followed, from then on, in my father's footsteps, attempting to find in motion what was lost in space—I traveled around a great deal. The cities swept about me like dead leaves, leaves that were brightly colored but torn away from the branches. I would have stopped, but I was pursued by something. It always came upon me unawares, taking me altogether by surprise. Perhaps it was a familiar bit of music. Perhaps it was only a piece of transparent glass—Perhaps I am walking along a street at night, in some strange city, before I have found companions. I pass the lighted window of a shop where perfume is sold. The window is filled with pieces of colored glass, tiny transparent bottles in delicate colors, like bits of a shattered rainbow. Then all at once my sister touches my shoulder. I turn around and look into her eyes. . . . Oh, Laura, Laura, I tried to leave you behind me, but I am more faithful than I intended to be! I reach for a cigarette, I cross the street, I run into the movies or a bar, I buy a drink, I speak to the nearest stranger—anything that can blow your candles out! *(Laura bends over the candles)*—for nowadays the world is lit by lightning! Blow out your candles, Laura—and so good-bye . . .

She blows the candles out.

(The Scene Dissolves.)

CONNECTIONS TO OTHER SELECTIONS

1. Discuss the symbolic significance of the glass menagerie in Williams's play and the piano in August Wilson's *The Piano Lesson* (p. 2031). How do the objects' symbolic values contribute to the theme of each play?

2. Compare and contrast the nonrealistic techniques that Williams uses with those used by Arthur Miller in *Death of a Salesman* (p. 1824).

3. Write an essay that compares Tom's narrative function in *The Glass Menagerie* with that of the Chorus in Sophocles' *Oedipus the King* (p. 1289) and *Antigone* (p. 1333).

PERSPECTIVES

TENNESSEE WILLIAMS (1911–1983)

Production Notes to The Glass Menagerie   1945

Being a "memory play," *The Glass Menagerie* can be presented with unusual freedom of convention. Because of its considerably delicate or tenuous material, atmospheric touches and subtleties of direction play a particularly important part. Expressionism and all other unconventional techniques in drama have only one valid aim, and that is a closer approach to truth. When a play employs unconventional techniques, it is not, or certainly shouldn't be, trying to escape its responsibility of dealing with reality, or interpreting experience, but is actually or should be attempting to find a closer approach, a more penetrating and vivid expression of things as they are. The straight realistic play with its genuine Frigidaire and authentic ice cubes, its characters that speak exactly as its audience speaks, corresponds to the academic landscape and has the same virtue of a photographic likeness. Everyone should know nowadays the unimportance of the photographic in art: that truth, life, or reality is an organic thing which the poetic imagination can represent or suggest, in essence, only through transformation, through changing into other forms than those which were merely present in appearance.

These remarks are not meant as a preface only to this particular play. They have to do with a conception of a new, plastic theater which must take the place of the exhausted theater of realistic conventions if the theater is to resume vitality as a part of our culture.

The Screen Device. There is *only one important difference between the original and acting version of the play* and that is the *omission* in the latter of the device which I tentatively included in my *original* script. This device was the use of a screen on which were projected magic-lantern slides bearing images or titles. I do not regret the omission of this device from the present Broadway production. The extraordinary power of Miss Taylor's° performance made it suitable to have the utmost simplicity in the physical production. But I think it may be interesting to some readers to see how this device was conceived. So I am putting it into the published manuscript. These images and legends, projected from behind, were cast on a section of wall between the front-room and dining-room areas, which should be indistinguishable from the rest when not in use.

The purpose of this will probably be apparent. It is to give accent to certain values in each scene. Each scene contains a particular point (or several) which is structurally the most important. In an episodic play, such as this, the basic structure or narrative line may be obscured from the audience; the effect may seem fragmentary rather than architectural. This may not be the fault of the play so much as a lack of attention in the audience. The legend or image upon the screen will strengthen the effect of what is merely allusion in the writing and allow the primary point to be made more simply and lightly than if the entire responsibility were on the spoken lines. Aside from this structural

Miss Taylor's: Laurette Taylor (1884–1946) played the role of Amanda in the original Broadway production.

value, I think the screen will have a definite emotional appeal, less definable but just as important. An imaginative producer or director may invent many other uses for this device than those indicated in the present script. In fact the possibilities of the device seem much larger to me than the instance of this play can possibly utilize.

The Music. Another extra-literary accent in this play is provided by the use of music. A single recurring tune, "The Glass Menagerie," is used to give emotional emphasis to suitable passages. This tune is like circus music, not when you are on the grounds or in the immediate vicinity of the parade, but when you are at some distance and very likely thinking of something else. It seems under those circumstances to continue almost interminably and it weaves in and out of your preoccupied consciousness; then it is the lightest, most delicate music in the world and perhaps the saddest. It expresses the surface vivacity of life with the underlying strain of immutable and inexpressible sorrow. When you look at a piece of delicately spun glass you think of two things: how beautiful it is and how easily it can be broken. Both of those ideas should be woven into the recurring tune, which dips in and out of the play as if it were carried on a wind that changes. It serves as a thread of connection and allusion between the narrator with his separate point in time and space and the subject of his story. Between each episode it returns as reference to the emotion, nostalgia, which is the first condition of the play. It is primarily Laura's music and therefore comes out most clearly when the play focuses upon her and the lovely fragility of glass which is her image.

The Lighting. The lighting in the play is not realistic. In keeping with the atmosphere of memory, the stage is dim. Shafts of light are focused on selected areas or actors, sometimes in contradistinction to what is the apparent center. For instance, in the quarrel scene between Tom and Amanda, in which Laura has no active part, the clearest pool of light is on her figure. This is also true of the supper scene, when her silent figure on the sofa should remain the visual center. The light upon Laura should be distinct from the others, having a peculiar pristine clarity such as light used in early religious portraits of female saints or madonnas. A certain correspondence to light in religious paintings, such as El Greco's,° where the figures are radiant in atmosphere that is relatively dusky, could be effectively used throughout the play. (It will also permit a more effective use of the screen.) A free, imaginative use of light can be of enormous value in giving a mobile, plastic quality to plays of a more or less static nature.

El Greco (1541–1614): Greek painter who worked primarily in Spain and is known for the unearthly lighting in his large canvases.

CONSIDERATIONS FOR CRITICAL THINKING AND WRITING

1. What was your response to the screen device as you read the play? Do you think the device would enhance a production of the play or prove to be a distraction?

2. How does Williams's description of music and lighting serve as a summary of the play's tone? Does this tone come through in your reading of the play or is it dependent upon the music and lighting? Explain your answer.

3. Explain whether you agree with Williams's assertion that "theater of realistic conventions" is "exhausted" (para. 2).

Tennessee Williams (1911–1983)
On Theme   *1948*

For a writer who is not intentionally obscure, and never, in his opinion, obscure at all, I do get asked a hell of a lot of questions which I can't answer. I have never been able to say what was the theme of my play and I don't think I've ever been conscious of writing with a theme in mind. I am always surprised when, after a play has opened, I read in the papers what the play is about. . . . I am thankful for these highly condensed and stimulating analyses, but it would never have occurred to me that that was the story I was trying to tell. Usually when asked about a theme, I look vague and say, "It is a play about life. . . ."

From *Where I Live: Selected Essays*, edited by Christine R. Day

Considerations for Critical Thinking and Writing

1. Williams's disclaimer invites the inevitable question: What is the theme of *The Glass Menagerie*? Write an essay that answers this question.

2. Discuss whether you think it is likely (or possible) to write a play without "a theme in mind."

50

An Album of
World Literature

Unveiling

Born in Prague, Czechoslovakia, Václav Havel has been writing plays since
he was in his twenties and has remained politically active in his country's
movement from communism to more democratic forms of government.
His plays typically probe relations between citizens and political environments that are threatening or oppressive. Among his plays are *The Garden
Party* (1963), *The Memorandum* (1965), *The Increased Difficulty of Concentration*
(1968), and three one-act plays from the seventies known as the Vaněk Trilogy that include *Unveiling*. Havel has also written several books about his
political imprisonment: *Living in Truth* (1989), *Disturbing the Peace* (1990),
and *Letters to Olga* (1990). In 1989 he was elected president of Czechoslovakia and in 1993 was elected president of the newly created Czech Republic.

In *Unveiling*, Havel explores the personal and political relations of
friends whose lives and values have moved in opposite directions in response to the tides of political change.

Research Václav Havel with LitLinks at
http://www.bedfordstmartins.com/meyer/bedintrolit

VÁCLAV HAVEL (CZECH / B. 1936)

Unveiling 1975

TRANSLATED BY JAN NOVAK

CHARACTERS

Vera
Michael
Ferdinand Vaněk

On stage is the apartment of Vera and Michael. It consists of a large living room, extending onto a step-up dining area upstage. A serving window connects the dining area with the kitchen behind the stage. Stage right, there is a door leading into a hallway; stage left, a large fireplace; at the center of the stage stands an antique table, surrounded by soft, modern seats. A mass of sundry antiques and curious objects decorates the room—for example, there is an Art Nouveau marquee, a Chinese vase, a limestone Baroque angel, an inlaid chest, a folkloristic painting on a glass pane, a Russian icon, old handmortars and grinders, and so on; a niche in the wall houses a wooden Gothic madonna; a rococo musical clock adorns the fireplace, and a Turkish scimitar hangs above it. The dining area is furnished in a "rustic style," with a wooden farm-cart wheel on the wall; the floor is covered with a thick, shaggy carpet, on it lie several Persian mats and, near the fireplace, a bear hide with a stuffed head; downstage left stands a filigreed wooden confessional. The room also has a hi-fi stereo and a bar cart standing near the fireplace and holding various bottles, glasses, ice cubes, as well as a bowl with stuffed oysters. As the curtain rises, Vaněk is standing at the door, evidently having just come in. Vera and Michael are facing him. Vaněk is holding a bouquet of flowers behind his back.

Vera: We're so glad that you've made it—

Michael: We were afraid that you might not make it any more—

Vera: We've been looking forward to seeing you so much—

Michael: What can I get you? A whiskey?

Vaněk: All right—*(Michael steps over to the bar cart and starts preparing three whiskeys; Vaněk is momentarily at a loss about what to do, then he hands the flowers to Vera.)*

Vera: Oh, they are lovely! *(She takes the bouquet and looks at it.)* And you never forget—*(She smells it.)* What a beautiful aroma! Thank you, Ferdinand—*(Vera walks upstage and puts the flowers into a vase; Vaněk looks around the apartment with curiosity. A short pause.)*

Vaněk: It looks different here somehow—

Vera: I hope so! Michael has poured a lot of sweat into it! You know how he is when he gets involved in something: He won't let go till he has everything just the way he's planned it—

Michael: I only finished the thing the day before yesterday: we haven't had anybody over yet, so this actually is sort of an unveiling. Ice?

Vaněk: All right—*(Vera comes back downstage; the surprised Vaněk is still looking around.)* Where did you get all this?

Michael: It wasn't easy, as you can imagine. I did have a few contacts among the antique dealers and collectors. I had to establish a few more. The most important thing was not to give up when I wasn't able to get my hands on what I wanted the first time around—

Vera: He did quite a job on this, didn't he?

Vaněk: I guess so—

Vera: I confess that even I didn't think it would come out this well! When you want to give your place some character, it's not merely enough to like old things—you have to know how to get them and how to present them and how to integrate them with your modern furnishings—but, it so happens that Michael is really good at that—that's why you won't find a single goof here—*(Michael hands the glasses to Vera and Vaněk, then he takes his glass, raises it, and turns to Vaněk.)*

Michael: Welcome, Ferdinand —

Vera: We've missed you —

Michael: As I was working on this, I thought about you often — what you were going to say when you saw it all.

Vaněk: Well, cheers — *(They all drink; a short pause.)*

Michael: Of course, if I didn't have Vera's full support, it would have never come out like this. And it wasn't just a matter of support and understanding either, she gave me direct assistance in this, too! Take that Turkish scimitar there — how do you like it?

Vaněk: It's nice —

Michael: And how does it fit in with everything here?

Vaněk: Very well —

Michael: You see, and it's something that Vera found on her very own, and she even put it up there, too — all the while not knowing that this was exactly the thing I had in mind for that spot over the fireplace! Isn't that awesome?

Vaněk: That's great — *(A short, awkward pause.)*

Vera: Have a seat —

Vaněk: Thank you — *(They all sit down in the soft seats. A short pause. Vaněk is looking around again; Vera and Michael watch him with satisfaction; Vaněk eventually notices the confessional.)* What's that?

Michael: It's what you see — a confessional —

Vaněk: Where did you get that?

Michael: You won't believe how lucky I was. I heard that they were going to liquidate a church that'd been closed down, so I dropped everything and jumped in the car. And this is the result. I managed to get it out of the sexton for three hundred —

Vaněk: That's all?

Michael: Not bad, is it? Pure Baroque!

Vaněk: What are you going to do with it?

Michael: What do you mean, what are we going to do with it? You don't like it?

Vaněk: Well I do —

Michael: Isn't that a fantastic object, we're really happy about it, aren't we, Vera?

Vera: It really is a superb piece of craftsmanship, I'd say that Michael really got another one of his steals there — *(A short pause.)* What do you think of the dining area?

Vaněk (turns around): It's cozy —

Vera: Wasn't that a nice idea — to do it so simply — as if on a farm —

Vaněk: Mmn — *(A short pause.)*

Michael: Do you know what I like best here?

Vaněk: What?

Michael: This Gothic madonna! I needed one that would fit into that niche, and they were all either bigger or smaller —

Vaněk: And there was no way to enlarge the niche?

Michael: But that's just what I didn't want to do. It strikes me that it's got the perfect dimensions the way it is —

Vera: See, that's Michael! He'd rather wear out his feet than simply enlarge the thing! *(Pause.)*

Michael: And what about you? When are you going to get started?

Vaněk: On what?

Michael: On your place —

Vaněk: I don't know —

Michael: You should finally do something about it! You can't go on living out of boxes forever —

Vaněk: I don't even pay any attention to it anymore —

Michael: If you don't feel like tackling it yourself, why doesn't Eva do something about it? She has plenty of time on her hands —

Vera: I think Eva actually needs to get involved in something like that — it would be a good way to get her back on her feet —

Michael: We would gladly come to the rescue if she found she couldn't handle something —

Vera: Michael has tons of experience with this now — he'd tell her what to do — where to start — what she'd need —

Michael: I'd tell her who's got what — where to go and who to see —

Vera: That's true, Ferdinand. Why don't you put Eva in charge of it anyway?

Vaněk: It's not really Eva's cup of tea —

Vera: We know that, but if you were to waken her interest somehow —

Michael: Damn it, you have to do something about that home of yours —

Vera: You know, Michael and I think that a person lives the way a person lives. When you have what we call a place with character, your whole life suddenly — like it or not — acquires a certain face, too — a sort of new dimension — a different rhythm, a different content, a different order — isn't that so, Michael?

Michael: She's right, Ferdinand! One really shouldn't be indifferent to what one eats, one shouldn't be indifferent to what one eats on, and what one eats with, what one dries oneself with, what one wears, what one takes a bath in, what one sleeps on. And once any of these things starts to matter, you'll find that something else suddenly matters, too, and then another thing gets you, and so a whole sort of a chain of things develops — and if you head down that road, what else can it mean but that you're upgrading your life to another, higher level of culture — and that you raise yourself to a kind of higher harmony — which then in effect translates itself into your relationships with other people! You tell him, Vera!

Vera: That is a fact, Ferdinand! If the two of you were to put a little more effort into the way you live, I'm sure that things would get smoother in your marriage, too —

Vaněk: But things are smooth —

Vera: Ferdinand!

Vaněk: But really —

Vera: You don't like to talk about it, I know. But you know, Michael and I have been talking about the two of you a lot lately; we've been thinking about you a lot — and we really care about how you two live!

Michael: We're only trying to help, Ferdinand!

Vera: You're our best friend — we like you a lot — you have no idea how happy we'd be for you if your situation finally got resolved somehow!

Vaněk: What situation?

Vera: Let's just drop it. Shouldn't I light the fireplace?

Vaněk: Not for me —

Michael: So I'll put on some music, all right?

Vera: Michael has just brought a ton of new records from Switzerland—

Vaněk: Maybe later, perhaps? *(Pause; then suddenly the musical clock on the mantelpiece breaks into a period tune, startling Vaněk. After a while, the clock falls silent. Pause.)*

Vera: So tell us—how is everything with you?

Vaněk: Well, you know—nothing's changed—

Vera: Is it true that you've got a job in a brewery now?

Vaněk: Yes—

Vera: That's horrible! *(Pause. Then Vera points at the bar cart.)* Michael, would you—

Michael: Oh yeah— *(Michael takes the bowl with oysters off the bar and stands it in front of Vaněk.)*

Vera: Help yourself—

Vaněk: What is it?

Michael: That's Vera's specialty: sauteed groombles—°

Vaněk: Groombles? I never heard of this—

Vera: We've really become very fond of them lately, Michael has just brought a whole box of them from Switzerland—

Michael: Because Vera really knows how to make them—

Vera: What you have to do is to watch for the precise moment, when they've just stopped puffing up and before they start falling—

Michael: Taste one! *(Vaněk takes one oyster and, using a spoon, begins to scoop out its contents. He concentrates on the taste; Vera and Michael watch him tensely.)* So what do you think?

Vaněk: It's good—

Michael: Isn't it?

Vaněk: You went to all the trouble of making this just for me?

Vera: We're having our unveiling today, right?

Vaněk: It sort of reminds me of blackberries a little bit—

Vera: That may be because I put in a few drops of woodpeak° to help the taste—

Vaněk: Drops of what?

Michael: Woodpeak—

Vera: That's my original contribution—

Vaněk: Really?

Michael: An excellent idea, isn't it? I can't help it, but Vera's really got a talent for cooking. A week doesn't go by without her making some novelty—and she always uses her imagination to improve it. Take this Saturday for example—what was it that we had now? Oh yeah, the liver with walnuts! And it was such a delicacy; anyway, would you ever think of putting woodpeak on groombles?

Vaněk: Never—

Michael: See what I mean! *(Vaněk puts away the empty oyster shell and wipes his mouth with a napkin.)*

Vera: Well, it's a joy cooking for Michael! He knows how to appreciate and praise even the most modest idea, and when something turns out well, he really gets off on it. If he just stuffed everything in like a mechanical

---

groombles: A made-up word.
woodpeak: Another made-up word.

pie-eater, not even knowing what it is that he's swallowing, then I probably wouldn't have so much fun with it either —

Vaněk: I can understand that —

Michael: But there's even more to it than that. When you know that an interesting dinner, some small gourmet surprise, is waiting for you at home, you look that much more forward to getting there and you have that much less reason to go bar-hopping with your buddies. Maybe it'll strike you as being petty, but I think that these things also represent a kind of cement that holds a family together and helps to create that important feeling that you've got something to back you up at home. Don't you think?

Vaněk: Yes, of course — *(Pause.)*

Vera: How's Eva doing? Has she learned to cook anything yet?

Vaněk: She's always cooked —

Vera: Granted, but how!

Vaněk: I pretty much like her cooking —

Vera: Because you got used to it already. Don't get offended, but those pepper steaks she made when we were over that time before Christmas — it was before Christmas, wasn't it?

Vaněk: Yeah —

Vera: Don't get offended, but they were dreadful! Do you remember, Michael?

Michael: How could I forget?

Vaněk: Eva was a little nervous that time —

Vera: I'm sorry, but something like that should never ever happen to a cook! What does she cook for you usually anyway?

Vaněk: We tend to have cold-plate dinners —

Vera: Even on Saturdays?

Vaněk: Sometimes we have something warm, too — breaded cutlets, for example —

Michael: Listen, Ferdinand, it's none of my business, but why don't you send Eva to some of those courses? She has plenty of time on her hands —

Vera: Eva? Come on! You think Eva would take any courses?

Michael: Well, that's true —

Vera: If she did learn how to cook though, it would immediately boost her self-confidence — but she won't see the connection: She's floating around somewhere, God knows where —

Vaněk: I think her cooking's fine —

Vera: Ferdinand!

Vaněk: Really, I —

Michael: You don't like to talk about it, I know. But you know Vera and I have been talking about the two of you a lot lately, we've been thinking about you a lot — and we really care about how you two live!

Vera: We're only trying to help, Ferdinand!

Michael: You're our best friend — we like you a lot — you have no idea how happy we'd be for you if your situation finally got resolved somehow!

Vaněk: What situation?

Michael: Let's just drop it. Shouldn't I light the fireplace?

Vaněk: Not for me —

Vera: So I'll put on some music, all right? Michael has just brought a ton of new records from Switzerland —

Vaněk: Maybe later, okay? *(Pause. Then suddenly the musical clock on the mantelpiece breaks into a period tune, startling Ferdinand. After a while, the clock falls silent. Pause.)*

Michael: So what do you actually do there, in that brewery?

Vaněk: I draw beer—

Michael: Into barrels?

Vaněk: Yes—

Michael: That's got to be pretty rough, doesn't it?

Vaněk: It's not that bad— *(Pause.)*

Michael: Are we going to show Pete to Ferdinand?

Vera: A little later, Michael, he might still wake up right now—

Vaněk: How is Pete doing?

Michael: He's fantastic! I'd only been gone to that Switzerland for ten days, but when I got back, I tell you I barely recognized him—that's how much of a jump he's made in that time!

Vera: He's extremely curious—

Michael: Bright—

Vera: Perceptive—

Michael: He has a superb memory—

Vera: And yet he's such a good-looking kid, too!

Michael: Just to give you an example. Do you know what he asked me this morning? *(To Vera)* I forgot to tell you about that! All of a sudden, he comes to me and says, "Daddy, can a frog drown?" What do you think about that? Isn't that awesome?

Vera: Did he really ask you that? If a frog can drown?

Michael: Imagine that! He comes to me and says, "Daddy, can a frog drown?"

Vera: Outstanding! I don't even know if I could have thought of that. Can a frog drown! Outstanding! Outstanding!

Michael: You know, Ferdinand, sometimes I say to myself that to have a child and to bring it up is the only thing that has any meaning in life! Because it is such an awesome encounter with the mystery of life—such a lesson in life appreciation! Unless you actually go through it, you can never even understand it—

Vera: Absolutely, Ferdinand, it's an awesomely strange and beautiful experience: One day this tiny being shows up here—and you know he is yours—that without you, he wouldn't even be here—that you've made him and now he's here—and he's living his own life—and is growing before your eyes—and then he starts to walk—and say things—and reason—and ask questions—now isn't that a miracle?

Vaněk: Certainly is—

Michael: You know a child really changes you a lot—suddenly you begin to understand everything differently, more deeply—life—nature—people—and all of a sudden your own life—like it or not—acquires sort of a new dimension—a different rhythm, a different content, a different order—isn't that so, Vera?

Vera: Exactly! Just take the responsibility you suddenly have. It's up to you what kind of a person he will turn out to be—what he'll feel—think—how he'll live—

Michael: But not only that: Because it was you who tossed him into this world, who offered it to him for his use and who provides him with some orientation in it, you suddenly start feeling a much greater responsibility for this world that now contains your child—do you know what I mean?

Vaněk: I guess so—

Michael: I never believed this, but now I see how a child gives you a brand new point of view, a brand new set of values—and suddenly it begins to dawn on you that the most important thing now is what you do for that child, what sort of a home you create for him, what sort of a start you give him, what openings you provide—and in the light of this awesome responsibility you start seeing the utter insignificance of most of the things you had once thought world-shattering—

Vera: How did he put it? Can a frog drown? Do you see what that tiny head can give birth to? Isn't that fantastic?

Vaněk: Mmn— *(Pause.)*

Michael: So what about you two?

Vaněk: What about us two?

Michael: Why don't you have a child yet anyway?

Vaněk: I don't know—

Vera: Eva probably doesn't want one, does she?

Vaněk: Oh no—she does—

Vera: I really don't understand that girl! Is she so afraid of all the worries that go along with having a child? Because if she really wanted a baby, you would have had one ages ago!

Michael: You are the ones who will lose out by not pursuing this—because for the two of you, a child would definitely be the best possible solution! It would help you, Ferdinand, to see many things far more sensibly, realistically, wisely—

Vera: It would straighten out your relationship, because it would give you a common purpose in life—

Michael: And what a good thing it would be for Eva!

Vera: You'd see how it would change her!

Michael: How it would suddenly bring out the woman in her again!

Vera: How it would teach her to pay attention to the house—

Michael: To cleanliness—

Vera: To routine—

Michael: To you—

Vera: To herself—

Michael: Seriously, Ferdinand, you ought to have child, believe us!

Vera: You have no idea how happy we'd be for you!

Michael: We really would, Ferdinand—

Vaněk: I believe you— *(Pause.)*

Vera: Of course, there are women who don't respond even to that—and then you really feel for the children—

Michael: Of course, just to rely on the kid as some sort of panacea that will solve all your problems, that wouldn't be right either—a certain aptitude probably already has to be there before anything else—

Vera: Absolutely! For example, Michael here makes an ideal father: He drives himself hard at the office, till I feel really sorry for him sometimes, just so that he brings home some money—and then he still devotes almost all of his free time to the family and to the home! Just take this remodelling he did. He came from the office and instead of stretching out and relaxing, he went right back to work—just so Pete can grow up in a nice environment from the very beginning, and learn to love nice things! And even while doing all that, he still found the time for Pete—

Michael: Of course, Vera is awesome, too. Do you know what it is—to shop, take care of the kid, cook, clean up, do the laundry—while the apartment is a disaster area—despite all that to look just the way she looks right now? That really is no joke! I have to say I admire her more and more as time goes on—

Vera: A lot of that is because our marriage is working—

Michael: Definitely! We get along just awesomely. I don't even remember us having any serious quarrels lately—

Vera: We are interested in one another, yet we don't limit or tie each other down—

Michael: We are kind and attentive to one another without tiring each other with too much thoughtfulness—

Vera: And we always have things to say to each other, because we're fortunate enough to have exactly the same sense of humor—

Michael: The same definition of happiness—

Vera: The same interests—

Michael: The same taste—

Vera: The same views on family life—

Michael: And what is extremely important: We also perfectly complement each other physically—

Vera: That's true, it is really extremely important! And Michael is awesome in that respect—he can be wild as well as tender—honestly selfish as well as awesomely attentive and giving—passionately spontaneous as well as inventively cunning—

Michael: But Vera deserves all the credit for that, because she manages to excite and stimulate me again and again—

Vera: You'd be surprised, Ferdinand, how often we do it! And that's only possible because we always approach it as though it were our very first time, so that it becomes something new, something different for us every time. Something unique, unforgettable. In short, we really invest ourselves fully into it, and, consequently, for us it can never become just a matter of a stereotype or a boring routine—

Michael: You see, Vera knows, too, that to be a good wife doesn't mean merely being a good homemaker and a good mother—she rightly feels that what it means more than anything else is to be a good lover! That's why she takes such wonderful care of herself. So that she keeps her sex appeal even while doing the heaviest chores—in fact, even more so then than at other times!

Vera: Do you remember the day before yesterday, Michael—when you got home early just as I was scrubbing the floor?

Michael: It was beautiful, wasn't it?

Vera: Why do you think Michael isn't drawn to other women? Because he knows that he doesn't have some mop-swinging wifey at home, but a real woman who knows how to take as well as give—

Michael: Of course, Vera is still just as attractive as always—I'd even say that now, after Pete, she has ripened even more—she has an astonishingly fresh and youthful body now—well, judge for yourself! *(Michael undoes Vera's clothes, uncovering her breasts.)* Not bad, right?

Vaněk: Great—

Michael: Do you know what I will do, for example?

Vaněk: No—

Michael: I'll kiss her, switching from her ear to her neck and back—which really turns her on and I like it, too—like this, look!

(*Michael starts to kiss Vera, alternating between her ear and her neck; Vera groans excitedly.*)

Vera: Don't darling, no—please—wait—a little later, okay—come on— (*Michael stops kissing Vera.*)

Michael: We'll talk a little more first, then we'll show you more—to give you an idea of the range of our technique—

Vaněk: Won't I make you nervous by being here?

Vera: You silly boy! You're our best friend, right?

Michael: And we'll be happy to show you how far you can take these things! (*Pause.*)

Vera: So what about you two?

Vaněk: How do you mean?

Vera: Do you still sleep with each other at all?

Vaněk: Oh yes—now and then—

Vera: Not too often, right?

Vaněk: That depends—

Vera: And how is it?

Vaněk: I don't know—it's normal—

Michael: I'm sure you don't put any effort into it—just go through the motions, so it's over and done with—

Vaněk: We do our best—

Vera: I don't understand that girl at all! Why wouldn't she try a little harder at least in this—

Michael: Is it really impossible for you to get her involved in this a little more?

Vaněk: We really don't pay that much attention to it—

Vera: See? That's where you go wrong, ignoring such an important thing! That's why you're in the shape you're in! Yet it would require so little effort—and maybe it would pull your relationship back up on its feet again!

Michael: And what a good thing it would be for Eva—you'd see how it would change her!

Vera: How it would bring out the woman in her again!

Michael: How it would teach her to pay attention to the house—

Vera: To you—

Michael: To herself—

Vera: And what a change it would effect in you! Just imagine, suddenly there are no more reasons to go bar-hopping with your cronies—

Michael: Chase waitresses—

Vera: Drink—

Vaněk: I don't chase waitresses—

Vera: Ferdinand!

Vaněk: I don't—

Vera: You don't like to talk about it, I know. But you know Michael and I have been talking about the two of you a lot lately, we've been thinking about you a lot—and we really care about how you two live!

Michael: We're only trying to help, Ferdinand!

Vera: You're our best friend — we like you a lot — you have no idea how happy we'd be for you if your situation finally got resolved somehow!

Vaněk: What situation?

Vera: Let's just drop it. Shouldn't I light the fireplace?

Vaněk: Not for me —

Michael: So I'll put on some music, all right?

Vera: Michael has just brought a ton of new records from Switzerland —

Vaněk: Maybe later, okay? *(Pause. Then suddenly the musical clock on the mantelpiece breaks into a period tune, startling Vaněk. After a while, the clock falls silent. Pause.)*

Michael: But anyway — that's what I call art!

Vaněk: What is?

Michael: That madonna —

Vaněk: Mmn —

Michael: Do you realize the dramatic tension that arises between her and that scimitar?

Vaněk: Mmn — *(Pause.)*

Vera: You probably don't use much woodpeak, do you?

Vaněk: Not really —

Vera: If you'd like, Michael could bring you some from Switzerland —

Vaněk: Oh yeah?

Michael: You know that'd be no trouble at all for me. *(Pause.)*

Vera: Have some more —

Vaněk: No, thank you — *(Pause.)*

Michael: Why didn't you bring Eva with you?

Vaněk: She didn't feel well —

Michael: It's not any of my business, of course, but you should take her out now and then — give her a reason to put some nice clothes on, put on some make-up, do her hair —

Vaněk: She does her hair —

Michael: Ferdinand!

Vaněk: She does —

Michael: You don't like to talk about it, I know. But we're only trying to help —

Vera: We like you a lot —

Michael: You're our best friend —

Vaněk: I know — *(Pause; the musical clock plays its tune.)*

Michael: Did you get my card from Switzerland?

Vaněk: That was from you?

Michael: You didn't figure that out?

Vaněk: Should have thought of it — *(Pause.)*

Vera (to Michael): What did Pete ask you now? Can a frog drown?

Michael: Right, imagine that —

Vera: Outstanding! Outstanding! *(Pause.)*

Michael (to Vaněk): Have some more —

Vaněk: No, thank you — *(Pause.)*

Vera: Do you know what we started to do again?

Vaněk: What?

Vera: Going to the sauna!

Vaněk: Really?

Vera: We've been going every week now, and you wouldn't believe how good it is for us. For the nerves, you know —

Michael: Do you want to start coming with us?

Vaněk: Not really —

Vera: Why not?

Vaněk: I wouldn't have the time —

Michael: Don't get offended, Ferdinand, but you're making a mistake! It would really get you into a better shape spiritually, psychically, as well as physically, and it would definitely be better for you and cost you less time, too, than the endless tongue-thrashing in bars with all those wise-guy cronies of yours —

Vaněk: Whom do you mean by that?

Michael: Well, all those various failures. Landovský and so on —

Vaněk: I wouldn't call them failures —

Vera: Ferdinand!

Vaněk: Not at all —

Vera: You don't like to talk about it, I know. But we're only trying to help you —

Michael: We like you a lot —

Vera: You're our best friend —

Vaněk: I know — *(Pause; the clock plays its tune.)*

Michael: Do you know what Vera promised me?

Vaněk: What's that?

Michael: That she'll give me another child next year!

Vaněk: That's nice —

Vera: I think Michael deserves no less — *(Pause.)* Do you know what Michael brought me from Switzerland?

Vaněk: What's that?

Vera: An electric almond peeler —

Michael: You'll have to take a look at it, it's a beautiful thing —

Vera: As well as practical —

Michael: Because Vera does a lot with almonds, so it saves her tons of time —

Vaněk: I believe it — *(Pause.)*

Vera: Have some more.

Vaněk: No, thank you — *(Pause.)*

Michael: Listen, Ferdinand —

Vaněk: Huh?

Michael: Do you ever write anything anymore?

Vaněk: Not a whole lot —

Michael: That's what we thought —

Vaněk: Now that I have that job, I don't have the time for it, nor the concentration —

Michael: But from what I hear, you weren't doing much writing anyway, even before you got this job —

Vaněk: Not all that much —

Vera: Listen, didn't you maybe take that job because in your own mind it gave you an excuse for not writing?

Vaněk: Not that —

Michael: So what is your real reason for not writing? Is it just that it's not pouring out? Or are you going through some kind of a crisis?

Vaněk: It's hard to say — the times, everything that is going on — you get this feeling of futility —

Michael: Don't get offended, Ferdinand, but I think that the times are just another excuse for you, just like the job at the brewery, and that the real problem is inside of you and nowhere else! You're just all bent out of shape, you've given up on everything, you find it too tedious to strive for anything, to fight, to wrestle with problems —

Vera: Michael is right, Ferdinand. Somehow you should finally pull yourself together —

Michael: Take care of problems at home — with Eva —

Vera: Start a family —

Michael: Give your place some character —

Vera: Learn how to budget your time —

Michael: Stop carousing —

Vera: Start going to the sauna again —

Michael: Simply begin to live a decent, healthy, rational life —

Vaněk: I don't feel that I'm doing anything irrational —

Michael: Ferdinand!

Vaněk: I don't —

Michael: You don't like to talk about it, I know. But we're only trying to help you —

Vera: We like you a lot —

Michael: You're our best friend —

Vera: You have no idea how happy we'd be for you if your situation finally got resolved somehow!

Michael: Shouldn't I light the fireplace?

Vaněk: Not for me —

Vera: So I'll put some music on, all right? Michael has just brought a ton of new records from Switzerland —

Vaněk: Maybe later, okay? *(Pause; the musical clock plays its tune.)*

Michael: Listen, Ferdinand —

Vaněk: Huh?

Michael: Listen, honestly now. Are you serious with that brewery?

Vaněk: What do you mean?

Michael: You know, don't get offended now, but we just don't understand what the purpose of the whole thing is —

Vera: To just throw yourself away like that — to bury yourself in a brewery somewhere — only to ruin your health —

Michael: All these gestures are completely senseless! What are you trying to prove? It's been a long time since that kind of thing impressed anybody —

Vaněk: I'm sorry, but it was the only thing I could do in my situation —

Michael: Ferdinand! Don't tell me that you couldn't do better than that — if only you really wanted to and tried a little harder — I'm convinced that with a little more effort and a little less ego on your part, you could've long been sitting in an editorial office somewhere —

Vera: You are, after all, basically an intelligent, hard-working person — you have talent — you have clearly proven that in the past with your writing — so why would you suddenly be afraid of confronting life?

Michael: Life is rough and the world is divided. The world doesn't give a damn about us and nobody's coming to our rescue — we're in a nasty predicament, and it will get worse and worse — and you are not going to change any of it! So why beat your head against the wall and charge the bayonets?

Vera: What I can't understand is how could you have got mixed up with those Communists —

Vaněk: What Communists?

Vera: Well, that Kohout and his crowd—you don't have anything in common with them! Don't be silly, forget about them and go your own way—

Michael: We're not saying that breaking out of that charmed circle is going to be easy, but it's your only chance and nobody's going to do it for you! In these things, it's every man for himself, but you're definitely strong enough to withstand that isolation!

Vera: Just take a look at us—you could be just as happy as we are—

Michael: You could have a home with character of your own—

Vera: Full of nice things and good family vibrations—

Michael: A well-coiffed and elegant wife—

Vera: A bright kid—

Michael: You could have a more appropriate job—

Vera: Make a few crowns—

Michael: Later they'd even let you go to Switzerland—

Vera: Eat decent food—

Michael: Dress better—

Vera: Go to the sauna—

Michael: Now and then you could have some friends over—

Vera: Show them your place—

Michael: Your kid—

Vera: Put on some music for them—

Michael: Make groombles—

Vera: In short, live a little more like humans! *(Vaněk has quietly got up and begun shyly to back up to the door. When Vera and Michael notice it, they stand up in surprise.)*

Michael: Ferdinand—

Vaněk: Mmn—

Michael: What's the matter?

Vaněk: Nothing's the matter—

Vera: You're leaving?

Vaněk: I have to go now—

Michael: Go where?

Vaněk: Home—

Vera: Home? How come? Why?

Vaněk: It's late—I get up early—

Michael: But you can't do this—

Vaněk: I really have to go—

Vera: I don't understand! Here we are in the middle of our unveiling—

Michael: We wanted to give you a tour of the place—

Vera: Show you everything we have here—

Michael: We thought you'd finish that bottle—

Vera: Eat the rest of the groombles—

Michael: Take a look at Pete—

Vera: Michael wanted to tell you about Switzerland—

Michael: Vera wanted to light the fireplace—

Vera: Michael wanted to play those new records for you—

Michael: We thought you'd stay the night—

Vera: See how we make love—

Michael: That we'd share a little of that family warmth you don't have at home—

Vera: Get into a different frame of mind—

Michael: Pull you out of that mess you're living in —

Vera: Get you back up on your feet —

Michael: Suggest some ways of how you can resolve your situation —

Vera: Show you what happiness is —

Michael: And love —

Vera: Family harmony —

Michael: A life that has some meaning —

Vera: You know that we're only trying to help you —

Michael: That we like you a lot —

Vera: That you are our best friend —

Michael: You cannot be this ungrateful!

Vera: We don't deserve this — not while we're trying to do so much for you!

Michael: Who did you think Vera has spent the whole afternoon baking the groombles for?

Vera: Who do you think Michael has bought that whiskey for?

Michael: Who do you think we wanted to play those records for? Why do you think I wasted all that hard currency on them, and dragged them halfway across Europe?

Vera: Why do you think I dressed up like this, put the make-up and the perfume on, got my hair done?

Michael: Why do you think we fixed this place up like this anyway? Who do you think we're doing all this for? For ourselves? *(Vaněk is by the door now.)*

Vaněk: I'm sorry, but I'll be off now —

Vera (agitated): Ferdinand! You can't just leave us here! You're not going to do that to us! You can't just pick up and go now; there's so much we still wanted to tell you! What are we going to do here without you? Don't you understand that? Stay, I beg you, will you stay here with us!

Michael: You haven't even seen our electric almond peeler yet!

Vaněk: See you later! And thank you for the groombles — *(Vaněk is leaving, but before he closes the door behind him, Vera breaks into hysterical sobs. Vaněk stops and looks at her, not knowing what to do.)*

Vera (crying): You're selfish! A disgusting, unfeeling, inhuman egotist! An ungrateful, ignorant traitor! I hate you — I hate you so much — go away! Go away! *(Vera runs to the bouquet that she got from Vaněk, tears it out of the vase, and throws it at Vaněk.)*

Michael (to Vaněk): See what you're doing? Aren't you ashamed? *(Vaněk is at a loss about what to do for a moment, then picks up the bouquet, carries it hesitantly to the vase, puts it back in, slowly returns to his seat, and sits down with some embarrassment. Vera and Michael watch tensely to see what he will do. As soon as they see that he has sat back down, they instantly return to their old selves, smiling as they sit down, too. A short pause.)*

Vera: Michael, won't we put some music on for Ferdinand?

Michael: That's a good idea — *(Michael walks over to the record-player and the instant he turns it on, music starts pouring forth out of all the speakers: preferably some international hit, such as Sugar Baby Love in the interpretation of Karel Gott.° The curtain falls; the music is booming on, the same tune over and over again, until the last spectator has left the theater.)*

Karel Gott: A popular, but not highly respected Czech singer who was favored by the government rather than by politically conscious artists.

CONNECTIONS TO OTHER SELECTIONS

1. In what sense can politics be thought of as the antagonist in *Unveiling* and in Jhumpa Lahiri's short story "When Mr. Pirzada Came to Dine" (p. 105)?

2. Explain how Michael in *Unveiling* and Willy Loman in Arthur Miller's *Death of a Salesman* (p. 1824) lack a fundamental sense of self-knowledge. Be sure to cite examples from the plays in your answer.

3. In an essay, discuss the tensions of the domestic life in this play and in Raymond Carver's "Popular Mechanics" (p. 286).

The Strong Breed

Born Oluwole Akinwande Soyinka in the western Nigerian town of Akinwande, Wole Soyinka has embodied in his life and art the contradictions and tensions that can often seem inevitable for the European-educated, English-speaking, African writer. "Selective eclecticism," he once said, is "the right of every productive being." Although he has written and published novels and poetry, Soyinka is most renowned as a playwright whose work often focuses on the tragic consequences of a clash between colonial and tribal values. Educated at Leeds University in England, he subsequently began an active career as a playwright as well as a political reformer and social critic. His autobiography *The Man Died* (1973) records his experiences as a political prisoner in Nigeria.

Soyinka's many plays include *The Swamp Dwellers* (1958), *The Invention* (1959), *The Lion and the Jewel* (1959), *A Dance of Forests* (1960), *The Strong Breed* (1963), *Madmen and Specialists* (1970), and *Death and the King's Horseman* (1976). He has also written two novels and three volumes of poetry. In 1986 he was awarded the Nobel Prize for Literature.

Like nearly all of Soyinka's writing, *The Strong Breed* is steeped in African tribal culture and tradition, but the play's abiding concern for human suffering and social justice invites all readers to step into the small village in which one "night's work" changes the lives of its inhabitants.

Web   *Research Wole Soyinka with LitLinks at*
        http://www.bedfordstmartins.com/meyer/bedintrolit

WOLE SOYINKA (NIGERIA / B. 1934)

The Strong Breed   1963

CHARACTERS

Eman, a stranger
Sunma, Jaguna's daughter
Ifada, an idiot
A Girl

Jaguna
Oroge
Attendant Stalwarts, the villagers

From Eman's past—

Old Man, his father
Omae, his betrothed
Tutor
Priest
Attendants, the villagers

> *The scenes are described briefly, but very often a darkened stage with lit area will not only suffice but is necessary. Except for the one indicated place, there can be no break in the action. A distracting scene-change would be ruinous. A mud house, with space in front of it. Eman, in light buba° and trousers, stands at the window, looking out. Inside, Sunma is clearing the table of what looks like a modest clinic, putting the things away in a cupboard. Another rough table in the room is piled with exercise books, two or three worn textbooks, etc. Sunma appears agitated. Outside, just below the window, crouches Ifada. He looks up with a shy smile from time to time, waiting for Eman to notice him.*

Sunma *(hesitant):* You will have to make up your mind soon, Eman. The lorry leaves very shortly.

> *As Eman does not answer, Sunma continues her work, more nervously. Two villagers, obvious travelers, pass hurriedly in front of the house, the man has a small raffia° sack, the woman a cloth-covered basket, the man enters first, turns, and urges the woman who is just emerging to hurry.*

Sunma *(seeing them, her tone is more intense):* Eman, are we going or aren't we? You will leave it till too late.

Eman *(quietly):* There is still time — if you want to go.

Sunma: If I want to go . . . and you?

> *Eman makes no reply.*

Sunma *(bitterly):* You don't really want to leave here. You never want to go away — even for a minute.

> *Ifada continues his antics. Eman eventually pats him on the head and the boy grins happily. Leaps up suddenly and returns with a basket of oranges, which he offers Eman.*

Eman: My gift for today's festival enh?

> *Ifada nods, grinning.*

Eman: They look ripe — that's a change.

Sunma *(she has gone inside the room. Looks round the door):* Did you call me?

Eman: No. *(She goes back.)* And what will you do tonight, Ifada? Will you take part in the dancing? Or perhaps you will mount your own masquerade?

> *Ifada shakes his head, regretfully.*

---

buba: Traditional long shirt.
raffia: Woven palm.

Eman: You won't? So you haven't any? But you would like to own one.

  Ifada nods eagerly.

Eman: Then why don't you make your own?

  Ifada stares, puzzled by this idea.

Eman: Sunma will let you have some cloth you know. And bits of wool . . .

Sunma (coming out): Who are you talking to, Eman?

Eman: Ifada. I am trying to persuade him to join the young maskers.

Sunma (losing control): What does he want here? Why is he hanging round us?

Eman (amazed): What . . . ? I said Ifada, Ifada.

Sunma: Just tell him to go away. Let him go and play somewhere else!

Eman: What is this? Hasn't he always played here?

Sunma: I don't want him here. *(Rushes to the window.)* Get away, idiot. Don't bring your foolish face here any more, do you hear? Go on, go away from here . . .

Eman (restraining her): Control yourself, Sunma. What on earth has got into you?

  Ifada, hurt and bewildered, backs slowly away.

Sunma: He comes crawling round here like some horrible insect. I never want to lay my eyes on him again.

Eman: I don't understand. It *is* Ifada you know, Ifada! The unfortunate one who runs errands for you and doesn't hurt a soul.

Sunma: I cannot bear the sight of him.

Eman: You can't do what? It can't be two days since he last fetched water for you.

Sunma: What else can he do except that? He is useless. Just because we have been kind to him. . . . Others would have put him in an asylum.

Eman: You are not making sense. He is not a madman, he is just a little more unlucky than other children. *(Looks keenly at her.)* But what is the matter?

Sunma: It's nothing. I only wish we had sent him off to one of those places for creatures like him.

Eman: He is quite happy here. He doesn't bother anyone and he makes himself useful.

Sunma: Useful! Is that one of any use to anybody? Boys of his age are already earning a living but all he can do is hang around and drool at the mouth.

Eman: But he does work. You know he does a lot for you.

Sunma: Does he? And what about the farm you started for him! Does he ever work on it? Or have you forgotten that it was really for Ifada you cleared that brush. Now you have to go and work it yourself. You spend all your time on it and you have no room for anything else.

Eman: That wasn't his fault. I should first have asked him if he was fond of farming.

Sunma: Oh, so he can choose? As if he shouldn't be thankful for being allowed to live.

Eman: Sunma!

Sunma: He does not like farming but he knows how to feast his dumb mouth on the fruits.

Eman: But I want him to. I encourage him.

Sunma: Well keep him. I don't want to see him any more.

Eman (after some moments): But why? You cannot be telling all the truth. What has he done?

Sunma: The sight of him fills me with revulsion.

Eman (goes to her and holds her): What really is it? *(Sunma avoids his eyes.)* It is almost as if you are forcing yourself to hate him. Why?

Sunma: That is not true. Why should I?

Eman: Then what is the secret? You've even played with him before.

Sunma: I have always merely tolerated him. But I cannot any more. Suddenly my disgust won't take him any more. Perhaps . . . perhaps it is the new year. Yes, yes, it must be the new year.

Eman: I don't believe that.

Sunma: It must be. I am a woman, and these things matter. I don't want a misshape near me. Surely for one day in the year, I may demand some wholesomeness.

Eman: I do not understand you.

Sunma is silent.

It was cruel of you. And to Ifada who is so helpless and alone. We are the only friends he has.

Sunma: No, just you. I have told you, with me it has always been only an act of kindness. And now I haven't any pity left for him.

Eman: No. He is not a wholesome being.

He turns back to looking through the window.

Sunma (half-pleading): Ifada can rouse your pity. And yet if anything, I need more kindness from you. Every time my weakness betrays me, you close your mind against me . . . Eman . . . Eman . . .

A Girl comes in view, dragging an effigy by a rope attached to one of its legs. She stands for a while gazing at Eman. Ifada, who has crept back shyly to his accustomed position, becomes somewhat excited when he sees the effigy. The Girl is unsmiling. She possesses, in fact, a kind of inscrutability which does not make her hard but is unsettling.

Girl: Is the teacher in?

Eman (smiling): No.

Girl: Where is he gone?

Eman: I don't really know. Shall I ask?

Girl: Yes, do.

Eman (turning slightly): Sunma, a girl outside wants to know . . .

Sunma turns away, goes into the inside room.

Eman: Oh. *(Returns to the girl, but his slight gaiety is lost.)* There is no one at home who can tell me.

Girl: Why are you not in?

Eman: I don't really know. Maybe I went somewhere.

Girl: All right. I will wait until you get back.

She pulls the effigy to her, sits down.

Eman (slowly regaining his amusement): So you are ready for the new year.

Girl (without turning round): I am not going to the festival.

Eman: Then why have you got that?

Girl: Do you mean my carrier? I am unwell you know. My mother says it will take away my sickness with the old year.

Eman: Won't you share the carrier with your playmates?

Girl: Oh, no. Don't you know I play alone? The other children won't come near me. Their mothers would beat them.

Eman: But I have never seen you here. Why don't you come to the clinic?

Girl: My mother said No.

Gets up, begins to move off.

Eman: You are not going away?

Girl: I must not stay talking to you. If my mother caught me . . .

Eman: All right, tell me what you want before you go.

Girl (stops. For some moments she remains silent): I must have some clothes for my carrier.

Eman: Is that all? You wait a moment.

Sunma comes out as he takes down a buba from the wall. She goes to the window and glares almost with hatred at the Girl. The Girl retreats hastily, still impassive.

By the way, Sunma, do you know who that girl is?

Sunma: I hope you don't really mean to give her that.

Eman: Why not? I hardly ever use it.

Sunma: Just the same don't give it to her. She is not a child. She is as evil as the rest of them.

Eman: What has got into you today?

Sunma: All right, all right. Do what you wish.

She withdraws. Baffled, Eman returns to the window.

Eman: Here . . . will this do? Come and look at it.

Girl: Throw it.

Eman: What is the matter? I am not going to eat you.

Girl: No one lets me come near them.

Eman: But I am not afraid of catching your disease.

Girl: Throw it.

Eman shrugs and tosses the buba. She takes it without a word and slips it on the effigy, completely absorbed in the task. Eman watches for a while, then joins Sunma in the inner room.

Girl (after a long, cool survey of Ifada): You have a head like a spider's egg, and your mouth dribbles like a roof. But there is no one else. Would you like to play?

Ifada nods eagerly, quite excited.

Girl: You will have to get a stick.

Ifada rushes around, finds a big stick, and whirls it aloft, bearing down on the carrier.

Girl: Wait. I don't want you to spoil it. If it gets torn I shall drive you away. Now, let me see how you are going to beat it.

Ifada hits it gently.

Girl: You may hit harder than that. As long as there is something left to hang at the end.

She appraises him up and down.

You are not very tall . . . will you be able to hang it from a tree?

Ifada nods, grinning happily.

Girl: You will hang it up and I will set fire to it. (*Then, with surprising venom.*) But just because you are helping me, don't think it is going to cure you. I am the one who will get well at midnight, do you understand? It is my carrier and it is for me alone. (*She pulls at the rope to make sure that it is well attached to the leg.*) Well don't stand there drooling. Let's go.

She begins to walk off, dragging the effigy in the dust. Ifada remains where he is for some moments, seemingly puzzled. Then his face breaks into a large grin and he leaps after the procession, belaboring the effigy with all his strength. The stage remains empty for some moments. Then the horn of a lorry is sounded and Sunma rushes out. The hooting continues for some time with a rhythmic pattern. Eman comes out.

Eman: I am going to the village . . . I shan't be back before nightfall.

Sunma (*blankly*): Yes.

Eman (*hesitates*): Well what do you want me to do?

Sunma: The lorry was hooting just now.

Eman: I didn't hear it.

Sunma: It will leave in a few minutes. And you did promise we could go away.

Eman: I promised nothing. Will you go home by yourself or shall I come back for you?

Sunma: You don't even want me here?

Eman: But you have to go home, haven't you?

Sunma: I had hoped we would watch the new year together — in some other place.

Eman: Why do you continue to distress yourself?

Sunma: Because you will not listen to me. Why do you continue to stay where nobody wants you?

Eman: That is not true.

Sunma: It is. You are wasting your life on people who really want you out of their way.

Eman: You don't know what you are saying.

Sunma: You think they love you? Do you think they care at all for what you — or I — do for them?

Eman: *Them?* These are your own people. Sometimes you talk as if you were a stranger too.

Sunma: I wonder if I really sprang from here. I know they are evil and I am not. From the oldest to the smallest child, they are nourished in evil and unwholesomeness in which I have no part.

Eman: You knew this when you returned?

Sunma: You reproach me then for trying at all?

Eman: I reproach you with nothing. But you must leave me out of your plans. I can have no part in them.

Sunma (*nearly pleading*): Once I could have run away. I would have gone and never looked back.

Eman: I cannot listen when you talk like that.

Sunma: I swear to you, I do not mind what happens afterwards. But you must help me tear myself away from here. I can no longer do it by myself. . . . It is only a little thing. And we have worked so hard this past year . . . surely we can go away for a week . . . even a few days would be enough.

Eman: I have told you, Sunma . . .

Sunma (desperately): Two days, Eman. Only two days.

Eman (distressed): But I tell you I have no wish to go.

Sunma (suddenly angry): Are you so afraid then?

Eman: Me? Afraid of what?

Sunma: You think you will not want to come back.

Eman (pitying): You cannot dare me that way.

Sunma: Then why don't you leave here, even for an hour? If you are so sure that your life is settled here, why are you afraid to do this thing for me? What is so wrong that you will not go into the next town for a day or two?

Eman: I don't want to. I do not have to persuade you, or myself, about anything. I simply have no desire to go away.

Sunma (his quiet confidence appears to incense her): You are afraid. You accuse me of losing my sense of mission, but you are afraid to put yours to the test.

Eman: You are wrong, Sunma. I have no sense of mission. But I have found peace here and I am content with that.

Sunma: I haven't. For a while I thought that too, but I found there could be no peace in the midst of so much cruelty. Eman, tonight at least, the last night of the old year . . .

Eman: No, Sunma. I find this too distressing; you should go home now.

Sunma: It is the time for making changes in one's life, Eman. Let's breathe in the new year away from here.

Eman: You are hurting yourself.

Sunma: Tonight. Only tonight. We will come back tomorrow, as early as you like. But let us go away for this one night. Don't let another year break on me in this place . . . you don't know how important it is to me, but I will tell you, I will tell you on the way . . . but we must not be here today, Eman, do this one thing for me.

Eman (sadly): I cannot.

Sunma (suddenly calm): I was a fool to think it would be otherwise. The whole village may use you as they will but for me there is nothing. Sometimes I think you believe that doing anything for me makes you unfaithful to some part of your life. If it was a woman then I pity her for what she must have suffered.

Eman winces and hardens slowly. Sunma notices nothing.

Keeping faith with so much is slowly making you inhuman. *(Seeing the change in Eman.)* Eman. Eman. What is it?

As she goes towards him, Eman goes into the house.

Sunma (apprehensive, follows him): What did I say? Eman, forgive me, forgive me please.

Eman remains facing into the slow darkness of the room. Sunma, distressed, cannot decide what to do.

I swear I didn't know. . . . I would not have said it for all the world.

A lorry is heard taking off somewhere nearby. The sound comes up and slowly fades away into the distance. Sunma starts visibly, goes slowly to the window.

Sunma (as the sound dies off, to herself): What happens now?

Eman (joining her at the window): What did you say?

Sunma: Nothing.

Eman: Was that not the lorry going off?

Sunma: It was.

Eman: I am sorry I couldn't help you.

 Sunma, about to speak, changes her mind.

Eman: I think you ought to go home now.

Sunma: No, don't send me away. It's the least you can do for me. Let me stay here until all the noise is over.

Eman: But are you not needed at home? You have a part in the festival.

Sunma: I have renounced it; I am Jaguna's eldest daughter only in name.

Eman: Renouncing one's self is not so easy — surely you know that.

Sunma: I don't want to talk about it. Will you at least let us be together tonight?

Eman: But . . .

Sunma: Unless you are afraid my father will accuse you of harboring me.

Eman: All right, we will go out together.

Sunma: Go out? I want us to stay here.

Eman: When there is so much going on outside?

Sunma: Some day you will wish that you went away when I tried to make you.

Eman: Are we going back to that?

Sunma: No. I promise you I will not recall it again. But you must know that it was also for your sake that I tried to get us away.

Eman: For me? How?

Sunma: By yourself you can do nothing here. Have you not noticed how tightly we shut out strangers? Even if you lived here for a lifetime, you would remain a stranger.

Eman: Perhaps that is what I like. There is peace in being a stranger.

Sunma: For a while perhaps. But they would reject you in the end. I tell you it is only I who stand between you and contempt. And because of this you have earned their hatred. I don't know why I say this now, except that somehow, I feel that it no longer matters. It is only I who have stood between you and much humiliation.

Eman: Think carefully before you say any more. I am incapable of feeling indebted to you. This will make no difference at all.

Sunma: I ask for nothing. But you must know it all the same. It is true I hadn't the strength to go by myself. And I must confess this now, if you had come with me, I would have done everything to keep you from returning.

Eman: I know that.

Sunma: You see, I bare myself to you. For days I had thought it over, this was to be a new beginning for us. And I placed my fate wholly in your hands. Now the thought will not leave me, I have a feeling which will not be shaken off, that in some way, you have tonight totally destroyed my life.

Eman: You are depressed, you don't know what you are saying.

Sunma: Don't think I am accusing you. I say all this only because I cannot help it.

Eman: We must not remain shut up here. Let us go and be part of the living.

Sunma: No. Leave them alone.

Eman: Surely you don't want to stay indoors when the whole town is alive with rejoicing.

Sunma: Rejoicing! Is that what it seems to you? No, let us remain here. Whatever happens I must not go out until all this is over.

There is silence. It has grown much darker.

Eman: I shall light the lamp.

Sunma (eager to do something): No, let me do it.

She goes into the inner room. Eman paces the room, stops by a shelf, and toys with the seeds in an "ayo" board,° takes down the whole board and places it on a table, playing by himself.

The Girl is now seen coming back, still dragging her "carrier." Ifada brings up the rear as before. As he comes round the corner of the house two men emerge from the shadows. A sack is thrown over Ifada's head, the rope is pulled tight rendering him instantly helpless. The Girl has reached the front of the house before she turns round at the sound of scuffle. She is in time to see Ifada thrown over the shoulders and borne away. Her face betraying no emotion at all, the Girl backs slowly away, turns, and flees, leaving the "carrier" behind. Sunma enters, carrying two kerosene lamps. She hangs one up from the wall.

Eman: One is enough.

Sunma: I want to leave one outside.

She goes out, hangs the lamp from a nail just above the door. As she turns she sees the effigy and gasps. Eman rushes out.

Eman: What is it? Oh, is that what frightened you?

Sunma: I thought . . . I didn't really see it properly.

Eman goes towards the object, stoops to pick it up.

Eman: It must belong to that sick girl.

Sunma: Don't touch it.

Eman: Let's keep it for her.

Sunma: Leave it alone. Don't touch it, Eman.

Eman (shrugs and goes back): You are very nervous.

Sunma: Let's go in.

Eman: Wait. *(He detains her by the door, under the lamp.)* I know there is something more than you've told me. What are you afraid of tonight?

Sunma: I was only scared by that thing. There is nothing else.

Eman: I am not blind, Sunma. It is true I would not run away when you wanted me to, but that doesn't mean I do not feel things. What does tonight really mean that it makes you so helpless?

Sunma: It is only a mood. And your indifference to me . . . let's go in.

Eman moves aside and she enters; he remains there for a moment and then follows. She fiddles with the lamp, looks vaguely round the room, then goes and shuts the door, bolting it. When she turns, it is to meet Eman's eyes, questioning.

Sunma: There is a cold wind coming in.

Eman keeps his gaze on her.

Sunma: It *was* getting cold.

ayo board: A game.

She moves guiltily to the table and stands by the ayo board, rearranging the seeds. Eman remains where he is a few moments, then brings a stool and sits opposite her. She sits down also and they begin to play in silence.

Sunma: What brought you here at all, Eman? And what makes you stay?

There is another silence.

Sunma: I am not trying to share your life. I know you too well by now. But at least we have worked together since you came. Is there nothing at all I deserve to know?

Eman: Let me continue a stranger — especially to you. Those who have much to give fulfill themselves only in total loneliness.

Sunma: Then there is no love in what you do.

Eman: There is. Love comes to me more easily with strangers.

Sunma: That is unnatural.

Eman: Not for me. I know I find consummation only when I have spent myself for a total stranger.

Sunma: It seems unnatural to me. But then I am a woman. I have a woman's longings and weaknesses. And the ties of blood are very strong in me.

Eman (smiling): You think I have cut loose from all these — ties of blood.

Sunma: Sometimes you are so inhuman.

Eman: I don't know what that means. But I am very much my father's son.

They play in silence. Suddenly Eman pauses, listening.

Eman: Did you hear that?

Sunma (quickly): I heard nothing . . . it's your turn.

Eman: Perhaps some of the mummers are coming this way.

Eman, about to play, leaps up suddenly.

Sunma: What is it? Don't you want to play any more?

Eman moves to the door.

Sunma: No. Don't go out, Eman.

Eman: If it's the dancers I want to ask them to stay. At least we won't have to miss everything.

Sunma: No, no. Don't open the door. Let us keep out everyone tonight.

A terrified and disordered figure bursts suddenly round the corner, past the window and begins hammering at the door. It is Ifada. Desperate with terror, he pounds madly at the door, dumb-moaning all the while.

Eman: Isn't that Ifada?

Sunma: They are only fooling about. Don't pay any attention.

Eman (looks round the window): That is Ifada. (Begins to unbolt the door.)

Sunma (pulling at his hands): It is only a trick they are playing on you. Don't take any notice, Eman.

Eman: What are you saying? The boy is out of his senses with fear.

Sunma: No, no. Don't interfere, Eman. For God's sake don't interfere.

Eman: Do you know something of this then?

Sunma: You are a stranger here, Eman. Just leave us alone and go your own way. There is nothing you can do.

Eman (he tries to push her out of the way but she clings fiercely to him): Have you gone mad? I tell you the boy must come in.

Sunma: Why won't you listen to me, Eman? I tell you it's none of your business. For your own sake do as I say.

Eman pushes her off, unbolts the door. Ifada rushes in, clasps Eman round the knees, dumb-moaning against his legs.

Eman (manages to rebolt the door): What is it, Ifada? What is the matter?

Shouts and voices are heard coming nearer the house.

Sunma: Before it's too late, let him go. For once, Eman, believe what I tell you. Don't harbor him or you will regret it all your life.

Eman tries to calm Ifada, who becomes more and more abject as the outside voices get nearer.

Eman: What have they done to him? At least tell me that. What is going on, Sunma?

Sunma (with sudden venom): Monster! Could you not take yourself somewhere else?

Eman: Stop talking like that.

Sunma: He could have run into the bush couldn't he? Toad! Why must he follow us with his own disasters!

Voices outside: It's here. . . . Round the back. . . . Spread, spread . . . this way . . . no, head him off . . . use the bush path and head him off . . . get some more lights . . .

Eman listens. Lifts Ifada bodily and carries him into the inner room. Returns at once, shutting the door behind him.

Sunma (slumps into a chair, resigned): You always follow your own way.

Jaguna (comes round the corner followed by Oroge and three men, one bearing a torch): I knew he would come here.

Oroge: I hope our friend won't make trouble.

Jaguna: He had better not. You, recall all the men and tell them to surround the house.

Oroge: But he may not be in the house after all.

Jaguna: I know he is here . . . *(To the men.)* . . . go on, do as I say.

He bangs on the door.

Teacher, open your door . . . you two stay by the door. If I need you I will call you.

Eman opens the door.

Jaguna (speaks as he enters): We know he is here.

Eman: Who?

Jaguna: Don't let us waste time. We are grown men, teacher. You understand me and I understand you. But we must take back the boy.

Eman: This is my house.

Jaguna: Daughter, you'd better tell your friend. I don't think he quite knows our ways. Tell him why he must give up the boy.

Sunma: Father, I . . .

Jaguna: Are you going to tell him or aren't you?

Sunma: Father, I beg you, leave us alone tonight . . .

Jaguna: I thought you might be a hindrance. Go home then if you will not use your sense.

Sunma: But there are other ways . . .

Jaguna (turning to the men): See that she gets home. I no longer trust her. If she gives trouble carry her. And see that the women stay with her until all this is over.

Sunma departs, accompanied by one of the men.

Jaguna: Now, teacher . . .

Oroge (restrains him): You see, Mister Eman, it is like this. Right now, nobody knows that Ifada has taken refuge here. No one except us and our men — and they know how to keep their mouths shut. We don't want to have to burn down the house, you see, but if the word gets around, we would have no choice.

Jaguna: In fact, it may be too late already. A carrier should end up in the bush, not in a house. Anyone who doesn't guard his door when the carrier goes by has himself to blame. A contaminated house should be burnt down.

Oroge: But we are willing to let it pass. Only, you must bring him out quickly.

Eman: All right. But at least you will let me ask you something.

Jaguna: What is there to ask? Don't you understand what we have told you?

Eman: Yes. But why did you pick on a helpless boy? Obviously he is not willing.

Jaguna: What is the man talking about? Ifada is a godsend. Does he have to be willing?

Eman: In my home, we believe that a man should be willing.

Oroge: Mister Eman, I don't think you quite understand. This is not a simple matter at all. I don't know what you do, but here, it is not a cheap task for anybody. No one in his senses would do such a job. Why do you think we give refuge to idiots like him? We don't know where he came from. One morning, he is simply there, just like that. From nowhere at all. You see, there is a purpose in that.

Jaguna: We only waste time.

Oroge: Jaguna, be patient. After all, the man has been with us for some time now and deserves to know. The evil of the old year is no light thing to load on any man's head.

Eman: I know something about that.

Oroge: You do? *(Turns to Jaguna, who snorts impatiently.)* You see I told you so, didn't I? From the moment you came I saw you were one of the knowing ones.

Jaguna: Then let him behave like a man and give back the boy.

Eman: It is you who are not behaving like men.

Jaguna (advances aggressively): That is a quick mouth you have . . .

Oroge: Patience, Jaguna . . . if you want the new year to cushion the land there must be no deeds of anger. What did you mean, my friend?

Eman: It is a simple thing. A village which cannot produce its own carrier contains no men.

Jaguna: Enough. Let there be no more talk or this business will be ruined by some rashness. You . . . come inside. Bring the boy out, he must be in the room there.

Eman: Wait.

The men hesitate.

Jaguna (hitting the nearer one and propelling him forward): Go on. Have you changed masters now that you listen to what he says?

Oroge (sadly): I am sorry you would not undertand, Mister Eman. But you ought to know that no carrier may return to the village. If he does, the people will stone him to death. It has happened before. Surely it is too much to ask a man to give up his own soil.

Eman: I know others who have done more.

Ifada is brought out, abjectly dumb-moaning.

Eman: You can see him with your own eyes. Does it really have meaning to use one as unwilling as that?

Oroge (smiling): He shall be willing. Not only willing but actually joyous. I am the one who prepares them all, and I have seen worse. This one escaped before I began to prepare him for the event. But you will see him later tonight, the most joyous creature in the festival. Then perhaps you will understand.

Eman: Then it is only a deceit. Do you believe the spirit of a new year is so easily fooled?

Jaguna: Take him out. *(The men carry out Ifada.)* You see, it is so easy to talk. You say there are no men in this village because they cannot provide a willing carrier. And yet I heard Oroge tell you we only use strangers. There is only one other stranger in the village, but I have not heard him offer himself. *(Spits.)* It is so easy to talk is it not?

He turns his back on him. They go off, taking Ifada with them, limp and silent. The only sign of life is that he strains his neck to keep his eyes on Eman till the very moment that he disappears from sight. Eman remains where they left him, staring after the group.

A blackout lasting no more than a minute. The lights come up slowly, and Ifada is seen returning to the house. He stops at the window and looks in. Seeing no one, he bangs on the sill. Appears surprised that there is no response. He slithers down on his favorite spot, then sees the effigy still lying where the Girl had dropped it in her flight. After some hesitation, he goes towards it, begins to strip it of the clothing. Just then the Girl comes in.

Girl: Hey, leave that alone. You know it's mine.

Ifada pauses, then speeds up his action.

Girl: I said it is mine. Leave it where you found it. *(She rushes at him and begins to struggle for possession of the carrier.)* Thief! Thief! Let it go, it is mine. Let it go. You animal, just because I let you play with it. Idiot! Idiot!

The struggle becomes quite violent. The Girl is hanging to the effigy and Ifada lifts her with it, flinging her all about. The Girl hangs on grimly.

Girl: You are spoiling it . . . why don't you get your own? Thief! Let it go, you thief!

Sunma comes in walking very fast, throwing apprehensive glances over her shoulder. Seeing the two children, she becomes immediately angry. Advances on them.

Sunma: So you've made this place your playground. Get away, you untrained pigs. Get out of here.

Ifada flees at once, the Girl retreats also, retaining possession of the carrier.

Sunma goes to the door. She has her hand on the door when the significance of Ifada's presence strikes her for the first time. She stands rooted to the spot, then turns slowly round.

Sunma: Ifada! What are you doing here?

Ifada is bewildered. Sunma turns suddenly and rushes into the house, flying into the inner room and out again.

Eman! Eman! Eman!

She rushes outside.

Where did he go? Where did they take him?

Ifada distressed, points. Sunma seizes him by the arm, drags him off.

Take me there at once. God help you if we are too late. You loathsome thing, if you have let him suffer . . .

Her voice fades into other shouts, running footsteps, banged tins, bells, dogs, etc., rising in volume.

    It is a narrow passageway between two mudhouses. At the far end one man after another is seen running across the entry, the noise dying off gradually.

    About halfway down the passage, Eman is crouching against the wall, tense with apprehension. As the noise dies off, he seems to relax, but the alert, hunted look is still in his eyes, which are ringed in a reddish color. The rest of his body has been whitened with a floury substance. He is naked down to the waist, wears a baggy pair of trousers, calf-length, and around both feet are bangles.

Eman: I will simply stay here till dawn. I have done enough.

A window is thrown open and a woman empties some slop from a pail. With a startled cry Eman leaps aside to avoid it and the woman puts out her head.

Woman: Oh, my head. What have I done! Forgive me, neighbor . . . Eh, it's the carrier! *(Very rapidly she clears her throat and spits on him, flings the pail at him and runs off, shouting.)* He's here. The carrier is hiding in the passage. Quickly, I have found the carrier!

The cry is taken up and Eman flees down the passage. Shortly afterwards his pursuers come pouring down the passage in full cry. After the last of them come Jaguna and Oroge.

Oroge: Wait, wait. I cannot go so fast.

Jaguna: We will rest a little then. We can do nothing anyway.

Oroge: If only he had let me prepare him.

Jaguna: They are the ones who break first, these fools who think they were born to carry suffering like a hat. What are we to do now?

Oroge: When they catch him I must prepare him.

Jaguna: He? It will be impossible now. There can be no joy left in that one.

Oroge: Still, it took him by surprise. He was not expecting what he met.

Jaguna: Why then did he refuse to listen? Did he think he was coming to sit down to a feast? He had not even gone through one compound before he bolted. Did he think he was taken round the people to be blessed? A woman, that is all he is.

Oroge: No, no. He took the beating well enough. I think he is the kind who would let himself be beaten from night till dawn and not utter a sound. He would let himself be stoned until he dropped dead.

Jaguna: Then what made him run like a coward?

Oroge: I don't know. I don't really know. It is a night of curses, Jaguna. It is not many unprepared minds will remain unhinged under the load.

Jaguna: We must find him. It is a poor beginning for a year when our own curses remain hovering over our homes because the carrier refused to take them.

They go. The scene changes. Eman is crouching beside some shrubs, torn and bleeding.

Eman: They are even guarding my house . . . as if I would go there, but I need water . . . they could at least grant me that . . . I can be thirsty too . . . *(He pricks his ears.)* . . . there must be a stream nearby . . . *(As he looks round him, his eyes widen at a scene he encounters.)*

An Old Man, short and vigorous looking, is seated on a stool. He also is wearing calf-length baggy trousers, white. On his head, a white cap. An attendant is engaged in rubbing his body with oil. Round his eyes, two white rings have already been marked.

Old Man: Have they prepared the boat?
Attendant: They are making the last sacrifice.
Old Man: Good. Did you send for my son?
Attendant: He's on his way.
Old Man: I have never met the carrying of the boat with such a heavy heart. I hope nothing comes of it.
Attendant: The gods will not desert us on that account.
Old Man: A man should be at his strongest when he takes the boat, my friend. To be weighed down inside and out is not a wise thing. I hope when the moment comes I shall have found my strength.

Enter Eman, a wrapper round his waist and a danski° over it.

Old Man: I meant to wait until after my journey to the river, but my mind is so burdened with my own grief and yours I could not delay it. You know I must have all my strength. But I sit here, feeling it all eaten slowly away by my unspoken grief. It helps to say it out. It even helps to cry sometimes.

He signals to the attendant to leave them.

Come nearer . . . we will never meet again, son. Not on this side of the flesh. What I do not know is whether you will return to take my place.
Eman: I will never come back.
Old Man: Do you know what you are saying? Ours is a strong breed, my son. It is only a strong breed that can take this boat to the river year after year and wax stronger on it. I have taken down each year's evils for over twenty years. I hoped you would follow me.
Eman: My life here died with Omae.
Old Man: Omae died giving birth to your child and you think the world is ended. Eman, my pain did not begin when Omae died. Since you sent her to stay with me, son, I lived with the burden of knowing that this child would die bearing your son.
Eman: Father.
Old Man: Don't you know it was the same with you? And me? No woman survives the bearing of the strong ones. Son, it is not the mouth of the boaster that says he belongs to the strong breed. It is the tongue that is red

danski: A garment.

with pain and black with sorrow. Twelve years you were away, my son, and for those twelve years I knew the love of an old man for his daughter and the pain of a man helplessly awaiting his loss.

Eman: I wish I had stayed away. I wish I never came back to meet her.

Old Man: It had to be. But you know now what slowly ate away my strength. I awaited your return with love and fear. Forgive me then if I say that your grief is light. It will pass. This grief may drive you now from home. But you must return.

Eman: You do not understand. It is not grief alone.

Old Man: What is it then? Tell me, I can still learn.

Eman: I was away twelve years. I changed much in that time.

Old Man: I am listening.

Eman: I am unfitted for your work, father. I wish to say no more. But I am totally unfitted for your call.

Old Man: It is only time you need, son. Stay longer and you will answer the urge of your blood.

Eman: That I stayed at all was because of Omae. I did not expect to find her waiting. I would have taken her away, but hard as you claim to be, it would have killed you. And I was a tired man. I needed peace. Because Omae was peace, I stayed. Now nothing holds me here.

Old Man: Other men would rot and die doing this task year after year. It is strong medicine which only we can take. Our blood is strong like no other. Anything you do in life must be less than this, son.

Eman: That is not true, father.

Old Man: I tell you it is true. Your own blood will betray you, son, because you cannot hold it back. If you make it do less than this, it will rush to your head and burst it open. I say what I know, my son.

Eman: There are other tasks in life, father. This one is not for me. There are even greater things you know nothing of.

Old Man: I am very sad. You only go to give to others what rightly belongs to us. You will use your strength among thieves. They are thieves because they take what is ours, they have no claim of blood to it. They will even lack the knowledge to use it wisely. Truth is my companion at this moment, my son. I know everything I say will surely bring the sadness of truth.

Eman: I am going, father.

Old Man: Call my attendant. And be with me in your strength for this last journey. A-ah, did you hear that? It came out without my knowing it; this is indeed my last journey. But I am not afraid.

Eman goes out. A few moments later, the attendant enters.

Attendant: The boat is ready.

Old Man: So am I.

He sits perfectly still for several moments. Drumming begins somewhere in the distance, and the Old Man sways his head almost imperceptibly. Two men come in bearing a miniature boat, containing an indefinable mound. They rush it in and set it briskly down near the Old Man, and stand well back. The Old Man gets up slowly, the attendant watching him keenly. He signs to the men, who lift the boat quickly onto the Old Man's head. As soon as it touches his head, he holds it down with both hands and runs off, the men give him a start, then follow at a trot. As the last man disappears Oroge limps in and comes face to face with Eman—as carrier—who is now seen still standing beside the shrubs, staring into the scene he has just witnessed. Oroge, struck by the look on Eman's face, looks anxiously behind him to see what has engaged Eman's attention. Eman notices him then, and the pair stare at each other. Jaguna enters, sees him and shouts, "Here he is," rushes at Eman, who is whipped back to the immediate and flees, Jaguna in pursuit. Three or four others enter and follow them. Oroge remains where he is, thoughtful.

Jaguna (reenters): They have closed in on him now, we'll get him this time.

Oroge: It is nearly midnight.

Jaguna: You were standing there looking at him as if he was some strange spirit. Why didn't you shout?

Oroge: You shouted didn't you? Did that catch him?

Jaguna: Don't worry. We have him now. But things have taken a bad turn. It is no longer enough to drive him past every house. There is too much contamination about already.

Oroge (not listening): He saw something. Why may I not know what it was?

Jaguna: What are you talking about?

Oroge: Hm. What is it?

Jaguna: I said there is too much harm done already. The year will demand more from this carrier than we thought.

Oroge: What do you mean?

Jaguna: Do we have to talk with the full mouth?

Oroge: S-sh . . . look!

Jaguna turns just in time to see Sunma fly at him, clawing at his face like a crazed tigress.

Sunma: Murderer! What are you doing to him? Murderer! Murderer!

Jaguna finds himself struggling really hard to keep off his daughter. He succeeds in pushing her off and striking her so hard on the face that she falls to her knees. He moves on her to hit her again.

Oroge (comes between): Think what you are doing, Jaguna, she is your daughter.

Jaguna: My daughter! Does this one look like my daughter? Let me cripple the harlot for life.

Oroge: That is a wicked thought, Jaguna.

Jaguna: Don't come between me and her.

Oroge: Nothing in anger—do you forget what tonight is?

Jaguna: Can you blame me for forgetting?

Draws his hand across his cheek—it is covered with blood.

Oroge: This is an unhappy night for us all. I fear what is to come of it.

Jaguna: Let's go. I cannot restrain myself in this creature's presence. My own daughter . . . and for a stranger . . .

They go off. Ifada, who came in with Sunma and had stood apart, horror-stricken, comes shyly forward. He helps Sunma up. They go off, he holding Sunma bent and sobbing.

Enter Eman—as carrier. He is physically present in the bounds of this next scene, a side of a round thatched hut. A young girl, about fourteen, runs in, stops beside the hut. She looks carefully to see that she is not observed, puts her mouth to a little hole in the wall.

Omae: Eman . . . Eman . . .

*Eman—as carrier—responds, as he does throughout the scene, but they are un-
aware of him.*

Eman (from inside): Who is it?

Omae: It is me, Omae.

Eman: How dare you come here!

*Two hands appear at the hole and, pushing outwards, create a much larger hole
through which Eman puts out his head. It is Eman as a boy, the same age as the girl.*

Go away at once. Are you trying to get me into trouble!

Omae: What is the matter?

Eman: You. Go away.

Omae: But I came to see you.

Eman: Are you deaf? I say I don't want to see you. Now go before my tutor
catches you.

Omae: All right. Come out.

Eman: Do what!

Omae: Come out.

Eman: You must be mad.

Omae (sits on the ground): All right, if you don't come out I shall simply stay
here until your tutor arrives.

*Eman (about to explode, thinks better of it and the head disappears. A moment later he
emerges from behind the hut):* What sort of a devil has got into you?

Omae: None. I just wanted to see you.

Eman (his mimicry is nearly hysterical): "None. I just wanted to see you." Do you
think this place is the stream where you can go and molest innocent
people?

Omae (coyly): Aren't you glad to see me?

Eman: I am not.

Omae: Why?

Eman: Why? Do you really ask me why? Because you are a woman and a most
troublesome woman. Don't you know anything about this at all? We are
not meant to see any woman. So go away before more harm is done.

Omae (flirtatious): What is so secret about it anyway? What do they teach you?

Eman: Nothing any woman can understand.

Omae: Ha ha. You think we don't know eh? You've all come to be circumcised.

Eman: Shut up. You don't know anything.

Omae: Just think, all this time you haven't been circumcised, and you dared
make eyes at us women.

Eman: Thank you—woman. Now go.

Omae: Do they give you enough to eat?

Eman (testily): No. We are so hungry that when silly girls like you turn up, we
eat them.

Omae (feigning tears): Oh, oh, oh, he's abusing me. He's abusing me.

Eman (alarmed): Don't try that here. Go quickly if you are going to cry.

Omae: All right, I won't cry.

Eman: Cry or no cry, go away and leave me alone. What do you think will happen if my tutor turns up now?

Omae: He won't.

Eman (mimicking): "He won't." I suppose you are his wife and he tells you
where he goes. In fact this is just the time he comes round to our huts. He
could be at the next hut this very moment.

Omae: Ha-ha. You're lying. I left him by the stream, pinching the girls' bottoms. Is that the sort of thing he teaches you?

Eman: Don't say anything against him or I shall beat you. Isn't it you loose girls who tease him, wiggling your bottoms under his nose?

Omae (going tearful again): A-ah, so I am one of the loose girls, eh?

Eman: Now don't start accusing me of things I didn't say.

Omae: But you said it. You said it.

Eman: I didn't. Look, Omae, someone will hear you and I'll be in disgrace. Why don't you go before anything happens.

Omae: It's all right. My friends have promised to hold your old rascal tutor till I get back.

Eman: Then go back right now. I have work to do. *(Going in.)*

Omae (runs after and tries to hold him. Eman leaps back, genuinely scared): What is the matter? I was not going to bite you.

Eman: Do you know what you nearly did? You almost touched me!

Omae: Well?

Eman: Well! Isn't it enough that you let me set my eyes on you? Must you now totally pollute me with your touch? Don't you understand anything?

Omae: Oh, that.

Eman (nearly screaming): It is not "oh that." Do you think this is only a joke or a little visit like spending the night with your grandmother? This is an important period of my life. Look, these huts, we built them with our own hands. Every boy builds his own. We learn things, do you understand? And we spend much time just thinking. At least, I do. It is the first time I have had nothing to do except think. Don't you see, I am becoming a man. For the first time, I understand that I have a life to fulfill. Has that thought ever worried you?

Omae: You are frightening me.

Eman: There. That is all you can say. And what use will that be when a man finds himself alone—like that? *(Points to the hut.)* A man must go on his own, go where no one can help him, and test his strength. Because he may find himself one day sitting alone in a wall as round as that. In there, my mind could hold no other thought. I may never have such moments again to myself. Don't dare to come and steal any more of it.

Omae (this time, genuinely tearful): Oh, I know you hate me. You only want to drive me away.

Eman (impatiently): Yes, yes, I know I hate you—but go.

Omae (going, all tears. Wipes her eyes, suddenly all mischief): Eman.

Eman: What now?

Omae: I only want to ask one thing . . . do you promise to tell me?

Eman: Well, what is it?

Omae (gleefully): Does it hurt?

She turns instantly and flees, landing straight into the arms of the returning tutor.

Tutor: Te-he-he . . . what have we here? What little mouse leaps straight into the beak of the wise old owl eh?

Omae struggles to free herself, flies to the opposite side, grimacing with distaste.

Tutor: I suppose you merely came to pick some fruits eh? You did not sneak here to see any of my children.

Omae: Yes, I came to steal your fruits.

Tutor: Te-he-he . . . I thought so. And that dutiful son of mine over there. He saw you and came to chase you off my fruit trees didn't he? Te-he-he . . . I'm sure he did, isn't that so, my young Eman?

Eman: I was talking to her.

Tutor: Indeed you were. Now be good enough to go into your hut until I decide your punishment. *(Eman withdraws.)* Te-he-he . . . now now, my little daughter, you need not be afraid of me.

Omae (spiritedly): I am not.

Tutor: Good. Very good. We ought to be friendly. *(His voice becomes leering.)* Now this is nothing to worry you, my daughter . . . a very small thing indeed. Although of course if I were to let it slip that your young Eman had broken a strong taboo, it might go hard on him, you know. I am sure you would not like that to happen, would you?

Omae: No.

Tutor: Good. You are sensible, my girl. Can you wash clothes?

Omae: Yes.

Tutor: Good. If you will come with me now to my hut, I shall give you some clothes to wash, and then we will forget all about this matter eh? Well, come on.

Omae: I shall wait here. You go and bring the clothes.

Tutor: Eh? What is that? Now now, don't make me angry. You should know better than to talk back at your elders. Come now.

He takes her by the arm, and tries to drag her off.

Omae: No no, I won't come to your hut. Leave me. Leave me alone, you shameless old man.

Tutor: If you don't come I shall disgrace the whole family of Eman, and yours too.

Eman reenters with a small bundle.

Eman: Leave her alone. Let us go, Omae.

Tutor: And where do you think you are going?

Eman: Home.

Tutor: Te-he-he . . . As easy as that eh? You think you can leave here any time you please? Get right back inside that hut!

Eman takes Omae by the arm and begins to walk off.

Tutor: Come back at once.

He goes after him and raises his stick. Eman catches it, wrenches it from him, and throws it away.

Omae (hopping delightedly): Kill him. Beat him to death.

Tutor: Help! Help! He is killing me! Help!

Alarmed, Eman clamps his hand over his mouth.

Eman: Old tutor, I don't mean you any harm, but you mustn't try to harm me either. *(He removes his hand.)*

Tutor: You think you can get away with your crime. My report shall reach the elders before you ever get into town.

Eman: You are afraid of what I will say about you? Don't worry. Only if you try to shame me, then I will speak. I am not going back to the village anyway.

Just tell them I have gone, no more. If you say one word more than that I shall hear of it the same day and I shall come back.

Tutor: You are telling me what to do? But don't think to come back next year because I will drive you away. Don't think to come back here even ten years from now. And don't send your children. *(Goes off with threatening gestures.)*

Eman: I won't come back.

Omae: Smoked vulture! But Eman, he says you cannot return next year. What will you do?

Eman: It is a small thing one can do in the big towns.

Omae: I thought you were going to beat him that time. Why didn't you crack his dirty hide?

Eman: Listen carefully, Omae . . . I am going on a journey.

Omae: Come on. Tell me about it on the way.

Eman: No, I go that way. I cannot return to the village.

Omae: Because of that wretched man? Anyway you will first talk to your father.

Eman: Go and see him for me. Tell him I have gone away for some time. I think he will know.

Omae: But, Eman . . .

Eman: I haven't finished. You will go and live with him till I get back. I have spoken to him about you. Look after him!

Omae: But what is this journey? When will you come back?

Eman: I don't know. But this is a good moment to go. Nothing ties me down.

Omae: But, Eman, you want to leave me.

Eman: Don't forget all I said. I don't know how long I will be. Stay in my father's house as long as you remember me. When you become tired of waiting, you must do as you please. You understand? You must do as you please.

Omae: I cannot understand anything, Eman. I don't know where you are going or why. Suppose you never came back! Don't go, Eman. Don't leave me by myself.

Eman: I must go. Now let me see you on your way.

Omae: I shall come with you.

Eman: Come with me! And who will look after you? Me? You will only be in my way, you know that! You will hold me back and I shall desert you in a strange place. Go home and do as I say. Take care of my father and let him take care of you. *(He starts going but Omae clings to him.)*

Omae: But, Eman, stay the night at least. You will only lose your way. Your father, Eman, what will he say? I won't remember what you said . . . come back to the village . . . I cannot return alone, Eman . . . come with me as far as the crossroads.

His face set, Eman strides off and Omae loses balance as he increases his pace. Falling, she quickly wraps her arms around his ankle, but Eman continues unchecked, dragging her along.

Omae: Don't go, Eman . . . Eman, don't leave me, don't leave me . . . don't leave your Omae . . . don't go, Eman . . . don't leave your Omae . . .

Eman — as carrier — makes a nervous move as if he intends to go after the vanished pair. He stops but continues to stare at the point where he last saw them. There is stillness for a while. Then the Girl enters from the same place and remains looking at Eman. Startled, Eman looks apprehensively round him. The Girl goes nearer but keeps beyond arm's length.

Girl: Are you the carrier?

Eman: Yes, I am Eman.

Girl: Why are you hiding?

Eman: I really came for a drink of water . . . er . . . is there anyone in front of the house?

Girl: No.

Eman: But there might be people in the house. Did you hear voices?

Girl: There is no one here.

Eman: Good. Thank you. *(He is about to go, stops suddenly.)* Er . . . would you . . . you will find a cup on the table. Could you bring me the water out here? The water pot is in a corner.

The Girl goes. She enters the house, then, watching Eman carefully, slips out and runs off.

Eman (sitting): Perhaps they have all gone home. It will be good to rest. *(He hears voices and listens hard.)* Too late. *(Moves cautiously nearer the house.)* Quickly, girl, I can hear people coming. Hurry up. *(Looks through the window.)* Where are you? Where is she? *(The truth dawns on him suddenly and he moves off, sadly.)*

Enter Jaguna and Oroge, led by the Girl.

Girl (pointing): He was there.

Jaguna: Ay, he's gone now. He is a sly one is your friend. But it won't save him forever.

Oroge: What was he doing when you saw him?

Girl: He asked me for a drink of water.

Jaguna: ⎤
            ⎬ Ah! *(They look at each other.)*
Oroge: ⎦

Oroge: We should have thought of that.

Jaguna: He is surely finished now. If only we had thought of it earlier.

Oroge: It is not too late. There is still an hour before midnight.

Jaguna: We must call back all the men. Now we need only wait for him — in the right place.

Oroge: Everyone must be told. We don't want anyone heading him off again.

Jaguna: And it works so well. This is surely the help of the gods themselves, Oroge. Don't you know at once what is on the path to the stream?

Oroge: The sacred trees.

Jaguna: I tell you it is the very hand of the gods. Let us go.

An overgrown part of the village. Eman wanders in, aimlessly, seemingly uncaring of discovery. Beyond him, an area lights up, revealing a group of people clustered round a spot, all the heads are bowed. One figure stands away and separate from them. Even as Eman looks, the group breaks up and the people disperse, coming down and past him. Only three people are left, a man (Eman) whose back is turned, the village Priest, and the isolated one. They stand on opposite sides of the grave, the man on the mound of earth. The Priest walks round to the man's side and lays a hand on his shoulder.

Priest: Come.

Eman: I will. Give me a few moments here alone.

Priest: Be comforted.

They fall silent.

Eman: I was gone twelve years but she waited. She whom I thought had too much of the laughing child in her. Twelve years I was a pilgrim, seeking the vain shrine of secret strength. And all the time, strange knowledge, this silent strength of my child-woman.

Priest: We all saw it. It was a lesson to us; we did not know that such goodness could be found among us.

Eman: Then why? Why the wasted years if she had to perish giving birth to my child? *(They are both silent.)* I do not really know for what great meaning I searched. When I returned, I could not be certain I had found it. Until I reached my home and I found her a full-grown woman, still a child at heart. When I grew to believe it, I thought, this, after all, is what I sought. It was here all the time. And I threw away my new-gained knowledge. I buried the part of me that was formed in strange places. I made a home in my birthplace.

Priest: That was as it should be.

Eman: Any truth of that was killed in the cruelty of her brief happiness.

Priest (looks up and sees the figure standing away from them, the child in his arms. He is totally still): Your father—he is over there.

Eman: I knew he would come. Has he my son with him?

Priest: Yes.

Eman: He will let no one take the child. Go and comfort him, priest. He loved Omae like a daughter, and you all know how well she looked after him. You see how strong we really are. In his heart of hearts the old man's love really awaited a daughter. Go and comfort him. His grief is more than mine.

> *The Priest goes. The Old Man has stood well away from the burial group. His face is hard and his gaze unswerving from the grave. The Priest goes to him, pauses, but sees that he can make no dent in the man's grief. Bowed, he goes on his way.*
>
> *Eman, as carrier, walks towards the graveside, the other Eman having gone. His feet sink into the mound and he breaks slowly on to his knees, scooping up the sand in his hands and pouring it on his head. The scene blacks out slowly.*

> *Enter Jaguna and Oroge.*

Oroge: We have only a little time.

Jaguna: He will come. All the wells are guarded. There is only the stream left him. The animal must come to drink.

Oroge: You are sure it will not fail—the trap, I mean.

Jaguna: When Jaguna sets the trap, even elephants pay homage—their trunks downwards and one leg up in the sky. When the carrier steps on the fallen twigs, it is up in the sacred trees with him.

Oroge: I shall breathe again when this long night is over.

> *They go out.*
>
> *Enter Eman—as carrier—from the same direction as the last two entered. In front of him is a still figure, the Old Man as he was, carrying the dwarf boat.*

Eman (joyfully): Father.

> *The figure does not turn round.*

Eman: It is your son. Eman. *(He moves nearer.)* Don't you want to look at me? It is I, Eman. *(He moves nearer still.)*

Old Man: You are coming too close. Don't you know what I carry on my head?

Eman: But, father, I am your son.

Old Man: Then go back. We cannot give the two of us.

Eman: Tell me first where you are going.

Old Man: Do *you* ask that? Where else but to the river?

Eman (visibly relieved): I only wanted to be sure. My throat is burning. I have been looking for the stream all night.

Old Man: It is the other way.

Eman: But you said . . .

Old Man: I take the longer way, you know now I must do this. It is quicker if you take the other way. Go now.

Eman: No, I will only get lost again. I shall go with you.

Old Man: Go back, my son. Go back.

Eman: Why? Won't you even look at me?

Old Man: Listen to your father. Go back.

Eman: But father!

> *He makes to hold him. Instantly the Old Man breaks into a rapid trot. Eman hesitates, then follows, his strength nearly gone.*

Eman: Wait, father. I am coming with you . . . wait . . . wait for me, father . . .

> *There is a sound of twigs breaking, of a sudden trembling in the branches. Then silence.*
> *The front of Eman's house. The effigy is hanging from the sheaves. Enter Sunma. Still supported by Ifada, she stands transfixed as she sees the hanging figure. Ifada appears to go mad, rushes at the object, and tears it down. Sunma, her last bit of will gone, crumbles against the wall. Some distance away from them, partly hidden, stands the Girl, impassively watching. Ifada hugs the effigy to him, stands above Sunma. The Girl remains where she is, observing. Almost at once, the villagers begin to return, subdued and guilty. They walk across the front, skirting the house as widely as they can. No word is exchanged. Jaguna and Oroge eventually appear. Jaguna, who is leading, sees Sunma as soon as he comes in view. He stops at once, retreating slightly.*

Oroge (almost whispering): What is it?

Jaguna: The viper.

> *Oroge looks cautiously at the woman.*

Oroge: I don't think she will even see you.

Jaguna: Are you sure? I am in no frame of mind for another meeting with her.

Oroge: Let's go home.

Jaguna: I am sick to the heart of the cowardice I have seen tonight.

Oroge: That is the nature of men.

Jaguna: Then it is a sorry world to live in. We did it for them. It was all for their own common good. What did it benefit me whether the man lived or died? But did you see them? One and all they looked up at the man and words died in their throats.

Oroge: It was no common sight.

Jaguna: Women could not have behaved so shamefully. One by one they crept off like sick dogs. Not one could raise a curse.

Oroge: It was not only him they fled. Do you see how unattended we are?

Jaguna: There are those who will pay for this night's work!

Oroge: Ay, let us go home.

They go off. Sunma, Ifada, and the Girl remain as they are, the light fading slowly on them.

CONNECTIONS TO OTHER SELECTIONS

1. Compare and contrast Eman's role as a scapegoat with that of Oedipus in Sophocles' *Oedipus the King* (p. 1289).

2. How does the use of flashbacks provide essential information about the two protagonists in *The Strong Breed* and in Miller's *Death of a Salesman* (p. 1824)?

3. Read the discussion of mythological criticism (p. 2107) in Chapter 52, "Critical Strategies for Reading." Explain what you think a mythological critic would have to say about *The Strong Breed*.

PERSPECTIVE

JAMES GIBB

Ritual Sacrifice in **The Strong Breed** 1986

The Strong Breed is a serious play of considerable substance, it shows a moment of spiritual growth in a community and provides excellent theater. Eman brings the growth, for when faced by moral choices he rises to the occasion and sacrifices himself for his convictions. He insults the men of the village and ridicules the practice of using a vulnerable and unwilling carrier. He argues that "the spirit of a new year [will not be] fooled" by an unwilling carrier. Challenged to be "a man" himself and discovering that Jaguna has captured Ifada, he offers himself: he becomes a willing sacrifice. In this there are deliberate parallels to the self-sacrifice of Christ and of the Yoruba deity Obatala, and the drama takes on the qualities of a passion play. From the reaction of the villagers it is clear that Eman's sacrificial death has an impact on the community. The final mood indicates that a climax has been reached and passed, those who have been part of it will never be the same again. This new year provides opportunities for a new beginning in Jaguna's village.

From *Wole Soyinka*

CONSIDERATIONS FOR CRITICAL THINKING AND WRITING

1. What parallels can you find between the self-sacrifice of Eman and that of Christ?

2. Use the library to learn about the Yoruba deity Obatala. How does the story of Obatala figure in the action of *The Strong Breed*?

3. Write an essay on the impact of Eman's death on the community.

4. Do you agree with Gibb's interpretation of the ending? Are there "opportunities for a new beginning in Jaguna's village"? Explain why or why not.

51

An Album of
Contemporary Plays

Stop Kiss

Raised in Dover, Delaware, Diana Son is a playwright as well as a screen-writer and acting teacher. "My life has been shaped by teachers," she says. "I have followed the path I was encouraged to follow. They are immensely powerful people." This love of teaching informs Son's work, which often seeks to create tolerance and understanding through the trials of her largely sympathetic characters. She is also inspired by her experience grow-ing up a second-generation Korean American: "As somebody who wears their ethnic identity on their face I feel like I walk through the world from the inside. So when people show that they have some expectation of me be-cause I have slanty eyes and black hair, I always feel jarred, and I fight it," Son says.

When *Stop Kiss* premiered in 1998, the play immediately won critical acclaim. The *New York Times* called it "a sweet, sad, and enchantingly sin-cere play." Although much attention is focused around the play's inclusion of homosexual themes, Son says *Stop Kiss* is primarily "about a woman who has never had to commit to anything in her life. Because of [a] traumatic event, she has the courage she didn't know she had, and she learns to commit." *Stop Kiss* won the 1999 Gay and Lesbian Association against Defamation Media Award for Outstanding New York Production and was nominated for an Outer Circle Critics Award. Son is also the author of *Fishes, Boy,* and *R.A.W.* (*'Cause I'm a Woman*), and is a prolific screenwriter as well, having written for the hit TV show *The West Wing* and Meg Ryan's pro-duction company, Prufrock Pictures.

Research Diana Son with LitLinks at
http://www.bedfordstmartins.com/meyer/bedintrolit

Diana Son (b. 1965)

Stop Kiss

1999

THE CHARACTERS

Callie, late 20s to early 30s.
Sara, mid-20s to early 30s.
George, late 20s to early 30s.
Peter, mid-20s to early 30s.
Mrs. Winsley, late 30s to mid-40s.
Detective Cole, late 30s to mid-40s.
Nurse, late 30s to mid-40s.
(The Nurse and Mrs. Winsley can be played by the same actor.)

TIME: *Current day.*
PLACE: *New York City.*

Scene 1

> *Callie's apartment. Callie puts on a CD: The Emotions, "Best of My Love." She ceremoniously closes all the blinds in her apartment, making sure each blade is turned over. She locks the front door and puts a piece of black tape over the peep hole. As the vocals begin, Callie lip-synchs to the song with the polish of someone who has their own private karaoke often. The phone rings. Callie turns off the music like a busted teenager, and picks up the phone.*

Callie: Hi George . . . yeah I know I'm late, I forgot this person is coming to my house at —*(Callie checks her watch)* — shit! . . . Well I would bring her along but I don't even know her. She's some friend of an old friend of someone I used to be frie — she just moved to New York and I said that I'd — I can't, what if she's some big dud and we all have a miserable time . . . Exactly, you'll all blame me. Give me half an hour, tops. *(She sets the phone down. Her buzzer buzzes)* Yes?

Sara *(Offstage, tentative):* It's Sara and —

Callie: Come on up! *(Callie buzzes her in and looks at all the junk on her sofa: newspapers, several pairs of dirty socks, a box of Kleenex, mail, a couple of videotapes and a bra. She picks up the bra and heads for the bedroom.)*

> *The doorbell rings. Callie hides the bra and opens the door. Sara is holding a pet carrier.*

Callie: Hi.

Sara: You're Callie.

Callie: Yes.

Sara: I'm Sara — *(She looks at the pet carrier)* This is Caesar and I can't believe you're doing this.

Callie *(Gestures at the couch, notices it's a mess):* Please uh, sit —

Sara: Some apartment.

Callie: I was cleaning.

Sara: It's huge — and the neighborhood — *(She sits on a pile of books)*

Callie: You can't be comfortable.

Sara: Oh, I am.
Callie: Are you sure?
Sara: Very.
Callie: Just . . . let me get rid of this stuff.

> *Callie gathers an armful of junk and heads toward her bedroom. As soon as she turns her back, Sara sits up and pulls out from under her a large key ring full of sharp, pointy keys and a candlestick as she silently mouths, "Ow." She moves the objects to another part of the sofa, covers them with leftover junk making sure the keys still show and makes a space for Callie. Callie reenters.*

Callie: Coffee!
Sara: Would be great. Listen, this is so nice of you —
Callie: I was thinking about getting a cat anyway. Oh, my keys! This'll give me a chance to see if I can hack it.
Sara: That's how I feel about New York.
Callie (Sounds familiar): Oh yes.

> *Sara hops up and approaches Callie.*

Sara: How long have you been here?
Callie: Eleven years.
Sara: I've lived in St. Louis my whole life. My parents live like, half an hour away. I go there for dinner when it's not even anybody's birthday. Things there — it's been, it *is* so —
Callie: Easy?
Sara: So easy.
Callie: It's hard here.
Sara: Good — Great, I can't wait.
Callie: Yeah, you uh — what do you . . . do?
Sara: I teach. Third grade.
Callie: Well it won't be hard finding a job.
Sara: I already have one.
Callie: Where?
Sara: P.S. 32 in the Bronx.
Callie: What was the school like that you came from?
Sara: Society of Friends, a Quaker school.
Callie (She bursts into laughter): I'm not — I'm not laughing *at* you, I'm laughing . . . *around* —
Sara: It's obviously — it's *very* . . . but I can do good work there.
Callie: I'm sure you're a good teacher.
Sara: No you don't know, but I am.

> *Pause.*

Callie: Where in the Bronx?
Sara: Tremont.
Callie: Is that where . . . Taft, is it Taft?
Sara: Taft High School?
Callie: You've heard of it?
Sara: Mm-hm.
Callie: You know there was a guy who taught there, this rich, white guy —
Sara: Yes I know.

Pause.

Callie: He got killed —
Sara: By a student. I'm here on a fellowship set up in his name.
Callie: How long is the fellowship?
Sara: Two years.

Callie offers Sara a coffee mug and raises hers in a toast.

Callie: Well, congratulations —
Sara: Thank you.
Callie: Best of luck —

Sara nods.

Callie: And . . . if it gets too rough — go home.

Callie touches her mug to Sara's but Sara does not reciprocate.

Sara: What brought *you* to New York?

Callie inhales to prepare for her long and interesting answer then realizes she has none.

Callie: College.
Sara: And what keeps you?
Callie: Keeps me from what?
Sara: What do you *do*?
Callie: I . . . ruin things for everyone else.
Sara: You're Rudolph Giuliani?
Callie: I'm a traffic reporter for a twenty-four-hour news radio station.
Sara (Impressed): Helicopters!
Callie: "The inbound lane at the Holland Tunnel is closed due to a car accident. The Brooklyn-bound lane of the Williamsburg Bridge is under construction through 1999. The D train is not running due to a track fire. You can't get in. You can't get out. You can't get around. I'll be back in ten minutes to tell you that nothing has changed."
Sara: Does that get to you?
Callie (She shrugs): It's a living.
Sara (Checking out the apartment): How long have you lived in this apartment?
Callie: Five years — well, two by myself — it's a funny — not ha ha — story.
Sara: It's OK. (*I.e., you don't have to tell me*)
Callie: I moved in here with my boyfriend Tom. This was his aunt's apartment, she lived here for twenty years.
Sara: Your rent must be —
Callie: Lucky.
Sara: You are.
Callie: Well, I got the apartment, he got . . . my sister.
Sara: Oh.
Callie: They live in L.A. now. It's perfect.
Callie: Well at least, I don't mean to be crass but —
Callie: Yes no, well I . . . like the apartment.
Sara: It's as big as mine and I'm sharing it with two other people.
Callie: Are they — did you . . . move here with any of them?
Sara: No, they came with the apartment. They're a couple. It's kind of awkward but, he's sweet, she's sweet, they seem to have a —
Callie: Sweet?

Sara: — relationship they're fine.
Callie (Nods): It's awkward.
Sara: Rents are *so* — everything is —
Callie: It's impossible to live here.

    Pause. Sara studies Callie.

Sara: You love it.
Callie: You know, Sara, I've actually been to St. Louis and it's a quaint, pretty
    city but — what's the point of that? Everyone's still got their cars all geared
    up with clubs and car alarms and computerized keys. And you have to
    drive all the way across town to get to the good, cheap places to eat. And
    drive, I mean you're in a city and you have to *drive* to get around?
Sara: Where did you grow up?
Callie: Tiny town upstate.
Sara: Industrial?
Callie: Countrified suburb. Tractor display in the middle of the mall.
Sara: Pretty, though?
Callie: I can't connect with mountains, trees, the little animals — they snub
    me. You know how you can be with two other people and you're all having
    a great time. Then the person sitting next to you says something in French
    and the two of them burst into laughter — best laugh anyone's had all
    night. And you're left out because you took Spanish in the seventh grade,
    not French. That's what nature does to me. Speaks French to the other
    people at the table.

    Slight pause.

Sara: I hate jazz.
Callie: You do?
Sara: I don't usually say that out loud because then people think I don't have a
    soul or something, but I don't like the way it sounds. I don't like saxo-
    phones.
Callie: My sister played the saxophone.
Sara: I'm sorry —
Callie: I hate my sister.
Sara: The one who —
Callie: Yeah!
Sara: I hate your sister too.

    Callie gives up a surprised smile, Sara does too. They hold it just a beat longer than
    normal, then Sara looks away.

Callie: So, do your friends think you're crazy?
Sara: Pff. Forget it. And my *parents* and Peter?
Callie: Huh?
Sara: — My ex. I mean, I've never lived away from them. Even when I was in col-
    lege I came home every weekend.
Callie: Close family.
Sara: It's . . . a cult. It's embarrassing, I should've moved . . . I mean, you were
    what, eighteen?
Callie: Don't look at me. I was going to go to one of those colleges that adver-
    tise on matchbook covers. My guidance counselor filled out my applica-
    tion to NYU.

Sara: I had to interview five times to get this fellowship. By the fourth one I had a rabbit's foot, rosary beads, crystals, a tiger's tooth and a Polynesian *tiki* all in my purse — now that I got this fellowship I have every god to pay.

Callie hands Sara a Magic 8-Ball.

Sara: What should I ask it?
Callie: Something whose answer you won't take too seriously.
Sara (Addressing the ball): Was moving to New York a good idea? *(She shakes the ball then looks at it)* It's sort of in between two of them.
Callie: That means yes.

Another shared smile. Sara stands up.

Sara: I should go, I'm taking up too much of your —

Callie looks at her watch.

Callie: I told some friends I would meet them, otherwise I wish —
Sara: You should've said —
Callie: No — no —
Sara: I didn't mean to keep —
Callie: What're you doing this weekend?
Sara: I don't know. Unpacking. But then I gotta do something New Yorky, don't I?
Callie: Do you want to come over and I'll take you around the neighborhood? Show you some fun places to go to and eat —
Sara: Yes!
Callie: And you can hang out here, spend some time with . . . is it Caesar?

Sara rushes to the pet carrier.

Sara: Caesar, forgive me. He hates being in this thing.
Callie: Let him out.

Sara does.

Sara: He may be a little shy at first, in a new place with a new person —
Callie: You could come and visit him. Just let me know. I hope you'll feel —
Sara: Thanks Callie.
Callie: For nothing, for what.

SCENE 2

A hospital examination room. Callie is sitting on an exam table buttoning the top button of her shirt. Detective Cole stands in front of her.

Detective Cole: Was he coming on to you, trying to pick you up?
Callie: He was just saying stuff, guy stuff, stupid kind of —
Detective Cole: What did you do?

She folds her arms protectively across her stomach as if it is tender.

Callie: I — I wanted to leave —
Detective Cole: Your girlfriend?
Callie: My friend — Sara . . . said . . . something —
Detective Cole: What.

Callie: "Leave us alone" or something.

Detective Cole: And that's what set him off?

Callie: N — n — yeah. Well, she said — but then he said something back and she told him . . . she said something — upset him.

Detective Cole: What'd she say?

Callie: . . . She sai — I think —

Detective Cole: What.

Callie: She told him to fuck off. Then he hit her.

Detective Cole: He hit her with his fist?

Callie: He hit her in her back then he grabbed her away —

Detective Cole: Grabbed her from you?

Callie: I — I was holding onto her arm with my hand like this — *(She puts her hand on her other elbow)* I wanted us to leave. But then he grabbed her and started banging her head against the building. And then he smashed her head against his knee — like one of those wrestlers — that's when she lost consciousness — and then he smashed her again. *(She refolds her arms across her stomach)*

> *Detective Cole looks at his report.*

Detective Cole: This was at Bleeker and West 11th — that little park.

Callie: Yes.

Detective Cole: At 4:15 in the morning?

Callie: Yes.

Detective Cole: What were you doing there?

> *Callie shakes her head.*

Callie: . . . Just . . . walking around.

Detective Cole: Which bar were you at?

Callie: Excuse me?

Detective Cole: Four-fifteen, honey, that's closing time.

Callie: Well, we had been . . . we were at the White Horse Tavern.

Detective Cole: The White Horse. On Hudson Street.

Callie: Yes.

Detective Cole: Was there a good crowd there?

Callie: . . . Yeah? Pretty crowded.

Detective Cole: Did anyone at the White Horse try to pick you up, buy you or your friend a drink?

Callie: No.

Detective Cole: Did you talk to anyone?

Callie: Just to each other mostly.

Detective Cole: What did the bartender look like?

Callie: Excuse me?

Detective Cole: Bartender.

Callie: . . . It was a man.

Detective Cole: Short, stocky guy? Salt and pepper hair?

Callie: No.

Detective Cole: Kind of tall, skinny guy with a receding hair line? I know a couple of guys there.

Callie: I didn't really get a good look at him — Sara ordered the drinks. But I think he was tall.

Detective Cole: I'll go talk to him. Could be someone followed you from the bar. Maybe there was someone suspicious acting that you didn't notice. Bartender mighta seen something you didn't or talked to someone. What'd the bad guy look like?

Callie: He was tall.

Detective Cole: Like the bartender.

Callie: He was big — sort of, like he worked out.

Detective Cole: Was he black?

> *Callie shakes her head no.*

Detective Cole: Hispanic?

Callie: It was dark, I couldn't —

Detective Cole: Short hair, long hair —

Callie: Short. Wavy, dark brown.

Detective Cole: You remember what he was wearing?

Callie: He had a leather jacket . . . jeans . . . some kind of boots. He was twenty-something, maybe mid.

Detective Cole: Like a college kid? Frat boy?

Callie: No.

Detective Cole: Like a punk?

Callie: No.

Detective Cole: Like what then?

Callie: . . . I don't know.

Detective Cole: Any markings on the jacket? A name or symbol?

Callie: No.

Detective Cole: So he sees a couple of good-looking girls walking — were you drunk? —

Callie: Not at all.

Detective Cole: He gives 'em a line, one of the women tells him to fuck off and he beats her into a coma. Anything else you want to tell me?

Callie: That's — that's what I . . . remember.

Detective Cole: Doctor done with you?

Callie: I think.

Detective Cole: Alright, I need you to go somewhere with me right now and look at some pictures.

Callie: Can you bring them here?

Detective Cole: I need to take you there.

Callie: Because, my friend — if my friend —

Detective Cole: They say she's out of the woods in terms of life or —

Callie: But if she wakes up —

SCENE 3

> *Callie's apartment. Callie hangs up her jacket and Sara's. Sara sits on the junk-free couch.*

Sara: I mean that's the way I am with the kids.

Callie: Sure, with kids it's OK.

Sara: Why just them? Listen, every day when I walk by this park, this guy, he's all cracked out, says something to me, you know, something nasty and I just lower my head and walk by.

Callie: Yep.

Sara: But yesterday, one of my students, Malik, is waiting for me outside the school and says he wants to walk me to the subway. So I say "sure" thinking maybe he has a problem he wants to tell me about. So, we're walking and we pass by the park and I'm worried. Is this crack head gonna mention my vagina in front of this eight-year-old boy? Sure enough, it's "pussy this" and "booty that" and Malik says, "This is my teacher, watch your mouth." And the guy shuts up.

Callie: Still —

Sara: Freaking eight-year-old boy. I should be able to do that for myself.

Callie: The best thing to do is walk on by.

Sara: But it worked.

The phone rings. Sara looks up but Callie does not.

Callie: Next time, just walk on by.

Sara: Why, what's ever happened to you?

Callie: Nothing and that's why.

The machine clicks on.

George (Voice on machine): Hey Callie, it's George. Your light is on, I know you're there.

Callie walks toward the phone then stops.

George (Voice on machine): Jasmine and Lidia and I are at the Sinatra bar, where are you? Anyway, we'll be here for a while so come hang out. 'Bye.

The machine clicks off.

Sara: I should go.

Callie: No no, they'll be there for hours.

Sara: I've taken up your whole —

Callie: Are you hungry? We could order in something. There's Polish, Indian, Cuban, there's a pretty good Vietnamese —

Sara: Are you sure you don't — I've never had Vietnamese —

Callie: I'll show you the menu. *(She hops up and goes into the kitchen)* Something to drink? Beer?

Sara: Yes to beer.

Callie returns and hands Sara a bottle. Sara leans her head toward the phone.

Sara: Were those friends from work?

Callie: Oh no, the people at my job are a bunch of stiffs — can you imagine? They listen to the same news reports every ten minutes for eight hours a day. They repeat themselves even in regular conversations. No, George — the guy on the phone — Lidia, Jasmine . . . Rico, Sally, Ben — we were all friends in college and now we're stuck to each other. I think we're someone's science experiment, we just don't know it. A study in overdependency.

Sara: Is George your boyfriend?

Callie hands a menu to Sara.

Callie: I like the noodle dishes, they're on the back.

Sara takes the menu.

Callie: George and I . . . are friends. Who sleep together. But date other people. Sometimes for long periods of time. We've been doing this since we were . . . twenty. Although he *never* likes anyone I'm dating, he's un-abashedly—and I admit I can get jealous when he's—but at least I try to hide it, I'm pretty good at it, too. It's only *after* they've broken up that I— Anyway, we'll probably get married.

Sara gets the 8-Ball and shakes it. She looks up at Callie.

Callie: Or not.
Sara: It's stuck between two again.
Callie: Why's that keep happening to you?
Sara: Me? I think you have it rigged.

Callie takes the ball and shakes it. She looks at the answer—it's stuck between two again. Sara tries to look—

Callie: OK, OK.
Sara: All my friends are married or getting engaged, having babies or wishing they were—and lately when I hear about it, I think—why?
Callie: Why not?
Sara: Marriage. Why would you say to anyone: "I will stay with you even if I outgrow you."

Pause.

Callie (Remembering): Peter.

Sara is unresponsive, then finally nods.

Callie: Did you leave him to come here?
Sara: . . . No.
Callie: Mm . . . "C-."
Sara: In what.
Callie: Acting.

Sara looks down.

Callie: I'm sorry—
Sara: No no—
Callie: I'm prying—
Sara: No, that's not why—
Callie: I hope I didn't—
Sara: No, it's OK.
Callie: Did you decide what you wanted to order?
Sara: I moved out from our apartment—we lived together—and moved in with my parents about a month ago. I came here from there.
Callie: How—how long—
Sara: Seven years.
Callie: Seven . . . so you must still be—
Sara: Finally. Finally where I want to be. I'll stay in New York for two years and then I'm going to take off.
Callie: Let me guess: India.
Sara: "A" for effort, but no. Australia, Malaysia, Indonesia, Micronesia—
Callie: All the countries that sound like skin rashes?

Sara: Peter said, "What about Anesthesia?" Mm. Speaking — what time is it?
Callie: Almost six.
Sara: Hm.
Callie: What?
Sara: Oh, he left a message on my machine saying he was going to call at six. He wants to come visit. He manages a restaurant in St. Louis so he wants to come and check out some of the special places here.
Callie: You'd better hurry.
Sara: I couldn't make it in fifteen minutes.
Callie: You could if you took a cab.

   Slight pause.

Sara: But then I wouldn't have Vietnamese food.
Callie: We could do it another time.
Sara: I just started this beer.

   Pause.

Callie: You wouldn't want to waste a beer.
Sara: That's what I was thinking.
Callie: Cheers.

   They tap glasses. There is a sudden loud and rhythmic clomping on the ceiling. Callie does not respond.

Callie: I always get this. It's not too spicy.
Sara: What is that?
Callie: Crispy squid in a little salt and —
Sara: No, what is *that*?
Callie: Huh? Oh. Every Thursday and Saturday at six.
Sara: What.
Callie: I think he teaches horses how to Riverdance.
Sara: Have you complained?
Callie: It happens at exactly the same time twice a week for an hour. I just make sure I'm out or doing something loud.
Sara: Let's go up there.
Callie: No, no —
Sara: Why not?
Callie: We gotta stay here and wait for the food.
Sara: We haven't ordered yet.
Callie (About the food): Yeah, so what do you want?
Sara: Chicken.
Callie: What kind of chicken?
Sara: You're chicken.
Callie: No I'm not, I'm smart.
Sara: Alright, I'll go.
Callie: Sara. Come on, don't. Please.

   Slight pause.

Sara: OK.
Callie: I'm gonna order. What do you want?
Sara: Come on, let's go!

SCENE 4

Police station. Mrs. Winsley sits behind a table that Detective Cole is sitting on. She's wearing a sharply tailored business suit.

Mrs. Winsley: He called them, "pussy-eating dykes."

Detective Cole: Come on, why would he call them that?

Mrs. Winsley: Two women in a West Village park at four in the morning? What's the chance they're *not* dykes?

Detective Cole: You tell me. You live in the West Village.

Mrs. Winsley: My husband and I have lived there for eight years.

Detective Cole: Like the neighborhood?

Mrs. Winsley: I sure do.

Detective Cole: Lot of clubs and bars there.

Mrs. Winsley: They even have ones for straight people.

Detective Cole: Is that why you live there?

Mrs. Winsley: My husband and I have a beautiful apartment, Detective Cole. In a safe building on an otherwise quiet street. The fact that it's Graceland for gay people doesn't matter to me.

Detective Cole: So, what were these girls doing?

Mrs. Winsley: I didn't see —

Detective Cole: Were they making out, rubbing up against each other? —

Mrs. Winsley: I didn't see anything till I heard the other one screaming. I went to the window then I called 911.

Detective Cole: What'd you see then?

Mrs. Winsley: He was beating on the both of them. I yelled down that I called the cops and I threw a couple flower pots at him. My spider plants —

Detective Cole: So the screams woke you up?

Mrs. Winsley: I was in bed but up. Reading.

Detective Cole: Four-thirty in the morning?

Mrs. Winsley: I'm a fitful sleeper.

Detective Cole: You ever take anything?

Mrs. Winsley: No.

Detective Cole: So, you weren't groggy or half asleep?

Mrs. Winsley: No.

Detective Cole: And you're sure you heard him call them dykes.

Mrs. Winsley: I'm sure.

Detective Cole: And your husband?

No response.

Detective Cole: Your husband.

Mrs. Winsley: He missed all the excitement.

Detective Cole: What'd he — sleep right through it?

Mrs. Winsley avoids his eyes.

Detective Cole: Oh . . . he wasn't home. Four-thirty in the — is he a doctor?

Mrs. Winsley: No.

Detective Cole: . . . Investment banker?

Mrs. Winsley: Ha!

Detective Cole: Fire chief?

Mrs. Winsley: He's a book editor, Detective Cole.

Detective Cole: I didn't know book editors worked so late.
Mrs. Winsley: They don't.
Detective Cole: Was he . . . out having drinks with some buddies?
Mrs. Winsley: He was obviously out, wasn't he.
Detective Cole: So, you were waiting up for him.
Mrs. Winsley: I'm a fitful sleeper, Detective. Have been since before I married
  him and those two girls are lucky that I am and that I was up and that I
  did something.
Detective Cole: You called 911.
Mrs. Winsley: And my flower pots.
Detective Cole: Did you hit him?
Mrs. Winsley: They fell near him. He stopped and took off.
Detective Cole: You stopped him.
Mrs. Winsley: Well, it wasn't the cops, took thirty minutes for someone to show
  up. You'd think it was Harlem, not the West Village.

Scene 5

*Callie's apartment. Callie walks on stage wearing jeans and carrying a fresh bou-
quet of flowers. She places the flowers in a vase. She goes into her bedroom and
reenters with several hangers with clothes on them. She looks at herself in the mirror
as she holds up a tube top in front of her—too slutty—she drops the top onto the
floor. She picks up a shirt and holds it up in front of her—too butch—she drops it
onto the floor. She tries on a short skirt which she can't get past her hips—she throws
it onto the floor—she puts her jeans back on. She puts on a third top—it looks like
something Sara would wear. The front door buzzer buzzes. Callie buzzes without
asking who it is. She fusses over the flowers and accidentally knocks the whole vase
over. She gets the disobedient skirt and uses it to wipe up the mess. There is a knock
on the door. Before Callie can get up, George walks in and stops in the puddle.*

George: Hey Cal, when did they paint the—whoops!

Callie is stunned to see George but plays it off like it's about the puddle.

Callie: George!

George looks down.

George: Did you get a puppy?
Callie: Yeah, right.

Callie stands up.

George: So you're alright, huh?
Callie: Yeah, what?
George: No, I haven't heard from you in a while.
Callie: I'm fine, I'm fine . . . busy.

Callie goes to the kitchen to throw away the skirt.

George: Lidia said she called you about that book you were looking for, you
  didn't call her back.
Callie: . . . I forgot.
George: She got that job, you know.
Callie: No, I didn't!

George stretches himself out on the couch, stacking a pile of pillows behind his head.

George: Yeah, she's really excited.

Callie looks disapprovingly at his move.

George: We're gonna take her out on Friday night so try not to be "fine but busy" that night, OK? *(He grabs the remote and clicks on the TV)*

Callie: I'll remember. Um, George —

He looks at his watch.

George: I know, I know, we can watch your show I just want to check to see what the score is.

Callie: I have plans for tonight.

George: Oh yeah, what?

Callie: I'm meeting someone for dinner.

George turns off the TV and sits up.

George: You have a date?

Callie: No!

George: With *who*?

Callie: It's not a date, I'm just meeting my friend Sara for dinner.

George: Who the hell is Sara?

Callie: I told you, that friend of a friend of a — *(Refreshing his memory)* She's new in town, I'm taking care of her cat —

George: I thought you said she was a big loser.

Callie: I said I didn't know, but now I do — she's not.

George: So what is she?

Callie: What.

George: What's she do?

Callie: She teaches up in the Bronx.

George: Oh, so she's a nut.

Callie: There's something wrong with us.

George: Why?

Callie: Because that's what I thought when she told me.

George: You have to wonder about people who want to do stuff like that. What does she want to do — save a life? Give a kid a chance? Or just feel good about trying.

Callie: She won a fellowship. She *competed* to get this job.

George: To teach in the Bronx? What'd the losers get?

The front door buzzer buzzes. Callie buzzes back.

George: You don't ask who it is anymore?

Callie: It's her.

George: You thought it was her when you buzzed me in.

Callie: You're right, that was a mistake.

Sara knocks at the door. Callie holds George's jacket open for him.

Callie: OK. Please leave now.

George: Why?

Callie: Because I gotta go.

He stands up.

George: I'll walk out with you.
Callie: But I'm not leaving yet.
George: Huh?

> *Callie growls at George then unlocks the door. Sara walks in.*

Callie: Hey.
Sara: Hi, here, these are —

> *Sara shyly hands Callie a small bouquet of baby roses. Callie takes them.*

Callie: Thank you. They're so —
Sara: They're — babies.

> *Callie goes to kiss Sara on the cheek but retreats. Sara takes the cue late and now her head is sticking out. Callie tries to respond but Sara has already reeled in like a turtle. Callie turns away, takes the other flowers out of the vase and puts the roses in.*

Callie: I was just going to throw these out. *(She crosses to the kitchen)*
Sara: Hey, did you see they're filming a movie or something on the next block? Do you think we could stop on our way to the restaurant and watch for a while?
George: It's *NYPD Bl* —

> *Sara starts. She had not noticed him.*

George: Oop — didn't mean to scare you.
Sara: No, no, you didn't.

> *He crosses to her and extends his hand.*

George: I'm George.

> *Sara shakes his hand.*

Sara: Oh, George, I heard so much about you!
George (Can't say the same thing): . . . Nice to meet you.
Callie (She comes out of the kitchen): Oh, sorry. Sara, this is George. George, this is —
George: We did this.
Callie: Good. *(To Sara)* We should go.
George: Where're you guys having dinner?
Callie (Tries to slip it past him): Vong.
George (He looks at Callie): Dressed like that?
Callie: I didn't have time —
Sara (Consoling): You look great.
George: Well, tell me what you get.
Sara: Have you ever been?
George: Out of my league.
Sara (To Callie): Is it expensive? I don't want you to —
Callie: It's not expensive.
George (To Callie): You're treating? Then I wanna —
Callie (To George): You still owe me for my birthday.
Sara: Let's go dutch, Callie.
Callie: It's *my* treat.
George: What's the occasion?

Silence. There is none.

Sara: Actually, we're celebrating the fact that today LaChandra, one of my students, wrote her name for the very first time.

Callie (*She looks down at her clothes*): I'm changing. (*She runs off*)

George: That's right, you're a teacher.

Sara: Mm-hm.

George: Kindergarten?

Sara: Third grade.

George: And this kid wrote her name for the first time?

Sara: Perfectly.

George: Isn't that —

Sara: Wonderful?

George: . . . Yeah, isn't it?

Callie reenters wearing the blouse she started off wearing.

Callie (*To Sara*): We should go, our reservation's at eight.

Sara: Do we have time to stop by? The *NYPD* —

Callie: Sure.

Sara starts for the door.

George: OK, well um, 'bye. Nice to meet you.

Sara: Don't you want to come with us and watch them filming?

George flashes Callie a furtive look.

George: Mm, I think I'll wait until it's on TV.

He looks at Callie, she ushers him out the door.

Callie: Meanie.

George: Never take *me* to Vong.

Callie closes the door and locks it.

SCENE 6

Police station. Callie sits in an interview room. Detective Cole enters.

Detective Cole: Hey, thanks for coming in. You want some coffee?

Callie: Thank you, I'm fine.

He flips through his report.

Detective Cole: We were talking about the White Horse Tavern last time, right? On Hudson Street?

Callie: Yes.

Detective Cole: That's a famous bar, you know? Has a long literary tradition. They say Dylan Thomas died waiting for a drink there.

Callie: . . . I hadn't heard.

Detective Cole: I talked to the bartender there. I told you I wanted to ask him if he noticed anyone suspicious there that night. Maybe someone paying attention to you and your friend that you didn't notice.

Callie: Yes, you said.

Detective Cole: I went in and talked to Stacy, she said she don't remember you and your friend coming in.

Callie: It was pretty crowded.

    Slight pause.

Detective Cole: Do you remember telling me that the bartender at the White Horse Tavern that night was a tall *guy*?

Callie: Sara ordered the drinks.

Detective Cole: So, you didn't get a good look at the bartender.

Callie: I didn't.

Detective Cole: Not even enough to tell if it was a girl or a guy.

Callie: I'm sorry.

Detective Cole: So after you leave the White Horse, you and your friend go for a walk. You end up in that park area outside the playground. And you're . . . doing what?

Callie: We were sitting on one of the benches, talking to each other . . . when this guy says something.

Detective Cole: What'd he say?

Callie: Something like, "Hey, you want to party—"

Detective Cole: What did you say?

Callie: I didn't.

Detective Cole: Sara said something.

Callie: Yes.

Detective Cole: So she provoked him.

Callie: What!?

Detective Cole: She told him to fuck off and that's when he hit her, right?

Callie: No.

Detective Cole: I mean, if the two of you had ignored him or walked away, this wouldn't have happened, would it?

Callie: If *he* hadn't started—

Detective Cole: But Sara had to say something and that's what got him pissed, that's why he wanted to hit her. Why did she say something?

Callie: He started it, he—

Detective Cole: Alright. *He* must have said something first—something that upset her. What upset her so much?

Callie: He was bothering—

Detective Cole: What did he say? She said, "Leave us alone," and then he said what?

    Callie does not respond.

Detective Cole: Did he call her something?

Callie: What?

Detective Cole: Did he call her something. Like a name?

Callie: No.

Detective Cole: What's a name that might upset her?

Callie: I don't know.

Detective Cole: How about "bitch"?

Callie: No.

Detective Cole: He didn't call her a bitch?

Callie: I don't—

Detective Cole: "A pussy-eating bitch"?

   Callie looks at Detective Cole.

Callie: No.
Detective Cole: What'd he say, then? —
Callie: He shouldn't've —
Detective Cole: What'd he call her?
Callie: He called —
Detective Cole: What?
Callie: A fucking —
Detective Cole: Say it!
Callie: "Fucking dykes! Pussy-eating dykes" — both of us.
Detective Cole: Why would he say that, why would he call you that? Two nice
   girls sitting on a park bench talking, why would he call you dykes?

   Pause.

Callie: Because we were kissing.

   Detective Cole gestures — there it is.

Callie: It was the first — We didn't know he was there. Until he said something:
   "Hey, save some of that for me." Sara told him to leave us alone. I couldn't
   believe she — then he offered to pay us. He said he'd give us fifty bucks if
   we went to a motel with him and let him watch. He said we could dry
   hump or whatever we like to do — turns him on just to see it. I grabbed her
   arm and started walking away. He came after us, called us "fucking
   dykes — pussy-eating dykes." Sara told him to fuck off. I couldn't believe —
   He came up and punched her in the back, then grabbed her and pulled her
   away. I yelled for someone to call the police. He pushed her against the
   building and started banging her head against the building. He told her to
   watch her cunt-licking mouth. But he had his hand over her jaw, she
   couldn't — she just made these mangled — she was trying to breathe. I
   came up behind him and grabbed his hair — he turned around and
   punched me in the stomach. I threw up, it got on him. Sara tried to get
   away but he grabbed her and started banging her head against his knee. I
   tried to hold his arms back but he was stronger — he knocked her out. He
   pushed me to the ground and started kicking me. Someone yelled something — "Cops are coming" — and he took off in the opposite direction.
   West. He was limping. He hurt his knee. *(She looks at Detective Cole)* That's
   what happened.

Scene 7

   *Callie's apartment. Sara is sprawled out on the couch holding several giant playing
   cards in her hand. She places a card on the discard pile and drains a glass of wine.
   Callie brings a bottle of red wine from the kitchen, an empty one stands on the
   table.*

Sara: OK. If you're in someone else's bathroom and they have the toilet paper
   coming out from the bottom instead of the top —
Callie: I hate that!
Sara: Do you change it or leave it the way it is.

Callie: What do you mean change it? You'd change somebody else's toilet roll?
Sara: If I was gonna use it a couple times.
Callie: Pfff.
Sara: Alright, you go next.
Callie: So, if you were driving down a highway and saw a pothole in the road ahead what would you do, straddle or swerve?
Sara: Mm, straddle. You?
Callie: Straddle.
Sara (About Callie): Swerve.
Callie: Nah-ah.
Sara: Yes you would.
Callie (A second scenario): Cat in the road.
Sara: Caesar! — say a rabbit.
Callie: OK, a rabbit. Straddle, swerve or brake?
Sara (This is clearly not an option): Straddle a rabbit.
Callie: Sport utility vehicle — four wheel drive, you could. *(She sits down, picks up her cards and discards)*
Sara: Screech to a brake, check the rabbit, then — smoke. You?
Callie: Brake.
Sara: Swerve.
Callie: Why do you keep saying that?
Sara: This is you — *(She grips her hands around an imaginary steering wheel. She fills her eyes with panic, turns the wheel a hard right then a fast left.)*

    Callie puts down her cards.

Callie: These cards are driving me nuts.
Sara: One more hand, please.

    Callie picks up the cards again.

Callie: Can I ask you something about your job?
Sara: Yep.
Callie: Why did you want it?
Sara: You mean this fellowship?
Callie: Public school, the Bronx — teaching.
Sara: Instead of private school, St. Louis — teaching?
Callie: That's what you're used to, right?
Sara: It's where I *worked* for five years, I never got used to it. I mean, I never went to private school. We all went to the cruddy public school — I mean, it was cruddy compared to the private school, it's the Sorbonne compared to where I teach now. But, in a private school . . . I mean, what am I giving them? They have more than everything.
Callie: And the Bronx?
Sara: These kids — you know who I was when I was their age? I was the kid who had the right answer, knew I had the right answer but would never raise my hand. Hoping the teacher would call on me anyway. Those are my favorite kids to teach. And here? Now? I got a classroom full of them.

    Callie looks at the discard pile.

Callie: Did you pick up a card? You have to pick up a card.

    Sara does.

Sara: You should come and meet them one day.

Callie: Yeah, OK.

Sara: I'll bet you've never even been to the Bronx.

Callie: I go every day.

Sara: Fly over.

Callie: That's more than most New Yorkers.

Sara: Can I ask you about your job?

Callie (Filled with dread): Go ahead.

Sara: Why the traffic?

Callie: Why the traffic indeed.

Sara: I mean, as opposed to news reporting or other kinds of journalism.

Callie: I'm not a journalist. I never worked in radio or TV before I got that job.

Sara: So how'd you get it?

Callie: My boyfriend Tom's uncle worked at the station.

Sara: Oh.

Callie: I mean, it's the traffic it's not even — *the weather.* You just ride around in a helicopter and tell people what the cars are doing.

Sara: The helicopter part is pretty great, right?

Callie: Yeah, how great?

Sara: Well, if you don't like it you should get another job.

Callie: I can't.

> *Sara imitates Callie swerving in her imaginary car again.*

Callie: I don't get that.

Sara: What time is it?

> *Callie looks at her watch.*

Callie: Two-thirty.

Sara: Already? Is the subway OK this time of night?

Callie: You should take a cab.

Sara: How much will that be?

Callie: About ten bucks?

Sara: I'll take the train.

Callie: I'll give you the money —

Sara: I have it, it's just too much. It's only four or five stops on the train.

> *Callie sits up a little.*

Callie: Listen you can . . . you know, you're welcome to stay . . . this pulls out to be a sofa bed . . . you can take a train in the morning, when it's safe. I'm not getting up for anything in particular.

Sara: Maybe Caesar will come sleep with me.

Callie: Yes! You can reconcile with your cat!

Sara: He's holding such a grudge. He never comes out when I'm here.

Callie: It took a few days before he started to sleep with me.

Sara: Lucky.

> *Slight pause.*

Callie: I'm sure he'll sleep with you tonight.

Sara: Yeah.

Callie: Here, let me just get these —

She pulls off the cushions. Sara helps. Together they pull out the bed.

Callie: I think it's comfortable, I haven't slept on it myself—because I live here, but if it's not comfortable enough then I'll switch beds with you. In fact, should we just do that? You sleep in my room and I'll sleep out here?

Sara: No, no, this'll be fine.

Callie: I think it's comfortable.

Callie bounces on it once then gets up.

Callie: Is there anything else you need?

Sara: I think I'm all set.

Callie: Alright. Sleep tight.

Sara: Good night.

They stand there. Finally, Callie smiles and walks off into her room. Sara takes off her shirt just as Callie reenters with a T-shirt.

Callie: Do you need a T—whoop.

Callie looks away.

Sara: Oh—I have one. (*She pulls one out of her bag*) We did face painting today so I—

Callie: I'm sorry.

Callie leaves. Sara puts on the shirt.

Sara: It's OK.

Callie (*Offstage*): Good night.

Sara: Sweet dreams. (*She gets in bed and shuts out the light. She lies there a minute*) Psss psss psss psss psss. (*She lifts her head up and looks for Caesar*) Caeeeesar. (*No sign of him. Sara lays there another minute*) Come on you grudge holder. Pssss psss psss. (*Nothing. Finally, to Callie in the other room*) Is he in there with you?

Callie: Uh-uh. He's not out there with you?

Sara: No.

Callie appears in her doorway.

Callie: Is he under your bed?

Sara leans over and looks.

Sara: No.

Callie shrugs at Sara.

Sara: Will you do me a favor? For just like, a minute?

Callie: Sure.

Sara: Would you just lay in bed here for just a minute to see if he comes?

Callie: OK.

Sara: Since he's been sleeping with you.

Callie gets in next to Sara and pulls up the covers.

Callie: I guess we have to convince him we're sleeping.

Sara: Oh, right.

They lie down.

Callie: This bed is comfortable.
Sara: Isn't it?
Callie: I never laid on it before.
Sara: It's comfortable.
Callie: I got it secondhand.
Sara: Really?
Callie: A hundred and fifty bucks.
Sara: That's cheap.
Callie: It's comfortable.

> *Pause.*

Sara: Are your feet hot?
Callie: What?
Sara: My feet get hot when I sleep.
Callie: Even in winter?
Sara: Yeah.
Callie: Take them out.
Sara: I usually move the sheet so that it goes the other way, you know, the short way —
Callie: OK.

> *Sara gets up and turns the sheet around so that both pairs of feet are exposed. She lies back down. Pause.*

Sara: Do you see him?
Callie: Who?
Sara: Caesar.
Callie: Not yet.

> *They both lie there staring at the ceiling. After a while —*

Callie: Huh? *(Pause)* Are you asleep? *(No response. Callie turns and looks at Sara)* You're not asleep already, are you?

> *No response. Callie draws her feet under the covers and turns her back to Sara. Sara opens her eyes.*

SCENE 8

> *Callie's apartment. There is loud banging on her door. Callie enters from her bedroom wearing pajamas. She looks through the peephole.*

Callie: Alright George, I hear you!

> *She unlocks the door and opens it. George bursts in wearing his bartender uniform.*

George: How long have you been home?
Callie: Lower your voice.
George: Why didn't you answer your phone?
Callie: I don't know.
George: You wanna know how fucked-up and worried about you everyone is right now?
Callie: No.
George: You wanna know how I heard?
Callie: No.

George: You wanna know exactly what drink I was making at the moment I heard your name on the goddamn TV?

Callie: No, I don't.

George: Dirty martini. TV's on in the background. I hear about this gay bashing, two women attacked and I sort of pay attention, not really. I'm making this drink and thinking about how I gotta run downstairs and get some more peanuts. And then I feel my ears close and my face gets all hot, like I just swallowed a mouthful of hot peppers. So I turn to the TV but now they're talking about some apartment fire. So, I switch the channel and they're just starting the story. Gay bashing. Woman in a coma. Callie Pax.

Callie: I'm not in a coma.

George: What?

Callie: Sara's in a coma.

George: How do I know that?

Callie: What was I —

George: How do I know anything but what I see on the goddamn —

Callie: What did you want — me to call you from the hospital?

George: Yes!

Callie: What would I say? On a pay phone. In the hospital. Sara lying in a room swollen and blue, face cracked open, knocked out, not responding to anything but the barest reflex — all because . . . because —

George: Come and get me. That's what you could've said.

Pause.

George: Are you hurt?

Callie does not respond.

George: Did a doctor look at you?

Callie: Sara's hurt.

George: Nothing happened to you?

Callie does not respond. He walks toward her, she walks away.

George: Callie —

Callie: Bruises.

George: Where.

Callie: Cracked rib.

George: Let me see.

Callie: It's nothing.

George: Let me see.

Callie: There's nothing to see.

Pause.

George: Do you want me to call anyone?

Callie: No.

Slight pause.

George: Do you want me to spend the night?

Callie: No.

George: Do you want me to go?

Slight pause.

Callie: No.

   Pause.

Callie: George, do you remember the first time we kissed?
George (Thinks about it): No.
Callie: Me neither.

   Pause.

Callie: You know, I would stand here at the door with Sara and say, "Good
   night," "Take care," "See ya tomorrow," "Get home safe . . ." — When what
   I *really* wanted to do was plant her a big, fat, wet one. Square on the lips.
   Nothing confusing about it. She wouldn't have to think, Maybe Callie
   meant to kiss me on the cheek and . . . missed. You know, just right there.
   Not between friends. Not a friendly kiss, at all. Bigger. So she'd know.
   She'd know for sure. That I was answering her. Sara is always asking me,
   "What do you *want*, Callie?" And finally, I let her know. I answered.

SCENE 9

   *Callie's apartment. Callie walks in from the kitchen carrying a roasting pan in two
   mittened hands. She pulls the top off and rears her head back as the smell assaults
   her. She reaches in and pulls out a drumstick, it's fossilized. She bonks it on the
   table, it sounds like a baseball bat. There's a knock on the door — Callie starts. She
   looks out the peephole and sees Sara. She hurries to hide the roasting pan and all
   signs of cooking. She opens the door and Sara steps in.*

Sara: The kids talked about you the rest of the day, you were hilarious.
Callie (Shady): How'd you get in?
Sara: Huh? Oh, there was this woman with a baby carriage. I held the door for
   her then squeezed in behind her. It smells like something in here.
Callie: Like what?
Sara: Like someone vomited in sawdust. Oh — I brought you this — *(She hands
   her a bottle of wine)* For coming in and talking to the kids.

   Callie silently takes it and sets it down.

Callie: It's a little early for me.
Sara: It's . . . almost six.
Callie: Go ahead, you have some.
Sara: Don't open it for me.
Callie: OK.
Sara (Trying to figure her out): So, what'd you do the rest of the day?
Callie: Nothing.
Sara: Nothing?
Callie: Nothing.
Sara: You know Michelle, the girl who had the sweater with the puppet on it
   today? She used to say, "Nothing" just like that. Until I squeezed an
   answer out of her.
Callie: Those kids adore you.
Sara: Do you think?
Callie: You have a knack for them.

Sara (As if this is the first time she's heard it): Thank you.
Callie: It was humiliating for me.
Sara: Why?
Callie: Standing up there talking about my idiotic job.
Sara: You ride in a helicopter, Callie, what could be cooler than that?
Callie: Have you noticed? The only thing you ever praise about my job is that I ride in a helicopter?

> *Pause.*

Callie: But that doesn't even matter. Standing up in front of those kids today telling them about what I do I thought—why should these kids care about traffic, their families don't have cars. *I* don't have a car. No one I care about has a car. Who am I helping?
Sara (Gently): People with cars.
Callie: Who are they? Why do they live in New York City? Why have a car when you hear every ten minutes on the radio that the traffic is so bad?
Sara: Maybe you should look for another job.
Callie: Whose uncle's gonna get it for me this time?
Sara: You could get a job based on your experience.
Callie: As a traffic reporter?
Sara: What do you want to do instead?
Callie: I don't know.
Sara: Alright. Come on, we can think about this. What do you like?
Callie: I don't want to do this.
Sara: You know a lot about food . . . you have great taste in restaurants—
Callie: I don't—I really don't want to do this.
Sara: You should become a chef!

> *The noise from upstairs starts again. Callie goes for her coat.*

Callie: Let's get the hell out of here.
Sara: You could go to cooking school—
Callie: Let's see what's playing at the three-dollar movie theatre.
Sara: You obviously have some kind of talent for food—
Callie: Come on, put your coat on, let's go.
Sara: God, what *is* that smell?
Callie: I think someone downstairs was trying to cook something.
Sara: Ugh, you think that smell is related to food?

> *Callie opens the door for Sara.*

Callie: Barely.

> *They exit.*

SCENE 10

> *Sara's hospital room. Callie walks in and stands at the foot of Sara's bed. What can she do? She thinks for a moment. She remembers. She untucks the sheet and rolls it back so that Sara's feet are exposed. She tucks the sides of the sheet in so that it'll stay that way.*

SCENE II

> *Callie's apartment. Callie, dressed up, is waiting impatiently for Sara. She refuses to sit—she paces across the apartment, picking up things, scowling at them then putting them down. Finally, there's a buzz. She buzzes back and puts on her coat. Sara knocks and Callie opens the door—Sara is holding a wet newspaper over her head.*

Sara: Wow, it's really starting to come down now.

Callie: That means it's gonna be hard to get a cab.

> *Sara looks at her watch.*

Sara: We still have time.

Callie: Not really.

Sara: We can be a little late, can't we?

Callie: Sara, I asked you to be here by 5:30.

Sara: I know, I'm sorry, I lost track of time. *(She takes off her coat)* Let me just stand next to the radiator for a second.

Callie: Is that what you're wearing?

Sara: . . . Yeah. *(She looks at her clothes)* What?

Callie: Nothing.

Sara: I mean, is this a dress up event?

> *Callie shrugs.*

Sara: What are you wearing?

Callie: Just . . . clothes.

Sara: Let me see.

Callie: It's just . . . what I wore to my hippie friend's wedding.

Sara: Let me see?

> *Callie opens her coat a little bit.*

Sara: Oh, you look great.

> *Callie shuts her coat.*

Sara: I'm underdressed.

Callie: We don't have time to stop by your place.

Sara: Can I borrow something of yours?

Callie: Let's just forget it, I don't want to go.

> *Callie sits with her coat on.*

Sara: I thought you had to.

Callie: Technically.

Sara: Isn't your station getting an award?

Callie: They are, I'm not.

Sara: So, do you want to go or not?

Callie: I have to.

Sara: OK, let's go.

> *Sara makes for the door. Callie remains seated.*

Sara: What's going on.

Callie: Nothing.

> *Pause.*

Sara: Why are you still sitting down?

    Callie shrugs.

Sara: Let me see what you've got in your closet.

    Sara goes to her bedroom and comes back holding a dress on a hanger.

Sara: Could I wear this?

Callie: I wore that to a reception last week.

Sara: You did, I didn't.

Callie: People will recognize it.

Sara: Do you care?

    Callie shrugs.

Sara: Callie, what the hell.

Callie: I don't know.

Sara: OK. Just tell me. What do you want?

Callie: I have to go to this thing.

Sara: Do you not want me to go? Is that it?

Callie: You don't have to go if you don't want to.

Sara: Callie, will you say what you want?

Callie: I have to go, I have to.

Sara: So, let's go.

Callie: What are you going to wear?

Sara: What?

    Callie gets up.

Callie: I have to go to this thing and I want you to go with me but I don't want you to wear what you're wearing and I don't want you to wear my clothes. What will people think if we walk in together and you're wearing my clothes?

    Sara sits down.

Sara: I'm not going.

Callie: Now this.

Sara: I'm tired, I'm underdressed, I'm not going to know anyone there except for you — forget it.

Callie: Sara, I asked you to go to this thing with me a week ago, I told you it was an awards ceremony, why did you dress like you were going camping?

Sara: You didn't make it sound like it was that big a deal.

Callie: An *awards ceremony*?

Sara: If you had wanted me to get dressed up you should've told me.

Callie: I told you to be here at 5:30, you couldn't manage that.

Sara: What's the big deal — you don't even like your job.

Callie: I don't like my job the way you love your job but that doesn't mean you shouldn't come at the time I asked you to, wearing something appropriate.

Sara: Obviously this is more important than you —

    The clomping from upstairs starts again.

Callie: There's my cue. I'm leaving now, I don't care what you do.

Sara: Yeah go, get chased out of your own apartment again.

Callie: What?

Sara: Better to plan your life around someone else's schedule than have to face them and tell them what you have every right —
Callie: What do you care? What do you care? This is my apartment —
Sara: You're pathetic, Callie —

Callie takes off her coat.

Callie: Fuck it, I'll stay right here then.
Sara: Perfect.
Callie: *You* can leave.
Sara: Glad to.
Callie: I'm busy tomorrow so forget about the museum.
Sara: Yeah, I'm busy too.

Callie opens the door for Sara. Sara grabs her coat and exits. Callie slams the door behind her.

SCENE 12

Hospital waiting room. Callie walks in, Peter is already sitting. She recognizes him. Callie sits one seat away from him. Peter continues to look straight ahead. Finally —

Callie: Her parents?
Peter: Anita and Joe are in there now, yeah.

Silence.

Callie: They're strict about that — the hospital. Two at a time.
Peter: Noah's ark.
Callie: Excuse me?
Peter: Two at a — *(He shakes his head at himself)* — stupid.

More silence.

Callie: Did you — was your flight OK?
Peter: There were like, six peanuts in the whole — *(He covers his eyes)* Flight was fine, fine. Thank you.
Callie: Her parents, are they — how are they?
Peter: Anita is . . . wrecked. *And* Joe — they're . . . I mean, Sara's their only daughter —
Callie: I know.
Peter: They never wanted her to come here —
Callie: I know.
Peter: The doctor said she can't be moved until she regains consciousness.
Callie: They want to move her?
Peter: Mm-hm.
Callie: Back to St. Louis?
Peter: To Chesterfield, where Anita and Joe live. It's about twenty minutes outside.

Pause.

Callie: But what — what if she doesn't want to go?
Peter: Why wouldn't she?
Callie: Because the fellowship, she wanted — she worked so hard to get and the kids —

Peter: Her old school would take her back in a heartbeat.
Callie: Her old school, but she —
Peter: But — I mean we have no idea when she'll be able to go back to work — or *if*. The doctors can't say. There could be permanent . . . she'll need rehabil-itation, maybe home care —
Callie: I know.
Peter: She needs her family. And they need to take care of her.

    Silence.

Peter: . . . There was a response.
Callie: Excuse me?
Peter: The doctor. He said Sara responded to — he told her to squeeze his hand and she . . . squeezed.
Callie: She did?
Peter: Yeah.
Callie: She did!
Peter: Fucking A.
Callie: Amazing!
Peter: I thought you'd want to know.

    Callie looks him in the eye.

Callie: Thank you. *(Pause)* Sara . . . Sara told me . . . nice things . . . about you — so many . . .

    Pause.

Peter: She didn't tell me about you.

    Callie looks down.

Peter: She said you were a friend.

    Pause.

Callie: I am her friend.

    Pause.

Peter: And that you knew good restaurants to go to — *(He looks at Callie)* That's all Sara told me about you.
Callie: I see.
Peter: Sara and I —
Callie: She told me.

    Pause.

Peter: We lived together for —
Callie: Yes.

    Pause.

Peter: I still —
Callie: Yes.

    Pause.

Peter: I'd like — I'd like you to tell me what happened that night.

    Silence. Peter waits long enough to figure out Callie's not going to answer.

Peter: Please.

> *Slight pause.*

Callie: I'm sorry.

Peter: What.

Callie: I can't.

Peter: Why can't you?

Callie: Everything you need to know has been in the papers, on the TV—

Peter: I've seen the newspapers and the TV.

Callie: Then you know every—

Peter: No, I don't know everything. I know what *time* it happened, I know *where* and I know that you were there. And now you're here and *Sara* is in there. That's the part I want to know about. Why is *she* in there.

Callie: I wish it was me but it isn't.

Peter: Why isn't it?

> *Callie doesn't respond.*

Peter: Were *you* hurt?

Callie: You don't know what fucking happened.

Peter: Tell me!

> *Callie doesn't answer.*

Peter: Why couldn't you protect her?

Callie: He was big, he was stronger—I tried—

Peter: How big?

Callie: I *tried*.

Peter: Bigger than me?

> *Callie turns away from him.*

Peter: Could I have—

> *He turns her back.*

Peter: Hey, was he bigger than me?

Callie: No!

> *Peter steps back.*

Peter: Why was she protecting you?

> *Callie holds on his eyes but does not answer.*

Scene 13

> *Callie's apartment. The phone rings. Her machine picks up. Callie runs in from the bedroom and picks it up.*

Callie: Hello?

> *Dial tone sounds over the speaker. She hangs up. She hovers over the phone for a moment. She jerks the receiver up to her ear, dials three numbers then abruptly hangs up. She stares at the phone. She picks up the phone, dials seven numbers then hangs up. She picks up the phone and places it on the floor in front of the sofa.*

Callie: Caesar, please? Come on, you've known her longer than I have. I'll dial her number for you. Tell her I—tell her I thought about—just tell her to come over.

Caesar doesn't come out.

Callie: If you were a dog you'd do it. *(Callie picks up the phone and dials seven numbers quickly)* Hi George, it's me — what. Did you just call here — why not. Yeah, Vong was great. I got the sea bass with cardamom, Sara got the grilled lamb chops with lemon grass — yeah she eats meat, why wouldn't she? So what? — Listen, what are you doing for dinner. 'Cause I just walked by Tomoe and noticed there's no line. Come on, I need a sushi fix. Alright, if you get there first just tell them — I know you know. OK 'bye.

Callie hangs up. She puts the phone back on the floor.

Callie: OK Caesar, second chance.

SCENE 14

Sara's hospital room. Callie walks in and stands at bedside.

Callie: They're finished building that building across from your apartment.

Sara doesn't respond.

Callie (Conversation volume): Wake up now.

No response.

Callie (A little stronger): Sara.

No response.

Callie: Can you hear me? *(She looks down. Nothing)* Open your eyes.

No response.

Callie: Open your eyes.

No response.

Callie: They're gonna start you on physical therapy tomorrow. Just little stuff, range of motion, something to get your blood moving. *(Pause)* You've gotten all these cards and letters, I'll read some to you later. *(Pause)* You know your parents are here. They're doing their best — I think they're doing OK, considering. You getting better makes them feel better — yeah. *(Pause)* They look at me . . . your parents look at me . . . like I'm some dirty old man. *(She waits for a response)* And the newspapers, the TV, the radio — my station, my own station, when they ran the news about the attack, they identified me — "Traffic reporter for this station." Now everybody — the guy at the deli — I used to be the blueberry-muffin lady, now I'm the lesbian traffic reporter whose lover got beat up. And I've gotten letters — from two women, their girlfriends were *killed* during attacks — and they wrote me these heartbreaking letters telling me what they've been through . . . and they tell me to speak truth to power and I don't know what that *means*, Sara. Do you? Do you know me? *(Callie leans in closer)* Do you know who I am?

Sara opens her eyes.

Callie: Oh my God. Hi.

SCENE 15

> *Callie's apartment. Callie walks in from the bedroom in her bare feet wearing a T-shirt and underwear. She pours two glasses of water and drinks from one. George enters from the bedroom wearing jeans and pulling on a T-shirt. Callie hands him the second glass of water. He takes a sip.*

George: Deer Park?

Callie: You can't tell.

George: Tastes like plastic.

Callie: You want Evian, you buy it.

George: Not Evian, *Vermont Natural Springs.*

Callie: It's Deer Park or Dos Equis, George. That's what I've got.

George: Dos Equis, please.

> *Callie hands him a beer.*

George: You got any snacks?

Callie: I think I have some wasabi peas.

George: Those green —

Callie: Taste like sushi —

George: Oh *shit.*

Callie: What.

George: I have to go.

Callie: Where?

> *He goes to get the rest of his clothes.*

George: It's someone's birthday at work so a bunch of people are going out to that Japanese tapas place on 9th Street afterwards, I promised I'd meet them.

Callie: Blow them off.

George: I can't.

Callie: Come on. We'll go to Aggie's in the morning for breakfast. Banana pancakes.

George: I'm sorry, Callie. I made these plans before you called.

Callie: Whose birthday?

George: This new girl at work. I don't think you've met her.

Callie: Let me guess. She's an actress.

> *He puts on his shoes.*

George: She's classically trained.

Callie: You gotta get out of the restaurant business, George. Broaden your dating pool.

George: I'll call — I'll see you on Wednesday, at Jasmine's, right? She's having everyone over for dinner.

Callie: Yeah, I'll put it down.

> *He gives her a quick kiss on the lips.*

George: 'Bye.

> *He exits and Callie closes the door behind him. She pours his beer down the drain. There's a knock on the door.*

Callie (Calling): I didn't lock it.

Sara opens the door halfway and takes a small step in.

Sara: I saw your light on —

Callie turns around, unconsciously pulling on the bottom of her T-shirt.

Callie: I — I'm not — I didn't know it was you.

Sara: I saw him — he didn't notice me.

Callie: Just . . . just give me a second.

Sara steps back into the hallway as Callie pushes the door closed and goes to her bedroom. She comes back out wearing a sweater over her T-shirt and a pair of sweat pants. She opens the door. Sara enters carrying a bottle of wine.

Sara: I think — I think you'll like this kind.

Callie takes it and gestures toward the couch. Sara steps in tentatively and sits down on the edge of it.

Callie: I'll get us some glasses. (*She starts toward the kitchen*)

Sara: You don't have to open it now — it's late, I just wanted to — (*She gets up and follows Callie*) — apologize, Callie. You've been so good to me since I came here. I'm embarrassed that I acted, that I said —

Callie: That I'm a loser?

Sara: I didn't —

Callie: That I'm pathetic?

Sara: You're not pathetic.

Callie: I do, I know — I sometimes . . . swerve. I was thinking . . . you know, when I was little, my parents made me take tennis lessons — I'm not an athlete — neither are my parents, I don't know why — because the lessons were free! And it was summer and my parents didn't want me sitting around the house doing nothing which is what they thought I was doing — which was . . . true. So, they made me take these lessons, even though I was a klutz, and I tried — but I was a natural klutz. Still, at the end of the summer we all had to play in these championships and compete against the kids from the other classes. So, for the first round, I get pitted against this kid who obviously took tennis lessons because she wanted to be a really good tennis player. I can't even return her serves. The match takes like, ten minutes. Afterwards, my parents can barely speak, they feel so bad. They take me to Dairy Queen, tell me to order whatever I want — I get the triple banana split and for the rest of the summer they let me sit around and watch *Love Boat* reruns which is all I wanted to do anyway. (*She hands Sara a glass of wine*)

Sara: It was a good show.

Callie: But lately, I feel like . . . there's something . . . worth . . . winning.

Sara: Callie, I know that neither you nor I have ever — well at least I know that I haven't, I've never really asked —

Callie: By the way, I did get an award.

Sara: What?

Callie: An award for traffic reporting — who knew?

Sara: Are you serious?

Callie: I'm sorry, I interrupted —

Sara: Did you know?

Callie: What.

Sara: You knew you were going to get an award, didn't you?
Callie: I swear, I didn't.
Sara: Is that why you were so? —
Callie: Sara, I could never have known. Trust me.
Sara: Did they call you up to the dais and everything?
Callie: Just like the Oscars.
Sara: I wish I had seen.

> *Sara touches Callie's hand.*

Callie: I wish you'da been there.

> *Callie squeezes Sara's hand. Slight pause.*

Callie: You want to see it?
Sara: Yes!

> *Callie roots through a pile of papers.*

Callie: I thought I stuck it in here.

> *Sara goes to the sofa and lifts the pillows.*

Sara (Sotto voce): Sometimes I find stuff in here. *(She pulls out a plaque and holds it in the air)* I found something.
Callie: There it is!

> *Sara looks at it. She walks over to the bookshelf and slides some photographs out of the way.*

Sara: Put it here, OK?
Callie: Not there.
Sara: Why not?
Callie: Everyone will see it.
Sara: Just keep it there.

> *Callie reaches for it.*

Sara: Stop it.

> *Callie takes her hand away but then reaches for it again.*

Sara: I mean it.

> *Callie takes her hand away. Sara takes the plaque, exhales on it, rubs it on her shirt, then puts it back.*

SCENE 16

> *Sara's hospital room. A nurse is writing on her chart. Callie walks in.*

Callie: Any good news?
Nurse: She's stable.
Callie: I guess that's good news.
Nurse: Her bruises are healing.

> *Callie looks at Sara's face.*

Callie: Yes.
Nurse: Can tell she's a pretty girl.
Callie: Yeah.

Nurse: She's a schoolteacher?

Callie: She is.

Nurse: Where?

Callie: In the Bronx. *(Makes eye contact with the nurse)* Third grade. She has thirty-five kids. She knew all of their names by the end of the first day.

Nurse: Takes a lot to be a public school teacher in New York City.

Callie: She's got it.

Nurse: Those kids are lucky.

Callie: They know it.

Nurse: I'm gonna give her her bath now.

Callie: Oh, alright. *(She starts to leave)*

Nurse: I'll show you so you can do it.

　　Callie stops. Slight pause.

Callie: Oh — that's very — but I don't think I should, I've never —

Nurse: You've seen the worst of her. Most of her bruises are on her face. Her body looks fine. If that's what you're afraid of.

Callie: I don't know if she'd want me to.

Nurse: It won't hurt my feelings, you know. I'm sure she'd like it better if you do it.

Callie: . . . Right now, though, I have to go. *(She taps on her watch face)* The time. But . . . thank you. *(She heads out)*

SCENE 17

　　Callie's apartment. Callie and Sara walk in. Sara carries groceries, Callie carries a bag from a record store.

Callie: Which airport is he flying into?

Sara: JFK.

Callie: At eleven in the morning?

Sara: Eleven-thirty.

Callie: Have the car service pick you up at around 10:30, tell them to take the BQE to the LIE to the Van Wyck — that'll get you to the airport by eleven. But tell the driver to take the Midtown Tunnel back, it'll cost you three-fifty but the Manhattan-bound traffic on the Williamsburg Bridge will be too heavy.

Sara: Check.

　　Sara looks through the CDs.

Sara: Do you ever go out dancing?

Callie: Sometimes I do — my friend Sheila goes to this club on Wednesday nights and sometimes she invites a bunch of us girls to go.

Sara: I'd like to go sometime.

Callie: . . . Sure . . .

Sara: Will you let me know next time you go?

Callie: A bunch of us girlfriends go . . . it's fun . . . the music's great and it's fun, you don't have to worry about guys trying to pick you up . . . 'cause it's all women. I like to go there and dance, there's this kind of warm — like when you go to the bathroom, there's only one line and everyone's really nice and smiles . . .

Sara: Have you ever . . . asked someone to dance?

Callie: We kind of stick to each other—us friends. Sheila usually knows a bunch of women there and I've met them.

Sara: You ever meet a woman there, that seemed . . . interesting . . . to you?

Callie: . . . No.

Pause.

Callie: Not there.

Pause.

Callie: Have you?—

Sara: What.

Callie: In St. Louis, do they—or have you been to?

Sara: We have a couple places like that but I've never been. My friend, Janet, says that only college girls go to the clubs and bars; older lesbians just stay home and read. That's what everyone in St. Louis does, stays home and brews their own beer or does their e-mail.

Slight pause.

Callie: But I mean, have you ever . . . ?

Sara: Of course, right? I mean, right? I mean I can't imagine any woman who's never felt attracted—

Callie: Right!

Sara: It's just, I mean if you've never—

Callie: You want a beer?

Sara: Love one.

Callie: I hope I have some.

Sara: What time is it?

Callie: Just about six.

Sara: Uh-oh.

Callie: What?

Sara: I promised my roommates I'd clean the apartment by the time they came back from their trip and they're gonna be home in an hour.

Callie: Just—wait here a couple more minutes.

Sara: I really should go.

Callie: Just wait one minute.

Sara: Why?

Callie: I wanna . . . show you something.

Sara: Callie—

Callie: Take my watch. *(She takes off her watch and hands it to Sara)* What time is it now?

Sara: 5:59.

Callie: And how many seconds?

Sara: Thirty-eight seconds.

Callie: And what day is today?

Sara: Thursday.

Callie: What time is it now?

Sara: 5:59 and fifty seconds.

Callie: So count 'em.

Sara: What?

Callie: Count 'em down. Five seconds, four—

Sara: Four, three, two, one—what.

Callie opens her hands toward Sara.

Sara: What?

Callie points toward the ceiling.

Sara: Yeah? It's quiet. Oh!

Callie gestures: Yes I did it.

Sara: It's Thursday at six! And it's quiet!

Sara opens her arms and they hold each other. They keep holding. Callie lets go.

Sara: I'll call you tomorrow.
Callie: OK.

Pause.

Sara: Um, see ya.
Callie: OK. 'Bye.

Sara opens the door and lets herself out. Callie ambles slowly over to the sofa, looks at the door, buries her head in a pillow and screams.

SCENE 18

A coffee shop. Mrs. Winsley is sitting at a table. Callie walks in.

Callie: Mrs. Winsley?
Mrs. Winsley: Yes.

Callie extends her hand, Mrs. Winsley shakes it.

Callie: I'm sorry I'm late. I came straight —
Mrs. Winsley: It's fine, it's fine. I don't have to meet my husband until eight. *(She gestures for Callie to sit)* Should we order something? Coffee or tea?
Callie: Coffee would be great.
Mrs. Winsley: How are you doing?
Callie: I'm OK.
Mrs. Winsley: Yeah?
Callie: I want to thank you for . . . what you did, Mrs. Winsley.
Mrs. Winsley: I only did what I should've.
Callie: Not everybody —
Mrs. Winsley: How's your girlfriend?
Callie: Sara — She's better. Alert and responding. We just have to wait to see what kind of effect. How much and what.
Mrs. Winsley: I read in the paper she's from Kansas or something.
Callie: St. Louis. Missouri. Kansas City is in Missouri but Sara's from St. Louis.
Mrs. Winsley: I'm from outside Cincinnati myself, although I've been here twenty years. When I first moved here I would smile at strangers on the subway, give quarters to beggars on the street.
Callie: Sara gives a dollar.
Mrs. Winsley: So, I can imagine what it must've seemed like to her. Small-town girl in the big city — seeing men dressed as women, women holding hands — must've seemed like gay paradise to her.

Slight pause.

Callie: St. Louis is not a small town.

Mrs. Winsley: She's at St. Vincent's, isn't she?

Callie: Yes.

Mrs. Winsley: How are the doctors there? Are you pleased with them?

Callie: It's hard to say. You want them to do everything, you just want them to make her better. But they do what they can, I think they're OK.

Mrs. Winsley: How do you find it—spending all your time there. I mean I know they have limited visiting hours but they probably let you stay all day.

Callie: I have to go to my job—

Mrs. Winsley: Of course. I didn't mean to imply—

Callie: But I do visit every day.

Mrs. Winsley: It must be exhausting for you.

Callie: Well, her family's here—

Mrs. Winsley: Are you close with them?

Callie: No . . . Not close.

Mrs. Winsley: I know what it's like with in-laws. It took years before mine . . . Have you and Sara been together long?

Callie: Um . . . no.

Mrs. Winsley: Oh, I'm sorry I thought you two were—

Callie: I know.

Mrs. Winsley: Here I've been going on and on as if—

Callie: Yes, you were.

Mrs. Winsley: So, you're not really—

Callie: No, like I said I go there every—

Mrs. Winsley: But, you're not really involved.

SCENE 19

> *Callie's apartment. George, wearing jeans and a dress shirt, checks himself out in the full-length mirror. Callie walks in from the bedroom wearing a dress.*

George: I'm a little strapped 'cause business was slow last night.

Callie: Just don't worry about it.

George: I brought fifty bucks.

Callie: That'll get you a salad.

George: How expensive is this place?

Callie: Expensive.

George: Why do we have to go to a place like that? Why can't we just go to Benny's Burritos and drink a bunch of margaritas.

Callie: I told you, I'm gonna pay for the whole thing so stop stressing out about it.

> *She pushes George out of the way with her hip and looks at herself in the mirror.*

George: OK. Miss Traffic Reporter of the Universe or whatever you are, I'm gonna get the lobster.

Callie: They have venison.

George (Even better): Ooo!

> *Callie turns toward him.*

Callie: Does this dress make me look fat?

George: I *cannot*, *will* not, *ever* answer that question.
Callie: I'm changing.

> *She heads for the bedroom.*

George: What are you so uptight about?
Callie (Offstage): I'm not uptight.
George: That's the third time you've changed. Who is this guy anyway?
Callie (Offstage): Sara's ex.
George: Why do you need to look so good for him?

> *Callie comes back on wearing a different dress. She stands in front of the mirror.*

Callie: It's a nice restaurant.
George: Is he gonna be dressed up? You told me I could wear jeans.
Callie: Because I knew you'd wear jeans anyway.
George (Has to admit she's right): Hm. *(He stands next to Callie and looks at their reflection. He puts his arm around her waist)*
Callie: So how was the birthday party the other night? *(She wriggles away)*
George: Fine.
Callie: Did the birthday girl get everything she asked for?
George: You want to talk about this?
Callie: No.
George: Cool.

> *Pause.*

Callie: Did you fuck her before or after midnight.
George: Nice.
Callie: I'm just wondering about the technicality—
George: Listen, I'm not like you and that guy—
Callie: Who?
George: Who was that, that guy with the nose ring that you—
Callie: Hey—
George: In the bathroom of the—
Callie: Hey—
George: With no protection.

> *The buzzer buzzes.*

Callie: I told you *that*?
George: I asked.
Callie: We should start keeping more to ourselves.
George: Too late.
Callie: Don't say that.
George: Why not?
Callie: Makes me feel old.
George: We are old.
Callie: You are.

> *There's a knock on the door. Callie opens it. Sara walks in alone. Callie looks behind her.*

Callie: . . . Hi.
George: Hey, how's it going?
Sara (In a small voice): Hi.

Callie: Where's Peter?

Sara: He . . . uh, left. You look beautiful. You too, George.

Callie: He left . . . New York?

Sara: Yeah, he changed his flight. He left a couple hours ago. I told him to tell the driver to take the Van Wyck.

Callie: Something happen at work?

Sara: No it — I asked him to leave.

Callie moves closer to her.

Callie: Oh, um — *(She looks at George then back at Sara)* Listen, we don't have to go out —

George: Yeah, no, if you're upset —

Sara: No, it's fine, I want to go out. I want to get to know George.

Callie: Are you — did something happen? — *(Again she looks at George; why can't he disappear?)* I mean, you don't have to —

George stands behind Callie and puts his hands on her shoulders. She looks at his hands like they are dead frogs.

Sara: He was being so — he was criticizing everything. "Your apartment's too small. It's in a bad neighborhood. Your school is dangerous. It's too far away." All he could talk about was how dirty and dangerous everything is.

Callie: . . . Well —

George: It *is*.

Sara: What? Compared to St. Louis? I don't want to live there. I've started something here and I — that's what — because it's . . . *(Pause)* I love . . . New York!

George (Nods): Mm.

Callie: Let's go eat.

George (To Sara): Are you sure?

Sara: Yeah.

George: Great! Let's go!

George offers Sara his arm. She takes it. He offers his other arm to Callie.

Callie: I'll catch up with you.

George: OK. *(To Sara, on the way out)* They have venison you know.

Sara: You mean Bambi?

George and Sara exit. Callie walks over to the Magic 8-Ball, shuts her eyes a moment then wiggles the ball. She looks at the answer.

Callie (Quietly): Yes!

She puts down the ball and hurries to catch up with them.

SCENE 20

Sara's hospital room. Sara's sitting in a wheelchair, eyes open. Peter sits next to her reading from a book.

Peter: "And then ninety-eight kilometers" — that's sixty-one miles — "north of Wilcannia is a lunar landscape." That looks lunar, doesn't it? "Some of the locals don't mind showing off the interiors of their white-walled, subterranean settlements" — You'll want to sign up early for *that* tour, gonna be a regular Who concert trying to get into — *(He looks at Sara, clears his throat, then goes back to the book)* As I was saying, "Looping around about a hundred and sixty kilometers" — a hundred miles to you and me — "a road leads to Mootwingee, a surprising patch of greenness in the barren Bynguano —" Australia *is* an English-speaking country, isn't it? *(He fingers the last few chapters of the book)* You know, I'm dying to see how this ends, but can we —

Sara nods. He kisses her hand.

Peter: Thank you. We'll save the big finish for after dinner. *(He puts the book away and picks up something)* Did you see this?

He holds a homemade greeting card in front of her. Callie steps into the room then steps back. She watches.

Peter: You got a card from your old class at Friends. See, there's Matthew and Sophia and Emily — your favorite, the anti-Christ. She writes, "I hope you feel bitter and come bark soon." I see your replacement is letting her spelling skills slip.

Sara tentatively takes the card in her hand.

Peter: Hey! Get you.
　　　I've been talking to Jenny and Steve a lot, keeping them updated. Jenny's been letting everyone know what's going on. Margaret's called, Jamie, Lisa — it's frustrating for them not to be able to see you. They picture the worst, all they have are the images in their heads from reading the newspaper articles. It'll be better for them when they can see you. The doctor says we can move you soon. Your parents and I have been talking. I agree that you should stay with them after you get out of rehab. You're *welcome* to stay at our old place, of course, if you want to, I would take off from work so that I could — Well, I'm going to take off from work anyway.

Pause.

Peter: Just because you're coming back home I'm not going to act like everything is going to be the way it was. I know you went to New York because you wanted to change things. *(He touches her face)* You do want to go home —

Tears drop from Sara's eyes.

Peter: Don't you?

Callie turns, walks toward Sara's nurse who is standing at her station.

Callie: Excuse me.
Nurse: You're back.
Callie: Do you have time now? To show me how to do it?

SCENE 21

Callie's apartment. Callie and Sara enter after having left the restaurant. Callie takes off her coat, Sara does not.

Callie: Uugggh, I'm so full it hurts to move. What do you want to do, we could watch a movie if you —

Sara: Let's uh . . . let's go out, let's go somewhere.
Callie: Where do you want to go?
Sara: There's a bar. In the West Village. Henrietta's, you ever been?
Callie: Once.
Sara: Will you go with me?
Callie (She looks at her dress): Like this?
Sara: We could change. Friday night, it's supposed to be a good night.
Callie: OK.

Slight pause.

Callie: Good for what?
Sara: There's supposed to be a lot of people there.
Callie (Nods though she doesn't quite understand): OK, let's go.
Sara: You change, and then we can stop by my place and then we'll go.
Callie: We don't — you can borrow some of my clothes.
Sara: Really? That's great. That's great!

They stand there.

Sara: You go ahead and change and I'll . . . change next. I'll wear whatever's leftover.
Callie: I'll go change.
Sara: Maybe we'll like it there — *(She looks helplessly at Callie)*
Callie (Trying to be helpful): Yeah, OK.
Sara: Let's just —
Callie: We'll go, we'll hang out, have a drink.
Sara: Yes! You know, maybe meet people.
Callie: Are you — I mean, do you . . . want to *meet* people?
Sara: Yes! — No! I want to meet people to — meet people, maybe make friends, but no, I don't want to meet *someone*, some stranger —
Callie: We'll just go.
Sara: It's just a bar.
Callie: With a whole bunch of lesbians in it.
Sara: And us.

They lock eyes hoping the other will say something perfect. They keep waiting.

SCENE 22

The hospital. Sara's sitting in a wheelchair. Callie enters carrying a bag.

Callie: Sara.

Sara turns to her.

Callie: I brought you stuff to change into. *(She pulls some clothes out of the bag)* Don't you think? *(She puts them in Sara's lap)* We're gonna do this. Watch me. You gotta listen to me too. *(She undoes Sara's gown)* OK, we're gonna start with the left side because we're taking things off. *(She takes off Sara's left sleeve)* And now the right. *(She helps Sara pull her arm out of the right sleeve. She takes out a bra)* This closes in front. Can you . . . go like this?

Callie lifts her arms at the elbows. Sara does it.

Callie: Good for you. I should tell — *(She looks around for the nurse)* Later. *(She puts on the bra)* So far so good. *(She takes the shirt off Sara's lap)* Nice shirt, huh? Did I pick out a nice shirt for you? OK, you're gonna need to sit up a little for me.

Sara sits up. Callie puts on the right sleeve.

Callie: If I can just — am I hurting you? I'm sorry, Sara — I'm sorry — *(To herself)* Relax. *(She puts on the left sleeve)* This one you can do. Push — push — keep breathing, and push —

Sara pushes her arm through the sleeve.

Callie: It's a girl! *(She buttons Sara's shirt)* Let's keep you warm. It's cold in this place. *(She takes the pants. She helps Sara's right foot off the foot rest)* We're gonna do this together. I'll do this one. *(She points to her left)* That one you can do.

Sara lifts her left leg off, it spasms.

Callie: Oh — oh. OK. OK. *(She flips up the foot pads. She scrunches up the right leg of the pants and wrangles it on)* We gotta work together on this one, OK?

Callie scrunches up the left leg. Sara lifts her leg.

Callie: Are you helping me? Yes. You are. Now, the shoes go last. Like this. *(She puts on the right shoe)* And like that.

Sara slips her left foot in the left shoe. Callie pushes Sara's feet closer to her. Callie stands up.

Callie: Now you're gonna stand up. I'm gonna help. One, two, three — *(She puts her hands under Sara's arms and lifts her up. She pulls her pants up)*

Callie and Sara sit back down.

Callie: I can do this, you see?

Sara nods.

Callie: Choose me.

Sara smiles.

SCENE 23

Sara and Callie are walking down the street, having just left Henrietta's. Finally, Sara turns to Callie.

Sara: What — was I thinking?

Callie: That was like — going to a birthday party when you don't know the person whose birthday it is.

Sara: I don't know why I was expecting . . . I don't know what I was expecting. What time is it?

Callie checks her watch.

Callie: Around four.

Sara: So late.

Callie: Should we . . . go somewhere — where do you want to go?

Sara: I don't know —
Callie: Let's just . . . keep walking.
Sara: Sure.

> They walk a few steps in silence. After a while —

Callie: How do you eat corn on the cob. Around the world or typewriter style?
Sara: Typewriter.
Callie: Me too.
Sara: What kind of person eats around the world?
Callie: I don't know.
Sara: I mean, what is that based on? You read left to right, right?
Callie: I do.
Sara: So you should eat your corn that way, too.
Callie: Do you think in Egypt they eat right to left?
Sara: I don't know.
Callie: Fascinating question, though.
Sara: Do you wait *in* line or *on* line?
Callie: Oh. Now I wait on line. But I used to wait in.
Sara: But physically, you're *in* a line, not *on* one, right?
Callie: Yeah, stick by your guns. I caved in.
Sara: You say on. I say in.
Callie: What about this? *(She plants her one)*

> They pull away.

Sara: Huh.
Callie: What?
Sara: You just did that.
Callie: Yes I did.
Sara: Nice.

> They come at each other but with their heads angled toward the same side. They
> bump noses.

Callie: Whoop —
Sara: Sorry —

> They back away. Callie puts her arms around Sara's waist and pulls her toward
> her.

Sara: Do you think we should —
Callie: I don't want to go anywhere, I don't want to change anything. Let's just —
Sara: OK.
Callie: Try again.

> They get their heads right, connect lips, put their arms around each other.
> And kiss.

> End of Play

CONNECTIONS TO OTHER SELECTIONS

1. Neither *Stop Kiss* nor William Faulkner's "A Rose for Emily" (p. 75) offers
   plots that are organized chronologically. Discuss the effects of this organization on your emotional response to the characters as the plots unfold.

2. Discuss *Stop Kiss* and David Ives's *Sure Thing* (p. 1254) as versions of love stories. What significant similarities and differences do you find in their respective themes?

3. Consider *Stop Kiss* and *Los Vendidos* by Luis Valdez (p. 1659) as works of literature that provide social commentary on contemporary issues. Which work do you find more effective? Explain why.

Tender Offer

Born in Brooklyn, New York, in 1950, Wendy Wasserstein studied at Mount Holyoke College, City College of New York, and the Yale School of Drama. A resident of Greenwich Village, she is also a resident playwright off-Broadway, at New York's Playwrights Horizon Theatre where many of her plays have been performed before audiences receptive to Wasserstein's humorous treatment of feminist issues. Among her plays are *Uncommon Women* (1977), *Isn't It Romantic* (1980), *The Sisters Rosenzweig* (1993), and the enormously successful *The Heidi Chronicles* (1988), which won numerous honors including a Tony Award, a Pulitzer Prize, and the New York Drama Critics' Circle Award. In 1990 her book of essays, *Bachelor Girl*, was published. She has received National Endowment for the Arts and Guggenheim grants in support of her work.

Tender Offer, which appeared in a special issue of one-act plays in the spring 1991 *Antaeus,* is a brief but absorbing treatment of the tentative relationship between a father and daughter. Characteristic of Wasserstein's work, this play uses humor deftly to present a serious moment that requires a "good deal" to resolve it.

b *Research Wendy Wasserstein with LitLinks at*
http://www.bedfordstmartins.com/meyer/bedintrolit

WENDY WASSERSTEIN (B. 1950)

Tender Offer   1991

A girl of around nine is alone in a dance studio. She is dressed in traditional leotards and tights. She begins singing to herself, "Nothing Could Be Finer Than to Be in Carolina." She maps out a dance routine, including parts for the chorus. She builds to a finale. A man, Paul, around thirty-five, walks in. He has a sweet, though distant, demeanor. As he walks in, Lisa notices him and stops.

Paul: You don't have to stop, sweetheart.

Lisa: That's okay.

Paul: Looked very good.

Lisa: Thanks.

Paul: Don't I get a kiss hello?

Lisa: Sure.

Paul (embraces her): Hi, Tiger.

Lisa: Hi, Dad.

Paul: I'm sorry I'm late.

Lisa: That's okay.

Paul: How'd it go?

Lisa: Good.

Paul: Just good?

Lisa: Pretty good.

Paul: "Pretty good." You mean you got a lot of applause or "pretty good" you could have done better?

Lisa: Well, Courtney Palumbo's mother thought I was pretty good. But you know the part in the middle when everybody's supposed to freeze and the big girl comes out. Well, I think I moved a little bit.

Paul: I thought what you were doing looked very good.

Lisa: Daddy, that's not what I was doing. That was tap-dancing. I made that up.

Paul: Oh. Well it looked good. Kind of sexy.

Lisa: Yuch!

Paul: What do you mean "yuch"?

Lisa: Just yuch!

Paul: You don't want to be sexy?

Lisa: I don't care.

Paul: Let's go, Tiger. I promised your mother I'd get you home in time for dinner.

Lisa: I can't find my leg warmers.

Paul: You can't find your what?

Lisa: Leg warmers. I can't go home till I find my leg warmers.

Paul: I don't see you looking for them.

Lisa: I was waiting for you.

Paul: Oh.

Lisa: Daddy.

Paul: What?

Lisa: Nothing.

Paul: Where do you think you left them?

Lisa: Somewhere around here. I can't remember.

Paul: Well, try to remember, Lisa. We don't have all night.

Lisa: I told you. I think somewhere around here.

Paul: I don't see them. Let's go home now. You'll call the dancing school tomorrow.

Lisa: Daddy, I can't go home till I find them. Miss Judy says it's not professional to leave things.

Paul: Who's Miss Judy?

Lisa: She's my ballet teacher. She once danced the lead in *Swan Lake*, and she was a June Taylor dancer.

Paul: Well, then, I'm sure she'll understand about the leg warmers.

Lisa: Daddy, Miss Judy wanted to know why you were late today.

Paul: Hmmmmmmmm?

Lisa: Why were you late?

Paul: I was in a meeting. Business. I'm sorry.

Lisa: Why did you tell Mommy you'd come instead of her if you knew you had business?

Paul: Honey, something just came up. I thought I'd be able to be here. I was looking forward to it.

Lisa: I wish you wouldn't make appointments to see me.

Paul: Hmmmmmmm.

Lisa: You shouldn't make appointments to see me unless you know you're going to come.

Paul: Of course I'm going to come.

Lisa: No, you're not. Talia Robbins told me she's much happier living without her father in the house. Her father used to come home late and go to sleep early.

Paul: Lisa, stop it. Let's go.

Lisa: I can't find my leg warmers.

Paul: Forget your leg warmers.

Lisa: Daddy.

Paul: What is it?

Lisa: I saw this show on television, I think it was WPIX Channel 11. Well, the father was crying about his daughter.

Paul: Why was he crying? Was she sick?

Lisa: No. She was at school. And he was at business. And he just missed her, so he started to cry.

Paul: What was the name of this show?

Lisa: I don't know. I came in in the middle.

Paul: Well, Lisa, I certainly would cry if you were sick or far away, but I know that you're well and you're home. So no reason to get maudlin.

Lisa: What's maudlin?

Paul: Sentimental, soppy. Frequently used by children who make things up to get attention.

Lisa: I am sick! I am sick! I have Hodgkin's disease and a bad itch on my leg.

Paul: What do you mean you have Hodgkin's disease? Don't say things like that.

Lisa: Swoosie Kurtz, she had Hodgkin's disease on a TV movie last year, but she got better and now she's on *Love Sidney.*

Paul: Who is Swoosie Kurtz?

Lisa: She's an actress named after an airplane. I saw her on *Live at Five.*

Paul: You watch too much television; you should do your homework. Now, put your coat on.

Lisa: Daddy, I really do have a bad itch on my leg. Would you scratch it?

Paul: Lisa, you're procrastinating.

Lisa: Why do you use words I don't understand? I hate it. You're like Daria Feldman's mother. She always talks in Yiddish to her husband so Daria won't understand.

Paul: *Procrastinating* is not Yiddish.

Lisa: Well, I don't know what it is.

Paul: Procrastinating means you don't want to go about your business.

Lisa: I don't go to business. I go to school.

Paul: What I mean is you want to hang around here until you and I are late for dinner and your mother's angry and it's too late for you to do your homework.

Lisa: I do not.

Paul: Well, it sure looks that way. Now put your coat on and let's go.

Lisa: Daddy.

Paul: Honey, I'm tired. Really, later.

Lisa: Why don't you want to talk to me?

Paul: I do want to talk to you. I promise when we get home we'll have a nice talk.

Lisa: No, we won't. You'll read the paper and fall asleep in front of the news.

Paul: Honey, we'll talk on the weekend, I promise. Aren't I taking you to the theater this weekend? Let me look. *(He takes out appointment book.)* Yes. Sunday. *Joseph and the Amazing Technicolor Raincoat* with Lisa. Okay, Tiger?

Lisa: Sure. It's *Dreamcoat*.

Paul: What?

Lisa: Nothing. I think I see my leg warmers. *(She goes to pick them up, and an odd-looking trophy.)*

Paul: What's that?

Lisa: It's stupid. I was second best at the dance recital, so they gave me this thing. It's stupid.

Paul: Lisa.

Lisa: What?

Paul: What did you want to talk about?

Lisa: Nothing.

Paul: Was it about my missing your recital? I'm really sorry, Tiger. I would have liked to have been here.

Lisa: That's okay.

Paul: Honest?

Lisa: Daddy, you're prostrastinating.

Paul: I'm procrastinating. Sit down. Let's talk. So. How's school?

Lisa: Fine.

Paul: You like it?

Lisa: Yup.

Paul: You looking forward to camp this summer?

Lisa: Yup.

Paul: Is Daria Feldman going back?

Lisa: Nope.

Paul: Why not?

Lisa: I don't know. We can go home now. Honest, my foot doesn't itch anymore.

Paul: Lisa, you know what you do in business when it seems like there's nothing left to say? That's when you really start talking. Put a bid on the table.

Lisa: What's a bid?

Paul: You tell me what you want and I'll tell you what I've got to offer. Like Monopoly. You want Boardwalk, but I'm only willing to give you the Railroads. Now, because you are my daughter I'd throw in Water Works and Electricity. Understand, Tiger?

Lisa: No. I don't like board games. You know, Daddy, we could get Space Invaders for our home for thirty-five dollars. In fact, we could get an Osborne System for two thousand. Daria Feldman's parents . . .

Paul: Daria Feldman's parents refuse to talk to Daria, so they bought a computer to keep Daria busy so they won't have to speak in Yiddish. Daria will probably grow up to be a homicidal maniac lesbian prostitute.

Lisa: I know what that word *prostitute* means.

Paul: Good. *(Pause.)* You still haven't told me about school. Do you still like your teacher?

Lisa: She's okay.

Paul: Lisa, if we're talking try to answer me.

Lisa: I am answering you. Can we go home now, please?

Paul: Damn it, Lisa, if you want to talk to me . . . Talk to me!

Lisa: I can't wait till I'm old enough so I can make my own money and never have to see you again. Maybe I'll become a prostitute.

Paul: Young lady, that's enough.

Lisa: I hate you, Daddy! I hate you! *(She throws her trophy into the trash bin.)*

Paul: What'd you do that for?

Lisa: It's stupid.

Paul: Maybe I wanted it.

Lisa: What for?

Paul: Maybe I wanted to put it where I keep your dinosaur and the picture you made of Mrs. Kimbel with the chicken pox.

Lisa: You got mad at me when I made that picture. You told me I had to respect Mrs. Kimbel because she was my teacher.

Paul: That's true. But she wasn't my teacher. I liked her better with the chicken pox. *(Pause.)* Lisa, I'm sorry. I was very wrong to miss your recital, and you don't have to become a prostitute. That's not the type of profession Miss Judy has in mind for you.

Lisa (mumbles): No.

Paul: No. *(Pause.)* So Talia Robbins is really happy her father moved out?

Lisa: Talia Robbins picks open the eighth-grade lockers during gym period. But she did that before her father moved out.

Paul: You can't always judge someone by what they do or what they don't do. Sometimes you come home from dancing school and run upstairs and shut the door, and when I finally get to talk to you, everything is "okay" or "fine." Yup or nope?

Lisa: Yup.

Paul: Sometimes, a lot of times, I come home and fall asleep in front of the television. So you and I spend a lot of time being a little scared of each other. Maybe?

Lisa: Maybe.

Paul: Tell you what. I'll make you a tender offer.

Lisa: What?

Paul: I'll make you a tender offer. That's when one company publishes in the newspaper that they want to buy another company. And the company that publishes is called the Black Knight because they want to gobble up the poor little company. So the poor little company needs to be rescued. And then a White Knight comes along and makes a bigger and better offer so the shareholders won't have to tender shares to the Big Black Knight. You with me?

Lisa: Sort of.

Paul: I'll make you a tender offer like the White Knight. But I don't want to own you. I just want to make a much better offer. Okay?

Lisa (sort of understanding): Okay. *(Pause. They sit for a moment.)* Sort of, Daddy, what do you think about? I mean, like when you're quiet what do you think about?

Paul: Oh, business usually. If I think I made a mistake or if I think I'm doing okay. Sometimes I think about what I'll be doing five years from now and if it's what I hoped it would be five years ago. Sometimes I think about what your life will be like, if Mount Saint Helens will erupt again. What you'll become if you'll study penmanship or word processing. If you speak kindly of me to your psychiatrist when you are in graduate school. And how the hell I'll pay for your graduate school. And sometimes I try and think what it was I thought about when I was your age.

Lisa: Do you ever look out your window at the clouds and try to see which kinds of shapes they are? Like one time, honest, I saw the head of Walter Cronkite in a flower vase. Really! Like look don't those kinda look like if you turn it upside down, two big elbows or two elephant trunks dancing?

Paul: Actually still looks like Walter Cronkite in a flower vase to me. But look up a little. See the one that's still moving? That sorta looks like a whale on a thimble.

Lisa: Where?

Paul: Look up. To your right.

Lisa: I don't see it. Where?

Paul: The other way.

Lisa: Oh, yeah! There's the head and there's the stomach. Yeah! *(Lisa picks up her trophy.)* Hey, Daddy.

Paul: Hey, Lisa.

Lisa: You can have this thing if you want it. But you have to put it like this, because if you put it like that it is gross.

Paul: You know what I'd like? So I can tell people who come into my office why I have this gross stupid thing on my shelf, I'd like it if you could show me your dance recital.

Lisa: Now?

Paul: We've got time. Mother said she won't be home till late.

Lisa: Well, Daddy, during a lot of it I freeze and the big girl in front dances.

Paul: Well, how 'bout the number you were doing when I walked in?

Lisa: Well, see, I have parts for a lot of people in that one, too.

Paul: I'll dance the other parts.

Lisa: You can't dance.

Paul: Young lady, I played Yvette Mimimeux in a *Hasty Pudding Show*.

Lisa: Who's Yvette Mimimeux?

Paul: Watch more television. You'll find out. *(Paul stands up.)* So I'm ready. *(He begins singing.)* "Nothing could be finer than to be in Carolina."

Lisa: Now I go. In the morning. And now you go. Dum-da.

Paul (obviously not a tap dancer): Da-da-dum.

Lisa (whines): Daddy!

Paul (mimics her): Lisa! Nothing could be finer . . .

Lisa: That looks dumb.

Paul: Oh, yeah? You think they do this better in *The Amazing Minkcoat*? No way! Now you go — da da da dum.

Lisa: Da da da dum.

Paul: If I had Aladdin's lamp for only a day, I'd make a wish . . .

Lisa: Daddy, that's maudlin!

Paul: I know it's maudlin. And here's what I'd say:

Lisa and Paul: I'd say that "nothing could be finer than to be in Carolina in the moooooooooooornin'."

CONNECTIONS TO OTHER SELECTIONS

1. Compare the fathers in *Tender Offer* and Sylvia Plath's poem "Daddy" (p. 1177). What conflicts are associated with the father in each work? To what extent are the conflicts resolved or not resolved?

2. *Tender Offer* and Jane Martin's *Rodeo* (p. 1656) are extremely brief dramatic works that present conflicts in which business serves as an antagonist. Write an essay on the nature of the conflicts in each play and how business is the source of those conflicts.

The Piano Lesson

August Wilson, who, as a young poet, "wanted to be Dylan Thomas," has become in recent years a major force in the American theater. He has projected a sequence of ten plays that will chronicle the African American experience in the United States in each decade of the twentieth century. *Ma Rainey's Black Bottom,* the first of these to be completed, premiered at the Yale Repertory Theatre in 1984, went to Broadway shortly thereafter, and eventually won the New York Drama Critics' Circle Award. The plays that have so far followed are *Fences* (1985), *Joe Turner's Come and Gone* (1986), *The Piano Lesson* (1987), *Two Trains Running* (1989), and *Seven Guitars* (1996).

Born in Pittsburgh, Pennsylvania, Wilson grew up in the Hill, a black neighborhood to which his mother had come from North Carolina. His white father never lived with the family. Wilson quit school at sixteen and worked in a variety of menial jobs, meanwhile submitting poetry to a number of local publications. He didn't begin to find his writing voice, however, until he moved to Minneapolis–St. Paul, where he founded the Black Horizons Theatre Company in 1968 and later started the Playwrights Center. He supported himself during part of this time by writing skits for the Science Museum of Minnesota.

The Piano Lesson — awarded a Pulitzer Prize in 1990 — offers comedy as well as serious examination of an African American family's spiritual heritage.

Research August Wilson with LitLinks at
http://www.bedfordstmartins.com/meyer/bedintrolit

AUGUST WILSON (B. 1945)

The Piano Lesson   1990

CHARACTERS

Doaker Charles	*Lymon*
Berniece, Doaker's niece	*Avery*
Maretha, Berniece's eleven-year-old daughter	*Wining Boy*
Boy Willie	*Grace*

SETTING: *The action of the play takes place in the kitchen and parlor of the house where Doaker Charles lives with his niece, Berniece, and her eleven-year-old daughter, Maretha. The house is sparsely furnished, and although there is evidence of a woman's touch, there is a lack of warmth and vigor. Berniece and Maretha occupy the upstairs rooms. Doaker's room is prominent and opens onto the kitchen. Dominating the parlor is an old upright piano. On the legs of the piano, carved in the manner of African sculpture, are masklike figures resembling totems. The carvings are rendered with a grace and power of invention that lifts them out of the realm of craftsmanship and into the realm of art. At left is a staircase leading to the upstairs.*

ACT I

SCENE I

The lights come up on the Charles household. It is five o'clock in the morning. The dawn is beginning to announce itself, but there is something in the air that belongs to the night. A stillness that is a portent, a gathering, a coming together of something akin to a storm. There is a loud knock at the door.

Boy Willie (offstage, calling): Hey, Doaker . . . Doaker! *(He knocks again and calls.)* Hey Doaker! Hey, Berniece! Berniece!

Doaker enters from his room. He is a tall, thin man of forty-seven, with severe features, who has for all intents and purposes retired from the world though he works full-time as a railroad cook.

Doaker: Who is it?

Boy Willie: Open the door, nigger! It's me . . . Boy Willie!

Doaker: Who?

Boy Willie: Boy Willie! Open the door!

Doaker opens the door and Boy Willie and Lymon enter. Boy Willie is thirty years old. He has an infectious grin and a boyishness that is apt for his name. He is brash and impulsive, talkative, and somewhat crude in speech and manner. Lymon is twenty-nine. Boy Willie's partner, he talks little, and then with a straightforwardness that is often disarming.

Doaker: What you doing up here?

Boy Willie: I told you, Lymon. Lymon talking about you might be sleep. This is Lymon. You remember Lymon Jackson from down home? This my Uncle Doaker.

Doaker: What you doing up here? I couldn't figure out who that was. I thought you was still down in Mississippi.

Boy Willie: Me and Lymon selling watermelons. We got a truck out there. Got a whole truckload of watermelons. We brought them up here to sell. Where's Berniece? *(Calls.)* Hey, Berniece!

Doaker: Berniece up there sleep.

Boy Willie: Well, let her get up. *(Calls.)* Hey, Berniece!

Doaker: She got to go to work in the morning.

Boy Willie: Well she can get up and say hi. It's been three years since I seen her. *(Calls.)* Hey, Berniece! It's me . . . Boy Willie.

Doaker: Berniece don't like all that hollering now. She got to work in the morning.

Boy Willie: She can go on back to bed. Me and Lymon been riding two days in that truck . . . the least she can do is get up and say hi.

Doaker (looking out the window): Where you all get that truck from?

Boy Willie: It's Lymon's. I told him let's get a load of watermelons and bring them up here.

Lymon: Boy Willie say he going back, but I'm gonna stay. See what it's like up here.

Boy Willie: You gonna carry me down there first.

Lymon: I told you I ain't going back down there and take a chance on that truck breaking down again. You can take the train. Hey, tell him Doaker, he can take the train back. After we sell them watermelons he have enough money he can buy him a whole railroad car.

Doaker: You got all them watermelons stacked up there no wonder the truck broke down. I'm surprised you made it this far with a load like that. Where you break down at?

Boy Willie: We broke down three times! It took us two and a half days to get here. It's a good thing we picked them watermelons fresh.

Lymon: We broke down twice in West Virginia. The first time was just as soon as we got out of Sunflower. About forty miles out she broke down. We got it going and got all the way to West Virginia before she broke down again.

Boy Willie: We had to walk about five miles for some water.

Lymon: It got a hole in the radiator but it runs pretty good. You have to pump the brakes sometime before they catch. Boy Willie have his door open and be ready to jump when that happens.

Boy Willie: Lymon think that's funny. I told the nigger I give him ten dollars to get the brakes fixed. But he thinks that funny.

Lymon: They don't need fixing. All you got to do is pump them till they catch.

> *Berniece enters on the stairs. Thirty-five years old, with an eleven-year-old daughter, she is still in mourning for her husband after three years.*

Berniece: What you doing all that hollering for?

Boy Willie: Hey, Berniece, Doaker said you was asleep. I said at least you could get up and say hi.

Berniece: It's five o'clock in the morning and you come in here with all this noise. You can't come like normal folks. You got to bring all that noise with you.

Boy Willie: Hell, I ain't done nothing but come in and say hi. I ain't got in the house good.

Berniece: That's what I'm talking about. You start all that hollering and carry on as soon as you hit the door.

Boy Willie: Aw, hell, woman, I was glad to see Doaker. You ain't had to come down if you didn't want to. I come eighteen hundred miles to see my sister I figure she might want to get up and say hi. Other than that you can go back upstairs. What you got, Doaker? Where your bottle? Me and Lymon want a drink. *(To Berniece.)* This is Lymon. You remember, Lymon Jackson from down home.

Lymon: How you doing, Berniece? You look just like I thought you looked.

Berniece: Why you all got to come in hollering and carrying on? Waking the neighbors with all that noise.

Boy Willie: They can come over and join the party. We fixing to have a party. Doaker, where your bottle? Me and Lymon celebrating. The Ghosts of the Yellow Dog got Sutter.

Berniece: Say what?

Boy Willie: Ask Lymon, they found him the next morning. Say he drowned in his well.

Doaker: When this happen, Boy Willie?

Boy Willie: About three weeks ago. Me and Lymon was over in Stoner County when we heard about it. We laughed. We thought it was funny. A great big old three-hundred-and-forty-pound man gonna fall down his well.

Lymon: It remind me of Humpty Dumpty.

Boy Willie: Everybody say the Ghosts of the Yellow Dog pushed him.

Berniece: I don't want to hear that nonsense. Somebody down there pushing them people in their wells.

Doaker: What was you and Lymon doing over in Stoner County?

Boy Willie: We was down there working. Lymon got some people down there.

Lymon: My cousin got some land down there. We was helping him.

Boy Willie: Got near about a hundred acres. He got it set up real nice. Me and Lymon was down there chopping down trees. We was using Lymon's truck to haul the wood. Me and Lymon used to haul wood all around them parts. *(To Berniece.)* Me and Lymon got a truckload of watermelons out there. *(Berniece crosses to the window to the parlor.)* Doaker, where your bottle? I know you got a bottle stuck up in your room. Come on, me and Lymon want a drink.

Doaker exits into his room.

Berniece: Where you all get that truck from?

Boy Willie: I told you it's Lymon's.

Berniece: Where you get the truck from, Lymon?

Lymon: I bought it.

Berniece: Where he get that truck from, Boy Willie?

Boy Willie: He told you he bought it. Bought it for a hundred and twenty dollars. I can't say where he got that hundred and twenty dollars from . . . but he bought that old piece of truck from Henry Porter. *(To Lymon.)* Where you get that hundred and twenty dollars from, nigger?

Lymon: I got it like you get yours. I know how to take care of money.

Doaker brings a bottle and sets it on the table.

Boy Willie: Aw hell, Doaker got some of that good whiskey. Don't give Lymon none of that. He ain't used to good whiskey. He liable to get sick.

Lymon: I done had good whiskey before.

Boy Willie: Lymon bought that truck so he have him a place to sleep. He down there wasn't doing no work or nothing. Sheriff looking for him. He bought that truck to keep away from the sheriff. Got Stovall looking for him too. He down there sleeping in that truck ducking and dodging both of them. I told him come on let's go up and see my sister.

Berniece: What the sheriff looking for you for, Lymon?

Boy Willie: The man don't want you to know all his business. He's my company. He ain't asking you no questions.

Lymon: It wasn't nothing. It was just a misunderstanding.

Berniece: He in my house. You say the sheriff looking for him, I wanna know what he looking for him for. Otherwise you all can go back out there and be where nobody don't have to ask you nothing.

Lymon: It was just a misunderstanding. Sometimes me and the sheriff we don't think alike. So we just got crossed on each other.

Berniece: Might be looking for him about that truck. He might have stole that truck.

Boy Willie: We ain't stole no truck, woman. I told you Lymon bought it.

Doaker: Boy Willie and Lymon got more sense than to ride all the way up here in a stolen truck with a load of watermelons. Now they might have stole them watermelons, but I don't believe they stole that truck.

Boy Willie: You don't even know the man good and you calling him a thief. And we ain't stole them watermelons either. Them old man Pitterford's watermelons. He give me and Lymon all we could load for ten dollars.

Doaker: No wonder you got them stacked up out there. You must have five hundred watermelons stacked up out there.

Berniece: Boy Willie, when you and Lymon planning on going back?

Boy Willie: Lymon say he staying. As soon as we sell them watermelons I'm going on back.

Berniece (starts to exit up the stairs): That's what you need to do. And you need to do it quick. Come in here disrupting the house. I don't want all that loud carrying on around here. I'm surprised you ain't woke Maretha up.

Boy Willie: I was fixing to get her now. *(Calls.)* Hey, Maretha!

Doaker: Berniece don't like all that hollering now.

Berniece: Don't you wake that child up!

Boy Willie: You going up there . . . wake her up and tell her her uncle's here. I ain't seen her in three years. Wake her up and send her down here. She can go back to bed.

Berniece: I ain't waking that child up . . . and don't you be making all that noise. You and Lymon need to sell them watermelons and go on back.

Berniece exits up the stairs.

Boy Willie: I see Berniece still try to be stuck up.

Doaker: Berniece alright. She don't want you making all that noise. Maretha up there sleep. Let her sleep until she get up. She can see you then.

Boy Willie: I ain't thinking about Berniece. You hear from Wining Boy? You know Cleotha died?

Doaker: Yeah, I heard that. He come by here about a year ago. Had a whole sack of money. He stayed here about two weeks. Ain't offered nothing. Berniece asked him for three dollars to buy some food and he got mad and left.

Lymon: Who's Wining Boy?

Boy Willie: That's my uncle. That's Doaker's brother. You heard me talk about Wining Boy. He play piano. He done made some records and everything. He still doing that, Doaker?

Doaker: He made one or two records a long time ago. That's the only ones I ever known him to make. If you let him tell it he a big recording star.

Boy Willie: He stopped down home about two years ago. That's what I hear. I don't know. Me and Lymon was up on Parchman Farm doing them three years.

Doaker: He don't never stay in one place. Now, he been here about eight months ago. Back in the winter. Now, you subject not to see him for another two years. It's liable to be that long before he stop by.

Boy Willie: If he had a whole sack of money you liable never to see him. You ain't gonna see him until he get broke. Just as soon as that sack of money is gone you look up and he be on your doorstep.

Lymon (noticing the piano): Is that the piano?

Boy Willie: Yeah . . . look here, Lymon. See how it got all cash money. He don't know I found out the most Stovall how it's carved up real nice and polished and everything? You never find you another piano like that.

Lymon: Yeah, that look real nice.

Boy Willie: I told you. See how it's polished? My mama used to polish it every day. See all them pictures carved on it? That's what I was talking about. You can get a nice price for that piano.

Lymon: That's all Boy Willie talked about the whole trip up here. I got tired of hearing him talking about the piano.

Boy Willie: All you want to talk about is women. You ought to hear this nigger, Doaker. Talking about all the women he gonna get when he get up here. He ain't had none down there but he gonna get a hundred when he get up here.

Doaker: How your people doing down there, Lymon?

Lymon: They alright. They still there. I come up here to see what it's like up here. Boy Willie trying to get me to go back and farm with him.

Boy Willie: Sutter's brother selling the land. He say he gonna sell it to me. That's why I come up here. I got one part of it. Sell them watermelons and get me another part. Get Berniece to sell that piano and I'll have the third part.

Doaker: Berniece ain't gonna sell that piano.

Boy Willie: I'm gonna talk to her. When she see I got a chance to get Sutter's land she'll come around.

Doaker: You can put that thought out of your mind. Berniece ain't gonna sell that piano.

Boy Willie: I'm gonna talk to her. She been playing on it?

Doaker: You know she won't touch that piano. I ain't never known her to touch it since Mama Ola died. That's over seven years now. She say it got blood on it. She got Maretha playing on it though. Say Maretha can go on and do everything she can't do. Got her in an extra school down at the Irene Kaufman Settlement House. She want Maretha to grow up and be a schoolteacher. She say she good enough she can teach on the piano.

Boy Willie: Maretha don't need to be playing on no piano. She can play on the guitar.

Doaker: How much land Sutter got left?

Boy Willie: Got a hundred acres. Good land. He done sold it piece by piece, he kept the good part for himself. Now he got to give that up. His brother come down from Chicago for the funeral . . . he up there in Chicago got some kind of business with soda fountain equipment. He anxious to sell the land, Doaker. He don't want to be bothered with it. He called me to him and said cause of how long our families done known each other and how we been good friends and all, say he wanted to sell the land to me. Say he'd rather see me with it than Jim Stovall. Told me he'd let me have it for two thousand dollars cash money. He don't know I found out the most Stovall would give him for it was fifteen hundred dollars. He trying to get that extra five hundred out of me telling me he doing me a favor. I thanked him just as nice. Told him what a good man Sutter was and how he had my sympathy and all. Told him to give me two weeks. He said he'd wait on me. That's why I come up here. Sell them watermelons. Get Berniece to sell that piano. Put them two parts with the part I done saved. Walk in there. Tip my hat. Lay my money down on the table. Get my deed and walk on out. This time I get to keep all the cotton. Hire me some men to work it for me. Gin my cotton. Get my seed. And I'll see you again next year. Might even plant some tobacco or some oats.

Doaker: You gonna have a hard time trying to get Berniece to sell that piano. You know Avery Brown from down there, don't you? He up here now. He followed Berniece up here trying to get her to marry him after Crawley got killed. He been up here about two years. He call himself a preacher now.

Boy Willie: I know Avery. I know him from when he used to work on the Willshaw place. Lymon know him too.

Doaker: He after Berniece to marry him. She keep telling him no but he won't give up. He keep pressing her on it.

Boy Willie: Avery think all white men is bigshots. He don't know there some white men ain't got as much as he got.

Doaker: He supposed to come past here this morning. Berniece going down to the bank with him to see if he can get a loan to start his church. That's why I know Berniece ain't gonna sell that piano. He tried to get her to sell it to help him start his church. Sent the man around and everything.

Boy Willie: What man?

Doaker: Some white fellow was going around to all the colored people's houses looking to buy up musical instruments. He'd buy anything. Drums. Guitars. Harmonicas. Pianos. Avery sent him past here. He looked at the piano and got excited. Offered her a nice price. She turned him down and got on Avery for sending him past. The man kept on her about two weeks. He seen where she wasn't gonna sell it, he gave her his number and told her if she ever wanted to sell it to call him first. Say he'd go one better than what anybody else would give her for it.

Boy Willie: How much he offer her for it?

Doaker: Now you know me. She didn't say and I didn't ask. I just know it was a nice price.

Lymon: All you got to do is find out who he is and tell him somebody else wanna buy it from you. Tell him you can't make up your mind who to sell it to, and if he like Doaker say, he'll give you anything you want for it.

Boy Willie: That's what I'm gonna do. I'm gonna find out who he is from Avery.

Doaker: It ain't gonna do you no good. Berniece ain't gonna sell that piano.

Boy Willie: She ain't got to sell it. I'm gonna sell it. I own just as much of it as she does.

Berniece (offstage, hollers): Doaker! Go on get away. Doaker!

Doaker (calling): Berniece?

Doaker and Boy Willie rush to the stairs, Boy Willie runs up the stairs, passing Berniece as she enters, running.

Doaker: Berniece, what the matter? You alright? What's the matter?

Berniece tries to catch her breath. She is unable to speak.

Doaker: That's alright. Take your time. You alright. What's the matter? *(He calls.)* Hey, Boy Willie?

Boy Willie (offstage): Ain't nobody up here.

Berniece: Sutter . . . Sutter's standing at the top of the steps.

Doaker (calls): Boy Willie!

Lymon crosses to the stairs and looks up. Boy Willie enters from the stairs.

Boy Willie: Hey Doaker, what's wrong with her? Berniece, what's wrong? Who was you talking to?

Doaker: She say she seen Sutter's ghost standing at the top of the stairs.

Boy Willie: Seen what? Sutter? She ain't seen no Sutter.

Berniece: He was standing right up there.

Boy Willie (entering on the stairs): That's all in Berniece's head. Ain't nobody up there. Go on up there, Doaker.

Doaker: I'll take your word for it. Berniece talking about what she seen. She say Sutter's ghost standing at the top of the steps. She ain't just make all that up.

Boy Willie: She up there dreaming. She ain't seen no ghost.

Lymon: You want a glass of water, Berniece? Get her a glass of water, Boy Willie.

Boy Willie: She don't need no water. She ain't seen nothing. Go on up there and look. Ain't nobody up there but Maretha.

Doaker: Let Berniece tell it.

Boy Willie: I ain't stopping her from telling it.

Doaker: What happened, Berniece?

Berniece: I come out of my room to come back down here and Sutter was standing there in the hall.

Boy Willie: What he look like?

Berniece: He look like Sutter. He look like he always look.

Boy Willie: Sutter couldn't find his way from Big Sandy to Little Sandy. How he gonna find his way all the way up here to Pittsburgh? Sutter ain't never even heard of Pittsburgh.

Doaker: Go on, Berniece.

Berniece: Just standing there with the blue suit on.

Boy Willie: The man ain't never left Marlin County when he was living . . . and he's gonna come all the way up here now that he's dead?

Doaker: Let her finish. I want to hear what she got to say.

Boy Willie: I'll tell you this. If Berniece had seen him like she think she seen him she'd still be running.

Doaker: Go on, Berniece. Don't pay Boy Willie no mind.

Berniece: He was standing there . . . had his hand on top of his head. Look like he might have thought if he took his hand down his head might have fallen off.

Lymon: Did he have on a hat?

Berniece: Just had on that blue suit . . . I told him to go away and he just stood there looking at me . . . calling Boy Willie's name.

Boy Willie: What he calling my name for?

Berniece: I believe you pushed him in the well.

Boy Willie: Now what kind of sense that make? You telling me I'm gonna go out there and hide in the weeds with all them dogs and things he got around there . . . I'm gonna hide and wait till I catch him looking down his well just right . . . then I'm gonna run over and push him in. A great big old three-hundred-and-forty-pound man.

Berniece: Well, what he calling your name for?

Boy Willie: He bending over looking down his well, woman . . . how he know who pushed him? It could have been anybody. Where was you when Sutter fell in his well? Where was Doaker? Me and Lymon was over in Stoner County. Tell her, Lymon. The Ghosts of the Yellow Dog got Sutter. That's what happened to him.

Berniece: You can talk all that Ghosts of the Yellow Dog stuff if you want. I know better.

Lymon: The Ghosts of the Yellow Dog pushed him. That's what the people say. They found him in his well and all the people say it must be the Ghosts of the Yellow Dog. Just like all them other men.

Boy Willie: Come talking about he looking for me. What he come all the way up here for? If he looking for me all he got to do is wait. He could have saved himself a trip if he looking for me. That ain't nothing but in Berniece's head. Ain't no telling what she liable to come up with next.

Berniece: Boy Willie, I want you and Lymon to go ahead and leave my house. Just go on somewhere. You don't do nothing but bring trouble with you everywhere you go. If it wasn't for you Crawley would still be alive.

Boy Willie: Crawley what? I ain't had nothing to do with Crawley getting killed. Crawley three time seven. He had his own mind.

Berniece: Just go on and leave. Let Sutter go somewhere else looking for you.

Boy Willie: I'm leaving. Soon as we sell them watermelons. Other than that I ain't going nowhere. Hell, I just got here. Talking about Sutter looking for me. Sutter was looking for that piano. That's what he was looking for. He had to die to find out where that piano was at . . . If I was you I'd get rid of it. That's the way to get rid of Sutter's ghost. Get rid of that piano.

Berniece: I want you and Lymon to go on and take all this confusion out of my house!

Boy Willie: Hey, tell her, Doaker. What kind of sense that make? I told you, Lymon, as soon as Berniece see me she was gonna start something. Didn't I tell you that? Now she done made up that story about Sutter just so she could tell me to leave her house. Well, hell, I ain't going nowhere till I sell them watermelons.

Berniece: Well why don't you go out there and sell them! Sell them and go on back!

Boy Willie: We waiting till the people get up.

Lymon: Boy Willie say if you get out there too early and wake the people up they get mad at you and won't buy nothing from you.

Doaker: You won't be waiting long. You done let the sun catch up with you. This the time everybody be getting up around here.

Berniece: Come on, Doaker, walk up here with me. Let me get Maretha up and get her started. I got to get ready myself. Boy Willie, just go on out there and sell them watermelons and you and Lymon leave my house.

Berniece and Doaker exit up the stairs.

Boy Willie (*calling after them*): If you see Sutter up there . . . tell him I'm down here waiting on him.

Lymon: What if she see him again?

Boy Willie: That's all in her head. There ain't no ghost up there. (*Calls.*) Hey, Doaker . . . I told you ain't nothing up there.

Lymon: I'm glad he didn't say he was looking for me.

Boy Willie: I wish I would see Sutter's ghost. Give me a chance to put a whupping on him.

Lymon: You ought to stay up here with me. You be down there working his land . . . he might come looking for you all the time.

Boy Willie: I ain't thinking about Sutter. And I ain't thinking about staying up here. You stay up here. I'm going back and get Sutter's land. You think you ain't got to work up here. You think this the land of milk and honey. But I ain't scared of work. I'm going back and farm every acre of that land.

Doaker enters from the stairs.

I told you there ain't nothing up there, Doaker. Berniece dreaming all that.

Doaker: I believe Berniece seen something. Berniece level-headed. She ain't just made all that up. She say Sutter had on a suit. I don't believe she ever seen Sutter in a suit. I believe that's what he was buried in, and that's what Berniece saw.

Boy Willie: Well, let her keep on seeing him then. As long as he don't mess with me. (*Doaker starts to cook his breakfast.*) I heard about you, Doaker. They say you got all the women looking out for you down home. They be looking to see you coming. Say you got a different one every two weeks. Say they be fighting one another for you to stay with them. (*To Lymon.*) Look at him, Lymon. He know it's true.

Doaker: I ain't thinking about no women. They never get me tied up with them. After Coreen I ain't got no use for them. I stay up on Jack Slattery's place when I be down there. All them women want is somebody with a steady payday.

Boy Willie: That ain't what I hear. I hear every two weeks the women all put on their dresses and line up at the railroad station.

Doaker: I don't get down there but once a month. I used to go down there every two weeks but they keep switching me around. They keep switching all the fellows around.

Boy Willie: Shakespeare can't turn that railroad loose. He was working the railroad when I was walking around crying for sugartit. My mama used to brag on him.

Doaker: I'm cooking now, but I used to line track. I pieced together the Yellow Dog stitch by stitch. Rail by rail. Line track all up around there. I lined track all up around Sunflower and Clarksdale. Wining Boy worked with me. He helped me put in some of that track. He'd work it for six months and quit. Go back to playing piano and gambling.

Boy Willie: How long you been with the railroad now?

Doaker: Twenty-seven years. Now, I'll tell you something about the railroad. What I done learned after twenty-seven years. See, you got North. You got West. You look over here you got South. Over there you got East. Now, you can start from anywhere. Don't care where you at. You got to go one of them four ways. And whichever way you decide to go they got a railroad that will take you there. Now, that's something simple. You think anybody would be able to understand that. But you'd be surprised how many people trying to go North get on a train going West. They think the train's supposed to go where they going rather than where it's going.

Now, why people going? Their sister's sick. They leaving before they kill somebody . . . and they sitting across from somebody who's leaving to keep from getting killed. They leaving cause they can't get satisfied. They going to meet someone. I wish I had a dollar for every time that someone wasn't at the station to meet them. I done seen that a lot. In between the time they sent the telegram and the time the person get there . . . they done forgot all about them.

They got so many trains out there they have a hard time keeping them from running into each other. Got trains going every whichaway. Got people on all of them. Somebody going where somebody just left. If everybody stay in one place I believe this would be a better world. Now what I done learned after twenty-seven years of railroading is this . . . if the train stays on the track . . . it's going to get where it's going. It might not be where you going. If it ain't, then all you got to do is sit and wait cause the train's coming back to get you. The train don't never stop. It'll come back every time. Now I'll tell you another thing . . .

Boy Willie: What you cooking over there, Doaker? Me and Lymon's hungry.
Doaker: Go on down there to Wylie and Kirkpatrick to Eddie's restaurant. Coffee cost a nickel and you can get two eggs, sausage, and grits for fifteen cents. He even give you a biscuit with it.
Boy Willie: That look good what you got. Give me a little piece of that grilled bread.
Doaker: Here . . . go on take the whole piece.
Boy Willie: Here you go, Lymon . . . you want a piece?

He gives Lymon a piece of toast. Maretha enters from the stairs.

Boy Willie: Hey, sugar. Come here and give me a hug. Come on give Uncle Boy Willie a hug. Don't be shy. Look at her, Doaker. She done got bigger. Ain't she got big?
Doaker: Yeah, she getting up there.
Boy Willie: How you doing, sugar?
Maretha: Fine.
Boy Willie: You was just a little old thing last time I seen you. You remember me, don't you? This your Uncle Boy Willie from down South. That there's Lymon. He my friend. We come up here to sell watermelons. You like watermelons? *(Maretha nods.)* We got a whole truckload out front. You can have as many as you want. What you been doing?
Maretha: Nothing.
Boy Willie: Don't be shy now. Look at you getting all big. How old is you?
Maretha: Eleven. I'm gonna be twelve soon.
Boy Willie: You like it up here? You like the North?
Maretha: It's alright.
Boy Willie: That there's Lymon. Did you say hi to Lymon?
Maretha: Hi.

Lymon: How you doing? You look just like your mama. I remember you when you was wearing diapers.

Boy Willie: You gonna come down South and see me? Uncle Boy Willie gonna get him a farm. Gonna get a great big old farm. Come down there and I'll teach you how to ride a mule. Teach you how to kill a chicken, too.

Maretha: I seen my mama do that.

Boy Willie: Ain't nothing to it. You just grab him by his neck and twist it. Get you a real good grip and then you just wring his neck and throw him in the pot. Cook him up. Then you got some good eating. What you like to eat? What kind of food you like?

Maretha: I like everything . . . except I don't like no black-eyed peas.

Boy Willie: Uncle Doaker tell me your mama got you playing that piano. Come on play something for me. (*Boy Willie crosses over to the piano followed by Maretha.*) Show me what you can do. Come on now. Here . . . Uncle Boy Willie give you a dime . . . show me what you can do. Don't be bashful now. That dime say you can't be bashful. (*Maretha plays. It is something any beginner first learns.*) Here, let me show you something. (*Boy Willie sits and plays a simple boogie-woogie.*) See that? See what I'm doing? That's what you call the boogie-woogie. See now . . . you can get up and dance to that. That's how good it sound. It sound like you wanna dance. You can dance to that. It'll hold you up. Whatever kind of dance you wanna do you can dance to that right there. See that? See how it go? Ain't nothing to it. Go on you do it.

Maretha: I got to read it on the paper.

Boy Willie: You don't need no paper. Go on. Do just like that there.

Berniece: Maretha! You get up here and get ready to go so you be on time. Ain't no need you trying to take advantage of company.

Maretha: I got to go.

Boy Willie: Uncle Boy Willie gonna get you a guitar. Let Uncle Doaker teach you how to play that. You don't need to read no paper to play the guitar. Your mama told you about the piano? You know how them pictures got on there?

Maretha: She say it just always been like that since she got it.

Boy Willie: You hear that, Doaker? And you sitting up here in the house with Berniece.

Doaker: I ain't got nothing to do with that. I don't get in the way of Berniece's raising her.

Boy Willie: You tell your mama to tell you about that piano. You ask her how them pictures got on there. If she don't tell you I'll tell you.

Berniece: Maretha!

Maretha: I got to get ready to go.

Boy Willie: She getting big, Doaker. You remember her, Lymon?

Lymon: She used to be real little.

There is a knock on the door. Doaker goes to answer it. Avery enters. Thirty-eight years old, honest and ambitious, he has taken to the city like a fish to water, finding in it opportunities for growth and advancement that did not exist for him in the rural South. He is dressed in a suit and tie with a gold cross around his neck. He carries a small Bible.

Doaker: Hey, Avery, come on in. Berniece upstairs.

Boy Willie: Look at him . . . look at him . . . he don't know what to say. He wasn't expecting to see me.

Avery: Hey, Boy Willie. What you doing up here?

Boy Willie: Look at him, Lymon.

Avery: Is that Lymon? Lymon Jackson?

Boy Willie: Yeah, you know Lymon.

Doaker: Berniece be ready in a minute, Avery.

Boy Willie: Doaker say you a preacher now. What . . . we supposed to call you Reverend? You used to be plain old Avery. When you get to be a preacher, nigger?

Lymon: Avery say he gonna be a preacher so he don't have to work.

Boy Willie: I remember when you was down there on the Willshaw place planting cotton. You wasn't thinking about no Reverend then.

Avery: That must be your truck out there. I saw that truck with them watermelons, I was trying to figure out what it was doing in front of the house.

Boy Willie: Yeah, me and Lymon selling watermelons. That's Lymon's truck.

Doaker: Berniece say you all going down to the bank.

Avery: Yeah, they give me a half day off work. I got an appointment to talk to the bank about getting a loan to start my church.

Boy Willie: Lymon say preachers don't have to work. Where you working at, nigger?

Doaker: Avery got him one of them good jobs. He working at one of them skyscrapers downtown.

Avery: I'm working down there at the Gulf Building running an elevator. Got a pension and everything. They even give you a turkey on Thanksgiving.

Lymon: How you know the rope ain't gonna break? Ain't you scared the rope's gonna break?

Avery: That's steel. They got steel cables hold it up. It take a whole lot of breaking to break that steel. Naw, I ain't worried about nothing like that. It ain't nothing but a little old elevator. Now, I wouldn't get in none of them airplanes. You couldn't pay me to do nothing like that.

Lymon: That be fun. I'd rather do that than ride in one of them elevators.

Boy Willie: How many of them watermelons you wanna buy?

Avery: I thought you was gonna give me one seeing as how you got a whole truck full.

Boy Willie: You can get one, get two. I'll give you two for a dollar.

Avery: I can't eat but one. How much are they?

Boy Willie: Aw, nigger, you know I'll give you a watermelon. Go on, take as many as you want. Just leave some for me and Lymon to sell.

Avery: I don't want but one.

Boy Willie: How you get to be a preacher, Avery? I might want to be a preacher one day. Have everybody call me Reverend Boy Willie.

Avery: It come to me in a dream. God called me and told me he wanted me to be a shepherd for his flock. That's what I'm gonna call my church . . . The Good Shepherd Church of God in Christ.

Doaker: Tell him what you told me. Tell him about the three hobos.

Avery: Boy Willie don't want to hear all that.

Lymon: I do. Lots a people say your dreams can come true.

Avery: Naw. You don't want to hear all that.

Doaker: Go on. I told him you was a preacher. He didn't want to believe me. Tell him about the three hobos.

Avery: Well, it come to me in a dream. See . . . I was sitting out in this railroad
yard watching the trains go by. The train stopped and these three hobos
got off. They told me they had come from Nazareth and was on their way
to Jerusalem. They had three candles. They gave me one and told me to
light it . . . but to be careful that it didn't go out. Next thing I knew I was
standing in front of this house. Something told me to go knock on the
door. This old woman opened the door and said they had been waiting on
me. Then she led me into this room. It was a big room and it was full of all
kinds of different people. They looked like anybody else except they all
had sheep heads and was making noise like sheep make. I heard somebody
call my name. I looked around and there was these same three hobos. They
told me to take off my clothes and they give me a blue robe with gold
thread. They washed my feet and combed my hair. Then they showed me
these three doors and told me to pick one.

     I went through one of them doors and that flame leapt off that can-
dle and it seemed like my whole head caught fire. I looked around and
there was four or five other men standing there with these same blue robes
on. Then we heard a voice tell us to look out across this valley. We looked
out and saw the valley was full of wolves. The voice told us that these
sheep people that I had seen in the other room had to go over to the other
side of this valley and somebody had to take them. Then I heard another
voice say, "Who shall I send?" Next thing I knew I said, "Here I am. Send
me." That's when I met Jesus. He say, "If you go, I'll go with you." Something told me to say, "Come on. Let's go." That's when I woke up. My head
still felt like it was on fire . . . but I had a peace about myself that was hard
to explain. I knew right then that I had been filled with the Holy Ghost
and called to be a servant of the Lord. It took me a while before I could accept that. But then a lot of little ways God showed me that it was true. So I
became a preacher.

Lymon: I see why you gonna call it the Good Shepherd Church. You dreaming
about them sheep people. I can see that easy.

Boy Willie: Doaker say you sent some white man past the house to look at that
piano. Say he was going around to all the colored people's houses looking
to buy up musical instruments.

Avery: Yeah, but Berniece didn't want to sell that piano. After she told me
about it . . . I could see why she didn't want to sell it.

Boy Willie: What's this man's name?

Avery: Oh, that's a while back now. I done forgot his name. He give Berniece a
card with his name and telephone number on it, but I believe she throwed
it away.

Berniece and Maretha enter from the stairs.

Berniece: Maretha, run back upstairs and get my pocketbook. And wipe that
hair grease off your forehead. Go ahead, hurry up.

Maretha exits up the stairs.

     How you doing, Avery? You done got all dressed up. You look nice. Boy
Willie, I thought you and Lymon was going to sell them watermelons.

Boy Willie: Lymon done got sleepy. We liable to get some sleep first.

Lymon: I ain't sleepy.

Doaker: As many watermelons as you got stacked up on that truck out there, you ought to have been gone.

Boy Willie: We gonna go in a minute. We going.

Berniece: Doaker. I'm gonna stop down there on Logan Street. You want anything?

Doaker: You can pick up some ham hocks if you going down there. See if you can get the smoked ones. If they ain't got that get the fresh ones. Don't get the ones that got all that fat under the skin. Look for the long ones. They nice and lean. *(He gives her a dollar.)* Don't get the short ones lessen they smoked. If you got to get the fresh ones make sure that they the long ones. If they ain't got them smoked then go ahead and get the short ones. *(Pause.)* You may as well get some turnip greens while you down there. I got some buttermilk . . . if you pick up some cornmeal I'll make me some cornbread and cook up them turnip greens.

Maretha enters from the stairs.

Maretha: We gonna take the streetcar?

Berniece: Me and Avery gonna drop you off at the settlement house. You mind them people down there. Don't be going down there showing your color. Boy Willie, I done told you what to do. I'll see you later, Doaker.

Avery: I'll be seeing you again, Boy Willie.

Boy Willie: Hey, Berniece . . . what's the name of that man Avery sent past say he want to buy the piano?

Berniece: I knew it. I knew it when I first seen you. I knew you was up to something.

Boy Willie: Sutter's brother say he selling the land to me. He waiting on me now. Told me he'd give me two weeks. I got one part. Sell them watermelons get me another part. Then we can sell the piano and I'll have the third part.

Berniece: I ain't selling that piano, Boy Willie. If that's why you come up here you can just forget about it. *(To Doaker.)* Doaker, I'll see you later. Boy Willie ain't nothing but a whole lot of mouth. I ain't paying him no mind. If he come up here thinking he gonna sell that piano then he done come up here for nothing.

Berniece, Avery, and Maretha exit the front door.

Boy Willie: Hey, Lymon! You ready to go sell these watermelons. *(Boy Willie and Lymon start to exit. At the door Boy Willie turns to Doaker.)* Hey, Doaker . . . if Berniece don't want to sell that piano . . . I'm gonna cut it in half and go on and sell my half.

Boy Willie and Lymon exit.

The lights go down on the scene.

SCENE II

The lights come up on the kitchen. It is three days later. Wining Boy sits at the kitchen table. There is a half-empty pint bottle on the table. Doaker busies himself washing pots. Wining Boy is fifty-six years old. Doaker's older brother, he tries to present the image of a successful musician and gambler, but his music, his clothes, and even his manner of presentation are old. He is a man who looking back over his life continues to live it with an odd mixture of zest and sorrow.

Wining Boy: So the Ghosts of the Yellow Dog got Sutter. That just go to show you I believe I always lived right. They say every dog gonna have his day and time it go around it sure come back to you. I done seen that a thousand times. I know the truth of that. But I'll tell you outright . . . if I see Sutter's ghost I'll be on the first thing I find that got wheels on it.

Doaker enters from his room.

Doaker: Wining Boy!

Wining Boy: And I'll tell you another thing . . . Berniece ain't gonna sell that piano.

Doaker: That's what she told him. He say he gonna cut it in half and go on and sell his half. They been around here three days trying to sell them watermelons. They trying to get out to where the white folks live but the truck keep breaking down. They go a block or two and it break down again. They trying to get out to Squirrel Hill and can't get around the corner. He say soon as he can get that truck empty to where he can set the piano up in there he gonna take it out of here and go sell it.

Wining Boy: What about them boys Sutter got? How come they ain't farming that land?

Doaker: One of them going to school. He left down there and come North to school. The other one ain't got as much sense as that frying pan over yonder. That is the dumbest white man I ever seen. He'd stand in the river and watch it rise till it drown him.

Wining Boy: Other than seeing Sutter's ghost how's Berniece doing?

Doaker: She doing alright. She still got Crawley on her mind. He been dead three years but she still holding on to him. She need to go out here and let one of these fellows grab a whole handful of whatever she got. She act like it done got precious.

Wining Boy: They always told me any fish will bite if you got good bait.

Doaker: She stuck up on it. She think it's better than she is. I believe she messing around with Avery. They got something going. He a preacher now. If you let him tell it the Holy Ghost sat on his head and heaven opened up with thunder and lightning and God was calling his name. Told him to go out and preach and tend to his flock. That's what he gonna call his church. The Good Shepherd Church.

Wining Boy: They had that joker down in Spear walking around talking about he Jesus Christ. He gonna live the life of Christ. Went through the Last Supper and everything. Rented him a mule on Palm Sunday and rode through the town. Did everything . . . talking about he Christ. He did everything until they got up to that crucifixion part. Got up to that part and told everybody to go home and quit pretending. He got up to the crucifixion part and changed his mind. Had a whole bunch of folks come down here to see him get nailed to the cross. I don't know who's the worse fool. Him or them. Had all them folks come down there . . . even carried the cross up this little hill. People standing around waiting to see him get nailed to the cross and he stop everything and preach a little sermon and told everybody to go home. Had enough nerve to tell them to come to church on Easter Sunday to celebrate his resurrection.

Doaker: I'm surprised Avery ain't thought about that. He trying every little thing to get him a congregation together. They meeting over at his house till he get him a church.

Wining Boy: Ain't nothing wrong with being a preacher. You got the preacher on one hand and the gambler on the other. Sometimes there ain't too much difference in them.

Doaker: How long you been in Kansas City?

Wining Boy: Since I left here. I got tied up with some old gal down there. *(Pause.)* You know Cleotha died.

Doaker: Yeah, I heard that last time I was down there. I was sorry to hear that.

Wining Boy: One of her friends wrote and told me. I got the letter right here. *(He takes the letter out of his pocket.)* I was down in Kansas City and she wrote and told me Cleotha had died. Name of Willa Bryant. She say she know cousin Rupert. *(He opens the letter and reads:)*

Dear Wining Boy: I am writing this letter to let you know Miss Cleotha Holman passed on Saturday the first of May she departed this world in the loving arms of her sister Miss Alberta Samuels. I know you would want to know this and am writing as a friend of Cleotha. There have been many hardships since last you seen her but she survived them all and to the end was a good woman whom I hope have God's grace and is in His Paradise. Your cousin Rupert Bates is my friend also and he give me your address and I pray this reaches you about Cleotha. Miss Willa Bryant. A friend.

(He folds the letter and returns it to his pocket.) They was nailing her coffin shut by the time I heard about it. I never knew she was sick. I believe it was that yellow jaundice. That's what killed her mama.

Doaker: Cleotha wasn't but forty-some.

Wining Boy: She was forty-six. I got ten years on her. I met her when she was sixteen. You remember I used to run around there. Couldn't nothing keep me still. Much as I loved Cleotha I loved to ramble. Couldn't nothing keep me still. We got married and we used to fight about it all the time. Then one day she asked me to leave. Told me she loved me before I left. Told me, Wining Boy, you got a home as long as I got mine. And I believe in my heart I always felt that and that kept me safe.

Doaker: Cleotha always did have a nice way about her.

Wining Boy: Man that woman was something. I used to thank the Lord. Many a night I sat up and looked out over my life. Said, well, I had Cleotha. When it didn't look like there was nothing else for me, I said, thank God, at least I had that. If ever I go anywhere in this life I done known a good woman. And that used to hold me till the next morning. *(Pause.)* What you got? Give me a little nip. I know you got something stuck up in your room.

Doaker: I ain't seen you walk in here and put nothing on the table. You done sat there and drank up your whiskey. Now you talking about what you got.

Wining Boy: I got plenty money. Give me a little nip.

Doaker carries a glass into his room and returns with it half-filled. He sets it on the table in front of Wining Boy.

Wining Boy: You hear from Coreen?

Doaker: She up in New York. I let her go from my mind.

Wining Boy: She was something back then. She wasn't too pretty but she had a way of looking at you made you know there was a whole lot of woman there. You got married and snatched her out from under us and we all got mad at you.

Doaker: She up in New York City. That's what I hear.

The door opens and Boy Willie and Lymon enter.

Boy Willie: Aw hell . . . look here! We was just talking about you. Doaker say you left out of here with a whole sack of money. I told him he wasn't going see you till you got broke.

Wining Boy: What you mean broke? I got a whole pocketful of money.

Doaker: Did you all get that truck fixed?

Boy Willie: We got it running and got halfway out there on Centre and it broke down again. Lymon went out there and messed it up some more. Fellow told us we got to wait till tomorrow to get it fixed. Say he have it running like new. Lymon going back down there and sleep in the truck so the people don't take the watermelons.

Lymon: Lymon nothing. You go down there and sleep in it.

Boy Willie: You was sleeping in it down home, nigger! I don't know nothing about sleeping in no truck.

Lymon: I ain't sleeping in no truck.

Boy Willie: They can take all the watermelons. I don't care. Wining Boy, where you coming from? Where you been?

Wining Boy: I been down in Kansas City.

Boy Willie: You remember Lymon? Lymon Jackson.

Wining Boy: Yeah, I used to know his daddy.

Boy Willie: Doaker say you don't never leave no address with nobody. Say he got to depend on your whim. See when it strike you to pay a visit.

Wining Boy: I got four or five addresses.

Boy Willie: Doaker say Berniece asked you for three dollars and you got mad and left.

Wining Boy: Berniece try and rule over you too much for me. That's why I left. It wasn't about no three dollars.

Boy Willie: Where you getting all these sacks of money from? I need to be with you. Doaker say you had a whole sack of money . . . turn some of it loose.

Wining Boy: I was just fixing to ask you for five dollars.

Boy Willie: I ain't got no money. I'm trying to get some. Doaker tell you about Sutter? The Ghosts of the Yellow Dog got him about three weeks ago. Berniece done seen his ghost and everything. He right upstairs. *(Calls.)* Hey Sutter! Wining Boy's here. Come on, get a drink!

Wining Boy: How many that make the Ghosts of the Yellow Dog done got?

Boy Willie: Must be about nine or ten, eleven or twelve. I don't know.

Doaker: You got Ed Saunders. Howard Peterson. Charlie Webb.

Wining Boy: Robert Smith. That fellow that shot Becky's boy . . . say he was stealing peaches . . .

Doaker: You talking about Bob Mallory.

Boy Willie: Berniece say she don't believe all that about the Ghosts of the Yellow Dog.

Wining Boy: She ain't got to believe. You go ask them white folks in Sunflower County if they believe. You go ask Sutter if he believe. I don't care if

Berniece believe or not. I done been to where the Southern cross the Yellow Dog and called out their names. They talk back to you, too.

Lymon: What they sound like? The wind or something?

Boy Willie: You done been there for real, Wining Boy?

Wining Boy: Nineteen thirty. July of nineteen thirty I stood right there on that spot. It didn't look like nothing was going right in my life. I said everything can't go wrong all the time . . . let me go down there and call on the Ghosts of the Yellow Dog, see if they can help me. I went down there and right there where them two railroads cross each other . . . I stood right there on that spot and called out their names. They talk back to you, too.

Lymon: People say you can ask them questions. They talk to you like that?

Wining Boy: A lot of things you got to find out on your own. I can't say how they talked to nobody else. But to me it just filled me up in a strange sort of way to be standing there on that spot. I didn't want to leave. It felt like the longer I stood there the bigger I got. I seen the train coming and it seem like I was bigger than the train. I started not to move. But something told me to go ahead and get on out the way. The train passed and I started to go back up there and stand some more. But something told me not to do it. I walked away from there feeling like a king. Went on and had a stroke of luck that run on for three years. So I don't care if Berniece believe or not. Berniece ain't got to believe. I know cause I been there. Now Doaker'll tell you about the Ghosts of the Yellow Dog.

Doaker: I don't try and talk that stuff with Berniece. Avery got her all tied up in that church. She just think it's a whole lot of nonsense.

Boy Willie: Berniece don't believe in nothing. She just think she believe. She believe in anything if it's convenient for her to believe. But when that convenience run out then she ain't got nothing to stand on.

Wining Boy: Let's not get on Berniece now. Doaker tell me you talking about selling that piano.

Boy Willie: Yeah . . . hey, Doaker, I got the name of that man Avery was talking about. The man's what's fixing the truck gave me his name. Everybody know him. Say he buy up anything you can make music with. I got his name and his telephone number. Hey, Wining Boy, Sutter's brother say he selling the land to me. I got one part. Sell them watermelons get me the second part. Then . . . soon as I get them watermelons out that truck I'm gonna take and sell that piano and get the third part.

Doaker: That land ain't worth nothing no more. The smart white man's up here in these cities. He cut the land loose and step back and watch you and the dumb white man argue over it.

Wining Boy: How you know Sutter's brother ain't sold it already? You talking about selling the piano and the man's liable to sold the land two or three times.

Boy Willie: He say he waiting on me. He say he give me two weeks. That's two weeks from Friday. Say if I ain't back by then he might gonna sell it to somebody else. He say he wanna see me with it.

Wining Boy: You know as well as I know the man gonna sell the land to the first one walk up and hand him the money.

Boy Willie: That's just who I'm gonna be. Look, you ain't gotta know he waiting on me. I know. Okay. I know what the man told me. Stoval already down tried to buy the land from him and he told him no. The man say he waiting on me . . . he waiting on me. Hey, Doaker . . . give me a drink. I see Wining Boy got his glass. (*Doaker exits into his room.*) Wining Boy, what you doing in Kansas City? What they got down there?

Lymon: I hear they got some nice-looking women in Kansas City. I sure like to go down there and find out.

Wining Boy: Man, the women down there is something else.

Doaker enters with a bottle of whiskey. He sets it on the table with some glasses.

Doaker: You wanna sit up here and drink up my whiskey, leave a dollar on the table when you get up.

Boy Willie: You ain't doing nothing but showing your hospitality. I know we ain't got to pay for your hospitality.

Wining Boy: Doaker say they had you and Lymon down on the Parchman Farm. Had you on my old stomping grounds.

Boy Willie: Me and Lymon was down there hauling wood for Jim Miller and keeping us a little bit to sell. Some white fellows tried to run us off of it. That's when Crawley got killed. They put me and Lymon in the penitentiary.

Lymon: They ambushed us right there where that road dip down and around that bend in the creek. Crawley tried to fight them. Me and Boy Willie got away but the sheriff got us. Say we was stealing wood. They shot me in my stomach.

Boy Willie: They looking for Lymon down there now. They rounded him up and put him in jail for not working.

Lymon: Fined me a hundred dollars. Mr. Stovall come and paid my hundred dollars and the judge say I got to work for him to pay him back his hundred dollars. I told them I'd rather take my thirty days but they wouldn't let me do that.

Boy Willie: As soon as Stovall turned his back, Lymon was gone. He down there living in that truck dodging the sheriff and Stovall. He got both of them looking for him. So I brought him up here.

Lymon: I told Boy Willie I'm gonna stay up here. I ain't going back with him.

Boy Willie: Ain't nobody twisting your arm to make you go back. You can do what you want to do.

Wining Boy: I'll go back with you. I'm on my way down there. You gonna take the train? I'm gonna take the train.

Lymon: They treat you better up here.

Boy Willie: I ain't worried about nobody mistreating me. They treat you like you let them treat you. They mistreat me I mistreat them right back. Ain't no difference in me and the white man.

Wining Boy: Ain't no difference as far as how somebody supposed to treat you. I agree with that. But I'll tell you the difference between the colored man and the white man. Alright. Now you take and eat some berries. They taste real good to you. So you say I'm gonna go out and get me a whole pot of these berries and cook them up to make a pie or whatever. But you ain't looked to see them berries is sitting in the white fellow's yard. Ain't got no fence around them. You figure anybody want something they'd fence it in. Alright. Now the white man come along and say that's my land. Therefore everything that grow on it belong to me. He tell the sheriff. "I want you to put this nigger in jail as a warning to all the other niggers. Otherwise first thing you know these niggers have everything that belong to us."

Boy Willie: I'd come back at night and haul off his whole patch while he was asleep.

Wining Boy: Alright. Now Mr. So and So, he sell the land to you. And he come to you and say, "John, you own the land. It's all yours now. But them is my berries. And come time to pick them I'm gonna send my boys over. You got the land . . . but them berries, I'm gonna keep them. They mine." And he go and fix it with the law that them is his berries. Now that's the difference between the colored man and the white man. The colored man can't fix nothing with the law.

Boy Willie: I don't go by what the law say. The law's liable to say anything. I go by if it's right or not. It don't matter to me what the law say. I take and look at it for myself.

Lymon: That's why you gonna end up back down there on the Parchman Farm.

Boy Willie: I ain't thinking about no Parchman Farm. You liable to go back before me.

Lymon: They work you too hard down there. All that weeding and hoeing and chopping down trees. I didn't like all that.

Wining Boy: You ain't got to like your job on Parchman. Hey, tell him, Doaker, the only one got to like his job is the waterboy.

Doaker: If he don't like his job he need to set that bucket down.

Boy Willie: That's what they told Lymon. They had Lymon on water and everybody got mad at him cause he was lazy.

Lymon: That water was heavy.

Boy Willie: They had Lymon down there singing *(sings):*

O Lord Berta Berta O Lord gal oh-ah
O Lord Berta Berta O Lord gal well

Lymon and Wining Boy join in.

Go 'head marry don't you wait on me oh-ah
Go 'head marry don't you wait on me well
Might not want you when I go free oh-ah
Might not want you when I go free well

Boy Willie: Come on, Doaker. Doaker know this one.

As Doaker joins in the men stamp and clap to keep time. They sing in harmony with great fervor and style.

O Lord Berta Berta O Lord gal oh-ah
O Lord Berta Berta O Lord gal well

Raise them up higher, let them drop on down oh-ah
Raise them up higher, let them drop on down well
Don't know the difference when the sun go down oh-ah
Don't know the difference when the sun go down well

Berta in Meridan and she living at ease oh-ah
Berta in Meridan and she living at ease well
I'm on old Parchman, got to work or leave oh-ah
I'm on old Parchman, got to work or leave well

O Alberta, Berta, O Lord gal oh-ah
O Alberta, Berta, O Lord gal well

When you marry, don't marry no farming man oh-ah
When you marry, don't marry no farming man well
Everyday Monday, hoe handle in your hand oh-ah
Everyday Monday, hoe handle in your hand well

When you marry, marry a railroad man, oh-ah
When you marry, marry a railroad man, well
Everyday Sunday, dollar in your hand oh-ah
Everyday Sunday, dollar in your hand well

O Alberta, Berta, O Lord gal oh-ah
O Alberta, Berta, O Lord gal well

Boy Willie: Doaker like that part. He like that railroad part.

Lymon: Doaker sound like Tangleye. He can't sing a lick.

Boy Willie: Hey, Doaker, they still talk about you down on Parchman. They ask me, "You Doaker Boy's nephew?" I say, "Yeah, me and him is family." They treated me alright soon as I told them that. Say, "Yeah, he my uncle."

Doaker: I don't never want to see none of them niggers no more.

Boy Willie: I don't want to see them either. Hey, Wining Boy, come on play some piano. You a piano player, play some piano. Lymon wanna hear you.

Wining Boy: I give that piano up. That was the best thing that ever happened to me, getting rid of that piano. That piano got so big and I'm carrying it around on my back. I don't wish that on nobody. See, you think it's all fun being a recording star. Got to carrying that piano around and man did I get slow. Got just like molasses. The world just slipping by me and I'm walking around with that piano. Alright. Now, there ain't but so many places you can go. Only so many road wide enough for you and that piano. And that piano get heavier and heavier. Go to a place and they find out you play piano, the first thing they want to do is give you a drink, find you a piano, and sit you right down. And that's where you gonna be for the next eight hours. They ain't gonna let you get up! Now, the first three or four years of that is fun. You can't get enough whiskey and you can't get enough women and you don't never get tired of playing that piano. But that only last so long. You look up one day and you hate the whiskey, and you hate the women, and you hate the piano. But that's all you got. You can't do nothing else. All you know how to do is play that piano. Now who am I? Am I me? Or am I the piano player? Sometime it seem like the only thing to do is shoot the piano player cause he the cause of all the trouble I'm having.

Doaker: What you gonna do when your troubles get like mine?

Lymon: If I knew how to play it, I'd play it. That's a nice piano.

Boy Willie: Whoever playing better play quick. Sutter's brother say he waiting on me. I sell them watermelons. Get Berniece to sell that piano. Put them two parts with the part I done saved . . .

Wining Boy: Berniece ain't gonna sell that piano. I don't see why you don't know that.

Boy Willie: What she gonna do with it? She ain't doing nothing but letting it sit up there and rot. That piano ain't doing nobody no good.

Lymon: That's a nice piano. If I had it I'd sell it. Unless I knew how to play like Wining Boy. You can get a nice price for that piano.

Doaker: Now I'm gonna tell you something, Lymon don't know this . . . but I'm gonna tell you why me and Wining Boy say Berniece ain't gonna sell that piano.

Boy Willie: She ain't got to sell it! I'm gonna sell it! Berniece ain't got no more rights to that piano than I do.

Doaker: I'm talking to the man . . . let me talk to the man. See, now . . . to understand why we say that . . . to understand about the piano . . . you got to go back to slavery time. See, our family was owned by a fellow named Robert Sutter. That was Sutter's grandfather. Alright. The piano was owned by a fellow named Joel Nolander. He was one of the Nolander brothers from down in Georgia. It was coming up on Sutter's wedding anniversary and he was looking to buy his wife . . . Miss Ophelia was her name . . . he was looking to buy her an anniversary present. Only thing with him . . . he ain't had no money. But he had some niggers. So he asked Mr. Nolander to see if maybe he could trade off some of his niggers for that piano. Told him he would give him one and a half niggers for it. That's the way he told him. Say he could have one full grown and one half grown. Mr. Nolander agreed only he say he had to pick them. He didn't want Sutter to give him just any old nigger. He say he wanted to have the pick of the litter. So Sutter lined up his niggers and Mr. Nolander looked them over and out of the whole bunch he picked my grandmother . . . her name was Berniece . . . same like Berniece . . . and he picked my daddy when he wasn't nothing but a little boy nine years old. They made the trade off and Miss Ophelia was so happy with that piano that it got to be just about all she would do was play on that piano.

Wining Boy: Just get up in the morning, get all dressed up and sit down and play on that piano.

Doaker: Alright. Time go along. Time go along. Miss Ophelia got to missing my grandmother . . . the way she would cook and clean the house and talk to her and what not. And she missed having my daddy around the house to fetch things for her. So she asked to see if maybe she could trade back that piano and get her niggers back. Mr. Nolander said no. Said a deal was a deal. Him and Sutter had a big falling out about it and Miss Ophelia took sick to the bed. Wouldn't get out of bed in the morning. She just lay there. The doctor said she was wasting away.

Wining Boy: That's when Sutter called our granddaddy up to the house.

Doaker: Now, our granddaddy's name was Boy Willie. That's who Boy Willie's named after . . . only they called him Willie Boy. Now, he was a worker of wood. He could make you anything you wanted out of wood. He'd make you a desk. A table. A lamp. Anything you wanted. Them white fellows around there used to come up to Mr. Sutter and get him to make all kinds of things for them. Then they'd pay Mr. Sutter a nice price. See, everything my granddaddy made Mr. Sutter owned cause he owned him. That's why when Mr. Nolander offered to buy him to keep the family together Mr. Sutter wouldn't sell him. Told Mr. Nolander he didn't have enough money to buy him. Now . . . am I telling it right, Wining Boy?

Wining Boy: You telling it.

Doaker: Sutter called him up to the house and told him to carve my grandmother and my daddy's picture on the piano for Miss Ophelia. And he
took and carved this . . . *(Doaker crosses over to the piano.)* See that right
there? That's my grandmother, Berniece. She looked just like that. And he
put a picture of my daddy when he wasn't nothing but a little boy the way
he remembered him. He made them up out of his memory. Only thing . . .
he didn't stop there. He carved all this. He got a picture of his mama . . .
Mama Esther . . . and his daddy, Boy Charles.

Wining Boy: That was the first Boy Charles.

Doaker: Then he put on the side here all kinds of things. See that? That's
when him and Mama Berniece got married. They called it jumping the
broom. That's how you got married in them days. Then he got here when
my daddy was born . . . and here he got Mama Esther's funeral . . . and
down here he got Mr. Nolander taking Mama Berniece and my daddy
away down to his place in Georgia. He got all kinds of things what happened with our family. When Mr. Sutter seen the piano with all them carvings on it he got mad. He didn't ask for all that. But see . . . there wasn't
nothing he could do about it. When Miss Ophelia seen it . . . she got excited. Now she had her piano and her niggers too. She took back to playing it and played on it right up till the day she died. Alright . . . now see,
our brother Boy Charles . . . that's Berniece and Boy Willie's daddy . . . he
was the oldest of us three boys. He's dead now. But he would have been
fifty-seven if he had lived. He died in 1911 when he was thirty-one years old.
Boy Charles used to talk about that piano all the time. He never could get
it off his mind. Two or three months go by and he be talking about it
again. He be talking about taking it out of Sutter's house. Say it was the
story of our whole family and as long as Sutter had it . . . he had us. Say we
was still in slavery. Me and Wining Boy tried to talk him out of it but it
wouldn't do any good. Soon as he quiet down about it he'd start up again.
We seen where he wasn't gonna get it off his mind . . . so, on the Fourth of
July, 1911 . . . when Sutter was at the picnic what the county give every
year . . . me and Wining Boy went on down there with him and took the
piano out of Sutter's house. We put it on a wagon and me and Wining Boy
carried it over into the next county with Mama Ola's people. Boy Charles
decided to stay around there and wait until Sutter got home to make it
look like business as usual.

    Now, I don't know what happened when Sutter came home and
found the piano gone. But somebody went up to Boy Charles's house and
set it on fire. But he wasn't in there. He must have seen them coming cause
he went down and caught the 3:57 Yellow Dog. He didn't know they was
gonna come down and stop the train. Stopped the train and found Boy
Charles in the boxcar with four of them hobos. Must have got mad when
they couldn't find the piano cause they set the boxcar afire and killed
everybody. Now, nobody know who done that. Some people say it was Sutter cause it was his piano. Some people say it was Sheriff Carter. Some
people say it was Robert Smith and Ed Saunders. But don't nobody know
for sure. It was about two months after that that Ed Saunders fell down
his well. Just upped and fell down his well for no reason. People say it was
the ghost of them who burned up in the boxcar that pushed him in his
well. They started calling them the Ghosts of the Yellow Dog. Now, that's

how all that got started and that why we say Berniece ain't gonna sell that
piano. Cause her daddy died over it.

Boy Willie: All that's in the past. If my daddy had seen where he could have
traded that piano in for some land of his own, it wouldn't be sitting up
here now. He spent his whole life farming on somebody else's land. I ain't
gonna do that. See, he couldn't do no better. When he come along he ain't
had nothing he could build on. His daddy ain't had nothing to give him.
The only thing my daddy had to give me was that piano. And he died over
giving me that. I ain't gonna let it sit up there and rot without trying to do
something with it. If Berniece can't see that, then I'm gonna go ahead and
sell my half. And you and Wining Boy know I'm right.

Doaker: Ain't nobody said nothing about who's right and who's wrong. I was
just telling the man about the piano. I was telling him why we say Berniece
ain't gonna sell it.

Lymon: Yeah, I can see why you say that now. I told Boy Willie he ought to stay
up here with me.

Boy Willie: You stay! I'm going back! That's what I'm gonna do with my life!
Why I got to come up here and learn to do something I don't know how to
do when I already know how to farm? You stay up here and make your
own way if that's what you want to do. I'm going back and live my life the
way I want to live it.

Wining Boy gets up and crosses to the piano.

Wining Boy: Let's see what we got here. I ain't played on this thing for a while.

Doaker: You can stop telling that. You was playing on it the last time you was
through here. We couldn't get you off of it. Go on and play something.

*Wining Boy sits down at the piano and plays and sings. The song is one which has
put many dimes and quarters in his pocket, long ago, in dimly remembered towns
and way stations. He plays badly, without hesitation, and sings in a forceful voice.*

Wining Boy (singing):

> I am a rambling gambling man
> I gambled in many towns
> I rambled this wide world over
> I rambled this world around
> I had my ups and downs in life
> And bitter times I saw
> But I never knew what misery was
> Till I lit on old Arkansas.
>
> I started out one morning
> to meet that early train
> He said, "You better work for me
> I have some land to drain.
> I'll give you fifty cents a day,
> Your washing, board and all
> And you shall be a different man
> In the state of Arkansas."
>
> I worked six months for the rascal
> Joe Herrin was his name

He fed me old corn dodgers
They was hard as any rock
My tooth is all got loosened
And my knees begin to knock
That was the kind of hash I got
In the state of Arkansas.

Traveling man
I've traveled all around this world
Traveling man
I've traveled from land to land
Traveling man
I've traveled all around this world
Well it ain't no use
writing no news
I'm a traveling man.

The door opens and Berniece enters with Maretha.

Berniece: Is that . . . Lord, I know that ain't Wining Boy sitting there.

Wining Boy: Hey, Berniece.

Berniece: You all had this planned. You and Boy Willie had this planned.

Wining Boy: I didn't know he was gonna be here. I'm on my way down home. I stopped by to see you and Doaker first.

Doaker: I told the nigger he left out of here with that sack of money, we thought we might never see him again. Boy Willie say he wasn't gonna see him till he got broke. I looked up and seen him sitting on the doorstep asking for two dollars. Look at him laughing. He know it's the truth.

Berniece: Boy Willie, I didn't see that truck out there. I thought you was out selling watermelons.

Boy Willie: We done sold them all. Sold the truck too.

Berniece: I don't want to go through none of your stuff. I done told you to go back where you belong.

Boy Willie: I was just teasing you, woman. You can't take no teasing?

Berniece: Wining Boy, when you get here?

Wining Boy: A little while ago. I took the train from Kansas City.

Berniece: Let me go upstairs and then I'll cook you something to eat.

Boy Willie: You ain't cooked me nothing when I come.

Berniece: Boy Willie, go on and leave me alone. Come on, Maretha, get up here and change your clothes before you get them dirty.

Berniece exits up the stairs, followed by Maretha.

Wining Boy: Maretha sure getting big, ain't she, Doaker. And just as pretty as she want to be. I didn't know Crawley had it in him.

Boy Willie crosses to the piano.

Boy Willie: Hey, Lymon . . . get up on the other side of this piano and let me see something.

Wining Boy: Boy Willie, what is you doing?

Boy Willie: I'm seeing how heavy this piano is. Get up over there, Lymon.

Wining Boy: Go on and leave that piano alone. You ain't taking that piano out of here and selling it.

Boy Willie: Just as soon as I get them watermelons out that truck.

Wining Boy: Well, I got something to say about that.

Boy Willie: This my daddy's piano.

Wining Boy: He ain't took it by himself. Me and Doaker helped him.

Boy Willie: He died by himself. Where was you and Doaker at then? Don't come telling me nothing about this piano. This is me and Berniece's piano. Am I right, Doaker?

Doaker: Yeah, you right.

Boy Willie: Let's see if we can lift it up, Lymon. Get a good grip on it and pick it up on your end. Ready? Lift!

> *As they start to move the piano, the sound of Sutter's Ghost is heard. Doaker is the only one to hear it. With difficulty they move the piano a little bit so it is out of place.*

Boy Willie: What do you think?

Lymon: It's heavy . . . but you can move it. Only it ain't gonna be easy.

Boy Willie: It wasn't that heavy to me. Okay, let's put it back.

> *The sound of Sutter's Ghost is heard again. They all hear it as Berniece enters on the stairs.*

Berniece: Boy Willie . . . you gonna play around with me one too many times. And then God's gonna bless you and West is gonna dress you. Now set that piano back over there. I done told you a hundred times I ain't selling that piano.

Boy Willie: I'm trying to get me some land, woman. I need that piano to get me some money so I can buy Sutter's land.

Berniece: Money can't buy what that piano cost. You can't sell your soul for money. It won't go with the buyer. It'll shrivel and shrink to know that you ain't taken on to it. But it won't go with the buyer.

Boy Willie: I ain't talking about all that, woman. I ain't talking about selling my soul. I'm talking about trading that piece of wood for some land. Get something under your feet. Land the only thing God ain't making no more of. You can always get you another piano. I'm talking about some land. What you get something out the ground from. That's what I'm talking about. You can't do nothing with that piano but sit up there and look at it.

Berniece: That's just what I'm gonna do. Wining Boy, you want me to fry you some pork chops?

Boy Willie: Now, I'm gonna tell you the way I see it. The only thing that makes that piano worth something is them carvings Papa Willie Boy put on there. That's what make it worth something. That was my great-granddaddy. Papa Boy Charles brought that piano into the house. Now, I'm supposed to build on what they left me. You can't do nothing with that piano sitting up here in the house. That's just like if I let them watermelons sit out there and rot. I'd be a fool. Alright now, if you say to me, Boy Willie, I'm using that piano. I give out lessons on it and that help me make my rent or whatever. Then that be something else. I'd have to go on and say, well, Berniece using that piano. She building on it. Let her go on and use it. I got to find another way to get Sutter's land. But Doaker say you ain't touched that piano the whole time it's been up here. So why you wanna stand in my way? See, you just looking at the sentimental value. See, that's good. That's alright. I take my hat off whenever somebody say my daddy's name. But I ain't gonna be no fool about no sentimental value. You can sit up here and look at the piano for the next hundred years and it's just gonna be a piano. You can't make more than that. Now I want to get Sutter's land with that piano. I get Sutter's land and I can go down and cash in the crop and get my seed. As long as I got the land and the seed then I'm alright. I can always get me a little something else. Cause that land give back to you. I can make me another crop and cash that in. I still got the land and the seed. But that piano don't put out nothing else. You ain't got nothing working for you. Now, the kind of man my daddy was he would have understood that. I'm sorry you can't see it that way. But that's why I'm gonna take that piano out of here and sell it.

Berniece: You ain't taking that piano out of my house. *(She crosses to the piano.)* Look at this piano. Look at it. Mama Ola polished this piano with her tears for seventeen years. For seventeen years she rubbed on it till her hands bled. Then she rubbed the blood in . . . mixed it up with the rest of the blood on it. Every day that God breathed life into her body she rubbed and cleaned and polished and prayed over it. "Play something for me, Berniece. Play something for me, Berniece." Every day. "I cleaned it up for you, play something for me, Berniece." You always talking about your daddy but you ain't never stopped to look at what his foolishness cost your mama. Seventeen years' worth of cold nights and an empty bed. For what? For a piano? For a piece of wood? To get even with somebody? I look at you and you're all the same. You, Papa Boy Charles, Wining Boy, Doaker, Crawley . . . you're all alike. All this thieving and killing and thieving and killing. And what it ever lead to? More killing and more thieving. I ain't never seen it come to nothing. People getting burned up. People getting shot. People falling down their wells. It don't never stop.

Doaker: Come on now, Berniece, ain't no need in getting upset.

Boy Willie: I done a little bit of stealing here and there, but I ain't never killed nobody. I can't be speaking for nobody else. You all got to speak for yourself, but I ain't never killed nobody.

Berniece: You killed Crawley just as sure as if you pulled the trigger.

Boy Willie: See, that's ignorant. That's downright foolish for you to say something like that. You ain't doing nothing but showing your ignorance. If the nigger was here I'd whup his ass for getting me and Lymon shot at.

Berniece: Crawley ain't knew about the wood.

Boy Willie: We told the man about the wood. Ask Lymon. He knew all about the wood. He seen we was sneaking it. Why else we gonna be out there at night? Don't come telling me Crawley ain't knew about the wood. Them fellows come up on us and Crawley tried to bully them. Me and Lymon seen the sheriff with them and give in. Wasn't no sense in getting killed over fifty dollars' worth of wood.

Berniece: Crawley ain't knew you stole that wood.

Boy Willie: We ain't stole no wood. Me and Lymon was hauling wood for Jim Miller and keeping us a little bit on the side. We dumped our little bit down there by the creek till we had enough to make a load. Some fellows seen us and we figured we better get it before they did. We come up there and got Crawley to help us load it. Figured we'd cut him in. Crawley trying to keep the wolf from his door . . . we was trying to help him.

Lymon: Me and Boy Willie told him about the wood. We told him some fellows might be trying to beat us to it. He say let me go back and get my thirty-eight. That's what caused all the trouble.

Boy Willie: If Crawley ain't had the gun he'd be alive today.

Lymon: We had it about half loaded when they come up on us. We seen the sheriff with them and we tried to get away. We ducked around near the bend in the creek . . . but they was down there too. Boy Willie say let's give in. But Crawley pulled out his gun and started shooting. That's when they started shooting back.

Berniece: All I know is Crawley would be alive if you hadn't come up there and got him.

Boy Willie: I ain't had nothing to do with Crawley getting killed. That was his own fault.

Berniece: Crawley's dead and in the ground and you still walking around here eating. That's all I know. He went off to load some wood with you and ain't never come back.

Boy Willie: I told you, woman . . . I ain't had nothing to do with . . .

Berniece: He ain't here, is he? He ain't here! *(Berniece hits Boy Willie.)* I said he ain't here. Is he? *(Berniece continues to hit Boy Willie, who doesn't move to defend himself, other than back up and turning his head so that most of the blows fall on his chest and arms.)*

Doaker (grabbing Berniece): Come on, Berniece . . . let it go, it ain't his fault.

Berniece: He ain't here, is he? Is he?

Boy Willie: I told you I ain't responsible for Crawley.

Berniece: He ain't here.

Boy Willie: Come on now, Berniece . . . don't do this now. Doaker get her. I ain't had nothing to do with Crawley . . .

Berniece: You come up there and got him!

Boy Willie: I done told you now. Doaker, get her. I ain't playing.

Doaker: Come on, Berniece.

Maretha is heard screaming upstairs. It is a scream of stark terror.

Maretha: Mama! . . . Mama!

The lights go down to black. End of Act I.

ACT II

SCENE I

The lights come up on the kitchen. It is the following morning. Doaker is ironing the pants to his uniform. He has a pot cooking on the stove at the same time. He is singing a song. The song provides him with the rhythm for his work and he moves about the kitchen with the ease born of many years as a railroad cook.

Doaker:

   Gonna leave Jackson Mississippi
   and go to Memphis
   and double back to Jackson
   Come on down to Hattiesburg

Change cars on the Y.D.
coming through the territory to
Meridian
and Meridian to Greenville
and Greenville to Memphis
I'm on my way and I know where

Change cars on the Katy
Leaving Jackson
and going through Clarksdale
Hello Winona!
Courtland!
Bateville!
Como!
Senitobia!
Lewisberg!
Sunflower!
Glendora!
Sharkey!
And double back to Jackson
Hello Greenwood
I'm on my way to Memphis
Clarksdale
Moorhead
Indianola
Can a highball pass through?
Highball on through sir
Grand Carson!
Thirty First Street Depot
Fourth Street Depot
Memphis!

Wining Boy enters carrying a suit of clothes.

Doaker: I thought you took that suit to the pawnshop.

Wining Boy: I went down there and the man tell me the suit is too old. Look at this suit. This is one hundred percent silk! How a silk suit gonna get too old? I know what it was he just didn't want to give me five dollars for it. Best he wanna give me is three dollars. I figure a silk suit is worth five dollars all over the world. I wasn't gonna part with it for no three dollars so I brought it back.

Doaker: They got another pawnshop up on Wylie.

Wining Boy: I carried it up there. He say he don't take no clothes. Only thing he take is guns and radios. Maybe a guitar or two. Where's Berniece?

Doaker: Berniece still at work. Boy Willie went down there to meet Lymon this morning. I guess they got that truck fixed, they been out there all day and ain't come back yet. Maretha scared to sleep up there now. Berniece don't know, but I seen Sutter before she did.

Wining Boy: Say what?

Doaker: About three weeks ago. I had just come back from down there. Sutter couldn't have been dead more than three days. He was sitting over there at the piano. I come out to go to work . . . and he was sitting right there. Had

his hand on top of his head just like Berniece said. I believe he broke his
neck when he fell in the well. I kept quiet about it. I didn't see no reason to
upset Berniece.

Wining Boy: Did he say anything? Did he say he was looking for Boy Willie?

Doaker: He was just sitting there. He ain't said nothing. I went on out the door
and left him sitting there. I figure as long as he was on the other side of
the room everything be alright. I don't know what I would have done if he
had started walking toward me.

Wining Boy: Berniece say he was calling Boy Willie's name.

Doaker: I ain't heard him say nothing. He was just sitting there when I seen
him. But I don't believe Boy Willie pushed him in the well. Sutter
here cause of that piano. I heard him playing on it one time. I thought it
was Berniece but then she don't play that kind of music. I come out here
and ain't seen nobody, but them piano keys moving a mile a minute.
Berniece need to go on and get rid of it. It ain't done nothing but cause
trouble.

Wining Boy: I agree with Berniece. Boy Charles ain't took it to give it back. He
took it cause he figure he had more right to it than Sutter did. If Sutter
can't understand that . . . then that's just the way that go. Sutter dead and
in the ground . . . don't care where his ghost is. He can hover around and
play on the piano all he want. I want to see him carry it out the house.
That's what I want to see. What time Berniece get home? I don't see how I
let her get away from me this morning.

Doaker: You up there sleep. Berniece leave out of here early in the morning.
She out there in Squirrel Hill cleaning house for some bigshot down there
at the steel mill. They don't like you to come late. You come late they won't
give you your carfare. What kind of business you got with Berniece?

Wining Boy: My business. I ain't asked you what kind of business you got.

Doaker: Berniece ain't got no money. If that's why you was trying to catch her.
She having a hard enough time trying to get by as it is. If she go ahead and
marry Avery . . . he working every day . . . she go ahead and marry him they
could do alright for themselves. But as it stands she ain't got no money.

Wining Boy: Well, let me have five dollars.

Doaker: I just give you a dollar before you left out of here. You ain't gonna take
my five dollars out there and gamble and drink it up.

Wining Boy: Aw, nigger, give me five dollars. I'll give it back to you.

Doaker: You wasn't looking to give me five dollars when you had that sack of
money. You wasn't looking to throw nothing my way. Now you wanna
come in here and borrow five dollars. If you going back with Boy Willie
you need to be trying to figure out how you gonna get train fare.

Wining Boy: That's why I need the five dollars. If I had five dollars I could get
me some money. *(Doaker goes into his pocket.)* Make it seven.

Doaker: You take this five dollars . . . and you bring my money back here too.

*Boy Willie and Lymon enter. They are happy and excited. They have money in all
of their pockets and are anxious to count it.*

Doaker: How'd you do out there?

Boy Willie: They was lining up for them.

Lymon: Me and Boy Willie couldn't sell them fast enough. Time we got one
sold we'd sell another.

Boy Willie: I seen what was happening and told Lymon to up the price on them.

Lymon: Boy Willie say charge them a quarter more. They didn't care. A couple of people give me a dollar and told me to keep the change.

Boy Willie: One fellow bought five. I say now what he gonna do with five watermelons? He can't eat them all. I sold him the five and asked him did he want to buy five more.

Lymon: I ain't never seen anybody snatch a dollar fast as Boy Willie.

Boy Willie: One lady asked me say, "Is they sweet?" I told her say, "Lady, where we grow these watermelons we put sugar in the ground." You know, she believed me. Talking about she had never heard of that before. Lymon was laughing his head off. I told her, "Oh, yeah, we put the sugar right in the ground with the seed." She say, "Well, give me another one." Them white folks is something else . . . ain't they, Lymon?

Lymon: Soon as you holler watermelons they come right out their door. Then they go and get their neighbors. Look like they having a contest to see who can buy the most.

Wining Boy: I got something for Lymon.

Wining Boy goes to get his suit. Boy Willie and Lymon continue to count their money.

Boy Willie: I know you got more than that. You ain't sold all them watermelons for that little bit of money.

Lymon: I'm still looking. That ain't all you got either. Where's all them quarters?

Boy Willie: You let me worry about the quarters. Just put the money on the table.

Wining Boy (entering with his suit): Look here, Lymon . . . see this? Look at his eyes getting big. He ain't never seen a suit like this. This is one hundred percent silk. Go ahead . . . put it on. See if it fit you. *(Lymon tries the suit coat on.)* Look at that. Feel it. That's one hundred percent genuine silk. I got that in Chicago. You can't get clothes like that nowhere but New York and Chicago. You can't get clothes like that in Pittsburgh. These folks in Pittsburgh ain't never seen clothes like that.

Lymon: This is nice, feel real nice and smooth.

Wining Boy: That's a fifty-five-dollar suit. That's the kind of suit the bigshots wear. You need a pistol and a pocketful of money to wear that suit. I'll let you have it for three dollars. The women will fall out of their windows they see you in a suit like that. Give me three dollars and go on and wear it down the street and get you a woman.

Boy Willie: That looks nice, Lymon. Put the pants on. Let me see it with the pants.

Lymon begins to try on the pants.

Wining Boy: Look at that . . . see how it fits you? Give me three dollars and go on and take it. Look at that, Doaker . . . don't he look nice?

Doaker: Yeah . . . that's a nice suit.

Wining Boy: Got a shirt to go with it. Cost you an extra dollar. Four dollars you got the whole deal.

Lymon: How this look, Boy Willie?

Boy Willie: That look nice . . . if you like that kind of thing. I don't like them dress-up kind of clothes. If you like it, look real nice.

Wining Boy: That's the kind of suit you need for up here in the North.

Lymon: Four dollars for everything? The suit and the shirt?

Wining Boy: That's cheap. I should be charging you twenty dollars. I give you a break cause you a homeboy. That's the only way I let you have it for four dollars.

Lymon (going into his pocket): Okay . . . here go the four dollars.

Wining Boy: You got some shoes? What size you wear?

Lymon: Size nine.

Wining Boy: That's what size I got! Size nine. I let you have them for three dollars.

Lymon: Where they at? Let me see them.

Wining Boy: They real nice shoes, too. Got a nice tip to them. Got pointy toe just like you want.

Wining Boy goes to get his shoes.

Lymon: Come on, Boy Willie, let's go out tonight. I wanna see what it looks like up here. Maybe we go to a picture show. Hey, Doaker, they got picture shows up here?

Doaker: The Rhumba Theater. Right down there on Fullerton Street. Can't miss it. Got the speakers outside on the sidewalk. You can hear it a block away. Boy Willie know where it's at.

Doaker exits into his room.

Lymon: Let's go to the picture show, Boy Willie. Let's go find some women.

Boy Willie: Hey, Lymon, how many of them watermelons would you say we got left? We got just under a half a load . . . right?

Lymon: About that much. Maybe a little more.

Boy Willie: You think that piano will fit up in there?

Lymon: If we stack them watermelons you can sit it up in the front there.

Boy Willie: I'm gonna call that man tomorrow.

Wining Boy (returns with his shoes): Here you go . . . size nine. Put them on. Cost you three dollars. That's a Florsheim shoe. That's the kind Staggerlee wore.

Lymon (trying on the shoes): You sure these size nine?

Wining Boy: You can look at my feet and see we wear the same size. Man, you put on that suit and them shoes and you got something there. You ready for whatever's out there. But is they ready for you? With them shoes on you be the King of the Walk. Have everybody stop to look at your shoes. Wishing they had a pair. I'll give you a break. Go on and take them for two dollars.

Lymon pays Wining Boy two dollars.

Lymon: Come on, Boy Willie . . . let's go find some women. I'm gonna go upstairs and get ready. I'll be ready to go in a minute. Ain't you gonna get dressed?

Boy Willie: I'm gonna wear what I got on. I ain't dressing up for these city niggers.

Lymon exits up the stairs.

That's all Lymon think about is women.

Wining Boy: His daddy was the same way. I used to run around with him. I know his mama too. Two strokes back and I would have been his daddy! His daddy's dead now . . . but I got the nigger out of jail one time. They was fixing to name him Daniel and walk him through the Lion's Den. He got in a tussle with one of them white fellows and the sheriff lit on him like white on rice. That's how the whole thing come about between me and Lymon's mama. She knew me and his daddy used to run together and he got in jail and she went down there and took the sheriff a hundred dollars. Don't get me to lying about where she got it from. I don't know. The sheriff *looked at that hundred dollars and turned his nose up.* Told her, say, "That ain't gonna do him no good. You got to put up another hundred on top of that." She come up *there and got me where I was playing at this saloon* . . . said she had all but fifty dollars and asked me if I could help. Now the way I figured it . . . without that fifty dollars the sheriff was gonna turn him over to Parchman. The sheriff turn him over to Parchman it be three years before anybody see him again. Now I'm gonna say it right . . . I will give anybody fifty dollars to keep them out of jail for three years. I give her the fifty dollars and she told me to come over to the house. I ain't asked her. I figure if she was nice enough to invite me I ought to go. I ain't had to say a word. She invited me over just as nice. Say, "Why don't you come over to the house?" She ain't had to say nothing else. Them words rolled off her tongue just as nice. I went on down there and sat about three hours. Started to leave and changed my mind. She grabbed hold to me and say, "Baby, it's all night long." That was one of the shortest nights I have ever spent on this earth! I could have used another eight hours. Lymon's daddy didn't even say nothing to me when he got out. He just looked at me funny. He had a good notion something had happened between me an' her. L. D. Jackson. That was one bad-luck nigger. Got killed at some dance. Fellow walked in and shot him thinking he was somebody else.

Doaker enters from his room.

Hey, Doaker, you remember L. D. Jackson?
Doaker: That's Lymon's daddy. That was one bad-luck nigger.
Boy Willie: Look like you ready to railroad some.
Doaker: Yeah, I got to make that run.

Lymon enters from the stairs. He is dressed in his new suit and shoes, to which he has added a cheap straw hat.

Lymon: How I look?
Wining Boy: You look like a million dollars. Don't he look good, Doaker? Come on, let's play some cards. You wanna play some cards?
Boy Willie: We ain't gonna play no cards with you. Me and Lymon gonna find some women. Hey, Lymon don't play no cards with Wining Boy. He'll take all your money.
Wining Boy (to Lymon): You got a magic suit there. You can get you a woman easy with that suit . . . but you got to know the magic words. You know the magic words to get you a woman?
Lymon: I just talk to them to see if I like them and they like me.
Wining Boy: You just walk right up to them and say, "If you got the harbor I got the ship." If that don't work ask them if you can put them in your pocket. The first thing they gonna say is, "It's too small." That's when you

look them dead in the eye and say, "Baby, ain't nothing small about me." If that don't work then you move on to another one. Am I telling him right, Doaker?

Doaker: That man don't need you to tell him nothing about no women. These women these days ain't gonna fall for that kind of stuff. You got to buy them a present. That's what they looking for these days.

Boy Willie: Come on, I'm ready. You ready, Lymon? Come on, let's go find some women.

Wining Boy: Here, let me walk out with you. I wanna see the women fall out their window when they see Lymon.

They all exit and the lights go down on the scene.

Scene II

The lights come up on the kitchen. It is late evening of the same day. Berniece has set a tub for her bath in the kitchen. She is heating up water on the stove. There is a knock at the door.

Berniece: Who is it?

Avery: It's me, Avery.

Berniece opens the door and lets him in.

Berniece: Avery, come on in. I was just fixing to take my bath.

Avery: Where Boy Willie? I see that truck out there almost empty. They done sold almost all them watermelons.

Berniece: They was gone when I come home. I don't know where they went off to. Boy Willie around here about to drive me crazy.

Avery: They sell them watermelons . . . he'll be gone soon.

Berniece: What Mr. Cohen say about letting you have the place?

Avery: He say he'll let me have it for thirty dollars a month. I talked him out of thirty-five and he say he'll let me have it for thirty.

Berniece: That's a nice spot next to Benny Diamond's store.

Avery: Berniece . . . I be at home and I get to thinking you up here an' I'm down there. I get to thinking how that look to have a preacher that ain't married. It makes for a better congregation if the preacher was settled down and married.

Berniece: Avery . . . not now. I was fixing to take my bath.

Avery: You know how I feel about you, Berniece. Now . . . I done got the place from Mr. Cohen. I get the money from the bank and I can fix it up real nice. They give me a ten cents a hour raise down there on the job . . . now Berniece, I ain't got much in the way of comforts. I got a hole in my pockets near about as far as money is concerned. I ain't never found no way through life to a woman I care about like I care about you. I need that. I need somebody on my bond side. I need a woman that fits in my hand.

Berniece: Avery, I ain't ready to get married now.

Avery: You too young a woman to close up, Berniece.

Berniece: I ain't said nothing about closing up. I got a lot of woman left in me.

Avery: Where's it at? When's the last time you looked at it?

Berniece (stunned by his remark): That's a nasty thing to say. And you call yourself a preacher.

Avery: Anytime I get anywhere near you . . . you push me away.

Berniece: I got enough on my hands with Maretha. I got enough people to love and take care of.

Avery: Who you got to love you? Can't nobody get close enough to you. Doaker can't half say nothing to you. You jump all over Boy Willie. Who you got to love you, Berniece?

Berniece: You trying to tell me a woman can't be nothing without a man. But you alright, huh? You can just walk out of here without me — without a woman — and still be a man. That's alright. Ain't nobody gonna ask you, "Avery, who you got to love you?" That's alright for you. But everybody gonna be worried about Berniece. "How Berniece gonna take care of herself? How she gonna raise that child without a man? Wonder what she do with herself. How she gonna live like that?" Everybody got all kinds of questions for Berniece. Everybody telling me I can't be a woman unless I got a man. Well, you tell me, Avery — you know — how much woman am I?

Avery: It wasn't me, Berniece. You can't blame me for nobody else. I'll own up to my own shortcomings. But you can't blame me for Crawley or nobody else.

Berniece: I ain't blaming nobody for nothing. I'm just stating the facts.

Avery: How long you gonna carry Crawley with you, Berniece? It's been over three years. At some point you got to let go and go on. Life's got all kinds of twists and turns. That don't mean you stop living. That don't mean you cut yourself off from life. You can't go through life carrying Crawley's ghost with you. Crawley's been dead three years. Three years, Berniece.

Berniece: I know how long Crawley's been dead. You ain't got to tell me that. I just ain't ready to get married right now.

Avery: What is you ready for, Berniece? You just gonna drift along from day to day. Life is more than making it from one day to another. You gonna look up one day and it's all gonna be past you. Life's gonna be gone out of your hands — there won't be enough to make nothing with. I'm standing here now, Berniece — but I don't know how much longer I'm gonna be standing here waiting on you.

Berniece: Avery, I told you . . . when you get your church we'll sit down and talk about this. I got too many other things to deal with right now. Boy Willie and the piano . . . and Sutter's ghost. I thought I might have been seeing things, but Maretha done seen Sutter's ghost, too.

Avery: When this happen, Berniece?

Berniece: Right after I came home yesterday. Me and Boy Willie was arguing about the piano and Sutter's ghost was standing at the top of the stairs. Maretha scared to sleep up there now. Maybe if you bless the house he'll go away.

Avery: I don't know, Berniece. I don't know if I should fool around with something like that.

Berniece: I can't have Maretha scared to go to sleep up there. Seem like if you bless the house he would go away.

Avery: You might have to be a special kind of preacher to do something like that.

Berniece: I keep telling myself when Boy Willie leave he'll go on and leave with him. I believe Boy Willie pushed him in the well.

Avery: That's been going on down there a long time. The Ghosts of the Yellow
Dog been pushing people in their wells long before Boy Willie got grown.

Berniece: Somebody down there pushing them people in their wells. They ain't
just upped and fell. Ain't no wind pushed nobody in their well.

Avery: Oh, I don't know. God works in mysterious ways.

Berniece: He ain't pushed nobody in their wells.

Avery: He caused it to happen. God is the Great Causer. He can do anything.
He parted the Red Sea. He say I will smite my enemies. Reverend Thompson used to preach on the Ghosts of the Yellow Dog as the hand of God.

Berniece: I don't care who preached that. Somebody down there pushing them
people in their wells. Somebody like Boy Willie. I can see him doing something like that. You ain't gonna tell me that Sutter just upped and fell in
his well. I believe Boy Willie pushed him so he could get his land.

Avery: What Doaker say about Boy Willie selling the piano?

Berniece: Doaker don't want no part of that piano. He ain't never wanted no
part of it. He blames himself for not staying behind with Papa Boy
Charles. He washed his hands of that piano a long time ago. He didn't
want me to bring it up here — but I wasn't gonna leave it down there.

Avery: Well, it seems to me somebody ought to be able to talk to Boy Willie.

Berniece: You can't talk to Boy Willie. He been that way all his life. Mama Ola
had her hands full trying to talk to him. He don't listen to nobody. He just
like my daddy. He get his mind fixed on something and can't nobody turn
him from it.

Avery: You ought to start a choir at the church. Maybe if he seen you was
doing something with it — if you told him you was gonna put it in my
church — maybe he'd see it different. You ought to put it down in the
church and start a choir. The Bible say "Make a joyful noise unto the
Lord." Maybe if Boy Willie see you was doing something with it he'd see it
different.

Berniece: I done told you I don't play on that piano. Ain't no need in you to
keep talking this choir stuff. When my mama died I shut the top on that
piano and I ain't never opened it since. I was only playing it for her. When
my daddy died seem like all her life went into that piano. She used to have
me playing on it . . . had Miss Eula come in and teach me . . . say when I
played it she could hear my daddy talking to her. I used to think them pictures came alive and walked through the house. Sometime late at night I
could hear my mama talking to them. I said that wasn't gonna happen to
me. I don't play that piano cause I don't want to wake them spirits. They
never be walking around in this house.

Avery: You got to put all that behind you, Berniece.

Berniece: I got Maretha playing on it. She don't know nothing about it. Let her
go on and be a schoolteacher or something. She don't have to carry all of
that with her. She got a chance I didn't have. I ain't gonna burden her with
that piano.

Avery: You got to put all of that behind you, Berniece. That's the same thing
like Crawley. Everybody got stones in their passway. You got to step over
them or walk around them. You picking them up and carrying them with
you. All you got to do is set them down by the side of the road. You ain't
got to carry them with you. You can walk over there right now and play

that piano. You can walk over there right now and God will walk over there with you. Right now you can set that sack of stones down by the side of the road and walk away from it. You don't have to carry it with you. You can do it right now. *(Avery crosses over to the piano and raises the lid.)* Come on, Berniece . . . set it down and walk away from it. Come on, play "Old Ship of Zion." Walk over here and claim it as an instrument of the Lord. You can walk over here right now and make it into a celebration.

Berniece moves toward the piano.

Berniece: Avery . . . I done told you I don't want to play that piano. Now or no other time.

Avery: The Bible say, "The Lord is my refuge . . . and my strength!" With the strength of God you can put the past behind you, Berniece. With the strength of God you can do anything! God got a bright tomorrow. God don't ask what you done . . . God ask what you gonna do. The strength of God can move mountains! God's got a bright tomorrow for you . . . all you got to do is walk over here and claim it.

Berniece: Avery, just go on and let me finish my bath. I'll see you tomorrow.

Avery: Okay, Berniece. I'm gonna go home. I'm gonna go home and read up on my Bible. And tomorrow . . . if the good Lord give me strength tomorrow . . . I'm gonna come by and bless the house . . . and show you the power of the Lord. *(Avery crosses to the door.)* It's gonna be alright, Berniece. God say he will soothe the troubled waters. I'll come by tomorrow and bless the house.

The lights go down to black.

SCENE III

Several hours later. The house is dark. Berniece has retired for the night. Boy Willie enters the darkened house with Grace.

Boy Willie: Come on in. This my sister's house. My sister live here. Come on, I ain't gonna bite you.

Grace: Put some light on. I can't see.

Boy Willie: You don't need to see nothing, baby. This here is all you need to see. All you need to do is see me. If you can't see me you can feel me in the dark. How's that, sugar?

He attempts to kiss her.

Grace: Go on now . . . wait!

Boy Willie: Just give me one little old kiss.

Grace (pushing him away): Come on now. Where I'm gonna sleep at?

Boy Willie: We got to sleep out here on the couch. Come on, my sister don't mind. Lymon come back he just got to sleep on the floor. He run off with Dolly somewhere he better stay there. Come on, sugar.

Grace: Wait now . . . you ain't told me nothing about no couch. I thought you had a bed. Both of us can't sleep on that little old couch.

Boy Willie: It don't make no difference. We can sleep on the floor. Let Lymon sleep on the couch.

Grace: You ain't told me nothing about no couch.

Boy Willie: What difference it make? You just wanna be with me.

Grace: I don't wanna be with you on no couch. Ain't you got no bed?

Boy Willie: You don't need no bed, woman. My granddaddy used to take women on the backs of horses. What you need a bed for? You just want to be with me.

Grace: You sure is country. I didn't know you was this country.

Boy Willie: There's a lot of things you don't know about me. Come on, let me show you what this country boy can do.

Grace: Let's go to my place. I got a room with a bed if Leroy don't come back there.

Boy Willie: Who's Leroy? You ain't said nothing about no Leroy.

Grace: He used to be my man. He ain't coming back. He gone off with some other gal.

Boy Willie: You let him have your key?

Grace: He ain't coming back.

Boy Willie: Did you let him have your key?

Grace: He got a key but he ain't coming back. He took off with some other gal.

Boy Willie: I don't wanna go nowhere he might come. Let's stay here. Come on, sugar. *(He pulls her over to the couch.)* Let me heist your hood and check your oil. See if your battery needs charging.

He pulls her to him. They kiss and tug at each other's clothing. In their anxiety they knock over a lamp.

Berniece: Who's that . . . Wining Boy?

Boy Willie: It's me . . . Boy Willie. Go on back to sleep. Everything's alright. *(To Grace.)* That's my sister. Everything's alright, Berniece. Go on back to sleep.

Berniece: What you doing down there? What you done knocked over?

Boy Willie: It wasn't nothing. Everything's alright. Go on back to sleep. *(To Grace.)* That's my sister. We alright. She gone back to sleep.

They begin to kiss. Berniece enters from the stairs dressed in a nightgown. She cuts on the light.

Berniece: Boy Willie, what you doing down here?

Boy Willie: It was just that there lamp. It ain't broke. It's okay. Everything's alright. Go on back to bed.

Berniece: Boy Willie, I don't allow that in my house. You gonna have to take your company someplace else.

Boy Willie: It's alright. We ain't doing nothing. We just sitting here talking. This here is Grace. That's my sister Berniece.

Berniece: You know I don't allow that kind of stuff in my house.

Boy Willie: Allow what? We just sitting here talking.

Berniece: Well, your company gonna have to leave. Come back and talk in the morning.

Boy Willie: Go on back upstairs now.

Berniece: I got an eleven-year-old girl upstairs. I can't allow that around here.

Boy Willie: Ain't nobody said nothing about that. I told you we just talking.

Grace: Come on . . . let's go to my place. Ain't nobody got to tell me to leave but once.

Boy Willie: You ain't got to be like that, Berniece.

Berniece: I'm sorry, Miss. But he know I don't allow that in here.

Grace: You ain't got to tell me but once. I don't stay nowhere I ain't wanted.

Boy Willie: I don't know why you want to embarrass me in front of my company.

Grace: Come on, take me home.

Berniece: Go on, Boy Willie. Just go on with your company.

> *Boy Willie and Grace exit. Berniece puts the light on in the kitchen and puts on the teakettle. Presently there is a knock at the door. Berniece goes to answer it. Berniece opens the door. Lymon enters.*

Lymon: How you doing, Berniece? I thought you'd be asleep. Boy Willie been back here?

Berniece: He just left out of here a minute ago.

Lymon: I went out to see a picture show and never got there. We always end up doing something else. I was with this woman she just wanted to drink up all my money. So I left her there and came back looking for Boy Willie.

Berniece: You just missed him. He just left out of here.

Lymon:. They got some nice-looking women in this city. I'm gonna like it here real good. I like seeing them with their dresses on. Got them high heels. I like that. Make them look like they real precious. Boy Willie met a real nice one today. I wish I had met her before he did.

Berniece: He come by here with some woman a little while ago. I told him to go on and take all that out of my house.

Lymon: What she look like, the woman he was with? Was she a brown-skinned woman about this high? Nice and healthy? Got nice hips on her?

Berniece: She had on a red dress.

Lymon: That's her! That's Grace. She real nice. Laugh a lot. Lot of fun to be with. She don't be trying to put on. Some of these women act like they the Queen of Sheba. I don't like them. Grace ain't like that. She real nice with herself.

Berniece: I don't know what she was like. He come in here all drunk knocking over the lamp, and making all kind of noise. I told them to take that somewhere else. I can't really say what she was like.

Lymon: She real nice. I seen her before he did. I was trying not to act like I seen her. I wanted to look at her a while before I said something. She seen me when I come into the saloon. I tried to act like I didn't see her. Time I looked around Boy Willie was talking to her. She was talking to him kept looking at me. That's when her friend Dolly came. I asked her if she wanted to go to the picture show. She told me to buy her a drink while she thought about it. Next thing I knew she done had three drinks talking about she too tired to go. I bought her another drink, then I left. Boy Willie was gone and I thought he might have come back here. Doaker gone, huh? He say he had to make a trip.

Berniece: Yeah, he gone on his trip. This is when I can usually get some peace and quiet, Maretha asleep.

Lymon: She look just like you. Got them big eyes. I remember her when she was in diapers.

Berniece: Time just keep on. It go on with or without you. She going on twelve.

Lymon: She sure is pretty. I like kids.

Berniece: Boy Willie say you staying . . . what you gonna do up here in this big city? You thought about that?

Lymon: They never get me back down there. The sheriff looking for me. All because they gonna try and make me work for somebody when I don't want to. They gonna try and make me work for Stovall when he don't pay nothing. It ain't like that up here. Up here you more or less do what you want to. I figure I find me a job and try to get set up and then see what the year brings. I tried to do that two or three times down there . . . but it never would work out. I was always in the wrong place.

Berniece: This ain't a bad city once you get to know your way around.

Lymon: Up here is different. I'm gonna get me a job unloading boxcars or something. One fellow told me say he know a place. I'm gonna go over there with him next week. Me and Boy Willie finish selling them watermelons I'll have enough money to hold me for a while. But I'm gonna go over there and see what kind of jobs they have.

Berniece: You shouldn't have too much trouble finding a job. It's all in how you present yourself. See now, Boy Willie couldn't get no job up here. Somebody hire him they got a pack of trouble on their hands. Soon as they find that out they fire him. He don't want to do nothing unless he do it his way.

Lymon: I know. I told him let's go to the picture show first and see if there was any women down there. They might get tired of sitting at home and walk down to the picture show. He say he wanna look around first. We never did get down there. We tried a couple of places and then we went to this saloon where he met Grace. I tried to meet her before he did but he beat me to her. We left Wining Boy sitting down there running his mouth. He told me if I wear this suit I'd find me a woman. He was almost right.

Berniece: You don't need to be out there in them saloons. Ain't no telling what you liable to run into out there. This one liable to cut you as quick as that one shoot you. You don't need to be out there. You start out that fast life you can't keep it up. It makes you old quick. I don't know what them women out there be thinking about.

Lymon: Mostly they be lonely and looking for somebody to spend the night with them. Sometimes it matters who it is and sometimes it don't. I used to be the same way. Now it got to matter. That's why I'm here now. Dolly liable not to even recognize me if she sees me again. I don't like women like that. I like my women to be with me in a nice and easy way. That way we can both enjoy ourselves. The way I see it we the only two people like us in the world. We got to see how we fit together. A woman that don't want to take the time to do that I don't bother with. Used to. Used to bother with all of them. Then I woke up one time with this woman and I didn't know who she was. She was the prettiest woman I had ever seen in my life. I spent the whole night with her and didn't even know it. I had never taken the time to look at her. I guess she kinda knew I ain't never really looked at her. She must have known that cause she ain't wanted to see me no more. If she had wanted to see me I believe we might have got married. How come you ain't married? It seem like to me you would be married. I remember Avery from down home. I used to call him plain old Avery. Now he Reverend Avery. That's kinda funny about him becoming a preacher. I like when he told about how that come to him in a dream about them sheep people and them hobos. Nothing ever come to me in a dream like that. I just dream about women. Can't never seem to find the right one.

Berniece: She out there somewhere. You just got to get yourself ready to meet her. That's what I'm trying to do. Avery's alright. I ain't really got nobody in mind.

Lymon: I get me a job and a little place and get set up to where I can make a woman comfortable I might get married. Avery's nice. You ought to go ahead and get married. You be a preacher's wife you won't have to work. I hate living by myself. I didn't want to be no strain on my mama so I left home when I was about sixteen. Everything I tried seem like it just didn't work out. Now I'm trying this.

Berniece: You keep trying it'll work out for you.

Lymon: You ever go down there to the picture show?

Berniece: I don't go in for all that.

Lymon: Ain't nothing wrong with it. It ain't like gambling and sinning. I went to one down in Jackson once. It was fun.

Berniece: I just stay home most of the time. Take care of Maretha.

Lymon: It's getting kind of late. I don't know where Boy Willie went off to. He's liable not to come back. I'm gonna take off these shoes. My feet hurt. Was you in bed? I don't mean to be keeping you up.

Berniece: You ain't keeping me up. I couldn't sleep after that Boy Willie woke me up.

Lymon: You got on that nightgown. I likes women when they wear them fancy nightclothes and all. It makes their skin look real pretty.

Berniece: I got this at the five-and-ten-cents store. It ain't so fancy.

Lymon: I don't too often get to see a woman dressed like that. *(There is a long pause. Lymon takes off his suit coat.)* Well, I'm gonna sleep here on the couch. I'm supposed to sleep on the floor but I don't reckon Boy Willie's coming back tonight. Wining Boy sold me this suit. Told me it was a magic suit. I'm gonna put it on again tomorrow. Maybe it bring me a woman like he say. *(He goes into his coat pocket and takes out a small bottle of perfume.)* I almost forgot I had this. Some man sold me this for a dollar. Say it come from Paris. This is the same kind of perfume the Queen of France wear. That's what he told me. I don't know if it's true or not. I smelled it. It smelled good to me. Here . . . smell it see if you like it. I was gonna give it to Dolly. But I didn't like her too much.

Berniece (takes the bottle): It smells nice.

Lymon: I was gonna give it to Dolly if she had went to the picture with me. Go on, you take it.

Berniece: I can't take it. Here . . . go on you keep it. You'll find somebody to give it to.

Lymon: I wanna give it to you. Make you smell nice. *(He takes the bottle and puts perfume behind Berniece's ear.)* They tell me you supposed to put it right here behind your ear. Say if you put it there you smell nice all day. *(Berniece stiffens at his touch. Lymon bends down to smell her.)* There . . . you smell real good now. *(He kisses her neck.)* You smell real good for Lymon.

He kisses her again. Berniece returns the kiss, then breaks the embrace and crosses to the stairs. She turns and they look silently at each other. Lymon hands her the bottle of perfume. Berniece exits up the stairs. Lymon picks up his suit coat and strokes it lovingly with the full knowledge that it is indeed a magic suit. The lights go down on the scene.

SCENE IV

It is late the next morning. The lights come up on the parlor. Lymon is asleep on the sofa. Boy Willie enters the front door.

Boy Willie: Hey, Lymon! Lymon, come on get up.

Lymon: Leave me alone.

Boy Willie: Come on, get up, nigger! Wake up, Lymon.

Lymon: What you want?

Boy Willie: Come on, let's go. I done called the man about the piano.

Lymon: What piano?

Boy Willie (dumps Lymon on the floor): Come on, get up!

Lymon: Why you leave, I looked around and you was gone.

Boy Willie: I come back here with Grace, then I went looking for you. I figured you'd be with Dolly.

Lymon: She just want to drink and spend up your money. I come on back here looking for you to see if you wanted to go to the picture show.

Boy Willie: I been up at Grace's house. Some nigger named Leroy come by but I had a chair up against the door. He got mad when he couldn't get in. He went off somewhere and I got out of there before he could come back. Berniece got mad when we came here.

Lymon: She say you was knocking over the lamp busting up the place.

Boy Willie: That was Grace doing all that.

Lymon: Wining Boy seen Sutter's ghost last night.

Boy Willie: Wining Boy's liable to see anything. I'm surprised he found the right house. Come on, I done called the man about the piano.

Lymon: What he say?

Boy Willie: He say to bring it on out. I told him I was calling for my sister, Miss Berniece Charles. I told him some man wanted to buy it for eleven hundred dollars and asked him if he would go any better. He said yeah, he would give me eleven hundred and fifty dollars for it if it was the same piano. I described it to him again and he told me to bring it out.

Lymon: Why didn't you tell him to come and pick it up?

Boy Willie: I didn't want to have no problem with Berniece. This way we just take it on out there and it be out the way. He wanted to charge twenty-five dollars to pick it up.

Lymon: You should have told him the man was gonna give you twelve hundred for it.

Boy Willie: I figure I was taking a chance with that eleven hundred. If I had told him twelve hundred he might have run off. Now I wish I had told him twelve-fifty. It's hard to figure out white folks sometimes.

Lymon: You might have been able to tell him anything. White folks got a lot of money.

Boy Willie: Come on, let's get it loaded before Berniece come back. Get that end over there. All you got to do is pick it up on that side. Don't worry about this side. You wanna stretch you' back for a minute?

Lymon: I'm ready.

Boy Willie: Get a real good grip on it now.

The sound of Sutter's Ghost is heard. They do not hear it.

Lymon: I got this end. You get that end.

Boy Willie: Wait till I say ready now. Alright. You got it good? You got a grip on it?

Lymon: Yeah, I got it. You lift up on that end.

Boy Willie: Ready? Lift!

The piano will not budge.

Lymon: Man, this piano is heavy! It's gonna take more than me and you to move this piano.

Boy Willie: We can do it. Come on—we did it before.

Lymon: Nigger—you crazy! That piano weighs five hundred pounds!

Boy Willie: I got three hundred pounds of it! I know you can carry two hundred pounds! You be lifting them cotton sacks! Come on lift this piano!

They try to move the piano again without success.

Lymon: It's stuck. Something holding it.

Boy Willie: How the piano gonna be stuck? We just moved it. Slide you' end out.

Lymon: Naw—we gonna need two or three more people. How this big old piano get in the house?

Boy Willie: I don't know how it got in the house. I know how it's going out though! You get on this end. I'll carry three hundred and fifty pounds of it. All you got to do is slide your end out. Ready?

They switch sides and try again without success. Doaker enters from his room as they try to push and shove it.

Lymon: Hey, Doaker . . . how this piano get in the house?

Doaker: Boy Willie, what you doing?

Boy Willie: I'm carrying this piano out of the house. What it look like I'm doing? Come on, Lymon, let's try again.

Doaker: Go on let the piano sit there till Berniece come home.

Boy Willie: You ain't got nothing to do with this, Doaker. This my business.

Doaker: This is my house, nigger! I ain't gonna let you or nobody else carry nothing out of it. You ain't gonna carry nothing out of here without my permission!

Boy Willie: This is my piano. I don't need your permission to carry my belongings out of your house. This is mine. This ain't got nothing to do with you.

Doaker: I say leave it over there till Berniece comes home. She got part of it too. Leave it set there till you see what she say.

Boy Willie: I don't care what Berniece say. Come on, Lymon. I got this side.

Doaker: Go on and cut it half in two if you want to. Just leave Berniece's half sitting over there. I can't tell you what to do with your piano. But I can't let you take her half out of here.

Boy Willie: Go on, Doaker. You ain't got nothing to do with this. I don't want you starting nothing now. Just go on and leave me alone. Come on, Lymon. I got this end.

Doaker goes into his room. Boy Willie and Lymon prepare to move the piano.

Lymon: How we gonna get it in the truck?

Boy Willie: Don't worry about how we gonna get it on the truck. You got to get it out the house first.

Lymon: It's gonna take more than me and you to move this piano.

Boy Willie: Just lift up that end, nigger!

Doaker comes to the doorway of his room and stands.

Doaker (quietly, with authority): Leave that piano set over there till Berniece come back. I don't care what you do with it then. But you gonna leave it sit over there right now.

Boy Willie: Alright . . . I'm gonna tell you this, Doaker, I'm going out of here . . . I'm gonna get me some rope . . . find me a plank and some wheels . . . and I'm coming back. Then I'm gonna carry that piano out of here . . . sell it and give Berniece half the money. See . . . now that's what I'm gonna do. And you . . . or nobody else is gonna stop me. Come on, Lymon . . . let's go get some rope and stuff. I'll be back, Doaker.

Boy Willie and Lymon exit. The lights go down on the scene.

Scene V

The lights come up. Boy Willie sits on the sofa, screwing casters on a wooden plank. Maretha is sitting on the piano stool. Doaker sits at the table playing solitaire.

Boy Willie (to Maretha): Then after that them white folks down around there started falling down their wells. You ever seen a well? A well got a wall around it. It's hard to fall down a well. You got to be leaning way over. Couldn't nobody figure out too much what was making these fellows fall down their well . . . so everybody says the Ghosts of the Yellow Dog must have pushed them. That's what everybody called them four men what got burned up in the boxcar.

Maretha: Why they call them that?

Boy Willie: Cause the Yazoo Delta railroad got yellow boxcars. Sometime the way the whistle blow sound like an old dog howling so the people call it the Yellow Dog.

Maretha: Anybody ever see the Ghosts?

Boy Willie: I told you they like the wind. Can you see the wind?

Maretha: No.

Boy Willie: They like the wind you can't see them. But sometimes you be in trouble they might be around to help you. They say if you go where the Southern cross the Yellow Dog . . . you go to where them two railroads cross each other . . . and call out their names . . . they say they talk back to you. I don't know, I ain't never done that. But Uncle Wining Boy he say he been down there and talked to them. You have to ask him about that part.

Berniece has entered from the front door.

Berniece: Maretha, you go on and get ready for me to do your hair. *(Maretha crosses to the steps.)* Boy Willie, I done told you to leave my house. *(To Maretha.)* Go on, Maretha.

Maretha is hesitant about going up the stairs.

Boy Willie: Don't be scared. Here, I'll go up there with you. If we see Sutter's ghost I'll put a whupping on him. Come on, Uncle Boy Willie going with you.

Boy Willie and Maretha exit up the stairs.

Berniece: Doaker — what is going on here?

Doaker: I come home and him and Lymon was moving the piano. I told them to leave it over there till you got home. He went out and got that board and them wheels. He say he gonna take that piano out of here and ain't nobody gonna stop him.

Berniece: I ain't playing with Boy Willie. I got Crawley's gun upstairs. He don't know but I'm through with it. Where Lymon go?

Doaker: Boy Willie sent him for some rope just before you come in.

Berniece: I ain't studying Boy Willie or Lymon — or the rope. Boy Willie ain't taking that piano out this house. That's all there is to it.

Boy Willie and Maretha enter on the stairs. Maretha carries a hot comb and a can of hair grease. Boy Willie crosses over and continues to screw the wheels on the board.

Maretha: Mama, all the hair grease is gone. There ain't but this little bit left.

Berniece *(gives her a dollar)*: Here . . . run across the street and get another can. You come straight back, too. Don't you be playing around out there. And watch the cars. Be careful when you cross the street. *(Maretha exits out the front door.)* Boy Willie, I done told you to leave my house.

Boy Willie: I ain't in you' house. I'm in Doaker's house. If he ask me to leave then I'll go on and leave. But consider me done left your part.

Berniece: Doaker, tell him to leave. Tell him to go on.

Doaker: Boy Willie ain't done nothing for me to put him out of the house. I told you if you can't get along just go on and don't have nothing to do with each other.

Boy Willie: I ain't thinking about Berniece. *(He gets up and draws a line across the floor with his foot.)* There! Now I'm out of your part of the house. Consider me done left your part. Soon as Lymon come back with that rope, I'm gonna take that piano out of here and sell it.

Berniece: You ain't gonna touch that piano.

Boy Willie: Carry it out of here just as big and bold. Do like my daddy would have done come time to get Sutter's land.

Berniece: I got something to make you leave it over there.

Boy Willie: It's got to come better than this thirty-two-twenty.

Doaker: Why don't you stop all that! Boy Willie, go on and leave her alone. You know how Berniece get. Why you wanna sit there and pick with her?

Boy Willie: I ain't picking with her. I told her the truth. She the one talking about what she got. I just told her what she better have.

Berniece: That's alright, Doaker. Leave him alone.

Boy Willie: She trying to scare me. Hell, I ain't scared of dying. I look around and see people dying every day. You got to die to make room for somebody else. I had a dog that died. Wasn't nothing but a puppy. I picked it up and put it in a bag and carried it up there to Reverend C. L. Thompson's church. I carried it up there and prayed and asked Jesus to make it live like he did the man in the Bible. I prayed real hard. Knelt down and everything. Say ask in Jesus' name. Well, I must have called Jesus' name two hundred times. I called his name till my mouth got sore. I got up and looked in the bag and the dog still dead. It ain't moved a muscle! I say, "Well, ain't nothing precious." And then I went out and killed me a cat. That's when I discovered the power of death. See, a nigger that ain't afraid to die is the worse kind of nigger for the white man. He can't hold that power over you. That's what I learned when I killed that cat. I got the power of death too. I can command him. I can call him up. The white man don't like to see that. He don't like for you to stand up and look him square in the eye and say, "I got it too." Then he got to deal with you square up.

Berniece: That's why I don't talk to him, Doaker. You try and talk to him and that's the only kind of stuff that comes out his mouth.

Doaker: You say Avery went home to get his Bible?

Boy Willie: What Avery gonna do? Avery can't do nothing with me. I wish Avery would say something to me about this piano.

Doaker: Berniece ain't said about that. Avery went home to get his Bible. He coming by to bless the house see if he can get rid of Sutter's ghost.

Boy Willie: Ain't nothing but a house full of ghosts down there at the church. What Avery look like chasing away somebody's ghost?

Maretha enters the front door.

Berniece: Light that stove and set that comb over there to get hot. Get something to put around your shoulders.

Boy Willie: The Bible say an eye for an eye, a tooth for a tooth, and a life for a life. Tit for tat. But you and Avery don't want to believe that. You gonna pass up that part and pretend it ain't in there. Everything else you gonna agree with. But if you gonna agree with part of it you got to agree with all of it. You can't do nothing halfway. You gonna go at the Bible halfway. You gonna act like that part ain't in there. But you pull out the Bible and open it and see what it say. Ask Avery. He a preacher. He'll tell you it's in there. He the Good Shepherd. Unless he gonna shepherd you to heaven with half the Bible.

Berniece: Maretha, bring me that comb. Make sure it's hot.

Maretha brings the comb. Berniece begins to do her hair.

Boy Willie: I will say this for Avery. He done figured out a path to go through life. I don't agree with it. But he done fixed it so he can go right through it real smooth. Hell, he liable to end up with a million dollars that he done got from selling bread and wine.

Maretha: OWWWWWW!

Berniece: Be still, Maretha. If you was a boy I wouldn't be going through this.

Boy Willie: Don't you tell that girl that. Why you wanna tell her that?

Berniece: You ain't got nothing to do with this child.

Boy Willie: Telling her you wished she was a boy. How's that gonna make her feel?

Berniece: Boy Willie, go on and leave me alone.

Doaker: Why don't you leave her alone? What you got to pick with her for? Why don't you go on out and see what's out there in the streets? Have something to tell the fellows down home.

Boy Willie: I'm waiting on Lymon to get back with that truck. Why don't you go on out and see what's out there in the streets? You ain't got to work tomorrow. Talking about me . . . why don't you go out there? It's Friday night.

Doaker: I got to stay around here and keep you all from killing one another.

Boy Willie: You ain't got to worry about me. I'm gonna be here just as long as it takes Lymon to get back here with that truck. You ought to be talking to Berniece. Sitting up there telling Maretha she wished she was a boy. What kind of thing is that to tell a child? If you want to tell her something tell her about that piano. You ain't even told her about that piano. Like that's something to be ashamed of. Like she supposed to go off and hide somewhere about that piano. You ought to mark down on the calendar the day that Papa Boy Charles brought that piano into the house. You ought to mark that day down and draw a circle around it . . . and every year when it come up throw a party. Have a celebration. If you did that she wouldn't have no problem in life. She could walk around here with her head held high. I'm talking about a big party!

    Invite everybody! Mark that day down with a special meaning. That way she know where she at in the world. You got her going out here thinking she wrong in the world. Like there ain't no part of it belong to her.

Berniece: Let me take care of my child. When you get one of your own then you can teach it what you want to teach it.

Doaker exits into his room.

Boy Willie: What I want to bring a child into this world for? Why I wanna bring somebody else into all this for? I'll tell you this . . . If I was Rockefeller I'd have forty or fifty. I'd make one every day. Cause they gonna start out in life with all the advantages. I ain't got no advantages to offer nobody. Many is the time I looked at my daddy and seen him staring off at his hands. I got a little older I know what he was thinking. He sitting there saying, "I got these big old hands but what I'm gonna do with them? Best I can do is make a fifty-acre crop for Mr. Stovall. Got these big old hands capable of doing anything. I can take and build something with these hands. But where's the tools? All I got is these hands. Unless I go out here and kill me somebody and take what they got . . . it's a long row to hoe for me to get something of my own. So what I'm gonna do with these big old hands? What would you do?"

    See now . . . if he had his own land he wouldn't have felt that way. If he had something under his feet that belonged to him he could stand up taller. That's what I'm talking about. Hell, the land is there for everybody. All you got to do is figure out how to get you a piece. Ain't no mystery to life. You just got to go out and meet it square on. If you got a piece of land you'll find everything else fall right into place. You can stand right up next to the white man and talk about the price of cotton . . . the weather, and anything else you want to talk about. If you teach that girl that she living at the bottom of life, she's gonna grow up and hate you.

Berniece: I'm gonna teach her the truth. That's just where she living. Only she ain't got to stay there. *(To Maretha.)* Turn you' head over to the other side.

Boy Willie: This might be your bottom but it ain't mine. I'm living at the top of life. I ain't gonna just take my life and throw it away at the bottom. I'm in the world like everybody else. The way I see it everybody else got to come up a little taste to be where I am.

Berniece: You right at the bottom with the rest of us.

Boy Willie: I'll tell you this . . . and ain't a living soul can put a come back on it. If you believe that's where you at then you gonna act that way. If you act that way then that's where you gonna be. It's as simple as that. Ain't no mystery to life. I don't know how you come to believe that stuff. Crawley didn't think like that. He wasn't living at the bottom of life. Papa Boy Charles and Mama Ola wasn't living at the bottom of life. You ain't never heard them say nothing like that. They would have taken a strap to you if they heard you say something like that. *(Doaker enters from his room.)* Hey, Doaker . . . Berniece say the colored folks is living at the bottom of life. I tried to tell her if she think that . . . that's where she gonna be. You think you living at the bottom of life? Is that how you see yourself?

Doaker: I'm just living the best way I know how. I ain't thinking about no top or no bottom.

Boy Willie: That's what I tried to tell Berniece. I don't know where she got that from. That sound like something Avery would say. Avery think cause the white man give him a turkey for Thanksgiving that makes him better than everybody else. That's gonna raise him out of the bottom of life. I don't need nobody to give me a turkey. I can get my own turkey. All you have to do is get out my way. I'll get me two or three turkeys.

Berniece: You can't even get a chicken let alone two or three turkeys. Talking about get out your way. Ain't nobody in your way. *(To Maretha.)* Straighten your head, Maretha! Don't be bending down like that. Hold your head up! *(To Boy Willie.)* All you got going for you is talk. You' whole life that's all you ever had going for you.

Boy Willie: See now . . . I'll tell you something about me. I done strung along and strung along. Going this way and that. Whatever way would lead me to a moment of peace. That's all I want. To be as easy with everything. But I wasn't born to that. I was born to a time of fire.

The world ain't wanted no part of me. I could see that since I was about seven. The world say it's better off without me. See, Berniece accept that. She trying to come up to where she can prove something to the world. Hell, the world a better place cause of me. I don't see it like Berniece. I got a heart that beats here and it beats just as loud as the next fellow's. Don't care if he black or white. Sometime it beats louder. When it beats louder, then everybody can hear it. Some people get scared of that. Like Berniece. Some people get scared to hear a nigger's heart beating. They think you ought to lay low with that heart. Make it beat quiet and go along with everything the way it is. But my mama ain't birthed me for nothing. So what I got to do? I got to mark my passing on the road. Just like you write on a tree, "Boy Willie was here."

That's all I'm trying to do with that piano. Trying to put my mark on the road. Like my daddy done. My heart say for me to sell that piano and get me some land so I can make a life for myself to live in my own way. Other than that I ain't thinking about nothing Berniece got to say.

There is a knock at the door. Boy Willie crosses to it and yanks it open thinking it is Lymon. Avery enters. He carries a Bible.

Boy Willie: Where you been, nigger? Aw . . . I thought you was Lymon. Hey, Berniece, look who's here.

Berniece: Come on in, Avery. Don't you pay Boy Willie no mind.

Boy Willie: Hey . . . Hey, Avery . . . tell me this . . . can you get to heaven with half the Bible?

Berniece: Boy Willie . . . I done told you to leave me alone.

Boy Willie: I just ask the man a question. He can answer. He don't need you to speak for him. Avery . . . if you only believe on half the Bible and don't want to accept the other half . . . you think God let you in heaven? Or do you got to have the whole Bible? Tell Berniece . . . if you only believe in part of it . . . when you see God he gonna ask you why you ain't believed in the other part . . . then he gonna send you straight to Hell.

Avery: You got to be born again. Jesus say unless a man be born again he cannot come unto the Father and who so ever heareth my words and believeth them not shall be cast into a fiery pit.

Boy Willie: That's what I was trying to tell Berniece. You got to believe in it all. You can't go at nothing halfway. She think she going to heaven with half the Bible. *(To Berniece.)* You hear that . . . Jesus say you got to believe in it all.

Berniece: You keep messing with me.

Boy Willie: I ain't thinking about you.

Doaker: Come on in, Avery, and have a seat. Don't pay neither one of them no mind. They been arguing all day.

Berniece: Come on in, Avery.

Avery: How's everybody in here?

Berniece: Here, set this comb back over there on that stove. *(To Avery.)* Don't pay Boy Willie no mind. He been around here bothering me since I come home from work.

Boy Willie: Boy Willie ain't bothering you. Boy Willie ain't bothering nobody. I'm just waiting on Lymon to get back. I ain't thinking about you. You heard the man say I was right and you still don't want to believe it. You just wanna go and make up anythin'. Well there's Avery . . . there's the preacher . . . go on and ask him.

Avery: Berniece believe in the Bible. She been baptized.

Boy Willie: What about that part that say an eye for an eye a tooth for a tooth and a life for a life? Ain't that in there?

Doaker: What they say down there at the bank, Avery?

Avery: Oh, they talked to me real nice. I told Berniece . . . they say maybe they let me borrow the money. They done talked to my boss down at work and everything.

Doaker: That's what I told Berniece. You working every day you ought to be able to borrow some money.

Avery: I'm getting more people in my congregation every day. Berniece says she gonna be the Deaconess. I get me my church I can get married and settled down. That's what I told Berniece.

Doaker: That be nice. You all ought to go ahead and get married. Berniece don't need to be by herself. I tell her that all the time.

Berniece: I ain't said nothing about getting married. I said I was thinking about it.

Doaker: Avery get him his church you all can make it nice. *(To Avery.)* Berniece said you was coming by to bless the house.

Avery: Yeah, I done read up on my Bible. She asked me to come by and see if I can get rid of Sutter's ghost.

Boy Willie: Ain't no ghost in this house. That's all in Berniece's head. Go on up there and see if you see him. I'll give you a hundred dollars if you see him. That's all in her imagination.

Doaker: Well, let her find that out then. If Avery blessing the house is gonna make her feel better . . . what you got to do with it?

Avery: Berniece say Maretha seen him too. I don't know, but I found a part in the Bible to bless the house. If he is here then that ought to make him go.

Boy Willie: You worse than Berniece believing all that stuff. Talking about . . . if he here. Go on up there and find out. I been up there I ain't seen him. If you reading from that Bible gonna make him leave out of Berniece imagination, well, you might be right. But if you talking about . . .

Doaker: Boy Willie, why don't you just be quiet? Getting all up in the man's business. This ain't got nothing to do with you. Let him go ahead and do what he gonna do.

Boy Willie: I ain't stopping him. Avery ain't got no power to do nothing.

Avery: Oh, I ain't got no power. God got the power! God got the power over everything in His creation. God can do anything. God say, "As I commandeth so it shall be." God said, "Let there be light," and there was light. He made the world in six days and rested on the seventh. God's got a wonderful power. He got power over life and death. Jesus raised Lazareth from the dead. They was getting ready to bury him and Jesus told him say, "Rise up and walk." He got up and walked and the people made great rejoicing at the power of God. I ain't worried about him chasing away a little old ghost!

There is a knock at the door. Boy Willie goes to answer it. Lymon enters carrying a coil of rope.

Boy Willie: Where you been? I been waiting on you and you run off somewhere.

Lymon: I ran into Grace. I stopped and bought her drink. She say she gonna go to the picture show with me.

Boy Willie: I ain't thinking about no Grace nothing.

Lymon: Hi, Berniece.

Boy Willie: Give me that rope and get up on this side of the piano.

Doaker: Boy Willie, don't start nothing now. Leave the piano alone.

Boy Willie: Get that board there, Lymon. Stay out of this, Doaker.

Berniece exits up the stairs.

Doaker: You just can't take the piano. How you gonna take the piano? Berniece ain't said nothing about selling that piano.

Boy Willie: She ain't got to say nothing. Come on, Lymon. We got to lift one end at a time up on the board. You got to watch so that the board don't slide up under there.

Lymon: What we gonna do with the rope?

Boy Willie: Let me worry about the rope. You just get up on this side over here with me.

Berniece enters from the stairs. She has her hand in her pocket where she has Crawley's gun.

Avery: Boy Willie . . . Berniece . . . why don't you all sit down and talk this out now?

Berniece: Ain't nothing to talk out.

Boy Willie: I'm through talking to Berniece. You can talk to Berniece till you get blue in the face, and it don't make no difference. Get up on that side, Lymon. Throw that rope around there and tie it to the leg.

Lymon: Wait a minute . . . wait a minute, Boy Willie, Berniece got to say. Hey, Berniece . . . did you tell Boy Willie he could take this piano?

Berniece: Boy Willie ain't taking nothing out of my house but himself. Now you let him go ahead and try.

Boy Willie: Come on, Lymon, get up on this side with me. *(Lymon stands undecided.)* Come on, nigger! What you standing there for?

Lymon: Maybe Berniece is right, Boy Willie. Maybe you shouldn't sell it.

Avery: You all ought to sit down and talk it out. See if you can come to an agreement.

Doaker: That's what I been trying to tell them. Seem like one of them ought to respect the other one's wishes.

Berniece: I wish Boy Willie would go on and leave my house. That's what I wish. Now, he can respect that. Cause he's leaving here one way or another.

Boy Willie: What you mean one way or another? What's that supposed to mean? I ain't scared of no gun.

Doaker: Come on, Berniece, leave him alone with that.

Boy Willie: I don't care what Berniece say. I'm selling my half. I can't help it if her half got to go along with it. It ain't like I'm trying to cheat her out of her half. Come on, Lymon.

Lymon: Berniece . . . I got to do this . . . Boy Willie say he gonna give you half of the money . . . say he want to get Sutter's land.

Berniece: Go on, Lymon. Just go on . . . I done told Boy Willie what to do.

Boy Willie: Here, Lymon . . . put that rope over there.

Lymon: Boy Willie, you sure you want to do this? The way I figure it . . . I might be wrong . . . but I figure she gonna shoot you first.

Boy Willie: She just gonna have to shoot me.

Berniece: Maretha, get on out the way. Get her out the way, Doaker.

Doaker: Go on, do what your mama told you.

Berniece: Put her in your room.

Maretha exits to Doaker's room. Boy Willie and Lymon try to lift the piano. The door opens and Wining Boy enters. He has been drinking.

Wining Boy: Man, these niggers around here! I stopped down there at Seefus. . . . These folks standing around talking about Patchneck Red's coming. They jumping back and getting off the sidewalk talking about Patchneck Red this and Patchneck Red that. Come to find out . . . you know who they was talking about? Old John D. from up around Tyler! Used to run around with Otis Smith. He got everybody scared of him. Calling him Patchneck Red. They don't know I whupped the nigger's head in one time.

Boy Willie: Just make sure that board don't slide, Lymon.

Lymon: I got this side. You watch that side.

Wining Boy: Hey, Boy Willie, what you got? I know you got a pint stuck up in your coat.

Boy Willie: Wining Boy, get out the way!

Wining Boy: Hey, Doaker. What you got? Gimme a drink. I want a drink.

Doaker: It look like you had enough of whatever it was. Come talking about "What you got?" You ought to be trying to find somewhere to lay down.

Wining Boy: I ain't worried about no place to lay down. I can always find me a place to lay down in Berniece's house. Ain't that right, Berniece?

Berniece: Wining Boy, sit down somewhere. You been out there drinking all day. Come in here smelling like an old polecat. Sit on down there, you don't need nothing to drink.

Doaker: You know Berniece don't like all that drinking.

Wining Boy: I ain't disrespecting Berniece. Berniece, am I disrespecting you? I'm just trying to be nice. I been with strangers all day and they treated me like family. I come in here to family and you treat me like a stranger. I don't need your whiskey. I can buy my own. I wanted your company, not your whiskey.

Doaker: Nigger, why don't you go upstairs and lay down? You don't need nothing to drink.

Wining Boy: I ain't thinking about no laying down. Me and Boy Willie fixing to party. Ain't that right, Boy Willie? Tell him, I'm fixing to play me some piano. Watch this.

Wining Boy sits down at the piano.

Boy Willie: Come on, Wining Boy! Me and Lymon fixing to move the piano.

Wining Boy: Wait a minute . . . wait a minute. This a song I wrote for Cleotha. I wrote this song in memory of Cleotha.

He begins to play and sing.

Hey little woman what's the matter with you now
Had a storm last night and blowed the line all down

Tell me how long
Is I got to wait
Can I get it now
Or must I hesitate

It takes a hesitating stocking in her hesitating shoe
It takes a hesitating woman wanna sing the blues

Tell me how long
Is I got to wait
Can I kiss you now
Or must I hesitate.

Boy Willie: Come on, Wining Boy, get up! Get up, Wining Boy! Me and Lymon's fixing to move the piano.

Wining Boy: Naw . . . Naw . . . you ain't gonna move this piano.

Boy Willie: Get out the way, Wining Boy.

Wining Boy, his back to the piano, spreads his arms out over the piano.

Wining Boy: You ain't taking this piano out the house. You got to take me with it!

Boy Willie: Get on out the way, Wining Boy! Doaker get him!

There is a knock on the door.

Berniece: I got him, Doaker. Come on, Wining Boy. I done told Boy Willie he ain't taking the piano.

Berniece tries to take Wining Boy away from the piano.

Wining Boy: He got to take me with it!

Doaker goes to answer the door. Grace enters.

Grace: Is Lymon here?

Doaker: Lymon.

Wining Boy: He ain't taking that piano.

Berniece: I ain't gonna let him take it.

Grace: I thought you was coming back. I ain't gonna sit in that truck all day.

Lymon: I told you I was coming back.

Grace (sees Boy Willie): Oh, hi, Boy Willie. Lymon told me you was gone back down South.

Lymon: I said he was going back. I didn't say he had left already.

Grace: That's what you told me.

Berniece: Lymon, you got to take your company someplace else.

Lymon: Berniece, this is Grace. That there is Berniece. That's Boy Willie's sister.

Grace: Nice to meet you. *(To Lymon.)* I ain't gonna sit out in that truck all day. You told me you was gonna take me to the movie.

Lymon: I told you I had something to do first. You supposed to wait on me.

Berniece: Lymon, just go on and leave. Take Grace or whoever with you. Just go on get out my house.

Boy Willie: You gonna help me move this piano first, nigger!

Lymon (to Grace): I got to help Boy Willie move the piano first.

Everybody but Grace suddenly senses Sutter's presence.

Grace: I ain't waiting on you. Told me you was coming right back. Now you got to move a piano. You just like all the other men. *(Grace now senses something.)* Something ain't right here. I knew I shouldn't have come back up in this house.

Grace exits.

Lymon: Hey, Grace! I'll be right back, Boy Willie.

Boy Willie: Where you going, nigger?

Lymon: I'll be back. I got to take Grace home.

Boy Willie: Come on, let's move the piano first!

Lymon: I got to take Grace home. I told you I'll be back.

Lymon exits. Boy Willie exits and calls after him.

Boy Willie: Come on, Lymon! Hey . . . Lymon! Lymon . . . come on!

Again, the presence of Sutter is felt.

Wining Boy: Hey, Doaker, did you feel that? Hey, Berniece . . . did you get cold? Hey, Doaker . . .

Doaker: What you calling me for?

Wining Boy: I believe that's Sutter.

Doaker: Well, let him stay up there. As long as he don't mess with me.

Berniece: Avery, go on and bless the house.

Doaker: You need to bless that piano. That's what you need to bless. It ain't done nothing but cause trouble. If you gonna bless anything go on and bless that.

Wining Boy: Hey, Doaker if he gonna bless something let him bless everything. The kitchen . . . the upstairs. Go on and bless it all.

Boy Willie: Ain't no ghost in this house. He need to bless Berniece's head. That's what he need to bless.

Avery: Seem like that piano's causing all the trouble. I can bless that. Berniece, put me some water in that bottle.

Avery takes a small bottle from his pocket and hands it to Berniece, who goes into the kitchen to get water. Avery takes a candle from his pocket and lights it. He gives it to Berniece, as she gives him the water.

Hold this candle. Whatever you do make sure it don't go out.

O Holy Father we gather here this evening in the Holy Name to cast out the spirit of one James Sutter. May this vial of water be empowered with thy spirit. May each drop of it be a weapon and a shield against the presence of all evil and may it be a cleansing and blessing of this humble abode.

Just as Our Father taught us how to pray so He say, "I will prepare a table for you in the midst of mine enemies," and in His hands we place ourselves to come unto his presence. Where there is Good so shall it cause Evil to scatter to the Four Winds.

He throws water at the piano at each commandment.

Get thee behind me, Satan! Get thee behind the face of Righteousness as we Glorify His Holy Name! Get thee behind the Hammer of Truth that breaketh down the Wall of Falsehood! Father. Father. Praise. Praise. We ask in Jesus' name and call forth the power of the Holy Spirit as it is written. . . . *(He opens the Bible and reads from it.)* I will sprinkle clean water upon thee and ye shall be clean.

Boy Willie: All this old preaching stuff. Hell, just tell him to leave.

Avery continues reading throughout Boy Willie's outburst.

Avery: I will sprinkle clean water upon you and you shall be clean: from all your uncleanliness, and from all your idols, will I cleanse you. A new heart also will I give you, and a new spirit will I put within you: and I will take out of your flesh the heart of stone, and I will give you a heart of flesh. And I will put my spirit within you, and cause you to walk in my statutes, and ye shall keep my judgments, and do them.

Boy Willie grabs a pot of water from the stove and begins to fling it around the room.

Boy Willie: Hey Sutter! Sutter! Get your ass out this house! Sutter! Come on and get some of this water! You done drowned in the well, come on and get some more of this water!

Boy Willie is working himself into a frenzy as he runs around the room throwing water and calling Sutter's name. Avery continues reading.

Boy Willie: Come on, Sutter! *(He starts up the stairs.)* Come on, get some water! Come on, Sutter!

The sound of Sutter's Ghost is heard. As Boy Willie approaches the steps he is suddenly thrown back by the unseen force, which is choking him. As he struggles he frees himself, then dashes up the stairs:

Boy Willie: Come on, Sutter!

Avery (continuing): A new heart also will I give you and a new spirit will I put within you: and I will take out of your flesh the heart of stone, and I will give you a heart of flesh. And I will put my spirit within you, and cause you to walk in my statutes, and ye shall keep my judgments, and do them.

There are loud sounds heard from upstairs as Boy Willie begins to wrestle with Sutter's Ghost. It is a life-and-death struggle fraught with perils and faultless terror. Boy Willie is thrown down the stairs. Avery is stunned into silence. Boy Willie picks himself up and dashes back upstairs.

Avery: Berniece, I can't do it.

There are more sounds heard from upstairs. Doaker and Wining Boy stare at one another in stunned disbelief. It is in this moment, from somewhere old, that Berniece realizes what she must do. She crosses to the piano. She begins to play. The song is found piece by piece. It is an old urge to song that is both a commandment and a plea. With each repetition it gains in strength. It is intended as an exorcism and a dressing for battle. A rustle of wind blowing across two continents.

Berniece (singing):

I want you to help me
I want you to help me
I want you to help me
I want you to help me
I want you to help me
I want you to help me
Mama Berniece
I want you to help me
Mama Esther
I want you to help me
Papa Boy Charles
I want you to help me
Mama Ola
I want you to help me

I want you to help me
I want you to help me
I want you to help me
I want you to help me
I want you to help me
I want you to help me
I want you to help me
I want you to help me

The sound of a train approaching is heard. The noise upstairs subsides.

Boy Willie: Come on, Sutter! Come back, Sutter!

Berniece begins to chant:

Berniece:
Thank you.
Thank you.
Thank you.

A calm comes over the house. Maretha enters from Doaker's room. Boy Willie enters on the stairs. He pauses a moment to watch Berniece at the piano.

Berniece:
    Thank you.
    Thank you.

Boy Willie: Wining Boy, you ready to go back down home? Hey Doaker, what time the train leave?

Doaker: You still got time to make it.

    Maretha crosses and embraces Boy Willie.

Boy Willie: Hey Berniece . . . if you and Maretha don't keep playing on that piano . . . ain't no telling . . . me and Sutter both liable to be back.

    He exits.

Berniece: Thank you.

    The lights go down to black.

Connections to Other Selections

1. Discuss the significance of custom and the past in *The Piano Lesson* and Wole Soyinka's *The Strong Breed* (p. 1956).

2. In an essay discuss the importance of African heritage in *The Piano Lesson* and Lorraine Hansberry's *A Raisin in the Sun* (p. 1731).

3. How might the narrator's experience in Ralph Ellison's "Battle Royal" (p. 231) be used to shed light on the conflicts in *The Piano Lesson?*

CRITICAL
THINKING
AND WRITING

52

Critical Strategies
for Reading

CRITICAL THINKING

Maybe this has happened to you: the assignment is to write an analysis of some aspect of a work—let's say, Nathaniel Hawthorne's *The Scarlet Letter*—that interests you and takes into account critical sources that comment on and interpret the work. You cheerfully begin research in the library but quickly find yourself bewildered by several seemingly unrelated articles. The first traces the thematic significance of images of light and darkness in the novel; the second makes a case for Hester Prynne as a liberated woman; the third argues that Arthur Dimmesdale's guilt is a projection of Hawthorne's own emotions; and the fourth analyzes the introduction, "The Custom-House," as an attack on bourgeois values. These disparate treatments may seem random and capricious—a confirmation of your worst suspicions that interpretations of literature are hit-or-miss excursions into areas that you know little about or didn't know even existed. But if you understand that the four articles are written from four different perspectives—formalist, feminist, psychological, and Marxist—and that the purpose of each is to enhance your understanding of the novel by discussing a particular element of it, then you can see that the articles' varying strategies represent potentially interesting ways of opening up the text that might otherwise never have occurred to you. There are many ways to approach a text, and a useful first step is to develop a sense of direction, an understanding of how a perspective—your own or a critic's—shapes a discussion of a text.

This chapter offers an introduction to critical approaches to literature by outlining a variety of strategies for reading fiction, poetry, or drama. These strategies include approaches that have long been practiced by readers who have used, for example, the insights gleaned from biography and history to illuminate literary works as well as more recent approaches, such as those used by gender, reader-response, and deconstructionist critics. Each of these perspectives is sensitive to point of view, symbol, tone, irony, and other literary elements that you have been studying, but each also casts those elements in a special light. The formalist approach emphasizes how the elements within a work achieve their effects, whereas biographical and psychological approaches lead outward from the work to consider the author's life and other writings. Even broader approaches, such as historical and cultural perspectives, connect the work to historic, social, and economic forces. Mythological readings represent the broadest approach because they discuss the cultural and universal responses readers have to a work.

Any given strategy raises its own types of questions and issues while seeking particular kinds of evidence to support itself. An awareness of the assumptions and methods that inform an approach can help you to understand better the validity and value of a given critic's strategy for making sense of a work. More important, such an understanding can widen and deepen the responses of your own reading.

The critical thinking that goes into understanding a professional critic's approach to a work is not foreign to you because you have already used essentially the same kind of thinking to understand the work itself. You have developed skills to produce a literary *analysis* that, for example, describes how a character, symbol, or rhyme scheme supports a theme. These same skills are also useful for reading literary criticism because they allow you to keep track of how the parts of a critical approach create a particular reading of a literary work. When you analyze a story, poem, or play by closely examining how its various elements relate to the whole, your *interpretation* — your articulation of what the work means to you as supported by an analysis of its elements — necessarily involves choosing what you focus on in the work. The same is true of professional critics.

Critical readings presuppose choices in the kinds of materials that are discussed. An analysis of the setting of John Updike's "A & P" (p. 606) would probably focus on the oppressive environment the protagonist associates with the store rather than, say, the economic history of that supermarket chain. (For a student's analysis of the setting in "A & P," see p. 2155.) The economic history of a supermarket chain might be useful to a Marxist critic concerned with how class relations are revealed in "A & P," but for a formalist critic interested in identifying the unifying structures of the story, such information would be irrelevant.

The Perspectives, Complementary Critical Readings, and Critical Case Studies in this anthology offer opportunities to read critics using a wide variety of approaches to analyze and interpret texts. In the Critical Case Study on Ibsen's *A Doll House* (Chapter 46), for instance, Carol Strongin Tufts (p. 1631) offers a psychoanalytic reading of Nora that characterizes her as a narcissistic personality rather than as a feminist heroine. The criteria she uses to evaluate Nora's behavior are drawn from the language used by the American Psychiatric Association. In contrast, Joan Templeton (p. 1633) places Nora in the context of women's rights issues to argue that Nora must be read from a feminist perspective if the essential meaning of the play is to be understood. Each of these critics raises different questions, examines different evidence, and employs different assumptions to interpret Nora's character. Being aware of those differences — teasing them out so that you can see how they lead to competing conclusions — is a useful way to analyze the analysis itself. What is left out of an interpretation is sometimes as significant as what is included. As you read the critics, it's worth reminding yourself that your own critical thinking skills can help you to determine the usefulness of a particular approach.

The following overview of critical strategies for reading is neither exhaustive in the types of critical approaches covered nor complete in its presentation of the complexities inherent in them, but it should help you to develop an appreciation of the intriguing possibilities that attend literary interpretation. The emphasis in this chapter is on ways of thinking about literature rather than on daunting lists of terms, names, and movements. Although a working knowledge of critical schools may be valuable and necessary for a fully informed use of a given critical approach, the aim here is more modest and practical. This chapter is no substitute for the shelves of literary criticism that can be found in your library, but it does suggest how readers using different perspectives organize their responses to texts.

The summaries of critical approaches that follow are descriptive, not evaluative. Each approach has its advantages and limitations. In practice, many critical approaches overlap and complement each other, but those matters are best left to further study. Like literary artists, critics have their personal values, tastes, and styles. The appropriateness of a specific critical approach will depend, at least in part, on the nature of the literary work under discussion as well as on your own sensibilities and experience. However, any approach, if it is to enhance understanding, requires sensitivity, tact, and an awareness of the various literary elements of the text, including, of course, its use of language.

Successful critical approaches avoid eccentric decodings that reveal so-called hidden meanings that are not only hidden but totally absent from the text. For a parody of this sort of critical excess, see "A Parodic Interpretation of 'Stopping by Woods on a Snowy Evening'" (p. 1026), in which Herbert R. Coursen Jr. has some fun with a Robert Frost poem and Santa Claus while making a serious point about the dangers of overly ingenious readings. Literary criticism attempts, like any valid hypothesis, to account for phenomena — the text — without distorting or misrepresenting what it describes.

THE LITERARY CANON: DIVERSITY AND CONTROVERSY

Before looking at the various critical approaches discussed in this chapter, it makes sense to consider first which literature has been traditionally considered worthy of such analysis. The discussion in the Introduction called The Changing Literary Canon (p. 5) may have already alerted you to the fact that in recent years many more works by women, minorities, and writers from around the world have been considered by scholars, critics, and teachers to merit serious study and inclusion in what is known as the literary canon. This increasing diversity has been celebrated by those who believe that multiculturalism taps new sources for the discovery of great literature while raising significant questions about language, culture, and society. At the same time, others have perceived this diversity as a threat to the established, traditional canon of Western culture.

The debates concerning who should be read, taught, and written about have sometimes been acrimonious as well as lively and challenging. Bitter arguments have been waged recently on campuses and in the press over what has come to be called *political correctness*. Two main camps have formed around these debates — liberals and conservatives (the appropriateness of these terms is debatable, but the oppositional positioning is unmistakable). The liberals are said to insist on encouraging tolerant attitudes about race, class, gender, and sexual orientation, and opening up the curriculum to multicultural texts from Asia, Africa, Latin America, and elsewhere. These revisionists, seeking a change in traditional attitudes, are sometimes accused of trying to substitute ideological dogma for reason and truth and to intimidate opposing colleagues and students into silence and acceptance of their politically correct views. The conservatives are also portrayed as ideologues; in their efforts to preserve what they regard as the best from the past, they fail to acknowledge that Western classics, mostly written by white male Europeans, represent only a portion of human experience. These traditionalists are seen as advocating values that are neither universal nor eternal but merely privileged and entrenched. Conservatives are charged with ignoring the political agenda that their values represent and that is implicit in their preference for the works of canonical authors such as Homer, Virgil, Shakespeare, Milton, Tolstoy, and Faulkner. The reductive and contradictory nature of this national debate between liberals and conservatives has been neatly summed up by Katha Pollitt: "Read the conservatives' list and produce a nation of sexists and racists — or a nation of philosopher kings. Read the liberals' list and produce a nation of spiritual relativists — or a nation of open-minded world citizens" ("Canon to the Right of Me . . . ," *The Nation*, Sept. 23, 1991, p. 330).

These troubling and extreme alternatives can be avoided, of course, if the issues are not approached from such absolutist positions. Solutions to these issues cannot be suggested in this limited space, and, no doubt, solutions will evolve over time, but we can at least provide a perspective. Books — regardless of what list they are on — are not likely to unite a fragmented nation or to disunite a unified one. It is perhaps more useful and accurate to see issues of canonicity as reflecting political changes rather than being the primary causes of them. This is not to say that books don't have an impact on readers — that *Uncle Tom's Cabin*, for instance, did not galvanize antislavery sentiments in nineteenth-century America — but that book lists do not by themselves preserve or destroy the status quo.

It's worth noting that the curricula of American universities have always undergone significant and, some would say, wrenching changes. Only a little more than one hundred years ago there was strong opposition to teaching English, as well as other modern languages, alongside programs dominated by Greek and Latin. Only since the 1920s has American literature been made a part of the curriculum, and just five decades ago including twentieth-century writers such as James Joyce, Virginia Woolf, Franz Kafka, and Ernest Hemingway in the curriculum was regarded with raised eyebrows. New voices do not drown out the past; they build on it and eventually become part of the past as newer writers take their place beside them. Neither resistance to change nor a denial of the past will have its way with the canon. Though both impulses are widespread, neither is likely to dominate the other because there are too many reasonable, practical readers and teachers who instead of replacing Shakespeare, Melville, and other canonical writers have supplemented them with neglected writers from Western and other cultures. These readers experience the current debates about the canon not as a binary opposition but as an opportunity to explore important questions about continuity and change in our literature, culture, and society.

FORMALIST STRATEGIES

Formalist critics focus on the formal elements of a work—its language, structure, and tone. A formalist reads literature as an independent work of art rather than as a reflection of the author's state of mind or as a representation of a moment in history. Historic influences on a work, an author's intentions, or anything else outside the work are generally not treated by formalists (this is particularly true of the most famous modern formalists, known as the *New Critics,* who dominated American criticism from the 1940s through the 1960s). Instead, formalists offer intense examinations of the relationship between form and meaning within a work, emphasizing the subtle complexity of how a work is arranged. This kind of close reading pays special attention to what are often described as *intrinsic* matters in a literary work, such as diction, irony, paradox, metaphor, and symbol, as well as larger elements, such as plot, characterization, and narrative technique. Formalists examine how these elements work together to give a coherent shape to a work while contributing to its meaning. The answers to the questions formalists raise about how the shape and effect of a work are related come from the work itself. Other kinds of information that go beyond the text—biography, history, politics, economics, and so on—are typically regarded by formalists as *extrinsic* matters, which are considerably less important than what goes on within the autonomous text.

Poetry especially lends itself to close readings because a poem's relative brevity allows for detailed analyses of nearly all its words and how they achieve their effects. For a student's formalist reading of how a pervasive sense of death is worked into a poem, see "A Reading of Dickinson's 'There's a certain Slant of light'" (p. 2150).

Formalist strategies are also useful for analyzing drama and fiction. In his well-known essay "The World of *Hamlet,*" Maynard Mack explores Hamlet's character and predicament by paying close attention to the words and images that Shakespeare uses to build a world in which appearances mask reality and mystery is embedded in scene after scene. Mack points to recurring terms, such as *apparition, seems, assume,* and *put on,* as well as repeated images of acting, clothing, disease, and painting, to indicate the treacherous surface world Hamlet must penetrate to get to the truth. This pattern of deception provides an organizing principle around which Mack offers a reading of the entire play:

> Hamlet's problem, in its crudest form, is simply the problem of the avenger: he must carry out the injunction of the ghost and kill the king. But this problem . . . is presented in terms of a certain kind of world. The ghost's injunction to act becomes so inextricably bound up for Hamlet with the character of the world in which the action must be taken — its mysteriousness, its baffling appearances, its deep consciousness of infection, frailty, and loss — that he cannot come to terms with either without coming to terms with both.

Although Mack places *Hamlet* in the tradition of revenge tragedy, his reading of the play emphasizes Shakespeare's arrangement of language rather than literary history as a means of providing an interpretation that accounts for various elements of the play. Mack's formalist strategy explores how diction reveals meaning and how repeated words and images evoke and reinforce important thematic significances.

For an example of a work in which the shape of the plot serves as the major organizing principle, let's examine Kate Chopin's "The Story of an Hour" (p. 12), a two-page short story that takes only a few minutes to read. With the story fresh in your mind, consider how you might approach it from a formalist perspective. A first reading probably results in surprise at the story's ending: a grieving wife "afflicted with a heart trouble" suddenly dies of a heart attack, not because she's learned that her kind and loving husband has been killed in a terrible train accident but because she discovers that he is very much alive. Clearly, we are faced with an ironic situation since there is such a powerful incongruity between what is expected to happen and what actually happens. A likely formalist strategy for analyzing this story would be to raise questions about the ironic ending. Is this merely a trick ending, or is it a carefully wrought culmination of other elements in the story so that in addition to creating surprise the ending snaps the story shut on an interesting and challenging theme? Formalists value such complexities over simple surprise effects.

A second, closer reading indicates that Chopin's third-person narrator presents the story in a manner similar to Josephine's gentle attempts to break the news about Brently Mallard's death. The story is told in "veiled hints that [reveal] in half concealing." But unlike Josephine, who tries to protect her sister's fragile heart from stress, the narrator seeks to reveal Mrs. Mallard's complex heart. A formalist would look back over the story for signs of the ending in the imagery. Although Mrs. Mallard grieves immediately and unreservedly when she hears about the train disaster, she soon begins to feel a different emotion as she looks out the window at "the tops of trees . . . all aquiver with the new spring life." This symbolic evocation of renewal and rebirth — along with "the delicious breath of rain," the sounds of life in the street, and the birds singing — causes her to feel, in spite of her own efforts to repress her thoughts and emotions, "free, free, free!" She feels alive with a sense of possibility, with a "clear and exalted perception" that she "would live for herself" instead of for and through her husband.

It is ironic that this ecstatic "self-assertion" is interpreted by Josephine as grief, but the crowning irony for this "goddess of Victory" is the doctors' assumption that she dies of joy rather than of the shock of having to abandon her newly discovered self once she realizes her husband is still alive. In the course of an hour, Mrs. Mallard's life is irretrievably changed: her husband's assumed accidental death frees her, but the fact that he lives and all the expectations imposed on her by his continued life kill her. She does, indeed, die of a broken heart, but only Chopin's readers know the real ironic meaning of that explanation.

Although this brief discussion of some of the formal elements of Chopin's story does not describe all there is to say about how they produce an effect and create meaning, it does suggest the kinds of questions, issues, and evidence that a formalist strategy might raise in providing a close reading of the text itself.

BIOGRAPHICAL STRATEGIES

A knowledge of an author's life can help readers understand his or her work more fully. Events in a work might follow actual events in a writer's life just as characters might be based on people known by the author. Ernest Hemingway's "Soldier's Home" (p. 152) is a story about the difficulties of a World War I veteran named Krebs returning to his small hometown in Oklahoma, where he cannot adjust to the pious assumptions of his family and neighbors. He refuses to accept their innocent blindness to the horrors he has witnessed during the war. They have no sense of the brutality of modern life; instead they insist he resume his life as if nothing has happened. There is plenty of biographical evidence to indicate that Krebs's unwillingness to lie about his war experiences reflects Hemingway's own responses on his return to Oak Park, Illinois, in 1919. Krebs, like Hemingway, finds he has to leave the sentimentality, repressiveness, and smug complacency that threaten to render his experiences unreal: "the world they were in was not the world he was in."

An awareness of Hemingway's own war experiences and subsequent disillusionment with his hometown can be readily developed through available biographies, letters, and other works he wrote. Consider, for example, this passage from *By Force of Will: The Life and Art of Ernest Hemingway*, in which Scott Donaldson describes Hemingway's response to World War I:

> In poems, as in [*A Farewell to Arms*], Hemingway expressed his distaste for the first war. The men who had to fight the war did not die well:
>
> > Soldiers pitch and cough and twitch —
> >   All the world roars red and black;
> > Soldiers smother in a ditch,
> >   Choking through the whole attack.
>
> And what did they die for? They were "sucked in" by empty words and phrases —
>
> > King and country,
> > Christ Almighty,
> > And the rest,
> > Patriotism,
> > Democracy,
> > Honor —
>
> which spelled death. The bitterness of these outbursts derived from the distinction Hemingway drew between the men on the line and those who started the wars that others had to fight.

This kind of information can help to deepen our understanding of just how empathetically Krebs is presented in the story. Relevant facts about Hemingway's life will not make "Soldier's Home" a better written story than it is, but such information can make clearer the source of Hemingway's convictions and how his own experiences inform his major concerns as a storyteller.

Some formalist critics — some New Critics, for example — argue that interpretation should be based exclusively on internal evidence rather than on any biographical information outside the work. They argue that it is not possible to determine an author's intention and that the work must stand by itself. Although this is a useful caveat for keeping the work in focus, a reader who finds biography relevant would argue that biography can at the very least serve as a control on interpretation. A reader who, for example, finds Krebs at fault for not subscribing to the values of his hometown would be misreading the story, given both its tone and the biographical information available about the author. Although the narrator never *tells* the reader that Krebs is right or wrong for leaving town, the story's tone sides with his view of things. If, however, someone were to argue otherwise, insisting that the tone is not decisive and that Krebs's position is problematic, a reader familiar with Hemingway's own reactions could refute that argument with a powerful confirmation of Krebs's instincts to withdraw. Hence, many readers find biography useful for interpretation.

However, it is also worth noting that biographical information can complicate a work. Chopin's "The Story of an Hour" presents a repressed wife's momentary discovery of what freedom from her husband might mean to her. She awakens to a new sense of herself when she learns of her husband's death, only to collapse of a heart attack when she sees that he is alive. Readers might be tempted to interpret this story as Chopin's fictionalized commentary about her own marriage because her husband died twelve years before she wrote the story and seven years before she began writing fiction seriously. Biographers seem to agree, however, that Chopin's marriage was evidently satisfying to her and that she was not oppressed by her husband and did not feel oppressed.

Moreover, consider this diary entry from only one month after Chopin wrote the story (quoted by Per Seyersted in *Kate Chopin: A Critical Biography*):

> If it were possible for my husband and my mother to come back to earth, I feel that I would unhesitatingly give up everything that has come into my life since they left it and join my existence again with theirs. To do that, I would have to forget the past ten years of my growth — my real growth. But I would take back a little wisdom with me; it would be the spirit of perfect acquiescence.

This passage raises provocative questions instead of resolving them. How does that "spirit of perfect acquiescence" relate to Mrs. Mallard's insistence that she "would live for herself"? Why would Chopin be willing to "forget the past ten years of . . . growth" given her protagonist's desire for "self-assertion"? Although these and other questions raised by the diary entry cannot be answered here, this kind of biographical perspective certainly adds to the possibilities of interpretation.

Sometimes biographical information does not change our understanding so much as it enriches our appreciation of a work. It matters, for instance, that much of John Milton's poetry, so rich in visual imagery, was written after he became blind; and it is just as significant — to shift to a musical example — that a number of Ludwig van Beethoven's greatest works, including the Ninth Symphony, were composed after he succumbed to total deafness.

PSYCHOLOGICAL STRATEGIES

Given the enormous influence that Sigmund Freud's psychoanalytic theories have had on twentieth-century interpretations of human behavior, it is nearly inevitable that most people have some familiarity with his ideas concerning dreams, unconscious desires, and sexual repression, as well as his terms for different aspects of the psyche — the id, ego, and superego. Psychological approaches to literature draw on Freud's theories and other psychoanalytic theories to understand more fully the text, the writer, and the reader. Critics use such approaches to explore the motivations of characters and the symbolic meanings of events, while biographers speculate about a writer's own motivations — conscious or unconscious — in a literary work. Psychological approaches are also used to describe and analyze the reader's personal responses to a text.

Although it is not feasible to explain psychoanalytic terms and concepts in so brief a space as this, it is possible to suggest the nature of a psychological approach. It is a strategy based heavily on the idea of the existence of a human unconscious — those impulses, desires, and feelings that a person is unaware of but that influence emotions and behavior.

Central to a number of psychoanalytic critical readings is Freud's concept of what he called the **Oedipus complex**, a term derived from Sophocles' tragedy *Oedipus the King* (p. 1289). This complex is predicated on a boy's unconscious rivalry with his father for his mother's love and his desire to eliminate his father in order to take his father's place with his mother. The female version of the psychological conflict is known as the **Electra complex**, a term used to describe a daughter's unconscious rivalry for her father. The name comes from a Greek legend about Electra who avenged the death of her father, Agamemnon, by plotting the death of her mother. In *The Interpretation of Dreams,* Freud explains why *Oedipus the King* "moves a modern audience no less than it did the contemporary Greek one." What unites their powerful attraction to the play is an unconscious response:

> There must be something which makes a voice within us ready to recognize the compelling force of destiny in the *Oedipus.* . . . His destiny moves us only because it might have been ours — because the oracle laid the same curse upon us before our birth as upon him. It is the fate of all of us, perhaps, to direct our first sexual impulse towards our mother and our first hatred and our first murderous wish against our father. Our dreams convince us that this is so. King Oedipus, who slew his father Laius and married his mother Jocasta, merely shows us the fulfillment of our own childhood wishes . . . and we shrink back from him with the whole force of the repression by which those wishes have since that time been held down within us.

In this passage Freud interprets the unconscious motives of Sophocles in writing the play, Oedipus in acting within it, and the audience in responding to it.

A further application of the Oedipus complex can be observed in a classic interpretation of *Hamlet* by Ernest Jones, who used this concept to explain why Hamlet delays in avenging his father's death. This reading has been tightly summarized by Norman Holland, a recent psychoanalytic critic, in *The Shakespearean Imagination.* Holland shapes the issues into four major components:

> One, people over the centuries have been unable to say why Hamlet delays in killing the man who murdered his father and married his mother. Two, psychoanalytic experience shows that every child wants to do just exactly that.

Three, Hamlet delays because he cannot punish Claudius for doing what he himself wished to do as a child and, unconsciously, still wishes to do: he would be punishing himself. Four, the fact that this wish is unconscious explains why people could not explain Hamlet's delay.

Although the Oedipus complex is, of course, not relevant to all psychological interpretations of literature, interpretations involving this complex do offer a useful example of how psychoanalytic critics tend to approach a text. (For Freud's discussion of *Hamlet*, see p. 1551.)

The situation in which Mrs. Mallard finds herself in Chopin's "The Story of an Hour" is not related to an Oedipus complex, but it is clear that news of her husband's death has released powerful unconscious desires for freedom that she had previously suppressed. As she grieved, "something" was "coming to her and she was waiting for it, fearfully." What comes to her is what she senses about the life outside her window; that's the stimulus, but the true source of what was to "possess her," which she strove to "beat . . . back with her [conscious] will" is her desperate desire for the autonomy and fulfillment she had been unable to admit did not exist in her marriage. A psychological approach to her story amounts to a case study in the destructive nature of self-repression. Moreover, the story might reflect Chopin's own views of her marriage — despite her conscious statements about her loving husband. And what about the reader's response? How might a psychological approach account for different responses in female and male readers to Mrs. Mallard's death? One needn't be versed in psychoanalytic terms to entertain this question.

HISTORICAL STRATEGIES

Historians sometimes use literature as a window onto the past because literature frequently provides the nuances of a historic period that cannot be readily perceived through other sources. The characters in Harriet Beecher Stowe's *Uncle Tom's Cabin* (1852) display, for example, a complex set of white attitudes toward blacks in mid-nineteenth-century America that is absent from more traditional historic documents, such as census statistics or state laws. Another way of approaching the relationship between literature and history, however, is to use history as a means of understanding a literary work more clearly. The plot pattern of pursuit, escape, and capture in nineteenth-century slave narratives had a significant influence on Stowe's plotting of action in *Uncle Tom's Cabin*. This relationship demonstrates that the writing contemporary to an author is an important element of the history that helps to shape a work. There are many ways to talk about the historical and cultural dimensions of a work. Such readings treat a literary text as a document reflecting, producing, or being produced by the social conditions of its time, giving equal focus to the social milieu and the work itself. Four historical strategies that have been especially influential are literary history criticism, Marxist criticism, new historicist criticism, and cultural criticism.

Literary History Criticism

Literary historians shift the emphasis from the period to the work. Hence a literary historian might also examine mid-nineteenth-century abolitionist attitudes toward blacks to determine whether Stowe's novel is representative of those views or significantly to the right or left of them. Such a study might even indicate how closely the book reflects racial attitudes of twentieth-century readers. A work of literature may transcend time to the extent that it addresses the concerns of readers over a span of decades or centuries, but it remains for the literary historian a part of the past in which it was composed, a past that can reveal more fully a work's language, ideas, and purposes.

Literary historians move beyond both the facts of an author's personal life and the text itself to the social and intellectual currents in which the author composed the work. They place the work in the context of its time (as do many critical biographers, who write "life and times" studies), and sometimes they make connections with other literary works that may have influenced the author. The basic strategy of literary historians is to illuminate the historic background in order to shed light on some aspect of the work itself.

In Hemingway's "Soldier's Home" we learn that Krebs had been at Belleau Wood, Soissons, the Champagne, St. Mihiel, and the Argonne. Although nothing is said of these battles in the story, they were among the bloodiest of the war; the wholesale butchery and staggering casualties incurred by both sides make credible the way Krebs's unstated but lingering memories have turned him into a psychological prisoner of war. Knowing something about the ferocity of those battles helps us account for Krebs's response in the story. Moreover, we can more fully appreciate Hemingway's refusal to have Krebs lie about the realities of war for the folks back home if we are aware of the numerous poems, stories, and plays published during World War I that presented war as a glorious, manly, transcendent sacrifice for God and country. Juxtaposing those works with "Soldier's Home" brings the differences into sharp focus.

Similarly, a reading of William Blake's poem "London" (p. 763) is less complete if we do not know of the horrific social conditions — the poverty, disease, exploitation, and hypocrisy — that characterized the city Blake laments in the late eighteenth century.

One last example: the repression expressed in the lines on Mrs. Mallard's face is more distinctly seen if Chopin's "The Story of an Hour" is placed in the context of "the women's question" as it continued to develop in the 1890s. Mrs. Mallard's impulse toward "self-assertion" runs parallel with a growing women's movement away from the role of long-suffering housewife. This desire was widely regarded by traditionalists as a form of dangerous selfishness that was considered as unnatural as it was immoral.

It is no wonder that Chopin raises the question of whether Mrs. Mallard's sense of freedom owing to her husband's death isn't a selfish, "monstrous joy." Mrs. Mallard, however, dismisses this question as "trivial" in the face of her new perception of life, a dismissal that Chopin endorses by way of the story's ironic ending. The larger social context of this story would have been more apparent to Chopin's readers in 1894 than it is to readers in the 2000s. That is why an historical reconstruction of the limitations placed on married women helps to explain the pressures, tensions, and momentary — only momentary — release that Mrs. Mallard experiences.

Marxist Criticism

Marxist readings developed from the heightened interest in radical reform during the 1930s, when many critics looked to literature as a means of furthering proletarian social and economic goals, based largely on the writings of Karl Marx. *Marxist critics* focus on the ideological content of a work — its explicit and implicit assumptions and values about matters such as culture, race, class, and power. Marxist studies typically aim at revealing and clarifying ideological issues and also correcting social injustices. Some Marxist critics have used literature to describe the competing socioeconomic interests that too often advance capitalist money and power rather than socialist morality and justice. They argue that criticism, like literature, is essentially political because it either challenges or supports economic oppression. Even if criticism attempts to ignore class conflicts, it is politicized, according to Marxists, because it supports the status quo.

It is not surprising that Marxist critics pay more attention to the content and themes of literature than to its form. A Marxist critic would more likely be concerned with the exploitive economic forces that cause Willy Loman to feel trapped in Miller's *Death of a Salesman* (p. 1824) than with the playwright's use of nonrealistic dramatic techniques to reveal Loman's inner thoughts. Similarly, a Marxist reading of Chopin's "The Story of an Hour" might draw on the evidence made available in a book published only a few years after the story by Charlotte Perkins Gilman titled *Women and Economics: A Study of the Economic Relation between Men and Women as a Factor in Social Evolution* (1898). An examination of this study could help explain how some of the "repression" Mrs. Mallard experiences was generated by the socioeconomic structure contemporary to her and how Chopin challenges the validity of that structure by having Mrs. Mallard resist it with her very life. A Marxist reading would see the protagonist's conflict as not only an individual issue but part of a larger class struggle.

New Historicist Criticism

Since the 1960s a development in historical approaches to literature known as *new historicism* has emphasized the interaction between the historic context of a work and a modern reader's understanding and interpretation of the work. In contrast to many traditional literary historians, however, new historicists attempt to describe the culture of a period by reading many different kinds of texts that traditional historians might have previously left for economists, sociologists, and anthropologists. New historicists attempt to read a period in all its dimensions, including political, economic, social, and aesthetic concerns. These considerations could be used to explain the pressures that destroy Mrs. Mallard. A new historicist might examine the story and the public attitudes toward women contemporary to "The Story of an Hour" as well as documents such as suffragist tracts and medical diagnoses to explore how the same forces — expectations about how women are supposed to feel, think, and behave — shape different kinds of texts and how these texts influence each other. A new historicist might, for example, examine medical records for evidence of "nervousness" and "hysteria" as common diagnoses for women who led lives regarded as too independent by their contemporaries.

Without an awareness of just how selfish and self-destructive Mrs. Mallard's impulses would have been in the eyes of her contemporaries, twentieth-century readers might miss the pervasive pressures embedded not only in her marriage but in the social fabric surrounding her. Her death is made more understandable by such an awareness. The doctors who diagnose her as suffering from "the joy that kills" are not merely insensitive or stupid; they represent a contrasting set of assumptions and values that are as historic and real as Mrs. Mallard's yearnings.

New historicist criticism acknowledges more fully than traditional historical approaches the competing nature of readings of the past and thereby tends to offer new emphases and perspectives. New historicism reminds us that there is not only one historic context for "The Story of an Hour." Those doctors reveal additional dimensions of late-nineteenth-century social attitudes that warrant our attention, whether we agree with them or not. By emphasizing that historical perceptions are governed, at least in part, by our own concerns and preoccupations, new historicists sensitize us to the fact that the history on which we choose to focus is colored by being reconstructed from our own present moment. This reconstructed history affects our reading of texts.

Cultural Criticism

Cultural critics, like new historicists, focus on the historical contexts of a literary work, but they pay particular attention to popular manifestations of social, political, and economic contexts. Popular culture — mass-produced and consumed cultural artifacts, today ranging from advertising to popular fiction to television to rock music — and "high" culture are given equal emphasis. A cultural critic might be interested in looking at how Baz Luhrmann's movie version of *Romeo + Juliet* (1996) was influenced by the fragmentary nature of MTV videos. Adding the "low" art of everyday life to "high" art opens up previously unexpected and unexplored areas of criticism. Cultural critics use widely eclectic strategies drawn from new historicism, psychology, gender studies, and deconstructionism (to name only a handful of approaches) to analyze not only literary texts but radio talk shows, comic strips, calendar art, commercials, travel guides, and baseball cards. Because all human activity falls within the ken of cultural criticism, nothing is too minor or major, obscure or pervasive, to escape the range of its analytic vision.

Cultural criticism also includes *postcolonial criticism,* the study of cultural behavior and expression in relationship to the formerly colonized world. Postcolonial criticism refers to the analysis of literary works written by writers from countries and cultures that at one time were controlled by colonizing powers — such as Indian writers during or after British colonial rule. The term also refers to the analysis of literary works written about colonial cultures by writers from the colonizing country. Many of these kinds of analyses point out how writers from colonial powers sometimes misrepresent colonized cultures by reflecting more their own values: Joseph Conrad's *Heart of Darkness* (published in 1899) represents African culture differently than Chinua Achebe's *Things Falling Apart* does, for example. Cultural criticism and postcolonial criticism represent a broad range of approaches to examining race, gender, and class in historical contexts in a variety of cultures.

A cultural critic's approach to Chopin's "The Story of an Hour" might emphasize how the story reflects the potential dangers and horrors of train travel in the 1890s or it might examine how heart disease was often misdiagnosed by physicians or used as a metaphor in Mrs. Mallard's culture for a variety of emotional conditions. Each of these perspectives can serve to create a wider and more informed understanding of the story. For a sense of the range of documents used by cultural critics to shed light on literary works and the historical contexts in which they are written and read, see the Cultural Case Studies on James Joyce's "Eveline" for fiction (p. 519), Julia Alvarez's "Queens, 1963" for poetry (p. 1084), and David Henry Hwang's *M. Butterfly* for drama (p. 1668).

GENDER STRATEGIES

Gender critics explore how ideas about men and women — what is masculine and feminine — can be regarded as socially constructed by particular cultures. According to some critics, sex is determined by simple biological and anatomical categories of male or female, and gender is determined by a culture's values. Thus, ideas about gender and what constitutes masculine and feminine behavior are created by cultural institutions and conditioning. A gender critic might, for example, focus on Chopin's characterization of an emotionally sensitive Mrs. Mallard and a rational, composed husband in "The Story of an Hour" as a manifestation of socially constructed gender identity in the 1890s. Gender criticism expands categories and definitions of what is masculine or feminine and tends to regard sexuality as more complex than merely masculine or feminine, heterosexual or homosexual. Gender criticism, therefore, has come to include gay and lesbian criticism as well as feminist criticism. Although there are complex and sometimes problematic relationships among these approaches because some critics argue that heterosexuals and homosexuals are profoundly biologically different, gay and lesbian criticism, like feminist criticism, can be usefully regarded as a subset of gender criticism.

Feminist Criticism

Like Marxist critics, *feminist critics* reading "The Story of an Hour" would also be interested in Charlotte Perkins Gilman's *Women and Economics: A Study of the Economic Relation between Men and Women as a Factor in Social Evolution* (1898) because they seek to correct or supplement what they regard as a predominantly male-dominated critical perspective with a feminist consciousness. Like other forms of sociological criticism, feminist criticism places literature in a social context, and, like those of Marxist criticism, its analyses often have sociopolitical purposes — explaining, for example, how images of women in literature reflect the patriarchal social forces that have impeded women's efforts to achieve full equality with men.

Feminists have analyzed literature by both men and women in an effort to understand literary representations of women as well as the writers and cultures that create them. Related to concerns about how gender affects the way men and women write about each other is an interest in whether women use language differently from the way men do. Consequently, feminist critics' approach to literature is characterized by the use of a broad range of disciplines, including history, sociology, psychology, and linguistics, to provide a perspective sensitive to feminist issues.

A feminist approach to Chopin's "The Story of an Hour" might explore the psychological stress created by the expectations that marriage imposes on Mrs. Mallard, expectations that literally and figuratively break her heart. Given that her husband is kind and loving, the issue is not her being married to Brently but her being married at all. Chopin presents marriage as an institution that creates in both men and women the assumed "right to impose a private will upon a fellow-creature." That "right," however, is seen, especially from a feminist perspective, as primarily imposed on women by men. A feminist critic might note, for instance, that the protagonist is introduced as "Mrs. Mallard" (we learn that her first name is Louise only later); she is defined by her marital status and her husband's name, a name whose origin from the Old French is related to the word *masle,* which means "male." The appropriateness of her name points up the fact that her emotions and the cause of her death are interpreted in male terms by the doctors. The value of a feminist perspective on this work can be readily discerned if a reader imagines Mrs. Mallard's story being told from the point of view of one of the doctors who diagnoses the cause of her death as a weak heart rather than as a fierce struggle.

Gay and Lesbian Criticism

Gay and lesbian critics focus on a variety of issues, including how homosexuals are represented in literature, how they read literature, and whether sexuality and gender are culturally constructed or innate. Gay critics have produced new readings of works by and discovered homosexual concerns in writers such as Herman Melville and Henry James, while lesbian critics have done the same for the works of writers such as Emily Dickinson and Toni Morrison. A lesbian reading of "The Story of an Hour," for example, might consider whether Mrs. Mallard's ecstatic feeling of relief—produced by the belief that her marriage is over owing to the presumed death of her husband—isn't also a rejection of her heterosexual identity. Perhaps her glimpse of future freedom, evoked by feminine images of a newly discovered nature "all aquiver with the new spring of life," embraces a repressed new sexual identity that "was too subtle and elusive to name" but that was "approaching to possess her" no matter how much she "was striving to beat it back with her will." Although gay and lesbian readings often raise significant interpretive controversies among critics, they have opened up provocative discussions of seemingly familiar texts.

MYTHOLOGICAL STRATEGIES

Mythological approaches to literature attempt to identify what in a work creates deep universal responses in readers. Whereas psychological critics interpret the symbolic meanings of characters and actions in order to understand more fully the unconscious dimensions of an author's mind, a character's motivation, or a reader's response, mythological critics (also frequently referred to as *archetypal critics*) interpret the hopes, fears, and expectations of entire cultures.

In this context myth is not to be understood simply as referring to stories about imaginary gods who perform astonishing feats in the causes of love, jealousy, or hatred. Nor are myths to be judged as merely erroneous, primitive accounts of how nature runs its course and humanity its affairs. Instead, literary critics use myths as a strategy for understanding how human beings try to account for their lives symbolically. Myths can be a window onto a culture's deepest perceptions about itself because myths attempt to explain what otherwise seems unexplainable: a people's origin, purpose, and destiny.

All human beings have a need to make sense of their lives, whether they are concerned about their natural surroundings, the seasons, sexuality, birth, death, or the very meaning of existence. Myths help people organize their experiences; these systems of belief (less formally held than religious or political tenets but no less important) embody a culture's assumptions and values. What is important to the mythological critic is not the validity or truth of those assumptions and values; what matters is that they reveal common human concerns.

It is not surprising that although the details of mythic stories vary enormously, the essential patterns are often similar because these myths attempt to explain universal experiences. There are, for example, numerous myths that redeem humanity from permanent death through a hero's resurrection and rebirth. The resurrection of Jesus symbolizes for Christians the ultimate defeat of death and coincides with the rebirth of nature's fertility in spring. Features of this rebirth parallel the Greek myths of Adonis and Hyacinth, who die but are subsequently transformed into living flowers; there are also similarities that connect these stories to the reincarnation of the Indian Buddha or the rebirth of the Egyptian Osiris. Important differences exist among these stories, but each reflects a basic human need to limit the power of death and to hope for eternal life.

Mythological critics look for underlying, recurrent patterns in literature that reveal universal meanings and basic human experiences for readers regardless of when or where they live. The characters, images, and themes that symbolically embody these meanings and experiences are called **archetypes.** This term designates universal symbols, which evoke deep and perhaps unconscious responses in a reader because archetypes bring with them our hopes and fears since the beginning of human time. Surely one of the most powerfully compelling archetypes is the death and rebirth theme that relates the human life cycle to the cycle of the seasons. Many others could be cited and would be exhausted only after all human concerns were cataloged, but a few examples can suggest some of the range of plots, images, and characters addressed.

Among the most common literary archetypes are stories of quests, initiations, scapegoats, meditative withdrawals, descents to the underworld, and heavenly ascents. These stories are often filled with archetypal images — bodies of water that may symbolize the unconscious or eternity or baptismal rebirth; rising suns, suggesting reawakening and enlightenment; setting suns, pointing toward death; colors such as green, evocative of growth and fertility, or black, indicating chaos, evil, and death. Along the way are earth mothers, fatal women, wise old men, desert places, and paradisal gardens. No doubt your own reading has introduced you to any number of archetypal plots, images, and characters.

Mythological critics attempt to explain how archetypes are embodied in literary works. Employing various disciplines, these critics articulate the power a literary work has over us. Some critics are deeply grounded in classical literature, whereas others are more conversant with philology, anthropology, psychology, or cultural history. Whatever their emphases, however, mythological critics examine the elements of a work in order to make larger connections that explain the work's lasting appeal.

A mythological reading of Sophocles' *Oedipus the King,* for example, might focus on the relationship between Oedipus's role as a scapegoat and the plague and drought that threaten to destroy Thebes. The city is saved and the fertility of its fields restored only after the corruption is located in Oedipus. His subsequent atonement symbolically provides a kind of rebirth for the city. Thus, the plot recapitulates ancient rites in which the well-being of a king was directly linked to the welfare of his people. If a leader was sick or corrupt, he had to be replaced in order to guarantee the health of the community.

A similar pattern can be seen in the rottenness that Shakespeare exposes in Hamlet's Denmark. *Hamlet* reveals an archetypal pattern similar to that of *Oedipus the King:* not until the hero sorts out the corruption in his world and in himself can vitality and health be restored in his world. Hamlet avenges his father's death and becomes a scapegoat in the process. When he fully accepts his responsibility to set things right, he is swept away along with the tide of intrigue and corruption that has polluted life in Denmark. The new order — established by Fortinbras at the play's end — is achieved precisely because Hamlet is willing and finally able to sacrifice himself in a necessary purgation of the diseased state.

These kinds of archetypal patterns exist potentially in any literary period. Consider how in Chopin's "The Story of an Hour" Mrs. Mallard's life parallels the end of winter and the earth's renewal in spring. When she feels a surge of new life after grieving over her husband's death, her own sensibilities are closely aligned with the "new spring life" that is "all aquiver" outside her window. Although she initially tries to resist that renewal by "beat[ing] it back with her will," she cannot control the life force that surges within her and all around her. When she finally gives herself to the energy and life she experiences, she feels triumphant — like a "goddess of Victory." But this victory is short lived when she learns that her husband is still alive and with him all the obligations that made her marriage feel like a wasteland. Her death is an ironic version of a rebirth ritual. The coming of spring is an ironic contrast to her own discovery that she can no longer live a repressed, circumscribed life with her husband. Death turns out to be preferable to the living death that her marriage means to her. Although spring will go on, this "goddess of Victory" is defeated by a devastating social contract. The old, corrupt order continues, and that for Chopin is a cruel irony that mythological critics would see as an unnatural disruption of the nature of things.

READER-RESPONSE STRATEGIES

Reader-response criticism, as its name implies, focuses its attention on the reader rather than the work itself. This approach to literature describes what goes on in the reader's mind during the process of reading a text. In a sense, all critical approaches (especially psychological and mythological criticism) concern themselves with a reader's response to literature, but there is a stronger emphasis in reader-response criticism on the reader's active construction of the text. Although many critical theories inform reader-response criticism, all ***reader-response critics*** aim to describe the reader's experience of a work: in effect we get a reading of the reader, who comes to the work with certain expectations and assumptions, which are either met or not met. Hence the consciousness of the reader—produced by reading the work—is the subject matter of reader-response critics. Just as writing is a creative act, reading is, since it also produces a text.

Reader-response critics do not assume that a literary work is a finished product with fixed formal properties, as, for example, formalist critics do. Instead, the literary work is seen as an evolving creation of the reader's as he or she processes characters, plots, images, and other elements while reading. Some reader-response critics argue that this act of creative reading is, to a degree, controlled by the text, but it can produce many interpretations of the same text by different readers. There is no single definitive reading of a work, because the crucial assumption is that readers create rather than discover meanings in texts. Readers who have gone back to works they had read earlier in their lives often find that a later reading draws very different responses from them. What earlier seemed unimportant is now crucial; what at first seemed central is now barely worth noting. The reason, put simply, is that two different people have read the same text. Reader-response critics are not after the "correct" reading of the text or what the author presumably intended; instead they are interested in the reader's experience with the text.

These experiences change with readers; although the text remains the same, the readers do not. Social and cultural values influence readings, so that, for example, an avowed Marxist would be likely to come away from Miller's *Death of a Salesman* with a very different view of American capitalism than that of, say, a successful sales representative, who might attribute Willy Loman's fall more to his character than to the American economic system. Moreover, readers from different time periods respond differently to texts. An Elizabethan—concerned perhaps with the stability of monarchical rule—might respond differently to Hamlet's problems than would a twentieth-century reader well versed in psychology and concepts of what Freud called the Oedipus complex. This is not to say that anything goes, that Miller's play can be read as an amoral defense of cheating and rapacious business practices or that *Hamlet* is about the dangers of living away from home. The text does, after all, establish some limits that allow us to reject certain readings as erroneous. But reader-response critics do reject formalist approaches that describe a literary work as a self-contained object, the meaning of which can be determined without reference to any extrinsic matters, such as the social and cultural values assumed by either the author or the reader.

Reader-response criticism calls attention to how we read and what influences our readings. It does not attempt to define what a literary work means on the page but rather what it does to an informed reader, a reader who understands the language and conventions used in a given work. Reader-response criticism is not a rationale for mistaken or bizarre readings of works but an exploration of the possibilities for a plurality of readings shaped by the readers' experience with the text. This kind of strategy can help us understand how our responses are shaped by both the text and ourselves.

Chopin's "The Story of an Hour" illustrates how reader-response critical strategies read the reader. Chopin doesn't say that Mrs. Mallard's marriage is repressive; instead, that troubling fact dawns on the reader at the same time that the recognition forces its way into Mrs. Mallard's consciousness. Her surprise is also the reader's because although she remains in the midst of intense grief, she is on the threshold of a startling discovery about the new possibilities life offers. How the reader responds to that discovery, however, is not entirely controlled by Chopin. One reader, perhaps someone who has recently lost a spouse, might find Mrs. Mallard's "joy" indeed "monstrous" and selfish. Certainly that's how Mrs. Mallard's doctors — the seemingly authoritative diagnosticians in the story — would very likely read her. But for other readers — especially late-twentieth-century readers steeped in feminist values — Mrs. Mallard's feelings require no justification. Such readers might find Chopin's ending to the story more ironic than she seems to have intended because Mrs. Mallard's death could be read as Chopin's inability to envision a protagonist who has the strength of her convictions. In contrast, a reader in 1894 might have seen the ending as Mrs. Mallard's only escape from the repressive marriage her husband's assumed death suddenly allowed her to see. A late-twentieth-century reader probably would argue that it was the marriage that should have died rather than Mrs. Mallard, that she had other alternatives, not just obligations (as the doctors would have insisted), to consider.

By imagining different readers we can imagine a variety of responses to the story that are influenced by the readers' own impressions, memories, or experiences with marriage. Such imagining suggests the ways in which reader-response criticism opens up texts to a number of interpretations. As one final example, consider how readers' responses to "The Story of an Hour" would be affected if it were printed in two different magazines, read in the context of either *Ms.* or *Good Housekeeping*. What assumptions and beliefs would each magazine's readership be likely to bring to the story? How do you think the respective experiences and values of each magazine's readers would influence their readings? For a sample reader-response student paper on "The Story of an Hour," see page 16.

DECONSTRUCTIONIST STRATEGIES

Deconstructionist critics insist that literary works do not yield fixed, single meanings. They argue that there can be no absolute knowledge about anything because language can never say what we intend it to mean. Anything we write conveys meanings we did not intend, so the deconstructionist argument goes. Language is not a precise instrument but a power whose meanings are caught in an endless web of possibilities that cannot be untangled. Accordingly, any idea or statement that insists on being understood separately can ultimately be "deconstructed" to reveal its relations and connections to contradictory and opposite meanings.

Unlike other forms of criticism, deconstructionism seeks to destabilize meanings instead of establishing them. In contrast to formalists such as the New Critics, who closely examine a work in order to call attention to how its various components interact to establish a unified whole, deconstructionists try to show how a close examination of the language in a text inevitably reveals conflicting, contradictory impulses that "deconstruct" or break down its apparent unity.

Although deconstructionists and New Critics both examine the language of a text closely, deconstructionists focus on the gaps and ambiguities that reveal a text's instability and indeterminacy, whereas New Critics look for patterns that explain how the text's fixed meaning is structured. Deconstructionists painstakingly examine the competing meanings within the text rather than attempting to resolve them into a unified whole.

The questions deconstructionists ask are aimed at discovering and describing how a variety of possible readings are generated by the elements of a text. In contrast to a New Critic's concerns about the ultimate meaning of a work, a deconstructionist is primarily interested in how the use of language — diction, tone, metaphor, symbol, and so on — yields only provisional, not definitive, meanings. Consider, for example, the following excerpt from an American Puritan poet, Anne Bradstreet. The excerpt is from "The Flesh and the Spirit" (1678), which consists of an allegorical debate between two sisters, the body and the soul. During the course of the debate, Flesh, a consummate materialist, insists that Spirit values ideas that do not exist and that her faith in idealism is both unwarranted and insubstantial in the face of the material values that earth has to offer — riches, fame, and physical pleasure. Spirit, however, rejects the materialistic worldly argument that the only ultimate reality is physical reality and pledges her faith in God:

> Mine eye doth pierce the heavens and see
> What is invisible to thee.
> My garments are not silk nor gold,
> Nor such like trash which earth doth hold,
> But royal robes I shall have on,
> More glorious than the glist'ring sun;
> My crown not diamonds, pearls, and gold,
> But such as angels' heads enfold
> The city where I hope to dwell,
> There's none on earth can parallel;
> The stately walls both high and strong,
> Are made of precious jasper stone;
> The gates of pearl, both rich and clear,
> And angels are for porters there;

The streets thereof transparent gold,
Such as no eye did e'er behold;
A crystal river there doth run,
Which doth proceed from the Lamb's throne.

A deconstructionist would point out that Spirit's language — her use of material images such as jasper stone, pearl, gold, and crystal — cancels the explicit meaning of the passage by offering a supermaterialistic reward to the spiritually faithful. Her language, in short, deconstructs her intended meaning by employing the same images that Flesh would use to describe the rewards of the physical world. A deconstructionist reading, then, reveals the impossibility of talking about the invisible and spiritual worlds without using materialistic (that is, metaphoric) language. Thus Spirit's very language demonstrates a contradiction and conflict in her conviction that the world of here and now must be rejected for the hereafter. Her language deconstructs her meaning.

Deconstructionists look for ways to question and extend the meanings of a text. A deconstructionist might find, for example, the ironic ending of Chopin's "The Story of an Hour" less tidy and conclusive than would a New Critic, who might attribute Mrs. Mallard's death to her sense of lost personal freedom. A deconstructionist might use the story's ending to suggest that the narrative shares the doctors' inability to imagine a life for Mrs. Mallard apart from her husband.

As difficult as it is controversial, deconstructionism is not easily summarized or paraphrased. For an example of deconstructionism in practice and how it differs from New Criticism, see Andrew P. Debicki's "New Criticism and Deconstructionism: Two Attitudes in Teaching Poetry" (p. 2119).

SELECTED BIBLIOGRAPHY

Given the enormous number of articles and books written about literary theory and criticism in recent years, the following bibliography is necessarily highly selective. Even so, it should prove useful as an introduction to many of the issues associated with the critical strategies discussed in this chapter. For a general encyclopedic reference book that describes important figures, schools, and movements, see *The Johns Hopkins Guide to Literary Theory and Criticism,* edited by Michael Grodin and Martin Kreiswirth (Baltimore: Johns Hopkins UP, 1994); and for its concise discussions, see Ross Murfin and Supryia M. Ray, *The Bedford Glossary of Critical and Literary Terms* (Boston: Bedford / St. Martin's, 1998).

Canonical Issues

"The Changing Culture of the University." Special Issue. *Partisan Review* 58 (Spring 1991): 185–410.

Gates, Henry Louis, Jr. *The Signifying Monkey.* New York: Oxford UP, 1988.

Greenblatt, Stephen, and Giles Gunn. *Redrawing the Boundaries: The Transformation of English and American Literary Studies.* New York: MLA, 1992.

Lauter, Paul. *Canons and Contexts.* New York: Oxford UP, 1991.

"The Politics of Liberal Education." Special Issue. *South Atlantic Quarterly* 89 (Winter 1990): 1–234.

Sykes, Charles J. *The Hollow Men: Politics and Corruption in Higher Education.* Washington, DC: Regnery Gateway, 1990.

Formalist Strategies

Brooks, Cleanth. *The Well Wrought Urn: Studies in the Structure of Poetry.* New York: Reynal and Hitchcock, 1947.

Crane, Ronald Salmon. *The Languages of Criticism and the Structure of Poetry.* Toronto: U of Toronto P, 1953.

Eliot, Thomas Stearns. *The Sacred Wood: Essays in Poetry and Criticism.* London: Methuen, 1920.

Fekete, John. *The Critical Twilight: Explorations in the Ideology of Anglo-American Literary Theory from Eliot to McLuhan.* London: Routledge, 1977.

Lemon, Lee T., and Marion J. Reis, eds. *Russian Formalist Criticism: Four Essays.* Lincoln: U of Nebraska P, 1965.

Ransom, John Crowe. *The New Criticism.* Norfolk, CT: New Directions, 1941.

Wellek, René, and Austin Warren. *Theory of Literature.* New York: Harcourt, Brace and World, 1949.

Biographical and Psychological Strategies

Bleich, David. *Subjective Criticism.* Baltimore: Johns Hopkins UP, 1978.

Bloom, Harold. *The Anxiety of Influence.* New York: Oxford UP, 1975.

Brennan, Teresa. *The Interpretation of the Flesh: Freud and Femininity.* New York: Routledge, 1994.

Crews, Frederick. *Out of My System: Psychoanalysis, Ideology, and Critical Method.* New York: Oxford UP, 1975.

——. *The Sins of the Fathers: Hawthorne's Psychological Themes.* New York: Oxford UP, 1966.

Felman, Shoshana. *Writing and Madness (Literature/Philosophy/Psychoanalysis).* Ithaca: Cornell UP, 1985.

——, ed. *Literature and Psychoanalysis: The Question of Reading: Otherwise.* Baltimore: Johns Hopkins UP, 1981.

Freud, Sigmund. *The Standard Edition of the Complete Psychological Works.* 24 vols. 1940–1968. London: Hogarth Press and the Institute of Psychoanalysis, 1953.

Holland, Norman. *The Dynamics of Literary Response.* New York: Oxford UP, 1968.

Jones, Ernest. *Hamlet and Oedipus.* New York: Doubleday, 1949.

Lacan, Jacques. *Écrits: A Selection.* Trans. Alan Sheridan. New York: Norton, 1977.

——. *The Four Fundamental Concepts of Psychoanalysis.* Trans. Alan Sheridan. London: Penguin, 1980.

Lesser, Simon O. *Fiction and the Unconscious.* Chicago: U of Chicago P, 1957.

Skura, Meredith Anne. *The Literary Use of the Psychoanalytic Process.* New Haven: Yale UP, 1981.

Zizek, Slavoj. *Looking Awry: An Introduction to Jacques Lacan through Popular Culture.* Cambridge: MIT P, 1991.

Historical Strategies, Including Marxist, New Historicist, and Cultural Strategies

Ang, Ien. *Watching Television.* New York: Routledge, 1991.

Armstrong, Nancy. *Desire and Domestic Fiction.* New York: Oxford UP, 1987.

Ashcroft, Bill, Ga Breth Griffiths, and Helen Tiffin, eds. *The Post-Colonial Studies Reader.* New York: Routledge, 1995.

Bhabha, Homi K. *The Location of Culture.* New York: Routledge, 1994.

Dollimore, Jonathan. *Radical Tragedy: Religion, Ideology and Power in the Drama of Shakespeare and His Contemporaries.* Brighton, Eng.: Harvester, 1984.

Frow, John. *Marxist and Literary History.* Cambridge: Harvard UP, 1986.

Geertz, Clifford. *The Interpretation of Cultures: Selected Essays.* New York: Basic, 1973.

Greenblatt, Stephen. *Renaissance Self-Fashioning: From More to Shakespeare.* Chicago: U of Chicago P, 1980.

——. *Shakespearean Negotiations: The Circulation of Social Energy in Renaissance England.* Berkeley: U of California P, 1985.

Lindenberger, Herbert. *Historical Drama: The Relation of Literature and Reality.* Chicago: U of Chicago P, 1975.

McGann, Jerome. *The Beauty of Inflections: Literary Investigations in Historical Method and Theory.* Oxford: Clarendon, 1985.

Storey, John, ed. *What Is Cultural Studies?* New York: St. Martin's, 1996.

White, Hayden. *Topics of Discourse: Essays in Cultural Criticism.* Baltimore: Johns Hopkins UP, 1978.

Williams, Raymond. *Marxism and Literature.* Oxford: Oxford UP, 1977.

Gender Strategies, Including Feminist and Gay and Lesbian Strategies

Ablelove, Henry, Michèle Aina Barale, and David M. Halperin, eds. *The Lesbian and Gay Studies Reader.* New York: Routledge, 1993.

Baym, Nina. *Feminism and American Literary History.* New Brunswick: Rutgers UP, 1992.

Beauvoir, Simone de. *The Second Sex.* Trans. H. M. Parshley. New York: Knopf, 1972. Trans. of *Le deuxième sexe.* Paris: Gallimard, 1949.

Benstock, Shari, ed. *Feminist Issues and Literary Scholarship.* Bloomington: Indiana UP, 1987.

Cixous, Hélène, and Catherine Clément. *The Newly Born Woman.* Trans. Betsy Wing. Minneapolis: U of Minnesota P, 1986.

Edelman, Lee. *Homographesis: Essays in Gay Literary and Cultural Theory.* New York: Routledge, 1994.

Fetterley, Judith. *The Resisting Reader: A Feminist Approach to American Fiction.* Bloomington: Indiana UP, 1978.

Flynn, Elizabeth A., and Patrocino P. Schweickert. *Gender and Reading: Essays on Readers, Texts, and Contexts.* Baltimore: Johns Hopkins UP, 1986.

Gilbert, Sandra M., and Susan Gubar. *The Madwoman in the Attic: The Woman Writer and the Nineteenth-Century Literary Imagination.* New Haven: Yale UP, 1979.

Irigaray, Luce. *This Sex Which Is Not One.* Ithaca: Cornell UP, 1985. Trans. of *Ce sexe qui n'en est pas un.* Paris: Éditions de Minuit, 1977.

Jagose, Annamarie. *Queer Theory.* Victoria: Melbourne UP, 1996.

Kolodny, Annette. "Some Notes on Defining a 'Feminist Literary Criticism.'" *Critical Inquiry* 2 (1975): 75–92.

Millett, Kate. *Sexual Politics.* New York: Avon, 1970.

Sedgwick, Eve Kosofsky. *Epistemology of the Closet.* Berkeley: U of California P, 1990.

Showalter, Elaine. *A Literature of Their Own: British Women Novelists from Brontë to Lessing.* Princeton: Princeton UP, 1977.

Smith, Barbara. *Toward a Black Feminist Criticism.* New York: Out and Out, 1977.

Mythological Strategies

Bodkin, Maud. *Archetypal Patterns in Poetry.* London: Oxford UP, 1934.

Frye, Northrop. *Anatomy of Criticism: Four Essays.* Princeton: Princeton UP, 1957.

Jung, Carl Gustav. *Complete Works.* Ed. Herbert Read, Michael Fordham, and Gerhard Adler. 17 vols. New York: Pantheon, 1953–.

Reader-Response Strategies

Booth, Wayne C. *The Rhetoric of Fiction.* 2nd ed. Chicago: U of Chicago P, 1983.

Eco, Umberto. *The Role of the Reader: Explorations in the Semiotics of Texts.* Bloomington: Indiana UP, 1979.

Escarpit, Robert. *Sociology of Literature.* Painesville, OH: Lake Erie College P, 1965.

Fish, Stanley. *Is There a Text in This Class? The Authority of Interpretive Communities.* Cambridge: Harvard UP, 1980.

Freund, Elizabeth. *The Return of the Reader: Reader-Response Criticism.* London: Methuen, 1987.

Holland, Norman N. *The Critical I.* New York: Columbia UP, 1992.

——. *Five Readers Reading.* New Haven: Yale UP, 1975.

Iser, Wolfgang. *The Implied Reader: Patterns of Communication in Prose Fiction from Bunyan to Beckett.* Baltimore: Johns Hopkins UP, 1974.

Jauss, Hans Robert. "Literary History as a Challenge to Literary Theory." *Toward an Aesthetics of Reception.* Trans. Timothy Bahti. Minneapolis: U of Minnesota P, 1982. 3–46.

Rosenblatt, Louise. *Literature as Exploration.* 1938. New York: MLA, 1983.

Suleiman, Susan, and Inge Crosman, eds. *The Reader in the Text: Essays on Audience and Interpretation.* Princeton: Princeton UP, 1980.

Tompkins, Jane P., ed. *Reader-Response Criticism: From Formalism to Post-Structuralism.* Baltimore: Johns Hopkins UP, 1980.

Deconstructionist and Other Poststructuralist Strategies

Barthes, Roland. *The Rustle of Language.* New York: Hill and Wang, 1986.

Culler, Jonathan. *On Deconstruction: Theory and Criticism after Structuralism.* Ithaca: Cornell UP, 1982.

de Man, Paul. *Blindness and Insight.* New York: Oxford UP, 1971.

Derrida, Jacques. *Of Grammatology.* 1967. Baltimore: Johns Hopkins UP, 1976.

——. *Writing and Difference.* 1967. Chicago: U of Chicago P, 1978.

Foucault, Michel. *Language, Counter-Memory, Practice.* Ithaca: Cornell UP, 1977.

——. *The Order of Things: An Archaeology of the Human Sciences.* 1966. London: Tavistock, 1970.

Gasche, Rodolphe. "Deconstruction as Criticism." *Glyph* 6 (1979): 177–216.

Hartman, Geoffrey H. *Criticism in the Wilderness.* New Haven: Yale UP, 1980.

Johnson, Barbara. *The Critical Difference: Essays in the Contemporary Rhetoric of Reading.* Baltimore: Johns Hopkins UP, 1980.

Martin, Bill. *Humanism and Its Aftermath: The Shared Fate of Deconstructionism and Politics.* Atlantic Highlands, NJ: Humanities, 1995.

Melville, Stephen W. *Philosophy Beside Itself: On Deconstruction and Modernism.* Theory and History of Literature 27. Minneapolis: U of Minnesota P, 1986.

Royle, Nicholas. *After Derrida.* Manchester: Manchester UP, 1995.

Said, Edward W. *The World, the Text, and the Critic.* Cambridge: Harvard UP, 1983.

Smith, Barbara Herrnstein. *On the Margins of Discourse: The Relation of Literature to Language.* Chicago: U of Chicago P, 1979.

PERSPECTIVES ON CRITICAL READING

SUSAN SONTAG (B. 1933)

Against Interpretation   1964

Like the fumes of the automobile and of heavy industry which befoul the urban atmosphere, the effusion of interpretations of art today poisons our sensibilities. In a culture whose already classical dilemma is the hypertrophy of the intellect at the expense of energy and sensual capability, interpretation is the revenge of the intellect upon art.

Even more. It is the revenge of the intellect upon the world. To interpret is to impoverish, to deplete the world — in order to set up a shadow world of "meanings." It is to turn *the* world into *this* world. ("This world"! As if there were any other.)

The world, our world, is depleted, impoverished enough. Away with all duplicates of it, until we again experience more immediately what we have. . . .

In most modern instances, interpretation amounts to the philistine refusal to leave the work of art alone. Real art has the capacity to make us nervous. By reducing the work of art to its content and then interpreting *that,* one tames the work of art. Interpretation makes art manageable, conformable.

This philistinism of interpretation is more rife in literature than in any other art. For decades now, literary critics have understood it to be their task to translate the elements of the poem or play or novel or story into something else.

From *Against Interpretation*

CONSIDERATIONS FOR CRITICAL THINKING AND WRITING

1. What are Sontag's objections to "interpretation"? Explain whether you agree or disagree with them.
2. In what sense does interpretation make art "manageable" and "conformable" (para. 4)?
3. In an essay explore what you take to be both the dangers of interpretation and its contributions to your understanding of literature.

ANNETTE KOLODNY (B. 1941)

On the Commitments of Feminist Criticism   1980

If feminist criticism calls anything into question, it must be that dog-eared myth of intellectual neutrality. For what I take to be the underlying spirit or message of any consciously ideologically premised criticism — that is, that ideas are important *because* they determine the ways we live, or want to live, in the world — is vitiated by confining those ideas to the study, the classroom, or the pages of our books. To write chapters decrying the sexual stereotyping of women in our literature, while closing our eyes to the sexual harassment of our women students and colleagues; to display Katharine Hepburn and Rosalind

Russell in our courses on "The Image of the Independent Career Women in Film," while managing not to notice the paucity of female administrators on our own campus; to study the women who helped make universal enfranchisement a political reality, while keeping silent about our activist colleagues who are denied promotion or tenure; to include segments on "Women in the Labor Movement" in our American studies or women's studies courses, while remaining willfully ignorant of the department secretary fired for efforts to organize a clerical workers' union; to glory in the delusions of "merit," "privilege," and "status" which accompany campus life in order to insulate ourselves from the millions of women who labor in poverty — all this is not merely hypocritical; it destroys both the spirit and the meaning of what we are about.

From "Dancing through the Minefield: Some Observations on the Theory, Practice, and Politics of a Feminist Literary Criticism," *Feminist Studies* 6, 1980

CONSIDERATIONS FOR CRITICAL THINKING AND WRITING

1. Why does Kolodny reject "intellectual neutrality" as a "myth"? Explain whether you agree or disagree with her point of view.

2. Kolodny argues that feminist criticism can be used as an instrument for social reform. Discuss the possibility and desirability of her position. Do you think other kinds of criticism can and should be used to create social change?

ANDREW P. DEBICKI (B. 1934)
New Criticism and Deconstructionism: Two Attitudes in Teaching Poetry   1985

[Let's] look at the ways in which a New Critic and a deconstructivist might handle a poem. My first example, untitled, is a work by Pedro Salinas, which I first analyzed many years ago and which I have recently taught to a group of students influenced by deconstruction:

Sand: sleeping on the beach today
and tomorrow caressed
in the bosom of the sea:
the sun's today, water's prize tomorrow.
Softly you yield
to the hand that presses you
and go away with the first
courting wind that appears.
Pure and fickle sand,
changing and clear beloved,
I wanted you for my own,
and held you against my chest and soul.
But you escaped with the waves, the wind, the sun,
and I remained without a beloved,
my face turned to the wind which robbed her,
and my eyes to the far-off sea in which she had
green loves in a green shelter.

My original study of this poem, written very much in the New Critical tradition, focused on the unusual personification of sand and beloved and on the metaphorical pattern that it engendered. In the first part of the work, the physical elusiveness of sand (which slips through one's hand, flies with the wind, moves from shore to sea) evokes a coquettish woman, yielding to her lover and then escaping, running off with a personified wind, moving from one being to another. Watching these images, the reader gradually forgets that the poem is metaphorically describing sand and becomes taken up by the unusual correspondences with the figure of a flirting woman. When in the last part of the poem the speaker laments his loss, the reader is drawn into his lament for a fickle lover who has abandoned him.

Continuing a traditional analysis of this poem, we would conclude that its unusual personification/metaphor takes us beyond a literal level and leads us to a wider vision. The true subject of this poem is not sand, nor is it a flirt who tricks a man. The comparison between sand and woman, however, has made us feel the elusiveness of both, as well as the effect that this elusiveness has had on the speaker, who is left sadly contemplating it at the end of the poem. The poem has used its main image to embody a general vision of fleetingness and its effects.

My analysis, as developed thus far, is representative of a New Critical study. It focuses on the text and its central image, it describes a tension produced within the text, and it suggests a way in which this tension is resolved so as to move the poem beyond its literal level. In keeping with the tenets of traditional analytic criticism, it shows how the poem conveys a meaning that is far richer than its plot or any possible conceptual message. But while it is careful not to reduce the poem to a simple idea or to an equivalent of its prose summary, it does attempt to work all of its elements into a single interpretation which would satisfy every reader . . . : it makes all of the poem's meanings reside in its verbal structures, and it suggests that those meanings can be discovered and combined into a single cohesive vision as we systematically analyze those structures.

By attempting to find a pattern that will incorporate and resolve the poem's tensions, however, this reading leaves some loose ends, which I noticed even in my New Critical perspective — and which I found difficult to explain. To see the poem as the discovery of the theme of fleetingness by an insightful speaker, we have to ignore the fanciful nature of the comparison, the whimsical attitude to reality that it suggests, and the excessively serious lament of the speaker, which is difficult to take at face value — he laments the loss of *sand* with the excessive emotion of a romantic lover! The last lines, with their evocation of the beloved/sand in an archetypal kingdom of the sea, ring a bit hollow. Once we notice all of this, we see the speaker as being somehow unreliable in his strong response to the situation. He tries too hard to equate the loss of sand with the loss of love, he paints himself as too much of a romantic, and he loses our assent when we realize that his rather cliché declarations are not very fitting. Once we become aware of the speaker's limitations, our perspective about the poem changes: we come to see its "meaning" as centered, not on the theme of fleetingness as such, but on a portrayal of the speaker's exaggerated efforts to embody this theme in the image of sand.

For the traditional New Critic, this would pose a dilemma. The reading of the poem as a serious embodiment of the theme of evanescence is undercut by an awareness of the speaker's unreliability. One can account for the conflict between readings, to some extent, by speaking of the poem's use of irony and by seeing a tension between the theme of evanescence and the speaker's excessive concern with an imaginary beloved (which blinds him to the larger issues presented by the poem). That still leaves unresolved, however, the poem's final meaning and effect. In class discussions, in fact, a debate between those students who asserted that the importance of the poem lay in its engendering the theme of fleetingness and those who noted the absurdity of the speaker often ended in an agreement that this was a "problem poem" which never resolved or integrated its "stresses" and its double vision. . . .

The deconstructive critic, however, would not be disturbed by a lack of resolution in the meanings of the poem and would use the conflict between interpretations as the starting point for further study. Noting that the view of evanescence produced by the poem's central metaphor is undercut by the speaker's unreliability, the deconstructive critic would explore the play of signification that the undercutting engenders. Calling into question the attempt to neatly define evanescence, on the one hand, and the speaker's excessive romanticism on the other, the poem would represent, for this critic, a creative confrontation of irresoluble visions. The image of the sand as woman, as well as the portrayal of the speaker, would represent a sort of "seam" in the text, an area of indeterminacy that would open the way to further readings. This image lets us see the speaker as a sentimental poet, attempting unsuccessfully to define evanescence by means of a novel metaphor but getting trapped in the theme of lost love, which he himself has engendered; it makes us think of the inadequacy of language, of the ways in which metaphorical expression and the clichés of a love lament can undercut each other.

Once we adopt such a deconstructivist perspective, we will find in the text details that will carry forward our reading. The speaker's statement that he held "her" against his "chest and his soul" underlines the conflict in his perspective: it juggles a literal perspective (he rubs sand against himself) and a metaphorical one (he reaches for his beloved), but it cannot fully combine them — "soul" is ludicrously inappropriate in reference to the former. The reader, noting the inappropriateness, has to pay attention to the inadequacy of language as used here. All in all, by engendering a conflict between various levels and perspectives, the poem makes us feel the incompleteness of any one reading, the way in which each one is a "misreading" (not because it is wrong, but because it is incomplete), and the creative lack of closure in the poem. By not being subject to closure, in fact, this text becomes all the more exciting: its view of the possibilities and limitations of metaphor, language, and perspective seems more valuable than any static portrayal of "evanescence."

The analyses I have offered of this poem exemplify the different classroom approaches that would be taken by a stereotypical New Critic, on the one hand, and a deconstructive critic on the other. Imbued with the desire to come to an overview of the literary work, the former will attempt to resolve its tensions (and probably remain unsatisfied with the poem). Skeptical of such a possibility and of the very existence of a definable "work," the latter will focus on the tensions that can be found in the text as vehicles for multiple readings. Given his or her attitude to the text, the deconstructive critic will not worry about going beyond its "limits" (which really do not exist). This will allow, of course, for more speculative readings; it will also lead to a discussion of ways in which the text can be extended and "cured" in successive readings, to the fact that it reflects on the process of its own creation, and to ways in which it will relate to other texts.

From *Writing and Reading DIFFERENTLY: Deconstruction and the Teaching of Composition and Literature,* edited by G. Douglas Atkins and Michael L. Johnson

CONSIDERATIONS FOR CRITICAL THINKING AND WRITING

1. Explain how the New Critical and deconstructionist approaches to the Salinas poem differ. What kinds of questions are raised by each? What elements of the poem are focused on in each approach?

2. Write an essay explaining which reading of the poem you find more interesting. In your opening paragraph define what you mean by "interesting."

3. Choose one of the critical strategies for reading discussed in this chapter and discuss Salinas's poem from that perspective.

PETER RABINOWITZ (B. 1944)

On Close Readings   1988

Belief in close reading may be the nearest thing literary scholars have to a shared critical principle. Academics who teach literature tend to accept as a matter of course that good reading is slow, attentive to linguistic nuance (especially figurative language), and suspicious of surface meanings.

Close reading is a fundamental link between the New Critics and the Yale deconstructionists. Indeed, deconstructionist J. Hillis Miller has gone so far as to characterize what he saw as an attack on close reading by Gerald Graff as "a major treason against our profession." Similarly, what Naomi Schor calls "clitoral" feminist criticism, and its "hermeneutics focused on the detail," is a variant of close reading. So is much reader-response criticism.

Despite its broad acceptance by scholars, however, close reading is not the natural, the only, or always the best way to approach a text. I'm not suggesting that it should never be taught or used. But I do want to argue that close reading rests on faulty assumptions about how literature is read, which can lead, especially in the classroom, to faulty prescriptions about how it *ought* to be read.

The fact is that there are a variety of ways to read, all of which engage the reader in substantially different kinds of activity. Which kind depends in part on the reader and his or her immediate purpose. Teasing out the implicit homoerotic tendencies in Turgenev's *Asya,* for instance, is a different activity from trying to determine its contribution to the development of first-person narrative techniques. In part, the way one reads also varies from text to text. Different authors, different genres, different periods, different cultures expect readers to approach texts in different ways.

The bias in academe toward close reading reduces that multiplicity. While all close readers obviously don't read in exactly the same way, the variations have a strong family resemblance. Their dominance in the aristocracy of critical activity—virtually undiminished by the critical revolutions of the last twenty years—can skew evaluation, distort interpretation, discourage breadth of vision, and separate scholars from students and other ordinary readers.

David Daiches was not being eccentric when he argued that literary value depends on the "degree to which the work lends itself" to the kind of reading demanded by New Critical theory. The schools in vogue may change, but we still assign value to what fits our prior conceptions of reading, and the academically sanctioned canon consequently consists largely of texts that respond well to close reading.

Once you give priority to close reading, you implicitly favor figurative writing over realistic writing, indirect expression over direct expression, deep meaning over surface meaning, form over content, and the elite over the popular. In the realm of poetry, that means giving preference to lyric over narrative poems, and in the realm of fiction, to symbolism and psychology over plot. Such preferences, in turn, devalue certain voices. A writer directly confronting brute oppression, for instance, is apt to be ranked below another who has the luxury minutely to explore the details of subtle middle-class crises. Thus, for a close reader, the unresonant prose of Harriet Wilson's *Our Nig* will automatically make the novel seem less "good" than Henry James's more intricate *What Maisie Knew*, although the racist brutality endured by Ms. Wilson's heroine is arguably more important for our culture—and thus more deserving of our consideration—than the affluent sexual merry-go-round that dizzies Maisie.

It would be bad enough if the preference for close reading simply meant that texts that didn't measure up were chucked onto a noncanonical pile—then, at least, the rebellious could rummage through the rejects. But close reading also has an insidious effect on interpretation. Not only do we reject many works that don't fit; more damaging, we also twist many others until they *do* fit.

Yet we fail to recognize the magnitude of this distortion. One of the major problems with much current critical practice is the tendency to underestimate the extent to which texts can serve as mirrors—not of the external world but of the reader, who is apt to find in a text not what is really there but what he expects or wants to find. . . .

When reading for class, many students read closely, but few continue the practice once they've left college. In fact, most people—including teachers—who really enjoy literature recognize that close reading is a special kind of interpretive practice. Literary scholars are apt to make a distinction between "real reading" and "reading for fun"; most nonacademic readers are likely to divide "real reading" from "reading for class." In either case, an artificial split is created between academe and "real life," which leads to theories that devalue the kinds of reading (and therefore the kinds of books) that engage most readers most of the time.

If I'm against close reading, then what am I for? The obvious alternative is pluralism.

We can legitimately show our students that different writers in different social, historical, and economic contexts write for different purposes and with different expectations. Likewise, we can teach our students that different readers (or the same reader under different circumstances) read for different reasons.

We must also give our students actual practice in various kinds of reading. For example, an introductory literature course should include many different sorts of texts: long novels as well as lyric poems; realistic (even didactic) works as well as symbolic ones; writing aimed at a broad audience as well as at a literate elite. The course should also include different kinds of tasks. Students should learn to approach a given text in several different ways, at least some of which arise out of their personal and cultural situations. Most important, we must help our students to be self-conscious about what they are doing, and to realize that every decision about how to read opens certain doors only by closing others.

It is not simply that learning new, less rigid ways of reading increases the number of works we can enjoy and learn from. More important, learning to read in different ways allows us to enjoy a wider range of texts and gain new perspectives on our cultural assumptions. Only such flexible reading leads to intellectual growth, for it is only that kind of reading that can enable us to be conscious of—and therefore able to deal effectively with—the narrowness of "standard" interpretive techniques.

> From "Our Evaluation of Literature Has Been Distorted
> by Academe's Bias toward Close Readings of Texts,"
> *Chronicle of Higher Education*, April 6, 1988

CONSIDERATIONS FOR CRITICAL THINKING AND WRITING

1. Why does Rabinowitz object to the bias toward close reading as the primary way to approach a literary work? Explain why you agree or disagree.

2. According to Rabinowitz, how does a critical emphasis on close reading affect the formation of the canon?

3. In an essay discuss Rabinowitz's observation that an emphasis on close reading "devalue[s] the kinds of reading (and therefore the kinds of books) that engage most readers most of the time" (para. 10).

HARRIET HAWKINS (B. 1939)

Should We Study King Kong *or* King Lear?   1988

There is nothing either good or bad, but thinking makes it so.
          —*Hamlet*

Troilus: *What's aught but as 'tis valued?*
Hector: *But value dwells not in particular will:*
   It holds its estimate and dignity
   As well wherein 'tis precious of itself
   As in the prizer.
          —*Troilus and Cressida*

To what degree is great literature—or bad literature—an artificial category? Are there any good—or bad—reasons why most societies have given high status to certain works of art and not to others? Could Hamlet be right in concluding that there is *nothing* either good or bad but thinking—or critical or ideological discourse — makes it so? Or are certain works of art so precious, so magnificent — or so trashy — that they obviously ought to be included in the canon or expelled from the classroom? So far as I know, there is not now any sign of a critical consensus on the correct answer to these questions either in England or in the United States.

In England there are, on the one hand, eloquent cases for the defense of the value of traditional literary studies, like Dame Helen Gardner's last book, *In Defence of the Imagination.* On the other hand, there are critical arguments insisting that what really counts is not what you read, but the way that you read it. You might as well study *King Kong* as *King Lear,* because what matters is not the script involved, but the critical or ideological virtues manifested in your own "reading" of whatever it is that you are reading. Reviewing a controversial book entitled *Re-Reading English,* the poet Tom Paulin gives the following account of the issues involved in the debate:

> The contributors are collectively of the opinion that English literature is a dying subject and they argue that it can be revived by adopting a "socialist pedagogy" and introducing into the syllabus "other forms of writing and cultural production than the canon of literature" . . . it is now time to challenge "hierarchical" and "elitist" conceptions of literature and to demolish the bourgeois ideology which has been "naturalised" as literary value. . . . They wish to develop "a politics of reading" and to redefine the term "text" in order to admit newspaper reports, songs, and even mass demonstrations as subjects for tutorial discussion. Texts no longer have to be books: indeed, "it may be more democratic to study *Coronation Street* [England's most popular soap opera] than *Middlemarch.*"

However one looks at these arguments, it seems indisputably true that the issues involved are of paramount critical, pedagogical, and social importance. There are, however, any number of different ways to look at the various arguments. So far as I am, professionally, concerned, they raise the central question, "Why should any of us still study, or teach, Shakespeare's plays (or *Paradise Lost* or *The Canterbury Tales*)?" After all, there are quite enough films, plays, novels, and poems being produced today (to say nothing of all those "other forms of writing," including literary criticism, that are clamoring for our attention) to satisfy anyone interested in high literature, or popular genres, or any form of "cultural production" whatsoever. They also raise the obviously reflexive question: "Assuming that all traditionally 'canonized' works were eliminated, overnight, from the syllabus of every English department in the world, would not comparable problems of priority, value, elitism, ideological pressure, authoritarianism, and arbitrariness almost(?) immediately arise with reference to *whatever* works — of whatsoever kind and nature — were substituted for them?"

If, say, the place on the syllabus currently assigned to *King Lear* were reassigned to *King Kong,* those of us currently debating the relative merits of the Quarto, the Folio, or a conflated version of *King Lear* would, *mutatis mutandis,*° have to decide whether to concentrate classroom attention on the "classic" version of *King Kong,* originally produced in 1933, or to focus on the 1974 remake (which by now has many ardent admirers of its own). Although classroom time might not allow the inclusion of both, a decision to exclude either version might well seem arbitrary or authoritarian and so give rise to grumbles about the "canon." Moreover, comparable questions of "canonization" might well

---

mutatis mutandis: Substituting different terms (Latin).

arise with reference to other films excluded from a syllabus that included either version (or both versions) of *King Kong*. For example: why assign class time to *King Kong* and not to (say) *Slave Girls of the White Rhinoceros*? Who, if any, of us has the right to decide whether *King Lear* or *King Kong* or the *Slave Girls* should, or should not, be included on, or excluded from, the syllabus? And can the decision to include, or exclude, any one of them be made, by any one of us, on any grounds whatsoever that do *not* have to do with comparative merit, or comparative value judgments, or with special interests—that is, with the aesthetic or ideological priorities, preferences, and prejudices of the assigners of positions on whatever syllabus there is? And insofar as most, if not all, of our judgments and preferences are comparative, are they not, inevitably, hierarchical?

Is there, in fact, any form of endeavor or accomplishment known to the human race—from sport to ballet to jazz to cooking—wherein comparative standards of excellence comparable to certain "hierarchical" and "elitist" conceptions of literature are nonexistent? Even bad-film buffs find certain bad films more gloriously bad than others. And, perhaps significantly given its comparatively short lifetime, the avant-garde cinema has, by now, produced snobs to rival the most elitist literary critic who ever lived, such as the one who thus puts down a friend who likes ordinary Hollywood films:

> Ah that's all right for you, I know the sort you are, but give me a private job that's shot on faded sepia sixteen millimetre stock with non-professional actors . . . no story and dialogue in French *any day of the week*.

What is striking about this snob's assumption is how characteristic it is of a long tradition of critical elitism that has consistently sneered at popular genres (e.g., romance fiction, soap operas, horror films, westerns, etc.) that are tainted by the profit motive and so tend to "give the public what it wants" in the way of sentimentality, sensationalism, sex, violence, romanticism, and the like.

From "*King Lear* to *King Kong* and Back: Shakespeare and Popular Modern Genres" in *"Bad" Shakespeare: Revaluations of the Shakespeare Canon,* edited by Maurice Charney

CONSIDERATIONS FOR CRITICAL THINKING AND WRITING

1. Do you agree or disagree that "great literature—or bad literature—[is] an artificial category" (para. 1)? Explain why.

2. Why would problems of "priority, value, elitism, ideological pressure, authoritarianism, and arbitrariness" (para. 3) probably become issues for evaluating any new works that replaced canonized works?

3. Write an essay in which you argue for (or against) studying popular arts (for example, the *Seinfeld* script on p. 1264) beside the works of classic writers such as Shakespeare.

MORRIS DICKSTEIN (B. 1940)

On the Social Responsibility of the Critic   1993

Many critics today, as if in violent reaction to the reading habits of the ordinary citizen, are haunted by the fear of becoming the passive consumer of ideological subtexts or messages. As the country grew more conservative in the eighties, many academic critics turned more radical, and this led to an onslaught by national magazines and media pundits on political correctness, the supposed left-wing and multicultural orthodoxy in American universities.

Here we encounter a number of puzzling paradoxes about "reading" in America today. As reading diminishes — not in absolute terms but in relation to other ways of receiving information — as reading loses its hold on people, the metaphor of reading constantly expands. Molecular biologists like Robert Pollack talk about "reading DNA," the structure of genetic transmission in each living cell. Students of urban life discuss "the city as text" and how to read it, as they did at a conference I attended in 1989. Film scholars publish books about "how to read a film" reflecting on our constantly expanding (and increasingly undifferentiated) notion of what constitutes a text. And literary critics over the past sixty years have developed ever more subtle and complex ways of reading those texts, often using obscure, specialized language that itself resists being read.

As educators worry about the role of video and electronic media in displacing the written word, as the skills of ordinary readers seem to languish, the sophistication and territorial ambition of academic readers continue to grow, widening a split that has been one of the hallmarks of the modern period. The common reader still exists, but many professional readers dissociate themselves on principle from the habits of the tribe: they deliberately read against the grain of the text, against common sense, against most people's way of reading — indeed, against their own way of reading in their ordinary lives. If the reader of *Scarlett* or *Gone with the Wind* reads passively, wanting to be possessed and carried away by a book, as by an old-fashioned movie or piece of music, the critical reader, influenced by theory and by the new historicism, has developed an active, aggressive, even adversarial approach to writing. What Paul Ricoeur in his book on Freud calls the "hermeneutics of suspicion" has become a primary feature of academic criticism, which aims above all to disclose the institutional pressures and ideological formations that speak through texts and influence us as we read.° . . .

Our advanced criticism is especially marked by the suspicion and the hostility with which it performs such operations: its failure to distinguish art from propaganda, literature from advertising; its fierce resistance to the mental framework of the works it examines. "All right, what's wrong with this book?" asks one programmatically suspicious instructor of the students in her humanities class, to make sure they don't get taken in by those "great" books. Some of our recent ideological criticism turns the social understanding of literature, which can be intrinsically valuable, into an all too predictable exercise in debunking and demystification. . . .

The role of the critic is not to read notionally and cleverly, and certainly not to castigate writers for their politics, but to raise ordinary reading to its highest power — to make it more insightful, more acute, without losing touch with our deepest personal responses. It is ironic to speak for the social responsibility of the writer while betraying the public sphere of reading. Criticism, even academic criticism, is neither a sect nor a priesthood but ultimately a public trust, mediating between artists or writers and their often puzzled audience. . . .

A naive reading, anchored in wonder, must remain an indispensable moment of a more self-conscious reading, not just a piece of scaffolding to be

What . . . read: Paul Ricoeur (B. 1913), a French philosopher and critic, author of *Freud and Philosophy: An Essay on Interpretation* (1970). Hermeneutics refers to the theory and method of perceiving and interpreting texts.

kicked away as our suspicion and professionalism take over. We need a better balance between the naive and suspicious readers in ourselves: between the willing suspension of disbelief and our ability to withhold ourselves and read skeptically; between our appreciation of art and our wary knowledge of its persuasive power; between a sympathy for the author as an individual like ourselves — working out creative problems, making contingent choices — and our critical sense of a literary work as the discursive formation of a cultural moment.

From "Damaged Literacy: The Decay of Reading," *Profession 93*

CONSIDERATIONS FOR CRITICAL THINKING AND WRITING

1. Do you think video and electronic media are "displacing the written word" (para. 3)? What evidence can you point to in your own experience that refutes or supports this claim?

2. What do you think Dickstein means when he refers to academic criticism as "a public trust" (para. 5)? What should the function of criticism be, according to Dickstein? In what sense is the role of the critic "to raise ordinary reading to its highest power" (para. 5)?

3. What criticism does Dickstein level against contemporary literary criticism? Explain why you agree or disagree with his perspective.

53

Reading and Writing

THE PURPOSE AND VALUE
OF WRITING ABOUT LITERATURE

Introductory literature courses typically include three components — reading, discussion, and writing. Students usually find the readings a pleasure, the class discussions a revelation, and the writing assignments — at least initially — a little intimidating. Writing an analysis of Melville's use of walls in "Bartleby, the Scrivener" (p. 116), for example, may seem considerably more daunting than making a case for animal rights or analyzing a campus newspaper editorial that calls for grade reforms. Like Bartleby, you might want to respond with "I would prefer not to." Literary topics are not, however, all that different from the kinds of papers assigned in English composition courses; many of the same skills are required for both. Regardless of the type of paper, you must develop a thesis and support it with evidence in language that is clear and persuasive.

Whether the subject matter is a marketing survey, a political issue, or a literary work, writing is a method of communicating information and perceptions. Writing teaches. But before writing becomes an instrument for informing the reader, it serves as a means of learning for the writer. An essay is a process of discovery as well as a record of what has been discovered. One of the chief benefits of writing is that we frequently realize what we want to say only after trying out ideas on a page and seeing our thoughts take shape in language.

More specifically, writing about a literary work encourages us to be better readers because it requires a close examination of the elements of a short story, poem, or play. To determine how plot, character, setting, point of view, style, tone, irony, or any number of other literary elements function in a work, we must study them in relation to one another as well as separately. Speed-reading won't do. To read a text accurately and validly—neither ignoring nor distorting significant details—we must return to the work repeatedly to test our responses and interpretations. By paying attention to details and being sensitive to the author's use of language, we develop a clearer understanding of how the work conveys its effects and meanings.

Nevertheless, students sometimes ask why it is necessary or desirable to write about a literary work. Why not allow stories, poems, and plays to speak for themselves? Isn't it presumptuous to interpret Hemingway, Dickinson, or Shakespeare? These writers do, of course, speak for themselves, but they do so indirectly. Literary criticism seeks not to replace the text by explaining it but to enhance our readings of works by calling attention to elements that we might have overlooked or only vaguely sensed.

Another misunderstanding about the purpose of literary criticism is that it crankily restricts itself to finding faults in a work. Critical essays are sometimes mistakenly equated with newspaper and magazine reviews of recently published works. Reviews typically include summaries and evaluations to inform readers about a work's nature and quality, but critical essays assume that readers are already familiar with a work. Although a critical essay may point out limitations and flaws, most criticism—and certainly the kind of essay usually written in an introductory literature course—is designed to explain, analyze, and reveal the complexities of a work. Such sensitive consideration increases our appreciation of the writer's achievement and significantly adds to our enjoyment of a short story, poem, or play. In short, the purpose and value of writing about literature are that doing so leads to greater understanding and pleasure.

READING THE WORK CLOSELY

Know the piece of literature you are writing about before you begin your essay. Think about how the work makes you feel and how it is put together. The more familiar you are with how the various elements of the text convey effects and meanings, the more confident you will be explaining whatever perspective on it you ultimately choose. Do not insist that everything make sense on a first reading. Relax and enjoy yourself; you can be attentive and still allow the author's words to work their magic on you. With subsequent readings, however, go more slowly and analytically as you try to establish relations between characters, actions, images, or whatever else seems important. Ask yourself why you respond as you do. Think as you read, and notice how the parts of a work contribute to its overall nature. Whether the work is a short story, poem, or play, you will read relevant portions of it over and over, and you will very likely find more to discuss in each review if the work is rich.

It's best to avoid reading other critical discussions of a work before you are thoroughly familiar with it. There are several good reasons for following this advice. By reading interpretations before you know a work, you deny yourself the pleasure of discovery. That is a bit like starting with the last chapter in a mystery novel. But perhaps even more important than protecting the surprise and delight that a work might offer is that a premature reading of a critical discussion will probably short-circuit your own responses. You will see the work through the critic's eyes and have to struggle with someone else's perceptions and ideas before you can develop your own.

Reading criticism can be useful, but not until you have thought through your own impressions of the text. A guide should not be permitted to become a tyrant. This does not mean, however, that you should avoid background information about a work — for example, that Joyce Carol Oates's story "The Lady with the Pet Dog" was based on a similar story by Anton Chekhov. Knowing something about the author as well as historic and literary contexts can help to create expectations that enhance your reading.

ANNOTATING THE TEXT AND JOURNAL NOTE TAKING

As you read, get in the habit of making marginal notations in your textbook. If you are working with a library book, use note cards and write down page or line numbers so that you can easily return to annotated passages. Use these cards to record reactions, raise questions, and make comments. They will freshen your memory and allow you to keep track of what goes on in the text.

Whatever method you use to annotate your texts — whether writing marginal notes, highlighting, underlining, or drawing boxes and circles around important words and phrases — you'll eventually develop a system that allows you to retrieve significant ideas and elements from the text. Another way to record your impressions of a work — as with any other experience — is to keep a journal. By writing down your reactions to characters, images, language, actions, and other matters in a reading journal, you can often determine why you like or dislike a work or feel sympathetic or antagonistic to an author or discover paths into a work that might have eluded you if you hadn't preserved your impressions. Your journal notes and annotations may take whatever form you find useful; full sentences and grammatical correctness are not essential (unless they are to be handed in and your instructor requires that), though they might allow you to make better sense of your own reflections days later. The point is simply to put in writing thoughts that you can retrieve when you need them for class discussion or a writing assignment. Consider the following student annotation of the first twenty-four lines of Andrew Marvell's "To His Coy Mistress" (p. 728) and the journal entry that follows it:

Annotated Text

If we had time . . .

Had we but world enough, and time, — *Waste life and you*
This coyness, lady, were no (crime.) — *steal from yourself.*
We would sit down, and think which way
To walk, and pass our long love's day.
Thou by the Indian (Ganges) side   5
Shouldst rubies find; I by the tide
Of (Humber) would complain.° I would — *Measurements* — *write love songs*
Love you ten years before the Flood, — *of time*
And you should, if you please, refuse
Till the conversion of the Jews.   10
My vegetable love should grow,° — *slow, unconscious growth*
Vaster than empires, and more slow;
An hundred years should go to praise
Thine eyes and on thy forehead gaze,
Two hundred to adore each breast,   15
But thirty thousand to the rest:
An age at least to every part,
And the last age should show your heart.
For, lady, you deserve this state,
Nor would I love at lower rate.   20

contrast river and desert images

(But) at my back I always hear
Time's wingèd chariot hurrying near; — *Lines move faster here —*
And yonder all before us lie — *tone changes*
(Deserts) of vast (eternity.) — *This eternity rushes in.*

Journal Note

> He'd be patient and wait for his "mistress" if they had
> the time--sing songs, praise her, adore her, etc. But they
> don't have that much time according to him. He seems to be
> patient but he actually begins by calling patience--her coy-
> ness--a "crime." Looks to me like he's got his mind made up
> from the beginning of the poem. Where's her response? I'm not
> sure about him.

This journal note responds to some of the effects noted in the annotations of the poem; it's an excellent beginning for making sense of the speaker's argument in the poem.

Taking notes will preserve your initial reactions to the work. Many times first impressions are the best. Your response to a peculiar character in a story, a striking phrase in a poem, or a subtle bit of stage business in a play might lead to larger perceptions. The student paper on John Updike's "A & P" (p. 2155), for example, began with the student writing "how come?" next to the story's title in her textbook. She thought it strange that the title didn't refer to a character or the story's conflict. That annotated response eventually led her to examine the significance of the setting, which became the central idea of her paper.

You should take detailed notes only after you've read through the work. If you write too many notes during the first reading, you're likely to disrupt your response. Moreover, until you have a sense of the entire work, it will be difficult to determine how connections can be made among its various elements. In addition to recording your first impressions and noting significant passages, characters, actions, and so on, you should consult the Questions for Responsive Reading and Writing about fiction (p. 44), poetry (p. 709), and drama (p. 1276). These questions can assist you in getting inside a work as well as organizing your notes.

Inevitably, you will take more notes than you finally use in the paper. Note taking is a form of thinking aloud, but because your ideas are on paper you don't have to worry about forgetting them. As you develop a better sense of a potential topic, your notes will become more focused and detailed.

CHOOSING A TOPIC

If your instructor assigns a topic or offers a choice from among an approved list of topics, some of your work is already completed. Instead of being asked to come up with a topic about *Antigone,* you may be asked to write a three-page essay that specifically discusses "Antigone's decision to defy Creon." You also have the assurance that a specified topic will be manageable within the suggested number of pages. Unless you ask your instructor for permission to write on a different or related topic, be certain to address yourself to the assignment. An essay that does not discuss Antigone's decision but instead describes her relationship with her sister would be missing the point. Notice too that there is room even in an assigned topic to develop your own approach. One question that immediately comes to mind is whether Antigone is justified in defying Creon's authority. Assigned topics do not relieve you of thinking about an aspect of a work, but they do focus your thinking.

At some point during the course, you may have to begin an essay from scratch. You might, for example, be asked to write about a short story that somehow impressed you or that seemed particularly well written or filled with insights. Before you start considering a topic, you should have a sense of how long the paper will be because the assigned length can help to determine the extent to which you should develop your topic. Ideally, the paper's length should be based on how much space you deem necessary to present your discussion clearly and convincingly, but if you have any doubts and no specific guidelines have been indicated, ask. The question is important; a topic that might be appropriate for a three-page paper could be too narrow for ten pages. Three pages would probably be adequate for a discussion of why Emily murders Homer in Faulkner's "A Rose for Emily." Conversely, it would be futile to try to summarize Faulkner's use of the South in his fiction in even ten pages; this would have to be narrowed to something like "Images of the South in 'A Rose for Emily.'" Be sure that the topic you choose can be adequately covered in the assigned number of pages.

Once you have a firm sense of how much you are expected to write, you can begin to decide on your topic. If you are to choose what work to write about, select one that genuinely interests you. Too often students pick a story, poem, or play because it is mercifully short or seems simple. Such works can certainly be the subjects of fine essays, but simplicity should not be the major reason for selecting them. Choose a work that has moved you so that you have something to say about it. The student who wrote about "A & P" was initially attracted to the story's title because she had once worked in a similar store. After reading the story, she became fascinated with its setting because Updike's descriptions seemed so accurate. Her paper then grew out of her curiosity about the setting's purpose. When a writer is engaged in a topic, the paper has a better chance of being interesting to a reader.

After you have settled on a particular work, your notes and annotations of the text should prove useful for generating a topic. The paper on "The A & P as a State of Mind" developed naturally from the notes (p. 2153) that the student jotted down about the setting and antagonist. If you think with a pen in your hand, you are likely to find when you review your notes that your thoughts have clustered into one or more topics. Perhaps there are patterns of imagery that seem to make a point about life. There may be scenes that are ironically paired or secondary characters who reveal certain qualities about the protagonist. Your notes and annotations on such aspects can lead you to a particular effect or impression. Having chuckled your way through "A & P," you may discover that your notations about the story's humor point to a serious satire of society's values.

DEVELOPING A THESIS

When you are satisfied that you have something interesting to say about a work and that your notes have led you to a focused topic, you can formulate a *thesis,* the central idea of the paper. Whereas the topic indicates what the paper focuses on (the setting in "A & P"), the thesis explains what you have to say about the topic (because the intolerant setting of "A & P" is the antagonist in the story, it is crucial to our understanding of Sammy's decision to quit his job). The thesis should be a complete sentence (though sometimes it may require more than one sentence) that establishes your topic in clear, unambiguous language. The thesis may be revised as you get further into the topic and discover what you want to say about it, but once the thesis is firmly established, it will serve as a guide for you and your reader because all the information and observations in your essay should be related to the thesis.

One student on an initial reading of Andrew Marvell's "To His Coy Mistress" saw that the male speaker of the poem urges a woman to love now before time runs out for them. This reading gave him the impression that the poem is a simple celebration of the pleasures of the flesh, but on subsequent readings he underlined or noted these images: "Time's wingèd chariot hurrying near"; "Deserts of vast eternity"; "marble vault"; "worms"; "dust"; "ashes"; and these two lines: "The grave's a fine and private place, / But none, I think, do there embrace."

By listing these images associated with time and death, he established an inventory that could be separated from the rest of his notes on point of view, character, sounds, and other subjects. Inventorying notes allows patterns to emerge that you might have only vaguely perceived otherwise. Once these images are grouped, they call attention to something darker and more complex in Marvell's poem than a first impression might suggest.

These images may create a different feeling about the poem, but they still don't explain very much. One simple way to generate a thesis about a literary work is to ask the question "why?" Why do these images appear in the poem? Why does Hamlet hesitate to avenge his father's death? Why does Hemingway choose the Midwest as the setting of "Soldier's Home"? Your responses to these kinds of questions can lead to a thesis.

Writers sometimes use freewriting to help themselves explore possible answers to such questions. It can be an effective way of generating ideas. Freewriting is exactly that: the technique calls for nonstop writing without concern for mechanics or editing of any kind. Freewriting for ten minutes or so on a question will result in fragments and repetitions, but it can also produce some ideas. Here's an example of a student's response to the question about the images in "To His Coy Mistress":

```
He wants her to make love. Love poem. There's little time.
Her crime. He exaggerates. Sincere? Sly? What's he want?
She says nothing--he says it all. What about deserts,
ashes, graves, and worms? Some love poem. Sounds like an
old Vincent Price movie. Full of sweetness but death
creeps in. Death--hurry hurry! Tear pleasures. What
passion! Where's death in this? How can a love poem be so
ghoulish? She does nothing. Maybe frightened? Convinced?
Why death? Love and death--time--death.
```

This freewriting contains several ideas; it begins by alluding to the poem's plot and speaker, but the central idea seems to be death. This emphasis led the student to five potential thesis statements for his essay about the poem:

1. "To His Coy Mistress" is a difficult poem.
2. Death in "To His Coy Mistress."
3. There are many images of death in "To His Coy Mistress."
4. "To His Coy Mistress" celebrates the pleasures of the flesh, but it also recognizes the power of death to end that pleasure.
5. On the surface, "To His Coy Mistress" is a celebration of the pleasures of the flesh, but this witty seduction is tempered by a chilling recognition of the reality of death.

The first statement is too vague to be useful. In what sense is the poem difficult? A more precise phrasing, indicating the nature of the difficulty, is needed. The second statement is a topic rather than a thesis. Because it is not a sentence, it does not express a complete idea about how the poem treats death. Although this could be an appropriate title, it is inadequate as a thesis statement. The third statement, like the first one, identifies the topic, but even though it is a sentence, it is not a complete idea that tells us anything significant beyond the fact it states. After these preliminary attempts to develop a thesis, the student remembered his first impression of the poem and incorporated it into his thesis statement. The fourth thesis is a useful approach to the poem because it limits the topic and indicates how it will be treated in the paper: the writer will begin with an initial impression of the poem and then go on to qualify it. However, the fifth thesis is better than the fourth because it indicates a shift in tone produced by the ironic relationship between death and flesh. An effective thesis, like this one, makes a clear statement about a manageable topic and provides a firm sense of direction for the paper.

Most writing assignments in a literature course require you to persuade readers that your thesis is reasonable and supported with evidence. Papers that report information without comment or evaluation are simply summaries. A plot summary of Shakespeare's *The Tempest*, for example, would have no thesis, but a paper that discussed how Prospero's oppression of Caliban represents European imperialism and colonialism would argue a thesis. Similarly, a paper that merely pointed out the death images in "To His Coy Mistress" would not contain a thesis, but a paper that attempted to make a case for the death imagery as a grim reminder of how vulnerable flesh is would involve persuasion. In developing a thesis, remember that you are expected not merely to present information but to argue a point.

ARGUING ABOUT LITERATURE

An argumentative essay is designed to make persuasive your interpretation of a work. Arguing about literature doesn't mean that you're engaged in an angry, antagonistic dispute (though controversial topics do sometimes engender heated debates; see, for example, Joan Templeton's comments in the Critical Case Study on Ibsen's *A Doll House* [p. 1633]). Instead, argumentation requires that you present your interpretation of a work (or a portion of it) by supporting your discussion with clearly defined terms, ample evidence, and a detailed analysis of relevant portions of the text.

If you have a choice, it's generally best to write about a topic that you feel strongly about. If you're not fascinated by Bartleby the Scrivener's haunting presence in Melville's short story, then perhaps you'll find chilling Emily Grierson's behavior in Faulkner's "A Rose for Emily," or maybe you can explain why Bartleby's character is so excruciatingly boring to you. If your essay is to be interesting and convincing, what is important is that it be written from a strong point of view that persuasively argues your evaluation, analysis, and interpretation of a work. It is not enough to say that you like or dislike a work; instead you must give your reader some ideas and evidence that can be accepted or rejected based on the quality of the answers to the questions you raise.

One way to come up with persuasive answers is to generate good questions that will lead you further into the text and to critical issues related to it. Notice how the Perspectives, Complementary Critical Readings, Critical Case Studies, and Cultural Case Studies in this anthology raise significant questions and issues about texts from a variety of points of view. Moreover, the Critical Strategies for Reading summarized in Chapter 52 can be a resource for raising questions that can be shaped into an argument, and the Questions for Writing: Incorporating the Critics (p. 513) can help you to incorporate a critic's perspective into your own argument. The following lists of questions for the critical approaches covered in Chapter 52 should be useful for discovering arguments you might make about a short story, poem, or play. The page number that follows each heading refers to the discussion in the anthology for that particular approach.

Formalist Questions (p. 2095)

1. How do various elements of the work—plot, character, point of view, setting, tone, diction, images, symbol, and so on—reinforce its meanings?
2. How are the elements related to the whole?
3. What is the work's major organizing principle? How is its structure unified?
4. What issues does the work raise? How does the work's structure resolve those issues?

Biographical Questions (p. 2097)

1. Are facts about the writer's life relevant to your understanding of the work?
2. Are characters and incidents in the work versions of the writer's own experiences? Are they treated factually or imaginatively?
3. How do you think the writer's values are reflected in the work?

Psychological Questions (p. 2099)

1. How does the work reflect the author's personal psychology?
2. What do the characters' emotions and behavior reveal about their psychological states? What types of personalities are they?
3. Are psychological matters such as repression, dreams, and desire presented consciously or unconsciously by the author?

Historical Questions (p. 2101)

1. How does the work reflect the period in which it is written?
2. What literary or historical influences helped to shape the form and content of the work?
3. How important is the historical context to interpreting the work?

Marxist Questions (p. 2103)

1. How are class differences presented in the work? Are characters aware or unaware of the economic and social forces that affect their lives?
2. How do economic conditions determine the characters' lives?
3. What ideological values are explicit or implicit?
4. Does the work challenge or affirm the social order it describes?

New Historicist Questions (p. 2103)

1. What kinds of documents outside the work seem especially relevant for shedding light on the work?
2. How are social values contemporary to the work reflected or refuted in the work?
3. How does your own historical moment affect your reading of the work and its historical reconstruction?

Cultural Studies Questions (p. 2104)

1. What does the work reveal about the cultural behavior contemporary to it?
2. How does popular culture contemporary to the work reflect or challenge the values implicit or explicit in the work?

3. What kinds of cultural documents contemporary to the work add to your reading of it?
4. How do your own cultural assumptions affect your reading of the work and the culture contemporary to it?

Gender Studies Questions (p. 2105)

1. How are the lives of men and women portrayed in the work? Do the men and women in the work accept or reject these roles?
2. Is the form and content of the work influenced by the author's gender?
3. What attitudes are explicit or implicit concerning heterosexual, homosexual, or lesbian relationships? Are these relationships sources of conflict? Do they provide resolutions to conflicts?
4. Does the work challenge or affirm traditional ideas about men and women and same-sex relationships?

Mythological Questions (p. 2107)

1. How does the story resemble other stories in plot, character, setting, or use of symbols?
2. Are archetypes presented, such as quests, initiations, scapegoats, or withdrawals and returns?
3. Does the protagonist undergo any kind of transformation such as a movement from innocence to experience that seems archetypal?
4. Do any specific allusions to myths shed light on the text?

Reader-Response Questions (p. 2109)

1. How do you respond to the work?
2. How do your own experiences and expectations affect your reading and interpretation?
3. What is the work's original or intended audience? To what extent are you similar to or different from that audience?
4. Do you respond in the same way to the work after more than one reading?

Deconstructionist Questions (p. 2111)

1. How are contradictory and opposing meanings expressed in the work?
2. How does meaning break down or deconstruct itself in the language of the text?
3. Would you say that ultimate definitive meanings are impossible to determine and establish in the text? Why? How does that affect your interpretation?
4. How are implicit ideological values revealed in the work?

These questions will not apply to all texts; and they are not mutually exclusive. They can be combined to explore a text from several critical perspectives simultaneously. A feminist approach to Kate Chopin's "The Story of an Hour" could also use Marxist concerns about class to make observations about the oppression of women's lives in the historical context of the nineteenth century. Your use of these questions should allow you to discover significant issues from which you can develop an argumentative essay that is organized around clearly defined terms, relevant evidence, and a persuasive analysis.

ORGANIZING A PAPER

After you have chosen a manageable topic and developed a thesis, a central idea about it, you can begin to organize your paper. Your thesis, even if it is still somewhat tentative, should help you decide what information will need to be included and provide you with a sense of direction.

Consider again the sample thesis in the section on developing a thesis:

> On the surface, "To His Coy Mistress" is a celebration of the pleasures of the flesh, but this witty seduction is tempered by a chilling recognition of the reality of death.

This thesis indicates that the paper can be divided into two parts — the pleasures of the flesh and the reality of death. It also indicates an order: because the central point is to show that the poem is more than a simple celebration, the pleasures of the flesh should be discussed first so that another, more complex, reading of the poem can follow. If the paper began with the reality of death, its point would be anticlimactic.

Having established such a broad and informal outline, you can draw on your underlinings, margin notations, and note cards for the subheadings and evidence required to explain the major sections of your paper. This next level of detail would look like the following:

1. Pleasures of the flesh
   Part of the traditional tone of love poetry
2. Recognition of death
   Ironic treatment of love
      Diction
      Images
      Figures of speech
      Symbols
      Tone

This list was initially a jumble of terms, but the student arranged the items so that each of the two major sections leads to a discussion of tone. (The student also found it necessary to drop some biographical information from his notes because it was irrelevant to the thesis.) The list indicates that the first part of the paper will establish the traditional tone of love poetry that celebrates the pleasures of the flesh, while the second part will present a more detailed discussion about the ironic recognition of death. The emphasis is on the latter because that is the point to be argued in the paper. Hence, the thesis has helped to organize the parts of the paper, establish an order, and indicate the paper's proper proportions.

The next step is to fill in the subheadings with information from your notes. Many experienced writers find that making lists of information to be included under each subheading is an efficient way to develop paragraphs. For a longer paper (perhaps a research paper), you should be able to develop a paragraph or more on each subheading. On the other hand, a shorter paper may require that you combine several subheadings in a paragraph. You may also discover that while an informal list is adequate for a brief paper, a ten-page assignment could require a more detailed outline. Use the method that is most productive for you. Whatever the length of the essay, your presentation must be in a coherent and logical order that allows your reader to follow the argument and evaluate the evidence. The quality of your reading can be demonstrated only by the quality of your writing.

WRITING A DRAFT

The time for sharpening pencils, arranging your desk, and doing almost anything else instead of writing has ended. The first draft will appear on the page only if you stop avoiding the inevitable and sit, stand up, or lie down to write. It makes no difference how you write, just so you do. Now that you have developed a topic into a tentative thesis, you can assemble your notes and begin to flesh out whatever outline you have made.

Be flexible. Your outline should smoothly conduct you from one point to the next, but do not permit it to railroad you. If a relevant and important idea occurs to you now, work it into the draft. By using the first draft as a means of thinking about what you want to say, you will very likely discover more than your notes originally suggested. Plenty of good writers don't use outlines at all but discover ordering principles as they write. Do not attempt to compose a perfectly correct draft the first time around. Grammar, punctuation, and spelling can wait until you revise. Concentrate on what you are saying. Good writing most often occurs when you are in hot pursuit of an idea rather than in a nervous search for errors.

To make revising easier, leave wide margins and extra space between lines so that you can easily add words, sentences, and corrections. Write on only one side of the paper. Your pages will be easier to keep track of that way, and, if you have to clip a paragraph to place it elsewhere, you will not lose any writing on the other side.

If you are working on a word processor, you can take advantage of its capacity to make additions and deletions as well as move entire paragraphs by making just a few simple keyboard commands. Some software programs can also check spelling and certain grammatical elements in your writing. It's worth remembering, however, that though a clean copy fresh off a printer may look terrific, it will read only as well as the thinking and writing that have gone into it. Many writers prudently store their data on disks and print their pages each time they finish a draft to avoid losing any material because of power failures or other problems. These printouts are also easier to read than the screen when you work on revisions.

Once you have a first draft on paper, you can delete material that is unrelated to your thesis and add material necessary to illustrate your points and make your paper convincing. The student who wrote "The A & P as a State of Mind" wisely dropped a paragraph that questioned whether Sammy displays chauvinistic attitudes toward women. Although this is an interesting issue, it has nothing to do with the thesis, which explains how the setting influences Sammy's decision to quit his job. Instead of including that paragraph, she added one that described Lengel's crabbed response to the girls so that she could lead up to the A & P "policy" he enforces.

Remember that your initial draft is only that. You should go through the paper many times — and then again — working to substantiate and clarify your ideas. You may even end up with several entire versions of the paper. Rewrite. The sentences within each paragraph should be related to a single topic. Transitions should connect one paragraph to the next so that there are no abrupt or confusing shifts. Awkward or wordy phrasing or unclear sentences and paragraphs should be mercilessly poked and prodded into shape.

Writing the Introduction and Conclusion

After you have clearly and adequately developed the body of your paper, pay particular attention to the introductory and concluding paragraphs. It's probably best to write the introduction — at least the final version of it — last, after you know precisely what you are introducing. Because this paragraph is crucial for generating interest in the topic, it should engage the reader and provide a sense of what the paper is about. There is no formula for writing effective introductory paragraphs because each writing situation is different — depending on the audience, topic, and approach — but if you pay attention to the introductions of the essays you read, you will notice a variety of possibilities. The introductory paragraph to "The A & P as a State of Mind," for example, is a straightforward explanation of why the story's setting is important for understanding Updike's treatment of the antagonist. The rest of the paper then offers evidence to support this point.

Concluding paragraphs demand equal attention because they leave the reader with a final impression. The conclusion should provide a sense of closure instead of starting a new topic or ending abruptly. In the final paragraph about the significance of the setting in "A & P," the student brings together the reasons Sammy quit his job by referring to his refusal to accept Lengel's store policies. At the same time she makes this point, she also explains the significance of Sammy ringing up the "No Sale" mentioned in her introductory paragraph. Thus, we are brought back to where we began, but we now have a greater understanding of why Sammy quits his job. Of course, the body of your paper is the most important part of your presentation, but do remember that first and last impressions have a powerful impact on readers.

Using Quotations

Quotations can be a valuable means of marshaling evidence to illustrate and support your ideas. A judicious use of quoted material will make your points clearer and more convincing. Here are some guidelines that should help you use quotations effectively.

1. Brief quotations (four lines or fewer of prose or three lines or fewer of poetry) should be carefully introduced and integrated into the text of your paper with quotation marks around them:

> According to the narrator, Bertha "had a reputation for strictness." He tells us that she always "wore dark clothes, dressed her hair simply, and expected contrition and obedience from her pupils."

For brief poetry quotations, use a slash to indicate a division between lines:

> The concluding lines of Blake's "The Tyger" pose a disturbing question: "What immortal hand or eye / Dare frame thy fearful symmetry?"

Lengthy quotations should be separated from the text of your paper. More than three lines of poetry should be double spaced and centered on the page. More than four lines of prose should be double spaced and indented ten spaces from the left margin, with the right margin the same as for the text. Do *not* use quotation marks for the passage; the indentation indicates that the passage is a quotation. Lengthy quotations should not be used in place of your own writing. Use them only if they are absolutely necessary.

2. If any words are added to a quotation, use brackets to distinguish your addition from the original source:

> "He [Young Goodman Brown] is portrayed as self-righteous and disillusioned."

Any words inside quotation marks and not in brackets must be precisely those of the author. Brackets can also be used to change the grammatical structure of a quotation so that it fits into your sentence:

> Smith argues that Chekhov "present[s] the narrator in an ambivalent light."

If you drop any words from the source, use ellipses to indicate the omission:

> "Early to bed . . . makes a man healthy, wealthy, and wise."

Use ellipses following a period to indicate an omission at the end of a sentence:

> "Early to bed and early to rise makes a man healthy. . . ."

Use a single line of spaced periods to indicate the omission of a line or more of poetry or more than one paragraph of prose:

> Nothing would sleep in that cellar, dank as a ditch,
> Bulbs broke out of boxes hunting for chinks in the dark,
> . . . .
> Nothing would give up life:
> Even the dirt kept breathing a small breath.

3. You will be able to punctuate quoted material accurately and confidently if you observe these conventions.

Place commas and periods inside quotation marks:

> "Even the dirt," Roethke insists, "kept breathing a small breath."

Even though a comma does not appear after "dirt" in the original quotation, it is placed inside the quotation mark. The exception to this rule occurs when a parenthetical reference to a source follows the quotation:

> "Even the dirt," Roethke insists, "kept breathing a small breath" (11).

Punctuation marks other than commas or periods go outside the quotation marks unless they are part of the material quoted:

> What does Roethke mean when he writes that "the dirt kept breathing a small breath"?

> Yeats asked, "How can we know the dancer from the dance?"

REVISING AND EDITING

Put some distance—a day or so if you can—between yourself and each draft of your paper. The phrase that seemed just right on Wednesday may be revealed as all wrong on Friday. You'll have a better chance of detecting lumbering sentences and thin paragraphs if you plan ahead and give yourself the time to read your paper from a fresh perspective. Through the process of revision, you can transform a competent paper into an excellent one.

Begin by asking yourself if your approach to the topic requires any rethinking. Is the argument carefully thought out and logically presented? Are there any gaps in the presentation? How well is the paper organized? Do the paragraphs lead into one another? Does the body of the paper deliver what the thesis promises? Is the interpretation sound? Are any relevant and important elements of the work ignored or distorted to advance the thesis? Are the points supported with evidence? These large questions should be addressed before you focus on more detailed matters. If you uncover serious problems as a result of considering these questions, you'll probably have quite a lot of rewriting to do, but at least you will have the opportunity to correct the problems — even if doing so takes several drafts.

A useful technique for spotting awkward or unclear moments in the paper is to read it aloud. You might also try having a friend read it aloud to you. If your handwriting is legible, your friend's reading — perhaps accompanied by hesitations and puzzled expressions — could alert you to passages that need reworking. Having identified problems, you can readily correct them on a word processor or on the draft, provided you've skipped lines and used wide margins. The final draft you hand in should be neat and carefully proofread for any inadvertent errors.

The following checklist offers questions to ask about your paper as you revise and edit it. Most of these questions will be familiar to you; however, if you need help with any of them, ask your instructor or review the appropriate section in a composition handbook.

Revision Checklist

1. Is the topic manageable? Is it too narrow or too broad?
2. Is the thesis clear? Is it based on a careful reading of the work?
3. Is the paper logically organized? Does it have a firm sense of direction?
4. Is your argument persuasive?
5. Should any material be deleted? Do any important points require further illustration or evidence?
6. Does the opening paragraph introduce the topic in an interesting manner?
7. Are the paragraphs developed, unified, and coherent? Are any too short or long?
8. Are there transitions linking the paragraphs?
9. Does the concluding paragraph provide a sense of closure?
10. Is the tone appropriate? Is it unduly flippant or pretentious?
11. Is the title engaging and suggestive?
12. Are the sentences clear, concise, and complete?
13. Are simple, complex, and compound sentences used for variety?
14. Have technical terms been used correctly? Are you certain of the meanings of all the words in the paper? Are they spelled correctly?
15. Have you documented any information borrowed from books, articles, or other sources? Have you quoted too much instead of summarizing or paraphrasing secondary material?
16. Have you used a standard format for citing sources (see p. 2173)?
17. Have you followed your instructor's guidelines for the manuscript format of the final draft?
18. Have you carefully proofread the final draft?

When you proofread your final draft, you may find a few typographical errors that must be corrected but do not warrant retyping an entire page. Provided there are not more than a handful of such errors throughout the page, they can be corrected as shown in the following passage. This example condenses a short paper's worth of errors; no single passage should be this shabby in your essay:

```
To add a letter or word, use a caret on the line where the
          is
addition needed. To delete a word draw a single line through
through it. Run-on words are separated by a vertical line,
and inadvertent spaces are closed like t his. Transposed
letters are indicated this way. New paragraphs are noted
with the sign ¶ in front of where the next paragraph is to
begin. ¶Unless you . . .
```

These sorts of errors can be minimized by using correction fluids or tapes while you type. If you use a word processor, you can eliminate such errors completely by simply entering corrections as you proofread on the screen.

MANUSCRIPT FORM

The novelist and poet Peter De Vries once observed that he very much enjoyed writing but that he couldn't bear the "paper work." Behind this playful pun is a half-serious impatience with the mechanics of it all. You may feel some of that too, but don't let your thoughtful, carefully revised paper trip over minor details. The final draft you hand in to your instructor should not only read well but look neat. If your instructor does not provide specific instructions concerning the format for the paper, follow these guidelines:

1. Papers (particularly long ones) should be typed on 8-1/2 by 11-inch paper in double space. Avoid transparent paper such as onionskin; it is difficult to read and write comments on. The ribbon should be dark and the letters on the machine clear. If you compose on a word processor with a dot-matrix printer, be certain that the dots are close enough together to be legible. And don't forget to separate your pages and remove the strips of holes on each side of the pages if your printer uses a continuous paper feed. If your instructor accepts handwritten papers, write legibly in ink on only one side of a wide-lined page.

2. Use a one-inch margin at the top, bottom, and sides of each page. Unless you are instructed to include a separate title page, type your name, instructor's name, course number and section, and date on separate lines

one inch below the upper-left corner of the first page. Double space between these lines and then center the title two spaces below the date. Do not underline or put quotation marks around your paper's title, but do use quotation marks around the titles of poems, short stories, or other brief works, and underline the titles of books and plays (for instance, Racial Stereotypes in "Battle Royal" and *The Piano Lesson*). Begin the text of your paper two spaces below the title. If you have used secondary sources, list them on a separate page at the end of the paper. Center the heading "Notes" or "Works Cited" one inch from the top of the page and then double space between it and the entries.

3. Number each page consecutively, beginning with page 2, a half inch from the top of the page in the upper-right corner.

4. Gather the pages with a paper clip rather than staples, folders, or some other device. That will make it easier for your instructor to handle the paper.

TYPES OF WRITING ASSIGNMENTS

The types of papers most frequently assigned in literature classes are explication, analysis, and comparison and contrast. Most writing about literature involves some combination of these skills. This section includes a sample explication, an analysis, and a comparison and contrast paper. For a sample research paper that demonstrates a variety of strategies for documenting outside sources, see page 2180. For genre-based assignments, see the sample papers for writing about fiction (p. 59), poetry (p. 712), and drama (p. 1278).

Explication

The purpose of this approach to a literary work is to make the implicit explicit. *Explication* is a detailed explanation of a passage of poetry or prose. Because explication is an intensive examination of a text line by line, it is mostly used to interpret a short poem in its entirety or a brief passage from a long poem, short story, or play. Explication can be used in any kind of paper when you want to be specific about how a writer achieves a certain effect. An explication pays careful attention to language — the connotations of words, allusions, figurative language, irony, symbol, rhythm, sound, and so on. These elements are examined in relation to one another and to the overall effect and meaning of the work.

The simplest way to organize an explication is to move through the passage line by line, explaining whatever seems significant. It is wise to avoid, however, an assembly-line approach that begins each sentence with "In line one (two, three) . . ." Instead, organize your paper in whatever way best serves your thesis. You might find that the right place to start is with the final lines, working your way back to the beginning of the poem or passage. The following sample explication on Dickinson's "There's a certain Slant of light" does just that. The student's opening paragraph refers to the final line of the poem in order to present her thesis. She explains that though the poem begins with an image of light, it is not a bright or cheery poem but one concerned with "the look of Death." Since the last line prompted her thesis, that is where she begins the explication.

You might also find it useful to structure a paper by discussing various elements of literature, so that you have a paragraph on connotative words followed by one on figurative language and so on. However your paper is organized, keep in mind that the aim of an explication is not simply to summarize the passage but to comment on the effects and meanings produced by the author's use of language in it. An effective explication (the Latin word *explicare* means "to unfold") displays a text to reveal how it works and what it signifies. Although writing an explication requires some patience and sensitivity, it is an excellent method for coming to understand and appreciate the elements and qualities that constitute literary art.

A SAMPLE EXPLICATION

A Reading of Dickinson's "There's a certain Slant of light"

The sample paper by Bonnie Katz is the result of an assignment calling for an explication of about 750 words on any poem by Emily Dickinson. Katz selected "There's a certain Slant of light."

EMILY DICKINSON (1830–1886)

There's a certain Slant of light
c. 1861

There's a certain Slant of light,
Winter Afternoons —
That oppresses, like the Heft
Of Cathedral Tunes —

Heavenly Hurt, it gives us —   5
We can find no scar,
But internal difference,
Where the Meanings, are —

None may teach it — Any —
'Tis the Seal Despair —   10
An imperial affliction
Sent us of the Air —

When it comes, the Landscape listens —
Shadows — hold their breath —
When it goes, 'tis like the Distance   15
On the look of Death —

This essay comments on every line of the poem and provides a coherent reading that relates each line to the speaker's intense awareness of death. Although the essay discusses each stanza in the order that it appears, the introductory paragraph provides a brief overview explaining how the poem's images contribute to its total meaning. In addition, the student does not hesitate to discuss a line out of sequence when it can be usefully connected to another phrase. This is especially apparent in the third paragraph, in her discussion of stanzas 2 and 3. The final paragraph describes some of the formal elements of the poem. It might be argued that this discussion could have been integrated into the previous paragraphs rather than placed at the end, but the student does make a connection in her concluding sentence between the pattern of language and its meaning.

Several other matters are worth noticing. The student works quotations into her own sentences to support her points. She quotes exactly as the words appear in the poem, even Dickinson's irregular use of capital letters. When something is added to a quotation to clarify it, it is enclosed in brackets so that the essayist's words will not be mistaken for the poet's: "Seal [of] Despair." A slash is used to indicate line divisions as in "imperial affliction / Sent us of the Air." And, finally, because the essay focuses on a short poem, it is not necessary to include line numbers, though they would be required in a study of a longer work.

Bonnie Katz

Professor Quiello

English 109-2

October 26, 20--

A Reading of Dickinson's

"There's a certain Slant of light"

Because Emily Dickinson did not provide titles for
her poetry, editors follow the customary practice of using
the first line of a poem as its title. However, a more appropriate title for "There's a certain Slant of light,"
one that suggests what the speaker in the poem is most
concerned about, can be drawn from the poem's last line,
which ends with "the look of Death." Although the first
line begins with an image of light, nothing bright, carefree, or cheerful appears in the poem. Instead, the predominant mood and images are darkened by a sense of
despair resulting from the speaker's awareness of death.

In the first stanza, the "certain Slant of light" is
associated with "Winter Afternoons," a phrase that connotes the end of a day, a season, and even life itself.
Such light is hardly warm or comforting. Not a ray or
beam, this slanting light suggests something unusual or
distorted and creates in the speaker a certain slant on
life that is consistent with the cold, dark mood that winter afternoons can produce. Like the speaker, most of us
have seen and felt this sort of light: it "oppresses" and
pervades our sense of things when we encounter it. Dickinson uses the senses of hearing and touch as well as sight
to describe the overwhelming oppressiveness that the
speaker experiences. The light is transformed into sound
by a simile that tells us it is "like the Heft / Of Cathedral Tunes." Moreover, the "Heft" of that sound--the slow,
solemn measures of tolling church bells and organ music--

weighs heavily on our spirits. Through the use of shifting imagery, Dickinson evokes a kind of spiritual numbness that we keenly feel and perceive through our senses.

By associating the winter light with "Cathedral Tunes," Dickinson lets us know that the speaker is concerned about more than the weather. Whatever it is that "oppresses" is related by connotation to faith, mortality, and God. The second and third stanzas offer several suggestions about this connection. The pain caused by the light is a "Heavenly Hurt." This "imperial affliction / Sent us of the Air" apparently comes from God above, and yet it seems to be part of the very nature of life. The oppressiveness we feel is in the air, and it can neither be specifically identified at this point in the poem nor be eliminated, for "None may teach it--Any." All we know is that existence itself seems depressing under the weight of this "Seal [of] Despair." The impression left by this "Seal" is stamped within the mind or soul rather than externally. "We can find no scar," but once experienced this oppressiveness challenges our faith in life and its "Meanings."

The final stanza does not explain what those "Meanings" are, but it does make clear that the speaker is acutely aware of death. As the winter daylight fades, Dickinson projects the speaker's anxiety onto the surrounding landscape and shadows, which will soon be engulfed by the darkness that follows this light: "the Landscape listens-- / Shadows--hold their breath." This image firmly aligns the winter light in the first stanza with darkness. Paradoxically, the light in this poem illuminates the nature of darkness. Tension is released when the light is completely gone, but what remains is the despair that the "imperial affliction" has imprinted on the

speaker's sensibilities, for it is "like the Distance / On
the look of Death." There can be no relief from what that
"certain Slant of light" has revealed because what has
been experienced is permanent--like the fixed stare in the
eyes of someone who is dead.

The speaker's awareness of death is conveyed in a
thoughtful, hushed tone. The lines are filled with fluid l
and smooth s sounds that are appropriate for the quiet,
meditative voice in the poem. The voice sounds tentative
and uncertain--perhaps a little frightened. This seems to
be reflected in the slightly irregular meter of the lines.
The stanzas are trochaic with the second and fourth lines
of each stanza having five syllables, but no stanza is
identical because each works a slight variation on the
first stanza's seven syllables in the first and third
lines. The rhymes also combine exact patterns with variations. The first and third lines of each stanza are not
exact rhymes, but the second and fourth lines are exact so that the paired words are more closely related:
Afternoons, Tunes; scar, are; Despair, Air; and breath,
Death. There is a pattern to the poem, but it is unobtrusively woven into the speaker's voice in much the same way
that "the look of Death" is subtly present in the images
and language of the poem.

Analysis

The preceding sample essay shows how an explication examines in detail
the important elements in a work and relates them to the whole. An analysis, however, usually examines only a single element—such as plot, character, point of view, symbol, tone, or irony—and relates it to the entire work.
An analytic topic separates the work into parts and focuses on a specific
one; you might consider "Point of View in 'A Rose for Emily,'" "Patterns of
Rhythm in Browning's 'My Last Duchess,'" or "The Significance of Fortinbras in *Hamlet*." The specific element must be related to the work as a

whole or it will appear irrelevant. It is not enough to point out that there are many death images in Marvell's "To His Coy Mistress"; the images must somehow be connected to the poem's overall effect.

Whether an analytic paper is just a few pages or many, it cannot attempt to discuss everything about the work it is considering. Only those elements that are relevant to the topic can be treated. This kind of focusing makes the topic manageable; this is why most papers that you write will probably be some form of analysis. Explications are useful for a short passage, but a line-by-line commentary on a story, play, or long poem simply isn't practical. Because analysis allows you to consider the central effect or meaning of an entire work by studying a single important element, it is a useful and common approach to longer works.

A SAMPLE ANALYSIS

The A & P as a State of Mind

Nancy Lager's paper analyzes the setting in John Updike's "A & P" (the entire story appears on p. 606). The assignment simply asked for an essay of approximately 750 words on a short story written in the twentieth century. The approach was left to the student.

The idea for this essay began with Lager asking herself why Updike used "A & P" as the title. The initial answer to the question was that "the setting is important in this story." This answer was the rough beginning of a tentative thesis. What still had to be explained, though, was how the setting is important. To determine the significance of the setting, Lager jotted down some notes based on her underlinings and marginal notations:

A & P
"usual traffic"
lights and tile
"electric eye"
shoppers like "sheep," "houseslaves," "pigs"
"Alexandrov and Petrooshki" — Russia

New England Town
typical: bank, church, etc.
traditional
conservative
proper
near Salem — witch trials
puritanical
intolerant

Lengel
"manager"

"doesn't miss that much" (like lady shopper)
Sunday school
"It's our policy"
spokesman for A & P values

From these notes Lager saw that Lengel serves as the voice of the A & P. He is, in a sense, a personification of the intolerant atmosphere of the setting. This insight led to another version of her thesis statement: "The setting of 'A & P' is the antagonist of the story." That explained at least some of the setting's importance. By seeing Lengel as a spokesman for "A & P" policies, she could view him as a voice that articulates the morally smug atmosphere created by the setting. Finally, she considered why it is significant that the setting is the antagonist, and this generated her last thesis: "Because the intolerant setting of 'A & P' is the antagonist in the story, it is crucial to our understanding of Sammy's decision to quit his job." This thesis sentence does not appear precisely in these words in the essay, but it is the backbone of the introductory paragraph.

The remaining paragraphs consist of details that describe the A & P in the second paragraph, the New England town in the third, Lengel in the fourth, and Sammy's reasons for quitting in the concluding paragraph. Paragraphs 2, 3, and 4 are largely based on Lager's notes, which she used as an outline once her thesis was established. The essay is sharply focused, well organized, and generally well written. In addition, it suggests a number of useful guidelines for analytic papers:

1. Only those points related to the thesis are included. In another type of paper the role of the girls in the bathing suits, for example, might have been considerably more prominent.

2. The analysis keeps the setting in focus while at the same time indicating how it is significant in the major incident in the story—Sammy's quitting.

3. The title is a useful lead into the paper; it provides a sense of what the topic is. In addition, the title is drawn from a sentence (the final one of the first paragraph) that clearly explains its meaning.

4. The introductory paragraph is direct and clearly indicates the paper will argue that the setting serves as the antagonist of the story.

5. Brief quotations are deftly incorporated into the text of the paper to illustrate points. We are told what we need to know about the story as evidence is provided to support ideas. There is no unnecessary plot summary. Because "A & P" is only a few pages in length and is an assigned topic, page numbers are not included after quoted phrases. If the story were longer, page numbers would be helpful for the reader.

6. The paragraphs are well developed, unified, and coherent. They flow naturally from one to another. Notice, for example, the smooth transition worked into the final sentence of the third paragraph and the first sentence of the fourth paragraph.

(Text continues on page 2157.)

Nancy Lager

Professor Taylor

English 102-12

April 2, 20--

The A & P as a State of Mind

The setting of John Updike's "A & P" is crucial to
our understanding of Sammy's decision to quit his job.
Although Sammy is the central character in the story and
we learn that he is a principled, good-natured nineteen-
year-old with a sense of humor, Updike seems to invest as
much effort in describing the setting as he does in Sammy.
The setting is the antagonist and plays a role that is as
important as Sammy's. The title, after all, is not "Youthful Rebellion" or "Sammy Quits" but "A & P." Even though
Sammy knows that his quitting will make life more difficult for him, he instinctively insists on rejecting what
the A & P comes to represent in the story. When he rings
up a "No Sale" and "saunter[s]" out of the store, he
leaves behind not only a job but the rigid state of mind
associated with the A & P.

Sammy's descriptions of the A & P present a setting
that is ugly, monotonous, and rigidly regulated. The fluorescent light is as blandly cool as the "checkerboard
green-and-cream rubber-tile floor." We can see the uniformity Sammy describes because we have all been in chain
stores. The "usual traffic" moves in one direction (except
for the swimsuited girls, who move against it), and
everything is neatly ordered and categorized in tidy
aisles. The dehumanizing routine of this environment is
suggested by Sammy's offhand references to the typical
shoppers as "sheep," "houseslaves," and "pigs." They seem
to pace through the store in a stupor; as Sammy tells us,
not even dynamite could move them.

The A & P is appropriately located "right in the middle" of a proper, conservative, traditional New England town north of Boston. This location, coupled with the fact that the town is only five miles from Salem, the site of the famous seventeenth-century witch trials, suggests a narrow, intolerant social atmosphere in which there is no room for stepping beyond the boundaries of what is regarded as normal and proper. The importance of this setting can be appreciated even more if we imagine the action taking place in, say, a mellow suburb of southern California. In this prim New England setting, the girls in their bathing suits are bound to offend somebody's sense of propriety.

As soon as Lengel sees the girls, the inevitable conflict begins. He embodies the dull conformity represented by the A & P. As "manager," he is both the guardian and enforcer of "policy." When he gives the girls "that sad Sunday-school-superintendent stare," we know we are in the presence of the A & P version of a dreary bureaucrat who "doesn't miss that much." He is as unsympathetic and unpleasant as the woman "with rouge on her cheeks and no eyebrows" who pounces on Sammy for ringing up her "HiHo crackers" twice. Like the "electric eye" in the doorway, her vigilant eyes allow nothing to escape their notice. For Sammy the logical extension of Lengel's "policy" is the half-serious notion that one day the A & P might be known as the "Great Alexandrov and Petrooshki Tea Company." Sammy's connection between what he regards as mindless "policy" and Soviet oppression is obviously an exaggeration, but the reader is invited to entertain the similarities anyway.

The reason Sammy quits his job has less to do with defending the girls than with his own sense of what it

Lager 3

means to be a decent human being. His decision is not an
easy one. He doesn't want to make trouble or disappoint
his parents, and he knows his independence and self-
reliance (the other side of New England tradition) will
make life more complex for him. In spite of his own hesitations, he finds himself blurting out "Fiddle-de-doo"
to Lengel's policies and in doing so knows that his
grandmother "would have been pleased." Sammy's "No Sale"
rejects the crabbed perspective on life that Lengel represents as manager of the A & P. This gesture is more than
just a negative, however, for as he punches in that last
entry on the cash register, "the machine whirs 'pee-pul.'"
His decision to quit his job at the A & P is an expression
of his refusal to regard policies as more important than
people.

7. Lager makes excellent use of her careful reading and notes by finding
   revealing connections among the details she has observed. The store's
   "electric eye," for instance, is related to the woman's and Lengel's
   watchfulness.
8. As events are described, the present tense is used. This avoids awkward
   tense shifts and lends an immediacy to the discussion.
9. The concluding paragraph establishes the significance of why the setting should be seen as the antagonist and provides a sense of closure
   by referring again to Sammy's "No Sale," which has been mentioned at
   the end of the first paragraph.
10. In short, Lager has demonstrated that she has read the work closely,
    has understood the relation of the setting to the major action, and has
    argued her thesis convincingly by using evidence from the story.

Comparison and Contrast

Another essay assignment in literature courses often combined with analytic topics is the type that requires you to write about similarities and differences between or within works. You might be asked to discuss "How
Sounds Express Meanings in May Swenson's 'A Nosty Fright' and Lewis

Carroll's 'Jabberwocky,'" or "Sammy's and Stokesie's Attitudes about Conformity in Updike's 'A & P.'" A *comparison* of either topic would emphasize their similarities, while a *contrast* would stress their differences. It is possible, of course, to include both perspectives in a paper if you find significant likenesses and differences. A comparison of Andrew Marvell's "To His Coy Mistress" and Richard Wilbur's "A Late Aubade" would, for example, yield similarities because each poem describes a man urging his lover to make the most of their precious time together; however, important differences also exist in the tone and theme of each poem that would constitute a contrast. (You should, incidentally, be aware that the term *comparison* is sometimes used inclusively to refer to both similarities and differences. If you are assigned a comparison of two works, be sure that you understand what your instructor's expectations are; you may be required to include both approaches in the essay.)

When you choose your own topic, the paper will be more successful — more manageable — if you write on works that can be meaningfully related to each other. Although Robert Herrick's "To the Virgins, to Make Much of Time" and Shakespeare's *Hamlet* both have something to do with hesitation, the likelihood of anyone making a connection between the two that reveals something interesting and important is remote — though perhaps not impossible if the topic were conceived imaginatively and tactfully. That is not to say that comparisons of works from different genres should be avoided, but the relation between them should be strong, as would a treatment of African American identity in M. Carl Holman's "Mr. Z" and August Wilson's *The Piano Lesson*. Choose a topic that encourages you to ask significant questions about each work; the purpose of a comparison or contrast is to understand the works more clearly for having examined them together. Despite the obvious differences between Henrik Ibsen's *A Doll House* and Gail Godwin's "A Sorrowful Woman," the two are closely related if we ask why the wife in each work withdraws from her family.

Choose works to compare or contrast that intersect with each other in some significant way. They may, for example, be written by the same author, in the same genre, or about the same subject. Perhaps you can compare their use of some technique, such as irony or point of view. Regardless of the specific topic, be sure to have a thesis that allows you to organize your paper around a central idea that argues a point about the two works. If you merely draw up a list of similarities or differences without a thesis in mind, your paper will be little more than a series of observations with no apparent purpose. Keep in the foreground of your thinking what the comparison or contrast reveals about the works.

There is no single way to organize comparative papers since each topic is likely to have its own particular issues to resolve, but it is useful to be aware of two basic patterns that can be helpful with a comparison, a contrast, or a combination of both. One method that can be effective for relatively short papers consists of dividing the paper in half, first discussing one work and then the other. Here, for example, is a partial informal outline for a discussion of Sophocles' *Oedipus the King* and Shakespeare's *Hamlet;* the topic is a comparison and contrast: "Oedipus and Hamlet as Tragic Figures."

1. Oedipus
   a. The nature of the conflict
   b. Strengths and stature
   c. Weaknesses and mistakes
   d. What is learned
2. Hamlet
   a. The nature of the conflict
   b. Strengths and stature
   c. Weaknesses and mistakes
   d. What is learned

This organizational strategy can be effective provided that the second part of the paper combines the discussion of Hamlet with references to Oedipus so that the thesis is made clear and the paper unified without being repetitive. If the two characters were treated entirely separately, then the discussion would be merely parallel rather than integrated. In a lengthy paper, this organization probably would not work well because a reader would have difficulty remembering the points made in the first half as he or she reads on.

Thus, for a longer paper it is usually better to create a more integrated structure that discusses both works as you take up each item in your outline. Here is the second basic pattern using the elements in the partial outline just cited:

1. The nature of the conflict
   a. Oedipus
   b. Hamlet
2. Strengths and stature
   a. Oedipus
   b. Hamlet
3. Weaknesses and mistakes
   a. Oedipus
   b. Hamlet
4. What is learned
   a. Oedipus
   b. Hamlet

This pattern allows you to discuss any number of topics without requiring that your reader recall what you first said about the conflict Oedipus confronts before you discuss Hamlet's conflicts fifteen pages later. However you structure your comparison or contrast paper, make certain that a reader can follow its elements and keep track of its thesis.

A SAMPLE COMPARISON

The Struggle for Women's Self-Definition in A Doll House *and* M. Butterfly

The following paper was written in response to an assignment that required a comparison and contrast — about 750 words — of two assigned plays. The student chose to write an analysis of how the women in each play resist being defined by men.

Although these two plays are fairly lengthy, Monica Casis's brief analysis of them is satisfying because she specifically focuses on the women's struggle for self-definition. After introducing the topic in the first paragraph, she takes up *A Doll House* and *M. Butterfly* in a pattern similar to the first outline suggested for "Oedipus and Hamlet as Tragic Figures." Notice how Casis works in subsequent references to *A Doll House* as she discusses *M. Butterfly* so that her treatment is integrated and we are reminded why she is comparing and contrasting the two works. Though this brief paper cannot address all the complexities and subtleties of gender definition in the plays, her final paragraph sums up her points without being repetitive and reiterates the thesis with which she began.

Monica Casis

Professor Matthews

English 105-4

November 4, 20--

The Struggle for Women's Self-Definition in

A Doll House and M. Butterfly

Though Henrik Ibsen's A Doll House (1879) and David
Henry Hwang's M. Butterfly (1988) were written more than
one hundred years apart and portray radically different
characters in settings and circumstances that are foreign to one another, both plays raise similar questions
about the role of women and how they are defined in
their respective worlds. Each play presents a woman who
initially seems to be without a strong identity as she
attempts to conform to her partner's ideals of the perfect

woman in an effort to be accepted and loved. However, at the same time Ibsen's Nora Helmer and Hwang's Song Liling are resourceful, cunning, and manipulative. Though the plays seem to be about the emergence of each woman's identity--Nora's refusal to be only a dutiful housewife and devoted mother and Song's refusal to be a woman at all(!)--these women are from the beginning stronger and more autonomous than their partners ever imagine them to be. Even so, that does not lead to their ability to define themselves as either completely autonomous or as women.

In A Doll House Nora is treated as her father's, then her husband's, doll. She is called "squirrel," "spend-thrift," and "lark" and is admonished for such things as eating sweets or asking her husband to take her ideas into consideration. Torvald's concept of the ideal woman is a showpiece who can dress up, recite, and dance. As a mother she only plays with her children, since she has Anne-Marie to take care of them. As a housewife, she has no control over the household finances and is given an allowance by her husband.

Although Nora externally conforms to her husband's expectations, she has the strength and resourceful courage to borrow money for a trip to Italy to save her husband's life and does odd jobs in order to pay the debt that she has committed forgery to secure. She is proud of her secret of sacrificing for the family. She refers to herself as a frivolous, helpless, dependent woman in order to coax her husband into giving her money or to steer him away from the mailbox carrying Krogstad's incriminating letter. Nora is constantly lying in order to please her husband. So although in one instance we see Nora as a woman trapped within her husband's definition of her, the reader is also aware that Nora uses his expectations to achieve her own goals. Once Nora sees and understands his superficiality and selfishness--that Torvald is concerned with only what might threaten him--she realizes she must abandon the confines of his definitions of her.

In a similar manner Song plays on the needs of Gallimard. To Gallimard, the perfect woman is one who is "beautiful" and "brave" but most important one whom he can dominate and control. Song is Asian, which underlies the cultural prejudice that she is expected to be subservient, quiet, faithful, and obedient. When Gallimard refers to her as Butterfly, she loses her individual identity as Nora loses hers within her pet names.

By the end of the play the reader is aware that Song is, in fact, a man working as a spy to obtain important military information from Gallimard. In order to keep hidden this secret identity, Song acts as he believes men desire women to be. As a woman Song refers to her "shame" or modesty so that Gallimard will not undress her. She pretends that she has a need to know everything he knows when in reality she is appeasing his ego and passing on military information to his enemies. Song tells Gallimard that she is trying to act "modern" and "manly" but cannot. In actuality Song is an actor who is acting the way a Chinese woman is assumed to act. When Song observes that "Once a woman submits, a man is always ready to become 'generous'" (1702; all page references are to the class text, The Bedford Introduction to Literature, 6th ed.), she is actually describing her method of control. Like Nora, the "woman" Song appeals to her mate's egotistical needs in order to fulfill her own personal goals and, in this case, the needs of her political allegiances. Just as Nora is Torvald's doll in need of care and protection,

Casis 4

Song is Gallimard's doll, beautiful and seemingly willing to accede to his every desire.

The turning point in these plays occurs when Nora and Song are faced with their dramatically changed relationships with their mates. Nora becomes convinced that she will corrupt her children and home with the guilt she bears--not for borrowing the vacation money but for being with a man she no longer knows. When Torvald learns of the truth from Krogstad, he regards her as a liar, hypocrite, and criminal and therefore repudiates her. Once Nora realizes the selfishness of her husband, she also realizes she cannot go on living the lie of being his ideal. Nora must leave her husband and children in order to search for an identity commensurate with her strengths. In M. Butterfly the controlling roles are switched when Gallimard admits that he loves Song and intends to marry her. It is when Song refuses marriage and determines the future of the child that Gallimard openly gives up control (which he never truly had). He supports Song and the child, divorces Helga, and passes classified information to Song. Once Song has total control, she emerges as a man, free from any of Gallimard's efforts to define her.

When Nora and Song come to terms with themselves, their situations are, however, no less problematic than when they falsely fulfilled the definition imposed on them. Nora leaves to pursue what may seem to some readers selfish desires, however necessary they are. In Ibsen's world, if a woman is not an obedient wife, mother, and nurturer, she defies definition. Similarly, Song's cruelty toward Gallimard and her revelation that she is not what he seems totally destroys Gallimard's image of Song as a woman, but we must understand that under the weight of that destruction Song's identity as a woman disappears,

just as Nora does when she slams the door of the doll
house she rejects. It seems that unless a man defines what
a woman is in these two plays, the strong and resourceful
woman must disappear rather than be allowed to redefine
herself.

54

The Literary
Research Paper

A close reading of a primary source such as a short story, poem, or play can give insights into a work's themes and effects, but sometimes you will want to know more. A published commentary by a critic who knows the work well and is familiar with the author's life and times can provide insights that otherwise may not be available. Such comments and interpretations — known as *secondary sources* — are, of course, not a substitute for the work itself, but they often can take you into a work further than if you made the journey by yourself.

After imagination, good sense, and energy, perhaps the next most important quality for writing a research paper is the ability to organize material. A research paper on a literary topic requires a writer to take account of quite a lot at once: the text, ideas, sources, and documentation techniques all make demands on one's efforts to present a topic clearly and convincingly.

The following list should give you a sense of what goes into creating a research paper. Although some steps on the list can be folded into one another, they offer an overview of the work that will involve you:

1. Choosing a topic
2. Finding sources
3. Evaluating sources
4. Taking notes
5. Developing a thesis
6. Organizing an outline
7. Writing drafts
8. Revising
9. Documenting sources
10. Preparing the final draft and proofreading

Even if you have never written a research paper, you most likely have already had experience choosing a topic, developing a thesis, organizing an outline, and writing a draft that you then revised, proofread, and handed in. Those skills represent six of the ten items on the list. This chapter briefly reviews some of these steps and focuses on the remaining tasks, unique to research paper assignments.

CHOOSING A TOPIC

Chapter 53 discussed the importance of reading a work closely and taking careful notes as a means of generating topics for writing about literature. If you know a work well and record your understanding of it in notes, you'll have impressions and ideas to choose from for potential topics. You may find it useful to review the information on pages 2130–32 before reading the advice about putting together a research paper in this chapter.

The student author of the sample research paper "How the Narrator Cultivates a Rose for Emily" (p. 2180) was asked to write a five-page paper that demonstrated some familiarity with published critical perspectives on a Faulkner story of his choice. Before looking into critical discussions of the story, he read "A Rose for Emily" several times, taking notes and making comments in the margin of his textbook on each reading.

What prompted his choice of "A Rose for Emily" was a class discussion in which many of his classmates found the story's title inappropriate or misleading because they could not understand how and why the story constituted a tribute to Emily given that she murdered a man and slept with his dead body over many years. The gruesome surprise ending revealing Emily as a murderer and necrophiliac hardly seemed to warrant a rose and a tribute for the central character. Why did Faulkner use such a title? Only after having thoroughly examined the story did the student go to the library to see what professional critics had to say about this question.

FINDING SOURCES

Whether your college library is large or small, its reference librarians can usually help you locate secondary sources about a particular work or author. Unless you choose a very recently published story, poem, play, or essay about which little or nothing has been written, you should be able to find out more about a literary work efficiently and quickly. Even if a work has been published recently, you can probably find relevant information on the Internet (see Electronic Sources, p. 2168). Here are some useful reference sources that can help you to establish both an overview of a potential topic and a list of relevant books and articles.

Annotated List of References

American Writers. 4 vols. New York: Scribner's, 1979–87. Chronological essays offer biography and criticism of major American writers.

Baker, Nancy L., and Nancy Huling. *A Research Guide for Undergraduate Students: English and American Literature.* 4th ed. New York: MLA, 1995. Especially designed for students; a useful guide to reference sources.

Bryer, Jackson, ed. *Sixteen Modern American Authors: A Survey of Research and Criticism.* New York: Norton, 1973. Extensive bibliographic essays on Sherwood Anderson, Willa Cather, Hart Crane, Theodore Dreiser, T. S. Eliot, William Faulkner, F. Scott Fitzgerald, Robert Frost, Ernest Hemingway, Eugene O'Neill, Ezra Pound, Edwin Arlington Robinson, John Steinbeck, Wallace Stevens, William Carlos Williams, and Thomas Wolfe.

Contemporary Literary Criticism. 106 vols. to date. Detroit: Gale, 1973–. Brief biographies of contemporary authors along with excerpts from reviews and criticism of their work.

Corse, Larry B., and Sandra B. Corse. *Articles on American and British Literature: An Index to Selected Periodicals, 1950–1977.* Athens, OH: Swallow, 1981. Specifically designed for students using small college libraries.

Dictionary of Literary Biography. Detroit: Gale, 1978–. A multivolume series in progress of American, British, and world writers that provides useful biographical and critical overviews.

Eddleman, Floyd E., ed. *American Drama Criticism: Interpretations, 1890–1977.* 2nd ed. Hamden, CT: Shoe String, 1979. Supplement 1984.

Elliot, Emory, et al. *Columbia Literary History of the United States.* New York: Columbia UP, 1988. This updates the discussions in Spiller (below) and reflects recent changes in the canon.

Harner, James L. *Literary Research Guide: A Guide to Reference Sources for the Study of Literature in English and Related Topics.* 3rd ed. New York: MLA, 1998. A selective but extensive annotated guide to important bibliographies, abstracts, databases, histories, surveys, dictionaries, encyclopedias, and handbooks; an invaluable research tool with extensive, useful indexes.

Holman, C. Hugh, and William Harmon. *A Handbook to Literature.* 8th ed. New York: Macmillan, 1999. A thorough dictionary of literary terms that also provides brief, clear overviews of literary movements such as Romanticism.

Kuntz, Joseph M., and Nancy C. Martinez. *Poetry Explication: A Checklist of Interpretation since 1925 of British and American Poems Past and Present.* Boston: Hall, 1980.

MLA International Bibliography of Books and Articles on Modern Language and Literature. New York: MLA, 1921–. Compiled annually; a major source for articles and books. Also available online and on CD-ROM.

The New Cambridge Bibliography of English Literature. 5 vols. Cambridge, Eng.: Cambridge UP, 1967–77. An important source on the literature from A.D. 600 to 1950.

Ousby, Ian, ed. *The Cambridge Guide to English Literature.* 2nd ed. Cambridge, Eng.: Cambridge UP, 1994. A valuable overview.

The Oxford History of English Literature. 13 vols. Oxford, Eng.: Oxford UP, 1945–, in progress. The most comprehensive literary history.

The Penguin Companion to World Literature. 4 vols. New York: McGraw-Hill, 1969–71. Covers classical, Asian, African, European, English, and American literature.

Preminger, Alex, and T. V. F. Brogan, eds. *The New Princeton Encyclopedia of Poetry and Poetics.* Princeton: Princeton UP, 1993. Includes entries on technical terms and poetic movements.

Rees, Robert, and Earl N. Harbert. *Fifteen American Authors before 1900: Bibliographic Essays on Research and Criticism.* Madison: U of Wisconsin P, 1971. Among the writers covered are Stephen Crane and Emily Dickinson.

Spiller, Robert E., et al. *Literary History of the United States.* 4th ed. 2 vols. New York: Macmillan, 1974. Coverage of literary movements and individual writers from colonial times to the 1960s.

Walker, Warren S. *Twentieth-Century Short Story Explication.* 3rd ed. Hamden, CT: Shoe String, 1977. A bibliography of criticism on short stories written since 1800; supplements appear every few years.

These sources are available in the reference sections of most college libraries; ask a reference librarian to help you locate them.

Electronic Sources

Researchers can locate materials in a variety of sources, including card catalogs, specialized encyclopedias, bibliographies, and indexes to periodicals. Many libraries now also provide computer searches that are linked to a database of the libraries' holdings; you can even access many of these databases from home. This can be an efficient way to establish a bibliography on a specific topic. If your library has such a service, consult a reference librarian about how to use it and to determine whether it is feasible for your topic. If a computer service is impractical, you can still collect the same information from printed sources.

In addition to the many electronic databases ranging from your library's computerized holdings to the many specialized CD-ROMs available, such as *MLA International Bibliography* (a major source for articles and books on literary topics), the Internet also connects millions of sites with primary sources (the full texts of stories, poems, plays, and essays) and secondary sources (biography or criticism). If you have not had practice with research on the Web, it is a good idea to get guidance from your instructor or a librarian. Browsing on the Net can be absorbing as well as informative, but unless you have plenty of time to spare, don't wait until the last minute to locate your electronic sources. You might find yourself trying to find reliable, professional sources among thousands of sites if you enter an unqualified entry such as "Charles Dickens." Once you are familiar with the Net, however, you'll find its research potential both fascinating and rewarding.

Do remember that your own college library offers a broad range of electronic sources. If you're feeling uncertain, intimidated, and profoundly unplugged, your reference librarians are there to help you to get started. Once you take advantage of their advice and tutorials, you'll soon find that negotiating the World Wide Web can be an efficient means of research for almost any subject.

Online Resources for Research and Writing

The details you'll need to conduct research on the Web go beyond the scope of this chapter, but Bedford/St. Martin's offers several online resources for researching and writing about literature that can help you find what you need on the Web — and then use it once you find it. Visit <**www.bedfordstmartins.com/meyer/bedintrolit**>, and explore the resources we offer to help you research online.

Citing sources correctly in a final paper is often a challenge, and the Web has made it even more complex. ***Research and Documentation Online,*** the online version of the popular booklet *Research and Documentation in the Electronic Age,* by Diana Hacker, provides clear, authoritative advice on documentation in every discipline. It also covers conducting library and online research and includes links to Internet research sources.

The English Research Room is a good starting place for any research project, large or small. *Research Web guides* will answer questions you may have about doing research, conducting electronic searches, using the Web and other online resources, and evaluating and citing sources. *Interactive tutorials* give you the opportunity to practice common electronic search techniques in a live environment. *Research links* make it easy to find hundreds of useful research sites, including search engines and reference sites.

Organized alphabetically by author within five genres, ***LitLinks*** offers links to sites about all the fiction writers, all the playwrights, and many of the poets in *The Bedford Introduction to Literature.* Clear, concise annotations and links to more than five hundred professionally maintained sites help you browse with direction, whether you're looking for a favorite text, additional biographical or critical information about an author, critical articles, or conversation with other students and scholars.

Once you're on the Web — or in the library — ***Research Assistant,*** a stand-alone application, can help you manage your research sources. Functioning as a smart file cabinet, *Research Assistant* helps you collect, evaluate, and cite your sources. It works not only with text but also with graphics, audio clips, and video clips. If you're writing a paper, *Research Assistant* will help you sort and organize your sources, moving you from researching into writing.

Finally, if your final research project will incorporate multimedia sources you may find it helpful to use the **Multimedia Project Guide.** While most useful as an aid to help you with the multimedia project assignments at the end of every case study chapter in this book, this guide can also be used generally to help you find, evaluate, and document multimedia sources.

EVALUATING SOURCES AND TAKING NOTES

Evaluate your sources for their reliability and the quality of their evidence. Check to see whether an article or book has been superseded by later studies; try to use up-to-date sources. A popular magazine article will probably not be as authoritative as an article in a scholarly journal. Sources that are well documented with primary and secondary materials usually indicate that the author has done his or her homework. Books printed by university presses and established trade presses are preferable to books privately printed. But there are always exceptions. If you are uncertain about how to assess a book, try to find out something about the author. Are there any other books listed in the card catalog that indicate the author's expertise? What do book reviews say about the work? Three valuable indexes to book reviews of literary studies are *Book Review Digest, Book Review Index,* and *Index to Book Reviews in the Humanities.* Your reference librarian can show you how to use these important tools for evaluating books. Reviews can be a quick means to gain a broad perspective on writers and their works because reviewers often survey previous approaches to the topic under discussion.

A cautionary note: assessing online sources can be more problematic than evaluating print sources because anyone with a computer and online access can publish on the Internet. Be sure to determine the nature of your sources and their authority. Is the site the work of a professional or an amateur? Is the information likely to be reliable? Is it documented? Before placing your trust in an Internet source, make sure that it warrants your confidence.

As you prepare a list of reliable sources relevant to your topic, record the necessary bibliographic information so that it will be available when you make up the list of works cited for your paper. (See the sample bibliography card on page 2171.) For a book include the author, complete title, place of publication, publisher, and date. For an article include author, complete title, name of periodical, volume number, date of issue, and page numbers.

Once you have assembled a tentative bibliography, you will need to take notes on your readings. If you are not using a word processor, use 3 by

5-, 4 by 6-, or 5 by 8-inch cards for note taking. They are easy to manipulate and can be readily sorted after you establish subheadings for your paper. Be sure to keep track of where the information comes from by writing the author's name and page number on each note card. If you use more than one work by the same author, include a brief title as well as the author's name. (See the sample note card below.)

The sample note card records the source of information (the complete publishing information is on the bibliography card) and provides a heading that will allow easy sorting later on. Notice that the information is summarized rather than quoted in large chunks. The student also includes a short note asking himself whether this will be relevant to the topic — the meaning of the title of "A Rose for Emily." (As it turned out, this was not directly related to the topic, so it was dropped.)

> Minter, David William
> _Faulkner: His Life and Work._
> Baltimore, MD: Johns Hopkins
> UP, 1980.

Sample bibliography card for a book.

> On the publication of "A Rose for Emily" Minter 116
>
> Minter describes "A Rose" as "one of Faulkner's finest short stories" yet it was rejected at _Scribner's_ when Faulkner submitted it.
>
> [Can I work this in?]

Sample note card.

Note cards can combine quotations, paraphrases, and summaries; you can also use them to cite your own ideas and give them headings so that you don't lose track of them. As you take notes, try to record only points relevant to your topic. Although the sample card on Scribner's rejection of "A Rose for Emily" wasn't used in the paper, it might have been. At least that fact was an interesting possibility, even if it wasn't, finally, worth developing.

DEVELOPING A THESIS AND ORGANIZING THE PAPER

As the notes on "A Rose for Emily" accumulated, the student sorted them into topics, including:

1. Publication history of the story
2. Faulkner on the title of "A Rose for Emily"
3. Is Emily simply insane?
4. The purpose of Emily's servant
5. The narrator
6. The townspeople's view of Emily
7. The surprise ending
8. Emily's admirable qualities
9. Homer's character

The student quickly saw that items 1, 4, and 9 were not directly related to his topic concerning the significance of the story's title. The remaining numbers (2, 3, 5, 6, 7, 8) are the topics taken up in the paper. The student had begun his reading of secondary sources with a tentative thesis that stemmed from his question about the appropriateness of the title. That "why" shaped itself into the expectation that he would have a thesis something like this: "The title justifies Emily's murder of Homer because . . ."

The assumption was that he would find information that indicated some specific reason. But the more he read, the more he discovered that it was possible to speak only about how the narrator prevents the reader from making a premature judgment about Emily rather than justifying her actions. Hence, he wisely changed his tentative thesis to this final thesis: "The narrator describes incidents and withholds information in such a way as to cause the reader to sympathize with Emily before her crime is revealed." This thesis helped the student explain why the title is accurate and useful rather than misleading.

Because the assignment was relatively brief, the student did not write up a formal outline but instead organized his stacks of usable note cards and proceeded to write the first draft from them.

REVISING

After writing your first draft, you should review the advice and revision checklist on pages 2144–46 so that you can read your paper with an objective eye. Two days after writing his next-to-last draft, the writer of "How the Narrator Cultivates a Rose for Emily" realized that he had allotted too much space for critical discussions of the narrator that were not directly related to his approach. He wanted to demonstrate a familiarity with these studies, but it was not essential that he summarize or discuss them. He corrected this by consolidating parenthetical references: "Though a number of studies discuss the story's narrator (see, for example, Kempton; Sullivan; and Watkins). . . ." His earlier draft had included summaries of these studies that were tangential to his argument. The point is that he saw this himself after he took some time to approach the paper from a fresh perspective.

DOCUMENTING SOURCES

You must acknowledge the use of a source when you (1) quote someone's exact words, (2) summarize or borrow someone's opinions or ideas, or (3) use information and facts that are not considered to be common knowledge. The purpose of this documentation is to acknowledge your sources, to demonstrate that you are familiar with what others have thought about the topic, and to provide your reader access to the same sources. If your paper is not adequately documented, it will be vulnerable to a charge of *plagiarism* — the presentation of someone else's work as your own. Conscious plagiarism is easy to avoid; honesty takes care of that for most people. However, there is a more problematic form of plagiarism that is often inadvertent. Whether inadequate documentation is conscious or not, plagiarism is a serious matter and must be avoided. Papers can be evaluated only by what is on the page, not by their writers' intentions.

Let's look more closely at what constitutes plagiarism. Consider the following passage quoted from John Gassner's introduction to *Four Great Plays by Henrik Ibsen* (New York: Bantam, 1959), p. viii:

> Today it seems incredible that *A Doll's House*° should have created the furor it did. In exploding Victorian ideals of feminine dependency the play seemed revolutionary in 1879. When its heroine Nora left her home in search of self-development it seemed as if the sanctity of marriage had been flouted by a playwright treading the stage with cloven-feet.

Rolf Fjelde, whose translation is included in Chapter 46, renders the title as *A Doll House* in order to emphasize that the whole household, including Torvald as well as Nora, lives an unreal, doll-like existence.

Now read this plagiarized version:

> *A Doll's House* created a furor in 1879 by blowing up Victorian ideals about a woman's place in the world. Nora's search for self-fulfillment outside her home appeared to be an attack on the sanctity of marriage by a cloven-footed playwright.

Though the writer has shortened the passage and made some changes in the wording, this paragraph is basically the same as Gassner's. Indeed, several of his phrases are lifted almost intact. Even if a parenthetical reference had been included at the end of the passage and the source included in "Works Cited," the language of this passage would still be plagiarism because it is presented as the writer's own. Both language and ideas must be acknowledged.

Here is an adequately documented version of the passage:

> John Gassner has observed how difficult it is for today's readers to comprehend the intense reaction against *A Doll's House* in 1879. When Victorian audiences watched Nora walk out of her stifling marriage, they assumed that Ibsen was expressing a devilish contempt for the "sanctity of marriage" (viii).

This passage makes absolutely clear that the observation is Gassner's, and it is written in the student's own language with the exception of one quoted phrase. Had Gassner not been named in the passage, the parenthetical reference would have included his name: (Gassner viii).

Some mention should be made of the notion of common knowledge before we turn to the standard format for documenting sources. Observations and facts that are widely known and routinely included in many of your sources do not require documentation. It is not necessary to cite a source for the fact that Alfred, Lord Tennyson, was born in 1809 or that Ernest Hemingway loved to fish and hunt. Sometimes it will be difficult for you to determine what common knowledge is for a topic that you know little about. If you are in doubt, the best strategy is to supply a reference.

There are two basic ways to document sources. Traditionally, sources have been cited in footnotes at the bottom of each page or in endnotes grouped together at the end of the paper. Here is how a portion of the sample paper would look if footnotes were used instead of parenthetical documentation:

```
As Heller points out, before we learn of Emily's bizarre be-
havior, we see her as a sympathetic--if antiquated--figure
in a town whose life and concerns have passed her by; hence,
"we are disposed to see Emily as victimized."¹

    ¹Terry Heller, "The Telltale Hair: A Critical Study of
William Faulkner's 'A Rose for Emily,'" Arizona Quarterly 28
(1972): 306.
```

Unlike endnotes, which are double spaced throughout under the title of "Notes" on separate pages at the end of the paper, footnotes appear four spaces below the text. They are single spaced with double spaces between notes.

No doubt you will have encountered these documentation methods in your reading. A different style is recommended, however, in the Modern Language Association's *MLA Handbook for Writers of Research Papers,* Fourth Edition (1995). This style employs parenthetical references within the text of the paper; these are keyed to an alphabetical list of works cited at the end of the paper. This method is designed to be less distracting for the reader. Unless you are instructed to follow the footnote or endnote style for documentation, use the parenthetical method explained in the next section.

The List of Works Cited

Items in the list of works cited are arranged alphabetically according to the author's last name and indented five spaces after the first line. This allows the reader to locate quickly the complete bibliographic information for the author's name cited within the parenthetical reference in the text. The following are common entries for literature papers and should be used as models. If some of your sources are of a different nature, consult the *MLA Handbook for Writers of Research Papers,* Fourth Edition (New York: MLA, 1995); or, for the latest updates, check MLA's Web site at < http://www.mla.org>.

A BOOK BY ONE AUTHOR

```
Hendrickson, Robert. The Literary Life and Other Curiosities.
     New York: Viking, 1981.
```

Notice that the author's name is in reverse order. This information, along with the full title, place of publication, publisher, and date, should be taken from the title and copyright pages of the book. The title is underlined to indicate italics and is also followed by a period. If the city of publication is well known, it is unnecessary to include the state. Use the publication date on the title page; if none appears there, use the copyright date (after ©) on the back of the title page.

A BOOK BY TWO AUTHORS

```
Horton, Rod W., and Herbert W. Edwards. Backgrounds of Amer-
     ican Literary Thought. 3rd ed. Englewood Cliffs: Pren-
     tice, 1974.
```

Only the first author's name is given in reverse order. The edition number appears after the title.

A Book with More than Three Authors

```
Abrams, M. H., et al., eds. The Norton Anthology of English
    Literature. 5th ed. 2 vols. New York: Norton, 1986.
    Vol. 1.
```

The abbreviation *et al.* means "and others." It is used to avoid having to list all fourteen editors of this first volume of a two-volume work.

A Work in a Collection by the Same Author

```
O'Connor, Flannery. "Greenleaf." The Complete Stories. By
    O'Connor. New York: Farrar, 1971. 311-34.
```

Page numbers are given because the reference is to only a single story in the collection.

A Work in a Collection by Different Writers

```
Frost, Robert. "Design." The Bedford Introduction to Litera-
    ture. Ed. Michael Meyer. 6th ed. Boston: Bedford/St.
    Martin's, 2002. 1018.
```

A Translated Book

```
Grass, Günter. The Tin Drum. Trans. Ralph Manheim. New York:
    Vintage-Random, 1962.
```

An Introduction, Preface, Foreword, or Afterword

```
Johnson, Thomas H. Introduction. Final Harvest: Emily Dick-
    inson's Poems. By Emily Dickinson. Boston: Little,
    Brown, 1961. vii-xiv.
```

This cites the introduction by Johnson. Notice that a colon is used between the book's main title and subtitle. To cite a poem in this book use this method:

```
Dickinson, Emily. "A Tooth upon Our Peace." Final Harvest:
    Emily Dickinson's Poems. Ed. Thomas H. Johnson. Boston:
    Little, Brown, 1961. 110.
```

An Encyclopedia

```
"Wordsworth, William." The New Encyclopedia Britannica.
    1984 ed.
```

Because this encyclopedia is organized alphabetically, no page number or other information is given, only the edition number (if available) and date.

AN ARTICLE IN A MAGAZINE

```
Morrow, Lance. "Scribble, Scribble, Eh, Mr. Toad." Time 24
    Feb. 1986: 84.
```

The citation for an unsigned article would begin with the title and be alphabetized by the first word of the title other than "a," "an," or "the."

AN ARTICLE IN A SCHOLARLY JOURNAL WITH
CONTINUOUS PAGINATION BEYOND A SINGLE ISSUE

```
Mahar, William J. "Black English in Early Blackface
    Minstrelsy: A New Interpretation of the Sources of
    Minstrel Show Dialect." American Quarterly 37 (1985):
    260-85.
```

Because this journal uses continuous pagination instead of separate pagination for each issue, it is not necessary to include the month, season, or number of the issue. Only one of the quarterly issues will have pages numbered 260–85. If you are not certain whether a journal's pages are numbered continuously throughout a volume, supply the month, season, or issue number, as in the next entry.

AN ARTICLE IN A SCHOLARLY JOURNAL WITH
SEPARATE PAGINATION FOR EACH ISSUE

```
Updike, John. "The Cultural Situation of the American
    Writer." American Studies International 15 (Spring
    1977): 19-28.
```

By noting the spring issue, the entry saves a reader looking through each issue of the 1977 volume for the correct article on pages 19 to 28.

AN ARTICLE IN A NEWSPAPER

```
Ziegler, Philip. "The Lure of Gossip, the Rules of History."
    New York Times 23 Feb. 1986: sec. 7: 1+.
```

This citation indicates that the article appears on page 1 of section 7 and continues onto another page.

A LECTURE

```
Stern, Milton. "Melville's View of Law." English 270 class
    lecture. University of Connecticut, Storrs, 12 Mar. 1992.
```

LETTER, E-MAIL, OR INTERVIEW

Vellenga, Carolyn. Letter to the author. 9 Oct. 1997.

Harter, Stephen P. E-mail to the author. 28 Dec. 1997.

McConagha, Bill. Personal interview [or Telephone
    interview]. 4 March 1998.

If a source appears in print as well as in an electronic format, provide
the same publication information you would for printed sources — the
title of the electronic source, the medium (such as "CD-ROM"), the name
of the distributor, and the date of publication. If it does not appear in
print form, or if you don't have all or some of the information, provide as
much as you have along with the date of access and the electronic address.
You need to provide all the information necessary for your readers to find
the source themselves.

CD-ROM ISSUED PERIODICALLY

Aaron, Belèn V. "The Death of Theory." Scholarly Book
    Reviews 4.3 (1997): 146-47. ERIC. CD-ROM. SilverPlatter.
    Dec. 1997.

CD-ROM ISSUED IN A SINGLE EDITION

Sideman, Bob, and Donald Sheehy. "The Risk of Spirit."
    Robert Frost: Poems, Life, Legacy. CD-ROM. Vers. 1.0.
    New York: Holt, 1997.

ELECTRONIC WEB SITE

Cody, David. "Dickens: A Brief Biography." World Wide Web.
    13 Feb. 1998. <http://www.stg.brown.edu/projects/
    hypertext/landow/victorian/dickens/dickensbio1.html>.

ELECTRONIC NEWSGROUP

Kathman, David. "Shakespeare's Literacy -- or Lack of." 3 Mar.
    1998. Newsgroup. <humanities.lit.authors.shakespeare>.

Parenthetical References

A list of works cited is not an adequate indication of how you have used
sources in your paper. You must also provide the precise location of quotations and other information by using parenthetical references within the
text of the paper. You do this by citing the author's name (or the source's
title if the work is anonymous) and the page number:

```
Collins points out that "Nabokov was misunderstood by early
reviewers of his work" (28).
```

or

```
Nabokov's first critics misinterpreted his stories (Collins
28).
```

Either way a reader will find the complete bibliographic entry in the list of works cited under Collins's name and know that the information cited in the paper appears on page 28. Notice that the end punctuation comes after the parentheses.

If you have listed more than one work by the same author, you would add a brief title to the parenthetical reference to distinguish between them. You could also include the full title in your text:

```
Nabokov's first critics misinterpreted his stories (Collins,
"Early Reviews" 28).
```

or

```
Collins points out in "Early Reviews of Nabokov's Fiction"
that his early work was misinterpreted by reviewers (28).
```

There can be many variations on what is included in a parenthetical reference, depending on the nature of the entry in the list of works cited. But the general principle is simple enough: provide enough parenthetical information for a reader to find the work in "Works Cited." Examine the sample research paper for more examples of works cited and strategies for including parenthetical references. If you are puzzled by a given situation, ask your reference librarian to show you the *MLA Handbook*.

A SAMPLE RESEARCH PAPER

How the Narrator Cultivates a Rose for Emily

The following research paper by Tony Groulx follows the format described in the *MLA Handbook for Writers of Research Papers*, Fourth Edition (1995). This format is discussed in the preceding section on documentation and in Chapter 53 in the section on manuscript form (p. 2146). Though the sample paper is short, it illustrates many of the techniques and strategies useful for writing an essay that includes secondary sources. (Faulkner's "A Rose for Emily" is reprinted on p. 75.)

Tony Groulx

Professor Hugo

English 109-3

December 3, 20--

How the Narrator Cultivates a Rose for Emily

William Faulkner's "A Rose for Emily" is an absorbing
mystery story whose chilling ending contains a gruesome
surprise. When we discover, along with the narrator and
townspeople, what was left of Homer Barron's body, we may
be surprised or not, depending on how carefully we have
been reading the story and keeping track of details such
as Emily Grierson's purchase of rat poison and Homer's
disappearance. Probably most readers anticipate finding
Homer's body at the end of the story because Faulkner
carefully prepares the groundwork for the discovery as the
townspeople force their way into that mysterious upstairs
room where a "thin, acrid pall as of the tomb seemed to
lie everywhere" (80). But very few readers, if any, are
prepared for the story's final paragraph, when we realize
that the strand of "iron-gray hair" (the last three words
of the story) on the second pillow indicates that Emily
has slept with Homer since she murdered him. This last
paragraph produces the real horror in the story and an
extraordinary revelation about Emily's character.

The final paragraph seems like the right place to
begin a discussion of this story because the surprise ending not only creates a powerful emotional effect in us but
also raises an important question about what we are to
think of Emily. Is this isolated, eccentric woman simply
mad? All the circumstantial evidence indicates that she is
a murderer and necrophiliac, and yet Faulkner titles the
story "A Rose for Emily," as if she is due some kind of
tribute. The title somehow qualifies the gasp of horror

that the story leads up to in the final paragraph. Why
would anyone offer this woman a "rose"? What's behind the
title?

   Faulkner was once directly asked the meaning of the
title and replied:

> Oh it's simply the poor woman had had no life at
> all. Her father had kept her more or less locked
> up and then she had a lover who was about to
> quit her, she had to murder him. It was just "A
> Rose for Emily"--that's all. (qtd. in Gwynn and
> Blotner 87-88)

This reply explains some of Emily's motivation for murdering Homer, but it doesn't actually address the purpose and
meaning of the title. If Emily killed Homer out of a kind
of emotional necessity--out of a fear of abandonment--how
does that explain the fact that the title seems to suggest
that the story is a way of paying respect to Emily? The
question remains.

   Whatever respect the story creates for Emily cannot
be the result of her actions. Surely there can be no convincing excuse made for murder and necrophilia; there is
nothing to praise about what she does. Instead, the tribute comes in the form of how her story is told rather than
what we are told about her. To do this Faulkner uses a
narrator who tells Emily's story in such a way as to maxi-
mize our sympathy for her. The grim information about
Emily's "iron-gray hair" on the pillow is withheld until
the very end and not only to produce a surprise but to
permit the reader to develop a sympathetic understanding
of her before we are shocked and disgusted by her
necrophilia.

   Significantly, the narrator begins the story with
Emily's death rather than Homer's. Though a number of

studies discuss the story's narrator (see, for example, Kempton; Sullivan; and Watkins), Terry Heller's is one of the most comprehensive in its focus on the narrator's effects on the readers' response to Emily. As Heller points out, before we learn of Emily's bizarre behavior we see her as a sympathetic--if antiquated--figure in a town whose life and concerns have passed her by; hence, "we are disposed to see Emily as victimized" (306). Her refusal to pay her taxes is an index to her isolation and eccentricity, but this incident also suggests a degree of dignity and power lacking in the town officials who fail to collect her taxes. Her encounters with the officials of Jefferson-- whether in the form of the sneaking aldermen who try to cover up the smell around her house or the druggist who unsuccessfully tries to get her to conform to the law when she buys arsenic--place her in an admirable light because her willfulness is based on her personal strength. Moreover, it is relatively easy to side with Emily when the townspeople are described as taking pleasure in her being reduced to poverty as a result of her father's death because "now she too would know the old thrill and the old despair of a penny more or less" (77). The narrator's account of their pettiness, jealousy, and inability to make sense of Emily causes the reader to sympathize with Emily's eccentricities before we must judge her murderous behavior. We admire her for taking life on her own terms, and the narrator makes sure this response is in place prior to our realization that she also takes life.

We don't really know much about Emily because the narrator arranges the details of her life so that it's difficult to know what she's been up to. We learn, for example, about the smell around the house before she buys the poison and Homer disappears, so that the cause-and-

effect relationship among these events is a bit slippery
(for a detailed reconstruction of the chronology, see
McGlynn and Nebecker's revision of McGlynn's work), but
the effect is to suspend judgment of Emily. By the time we
realize what she has done, we are already inclined to see
her as outside community values almost out of necessity.
That's not to say that the murdering of Homer is justified
by the narrator, but it is to say that her life maintains
its private--though no longer secret--dignity. Despite the
final revelation, Emily remains "dear, inescapable, impervious, tranquil, and perverse" (80).

The narrator's "rose" to Emily is his recognition that
Emily is all these things--including "perverse." She evokes
"a sort of respectful affection for a fallen monument" (75).
She is, to be sure, "fallen" but she is also somehow cen-
tral--a "monument"--to the life of the community. Faulkner
does not offer a definitive reading of Emily, but he does
have the narrator pay tribute to her by attempting to provide a complex set of contexts for her actions--contexts
that include a repressive father, resistance to a changing
South and impinging North, the passage of time and its influence on the present, and relations between men and women
as well as relations between generations. Robert Crosman
discusses the narrator's efforts to understand Emily:

> The narrator is himself a "reader" of Emily's
> story, trying to put together from fragments a
> complete picture, trying to find the meaning of
> her life in its impact upon an audience, the
> citizens of Jefferson, of which he is a member.
> (212)

The narrator refuses to dismiss Emily as simply mad or to
treat her life as merely a grotesque, sensational horror
story. Instead, his narrative method brings us into her

Groulx 5

life before we too hastily reject her, and in doing so it
offers us a complex imaginative treatment of fierce determination and strength coupled with illusions and shocking
eccentricities. The narrator's rose for Emily is paying
her the tribute of placing that "long strand of iron-gray
hair" in the context of her entire life.

Works Cited

Crosman, Robert. "How Readers Make Meaning." College
    Literature 9 (1982): 207-15.

Faulkner, William. "A Rose for Emily." The Bedford
    Introduction to Literature. Ed. Michael Meyer.
    6th ed. Boston: Bedford/St. Martin's, 2002. 75.

Gwynn, Frederick, and Joseph Blotner, eds. Faulkner
    in the University: Class Conferences at the
    University of Virginia, 1957-58. Charlottesville:
    U of Virginia P, 1959.

Heller, Terry. "The Telltale Hair: A Critical Study
    of William Faulkner's 'A Rose for Emily.'" Ari-
    zona Quarterly 28 (1972): 301-18.

Kempton, K. P. The Short Story. Cambridge: Harvard UP,
    1954. 104-06.

McGlynn, Paul D. "The Chronology of 'A Rose for Emily.'"
    Studies in Short Fiction 6 (1969): 461-62.

Nebecker, Helen E. "Chronology Revised." Studies in
    Short Fiction 8 (1971): 471-73.

Sullivan, Ruth. "The Narrator in 'A Rose for Emily.'" The
    Journal of Narrative Technique 1 (1971): 159-78.

Watkins, F. C. "The Structure of 'A Rose for Emily.'" Mod-
    ern Language Notes 69 (1954): 508-10.

55

Taking Essay
Examinations

PREPARING FOR AN ESSAY EXAM

Keep Up with the Reading

The best way to prepare for an examination is to keep up with the reading. If you begin the course with a commitment to completing the reading assignments on time, you will not have to read in a frenzy and cram just days before the test. The readings will be a pleasure, not a frantic ordeal. Moreover, you will find that your instructor's comments and class discussion will make more sense to you and that you'll be able to participate in class discussion. As you prepare for the exam, you should be rereading texts rather than reading for the first time. It may not be possible to reread everything, but you'll at least be able to scan a familiar text and reread passages that are particularly important.

Take Notes and Annotate the Text

Don't rely exclusively on your memory. The typical literature class includes a hefty amount of reading, so unless you take notes, annotate the text with your own comments, and underline important passages, you're likely to forget material that could be useful for responding to an examination question (see pp. 2131–33 for a discussion of these matters). The more you can retrieve from your reading, the more prepared you'll be for reviewing significant material for the exam. These notes can be used to illustrate points that were made in class. By briefly quoting an important phrase or line from the text you can provide supporting evidence that will make your argument convincing. Consider, for example, the difference between writing that "Marvell's speaker in 'To His Coy Mistress' says that they won't be able to love after they die" and writing that "the speaker intones that 'The grave's a fine and private place / But none, I think, do there embrace.'" No one expects you to memorize the entire poem, but recalling a few lines here and there can transform a sleepy generality into an illustrative, persuasive argument.

Anticipate Questions

As you review the readings, keep in mind the class discussions and the focus provided by your instructor. Class discussions and the instructor's emphasis often become the basis for essay questions. You may not see the exact same topics on the exam, but you might find that the matters you've discussed in class will serve as a means of responding to an essay question. If, for example, class discussion of John Updike's "A & P" (see p. 606) centered on the story's small-town New England setting, you could use that conservative, traditional, puritanical setting to answer a question such as "Discuss how the conflicts that Sammy encounters in 'A & P' are related to the story's theme." A discussion of the intolerant rigidity of this New England town could be connected to A & P "policy" and the crabbed values associated with Lengel that lead to Sammy's quitting his job in protest of such policies. The point is that you'll be well prepared for an essay exam when you can shape the material you've studied so that it is responsive to whatever kinds of reasonable questions you encounter on the exam. Reasonable questions? Yes, your instructor is more likely to offer you an opportunity to demonstrate your familiarity with and understanding of the text than to set a trap that, for instance, demands you discuss how Updike's work experience as an adolescent informs the story when no mention was ever made of that in class or in your reading.

You can also anticipate questions by considering the generic Questions for Responsive Reading and Writing about fiction (p. 44), poetry (p. 709), and drama (p. 1276) and the questions in Arguing about Literature (p. 2137), along with the Questions for Writing about an Author in Depth (p. 988). Not all of these questions will necessarily be relevant to every work that you read, but they cover a wide range of concerns that should allow you to organize your reading, note taking, and reviewing so that you're not taken by surprise during the exam.

Studying with a classmate or a small group from class can be a stimulating and fruitful means of discovering and organizing the major topics and themes of the course. This method of brainstorming can be useful not only for studying for exams but throughout the semester for understanding and reviewing course readings. And, finally, you needn't be shy about asking your instructor what types of questions might appear on the exam and how best to study for them. You may not get a very specific reply, but almost any information is more useful than none.

TYPES OF EXAMS

Closed-Book versus Open-Book Exams

Closed-book exams require more memorization and recall than open-book exams, which permit you to use your text and perhaps even your notes to answer questions. Dates, names, definitions, and other details play less of a role in an open-book exam. An open-book exam requires no less preparation, however, because you'll need to be intimately familiar with the texts and the major ideas, themes, and issues that you've studied in order to quickly and efficiently support your points with relevant, specific evidence. Since every student has the same advantage of having access to the text, preparation remains the key to answering the questions. Some students find open-book exams more difficult than closed-book tests because they risk spending too much time reading, scanning, and searching for material and not enough time writing a response that draws on the knowledge and understanding that their reading and studying has provided them. It's best to limit the time you allow yourself to review the text and notes so that you devote an adequate amount of time to getting your ideas on paper.

Essay Questions

Essay questions generally fall within one of the following categories. If you can recognize quickly what is being asked of you, you will be able to respond to them more efficiently.

1. **Explication** Explication calls for a line-by-line explanation of a passage of poetry or prose that considers, for example, diction, figures of speech, symbolism, sound, form, and theme in an effort to describe how language creates meaning. (For a more detailed discussion of explication, see p. 2147.)

2. **Definition** Defining a term and then applying it to a writer or work is a frequent exam exercise. Consider: "Define *romanticism*. To what extent can Hawthorne's *The Scarlet Letter* be regarded as a romantic story?" This sort of question requires that you first describe what constitutes a romantic literary work and then explain how *The Scarlet Letter* does (and doesn't) fit the bill.

3. **Analysis** An analytical question focuses on a particular part of a literary work. You might be asked, for example, to analyze the significance of images in Diane Ackerman's poem "A Fine, a Private Place" (p. 732). This sort of question requires you to discuss a specific element of the poem and also to explain how that element contributes to the poem's overall effect. (For a more detailed discussion of analysis, see pp. 2152–53.)

4. **Comparison and Contrast** Comparison and contrast calls for a discussion of the similarities and/or differences between writers, works, or elements of works — for example, "Compare and contrast Lengel's sensibilities

in John Updike's 'A & P' (p. 606) with John Wright's in Susan Glaspell's *Trifles* (p. 1238)." Despite the obvious differences in age and circumstances between these characters, a discussion of their responses to people — particularly to women — reveals some intriguing similarities. (For a more detailed discussion of comparison and contrast, see pp. 2157–59.)

5. **Discussion of a Critical Perspective** A brief quotation by a critic about a work is usually designed to stimulate a response that requires you to agree with, disagree with, or qualify a critic's perspective. Usually it is not important whether you agree or disagree with the critic; what matters is the quality of your argument. Think about how you might wrestle with this assessment of Robert Frost written by Lionel Trilling: "The manifest America of Mr. Frost's poems may be pastoral; the actual America is tragic." With some qualifications (surely not all of Frost's poems are "tragic") this could provide a useful way of talking about a poem such as "Mending Wall" (p. 1004).

6. **Imaginative Questions** To a degree every question requires imagination regardless of whether it's being asked or answered. However, some questions require more imaginative leaps to arrive at the center of an issue than others do. Consider, for example, the intellectual agility needed to respond to this question: "How do you think Dickens's Mr. Gradgrind from *Hard Times* and the narrator of Frost's 'Mending Wall' would respond to Sammy's character in Updike's 'A & P'?" As tricky as this triangulation of topics may seem, there is plenty to discuss concerning Gradgrind's literal-mindedness, the narrator's imagination, and Sammy's rejection of "policy." Or try a simpler but no less interesting version: "How do you think Frost would review Marvell's 'To His Coy Mistress' and Ackerman's 'A Fine, a Private Place'?" Such questions certainly require detailed, reasoned responses, but they also leave room for creativity and even wit.

STRATEGIES FOR WRITING ESSAY EXAMS

Your hands may be sweaty and your heart pounding as you begin the exam, but as long as you're prepared and you keep in mind some basic strategies for writing essay exams, you should be able to respond to questions with confidence and a genuine sense of accomplishment.

1. Before you begin writing, read through the entire exam. If there are choices to be made, make certain you know how many questions must be answered (only one out of four, not two). Note how many points each question is worth; spend more time on the two worth forty points each, and perhaps leave the twenty-point question for last.

2. Budget your time. If there are short-answer questions, do not allow them to absorb you so that you cannot do justice to the longer essay questions. Follow the suggested time limits for each question; if none is of-

fered, then create your own schedule in proportion to the points allotted for each question.

3. Depending on your own sensibilities, you may want to begin with the easiest or hardest questions. It doesn't really matter which you begin with as long as you pace yourself to avoid running out of time.

4. Be sure that you understand the question. Does it ask you to compare and/or contrast, define, analyze, explicate, or use some other approach? Determine how many elements there are to the question so that you don't inadvertently miss part of the question. Do not spend time copying the question.

5. Make some brief notes about how you plan to answer the question; even a simple list of what you'll need to cover can serve as a useful outline.

6. Address the question; avoid unnecessary summaries or irrelevant asides. Focus on the particular elements enumerated or implied by the question.

7. After beginning the essay, write a clear thesis that describes the major topics you will discuss: "*The Scarlet Letter* is typical of Hawthorne's concerns as a writer owing to its treatment of sin, guilt, isolation, and secrecy."

8. Support and illustrate your answer with specific, relevant references to the text. The more specificity — the more you demonstrate a familiarity with the text (rather than simply provide a plot summary) — the better the answer.

9. Don't overlap and repeat responses to questions; your instructor will recognize such padding. If two different questions are about the same work or writer, demonstrate the breadth and depth of your knowledge of the subject.

10. Allow time to proofread and to qualify and to add more supporting material if necessary. At this final stage, too, it's worth remembering that Mark Twain liked to remind his readers that the difference between the right word and the almost right word is the difference between lightning and a lightning bug.

Glossary of Literary Terms

Accent The emphasis, or STRESS, given a syllable in pronunciation. We say "*syl*-lable" not "syl*lable*," "*em*phasis" not "em*pha*sis." Accents can also be used to emphasize a particular word in a sentence: *Is* she con*tent* with the *contents* of the *yel*low *pack*age? See also METER.

Act A major division in the action of a play. The ends of acts are typically indicated by lowering the curtain or turning up the houselights. Playwrights frequently employ acts to accommodate changes in time, setting, characters onstage, or mood. In many full-length plays, acts are further divided into scenes, which often mark a point in the action when the location changes or when a new character enters. See also SCENE.

Allegory A narration or description usually restricted to a single meaning because its events, actions, characters, settings, and objects represent specific abstractions or ideas. Although the elements in an allegory may be interesting in themselves, the emphasis tends to be on what they ultimately mean. Characters may be given names such as Hope, Pride, Youth, and Charity; they have few if any personal qualities beyond their abstract meanings. These personifications are not symbols because, for instance, the meaning of a character named Charity is precisely that virtue. See also SYMBOL.

Alliteration The repetition of the same consonant sounds in a sequence of words, usually at the beginning of a word or stressed syllable: "*descending dew drops*"; "*luscious lemons*." Alliteration is based on the sounds of letters, rather than the spelling of words; for example, "*keen*" and "*car*" alliterate, but "*car*" and "*cite*" do not. Used sparingly, alliteration can intensify ideas by emphasizing key words, but when used too self-consciously, it can be distracting, even ridiculous, rather than effective. See also ASSONANCE, CONSONANCE.

Allusion A brief reference to a person, place, thing, event, or idea in history or literature. Allusions conjure up biblical authority, scenes from Shakespeare's plays, historic figures, wars, great love stories, and anything else that might enrich an author's work. Allusions imply reading and cultural experiences shared by the writer and reader, functioning as a kind of shorthand whereby the recalling of something outside the work supplies an emotional or intellectual context, such as a poem about current racial struggles calling up the memory of Abraham Lincoln.

Ambiguity Allows for two or more simultaneous interpretations of a word, phrase, action, or situation, all of which can be supported by the context of a work. Deliberate ambiguity can contribute to the effectiveness and richness of a work, for example, in the open-ended conclusion to Hawthorne's "Young Goodman Brown." However, unintentional ambiguity obscures meaning and can confuse readers.

Anagram A word or phrase made from the letters of another word or phrase, as "heart" is an anagram of "earth." Anagrams have often been considered merely an exercise of one's ingenuity, but sometimes writers use anagrams to conceal proper names or veiled messages, or to suggest important connections between words, as in "hated" and "death."

Anapestic meter See FOOT.

Antagonist The character, force, or collection of forces in fiction or drama that opposes the PROTAGONIST and gives rise to the conflict of the story; an opponent of the protagonist, such as Claudius in Shakespeare's play *Hamlet*. See also CHARACTER, CONFLICT.

Antihero A protagonist who has the opposite of most of the traditional attributes of a hero. He or she may be bewildered, ineffectual, deluded, or merely pathetic. Often what antiheroes learn, if they learn anything at all, is that the world isolates them in an existence devoid of God and absolute values. Yossarian from Joseph Heller's *Catch-22* is an example of an antihero. See also CHARACTER.

Apostrophe An address, either to someone who is absent and therefore cannot hear the speaker or to something nonhuman that cannot comprehend. Apostrophe often provides a speaker the opportunity to think aloud.

Approximate rhyme See RHYME.

Archetype A term used to describe universal symbols that evoke deep and sometimes unconscious responses in a reader. In literature, characters, images, and themes that symbolically embody universal meanings and basic human experiences, regardless of when or where they live, are considered archetypes. Common literary archetypes include stories of quests, initiations, scapegoats, descents to the underworld, and ascents to heaven. See also MYTHOLOGICAL CRITICISM.

Aside In drama, a speech directed to the audience that supposedly is not audible to the other characters onstage at the time. When Hamlet first appears onstage, for example, his aside "A little more than kin, and less than kind!" gives the audience a strong sense of his alienation from King Claudius. See also SOLILOQUY.

Assonance The repetition of internal vowel sounds in nearby words that do not end the same, for example, "asleep under a tree," or "each evening." Similar endings result in rhyme, as in "asleep in the deep." Assonance is a strong means of emphasizing important words in a line. See also ALLITERATION, CONSONANCE.

Ballad Traditionally, a ballad is a song, transmitted orally from generation to generation, that tells a story and that eventually is written down. As such, ballads usually cannot be traced to a particular author or group of authors. Typically, ballads are dramatic, condensed, and impersonal narratives, such as "Bonny Barbara Allan." A **literary ballad** is a narrative poem that is written in deliberate imitation of the language, form, and spirit of the traditional ballad, such as Keats's "La Belle Dame sans Merci." See also BALLAD STANZA, QUATRAIN.

Ballad stanza A four-line stanza, known as a QUATRAIN, consisting of alternating eight- and six-syllable lines. Usually only the second and fourth lines rhyme (an *abcb* pattern). Coleridge adopted the ballad stanza in "The Rime of the Ancient Mariner."

All in a hot and copper sky
The bloody Sun, at noon,
Right up above the mast did stand,
No bigger than the Moon.

See also BALLAD, QUATRAIN.

Biographical criticism An approach to literature which suggests that knowledge of the author's life experiences can aid in the understanding of his or her work. While biographical information can sometimes complicate one's interpretation of a work, and some formalist critics (such as the New Critics) disparage the use of the author's biography as a tool for textual interpretation, learning about the life of the author can often enrich a reader's appreciation for that author's work. See also CULTURAL CRITICISM, FORMALIST CRITICISM, NEW CRITICISM.

Blank verse Unrhymed iambic pentameter. Blank verse is the English verse form closest to the natural rhythms of English speech and therefore is the most common pattern found in traditional English narrative and dramatic poetry from Shakespeare to the early twentieth century. Shakespeare's plays use blank verse extensively. See also IAMBIC PENTAMETER.

Cacophony Language that is discordant and difficult to pronounce, such as this line from John Updike's "Player Piano": "never my numb plunker fumbles." Cacophony ("bad sound") may be unintentional in the writer's sense of music, or it may be used consciously for deliberate dramatic effect. See also EUPHONY.

Caesura A pause within a line of poetry that contributes to the rhythm of the line. A caesura can occur anywhere within a line and need not be indicated by punctuation. In scanning a line, caesuras are indicated by a double vertical line (‖). See also METER, RHYTHM, SCANSION.

Canon Those works generally considered by scholars, critics, and teachers to be the most important to read and study, which collectively constitute the "masterpieces" of literature. Since the 1960s, the traditional English and American literary canon, consisting mostly of works by white male writers, has been rapidly expanding to include many female writers and writers of varying ethnic backgrounds.

Carpe diem The Latin phrase meaning "seize the day." This is a very common literary theme, especially in lyric poetry, which emphasizes that life is short, time is fleeting, and that one should make the most of present pleasures. Robert Herrick's poem "To the Virgins, to Make Much of Time" employs the *carpe diem* theme.

Catharsis Meaning "purgation," *catharsis* describes the release of the emotions of pity and fear by the audience at the end of a tragedy. In his *Poetics,* Aristotle discusses the importance of catharsis. The audience faces the misfortunes of the protagonist, which elicit pity and compassion. Simultaneously, the audience also confronts the failure of the protagonist, thus receiving a frightening reminder of human limitations and frailties. Ultimately, however, both these negative emotions are purged, because the tragic protagonist's suffering is an affirmation of human values rather than a despairing denial of them. See also TRAGEDY.

Character, characterization A character is a person presented in a dramatic or narrative work, and characterization is the process by which a writer makes that character seem real to the reader. A **hero** or **heroine,** often called the PROTAGONIST, is the central character who engages the reader's interest and empathy. The ANTAGONIST is the character, force, or collection of forces that stands directly opposed to the protagonist and gives rise to the conflict of the story. A **static character** does not change throughout the work, and the reader's knowledge of that character does not grow, whereas a **dynamic character** undergoes some kind of change because of the action in the plot. A **flat character** embodies one or two qualities, ideas, or traits that can be readily described in a brief summary. They are not psychologically complex characters and therefore are readily accessible to readers. Some flat characters are recognized as **stock characters;** they embody stereotypes such as the "dumb blonde" or the "mean stepfather." They become types rather than individuals. **Round characters** are more complex than flat or stock characters, and often display the inconsistencies and internal conflicts found in most real people. They are more fully developed, and therefore are harder to summarize. Authors have two major methods of presenting characters: **showing** and **telling. Showing** allows the author to present a character talking and acting, and lets the reader infer what kind of person the character is. In **telling,** the author intervenes to describe and sometimes evaluate the character for the reader. Characters can be convincing whether they are presented by showing or by telling, as long as their actions are motivated. **Motivated action** by the characters occurs when the reader or audience is offered reasons for how the characters behave, what they say, and the decisions they make. **Plausible action** is action by a character in a story that seems reasonable, given the motivations presented. See also PLOT.

Chorus In Greek tragedies (especially those of Aeschylus and Sophocles), a group of people who serve mainly as commentators on the characters and events. They add to the audience's understanding of the play by expressing traditional moral, religious, and social attitudes. The role of the chorus in dramatic works evolved through the sixteenth century, and the chorus occasionally is still used by modern playwrights such as T. S. Eliot in *Murder in the Cathedral.* See also DRAMA.

Cliché An idea or expression that has become tired and trite from overuse, its freshness and clarity having worn off. Clichés often anesthetize readers, and are usually a sign of weak writing. See also SENTIMENTALITY, STOCK RESPONSES.

Climax See PLOT.

Closet drama A play that is written to be read rather than performed on-stage. In this kind of drama, literary art outweighs all other considerations. See also DRAMA.

Colloquial Refers to a type of informal diction that reflects casual, conversational language and often includes slang expressions. See also DICTION.

Comedy A work intended to interest, involve, and amuse the reader or audience, in which no terrible disaster occurs and that ends happily for the main characters. **High comedy** refers to verbal wit, such as puns, whereas **low comedy** is generally associated with physical action and is less intellectual. **Romantic comedy** involves a love affair that meets with various obstacles (like disapproving parents, mistaken identities, deceptions, or other sorts of misunderstandings) but overcomes them to end in a blissful union. Shakespeare's comedies, such as *A Midsummer Night's Dream*, are considered romantic comedies.

Comic relief A humorous scene or incident that alleviates tension in an otherwise serious work. In many instances these moments enhance the thematic significance of the story in addition to providing laughter. When Hamlet jokes with the gravediggers we laugh, but something hauntingly serious about the humor also intensifies our more serious emotions.

Conflict The struggle within the plot between opposing forces. The PROTAGONIST engages in the conflict with the ANTAGONIST, which may take the form of a character, society, nature, or an aspect of the protagonist's personality. See also CHARACTER, PLOT.

Connotation Associations and implications that go beyond the literal meaning of a word, which derive from how the word has been commonly used and the associations people make with it. For example, the word *eagle* connotes ideas of liberty and freedom that have little to do with the word's literal meaning. See also DENOTATION.

Consonance A common type of near rhyme that consists of identical consonant sounds preceded by different vowel sounds: *home, same; worth, breath.* See also RHYME.

Contextual symbol See SYMBOL.

Controlling metaphor See METAPHOR.

Convention A characteristic of a literary genre (often unrealistic) that is understood and accepted by audiences because it has come, through usage and time, to be recognized as a familiar technique. For example, the division of a play into acts and scenes is a dramatic convention, as are soliloquies and asides. FLASHBACKS and FORESHADOWING are examples of literary conventions.

Conventional symbol See SYMBOL.

Cosmic irony See IRONY.

Couplet Two consecutive lines of poetry that usually rhyme and have the same meter. A **heroic couplet** is a couplet written in rhymed iambic pentameter.

Crisis A turning point in the action of a story that has a powerful effect on the protagonist. Opposing forces come together decisively to lead to the climax of the plot. See also PLOT.

Cultural criticism An approach to literature that focuses on the historical as well as social, political, and economic contexts of a work. Popular culture — mass produced and consumed cultural artifacts ranging from advertising to popular fiction to television to rock music — is given equal emphasis with "high culture." Cultural critics use widely eclectic strategies such as new historicism, psychology, gender studies, and deconstructionism to analyze not only literary texts but everything from radio talk shows, comic strips, calendar art, commercials, to travel guides and baseball cards. See also HISTORICAL CRITICISM, MARXIST CRITICISM, POSTCOLONIAL CRITICISM.

Dactylic meter See FOOT.

Deconstructionism An approach to literature which suggests that literary works do not yield fixed, single meanings, because language can never say exactly what we intend it to mean. Deconstructionism seeks to destabilize meaning by examining the gaps and ambiguities of the language of a text. Deconstructionists pay close attention to language in order to discover and describe how a variety of possible readings are generated by the elements of a text. See also NEW CRITICISM.

Denotation The dictionary meaning of a word. See also CONNOTATION.

Dénouement A French term meaning "unraveling" or "unknotting," used to describe the resolution of the plot following the climax. See also PLOT, RESOLUTION.

Dialect A type of informational diction. Dialects are spoken by definable groups of people from a particular geographic region, economic group, or social class. Writers use dialect to contrast and express differences in educational, class, social, and regional backgrounds of their characters. See also DICTION.

Dialogue The verbal exchanges between characters. Dialogue makes the characters seem real to the reader or audience by revealing firsthand their thoughts, responses, and emotional states. See also DICTION.

Diction A writer's choice of words, phrases, sentence structures, and figurative language, which combine to help create meaning. **Formal diction** consists of a dignified, impersonal, and elevated use of language; it follows the rules of syntax exactly and is often characterized by complex words and lofty tone. **Middle diction** maintains correct language usage, but is less elevated than formal diction; it reflects the way most educated people speak. **Informal diction** represents the plain language of everyday use, and often includes idiomatic expressions, slang, contractions, and many simple, common words. **Poetic diction** refers to the way poets sometimes employ an elevated diction that deviates significantly from the common speech and writing of their time, choosing words for their supposedly inherent poetic qualities. Since the eighteenth century, however, poets have been incorporating all kinds of diction in their work and so there is no longer an automatic distinction between the language of a poet and the language of everyday speech. See also DIALECT.

Didactic poetry Poetry designed to teach an ethical, moral, or religious lesson. Michael Wigglesworth's Puritan poem *Day of Doom* is an example of didactic poetry.

Doggerel A derogatory term used to describe poetry whose subject is trite and whose rhythm and sounds are monotonously heavy-handed.

Drama Derived from the Greek word *dram*, meaning "to do" or "to perform," the term *drama* may refer to a single play, a group of plays ("Jacobean drama"), or to all plays ("world drama"). Drama is designed for performance in a theater; actors take on the roles of characters, perform indicated actions, and speak the dialogue written in the script. **Play** is a general term for a work of dramatic literature, and a **playwright** is a writer who makes plays.

Dramatic irony See IRONY.

Dramatic monologue A type of lyric poem in which a character (the speaker) addresses a distinct but silent audience imagined to be present in the poem in such a way as to reveal a dramatic situation and, often unintentionally, some aspect of his or her temperament or personality. See also LYRIC.

Dynamic character See CHARACTER.

Editorial omniscience See NARRATOR.

Electra complex The female version of the Oedipus complex. *Electra complex* is a term used to describe the psychological conflict of a daughter's unconscious rivalry with her mother for her father's attention. The name comes from the Greek legend of Electra, who avenged the death of her father, Agamemnon, by plotting the death of her mother. See also OEDIPUS COMPLEX, PSYCHOLOGICAL CRITICISM.

Elegy A mournful, contemplative lyric poem written to commemorate someone who is dead, often ending in a consolation. Tennyson's *In Memoriam*, written on the death of Arthur Hallam, is an elegy. *Elegy* may also refer to a serious meditative poem produced to express the speaker's melancholy thoughts. See also LYRIC.

End rhyme See RHYME.

End-stopped line A poetic line that has a pause at the end. End-stopped lines reflect normal speech patterns and are often marked by punctuation. The first line of Keats's "Endymion" is an example of an end-stopped line; the natural pause coincides with the end of the line, and is marked by a period:

A thing of beauty is a joy forever.

English sonnet See SONNET.

Enjambment In poetry, when one line ends without a pause and continues into the next line for its meaning. This is also called a **run-on line.** The transition between the first two lines of Wordsworth's poem "My Heart Leaps Up" demonstrates enjambment:

My heart leaps up when I behold
A rainbow in the sky:

Envoy See SESTINA.

Epic A long narrative poem, told in a formal, elevated style, that focuses on a serious subject and chronicles heroic deeds and events important to a culture or nation. Milton's *Paradise Lost*, which attempts to "justify the ways of God to man," is an epic. See also NARRATIVE POEM.

Epigram A brief, pointed, and witty poem that usually makes a satiric or humorous point. Epigrams are most often written in couplets, but take no prescribed form.

Epiphany In fiction, when a character suddenly experiences a deep realization about himself or herself; a truth which is grasped in an ordinary rather than a melodramatic moment.

Escape literature See FORMULA LITERATURE.

Euphony *Euphony* ("good sound") refers to language that is smooth and musically pleasant to the ear. See also CACOPHONY.

Exact rhyme See RHYME.

Exposition A narrative device, often used at the beginning of a work, that provides necessary background information about the characters and their circumstances. Exposition explains what has gone on before, the relationships between characters, the development of a theme, and the introduction of a conflict. See also FLASHBACK.

Extended metaphor See METAPHOR.

Eye rhyme See RHYME.

Falling action See PLOT.

Falling meter See METER.

Farce A form of humor based on exaggerated, improbable incongruities. Farce involves rapid shifts in action and emotion, as well as slapstick comedy and extravagant dialogue. Malvolio, in Shakespeare's *Twelfth Night*, is a farcical character.

Feminine rhyme See RHYME.

Feminist criticism An approach to literature that seeks to correct or supplement what may be regarded as a predominantly male-dominated critical perspective with a feminist consciousness. Feminist criticism places literature in a social context and uses a broad range of disciplines, including history, sociology, psychology, and linguistics, to provide a perspective sensitive to feminist issues. Feminist theories also attempt to understand representation from a woman's point of view and to explain women's writing strategies as specific to their social conditions. See also GAY AND LESBIAN CRITICISM, GENDER CRITICISM, SOCIOLOGICAL CRITICISM.

Figures of speech Ways of using language that deviate from the literal, denotative meanings of words in order to suggest additional meanings or effects. Figures of speech say one thing in terms of something else, such as when an eager funeral director is described as a vulture. See also METAPHOR, SIMILE.

First-person narrator See NARRATOR.

Fixed form A poem that may be categorized by the pattern of its lines, meter, rhythm, or stanzas. A sonnet is a fixed form of poetry because by definition it must have fourteen lines. Other fixed forms include LIMERICK, SESTINA, and VILLANELLE. However, poems written in a fixed form may not always fit into categories precisely, because writers sometimes vary traditional forms to create innovative effects. See also OPEN FORM.

Flashback A narrated scene that marks a break in the narrative in order to inform the reader or audience member about events that took place before the opening scene of a work. See also EXPOSITION.

Flat character See CHARACTER.

Foil A character in a work whose behavior and values contrast with those of another character in order to highlight the distinctive temperament of that character (usually the protagonist). In Shakespeare's *Hamlet*, Laertes acts as a foil to Hamlet, because his willingness to act underscores Hamlet's inability to do so.

Foot The metrical unit by which a line of poetry is measured. A foot usually consists of one stressed and one or two unstressed syllables. An *iambic foot*, which consists of one unstressed syllable followed by one stressed syllable ("away"), is the most common metrical foot in English poetry. A *trochaic foot* consists of one stressed syllable followed by an unstressed syllable ("lovely"). An *anapestic foot* is two unstressed syllables followed by one stressed one ("understand"). A *dactylic foot* is one stressed syllable followed by two unstressed ones ("desperate"). A *spondee* is a foot consisting of two stressed syllables ("dead set"), but is not a sustained metrical foot and is used mainly for variety or emphasis. See also IAMBIC PENTAMETER, LINE, METER.

Foreshadowing The introduction early in a story of verbal and dramatic hints that suggest what is to come later.

Form The overall structure or shape of a work, which frequently follows an established design. Forms may refer to a literary type (narrative form, short story form) or to patterns of meter, lines, and rhymes (stanza form, verse form). See also FIXED FORM, OPEN FORM.

Formal diction See DICTION.

Formalist criticism An approach to literature that focuses on the formal elements of a work, such as its language, structure, and tone. Formalist critics offer intense examinations of the relationship between form and meaning in a work, emphasizing the subtle complexity in how a work is arranged. Formalists pay special attention to diction, irony, paradox, metaphor, and symbol, as well as larger elements such as plot, characterization, and narrative technique. Formalist critics read literature as an independent work of art rather than as a reflection of the author's state of mind or as a representation of a moment in history. Therefore, anything outside of the work, including historical influences and authorial intent, is generally not examined by formalist critics. See also NEW CRITICISM.

Formula literature Often characterized as "escape literature," formula litera-ture follows a pattern of conventional reader expectations. Romance novels, westerns, science fiction, and detective stories are all examples of formula literature; while the details of individual stories vary, the basic ingredients of each kind of story are the same. Formula literature offers happy endings (the hero "gets the girl," the detective cracks the case), entertains wide audi-ences, and sells tremendously well.

Found poem An unintentional poem discovered in a nonpoetic context, such as a conversation, news story, or advertisement. Found poems serve as re-minders that everyday language often contains what can be considered po-etry, or that poetry is definable as any text read as a poem.

Free verse Also called OPEN FORM poetry, free verse refers to poems character-ized by their nonconformity to established patterns of meter, rhyme, and stanza. Free verse uses elements such as speech patterns, grammar, empha-sis, and breath pauses to decide line breaks, and usually does not rhyme. See OPEN FORM.

Gay and lesbian criticism An approach to literature that focuses on how homosexuals are represented in literature, how they read literature, and whether sexuality, as well as gender, is culturally constructed or innate. See also FEMINIST CRITICISM, GENDER CRITICISM.

Gender criticism An approach to literature that explores how ideas about men and women — what is masculine and feminine — can be regarded as so-cially constructed by particular cultures. Gender criticism expands cate-gories and definitions of what is masculine or feminine and tends to regard sexuality as more complex than merely masculine or feminine, heterosexual or homosexual. See also FEMINIST CRITICISM, GAY AND LESBIAN CRITICISM.

Genre A French word meaning kind or type. The major genres in literature are poetry, fiction, drama, and essays. Genre can also refer to more specific types of literature such as comedy, tragedy, epic poetry, or science fiction.

Haiku A style of lyric poetry borrowed from the Japanese that typically pre-sents an intense emotion or vivid image of nature, which, traditionally, is designed to lead to a spiritual insight. Haiku is a fixed poetic form, consist-ing of seventeen syllables organized into three unrhymed lines of five, seven, and five syllables. Today, however, many poets vary the syllabic count in their haiku. See also FIXED FORM.

Hamartia A term coined by Aristotle to describe "some error or frailty" that brings about misfortune for a tragic hero. The concept of hamartia is closely related to that of the tragic flaw: both lead to the downfall of the protagonist in a tragedy. Hamartia may be interpreted as an internal weak-ness in a character (like greed or passion or HUBRIS); however, it may also refer to a mistake that a character makes that is based not on a personal fail-ure, but on circumstances outside the protagonist's personality and con-trol. See also TRAGEDY.

Hero, heroine See CHARACTER.

Heroic couplet See COUPLET.

High comedy See COMEDY.

Historical criticism An approach to literature that uses history as a means of understanding a literary work more clearly. Such criticism moves beyond both the facts of an author's personal life and the text itself in order to examine the social and intellectual currents in which the author composed the work. See also CULTURAL CRITICISM, MARXIST CRITICISM, NEW HISTORICISM, POSTCOLONIAL CRITICISM.

Hubris or Hybris Excessive pride or self-confidence that leads a protagonist to disregard a divine warning or to violate an important moral law. In tragedies, hubris is a very common form of hamartia. See also HAMARTIA, TRAGEDY.

Hyperbole A boldly exaggerated statement that adds emphasis without intending to be literally true, as in the statement "He ate everything in the house." Hyperbole (also called **overstatement**) may be used for serious, comic, or ironic effect. See also FIGURES OF SPEECH.

Iambic meter See FOOT.

Iambic pentameter A metrical pattern in poetry which consists of five iambic feet per line. (An iamb, or iambic foot, consists of one unstressed syllable followed by a stressed syllable.) See also FOOT, METER.

Image A word, phrase, or figure of speech (especially a SIMILE or a METAPHOR) that addresses the senses, suggesting mental pictures of sights, sounds, smells, tastes, feelings, or actions. Images offer sensory impressions to the reader and also convey emotions and moods through their verbal pictures. See also FIGURES OF SPEECH.

Implied metaphor See METAPHOR.

In medias res See PLOT.

Informal diction See DICTION.

Internal rhyme See RHYME.

Irony A literary device that uses contradictory statements or situations to reveal a reality different from what appears to be true. It is ironic for a firehouse to burn down, or for a police station to be burglarized. **Verbal irony** is a figure of speech that occurs when a person says one thing but means the opposite. **Sarcasm** is a strong form of verbal irony that is calculated to hurt someone through, for example, false praise. **Dramatic irony** creates a discrepancy between what a character believes or says and what the reader or audience member knows to be true. **Tragic irony** is a form of dramatic irony found in tragedies such as *Oedipus the King,* in which Oedipus searches for the person responsible for the plague that ravishes his city and ironically ends up hunting himself. **Situational irony** exists when there is an incongruity between what is expected to happen and what actually happens due to forces beyond human comprehension or control. The suicide of the seemingly successful main character in Edwin Arlington Robinson's poem "Richard Cory" is an example of situational irony. **Cosmic irony** occurs when a writer uses God, destiny, or fate to dash the hopes and expectations of a character or of humankind in general. In cosmic irony, a discrepancy exists between what a character aspires to and what universal forces provide. Stephen Crane's poem "A Man Said to the Universe" is a good example of cosmic irony, because the universe acknowledges no obligation to the man's assertion of his own existence.

Italian sonnet See SONNET.

Limerick A light, humorous style of fixed form poetry. Its usual form consists of five lines with the rhyme scheme *aabba*; lines 1, 2, and 5 contain three feet, while lines 3 and 4 usually contain two feet. Limericks range in subject matter from the silly to the obscene, and since Edward Lear popularized them in the nineteenth century, children and adults have enjoyed these comic poems. See also FIXED FORM.

Limited omniscience See NARRATOR.

Line A sequence of words printed as a separate entity on the page. In poetry, lines are usually measured by the number of feet they contain. The names for various line lengths are as follows:

monometer: one foot	pentameter: five feet
dimeter: two feet	hexameter: six feet
trimeter: three feet	heptameter: seven feet
tetrameter: four feet	octameter: eight feet

The number of feet in a line, coupled with the name of the foot, describes the metrical qualities of that line. See also END-STOPPED LINE, ENJAMBMENT, FOOT, METER.

Literary ballad See BALLAD.

Literary symbol See SYMBOL.

Low comedy See COMEDY.

Lyric A type of brief poem that expresses the personal emotions and thoughts of a single speaker. It is important to realize, however, that although the lyric is uttered in the first person, the speaker is not necessarily the poet. There are many varieties of lyric poetry, including the DRAMATIC MONOLOGUE, ELEGY, HAIKU, ODE, and SONNET forms.

Marxist criticism An approach to literature that focuses on the ideological content of a work — its explicit and implicit assumptions and values about matters such as culture, race, class, and power. Marxist criticism, based largely on the writings of Karl Marx, typically aims at not only revealing and clarifying ideological issues but also correcting social injustices. Some Marxist critics use literature to describe the competing socioeconomic interests that too often advance capitalist interests such as money and power rather than socialist interests such as morality and justice. They argue that literature and literary criticism are essentially political because they either challenge or support economic oppression. Because of this strong emphasis on the political aspects of texts, Marxist criticism focuses more on the content and themes of literature than on its form. See also CULTURAL CRITICISM, HISTORICAL CRITICISM, SOCIOLOGICAL CRITICISM.

Masculine rhyme See RHYME.

Melodrama A term applied to any literary work that relies on implausible events and sensational action for its effect. The conflicts in melodramas typically arise out of plot rather than characterization; often a virtuous individual must somehow confront and overcome a wicked oppressor. Usually, a melodramatic story ends happily, with the protagonist defeating the antagonist at the last possible moment. Thus, melodramas entertain the reader or audience with exciting action while still conforming to a traditional sense of justice. See also SENTIMENTALITY.

Metaphor A metaphor is a figure of speech that makes a comparison between two unlike things, without using the word *like* or *as*. Metaphors assert the identity of dissimilar things, as when Macbeth asserts that life *is* a "brief candle." Metaphors can be subtle and powerful, and can transform people, places, objects, and ideas into whatever the writer imagines them to be. An **implied metaphor** is a more subtle comparison; the terms being compared are not so specifically explained. For example, to describe a stubborn man unwilling to leave, one could say that he was "a mule standing his ground." This is a fairly explicit metaphor; the man is being compared to a mule. But to say that the man "brayed his refusal to leave" is to create an implied metaphor, because the subject (the man) is never overtly identified as a mule. Braying is associated with the mule, a notoriously stubborn creature, and so the comparison between the stubborn man and the mule is sustained. Implied metaphors can slip by inattentive readers who are not sensitive to such carefully chosen, highly concentrated language. An **extended metaphor** is a sustained comparison in which part or all of a poem consists of a series of related metaphors. Robert Francis's poem "Catch" relies on an extended metaphor that compares poetry to playing catch. A **controlling metaphor** runs through an entire work and determines the form or nature of that work. The controlling metaphor in Anne Bradstreet's poem "The Author to Her Book" likens her book to a child. **Synecdoche** is a kind of metaphor in which a part of something is used to signify the whole, as when a gossip is called a "wagging tongue," or when ten ships are called "ten sails." Sometimes, synecdoche refers to the whole being used to signify the part, as in the phrase "Boston won the baseball game." Clearly, the entire city of Boston did not participate in the game; the whole of Boston is being used to signify the individuals who played and won the game. **Metonymy** is a type of metaphor in which something closely associated with a subject is substituted for it. In this way, we speak of the "silver screen" to mean motion pictures, "the crown" to stand for the king, "the White House" to stand for the activities of the president. See also FIGURES OF SPEECH, PERSONIFICATION, SIMILE.

Meter When a rhythmic pattern of stresses recurs in a poem, it is called *meter*. Metrical patterns are determined by the type and number of feet in a line of verse; combining the name of a line length with the name of a foot concisely describes the meter of the line. **Rising meter** refers to metrical feet which move from unstressed to stressed sounds, such as the iambic foot and the anapestic foot. **Falling meter** refers to metrical feet which move from stressed to unstressed sounds, such as the trochaic foot and the dactylic foot. See also ACCENT, FOOT, IAMBIC PENTAMETER, LINE.

Metonymy See METAPHOR.

Middle diction See DICTION.

Motivated action See CHARACTER.

Mythological criticism An approach to literature that seeks to identify what in a work creates deep universal responses in readers, by paying close attention to the hopes, fears, and expectations of entire cultures. Mythological critics (sometimes called *archetypal critics*) look for underlying, recurrent patterns in literature that reveal universal meanings and basic human experiences for readers regardless of when and where they live. These critics attempt to explain how archetypes (the characters, images, and themes that symbolically embody universal meanings and experiences) are embodied in literary works in order to make larger connections that explain a particular work's lasting appeal. Mythological critics may specialize in areas such as classical literature, philology, anthropology, psychology, and cultural history, but they all emphasize the assumptions and values of various cultures. See also ARCHETYPE.

Naive narrator See NARRATOR.

Narrative poem A poem that tells a story. A narrative poem may be short or long, and the story it relates may be simple or complex. See also BALLAD, EPIC.

Narrator The voice of the person telling the story, not to be confused with the author's voice. With a **first-person narrator,** the *I* in the story presents the point of view of only one character. The reader is restricted to the perceptions, thoughts, and feelings of that single character. For example, in Melville's "Bartleby, the Scrivener," the lawyer is the first-person narrator of the story. First-person narrators can play either a major or a minor role in the story they are telling. An **unreliable narrator** reveals an interpretation of events that is somehow different from the author's own interpretation of those events. Often, the unreliable narrator's perception of plot, characters, and setting becomes the actual subject of the story, as in Melville's "Bartleby, the Scrivener." Narrators can be unreliable for a number of reasons: they might lack self-knowledge (like Melville's lawyer), they might be inexperienced, they might even be insane. **Naive narrators** are usually characterized by youthful innocence, such as Mark Twain's Huck Finn or J. D. Salinger's Holden Caulfield. An **omniscient narrator** is an all-knowing narrator who is not a character in the story and who can move from place to place and pass back and forth through time, slipping into and out of characters as no human being possibly could in real life. Omniscient narrators can report the thoughts and feelings of the characters, as well as their words and actions. The narrator of *The Scarlet Letter* is an omniscient narrator. **Editorial omniscience** refers to an intrusion by the narrator in order to evaluate a character for a reader, as when the narrator of *The Scarlet Letter* describes Hester's relationship to the Puritan community. Narration that allows the characters' actions and thoughts to speak for themselves is called **neutral omniscience.** Most modern writers use neutral omniscience so that readers can reach their own conclusions. **Limited omniscience** occurs when an author restricts a narrator to the single perspective of either a major or minor character. The way people, places, and events appear to that character is the way they appear to the reader. Sometimes a limited omniscient narrator can see into more than one character, particularly in a work that focuses on two characters alternately from one chapter to the next. Short stories, however, are frequently limited to a single character's point of view. See also PERSONA, POINT OF VIEW, STREAM-OF-CONSCIOUSNESS TECHNIQUE.

Near rhyme See RHYME.

Neutral omniscience See NARRATOR.

New Criticism An approach to literature made popular between the 1940s and the 1960s that evolved out of formalist criticism. New Critics suggest that detailed analysis of the language of a literary text can uncover important layers of meaning in that work. New Criticism consciously downplays the historical influences, authorial intentions, and social contexts that surround texts in order to focus on explication — extremely close textual analysis. Critics such as John Crowe Ransom, I. A. Richards, and Robert Penn Warren are commonly associated with New Criticism. See also FORMALIST CRITICISM.

New historicism An approach to literature that emphasizes the interaction between the historic context of the work and a modern reader's understanding and interpretation of the work. New historicists attempt to describe the culture of a period by reading many different kinds of texts and paying close attention to many different dimensions of a culture, including political, economic, social, and aesthetic concerns. They regard texts not simply as a reflection of the culture that produced them but also as productive of that culture playing an active role in the social and political conflicts of an age. New historicism acknowledges and then explores various versions of "history," sensitizing us to the fact that the history on which we choose to focus is colored by being reconstructed from our present circumstances. See also HISTORICAL CRITICISM.

Objective point of view See POINT OF VIEW.

Octave A poetic stanza of eight lines, usually forming one part of a sonnet. See also SONNET, STANZA.

Ode A relatively lengthy lyric poem that often expresses lofty emotions in a dignified style. Odes are characterized by a serious topic, such as truth, art, freedom, justice, or the meaning of life; their tone tends to be formal. There is no prescribed pattern that defines an ode; some odes repeat the same pattern in each stanza, while others introduce a new pattern in each stanza. See also LYRIC.

Oedipus complex A Freudian term derived from Sophocles' tragedy *Oedipus the King*. It describes a psychological complex that is predicated on a boy's unconscious rivalry with his father for his mother's love and his desire to eliminate his father in order to take his father's place with his mother. The female equivalent of this complex is called the **Electra complex.** See also ELECTRA COMPLEX, PSYCHOLOGICAL CRITICISM.

Off rhyme See RHYME.

Omniscient narrator See NARRATOR.

One-act play A play that takes place in a single location and unfolds as one continuous action. The characters in a one-act play are presented economically and the action is sharply focused. See also DRAMA.

Onomatopoeia A term referring to the use of a word that resembles the sound it denotes. *Buzz, rattle, bang,* and *sizzle* all reflect onomatopoeia. Onomatopoeia can also consist of more than one word; writers sometimes create lines or whole passages in which the sound of the words helps to convey their meanings.

Open form Sometimes called "free verse," open form poetry does not conform to established patterns of METER, RHYME, and STANZA. Such poetry derives its rhythmic qualities from the repetition of words, phrases, or grammatical structures, the arrangement of words on the printed page, or by some other means. The poet E. E. Cummings wrote open form poetry; his poems do not have measurable meters, but they do have rhythm. See also FIXED FORM.

Organic form Refers to works whose formal characteristics are not rigidly predetermined but follow the movement of thought or emotion being expressed. Such works are said to grow like living organisms, following their own individual patterns rather than external fixed rules that govern, for example, the form of a SONNET.

Overstatement See HYPERBOLE.

Oxymoron A condensed form of paradox in which two contradictory words are used together, as in "sweet sorrow" or "original copy." See also PARADOX.

Paradox A statement that initially appears to be contradictory but then, on closer inspection, turns out to make sense. For example, John Donne ends his sonnet "Death, Be Not Proud" with the paradoxical statement "Death, thou shalt die." To solve the paradox, it is necessary to discover the sense that underlies the statement. Paradox is useful in poetry because it arrests a reader's attention by its seemingly stubborn refusal to make sense.

Paraphrase A prose restatement of the central ideas of a poem, in your own language.

Parody A humorous imitation of another, usually serious, work. It can take any fixed or open form, because parodists imitate the tone, language, and shape of the original in order to deflate the subject matter, making the original work seem absurd. Anthony Hecht's poem "Dover Bitch" is a famous parody of Matthew Arnold's well-known "Dover Beach." Parody may also be used as a form of literary criticism to expose the defects in a work. But sometimes parody becomes an affectionate acknowledgment that a well-known work has become both institutionalized in our culture and fair game for some fun. For example, Peter De Vries's "To His Importunate Mistress" gently mocks Andrew Marvell's "To His Coy Mistress."

Persona Literally, a *persona* is a mask. In literature, a *persona* is a speaker created by a writer to tell a story or to speak in a poem. A persona is not a character in a story or narrative, nor does a persona necessarily directly reflect the author's personal voice. A persona is a separate self, created by and distinct from the author, through which he or she speaks. See also NARRATOR.

Personification A form of metaphor in which human characteristics are attributed to nonhuman things. Personification offers the writer a way to give the world life and motion by assigning familiar human behaviors and emotions to animals, inanimate objects, and abstract ideas. For example, in Keats's "Ode on a Grecian Urn," the speaker refers to the urn as an "unravished bride of quietness." See also METAPHOR.

Petrarchan sonnet See SONNET.

Picture poem A type of open form poetry in which the poet arranges the lines of the poem so as to create a particular shape on the page. The shape of the poem embodies its subject; the poem becomes a picture of what the poem is describing. Michael McFee's "In Medias Res" is an example of a picture poem. See also OPEN FORM.

Plausible action See CHARACTER.

Play See DRAMA.

Playwright See DRAMA.

Plot An author's selection and arrangement of incidents in a story to shape the action and give the story a particular focus. Discussions of plot include not just what happens, but also how and why things happen the way they do. Stories that are written in a **pyramidal pattern** divide the plot into three essential parts. The first part is the **rising action,** in which complication creates some sort of conflict for the protagonist. The second part is the **climax,** the moment of greatest emotional tension in a narrative, usually marking a turning point in the plot at which the rising action reverses to become the falling action. The third part, the **falling action** (or RESOLUTION) is characterized by diminishing tensions and the resolution of the plot's conflicts and complications. *In medias res* is a term used to describe the common strategy of beginning a story in the middle of the action. In this type of plot, we enter the story on the verge of some important moment. See also CHARACTER, CRISIS, RESOLUTION, SUBPLOT.

Poetic diction See DICTION.

Point of view Refers to who tells us a story and how it is told. What we know and how we feel about the events in a work are shaped by the author's choice of point of view. The teller of the story, the narrator, inevitably affects our understanding of the characters' actions by filtering what is told through his or her own perspective. The various points of view that writers draw upon can be grouped into two broad categories: (1) the third-person narrator uses *he, she,* or *they* to tell the story and does not participate in the action; and (2) the first-person narrator uses *I* and is a major or minor participant in the action. In addition, a second-person narrator, *you,* is also possible, but is rarely used because of the awkwardness of thrusting the reader into the story, as in "You are minding your own business on a park bench when a drunk steps out and demands your lunch bag." An **objective point of view** employs a third-person narrator who does not see into the mind of any character. From this detached and impersonal perspective, the narrator reports action and dialogue without telling us directly what the characters think and feel. Since no analysis or interpretation is provided by the narrator, this point of view places a premium on dialogue, actions, and details to reveal character to the reader. See also NARRATOR, STREAM-OF-CONSCIOUSNESS TECHNIQUE.

Postcolonial criticism An approach to literature that focuses on the study of cultural behavior and expression in relationship to the colonized world. Postcolonial criticism refers to the analysis of literary works written by writers from countries and cultures that at one time have been controlled by colonizing powers — such as Indian writers during or after British colonial rule. Postcolonial criticism also refers to the analysis of literary works written about colonial cultures by writers from the colonizing country. Many of these kinds of analyses point out how writers from colonial powers sometimes misrepresent colonized cultures by reflecting more their own values. See also CULTURAL CRITICISM, HISTORICAL CRITICISM, MARXIST CRITICISM.

Problem play Popularized by Henrik Ibsen, a problem play is a type of drama that presents a social issue in order to awaken the audience to it. These plays usually reject romantic plots in favor of holding up a mirror that reflects not simply what the audience wants to see but what the playwright sees in them. Often, a problem play will propose a solution to the problem that does not coincide with prevailing opinion. The term is also used to refer to certain Shakespeare plays that do not fit the categories of tragedy, comedy, or romance. See also DRAMA.

Prologue The opening speech or dialogue of a play, especially a classic Greek play, that usually gives the exposition necessary to follow the subsequent action. Today the term also refers to the introduction to any literary work. See also DRAMA, EXPOSITION.

Prose poem A kind of open form poetry that is printed as prose and represents the most clear opposite of fixed form poetry. Prose poems are densely compact and often make use of striking imagery and figures of speech. See also FIXED FORM, OPEN FORM.

Prosody The overall metrical structure of a poem. See also METER.

Protagonist The main character of a narrative; its central character who engages the reader's interest and empathy. See also CHARACTER.

Psychological criticism An approach to literature that draws upon psychoanalytic theories, especially those of Sigmund Freud or Jacques Lacan to understand more fully the text, the writer, and the reader. The basis of this approach is the idea of the existence of a human unconscious — those impulses, desires, and feelings about which a person is unaware but which influence emotions and behavior. Critics use psychological approaches to explore the motivations of characters and the symbolic meanings of events, while biographers speculate about a writer's own motivations — conscious or unconscious — in a literary work. Psychological approaches are also used to describe and analyze the reader's personal responses to a text.

Pun A play on words that relies on a word's having more than one meaning or sounding like another word. Shakespeare and other writers use puns extensively, for serious and comic purposes; in *Romeo and Juliet* (III.i.101), the dying Mercutio puns, "Ask for me tomorrow and you shall find me a grave man." Puns have serious literary uses, but since the eighteenth century, puns have been used almost purely for humorous effect. See also COMEDY.

Pyramidal pattern See PLOT.

Quatrain A four-line stanza. Quatrains are the most common stanzaic form in the English language; they can have various meters and rhyme schemes. See also METER, RHYME, STANZA.

Reader-response criticism An approach to literature that focuses on the reader rather than the work itself, by attempting to describe what goes on in the reader's mind during the reading of a text. Hence, the consciousness of the reader — produced by reading the work — is the actual subject of reader-response criticism. These critics are not after a "correct" reading of the text or what the author presumably intended; instead, they are interested in the reader's individual experience with the text. Thus, there is no single definitive reading of a work, because readers create rather than discover absolute meanings in texts. However, this approach is not a rationale for mistaken or bizarre readings, but an exploration of the possibilities for a plurality of readings. This kind of strategy calls attention to how we read and what influences our readings, and what that reveals about ourselves.

Recognition The moment in a story when previously unknown or withheld information is revealed to the protagonist, resulting in the discovery of the truth of his or her situation and, usually, a decisive change in course for that character. In *Oedipus the King,* the moment of recognition comes when Oedipus finally realizes that he has killed his father and married his mother.

Resolution The conclusion of a plot's conflicts and complications. The resolution, also known as the **falling action,** follows the climax in the plot. See also DÉNOUEMENT, PLOT.

Revenge tragedy See TRAGEDY.

Reversal The point in a story when the protagonist's fortunes turn in an unexpected direction. See also PLOT.

Rhyme The repetition of identical or similar concluding syllables in different words, most often at the ends of lines. Rhyme is predominantly a function of sound rather than spelling; thus, words that end with the same vowel sounds rhyme, for instance, *day, prey, bouquet, weigh,* and words with the same consonant ending rhyme, for instance *vain, feign, rein, lane.* Words do not have to be spelled the same way or look alike to rhyme. In fact, words may look alike but not rhyme at all. This is called **eye rhyme,** as with *bough* and *cough,* or *brow* and *blow.*

End rhyme is the most common form of rhyme in poetry; the rhyme comes at the end of the lines.

It runs through the reeds
    And away it proceeds,
Through meadow and glade,
    In sun and in shade.

The **rhyme scheme** of a poem describes the pattern of end rhymes. Rhyme schemes are mapped out by noting patterns of rhyme with small letters: the first rhyme sound is designated *a,* the second becomes *b,* the third *c,* and so on. Thus, the rhyme scheme of the stanza above is *aabb.* **Internal rhyme** places at least one of the rhymed words within the line, as in "Dividing and gliding and sliding" or "In mist or cloud, on mast or shroud." **Masculine rhyme** describes the rhyming of single-syllable words, such as *grade* or *shade*. Masculine rhyme also occurs when rhyming words of more than one syllable, when the same sound occurs in a final stressed syllable, as in *defend* and *contend, betray* and *away*. **Feminine rhyme** consists of a rhymed stressed syllable followed by one or more identical unstressed syllables, as in *butter, clutter; gratitude, attitude; quivering, shivering*. All the examples so far have illustrated **exact rhymes**, because they share the same stressed vowel sounds as well as sharing sounds that follow the vowel. In **near rhyme** (also called **off rhyme**, **slant rhyme**, and **approximate rhyme**), the sounds are almost but not exactly alike. A common form of near rhyme is CONSONANCE, which consists of identical consonant sounds preceded by different vowel sounds: *home, same; worth, breath*.

Rhyme scheme See RHYME.

Rhythm A term used to refer to the recurrence of stressed and unstressed sounds in poetry. Depending on how sounds are arranged, the rhythm of a poem may be fast or slow, choppy or smooth. Poets use rhythm to create pleasurable sound patterns and to reinforce meanings. Rhythm in prose arises from pattern repetitions of sounds and pauses that create looser rhythmic effects. See also METER.

Rising action See PLOT.

Rising meter See METER.

Romantic comedy See COMEDY.

Round character See CHARACTER.

Run-on line See ENJAMBMENT.

Sarcasm See IRONY.

Satire The literary art of ridiculing a folly or vice in order to expose or correct it. The object of satire is usually some human frailty; people, institutions, ideas, and things are all fair game for satirists. Satire evokes attitudes of amusement, contempt, scorn, or indignation toward its faulty subject in the hope of somehow improving it. See also IRONY, PARODY.

Scansion The process of measuring the stresses in a line of verse in order to determine the metrical pattern of the line. See also LINE, METER.

Scene In drama, a scene is a subdivision of an ACT. In modern plays, scenes usually consist of units of action in which there are no changes in the setting or breaks in the continuity of time. According to traditional conventions, a scene changes when the location of the action shifts or when a new character enters. See also ACT, CONVENTION, DRAMA.

Script The written text of a play, which includes the dialogue between characters, stage directions, and often other expository information. See also DRAMA, EXPOSITION, PROLOGUE, STAGE DIRECTIONS.

Sentimentality A pejorative term used to describe the effort by an author to induce emotional responses in the reader that exceed what the situation warrants. Sentimentality especially pertains to such emotions as pathos and sympathy; it cons readers into falling for the mass murderer who is devoted to stray cats, and it requires that readers do not examine such illogical responses. Clichés and stock responses are the key ingredients of sentimentality in literature. See also CLICHÉ, STOCK RESPONSES.

Sestet A stanza consisting of exactly six lines. See also STANZA.

Sestina A type of fixed form poetry consisting of thirty-six lines of any length divided into six sestets and a three-line concluding stanza called an ENVOY. The six words at the end of the first sestet's lines must also appear at the ends of the other five sestets, in varying order. These six words must also appear in the envoy, where they often resonate important themes. An example of this highly demanding form of poetry is Elizabeth Bishop's "Sestina." See also SESTET.

Setting The physical and social context in which the action of a story occurs. The major elements of setting are the time, the place, and the social environment that frames the characters. Setting can be used to evoke a mood or atmosphere that will prepare the reader for what is to come, as in Nathaniel Hawthorne's short story "Young Goodman Brown." Sometimes, writers choose a particular setting because of traditional associations with that setting that are closely related to the action of a story. For example, stories filled with adventure or romance often take place in exotic locales.

Shakespearean sonnet See SONNET.

Showing See CHARACTER.

Simile A common figure of speech that makes an explicit comparison between two things by using words such as *like, as, than, appears,* and *seems:* "A sip of Mrs. Cook's coffee is like a punch in the stomach." The effectiveness of this simile is created by the differences between the two things compared. There would be no simile if the comparison were stated this way: "Mrs. Cook's coffee is as strong as the cafeteria's coffee." This is a literal translation because Mrs. Cook's coffee is compared with something like it — another kind of coffee. See also FIGURES OF SPEECH, METAPHOR.

Situational irony See IRONY.

Slant rhyme See RHYME.

Sociological criticism An approach to literature that examines social groups, relationships, and values as they are manifested in literature. Sociological approaches emphasize the nature and effect of the social forces that shape power relationships between groups or classes of people. Such readings treat literature as either a document reflecting social conditions or a product of those conditions. The former view brings into focus the social milieu; the latter emphasizes the work. Two important forms of sociological criticism are Marxist and feminist approaches. See also FEMINIST CRITICISM, MARXIST CRITICISM.

Soliloquy A dramatic convention by means of which a character, alone onstage, utters his or her thoughts aloud. Playwrights use soliloquies as a convenient way to inform the audience about a character's motivations and state of mind. Shakespeare's Hamlet delivers perhaps the best known of all soliloquies, which begins: "To be or not to be." See also ASIDE, CONVENTION.

Sonnet A fixed form of lyric poetry that consists of fourteen lines, usually written in iambic pentameter. There are two basic types of sonnets, the Italian and the English. The **Italian sonnet,** also known as the **Petrarchan sonnet,** is divided into an octave, which typically rhymes *abbaabba,* and a sestet, which may have varying rhyme schemes. Common rhyme patterns in the sestet are *cdecde, cdcdcd,* and *cdccdc.* Very often the octave presents a situation, attitude, or problem that the sestet comments upon or resolves, as in John Keats's "On First Looking into Chapman's Homer." The **English sonnet,** also known as the **Shakespearean sonnet,** is organized into three quatrains and a couplet, which typically rhyme *abab cdcd efef gg.* This rhyme scheme is more suited to English poetry because English has fewer rhyming words than Italian. English sonnets, because of their four-part organization, also have more flexibility with respect to where thematic breaks can occur. Frequently, however, the most pronounced break or turn comes with the concluding couplet, as in Shakespeare's "Shall I compare thee to a summer's day?" See also COUPLET, IAMBIC PENTAMETER, LINE, OCTAVE, QUATRAIN, SESTET.

Speaker The voice used by an author to tell a story or speak a poem. The speaker is often a created identity, and should not automatically be equated with the author's self. See also NARRATOR, PERSONA, POINT OF VIEW.

Spondee See FOOT.

Stage directions A playwright's written instructions about how the actors are to move and behave in a play. They explain in which direction characters should move, what facial expressions they should assume, and so on. See also DRAMA, SCRIPT.

Stanza In poetry, *stanza* refers to a grouping of lines, set off by a space, that usually has a set pattern of meter and rhyme. See also LINE, METER, RHYME.

Static character See CHARACTER.

Stock character See CHARACTER.

Stock responses Predictable, conventional reactions to language, characters, symbols, or situations. The flag, motherhood, puppies, God, and peace are common objects used to elicit stock responses from unsophisticated audiences. See also CLICHÉ, SENTIMENTALITY.

Stream-of-consciousness technique The most intense use of a central consciousness in narration. The stream-of-consciousness technique takes a reader inside a character's mind to reveal perceptions, thoughts, and feelings on a conscious or unconscious level. This technique suggests the flow of thought as well as its content; hence, complete sentences may give way to fragments as the character's mind makes rapid associations free of conventional logic or transitions. James Joyce's novel *Ulysses* makes extensive use of this narrative technique. See also NARRATOR, POINT OF VIEW.

Stress The emphasis, or accent, given a syllable in pronunciation. See also ACCENT.

Style The distinctive and unique manner in which a writer arranges words to achieve particular effects. Style essentially combines the idea to be expressed with the individuality of the author. These arrangements include individual word choices as well as matters such as the length of sentences, their structure, tone, and use of irony. See also DICTION, IRONY, TONE.

Subplot The secondary action of a story, complete and interesting in its own right, that reinforces or contrasts with the main plot. There may be more than one subplot, and sometimes as many as three, four, or even more, running through a piece of fiction. Subplots are generally either analogous to the main plot, thereby enhancing our understanding of it, or extraneous to the main plot, to provide relief from it. See also PLOT.

Suspense The anxious anticipation of a reader or an audience as to the outcome of a story, especially concerning the character or characters with whom sympathetic attachments are formed. Suspense helps to secure and sustain the interest of the reader or audience throughout a work.

Symbol A person, object, image, word, or event that evokes a range of additional meaning beyond and usually more abstract than its literal significance. Symbols are educational devices for evoking complex ideas without having to resort to painstaking explanations that would make a story more like an essay than an experience. **Conventional symbols** have meanings that are widely recognized by a society or culture. Some conventional symbols are the Christian cross, the Star of David, a swastika, or a nation's flag. Writers use conventional symbols to reinforce meanings. Kate Chopin, for example, emphasizes the spring setting in "The Story of an Hour" as a way of suggesting the renewed sense of life that Mrs. Mallard feels when she thinks herself free from her husband. A **literary** or **contextual symbol** can be a setting, character, action, object, name, or anything else in a work that maintains its literal significance while suggesting other meanings. Such symbols go beyond conventional symbols; they gain their symbolic meaning within the context of a specific story. For example, the white whale in Melville's *Moby-Dick* takes on multiple symbolic meanings in the work, but these meanings do not automatically carry over into other stories about whales. The meanings suggested by Melville's whale are specific to that text; therefore, it becomes a contextual symbol. See also ALLEGORY.

Synecdoche See METAPHOR.

Syntax The ordering of words into meaningful verbal patterns such as phrases, clauses, and sentences. Poets often manipulate syntax, changing conventional word order, to place certain emphasis on particular words. Emily Dickinson, for instance, writes about being surprised by a snake in her poem "A narrow Fellow in the Grass," and includes this line: "His notice sudden is." In addition to the alliterative hissing *s*-sounds here, Dickinson also effectively manipulates the line's syntax so that the verb *is* appears unexpectedly at the end, making the snake's hissing presence all the more "sudden."

Telling See CHARACTER.

Tercet A three-line stanza. See also STANZA, TRIPLET.

Terza rima An interlocking three-line rhyme scheme: *aba, bcb, cdc, ded,* and so on. Dante's *The Divine Comedy* and Frost's "Acquainted with the Night" are written in *terza rima*. See also RHYME, TERCET.

Theme The central meaning or dominant idea in a literary work. A theme provides a unifying point around which the plot, characters, setting, point of view, symbols, and other elements of a work are organized. It is important not to mistake the theme for the actual subject of the work; the theme refers to the abstract concept that is made concrete through the images, characterization, and action of the text. In nonfiction, however, the theme generally refers to the main topic of the discourse.

Thesis The central idea of an essay. The thesis is a complete sentence (although sometimes it may require more than one sentence) that establishes the topic of the essay in clear, unambiguous language.

Tone The author's implicit attitude toward the reader or the people, places, and events in a work as revealed by the elements of the author's style. Tone may be characterized as serious or ironic, sad or happy, private or public, angry or affectionate, bitter or nostalgic, or any other attitudes and feelings that human beings experience. See also STYLE.

Tragedy A story that presents courageous individuals who confront powerful forces within or outside themselves with a dignity that reveals the breadth and depth of the human spirit in the face of failure, defeat, and even death. Tragedies recount an individual's downfall; they usually begin high and end low. Shakespeare is known for his tragedies, including *Macbeth, King Lear, Othello,* and *Hamlet.* The **revenge tragedy** is a well-established type of drama that can be traced back to Greek and Roman plays, particularly through the Roman playwright Seneca (c. 3 B.C.–A.D. 63). Revenge tragedies basically consist of a murder that has to be avenged by a relative of the victim. Typically, the victim's ghost appears to demand revenge, and invariably madness of some sort is worked into subsequent events, which ultimately end in the deaths of the murderer, the avenger, and a number of other characters. Shakespeare's *Hamlet* subscribes to the basic ingredients of revenge tragedy, but it also transcends these conventions because Hamlet contemplates not merely revenge but suicide and the meaning of life itself. A **tragic flaw** is an error or defect in the tragic hero that leads to his downfall, such as greed, pride, or ambition. This flaw may be a result of bad character, bad judgment, an inherited weakness, or any other defect of character. **Tragic irony** is a form of dramatic irony found in tragedies such as *Oedipus the King,* in which Oedipus ironically ends up hunting himself. See also COMEDY, DRAMA.

Tragic flaw See TRAGEDY.

Tragic irony See IRONY, TRAGEDY.

Tragicomedy A type of drama that combines certain elements of both tragedy and comedy. The play's plot tends to be serious, leading to a terrible catastrophe, until an unexpected turn in events leads to a reversal of circumstance, and the story ends happily. Tragicomedy often employs a romantic, fast-moving plot dealing with love, jealousy, disguises, treachery, intrigue, and surprises, all moving toward a melodramatic resolution. Shakespeare's *Merchant of Venice* is a tragicomedy. See also COMEDY, DRAMA, MELODRAMA, TRAGEDY.

Triplet A tercet in which all three lines rhyme. See also TERCET.

Trochaic meter See FOOT.

Understatement The opposite of hyperbole, understatement (or litotes) refers to a figure of speech that says less than is intended. Understatement usually has an ironic effect, and sometimes may be used for comic purposes, as in Mark Twain's statement, "The reports of my death are greatly exaggerated." See also HYPERBOLE, IRONY.

Unreliable narrator See NARRATOR.

Verbal irony See IRONY.

Verse A generic term used to describe poetic lines composed in a measured rhythmical pattern, that are often, but not necessarily, rhymed. See also LINE, METER, RHYME, RHYTHM.

Villanelle A type of fixed form poetry consisting of nineteen lines of any length divided into six stanzas: five tercets and a concluding quatrain. The first and third lines of the initial tercet rhyme; these rhymes are repeated in each subsequent tercet (*aba*) and in the final two lines of the quatrain (*abaa*). Line I appears in its entirety as lines 6, 12, and 18, while line 3 reappears as lines 9, 15, and 19. Dylan Thomas's "Do not go gentle into that good night" is a villanelle. See also FIXED FORM, QUATRAIN, RHYME, TERCET.

Well-made play A realistic style of play that employs conventions including plenty of suspense created by meticulous plotting. Well-made plays are tightly and logically constructed, and lead to a logical resolution that is favorable to the protagonist. This dramatic structure was popularized in France by Eugène Scribe (1791–1861) and Victorien Sardou (1831–1908) and was adopted by Henrik Ibsen. See also CHARACTER, PLOT.

Acknowledgments (continued from p. iv)

Margaret Atwood. "There Was Once" from *Good Bones and Simple Murders* by Margaret Atwood. Copyright © 1983, 1992, 1994 by O. W. Toad Ltd. A Nan A. Talese Book. Used by permission of Doubleday, a division of Random House, Inc. Also from *Good Bones* by Margaret Atwood, used by permission of McClelland & Stewart, Ltd., The Canadian Publishers of *Good Bones* by Margaret Atwood.

Alison Baker. "Better Be Ready 'Bout Half Past Eight" from *How I Came West and Why I Stayed* by Alison Baker. Copyright © 1993 by Alison Baker. Reprinted by permission of Brandt & Hochman Literary Agents, Inc.

John Barth. "On Minimalist Fiction" from "A Few Words about Minimalism" by John Barth, *New York Times*, December 28, 1986. Copyright © 1986 by The New York Times Company. Reprinted by permission.

Amy Bloom. "Hold Tight" from *A Blind Man Can See How Much I Love You* by Amy Bloom. Copyright © 2000 by Amy Bloom. Used by permission of Random House, Inc.

Tadeusz Borowski. "This Way for the Gas, Ladies and Gentlemen" from *This Way for the Gas, Ladies and Gentlemen* by Tadeusz Borowski, translated by Barbara Vedder. Translation copyright © 1967 by Penguin Books Ltd. Original text copyright © 1959 by Maria Borowski. Used by permission of Viking Penguin, a division of Penguin Putnam, Inc., and Penguin Books Ltd.

George Bowering. "A Short Story" from *A Place to Die* by George Bowering. Reprinted by permission of Oberon Press.

T. Coraghessan Boyle. "Carnal Knowledge" from *Without a Hero* by T. Coraghessan Boyle. Copyright © 1994 by T. Coraghessan Boyle. Used by permission of Viking Penguin, a division of Penguin Putnam Inc.

Matthew C. Brennan. "Point of View and Plotting in Chekhov's and Oates's 'The Lady with the Pet Dog' " excerpted from "Plotting against Chekhov: Joyce Carol Oates and 'The Lady with the Pet Dog.' " *Notes on Modern American Literature* (Winter 1985). Reprinted by permission of the author.

Edgar Rice Burroughs. Excerpt from *Tarzan of the Apes* by Edgar Rice Burroughs. Copyright © 1912 by Frank A. Munsey Company, used by permission of Edgar Rice Burroughs, Inc.

Angela Carter. "A Souvenir of Japan" from *Burning Your Boats: The Collected Stories* by Angela Carter. Copyright © 1981 by Angela Carter. Reproduced by permission of the Estate of Angela Carter c/o Rogers, Coleridge & White Ltd., 20 Powis Mews, London W11 1JN.

Raymond Carver. "Popular Mechanics" from *What We Talk about When We Talk about Love* by Raymond Carver. Copyright © 1981 by Raymond Carver. Used by permission of Alfred A. Knopf, a division of Random House, Inc.

Anton Chekhov. "A Lady with a Dog" from *The Oxford Chekhov* translated by Ronald Hingley, Vol. IX (1975). Reprinted by permission of Oxford University Press. "The Lady and the Dog" from *The Image of Chekhov* by Anton Chekhov. Copyright © 1963 and renewed 1991 by Alfred A. Knopf, Inc. Used by permission of Alfred A. Knopf, a division of Random House, Inc. "The Lady with the Pet Dog" from *The Portable Chekhov* by Anton Chekhov, edited by Avrahm Yarmolinsky. Copyright 1947, © 1968 by Viking Penguin, Inc. Renewed © 1975 by Avrahm Yarmolinsky. Used by permission of Viking Penguin, a division of Penguin Putnam Inc.

Colette. "The Hand" from *The Collected Stories of Colette*, edited by Robert Phelps, and translated by Matthew Ward. Translation copyright © 1983 by Farrar, Straus & Giroux, Inc. Reprinted by permission of Farrar, Straus & Giroux, LLC.

A. R. Coulthard. "On the Visionary Ending of 'Revelation' " from "From Sermon to Parable: Four Conversion Stories by Flannery O'Connor," *American Literature* 55:1 (March 1983). Copyright 1983, Duke University Press. All rights reserved. Reprinted with permission.

E. E. Cummings. "my sweet old etcetera" from *Complete Poems: 1904–1962* by E. E. Cummings, edited by George James Firmage. Copyright © 1923, 1925, 1926, 1931, 1935, 1938, 1939, 1940, 1944, 1945, 1946, 1947, 1948, 1949, 1950, 1951, 1952, 1953, 1954, © 1955, 1956, 1957, 1958, 1959, 1960, 1961, 1962, 1963, 1966, 1967, 1968, 1972, 1973, 1974, 1975, 1976, 1977, 1978, 1979, 1980, 1981, 1982, 1983, 1984, 1985, 1986, 1987, 1988, 1989, 1990, 1991 by the Trustees for the E. E. Cummings Trust. Copyright © 1973, 1976, 1978, 1979, 1981, 1983, 1985, 1991 by George James Firmage. Reprinted by permission of Liveright Publishing Corporation.

Edwidge Danticat. "New York Day Women" from *Krik? Krak!* by Edwidge Danticat. Copyright © 1995 by Edwidge Danticat. Reprinted by permission.

Don DeLillo. "Videotape" from *Underworld* by Don DeLillo. Copyright © 1994, 1997 by Don DeLillo. Reprinted with the permission of Scribner, a division of Simon & Schuster, Inc.

Benjamin DeMott. "Abner Snopes as a Victim of Class" from *Close Imaginings: An Introduction to Literature* by Benjamin DeMott, copyright © 1988. Reprinted with permission of Bedford/St. Martin's. "On Munro's Female Protagonists," *New York Times*, January 1, 1983. Copyright © 1983 by The New York Times Company. Reprinted by permission.

Emily Dickinson. "A narrow Fellow in the grass." Reprinted by permissions of the publishers and the Trustees of Amherst College from *The Poems of Emily Dickinson*, Thomas H. Johnson, ed., Cambridge, Mass.: The Belknap Press of Harvard University Press. Copyright © 1951, 1955, 1979 by the President and Fellows of Harvard College.

Andre Dubus. "Killings" from *Finding a Girl in America* by Andre Dubus. Copyright © 1980 by Andre Dubus. Reprinted by permission of David R. Godine, Publisher, Inc.

Ralph Ellison. "Battle Royal" from *Invisible Man* by Ralph Ellison. Copyright © 1948 by Ralph Ellison. Used by permission of Random House, Inc.

William Faulkner. "A Rose for Emily" from *Collected Stories of William Faulkner* by William Faulkner. Copyright 1930 and renewed 1958 by William Faulkner. Used by permission of Random House, Inc. "Barn Burning" from *Collected Stories of William Faulkner* by William Faulkner. Copyright 1950 by Random House, Inc. Reprinted by permission of Random House, Inc. "On 'A Rose for Emily' " from *Faulkner in the University*, edited by Frederick L. Gwynn and Joseph L. Blotner (Charlottesville: Virginia, 1995). Reprinted with permission of the University Press of Virginia.

James Ferguson. "Narrative Strategy in 'Barn Burning' " from *Faulkner's Short Fiction* by James Ferguson, copyright © 1991. Reprinted by permission of the University of Tennessee Press.

Judith Fetterley. "A Feminist Reading of 'The Birthmark' " from *The Resisting Reader: A Feminist Approach to American Fiction* by Judith Fetterley. Copyright © 1978. Reprinted by permission of Indiana University Press.

Marshall Bruce Gentry. "On the Revised Ending of 'Revelation' " from *Flannery O'Connor's Religion of the Grotesque*. Copyright © 1986. Reprinted by permission of the University Press of Mississippi.

Graeme Gibson. "An Interview with Munro on Writing" from *Eleven Canadian Novelists* by Graeme Gibson. Copyright © 1973 by Graeme Gibson. Reproduced by permission of Stoddart Publishing Company, Ltd., Toronto.

Dagoberto Gilb. "Love in L.A." from *The Magic of Blood* by Dagoberto Gilb. Copyright © 1993 by the University of New Mexico Press. Story originally published in *Buffalo*. Reprinted by permission.

Gail Godwin. "A Sorrowful Woman," published in 1971 by *Esquire* Magazine. Copyright © 1971 by Gail Godwin. Reprinted by permission of John Hawkins & Associates, Inc.

Robert Hampson. "On the Reader's Expectations in 'How I Met My Husband' " from "Johnny Panic and the Pleasures of Disruption" in *Re-Reading the Short Story*, Claire Hanson, editor. Copyright © Claire Hanson. Reprinted with permission of St. Martin's Press, LLC.

Ron Hansen. "Nebraska" from *Nebraska: Stories* by Ron Hansen. Copyright © 1989 by Ron Hansen. Used by permission of Grove/Atlantic, Inc.

Bessie Head. "The Prisoner Who Wore Glasses" from *Tales of Tenderness and Power* (Heinemann International, 1990). Copyright © the Estate of Bessie Head. Reprinted by permission of John Johnson Limited.

Ernest Hemingway. "Soldier's Home" from *In Our Time* by Ernest Hemingway. Copyright © 1925 by Charles Scribner's Sons. Copyright renewed 1953 by Ernest Hemingway. Reprinted with the permission of Scribner, a division of Simon & Schuster, Inc.

Jane Hiles. "Blood Ties in 'Barn Burning' " from "Kinship and Heredity in Faulkner's 'Barn Burning.' " *Mississippi Quarterly* 38.3 (Summer 1985), pp. 329–37. Copyright © 1985 Mississippi State University, Mississippi State, Mississippi. Reprinted by permission of *Mississippi Quarterly: The Journal of Southern Culture*.

Langston Hughes. "On the Road" from *Short Stories* by Langston Hughes. Copyright © 1996 by Ramona Bass and Arnold Rampersad. Reprinted by permission of Hill and Wang, a division of Farrar, Straus & Giroux, LLC.

Gish Jen. "Who's Irish?" from *Who's Irish? Stories* by Gish Jen. Copyright © 1999 by Gish Jen. Used by permission of Alfred A. Knopf, a division of Random House, Inc.

Franz Kafka. "A Hunger Artist" from *Franz Kafka: The Complete Stories* by Franz Kafka, edited by Nahum N. Glatzer, translated by Willa and Edwin Muir. Copyright © 1946, 1947, 1948, 1949, 1954, 1958, 1971 by Schocken Books, Inc. Used by permission of Schocken Books, a division of Random House, Inc.

Claire Kahane. "The Function of Violence in O'Connor's Fiction" from "Flannery O'Connor's Rage of Vision," *American Literature* 46.1 (March 1974). Copyright 1974, Duke University Press. All rights reserved. Reprinted with permission.

Thomas E. Kennedy. "On Morality and Revenge in 'Killings' " from *Andre Dubus: A Study of the Short Fiction* by Thomas E. Kennedy. Copyright © 1988 by G. K. Hall & Company. Reprinted by permission of The Gale Group.

Jamaica Kincaid. "Girl" from *At the Bottom of the River* by Jamaica Kincaid. Copyright © 1983 by Jamaica Kincaid. Reprinted by permission of Farrar, Straus & Giroux, LLC.

Jhumpa Lahiri. "When Mr. Pirzada Came to Dine" from *Interpreter of Maladies* by Jhumpa Lahiri. Copyright © 1999 by Jhumpa Lahiri. Reprinted by permission of Houghton Mifflin Company. All rights reserved.

"A Letter Home from an Irish Emigrant in Australia" from *Oceans of Consolation: Personal Accounts of Irish Migration to Australia* by David Fitzpatrick (Cornell UP, 1994). Reprinted by permission of David Fitzpatrick and Nancy Lunch.

Naguib Mahfouz. "The Answer Is No" from *The Time and the Place and Other Stories* by Naguib Mahfouz. Copyright © 1991 by the American University in Cairo Press. Used by permission of Doubleday, a division of Random House, Inc.

Mordecai Marcus. "What Is an Initiation Story?" from *The Journal of Aesthetics and Art Criticism* 19.2, pp. 222–23. Reprinted by permission of Blackwell Publishers.

Gabriel García Márquez. "The Handsomest Drowned Man in the World" from *Leaf Storm and Other Stories* by Gabriel García Márquez. Copyright © 1971 by Gabriel García Márquez. Reprinted by permission of HarperCollins Publishers, Inc.

W. R. Martin. "On Prue's Suppressed Passions" from *Alice Munro: Paradox and Parallel* (Edmonton: The University of Alberta Press, 1987). Reprinted by permission of The University of Alberta Press.

Dan McCall. "On the Lawyer's Character in 'Bartleby, the Scrivener' " from *The Silence of Bartleby* by Dan McCall (Cornell UP, 1989). Reprinted by permission of Cornell University Press.

Alice McDermott. "Enough," *New Yorker*, April 10, 2000. Copyright © 2000 by Alice McDermott. Reprinted by permission of the Harriet Wasserman Literary Agency, Inc.

Lorraine McMullen. "On Munro's Ironic Humor in 'An Ounce of Cure' " from " 'Shameless, Marvellous, Shattering Absurdity': The Humour of Paradox in Alice Munro" in *Probable Fictions: Alice Munro's Narrative Acts*, edited by Louis K. MacKendrick. Reprinted by permission of ECW Press.

Susan Minot. "Lust" from *Lust and Other Stories* by Susan Minot. Copyright © 1989 by Susan Minot. Reprinted by permission of Houghton Mifflin Company. All rights reserved.

POETRY

Claribel Alegría. "I Am Mirror" from *Sobrevito* by Claribel Alegría. Reprinted by permission of the author.

Paula Gunn Allen. "Hoop Dancer" from *Shadow Country* by Paula Gunn Allen, University of California Publication in American Indian Series © 1982. Reprinted with permission of the University of California Press.

Julia Alvarez. "Queens, 1963" from *The Other Side/El Otro Lado*. Copyright © 1995 by Julia Alvarez. Published by Plume Penguin, an imprint of Dutton, a division of Penguin USA, and originally in hardcover by Dutton Signet. Reprinted by permission of Susan Bergholz Literary Services, New York. All rights reserved.

Yehuda Amichai. "Jerusalem" from *The Selected Poetry of Yehuda Amichai*, trans./ed. by Bloch, Chana and Stephen Mitchell. Copyright © 1996 by The Regents of the University of California.

A. R. Ammons. "Coward" from *Diversifications* by A. R. Ammons. Copyright ©1975 by A. R. Ammons. Reprinted by permission of W. W. Norton & Co., Inc.

Charles R. Anderson. "Eroticism in 'Wild Nights – Wild Nights!'" from *Emily Dickinson's Poetry: Stairway of Surprise* (Holt, Rhinehart, and Winston, 1960). Reprinted with permission of the estate of Charles R. Anderson.

Maya Angelou. "Africa" from *Oh, Pray My Wings Are Gonna Fit Me Well* by Maya Angelou. Copyright © 1975 by Maya Angelou. Reprinted by permission of Random House, Inc.

Richard Armour. "Going to Extremes" from *Light Amour* by Richard Armour. Permission to reprint this material is given courtesy of the family of Richard Armour.

Margaret Atwood. "Bored" and "February" from *Morning in the Burned House* by Margaret Atwood. Copyright © 1995 by Margaret Atwood. Used by permission by McClelland & Stewart, Inc., The Canadian Publishers. "Bored" from *Morning in the Burned House*. Copyright © 1995 by Margaret Atwood. Reprinted by permission of Houghton Mifflin Company. All rights reserved. "February" from *Morning in the Burned House*. Copyright © 1995 by Margaret Atwood. Reprinted by permission of Houghton Mifflin Company. All rights reserved. "February" from *Morning in the Burned House* by Margaret Atwood. Copyright © 1995 by Margaret Atwood. Used by permission, McClelland & Stewart, Inc. The Canadian Publishers. "you fit into me" from *Power Politics* by Margaret Atwood (Toronto: House of Anansi Press, 1971). Reprinted with permission of Stoddard Publishing Co., Limited, Canada.

W. H. Auden. "The Unknown Citizen" from *W.H. Auden: Collected Poems* by W. H. Auden, ed. by Edward Mendelson. Copyright © 1940 and renewed 1968 by W. H. Auden. Reprinted by permission.

Jimmy Santiago Baca. "Green Chile" from *Black Mesa Poems*. Copyright © 1989 by Jimmy Santiago Baca. Reprinted by permission of New Directions Publishing Corp.

David Barber. "A Colonial Epitaph Annotated" first appeared in Parnassus, vol. 24, no. 1. Reprinted with permission of the author.

Richard K. Barksdale. "On Censoring 'Ballad of the Landlord'" from *Langston Hughes: The Poet and His Critics* by Richard K. Barksdale. American Library Association, 1977.

Jeanette Barnes. "Battle-Piece" reprinted from *Shenandoah: The Washington and Lee University Review*, with the permission of the Editor.

Regina Barreca. "Nighttime Fires" from *The Minnesota Review* (Fall, 1986). Reprinted by permission of the author.

Matsuo Bashō. "Under cherry trees" from *Japanese Haiku*, trans. by Peter Beilenson, Series I, Copyright © 1955–56, Peter Beilenson, Editor. Reprinted by permission of Peter Pauper Press.

Michael L. Baumann. "The 'Overwhelming Question' for Prufrock" excerpted from "Let Us Ask 'What Is It?'" *Arizona Quarterly* 37 (Spring 1981): 47–58.

Paula Bennett. "On 'I heard a Fly buzz – when I died –'" reprinted from *Emily Dickinson: Woman Poet* by Paula Bennet by permission of the University of Iowa Press.

Elizabeth Bishop. "Manners" "Sestina," and "The Fish" from *The Complete Poems 1927–1979* by Elizabeth Bishop. Copyright © 1979, 1983 by Alice Helen Methfessel. Reprinted by permission of Farrar, Straus & Giroux, Inc.

Sophie Cabot Black. "August" copyright © 1994 by Sophie Cabot Black. Reprinted from *The Misunderstanding of Nature* with the permission of Graywolf Press, Saint Paul, Minnesota.

Robert Bly. "Snowbanks North of the House" from *The Man in the Black Coat Turns* by Robert Bly. Copyright © 1981 by Robert Bly. Used by permission of Doubleday, a division of Bantam Doubleday Dell Publishing Group, Inc. "Snowfall in the Afternoon." Reprinted from *Silence in the Snowy Fields*, by Robert Bly, Wesleyan University Press, Middletown, CT, 1962. Copyright © 1962 by Robert Bly. Reprinted with his permission. "On 'Snowbanks North of the House'." Reprinted with permission of the author.

Laure-Anne Bosselaar. "The Bumper-Sticker" copyright © by Laure-Anne Bosselaar. Reprinted from *The Hour Between Dog and Wolf*, by Laure-Anne Bosselaar, with the permission of BOA Editions, Ltd.

Gwendolyn Brooks. "The Mother," "We Real Cool," and "Sadie and Maud" from *Blacks* (Chicago, IL: Third World Press, 1991). Copyright © 1991 by Gwendolyn Brooks Blakely.

Diane Burns. "Sure You Can Ask Me a Personal Question" from *Riding the One-Eyed Ford* (1981), reprinted in Lavinia Trout ed. *Native American Literature*, NTL Publishing, 1999.

Rosario Castellanos. "Chess" as translated by Maureen Ahern, from *A Rosario Castellanos Reader* by Rosario Castellanos, edited and translated by Maureen Ahern and others. Copyright © 1988. Reprinted with permission of the University of Texas Press and the author.

Keith Casto. "She Don't Bop" from *Light Year '87* Robert Wallace, ed. Brits Press, Cleveland, 1986.

Helen Chasin. "The Word *Plum*" from *Coming Close and Other Poems* by Helen Chasin. Copyright © 1968 by Yale University Press. Reprinted with permission of Yale University Press.

Kelly Cherry. "Alzheimer's" from *Death and Transfiguration*. Copyright © 1997 by Kelly Cherry. Reprinted with permission of Louisiana State University Press.

David Chinitz. "The Romanticization of Africa in the 1920s" from *Rejuvenation through Joy: Langston Hughes, Primitivism, and Jazz.* American Literary History Spring 1997. vol. 9, no. 1, pp. 60-78. Reprinted by permission of Oxford University Press.

Ann Choi. "The Shower" from *The Asian American Literary Reader,* 4, 1991. Used with permission of NTC/Contemporary Publishing Group.

John Ciardi. "Suburban" from *For Instance* by John Ciardi. Copyright © 1979 by Jon Ciardi. Reprinted by permission of W. W. Norton & Company, Inc.

Judith Ortiz Cofer. "Common Ground" is reprinted with permission from the publisher of *Silent Dancing: A Partial Remembrance of a Puerto Rican Childhood* (Houston: Arte Publico Press—University of Houston, 1991).

Michael Collier. "The Barber" from *The Neighbor.* Copyright © 1995 by the University of Chicago Press and Michael Collier. Reprinted with permission of the author.

Billy Collins. "Marginalia" from *Picnic, Lightning,* by Billy Collins. Copyright © 1998. Reprinted by permission of the University of Pittsburgh Press.

Emund Conti. "Pragmatist" from *Light Year '86.* Reprinted by permission of the author.

Herbert R. Coursen Jr. "A Parodic Interpretation of 'Stopping by Woods on a Snowy Evening.'" Excerpted from the "Ghost of Christmas Past: 'Stopping by Woods on a Snowy Evening'" by Herbert R. Coursen Jr., from *College English,* December 1962. Originally published by the National Council of Teachers of English.

Sally Croft. "Home-Baked Bread" from *Light Year '86.* Reprinted by permission of the author.

Pam Crow. "Meat Science" first appeared in *Ploughshares,* Spring 1998, vol. 24, no. 1. Reprinted by permission of the author.

Victor Hernandez Cruz. "Anonymous" from *Rhythm, Content and Flavor.* Copyright © 1969. Reprinted by permission of the author.

Countee Cullen. "On Racial Poetry" reprinted by permission of GRM Associates, Inc., Agents for the Estate of Ida M. Cullen from *Opportunity: A Journal of Negro Life;* February 1926 issue. Copyright © 1926 by *Opportunity* Magazine; copyright renewed 1954 by Ida M. Cullen. "Yet I Do Marvel" reprinted by permission of GRM Associates, Inc., Agents for the Estate of Ida M. Cullen from *Color* by Countee Cullen. Copyright © 1925 by Harper & Brothers; copyright renewed 1953 by Ida M. Cullen.

E. E. Cummings. "Buffalo Bill 's," "in Just-," "l(a," "next to of course god america i," "she being Brand," and "since feeling is first" from *Complete Poems: 1904–1962* by E. E. Cummings, edited by George J. Firmage. Copyright 1923, 1925, 1926, 1931, 1935, 1938, 1939, 1940, 1944, 1945, 1946, 1947, 1948, 1949, 1950, 1951, 1952, 1953, 1954, © 1955, 1956, 1957, 1958, 1959, 1960, 1961, 1962.

Peter De Vries. "To His Importunate Mistress." Reprinted by permission of the Estate of Peter De Vries and the Watkins/Loomis Agency.

Mary di Michele. "As in the Beginning" from *Necessary Sugar.* Originally published by Oberon Press, 1984. Reprinted by permission of the author.

Andrew P. Debicki. "New Criticism and Deconstructionism: Two Attitudes in Teaching Poetry" from *Writing and Reading Differently: Deconstruction and the Teaching of Composition and Literature,* ed. G. Douglas Atkins and Michael L. Johnson. Copyright © 1985 by the Unviversity Press of Kansas. Reprinted by permission.

James Dickey. "Deer Among Cattle" from *Poems, 1957–1967* by James Dickey. Wesleyan UP, 1978. Reprinted by permission of University Press of New England.

Emily Dickinson. "Heaven—is what I cannot reach!," "Faith is a fine invention," "A Bird came down the Walk—," "After great pain a formal feeling comes—," "Apparently with no surprise," "Because I could not stop for Death—," "From all the Jails the Boys and Girls," "I dwell in Possibility—," "I felt a Cleaving in my Mind—," "I heard a Fly buzz—when I died—," "I know that He exists," "I never saw a Moor—," "I read my sentence—steadily," "If I can stop one Heart from breaking," "If I shouldn't be alive," "Much Madness is divinest Sense—," "One need not be a Chamber—to be Haunted—," "Portraits are to daily faces," "Presentiment—is that long Shadow—on the lawn—," "Safe in their Alabaster Chambers —" (1859 version), "Safe in their Alabaster Chambers—" (1861 version), "Some keep the Sabbath going to Church—," "Success is counted sweetest—," "Tell all the Truth but tell it slant—," "The Bustle in a House," "The Soul selects her own Society—," "The Thought beneath so slight a film—," "There's a certain Slant of light," "This was a Poet—it Is That," "To make a prairie it takes a clover and one bee," "What Soft—Cherubic Creatures—," "Wild Nights—Wild Nights!," "A loss of something ever felt I—," "How many times these low feet staggered," "I like a look of Agony," "I would not paint—a picture—," "Nature—sometimes sears a Sapling—," "Oh Sumptuous moment," "The Wind begun to knead the Grass—," "These are the days when Birds come back—," reprinted by permission of the publishers and the Trustees of Amherst College from *The poems of Emily Dickinson,* Thomas H. Johnson, ed., Cambridge, Mass.: The Belknap Press of Harvard University Press, copyright © 1951, 1955, 1979, 1983 by the President.

Morris Dickstein. "On the Social Responsibility of the Critic" reprinted by permission of the Modern Language Association of America from *Damaged Literacy: The Decay of Reading.* Originally appeared in *Profession 93.* Copyright © 1993 by the Modern Language Association.

Chitra Banerjee Divakaruni. "Indian Movie New Jersey" from the *Indiana Review,* 1990. Copyright © by Chitra Banerjee Divakaruni. Reprinted by permission of the author.

Gregory Djanikian. "When I First Saw Snow" reprinted from *Gregory Djanikian: Falling Deeply Into America* by permission of Carnegie Mellon University Press. Copyright © 1989 by Gregory Djanikian.

David Donnell. "The Canadian Prairie's View of Literature" from *Settlements* by David Donnell. Used by permission of McClelland & Stewart, Ltd. The Canadian Publishers.

Mark Doty. "Golden Retrivals" from *Sweet Machine* by Mark Doty. Copyright © 1998. Reprinted with permission of HarperCollins Publishers.

Stephen Dunn. "John & Mary" from *Different Hours* by Stephen Dunn. Copyright © 2000 by Stephen Dunn. Used by permission of W. W. Norton & Company, Inc.

Bernard Duyfhuizen. "'To His Coy Mistress': On How a Female Might Respond" excerpted from "Textual Harassment of Marvell's Coy Mistress: The Institutionalization of Masculine Criticism," *College English* (April 1988). Copyright © 1988 by the National Council of Teachers of English.

Cornelius Eady. "The Supremes" reprinted from *Cornelius Eady: The Gathering of My Name* by permission of Carnegie Mellon University Press. Copyright © 1991 by Cornelius Eady.

George Eliot. "In a London Drawingroom" from *George Eliot, Collected Poems.* Reprinted with permission of Skoob Books, Ltd.

James A. Emanuel. "Hughes's Attitudes toward Religion" from "Christ in Alabama: Religion in the Poetry of Langston Hughes" in *Modern Black Poets,* ed. Donald B. Gibson.

Martín Espada. "Coca-Cola and Coco Frío" from *City of Coughing and Dead Radiators* by Martín Espada. Copyright © 1993 by Martín Espada. Reprinted by permission of W. W. Norton & Company, Inc. "Latin Night at the Pawnshop" from *Rebellion is the Circle of a Lover's Hands* by Martín Espada. Curbstone Press, 1990. Reprinted by permission of Curbstone Press, Inc. Distributed by Consortium.

Barbara Everett. "The Problem of Tone in Prufrock" excerpted from "In Search of Prufrock," *Critical Quarterly* 16 (Summer, 1974). Reprinted by permission of Critical Quarterly, Ltd.

Faiz Ahmed Faiz. "If You Look at the City from Here" from *Faiz Ahmed Faiz, The True Subject,* trans. Naomi Lazard. Copyright © 1988 Princeton UP. Reprinted with permission of Princeton University Press.

Blanche Farley. "The Lover Not Taken" from *Light Year '86.* Reprinted by permission of the author.

Kenneth Fearing. "AD" from *New and Collected Poems by Kenneth Fearing* (Indiana University Press, 1956).

Robert Francis. "Catch" copyright © 1950, 1953 by Robert Francis. From *The Orb Weaver,* copyright 1950, 1953 by Robert Francis. Wesleyan University Press. Reprinted by permission of the University Press of New England. "The Pitcher" copyright © 1950, 1953 by Robert Francis. From *The Orb Weaver,* copyright 1950, 1953 by Robert Francis. Wesleyan University Press. Reprinted by permission of the University Press of New England. "On 'Hard' Poetry" reprinted from *The Satirical Rogue of Poetry* by Robert Francis (Amherst: University of Massachusetts Press, 1968), copyright © 1968 by Robert Francis.

Robert Frost. "Acquainted with the Night," "Design," "Fire and Ice," "Neither Out Far nor In Deep," "Nothing Gold Can Stay," "Stopping by Woods on a Snowy Evening," "The Pasture," "The Silken Tent," "A Girl's Garden," "The Investment," "Spring Pools," "The Armful" from *The Poetry of Robert Frost* edited by Edward Connery Lathem, copyright 1936, 1942, 1951, © 1956 by Robert Frost, copyright 1923, 1928, 1969 by Henry Holt and Co., copyright 1964, 1970 by Lesley Frost Ballantine. Reprinted by permission of Henry Holt and Company, LLC. "The Figure a Poem Makes" from *The Selected Prose of Robert Frost,* edited by Hyde Cox and Edward Connery Lathem. Copyright 1946, © 1956, 1959 by Robert Frost. Copyright 1949, 1954, © 1966 by Henry Holt & Co., Inc. Reprinted by permission of Henry Holt & Co., Inc. "On the Living Part of a Poem" from *A Swinger of Birches: A Portrait of Robert Frost* by Sidney Cox. Copyright © 1957 by New York University Press. Reprinted with permission of New York University Press. "On the Way to Read a Poem" from *Poetry and School* by Robert Frost in *The Atlantic Monthly,* June, 1951. Reprinted by permission of the Estate of Robert Frost.

Xu Gang. "Red Azalea on the Cliff" from *The Red Azalea,* Edited by Edward Morin. Copyright © 1990 University of Hawaii Press. Reprinted with permission.

Deborah Garrison. "The Boss" from *A Working Girl Can't Win* by Deborah Garrison. Copyright © 1998 by Deborah Garrison. Reprinted by permission of Random House, Inc.

Donald B. Gibson. "The Essential Optimism of Hughes and Whitman" excerpt from *The Good Black Poet and the Good Gray Poet: The Poetry of Hughes and Whitman in Langston Hughes—Black Genius: A Critical Evaluation* by Donald B. Gibson. William Morrow, 1971. Reprinted with permission of the author.

Sandra M. Gilbert and Susan Gubar. "On Dickinson's White Dress" excerpted from *The Madwoman in the Attic,* Yale University Press, 1979. Reprinted by permission of Yale University Press.

Sandra M. Gilbert. "Mafioso" reprinted with permission of the author.

Allen Ginsberg. "First Party at Ken Kesey's with Hell's Angels" from *Collected Poems 1947–1980* by Allen Ginsberg. Copyright © 1965 by Allen Ginsberg. Reprinted by permission of HarperCollins Publishers, Inc.

Nikki Giovanni. "Clouds" from *Blues: For All the Changes* by Nikki Giovanni. Copyright © by Nikki Giovanni.

H. D. [Hilda Doolittle]. "Heat" from *Collected Poems, 1912–1944.* Copyright © 1982 by The Estate of Hilda Doolittle. Reprinted by permission of New Directions Publishing Corp.

Rachel Hadas. "The Red Hat" from *Halfway down the Hall: New and Selected Poems.* Copyright © 1998 by Rachel Hadas, Wesleyan University Press by permission of University Press of New England.

Donald Hall. "Letter with No Address." An earlier version of this poem appeared in *Ploughshares,* Winter 1996–97, vol. 22, no. 4, pp. 109–113. Reprinted with permission of the author.

Joy Harjo. "Fishing" from June 21, 1991 Op-Ed page of the *New York Times.* Copyright © 1991 by The New York Times Company. Reprinted by permission.

Jeffrey Harrison. "Horseshoe Contest" first appeared in the *Kenyon Review.* Used with permission of the author.

Robert Hass. "Happiness" from *Sun Under Wood* by Robert Hass. Copyright © 1996 by Robert Hass. Reprinted by permission of HarperCollins Publishers, Inc. "A Story about the Body" from *Human Wishes* by Robert Hass. Copyright © 1989 by Robert Hass. Reprinted by permission of HarperCollins Publishers, Inc.

William Hathaway. "Oh Oh" from *Light Year '86.* This poem was originally published in *The Cincinnati Poetry Review.*

Robert Hayden. "Those Winter Sundays" copyright © 1966 by Robert Hayden, from *Angle of Ascent: New and Selected Poems* by Robert Hayden. Reprinted by permission of Liveright Publishing Corporation.

Seamus Heaney. "Mid-term Break" from *Death of a Naturalist* by Seamus Heaney. Reprinted by permission of Faber & Faber, Ltd. "Mid-term Break" from *Poems 1965–1975* by Seamus Heaney. Copyright © 1980 by Seamus Heaney. Reprinted by permission of Farrar, Straus & Giroux, Inc.

Anthony Hecht. "The Dover Bitch" from *Collected Earlier Poems* by Anthony Hecht. Copyright © 1990 by Anthony D. Hecht. Reprinted by permission of Alfred A. Knopf., Inc.

Judy Page Heitzman. "The Schoolroom on the Second Floor of the Knitting Mill" first appeared in *The New Yorker*, 1992. Reprinted by permission of the author.

William Heyen. "The Trains" from *The Host: Selected Poems 1965–1990*, by William Heyen. Reprinted by permission of Time Being Books. Copyright © 1994 by Time Being Press. All Rights Reserved.

Thomas Wentworth Higginson. "On Meeting Dickinson for the First Time" reprinted by permission of the publishers from *The Letters of Emily Dickinson* edited by Thomas H. Johnson, Cambridge, Mass.: The Belknap Press of Harvard University Press. Copyright © 1958, 1986 by the President and Fellows of Harvard University.

Edward Hirsch. "Fast Break" from *Wild Gratitude* by Edward Hirsch. Reprinted by permission of Alfred A. Knopf, Inc.

Jane Hirshfield. "The Lives of the Heart" from *The Lives of the Heart* published by HarperCollins. Copyright © 1997 by Jane Hirshfield. First appeared in *The Yale Review*, January, 1997, vol 85, no. 1. Used by permission.

Li Ho. "A Beautiful Girl Combs Her Hair" translated by David Young, from *Five T'ang Poets: Field Translation Series #15*. Copyright © 1990 Oberlin College Press. Reprinted by permission of Oberlin College Press.

Linda Hogan. "Hunger" from *The Book of Medicines* by Linda Hogan, Coffee House Press, 1993. Copyright © 1993 by Linda Hogan. Used by permission of the publisher. "Song for My Name" from *Calling Myself Home* by Linda Hogan. Reprinted by permission of Greenfield Review Press.

Jonathan Holden. "Cutting Loose on an August Night" from *The Names of the Rapids*. Copyright © 1985 by Jonathan Holden. Reprinted by permission of the author.

M. Carl Holman. "Mr. Z." Reprinted by permission of the Carl Holman Estate.

Carolynn Hoy. "In the Summer Kitchen" from *Ariel*, vol. 24:2, April 1993. Reprinted with permission of The Board of Governors, University of Calgary.

Andrew Hudgins. "Seventeen" from *The Glass Hammer*. Copyright © 1994 by Andrew Hudgins. Reprinted by permission of Houghton Mifflin Company. All rights reserved. "Elegy for my Father, Who is Not Dead" from *The Never-Ending*. Copyright © 1991 by Andrew Hudgins. Reprinted by permission of Houghton Mifflin Company. All rights reserved.

Langston Hughes. "Ballad of the Landlord," "Cross," "Danse Africaine," "Dinner Guest: Me," "doorknobs," "Dream Boogie," "Dream Variations," "Formula ," "Frederick Douglass: 1817–1895," "Harlem," "I Too," "Jazzonia," "Lenox Avenue: Midnight," "Negro," "Old Walt," "Red Silk Stockings," "Rent-Party Shout: For a Lady Dancer," "The Negro Speaks of Rivers," "The Weary Blues," "Theme for English B," "Un-American Investigators," "Bad Man," "Democracy," "Drum," "Madam and the Census Man," "Mother to Son," "Song for a Dark Girl," and "Uncle Tom," from *Collected Poems* by Langston Hughes. Copyright © 1994 by the Estate of Langston Hughes. Reprinted by permission of Alfred A. Knopf, Inc. "On Harlem Rent Parties" text excerpt from "When the Negro Was in Vogue" from *The Big Sea* by Langston Hughes. Copyright © 1940 by Langston Hughes. Copyright renewed © 1968 by Arna Bontemps and George Houston Bass. Reprinted by permission of Hill and Wang, a division of Farrar, Straus & Giroux, Inc. "On Racial Shame and Pride" excerpt from *The Negro Artist and the Racial Mountain* by Langston Hughes. Reprinted with permission from the June 23, 1926 issue of *The Nation*.

Paul Humphrey. "Blow" from *Light Year '86*. Reprinted with permission of the author.

Mark Jarman. "Unholy Sonnet" from *Questions for Ecclesiastes* by Mark Jarman, Storyline Press, 1997. Reprinted with permission of the author.

Randall Jarrell. "The Death of the Ball Turret Gunner" from *The Complete Poems*. Copyright © 1969 by Mrs. Randall Jarrell. Reprinted by permission of Farrar, Straus & Giroux, Inc.

Onwuchekwa Jemie. "On Universal Poetry" from *Langston Hughes* by Onwuchekwa Jemie. Copyright © 1985 by Columbia University Press.

Alice Jones. "The Foot" from *Anatomy*, Bullnettle Press, San Francisco, 1997. Reprinted by permission of the author. "The Larynx" from *Anatomy*, Bullnettle Press, San Francisco, 1997. Reprinted by permission of the author.

Donald Justice. "Order in the Streets" from *Loser Weepers* by Donald Justice. Reprinted by permission of the author.

Katherine Kearns. "On the Symbolic Setting of 'Home Burial'" excerpt from "The Place Is the Asylum: Women and Nature in Robert Frost's Poetry" in *American Literature 59* (May 1987). Copyright © 1991 by Duke University Press. Reprinted by permission of Duke University Press.

Aron Keesbury. "Song to a Waitress." Copyright 1997 by Aron Keesbury, Boston, MA. Reprinted by permission of the author.

Karl Keller. "Robert Frost on Dickinson" from *The Only Kangaroo among the Beauty: Emily Dickinson in America*. Copyright © 1979. The Johns Hopkins University Press.

X. J. Kennedy. "A Visit from St. Sigmund." Copyright © 1993 by X. J. Kennedy. First printed in *Light, The Quarterly of Light Verse*. Reprinted with permission of *Light*.

Jane Kenyon. "The Blue Bowl." Copyright © 1996 by Jane Kenyon. Reprinted from *Otherwise: New & Selected Poems* with the permission of Graywolf Press, Saint Paul, Minnesota. "Surprise" copyright 1996. Reprinted from *Otherwise: New & Selected Poems* with the permission of Graywolf Press, Saint Paul, Minnesota.

Willyce Kim. "In This Heat" from *Asian American Literature*, 2000. Used by permission of NTC/Contemporary Publishing Group.

Maxine Hong Kingston. "Restaurant" from *The Iowa Review 12* (Spring/Summer, 1981). Reprinted by permission of the author.

Galway Kinnell. "After Making Love We Hear Footsteps" from *Three Books*. Copyright © 1993 by Galway Kinnell. Originally published in *Mortal Acts, Mortal Words* (1980). Reprinted by permission of Houghton Mifflin Company. All rights reserved. "Blackberry Eating" from *Three Books*. Copyright © 1993 by Galway Kinnell. Originally published in *Mortal Acts, Mortal Words* (1980). Reprinted by permission of Houghton Mifflin Company. All rights reserved. "The Deconstruction of Emily Dickinson" from *Imperfect Thirst*. Copyright © 1994 by Galway Kinnell. Reprinted by permission of Houghton Mifflin Company. All rights reserved.

Carolyn Kizer. "After Basho" copyright © 1984 by Carolyn Kizer. Reprinted from *Yin: New Poems*, by Carolyn Kizer, with the permission of BOA Editions, Ltd.

Etheridge Knight. "A Watts Mother Mourns While Boiling Beans" from *Belly Song and Other Poems* by Etheridge Knight. Copyright © 1973 by Broadside Press. Reprinted with their permission.

Ron Koertge. "1989" copyright © 1999 by Ronald Koertge. Reprinted by permission of John Hawkins & Associates, Inc.

Philp Larkin. "A Study of Reading Habits" from *The Whitson Weddings* © 1964 by Philip Larkin. Reprinted by permission of Faber & Faber, Ltd. "A Study of Reading Habits" from *Collected Poems* by Philip Larkin. Copyright © 1988, 1989 by the Estate of Philip Larkin. Reprinted by permission of Farrar, Straus & Giroux, Inc. "This Be the Verse" from *The Whitson Weddings* © 1964 by Philip Larkin. Reprinted by permission of Faber & Faber, Ltd. "This Be the Verse" from *Phillip Larkin, Collected Poems,* ed. Anthony Thwaite © 1988 by the Estate of Philip Larkin.

Richard Lattimore. "Invocation to Aphrodite" (translation of Sappho) from *Greek Lyrics* tr. Richard Lattimore, 2 ed. University of Chicago Press, pp. 38–39. Reprinted by permission of the University of Chicago Press.

Tato Laviera. "AmeRícan" from *AmeRícan*. Copyright © 1985. Reprinted by permission of Arte Publico Press — University of Houston.

Norman Lear. "Meet the Bunkers." "All in the Family" written by Norman Lear from the television series *All in the Family*. "All in the Family," copyright © 1971, Columbia TriStar Television.

Li-Young Lee. "Eating Together" copyright © 1986 by Li-Young Lee. Reprinted from *Rose*, by Li-Young Lee, with the permission of BOA Editions, Ltd.

David Lenson. "On the Contemporary Use of Rhyme" from *The Chronicle of Higher Education* (February 24, 1988).

Phillip Levine. "Reinventing America" from *The Mercy* by Phillip Levine. Copyright © 1999 by Phillip Levine. Reprinted by permission of Alfred A. Knopf, a division of Random House, Inc.

J. Patrick Lewis. "The Unkindest Cut" from *Light 5* (Spring 1993). Reprinted with permission of the author and *Light*.

Sarah Lindsay. "Aluminum Chlorohydrate" from *Primate Behavior,* copyright © 1997 by Sarah Lindsay. Published with permission of Grove/Atlantic, Inc.

Audre Lorde. "Hanging Fire" from *The Black Unicorn* by Audre Lorde. Copyright © 1978 by Audre Lorde. Reprinted by permission of W. W. Norton & Company, Inc.

Robert Lowell. "For Sale" from *Selected Poems* by Robert Lowell. Copyright © 1976 by Robert Lowell. Reprinted with permission of Farrar, Straus & Giroux.

Thomas Lynch. "Liberty" from *Still Life in Milford* by Thomas Lynch. Copyright © 1998 by Thomas Lynch. Used by permission of W. W. Norton & Company.

Katharyn Howd Machan. "Hazel Tells LaVerne" from *Light Year '85*. Reprinted by permission of the author.

Archibald MacLeish. "Ars Poetica" from *Collected Poems 1917–1982* by Archibald MacLeish. Copyright © 1985 by The Estate of Archibald MacLeish. Reprinted by permission of Houghton Mifflin Company. All rights reserved.

Elaine Magarrell. "The Joy of Cooking" from *Sometime the Cow Kick Your Head, Light Year 88/89*. Reprinted with permission of the author.

Kathy Mangan. "An Arithmetic" first appeared in *Ploughshares*. Reprinted with permission of the author.

Julio Marzán. "The Translator at the Reception for Latin American Writers." Reprinted with permission of the author. "Ethnic Poetry" originally appeared in *Parnassas: Poetry In Review*. Reprinted by permission of the author.

Florence Cassen Mayers. "All-American Sestina." Copyright © 1996 Florence Cassen Mayers, as first published in *The Atlantic Monthly*. Reprinted with permission of the author.

Gail Mazur. "Snake in the Grass" from *The Common,* University of Chicago Press, 1995. Copyright © Gail Mazur. Reprinted with permission of the author.

David McCord. "Epitaph on a Waiter" from *Odds without Ends* copyright © 1954 by David T. W. McCord. Reprinted by permission of Arthur B. Page, executor of the estate of David McCord.

Michael McFee. "In Medias Res" reprinted from *Colander* by Michael McFee, by permission of the author. Copyright © 1996 by Michael McFee.

Rennie McQuilkin. "The Lighters" reprinted by permission from *The Hudson Review*.

Jay Meek. "Swimmers" first appeared in *Windows,* Carnegie Mellon University Press: Pittsburgh, PA, 1994. Reprinted with permission of the author.

Peter Meinke. "The ABC of Aerobics" from *Night Watch on the Chesapeake,* by Peter Meinke, © 1987. Reprinted by permission of the University of Pittsburgh Press.

James Merrill. "Casual Wear" from *Selected Poems 1946–1985* by James Merrill. Copyright © 1992 by James Merrill. Reprinted by permission of Alfred A. Knopf Inc.

W. S. Merwin. "For the Anniversary of My Death" from *The Lice* by W. S. Merwin, 1970.

Edna St. Vincent Millay. "I will put Chaos into fourteen lines" from *Collected Poems,* HarperCollins. Copyright © 1923, 1951, 1954, 1982 by Edna St. Vincent Millay and Norma Millay Ellis. All rights reserved. Reprinted by permission of Elizabeth Barnett, literary executor.

Janice Mirikitani. "Recipe" excerpted from *Shedding Silence,* copyright © 1987 by Janice Mirikitani. Reprinted by permission of Celestial Arts, P.O. Box 7123, Berkeley, CA 94707.

Elaine Mitchell. "Form" from *Light 9* (Spring 1994). Reprinted by permission of the author.

N. Scott Momaday. "Crows in a Winter Composition" from *In the Presence of the Sun* by N. Scott Momaday. Copyright © 1992 by N. Scott Momaday. Reprinted by permission of St. Martin's Press, LLC.

Janice Townley Moore. "To a Wasp" first appeared in *Light Year,* Bits Press. Reprinted by permission of the author.

Marianne Moore. "Poetry" reprinted with permission of Simon & Schuster from *Collected Poems of Marianne Moore.* Copyright 1935 by Marianne Moore; copyright renewed © 1963 by Marianne Moore and T. S. Eliot.

Pat Mora. "Another Brown Man" from *Agua Santa/Holy Water* by Pat Mora. Copyright © 1995 by Pat Mora. Reprinted by permission of Beacon Press, Boston.

Robert Morgan. "Mountain Graveyard" from *Sigodlin,* copyright © 1990 by Robert Morgan. Wesleyan University Press. Reprinted by permission of the University Press of New England. "On the Shape of a Poem" from *Epoch* (Fall/Winter 1983). Reprinted by permission of the author. "Time's Music" from "Poetry and School" by Robert Frost in *The Atlantic Monthly,* June, 1951. Reprinted by permission of the Estate of Robert Frost. "Wind from a Waterfall" from *The Atlantic Monthly,* Sept. 1999. Reprinted by permission of the author.

Robin Morgan. "Invocation" included in *A Hot January: Poems 1996–1999* by Robin Morgan. Copyright © by Robin Morgan. Reprinted by permission of the author.

Joan Murray. "Play-By-Play" reprinted by permission from *The Hudson Review,* Vol. XLIX, No. 4 (Winter 1997). Copyright © 1997 by Joan Murray.

Pablo Neruda. "Sweetness Always" from *Extravagaria* by Pablo Neruda, trans. by Alastair Reid. English translation copyright © 1974, by Alastair Reid. Reprinted by permission of Farrar, Straus & Giroux, Inc.

John Frederick Nims. "Love Poem" from *Selected Poems.* Copyright © 1982 by the University of Chicago. Reprinted by permission of the Publisher.

Alden Nowlan. "The Bull Moose" from *An Exchange of Gifts* by Alden Nowlan. Reprinted with the permission of Stoddart Publishing Co. Limited, Canada.

Sharon Olds. "Rite of Passage" from *The Dead and the Living* by Sharon Olds. Copyright © 1983 by Sharon Olds. Reprinted by permission of Alfred A. Knopf, Inc. "Sex without Love" from *The Dead and the Living* by Sharon Olds. Copyright © 1983 by Sharon Olds. Reprinted by permission of Alfred A. Knopf., Inc. "Poem for the Breasts" first appeared in *Ploughshares.* Reprinted with permission of the author.

Mary Oliver. "Seven White Butterflies" from *West Wind* by Mary Oliver. Copyright © 1997 by Mary Oliver. Reprinted by permission of Houghton Mifflin Company. All rights reserved.

Eric Ormsby. "Nose" from *For a Modest God.* Copyright © 1997. Reprinted by permission of ECW Press.

Sue Owen. "Zero" from *The Book of Winter,* Columbus: Ohio State University Press, 1988. Copyright © 1988 by Sue Owen. Reprinted with permission from the author.

Wilfred Owen. "Dulce et Decorum Est" from *The Collected Poems of Wilfred Owen.* Copyright © 1963 by Chatto & Windus, Ltd. Reprinted by permission of New Directions Publishing Corp.

Lisa Parker. "Snapping Beans" from *Parnassus 1998,* vol. 23, no. 1 and 2.

Linda Pastan. "Marks" copyright © 1978 by Linda Pastan from *PM/AM: New and Selected Poems by Linda Pastan.* Reprinted by permission of W. W. Norton & Co., Inc.

Octavio Paz. "The Street" from *Early Poems 1935–1955.* Reprinted with permission of Indiana University Press.

Molly Peacock. "Desire" from *Molly Peacock, Raw Heaven,* Random House, 1984.

Laurence Perrine. "The limerick's never averse" from *A Limerick's always a verse: 200 original limericks* by Laurence Perrine. Copyright © 1990 by Laurence Perrine.

Stephen Perry. "Blue Spruce" copyright © 1991 by Stephen Perry. Originally in *The New Yorker,* January 28, 1991, p. 34–35.

Marge Piercy. "The Secretary Chant" from *Circles on the Water* by Marge Piercy. Copyright © 1982 by Marge Piercy. Reprinted by permission of Alfred A. Knopf, Inc.

Sylvia Plath. "Daddy" from *The Collected Poems* by Sylvia Plath, ed. Ted Hughes. Reprinted by permission of Faber & Faber, Ltd. "Daddy" from *Ariel* by Sylvia Plath. Copyright © 1963 by Ted Hughes. Reprinted by permission of HarperCollins Publishers, Inc. "Mirror" from *The Collected Poems* by Sylvia Plath, ed. Ted Hughes. Reprinted by permission of Faber & Faber, Ltd. "Mirror" from *Crossing the Water* by Sylvia Plath. Copyright © 1963 by Ted Hughes. Originally appeared in *The New Yorker.* Reprinted by permission of HarperCollins Publishers, Inc. "Mushrooms" from *The Colossus and Other Poems* by Sylvia Plath. Copyright © 1960 by Sylvia Plath. Reprinted by permission of Alfred A. Knopf, Inc.

Ezra Pound. "In a Station of the Metro" from *Personae.* Copyright © 1926 by Ezra Pound. Reprinted by permission of New Directions Publishing Corp.

Jim Powell. "[Artfully adorned Aphrodite, deathless] (translation of Sappho fragment)" from *Sappho A Garland: The Poems and Fragments of Sappho.* Copyright © 1993 by Jim Powell. Reprinted by permission of Farrar, Straus & Giroux, Inc.

Wyatt Prunty. "Elderly Lady Crossing on Green" from *The Run of the House,* page 18. Copyright © 1993. Used by permission of The Johns Hopkins University Press.

"Queens: The 'Fair' Borough" (originally titled "Cariello Glorifies Queens as Example of Gracious Living"), *New York Times,* July 18, 1963. Copyright © 1963 by The New York Times Company. Reprinted by permission.

Henry Reed. "Naming of Parts 'Lessons of War' (1. Naming of the Parts)" from *Henry Reed: Collected Poems,* ed. Jon Stallworthy. Copyright © 1991 by the Executor of Henry Reed's Estate.

Marny Requa. "From an Interview with Julia Alvarez" from "The Politics of Fiction," *Frontera 5* (1997):n. pdg. World Wide Web. 29 Jan. 1997. Reprinted with permission of Marny Requa.

David S. Reynolds. "Popular Literature and 'Wild Nights—Wild Nights!'" from *Beneath the American Renaissance* by David S. Reynolds, copyright © 1988 by David S. Reynolds. Reprinted by permission of Alfred A. Knopf, Inc.

Oliver Rice. "The Doll House." Reprinted with permission of the author.

Adrienne Rich. "Living in Sin." Copyright © 1993, 1955 by Adrienne Rich, from *Collected Early Poems: 1950–1970* by Adrienne Rich. Reprinted by permission of W. W. Norton & Company, Inc.

Rainer Maria Rilke. "The Panther" from *The Selected Poetry of Rainer Maria Rilke* by Rainer Maria Rilke, edited & translated by Stephen Mitchell copyright © 1982 by Stephen Mitchell. Reprinted by permission of Random House, Inc.

Alberto Ríos. "Seniors" from *Five Indiscretions*. Copyright © 1985 by Alberto Ríos. Reprinted by permission of the author.

Theodore Roethke. "My Papa's Waltz" copyright © 1942 by *Hearst Magazines, Inc.* From *The Collected Poems of Theodore Roethke* by Theodore Roethke. Used by permission of Doubleday, a division of Bantam Doubleday Dell Publishing Group, Inc. "Root Cellar" copyright © 1943 by Modern Poetry Association, Inc. From *The Collected Poems of Theodore Roethke* by Theodore Roethke. Used by permission of Doubleday, a division of Bantam Doubleday Dell Publishing Group, Inc.

Frederik L. Rusch. "Society and Character in 'The Love Song of J. Alfred Prufrock,'" "Approaching Literature through the Social Psychology of Erich Fromm" in *Psychological Perspectives on Literature: Freudian Dissidents and Non-Freudians*, edited by Joseph Natoli. Copyright © 1984. Reprinted by permission of the author.

Kate Rushin. "The Black Back-Ups" from *The Black Back-Ups* by Kate Rushin. Copyright © 1993 by Kate Rushin. Reprinted by permission of Firebrand Books.

Indira Sant. "Household Fires" from *Sixteen Modern Indian Poems* ed. A. K. Ramanujan and Vinay Dharwadker © 1989. Reprinted by permission of *Daedalus, Journal of the American Academy of Arts and Sciences* from the issue entitled "Another India," Fall 1989, vol. 118, no. 4.

Robyn Sarah. "Villanelle for a Cool April" reprinted from *Shenandoah: The Washington and Lee University Review*, with the permission of the editor and author. Copyright 1998 by Robyn Sarah.

Elisabeth Schneider. "Hints of Eliot in Prufrock" reprinted by permission of the Modern Language Association of America from "Prufrock and After: The Theme of Change," PMLA 87 (1982): 1103–1117.

Saundra Sharp. "It's the Law: A Rap Poem" from *Typing in the Dark* 1991, Writers and Readers Publishing, Inc. Reprinted in *African American Literature* 1998. Used by permission of NTC/Contemporary Publishing Group.

Charles Simic. "Filthy Landscape" from *Jackstraws*. Copyright © 1999 by Charles Simic. Reprinted by permission of Harcourt, Inc.

Louis Simpson. "In the Suburbs" from *At the End of the Open Road* by Louis Simpson. Wesleyan UP, 1963. Reprinted by permission of the author.

David R. Slavitt. "Titanic" from *Big Nose* by David R. Slavitt. Copyright © 1983 by David R. Slavitt. Reprinted by permission of Louisiana State University Press.

Ernest Slyman. "Lightning Bugs" from *Sometime the Cow Kick Your Head, Light Year 88/89*. Reprinted by permission of the author.

Patricia Smith. "What It's Like to Be a Black Girl (For Those of You Who Aren't)" reprinted with permission of the author.

David Solway. "Windsurfing" reprinted by permission of the author.

Cathy Song. "The White Porch" from *Picture Bride*. Copyright © 1983 by Yale University Press. Reprinted with permission. "The Youngest Daughter" from *Picture Bride*. Copyright © 1983 by Yale University Press. Reprinted with permission.

Gary Soto. "Behind Grandma's House," "Black Hair," and "Mexicans Begin Jogging" from *New and Selected Works* by Gary Soto. Copyright © 1995, published by Chronicle Books, San Francisco.

Wole Soyinka. "Future Plans" from *A Shuttle in the Crypt* by Wole Soyinka. Copyright © 1972 by Wole Soyinka. Reprinted by permission of Hill and Wang, a division of Farrar, Straus & Giroux, Inc. "Telephone Conversation" from *Ibadan*, volume 10, November 1960, p. 34.

Bruce Springsteen. "The Streets of Philadelphia" reprinted with permission.

William Stafford. "Traveling through the Dark" copyright © 1962, 1998 by the Estate of William Stafford. Reprinted from *The Way It Is: New & Selected Poems* with the permission of Graywolf Press, Saint Paul, Minnesota.

Timothy Steele. "Waiting for the Storm" from *Sapphics Against Anger and Other Poems*. Copyright © 1986 by Timothy Steele. Reprinted with permission of the University of Arkansas Press.

Jim Stevens. "Schizophrenia" originally appeared in *Light: The Quarterly of Light Verse* (Spring 1992). Copyright © 1992 by Jim Stevens.

Wallace Stevens. "The Emperor of Ice-Cream" from *Collected Poems* by Wallace Stevens. Copyright © 1923 and renewed 1951 by Wallace Stevens. Reprinted by permission of Alfred A. Knopf., Inc.

Robert Sward. "A Personal Analysis of 'Love Song of J. Alfred Prufrock'" from *Touchstones: American Poets on a Favorite Poem* eds. Robert Pack and Jay Parini. Middlebury College Press. Published by UP New England.

May Swenson. "A Nosty Fright" from *In Other Words* by May Swensen. Copyright © 1984 by May Swenson. Reprinted by permission of the Estate of May Swenson.

Wislawa Szymborska. "Maybe All This" from *View Within a Grain of Sand*. Copyright © 1993 by Wislawa Szymborska, English translation by Stanislaw Baranczak and Clare Cavanagh. Copyright © 1995 by Harcourt, Inc., reprinted by permission of the publisher.

Diane Thiel. "The Minefield" from *Echolocations*, copyright © 2000 by Diane Thiel. Reprinted with permission of Story Line Press.

Arthur Miller. *Death of a Salesman*. Copyright 1949, renewed © 1977 by Arthur Miller. Used by permission of Viking Penguin, a division of Penguin Putnam Inc. "On Biff and Willy Loman," *New York Times* (February 5, 1959). Copyright © 1959 by Arthur Miller. Reprinted by permission of International Creative Management, Inc. "Tragedy and the Common Man." Copyright © 1959 by Arthur Miller. Reprinted by permission of International Creative Management, Inc. Copyright © 1949, renewed © 1977 by Arthur Miller, from *The Theater Essays of Arthur Miller*, edited by Robert A. Martin. Used by permission of Viking Penguin, a division of Penguin Putnam Inc.

Louis Adrian Montrose. "On Amazonian Mythology in *A Midsummer Night's Dream*" from " 'Shaping Fantasies': Figurations of Gender and Power in Elizabethan Culture," *Representations* 2 (Spring 1983). Copyright © 1983 by The Regents of the University of California. Reprinted by permission of the publisher and the author.

Geoffrey O'Brien. "On *Seinfeld* as Sitcom Moneymaker" excerpted from "Sein of the Times," *New York Review of Books*, August 14, 1997. Reprinted with permission from *The New York Review of Books*. Copyright © 1997 NYREV, Inc.

Frank Rich. "A Theater Review of *M. Butterfly*" from "*M. Butterfly*, a Story of a Strange Love and Betrayal," *New York Times*, March 21, 1988. Copyright © 1988 by The New York Times Company. Reprinted by permission.

Harold Rosenthal. "A Plot Synopsis of *Madame Butterfly*" from *The Concise Oxford Dictionary of Opera* by Harold Rosenthal and John Warrack (1964). Reprinted by permission of Oxford University Press.

Muriel Rukeyser. "On *Oedipus the King*." Originally titled "Myth," from *Out of Silence* (Evanston, IL: TriQuarterly Books, 1992). Copyright © 1992 Muriel Rukeyser. Reprinted by permission of International Creative Management, Inc.

Maurice Sagoff. "A Humorous Distillation of *Antigone*" excerpted from *Shrinklits*. Copyright © 1970, 1980 by Maurice Sagoff. Used by permission of Workman Publishing Company Co., Inc., New York. All Rights Reserved.

David Savran. "An Interview with David Henry Hwang" from *In Their Own Words: Contemporary American Playwrights* by David Savran. Copyright © 1988 by David Savran. Used by permission of Theatre Communications Group.

William Shakespeare. *A Midsummer Night's Dream* and *Hamlet, Prince of Denmark* with notes from *The Complete Works of Shakespeare*, 4th ed., edited by David Bevington. Copyright © 1992 by HarperCollins Publishers, Inc. Reprinted by permission of Pearson Education, Inc. *Othello*, edited by Gerald Eades Bentley. Copyright © 1958, 1970 by Penguin Books, © 2000 Penguin Putnam Inc. Used by permission of Penguin, a division of Penguin Putnam Inc.

Diana Son. *Stop Kiss*. Copyright © 1999 by Diana Son. Reprinted by permission of The Overlook Press.

Sophocles. "Antigone" and "Oedipus the King" from *Three Theban Plays* by Sophocles, translated by Robert Fagles. Translation copyright © 1982 by Robert Fagles. Used by permission of Viking Penguin, a division of Penguin Putnam Inc.

Wole Soyinka. *The Strong Breed*. Copyright © Oxford University Press 1964. Reprinted from *Collected Plays 1* (1973) by permission of Oxford University Press.

Joan Templeton. "Is *A Doll House* a Feminist Text?" excerpted from "The *Doll House* Backlash: Criticism, Feminism, and Ibsen." Reprinted by permission of the Modern Language Association of America from *PMLA* 104. Copyright © 1989 by the Modern Language Association.

Carol Strongin Tufts. "A Psychoanalytic Reading of Nora" excerpted from "Recasting *A Doll House*: Narcissism as Character Motivation in Ibsen's Play." Originally published in *Comparative Drama* (Summer 1986). Reprinted by permission of the publisher.

Luis Valdez. *Los Vendidos*. From *Luis Valdez—Early Works: Actos, Bernabé, and Pensamiento Serpentino* (Houston: Arte Público Press—University of Houston, 1990). Copyright © 1971 by Luis Valdez. Reprinted with permission from the publisher.

Wendy Wasserstein. *Tender Offer*. Copyright © 1991 by Wendy Wasserstein. First appeared in *Antaeus* 66, *Plays in One Act*. No part of this material may be reproduced, in whole or in part, without the express written permission of the author or her agent.

Tennessee Williams. *The Glass Menagerie* (play and production notes). Copyright 1945 by Tennessee Williams and Edwina D. Williams. Copyright renewed 1973 by Tennessee Williams. Used by permission of Random House, Inc. "On Theme" from *Where I Live*. Copyright © 1978 by Tennessee Williams. Reprinted by permission of New Directions Publishing Corporation.

August Wilson. *The Piano Lesson*. Copyright © 1988, 1990 by August Wilson. Used by permission of Dutton Signet, a division of Penguin Putnam Inc.

Barry Witham and John Lutterbie. "A Marxist Approach to *A Doll House*." Reprinted by permission of the Modern Language Association of America from *Approaches to Teaching Ibsen's "A Doll House"* edited by Yvonne Shafer. Copyright © 1985 by the Modern Language Association.

CRITICAL THINKING AND WRITING

Andrew P. DeBicki. "New Criticism and Deconstructionism: Two Attitudes in Teaching Poetry" from *Writing and Reading Differently: Deconstruction and the Teaching of Composition and Literature*, edited by G. Douglas Atkins and Michael L. Johnson. Copyright © 1985 by the University Press of Kansas. Reprinted by permission.

Emily Dickinson. "There's a certain Slant of light." Reprinted by permissions of the publishers and the Trustees of Amherst College from *The Poems of Emily Dickinson*, Thomas H. Johnson, ed., Cambridge, MA: The Belknap Press of Harvard University Press. Copyright © 1951, 1955, 1979, 1983 by the President and Fellows of Harvard College.

Index of First Lines

Index of Authors and Titles

2236

On Narration in "An Ounce of Cure," 489
On Nathaniel Hawthorne's Tragic Vision, 374
On "Nebraska" as an Unconventional Short Story, 164
On O'Connor's Refusal to "Do Pretty," 441
On O'Connor's Use of History, 443
On *Oedipus* and Human Freedom, 1379
On *Oedipus the King*, 1375
On Producing *Hamlet*, 1552
On Prue's Suppressed Passions, 487
On Racial Poetry, 1064
On Racial Shame and Pride, 1058
On Repression in *Hamlet*, 1551
On Rhyme and Meter, 915
On *Seinfeld* as a Sitcom Moneymaker, 1273
On Shakespeare's Characters, 1550
On Snowbanks North of the House, 815
On Solitude, 371
On Symbolism in Munro's Fiction, 488
On Symbols, 831
On the Commitments of Feminist Criticism, 2118
On the Contemporary Use of Rhyme, 842
On the Dangers of Reading Fiction, 41
On the Differences between Poetry and Prose, 775
On the Figure a Poem Makes, 1021
On the Importance of Place in "IND AFF," 171
On the Late Massacre in Piedmont, 1174
On the Lawyer's Character in "Bartleby, the Scrivener," 142
On the Living Part of a Poem, 1020
On the Many Voices in Dickinson's Poetry, 982
On the Materials of Fiction, 438
On the Oedipus Complex, 1371
On the Power of the Writer's Imagination, 372
On the Reader's Experience in Reading Munro's Stories, 487
On the Revised Ending of "Revelation," 445
On the Road, 574
On the Shape of a Poem, 911
On the Social Responsibility of the Critic, 2126
On the Symbolic Setting of "Home Burial," 1030
On the Theater of the Absurd, 1655
On the Use of Exaggeration and Distortion, 439
On the Value of Comedy in the Face of Tragedy, 1558
On the Visionary Ending of "Revelation," 443
On the Way to Read a Poem, 1023
On the Words in Poetry, 861
On Theme and Symbol, 440
On Theme, 1940
On Tragic Character, 1369
On Universal Poetry, 1065
On What Artists Do Best, 1625
On What Every Writer Needs, 159
One need not be a Chamber—to be Haunted, 970
One's-Self I Sing, 1188
Ophelia's Desperation, 1559
Ophelia's Mad Speeches, 1561
Order in the Streets, 935
ORMSBY, ERIC
  Nose, 744
Ounce of Cure, An, 451
"Out, Out—," 1012
Overwhelming Question for "Prufrock," The, 1074
OWEN, SUE
  Zero, 786
OWEN, WILFRED
  Dulce et Decorum Est, 764
Ozymandias, 1182

Panther, The, 768
PARKER, LISA
  Snapping Beans, 700
Parker's Back, 424
Parodic Interpretation of "Stopping by Woods on a Snowy Evening," A, 1026
Parting at Morning, 1150
Passionate Shepherd to His Love, The, 1099
PASTAN, LINDA
  Marks, 794
Pasture, The, 1002

Index of Terms

Boldface numbers refer to the Glossary of Literary Terms